REESE CHRONOLOGICAL
Encyclopedia of
Christian Biographies

Ed Reese

Advancing the Ministries of the Gospel
AMG *Publishers*

God's Word to you is our highest calling.

Reese Chronological Encyclopedia of Christian Biographies
Copyright © 2007 by Edward Reese

Published by AMG Publishers
6815 Shallowford Rd.
Chattanooga, Tennessee 37421

All rights reserved. Except for brief quotations in printed reviews, no part of this publication may be reproduced, stored in a retrieval system, or transmitted in any form or by any means (printed, written, photocopied, visual electronic, audio, or otherwise) without the prior permission of the publisher.

All Scripture quotations, unless otherwise noted, are taken from the Holy Bible, King James Version, which is in the public domain.

ISBN 13: 978-089957397-7
ISBN 10: 0-89957-397-5

Second printing—May 2008

Cover designed by ImageWright, Chattanooga, Tennessee
Interior design and typesetting by Ryan Keiter, Knoxville, Tennessee
Edited and Proofread by Dan Penwell, Sharon Neal, Lois Lohman, and Rick Steele

Printed in Canada
13 12 11 10 09 08 –T– 8 7 6 5 4 3 2

Table of Contents

Introductory Pages

    "God's Hall of Fame" (poem) — iv

    A word about the Compiler/Editor — v

    Foreword: Ted W. Engstrom — vii

    Preface — ix

    In Appreciation — xi

    Overview of the Project — xiii

    Dedication — xv

    "Valiant–for–the–Truth Goes Home" (poem) — xvii

Section I

Chronological Encyclopedia of Biographies 1–1252

General Alphabetical Index 1253–1306

Section II

Other Influential Personalities 1307–28

Abbreviations 1329–32

Glossary 1333–40

Acknowledgments 1341–90

God's Hall of Fame

Your name may not appear down here
In this world's Hall of Fame;
In fact, you may be so unknown,
That no one knows your name.
The Oscars here may pass you by,
And neon lights of blue;
But if you love and serve the Lord,
Then, I have news for you!

This Hall of Fame is only good
As long as time shall be;
But keep in mind, God's Hall of Fame
Is for eternity!
To have your name inscribed up there
Is greater, yes, by far,
Than all the Halls of Fame down here,
And every man-made star.

This crowd on earth they soon forget
The heroes of the past,
They cheer like mad until you fall,
And that's how long you last!
But God, He never does forget,
And in His Hall of Fame,
By just believing in His Son,
Inscribed you'll find your name.

I tell you, friend, I wouldn't trade
My name, however small,
That's written there beyond the stars
In that celestial Hall!
For every famous name on earth
Or glory that they share:
I'd rather be an unknown here,
And have my name up there!

—Anonymous

A Word about the Compiler/Editor

Edward Reese was born in Grand Rapids, Michigan, May 7, 1928. He was born again March 11, 1941 through the prayers of his mother, the influence of the youth work at the MEL TROTTER Mission and its youth director, MERLE (MEL) JOHNSON. Reese is a 1950 graduate of Moody Bible Institute. He has spent a lifetime in Christian service and has had much experience in several major fields: pastor, evangelist, musician, missionary, educator, writer—and thus has a heart for all. He has maintained friendships and contacts in multiple facets of the evangelical/fundamental world. Reese has worked with many Christian organizations and leaders such as Youth for Christ (TED ENGSTROM), Christian Aid Mission (Bob Finley), World Literature Crusade (JACK MCALISTER), Second Coming (Salem Kirban), Hyles Anderson College (JACK HYLES), Jack VanImpe Ministries, Church League of America (Edgar Bundy), among others. He began teaching at Crown College, Powell, TN in 1996. Reese has accumulated an impressive information base called Reese Religious Research (RRR) and has been of help to a number of organizations and individuals through the years. He pastored in East Hazel Crest, IL and Bangor, MI and did evangelistic work in twenty-six states and four foreign countries.

Studying Christian biographies for a lifetime, he may be the foremost authority on the subject in the world. The 5,000-plus sketches, 4,000-plus photos, numerous autographs and the cooperation of 1,000-plus organizations attest to his thoroughness.

Ed Reese would welcome communications from readers: especially corrections, additional material (birth and death dates) and missing photos or people for possible future editions.

AMG Publishers
6815 Shallowford Rd.
Chattanooga, TN 37421
Telephone (423) 894-6060
Fax (423) 894-9511
Web - www.amgpublishers.com

Ed Reese
7801 Ember Crest Trail
Knoxville, TN 37938
Telephone (865) 922-8056
Fax (865) 922-8162
Email - reesrelresch@earthlink.net
Web - www.christiandata.org

Foreword

By Ted W. Engstrom

It was over a half century ago that I first met my friend, Ed Reese—in the dramatic post-world war days of the late 1940s. He first attended, briefly, the youth meetings at Mission (Evangelical) Covenant Church in Grand Rapids where I was youth director. Then I was the volunteer director of the Youth for Christ program in Grand Rapids, Michigan, where he was very active, while a student at Moody Bible Institute (summer vacations, some weekends, etc).

From those earliest days, I recall his intense interest in the ministry of the Church, Evangelism and Missions. Like so many young men and women of that genre, he wanted to make a difference in his world, part of a wonderful group of young people who were known for their zeal and vision. He always had the unique ability to ask penetrating questions concerning individuals, events, and circumstances in our Christian witness.

This tremendously significant volume you hold in your hands is a result of fifty years of research, an examination of the Church historically and the biographical sketches of its key players. I can think of no one who could have gathered together this type of material better than, or more extensively than, my friend, Ed Reese, who, incidentally, compiled the Reese Chronological Bible (1978). Normally a research book like this has dozens of editors, but one man working on a shoestring has put the whole thing together.

This is a treasure trove of significant and valuable biographical material regarding those who, historically, have made a difference in the world because of their Christian leadership and investment in the cause of Christ during their day and time. You will be hard-pressed to find someone of note that he has omitted.

Ed Reese is a college professor, evangelist, musician, and researcher par excellence. He continues in his passion to use talent and time to help reach the world with the message of the risen Christ. *Reese Chronological Encyclopedia of Christian Biographies* is a labor of love on the part of one of the most committed men to the task of evangelism I've known over a lifetime.

The Christian community is indebted to this gentleman for this remarkable contribution to the legacy of the cause of Christ. The marvelous collection of photos contained in this volume will ignite memories in readers of all ages. It is not often you can say about a research book, "A true blessing awaits you," but it does.

Ted W. Engstrom

[signature]

President Emeritus
World Vision

Note: I know of no one more respected in Christian work than Dr. Ted. Over fifty years ago, I visited his cottage in Muskegon, Michigan. We sat on the porch and I asked him about his knowledge of a list of people I had compiled. In essence, that was the beginning of my information base. Ted served as editor for Zondervan Publishers, president of Youth for Christ, president of World Vision, and has been on numerous boards of major Christian works. His six decades of service as a compassionate communicator has left an impact around the world. He died on July 14, 2006.

—*Ed Reese*

Preface

While still a student at Moody Bible Institute, it seems the Lord inspired me to consider two great writing projects. One was a chronological Bible, and the other, a Christian biography encyclopedia—this book you hold in your hands.

When I learned that, chronologically, Ezra and Nehemiah really belonged with the Minor Prophets, I wondered, "Why hasn't someone arranged the Bible in the flow of history?" Twenty-five years later, while a teacher myself, I finally finished the *Reese Chronological Bible* (Bethany/Baker Bookhouse), first of its kind, and now some 250,000 copies are in circulation. Everett Gaddy helped give it a wide circulation in its early days.

Likewise, as my young, inquisitive mind poured over a newly purchased, two-volume *Twentieth Century Encyclopedia of Religious Knowledge*, a great Baker publication, I was disappointed. With 500 contributors, I found great holes in the biography section. I was non-plussed. There was Wilbur M. Smith…but no Gypsy (Rodney) Smith. There was Walter A. Maier…but no Charles E. Fuller…and "Why isn't Harry Ironside in here?" I counted 722 biographical entries and found 20 who could be considered evangelical or conservative. Was this fair and balanced? I said to myself, "Someday I'll do a book that will include the whole spectrum of Christianity." That was some 50 years ago and it took another 25 years, after the release of the *Reese Chronological Bible*, to complete it. Fifty years of "Reese Religious Research" has gone into making this "fair and balanced," with only one compiler—me.

Christian biographies have been a lifelong interest for me. I began to amass information with my card files with interest growing to great proportions. Forty years ago, I began sending questionnaires to Christian leaders. Hundreds responded. My biography library grew rapidly. So, with an old-fashioned typewriter and shoeboxes full of card files, I doggedly began considering every notable Christian in history, as I continued to add data to my existing information base.

I was soundly converted (born again) at age 13. I was raised in a church that did not stress this, so I was glad for the youth program of the Mel Trotter Mission in Grand Rapids, that introduced me to Christ. Some seminaries left historic Christianity at the turn of the twentieth century to espouse a more liberal theology. For those outside the realm of mainstream Christianity, I have produced a section of "one-liners" listing many influential people in various categories.

Many people have helped me, and I list them in the acknowledgment section. In addition, I thank my lifelong friend, the respected, Ted W. Engstrom, who wrote the foreword to this effort. I thank Larry Wallace of Trinity Baptist Church, Lake Wales, FL who allowed me to store all my research books and files there. I thank Mike Stranahan, who financed me substantially during some difficult days. I thank Clarence Sexton, pastor of Temple Baptist Church and president of The Crown College, Powell, TN for encouraging me and for giving me a light teaching load these past few years, in consideration of my research and writing and the need to finish this volume.

Of course, you are going to wonder why your particular Christian "hero" isn't in here, and why certain others are included, I've simply done the best I could with the criteria I established, and as I understood Church history with it's participants.

You may also wonder why I have arranged these entries in chronological order according to their death date. Two reasons: First, so that you can appreciate the flow of history, with all its wonder and foibles, as you see how God used men and women to accomplish His purposes through the years. Secondly, I have for years intended to entitle this work, "The Saints Go Marching In," thinking of the joyful, mixed emotions as each Christian "soldier" laid down his sword and rose to meet his Savior in that Heavenly Kingdom.

May this book be a blessing to you as you take a walk through Church history led by its participants.

Sincerely,

Edward Reese

Edward Reese
Psalm 35:28

In Appreciation

I could not have made this journey without my wife, Margaret, a Proverbs 31 lady. At times, working double shifts, Christian and secular, to make ends meet, I had limited time to give to the family. If I could squeeze in a few hours to work on this project, I would count it a bonus. This is why it took so long. No funding or help for years, just like the tortoise,…plod,…plod,… plodding along. Margaret was always there, in step, beside me, glad that I was happy, helping me, encouraging me, and leading in the raising of our five children. I also appreciate the support of these children: Becky (Mrs. Tom Porter), Scott, Lane, Philip, and Donna (Mrs. Jeff Twilla). They are all Christians and that means so much to us. Scott, of Chicago Heights, IL, is an urban missionary and internet minister. My parents, Ed and Anna Reese, and my brother, Melvin, also contributed much to my life. This book was compiled while I worked in other ministries. The same is true of these fine people listed below, all working intermittently, while involved in various pursuits at home or employed elsewhere. From Flavia to Ryan, God sent us special people. This book could not have happened without their help.

Other key participants who aided me in this work:

1) **Flavia Horne Mullen**. Original Database Architect. Flavia introduced me to the computer age. She took my ancient card files and designed a database capable of expanding with my research. From 1977-2003, she assisted in many areas - including data entry and conversion, research, and editing. She continued to be available as a consultant thereafter. I am grateful for her dedicated work and belief in this project. Flavia managed one of the largest public relations databases in the country, and continues to consult on database and editorial projects. The Mullens have three children, whom she homeschooled, and nine grandchildren. Flavia lives in the Atlanta, GA area with her husband, Dr. John W. Mullen of Energetic Health.

2) **Rebekah Hanks**. In 1997, we hired Rebekah Hanks. She was available four years, full-time summers and part-time the rest of the year, while teaching English and mathematics at The Crown College, Powell, TN. She inserted considerable new material into the older sketches, and entered the bulk of the rest of the sketches into the database. She also helped me move my library and did another round of editing of about three-fourths of the book. She continues in a teaching career in the Minneapolis area.

3) **Dylan and Leah Saunders**. Specialists in graphics. God then brought the ideal couple along to add the dimension of photos and design. They transferred the database into the Quark program, inserted thousands of photos, and ran the chronological order of these 5,000 sketches. They helped, 2001–03, volunteering much of their time and effort. They also inserted some photos I never knew existed. They went into missionary work in Alaska and continue graphics under Saber Design.

4) **Ryan Keiter** produced the finished redesigned product, text, and photos for the publisher. He converted the old Quark files to Adobe InDesign, entered final corrections and helped convert and redesign the various indexes. Special thanks to Josh Tangeman, Brian Allison, Stephen Troell for significant help prior to Ryan's involvement. Also, thanks to Lois Lohman for her assistance to Ryan in helping make the final corrections from the proofreader.

Appreciation (*cont.*)

There have been so many more: Stephanie Smith Alford, Shauna Brockman, Dianne Cannon, Pollie Deeringer, David Evans, Pat Forseth, Melody Frederick, Terri Hamby, Jamie Divens Huling, Christine Jennette, Holly Johnson, Rachel Jones, Karen Keiter, Robin Kent, Doug Koepple, Rebekah Gordon Lowen, Mitch Martin, Brian and Kellie Mullen, Jeremiah Nitz, Tami Orick, Marlina Reese, Cindi Shane, and Sandy Van Vlyman, among others.

Special recognition must go to **Greg Pratt**, computer specialist, to whom we turned for help with technical problems, including the critical database conversion.

My faithful friend, **Kay Griffin**, has helped me for thirty years in many, many ways. Because she has kept my small publishing business alive in Munster, IN, I have been free to concentrate on this work. I cannot thank her properly for her loyalty.

Thousands of people have provided me with data: by telephone, letters, email, faxes, etc. I had hundreds of phone conversations with widows, children, and colleagues of the deceased. I thank them collectively here.

I am grateful for AMG Publishers, Chattanooga, TN for accepting this project for publication.

Overview of the Project
How did I determine who would be included?

1) I have a biography library of over 1,000 books. Some are single volumes on one individual; others have multiple entries. If anyone surfaced in two or more of these books, they were included. Occasionally, as an editorial choice, I would include an individual with only one source.

2) I contacted every Christian organization of major significance, some 1,400, enclosing a questionnaire asking for their listing of CEOs, presidents, directors, etc. With additional follow-up calls, we received data from 90 percent of them.

- Bible schools, seminaries, and a few Christian liberal arts colleges: if the president/deans served 10 or more years, they were included.
- Missionary societies: if the CEOs served fifteen or more years, they were included.
- If it were a denomination, I would determine (by size of denomination) which leaders to include

For example:

Every president of the Southern Baptist Convention is included even though a few served just one year. Other major denominational leaders who served five or more years are included. For smaller denominations, we used the criteria of ten or fifteen years of leadership.

- All presidents of major organizations, such as National Association of Evangelicals, National Council of Churches, Evangelical Foreign Missions Association, Accrediting Association of Christian Schools, Association of Theological Schools, etc. are included.
- For other organizations, we used five-year or ten-year leadership criteria
- I regret that I have neglected the Independent Christian Churches/Churches of Christ in my research. In a future edition, I hope to include some of their leaders.

3) Reese Religious Research has a large division featuring songwriters/composers and their compositions. Using editorial choice, I selected those I felt were most familiar.

4) Then there were those whom I entered simply because they were high profile in the news: such as Tom Landry, Johnny Cash, etc.

5) About two dozen others were recommended.

6) Please note that any name mentioned within a biographical entry in all-capital letters indicates that a separate biographical entry for that person is included in this volume. For example, on page 1 in the entry, "Dionysius the Areopagite," you will see the name "Eusebius of Caesarea." The all-caps style of the name indicates that a full biographical entry also exists in this volume for Eusebius of Caesarea, and you can consult the General Alphabetical Index in the back of the volume for the exact location of this entry.

Educational Data

Because we could not provide stats of education and degrees earned on all, we felt it would be better to concentrate on accomplishments, places of service, and the other biographical information available to us. *Who's Who in America* and *Who Was Who in America* provide excellent material in that field.

Why Study Biographies?

1) Biographies have always been used of God to stimulate more service for Christ. Paul said, "Be ye followers of me as I am also of Christ." Only eternity will reveal how many have been inspired to enter Christian service or to a deeper walk with God as a result of reading such as David Brainerd's journal.

2) Biographies keep the wonderful ministries of many people alive and fresh before us. Many might soon be forgotten unless their challenging stories are brought to the attention of the Christian world afresh.

3) Biographies introduce people to us whom we might not know, or perhaps have misunderstood. In a day when Christians seem to be divided into many "camps," it is hoped that this book will help give all true believers a new appreciation of ministries other than their own.

4) Biographies introduce us to people we will soon be living with for all eternity. The "family of God" is a wonderful family.

"LIVES OF GREAT MEN ALL REMIND US, WE CAN MAKE OUR LIVES SUBLIME, AND DEPARTING — LEAVE, BEHIND US, FOOTPRINTS IN THE SANDS OF TIME..."

- Henry W. Longfellow

Dedication

To the Saints That I Have Missed because there was no reporter or photographer on hand recording their selfless offerings for the cause of Jesus Christ in this world. Three groups stand out.

To the Martyrs

Whether they were fed to lions, beheaded, burned at the stake, tortured, shot, or drowned, they are a noble lot. Some of the more visible individuals are in this volume. But there are many more, seen only by God as they came marching prematurely into heaven. Their memory is sacred to us also. They have provided a heritage and legacy for us.

Recent examples come to mind: the New Tribes missionaries, captured on January 31, 1993, by armed guerrillas in Pucuro, Panama. Dave Mankins, Mark Rich, and Rick Tenenoff were never to be seen alive again by their loved ones.

Another is Nelseev Livan Vasileivich, born in 1952, martyred on July 18, 1972, serving in the Soviet Army. Singled out as a Christian, he was burned with red-hot irons, beaten and forcibly drowned in the Black Sea.

Similar incidents, unknown to the world in general, have been carried out by the thousands throughout history and will continue until our Savior returns. We are debtors to their memories.

World Christian Trends, by David B. Barrett and Todd M. Johnson, lists some of the martyrs (2,550 of them) from all over the world (AD 30–2000 AD).

To God's Hidden People

Especially found in third world nations. We have been unable to even begin to recognize these faithful national pastors and evangelists serving the Lord, traveling the length and breadth of their lands on foot or bicycle, often hungry, living and dying in obscurity. Some are even in America—faithful home missionaries in the mountains of such as Kentucky or working on Indian reservations in such as Arizona. They have sought the favor of God alone and are the true "heroes of the faith." God bless them.

They will all be acknowledged one day, sitting in the front rows of Heaven, receiving their recognition… from the Savior Himself.

To the Unknown

This Christian never made the headlines as a great theologian or a silver-tongued orator. He (or she) is a faithful, consecrated, born-again layman: a foot soldier in the gospel army as a Sunday school teacher, an usher, a singer, a bus worker, a nursery helper, a parking lot attendant, or a prayer warrior—some service unheralded, but vital, in the cause of Christ. His (or her) testimony adorns the Gospel, faithfully witnessing daily "in the temple, and in every house," gladly giving time, talent, and tithe to the Lord.

Having served the Lord in the home, the church, and the world, this Christian will one day hear the Master say, "Well done, thou good and faithful servant: thou hast been faithful over a few things, I will make thee ruler over many things: enter thou into the joy of thy Lord." (Matthew 25:21)

Valiant-for-the-Truth Goes Home

"So he passed over,
and all the trumpets sounded for him on the other side."
(*The Pilgrim's Progress*)

The silver cord is loosened within the holy mount,
The golden bowl is broken, and the pitcher at the fount;
A spirit soars triumphant across Death's swelling tide,
And the trumpets all are sounding on the other side.

He is going to his Father: his courage and his skill,
His sword, he leaves behind him – let him gather them who will;
His marks and scars he carries, witnesses of work well done;
And the trumpets all are sounding for his battles won.

And Christ, his Lord and Master, the One his soul adored,
For whose dear sake he laboured, is now his great Reward;
Forever shall he serve Him, forever see His face;
And the trumpets all are sounding the glories of His grace.

The trumpets all are sounding, with harps' exultant voice
In heavenly music mingling, as many waters' noise;
Through toil and tribulation in triumph has he come,
And the Father's House is ringing with his welcome Home.

And all the holy angels, and all the ransomed, sing:
"O Grave, where is thy victory? O Death, where is thy sting?"
The Lord of Life swings wide the gates of Paradise again,
And all the trumpets answer with an infinite "AMEN!"

- E. Margaret Clarkson

Veronica

c 54
Rome, Italy

Jerusalem, Palestine (Israel)

Woman whose veil retained impression of Christ. Veronica was a legendary, pious, and renowned woman of Jerusalem. According to French legend (thirteenth century), she took the cloth wrapped around her head and gave it to Jesus that He might wipe His face as He carried the cross to His crucifixion on Calvary. When Jesus returned it to her, the impression of His features were upon it. Emperor Tiberius (ruled: 14–37), falling sick, requested Veronica to produce the famed veil, which, when he touched it, cured him. After responding to this summons, Veronica remained in Rome where she bequeathed the cloth to Bishop CLEMENT I OF ROME. It is said to be preserved in St. Peter's Church in Rome. A "Veronica" has become a dictionary noun describing "a cloth (veil or handkerchief) bearing an impression of Christ and resembling the legendary one belonging to St. Veronica." The origin of the legend may spring from a misapplication of a story in EUSEBIUS' *Historia Ecclesiastica*.

Anastasia and Basilissa

April 15, 65–68
Rome, Italy

Martyrs. Anastasia and Basilissa were noble Roman Christian women who were converted to Christianity by the teachings of Apostles Peter and Paul. After the martyrdom of the Apostles, the women allegedly removed the bodies by night and proceeded to give them an honorable burial. When accused of their actions under the persecutions of Christians by Emperor Nero (ruled: 54–68), they proclaimed their Christianity, were cruelly mutilated, and then beheaded.

Linus

Sept. 23, 76
Italy

Volterra, Tuscany, Italy

"Second" bishop of Rome, 67–76. Linus was actually the first bishop of the Christian Church in Rome and predecessor to ANACLETUS I (Many Catholics list Peter as the first bishop of Rome, while most Protestants do not. However, we will follow the official list because of its impact on history. Peter was not identified as the first Roman bishop until the beginning of the 3rd century.) Tradition says Linus was known to Apostles Paul and Timothy, as stated in Scripture (II Tim. 4:21). He appointed the first 15 bishops. Linus also forbade women to enter church with uncovered heads. Mark and Luke were martyred during his tenure. Legend indicates he was martyred under Emperor Vespasian (ruled: 69–79).

Dionysius the Areopagite

c 85
Athens, Greece

Athens, Greece

Greek convert, first bishop of Athens and martyr. Dionysius was led to Christianity by the Apostle Paul (c. 50) and was referred to by Paul in Acts 17:34. He was extolled for his literary attainments and for being a judge of the Areopagus (Supreme Court of Athens that met on a hill named Areopagus). His mystical writings were valued in later eras. Sixth century writings by another Dionysius were wrongly credited to him in the fourteenth century. According to the historian, K353 , Dionysius was the first bishop of Athens and suffered martyrdom under Emperor Domitian (ruled: 81–96).

Anacletus I
Anencletus/Cletus

Rome, Italy

April 26, 88
Rome, Italy

Third bishop of Rome, 76–88. Some claim Linus (second bishop), Anacletus I, and CLEMENT I (fourth bishop) were all consecrated by the Apostle Peter or by Apostles Peter and Paul. Anacletus I is mentioned in the Canon of the Mass (central, unchanging part of the religious service of the Latin church) with respect to the ordination of priests. He drew up rules for the consecration of bishops. Anacletus I had an oratory (chapel or room for private devotions) built for the burial of martyrs. He also was responsible for rules governing ecclesiastical dress. Anacletus I may have died a martyr under Emperor Domitian.

Antipas
Like the Father

90
Pergamus (Bergama), Mysia, Asia Minor (Turkey)

Martyr and first bishop of Pergamus (city in Mysia, Asia Minor that became major Greek kingdom of Pergamum, rising to prominence in the third century). Antipas is the "faithful martyr" referred to by John in Revelation 2:13. Tradition says he was roasted to death in a brazen ox during the persecutions under Emperor Domitian.

Flavia Domitilla

c 100
Pandataria, Ponza Island, Italy

Persecuted matron. Flavia Domitilla was a member of the Roman Domitian imperial family. She was banished for her Christian faith by her cruel uncle, Emperor Domitian, in AD 95, to Pontia (Pandataria) in the Tyrrhenian Sea (west of Naples, Italy). Flavia's husband, Titus Flavius Clemens, Domitian's cousin and nephew by marriage, was beheaded (c 95). One of the oldest catacombs (Christian underground burial chambers, 20 feet—65 feet below ground, covering some 600 acres beneath Rome) on the Via Ardeatina, near Terracina, is known as the Cemetery of Domitilla. This may have been her gift to her Christian brothers. She was the daughter of Emporer Vespasian.

Clement I of Rome

c 30
Rome, Italy

Nov. 23, 100

Fourth bishop of Rome, 88–97. Clement I was converted by the Apostle Paul and possibly mentioned in Philippians 4:3. His *Epistle to the Corinthians* (97) is the oldest specimen of post-Apostolic literature. It is one of the most valuable sources of early church history and the events chronicled in the New Testament, including his testimony regarding the martyrdom of Peter and Paul in Rome. This epistle addressed a need for order in the Church. IRENAEUS wrote that Clement I was a contemporary of the Apostles. He originated the use of "amen" in religious ceremonies and restored the sacrament of confirmation. Tradition says he was banished to Pontus by Emperor Trajan (ruled: 98–117) and martyred by being cast into the sea while tied to an anchor. He was the first of the apostolic fathers (personal associates of the original twelve Disciples of Christ) to die. Early authorities say he died in 97. He believed in spiritual gifts among Christians.

"Prayer is conversation with God."

Evaristus

Greece

Oct. 26, 105
Rome, Italy

Fifth bishop of Rome, 97–105. Evaristus was the son of a Hellenstic Jew of Bethlehem. Because of the increase in the number of Christians, he divided the city into parishes. He organized the first seven diaconates (body of deacons) entrusted to senior priests, which is considered the origin of the present College of Cardinals. Tradition says he was possibly a martyr. He was the first of eleven Greek bishops of Rome.

Ignatius—Theophoros ("God-Bearer")

c 30
Antioch (Antakya), Syria (Turkey)

Oct. 17, 107
Rome, Italy

Martyr, Apostolic Father and third bishop of Antioch, serving c. 69–107. Ignatius was a pupil of John the Apostle. He was among the first to use the term "catholic church" (universal church of Christ), was the first to stress the virgin birth, and to distinguish between bishops and elders. He opposed the Docetists (denied Jesus' life and death for God cannot die) and the Judaizers (Old Testament extreme sabbath keepers). When asked by Emperor Trajan to sacrifice to heathen gods, Ignatius refused. He was arrested and led to Rome by ten soldiers. Christian churches along the way greeted him with love and visited him in prison. He wrote seven important letters while traveling to Rome to face martyrdom. Ignatius passionately embraced his martyrdom as the ultimate godly gift. His epistles to the church at Ephesus, to the church at Rome, and to Greek Bishop, POLYCARP of Smyrna, were invaluable testimonies of the beliefs and internal organization of the early Christians, freely quoting from NT Scripture. When thrown to the lions in the Roman Coliseum, he said, "I would rather die for Christ than rule the world," and "I am the wheat of Christ...that I may be found pure bread."

Alexander I

Rome, Italy

May 3, 115
Rome, Italy

Sixth bishop of Rome, 105–115. Alexander I introduced holy water to bless various objects, including Christian homes. He conceived the usage of holy water mixed with salt in churches and homes to guard against evil spirits. Additionally, Alexander I promoted changes in the ancient service of the Lord's Supper by using bread without leaven and mixing water with wine, moving the ceremony toward the Roman Mass. Some believed he died a martyr, along with two companions, under Emperor Trajan, but this is unlikely.

Eustace

c 118

Roman officer under Emperor Trajan. Eustace stated he was converted while hunting, when confronted with the vision of a stag bearing a crucifix between its antlers. He refused to make sacrifices to pagan deities and was thus martyred with his family, under Emperor Hadrian (ruled: 117–138). Tradition says that he was originally a Roman general, Placidas.

Sixtus I
Xystus I

c 75
Rome, Italy

125

Seventh bishop of Rome, 115–125. Sixtus I was a Roman citizen by birth. His family home covered the location now occupied by the St. Mary-in-Broad-Street Church. His contri-

The Saints Go Marching In

bution relates to the celebration of communion. He established ordinances directing that only the clergy should touch the sacred vessels used in communion and ordered the hymn "Holy, Holy, Holy, Lord God of Sabbath" be sung during the observance. Sixtus I governed during the time when church leadership was the common prelude to martyrdom. It cannot be verified that he was a victim of Emperor Hadrian's persecutions, although some believe he suffered martyrdom.

Symphorosa
c 127

Female martyr and rebel against widow burning. After her husband suffered martyrdom, Symphorosa refused to obey the command of Emperor Hadrian to sacrifice herself and thus take part in the pagan practice of widow burning. This heathen rite was consecrated by the imperial palace at Tibur (Tivoli), 15 miles northeast of Rome. Symphorosa was cruelly tortured and then killed with her seven sons.

Papias
c 60
c 130
Hierapolis, Phrygia, Asia Minor (Turkey)

Apostolic Father and bishop of Hierapolis. IRENAEUS states that Papias was a friend of POLYCARP and thought to have been a disciple of the Apostle John. He was among the first to write about the origins of the Gospels. Papias testified that Mark was the earliest of the four Gospels and affirmed that Matthew wrote in his native Hebrew tongue (this has been doubted since the Reformation), although the majority of the New Testament was written in Greek. His five-volume work, *Exposition of the Lord's Oracles* (explanation of the sayings of the Lord), has been lost since 1218. It was a collection of the words and works of Christ. Papias was a fervent believer in Christ's imminent return. His martyrdom, during Emperor Hadrian's tenure, has been questioned.

Quadratus
c 130

Asia Minor (Turkey)

Christian apologist in Asia Minor. Quadratus was one of the first apologists (literary defenders of Christianity). He claimed to have been a disciple of the Apostles, and was a student of IGNATIUS and POLYCARP. He wrote a carefully reasoned apology, presenting the Christian faith to Emperor Hadrian, in which he contrasted Christianity to Jewish and pagan worship. This *Apology of Christianity* was presented during the era of Christian persecutions, 124–29, when Quadratus was probably bishop of Athens. Although only fragments of his writings are preserved, his intellectual insight is credited with the logical foundation of his appeal and its acceptance.

Telesphorus
Jan. 5, 136

Greece

Eighth bishop of Rome, 125–136. Telesphorus took the reins of the church at a time when it was reeling from the havoc of Hadrian's persecutions. Some historians falsely credit him with establishing the 40 days of Lent celebration and the midnight Christmas mass, among three masses on Christmas night. These probably started later. He inserted new prayers into the mass. He composed the "Gloria in Excelsis Deo" and, according to EUSEBIUS OF CAESAREA, Telesphorus was referenced as a martyr—dying during the reign of Emperor Hadrian. He is the first Roman bishop whose martyrdom is verified.

Hyginus

140

Athens, Greece

Ninth bishop of Rome, 136–140. He determined the different prerogatives of the clergy and defined the levels of the ecclesiastical hierarchy. Hyginus instituted the use of godparents at baptism, to assist the newly born, and decreed that all churches be consecrated. Tradition says he died a martyr. He was a philosopher.

Marcianus Aristides
Aristrides/Aristeides

Aug. 31, 141

Greek apologist and philosopher. Aristides was an eloquent Athenian philosopher who continued to wear his philosopher's robe even after his conversion. His apology for the Christian faith protested anti-Christian slanders and persecutions. This treatise was highly esteemed by the ancient church as the earliest defense of the faith. It sought to prove that Christians understood the eternity of God, were in possession of the full truth, and had guidelines by which they endeavored to live their lives. The *Apology of Aristides* (c 139) was written to Emperor Hadrian (ruled: 117–38) or Antonius Pius I (ruled: 138–61).

Hermas

c 60
Rome, Italy

c 150

Apostolic Father and writer. Hermas wrote the often-quoted, near-canonical *Shepherd of Hermas*, which was a description of contemporary Christian life. It was highly regarded by the Eastern church for its early teaching on the need for repentance. Hermas transformed his personal religious experiences into a series of ten parables that contain twelve moral "commandments." He appears to have been a freed slave-turned-merchant who repented of evil practices after a series of visions. Hermas probably was the brother of bishop Pius I.

Polycarp

c 69 (or before)
Smyrna (Izmir), Asia Minor (Turkey)

Feb. 23, 155
Smyrna (Izmir), Asia Minor (Turkey)

Apostolic Father and martyred Greek bishop of Smyrna. Polycarp was believed to have been a disciple of the Apostle John, who appointed him bishop. Polycarp's sanctity of life and attacks on heresies made him a very influential figure. He visited Rome, disagreeing with Bishop ANICETUS over the correct date to celebrate Easter. One of his epistles survived, the *Epistle to the Philippians* (150 or earlier), in which he quotes from 19 NT books. He also compiled and preserved the *Epistles of Ignatius*. He contributed greatly to the development of the church and the formation of the Canon of the New Testament. Polycarp defended Christianity against the following: Marcionism (rejected OT, incarnation, resurrection), calling Marcion (wealthy ship owner snubbed by orthodoxy), "the first born of Satan;" the Valentinians (Valentinus: Gnostic philosopher); and the Gnostics (salvation through knowledge, rather than faith; believed they had secret knowledge of religious mysteries, "lodge" mentality). Polycarp was arrested during the tenure of Emperor Antonius Pius I in Smyrna, tried and condemned by an angry mob, and burned to death for his faith. His dying statement immortalized him, "Eighty-six years I have served Him, and He hath done me no wrong. How can I speak evil of (blaspheme) my King?"

Pius I

c 90
Aquilia, Italy

July 11, c 155
Rome, Italy

Tenth bishop of Rome, 140–155. Pius is believed to have been the brother of HERMAS of Rome making them both freed slaves. He was forced to deal with a mounting number of heretical sects espousing a diversity of peculiar doctrinal options. Cerdo of Syria (a Gnostic teacher and forerunner to Marcion), professed orthodoxy, but actually was teaching heresy in secret (The Old Testament God is known and righteous while the Father of Jesus is unknown). Marcion arrived in Rome spouting his Marcionism in harmony with the Gnostic heresies, while Valentinus (Valentinians) chimed in with intellectual questions twisting the vague points in Scripture to create doctrinal doubts. It was left to Pius I to sort through this stormy hodge-podge of activity, such as excommunicating Marcion. JUSTIN MARTYR proved to be a great encourager and wise friend to him. His *Rules for the Conversion of Jews* was considered important. He is alleged to have established the date of Easter on the first Sunday after the full moon in March. Tradition says he died a martyr, but no evidence supports this. He was the first sole bishop of Rome. Prior, it was collective responsibility shared with others.

Justin Martyr
The Philosopher

c 100
Flavia Neapolis/Shechem (Nablus), Jordan

c 165
Rome, Italy

Converted Platonic philosopher and apologist. Upon Justin's conversion, through the witness of an old man on the seashore (c 133), he became a teacher and author who defended his faith against scornful critics. He went to Rome (c 150). His writing explained his stand: *First Apology* [dedicated and addressed to Emperor Antoninus PIUS I (c 150–55)], *Second Apology*, and *A Dialogue with Trypho the Jew* (c 160). Justin was active in Palestine and Ephesus as a lay teacher. He opened the first school of Christian philosophy in Rome and continued his written messages, *Against Heresies* and *Against Marcion*. Justin attempted to reconcile Christian doctrines with pagan culture on the basis of prophecy, miracles, and ethics. His writings show familiarity with 13 New Testament books, quoting from Matthew 43 times. In Rome, when he refused to sacrifice to pagan gods, Justin was scourged and beheaded for his faith—martyred with six others during the reign of Emperor Marcus Aurelius (ruled: 161–80). After his death, the title of "Martyr" was added to his name.

Anicetus

Syria

166
Rome, Italy

Eleventh bishop of Rome, 155–166. Anicetus conferred with the visiting POLYCARP and leaders of the Church in the East regarding when Easter should be observed. Anicetus and those at Rome held Easter services on Sunday—the date varying with regard to the vernal full moon. POLYCARP and the Easterners proposed a celebration on the evening of the fourteenth of Nisan (April) regardless of what day it was, even if that day might be the Jewish Passover or a Sunday. The Easter date conflict was further defined at the Council of Nicea in 325, with the Western view (dating back to Anicetus) becoming the accepted global date, though never embraced by Eastern Orthodox churches. Anicetus was the first bishop who commanded priests to shave their heads in the form of a crown, opposing long hair on clergy. He devoted much of his administration to fighting the heresies of the Marcionites and Gnostics. Anicetus died a martyr during the reign of Emperor Marcus Aurelius. He was the first of six Syrian bishops of Rome.

Sylvanus

c 170
Rome, Italy

One of seven martyred brothers. Sylvanus was a persecuted Christian under Emperor Marcus Aurelius. He was cast from a cliff to his death while his soon-to-be martyred mother, Felicitas, stood by, exhorting him to remain faithful to Christ.

Felicitas

c 170
Rome, Italy

Martyred Roman widow. Felicitas was a lady of high rank. She was martyred along with her seven sons at Rome during the reign of Emperor Marcus Aurelius. Felicitas, who publicly practiced the Christian religion, took many from the worship of the immortal gods, who were the guardians and protectors of the empire. Publius, the prefect of Rome, caused the mother and her sons to be apprehended and brought before him, and, addressing her, said, "Take pity on your children." Then, turning herself towards her children, she said to them, "My sons, look up to heaven, where Jesus Christ with His Saints expect you. Be faithful in His love, and fight courageously for your souls." Januarius was scourged to death with whips loaded with plummets of lead. The next two, Felix and Philip, were beaten with clubs till they expired. Sylvanus, the fourth, was thrown headlong down a steep precipice. The three youngest, Alexander, Vitalis, and Martialis, were beheaded, and the same sentence was executed upon the mother four months after.

Aristo

c 171

Pella, Macedonia (Greece)

Jewish Christian apologist. Aristo was the reputed author of *Dialogue Between Jason and Papiscus Concerning Christ*. This literary creation presented a discussion between a Jewish Christian and an Alexandrian Jew, whom the Christian wins to Christ. It was written between 140 and 170, using the Aquila Version of the Bible (Jewish translation of Old Testament from Hebrew into Greek: c 140). Aristo may be the first apologist against Judaism.

Soter

Soterus

April 22, 174

Fondi, Campania, Italy

Twelfth bishop of Rome, 166–74. Soter originated the practice of priests fasting before officiating at services. He also mandated that women were not to touch sacred vessels nor approach the altar. During his tenure, Easter became an annual church feast. He ratified marriage a sacrament valid only if blest by a priest. Soter was one of the earliest written opponents of Montanism. DIONYSIUS OF CORINTH referenced Soter as a bishop flowing with fatherly kindness. Some believe he died a martyr, but evidence lacks.

Montanus

c 175
Phrygia, Asia Minor (Turkey)

Founder of Montanism (extreme prophecy and ridged moral norms) and reformer. Upon conversion, Montanus felt his duty was to recall the church to primitive purity and holiness (c 157). This movement (Montanism) gained a large following among the excitable and religiously-sensitive people of Asia Minor. Prophecy and spiritual gifts were stressed, along with severe asceticism and strict church discipline, sharing many elements with modern Pentecostalism. Montanus proclaimed himself to be the Paraclete (Comforter) promised by Jesus Christ (John 14:16), and his followers, the spiritually "elite" Christians. Montanus further claimed divine inspiration and prophesied a rapid Second Coming. Montanism spread rapidly, reaching Rome in 170, and producing from among its followers, the illustrious theologian TERTULLIAN. Its message eroded into vigorous legalism. He and his followers were excommunicated around 175. Although suppressed by Byzantine Emperor JUSTINIAN I (ruled: 527–65), it continued into the Reformation era as an underground movement protesting the formalism and worldliness of the official church. Montanus was one of the earliest leaders that recognized the church's drift from the New Testament.

Blandina

Lyons, Gaul (France)

June 2, 177
Lyons, Gaul (France)

Roman slave girl and martyr. Blandina refused to renounce her faith and was hideously tortured. As one of the 48 Martyrs of Lyons, she was forced to watch as her companions were slain. Blandina was put through a slow, gruesome execution in the town amphitheater. When the goring of wild beasts failed to kill her, she was bound to a stake, continued to be gored alive, then stabbed and burned. The historian, EUSEBIUS OF CAESAREA, preserved the account of her death, along with the tragic martyrdom of the city's leading pastor. This persecution befell them for refusing allegiance to pagan gods and was sanctioned during the reign of Emperor Marcus Aurelius. Her dying words were, "I am a Christian, and no evil is among us."

Pothinus

87
Asia Minor (Turkey)

June 2, 177
Lyons, Gaul (France)

First bishop of Lyons. Pothinus is believed to have been a disciple of POLYCARP who sent him from Smyrna to minister in Gaul. He was mistreated in prison, and finally stoned. Pothinus was one of the 48 martyrs of Lyons, bitterly persecuted under Emperor Marcus Aurelius. He was reputed to have been past age 90 at the time of his death in prison. IRENAEUS succeeded him as bishop.

Prisca (Priscilla)

c 178

Leader of the New Prophets and fanatical Phrygian prophetess. Prisca proclaimed the speedy end of the world and the coming of Christ. She and another woman, MAXIMILLA, abandoned their husbands to follow MONTANUS (c. 175). Their headquarters were in Perpuza, Phrygia, Asia Minor. They capitalized on the popular dissatisfaction with the church's wealth and worldliness. Prisca was a woman of high noble character, earnestly seeking to help restore the discipline of the early Church.

Maximilla

179

Leader of the New Prophets and fanatical Phrygian prophetess. Maximilla claimed to have special communication directly from the Holy Spirit. She and another woman, PRISCA, abandoned their husbands to follow the reformer, MONTANUS. She gave her wealth to the church and lived on freewill offerings. Maximilla prophesied in Perpuza, Phrygia, Asia Minor, proclaiming the imminent end of the world.

Hegesippus
Father of Church History

c 180

Greek Church historian. Hegesippus was a Jewish convert to Christianity who, after 20 years (157–177) in Rome and visiting most of the important centers of Christianity, wrote the history of the first 150 years of the church: *The Memorials* (133). It was considered more a historical apology than a history of the church, although it was the first attempt to chronicle events after the Book of Acts. Hegesippus' message supported orthodoxy and denounced Gnosticism. He ministered in Syria, Greece, and Rome—blaming all heresies on Judaism. Next to EUSEBIUS OF CAESAREA, who used this work extensively, he was the foremost early church historian.

Tatian

110   180
Assyria (Iraq)   Edessa (Urfa), Mesopotamia (Turkey)

Syrian writer and philosopher. Tatian was converted at Rome (c 150) by the teachings of JUSTIN MARTYR, and became his disciple and pupil. He also ministered in Syria. He combined a harmony of the four Gospels into his widely read *Diatessaron*—for a long time the only life of Christ available in Syria. He wrote a noted apology, *Address to the Greeks* (176), denouncing Greek mythology and philosophy. Tatian later went to the East and lapsed into heresy following the doctrines of the Encratites (no marriage, meat eating or wine) and participated in Gnostic teachings, entering a school in Mesopotamia (Iran/Iraq). He finally escaped to a celibate life of asceticism (c 173). Tatian was one of the earliest apologists.

Theophilus

c 130   183
Persia (Iran)   Persia (Iran)

Apologist and sixth bishop of Antioch, Syria, 169–83. Theophilus was an Eastern philosopher who was converted from paganism by reading the Scriptures. He addressed his *Apology of Christianity* to Autolycus, his learned heathen friend. Theophilus' writings sought to show the falsity of idolatry and the truth of Christianity. His writing fame surfaced after he gained prominence as the bishop of Antioch. He was the first known writer to use the term "Trinity" to reference "the Godhead." Theophilus is considered one of the early Church Fathers.

Claudius Apollinaris

c 185

Hierapolis, Phrygia, Asia Minor (Turkey)

Bishop of Hierapolis, 171– c 185. Apollinaris was an active and esteemed Christian writer. He used his knowledge of heathen literature to refute heresy, especially Phrygian Montanism. He also took a leading part in the Paschal Controversy (disagreement over the date of Passover and Easter celebrations). His chief writing was *Apology*, addressed to Emperor Marcus Aurelius some time after 174. Only fragments remain of this great work. His other three apologies were *Against Greeks*, *Against the Montanists*, and *Concerning Truth*. Apollinaris remained loyal to the Roman Empire.

Publius A. Aristides
Theodorus

117   189
Adriani, Mysia, Asia Minor (Turkey)   Smyrna (Izmir), Asia Minor (Turkey)

Greek philosopher and rhetorician (teacher of oration). Aristides, living in Athens about 140, wrote a stirring appeal in his *Apology to Emperor Antoninus Pius* about the Christian faith. He pointed out the helplessness of ancient cults to meet human aspirations and impressively stated the meaning of the Gospel, the idea of God, and the moral superiority of Christians. Later, Aristides was a priest at Smyrna, and became a trusted friend and advisor to Emperor Marcus Aurelius. This relationship may have so impacted Aurelius that it shortened and localized the duration of his persecution of Christians, 177–78. When an earthquake destroyed Smyrna in 178, Aristides persuaded Aurelius to rebuild the city. Little was known of Aristides' work until, 1889, when it was discovered in a monastery on Mt. Sinai (Mt. Horeb), Sinai Peninsula (Arabia).

Eleutherius

189
Rome, Italy

Nicopolis (Epirus), Greece

Thirteenth bishop of Rome, 175–89. Eleutherius was a deacon of the Roman Church, 154–75 and abolished some Jewish customs concerning the purity of foods. He was an opponent of the Montanists, Marcionites, and Valentinians. There are several legends, supported by English historian, BEDE, tied to Eleutherius regarding a Lucius, British king, who requested teachers be sent to assist many subjects, such as himself, who were ready to embrace Christianity. Some historians assert that the legend was invented to corroborate the Roman origin of British Christianity. It can be substantiated that Eleutherius received two emissaries, Elfan and Medwy from the West. He made Elfan, who founded the first church in the British Isles, a bishop at Llandaff (smallest British city, near Cardiff, South Wales). Eleutherius is also said to have sent missionaries, Damian and Fugatius, to evangelize and help establish the first schools in the British Isles. This whole account is doubted by others. Eleutherius was said to have shared counsel with IRENAEUS. He died a martyr, says an unreliable ninth-century list.

Melito

190

Asia Minor (Turkey)

Martyr, apologist, theologian and bishop of Sardis (capital of Lydia, Asia Minor). Melito was one of the earliest apologists and a great theologian. He wrote his Apology between 169 and 180, to refute the accusations made against the Christian Church by the Roman government. He never married. Melito produced several works, including *On the Pasch*. He leaned toward Montanism, which emphasized emotional spirituality. Although an ascetic, Melito was significantly knowledgeable to address current dogmatic questions. He was considered the first "pilgrim," since his travels were motivated by a desire to personally experience locations having historic Christian significance. He died a martyr, during the reign of Emperor Commodus (ruled: 180–92).

Athenagoras

c 190

Athens, Greece

Apologist, philosopher, and educator. Athenagoras attempted to refute charges made against Christians and to soften the hostility of the Roman government. He wrote *Apology for the Christians* (c 177) to Emperor Marcus Aurelius, and later *On the Resurrection of the Dead*, using a classical style. Through his writings, Athenagoras defended Christians against charges of atheism (ignoring Roman gods), incest, and cannibalism (some sects were accused of drinking blood "in secret" during the communion). He was a converted Greek Platonistic philosopher. Athenagoras is thought to have been the first head of the Catechetical School (religious training before baptism or church membership) in Alexandria.

Dionysius of Corinth

Corinth, Greece   c 195
                       Corinth, Greece

Bishop of Corinth, 170–95. Dionysius was a famous preacher and apologist who gained distinction for his zeal, moderation, and peaceful spirit. His piety, learnedness, and eloquence were well known. Dionysius wrote seven pastoral letters to various congregations. Many of his epistles were lost, although fragments were preserved by the historian, EUSEBIUS OF CAESAREA. Dionysius died a martyr under Emperor Septimus Severus (ruled: 193–211).

Polycrates

c 120   c 195

Bishop of Ephesus, Lydia, Asia Minor. Polycrates led the Eastern churches in their squabble with Rome and the Western churches over the dates for Easter celebrations. He called a council (synod) Dec. 31, 192, to consider the matter. As a result, Polycrates was excommunicated by VICTOR I, bishop of Rome—increasing the bitterness of the controversy. The Asia Minor churches continued their observances of Easter on the fourteenth of Nisan (April) in defiance of Rome.

Victor I

Africa   July 28, 199
                       Rome, Italy

Fourteenth bishop of Rome, 189–99. One of the main accomplishments of Victor I's incumbency was the acceptance of Latin as the official language of the church, replacing Greek. His challenges included answering the Valentinian heretical writings and discrediting the message of Theodotus of Byzantium (questioning divinity of Christ: Jesus seen as only a supernaturally endowed man). The major conflict revolved around resolving the Easter date controversy. Victor I grew weary over the arrogant stand of the Eastern churches (bishops of Asia and Africa who celebrated according to the Jewish view and not the Roman) and threatened to excommunicate the vocal elements. He did excommunicate POLYCRATES. IRENAEUS represented a strong faction of clerics who protested Victor I's brash response. The fact that Victor I withdrew his position indicates that he did not have supremacy over other churches, although there was a notable development of his claim to exercise jurisdiction over all other churches, the first to assert such authority beyond his local diocese (Easter date celebration pronouncement). He secured the release of Christians condemned to the mines of Sardinia by having dealings with the imperial household. Victor I also decreed that any kind of water could be used in baptism in an emergency. Some say he died a martyr, but no evidence supports this. He was the first of three African bishops of Rome.

Militiades

                       c 200

Apologist. Miltiades was a philosopher in Asia Minor who became a Christian (c 160–170). He wrote, *Apology of Christian Philosophy* to Emperor Marcus Aurelius, defending Christianity against pagans and Jews. There is evidence that he also wrote against the Montanists and the Gnostics. Scant excerpts of his writings are in historian EUSEBIUS' work. Miltiades also opposed the Valentinians.

Noetius

                       c 200

Smyrna or Ephesus, Asia Minor (Turkey)

Teacher in Asia Minor, 180–200. Noetius originated a somewhat heretical theological viewpoint whose adherents were called Modalistic Monarchians (God is unknowable, except for his manifestations of which Christ is one. Monarchianism means rule of one: God has sole authority over Christ, a "power" or "mode" of God, and the Holy Spirit. This denies the Trinity and causes conflict in accepting the deity of Christ while maintaining the unity of God.) Surrounded by a heathen polytheism (more than one god), he tried to emphasize the unity of God the Father through his misdirected approach. Noetius also feared that Logos Christianity (a divine force which connects God to man—the "Logos" (word) is Jesus, a term which was later replaced by "son," when the Trinity was referenced), then gaining acceptance, undermined his Monarchianistic unity. A similar cult was Sabellianism [denies equality of Trinity; God's names (Father, Son, Holy Spirit) change with His roles].

Leonides

c 155 *April 22, 202*
Alexandria, Egypt

Philosopher, father of Origen, and martyr. Leonides must have been a prominent rhetorician and Christian philosopher to be considered a threat by Laetus, governor of Egypt. In 202, when Roman Emperor Septimus Severus enacted a rigid law against the spread of Christianity and Judaism, Leonides was one of the early victims. His eldest son, ORIGEN, was 17 when Leonides was imprisoned. As a loving tutor to his son, who became one of the greatest early church theologians, Leonides instilled the desire to be a worthy Christian. Later, ORIGEN wrote his father, Leonides, a touching letter, encouraging him to accept with courage and joy, the crown before him—exhorting him to be faithful to the end. Leonides was beheaded, his property confiscated and his family reduced to severe poverty. ORIGEN assumed the support of his mother and six brothers after his father's martyrdom.

Irenaeus

c 125/130 *June 28, 202*
Smyrna (Izmir), Asia Minor (Turkey) Lyons, Gaul (France)

Greek Church Father, apologist, apostle to Gaul, and second bishop of Lyons. Irenaeus was the spiritual son of POLYCARP. As a missionary to Gaul, he settled in Lyons where, after the terrible persecutions of 177 by Emperor Marcus Aurelius, he succeeded POTHINUS, as bishop. He describes charismatic gifts, especially prophecy. He warned against Gnostics who fabricated the gifts to win the naive. Irenaeus dealt with the dangerous Gnostic sects in his great work, *Against the Heresies* (180) and continued to write extensively for the next ten years. In his famed book, he made 1800 quotations from the New Testament, implying they had for some time been considered Scripture. He defended Eastern Christianity during the Easter date controversy. Irenaeus is considered the first writer to deserve the title of theologian, using both the Old Testament and New Testament in building his theology. Irenaeus presented the premillennial view that Christ would return to rapture the church before the tribulation and prior to His triumphant Millennial Rule. Irenaeus is thought to have died a martyr under Emperor Septimus Severus. He evangelized most of Lyons, France. His favorite Bible verse was II Timothy 2:2.
"He became what we are, to make us what He is."

Pantaenus

 c 203
Sicily, Italy Carthage (near Tunis), North Africa (Tunisia)

Greek philosopher, missionary, teacher, and presbyter (in Scripture, it meant elder/mature Christian. By later second century it began hierarchical climb to "bishop." By Middle Ages it was translated to "priest." CALVIN restored true "presbyter/elder" role later adopted by Reformed and Presbyterian churches). Pantaenus was the head and first catechetical teacher at a school in Alexandria, Egypt, 180–90, until he was replaced by CLEMENT OF ALEXANDRIA, whom he had mentored along with ORIGEN. Historian EUSEBIUS OF CAESAREA wrote that he was an enthusiastic and ardent preacher, gaining the nickname "Sicilian bee," indicating his industriousness and sweet countenance. Pantaenus was also a zealous missionary who traveled to Yemen and across the Gulf of Aden to Ethiopia, Africa. According to JEROME, Pantaenus wrote several commentaries; but, with the exception of two small fragments, his works have all been lost. He was not heard of after 203. Pantaenus was trained under the Stoics (philosophy started by Zeno of Citium in 300 BC—which taught that wise men should be free of emotion, indifferent to pain or pleasure and submissive to laws of nature) and influenced by Emperor Commodus. Some historians place his death at 213 or 216.

Felicity
Felicitas

March 7, 203
Carthage (near Tunis), North Africa (Tunisia)

Slave and martyr. Felicity, Revocatus (also a slave), Secundulus, Saturus, and PERPETUA were consigned to prison for becoming Christians. Their faith and heavenly visions sustained them through many accusing interviews and mistreatments. Felicity refused to deny her faith and to sacrifice to Emperor Septimus Severus. Her daughter was born in prison shortly before her martyrdom and adopted by fellow believers. Felicity's death resulted from cruel blows from a gladiator's sword after being gored by an enraged cow in the amphitheater.

Viba Perpetua

c 180
North Africa

March 7, 203
Carthage (near Tunis), North Africa (Tunisia)

Martyr. Perpetua was the 22-year-old wife of a prominent merchant and the mother of a young son. Her mother and one brother were Christians. Her father and the other living brother were pagans. An edict of 202 forbade conversion to Judaism or Christianity. As a result, Perpetua was condemned for treason, since her belief prevented her from sacrificing to Emperor Septimus Severus or his son, Geta. She was initially imprisoned in a house and received visitors, including her elderly father with his pleas to forsake the "absurd religious views" which she had recently adopted. Saturus, who had introduced Christianity to Perpetua and her slave girl, FELICITY, voluntarily joined them, baptizing them while they were all awaiting martyrdom in prison. After being exposed to the ravaging of wild beasts, Perpetua died from sword piercings in the Gladiator Arena. She left a beautifully written text in Latin, *The Acts of Perpetua and Felicity*, describing her beliefs, spiritual vision and imprisonment. TERTULLIAN later edited and validated her testimony.

Clement of Alexandria
Titus Flavius Clemens—Alexandrinus

c 150–155
Athens, Greece

Dec. 5, 215
Palestine (Israel)

First known Christian scholar. Clement was converted from paganism and became the leader in the Catechetical School in Alexandria, Egypt. He taught ORIGEN, who later assumed Clement's role as the school's leader. Under Clement's leadership, 190–203, the school became the center of Christian scholarship. He was the first to attempt to reconcile Platonism (physical objects are transitory representations of unchanging ideas which alone give true knowledge) with Christian doctrines. Clement endeavored to intellectually achieve a unity of all truth and claimed knowledge to be the goal of Christian perfection. He reasoned that as the law brought the Jews to God, so Christian philosophy brought the Greeks to Christ. Clement wrote several distinguished books including *Exhortation to the Greeks* (apology for Christianity) and one of the oldest hymns still sung, "Shepherd of Tender Youth" (music by FELICE DE GIARDINI, 1,550 years later). Other works were *Tutor* (exposition of Christian ethics), *Miscellanes* (higher life of Christian knowledge), and *The Rich Man's Salvation* (exegete on Mark 10:17–31). He fled to Jerusalem in 202 during the persecution of Emperor Septimus Severus. He called the New Testament books "The Divine Scriptures," and quotes from nearly all these books in his writings.

"We cannot be friends both to the world that is, and the world to come."
"Philosophers are children until they have been made men by Christ."

Zephyrinus

Rome, Italy

217
Rome, Italy

Fifteenth bishop of Rome, 199–217. Zephyrinus was an indecisive bishop who tried ineffectively to slow down the hot disputes over Christology (theological interpretation of the person and work of Christ). The conflict between learned apologist HIPPOLYTUS and the Monarchians was hurting the church. Zephyrinus issued an edict allowing unchaste sinners into the legalistically prone community. To many, Zephyrinus seemingly favored the heretics, further entangling him in controversies over doctrinal matters, such as excommunicating TERTULLIAN. HIPPOLYTUS and TERTULLIAN were frustrated with his weakness and vacillation in answering the challenges of Montanism, adoptionism, and Sabellianism. He also encouraged young people 14 years of age and over to receive Communion at Easter. He died a martyr. He was the first Roman bishop to be buried in the catacombs.

Hermogenes

c 150
Tarsus, Cilicia, Asia Minor (Turkey)

c 220

Greek philosopher and rhetorician. Hermogenes was a painter by profession. Emperor Marcus Aurelius sent for him when Hermogenes was but 15 years old; his fame as a precocious, extemporaneous speaker preceded him. When introduced to the emperor he said, "Behold I am come to you. . .an orator requiring a pedagogue, an orator still looking forward to maturity." He was appointed an instructor in oratory at age 17. Hermogenes taught in Rome and his rhetorical treatises were widely used as textbooks. His *Manual of Rhetoric* was a standard work on the subject. He did all his writing before the age of 25, when his health plunged. Considering that he lived close to 70 years, it is valuable to note that his intellectual prowess gave him wisdom beyond his years. Although he believed that matter in itself was evil, he still put forth his theory of the "Eternity of Matter" in order to reconcile the goodness of God with the existence of evil, which TERTULLIAN refuted in a treatise. It was believed that Hermogenes had Gnostic tendencies. Around 200, Hermogenes arrived in Carthage, North Africa. He did not teach a thorough going Gnostic system, but probably in the belief that he was not contradicting the Church's faith, attempted to complement it by certain propositions taken from philosophy. He denied the creation of the world out of nothing.

Calixtus I

July 11, 154
Rome, Italy

Oct. 14, 222

Sixteenth bishop of Rome, 217–222. In his early years, Calixtus I was the slave of a Christian master who had put him in charge of a bank. Deposits were lost due to carelessness, rather than dishonesty. Calixtus I fled, thinking he would be the scapegoat, but was caught and sent to labor in the mines on the Island of Sardinia. Bishop ZEPHYRINUS recalled Calixtus I, made him a deacon/counselor, and put him in charge of the public Christian burial grounds. He was responsible for the excavation of the famed catacombs on the Via Appia, where 46 Roman bishops (popes) and some 200,000 martyrs were buried. He excelled, unifying the surrounding land and defining the property so that it became the first land claim held by the Church. Upon the death of ZEPHYRINUS, he was made bishop. Calixtus I excommunicated Sabellius, a false teacher, about 220, for promoting heresy. Calixtus I was criticized for his tolerance toward converted heretics. His relaxed discipline policy against sexual indiscretions, and permitting married priests and remarried bishops to remain active clerics, caused the wise apologist, Hippolytus, to set himself up as an antipope. Tertullian, as a Montanist, also reacted harshly to Calixtus I's liberal tendencies. It is alleged that his martyrdom, under Emperor Alexander Severus (ruled: 222–35), was triggered by his tendency to pronounce judgments contrary to Roman civil law. He is alleged to have been beaten to death with clubs, and his remains were thrown into a well. His name appears in the oldest Roman martyrology, but there was no persecution during his bishopric, so his martyrdom is questionable.

Bardesanes

July 11, 154
Edessa (Urfa), Mesopotamia (Turkey)

223
Edessa (Urfa), Mesopotamia (Turkey)

Syrian hymn writer and first missionary in the East. As one of the first missionaries after apostolic days, Bardesanes may have led Agbar Mar-Manu, ruler of Edessa, to Christ. When Edessa fell to Rome, Bardesanes maintained his bold confession. He also went to Armenia; preaching and writing. Bardesanes wrote against the heresy of Marcion. The hymns of Bardesanes were widely used until the many new hymns of the Syrian father, Syrus Ephraim, were introduced to the Edessa community in the fourth century. Harmonius, his son, also wrote hymns—a total of 150 from both men. At times he was influenced by Valentinus' (died: 160) gnosticism.

Tertullian
Quintus Septimius Florens Tertullianus
Father of Latin Theology

c 160
Carthage, North Africa

c 225
Carthage (near Tunis), North Africa (Tunisia)

Theologian and first Latin ecclesiastical writer. Tertullian was the son of a Roman army officer. Before his conversion, he was a lawyer. He married and was converted (c 197) after observing the courage of Christian martyrs. Tertullian is celebrated as the first important Christian Latin writer. He devoted himself to the mastery of the Scriptures and became a presbyter. Many of his words, such as "person, Trinity, New Testament, etc.," were adopted into our English usage. He attacked Modalistic Monarchianism/Sabellianism. Tertullian's *Apologeticus*, written around 197 to the governors of the empire provinces, is a pungent defense of Christianity. He also wrote *Persecution of Heretics*. More than 30 of his works have survived. In 203, he joined the Montanists, but in 207, he formed his own sect, the Tertullianists, which lasted until the fifth century. He practiced healing, prophecy, and tongues. He separated "apostles" (spirit fully) from "believers" (spirit partially). He lived in Rome and Carthage. He was excommunicated by Bishop Zephyrinus of Rome. Tertullian's wisdom was hampered by his propensity toward exaggeration. He wrote extensively from 196, until his death. He quotes more than 1,800 different passages from the New Testament, making 7,200 references, 3,800 from the Gospels, 200 from John, etc. He uses 22/23 NT books as inspiration.

"The blood of the martyrs is the seed of the church."

Tibertius

April 14, 230/232
Rome, Italy

Martyr. Tibertius was converted to the Christian faith by Valerian, his brother, who had been led to the Lord by his virgin wife, Cecilia. Tibertius steadfastly refused to burn the required pinch of incense in reverence to Roman deities as decreed by Emperor Alexander Severus. After their conversion, the brothers assumed the job of burying the bodies of the martyrs, another violation for which they were subsequently arrested. As a result, Tibertius and Valerian were both beheaded at Rome on the Via Labicana ("way through" or "main street" in the ancient Latin town of Labici) for their allegiance to Christ. Their remains, plus those of

CECILIA, were found in a burying ground later named Cemetery of Tibertius, believed to have been where the brothers had previously labored.

Urban I of Rome

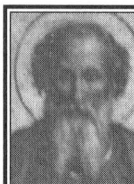

Rome, Italy

May 23, 230

Seventeenth bishop of Rome, 222–30. Urban was the son of Pontianus. a Roman nobleman. Little is known of his tenure. He was not persecuted as were his predecessors since the emperor was the tolerant Alexander Serverus, whose mother was a Christian. He was responsible for CECILIA's conversion. Urban consented to the acquiring of property by the church.

Cecilia
Cecily

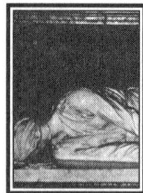

c 170
Rome, Italy

Nov. 22, 230
Rome, Italy

Martyr. Cecilia was a Roman citizen, educated as a Christian. In spite of her vow of celibacy, Cecilia was compelled to marry Valerian, a young nobleman. She converted Valerian—who respected her celibate vow—and who, in turn, won his brother, TIBERTIUS to the Lord. Cecilia also converted Maximus, a would-be executioner. In defiance of the Christian witness established there, the Roman soldiers attempted to martyr her in her own home. When an over heated bath failed to suffocate her, she was taken out and beheaded. After her martyrdom, bishop URBAN I baptized over 400 converts in Cecilia's home. Her martyrdom occurred during the reign of Emperor Alexander Severus. Cecilia was a patroness of music; writing hymns herself, singing beautifully and playing several musical instruments. The Church of St. Cecilia was established where her home once stood. Some historians have her death on Sept. 16, 177.

Demetrius

c 126
Alexandria, Egypt

Oct. 9, 231
Alexandria, Egypt

Bishop of Alexandria, 189–231. Demetrius headed the church during the rise of the great scholar, ORIGEN. He permitted ORIGEN, in 203, to gather students and reorganize the Catechetical School. Demetrius, however, was perturbed when, as a layman, ORIGEN preached in Caesarea, Palestine in 215 to a group of bishops. As ORIGEN's fame increased, Demetrius, who had stood by him through several earlier conflicts, felt snubbed and was jealous when ORIGEN chose to be ordained in Caesarea in 230. As a result, Demetrius banished him from Alexandria. Demetrius appointed HERACLAS to succeed ORIGEN as head of the school at Alexandria. Around 200, Demetrius sent forth PANTAENUS as a missionary to Yemen and to nearby Ethiopia. Demetrius was known for his intuitive spirit and lived for 105 years. HERACLAS succeeded him as bishop.

Felix M. Minucius

c 235/250

North Africa

First Latin apologist. Born a pagan, Minucius remained a layman after his conversion. His chief apology, *Octavius*, was a dialogue between a pagan (Caecilius) and a Christian (Octavius). The pagan confesses his error and asks for Christian instruction. In this work, educated paganism is refuted. His treatise is one of the earliest known examples of Latin Christian literature (other than TERTULLIAN), although it had limited doctrinal input. Minucius lived most of his life in Rome, serving as a Roman legal advocate. He wrote before 200.

Pontian
Pontianus

Rome, Italy

Oct. 235
Tavarolia, Sardinia, Italy

Eighteenth bishop of Rome, 230–35. Pontian called a synod in 232 to confirm the decrees of Demetrius against Origen's teachings. He ordered the chanting of the Psalms. Pontian was condemned to a life of slavery in the Sardinian mines when Emperor Maximinus issued an edict against Christians. While exiled on Sardinia, Pontian was reconciled to Hippolytus (his rival and antipope), and was also able to bring his former adversary back to "The Church." Suffering in the slave camp, Pontian abdicated his religious position to Anterus, September 28, 235, the first Roman bishop to do so.

Anterus

Magna Grecia, Italy

Jan. 3, 236
Rome, Italy

Nineteenth bishop of Rome, 235–36. It is alleged he reigned for only 40 days. He ordered that the acts and relics of the martyrs, called the "scrinium," be gathered together and kept in churches. He, himself, died a natural death. He is buried in the papal crypt of the Catacomb of Calixtus I.

Hippolytus

c 170

Aug. 13, 236
Sardinia, Italy

Apologist, teacher, writer, and bishop of Porto, Italy. Hippolytus was a pupil of Irenaeus. As a philosophical and literary teacher, he refuted many ancient heresies. Hippolytus was considered the West's theological equivalent to Origen in the East. When Calixtus I was chosen bishop in 217, Hippolytus clashed with the laxity of the church's position regarding heresies and degenerate Christians. He withdrew from the Roman Church, creating the first schism, and supporters made him the first antipope (rival to pope) (217–35) through the reigns of Calixtus I (217–22), Urban I (222–30), and Pontian (230–35). Hippolytus was exiled with Bishop Pontian to the Island of Sardinia (c 235) by Emperor Maximinus (ruled: 235–38), where they both died from their sufferings. He wrote several books: *Philosphumena or A Refutation of all Heresies* (discussed pagan origin of all heresies) in ten books, and *The Apostolic Tradition* (contained an early form of The Apostles' Creed). He accused Zephyrinus and Calixtus I, Roman bishops, of Sabellian heresy.

Sextus J. Africanus

c 160
Jerusalem, Palestine (Israel)

c 240
Nicopolis (near Alexandria), Egypt

Historian, scholar, and apologist. Africanus made his home for years at Emmaus, Palestine, 195–240, but traveled extensively throughout Asia Minor. Impressing Emperor Alexander Severus, Africanus was commissioned to organize his public library in Rome. His greatest writing was *Chronographia*, a history of the world covering the 5,700-year period from Creation (dated at 5499 b.c.) to the reign of Emperor Heliogabalus (ruled: 218–22), skillfully combining both sacred and secular history. Unfortunately, most of his works have been lost, including his 24-volume *Cesti* (encyclopedic work covering a full range of topics). The majority of Eastern churches adopted Africanus' chronology of the Ancient World, called "The Alexandrian Era." He studied under Origen.

His work was greatly used by historians. There were cities named Nicopolis in Cappadocia, Egypt, Greece, and Palestine at this time, giving rise to speculation as to his precise place of death.

Heraclas

c 170

248

Scholar and bishop of Alexandria, 233–48. Heraclas and his brother, Plutarch, were converted sons of pagan parents. They lived in Egypt, 204–248, and were taught by ORIGEN. Heraclas was appointed by ORIGEN as his assistant and then for two years became his successor at the Catechetical School in Alexandria. Heraclas later joined Bishop DEMETRIUS in opposing ORIGEN and followed DEMETRIUS in the Alexandrian excommunication of ORIGEN. DIONYSIUS OF ALEXANDRIA succeeded him as bishop.

Apollonia

249
Alexandria, Egypt

Martyr. Apollonia suffered martyrdom during the Decian persecution (Emperor Decius, ruled: 249–51). She was seized and, together with other Christians, lost all of her teeth as a result of severe blows to her jaws. The pagans who lit a death pyre asked her to curse Christ. She paused briefly, and then leaped directly into the fire. Apollonia had been very active in the Church at Alexandria. This persecution was ignited by secular events stemming from the celebration of Rome's 1,000-year anniversary (founded in 753 BC) commencing in 247.

Alexander of Comana

c 250

Comana, Pontus, Asia Minor (Turkey)

Bishop of Comana. Alexander was known as the "charcoal burner" because of his preference for menial assignments to escape worldly honors. His merits were discovered by GREGORY THAUMATURGUS resulting in Alexander's reluctant acceptance of the bishopric of Comana. Alexander was considered a learned philosopher. He was martyred by fire during Emperor Decius' persecution.

Polyeuctes

c 250
Melitene, Cappadocia, Asia Minor (Turkey)

Converted Roman military officer and martyr. Polyeuctes served with the famous Twelfth Thunder Legion of the Roman army. He was attracted to the Gospel by Nearchus, a friend. While stationed at Melitene, he became a victim of Emperor Decius' harsh reprisals against Christians. Polyeuctes refused to worship Roman idols and consequently destroyed several Roman temples. He and Nearchus were both beheaded on the orders of Polyeuctes' father-in-law, Emperor Decius. Beginning in Paris, France in 1643, their tragedy became the subject of several operas and plays, bringing the biography of Polyeuctes out of historical obscurity. Polyeuctes was greatly venerated by Greek Orthodox followers.

Fabian

Jan. 20, 250
Rome, Italy

Rome, Italy

Twentieth bishop of Rome, 236–50. Fabian reputedly was elected when a dove landed on his head, which was interpreted by the electorate as a divine sign. He quickly showed organizational genius by dividing Rome into seven districts and assigning deacons to look after each area. Fabian also appointed notaries to record the deeds of the martyrs and had many of the catacombs repaired. Fabian served during the days of Emperor Philip (the Arabian) (ruled: 244–49), but died a martyr under his successor, Roman Emperor Decius, as a result of brutal treatment in prison. The exodus of so many Christians from Rome under Decius encouraged an increase in monastic living. He was greatly respected.

Christopher
Christ Bearer

July 25, 250

Syria

Martyr embodying legend. Christopher was a Syrian baptized by Babylas, bishop of Antioch (reigned: 237–50). Few actual facts are known about his life, but dozens of legends have developed. Roman Martyrology testifies of a man named Christopher, a Canaanite of great stature, who sought to serve the "greatest-biggest" king. While searching, he came across a child needing to cross a swollen stream. Christopher hoisted him on his shoulders to take him across. As they progressed, the water got deeper and faster and the child got heavier and heavier. Upon reaching the other side, Christopher said, "Child, it felt as if the weight of the world were upon my shoulders." The child replied, "Thou hast borne Him that created and made all the world. . . I am Jesus Christ, the King whom you are seeking to serve." This third century Christopher was a large person with a strong build who was remembered for carrying travelers across rivers where there were no bridges. Emperor Decius had Christopher shot with arrows and beheaded when flames failed to kill him. The concept of "looking to Christopher—looking to Christ" for sustaining help influenced the Roman custom of making large statues.

Anastasius (1)

251

Martyr and former tribune (defender of the Roman people) in Emperor Decius' army. Anastasius was assigned to the execution squad that put Christians to death. He was so impressed with the courage and conviction of the would-be martyrs that he became a Christian. His family was beheaded along with him.

Agatha

c 216
Palermo or Catania, Sicily, Italy

Feb. 5, 251
Catania, Sicily, Italy

Martyr. Agatha was born into a noble Sicilian family and was famous for her beauty and gentleness. She refused the advances of Quintianus, the Roman governor of Sicily, which resulted in her torture at Palermo. Remaining true to the Christian faith, Agatha, a virgin, was martyred during the Decian persecution at Catania while imprisoned there. It is recorded that she was scourged, burnt with hot irons, torn with hooks and placed on a bed of live coals and glass. Agatha is mentioned in the Canon of the Mass and is the patroness of Malta. She said as she died, "Our nobility lies in this, that we are servants of Christ."

Alexander of Jerusalem

c 175
Cappadocia, Asia Minor (Turkey)

March 18, 251
Caesarea, Palestine (Israel)

Martyr, bishop of Cappadocia and later bishop of Jerusalem in 222. Alexander went to school with ORIGEN in Alexandria. He became a bishop in Asia Minor at the beginning of the third century, and was imprisoned in 204 under Emperor Septimus Severus' persecutions. CLEMENT OF ALEXANDRIA visited him there. When released in 212, Alexander was made co-adjutor (assistant) bishop and then sole bishop of Jerusalem. He was the gatherer of an excellent library in Jerusalem. Alexander defended ORIGEN against attacks by DEMETRIUS, offering him safe refuge in Jerusalem and ordaining him. ORIGEN then served in Alexander's diocese as a theology teacher. Emperor Decius attempted to have Alexander killed, but the wild beasts could not be induced to attack him. He died in chains in a Caesarean prison.

Cornelius

Rome, Italy

June 14, 253
Civita Vecchia, Italy

Twenty-first bishop of Rome, 251–53. (Prior to Cornelius taking the bishopric, there was a 15-month papal vacancy as the church regrouped from the violent Decian persecutions.) During his short reign, Cornelius was harassed by religious controversies and the appearance of the rival bishop, NOVATIAN, who became the second antipope. NOVATIAN challenged him for being too lenient to those who had lapsed from the faith during persecutions and by allowing them to return to the church. Cornelius died a martyr with 21 others, having been banished by Emperor Gallus (ruled: 251–53) for refusing to offer sacrifices to pagan gods. Cornelius was a friend of CYPRIAN.

Origen
Father of Systematic Theology—Adamantius

c 185
Alexandria, Egypt

254
Tyre, Caesarea, Palestine (Israel)

Greek Christian writer and teacher. Origen was a voluminous writer (c. 205 on) and an influential Biblical scholar. His father, LEONIDES, was martyred in 202. At age 18, Origen, the intellectual protégé, became a teacher, following his mentor, CLEMENT, as the sporadic head of the Catechetical School at Alexandria, 211–32. A popular uprising with soldiers plundering the city and shutting the schools caused him to flee to Caesarea in 215. He returned in 219 with a stronger ascetic orientation and a renewed determination to concentrate on his writing full-time. His unique teaching style placed difficult Scriptures within an allegorical setting. He required the services of several secretaries, hired by a wealthy convert, to copy and publish his lectures. Origen defined amillennial views (no literal 1,000 year rule). His book, *On First Principles*, was the first major attempt to define theology. Origen lectured, wrote, and later founded a school at Caesarea, after being ordained a presbyter by ALEXANDER OF JERUSALEM in 228. Origen's masterful *Hexapla* (c. 250) was a six-column Bible with various texts resembling the modern parallel study Bibles. His most famous work was *Contra Celsum*, a defense of Christianity against Celsus, a platonist philosopher. As he proceeded to clarify his theology, it translated into a disbelief in the physical resurrection and an eternal hell. This unorthodox interpretation caused his expulsion from Alexandria in 231 and from Palestine in 235. He returned to Palestine (238), suffered persecution (250), was imprisoned during the Decian persecution and tortured to death under Emperor Valerian (ruled: 253–59). The question of his orthodoxy has been bitterly discussed ever since. He claimed 21 NT books were genuine, because they were received everywhere.

Lucius I

Rome, Italy

March 5, 254
Rome, Italy

Twenty-second bishop of Rome, 253–54. Lucius I was deported shortly after his election in 253, but returned after Emperor Gallus died. He won the people's approval for his leniency toward those who had lapsed from the faith during Emperor Decius' persecution, but who were penitent. He forbade men and women, not related, to live together, and that clergy should not live with deaconesses. His tombstone is in the catacomb of CALIXTUS I. He was put to death by Emperor Valerian. Though honored as a martyr, some say Lucius I could have died a natural death.

Stephen I of Rome

Rome, Italy

Aug. 2, 257
Rome, Italy

Twenty-third bishop of Rome, 254–257. Stephen I engaged in a heated controversy regarding the subject of baptism with CYPRIAN. Stephen I insisted that the meaning of the baptism ordinance lay not in the purity or orthodoxy of the priests, but in the faith of the believer—hence re-baptism of heretics is valid. Stephen I upheld Rome's teaching authority against CYPRIAN's views, and the three North African Church Councils supported him. Several times, however, CYPRIAN and other bishops over-ruled Stephen I, indicating the Roman bishop lacked widespread authority over other bishops. He also had continuous strife with the followers of NOVATIAN. Stephen I died a martyr during Emperor Valerian's persecutions. He was beheaded during a religious gathering in the Catacombs of CALIXTUS I.

Novatian

Phrygia, Asia Minor (Turkey)

258
Rome, Italy

Roman presbyter, theologian, and martyr. Novatian was converted from Stoicism after a near-fatal illness. He started a schismatic movement, the Novatians, which in reality was a continuation of Montanism. History credits Novatian as beginning the "Puritan Party" in the church. He was the first Roman theologian to publish treatises in Latin and was offended when CORNELIUS, a man of lesser ability, was elected as Roman bishop in 251. In opposition, Novatian had himself consecrated by his sympathizers, the second antipope. He opposed the easy reception of those who had lapsed during the time of persecution back into what he called "The Church of Compromisers." Novatian was excommunicated (c 257) at a Council held in Rome. He died a martyr under Emperor Valerian. His important work, *On the Trinity*, refuted the Monarchians/Sabellians. Novatianism (Separatist movement championing true Christology and doctrinally accurate treatment of the Trinity) continued until the sixth century. His successors were called Cathari (the clean) in the eleventh century.

Sixtus II

Greece

Aug. 6, 258

Twenty-fourth bishop of Rome, 257–58. Dispite a meek disposition, he settled the disputes that had risen under his three predecessors, the reconciling of the churches of North Africa and Asia Minor on the question of baptizing "heretics." He affected the final burial of the mortal remains of Paul and Peter. He died a martyr during the reign of Emperor Valerian. Of all the Roman bishops included in this book, he was the best and most revered.

Lawrence of Rome

Huesca, Aragon (Spain)

Aug. 10, 258
Rome, Italy

Martyred deacon of Rome. Lawrence, while serving under Bishop SIXTUS II, was martyred three or four days after the bishop. This event occurred during the persecutions of Emperor Valerian. According to legend, his heroic death—from slowly being roasted on an iron bed over an open fire—resulted in many conversions. Lawrence was martyred because of his faithful administration of church funds in contradiction to secular direction. When asked for the church treasures, he gathered a crowd of the old, poor, sick, and crippled.

Thascius Cyprian

c 200
Carthage, North Africa

Sept. 14, 258
Carthage (near Tunis), North Africa (Tunisia)

Martyred bishop of Carthage, 248–58. Trained in rhetoric, Cyprian was a gifted and wealthy lawyer who was converted in 246, after talking to a church elder. He wrote on theology and practical matters, being influenced by TERTULLIAN. He took a strict stand against those who had faltered in persecution under Emperor Valerian. Cyprian, however, did allow those who recanted to return to the church. Unfortunately, he advanced some non-Biblical teachings (authority of bishops over an area, Rome as the principle Church, importance of infant baptism and doing penance, etc.). The Decian persecution, 249–51, forced him into hiding, but he returned in 251. He conducted seven councils, the last one in 256. He produced over 65 letters, one of which, *De Mortalitate*, was written to comfort and fortify his flock during the terror and desolation of the plague that ravaged North Africa, 252–54. Cyprian organized Christians to help others during this bleak time, exhorting them that it was their duty to show "mercy and charity to all." His other writings included *Outside the Church, No Salvation*, and *On the Unity of the Church* (251). Cyprian was banished to Curubis (pleasant, healthy desert city on the peninsula, 50 miles from Carthage) in 257. He quoted from Scripture largely in his 81 letters and 12 treatises. He was beheaded a year later outside of Carthage. Cyprian said as he died, "I am a Christian and cannot sacrifice to the gods."

"Outside the church, no salvation."

Denis
Dionysius of Paris—Denys—Apostle to the Gauls

Italy

Oct. 9, c 258
Paris, Gaul (France)

First bishop of Paris. Denis and six other bishops were sent to Gaul as missionaries from Rome. Having made many converts in Paris (c 250) and establishing a church on an island in the Seine River (known as La Cite in Paris), he was brought before the Roman governor. After cruel tortures, Denis was beheaded along with his preacher, Rusticus, and his deacon, Eleutherius, during the reign of Emperor Valerian. To further insult the magnitude of his ministry, those pronouncing the death sentences had the martyrs thrown into the Seine River, putting other Christians at risk if they tried to rescue them for proper burial. A basilica and a monastery were erected over his tomb at Catulliancus (a suburb of Paris), later known as St. Denis. In modern times a department (state/province) in France was named Seine-Saint-Denis. Some historians place his death at 272 or 290.

Patroclus

Jan. 21, c 259

Martyr. Patroclus staunchly stood by his commitment to Jesus Christ during Emperor Valerian's persecution. He was a respected citizen and beloved churchman of Troyes, Gaul (France). Under Governor Aurelian, he escaped when authorities attempted to drown him in the Seine River. He was recaptured, suffered ghastly torture, and finally beheaded.

Dionysius of Alexandria
Dionysius the Great

c 190 / 195
Alexandria, Egypt

265
Alexandria, Egypt

Bishop of Alexandria, 247–65. Dionysius received a philosophical education, was converted after reading the Apostle Paul's Epistles and attributed his growth in Christian thought to ORIGEN. Dionysius headed the well-known Catechetical School at Alexandria (232) before becoming bishop (247). He fled in 251 to avoid persecution under Emperor Decius, was banished, 257–60, under Emperor Valerian, but returned to his see (jurisdiction of a bishop) in 260. His bishopric was troubled by revolts, the plague, and famine. Dionysius was considered more an ecclesiastical administrator than a theologian. His writings, *On Nature* and *On Promises*, popularized ORIGEN's teachings. Dionysius corresponded widely with the clergy and was a foe of Sabellianism. In the third century, he was the most eminent prelate besides CYPRIAN. He accepted all the NT books except II Peter and Jude.

Eusebius of Laodicea

Asia Minor (Turkey)

c 268
Laodicea, Asia Minor (Turkey)

Bishop of Laodicea, 263–68. Eusebius spent most of his career, 247–63, as a deacon in Alexandria under DIONYSIUS OF ALEXANDRIA. After a siege in 260 by Emperor Gallienus (Valerian's son; co-emperor, 253–60, ruled alone: 260–68), Eusebius helped the needy through their hardships and an accompanying plague. He also risked his life to help Christian martyrs during the persecutions of Emperors Decius and Valerian. Revered for his saintliness, Eusebius participated at the Roman Church Council that condemned Paul of Samosata (Monarchian heretic), bishop of Antioch (reigned: 260–72), for teaching Christ was a "mere man."

Dionysius of Rome
Denis

Turio, Greece

Dec. 26, 268
Rome, Italy

Twenty-fifth bishop of Rome, 259–68. Dionysius was a precise thinker and an outstanding theologian. In 262, he summarized doctrinal issues from a synod at Rome, which became the basis for orthodox Christology. His efforts toward defining the nature of Christ and the Trinity saved the Western church many bitter wrangles over semantics (word usage to produce a specific effect or definition) at the Council of Nicea in 325. He was also involved in the Subordinationism Controversy (anti-Trinitarian doctrine) and was in dispute with DIONYSIUS OF ALEXANDRIA on doctrinal matters. Dionysius of Rome reorganized the church after the Valerian persecutions and sent help to the Church of Caesarea when it was invaded by barbarians (c 268). The barbarians also stormed the gates of the Roman Empire during his tenure. He reorganized the parishes of Rome and obtained liberty for Christians from Emperor Gallienus. Also, in 268, he was among those who condemned Paul of Samosata.

Valentine

Feb. 14, 269
Rome, Italy

Martyred Roman priest. Valentine was active on behalf of the martyrs during the persecutions under Emperor Claudius II (ruled: 268–70). As a result, Valentine was arrested and beheaded. He was famous for the love and charity he spread to others. The Valentine's Day association was of pagan origin, though it can be assumed that his many kind and gracious acts caused the equating of his name with this lovers' festival. Sending Valentines on February 14 (Valentine's death date), somehow originated in a heathen rite celebrating the worship of mythological characters Juno (Roman goddess—protector of women) and Jupiter (Juno's sister/wife). Another legend cites his deathdate as the day of note when birds begin to pair—hence the reference to "love birds" in association with Valentine's Day.

Gregory Thaumaturgus
Theodorous—Gregory of Neocaesarea

c 210/213
Neocaesarea, Asia Minor

c 270
Neocaesarea (Niksar), Pontus, Asia Minor (Turkey)

Greek Eastern Church father and bishop of Neocaesarea, 244–70. The name Thaumaturgus means "wonder-worker" and was given Gregory because of reputed miracles associated with his efforts. Though raised in a pagan home, he was converted at Caesarea by the teachings of ORIGEN. He returned to Pontius in 238/39, where there were only 17 Christians. By the time he died, some 30 years later, there were only 17 non-Christians there. He wrote *Declaration of Faith* and *Eulogy on Origen*, along with several other worthy writings that solidified him as an ardent defender of the Trinity. He attended the Synod of Antioch in 265. Gregory introduced martyrs' commemorations in place of pagan festivals.

Felix I

Rome, Italy

Dec. 30, 274
Rome, Italy

Twenty-sixth bishop of Rome, 269–74. During the controversy with Paul of Samosata over the Trinity, Emperor Aurelian (ruled: 270–75) backed Felix I with a decree stating that church buildings in Antioch should be given only to those whom the Roman bishop decrees. This support demonstrated Rome's expanding influence. He asserted the divinity and humanity in Christ, two natures in one person. He began the custom of burying martyrs under church altars and of celebrating mass on their tombs. He also wrote an important letter defining the unity of Christ (God-man). Felix I at one time was believed to have been martyred under the persecutions of Emperor Aurelian, however, others say he died a natural death. He is buried in a catacomb of CALIXTUS I. He was one of the least-known bishops of Rome.

Commodianus

c 200

c 275

Oldest known Christian Latin poet. Commodianus was born in a pagan home and most likely lived in North Africa. He accepted Christ through his personal study of the Scriptures. He was a scholar of the Western school of thought and may have become a bishop. The apologetic nature (defensive stand) of his work has value to church history, although his theology is often unreliable. *Doctrines in Verse* and *Against Heathen Gods* were some of his works.

Eutychian(us)

Luni, Tuscany, Italy

Dec. 7, 283
Rome, Italy

Twenty-seventh bishop of Rome, 275–83. Eutychian is reputed to have established regulations for the burial of the dead. He had ordered martyrs' remains be covered with a cloak. He also instituted the blessing of the crops. Since he served in an era lacking military conflict or religious persecution, he was able to concentrate on the status of the church, bringing it stability and organization. At this time, Christian cemeteries began. Previously, the catacombs, built under the city, were required for Christian tombs. After martyrdom, he was buried in the catacomb of CALIXTUS I on the Appian Way.

Novatus

c 285

Lenient presbyter at Carthage, North Africa. The total focus of Novatus' career revolved around how the church dealt with Christians who "hid their faith" to save their lives during the time of persecution. He became irate when CYPRIAN was elected bishop of Carthage in 248, because he regarded CYPRIAN entirely too severe with those who had lapsed from the Church. Novatus appointed Felicissimus (a wealthy layman), as deacon in Carthage, enabling him to gain control of funds to assist the "lapsed." They formed a schismatic group in 250, who welcomed any and all. Novatus was excommunicated in 251, but later moderated his stand and embraced Novatianism.

Maurice Tiberius

286
Agaunum, Switzerland

Martyred commander of the Theban Legion (a group of Egyptian Christians serving in the Roman army). Maurice was the son of Chromatius, a prefect {chief administrative officer} of Rome. He refused to follow an order from the future emperor, Maximian (co-emperor; ruled: 286–305, co-emperor in the West; ruled: 306–308) to subdue a revolt by Christian peasants in Gaul (France). Maurice and his entire legion, including Vitalis, Candidus, and Exuperius, were executed at Agaunum (St. Maurice-en-Valais) during Emperor Diocletian's reign (ruled alone: 284–86; co-emperor: 286–305). St. Maurice and the Theban Legion still exist in Switzerland and northern Italy.

Vitus

c 274
Sicily, Italy

c 286/303
Lucania, Italy

Martyred boy with healing power. Vitus' life story is clouded in the mist of legend. He was baptized a Christian without his parents' knowledge. His father Hylas, a senator in Sicily, tried to dissuade him and threatened harm unless he renounced his faith. Vitus, a young boy of seven to twelve years of age, along with his tutor, Modestus, and his nurse, Crescentia, escaped to Lucania; guided by an "angel." Everywhere he went he cured people, especially those with strange neurological disorders, and led many to Christianity. In Rome, he cured the son of Emperor Diocletian. Since he wouldn't sacrifice to pagan gods, his healing powers were attributed to sorcery. Many tortures were unsuccessfully afflicted on Vitus and his guardians. Debilitated from their suffering, an "angel" is said to have intervened and led them back to Lucania where they expired peacefully. Vitus became the protector of epileptics and the patron of sufferers from many illnesses, especially chorea (a disease causing erratic movements of the limbs – St. Vitus' Dance). Vitus and his companions were logged as martyrs under the Diocletian persecution.

Crispin and Crispinian

Oct. 25, 287
Soissons, Gaul (France)

Lay missionary martyrs. Crispin and Crispinian were brothers of a noble Roman family who went to Gaul to labor for the conversion of the pagans. They lived at Soissons and supported themselves through their shoemaking trade at night, devoting most of their energies to preaching during the day. They were successful missionaries who were beheaded during Emperor Diocletian's persecution, suffering cruel tortures administered by his colleague, co-emperor Maximian.

Sebastian

c 255
Narbonne, Gaul (France)

Jan. 20, 288
Rome, Italy

Healer and Roman soldier martyr. Sebastian was raised in Milan where he became a Christian. Although he was averse to military life, in 283 he joined the ranks hoping that, as a soldier, he could bear a strong testimony and assist martyrs in their suffering. Sebastian's excellent record and strong character gained him posting as an officer in the Praetorian Guard (imperial bodyguards). He is alleged to have worked many miraculous cures: restoring lost speech, curing gout, and healing plague victims. He quietly spread the faith, leading many soldiers to Christ. During an attempt to execute him in the Roman Coliseum, he was horribly wounded with arrows. He was finally clubbed to death by command of the irate Emperor Diocletian, who had ordered him to desist from witnessing. Sebastian's body was cast into the city sewer.

Faith

Oct. 6, 290
Agen, France

Young martyr. Faith could be the embodiment of a multitude of faithful martyrs whose strength became the source of numerous embellished stories that, through the years, have encouraged many. Faith was a young woman who was very strong in her Christian belief. She was summoned to answer for her faith before Dacian, the local procurator (officer in the Roman Empire having administrative responsibilities). She answered, "My name is Faith and I endeavour to have that for which I am named." When asked to explain her religion, she replied, "I have served Christ from my infancy and to Him I have consecrated myself." Faith remained steadfast, refused to sacrifice to Diana (goddess in Roman mythology) and was burned to death during Emperor Diocletian's reign.

Caius

April 22, 296
Rome, Italy

Dalmatia, Illyricum (Croatia + Bosnia/Herzegovina)

Twenty-eighth bishop of Rome, 283–96. He made strict requirements for being ordained a bishop. Although a nephew of Emperor Diocletian, Caius was believed to have died during the emperor's bloody persecution of Christians, though not at the hands of Diocletian. He is believed to have suffered for eight years, surviving in the catacombs before being martyred. He is buried in the catacomb of CALIXTUS I.

Cosmas and Damian

Sept. 27, 302/303
Aegeae, Cilicia, Asia Minor (Turkey)

Physicians and martyred laymen. Cosmas and Damian were twin brothers who came from the Eastern church in Arabia to the Aegeae on the Bay of Alexandretta (south coast of Turkey) where they practiced their profession as physicians and missionaries. They labored to advance the Christian faith, and it is said they accepted no money for their services. They refused to denounce their faith at the bidding of Governor Lysias. The brothers suffered martyrdom under Emperor Diocletian, being tortured and then bound hand and foot and cast into the sea. Churches were built in their honor in Constantinople and Rome.

George
Protector of the Kingdom of England
Christian Hero of the Middle Ages

Cappadocia, Asia Minor (Turkey)

April 23, 303
Nicomedia (Izmit), Bithynia, Asia Minor (Turkey)

Military leader and martyr. George entered the Roman army, but left when the persecutions under Diocletian and Maximian (co-emperors) began. George is one of those half legendary, half historical figures about whom reliable data is lacking. The legend of George slaying the dragon began in the sixth century and attached George to the area where Perseus had slain the sea monster that threatened the virgin Andromeda. George's bravery became an "Emblem of the Faith" that encouraged the Crusaders in their mission to rid the Holy Land of the Muslims. This warrior "saint" became very popular in England during the reign of King Edward III (ruled: 1327–77) and was adopted as the patron (special guardian) of England. It is believed that George was arrested and tortured, after testifying to his faith before Emperor Diocletian.

Florian

c 230

c 304
Lorch, Austria

Military martyr. While a soldier in the army of Emperor Diocletian, Florian, known for his miracles of healing, was confronted as to the source of his power. He promptly confessed his Christian faith. He was severely beaten and then drowned in the Enns River at the junction where it meets the Danube River. His body, found with a stone tied around his neck, was later taken to Rome. In 1183, Pope Lucius III (reigned: 1181–85) related Florian's martyrdom to King Casimir of Poland who in turn made Florian the patron of Poland. He is buried under an AUGUSTINE monastery in Scharding, Austria.

Anastasius (2)
The Younger

304

Venice, Italy

Martyr. Anastasius was a cloth cleaner from a city near Venice who moved to Dalmatia, a city in the Roman province of Illyricum (Croatia and Bosnia/Herzegovina—formerly Yugoslavia). He refused to conceal his faith and proudly painted a cross on his door. Anastasius was put to death by drowning during the persecutions of Emperor Diocletian.

Agnes

c 292
Italy

Jan. 21, 304
Rome, Italy

Young martyr. Agnes was a young, beautiful, Roman Christian who was exposed and tormented in brothels, because she refused to abandon her faith and marry the son of the prefect of Rome. She steadfastly refused all offers of marriage, claiming she was the "Bride of Christ." When flames failed to kill her, she was taken out and beheaded under the persecutions of co-emperors Diocletian and Maximian; her chastity preserved. Agnes is believed to have lived a mere twelve years. She said as she died, "I will willingly receive into my bosom the length of this sword that thus married to Christ, my spouse, I may surmount and escape all the darkness of this world." Her grave is near the Via Nomentana (Road of the Saints/Way of Great Names).

Vincent of Saragossa

Osca (Huesca), Spain

Jan. 22, 304
Valencia, Spain

Martyred Spanish cleric. Vincent was a deacon at the Church of Saragossa, Spain. By age 20, Vincent was serving under Valerius, bishop of Saragossa. His unswerving Christian faith caused him to undergo horrible tortures under co-emperors Diocletian and Maximian's persecutions. The account of his sufferings, known as *Acts*, was widely circulated, especially in the Mediterranean countries. Vincent was one of the earliest Spanish clerics to suffer martyrdom and defend the faith at Valencia. A raven perched upon a millstone is often the symbol of Vincent.

Alban

Hertfordshire, England

June 22, 304
Verulamium (St. Albans), England

First known British martyr. Alban was a pagan serving in the Roman army. He sheltered a fugitive Christian priest/clerk, possibly named Amphibalus who had been influential in Alban's conversion and helped him to escape. The fury of the pagans turned on Alban since he was disguised in the priest's cloak. Asclepiodotus, the prefect, demanded his death in submission to the persecution decrees of Emperor Diocletian. Alban was arrested and put to death in the priest's place. He was beheaded near the city of Verulamium, which now bears his name. His courage as a new convert so impressed his executioner that he too accepted Christ and asked to be martyred. Alban performed many miracles en route to his execution. He said as he died, "The sacrifices you offer are made to devils ... I worship the true and living God ..." In 793, Mercian King Offa (ruled: 757–96) founded a large monastery upon his place of death.

Marcellinus

Rome, Italy

Oct. 25, 304

Twenty-ninth bishop of Rome, 296–304. The last Roman bishop to be martyred. Marcellinus was falsely accused by the Donatists of apostasy (renouncing one's faith). He was a seemingly faithful churchman, although he may have yielded to offer incense to pagan gods and hand over Scriptures to forestall persecution. It is believed that after repentance for his act of weakness he sought execution, a holy death, to atone for his transgression. Marcellinus was beheaded under the reign of Emperor Diocletian, when churches and sacred text were destroyed with great fervor. During his tenure, the Roman catacombs were fortified, several Christian cemeteries were enlarged and new ones were dedicated. The theologian AUGUSTINE believed that Marcellinus was unfairly discredited and dismissed the account of his regression. However, he also erroneously denied his martyrdom. Marcellinus' death left the Church of Rome without a leader for more than four years.

Anastasia (1)
The Younger

Dec. 25, 304
Sirmium, Pannonia (Hungary)

Prison missionary and martyr. Anastasia was a Roman noblewoman who was kind to the poor and ministered to those in prison. This brave woman was the wife of Publius, a pagan, who, according to one version of her life, betrayed her to the authorities. Another story relates how Publius forbade her to visit the prisoners, and then he was killed while traveling to Persia. After his death, Anastasia followed Chrysogonus, her Christian "counselor" to Aquileia in the Roman province of Venetia, Italy. As she continued her prison ministry, her faith was brought to the attention of the jailers. She was arrested, wrote two poignant letters (that have been preserved) from prison and was martyred under Emperor Diocletian.

Januarius

272
Benevento or Naples, Italy

Sept. 19, 305
Puteoli (Pozzuoli), Italy

Martyred bishop of Benevento, Italy, 303–05. Januarius went to visit Christian prisoners in Naples, was found guilty of sharing their faith, and sentenced to destruction by the mauling of wild beasts. When the starved animals could not be induced to attack, Januarius and two companions were beheaded in compliance with the persecution decrees of Emperor Diocletian. His head and two vials containing his blood are kept in the chapel of the cathedral in Naples, Italy, and are exhibited at specified holy festivals throughout the year. The blood allegedly liquefies, changes from a dark brown to red, stirs, sometimes froths and bubbles and increases in volume. This phenomenon has been observed with great scrutiny by the scientific community and determined to be without an earthly explanation.

Theodore Tyro

306

Martyred Roman soldier. Tyro was a Christian soldier in the Roman army. He set fire to the temple of Cybele (nature goddess—"Mother of the Gods," in ancient religious sects of Phrygia and Lydia). His judge entreated him to renounce his faith and save his life; but Theodore made the sign of the cross, and answered: "As long as I have breath, I will confess the name of Christ." After cruel torture, the judge bade him think of the shame to which Christ had brought him. "This shame," Theodore answered, "I and all who invoke His name take with joy." He was condemned to be burnt. Tyro was a victim of Emperor Maximian.

Barbara

Dec. 4, 306
Nicomedia (Izmit), Bithynia, Asia Minor (Turkey)

Virgin martyr. Barbara was the beautiful daughter of Dioscorus, a rich man. She continually denied marital suitors, greatly exasperating her father. She lived a reclusive life in the tower of their vast home. After her conversion, she sought to convert her father, but he reproved her. Barbara further revealed her faith when she altered the design of her bathhouse (a gift from her father) with three windows (Trinity reminder) instead of the usual two. He was irate, demanding she recant her belief, causing her humiliating pain and finally turning her over to authorities to be executed. At the scene of her beheading, lightning allegedly killed her father. Barbara is depicted on the left of the Virgin Mary in Raphael's (1483–1520) Sistine Chapel's "Madonna." Some of her story is hard to validate, but she remains a "holy" maid, martyred under Emperor Maximian. Another Christian, Juliana, was martyred with her.

Catherine of Alexandria

c 289
Alexandria, Egypt

Nov. 25, 307
Alexandria, Egypt

Scholarly martyr. Catherine was a young lady of royal descent in Alexandria who publicly shared the Gospel at a sacrificial feast appointed by Maximinus, governor of Syria and Egypt, urging him to cease worshiping pagan gods. While in prison, at the age of 18, she vanquished her pagan adversaries (50 philosophers) in a debate. This so enraged the Emperor that he ordered them all burned. Maximinus was so intrigued with Catherine's intellect and beauty that he proposed a liaison that would pardon her. She rebuked him, greatly offending him, which resulted in her being tortured while in prison. Legend states that while the Emperor was away, the empress, General Porpherius, and 200 soldiers came out of curiosity to visit Catherine and were converted. Maximinus had them all slain and ordered Catherine put to death on a machine of spiked wheels. It blew apart, its spikes killing many onlookers. She was finally beheaded. Reality and emotion become confused as it is related that angels carried her body to the great monastery on Mt. Sinai, where her relics remain today. Catherine's voice is said to be one of those encouraging JOAN OF ARC during her martyrdom.

Margaret of Antioch
Marina

c 255
Antioch (Antakya), Syria (Turkey)

July 20, c 308
Antioch (Antakya), Syria (Turkey)

Virgin martyr. Margaret, the daughter of a pagan priest of Antioch, was led to the Lord by her nurse/nanny. She was banned from her father's house, sought refuge in the home of her old Christian nurse, became a shepherdess and was often called upon to minister to women giving birth. Though fact and fiction may have been mixed through the years, fragments of her story contain struggles with an evil dragon—over which she triumphed. Margaret is attributed to be one of the "angelic voices" that spoke to JOAN OF ARC as she was burned at the stake. Margaret endured much persecution because of her faith, but remained true. She became a revered figure in the Eastern Greek Church after she allegedly worked many miracles and died a martyr. She was tortured on the wheel and beheaded by order of Maximinus (co-emperor in the East; ruled: 308–14). She is thought to be the same person as Pelagia.

Marcellus I

Jan.16, 309

Rome, Italy

Thirtieth bishop of Rome, 308–309. Marcellus I, who was elected after the severe persecution of the Church by Emperor Diocletian, left the papal position empty for over four years. He organized the city of Rome into 25 districts and appointed a presbyter to take charge of each area. Marcellus I's administrative change revived the teaching and discipleship of the Church. He decreed a Council could not be held without the Roman bishop's authority. He believed that those who lapsed during persecution needed to do penance, which caused riots among the people. This was a difficult problem to deal with. Marcellus I was banished by Emperor Maxentius (co-emperor in the West; ruled: 308–12), supposedly performing his own penance by grooming horses/tending cattle. He died from the drudgery while in exile.

Eusebius of Rome

Aug. 17, 309
Sicily, Italy

Cassano, Greece

Thirty-first bishop of Rome, 309. Eusebius was the son of a physician. Although bishop for only four months (April 18—August 17), Eusebius supported the stand of his predecessor, MARCELLUS I, insisting that those who had forsaken the faith during the Diocletian persecution should do penance before reinstatement in the Church. There was increased discord (almost a schism) among the lapsed parishioners that now broke into violent strife. Heraclius, a moderate, represented the frustrated offending believers and favored readmission without penance. In order to restore order, Emperor Maxentius had them both exiled from the city. Eusebius was shipped off to Sicily, where he died shortly thereafter as a martyr. Eusebius' administration was noteworthy for the advent of prayers for the dead and the act of making the sign of the cross. Some believe his death could be August 17, 310.

Pamphilus

c 240
Beirut, Phoenicia (Lebanon)

Feb. 16, 310
Caesarea, Palestine (Israel)

Christian teacher and scholar. Pamphilus amassed one of the finest libraries of his time. He enjoyed an excellent reputation as a teacher in the famed Catechetical School, Alexandria, Egypt; and in Caesarea, where he founded a theological school and his famous library. One of his students, EUSEBIUS OF CAESAREA, became the brilliant Father of Church History. Pamphilus aided poor students, distributed the Scriptures, and defended the orthodoxy of Greek Church Father, ORIGEN. Pamphilus wrote *An Apology for Origen* (five books), collaborating with EUSEBIUS on the project. He also helped in an edition of the Septuagint (Greek version of the Old Testament). Pamphilus was imprisoned, 307–309, and tortured for refusing to sacrifice to pagan deities. He was beheaded, along with eleven others, under Emperor Maxentius. Some historians describe his death as follows: His flesh was torn off to the very bones, and his bowels exposed to view, and the torments were continued a long time without intermission, but he never once opened his mouth so much as to groan. He finished his martyrdom by a slow fire, and died invoking Jesus, the Son of God.

Dorothea (Dorothy)

267
Caesarea, Asia Minor

Feb. 6, 311
Caesarea (Kayseri), Cappadocia, Asia Minor (Turkey)

Martyred virgin. Dorothea was noted for her beauty and piety. This maiden, refusing to sacrifice to idols, was tortured and beheaded during the persecution of Christians. Her fame was preserved through the ages because of the incredible story attached to her execution. Theophilus, a young lawyer, mocked her, suggesting that she send him a basket of fruit from the beautiful garden in the "heaven" to which she said she was gloriously going. As the moment of her execution approached, it is recorded that an angel appeared with a basket of fruit, which Dorothea requested be given to Theophilus. As a result of this miraculous act, he was converted to Christianity, later tortured for his faith and decapitated, sharing her same fate. Her *Acta* is mostly apocryphal (doubtful, false) according to *Aldhelm*.

Peter of Alexandria

Alexandria, Egypt

Nov. 24–26, 311
Alexandria, Egypt

Martyred bishop of Alexandria, 300–311. As head of the great Catechetical School at Alexandria, Peter was greatly respected for his knowledge of the Scriptures. He became metropolitan/patriarch (Eastern/Greek Orthodox head of the ancient territories, cities, sees) of Alexandria in 300. He issued decrees to receive lapsed members back into the Church. Peter continued to beg God for himself and for his flock the necessary grace and courage, "... to die daily to their own wills that they might be prepared to die for Christ." Peter opposed Arius and ORIGEN, and excommunicated Bishop MELITIUS OF LYCOPOLIS for stirring up a schism. Upon returning to supervise his see, Peter was seized, imprisoned, and put to death without a trial under the persecution of Emperor Maximinus. Roman Martyrology names four bishops and over 600 others who "were raised to Heaven by the sword of persecution" in Egypt at this time. Peter was the last martyr put to death by public authority at Alexandria.

Tiridates III
Tiridates the Great

c 238

314
Armenia

First Christian king of Armenia, 259–314. The Persians conquered Armenia in 252. Tiridates III became king in 259 but saw his country again defeated by the Persians. He regained the throne in 286 with the aid of Emperor Diocletian. The conquests of Tiridates were widespread. He was led to Christ by GREGORY THE IL-

LUMINATOR and baptized by him in 303. Tiridates fathered the growth of a strong Armenian Church, which had a powerful impact on the spread of the Gospel.

Miltiades of Rome
Meltiades/Melchiades

Jan. 11, 314

Africa

Thirty-second bishop of Rome, 311–314. At the request of Emperor CONSTANTINE I, Meltiades presided at the Lateran Council (held in the house of Empress Fausta, 289–326) in Rome on October 2, 313. The council heard protests from angry rigorists who thought the Church was being too lenient in readmitting compromisers who had wavered in their faith during the persecutions. Miltiades and the Synod, unable to pacify the protesters, saw them form a rival faction known as the Donatists. He constructed the Church of St. John Lateran. Blessed bread dates from his time. The state persecution of Christendom ended during his reign in 312, when CONSTANTINE I defeated Maxentius, because of Miltiades' invitation for him to come to Italy to drive out the worthless emperor.

Blaise

Feb. 3, 316

Hermit, healer, and martyred bishop of Sebaste (Sivas), Armenia. Blaise, the son of rich and noble parents, received a Christian education and became a bishop at a very young age. When the persecutions of Emperor Licinius (co-emperor in the East; ruled: 308–24) reached his area, he followed divine direction and retreated to a cave in the mountains, sharing it with wild beasts. Legend relates that he lived as a hermit, ministering to the needs of these wild creatures. Hunters reported his Christian actions to Governor Agricolaus of Cappadocia and Lesser Armenia, who had Blaise tracked down and arrested. While en route to his fate, he performed several healing miracles: rescuing a woman's pig and saving the life of a child by removing a fishbone stuck in his throat. Blaise was sustained in prison with food smuggled in by the woman whose pig he had freed. He suffered torture by having his flesh hideously torn with iron combs used by wool-combers, before he was beheaded. Blaise became a Christian hero among the French and German herdsmen.

Melitius of Lycopolis

c 325/326

Egypt   Lycopolis, Egypt

Bishop of Lycopolis and founder of the Melitians. Melitius felt that PETER OF ALEXANDRIA was too lenient toward those who renounced their faith during the Diocletian persecutions, 284–305, and created the Melitian Schism in 305. Melitius was banished to the Petraea mines in Arabia and, upon his release, founded the rigorist group known as the Melitians (tenets focused on strict rules for believers). The Council of Nicea permitted Melitians to operate only in Lycopolis. They were not granted their own religious see, but could replace Orthodox bishops if they were duly elected. This arrangement proved unsatisfactory, resulting in his faction breaking off from the rest of the Church in 328 and becoming Arians.

Alexander of Alexandria

c 250 – 273   April 17, 326
Alexandria, Egypt   Alexandria, Egypt

Patriarch of Alexandria, 312–26. Alexander was the proponent for Orthodoxy when the Arian controversy (Christ was neither God nor man, but someone in between) broke out between himself and Arius (an eloquent parish presbyter in the Alexandria Church), who developed this heretical doctrine, 256–336.

His appointment as patriarch eliminated Arius as a contender for this post. Alexander, being a man of mild disposition, tried to appeal to Arius through sound doctrinal arguments, but to no avail. This was the first liberal theological challenge. At a Synod called by Alexander in 320, Arius was condemned and excommunicated. Alexander was one of the Orthodox leaders against Arius at the Council of Nicea, Bithynia, Asia Minor (gathering of 318 bishops: 313 from the East and 5 from the Latin West) in 325. Alexander mentored ATHANASIUS, his deacon, to be his replacement.

Arnobius the Elder
Arnobius Afer

c 327

Sicca, Numidia (Algeria)

Latin philosopher, teacher of rhetoric, and apologist. Arnobius' early years found him to be a fierce opponent of Christianity. As a young man he was a fellow student with LACTANTIUS at Sicca Veneria (Le Kef, Tunisia). He was a teacher of rhetoric at Sicca during Emperor Diocletian's reign. His skill as a satirist was superb. The plight of Christian martyrs greatly affected Arnobius and precipitated his conversion (after 300). After becoming a Christian, Arnobius used his scholarship for the furtherance of Christianity. He wrote a seven-volume treatise called *Against the Gentiles*, defending Christians against their enemies. Arnobius was more successful in his refutation of error, however, than in the defense of the truth because he had limited Bible knowledge, though he excelled in religious zeal.

Helena
Flavia Julia Helena

c 248/255
Drepanum/Helenapolis, Bithynia, Asia Minor (Turkey)

Aug. 18, 330
Palestine (Israel)

Mother of Constantine and church founder. Helena's life radiated a true Christian spirit, as attested to by the historian EUSEBIUS, "...though Empress of the world and mistress of the empire, she looked upon herself as a servant of the handmaids of Christ..." She was the daughter of King Cole of Colchester, England. She met her husband while he was commander-in-chief of the Roman army, occupying Britain. Helena's husband, Constantius I Chlorus (co-emperor in the West; ruled: 305–6), divorced her in 292, after 22 years of marriage when he became Caesar (emperor, tyrant or dictator; temporal ruler). He felt that her humble background as the daughter of an inn keeper was a deficit to his elevated position. He then married Empress Theodora. However, in 306, after Helena's son, Constantine, became co-emperor, he renamed her birth city in her honor, and had coins produced with her mark. In 313, Helena was converted and encouraged her son in their newfound faith. On a trip to the Holy Land, she allegedly discovered Calvary's true cross on May 3, 325 in Jerusalem. With CONSTANTINE's backing, she personally supervised the building of the Church of the Nativity in Bethlehem (oldest Christian church in the world) and the Church of the Holy Sepulcher. She also built a church on the Mount of Olives. When Helena died, her body was taken to Rome for burial.

Gregory the Illuminator

c 257
Valarshabad, Armenia (Russia)

Sept. 30, 332
Ashtishat/Thortan, Taran (Iran)

Founder of the Armenian Church. Gregory had been taken by his nurse to Caesarea, Cappadocia to spare his life after Anak, his father, had killed Armenian King Khosrov I. While in exile, he accepted Christianity, received a Christian education, married, had two sons, and miraculously healed people. Upon his return to Armenia, King TIRIDATES III (whose father Gregory's father had murdered) demanded that he participate in pagan sacrifices. Gregory refused, was horribly tortured, thrown into a pit to die and forgotten for 15 years. A widow threw him bread to sustain him. The king had a

The Saints Go Marching In

severe mental collapse after a thwarted love affair and his sister speculated that perhaps Gregory, the Christian, could "save" him. All were amazed to see that Gregory was still alive.

Macarius of Jerusalem

Palestine? (Israel)

March 10, c 335

Bishop of Jerusalem, 312–35. Macarius' piety and zeal are mentioned by Theodoret and others. Arius refers to him as one of his opponents, a position that Macarius maintained at the Council of Nicea. It was during his pastorate that CONSTANTINE's mother, HELENA, is said to have discovered the cross of Christ. Macarius actually assisted in establishing which of the three crosses excavated bore Christ's body. In 326 CONSTANTINE commissioned Macarius to erect a basilica (religious meeting place) on the site of Christ's sepulchre, also located by HELENA and others. It was named the Church of the Holy Sepulchre.

Sylvester I

Rome, Italy

Dec. 31, 335
Rome, Italy

Thirty-third bishop of Rome, 314–35. Sylvester I served during a crucial time in church history. He called an early Church Council at Rome, warning against the teachings of Arianism and Donatism, laying the groundwork for the Council of Nicea. Due to his advanced age, Sylvester I was not among the 318 bishops attending this gathering, but was honored for his efforts toward establishing a Christian Roman Empire. According to the Sixth Canon from the Nicene Council, the administrative areas of the church were defined: Alexandria (Egypt), Antioch (Asia Minor), and Rome (the seven middle and lower provinces of Italy only), with each sharing equal authority; none being superior to the other. Many historians consider this time period under Sylvester I, when construction of the Church of St. Peter was begun, to be the foundation for the Vatican City complex. Sylvester I consecrated many famous local churches and participated in the first use of wax candles in 320. He was the first bishop to wear the tiarae (papal crown) and also declared Sunday a holy day. During his tenure, CONSTANTINE moved the capital of the Roman Empire from Rome to Byzantium in 330, later changing the city's name to Constantinople (Istanbul). His was the tenth longest pontificate: 20 years, 11 months.

Mark

Rome, Italy

Oct. 7, 336

Thirty-fourth bishop of Rome, 336. Mark decreed that the bishop of Rome be consecrated by the bishop of Ostia (14 miles south west of Rome). He insituted the pallium (woolen vestment worn by popes, archbishops), made from the wool of a blessed lamb and decorated with black crosses. He also instituted a calendar of religious feast days.

Constantine I
Constantine the Great – Flavius Valerius Aurelius Constantinus

Feb. 27, 280
Naissus (Nis), Serbia (Yugoslavia)

May 22, 337
Nicomedia (Izmit), Bithynia, Asia Minor (Turkey)

First Christian Emperor of Rome, 312–337. As sole emperor, Constantine I reunited the Roman Empire from 324 until his death. He was married twice, the second time, in 307, to Fausta, daughter of Maximian. A vision of a flaming cross in the sky with the words "In this sign, conquer" led to his military victories over Emperor Maxentius on October 27, 312 and caused his conversion. Thus the cross became his monogram. He had served as co-emperor, 306–12 and ruled alone, 312–24 in the East. During his leadership, Christianity began to replace paganism. His Edict of Toleration (Edict of Milan) in 313 gave freedom to Christians for the first time, granting them the right to legally own property. This decree called for all to join the church rather than fight it. To some, this signifies the beginnings of the Roman Catholic Church. This is the same year that Constantine's mother, HELENA, was converted. Constantine I encouraged the copying of the Scriptures and called the first great Church Council at Nicea in 325. About this time, Fausta, his wife, caused that Crispus, his eldest son by his first marriage, be put to death. Constantine I, in turn, ordered that she be killed also in 326. Circumstances regarding this interlude are uncertain. In 330, he moved the capital of the empire to Byzantium and renamed the city Constantinopolis (Constantinople), dedicating it with both Christian and pagan ceremonies. Constantine I set aside December 25 to celebrate the birth of Christ. While he certainly embraced Christianity, he put off his baptism until his death bed where scribes record he believed his sins would be washed away. Therefore his orthodoxy has been questioned by many. He was a slave holder.

Eusebius of Caesarea
Eusebius Pamphili—Father of Church History

c 260–265
Caesarea, Palestine (Israel)

May 30, 339
Caesarea, Palestine (Israel)

Theologian, scholar, and bishop of Caesarea, 314–39. Eusebius was a student of PAMPHILUS, imprisoned in Egypt for his faith, and greatly influenced by ORIGEN. Eusebius had the honor of giving the official welcome to Emperor CONSTANTINE I at the opening of the Council of Nicea and submitted the first draft of The Nicene Creed which, after several rounds of changes, was finally adopted. Eusebius baptized CONSTANTINE I in 337 and wrote *Life of Constantine*. His principal work was *Ecclesiastical History* (originally in seven volumes and later extended to ten). It was the first written history of Christianity and has remained the primary source of documentation for the Eastern church from Apostolic times. In many ways Eusebius was an enigma. A strong supporter of the Nicene Creed (whose main focus was substantiating Orthodoxy over Arianism and belief in the Trinity as the keystone for the Christian faith), yet he was a moderate in mediating the differences with the Arians. This vacillation led him to take part in the condemnation of Athanasius (who held a life long, adamant stand against Arianism) at Tyre in 335, where he read *The Semi-Arians* (encouraged fellowship between Arians and Orthodox). Eusebius also attended the Synod of Antioch in 330, which deposed the godly Eustathius. Some have concluded that Eusebius was better at documenting history than at making it. He gave some attention to sorting Scripture and spurious books. He described mass executions of Christians by beheading under Emperor Diocletian.

Firmianus Lactantius
The Christian Cicero —Lucius Caelius

c 250/260
Proconsular, North Africa

c 340
Treves (Trier), Gaul (Germany)

Latin apologist and writer. As a young man, Lactantius studied with ARNOBIUS. He was converted at age 30 while serving as a teacher of rhetoric in Roman Emperor Diocletian's school at Nicomedia, Asia Minor. He moved to the West in 305. Lactantius was protected from Christian persecution by Emperor CONSTANTINE, whose son, Crispus, he tutored in Gaul (c 313). JEROME called Lactantius the most learned man of his time. His *Seven Books of the Divine Institutions* stated that pagan religion and philosophy were weak disciplines upon which to create a foundation of knowledge, whereas Christianity puts all attitudes and wisdom in balanced perspective. He died at CONSTANTINE's Imperial Court.

Caecilian

c 340/350

Bishop of Carthage, 311–40/50. Caecilian served as deacon of the Church in North Africa during the Diocletian persecution, 284–305. Some refused to acknowledge his bishopric since he was ordained by a compromiser during persecution days. MAJORINUS was chosen an alternate bishop and later was succeeded by DONATUS. It is said that Caecilian's obnoxious personality contributed to his lack of acceptance. He led in synods from 313–16 and was the only bishop from Africa at the Council of Nicea.

Eustathius of Antioch

270   July 16, c 340
Side, Pamphylia, Asia Minor (Turkey)   Trajanopolis, Thrace, Macedonia (Bulgaria, Greece)

Greek prelate and patriarch at Antioch, 324–30. Eustathius was the first bishop of Beroea (Aleppo), Syria (c 320). He earnestly opposed the Arians at the Council of Nicea, and when they came into power in 331 he was deposed. Since Arianism grew in spite of the efforts of the Council of Nicea to discredit it, life in the East became increasingly difficult for Eustathius. Although it seemed inconsistent, Emperor CONSTANTINE supported a Synod in Antioch, Syria, 330, which demanded Eustathius' exile and banishment. CONSTANTINE's goal was not to suppress Arians but rather to unite them with the church in one common belief. In exile, followed by many of his loyal clergy, Eustathius exhorted the church at Antioch to remain faithful to truth. He maintained followers, the Eustathians, until 413. As leader of the most prominent see next to Alexandria, Eustathius is extolled for the great patience he exhibited in the face of lying accusations and his unjust dismissal. Of his writings, only one work against ORIGEN remains, in addition to a historic record which chronicles his literary debate against the esteemed EUSEBIUS OF CAESAREA. One source claims that he died about 360.

Paul of Thebes
The Hermit

c 228–234   Jan. 15, 342
Thebes, Egypt   Egypt

Early Hermit. Paul was orphaned at age 15. He fled from Emperor Decius' persecution and subsisted in the desolate vastness of Upper Egypt for nearly a century. Those who chose to flee were not necessarily cowards, but dedicated souls directed by God to fulfill the needs of His earthly flock through prayer. At the age of 22, Paul began daily communion with God, living in a series of caves. At their entrances, a clear spring and a palm tree provided his raiment and food. According to JEROME, ANTHONY OF EGYPT, nearing age 90, was told in a dream to seek another kindred soul living in the desert. He was miraculously led to Paul who had been "told" to expect him. That same day, Paul, like Elijah, was miraculously fed bread brought by a raven, indicating God's blessing. Nearing 113 years of age, Paul requested that Anthony bury him in the cloak of Bishop ATHANASIUS OF ALEXANDRIA. JEROME called Paul of Thebes the "Founder of Monasticism."

Nicholas of Myra
The First Santa Claus—Old St. Nick

Dec. 6, 345
Pararia, Lycia, Asia Minor (Turkey)   Myra, Lycia, Asia Minor (Turkey)

Bishop of Myra and patron of the Russian Orthodox Church. Although Nicholas was raised in a privileged environment, he displayed an inquisitiveness for spiritual things. He was orphaned young, receiving a great inheritance yet served as a shepherd. He vowed to use his financial legacy for the charitable benefit of others. His many generous and timely gifts stimulated the legend of Santa Claus, beginning the custom of distributing gifts at Christmas. When the episcopal see was vacant in Myra, he was the unanimous choice. Nicholas suffered during the Diocletian persecution, and was imprisoned. However, it is alleged that he later attended the Council of Nicea. His influence so strengthened Myra that it was one of the few cities free from Arianism.

Pachomius
The Elder

c 292
Esneh (Esna), Lower Egypt

May 9, 348
Prou/Peboou, Egypt

Founder of first monastic community in Egypt. Pachomius was touched by the kindness of Christians while serving as a soldier at Thebes. This benevolence influenced his decision to be baptized after his army service. In 318, in response to a vision, he gathered other monks into an organized community on the Island of Tabenna (Ennisi) in the Nile River near Dendera (Upper Egypt). The members agreed to observe rules of life and conduct established by Pachomius. This was the first example of communal monasticism in the West. His brother, John, was the first to commit to his monastic regime. His unique disciplined organization registered each monk in one of 24 categories, relative to their spiritual weaknesses, and housed them in "support" groups of three. His ministry used the Nile River to reach remote areas and included nine monasteries with 7,000 monks and two convents at the time of his death. Pachomius' gift of healing ministered to many, although he himself died from an epidemic disease.

Paphnutius

c 275

Sept. 11, c 350–360

Bishop of Thebes (Thebaid), Upper Egypt. Paphnutius spent many years in the desert as a disciple of ANTHONY OF EGYPT. Under Emperor Maximinus' persecution, he suffered mutilation (one eye was removed and a knee tendon severed) and in this crippled condition was condemned to labor in the mines. When peace returned to the church, he was freed to return to his flock. Paphnutius took a prominent part in the Council of Nicea where Emperor Constantine I was so grieved by his physical plight that out of reverence he kissed Paphnutius' seared eye. Paphnutius opposed the Arians and urged that clergy be permitted to keep their wives if married before their ordination. The church was attempting to force clergy to make a choice between clerical or marital vows. The strength of his argument led the Eastern churches to follow his direction from that day forward, allowing married men to receive holy orders. Paphnutius attended the Synod of Tyre in 335 and bonded with Maximus of Jerusalem, Greek church writer, a fellow tortured man of God, to defend ATHANASIUS OF ALEXANDRIA, whom they both extolled.

Majorinus

c 350

Bishop of Carthage, 311–15. Elected by the schismatics (those seeking separation from the norm—not always relevant to doctrinal issues), Majorinus tried to undermine the rightfully elected CAECILIAN. He was a rigorist who refused to recognize the more lenient CAECILIAN. Majorinus and his party proclaimed the sacraments were invalid when administered by anyone who had once forsaken the faith. His group eventually joined the Donatists when DONATUS replaced him as bishop.

Julius I

Rome, Italy

April 12, 352
Rome, Italy

Thirty-fifth bishop of Rome, 337–52. Julius I tried to unite the West against Arianism. He provoked resentment among leaders in the Eastern church by welcoming ATHANASIUS who had just been exiled from Alexandria by the Arians, and by calling 50 Italian bishops together in 340 to vindicate him. At the request of the joint Emperors, the sons of the deceased CONSTANTINE THE GREAT, JULIUS I assembled the Council of Sardica (Sofia), Thracia (Bulgaria), in 343. The emperors were divided and wanted to hear both sides: Constans (ruled: 337–50) opposed Arianism and Constantius II (ruled: 337–61) favored it. The Eastern church and leaders in Constantinople boycotted the council. The council's consensus favored Julius I's "letter of position" which stated that any deposed bishop had the right to appeal to the bishop of Rome. (The position of the bishop of Rome under the rule of JULIUS I was anti-Arian.) This event established the supremacy of Rome in Christian history and provided the foundation for the Roman Catholic Church. JULIUS I founded the archives of the Holy See. He ordered the Oriental Church to celebrate Christmas on December 25 instead of January 6. He was responsible for building the Church of the Twelve Apostles in Rome and the Church of Santa Maria in Trastevere.

Donatus

c 270   355
Casae Nigrae (Tunisia)

Founder of the Donatists (African Separatist Church) **and bishop of Carthage, 315–55**. Donatus was energetic and eloquent of speech. He was the founder of a new, puritanical, rigorist movement—similar to Montanism and Novatianism. His followers took a stringent stand against taking lapsed Christians back into the church after a persecution era ended. Donatus was elected by a spiritual group in North Africa, succeeding MAJORINUS alternate bishop. The majority of African Christians accepted him as their bishop. The Donatists surfaced in 311 in protest against the consecration of CAECILIANUS as bishop of Carthage, by Bishop FELIX I. They believed that sanctity and godliness was essential for the administration of sacraments and church membership. The movement remained localized in North Africa and, by the fifth century, tended to gather economic and social discontents, dissipating when other religious options became available.

Anthony of Egypt
Antonius/Antony the Great

251   Jan. 17, 356
Coma, Upper Egypt   Pispir, Egypt

Healer and founder of Monasticism (act of living alone). As a rich young man, too shy for school, Anthony gave all his wealth away. Desiring to live a more devout Christian life, he retired to the Egyptian desert in 270 to live in solitude. His first dwelling was a sepulchre. He then spent 20 years in the ruins of a castle and finally settled on Mount Colzim. He practiced severe self-torment and resisted fleshly temptations. Other ascetics, attracted by reports of his discernment, powers of sanctity, and signs and wonders, took up residence near him. Although they all lived separately, they met together for prayer. Anthony organized them into communities of monks (c 305). By the time of his death, reportedly there were 15,000 devotees. In 338, he followed God's leading and went into the "world," to Alexandria, to disavow Arianism and support ATHANASIUS. Anthony was known to intercede for and heal people of "the burning sickness" (named St. Anthony's fire in the 1030s) or "erysipelas," a contagious skin disorder causing feverish blisters. He left no written rule, but several letters have survived which contain many of his wise maxims, such as "knowledge of ourselves is the necessary and only step by which we can ascend to the knowledge and love of God."

Hosius
Osius

256   358
Cordova, Spain   Cordova, Spain

Chairman of the Nicene Council and bishop of Cordova, 300–58. For several years, Hosius was the chief ecclesiastical advisor to Emperor CONSTANTINE I. Throughout his career he was selected to mediate between dissenting factions—beginning in 318 with disgruntled bishops. Hosius attempted to intercede in the ALEXANDER/Arius dispute of 324. He also chaired the Council of Nicea and participated in the preparation of the Nicene Creed. He played important roles in the Councils of Antioch (324) and Sardica, Spain (343). Hosius was one of the first ecclesiastics to argue for a separation of church and state, as outlined in a letter he sent to Constantius II. He was over 100 years old in 357 when Arian co-emperor Constantius II tortured him into signing a compromising "formula" at Sirmium, Lower Pannonia (Yugoslavia), which he retracted before his death.

Jacob Aphraates
The Persian Sage

c 230–256　　　*c 360*

Earliest Persian Christian writer. Aphraates was a pupil of Bishop JULIUS I. After his conversion, he moved to Edessa, Mesopotamia (Urfa, Turkey) seeking the most perfect way to serve God. Deciding this would be best accomplished in solitude, he became an ascetic monk. Between 337–45 he composed 23 Biblical homiletical commentaries (informal exposition of Scriptures) on Christian doctrine and practice. His writings are without Western influence, revealing the isolation of the Persian Church and indicating that the Bible may well have been his only written source. Aphraates later went to Antioch. He was allowed to move freely about the city because he had found favor by healing Emperor Valen's (ruled in the East: 364–78) favorite horse. When he was questioned why he was moving about the city dressed as an ascetic monk, he responded that he had to go where the needs of the people were. He was a strong opponent of Arius, and, since the Arians had taken possession of most of the churches, he saw the need to quietly strengthen and encourage believers—often meeting in small groups by the river or open spaces outside of town. Though he met the people's spiritual needs, he was equally popular as a faith healer, meeting their physical needs. Aphraates lived to be over 100 years of age.

Sarapion

c 361

Egyptian monk, theologian and bishop of Thmuis in the Nile Delta. Sarapion was a key figure in early Monasticism. With his friend, Bishop ATHANASIUS, he championed orthodox teaching against the Arians and wrote his famed *Against the Manichees* (Manichaeans). His other well-known work, discovered in 1894, is the *Euchologion*, which contains prayers and liturgical texts.

Jovianus
Flavius C. Jovianus

c 331　　　*Feb. 17, 364*
Singidunum (Belgrade), Illyricum (Yugoslavia)　　　　　　　　　　　Dadastana, Bithynia, Asia Minor (Turkey)

Roman emperor, 363–364. Jovianus was a general when Emperor Julian the Apostate (ruled: 361–63) died in Persia. The troops chose Jovian to be their new leader, and thus Julian's successor. Jovianus made a hasty and humiliating treaty with the Persians to save his army, giving up the five Roman provinces beyond the Tigris River. When he arrived at Antioch, Syria, he rescinded the edicts of Julian against the Christians, revived the monogram of Christ on the imperial standards and restored to the clergy their privileges and revenues. Above all, Jovianus restored religious toleration and supported the Nicene Creed against Arianism. He died suddenly while traveling on a remote road, enroute to Constantinople.

Liberius

Rome, Italy

Sept. 24, 366
Rome, Italy

Thirty-sixth bishop of Rome, 352–66. As a Roman deacon, Liberius showed theological agility in clinging to his title. Accused of heresy while bishop, he was banished by Emperor Constantius II for refusing to agree with the Arian-controlled Council of Arles in 353. Liberius was exiled to Thrace in 355 for supporting ATHANASIUS—being one of the few bishops who refused to sign the condemnation toward him. Liberius was reinstated in 358 when, in an act of cowardice, he finally excommunicated ATHANASIUS, yielding to Arian pressure. His bad, compromising leadership resulted in him being the first Roman bishop not listed among the saints. As a result, antipope Felix II was elected and established in the suburbs. Outwardly compromising until Constantius II's death in 361, he later resumed his orthodox position. Liberius laid the foundation for the Church of St. Mary Major.

Hilary of Poitiers
The Athanasius of the West

c 300–315
Poitiers, France

Jan. 13, 368
Poitiers, France

Bishop of Poitiers, 353–68 intermittently. Following his conversion in 350, Hilary devoted his tongue and pen to fighting the Arian heresy. He spoke Latin, had knowledge of Jewish customs and disdained by Greek Christian leaders. For his religious zeal, he suffered banishment to Phrygia, Asia Minor, in 356 by Emperor Constantius II. While exiled in Phrygia, Hilary wrote his main work, the twelve-volume *On the Trinity*. He was recalled to France in 361, only to be banished once again. He lost favor while on a trip to Italy in 364, when he found it necessary to impeach Auxentanius, bishop of Milan, who had embraced Arianism. The remainder of his life was lived in rural exile. He was the first exegete (one who gives an explanation or an interpretation of a Scripture text) among the Latin writers. Hilary was married and, along with being an esteemed theologian, was also a great lyric poet—composing hymns of beauty and power. He established a monastery in France.

Eusebius of Vercelli

c 283
Sardinia, Italy

Aug. 1, 371
Vercelli, Italy

First bishop of Vercelli, 340–71. When Eusebius' father died in chains for the faith, his mother took the family to Rome. He became an outstanding bishop; combining monastic discipline, religious education and administrative training. He staunchly defended the orthodox Nicene position to the extent that he suffered imperial and ecclesiastical political criticism. At the Council of Milan in 335, he declined to join in condemning ATHANASIUS. He was banished by Emperor Constantius II to Palestine; tortured by the Arians; confined in Cappadocia, Asia Minor; and finally settled in the Upper Thebaid region of Egypt. Emperor Julian reinstated Eusebius in 362. He visited churches in the East, attempting to restore peace, but immediately fell out of favor for challenging the Council of Alexandria's tolerance toward ex-Arian bishops. Eusebius is credited with the composition of the Athanasian Creed, a careful Latin translation of EUSEBIUS OF CAESAREA's *Commentary on the Psalms* and a manuscript copy of the Gospels—the oldest surviving Latin version of the codex (manuscript volume) which is displayed in the cathedral of Vercelli.

Hilarion

291
Tabatha, Palestine (Israel)

Oct. 21, 371
Cyprus

Hermit and healer. Hilarion was converted at age 15 and studied for a brief, but profoundly impressionable, time with ANTHONY OF EGYPT in the desert. He worked the soil, meditated on spiritual things, lived an ascetic life and went 20 years before he performed his first miracle: curing a barren woman. When he settled in the Gaza area about 329, large crowds began seeking his healing power. In search of more solitude, he went to Majuma, a remote area where he lived in a hut. He went back to his homeland where he became the first to introduce monasticism to Palestine. Hilarion fasted for seven days, beseeching the people to let him go back to Egypt. In response to a vision that ANTHONY was soon to die, he returned in 356. After ANTHONY's death, there were three years of drought. In 359, he obliged the people, raised his arms to heaven and brought rain to the land. Hilarion could not escape the great crowds. With the help of his disciple, HESYCHIUS, he moved to Sicily, where he expelled menacing serpents. Again the multitudes recognized him, so he traveled to Dalmatia (Croatia), and then to the Island of Cyprus finally having to trudge twelve miles inland to reach a spot of tranquility and quietness. His last retreat at Cyprus was broken by a paralytic, who was cured by Hilarion, and then spread his fame. He died with the words, "Go forth, my soul; why dost thou doubt? Nigh seventy years hast thou served God, and dost thou fear death?"

Athanasius of Alexandria
Father of Orthodoxy

c 293–296
Alexandria, Egypt

May 2, 373
Alexandria, Egypt

Greek theologian and bishop of Alexandria, 326–73. Athanasius waged a life long battle against Arianism. He suffered five exiles, which resulted in banishment for 20 of his 46 years, starting in 335–37. One of these exiles was in Rome 339–46, where he cemented firm links with the established Church. One exile was in the desert, 356–62. Athanasius was finally restored permanently in 366, having lived a basically ascetic life. In 319, Bishop ALEXANDER of ALEXANDRIA ordained him a deacon. He served as ALEXANDER's "secretary" at the Council of Nicea in 325. Athanasius impressed many by the clarity of his journalistic style in recording the proceedings and adding insightful commentary as to the ramifications of the proposed actions. Historians uphold him as the one most responsible for the important triumph of Orthodoxy at the Council. Athanasius succeeded Alexander and under his seal, the heathen temples were emptied. Athanasius wrote voluminously, gaining the title "Father of Orthodoxy" for his firm stand on Christ's divinity, for saving the church from pagan intellectualism, and for giving unity and integrity to the Christian faith. His treatises included *History of the Arians, On the Decrees of the Nicene Council,* and *On the Incarnation of the Divine Word* (318). His "Letter of 367," defining key doctrines, gives final clarity to the canon of the Scriptures by being the first document to name the 27 books of the New Testament as exclusively canonical. He wrote, "Let no man add to these wells of salvation, and let nothing be taken away." His works were apologetic, dogmatic, controversial, personal defense, exegetical, ascetic, and practical.

Syrus Ephraem
Ephrem the Syrian—Ephraim/Aphrem—Ephraem Syrus

c 306
Nisibis, Mesopotamia (Syria)

June 9/10/18, 373
Edessa (Urfa), Mesopotamia (Turkey)

Most famous of the Syrian Fathers: hermit, poet, hymnist, apologist, and preacher. After being ordained a deacon in 338, Ephraem settled at Odessa Saramate (Ukraine) on the Black Sea, later moving to Edessa in 363. Most of his works were written from Syria. His commentaries, theological treatises, homilies, and 70 hymns were widely used. Ephraem was a pioneer in introducing sacred songs into the Church's public services. A harp probably accompanied the singing. His sermons, combating Arianism and the other heresies of his day, were publicly read in many churches. Ephraem was considered the most distinguished theologian, orator, and hymn writer of the ancient Syrian Church.

Anthusa
c 330   c 374

Mother of JOHN CHRYSOSTOM. As a widow at age 20, Anthusa attracted many suitors, but devoted herself to rearing John and a daughter. She gave him the best public education in Antioch, Syria, and the best religious training at home. John remained with his mother as long as she lived. Her brief marriage was to a military officer.

Valentinian I
Flavius Valentinianus

321   Nov. 17, 375
Cibalis, Pannonia (Hungary)   Bregetio, Pannonia (Hungary)

Roman emperor in the West, 364–75. Valentinian I succeeded JOVIAN and was elected ruler by the Roman army. Almost immediately after gaining the throne, Valentinian I appointed his younger brother Valens, an Arian, as co-ruler; giving him the East. Valentinian I was forced to contend with many barbarian invasions in Gaul, Illyricum (Roman Empire prefecture), and Africa, 365–70. His rule allowed the people to have complete religious freedom, with interventions only when there were infractions against the state. He punished clergy when it was merited. Valentinian I was married twice, first to Valeria Severa and then to Justina. One of their daughters was Galla, who married Theodosius I. He brought about reforms in religion, law, and education. He reduced taxes, promoted education and provided medical care for the poor. When Valentinian I died of a stroke, he was succeeded by his sons who reigned jointly in the West: Gratian (age 16, ruled: 367–83 also in the East: 378–83) and Valentinian II, an infant of four (ruled: 375–92) years of age.

Eustathius of Sebaste
c 300   c 378–380
Sebaste (Sivas), Armenia (Turkey)   Sebaste (Sivas), Armenia (Turkey)

Semi-Arian bishop of Sebaste, 356–378 intermittently. Eustathius changed his views so often from orthodoxy to different phases of Arianism that he was condemned by several synods. He introduced Monasticism in Armenia and the Roman provinces of Pontus and Paphlagonia. In addition, he organized an ascetic party called the Eustathians, which practiced celibacy. Eustathius' interests were more ascetic than theological. He was a prominent member of the Synod of Ancyra/Militene in 358, and was subsequently deposed in 360 for his Arian stand. He was a formative influence on Basil the Great, but that relationship dissolved in 366, when Eustathius became a leader in the Macedonian heresy (begun by Macedonius, bishop of Constantinople—denying the distinct existence and Godhead of the Holy Spirit). Eustathius was widely respected for his care of refugees, and the building of almshouses and hospitals. He later identified with the Homoiousians (essence of the Son is similar to, but not the same as, the Father).

Basil
The Great Church Father

c 329–330   Jan. 1, 379
Caesarea, Asia Minor   Caesarea (Kayseri), Cappadocia, Asia Minor (Turkey)

Ascetic theologian and bishop of Caesarea, 370–79. Basil was the older brother of GREGORY OF NYSSA. He was educated in a Christian home. Basil attended the University of Athens, majoring in philosophy, where his closest friends were Emperor Julian and GREGORY OF NAZIANZUS. He studied philosophy in Athens, then worked tirelessly to strengthen the delicate ties between leaders of the Western church and the anti-Arians in the East. He taught philosophy in Caesarea. He founded Eastern Communal Monasticism and adopted this way of life, 357–64, establishing small monastic communities in Syria, Egypt and Pontus, Cappadocia in 358. He was ordained a presbyter in 364. Basil founded the first hospice (hospital, school, hotel, and monastery) for lepers. He stressed that hard work, charitable services, and communal life were quality replacements for the ascetic life and the isolated existence of a hermit. From 364–70, he wrote *Five Books Against Eunomius* (leader of the extreme Arians, died 395), as well as commentaries on Scriptures. Basil said as he died: "Hold my head that I may have the pleasure of looking towards my little oratory, where I used to pray, and that I may once more call upon my Heavenly Father."

Frumentius
Apostle to Ethiopia—Abba Salamah (Father of Peace)

c 300
Tyre, Phoenicia (Lebanon)

April 23, 380

First bishop of Ethiopia. On his way to India (c 326), after surviving a shipwreck, Frumentius was captured by Ethiopian pirates on the shores of the Red Sea. He was sold as a slave to the king of Aksum, Ethiopia; and, like Joseph of old, he was elevated to a prominent position. On his deathbed, the king gave Frumentius his freedom, but at the queen's request, he stayed on to assist in the royal household having established a special bond with the two princes. Upon the queen's demise, Frumentius left and went to Alexandria to petition ATHANASIUS for missionaries to be sent to Ethiopia. The wise ATHANASIUS said no one was more qualified than Frumentius, ordaining him a bishop of Aksum in 328. Frumentius formed a Christian congregation, baptized the two princes and built many churches. His legacy speaks through the 40 per cent of Ethiopia's 66 million population that belong to the Ethiopian Coptic/Orthodox Church.

Eusebius of Samosata

Samosata (Samsat), Asia Minor (Turkey)

June 22, 380
Dolica, Syria

Bishop of Samosata, 361–380. Eusebius helped orthodoxy by his support of the Nicene Creed, for which he was banished, 371–78, during Valens' reign. In 374, he was specifically exiled to Thrace (Bulgaria) but was reinstated by Emperor Gratian. He traveled through Syria, Phoenicia, and Palestine, disguised as a soldier, preaching and consecrating priests. An Arian woman threw a tile at him from a roof and he died several days later from head trauma.

Melitius of Antioch

Melitene (Malatya), Cappadocia, Asia Minor (Turkey)

381
Constantinople (Istanbul), Asia Minor (Turkey)

Bishop of Antioch, Syria, 361–81. Melitius succeeded EUSTATHIUS as bishop of Sebaste, Armenia, 357–61. He was exiled three different times by Arian Emperor Constantius II before the non-Arian Emperor Gratian finally declared him to be the duly installed bishop of Antioch in 378. He had been banished a few times prior to this by Emperor Valens. He was a good friend of BASIL THE GREAT and an early opponent and rival of EUSTATHIUS OF SEBASTE. Melitius died suddenly while presiding at the second Council of Constantinople.

Priscillian

c 340
Emeritta Augusta (Merida), Spain

c 384/385
Treves (Trier), Gaul (Germany)

Mystical Spanish ascetic reformer. Priscillian headed a reform movement in the ancient Spanish Church. His followers were called Priscillianists (sects in Spain and Gaul (France), who rejected the world, considered material things evil and had mystical leanings). Priscillianists mixed Gnosticism and Manichaeanism (Persian roots: belief in releasing the spirit from matter through asceticism, founded by Mani, last of the Gnostics) with Christianity. Ordained a priest, Priscillian was excommunicated by the Synod of Saragossa in 380 as a heretic. Although he had served as bishop of Avila, Spain, he was condemned for sorcery, tortured, and executed by fellow bishops. Priscillian was the first professing Christian put to death by a "Christian" state. Other leaders who embraced his extreme views shared his fate.

The Saints Go Marching In

Damascus I

c 304　　　　　　　　　　　　　　　　　　　　　　　　Dec. 11, 384
Spain　　　　　　　　　　　　　　　　　　　　　　　　Rome, Italy

Thirty-seventh bishop of Rome, 366–84. Damascus I became bishop by fighting Ursin antipope (reigned: 366–84), who had been chosen bishop by an opposing faction. The troops of Damascus I broke down the gates of the rival church and burned it, killing 137 people. Emperor Valentinian I validated Damascus I as the presiding bishop. He was energetic in suppressing various heresies. Damascus I held two Roman synods, 368 and 370, at which Arianism was condemned. Because of his anti-Arian views, he was not invited in 381 to the Church Council of Constantinople, which, at the time, had surpassed Rome as the religious hub. Damascus I, in 382, was the first to call Rome the Apostolic See, thus attempting to connect it to the Apostle Peter as a means to elevate its position above the growing strength of Constantinople. He also opposed Apollinarianism, condemning it in the Roman Councils of 377 and 381. He authorized the singing of the Psalms by alternate choirs (Ambrosian Rite) and introduced the use of the Hebrew word "Alleluia." Damascus I commissioned JEROME his secretary, in 382, to translate the Biblical text which became known as the Latin Vulgate. He also restored the catacombs and decorated the tombs of martyrs for shrines. In 375, the veneration of angels and dead saints began.

Cyril of Jerusalem

c 310/315　　　　　　　　　　　　　　　　　　　　　　March 18, 386
Jerusalem, Palestine (Israel)　　　　　　　　　　　　Jerusalem, Palestine (Israel)

Bishop of Jerusalem, 350–86. Sixteen years of Cyril's 35-year term were spent in exile for opposing Arianism and offending his Arian superior, Bishop Acacius of Caesarea (reigned: 340–66), who deposed him. In 357, Emperor Constantius II expelled him for selling ornaments of the church to provide food for the poor. Cyril regained his religious privileges and his see in 379, though some in Orthodoxy still considered him to be a Semi-Arian. His sermons, after his ordination as a priest in Jerusalem 347–48, comprised an important part of Christian history. At the Second Ecumenical Council of Constantinople in 381, however, he was honored and proclaimed a "Confessor of Faith." Cyril was entrusted to write instructions on Christian doctrine for catechumens (people training for church membership) in preparation for baptism. His 23 *Catechetical Lectures on Christian faith* and practice are strong reference works that give valuable insight into the liturgy of the Palestinian Church. Cyril developed Jerusalem into a pilgrimage center. He acknowledged every NT book as Scripture, except Revelation.

Monica
Monnica

c 331　　　　　　　　　　　　　　　　　　　　　　　　May 4, 387
Tagaste (Souk-Ahras), Numidia (Algeria)　　　　　　　Ostia, Italy

Mother of AUGUSTINE OF HIPPO. Married to Patricius, a pagan government official, Monica struggled for years to bring her husband to the Lord. He finally responded in 370. A year later, she was widowed, at age 40, and followed her lost son, AUGUSTINE, to Rome in 383. AMBROSE comforted her by saying, "It is impossible that a son of so many prayers can be lost." Her prayers and AMBROSE's preaching won AUGUSTINE to the Lord in Milan, Italy, in 386. She died preparing for the return trip to Africa. As she died, she said, "In peace I will sleep with Him and take my rest." She had two other children—Navigius and Perpetua.

Adeotatus

372
Italy

389
Tagaste, Numidia (Algeria)

Son of AUGUSTINE OF HIPPO. Adeotatus was deeply loved by his father. His mother, a mistress of AUGUSTINE, separated from him after his conversion. Adeotatus showed early signs of brilliance, but died tragically at age 17; two years after he and his father were baptized.

Gregory of Nazianzus
Gregory the Theologian —Theologus

c 325
Arianzus, Asia Minor

May 9, 389
Arianzus, Cappadocia, Asia Minor (Turkey)

Eastern church father and patriarch of Constantinople, 379–81. Gregory received an excellent education, but after meeting BASIL of Caesarea, he changed his legal focus, studied in Alexandria, and spent ten years with him in Athens. He was baptized there in 358. A theological brain trust was formed with Gregory, BASIL, and GREGORY OF NYSSA—being known together as "The Three Cappadocians." Around 368, Gregory's father, then in his eightieth year, needed to retire as bishop of Nazianzus and desired him to help manage his diocese. His father insisted on ordaining him. Gregory fled to Basil, but returned ten weeks later to shoulder his responsibility and became the new bishop of Nazianzus 372–79. With THEODOSIUS I as the newly baptized emperor, Gregory witnessed the return to Orthodoxy. As patriarch and a seasoned orator, he was prominent at the Council of Constantinople of 381. That same year, Gregory returned to the bishopric of Nazianzus, and in 383 handed over its leadership to Eulalius, his cousin. He then retired to his family estate in nearby Arianzus. He wrote *Defense of the Trinity* and *Five Theological Orations*. His other works are divided into descants (religious discussions), letters, and poems. They include 45 orations, 243 letters, and a large number of poems.

Apollinaris of Laodicea

c 300–310
Laodicea (Denizli), Asia Minor (Turkey)

c 390

Rhetoric teacher and bishop of Laodicea, 362–82. Apollinaris was an active opponent of Arianism and swung the pendulum too far the other way, actually denying the humanity of Christ. This teaching was condemned as Docetism in 381. It prepared the way for Monophysitism (humanity and divinity of Christ = one nature), causing Apollinaris to secede from the Orthodox Church in 375. His stand was condemned at councils from 362–81. Apollinaris wrote against many of Christianity's enemies and was the founder of the Apollinarians (attributed human soul to Christ, but no human spirit—Christ is one person with one nature, not equally human and divine). His teachings were widely accepted in Syria. Apollinaris authored poems and religious works. When Emperor Julian forbade the Christians to teach the pagan classics, Apollinaris produced stories based on sacred Scriptures, prepared in classical form. These restyled Biblical texts became poetic/philosophical dialogues.

Macarius of Egypt
Macarius the Elder—The Great Macarius

c 300
Upper Egypt

c 390
Scete Desert, Lower Egypt

Hermit and writer. Macarius was an extreme ascetic who was constantly attempting greater degrees of abstinence in his quest for "perfect communion with God." Macarius and his following all lived in separate "hermitages" in the Scete Desert which, of the three deserts in Lower Egypt, was the one closest to Libya. The extremes of desert life seemed to attract other ascetics, which made Egypt a center for Monasticism. Macarius, who became a monk at age 30, was renowned for his sanctity and influenced others to mimic his extreme existence. Evagrius served as his disciple and "assistant." Macarius was ordained at age 40, to fulfill the "hierarchical duty of a monk," though he preferred to be considered a hermit. During Emperor Valens' persecution of Orthodoxy, Macarius was banished to an island in the Nile Delta. When released, he visited the monks in the Nitria Desert and had his only known meeting with MACARIUS OF ALEXANDRIA, when they shared a boat at a river crossing. His sole authentic work is *To the Friends of God*, although 50 homilies (sermons) are attributed to him.

Diodorus
Diodore

Antioch (Anatyka), Syria (Turkey)

c 393
Tarsus, Cilicia, Asia Minor (Turkey)

Teacher and bishop of Tarsus, c 378–c 393. In his early years, Diodorus served as a model priest and monk in Antioch. He wrote many commentaries and opposed Monophysitism and Arianism. Diodorus taught THEODORE OF MOPSUESTIA and JOHN CHRYSOSTOM. In 372, he was banished from Antioch to Armenia by Emperor Valens. Diodorus was active in the Council of Constantinople in 381. Some of his views were considered forerunners of Nestorianism and, at some point, he may have opposed the doctrine of everlasting punishment. He opposed the Alexandrian school of thought (Neoplatonism: Hellenistic and Christian theology – highest point under ORIGEN (230s) objectives: exhortation to the heathen, instruction in Christian morals, training in Divine Wisdom). He and his followers met with FLAVIAN I and his followers outside the walls of Antioch to worship.

Didymus
Didymus the Blind

c 309
Alexandria, Egypt

394–395
Alexandria, Egypt

Scholar, prolific writer, and theologian. Didymus lost his sight at the age of four, yet became one of the most learned men of his time. ANTHONY OF EGYPT gave spiritual insight as to what might have been a learning disability. "Let nothing move you, O Didymus, that your bodily eyes are lost, for you are deprived only of the same kind of eyes as serve the basest insects for vision; but rather rejoice that you possess those with which angels are seen, and God himself is discerned." Under ATHANASIUS' appointment Didymus became one of the last to head and teach at the Alexandrian Catechetical School. He was a prolific writer, scholar, and theologian, producing commentaries on Micah, Hosea, and Zechariah. His teaching spanned 50 years and included famous pupils such as ANTHONY, AMBROSE, and JEROME, who translated his *On the Holy Spirit* into Latin. Didymus strongly opposed Arianism, but supported ORIGEN which generated criticism against him at the Council of Constantinople in 381. He was to the theological world what FANNY CROSBY later became to the Christian music world.

Gregory of Nyssa

c 331
Caesarea (Kayseri), Cappadocia, Asia Minor (Turkey)

March 9, 395–396
Nyssa, Cappadocia, Asia Minor (Turkey)

Theologian and reluctant bishop of Nyssa, 372–c 394. Influenced by ORIGEN, Gregory became an excellent theologian. He was the younger brother of BASIL THE GREAT. They, with GREGORY OF NAZIANZUS, were known as the "Three Cappadocians"—Gregory of Nyssa being the philosopher in the trio. He wrote against paganism and heresies, including Arianism, and defended Nicene doctrines. Gregory attended the Councils of Antioch (379) and Constantinople (381). Arian accusations caused him to be deposed (376), at the Synod of Nyssa, under Emperor Valens, but he was reinstated (378) by Emperor Gratian, who also called upon him to preach the funeral for his wife and daughter. He wrote several books, including *Catechetical Discourse* (after 381) and *Life of Moses*. Although Gregory was inferior to BASIL as a bishop, he surpassed him as a theologian. Their sister, Macrina the Younger, founded a monastery on their family estate. Gregory's wife's name was Theosebeia.

Theodosius I

346
Cauca, Spain

Jan. 17, 395
Milan, Italy

Roman emperor of the East, 379–95, and of the West, 394–95. Theodosius has been called the first great ruler with strong Christian convictions. Upon his baptism in 380, he re-established Christianity as the state religion. Under him, Rome hosted the Council of Constantinople in 381, reaffirming the Nicene Creed. In 390, he yielded to Bishop AMBROSE and gave a public confession, showing religious humility for over-reacting and allowing the massacre of 7,000 people attending a circus in Thessalonica. This slaughter was in response to a public mob slaying of the governor, his family, staff, and attending officers. His confession vindicated Christianity to the world as being no respecter of persons. Theodosius opposed the Arians and pacified the Goths (barbarian Teutonic German people). His career started when he accompanied his father, General Flavius Theodosius (executed at Carthage, 376) into Britain in 368 and ended in 394 when he defeated Eugenius (emperor in the West; ruled: 392–94) and Frankish General Arbogast (responsible for the murder of co-emperor Valentinian II in the West, died: 394) near Aquileia, Italy. He destroyed pagan temples and terminated the Olympic games (resumed in 1896) in 393 as pagan shows. He married Galla, daughter of VALENTINIAN II of Rome. He permanently divided the Roman Empire at his death, giving sons Arcadius, the East (ruled: 395–408) and Honorius, the West (ruled: 395–423). The West spoke Latin until it fell to Istanbul in 1453. The East (Byzantine) led in art and culture for 1,000 years.

Ambrosiaster
Divine or Immortal One

c 315

c 397

Writer. Ambrosiaster was a Latin name given to the unknown author of *Commentary on the Epistles of St. Paul* —at one time attributed to AMBROSE. It is a work of high value relating an early interpretation of Paul's writings, and preserved many quotations from the ancient Vulgate (commonly used) Bible, popular before JEROME's translation into Latin. It was written between 366 and 384. Ambrosiaster is sometimes identified with bishop HILARY OF POITIERS.

Philaster

c 397

Egypt

Expository writer and bishop of Brescia, Lombardy, Italy. As bishop, Philaster was present at the Synod of Aquileia, Italy in 381. About 384, he wrote *Diversarum Haereoseon Liber*, a book exposing 156 heresies: 28 before Christ and 128 after Christ's Resurrection. Philaster was an ordained priest and traveled widely, preaching against pagans, Jews, and Arians. AUGUSTINE endorsed him, which gave more importance to Philaster's work.

Ambrose
Father of Church Music

c 339–340
Treves (Trier), Gaul (Germany)

April 4, 397
Milan, Italy

Hymn writer, theologian and bishop of Milan, 373–97. Ambrose, of noble birth, studied law and was appointed governor of Northern Italy in 370, while living in Milan. Upon the death of the local bishop, Ambrose was unanimously chosen to the post. He sold his property, distributing the profits to the poor and studied theology. He was baptized and ordained December 7, 374. Ambrose presided at the Church Synod in Aquileia, 381, which deposed Arian leaders. In 384, he revised the music of the Church, writing simple hymns that congregations could sing, and developed the "Ambrosian Chant." His hymns were organized into topics. Ambrose defied the Empress Justina (mother of Emperor Valentian) an ardent Arian. The troops she sent to besiege the cathedral in Milan dispersed as singing was heard. He was instrumental in both the conversion and baptism of AUGUSTINE OF HIPPO in 387. He extracted a humbling public confession from Emperor THEODOSIUS I in 390, for over reacting and killing thousands in Thessalonica in retaliation for the mob killings of his officers and the Roman governor. This act established the Church as a powerful, independent force, above state control. He remained in Milan during its occupation by the barbaric Visigoths (Western branch of the Goths—which settled in southern France and Spain, flourishing 375–711) but was forced to flee in 392. Ambrose steadfastly opposed Arianism. His hymns gained widespread recognition when Empress Justina sent soldiers to arrest him for not surrendering his church to be used for Arian congregations. Ambrose and his faithful flock stayed in the sanctuary of the church for days, singing and praying. The empress lost the standoff. His main work, *Decificiis Ministrorum* (Of the Offices of Christian Ministers) was a book on Christian ethics, written for the clergy. He also wrote *On Faith, On the Holy Ghost, On the Sacraments* and many homiletic commentaries. Pagans and Jews joined the Christian multitude that attended his funeral and viewed his body that was enclosed in a glass coffin.

Nectarius

Tarsus, Cilicia, Asia Minor (Turkey)

Sept. 27, 397
Constantinople (Istanbul), Asia Minor (Turkey)

Patriarch of Constantinople, 381–97. At the Second Ecumenical Council of Constantinople in 381, Nectarius visited his old bishop, DIODORUS, who informed him that GREGORY OF NAZIANZUS had resigned the Constantinople high office position. DIODORUS, impressed by Nectarius' mannerisms, submitted his name even though he was married and the father of a son. When Emperor THEODOSIUS I declared him elected, many in the episcopacy were shocked, especially since Nectarius had neither been baptized nor ordained. Once ordained, he was a dutiful bishop, though his lack of credentials further strengthened Rome's position over that of Constantinople. Nectarius abolished public confession as a form of penance and the practice of a secret confessionary. He was succeeded by JOHN CHRYSOSTOM.

Martin of Tours

Nov. 11, 335
Sabaria (Szombathely), Pannonia (Hungary)

Nov. 8, 397
Tours, Gaul (France)

Bishop of Tours, 371–97. Martin served with the Roman army, until 356, when Julian (soon to be emperor in 361) prepared the troops for battle against a barbarian invasion of Gaul. Martin, who had accepted Christ at age ten, became a "conscientious objector" and fled to sanctuary at the monastery of HILARY OF POITIERS. He was baptized into the church in 362, led his family (except his father) to Christianity, and then served as a monk in Milan until expelled by the Arians. He sought counsel with HILARY, who gave him land at Liguge, near Poitiers where Martin established his famous monastery—the first in the West. He gained a reputation for his kind generosity and helpful miracles that touched the lives of many. Often Martin's very presence weakened would-be attackers and it is documented that he cured PAULINUS OF NOLA of a severe eye problem. Sulpicius Severus states that Martin's miracles were extraordinary and visible to the multitude, yet "wretched, degenerate and slothful men denied the truth." He led the bishopric from within the protective walls of his monastery. Martin conducted church reforms and encouraged the spread of monastic communities throughout France. Hundreds of French villages are named after him, as was MARTIN LUTHER. Martin of Tours died in a monastery he had founded. He said to Satan as he died, "What doest thou here, thou cruel beast?" He destroyed paganism, won the masses, planted monasteries, and trained a clergy with a passion for holiness.

Evagrius
Evagrius Ponticus

346
Pontus, Asia Minor (Turkey)

399
Egypt

Monk and writer. Evagrius was ordained a deacon by GREGORY OF NAZIANZUS. He was active in the church at Constantinople, attending the council of 381. Evagrius then went to Jerusalem where he was influenced to live an ascetic life. He was a gifted preacher and was highly regarded in his day as a spiritual guide and one of the first monks to write about spirituality. His writings were a formative influence on later spiritual writers, although his credence was hurt by his alignment with ORIGEN's theology, which contained Neoplatonic teachings (dualistic view of reality bordering on transcendental meditation; all existence originates from the One with whom the soul may be reunited). An illness sent him to recover in the dry climate of the Nitrian Desert in Egypt, which proved in keeping with his desire for a monastic life. Evagrius became a disciple of MACARIUS OF EGYPT and lived in various monastic communities from 382 until his death.

Fabiola

Rome, Italy

399
Rome, Italy

Founder of the first public hospital in Western Europe. Fabiola came from a distinguished noble family in Rome that had been converted. She divorced a vicious first husband, losing the approval of the local Christian community, and dedicated herself to the care of the sick, especially after the death of her second husband. She gave away her wealth, worked closely with JEROME, and even went to the Holy Land in 395. Fabiola, concerned about the barbaric Visigoths and Vandals, (Germanic people who ravaged Gaul, Spain, and Rome) returned to her hospital in Rome and the furtherance of her desire to continue God's work.

Siricius

Nov. 26, 399

Rome, Italy

Thirty-eighth bishop of Rome, 384–99. In 386, Siricius called a synod in Rome issuing the first church decree (local churches were bound by "official" mandate). His statement dictated how to deal strongly with reactionary classes within the church: converted Arians, penitents, undisciplined monks, and especially married priests—decreeing that they had to leave their wives and commence living celibate lives. Siricius excommunicated the unorthodox and vocal monk, JOVINIAN, and eight associates for promoting marital union for the clergy in 390. He seriously regarded his rights and duties as overseer of the Church and demanded that his decisions be preserved. He was the first to use the title of Pope (Papa from the Greek, "Father"), and laid the groundwork for Pope Leo I the Great (reigned: 440–61), who was the first to have authority as the leader of the church throughout the West. Though his stand was severe, Siricius elevated the level of the clergy through ecclesiastical discipline. He was the first Roman bishop to issue decretals in the style of imperial edicts.

Telemachus
Almachius

Syria

c 400
Rome, Italy

Martyred Syrian monk. Telemachus ended the grisly sport of forcing combatants to fight to the death in the arenas. He leaped into the ring in Rome's Colosseum to register his protest. His act infuriated the sports fans, who poured out of the stands and stoned him to death. This persuaded Western Roman Emperor Honorius to do away with such gladiatorial contests.

Tyconius

c 400

Proconsular, North Africa

Moderate Donatist lay theologian. In his two works, now lost, *On Internal War* and *Expositions of Various Causes*, Tyconius expressed a philosophy that the Church must be a society spread over the whole earth, and must contain both good and bad—the concept of the "universal" catholic church. Tyconius stressed that the Church was the institution to enter for salvation. His *Book of Rules*, published about 382, is the first attempt at hermeneutics (methodological principles of Bible interpretation). Many of its principles are still used. Tyconius opposed those who followed Pelagianism. Tyconius had a strong influence on the work of AUGUSTINE OF HIPPO.

Anastasius I

Dec. 19, 401

Rome, Italy

Rome, Italy

Thirty-ninth bishop of Rome, 399–401. Anastasius condemned the teachings of the Donatists and ORIGEN. He excommunicated RUFINUS (ORIGEN supporter), who did not understand the controversy. He resolved the schism between Rome and the Church of Antioch. Anastasius I was renown for his charity, holiness and poverty, as well as his orthodoxy. At a synod in Carthage, on September 13, 401, he exhorted African bishops to expose misrepresentations perpetrated by the Donatists. Anastasius I also clashed with JEROME. He fought immorality and decreed priests should remain standing during the reading of the Gospel. His son, Innocent I, succeeded him, the only time in the history of the Roman bishops (popes).

Epiphanius

c 315

May 12, 403

Besandouk (Beit-Jibrin), Palestine (Israel)

At sea near Cyprus

Orator and bishop of Salamis (Constantia), Cyprus, 367–403. Epiphanius was a disciple of HILARION, who introduced monasticism to Palestine. He was highly esteemed for his monastic ascetic learning, skill as a pulpit orator, piety, self-denying care for the poor, and his zeal for Orthodoxy. He headed a monastery in Besandouk (Bet-Jibrin, 23 miles southwest of Jerusalem) 335–67, and denied any place for Greek learning in the church. Epiphanius attended the Synods of Antioch (376) and of Rome (382). He retired to Cyprus in 385. In his fervor to attack heretics, he managed to tangle with most of his leading contemporaries, including ORIGEN and CHRYSOSTOM. His major work *Panarion* (revealing 80 heresies) was called the "medicine chest" against all heresies. Epiphanius was a violent partisan—being quick to judge others "guilty by association". Then, on several occasions, he was forced to apologize, admitting that he hadn't even read the written words of his self-proclaimed adversaries. His *Book of Weights and Measures* is an excellent history of Jewish customs. JEROME, in his comments, said, "Epiphanius was a last relic of ancient piety." Epiphanius died on his return from Constantinople where he sought, once again, to denounce JOHN CHRYSOSTOM for favoring ORIGEN, whom he obsessively opposed.

Paula

May 5, 347

Jan. 26, 404

Rome, Italy

Bethlehem, Palestine (Israel)

Wealthy Roman lady, monastery founder, and assistant to JEROME. Paula was a lady of society who, following the example of the widowed MARCELLA, relinquished all material goods in favor of a spiritually focused life. After the death of her husband, Senator Toxotius, in 380, Paula became driven to find an environment to support her religious desires. She raised a godly family of five children and suffered when daughters, Blesilla and Rufina, died in their youth. Daughter Eustochium became her mother's inseparable companion, and joined her with the group that went with JEROME to the Holy Land in 385. They stopped enroute to visit EPIPHANIUS on the Island of Cyprus. Although she initially lived in a cave in Bethlehem, she established a monastery in 386, a nunnery, and a hospital. Her excellent education, which included Greek and Hebrew, were assets, as she became an assistant to JEROME in his translations and writings. Paula spent her life in poverty and devotion. It is felt that the austerity of her life hastened her death.

Flavian I

c 320
Antioch (Antakya), Syria (Turkey)

June 404
Antioch (Antakya), Syria (Turkey)

Bishop of Antioch, 381–404. Flavian was an advocate and supporter of the Orthodox Party, opposing Arianism. He succeeded MELITIUS OF ANTIOCH. The bishops of Rome and Egypt did not recognize Flavian's appointment and, in 398, raised a furor, which widened the schism between these ecclesiastical centers. He was troubled by a dissident sect, the Eustathians {though anti-Arian, raised questions on the divinity and humanity of Christ}. CHRYSOSTOM and Emperor THEODOSIUS I supported his orthodox stand and acknowledged him as the legitimate bishop, even though they initially chose PAULINUS OF NOLA for that post. Flavian originated the art of antiphonal singing (responsive alternation between two choral groups) when he and his followers sang with DIODORUS and his followers outside the walls of Antioch in worship, prior to 372.

Jovinian

Italy

c 406
Island of Boa

Unorthodox Italian monk. Jovinian wrote and argued against certain phases of monasticism and Orthodox theology. Through his writings, which conveyed that marriage is a sanctified union and of equal esteem to virginity, many monks and nuns left their celibate life and married. He stated that fasting had no greater merit than eating with thankfulness, and that heavenly rewards were equally available to all and thus not in proportion to earthly status. Jovinian's more radical views caused Western Emperor Honorius to oppose and banish him for heresy (c 390) after he was excommunicated by SIRICIUS. Jovinian stated that a born-again, baptized person could not be led into sin, and opposed the perpetual virginity of Mary, stating that Jesus had earthly siblings. Jovinian then went to Milan, where AMBROSE held a council against him in 391. JEROME vehemently opposed him, devoting three major works to defining the reasons for his ostracism and called him a "dangerous heretic," leaving him to die in exile. He was unmarried.

Macarius of Alexandria
Macarius the Younger

c 320
Alexandria, Egypt

Jan. 2, 406
Nitria Desert, Egypt

Godly hermit. Macarius was a baker in the Alexandria/Thebaid region until 346, when he felt called to a "better life with God." He spent the next 60 years in the desert of Lower Egypt. He had a "cell" in each of the three deserts: the Skete (near Libya), the Cellia (named for the presence of many hermit huts and the Nitria (near the western branch of the Nile). The monks lived alone in their small huts, not in sight of one another, assembling on Saturdays and Sundays for worship and instruction. Macarius trained some 5,000 monks. They performed manual labor (basket/mat weaving) to meet their bare sustenance needs. It is said though many were present, there existed a "profound silence" in the land. Macarius is the reputed author of *The Rules of the Monks*, consisting of 30 chapters. When advanced in age he visited Pachomius' monastery in disguise, to learn about their regime. When someone commented on his cheerfulness, observing that he must be happy in his poverty, he replied, "You have reason to call us happy for that is our name" (Macarius: "happy" in Greek). Some feel he may have died in 394.

Vigilantius

c 370
Calagurris, Martres, Gaul (Spain)

c 407

Presbyter of Aquitaine, Gaul (France). Vigilantius was theologically consistent and courageous. Vigilantius was ordained in 395 in Barcelona, Spain, and later visited JEROME in Bethlehem. He wrote *Contra Vigilantium* around 403, denouncing superstitions associated with the veneration of relics and saints. This work also opposed the double set of standards in the church, one for the laity and another for the clergy. His views resulted in bitter exchanges between himself and JEROME, although they respected each other. Vigilantius also denounced priestly celibacy, excessive asceticism, and purposeful impoverishment.

John (Chrysostom) of Antioch
Chrysostomos (Golden Mouthed)

c 347
Antioch (Antayka), Syria (Turkey)

Sept. 14, 407
Comana, Pontus, Asia Minor (Turkey)

Outstanding preacher and patriarch of Constantinople, 398–404. Chrysostom was the best preacher of the Greek Church, being both eloquent and popular. He studied rhetoric under Libanius (314–93), a pagan professor, around 365, was baptized around 369, and studied in an ascetic school under DIODORUS. His reforming zeal and plain speaking pleased the common people, but angered the powerful and wealthy. From 373–81, he became a hermit in the mountains. He then returned to Antioch where he wrote *On the Priesthood*, was ordained a deacon by MELITIUS OF ANTIOCH and a priest by Bishop Flavian in 386. When Chrysostom was chief preacher in Antioch, 386–97, he delivered his famous message, "Homilies on the Statues" (387), after which he was invited to the main see in Constantinople. His speech vindicated actions by the populace who had destroyed statues in protest of levied taxes. For challenging imperial authority, Queen Eudoxia, wife of Eastern Emperor Arcadius, banished him to Cucusus, Armenia, by the Synod of the Oak in 403. She recalled him when an earthquake hit but banished him again in 404 for attacking the immorality of the Byzantine court and his "control" over the people. Chrysostom's preaching was said to be so absorbing that it produced wild applause and mesmerized the crowd so that pickpockets thrived. As he left on his trek into exile, he exclaimed, "Glory to God for all events." He died under the piercing hot sun of the desert by the Black Sea, en route to his exile in Pityus. His remains were exhumed and returned to Constantinople for burial in 438. Chrysostom held to 22 books of the New Testament as Scripture, omitting II Peter, II and III John, Jude, and Revelation. He reported numerous divine healings. His "golden mouthed" (Chrysostom) name came in the seventh century, 300 years after his death.

Tyrannius Rufinus

c 345
Concordia (near Aquileia), Italy

410
Messina, Sicily, Italy

Latin theologian and Church historian. Rufinus was an Italian pagan converted around 370. He translated many Greek works into Latin, which saved countless texts from being lost. He and JEROME were both pupils of DIDYMUS of Alexandria. Living as a monk in Egypt until 375, Rufinus founded a monastery (c 379) on the Mount of Olives in Jerusalem, where he wrote and translated. In 394, he was made a presbyter of JerusalemHis last years were spent in Aquileia, 398–410. He attempted one last trip to the Holy Land, but got no further than Sicily when he died. Rufinus turned against JEROME when he publicly expressed his opposition to ORIGEN ANASTASIUS I excommunicated him for his support of ORIGEN.

Asterius

c 350
Cappadocia, Asia Minor (Turkey)

c 410/430
Amasia, Pontus, Asia Minor (Turkey)

Bishop of Amasia, 378 on. Asterius' fame rests upon his homilies (short religious, moral sermons), which had a great reputation in the Eastern church. Eleven of them have been preserved, along with the fragments of 22 others. Asterius was a famous pulpit orator of the ancient Church. His works are a valuable contribution to the history of preaching.

Aurelius C. Prudentius

348
Saragossa, Spain

c 410
Calahorra, Spain

Chief Latin poet and hymnodist. Prudentius was a lawyer and provincial governor in Spain before being called to occupy a military post at the court of Emperor THEODOSIUS I. After his conversion, he became a poet. He wrote 28 hymns, about the same time that AMBROSE was creating his, but with more warmth and less liturgical usage. Prudentius produced the earliest religious allegory (use of symbolic fictional figures to portray a truth). He retired to a monastery around 405, ending secular employment at age 57, to write about Christ and His church. MARTIN LUTHER desired that his writings be studied in schools.

Marcella

325

Jan. 31, 410
Rome, Italy

Martyred widow. Marcella was an ascetic whose husband died after seven months of marriage. Vowing perpetual celibacy, she gave her goods to relatives and to the poor. She encouraged others to follow her example, among whom was the widowed PAULA, and her family. Marcella studied the Scriptures with JEROME when he came to Rome in 382. Her home became a convent dedicated to the study of Scripture. After the sack of Rome in 410, she was tortured by the Goths, but through her pleadings, her virgin pupil, Principia, was protected. The barbarians (uncivilized people) tried many hideous means to make Marcella reveal her supposed wealth—not listening when she attempted to explain that her "wealth" awaited her in heaven. Although finally granted sanctuary, she died in Principia's arms, exhausted and fatally injured from her ordeal. She may have died in late August.

Synesius

c 370
Cyrene, Cyrenaica (Libya)

c 413/414
Ptolemais, Cyrenaica (Libya)

Bishop of Ptolemais, 410–14. Synesius lived during the time of the sack of Rome in 410. He was a Neoplatonic philosopher until his baptism in 409. He loved hunting (sports) as well as his bishopric. Synesius was an efficient administrator and a prolific writer. He interceded to Emperor Honorius for aid to Cyrene when the Vandals came. His writings during the political turmoil expressed a longing for a closer communion with God. He lived in Constantinople, 397–400, and then moved to Ptolemais.

Innocent I

Albano, Rome, Italy

March 12, 417
Rome, Italy

Fortieth bishop of Rome, 401–17. Innocent I guided the Church during the days of the barbarians crossing the Rhine in 406 and again when the Visigoths sacked Rome under King Alaric I (ruled: 395–410) in 410. Innocent I then deserted his flock and fled to Ravenna, Italy. He advocated celibacy among all clergy, expecting already married priests to live apart from their wives. Innocent I took a strong stand against Pelagianism. He enhanced the power of his position by insisting that other bishops refer important questions to Rome and follow Roman customs. His policies and leadership enhanced the power of the papacy in its formative years. He persuaded Emperor Honorius to prohibit gladiatorial contests in the arenas, and he supported CHRYSOSTOM in his difficulties at Constantinople.

Zosimus

Greece

Dec. 26, 418
Rome, Italy

Forty-first bishop of Rome, 417–18. Tactless, tricky, and tyrannical, Zosimus ineptly handled the North African clergy during the Pelagian controversy so that Emperor Honorius finally had to intervene. Zosimus' problems began when he cancelled the condemnation of PELAGIUS and Celestius, his zealous follower, in 418. He later condemned PELAGIUS and his doctrine, while Celestius retracted his position. Zosimus upset the French clergy by appointing Patrocles, bishop of Arles, papal vicar of Gaul, and metropolitan over Vienne and Narbonne, disrupting the status quo of the religious hierarchy among the Franks in the region. He insisted on the rights of the Church against foreign interference. He had strict morals.

Pelagius

c 339
Ireland or England

c 419
Palestine (Israel)

British monk and theologian. Pelagius was an Irish monk who settled in Britain. When he visited Rome in 384, as a Christian moralist, he was deeply shocked by what he considered to be the tone of behavior there. Pelagius preached in Rome in 400 (challenging AUGUSTINE's doctrine of predestination, arguing for freedom of the will) holding out the hope of heaven to all men, not merely to the elect. Accused of heresy in 415, he was acquitted, but banished from Rome in 418 by Bishop ZOSIMUS. He rejected the doctrine of original sin and said people were sinners because they followed their own free choice to do evil—so each person should simply choose "good." In 410, he went to Carthage and in 411 to Palestine. Although cleared of charges of heresy at a Jerusalem Synod, he was condemned and excommunicated by African bishops in 416. His followers embraced the concepts of an aristocratic, adult-baptized religious community that discouraged asceticism; were committed to perfectionist ideals, believing that godly grace forgave sins; and that infants were baptized for sanctification, not for forgiveness of sins, since they were born sinless. Pelagianism (salvation by works, denying original sin, stressing man has perfect freedom of will) sparked a major controversy, that was a forerunner to the CALVIN-ARMINIUS debates centuries later.

Jerome of Bethlehem
Eusebius Hieronymus

c 345
Stridon, Palmatia, Italy

Sept. 30, 420
Bethlehem, Palestine (Israel)

Translator of the Latin Vulgate Bible. Jerome was a monk, and the foremost Christian scholar of his day, giving the Christian community the Latin Bible text in 405/406. Raised in a Christian home, he went to Rome and studied philosophy, rhet, and the classic languages under DONATUS. It was said that he spent his Sundays in the catacombs, translating the burial inscriptions. He had an extensive knowledge of Greek and Hebrew. He was baptized in 360, and ordained without pastoral responsibilities by Bishop PAULINUS so that he would have greater religious/academic access for his historical/ecclesiastical research. He lived in Gaul; Antioch, Syria; Aguileia, Italy; and then, in 374, became an aesthetic in the Chalcis Desert (Euboea Island, Greece), teaching the hermits. He journeyed through the Eastern Roman Empire, 374–90, and in 378 was ordained a presbyter in Antioch. In 381, he attended the Second Ecumenical Council in Constantinople. While serving in Rome as administrative secretary to Bishop

Damascus I, 382–85, he encouraged many Roman women toward asceticism. Many, including Paula and her daughter Eustochium, went with him, in 386, to Bethlehem, participating in his editorial work and the founding of several monasteries and a convent. It was during this time that Jerome produced his Bible commentaries and church histories, as well as his translation of the Bible from the original Hebrew language. He was involved in the church controversy over Origen's stand and also wrote against Gnostic and Pelagian heresies, 393–410. Jerome died after spending many years in desert seclusion. He accepted the same 27 New Testament books that Athanasius stated were Scripture. His favorite Bible verse was Psalm 1:2.

"May the devil always find you employed."

Sulpicius Severus

c 360
Aquitaine, Gaul (France)

c 421
Aquitaine, Gaul (France)

Latin church historian, ascet, and hagiographer (biographer of saintly persons). Severus was an authority on the Christian life in Gaul and rejoiced in giving his worldly goods to the poor. Early in his career, he was a lawyer. He chronicled the life of his friend, Martin of Tours, in *Vita S. Martini*, and was baptized with his friend Paulinus of Nola. After his wife died in 392, when Severus was only 32, he retired to a monastic life in Aquitaine. His *Dialogue* (404) revealed his interest in the development of Monasticism. His works included *Historia Sacra* and *Chronicle* (resume of Church History).

Boniface I

c 350
Rome, Italy

Sept. 4, 422
Rome, Italy

Forty-second bishop of Rome, 418–22. Boniface I was old and frail when, as a papal representative to Constantinople, he was selected in a disputed election. Eulalius was his rival, but Emperor Honorius ultimately decided in favor of Boniface I for this high position. Charles of Ravenna (city in northeast Italy) began the secular powers' interference in the elections of the popes. Boniface I supported Augustine in his stand against the Pelagians. He sought to establish and defend Roman authority in the West. He persuaded Theodosius II, the Eastern Roman emperor, to leave Illyricum (Yugoslavia). Boniface I was a gifted organizer and known for his justice and moderation. At the Council of Carthage, North Africa, in 414, he was urged to accept appeals from bishops, not from clerics.

Theodore of Mopsuestia

c 350
Antioch (Antakya), Syria (Turkey)

428
Mopsuestia, Cilicia, Asia Minor (Turkey)

Theologian and Greek bishop of Mopsuestia, 392–428. Theodore came from wealthy parentage and abandoned a secular career to attend the monastic school of bishop Diodorus of Tarsus. There he became the close friend of the famous preacher, John Chrysostom. In 383, he became a presbyter in Antioch. Theodore attended the second Council of Constantinople in 394 and was unjustly condemned for his theological association with his pupil Nestorius. Theodore preached before emperor Theodosius I. He wrote a number of Biblical commentaries and treatises, including *Against the Allegorists* and *Against Defenders of Original Sin*. However his nationalist mode of interpretation caused them to be condemned posthumously at the Council of Constantinople in 553. Theodore's Orthodox position was strong and his writings gave modern-day scholars great insight into the Antiochene Church. Theodore was a theologian, preacher, later an exegete of the Nestorian Church, and writer of considerable renown—being the first to present the Psalms historically. Theodore was entangled in the Pelagian and Monophysite controversies later in life.

Nilus
Nilus of Sinai–Nilus the Wise

c 430
Asia Minor (Turkey)

Greek Byzantine (Eastern Roman Empire c 476–1453) **abbot** (head of a monastery), **and author of ascetic literature**. Nilus became a hermit on Mt. Sinai, with his son. He later moved to Asia Minor where he eventually served as abbot of a monastery near Ancyra, Galatia, Asia Minor. Nilus was a disciple and supporter of JOHN CHRYSOSTOM. He wrote many tracts on moral and monastic subjects. His writings show him to have been a quality example of Christian spirituality. Nilus refuted Arianism, and greatly influenced the direction of Monasticism.

Palladius of Helenopolis

c 363
Galatia, Asia Minor (Turkey)

c 430
Asperna, Galatia, Asia Minor (Turkey)

Writer and Greek desert monastic bishop of Helenopolis, Bithynia, Asia Minor, 400. Palladius suffered imprisonment twice for supporting JOHN CHRYSOSTOM. He was finally banished to Ancyra, Galatia, where he wrote the *Historia Lausiacav* (419–20), which described monastic life in Egypt and Palestine. It became a valuable source on the origins of Christian asceticism. *Friends of God* (c 419) is another work by Palladius. He was recalled out of banishment, and made bishop of Asperna.

Aurelius Augustine
Augustine of Hippo—Founder of Theology

Nov. 13, 354
Tagaste (Souk Ahras), Numidia (Algeria)

Aug. 28, 430
Hippo Regius, Numidia (Algeria)

Esteemed theologian and bishop of Hippo, 396–430. Augustine was the leading theologian between the Apostle Paul of Tarsus and JOHN CALVIN. Both Catholics and some Protestants claim him to be one of the greatest of the Latin Fathers. He advocated that salvation is totally by the grace of God, given only to the elect. His views are expressed in 200 treatises, 70 books, and 300 letters. He studied in Madaura (365) and in Carthage (370), but never mastered Greek. His unofficial marriage, 372–85, gave him a son, ADEOTATUS. From 373 to 382 Augustine was a Manichean. He taught grammar in Tagaste (375–76), rhetoric in Carthage (376–80) and Rome (380–83), and was a public orator in Milan (384–87). He was converted in 386 via his mother MONICA's prayers, AMBROSE's preaching, and by literature witness (Romans 13:13–14). He was baptized by AMBROSE on Easter Sunday in 387. After his return to North Africa in 388, Augustine was ordained a priest in 391, and was made bishop of Hippo Regius. His *Confessions* (397–400) and *City of God* (413–26) are classics. His theology was between the Donatists and Pelagians. Augustine died as the city of Hippo was being besieged by the barbaric Vandals. Some of his last words were: "Oh Lord, shall I die at all? Shall I die at all? Yes! Why, then, Oh Lord, if ever, why not now?" He held to the canonicity of the 27 New Testament books.

Marcus Eremita

c 330

c 431

Egyptian monk. He lived in the desert of Scete (Scetis) in Libya. Eremita was first known by a series of treatises later described by PHOTIUS. Nine treatises bearing his name have come down to us. They cover such topics as the spiritual law, justification, penitence and baptism. They were published in Latin and Greek. Some have unsuccessfully tried to prove different authorship. He lived over 100 years.

Paulinus of Nola
Pontius Meropius Anacius Paulinus

353
Bordeaux, Gaul (France)

June 22, 431
Nola, Italy

Bishop of Nola, 409–31. Paulinus was a Roman consul who, after the death of his son, turned his back on wealth and position to become a monk. He won wide approval for his asceticism and generosity to pilgrims and the poor. Paulinus used his wealth to help the entire area, even going so far as to repair the water duct. He went to Barcelona, Spain where he was ordained a priest by the bishop of Barcelonia on December 23, 393. His Spanish wife, Therasia, was also wealthy. He authored 32 songs in various meters, penned over 50 letters in his *Epistles* and was recognized as a gifted poet. MARTIN OF TOURS cured him of a severe eye problem. Paulinus was briefly the bishop of Antioch (Antakya), Syria (Turkey).

Alypius

c Dec. 431

Tagaste (Souk-Ahras), Numidia (Algeria)

Bishop of Thagaste, 394–430. Alypius went with AUGUSTINE OF HIPPO to Rome to study law. Moving on to Milan, he was converted along with AUGUSTINE. He was abbot of the monastery that AUGUSTINE established at Hippo, prior to his bishopric. Alypius attended a council at Carthage in 411, as a spokesman for the bishops confronting Donatism, and another synod in 418, where the view of original sin and grace was presented in nine canons (body of church law determined by church consuls or pope). He was believed to have been present at the death of his friend and colleague, AUGUSTINE OF HIPPO, and to have made a trip to the Holy Land where he met JEROME.

Celestine I

July 27, 432
Rome, Italy

Campania, Italy

Forty-third bishop of Rome, 422–432. He opposed heresy and irregularity. Celestine became involved in a heated doctrinal battle between NESTORIUS of Antioch and CYRIL OF ALEXANDRIA. Celestine condemned Nestorianism at the Third Ecumenical Council of Ephesus in 431, and also fought against Pelagianism by sending emissaries to Britain to root it out. Celestine also had problems in Southern France (opposing Augustinian doctrines) and with his bishops in North Africa. He was reputed to have sent PALLADIUS OF HELENOPOLIS (431) and PATRICK (432) as missionaries to Scotland and Ireland. He closed Novatianist churches in Rome. During his tenure, the worship of Mary originated at the Council of Ephesus in 431. He condemned bishops who wore distinctive dress. He wrote, "You should be known for your doctrine and morals, not your dress." The pastoral "staff" is first mentioned in his tenure.

Ninian
Apostle of the Southern Picts

c 360
Cumberland, England

Sept. 16, 432
Cumberland, England

First missionary and monastic bishop to Scotland. Ninian visited Rome in 380 and spent 15 years there. He was ordained a bishop in 394. Returning to Britain, Ninian built a stone church in Candidicasa, which was later called Whithorn, in 397, and dedicated it to MARTIN OF TOURS. This church became a monastic mission center from which he worked among Picts (early clans of Scotland) and Britons. For centuries it was an education center for Welsh and Irish missionaries. He went to Ireland in 420, where he founded a monastery at Clonconnor and ministered as far north as Grampian Hills.

John Cassianus
Johannes Eremita—Johannes Massiliensis

36
Dobrudschia, Scythih, Gaul (France)

435
Marseilles, Gaul (France)

Writer and theologian. One of the first founders of monastic institutions in western Europe. Cassianus was probably raised in modern Romania. He spent his formative years in a monastery in Bethlehem and lived in solitude among the desert hermits in Egypt 385–400. Cassianus was in Rome, 405–15. He later returned to his native France to found what became the large, influential religious order at St. Victor Monastery, Marseilles, in 415. Cassianus, a theologian, was the founder and first representative of Semi-Pelagianism (every soul was created sinless by God). He wrote *The Institutes* (425–30), which greatly influenced the Benedictine Rule developed by Benedict of Nursia. He opposed both Augustine and Pelagius.

Isaac
The Great

345

Sept. 7, 439
Ashtishat, Asia Minor (Turkey)

Leader of the Armenian Orthodox Church. In 390, Isaac negotiated the severance of the Armenian Church from submission to the see of Caesarea in Cappadocia. After his wife's death, he led the life of an Orthodox monk. He fostered Armenian ecclesiastical independence and culture. Isaac produced the first translation of the Bible into Armenian and is credited with many Armenian hymns.

Sixtus III

Rome, Italy

Aug. 19, 440

Forty-fourth bishop of Rome, 432–40. Sixtus III enlarged and embellished the Basilicas of Liberius (St. Mary Major) and St. Lawrence. He was the author of several epistles and upheld the jurisdiction of Rome over Illyria against the Eastern Emperor who wanted it to be dependent on Constantinople. He approved the acts of the Council of Ephesus in 451. He sought to reconcile John of Antioch and Cyril of Alexandria. He is the last Roman bishop ("pope") mentioned in this compilation. The next bishop, Leo I the Great, (reigned: 440–61) was declared by Valentinian III, emperor in the West, as primate of all the West, thus giving the papacy widespread authority and the bonafide use of the word "pope."

John of Antioch

c 403

441
Antioch (Antakya), Asia Minor (Turkey)

Patriarch of Antioch. John supported his friend Nestorius during the ecclesiastical, political, and theological disputes at the Council of Ephesus in 431. History portrays John as the force representing the moderate Easterners in the Nestorian controversies. Each side condemned members of the opposing faction in the Church, while arguing over the nature of Christ and being somewhat at odds with Cyril of Alexandria.

Socrates

380
Constantinople, Asia Minor

c 441/450
Constantinople (Istanbul), Asia Minor (Turkey)

Greek Church historian. He lived in Constantinople most of his life. Socrates continued the writing of Church history (306–439) where Eusebius of Caesarea left off. Seven books are still in existence. He wrote as a layman, not a cleric. His work is fair, comprehensive, orthodox in nature and indicative of his independent style, although it leans toward Novatianism. This Socrates (not the Greek philosopher) traveled greatly in his later years.

Salaminius H. Sozomen
Hermius Sozomenus

c 400
Bethella, Palestine

c 443
Bethella (near Gaza), Palestine (Israel)

Greek Church historian. Like Socrates, Sozomen continued tracing history since the time of Eusebius of Caesarea, concentrating on the years between 312–439 and dedicating it to Emperor Theodosius II. His book is similar to the work of Socrates, except that he gives more attention to the history of monasticism of this period. This emphasis came about because his father, a Palestinian, was a convert of Hilarion. Sozomen wrote much in favor of desert ascetics and opposed religious heresies.

Cyril of Alexandria

c 375/376
Alexandria, Egypt

June 27, 444
Alexandria, Egypt

Patriarch of Alexandria, 412–44. Successor of Theophilus, his uncle, Cyril was considered a brilliant theologian with an intemperate zeal. He immediately waged war upon Novatianism and had the Jews expelled from the city. In 431, he presided over the third General Council at Ephesus, which again condemned Nestorius. He opposed Chrysostom, Theodore of Mopsuestia and Nestorius, and advocated the veneration of Mary. Cyril gave much of his life to defending Christ's divinity, teaching on the Trinity and the incarnation, although much of his theology was essentially Platonism.

Germain of Auxerre

378
Auxerre, Gaul (France)

July 31, 448
Ravenna, Italy

Bishop of Auxerre, 418–48. Germain studied law at Rome, gaining a reputation as an orator and a lawyer. He was military governor of his native district. Twice he visited Britain (429 and 440) to combat Pelagianism. Germain established numerous schools for monks in Britain and led an army against the invading Picts and Saxons [Germanic tribe, some of whom settled in southern England; Wessex (southwest), Sussex (south), Essex and Kent (southeast)]. Although he was married, he put his wife away in 418 when he adopted the ascetic life. In 448, he set out for Ravenna. Germain died before he could return to Britain, after interceding on behalf of the rebellious Armoricans (Northwest France/Brittany) to Galla Placilia, the empress mother.

Flavian of Constantinople

c 390
Turkey

Aug. 11, 449
Hypepe, Lydia, Asia Minor (Turkey)

Bishop of Constantinople, 447–49. Known for his piety, Flavian earnestly opposed the Eutychian heresy (Christ's humanity was absorbed in His one Divine nature). He excommunicated Eutychius (founder of Monophysitism, opposite of Nestorianism, c 384–454) at a synod at Constantinople in 448. Flavian was deposed for this stand, in 449, by the Council of Ephesus (known as the Robber Council). He died soon after of bodily injuries delivered by theological opponents while he was on his way into exile at Hypepe. His remains were brought back and buried at Constantinople. The Council of Chalcedon in 451 exonerated him and declared him a martyr.

Peter Chrysologus
Golden Orator

c 406
Imola, Italy

c 450
Ravenna, Italy

Archbishop of Ravenna, residence of the Western Roman Emperor, 433–50. Chrysologus erected many church buildings. His reputation for eloquence and orthodoxy reached even to the East where Eutychius, the Monophysite, appealed to Chrysologus to intercede in his behalf to Pope Leo I. He presided over the Council of Ephesus in 431 when NESTORIUS was condemned as a heretic. He was a writer and opposed Monophysitism. He also persecuted Novationists and expelled Jews from Alexandria.

Vincent of Lerins

Toul, Gaul (France)

c 450
Lerins, France

Gallic theologian and monk. Vincent came from an aristocratic family on the island of Lerins (St. Honorat), near Cannes. At that time, Lerins was a monastic center of education and culture. Vincent had a reputation for vast scriptural knowledge and theology. In 434, he wrote his *Commonitorium (Commonitoria) Against Heretics* which was a reply to the current heresies—especially Nestorianism. He spent some years in the army before retiring to the monastery where he later died. A disciple of Johannes Cassianus, he was a strong defender of the faith which was now developing Roman Catholic trends.

Theodosius II

April 10, 401
Constantinople (Istanbul), Asia Minor (Turkey)

July 28, 450
Constantinople (Istanbul, Asia Minor (Turkey)

Byzantine emperor, 408–50. The empire was actually ruled by Antheius (408–14) and then jointly between Theodosius II and his sister, PULCHERIA (414–50). Theodosius II served during a most exasperating episode, when the churches of Alexandria and Constantinople were battling over the wording to define the nature of Jesus and the role of Mary. He and Valentinian III (Western Roman Emperor; ruled: 425–55) called for the Council of Ephesus in 431. Theodosius II carried on two wars with Persia (421 and 441), when the empire was also suffering attacks by the Huns (pagan tribesmen), paying tribute to them after 440. His rule could be called a triumvirate, since his wife EUDOCIA, whom he married June 7, 421, and sister, PULCHERIA, controlled him. His *Thessodian Code* was published in 438, the first official codifications of laws issued by Roman emperors since CONSTANTINE. He founded the University of Constantinople in 425.

Nestorius

c 381
Maras, Asia Minor (Turkey)

c 452
Egypt

Patriarch of Constantinople, 428–431. Nestorius was formerly a presbyter and monk from Antioch (Antakya), Syria (Turkey). As a result of his leadership, his followers were named Nestorians. His teachings on Christ caused controversy and schism. Some called him a heretic. Nestorius stated that Mary should be called the "Mother of Christ," but not the "Mother of God," stressing Christ's two separate natures of humanity and divinity. Christ was a God-bearing man, not the God-man. Nestorius was deposed by the Council of Ephesus in 431 and banished to the Libyan desert, breaking with the Monophysites on the one hand, and with the Orthodox churches of West Syria on the other. Nestorianism (Christ's divine and human persons remain separate; the divine Christ and the human Christ lived together in Jesus) became a mighty missionary church party and spread to the Far East, still existing in some places. He wrote *The Bazaar of Heracleides* in Greek in his last year, defending himself and his beliefs.

Eusebius of Dorylaeum

c 452
Asia Minor (Turkey)

Bishop of Dorylaeum, Phrygia, 448–52. Eusebius was a Greek theologian and lawyer. He was the first to publicly challenge the teaching of NESTORIUS, his superior, c. 428. Serving as bishop of Constantinople and later as bishop in Phrygia, he accused Eutyches, a local monk, of the heresy of Monophysitism in 448. Because of this, Eusebius was condemned, deposed, and imprisoned at the Council of Ephesus in 449. The Council of Chalcedon reinstated him to his see in 451. After his death, he was vindicated.

Pulcheria

Jan. 19, 399
Constantinople, Asia Minor

Sept. 10/11, 453
Constantinople (Istanbul), Asia Minor (Turkey)

Empress of the Byzantine empire, 450–53. Daughter of Emperor Arcadius. Pulcheria reigned jointly with her brother THEODOSIUS II (414–50) and, upon his death, married a little-known general named Marcian, making him Eastern Roman Emperor (ruled: 450–57). Pulcheria ruled firmly but fairly until her death. She sponsored the Council of Chalcedon in 451, which denounced Monophysitism. They built many churches and helped open the University of Constantinople. Pulcheria was also an enemy of Nestorianism.

Ursula

c Oct. 453/454
Cologne, Austrasia (Germany)

Britain

Martyred British princess. The story of Ursula and her massacred maidens was embellished in the eleventh and twelfth centuries, but was based upon massive graves in Cologne, Germany. Supposedly a Christian, British princess, Ursula was betrothed to a pagan king (a barbaric Hun). She gained a reprieve for three years and set sail in eleven ships, taking her ten ladies-in-waiting and a large number of companions with her. A peculiar storm blew them from the North Sea up the Rhine River to Cologne. They then journeyed over the Alps to visit the tombs of the Apostles in Rome. Since the three years had passed and she was obviously attempting to evade her marriage commitment, the Huns planned an ambush on the group's return trip to avenge their jilted king. The virgins were massacred and "angels" dispersed the Huns (history states they left the area abruptly in 451) so that townspeople could properly bury the young martyrs. GEOFFREY supposedly enhanced the legend to include 11,000 attendants who helped colonize Armorica (Brittany, France).

Hesychius

c 455
Jerusalem, Palestine (Israel)

Greek writer and monk of the Eastern Orthodox Church. Hesychius was revered not only as a theologian but also as a Biblical commentator and preacher. Most of his writings, including a history of the church, have been lost, but he is said to have written a commentary on the whole Bible. Hesychius was highly regarded by his contemporaries. He was also a presbyter of Jerusalem in 412. He wrote a history of the Council of Ephesus in 431 and opposed the Council of Chalcedon in 451. He was a disciple of HILARION.

Theodoret

c 390/393
Antioch (Antakya), Syria (Turkey)

c 457
Cyrus/Cyrrhus, Syria

Greek theologian, historian, and bishop of Cyrus, 423–48 and 451–60. Drawing upon his monastic background, Theodoret was energetic in fighting heresy. He wrote several apologetic treatises, the most famous being

Therapeutike. Because he befriended NESTORIUS, Theodoret was deposed at the Council of Ephesus in 449. He was later restored at the Council of Chalcedon in 451. He wrote *Ecclesiastical History* along with several commentaries, exegeses, controversial treatises, and biographies.

Ibas

c 380

Oct. 28, 457
Syria

Bishop of Edessa, Syria, 435 on. Ibas stood with NESTORIUS during the Church squabble over the proper wording to define the nature of Christ. He was deposed by the notorious Synod of Ephesus in 449, which was manipulated by the Alexandrians. He was restored again at the Council of Chalcedon in 451, on condition of his anathematizing (vigorously denouncing) NESTORIUS and Eutyches, Monophysitism founder. Ibas translated writings into Syrian and wrote a letter to the heathen Persians of Mari, Mesopotamia (Iraq), for which he was later condemned by Emperor JUSTINIAN.

Anatolius

c 400
Alexandria, Egypt

July 3, 458
Constantinople (Istanbul), Asia Minor (Turkey)

Bishop of Constantinople, 450–58. Anatolius is the author of several hymns. The best known begins, "Fierce was the wild billow...," translated by JOHN M. NEALE. During a time of conflict, he was often accused of heresy, ambition, and injustice. At the Council of Chalcedon in 451, Anatolius reaffirmed the equality of Constantinople with Rome. He crowned Eastern Roman Emperor Leo I (ruled: 457–74), making him the first churchman whose actions bestowed power over secular rule. He received clerical support for the Chalcedonian party (leaders in Chalcedon, a city in northwest Asia Minor on the Bosporus) against a violent Monophysite leader of Alexandria, Timothy Aelurus.

Simeon Stylites

c 389
Sisan, Syria

Sept. 2, 459
Telanissos(us) (Dair Sem'an), Syria

First known and most famous of the pillar hermits (the Stylites). This fanatical Syrian monk lived 36 years, 423–59, on the top of an increasingly taller pillar, three feet in diameter and finally 60 feet high, as an exercise of religious contemplation. Simeon preached from his post and had many converts. His meager wants were hoisted up in a basket. Others followed his example. By way of preparation, he lived in an enclosed cell near Antioch (Antakya), Syria (Turkey), 413–23, prior to his pillar activity.

Marius Mercator

c 390
North Africa

c 460

Latin ecclesiastical writer. Mercator was a cultivated layman who knew the Scriptures and was proficient in polemics {disputation, controversies, arguments}. He wrote tracts against the Pelagians and opposed the Nestorians. Mercator was an admirer of AUGUSTINE OF HIPPO and CYRIL OF ALEXANDRIA. He later lived in Rome, then Constantinople, 429–51. He was considered a "young author" in 418.

Eudocia

c 394
Athens, Greece

Oct. 20, 460
Jerusalem, Palestine (Israel)

Byzantine empress and wife of Emperor THEODOSIUS II. Through the training of her father, Leontius, a learned sophist (professional teacher of philosophy), Eudocia developed remarkable intellectual powers. Captivated by her varied accomplishments, THEODOSIUS II married her June 7, 421, making her a political rival to his sister

PULCHERIA. After they were divorced, Eudocia retired to Jerusalem in 443. She was devoted to works of piety and charity and wrote poetry and prose. Their daughter, Eudoxia, became the wife of Emperor Valentian III.

Patrick
Apostle of the Irish

May 24, 389/396
Severn, England

March 17, 461/469/491
Saul, Ireland

First missionary to Ireland. The dates and his life story often vary—some, perhaps, being legend. Patrick was captured by Irish pirates at age 16 and sold as a slave in northern Ireland in 405. After six years, he escaped and wandered for 38 days, until he found refuge in a monastery. Returning to Scotland, he received a vision saying, "Child of God, walk amongst us." Apparently he went to France for 14 years of study and preparation, returning to Ireland in 432. He built 365 churches and baptized some 12,000 converts by immersion. He visited Pope Leo I in Rome, 441–43, returning to evangelize against the bitter opposition of the Druids (religious order of priests among ancient Celts). He settled in Armagh, founding the Cathedral Church and a number of great schools. During his lifetime ministry, the nation changed from paganism to 100,000 believers. He retired in 457. His grave at Downpatrick is marked with a cross. His confessions tell his story. Both Catholics and Protestants claim him, but history shows the Celtic (branch of the Indo-European family of languages) Church did not become Catholic until AD 664. The celebration of St. Patrick's Day continues on March 17th, a tribute to one whose doctrine was much like a modern-day Baptist. His favorite Bible verse was Matthew 24:14.

Prosper

c 403
Aquitane, Gaul (France)

c 464
Rome, Italy

Monk, poet, and theologian of Marseilles, 429–40. Prosper was known for his defense of orthodoxy against Semi-Pelagianism, his support of AUGUSTINE OF HIPPO and especially for his teachings on grace and predestination. Prosper also criticized the writings of CASSIAN. He was secretary to Pope Leo I, 440 on. He wrote *The Book of the Sentences of St. Augustine* and other polemical literature, including a dogmatic poem, "On The Ungrateful" (chiding Semi-Pelagians for being ungrateful for divine grace).

Julia

c 485

Martyred slave girl. Owned by a pagan master who respected her faith and goodness. When visiting a foreign country, however, a pagan governor ordered her to sacrifice to the gods. Her refusal brought swift crucifixion.

Valentinus

c 485

Bishop of Passau, Bavaria (Austria). He was one of the first Christian missionaries in southeastern Germany in the fifth century. He is buried in the church at Zenoburg near Meran, Italy. There are some churches in Tirol, Austria, dedicated to him.

Acacius

489

Patriarch of Constantinople, 471 on. Acacius was involved in the divisions between Rome and Constantinople after the Council of Chalcedon meeting in 451. Acacius tried to modify some of the Western church emphasis in the Chalcedonian Creed in order to make it more palatable to Eastern believers. The first real schism between

Eastern and Western believers was Acacius' excommunication by Pope Felix III (reigned: 483–92) in 484, for encouraging Byzantine Emperor Zeno (ruled: 474–91) to promulgate the *Henoticon* (482) in the interests of theological peace.

Faustus

c 407–410
England

c 490/495
Riez, France

Bishop of Riez, 452 on. Faustus was abbot on the island of St. Honorat off Cannes, 433–37, and at Lerins, 437–52. He was exiled, 477–85, by Visigoth King Euric (ruled: 466–84), for being anti-Arian and restored after Euric's death. Faustus held a Semi-Pelagian view expressed in his book, *Grace and Free-Will*. He states that God's grace saves man only when man allows his impulse toward salvation to utilize that grace. He was condemned posthumously by the Synod of Orange in 529, for his support of a Semi-Pelagian position at the Synod of Arles, about 471. He was known for his piety and asceticism.

Clovis I

c 465–466
Tournai, France

Nov. 27, 511
Paris, France

King of the Salian Franks, 481–511. Clovis I founded the Frankish Empire (ancient Germanic people dwelling in regions of the Rhine) in ancient Gaul, beginning the royal Merovingian line (Frankish dynasty established by Clovis I in Gaul and Germany, 500–751). Clovis I was a heathen when he was invited by the Christian clergy to invade Gaul, sharing their desire to extinguish Arianism in the region. In 486, he overthrew the last Roman governor of Gaul and united all Frankish people. Clovis I, along with 3,000 others, was baptized by Archbishop REMIGIUS at Rheims on December 25, 496. The Franks ("Spear–men") became the first German tribe to accept Christianity. Clovis I invoked God's help to win a decisive victory at the battle of Vouille in 507, killing Visigoth King, Alaric II, with his own hands, establishing his court in Paris. In 493, he married CLOTILDA, a Christian Burgundian (region in central France) princess, and later divided his territory among their four sons. He built the Church of Holy Apostles (St. Genevieve) at Paris and convoked the Council of Orleans, July 10, 511, attended by 32 bishops.

Genevieve

c 422
Nanterre, France

Jan. 3, 512
Paris, France

Patroness of Paris who predicted the invasion of the Huns. At age seven, a sermon inspired Genevieve to dedicate her life to God. At age 15, she became a nun, going to Paris in 437 after her parents' death. When the invading army appeared on the outskirts of Paris, she sustained the courage of the people through her prayers, encouraging them not to abandon the city and assuring them that all would be well. Attila the Hun (leader of this cruel Mongolian tribe of invaders, 406–53) abruptly changed the direction of his attack and was crushed at Orleans in 451. She supported the Parisian resistance against CLOVIS I (prior to his conversion in 496). Genevieve further met the needs of the people during a famine by bringing twelve boatloads of grain to Paris, via the Seine River. She urged CLOVIS I to build a church dedicated to the Apostles Peter and Paul. It was later named St. Genevieve's Church and housed the tombs of CLOVIS I, his wife CLOTILDA and Genevieve. From age 15 to 50, Genevieve ate only twice a week—being sustained solely by barley bread, with the addition of fish and milk after age 50.

Flavian II

July 18, 518
Petra, Palestine (Jordan)

Patriarch of Antioch (Antakya), Syria (Turkey), 498–512. Flavian II was a bland leader who tried unsuccessfully to appease all theological parties, but provoked riots in 511 during the disgraceful Church quarrels over Christology. He also opposed the Monophysite heresy and accepted the decree of union issued in 482 by Byzantine Emperor Zeno. The patriarch of Constantinople was his enemy. Flavian II was deposed in 512 and banished to Petra by Eastern Roman Emperor ANASTASIUS I (ruled: 491–518) for objecting to the Chalcedon Council decrees in 451, which split the church over the Monophysite heresy, which he opposed.

Magnus F. Ennodius

474
Arles, France

July 17, 521
Ticinum (Pavia), Italy

Bishop of Pavia (Padua), about 515. Ennodius' major interest for many years was the rhetorical, stylish literature of Latin poets. He married (489), was ordained (493), and continued to indulge in his literary activities. A serious illness changed his values. He taught rhetoric in Milan, 494 on, during the struggles between the Arian King of the Ostrogoths (eastern division of the Goths, maintaining monarchy in Italy), Theodoric of Italy (ruled: 493–526) and Pope Symmachus (reigned: 498–514). Theodoric, in 502, urged that the Pope be judged only by God, which boosted the claims of the papacy. Ennodius headed two missions to Eastern Roman Emperor ANASTASIUS I of Constantinople (515 and 517) to oppose Monophysite error and affect a reconciliation between Rome and the East.

Anicius M. S. Boethius

c 480
Rome, Italy

524
Ticinum (Pavia), Italy

Scholar, philosopher, and statesman, converted to Christianity. Boethius felt philosophy could lead mankind to God and introduced people to Aristotle. He has been called the last of the Roman philosophers and the first of the scholastic (educated) theologians. Boethius married the daughter of Pope Symmachus. He wrote several works on art, math, music, theology, and philosophy. *On the Consolation of Philosophy* (523) was written in prison while he was awaiting execution. He was exiled to Pavia, imprisoned and beheaded by Arian King Theodoric of the Ostrogoths, whom he had served as a government official since 510, for alleged treasonable relations with Byzantine Emperor Justin (ruled: 518–27) of Constantinople. His book, *The Trinity*, affirms his Christian faith. He bridged the gap between the antique and medieval science of music.

Brigit
Bride of Ireland, Brigid

451
Offaly/Fochart, Ireland

Feb. 1, 525
Kildare, Ireland

Founded the first nunnery in Ireland, located in Kildare. Brigit founded four nunneries, the one at Kildare, Convent of Cill-Dara (Church of the Oak), remaining the primary one. It became a model and pattern for monasteries and nunneries throughout the country. Brigit was beautiful and intelligent but wanted to devote her life to God without being bothered by suitors or a husband. The King of Ulster freed her from the marital ambitions of her parents. Brigit settled under a big oak tree as a nun. She was very generous and showed mercy and pity for the poor. Her remains were placed beside PATRICK and COLUMBA. Some say she died in 521 or 523.

Pseudo-Dionysius the Areopagite

c 531

Philosophical writer whose Neo–platonic references became a catalyst for later Christian metaphysical theology. Historic research has failed to reveal the identity of this writer who assumed the pseudonym of one of Paul's converts (Acts 17:34), Dionysius the Areopagite. Pseudo-Dionysius was probably a Syrian monk who wrote his four treatises and ten letters in an attempt to unify philosophy and theology through Christian, Greek, Oriental and Jewish dogma. His works were considered mystical and his theology speculative. Those works included, *Concerning the Celestial Hierarchy* and *Concerning Mystic Theology*. Pseudo-Dionysius' influence pervaded from BEDE (eighth century) to the sixteenth century Spanish mystics and exerted lasting influence on the development of scholasticism. Through the translation of the treatises by Erigena, Irish philosopher and theologian (c 815–91), in 860 into Latin, Western culture was provided a vehicle to explain the concepts of Neo-platonism.

Sabas

439   Dec. 5, 532
Mutalask (near Caesarea), Cappodocia, Asia Minor (Turkey)   Mar Saba, Palestine (Israel)

Founder of a group of monks, the Sabaites, named after him. Sabas inherited wealth and gave it up to become a hermit in Palestine. He entered a monastery at the age of eight, becoming a hermit at age 18. Joined by others, he was made an abbot of an order of monks in 484. His discipline was very severe. Sabas founded Mar Saba (Kedron Valley three miles from Jerusalem) convent. In 491 he was ordained a priest and made exarch (patriarch's deputy) of all hermits in southern Palestine.

Fulgentius

468   Jan. 1, 533
Telepte, Byzacene (North Africa)   Ruspe, North Africa

Bishop of Ruspe, 508 on. Fulgentius was driven from his home to Rome and then to Sicily about 500. Upon his return, he became abbot of Ruspe (a small island cloister) on the African coast (until c. 508). In 510, he was banished from Africa by the Vandal King Thrasimund, an Arian, to Cagliari, Sardinia, but was allowed to return in 523. Fulgentius retired to a monastery in 532 and committed his strong opposition to Arianism and Semi-Pelagianism to writing. He was a strong follower of AUGUSTINE.

Remigius
(Remi/Remy)—Apostle of the Franks

c 437   Jan. 13, 533
Laon, France   Rheims (Reims), France

Frankish archbishop of Rheims, 459 on. Remigius witnessed the collapse of Roman rule December 25, 499 in Gaul and the emergence of new kingdoms. He was the catalyst in the conversion and baptism of CLOVIS I, King of the Franks, in 496. Remigius left only four letters of testimony to his era. Many years later, for political reasons, HINCMAR OF RHEIMS invented some untruths about him: (1) that he anointed CLOVIS I with oil and (2) that he received a letter from Pope Hormisdas (reigned: 514–23) recognizing him as primate of France. Pope Hormisdas was the proud father of Pope Silverius (reigned: 536–38). Remigius tried to raise the moral level of the clergy. Through his untiring efforts and the example of CLOVIS I, most of Gaul was Christianized.

Severus

c 460/465   Feb. 8, 538
Sozopolis, Pisidia, Asia Minor (Turkey)   Xois, Egypt

Bishop of Antioch (Antakya), Syria (Turkey), 512–18. Severus was forced out of his position because of his Monophysite sympathies. In 518, he fled to Egypt, where he spent his last 20 years. As head of the Monophysites, he regarded the Chalcedonian Council and Creed with suspicion, thus perpetuating the controversy in the Eastern church. His excommunication in 536 led him to a lonely desert south of Alexandria.

Leontius

c 485
Asia Minor (Turkey)

543
Constantinople (Istanbul), Asia Minor (Turkey)

Greek theologian who was a Nestorian Christian in his youth. He converted to orthodoxy and later penned theological works trying to explain the union of the human and divine natures in Jesus Christ. His teachings delighted Emperor JUSTINIAN who was trying to satisfy Eastern churchmen (CYRIL OF ALEXANDRIA's views) and Western churchmen (Nicene Christianity). He was a devotee of Aristotle, applying his philosophies to Christological problems. Leontius wrote against Monophysites and Nestorians. He lived at various times in Constantinople.

Benedict of Nursia
The Patriarch of Western Monasticism

480
Norica (Nursia), Italy

March 21, 543
Monte Cassino, Italy

Founder of monasteries in western Europe—the Benedictine Order (first monastic order noted for strict rules). Benedict's monastic way of life was based upon his celebrated rule. He gave his life to improve monastery life after living in a cave for three years. About 529, he founded a new monastery on Monte Cassino (between Rome and Naples), where he lived out his days. In 73 chapters of his *Rule*, he deals with work, worship, study, and discipline. Benedict founded twelve monastic communities in Subiaco. His monks were governed by strict rules. His was the first monastic order and his *Rule* of 529 was almost universally adopted in the Middle Ages by Western monasteries. A pet raven snatched a poison slice of bread from Benedict's hand, just in time to save his life. The tame bird was kept as a pet and its progeny in an unbroken line has been befriended by this monastery ever since.

Clotilda

c 475
Lyons, France

June 3, 545
Tours, France

Queen of the Franks who married CLOVIS I the king in 493. Clotilda was a devout Christian and influenced CLOVIS I to be baptized. After his death in 511, she lived an exemplary life, living out her days at the Monastery of St. Martin at Tours, France. Her father Burgundian King Chilperic of Neustria (western kingdom of the Franks; ruled: 561–84), mother, and two brothers were murdered. Her daughter, also named Clotilda, married Amalaric (502–31), king of the Visigoths (ruled: 526–31).

Dionysius Exiguus

c 470–500
Dobrudscha, Scythia (Russia)

c 550
Rome, Italy

Exegete, theologian, writer and canonist, also an abbot of a monastery in Rome. Exiguus was a monk, scholar, and monastic expert on canon law and church chronology. In 525, at the request of Pope John I (reigned: 523–26) of Rome, he worked out the Christian calendar still used today. Unfortunately, he wrongly dated the year of Christ's birth (4 BC). He collected church laws and council decrees. Exiguus acquainted the West with Greek learning, translating their works into Latin. Exiguus means "little," and it is thought the surname was given because of his humility.

Placidus

c 515
Rome, Italy

c 550
Sicily (Placidas, Italy)

Founded the monastery of St. John at Messina, Sicily. As a boy he was miraculously saved from drowning and sent to live at the famous monastery of Monte Cassino in Italy with BENEDICT OF NURSIA. Placidus was the son of Tertellus, a Roman patrician (noble, high-rank aristocrat). According to some legends, he, his two brothers, a sister, and 33 others were martyred by pirates invading the monastery.

Finnian

c 470
Leinster, Ireland

Dec. 12, 552
Clonard, Ireland

Irish monk during an amazing surge of piety and learning which made Ireland's Celtic Church the center for saints and scholars during the early Middle Ages. He was head of the monastery at Clonard and became the teacher of COLUMBA. He founded churches, monasteries and schools.

Cloud

c 522

c 560
Nogent (near Paris), France

Monastery founder. Cloud was a grandson of the CLOVIS I/CLOTILDA union, who barely escaped being murdered when two uncles (Clotaire & Childebert) killed two of his brothers. He became a monk and lived in Provence (province, later a region). He founded the well known monastery near Paris at Nogent. The monastery later became known as St. Cloud's.

Procopius of Caesarea

c 500
Caesarea, Palestine

c 564
Constantinople (Istanbul), Asia Minor (Turkey)

Byzantine historian. In 527, Emperor JUSTINIAN sent Procopius as secretary and counselor to Belisarius (general of the Eastern Roman Emperor, 529–59) in an expedition against the Persians. He was in North Africa during the war against the Vandals in 533, then went to Sicily in 536 to join in the war against the Goths. He wrote histories of these expeditions after returning to Constantinople in 542. His Christian commitment has been questioned.

Justinian I
Flavius Justinianus—The Great Justinian

May 11, 483
Tauresium (Skopje), Illyricum (Croatia and Bosnia/Herzegovina)

Nov. 14, 565
Constantinople, Asia Minor

Roman Emperor of the East, 527–65. Justinian I's armies won many victories because of qualified generals, recovering lost territories. His armies defeated the Vandals in North Africa, and a year later he drove the Goths from Italy. He married Theodora in 523. His fame rests upon his codification (compiling and systematizing) of existing Roman law, *Corpus Juris Civilis*. The Roman law as now received in jurisprudence, formed the foundation of law in most of western Europe. His many public works included the commissioning of the famous church of Hagia Sophia in Constantinople. He oppressed the people with taxes. In 562, a civil conflict destroyed most of Constantinople.

Gildas
The Wise One

c 516
Clwyd, Wales/Dumbarton, Scotland

c 570
near Glastonbury, England/Houat, Brittany (France)

Welsh monk and British historian. His history is somewhat uncertain. Gildas spent seven years in France 549–56, went to Ireland, and then returned to England, becoming an earnest preacher. He wrote a history of Britain, *On the Destruction and Conquest of Britains* (first published in 1525), which is the oldest historical work on Christian Britain. Some say he lived out his days in the St. Gildas de Ruys monastery of Brittany, near Vannes, that he founded, and others say that he died near Glastonbury.

Germain of Paris

469   *May 28, 576*
Autun, France   Paris, France

Bishop of Paris, 555–76. Germain was abbot of St. Symphorien near Autun, 530–55. He participated in the third and fourth Councils of Paris (557 and 573) and the second Council of Tours (566). He consecrated the Church of St. Vincent in Paris in 558, and in 568, he excommunicated the licentious Charibert, Frankish ruler of Paris. Germain is revered as a famous French Christian leader. His bones are buried in the Paris church which was named for him, St. Germaine des Pres.

Brendan

c 484   *May 16, 578*
Near Tralee, Ireland   Annadown/Clonfert, Ireland

Founder of many monasteries in Ireland and Scotland. Brendan became a monk and was ordained a priest. For 20 years he was abbot of a monastery which he founded in Galway, western Ireland. He sailed in a leather craft with 17 other monks. Legend says he even crossed the Atlantic 565–73 and landed on "St. Brendan's Island," Newfoundland. Authorities are divided as to the validity of these trips which took seven years. In 557, he founded the Monastery of Clonfert, where he ruled for 20 years. He was a good friend of Comgall, with whom he made several tours to Europe.

Jacobus Baradaeus
Jacob Baradai

c 490   *July 30, 578*
Tella, Syria (Turkey)   Cassianus (Kaison), Egypt

Syrian Monophysite missionary bishop of Edessa, 542 on. Baradaeus served as a monk in Constantinople for 15 years. He devoted all his energies to the defense of Monophysitism. Baradaeus traveled extensively in ragged horsecloth from Nisibis, Mesopotamia to Alexandria, Egypt, from 543 on. The Jacobite (branch of Monophysites) Church, which he founded, is still known–sometimes referenced as the Syrian Monophysite Church, indicating its religious roots. It is said he consecrated and ordained two patriarchs, 89 bishops, and 100,000 priests and deacons. He died at a monastery on the Egyptian border.

Flavius M. A. Cassiodorus

c 485   *c 580*
Scylacium (Squillace), Calabria, Italy   Vivarium (Viviers), Italy

Roman historian, statesman, writer, and monk. After the collapse of Gothic rule at about 540, Cassiodorus withdrew from Ravenna. Cassiodorus built a monastery at Vivarium in Calabria in 550 to perpetuate early Greek culture. He was very successful in inciting the monks of his time to literary work, requiring them to copy and translate Greek works. His *Historia Ecclesiastica Tripartita*, a manual of church history for the Latin Church of his day became an important work. Cassiodorus also wrote books on the liberal arts, music, and theology, plus imperial edicts and decrees, such as Variae. He lived nearly a century.

Martin of Braga

c 510   *March 20, 580*
Pannonia (Hungary)

Archbishop of Braga, northwest Portugal, 559 on. Martin went to Spain in 551 as a missionary. He founded the monastery of Dumio, of which he was the first abbot and then bishop in 561. His principal work is a collection of canons of Greek and Spanish synods, published by Mansi and others. He also wrote on canon law and ethics. Some of his letters and verses are still available.

Fridolin

Ireland

March 6, 585
Sackingen Island, France

First Celtic missionary of the Alemanni (Germanic tribes of modern southwestern Germany, Switzerland; also known as Swabia). Fridolin went to the Upper Rhine in France as a missionary, serving at Poitiers. He occupied himself with collecting relics of HILARY OF POITIERS and was made abbot of Hilary's monastery. After years of preaching, he founded a number of churches and monasteries along the Rhine River, such as the one on the island of Sackingen (in the Upper Rhine).

John of Asia

c 506/507
Amida (Diyarbakir), Asia Minor (Turkey)

586

Monophysite bishop of Ephesus and noted historian. John was driven by plagues and persecutions from Palestine to Constantinople (c 535). He was put in charge of the finances of the Monophysite Church. He was appointed bishop by Emperor JUSTINIAN I, who employed him to combat heathenism in Asia Minor. John established 96 monasteries and churches and baptized over 70,000 converts in Asia Minor. He also produced a three-part church history.

Gregory of Tours
Georgius Florentius Gregorius

Nov. 30, 538
Averm (Clermont-Ferrand), France

Nov. 17, 594
Tours, France

Frankish historian and bishop of Tours, 573–94. Tours was the religious center of Gaul. A dangerous illness induced him to make a pilgrimage to the Shrine of St. Martin at Tours in 573. His recovery started his interest in Christian work. He participated in the political and civil life of his time. Except for 576–84, when he was at odds with King Chilperic, he was on good terms with all four rulers of Tours during his bishopric. Of noble descent, Gregory showed great ability in the conduct of his diocese. Besides producing several books on miracles, he wrote a *History of the Franks*, exposing many violent family feuds causing the political decline of the Merovingians. His writings reveal moral, social, and political corruption in his day.

Asaph

Wales

c 595/ 600

Celtic missionary and first bishop of Wales at the monastery in Llanelwy in 590. He later established a monastery at Llanasa, Flintshire. Asaph was distinguished for his learning, piety, and earnest preaching. Asaph became a pupil of KENTIGERN. Asaph wrote *The Ordinations of His Church* and *A Life of St. Kentigern*. His diocese was later named after him.

John IV
John the Faster

Constantinople (Istanbul), Asia Minor (Turkey)

Sept. 2, 595

Patriarch of Constantinople, 582 on. An extreme ascetic, he went long periods without food. He insisted on the title "Ecumenical Patriarch," which infuriated the popes of Rome who maintained that this title may never be used by any bishop outside of Rome. He was denounced by Popes Pelagius II (reigned: 579–90) and Gregory I (reigned: 590–604).

Anastasia (2)

c 597

Greek woman who lived in Constantinople. Anastasia fled to Alexandria, Egypt, to avoid being dragged into Emperor JUSTINIAN I's harem. She lived, disguised as a monk, for 28 years in Egypt.

Columba
Apostle of the Picts

Dec. 7, 521
Gartan, Ireland

June 8, 597
Iona, Scotland

Renowned Celtic missionary. Columba founded his first monastery in 545. He was ordained a priest around 551 in a monastery at Clonnard. In 561 he involved himself in a quarrel over a disputed book and the Battle of Culdrevney. He founded churches and monasteries in Ireland (Londonderry, Darrow, and Kells) before building a monastery and missionary community on Iona Island in May 563, when he became abbot. He and twelve companions set out to convert Scotland. Columba's preaching led to the conversions of two kings, AIDAN and Brude, and many of the northern Picts in 564. His lifestyle led to the founding of numerous monasteries throughout the Highlands. From his headquarters, he evangelized both Ireland and Scotland. In 575, Columba hosted a national convention at Brumceatt near Derby, Ireland. Columba operated independent of papal supervision and wrote three hymns. The day before he died, he was busy copying the Psalms and the next day he was found dead before the altar of the church. He was reportedly one of the first to see the so-called Loch Ness Monster.

Leander

c 540/550
Cartagena, Spain

March 13, 600
Seville, Spain

Spanish monk and bishop of Seville, 584–600. Leander spent 579–82 in Constantinople with his friend Gregory I (later pope). He was used to convert King RECARED I of the Visigoths and his people from Arianism to Catholicism. In 589, he presided over the famous Council of Toledo, Spain, where "Filioque" (controversy over origin of the Holy Spirit which divided Western and Eastern church thought) was added to the Creed, stating that the Holy Spirit came from the Father and the Son. This position condemned Arianism. Leander's brother was Isidore of Seville.

Recared I

601

King of the Visigoths, 586–601. LEANDER of Seville influenced King Recared's conversion from Arianism. At the Council of Toledo, Spain, in 589, Recared formally renounced Arianism and was followed by many of his bishops and nobles. Recared I made Catholicism the official Visigoth religion. He restricted Jews and commanded baptism of children of mixed marriages.

David

c 520
Wales

March 1, 601

Ascetic monk and bishop of St. David's, Menevia. David was an important leader of the Welsh Church and the founder of many of its churches. No reliable account of his life exists. It is believed he descended from Welsh royalty and evangelized South Wales, where 53 churches are named for him. He founded twelve monasteries, the most famous being St. David's, and declared St. David's to be the seat of church government. His eloquence silenced Pelagianism at the Welsh Synod of Llandeewi-Brefi. David also presided over the Synod of Victory at Caerleon-on-Usk. He wrote several theological treatises and presided over two synods.

Comgall

517
Dalriada (Antrim), Northern Ireland

May 10, 602
Bangor, Northern Ireland

Monk who emphasized evangelism and missionary outreach. Comgall was a part of the great upsurge of learning and evangelizing in the Irish Church in the sixth century. In 558, he founded the great monastery at Bangor. Many missionary scholars were sent out from here during the zenith of the Celtic Church. He established several monasteries throughout Ireland, Scotland, and the Scottish Isle of Iona. At one time he had 3,000 student monks under him, including COLUMBA. Comgall was a close friend of BRENDAN with whom he made several tours to Europe.

Kentigern
Head Chief

c 518
Culross, Scotland

Jan. 13, 603
Glasgow, Scotland

Celtic missionary. Kentigern was baptized and educated in a monastic school at Culross. He was brought up by Serramis, initially lived as a hermit at Glasgow, and then became a missionary. Kentigern preached in Cumbria and Wales, eventually returning to Glasgow in 570. After religious persecution again sent him away, Kentigern reappeared in Scotland to reclaim the Picts of Galloway (division of southwestern Scotland) from idolatry (c 573). He established a bishopric see at Hoddam in 573. After preaching and teaching for 13 years in Cathures (Glasgow), Kentigern returned in 580, to finally become the area's bishop. The college for monks and the churches planted by Kentigern's efforts, greatly contributed to establishing Glasgow as the Christian center for Britons. Kentigern was influential in sending many missionaries to Norway, Iceland, and other Scandinavian countries.

Augustine of Canterbury
Apostle to the English

May 26, 604
Canterbury, England

First Archbishop of Canterbury, 597–604. After serving as prior of the Benedictine Monastery of St. Andrew's in Rome, he was sent by Pope Gregory I with 40 Frankish monks as missionaries to England in 596/597. He was well received by King ETHELBERT I of Kent. A year later on Christmas Day, the King and 10,000 subjects were baptized in the river Swale. Augustine was unable to persuade Celtic clergy in Wales and northern England to join Catholicism. A monastery (St. Peter and Paul) and cathedral (Christ Church) were founded at Canterbury. Augustine was consecrated as an English bishop in 597 at Arles, France. His ministry brought ancient British churches under Catholicism.

Damianus

c 520
Syria

June 12, 605

Jacobite patriarch of Alexandria, Egypt, 578 on. Damianus held views similar to those of Sabellius. He explained the doctrine of the Trinity on philosophical principles—a temporal Trinity. His reign was very turbulent, since he opposed the Paulites. He journeyed through Syria and Constantinople, endeavoring to frustrate budding peace negotiations. The Jacobite patriarch, Peter of Antioch, was consecrated by Damianus in Alexandria (c. 580), but later they split over tritheism (the trinity is three distinct Gods).

Ventantius H. C. Fortunatus

c 530
Ceneda (near Treviso), Italy

c 609
Poitiers, France

Bishop of Poitiers, 597 on, and chief Latin poet. Fortunatus was converted at an early age at Aquileia. While a student at Ravenna, he became almost blind. Miraculously his sight was restored by the anointing of his eyes with oil from a lamp that burned before the altar of MARTIN OF TOURS. Hence, he made a pilgrimage to the shrine of MARTIN OF TOURS in 565, remaining in Gaul the rest of his life. He was a friend, protègè of and chaplain to Frankish Queen Rahegunda (Rhadegunda) (510–57) of the Franks, who helped him get established at Poitiers. Fortunatus served the community as steward, then as chaplain, before his appointment as a bishop. He produced a considerable amount of literary work, including 11 books, 250 poems, and 300 hymns. He wrote many hymns, such as "Welcome Happy Morning" and "The Royal Banners Forward Go." Early in his career in 565, he served at the court of Sigebert I, king of Austrasia (eastern kingdom of the Franks, covering both sides of Rhine River). His hymns are rich in romantic symbolism which marks the beginning of the medieval way of thought.

Columbanus/Columban

c 543
Leinster, Ireland

Nov. 21, 615
Bobbio, Italy

Missionary and scholar to the European continent. At about 45 years of age, Columbanus sailed to France (c. 585) with twelve monks, including GALL, founding the monasteries of Annegray, Luxeuil, and Fontaine, and settled in Vosges, 590–95. He came to France hoping to eradicate the impiety and immorality in the Frankish courts. Columbanus was involved in controversy with French bishops over tenure and the dating of Easter. Finding the situation hopeless, he was expelled in 610 and withdrew to Switzerland in 612, then on to Italy, where he founded the monastery of Bobbio in the Appennines Mountains. Columbanus was a man of wide learning.

Aethelbert of Kent
Athelbert - Ethelbert

c 550/552

Feb. 24, 616
Canterbury, England

King of Kent, 560–616, England's first Christian king. Aethelbert was defeated by the West Saxons in 568. Although named king at a very young age, he rapidly grew into an effective monarch. He married Bertha, a Christian and daughter of Charibert, Frankish king who ruled in Paris. When AUGUSTINE came to Kent in 596, Aethelbert was converted and established Christianity among his pagan Saxons. AUGUSTINE baptized him in 597. Aethelbert promulgated the English legal code after Roman law and produced the first written code of British laws around 600. He founded the important archbishopric of Canterbury (his headquarters) in 602, which became a center of Christianity. Aethelbert also built a church at Rochester. His daughter, Ethelburg, married King EDWIN of Northumbria. It appears to the editor that becoming king at age eight is unusual, but this is what the *Encyclopedia Americana* portrays.

Lawrence of Canterbury
Laurentus

England

Feb. 2, 619

Second archbishop of Canterbury, 604–19. Lawrence was one of the Benedictine monks who accompanied AUGUSTINE, whom he succeeded, to England in 597. He never received the pallium. Lawrence tried to convert the Celtic Church bishops, and consecrated a church in Canterbury in 613.

Justus

Rome, Italy?

Nov. 10, 627
Canterbury, England

Fourth Archbishop of Canterbury, 624–27. Justus was sent to England in 601 by Pope Gregory I to help AUGUSTINE. Justus was also consecrated by AUGUSTINE as the first bishop for Rochester, West Kent, in 604. ETHELBERT, the king of Kent, built him a church at Rochester. In 617 he fled to France during a heathen uprising. Justus later dispatched PAULINUS to convert Northumbria (northeast England).

Edwin

585
Northumbria, England

Oct. 12, 633
Hatfield, England

King of Northumbria, 617–633. Edwin was the most famous convert of missionary PAULINUS OF YORK, who baptized him in 627. Ethelburga, a Christian princess, became King Edwin's wife in 625. (She was the daughter of King AETHELBERT OF KENT.) With the support of East Anglia, Edwin defeated Aethelfirth in 617 and formed a united Northumbria. He encouraged the work of PAULINUS and installed him as bishop of York in 627. A coalition of the Mercians (central England) under King Penda (ruled: 626–55), a pagan, and the North Wales forces under King Caedwalla against Northumbria caused his death. Edwin was slain in the Battle of Heathfield, where Anglo-Saxon kingdoms rose up against one another.

Isidore

c 560
Cartagena, Spain

April 4, 636
Seville, Spain

Archbishop of Seville, 600–36. Isidore was by far the most learned man of his time. As archbishop, he founded schools, planned for the conversion of Jews, and presided over church councils. He was a strong orthodox leader, praising monasticism, and heading the Spanish Church; thereby influencing others by his writings. He headed the Council of Toledo in 633 and was allegedly said to have completed the *Pseudo-Isodorean Decretals*. He was the brother of LEANDER of Seville. His *Three Books of Sentences* was the standard theological textbook in the Latin Church until the twelfth century. His *Etymologiae* was an outstanding encyclopedia used for many centuries. He also wrote on archaeology, dogmatics, and ethics. His learning embraced the entire range of the arts and sciences.

Sergius of Constantinople

Syria (Turkey)

c 638/ 641

Patriarch of Constantinople, 610–38. Sergius tried to help Byzantine Emperor Heraclius (ruled: 610–41) knit feuding fragments together in the empire and church. In the throes of dissension, Sergius defended his city in 626 against the Avars (lived in area now known as Hungary and Romania) and the threatened invasions by the fanatic Arab Moslems and Persians. Sergius wrote *Ecthesis* (638), a compromise formula to end the division over Christ's divinity. The Monothelite controversy (belief in one nature of Christ, instead of two natures, divine and human) began during Sergius' days. Sergius also wrote a Greek hymn and developed liturgy.

Oswald of Northumbria

c 605
England

Aug. 5, 642
Maserfield, England

King of Northumbria, 634–42, following his Uncle Edwin to the throne. Oswald was converted to Christianity on the Isle of Iona, Scotland, where he had taken refuge during a civil upheaval in 617. While there, he established himself as king. Oswald helped to drive out Anglican invaders, defeating and killing King Caedwalla of North Wales in 634. His political power extended to Strathclyde (northwest England), Scotland and Wessex. King Oswald appealed to Iona for monks to establish Christianity on the British mainland. Aidan and others responded to his plea. Oswald was killed in a battle against King Penda of Mercia. His brother, Oswy, followed him to the throne.

Paulinus of York

c 584
Rome, Italy

Oct. 10, 644
Rochester, England

First bishop of Northumbria, 625, and archbishop of York, 627. Paulinus was a Roman missionary to Britain in 601, joining AUGUSTINE in Kent by the command of Pope Gregory I. He was successful in working with British nobility, baptizing King EDWIN of Northumbria at York in a wooden church in 627 and advancing the cause of Catholicism in the North. When EDWIN was killed in 633, Paulinus fled to Kent and became bishop of Rochester, 633–44. HILDA was one of his converts.

Gall

c 550
Ireland

Oct. 16, 645
Arbon, Switzerland

Monk and missionary to Alemanni, 585. Gall was the companion of COLUMBANUS, missionary to Gaul until 612, when they separated at Bregenz, Austria, and he returned to Switzerland. He lived a hermit's life in the Swiss Alps for many years. In 613, Gall established a cell (small religious house dependent on a monastery) on the shores of the Steinach River, then he established a town and monastery, both of which bear his name to this day. He left behind a Christianized nation. Gall was also known as "the Apostle to the Suevi" (people of Alemanni). He was known for preaching personal holiness and miracle-working power.

Felix of Dunwich

March 8, 648

Burgundy, France

Bishop of Dunwich, 631 on. Felix was an early missionary in ancient England to the East Anglia (eastern England) area. He was sent by HONORIUS to convert Sigebert II, king of the East Saxons (ruled: 636–56), and organize the church there. He was successful. From his Dunwich, Suffolk headquarters, Felix spent 17 years converting the heathen of East Anglia and introducing monastic life.

John Climacus
John of the Ladder

c 579

c 649

Byzantine hermit. Climacus was a monk (c. 600) and later, an abbot (639) of St. Catherine's on Mount Sinai in Arabia. His nickname is derived from his work, *The Ladder of Divine Ascent*. As a handbook on the ascetical and mystical life, it has been regarded a spiritual classic and guide toward perfection. The renunciation of the world is the first of 30 steps in his ladder.

Winifred

c 650

Wales

Gwytherin, Wales

Welsh heroine and martyr. Winifred was the beautiful daughter of a wealthy family living in Northern Wales. Refusing the advances of Prince Caradog (Caractacus) of Hawarden, she was wounded ("beheaded") by him. Legend says she was healed by her Uncle Beuno. Winifred spent her last 15 years as a nun, becoming abbess of the convent at Gwytherin, Wales. The place of her restoration (cure), Holywell or St. Winifred's Well, became a pilgrimage center. It is also referred to as The Holy Well in Flintshire.

Birinus

Dec. 3, 650
Dorchester, England

Bishop in Genoa, Italy. He landed in Wessex (634) and converted the local king Cynegis (635). Birinus also baptized the king's son and grandson. He was the first bishop of Dorchester and is regarded as the Apostle of the West Saxons. Birinus was a Benedictine monk at Rome and was commissioned as a missionary by Pope Honorius I (reigned: 625–38). He gained influence in Wessex and Mercia through the help of OSWALD OF NORTHUMBRIA.

Aidan

c 605
Ireland

Aug. 31, 651
Bamburgh, England

Celtic monk and missionary. Aidan began as a monk on Iona Island, Scotland, then served as a missionary in Northumbria. At the request of OSWALD OF NORTHUMBRIA, Aidan went to the Isle of Lindisfarne, England to introduce Christianity and founded a famous monastery there. He became the first bishop of Lindisfarne, England, 635–51. From this monastic center, Aidan evangelized Northumbria, founding churches and monasteries. He was well known for his learning and charity. Aidan ordained many slaves as priests and helped the poor. He later won the favor of King Oswin, the last Deira (Anglican kingdom of Yorkshire, England) king. His leadership for the Celts balanced that of AUGUSTINE OF CANTERBURY who was introducing Catholicism. One of his pupils was CHAD.

Honorius

Sept. 30, 653

Fifth Archbishop of Canterbury, 627–53. Honorius was sent by Pope Gregory I to Kent. He arrived in England around 601 with the second group of Roman monks sent as missionaries to the West. The key accomplishment of Honorius' tenure was to consolidate the smaller bishoprics and to establish an administrative leadership flow. He was instrumental in sending FELIX OF DUNWICH to evangelize the East Angles. During his reign, the first appointment of an English bishop occurred in 644, establishing Itham of Rochester as a ruling cleric. Itham in turn consecrated DEUSDEDIT, as archbishop of Canterbury in 655.

Eligius

c 588
Cadillac/Chatelat, Limousin, France

Nov. 30, 660
Limoges/Noyon, France

Missionary in Flanders (ancient country including parts of Belgium, Netherlands, and France), **philanthropist, and bishop of Noyon and Tournai, France, 639–59**. Under the influence of COLUMBANUS in Paris in 610, Eligius devoted himself to charitable works. He purchased hundreds of young Saxon slaves and gave them their freedom. Eligius founded several monasteries and churches. He was a recognized leader at the Synod of Chalons (644) and at Orleans (650). Eligius learned the goldsmith's metal work trade. He gained the favor of the Frankish king, Clotaire II (ruled: 613–28) by making him a throne. He built abbeys and churches, including the Abbey of St. Rome in Paris. He was also the chief counselor to Frankish king, Dagobert I (ruled: 628–38). He preached in the regions of Antwood, Covrtrai, and Ghent.

Finan
Finnan

Feb. 9, 661
Lindisfarne Island, England

Ireland

Second bishop of Lindisfarne, 652–61. Finan was an Irish Celtic monk of Iona Island, Scotland, who succeeded AIDAN at the see of Lindisfarne, England. He was a fruitful missionary—consecrating CAEDMON, baptizing kings Penda of Mercia and Siegbert of the East Saxons. He strongly opposed the Roman Church, especially its rituals and observance of Easter. He was aided by King Oswy.

Maximus
The Confessor

c 580
Constantinople (Istanbul), Asia Minor (Turkey)

Aug. 13, 662
Skhemaris/Lazica, Russia

Noted writer, theologian, and Byzantine Church leader. After 20 years of service as secretary to Byzantine Emperor Heraclius (ruled: 610–41), he embraced the monastic life in 630. He soon became abbot at Chrysopolis near Constantinople. Maximus participated in the Monothelite controversy, defending the orthodox position and the supremacy of Rome. He helped Pope Theodore I (reigned: 642–49) call the First Lateran Council in 649. He was imprisoned (653), banished to Thrace (655), then recalled to Constantinople (662). Still refusing to accept Monothelite heresy, Maximus was tortured and again banished, dying soon afterward. His tongue and right hand were cut off.

Deusdedit

July 14, 664
Canterbury, England

Archbishop of Canterbury, 655–64. Deusdedit was a West Saxon whose native name was Frithona. He took the post of archbishop, after a vacancy of one and a half years. He consecrated only one English bishop, and was not present at the Synod of Whitby. The see remained vacant for some time after his death.

Cedd

Oct. 26, 664
Northumbria, England   Lastingham, England

Bishop of Essex to the East Saxons, 654 on. Cedd was brother to CHAD. They were brought up on the Isle of Lindisfarne, England, under AIDAN. In 653, Cedd was sent by King Oswy of Northumbria to evangelize Mercia. He worked among the people of Mercia and then at Essex. He founded monasteries at West Tilbury, Bradwell-on-Sea, and in Yorkshire at Lastingham. At the Synod of Whitby in 664, he acted as doctrinal interpreter. Although Cedd favored the Celtic position, he acquiesced when the Roman stand prevailed. He died during a plague.

Fiacre

c 600–610
Ireland

Aug. 18, 670
Breuil, Gaul (France)

Irish nobleman and leader in France. He is considered by some as patron of gardeners. Fiacre came to Meaux, France, in 628, lived many years in Breuil, and erected an oratory there to the Virgin Mary. Seeking seclusion, he also erected a small monastery in the woods near Meaux. As early as the ninth century, his fame grew. Fiacre was considered a miracle worker (claimed to have been miraculously cured from a tumor), which encouraged pilgrims to flock to his shrine.

Oswy

c 612   Feb. 15, 671

King of England, 642–671. Oswy summoned and presided at the Synod of Whitby to resolve the conflict over the authority of the Pope, that had risen between the ancient Celtic Church and the newer Roman Christianity. The Romanists insisted that all practices and types of administration conform with Rome. This Synod of 664 decided in favor of Rome. Oswy (brother of OSWALD) defeated Penda, the heathen champion, in 655, with whom he warred constantly. This victory gave Oswy supremacy over the contested areas and all of Teutonic (northern European tribe, particularly East German) Celtic Britain except for Wessex, Kent, and Sussex.

Chad

Northumbria, England

March 2, 672
Lichfield, England

Bishop of the Northumbrians. Chad was the brother of CEDD. They were brought up on the Isle of Lindisfarne, England, under AIDAN. He succeeded CEDD as abbot of Lastingham in 664 but moved the see to York (c 665). When WINIFRED returned to York, Chad was sent as a bishop to the Mercians, settling himself at Lichfield (669). He preached as a missionary throughout Northumbria and founded two monasteries. Like his brother, Chad died during yet another plague.

Colman

c 605
Connacht, Ireland

Aug. 8, 676
Inishbofin Island, Ireland

Bishop of Lindisfarne, 661–64. Colman succeeded FINAN. He had been a monk at Iona Island, Scotland. In the clash between Celtic and Roman liturgical customs (date of Easter), he supported the Celtics. When the Whitby Synod in 664 did not, he resigned and went to Ireland in 668, with Irish and English monks, carrying the bones of AIDAN. He then built a monastery at Inishbofin.

Caedmon

658
Northumbria, England

c 678/680
England ?

The first Christian poet in England. According to BEDE, Caedmon was an illiterate pig-keeper at Whitby Abbey (group of buildings comprising a monastery). He had a vision in which he claimed he was told to sing verses in praise of God—to sing of "The beginning of created things." When he awoke, he remembered his dream poem: the nine-line "Hymn." HILDA, the abbess (female superior of convent), ordered him received as one of the brethren. *Paraphrase* is his best known work. Caedmon turned simple Bible stories into poetic verse and was also the reputed author of metrical paraphrases found in versions of the Old Testament. His amazing poetical gift from God was unequalled at that time. BEDE said he composed the first story of the Bible in Old English verse.

Amandus

c 584
Poiton/Aquitaine, France

Feb. 6, 679
Elnon, France

Founder of Belgian monasticism and apostle of Flanders. Amandus was a bishop and missionary to the Franks. He founded eight abbeys, five in southern Netherlands, and spread the teachings of COLUMBANUS. He became a monk at age 20, living as a hermit. Amandus began his ministry, preaching, and baptizing near Ghent in 629, with the haughty Frieslanders hindering his work. His permanent field was the region of Antwerp. Once monasteries were founded, his work became more successful. Amandus retired to his Elnon abbey (c 675), where he continued to work fervently for the conversion of the Frankish and Basque (people of West France and Spain) heathen.

Aethelthryth (Etheldreda)

c 630
Exning, England

June 23, 679
Ely, England

East Anglican princess and later queen of Northumbria. Aethelthryth was espoused to Tondbert (died: 655) and married to him in 650. By refusing to consummate the marriage, she persuaded her husband to permit her to become a nun. Her second husband, Egfrid, king of Northumbria, to whom she was married in 660, was 14 years of age at the time and also consented to her becoming a nun. She founded a convent at Ely in 673 where espoused men and women could live separately. She became a well-known abbess through her work there. She died of the plague.

Hilda

614
West Riding, England

Nov. 17, 680
Whitby, England

Anglo-Saxon abbess. Converted in 627, when she was eleven years old, Hilda served in a French monastery until 650. She then served as head of the abbey at Hartlepool and became known for her piety and holy life. Founding a convent in Whitby, England, Hilda headed that work, as abbess, for the rest of her life, 657–680. Hilda made this the strongest and most influential abbey in England. It was known for its stand against Celtic religious rituals (decided at the Synod of Whitby in 664). Her influence also helped secure unity in the English Church at that synod. It was there she encouraged CAEDMON to dictate his epics.

Alopen (Olopun)

c 685

Syria/Persia

Nestorian missionary who went to China around 635. Alopen's ministry resulted in great numbers adhering to the Christian faith. He translated sacred books into native languages and established a church that lasted for about 150 years, greatly influencing Mongol and Chinese Christianity. Tolerance and acceptance of Christianity came and went in China until JOHN OF MONTE CORVINO reached Peking in 1291. Alopen's activities were discovered in 1625, on a Nestorian tablet written originally in 781.

Cuthbert of Lindisfarne

c 635/636
Melrose, Scotland

March 20, 687
Farne Island, England

English monk and bishop of Lindisfarne, 685 on. Cuthbert was a shepherd boy who embraced the monastic life 651–76; sequestered first at Old Melrose in 651; and then on Lindisfarne Island, England in 664. Cuthbert had retired to a hermit's life at Farne (676), when he was recalled to become a bishop—first at Hexham (684), and then at Lindisfarne (685). He was well known for his piety, diligence, and obedience. Cuthbert became a faithful preacher and missionary to the wild and untamed mountain people on Lindisfarne Island. In 687, Cuthbert once again retired to his cell at Farne Island. His body was transferred to Durham Cathedral in England in 1104.

Kilian

640
Ireland

July 8, 689
Wurzburg, Germany

Irish missionary to Germany, who became bishop of Thuringia and Franconia. He appears to have begun his work there in 685. Within a short time, a large part of the population was converted. After a pilgrimage to Rome he became the first bishop of Wurzburg. He won Duke Gosbert and many of his subjects to Christianity. Kilian's murder was instigated by Geilana, the pagan wife of Gosbert.

Benedict Biscop

c 628
Northumbria, England

Jan. 12, 690
Wearmouth, England

English Benedictine scholar and church builder. Biscop made five trips to Rome from England, his first in 653. He was made a monk at Lerins, France in 666. Biscop is credited with bringing back treasures, relics, and the art of stained-glass window making and stone masonry for erecting lovely church buildings. He also brought the precentor (song leader) from St. Peter's in Rome to teach Gregorian chants. Biscop built the monasteries at

Wearmouth (674) and at Jarrow (682). He was also abbot of St. Peter's in Canterbury in 669. Biscop struggled through the last four years of his life as a cripple, suffering from palsy. His famed pupil was the VENERABLE BEDE, for whom Biscop served as guardian from the time BEDE was seven years old.

Theodore

c 602
Tarsus, Cilicia, Asia Minor (Turkey)

Sept. 19, 690
Canterbury, England

Greek Archbishop of Canterbury, 668–90. Theodore was the last foreign missionary to occupy this position and the first archbishop of Canterbury that all Britons respected. He also founded a Greek school at Canterbury. Theodore was an outstanding monastic scholar and ecclesiastical administrator. He tied the English Church firmly to Rome and convened the first synod of clergy at Hertford in 673, which was the first synod of the whole English Church, establishing papal supremacy in England. Theodore was reconciled to WILFRID in 686. In 678 he had sought to divide his York bishopric without consulting him.

Adamnan

c 624/625
Drumhome, Ireland

Sept. 23, 704
Iona, Inner Hebrides, Scotland

Abbot of Iona, 679–704. Adamnan was converted during a visit to Northumbria around 676 and became an Irish monastic, carrying Celtic Christianity to distant places. As a result of visiting England in 685, Adamnan became one of the first Celtic churchmen to be won over to the Roman way of setting the date for Easter. At the Synod of Tara, Ireland, Adamnan had the rules of warfare changed so that women and children would no longer be fighting and taken as prisoners. He wrote *De Locis Sanctis*, an account of a visit to the Holy Land about 690, and *Life of Saint Columba*, which began Scottish literature. Despite the fact that his monastery emphasized independence from Rome, Iona would later acknowledge Rome's authority in 716.

Jacob of Edessa

c 633
Indaba, Syria (Iraq)

June 5, 708
en route to Edessa, Mesopotamia (Turkey)

Syrian theologian, historian, and bishop of Edessa, 684–700 and 708. Jacob of Edessa was best known for his work on the Syriac version of the Old Testament and Greek theology, which greatly influenced the area at this time. Jacob resigned from his Edessa bishopric over disputes with his clergy. He lived 11 years in the monastery of Eusebona, then nine years in the monastery of Tell'eda. In 708, he reaccepted his position but died on the way there while transporting his library. Jacob wrote on theology, history, philosophy, and grammar. He was proficient in Syriac, Greek, and Hebrew.

Aldhelm

c 640
Brokenborough, England

May 25, 709
Doulting, England

Bishop of Sherborne, 705 on. Aldhelm belonged to the royal family of Wessex. He founded many centers of learning, monasteries and built churches in England, serving as abbot of Malmesbury in 675. Aldhelm was a poet and highly regarded as the most learned teacher of his time. He was the first English Latin scholar and a pioneer in Latin verse among the Saxons and was known as the first translator of the Psalms around 705. Aldhelm wrote a treatise on Latin prosody (study of poetic metric structure), which included his famous 101 riddles, as well as several English songs. He introduced Benedictine rules in his various places of service. He was esteemed by BEDE.

Wilfrid
Wilfrith

634
Ripon, Northumbria, England

Oct. 3, 709
Oundle, England

Bishop of York, 669–709. Wilfrid traveled widely in his missionary labors, establishing, building, and strengthening churches throughout England, 669–78. He promoted papal authority. Wilfrid established the Benedictine Rule at the Hexham Monastery as abbot at Ripon (660) and York (666), and improved both the physical structures and the liturgy. Wilfrid was a leader at the Synod of Whitby in 664, taking the Roman side to overthrow the Celts. Several times he was driven from his see and then restored. He was reconciled to THEODORE in 686. He traveled to Rome to recover his divided bishopric in 703, establishing a precedent. Wilfrid spent his last years at the monastery in Ripon, but died at Oundle, England.

Giles (Gilles) of Provence

640
Athens, Greece

c 712/ 720
St. Gilles/ Rhone, France

French hermit. Giles was a Greek who chose to live as a hermit in a cave before emigrating to Provence, France (possibly in the desert region near Arles). While there, he was discovered in the forest by Wamba (Flavius) Visigoth king of Spain and brought back there later. Giles soon founded a monastery eleven miles southeast of Nimes, where the town of Saint-Gilles was located. He was a cripple who refused any attempts at healing in order to mortify his pride.

Guthlac

c 673
Mercia, England

April 11, 714
Crowland, England

Presbyter and hermit of Crowland. In his youth, Guthlac led a band of soldiers against the Britons. He was converted in 697 and entered a monastery at Repton. He left for Crowland, a wild and desolate island south of Lincolnshire, taking a few companions in 699. He lived on one meal a day after sunset, barley bread and water. His fame spread and many flocked to him. The island was finally reclaimed and brought under cultivation and a monastery was erected on his cell's site.

Hubert

c 656
Maestricht, Frisia (Netherlands)

May 30, 728
Tervueren, Belgium

Bishop of Maestricht and Liege, 704 on. Hubert was converted and challenged to Christian service by a vision of a stag with a crucifix between its antlers, which he saw while hunting in the forest in the Ardennes in France. He immediately won over a band of brigands (bandits) he met in the forest to a better life. Hubert reportedly performed many miracles, especially relating to protection against mad dogs.

John of Odzun (Otzun)
Hovhannes IV Otznetzi

650
Odzun (Otzun) Armenia (Russia)

729
Diorin, Armenia (Russia)

Learned theologian and leader of the Armenian Church. In 718, he became the leader of that church and encouraged orthodox Christology in the Eastern church. His principal work in defense of the human nature of Christ was *Against the Fantastic*.

Gerald of Northumbria
Gerald of Mayo

Winchester, England?

March 13, 732
Mayo, Ireland

Northumbrian monk. He followed Bishop Colman from Lindisfarne Island, England to Ireland. Gerald joined COLMAN in supporting King OSWY's defense of the Celtic tradition over the press to accept Romanizing trends. Their efforts were unsuccessful. He became COLMAN's successor and resided in the English house built at Mayo for the English Monastic Colony.

Bede
The Venerable Bede

c 673
Monkton, Northumbria (England)

May 27, 735
Jarrow, England

English scholar, historian, and theologian known as the "Father of English History." Bede lived from the age of seven in the monasteries of Wearmouth (est. 674) and Jarrow (est. 681), never traveling more than a few miles from his birthplace. He became an instructor of Greek, Latin, Hebrew, and theology, having taught himself through the monastery's libraries. Bede was ordained at the age of 30, taking his final priestly vows in 702. He spent his time reading, studying Scripture, praying, teaching, and writing voluminous scientific and theological treatises (including 24 allegorical commentaries), two books of hymns and several epigrams (concise satirical poem emphasizing a single concept and ending with an ingenious twist of thought. He combined missionary zeal, unaffected piety, and a passion for learning. His epic work was *Ecclesiastical History of the English Nation* (731). Bede was the first historian to date events, "Anno Domini" (AD—in the year of our Lord). His hymns include "A Hymn of Glory," "Let us Sing" and "Sing We Triumphant Hymns of Praise." He finished his Anglo-Saxon translation of the Gospel of John shortly before his death. As an inflammation in his lungs brought death near, Bede said, ". . .nor am I afraid to die because we have a gracious God," repeated the Benediction (Gloria chant), and immediately expired, after giving his scribe the last sentence of his translation. His relics were brought to Durham in the eleventh century, along with those of CUTHBERT, but moved to Galilee Chapel in 1370.

Willibrord
Apostle of Frisia

c 658
Northumbria, England

Nov. 7, 739
Echternach, Luxemburg

First missionary to the Frisians of the Netherlands, in 690. Willibrord was one of the earliest English Benedictine missionaries to the Continent. He was made a missionary bishop by Pope Sergius I (reigned: 687–701) on a trip to Rome in 695, and was installed as the first archbishop of Utrecht, Netherlands. Willibrord founded a monastery at Echternach. His 45 years of labor thoroughly established Christianity in what is now known as The Netherlands. Willibrord also served as a missionary to Denmark. BONIFACE, his assistant for many years, continued his work.

Andrew of Crete

c 660
Damascus, Syria

July 4, 740
Erissos, Mytilene, Lesbos, Aegean Islands, Greece

Theologian, hymn writer and archbishop of Crete (c 692), in Gortyna. Andrew took up monastic life in Jerusalem at age 15 and attended the Sixth General Council at Constantinople in 680. He became the metropolitan of Gortyna (c 711). From 712–13, he followed the Monothelite heresy, later becoming a vigorous opponent of it. Andrew was a prominent hymn writer and invented the so-called musical or Greek canon (note for note imitation of one melodic line by another). His penitential canon of 250 stanzas is especially famous. Many of his hymns are still sung in the Greek Church, and a number were translated into English. He was also a deacon in Constantinople, early in his career.

Leo III

c 680   June 18, 741
Germanicia (Maras), Asia Minor (Turkey)

Byzantine emperor, 717–41. Leo III overthrew Byzantine Emperor Theodosius III (ruled: 716–17) and began the Isaurian (district in Asia Minor) dynasty. Employing Greek fire power and assisted by a violent storm, he sank or dispersed a fleet of 1,800 Arab ships, blockading Constantinople, 717–18. He defended Constantinople against the Arabs who besieged the city 717–20. From 726–39, he fought the Moslems, finally defeating them at Acronium, Phrygia. Leo III is best known for his long struggle against the superstitious worship of icons in the churches, banning them in 726. Leo III was excommunicated by Pope Gregory III (reigned: 731–41) in 731, whereupon he confiscated the papal lands within his empire (south Italy and Greece).

Charles Martel
The Hammer

689   Oct. 22, 741
Quierzy-sur-oise, France

Carolingian (Frankish dynasty in France, 751–987) **ruler, 714–41**, who stopped the 60,000 Muslims at the Battle of Tours in 732. Martel was ruler of the Franks of Austrasia, 715 on. He stopped the Saracen (nomadic tribe, usually Arab, Turkish Muslims) Muslim tide from engulfing Europe by stopping them near Poitiers, October 25, 732, defeating the Arab Emir from Spain. This was one of the greatest victories in history, allowing Europe to remain Christian rather than Muslim. His rule subsequently developed the feudal system. Charles supported the missionary work of WILLIBRORD and BONIFACE. He was the grandfather of CHARLEMAGNE.

John of Damascus
John Damascene—The Golden Speaker

c 675   Dec. 4, 749
Damascus, Syria   Mar-Saba, Palestine (Israel)

Greek theologian and hymn writer of "The Day of Resurrection." He was considered by some as the greatest of the Greek church poets and was the last of the great Eastern Fathers. John also wrote an *Encyclopaedia of Christian Theology*, among other works. After 700 he resided and worked mostly at the monastery of St. Sabas, near Jerusalem, where he was ordained. He favored the use of pictures and images. Before his monastery years, John was the financial officer under a Muslim caliph (spiritual ruler) of Damascus. He organized the liturgical chants and reformed musical notation for the Eastern church. He became a monk after 730. His chief dogmatic work was *Fount of Knowledge*.

Boniface
Apostle of Germany—Wynfrith, Winfrid, Winfrith

680   June 5, 754
Crediton, Devon, England   Dokkum, Friesland (Netherlands)

Benedictine monk, missionary, martyr and reformer of the Franks, 716–54. Boniface began his ministry in the Netherlands in 716. He was commissioned by Rome as a missionary to central Germany in 718. He became a bishop in 722. From 723–35, he founded churches in Hesse and Thuringia. Boniface was made archbishop (732) by Pope Gregory III and papal legate (emissary) (739), appointed to reorganize the Frankish church (741). He then served as bishop of Mainz, Germany (746–48), and as the area's archbishop (748–54). Boniface worked closely with popes and kings to evangelize and educate the people and was the first to be sent beyond the Alps. Boniface helped STURMI begin the first monastery of Fulda in 744, which was the center of German missionary activity. Three trips to Rome made him a powerful personality. When going to Friesland to continue the work, Boniface was killed by a drunken mob of pagans. It was under Boniface that unity in the Western church and the empire took form.

Cuthburt of Canterbury
Oct. 25, 758

Archbishop of Canterbury, 740–60. Cuthburt was from a noble English family. He served as abbot of Lyminge in Kent and bishop of Hereford before being appointed archbishop. His friend BONIFACE encouraged him, through their correspondence, to emphasize moral standards and dissuade women from making solo pilgrimages to Rome. Continuing with this ethical theme, Cuthburt, in 747, called a synod at Clovesho (Cliff, Kent) to further define the duties of the clergy and outline moral guidelines for their conduct. In 754, Cuthburt established a feast day to honor BONIFACE's martyrdom. Cuthburt was the first archbishop of Canterbury to be buried in his own church rather than in St. AUGUSTINE's Abbey.

Pepin III
The Short

714
Paris, France

Sept. 24, 768
St. Denis, France

King of the Franks, 751–68. Pepin was the father of King CHARLEMAGNE and son of CHARLES MARTEL. He supported BONIFACE in his baptism of German chieftans and tribesmen into Christianity. Then Pepin defended Pope Gregory III from the invading Lombards (Teutonic invaders, Germanic tribe in north Italy) and was rewarded by being crowned king of France. He also aided Pope Stephen III (reigned: 752–57) against the Lombards 754–55. He deposed Childeric III (last of the Merovingians) 751 and founded the Carolingian dynasty, when he was mayor of the palace 747–51. This started the struggle between the papacy and the empire which dominated history in the Middle Ages. His wife was named Bertha. Pepin also fought against the Saxons, the army CHARLEMAGNE finally subdued.

Gregory of Utrecht

707
Treves (Trier), Germany

Aug. 25, 776
Utrecht, Friesland (Netherlands)

Frankish missionary and abbot. Gregory became an abbot at St. Martin's Monastery in Utrecht in 750. He had been the disciple and companion of BONIFACE during many of BONIFACE's missionary journeys to Germany and Rome. In 744 he came to Utrecht at BONIFACE's request. Gregory's famed school sent out preachers and missionaries by the scores. He declined the bishopric in order to continue counseling and teaching until his death. St. Martin's became a well-known missionary seminary, attracting students from all over Europe.

Walpurgis
Waloutga —Walburga

c 710
Sussex, England

Feb. 25, 779
Heidenheim, Germany

Missionary to the Germans, abbess, and missionary assistant. Walpurgis spent her life in Germany assisting her brother Willibald and her uncle BONIFACE in their missionary labors. She became abbess of a convent at Heidenheim in Franconia, Bavaria in 761. She came to Germany about 750 via Antwerp and Mainz. Her remains were moved to Eichstatt, Bavaria.

Sturm of Fulda
Sturmi

710
Bavaria, Germany

Dec. 17, 779
Fulda, Germany

First German Benedictine monk. Sturm founded the great monastery of Fulda in 744. He developed it into one of the finest schools in Europe, which trained many of the brightest minds of the Medieval Church. CHARLEMAGNE sent him as a missionary among the Saxons and also employed him in diplomatic affairs. Sturm buried the remains of his beloved teacher, BONIFACE, at his monastery in Fulda.

Lioba

700
Wessex, England

Sept. 28, 780
near Mainz, Germany

Nun and missionary to south Germany. Lioba was called to Germany by BONIFACE in 738, who gave her a convent. She was outstanding in piety, humility, and good works—an honored friend of kings and queens. Her conversion was at Tauberbischofsheim. At a time when women in Christian service were few, she was a protective, effective, Christian worker. She was engaged in charity and evangelism endeavors.

Virgilius

c 710
Ireland

Nov. 27, 784
Salzburg, Austria

Educator and bishop of Salzburg, Austria, 767 on. Virgilius was one of the greatest teachers of his age. He left Ireland for the European continent where he established a career as an abbot, evangelist, administrator, and eminent scholar. Virgilius taught that the earth is a sphere and spoke of the existence of antipodes (opposite poles). He helped convert the Alpine Slavs in 772.

Willibald

c 700
England

July 7, 786
Eichstadt, Bavaria, Germany

Missionary in Thuringia, travele, and bishop of Eichstatt, 741–86. Willibald made a pilgrimage to Rome and the Holy Land in 720–22. This was the first recorded trip by an English pilgrim. From this, Willibald wrote the first travel book in English. He traveled east for more than seven years, visiting Sicily, Cyprus, Palestine, Tyre, and Constantinople. He stayed at Monte Cassino Abbey, Italy (730–39), then served in Germany (740–86) under his uncle BONIFACE as a missionary and built a monastery at Eichstatt. His sister, WALPURGIS, assisted him in Germany.

Athelbert of East Anglia
Ethelbert

May 20, 794

King of East Anglia. Ethelbert lived a saintly life, with over 20 Anglican Churches dedicated to him, including Hereford Cathedral. Ethelbert was beheaded by the order of Mercian king Offa (ruled: 757–96) and is venerated at Hereford Cathedral.

Paul the Deacon
Paulus Diaconus

c 720–722
Frioul/Cividale, Austria

April 13, 799
Monte Cassino, Italy

Italian Benedictine monk and historian. Paul devoted his life to writing. He served at the Court of CHARLEMAGNE, 782–86, and then returned to Monte Cassino Abbey in Italy, 787. Among his works are *Life of*

Gregory the Great, History of the Lombards, and six books on Roman history. From one of Paul's poems on John the Baptist, the names of the notes in the musical scale were derived by GUIDO. He was called "The Deacon" from 782 on.

Flaccus A. Alcuin
Albinus Flaccus—Ealhwine

c 735
York, England

May 19, 804
Tours, France

Educator, theologian, scholar, poet, and deacon. Alcuin worked with Emperor CHARLEMAGNE to introduce the Latin language and culture to the rough Franks. At the onset of his career, he was headmaster at the English Yorkminster School in 767. In 780, he met CHARLEMAGNE in Parma, Italy, and at his request, Alcuin founded an educational center-court school system at Aachen in western Germany, 782–96. Alcuin left the service of the court to become abbot of St. Martin's monastery at Tours in 796. Alcuin's influence helped the Franks build a Christian state. He further upheld orthodoxy against the Adoptionist Heresy [taught God adopted the human Jesus as His special Son at birth (not conception) or baptism, and gave Him an extra measure of divine power] at the Council of Frankfurt in 796, opposing FELIX OF URGEL. His writings were comprised of histories, poetry, educational manuals, and theological texts, including, *The Trinity and Life of St. Willibrord*. In 802, Alcuin led a group of scholars in revising JEROME's Latin Vulgate Bible. He sought to convert and civilize invaders through the power of the Gospel. Alcuin was the greatest scholar of his time.

Aethelheard
Adelard—Aethelhard—Eaethelhard—Edelred—Ethelhard

May 12, 805
Canterbury, England

Archbishop of Canterbury, 793–805. Aethelheard's consecration was delayed until 793 due to opposition from the Kent nobility who opposed having an archbishop selected from Mercia. Upon the death of his patron, King Offa of Mercia in 796, Aethelheard was banished to Mercia. Pope Leo III (reigned: 795–816) restored him to Canterbury in 798, and in the process, the see of Canterbury gained primacy over the other Anglican bishoprics.

Liudger
Ludger

c 744
Zeilen, Friesland (Netherlands)

March 26, 809
Billerbeck, Friesland (Netherlands)

Missionary to the Saxons in Frisia and Westphalia. Liudger was the first bishop of Munster, Germany. He was ordained a priest in 777. For seven years, 777–84, he labored as a missionary in Frisia when the Saxons forced him to move. Liudger wrote *Life of St. Gregory* (the Great). During 789 a revolt forced him to flee to Rome, living at the monastery of Monte Cassino for two and one half years. On his return, CHARLEMAGNE gave him an enlarged field in Doccum, Frisia. Between the years 802–05, he was consecrated bishop of southern Westphalia with headquarters in Munster where he built 90 parishes.

Charlemagne

Charles the Great

April 2, 742
Liege, Belgium

Jan. 28, 814
Aix-la-Chapelle (Aachen), Germany

King of the Franks, 768–814, and first emperor of the Holy Roman Empire, 800–14. Charlemagne was the first German to bear the title "Emperor of the West" and was the first medieval

Roman emperor. In 774 he defeated the Lombards and annexed North Italy. He undertook a long-term effort to subdue and Christianize the Saxons in 775. He was crowned Emperor on December 25, 800, by Pope Leo III, with the church and state being united. Charlemagne introduced Christianity into every province of Germany, expanding and unifying the kingdom. In 804, under his rule, Saxony was conquered and Christianized. Schools and monasteries appeared throughout Europe, even though he, himself could not write. Fighting 52 campaigns, Charlemagne welded western Europe's wild, warring tribes into a cohesive empire. This Holy Roman Empire, a Germanic empire of Central European states, lasted until 1806. He saw himself as the protector of the Pope instead of his rival. Charlemagne married Hildegarde of Swabia (district in southwest Germany), although it is reported that he had many wives, divorcing them at will. His morals indicated his weak Christian commitment. He was the son of PEPIN THE SHORT and the father of Louis I, from his second wife, Hildegarde of Kempten (758– April 30, 783). His autograph is worth at least $75,000. He said as he died of pneumonia, "Lord, into Thy hands I commend my spirit." He is buried in Aix-la-Chapelle. His favorite Bible verse was II Kings 23:3.

Angilbert
Homer of His Age

740
Feb. 18, 814
Centula (St. Riquier), France

Frankish Latin poet. Angilbert was considered the most distinguished poet of his age. He married Bertha, daughter of CHARLEMAGNE, and had two sons. In 790, he retired to the monastery of St. Centula. He became its abbot in 794 and rebuilt it with much splendor. Angilbert was also a historian, diplomat, counselor to CHARLEMAGNE, and was involved in many difficult negotiations. Angilbert was a friend of ALCUIN.

Theophanes
The Confessor

c 758/760
Constantinople (Istanbul), Asia Minor (Turkey)
March 12, 817
Samothrace (island in Aegean Sea), Greece

Greek monk. Theophanes founded and headed a monastery at Sigriano in Marmora (island in Sea of Marmora, 70 miles southwest of Constantinople). He was a pious partisan of icon (religious picture/image painting) veneration and became deeply involved in the controversy over the use of images. He advocated image worship at The Second Council of Nicea in 787. Theophanes suffered imprisonment in Constantinople and banishment to Samothrace in 815, by Byzantine Emperor, Leo V (ruled: 813–17), where he died in prison after a brief exile. His main work was a historical chronicle. Compelled to marry at age twelve, he and his wife separated ten years later.

Felix of Urgel

c 748
Spain
818

Spanish bishop of Urgel, Spain. Felix was a devoted friend of Elipandus of Toledo, the Adoptionist theologian. He promoted Elipandus' view in the Adoptionist controversy. This doctrine was condemned at the Synod of Regensburg, Germany in 792, where he defended his views in front of CHARLEMAGNE. In 798, at the Council of Aix-la-Chapelle, he recanted, and was placed under the archbishop of Lyons until his death.

Benedict of Aniane

750
Languedoc, France
Feb. 11, 821
Aachen, Germany

Founder of a monastery at Aniane, in southern France, 779. Benedict was a strict, Visigothic, ascetic reformer who brought monasticism back to its original purposes of worship, contemplation, and self-denial. He was instrumental in bringing the rule of BENEDICT OF NURSIA (the Benedictine order) back to the convents. He discouraged monks who became involved in educational and cultural activities. Manual labor was emphasized more than study. Benedict became an advisor to CHARLEMAGNE and founded the monastery of Juda. In 814, he became a monastic advisor to Emperor LOUIS I and founded a monastery in Aix-la-Chapelle. He compiled monastic rules and was general supervisor of Frankish monasteries.

Theodulf
Theodulph

c 760
Spain

Sept. 18, 821
Angers, France

Theologian, scholar, and hymn writer. Theodulf wrote the famous hymn, "All Glory, Laud, and Honor." Teschner composed the music in 1615. He was brought to France by CHARLEMAGNE and served as bishop of Orleans from 781–818. He was the Emperor's chief theologian and one of his counselors. Theodulf introduced reform to French monasticism. He advanced education and culture. He was renown as one of the cultural leaders in the Carolingian renaissance. Having been accused of conspiracy with the king of Italy, Theodulf came into disfavor with Emperor LOUIS I, resulting in his imprisonment at Angers in 818. Theodulf died of poisoning.

Cynewulf
Cynwulf

c 750
Northumbria or Mercia, England

825

Anglo-Saxon poet. As a scholar, Cynewulf was familiar with both Latin and religious literature. He may have studied in a monastery, prior to traveling widely, then settled again into monastery life. Cynewulf produced four religious poems, *Juliana* (his martyrdom account), *Elene* (legend of cross discovery), *Christ* (His coming, ascension, etc.), and *The Fates of the Apostles* (thought to be a Northumbrian minstrel). He may have also been the Bishop Cynewulf of Lindisfarne Island, England, who died in 783.

Theodore of Studius

759
Near modern Pirusa, Turkey

Nov. 11, 826
Island of Chalcis, Greece

Abbot of the great monastery of the Studion (Studium/Studius) in Constantinople, 797 on. Theodore triggered a monastic revival which spread throughout the East, as far as Russia. Theodore fought for church independence from imperial power, which caused him to be exiled twice. He spent his remaining years in various monasteries, 824–26. Theodore became a monk in 787, and reformed monastic life. He published homilies and nearly 600 letters. His penmanship and manuscript copies were well known. Theodore was also the author of hymns and controversial treatises. He championed the worship of images. This image emphasis and his charges of adultery against Byzantine Emperor Constantine VI (ruled: 780–97) brought him frequent persecutions and banishment.

Nicephorous

758
Constantinople (Istanbul), Asia Minor (Turkey)

June 2, 828
Tou Agathou, Asia Minor (Turkey)

Greek Orthodox historian, theologian and patriarch of Constantinople, 806–15. Nicephorous wrote about and struggled in the cause of the Byzantine controversy over the veneration of images. He opposed iconoclasts (dispute between church and state, 717–843, the latter attempting to legislate against pictures/statuary in churches, stating that it encouraged image worship) at the Second Nicene Council in 787. He refused to obey Byzantine Emperor Leo V's edict (814), and thus was deposed (815). Nicephorous supported icon usage in his *Apologeticus Minor* and *Apologeticus Major* (817). His works of history (on Constantinople and a chronology) were highly regarded. Nicephorous died in a monastery.

Oengus
The Culdee

Ireland

c 835

Monk at Clon Enagh in Leix. He was later a student at Tallaght near Dublin. Oengus was closely connected with the reform movement among Irish monastics which was known as "Fellows of God." About 800, he assembled his "calendar" in Irish, *The Felire*, a type of prayer book listing names under each day of the year which became an important part of Irish liturgy.

Amalarius

c 775/780
Metz, Germany

c 837/850
Metz, Germany

Liturgical writer. Amalarius influenced the formation of Roman worship patterns in western Europe by describing the order of service being observed at that time. He studied under ALCUIN, served as bishop of Treves, Germany, and briefly acted as envoy to Constantinople. He also was abbot of Hornbach and head of the Church of Lyons, France, 835–37. He is responsible for the medieval Mass which gave every prayer chant and ceremony a symbolic reference to the life and work of Christ. Some of his views were condemned by the Synod of Quiercy in 838.

Einhard
Eginhard

c 775
Franconia, Germany

March 14, 840
Seligenstadt-on-the-Main, Germany

Frankish historian, architect and biographer of CHARLEMAGNE. Einhard was with CHARLEMAGNE almost constantly, being part of his court, 791–92. Einhard was educated under ALCUIN, appointed secretary to Emperor CHARLEMAGNE, and superintendent of public buildings in 796. In 806, he became the imperial legate to Rome. In 829, he became abbot of the Benedictine Monastery at Seligenstadt, which he had founded. He continued in the court with Emperor LOUIS I OF AQUITANE, until he opposed the wickedness of the Empress in 830. He married Emma (died: 836), sister of the bishop of Worms. He also wrote a famous biography on CHARLEMAGNE.

Louis I of Aquitane
The Pious

778
Chassenevil, France

June 20, 840
Island near Mainz, Germany

Holy Roman Emperor, 816–40, and King of the Franks, 814 on. Louis I was from Aquitaine (southwestern region of France). Louis was the youngest son and successor of CHARLEMAGNE who earned his title of "The Pious" by banishing his sisters and others of immoral life from the court and giving aid to the poor. Deeply religious, he did not possess the administrative strength of his father. The empire was divided among his three sons, Lothar, Louis II, and Charles the Bald. This fragmenting of the unified power, which might have resisted the Norsemen, created many quarrels among the royal family and changed the direction for the future of France, resulting in civil war, 838–40. Judith of Bavaria became Louis I's second wife in 819, but evidently she was wicked. He encouraged ANSKAR to be a missionary to Scandinavia.

Walafrid Strabo

c 808/809
Swabia, Germany

Aug. 18, 849
Reichenau (Island in Lake Constance), Germany

Theologian, abbot, and author. Strabo headed the monastery at Reichenau, 838–49, wrote much of *Glossa Ordinaria* and penned liturgical material and biographies of the saints. Once a monk at Fulda, under the distinguished *Rabanus Maurus*, Strabo combined his skills as a Latin scholar/poet with statecraft (art of government and diplomacy) and served as advisor to LOUIS I. He was also chaplain to Empress Judith and tutor to their son, Charles the Bald.

Rabanus Maurus

c 780
Mainz, Germany

Feb. 4, 856
Winkel, Germany

Benedictine abbot and theologian. Maurus served as abbot of Fulda (822–42) and as archbishop of Mainz (847–56). He was prominent in the resurgence of learning spurred by CHARLEMAGNE. His *Excerpito* was the most popular textbook for several centuries. Maurus' school at Fulda, founded in 803, was one of the greatest monastery schools in Europe. He wrote a 22-volume encyclopedia, *On the Nature of Things*, and was a pupil of ALCUIN. He opposed GOTTSCHALK's defense of predestination advocated by AUGUSTINE. Maurus authored poetry and commentaries and produced theological and pedagogical writings on most books of the Bible. Some called him "The First Teacher of Germany." He compiled a Latin-German Glossary of the Bible.

Prudentius of Troyes
Prudentius Galindo

Spain

April 6, 861
Troyes, France

Bishop of Troyes, 847–61. Prudentius was a native of Spain. He supported GOTTSCHALK in the Predestination Controversy and wrote a couple of treatises. Prudentius was a bitter opponent of HINCMAR OF REIMS. His part of the *Annales Bertiniani*, which was produced between 835 and 861, is considered his chief contribution to history.

Swithun

c 800

July 2, 862
Winchester, England

Bishop of Winchester, England, 852–62. Swithun was a priest at Wessex, who went from chaplain and counselor to West Saxon King Egbert (ruled: 802–39), to become a bishop. He then became one of King Ethelwulf's (of Kent 828–58, and Wessex 839–56) chief counselors. Swithun built several churches and was renowned for both his humility and his concern for the needy. He allegedly worked many miracles. He asked to be buried in the churchyard where rain could fall on his grave. On July 15, 971, his remains were moved inside the cathedral and deemed church relics.

Ansgar (Anskar)
Apostle to the North

Sept. 9, 801
Amiens/Corbie, France

Feb. 3, 865
Bremen, Germany

Fearless and tireless missionary to Scandinavia. Ansgar was a monk from Corbie who eventually became the first archbishop of Hamburg (831) and of Bremen (847). Ansgar labored amidst great discouragement and hostile tribes in a valiant effort to organize the Church in Jutland (Denmark) (826–27) and in Sweden (829–31). Ansgar combatted the slave trade (852) and converted the King of Jutland (854). In 864 he was made archbishop of Scandinavia. This gave him the right to send missionaries to all northern lands. He said as he died, "Into Thy hands do I commend my spirit, for Thou hast redeemed me, O Lord!" He was buried in his cathedral.

Paschasius Radbertus

c 785–786
Soissons, France

April 26, 865
Corbie, France

French Benedictine abbot and monk of Corbie, 842–51. Orphaned, Radbertus entered into a Benedictine monastery. He is best known for his *Body and Blood of the Lord* (831), the first comprehensive treatise on the sacrament of the Lord's Supper. Although he did not use the term "transubstantiation", he taught that by divine miracle, the elements became the very body and blood of Christ. Radbertus retired to the abbey at St. Requier but returned to Corbie just before his death. He was a friend of Louis I of Aquitaine and Gottschalk. He was distinguished for learning and for piety as a writer.

Gottschalk

803
Mainz, Germany

Oct. 30, 868
Hautvilliers, France

Benedictine monk, poet, and theologian who was ordained at the convent of Orbais. Gottschalk was sent to a monastery as a child by his parents. He tried to leave when he was an adult but was not permitted to do so. He spent most of his life in a Franciscan monastery at Orbais (diocese of Soissons). He was the originator of the predestination controversy that today would be called by some "extreme Calvinism." Gottschalk advocated that God predestined some to eternal life, others to eternal death. His teachings were condemned by a succession of synods, the last being at Mainz in 828. Gottschalk was imprisoned in a monastery at Hautvilliers where he was beaten brutally and so died, having become insane in the latter years of his life. He was denied a Christian burial. He wrote *The Eclogue of Theololus*.

Ratramnus

798

c 869
Corbie, France

Theological writer and monk of the famed monastery of Corbie. Around 844, Ratramnus wrote and answered the argument advocated by Radbertus on transubstantiation (elements become actual body and blood of the Lord during communion). His view would later be called consubstantiation, a view to which Luther would hold (body and blood are mysteriously present, but not the same as that on the cross). Ratramnus' opinions were frequently sought by Frankish Emperor Charles the Bald (ruled: 840–77).

Constantius Cyril of Thessalonica

c 826
Thessalonica (Salonik), Greece

Feb. 14, 869
Rome, Italy

"Apostle of the Slavs" (Southeast European family), **along with his older brother Methodius**. He began his public life as secretary to the patriarch of Constantinople. When the duke of Moravia asked for missionaries in 86, the Byzantine Emperor, Michael III (ruled: 842–67) sent them. Cyril invented the Cyrillic (script from Greek unicals) alphabet used by Slavs and Russians and translated the Gospels and liturgical books into the Slavic language. Tradition says he discovered the bones of Clement of Rome and carried them with him. In 868 Constantius Cyril sought Pope Adrian II's (reigned: 867–72) approval for religious messages given in the Slavic language. Adrian II was the last married pope. His wife, Stephania, and their daughter lived in the Lateran Palace with him for a short time. Later, one of his rivals abducted his daughter and married her by force. Cyril entered a monastery in Rome in late 868 and died less than two months later.

Edmund

c 840
Nuremberg, Germany

Nov. 20, 870
Oxen (Hoxon), Norfolk, England

Martyr and king of East Anglia, 855–70. In 870, Edmund's kingdom was invaded by the Danes, who wanted him to share his kingdom with their leader. He refused to deny his Christian faith and collaborate with a pagan. Edmund was captured at Hoxon, then either shot to death with arrows or beheaded for refusing to renounce Christianity. Devout and dedicated, his body was moved, in the tenth century, to a place called Bury St. Edmund's.

Hincmar of Laon

c 830
Laon, France

879

Bishop of Laon, 858 on. Hincmar received his office through his uncle's (HINCMAR OF RHEIMS) influence. He was deposed by the Synod of Douzi in 871, over which his uncle presided, because he opposed the king and took the side of Pope Adrian II in his contention with the French church. Hincmar was taken prisoner and blinded. The next pope, John VIII (reigned: 872–82) restored him, and gave him half of the bishopric's revenue.

Hincmar of Rheims

c 806
Rheims, France ?

Dec. 21, 882
Epernay, France

Archbishop of Rheims, 845 on. From 822–45, Hincmar was at the imperial court of Aachen. He was a most influential churchman who defended the French Church's independence against Pope Nicholas I's (reigned: 858–67) claims. He also defended the orthodox view of divine predestination in a controversy with GOTTSCHALK. Hincmar directed the course of the entire Frankish kingdom during his lifetime. He was driven from Rheims, not long before his death, by the Normans (Scandinavians who conquered and settled in Normandy in 911). Hincmar's education took place at the abbey of St. Denis. He was the author of treatises which were inspired by religious controversies. His chief work was *Annales Bertiniani*. In 869, he crowned Charles the Bald and became his advisor despite papal (Adrian II) objection.

Joseph
The Hymnographer

April 3, 883

Sicily, Italy

Voluminous Greek hymn writer. Joseph left Sicily in 830, going first to Thessalonica, Greece and then Constantinople, Turkey in search of a purer monastic life. He left Constantinople during the iconoclastic persecutions. While en route to Rome, Joseph was captured by pirates who forced him into slavery on the Island of Crete. When freed, he returned to Constantinople where he established a monastery for inmates that was aligned with the church named in honor of JOHN CHRYSOSTOM. Joseph was once again in turmoil, having been banished for his defense of icons. Finally in 843, the policy of iconoclasm was reversed under the widowed Empress Theodora (810–62), who recalled Joseph. Joseph was very old when he died. During his lifetime he is believed to have written close to 1,000 hymns, 200 of which are presented in his collection, *Menaea*. Three of his more notable hymns are: "Let Us Now Our Voices Raise," "O Happy Band of Pilgrims," and "Stars of the Morning."

Christian Druthmar

c 835

c 885

Learned Benedictine monk of Corvey (German Benedictine abbey). While in the monastery at Stavelo (Stablo), in the diocese of Liege, Belgium, Druthmar prepared a famous commentary on the Gospel of Matthew.

Druthmar stressed historical sense and following true exegetical principles, appears to have rejected the doctrine of transubstantiation. His writing reveals that the Bulgarians were converting to Christianity during his lifetime which dates the thrust of his ministry around 865. He was distinguished for his linguistic learning.

Harold Klak

c 885
Friesland (Netherlands)

King of Denmark who introduced the Gospel to Denmark, while still clinging to the throne. He was then banished by a usurper. Around 826, he was baptized at Ingleheim. Returning to power, Klak brought back ANSGAR and established the Danish Church. He died in exile, having been once again forced out of office. Klak suffered the ups and downs of being a feudal (holding of land estate) leader.

Methodius

c 815
Thessalonica, Greece

April 6, 885
Velehrad, Czechoslovakia

"Apostle of the Slavs" along with his younger brother, CYRIL. When the Duke of Moravia asked for missionaries in 864, the Eastern emperor, Michael III, sent them. While in consultation in Rome about the work, CYRIL died, and Methodius returned to Moravia becoming archbishop there. As key people (Ratislav and Pope Adrian II) passed on, the work became insecure. They won King BORIS I to the Christian faith. Methodius became archbishop of Surinium, Pannonia. Opposed by a German bishop, he was imprisoned for two years, then returned to Moravia and worked with such things as the Slavonic liturgy. He (and CYRIL) were respected by both the church in the West and in the East.

Photius

c 820
Constantinople (Istanbul), Asia Minor (Turkey)

Feb. 6, 891
Bordi, Armenia

Patriarch of Constantinople, 858–86. Photius held this position while still a layman and professor of philosophy. He was excommunicated in 863 by Pope Nicholas I. He defended his church against the papacy. Photius is remembered for objecting to the insertion of the "filioque" clause in the Nicene Creed, which precipitated the 1054 schism (break with Rome). Photius was deposed 869–77 for refusing to serve communion to Byzantine Emperor Basil I (ruled: 867–86), on account of his murder of Byzantine Emperor, Michael III. He was banished by Byzantine Emperor, Leo VI (ruled: 886–911) to an Armenian cloister. He promoted Christian missions in Monrovia, Bulgaria and Russia, and finalized the defeat of iconoclasm.

Alfred
The Great

849
Wantage, England

Oct. 28, 901
Winchester, England

King of West Saxons, Wessex, 871–901, and all England, 886–99. He first appears in public in 866 helping repel attacks of the Danes. He married in 868. Alfred captured London in 885–86, subduing the Angles and the Saxons. As King of Wessex, he saved England from conquest by the Danes in 897, and was successful in promoting a great revival of learning. Alfred compiled a code of laws, rebuilt schools, founded monasteries, and invited scholars to his court, making him a champion of England and of Christianity. He translated many Latin works that were vital to the English knowledge of theology, philosophy, and history. This effort included the works of BEDE and Orosius, Latin historian and theologian, plus BOETHIUS' *Consolation of Philosophy*, AUGUSTINE's *Soliloquies*, and Pope Gregory I's *Pastoral Care*. He translated the ten commandments and other Old Testament laws, placing them at the head of his laws for England. He also translated the Psalms and started on the Gospels until death.

Boris I

c 827   May 2, 907
Constantinople (Istanbul), Asia Minor (Turkey)

King of the Bulgars (Bulgaria), 852–88, a tribe in the Balkans from eastern Russia. Boris was converted through the persuasion of Byzantine Emperor Michael III. Following his baptism in 865 by the patriarch of Constantinople, he introduced Christianity to the Bulgarians. For some time he wavered, deciding whether to have spiritual loyalty to Constantinople or Rome. Constantinople prevailed in 870, since it promised to the Bulgarian Church a greater degree of autonomy. From that time on, eastern Europe gravitated to Greek rather than Latin tradition. Boris I abdicated his throne in 889 and retired to a monastery. He returned in 893 to depose his son Vladimir, a vicious ruler, and enthroned his youngest son, Simeon I. He died at the Saint Pantaleon (martyr, died: 305) Monastery.

Asser

c 909
Wales   Sherborne, England

Welsh monk, saint, and bishop of Sherborne before 900. Asser was a noted churchman in medieval England. He was the tutor-companion and scholar at the court of the esteemed English king, ALFRED, as of 885. He also wrote *Life of Alfred* (c 893). The chronology of the book is confusing and the style bad. He was a monk at St. David's in Wales before coming to England.

Gerald of Aurillac

855   Oct. 13, 909
Aurillac, France   Aurillac, France

Nobleman and religious cleric. Gerald lived a very holy life at a time of great moral degeneracy. Although he was a nobleman, he chose to leave his titled heritage of aristocracy behind and enter religious life. He lived according to a very strict rule. Gerald was renowned for his justice, devotions and gift of healing. After several pilgrimages to Rome, he founded a monastery for the Benedictine monks at Aurillac.

Plegmund

914

Archbishop of Canterbury, 890–914, noted prelate who flourished at this time, a friend and fellow student of ALFRED. Plegmund exerted great influence on ecclesiastical affairs through him.

William I the Pious

886   918

Duke of Aquitaine, 898–918, and as William II, Count of Auvergne (former province in central France), **886–918**. William founded, for the purpose of reform, the great monastery at Cluny by 910, placing it directly under Pope Sergius III (ruled: 904–11). It became the center of a reform movement in the years to come. William was disturbed about the laxity in Medieval monasticism and sought to reform it.

Berno

c 850   Jan. 13, 927
Burgundy, France

Burgundian Benedictine monk. Berno became the first abbot of the monastery at Cluny, being appointed by WILLIAM I THE PIOUS in 910. He enforced the strictest observance of the rules of BENEDICT. Berno soon had six satellite monasteries. He energetically reformed and reshaped monasticism. Trained at the monastery of Dijon, France, Berno served as a successful pastor in several abbeys.

Wenceslaus

c 907

Sept. 28, 929
Alt-Bunzlau (Stara Boleslav), Bohemia (Czechoslovakia)

Prince and duke of Bohemia, 922–929. As a Christian, Wenceslaus took over the reins of government when paganism had a stronghold on the people. He was a man of deep piety, having been raised a Christian by his grandmother, Ludmilla. They both were murdered by Wenceslaus' pagan mother, Drahomira. His brother, Boleslav, also participated in his murder which occurred on the church steps, while visiting his brother's castle. Wenceslaus' spirituality and friendship with Germany were the roots behind his murder. A Czech hero, his virtues are extolled in the Christmas hymn, "Good King Wenceslaus," which is based on a native legend.

Odo of Cluny

Dec. 24, 877/879
Tours/Lemans, France

Nov. 18, 942
Cluny, France

Second abbot of the famed Cluny Monastery in 927, succeeding BERNO. Odo's excellent leadership influenced some 65 "congregations" to become obedient to the Cluny discipline. He traveled extensively in France and Italy, usually taking monks in training with him. Odo was noted for his learning, wisdom, piety, and character. A century later Cluny-trained monks were becoming popes.

Odo of Canterbury

c 875
North England

June 2, 959
Canterbury, England

Archbishop of Canterbury, 942–58. Odo was a Dane, and rejected by his family when he was converted, and adopted by a nobleman in the entourage of King ALFRED. He headed the see of Ramsbury 927–42. King Edmund of the West Saxons and Mercians (ruled: 940–46) offered him the high post, which he at first declined, because he was not a monk, but later accepted. He was active in renovating buildings and restoring the morals of the clergy.

Haakon I
The Good

c 914

June 2, 961

King of Norway, 935–61. Haakon was raised a devout Christian by King Aethelstan of England (ruled: 924–40). After his father's death (933), he sailed with a fleet to Norway to fight his half brother Eric Bloodace, who had seized the throne (930). Haakon was not notably successful, but at least a start was made at introducing Christianity to Norway when he built a church at Drontheim. The sons of Eric (his half brother) and their Danish allies fought him, resulting in Haakon's death from wounds received in battle.

Bruno I
Bruno the Great

Spring 925

Oct. 11, 965
Rheims, France

Archbishop of Cologne and duke of Lorraine, 953–65. Bruno was the youngest son of King Henry I of Germany (ruled: 919–36). He exercised considerable influence over his brother, OTTO I, in reviving peace and learning in the empire. This German prince was noted for his piety, statesmanship, and scholarship, often representing his brother in trying diplomatic situations, showing a successful union of church and state. He was appointed imperial chancellor (939), and was instrumental in making the court the cultural center of Germany (940). In 941, Bruno was made abbot of monasteries (Lorsch near Worms and of Carvei on the Weser). He then became arch-chaplain to OTTO I in 951. He was victorious in 953 over Conrad of Lorraine. He was made regent in Germany in 961.

Olga
Helga—Helena

c 890
Pskov, Prussia (Germany)

July 11, 969
Kiev, Russia

Queen of Kiev, Ukraine, 945–55. Olga was a peasant who became a princess by marrying Prince Igor of Kiev and became queen after his sudden death in 945. Olga ruled Russia until her son, Sviatoslaf, came of age in 955. In 957 she went to Constantinople to be baptized by Patriarch Theophilaxtes and took the name Helena. Upon her return, she worked tirelessly to promote Christianity, even to the point of requesting missionaries to assist in spreading the Gospel. She was the grandmother of VLADIMIR I.

Otto I
Otto the Great

Nov. 23, 912

May 7, 973
Memleben, Prussia (Germany)

King of Germany, 936–73, and emperor of the Holy Roman Empire, 962–973. Otto was crowned by Pope John XII (reigned: 955–63) and revived the empire of CHARLEMAGNE. He was considered the founder of the Holy Roman Empire, raising the authority of the throne, rivaling that attained by CHARLEMAGNE two cenuries earlier. In his early years, he was instrumental in suppressing revolts by the nobles (Bohemians, Wends and Danes). Otto was the greatest military and political figure in Europe during the latter part of the tenth century. Annexing northern Italy, he restored it to its former power. Otto unified the feuding German duchies, shoving out the invading Magyars and Slavs on the Lechfeld (large plain in Bavaria) on October 10, 955. Otto the Great installed Leo VIII (reigned: 963–64) as Pope, deposing John XII in 963, which began the long pope/emperor struggles. His wife was Adelaide, Queen of Lombard, Italy, whom he aided against King Berengar II of Italy (ruled: 950–61) in 951. Their son, OTTO II, became joint emperor in 967.

Ulrich

890
Augsburg, Germany

July 4, 973
Augsburg, Germany

Reforming bishop of Augsburg, 923–73. Ulrich discharged his duties with great vigor and ability. His wealth was used in the construction of churches and religious houses. He enforced the rules regarding hours of worship with great rigor. Ulrich insisted upon the celibacy of the clergy, strict observance of their duties, and enforced a peculiar reverence for religious relics. He made three pilgrimages to Rome.

Edward the Martyr

963
England

March 18, 978
Corfe Castle, England

Martyr and child king of The West Saxons, 975–78, at the age of 13, succeeding his father, Edgar the Peaceful (ruled: 959–75). Edward was allegedly stabbed to death by his stepmother, Elfrida, who wanted the throne for her own son, Aethelred II the Unready (ruled: 978–1016). DUNSTAN (Archbishop of Canterbury) had influenced Edward's election; however, a reaction against this monastic policy developed along with disputes with secular clergy. He tried to defend churches and monasteries against a growing anti–monastic reaction. He died at age 15.

Otto II

late 955
Rome, Italy

Dec. 7, 983
Rome, Italy

King of Germany and emperor of The Holy Roman Empire, 973–83. Otto II followed the same supportive policies toward the Church of his gifted father, OTTO I, but lacked his firm touch. Otto II regarded Germany and Italy as a united realm. He defeated the Danes (974), subdued a revolt in Bavaria in 976 and defeated the Bohemians (977). Otto fought France, 978–80, but was unsuccessful in his siege of Paris. He further attempted to enlarge his domain in Italy, but was finally defeated by the Greeks and the Saracens, July 13, 982, near Crotone in Calabria, southeast Italy, barely escaping by boat. Theophano (c. 955–91), daughter of the Byzantine emperor, became his wife in 972.

Aethelwold
Adelwold—Ethelwold

908

Aug. 1, 984
Beddington, England

Bishop of Winchester, 963 on. Aethelwold was a reform–minded English monastic. He was instrumental in the building of the famed Winchester Cathedral. Prior to his Winchester appointment, he was abbot of Abington (c 954), where he re-established a monastic house and introduced strict Benedictine rule.

Harold Blaatand
Harold Bluetooth

c 985

King of Denmark, 940–85. Blaatand was converted to Christianity (c 960), through the influence of Emperor Otto I. He succeeded in establishing a strong church with its own bishopric in his territory of the Jutland Peninsula (Denmark). Responding to a Norwegian appeal, he dispatched missionaries to help King HAAKON I (c 974), but they could not restrain Norway from the heathen. In 983, he freed Denmark from German occupation, but his son, Sweyn Forkbeard, on the Danish throne, led an anti–Christian revolt to force him off his throne. Blaatand was killed when he attempted to flee from the war. He tried unsuccessfully to reach friendly Slavic tribes for refuge. He was the grandfather of CANUTE II.

Adaldag

900

April 28, 988
Bremen, Germany

Archbishop of Hamburg-Bremen, 937–988. Adaldag was an energetic and persuasive Scandinavian missionary. He influenced HAROLD BLAATAND, king of Denmark, to be baptized as a Christian. Denmark's religion changed to Christianity, and bishoprics were established throughout the country under his leadership. Originally a canon (member of a religious order) of Hildesheim, Germany, he resisted the city of Cologne's claims of jurisdiction over Bremen. Adaldag served as counselor to Holy Roman Emperor OTTO I and accompanied him on his journey to Rome in 961 to strengthen his political position.

Dunstan

c 910
near Glastonbury, England

May 19, 988
Canterbury, England

Archbishop of Canterbury, 961–88. Dunstan was a Benedictine monk and abbot of Glastonbury (c 932), which he reformed and made famous as a center of learning. He was treasurer of the kingdom under King Edmund, chief advisor to King Edward (ruled: 946–55), banished by King Eswy (ruled: 955–59) but brought back Benedictine traditions from Ghent, Netherlands (and the abbey of St. Peter), and carried through sweeping state and church reforms as the chief minister of King Edgar, having been appointed bishop of Winchester in 957. He was also bishop of London, 959–61 and of Canterbury in 961 and influenced the election of Edgar's son, EDWARD THE MARTYR. Dunstan restored monastic life in England and is said to have been a worker of miracles. Under Edgar, a weak ruler, Dunstan was all but in name, a wise and vigorous ruler of the kingdom. He retired to Canterbury in 978, upon the death of the child-king, EDWARD THE MARTYR. Dunstan said as he died, "He hath given meat to them that fear Him."

Oswald of York

c 925   *Feb. 29, 992*
Denmark   Worcester, England

Archbishop of York, 972–92, and bishop of Worcester, 962–92. Oswald came from a Danish family. His early days were spent in Fleury, France, where he was a Benedictine monk. He established many monastic houses, particularly at Ramsey in Huntingdonshire. Oswald labored to upgrade the moral tone among the clergy by restoring church discipline and cooperating with the reforming efforts of DUNSTAN and AETHELWOLD. He was renowned for his energetic emphasis toward clerical education, stressing the importance of building upon a solid knowledge of theology. Oswald died while washing the feet of the poor.

Adalbert of Prague
Apostle of the Prussians

c 938   *April 23, 997*
Prague, Bohemia (Czechoslovakia)   Gnesen (Danzig) (Gdansk), Prussia (Poland)

Martyred missionary to Slavs and apostle of Bohemians and Prussians. Adalbert was the second bishop for the Prussians, serving as bishop of Prague 982–97. He retired to a Benedictine monastery near Rome (988) but was sent back to his bishopric in Prague (992) by Pope John XV (reigned: 985–96). However, he was repulsed as he sought to remove heathen customs and institute moral reforms. He went as a missionary to Germany with OTTO III and met with great success in Prussia, Poland, and Hungary, where he baptized STEPHEN (later king of Hungary). Adalbert became archbishop of Gnesen, but was killed by an angry pagan priest's instigation along the Nogat River on a trip to Prussia. His bones were transferred from Gnesen to Prague in 1039.

Olaf I of Norway
Olav Tryggvesson

969   *1000*
                                                          off Swold Island (in Baltic Sea), Scandinavia

King of Norway, 995–1000. At age nine (978), he avenged the murder of his foster father by slaying the killer with a hatchet. In his early years, Olaf participated in the raiding of England, Ireland, and France, but changed his behavior after being baptized by a hermit on the Scilly Islands (off southwest England) where he was converted around 994. He married Gyda, a Christian Irish princess, while in Ireland, 990–93. Olaf then returned to Norway in 995 and pushed out Earl Haakon, the pagan ruler. He introduced Christianity to the country. Olaf made Trondheim his capital and erected the earliest Norwegian cathedral. He sought to unite Scandinavia into one kingdom but, when waylaid at sea by King Sweyn of Denmark (ruled: 1024–32) and the king of Sweden, he jumped overboard and presumably drowned.

Otto III
The Wonder of the World

July 980   *Jan. 23, 1002*
near Cleves, Germany   Paterno, Italy

Holy Roman Emperor, 996–1002. Otto III took the reins of the empire in 996, at the age of 16, and was the last of the Saxon ("Sword-men") line of kings. Having inherited the throne in infancy, his mother, Theophano, initially served as co-regent (983–91) until she died when he was eleven; at which time his Italian grandmother, Adelaide, assumed the regency with the archbishop of Mainz, Germany (991–96). Otto III subdued the troublesome Roman nobles who tried to control the papacy and, in 996, installed his cousin BRUNO in the papal chair as Gregory V, the first German pope (reigned: 996–99). Another wise decision was Otto III's appointment of the honest and pious archbishop Gerbert of Aurillac, who became the first French pope: Sylvester II (reigned: 999–1003). Otto III exhibited so much missionary zeal, that ROMAULD of Ravenna wanted him to join his Camaldoli Monastic Order (observed two lents in the year, abstained from meat, lived on bread and water three days a week). In an attempt to make Rome the new capital of a revived Roman Empire, Otto III moved his seat of government there in 998. Otto III was successful in bringing Christianity to Hungary and Poland, and was crowned king of Hungary in 1001. Otto III's goal was to promote a Christian dominion in which the emperor and pope would jointly rule. Although he died from malaria at only 21 years of age, he had spent his brief life attempting to make the Holy Roman Empire truly holy. His intellectual endowment gave him his nickname.

Athanasius the Athonite

c 920
Athos, Greece

1003

Byzantine founder of Cerobite (communal) monasticism. Originally named Abraham, Athanasius left urban monastic life in Constantinople to establish a unique monastery in northeast Greece in 961. It was the first communal monastery on Mt. Athos, which was already populated with scattered hermits. He succeeded, despite fierce opposition. The writing of the rule for the monastery was supported by the emperors, Nicephorus Phocas and John Tzimisces. He died in a building accident.

Abbo(n)

c 945
near Orleans, France

Nov. 13, 1004
Fleury-sur-Loire, France

Chronicler, theologian, diplomat and Benedictine abbot of Fleury where he built a thriving school on his return to France in 988. During the decay of Anglo-Saxon culture, he kept intellectual pursuits alive. Abbo was a French theologian who made two trips to Rome, 986 and 996, for King Robert II (ruled: 996–1031) to ward off papal interdicts (forbidding to participate in sacred acts). Abbon, a reform-minded monk, directed theology toward scholasticism. In 986, he helped found the Ramsey Abbey in England, at the request of OSWALD OF YORK. He served as director of the newly founded Ramsey Monastery School in Huntingdon, England, 965–67. While visiting a monastery in Reole, Gascony while attempting to separate two local groups of quarreling monks. He died in the arms of his disciple, Almoin. His most important work was *Collectio Cannonum*. Abbo was known for learning and sanctity. He calmed those who foresaw the end of the world in 1000.

Aelfric of Canterbury

c 940
Canterbury, England (?)

Nov. 16, 1005

Archbishop of Canterbury, 995–1005. When Aelfric was a canon monk of Winchester, he undertook the translation of the Bible into English. Many of his works and homilies have been preserved along with the following sections of the Bible: the Pentateuch, Joshua, Judges, the four Gospels, Esther, Job, and a part of Kings. Originally a monk at Abingdon, he became abbot of St. Albans and bishop of Ramsbury and Wilton around 990. In 1067 his remains were transferred to St. Jolius, Canterbury. He removed diocesan clergy from Canterbury Cathedral in favor of monks.

Bernard of Menthon
Bernard of Montjoux —Bernard of Aosta

923
Menthon, France

May 28, 1008
Novara, Italy

Missionary to the mountaineers. Bernard was vicar general (assistant to bishop) of the Aosta Diocese in the Italian Alps. He was concerned for travelers going through two mountain passes and established hospices to care for them. The dogs used by the hospices and, in time, the passes themselves were named after him. Since the seventeenth century, the St. Bernard dog breed has been used to rescue travelers lost in the snow. The Augustinian (followers of AUGUSTINE OF HIPPO) monks rescued many distressed travelers.

Bruno (Boniface) of Querfurt
Apostle to the Prussians

c 970
Querfurt, Prussia (Germany)

Feb. 14, 1009
Braunsberg, East Prussia (Lithuania)

German monk and Saxon nobleman. Bruno was sent by Pope Sylvester II as a missionary to the Slavs. He served as an effective missionary to Poland, Hungary, and Russia, after serving at Magdeburg, Germany, as a Benedictine monk. Bruno was also a successful preacher. He was a cousin to Emperor OTTO III and went to Rome with him in 996, where OTTO received religious direction. Bruno became an archbishop to the Prussians in 1004, zealously evangelizing Hungary, Poland, and Russia. He died a martyr's death with 18 companions while trying to reach the pagan Prussians. Bruno's death was similar to that of ADALBERT OF PRAGUE, a friend and model.

Simeon Metaphrastes

1010
Constantinople (Istanbul), Asia Minor (Turkey)

Most illustrious of the Byzantine hagiographers. Metaphrastes compiled a famous collection of the *Lives of the Saints in the Eastern Church*, arranging them for the twelve months of the year. More than 700 of his original manuscripts have survived from antiquity. Much of our knowledge of the biographies of early Eastern churchmen is due to his careful research and records. Toward the end of his long life, he became a monk and was buried in the Church of Mother of God at Hodigi.

Alphege
Godwine Elphege

954

April 19, 1012
Greenwich, England

Archbishop of Canterbury, 1005–12. Alphege was a Benedictine monk and anchorite (one living in seclusion for religious reasons) who was chosen abbot of Bath, and then in 984, bishop of Winchester. He obtained a promise from OLAF I (king of Norway), in 994, not to invade England. When the Danes sacked Canterbury in 1011, they seized him for ransom. Alphege refused to appeal to his poor tenants, so he was pelted with ox bones and killed. His remains were brought to Canterbury for proper burial in 1023.

Vladimir I
Vladimir the Great

c 956

July 15, 1015
Berestovoe, Russia

Early Christian ruler and emperor of Russia, 980–1015. Vladimir is credited with popularizing the Christian faith in Russia. His grandmother, OLGA, was the first Christian ruler there, 945–62. He married Princess Anna Porphyrogenta (daughter of Byzantine Emperor Basil II of Constantinople; ruled: 976–1025) in 987, which led to his contact with Christian Byzantium. Vladimir's conversion (988) is said to have produced a complete change of heart in the ruler. Although his conversion was initially politically motivated to further his military conquests and ambitions, he rapidly became an ardent promoter of his new faith. He sought to make the Greek Orthodox Church the state religion. Vladimir forced mass conversion on his subjects. He erected churches and monasteries in the Byzantine style, promoted education, aided the poor, and treated criminals fairly. Through the help of Greek missionaries, Vladimir influenced the conversion of the majority of the nobility and well-to-do merchants of Kiev, his home city, where he became Grand Duke (sovereign of a small state or territory) in 978. He is highly revered by the Russian Orthodox Church. His sons, Boris and Gleb, became martyrs for the faith.

Aelfric the Grammarian
Grammaticus

c 940
England

1020

Anglo-Saxon monk, writer and priest at Cerne Abbas, 987–1005, and abbot of the Benedictine community in Eynsham, Oxfordshire, 1005. He was considered to be the greatest scholar of the English Benedictine revival. Aelfric created a new level of grammatical Anglo-Saxon prose. His *Catholic Homilies* (two books) (c. 991) were sermons based on the church fathers, and his prose is considered to be some of the best of his time. He wrote *Lives of the Saints*. He spent his life educating the clergy in church doctrine before 998. Aelfric denied the Immaculate Conception (Virgin Mary conceived without original sin). He translated parts of the Old Testament into English, and openly condemned the doctrine of transubstantiation. His writings included a Latin and English grammar and glossary.

Simeon the New Theologian

c 949
Galate, Paphlagonia, Asia Minor (Turkey)

March 12, 1022
Chrysopolis (near Chaledon), Asia Minor (Turkey)

Byzantine monk, mystic, and spiritual writer. Simeon served as a monk at Studios and priest/abbot of St. Manas monastery near Constantinople until 1009. He was the most outstanding mystic in the Greek Church of his century. He asserted that a vision of God is possible for a believer. Simeon's works were of devotional beauty. His *Hymns of the Divine Loves* describes his spiritual experiences. Some say he died between 1032 and 1041. He reports his most intimate spiritual experiences, including a "baptism in the Holy Spirit" distinct from those graces received in the sacraments.

Notker
Thicklipped—Labeo—Teutonicus—The German

c 950
Germany

June 29, 1022
St. Gall, Switzerland

Learned monk at St. Gall. Notker was one of the most important contributors to German literature, and headed an abbey school most of his life, teaching at the monastery at St. Gall, Switzerland. He translated many Latin and Greek classics into Old High German, enhancing the development of German literature and language. The biblical books of Psalms and Job were among his translations.

Wulfstan of London

May 28, 1023
York, England

Bishop of London, 996–1002; archbishop of York, 1003–16; and bishop of Worcester, 1003–16. Wulfstan was a monk and author of many sermons, treatises, and codes of law. His most famous work was his call to reform, *Sermo Lupi and Anglos*. Wulfstan was an advisor to Kings Aethelred II and CANUTE II, drafting their codes of law. Several homilies are attributed to him, one of which described the desperate conditions after the Danish raids. He is buried at Ely.

Olaf I of Sweden
Skottkonung

Sweden

c 1024

First Christian King of Sweden, 993–1024. Olaf was baptized in 1008 and established the church in his kingdom. He encouraged the spread of the faith without resorting to threats or cruelty to his subjects. Wary of the powerful Norwegian kingdom, he joined with the Danes to defeat Norway in 1000.

Romauld

c 950/952
Ravenna, Italy

June 19, 1027
Val di Castro, Italy

Italian monk. Romauld was a leading ascetic and reformer. He promoted reform by organizing groups of hermits into settlements known as "deserts." His best known "desert", was Camaldoli, located near Arezzo (in Tuscany Province south of Florence). Romauld demanded discipline and dedication from his monks, dispatching them as missionaries and preachers. He founded the Camaldolese Order in 1012. He was an abbot of several Benedictine monasteries, but was expelled by monks unable to meet his rigorous demands.

Fulbert

c 960
Reims, France

April 10, 1028
Chartres, France

French writer, priest and bishop of Chartres, 1006–28. Fulbert was the architect and laid the foundation for the Chartres Cathedral in 1020, which became a Gothic (style of architecture, pointed arch, ribbed vault) masterpiece after a fire destroyed the earlier structure. Fulbert originated new forms of education and opened the outstanding Cathedral School of Chartres in 990, which drew students from all over Europe. He raised funds to have it rebuilt in 1026 after it burned. He wrote extensively and practiced medicine. Many of his poems appear in hymnbooks. His *Lettres* are a valuable source of history. Fulbert advocated reform of the clergy and upheld the church against nobles.

Olaf II
Olav Haraldsson—Olaf the Fat

995

July 29, 1030
Stiklestad, Norway

King of Norway, 1016–28, a result of a decisive victory at Nesjar. As a youth, Olaf II lived a wild life, taking part in Viking expeditions. He fought the Danes for the English. He accepted baptism, however, in Roven, France, in 1015, and summoned missionaries from England to Christianize his country once he was king. In 1028, when CANUTE II of Denmark attacked, King Olaf was forced to flee to Russia. During an attempt to regain his throne, Olaf II was killed in battle against Danes and revolting Norwegians. After his death, Olaf II's fame grew to sainthood for his efforts in uniting Norway politically and for introducing Christianity there. He became a national hero. He punished his own hand by fire for desecrating the Sabbath. Absentmindedly whittling wood one Sunday, he was smitten with guilt, picked up a pile of chips, placed them in his palm, set fire to it until the chips were completely consumed.

Canute II
Canute the Great

c 994

Nov. 12, 1035
Shaftesbury, England

King of England, Denmark and Norway. Canute became one of the most popular and mighty rulers of his age. His rule included: England (1016–35); Denmark (inheriting the throne after his brother Harold's death); Baltic states and Poland (1018–35); and upon conquering it, Norway (1028–35). After the sudden death of his father, King Sweyn of Denmark in 1014, he had to reconquer England. Under him, the conversion of Denmark was practically completed, with bishops and monks coming from England to aid. He had a semi-cordial relationship with Pope John XIX (reigned: 1024–32), making a pilgrimage to Rome 1026–27. Although the early part of his career was marked by great barbarity (overthrowing King OLAF II and his Christian work in Norway), Canute's later reign was that of a statesman and patriot. In 1017, he married his wife, Emma, of Normandy, widow of English King Aethelred II. There was constant strife in ruling his expanding empire. On January 7, 1030, he demanded through law, that adulterous women lose not only all their possessions, but their nose and ears as well. Canute created the "Tinglid," a military brotherhood (royal bodyguard) of over 3,000 members from the richest, noble families and also was the first Danish king to coin money. He was buried at Winchester Cathedral in England. He was the grandson of HAROLD BLAATAND.

Stephen I of Hungary
Apostle of Hungary

975
Gran, Hungary

Aug. 15, 1038
Esztergom, Hungary

First king and founder of Hungary, 1001–38. Stephen was converted as a youth in 985, along with his father, Geza, and was baptized by ADALBERT OF PRAGUE. Stephen established Christianity in his kingdom after several previous unsuccessful attempts by others. He withstood the Pagan Party, and defeated them in battle. Gisela (sister of Holy Roman Emperor HENRY II (ruled: 1014–24) and daughter of Duke Henry II of Bavaria) became his wife in 997. After serving as duke in 997, Stephen received a crown in December, 1000 for his coronation from Pope Sylvester II, which remained the sacred symbol of Hungarian nationality for 900 years. He built schools and churches, and divided his territory into ten bishoprics. For the betterment of Hungary, Stephen called in foreign priests, endowed abbeys and formed a council of nobles and churchmen. Stephen also drew up the code of laws which form the present Hungarian Constitution. He liberated his slaves and asked for missionaries from other lands.

Aethelnoth

Oct. 29, 1038
Canterbury, England

Archbishop of Canterbury, 1020–38. Aethelnoth first served as a monk at Glastonbury and then dean at Canterbury College. He was chief advisor to CANUTE II who bestowed on Ethelnoth the earliest known writ of judicial and financial authority given to an English prelate. Ethelnoth was instrumental in recovering the remains of the martyred Alphege and bringing them to Canterbury.

Odilo

c 962
Auvergne, France

Dec. 31, 1048
Souvigny, France

Abbot of the great monastery at Cluny, France, 999–1048. Odilo was a master organizer/administrator. History extolls his great virtue and gentle manner. He advanced the centralized control of other monasteries founded or reformed by Cluny leadership, bringing them under the complete supervision of the abbot of Cluny. Odilo served there for 50 years, increasing the Cluniac houses from 37 to 65. He made Cluny a separate order, rivaling other monastic groups. The observance of All Souls Day (a day of solemn prayer for all dead persons), November 2, was believed to have been started by Odilo.

Guido of Arezzo

c 992–995
Arezzo, Italy

1050
Avellino, Italy

French Benedictine monk and inventor of "The Great Musical Scale." Guido first reduced music to a system of symbols – "do, re, mi, fa, sol, la, ti, do," inventing the medieval "great scale" or gamut. He derived this somehow from a poem by Paul the Deacon. Guido has been called "the Father of Modern Music." He went to Rome in 1022 and later taught Pope John XIX his musical scales. Guido also wrote several books on musical theory in 1028 and originated the hexachord (diatonic series of six tones) and four-line staff. His musical structuring ideas spread throughout Italy and the Catholic Church. Although tradition lists his birthplace as Arezzo, Italy, he began his ascetic life as a monk near Paris, then lived near Ferrara (northern Italy). Finally he became an abbot of Santa Croce at Avellino near Arellano and a prior of Avellino in 1029.

Aelfric of York

1050

Archbishop of York, 1023 on. Aelfric assisted at the coronation of Canute II, Edward the Confessor, and other kings. He has sometimes received undue credit as the author of works that were written by Aelfric of Canterbury.

Wipo

c 1050

Priest and chaplain to Roman Emperor Conrad II (ruled: 1027–39) and his son Henry III of Germany and the Holy Roman Empire. Wipo wrote poetry but is best remembered for his Easter hymn, "Victimae Paschali Laudes."

Robert of Jumieges

Normandy, France

May 26, 1055
Jumieges, France

Archbishop of Canterbury, 1051–52. Robert was a French Norman prelate, 1037–41, who left Jumieges Abbey in France for England in 1041 when King Edward the Confessor seized the English throne. As Edward's most trusted and prominent foreign friend, Robert of Jumieges was rewarded with titles and honors, including bishop of London in 1044. He led the hostile party to Godwine (died: 1053), earl (governor) of the West Saxons, but fled to Normandy on Godwine's return from exile in 1052 and was stripped of his titles.

Henry III
Henry the Black

Oct. 28, 1017
Osterbeck, Netherlands

Oct. 5, 1056
Bodfeld, Germany

King of Germany, 1039–56, and Holy Roman Emperor, 1046–56. Henry was responsible for cleansing the papacy in his day. At age 22, he succeeded to the throne after his father's death. During his reign, he subdued the Bohemians in 1041 and the Hungarians, 1043–45. Henry III made an expedition to Rome and deposed three rival popes, appointing Clement II (reigned: 1046–47). Clement II then crowned him emperor Dec. 25, 1046. During his short lifetime, Henry appointed four German popes. He was a deeply religious person who was educated by bishops Bruno and Egilbert. Henry supported ecclesiastical reforms, such as the monastical reforms at Cluny. He was also a patron of learning, founding schools and completing a number of cathedrals (Worms, Mainz, and Speyer). He checked clerical abuses in the Church. His later years were plagued by revolts throughout Germany. Henry first married Gunhilda (Queen Kunigunde, daughter of CANUTE THE GREAT) in 1036 and then Agnes (daughter of William I, Duke of Guisse) in 1043.

Michael Cerularius

c 1005
Constantinople (Istanbul), Asia Minor (Turkey)

Jan. 21, 1059
Hellespont (Strait of Dardanelles)/Asia Minor

Patriarch of Constantinople, 1043–59. Cerularius was fiercely opposed to the Western church (Catholic Church at Rome). He was so energetic in defense of the Eastern (Greek) church that a major schism became a permanent separation in 1054, when he and Pope Leo IX (reigned: 1049–54) excommunicated each other. This conflict began when he closed Latin churches in Constantinople in 1052 for not using Greek languages and practices. Cerularius was powerful for several years, dethroning one emperor and crowning another, but he was banished by Byzantine Emperor Issac I Commenus (ruled: 1057–59) in 1059. Cerularius died in exile.

Ferdinand I
El Magno – The Great

c 1000–1018

Dec. 27, 1065
Leon, Spain

King of Castile, in 1028, and of Leon, 1038–65. This powerful Spanish ruler led his own troops to recover Spain from the Moslems, 1058–65, beginning a period of reconquest, as far as Portugal. In 1054, he fought against his brother, Garcias IV, King of Navarre (former kingdom in parts of France and Spain), and won. He assumed the title of emperor of Spain in 1056, which was considered a threat by some to the headship of Christendom, diverting prestige from the Holy Roman Empire. Ferdinand's success caused Pope Urban II (reigned: 1088–99) to call a crusade in 1096 to expel Moslems (Moors) from the Holy Land. Ferdinand's marriage to Sancha, sister of Bermudo III of Leon, secured succession to that area. His sons, Garcia, Sancho, and Alphonso, divided the kingdom between themselves.

Edward
The Confessor

1003
Islip, England

Jan. 5, 1066
Westminster, London, England

King of West Saxons, 1042–66. Edward was recalled from Normandy and placed on the throne after the death of CANUTE II's son. Edward was the last of the Anglo-Saxons, restoring the old Saxon line after a quarter century of Danish rule. He married Edith Godwine of Wessex in 1045. Edward was primarily occupied with building monasteries (which also served as inns and schools) and churches. He founded Westminster Abbey in 1065, where he was buried a year later. Edward is also noted for codifying and compiling Anglo/Saxon laws—*The Laws of Edward the Confessor* (1070). Throughout his reign, Edward put spiritual matters over kingly responsibilities, neglecting many of his duties and remaining dependent on others. He was a mild-mannered ascetic. His sanctity gave him his nickname. He was an albino (red eyes, white skin, hair, and beard).

William Stigand

1002
East Anglia, England

c Feb. 22, 1072
Winchester, England

Archbishop of Canterbury, 1052–70. Stigand served as bishop of Elmham in 1043 and as chaplain to CANUTE IV, supporting the platform of Godwine. He loyally backed English leaders when the Normans invaded.

He was dismissed by an ecclesiastical investigation committee from Rome at the behest of the Norman leader, WILLIAM I OF ENGLAND. Stigand submitted to WILLIAM I in 1066, after voting for a rival. Under charges of usurpation (illegal seizure) and plurality (excessive votes, holding more than one benefice), a commission of cardinals sentenced him to life in prison, where he died of starvation.

Adalbert of Hamburg/Bremen

c 1000

March 16, 1072
Goslar, Germany

Archbishop of Hamburg and Bremen, 1045–72 with jurisdiction over Scandinavian churches. Adalbert became a tyrannical and powerful prelate (high order church officials). He became papal cleric and legate of Nordic (north European) nations in 1053. Saxon dukes opposed his leadership, controlled King HENRY IV OF GERMANY, and after the death of righteous HENRY III, ruled much of northern Europe for a short time. He attempted to form a northern patriarchate (religious headquarters), which would have included Germany, England and Scandinavia, seeking independence for the Church in Denmark from Hamburg . The papacy frustrated this plan and the Saxon leaders banished him from court 1066–69. He regained his former power, 1069–72. His injustice and tyranny caused confusion and calamity. Adalbert spread Christianity among the Wends (Slavic people of eastern Germany). He died of dysentery.

Anthony of Kiev

July 10, 1073

Founder of monasticism in Russia. Anthony introduced the solitary life at a Greek Orthodox monastery on Mt. Athos. He returned to Kiev and settled in a cave on Mt. Berestov. This became a center which grew into a community. By 1250, 50 of its monks had become bishops in the Russian Orthodox Church.

Stanislaus
Stanislav

July 26, 1030
Szczepanow, Poland

May 8, 1079
Cracow, Poland

Bishop of Cracow, 1071–79. Stanislaus came from a noble family and was a just Polish prelate. He excommunicated Boleslav II, King of Poland for his outrageous conduct. As a result, Stanislaus was brutally murdered on the trumped-up charges of treason by the vengeful monarch's orders during Mass (celebration of the Eucharist) at the Church of St. Michael. He was the first Pole to be canonized (1253).

Lady Godiva

c 1085

Honorable and compassionate member of the English nobility, wife of Leofric (earl of Mercia). She generously aided many English monasteries. In 1040, Lady Godiva built a monastery in Stow and in 1043 a Benedictine monastery in Coventry. There is a legend of her riding naked through the streets of Coventry, covered only by her flowing hair. It is alleged that this happened on January 6th. The term "peeping Tom" was to have originated for a townsperson who was miraculously blinded for looking upon her during this ride. However, this story is presumed to be false. Supposedly she was carrying out an ill-advised agreement with her husband to lower burdensome taxes.

Canute IV
The Saicret

c 1040

July 10, 1086
Odense, Denmark

King of Denmark, 1080–86, who was murdered by rebels among his own troops during a campaign against England's WILLIAM I OF ENGLAND, which started in 1085. He died while kneeling at an altar and was made the patron saint of Denmark. Although an unpopular king, he built and supported many churches.

William I of England
William the Conqueror

c 1027/1028
Falaise, France

Sept. 9, 1087
Rouen, France

Duke of Normandy, 1035–87, and King of England, 1066–87. William invaded England upon the death of Edward (the Confessor), and the installation of King Harold II of England (ruled: 1066). He defeated Harold II at the Battle of Hastings in 1066 and was crowned in Westminster Abbey on Christmas Day. He regarded himself not as a conqueror but a legitimate heir. He was ruthless, unscrupulous, masterful, and indomitable. He spent one-third of his reign outside of England as the country was not directly involved in the politics of Europe. He refused to pay homage to Pope Alexander II (reigned 1061–73) and organized the church as a dependency of the English crown. He married Matilda of Flanders in 1053 and had nine children. He was the father of HENRY I of England. He died from a fatal injury when his horse stumbled during fighting in France.

Berengar

c 1000
Tours, France

Jan. 6, 1088
Saint-Cosmas/Come Island (near Tours), France

Theologian. Berengar was archdeacon (ranked below a bishop, with administrative responsibilities for a diocese) of Angers in 1040. He headed a school and was canon of the cathedral at Tours 1031–40. His fame rests upon his independent challenge in 1045, attacking the popular view of transubstantiation. Popes and contemporary theologians condemned and argued with him. Berengar was condemned at several synods: Vercelli (1050), and Rome (1059 and 1079). After being condemned for heresy, he ended his days in solitude as an ascetic on an island. He eventually recanted and died reconciled with the Church. His teaching as expressed in his work, *De Sacra Coena*, was known as consubstantiation, which LUTHER believed.

Lanfranc

c 1005
Pavia, Italy

May 24, 1089
Canterbury, England

Archbishop of Canterbury, 1070–89. Lanfranc was a Benedictine theologian from northern Italy and a trusted counselor of WILLIAM I OF ENGLAND. He became a Benedictine in Bec, France, in 1042, where he established the illustrious school (c 1040) and served as a prior (ranked below an abbot in monastic order), teacher, and administrator, 1042–45. At the Council of Tours, in 1055, he opposed BERENGAR's views on transubstantiation. Lanfranc became abbot of St. STEPHEN's at Caen, France, 1066–70. After serving in France, 1039–70, he went to England after the Norman invasion and soon dominated church affairs. He reformed ecclesiastical courts, strengthened monasteries, rebuilt cathedrals (Canterbury included, destroyed in the fire of 1067), and shifted bishoprics from small towns to important cities. An associate of WILLIAM I, he reluctantly became archbishop of Canterbury. In 1087, he crowned King William II of England (ruled: 1087–1100). His *Concerning the Body and Blood of the Lord* became a medieval classic, providing valuable information on English monasticism.

Margaret of Scotland

c 1045
Hungary

Nov. 16, 1093
Edinburgh, Scotland

Queen of Scotland. In 1070, Margaret became the second wife of King Malcolm III MacDuncan (Canmore) of Scotland (ruled: 1059–93). Margaret brought the Church in Scotland into conformity with the Roman Church of Europe. She instigated church reform and inspired many with her own personal devotion and benefactions, such as cleansing lepers' sores and washing beggars' feet. This pious and pure queen's (Saxon birth's) marriage provoked retaliation by WILLIAM I OF ENGLAND in 1072.

Wulfstan of Worcester

c 1012
Litle/Long Itchton, England

Jan. 18, 1095
Worcester, England

Bishop of Worcester, London, 1062–95. Wulfstan was the last English bishop to be selected by a Saxon king. He was a Benedictine monk who helped to suppress the slave trade practiced at Bristol upon English subjects by Ireland. Wulfstan also assisted in compiling the *Domesday (Doomsday) Book* which was ordered by WILLIAM I OF ENGLAND, and completed in 1086. It is a valuable record of the ownership, tenants, livestock and value of the lands of England and is still considered a worthy ancestral reference. Wulfstan oversaw the rebuilding of Worcester Cathedral, 1084–89. He supported his son, King William II, against the Welsh. It is said that he was the only bishop who obtained his position because he was spiritual.

William of St. Carilef

St. Carilef, England

Jan. 2, 1096
Windsor, England

Norman-French bishop of Durham, England, 1081 on. William won this position by appointment from WILLIAM I of England after the Norman invasion. He then assisted in Bishop Odo's (Norman prelate of Bayeux, died in 1097) rebellion against William II in 1088. He took refuge in Normandy and finally returned to England after a pardon was given in 1091. William of St. Carilef escaped charges and prudently thereafter took the king's side against all troublesome churchmen, including Archbishop ANSELM. William began the rebuilding of the Durham Cathedral in 1093.

Walter the Penniless

1097
Nicea, Asia Minor (Turkey)

French knight who led the Peasants' Crusade, a forerunner of the First Crusade in 1096. Masses of disorderly French peasants clamored for someone to lead them against the Turks. Walter started out with about 20,000 on their crusade to liberate the Holy Land from the Mohammedans. Many of these Christian crusaders were destroyed at the storming of Belgrade, Serbia (Yugoslavia), and many more were lost in Bulgarian forests. He united with PETER THE HERMIT's, beleaguered survivors in Constantinople. They crossed the Bosphorous, and were utterly defeated by the Turks at Nicea. Walter was slain in battle.

Ademar
Adehemar

988

Aug. 1, 1098

Bishop of Puy, France, 1080 on. Ademar made a pilgrimage to the Holy Land (c 1086–87). In 1095 he was appointed legate and deputy to two of his armies by Pope Urban II, who proclaimed the First Crusade at Clermont. Ademar designated Constantinople as the gathering place for the Crusaders' three great armies and mediated between rival Christian princes and Eastern and Western churchmen.

Osmund

c 1006
Normandy, France

Dec. 3, 1099

Norman prelate and bishop of Salisbury, England, 1078–99. Osmund became chancellor {chief administrator of state} of England after following his uncle, WILLIAM I OF ENGLAND, from Normandy to England. He helped compile the *Domesday Book* and is credited with the introduction of the Sarum (Salisbury) Rite (liturgy used before the Reformation of the Church of England; adapted in 1085, it became very popular in England).

Wilbert

1100

Archbishop of Ravenna, Italy. Wilbert allowed himself to be duped by Emperor HENRY IV OF GERMANY into being elevated as a counter-pope to oppose Pope Gregory VII (Hildebrand; reigned: 1073–85). Wilbert actually resided in Rome from 1084 to 1093, until he was driven out by the legitmate Pope Urban II. When the emperor was overthrown, Wilbert too, lost his position.

Godfrey
Protector of the Holy Sepulcher

1060/ 1061
Baisi-Thy, Lorraine (Belgium)

July 18, 1100
Jerusalem, Palestine (Israel)

One of the leaders of the First Crusade, 1096–99. Godfrey was made duke of the Lower Lorraine (French duchy {territory ruled by a duke}) by HENRY IV in 1088. He was a French nobleman who marched in 1095 at the head of 25,000 infantrymen and 5,000 horsemen. The logistics such as eating, sleeping, etc. must have been staggering. In the wake of many adventures, The Crusaders with an army of 15,000, arrived at Jerusalem and took the city on July 15, 1099, after a five-week siege. Godfrey completed the conquest of the Holy Land by defeating the Sultan of Egypt on Aug. 12, 1099 at Ascalon. Godfrey has been idealized in legends and literature as the perfect Christian knight. However, he was responsible for many innocent deaths, which Moslems resent until this day. He died of the plague a year later, before he was able to carry out his plans for reconstruction. Godfrey was buried in the Church of the Holy Sepulcher in Jerusalem.

Bruno of Cologne

1030
Cologne, Germany

Oct. 6, 1101
La Torre, Italy

Founder of the Carthusian (austere monastic) **order of monks, 1084**, a very strict order of monks. Bruno was director of the schools in the diocese of Rheims, France in 1057. A canon of Rheims, he taught arts and theology. He then became chancellor of the archdiocese (c. 1075). In 1084, Bruno withdrew to seclusion in the wild mountains of the Chartreuse Valley, near Grenoble, to start a monastery with the help of Hugh, a local bishop. His monks were distinguished for their solitude and silence. In 1090, Bruno became advisor to Pope Urban II, but he soon retired to the desert area in Calabria, where he established a second monastery at Della Torre called Santa Maria (c. 1094).

Benno
Apostle of the Wends

1010
Hildesheim, Germany

June 16, 1106
Meissen, Germany

Bishop of Meissen, Saxony, 1066–1106. Benno was a canon in the imperial church at Goelar before 1066. Benno was twice imprisoned by HRE HENRY IV on suspicion of disloyalty in 1075–76 and 1085–88 for non-support during the Saxon noble's revolt and his support of Pope Gregory VII against the Holy Roman Emperor. Benno also did missionary labors among the Wends. He authored *Teaching and the Sunday Gospels*. MARTIN LUTHER violently criticized Pope Adrian VI (reigned: 1522–23) for canonizing Benno in 1523.

Henry IV of Germany

Nov. 11, 1050
Goslar, Germany

Aug. 7, 1106
Liege, Belgium

Holy Roman Emperor and German King, 1056–06. Henry IV defeated the Saxons in 1075 and imprisoned their rebellious bishops. He was engaged in a lifelong feud with Pope Gregory VII over the question of lay investiture (political/secular power making ecclesiastical appointments), as demonstrated by Henry IV's appointment and control over Saxon bishops. On July 22, 1076, Pope Gregory VII (Hildebrand) excommunicated him. Henry IV will always be remembered as the ruler who, in Canossa, Italy, was forced to wait barefoot in the snow to beg Gregory VII for restoration from excommunication, eventually granted on January 28, 1077. Henry IV later besieged Rome and deposed Gregory VII in 1084, setting up antipope Clement III. Henry IV's last years were marked by conflict from his rebellious sons, Conrad and Henry V, who were papal loyalists. He defeated his sons while on a second expedition to Italy, 1090–97. After fresh revolts broke out in Germany, he deposed son Conrad (1098). Son, HENRY V, dethroned and imprisoned him in 1105, although he escaped in 1106. Henry IV's rule is important for the power lines it ignited between church and state.

Theophylactus

c 1050
Achrida (Ochrida), Albania

c 1107/1109

Greek prelate and scholar. Theophylactus was archbishop of Achrida and the area of Bulgaria, 1078–1107. Theophylactus led his flock of rough Bulgars in a manner independent of high church control from Constantinople. He was instrumental in developing the native Bulgarian Orthodox Church and Balkan Slavic literature. Theophylactus was a learned Greek exegete who wrote commentaries on the Minor Prophets and much of the NT. His works were the best produced at this period in the Latin Church. As an exegete, Theophylactus was credited as being skillful and sensible.

Anselm of Canterbury
Father of Schoolmen/Scholasticism

c 1033
Aosta, Italy

April 21, 1109
Canterbury, England

Philosopher ("Faith before Reason"), **theologian, and Archbishop of Canterbury, 1093–1109.** Anselm was the most original thinker since AUGUSTINE. He opposed lay investiture and was trained in the Benedictine order of the abbey at Bec, France (1060–63), where he became a prior (1063–78), and an abbot, (1078–92). In 1092, he began to help St. Werburg's monastery in Chester, England. Loyal to Pope Gregory VII's policies, Anselm was embroiled with William II (Rufus) over Anselm's refusal to accept lay investiture from the king and with HENRY I OF ENGLAND over Anselm's refusal to consecrate prelates invested by the king. He favored dominance of the popes of Rome. He was exiled in 1103 after these refusals but was reconciled to HENRY I OF ENGLAND by the Compromise of 1107. His greatest theological work was *Why Did God Become Man?* His writings consisted of systematic works, prayers, meditations, and letters. He argued, "I believe in order to understand." He said as he died, "I shall gladly obey His call..."

Hugh of Cluny

1024
Burgundy, France

April 29, 1109
Cluny, France

Abbot of the Benedictine Monastery of Cluny, 1049 on. Under him, Cluny Abbey reached the highest point of its power and influence. He attended many councils and synods. Hugh supported the Gregorian reforms within the church, and nine successive popes turned to him for advice. A Benedictine church was erected and the altar dedicated by Pope Urban II in 1095. He supported Latin liturgy development and championed orthodox doctrine at church councils.

Marc Bohemund I

c 1056

March 1111
Canossa, Italy

Norman prince of Antioch (Antakya), Syria (Turkey). Commander of the Normans from Italy, which was the finest fighting outfit to set out on the First Crusade in 1096. He was prince of Tarentum (Taranto), Italy, 1085–89 and participated in the recapture of Antioch (1098) and of Jerusalem (1099) from the Moslems. Bohemund was captured and imprisoned by Moslems, 1100–3, and defeated at Haran in 1104 before being returned to Europe. Bohemund married Constance, daughter of King Philip I of France (ruled: 1060–1108), and was the prince of Antioch, 1108–11.

Robert of Molesme

c 1027–1029
Troyes, France

April 17, 1111
Molesme, France

Cofounder of the Cistercian order of monks. This order became a monastic community in the forest of Molesme in southern France. Robert advocated six hours each for sleep, singing, manual labor, and study. He moved to the monastery at Citeaux near Chalons (south of Dijon) in 1098, where the first abbey of the Cistercian order (order of monks and nuns founded in 1098 under Benedictine rule) was established by him and STEPHEN HARDING. BERNARD OF CLAIRVAUX made the Cistercian Order famous.

Sigebert

c 1030
Gembloux, Belgium

Oct. 5, 1112
Gembloux, Belgium

Historian and biographer. Sigebert was a Benedictine monk who wrote *Chronographia*, a carefully documented history of world events from 381 until 1111. He chose to stand by his Emperor, HENRY IV OF GERMANY, rather than Pope Gregory VII during the monumental struggles between the papacy and the crown. Sigebert also wrote biographies of illustrious men. He taught for some years at St. Vincent Abbey in Metz, then returned about 1070 to Gembloux to devote the rest of his life to teaching and writing.

Tancred

c 1075
Sicily

Dec. 5, 1112
Antioch, Turkey

Norman hero in the bloody First Crusade, 1096–99. Tancred's courage was revealed as he led the advance wave of troops and was the first to storm the walls of Jerusalem. He also assisted in the capture of Nicaea (Isnik) and Tarsus in the seven-month siege of Antioch in 1097. The Battle of Ascalon also saw his skilled leadership. Tancred showed restraint and refused to revel in the orgy of bloodletting that followed the Christian victory over the Moslems in 1099. He became prince of Galilee and in later years of Edessa (Urfa), Asia Minor (Turkey). He obtained the principality of Antioch (Antakya), Syria (Turkey), in 1111, following BOHEMUND I's death.

Peter the Hermit

c 1050
Amiens, France

July 8, 1115
near Neufmoutier, Belgium

Influential preacher and monastic founder. Peter was the person who first suggested, to Pope Urban II, the idea of a Crusade to recapture the Holy Land from the Moslems. He became a wandering preacher promoting this concept in 1095 with WALTER THE PENNILESS. Peter led a people's division (40,000) of the crusades, months ahead of the military insertion, with disastrous results, from Amiens, France, to Asia Minor in 1096. Only 7,000 reached Constantinople. He met up with WALTER's section in Constantinople, where they joined forces. Peter's followers were destroyed by the Turks. He returned to Constantinople, joined the army of princes in 1097, helped in the Jerusalem conquest under GODFREY of Bouillon and preached on the Mount of Olives, July 8, 1099. He returned to Europe after Jerusalem was taken. He founded the abbey of Neufmoustier (near Huy), where he died.

Ivo/Ives of Chartres
Yves of Chartres

c 1040
Beauvais, France

Dec. 23, 1116
Chartres, France

Bishop of Chartres, 1090–1116. Yves studied theology at Bec under LANFRANC. He was prominent in several controversies, the most important of which regarded the right of investiture. He especially attacked the faults and failings of Roman church leaders, and stressed the importance of maintaining standards of conduct among the clergy. Yves' important works are two collections of canon law.

Anselm of Laon
Doctor Scholasticus

c 1040
Laon, France

July 15, 1117
Laon, France

Frankish theologian. Anselm studied at Bec under ANSELM OF CANTERBURY. PETER ABELARD was one of his students when he taught in Paris beginning in 1076. Anselm made the first interlinear gloss (margin explanations) of the Latin Vulgate Bible, a widely used aid to Bible study for many centuries, which enjoyed frequent reprintings. He also headed a school of theology at Laon, which became very famous.

Baldwin I

1058
Boulogne, France

April 2, 1118
El Avish, Egypt

First king of the Latin Kingdom of Jerusalem, 1100–18. Baldwin I was an impetuous adventurer and warrior in the First Crusade. Baldwin took up the leadership void after the death of GODFREY of Bouillon, his brother. Baldwin increased the Latin Kingdom by taking Acre (1104), Beirut, Lebanon (1109), and Sidon (1110).

Euthymius Zigabenus

c 1119

Byzantine theologian, exegete, and monk. Zigabenus lived in a cloister near Constantinople. He wrote against all heresies in his *Panoplia Dogmatics*. Zigabenus attacked the Catholic doctrines of the procession of the Holy Spirit and the use of unleavened bread. He also wrote extensive commentaries.

Tenque Gerard
The Blessed

c 1040
Amalfi, Italy

1120

Italian monk who joined the Crusades. He founded the famous order of the Knights Hospitallers of St. John of Jerusalem to provide safety and shelter for pilgrims to the Holy Land (c. 1100). This movement achieved fame and power during the Middle Ages and was recognized by Pope Paschal II (reigned: 1099–1118) in 1113.

William of Champeaux
Guillaume de Champeaux

c 1070
Champeaux, France

1121/1122
Chalons-sur-Marne. France

Scholastic philosopher, theologian, and reforming bishop of Chalons, 1113 on. William was a great advocate of realism (an abstract term meaning an independent reality, realities come from the specifics of life, not the generals). William was an eminent medieval schoolman and educator. He headed the noted Cathedral (Notre Dame) school of St. Victor near Paris, making it a mecca for Europe's brightest students, 1110–13. He taught dialectics (logical discussions). ABELARD was educated there by William, but later became his rival.

Roscellinus
Rucelinus

c 1050
Compiegne, France

1122

Scholastic philosopher, theologian and founder of nominalism (no single concept corresponding to any universal or general term) **opposing realism.** Roscellinus was a canon at Compiegne, after being educated at Rheims. While a canon at Loches, he had a famous pupil, PETER ABELARD. He held some heretical views on the doctrine of the Trinity, insisting they were three individual Gods. Roscellinus was condemned at a Council of Soissons in 1092, where he recanted. He fled to England and attacked ANSELM OF CANTERBURY. Roscellinus then returned to France and was involved in a controversy with his former student, ABELARD.

Henry V

Jan. 8, 1081

May 23, 1125
Utrecht, Netherlands

King of Germany, in 1106, and Holy Roman Emperor, 1111–25. Henry V was another German monarch who tried to control the papacy over lay investiture. He restored peace at home, was successful in wars against Flanders, Bohemia, Hungary and Poland. Henry V invaded Italy in 1110 and 1116, seizing Pope Paschal II for two months. On September 23, 1122, at the Concordat (official agreement) of Worms, he agreed to permit his German churchmen to elect their own bishops. Bishops and abbots, henceforth, had to be acceptable to both the emperor and the church. He was the son of HENRY IV OF GERMANY (whom he imprisoned), and married Matilda (daughter of HENRY I OF ENGLAND) in 1114.

Peter of Bruys
Pierre de Bruis

Bruys, (Bruis) France

c 1126
St. Gilles, France

Martyr, French reformer and founder of Petrobrusians (followers of Peter of Bruys.) His stern, simplistic, and radical preaching in southern France aroused immense controversy. He was one of the first to preach a return to Biblical truths. Peter was a student of ABELARD. He sought to abolish transubstantiation, the use of images in churches, the mass and infant baptism. Unfortunately, he was seized, arrested, and burned alive.

Baldwin II

Aug. 21, 1131
Jerusalem, Palestine

King of Jerusalem, 1118–31. Baldwin first served as Count of Edessa and was a nephew of BALDWIN I. He stretched the kingdom of Jerusalem to its largest size. Baldwin II used the military orders of the Knights Templars (military religious order formed in 1119 to protect pilgrims, especially the sickly, en route to holy shrines in Jerusalem) for the defense of the Holy Land. He was captured by the Arabs on his way to Edessa (1124) and released (1125). He left his greatly enlarged kingdom to his son-in-law, Fulk V, of Anjou, France.

Hugh of Grenoble

1052
Chateauneuf d'Isere, France

April 1, 1132
Grenoble, France

Bishop of Grenoble, c. 1080 on. Hugh was elected to the bishopric at the age of 27, before he was formally ordained. He served there for 52 years and brought much needed reform to the episcopate (office of bishop). Hugh believed he was inefficient and retired to an austere abbey for discipline. Pope Innocent II (reigned: 1130–43), however, impressed by Hugh's holy life, recalled him to his former bishopric where he served till death.

Stephen Harding

c 1048/1050
Sherborne, England

March 28, 1134
Citeaux/Ghent, France

Cofounder of the Cistercian order of monks. Harding was an austere English monk who served as the third abbot of the great monastery at Citeaux, 1110–33. This was the first abbey of the Cistercian order. He cofounded the order with ROBERT DE MOLESME in 1098, and founded at least 13 various branches of it in the ensuing years. The community was faced with extinction (for lack of novices) when BERNARD OF CLAIRVAUX arrived with 30 companions in 1113. Harding was a superb organizer and administrator. He wrote *Rule of Love* and the *Rule of the Cistercian Order*.

Norbert

c 1082/85
Cleves, Germany

June 26, 1134
Magdeburg, Prussia (Germany)

Archbishop of Magdeburg, 1126–34. Norbert, a French churchman, also founded the Premonstratensian Order (dedicated to penitence and preaching) at Premontre (near Laon, France). Norbert was known for his eloquence and traveled throughout Europe (Germany, France, Belgium) spreading his message. He exerted great influence in church affairs.

Henry I
Henry Beauclerc – The Scholar

1068
Selby, England

December 1, 1135
near Gisors, France

King of England, 1100–35. Henry I usurped the monarchy in the absence of his elder brother, Robert II, duke of Normandy (ruled: 1087–1134), who was on his way home from the First Crusade. The resultant war between the two brothers was won by Henry I, 1105–6. He contested with the Church leaders for power and grew irritated when the famous ANSELM refused to be installed as Archbishop of Canterbury until Henry I relinquished his claim to invest that position with spiritual authority. Henry I, infuriated, was forced to back down. Wars with France occurred, 1109–13 and 1116–20. He was the fourth son of WILLIAM I OF ENGLAND and Matilda of Flanders. His two marriages were to Matilda (daughter of King Malcolm III of Scotland) and Adela. His daughter, Matilda, married KING HENRY V.

William of Corbeil
William of Corbail/Corbeuil/Curbuil

c 1070
Corbeil, France

Nov. 21, 1136
Canterbury, England

Archbishop of Canterbury, 1123–36. William was the first archbishop after the Norman conquest who was not a monk. He studied under theologian, ANSELM OF LAON. He became an Augustinian canon and then a prior in Essex. As archbishop during three important councils at Westminster, William pressed for reforms prohibiting clerical marriage, fornication, and inheritance of clerical benefits. His support for crowning King Stephen I of England (ruled: 1135–54) over Matilda, thus countermanding a sworn oath, earned him criticism from church historian, Henry of Huntingdon, among others. In his defense, he thought he was making the best decision for the future of the country. William dedicated the cathedral in Canterbury in 1130.

Otto of Bamberg

1060
Suabia (Swabia), Bavaria (Germany)

June 30, 1139
Bamberg, Germany

Apostle of Pomerania (northwest Poland) and bishop of Bamberg, 1102 on. He was a teacher in Poland before entering the service of HENRY IV OF GERMANY. It was Duke Boleslaus who requested he go to Pomerania in 1124 to preach Christianity to the Slavs. He baptized 22,165 converts and established 11 churches in 9 cities. Even after his return to Bamberg, he continued to supervise the newly established Pomeranian Church.

Thurstan
Turstin

Bayeux, France

Feb. 6, 1140
Pontefract, England

Bishop of York, 1114–21, who determined to keep his see independent, refusing to give submission to Ralph d'Escures, Archbishop of Canterbury (reigned: 1114–22) and was therefore denied consecration for a long time. He is best remembered as the north country patriot who raised an army which staved off the attacking Scots in 1138 at the Battle of the Standard. He died as a Cluniac (Benedictine) monk.

Hugh of St. Victor

c 1096
Ypres, Flanders (Belgium) or Saxony, Germany

Feb. 11, 1141
Paris, France

French mystic, schoolman, and theologian who headed the abbey school of St. Victor's at Paris, 1133 on. Hugh had roots in Blantonburg. His works covered a wide field of exposure from geometry to Scripture commentaries. To Hugh, everything was subordinate to the life of contemplation, and his success was gained through personal mysticism. His theology clashed with ABELARD's. He said, "Faith is a certainty above opinion and below science." He suffered from continual ill health.

Peter Abelard
Pierre du Pallet

1070
Le Pallet (near Nantes), France

April 21, 1142
Chalon-sur-Saone, France

Scholastic philosopher ("Nothing is to be believed until it is understood."), **monk and theologian**. Abelard was a student of ANSELM OF LAON. He taught rhetoric and dialect at Notre Dame School of Paris, 1115–18. While in college, he adopted the surname, Abelard, replacing his birth name of Pierre du Pallet. He wrote several hymns and chants, including "O What Their Joy and Their Glory Must Be." In 1118, he secretly married a young lady named HELOISE (a beautiful love affair), whom he tutored. They had a son. Her enraged uncle, whom he met in Paris in 1115, had him castrated and disgraced. Their letters of adoring love are legendary. Abelard retired to a monastery in St. Denis in 1119. In 1121, he was condemned by the Council of Soissons. Abelard served briefly as an abbot of St. Gildas in Britany (1125), but his zeal offended many monks, who turned against him, so he fled (1132). He publicly disputed with BERNARD OF CLAIRVAUX (1129), who later denounced some of Abelard's teachings on the Trinity at the Council of Sens (1141). Condemned by French bishops then by the Pope, he was defended by Peter of Cluny and allowed his freedom. He returned to Paris in 1136 to lecture and became very popular. Abelard wrote *Christian Theology* (1123–24). He died in the Cluniac priory (religious house) of St. Marcel, saying, "I do not know." He used logical analysis to arrive at religious realities claiming "Faith" and "Reason."

Henry of Lausanne
Henry of Cluny/Henry the Deacon/Henry the Hermit

Italy

c 1145–1146
Toulouse, France

Monk, theologian, reformer, and evangelist who was the originator of the Henricians, reformers in Switzerland and southern France. His followers were largely absorbed by the Waldensians. Henry, a medieval dissenter, was the second (see PETER OF BRUYS) to push reformation preaching. He called for a return to apostolic poverty and simplicity. Although his message attracted large throngs, it enraged the Church hierarchy. In 1101, he left Lausanne and went to Le Mans to preach. Henry was arrested by the bishop of Arles in 1135 and given lifelong imprisonment for his Biblical stand and banished to southern France.

William of St. Thierry

c 1085
Liege, Belgium

Sept. 8, 1148
Signy, France

Monk, theologian and mystical writer. After entering the Benedictine monastery at Rheims in 1113, William became a specialist in Scripture and patristic (church fathers) writings. William was elected abbot of St. Thierry, near Rheims, 1119–35, after which he joined the Cistercians in 1135. His written works included *On the Nature and Dignity of Love* and *On the Contemplation* plus several doctrinal, exegetical, practical, and historical works. He wrote against ABELARD. William was encouraged by BERNARD OF CLAIRVAUX.

O'Morgair Malachy

1094
Armagh, Ireland

Nov. 2, 1148
Clairvaux, France

Archbishop of Armagh, Ireland, 1132–36, and bishop of Down, 1136–48. Malachy promoted reform in the Irish Church. He brought the Celtic Church into conformity with Roman Catholic practices and increased discipline among the monks. He was the abbot of Bangor (1123–24), and bishop of Connor (1124–32). On a pilgrimage to Rome in 1140, he met BERNARD OF CLAIRVAUX who influenced Malachy to introduce the Cistercian order into Ireland. Malachy also served as the papal legate in Ireland. He died in the arms of BERNARD on his journey to Rome.

Thierry
Thierry the Breton

c 1100
France

c 1151/1156
Chartres, France

Theologian, medieval philosopher, and eminent teacher who taught at Chartres (1121) and then at Paris (1124). He was one of the first to introduce Arabian knowledge of science into the West. In 1141, Thierry became chancellor of Chartres. His unpublished *Heptateuchon* and *Genesis Commentary* reveal him as an exponent of the application of Platonist philosophy to Christianity.

Bernard of Clairvaux

c 1090
Les Fontaines, France

Aug. 20, 1153
Clairvaux, France

Monastic reformer, mystic, and theologian. Bernard was the founder (1112) and abbot (1115) at a now-famous Cistercian monastery at Clairvaux. He subsequently founded 68 other monasteries and 72 branches of his order. His pupils included one pope, six cardinals, and 30 bishops. MARTIN LUTHER said Bernard was the greatest monk that ever lived. Bernard settled church quarrels, advised popes, prosecuted heretics, and wrote extensively, including *Praise to the New Chivalry* (1128). He was the principal opponent in public disputes with scholastic philosopher Peter ABELARD's rationalistic theology, 1139–40. Bernard preached the Second Crusade, 1146–47. His hymn creations include, "Jesus, the Very Thought of Thee" (1150) (music by JOHN DYKES), "O Sacred Head Now Wounded" (music by HANS HASSLER), and "Jesus, Thou Joy of Loving Hearts" (music by Henry Baker). He said as he died, "May God's will be done."
"God is known so far as He is loved."

Geoffrey

1100
Monmouth, Wales

1154
Llandaff, Wales

Bishop of St. Asaph, Wales, 1152 on. He was a noted English chronicler and, earlier in his career, archdeacon of Monmouth. Geoffrey was the creator of the Arthurian legend so prominent in English literature. He also wrote *Historia Britanniae* (1147), a skillful mixture of history, legend, and imagination. It traced the history of early British kings and included a collection of Arthurian legends. He was archdeacon of Llandaff, 1140–52.

Arnold of Brescia

1100
Brescia, Italy

June 1155
Rome, Italy

Monk and church reformer who was the originator of the Arnoldists; the third voice to push pre-Reformation Biblical teaching. Arnold studied under Peter ABELARD. He was in Sens, Paris, Zurich, and Bohemia. He denounced the corruption of the clergy, stating that they should renounce all property and power. This won him a large following among the poor in Brescia. Arnold was excommunicated in 1139 and banished 1141–45, although later allowed to return. He preached in Switzerland during his banishment. He led a six-year rebellion 1146–52. Arnold was idolized by the people, condemned by BERNARD OF CLAIRVAUX, forced into exile by Popes Eugene III (reigned: 1145–53) and Adrian IV (reigned: 1154–59), then arrested by order of FREDERICK I (BARBAROSSA). He returned to Rome and was later hung and his body burned.

Bernard of Cluny
Bernard of Morlaix

c 1100
Morlaix, France

c 1156
Cluny, France

Benedictine monk and poet at the famed monastery of Cluny, 1122–56. Bernard was famous as a preacher and writer. To fully appreciate his work, it is valuable to glimpse the splendor of his environment at the abbey of Cluny, the largest and most opulent of all similar institutions of this era. The abbey was elaborate, the services were steeped in decorum, and the accommodations were luxurious. Here Bernard was moved to create his venerable satirical 3,000-line poem, "Condemning the World." This work attacks the monastic vices and follies, stressing the transitory nature of life. This poem is the source of famous hymns such as "Jerusalem the Golden," "For Thee, O Dear, Dear Country," and "The World Is Very Evil." Hymnodist JOHN MASON NEALE, who translated the hymns (1851–58), writes of Bernard's great poem, "As a contrast to the misery and pollution of earth, this poem opens with a description of the peace

Peter the Venerable

c 1092
Montboissier, Auvergne, France

Dec. 25, 1156
Cluny, France

Abbot of the famed monastery at Cluny, 1122–56. From 1121 on, this Cistercian monk tightened the discipline in an order which had grown lax, bringing new luster and power to Cluny. In 1122, he was chief abbot over 2,000 dependent houses across Europe. Peter wrote against the Petrobrusians, the Jews, and the Mohammedans. He was present at the Council of Pisa in 1134, helped get Innocent II on the papal throne, and befriended ABELARD. He was a scholar of great ability. The glory of Cluny declined after his death. He was an advocate of a peaceful mission to Islam. He initiated the Latin Church's first missionary study programs, located in Toledo, Spain. He criticized the Crusades calling for conversion rather than extermination of Muslims. FREDERICK I (BARBAROSSA) and BERNARD OF CLUNY called him "The Venerable."

Gratian
Franciscus Gratianus

1090
Orvieto, Italy

c 1158/ 1160
Bologna, Italy

Lawyer and theologian who established canon law. Gratian was an Italian monk of the Camaldolensian order who taught theology at San Felice in Bologna, and compiled the *Decretum Gratiani* (c. 1150). This tome (heavy large book) contained nearly 3,800 texts touching all areas of church discipline. It became the textbook for canon law for centuries. The *Decretum Gratiani* was also an important source for the Roman Catholic *Code of Canon Law* (1917). He lived in the monastery of St. Felix de Bologna.

Raymond du Puy

c 1120
France

c 1160

General and Master of the Knights Hospitallers of St. John (caregivers formed into a military order). Du Puy supervised the work of the ancient hospital in Jerusalem during the Crusades of the twelfth century. They came to have immense influence and were keen rivals to the Knights Templars. Hospitallers were medieval men and women caring for the sick. Both they and their patients usually observed religious vows. Monasteries were often the first "hospitals." The need to provide for the pilgrims and crusaders coming to Jerusalem during the religious crusades was intensified. Modern-day hospices are fashioned after the original institutions established by the Hospitallers of which there were several orders.

Theobald

c 1090
near Bec, France

April 18, 1161

Archbishop of Canterbury, 1139–61. From 1127–38, Theobald was originally a Benedictine monk and then abbot at Bec. Theobald persistently defied King Stephen I of England, after he was crowned. He suffered banishment twice—once for attending the papal conference at Rheims in 1130, and later for refusing to recognize the King's son, Eustace, as successor. He took young theologians into his home as students and was also credited as being Thomas à Becket's (controversial archbishop of Canterbury; reigned: 1162–70) mentor. Theobald also introduced the study of Roman law to the clergy of England.

Heloise
Eloise

c 1100
Drepanum Helenopais/Nicodemia (Izmit), Turkey

May 15, 1164
Nogent-sur-seibe, France

Wife of the famous scholastic, Peter Abelard. Heloise was the learned and lovely niece of Canon Fulbert of Notre Dame (Paris) who hired Abelard (20 years her senior) as her tutor, offering him lodging in their home. Abelard seduced her and became the love of her life. When Heloise was seventeen they were secretly married and shortly thereafter, in 1118, she bore him a son, Peter Astralabe. Her uncle was so enraged by this deception that he banished her to a convent and in a moment of ignorant rage, had Abelard castrated. Her uncle continued to move Abelard from monastery to monastery to ensure that the lovers were never together again. Heloise joined the convent of St. Argentevil (six miles north of Paris) as a nun, and in 1129 became the prioress (woman holding position corresponding to prior) of the Paraclete (60 miles southeast of Paris) nunnery, which her uncle founded. After twenty monastic years, Abelard returned to Paris as a teacher. The movingly beautiful love letters exchanged between Abelard and Heloise are classics. They were buried beside each other and, in 1817, properly entombed together in Paris.

Peter the Lombard
Peter of Lombardy—Petrus Lombardus
Master of Sentences

c 1100
Lugelogno (near Novara), Italy

July 20, 1164
Paris, France

Theologian and bishop of Paris, 1159 on. Peter's fame rests upon his *Four Books of Sentences*, of which four volumes are a clear systematic presentation of theology with emphasis on the seven sacraments (baptism, Eucharist/Lord's Supper, confirmation, marriage, penance, Holy Orders/Ordination, anointing of the sick/dying). They were widely studied and quoted until the Reformation. This work was a collection of the opinions of the early fathers of the church. Peter was considered the father of systematic theology in the Catholic Church. The Church was won over to the speculative system of *The Scholastics*. He was a scholar of Abelard and the first doctor of the University of Paris. His philosophy was: "Dilemmas of faith to be resolved by reason."

Aethelred
Ethelred

c 1109
Hexham, England

Jan. 12, 1166
Rievaulx, England

Theologian, historical writer, and Cistercian abbot. Aethelred was the abbot of Revesaby (1142–46) and of Rievaulx, Yorkshire (1146–66). Aethelred wrote some 20 works in Latin, including a biography of Edward the Confessor. His most important spiritual writing is *Mirror of Love*. Aethelred also did missionary work among the Galloway Picts of Scotland, persuading the chief to become a monk.

Richard of St. Victor

1103
Scotland

March 10, 1173
Paris, France

Mystic and theologian. Richard was one of the great teachers of his time who became a prior of the Augustine Abbey of St. Victor in Paris in 1162. He also began his writing career in 1162. Richard wrote a six-volume *De Trinitate*. He also wrote numerous books of Scriptural exegesis and works on Christian mysticism.

Hildegard

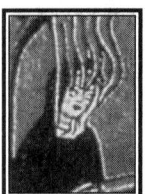

1098
Benershem/Bockelheim, Germany

Sept. 17, 1179
Rupertsberg (near Bingen), Germany

Benedictine nun, abbess, prophetess, writer and mystic. Hildegard became abbess at the convent of Disibodenberg in 1136. In 1148, she founded the Benedictine Monastery of Rupertsberg, near Bingen. Her prophetic visions were approved by the pope. These ecstatic, mystical experiences, which began in 1141, were published in *Scivias* (1141–50) and were widely read. Her experiences included visions, gifts of tears and compuction, wisdom, knowledge, and prophecy. Numerous miracles were attributed to her. It is also claimed she sang "concerts" in the spirit and wrote entire books in languages unknown to her.

Louis VII
The Young – The Pious

1120

Sept. 18, 1180
Paris, France

King of France, 1137–80. Louis VII acquired Aquitaine (ancient division of southwestern France) temporarily by marrying Eleanor, the heiress of the Duchy in 1137. He conquered Champagne (ancient government of Southwestern France), 1142–44. He quarreled with the papacy over the right of royal nomination to vacant bishoprics and was excommunicated by Pope Innocent II. Louis left on his second crusade in 1147, returning in shame after sustaining great losses in just two years. His marriage was annulled in 1152. HENRY II OF ENGLAND then married Eleanor of Aquitaine. Louis VII carried on long wars with HENRY II, finally giving up Aquitaine in 1154 and many other parts of France, outmaneuvered both in battle and diplomacy. Louis had an heir, Philip Augustus, by his third wife in 1165.

John of Salisbury

c 1115
Salisbury, England

Oct. 25, 1180
Chartres, France

Theologian and philosopher. John studied under ABELARD. He knew many popes and church leaders and authored *Policraticus* (1159), a book that describes the ideal state ruled by clergy, and *Metalogicus* (1159), which means "causing formal scholasticism". He taught that the prince received his power from the church. In England, John became chaplain and secretary to THEOBALD, 1150–61. He then returned to Rheims, France, in 1164. Returning again to England in 1170, he saw his close friend, Thomas à Becket, murdered in the cathedral. He finished his life 48 miles southwest of Paris as bishop of Chartres.

Benezet

1165
Hermillon, France

April 14, 1184
Avignon, France

Bridge builder. In an age when it was believed to be a great act of piety to erect a bridge across a river, Benezet mobilized a crew of workmen to begin a bridge across the Rhone River at Avignon, France, in 1177. The plans were supposedly revealed to him in a vision and voice at age twelve and the engineering and construction were all under his supervision. Benezet died when he was only 19, before this bridge was completed. He is supposed to have founded or inspired the Brotherhood of Bridgebuilders who were very active in this era in southern France.

William of Tyre

c 1130
Tyre, Palestine (Lebanon)

Oct. 17–21, 1186
Tyre, Palestine (Lebanon)

French Archbishop of Tyre, 1175 on. William served in Jerusalem as chancellor, 1174–83. He wrote a 23-volume history of the *Latin Kingdom of Jerusalem* (1127–84). In addition to telling the story of the French Crusaders, he attended the third Lateran (ecumenical church councils held in Church of St. John Lateran in Rome) in 1179. This particular council, under Pope Alexander III (reigned: 1159–81), declared that popes should be elected exclusively by the college of cardinals and that a two-thirds vote was necessary for an election to be validated.

Gilbert

c 1083
Sempringham, England

Feb. 4, 1189
Sempringham, England

Founder of the Gilbertine order. Gilbert was a parish priest of Sempringham and then Tyrington in 1123. He founded the only English, medieval, religious order of sisters and brothers, which lived under Augustinian rule and were called the Gilbertines or Sempringenses. His monasteries housed 700 males and 1,500 females. There were only 25 left when they were suppressed by King Henry VIII of England (ruled: 1509–47) in the sixteenth century. He supported Becket against HENRY II OF ENGLAND, despite being held in high regard by the king. Gilbert founded a house for seven destitute girls in 1135, which began his outreach of hospitals and orphanages. He lived to be 106 years old.

Henry II
Curtmantle

March 5, 1133
Le Mans, France

July 6, 1189
Chinon, France

King of England, 1154–89. Henry II sought to bring the Church of England under his secular control. He married Eleanor of Aquitaine (1122–1204) in 1152 and fathered RICHARD THE LION HEARTED. He imprisoned his wife 1173–89. He had successful conflicts with Scotland and Wales. His reforms at the Constitutions of Clarendon in 1164, putting bishops under his control, were vehemently opposed by Thomas à Becket, Archbishop of Canterbury. Henry II engineered Becket's murder on the steps of the cathedral in 1170, which obliged him to come to terms with the church. Henry sought to suppress the rebellion headed by his sons Henry, RICHARD, and Geoffrey but was compelled to walk barefoot through the streets while being flogged by monks. Henry died in 1183, Geoffrey in 1186, but RICHARD enlisted the support of KING PHILIP II of France in a conflict 1188–89. Henry II was succeeded by his son, RICHARD I. In a campaign to wipe out robber barons, he destroyed 1,115 castles.

Frederick I
Barbarossa–Italian for Red Beard

1122
Waiblingen, Germany

June 10, 1190
Cilicia, Turkey

German King, 1152; King of Italy, 1154–90; and Holy Roman Emperor, 1155–90. Frederick controlled his German bishops and ruled peacefully in Germany but ran into problems when he sought to control the papacy as well. He captured the reformer, ARNOLD OF BRESCIA, about 1154. He was defeated by Pope Alexander III's Lombard League (association of northern Italian cities) in 1176 at Legnano (18 miles northwest of Milan). He was highly esteemed by the Germans. He drowned in a Cilician river (Kalykadnos) en route to the Holy Land on the ill-fated Third Crusade (1189–92), which failed to recover Jerusalem from the Muslim's occupancy in 1187. His death caused the Crusade to falter because he was the best strategist of the three armies.

Baldwin

Exeter, England

Nov. 19, 1190
Acre, Syria

Archbishop of Canterbury, 1185–90. This Cistercian monk, supported by the king, was constantly opposed by the monks of Christ Church, Canterbury, which was supported by the pope. Baldwin was a scholar and writer who took part in one of the Crusades. He apparently died of grief at the lack of discipline and conduct of the Christian armies. From 1180–85 (through the Third Crusade), he was bishop of Worcester, England. He preached this crusade following Saladin's (ruled: 1174–93) capture of Jerusalem in 1187, going to the Holy Land himself. Saladin was the sultan (sovereign of an Islamic country) of Egypt and Syria who led the Moslems.

Adam of Saint Victor

c 1110
England or France

c 1192
Paris, France

Liturgical poet and premier medieval hymnologist. Adam wrote more and better hymns than anyone else of his time. He was educated in Paris and entered the abbey of St. Victor (c 1130), staying there until his death. He was the greatest Latin poet of the Middle Ages. Some of his hymns were originally used in the Roman liturgy of the Mass and preceded the presentation of the Gospel. Thanks to the translation work of JOHN M. NEALE, many of his original Latin hymns are still being sung: "Jesus, Word of God Incarnate," "Yesterday, with Exultation," and "Joy and Triumph Everlasting." This Augustinian composed some 45 liturgical sequences that were approved by Pope Innocent II.

Eustathius of Thessalonica

Constantinople (Istanbul), Turkey

1194
Thessalonica, Greece

Bishop of Myra, Lycia (SE Asia Minor) and metropolitan of Thessalonica, 1175 on. An outstanding classical scholar and Byzantine reformer, Eustathius upheld the rights of the Church, defended his people against greedy tax-collectors, and stayed with his flock during the Norman siege of 1185 by King William II of Sicily (ruled: 1166–89). He opposed laxness among monks and formalism in the Church. As the best Greek author of his age, he authored commentaries on Homer, Pindar, and JOHN OF DAMASCUS. He had strong evangelical feelings.

Theodore Balsamon

1105
Constantinople (Istanbul), Turkey

c 1195/1204
Constantinople (Istanbul), Turkey

Ecclesiast and writer of the Greek Church. Balsamon was the librarian of the Cathedral of St. Sophia, Constantinople. His works consist of commentaries on the canon law. Balsamon opposed the claims of the papacy and was a patriarch of Antioch from 1193 on.

Richard I
Richard the Lion Hearted

Sept. 8, 1157
Oxford, England

April 6, 1199
Chaluz, France

King of England, 1189–99. Richard was a key figure in the Third Crusade of 1191 recovering some of the Holy Land: Cyprus Acre (1191) and Jaffa (1192) but not Jerusalem. He married Berengaria of Navarre in Cyprus (c 1189). Conflict with Saladin over treatment of Moslem prisoners resulted in renewed hostilities, a stalemate, and finally a truce. He had slaughtered 2,700 defenseless Islamic prisoners of war. Richard I was seized in Austria, imprisoned by Holy Roman Emperor Henry VI (ruled: 1191–97), and returned to England in payment of a ransom (100,000 pounds and his kingdom) in 1194. King Richard waged war in France from 1194 onward, never returning to England. His great passion was war, so he did very little for his country. He was mortally wounded by an arrow in his shoulder while besieging Chaluz Castle, near Limoges, France.

Hugh of Lincoln

c 1135–1140
Avalon, France

Nov. 16, 1200
London, England

Bishop of Lincoln, England, 1186 on. He joined the French Carthusian monks in 1160, winning a reputation as a skillful and tactful administrator. Hugh was known for his courage, wisdom, and justice. He served King Henry II of England as a special envoy, 1175, personal advisor, ambassador to France, and prior of a faltering monastery in Witham. Hugh was capable of disagreeing with the king and yet remaining in his royal favor. He took the lead in 1198 in the first refusal of a money grant. He braved rioting mobs to defend the Jews of Lincoln. On a return trip, he contracted a fever and never recovered.

Axel Absalon

Oct. 1128
Fjenneslev, Denmark

March 21, 1201
Soro, Denmark

Archbishop of Lund, 1178 on, this national hero was also a soldier and statesman. Absalon functioned as esteemed advisor and general to King Valdemar I (Waldemar) (ruled: 1157–82) and Canute VI. He became primate of Denmark and Sweden and eventually papal legate. Early on he taught at St. Genevive School in Paris. He returned to Denmark to become bishop of Roskilde, 1158–78. He introduced customs of clerical celibacy and monasticism in Denmark and built a fort, where Copenhagen is now located in 1167, eliminating piracy from the Baltic Seas. He destroyed the Pomeranian (province northeast Germany, now mostly northwest Poland) fleet from Prussia, which had attacked Rugen in 1184. He also conquered Mecklenburg (northern Germany) and Estonia. He waged war on paganism in Scandinavia, once overturning idols in a Wendish temple. Absalon died in the abbey of Soro, which he founded on the island of Zealand, Denmark.

Joachim

c 1145
Celico, Italy

March 20, 1202
San Giovanni, Italy

Italian mystic, theologian, Biblical commentator, and abbot of Fiore. He lived first as a Cistercian monk and then formed his own local religious order in San Giovanni, 1192. The Joachimites, with a monastery founded in Fiore (1196), were later absorbed by the Cistercians (1505). Joachim exemplified great personal sanctity. He wrote against Peter the Lombard, with whom he disagreed on the subject of the Trinity. The writings were condemned at the Fourth Lateran Council in 1215. He divided time (1–1260) into three ages (Father, Son, and Holy Spirit). He opposed many of the abuses in the church, the Crusades, indulgences, and temporal power.

Alain
The Universal Doctor

c 1125
Lille, France

c 1202–1203
Citeaux, France

Philosopher, alchemist (medieval form of chemistry) **and theologian**. Alain's work, *The Art of the Catholic Faith*, reveals the mystic slant of his theology. He taught in Paris, 1157–70, then in Montpelier, 1171–85, and combatted the Catharist "heresy" (Catharians were an aesthetic sect in northern Italy in the twelfth century, denying infant baptism and purgatory, Catholic sacraments, replaced by baptism with fire and the Holy Spirit). He took part in the Third Lateran Council in 1179. Alain later joined the Cistercians at Citeaux and authored the encyclopedic poem *Antclaudianus* (c. 1184), a treatise on morals which inspired Dante and Chaucer and *De Dlanctu Narurae*, a satire on Roman vices. His outlook was largely Neo–platonic. He also wrote *The Articles of the Catholic Faith*.

Walter Hubert

c 1150
Dereham, England

July 13, 1205

Archbishop of Canterbury, 1193–1205. Hubert was raised by his uncle, the renowned lawyer, Ranulf de Glanville, who inspired the lad to follow a legal career. Instead, Hubert applied his legal training to clerical positions. Early on, as bishop of Salisbury, Hubert accompanied RICHARD I on the Third Crusade and raised the ransom when the King was imprisoned. Hubert as justiciar (high judicial officer), was in virtual charge of the kingdom in 1194 upon RICHARD I's absence. Pope Celestine III (reigned: 1191–98) appointed him papal legate. King John (Lackland) of England (ruled: 1199–1216) chose him to be England's chancellor in 1199. While at this post, he organized the judicial matters, insisting on enforcement of law and order, and instituted the national customs system in 1202. Hubert's position in the church/state was unrivaled until Cardinal Wolsey's (1475–1536) post in the 1515s. Hubert faithfully served three kings: HENRY II, RICHARD I, and John (Lackland). There is a three-year gap, 1190–93 between archbishops.

Didacus
Diego de Acebes

Acevedo, Spain

Dec. 30, 1207
Osman, Spain

Bishop of Osman. Didacus was a close friend and supporter of Dominic (founder of the Dominicans, 1170–1221). In 1203, these two friends went to France and were exposed to the Cathari, an underground movement of the "pure." Didacus was shocked. He returned to Spain to devise a new strategy for Roman preachers and missionaries. Didacus applauded their emphasis on purity, but rejected their doctrine which contained strong elements of dualism and universalism. He ended up preaching against the Cathari—stressing the foundation of Christ and the Apostles. With corruption being a constant challenge among the clergy, Didacus wisely incorporated the non-extreme elements of the Cathari's asceticism into a new sect called the Order of Preachers. He further strengthened his stand on morality by establishing a separate community of women at Prouille, which later became the first monastery for the Order of Preachers.

Peter of Blois
Petrus Blesensis

c 1135
Blois, France

c 1208

Well-known scholar and writer who spent his early years in Sicily followed by several church appointments in France. During the reign of HENRY II, he went to England in 1173, filling various church posts. He was secretary to Richard of Dover and BALDWIN, archbishops of Canterbury (1174–90) and to Queen Eleanor (1191–95). Peter wrote sermons, histories, and commentaries. He may have been the first writer to use the word "transubstantiation." Peter spoke out against abuses in schools, churches, and secular bodies.

Felix of Valois

April 19, 1127
Valois, France

Nov. 4, 1212
Cerfroid, France

French hermit. Felix lived as a hermit monk in the French forests. He retired to a monastery at Cerfroid, near Paris, where John of Matha (1160–1213) joined him and they founded the Trinitarians (strong believers in Trinity) in 1198. They devoted their lives to rescuing Christians captured by the Saracens. The Christians had to be purchased from their life of slavery. This order of Trinitarians grew to over 800 houses and was sanctioned by Pope Innocent III (reigned: 1198–1216).

Peter Waldo
Pierre Valdes/Valdo/Waldo of Lyons

c 1140
Lyons, France

c 1218

Founder of the Waldenses/Waldensians. The Waldensians were reformationists before Luther, emphasizing Scripture and rejecting such church practices as indulgences, purgatory, and masses for the dead. Witnessing the sudden death of a prominent citizen in 1173 awakened Waldo's spiritual needs. A respected merchant from Lyons, he abandoned his wealth and determined to live a life of poverty that was focused on evangelical perfection, modeled after the Apostles whom he championed as the true "successors of Scripture." His followers were known as the "Poor men of Lyons." Waldo commissioned the translation of several books of the Bible and renowned theological works into the common dialect, French-Provincial. He trained his followers and sent them out "to preach to the public." He opposed oath-taking, war service, and capital punishment; crying out against the lust and greed of the clergy. Waldo witnessed in Lyons, Metz, Lombardy, and Bohemia; was often expelled for his brazen tactics and message; but undauntedly gave the response: "It is better to obey God than man" (Acts 4:19). Some believe his constant reference to the Apostle Peter is how "Waldo of Lyons" became known as Peter Waldo. They were initially not considered a threat to the "establishment" since they were seen as a movement rather than a sect/denomination. Through the Dark Ages, this scattered group remained the strongest evangelical witness, facing various forms of excommunication (beginning in 1184), and for centuries withstood severe repression. He was widely effective and the first to make use of the Bible while preaching.

Giraldus Cambrensis

c 1146
Pembroke, Wales

c 1220

Cleric and historian. Cambrensis toured Wales to enlist troops for the Third Crusade. He wrote a well-known account of his tour of Ireland in 1185: *Itinerarium Cambriae*. He was chaplain to Henry II in 1184. In 1198, Cambrensis was appointed bishop of St. David's, a city in Pembrokeshire, Wales.

Philip II
Augustus

Aug. 21, 1165
Gonesse, France

July 14, 1223
Mantes, France

King of France, 1180–1223. Philip joined King Richard I and King Frederick I (Barbarossa) in the Third Crusade to the Holy Land in 1190. He pouted and squabbled with the others and quickly found an excuse to return to France. In 1199, Philip annexed Normandy, Brittany, and Anjou from King John (Lackland) of England, a great victory, occuring July 27, 1214, at Bouvines (seven miles southeast of Lille). This military action doubled the size of France. Philip built the Louvre, issued the first charter for the University of Paris and made Paris the official royal residence. Religiously, he banished Jews and opposed Albigensians (derived from teaching of Mani in third century, and did not believe in hell or purgatory but believed human government was wicked and evil.) He married Isabella in April, 1180, and upon her death, Ingeborg, 1193. After a separation, he married Agnes in 1196, and upon excommunication for this, he recognized Ingeborg, but kept her imprisoned until 1213.

Francis of Assisi

1182
Assisi, Italy

Oct. 3, 1226
Assisi, Italy

Founder of the Franciscan order (observed vows of poverty and austerity) in 1210 and hymn writer of "All Creatures of Our God and King" (1226). Francis enlisted in the army, became a prsioner of war and became gravely ill in 1202. This brought about his conversion and rejection by his wealthy cloth merchant father. On February 24, 1208, while meditating on Matthew 10:7–10, he was challenged to devote his life to helping the poor, the lepers, the sick, and the suffering. In 1208, he repaired the chapel of St. Damian and began to work at Portiuncula in Assisi. He prayed in caves and decaying chapels. In 1209, he felt the call to preach and organized the Franciscan movement, drafting its values and receiving approval from Pope Innocent III the following year. In a great effort to reach Moslems, he preached in Rome, France, Spain, eastern Europe, Syria, Egypt and the Holy Land, returning to Italy in 1220. He abdicated his leadership in 1223 because it had been taken from him in his absence. From 1224 on, he spent his time in solitude and prayer. It is said that Francis was married to poverty and considered the birds as his family. Some of his last words were, "Welcome, Sister Death." We still sing his prayer, "Eternal Life." He died at the Chapel of Portiuncula. His favorite Bible verse was Galatians 6:14. He was 5 feet 1 inch tall.

"Lord, make me an instrument of thy peace."

Anthony of Padua

Aug. 15, 1195
Lisbon, Portugal

June 13, 1231
Arcella (near Padua), Italy

Missionary preacher to Africa and Italy. He was a faithful and eloquent preacher against doctrinal errors and civil wickedness. Anthony was a follower of Francis of Assisi and began his ministry as a missionary to the Moors (Muslims of northwest Africa) in Morocco, when bad health stopped him. Returning to Padua, he denounced corruption; and the city was reformed. His ability as a preacher was made known during the consecration of a priest at Forli, and his lecture series in 1231 in Padua, which had 30,000 hearers in an oxen field. Anthony devoted himself to the care of the poor and was credited as a miracle worker. He taught in Bologna, Italy (1222); Montpellier (1224); Toulouse, France, and Padua, Italy, working out of his monastery at Montepaolo.

Elizabeth

1207
Pressburg (Bratislava), Hungary (Czechoslovakia)

Nov. 17, 1231
Marburg, Germany

Franciscan ascetic who devoted her short life to the underprivileged. Elizabeth married Louis IV, Landgrave of Thuringia, at the age of 14, when he was 21. He died of the fever (plague) on his way to the Sixth Crusade when she was 20. Now a widow with three children, she built a hospice at Marburg and devoted her life and fortune to caring for the ill, elderly, unwanted, and indigent, joining the Third Order of St. Francis in 1228. Elizabeth was the daughter of King Andrew. Her unnatural asceticism hastened her death due to exhaustion.

Edmund of Abingdon
Edmund Rich

Nov. 20, 1175
Abingdon, England

Nov. 16, 1240
Soisy, France

Archbishop of Canterbury, 1233–40. Edmund was educated at Oxford and Paris. Throughout his life, he preferred the life of a scholar. Edmund taught theology and logic after 1205 at Oxford. He preached in the Sixth Crusade throughout England around 1227. He sought reformation for clergy, people, and monasteries. As archbishop, he showed a stubbornness which quickly brought him into conflict with King Henry III of England (ruled: 1216–72) over bishopric appointments and revenues from vacant sees. Not only the king, but the monks of Canterbury opposed him. His life ended in exile in Soissy and Pontigny, France.

Hedwig

c 1174
Castle of Andechs, Germany

Oct. 12–16, 1243
Trebnitz, Silesia (Poland)

Founded the first Cistercian convent in Trebnitz, near Breslau (Wroclaw, Poland), where she returned in 1209 for some 30 years. Hedwig was the daughter of a Bavarian count (Berthold) and was reared in a convent. She married Henry I, duke of Silesia, at age 12 and had six children. Her husband encouraged her and helped her build or rebuild many monasteries and convents. After his death, Hedwig moved to Trebnitz.

Alexander of Hales
Monarch of Theologian—Doctor Irrefragabilis.

c 1170–85
Halesowen, England

Aug. 21, 1245
Paris, France

Franciscan schoolman, theologian, and philosopher. He began to teach in Paris (1220), and joined the Franciscans (1232), which caused a sensation, and helped foster the rise of scholasticism in the Middle Ages. He held Scripture as the only final truth. He said, "Faith precedeth knowledge." Alexander's work (though uncompleted) is entitled *System of Universal Theology* (published 1475). It was completed by his pupil in 1252. He taught until 1238. He sought to combine Augustinian theology with the writings of Aristotle and the Arab commentators.

William of Auvergne
William of Paris

c 1185
Aurillac (Cantal), France

March 30, 1249
Paris, France

Scholastic theologian and philosopher. William was the canon of Notre Dame (1223), then archbishop of Paris (1228). He lectured on divinity at the University of Paris. Pope Gregory IX (reigned: 1227–41) rebuked him for his laxity in dealings with problems at the University of Paris. He authored the monumental work, *Magisterium Divinale* (1223–40). He was active in the affairs of King Louis IX (ruled: 1226–70). His writings influenced the rise of scholasticism (philosophical and theological teaching). Auvergne was a province and ancient government in central France.

Rose of Viterbo

1235
Viterbo, Italy

March 6, 1252
Viterbo, Italy

Franciscan tertiary (third monastic order of laypeople). She began preaching on the streets at age twelve for support of the papacy and to throw off the aristocratic Ghibelline (party that supported claims of German emperors against the papacy) control. Rose was driven from the town by Holy Roman Emperor and King Frederick II of Germany (ruled: 1220–50) in January, 1250, but returned a year later, after his death, to her father's peasant home. She practiced penitence and prayer until her death.

Richard of Chichester

c 1197/1198
Droitwich (Wyche), England

April 3, 1253
Dover, England

Bishop of Chichester, 1244–53. Richard's unswerving moral standards and church discipline irritated King Henry III. He was chancellor at Oxford (c 1235). He proved to be a model bishop and was renowned for his sanctity of life. He authored profound prayers which were sometimes set to music. Early in his life, Richard studied at Oxford, Paris, and Bologna. He died the day after consecrating a new church in honor of EDMUND OF ABINGDON.

Elias

c 1180
near Assisi, Italy

April 22, 1253
Cortona, Italy

Church builder and establisher. Elias was one of the early companions of FRANCIS OF ASSISI. He built a basilica at Assisi. Elias was also the third minister-general of the Franciscan order but was deposed in 1239 by Pope Gregory IX. Eventually the order expelled him. Officials disliked him because he favored laymen to be equal with clerics (as did FRANCIS). He went back to Cortona and established a monastery of his own.

Clare Sciffi

July 16, 1194
Assisi, Italy

Aug. 11, 1253
Assisi, Italy

Founder of the Order of the Poor Clares. Clare, moved by the influence of FRANCIS OF ASSISI, gave herself to charity and monastic life, beginning on March 18, 1212. She supervised the activities of the Order and at one point, took a stand to protect it against raids by soldiers of FREDERICK II OF GERMANY. The headquarters for the Poor Clares was first at San Argelo, then at San Damien (Damiano) near Assisi. Clare's great charity and spiritual devotion won her the admiration of all. In 1228, they adopted the Rule of ST. BENEDICT.

Robert Grosseteste
Harbinger of the Reformation

c 1175
Stradbrook, England

Oct. 9, 1253
Buckden, England

Learned bishop of Lincoln, 1235–53. Grosseteste excelled in three national areas: Episcopalian administration and participation, papal polities, and scholarly scientific work. He was the first rector of the Franciscan School, Oxford, 1224–35, with ROGER BACON being one of his pupils. Grosseteste excelled in math, astronomy and science. He defended the Jews against Henry III (ruled: 1216–72) in 1232 and insisted on high moral standards for the clergy. Grosseteste refused to install a relative of Pope Innocent IV (reigned: 1243–54) as a canon of the Lincoln Cathedral in 1253. Grosseteste, the first English scholar of his time, knew Hebrew, Latin, Greek, French, mathematics, medicine, and music. He said, "The Roman pope and his court were the origin of all the evils of the Church."

Peter Nolasco

c 1189
Le Mas Des Santas Puelles, France

c Dec. 24–Jan. 28, 1256
Valencia, France

Founder of the Order of Our Lady of Mercy for the Redemption of Captives in 1228. He spent most of his inheritance and energies ransoming Christians held as slaves in Spain by the Moors. His order raised funds and bought freedom for hundreds of captured Christians. Peter personally made two trips to Africa for this cause. RAYMOND OF PENAFORT helped him found this order.

Juliana of Liege

1191
Liege ?, Belgium

1258

Prioress of the Canonesses Regular of Mont-Cornillon in 1222. In 1209 Juliana had a vision which encouraged her to work for a special church feast of the Blessed Sacrament (consecrated host). Pope Urban IV (reigned: 1261–64) extended this celebration of Corpus Christi (festival in honor of the Eucharist) to the whole church in 1264.

Adam of Marsh
Doctor Illustris

1180
Bath, England

Nov. 18, 1259

Franciscan monk and theologian who was a student, friend, and spiritual advisor of Robert Grosseteste and Simon de Montfort (founder of the House of Commons, 1208–65). Adam of Marsh was bishop of Lincoln in 1235 and a monk at Worcester, (c 1232–57). He also attended the Council of Lyons, 1244–46. Men such as King Henry III, Boniface of Savoy, and the pope sought his advice because Adam's influence was greatly felt on the political and social life of the period. He was the master regent (president) at Oxford University, 1247–59, and one of the most learned men of his time.

Matthew

c 1195–1200
Paris, France

June 1259
St. Albans, England

Benedictine monk of St. Albans who was one of the most learned men of his day. He entered the Cluniac Monastery at St. Albans in 1217 and secured certain privileges for the University of Oxford. His greatest work was the *Historia Anglica Major*, a history of England, 1066–1259. The earlier part of this work was produced by Roger of Wendover (English Chronicler, died: 1236). Matthew reorganized the affairs of the abbey in the Trondhjem Province in Norway, 1248–49. Besides being a historian, he was an artist.

Alexander Nevski

May 30, 1220
Vladimir, Russia

Nov. 19, 1263
Gorodetz, Russia

Prince and general who was one of the best-known Russian heroes. He defeated the invading Swedes at the decisive battle on the site of present-day Leningrad (on the Neva River, hence his name of Nevski) (1240), where he also opposed the Teutonic knights (1242). Alexander was a loyal churchman who was deeply venerated in traditional Orthodox Church lore. He became Prince Novgorod (1238), grand duke of Kiev (1246) and of Vladimir (1252). He repulsed the Teutonic knights in 1246. He died returning from a journey to Sarai (ruins near Zareuka), where he won substantial concessions.

Simon Stock

c 1165
Aylesford, England

May 16, 1265
Bordeaux, France

Hermit. Legend states that when a young boy of twelve, he began living in a tree trunk. Stock studied at Oxford. On a pilgrimage to Jerusalem, Simon joined the Carmelite order in 1201. He became vicar-general of the far West, serving in Palestine for the order in 1215. Stock returned to England in 1244, and introduced the Carmelite (religious order founded at Mount Carmel in twelfth century) order to England, promoting its expansion and becoming its superior general, 1245–47.

Boniface of Savoy

c 1207

July 14, 1270
Savoy, France

Archbishop of Canterbury, 1241–70. Elected archbishop through influence of his niece (Queen Eleanor wife of Henry II of England), he was not consecrated until 1245. Boniface was the son of the Count of Savoy and joined the Carthusian order while still a young boy. He visited his province only twice during his tenure, creating hostility among his clergy. Boniface was not disuaded in his actions and is credited with a number of financial reforms during his tenure. He sided with what appeared "right" to him, not often what was "popular."

He did support excommunication of rebel barons (feudal vassal holding lands under direct grant from the king). He loved the Savoy area, and was often criticized for the excessive time he spent there.

Louis IX

April 25, 1214
Poissy, France

Aug. 25, 1270
near Tunis, Tunisia, North Africa

King of France, 1226–70, creating a long reign of peace and prosperity. He was a brave warrior, considerate to his people, and especially cognizant of the needs of the poor. Louis was called the perfect knight-chivalrous, being just and courageous. His life was more austere and prayerful than that practiced by many a religious cleric. Louis saw the completion of Gothic cathedrals at Chartres, Rheims, and Paris. He also participated in the Crusades during the last gasps of the crusading spirit in Europe, 1248–49. He came home in 1254. His entire army of 50,000 was captured at Damienta in Egypt in the Sixth Crusade. A large ransom brought freedom. Pestilence (probably bubonic plague) killed Louis while he was preparing to besiege Tunis as he led the Seventh (and last) Crusade within two months of landing. His last words were: "I will enter now the house of the Lord. . ."

Berthold von Regensburg
Ratisbon

c 1220
Regensburg, Germany

Dec. 14, 1272
Regensburg, Germany

Famous Franciscan preacher who used his eloquence to insist that true repentance comes from the heart and all other actions are merely outward symbols. Beginning in 1250, he preached in monasteries in Regensburg. Berthold often spoke to as many as 60,000 people; most churches could not hold the crowds. He constantly preached against vices that would destroy homes. Berthold opposed indulgences and prayers to saints and to Mary. He was from Bavaria, but traveled as a missionary to Austria, Thuringia, Moravia, Switzerland, and Hungary. In 1263, Pope Urban IV ordered him to preach against heresy as well.

Arsenius Autorianus

c 1200
Constantinople (Istanbul), Turkey

Sept. 20, 1273
Proconnesus, Turkey

Patriarch of Constantinople, 1261–64. Autorianus was earlier patriarch of Nicaea, 1255–61. He excommunicated his Byzantine emperor, Michael VIII (ruled: 1261–82), in 1261 for cruelty. The vindictive emperor, however, got the last word as Arsenius was deposed and exiled (c. 1264) to a monastery on the isle of Proconnesus. His irate supporters organized themselves into a schismatic group in 1264, the schism continuing until 1315.

Robert of Sorbon

1201
Sorbon, France

1274
Paris, France

French theologian and founder of the Sorbonne (Theological College of the University of Paris). The Sorbonne started out as the residence for poor theological students in Paris' Latin Quarter and grew into the distinguished university that it is today. What was intended to be a simple dormitory and reading room became one of Europe's outstanding centers of theology.

Raymond of Penafort

c 1175/1180
Penafort, Spain

Jan. 6, 1275
Barcelona, Spain

Spanish Dominican monk, 1222 on, and theologian who studied and taught church law at Barcelona. Pope Gregory IX asked Raymond to come to Rome to codify canon law in 1230. He consented, and his work (*Peoretals*, 1234) became the authority for over 700 years. He returned to Barcelona in 1235. Raymond devoted his time to missionary work among the Jews and Moors; furthermore, he revised the constitutions of the Dominicans (order founded by Dominic in 1204; foe of the Albigensians) and became their master general, 1238–40, but resigned in order to convert heretics and unbelievers. Raymond also helped Peter Nolasco found the Order of Our Lady of Mercy for the Redemption of Captives (c 1228).

Albertus Magnus
Doctor Universalus

1193
Lauingen, Swabia (Germany)

Nov. 15, 1280
Cologne, Germany

Dominican philosopher, theologian, scientist and schoolman. Magnus wrote books on Aristotle, philosophy, chemistry, botany, zoology, astronomy, geography, and science. He taught at Paris (1245–48) and at Cologne (1248–55). Thomas Aquinas (Catholic scholar, 1225–74) was one of his pupils. He also was briefly a bishop at Regensburg 1260–62. He retired to the Dominican Convent in Cologne, 1262–80, to teach and study. Magnus sought to reconcile philosophy and Christianity. He wrote *System of Nature* and *The Praise of Mary*. He advanced the veneration of Mary. He paved the way for modern conflict between theology and science. He also wrote *Summa Theologiae* (two volumes).

Thomas of Cantelupe

c 1218
Cantelupe ?, England

Aug. 25, 1282
Orvieto, Italy

English reforming bishop of Hereford whose reforming spirit and ascetical life enabled him to become a confidential advisor to King Edward I. Thomas taught canon law at Oxford in 1279, and led the opposition to John Peckham, the archbishop of Canterbury. Thomas appealed to Rome against Peckham over jurisdiction, causing his excommunication by Peckham. Pope John XXII (reigned: 1316–34) later canonized Thomas of Cantelupe.

Machtild

c 1210

1285

German mystic who became a Beguine (a philanthropic community of women not under vows) at Magdeburg and recorded the visions she experienced 1250–69. Machtild stayed there for 40 years under the spiritual direction of Dominican friars. She retired to a convent in Helfta, Germany. Machtild's mystical experiences are written in her book *The Flowing Light of the Godhead*.

Raymond Martini

c 1220
Sobirats, Spain

1285
Barcelona, Spain

Dominican monk and learned Orientalist. At this time in history, Spain had become a center for Jewish and Mohammedan scholarship. The Dominicans saw this as a threat. In 1250, the Dominicans selected Martini as the most promising and talented of the order to be educated as a defender of the faith. With financial backing from the kings of Castile and Aragon, Martini spent the next 25 years gaining a mastery of Semitic, Hebrew, and Arabic. His comparison of Jewish beliefs was completed in 1278, and was called *Pugio Figei*. His other works included a book refuting the *Koran*, *Confutation of the Alcoran*. Many of his writings were expanded upon and altered up through 1650 as a means to clarify "heretic belief."

William de la Mare
1290

English Franciscan theologian and philosopher who criticized the Aristotelian thought of Thomas Aquinas. William's *Correctorium Fratris Thomae* expressed his opposition. The premise of this book was accepted as doctrine for the whole Franciscan order in 1282.

John Peckham

1225
Patcham/Lewes, England

March 20, 1292
Mortlake, England

Archbishop of Canterbury, 1279–92. Theologian and poet who joined the Franciscan order at Oxford where he studied and later taught, 1270 on. After a period in Rome, he came to his English high post and immediately promoted church reform. His works included Bible commentaries and his poetic creation *Philomena*.

Henry of Ghent
Doctor Solemnis

c 1217
Mude (near Ghent), Belgium

June 29, 1293
Tournai, Belgium

Scholastic philosopher and theologian who was considered one of the most illustrious teachers of his time. He supported Augustianianism against Thomas Aquinas in Paris (1277) and, as a priest, fount against the privileges of the Mendicant orders (friars who depended on begging for their sustenance) in 1252. Henry's theological teaching is seen in his *Quodlibeta* and *Summa Theologica*. Henry was canon of Tournai (1267) and archdeacon of Bruges (1276). He was master of Sorbonne theology and a distinguised professor theology at the University in Paris, 1276 on.

Roger Bacon
Doctor Mirabilis

c 1214
near Ilchester, England

June 11, 1294
Oxford, England

Franciscan philosopher and scientist. Bacon opposed scholasticism and insisted on the supreme authority of the Scriptures. This friar was a thinker far ahead of his time. He was a teacher in Paris in the 1240s and 50s. He joined the Franciscans about 1257, then returned to Paris to stay until the late 1260s. He demanded rational proofs for theories then in vogue. He was imprisoned twice, allegedly without books or writing instruments for 10 and 14 years, respectively. He advocated Bible study in its original languages and vehemently opposed Church corruptions of the priests and monks. His discoveries (which included black gunpowder) were primarily in chemistry, alchemy, optics, physics, and astronomy. Bacon wrote *Opus Majus*, one of the first in-depth encyclopedias: encompassing grammar, logic, mathematics, physics, philology, comparative linguistics, and philosophy.

Gertrude
The Great

Jan. 6, 1256
Eisleben, Germany

Nov. 17, 1302
Helfta, Thuringia (Germany)

Mystic. At age five she was placed in the Benedictine convent of Helfta. Gertrude was converted at age 25. Her book, *Legatus Divinae Pietatis*, was considered a spiritual classic. She was one of the first exponents of devotion to the Sacred Heart of Jesus (special devotion of the Lord's heart, a symbol of His love), which she believed was revealed to her in the supernatural visions she experienced beginning in 1284, followed by a life of contemplation.

Yves of Brittany
Ivo Helory of Kermartin

Oct. 17, 1253
Kermartin, France

May 19, 1303
Louannec, France

Lawyer and theologian. Ivo distinguished himself during ten years of studies in Paris, gaining distinction in philosophy, theology, and canon law. He was a saintly and able defender of the indigent and deprived, becoming known as "the poor man's advocate." He gravitated toward ecclesiastical court cases, was above the prevalent bribe system, encouraged out-of-court reconciliation of grievances rather than costly lawsuits, and was greatly extolled as a skilled arbitrator. His wise counsel and mastery of canon and civil law at Rennes, 1280 onward, was noticed by his bishop who encouraged him to pursue clerical orders. Ivo was ordained (1284), became a parish priest at Tredrez (1285), resigned his legal position (1287), and later served at Louannec (1292). He built a hospital, personally ministered to the ill and poor, and acquired a reputation as a preacher who was just as solicitous about people's temporal needs as their spiritual condition. Ivo spoke in many pulpits.

John of Paris
John Quidort

1250
Paris, France

Sept. 22, 1306
Bordeaux, France

Dominican preacher and controversialist who taught philosophy and theology at Paris. He took a stand against transubstantiation in his conflict with Pope Boniface VIII (reigned: 1294–1303). In his tract, *Authority of the Pope and the King*, he stated that neither power had a right to interfere in the sphere of the other. John was prohibited by the bishop of Paris from preaching, lecturing, and hearing confessions because of his writings on the Eucharist (Lord's supper, mass, holy communion) and the papacy. Undoubtedly his writings influenced MARSILIUS and DANTE. He died while appealing his suspension to Pope Clement V (reigned: 1305–14).

Jacopone da Todi

c 1230
Todi, Italy

Dec. 25, 1306
Collazone, Italy

Franciscan monk, hymn writer and poet. He is remembered for more than 100 mystical poems of great power: originally for the hymn, "Stabat Mater Dolorosa" (A Sorrowing Mother Stood) and "Laude" (Hymns of Praise). His wife died suddenly from a fall in a theater gallery in 1268. In 1278, he became a Franciscan friar. Jacopone was imprisoned, 1298–1303, and excommunicated for writing satirical verse against Pope Boniface VIII. He was fearless in his attacks on abuses of his day, and gave Italian poetry religious expression. He died in a monastery.

Dolcino

Novara, Italy

June 1, 1307
Vercelli, Italy

Leader of the Apostolic Brethren or Dulcinists, successor of the martyred Segrarelli. Dolcino had joined the apostolic Brethren (1291) and became their leader (1300). He was concealed at Dalmatia (Austria/Hungary), until 1304, when he led an army against troops that opposed him in Novara and Vercelli. Attempts were made to arrest him, but it was not until March 23, 1307, that he was defeated. Dolcino was a well-meaning religious enthusiast but was considered fanatical and ill-balanced in mind. He was burned at the stake.

Edward I
Longshanks

June 17, 1239
Westminster, England

July 7, 1307
Burgh-on-Sands, England

King of England, 1272–1307 known for "No taxation without representation." Edward I is remembered as the leader of the last major expedition of the Crusades in 1272 to free the Holy Land from the Moslems. Edward I landed at Acre (70 miles north of Jerusalem, the last Christian stronghold to fall: 1291), narrowly escaping assassination. While returning from the Eighth Crusade, he learned of his accession to the throne. He married Eleanor of Castile (1254, Spanish alliance, died 1290) and Phillip IV's sister, Margaret (1299, French alliance). Together they gave him 15 children, only two of which were sons. England's conquest of Wales began (1277), and culminated in its annexation (1284). Edward I carried through legislation, 1275–90, eliminating feudalism, ending papal over lordship, and refusing tribute to Rome. One of his lasting contributions was the establishment of a "Model Parliament" in which all sectors of the kingdom had representation. In 1290, he banished 16,000 Jews charged with organized extortionate usury. He defeated the Scots in 1296 and later gave Scotland a new constitution and representation in the newly organized English Parliament. Attempting to annex Scotland, he died while marching north to suppress a revolt by King Robert Bruce (Robert I of Scotland, ruled: 1306–29).

John (Johannes) Duns Scotus
Doctor Subtilis

1265
Maxton, Scotland

Nov. 8, 1308
Cologne, Germany

Medieval philosopher and scholastic theologian who joined the Franciscan order and taught at Oxford and Paris, 1296–1304, before transferring to Cologne. His belief was, "Something may be true in philosophy and false in religion." He criticized such men as Thomas Aquinas and developed a scholastic system called Scotism which stated that "Faith was not speculative but an act of will." He was banished from Paris for taking the side of Pope Boniface VIII against the king. John strongly opposed humanists, and his opposition to classical studies caused scoffers to coin the word "dunce" meaning a blockhead or sophist. He defended the doctrine of the Immaculate Conception. John authored several commentaries on the Bible and Aristotle, with his *Commentary on the Sentences of Peter Lombard* (12 volumes) being his most poignant work.

Athanasius I

1230
Adrianople, Turkey

Oct. 28, 1310
Xerolophus, Turkey

Monk and patriarch of Constantinople who opposed the work for reunion between Eastern and Western churches at the Second Council of Lyons in 1274. His own severe reforming measures for his clergy failed and brought about his resignation.

Guillaume Nogaret

c 1265
Toulouse, France

April 11, 1313
Schonen, Paris, France

Political leader, jurist, and statesman for King Philip IV of France during the French power struggles with Pope Boniface VIII. He humiliated Boniface by forcibly preventing him from sending a bull (papal letter sealed with a bull-round, lead, red-inked papal seal) to curb Philip's authority in France. Nogaret arranged to have Clement V elected pope, starting the French Avignon papacy (70 years of counter popes in Rome) in 1305. Pope Clement V moved the headquarters in 1309. He was hostile to the Knight Templars, desiring to seize the enormous wealth of the order, which had immunity from taxes.

Robert Winchelsey
Robert de Winchelsea

c 1240–1245
Winchelsea, England

May 11, 1313
Oxford, England

Archbishop of Canterbury, 1294–1313. Theologian who championed ecclesiastical rights and found himself in constant opposition to both EDWARD I and EDWARD II. Through a papal mandate in 1300, Winchelsey specifically forbade EDWARD I's attack on the Scots. He also aided the barons in their struggle with King Edward II (ruled: 1307–27). Of all the English religious primates, none was as unpopular as Winchelsey. He was considered self-willed and haughty. At a time when the English nation was rising to national independence, Winchelsey put himself in opposition to the country. Some felt his distractions to the growth of England were grounds for high treason. Winchelsey's private life—giving boundless charities to the poor—was more in keeping with the role of a benevolent cleric.

Jacques de Molay

c 1243
Molay, France

March 11, 1314
Paris, France

Last Grand Master of the Knights Templars, 1298 on. De Molay tried to reequip in 1306 after the Templars had been driven from Palestine. While in Cyprus in 1310, he was busy raising new troops to defend against the Saracens. At this time, he was summoned to France by Pope Clement V, who was determined to end the feuding between the Knights Templars and the Knights of St. John. He was turned over to French King PHILIP IV, who feared and resented the strength of the Knights. De Molay was tried, tortured by NOGARET, imprisoned, and finally burned at the stake after five years of imprisonment. Pope Clement V dissolved the Templars in 1312.

Philip IV
Philip the Fair

1268
Fontainebleau, France

Nov. 29, 1314
Fontainebleau, France

King of France, 1285–1314, responsible for the most momentous reign in medieval history. He married Jeanne de Navarre in 1284, daughter of King Henry II of Navarre. His reign marked the beginning of papal decline. The pope wanted permission granted to tax church properties. King Philip refused to let church money leave France which stirred the pope to issue a papal bull. Philip made Pope Benedict XI (reigned: 1303–4) his prisoner and required the new pope, Clement V, to live in Avignon, France, beginning what is termed the Babylonian captivity of the Middle Ages, 1305–78. His rule is blotted with Jewish persecution in 1306 and cruel suppression of the Order of Knights Templars in France, 1307–12.

Raymond Lull

c 1232–35
Palma, Balearic Islands

June 29, 1315
off coast of Algiers (Algeria)

Martyred Spanish missionary to Muslims. He was also a scholar, alchemist, mystic, and theologian. He wrote over 300 works. Converted around 1263, Lull sought to establish language schools for missionaries and also served as a missionary to Spanish Mallorca (one of the Balearic Islands) near his home, founding a Franciscan missionary school in 1276. He traveled and lectured extensively in Italy and France the next 30 years. He tried three times to preach to Muslims at Tunis (1291), Algeria (1305), and North Africa (1314), but was imprisoned, cast out of the city twice, and finally left for dead after being savagely stoned the third time. He died on board a "rescue ship," at sea in sight of Palma. His *Contemplations* helped many people.

Alighieri Dante

May 14, 1265
Florence, Italy

Sept. 14, 1321
Ravenna, Italy

Poet, reformer, prose writer, moral philosopher, and political thinker. Dante's epic, *The Divine Comedy* (1321), is a literary masterpiece demanding reformation, and condemning the corruption of the church. There are more than 500 manuscript copies, the original being lost. It is divided into three journeys: the first two, Hell and Purgatory, are led by Virgil, and the final journey through Paradise led by Beatrice, the love of Dante's life. Much of his work which began around 1273, when he was a mere nine years old, was inspired by his love for Beatrice Portinari (died: 1290). He married Gemma Donati (c. 1287), and they had four children. He lived in such places as Lucca, Verona, and Ravenna. Dante was entrusted with various diplomatic missions, banished from Florence in 1302 (he never saw his wife again), then died in political exile at the court of Guido da Polenta of malaria. The statue, "The Thinker," by Auguste Rodin, is a portrait of Dante. Longfellow said his work was "a medieval miracle of song."

Meister (Johann) Eckhart

c 1260
Hochheim, Thuringia (Germany)

1327
Cologne, Germany

Dominican theologian, preacher, and mystic. His writings were very influential and initiated a popular, mystical movement in Germany. In 1307, he was appointed vicar-general of Bohemia with the task of reforming monastic houses. His movement was called the Brethren of the Free Spirit. He taught in Paris, 1311–14, went to Strasbourg as a professor of theology, and finally traveled to Rome. In 1326, 17 of his written propositions were judged to be heretical at the Inquisition at Cologne. Some say he was pantheistic (identifies God with the universe, part of everything in the universe), but this charge is generally discounted. Some of his followers included HENRY SUSO and JOHANN TAULER. He taught salvation through perfect love for God and self-denial.

Roch

c 1295
Montpelier, France

Aug. 16, 1327
Montpelier, France

Healer of the plague-stricken. At the age of twelve Roch began to manifest strict asceticism and great devoutness. After his parents' death when he was 20, Roch gave away his possessions and joined the Franciscans. Coming to Italy during an epidemic, he diligently tended the sick, bringing about many miraculous cures through prayer. There is a legend that he fell ill while traveling through a forest, and that the dog of a nobleman Roch had healed, brought him bread daily which sustained him. When he returned to Montpelier, he was arrested as a spy and thrown into prison where he died. Roch had shared with many, that by calling upon God, plague-stricken persons would be healed. His life was devoted to the service of the ill, especially those who were abandoned. Many churches and hospitals were dedicated to him.

John of Monte Corvino

1246
Monte Corvino, Italy

1328
Khanbaligh (Peking), China

Franciscan missionary to China, commissioned by Pope Nicholas IV (reigned: 1288–92) in 1291. In the beginning of his ministry, John labored in Armenia, Persia, and India. He founded the first Christian mission in China upon entering Peking in 1294. He was appointed archbishop over six bishops in China in 1307. He translated the New

Testament and Psalms. Later, John founded a congregation of about 1,300. He had 6,000 converts. This work flourished until 1368. When the Mongol dynasty fell, Nestorian Christians opposed him.

John of Jandun

c 1275–1286
Jandun, France

Sept. 15, 1328
Montalto, France

Controversial theologian and political writer who helped to write *Defender of the Peace* with MARSILIUS of Padua in 1324. They stated that popes and kings are granted their rights to rule by the consent of the governed. They were excommunicated in 1327 by Pope John XXII, but were protected by Holy Roman Emperor Louis IV (the Bavarian) (ruled: 1314–47). John of Jandun was a professor of theology and philosophy in Paris. He championed the king against the claims of the papacy.

Odoric

c 1286

Jan. 14, 1331

Franciscan monk who served as a missionary in Asia, 1316–29. He traveled extensively through China penetrating as far north as Peking. Odoric returned home via Tibet. Although regarded with indifference by his fellow Franciscans, he was treated as something of a popular hero among the laity.

Bartholomew
Apostle of Armenia

Bologna, Italy

1333

Apostle of Armenia (Turkey/USSR). Bartholomew was a Dominican who became bishop of Maraga and archbishop of Nakschiwan in Armenia. He translated the *Missal*, the *Psalter*, and other liturgical books into Armenian.

William Durand

1275
St. Pourcain, France

Sept. 10, 1334
Meaux, France

Schoolman, 1303–34, who asserted that there was no human authority above human reasoning. Breaking with ANSELM OF CANTERBURY and Aquinas, he made man the center of his theology and the Scriptures a help to gain a better life. Durand denied sacramental salvation, thus preparing the way for the Reformation.

Giotto Bondone

c 1267
Vespignino, Italy

Jan. 8, 1337
Florence, Italy

One of the most important artists before the Renaissance. Bondone is well known for his frescoes and altarpieces in Rome, Padua, and Florence. He was also a painter, sculptor, and architect. Bondone decorated part of the Church of St. Francis and part of St. Peter's in Rome. He used artistic paintings for most of his decor. Bondone is best known for his four allegorical frescoes (painting on a moist lime plaster surface with pigments, colors, ground in water) in honor of FRANCIS OF ASSISI. His scenes include "Last Supper" and "Presentation of Christ in the Temple." He drew a perfect circle with one free-arm movement.

Juliana Falconieri

1270
Florence, Italy

June 19, 1341
Florence, Italy

Founder of the Servite order (service of Mary) **of Nuns**. Juliana was of a Florentine heritage, who rejected her family's marriage plans and instead became a tertiary of the Servite order at age sixteen. After her mother's death in 1304, she headed a group of women dedicated to prayer and charitable works.

Marsilius

c 1270
Padua, Italy

1342
Munich, Germany

Scholar and professor of philosophy. Marsilius was one of the first to speak out against the power of the papacy. He served as a rector of the University of Paris 1313 on. Marsilius wrote *Defender of the Peace* with JOHN OF JANDUN in 1324. This work proved to be a juridical treatise against temporal powers of the pope. For this work, Pope John XXII excommunicated Marsilius in 1327. Holy Roman Emperor Louis IV (the Bavarian) protected Marsilius until his death. WYCLIFFE and LUTHER benefited from his work.

John Stratford

Stratford-upon-Avon, England

Aug. 23, 1348
Mayfield, England

Archbishop of Canterbury, 1333–48. Stratford was chancellor of England and counselor of the young King Edward III (ruled: 1327–77). He admired Thomas à Becket and later imitated Thomas' style in standing up to the king over a peer's right to be judged by his equals in Parliament. Stratford also gave generously of his time and money to his native town.

William of Ockham
William of Occam—Doctor Invincibilis—Venerabilis Inceptor

c 1285
Ockham, England

April 10, 1349
Munich, Germany

Franciscan monastic Oxford scholar and medieval scholastic philosopher, William divorced philosophy from theology, lecturing on both at Oxford, 1315–19. He maintained that the pope was not infallible and that the Bible was the only source of authority causing his excommunication. He was imprisoned from 1322–28 by Pope John XXII at Avignon. William escaped and took refuge with Holy Roman Emperor Louis IV (the Bavarian) at Pisa and followed him to Munich. He was a nominalist. In William's work *Dialogues*, he suggested separation of church and state. He studied under DUNS SCOTUS and taught in Paris for some years. He said, "God must be believed by faith." Luther highly valued some of his works.

"Doctrines peculiar to theology are not suspect to proof by pure reason."

Thomas Bradwardine
Profound Doctor

c 1290
Hartfield, England

Aug. 26, 1349
Lambeth, London, England

English prelate, theologian, and mathematician. Bradwardine was chancellor and professor of divinity at Oxford University, and chaplain and fearless confessor of King Edward III, whom he accompanied abroad on his French campaign. Bradwardine was appointed archbishop of Canterbury in 1349 but died of the Black Death (40-day illness) before being officially enthroned. His principal work was *De Cause Dei* (1316), which emphasized the grace of God in salvation and was directed against Pelagianism. This prepared WYCLIFFE for his work.

Richard Rolle de Hampole

c 1290
Thorton, England

Sept. 29, 1349
Hampole, England

English mystic, hermit, and author of tracts on Christian mysticism. Rolle studied at Oxford but broke off his studies at age 19 to become a hermit. His last years were spent near a convent at Hampole near Doncaster. Here, Rolle acted as a spiritual advisor to nuns. He was highly regarded for his sanctity and spiritual writings. Rolle is known for his 9,624-line poem, *The Price of Conscience*. He wrote in Latin and English. Rolle translated the Psalms with a verse-by-verse commentary. This created hunger for more portions of the Bible, and prepared the way for Wycliffe.

Jordanus (Jordan)

c 1350

Dominican missionary. About 1319, Jordanus left Avignon, France for the Far East. In India, he found a few Nestorian Christians where he won more than 10,000 people there to the Latin Church. Jordanus' companions were murdered by Moslems. Later, he was made bishop of Quilon by Pope John XXII upon his return to Europe in 1330.

Gregory Palamas

c 1296
Constantinople (Istanbul), Turkey

Nov. 14/15, 1359
Thessalonica, Greece

Greek theologian and archbishop of Thessalonica in 1349. Palamas became a monk at Mount Athos after being brought up in the court of Byzantine emperor John Cantacuzenus (ruled: 1347–54). The people of Thessalonica refused to accept Palamas so he retired to the island of Lemnos (in Aegean Sea, belonging to Turkey). He made much of meditation with God. "God's essence could not be known," he said, "but God's energies could." He related his doctrine of uncreated light to the divine energy, which was upheld at the Council in Constantinople in 1341. His work *Prosopopoeia* opposed the Latin Church. He emphasized laying on hands for gifts of healing, miracles, foreknowledge, wisdom, and tongues.

Johann Tauler

c 1300
near Strasbourg, Germany

June 16, 1361
Strasbourg, Germany

German Dominican mystic and preacher. Tauler was ordained to preach around 1316. He was more practical, devotional, and evangelistic than his contemporaries, such as Eckhart and Suso. After being driven from his native town of Strasbourg, Tauler settled in Basel. Twelve years later, he returned to Strasbourg and continued to preach with great power after experiencing a personal religious awakening (conversion) around 1348. He condemned external ceremonies, longing for revival. Tauler fellowshiped with and popularized the Friends of God (German mystics) movement, preaching in German mingled with Latin. He was considered the greatest preacher of his time.

Heinrich (Henry) Suso

March 21, 1295
Constance/Uberlinger, Germany

Jan. 25, 1366
Ulm, Germany

Dominican monk and mystic. Converted at age 18, Suso studied under Meister Eckhart and was closely associated with the Friends of God movement. His strict self-denial caused numerous health problems. In 1348, he settled in the Dominican convent at Ulm. At age 40, he abandoned extreme asceticism to be pastor and preacher. Suso is most known for his devotional books: *Little Book of Truth* (1329), *Horologe* (instrument to measure time) *of Wisdom* (1337), *The Little Book of Eternal Wisdom* (1348), and the important *The Life of the Servant*. He used poetic language and symbolism. Suso died after much persecution and slander.

Simon Islip

April 26, 1366

Islip, England

Archbishop of Canterbury, 1349–66. Simon was named for the village of Islip near Oxford. He first served as a member of the privy council to King Edward III of England. Islip was well respected for his efforts in founding Canterbury College which later became Christ Church at Oxford. Also noteworthy is his conduct toward the reformer, JOHN WYCLIFFE, who he appointed as overseer of Canterbury College. Islip said he selected WYCLIFFE because he was "A man in whose circumspection, fidelity, and activity he had the utmost confidence, and to whom he gave this post on account of his honorable deportment and his learning."

Conrad of Waldausen

1369

Waldausen, Bohemia

Stirring preacher from Bohemia. Conrad rigorously opposed the corruption in the Church and insisted that Scripture, not the Vatican, was the rule of life. He prepared the groundwork for the coming of JOHN HUSS.

Bridget
Birgitta—Brigit

June 1303
Upland/Finstad, Sweden

July 23, 1373
Rome, Italy

Founder of the Brigittine monastic Order of Sisters in 1370. She was a mystic whose published *Revelations* (evangelical tendencies) in 1346 were influential in the Middle Ages. Bridget married a wealthy nobleman, Ulf Gudmarson (1316), had eight children, and upon his death (1344), retired into a monastery. She went to Rome in 1349, was considered a prophetess, became the patroness of Sweden and was known as the mother of CATHERINE OF SWEDEN. She made several pilgrimages, one to the Holy Land in 1372. Her monasteries were divided, with one portion for monks, the other for nuns.

Jan Milic(z)

June 29, 1374

Kremsier, Moravia (Germany)

Avignon, France

Bold preacher, who like CONRAD OF WALDAUSEN, stirred Bohemia prior to the days of JOHN HUSS. Milicz lived and taught at Kremsier and lamented the corruption among the clergy. He pleaded for more frequent communion services and insisted that the Bible was sufficient authority for belief. Milicz further stated that unworthy clergy were evidence of the coming of the Antichrist. He began his crusading evangelism in 1363, preaching in the Czeck tongue. In 1367, he was briefly in Rome, where he was imprisoned by the Inquisition, but later released, and received by Pope Urban V (reigned: 1362–70). From 1369 on, he lived in Prague. He was denounced as a heretic by the Mendicants, whom he attacked.

Francesco Petrarch

July 20, 1304
Arezzo, Italy

July 18, 1374
Arqua, Italy

Foremost humanist scholar and poet. Petrarch's talent for Latin poetry commended him to the court of Pope John XXII, where he took minor orders in the church. He had a consuming passion for the spirit of the Renaissance. Petrarch was known for his sonnets and odes in the vernacular. He dominated the international literary scene for many years. Petrarch revived interest in Latin literature by library research for the manuscripts. His poetry meditates on life's transitory nature. He spent most of his life up to 1340 in Avignon, France, where his family moved after his birth. From 1341 on, he lived mostly in Italy: Milan, Padua, and Venice. He was married to an Avignon lady and had two children. He was highly interested in classical antiquity, which he sponsored at Arqua. At the age of 40, he "died" and was laid out for mourners to visit. Local law said corpses had to lie in public view for 24 hours before burial. After 20 hours a sudden change of temperature made him sit up in bed complaining about the draft and scolding his attendants for not looking after him properly. Instead of being buried alive, he went on to live for 30 more years.

John of Chur

c 1380

Chur, France

Leader among the Friends of God. John became a mystic and distributed his fortune in benevolence. This pious hermit lived in a cell/chapel on the Rutburg in the canton of St. Gaul, France. His writings are often vague with confusing contradictions. John of Chur did not express any specific doctrines.

Catherine of Siena

March 25, 1347
Siena, Italy

April 29, 1380
Rome, Italy

Italian Dominican mystic. Catherine was responsible for the return of the papacy from Avignon, France, to Rome in 1377. Taking the vows of the Church, she dedicated herself to help the poor and work for conversions. Catherine claimed to have visions and prophecies. In 1354, she saw a vision of Jesus with Peter, Paul, and John, and vowed a spiritual life. In 1363, she became a member of the Sisters of Penitence. Catherine saw a vision of her celestial marriage, which began her ministry in 1367. She wrote many letters beginning in 1370. She denounced the clergy for greed and immorality and was the confidante of kings and feuding Italian princes. Fearlessly confronting and swaying mercenary warlords, she advised popes, criticized weak-willed cardinals, comforted the poor, and gave direction to many of the abbots and soldiers of Europe. Catherine lived in Siena, 1368–74, then was tried for heresy by the Dominicans in Florence. She received Raymond of Capua as a spiritual guide. In 1375, interest in crusades took her to Pisa. She traveled to Avignon and persuaded Pope Gregory XI (reigned: 1370–78) to return with curia (papal court) to Rome in 1376. Beginning in 1378, she lived in Rome, working toward unity and the support of the new pope, Urban VI (reigned: 1378–89). She lived on a handful of herbs each day and on two hours of sleep each night.

Catherine of Sweden

1331
Sweden

March 24, 1381
Vadstena, Sweden

Abbess of the convent at Vadstena in 1373, succeeding her famous mother, Bridget of Sweden. Catherine performed many charitable deeds throughout the country of Sweden. The Brigittine Order was confirmed under her. She was an ally of Catherine of Siena. She was married at age 13 to Egard van Kyven, who died while she and her mother were on a pilgrimage to Rome and the Holy Land.

Walter Tyler
Wat Tyler

June 15, 1381
Smithfield, London, England

Leader of the Peasant's Revolt. Tyler headed the angry mob (rebels from Kent) which poured from the countryside into London on June 13, 1381 in protest against the Statute of Laborers, imposition of poll tax, and overall economic distress. Two days later, Tyler took his case all the way to King Richard II (ruled: 1377–99), demanding abolishment of serfdom, removal of restrictions on labor and trade, and amnesty for the rebels representing the cause. Lord Mayor William Walworth was so incensed that he stabbed Tyler to death. Tyler had a passion for justice and was an able orator, though a roof tiler by trade.

John Ball (1)

July 15, 1381
St. Albans, England

Reforming priest and follower of JOHN WYCLIFFE. Ball was frequently imprisoned and eventually excommunicated twice for teaching ownership of property. Later in his life, Ball was excommunicated again for his extreme political and religious views; however, he remained popular with the people. He was forbidden to preach (1366) and jailed (1381). WALTER TYLER, the leader of the Peasant's Revolt in 1381, was a close friend to Ball. King Richard II finally hanged Ball as a traitor to the state for his support of the revolution, which was surprising since WYCLIFFE, his leader, condemned the rebellion. Ball was called the "Mad Priest," although his views had no doctrinal grievances.

Jan van Ruysbroeck

1293
Ruysbroeck, Brabant (Belgium)

Dec. 2, 1381
Groenendael, Brabant (Belgium)

Dutch mystic and literary figure. Van Ruysbroeck was a compatriot of the band of mystics who called themselves Friends of God. He served as a priest for a time, then he organized the abbey at Groenendael. His writings spread rapidly throughout the Netherlands. Van Ruysbroeck's classic, *The Adornment of the Spiritual Marriage* (1350), is a guide for the soul. His mysticism is related to Platonic concepts, and some of his writings are a reaction to the myticism of ECKHART and pantheistic tendencies of Bloemardinne (popular woman writer).

Rulman Merswin

1307/1308
Strasbourg, Germany

1382

Leader of the Friends of God. Merswin wrote numerous letters and tracts. He held a wide range of readers. His background was in banking and mercantile at Strasbourg. Merswin became a friend of TAULER and left his business to help the spiritual cause. He signed his letters: "Great Friend of God."

Gerhard Groote
Father of Modern Devotion

Oct. 1340
Deventer, Netherlands

Aug. 20, 1384
Deventer, Netherlands

Founder of the Brethren of the Common Life in 1384 at Zwole. Groote was a brilliant and well-respected professor who renounced his scholarly position to become a missionary in 1374, the time of his conversion, influenced by RUYSBROECK. He had taught philosophy and theology at Cologne till then. He then "retired" to a monastery at Munnikhuizen, 1374–77. Groote traveled widely as a reformer and founded the houses of the Brethren and Sisters of the Common Life (mystical lay piety in Germany and Netherlands), where he basically headquartered at Deventer in 1380 and Zwolle. He focused his energy on preaching against the laxity of the clergy. He favored meditation rather than hollow rituals. Groote proved to be an extremely popular Dutch preacher, missionary, educator, and reformer. His impressive sermons stressed the repentance theme. He died of the plague. FLORENTIUS RADEWYN was his co-worker and successor.

John Wycliffe
John Wickliffe/Wyclif/Wiclif
Morning Star of the Reformation

c 1320
Ipreswell (Hipswell), England

Dec. 31, 1384
Lutterworth, England

Reformer, theologian, philosopher, and Bible translator. Wycliffe, Huss, and Savonarola paved the way for the Reformation. He believed that Scripture should be the ultimate authority over the papacy. In 1360, he was the Master of Balliol College, Oxford, where he served as professor and priest. He began his career as a reformer in 1374 serving as rector of a church in Lutterworth where he established his headquarters. He sent out Lollards (Wycliffe's poor preachers) in 1378. Wycliffe was the first to translate most of the Bible from the Latin Vulgate into English. He strongly denied transubstantiation and purgatory, and objected to the pope's interference in English politics as well as the church's wealth and sale of indulgences. He was condemned in papal bulls before a tribunal of bishops in St. Paul's Cathedral, London. Wycliffe's Tenets expressed his opposition to Pope Urban VI. He was forced into retirement as a result of the Peasant Revolt in 1381. His ideas were condemned in 1382 and he suffered his first stroke. Wycliffe died of a stroke while saying Mass, only to have his bones dug up in 1428 to be burned for his "heretical" views. His doctrines had been condemned at the Council of Constance in 1415.

Sergius of Radonezh

May 3, 1314
Rostov, Russia

Sept. 25, 1392
Zagorsk, Russia

Orthodox monk from 1337 until his death. Sergius incited the Muscovites to attack their overlords, the Mongols. This surprise attack proved successful for the Russians. Sergius founded Russia's greatest monastery, Holy Trinity, which is located near Moscow. He built a chapel in honor of the Trinity in the Forest of Radonezh, which later became the famous monastery. This great ediface became the inspiration for 75 other monasteries across Russia. Sergius is credited with stopping four civil wars from erupting. He is remembered for his asceticism, compassion, and humility, demonstrated by rejecting the Moscow patriarchate in 1379. He died at the Holy Trinity Monastery of Zagorsk.

John of Nepomuk

1340
Nepomuk (Czechoslovakia), Bohemia (Pomok)

March 20, 1393
Prague, Czechoslovakia

Canon and vicar-general of the Cathedral of Prague in 1393. John was tortured and drowned in the Moldau River by King Wenceslaus IV of Bohemia when he refused the king's demand to turn an abbey into a cathedral. He also did not endear himself to the king when he refused to "share" the Queen's confession.

Matthias

Janov, Bohemia (Czechoslavakia)

1394

Stirring preacher from Bohemia. Matthias ministered in the pre-Huss era. He denounced the corruption, immorality, and greed of the church. Furthermore, Matthias emphasized the Bible as the only authority for belief. He warned that the Antichrist was near and could be seen in wicked clergy.

Nicholas of Basel

1308
Basel, Switzerland

C 1396
Vienna, Austria

Martyr, known as "the friend of God". Nicholas was from the Oberland (high Alps). He spread the evangelical message for over half a century under the very eye of Rome. At the age of 13, he was touched by preaching on the sufferings and death of Christ. He bought himself a crucifix and somehow gained access to a Bible. At age 24, he became wealthy when his merchant father died. Rejecting marriage, he lived under bondage for years in self-inflicted penance. Nicholas was suddenly delivered from all this when he came under the influence of the Waldensians. He built a home, in a hidden spot, high in the Alps. There, five men and two servants devoted themselves to lives of prayer. Under his guidance, a resulting ministry reached out along the Rhine to Holland, the lower cantons of Switzerland, and in Alsace and Bavaria as far east as Hungary. He had a big influence on JOHN TAULER. When two of his friends were seized in Vienna, Nicholas was also detained and asked to renounce the condemned pair as heretics. When he refused to do so, the three were burned to death.

Walter Hilton

c 1340

March 24, 1396
Thurgarton, England

English mystic and devotional writer. Hilton studied at Cambridge; and after a period as a hermit, joined the Augustinian canons at Thurgarton priory in Nottinghamshire. Hilton's writings were well read, his most famous work being *The Scale of Perfection*.

John of Gaunt

March 1340
Ghent (Gaunt), Belgium

Feb. 3, 1399
London, England

Prominent duke in domestic affairs of England during his father's (Edward III) senile years. John was involved in English wars and was a self-seeking, chivalrous knight. He supported WYCLIFFE, although he did not support his religious views, and protected him from the attacks of the bishop of London. John enjoyed art and was a patron of CHAUCER's literature. John of Gaunt married Blanche of Lancaster (1359) (died of the plague in September, 1369), Constance Cruel (1372), and Catherine Swynford (1396). John led armies of English forces in France 1369–70. From 1386–89, he tried to take the Spanish throne but failed. He founded the House of Lancaster which gave several kings to England and was duke of the same (1361) and duke of Aquitaine (1390). His son, King Henry IV of England, began his reign in the year of his death.

Florentius Radewyn

1350

1400

Cofounder of the Brethren of the Common Life, along with GERHARD GROOTE, who inspired him to a consecrated life. Radewyn established the first house at Deventer, Netherlands, where those who wanted a warmer, personal religious experience could come. Although Radewyn was a mystic, he abhorred radical excesses and insisted that his disciples maintain churchly forms. After GROOTE's death in 1384, he became the leader and organizer.

Geoffrey Chaucer
Knight of Kent

c 1340
London, England

Oct. 25, 1400
London, England

Father of English poetry. Chaucer studied the Latin classics and composed poetry to enrich the English language. His *Canterbury Tales*, 23 stories in verse told by pilgrims, reveals the regimen of everyday life in fourteenth century England. Chaucer was the son of a well-to-do merchant whose connections landed him a variety of jobs in the royal household, 1357–70. In 1386, Chaucer was elected to Parliament. He represented England to various embassies, which accounted for his nine visits to the European Continent, 1368–87. Finances were often a challenge for Chaucer, especially when his benefactors were out of current political favor. Prince JOHN OF GAUNT, and later, his widow Catherine Swynford, were Chaucer's greatest patrons. Through John's influence, both kings Richard II and Henry IV (ruled: 1399–1413) granted Chaucer state pensions. Chaucer embraced JOHN WYCLIFFE's writings and suffered imprisonment as a result. He married Philippa de Roet in 1366. She died in August 1369 from the plague. Chaucer is buried in Poet's Corner in Westminster Abbey. Other writings were *Book of the Duchess, Legends of Good Women, Troilus and Criseyde, House of Fame* and *The Parliament of Birds*.

Thomas of Sitney

1331
Sitney, Bohemia (Czechoslovkia)

1401

Pre-reformation preacher of reform in Bohemia (westeern Czechoslovakia). Thomas denounced corruption rampant among the clergy. He stressed the centrality of the Bible and urged regular observance of the Lord's Supper. Thomas was another one of those powerful preachers who aroused Bohemia by his oratory and prepared the way for JOHN HUSS.

William of Wickham
William of Wykeham

Summer 1324
Wickham, England

Sept. 27, 1404
South Waltham, England

Bishop of Winchester, 1367 on, and Lord Chancellor, 1368–71 and 1389–91. He encountered the enmity of the anti-clerical party of JOHN OF GAUNT in a bitter power struggle during King Edward III's last days when, because of the king's senility, William virtually led the government. Impeached and punished, William won a pardon when King Richard II took the throne. William of Wickham founded New College of Oxford (1380) and St. Mary's College at Winchester (1387), the first public school. He rebuilt Winchester Cathedral, 1395–1404, making it a Gothic masterpiece.

Juliana of Norwich

c 1342
Norwich, England

c 1413
Norwich, England

English mystic, who lived as an anchoress (female recluse) outside St. Julian's Church in Norwich. Juliana claims to have received 15 revelations in five hours, May 8, 1373. These visions of Christ's death and the Holy Trinity were put together in her influential book, *Revelations of Divine Love*. Juliana believed that God revealed Himself in life, light, and love.

John Huss
Jan Hus

July 6, 1369
Husinec, Bohemia (Czechoslovakia)

July 6, 1415
Constance, Germany

Bohemian reformer. Huss, along with WYCLIFFE and SAVONAROLA, paved the way for the Reformation that followed 100 years later. At the University of Prague he was dean of the philosophical faculty (1401) and chaplain of the Bethlehem Chapel (1402) and rector (1403). Huss was a fearless preacher who cried out against the sins of the clergy and the Church. He exalted the Scriptures, translated some of WYCLIFFE's sermons, and felt that the Church should be known for Christ-like living rather than by its sacraments. His opposition to the sale of indulgences resulted in his being forbidden to preach. Excommunication followed in 1410, which forced him to retire from his rectorship at the University of Prague. In 1412, Huss was exiled from the city after calling Pope Gregory XII (reigned: 1406–15) the Antichrist. With the end of his formal religious responsibilities, Huss used the written word producing *The Church and Simony* (1413). The Bohemian nation rallied behind him. Huss was promised protection, if he would present his case to the Council of Constance (called to end the multiple papal offices/conflicts, and deal with heretical views, 1414–18). Once he arrived in Germany in 1414, he was arrested. The Council thought the Reformation of the Church included the suppression of Bohemian "heresy." Huss was not permitted to present and defend his own views, but instead was expected to answer the voluminous (65+) false charges drummed up against him. Huss was imprisoned, named a heretic, condemned, and burned at the stake. As he died, he said, "What I have taught with my lips, I now seal with my blood." He then repeated Psalm 31 and said, "Into Thy hands, I commend my spirit."

Jerome of Prague

c 1370/ 1371
Prague, Czechoslovakia

May 30, 1416
Constance, Germany

Bohemian reformer and companion of JOHN HUSS. Jerome visited Oxford and copied some of the works of WYCLIFFE. He frequently aroused the Prague populace to public disturbances by his intemperate oratory. He was asked by the King of Poland to set up the University of Cracow and by the King of Hungary to preach at the palace. He was excommunicated in 1409. In 1410, he was imprisoned in Vienna for his support of WYCLIFFE, but escaped into Monrovia. In 1411, he publicly burned the bull for a crusade against Ladislaus of Naples (ruled: 1386–1414) and the papal indulgences. In 1414, Jerome followed HUSS to the Council of Constance, to aid if possible, but he was captured and tortured for 18 months before being burned at the stake. Jerome was well educated and eloquent in his oratory. As he died, he sang, "This soul in flames I offer, Christ, to Thee. Bring thy torch, had I feared death, I'd have avoided it."

John Oldcastle
The good Lord Cobham

c 1378
Almeley, England

Dec. 14/25, 1417
London, England

Leader and the most prestigious martyr of the Lollard movement. He was a strong follower of WYCLIFFE. Oldcastle held a series of prominent posts in the English government including the rank of general in the French wars. In 1395, he wrote a book exposing the corruptions of the Church. He married his third wife Joan, granddaughter of Lord Cobham, in 1409 to obtain his peerage. He espoused the Lollard cause in 1410 and was accused of heresy in 1413. Oldcastle was captured, hanged, and buried alive. He was transformed by SHAKESPEARE into the character of Falstaff.

Euthymius

1419
Backovo, Bulgaria

Slavic author who started Bulgarian religious writings which influenced the Christian development of Serbia, Romania and Russia. Euthymius established a monastery near Trnovo, in northern Greece in 1376. Euthymius was the last patriarch of Trnovo. He was an eloquent and effective preacher. When the area was overrun by the Turks in 1393, he was exiled to a monastery in southern Bulgaria, where he completed his translation of the Greek liturgy and died.

Vincent Ferrer
Vincent Ferrier

Jan. 23, 1350
Valencia, Spain

April 5, 1419
Vannes, France

Spanish Dominican priest and famous preacher. Ferrer taught at the local Cathedral school, 1384–99. He held huge, open-air church rallies throughout southern and central Europe. Enormous crowds heard him in France, Switzerland, and northern Italy, 1399 on. He worked from 1408–16 to revitalize the spiritual life of Spain. Ferrer was confessor and supporter of antipope Benedict XIII (reigned: 1394–1409) and saw many Jewish and Moslem converts, 1394–1417.

Wenceslaus IV
Wenzel

Feb. 26, 1361
Nuremburg, Germany

Aug. 16, 1419
Prague, Czechoslavakia

King of Bohemia, 1378–1417, and Holy Roman Emperor and emperor of Germany, 1378–1400, when he came into full power in Bohemia. Wenceslaus had to abdicate as emperor (1400), but regained the throne (1404). He was seized and imprisoned at least two times, 1393–94 and 1402, and had a dubious reputation as a tyrannical and cruel leader. Wenceslaus favored JOHN HUSS, but, because of his tenuous position and vacillating attitude, he was unable to save HUSS from martyrdom.

Nicholas of Hereford

1350
Hereford, England

1420
Coventry, England

Lollard writer and early English translator of the Scriptures. He worked with WYCLIFFE to translate the Bible from the Latin Vulgate to English. Most scholars believe Nicholas did most of the Old Testament, while WYCLIFFE did the New Testament. Nicholas was made chancellor of Hereford Cathedral and became a Carthusian monk at Coventry. He began to preach Lollard doctrines in 1382 and was excommunicated. He was imprisoned in Rome (1385) and Nottingham, England (1391). He died in St. Anne's Monastery.

Dorothy of Prussia

c 1350
Prussia?

c 1420

Prussian (Hungarian) lady who devoted herself to an ascetic life in 1394. Prior to her reclusive life, Dorothy gave birth to nine children. After her death, many miracles were reported at her grave.

Jan Zizka
John Ziska

c 1358–1360
Trocnov, Bohemia (Czechoslovakia)

Oct. 11, 1424
Pribyslav, Poland

Military leader of the Hussites (a politico-religious party organized after JOHN HUSS' death who waged fierce civil war from 1419–1434). They were divided between the Taborites (Hussite spin-off led by Zizka till 1423) who merged with the Bohemian Brethren and the Calixtines (Hussite spin-off who leaned toward Lutheranism). Zizka distinguished himself at the Battle of Tannenberg (1410) and captured Prague (1421), winning battle after battle for the cause of religious freedom. He was blinded at the Battle of Rabi in 1421. The bubonic plague (inflammatory swelling of a lymphatic gland, in groin or armpit) snuffed out his life.

Hubert van Eyck

c 1366/1370 — Sept. 18, 1426
Maeseyck, Belgium — Ghent, Belgium

Flemish painter. Hubert tutored his younger brother, Jan, and both of them settled in Bruges. Hubert started the famous, "Adoration of the Lamb" altarpiece for the St. Bavon Cathedral in Ghent. JAN finished this work in 1432.

John Purvey

c 1353–1354 — c 1428
Lathbury, England

Bible translator who was associated with JOHN WYCLIFFE at Lutterworth and became a leader of the Lollard party. While imprisoned in 1390, he wrote a commentary entitled *Revelation*. He was imprisoned in 1390 and briefly in 1421. Purvey revised The Wycliffe/Nicholas of HerefordBible into a literal and unidiomatic (no expression peculiar to a language) style in 1388. He also wrote against the corruption of the Church in a work called *Ecclesiae Regimen*.

Andrei Rublev

c 1360 — Jan. 29, 1430
Muscow (Moscow), Russia

Renowned painter of the Russian Church. Rublev was honored by the Russian Orthodox Church and is best remembered for his famous icon, "The Hospitality of Abraham" (also known as "The Old Testament Trinity"). He became a monk and learned iconography (symbolic representation by means of an image) from the famed artist, Theophanes the Greek. Rublev died at the Spasso-Andronikon Monastery.

Joan of Arc
Jeanne d'Arc or Darc—Maid of Orleans

Jan. 6, 1412 — May 30, 1431
Domremy, France — Rouen, France

National heroine of France. Joan was one of history's most remarkable women, despite not being either beautiful or cultured. A peasant girl who, with common sense, devotion to principle, natural intelligence, and patriotism, led her French king's army of 6,000 at age 17 against the British invaders. She persuaded CHARLES VII of her mission, February 27, 1429, revealing her spiritual calling at age 13. She was given command of an army which forced the English to retreat, giving the French a victory at the Battle of Orleans, May 8, 1429. As a result, CHARLES VII was crowned at Rheims, July 17, 1429. Joan was captured by the British, May 24, 1430, tried for heresy and sorcery, and burned at the stake at age 19. In 1456, a court declared her innocent. May 30 is a national holiday in France in her honor. There is a 90-mile Arc River in France. It still is not clear as to what "of Arc" means. She never married. Her autograph is worth at least $125,000.

Nicholas of Clamanges
Nicholas de Clamanges—Nicholas Poille-vilain

c 1360 — c 1434
Clamanges, Champagne, France — Paris, France

French theologian. Nicholas was an evangelical Bible-loving Catholic who tried to end the scandalous division in the papacy. He was a professor of theology (1391) and rector (church leader in charge of a university or a congregation) at the University of Paris (1393). While serving as papal secretary at Avignon papacy headquarters, 1397–1405, he witnessed the weakness and corruption prevalent in the system. Nicholas emphasized the importance of Scriptural study and outwardly expressed his conviction that much of the problems facing the church resulted from a neglect of Bible study. He was later canon at Langres. In his writings, he turned against the excessive feast days in the church and simony among the higher clergy. He lived in voluntary exile with Carthusian monks, 1407–25. He returned to Paris to lecture at the College of Navarre. He died while retiring to a Cistercian cloister to pursue Biblical studies.

Andrew Procopius

c 1380
Bohemia (Czechoslovakia)

May 30, 1434
Lipnik (Lipany), Bohemia (Czechoslovakia)

Bohemian priest who succeeded ZIZKA as leader of the Hussite army. Andrew waged civil war to overthrow Holy Roman Emperor Sigismund (ruled: 1411–37). His branch of the Hussites known as Taborites, which he commanded after JAN ZISKA's death in 1424, continued the civil war after the rest of the Hussites agreed to the terms of the Council of Basel. On June 16, 1426, he won a huge victory over the imperial troops at Usti and-Labem (Au-Sig) and soon drove them south across the Danube. Procopius was killed at the Battle of Lipnik. This defeat of the Taborites left affairs in the hands of the moderate party, the Calixtines.

Joseph II

1439

Patriarch of Constantinople. Joseph sought reunion with Rome, but he failed in all his attempts. He was threatened by an invasion of the Muslim Turks and was pressed by the Eastern Emperor John VIII (ruled: 1425–48) and archbishop of Nicea, Bessarian to find allies. In order to combat these terrors, Joseph offered to start negotiations with Pope Nicholas V (reigned: 1447–55). Mark of Ephesus scuttled these plans, and Constantinople was eventually captured in 1453.

Margery Burnham Kempe

c 1373
Lynn, England

c 1440
Lynn, England

English visionary and mystic. Kempe's autobiography is one of the earliest in English literature. In the dedication of her *Book of Margery Kempe*, she describes her pilgrimages to Jerusalem, Rome, and Germany as well as her many mystical experiences. Kempe was the faithful mother of 14 children. She married John Kempe in 1393. They took a vow of chastity in 1413.

Jan van Eyck

c 1390
Maeseyck, Belgium

July 9, 1440
Bruges, Belgium

Flemish painter. Jan was a pupil of his older brother, HUBERT. Both of them settled in Bruges. Jan finished the famous altarpiece, "Adoration of the Lamb" (left uncompleted upon his brother's death in 1426), 1430–32. Jan's works were known for their realism. The "Madonna of Chancellor Rolin," located today in the Louvre Museum in Paris, is an outstanding example of his work. Jan also was court painter to Philip the Good (Burgundy duke ruled: 1419–67), 1425–40. He came to Bruges in 1430.

Henry Chichele

c 1362

April 12, 1443

Archbishop of Canterbury, 1414–43. Chichele had a solid upper-class home and quality education. He studied at Winchester and Oxford with an emphasis in law. He became known as one of the lawyer-bishops of the Middle Ages. He first served as a bishop at St. David's in 1408 and participated in several missions abroad. He attended the Council of Pisa, 1409 (called by cardinals to end the Great Schism—three popes claiming to head the church). Chichele upheld England's antipapal Statutes of Provisors and Praemunire (writ charging the offense of resorting to a foreign court, pope, etc.) and as a result was denied envoy authority from 1427–29. He turned his focus on education, promoting graduate studies for clergy and founded All Souls College and St. Bernard's (St. John's) at Oxford in 1437.

Bernardino

Sept. 8, 1380
Massa Marittima, Italy

May 20, 1444
Aquila, Italy

Famed Franciscan preacher who sought to bring about moral reform through emphasizing a deep personal love of Jesus Christ. Bernardino was a member of the Observants (a strict Franciscan branch), becoming a friar in 1402, and elected vicar-general, 1438–44. He preached moral rather than religious sermons calling for outward change over a spiritual change. His strong delivery frequently caused gamblers to throw away their dice and to destroy their cards. Bernardino is said to have founded or reorganized over 300 monasteries. His sermons promoted the Virgin Mary and doctrine of purgatory, along with his devotion to the holy name of Jesus. He died while on one of his many preaching tours. Siena was 33 miles southwest of Massa and evidently a headquarters for him.

Marcus (Mark) Eugenicus

1391
Constantinople (Istanbul), Turkey

c 1447

Archbishop of Ephesus and one of the representatives of the Greek Orthodox Church at the Council of Ferrara-Florence in 1438. He was unyielding in his opposition to papal demands. For the rest of his life, Eugenicus continued to oppose any union with Rome.

Fra Angelico
Guido di Pietro—Fra Giovanni da Fiesole

1387
Vicchio, Italy

March 18, 1455
Rome, Italy

Florentine painter and Dominican monk. Angelico was an outstanding painter representing the early Renaissance. His works were religious frescos of saints and angels with a distinctive intense use of pink and blue hues. He was convinced that painting Christ demanded a painter to be Christ-like. Angelico performed his work prayerfully. The Great Western Schism (three papal divisions rallying for control, 1409–18) forced him to go first to Foliano and then Cortina, where some of his greatest paintings are found. He produced brilliant works in Florence (1439–45), Rome (1445–50) and finally in Fiesole, living out the last years of his life in a monastery. Two of his most notable works are *The Coronation of the Virgin* and *The Last Judgment*. Angelico also did frescoes in two chapels of the Vatican and decorated the convent of San Marco in Florence with murals and an elaborate altarpiece.

Jacob of Misa

c 1351
Misa, Bohemia (Czechoslovakia)

Aug. 9, 1459
Prague, Czechoslovakia

Maverick pastor who insisted that withholding the cup from the laity was unwarranted during a Lord's Supper observance. Jacob was a pastor at Tina, then at the Church of St. Michael in Prague, Bohemia. He defended his views publicly in 1414 and soon after began to administer the cup to the members of his parish. Despite opposition from bishops and the university, Jacob continued to follow his beliefs. Although he believed in purgatory, his support of JOHN HUSS showed the gradual weakening of the Catholic stronghold in Europe.

Charles VII
Charles the Victorious—Charles the Well Served

Feb. 22, 1403
Paris, France

July 22, 1461
Mehun-sur-Yevre, France

King of France, 1422–61. Charles' throne was disputed by the English in 1422, and Orleans was soon besieged by the same. JOAN OF ARC came to the rescue and saved the king's cause. Charles entered Paris triumphantly in 1436. In 1438, he profited from a quarrel with Pope Nicholas V by appropriating some French tax money and putting an end to papal interference in French government. By 1453, Charles had recovered all his lands but the city of Calais. His last years saw domestic difficulties, in which his son and successor, King Louis XI (ruled: 1461–83), opposed him.

Catherine of Bologna

Sept. 8, 1413
Bologna, Italy

March 9, 1463
Bologna, Italy

Founder of the Convent of the Holy Sacrament of the Order of Poor Clares. Catherine was reared in luxury at Ferrara and was a lady of honor to Margaret d'Este for two years before entering the order of Poor Clares at Ferrara in 1430. She then began the convent in her hometown of Bologna and was the Prioress of her convent.

John Capgrave

April 21, 1393
Lynn, England

Aug. 12, 1464
Lynn, England

English historian and theologian who lectured at Oxford University. Capgrave was an ordained priest who later became a hermit of the Augustinian order at the local friary (monastery of brotherhood friars). He is credited with many theological works and is especially remembered for his *New Legends of England* (catalog of English saints) and *Life of St. Catherine* .

Johann Gutenberg

Feb. 23, 1396
Mainz, Germany

Feb. 23, 1468
Mainz, Germany

Inventor of printing from movable type. It is believed that Gutenberg's invention began while he lived in Strasbourg. His printing experiments were probably done there between 1436–46 and included the use of molds, metal type, special press methods, and oil-based inks, which became the prototype for modern printing. He then returned to Mainz in 1448, where the actual printing was accomplished. Gutenberg's work is considered one of the key inventions in history. The first example of printing was his masterpriece, the 42-line *Gutenberg Bible* (1450–55). The 42-line *Latin Gutenberg* (Mazarin) *Bible* (first book printed with movable types) appeared in 1455. It was later called the *Mazarin Bible* when it was discovered in the library of Cardinal Jules Mazarin in 1760 in Paris. It was JEROME's Latin Vulgate Edition. In 1456, 200 copies were printed. Duplicating the written word in an affordable and rapid manner introduced literacy and the truth of Scripture to the common man. Gutenberg also published a *Psalter* (1457). Unfortunately, Johann Faust (died: c 1466), a goldsmith (makes and sells gold) with whom Gutenberg had formed a partnership (1450), demanded repayment of money advanced to further the printing enterprise (1455). A settlement was reached whereby Gutenberg was forced to abandon his claims to his invention. With the help of Conrad Humery, Gutenberg again established himself in the printing business. The first German Bible was not printed until 1462 in Strasbourg. In 1465, recognition was restored to Gutenberg by Archbishop Adolph of Nassau, elector of Mainz. One poll shows him as the most influential person of the fifteenth century.

Fra Filippo Lippi

1406
Florence, Italy

Oct. 9, 1469
Spoleto, Italy

Florentine painter of religous subjects. Lippi was a Carmelite monk in Florence, 1421–31. In 1437, he produced his first well-known painting, *Madonna*. Early in his career, he created a series of frescoes in the Prato Cathedral where he became prior. The most noted of his frescos were *Life of St. John the Baptist* and *Life of St. Stephen*. At the age of 56, he was freed from his vows as a Carmelite monk and eloped with a nun, Lucrezia Buti, who bore him two children. Lippi's most famous paintings are *Coronation of the Virgin, Adoration of the Magi,* and *The Annunciation*. He died while working on the *Death and Coronation of the Virgin* in the Spoleto Cathedral. His most important pupil was ALESSANDRO BOTTICELLI. His paintings are some of the best in history.

Thomas à Kempis
Thomas Hemerken or Hammerlein—Haemmerken (Maleclus)

c 1380
Kempen, Prussia (Germany)

July 25, 1471
near Zwolle, Netherlands

Ecclesiastic, mystic, and writer. Kempis wrote *The Imitation of Christ*. This Latin work was the most famous book until *Pilgrim's Progress*. In 1407, he entered the Augustine convent at Mount St. Agnes which is near Zwolle. Thomas lived a simple, mystic life. He was ordained priest (1413) and a subprior (1429). Thomas spent the rest of his life directing novices, writing, and preaching. Some advocate that his famed book was a collection of sayings from several monks, with Thomas only the editor. Some have alleged GERHARD GROOTE wrote it in Dutch and Kempis translated it into Latin. Most contend however that the entire work was authored by Thomas alone.

"Man proposes but God disposes."

Gennadius II
Georgius Scholarius

1405
Constantinople (Istanbul), Turkey

1472
Mount Menoikeion, Greece

Greek scholar and prelate. Gennadius was the patriarch of Constantinople, 1453–59, and he was one of the most prolific writers of his age. Gennadius wrote more than 100 works, many in manuscript only. At first, he favored a projected union of the Greek and Latin Churches when he served as an imperial counselor to Emperor Johannes. Later Gennadius opposed this plan. He died at a monastery in Macedonia where he retired in 1459.

Dionysius the Carthusian

1402
Ryckel, Belgium

March 17/21, 1472
Roermonde, Netherlands

Writer and member of the Carthusian order in 1423 who wrote accurate Old Testament and New Testament commentaries. These and his other theological works were very popular. As a mystic, he was one of the bright lights of the Rhenish (regions bordering Rhine River) school of spirituality, and his *De Contemplatione* was considered a spiritual classic. He was at the Carthusian monastery at Roermond, 1424–51. He assisted Cardinal Nicholas of Cusa (served: 1448–64) in reform visitation in the Rhineland (1451–52) and on a trip to monasteries that needed reformation (1452–64). From 1465–69, he founded a monastery at Herzogenbuech. He was known for his saintly life, great learning and work capacity. Dionysius was later in charge of the order at Bois Le Dec.

Johann Goch

c 1400
Goch, Prussia (Germany)

March 28, 1475
near Mechlin, Germany

Pre-Reformation orthodox clergyman who spent his life teaching the supreme authority of the Bible. He was an opponent of scholasticism. He seems to have been trained in one of the schools of the Brethren of the Common Life, then studied at Cologne, followed by educational pursuits in Paris. Goch was a member of the house established by Brethren of the Common Life at Harderwijk and rector of the house in Gouda. In 1451, he arrived in Mechlin, where he stayed until his death. Goch founded the priory of Thabor for canoness' (woman living under a rule, but not under a vow) of St. Augustine in 1459, over which he presided. He was a mystic who sought an intimate union with God. His major work was *De Liberatate Christian* (1473, published in 1521). His theological convictions are summarized in the statement: "From God, through God, to God."

John of Wesel

1400
Oberwesel am Rhein, Germany

c 1481
Mainz, Germany

Pre-Reformation Catholic reformer and preacher. John was a student, rector, and a professor at the University of Erfurt, where he distinguished himself. After 1450, he published a treatise against indulgences. He preached at Worms, Germany, 1463–80, after serving at Basel, Switzerland, and Mainz. John was seized, tried, imprisoned, and brought before the Inquisition (Catholic tribunal engaged to combat, supress, and punish heresy) in 1479 for denying the authority of the pope and the councils. He was confined in the Augustinian monastery in Mainz. He died there from the after-effects of torture and maltreatment.

Nicholas of Flue

March 21, 1417
Flueli (near Sachseln), Switzerland

March 21, 1487
Sachseln, Switzerland

Famed Swiss political leader who served with distinction as a soldier in 1439, cantonal (state or division of Switzerland) counselor, and judge. Nicholas was happily married with ten children but, at the age of 50, he left his family with their approval and became a hermit at Ranft. He was known for his holiness and wise counsel and was instrumental in averting a civil war between Swiss cantons in 1481.

Johann (John) Wessel

c 1420
Groningen, Netherlands

Oct. 4, 1489
Groningen, Netherlands

Teacher, theologian, mystic, and pre-Reformation reformer belonging to the Brethren of Common Life. Wessel lived part of the time near Zwolle and part of the time at Groningen after 1479. Prior to that, he was at Paris, Rome, and Basel. Wessel was influential in building up the University of Heidelberg and was active in German circles. Many of his teachings and writings were against the philosophies of the Roman Catholic Church. Said to be a forerunner of Luther, who said of him, "Our two minds agree." He denied transubstantiation, opposed the sale of indulgences and priestly celibacy, and emphasized the authority of Scripture. Wessel also denied the pope's infallibility. He died in prison after being convicted of heresy. He was a strong humanist.

Giovanni Pico della Mirandola

Feb. 24, 1463
Mirandola, Italy

Nov. 17, 1494
Florence, Italy

Philosopher and scholar of Hebrew and the Cabala (occult, secret doctrine or science). In 1484, Pico went to Florence. He offered to debate anyone on any of 900 subjects, but when forbidden by the pope to do so, because some of his views were considered heretical, he returned to France. Pico was famous as a Platonist and humanist who tried to combine Greek and Christian ideas. His Hebrew studies influenced the Italian Renaissance. Under SAVONAROLA, Pico was led to become a missionary preacher, but he died suddenly at the age of 31.

Gabriel Biel

c 1425
Speyer, Germany

Dec. 7, 1495
Schonau (near Tübingen), Germany

Scholastic philosopher and theological professor, who was also a diligent preacher. In 1462, Biel was a cathedral preacher in Mainz. In 1468, he joined the Brethren House Marlenthal near Grieslyein, and soon became prior of St. Mark's in Butzbach. He transformed St. Amandus Church in Urich to a Brethren of Common Life Church in 1477. Biel was a professor of theology at the Unversity of Tübingen, 1484–95, which he had helped found in 1477. He wrote on the limits of human reason and the need for revelation, which later influenced LUTHER and MELANCHTHON. Biel believed that church councils were above the pope. He also opposed transubstantiation. He wrote *Epitome of Ockham's Writings* (1445), *Lecture and Exposition of the Canon of the Mass* (1488, 1499), and *Sermons* (1499).

Girolamo Savonarola

Sept. 21, 1452
Ferrara, Italy

May 23, 1498
Florence, Italy

Florentine Dominican friar and monk, preacher, and reformer who followed in the footsteps of WYCLIFFE and HUSS. Savonarola entered a Dominican Monastery in 1474–81 and became a famous preacher and teacher. He preached in Brescia (1484–85), and then went to Florence in 1490. In 1492, Savonarola replaced Lorenzo as mayor of Florence, becoming political as well as spiritual leader of the city, serving as prior of San Mark, 1491 onward. He named Christ king of the city and ruled as a virtual dictator condemning its evils, 1494–96. Refusing a papal summons and bribery, Savonarola proceeded to denounce Pope Alexander VI (reigned: 1492–1503) and his nobles for corruption and immorality. As a result, he was forbidden to preach (1495), excommunicated (1496), lost his base of support, imprisoned, tried, hanged, and his body burned. His favorite Bible verses were Matthew 3:2, 10.

Marsilio Ficino

Oct. 19, 1433
Figline, Italy

Oct. 1, 1499
Careggi (near Florence), Italy

Philosopher, physician, and priest. Ficino was the leader of the Platonic Academy at Florence, famous for its part in the classical studies of the Renaissance. After 1462, his villa at Careggi became the site of the Florentine Academy. In 1473, he became rector of two Florentine Churches and enjoyed a canonry (office or benofice of a canon) in the cathedral. An expert of Plato's, (Greek philosopher, 423–337 b.c.) writings, Ficino revived stern European interest in classical origins which influenced scholars such as LEFEVRE and John Colet, (dean of St. Paul's, London 1505–19). He upheld the superiority of Christianity but saw a harmony among all religions directed to one, true God. His chief philosophical works were *De Christiana Religione* (1474) and *Theologia Platonica* (1482).

"All souls possess a desire for truth and virtue."

John Alcock

1430
Beverly, England

Oct. 1, 1500
Wisbeach Castle, England

Catholic bishop of Rochester, 1472; of Worcester, 1476; and of Ely 1486; and for a time, chancellor of England. Alcock was educated at Cambridge, where he later founded Jesus College in 1496. His most important work was *The Hill of Perfection*. In 1476, he became Lord President of Wales and tutor to future king of England,

Edward V (ruled: 1483). He was appointed by Richard III (ruled: 1483–85) as a commissioner for liaison with Scotland (1484) to negotiate a treaty beween the two countries (1486).

Christopher Columbus

Oct. 12, 1451
Genoa, Italy

May 20, 1506
Valladolid, Spain

Founder of the Americas – the most famous traveler in history. Columbus was a skilled navigator and sailor, who discovered the "New World." He was devoutly committed to Christ. He was married to Felipe Perestrello around 1478. On August 3, 1492, he set sail from Portugal with 90 men in three vessels: *The Nina, The Pinta,* and *The Santa Maria.* Upon landing on the island of San Salvador ("Holy Savior") in the Caribbean, October 12, 1492, he first "thanked God for His goodness" and then planted the "sacred cross." Cuba (October 28) and Hispaniola (Haiti; December 6) followed. He followed this exploration with three other trans–Atlantic trips in 1493, 1498, and 1502. These four voyages to the New World cost less than a modern–day new car. The gold he brought back from the Americas gilded the ceiling of the church of Santa Maria Maggiore in Rome. Columbus established a colony of 40 men on the island of Hispaniola and built the first church in the New World in 1494. Evangelizing an area was as important to Columbus as was the initial discovery process. He signed his will, "Christ Bearer." Columbus' last words were: "O, Lord, into Thy hands I commend my spirit." He died alone in poverty and neglected. He is buried in the cathedral in Seville. He was a slaveholder. His autograph is worth at least $500,000.

Francis of Paola

March 27, 1416
Paola, Italy

April 2, 1507
Plessis–les–Tours, France

Founder of the Order of the Hermits of St. Francis of Assisi (Order of Minims in 1493) (order of friars who regarded themselves as the least religious of all), approved by Pope Sixtus IV (reigned: 1471–84) in 1474. This ascetic Franciscan became a hermit, and started his unofficial order (1435) building a church and house (1453). Francis endeavored to outdo Francis of Assisi through his commitment to a life of austerity. He was known for his holiness and was sought by kings for spiritual guidance. His vows included abstaining from all meat, fowl, eggs, and dairy products. He evidently lived to age 91 as a vegetarian.

Henry VII

Jan. 28, 1457
Pembroke Castle, Wales

April 21, 1509
Richmond, England

King of England, 1485–1509. Henry invaded England from Brittany, France, defeated King Richard III at Bosworth Field, and was made king. He was the first of the Tudor kings and achieved immense control over church affairs in England, paving the way for his son, King Henry VIII (ruled: 1509–47), to sever the ties with Rome. Henry VII married Elizabeth, the eldest daughter of King Edward IV (ruled: 1461–83), on January 18, 1486. He died a wealthy man with his dynasty well established.

Johann Geiler Von Kaysersberg

March 16, 1445
Schaffhausen, Switzerland

March 10, 1510
Strasbourg, Germany

Pre–Lutheran reformer and forceful preacher. Geiler became known as the "German Savonarola." Geiler began his career as a scholar and lecturer at Freiburg University in 1476. From his pulpit in the Cathedral of Strasbourg, 1478 onward, he denounced the evils of his day, earning him wide acclaim. His sermons were mystical yet they dealt with everyday life. However he shared in the witch hunt and hatred of the Jews.

Alessandro Botticelli
Alessandro di Mariano del Filipepi Botticelli

1445
Florence, Italy

May 17, 1510
Florence, Italy

Gifted painter of the Renaissance era. Botticelli studied under FRA FILIPPO LIPPI and LEONARDO DA VINCI. His paintings include: *The Adoration of the Magi, The Annnunciation, Magnificat, The Burial of the Crucified*, and *The Nativity*. Botticelli's frescoes entitled, *Life of Moses* were painted in the Sistine Chapel. His two most famous works are considered to be *Primavera* and *The Birth of Venus* (1485). These works are still on display in the Florence Gallery. Botticelli's conversion took place at one of the meetings led by the Italian Dominican reformer, SAVONAROLA in Florence. After this experience, Botticelli concentrated on religious topics—rejecting pagan themes. His talents were greatly used to glorify the Lord.

Catherine of Genoa

1447
Genoa, Italy

Sept. 14, 1510
Genoa, Italy

Italian mystic who claimed to see visions. Catherine was married in 1463 to Giuliano Adorni (died 1474). She was converted in 1473. While a very young widow, she responded to one of her visions and devoted the rest of her life caring for the poor and ill. She was especially helpful during the plagues that decimated Genoa (1497–1501). Catherine's deeds of mercy and her many writings were well received and appreciated. She worked with the Ladies of Mercy in the hospital of St. Lazarus in Genoa as rector, nursing her second husband's fatal illness in 1497–98. Her teachings were contained in her *Dialogues on the Soul and Body* and *Treatise on Purgatory*.

Joseph of Volokolamsk
Joseph Panin

1439

Sept. 9, 1515

Orthodox theologian and monk, known as the "Father of Medieval Russia." In 1477, Joseph became abbot at Borovsk and attempted to initiate ascetical reforms. He clashed with royal patrons, especially Prince Ivan III Vasilyevich (grand duke of Moscow, ruled: 1462–1505). Joseph resigned and then founded the celebrated monastery of Volokolamsk near Moscow. Here he finally was able to apply his ideas for reorganization in the church. This monastery became a center for social improvement and popular devotion, with doctrine opposing Judaizing and Christian sects and standing strong against Westernizing influences. He authored *Prosvetitel*. Joseph's monastic reforms emphasized community life and inspired a spiritual renewal in the Russian Orthodox Church.

Fra Bartolommeo
Baccio della Porta

c March 28, 1472
Soffignano, Italy

Oct. 31, 1517
Florence, Italy

Great Renaissance painter. Bartolommeo was a student of DA VINCI, yet he also learned from MICHAELANGELO. He influenced Raphael (fellow painter), with his unique style of handling drapery, creating a flowing fullness. He admired SAVONAROLA, was converted by him, and joined the Dominican order in 1500–04 in a Florence monastery (San Marco). Bartolommeo's works extended from the early *Annunciation* in 1497 to his more gentle *Pieta* in 1515. In 1509 he assumed a leader's role within the Contemporary School of Painting in Florence. His most noted work was *Saint Mark*. He died of malaria.

Leonardo da Vinci

April 15, 1452
Vinci, Italy

May 2, 1519
Cloux (near Amboise), France

Scientist, inventor, Renaissance painter, sculptor, architect, musician and art critic. In 1482, da Vinci left Florence and entered the service of the Duke of Milan as an engineer and architect until 1499. During this time, he painted his famous *Last Supper* (1495–98), a fresco which still hangs in Milan in the chapel of Santa Maria delle Grazie and is considered the grandest monument of religious art. During the Napoleonic Wars, French soldiers used the painting in target practice, shooting at Christ's head, explaining why the face of Christ is almost obliterated. He also painted *Mona Lisa* which hangs in the Louvre. The real name of the painting is *La Gianconda* and it is a portrait of a middle-class woman (Fran Cesco Gioconda), wife of a merchant named Goacondo Leonidas. The painting is less than 2 feet by 2 feet. Da Vinci was one of the greatest minds of the Renaissance-also being an accomplished inventor, botanist, astronomer, geologist, and anatomist. One of his most practical inventions was the scissors. From 1500–17, he lived in Florence, and then returned to France at the invitation of King Francis I (ruled: 1515–47). He was number one on one pollster's all-time genius list.

William Grocyn

c 1446
Colerne, England

Oct. 1519
Maidstone, England

English humanist and Renaissance scholar. Grocyn served as prebendary (honorary canon with stipend or land grant) at Lincoln Cathedral in 1485, and studied in Italy, 1488–91. In 1491, he began to lecture on the classics at Exeter College, Oxford. He eventually became the first professor of Greek at Oxford. Thomas More (Lord Chancellor, 1478–1535), was one of his pupils, and the famed philosopher, Erasmus (humanist, 1466–1538), lived with Grocyn while Grocyn was a rector at Shepperton. Grocyn became paralyzed in 1518.

Franz von Sickingen

March 2, 1481
Ebernburg (near Kreuznach), Germany

May 7, 1523
Castle Landstuhl, Germany

Lutheran knight of the German Empire who devoted his life to military activity and seemed to have a passion to protect the oppressed. Von Sickingen was constantly repressing the despotism of princes and the arrogance of priests. He and ULRICH VON HUTTEN headed a league to forcibly introduce the Reformation. In 1522–23, he headed a league to extend the Reformation throughout Germany and to secularize the land of ecclesiastic princes. He hurt the Reformation more than helping it, as his goals were for political advantage. Von Sickingen died of wounds received in the Knight's War as his fortress was besieged by the elector of Treves. The coalition that defeated him was the elector archbishop in Treves, the Landgrave of Hesse, and the Count Palatine of the Rhine. His castles were used for persecuted reformers. He died near Kaiserslautern.

Ulrich von Hutten

April 21, 1488
Castle Steckelberg (near Zulda), Germany

Aug. 29, 1523
Ufenau Island, Lake Zurich, Switzerland

Humanist, poet, satirist, and Lutheran knight of the German Empire. About 1505, Von Hutten fled from the Benedictine monastery in Fulda, and began a scholars and soldiers vagabond life. As such, Hutten spent time in Germany, Italy, and Switzerland. Holy Roman Emperor Maximilian I (ruled: 1493–1519) crowned him poet laureate in 1517. The assassination of his father by the Duke of Wurtemburg stirred his revengeful pen. Hutten's pamphlets gained him popularity as he urged freedom from the power of Rome, which caused his dismissal from the archbishop's service in 1520. He offered his help to LUTHER in 1520, but was declined. Von Hutten was a Latin satirist under Maximilian I and joined FRANZ VON SICKINGEN in his physical battle with the elector of Treves. Von Hutten favored a union of the German princes against the pope. He fled to Switzerland after SICKINGEN's death. Erasmus refused to help him, because of his excesses, in Basel in 1522. Going to Zurich, ZWINGLI befriended him and found him a flock to lead. He died from venereal disease.

Johann von Staupitz

c 1469
Motterwitz/Moderwitz, Germany

Dec. 28, 1524
Salzburg, Austria

Mentor who helped LUTHER find the truth. A scholar in head and heart, Staupitz was asked by FREDERICK III OF SAXONY to help found the new university at Wittenberg. In 1502 he was made professor and dean, and in 1503 was chosen vicar general of all Augustinians in Germany. Staupitz ordered them to read the Bible at meal time. He met LUTHER at Erfurt in 1505 and became his spiritual advisor. When LUTHER was distressed, he said, "Your thoughts are not of Christ, for Christ does not terrify, but console." LUTHER in a letter said of him "through whom the light of the gospel was first made to shine from the darkness into our hearts." From 1509–14, he gave LUTHER valuable advice, so that LUTHER said, "I owe everything to Staupitz." He stressed the doctrine of election. When the papal see suspected him of being an adherent of LUTHER and pressed him for action against LUTHER, he relinquished his office as vicar general, in 1520, and went to Salzburg as court chaplain, joining the Benedictines.

Allessandro Geraldini

1455
Italy

March 8, 1525
Santo Domingo, Dominican Repulic

Bishop and historian. Geraldini was a Catholic churchman who presented the idea of sending COLUMBUS to the New World. He was later the first Catholic bishop of Santo Domingo from 1520 until his death. Geraldini built the first cathedral in the Americas. This church became a tribute to CHRISTOPHER COLUMBUS. His bones were later entombed there along with crowns and jewels from the court of Queen Isabella of Castile (ruled: 1474–1504) and King Ferdinand V of Castile (ruled: 1474–1516). Geraldini set up orderly procedures of government on the island of Hispaniola after the chaos left by the Spanish conquest. He recorded his journeys and wrote about the island.

Frederick III of Saxony
Frederick the Wise

Jan. 17, 1463
Torgau, Germany

May 5, 1525
Lochav (near Annaburg), Germany

Lutheran elector (German prince entitled to help elect the Holy Roman Emperor); **duke of Saxony in 1486–1525, and founder of the University of Wittenberg in 1502**. Frederick later appointed LUTHER and MELANCHTHON as professors in 1511. He did not commit himself to the Reformation but made it happen, shielding LUTHER from harm. His secretary, GEORG SPALATIN, informed him of LUTHER's actions. He actually saved him and the Protestant Reformation (1518) when he shifted the hearing of LUTHER's case from Rome to Augsburg and again by removing him to Wartburg after the Diet of Worms (1521). Frederick III was mostly opposed to Rome's money hungry agents. He remained a Catholic; but on his deathbed, with SPALATIN's help, he accepted evangelical doctrines, the Lord's Supper, and fasts. He died at Lochau Castle, with LUTHER preaching his funeral and MELANCHTHON giving an oration. Strangely, he never met LUTHER.

Thomas Muntzer

Dec. 20, 1488
Stolberg am Harz, Germany

May 30, 1525
Muhlhausen, Germany

German Anabaptist demagogue. Muntzer served briefly with MARTIN LUTHER, 1519–20, before breaking with him. He wanted the Reformation to be more radical. He outraged both Protestants and Catholics by his senseless destruction of church property. From 1514–20, he was provost at Frohse. Muntzer inspired the Peasant's War 1524–25 and disliked LUTHER for his condemnation of it. Muntzer preached in Zwickau, 1520–23, associated with the Zwickau prophets and also in Alstedt in 1523 before the battle of Frankenhausen. He emphasized the "inner word" and baptism of the Holy Spirit, direct revelation in visions, Holy Spirit possession and guidance, as well as radical social reform and the imminent return of Christ. He was defeated by PHILIP OF HESSE at the battle of Frankenhausen, May 15, 1525, and beheaded.

Peter M. Aughiera
Pietro via Aughiera

Feb. 2, 1455
Aughiera, Italy

1526
Granada, Spain

Cleric stationed at the Spanish Court from 1517 on, at the time of Ferdinand and Isabella's reign and the epochal voyages of COLUMBUS. In 1505, he was appointed dean of the Cathedral at Granada. Peter wrote the first account of the discovery of America, *De Rebus Oceanicis et Novo Orbe* (1516). He is sometimes known as "Peter Martyr." Only three people have been given this distinction.

Thomas Wyttenbach

1472
Biel, Switzerland

1526
Biel, Switzerland

Pre–Reformation Church humanist and reformer who taught at Basel. ZWINGLI was one of his converts and pupils. A one time priest from Biel, Wyttenbach was one of the earliest to advocate the sole authority of the Bible. He also believed that indulgences were useless and that Christ's sacrifice on the cross was sufficient for forgiveness of sins. His marriage in 1524 led to his deposition.

Conrad Grebel

1498
Zurich, Switzerland

August, 1526
Maienfeld, Switzerland

Swiss Anabaptist leader during the tragic days of the movement's beginning in Zurich. Grebel returned to Zurich in 1520, after completing his education at Basel, Vienna, and Paris. Converted (1522), he was greatly influenced by ULRICH ZWINGLI, but separated from him (1523). The Anabaptist movement was founded by the Swiss Brethren who opposed ZWINGLI. The dispute was over infant vs. adult believers' baptism and a state-type church vs. believers only. On January 21, 1525, he performed the first adult baptism in modern history, when he baptized GEORGE BLAUROCK (BLAUROCK, in turn, baptized others). This was by sprinkling in the home of FELIX MANZ. A NT church was founded as a result. He became an Anabaptist evangelist, 1525–26. Weakened by imprisonment, he died of the plague soon after.

Hans Hut

c 1490
Hain, Franconia/Bavaria, (Germany)

1527
Augsburg, Germany

German Anabaptist evangelist and demagogue who was a self–appointed "prophet." Hut came into conflict with the Anabaptists in Weissenfels in 1524. He preached a terrifying message of speedy final judgment executed by a Turkish invasion that would end the Holy Roman Empire and usher in the final days. His message met with disagreement by HUBMAIER and others. Hut was imprisoned at Augsburg on September 15, 1527 and following torture, was returned unconscious to his cell. He tried to escape by lighting the straw where he laid in prison, but died eight days later from burns he received.

Felix Manz

c 1490–98
Jan. 5, 1527
Zurich, Switzerland

Swiss Anabaptist reformer whose drowning made him the first Protestant to be martyred at the hands of other Protestants. Manz was a member of the Swiss Brethren who insisted upon believers' baptism. The first adult baptism in modern history took place in his home, January 21, 1525, with GREBEL baptizing BLAUROCK. He was imprisoned numerous times before the Zurich Council condemned him to death by drowning in the Limmat River.

Johannes Denck

Nov. 1495
Heybock, Bavaria (Germany)
Nov. 1527
Basel, Switzerland

Mystic and Anabaptist reformer, he taught an innerlight superior to all Scriptures and saw in Christ the highest human example of love. In Augsburg in 1525, he was baptized by HUBMAIER and joined the Anabaptists. Many others soon followed. In 1526, he moved to Strasbourg where he was forced into disputation with BUCER and CAPITO. He was driven from the city and went to Worms, only to be met with the same fate. At Augsburg, in 1517, he presided over the Synod of the Austrian Anabaptists, referred to as the Martyr's Synod because so many of them lost their lives.

Patrick Hamilton

1504
Stanehouse/Kincavel (near Glasgow), Scotland
Feb. 29, 1528
St. Andrews, Scotland

Pre–Presbyterian reformer and martyr. Hamilton was won to the reformation while a student in Germany. He met LUTHER and MELANCHTHON as well as TYNDALE. Following this experience, he returned and preached at Linlithgow, 1517–22. He began to preach Lutheran doctrine in 1526. Hamilton was lured to St. Andrews by the wily, future cardinal, David Beaton (served: 1537–46) under the guise of safety. When persecuted, he fled to the continent (Wittenberg and Marburg) in 1527. He married late in the year of 1527. After one month, he was seized and burned at the stake. As he died, he said, "How long wilt Thou suffer this tyranny of men? Lord Jesus, receive my spirit." His death was the challenge that inspired JOHN KNOX.

Balthasar Hubmaier

1485
Friedberg, Germany
March 10, 1528
Vienna, Austria

Anabaptist evangelist who was converted from the Catholic priesthood in 1522. For a while, Hubmaier professed the Reformers' faith and later became the leading spokesman for the Anabaptists. He pastored at Waldshut, Switzerland, 1521–24, and was imprisoned in Zurich for his new beliefs. He escaped to Moravia and was baptized by WILHELM REUBLIN in 1525. In turn, he baptized 300 others out of a milk pail filled with water. He averaged over 6,000 baptisms a year and established an Anabaptist community at Nikolsburg in Moravia. Hubmaier rejected princes and governments, upset both Lutherans and Catholics and preached to great crowds before being burned at the stake. His faithful wife was drowned eight days later for being too critical of Rome.

Albrecht Dürer

May 21, 1471
Nuremberg, Germany

April 6, 1528
Nuremberg, Germany

Outstanding engraver (copperplate work) and woodcut designer. Dürer was also a painter. He lived briefly in Colmi, Basel, Csuitz, and Strasbourg before marrying Agnes Frer in 1494. He visited Italy 1505–7. He never renounced Catholicism, but showed sympathy with the Reformation, being a friend of LUTHER and MELANCHTHON. His painting, *Four Evangelists*, was his greatest work of art.

Matthias Grunewald

c 1470–1475
Wurzburg, Germany

Aug. 1528
Halle, Germany

Artist, painter and engraver whose altarpiece in several panels now stands in the museum at Colmar, France. His altar piece, *Crucifixion*, named and painted for the church in a Palsatian (region of northeast France) village, is his masterpiece. The vivid dramatic power of this depiction of Christ's suffering gave him much fame. He was the last Gothic painter—the court painter and architect to two archbishops of Mainz—his chief patron being ALBERT.

Louis de Berquin

June 1490
Paris, France

April 17, 1529
Paris, France

Lutheran martyr who was the first Protestant martyr in modern France. He was a pupil of the humanist churchman LEFEVRE but later left Catholicism. Berquin was twice imprisoned for heresy by openly attacking the Sorbonne. In 1522, officials found his writings heretical, so he was sentenced to life in prison. When he appealed to the king, the judges became enraged and burned him alive.

Georg Blaurock

c 1492

Sept. 5, 1529
Innsbruck, Austria

Swiss Anabaptist evangelist and reformer who was the first adult in modern history to be baptized. Blaurock responded to ZWINGLI's preaching sometime before 1523. GREBEL baptized him in the home of MANZ on January 21, 1525. He then founded an Anabaptist congregation at Zollikon, winning some 150 converts. Blaurock instituted modern believer's baptism, baptized by sprinkling or pouring at first, as the mode was not important at this time. Exiled from Zurich in 1527, he became an evangelist and won thousands to Christ. Blaurock was captured in Tyrol and burned at the stake.

Francois Lambert

1486
Avignon, France

April 18, 1530
Marburg, Germany

Lutheran reformer of Hesse who was one of the first Reformation monks to marry, going to Wittenberg in 1523. He was converted out of the Franciscan Observants at Avignon in 1522 and was one of the first French Protestants. He preached in Strasbourg from 1524–26. In 1527, Lambert became a professor of theology/exegesis at the University of Marburg and had a large role in establishing the Reformation in Hesse. Lambert translated several Protestant works into French and Italian, and in 1529, favored ZWINGLI's views. He died of the plague.

Thomas Bilney

c 1495
Norfolk, England

Aug. 19, 1531
Norwich, England

Pre–Church of England reformer and martyr. Bilney was converted through reading Erasmas' New Testament (I Timothy 1:15) and LUTHER's works. He was ordained in 1519. Bilney questioned such tenets as salvation by works and the work of the saints. He converted HUGH LATIMER to the Reformation doctrine. Bilney preached in London and East Anglia. He was arrested for heresy in 1527 and tried by Cardinal Thomas Wolsey (served: 1515–30). Bilney recanted, resumed preaching (tour of Norfolk), was rearrested, tried again, and burned at the stake.

Ulrich Zwingli

Jan. 1, 1484
Wildhaus, Switzerland

Oct. 11, 1531
Kappel am Albis, Switzerland

Reformation leader in Switzerland, 523 on, and former Catholic priest in Glarus (1506–16), Einsiedeln (1516–19), and Zurich (1519–31). Influenced by Erasmus, he was converted in 1507 by the witness of WYTTENBACH. He became the pastor of Great Minster Church in Zurich, 1518–23. Zwingli built the foundation for CALVIN. He supported laypeople and the government and opposed the selling of mercenaries by the Swiss. He secretly married Anna Reinhard in 1522. In 1524, a complete break with Rome occurred as he stated his 67 disputations. The Council of Zurich, however, stood firm on infant baptism, meaning Zwingli was a silent partner in Anabaptist persecutions. In 1529, he met with LUTHER and MELANCHTHON in Marburg, where they disagreed on the ordinance of the Lord's Supper. In violent conflict with Catholics, Zwingli acted as chaplain of the Zurich troops and, in the second Cappel war, was killed in battle. He wrote *67 Conclusions* (1523), a summary of his doctrines, *Concerning Freedoms and Choice of Food* and *Fidel Ratio* (1530). He was involved in the Baden Disputation (1526), the Bern Disputation (1528), the first Cappel War, and the Marburg Coloquy (1529).

"They can kill the body, but not the soul."

Johannes Oecolampadius

1482
Weinsberg, Germany

Nov. 24, 1531
Basel, Switzerland

Pre-Reformed Swiss reformer who would have been the logical successor to ZWINGLI but died in the same year. Oecolampadius was the pastor of the Church of St. Martin, Basel, 1522–31. In 1525, he wrote a work seeking to win Protestants in Swabia away from LUTHER. In 1529, he and ZWINGLI attended the Colloquy at Marburg, dissenting with LUTHER and MELANCHTHON on the Lord's Supper. He was also a professor of theology at the University in Basel. Oecolampadius was respected for his charity and cheerfulness. He aided Erasmus in the publication of his Greek New Testament. He married Wilibrandis Rosenblatt, aided the Reformation at Baden (1526), Bern (1528), and Ulm (1551). He worked with MARTIN BUCER in Ulm during his last year.

John the Constant

June 30, 1468
Messen, Saxony (Germany)

Aug. 16, 1532
Schweinitz, Germany

Lutheran Elector of Saxony, 1525–32. John succeeded his brother, FREDERICK THE WISE, with whom he served as co-ruler, 1486–1525. John was a close friend and admirer of LUTHER. In 1526, he joined the League of Torgau (Protestant powers against Catholic states). At the Diet of Spires in 1529, he was one of the first to be called a Protestant. In 1530, he signed the Augsburg Confession. In 1531, John helped PHILIP OF HESSE organize the Schmalkaldic League (Lutheran princes formed to protect their interest, basically Protestants against Holy Roman Emperor Charles V (ruled: 1520–58). He was the father of JOHN FREDERICK I. Throughout his life he was loyal to the Bible, with LUTHER preaching his funeral. When theologians offered to present the Augsburg Confession without him, he replied, "I too, will confess my Christ."

Frederick I

Oct. 7, 1471

April 10, 1533
near Schleswig, Germany

Lutheran King of Denmark and Norway, who in 1523 introduced Lutheranism to Denmark. Frederick I won a war with Norway in 1524. In 1526 he arranged to have Danish bishops appointed by the king. In 1527, Frederick I granted toleration to Lutherans. Finally, he encouraged TAUSEN to present the 43 Copenhagen Articles to the Danish Parliament. He died at Gottorp Castle.

John Frith

1503
Westerham, England

July 4, 1533
London, England

Pre–Church of England reformer and martyr. Frith's works in reform began at Cambridge when he was but age 15. He was a promising scholar who distinguished himself by assisting TYNDALE with the translation of the New Testament in Antwerp, Belgium. He promoted ideas about the Lord's Supper, which became part of the Church of England's liturgy in 1559. He fled to the continent in 1528 to escape persecution. There he attacked transubstantiation and purgatory, chiefly at the University of Marburg. He was later burned at the stake at Smithfield, London, after returning to England in 1532. One of his judges was THOMAS CRANMER.

Jan Mathys

1534

Anabaptist iconoclast who tried to bring in the New Age by armed force in the city of Munster in 1533. Mathys moved his headquarters from Strasbourg to Munster, Germany. Three months later he was killed in a skirmish with soldiers who recaptured the city for the bishop. Mathys claimed to be Enoch, the witness listed in Revelation 11:3.

Guillaume (William) Briconnet

1471
Tours, France

Jan. 24, 1534
Montereau, France

Bishop of Meaux, beginning in 1516, who leaned strongly toward the Reformers. Briconnet never broke from Catholicism, but he agreed intellectually with the reformers. He believed salvation was a free gift not earned through works. Briconnet denied the authority of the pope and the worship of Mary and the saints. Briconnet even allowed fiery WILLIAM FAREL to preach in his diocese in 1521, and associated with CALVIN and CALVIN's friends.

Bernhard Rothman

c 1495

June 24, 1535
Munster, Germany

Radical Anabaptist, 1533–1535, who introduced the Reformation to the city of Munster. Rothman was a German evangelical preacher and friend of MELANCHTHON. However, he was influenced by MATHYS and joined in the endeavor to bring in the kingdom by force. He probably died following the siege of Munster when the city was taken.

Nikolaus Storch

1490
Stockberg, Germany

1536
Munich, Germany

Radical Anabaptist. He was a weaver from Zwickau in Germany, who steeped himself in the Scriptures and became one of the "prophets," claiming direct revelation from God. Storch and his friend, Markus Stubner, stormed into Wittenberg, Germany, in 1521, and unsettled PHILIP MELANCHTHON by their shrill denunciations of infant baptism and end of the world predictions.

John of Leyden
Johann Bockelson—Bockold

c 1508–1510
Leyden, Netherlands

Jan. 23, 1536
Munster, Germany

Radical Anabaptist who was a follower of JAN MATHYS, whom he succeeded. He originally was a tailor from Leyden. Seeking to set up an earthly New Jerusalem, he was elected "king" of the polygamous, communal group. Fanaticism, cruelty, and licentiousness ruled in Munster. He was imprisoned by the bishop of Munster in 1535. John died when Protestant nobles (Lutherans) joined Catholic troops recapturing the city. He was tortured to death by red-hot pincers, and then hung up in an iron cage on St. Lambert steeple, as a terror to all rebels.

Berthold Haller
Bertold—Berchtol

1492
Aldingen, Germany

Feb. 25, 1536
Bern, Switzerland

Reformed Swiss schoolmaster and canon of Bern Cathedral, 1519 on, who became the leader of the Reformation movement in Bern, Switzerland, establishing Protestantism there in 1528. Haller was greatly influenced by ZWINGLI, whom he had met in 1521. He helped to develop a Protestant liturgy. He taught in Bern's gymnasium, served as assistant preacher at St. Vincent's Church (1517), then was appointed people's priest (1520). He often conflicted with Anabaptists.

Jacob Hutter

Moos, Austria

Feb. 25, 1536
Innsbruck, Austria

Anabaptist leader and founder of the Hutterites, 1531–36. Hutter was a Swiss Brethren who went to Moravia to determine the difference between him and the Anabaptists. Hutterites are descendants from the Anabaptists, believing in communal living and pacifism. He died at the stake.

William Tyndale

c 1494
North Niblely, England

Oct. 6, 1536
Vilvorde, Belgium

Reformer, Bible translator, and martyr, who was influential in shaping the thought of the Puritan Party in England. He was a Greek scholar while at Oxford and Cambridge. In 1521, he stayed at Little Sodbury Manor. He had an interview (1523) with Cuthbert Tunstall (bishop of London, 1474–1559), then went to Germany (1524). The first complete reprinting of the New Testament occurred at Worms in 1526. When in Cologne, Germany, he translated Erasmus' Greek New Testament (LUTHER's German Testament) into English (c. 1525—revised version 1534). Tyndale had 3,000 copies smuggled into England in 1526. He also translated the Pentateuch (published c. 1530 at Antwerp) and Jonah. His translation was the basis for 75 per cent of the future King James Version of the NT. From 1531 on, he was in Antwerp, revising the New Testament translation. In 1535, he was betrayed by a spy named Philipp, tried, condemned, and later strangled and burned in Belgium. Tyndale's last requesting words were, "Open the eyes of the King of England;" his prayer was answered two years later as Bibles became welcomed in England. His favorite Bible verse was I John 4:19. He was a significant person in developing the English language.

Jacques Lefevre D'Etaples
Jacobus Faber/Fabri

c 1450–60
Etaples, France

Jan. 1537
Nerac, France

Humanist, theologian, reformer, scholar, and teacher in Paris. He influenced FAREL, his pupil, and also reformer JOHN CALVIN. In 1491 his interest in spiritual things developed after reading Raymond Lull's *Contemplations*. In 1507, after two visits to Italy, he was invited to reside in St. Germain des Pres. He served as librarian of the abbey until 1521. He collected German manuscripts of mystics (1510), and became vicar (1523) to the bishop of Meaux, where he instigated a reform, after which he served as librarian and tutor to the royal family at Blois (1526). Lefevre translated the whole Bible into French 1523–30. His last days were spent at the court of the future queen, Margaret of Navarre (ruled: 1544–49), going to Nerac in 1531. D'Etaples frequently had to flee for his life, because he believed in the supreme authority of the Scripture and justification by faith. However he kept purgatory, transubstantiation, and celibacy of clergy, never fully breaking from the trappings of Catholicism.

Pierre R. Olivetan

c 1506
Noyon, France

1538
Ferrera, Italy

French Biblical scholar who, upon his conversion, influenced JOHN CALVIN, his cousin, to accept evangelical doctrine. Olivetan fled to Strasbourg, Germany (1528, and then to Geneva, Switzerland (1531). He taught in Geneva 1533–35. With the help of LEFEVRE's earlier translation and CALVIN's later corrections, Olivetan produced a translation of the Bible in French, which became the foundation for the Geneva Bible (1560).

Robert Barnes

1495
near Lynn, England

July 30, 1540
London, England

Reformer and martyr. This Augustinian monk was converted by LUTHER's writings and helped spread Lutheranism throughout England. Barnes was prior of the Austin Friars at Cambridge in 1523. He was forced to stand trial under Cardinal Thomas Wolsey in 1526, was condemned, then escaped to Antwerp, where he served as Henry VIII's emissary before losing favor with him. In 1528 he met with LUTHER in Wittenberg. Barnes then traveled freely between England and Germany. He returned to England in 1531, as an agent of Thomas Cromwell (minister of King Henry VIII), whose policy was to establish better relations between the king and the Protestant princes of Germany. He arranged meetings of the English divines with those of Wittenberg (1536), and those of the Lutherans with the English at Langbuth (1538). After his protector, Thomas Cromwell (statesman, c 1485–1540), fell from favor (beheaded), Barnes was burned at the stake with two others. He said as he died, "I trust in no good works that ever I did, but only in the death of Christ..."

Guillaume (William) Bude

Jan. 26, 1467
Paris, France

Aug. 23, 1540
Paris, France

Reformed French scholar and friend of Erasmus who became an eminent Greek scholar and man of great influence. He was a secret adherent of the Reformation before LUTHER wrote against the corruption of the clergy and the papacy. Bude knew philosophy, theology, law, medicine, and science. His family joined the Reformed Church in Geneva after his death. Bude served as royal librarian in Rome from 1522 on. He married Roberte

Lelieur. His books spanned the years 1508 to 1535 and had humanistic tendencies. Bude never did officially support the Reformation.

Heinrich
1541

Fervent German Lutheran who made Saxony completely Protestant during his brief two year reign, 1539–41, as duke of Saxony.

Wolfgang F. Capito

1478
Hagenau, France

Nov. 4, 1541
Strasbourg, Germany

Clergyman and reformer who was a Benedictine monk. He was attracted to the Reformation by ZWINGLI's preaching and LUTHER's personal letters. Capito became a cathedral preacher and professor of theology in Basel (1515), and chancellor and preacher in Mainz (1519). In 1523 he moved to Strasbourg where he took an active part in the Reformed Church (provost of Church of St. Thomas, and pastor of New St. Peters). He was married in 1524 (his wife died in 1531). He then married OECOLAMPADIUS's widow in 1532, taking part in the Synod of Bern the same year. Capito sought to reconcile Swiss/German reformers and also helped to write various confessions of faith, including the *Wittenberg Concordia* in 1536. He died of the plague.

Andreas R. B. Carlstadt

c 1480
Karlstadt, Germany

Dec. 24, 1541
Basel, Switzerland

Radical reformer who was the friend, and afterward, an opponent of LUTHER. Converted in 1516, he taught at Wittenberg 1513–23. He was condemned with LUTHER in a papal bull in 1520. In 1521–22, during LUTHER's absence from Wittenberg, Carlstadt sought to turn reform efforts into a revolution. He was one of the first priests to marry, January, 1522. Riots against the Catholic Mass and much needless destruction of church art and property took place. From 1521–24, he was in Zurich, Switzerland. From 1525–29, he was back in Saxony, but not allowed to lecture. He pastored and taught at the University of Basel, working with Zwinglian reformers (especially Swiss Anabaptists), beginning in 1534 giving up his political agitation. Carlstadt was a powerful influence on the Anabaptists and other Reformers, opposing infant baptism and supporting communion as a memorial service.

Leo Jud

1482
Germar, France

June 19, 1542
Zurich, Switzerland

Swiss reformer. In Basel, Switzerland, Jud studied theology because of the influence of ZWINGLI. In 1519, he succeeded ZWINGLI as pastor at Einsiedeln. In 1523, he pastored at St. Peter's in Zurich and married a former nun. He was called to succeed ZWINGLI, but declined and passed the torch to BULLINGER. Jud was actively involved in translating the Bible into French to benefit the Swiss people. He preached against images and introduced a German baptismal liturgy. His Protestant *Catechism* (1538) remained in use for a long time. He helped formulate the Helvetic (region in western and central Switzerland) Confessions (two creedal standards of the Swiss Reformed Churches).

Melchior Hof(f)mann

1498
Schwabisch–Hall, Germany

1543
Strasbourg, Germany

Radical Anabaptist who believed he was divinely appointed to lead the faithful to Strasbourg to await the end of the world in 1533. Earlier, he was a Lutheran who attracted a following in his native Netherlands c. 1530. He traveled widely 1523–33. Hoffmann was arrested in May, 1533, imprisoned, and kept in a dungeon until his death. He had predicted this six–month confinement in the "New Jerusalem." He was the spiritual father of the Munster tragedy. This fanaticism helped restore Catholicism in Westphalia.

George of Brandenberg
George the Pious Confessor

March 4, 1484
Onolzbach, Germany

Dec. 17, 1543
Onolzbach, Germany

Prince and margrave (hereditary title of ruler of certain states) **of Brandenberg–Ansbach–Kulmbach** who was one of the first to espouse the cause of the Reformation. No other German prince did more than he to secure its success. George was an intimate friend with LUTHER and helped Lutheranize Prussia, 1524 on. His boldness in speaking and energy in laboring for the Reformation were awesome, defending it at the Diet of Speyers (1529) and Augsburg (1530). In 1523, he obtained the town of Jagerndorf in Silesia which he developed. He also aided the Reformation in Ansback.

Clement (Clemens) Marot

c 1495–1497
Cahors, France

Sept. 1544
Turin, Italy

French poet and hymnist whose hymns were popular and helpful in the Reformation. Many of his translated Psalms in poetic meter found their way into JOHN CALVIN's French Protestant hymnal. Marot was a resident for some time in the court of King Francis I of France (ruled: 1515–47). Attacking the abuses of the Roman Church, he was imprisoned (1527), fled to Ferrara, Italy, (1534), then returned to Lyons, France, fleeing (1542) to Geneva. Unable to submit to the ecclesiastical discipline of Geneva, he returned to Italy. In 1562, THEODORE BEZA completed the hymnbook with 101 of his Psalms added to Marot's 49. He was the first French poet of the Renaissance. He was a worldly minded courtier encouraged by Holy Roman Emperor Charles V and Catherine de Medici, (future queen of France, ruled: 1560–63).

Matyas B. Devay

c 1500
Deva, Transylvania, Austria (Hungary)

c 1545
Debreczin, Hungary

Hungarian reformer. After being with LUTHER at Wittenberg in 1529, he returned to Hungary, preaching and writing about the Reformation. He was twice imprisoned in 1531 and 1534. Upon his release, he published a grammar book which included some of LUTHER's catechism. He met LUTHER for the second time in Wittenberg in 1541. This was the first book printed in Hungary. As a result, Devay was driven into Switzerland where he adopted the Reformed (ZWINGLI's) view of the Lord's Supper, thus turning from Lutheranism to Reformed Calvinism. He was originally a Catholic.

Georg Spalatin

Jan. 17, 1484
Spalt, Germany

Jan. 16, 1545
Altenburg, Germany

German reformer, friend and associate of LUTHER. Ordained as a priest in 1508, he became a trusted advisor, chaplain, and secretary of FREDERICK III (the Wise) OF SAXONY. Spalatin won for LUTHER the sympathy and support of FREDERICK. He married in 1525. He was canon at Altenburg, 1525–45. Later he became a preacher. He attended the Diet of Spires (1526) and the Diet of Augsburg (1530). His literary and political labors were valuable, being the translator of the Latin writings of LUTHER, MELANCHTHON, and Erasmus. LUTHER wrote him over 400 letters. He bought a Bible at a high price.

Peter Brully

c 1518
near Metz, Germany

Feb. 19, 1545
Tournay, Belgium

Successor of CALVIN **in Strasbourg and a martyr for his faith**. Brully started as a Dominican lecturer in Metz, but he met CALVIN in Strasbourg and succeeded him as pastor when CALVIN returned to Geneva in 1541. In September 1544, he took a tour to Flanders and preached Reformationist doctrine, which caused his arrest in November, 1544. He was burned at the stake.

Martin Luther

Nov. 10, 1483
Eisleben, Saxony (Germany)

Feb. 18, 1546
Eisleben, Saxony (Germany)

Reformer and Bible translator. After completing his law studies, 1501–5 at the University of Erfurt, he taught briefly but found himself drawn to the Augustinian order of monks (Oct. 17, 1505), which led to his ordination as a priest in 1507. His disappointing trip to Rome in 1510, on business for his monastic order, opened his eyes to the need for church reform. Luther lectured to eager students at the University of Wittenberg, 1512–17. In early 1514 in Leipzig, he came upon the truth of Romans 1:17 and was converted. On October 31, 1517 he posted the famed Ninety-Five Theses against papal abuses and corruption on the church door at Wittenberg, which ushered in the Protestant Reformation. He went to the Augsburg hearing (1518), debated with Johann von Eck (1519), was excommunicated (1520) by Pope Leo X (reigned: 1513–22), whose papal bull Luther burned. Luther presented his stand before Charles V at the Diet of Worms, April 17–18, 1521. He was declared an outlaw by the Edict of Worms, May 25, 1521, so was taken into protective custody at the Wartburg Castle to ensure his safety for several months. KATARINA VON BORA became his wife on June 13, 1525. They had six children. His translation of the whole Bible into German was published in 1534. He also wrote the lyrics and music for "A Mighty Fortress Is Our God" in 1527. He did not write "Away in a Manger." Luther is acknowledged as the real creator of the present universal language of Germany and wrote until c. 1534. He died of a heart attack. As he died, he quoted John 3:16 and Psalm 68:20. He became the most renowned individual in the history of the church. He is buried at Castle Church, Wittenberg, Germany.

"Here I stand, God help me, I cannot do otherwise."

George Wishart

c 1513
Montrose, Scotland

March 1, 1546
St. Andrews, Scotland

Pre–Presbyterian Scottish reformer and martyr. For teaching the Greek New Testament, 1538–39, Wishart had to flee for his life to England, and then to the European Continent. In 1544, he returned to Scotland to engage in evangelistic endeavors. Among his converts was JOHN KNOX, who witnessed Wishart's death. Wishart was arrested by emissaries of Cardinal David Beaton in 1545, tried for heresy against the Catholic Church in February, 1546 and burned at the stake.

Friedrich Myconius

Dec. 26, 1490
Lichtenfels, Thuringia (Germany)

April 7, 1546
Gotha, Germany

Lutheran reformer. Early in his life, Myconius entered the Franciscan order of monks but found no peace in scholastic theology. In 1524, he left the order and married. Myconius became a great leader of the Reformation in Thuringia. He was an influential preacher in Gotha and other Thuringian cities. Myconius took part in several important Lutheran conferences, first traveling to Zwickau, then to Gotha.

Anne Askew

1521
Stallingborough, England

July 16, 1546
London, England

Protestant martyr. Anne was denounced by her husband for her religious views. She had been married against her will to her wealthy Catholic neighbor, Thomas Kyne. She was primarily charged for interpreting Scripture contrary to the Catholic faith, refusing to go to confession, and for her critical views on the sacraments. In March 1545, she was examined for heresy and imprisoned. Acquitted, she was rearrested in June 1546. Anne was tortured on the rack and then burned at the stake at Smithfield. She said as she died, "I came not thither to deny my Lord and Master."

Matthew Zell

Sept. 21, 1477
Kaiersburg, Germany

Jan. 9, 1548
Strasbourg, France

Zealous reformer who preached doctrines espoused by ZWINGLI. From 1517–23, Zell served as pastor of the Cathedral in Strasbourg, planting the Reformation there. After 1521, he preached primarily on the Book of Romans, which emphasizes salvation by faith and Christian duties. He married Catrina in 1523 which caused his excommunication from Rome. Zell was practical, avoided controversies, and sought to unite, rather than divide the Protestant world. He issued catechisms (a summary of religious doctrine lessons, often in question and answer format) for teachers (1536) and for children (1537). He was won to the Lord by the influence of the Bible, LUTHER, and John Tyler.

Thomas Sternhold

c 1500
Blakeney, England

Aug. 23, 1549

English writer. Sternhold, and a man named John Hopkins, were the musical authors of the old "Metrical Versions" (meter/rhythmical pattern of verse) of the Psalms (1547). Their rendition was the first introduced into England. *51 Psalms*, whose meter was verified by Sternhold, was printed in 1549, the year of his death. These Psalms were later sung in churches. The collection was enlarged and printed as *The Whole Book of Psalms* (1561). Sternhold was a groom (valet) of the chambers to King Henry VIII and EDWARD VI.

Peter Magni

c 1550

Swedish bishop of Vasteras, Sweden. Magni agreed to consecrate Sweden's newly appointed Lutheran bishops in 1528, which was the time of the Swedish Reformation, led by King VASA GUSTAVUS I.

Nicholas Cop

c 1550

Scholar and leader of the humanist circle of intellectuals in Paris. Cop was a close friend of CALVIN, during CALVIN's student days in Paris. In November 1533, he gave his inaugural address (on Matthew 5:3) as the newly elected rector of the University of Paris. CALVIN helped him write it. Cop's speech was so full of evangelical truth that both he and CALVIN had to flee to Basel, Switzerland, to avoid arrest.

The Saints Go Marching In

George of Polentz

1478
Polentz, Saxony (Germany)

April 28/Oct. 1, 1550
Balga, Prussia (Russia)

Bishop of Sambia/Samland, 1519 on. George had studied canon law in Italy. In the summer of 1523, he allowed Reformation doctrines to be preached in the Cathedral Church at Konigsberg, Prussia (Kaliningrad, Russia). Before the year was over, George had joined the followers of LUTHER. By 1525, the Prussian State Church was organized and he also married. He founded and developed the University of Konigsberg in 1544 and died near there.

Martin Bucer
Kuhhorn

Nov. 11, 1491
Schlettstadt (Selestat), France

Feb. 28, 1551
Cambridge, England

German reformer and Dominican monk. Bucer was converted and helped the Reformation everywhere, especially in Strasbourg, France. He was influenced by MARTIN LUTHER at the Disputation in Heidelberg (theology defined as faith alone, grace alone, and the Bible alone), 1518. Bucer met LUTHER personally in April, 1518, and replaced Swiss reformer Erasmus as the movement's spokesperson. After being released from his monastic vows in 1521, he preached Lutheranism as pastor of St. Aurelias in Strasbourg, 1523–49. Bucer was one of the first Reformers to marry. Elizabeth Palass, a former nun, became his wife in 1522. The Wittenberg Concord (uniting southern Germans under moderate Lutheranism) was obtained by Bucer in 1536. From 1538–41, Bucer became the leader of the Reformed Church in Switzerland. He attempted, with moderate success, to unite the opposing Protestant groups represented by LUTHER and ZWINGLI. Bucer greatly influenced JOHN CALVIN. Bucer refused to sign the Regensburg Interim (Charles V's attempt to reconcile Roman Catholics with Lutheranism, 1541), but with MELANCHTHON, presented a rebuttal compromise of 23 articles which the other side rejected—making this Colloquy (Conference) of Ratisbon meritless. When Bucer returned to Strasbourg, he found that his wife, children, and many close associates had died from the plague. In 1549, Bucer went to England to teach theology at Cambridge and advise THOMAS CRANMER. The effects of his Reformation efforts were so encompassing that Catholic Tudor Queen Mary I of England (ruled: 1553–58) had his bones dug up and his body publicly burned in 1557, thus beginning her Protestant Persecutions. Three years later, under QUEEN ELIZABETH, Cambridge University was instructed to restore all honors to him.

Joachim Vadianus

Dec. 28, 1484
St. Gall, France

April 6, 1551
St. Gall, France

Swiss poet and humanist. He rose to be mayor of St. Gall (1526), where he also practiced medicine (1518) and was a popular preacher. Vadianus was a great help in establishing the Reformation in Switzerland. He wrote against the radical Anabaptists, was an able historian, and held his own as Catholics regained strength after ZWINGLI's death in 1531.

Olaus Petri

Jan. 6, 1493
Orebro, Sweden

April 19, 1552
Stockholm, Sweden

Along with brother, LAURENTIUS, he brought the Reformation to Sweden. After studying at the University of Wittenberg in Germany, Peter returned to Sweden with the tenets of Lutheranism in 1520. He was appointed chancellor to King VASA GUSTAVUS of Sweden in 1531. He was removed in 1539 because of his ruthless methods of reform when the king sought to control the state church. He was condemned to death in 1540 by Vasa Gustavus I but was pardoned. He published a Swedish Bible in 1541. He pastored again in 1542 after his imprisonment. He became the first Lutheran pastor in Stockholm, Sweden. His public Protestant marriage caused opposition. Petri is considered the Father of Swedish Hymns.

Lars Anderson
Laurentius Andreae

1482
Stengnas, Sweden

April 29, 1552
Stengnas, Sweden

Leader of the Reformation in Sweden. He was originally a Catholic archdeacon but was converted to Lutheranism by the persuasive preaching of the Petri brothers. Anderson was chancellor under King Vasa Gustavus I of Sweden, encouraging the Crown to take possession of Catholic Church lands in Sweden. With Olaus Petri, he translated the Bible into Swedish in 1526.

Alexander Barclay

c 1475
Scotland

Buried-June 10, 1552
Croydon, England

Priest with gifts as a satirist. Barclay wrote the stinging *The Shyp of Folys of the World* (Ship of Fools) (1508), which indicted most of society, including the Church. He was a monk of Ely and Canterbury, a priest at the College of Ottery St. Mary, a vicar (clergyman in charge of parish, similar to pastor) of Much Naden Church in Essex, and a rector of All Hallows Church on Lombard Street in London. He was buried on June 10th at Croydon, Surrey, England, which indicates that his death date was probably slightly earlier.

Oswald Myconius

Oct. 14, 1488
Lucerne, Switzerland

Oct. 14, 1552
Basel, Switzerland

Reformer, theologian, and Reformed minister. Myconius was a friend of Erasmus, Zwingli, and Jud. Early in his life he was considered a "Lutheran heretic." He succeeded Oecolampadius, serving 1531–51 as pastor of St. Martin Church in Basel. Myconius also taught New Testament exegesis at the University of Basel in Switzerland. He was a strong leader of the Church in Basel: reforming schools and writing the First Basel Confession of Faith in 1534. Myconius tried to mediate between the Reformed followers and the staunch Lutheran partisans on the Communion problem.

Andreas Osiander
Hosemann

Dec. 19, 1498
Gunzenhausen, Germany

Oct. 17, 1552
Konigsberg (Prussia), Kaliningrad (Russia)

German Lutheran theologian and reformer. Osiander was the first scholar to publish a Harmony of the Gospels (1537). He became a priest in Nuremberg, Germany (1520) and brought the Reformation as the first evangelical preacher there (1522). Osiander was involved in doctrinal disputes on such topics as justification but for the most part was in agreement with Luther whom he met in 1529. He strongly opposed Romanism and Calvinism. He refused to support the Augsburg Interim (provisional arrangement for settlement of differences between Roman Catholics and Protestants) (May 15, 1548) and was therefore forced to leave Nuremberg. He became a pastor and professor at Konigsberg in 1549, his teaching concerning justification being questionable.

Katherine Bora Luther
Katharina von (meaning "from") Bora

Jan. 29, 1499
Klein–Laussig, Germany

Dec. 20, 1552
Torgau, Germany

Wife of MARTIN LUTHER. Katherine married LUTHER June 13, 1525 (eight years after he had posted his ninety five theses in Wittenberg); she was 26, and he was 41. Besides rearing their six children (3 girls and 3 boys), she managed to care for several orphaned nieces and nephews, plus a constant house full of poor students and student boarders. Katherine was a former Cistercian nun from Nimptschen, Saxony, 1515–23. She was affectionately called by her husband, "Katy my rib." Going to Torgau to escape the plague, she died tragically in an accident at the age of 53, having been a widow for six years.

Edward VI

Oct. 12, 1537
Hampton Court, England

July 6, 1553
Greenwich, England

King of England, 1547–53. Edward was the frail and sickly son of Henry VIII and his third wife, Jane Seymour. As a Protestant boy–king, he ruled only six years before his death at age 15 from tuberculosis. In his name, most of the English Reformation came to fruition, which included the introduction of *The Book of Common Prayer* (1549), and a compromise between Lutherans and Calvinists. Reformers from the continent came to England during his reign. Unfortunately, he was succeeded by Queen "Bloody" Mary (daughter of Henry VIII and Catherine of Aragon), his half sister who restored papal power, murdering over 300 believers during her reign, 1555–58. He said as he died, "Oh, Lord God, defend this realm and maintain Thy true religion. Lord, have mercy upon me, and receive my spirit."

Maurice

March 21, 1521
Freiberg, Saxony (Germany)

July 11, 1553
near Sievershausen, Germany

Duke and elector of Saxony, 1547 on. Maurice succeeded his father, Henry the Pious, as duke in 1541. Early on, bribed by promise of territory and the electoral hat, he helped the emperor, Charles V, crush the Lutheran elector of Saxony, JOHN FREDERICK I, his cousin. Knowing the emperor hated the Lutherans, he embraced the Reformation and signed the Articles of Schmalkalden but did not join the Schmalkaldic League. In 1552, Maurice forced the aging emperor, Charles V of Germany, to sign the Treaty of Passau, which gave religious freedom to the Lutherans at Innsbruck. Maurice died in battle fighting against ALBERT OF BRANDENBURG. His father–in–law was PHILIP OF HESSE.

Jakob Sturm

Aug. 10, 1489
Strasbourg, Germany

Oct. 30, 1553
Strasbourg, Germany

German reformer and statesman. Respected by all parties, he was chief magistrate of his native city, Strasbourg: representing it 91 times at religious and political conferences. In 1529, he was one of the original protesters, who formed a "protestation" (from which the word "Protestant" was derived) at the Diet of Speyers, the capital city of Bavaria. He also influenced Strasbourg to join the Schmalkaldic League in 1531. Sturm founded the Protestant Gymnasium in Strasbourg in 1538, which later became the University of Strasbourg, 1525–52.

Antonio Brucioli

c 1500
Florence, Italy

c 1554

Italian Protestant reformer and scholar. Brucioli was implicated in a conspiracy against Cardinal de Medici (served: 1511–35) of Florence and had to flee to France. He eventually resided in Venice, where he published a number of works, including a translation of the Bible into Tuscan (literary dialect of Italy). This translation and his Bible commentaries were considered heresy.

Jane Grey

c 1537
Bradgate, England

Feb. 12, 1554
London, England

Martyred English princess. This highly intelligent young woman at the age of twelve was able to write Greek and Latin, speak French and Italian, and was rapidly grasping a knowledge of Hebrew, Chaldee, and Arabic. She was the great–granddaughter of King HENRY VII and a victim of a plot to wrestle the throne away from the Tudors and into the family line of the Dudleys. Her father, Earl Grey of Dorset, and the duke of Northumberland, plotted the deception by marrying Jane to the duke's youngest son, Lord Guildford Dudley, May 1553 and by persuading the dying King EDWARD VI to deed Jane into the line of succession. Upon Edward's death, Jane briefly became queen on July 10, 1553, at the age of 16. However the council repudiated the action and Mary I was crowned nine days later. Jane and her husband were imprisoned in the Tower of London. At age 17 she pleaded guilty to treason—not wanting to shame her Lord—even though she was the victim of political intrigue, her father's participation in the abortive insurrection led by Sir Thomas Wyatt. After seven months in prison, Jane was beheaded along with her husband. Her martyrdom was also the result of her faith. She could have converted to Catholicism and maybe became queen. Instead she gave a short testimony and laid her head on the block.

John Frederick I
The Magnanimous

June 30, 1503
Torgau, Germany

March 3, 1554
Weimar, Germany

Elector of Saxony, 1532–47, succeeding his father, JOHN THE CONSTANT. He was educated as a Lutheran and was a champion of the Protestant faith. His support of LUTHER began in 1530. Frederick I was defeated at the Battle of Muehlberg on April 24, 1547, by MAURICE OF SAXONY (cousin) and Emperor Charles V in the Schmalkaldic War. He was in prison, 1547–52. His death sentence was cancelled when he renounced electorship and when MAURICE (his successor) defeated the emperor in 1552. Frederick founded the University of Jena, Prussia, which later opened in 1558. He remained devoted to the evangelical faith. He was wounded and taken prisoner refusing to recognize the Council of Trent (held to seek ways to halt Protestantism).

John Rogers

c 1500
Deritend, England

Feb. 4, 1555
Smithfield, London, England

English Lutheran reformer and the first Protestant martyr under the persecution of Queen "Bloody" Mary I. He wrote the first Bible commentary published in English. Rogers took the Bible translations of TYNDALE and COVERDALE, adding marginal notes, and produced Matthew's Bible in 1537 (his pen name being Thomas Matthew). Rogers was in Antwerp and Wittenberg till 1548, then returned to England. His denunciation of Catholicism soon caused him to be imprisoned in Newgate, January 29, 1554, and burned at the stake in the presence of his wife and eleven children.

John Hooper

c 1495
Somersetshire, England

Feb. 9, 1555
Gloucester, England

Bishop of Gloucester in 1549 and of Worcester in 1552. Hooper was a stubborn English martyr. He was exiled to Zurich, Switzerland 1539–49. He was freed for a time during this period,

The Saints Go Marching In

so he returned to England and resumed his preaching. He married in Basel in 1546, then was re-exiled to Zurich, 1546–48. Hooper wrote *A Godly Confession and Protestation of the Christian Faith*. At Gloucester he refused to wear the vestments at his consecration as bishop. He was bishop of Gloucester (1550), and of Worcester (1552). When Queen Mary I arrived on the throne in 1553, he remained in jail until she passed laws against heresy, allowing her to have Hooper burned alive. As he died, he said, "Lord Jesus, have mercy on me; Lord Jesus, receive my spirit," as he beat his chest with one hand until it was burned to a stump.

Robert Ferrar

c 1508
near Halifax, England

March 30, 1555
Carmarthen, Wales

Bishop of St. David's Church, Wales, 1548–54, and martyr under Queen Mary I. He was martyred for denying the Catholic doctrine on the Lord's Supper (transubstantiation). In 1528, Ferrar turned from Catholicism influenced by Lutheran literature. He was imprisoned, transferred to a London jail temporarily, then returned to Wales to be burned at the stake.

John Bradford

c 1510
Manchester, England

July 1, 1555
London, England

Popular preacher martyred under Queen Mary I. He studied law and then theology. Bradford was appointed secretary to Nicholas Ridley (1550), prebendary of St. Paul's (1551–53), and chaplain to King Edward VI (1552). Bradford was arrested in August, 1553 for seditious utterances and heresy. On June 30, great crowds of people lined the road to Smithfield, weeping and praying for him. He refused to recant and met the death of a martyr with courage, being burned at the stake in Smithfield for his beliefs. He said as he died to John Leaf, a fellow companion who was likewise martyred: "Be of good comfort, brother, for we shall have a merry supper with the Lord this night."

Justus Jonas
Jobst Koch

June 5, 1493
Nordhausen, Germany

Oct. 9, 1555
Eisfeld, Germany

Lutheran reformer and scholar, converted in 1521. Early on, Jonas was canon, professor, and rector of Erfurt University. He was dean of the theological faculty of Wittenberg University (1523–33), where he taught canon law (1521–41). For twenty years he was an able assistant of Reformation leaders LUTHER and MELANCHTHON, accompanying LUTHER to the Diet of Worms in 1521 and helping to translate the OT. Jonas was with LUTHER when he died and gave the funeral oration at Eisleben, Germany. In 1541, Jonas went to Halle and later pastored at Eisfeld. He wrote the hymn, "If God Were Not Upon Our Side" (1524).

Nicholas Ridley

c 1500
Unthanx, England

Oct. 16, 1555
Oxford, England

Martyr with HUGH LATIMER. They were burned at the stake by Queen Mary I. Ridley was a bishop of Rochester (1547), and of London (1550). His zeal sometimes caused him to commit acts of vandalism against Catholics. Ridley helped to complete the *Book of Common Prayer* (1549), and helped to establish Protestantism at Cambridge University. He supported Lady JANE GREY's bid for the English throne, but when Mary prevailed, Ridley's fate at the stake was sealed. He was arrested and sent to the Tower, July 20, 1553.

Hugh Latimer

c 1485
Thurcaston, England

Oct. 16, 1555
Oxford, England

Reformer and martyr with NICHOLAS RIDLEY, who were both burned at the stake at Queen Mary I's behest. He was converted through the influence of THOMAS BILNEY. Latimer had great influence at Cambridge University, 1520–30. He was a bishop of Worcester, 1535–39. He lived in privacy (1539–47), then became a court preacher during EDWARD VI's reign (1547–53). His preaching helped spread the Reformation. Latimer nullified Henry VIII's marriage to Catherine of Aragon in 1530, revised the *Book of Common Prayer*, and put the Bible into every church in England during EDWARD VI's reign. In 1534, he preached a weekly sermon before the king. He was found guilty of "heresy" after disputing with Catholic theologians at Oxford, during Queen Mary's reign. He was imprisoned in the Tower (Sept. 13, 1553), and sentenced to death (October 1, 1555). As he died, Latimer said, "We shall this day light such a candle, by God's grace, in England, as I trust shall never be put out." His favorite Bible verse was I Timothy 1:15.

Thomas Cranmer

July 2, 1489
Aslocton, England

March 21, 1556
Oxford, England

First Protestant archbishop of Canterbury, appointed by Henry VIII, 1533–56, who was martyred under Queen Mary I. Margarette, niece of ANDREAS OSIANDER, became his wife in 1532 in Germany. One source states his second wife, Joan, died in childbirth. In 1536, he preached at St. Paul's against Pope Paul III (reigned: 1534–49), purgatory, and indulgences. Cranmer allowed King Henry VIII a divorce from Catherine of Aragon in 1533, which gained him the archbishopric, temporarily discounting Mary's bid for the throne and strengthening Lady JANE GREY's right of ascendency to the throne after EDWARD VI. Cranmer encouraged Bible circulation (Great Bible 1539), sanctioned marriage for priests, and replaced the Mass with the Lord's Supper. In 1549 he wrote *Book of Common Prayer* (revised 1552). He was tried for treason and heresy, imprisoned, condemned to death, and burned at the stake, once Mary Tudor (English dynasty starting with JOHN OF GAUNT) was queen. He said as he died, "Lord Jesus, receive my spirit."

Johann D. Joris

1501
Ghent/Bruges, Netherlands

Aug. 25, 1556
Basel, Switzerland

Radical Anabaptist leader. He became the head of a sect which recognized him as their Messiah. Many disbelievers were burned at the stake, and others suffered as a result. Joris personally accumulated a fortune and moved to Basel in 1544, functioning as a rich and pious citizen. The deception was not known until after his death. His distorted sect existed for about one hundred years.

Gabriel Zwilling

c 1487
Annaberg, Germany

1558
Torgau, Germany

Fiery fellow monk in the Augustinian monastery with LUTHER. Zwilling followed LUTHER out of the monastery, but adopted a more radical stance. Zwilling's views were similar to CARLSTADT: fiercely attacking the Mass, adoration of the sacrament, monasticism and images. LUTHER was incensed at the civil disorder Zwilling, CARLSTADT, and other would-be reformers stirred up at Wittenberg, Germany, 1521–22. He pastored at Zwickau later in life.

Johann Bugenhagen
Dr. Johannes Pomeranus

June 24, 1485
Wollin, Germany

April 20, 1558
Wittenberg, Germany

Reformer who switched from Catholicism to Lutheranism in 1520. Bugenhagen organized the Lutheran Church in North Germany and Denmark, 1537–42, at the invitation of King Christian III of Denmark and Norway (ruled: 1534–39). He was rector in Treptow (1504–17), taught in Belbuck (1517–21), pastored in Wittenberg (1522–58) and was professor of biblical exegesis at the University of Wittenberg in 1525. Bugenhagen married (1522), officiated at LUTHER's wedding (1525) to KATHARINA VON BORA and preached LUTHER's memorial service in Wittenberg (1546). LUTHER had often sought counsel from him. He also helped MELANCHTHON draft the Augsburg Confession (summary of Lutheran faith), which was read before the Diet of Augsburg, Germany, in 1530. Bugenhagen wrote *Brunswick Church Order* and translated the Bible into Low German (dialect spoken along the North Sea).

"If you know Christ well, it is enough...if you do not know Christ, it is nothing..."

Christian II
The Cruel

July 1, 1481
Nyborg, Denmark

Jan. 25, 1559
Kalundborg, Denmark

King of Norway, Denmark, and Sweden, 1513–23. In 1515, Christian married Isabella (sister of Charles V of The Holy Roman Empire). He was driven from Sweden by VASA GUSTAVUS I when he executed 82 Swedish noblemen in 1520. Christian II sought to introduce the Reformation to Denmark, but he wanted a state Protestant church under the control of his uncle, King FREDERICK I, in 1522. Denmark revolted, forcing Christian II to flee to the Netherlands, where he continued to favor society's lower classes. While trying to recapture Norway, he was imprisoned from 1532 until his death, first at Sonderburg Castle, then Kalundborg Castle. He was known as Christian "The Cruel" for his massacre of Scandinavian nobility.

Obbe Philips

c 1500
Leuwarden, Netherlands

1560

Anabaptist preacher. Philips opposed MELCHIOR HOFFMANN's (radical Anabaptist who predicted the end of the world) extravagant views, banning any people associated with him or the town of Munster, Germany. Philips organized the first Anabaptist congregation in West Friesland, Netherlands, and in 1536 baptized MENNO SIMONS. Obbe left the Mennonite movement, but his brother Dirck, whom he won to the faith, was co–laborer with SIMONS.

Wilhelm Reublin

c 1480
Rottenburg, Swabia (Germany)

1560
Znaim, Austria

Anabaptist who suffered much persecution. Reublin opposed the carrying of relics, preferring to carry the Bible. He was one of the early advocates of believer's baptism and was banished from Zurich for this belief. He married Abelheid Leemann on April 28, 1523. He later traveled to Waldshut where he met and baptized HUBMAIER about Easter, 1525. Reublin constantly opposed and attacked the superstitions of the Church. He was imprisoned in Strasbourg in 1528. In 1535, Reublin withdrew from Anabaptist circles. Reublin returned to Basel in 1554, then disappeared somewhat friendless and persecuted.

Peder Palladius
Peter E. Palladius

1503
Ribe, Denmark

Jan. 3, 1560

Danish leader of the Reformation. Palladius was the rector of a church in Odense in 1530, when he became a Reformation convert. He studied in Wittenberg, 1531–37, after which he introduced the Lutheran Reformation to Denmark, Norway, and Iceland. He was appointed by King Christian III as the first Protestant bishop of Zealand (Denmark's largest island containing the capital Copenhagen) in 1537, where he later served as professor of theology at the University of Copenhagen. He wrote 65 works, made frequent visits to more than 300 churches, and preached against saints and pilgrimages.

Jan Laski (Johannes a Lasco)

1499
Lask or Warsaw, Poland

Jan. 8, 1560
Pinczow, Poland

Political friend of the Reformation in several European locations. Early on, Laski was sent on diplomatic missions for the Catholic Church. In 1525, he joined the Reformation movement while living with Erasmus in Basel. He was bishop in Veszprem, Hungary, 1529–38. Converted in 1538, he lived in Cracow, Poland (1538–43), after which he helped to introduce the Reformation in Emden, Germany (1543–50), superintending the work in East Frisia. He was married at Louvain shortly thereafter. Laski was asked by Archbishop THOMAS CRANMER to help organize the Anglican Church in England in 1550. He wisely left England when Queen Mary I came to the throne in 1553. He ended his days as superintendent of the Reformed Church in South Poland. Laski sought to unite Lutherans, Calvinists, and Hussites in Poland. This happened in 1570 after his death. He composed the famous *Emden Catechism* (1546) and, with 17 others, he prepared the Polish version of the Bible.

Philip Melanchthon

Feb. 16, 1497
Bretten, Germany

April 19, 1560
Wittenberg, Germany

Second only to LUTHER in importance as a reformer. His knowledge of Greek made him valuable to LUTHER in Bible translation work. Melanchthon wrote the first great work of Protestant dogmatic theology: *Loci Communes* (1521). He also authored the Lutheran statement of faith, the Augsburg Confession of 1530. Beginning in 1518, he taught Greek for many years at the University of Wittenberg. Katharina Krapp became his wife on November 25, 1520, giving him four children. She died in 1557 when Melanchthon was defending the Reformation in the town of Worms, Germany. From 1528–46, he was at odds with LUTHER, taking a milder stand on Reformation matters. Additionally, he wrote many Latin hymns and founded many schools. Melanchthon favored reconciliation between Protestant sectors to preserve Christian unity. He died as a result of a severe cold followed by a fever contracted on a journey to Leipzig in March. His favorite Bible verse was Romans 8:31.

Vasa Gustavus I

May 12, 1496
Lindholmen, Sweden

Sept. 29, 1560
Stockholm, Sweden

King of Sweden, 1523–60. Gustavus was a prior in Denmark (1517–19) and drove the Danes out of Sweden, defeating King CHRISTIAN II (1521–23). He sought to bring the Church in his realm under the control of the crown. During his 37-year reign, the Lutheran Church was thoroughly established in 1529, and the property of the Catholic Church confiscated. Gustavus I was a civil as well as a religious reformer. He is venerated as the founder of Swedish independence and was the grandfather of GUSTAVUS ADOLPHUS II. In 1559, he sent the first Lutheran missionaries to the despised pagan laplanders (northern Scandinavian inhabitants).

Diebold Schwarz

1485   *1561*

Conducted the first Reformed Mass in the German language in 1524. Schwarz was an early follower of LUTHER who translated the old Roman service into simple German, eliminating its Catholic doctrine. He pastored Old St. Peter's Church in Strasbourg and was associated with CALVIN during CALVIN's stay there.

Louis Bourgeois

1510   *c 1561*
Paris, France   Paris, France

CALVIN's choirmaster at Geneva, Switzerland, 1545–52. Bourgeois came to Geneva about 1541 and was chief musician of the city. He composed the music for what is commonly known as the "Doxology" (1545–47), when he returned to Paris. THOMAS KEN wrote the lyrics in 1674. Bourgeois compiled the *Geneva Psalter* (1547), which was the earliest and best collection of words and music for congregational singing. His published tunes put him in prison in 1551, but he was released by CALVIN's pleas. He was one of the first to harmonize the melodies of the French version of the Psalms and was the chief founder of Huguenot (French Protestants named after Besancon Hugues, Swiss political leader from Eidgnot) melody. In 1557 he returned to Paris. He also composed music for "All People That on Earth Do Dwell" (lyrics by WILLIAM KETHE).

Menno Simons

c 1492–1496   *Jan. 31, 1561*
Witmarsum, Friesland (Netherlands)   Wustenfelde, Prussia (Germany)

Leader of the Dutch Anabaptists from 1537 on, the same year he was ordained an elder by OBBE PHILLIPS. Simons gave the somewhat leaderless and unstable Anabaptists credibility with his wise, moderate, and spiritual direction. Simons served as a popular evangelical Catholic preacher, 1526–30, until his conversion. In Bolsward, 1535, a slaughter of 300 Anabaptists, including his brother, at Old Cloister led to his conversion. In January, 1536, he left the Catholic Church and was baptized as an Anabaptist. Simons was a pacifist and rejected a state church. For 12 years he was in constant danger as a heretic and forced to move from place to place. He married and travelled as an evangelist in Holland and Germany. He finally found refuge on an estate in Wustenfelde, Germany, between Hamburg and Luebock (near Oldsloe), 1554 on. Simons developed the teaching that led to the formation of the Mennonite Church, named in his memory. He published *The Foundation of Christian Doctrine* (1539).

Hans Tausen

1494   *Nov. 11, 1561*
Birkende, Fyn Island, Denmark   Ribe, Denmark

Father of the Danish Reformation. Tausen was a monk and language scholar who converted to Lutheranism. In 1525, he was imprisoned at Viborg for preaching "heretical" doctrines; and upon his release, he left the Franciscans. He translated the Pentateuch into Danish, 1535. After the Reformation triumph in Denmark (1536), he became bishop of Ribe (1542). Tausen was the first to use the Danish tongue in worship, the first to preach Lutheranism in Denmark, and the first Danish cleric to marry. He was professor and pastor at Copenhagen. He gave Denmark the Lutheran Confession, Danish Bible, Lutheran hymnbook, and a school.

Caspar Schwenkfeld

Dec. 1489
Ossig, Germany

Dec. 10, 1561
Ulm, Germany

Silesian (N Czechoslovakia - SW Poland) Reformation theologian, writer, and preacher who enthusiastically embraced the Lutheran Reformation. He developed doctrines different from others, opposing war, secret societies, and oath taking. Schwenkfeld rejected all ceremonies which left him estranged from the Lutherans, the Reformed, and the Anabaptists. He was in various towns of Swabia, traveling in exile—a homeless wanderer (1529) going to Strasbourg (1534). He withdrew from the Lutheran Church in 1540. His Schwenkelder Church, which he did not wish to organize, embraced the views later representative of the Quakers. He had a strong emphasis on inward mystical religion.

Augustin Marlorat

1506
Bar-le-Duc, France

Oct. 31, 1562
Rouen, France

Reformed Church martyr who pastored in Paris (1559) and then in Rouen (1561), where he was eventually hanged. He was educated in an Augustinian convent but later sympathized with the Reformation. The succession of King Charles IX (ruled: 1560–74) to the throne brought persecution to the Protestants. After the Catholics recaptured Rouen October 26, 1562, Marlorat was condemned, and then executed in front of his church. He wrote commentaries on various books of the Bible.

Pietro Vermigli

May 8, 1500
Florence, Italy

Dec. 12, 1562
Zurich, Switzerland

Italian reformer. Vermigli was an Augustinian monk who changed from Catholicism after reading the works of LUTHER and ZWINGLI. In 1526, he sought to preach throughout Italy. He left Catholicism in 1542 and taught at Strasbourg, 1543–47. At the invitation of CRANMER, he emigrated to England (1547) and taught theology at Oxford University (1549). Persecution in 1553 forced him out, so he resumed his position as professor of theology at Strasbourg University, 1553–56. In 1556, he served as professor of Hebrew at Zurich, at the bidding of BULLINGER. In 1561, his wife died at Oxford. He was a strong Calvinist, and the author of many works on theology and commentaries on the Bible.

John Bale

Nov. 21, 1495
Cove, England

Nov. 1563
Canterbury, England

Controversial churchman. Raised a Catholic, Bale became an Anglican while studying at Cambridge University. He fled to Basel, Switzerland and Germany, 1540–47. Returning to England (1547), he was appointed bishop of the Irish see of Ossory (1552). During Queen Mary I's reign, he fled to Holland. Then Bale returned to England upon the accession of Protestant Queen ELIZABETH and was made prebendary of Canterbury Cathedral in 1560. He was learned, but abrasive in his controversial attacks against Catholicism. Bale wrote 21 miracle plays based on the life of Christ. He also wrote *Illustrium Majoris . . . Summarium* and other prose pieces.

Bernardino Ochino

1487
Sienna, Italy

1564
Slavkow, Moravia (Czechoslovakia)

Unstable Italian reformer whose radical views, such as advocating polygamy, made him a fugitive most of his life. He began his career as a Franciscan monk and in 1538 was a general of the Capuchin (mendicant order of Franciscans that observed poverty and austerity, 1525) order. Influenced by Valdes, (Spanish humanist and reformer, c 1500–41), he became a Calvinist in

1542 at the beginning of the Roman Inquisition. He fled to Geneva and married. He was minister of an Italian Protestant congregation at Augsburg, 1545–47, but had to flee before the city was occupied. Ochino became a Lutheran pastor, when the Schmalkald War (Protestants against Holy Roman Emperor Charles V) forced him to England to help CRANMER, 1547–53. Ochino fled to Zurich upon Queen Mary I's accession, pastoring a congregation of Italian refugees, 1553–63. He was banished from Switzerland for his extreme views and fled to Cracow, Poland, in 1563, but was not welcomed there. Ochino died of the plague the next year.

Michelangelo Buonarroti

March 6, 1475
Caprese, Italy

Feb. 18, 1564
Rome, Italy

Sculptor, painter, and architect. This Catholic showed his love for the Lord through his multi-talented accomplishments. He, like Shakespeare was among the dramatists, that had no rival in his field, as he painted such as the *Conversion of St. Paul*, and sculpted the *David* (1501–04) and *Moses* (1513–16). He was best known for painting the ceiling (10,000 square feet) of the Sistine Chapel, 1508–12 and 1535–41. After his last painting, *The Last Judgment* (1537–41), he worked as chief architect of St. Peter's, in 1547, designing the great central dome. In writing to his father, he said, "Live on, and if you are to share in the honors of this world like other citizens, it is enough to have bread and to live in the faith of Christ, even as I do here,". . .In his will he said, "I commit my soul to God. . .I die in the faith of Jesus Christ and in the firm hope of a better life." His activity was basically in Florence (1520–34) and Rome (1534–64). His nose was squashed against his face as a result of a beating he received as a child when he taunted Pietro Torrigiano, a painter. At age 88 he prepared architectural plans for the church of Santa Maria degli Angeli. Although he was rich, he lived as frugally as a poor man, living for years on bread and wine. He was number two on one pollster's all-time genius list. He received double pay for overtime at night. He made himself a hood into which he placed a lighted candle, so he could see his work as he labored. His last words were: "Through life remember the sufferings of Jesus."

John Calvin

July 10, 1509
Noyon, France

May 27, 1564
Geneva, Switzerland

Theologian and reformer who founded the doctrinal system called Calvinism. This led to the formation of the Reformed Church in the Netherlands and the Scottish Presbyterian Church, among others. Originally, he began to pursue a career in law in 1528, but became a priest instead. He was converted in April, 1534 after a visit to LEFEVRE. He fled from Paris with NICHOLAS COP to Basel (1535), then detoured through Geneva (1536). FAREL successfully begged him to stay in Geneva to help establish a theocratic government and provide leadership for the Reformation, 1536–64. He resided in Strasbourg, 1538–41, being briefly exiled from Geneva. Calvin's *Institutes of the Christian Religion* (Basel, Switzerland: 1536–59) is the basis of theology for his movement. Idelette de Bure (Anabaptist widow) became his wife in August, 1540 (died: March 29, 1549). They had one son, who lived only a few days. Calvin introduced congregational singing to Protestant services. In his fight against heretics, Calvin proceeded to have Michael Servetus (a man with unorthodox, anti-Trinitarian, Arian, and Anabaptist views), burned at the stake, 1553, a blot on his life. He helped establish the Academy (University) of Geneva in 1559. His Genevan government became a focal point of French Protestantism. Calvin built the "building" after ZWINGLI had laid the foundation. Refugees from all over Europe came to Geneva, studied and returned, spreading his doctrinal "ideas." He said as he died, "This intervening wall will not prevent me from being present with you in spirit, though absent in body." He died in BEZA's arms. He was a slaveholder.

"Until He is united with us, Jesus considers Himself incomplete."

Alexander Alesius

April 23, 1500
Edinburgh, Scotland

March 17, 1565
Leipzig, Germany

Lutheran reformer. As a young man, Alesius sought a recantation from PATRICK HAMILTON, but found himself converted to Protestantism instead. Alesius signed the Augsburg Confession in 1530. After imprisonment in Scotland for his Reformation sympathies, he fled to Germany in 1532, meeting LUTHER and MELANCHTHON. He lived in England, 1535–40, then returned to Germany (1540), becoming a professor of theology at Frankfurt on the Oder and dean at the University of Leipzig (1543).

Nikolaus von Amsdorf

Dec. 3, 1483
Torgau, Germany

May 14, 1565
Eisenach, Germany

Lutheran theologian and reformer. He, along with FLACIUS, sought to retain the purity of LUTHER's teachings as liberal elements came on the scene. He said, "good words are harmful to salvation." Amsdorf was one of the first students at Wittenberg in 1502. He was a professor there, 1511–24. He was a pastor at Magdeburg (1524–31), then helped reform Goslar (1531–34), and Einbeck (1534–42). Amsdorf was made bishop of Naumburg (1542), but lost this appointment as a result of the Smalkaldic War (1547). He went to Madgeburg in that year. In 1552, he was appointed general superintendent and counsellor to the dukes of Eisenach residing there. Amsdorf helped found the University of Jena and aided LUTHER in translating the Bible into German. After LUTHER's death, he opposed MELANCHTHON and his pupils.

Guillaume Farel

1489
near Gap/Fareaux, France

Sept. 13, 1565
Neuchatel, Switzerland

Dynamic French Reformation pioneer who broke ground for the Reformation in many French and Swiss cities. He was driven from Paris for being a Lutheran in 1521. It was in 1523 that Farel became interested in the work of Hinne Rode, rector of the Brethren of Common Life at Utrecht. Farel turned from Catholicism to Christ in 1524. After being driven from Basel, Switzerland, he became a traveling preacher for eight years, 1524–32, before settling down in Geneva in 1532. In 1530, he secured public adoption of Reformed doctrines in Neuchatel, Switzerland. When CALVIN stopped there in 1536, Farel convinced him to stay on and serve the Reformation cause there. He was banished from Geneva because of his attempt to enforce a stricter moral discipline, 1538–41. Farel lived out his days in Neuchatel, Switzerland, where he began pastoring in 1541. At age 69, he married a very young lady. Farel had the privilege of being with CALVIN at the time of CALVIN's death.

Johann Agricola
Johannes Sneider

April 20, 1494
Eisleben, Germany

Sept. 22, 1566
Berlin, Germany

Lutheran reformer who originally supported LUTHER and was one of the signers of the Augsburg Confession. After studying at Wittenberg University, he introduced the Reformation at Frankfurt in 1525 then went to Eisleben, where he was a preacher at St. Nicolai. In 1526, he was a chaplain to Elector JOHN THE CONSTANT OF SAXONY at the Diet of Spires. In 1527, he had a dispute with MELANCHTHON over the relationship between repentance and faith. Agricola was a professor at the University of Wittenberg in 1537. He then served as a court preacher and general superintendent in Brandenburg (Berlin) from 1540 on. Agricola espoused antinomianism (Mosaic law had no place in the Christian life). He was one of the authors of the Augsburg Interim in 1548.

Philip of Hesse
Philip the Magnanimous

Nov. 13, 1504
Marburg, Germany

March 31, 1567
Kassel, Germany

Landgrave (German count having territorial jurisdiction) **of Hesse, 1509–67**. Philip did much to advance the Reformation. At the Council at Worms in Germany in 1521, he insisted that LUTHER should receive full protection. Philip tried to unite German and Swiss Protestants. He defeated THOMAS MUNZER in the Peasants War, 1524–25. In 1531, he formed the Schmalkaldic League. He began to sabotage it (1538) and blocked the demand for a civil war (1539). His bigamous marriage in 1540 hurt the Reformation cause when he married 17-year-old Margaret van der Sale (Soale) with the consent of LUTHER. He was already married to Christina, daughter of Henry the Pious, the Duke of Saxony. Philip won a diplomatic war (1539–44), after which he was treacherously seized by Emperor Charles V and imprisoned (1547–52). The treaty of Passau gave him freedom. Philip was denounced as a Zwinglian radical. Returning to Hesse, he sent aid to the French Huguenots, and aided the insurgents in the Netherlands. He founded the University of Marburg. His daughter married MAURICE of Saxony.

Guido De Bres

c 1522
Mons, Belgium

May 31, 1567
Valenciennes, Netherlands

Preacher, reformer, author of the Belgic Confession and martyr. Brought up in a Christian home, De Bres fled to England in 1548, and joined a refuge colony in London. In 1552, he was back home assisting Protestant churches in Lille and Tournai. His Belgic Confession (a basic statement of faith in Calvinism written in French) of 1559 was sought to convince the secular authorities and to serve as a standard for Reformed churches. In 1561, he fled again from Spanish authorities and went to Sedan, France. De Bres had mastered Latin, Greek, and Hebrew and was a follower of CALVIN. This document won thousands to the cause of the Reformation. In 1566, he came to Antwerp, Belgium, where he opposed the Anabaptists. He was arrested and imprisoned, at Tournai and then at Valenciennes, where he was executed by hanging in front of the town hall. His last words were an exhortation to obey the magistrates.

Albert

May 16, 1490
Ansbach, Germany

March 20, 1568
Tapiau (Guardersk), Prussia (Lithuania/Russia)

Last Grand Master of the Teutonic Order of Knights (which he dissolved under the advice of LUTHER), in 1511; first duke of Prussia, 1525 on; and Margave of Brandenburg. Being recognized by Poland, Albert proceeded to Konigsberg, and assumed the government in 1512. LUTHER influenced his conversion in 1520. In 1522, at Nuremberg, he came under the influence of ANDREAS OSIANDER, who won him over to the Reformed faith. Albert actively encouraged the Reformation in Prussia (1525), although being somewhat banned (1532). In 1527, he married Dorothea, daughter of King FREDERICK I of Denmark. His rule was disturbed by peasant uprisings and theological quarrels. Albert founded the University of Konigsberg in 1544, the third Protestant university. He was responsible for the strict Lutheranism that prevailed there. He did much to make Prussia a Protestant state.

Miles Coverdale

1488
North Riding, York, England

buried— Jan. 20, 1569
London, England

Translator of the first complete English Bible in 1535 known as the Coverdale Bible. This was most of WILLIAM TYNDALE's work, supplemented by Latin and German versions. Coverdale was a former Augustinian friar (member of Mendicant order, whose orders are not attached to a monastery and own no communal property) who left the order in 1528 because he found Christ on his own. He preached against images, the mass, and intercessory confession. He was exiled to the continent (1528–34 and 1540–48), pastoring a Lutheran congregation at Bergzabern, Germany (1545–48). In 1539, he produced the Great Bible (depending on German and Latin versions), which was a revision of Matthew's Bible (Old Testament and TYNDALE's New Testament). It appeared in several editions, 1540–41. Much of Coverdale's phraseology was incorporated into the King James Version (1611). Coverdale served as bishop of Exeter, 1551–53, until imprisoned by Queen Mary I. Escaping, he lived on the Continent, 1555–59. He became a Puritan leader, returning to England and serving as rector of St. Magnus, London Bridge, 1559–66. He also assisted in preparing the Geneva Bible, published in 1560, the first English Bible translated from the original text. His date of death is controversial. *Encyclopedia Americana* gives his burial date as Feb. 19, 1568. The parish register of St. Bartholomew's, behind the Royal Exchange, states January 20, 1569 as his burial date.

Louis de Bourbon

May 7, 1530
Vendome, France

March 13, 1569
Jarnac, France

Prince of Conde, France. Louis was the first great leader of the Huguenots, joining them in 1559. He was the French general in charge of the Huguenot Army after their massacre at Vasse in 1562. From 1551–58, he participated in many battles in France and Italy. In 1555, on his way back from an Italian campaign, he stopped at Geneva to attend a Calvinistic service. When the Guises (chief royal bulwark of Catholic prior) gained control, Louis engaged in three battles against them, 1562–63, 1567–68, and 1569. Louis was captured at the Battle of Jarnac, and treacherously shot by a Catholic Swiss officer when he was in the process of surrendering his sword. He will be remembered for making French Calvinism a political power. He was a contemporary and colleague of COLIGNY.

Paul Eber

Nov. 8, 1511
Kitzingen, Bavaria (Germany)

Dec. 10, 1569
Wittenberg, Germany

Lutheran theologian and Bavarian poet. Eber is ranked second only to LUTHER among the Wittenberg poets. Eber was a professor of Latin (1541), of physics (1545), and Hebrew (1550) at Wittenberg University. He was a preacher at Castle Church in Wittenberg and, in 1558, of the City Church (succeeding BUGENHAGEN) and was secretary to MELANCHTHON at the Worms Colloquy (Conference) in Germany. He also wrote several hymns, including, "When in the Hour of Utmost Need" and "Lord Jesus Christ, True Man and God."

Antonio Paleario
Aonio della Paglia

c 1503
Veroli, Italy

July 3, 1570
Rome, Italy

Catholic reformer, humanis, and martyr who was hanged, then burned at the stake for teaching justification by faith. He was a teacher at Siena, Italy, and gained fame as a poet. He was a professor at Lucca (1546–55) and then at Milan (1555–67). Three times he was charged with "heresy," at Siena (1542), at Milan (1559 and 1567). He strongly attacked the doctrine of purgatory. Paleario was sent to Rome for two years of imprisonment before his conviction and death. He was hanged, and his body burned. He wrote a book on the sufficiency of the passion of Christ.

Johannes Brentz

June 24, 1499
Weilderstadt, Wurttemberg-Baden (Germany)

Sept. 11, 1570
Stuttgart, Germany

Lutheran reformer. Brentz saw LUTHER at Heidelberg in 1518 and became his follower. In 1522. he went to Halle. By 1523, he had stopped serving mass and had begun to support the work of the Reformers. He authored the first Protestant cathechism (a year before LUTHER's). Brentz expounded on LUTHER's view of the Real Presence in the Lord's Supper (consubstantiation) and published these sentiments in 1524 and helped to realign the constitution of the University of Tubingen. In 1548, he fled from Halle when it was captured by imperial forces. Brentz later was the chief pastor in Stuttgart beginning in 1553. He refused presents from great lords and lucrative places in Magdeburg, Prussia, and England.

Pierre Viret

May 4, 1511
Orbe, Switzerland

April 4, 1571
Orthez, France

Eloquent member of the great trio of reformers in Switzerland which, along with himself, included CALVIN and FAREL. Upon Viret's ordination by FAREL in 1531, he returned to his hometown of Orbe, Switzerland, where he began pastoring. Viret joined FAREL in Geneva in 1534, where he was almost poisoned by a Catholic priest inspired plot. From 1536–59, he led the Reformation movement in Lausanne and founded a Reformed church. Viret helped CALVIN overcome opposition and return to Geneva in 1541. He was an able preacher and writer.

John Jewel

May 24, 1522
Buden, England

Sept. 23, 1571
Monkton Farleigh, England

Bishop of Salisbury, as of 1560. In 1541, he became vicar of Sunningwell. Jewel was a fellow (graduate student who is allowed additional, special study) at Corpus Christi College, Oxford, 1542 on. He became one of the intellectual leaders and great apologetical writers of the Church of England. After Queen Mary I's death, he emerged as a major Anglican leader, having spent 1553–58 on the Continent. His *Apologia pro Ecclesia Anglicana* (1562) refuted Catholic attacks on his church. Jewel also opposed Puritanism and built a library of note.

Jeanne D'Albret

Jan. 7, 1528
Pau, France

June 9, 1572
Paris, France

Queen of Navarre. She was a devoted follower of the Reformation. Jeanne was the daughter of Henry d'Albret and mother of HENRY IV, French king. Upon her father's death in 1555, she inherited the throne. CALVIN was her devoted counselor. She married Duke Antoine Bourbon (1518–62) on October 20, 1548, sharing the throne with him until his death. After the battle of Jarnac, France (Catholics defeated Protestants) in 1569, she did all in her power to help the Huguenot cause. Queen d'Albret died while visiting to attend her son's wedding, which instigated St. Bartholomew's Day Massacre. She said as she died, "...God by this sickness calls me hence to enjoy a better life..."

Gaspard de Coligny

Feb. 16, 1519
Chatillon-sur-Loing, France

Aug. 24, 1572
Paris, France

Statesman and military admiral who became the spokesman for the Huguenots. At age 35, he was the highest military officer of the land, becoming the French admiral in 1552. Coligny was converted sometime between 1555–60 and joined the Reformed Church. He defended San Quentin for 17 days against the superior force of King Philip II of Spain (ruled: 1556–98) in 1557 but was finally forced to surrender. From 1557–59, he was in a Flemish prison. He encouraged colonization in Brazil (1555) and Florida (1562) to provide refuge for the Huguenots. Coligny defended the Protestants in the fierce "Wars of Religion," beginning in 1562. Always willing to negotiate, he frequently returned to court on their behalf. He was the first to be killed in the bloodbath known as the St. Bartholomew's Day Massacre in France when Catholics attacked the many Huguenots assembled in Paris for the Protestant wedding of HENRY IV OF NAVARRE. Some 25,000 were killed. His head was sent to Pope Gregory XIII (reigned: 1572–85) at Rome.

John Knox

c 1514–1515
Haddington, Scotland

Nov. 24, 1572
Edinburgh, Scotland

Father of the Reformation in Scotland and founder of Presbyterianism. Knox entered the Catholic priesthood (1536) but was converted (c. 1543). In 1547, he joined a rebel group of Protestants in the Castle of St. Andrew's. This was captured by the French, and he was imprisoned for 19 months in France until February, 1549. He pastored in Berwick Tweed, England, 1549–53, preaching until the Queen of Scots, Mary Stuart (ruled: 1543–67), ascended to the throne. He fled in exile to Geneva in 1553 and for the next four years assisted CALVIN there. He married Marjorie Bowes while revisiting Scotland (1555), then pastored an English-speaking church in Geneva (1556). In 1559, he made his final return to Scotland and his dynamic preaching of Bible doctrine completely turned the country around. Knox also excelled in educational reforms. His wife died in December, 1560 (about age 28), and he (age 59) married 17-year-old Margaret Stewart in 1564 and had three daughters. Knox ignored the Catholic proclamations of Mary, Queen of Scots, who had returned in 1561. She was forced to abdicate the throne in 1567. Suffering a paralytic stroke in 1570, he died two years later, while his wife read John 17 (favorite verses, John 17:2–3) and a part of CALVIN's Ephesian sermons. He went peaceably saying, "Now, it is come."

Richard Grafton

c 1513

1573

Chronicler (one who lists historical events) **and printer**. Grafton was a London merchant who was an energetic supporter of the Reformation. He is remembered as the printer of Matthew's Bible (1537), the Great Bible (1539) and the *Book of Common Prayer* (1st ed. 1549; 2nd ed. 1552). Grafton suffered imprisonment briefly and lost his title of "King Printer" under Queen Mary I. Later he was a member of Parliament for London and then for Coventry. Some of his business methods were questioned.

Laurentius Petri

1499
Orebro, Sweden

Sept. 22, 1573

Church of Sweden primate (archbishop, high church leader). He was one of two brothers that brought the Reformation to Sweden in 1518. With his brother OLAUS, he was a student of Luther's at the University of Wittenberg in Germany. He served as theology professor at Upsala, and then became the first Lutheran archbishop of Sweden in 1531. Petri produced a translation of the New Testament in Swedish, at the request of the Swedish King, VASA GUSTAVUS I. He also translated many Psalms into the Swedish liturgy.

Matthias Flacius
Matija Vlacic, the Illyrian

March 3, 1520
Labin, Austro-Hungary (Yugoslavia)

March 11, 1575
Frankfurt am Main, Germany

Lutheran theologian and church historian. Flacius' academic posts began as a professor of Hebrew at Wittenberg (1544), and then continued at universities in Jena (1558), Antwerp (1566), Frankfurt, and Magdeburg. In 1541, he arrived in Wittenberg where contact with MARTIN LUTHER convinced him of evangelical truths. Flacius opposed Augsburg and Leipzig Interims (statements by German Protestant theologians, in which important concessions were made to pacify the Catholics). His intermittent conflict with civil and ecclesiastical authorities reduced his welcome everywhere as evidenced by his temporary residence in nine German cities, including Regensburg (1562–66) and Strasbourg (1567–73). Flacius first married (1545), but after his wife and children's death, he married Magdalena Illbeck (1564). His stubborn refusal to admit defeat to the Catholic cause in Magdeburg, kept Lutheranism alive in that part of Germany. Flacius finally found asylum in a cloister at Frankfurt, where he was protected until his death. He was strong on verbal inspiration.

Matthew Parker

Aug. 6, 1504
Norwich, England

May 17, 1575
Canterbury, London, England

Archbishop of Canterbury, 1559–75. Parker was chosen from obscurity by Queen ELIZABETH because of his common sense, scholarship, and spirituality. He made a distinct Protestant identity apart from Catholicism, was involved in the formulation of the 39 Articles and aided in the preparation of the Bishop's Bible (1560). He chaired a revision committee of about 17 bishops (scholars). Parker also helped to care for Elizabeth when she was a child. He was vice-chancellor of Cambridge (1545) and dean of Lincoln (1552), which was nullified when Catholic Mary I came to the throne (1553). He married Margaret Harlestone in June, 1547. Parker was a strong opponent of Puritanism. A fall from his horse gave him permanent injuries. Parker was the second Protestant archbishop, CRANMER being the first.

Renee
Renata

Oct. 25, 1510
Blois, France

June 12, 1575
Montargis, France

Huguenot Duchess of Ferrara, Italy. She espoused the Reformation. Renee was the daughter of King Louis XII (ruled: 1498–1515) of France. She was married to Ercole II of Este (Duke of Ferrera) in April, 1520. When she came to Ferrara in 1535, they began a lifelong friendship. Renee was influenced by Queen Margaret d'Albret (ruled: 1544–49) of Navarre toward evangelical truths. Renee's unbelieving husband persecuted her and imprisoned her until he died on October 3, 1559, whereupon she returned to France. She had also been threatened with banishment by her own son. Later, she lived in Montargis, France, where she held church services in her home and was distinguished for piety and learning.

Richard Taverner

1505
Brisley, England

July 14, 1575
Wood Eaton, England

Bible translator. He issued the first translation of the Bible to be printed in England. His translation was a revision of Matthew's Bible and was known as Taverner's Bible (London, 1539). He was clerk of the Privy Seal in England, 1536–53, under Thomas Cromwell. Taverner was licensed to preach by King EDWARD VI (1552) but was removed from office (1553) upon the accession of Queen Mary I. Later under ELIZABETH I, he served as sheriff of Oxford. Taverner also wrote commentaries on New Testament books. He translated the Ausburg Confession into English (1536) and published the first book of English Lutheran *Dogmatics* (1538).

J. Heinrich Bullinger

July 18, 1504
Bremgarten (near Zurich), Switzerland

Sept. 17, 1575
Bremgarten, Switzerland

Reformer and powerful supporter of Zwingli. Bullinger left Catholicism in 1522. Leaving Cologne, he returned to Switzerland in 1523. In 1529, he married a former nun who gave him eleven children. He fled from Bremgarten to pastor the church in Zurich, vacated by Zwingli's death, serving 1531–71. Bullinger helped draft Zwingli's First Helvetic Confession (1536) and the Second Helvetic Confession (1566). In 1549, he reached an agreement with Calvin on the Lord's Supper, which united the Churches of Zurich and Geneva. He was close to Cranmer, Melanchthon, Calvin, and Beza. Bullinger corresponded with three monarchs of England: Henry VIII, Edward VI, and Elizabeth I. He was also an able historian, writing works such as *History of the Reformation*.

"The best prayers have often more groans than words"

Hans Sachs
The Poet-Shoeman

Nov. 5, 1494
Nuremburg, Germany

Jan. 19, 1576
Nuremburg, Germany

Poet and singer. He was known as "The Prince and Patriarch of the Master-singers." The "master singers" that he organized were simply mechanics and trades-people who sang the poems they composed. Sachs visited the principal cities of Germany, 1510–15; cultivating these experiences into the art of poetry. Sachs composed some 6,636 poems himself, also writing songs and plays. In 1519, he married. His famous poem about Luther was called, "The Nightingale of Wittenberg" (1523). He influenced the Reformation in Nuremberg. He was a shoeman by trade.

Frederick III
The Pious

Feb. 14, 1515
Simmern, Prussia (Germany)

Oct. 26, 1576

Elector of the Palatinate (German areas around the Rhine River), **1559**. Frederick married pious princess, Maria Casimir of Brandenburg (1537) and was converted (1546). Embracing Lutheranism, he was one of the few rulers to make a personal study of theological issues during the Reformation. Adopting a Calvinist position, from 1548–61, he imposed Reformed doctrines on Catholics and Lutherans as well, aiding French Huguenots and Dutch Calvinists. Frederick instructed theologians to prepare the Heidelberg Catechism (summary of religious doctrine in question and answer format) in 1562. from 1548–61, he imposed Reformed doctrines on Catholics and Lutherans as well, aiding French Huguenots and Dutch Calvinists.

Johannes Stumpf

April 23, 1500
Bruchsal, Switzerland

1578
Zurich, Switzerland

Chronicler. He was one of the most important figures of the Swiss Reformation. As a friend of Zwingli, Stumpf dedicated his life to the work of building up the Reformation in Switzerland. His earlier years were spent as a prior of the monastic order, Knights of St. John.

John I. Tremellius

1510
Ferrara, Italy

Oct. 9, 1580
Sedan, France

Bible translator. Of Jewish origin, he was converted in 1540 to Catholicism and became a Protestant a year later. Upon leaving Italy as a Hebrew scholar, he taught successively at Strasbourg, Germany (1542); Cambridge, England (1549–53); Heidelburg, Germany (1561); and Sedan, France (1577). His greatest achievement was his translation of the Bible into Latin. For some time Tremellius' work was considered the standard Protestant Latin translation. From 1553–61, he was on the Continent in various places.

Richard Cox

c 1500
West Haddon, England

July 22, 1581
Ely, England

Bishop of Ely, 1559–80. Cox was also the first chancellor of Christ Church in Oxford (1547), then of Westminster Abbey (1549). He made important contributions to the prayer books of 1549 and 1552. Cox was a zealous supporter of Reformed views in England. He was imprisoned and then exiled to Frankfurt during Queen Mary I's reign. On his return, Cox was briefly bishop of Norwich to 1559. He also contributed to the Bishop's Bible. He opposed both Catholics and Puritans and resigned in 1580 because of candles and crucifixes in the queen's chapel.

Antoine Froment

1508
Mens, France

Nov. 6, 1581
Geneva, Switzerland

Genevan reformer. He was an associate of FAREL. Froment was the first person to come to Geneva in 1532 and preach Reformed doctrine. He became pastor of St. Gervais Church in 1537, although he had trained as a schoolmaster and had come to teach. Froment built up a following and paved the way for FAREL to come to Geneva. His French language school used the Bible as a textbook. He gave up the ministry for a while, but later was restored. He was imprisoned 1562–72, returning afterwards to Geneva.

George Buchanan

Feb. 1, 1506
near Killearn, Scotland

Sept. 28, 1582
Edinburgh, Scotland

Author, teacher, historian, scholar and tutor of King of Scotland, JAMES VI, in 1570. Buchanan's humanist views got him into difficulty with the Catholic zealots. He was arrested in 1539 for writing against Franciscans but escaped to France and later switched to Reformed Church doctrine. Buchanan returned to Scotland in 1560 and took an active role in the Presbyterian Church. In 1566, he was principal of St. Leonard's College, St. Andrews, Glasgow. He gained fame as a tutor to the child, King JAMES VI, in 1570. His famous treatise stated that all political power is the people.

Bernard Gilpin
Apostle of the North

1517
Kentmere, England

March 4, 1583
Houghton-le-Spring, England

Anglican who worked among the poor. Gilpin lived in France, 1552–56, and declined several important pastorates to continue his long missionary journeys to the North to neglected areas comforting many. He served in desolate north country villages in Yorkshire, Cumberland, and Northumbria, England, from 1556 until his death. In 1556, he was rector of Easington and archdeacon of Durham. As rector of Houghton, Gilpin was able to influence many people, especially through the large grammar school he founded. He was arrested in 1558 for his religion, but the death of Queen Mary I saved his life.

Zacharias Ursinus

July 18, 1534
Breslau, Germany

March 6, 1583
Neustadt, Germany

Reformed theologian and writer. He was one of the authors of the Heidelberg Cathechism in 1562. As professor of theology at Heidelberg University, 1561–77, he and OLEVIANUS prepared the catechism. Ursinus was forced to leave Heidelberg when his patron, FREDERICK III, died in 1576. The remainder of Ursinus' days were spent as a professor at Neustadt.

John Copping

June 5, 1583

Congregational layman to Bury St. Edmunds. He was hanged for "dispersing of ROBERT BROWNE's books and ROBERT HARRISON's books." Copping suffered imprisonment for seven years with fellow prisoner Thacker for circulating these books, which were adverse to the Church of England, because of the Congregationalist roots they were developing.

Edmund Grindal

1519
near Bees, England

July 6, 1583
Croydon, England

Archbishop of Canterbury, 1576–83. He held strong Puritan sympathies in his high post, thus displeasing Queen ELIZABETH and his fellow bishops for being too lenient toward non-conformists. Prior to being head of the Church of England, he served as prebendary of Westminister (1552), bishop of London (1559), and archbishop of York (1570). Grindal was strong anti-Catholic. ELIZABETH suspended his leadership 1577–82 as she sought the goodwill of Catholic powers. He died blind.

Thomas Erastus

Sept. 7, 1524
Baden, Switzerland

Dec. 31, 1583
Basel, Switzerland

Disciple of ZWINGLI, **physician and theologian**. Erastus opposed the Calvinistic Party for adopting a Presbyterian form of church government and discipline. His Lord's Supper and church polity were orthodox. He lived in Heidelberg, 1558–80, serving as professor of medicine at the university. Erastus was excommunicated for Unitarianism but was restored three years later. He wrote extensively against the punishment of excommunication.

William I of the Netherlands
William the Silent (Stadholder, Count of Nassau and Orange)

April 24, 1533
Dillenburg, Prussia (Germany)

July 10, 1584
Delft, Netherlands

Founder of the Dutch Republic. He was educated in the Lutheran faith at home until his fifteenth year, then in the Catholic faith at the Spanish court. He spoke seven languages. William married Anna van Buren in 1551 (died: 1558) and Anna of Saxony in 1561. He was the hero of the Dutch independence, and he courageously rallied the Dutch against King Philip II of Spain, in the "War of Liberation." In 1567, they revolted against Spain. He publicly declared himself a Calvinist in 1573. Although William was defeated several times, he was finally victorious (1576), and the republic was founded (1579) as a Protestant state. William was murdered by Philip's agent, Balthasar Gerard. Orange is a town in southeast France (13 miles north of Avignon), a principality he inherited. The House of Nassau was a princely European family. He was the grandfather of WILLIAM III.

Robert Harrison

1585
Middelburg, Netherlands

English Puritan separatist preacher. He is one of the fathers of Congregationalism. Harrison was a disciple of ROBERT BROWNE, and they were co-founders of the Congregational Church in Norwich, England, in 1580, where he had been master of a local hospital. When the pressures came, the entire congregation moved to Middelburg in 1581. He wrote numerous books.

Gisser Einarsen

1508

c 1585

Father of the reformation in Iceland. Einarsen studied in Germany where he absorbed Lutheran ideas. Upon returning to Iceland in 1540, he began a Lutheran Reformed movement at Skalholt. Einarsen became the bishop of the Danish State Church in Iceland, 1540–48. He was instrumental in subduing the uprising led by a fiery nationalist Catholic, Bishop Jon Arason. He reformed Iceland according to BUGENHAGEN's church order for Denmark.

Thomas Tallis

c 1505–1510
Leicestershire, England

Nov. 23, 1585
Greenwich, England

Important composer of sacred music. Tallis and William Byrd had a monopoly on printed music for over 20 years. Tallis' first printed works appeared in 1560. His Cantiones Sacrae (1575) included 16 of his motets. His *Responses* are his best-remembered compositions. Early in his career, Tallis was an organist at Waltham Abbey until 1540, then of the chapel royal in the reigns of three monarchs until his death. Tallis' "Canon" is a most famous hymn tune. He authored some of the finest chants in the cathedral service of the Anglican Church.

Martin Chemnitz

Nov. 9, 1522
Treuenbrietzen, Germany

April 8, 1586
Brunswick, Germany

Lutheran theologian. He was a principal influence in consolidating and defending LUTHER's doctrines after his death, having studied under MELANCHTHON. Chemnitz was a professor of philosophy at Wittenberg, 1553–54. In 1554, he went to Brunswick, staying active in church and civic affairs. He became superintendent of the city in 1567. Later in life, he did pastoral work and administrative work and writing in Brunswick. He attacked the Jesuits in a book, which was published in 1562. Chemnitz helped write the Formula of Concord (Lutheran confession which settled doctrinal controversies after LUTHER's death) in 1577. He defended consubstantiation, and he attacked decrees of the Council of Trent. He was the most learned theologian of his time. Catholics said, "If Chemnitz had not come, LUTHER had not stood."

Kasper Olevianus
Casper Olevianus

Aug. 10, 1536
Treves, Prussia (Germany)

March 15, 1587
Herborn, Prussia (Germany)

Theologian and founder of the Reformed Church in Germany. Olevianus taught reformation doctrine in 1559 and taught at the Latin School at Treves (Trier) but was imprisoned. When released, he taught theology at Heidelberg in 1561 where he wrote the Heidelberg Catechism with URSINUS. Lutheran elector Louis II acceded to power in 1576, and banished Olevianus.

He went to Berleberg where he wrote his commentaries, 1576–84, then to Herborn in 1584. He Calvanized the Palatinate.

John Foxe

1516
Boston, England

April 18, 1587
London, England

English Puritan clergyman and historian. He wrote the famous *Foxe's Book of Martyrs* in 1563. At that time, it was in eight volumes. John Day, a printer, played an important role in the publishing of the book. He was a fellow of Magdalen, 1539–45. From 1553–58 (during Queen Mary I's reign), Foxe was in Strasbourg, Frankfurt, and Basel, working as proofreader to writers and printers. The Latin Version of the famed book was published in 1559. Upon ELIZABETH's succession, Foxe was appointed prebendary of Salisbury Cathedral. The queen even helped promote the book.

John Field

1588

Presbyterian Puritan. Field was convinced that Presbyterianism was the correct way of governing the church. Field was the co-author with Thomas Wilcox of *An Admonition to the Parliament*. This demand in 1572 was designed to change the Church of England from episcopacy to Presbyterianism.

Bernard Palissy

c 1510
La Capella Biron, France

1589
Paris, France

Huguenot artist famous for his glass painting and beautiful figured pottery. Palissy journeyed through France and Germany in chemical research, supporting himself by doing land surveys. His family nearly starved while he was creating his beautiful ceramic designs, 1538–54. Success came, and he embellished the king and nobility with his art specimens. Palissy was first imprisoned at Bordeaux on charges of being a Calvinistic preacher (1562), then was arrested (1588) and thrown into the Bastille where he died a year later. He also wrote on subjects such as natural history, chemistry, and religion. In one article, he wrote, "Take refuge when under the shelter of our protecting Chief and Captain, our Lord Jesus Christ, who in time and place will know how properly to avenge the wrong that He has suffered and your sorrows."

Johannes Sturm

Oct. 1, 1507
Schlesden (Sleida), Germany

March 3, 1589
Strasbourg, Germany

German humanist and educational reformer. Sturm was influenced by BUCER, and he adopted Reformation principles. He supported the Reformed Church. In 1537, Sturm founded the Gymnasium (high school) of Strasbourg which he directed for over 40 years. Many consider Sturm to be the greatest Reformed Church educator ever. He emphasized discipline and the classics.

"Education should have piety, knowledge and eloquence."

Thomas Sampson

1517
Playford, England

April 9, 1589
Leicester, England

Puritan divine. Sampson was one of the earliest members of the Church of England who wanted to purify the Church. He held pastoral positions in London (1551), Chicester (1554), and Durham (1560). During the reign of Queen Mary I, he wisely lived in Strasbourg, Germany, 1555–58. He also was the dean (head of a collegiate church) of Christ Church, Oxford, 1561. Sampson married the niece of martyred reformer, HUGH LATIMER.

Sampson and LAURENCE HUMPHREY opposed the use of vestments in 1564. By 1568, he was religious director at Wigston Hospital in Leicester and prebendary at St. Paul's Cathedral. Sampson's stand was so zealous that he was imprisoned for his views. The debate over clerical attire led to his followers being called Puritans (movement to purify the Church of England, mostly Calvinistic, but divided into many denominations. In England, most became known as Nonconformists, many eventually leaving for America, where they were mostly known as Congregationalists).

William Fulke

1538
London, England

Aug. 28, 1589
Pennington, England

Puritan divine. He was educated at Cambridge, then served there, 1564–69. He resided in France, 1572–78. Fulke was elected master (male teacher tutor, or school head) of Pembroke College Hall, Cambridge University and professor of divinity in 1578. He was one of the most able clerics of his time and one of the principal opponents of Catholicism. Fulke was also a prolific writer. He wrote a defense of the translation of Scriptures into English.

Laurence Humphrey

1527

1590

Puritan intellectual in the Church of England. He headed Magdalen College in Oxford and had to flee to the continent to escape Queen Mary I's death sentence. Upon returning, Humphrey led the discussions in the Church over the use of vestments prescribed by Archbishop MATTHEW PARKER. In spite of severe pressure, he would not wear these vestments. THOMAS SAMPSON supported him.

Jacob (James) Andreae

March 25, 1528
Weiblingen, Germany

Jan. 7, 1590
Tübingen, Germany

Lutheran scholar, writer, and theologian. In 1562, he was appointed professor of theology, provost, and chancellor of the University of Tübingen. He was an active reformer in all of southern Germany. Andrae pastored at Stuttgart (1516–48), Tübingen (1548–53), and Gottingen (1553–61). From 1567–80, he was an advisor to Elector August Augustus of Saxony (ruled: 1553–86). In 1577, along with MARTIN CHEMNITZ, he helped draw up the last great Lutheran creed, the Formula of Concord (published June 25, 1580). He wrote more than 200 works, chiefly polemical writings against Calvinism. Andreae helped unite the Lutherans. He was the grandfather of JOHANN V. ANDREAE.

Dirck V. Coornhert
Restorer of the Dutch Language

1522
Amsterdam, Netherlands

Oct. 29, 1590
Gouda, Netherlands

Dutch copper-engraver, politician, theologian, and translator. In 1562, he was secretary of the city of Harlem. Coornhert opposed Spanish authorities, so was imprisoned in The Hague in 1568. He escaped and took refuge in Cleves. In 1572, after the Dutch Revolt, he served in the capacity of Secretary of State for Holland. Coornhert disturbed many of his contemporaries by his tolerance, refusing to endorse capital punishment of heretics. He wrote critically of the Heidelberg Catechism and won ARMINIUS to his views when Arminius was sent to refute him. He developed Dutch literary language.

John Erskine

1509
Dun, Scotland

March 12/June 17, 1591

Intermediary between Mary, Queen of Scots, and the Reformers. Erskine was educated at King's College, Aberdeen, where he was made Lord (master, chief) of Dun and became a close friend of reformers WISHART and KNOX. Four times, he was elected moderator of the general assembly of the Presbyterian Church of Scotland. He was one of the superintendents of the Reformed Church of Scotland in 1560. He introduced Greek into the country, opened his home for Knox's preaching, and championed the Reformation cause many times, winning even the respect of Mary, Queen of Scots.

Patrick Adamson

Feb. 15, 1536
Perth, Scotland

Feb. 19, 1592
St. Andrews, Scotland

Archbishop of St. Andrew's, Scotland, 1576 on. Recalled to Scotland from France (c. 1571), he later became a prominent minister. Adamson was involved in a long controversy with the Presbyterian Party in the Scottish Church. His writings and oratory caused much hostility, so he was excommunicated by the Synod of Fife in 1586. Having lost the favor of King JAMES I, he ended his days in poverty, because JAMES deprived Adamson of revenues from his see after the king was accused by Adamson of severe measures against the Puritans in 1588.

Nickolaus Selnecker

Dec. 6, 1528
Hersbruck, Germany

May 12, 1592
Leipzig, Germany

Lutheran theologian at Leipzig, most of his life. In 1577, Selnecker helped prepare the Formula of Concord. As a Lutheran scholastic, Selnecker assisted in introducing the era of high orthodoxy in Lutheranism. He lectured at the University of Wittenberg, was court preacher at Dresden, professor of theology at Jena, professor at Leipzig, pastor of St. Thomas Church where he defended the motet (vocal composition on a Biblical or similar prose text) choir and court preacher at Wolfenbvette, among other activities. He was organist in the church of Nuremberg at age twelve.

Henry Barrow(e)

1550
Shipdam, England

April 6, 1593
Tyburn, London, England

Church reformer and separatist attorney. Considered by some to be the founder of Congregationalism, but his precise beliefs seem uncertain. Barrowe was converted through "loud-mouthed preaching" to lead a strict Puritan life. The writings of JOHN BROWNE influenced him. He and JOHN GREENWOOD were imprisoned for holding meetings in London. Barrow's writings opposed both Anglicans and Puritans. He was arrested again in 1590 for circulating seditious books, *A True Description of the Visible Congregation of the Saints* (1598) and *A Brief Discount of the False Church* (1590). He was hanged with GREENWOOD.

John Greenwood

c 1560
England

April 6, 1593
Tyburn, London, England

Considered by some to be the father of Congregationalism. Greenwood became a zealous Puritan and chaplain in the Essex home of Lord Robert Rich. Moving to London, he associated himself with separatists who were critics of a state church. Greenwood left the Church of England in 1581 and was imprisoned (for holding an illegal meeting) and denying episcopacy, 1586–92. Imprisoned with HENRY BARROW and JOHN PENRY, they composed tracts defending separatism, some of them printed in Holland. Released in 1592, he founded an independent congregation (called the ancient church) at Nicholas Lane, London, which later migrated to Holland. This action started Congregationalism in England. Arrested on December 5, 1592, Greenwood was imprisoned in the Fleet Prison for writing and publishing seditious books and hanged with HENRY BARROW.

John Penry

c 1559–1563
Llangamarch, Wales

May 29, 1593
St. Thomas-a-Watering, London, England

Congregational martyr. He became a Puritan while a student at Cambridge. In 1587, Penry published a plea for gospel preaching in Wales and had charge of a Puritan press. He fled to Scotland, 1589–92, when Queen ELIZABETH was upset with his "Martin Marprelate" signature on tracts. Upon returning to England in 1590, Penry was unjustly condemned and hanged, as JOB THROCKMORTON was the real author.

William Kethe

c 1538
Scotland

June 6, 1594
Childe, England

Calvinist Presbyterian musician. Kethe wrote a well-known response, "All People That on Earth Do Dwell" in 1561 (music by Louis Bourgeois). While exiled from England 1555–59, Kethe lived in Frankfurt and Geneva. In 1556, he and William Whittingham published a service book containing 51 metrical psalms in English. From 1561 until his death, Kethe served as a pastor in Childe.

Gerhardus Mercator
Gerhard Kremer

March 5, 1512
Rupelmonde, Belgium

Dec. 2, 1594
Duisburg, Prussia (Germany)

Mathematician, cartographer and creator of celestial globes. Mercator was a Protestant in Catholic Flanders, later moving to Duisburg. Although he excelled in philosophy and math at the University of Lorraine, he was drawn to geography. He received a commission from Charles V to produce terrestrial (1541) and celestial (1551) globes. He exclaimed, "What a privilege to map the heavens of the Almighty." His work is said to have been superior to all previous efforts. In 1544, he was arrested for heresy, but escaped. He invented the Mercator system of projection in 1552 with the parallels and meridians at right angles, which made his maps especially valuable for ship navigation. He compiled the first collection of maps and named them an "atlas" (1554). The first world Mercator Map was completed in 1569.

David Ferguson

1525
Dundee, Scotland

Aug. 13, 1598
Dunfermline, Scotland

Scottish reformer. He was appointed pastor of Dunfermline (the seat of the royal palace) by Parliament (1560), in Rosyth (1567), and Cumnock and Beith (1574). Here Ferguson preached the Reformed faith at great personal sacrifice. He influenced King JAMES VI of Scotland (James I) greatly in his duties. Ferguson published two tracts which met the approval of JOHN KNOX and was a prominent church leader.

Edmund Spenser

c 1552
London, England

Jan. 16, 1599
Westminster, London, England

English poet. He was ranked next to SHAKESPEARE in that era. Spenser was appointed secretary to the new Lord Deputy of Ireland (1580), and he became sheriff of Cork (1598). His *Faerie Queen*, and *Hymnes of Heavenly Love and Beautie* won him a place in religious literature. The former was a defense of Puritanism. He married Elizabeth Boyle in 1592. The Irish burned his castle (causing death to his youngest child), and Spenser died penniless three months later.

Richard Hooker

March 1554
Heavitree, England

Nov. 2, 1600
Bishopsbourne, England

Church of England theologian and apologist. Hooker authored the famed *Laws of Ecclesiastical Polity* (eight books, 1593–97). Although the last three books were published after his death, this work remained a great classic of Anglican Church government, especially in reply to the Puritans and Presbyterians. He also did not support the Calvinists. Hooker appealed to Scripture, reason, and tradition—distinguishing between the laws of the state and the law of nature. He held the key post at the Inns of Court, 1585–91, a distinguished legal society. He went to Boscombe (1591) and to Bishopsbourne (1595). Hooker died after a long and painful illness, saying, " . . .for I am at peace with all men, and He is at peace with me. . . .My days are past as a shadow that returns not."

John Craig

c 1512
Aberdeenshire, Scotland

Dec. 12, 1600
Edinburgh, Scotland

Reformer. Craig began as a Dominican monk who was forced to leave Scotland for his radical views. Imprisoned for heresy in 1536, he escaped to become rector of the Dominican convent in Bologna, Italy. There he was converted while reading CALVIN's *Institutes*. After 24 years of wandering, he returned to Scotland in 1560. He became KNOX's assistant at St. Giles (1562), and upon KNOX's death (1572), Craig became the leader of the Scottish Presbyterian Church. From 1572–79, he preached and taught at Montros and Aberdeen. Craig returned to Edinburgh in 1579, as chaplain to young King JAMES VI. When Catholics attempted to regain hold of Scotland in 1580, Craig drafted the National Covenant in 1597–the first of the "Covenants." In 1581, he had the episcopy abolished.

Job Throckmorton

1545

1601

English Puritan layman and tract author. Throckmorton is believed to have been the author of tracts published between 1588–1589 carrying the signature, "Martin Marprelate." These tracts spoke in stinging satire against Anglican bishops, particularly Archbishop of Canterbury JOHN WHITGIFT. Anglicans were infuriated, but Puritans were delighted. JOHN PENRY, Congregational martyr, was his associate.

Alexander Nowell

1507
Read Hall Whalley, England

Feb. 13, 1602
London, England

Anglican priest and scholar. Nowell was dean of St. Paul's Cathedral, London, 1560–1602. During Queen Mary I's reign, he fled to the Continent. Upon his return, Nowell was made canon of Canterbury in 1560, even though he often offended Queen ELIZABETH I. He was active in the 1563 Convocation of Canterbury that reduced the 42 Church of England Articles of Faith to 39. Nowell wrote three cathechisms, the Large, the Middle, and the Short, the last of which is still used by the Church of England (pub. 1570 and 1572). He was inclined toward Calvinism.

William Perkins

1558
Marston Jabbet, England

Oct. 22, 1602
Cambridge, England

English Puritan theologian. Perkins was famed for his powerful, anti-Romanist preaching and systematic exposition of Puritan theology. He was a fellow of Christ's College, Cambridge, 1584–94, where he was converted. Perkins was rector at St. Andrew's, Cambridge, 1585–1602, following years of preaching at the Cambridge jail. His works included *Reformed Catholike* (1597), and many of them were translated into other languages. He married in 1590. Through his speaking, JOHN COTTON was brought under great conviction. He protested liturgical formalities in the Church of England and the theology of the "semi-Pelagian Baptists."

Elizabeth I

Sept. 7, 1533
Greenwich, England

March 24, 1603
Richmond, England

Queen of England and Ireland, 1558–1603. Elizabeth succeeded her half-sister, "Bloody" Mary I. A very educated young lady, Elizabeth spoke French, Latin, and Italian fluently. She had been imprisoned at age 21 by her sister, in the tower of London, but became queen at age 25. They were both daughters of Henry VIII, with the red headed Elizabeth being the only child of his union with Anne Boleyn. She quickly reversed the direction of the country and became a strong defender and strengthener of the Church of England, making it the state church. Elizabeth was vain and capricious, but she was also very popular with the people. Upon her coronation she issued a proclamation that the English litany was to be read in all London churches. She further sent help to the French Huguenots against the Duke of Guise, Francois de Lorraine (ruled; 1550–63), aided Protestants in Scotland and the Low Countries, and promulgated EDWARD VI's 39 Articles of Religion (1563) with the extension of the Act of Supremacy (Queen's power over papal control). She did consent to the execution of Mary, Queen of Scots in 1587. Catholic Spain declared war, but Elizabeth had built a 34-ship fleet which defeated the Spanish Armada and King Philip II in July, 1588, whose marriage offer she declined. Although a violent storm contributed to the Armada's defeat, this victory positioned England as the new, world power. Elizabeth restored the policies of Archbishop of Canterbury THOMAS CRANMER, and repressed Catholicism—persecuting those who hindered the Protestant progression. She never married and said as she died, "All my possessions for one moment of time." One poll shows her as the most influential person of the sixteenth century. She was completely bald, losing her hair after suffering smallpox at age 29. She always wore a wig.

Thomas Cartwright

1535
Royston, England

Dec. 27, 1603
Warwick, England

Persecuted scholarly leader of the Puritans and early Presbyterian leader. Cartwright was a professor of divinity at Cambridge University, 1569–70, until his dismissal by his enemy, JOHN WHITGIFT. He lectured against the Constitution of the Church of England and was imprisoned. Cartwright fled to the European Continent and pastored at Antwerp and Middelburg. His mentor was THEODORE BEZA in Geneva. After ten years, he returned to England (1585), only to be imprisoned twice and released (1592). Ironically, Cartwright opposed separating from the Church of England. He envisioned a reformed church functioning within an umbrella of Anglicanism (state controlled: episcopacy), insisting a local parish should call their own pastor. Cartwright authored several exegetical treatises. His remaining years were spent quietly on the island of Guernsey, with the exception of some years in Warwick. He wrote *Holy Discipline for Presbyterian Congregations*.

John Whitgift

c 1530
Great Grimsby, England

Feb. 29, 1604
Lambeth, London, England

Archbishop of Canterbury, 1583–1604. Whitgift first served as prebendary of Ely, then as dean of Lincoln (1571), and finally as bishop of Worcester (1577) until his appointment at Canterbury. He sought to strengthen and unify the Church of England, opposing both papal and Puritan influences. Whitgift enforced Queen

Elizabeth's policy of religious uniformity and, in the process, suspended and mistreated hundreds of Puritan pastors. He went so far as to get a law passed (1593) which made Puritanism a statutory offense and helped to draft the Lambeth Articles (supported Calvinism) (1595). They met with disapproval by Queen Elizabeth and were withdrawn. Whitgift did take part in the Hampton Court Conference of 1604 (called by James I to discuss differences between Puritans and high church supporters). He founded alms-houses and a school at Croydon. Whitgift also served as vice-chancellor of Trinity College at Cambridge (1570) after having taught divinity there (1563–70). He never married. Whitgift attended Elizabeth on her deathbed and also crowned James I in 1603.

Theodore Beza

June 24, 1519
Vezelay, France

Oct. 13, 1605
Geneva, Switzerland

Calvinist theologian, author and Bible translator. Beza secretly married Claudine Denosse in 1544 (died 1588). Beza adopted Protestantism after his conversion due to a serious illness in Geneva in 1548, where he fled from Catholic persecution with his wife. He became a professor of Greek in the academy at Lausanne, Switzerland (1549–58) and then went to Geneva (1559–97) to pastor and teach. Calvin died in Beza's arms in 1564 and passed the presidency of the Geneva College on to him, along with the mantel of leading the Reformed Church. He opposed Lutheran doctrines and was a power among the Huguenots. Beza presented the famous Codex D (Greek-Latin manuscript on the New Testament) to Cambridge University in 1565. His work was the basis for the Geneva Bible and the King James Version and was the real origination of the Textus Receptus (Greek Text). He presided at various synods and defended the death of Servetus, who was accused of heresy. In 1589, he married Catherine del Piano, a widow. He said on his deathbed, "Cover, Lord, what has been; govern what shall be. Oh, perfect that which Thou hast begun, that I suffer not shipwreck in the haven." His written works appeared in French, English, and Latin.

Stephen Bocskay

1557
Kolozsvar (Cluj), Transylvania (Romania)

Dec. 29, 1606

Prince of Transylvania, 1604–06, and leader of the Reformation in Hungary. Bocskay's struggle with civic authorities to protect his rights and to preserve his properties culminated in the Peace of Vienna which guaranteed constitutional rights and religious freedom throughout Hungary. He led Hungarian revolutionists against Holy Roman Emperor Rudolf II (ruled: 1576–1612), 1604–6. With Archduke {sovereign prince of former ruling house of Austria, Matthias, he secured the Treaty of Vienna in 1606, which gave religious freedom to Protestants. Bocskay was said to have been poisoned by his chancellor, Mihaly Katay, who subsequently was hacked to pieces by Bocskay supporters.

John Reynolds

1549
Pinhoe, England

May 21, 1607
Oxford, England

Biblical scholar. Reynolds was dean of Lincoln in 1593 and then president of Corpus Christi College, Oxford, 1598–1607. Reynolds was one of the four Puritans who represented their party at the Hampton Court Conference. He is said to have been the first to propose the need for an authorized version of the Bible. From his direction came the King James Version Bible. Reynolds also translated most of the books by Old Testament prophets for the King James Version Bible.

Robert Hunt

1568
June 12, 1608
Jamestown, Virginia

First pastor in America. He married Elizabeth Edwards in 1597, and they had two children. He was vicar in Riculver, England (1594–1602) and Heathfield (1602–6). In 1607, 144 men, led by Captain John Smith, arrived (including Hunt, the Anglican chaplain) in Jamestown. The first service was held May 14, 1607. Were it not for the example of this godly minister, the hapless colony might not have survived. Every Sunday, from behind a plank nailed between two trees, he preached to a small congregation shaded under the canopy of an old sail cloth. During the week, he cared for the sick and dying that first year. A fire in January of 1608 destroyed the church and all of Hunt's books and possessions.

Jacobus Arminius
Jacob Harmensen—Hermansz

Oct. 10, 1560
Oudewater, Netherlands
Oct. 19, 1609
Leyden, Netherlands

Dutch theologian and founder of Arminianism. This brand of Reformed theology was a reaction to the sternness of the strict predestination of Calvinism. JOHN WESLEY later preached the "free choice salvation" that Arminius taught. He urged the State to tolerate all religions. Arminius pastored in Amsterdam (1587–1603) and also was a professor at Leyden University (1603–9). From 1604–9, he was engaged in bitter controversy with his colleague, FRANCIS GOMARUS. This was the beginning of a major doctrinal division (whosoever will vs. God's call) that still exists today. Years of tense and disputing persecution wore him out, although attempts to bring him to trial always failed. Arminius' complete works were published in Latin in 1629. His disciples were later called Remonstrants (followers of Arminianism which taught salvation is for all who believe).

"Redemption is for all, but only those who believe will be saved."

Henry IV of France
Henry the Great—Henry of Navarre

Dec. 14, 1553
Pau, France
May 14, 1610
Paris, France

First Bourbon (French royal family that ruled, 1589–1793) **king, 1589–1610.** He also served as king of Navarre as Henry III from 1572–89. Henry was a Protestant-born noble warrior who became a Catholic on July 25, 1593, in order to consolidate his kingship. He said, "Paris is worth a mass." Upon the death of his mother, JEANNE D'ALBRET (queen of Navarre), he married Margaret of Valois on August 18, 1572. This political move stopped impending religious wars, although it was through feigning Catholic conversion that he escaped the Protestant massacre of St. Bartholomew's Day, which started four days after his wedding date, as many Protestants came to Paris for the event. He was under house custody for nearly three years. In 1576, he escaped and placed himself at the head of Huguenot armies. He was not recognized by the Holy League, which received assistance from Philip II of Spain. Unable to take Paris, he became a Catholic (1593), giving him Paris (1597). On April 13, 1598, he issued the Edict of Nantes, (giving Huguenots religious liberty). He became a popular king. Divorced in 1599, he married Marie de' Medici who gave him five children, including his successor, King Louis XIII (ruled: 1610–43). He also had three children out of wedlock. His final years (1600–10 were devoted to France's recovery from its wars. As a result of favoring Protestant foreign policy, Henry IV was assassinated by a former Jesuit named Francois Ravaillac (1578–1610), who was executed May 27.

Frederick IV
Frederick the Upright

March 5, 1574　　　　　　　　　　　　　　　　　　　　　　　　　　　　　　　　　　Sept. 19, 1610

Amberg, Germany

Palatine elector, 1592–1610. Frederick organized and headed a group of northern German states determined to safeguard Protestantism in their territories. Frederick married Louise, daughter of WILLIAM I OF THE NETHERLANDS in 1593. In May of 1608, he founded the Union of Evangelical States. This "union" was soon opposed by the "league," a band of southern German, Catholic rulers. Bitter religious conflict and sporadic warfare ensued with both sides seeking unity.

Richard Bancroft

Sept. 1544　　　　　　　　　　　　　　　　　　　　　　　　　　　　　　　　　　　　Nov. 12, 1610
Farnworth, England　　　　　　　　　　　　　　　　　　　　　　　　　　Lambeth, London, England

Archbishop of Canterbury, 1604–10. Early on, he was the rector of St. Andrews in Haborn, treasurer at St. Paul's Cathedral, and canon of Westminster. Bancroft was an outspoken defender of Episcopalianism during the struggle between the Anglicans and the Presbyterian Puritans. He sponsored canons against Puritanism and claimed his views existed by "Divine Right." He encouraged repression of Separatists and Puritans and created strife among the clergy. In 1575–84, he was the rector of Teversham, Cambridge. King JAMES I appointed him supervisor of Bible translations for the KJV project. He was prebendary of St. Paul's Cathedral, London (1590–97) and then bishop in London (1597–1604). Bancroft also attended the Hampton Court Conference of 1604 and all but wrecked it with his belligerence. Bancroft died at the residence of the archbishops of Canterbury.

Charles IX

Oct. 4, 1550　　　　　　　　　　　　　　　　　　　　　　　　　　　　　　　　　　　Oct. 30, 1611
Stockholm, Sweden　　　　　　　　　　　　　　　　　　　　　　　　　　　　　　Nykoping, Sweden

King of Sweden, 1604–11. As regent (one who exercises ruling power in absence of ruler) from 1599–1604, Charles restored the Protestant faith and forced his nephew, King Sigismund III (ruled: 1587–1632), to retire to Poland. A long war resulted with Poland (1600) and then with Denmark (1611). Charles suffered years of humiliation at the hands of his brother, who tried unsuccessfully to have him renounce his Calvinistic faith. Charles was kept busy holding off attacks by Poland, Russia, and Denmark. He firmly planted Protestantism in Sweden, preparing the way for ADOLPHUS GUSTAVUS II (champion of northern Protestantism). Charles IX was the fourth son of VASA GUSTAVUS I.

Hans L. Hassler

Oct. 26, 1564　　　　　　　　　　　　　　　　　　　　　　　　　　　　　　　　　　June 8, 1612
Nuremberg, Germany　　　　　　　　　　　　　　　　　　　　　　　　　　　Frankfurt, Germany

Lutheran composer and noted organist. Hassler composed the music for "O Sacred Head, Now Wounded" (lyrics by BERNARD OF CLAIRVAUX). Hassler studied music in Venice. Upon returning to Germany (c. 1586), he became organist to Count Octavian Fugger at Augsburg, Frauenkirche, Nuremberg, and at the court of Prince Christian II of Saxony. In 1605, he married Cordula Claus, then moved to Ulm, continuing to manufacture mechanical musical instruments. Hassler was the most prominent organist of his time. He ardently composed church music and songs with melodic charm. Turberculosis set in, and he died en route to Frankfurt to participate in an election.

John Smythe (Smith)

c 1570

Aug. 8, 1612
Amsterdam, Netherlands

Founder of General Baptists. Smythe began as a Puritan and then was a Separatist pastor after being ordained by the Church of England. Having been influenced by the Brownists, he became pastor of an independent church in Gainsborough, England in 1606. Fleeing to Amsterdam (1607), he organized the first modern Baptist Church called the Second English Church (1608), which contained Mennonite influence. Smythe accepted Arminian and Baptist views, baptizing himself, then HELWYS, then others, 1608–09. He considered infant baptism as an option. He and THOMAS HELWYS wrote a *Confession of Faith* that contained 26 articles. He was buried on September 1, 1612.

Nicholas Bownde

1613

Puritan legalist. Bownde emphasized Sunday observance, writing an influential Doctrine of the Sabbath (1595). He also helped Puritanism to lay immense importance on the proper keeping of the Lord's Day (Sunday) and was indirectly responsible for the idea of "Blue Laws" (no alcohol sold or served on Sundays) in the colonies. Bownde sought to preserve the fourth commandment ("Keep the Sabbath day") in a strict way.

Adrian Saravia

c 1531/1532
Vielil-Hesdin, Belgium

Jan. 15, 1613
Kent, England

Walloon (Celtic people of South Belgium) **theologian**. Saravia moved to England in 1587 where he became an Anglican defender of the Episcopal system and a rector at Tattenhill. He affirmed that episcopacy was ordained by God and denounced Puritanism, which he felt flaunted divine law. Saravia helped lay the foundations for the High Church Party in the Church of England. He was a professor of divinity at the University of Leyden, 1584–87. He was a prebendary in churches at Gloucester (1591), Canterbury (1595), Worcester and Westminster (1601). During this time, he was also a vicar at Lewis Ham (1595–1609), moving to Great Chart (1609–13). He was the earliest modern advocate of worldwide evangelization. He was one of King James Version translators.

Isaac Casaubon

Feb. 18, 1559
Geneva, Switzerland

July 12, 1614
London, England

Classical scholar and liberal Reformed theologian. Casaubon was considered the greatest scholar of his era. In 1586, he married the daughter of Henri Estienne (a famous printer 1528–98). He was professor of Greek at Geneva (1582–96), then at Montpelier (1596–1600). He edited *Novum Testamentus Graecum* in Geneva in 1587. From 1600 on, Casaubon was the royal librarian in Paris to King HENRY IV of France. After HENRY IV's assassination in 1610, Casaubon moved to London, resisting the pressure to become a Catholic. He was welcomed by Anglican bishops but was persecuted by Jesuit tracts after he failed to recant his previous religious views. Casaubon was prebendary of Canterbury and Westminster and a pensioner of JAMES I from 1611 on. Intense studies wore him out prematurely.

Thomas Helwys

1550
Askam, England

1616
London, England

Founder of the first English (General) Baptist Church. Helwys married Joan Ashmore in 1595. He was a member of SMYTHE's church that fled to Amsterdam, Netherlands. SMYTHE wavered on infant baptism. This difference led Helwys and JOHN MURTON to return to England in 1611 to found a General Baptist congregation on Newgate Street. They believed in pouring and baptizing adults only, supported Arminian theology, and were later imprisoned in England.

William Shakespeare

April 23, 1564
Stratford-on-Avon, England

April 23, 1616
Stratford-on-Avon, England

Poet, dramatist, playwright, and actor. Shakespeare wrote 38 plays, 154 sonnets, and two narrative poems. He was "baptized" on April 26, 1564. At the age of eighteen, Shakespeare married Anne Hathaway November 28, 1582 (died: 1623), eight years his senior. Their children were Susanne (1583) and twins, Hamnet and Judith (1585). They lived in London until 1610, then moved to Stratford-on-Avon where they purchased the largest house available. This famous redhead was established in London as an actor/playwright in 1592 and produced plays until his death. Shakespeare's 38 plays were never equaled in popular appeal: *Merchant of Venice, Romeo and Juliet, MacBeth, Hamlet, King Lear, Henry IV*, etc. His last one was *The Tempest* (1611). In 1599, he and others built the 1,500-seat Globe Theatre in Southwark, where many of his plays were performed. His will testified to his Christian commitment. He retired in 1612. Bob Jones University, Greenville, SC perpetuates his memory through their Artist Series elaborate productions. He is buried at the local Holy Trinity Church. A few historians have doubted his writing of the plays.

"There sits a judge what no king can corrupt."
"The devil can cite Scripture for his purpose."

Thomas Bilson

1547
Winchester, England

June 18, 1616
London, England

Church of England bishop and writer. In addition to being warden (college administrator, president, governor) of Winchester College in 1576, Bilson became bishop of Worcester (1596) and of Winchester (1597). He wrote *Christian Subjection and Unchristian Rebellion* (1585). He attacked Puritan and Separatist views in his *Perpetual Government of Christ's Church* (1593). Bilson led in the final revision of the King James Version, and prepared the Bible's chapter headings. He preached the coronation sermon before JAMES I in 1603.

Leonhard Hutter

Jan. 1563
Helligen, Germany

Oct. 23, 1616
Wittenberg, Germany

Lutheran professor of theology at Wittenberg, 1596–1616. Hutter was a voluminous, strong orthodox writer whose *Compendium Locorum Theologicorum* (1610) superceded MELANCHTHON's *Loci* as a theology textbook. Hutter's book was translated into many languages. In 1594, he was the private tutor at Jena University. He married Barbara Manlich in 1599. Hutter studied philosophy, philology (writings, linguistics in original languages), and theology at four universities.

Richard Field

Oct. 15, 1561
Hempstead, England

Nov. 21, 1616
Windsor, England

Anglican preacher and writer. Field was chaplain in the ordinary to ELIZABETH I (1598), canon of Windsor (1604), and dean of Gloucester (1610). He is most remembered for *Of the Church* (1606–10), consisting of five books. It has been republished by the Ecclesiastical History Society (Cambridge, 1847) in four volumes.

Pocahontas

c 1595
Virginia

March, 1617
near Gravesend, England

First Indian convert in America. Pocahontas helped maintain peace between English colonists and Native Americans by befriending the settlers and eventually marrying one of them. She saved Captain John Smith's (1579–1631) life in 1608, by interceding on his behalf with her father (Powhatan warrior). Smith was president of Virginia Colony, 1608–9. She was taken prisoner by the English in 1612. Pocahontas was baptized as "Rebecca" in Jamestown and married John Rolfe (1585–1622), the colonist who discovered how to cure tobacco in April, 1614. This union was regarded as a bond of friendship between the races. The couple returned to England (1615) where she was treated as a princess (1616) and presented to King JAMES I. Their son, Thomas, was educated in England. She died of smallpox on board a ship, preparing to return to America.

William Bradshaw

1571
Market Bosworth, England

May 1618
Chelsea, England

Puritan clergyman. Bradshaw settled at Chatham, 1601, but was suspended for refusing to sign the 39 Articles (doctrinal statement of the Church of England). Bradshaw lectured at Christ Church of Newgate Street, London, but his opposition to "ceremonies" continued to cause problems. He moved to the country, in Derbyshire. Bradshaw's most important work was *English Puritanisme: In the Realme of England* (1605), in which he advocated independence of congregations. He also wrote *A Treatise of Justification* (1615).

Sir Walter Raleigh

1552
Hayes, England

Oct. 29, 1618
Westminster, England

Explorer, soldier, sailor, historian, poet, and author. He sent expeditions to the North American coast from Florida to North Carolina, 1584–89, but failed in colonization efforts. From 1595–97, he personally led expeditions to South America. When ELIZABETH I died, his enemies made JAMES I believe he was against his accession. Charged with conspiracy, he was sent to the Tower, where he lived with his wife, Elizabeth Throckmorton, and son, 1603–16, and wrote *History of the World*. He introduced tobacco and the potato into England and Ireland. Raleigh undertook another expedition in 1616 and was beheaded two years later on demand of the Spanish ambassador for destroying the Spanish settlement of St. Thomas, Guiana. In his *Treatise on the Soul* he writes, "And the immortality of the soul of Christ maketh much for the immortality of our souls, for he hath promised that where he is there his servants shall be also." He was buried with his favorite pipe and a tin of tobacco. Everyone attending his funeral received ten pounds of tobacco and two pipes.

Johann van Oldenbarneveldt

Sept. 25, 1547
Amersfoort, Netherlands

May 13, 1619
The Hague, Netherlands

Statesman who championed Dutch independence. Earlier, he helped throw off the Spanish yoke and later broke with Prince Maurice (1567–1625) of Orange, who supported Calvinism. As Grand Pensionary of the province of Holland (1586), he negotiated a Spanish Treaty (1609). Oldenbarneveldt sided with the Arminian-leaning Remonstrants during the power struggle against the strict Dutch Calvinists, such as the Gomarists, in 1617. Johann was illegally arrested on August 23, 1618 by the State General, condemned as a traitor, and beheaded, as Maurice advanced into Holland.

John Carver

c 1575
Nottinghamshire, England

April 5, 1621
Plymouth, Massachusetts

Pilgrim (Bible Christians who fled from England, looking for freedom of worship) **father and first governor of Plymouth Colony, 1620–21**. Carver was a wealthy London merchant who migrated with the Separatists to Leyden, Netherlands in 1609. He became a deacon in JOHN ROBINSON's church and agent for the American Pilgrim expedition, 1617–20. Carver secured financial backing, chartered a boat, and equipped the *Mayflower*. The Pilgrims left London on July 15th; Plymouth, England on September 16; sighted land on November 19; and arrived at Plymouth on December 26, 1620. Carver was elected governor under the Mayflower Compact (document signed prior to disembarking, describing the new land) signed on November 11, 1620. He made the treaty with the Indian chief, Massasoit. Carver died from sunstroke just a few months later.

Johann Arndt

Dec. 27, 1555
Ballenstedt, Germany

May 11, 1621
Celle, Germany

German Lutheran theologian and mystic. Arndt pastored, 1583–1611, in several locations: Badeborn (1583), Quedlinburg (1590), Brunswick (1599), and Eisleben (1608, but was compelled to move on by Calvinistic hostility. He authored *True Christianity* (1609), a widely translated treatise on a personal mystical piety between the believer and God. Arndt was the general superintendent of the Luneburg Church and court preacher at Celle, 1611–21. His writings influenced SPENSER and the Pietist Movement.

Daniel Chamier

1565
Le Mont Castle, France

Oct. 17, 1621
Montauban, France

French Protestant preacher. Chamier was a professor and pastor at Montauban in 1612. He was also a skilled conversationalist and became a trusted leader of the Huguenots. It is thought that he wrote the Edict of Nantes, a milestone toward a free church in a free state, favoring the Huguenots over the Catholics, but revoked in 1685 by King Louis XIV (ruled: 1643–1715). Chamier's chief work was a four-volume *Panstratiae Catholicae* (Geneva, 1626). When Louis XIII besieged the city, Chamier died from a cannonball wound.

Henry Ainsworth

March 1570/1571
Swanton Morley, England

1622
Amsterdam, Netherlands

Congregational Puritan pastor and scholar. Ainsworth's independent thinking as a Separatist forced him to flee to Amsterdam (1593), where he became a bookseller and then a teacher to a group of Brownists (1596), who had moved from London. Ainsworth authored a Brownist confession of faith in 1596 and co-authored *A Defense of Brownists* (1604) with Francis Johnson (see` ROBERT BROWNE biography). He pastored this new congregation 1610–22. He gained a profound knowledge of Hebrew and wrote *Annotation on Several Books of the Bible*, an exegetical work on the Old Testament. Ainsworth was a profound rabbinical and Oriental scholar, best known for his annotations on the *Psalms* (1612) and the *Pentateuch* (1616–19).

Andrew Melville

Aug. 1, 1545
Baldovie, Scotland

1622
Sedan, France

Reformer, scholar, and educator. Melville followed KNOX in carrying the Presbyterian torch. He studied under BEZA in Geneva in 1564. Upon his return to Scotland, Melville became the principal of Glasgow University (1574–80) and then of St. Mary's College at St. Andrews (1580–1606), becoming its rector in 1590. He reorganized Scottish universities and emphasized his taste for Greek learning by promoting the study of Aristotle (384–322 BC). Melville gave the Reformed Church its Presbyterian character. He preached boldly before the General Assembly against spiritual authority emanating from the king and against the woes of imperial hierarchy. He escaped to England, 1582–1585. In 1606, his preaching emphasis was against the papacy and its superstructure. He opposed the efforts of the kings to introduce Episcopalian doctrine into Scotland. Melville was then exiled and imprisoned in the Tower of London, 1607–11, under King JAMES I. Upon his release, he retired to France as professor of Biblical theology at the University of Sedan.

Henry Savile

Nov. 30, 1549
Bradley, England

Feb. 19, 1622
Eton, England

English mathematician and classical scholar. Savile helped in the preparation of the King James Version, working on parts of the Gospels, Acts, and Revelation. He collected and published the *Works of Chrysostom* (8 volumes, 1610–13) and produced *Cylopaedia* (1613). He also founded two Savilian professorships in astronomy and mathematics at Oxford University in 1619. Savile was warden of Merton College, Oxford University (1585), and provost (officer of college dealing with curriculum and faculty) of Eton (1596). In 1619 he founded two professorships in geometry and astronomy at Oxford.

Paolo Sarpi

Aug. 14, 1552
Venice, Italy

Jan. 15, 1623
Venice, Italy

Catholic historian, scientist, statesman, and churchman. Sarpi urged reformation of his church and corresponded with Reformation leaders. When he was summoned to an inquisition, he refused to attend, which resulted in his excommunication. Sarpi specifically opposed the temporal power of the pope. He entered the Servite order (1565), and became professor of philosophy in a Servite monastery in Venice (1570). From 1588, he devoted himself to scientific and philosophical studies and attainments. He was noted for his "letters" (written communiques). Sarpi's status in the church was restored in 1607, but persecution and attempts on his life continued. He wrote *History of the Council of Trent* (1619). His hatred of the Jesuits and patriotism of Venice caused Rome's influence to diminish there. He said, "I wear a mask, but only of necessity, because without it no one can live in Italy."

Philippe de Mornay
DuPlessis—Mornay

Nov. 5, 1549
Chateau Buhy, France

Nov. 11, 1623
La Foret-sur-Sevre, France

Statesman, diplomat, writer, and leader of the Huguenots. Converted through his mother, Mornay sought toleration for the French Protestants. He barely escaped death in the St. Bartholomew Day massacre in August, 1572. When HENRY IV turned from Protestantism in 1593, Mornay disappointedly left the court and devoted himself to writing. Mornay wrote *Institution of the Lord's Supper*, which opposed the mass, and *The Mystery of Iniquity*. As counselor to King Henry IV, he was successful in bringing about the Edict of Nantes in 1598. After Prince Conde's (1552–88) (Huguenot general) death, Mornay's power and influence gained him the nickname of "Huguenot Pope." His wife died in 1606. Mornay was forced out of his Saumur governorship in 1620 because of his Protestant views. He had founded a Protestant university there. His *Memoires* were published in 1624. He said as he died, ". . .I laboured. Yet not I, but the grace of God which was in me. Away with all merit, either in me or any other man whatsoever. I call for nothing but mercy."

Henry Jacob

1563
Kent, England

1624
Virginia

English Congregationalist. Jacob replanted the movement after earlier congregations had been uprooted by authorities. He was a member of Robinson's congregation of Separatists at Leyden, Netherlands, but he returned to England and founded a church at Southwark in 1616. This church became the first permanent independent Congregational Church. In 1624, Jacob emigrated to Virginia. He died soon after his arrival.

Jakob Boehme

April 24, 1575
Alt-Seidenburg, Prussia (Germany)

Nov. 17, 1624
Gorlitz, Prussia (Germany)

Silesian shoemaker who became a Lutheran mystic and theosophist (mystical insight into divine nature). He married in 1599 and had six children. He attempted to explain the origin of evil. His most important mystical experience was in 1600 when he looked at a dish reflecting sunlight, where in ecstasy he declared that he saw the eternal Godhead. Boehme had limited education, but he used the Bible and Phillipus Paracelsus (physician) (1493–1541) as his sources. Boehme later wrote some 30 works, two of which brought him persecution. His theology stated that God was the source of both good and evil. He fled to Dresden, then to Silesia, where illness finally caught up with him. His modern heirs are Quakers. He published *Aurora [or] The Rising of the Dawn* (1612) and *The Way to Christ* (1623). He said as he died, "Now I go hence to paradise." He influenced Hegel (1770–1831) and Schopenhauer (1788–1860).

John Murton

1625

Early Baptist pastor. Murton and Thomas Helwy founded the first permanent Baptist congregation in England. Murton was won to the Separatist movement by Smythe and others of the Gainsborough, England congregation. This entire congregation was forced to flee to Amsterdam in 1607. When Smythe quarreled with the Netherlands congregation over petty issues, Murton and Helwys led the congregation back to England in 1611, founding a General Baptist Church on Newgate Street. Murton remained a loyal member.

John Robinson

c 1575
Sturton Steeple, England

March 3, 1625
Leyden, Netherlands

Separatist leader and pastor. Robinson was the leader of the Separatists at Norwich, England, in 1604, the same year he was married. He was suspended from the ministry in 1605. He then moved on to pastor in Scrooby in 1606. Robinson moved to the European Continent to pastor in Amsterdam (1608) and then in Leyden (1609), where he was formally ordained and where he served until his death. Although he chose to stay with the exiled congregation in Leyden, Robinson did assist in the Pilgrims' removal on the Speedwell to Plymouth, England, July 21, 1620, where they met up with the *Mayflower*. When the Leyden congregation had stabilized, Robinson had intended to follow the Pilgrims to America but died before another pilgrimage was made. His writings range from *Justification of Separation from the Church of England* (1610) to *Essays or Observations, Divine and Moral* (1625). His Separatism was a forerunner of Congregationalism.

James I

June 19, 1566
Edinburgh Castle, Scotland

March 27, 1625
Theobalds, England

King of England, Ireland, 1603–1625, and James VI of Scotland, 1567–1625. James I lent his name to the English translation of the Bible, known as the King James Version in 1611, which he authorized and financed. Forty–seven scholars worked on this, 1607–11, which was basically TYNDALE's work, and a revision of the Bishop's Bible ("The Bishop's Bible shall be followed and as little altered as the truth of the original shall permit"—one of 15 rules guiding the scholars.) The Bishop's Bible was the 4th edition of TYNDALE's revision in 1568. The text was later (1633) called the *Textus Receptus* (Stephen's 3rd edition of 1550, based on Erasmus' 5th edition of 1535 with marginal readings from 15 manuscripts, one of which was Codex D-Beza). To pacify Rome and Catholic factions, he married Anne, daughter of the Catholic king of Denmark, Frederick II, on November 23, 1589. By 1594, James had broken the power of Catholic nobles in Scotland. He began the Stuart line of kings [in England (1603–1714), already in Scotland, (1371–1714)]. His ego put him at odds with nearly every subject. His religious stand vacillated, depending on which alliance benefited him most. James was not pleased with either the Parliament Catholics or the Puritans, then he confused Puritans with the Presbyterians. He did stimulate colonization of the New World, resulting in the Jamestown Colony bearing his name (est. 1607). He was also a patron of SHAKESPEARE's Globe Theatre. James I wrote treatises on the evils of tobacco usage, *Counterblast to Tobacco* (1604) and another advocating severe measures against witchcraft, *Demonology* (1597). His Catholic mother was Mary, Queen of Scots. He once was so delighted with a loin of beef served to him at dinner, that he knighted it and said, "Arise, Sir Loin." His favorite Bible verse was Exodus 1:17.

Francis Bacon

Jan. 22, 1561
London, England

April 9, 1626
Highgate (near London), England

Philosopher, scientist, lawyer, statesman, and writer. Bacon developed the inductive method of reasoning. He separated religion and philosophy, saying that faith is nobler than the wisdom of philosophers, and also separated natural science from supernatural theology. His sentiments appear to parallel moderate Calvinism, as demonstrated in his *Confessions of Faith*. Bacon's thinking influenced subsequent thought in theological circles and reformed the methods of scientific investigation. Alice Barnham became his wife in 1606. His career included posts as solicitor general (1607), attorney general (1613), lord chancellor/barron (1618), and viscount (1621). He was deposed from public office (Parliament and court) for alleged bribery and corruption on May 3, 1621. This allowed him to retire and focus on science and literature. Bacon authored *New Atlantis* and *Novum Organum* but is best known for his essays on practical wisdom. Francis Bacon is listed as the sixth greatest thinker of all time. He said as he died, "Thy Creatures, O Lord, have been my books, but Thy Holy Scriptures much more." He died on Easter as a result of a chill; taking refuge in the house of Lord Arundel, Thomas Howard (1586–1646).
"*I believe that Jesus...became...a sacrifice for sin.*"

Lancelot Andrewes

Sept. 25, 1555
Barking, Essex England

Sept. 26, 1626
Southwark, London, England

Anglican leader and intellectual giant. He was chaplain to Queen ELIZABETH and Archbishop of Canterbury John Whitgift, around 1587. Andrewes' name was first on the list of those appointed to help make the King James Version translation of the Bible in 1611. He translated the Pentateuch and Joshua through I Chronicles, 1607–11. Andrewes was privy councilor (private advisor) to the crowns of Scotland and England, and a favorite preacher to ELIZABETH I, JAMES I, and CHARLES

I. He served as bishop of Chichester (1605), of Ely (1609, and of Winchester (1609). Andrewes was critical of both Catholicism and Calvinism. He wrote *Private Devotions* (1648), taken from the complexities of court problems in England and written in Hebrew, Latin, and Greek, and *Tortura Tori* (1609). In all, he mastered 15 languages. Andrewes died at Winchester House, a town house for bishops since 1107.

Gudbrandur Thorlaksson

c 1541/1542

1627

Lutheran bishop of Iceland. Through the use of tact and firmness, Thorlaksson brought the Reformation to his country. He translated many hymns from German and Danish into Icelandic, and printed an excellent translation of the Bible at Holar in 1584. He had 84 published works.

Johannes Kepler

Dec. 27, 1571
Weilder Stadt, Germany

Nov. 15, 1630
Regensburg, Bavaria (Germany)

Mathematician and founder of physical astronomy. Kepler was court mathematician and astronomer to Holy Roman Emperor Rudolf II (ruled: 1576–1612). He taught in Austria, then taught math at Gratz (1593), at Linz (1612); moved to Ulm, Germany, (1626); and then lived in Sagen, Silesia, Germany (Poland), (1628). He also was in Prague in 1599. Barbara von Muhleck became his wife on April 27, 1597 (died: 1611). He then married Susanna Reutlinger, a poor orphan girl, in 1613. In 1606, he wrote a book which proposed a theory to explain the star which led the Magi to the Christ child. Kepler, crippled and with impaired eyesight from childhood smallpox, originally studied to enter the Lutheran ministry and never lost sight of God's position as the Creator of the heavens and earth. At the Diet of Ratisbon (general assembly of the estates of the Holy Roman Empire) in 1613, Kepler scientifically defended the Gregorian Calendar. Kepler wrote on optics, approximated the law of refraction and pioneered work that led to the invention of calculus. He discovered the three laws of planetary motion, 1609 and 1618, elliptical orbits, gravity, tides, and harmony among motions of planets with the sun being the controlling/central force as the center of the universe. His understanding of nature was pantheistic. He opposed the doctrine of predestination.

John Donne

Jan. 24, 1573
London, England

March 31, 1631
London, England

Church of England preacher and poet. In 1592, he renounced Catholicism. Donne was ordained at the age of 41. He married Anne More in 1601 (died: December, 1617), leaving him to rear his seven children alone. He served as royal chaplain, 1615–21. Donne preached riveting sermons before CHARLES I and Princess Elizabeth in 1619. Donne became known as a persuasive preacher of great power, which led to his appointment as dean of St. Paul's Church in London, 1621–31. His famous phrase "For whom the bell tolls" and his most famous poem "Go, and Catch a Falling Star" are both found in his book, *Devotions Upon Emergent Occasions* (1624), which he wrote after recovery from a near fatal illness. His last sermon was titled "Death's Duel." His work, *Pseudo-Martyr*, gained approval from King JAMES I of England. Donne's published works included *Divine Poems* (1607), *Cycle of Holy Sonnets* (1618), and many theological writings.

Adolphus Gustavus II
Lion of the North

Dec. 9, 1594
Stockholm, Sweden

Nov. 16, 1632
Lutzen, Germany

King of Sweden, 1611–32. Gustavus was a mighty warrior having 80,000 well-disciplined troops to fight against modern-day Poland, Denmark, and Russia. He was a devout Lutheran believer. His military exploits included winning Swedish territory back from Denmark (1611–13), winning victories against Russia by cutting off their access to the Baltic Sea, (1613–17), and leading in a defensive war with Poland (1621–29). Landing in Pomerania in 1630, Gustavus led 16,000 troops into Germany as the champion of northern Protestantism. Although a brilliant strategist throughout this three-year conflict, Gustavus was killed in a final victorious battle, struck by a cannonball, and fell from his horse. With the aid of France, he had saved Protestantism in Germany from the clutches of the Holy Roman Empire. His daughter, Christina, by his wife, Marie Eleonoira (married: 1620), succeeded him on the throne. Gustavus II was the grandson of VASA GUSTAVUS I and one of history's greatest generals. He said as he died, "...I seal with my blood the Protestant religion and the liberty of Germany! Alas! my poor Queen. My God! My God!"

George Herbert

April 3, 1593
Montgomery Castle, Wales

March 1, 1633
Bemerton, England

Anglican, metaphysical poet, preacher, and composer. Herbert wrote the hymn, "Let All the World in Every Corner Sing" (music by ROBERT MCCUTCHAN). In 1629, he married Jane Danvers. He was ordained in 1630, after serving as public orator at Cambridge, 1619–27. Herbert lived a holy and exemplary life. Toward the end of his life, Herbert was a country parson of Fuggelston St. Peter's at Bemerton, 1629–33. Most of his devotional hymns were published in 1633. Herbert's prose work, *A Priest to the Temple* (published 1652), was also well received. He died of tuberculosis. His devotional poems were noted for their precise diction. As he died, he repeated Ps. 71:8, among other statements such as the following: "...I shall dwell with men made perfect, dwell where these eyes shall see my Master and Saviour."
"He that fears death, lives not."

George Abbot

Oct. 29, 1562
Guildford, England

Aug. 4, 1633
Croydon, England

Archbishop of Canterbury, 1611–33. Abbot possessed Puritan sympathies and was the recognized leader of the English Calvinists. He served as dean of Winchester (1600), vice-chancellor of Oxford University, 1600–9, and bishop of London (1609). His rise to power followed his defense of the hereditary monarchy (1606), and his efforts to combine the English and Scottish churches (1608). Abbot disagreed with King CHARLES I of England, which caused him to be briefly suspended from his duties. He also helped translate the New Testament, excluding the Epistles, for the King James Version Bible.

Robert Browne

1550
Tolethorp, England

Oct. 1633
Northampton, England

Pioneer of English separatism, often called "The Father of English Congregationalism." Browne began a movement known as the Brownists (term of abuse), (who were predecessors of the Pilgrims, Congregationalists, Independents, Nonconformists, Separatist). Believing that all true Christians should withdraw from the Church of England and form new churches composed of only serious believers, Browne led a church at Norwich in 1580. For this pastorship and similar activities, he was imprisoned 32 times and exiled in 1581. Browne emigrated to Middelburg, Netherlands, and established a pastorate there, 1581–83. Finally, he submitted to the Church of England in 1584 but was excommunicated. He then regrouped and served as schoolmaster of the Stamford School, 1586–91. He was ordained as an Anglican in 1591 and became rector in a church. He died in jail at age 80, being held for assaulting a constable.

William Ames

1576
Ipswich, England

Nov. 14, 1633
Rotterdam, Netherlands

Puritan theologian. Ames supported strict Calvinism, which compelled him to leave England in 1610 and settle in Rotterdam, Netherlands, as chaplain in an English church. There he wrote and lectured on theology and was an English chaplain to The Hague (seat of government), as well as a divinity professor at the University of Franeker in Friesland, Netherlands, 1622–32. He also became rector of the University in 1626. He next moved to Rotterdam in 1632. Ames is considered to be one of the greatest Calvinistic theologians with his work *Marrow of Theology* (1623), summing up Calvinism. He died suddenly as he was about to leave for America. His book *Conscience* (1632), written in Latin and English, was widely read.

Walter Travers

c 1548
Nottingham, England

1635

English Puritan writer. Travers quit Cambridge after an argument with JOHN WHITGIFT, and soon thereafter wrote an inflammatory *Declaration of Ecclesiastical Discipline*. He was provost of Trinity College, Dublin, 1594–98. He severely criticized English universities and the established church, which forced him to live in cities such as Geneva, Switzerland, and Antwerp, Belgium, which were areas more tolerant to freedom of religious thought. Travers became a close friend of THEODORE BEZA. His life exemplified firm Puritan convictions and his work summed up a strong Puritan position.

Melchior Teschner

April 29, 1584
Fraustadt, Silesia (Poland)

Dec. 1, 1635
Oberprietschen, Germany

Pastor and composer. Teschner composed the music for "All Glory, Laud, and Honor" (1615). THEODULF OF ORLEANS wrote the lyrics in 820. In 1609, Teschner was appointed cantor (one who sings or chants prayers) of the Lutheran Church at Fraustadt, and taught in the parish school. He next became pastor at Oberprietschen, 1614. His son and grandson followed Teschner in pastoring at the same church.

Johann Gerhard

Oct. 17, 1582
Quedlinburg, Prussia (Germany)

Aug. 20, 1637
Jena, Germany

Lutheran theologian and writer. In 1608, he married 13-year-old Barbara Neumeier (who died two years later). He then married Mary Mattenberg in 1614, who bore him ten children. Gerhard wrote and taught at the University of Jena, 1616–37. He solidified LUTHER's thoughts into a tight system of high Lutheran orthodoxy. In the early years of his career, Gerhard was influenced by JOHANN ARNDT. Gerhard's nine-volume *Loci Theologici* (1610–22) was a most important and influential theological work which eventually became a classic of the Lutheran scholasticists. He also wrote *Meditationes Sacrae* (1606), *Confessio Catholicae* (1634) and 51 commentaries. He was offered teaching positions at some 24 universities, but stayed at Jena where students flocked.

Nicholas Ferrar

Feb. 22, 1592
London, England

Dec. 4, 1637
Little Gidding, England

Church of England theologian and educator. Ferrar was active in the affairs of the Virginia Company (until 1623), then served in Parliament (1624–25). He set up a Christian community of about 30 people, composed largely of his own family, in Little Gidding, in 1625. It functioned as a mini-monastery, providing a free school for the neighborhood, with bookbinding as its main industry. King CHARLES I visited the community three times. It was destroyed by Puritans (1646) and by Parliament (1647), which was at odds with CHARLES I.

Cyril Lucar(is)

Nov. 13, 1572
Candia, Crete

June 27, 1638
Constantinople, Turkey

Martyred Greek Orthodox theologian and patriarch of Constantinople, 1621–38. He was in Alexandria prior to 1621. Lucar sympathized with Calvinism and opposed the Roman papacy. He sought to introduce the doctrines of the Reformed Church into the Greek Church. Lucar sent the Codex Alexandrinus (Codex A) (Greek document found about 450 containing the Old Testament (Septuagint), with the Apocrypha and the New Testament) to King CHARLES I of England in 1628, too late for use in the King James Version. This contained the third oldest Bible in existence at that time. Opposed by his own church, Lucar was hung on a political charge by the Turkish Sultan Murad (Amurath IV) (ruled: 1636–40), who accused him of instigating rebellion among the Cossacks [tribes (horseman) of Slavic warriors].

John Harvard

Nov. 26, 1607
Southwark, London, England

Sept. 14, 1638
Charlestown (Boston), Massachusetts

Congregational minister and benefactor to Harvard College (University). He was "baptized" November 29, 1607. John Harvard married Anne Sadler (1636), and came to America (1637) as a teaching elder in Boston. For a while he was the assistant pastor at the First Church in Charlestown. John Harvard bequeathed his library (started in 1636) of 320 books and half his estate (700 pounds) to the struggling new Cambridge College in Massachusetts, which became the famed Harvard University. The Massachusetts General Court named the college in his honor on March 13, 1639, for his property was a big improvement over the tall stockade surrounding Cambridge to keep out prowling wolves and hostile Indians. He died of consumption (tuberculosis).

John Spotswood

1565
Mid-Calder, Scotland

Nov. 26, 1639
London, England

Episcopalian theologian. Spotswood went to Mass in France with the Catholic duke of Lennox in 1601, then embraced Episcopalianism under King JAMES VI of Scotland. He was made archbishop of Glasgow (1603) and of St. Andrews, then became primate of Scotland (1615), and finally chancellor of Scotland, 1635–38. Spotswood's immense quest for the satisfying of his personal ambitions, fostered such intense dislike among fellow Scots that he was removed from office, and excommunicated in 1638, fleeing to London. Spotswood's most valuable contribution was his work, *History of the Church and State of Scotland* (published in London: 1655).

Robert Burton

Feb. 8, 1577
Lindley, England

Jan. 25, 1640
Oxford, England

Clergyman and author. Burton was a graduate of Christ's Church College, Oxford University, in 1599. He served as vicar at St. Thomas Parish in Oxford, and as rector of Walesby (1624–31) and Seagrave (1633–40).

He wrote a Latin comedy called *Philosophaster* (1606). Burton wrote *The Anatomy of Melancholy* (1621), which was full of wit and learning and was highly praised by Charles Lamb (essayist and critic: 1735–1834) and JOHN MILTON. Burton never married.

John Ball (2)

Oct. 1585
Cassington, England

Oct. 20, 1640
Whitmore, England

Zealous Puritan and one of the founders of Presbyterianism in England. Ball was educated at Oxford and ordained in 1610, after which he became a minister at Whitmore. There he established a small school and spent his life in poverty. He was imprisoned at times for his zealous action. His chief literary work, *A Treatise of the Covenant of Grace*, was published after his death. His writings held great influence on the covenants in the Westminster Confession of Faith [an evangelical summary of Christian faiths and doctrine expressed in 33 chapters (1645–47), a new reformed church policy after the defeat of episcopacy]. This became a hallmark for Presbyterianism. Ball also attacked the new independent church (Congregationalism), as well as Romanism.

Laurence Chaderton

Sept. 14, 1536
near Oldham, England

Nov. 13, 1640
Cambridge, England

Puritan theologian and King James Version Bible translator (II Chronicles to Song of Solomon). Chaderton was a fellow of Christ's College, Cambridge, and a favorite preacher there for many years. He was the first master of Emmanuel College of Cambridge, 1584–1622. From 1598–1640, he was a prebendary of Lincoln. For nearly 50 years, he served as an afternoon lecturer at St. Clement's. Chaderton was one of the five Puritan representatives at the Hampton Court Conference in 1604. He lived to be 104.

Francis Gomarus

Jan. 30, 1563
Brugge (Bruges), Belgium

Jan. 11, 1641
Groningen, Netherlands

Uncompromising Calvinist theologian. He pastored a Reformed church in Frankfurt Ammain 1587–93. Gomar taught theology at Leyden, 1594–1611. Here he was the chief opponent of fellow university educator, JACOB ARMINIUS, who arrived in 1603. Gomarus engaged in several caustic public debates. When Leyden University later appointed Konrad Vorst, a follower of ARMINIUS to succeed him (ARMINIUS) in the theology department, Gomarus resigned. He then taught in the universities of Middlesburg (1611), Saumur (1614), and Groningen (1618). He attended the Synod of Dort, 1618–19 (excluded the Arminians from the Reformed Church).

Galileo A. Galilei

Feb. 15, 1564
Pisa, Italy

Jan. 8, 1642
Arcetri, Florence, Italy

Astronomer, physicist, philosopher, and mathematician. Galileo prepared the path for modern science by establishing that the sun is the central body around which the earth (not the commonly accepted belief that the earth is the center of the universe, Isaiah 40:21–22), and planets revolve, and that the moon only reflects light. In essence, he discovered the first two of ISAAC NEWTON's three laws of motion (uniform motion, acceleration). He studied medicine, was a talented musician, and a skillful painter. In 1616 he was condemned at Rome for showing the Scriptural confirmation for the Copernican System (1512: sun-centered theory of planetary motion). Galileo was tried by the Inquisition at Rome (1632), was publicly humiliated (1633), but allowed to retire to Arcetri, where he spent his remaining years in his own house. The Vatican's censure started distrust between science and the Church. He was professor of math at the universities of Pisa (1589–91), Padua (1592–1610), and Florence (1610 on). Galileo, who had an IQ of 145, defined the first principles of dynamics (pendulum: 1585), developed a thermometer, (1597) and a telescope (1609). Through his telescope, in addition to defining planetary motion around the sun, he found Jupiter's moons, Saturn's rings, sunspots, and the grouping of the Milky Way Galaxy. Galileo was blind the last five years of his life. The treatment he received was a great blunder of Catholicism. He sought to harmonize the Bible (Joshua 10:13) with science.

William Bedell

Dec. 25, 1571
Black Notely, England

Feb. 7, 1642
Drum Corr, Ireland

Prelate of the English Church. From 1604–8, he was in Venice, Italy, as chaplain of the Ambassador, Sir Henry Wotton. He ministered at Horningsheath, Suffolk (1615–27), followed by the provost position at Trinity College in Dublin, Ireland (1627–29). Bedell was elected bishop of Kilmore and Ardagh, Ireland, in 1629. In 1633, he resigned his see at Ardagh over his disapproval of the inconsistencies he found in church doctrine finding refuge in a minister's home. He was imprisoned in the castle of Cloughboughter during a 1641 rebellion in Ulster, Ireland, where 30,000 Protestants were killed. Bedell died as a consequence of his treatment while imprisoned there. He directed the translation of the Old Testament into Irish. He said as he died, "...I have finished my ministry and life together. I have kept the faith."

Simon Episcopius
Simon Biscop—Bischop

Jan. 1, 1583
Amsterdam, Netherlands

April 4, 1643
Amsterdam, Netherlands

Arminian theologian. Episcopius studied at Leyden, taught theology there, 1612–18, replacing FRANCIS GOMARUS as chair for the theology department, and became successor to Arminius in 1609 as head of the Arminian (Remonstrant) movement. He was stoned by fanatic Calvinists in the streets and almost killed in 1612. At the Synod of Dort, 1618–19, Episcopius was condemned and banished from the country. He lived at Brussels, Paris, and Rouen (1618–26), before returning to pastor in 1626 and teach in the Remonstrant Seminary in Amsterdam (1634–43). His writings included *Confessio* (1622) and *Apologia* (1629). His views would be considered liberal today. He was a tolerant reformer opposing both Calvinists and Catholics.

Anne Marbury Hutchinson

July 20, 1591—Baptized
Alford, England

Aug. 1643
Westchester County, New York

Nonconformist favoring commonsense religious toleration. Anne came to Boston in May of 1634 and organized weekly women's Bible-teaching groups. These attempts to expand women's Bible knowledge and community involvement increased her disfavor with Puritan authorities. Anne was excommunicated from JOHN COTTON's Boston church and banished from the colony in 1637 for holding meetings and teaching "heretical views" (Covenant of Grace over Covenant of Works). She was dubbed an antinomian. Anne married William Hutchinson, August 9, 1612 (died: 1642), and they had 14 children. They moved to Rhode Island, March 28, 1638 and then on to Westchester County (near the Bronx) in 1642. Anne and the children were murdered by Indians a year after the death of her husband near the shore of Pelham Bay.

Johan Wtenbogaert

1557

1644

Dutch Reformed Arminian preacher. Wtenbogaert sided with ARMINIUS which helped cause the furious controversy to surface which doubted the extreme Calvinist doctrine of unconditional predestination. For many years, Wtenbogaert held the post of court preacher in the Netherlands, and he became the chief spokesman for Arminianism after the death of JACOB ARMINIUS.

William Chillingworth

Oct. 22, 1602
Oxford, England

Jan. 30, 1644
Chicester, England

Church of England theologian and writer. Chillingworth left his strong Catholic background in 1634, advocating that God was the sole authority of the Bible and that all men had the right to interpret it. He was ordained into the Church of England in 1638 and was appointed chancellor of Salisbury. Chillingworth's writings presented a strong defense for the merits of Protestantism. The year 1638 saw the appearance of his famous work, *The Religion of Protestants–A Safe Way to Salvation*. His *Works* (1637) were last published at Oxford in three volumes in 1838. Chillingworth served in the Royalist Army during England's Civil War, was captured on December 9, 1643, and died six weeks later.

William Brewster

Jan. 1567
near Scrooby, England

April 10, 1644
Plymouth, Massachusetts

Plymouth elder and Pilgrim leader on the Mayflower. He and his wife Mary, whom he married in 1591, had six children. Brewster began a life of community service in Scrooby (1589), where he was a bailiff and postmaster, 1594–1607, and a leading member of a small Puritan congregation which separated from the established church (1606). During this time, Puritans and Brownists met in Brewster's home, where he served as a ruling elder. These Separatist beliefs caused him to flee to the Netherlands (Amsterdam and Leyden, 1609–19, where he pursued religious freedom but was persecuted for the books his printing business produced, which revealed fallacies in the English governmental system. In 1620 Brewster became the spiritual leader for the Pilgrims embarking for America on the *Mayflower*. Brewster preached regularly in Plymouth Colony, 1620–29, before the arrival of the first official pastor (Ralph Smith). For the duration of his life, he remained a ruling elder, and to many, "The leader of the Pilgrims."

Daniel Featley (Fairclough)

March 15, 1582
Charlton-upon-Otmoor, England

April 17, 1645
Chelsea, London, England

Anglican pastor. He was chaplain to the Ambassador at Paris, 1610–13, and then to GEORGE ABBOT (Archbishop of Canterbury). Featley held pastorates at Lambeth (1619–27) and then Acton (after 1627). Featley was a member of the Westminster Assembly (Parliament convened 121 divines, ten lords, and 20 commoners to bring the Church of England closer to the Bible—met 1643–49) in 1643, and the last Episcopal member who remained in the assembly. During the English Civil War in 1644, he was suspected of spying for King CHARLES I. He wrote a set of sermons on hard texts and also wrote *Private Devotion*. Featley died at Chelsea College, being imprisoned for 18 months by CROMWELL.

Hugo Grotius

Oct. 10, 1583
Delft, Netherlands

Aug. 28, 1645
Rostock, Germany

Brilliant jurist, statesman, and theologian. Grotius was active in politics and religion. Established as a lawyer in 1599, he is known as the founder of International Law, as substantiated by his *The Law of War and Peace* (1625). His most famous work was *Truth of the Christian Religion* (Latin, 1627). It was translated into English, German, and French. After his death 144 editions and translations were published. He also wrote three dramas in Latin. Grotius sided with the Arminians; hence, he was jailed in 1618 by the GOMARIST Calvinists. He escaped to France in 1621 with the help of his brave wife, Maria van Reigerebergh, and became an ambassador to Sweden, 1634–45. Finally, in 1645, Grotius was granted permission to return to the Netherlands, but his boat was shipwrecked, and he arrived in Rostock seriously ill and died. He knew Latin, Greek, Hebrew, and Arabic. He sought to unite all Christian denominations.

William Twisse

c 1575/1578
Speenham-Land, England

July 20, 1646
London, England

First moderator of the Westminster Assembly, 1643. Twisse was chaplain to princess Elizabeth Stuart, later Queen of Bohemia (1596–1622), daughter of JAMES I. Twisse was educated at Oxford and then became vicar of Newbury in 1620, where he remained until the opening of the English Civil War, 1642–46. He was a high Calvinist and distinguished himself by his writings against the Arminians. He was a student of theology and produced numerous works.

Alexander Henderson

1583
Criech, Scotland

Aug. 19, 1646
Edinburgh, Scotland

Clergyman and diplomat. Henderson was second only to JOHN KNOX, in developing the Church of Scotland. He ministered at Leuchars, 1613–38. Henderson's background was Episcopalian, but he changed as a result of the resistance to the mandatory Prayer Book of 1637. He was moderator of the General Assembly of Glasgow in 1638, which deposed Scottish bishops and formally began Presbyterianism. He was appointed rector of Edinburgh University in 1640, where he introduced the teaching of Hebrew. Henderson drafted the National (Scottish) Covenant (1638) and the Solemn League and Scottish Presbyterian Covenant adopted by the Westminster Assembly (1643). Henderson then became a leader of the Covenanters (defenders of Presbyterians, and signers of Scottish National Covenant), which contributed to the defeat of King CHARLES I. Henderson wrote *The Bishop's Doom* (1638).

Thomas Hooker
Father of Congregationalism

July 7, 1586
Marfield, England

July 7, 1647
Hartford, Connecticut

Puritan theologian and founder of Connecticut, specifically the colony of Hartford, 1639. After pastoring in England, 1620–30, Hooker fled to Holland (1630) and then immigrated as a refugee to Boston (1633) with JOHN COTTON. He pastored in Newtown (Cambridge) MA, until 1636, when he migrated with his congregation to found the colony of Hartford. He clashed with COTTON over the order of salvation in the Antinomian controversy of 1637–38. He was a devout believer, and eloquent preacher. His Connecticut Constitution established him as a "Father of Democracy." Hooker also organized the United Colonies of New England in 1643, a defensive alliance. He coauthored (with JOHN COTTON) a book entitled *Church Discipline* (1648). Thomas and Susanna Hooker had at least three children. His writings range from *The Soul's Preparation for Christ* (1632) to *The Poor Doubting Christian* (pub. 1648).

Herbert Palmer

March 29, 1601
Wingham, England

Aug. 13, 1647

Pastor and writer of Presbyterian doctrine. One of Palmer's catechisms was the basis for the Westminster Catechism. He was a moderate Presbyterian who favored presiding bishops. Palmer was a pastor at Ashwell (1632), then was a member of the Westminster Assembly (1643), and a master of Queen's College, Cambridge (1644). As a pastor, Palmer was devout and eloquent. He used his inherited wealth for the furtherance of Christ's message.

Christian IV

April 12, 1577
Frederiksborg, Denmark

Feb. 28, 1648
Copenhagen, Denmark

King of Denmark and Norway, 1588–1648. Christian succeeded his father, Frederick II. The young king's court was one of the most joyous and magnificent in Europe. Christian founded the Danish Navy, defeated Sweden (1611–13) and increased Scandinavian influence along the Baltic coast of Germany (1613–21). In the Thirty Years' War, he was the Chief of the Protestant Union (1625), before yielding to ADOLPHUS GUSTAVUS II of Sweden (1629). Christian IV's policies irritated Sweden, which declared war against him 1643–45, and defeated him, forcing him to yield more power to the ruling nobles of his own country. In 1624, the present town of Oslo was rebuilt and named Christiania in honor of Christian. Copenhagen was also enlarged under his rule.

George Gillespie

Jan. 21, 1613
Kirkcaldy, Scotland

Dec. 17, 1648
Kircaldy, Scotland

Presbyterian minister. Gillespie pastored in Wemyss (1638–42) and at Greyfriars Church in Edinburgh (1642 on). He was one of the four commissioners sent from the Church of Scotland to the Westminster Assembly to negotiate with the Church of England for the freedom to deviate from the church's form of worship in 1640. Later, Gillespie drafted the church legislation sanctioning the Presbyterian form of worship in 1645. He wrote *The Divine Ordinance* (1646) and *Aaron's Rod Blossoming* (1646), among other theological and controversial works.

Charles I

Nov. 19, 1600
Dunfermline, Scotland

Jan. 30, 1649
London, England

King of Great Britain and Ireland, 1625–49. He became Prince of Wales in 1616 and plunged England into five disastrous years, 1624–28, of war with France. Charles I, son of JAMES I, married Henrietta Maria of France in 1625. Charles I dismissed three Parliaments in four years because they refused to submit to him. He ruled without a Parliament for eleven years, 1629–40. His autocratic rule caused large migrations to America and brought on "The Great Rebellion," the English Civil War, 1642–46. Charles tried to force the Church of England style of worship on the Scots, which resulted in defeat for his Royalist Army in 1645 at Nasby. CROMWELL and the Puritans took over the government, and Charles was captured in 1647, tried by 67 judges as a tyrant and enemy, and finally beheaded at Whitehall, the royal palace in London. His religious affiliations waffled according to his political needs. At various times he was pro-Catholic, pro-Anglican, and even pro-Presbyterian.

Gerhard J. Voss
Gerardus Johannes Vossius

Spring, 1577
Near Heidelberg, Germany

March 17, 1649
Amsterdam, Netherlands

Dutch theologian, church historian, classical scholar, philologist, and humanist. Voss directed the College of Theology at Leyden, 1615–19, but resigned under suspicion of heresy. He then held professorships at Dort (1619–22), the University of Leyden (1622–31), and at Amsterdam Athenaeum in 1631. Voss had a long friendship with HUGO GROTIUS and leaned toward Remonstrant teachings. He was invited to England and accepted a post at Canterbury offered by Archbishop of Canterbury William Laud (served: 1633–45). Voss' works, such as *Historia Pelagiana* (1618), made a solid contribution to refined scholarship. His main study was history of dogma.

John Winthrop

Jan. 12, 1588
Edwardstone, England

March 26, 1649
Boston, Massachusetts

First governor of Massachusetts Bay Colony, 1629–49. Winthrop was unhappy with the anti-Puritan policies of King CHARLES I of England. He sold his estates and sailed on the *Arabella* (April 8–June 12, 1630), with a convoy of ships carrying 1800 people to the New World. They arrived in Salem, MA with Winthrop, soon settling in the Boston area. Winthrop led the colony through the perils and difficulties of infancy, and eventually the colony became Boston. He was responsible for the early success and prosperity even though he did not believe in democracy or religious freedom, serving as governor twelve times. He opposed HENRY VANE, ANNE HUTCHINSON, and the Antinomians, 1636–37. Winthrop organized The Confederation of New England Colonies, 1645. His most noted work was a two-volume reference, *History of New England* (1630–49). Disease and childbirth took many young wives in the 1700s. Winthrop was married to Mary Forth on April 16, 1605 (died: 1615), Thomasine Clopton in December, 1615 (died: December 8, 1616), Margaret Tyndal April, 1618 (died: 1647), and Martha Cotymore, who gave him a total of seven children.

Thomas Shepard

Nov. 5, 1605
Towcester, England

Aug. 25, 1649
Cambridge, Massachusetts

Pastor and educator. Shepard came to America in 1635, after being silenced for nonconformity by Archbishop of Canterbury William Laud. Shepard was a friend of JOHN HARVARD and influential in establishing Harvard College in 1636. He became pastor of the church in Cambridge, 1636–49, and was prominent in the Cambridge Synod (New England model of Congregational church government). Shepard's prolific writing included, *The Parable of the Ten Virgins*. Seven children came from his three marriages: Margaret Tauteville (1632); Joanna Hooker (1637); and Margaret Boradel (September 8, 1647). He initiated public confessions of faith.

J. Giovanni Diodati

June 6, 1576
Lucca, Italy

Oct. 3, 1649
Geneva, Switzerland

Calvinist theologian. Diodati was professor of Hebrew (1597) and of theology (1609) in Geneva. He taught until 1645. In 1607, he published a translation of the Bible in Italian. Diodati attended the Synod of Dort, 1618–19. He was unsuccessful in an attempt to spread Reformed doctrine into Italy. He also translated the Bible into French in 1644, and pastored at Nimes. He wrote *Annotations Upon the Bible*.

Martin Rinkhart

April 24, 1586
Eilenburg, Germany

Dec. 8, 1649
Eilenburg, Germany

Pastor and hymn writer. Rinkhart wrote the famous hymn, "Now Thank We All Our God" (1636). CRUGER composed the music in 1647. He was a German Lutheran pastor in Eilenburg when war, famines, and plagues ravaged Germany. Eighty thousand people died, 4,000 of whom succumbed to the plague in 1637, including his wife on May 8. His congregation ate cats and dogs in 1638. They buried up to 45 people each day. The singing of his hymn at the end of the Thirty Years' War in 1648 was with great feeling. Rinkhart possessed unusual strength and steadfastness. He previously pastored at Erdeborn and Lyttichendorf.

Janet Geddes

c 1650

Scottish Presbyterian. Janet Geddes led a popular uprising that proved to be the deathblow of liturgy in Scotland. Catholic Archbishop of Canterbury, William Laud, had tried to introduce English liturgy into Scotland. When the bishop of the St. Giles Cathedral Church of Edinburgh attempted to read it on July 23, 1637, Geddes hurled the stool on which she was sitting at his head. A riot resulted and street marchers cried, "A pope or the sword of the Lord." Some historians are skeptical about the incident.

David Calderwood

1575
Dalkeith, Scotland

Oct. 29, 1650
Jedburgh, Scotland

Church of Scotland Presbyterian minister, historian, and apologist. Calderwood was so opposed to Episcopal authority that he was banished by JAMES VI in 1617 for refusing to surrender a roll of signatures to a remonstrance (document formally stating opposition or grievances). Calderwood was ordered to leave the country in 1619, so spent several years in Holland and worked on the Scottish Church's *Directory for Public Worship*. He further defended Presbyterianism in *The Altar of Damascus* (1623). After King JAMES VI's death in 1625, he returned to Scotland. His *History of the Kirk (church) of Scotland* was published, posthumously, in 1678.

Nathaniel Ward

1578
Haverhill, England

Oct. 1652
Shenfield, England

Minister, legal scholar and Puritan writer. Ward's career as a Puritan, 1618 on, took him to both sides of the Atlantic. He served in England as an Anglican rector in Stondon Massey 1628–33, until archbishop of Canterbury, William Laud, excommunicated him for his ardent Puritanism. Ward became pastor at Ipswich, MA from 1634–38. He helped write the first set of laws for the Massachusetts Colony, *The Body of Liberties*, which were formally adopted in 1641. Ward returned to England in 1647, and pastored in Shenfield, 1648–52. His first and best-known book was *The Simple Cobbler* (1647), a rebuke of English Puritanism for yielding to the pressures of toleration, and his last, *Discolliminium* (1650).

John Cotton
Patriarch of New England

Dec. 4, 1584
Derby, England

Dec. 23, 1652
Boston, Massachusetts

Puritan Congregational minister and author. Cotton was ordained in 1610 and pastored at St. Botolph's in Boston, England, 1612–33. He then went to Charlestown (Boston), where he was the spiritual leader and teacher at the First Congregational Church, 1633–52. The city of Boston (MA) was named in his honor as a memorial for his first pastorate. Cotton married Elizabeth Harrocks (July 3, 1613), and then Sarah Story (April 25, 1632), who when widowed, married RICHARD MATHER in 1657. Of Cotton's six children, daughter, Maria, married INCREASE MATHER. John Cotton became the head of Congregationalism in America, a position that upheld authority of the magistrates over religious as well as secular affairs of the citizens. Freedoms of speech, thought, and religion were forbidden. As a result, Cotton helped to banish ANNE HUTCHINSON and ROGER WILLIAMS from their colony for spouting a "Covenant of Grace," rather than the Puritan belief of a "Covenant by Works." His writings included *The Keys of the Kingdom of Heaven* (1644), and *The Way of the Congregational* (1648). John Cotton introduced the practice of keeping the Sabbath from Saturday evening to Sunday evening. He published 50 volumes of theological works.

Thomas Adams

c 1580–92   *1653*

Pious and learned Puritan minister. Robert Southey (English author and poet laureate, 1774–1843) called him "The prose SHAKESPEARE of the Puritan theologians." Adams served as pastor at Willington (1612–14), Wingrave–Bucks (1614–15) and St. Gregors (1618–23). Adams wrote a commentary on *II Peter*. He was probably a Royalist in the Civil War. JOSEPH ANGUS edited and Thomas Smith published a three-volume collection of his works (1862, London).

Roger Manwaring

1590   *1653*

Supporter of the monarchy. Manwaring was the Church of England cleric who served as royal chaplain to King CHARLES I. He preached that the king rules as God's representative, and that refusing to pay taxes could cause damnation. Parliament fined and imprisoned Manwaring, but CHARLES I protected him and promoted him to bishop.

William Gouge

Nov. 1, 1575   *Dec. 12, 1653*
Stratford Bow, England   London, England

Puritan pastor. For 45 years, Gouge served at St. Ann's Blackfriars Parish, London, 1606–51. Early in his life, Gouge lectured on logic and philosophy at King's College, Cambridge University. Beginning in 1643, he was a member of the Westminster Assembly, often serving as its moderator. Through the Assembly, he assisted in preparing the Westminster Confession of Faith. Just prior to death, he finished his *Commentary on Hebrews*. He was imprisoned nine weeks for republishing *The Calling of the Jews*. His last words were, "I am sure I shall be with Christ when I die."

Johann V. Andreae

Aug. 17, 1586   *June 27, 1654*
Herrenberg, Germany   Stuttgart, Germany

Lutheran theologian and satirist. During the Thirty Years' War, 1618–48, Andreae served as a physician, minister, and grave digger. He served as superintendent and minister at Cal, 1620–39. In 1639, Andreae was called to Stuttgart to be court preacher. In 1650, he became general superintendent (clergyman having oversight of specific area) of Bebenhausen (outside Wurttemberg) until his health failed. In 1654, he became abbot of Adelberg. Andreae wrote as many as 150 books and pamphlets, mostly in Latin, including *Christianapolis*, *Theophilus*, and *Menippus* (a satire: 1648). He was the grandson of JACOB ANDREAE. He insisted on pure morals as well as pure doctrine. He labored to educate ministers and to introduce church discipline. Some claim he founded a secret organization, The Rosicrucian Society.

Thomas Gataker

Sept. 4, 1574   *July 27, 1654*
Salvington, England   Rotherhithe, *England*

Writer and member of the Westminster Assembly, 1643. Gataker was preacher of Lincoln's Inn in 1601 and rector of Rotherhithe, 1611–54. Gataker's first book was *Of the Nature and Use of Lots* (1619), defining unlawful games of chance. He was also a learned author who specialized writing on transubstantiation. His works included *Annotation on Isaiah and Jeremiah* (1645, 1651) and *Meditations on Aurelius* (1652), besides the editing of several classics.

John Selden

Dec. 16, 1584
Salvington, England

Nov. 30, 1654
London, England

Lawyer, jurist, statesman, antiquarian (study of old history, antiquities, books**) and controversial author**. His *History of Tithes* (1618), so angered King CHARLES I, that Selden had to re-write the book. His stand denied that tithes were a "divine institution." Selden was imprisoned in the Tower of London (1621) for rejecting the premise that privileges of Parliament were royal grants but later was elected to the House of Commons (1623). In 1629, he was again imprisoned for his judicial stand, which affected the intake of funds for the royal treasury. This controversy related to a discussion of tonnage (duties/fees based on weight of goods) and poundage (commissions). Selden represented Lancaster in several Parliaments. In 1643, he sat in the Westminster Assembly as a moderate and was made keeper of the Records of the Tower of London. His most popular work was *Table-Talk* (1689). He joined the Presbyterians in later days.

Edward Winslow

Oct. 18, 1595
Droitwich, England

May 8, 1655
Caribbean Sea between islands of Hispaniola and Jamaica

Liaison, explorer, and statesman in America. As a *Mayflower* pilgrim, Winslow came to America in 1620 and was delegated to build relations with local Indians, engage in trade opportunities, and explore the New England coast. Winslow was married to Elizabeth Barker on May 16, 1618, (died during the first hard winter), and Susanna F. White on May 12, 1621. This was the first marriage performed in New England. Winslow formed a trusted friendship with Indian chief Massasoit (leader of Wampanoag tribe in region of Bristol, Rhode Island, 1588–1662). He went back and forth, several times to England on behalf of the needs of the Plymouth Colony to whom he served as governor, 1633, 1634, and 1644. He returned to England in 1646. In London, in 1649, he was instrumental in the founding of the Society for the Propagation of the Gospel in New England. Winslow helped the English to seize the island of Jamaica from the Spanish in 1655, but died of a fever on a return trip to England. His writings range from *Good News From New England* (1624) to *Platform of Church Discipline* (1653).

Edward Fisher

c 1597
Godmanchester, England

Nov. 1655
Ireland

Controversial theological writer. Fisher was probably, but not certainly, the author of the theological tract, *The Marrow of Modern Divinity* (1644), which became a great favorite with the Puritans. He personally was an ardent Royalist and a strong Calvinist. Fisher taught school in Caermarthen, Wales and wrote theological pieces, but he fled to Ireland to escape creditors. Marrowme (later Scottish Evangelical Group) printed his tract in 1718.

Stephen Marshall

1594
Godmanchester, England

Nov. 1655

Popular Puritan pastor and doctrinal writer. As a member of the Westminster Assembly (1643), he also worked on the Shorter Westminster Catechism (1647). Marshall pastored at Wethersfield, and at Finchingfield, Essex. Marshall wrote in defense of infant baptism. His position as a powerful preacher, influenced the elections of the Short Parliament (lasted 3 weeks in 1640). He swayed the House of Commons through his eloquent sermons to accept episcopal (relating to bishops) and liturgical reform. He died of consumption (tuberculosis).

Justus Heurnius

c 1585
Netherlands

1656
Netherlands

Dutch missionary to Indonesia. Heurnius was sent by the East India Company to the Indonesian Islands, especially the Netherlands-owned city of Batavia (Djakarta) on the island of Java. He worked among both the Malayans and the Chinese. He prepared a Dutch-Latin-Chinese dictionary. On the Indonesian island of Ambona (Moluccas/Spice Islands), his food was poisoned by the Mohammedans. He returned to the Netherlands to write and translate various works into Malayanese.

Georg Calixtus

Dec. 14, 1586
Medelby, Germany

March 19, 1656
Konigsluter/Helmstedt, Germany

Lutheran ecumenical theologian. From 1609–13, he advocated that the Christian life was more important than purity of doctrine, and made Christian morality a distinct branch of science. Calixtus was a divinity (theology) professor at Helmstedt, after 1614, spending over 40 years in laborious literary work. He attempted to develop a theology which would reconcile Lutherans, Calvinists, and Catholics. His philosophy was called syncretism (Greek roots meaning a combination of different religious beliefs). Calixtus was regarded as an influential religious independent who traveled extensively throughout England and the European Continent.

James Ussher

Jan. 4, 1581
Dublin, Ireland

March 21, 1656
Reigate, England

Chronologist, archbishop of Armagh, and primate of Ireland, 1625–40. Ussher began his career as chancellor of St. Patrick's Cathedral, Dublin, 1605–21, while teaching divinity at the University of Dublin, 1607–20. He then served as bishop of Meath (1621–24), He prepared a chronology of Biblical events based on his studies, and he concluded that creation occurred 4004 BC. Ussher had strong sympathies toward the Calvinist Puritans, in spite of his Anglicanism, and worked for reconciliation between these two groups. Through his correspondence with Archbishop of Canterbury William Laud, 1628–40, it is recorded that he was unsuccessful in his attempts to make doctrinal standards of the Irish Church conform to the Church of England. Since Ussher sided with CHARLES I, Ussher lost nearly all his property in Ireland and was never able to return there after 1641, when rebellion broke out. He ended his career with a preaching post at the Society of Lincoln's Inn in London (1647–56). Ussher received a state funeral in Westminster Abbey, London, conducted by OLIVER CROMWELL.

Joseph Hall

July 1, 1574
Ashby-de-la-Zouch, England

Sept. 8, 1656
Higham, England

Bishop of Exeter, 1627–41, and Norwich, 1641–47. He was the dean of Worcester, 1616–27. Hall defended the episcopacy when it was attacked by Parliament. He was accused of puritanical views and was impeached. He and eleven other bishops were imprisoned in the Tower of London for six months in 1642. His cathedral was desecrated in 1643. After this, Hall retired to live in poverty at Higham. One of his many works, *Heaven Upon Earth*, was reprinted by WESLEY. Hall authored verses, devotional works, satires, and controversial treatises such as *Epistles* (1608–11) and *Contemplations* (1612–26). He was a pulpit orator and prolific writer and sought a balanced tolerant ministry to all. He published *Divine Right of Episcopacy* (1640).

Myles Standish

1584
Lancashire, England

Oct. 3, 1656
Duxbury, Massachusetts

American colonist and soldier. He joined the Pilgrim/Separatist Colony at Leyden, Netherlands in 1609. Standish came over on the *Mayflower* in 1620. His wife, Rose, died during the first winter in Massachusetts. He was made military defender of the Plymouth Colony. Standish gained acclaim for defeating the Indians at Weymouth in 1623. He and his second wife, Barbara, married in 1624, and had six children. During the first five years, Standish was the principal military leader for the Plymouth colonies. He represented them in England, negotiating for land ownership and supplies. Upon his return to America, Standish became magistrate of Duxbury, the colonial city he founded with John Alden (1599–1687) in 1631. Longfellow later wrote a poem about Standish, *The Courtship of Miles Standish*.

Robert Abbot

c 1588

c 1657
London, England

Puritan pastor and writer. Abbot served as a vicar in Cranbrook, Kent, 1616–43, and as a pastor in Southwick, before going to London to serve as pastor of St. Austin's of Watling Street until his death. He was a Puritan of earnest convictions who vigorously opposed the Brownists in the controversies flaring at that time. Abbot's popularity as a writer was evidenced through his work, *A Mother's Catechism for Her Children* (1646).

Henry Whitfield

1597
near London, England

c 1657
Winchester, England

Puritan sympathizing rector of the Church of England. He went to Oculey in 1616. Dorothy Sheaffe became his wife in 1618. Whitfield later brought down the wrath of Archbishop of Canterbury William Laud by protecting several Puritan preachers. Therefore, in 1639, he fled to New England. Whitford helped to found Guilford, CT. He bought the land from the Indians and settled there to work among them. In 1650, Whitfield returned to England, where he pastored at Winchester until his death. One of his works was *Strength Out of Weakness* (1652).

William Bradford

March 19, 1589
Austerfield, England

May 9, 1657
Plymouth, Massachusetts

Pilgrim father, historian and second governor of Plymouth Colony, 1621–57 (except for five years). Bradford succeeded JOHN CARVER as governor and maintained Plymouth's independence from the nearby Massachusetts Bay Colony for a while. He was instrumental in developing fishing, trade, and agriculture. Bradford first joined the Brownists in England (1606), went to Amsterdam (1609), then to Leyden (1611), in search of religious freedom. Bradford arrived in America on the *Mayflower* in 1620. Only 56 of the 102 passengers survived the first winter. He was highly regarded by both Pilgrims and Indians. One son came from his marriage to Dorothy May on Dec. 10, 1613. She drowned after falling from the *Mayflower* deck in Plymouth harbor. He had three children from his marriage to Alice Carpenter on Aug. 14, 1623. Bradford wrote *History of Plymouth Plantation* (1630–31, 46–50), a key source of information on the colony. His farewell poem tells of his faith in Christ. His grave in Plymouth, MA states he was 69 years of age. Perhaps he was born in 1588.

William Harvey

April 1, 1578
Folkestone, England

June 3, 1657
London, England

Physician and anatomist. Harvey discovered the circulation of the blood. He received his doctor of medicine degree from Cambridge University in 1602. He was the head of three departments of science at the College of Physicians, 1615–56: comparative anatomy, physiology, and medicine. The function of the heart as a pump was first stated in his lectures in 1616 and later published, in Latin, in "Essay on the Motion of the Heart and the Blood" (1628). He was the physician of JAMES I, CHARLES I, and FRANCIS BACON. In his will he said, "I do most humbly render my soul to him that gave it, and to my blessed Lord and Saviour, Jesus Christ."

Robert Blake

Aug. 15, 1599
Bridgewater, England

Aug. 17, 1657
off the coast of England

Admiral who sided with the Puritans and became one of their most celebrated military commanders. His energy and persistent courage has been seldom, if ever, excelled in any war or at any time. He won notable victories over the pirates off the coast of Barbary, which taught Portugal, Spain, France, and Italy to fear him, again and again. He defeated the Dutch, and for the first time established the naval supremacy of the English. Upon a victory, he said "...for which we, in our gratitude, have great cause everlastingly to praise the Lord for his wonderful goodness and to rejoice in these, his salvations, with fear and trembling." He served in the Parliamentary forces during the Civil War, 1643–45. In 1649, he began his naval career. After a final defeat of a Spanish fleet, he died while the fleet was entering Plymouth Sound.

Pierre Du Moulin
Pierra Molinaeus

Oct. 18, 1568
Buhin, France

March 10, 1658
Sedan, France

Huguenot leader, preacher and lecturer. Moulin was a pastor at the French Reformed Church in Charenton near Paris and then chaplain to Catherine of Bourbon. His home served as a resort, a place of restful refuge for many Huguenot leaders of the day. Several universities offered him positions, but he refused to leave his Paris church until he taught at Leyden in 1593–99. Moulin also served as advisor to JAMES I of England for many years and received a D.D. degree from Cambridge. In 1620, he accepted the professorship of theology at Sedan, where he spent the rest of his life.

Oliver Cromwell

April 25, 1599
Near Huntingdon, England

Sept. 3, 1658
Whitehall, London, England

English statesman, cavalry leader in civil wars, and Lord Protector of England (refused to be called king), 1653–58. He was "baptized" (Apr. 29, 1599), and converted (c 1627). The red-headed Cromwell married Elizabeth Bourchier (1620) and served as a member of Parliament (1624). As a member of Parliament, his first recorded statement in the House of Commons was against "papacy." He became an independent and led an army of farmers and common people with so much courage that they were known as "The Ironsides." From 1645–51, he won victories everywhere he went. Cromwell defeated CHARLES I, and later had him executed, and also defeated the Scots at Dunbar in 1650. He was hostile to both the bishops of the Church of England and Catholicism and sought to bring Baptists, Presbyterians, and Independents together. Cromwell enforced the ban against theatres and dancing, among other things. He died of the plague (a slow fever). As he died, he asked if it were possible to fall from grace. When told "no," he said, "Then I am safe, for I know that I was once in grace." His favorite Bible verse was Philippians 4:13. His brain weighed 82.25 ounces. This is the highest ever recorded.

"Trust in God and keep your powder dry."

Francis Rous

1579
Dittisham, England

Jan. 7, 1659
Acton, England

English Puritan composer. Rous set many of the Psalms to music and gathered them in a collection for congregational singing in 1643 for Scotland and England. Many of the Psalm tunes and words that were set to English meter became classics. Rous began as a Presbyterian, but later became a Congregationalist. From 1601–25, he wrote from Landrake in Cornwall. He was also a member of Parliament in 1625 who backed CROMWELL's activities. In 1643, Rous was appointed provost of Eton College. His *Psalms of David in English Metre* (1643) is still used in a revised version in some Scotch Presbyterian churches.

Henry Dunster

Nov. 26, 1609 – baptized
Bury, England

Feb. 27, 1659
Scituate, Massachusetts

First president of Harvard College (University in 1780), **Cambridge, MA 1640–54.** Dunster came to New England in 1640 to escape high church tyranny. Elizabeth Glover became his wife on June 22, 1641 and later Elizabeth Atkinson in 1644. He taught Oriental languages at Harvard. He acted as a one-man faculty, without regular salary, though he was allowed to collect certain taxes for his support. Dunster was forced to resign (October 24, 1654) for refusing to have his infant son baptized in 1653, and for preaching against infant baptism. He was indicted, tried, convicted, and publicly admonished for his "error." Dunster next took a Congregational Church pastorate in Scituate, where he served until his death. Dunster is known for his piety and learning.

Mary Barret Dyer

c 1605–1610
Somersetshire, England

June 1, 1660
Boston, Massachusetts

Quaker martyr. Mary married William Dyer and had seven children. She came to Boston in 1635 and supported ANNE HUTCHINSON's beliefs (Covenant of Grace). Moving to Rhode Island, 1637–38, the Dyers helped found Portsmouth. Mary became a Quaker during a trip to England in 1650. She returned with ten Quakers to Boston in 1657, was arrested, then banished. After twice returning to Boston, 1659, 1660, to visit imprisoned Quakers, she was condemned for sedition (insurrection against lawful authority) and hanged in Boston Common (the town square). When the news reached England, King Charles II (ruled: 1660–85) banned further executions of Quakers in Massachusetts.

James Naylor (er)

Oct. 1616–1618
Ardsley, England

Oct. 1660
Holme, England

Quaker leader. In his early years, Naylor served in the Parliamentary Army 1642–50. Upon Naylor's conversion in 1651, he became GEORGE FOX's associate. He preached widely in northern England and led the London Society of Friends in 1655. He said publicly that he was the reincarnation of Christ in 1656 and was imprisoned for blasphemy, after which he suffered cruel punishment. In 1659, he openly confessed his error. Upon his release, he labored with both pen and voice on behalf of Fox and the Society of Friends (Quakers).

Hugh Peter

June 29, 1598
Fowey, England

Oct. 16, 1660
Charing Cross, London, England

Puritan activist in England and pastor in America. He married Elizabeth Reade (1624) and Deliverance Sheffield (1639). Peter was a noted Puritan who immigrated to New England in 1636 and became the successor to ROGER WILLIAMS's pastorate in Salem, MA from 1636–41. He returned to England to be a chaplain for Parliamentary forces loyal to OLIVER CROMWELL, 1642–49. Early in his life, Peter preached in London and Rotterdam. Peter was reprimanded for his attempts to mediate the English/Dutch War (conflict over English Navigation Act of 1651), 1652–53. At the Restoration (under Charles II, the restoring of the Catholic monarch to England, 1660), Peter was arrested and hanged for being an accomplice in the death of CHARLES I, after Royalists returned to power.

Samuel Rutherford

c 1600
Nisbet (Crailing), Scotland

March 20, 1661
St. Andrews, Scotland

Scotch theologian and Covenanter. Rutherford was a professor at Edinburgh (1623–27) and then pastored at Anworth (1627–36), where he defended the Presbyterians rather than the Arminians. He was banished from the pastorate, 1636–38, for nonconformity to the Acts of Episcopacy. Rutherford next served as professor at St. Andrews (1639), was a representative at the Westminster Assembly in London (1643), and engaged in controversies with non-Covenanters, then was appointed principal of New College (1649). Rutherford was the rector of the University of St. Andrews (1651) but was forced to resign (1660) and was scheduled to appear before Parliament on charges of treason when he died of severe illness. He authored *Lex Rex* (The Law and the Prince) (1644), which was burned in 1661. Rutherford is remembered for the letters he wrote during his period of banishment (published: 1664).

"The plough of my Lord maketh deep furrows on my soul...He prospereth a crop."

Thomas Fuller

June 19, 1608
Aldwincle, England

Aug. 16, 1661
London, England

Anglican scholar, historian, writer and preacher. Fuller held various pastoral assignments including curate (clergyman or parish priest or assistant to vicar or rector) of St. Benet's, Cambridge (1630), prebendary of Salisbury (1631–33), rector of Broadwindsor (1634–42), curate of Savoy, London (1642), and rector of Crawford (1658). He is remembered for his sermons advocating peace between the king and Parliament and for his historical accounts of this period, such as *Church History of Britain*. Fuller was a chaplain to kings, CHARLES I (1643) and Charles II (1660). He was also a prolific and witty writer, with his writings ranging from *David's Heinous Sinne* (1631) to *History of the Worthies of England* (published 1662). He died of typhoid fever.

Brian Walton

1600
Seymour, England

Nov. 29, 1661
London, England

Bible compiler. Walton is noted for his six-volume *London Polyglot Bible* (1654–57), produced at Oxford University, which contained the Bible in nine languages. In the fifth volume, he added to the Greek text the headings of Codex A. It has never been superseded. In addition to the usual Hebrew and Greek, it contained the Samaritan Pentateuch, Syriac, Ethiopiac, Arabian (Castell's contribution), and Persian versions. Walton lost his living and was imprisoned for supporting Archbishop of Canterbury William Laud and the clergy in demand for city tithes around 1641. He was later made chaplain to Charles II. He was the Anglican bishop of Chester, only a few months before his death, 1660–61.

Edward Burrough

1633
Near Kendal, England

1662
London, England

Quaker preacher. Burrough defended Quaker doctrines against the Baptist platform of JOHN BUNYAN and others. He was initially a Presbyterian, then heard GEORGE FOX preach (1652) and went to London, where he was first imprisoned (1654) for expressing his beliefs. Upon his release, he went to Ireland and labored there. Afterward, he returned to London and was again arrested in 1662 for holding illegal meetings, and died in Newgate Prison during the reign of Charles II. His writings included *The Trumpet of the Lord*.

Johann Cruger

April 9, 1598
Grosbreesen, Germany

Feb. 23, 1662
Berlin, Germany

Composer of choral music and an organist. Cruger composed the music for "Now Thank We All Our God" in 1647. RINKHART wrote the lyrics in 1636. He became a cantor and organist of the Lutheran Cathedral of St. Nicholas in Berlin, 1622–62, where he remained until his death. His *Praxis Pietatis Melica* (hymn collection) went through 44 editions (1644–1736). Cruger also authored treatises on musical theory. He set a large number of PAUL GERHARDT's hymns to music.

Peter Heylyn

Nov. 29, 1600
Burford, England

May 8, 1662
London, England

Anglican Church historian. Heylyn was a supporter of Archbishop of Canterbury William Laud and was appointed chaplain to CHARLES I in 1629. He served as a Royalist during the English Civil War, 1642–46. He was subdean of Westminster in the pre- and post-CROMWELL era. His controversial works included bitter attacks on the Presbyterians, and was persecuted by the Puritans as a result. On May 29, 1661, he preached a jubilant sermon at Westminster Abbey on the return of Charles II. Heylyn also wrote *The History of the Reformation of the Church of England* (1661) and *Cosmography* (1662).

Henry Vane
Sir Henry Vane the Younger

May 23, 1613
Debden, England

June 14, 1662
Tower Hill, London, England

English Puritan and worldwide traveler. He was "baptized" May 26. Vane went to New England (1635), where he served as governor of Massachusetts (1636) for one year. He lost popularity for siding with ANNE HUTCHINSON against legalistic Puritanism, and returned to England in 1637. In 1640, Vane became a member of Parliament and was knighted by CHARLES I. Thirteen children came from his marriage on July 1, 1640 to Francis Wray. In 1653, he opposed CROMWELL's expulsion of the Long Parliament. Vane wrote *Retired Man's Meditations* (1655). Vane was imprisoned in the Tower in 1656 for his attacks on CROMWELL's Protectorate. At the Restoration (1660), he was transferred to Scilly Isles, then brought back to the Tower in April, 1662, tried, and sentenced to death on June 11. He was beheaded for his alleged traitorous Parliamentary activities.

Robert Baillie (1)

April 30, 1599
Glasgow, Scotland

July 1662
Glasgow, Scotland

Presbyterian minister and theological scholar. Baillie led the Scottish Church in 1637 to reject England's *Book of Common Prayer*. He also participated in the Glasgow Assembly (re-establishing Presbyterianism) in 1638, protesting the thrusting of episcopacy on an unwilling people. He was appointed professor of divinity at

Glasgow University (1642) and then its principal (1661). Baillie was sent to the Westminster Assembly in 1643 as one of the five Scots to draw up the Westminster Confession of Faith. He died disillusioned after episcopacy was once more forced upon the country. In 1649, he was sent to the Netherlands (where the new English king was seeking refuge after his father's execution) to invite King Charles II to sign the National Covenant of Scotland (updated oath to keep Presbyterian/Reformed doctrine in Scotland instead of Roman Catholicism—first drawn up in 1557), after which he went to Scotland. He also published *Letters and Journals* (1637-62), which are of historic importance.

Blaise Pascal

June 19, 1623
Clermont-Ferrand, France

Aug. 19, 1662
Paris, France

Catholic layman, mystic, philosopher, scientist, mathematician, and physicist. When only twelve years old, he defined the basis for differential calculus. He revealed his beliefs in his *Thoughts*. Pascal was converted Nov. 23, 1654, when his theology openly centered on Christ. His significant literary work began with his entrance into the Jansenist Monastic Community of Port Royal in 1655. His *Eighteen Provincial Letters* (1656–57) defended Jansenism because it attacked the Jesuits. They were banned in 1789 by the Catholic index of forbidden books. He invented the first mechanical calculator (adding machine: 1642–44) and excelled in math and natural philosophy. Pascal originated, with Pierre de Fermat (mathematician, 1601–65), the number and probability theory. His *Pensees* (1657–58, published 1670), is a well-known work on Christian apologetics. Pascal was shy and sickly (1658–62) because of his ascetic/self-denying lifestyle. During his illness (malignant ulcer of the stomach) of February, 1659, he composed his "prayer of conversion" that the WESLEYS came to regard so highly. Near the end of his brief sojourn of 39 years on earth, Pascal focused on meeting the needs of the poor. The Pascal personal computer programming language was named after him. He also invented roulette, a by-product of his experiments with perpetual motion. He said, "The heart has its reasons which reason cannot know." His favorite Bible verse was Jeremiah 2:13. Pascal was an epileptic. As he died, he said, "May God never abandon me." The pascal is a unit of measure.

"There are only two kinds of men: the righteous who believe themselves sinners;
the rest, sinners, who believe themselves righteous."

John E. Gauden

1605
Mayland, England

Sept. 20, 1662
Worcester, England

Theologian, Anglican bishop of Exeter, 1660, and of Worcester, 1662. Gauden first served as chaplain to the Earl of Warwick (1640) and then as vicar of Chippen Row and dean of Bocking (1641). He was chosen to be a member of the Westminster Assembly in 1643, but was not allowed to participate. During the days of religious conflict, he sided with the Royalists. At the Catholic Restoration, he was made chaplain to Charles II. Gauden wrote an account of the life of CHARLES I. He was also a member of the Savoy Conference (Puritan–Church of England conclave) of twelve Puritans and twelve bishops of the Church of England. This was an unsuccessful attempt to find common ground in revising the *Book of Common Prayer* (1661), and settle liturgical differences, held at the Savoy Chapel in London. Among Gauden's works were *Eikon Basilike* and *Tears of the Church* (1659).

Samuel Stone

July 30, 1602— baptized
Hertford, England

July 20, 1663
Hartford, Connecticut

Puritan pastor. Stone immigrated to Massachusetts in 1633. He and THOMAS HOOKER later took some colonists to Hartford from Cambridge, MA, where he pastored, 1633–36. After HOOKER's death, Stone practically ruled Hartford, pastoring there for 27 years, 1636–63. He was a strong believer in Congregationalism. Stone married before 1640 and then Elizabeth Allen in 1641. They had at least five children.

Moise (Moses) Amyraut

Sept. 1596
Bourgueil, France

Jan. 8, 1664
Saumur, France

Calvinist theologian. Amyraut courageously told the French king, Louis XIII, at the Synod of Alencon (1637) how the Edict of Nantes (1598) was widely disregarded as Protestants were still being persecuted. He made many attempts to foster a reunion between Catholics and Protestants but failed. Amyraut was a professor at the Theological Seminary in Saumur, 1633–64, where he made the city a Protestant center. He was a notable Bible commentator and preacher. He was once accused of Arminianism but was acquitted. His Amyraldism (liberal form of Calvinism) had many followers in colonial New England. He also wrote many books including one on Christian ethics.

Isaac Ambrose

May 29, 1604—baptized
Ormskirk, England

Buried – Jan. 25, 1664
Preston, England

Non-conformist minister and devotional writer. Ambrose was a former Anglican priest who became a Presbyterian in 1641 and ministered in the Leeds area. Ambrose was caught up in the English Civil War, 1642–46, being twice imprisoned by the Royalists. He spent his last year in Preston, where he had formerly pastored, 1634–54. From 1654–62 he filled a pastorate at Garstang but was stopped by the Act of Uniformity (license needed to preach: 1662). His devotional writings were quite famous, *Looking Unto Jesus* (1658), being the most well known.

John Goodwin

1594
Norfolk, England

1665
London, England

Learned Arminian preacher. He pastored at East Rainham, 1625–33, then was vicar at St. Stephens, London, (1633), from which he was rejected for writing against the Presbyterians (1645) and for requiring high standards for those participating in the ordinances of the church. Goodwin wrote two tracts endorsing OLIVER CROMWELL's political actions and was subsequently restored to the pastorate by CROMWELL in 1649. At the Restoration (1660), his works were burned. Goodwin has been called the "WYCLIFFE of Methodism." JOHN WESLEY republished his first work, *Justification* (1642). His last work was *Triumviri* (1658), a reply to his critics. He was one of the few Arminian Puritans.

John Endecott (Endicott)

c 1589
Chagford, England

March 15, 1665
Boston, Massachusetts

Puritan colonial governor and military leader of Massachusetts Bay Colony. Endecott arrived in America on the *Abigail* (September 6, 1628), just before the main body of colonists came in 1630. He served as governor until JOHN WINTHROP. In 1636, he fought against the Pequot Indians. Endecott married Anne Gower and Elizabeth Gibson, who gave him at least two sons. He defended ROGER WILLIAMS, but mistreated the Quakers, putting four to death. Endecott enforced his belief that women should wear veils. He served the colonies as assistant governor, deputy governor, and governor (1644, 1649, 1651–53, 1655–64).

William Caton

1636
England

Nov. 1665
Netherlands

Itinerant Quaker preacher and missionary. Caton's life was greatly influenced, beginning in 1652, by GEORGE FOX. He was imprisoned in Maidstone briefly but traveled through France and the Netherlands, where he was, at times, mistreated. In 1656, Caton was arrested in Middelburg, Netherlands and sent back to England. He made additional trips to France, the Netherlands (1657, 1659), and Scotland, venturing into Germany (1661). Caton wasted away in an English prison at Yarmouth, 1663–64. His *Journal* is still read in Quaker circles.

Adam Borel

1603
Middelburg, Netherlands

1666
Amsterdam, Netherlands

Pastor and founder of Borelists. Borel initially pastored in the Reformed Church, but he resigned and became a Remonstrant, influencing many followers to continue in their allegiance to its founder ARMINIUS. Borel still saw a need for change and became the leader of a party bearing his name, the Borelists (c. 1645). He acknowledged no other authority than the Bible, without note or comment. Their tenets were similar to those of the Quakers, and they confined themselves to private devotion.

Edmund Calamy

February 1600
London, England

Oct. 29, 1666
London, England

Presbyterian Puritan minister. He was active in the religious and political turmoils of his day. Calamy originally identified with the Calvinist Party, but resigned his church office upon the enforcement of ceremonial observances in 1636. He was a lecturer, 1626–39, at Bury Stedmunds. He was elected to the curacy of St. Mary's Aldermanbury Church, London, 1639–62. Calamy became an active defender of the Presbyterian cause in 1641. He shared OLIVER CROMWELL's views against the divine right of episcopacy and was a member of the Westminster Assembly in 1643. Calamy opposed the execution of CHARLES I. After the Restoration (1660), he was briefly imprisoned with others for illegally preaching in his church after the Act of Uniformity (1662). He was the first of the Nonconformists to be penalized under the new act.

Jeremy Taylor

Aug. 15, 1613
Cambridge, England

Aug. 13, 1667
Lisburn, Ireland

Church of England theologian and writer of devotional books. Taylor served as chaplain to the Royalist Army and was imprisoned for being chaplain to Archbishop of Canterbury William Laud and CHARLES I, who gave him his watch and some jewels prior to execution. Taylor took refuge in Wales in 1645 and concentrated on his writing from 1646–60. After the Restoration (1660), he was made bishop of Down and Connor in North Ireland (1661), but continued to have conflicts with the Presbyterian Church there. His *Holy Living* (1650) and *Holy Dying* (1651) were classics. Taylor also wrote *The Golden Grove* (1655), a devotional manual. He was a renowned preacher.

Joseph Alleine

April 8, 1634
Devizes, England

Nov. 17, 1668
near Taunton, England

Oxford scholar who became a Puritan preacher. He married Theodosia in 1655, and received Presbyterian ordination. Alleine served as an assistant in the St. Mary Magdalene Church of Taunton, 1655–62. Alleine suffered repeated imprisonments and fines for refusing to stop his evangelical preaching after the Act of Uniformity (1662). In 1663, he was imprisoned in Ilchester for singing in his home and preaching to his family. Alleine carried on his pastoral work after his last release from prison. He also authored the best seller *An Alarm to the Unconverted* (1655–62), published in 1672, selling 70,000 copies. He said as he died, "This vile body shall be made like Christ's glorious body…My life is hid with Christ in God."

Richard Mather

1596
Lowton, England

April 22, 1669
Dorchester, Massachusetts

Congregational leader in Massachusetts. He was an ordained Anglican (1618) and was eventually suspended from his ministry (1633) in Toxteth Park, Liverpool, for his Puritanism. Mather was a Puritan clergyman when he emigrated to Massachusetts in 1635. He pastored the Congregational Church, Dorchester, MA from 1636–69. His son, INCREASE MATHER, his grandson, COTTON MATHER, and great-grandson, Samuel Mather, dominated church and civic affairs for many years. He married Katherine Holt (1624) and Sarah Cotton, widow of JOHN COTTON (1657). Mather fathered a total of six children. He participated in the publishing of *The Bay Psalm Book* (1640) and *A Platform of Church Discipline—"The Cambridge Platform"* (1649) became the basic document defining and defending New England Congregationalism.

Rembrandt van Rijn

July 15, 1606
Leiden, Netherlands

Oct. 4, 1669
Amsterdam, Netherlands

Great painter. Rembrandt painted religious scenes, portraits, genre pictures, and landscapes. He was also an accomplished etcher and draftsman. He was popular as a portrait painter in Amsterdam, 1631–42. Rembrandt settled in Amsterdam in 1631, as portrait painter and teacher at Uy-len-burgh (Ulenburg) and became famous through his portrait of his mother. On June 10, 1634, he married the wealthy Saskia van Uylenborch (died: 1642). Upon her death, he had financial difficulties and loss of favor, making him neglected and poor in latter years. Of their four children, only Titus (1641–68) reached adulthood. Rembrandt went bankrupt in 1656, causing his collections to be seized and sold for a paltry 500 florins (5,000 guilders: gold coins). He then set up a studio in an art shop in 1660, spending his last years in poverty and semi-seclusion. This master of light and shadow, always dignified Christ in his works, presenting a strong and winsome testimony. Rembrandt painted nearly 50 portraits of himself. Nearly 600 paintings, 2,000 drawings, and 300 etchings still survive. Some of Rembrandt's most famous works include *The Night Watch* (1642) and the great portraits of *Syndics* (magistrates) *of the Cloth Hall* (1661). Other famous paintings were *Portrait of Artist's Son, Titus* (1653–54) and the *Return of the Prodigal Son* (1668). His favorite Bible verses were Luke 15:20–21.

John Trapp

June 5, 1601
Croome d'Abetot, England

Oct. 16, 1669
Weston-on-Avon, England

English Puritan theologian. Trapp pastored at Weston, was rector of Welford, 1646–60, and then returned to his post at Weston until his death. He was an extremely industrious and excellent preacher. His fame rests upon his *Commentary of the Whole Bible*, which provides Puritan Bible study at its best (a combination of quaint humor and profound scholarship). Trapp also wrote *God's Love Tokens*.

William Prynne

1600
Swainswick, England

Oct. 24, 1669
London, England

Puritan lawyer. Prynne was a member of Parliament who, through controversial pamphlets, expressed his strong Puritan beliefs and assailed Arminianism and ceremonialism in 1627. His denunciation of the theater and Archbishop of Canterbury William Laud led to persecution, imprisonment, and disfigurement (loss of his ears in 1634). Prynne was expelled from the House of Commons because of opposition to CROMWELL. He was imprisoned again, 1650–53, and continued to write his tracts which showed his opposition to the Independents, the Catholics, the Quakers, and later to the execution of CHARLES I. He became the keeper of the Records of the Tower of London around 1653. In 1661, Prynne was readmitted to Parliament as a Royalist.

Charles Drelincourt

July 10, 1595
Sedan, France

Nov. 3, 1669
Paris, France

Pastor and writer. Drelincourt ministered at Charenton, near Paris for 50 years, 1620–69. He was a prolific writer with his most renowned work being *Christian's Defense Against the Fear of Death* (1651). He was active in the Reformed Church of France and educated at the Theological Seminary of Saumur, France. Drelincourt gave twelve points on how to die well.

Johannes Cocceius

Aug. 9, 1603
Bremen, Germany

Nov. 5, 1669
Leiden, Netherlands

Theologian of the Reformed Church. As a German, Cocceius never felt at home in the precision of strict Dutch Calvinism. Although he embraced some of the tenets of covenant theology, his educational and religious beliefs were summed up in Cocceianism (The covenant was the basis of all theology). His viewpoint stimulated the study of the Scriptures in the original languages. Cocceius taught at Bremen (1629–36), at Franeker (1636–50) and theology dogmatics at the University of Leyden (after 1650). His collective works were published as *Opera Omnia* (12 vols). He was the author of the first acceptable complete *Hebrew Dictionary* (1669). He was the founder of Federal Theology (covenant of works before man's fall, covenant of grace after man's fall).

John Davenport

April 9, 1597 – baptized
Coventry, England

March 13, 1670
Boston, Massachusetts

Pastor and founder of the colony of New Haven, CT in 1638. One son came from his marriage to Elizabeth Wolley. From 1619–33, he had two congregations in London. The Davenport family fled from the wrath of Archbishop of Canterbury William Laud (1633), went to the Netherlands, then on to Boston (1637) with 250 settlers, then to New Haven (1638). Davenport pastored a Congregational church there for nearly 30 years, 1638–67. He opposed the 1665 union of New Haven with other Connecticut colonies. The last three years of his life, Davenport pastored the First Congregational Church of Boston, 1668–70. He also gave refuge to the regicide judges who ordered the execution of King CHARLES I. He was an early advocate of premillennialism. His writings include *Discourse About Civil Government in a New Plantation Whose Design Is Religion* (1663) and *The Power of Congregational Churches Asserted and Vindicated* (published 1672).

John (Jay) A. Comenius

March 28, 1592
Niwnitz (Ungarisch-Brod), Moravia (Czechoslovia)

Nov. 15, 1670
Amsterdam, Netherlands

Bohemian theologian, priest, and innovative educational reformer. Comenius first pastored in Fulneck, Germany, 1618–21. Here he lost his wife and children in 1621 and was driven by the Spanish into Poland. Initially, he was influenced by German Protestant millennialists and FRANCIS BACON. He then was expelled from Bohemia and settled in Lissa (Leszno), Poland (1628). Comenius was rector of the gymnasium (German secondary school) and bishop in Lissa, 1636–38,

1654–56, and gained fame by his innovative teaching methods. Comenius emphasized a universal system of education which included equal opportunities for women, and pioneered an educational teaching method for children. He also reorganized Sweden's school system (1638–40, 1642–48), after a brief sojourn in England (1641–42). Comenius was the last bishop of the Moravian Church in Lissa, 1648–56, when the city was burned by the Poles. During this time, his area of service included four years in Saros-Patak, Hungary, 1650–54. After 1656, Comenius made his home in Amsterdam. Comenius authored *Gates of Languages Unlocked* (1631) and the first early learning textbook with pictures in 1658 which was published in Latin and Hungarian. Comenius was the first educator to stress teaching in the vernacular, rather than in the traditional Latin. His complete educational system is published in his book, *The Great Didactic*.

John Livingstone

1603
Kilsyth, Scotland

1672
Rotterdam, Netherlands

Known for one sermon that created an awakening of great proportions. In 1630, he preached for an hour and a half at Kirk O'Shott's on a Monday at a special meeting with 500 people listening. The text was Ezekial 36:25–26. It began to rain and the crowd was a bit agitated, so he said, "What mercy it is…that the Lord does not rain down fire and brimstone as he did upon Sodom and Gommorah." Revival came and he preached another hour. As a result, he preached before OLIVER CROMWELL and became a leader of the Covenanters. When Charles II was restored, he was exiled, 1633–72, from Edinburgh to Rotterdam.

John Cosin

Nov. 30, 1594
Norwich, England

Jan. 15, 1672
Westminster, London, England

Church of England clergyman. Cosin stood for strict enforcement of state church conformity. While chaplain at Durham Cathedral, 1619 on, he wrote a daily prayer book, *Collection of Private Devotions* (1627), at the request of King CHARLES I. He was appointed bishop of Durham in 1624, archdeacon of East Riding (1625–35), master of Peterhouse and dean of Cambridge, and vice-chancellor of Cambridge Church (1639–40). From 1642–60, Cosin was chaplain to the royal household while in exile in Paris, when the Puritans were in power. After the Restoration (1660) he was made bishop of Durham. He repressed both Puritans and Catholics using the militia to coerce church attendance. Cosin was one of the revisers of the English *Book of Common Prayer* (1662) and strongly supported the revival of Gothic art and architecture.

Charles Chauncy

Nov. 5, 1592—baptized
Yardley-Bury, England

Feb. 19, 1672
Cambridge, Massachusettsv

Second president of Harvard College (University in 1780), **Cambridge, MA 1654–1672**. Chauncy was silenced by Archbishop of Canterbury William Laud for his Puritan views. Later at Harvard, he served under an agreement preventing him from promoting some of his doctrinal views. He first taught Hebrew and Greek at Cambridge University, earned a degree in medicine, and then pastored in Ware, England, 1626–37. Chauncy married Catharine Eyre on March 17, 1630. They had six sons, all of whom became ministers. Chauncy fled to New England in 1638, after imprisonment for criticizing the Church. He pastored at Plymouth, MA (1638–41) and then at Scituate, MA (1641–54), where he openly expressed his beliefs (strict/legalistic Puritanism), causing dispute and schism. For example, he insisted on baptizing babies by immersion.

Anne Dudley Bradstreet

1612
Northampton, England

Sept. 16, 1672
Andover, Massachusetts

Puritan poet who was the first important woman writer in America. She married Simon Bradstreet (1671–1741) at age 16, and they came to Massachusetts in 1630. They lived in Ipswich, then at North Andover and had eight children. Her poetry written in the intervals between household chores shows a sovereign and loving God and reveals much of early Puritan New England society. A collection of her poems, first distributed in manuscript form, was published in London under the title, *The Tenth Muse Lately Sprung Up in America* (1650). Both her father, Thomas Dudley (served: 1634–35, 40–41, 45–46, 50–51, 79–86, 89–92), and her husband were governors of the Massachusetts Bay Colony.

John Wilkins

1614
Fausley, England

Nov. 19, 1672
London, England

Anglican bishop of Chester and a founder of the Royal Society. Wilkins married Robina Cromwell, sister of English leader OLIVER CROMWELL, in 1656. As bishop, Wilkins advocated tolerance for dissenters during the Protestant uprising prior to 1660. Wilkins greatly helped the Copernican System gain credibility in England. The Royal Society, which he helped to found in 1660, was conceived as a scientific discussion center for scientific research and publication. It was granted a royal charter in 1662, and still advises the British government on scientific matters. Wilkins died at the home of JOHN TILLOTSON. His many research works include *The Discovery of a World in the Moone* (1638), *On the Principles and Duties of Natural Religion* (1675/78) and *A Discourse Tending to Prove That 'Tis Probably Our Earth is One of The Planets* (1640).

Jean de Labadie

Jan. 13, 1610
Bourg-en-Guienne, France

Jan. 13, 1674
Altona, Germany

French religious reformer. Labadie was trained as a Jesuit but left them to follow Pietism (Lutheran movement stressing piety}). In 1645, he was brought to trial and ordered to cease preaching. He then converted to Calvinism in 1650, pastored in Montauban before becoming a Reformed pastor at Geneva. Because of his unusual beliefs, he had to change the location of his headquarters to Amsterdam, Netherlands. His communal group was called Labadists (Lutheran movement stressing piety over orthodoxy and formality). Because of his doctrines (zealously preached a return to primitive Christianity), he was deposed by the Protestant Synod of Netherlands in 1668. Labadie took his Separatist group of Pietists to Westphalia, Germany, in 1670 and finally to Denmark. The last Labadish colony at Wiewert was dissolved in 1732.

Thomas Traherne

1637
Hereford, England

Sept. 27, 1674
Teddington, England

Anglican pastor, metaphysical poet and religious writer. In 1657, Traherne became pastor of Credenhill and later served at Teddington. He was also chaplain to the Lord Keeper of the Seals (officer of state, responsible for important documents issued under the Seal of England) at Teddington. Traherne authored *Roman Forgeries* (1673), *Christian Ethicks* (1675). His *Poems* (1903) and *Centuries of Meditations* (1908), published after his death, were his best known works.

Robert Herrick

Aug. 20, 1591
Cheapside, London, England

buried— Oct. 15, 1674
Dean Prior, England

Lyric poet and Church of England cleric. He was "baptized" August 24, 1591. Herrick pastored at Dean Prior, Devonshire, 1629–47, 1662–74. He was ejected for his Royalist sympathies (1647) and retired to London, but was reinstated after the Restoration (1660). He wrote over 1,300 poems, "The Littany" being his masterpiece. His collection of sacred poems is called *Noble Numbers* or *Pious Pieces* (1647). Herrick coined the phrase, "Gather ye rosebuds while ye may." His collected verses, W*orks Both Human and Divine of Robert Herrick, Esq.*, were published in 1648.

John Milton

Dec. 9, 1608
London, England

Nov. 8, 1674
London, England

Poet. In his youth, Milton felt called to a high vocation in the service of God. His earliest important poem, "On the Morning of Christ's Nativity" (1629), speaks of the Incarnation as well as Christmas. Then came "Comus" (1634) and "Lycidas" (1637). After the outbreak of the Civil War he was occupied with pamphleteering in the parliamentary cause and then in the service of government as Latin Secretary under the Commonwealth serving in Italy, 1638–42. In the spring of 1642, he married 17-year-old Mary Powell. She died in 1652, three days after giving birth to her third child, the same year he went partially blind at age 44, leaving him one-eyed. On Nov. 12, 1656, he married Katherine Woodcock (who died in the winter of 1657–58). With the Restoration (1660), Milton was an apologist for killing the king, which endangered his life. During the Restoration, he was arrested, fined, and imprisoned. In February, 1663, he married Elizabeth Minshull (age 24). "Paradise Lost" appeared (1667) follwed by "Paradise Regained" (1671). He rejected the doctrine of the Trinity but otherwise seemed orthodox. He died of gout. His final words were, "Death is the great key that opens the palace of Eternity." His favorite Bible verses were Psalms 107:1, 118:1, and Romans 5:18. His state papers were banned by the Catholic's index of forbidden books in 1694.

John Lightfoot

March 29, 1602
Stoke-Upon-Trent, England

Dec. 6, 1675
Ely, England

Hebrew scholar. Lightfoot pastored at St. Bartholomew's, London, in 1642 and attended the Westminster Assembly the next year. He also pastored in Stafford and Shrodshire (1630–42), was master of Catherine Hall in Cambridge (1643–54) and was appointed vice-chancellor of Cambridge in 1654. Having acquiesed to the Act of Uniformity (1662). Lightfoot became a prebendary of Ely (1668). Lightfoot also assisted BRIAN WALTON with the London or WALTON's *Polyglot Bible* (1653–57) and wrote *Harmony of the Four Evangelists* (1644), *Harmony of the OT* (1647), and *Harmony of the NT* (1655). He wrote six volumes of *Hebraic and Talmudic Hours* (1658–78).

Edward Reynolds

Nov. 1599
Southampton, England

Jan. 16, 1676
Norwich, England

Maverick Anglican cleric. Reynolds did all that he could to advance Presbyterianism. Reynolds attended the Westminster Assembly in 1643, and helped to frame the Presbyterian Confession. He was a Puritan during CROMWELL's reign, and he supported the Restoration (1660), hoping that Presbyterianism would become the state religion. Also in 1660, he drew up proposals for reconciling Episcopalians and Presbyterians. He was vicar of St. Lawrence Jewry in London, 1645–62 and was made the bishop of Norwich without having to change his views in 1661.

John Clarke

Oct. 8, 1609
Suffolk/Westhorpe, England

April 28, 1676
Newport, Rhode Island

English Baptist physician, preacher, and cofounder of Rhode Island Colony, 1638. He came to Boston (1637) but was driven from Massachusetts (1638). Clarke was one of the purchasers of Rhode Island from the Indians. It was initially called Aquidneck. In 1639, he helped to found the Newport area. In 1644, while practicing medicine to support himself, Clarke started America's second Baptist church, which was located in Newport, RI. He served there for 32 years, until his death. He was arrested and fined in July, 1651 in Lynn, MA for holding a service in the house of a friend. Clarke returned to England as a colony agent, 1651–64. He obtained the Rhode Island Charter of 1663, which was unique from the Providence, RI, settlement. He was most influential in developing Baptists in the colony. His views were similar to those of ROGER WILLIAMS, a non-legalistic democratic approach. Clarke married Elizabeth Harris, Jane Flecher in 1671, then Sarah Davis.

Paul Gerhardt

March 12, 1607
Grafenheinchen, Saxony (Germany)

June 7, 1676
Lubben, Brandenburg (Germany)

Greatest of the German hymnwriters. He served at the University of Wittenburg (1628–42) and lived in Berlin as a tutor of theology (1643–51). Gerhardt was a Lutheran pastor who served at Mittenwalde (1651–57), dean at St. Nicholas in Berlin (1657–66), and then archdeacon at Lubben (1669–76). Gerhardt was dismissed from The Berlin Church position in 1666 because of his unwillingness to consider a union with the Reformed Church. Gerhardt wrote some 125 hymns, with his first being published in 1648. One of his most well-known compositions is "Jesus, Thy Boundless Love to Me" (1653). He also translated BERNARD's famous hymn, "O Sacred Head Now Wounded" (1656), from Latin into German. Four of his children died in infancy, and his wife died after 13 years of marriage. As he died, he said, "Him no death has power to kill, . . .bears His spirit safe away."

Gisbert Voetius

March 3, 1588
Heusden, Netherlands

Nov. 1, 1676
Utrecht, Netherlands

Calvinist theologian. Voetius carried the doctrine of predestination farther than his mentor (Calvin) ever intended. From 1611–34, he preached at Vlijmen, Heusden, Gouda, and Bois Le Duc. He served 40 years, 1634–74, as professor of theology at the University of Utrecht, also becoming pastor there in 1637. Voetius strongly opposed Catholicism, Arminianism, and the rationalistic thought of Rene Descartes (French philosopher, 1596–1650). He also was an adversary of Cocceianism. He was the first Protestant to write a comprehensive theology of missions.

Matthew Hale

Nov. 1, 1609
Alderley, England

Dec. 25, 1676
Alderley, England

Jurist whose Christian faith made him an exceptional judge. As a youth at Oxford, Hale called on the Lord as a fellow student appeared to be dying from overdrinking. He studied 16 hours a day in fields of natural philosophy, mathematics, history, and divinity, as well as subjects relating to his field. During the Civil War, his personal integrity and skill in his profession secured him the esteem of both Royalists and Parliamentarians. In 1654, he became a justice of common pleas. He was a member of the Parliament that restored Charles II. In 1671, he was raised to the lord chief justiceship of the King's Bench. Hale was the last English judge who sanctioned the conviction of culprits for witchcraft. He had ten children with his first wife who died, after which he remarried. He opened his home to the poor. Often, he returned half of his income that had been paid to him. He daily met with God, which helped make him a lawyer, judge, and legal scholar seldom matched.

Isaac Barrow

Oct. 16, 1630
London, England

May 4, 1677
near Charing Cross, London, England

Mathematician and Anglican theologian. Barrow was appointed professor of Greek (1660) and of math (1663) at Cambridge University but resigned (1664) in favor of his pupil, ISAAC NEWTON. After serving as chaplain to Charles II (1670), Barrow was appointed master of Trinity College, Cambridge (1672) and then vice-chancellor of Cambridge (1675). Barrow's court sermons were well received, and his works were published in nine volumes in 1859 at Cambridge. His writings included *Methods of Tangents, Pope's Supremacy* (1680), and *Sermons*.

Thomas Manton

March 31, 1620
Lydiard/St. Lawrence, England

Oct. 18, 1677
London, England

Puritan preacher and theologian. Manton was one of CROMWELL's chaplains who preached frequently before Parliament. He favored the Restoration (1660) and became one of Charles II's chaplains. Manton took part in the Savoy Conference. In 1662, he left St. Paul's and held meetings in his own house and elsewhere. This led to his imprisonment for six months in 1670.

Gilbert Sheldon

July 19, 1598
Ashbourn, England

Nov. 9, 1677
Lambeth, England

Archbishop of Canterbury, 1663–77. Sheldon was an active supporter of Archbishop of Canterbury William Laud's reforms, particularly at his old college, Trinity of Oxford. Sheldon served as warden of All Souls College at Oxford, 1626–48, until he was ejected and imprisoned by Parliament for his Royalist activities. Prior to his archbishopric selection, Sheldon was bishop of London in 1660. During the Restoration (1660), he treated previous dissenters of the monarchy and the Church of England very severely. He was a strong anti-Puritan. Sheldon used his own funds to build the Sheldonian Theatre at Oxford University, being a chancellor there, 1669–77.

Theophilus Gale

Feb. 1628
Kingsteignton, England

March 1678
Newington, London, England

Puritan and Nonconformist writer. Gale refused to submit to the Act of Uniformity (1662). As a result, he lost his fellowship and curacy at Winchester Cathedral where he had served since 1657. Gale then became a tutor to Lord Thomas Wharton's (English Whig politician: 1648–1715) firstborn son and traveled with his student on the European continent, 1662–65. After serving as associate pastor, 1666–77, he became pastor of an independent congregation in 1677 in Holborn. He wrote *The Court of the Gentiles* (1669–77). The premise was that heathen philosophers corrupt divine truth. He willed his library to Harvard College.

Matthew Poole

1624
York, England

Oct. 1679
Amsterdam, Netherlands

Biblical commentator and Nonconformist clergyman. Poole became a Presbyterian pastor at St. Michael-le Quernes, London, in 1648. He lost his position when he would not comply with the Act of Uniformity (1662), hence he devoted himself to Biblical studies and writings. Poole left an uncompleted *Annotations of the Holy Bible*, which was completed by friends. He wrote against Catholicism with considerable vigor.

Isaac Pennington

1616
London, England

Oct. 8, 1679
Goodnestone Court, England

Quaker mystic. After Pennington heard GEORGE FOX speak in 1657, he joined the Society of Friends (Quakers). He was imprisoned for his beliefs and lost his property. After 1658, Quakers met in his house at Chalfont Grange to worship. Pennington preached powerful sermons and wrote many books, pamphlets, and letters. He died due to mistreatment and exposure sustained during one of his prison stays. He married Mary Springatt, who by previous marriage was mother of William Reure. His stepdaughter, Guelma Springatt, married WILLIAM PENN.

William Gurnall

1617
Walpole, England

Oct. 12, 1679
Lavenham, England

English clergyman and writer of book on practical divinity. Gurnall was the pastor at Lavenham for 35 years, 1644–79, but was not ordained until the Restoration (1660). His book, *The Christian in the Complete Armor or A Treatise on the Saint's War With the Devil* (3 vols., 1655–62), expounded on Ephesians 6:6–20. It was published (1655) and again (1865) with an introduction by Bishop JOHN C. RYLE.

Praisegod Barbon
PraiseGod Barebone(s)

c 1596

c late 1679
England

Fleet Street (London, England's center of newspaper district) **leather merchant and Baptist preacher**. Barebone achieved immortality by lending his unusual name to CROMWELL's short-lived "Little (Short) Parliament" of July-December 1653. It was known as "Barebone's Parliament." His main published work was a defense of pedo-baptism (child baptism) in 1642. Barebone vocally opposed the restoration of Charles II (1660) and as a result was imprisoned in the Tower of London until 1662. He was a fifth monarchy man (fanatic religious and political group who believed Christ's return was imminent, so the fifth monarchy would begin after Assyria, Persia, Greece, and Rome) who offered his house as a secret rallying point and barely escaped being lynched by an angry mob. He was buried on January 5, 1680.

Thomas Goodwin

Oct. 5, 1600
Rollesby, England

Feb. 23, 1680
London, England

Independent English cleric. Goodwin left the Church of England to initially embrace JOHN COTTON's Separatist beliefs in 1633, after which he preached in London, 1633–39. He later preferred Congregational policy and participated in the Westminster Assembly, by drafting the Westminster Confession of Faith. Goodwin headed the "Dissenting Brethren" (Congregationalists) who were in opposition to the Church of England, then was exiled briefly in the Netherlands before returning to England in 1640. He pastored at St. Dunstan's in London (1640–49) and was also president of Magdalen College, Oxford (1650–60). His works were published from 1681–1704. As he died, he said, "Ah, is this dying? How I have dreaded as an enemy this smiling Friend."

Joachim N. Neander

1650
Bremen, Germany

May 31, 1680
Bremen, Germany

Greatest of the Reformed hymn writers. Neander's most famous hymn is "Praise Ye the Lord, the Almighty" (1679). In all, he wrote over 60 hymns and was a noted German Reformed poet as well. Neander was also the rector of the Latin School at Dusseldorf (1671), until his suspension (1679), due to his association with the Pietists, led by PHILIP SPENER. He pastored at St. Martin's in Bremen the year prior to his death. Neander died of tuberculosis at age 30. His collection contained 57 hymns, many adopted by the Lutheran Church.

Richard Cameron

1648
Falkland, Scotland

July 22, 1680
Ayrdsmoss, Scotland

Founder of the Cameronians (a group of stern Reformed Presbyterians). They rejected the authority of Charles II. Cameron led this group of Covenanters to resist the British government, as they attempted to reinstate the Episcopal Church in Scotland. Converted (after 1679 ordination in Rotterdam) by the "field preachers," he was licensed as one of them and became known for his eloquence as he spoke to those laboring in the Scottish fields. Then returning from Holland, he and his Cameronians were brutally murdered by British troops in the battle of Ayrdsmoss, which occurred in the Hills of Ayrshire, Scotland, July 20–22, 1680. His hands and head were cut off and carried to Edinburgh, along with other prisoners. By 1743 the Cameronians became the Reformed Presbyterians (still found in Scotland, northern Ireland, and North America). The majority united with the Free Church of Scotland in 1876.

Stephen Charnock

1628
London, England

July 27, 1680
London, England

Puritan divine and theologian. Charnock's fame rests on his work, *Discourses on the Existence and Attributes of God*. In 1653, he went to Dublin as chaplain to Henry Cromwell (lord deputy and lieutenant of Ireland: 1628–74, son of OLIVER CROMWELL), but was rejected under the Act of Uniformity (1662). He preached as an evangelist for 15 years. Charnock did receive a London Presbyterian church in 1675 and pastored there until his death. He was known for his piety and learning.

Donald Cargill

c 1619
Rattray, Scotland

July 27, 1681
Edinburgh, Scotland

Covenanter. Cargill led an outlaw band around the bleak moors of southwestern Scotland. They criticized episcopacy and the Stuart kings. He pastored at Barony Church of Glasgow 1655–61 until the episcopacy was re-established. Cargill was ejected from his parish for rebuking Charles II's conduct, along with many other Presbyterian ministers in 1662. He was wounded at Bothwell Bridge in 1679 during an insurrection by his comrades. Later he joined RICHARD CAMERON, fled to the Netherlands briefly, then returned and declared Charles II deposed and excommunicated in 1680. Cargill was finally tracked down as one of the Covenanters in May, 1681, tried at Edinburgh, and beheaded for treason. He said as he died, ". . .Farewell, reading and preaching, praying and believing, wondrous reproaches and suffering. Welcome, joy unspeakable and full of glory."

John Pordage

1607
London, England

Dec. 1681
London, England

One of the founders of the Philadelphia Society. Pordage studied theology and medicine at Oxford University, was a curate in the city of Reading, and pastored in Bradfield, England. While there, Pordage became a convert of JAKOB BOEHME's views. Pordage and a few disciples moved to London in 1670, where he aided in the formation of the Philadelphia Society, which was a circle of mystics associated with Jean Lead, who kept in touch with others of the same experience in Germany and Holland. As the result of a vision, Pordage believed that his mission was to restore the primitive (early Biblical) church.

Thomas Browne

Oct. 19, 1605
Cheapside, London, England

Oct. 19, 1682
Norwich, England

English physician and author. Browne is best known for his book, *The Religion of a Doctor* (1642). The book describes his religious outlook and expressed a religious tolerance unknown at the time. The book was widely read throughout Europe. When Charles II visited Norwich, Browne was knighted in September, 1671, for his antiquarian scholarship. It was primarily his mode of expression that made him one of the outstanding figures in the history of English literature. Browne practiced medicine at Norwich (1637–82), after serving as a doctor of medicine at Leyden, Netherlands (1633–37). He married Dorothy Mileham in 1641 (died: 1684), and they had twelve children. He also wrote *Urn Burial* on death, immortality, and burial customs.

Roger Williams

Jan. 27, 1603
London, England

March 1683
Providence, Rhode Island

Founder of the colony of Providence, Rhode Island, 1636, and of the first Baptist Church in America, 1639. Williams came to New England in 1630 as a Puritan, in search of religious liberty. While still in England, Williams married Mary Barnard on December 15, 1629. Initially, Williams pastored the First Congregational Church in America, Salem, MA from 1631–35 but sustained hostility from civil authorities who refused to acknowledge a separation from the Church of England. He had a brief ministry in Plymouth, MA from 1632–33, where he made friends with the Narragansett Indians. Williams was banished from Massachusetts in 1635 for his views on separation of church and state, later expressed in his book *Queries of Highest Consideration* (1644). The Providence Colony was built on land purchased from them. In 1639 Williams was baptized and organized a Baptist church, after which he withdrew from all formal church connections and formed his own group who accepted no formal creed but maintained a fundamental belief in Christianity and the Bible. He agreed with Baptist insistence on religious liberty, but could not accept "the true church" which could only be entered through their "true baptism." He went to England, 1642–44, and in 1651 to procure and confirm a charter for the Providence Plantations, which was reaffirmed in 1663 as a "patent granting absolute liberty of conscience." Williams became president of this colony, 1654–57. His work, *Key into the Language of America* (1643), explained the native Indian dialect. He was perhaps the purest of American Puritans, and died as an independent evangelical Christian without a denomination.

Benjamin Whichcote

March 11, 1609
Stoke, England

May 1683
Cambridge, England

Philosophical theologian and prominent Cambridge Platonist. In 1644, Whichcote was made provost of King's College at Cambridge. At the Restoration (1660), he was removed by the king because he was appointed under the Commonwealth. Whichcote began pastoring at St. Ann's of Blackfriar, London (1662) until the great fire of London (1666). Later, he pastored St. Lawrence Jewry, London, 1668–83.

John Owen

1616
Stadhampton, England

Aug. 24, 1683
Ealing, England

Puritan minister, writer, and preacher. Ordained in the Church of England (1637), he was vicar of Fordham, Essex (1643), then became a Congregationalist (1646). He held pastorates at Fordham, Coggeshall, and Essex, 1646–51. His message to Parliament as chaplain with CROMWELL's armies (1649–51), the day after King CHARLES I's execution (1649) led to his appointment as dean (1651) and then vice-chancellor (1652–58) at Christ Church College, Oxford. He remained at Oxford until the Restoration (1660). Owen was originally an English Calvinist but became an independent minister in 1660. Owen then devoted himself to preaching, controversial writings, and theological tracts. He was a Nonconformist leader, 1660–83, pastoring a large congregation in Leadenhall Street, London (1673), after declining a call to be president of Harvard College (1670). From 1675 on, he pastored an independent church in London. His last words were "I am going to Him whom my soul loveth, or rather who has loved me with an everlasting love." His favorite Bible verse was Psalm 130:4.

John Campanius

Aug. 15, 1601
Stockholm, Sweden

Sept. 17, 1683
Sweden

Lutheran clergyman and missionary. He came to America on Februray 15, 1643, with Governor Johan Printz to minister to the Swedes on the Delaware River. Campanius stayed until 1648 pastoring at Ft. Christina (Wilmington, DE). He also ministered to Delaware Indians and translated LUTHER's small Catechism into their language. He was chaplain to the governor of Tinieum Island, just below Philadelphia, where the first Lutheran Church building in America was dedicated, Sept. 4, 1646. Campanius returned to Sweden and pastored at Frosthult and upland Hernevi, 1649–83.

Louis I. L. Sacy

March 29, 1613
Paris, France

Jan. 4, 1684

French director of the recluses of Port Royal. In addition to being a retreat, Port-Royal-de-Paris became the center of Jansenism (strong Calvinist teachings led by Catholic theologian, Cornelius Jansen: 1585–1638.) This flourished, 1640–1801. It was a noted institution of higher learning, with knowledge being treated as a means rather than an end and the application of "natural" methods of learning. During the persecution of the Jansenists, Sacy was imprisoned in the Bastille in 1666. After his release in 1668, he returned to Port Royal. However, he was compelled to leave the monastery (17 miles west of Paris: founded in 1204) in 1679. Although Roman Catholic in belief, the Jansenists favored the original premises of St. Augustine and discounted the papal hierarchy. Sacy spent the rest of his life in a house with his cousin. His translation of the New Testament was condemned by Pope Clement IX (reigned: 1667–69).

Robert Leighton

1611
London, England

June 25, 1684
London, England

Presbyterian preacher and theologian. Leighton lived in Edinburgh (1631–40), then pastored in Newbattle, Scotland (1641–53). Although he signed the Scottish Presbyterian Covenant of 1643, he was neither a consistent Presbyterian nor a typical Anglican. Leighton was named principal and professor of divinity at the University of Edinburgh in 1653 and bishop of Dunblane, 1661–70, following the Restoration (1660). He then served as Anglican archbishop of Glasgow, 1670–74. Failing to achieve unity in the Church of Scotland and unable to prevent harsh treatment of Presbyterians, he retreated to Sussex in 1674 to engage in works of charity. As a result of Leighton's weak stand and the growing persecution against Covenanters, he failed in harmonizing the two systems, Presbyterians and Episcopalians. His main work was entitled *Rules and Instructions for a Holy Life*.

Robert Baillie (2)

c 1634
Jerviswood, Scotland

Dec. 24, 1684
Edinburgh, Scotland

Scottish nationalist leader and Covenanter. After 1667, Baillie was actively associated with the struggle to free Scottish Presbyterianism from the control of the Anglican Church of England. Baillie was executed for allegedly conspiring to assassinate King Charles II (evidence was inconclusive) and his brother James, duke of York, later James II (ruled: 1685–88). This was known as the Rye House Plot (foiled assassination to have taken place by Rumbold's Rye House in Hertfordshire on the road between London and Newmarket: 1683).

Edmund Castell

1606
East Hatley, England

1685
Higham Gobion, England

Learned English Orientalist (knowledge and study of Oriental langauges and literature) and reference compiler. Castell aided BRIAN WALTON in the preparation of his Polyglot Bible (1657), by giving him the Arabic version. There were several famous *Polyglot Bibles*, (different versions, often in different languages, presented in parallel columns). Castell prepared his *Lexicon Heptaglotten* (1669), while teaching at Cambridge University as a professor of Arabic since 1667. He spent 18 years and $60,000 on this work, which left him with depleted health and funds. Castell was a canon at Canterbury in 1667, a vicar of Hatfield Peverell, and rector of Wodeham Walter and Higham Gobion.

John Fell

June 23, 1625
Longworth, England

July 10, 1686
Oxford, England

Bishop of Oxford, 1675–86. Fell was educated at Christ Church College in Oxford, and supported the Royalist cause during the Civil War, 1642–49. He was ordained in 1647 and kept the Anglican services alive at Oxford during the Commonwealth (Government by the consent of the people: 1649–60). Fell held the posts of dean at Christ Church College, chaplain to Charles II in 1660, vice-chancellor of Oxford (1666–69), and bishop of Oxford (1675–86). He used his influence to revitalize or rebuild many Oxford structures along with restoring the school's traditions. He updated the University's press, setting up a type foundry and designed a special "Fell" type for it. Fell's chief works were *Interest of England Stated* (1659) and a paraphrase on the *Epistles of St. Paul* (1675). In 1675 he published a Greek Testament utilizing more than 100 manuscripts.

John Pearson

Feb. 28, 1612
Great Snoring, England

July 16, 1686
Chester, England

Church of England bishop and scholar. Pearson was bishop of Chester, 1673–86, and one of the most learned theological scholars of his century. He pastored at St. Clement's in 1650 in London. He published *Exposition of the Creed* (1659), which dealt with dogmatic theology. At the Restoration (1660), Pearson was highly honored. In 1661, Pearson participated in the Savoy Conference. Pearson then became rector of St. Christopher's, London, prebendary of Ely, and master of Jesus/Trinity College of Cambridge University in 1662. He defended the Anglican Church against Catholic and Puritan attacks and promoted the London (WALTON) *Polyglot Bible*.

Jean Claude

1619
La Sauvetat-du Dropt, France

Jan. 13, 1687
The Hague, Netherlands

Prominent Huguenot preacher. Claude pastored at La Treine (1645), at Saint-Affrique (1646), at Nimes (1654) (where he was also professor of theology), at Montauban (1662) and at Charenton, near Paris (1666). He was considered the leader of the French Reformed Church. Claude wrote *Essay On Composition of a Sermon*, *Account of the Protestants*, and *Defense of the Reformation* (1673). The revocation of the Edict of Nantes obligated him to flee to The Hague in 1685. As he died of a fatal illness, he said to his wife and son, "…My whole resource is the mercy of God. I expect a better life than this; our Lord Jesus Christ is my only rightcousness."

Henry More

Oct. 12, 1614
Grantham, England

Sept. 1, 1687
Cambridge, England

Poet and philosopher of religion. More was a Cambridge Platonist who argued against philosophers, Descartes (1596–1650) and Hobbes (1588–1679). He lectured as a fellow in 1639 and spent his whole life at Cambridge University. His writings emphasize the mystical and theosophic phases of Platonism. Sir Isaac Newton studied under him and was greatly influenced by More's works, which included *Philosophical Poems* (1647) and *The Immortality of the Soul* (1659). More was also fascinated with Neoplatonism which influenced his books in verse and prose including "Song of the Soul." His best-known work was *Divine Dialogues* (1668). More considered Christianity's enemies to be atheism, Catholicsm, and "enthusiasm."

Justinian F. von Weltz

1621
Chemnitz, Germany

1688
Dutch Guiana (Surinam)

Lutheran missionary pioneer to Dutch Guiana. In 1664, Weltz published an appeal to a lethargic Lutheran church soliciting for a school and missionary society to train people and send them prepared for service on the mission field. Failing to interest others, Weltz went to the Netherlands and was ordained by a Lutheran preacher and sailed to Dutch Guiana (Surinam). He fell victim to the inhospitable climate (or to wild beasts) and died. A wealthy baron, he gave much of his wealth to the Lord.

James Renwick

Feb. 15, 1662
near Moniaive, Scotland

Feb. 17, 1688
Edinburgh, Scotland

Scottish Covenanter. Renwick joined Richard Cameron and others to protest King Charles II's attempts to impose episcopacy on Presbyterian-minded Scots in 1681. Renwick sojourned in the Netherlands, then returned to Scotland and ignored the crown and continued to hold illegal meetings. He was ordained in 1683 in Groningen, Holland, and became a field preacher. Renwick was outlawed for his Apologetic Declaration in 1684, which disavowed the authority of Charles II. He and his band of Cameronians were tracked down, condemned, and hanged at Edinburgh (the last of the Covenanter martyrs).

Frederick William
The Great Elector

Feb. 16, 1620
Berlin, Germany

May 9, 1688
Potsdam, Germany

Elector of Brandenburg, 1640–88. Frederick proved to be a staunch defender of the Reformation and a strong supporter of education and religion. For his actions, Frederick was accorded recognition in the Treaty of Westphalia (ending Thirty Years' War: 1648). On June 6, 1673, he concluded a treaty in France at Vossem, by which France promised to evacuate Westphalia and pay 800,000 livres to the elector, who in return broke off his treaty with Holland and promised not to render any aid to the enemies of France. When the Edict of Nantes was revoked by King Louis XIV of France in 1685, and the Huguenot Protestants were forbidden to flee from the country, Frederick offered them freedom and refuge. He saved thousands from being destroyed. He spent his last years improving conditions of the electorate, aiding education, improving Prussian finances, and developing a strong army.

Ralph Cudworth

1617
Aller, England

June 26, 1688
Cambridge, England

Church of England philosopher and chief Cambridge Platonist. At Cambridge, Cudworth served as master of Clare Hall College (1644–54), professor of Hebrew (1645–54), and master of Christ's College (1654–88). He stood against deism (natural religion based on human reason rather than divine revelation), fatalism (predestination), and irreligion (lacking religious emotion, doctrines, or practices) of the age. In his chief work, *The True Intellectual System of the Universe* (1678), Cudworth shows the folly of atheism and reveals the true source of knowledge found in Christianity. He was a rector at Ashwell, and a prebendary of Gloucester.

John Bunyan

Nov. 25/28, 1628
Elstow, England

Aug. 31, 1688
Swan Hill, London, England

Puritan writer and preacher. Bunyan authored the most recognized book in Christian history, *Pilgrim's Progress* (1678). His parents had him "baptized" on Nov. 28, 1628, In 1649, Bunyan married the young girl that won him to Christ. He was converted one evening as he sat by the fireside reflecting on Hebrews 2:14–15. This was preceeded by the preaching of Christopher Hall and John Gifford, plus the prayers of his wife. His wife died in 1655, leaving him with four children, one (Mary) who was blind. Bunyan remarried a girl named Elizabeth in 1659. He joined the Baptist Church in Bedford (1653), began to preach (1655), and became the pastor of his church before he was imprisoned, (1660–72, except for a few weeks in 1666) for preaching without a license. Bunyan wrote nine books during his twelve-year confinement and was finally released by Charles II's Declaration of Indulgence (penal laws against nonconformists lifted: 1672), Bunyan began to pastor the Bedford Church again in 1675. His wife and children suffered greatly during this time. In 1675–76, he was imprisoned again for six months, during which time he wrote two thirds of his epic work, *Pilgrim's Progress*, an allegory describing the Christian's journey from the City of Destruction to the Celestial City. Bunyan pastored for 16 more years after his release. His testimony is recorded in his autobiography, *Grace Abounding* (1666). The second part of *Pilgrim's Progress* came out in 1684. He endured another imprisonment in 1685. Bunyan was visiting a friend in London in 1688 and suffered exposure from a rainstorm, which gave him a fever, from which he died. He said as he died, "Weep not for me but for yourselves. I go to the Father of our Lord Jesus Christ . . ." His favorite Bible verses were John 6:37 and I Corinthians 1:30.

John Durie

1596
Edinburgh, Scotland

Sept. 26, 1689
Cassel, Germany

Minister devoted to uniting Lutheran and Calvinist churches. In 1634, Durie was ordained a priest in the Church of England and became a chaplain to CHARLES I. He espoused the royalist cause, then he wavered and was not acceptable to either party. Durie spent most of his time on the European Continent, striving for unity, especially in Sweden, 1636–38.

John Eliot
Apostle to the Indians

Aug. 5, 1604
Widford, England

May 20, 1690
Roxbury, Massachusetts

Missionary to the Indians. Eliot served the Congregational Church in Roxbury, MA, for nearly 60 years while also ministering to Indians within a 50-mile radius, 1632–90. He came to America in 1631 as a Puritan. Eliot then married Ann Mumford in October, 1632. They raised six children. His *Bay Psalm* (1640) was the first book printed in New England. Eliot began his ministry to the Indians (1646), starting his first church in Natick, MA, (1660), which continued until 1716. He learned their language, preached to them, and translated the Bible into Algonquin/Natick, 1649–63. This was the first printed Bible in America, 1661–63. By 1674, there were 14 communities of praying Indians with over 3,600 Christian natives. Wars seriously impacted his work. In 1689, he gave 15 acres in Roxbury for teaching Indians and Negroes. He said as he died, "The Lord Jesus, whom I have served for 80 years like POLYCARP, forsakes me not . . . Oh, come in glory! I have waited long for Thy coming. Pray! Pray!"

"We must not sit down and look for miracles, be up and doing."

Robert Barclay

Dec. 23, 1648
Gordonstown, Scotland

Oct. 3, 1690
Ury, Scotland

Quaker theologian and apologist. Barclay became the earliest defender of Quakerism by putting their beliefs in writing. He joined the movement in 1667. In 1670, he married Christina Mollison, settled at his estate at Ury, and began to write. He suffered arrest and imprisonment several times for his zealous voice and pen, 1672–77. Barclay wrote *Apology for the Quakers* (1676), which presented 15 propositions. James II of England granted a patent for East New Jersey to the Society of Friends and made Barclay the nominal governor, 1682–88, although he never went to America. He was a friend of WILLIAM PENN, governor of East New Jersey. Barclay was known for his gentle spirit and deep integrity. He wrote three books (1673–78) on his beliefs, chiefly *An Apology for the True Christian Divinity in Latin* (1675).

George Fox

July 19, 1624
Drayton-in-the-Clay, England

Jan. 13, 1691
London, England

Founder of the Society of Friends (Quakers), 1648. In 1643, he left home to engage in religious search. Fox was an apprentice shoemaker and visionary who was grieved by the hypocrisy in the church, even among the Puritans. His public ministry began in 1648. In 1650, Justice Bennet gave them the derisive title of "Quakers" (shaking, excited people). He met with OLIVER CROMWELL to urge religious liberty, 1655–57. He suffered eight hard imprisonments for his faith, some of which were at Lancaster and Scarborough Castle (his longest, 1664–66), at Worcester and London (1674), causing serious illness. Fox married one of his converts, MARGARET FELL (1669), and she joined him on some of his missionary journeys: Scotland (1657), Ireland (1669), North America and the West Indies (1671–73), Holland (1677), Europe (1678), and Holland (1684). The Quakers also found refuge in Rhode Island and in WILLIAM PENN's colony in Pennsylvania in 1682. Visiting Quaker families and meetings, he felt more at home in "house churches," than in "steeple churches." Fox was an outstanding evangelist and organizer. His *Journal* and other writings were published 1694–1706, in which he taught that the "Inner Light of the Holy Spirit" should guide one's faith and actions, so silent meditation became a part of the meetings. They refused to participate in the Church of England services, take oaths, or bear arms. He said as he died, "All is well, and the seed of God reigns over all, and over death itself." His favorite Bible verse was John 8:12.

Nicholas Herman
Brother Lawrence

1605
Lorraine, France

Feb. 12, 1691
Paris, France

Mystic. After 50 years of age, Herman entered into the Carmelite monastery in Paris where he died. He spent most of his life doing menial tasks to the glory of God in a monastery, such as serving in the kitchen, and writing about his love for the Lord, both of which have been captured in his famous *The Practice of the Presence of God*. Early on, he spent many years as a soldier and then as a footman—"an awkward fellow who broke everything". His last words were "I am doing what I shall do, through all eternity—blessing God, praising God, adoring God, giving Him the love of my whole heart. It is our one business, my brethren, to worship Him and love Him, without thought of anything else."

John Flavel

1627
Bromsgrove, England

June 26, 1691
Exeter, England

Puritan (Presbyterian) and Nonconformist pastor. Flavel pastored in Diptford (1650) and Dartmouth (1656) until the Act of Uniformity (1662). Flavel was supported by wealthy friends, and he preached in secluded places until he was able to return to Dartmouth in 1671. He was prolific on practical religion and piety. While in Devon, he helped unite Presbyterians and Congregationalists, 1690–91. His writings range from *Husbandry Spiritualized* (his best-known work: 1669) to *An Exposition of the Assembly's Catechism* (published: 1693).

Hanserd Knollys

1599
Cawkwell, England

Sept. 19, 1691
London, England

Baptist pastor. He left the Anglican Church. After his English imprisonment in Boston because of his Separatist views 1636–38, Knollys changed his views on infant baptism and went to America. He was the first minister at Dover, NH from 1638–41. Knollys returned to England in 1641 to start and pastor a Baptist church in London, 1645–60 and 1663–91. Knollys fled to Holland and Germany in 1661–63 following the Restoration (1660), then was imprisoned again in 1670 and later freed. He published three books.

Richard Baxter

Nov. 12, 1615
Rowton, England

Dec. 8, 1691
London, England

Beloved Puritan (Presbyterian) pastor. After his conversion (1630) Baxter was ordained (1637) in Worcester Cathedral. He was a model of pastoral care, at Kidderminster, 1640–60, although he lacked a university education. During the English Civil War, he was a chaplain in CROMWELL's army, 1645–46, and later chaplain to Charles II. His moderation sought continual reconciliation and in 1660 he found himself helping to restore the monarchy. At the Savoy Conference of 1661, Baxter attempted to provide a means for moderate dissenters to be allowed to stay in the Church of England. His stand brought him persecution and numerous imprisonments. As the leader of some 2,000 Nonconformists, he faced a huge burden, since these clerics would be denied their state-supported living. Baxter was forced out of his Presbyterian Church, because of the Act of Uniformity (1662). Initially, Baxter retired to Acton (suburb of London). Baxter married Margaret Charlton in 1662 (died, 1681). In 1685, at the age of 70, he served 18 months in prison for libeling the Church of England in his *Paraphrase of the New Testament*. Baxter did much work in early English hymnody, constantly striving to revise the English Psalters. His hymns included "He Lacks Not Friends That Hath Thy Love," "Lord, It Belongs Not to My Care," and "Ye Holy Angels Bright". In 1689, he compiled the largely autobiographical book, *Seventeen Years of Silence*. It was during his frequent spells of infirmity that he produced some of his greatest works: *Aphorisms of Justification* (1649), *The Saint's Everlasting Rest* (1650), and *Call to the Unconverted* (1657). He preached as a "dying man to dying men." He said as he died to a fellow minister, "The Lord teaches you to die." His favorite Bible verse was Luke 18:13.

"In neccesary things, unity; doubtful things, liberty; in all things, charity."

Robert Boyle
Father of Modern Chemistry

Jan. 25, 1627
Lismore Castle, Ireland

Dec. 30, 1691
London, England

Outstanding scientist. Boyle was a natural philosopher, heir to the methods and abilities of FRANCIS BACON. A violent storm in Geneva in 1641 led to his conversion. He lived first on his estate, Stalbridge, in Oxford (1654–68), and then in London (1668–91). He wrote many theological, moral and religious essays, and gave freely for the translation of the Bible into various languages. He was leader of the Corporation for the Spread of the Gospel in New England. He left an endowment of 50 pounds annually for the Boyle Lectures, a series of eight sermons to be delivered each year, in some churches against unbelievers, proving Christianity. Boyle wrote on science, philosophy, and theology and sought to reconcile God and science. He was influential in establishing the Royal Society of London. A majority of its first members were Christians who saw science as a means of understanding God's workings in nature. He wrote *Some Considerations Touching the Style of the Holy Scriptures*.

Bridget Bishop

June 10, 1692
Salem, Massachusetts

First person hanged in Salem for witchcraft during the 20-month ordeal known today as the "Salem Witch Trials" (all victims were innocent). Nineteen people were hanged, two died in jail, and one man was pressed to death in the Puritan community of Salem, MA. Thirty-one were tried in 1692 (6 men, 25 women).

William Sancroft

Jan. 30, 1617
Fressingfield, England

Nov. 24, 1693
Fressingfield, England

Archbishop of Canterbury, 1678–91. Early in his ministry, Sancroft was dean of York (1663), dean of St. Paul's in London (1664) and archdeacon of Canterbury (1668). He crowned James II in 1685. As leader of the seven bishops who opposed James II's Declaration of Indulgences (which exempted Catholics and Protestant nonconformists from penal statutes and abolished religious tests for office: 1688), Sancroft was imprisoned in the Tower of London. After his acquittal, he refused to recognize WILLIAM III (and Mary) of Orange's claim to the throne and was deprived of his see in 1690.

John Tillotson

Oct. 10, 1630
Sowerby, England

Nov. 22, 1694
London, England

Archbishop of Canterbury, 1691–94. Tillotson fiercely opposed Catholics, Puritans, and atheists. He was successful in his plans to include English Presbyterians within the Church of England. He was attacked by extreme Anglicans, but esteemed by most Protestants for his evangelical sermons. Tillotson submitted to the Act of Uniformity (1662). He was preacher at Lincoln's Inn (1664), chaplain to Charles II and dean of Canterbury (1670), canon of St. Paul's, London (1675), and then its dean (1689). Tillotson ably defended his position against non-jurors (pensioned clergy in England and Scotland who refused to take an oath of allegiance to WILLIAM III and Mary or to their successors after the revolution of 1688). He reluctantly accepted the archbishopric of Canterbury, left vacant when the nonjuror WILLIAM SANCROFT was deposed in 1690.

Henry Vaughan

April 17, 1622
Llansantffraed/Newton-by-Usk, Wales

April 23, 1695
Llansantffraed/Newton-by-Usk, Wales

Metaphysical (philosophy that treats the first principles on ultimate nature of existing, reality and experience) **poet and doctor.** Vaughn practiced medicine in Skethiog, South Wales, 1645 on. After a spiritual experience in 1650, he produced religious poetry of great depth. Vaughan's, "The Mount of Olives" (1652), was a wonderful prose work. Another volume of poetry was produced in 1655. His poems were written in the style of GEORGE HERBERT (emphasis on institution of the church), but Vaughan's work affirmed a mystical communion with nature. Vaughan, in turn, had great influence upon WILLIAM WORDSWORTH. One often quoted line of Vaughan's was, "I saw Eternity the other night." His noted work, *Poems* (1646), included a few nonreligious poems.

Henry Purcell

c 1659
Westminster, London, England

Nov. 21, 1695
Westminster, London, England

Composer, organist, and father of Anglican Church music. Purcell was the resident composer, (1672 on) and organist (1676 on) at Westminster Abbey and later at Chapel Royal, St. James (1682–95). In 1683, he began to compose chamber music. Purcell was famous for both vocal and instrumental music. He wrote numerous anthems, cantatas, and chants for the Church of England. In honor of King James II's birthday, Purcell composed the music for "Benedicite," "Magnificient," and "Sound the Trumpets" (a popular choice for American Christian wedding processionals). In addition to writing the music for 43 plays and 33 dramas, he produced the opera, *Dido and Aeneas,* perhaps England's best (c 1689). During his lifetime, Purcell composed an ode or anthem for every public event in London. His greatest works were "Te Deum" and "Jubilate" (1694), composed for the celebration of St. CECILIA's Day.

Philip Henry

Aug. 24, 1631
London, England

June 24, 1696
Broad Oak, Wales

Puritan (Presbyterian) and Nonconformist cleric. Henry pastored at Worthenbury (1658), but he gave up his parish (1660) when he refused to agree to the Act of Uniformity (1662). He then made his home at Broad Oak, preaching there from 1687 on. The poet WILLIAM WORDSWORTH later said, "I could nowhere find nonconformity united with more Christian graces than in Philip Henry." Henry's *Memoirs* was written by his son MATTHEW HENRY. He was born in the royal palace (Whitehall Estate).

Miguel de Molinos

June 29, 1628
Minozzi (Muniesa), (near Saragossa), Spain

Dec. 28, 1696
Rome, Italy

Mystic priest and founder of the Quietists (meditation and spiritual worship by waiting on the Spirit, so that God might speak directly). Molinos went to Rome in 1663, as a celebrated confessor, became the city's spiritual director and published his *Spiritual Guide* (1675). Molinos advocated a perpetual union with God and taught that perfection was obtained by abandonment of the will. This extreme Quietism movement, which he developed within the Spanish Catholic Church, spread rapidly to France and resulted in his arrest in 1685. He recanted for his "heresy," but was imprisoned for life for his "immorality." Molinos was condemned by the Inquisition of Pope Innocent XI (reigned: 1676–89) in 1687. This produced Protestant sympathy and anti-Jesuit feeling among Catholics. He lived a pure life without priests and confessionals.

Johann B. Carpzov

April 24, 1639
Leipzig, Germany

March 23, 1699
Leipzig, Germany

Lutheran professor of Hebrew and theology. Carpzov descended from a distinguished German family of jurists, educators, and theologians. He was a preacher at St. Nicholas's (1662), a deacon (1674) and later pastor of St. Thomas's (1679). Carpzov began as professor of ethics at Leipzig University (1665), then became professor of Hebrew (1674) and of theology (1684). To some, he was considered an arrogant Hebrew expert who, as a Lutheran orthodox preacher, mercilessly harassed the gentle German pietists, HERMANN FRANCKE and PHILIP SPENER.

Edward Stillingfleet

April 17, 1635
Cranborne, England

March 28, 1699
Westminster, England

Church of England prelate and theologian. Stillingfleet began his career as chaplain to Charles II (1667), then served as canon in Canterbury Cathedral (1669) and dean of St. Paul's, 1678–88. In 1677, he served as archdeacon of London. After the Glorious Revolution (WILLIAM III replacing James II in 1688), Stillingfleet became bishop of Worcester, 1689–99. In 1659, he wrote *Irenicum* which, as a treatise on church government sought to reach a compromise between Episcopacy and Presbyterianism. He attacked Catholics, Nonconformists, Deists and Socinians (Italian sect denying Trinity, original sin, and divinity of Christ: unitarian views). His collected works were published in London in six volumes (1710). His writings were apologetic, controversial and metaphysical.

William Kiffin

1616

Sept. 29, 1701
London, England (?)

Particular Baptist leader. Originally a merchant, Kiffin used his wealth to exert influence at the courts of King Charles II (ruled: 1660–85) and James II (ruled 1685–88). Both parents died of the great plague when he was nine. He married at age 19 and became a Baptist at 22, when he joined the church at Whapping. He began to pastor two years later at the Baptist Church of Devonshire Square in London, 1639–1701 (62 years). He is regarded as the father of the Particular Baptists. He was arrested for the first time in 1641 for holding a public service, and confined for six months. He wrote in favor of strict communion in reply to JOHN BUNYAN and opposed DAN FEATLEY in the famous disputation at Southwark. MacAulay, in his *History of England* said, "Great as was the authority of Bunyan with Baptists, that of Kiffin was still greater. He was the first man among them in wealth and station."

Margaret Fell Fox

1614

1702

Wife of GEORGE FOX, founder of the Quakers. In 1652, Margaret was an early convert of Fox's "Society of Friends" and became one of the movement's most distinguished followers. She married Fox in 1669, following her first husband's (Thomas Fell, 1598–1658) death. Margaret and Judge Thomas Fell, Cromwell's chancellor for Lancaster County, had generously offered the hospitality of their comfortable estate, Swarthmore Hall, in northern England, as the early headquarters for Quakerism. Margaret had often provided her residence as a house of refuge for persecuted Quakers. She was a strong helpmate to her husband's ministry and many times accompanied him on missionary journeys including North America (1671–73), Holland (1677) and throughout Europe (1678).

William III
William of Orange

Nov. 4, 1650
The Hague, Netherlands

March 8, 1702
Kensington, England

Stadholder (CEO) of The Netherlands, 1672–1702, and King of England, Scotland, and Ireland, 1689–1702. After success in the Dutch Wars against France, 1672–74, William made peace with England. William married Mary II (1662–94), Protestant daughter of Catholic James II of England, his cousin, on November 4, 1677. She died childless, allowing the crown to pass, after William's death, to her sister Anne (ruled: 1702–14). She was the last of the Stuart rulers in England and Scotland. Because of William's Protestant position, he was invited by important nobles to vie for the English throne, crossing the English Channel in 1688 with a show of 15,000 troops. James II was allowed to escape to France. This was known as the "Glorious Revolution" in which Parliament triumphed over the crown without bloodshed. On February 13, 1689, William accepted the Declaration of Rights (limiting royal power and defining the rights of succession) and the English throne, serving jointly with his wife. He was victorious over the Jacobites in Scotland, making Scottish Presbyterianism secure. After defeating the exiled James II at the Battle of Boyne in 1690, William III increased the political, economic, and civil discrimination (land transferred to English absentee owners) against Roman Catholics in Ireland, laying the groundwork for many of the conflicts experienced there today. His war in the US was limited to Indian raids on the frontier, 1688–97. William and Mary College (University, 1779), chartered in 1692 (opened in 1725) by Episcopalians in Williamsburg, Virginia, was named in their honor and became the second oldest institution of higher learning in America. He died after a fall from his horse. He was the grandson of William I. Technically he was William I of Ireland, William II of Scotland, William III of England, and William IV of Normandy.

Benjamin Keach

Feb. 29, 1640
Stoke Hammond, England

July 18, 1704
Southwark, England

Calvinistic "Particular" Baptist leader. Keach was self-taught. He entered the ministry (1659) and married Jane Grove (1660). She died ten years later, leaving him to raise their five children. In 1664, he was tried at Aylesbury for having taken "certain damnable positions" regarding the Second Coming, resulting in two weeks' imprisonment and the burning of his book. In 1668, he came to London to pastor the Baptist church on Tooley Street, Southwark. In 1672, his congregation moved to a large wooden structure at Horsleydown. He was a well-known preacher and defender of Baptist doctrines. That year, he changed from General Baptist to Particular Baptist (begun in 1633 by Calvinistic London Separatists who believed in a "particular" atonement in which Christ died only for His elect people). In 1688, Keach was perhaps the first Baptist pastor to introduce congregational singing into the church service.

John Locke

Aug. 29, 1632
Wrington, England

Oct. 28, 1704
Oates, England

Influential philosopher and founder of British empiricism (all knowledge is derived from sense experience). Locke taught at Oxford (1660–66), traveled, studied, and practiced medicine in France and Italy (1675–79) and held various public offices. His diplomatic posts, 1675–89, expanded his horizons through travel and allowed him the time to pursue his writing. After being suspected of radicalism, he fled to Holland, 1683–88. Locke also validated the Glorious Revolution (1688) in his *Two Treatises on Civil Government*, which increased his fame as the leading philosopher of freedom. His political theory declared that all men were equal and independent, and none had a right to harm another in his "life, health, liberty, or possessions." He argued for broad religious freedom and wrote the policy of checks and balances as followed in the Constitution of the United States. He returned exonerated to England, where he did his writing and was Commissioner of Appeals, 1689–1704. He is famous for his *An Essay Concerning Human Understanding* (1690), which states that God's existence and morality can be demonstrated based on experience, and that religion is reasonable. At the time of death, he asked for the Psalms to be read. He then said: "Oh, the depth of the riches of the goodness and knowledge of God . . ."

Philip J. Spener
Father of Pietism

Jan. 13, 1635
Rappoltswieler, France

Feb. 5, 1705
Berlin, Germany

Lutheran pastor, teacher, and pietist. The Pietists aimed to thaw out the cold, formal, dogmatic character of Lutheranism through prayer groups, Bible study, and personal holiness. This approach later influenced Moravianism and Methodism. Spener pastored in Frankfort (1666–86), was court chaplain of the elector of Saxons in Dresden (1686–91) and then became rector of St. Nicholas' in Berlin (1691–1705). In 1694, at the University of Halle he founded the Halle Foundation, a complex including a school, printing press, orphanage, and medical dispensary. In 1698, he renounced all controversy. The orthodox Lutheran clergy of Wittenberg University (which in 1817 was absorbed by the University of Halle) brought charges against Spener's theological stand, accusing him of having 264 theological errors in his writing. Spener was also a genealogist and heraldic (tracing records of insignias, family seals, coat-of-arms, etc.) scholar. He published *Pia Pesideria/Heartfelt Desire for God-pleasing Reform* (1675).

John Howe

May 17, 1630
Loughborough, England

April 2, 1705
Smithfield, London, England

Puritan divine and author who had a diversified career. Howe pastored in Great Torrington (1654), was domestic chaplain to Oliver Cromwell (1656) and his son Richard Cromwell (1626–1712), and then served again at Great Torrington. Howe led the effort to unite Presbyterians and Congregationalists in 1659. After losing his right to preach in England (Act of Uniformity: 1662), he traveled across the country, preaching and writing. From 1670–76, he was chaplain at Antrim Castle in Dublin, Ireland, then returned to England. Here he took a Presbyterian pastorate in London (1676–1705), except for two years (1685–87), while he served at an English chapel in Utrecht. His writing absorbed much of his later years. Howe's principal work was *The Living Temple of God* (1675), which was a noble expression of Puritanism, along with *The Redeemer's Tears* (1684).

Michael Wigglesworth

Oct. 18, 1631
Yorkshire, England

May 27, 1705
Malden, Massachusetts

New England Puritan clergyman. Wigglesworth went to America in 1638, and was converted at Harvard College. He pastored for nearly 50 years, 1656–1705, in Malden, MA. For 20 years, ill health kept him out of the pulpit. He first married Mary Reyner (May 18, 1655), then Martha Mudge (1679) and finally Sybil Avery (June 23, 1691). He had eight children. Wigglesworth is best remembered for his poem, "The Day of Doom" (1662), which, as a ballad of Puritan theology, depicted the Last Judgment in horrifying, lurid details. It was the first American "best seller." Wigglesworth practiced medicine and ably wrote didactic poetry. His other major works were *God's Controversy with New England* (c. 1662) and *Meat Out of the Eater* (1669).

Simon Patrick

Sept. 8, 1626
Gainsborough, England

May 31, 1707
Ely, England

Anglican bishop. Originally a Presbyterian, Patrick was ordained in the Anglican ministry in 1654 and became a bishop after a succession of pastoral posts in Westminster and Peterborough. He served as bishop of Chichester (1689) and then of Ely (1691). Patrick helped THOMAS BRAY to found the Society for Promoting Christian Knowledge (tract society: 1698) and the Society for the Propogation of the Gospel (mission society: 1701). He wrote *The Parable of the Pilgrim* (1664), and a commentary of the Old Testament through the Song of Solomon. His favorite Bible verse was Philippians 1:21.

William Sherlock

1641
Southwark, London, England

June 19, 1707
Hampstead, London, England

Church of England clergyman and nonjuror. Sherlock pastored at St. George's of Botolph Lane in London in 1669. He got into a heated controversy with JOHN OWEN. Sherlock was later made prebender of St. Paul's (1681) and master of the Temple (1685). Sherlock refused an allegiance oath to Protestant rulers WILLIAM III and Mary (after the Glorious Revolution of 1688) causing him to be classified as a nonjuror and suspended of his clerical positions in 1689. In 1691, he submitted to the crown and was restored. Sherlock was made dean of St. Paul's Cathedral in London, 1691–1698, and then pastored in Therfield in 1698. He wrote *A Vindication of the Doctrine of the Trinity* (1690).

John Mill
John Milne (till 1673)

c 1645
Hardendale, England

June 23, 1707
Canterbury, England

Biblical commentator. Mill's fame rests upon his critical edition of the Greek Testament. It was the result of 30 years of labor and contains 30,000 various readings from manuscripts, commentaries, and writings of the Church Fathers using 78 new manuscripts. The work was published June 9, 1707, two weeks before his death. He married Priscilla Palmer in 1684. Mill also served as a fellow of Queen's College, Oxford (1670–82); prebendary of Exeter (1677–1705); rector of Blechinodon (1681–1707); principal of St. Edmund's Hall College, Oxford (1685–94); protector of clergy of Canterbury (1694–1704); and prebendary of Canterbury (1704 on).

Francis Makemie

1658
Ramelton, Northern Ireland

Summer 1708
Accomack County, Virginia

Founder of Presbyterianism in America. He was a Scotch Presbyterian and served as an evangelist to the areas from South Carolina to New York 1683–1707. In 1683, Makemie went to America and in that same year founded the first Presbyterian church in America in Snow Hill, MD. Two children came from his marriage to Naomi Anderson (before 1698). From 1692–1698, Barbados was his base while establishing churches in Virginia and Maryland. In 1699, he selected eastern Virginia for his homestead. In 1704–5 he was in Britain to raise funds and recruit pastors for Maryland churches. He organized the first American presbytery (district of Presbyterian leaders) in 1706 in Philadelphia, PA. In 1707, he was imprisoned in Long Island, NY for preaching without a license.

Bernard Smith
Bernhard Schmidt

1630
Germany

1708

English organ builder. Known as "Father Smith," he established a reputation as a master organ builder during the English Restoration. In 1681, Smith was appointed the king's organ maker. He built many important instruments, including the organ at St. Paul's Cathedral in London.

William Beveridge

Feb. 21, 1637
Barrow, England

March 5, 1708
London, England

Anglican bishop and historical writer. Beveridge's career included being vicar of Ealing (London), rector of St. Peter's in Cornhill (London) (1672), prebendary of St. Paul's in Chiswick (London) (1674), archdeacon of Colchester (1681), president of Sion College (1689), and bishop of St. Asaph's, Wales, 1704–8. Beginning at the age of 20, Beveridge authored many theological works. He also wrote about church history and the canon law. He said as he died, "Precious Savior! I have known him these 40 years. He is my only hope."

George Bull

March 25, 1634
Wells, England

Feb. 17, 1710
Brecon, Wales

Church of England bishop and theologian. He pastored at St. George's (near Bristol), Suddington (1662), and at Avening (1685). Bull became archdeacon of Llandaff (1687) and then bishop of St. David's in Wales (1705). He also wrote *Defensio Fidei Nicenae* (1685), showing that the doctrine of the Trinity was held by early Church Fathers (prior to 300s). Bull attacked the Catholic theory of justification, as defined in his book, *The Corruption of the Church of Rome* (1705).

Jacob (Joseph) Amman

c 1644

c 1711/1730

Founder of Amish Mennonites. Amman was a stern, schismatic, Swiss Anabaptist–Mennonite elder. He split the German–speaking Anabaptist-Mennonite group, 1693–97, in Switzerland and Alsace (region in NE France) which resulted in the formation of his Old Order of Amish. The split ensued over the issue of "shunning," with Amman demanding of his congregation at Erlenbach that all nonbelievers be avoided. He ostracized lapsed members, instituted uniformity of dress, untrimmed beards, foot washing, etc. Current Amish are recognized for their strong communal values enforced by strict nonconformity to the world in matters of dress and use of technology. Around the 1720s, the Amish settled in America, locating primarily in Lancaster County, PA, Holmes County, OH, and in Indiana.

Thomas Ken

July 1637
Little Berkhampstead, England

March 19, 1711
Longleat, England

Bishop of Bath and Wells, remembered for writing the "**Doxology**" (music by Louis Bourgeois, c 1546). Ken was educated at Winchester College. He returned there with duties (prebendary of Winchester) at the Cathedral in 1669, at the college, and as the bishop's chaplain. He was chaplain to Charles II in 1680. Ken attended Charles II at his deathbed and at his execution in 1685 while serving as bishop of Bath and Wells, 1684–91. Ken and six other bishops refused James II's Declaration of Indulgence in 1688, and he was imprisoned for three years. He refused the oath of allegiance to William III and Mary (1689), resigned his bishopric (1691) for maintaining allegiance to James II, and lived out his days in Longleat from 1703 on. In addition to writing "Praise God, From Whom All Blessings Flow" (1674: "Doxology"), he wrote, "Awake, My Soul" and "Glory to Thee, My God, This Night." As he died, he said, "God's will be done."

Christian F. G. Richter

Oct. 5, 1676
Sorau, Silesia (Germany)

Oct. 5, 1711
Halle, Germany

Writer, hymn writer, and physician. Richter was appointed by AUGUSTUS FRANCKE to be the principal of the Halle Academy and later physician to the Halle Orphan House. Richter wrote 33 hymns. His four remarkable treatises on the physical suffering of Christ during the crucifixion were contained in his three-volume *Opuscula Medica*. Richter gave the profits from a medicine he discovered to the Halle orphanage, started by FRANCKE.

Henry Compton

1632
Compton Wynyates, England

July 7, 1713
Fulham, London, England

Church of England bishop. Compton was appointed bishop of Oxford (1674) and of London (1675). He was broad-minded about dissenters and was concerned about nonbelievers in remote areas. This attitude was in disobedience to the direction of King James II and resulted in Compton's suspension, 1685–88. He became a leader in the Glorious Revolution (1688) and protested James II's illegal acts, being the only churchman to vote for declaring the throne vacant. Compton had previously been the religious instructor to James II's daughters, Mary and Anne. Mary became a Protestant, sharing Compton's religious sympathies, and Compton was pleased to perform her coronation with WILLIAM III, Prince of Orange, as the new rulers of England in 1689. He also appointed THOMAS BRAY to organize the first Episcopal church work in the American colonies of Maryland and Virginia in 1696. Compton's hobby was the collection of exotic and rare botanical specimens.

Joseph Stennett

1663
Abingdon, England

July 11, 1713
Knaphill, England

English hymn writer and pastor. Stennett was ordained in 1690 as pastor of the Baptist church, Devonshire Square in London where he served, 1690–1713. His *Hymns for the Lord's Supper* appeared in 1697. Stennett published *Version of Solomon's Song with the 47th Psalm* (1700) and *Twelve Hymns on Believer's Baptism* (1712). He knew French, Italian, Hebrew and Oriental languages. His grandson, SAMUEL STENNETT, followed in his hymn-writing footsteps.

Gottfried Arnold

Sept. 5, 1666
Annaberg, Saxony (Germany)

May 30, 1714
Perleberg, Prussia (Germany)

Lutheran theologian, devotional writer, and church historian. Although educated in Lutheran Orthodoxy at Wittenberg University, he would represent the radical wing of Pietism. Early in his career, influenced by PHILIP SPENER, he taught at Quedlinburg, and attacked the established churches in his *A History of Heresy* (1699–1700). He married Anna Sprogel in 1701. They had a delinquent child, who proved to be a distraction to Arnold's attempts to reach a higher spiritual plain. Arnold further believed that "true Christianity" involved an experience of rebirth. He served as a pastor in Werben, Prussia (1704) and as inspector in Perleberg (1707). Later in life, Arnold tempered his position and urged reform of Lutheranism from within his previously defined structure. Arnold was the first to use the German language instead of Latin in teaching history.

Matthew Henry

Oct. 18, 1662
Broad Oak, Wales

June 22, 1714
Nantwich, England

Presbyterian clergyman, Bible expositor, and commentator. Henry is famous for his *Exposition of the Old and New Testament*, later known as the five-volume *Matthew Henry's Commentaries* (1708–10). His father was PHILIP HENRY, a gracious Nonconformist pastor. Converted in 1672, Henry pastored in Chester (1687–1712), then spent two years serving in Hackney, London (1712–14). Ten children (nine daughters) came from his two marriages. In 1710, he wrote *A Method for Prayer*. Henry's many unfinished works (including his commentary which he had completed up to Acts) were completed posthumously by 13 of his fellow clergymen, and was published in full in 1811. He visited Chester in May, 1714, and on his return journey, was seized with a stroke, and died. His dying words were, "A life spent in the service of God . . . is the most comfortable life that anyone can lead . . ."

"Man's extremity is God's opportunity."

Francois S. M. Fenelon

Aug. 6, 1651
Chateau de Fenelon, Perigord, France

Jan. 7, 1715
Cambrai (Cambrey), France

Author, mystic, philosopher, and Catholic archbishop of Cambrai, 1695–97. Fenelon was known for his wise and gentle counsel and for his mystical writings. He defended Semiquietism and MADAME GUYON in a controversy with Jaques Bossuet (great French Catholic prelate and orator: 1627–1704). In 1668, he began service in the parish of St. Sulpice, Paris. Fenelon was director of a college for women, 1678–89, which was designed to train young Protestant women to be Catholics. Fenelon preached at Saintonge (1685), in Avnis (1687), served as preceptor to the Duke of Burgundy (1689) and was preceptor (teacher) to Louis XIV's grandson, 1689–97. His *Maxims of the Saints* (1697) drew the damnation of Pope Innocent XII (reigned: 1691–1700) for teaching mysticism and associating with followers of MADAME GUYON. Fenelon was disgraced and banished from the French Court upon publication of his *Telemaque* (1699), which was thought to satirize the king and his policies. Fenelon's collected works number over 38 volumes. He was a missionary to Huguenots and an opponent of Jansenists.

Gilbert Burnet

Sept. 18, 1643
Edinburgh, Scotland

March 17, 1715
Salisbury, London, England

Theologian, historian, and Church of England bishop of Salisbury, 1689–1715. Burnet earnestly sought church union with Nonconformists when most Anglicans would not tolerate them, but he remained outspoken against the Catholics. He was a professor of divinity in Glasglow, Scotland (1669–74) and in London, where he became chaplain at Rolls Chapel and lecturer of St. Clement's (1675–84) until the accession of James II in 1685 in England caused him to flee to Holland. Burnet counseled WILLIAM III and Mary. He came with them to England in 1688, and preached their coronation sermon. He was bishop of Salisburg in 1689. After Mary of Modena's (Queen of James II; 1658–1718) death, Burnet devised a plan (Queen Anne's Bounty) to use vacant church livings to augment the income of poorer clergymen. Burnet wrote *Doctrines of the Church of England Established Under Queen Elizabeth* (1663), *History of the Reformation in England* (1679–1714) and *The Exposition of the Thirty-nine Articles* (1699), plus numerous lesser works on history and theology. He married Margaret Kennedy in the late 1670s (died: mid-1680s), Mary Scott (died: 1698), and Elizabeth Berkley in 1700.

Charles Ancillon

July 28, 1659
Metz, Germany

July 5, 1715
Berlin, Germany

French Protestant jurist, writer, and historian. Ancillon fled to Berlin in 1685, after the revocation of the Edict of Nantes. He directed the colony of Huguenot exiles residing in Berlin, 1686. Ancillon became counsellor and historiographer to King Frederick I of Prussia (ruled: 1701–13). Ancillon is remembered in academic circles as being a cofounder, with GOTTFRIED LEIBNIZ, of an Academy of Sciences in Berlin in 1700. Ancillon was also a distinguished political writer, and a great educator in Prussia.

Nahum Tate

1652
Dublin, Ireland

Aug. 12, 1715
Southwark, London, England

Psalmist, playwright, and poet laureate, 1690 and 1692. He was poet laureate of England, 1692–1715. Tate wrote the lyrics of the Christmas carol, "While Shepherds Watched Their Flocks By Night," 1700 (music by GEORGE F. HANDEL). He was known for his metrical version of the Psalms, *A New Version of the Psalms of David* (1696), which he prepared in conjunction with NICHOLAS BRADY. This was appended to the Church of England *Book of Common Prayer*. In 1702, Tate was made Historiographer Royal. He also wrote the hymn, "As Pants the Hart" (1696).

Thomas Tenison

Sept. 29, 1636
Cottenham, England

Dec. 14, 1715
Lambeth, London, England

Archbishop of Canterbury, 1696–1715. Tenison also was rector of St. Martin's, the Fields, London (1680–91) and bishop of Lincoln (1692–95). Tenison, a noted author of his day, is also credited with establishing the first public library in London in 1695. He displayed remarkably tolerant views toward non-Anglicans for his times. In 1701, Tenison helped found the illustrious early mission board, the Society for the Propagation of the Gospel. He was one of the first archbishops to favor missions. Tenison championed Protestantism during the reign of Catholic James II. He crowned King George I of Great Britain and Ireland (ruled: 1714–27) in 1714.

William Carstares

Feb. 11, 1649
Cathcart, Scotland

Dec. 28, 1715
Edinburgh, Scotland

Presbyterian theologian, pastor and statesman. Carstares was imprisoned, 1674–79, for distributing seditious literature. In 1683, he was arrested and tortured for plotting to overthrow Charles II of England. While studying theology at Utrecht University, he became friends with the stadholder, WILLIAM III. Carstares served as WILLIAM's chaplain and advisor (1686), accompanying him to accept the English throne with his wife, Mary (1688). Carstares was also WILLIAM III's chief advisor on Scottish affairs and served as the royal chaplain, 1688–1715. He was principal of Edinburgh University, 1703–15, and moderator of the Church of Scotland. Carstares was able to strengthen the independence of the Scottish Church. Later, during Queen Anne's reign, he sought to keep the position of the Episcopalian Jacobites in check and was nicknamed "the Cardinal" for his efforts. In 1707, he used his influence in Scotland to secure union with England.

George Keith

c 1638
Peterhead, Scotland

March 27, 1716
Edburton, England

Founded Christian Quaker sect in America. Keith, raised a Presbyterian, became a Quaker in 1664. His association with ROBERT BARCLAY and GEORGE FOX resulted in Keith's imprisonment in 1664, 1667 and 1675. He married Elizabeth Johnston and moved to America, 1688–94.

He became survey-general of East New Jersey. Keith was involved in a doctrinal controversy that led to his founding a new sect known as Christian Quakers or "Keithians" in 1692. He returned, disillusioned, to England. He was dismissed from the Quakers in 1694/1695. He preached to his own followers at Turner Hall, London, 1695–1700. He was ordained an Anglican in 1700. When Keith made a second trip to America 1702–04, he came as an Anglican missionary and school teacher. He served in the area of Pennsylvania. After returning to England, Keith served as rector at Edburton, 1706–16. Some attribute the lyrics of "How Firm a Foundation" to him, but many historians disagree. He wrote two books.

Robert South

Sept. 4, 1634
Hackney, England

July 8, 1716
Westminster, London, England

Church of England prelate and court preacher. South became famous for his pithy, vigorous sermons. He was the public orator of Oxford University, 1660–77. He was prebendary of St. Peter's in Westminster (1663), chaplain to the Duke of York (later James II) (1667), canon of Christ Church College at Oxford University (1670), pastor of Islip (1678) and chaplain to Charles II. South opposed the Toleration Act (attempted union of English Protestants under rule of WILLIAM III and Mary: 1689) and was a staunch adherent of the established church. He waged a verbal war against Catholicism and Puritanism, and preached in favor of the divine right of kings. He entered into his great controversy with WILLIAM SHERLOCK (1693) over the latter's book vindicating the Trinity (1690). His sermons were direct and rigorous in expression, and often contained wit and sarcasm.

Gottfried W. Leibniz

July 1, 1646
Leipzig, Germany

Nov. 14, 1716
Hanover, Germany

Philosopher and mathematician. Leibniz also received recognition as a statesman, doctor of law, historian, librarian and tireless promoter of a reunion between Protestants and Catholics, Lutherans and Reformers. Raised as a Lutheran, his attempt to find a common theological ground is expounded in his *Systema Theologicum* (1686). Leibniz was a deep metaphysical philosopher who explained the flow of life in terms of "monads" with God as the original monad (center of energy) or powercenter. Leibniz was in the diplomatic service of the elector of Mainz (1666–76) and then privy councilor to the duke of Brunswick, 1676–1716. He settled in Hanover as librarian and historiographer, 1676–87. His last 30 years, from 1687–1716, were spent in the study and composition of his philosophical works. In 1700, Leibniz became the first president of the scientific academy at Berlin. Leibniz's principal theological work was *Theodice* (1710), which addresses the problem of evil and yet artfully presents a defense of optimistic thought. He considered himself a Christian philosopher. He had interest in China and the possibility of using science as a mission outreach.

Jeanne M. B. Guyon
Jeanne Marie Bouvieres de la Motte Guyon

April 13, 1648
Montargis, France

June 9, 1717
Blois, France

French mystic who introduced Quietism to France. She was a young widow (married in 1664 when she was 16 to Jacques de la Motte Guyon who was 38). Her husband died in 1676. She was converted July 22, 1668. Although a Roman Catholic, Madame Guyon's heretical opinions and her correspondence with MIGUEL DE MOLINOS resulted in the government confining her to a convent in Paris, 1688–94, the Seminary of St. Cyr. She was defended by her student, FRANCOIS FENELON, but she still received harsh treatment from Catholic clergy in Paris. She furthered the spread of Quietism from Spain to France. In 1695, Jeanne was sentenced to the Bastille (prison cell at Vincennes)

for seven years. She was later banished from Paris to Blois, 1702–17. Jeanne Guyon wrote a translation of the Bible, 1713–15 and 40 other volumes (published 1767–91). Some of her last words were, "If my work is done, I think I am ready to go."

Adrian Reland

July 17, 1676
Rijp, Netherlands

Feb. 5, 1718
Utrecht, Netherlands

Greatest Orientalist of his day. Reland was a professor at Utrecht in 1701, where he taught Oriental languages and church history. He was a Dutch authority on Oriental (biogeographic area of Asia south, southeast of the Himalayas, and part of Malay Archipelago) languages and ecclesiastical antiquities which he studied at Amsterdam and Leyden University. His chief work was *Palaestina ex Monumentis Veteribus Illustrata* (1714), an authoritative text on ancient Palestine. Reland died of smallpox.

William Penn

Oct. 14, 1644
Tower Hill, London, England

July 30, 1718
Ruscombe, England

English Quaker and founder of Pennsylvania. Penn was expelled from Oxford for his religious extremism in 1662. While overseeing family estates in Ireland, he became a staunch member of the Society of Friends and began preaching in 1668. Penn was imprisoned for short periods throughout his life for his nonconformity and powerfully written religious tracts. In payment for back wages owed his father, Penn obtained from King Charles II in 1681, a charter to establish in Pennsylvania his "holy experiment" of a colony set aside as a haven for persecuted co–religionists. He was a friend of the Indians and created peace treaties with them as he organized the colony. He laid out the city of Philadelphia shortly after his arrival in America on Oct. 27, 1682. Within two years, Philadelphia, "The Christian state on a Quaker Model," had 300 houses and a population of 2,500. Penn made three missionary journeys to Germany and Holland. On April 4, 1672, he married Guljelma Springett (died: Feb. 23, 1694), and they had five children. In January, 1696, he married Hannah Callowhill (died: 1726) who gave him four sons. His was one of the first houses in the American Colonies built from bricks used as ballast in the holds of ships. Family stress coupled with stress from within England courts and from unrest in the New World, brought on a series of apoplectic fits (strokes) in 1712–13, which shattered his understanding and memory. His favorite Bible verse was I John 5:4.
"I owe my conscience to no mortal man."

Bartholomew Ziegenbalg
Bartholomaus Ziegenbalg

June 14, 1683
Pulsnitz, Saxony (Germany)

Feb. 23, 1719
Tranquebar, India

First German Lutheran Pietist missionary to India. He was converted in high school after the loss of his parents. Ziegenbalg left the University of Halle in 1706 to respond to Danish King FREDERICK IV's appeal for a Christian witness in India. He settled at Tranquehar. He was the first to translate the NT into the Indian language of Tamil (language of south India and Sri Lanka) in 1711. Ziegenbalg also founded a church and seminary and wrote catechetical materials. The rough Asian climate took his life at age 35, following a health break in Europe, 1715–19. The Danish-Halle-Mission, which he helped found, was the first modern mission society. He worked closely with HEINRICH PLUTSCHAU.

Joseph Addison

May 1, 1672
Milston, England

June 17, 1719
Holland House, London, England

Anglican essayist (master of English prose), **poet, hymn writer and statesman**. He traveled throughout Europe (1699–1703) in preparation for diplomatic service to Ireland (1710, 1715, 1717–18) and held a membership in Parliament (1708–19). Returning from an Italian trip in 1702, he published his *Travels* with great profit. In 1710, his essays began appearing in the premier periodicals of the day: the *Tatler*, the *Spectator*, and the *Guardian*. Many of these were later republished as *Evidences of the Christian Religion*. He also received recognition for his poem "The Campaign" (1704), his play *The Drummer* (1716), and his dramatic tragedy *Cato*, a stage play (1713). Addison's hymns of note included "The Spacious Firmament on High" and "When All Thy Mercies, O My God" (music by WILLIAM GARDNER), both in 1712. His marriage to Dowager Countess Charlotte of Warwick on August 3, 1716 proved to be an unhappy union. At the place of his death, Holland House, he said to his stepson as he died, "See in what peace a Christian can die." Addison was buried in Westminster Abbey, London. His favorite Bible passage was Psalm 23. His "remarks on several parts of Italy" were banned by the Catholic index of forbidden books in 1729.

Karl H. Canstein

Aug. 4, 1667
Lindeberg, Germany

Aug. 19, 1719
Berlin, Germany

Founder of the Canstein Bible Institute and Bible Publishing House, 1710. Canstein was called the "Father of All Bible Societies," whose purpose was to publish and circulate inexpensive copies of the Bible. In his lifetime, there were 40,000 Bibles and 100,000 copies of the New Testament distributed under his ministry. He was a good friend of FRANCKE. Canstein lived in Halle during the great upsurge of awareness for social needs, and headquartered his ministries there. He was a baron and one of the many nobles enlisted for philanthropic service by FRANCKE.

J. Thorkelsson Vidalin

1666
Gardar, Iceland

1720
Icelandic Mountains

Eloquent Lutheran Icelandic bishop, 1697 on, and prose writer. Vidalin was both a talented poet and preacher. He pastored in Skalholt, 1691–96. He wrote a popular piece which became a classic of Icelandic Church literature and which was set to music. His *Huspostilla* (1715–20) was sermons for the Christian home.

Samuel Parris

1653
London, England

Feb. 27, 1720
Sudbury, Massachusetts

Superstitious Congregational cleric. Parris touched off the disgraceful episode known as the Salem witch hunts, 1692–94. Five children came from his marriages to wives Elizabeth and Dorothy. He came to America, before 1674, and began pastoring (1689) in Salem Village (Danvers), until the congregation dismissed him (1696). He engaged in business activities, 1696–1720. Parris and ten young girls accused his West Indian slave girl, Titubain 1692, and two old women of bewitching activities, which resulted in a serious illness falling upon one of Parris' daughters. He extorted (to obtain by force or illegal means: literally to "wrench/twist out") a "confession" which ignited the hysteria known later as the Salem Witch hunt. His family's accusations began the witchcraft delusions, which were responsible for the trials, under Judge Samuel Sewall (1652–1730), against many innocent persons, the execution of 20, and the torture of 50 others. By May 1693, Governor Phelps ordered the release of all prisoners held on the charge of witchcraft. Parris was required to leave Salem in 1697.

Ernest C. Hochmann

1670
Lauenburg, Germany

1721

Wandering radical Pietist and mystic. Hochmann's eccentric views expelled him from Halle University in 1693. He went to Frankfurt as a missionary to the Jews, but turned his attention to preaching against the emphasis on the church. Hochmann opposed the status quo in orthodoxy. From 1700–11, he was a homeless, persecuted, wandering preacher, stumbling through Germany. He worked with ALEXANDER MACK in the Palatinate in 1706 and played a major role in founding the Brethren movement. He often suffered imprisonment, not as much for what he said or wrote, but "how" he conveyed his message. Hochmann advocated separation of church and state. As a writer, he followed the theme of "replacing ecclesiastical forms with genuine personal experiences."

Henri Arnaud

Sept. 30, 1641
Embrun, France

Sept. 8, 1721
Schonenberg, Germany

Persistent and fearless Waldensian leader, soldier, and preacher. Arnaud organized the hapless Waldensians who had been driven by the French from their Piedmont (remote corner of Italy in the Cottian Alps) homes in 1686 into exile in Switzerland, Germany, and Savoyards (Savoy duchy, northern Italy under mercurial leader Victor Armedeus II), where he pastored. Arnaud began his mission as a well-educated young pastor who made a stirring plea on April 18, 1688, advocating armed resistance. Repeated heroic, but futile, attempts to return to their home territory led to harsh reprisals and bloody defeats. Arnaud led the remaining band of 300 Waldensians trapped on high cliffs, against the final assault by 4,000 French Dragoons (heavily armed mounted troops) on May 2, 1689. A deep fog, sent by God, descended in the valley and allowed the Waldensians to escape and rebuild in their native Vaudois (canton in Switzerland) valleys. After securing the repartition of the Waldensians (1690–98), Arnaud pastored a Waldensian group of exiles in Durrnenz-Schonenberg, Germany (1698–1721).

Campegius Vitringa

May 16, 1659
Leenwarden, Netherlands

March 31, 1722
Franeker, Netherlands

Reformed OT scholar and professor at the University of Franeker. Vitringa started teaching there (1681), focusing on Oriental languages, then theology (1683), and finally church history, 1693–1722. He is best known for his two-volume *Commentary on Isaiah* (1714–20). He is the founder of historical exegesis. Besides this reference, Vitringa wrote an important work entitled, *Old Synagogue/Synagogue in the Church* (1694). He died of a stroke, leaving five children.

Charles Leslie

July 17, 1650
Dublin, Ireland

April 13, 1722
Glasslough, Ireland

Jacobite, Anglican divine, and writer. Leslie wrote many highly regarded apologetical works against the Deist philosophy, the Quakers, the Jews and the Catholics. He was an opponent of WILLIAM III (William and Mary) and their Protestant tendencies. Leslie returned to England in 1689 and continued his writings against various groups while supporting nonjuring (Jacobite) interests. Many were Catholics supporting the high church doctrine of nonresistance and the divine right of kings. His work in 1694, *Short and Easy Method with the Deists*, received much acclaim. Leslie was forced to leave England in 1711. He remained an ardent Jacobite (loyal to James II), and accompanied the Old Pretender (Francis Edward Stuart, son of James II, 1688–1766) to Rome after the Jacobite Rebellion of 1715.

Christopher Wren

Oct. 20, 1632
East Knoyle, England

Feb. 25, 1723
Hampton Court, London, England

Architect and famous designer of churches and cathedrals. Wren's career began as a professor of astronomy at Oxford, 1661–73, where he became a noted scientist and mathematician. His architectural pursuits commenced around 1663. During the 40 years following the great fire of London, 1666, Wren's architectural imprint was the most prominent. His masterpiece is St. Paul's Cathedral in London which he rebuilt, 1675–1716, and where he is buried. He also designed over 52 other churches, each with his trademark of a spire in receding stages. Among the notable buildings to his credit are: the library of Trinity College at Cambridge University (1677–92), Sheldonian Theatre (1664–69) and Queen's College Library (both at Oxford University), Chelsea Hospital (1682–85), Kensington Palace, and Hampton Court Palace (1696–1704).

William Fleetwood

Jan. 1, 1656
London, England

Aug. 4, 1723
Tottenham, England

Anglican bishop and eloquent preacher. After completing his education at Cambridge and Eton, Fleetwood became rector of St. Augustine and St. Faith, 1689–1702. This was followed by a canon post at St. George's at Windsor Castle (1702), and bishoprics at St. Asaph (1708) and Ely (1714). Fleetwood held liberal political views, favored the Glorious Revolution (1688), and became a zealous Whig (limited royal authority and increase in Parliamentary power, low church segment). In 1712, his opposition to nonresistance put him in conflict with JONATHAN SWIFT and the Tories {favored royal authority and Established Church over Parliament}. Fleetwood became the chaplain to King WILLIAM III. He was the most eloquent preacher of his day. Fleetwood's *Chronicon Preciosum* (1707) was a pioneer work in economic history. His *Complete Works* (three vol.) published at Oxford in 1854.

Increase Mather

June 21, 1639
Dorchester, Massachusetts

Aug. 23, 1723
Boston, Massachusetts

President of Harvard College (University in 1780), **Cambridge, MA 1685–1701**. He is the first American-born Christian leader in this book (except for POCAHONTAS). Increase was the son of RICHARD MATHER and the father of COTTON MATHER. Increase Mather preached in England, until 1660 (ascension of Charles II), then came to America in 1661. He pastored the Second (North) Congregational Church, Boston, MA from 1664–1723 (59 years). Mather returned to England, 1688–92, to represent Massachusett's colonial interests. He married Maria Cotton (daughter of JOHN COTTON; February 16, 1641–April 4, 1714) on March 6, 1662. They had ten children. He then married Ann Lake in 1715 (died: March 29, 1737). Mather studied for 16 hours a day and wrote 130 books. His book, *Cases of Conscience Concerning Evil Spirits* (1693), is credited with ending the Salem (MA) witchcraft executions. He also wrote *A Brief History of the War with the Indians* (1676) and *The Surest Way to Greatest Honor* (1699). Increase Mather was the first honorary degree recipient in America.

John Leverett

Aug. 25, 1662
Boston, Massachusetts

May 3, 1724
Cambridge, Massachusetts

President of Harvard College (University in 1780), **Cambridge, MA 1707–24**. Leverett married Margaret Berry (Feb. 18, 1664–June 7, 1720) on Nov. 25, 1697, and later, Sarah Crisp Harris (Sept. 15, 1672–April 24, 1744), giving him a total of nine children. Leverett first served as a fellow and a tutor at Harvard, 1685–1700. His legal/political career began as an elected representative to the Massachusetts General Court from Cambridge, 1696–97. This was followed by the office of Justice of the Peace (1699), and then speaker of the Massachusetts House of Delegates (1700). He started the Brattle St. Church, Boston, MA in 1699 as an alternative to Congregationalism. Leverett was judge of the superior court and then judge from Middlesex County, Massachusetts, 1700–7. Leverett was responsible for the liberal direction of Harvard University, introducing Anglican doctrine, secular literature and a freer style of campus life. His administration incurred the wrath of COTTON MATHER and other conservatives.

Henry Sacheverell

1674
Marlborough, England

June 5, 1724
Highgate, London, England

Anglican pulpit idol and political preacher. Sacheverell incited strong feelings against nonconformist groups by polemical preaching at his church, St. Saviour's in Southwork, in 1709. In two sermons he specifically attacked the Whig ministry for neglect of the interests of the church and condemned their religious toleration. He was censored by Parliament, but was a hero to his high-church clientele and the Tory Party. Sacheverell rode the crest of a wave of adulation for a time, gained a good paying parish and distributed 40,000 copies of these sermons. He was at Southwork, 1705–13, then at St. Andrew's at Holborn till his death. Although suspended for three years, 1710–13, under the Tory political machine of Sidney Godophin (1645–1712), the subsequent Tory ministry called upon Sacheverell for a Restoration sermon in 1713.

John Wise

Aug. 15, 1652—baptized
Roxbury (Boston) Massachusetts

April 8, 1725
Ipswich, Massachusetts

Congregational clergyman. After Harvard graduation in 1673, Wise settled in Ipswich. He married Abigail Gardner on December 5, 1678 and they had seven children. He pastored the Chebacco Congregational Church there, 1680 till death (45 years). He was a militant champion of the rights of the colonists. His ideas of democracy in church and state had considerable influence on the political thinking of the revolutionary period. His *The Churches Quarrel Espoused* was used to defeat INCREASE MATHER's proposal for a Presbyterian form of government in New England churches. His *A Vindication of the Government of New England Churches* (1717) details his ideas about civil and ecclesiastical government, several passages of which are paraphrased in the Declaration of Independence.

Nicholas Brady

Oct. 28, 1659
Bandon, Ireland

May 20, 1726
Richmond, England

Anglican clergyman and author of a new metrical version (varied meter: applicable for hymns) **of the Psalms**. With NAHUM TATE, Brady produced *A New Version of the Psalms of David* (1696). This form replaced the ballad version (poetic form) presented in *Psalms of Sternhold and Hopkins*. Brady was an Anglican priest and poet whose later pastoral ministry was at St. Catherine Free Church, Clapham (London) 1691–96 and in Richmond, England. He was an earnest advocate of the Glorious Revolution (1688), prebendary in Cork, and chaplain to King WILLIAM III (William and Mary) and Queen Anne. He also translated classics such as Virgil's (70–19 BC) works.

Isaac Newton

Dec. 25, 1642
Woolsthrepe, England

March 20, 1727
Kensington, London, England

Renowned mathematician, astronomer and physicist. His exploits caused the French mathematician, Adrian Legendre (1752–1833), to say, "Newton was the greatest genius that ever existed." Basically he showed order in the universe and discovered how gravity holds the universe together.

He was converted as a student at Cambridge and his paramount goal was to understand Scriptures. In earlier years he helped in the distribution of Bibles to the poor. It was in 1665, at age 23, that he supposedly watched an apple fall from a tree, which suggested to him the law of gravitation and started a lifetime of research. In July, 1668, he made the first reflecting telescope. He was professor of mathematics at Cambridge, 1669–99. His great work *Principia* (1687) discussed mathematical questions that few could comprehend. Newton never married. When he died, he left more than 1 million words of notes on the Bible. In his short scheme of *True Religions*, he says, "we are to worship the Father alone as God Almighty, and Jesus alone as the Lord, the Messiah, the great King, the Lamb of God, who was slain, and hath redeemed us with his blood, and made us kings and priests." A bladder infection hastened his death. His favorite Bible verse was Isaiah 45:3.

August H. Francke

March 22, 1663
Lubeck, Germany

June 8, 1727
Halle, Germany

Lutheran Pietist educator, pastor, and philanthropist. Francke was noted for his leadership in founding charitable institutions upon a strong foundation of faith that God would provide for every need. Converted in 1687, Francke began to conduct Bible classes in Leipzig. Francke lectured in philosophy at Leipzig University (1684), served as a pastor at Glancha (1692), was professor of Oriental studies and philosophy (1692–98), and then theology at the University of Halle (1698–1727). He also assisted PHILIP SPENER in founding the University of Halle in 1694. In 1695, he started an orphanage out of his home which grew to be responsible for sheltering over 2,000 children. Francke explored practical avenues of education, which led him to establishing a vocational training school, a Latin school, and a boarding school. The core of his curriculum was intensive Bible study in conjunction with membership in a Bible club for fellowship and prayer. These endeavors were combined to form the Francke Institute, which was augmented by the Halle Foundation that coordinated all his activities. Francke also owned a printing press and used it for the furtherance of the Lutheran Pietist movement. Francke was keenly interested in foreign missions.

"Greek and Hebrew, the two eyes of theological study."

William Croft

Dec. 30, 1678—baptized
Netherettington, England

Aug. 14, 1727
Bath, England

Composer and organist. Croft composed music for works to be adapted for use in worship services. Some of his major contributions were, "O God, Our Help in Ages Past," 1708 (WATTS), "God Moves in a Mysterious Way" and "O Where Are Kings and Empires Now?" (COXE). Croft was also an organist at St. Anne's in Soho, London, 1700–12 and at Chapel Royal (1704), followed by filling the organist post at Westminster Abbey, London (1708). His *Musica Sacra* (published 1724, 2 vols.), contained his choral works and was the first edition of English church music in full score. It also contained his majestic burial service arrangement. He was considered the foremost church musician of his time.

James Abbadie

c 1656
Nay, France

Sept. 25, 1727
Marylebone (near London), England

French Reformed pastor and apologist. Abbadie initially pastored the French Protestant Church of Berlin in 1680. Abbadie was an earnest supporter of the Glorious Revolution (1688). He then ministered to the French in the Savoy (section of London) (1689) and then became nonresident dean of Killaloe, Ireland (1699). He was also a prolific, apologetical writer. He is noted for his books *On the Truth of the Christian Religion* (1684–89) and *On the Divinity of Jesus Christ*.

Eberhard L. Guber

1665   1728

Lutheran clergyman and cofounder of the Amana Church Society. Guber joined JOHANN F. ROCK in defining a movement among German Pietists called "Inspirationism." The Amana Church Society was a radical arm of Communal Pietism which began (1714) in central Germany but soon immigrated to New York (1742). They were considered a "Community of the True Inspiration." The Amana Church Society still survives today.

Cotton Mather

Feb. 12, 1663   Feb. 13, 1728
Boston, Massachusetts   Boston, Massachusetts

Third generation of famous Puritan (Congregational) family. Cotton worked with his father, INCREASE MATHER, at the Second Congregational Church, 1685–1723. Upon his father's death in 1723, Cotton assumed the pastorate, which was then passed on to his son, Samuel in 1728. He initially supported the Salem witchcraft trials and executions, 1692–93, but later realized the accusations were ungrounded and the trials grossly unfair. Mather was the first American minister to organize clubs for young people, to initiate regular calls upon parishioners and to establish a prison ministry. Mather married Abigail Phillips in 1686, Elizabeth Hubbard, and Lydia George. He had 15 children. Mather was a strong supporter of science and education. He was elected to the Royal Society in 1713. After the smallpox epidemic hit Boston in 1720, he supported smallpox innoculations (helpful, but very risky). In 1721, he declined the offer to be president of Yale University. He gave much time, thought, and written works to reach American Indians. He welcomed blacks in his home and church. Mather published 469 works on religious, historical, scientific, and moral subjects, including *Wonders of the Invisible World* (1693) and *Cusiosa Americana* (1712–24). His key works were *Magnalia Christi Americana* (church history of New England, 1702) and *The Christian Philosopher* (1721). He is buried in Copp's Hill Burying Ground. As he died, he said, "Oh, I can bear this! I can bear it."

Christian Thomasius

Jan. 1, 1655   Sept. 23, 1728
Leipzig, Germany   Halle, Germany

Jurist and philosopher. His style was a departure from the traditional scholastic curriculum, believing that philosophy and theology should be taught as independent disciplines with the instruction conducted in the vernacular German, rather than Latin. Thomasius also opposed the persecuting of the Pietists. This posture caused him to be driven, in 1691, from the University of Leipzig, where he taught since 1684, by reactionary theologians. As a legal scholar, Thomasius helped to establish the academic reputation at the newly formed University of Halle, where he taught from 1694 on as professor of jurisprudence. Thomasius also scorned the popular belief in the use of trial and torture in the court system for witchcraft. He was instrumental in framing German jurisprudence. He substituted the German language for Latin in his lectures (1687) and established a German scientific magazine (1688).

Solomon Stoddard

Sept. 27, 1643   Feb. 11, 1729
Boston, Massachusetts   Northampton, Massachusetts

Congregational pastor at Northampton, MA 1672–1729. In the early years of his ministry, Stoddard was a chaplain on the British Island of Barbados in the western Caribbean and then was the first librarian at Harvard University, 1667–72. For the next 57 years, he pastored at Northampton. He introduced the doctrine of Stoddardeanism (often called the Half-Way Covenant of 1662) (in which a person's profession of faith, rather than an experience of grace, was sufficient for church membership and communion). To many this avenue of belief, was unacceptable. Stoddard married Esther Mather and they had twelve children. His grandson, JONATHAN EDWARDS, Sr., became his associate pastor (1727) and successor (1729). Stoddard wrote several theological works ranging from *Day of Judgment* (1687) to *An Answer to Some Cases of Conscience* (1722). He opposed excessive drinking, extravagant dress, including wigs and long hair.

Johann F. Budde

June 25, 1667
Anclam, Prussia (Germany)

Nov. 19, 1729
Gotha, Germany

Lutheran theologian and scholar. Budde was well respected as a writer on moral issues and a man of genuine piety and immense learning. He was a professor at Wittenberg and Jena, often serving as a mediator between orthodox Lutheranism and Lutheran Pietism. Budde was considered the most outstanding theologian of his time. He wrote several books on history and philosophy, including the esteemed *Institutiones Theologiae Dogmaticae* (1724) and *Isagoge Historic-Theologica ad Theologiam Universam* (1730).

Johann C. Schwedler

Dec. 21, 1672
Krobsdorf, Silesia (Poland)

Jan. 12, 1730
Niederwiese, Silesia (Poland)

Prolific hymn writer. Schwedler studied at Leipzig and then pastored for 30 years at Niederwiese, 1701–30. Great throngs attended his church, and it is said that sometimes services began at five or six in the morning and would continue all day until mid afternoon with groups of worshipers coming and going. He was a gifted preacher and founded an orphanage. He wrote over 500 hymns, including "Ask Ye What Great Things I Know." Schwedler was a good friend of ZINZENDORF.

Thomas Bray

1656
Marton, England

Feb. 15, 1730
London, England

Anglican philanthropist, missionary promoter, and clergyman. Bray was "baptized," May 3, 1658, in Chirury, England. In his early years, he served at several country parishes, 1682–95. Bray was commissioned by the bishop of London to organize the American branch of the Anglican Church (Episcopalian Church) in America 1695–1704. Bray founded the Society for Promoting Christian Knowledge in 1698, to carry out this ministry, which proved equally effective in England and Wales. Bray recruited missionaries and assembled literature for Christian libraries in each parish. Through his efforts the Episcopal Church had its first roots in Virginia (1699) and Maryland, where he personally served for three months (1700). He also founded the Society for the Propagation of the Gospel in 1701, which initially was a ministry to American Indians. While overseeing his philanthropic endeavors, Bray pastored at St. Botoph's, Aldgate, MD from 1706–30. In 1723 he founded "Dr. Bray's Associates," a charity society for assisting General James Oglethorpe (1696–1785) in settling the area of Georgia for the evangelization of African-American slaves and the relief of indentured English prisoners. He wrote, *Catechetical Lectures, Martyrology*, among others.

Frederick IV

Oct. 11, 1671
Copenhagen, Denmark

Oct. 12, 1730
Odense, Denmark

King of Denmark and Norway, 1699–1730. Frederick IV was a devout Lutheran and sent the first Protestant missionaries to India in 1705. The missionaries established a mission outpost at Transquebar, then owned by Denmark. Frederick IV also established a college of missions, sent missionaries to Lapland (1716), and sent HANS EGEDE to Greenland (1718). Although he was defeated by Sweden (1700) and by Charles XII (1710), king of England (ruled: 1697–1718), he did rebuild Copenhagen and freed peasants from serfdom during his reign. He was the grandson of CHRISTIAN IV.

Jacques Saurin

Jan. 6, 1677
Nimes, France

Dec. 30, 1730
The Hague, Netherlands

French Reformed preacher and pulpit orator. After a four-year ministry in London, Saurin became pastor of the French Reformed Walloon Church at The Hague in 1705. His eloquent preaching attracted large congregations. The vigor of his preaching often left him speechless and exhausted before the closing prayer. Saurin wrote *Discourses Upon the More Memorable Events in the Bible*. He was charged with heresy (moderate Calvinist), his magnificence stirring up much jealousy among his colleagues. Saurin was tried before the Synod of The Hague. These petty persecutions shortened his life.

Francis Atterbury

March 6, 1662
Bedford/Middleton (Milton), England

Feb. 15, 1732
Paris, France

Anglican bishop, politician and staunch Jacobite. Ordained in 1687, Atterbury was a lecturer at St. Bride's in 1691 and then chaplain to WILLIAM III and Mary. He began his career as archdeanory of Totnes at Exeter Cathedral, 1701–4, dean of Carlisle (1704), and became concurrently bishop of Rochester and dean of Westminster (1713). His temper and love of politics launched him into many difficulties. He became involved with the Jacobite plots to restore the Stuarts to the English throne. Atterbury was a visible leader of the Tory High Church Party. These actions resulted in his imprisonment at the Tower of London (1722) and eventual banishment (1723) to Brussels and then Paris during the last nine years of his life.

Thomas Boston

March 17, 1677
Duns, Scotland

May 20, 1732
Ettrick, Scotland

Presbyterian pastor and scholar. The early years of Boston's ministry were at Simprin, Berkwickshire, 1699–1707. His main pastorate was at Ettrick, 1707–32. Boston was the center of controversies between Calvinists and Evangelicals. His preaching stressed salvation and de-emphasized repentance. The stir became more volatile when Boston promoted the publication of *The Calvinist: The Marrow of Modern Divinity* (1645) in Scotland in 1718. In 1720, the Scottish General Assembly charged Boston saying Calvinism was too free in offering salvation. Boston authored *Human Nature in Its Fourfold State* (1720), *Crook in the Lot*, and *An Illustration of the Doctrines of Christian Religion* (1773). Too feeble for the pulpit, he preached his last two Sundays from the manse window. He had 19 children, nine of whom died in infancy. His sermon, "The Nature of Regeneration," is in *The Fundamentals* (1910–15). His favorite Bible verse was John 1:29.

Alexander Mack

July 27, 1679 – baptized
Schriesheim, Germany

Feb 19, 1735
Germantown, Pennsylvania

Founder of the New Baptists or Brethren. Mack became a Separatist early in life. He made many preaching trips along the Rhine River and felt that right living was as important as right doctrine. In 1708, he and seven others organized the first "Brethren" assembly, which were called "Dunkards, Dunkers, or Tunkers," from the German word "to dip," which referred to their method of baptizing by immersion. The first church in Schwarzenau (Black Forest region) was sorely persecuted. Peter Becker led the group to America (1719), where they settled in Germantown (1729) as the second party of 250 with Mack arrived. The Brethren opposed war and advocated temperance, the simple life, plain dress, and stressed "obedience to Christ rather than obedience to creeds and cults." In 1871, the adapted name was German Baptists Brethren (Dunkers). The Church of the Brethren ("Conservative Dunkers") is the main denomination today from the group.

Samuel Wesley Sr.

Dec. 17, 1662
Winterborn, England

April 25, 1735
Epworth, England

Church of England pastor. Samuel Wesley Sr. married Susannah Annesley in 1688, and they had 19 children, including the famous Charles Wesley (child number 18) and John Wesley (child number 15). Nine children died in infancy. From 1690–95, he pastored at South Ormsby. For 40 years, Samuel pastored at Epworth, 1695–1735. Fires (1702 and February 9, 1709) destroyed his rectory and nearly took the life of his famous young sons when the parsonage also was engulfed. After 13 years, only half of it had been refurbished. His parson's pay was scant and its regularity often unpredictable which caused Wesley to face imprisonment a few times for mounting debts. Wesley wrote *A Life of Christ in Verse* (1693), and dedicated the book to Protestant Queen Mary II (ruled England with William III: 1689–94). The original Irish family name was "Westley", but was changed by Samuel to the English spelling "Wesley". His pamphlet war with the Dissenters resulted in his being jailed in 1705. In 1710, he was active in the defense of Henry Sacheverell and the High-Church party.

William Wake

Jan. 26, 1657
Blandford, England

Jan. 24, 1737
Lambeth, London, England

Archbishop of Canterbury, 1716–37. In his early career, Wake was bishop of London, 1705–16. Wake engaged in negotiations for reunion of the Church of England with the French Roman Catholic Church (Jansenists), represented by the Gallican theologian, Dupin, 1717–20. Wake sympathized with the Nonconformists and advocated changes to accommodate them within the sphere of English religious toleration. His book *Principles of the Christian Religion* (1700) was very popular.

Benjamin Schmolck

Dec. 21, 1672
Brauchitschdorf, Germany

Feb. 12, 1737
Schweidnitz, Germany

Popular hymn writer. Schmolck was ordained into the Lutheran ministry (1701) and married (1702). One year after his ordination, he began pastoring Friedenskirche in Schweidnitz, one of three Protestant churches in Catholic Silesia. Schmolck remained at that church until his death. He suffered from blindness and paralysis his last two years. His church served 36 villages whose religious pursuits were under strict Catholic restrictions. Schmolck wrote over 1,180 hymns, including the well known, "My Jesus, As Thou Wilt" 1718 (music by Karl Weber).

Benjamin Wadsworth

Feb. 28, 1669
Milton, Massachusetts

March 16, 1737
Cambridge, Massachusetts

President of Harvard College (University in 1780), **Cambridge, MA 1725–37**. When Wadsworth was six, his father was killed by Indians. On December 30, 1695, he married Ruth Bordman. Since they had no children of their own, many young people through the years boarded with the couple. From 1697–1725, Wadsworth pastored the First Congregational Church of Boston. Wadsworth maintained the liberal tradition established by his predecessor, John Leverett.

Samuel Andrew

Jan. 29, 1656
Cambridge, Massachusetts

Jan. 24, 1738
Milford, Connecticut

Founder and second rector (CEO) of Collegiate School, Brantford, CT 1707–16, renamed and relocated, Yale College (University in 1887), New Haven, CT 1716–19. Andrew's career began as a tutor at Harvard, 1675–84. He then filled a pastorate at the Congregational Church of Milford, 1685–1738. He participated as a member of the Saybrook Synod (confessional of Congregational Churches of Connecticut) of 1708. Andrew served as a trustee of Yale, 1701–38. He married Abigail Treat on December 25, 1697 (died: December 25, 1727). His second wife was also an Abigail (died: Sept. 9, 1742).

Isaac de Beausobre

March 8, 1659
Niort, France

June 5, 1738
Berlin, Germany

Eminent French writer. Beausobre became the minister at Chatillon-sur-Indre in Touraine, France, 1683. His loyalty to the Huguenots compelled him to seek refuge first at Rotterdam, Netherlands, and then at Dessau, Germany. Isaac then served as a French pastor in Berlin, 1694–1738. He wrote several histories with a theme of opposition against Lutherans and Catholics. Beausobre also authored a two-volume translation of the New Testament into French from the original Greek, 1734–44.

Thomas Shepherd

1665
England

Jan. 29, 1739
Bocking, England

Hymn writer. Although ordained in the Church of England, Shepherd later pastored two independent churches, one at Nottingham (1694–1700) and the other at Bocking (1700–39). For several years he preached in a barn, before his Nonconformist congregation was evicted and built a chapel. Shepherd wrote the first stanza for "Must Jesus Bear the Cross Alone." The original song's form was "Shall Simon Bear the Cross Alone, and Other Saints Be Free…"

Johann A. Freylinghausen

Dec. 2, 1670
Gandersheim, Germany

Feb. 12, 1739
Halle, Germany

German hymn writer, teacher, pastor, and prominent Pietist leader. Freylinghausen studied theology at Jena and then became vicar at Glaucha, a suburb of Halle, 1695–1715. Freylinghausen was a colleague of AUGUST FRANCKE at Halle University, marrying FRANCKE's only daughter in 1715. Upon FRANCKE's death in 1727, he became superintendent of the school and orphan house, and pastor of St. Ulrich's. He also wrote several works on theology. In addition to writing 44 hymns, Freylinghausen was the editor of the first hymnal Gesangbuch, with hundreds of hymns used by the Pietists.

Jean Cavalier

Nov. 28, 1681
Ribaute, France

May 17, 1740
Chelsea, London, England

French insurgent general and leader of the Camisards (Protestant resistance fighters). Following the revocation of the Edict of Nantes in 1685, Cavalier took refuge in Geneva, Switzerland. He fought for the Camisards in the Cevennes Mountains (Southern France) until defeated, 1702–4, failing to obtain "liberty of conscience" (freedom of religion). After serving with the English in Spain in 1706, Cavalier went back to Switzerland, then to the Netherlands, where he married. He settled in the French colony in Portar Lington, Ireland, 1709–27, returning to England for the remainder of his life, being lieutenant general of the island of Jersey in 1738.

Daniel Waterland

Feb. 14, 1683
Walesby, England

Dec. 23, 1740
Twinkenham, England

Anglican theologian and writer. Waterland rose through ecclesiastical seniority to become a learned theologian defending trinitarian orthodoxy. He was an assailant of Arianism and Deism, 1719–37. Waterland was chaplain to the King of Great Britian and Ireland George I (1717), chancellor of York (1722), canon of Windsor (1724) and vicar of Twinkenham (1730). He wrote *History of the Athanasian Creed* (1715), and authored several other books, including *Eight Sermons in Defense of the Divinity of Our Lord Jesus Christ* (1719), attacking Samuel Clarke (1675–1729) and Daniel Whitby (1638–1726), contemporary scholars.

Daniel E. Jablonski

Nov. 20, 1660
Nassenhuben, Germany

May 25, 1741
Berlin, Germany

German Reformed theologian and bishop of the Moravians (Unitas Fratrum), 1699. Jablonski was appointed court preacher in Konigsberg, Prussia (1691) and to Frederick III, elector of Brandenburg (served 1688–1700) in Berlin (1693). He was elected bishop of the Moravians in 1699, becoming the last to serve at the old Hussite Bohemian Church. He failed in his attempt with GOTTFRIED LEIBNIZ to unite various groups into one German Protestant body. Jablonski was successful in uniting together remnants of the exiled Bohemian Hussite groups in Poland and Germany and passed on the torch by consecrating Bishop ZINZENDORF in 1737.

Richard Bentley

Jan. 27, 1662
Oulton, England

July 14, 1742
Cambridge, England

Scholar, critic and philologist. Bentley was master of Trinity College, Cambridge University (1700–42) and professor of Divinity there (1717 on). He edited many classics, with his most critical exposè being on the fourteenth century forgery *Dissertation on the Epistles and Pharlaris*. His "Boyle Lectures" (sermon truths endowed annually by scientist ROBERT BOYLE since 1627) of 1692; and his book, *A Confutation of Atheism* (1713), were master attacks against atheism. Bentley was instrumental in helping to reform Cambridge, although his tyrannical style of rule nearly got him ejected from his post. He was the founder of historical philology. Bentley was largely responsible for the high standards of textual criticism which followed and is generally considered the greatest of English classical scholars.

Susannah Annesley Wesley
Mrs. Samuel Wesley Sr.

Jan. 20, 1669
London, England

July 23, 1742
London, England

Mother of JOHN and CHARLES WESLEY and 17 others. Susannah married Church of England preacher, Samuel Wesley Sr., in 1688. She was of fine intellect and good education, ruling her house with diligence, organization, and piety. She was the twenty-fifth child of her preacher father. Susannah joined the Church of England at age 13, and later became a member of the Methodist Church (c. 1739), established by her son, JOHN, who preached her funeral discourse. Although nine children died in infancy, Susannah had time to give each child the groundwork for future conversion. She spent 39 of her 46 married years in Epworth. Her dying words were, "Children, as soon as I am released, sing a psalm of praise to God."

"The best help for suffering is a regular and exact performance of duty."

Hugh Boulter

Jan. 14, 1672 — *Sept. 27, 1742*

English archbishop of Armagh, Ireland, 1724, and Lord Justice of Ireland, 1724–42. Boulter became the virtual ruler of Ireland, representing the Protestant cause and ascendancy. He believed England's interests in Ireland were threatened by the large Catholic majority, so he applied penal laws with energy and deprived Catholics of the vote. Early in his career, he was chaplain to King George I of Great Britain and Ireland in 1719. Boulter was concerned with the needs of the poor, feeding 2,500 people daily during the famine of 1740.

Daniel Neal

Dec. 14, 1678
London, England

April 4, 1743
Bath, England

Clergyman, historian, and famed author of *History of the Puritans* (4 vols. 1732–38). Neal's work presented a nonconformist approach to the sect's development, 1517–68, and an historical chronology, through 1689. Neal went to the Netherlands (1700) to study at Utrecht and Leyden, then returned to England (1703). He pastored the Aldersgate Street Church (independent), later on Jewin Street 1706–42. In 1720 he published *A History of New England* (2 vols.), which met with much favor.

James Blair

c. 1655
Aluah, Scotland

April 18, 1743
Williamsburg, Virginia

Episcopal clergyman who founded and was first president of William and Mary College, Williamsburg, VA 1729–43. Blair immigrated to Virginia in 1685 after being deprived of his Edinburgh parish for refusing to support the Catholic duke of York as heir to the Scottish throne. He was then asked by the bishop of London to become an Anglican Church missionary to colonial Virginia with the goal to revive and reform the Episcopal Church there. Blair served as rector at Varina Parish, Henrico (1685–94), in Jamestown (1694–1710) and then at the Bruton Parish Church, Williamsburg (1710–43). Sarah Harrison became his wife on June 2, 1687. He warmly welcomed GEORGE WHITEFIELD. Blair petitioned the English monarchs, King WILLIAM III and Mary, for a charter (obtained Feb. 14, 1692) to start the second college in the New World (Harvard being the first). Opening William and Mary College was delayed until 1729. In conjunction with Henry Hartwell and Edward Chilton, Blair wrote *The Present State of Virginia and the College* (1727). His major work was *Our Saviour's Divine Sermon on the Mount* (1722).

James Gardiner

Jan. 11, 1688
Carriden, Scotland

Sept. 21, 1745
Prestonpans, Scotland

Colonel of Dragoons. In 1702, Gardiner joined the English army and distinguished himself in the campaigns of John Churchill, duke of Marlborough (1650–1722). He became a part of the Dragoons. They were the main harassers of the French Huguenots after the revocation in 1685 of the Edict of Nantes by Louis XIV. From their behavior, came the term "to dragoon" (meaning to force into submission by violent measures). The story of Gardiner's early life of sin and his remarkable conversion to Presbyterianism (July or October of 1719) is told in DODDRIDGE's *Life of Colonel Gardiner*. He picked up a Christian book at a time of great temptation and was saved. Gardiner had a strong devotional life and was said to fear sinning more than fighting. He was killed at the Battle of Prestonpans, near his Scottish home, when his own regiment deserted him.

Jonathan Swift

Nov. 30, 1667
Dublin, Ireland

Oct. 19, 1745
Dublin, Ireland

Anglican author, poet, and master of English satire and prose. In 1688 he went to England and over the next ten years performed various services for the Moor Park Residence of Sir William Temple (retired English diplomat and essayist: 1628–99). When 22, Swift became the tutor of a servant's child, Esther Johnson, then eight years old. She was the infamous "Stella" of his journals, which began in 1710. Their friendship and romance were interrupted by her death (Jan. 18, 1728) It was complicated by his passionate involvement with one Esther "Vanessa" Vanhomrigh, whose death (1723). came unexpectedly after Swift scolded and rejected her for revealing their relationship to his beloved "Stella," next to whom he was buried 17 years later at St. Patrick's Cathedral in Dublin. Swift's career began in 1695 as an Anglican clergyman of a small country church at Kilroot. By 1710 Swift was the leading writer for the English Tory Party. In 1713, Swift became dean of St. Patrick's in Dublin until his death. Of his more than 100 writings, the most famous is *Gulliver's Travels* (1726), a children's classic and a satire on courts, parties, and statesmen. Dementia followed a stroke in 1742, completely incapacitating Swift.

William Tennent Sr.

1673
Ireland

May 6, 1746
Neshaminy, Pennsylvania

Presbyterian clergyman and educator. He married Catharine Kennedy on May 15, 1702. They had five children including the well-known GILBERT TENNENT, whose religious zeal paved the way for the Great Awakening (1720's–1760's) in America under GEORGE WHITEFIELD and WILLIAM, TENNENT JR. His family immigrated to Philadelphia in 1718. He first pastored in Bedford, NY (1720–26) and then in Neshaminy (1726–46). In 1728, Tennent established a school in a little log house on his estate for training his four sons and others of his church. It became known as the "log college" in 1736 and developed into the College of New Jersey (Princeton University/Seminary). He trained ministers to have an evangelistic approach.

Heinrich Plutschau

1678
Wesenberg, Germany

1747
Itzehoe, Germany

Lutheran Pietist missionary to India. While a student of AUGUST FRANCKE, Plutschau was sent to Tranquebar, India, in 1705 by King Frederick IV of Denmark. In addition to bringing a Christian witness to southern India, he and BARTHOLOMEW ZIEGENBALG, also from Halle University, translated Lutheran hymns, prayers, and catechism into Tamil and Portuguese. Plutschau's efforts produced many Hindu converts. In 1711, he was sent home to defend the mission against critics in Europe, including some of the royal court at Copenhagen. In 1714, he pastored in Itzehoe. The Danish-Halle Mission, which they founded, is the oldest Protestant mission board.

Jean F. Osterwald

Nov. 16, 1663
Neuchatel, Switzerland

April 14, 1747
Neuchatel, Switzerland

Theologian. Osterwald was educated at Swedish universities in Zurich and Saumur, after which he pursued his theological studies in France (at Orleans and Paris) and completed his educational career at Geneva. He was ordained in his hometown of Neuchatel in 1683. From 1702 on, as a preacher, lecturer, and author, Osterwald attained a position of great influence in his day. With friends J. A. Surretin of Geneva and S. Werenfels of Basil, he formed the "Swiss Tri-umvirate."

Theodorus J. Frelinghuysen

c 1691
Lingen, Germany

after May, 1747
New Jersey

Instrumental in creating Dutch Reformed Churches in America. Frelinghuysen was a Reformed revivalist and Pietist pastor whose stirring preaching in New Jersey kindled the beginning of the Great Awakening in the American colonies. He came from Amsterdam, Netherlands, to pastor in Raritan, NJ in 1720. Theodorus married Eva Terhune and had seven children. His ministry was to Dutch congregations and in 1737 he initiated the move toward creating Dutch Reformed Churches in America, which happened around the time of his death. He greatly influenced his Presbyterian neighbor, GILBERT TENNENT.

Jonathan Dickinson

April 22, 1688
Hatfield, Massachusetts

Oct. 7, 1747
Elizabethtown, New Jersey

Founder and first president of College of New Jersey (Princeton University in 1898), **Elizabeth, NJ 1746–47**. After graduating from Yale in 1706, Dickinson pastored in Elizabeth, NJ from 1709–47. In 1717, he led his church from Congregationalism to Presbyterianism. When WILLIAM TENNENT Sr.'s Log Cabin School closed in 1746, Dickinson started a small school which originally met in his home, May–October, 1747. He married Joanna Melyen (around 1709) and Mary Crane (April, 1747). He was keenly interested in reaching Indians and once lodged DAVID BRAINERD. Dickinson was considered the leading theologian for the Great Awakening in the middle colonies, and was the moderator of Presbyterianism. He wrote *The Reasonableness of Christianity* (1732).
"Cursed be all that learning that is contrary to the cross of Christ."

David Brainerd

April 20, 1718
Haddam, Connecticut

Oct. 9, 1747
Northampton, Massachusetts

Missionary to the Indians. Converted on July 12, 1739 while taking a walk, Brainerd had an abbreviated Yale (expelled 1742) education before yielding to his missionary calling. He endured incredible hardships to reach the Seneca, Susquehanna, and Delaware tribes in Kaunaumeek, NY; near Easton, PA; and in Crossweeksung, NJ 1743–47, the latter known as NJ Bethel Mission near Cranbury. He was ordained a Presbyterian in 1744. In Brainerd's short years of ministry, he rode over 3,000 miles on horseback and saw over 130 Indians converted, mostly the Delaware Indians, near Trenton, NJ. His famed *Journal* has moved many to missionary service. Both the *Journal* and his biography were published in 1749 by JONATHAN EDWARDS SR., with assistance from John Brainerd (1720–81), David's brother. Brainerd was associated with the Scottish Society for Propagation of Christian Knowledge, 1742–47. He was engaged to Jerusha Edwards (also known as Jemima, daughter of JONATHAN EDWARDS). He died from tuberculosis at the Edwards' home, followed in death six months later by his fiance on February 14, 1748. He said as he died, "He will come and will not tarry. I shall soon be in glory; soon be with God and His angels." His favorite Bible verse was John 7:37.

John Potter

1674
Wakefield, England

Oct. 10, 1747
Lambeth, England

Archbishop of Canterbury, 1737–47. Potter was a classical scholar who graduated from Oxford and then became regus professor of divinity there in 1707. From 1708–15, he was professor of divinity and canon of Christ Church, Oxford. He served as bishop of Oxford, 1715–37. Potter wrote an excellent work on Greek antiquities

Archaeologica Graeca (2 vols. 1697–99) and *A Discourse on Church Government* (1707). Potter was considered an unlikely choice for archbishop since, from a religious point of view, he opposed a faction of the Whig party represented at that time by Bishop Benjamin Hoadly (1676–1761). Potter strongly opposed their views which justified generous inclusion of all groups within the church, including Arians and also denied that there was a visible Church of Christ. Potter's Whig political views, however, ensured his favor with the government.

Isaac Watts

July 17, 1674
Southampton, England

Nov. 25, 1748
Stoke Newington, London, England

First great hymn writer to date. Watts and CHARLES WESLEY phased out metrical Psalm singing and began to write hymns for use in church services. He gave us such memorable hymns as: "At the Cross," 1707 (HUDSON), "When I Survey the Wondrous Cross," 1707 (MASON), "We're Marching to Zion," 1709 (LOWRY), "Joy to the World," 1719 (HANDEL), "Jesus Shall Reign," 1719 (HATTON), "Our God, Our Help in Ages Past," 1719 (CROFT), "Alas and Did My Saviour Bleed," (WILSON), "When the Battle's Over," (BLAKE), and "Am I a Soldier of the Cross?" 1724 (ARNE). He began to write poems at age seven and wrote the bulk of his hymns 1694–96, which would be published some 15 years later. He learned Greek, Latin, and Hebrew. Watts pastored at Mark Lane Independent Chapel in London (1702–12), after being an assistant (1697–1702). Unmarried, he was an invalid for his last 36 years (1712–48), living at the Thomas Abney home (in Herts 1712–35 and Stoke Newington 1735–48) where he composed an additional 600 hymns. Watts authored sacred poems, catechisms, metrical psalms, philosophical and theological works which embodied the stern doctrines of Calvinism cloaked in sympathy and gentleness. His *Logic* was a textbook at Oxford for a considerable time. His *Hymns and Spiritual Songs* (1707) and *Psalms of David Imitated* (1719) were his chief works. He is buried in Bunhills Fields Cemetery. Various individuals added to his hymns. His favorite Bible verse was Revelation 5:9.

Johann F. Rock

1678
Oberwalden, Germany

1749
Iowa

Leader of "Inspirationists" who became Amana Church Society. This was initially a movement within German Lutheran Pietism. Rock advocated that inspiration had not ended and that God spoke directly to men, including himself in 1707. Greatly persecuted, he and his followers emigrated to America, settling briefly in New York (1742) and then moving to southeastern Iowa (1745). His group was known as the Amana Church Society. The Amana Colonies are still found in Iowa and the appliances produced by the Amana Corporation are among the leaders in the industry today. He rejected preaching and the sacraments. He was assisted by EBERHARD GUBER.

Johann S. Bach

March 21, 1685
Eisenach, Germany

July 28, 1750
Leipzig, Germany

Choirmaster, composer of church music, and one of history's greatest organists. Bach began as a child soprano, and progressed to an accomplished violinist. He first branched into his expertise as organist at Arnstadt (1704), at Muhlhausen (1707), court organist at Weimar (1708–17), court kapellmeister (director of choir, orchestra, etc.) at Anhalt-Cothen (1718–23) and cantor and organist at the Thomas School in Leipzig (1723–50). Bach married Maria Barbara (a cousin, 1684–1720) in 1707 and later, Anna Wulken (1701–60), in December, 1721. They gave him twenty children, all of whom shared his talent and love for music. He also wrote over 370 oratorios (chorales) for the Lutheran Church, including *St. John's Passion* and *St. Matthew's Passion*. Bach went blind in 1749. His music remained undiscovered until 70 years later in 1821. Other renowned works are: *Mass in B Minor, The Art of Fugue,* and *Well-Tempered Clavier.* Bach's music has generated more recordings than any other composer. He was initially buried in St. John's Church, but after it was destroyed in World War II, he was re-interred in 1949, in St. Thomas' Church, Leipzig where he had served as an organist 200 years earlier. He wrote the harmony for BERNARD's "O, Sacred Head Now Wounded."

"The aim and final end of all music should be none other than the glory of God . . ."

Christian David

Dec. 31, 1690
Senftleben, Moravia (Germany)

Feb. 3, 1751
Herrnhut, Germany

Evangelist and renewal leader of the Moravian Brethren Church. David's conversion at age 27 was influenced by his dissatisfaction with his Catholic upbringing, by the testimony of the Christian carpenter who taught him his trade, and through the German Bible he had obtained at age 20. In 1717, David married and embarked on trips into Moravia, where he discovered Moravian Brethren longing for the rebirth of their church. Persecution against non-Catholics was raging in Silesia (north Czechoslovakia, southwest Poland), Bohemia (west Czechoslovakia), Moravia (central Czechoslovakia), Austria, and Hungary. Beginning in 1722, David led ten dangerous missions to bring German-speaking Moravians to freedom on the estate of Count NICHOLAS VON ZINZENDORF. These refugees became the Herrnhut Community, where a spiritual reawakening of the Moravian Brethren Church triumphed. In 1733–35, Christian David and three Brethren assisted a Danish missionary struggling among the Eskimos of Greenland. He continued to travel extensively helping to further the Moravian outreach, especially in Germany (1741) and in the Pennsylvania Colony (1748) in North America.

Samuel Blair

June 14, 1712
Ulster, Ireland

July 5, 1751
(New) Londonderry, Pennsylvania

Evangelical Presbyterian who became the chief spokesman for the "New Side," after colonial Presbyterianism split over the impact of the Great Awakening. He studied at TENNENT's Log College, then established his own similar school at Fagg's in Manor (Londonderry), Chester County, PA, where he is buried. He pastored at Londonderry, PA 1739–51 after pastoring in Middletown and Shrewsbury, NJ from 1733–39. He strongly supported WHITEFIELD.

Philip Doddridge

June 26, 1702
London, England

Oct. 26, 1751
Lisbon, Portugal

Nonconformist minister and noted hymn writer. Doddridge wrote the lyrics for about 370 hymns, including: "O Happy Day" (1735: best known, music by EDWARD RIMBAULT in 1854), "Awake My Soul" (music by HANDEL), and "Grace, 'Tis a Charming Sound" (coauthor with TOPLADY, music by SANKEY). He was the youngest of 20 children, 18 of whom died in infancy. He pastored in Kibworth, 1723–29, and was identified with the dissenting/Nonconformist clergy. In 1729, Doddridge began his lifelong pastorate of an independent congregation at Castle Hill Congregational Chapel of Northampton, England. He also established an academy there. Doddridge wrote *The Rise and Progress of Religion in the Soul* (1745), which had a wide circulation, and *The Family Expositor* (6 vols., 1734–56). He died from tuberculosis contracted while in Portugal recuperating from exhaustion. He is buried in the English Protestant Cemetery in Lisbon.

Joseph Butler

May 18, 1692
Wantage, England

June 16, 1752
Bath, England

Anglican bishop, scholar and moralist. Butler began his ministry as a preacher at Rolls Chapel, London (1719–26), prebendary of Salisbury (1721–38), and rector of Stanhope (1725–40). He was also clerk of the closet (1736) to Queen Caroline (ruled: 1727–37) (1683–1737, wife of George II) and later (1746) to King George II of Great Britian and Ireland (ruled: 1727–60). He was a bishop in Bristol (1738), bishop in Durham (1750) and dean of St. Paul's Cathedral (1740). Butler was a moral philosopher and preacher in the royal court. By discrediting deism and advocating theism, Butler defended the truth against the rationalists of his time. He also stressed that their "God of Nature" was the God of Revelation. Butler wrote *Analogy of Religion* (1736). He never married.

Johann A. Bengel

June 24, 1687
Winnenden, Germany

Nov. 2, 1752
Alpirsbach, Germany

Lutheran theologian, scholar and great expert on original texts of the Bible. Bengel was a man of eminent piety and of vast, sound learning. He was considered the "Father of Modern Methods of New Testament Exegesis" and founder of "Biblical Realism." He was a tutor in theology at Tübingen, 1708–13. He headed a seminary and pastored the Village Congregation at Denkendorf (1713–41), then served as general superintendent at Herbrechtingen in 1741, prelate of Alpirsbach (1749–52), and was consistorial counselor with residence at Stuttgart. Bengel authored a critical study of the New Testament in 1734, and wrote *Ordo Temporum* (1741). In 1742 he wrote his *Gnomon Novi Testamenti* (Index), a commentary on Scripture, in which he explained the New Testament Greek text. He mainly used the Textus Receptus for his NT. Bengal was the founder of Swabian (southwest Germany) Pietism and was also responsible for preserving sound doctrine in southern Germany. He set the date of the beginning of the millennium at 1836.

George Berkeley

March 12, 1685
Dysert Castle, (near Kilkenny), Ireland

Jan. 14, 1753
Oxford, England

Anglican philosopher and bishop of Cloyne, 1734–52. As one of the foremost modern idealists, he stressed that ideas in the mind are products of the mind of God and that external objects exist only as they are perceived in the mind. This was basically advancing JOHN LOCKE's ideas. From 1713–20, Berkeley traveled in England and on the European continent, absorbing a potpourri of ideas, including his universal remedy for all ills: tar-water. He lectured at the University of Dublin, 1721–24 and was dean of Derry in 1724. On August 1, 1728, Berkeley married the daughter of John Foster. They lived in Rhode Island, 1728–31, in an attempt to found a missionary college on the island of Bermuda to evangelize the American Indians there. He wrote *A Treatise Concerning the Principles of Human Knowledge* (1710) to counter the deists. His major work was *Alciphron* (1732). His work *The Minute Philosopher* (1733), stressed that all nature is the language of God. Berkeley basically demonstrated that the church could outlive its critics. He died of a heart attack while his wife was reading a sermon to him.

Ebenezer Erskine

June 22, 1680
Dryburgh, Scotland

Stirling, Scotland

Secession Church founder. Erskine pastored at Portmoak, 1703–31 and then was transferred to Stirling where he served until 1740. He married Alison Turpie in 1704. He was deposed

(1733) for suggesting, in a sermon (1732), that a congregation has the right to choose their own ministers and for his endorsement of a strong evangelical book, *The Marrow of Modern Divinity* (1718). As a result, Erskine led the Seceders out of the Established Church of Scotland, forming with James Fisher (his son-in-law), William Wilson, and Alexander Moncrieff, the Associate Reformed Presbytery (1733) at Gairney Bridge (near Kinross) which became the Secession Church (1740). In 1747, Erskine headed the Burghers (Scottish Presbyterian successionist group) in the split of the Seceders against the antiburghers (General Associated Synod). The Secession Church divided over the question of subscribing to the Civil Oath (acknowledging true religion publicly preached and authorized by law) taken by the burgesses (citizens) of Edinburgh, with Erskine leading the Burghers who assented its legality. His favorite Bible verse was Exodus 20:2.

Thomas Wilson

Dec. 20, 1663
Burton, England

March 7, 1755
Isle of Man, England

Bishop of Sodor and Man, 1697–1755. Through his earnest labors, a great change for the better was brought about in his diocese. Wilson also wrote well–known devotional works. His sincere piety and fervent missionary spirit made him a model bishop. He was curate at Newchurch, Kenyon (1687–92) and chaplain to the Earl of Derby (1692–97). Wilson was educated in Dublin, Ireland. He died at Bishop's Court.

John Cennick

Dec. 12, 1718
Reading, England

July 4, 1755
London, England

Evangelist and hymn writer. Cennick was born of Quaker stock, brought up in the Church of England, and converted on September 6, 1737, via Methodism. He became a teacher in Kingswood in 1740. In 1745, he joined the Moravian Brethren, traveling and preaching in Germany and Ireland as an evangelist, after being ordained in 1739. He married about 1747. "Be Present at Our Table, Lord" is one of the most well-known hymns that Cennick published. He is buried in the Moravian Burial Ground, Chelsea, England.

Elisha Williams

Aug. 24, 1694
Hatfield, Massachusetts

July 24, 1755
Wethersfield, Connecticut

Rector (CEO) of Yale College (University in 1887), **New Haven, CT 1726–39**. Williams studied theology under his father, began teaching at Yale (1716) and was ordained a Congregationalist (1722). Six children came from his marriages to Eunice Chester (February 23, 1714) and then to Elizabeth Scott (January 29, 1751). He initially held pastorates in Wethersfield and then served in Nova Scotia before returning to Connecticut. Williams was also a Connecticut judge (1740–43) and made a trip to England (1749–51).

Johann L. Mosheim
Father of Modern Church History

Oct. 9, 1694
Lubeck, Germany

Sept. 9, 1755
Gottingen, Germany

Lutheran theologian, church historian, and pulpit orator. This noted scholar and theologian taught at Kiel and preached at Helmstadt, Brunswick (1723–45), while filling a pastorate at Marienthal and Michaelstein (1726–45). He was a preacher and professor at Gottingen University, 1747–55, which he helped to found. His *Institutiones* (1726), told the entire sweep of church history. He was considered the most learned Lutheran of his time and was objective without bias in his work. Mosheim was a pioneer in modern preaching methods and a founder of modern pragmatic ecclesiastical historical writing in Germany.

Thomas Herring

1693
Walsoken, England

1756
Croyden, England

Archbishop of Canterbury, 1747–56. Herring took the see in Bangor (1737–43) and of York (1743–47). After the defeat of the king's troops at Preston Pans in 1745, Herring exerted himself in his diocese with so much patriotism and zeal that he repressed the disaffected, inspired the desponding and procured, at a county meeting, a subscription of 40,000 pounds toward the defense of the country. His zeal earned him the title of "the red herring."

Erdmann Neumeister

May 12, 1671
Uechteritz, Germany

Aug. 18, 1756
Hamburg, Germany

Hymn writer. Neumeister wrote about 650 hymns, the most famous being the gospel song, "Christ Receiveth Sinful Men" (1718). JAMES MCGRANAHAN composed the music over 200 years later. Neumeister is considered the originator of church cantatas. A couple of his hymns were texts for BACH's cantata creations. He also wrote a history of Germany in 1695. He was senior court preacher in Soraw (1706–15), after pastoring in Bibraa (1698–1704). In 1715, Neumeister became pastor of St. James' Church, Hamburg, where he served until his death. Being a strong, conservative, Lutheran theologian, he felt the reforming efforts of Pietists and Moravians were unnecessary. He became blind later in life.

Aaron Burr Sr.

Jan. 4, 1716
Fairfield, Connecticut

Sept. 24, 1757
Princeton, New Jersey

Second president of the College of New Jersey, 1748–56 (Newark, 1748–52, Princeton, 1752–56), **renamed and relocated, Princeton (NJ) College** (University in 1898), **1756–57**. Burr was ordained to the Presbyterian Church in 1736 and soon pastored at First Presbyterian Church, Newark, NJ. He married Esther Edwards (daughter of JONATHAN EDWARDS) on June 29, 1752, and had two children, one of whom (Aaron Jr.) became vice president of the United States (served: 1801–5) under President Thomas Jefferson (served: 1801–9). He also served as trustee of CNJ/PC.

Jonathan Edwards Sr.

Oct. 5, 1703
East Windsor, Connecticut

March 22, 1758
Princeton, New Jersey

Congregationalist revivalist preacher and Calvinistic theologian. Edwards knew Latin, Greek, and Hebrew by age 13. During his devotions one day in 1716 while a student at Yale, I Tim.1:17 convicted him, resulting in his conversion. After graduation in 1720, he tutored there, 1724–26, then married Sarah Pierpont (1710–58) on July 28, 1727. They had twelve children. Edwards was ordained as a Congregationalist, served (1727–29) as an associate and then pastored in Northampton, MA (1729–50), where a revival (1734–37) sparked the Great Awakening, 1735. He gave his most famous sermon "Sinners in the Hands of an Angry God" on July 8, 1741, in Enfield, CT. He was later dismissed from the Northampton church because of his convictions for a converted membership to take communion, opposing the Half-Way Covenant. Edwards then pastored (missionary) at a Native American Mission (Mohawk Indians) in Stockbridge, MA from 1750–57, where he wrote more than he preached, followed by a brief five-week third presidency at Princeton College (University in 1898) preceding his death. His death was a result of an ill-prepared smallpox vaccination. His work, *Freedom of the Will* (1754), is a classic, although he seemingly denied this same concept. Edwards influenced many spiritual leaders, including

BRAINERD, WHITEFIELD, and THOMAS CHALMERS. He said as he died, "Where is Jesus, my never failing Friend?" His wife died six months later of dysentery.

Johann A. Rothe

May 12, 1688
Lissa, Germany

July 6, 1758
Thommendorf, Germany

Lutheran Pietist pastor of the church on ZINZENDORF's estate at Berthelsdorf in 1722. He was a close associate of ZINZENDORF. They welcomed a colony of Hussites exiled from German-speaking Moravia and tried to incorporate these Moravians into the Saxony Lutheran Church. He was the chief pastor of the Herrnhut Colony, 1722–37, when a break occurred. He then pastored in Hermsdorf (1737) and Thommendorf (1742).

Christopher Sower

1693
Laasphe, Germany

Sept. 25, 1758
Germantown, Pennsylvania

Printer and publisher in the colonies. He was originally with the Reformed Church, later the German Baptist Brethren (Dunkers). Sower married Maria Christina sometime before 1721, and they had one son. His wife left him, 1730–44. He came to Germantown, PA (1724) and established a print shop (1738). In 1743, he published, in the German language, the second Bible printed in America. He also published a German hymnbook and newspaper.

Hans Egede

Jan. 31, 1686
Harstad, Senjen Isle, Norway

Nov. 5, 1758
Stubbekobing, Falster Isle, Denmark

Norwegian Lutheran minister and missionary who was the first to preach the gospel to the Eskimos of Greenland as part of a group of 46, which included some of Egede's family. Early in his ministry he pastored in Vagan, Lofoten Islands, 1706–19. Egede arrived in Greenland on July 3, 1721, under the support of the Danish government, founding the colony of Godthaab. His wife, Giertrud (Gertrude), died in 1735. He saw many converts until his ill health compelled him to return to Copenhagen in 1736. There in Copenhagen, he founded a seminary to train missionaries for the work in Greenland. In 1740, he became superintendent of the Greenland Mission and bishop of Greenland. Egede wrote a book on Greenland's natural history. His son, Paul (1708–1789), translated the NT into the Greenlandic language.

Experience Mayhew

Jan. 27, 1673
Chilmark, Massachusetts

Nov. 29, 1758
Martha's Vineyard, Massachusetts

Pastor and missionary to the Massachusetts Indians, 1694–1758. Mayhew pastored six congregations of Indians and English. He married Thankful Hinkley (1695) and Remember Bourne (1711) and had at least one son. In 1709, he translated the gospel of John and Psalms into Indian dialects. He opposed GEORGE WHITEFIELD because of fears that antinomian notions of direct revelation would take hold among the Indians. He wrote *Indian Converts* (1727). He was the fourth Mayhew in five generations to give continuous missionary service to the Indians in Massachusetts: Governor Thomas (1593–1681), Thomas, Jr. (1620–57), John (1652–88), and later Zechariah (1718–1806).

James Hervey

Feb. 26, 1714
Hardingstone, England

Dec. 25, 1758
Weston-Favell, England

Anglican clergyman and devotional writer. He was a college friend of Wesley at Oxford. Hervey pastored in Weston-Favell, Dummer, Biddeford, among others. WHITEFIELD was influential in his conversion in Collintree, which came at age 27, after he had been pastoring for several years. He broke with WESLEY in 1755 over

Hervey's insistence of the imputed righteousness of Christ. His *Meditations Among the Tombs* is considered his most famous work. He died of tuberculosis.

Robert Seagrave

Nov. 22, 1693
Twyford, England

c 1759

Evangelist and hymn writer. He wrote some 50 hymns of which "Rise, My Soul, and Stretch Thy Wings" was the most well known. Ordained in the Church of England, he became interested in the work of WESLEY and WHITEFIELD. Seagrave was appointed Sunday evening lecturer at Lorimer's Hall in London, 1739–50. He also frequently preached at Whitefield's Tabernacle.

George F. Handel

Feb. 23, 1685
Halle, Germany

April, 14, 1759
London, England

Composer of the greatest piece of Christian music ever written, "The Hallelujah Chorus" *("Messiah")*. It was at age 55 in August of 1741, that Handel shut himself up in a room for 24 days, inspired by the Scriptures: Revelation 11:15; 19:6, 16. What transpired was to move millions until the Lord's return. The *Messiah* was first performed April 23, 1742, before 700 people with Handel at the organ in London. It was last conducted by him April 6, 1759. He became ill afterwards and died eight days later. He was in the orchestra of the Hamburg opera (1703) and created his first opera, *Almira* (1704). He wrote some 420 compositions, including the music for "Joy to the World" (lyrics by ISAAC WATTS), "I Know That My Redeemer Liveth" (lyrics by CHARLES WESLEY), and "While Shepherds Watched Their Flocks" (lyrics by NATHAN TATE). Twenty oratorios and 49 operas were created by Handel. His "Esther" and "Israel in Egypt" were some of his best. The oratorios spanned from "Esther" (1720) to "Jephthah" (1752). He left the position of court conductor to be the Elector (1712), settled in London (1713), and became a British citizen (1726), leaving the Lutheran Church then. He was the director of the Royal Academy of Music (1720–28) and a partner in the King's Theater (1729–34). He gave up operatic management entirely (1740), after he lost a fortune in the business, going bankrupt (1737). Handel became blind in 1752. He suffered a stroke in 1737, five years before *Messiah* was first performed. Handel never married. He conducted ten concerts during the last month of his life.

Nicholas L. von Zinzendorf

May 26, 1700
Dresden, Germany

May 9, 1760
Herrnhut, Germany

Founder of the Moravian Church and of Bethlehem, PA in 1741 which became its American headquarters. Zinzendorf married Countess Erdmuth Dorothea von Reuss on September 7, 1722, and they had at least one daughter. He later married Anna Nitschmann in June, 1757. He left politics (Saxon civil service since 1721) in 1727, and devoted himself to his growing Herrnhut (The Lord's Shelter) community on his estate which grew into the Moravian Brethren (originally Bohemian Brethren). It began, when in 1722, he permitted some members of the Moravian sect, fleeing from persecution in Austria, to settle on his estate near Dresden. In August, 1727, a powerful prayer meeting began that lasted for 100 years. A chance meeting of a West Indian Negro in Copenhagen in 1731 rekindled his interests in foreign missions. In 1732, Herrnhut had grown to over 600 and also sent out their first two missionaries. In 1734, he was ordained Lutheran. After Zinzendorf was made bishop of the Moravian Church in 1737, he was expelled from Saxony, 1737–48. He was in London (1737), but welcomed by JOHN WESLEY in America (1741), establishing churches in several Pennsylvania towns and back to England, 1747 and most of 1749–55. His vision was "I have one passion. It is He." He wrote 2,000 hymns, including "Jesus Thy Blood and Righteousness" (1739).

Antoine Court

May 17, 1696
Villeneuve-de-berg, France

June 12, 1760
Lausanne, Switzerland

Reformed Church minister and evangelist who devoted his life to the restoration of Protestantism in France. He was ordained November 21, 1718, and his followers were known as the Church in the Desert. Defying King Louis XIV's decrees, Court convened synods and prepared ministers. Persecutions broke out in 1724. In 1730, he fled from the king's wrath to Lausanne, where he headed up a seminary which trained pastors for the Reformed Church of France until his death.

Samuel Davies

Nov. 3, 1723
Summit Ridge (Newcastle), Delaware

Feb. 4, 1761
Princeton, New Jersey

President of Princeton (NJ) College (University in 1898), **1759–61**, succeeding Jonathan Edwards Sr. Davies married Sarah Kirkpatrick (Oct. 23, 1746) and Jean Holt (Oct. 4, 1748). His first wife and son died in 1747. As a Presbyterian preacher/evangelist to Hanover County, VA, his eloquence of speech assisted the Great Awakening. Davies took a trip to Scotland and England in 1753 to raise funds for the college. He wrote the hymn "Great God of Wonders" (music by JOHN NEWTON), making him the first American hymn writer of note. He said a sermon should be prepared with at least four days of hard labor. Davies contracted pneumonia and blood poisoning from being bled. He was called the founder of southern Presbyterianism.

William Law

1686
King's Cliffe, England

April 9, 1761
King's Cliffe, England

Anglican clergyman and devotional writer. Law gave most of his life to organizing schools and almshouses (poorhouses). He lived a life of prayer and had several published works. He was a tutor in Cambridge (1711), a cleric and tutor in London (1727), then came back to King's Cliffe (1740). About 1737, he came under the mysticism of JACOB BOHME. His famed book, *A Serious Call to a Devout and Holy Life* (1728), is a devotional masterpiece, which greatly impressed the WESLEYS. He also wrote *Christian Perfection* (1726) and *Divine Knowledge* (1752). His favorite Bible verse was I John 4:19.

William Grimshaw

Sept. 14, 1708
Brindle, England

April 7, 1763
Haworth, England

Evangelical cleric and revivalist. He was curate of Haworth, 1742–63. The illness and death of Grimshaw's wife of four years brought him to Christ. Following his ordination in 1731, Grimshaw briefly served as curate at Littleborough near Rochdale. At Todmorden, he was greatly influenced by William Darney in 1744. He became JOHN WESLEY's chief assistant in establishing Methodism in the north of England, creating and regulating the "Great Haworth Round." On October 18, 1748, he conducted the first Methodist Circuit Quarterly Meeting, an idea put forward by John Bennet. Grimshaw was known for his indefatigable labor. His intercessory prayer life was unmatched in his day and his fervent sermons brought a sweeping revival to a desolate and degenerate sector of England.

John Byrom

Feb. 29, 1692
Kersall Cell, England

Sept. 26, 1763
Manchester, England

Anglican poet and stenographer. Byrom's training included medical college at Montpelier University in France. He decided against being a doctor but also declined ordination. In France he studied mysticism and wrote religious studies, poems, and humorous verse. Upon his return to England in 1718, he began writing hymns. Converted (1738) as a result of his friendship with JOHN WESLEY, he settled at his family estate in Kersall (1740). In addition to his accomplishments with verse, he also invented a system of shorthand in 1742. He married his cousin, Elizabeth Byrom. His most well-known hymn was "Christians, Awake, Salute the Happy Morn." He is buried at Manchester Cathedral.

Hans A. Brorson

June 20, 1694
Randrup, Denmark

June 3, 1764
Ribe, Denmark

Danish hymn writer. Ordained (1722), Brorson became a pastor in Randrup (1727), deacon in Tondern (1729), and dean at the Cathedral at Ribe (1739), then bishop of the latter (1741). Nearly one-third of the hymns in use in the Danish Church come from his pen. An edition of his hymns was published in Copenhagen in 1867, where he studied theology early in life. He was a popular preacher. He had 357 of his best hymns published in 1901.

Gilbert Tennent

Feb. 5, 1703
County Armagh, Ireland

July 23, 1764
Philadelphia, Pennsylvania

Scholarly Biblical preacher and powerful Presbyterian evangelist. He emigrated to Philadelphia (1717), then pastored in New Brunswick, NJ from 1726–43, with revival breaking out (1729). He married Cornelia Clarkson in 1741 and Sarah Spofford later and had three children. He was an outspoken defender of WHITEFIELD, whose coming in 1740–42 he prepared with great zeal. He made a preaching tour of Massachusetts and Connecticut, giving his famous sermon "The Danger of an Unconverted Ministry" on March 8, 1740, in Nottingham, PA. Tennent pastored in New Brunswick, NJ (1726–43), then at Second Presbyterian Church, Philadelphia (1743–53), after which he traveled to England with SAMUEL DAVIES to raise funds for Nassau Hall at the College of New Jersey (Princeton University in 1898). WHITEFIELD said, "He is the son of thunder. Hypocrites must either be converted or enraged at his preaching." He is buried in Abington, PA.

Katharina von Schlegel

Oct. 22, 1697
Germany

1765

Wrote famed devotional hymn, "Be Still My Soul." JEAN SIBELIUS added the music over 220 years later. She was the head of a Woman's House of the Evangelical Lutheran Church at Cothen, Germany. She was also attached to the ducal court there. Of her 29 hymns, this was the only one translated into English via JANE BORTHWICK.

Edward Young

June 30, 1683
Upham, England

April 5, 1765
Welwyn, England

Anglican poet, pastor, and writer. Young was "baptized" July 3, 1683. He was ordained (1727) and served as pastor of Welwyn (1730). He married Elizabeth Lee in 1731. Known for his melancholy meditation in blank verse, he published three tragedies, letters, essay, and many poems. Young is remembered for his popular *Night Thoughts* (1742–50). A worthy quote from him is, "Procrastination is the thief of time."

Timothy Cutler

May 31, 1684
Charleston (Boston), Massachusetts

Aug. 17, 1765
Boston, Massachusetts

Congregational and Episcopalian cleric. Upon his ordination, he became pastor of the Congregational Church in Stamford, CT from 1710–19. Cutler married Elizabeth Andrew on February 1, 1711. Cutler was the third rector (CEO) of Yale College (University in 1887) in 1719. He caused a major sensation when, in 1722, he announced his switch to Episcopalianism. He traveled to London to be ordained in the Church of England. He then was rector of Christ's Old North Church in Boston, MA from 1723–65. He was against the revival endeavors of such as WHITEFIELD.

J. Leonhard Dober

1706
Munchsroth, Germany

1766

First Moravian missionary. He was a Moravian refugee at ZINZENDORF's estate in 1725. Dober became a leader and missionary for the group. In 1732–34, he and DAVID NITSCHMANN ministered to the Negroes of St. Thomas in the Danish West Indies. They walked 600 miles to Copenhagen to depart. To earn his livelihood, he became a watchman on a plantation. He married Anna Schindler in 1737. After returning to Europe, he assisted at Hernnhut (1734–38), being last chief elder (1735–41), then served as a missionary to the Jews in Amsterdam (1748–51). Dober was made a bishop in 1747.

Thomas Clap

June 26, 1703
Scituate, Massachusetts

Jan. 7, 1767
New Haven, Connecticut

Rector (CEO) 1740–45 and first president of Yale College (University in 1887), **New Haven, CT 1745–66**. He married Mary Whiting (November 23, 1727) and Mary Haynes (February 5, 1740). Clap pastored the Congregational Church, Windham, CT from 1727–39. A strong Calvinist, he was considered one of the most learned men of his time and was a controversial personality, because of his orthodoxy. A liberal charter was granted in 1745. He wrote about his opposition to WHITEFIELD (1755), which led to his resignation from Yale (1766). He also opposed the methods of JONATHAN EDWARDS. His expulsion of DAVID BRAINERD created a furor.

Lawrence Sterne

Nov. 24, 1713
Clonmel, Ireland

March 18, 1768
London, England

Clergyman, novelist, and humorist. Sterne was ordained an Anglican priest in 1738. He served as a country clergyman near York, while living in a strange manner, 1740–60. His unconventional habits drove his wife, Elizabeth Lumley (married in 1742), insane in 1758. He farmed for a while and then concentrated on writing his nine-volume tome, *The Life and Opinions of Tristram Shandy* (1760–67). He rose to literary fame in 1760 as a result. He also wrote *Sentimental Journey Through France and Italy*.

Joseph Hart

1712
London, England

May 24, 1768
London, England

Powerful preacher remembered for his hymns. Hart wrote the words of "That Dreadful Night" and "Come Ye Sinners, Poor and Needy." Hart was converted in 1757, in the Moravian Chapel, Fetter Lane, London. In 1759 he became pastor of Jewin St. Independent Chapel in London. An ardent Calvinist, he was widely known and loved. Over 20,000 people attended his funeral at Bunhill Fields Cemetery.

Thomas Secker

1693
Aug. 3, 1768
Sibthorpe, England

Archbishop of Canterbury, 1758–68. Secker belonged to a family of Dissenters, but was influenced to conform. He had studied for the practice of medicine, but entered Exeter College, Oxford, in 1721. In 1722, he was ordained deacon, then priest. Secker was rector of Houghton le Spring (1724–27) and Durham (1727–32). He took the rectory of St. James (1733) and was made bishop of Bristol (1735). He was then made bishop of Oxford (1737) and dean of St. Paul's (1750).

Joseph Grigg

c 1720
London, England
Oct. 29, 1768
Walthamstown, England

Presbyterian hymn writer. Grigg's 40 hymns are highlighted by the words for "Behold a Stranger at the Door," "Jesus, Shall It Ever Be?" and "Ashamed of Jesus." He trained for mechanical pursuits but at an early age forsook his trade to become assistant pastor at Silver Street Presbyterian Church in London, retiring in 1747. He then married and took up residence at St. Albans.

Gerhard Tersteegen

Nov. 25, 1697
Moers, Germany
April 3, 1769
Mulheim, Germany

Reformed mystic and noted hymn writer, writing some 111 hymns. Tersteegen was converted at age 16, and in 1724, he wrote out a solemn covenant with God, signed with his own blood. He worked in his business of weaving with a loom for many years. He then left the business world and opened his home as a refuge to the physical and spiritual needs of people at Otterbeck in the Niedervhein region. Tersteegen translated devotional works and directed his mission, Pilgrim's Hut. He led a life of seclusion and self-denial for many years. He ministered in Denmark, Sweden, Pennsylvania, and the Netherlands. He was a mystic and a separatist from established groups.

Edward Holyoke

June 25, 1689
Boston, Massachusetts
June 1, 1769
Cambridge, Massachusetts

President of Harvard College (University in 1780), **Cambridge, MA 1737–69.** He was ordained April 25, 1716. Holyoke married Elizabeth Browne August 8, 1717 (died: August 15, 1719), Margaret Appleton November 9, 1725 (died June 25, 1740) and Mary Epes March 17, 1742 (died: March 23, 1790). He served the Marblehead, MA Congregational Church until 1737. Holyoke was very negative to GEORGE WHITEFIELD's ministry in the area.

Christian F. Gellert

July 4, 1715
Hainichen, Saxony (Germany)
Dec. 13, 1769
Leipzig, Germany

Theologian, philosopher, poet, and hymn writer. His most well-known composition was "Jesus Lives, and I With Him." Gellert studied theology at Leipzig and became a professor of poetry, rhetoric, literature, and moral philosophy there in 1751. Definitely a versatile writer, his most popular book was *Fables* (2 vols., 1746–48). He suffered from hypochondria after 1752. His *Spiritual Odes and Songs* was published in 1757. Many of his hymns were translated into other languages.

His complete works were published in ten volumes, 1769–74. As he died, he said, "Only repeat to me the name of Jesus . . . God be praised, only one hour more." He is buried at St. John's Church, Leipzig.

George Whitefield

Dec. 16, 1714
Gloucester, England

Sept. 30, 1770
Newburyport, Massachusetts

Powerful evangelist whose preaching won many converts in England and America. Whitefield, son of an innkeeper, met the WESLEYS at Oxford. He was converted in March, 1735, at Oxford University and became a "boy preacher." In 1736, he graduated, was ordained a deacon, and began his ministry. He broke with Wesley over predestination and perfectionism. Whitefield came to America in 1738 and began open-air preaching, which was later adopted by the WESLEYS. He became the core of the Great Awakening of 1740. That very same year he condemned WESLEY's "free grace." His marriage to Elizabeth James on November 14, 1741 (died: August 9, 1768), brought one child who died shortly after birth. In 1743, he started the Calvinistic Methodist Society. Whitefield had a regular ministry to the nobility in London. In 1753, he opened his tabernacle in London. He also started an orphanage in Savannah, GA and a seminary in Trevecca, Wales, and then Trevecca College in 1768. At one meeting, Whitefield spoke to over 100,000 people in Glasgow, Scotland. While in America on his seventh visit, he died after preaching from the parsonage balcony of the First Presbyterian Church, where he is buried. He sometimes preached 40 hours a week. Some 18,000 sermons were preached in his lifetime. He made seven trips to America as well as preaching in Wales, Scotland, and Ireland. His favorite Bible verses were John 3:3, 7.

Alexander Cruden

May 31, 1701
Aberdeen, Scotland

Nov. 1, 1770
Islington, London, England

Eccentric Presbyterian and author of a famous concordance. His actions bordered on insanity, yet he was a humble and devout worker in London as a bookseller and corrector of the press from 1732 on. He believed that he was appointed of God to correct the ills of the nation. He is most famous for his *Cruden's Concordance* (1737), which has remained worthy and popular, going through many editions. Cruden never married. He was confined to mental institutions three times.

Christopher Dock

1698
Germany

1771
Pennsylvania

Mennonite schoolmaster who spent most of his life teaching in schools at Skippack, 1718–28, and Salford, PA 1738–71. He came to Pennsylvania around 1712. Dock emphasized religious education and Christian character. He returned to farming 1728–38. He taught both schools in three-day intervals for 33 years, 1738–71. Dock used modern teaching methods and composition exercises, and stressed the importance of constructive writing techniques. He also composed ten hymns.

John Gill

Nov. 23, 1697
Kettering, England

Oct. 14, 1771
London, England

Eminent Baptist pastor and learned Rabbinical scholar. He married Elizabeth Megus in 1718. Converted at age twelve, Gill became pastor in Horsleydown, near London, in 1719, ministering there for 52 years. The church later moved to become Carter Lane Baptist Church in 1757. He was a hyper-Calvinist scholar and theologian. His most important work was his *Exposition of the Old and New Testament* (9 vols., pub. 1746–66). His writings range from *The Doctrine of the Trinity* (1731) to *A Body of Practical Divinity* (1770).

Samuel Johnson (1)

Oct. 14, 1696
Guilford, Connecticut

Jan. 6, 1772
Stratford, Connecticut

First president of King's College (Columbia University in 1784), **NYC 1754–63.** He entered the Congregational ministry (1720), but went to England to receive his Anglican (Episcopal) ordination (1723). Returning to America, he settled in Stratford, CT from 1723–54 and 1763–72. Johnson married Charity Nicoll (September 26, 1725) and Mrs. Sarah Beach (June 18, 1761), and had a family of three children. In 1746, he published *The First Principles of Moral Philosophy*. His last work was *An English and Hebrew Grammar* (1767).

John Woolman

Oct. 19, 1720
Ancocas (Rancocas), New Jersey

Oct. 7, 1772
York, England

Quaker preacher and campaigner against slavery. Woolman was troubled by the wretched condition of the poor and the spiritual condition of the rich. He was a farmer and tailor who traveled widely to rally Quakers to release slaves, 1743–58. He married Sarah Ellis on October 18, 1749. His *Journal* (1774) is recognized as a spiritual classic. He died of smallpox during a trip to England and is buried in York. Woolman wrote a sensitive appeal, *Some Consideration for. . .Negroes* (1754), which created a new look at "slavery." His favorite Bible verse was Revelation 22:1.

David Nitschmann

Dec. 27, 1696
Zauchtenthal, Moravia (Czechoslovakia)

Oct. 8, 1772
Bethlehem, Pennsylvania

Bishop of the Moravian Church in 1735 and pioneer missionary. Nitschmann came to Herrnhut in 1724. He married Rosina Schindler on November 12, 1726 (died: 1753), and later Mary L. Martin in 1754. On a trip to Georgia in 1731, he and 15 others made a deep impression on JOHN WESLEY during the boat trip. He was in charge of the Moravian settlers in Georgia at that time. In 1732, he and LEONARD DOBER went to the Danish West Indies. He organized a settlement in Savannah, GA in 1735 and Bethlehem, PA in 1740. He was at Lititz (1756–61) and Bethlehem (1761–72), PA. His missionary endeavors were in Germany, Denmark, Sweden, Norway, England, and several states in the United States. Nitschmann made at least 50 sea voyages to further the cause of Christ.

Benjamin Ingham

June 11, 1712
Ossett, England

1772
Abberford, England

Evangelist and founder of the sect of Inghamites. He joined the WESLEYS and traveled to Georgia and Germany with JOHN. In 1738, he organized the Moravian Methodists. He married Lady Margaret Hastings of Huntingdon, a distant relative, in 1741. He switched from Methodism to Moravianism (1742), later withdrawing from them (1753). His Inghamite sect grew to some 80 congregations but only 13 remained loyal to him. Sandemanians (founded by Robert Sandeman (1718–71), son-in-law of JOHN GLAS: community of goods, love–feasts, weekly communion, etc.) siphoned off most of these. The defections from his sect was disheartening and, many felt, a factor that hastened his death.

Howell Harris

Jan. 14, 1714
Talgarth, Wales

July 21, 1773
Trevecca, Wales

Renowned evangelist. After Harris' conversion as a village schoolmaster in Talgarth, he preached fervent evangelical sermons to Welsh miners and villagers, often in open–air gatherings. He was converted on May 25, 1735, while taking communion in a church in Talghrai. He married Anne Williams in May, 1744 (died: 1770). He later formed the Welsh Calvinistic Methodist Church. By 1739, some 30 societies were in South Wales and two years later, there were 300. Harris was frequently attacked by the Church of England. WHITEFIELD considered him a good friend, as did WESLEY. He was repeatedly assaulted by mobs, continually persecuted by magistrates and the clergy, and denied ordination on account of the irregularity of his methods. From 1771–73, he was confined to Trevecca.

Philip Embury

c Sept. 1, 1728
Ballingrane, Ireland

Aug. 9, 1773
Camden, New York

First Methodist minister in America. Raised a Lutheran ("baptized" on September 29, 1728), he was converted by WESLEY's preaching on Christmas Day, 1752. He married Margaret Switzer on November 27, 1758. Embury came to New York City (1760) and preached his first New York sermon to five people in his living room (1766), encouraged by his cousin, BARBARA HECK. Being a carpenter, he erected Wesley chapel in 1768 on the present-day site of St. John's Methodist Church. In 1770, Embury moved upstate to a farm in East Salem, NY, then moved to Camden, NY, where he worked as a carpenter and preached. A mowing accident caused his death. He was buried in Cambridge, NY.

George Lyttelton

Jan. 17, 1709
Hagley, England

Aug. 22, 1773
Hagley, England

Statesman and man of letters. He was elected to the House of Commons in 1735–56, after which he was elevated to the House of Lords. Lyttelton was converted about age 38 and had strong religious convictions thereafter. He wrote *Observations on the Conversion and Apostleship of St. Paul* (1747), maintaining that Paul's conversion was proof of his Christianity. As he died, he said, "The evidence of Christianity...made me a firm believer..."

John Glas(s)

Oct. 5, 1695
Auchtermuchty, Scotland

Nov. 2, 1773
Perth, Scotland

Founder of a sect known in Scotland as Glassites, but in America as the Sandemanians. The movement flourished, 1725–1900, and emphasized salvation as the work of Christ. The book was *Testimony of the King of Martyrs* (1727). His congregations had an independent form of government. While pastoring at Tealing, he was deposed by the General Assembly of the Church of Scotland because of a book he published in 1730 that maintained that an "established church" was contrary to Scripture. Glas founded an independent church in Dundee, then built a church in Perth (first to be built there) in 1733. Many Inghamites (Moravian Methodists) joined his group. His writings are scholarly, kindly, and devout.

Thomas Gillespie

1708
Clearburn, Scotland

Jan. 19, 1774
Dunfermline, Scotland

Church of Scotland pastor and founder of the Relief Church in Scotland, October 22, 1761. Gillespie insisted on the independence of a congregation from civil control. His work united with the Secession Church in 1847 to form the Scottish United Presbyterian Church of Scotland. He pastored at Carnock until replaced in 1752, when he formed a congregation in Dunfermline. He promoted missions and welcomed all to his pulpit.

Karl H. Bogatzky

Sept. 7, 1690
Jankowe, Silesia (Poland)

June 15, 1774
Halle, Germany

Pietist author. He served as spiritual advisor in circles of the nobility in Silesia, 1718–40. From 1740–46, he lived at the ducal court of Saalfeld. From 1746 on, by Francke's invitation, Bogatzky lived at the Halle orphanage, and devoted his time to the preparation of devotional literature. Poor health prevented him from taking up active church work. His book, *The Golden Treasury for the Children of God* (1718), had over 60 editions, including one from London in 1888. Bogatzky also wrote several hymns. Later, he combined the pastorate with a small seminary for training ministers. From 1800 on, his seminary undertook the training of 115 missionaries.

Thomas Scott (1)

1705
Hopton, England

1775

Pastor and poet. English dissident minister at Suffolk, 1737–74, Hopton and Ipswich. He published several poetical works. A couple of his well-known hymns were "Hasten, Sinner, to Be Wise," "Angels, Roll the Rock Away," and "Return, O Wanderer, Return."

Peter Boehler

Dec. 31, 1712
Frankfurt-am-Main, Germany

April 27, 1775
London, England

Moravian minister and missionary. He escorted Wesley at sea en route to America in 1735. Boehler had switched from Lutheranism to Moravianism in 1737. Boehler established the Fetter Lane Society in 1738 and traveled to Savannah, GA that same year. Boehler had deeply influenced the Wesleys (led Charles to Christ) who had joined his "Society" in London and who had stayed with him until 1740. He led his followers to Bethlehem, PA (1740), then returned to England (1741). He married Elizabeth Hobson on February 29, 1742. He returned again to England, 1747–53, becoming a bishop in 1748. He served in Bethlehem once again (1753–64) and was made assistant superintendent of the Moravians in America in 1756, after serving as third president of the Moravian Church in North America (1753–54). Boehler died of a stroke and was buried in a Moravian cemetery in Chelsea, England.

Aaron Williams

1731
London, England

1776
London, England

Hymn writer. Composer of the music for such hymns as, "I Love Thy Kingdom, Lord" (lyrics by William Merrill) (same tune as "Rise Up, O Men of God" (Dwight), "Holy Ghost Is Here" (Spurgeon), and "Come, We That Love the Lord" (Watts). He taught music in London, and was a music engraver and publisher. He served as clerk at the Scottish Church, London Wall. His first publication was *Universal Psalmodist* (1763).

Nathan Hale

June 6, 1755
Coventry, Connecticut

Sept. 22, 1776
New York, New York

American patriot. He was sent by General George Washington in September of 1776, to gather intelligence on the British position. Hale was raised in the First Congregational Church. He entered college at age 14. In 1776, Hale went to gather information on Long Island, NY (disguised as a schoolteacher), and was captured on his return trip on September 21, 1776. Hale served well as a ranger and a spy. He died at age 21. His execution was ordered by General William Howe (1729–1814). Prior to his hanging by the British, this faithful and godly young man said:

"I only regret that I have but one life to lose for my country"

William Tennent, Jr.

Jun. 3, 1705
County Armagh, Ireland

March 8, 1777
Freehold, New Jersey

Pastored the Presbyterian Church of Freehold, NJ 1732–77. William studied under his father at their "log college" with his famed brother, GILBERT. Sometime before 1730, he was almost buried alive, but an alert physician saw a slight tremor from the presumed dead body and after three days, William revived completely. He had at least three children by Catherine Noble, whom he married on August 23, 1738.

Carl Linnaeus

May 23, 1707
Rashult, Sweden

Jan. 10, 1778
Upsala, Sweden

Swedish botanist. He was the son of a Lutheran clergyman. Called the father of modern taxonomy (scientific technique of classification), Linnaeus invented the binomial (general and specific) method of plant and animal classification (and also minerals). In 1739, he married Sara E. Moraea. In 1741 he became professor of medicine and botany at Upsala University, remaining there the rest of his life. King Gustavus III (ruled: 1771–92) honored him in 1761 with a patent of nobility. All of his most important works begin and end with some verse of Scripture. His diary contains many indications of his reverence for and gratitude to God. In 1774 he suffered a stroke and eventually was almost reduced to poverty.

Thomas A. Arne

March 12, 1710
London, England

March 5, 1778
London, England

Composed the music for ISAAC WATTS' great hymn, "Am I a Soldier of the Cross," (1762). Arne married Celia Young in 1740, and after completing a law course, he turned his efforts to music. Arne composed two oratorios, *Judith* (1764) and *Abel* (1774), plus 13 masques (dramatic presentation with mythological theme) and operas, including *Alfred* (1740) with the famed finale, "Rule Britannia" and "Artaxerxes." He was among the first to introduce women's voices into choral writings and oratoric chorus. Arne set many of SHAKESPEARE's lyrics to music. His sister, Susanna Arne Cibber (1714–66), was a solo singer in HANDEL's *Messiah* and a strong supporter of her brother's efforts. He is buried at St. Paul's Cathedral, Covent Garden, London.

Augustus M. Toplady

Nov. 4, 1740
Farnham, England

Aug. 14, 1778
Kensington, London, England

Anglican priest and vicar, hymn writer of "Rock of Ages," (1775) (music by THOMAS HASTINGS in 1830). James Morris, a Methodist lay preacher, was responsible for his conversion in 1755. Augustus Toplady pastored in Blagdon (1762), Fareligh (1764), Harpford (1766), Broad Hembury (1768), and a French Calvinist Church, Leicester Fields, London (1775). As an ardent Calvinist, he was an outspoken critic of Wesleyan theology from 1770 onward, writing such works as historic proof of *The Doctrinal Calvinism of the Church of England* (1774). He was a popular and powerful preacher. He died from tuberculosis, and was buried at Whitfield's Tabernacle, London. His favorite Bible verse was Ephesians 2:8. He co-authored with DODDRIDGE, "Grace 'Tis a Charming Sound" (music by SANKEY).

Anne Steele

1716
Broughton, England

Nov. 11, 1778
Broughton, England

Author of many well-known hymns. Anne was the daughter of a local Baptist minister, who was baptized on July 9, 1732. She became a life long invalid as a result of a severe hip injury at age 19. Two years later, her fiance´ drowned the day before they were to be married. Her poems were in *Poems on Subjects Chiefly Devotional* (2 vol. in 1760) and *Miscellaneous Pieces in Verse and Prose* (1780) when a third volume was added. Among her well-known hymns were, "Lord of My Life" and "To Jesus, Our Exalted Lord." She wrote 144 hymns and 34 versified Psalms.

James C. Cook

Oct. 28, 1728
Marton, England

Feb. 14, 1779
Kealakekua, Hawaii

Navigator and explorer. Cook made three unparalleled expeditions: first, to Australia, New Zealand, and much of the South Pacific including Tahiti (1768–71), claiming the land masses for England; second, to Antarctica (1772–75), and thirdly to the Arctic regions (1776–79). He also charted the Pacific Coast of North America from Oregon to the Bering Strait on the final tour. On this last trip, he also rediscovered the Sandwich Islands (Hawaii) where he was killed by natives, when he went ashore, armed to recover one of his stolen vessels.

Eleazar Wheelock

April 22, 1711
Windham, Connecticut

April 24, 1779
Hanover, New Hampshire

Clergyman, missionary, founder and first president of Dartmouth College (University in 1816), **Hanover, NH 1770–79.** He married Mrs. Sarah Malty (April 29, 1735) and Mary Brimstead (Nov. 21, 1747) and had eleven children. As the second Congregational minister, 1735–70, at Lebanon, CT, he had specific concerns for education of the Indians. Wheelock also had a burden to train white missionaries. He tutored youths in his Massachusetts home and opened a private academy known as Moors Indian Charity School, 1754–68. In 1767 he raised 12,000 pounds in England and Scotland for his school. In 1769 it was moved to Hanover and renamed Dartmouth. Dartmouth was the only college in New England to stay open during the Revolutionary War and was named for the Earl of Dartmouth.

William Warburton

Dec. 24, 1698
Newark, England

June 7, 1779
Gloucester, England

Church of England bishop of Gloucester, 1760 on. He was chaplain to the king (1754), prebendary of Durham (1755) and dean of Bristol (1757). Warburton authored *The Alliance Between Church and State* (1736—defending the primacy of episcopacy), and *The Doctrine of Grace* (1762—fiercely attacking Methodism). He also was an opponent of slavery and the deists.

William E. Blackstone (1)

July 10, 1723
London, England

Feb. 14, 1780
London, England

Jurist and first professor of English law at Oxford University, 1758. He wrote *Commentaries on the Laws of England* (4 vol. 1765–69), the basic legal textbook in Britain for over a century. In 1746 he began his law practice. Blackstone married (1761) and also became a member of Parliament, and then became solicitor general to the queen (1763). After leaving Parliament the last time in 1770, he was made a justice of common pleas. He said, "The belief in a future state or rewards and punishments…and a firm persuasion that He superintends and will finally compensate every action in human life (all of which are clearly revealed in the doctrines and precepts of our Saviour Christ)—these are the grand foundations of all judicial oaths…"

John Andre

May 2, 1750
London, England

Oct. 2, 1780
Tappan, New York

Executed by hanging as a spy during the Revolutionary War. Two days before his execution, he was converted, and in his last two days, wrote a poem entitled "My Hiding Place." One verse states, "A few more setting suns at most, Shall land me on fair Canaan's coast, Where I shall sing the song of grace, and see my glorious Hiding Place." In November 1776, he joined the British army in New York City. He participated in 1777, in the Bloody Padi, PA bayonet massacre of American troops. In April 1779, he was put in charge of intelligence. He took a leading part in the capture of Charleston, SC. He was caught near Tarrytown, NY on Sept. 23 by three American military personnel. He had just spent time with traitor, Benedict Arnold (1741–1801), behind American lines. His gallant behavior caused even his enemies to mourn for him. He was reinterred in Westminster Abbey in London in 1821. He was single. On the scaffold, he said, "It will be but a momentary pang."

Naphtali Daggett

Sept. 8, 1727
Attleboro, Massachusetts

Nov. 25, 1780
New Haven, Connecticut

Second president of Yale College (University in 1887), **New Haven, CT 1766–77.** He married Sarah Smith on December 19, 1753. After being ordained in the Presbyterian church, he pastored on Long Island. He began teaching at Yale, in 1756, as the first professor, when only tutors and the president taught. He resigned after students petitioned for his removal. Daggett took part in the defense of New Haven, CT and was captured by the British in 1779. Daggett also wrote three books.

Robert Strawbridge

Drumsna, Ireland

Aug. 1781
Near Townson, Maryland

Independent Methodist preacher in the American colonies. Strawbridge came to America sometime between 1759–66, and settled on Sam's Creek in Maryland. He erected a log chapel, thought by many to be the first Methodist meetinghouse built in America. He refused to submit to the rules of the Conference, moderated by THOMAS RANKIN in 1773. In 1776, he moved his family to a farm and continued to preach. He worked independently of the Conference and of the superintendent (feeling no need of ecclesiastical approval) preaching with great success in Sam's Creek and Bush Forest societies. Independent all the way, his influence for the growth of the Methodist Church seems to have been far-reaching.

Johann A. Ernesti

Aug. 4, 1707
Tennstadt, Germany

Sept. 11, 1781
Leipzig, Germany

Lutheran philologist and theologian. Ernesti gave a great impetus to serious Biblical scholarship. He was rector of the Leipzig Thomasschule, 1734–59. He began his illustrious career as professor of ancient literature (1742), adding rhetoric (1756) and theology (1758) at the University of Leipzig. He taught until 1780. Ernesti insisted that careful rules of interpretation be used in biblical studies (grammatical analysis over symbolic interpretation). He tried to reconcile traditional Lutheran beliefs with biblical scholarship holding to the inspiration of the Bible, but, nevertheless, made concession to the rationalistic tendency of his time. His principal theological work is *Institution Interpretis of the New Testament* (1761), thought in Latin and wrote in German.

Nathaniel Seidel

Oct. 2, 1718
Lauban, Silesia (Germany)

May 17, 1782
Bethlehem, Pennsylvania

President of Moravian Church in NA (North), Bethlehem, PA 1766–82. Upon his conversion, Seidel joined the Moravian church at Herrnhut, Germany (1739), then came to Bethlehem, PA (1742), to engage in evangelistic work. He ministered amongst the Indians and white settlers. In 1758, he was consecrated a bishop, and after ZINZENDORF's death, followed him in the above-mentioned positions. He married Anna J. Piesch on October 30, 1760. He also ministered in the West Indies.

Richard Boardman

1738
Ireland

Oct. 4, 1782
Cork, Ireland

Evangelist. He came to America in 1769 with JOSEPH PILMOOR. Boardman began a mission in New York in the John Street Church, which was established a year earlier by PHILIP EMBURY. Although he did his chief work there, he was an evangelist and often exchanged pulpits with PILMOOR of Philadelphia. Boardman returned to England in 1774 and continued evangelistic work in England and Ireland.

Benjamin F. Kennicott

April 4, 1718
Totnes, England

Aug. 18, 1783
Oxford, England

English Biblical scholar. Kennicott's fame rests upon his lifework, a critical study of the Hebrew text/manuscripts of the Old Testament. He had numerous positions, some of them overlapping: fellow of Exeter College (1747–71), vicar of Culham (1753–83), librarian at Oxford (1767–83), canon of Christ Church Oxford (1770–83), and vicar of Menheniot (1771–81). His research (Hebrew Bible) was published between 1776–80 in two volumes. His dissertations at Oxford were so highly received there, that he was made a fellow of Exeter College. He preferred studying from the Samaritan Pentateuch.

Henry Alline

June 14, 1748
Newport, Rhode Island

Feb. 2, 1784
New Hampton, New Hampshire

Leader of a great awakening in Nova Scotia. His family moved in 1760 to Falmouth. Converted, March 26, 1775, he became an evangelist and reached much of the Maritime Provinces. This stimulated the growth of New Light Congregational Churches as well as Baptist churches. Returning to New England in 1783, he made an extensive preaching tour before he died of tuberculosis. He wrote *The Anti-Traditionalist* (1783) and *Two Mites* (1802), showing the influence of WILLIAM LAW. He wrote some 500 hymns, and his *Hymns and Spiritual Songs* (1786) was reprinted by the Free Will Baptists of New England.

Thomas Maxfield

c 1720

March 18, 1784

First regular lay preacher enlisted by JOHN WESLEY. Maxfield was converted under JOHN WESLEY's preaching on May 21, 1739. He helped set the pattern in Methodism in which laymen were widely used. His visions included an end-of-the-world prediction for February 22, 1763. His wife, Elizabeth Branford died in 1777. Maxfield grew ambitious and made life miserable for the WESLEYS by denouncing and opposing them.

Ann Lee Standerlin
Mrs. Abraham Standerlin

Feb. 29, 1736
Manchester, England

Sept. 8, 1784
Watervliet, New York

Founder of the Shaker movement which spread throughout New England. Ann was an illiterate factory worker and daughter of an English blacksmith. She was married to Abraham Standerlin on January 5, 1762, and had four children, all of whom died in infancy. Once she embraced the tenets of a segmented Quaker faction (1758), she took an oath of celibacy and thus negated her marriage vows (1766). She was often imprisoned in England for performing peculiar "shaking" behavior while witnessing on behalf of her faith. In 1774, she and seven followers emigrated to America and founded a settlement, called Watervliet, near Albany, NY in 1775–76.

Phyllis Wheatley
Mrs. John Peters

c 1753
Senegal, Africa

Dec. 5, 1784
Boston, Massachusetts

African-American poet. In 1761, John Wheatley purchased a seven-year old slave girl, christened her Phyllis, and treated her as a family member. Encouraged to read the Bible and classical literature, she learned how to write poetry. She studied JOHN MILTON and copied his style, writing her first verses when she was but 13. In 1770, she published her first work *On the death of George Whitefield*. In 1773, the Wheatleys gave her freedom and took her to London where she astonished the British aristocracy with her poetry. She was invited to the court of King George II (reigned: 1727–60). GEORGE WASHINGTON would read her poetry. In 1778, she married John Peters, a free black, but it was not a happy marriage. She had three children and ended up in poverty working in a boardinghouse.

Samuel Johnson (2)

Sept. 18, 1709
Lichfield, England

Dec. 13, 1784
London, England

Moralist, essayist and lexicographer dictionary compiler. His colorful character is revealed in James Boswell's (1740–95) biography of him. He married Elizabeth Porter on July 9, 1735. In 1737 he began to write for the *Gentleman's Magazine*. Johnson's greatest accomplishments were *Dictionary of English Language* (40,000 definitions, 1755) and the ten-volume *The Lives of the Poets* (1781). His *Prayers* reveal his depth as a Christian. He was a Tory and an Anglican. This famed critic and lexicographer was blind in one eye. Some of his last words were, "I have prayed that I may render up my soul to God unclouded". His favorite Bible verse was Luke 12:48.

John W. Fletcher

Sept. 12, 1729
Nyon, Switzerland

Aug. 14, 1785
Madeley, England

Wesley's closest associate (besides his brother Charles). He was known for his saintly life and diligent pastoral labors. He was converted in England, Jan. 24, 1755, at age 26, via a dream (standing before God). He later became a strong Arminian and zealous Methodist evangelist in the Anglican Church in 1757. From 1760–85, he pastored at Madeley. Fletcher also presided over Selina Hastings College, Trevecca, Wales, 1768–70, and established Sunday schools there. He married Polly (Mary) Bosanquet (Sept. 12, 1739–Sept. 4, 1815) on Nov 12, 1781, who was exactly ten years younger than he. His wife was known as a shepherdess of orphans. Poet Robert Southey (1774–1843) said of Fletcher, "No age or country has ever produced a man of more fervent piety." An epidemic of fever was raging locally and took his life. Wesley said, "So unblameable a man in every respect I have not found either in Europe or America".

John Brown
Brown of Haddington

1722
Carpow, Scotland

June 19, 1787
Haddington, Scotland

Pastor and educator. He served as pastor of the Burgher branch of the Secession Church in Haddington (1751–87) and taught in a school of theology (1769–87). Brown taught himself Hebrew, Latin, and Greek. His works range from *A Short Catechism* (1764) to *Compenduous History of the British Churches* (1788). He wrote a *Dictionary of the Bible* (1769). He said as he died, "My Christ!" His *Self-Interpreting Bible* (1778) is still being reprinted.

Henry M. Muhlenberg

Sept. 6, 1711
Einbeck, Germany

Oct. 7, 1787
New Providence (Trappe), Pennsylvania

Founder of the Lutheran Church in America. Sent by August Francke, he emigrated to Philadelphia in 1741. and married Anna M. Weiser on April 22, 1745, who gave him eleven children —six of which were sons. Muhlenberg organized the first Lutheran synod in America on August 14, 1748, and reorganized the Philadelphia congregation in 1762 under a constitution adopted by most later Lutheran congregations. Muhlenberg died with Paul Gerhardt's hymn "Commit Thou All Thy Griefs" on his lips and was buried in New Providence, NJ. He had three well-known sons.

Charles Wesley

Dec. 18, 1707
Epworth, England

March 29, 1788
London, England

Writer of over 7,270 hymns, second only to Fanny Crosby in number of songs created. Along with Issac Watts, Wesley was instrumental in introducing hymn singing to the world. In 1729, he helped organize "The Holy Club" at Oxford. Charles was converted via Peter Boehler, in his home following his attending a Moravian service on May 21, 1738, a few days before his brother, John Wesley's conversion. He was the 18th child of Susannah and Samuel Wesley. He married Sarah Gwynne (1726–1822) on April 8, 1749, and they had eight children. He traveled constantly until 1756. They lived in Bristol (1756–71) and then in London (1771–88). Charles gave the world such memorable hymns as: "And Can it Be," "Jesus, Lover of My Soul" (1738), "O for One Thousand Tongues," "Christ the Lord Is Risen Today" (1739), "Love Divine" (1747) "I Do Believe," and "A Charge to Keep" (1762). He wrote "Hark, The Herald Angels Sing" (1730) from the inspiration of walking to church and hearing bells ring on Christmas morning. John was unable to attend his funeral as he got the message too late. His last hymn was on Hosea 14:2. He is buried at Marylebone Parish Church, London.

John Darwall

Jan. 13, 1731
Haughton, England

Dec. 18, 1789
Walsall, England

English composer, who wrote the music for "Rejoice, the Lord is King". In 1769, Darwall became the pastor of St. Matthew's Parish Church in Walsall, serving there until his death. In addition to two volumes of piano sonatas, he composed tunes for all of the 150 Psalms of Tate and Brady's New Version. Unfortunately, only his musical setting of Psalm 148 (mentioned above) has survived.

John Howard
The Philanthropist

Sept. 2, 1726
Hackney, London, England

Jan. 20, 1790
Kherson, Russia

Congregational layman who is revered as the Father of Prison Reform. Howard was shocked at the conditions in jails. In 1773, he was the sheriff of Bedfordshire. He pushed Parliament to improve prison conditions in 1774 and founded a Penal Reform League. He toured Europe in 1778, 1781, 1783 and 1785. Howard also championed the fight against the deadly bubonic plague (camp fever), which killed him by the Black Sea, as he was studying Russian military hospitals. As he died, he said, "Place a sundial over my grave, and let me be forgotten." He wrote about his discoveries. His favorite Bible verse was Psalms 17:15.

Joseph Bellamy

Feb. 20, 1719
Cheshire, Connecticut

March 6, 1790
Bethlehem, Connecticut

Congregational theologian, educator and pastor in Bethlehem, CT from 1738 until his death, 52 years later. He married Frances Sherman on April 27, 1744 and Abiah Burbank in 1786. Next to JONATHAN EDWARDS, he was the most influential churchman in colonial times. He also wrote *True Religion Delineated* (1750) and *The Halfway Covenant* (1769). His most famous work was *The Wisdom of God in The Permission of Sin* (1758). JONATHAN EDWARDS, JR., SAMUEL HOPKINS, and Bellamy promoted New England theology, which said, "God inclines the will to man able to respond to salvation." His last words were, "I will tell them there forever 'Jesus is precious'."

Robert Robinson

Sept. 27, 1735
Swaffham, England

June 8, 1790
Showell Green/Birmingham, England

Hymnwriter and pastor. He wrote, "Come Thou Fount of Every Blessing," 1758 (music by John Wyeth). He was converted (as a cleric) in 1755, three years after hearing WHITEFIELD. Next, he pastored a Calvinistic Methodist Chapel in Mindenhall, Suffolk, before taking the Stone Yard Church, Cambridge, 1761–90. Later he turned toward Socinianism. Late in life while talking to a lady about his famed hymn, he said, ". . . I am the poor unhappy man who wrote that hymn. . . I would give 1,000 worlds . . . to enjoy the feelings I had then".

Michael Schlatter

July 14, 1716
St. Gall, Switzerland

Oct. 31, 1790
Chestnut Hill, Philadelphia, Pennsylvania

German Reformed minister who pioneered and organized the German Reformed Church in America, bringing twelve congregations together in 1747. This movement is now part of the United Church of Christ. He came to Pennsylvania in 1746, married Maria Schleidorm, and raised nine children. He was superintendent of schools in Philadelphia (1754–56), then a British army chaplain (1756–59) after his capture by the British. He then pastored in Philadelphia. Several times Schlatter returned to Europe to raise funds for the fledgling ministry. His support of the American Revolution put him in prison in 1777.

William Williams

Feb. 11, 1717
Cefn-y-coed, Wales

Jan. 11, 1791
Pant-y-Celyn, Wales

Calvinistic Methodist evangelist and hymn writer of about 800 Welsh hymns. They include the famed "Guide Me, O Thou Great Jehovah" (music by John Hughes), 1745. Ordained deacon in the Anglican Church in 1740, he soon left it upon hearing HOWELL HARRIS preach, and became identified with the WESLEYS, then the Calvinist Methodists. Williams traveled over 96,000 miles during his 43 years of preaching. He lived in Pant-y-Celyn, 1749–91. Outside of CHRISTMAS EVANS and EVANS ROBERTS, he was the most outstanding Welsh revivalist in history. He is buried at the Church of Llamfair one mile north of Llandovery.

John Wesley

June 17, 1703
Epworth, England

March 2, 1791
London, England

Father of Methodism, renowned evangelist and one of the hardest working men in history. As the fifteenth of 19 children, he barely escaped a parsonage fire at age six. After some early religious activity at Oxford ("Holy Club"), he tutored there (1729–35), then went to Georgia in America, along with 26 German Moravians (1735–37). He returned to London where he was converted on May 24, 1738 at a Moravian meeting at St. Pauls on Aldersgate Street. John began to preach and organize "societies" wherever he went, throughout England, Scotland, and Ireland. On June 25, 1744, the first Methodist Conference in London was held. He kept a daily diary for over 50 years (longest on record). His February 18, 1751 marriage to Mary Vazeille (1710–October 8, 1781) was an unhappy one. She left him in 1776. He organized Methodist societies (1740) which officially left the Church of England (1784). He founded the *Arminian Magazine* (1778). As an evangelist, he traveled over 250,000 miles on horseback and preached 40,000 sermons, and wrote over 200 works. His favorite Bible verses were Mark 12:34 and Romans 8:1–2. He is buried in City Road Chapel, London.

"Cleanliness is next to godliness."

Selina Shirley Hastings
Mrs. Theophilus Hastings, Lady Huntingdon

Aug. 24, 1707
Stanton Harold, England

June 17, 1791
London, England

Methodist, Calvinist philanthropist. Selina married Thomas Hastings, Earl of Huntingdon, in June of 1728, and they had six children. She was converted, after her marriage, as a result of an almost fatal illness and by the witness of her sister-in-law, Margaret Hastings. The first Methodist Conference was held at her house in 1744. Upon her husband's death in 1746, she devoted herself completely to spreading WHITEFIELD's message, considering him as her private chaplain. Selina embraced Calvinism after correspondence with HOWELL HARRIS, which shifted her support from WESLEY, whose meetings she attended in Fetter Lane, to WHITEFIELD. Through her social position she was able to bring WHITEFIELD into contact with men of the upper classes. She founded schools for clergy (including the seminary at Trevecca, Wales, in 1768), built 64 chapels (which in 1781 were registered as dissenting places of worship), and supported them. She also wrote hymns. She had a ruptured blood vessel and lingered from November to June. After eight months of illness, she whispered, "I shall go to my Father tonight." Her favorite Bible verse was I Corinthians 3:11. She is buried at St. Helens Church, Leicester, England.

James Manning

Oct. 22, 1735
Piscataway, New Jersey

July 29, 1791
Providence, Rhode Island

Baptist minister who founded Rhode Island (Brown University in 1804) **University, Providence, Rhode Island, and was its first president, 1765–91.** Beginning with one student, the school started as a Baptist seminary in Warren, RI from 1760–65. He married Margaret Stites on March 23, 1763. Converted in a Baptist church in his hometown, he pastored Baptist churches in Warren, and at FBC, Providence. Manning founded the Warren Association of New England Baptists in 1767. In 1786, he was elected to represent the state at the Continental Congress for the framing of the federal constitution.

Edward Perronet

Aug. 2, 1721
Shoreham/Sundridge, England

Jan. 2, 1792
Canterbury, England

Independent evangelist who wrote the hymn, "All Hail the Power of Jesus' Name" (1779). In 1749, he traveled with WESLEY in northern England, serving as an evangelist for eight years. Ridiculed by the Church of England, Perronet became one of SELINA HASTINGS' chaplains. Having tendencies toward the extreme and sensational, Perronet chose to end his preaching career at a Congregational chapel in Canterbury, ground "sacred" to the Church of England crowd. He is buried in Canterbury Cathedral, Kent.

Samson Occom

c 1723
Mohegan, Connecticut

July 14, 1792
New Stockbridge, New York

Presbyterian Mohegan Indian evangelist. Occom was converted at age 17 upon hearing WHITEFIELD. He married Mary Fowler in 1751, and had ten children. Occom labored with the Montauk Indians of Long Island, NY from 1749–64, and was ordained a Presbyterian in 1759. Occom visited England, 1765–68 and raised 45,000 pounds for ELEAZAR WHEELOCK's Indian school (later incorporated as Dartmouth College) in Lebanon, CT. He published *Choice Collection of Hymns and Spiritual Songs* (1774). He traveled as an evangelist 1768–89. From 1789–92, he pastored in Brothertown which was in Oneidas Indian territory. He is buried southwest of Kirkland, NY.

August G. Spangenberg

July 15, 1704
Klettenberg, Prussia, Germany

Sept. 18, 1792
Herrhut/Berthelsdorf, Germany

First president of Moravian Church in NA (North), Bethlehem, PA 1744–1748, 1751–1753, and 1754–1762 and successor of Zinzendorf in Germany in 1762. He was ZINZENDORF's assistant (1733) then became bishop (1744). He traveled the world and went to America, (1735–39); to Germany, (1739–41); to England (1741–44), to Pennsylvania (1744–52), to North Carolina (1752–62) and back to Germany, (1762–93). Spangenberg was active in missionary work among colonists and Indians. He stabilized the Moravian movement from some of ZINZENDORF's oddities. Two children resulted from his marriages to Eva Immig and Mary Miksch on March 5, 1740. In 1782 he produced the first summary of Moravian mission work.

John Hatton

c 1710
Warrington, England

Buried—Dec. 13, 1793
St. Helens, England

Song composer of "Jesus Shall Reign" (1793) (lyrics by ISAAC WATTS). Hatton lived on Duke Street in Windle. His funeral was held in the Presbyterian Chapel, his death possibly occurring a couple of days earlier.

Anne Cutler

1759
Preston, England

1794

Prayer warrior. Anne was used to bring revivals in the mining and weaving towns of North England. WILLIAM BRAMWELL, revivalist, credits her intercessory prayers as a vital part of his endeavors. She was converted under him. She would pray from midnight to 4 or 5 AM pleading for herself, the society, the preachers, and the Church. Her last words were, "I am going to die. Glory be to God and the Lamb forever" and at 35, she was in heaven.

Paul Rabaut

Jan. 29, 1718
Bedarieux, France

Sept. 25, 1794
Nimes, France

Reformed pastor of "The Church of the Desert." In 1739, he married Madeleine Gaidan. He assumed leadership of the Huguenots on the death of ANTOINE COURT in 1760. His patient restraint helped to achieve the Edict of Toleration of 1787 {statute of William and Mary to grant Protestant dissenters from Church of England freedom of worship}. Because a large price was on his head if captured, Rabaut performed pastoral duties under utmost secrecy, still preaching to over 10,000 people. He was associated with the church in Nimes all his life.

John Witherspoon

Feb. 5, 1723
Gifford, Scotland

Nov. 15, 1794
near Princeton, New Jersey

President of Princeton (NJ) College (University in 1898), 1768–94. Prior to his work in America, Witherspoon pastored in Scotland: Beith (1744–57) and Paisley (1757–68). He was a Presbyterian minister and the only clergyman to sign the Declaration of Independence. He married Elizabeth Montgomery (September 2, 1748) and Ann Dill (May 30, 1791), having a family of twelve children. Witherspoon's quiet, direct manner had tremendous influence on others. He was the New Jersey representative to the Continental Congress, 1776–82. The last four years of his life were spent in total blindness. His favorite Bible verse was Ephesians 5:16.

"Only the fear of God can deliver from the fear of men"

Ezra Stiles

Dec. 15, 1725
North Haven, Connecticut

May 12, 1795
New Haven, Connecticut

Third President of Yale College (University in 1887), **New Haven, CT 1777–95.** He raised academic standards and helped reconcile warring factions. Prior to his years at Yale, he had a law practice and pastored Second Congregational Church in Newport, RI (1755–77), after tutoring at Yale, (1749–55). He married Elizabeth Hubbard (Feb. 10, 1757) and Mary Checkley (Oct. 17, 1782), resulting in eight children. Stiles was an ardent patriot during the Revolution. Stiles was professor of divinity and church history at Yale from 1780–95. He helped found what is now Brown University.

William Romaine

Sept. 25, 1714
Hartlepool, England

July 26, 1795
London, England

Church of England evangelical divine who became a popular preacher. After 1755, he followed WHITEFIELD. For many years Romaine drew large congregations in London, first at St. Anne's, Blackfriars (1762), and then at St. Andrews of the Wardrobe (1764), where he was a popular preacher until his death. His extreme Calvinism was expounded in *The Life of Faith*, *The Walk of Faith*, and *The Triumph of Faith*.

Samuel Stennett

June 1, 1727
Exeter, England

Aug. 24, 1795
London, England

Baptist pastor and hymn writer. He wrote the lyrics for two beloved hymns in 1787, "Majestic Sweetness" (music by THOMAS HASTINGS) and "On Jordan's Stormy Banks I Stand" (music by RIGDON MCINTOSH). He pastored a Baptist church on Little Wild Street in London from 1758–95. Then, he preached for 20 years at a Seventh Day Baptist Church, while still continuing his Sunday services at his regular church. Samuel was the grandson of hymn writer, JOSEPH STENNETT.

Samuel Seabury

Nov. 30, 1729
North Groton (Ledyard), Connecticut

Feb. 25, 1796
New London, Connecticut

First presiding bishop of Protestant Episcopal Church (Episcopal Church in 1967), **1785–96.** He married Mary Hicks on October 12, 1756, and had at least six children. After his ordination in England, he served Christ Church in New Brunswick, NJ from 1753–57. He served at Grace Church in Jamaica, NY (1757–66), and at St. Peter's in Westchester, NY, (1766–75). He was a guide to the British army in 1776. He was made bishop on Nov. 14, 1784, with a diocese including Connecticut and Rhode Island. He served as rector of St. James' Church in New London, 1784–96.

Felice de Giardini

April 12, 1716
Turin, Italy

June 8, 1796
Moscow, Russia

Musical composer for "Come Thou Almighty King," (1769) **and "Shepherd of Eager Youth"** (lyrics by Clement of Alexandria). Giardini played violin in opera orchestra in Rome and Naples. He became well known through concerts (voice and violin) in Italy, a Germany tour (1748), and concerts in London (1750). From 1752–84, he lived in London as a violinist, teacher, and conductor, befriended by SELINA HASTINGS. He died in the third month of a concert tour in Russia.

Peter Williams

Jan. 7, 1722
Llansadurnin, Wales

Aug. 8, 1796
Llandyfeilog, Wales

Calvinistic Methodist evangelist. He was converted under WHITEFIELD as a boy. He left the Church of England because of their objections to his fervent preaching in 1746. After being expelled by the Welsh Calvinist Methodists for heresy, he formed his own chapel on Water Street, Carmarthen in 1791. Williams published a Welsh hymnbook, a Welsh Bible, a concordance and *Hymns on Various Subjects*.

Benjamin V. Abbott

1732
Pennsylvania

Aug. 14, 1796
Salem, New Jersey

Methodist evangelist. Although he was unlearned, Abbott possessed great natural speaking ability, which he used to convert thousands. On October 12, 1772, he was converted by the preaching of Abraham Whitworth and became a spellbinding frontier evangelist who drew great crowds. Abbott strongly attacked Calvinism and was responsible for the conversion of much of southern New Jersey to Methodism. He was a local preacher (1773–89), then went on various circuits (1789–93), before going to Maryland in 1793.

Thomas Webb

1724
England

Dec. 20, 1796
Bristol, England

Methodist preacher and soldier. He served as a captain in the British army and was badly wounded (lost an eye) in the Battle of Quebec in 1759. He was married twice, once to Mary Arding in 1760. After he was converted in Bristol under JOHN WESLEY (1765), he came to America (1766). Webb became a fervent evangelist and helped Methodism, especially in New York and Philadelphia. Webb built the Portland Chapel in Bristol from his own expense and settled there in 1783.

Henry Venn

March 2, 1724
Barnes, England

June 24, 1797
Yelling, England

Prominent leader of the evangelical revival in the Church of England. Known for his piety and earnestness, he pastored in Clapham (1754), Huddersfield (1759), and Yelling (1771). Venn engaged in evangelistic efforts with his friend WHITEFIELD and shared in LADY HUNTINGDON's outreach endeavors. His most popular book was *The Complete Duty of Man*. He gave a funeral oration for GEORGE WHITEFIELD (1770) and often preached as much as ten times a week.

Joseph Milner

Jan. 2, 1744
Leeds, England

Nov. 15, 1797
Hull, England

Church historian and evangelical clergyman. As headmaster of the Latin school and evening preacher in Hull, Milner made the city a center for evangelism. Milner was also a founder of the "Evangelical School" of the Church of England, begun about 1770, when he became a recluse. However, he exhorted constantly the themes of repentance and revival. He wrote the first three volumes of *History of the Church of Christ* (1794–97) with his brother ISAAC, who completed the last two in 1798.

Christian F. Schwartz

Oct. 26, 1726
Sonnenburg (Stonsk), Prussia (Poland)

Feb. 13, 1798
Tanjore (Thanjavur), India

Lutheran missionary evangelist to India. Upon leaving the University of Halle, he went to South India in 1750, and served there for 48 years (without furlough) until his death. He never married. He won multiple converts yet maintained esteem from both Muslim and Hindu leaders. Schwartz spent ten years in Tranquebar (1750–60), visited Ceylon (Sri Lanka, 1760) then 16 years at Trichinopoli (1762–78), before leaving the Danish Mission and ministering on his own. He became an English chaplain in 1767. He went to Tanjore in 1778.

Jeremy Belknap

June 4, 1744
Boston, Massachusetts

June 20, 1798
Boston, Massachusetts

Congregational Pastor and one of the founders of the Massachusetts Historical Society, 1794. Belknap was a Harvard graduate in 1762, noted historian and author, producing theological, historical, and biographical material. Belknap held two pastorates, one in Dover, NH (1766–86) and the other at the Federal Street Church, Boston (1787–98). He married Ruth Eliot in 1767. His books included: *History of New Hampshire* (1784–92), *Sacred Poetry: Consisting of Psalms and Hymns Adapted to Christian Devotion in Public and Private* (1795), and *American Biographies* (2 vol. 1794–98) which established his research credibility. Belknap's primary hymn contribution was, "O'er Mountain Tops, the Mount of God."

John Barclay

1734
Muthill, Scotland

July 29, 1798
Edinburgh, Scotland

Berean founder. This eccentric Church of Scotland minister was dismissed from his congregation (assistant minister at Fettercairn) because of his peculiar traits and interpretations of Scripture. He was an assistant minister in Errol and Fettercairn, 1759–72. He founded a sect known as "Bereans" (Acts 17:2) or, more popularly, "Barclayites", which flourished for a time at Edinburgh (1766) and London (1776). His book *Christ All in All* (1766) expresses his views. The group later merged with the Congregationalists.

Alexander Kilham

July 10, 1762
Epworth, England

Dec. 20, 1798
Nottingham, England

Methodist evangelist. After Wesley's death, Kilham became leader of the Methodist New Connection, often called the "Kilhamites." He was a Methodist preacher, 1785–96. He was expelled from the London Methodist Conference in 1796, which prompted his new organization. Kilham earnestly sought to separate the Methodists from the Church of England. He and three others formed the Methodist New Connections in 1797, which continued until 1907. This movement demanded complete separation from the Church of England. Kilham married Hannah Scurr (August 12, 1774 –March 31, 1832) shortly before his death.

Thomas Olivers

Sept. 8, 1725
Tregynon, Wales

March 7, 1799
London, England

Methodist evangelist and hymn writer who wrote "The God of Abraham Praise". He was converted at a Whitefield meeting in Bristol and traveled throughout Scotland in (1750), England, 1753–75 and Ireland (1772). He remained with the Wesleys after Whitefield's separation, becoming supervisor of all publications, 1775–79, until discharged by Wesley. He co-edited the *Arminian Magazine* for some time. He was buried in Wesley's tomb at City Road Chapel.

Patrick Henry

May 29, 1736
Studley, Virginia

June 6, 1799
Red Hill, Virginia

Governor of Virginia, 1776–79 and 1784–86, and member of the First Continental Congress, 1774–76. He was raised in Pastor Samuel Davies' Fork Presbyterian Church, Hanover County. Henry married Sarah Shelton (1754) and Dorothea Dandridge (1770). Henry claimed legislative independence for Virginia in response to the Stamp Act of 1765, saying "If this be treason, make the most of it." He was a lawyer, statesman, and Bill of Rights supporter who was remembered for his famed speech at St. John's Church, Richmond, VA March 23, 1775: "Give me liberty, or give me death!" He was a member of the Episcopal Church and a warm friend of Christianity. He may have been the greatest orator in congress history, save for Daniel Webster. He retired in 1794. Just before his death, he said, "The Bible is worth more than all the other books which were ever printed." He thanked God for all his blessings just before he stopped breathing. He died following a dose of liquid mercury. He owned 65 slaves at the time of his death. In his will he said, "There is one thing more I wish I could give them, and that is faith in Jesus Christ."

Samuel Medley

June 23, 1738
Cheshunt, England

July 17, 1799
Liverpool, England

Baptist hymn writer of "O Could I Speak," (music by Lowell Mason) **(1789) and "His Loving Kindness"** (music by William Caldwell). Medley joined the British Royal Navy and was severly wounded in a battle off Port Lagos in 1759. Converted by reading a Watts sermon in the home of his grandfather, he studied for the ministry under Dr. Gifford in London. He pastored first in Watford, Hertfordshire (1767–72) and then at Byrom St. Baptist Church, Liverpool (1772–99). Under his pastorship this church built a new building in 1790. Two books were published containing Medley's hymns. Some of his last words were, "Dying is sweet work! Sweet work! . . . Glory, Glory, Home, Home."

John B. Smith

June 12, 1756
Pequea, Pennsylvania

Aug. 22, 1799
Philadelphia, Pennsylvania

President of Hampden–Sydney (VA) College (Union Theological Seminary, Richmond, VA in 1898), **1779–89.** The school opened in 1776 and was named for two English patriots, John Hampden (1594–1643) and Algernon Sidney (1622–1683). He tutored at Hampden, 1775–79. Smith married Elizabeth Nash in 1779; they had six children. Smith was ordained Presbyterian; and served as the denomination leader in the Virginia revival movement, 1789–91. He also pastored the Third Presbyterian Church in Philadelphia (1791–95) and was the president of Union College, Schenectady, NY (1795–99). He was an early supporter of American independence.

Samuel Pearse

July 20, 1766
Plymouth, England

Oct. 10, 1799

Outstanding cleric. Pearse was converted at Bristol College around 1782. He took the pastorate of the Cannon Street Baptist Church in Birmingham, in 1790. He wrote several hymns and married Sarah Hopkins in February, 1791. He was one of the founders of the Baptist Missionary Society in Kettering in 1792. In his ten-year ministry at Cannon Street, he baptized some 335 and saw a Sunday school grow to 1,200. His daughter, Anna, married WILLIAM CAREY's son, Jonathan. WILLIAM JAY said Pearse reminded him of the Lord in his preaching. He died of consumption.

George Washington
Father of Our Country

Feb. 22, 1732
Bridges Creek, Virginia

Dec. 14, 1799
Mount Vernon, Virginia

First president of the United States, 1789–96. Washington began military activity in 1752 when hostilities with England commenced. He married Martha Curtis (June 2, 1731–May 22, 1802), a widow, on Jan. 6, 1759, adopting her two children. He inherited his brother's estate at age 20 and lived as a farmer from 1759–75, owning 216 slaves in 1773. Washington actually grew marijuana (hemp) on his plantation to make rope. He was made Commander-in-Chief of the Colonial army from 1775–81. Washington did not swear, observed the Lord's Day, and prayerfully led his troops during the austere and bitter Valley Forge winter of 1777–78. An aristocrat, he distrusted the wisdom of average people, believing them incapable of self-government. Early on, he was an Episcopalian (see MASON WEEMS), but upon his presidency and residence in NYC he was baptized by John Gano at the FBC there. When he was sworn in as first president he added, "so help me God" and kissed the Bible. Washington, a Federalist, won both elections (1789, 1792) unopposed. He laid the cornerstone of the capital on Sept 18, 1793. He was 6'4" and weighed 225 pounds. His annual salary was $25,000. He was a redhead and never went to high school. Before death he had a dull sore throat, and doctors bled him twice. He said as he died, "Doctor, I die hard, but I am not afraid to go."

William Cowper

Nov. 15, 1731
Great Berkhamstead, England

April 25, 1800
East Dereham, England

Eccentric and sometimes unstable poet, who gave the world one of its greatest hymns, "There Is a Fountain Filled with Blood," (1771) (music by LOWELL MASON). Other hymns he wrote include "O For a Closer Walk With God" (music arranged by WILLIAM GARDINER) and "God Moves in a Mysterious Way." Cowper's father was a clergyman, and his mother died when he was six, prompting him to be sent to a boarding school. At school, he was beaten by other boys, which caused

The Saints Go Marching In

suicide attempts later. After briefly studying law, he was admitted to the bar in 1754, although he never practiced law. Converted, he later was in an asylum where he remained for five months in early 1764. He made his home with Pastor Morley Unwin. From 1765–96, the pastor's wife, Mary Unwin, ministered to him and did much to keep him happy. In 1767, they moved to Olney where he worked with JOHN NEWTON, Church of England cleric, in producing *Olney Hymns* (1779), which included 67 hymns of his own. He never married. After attempting suicide in 1783, he was confined to an asylum for 18 months. His works included a long poem of 5,000 lines, *The Task,* and a ballad, "The Diverting History of John Gilpin". His favorite Bible verse was Rom. 3:24–25. NEWTON conducted his funeral service.

"Satan trembles when he sees the weakest saint upon his knees."

Johann K. Lavater

Nov. 15, 1741
Zurich, Switzerland

Jan. 2, 1801
Zurich, Switzerland

Poet, mystic and theologian. Lavater was pastor of the Church of St. Peter in Zurich beginning in 1786, following previous Zurich pastorates, 1775–86. He was a pioneer in personal counseling and pastoral ministry. While he served there, he wrote many devotional works. Evangelical in doctrine, he was imprisoned for preaching against French rule in Switzerland. He was shot by a French grenadier at the capture of Zurich in 1799 and died a little over a year later from its effect. He wrote *Views of Eternity* (4 vols., 1768–78). In 1775 he published *Physiognomic Fragments* (4 vols).

Devereaux Jarratt

Jan. 17, 1733
New Kent County, Virginia

Jan. 29, 1801
Dinwoodie County, Virginia

Episcopal pastor and evangelist who ministered in Bath, VA 1763–1801. He married Martha Claiborne. Jarratt was friendly with many Methodist leaders and was greatly influenced by them. Fellow Anglicans considered him a fanatic. He won thousands of converts to the Lord and was used by the Methodists to administer ordinances to them, reaching out to 29 nearby counties. Jarratt wrote *Revival of Religion in Virginia* (1773), to *Argument* (Anabaptists vs. Methodists) *on Baptism* (1814).

Friedrich L. von Hardenberg
Georg Friedrich Philipp von Hardenberg/Novalis

May 2, 1772
Oderwiedelstedt, Germany

March 25, 1801
Weissenfels, Germany

Poet. Hardenberg had a remarkable literature career as a poet. He served early on as auditor of the Saxon salt-works. His best works are his *Spiritual Songs,* which show beautiful simplicity and devotion. Other works include *Heinrich von Ofterdingen, The Pupils at Sais,* and *Hymns to the Night.* He died of tuberculosis at age 28.

Frederick A. C. Muhlenberg

Jan. 1, 1750
New Providence (Trappe), Pennsylvania

June 4, 1801
Lancaster, Pennsylvania

Lutheran clergyman and congressman. Muhlenberg pastored, 1770–79, including nearly three years at Christ Lutheran Church, NYC. Catherine Schaefer became his wife on Oct. 15, 1771, and gave him seven children. A fervent patriot, he was compelled to leave New York City when the British entered in 1776. Muhlenberg became a member of the Continental Congress in Pennsylvania, 1779–80. He was a Federalist and the first Speaker of the House of Representatives, 1789–97. His brother-in-law stabbed him after he cast the tie-breaking vote to implement the controversial Jay Treaty in 1795 between America and Great Britain. This imposed severe restrictions on U.S. trade in West Indies, allowing unrestricted navigation on the Mississippi, and failed to secure recognition of the principles of international maritime law. He was the son of H. M. MUHLENBERG.

Jonathan Edwards Jr.

May 26, 1745
Northampton, Massachusetts

Aug. 1, 1801
Schenectady, New York

Congregational theologian. Edwards was the ninth child of the famed JONATHAN EDWARDS. He married Mary Porter (1770) and Mercy Sabin (1783). He pastored the White Haven Church in New Haven, CT (1769–95), and in Colebrook, CT (1796–99). In 1799, he was elected president of Union College, Schenectady, NY. His modified Calvinism became known as "New England theology". He was dismissed, like his father, over the issue of qualifications for church members. His major work was *Discourses on the Atonement* (1785). He was a follower of GROTIUS in his atonement views. His last words were, "Trust in God, and you have nothing to fear."

John Ettwein

June 29, 1721
Freudenstadt, Germany

Jan. 2, 1802
Bethlehem, Pennsylvania

President of Moravian Church in NA (North), Bethlehem, PA 1782–1802. Ettwein joined the Moravian Church at Marienborn, Germany, in 1738, and soon was doing missionary work in the Netherlands and England. He married Johanna Kymbel in 1746 (died: 1789). Ettwein came with SPANGENBERG to the colonies in 1754. He moved to Bethlehem, PA, and served as a Moravian missionary to the Indians on the frontiers (1766), prior to becoming bishop of Ohio (1772), when he led a colony of Indian converts from Pennsylvania to the Tuscarawas Valley in Ohio, where DAVID ZEISBERGER was a year before. By 1784 he was the head of the movement. Ettwein represented the Moravians in their relations with the American government. He was a Moravian bishop, 1781–1801.

Frederic W. Marshall

Feb. 15, 1721
Dresden, Germany

Feb. 11, 1802
Salem, North Carolina

First president of Moravian Church in NA (South), Salem, NC 1785–1802. As an older teenager, Marshall visited ZINZENDORF's Herrnhut Community and was converted. He went to London in 1741 and was with ZINZENDORF when the first Moravian church was started there. He married Hedwig E. Schweinitz in 1750 (died: 1795). He helped in Herrnhut, advising ZINZENDORF on business matters. He arrived in Bethlehem, PA in October, 1761. In 1765, he picked a place which would be called Salem (NC), where he settled, built a church, and designed other buildings. He was in Europe during the Revolutionary War but returned in 1779.

Friedrich G. Klopstock

July 2, 1724
Quedlinburg, Germany

March 14, 1803
Hamburg, Germany

Lutheran poet and hymn writer. Klopstock was the oldest of 17 children. It was said he helped to inaugurate the golden age of German literature. Many of his odes were set to music by BEETHOVEN, Franz Schubert (1797–1828), and others. His epic work was *The Messiah* (1748–73), the first important work of modern German literature. From 1751–70, he lived on a pension in Copenhagen in the court of King Frederick V of Norway and Denmark (ruled: 1746–66). He married Meta (Margarethe) Maller in 1754 (died: 1758). From 1771 on, he lived in Hamburg. He remarried in 1791 to a niece of his first wife. In an age of infidelity he gave strong expression to his faith in Christ.

Samuel Hopkins

Sept. 17, 1721
Waterbury, Connecticut

Dec. 20, 1803
Newport, Rhode Island

Congregational theologian, pastor, and writer. He married Joanna Ingersoe on January 13, 1748, and they had eight children. Hopkins pastored in Great Barrington, MA (1743–69), growing from five to 121, and at First Church in Newport, RI (1770–1803), where he was one of the first church leaders to fight slavery. He started the Hopkinsian Controversy by opposing current attitudes of original sin and the atonement. JOSEPH BELLAMY was his partner in all this. His views were expressed as A *System of Doctrines Contained in Divine Revelation* (2 vols., 1793). His first work was *The Wisdom of God* (1759). He basically rejected the implication of Christ's righteousness. He was a great enthusiast for African missions. This gave Calvinism the missionary spirit it needed.

Barbara Ruckle Heck
Mrs. Paul Heck

1734
Ballingarry/Ruckle Hill, Ireland

Aug. 17, 1804
near Augusta, Ontario, Canada

Mother of American Methodism. Barbara was a Wesleyan convert in Ireland. She immigrated to NYC on April 11, 1760, and that same year married Paul Heck (died: 1795). Barbara urged her cousin, PHILIP EMBURY, to develop Methodism in NYC. In 1766, the first service was held in his home. Because of her Loyalist views (favored British rule on American soil) the family moved often, starting Methodist societies along the way: Camden in upstate NY (1770), Sorel near Montreal (1774), and then Augusta township in northern Ontario. Two years later in 1778, she whitewashed the walls of the first Methodist church in America—Wesley Chapel. This became the well-known John Street Methodist Church in New York City.

Joseph Willard

Dec. 29, 1738
Biddeford, Maine

Sept. 25, 1804
New Bedford, Massachusetts

President of Harvard University, Cambridge, MA 1781–1804. He married Mary Sheaffer on March 7, 1774, and they had 13 children. He was a tutor of Greek at Harvard (1766–72), and pastored the Congregational Church, Beverly, MA (1772–81). Willard founded the American Academy of Arts and Sciences in 1780 and the Harvard Medical School. He was also a member of the Medical Society of London. Willard devoted himself to the task of repairing the damage to the university wrought by the Revolutionary War, and was the first president after it changed from a college to university status in 1780.

John Moore

1733
Gloucester, England

1805

Archbishop of Canterbury, 1783–1805. After ordination, Moore became chaplain to the Duke of Marlborough and tutor to one of his sons, obtaining by that position a prebendary stall in the cathedral of Durham. Moore was made dean of Canterbury (1771–76) and bishop of Bangor (1776–83). He was recommended highly for the position of archbishop by bishops Lowth and Hurd, who had both been offered that high position themselves, but who esteemed Moore more deserving.

Johann C. F. Schiller

Nov. 10, 1759
Marbach, Germany

May 9, 1805
Weimar, Germany

Dramatist, poet, philosopher and historian. He became professor of history at Jena from 1789 onward. While there, he formed a friendship with Johann Goethe (poet; 1749–1832), whom he is considered second to in German literature. He married Dotte (Charlotte) von Lengefeld on February 22, 1790. His works, *History of 30 Years* and *Defection of Netherlands*, hail Protestantism as a defender of religious and German freedom.

William Paley

July 1743
Peterborough, England

May 25, 1805
Lincoln, England

Anglican priest, theologian, writer and philosopher. He married in 1776. In 1780, he was prebendary of Carlisle and five years later, chancellor of the diocese. Paley had several church appointments, his last two being subdean of Lincoln and rector of Wearmouth in 1795. He was also a Cambridge lecturer. Paley wrote *National Theology*, an argument for the existence of God. His *Principles of Moral and Political Philosophy* (1785) became a textbook. His most famous work, *View of Evidences of Christianity* (1794), was required reading for Cambridge entrance.

James Waddel

July 1739
Newry, Ireland

Sept. 17, 1805
Gordonsville, Virginia

Presbyterian home missionary. Waddel came to America as an infant. He was educated at Samuel Finley's (1715–1766) Academy at Nottingham, PA, receiving his license to preach in 1761. Mary Gordon became his wife in 1768. They had ten children. He served in Northumberland, Lancaster, and Augusta Counties in Virginia, prior to his ministry in the Shenandoah Valley in 1778. His last 20 years were spent in blindness.

William Shrubsole

Jan. 13, 1760
Sheerness (Isle of Shippey), England

Jan. 18, 1806
London, England

Composer of music for "All Hail the Power of Jesus Name" (lyrics by EDWARD PERRONET). It is not the most familiar tune (OLIVER HOLDEN's), but it is used often as an alternative. He started as an Anglican organist at Bangor Cathedral, but was dismissed because of sympathies with the Dissenters. In 1784, he became organist at Spa Fields Chapel in London until his death, and was active in a Congregational Church benevolence and reformatory institution.

Richard Whatcoat

Feb. 23, 1736
Quinton, England

July 5, 1806
Dover, Delaware

Bishop in the Methodist Episcopal Church, 1800–06. He was the second elected bishop in American Methodism. After 16 years as a lay preacher in England, Wales, and Ireland, he was dispatched by WESLEY to America in 1784 to bolster the fledgling movement. As an evangelist, he traveled all over the eastern seaboard, 1785–1800. He was a devout man, not strong physically, but universally beloved. He was empowered to ordain others. Whatcoat preached his last sermon on April 8, 1806, at Milford, DE.

Samuel Horsley

Sept. 15, 1733
London, England

Oct. 4, 1806
Brighton, England

Anglican bishop of St. David's, 1788, of Rochester, 1793, and of St. Asaph's, 1803. Samuel was curate in 1758 to his father at Newington Butts, and later succeeded him as rector, then archdeacon of St. Alban's, 1781–88. In 1788, he was promoted to the see of St. David's, then bishop of St. Rochester (1793–1802), and of St. Asaph's (1802–6). Horsley was considered one of the greatest pulpit orators of his time. He was also a fellow of the Royal Society. In addition to writing many scientific books, he wrote theological works as well. The message in his *Seventeen Letters to Dr. Priestley* helped to subdue Socinianism. He was mentally unbalanced when he died.

Benjamin Banneker

Nov. 9, 1731
Ellicott's Mills, Maryland

Oct. 9, 1806
Baltimore, Maryland

Black essayist, inventor, mathematician, and lay astronomer. He helped survey and lay out the nation's capital, known as Federal City (Washington, D.C.) in 1790. Banneker reputedly made the first clock in America. In astronomy he made calculations for his annual almanacs. Banneker was a genius when it came to difficult math problems. He studied bees, locust cycles, and wrote a famous letter to President Jefferson on segregation trends. He never married and was a devoted Christian.

Henry K. White

March 21, 1785
Nottingham, England

Oct. 19, 1806
Cambridge, England

Hymn writer and poet. White became a devout Christian through the appeals of a friend, and reading WALTER SCOTT's *Force of Truth*. His poem, "The Star of Bethlehem," describes his conversion. In 1802, he published a little volume of poems which attracted Robert Southey. Some of them have found a place in hymn collections, in addition to his published work entitled *Remains*. He left a mass of manuscripts upon his death. He is buried in a graveyard opposite St. John's College, Cambridge, which he was attending, planning to become a minister before he fell ill from tuberculosis and died at the age of 21.

Isaac Backus

Jan. 9, 1724
Norwich, Connecticut

Nov. 20, 1806
Middleborough, Massachusetts

Baptist evangelist, minister, historian and champion of religious liberty in New England. Backus was converted on August 24, 1741, during the Great Awakening. His marriage to Susannah Mason on November 29, 1749 (died: 1800), resulted in nine children. Originally a Congregationalist, he was a New Light or Separatist minister (1748–56), after which he organized the FBC in 1756 in Middleborough where he pastored for 50 years. He changed because of his objections to infant baptism. In 1751 he adopted Baptist views and was baptized (August 22) with his wife in the church he soon would pastor. His *Appeal to the Public for Religious Liberty* tract, circulated in 1773, influenced many people. Backus, a dedicated and fervent evangelist, made over 1,000 trips (over 68,000 miles) on horseback and preached over 10,000 sermons. He fought for religious freedom, arguing his point before the First Continental Congress in 1774. In 1833 (27 years after his death), religious liberty came to his region. He wrote the three-volume *A History of New England Baptists* (1777–96).

John C. Kunze

Aug. 5, 1744
Artern, Germany

July 24, 1807
New York, New York

Lutheran clergyman and educator. He came to America in 1770. Kunze married Margaretta Muhlenberg on July 23, 1771, and they had five children. He pastored in Philadelphia, PA (1779–84) and then was pastor of Trinity and Christ Churches, NYC (1784–1807). He was a professor of Oriental languages and literature at Columbia University, 1784–87 and 1792–99. He aided in founding the University of New York, where he served as regent and professor. Kunze's purpose at this time was to teach English to Lutheran clerics. He produced the first Lutheran hymnbook in English in 1797. He grieved over the inroads of rationalism.

John P. G. Muhlenberg

Oct. 12, 1746
New Providence (Trappe), Pennsylvania

Oct. 1, 1807
near Philadelphia, Pennsylvania

Clergyman, military officer and politician. Muhlenberg was a major general in the Revolutionary War and was considered a maverick in his day. Six children came from his marriage to Anna B. Meyer on November 6, 1770. Although raised a Lutheran, he accepted an Episcopalian ordination in order to collect tithes in his parishes. In June, 1775, after he heard General GEORGE WASHINGTON's call to arms, Muhlenberg preached a farewell sermon on Ecclesiastes 3:1–8 in his Woodstock, VA church. He removed his clerical gown and stood in full military uniform. By the day's end, 300 members of his congregation enlisted with him. During the war, he was promoted to major general, participating in several battles. He was a leader in the decisive Battle of Yorktown. Muhlenberg was involved in politics in his later years, serving in Congress as a representative, 1789–95 and 1799–1801. From 1802–7, he was the customs collector of the port of Philadelphia. He was buried in his hometown of New Providence (Trappe).

Joseph Brant
Thayendanega

1742
(River Banks) Ohio

Nov. 24, 1807
Wellington Square, Ontario, Canada

Anglican Mohawk Indian chief. He became a Christian at ELEAZER WHEELOCK's Moor's Charity School in Lebanon, CT in 1770. Brant was a fearless military ally of Britain in the War of Independence, leading some 3,000 Indians on the Royalist side. He built the first Episcopal Church in upper Canada in 1786, after the King gave him an estate at the head of Lake Ontario while in England earlier that year. Brant was an effective missionary who helped to translate the *Book of Common Prayer* and the Gospel of St. Mark into the Mohawk language.

John Newton

July 24, 1725
London, England

Dec. 21, 1807
London, England

Wrote the beloved hymn, "Amazing Grace" (1779) (music unknown). This hymn was a description of his conversion. Newton's godly mother died when he was seven. With only two years of schooling, Newton went to sea with his father at age eleven and spent the next 20 years as a sailor. While in port in 1742, at the age of 17, he fell in love with Mary Catlett, who for years continued to pray for him. He lived a profane, rough, and reckless life—surviving harsh treatment as a naval deserter and as a captured slave for 15 months in Africa in 1743–44. He was nearly killed many times. Newton was converted during a horrendous storm at sea in March, 1748. When his ship, *The Greyhound*, limped into a harbor in Ireland a month later, Newton hurried to the first church he could find, to publicly profess his faith. In January, 1750, while docked in England, he finally married Mary Catlett. Newton continued to command a slave ship, as his faith slowly matured over the next six years. Finally in 1754, he left the sea, and became a surveyor of tides at Liverpool, England, 1755–64, studied Hebrew and Greek, and mingled with Nonconformists like GEORGE WHITEFIELD and CHARLES WESLEY. He became a Church of England pastor serving first at Olney (1764–79), and then at St. Mary's in Woolnoth, London (1779–1807). This church contains a plaque bearing the epitaph he wrote: "John Newton, clerk—Once an infidel and libertine—A servant of slaves in Africa—Was, by the rich mercy of our Lord and Saviour JESUS CHRIST—Restored, pardoned, and appointed to preach the Gospel which he had long laboured to destroy. . . ." Newton's *Olney Hymns*, published in 1779, contained 280 of his hymns and 60 of WILLIAM COWPER'S. His other well-known hymns include: "Glorious Things of Thee Are Spoken" (1799), "Safely Through Another Week," "How Tedious and Tasteless the Hours," "He Died for Me," "How Sweet the Name of Jesus Sounds," and "Christ a Redeemer and Friend," and the music for "Great God of Wonders." His favorite Bible verse was Deuteronomy 15:15. He and his wife are buried in the graveyard at St. Peter and St. Paul's Church, Olney.

"And thou shalt remember that thou wast a bondman in the land of Egypt, and the Lord thy God redeemed thee: therefore I command thee this thing today."

Samuel Kirkland

Dec. 1, 1741
Norwich, Connecticut

Feb. 28, 1808
Clinton, New York

Congregational missionary to the Iroquois Indians beginning in 1766. Kirkland married Jerusha Bingham on September 19, 1769. Kirkland persuaded many tribesmen (Seneca and Oneida Indians) to join the cause of the colonies during the American Revolution. He founded the Hamilton (NY) Oneida Academy (Hamilton College in 1812) in 1793 for the education of Indian boys. His conversion came as the result of the death of several of his children.

Jacob Albright

May 1, 1759
Pottstown, Pennsylvania

May 18, 1808
Pottstown, Pennsylvania

Evangelist and founder (first bishop) of the Evangelical Association of North America, (EANA) 1813, for the purpose of providing a movement among the Germans in America. Albright was a farmer and tilemaker. Catherine Cape became his wife in 1785. He was raised a Lutheran, but the death of his three children in 1790 led to his conversion. He then switched to Methodism (1791) and began his Methodist ministry (1796). However, he could not attend weekly class meetings so he founded the first EANA Church in 1800 and organized it (1807). His church (renamed the Evangelical Church in 1922) merged with the United Brethren in 1946 to form the Evangelical United Brethren Church. He died at the home of a friend.

Benjamin Randall

Feb. 7, 1749
New Castle, New Hampshire

Oct. 22, 1808
New Durham, New Hampshire

Founder of the Free Will Baptist movement. Randall was greatly influenced by WHITEFIELD'S preaching, and when WHITEFIELD died in 1770, Randall was converted. He married Joanna Oram on Nov. 28, 1771, and they had nine children. He was a Congregationalist, 1770–76, then became associated with the Regular Baptists until he was disfellowshiped for rejecting strict Calvinist Baptist emphasis on predestination. He moved to New Durham, NH and organized a Free Will Baptist Church with seven members in 1780 where he was ordained as an evangelist and the new movement began. As an Arminian, he chose to serve open communion. By 1792 the organization was complete with the addition of a yearly meeting.

David Zeisberger

April 11, 1721
Zauchtenthal, Moravia (Czechoslovakia)

Nov. 17, 1808
Goshen, Ohio

Dedicated Moravian missionary to the American Indians, 1743–1808. He came to Georgia in 1738, worked there with the Delaware, Iroquois and Creek Indians (1743–45) and then helped establish Bethlehem and Nazareth, PA (1745–72). He preached in Ohio, 1772–82, Michigan, Canada, then back to Ohio, founding Goshen in 1798. In 1772, he founded a Christian Indian village, Schoenbrunn, Ohio's first town. After living so closely with Indians, it was said that he even began looking like them. On June 4, 1781, he married Susan Lecron. Most of the Indian towns that he founded were destroyed.

Thomas Rankin

1738
Dunbar, Scotland

May 17, 1810
London, England

Methodist evangelist in America. Rankin came under the influence of WHITEFIELD, then was an evangelist for WESLEY for eleven years. In 1773, he was sent to America to help the work of Methodism. Rankin called the first American Methodist Conference on July 4, 1773. He traveled as an evangelist, returning to England in 1778, pious, but too stern to succeed as a leader. He retired in 1783.

Richard Cecil

Nov. 8, 1748
London, England

Aug. 15, 1810
Hampstead, London, England

Key leader of the Evangelical Party of the Church of England. Cecil was converted as a result of his mother's influence. After graduating from Oxford, he was ordained (1776) and became the pastor of St. John's Chapel, Bedford Row, London (1780). The places in which he preached gained a high reputation for eloquence. His *Works*, along with *Memoir*, was reprinted in New York City (3 vols., 1845).

Sarah Trimmer

Jan. 6, 1741
Ipswich, England

Dec. 15, 1810

Authoress. Mother of twelve children who promoted the Sunday school movement by writing and producing religious textbooks for charity schools. A woman of great piety and charity, Sarah is best remembered for her children's book *The History of the Robins* (1786).

Robert Raikes

Sept. 14, 1735
Gloucester, England

April 5, 1811
Gloucester, England

Founder of the modern Sunday school movement. Greatly influenced by WESLEY and WHITEFIELD, he was concerned about prison reform (1768–73). However, seeing ragged children who could not read consumed him to seek reforms and burdened him to reach and teach them. In July of 1780, in Gloucester, England, Raikes started a Sunday school class for underprivileged children. By 1786, his efforts had brought some 200,000 children to English Sunday schools. He was the heir to a successful printing business which he worked until 1802. By 1803, a SS Union was founded. His favorite Bible verses were Matthew 12:11–12.

John Rodgers

Aug. 5, 1727
Boston, Massachusetts

May 7, 1811
New York, New York

Presbyterian pastor, primarily in NYC from 1765–1810, with the exception of the Revolutionary War time. Prior to this, Rodgers ministered at St. George's, Newcastle, DE 1749–65. He married Elizabeth Bayard (September 19, 1752), and Mary Grant (August 15, 1764), giving him a total of five children. Rodgers was an earnest patriot and was often consulted by GEORGE WASHINGTON.

Johannes T. Vanderkemp

1747
Rotterdam, Netherlands

Dec. 15, 1811
Cape Town, South Africa

Missionary to the Hottentots in South Africa. After years in medical practice at Rotterdam, Vanderkemp was converted after his wife and daughter drowned in 1791. He organized the first missionary society in the Netherlands, then left for Africa, arriving at Capetown in March 1799 through the London Missionary Society. He ministered in new areas removing his adherents to Algoa Bay (1802) and founded the Mission Institute at Bethelsdorf (1803). He (at age 60) married a Malagasy slave girl who was 17 years old. He redeemed many slaves with his private funds from cruel Boer (South African of Dutch extraction) masters.

Martin Boehm

Nov. 30, 1725
Conestoga, Pennsylvania

March 23, 1812
Conestoga, Pennsylvania

Cofounder, with Philip Otterbein, of the Church of the United Brethren in Christ (CUBC) in 1789. Boehm married Eve Steiner in 1753, who gave him eight children, seven of which were girls. Converted (1758), he became a bishop (1759) and preached as a Mennonite evangelist for 15 years to German–speaking people in Pennsylvania, Maryland, and Virginia. He met OTTERBEIN at a great preaching meeting near Lancaster in 1768. He was excommunicated by the Mennonites around 1775 because of his association with Christians "walking on the broad way." By 1789, they unofficially started the movement. The many converts formed the new CUBC group. They became bishops of the first conference in 1800, Boehm serving until death.

Franz V. Reinhard

March 12, 1753
Vohenstrauss, Germany

Sept. 6, 1812
Dresden, Germany

Lutheran preacher who was professor and preacher at the University of Wittenberg, 1782–92. In 1792, Reinhard began as court preacher, ecclesiastical counselor, and member of the supreme consistory of Dresden. He defended the Bible and the deity of Christ but explained away much of the miraculous content of the Bible. His collection of sermons comprise 35 volumes. Reinhard's *System of Christian Morals* (1788–1815) was five volumes.

Henry Martyn

Feb. 18, 1781
Truro, England

Oct. 16, 1812
Tokat, Turkey

Missionary to India and Persia, and Hindu and Arabic Bible translator. Martyn was an outstanding Anglican missionary who died, unmarried, at age 31. For years his sister, Sally, had been praying for him and encouraging him to read his Bible. It took the unexpected death of his father, during the Christmas season of 1799, to jolt him into the Scriptures, leading to his salvation. Martyn went to India in 1806, serving as chaplain of the East India Company (trading), leaving the lady he loved behind. He ministered in the Indian cities of Dinapore (1806) and then at Cawnpore (1809).

While there, he translated the New Testament into Hindustani. Suffering from consumption (tuberculosis), he traveled on to a drier climate, settling in Persia (Iran) in 1811. While at Shiraz, Martyn greatly tested his Arabic translators when he tackled translating the New Testament into Persian—completing the process he had begun in India. Fighting a debilitating fever and other traveling challenges, Martyn died in the desert while walking home to England (possibly with a horse). His diary said, "Now let me burn myself out for God." The day before he died he wrote, "...my Companion, my Friend, and my Comforter! O, when shall time give place to Eternity?..." His favorite Bible verse was Zechariah 3:2, "...is not this a brand plucked out of the fire?"

"The foes of missions are ignorance and prejudice."

Harriet Atwood Newell

Oct. 10, 1793
Haverhill, Massachusetts

Nov. 30, 1812
Port Louis, Isle de France (Mauritius)

Young missionary heroine who died at age 19. Harriet was converted at Bradford Academy and joined the Congregational Church in 1809. Shortly after her marriage to SAMUEL NEWELL on February 9, 1812, she and her husband sailed with the JUDSONS to Calcutta, India. Soon after arrival they were ordered to leave India, so they went to the Isle of France (Mauritius—island in Indian Ocean), where she became the first American missionary to die on a foreign field. Her premature baby, born at sea, also died. Her early death did much to quicken sympathy for the missionary's cause.

Joel Barlow

March 24, 1754
Redding, Connecticut

Dec. 14, 1812
Zarnavica (Zarnowiec), Poland

Poet and diplomat. After graduation from Yale, Barlow fought in the American Revolution, and became a well known author and politician. He married Ruth Baldwin on January 26, 1781. After serving as a New England lawyer, he went on a diplomatic mission to London where he met future American political philosopher, Thomas Paine (1737–1809). Barlow was next sent as U.S. Consul to Algiers, North Africa, negotiating treaties with Tunis, Algiers, and Tripoli, 1795–97. He moved back to America, but returned to Europe under U.S. President James Madison's appointment as the American Ambassador to France in 1811. His writings included the epic poem, "The Vision of Columbus" (1787), an essay "Advice to the Privileged Orders " (1792), and the mock epic "Hasty Pudding" that later gave rise to the irreverent Hasty Pudding Society at Harvard University. He wrote several hymns. Barlow's unique historical contribution was the editing of the *Psalms of David Imitated* written in 1719 by the famed ISAAC WATTS. Barlow was commissioned by the Congregational General Association of Connecticut to enlarge the work and adapt it to the imitated American culture. While traveling, he caught cold, dying of pneumonia 20 miles north of Kracow in a peasant's cottage.

Friedrich F. Flemming

Feb. 28, 1778
Neuhausen, Germany

May 27, 1813
Berlin, Germany

Musician. He settled in Berlin after completing his musical education at Wittenberg, Jena, Vienna, and Trieste. Flemming became a successful physician and maintained a keen interest in music as a vocation, composing songs with many parts for men's choral groups. Flemming wrote, "O Holy Saviour, Friend Unseen."

John Venn

1759
Claphall, England

July 1, 1813
Claphall, England

Anglican co-founder of The Church Missionary Society in 1799 and zealous missions leader. Venn was rector of Little Dunham, Norfolk, VA from 1783–92. For many years he served as rector at Clapham, 1792–99, where he attracted a group of like-minded Evangelicals who came to be known as the "Clapham sect." He persistently worked for the organization of a mission board and finally, helped by THOMAS SCOTT, formed the Church Missionary Society. He had bad health all his life.

Philip W. Otterbein

June 3, 1726
Dillenberg, Prussia (Germany)

Nov. 17, 1813
Baltimore, Maryland

Cofounder, with Martin Boehm, of the Church of the United Brethren in Christ in 1789. Otterbein was a German Reformed evangelist who went to America in 1752 to work with the German-speaking people there. In Lancaster, PA he was converted and cast his lot with the Methodists and Mennonites. He married Susan LeRoy on April 19, 1762 (died: April 27, 1768). He never remarried. Otterbein was pastoring in York, PA where evangelist BOEHM was holding a revival in Isaac Long's barn, near Lancaster, PA, in 1768. After the service they embraced each other saying, "We are brethren." Otterbein pastored in Lancaster, PA (1752–58); Tulpehocken, PA (1758–60); Frederick, MD (1760–65); York, PA (1765–74) and an Evangelical Reformed congregation in Baltimore (1774–1813). They actually started the movement in 1789 with six lay evangelists. They became bishops at the first conference in 1800, Otterbein serving until death.

Thomas Coke

Sept. 9, 1747
Brecon, Wales

May 3, 1814
Indian Ocean

First bishop of the Methodist Episcopal Church, 1784. Coke was associated with WESLEY since 1777. A dissenting preacher led him to Christ after he was already ordained as an Anglican. He was sent by WESLEY to America in 1784 to lead in the work. Coke helped to organize the Baltimore Conference (1784) and was placed in charge of all foreign work (1789). He made nine trips altogether to America, 1784–1803, at his own expense. He founded Cokesbury College, Abingdon, MD in 1787. Beginning in 1792, he led in sending pioneer missionaries to the West Indies, Sierra Leone, Nova Scotia, Ireland, and France. He ordained FRANCIS ASBURY to carry on his work. Since the American Church remained strong, he returned to England in 1803. Coke was interested in starting a missionary endeavor to Ceylon, but he died of a stroke on his way there. He was buried at sea in the Indian Ocean near southern Asia by the party of missionaries accompanying him.

Isabella Marshall Graham

July 29, 1742
Lanark, Scotland

July 27, 1814
New York, New York

Pioneer in woman's work for the benefit of women in America. Isabella married Dr. John Graham in 1765, and they had four children. After her surgeon husband died in Antigua, she returned to Scotland (1773) and then to New York (1789), where she established a successful school for young ladies. Isabella organized the New York Missionary Society for Indians (1796), and the Society for the Relief of Poor Widows and Children (1797). Pessimistic about social reform, she remained hopeful about the impact of early instruction.

Claudius Buchanan

March 12, 1766
Cambuslang, Scotland

Feb. 9, 1815
Broxbourne, England

Church of England clergyman and missionary to India in 1796. Buchanan was an excellent linguist and persuasive organizer for the Anglican church. He was chaplain for the East India Company at Barrackpur for two years before becoming chaplain in Calcutta and vice-principal of Ft. William College, 1800–6. Buchanan translated the Bible into Hindustani and Persian and arranged to have the first bishop appointed to India. In

1809 he returned to Great Britain to recuperate and to campaign for Christian missions in India. He wrote *Christian Researches in India* (1811).

Andrew Fuller

Feb. 6, 1754
Wicken, England

May 7, 1815
Kettering, England

Baptist theologian. Fuller was converted in November, 1769. He became a pastor in Soham at a hyper-Calvinistic Baptist Church, 1775–82. Fuller pastored at Kettering 1782–1815. He cooperated with JOHN RYLAND and John Sutcliff in assisting WILLIAM CAREY in the foundation and support of the Baptist Missionary Society of which he was the first secretary. This was founded October 2, 1792 in the home of one of his deacons in Hettering. He wrote *The Calvinist and Socinian Systems Compared* (1795) and *The Gospel, Its Own Witness* (1799). His greatest work was *The Gospel Worthy of All Acceptation*, denouncing hyper-Calvinist theology. Fuller died of tuberculosis and said as he died, "By great and sovereign grace." His favorite Bible verse was Matthew 11:28.

Gotthilf H. E. Muhlenberg

Nov. 17, 1753
New Providence (Trappe), Pennsylvania

May 23, 1815
Lancaster, Pennsylvania

Lutheran clergyman and first president of Franklin and Marshall College, Lancaster, PA 1787. Muhlenberg assisted his father, HEINRICH, in Philadelphia. He married Mary Hall on July 26, 1774. Beginning in 1779, he pastored the Church of the Holy Trinity at Lancaster until his death. Muhlenberg was an eminent naturalist and studied botany independently, discovering more than 100 new plants. He was an honored member of several philosophical societies.

Charles Buck

1771
Hillsley, England

Aug. 11, 1815
London, England

Pastor and writer. Buck spent his life in the ministry of the Independents in England, pastoring in Sheerness and London. He published *Anecdotes: Religious, Moral, and Entertaining* (1799), which was very popular in its day. His fame rests upon his *Theological Dictionary* (1802), first published in London. It had an immense sale both in England and America.

Samuel Provoost

March 9, 1743
New York, New York

Sept. 6, 1815
New York, New York

First Episcopal bishop of New York in 1786 until his death in 1815. Provoost was consecrated at Canterbury, England in 1766. Four children came from his marriage to Maria Bousefield on June 8, 1766. Provoost was rector at Trinity Church, New York City (1784–1800), having served as an assistant there (1766–71). Political conditions caused him to retire to a small estate in 1774. He was chaplain to the Continental Congress (1785) and to the U.S. Senate (1789). Provoost conducted the service at St. Paul's Chapel, following GEORGE WASHINGTON's inauguration (1789), and also officiated at his memorial service (1799). His poor health limited him after 1801. He is buried at Trinity Parish churchyard.

Mary Bosanquet Fletcher

Sept. 12, 1739
Essex, England

Sept. 9, 1815
Madeley, England

Shepherdess to orphans. Raised in a worldly home, Mary chanced upon a godly Methodist woman and came to Christ as a teenager. At age 21, she was put out of her home because of her faith. In 1768, with a legacy left her by her grandparents, she was able to take over a farm in Yorkshire where she provided for destitute and ill orphans under her roof, although she struggled financially. On November 12, 1781, 52 year old JOHN FLETCHER and 42-year-old Mary Bosanquet re-met and married after a 25-year friendship. Little did they know they would have only three years, nine months and two days together. When he died, she remained on at his parish at Madeley for 30 more years, encouraging the new vicars and carrying on Christian work in her neighborhood, having close to 100 members in her teaching classes.

Charles Inglis

1734
Glencolumbkille, Donegal, Ireland

Feb. 24, 1816
Halifax, Nova Scotia, Canada

First colonial bishop from the Church of England. Coming to the Colonies in 1757 as a teacher, Inglis was also a missionary in Dover, DE from 1759–64. He married Mary Vining (February, 1764) and Margaret Crooke (May 31, 1773), and had four children. Inglis served at Trinity Church, NYC in 1764, before the American Revolution forced him, an unswerving Tory, to flee first to England, then back to Halifax, Nova Scotia. In fact, his church was burned in 1777. After living in England from 1784–87, he was bishop in Nova Scotia from 1787 until his death.

Francis Asbury

Aug. 20, 1745
Handsworth, England

March 31, 1816
Spotsylvania, Virginia

Father of Methodism in America. Converted in his family's barn at age 16, he later traveled as an evangelist, 1766–71. The barn in Wednesbury was used for preaching and Alexander Nathan, Wesleyan evangelist, was instrumental in his decision. Upon WESLEY's appointment, August 7, 1771, Asbury came to America, never to return to Europe. He began preaching, November 24, 1771. He was made the first bishop in America, ordained by THOMAS COKE on December 25, 1784, at Baltimore in the historic conference, which formed Methodism in America. Asbury never married, never had a place to call "home," evangelizing until his death. His last sermon was in Richmond, VA on March 24, using Romans 9:28 as his text. He saw his work grow to 3,000 preachers ordained by him, and 13,790 to 214,235 members. Asbury presided over 224 annual conferences, and preached 17,000 sermons. Asbury traveled over 300,000 miles in his ministry and some 6,000 miles on horseback each year. Asbury College in Wilmore, KY was named for him. His journals reveal his zeal and wide missionary activity. He died in the home of his friend, George Arnold. He is buried in Mt. Olivet Cemetery, Baltimore (25,000 people gathered for his funeral). One source says he is buried in Eutau Methodist Church, Baltimore.

*"Where am I going? To the New World. To gain honor or money?
No, I am going to live to God and bring others to do so."*

Richard Watson (1)

Aug. 9, 1737
Heversham, England

July 4, 1816
Calgarth Park, England

Anglican theologian, chemist and pastor. At Cambridge, Watson was professor of divinity, 1771–79. He also served as rector of Somersham in 1771, archdeacon of Ely, 1779–82, and bishop of Llandaff, 1782. He wrote

Apology for Christianity (1776—to Edward Gibbon [1737–94]), *Apology for the Bible* (1796—to Thomas Paine), plus a six-volume Collection of Theological Tracts. Watson also served as a professor of chemistry at Trinity College, Cambridge, 1764–71. His experiments with salt solutions won him election to the Royal Society in 1769. In 1772, he invented the black-bulb thermometer.

Jesse Lee

March 12, 1758
Prince George County, Virginia

Sept. 12, 1816
near Hillsboro, Maryland

Methodist circuit riding preacher, beginning in 1783. Converted just before the American Revolution, Lee served as FRANCIS ASBURY's assistant, 1785–87 and 1797–1800, working out of Stanford CT (c. 1789–1800), as an evangelist. He left New England in 1800, leaving 50 preachers and 6,000 members. From 1801–15, he was the presiding elder of the Southern District of the Methodist Churches in Virginia. Later he was the chaplain for the U.S. House of Representatives, 1809–14, and of the U.S. Senate in 1814. Lee published *A History of Methodists* (1810). He died while attending a short camp meeting. Outside of ASBURY, he is regarded as the greatest early influence for Methodism in the East.

Dan Taylor

Dec. 21, 1738
Northowram, England

Dec. 2, 1816
London, England

Founder of the New Connection of General Baptists in June, 1770, after he discovered there was a Unitarian drift among some General Baptists. Taylor pastored in Birthcliffe (1763–83), Halifax (1783–85), and at Church Street, Whitechapel, London (1785 on). Taylor founded a college (1797), and became editor of its magazine (1798).

Nathan Strong

Oct. 16, 1748
Coventry, Connecticut

Dec. 25, 1816
Hartford, Connecticut

Congregational minister who served the First Church of Hartford, CT 1774 onward (42 years, except for the years as army chaplain during the Revolutionary War). Strong was a missions pioneer and a founder of the Connecticut Missionary Society (for home missions) in 1801. Strong also founded the *Connecticut Evangelical Magazine* and wrote several hymns.

Timothy Dwight (1)

May 14, 1752
Northampton, Massachusetts

Jan. 11, 1817
New Haven, Connecticut

President of Yale College (University in 1887), **New Haven, CT 1795–1817, Congregational clergyman, theologian, poet, and educator.** Dwight was converted following a serious illness while a student at Yale. He became professor of divinity, as well as pastoring there, 1771–77. He turned the school back around from French enlightenment infidelity to the evangelical faith. He married Mary Woolsey on March 3, 1777. While Dwight pastored the Congregational Church in Greenfield Hill, CT from 1783–95, he also started a school on the church property. At Yale, his preaching converted 1/3 of the students in 1802. He wrote 33 hymns, including "I Love Thy Kingdom, Lord" (music by AARON WILLIAMS). His college chapel sermons were published in *Theology Explained and Defended* (5 vols., 1818–19). His mother was a daughter of JONATHAN EDWARDS. When Dwight served as chaplain in the Revolutionary army 1777–78, he became a good friend of GEORGE WASHINGTON. He wrote five volumes of theology, 1818–19.

"Faith sees the bright eternal doors unfold, to make His children's way."

James McGready

c 1758–1760　　　　　　　　　　　　　　　　　　　　　　　　　　　　　　　　Feb. 1817
Western Pennsylvania　　　　　　　　　　　　　　　　　　　　Henderson County, Kentucky

Presbyterian revivalist and frontier preacher. He originated the idea of the outdoor camp meeting, which sparked a revival in Logan County, KY, and then led to a national awakening, 1800–5. On the first Sunday after recovery from smallpox, he was converted, about 1787, as a result of friends debating Christianity. McGready pastored in Orange County, NC from 1790–96, when he moved to Logan County, KY. He devoted his ministry to reaching lonely families and unchurched villages in raw frontier areas. In 1796 his three small congregations, which became known as the Gasper River Camp Meeting in July, 1800, laid the foundation for the awakening. Many people came from 100 miles away. In August, 1801, at Cane Ridge, KY, crowds were in the thousands. He established churches in southern Indiana, 1811–16, following the establishment of the Cumberland Presbyterian Church denomination in 1810. One of his converts was BARTON W. STONE.

John Fawcett

Jan. 6, 1740　　　　　　　　　　　　　　　　　　　　　　　　　　　　　　　July 25, 1817
Lidget Green, England　　　　　　　　　　　　　　　　　　　　　　Hebden Bridge, England

Beloved Baptist pastor who wrote "Blest Be the Tie" (music by JOHANN NAGELI). Converted at age 16 through the preaching of GEORGE WHITEFIELD, he conducted an academy (Rawdon College) at Brearley Hall, besides taking some pastorates. Fawcett settled in Wainsgate and Hebden Bridge in 1764, where he remained until his death 53 years later. Fawcett's great hymn was published in 1782 before NAGELI found it. This hymn resulted from his decision to decline a call to the famous Carter Lane Baptist Church, London, in 1772. He wrote hymns to go along with many of his sermons, one such being "How Precious Is the Book Divine" (music by WILLIAM GARDINER). He wrote *Devotional Commentary on the Holy Scripture* (1811).

Johann L. Burckhardt
John Lewis or Johann Ludwig Burckhardt

Nov. 24, 1784　　　　　　　　　　　　　　　　　　　　　　　　　　　　　　　Oct. 17, 1817
Lausanne, Switzerland　　　　　　　　　　　　　　　　　　　　　　　　　　　Cairo, Egypt

Celebrated Eastern traveler. He came to England in 1806. Burckhardt received aid from the Association for Promoting the Discovery of the Interior Parts of Africa in order to travel in Syria, Palestine, Egypt, and Arabia. He started traveling in 1810, impersonating a Moslem pilgrim, which succeeded in smuggling him into many "closed areas." His early death prevented exploration of the sources of the Niger River. Burckhardt wrote several books, all published after his death, from *Travels in Nubia* (northeast Africa) (1819) to *Arabic Proverbs* (1830).

Henry Obookiah
Henry Opukahaia

c 1792　　　　　　　　　　　　　　　　　　　　　　　　　　　　　　　　　　Feb. 17, 1818
Kau, Hawaii　　　　　　　　　　　　　　　　　　　　　　　　　　Cornwall, Connecticut

Missionary student. Obookiah witnessed the slaying of his parents when he was about eleven. Through a kindhearted ship captain, he arrived in New Haven, CT as a 15-year-old orphan. Converted in 1812, he was discipled by missionary SAMUEL J. MILLS, sent to Andover (MA) Seminary, and was converted and received into the Congregational Church in Torringford, CT in 1815. Obookiah then went to a mission school in Cornwall, CT in 1817. He always had a desire to return to Hawaii, but typhoid fever caused his early death. His memoirs (by Edwin Dwight) inspired the organization of a mission, which started in 1819 becoming a formative influence in the history of Hawaii.

Samuel J. Mills

April 21, 1783
Torringford, Connecticut

June 16, 1818
Atlantic Ocean off Africa

Father of foreign missions movement in the United States. He was converted during a revival in 1801. Mills was a Williams College (Williamstown, MA) student and leader of the "Hay Stack Prayer Meeting" in 1806. Mills led in the formation of the American Board of Commissioners for Foreign Missions in 1810. They sent their first missionaries to India in 1812. He gave impulse to the organization of the American Bible Society in 1816. He died at sea (of an illness) while returning from Liberia, Africa, after a year's work there. During his brief lifetime, he inspired, as few others, individuals, churches, and denominations to be part of the world mission endeavor. He was the driving force behind the spread of the missionary movement from America.

William Bramwell

Feb. 1759
Elswick, England

Aug. 13, 1818
Leeds, England

Methodist preacher and revivalist. As the tenth child of eleven children, Bramwell was converted while taking the Lord's Supper in the Church of England. He soon joined the Methodist Church. About 1786 he became an earnest preacher and evangelist. In 1787, he married E. Byrom. In his ministry of more than 30 years, thousands were converted, and many sick were healed in answer to prayer. Bramwell was a great man of prayer and faith. He died suddenly of apoplexy (stroke).

Abigail Smith Adams

Nov. 11, 1744
Weymouth, Massachusetts

Oct. 28, 1818
Quincy, Massachusetts

Wife of President John Adams and mother to President John Quincy Adams. Abigail was a spiritual powerhouse in the home. These two presidents are not in this compilation because they were Unitarians, and their Christian commitment is clouded as a result. She married John Adams on Oct. 25, 1764, and bore him three sons and a daughter. In 1801, during the last three months of Adam's presidency, she became the first mistress of the newly built White House. While her husband was gone on government business, she began writing her letters, which have made her famous. At least three collections of her letters have been published which have strong spiritual insights. She died of typhoid fever.

Johann M. Hahn

Feb. 2, 1758
Altdorf, Germany

Jan. 20, 1819
Sindlingen, Germany

Lutheran preacher and writer. His views were held by followers called Michalians. Hahn was widely esteemed in Wurtemburg and drew great crowds. Hahn stressed sanctification more than justification. As a result, he was rebuked, and so he left his native town of Altdorf. He was greatly influenced by the writings of Jacob Bohme and Friedrich Oetinger, German theosophist theologian (1702–82).

John Bakewell

1721
Brailsford, Derbyshire, England

March 18, 1819
Lewisham, Kent, England

Methodist evangelist and hymn writer. Bakewell wrote "Hail, Thou Once Despised Jesus." At age 18, he was converted and called to preach as a result of studying Thomas Boston's, *Human Nature in Its Four-fold State*. After the first Methodist Conference in 1744, Bakewell moved to London, and became acquainted with the evangelical leaders of the day, John and Charles Wesley, Augustus Toplady, and John Fletcher. For many years he conducted the Greenwich Royal Park Academy, introducing Methodism there. His post was filled by his son-in-law, James Egan, when Bakewell focused full-time on preaching for the Wesleyans. Bakewell is buried at City Road Chapel in London.

Stephen West

Nov. 2, 1725
Tolland, Connecticut

May 15, 1819
Stockbridge, Massachusetts

Congregational cleric. He followed JONATHAN EDWARDS at Stockbridge, MA from 1755–75. For 16 years West preached to the Indians via an interpreter and also in English. He was an able teacher and scholar, and trained many young men for the ministry. A sample of West's writing would be *An Essay on Moral Agency* (1772) and *Scripture. . .Doctrine of the Atonement* (1785).

Samuel S. Smith

March 16, 1750
Pequa, Pennsylvania

Aug. 21, 1819
Baltimore, Maryland

President of Princeton (NJ) College (University in 1898), **1795–1812.** This Presbyterian pastor and educator was also the first president of Hampden Sydney (VA) College, 1775–79. Smith rebuilt Princeton College, which was badly wrecked by the Revolutionary War. He taught philosophy, 1779–95, theology (1783) and was vice-president (1786). He married Ann Witherspoon and had nine children. Smith helped to develop the Book of Government of the Presbyterian Church.

Afrikaner

South Africa

c 1820
South Africa

Hottentot Chief in Namaqualand, South Africa. He was the sensational convert of ROBERT MOFFAT, a missionary to his region. Afrikaner was a robber and an outlaw, bringing terror to native tribes and colonists. To everyone's surprise, 20-year-old MOFFAT gained his confidence and won him to complete Christian dedication in 1815. Unfortunately, Afrikaner died before he could work extensively with his new friend.

Thomas Haweis

Jan. 1, 1734
Redruth, England

Feb. 11, 1820
Bath, England

Cofounder of the London Missionary Society in 1795 with Congregationalist David Bogue. Haweis was converted under Samuel Walker, curate of St. Mary's in 1764. He held deep convictions about proclaiming the gospel everywhere. Haweis was a Christian service assistant who practiced medicine for a time. He then became a chaplain at a local hospital in London, then a Church of England rector at All Saints Church in Aldwinkle, 1764–1820. In 1774, he was chaplain and trustee executive to SELINA HASTINGS. Haweis was also a chaplain in Bath when he retired in 1809. His hymns include "Oh Thou from Whom All Goodness Flows." He was a prodigious writer in prose and poetry.

Lewis Edson

Jan. 22, 1748
Bridgewater, Massachusetts

Spring 1820
Woodstock, Connecticut

Musician and composer of hymns. Edson wrote the music for "How Tedious and Tasteless the Hours" (lyrics by JOHN NEWTON) He was a blacksmith by trade. He married in 1770. Because of his Tory tendencies during the Revolutionary War, he moved his family to western Massachusetts in 1776 and then to New York. Following the war, he conducted singing schools, finally settling in Woodstock, CT in 1817.

Isaac Milner

Jan. 11, 1750
Leeds, England

April 1, 1820
London, England

Evangelical mathematician, clergyman and church historian. Milner was a Cambridge professor who taught natural philosophy, 1783–88. In 1788 he became president of Queen's College. He and his brother JOSEPH, worked together on *History of the Church of Christ* until Joseph died in 1797, after which Isaac completed the work. Milner succeeded ISAAC NEWTON in the chair of mathematics in 1798. Like his brother, he was an evangelical Anglican. He also wrote *An Ecclesiastical History*. He died in the home of WILLIAM WILBERFORCE, one of his disciples.

John Smalley

June 4, 1734
Lebanon (Columbia), Connecticut

June 1, 1820
New Britain, Connecticut

Pastor of the Congregational Church in New Britain, 1757–1813 (56 years). Converted after graduation from Yale in 1756, Smalley trained many other young ministers for the ministry. Smalley held strong Calvinistic views, and defended New England theology. He published a volume of *Discourses* (1803), and a second volume in 1815. Among his pupils were NATHANIEL EMMONS and Ebenezer Porter (1772–1834), Congregational president of Andover (MA) Theological Seminary in 1827.

Moses D. Hoge

Feb. 15, 1752
Cedargrove, Virginia

July 5, 1820
Philadelphia, Pennsylvania

President of Hampden-Sydney (VA) College (Union Theological Seminary, Richmond, VA in 1898), 1807–1820. Hoge married Elizabeth Poage (Aug. 23, 1783) and Susan W. Hunt (Oct. 25, 1803) and had two sons. He was ordained to the Presbyterian ministry in 1782, followed by a trusteeship of Washington College, Chestertown, MD from 1791–1807. Hoge fought in the Revolutionary War and wrote several books. His grandson was a famous Southern Presbyterian preacher, Moses D. Hoge (1819–99).

Joseph Benson

Jan. 25, 1749
Melmerby, England

Feb. 16, 1821
London, England

Eminent Methodist minister. Benson was converted at age 16 by the witness of a cousin, reading WESLEY's sermons, and hearing Methodist preaching. An earnest student throughout his life, Benson was a popular itinerant evangelist after 1771. He married in 1780 (she died: 1810). He was editor of *Methodist Magazine* (1804–21). A commentary on the Holy Scriptures was prepared by him in five volumes from 1815–18. Benson is quoted as saying, "I could and did devote my soul and body and health and strength to His glory and service."

Samuel Newell

July 25, 1785
Durham, Maine

March 30, 1821
Bombay, India

Missionary to India. Newell was one of the famed five men ordained February 6, 1812 (JUDSON, NOTT, RICE and HALL). He married HARRIET ATWOOD on February 9, then sailed with the JUDSONS to India. When not allowed in Calcutta (June), they went on to the Isle of France (his daughter was buried at sea), where he lost his young wife HARRIET on November 30, 1812. Newell ministered with HALL and NOTT in Bombay until he fell victim of the cholera epidemic.

Thomas Scott (2)

Feb. 4, 1747
Braytoft, England

April 16, 1821
Aston Sandford, England

Anglican cofounder of the Church Missionary Society in 1799 and Bible commentator. He was ordained (1773) and after several positions, followed JOHN NEWTON as curate of Olney (1781). Scott was dismissed as a surgeon trainee, but in 1785, he became a hospital chaplain in London. In 1801, he assumed the vicarship of Aston Sandford, Buckinghamshire. Scott, along with JOHN VENN, was instrumental in forming the Church Missionary Society, and served as its first secretary. He was a convert from Unitarianism to Calvinism. Scott's most famous work was *The Holy Bible with Notes* (4 vols., 1788–92).

Elias Boudinot

May 2, 1740
Philadelphia, Pennsylvania

Oct. 24, 1821
Burlington, New Jersey

First president of American Bible Society, 1818–21. Boudinot began a law practice in Elizabethtown, NJ in 1760. Boudinot married Hannah Stockton on April 21, 1762. He was a Continental Congressman, 1777–78, 81–84, being a New Jersey delegate. He was a lawyer by profession and president of Congress in 1782, when an early peace treaty was signed with England. He was elected to the House of Representatives, 1789–95, and a trusted friend of GEORGE WASHINGTON. He served as director of the U.S. Mint from 1795–1805, and will be remembered as a patriot and philanthropist.

Krishan Pal

1763
Barigram, India

Aug. 1822
Sylhet, India

One of India's great evangelists, he heard the gospel because of a broken limb, which a missionary set for him. Soon he was baptized in the River Ganges, near Serampore, where the hymn "Jesus and Shall it Ever Be" was sung in Bengali. In 1804, he entered Christian work. He baptized hundreds of converted idolaters, and then died from cholera, triumphant in Christ. He wrote two or three hymns, most well-known, " O Thou, My Soul, Forget No More." CAREY said of him, "A steady, zealous, well-informed…eloquent minister of the gospel, averaging 13 sermons a week." He did this for over 20 years on $6 a month budget.

Levi Parsons

July 18, 1792
Goshen, Massachusetts

Feb. 10, 1822
Alexandria, Egypt

Missionary to Palestine. Parsons was one of the finest to graduate from Andover (MA) Theological Seminary in 1817. He went with PLINY FISK, in 1819, to survey the field. They arrived in Jerusalem on February 17, 1821, becoming the first Protestant missionaries to enter that city, distributing tracts and Bibles. Ill health overtook him. In May, 1821, he left for Smyrna, suffering a serious illness en route, rejoined FISK, and with him started again for Jerusalem via Egypt. At Alexandria his illness caused him to die at age 29. He served under ABCFM.

William Milne

April 22, 1785
Kinnethmont, Scotland

May 27, 1822
Malacca, Malaysia

Missionary to China. Milne was the second Protestant missionary there. In 1813 he went to Macao (Portuguese Island, southeast China); then, with ROBERT MORRISON, he went to Canton, ministering throughout the Malay Archipelago. Milne served under the London Missionary Society. Milne set up a printing press and assisted MORRISON in translating the NT into Chinese. Milne founded the Anglo-Chinese College of Malacca,

Malaysia. He married Rachel Cowie (1783–1819). She had three children during their marriage. After his wife died, he accepted the responsibility of raising all their children. He also visited the islands of Singapore and Penang. He lived also in Java for a time.

John Burton

Feb. 26, 1773
Nottingham, England

June 24, 1822
Leicester, England

Baptist layman and hymn writer of "Holy Bible, Book Divine" (1803) (music by WILLIAM BRADBURY). He married (1805), then moved to Leicester (1813). Burton became interested in Sunday school work and even wrote hymns for children. A volume of his hymns was published in 1802 under the title, *The Youth's Monitor in Verse,* in a Series of Little Tales, Emblems, Poems, and Songs.

Thomas F. Middleton

Jan. 26, 1769
Kedleston, England

July 8, 1822
Calcutta, India

Anglican missionary and first bishop of Calcutta in 1814. Middleton served in various churches, 1792–1814. He founded the Bishop's College in 1820. Known for his Biblical scholarship. His bishopric included all of India and Australia. Middleton published *Doctrine of the Greek Article* (1808).

David Osgood

Oct. 14, 1747
Andover, Massachusetts

Dec. 12, 1822
Medford, Massachusetts

Congregational pastor at Medford for fifty years following his graduation from Harvard in 1771. Osgood was a zealous Federalist. In 1794, he preached a sermon which attracted wide attention, denouncing Edmond Genet's (1765–1834), French diplomat to the United States, appeal to the people against the government. A volume of his sermons, which passed through several editions, was published in 1824.

Edward Jenner

May 17, 1749
Berkeley, England

Jan. 26, 1823
Berkeley, England

Discoverer of vaccination as a preventative of smallpox. Jenner studied under the famed anatomist, John Hunter (1728–93). Jenner began practicing medicine in 1772. Having observed that dairymaids did not get smallpox, he inoculated a small boy with cowpox in 1796 and thus demonstrated his immunity to smallpox. In 1798, he published his findings. In 1802, he received parliamentary grants to further his work. Hospitals slowly began using his inoculation vaccine. Emperor Napoleon (1769–1821) said, "We can refuse nothing to that man." In his lifetime, Jenner saw many countries, including the United States, adopt his vaccination protocol. He traveled widely, fulfilling many illustrious speaking opportunities and was awarded many medals from learned societies. Jenner had great reverence for the Bible, giving copies to many. He said, "...The sacred Scriptures form the only pillow on which the soul can find repose and refreshment."

William Ward

Oct. 20, 1769
Derby, England

March 7, 1823
near Calcutta, India

Missionary to India. He was apprenticed to a printer of a large printing establishment and trained in journalism. In 1799, he followed the call for people to help WILLIAM CAREY bring the Word to India. Ward became the printer at the Serampore Mission established in India. He was part of the famed missionary trio of CAREY, MARSHMAN, and Ward. He married Mary

The Saints Go Marching In

Fountaun, a widow, in India. From 1800–23 he was indispensable to the mission as an administrator, printing press manager, cross-cultural pastoral counselor, and peacemaker.

Thomas Erskine

Jan. 21, 1750
Edinburgh, Scotland

Nov. 17, 1823
Almondell (near Edinburgh), Scotland

Well-known lawyer. Erskine served in the navy and army, and while on duty in the latter service attracted the attention of Justice Lord Mansfield, who led him to study law. In his first plea, he achieved notable success. In a speech on the prosecution of a publisher (Williams) for publishing Thomas Paine's *Age of Reason*, he said, "For my own part, Gentlemen, I have been ever deeply devoted to the truths of Christianity, and my firm belief in the holy Gospel. . .has arisen from. . .reflections of my riper years and understanding." He was a member of the House of Commons, 1790–1806.

Queen Kapiolani

c 1798
Hawaii

1824
London, England

Queen of Hawaii that overthrew native pagan customs. Kapiolani was the wife of Kamehameha II (Liholiho; 1797–1824) who reigned 1819–24. She was greatly influenced by her mother-in-law, Kaahumanu (c 1772–1832), wife of Kamehameha I who served as premier during her son's administration. Kapiolani became a Christian, gave up her drinking habits, and committed herself to one husband. New Christians, like everyone else, shuddered at the great goddess—Pele—who, according to legend, lived up in the mountains in the boiling crater of the fiery volcano, on Hawaii. The native priests were angry because the preaching of the missionaries had led many away from the worship of Pele, and they were thus receiving fewer hogs (popular means of tribute payment) to keep Pele at bay. Kapiolani was determined not to let the "Pele Legend" distract others from knowing the one true God. She said, "Pele is naught. I will go to Kilauea, the mountain of the fires where the smoke and stones go up, and Pele will not touch me. My God made the mountain and fires within it too, as He made us all." Eighty believers went with her. She read the New Testament to a native priestess at the crater's edge, stepped into the crater, returned, called on the group to sing, and from that time on, the power of the priests was gone, and Christ replaced Pele as the object of worship. Both she, and her husband king, received the first American missionaries to the islands. They went to England in 1824 and both were victims of the measles epidemic and died there.

Hans N. Hauge

April 3, 1771
Thun, Norway

March 29, 1824
Bredtvedt, Norway

Pietist evangelist and peasant lay preacher. He greatly influenced his nation, despite opposition from the state church. Hauge was converted April 5, 1796, in his room while reading LUTHER's works. From 1798–1804, he formed little brotherhoods for prayer, conversation, and exhortation, walking over 7,000 miles. Hauge was imprisoned, 1804–11 and 1814–16, for lay preaching, being arrested ten times. He traveled extensively, and often preached twice a day. He lived on his estate in Bredtvedt from 1816 on. He was later greatly honored as his health declined. He did much to counteract rationalism in Norway.

Charles Strong

Aug. 4, 1788
Chester County, South Carolina

July 20, 1824
near Newberry, South Carolina

Stated Clerk of Associate Reformed Presbyterian Church, Greenville, SC 1815–24. During this time, Strong served the pastorates of Cannon Creek, Kings Creek, and Prosperity, SC. He was married on Feb. 13, 1817 to

Nancy Harris (died: November 8, 1842). He is remembered as a man of vigorous intellect, amiable manners, unassuming and dignified deportment, solid and extensive learning, firm attachment to evangelical truth, and fervent, consistent piety.

Hugh Wilson

1766
Fenwick, Scotland

Aug. 14, 1824
Duntocher, Scotland

Musician whose trade was that of a shoemaker. Wilson studied mathematics, music, and designed sundials. He often led the psalm singing in the Secession Church of Scotland. After 1800, he became a calculator and draftsman in the mills at Pollokshaws and then in Duntocher where he founded a Sunday school. Wilson composed many tunes, the most famous being, "Alas, and Did My Saviour Bleed" (lyrics by Isaac Watts).

John H. Livingston

May 30, 1746
Poughkeepsie, New York

Jan. 20, 1825
New Brunswick, New Jersey

Father of the (Dutch) Reformed Church of America, 1771; and president of Theological Seminary of the Reformed (Dutch) Church in America, 1784–1810, renamed and relocated, New Brunswick (NJ) Theological Seminary, 1810–25; and first President of Queen's (Rutgers in 1825) College, 1810–25. This seminary was located in NYC from 1784–96; Flatbush, NY from 1769–99; Manhattan, NY from 1799–1810; moving to Queens facilities in New Brunswick in 1810. Livingston married Sarah Livingstone on Nov. 26, 1775, and they had one child. He pastored the Collegiate Reformed Church in NYC from 1770–76, but was driven from the city by the Revolution. He pastored in upstate NY from 1776–83 at four different locations until 1784, then back to his New York City church until 1810. He wrote the first hymnbook in English for the Dutch Reformed Church, as well as its constitution. His books included *Latin Work* (1785) and *Marriage of a Man with His Sister-in-Law* (1816).

John J. Husband

1760
Plymouth, England

March 19, 1825
Philadelphia, Pennsylvania

Music teacher and composer for "Revive Us Again" (lyrics by William MacKay). Husband came to America in 1809 and settled in Philadelphia where he taught music. He served as a clerk at St. Paul's Episcopal Church until his death. On Tuesday and Friday evenings he conducted a singing school. He is buried in the churchyard of the parish he loved so dearly.

Mason L. Weems
Parson Weems

Oct. 11, 1759
Anne Arundel County, Maryland

May 23, 1825
Beaufort, South Carolina

Church of England cleric, writer and bookseller. He served Episcopal parishes from 1784–1794, at which time he embarked on his career as an itinerant bookseller and pamphleteer. Weems's moral pamphlets attacked murder, adultery, gambling, and drunkenness. He married Frances Ewell on July 2, 1795, and had ten children. Weems authored 26 titles, including a biography of George Washington who was a member of his Pohick Church in Mt. Vernon, VA. He traveled from New York to Georgia for 30 years.

John Ryland

Jan. 29, 1753
Warwick, England

May 25, 1825
Bristol, England

Baptist minister and hymn writer. He pastored College Lane Baptist, Northampton 1781–93. Ryland was one of the founders of the Baptist Missionary Society in 1792, and second secretary from 1812–25. From 1794 until his death, he was president of Bristol Baptist Academy (breaking the grip of the Church of England on higher education) and in charge of Broadmead Baptist Chapel where he baptized WILLIAM CAREY. His hymns and verses were collected in an 1862 volume.

John Summerfield

Jan. 31, 1798
Preston, England

June 13, 1825
New York City, New York

Methodist evangelist. This eloquent pulpiter entered the Methodist Conference in Ireland (1819) and came to America (1821). Converted in 1817, Summerfield preached to great congregations in Philadelphia, Baltimore, and Washington in 1822, but poor health sent him to France for treatment. Summerfield returned to New York in 1824, but he was never able to resume a full evangelistic schedule. He helped found the American Tract Society. He died at the young age of 27.

Joseph Pilmore

Nov. 11, 1739
Tadmouth, England

July 24, 1825
Philadelphia, Pennsylvania

Early preacher of Methodism. Pilmore was converted by WESLEY's preaching (1755) and became an evangelist (1765). He labored in Philadelphia (1769–74), then went to England (1774–84). Unable to agree with WESLEY, Pilmore spent his last 40 years pastoring Episcopal churches: St. Thomas', Philadelphia (1785–93), Christ Church, New York City (1793–1804), and then St. Paul's, Philadelphia (1804–25). One child came from his union to Mary Wood in 1790.

Richard Furman

Oct. 9, 1755
Espus, New York

Aug. 25, 1825
South Carolina

Pastor and Baptist pioneer in the South. Furman was a southern embodiment of the best of Puritanism. He was converted under the influence of Evangelist Joseph Reese, in High Hills, South Carolina. Furman was ordained in 1774, then pastored in High Hills until 1787. He married Elizabeth Haynesworth in November, 1775 and Dorthea Burn on May 5, 1789. He went to FBC, Charleston, SC where he ministered for 37 years. The Baptist Convention of South Carolina was formed in 1821, the first state convention in Baptist circles, with Furman the chief advocate. He died a few months before the convention authorized establishment of a school, later known as Furman University, Edgerfield, SC (Greenville, SC), in 1851.

Pliny Fisk

June 24, 1792
Shellburne, Massachusetts

Oct. 23, 1825
Beirut, Syria (Lebanon)

Congregational (ABCFM) missionary and part of the first American mission to the Near East. Fisk and LEVI PARSONS were appointed in 1818 to consider opening a work in Palestine and Syria. They left November 3, 1819, and arrived in Smyrna, Turkey in 1820 and then went on to Egypt. After PARSON's death, Fisk traveled to Jerusalem through Egypt, Greece, Palestine, and Syria, surveying, distributing Bibles, and conducting language studies. He died of a malignant fever, having nearly completed an Arab and English dictionary.

David Bogue

Feb. 18, 1750
Coldingham, Hallydown, Scotland

Oct. 25, 1825
Brighton, England

Cofounder of the London Missionary Society, 1795 with Anglican THOMAS HAWEIS. Bogue was a Presbyterian, later turned Congregationalist minister, who was an early leader of modern missions. Bogue had hoped to serve in India but was blocked from going by the powerful East India Company. He also helped found a Bible and Tract Society. He pastored in Gospert, 1771–80, then tutored young men preparing for Congregational ministries. He wrote *An Essay on the Divine Authority of the New Testament* (1801) which was translated into many languages.

Paul Henkel

Dec. 15, 1754
Rowan County, North Carolina

Nov. 27, 1825
New Market, Virginia

Lutheran evangelist. In 1776, Henkel heard GEORGE WHITEFIELD preach and was converted. He married Elizabeth Negeleyon Nov. 20, 1776 and had nine children. Self-trained and self-supporting, Henkel was licensed (1783) and ordained in (1792) by the Pennsylvania Ministerium. Preaching in both English and German, he became an itinerant evangelist to Virginia, West Virginia, North and South Carolina, Tennessee, Kentucky, Indiana, and Ohio. He fathered three synods (North Carolina, 1803; Ohio, 1818; and Tennessee, 1820), and had six sons who entered the ministry. Henkel helped his sons establish a printing press and also authored numerous German and English books. He pastored in New Market, VA (twice), and in Salisbury, NC.

Gordon Hall

April 8, 1784
Tolland, Massachusetts

March 20, 1826
Bombay, India

First American missionary to Bombay, India. He was one of the first missionaries sent out by the ABCFM. Hall was converted at Williams College (1808), the same year he graduated from there, and was ordained to be a missionary (1812). He sailed with NOTT and RICE in 1812 to Bombay. He married Margaret Lewis on December 19, 1816. Hall served in India for 13 years where he labored with great diligence and success. After two children died, Mrs. Hall and two sons returned to America in 1825. Just before he died (from cholera he contracted as he ministered to stricken natives), he completed the revision of the Mahratta (Hindu people of south central India) Version of the New Testament. He evangelized, provided medical services, opened 35 schools, and distributed literature.

Reginald Heber

April 21, 1783
Malpas, England

April 3, 1826
Trichinoply, India

Anglican bishop of Calcutta, India, 1823–26, and hymn writer. Heber was rector of the village church in Hodnet, 1807–13. He completed the establishment of Bishop's College in Calcutta. He gave Christendom the great hymns, "Holy, Holy, Holy," 1809 (music by JOHN DYKES), "The Son of God Goes Forth to War" (music by HENRY CUTLER), and "From Greenland's Icy Mountains" (music by LOWELL MASON). While he was in the water (his outside spring bath) one day, he suffered a fatal stroke. His 57 hymns were published (1827), as well as his poetical works (1841).

Jean F. Oberlin

Aug. 31, 1740
Strasbourg, France

June 1, 1826
Ban-De-La-Roche, France

Teacher who became a Lutheran pastor at Walderbach in the Vosges (low mountains in NE France) and at Steinthal in 1767. Oberlin dedicated his life to raising the living standards of five isolated villages. Oberlin practiced medicine, founded a savings and loan bank, introduced cotton manufacturing, built roads, encouraged agriculture, and founded children's classes, showing competence and compassion. Oberlin (OH) College was founded and named after him in 1833. Each month he preached three sermons in French and one in German. His wife, Magdalena Salome, was a great help to him.

Karl M. Weber

Nov. 18, 1786
Eutin, Germany

June 5, 1826
London, England

Composed the music for "My Jesus, as Thou Wilt" (lyrics by BEN SCHMOLCK) and "Softly Now the Light of Day" (lyrics by GEORGE DOANE). In 1804, Weber became the conductor of operas at the Municipal Theater at Breslau, and later held similar positions at Stuttgart, Prague (1813), and Dresden (1815) until 1826. He is considered the founder of the German Romantic opera, of which he wrote ten. Of his instrumental music, *Invitation to the Dance* for piano is the best known. He was a noted concert pianist. Weber died from tuberculosis and was found dead in his bed.

Jedediah Morse

Aug. 23, 1761
Woodstock, Connecticut

June 9, 1826
New Haven, Connecticut

Pastored the First Congregational Church, Charlestown (Boston), MA 1789–1819. Morse prepared the first geography book ever published in America for use in schools in 1784. Eleven children came from Morse's marriage to Elizabeth Breese on May 14, 1789 (SAMUEL F. B. MORSE being one of them). He served on many boards. Andover was founded after an incident in 1805 at Harvard when a liberal Unitarian, Henry Ware (1764–1845), was appointed instead of him for a divinity teaching post. He founded and edited the *Panoplist*, which meant "a magnificent, complete covering," (1806–11), which was orthodox and anti-Unitarian. He helped found Andover (MA) Theological Seminary (1808) and the American Bible Society (1816).

Eliphalet Pearson

June 11, 1752
Newbury, Massachusetts

Sept. 12, 1826
Greenland, New Hampshire

One of the founders of Andover (MA) Theological Seminary. Pearson married Priscilla Holyoke (July 17, 1780), and Sarah Bromfield (Sept. 29, 1785), giving him a total of five children. From 1778–86, he was principal of Philips Academy, Andover, MA. Prior to his Andover days, he was professor of Hebrew and Oriental languages at Harvard, 1786–1806. He prepared a constitution for Andover and served as a professor during its first years, 1808–09.

James O'Kelly

c 1735
Ireland

Oct.16, 1826
Southern Virginia/North Carolina

Methodist minister. O'Kelly married Elizabeth Meeks in 1760. He came to America in 1778. O'Kelly was an elder in the Methodist Episcopal Church in 1789. He opposed the Church's stand on matters of life tenure and powers of the bishops, so in 1792, he withdrew and formed a Republican Methodist Church, and later helped form the Christian Church. He was an active opponent of slavery. O'Kelly wrote *Essays on Negro Slavery* (1784). Remnants of his work later merged with the Congregationalists.

Ann Hasseltine Judson

Dec. 22, 1789
Bradford, Massachusetts

Oct. 24, 1826
Amherst, Burma

Beloved first wife of ADONIRAM JUDSON and a missionary heroine. Ann, along with HARRIET NEWELL, was the first woman to leave America as a missionary. She was converted Sept. 14, 1806 as a result of HANNAH MORE's writings. She married JUDSON on February 5, 1812, and had three children, all of whom died in infancy. She accompanied her husband to India, then to Burma. After a brief furlough, 1822–23, she rejoined her husband and supported him during his days of imprisonment for preaching the gospel during the English/Burmese War of 1824. She translated Matthew, Daniel, and Jonah into Burmese. When Judson was finally released he found her in a coma, after which he cared for her as much as possible. She died of tropical fever and was buried while Judson was away at a court hearing in Ava, Burma.

"Shall we sit down in ease and leave beings like ourselves of our own sex to perish? No! By all our tender feelings and by the blood of Him who died, enlighten and save (them)."

Thomas Vasey

1745
England

Dec. 27, 1826
Leeds, England

Methodist circuit-riding preacher and evangelist. He was an early follower of WESLEY. Vasey was ordained in 1784 by WESLEY, and was sent to the American colonies. He worked diligently on the frontiers organizing congregations and visiting isolated farms. He planted Methodism abroad for a couple of years and then returned to England, traveling and preaching throughout the country, after a brief ministry in the Episcopal/Anglican world, 1786–89. He attended Wesley Chapel, London, 1811–25.

Johann H. Pestalozzi

Jan. 12, 1746
Zurich, Switzerland

Feb. 17, 1827
Brugg, Switzerland

Educational reformer who established an industrial school for poor children on his estate, Neuhof, in 1775. Pestalozzi married Anna Schulthess in 1769. After five years, he turned to writing educational novels, 1779–98. When France invaded Switzerland in 1798, he took care of 80 orphans at Unterwalden. He taught school at Yverdon for 20 years until 1825. Pestalozzi's "object-lesson" style of teaching became famous. He emphasized education must be essentially religious, developing man as a whole, among other convictions.

Leigh Richmond

Jan. 29, 1772
Liverpool, England

May 8, 1827
Turvey, England

Church of England pastor who was curate at Brading on the Isle of Wight (1798–1805) and then rector of Turvey (1805–27). Richmond was a convert of WILBERFORCE's writings. Richmond's popular tract, "The Dairyman's Daughter" (1809), saw over four million copies circulated in 19 languages. Other worthy tracts were "The Negro Servant" and "The Young Cottager."

James Varick

Jan. 10, 1750
Newburgh, New York

June 9 or July 22, 1827
New York City, New York

First senior bishop of African Methodist Episcopal Zion Church, 1820–28. Varick served unofficially for the first two years. He organized the Zion Society in 1796, and an African Church in Methodism from 1799–1816. He married Aurelia Jones in 1798 and they had seven children. He declared his independence from the Methodist Church in 1820. He died two weeks after New York abolished slavery. The name Zion was added in 1848 after his death. Some say he died in 1828.

Freeborn Garrettson

Aug. 15, 1752
Hartford County, Maryland

Sept. 26, 1827
Rhinebeck, New York

Methodist evangelist and abolitionist. Upon his conversion, he became involved in freeing slaves along with pursuing his passion for lost souls. Garrettson became a Methodist in 1775, converted under the preaching of Daniel Ruff. He spent 50 years as an evangelist. He and another person were sent to Nova Scotia and New Brunswick, becoming the first missionaries of American Methodism. Garrettson married Catharine Livingston on June 30, 1793, and they settled in Rhinebeck in 1800. He would be considered a pacifist today. He said as he died, "Holy, Holy, Holy, Lord God Almighty! Hallelujah! Hallelujah!"

Edward Payson

July 25, 1783
Rindge, New Hampshire

Oct. 22, 1827
Portland, Maine

Congregational pastor at Second Church, Portland, ME 1807–27. During Dawson's 20 years there, he received more than 700 converts. He also traveled, conducting large evangelistic endeavors. He married Anna Shipman on May 8, 1811, and had eight children, including Elizabeth (Prentiss - novelist and hymn writer). Payson was known for his devotional life and prayer time. He wrote *The Bible Above All Price* (1814).

George Liele

1751
Virginia

1828

America's first missionary to a foreign land. He was probably the first ordained black preacher in America. This slave was converted in 1773 in a Baptist Church where his master was a deacon. The congregation was amazed at Liele's ability to explain the Scriptures and ordained him. He preached in Georgia during the Revolutionary War. In 1779, he, and his friend, Andrew Bryan, founded what many believe to be America's first black Baptist Church in Savannah, GA. In September of 1784, he went to Jamaica and started the FBC there. It grew from four to 500 in eight years. In 1793, he baptized 500 converts, established congregations in other towns, and recruited other preachers. He was jailed in 1797, falsely charged with encouraging rebellion by preaching. He organized a missionary society in Jamaica that sent 50 Jamaican missionaries to Africa and 20 more to the US to minister to blacks. This was 33 years before JUDSON sailed for India/Burma!

Charles Manners-Sutton

Feb. 14, 1755
England

July 21, 1828
Lambeth, England

Archbishop of Canterbury, 1805–28. Manners was the name of an English family possessing earldom and dukedom of Rutland and marquisate {marquis is a nobleman above count or earl, but below a duke—marquisate is the territory ruled} of Granby who had many distinguished members. Charles Manners-Sutton, Sr. was the fourth son of Lord George Manners-Sutton, and the grandson of John, third duke of Rutland. Charles Sr. was educated at Cambridge. He held a pastorate in Nottingham and then served as bishop of Norwich, 1792–1805. His son, Charles was first Viscount of Canterbury (1780–1845) and an English politician representing the Tory Party.

Lott Cary

c 1780
Charles City County, Virginia

Nov. 10, 1828
Liberia

Baptist missionary, the first African American to Africa. Cary was a slave, who purchased the freedom for his two children in 1813 ($850) after his wife's death. After his conversion in 1807, upon hearing a sermon on John 3:16, he learned to read and became a strong Baptist preacher. He later married again. He founded Richmond Foreign Missions Society (1813) and Richmond African Baptist Missionary Society (1815). He went to Liberia in 1821 as a missionary with five companions and was the pastor of a Baptist church organized there. Cary is considered one of the founders of the nation of Liberia in 1822 and became its governor. He pastored at Cape Montserado, 1822–28. An accidental explosion of gunpowder killed him while he was helping to fortify the colony against a threatened attack by natives.

Felix Neff

Oct. 8, 1798
Geneva, Switzerland

April 12, 1829
Geneva, Switzerland

Leader among the brave Waldensians. After his conversion, Neff became a Swiss soldier in the garrison of his native city in Geneva. He went to London (1819), was ordained (1823), and then returned to Switzerland. He began a ministry in the Hautes-Alpes, creating a place of refuge. Neff endured much hardship but had a vital ministry to the Waldensians from those secluded valleys.

Carl G. Glaser

May 4, 1784
Weissenfels, Germany

April 16, 1829
Barmen, Germany

Hymn composer for "O for a Thousand Tongues to Sing" (lyrics by CHARLES WESLEY) and wrote the lyrics for "Come Holy Spirit, Heaven Dove" (music arranged by LOWELL MASON). Glaser received musical training from his father and violin training from Campagnoli in Leipzig. Glaser moved to Barmen, where he taught voice, piano, and violin. He was also a gifted choral conductor, composer, and publisher.

Elizabeth King Mills

1805
Stoke Newington, England

April 21, 1829
London, England

Hymn writer who wrote the spirited hymn "We'll Work 'Till Jesus Comes." William Miller wrote the music. It is not conclusive if he was the Adventist leader (1782–1849) of his time. Elizabeth was the daughter of Philip King and the wife of Thomas Mills, a member of Parliament.

John Jay

Dec. 12, 1745
New York, New York

May 17, 1829
Bedford, New York

President of American Bible Society, 1821–28, and the first chief justice of the United States, 1789–95. As chief justice, he wrote a decision that resulted in the eleventh Amendment to the U.S. Constitution and settled many disputes. Jay married Sarah Livingston on April 28, 1774 (died: May 28, 1802), and they had seven children. Jay was admitted to the bar in 1768, served as a delegate to the Continental Congress (1774–79), and was president of this Congress (1778–79). He was governor of New York, 1795–1801. Jay was in complete retirement after this.

John M. Mason

March 19, 1770
New York, New York

Dec. 26, 1829
New York, New York

Pastor of Scotch Presbyterian Church on Cedar St. in NYC 1793–1810. Mason married Ann Lefferts on May 13, 1793 and had eight children. In 1804, he founded a seminary to educate Scotch Presbyterians which opened in his home in 1805. It later became Union Theological Seminary of New York. Mason served as provost of Columbia University, NYC (1811–16) and then was president of Dickinson College, Carlisle, PA (1821–24). He edited the *Christian Herald*. Early on, he was in the Associate Reformed denomination.

John Anderson

1748
England

April 6, 1830
North Buffalo, New York

Founder, teacher and first president of Associate Presbyterian Synod (Pittsburgh Theological in 1959) Seminary, Service, PA 1794–1819. Anderson was an Associate Reformed Church pastor. In 1783 he came to America in answer to a plea for ministers. He gathered an 800-volume library from Scotland and moved to western Pennsylvania, where he founded his seminary. It was the first seminary west of the Alleghenies.

John H. Hobart

Sept. 14, 1775
Philadelphia, Pennsylvania

Sept. 12, 1830
Auburn, New York

Protestant Episcopal bishop of New York and rector of Trinity Church, 1816–30. Hobart was a zealous conservative. He married Mary Chandler on May 6, 1800. By 1806, Hobart was active in founding the General Theological Seminary, NYC, where he became a professor of pastoral theology in 1821. He was one of the first Protestants to preach in Rome. Hobart also founded the Episcopal Tract Society in 1810. He was bishop-co-adjutor in the New York diocese (1811) and rector of Trinity Church there (1816). He founded an Episcopal college in Geneva, NY, which in 1860 changed its name to Hobart College. His most famous work was *An Apology for Apostolic Order and Its Advocate* (1807) which caused much controversy, claiming continuing succession from the apostles is the only valid Christian ministry. He is buried in NYC.

John Smith

Jan. 12, 1794
Cudworth, England

1831

Prayer warrior, known as the man with callused knees. At 18, Smith attended a revival in his home area and was soundly converted. He attended Leeds Academy and began to pray much and witness. He itinerated in York for nine months, rapidly growing spiritually. He often prayed and studied the Bible seven to eight hours a day. Smith married a Miss Hamer. He labored amongst the Wesleyan Methodist in England, beginning in 1816. He contracted consumption (TB) and, after his last preaching appointment in Lincoln, his lungs gave out. He died at 37. Along with "Praying HYDE," Smith is remembered as one of the greatest prayer warriors of all time. His last word was "Amen."

George D. Boardman, Sr.

Feb. 8, 1801
Livermore, Maine

Feb. 11, 1831
Tavoy, Burma

Baptist missionary to Burma. Boardman went there in 1827 and labored successfully among the Karens until his early death at age 30. After a year at Moulmein, he opened a new station at Tavoy, 125 miles south of there. In 1829, he began his ministry to the Karens. Boardman had much physical suffering, "ever an invalid," and died of pulmonary disease (tuberculosis). His widow, SARAH HALL, became the second Mrs. ADONIRAM JUDSON. The Boardmans lost two of their three children to disease.

Robert Hall

May 2, 1764
Arnesby, England

Feb. 21, 1831
Bristol, England

Baptist preacher and social reformer. He was famous for his commanding oratory and defense of workers' rights, particularly the Leicestershire lace workers. Hall was baptized into the Baptist denomination at age 14. In 1783, he began his ministry in Bristol as assistant pastor until 1791. Hall then pastored in Cambridge (1791–1805), at Harvey Lane, Leicester (1807–25), and back at Broadmeade, Bristol (1825–31). He also married after 1807. Despite frail health, he was considered to be a giant in English Baptist circles. He was subject to attacks of insanity and had a spine disease. He wrote from *Freedom of the Press* (1793) to *Reflections on War* (1802). He appears to have been the ROBERT G. LEE of the 1800's in majesty of thought and expression—the foremost preacher of his time. He also wrote *Modern Infidelity*.

Richard Allen

Feb. 14, 1760
Philadelphia, Pennsylvania

March 26, 1831
Philadelphia, Pennsylvania

Founder and first bishop of the African Methodist Episcopal Church, 1816–31, a denomination which he himself founded. Allen grew up a slave on a farm in Dover, DE. As a Methodist convert at age 17, he joined the church in Philadelphia; but in 1787, he founded his own church (St. George Methodist) for blacks because of prejudice. It was called the Free African Society. By 1794, his African Methodist Episcopal Church was dedicated by FRANCES ASBURY. In 1816 some 16 black Methodist churches expanded to found the AMEC. Allen's wife, Sara, died on July 16, 1849.

Benjamin Carr

Sept. 12, 1769
London, England

May 24, 1831
Philadelphia, Pennsylvania

Singer, composer, arranger, organist, pianist, publisher, and editor. Carr edited the *Musical Journal* and was one of the founders of the Musical Fund Society of Philadelphia in 1820. Carr came to America in 1793 and operated the first music store in Philadelphia, 1793–1831. He encouraged other musicians and also published collections of sacred music. He became organist at St. Peter's Church in Philadelphia in 1820.

Willem Bilderdijk

Sept. 7, 1756
Amsterdam, Netherlands

Dec. 18, 1831
Haarlem, Netherlands

Poet, grammarian, critic and scholar who became state librarian under Emperor Napoleon (ruled: 1806–14). In 1802, Bilderdijk married Katherina Schweikhardt. Early in his life, he practiced law at The Hague until he was exiled (1795), moving to Hamburg, Germany, then to London before returning to the Netherlands (1806). From 1817–27, he lectured on history in Leyden. After 1827, he lived at Haarlem. He and ISAAK DA COSTA, his convert, started a strong evangelical revival in the Netherlands. His famous poem was "The Destruction of the First World".

Jacob Engle

1753
Switzerland

1832

First overseer of the Brethren in Christ Church (first known as River Brethren) **in Pennsylvania.** Engle's family immigrated to America in 1759 when Jacob was a child. He later settled near Marietta in Lancaster County,

PA and worked with a weaver named Witmer. They shared the conviction that immersion was the proper mode of baptism, and in 1778, they immersed each other. Shortly thereafter, they met in the home of Henry Engle and organized a new movement, over which Jacob was appointed bishop in Pennsylvania. BCC was a combination of Pietist and Mennonite beliefs. He made one horseback trip to Ontario to organize those that moved there.

Adam Clarke

April 1762
Moybeg, Ireland

Aug. 16, 1832
London, England

Theologian and writer who was perhaps the greatest Methodist since WESLEY. Clarke was converted in 1779 while praying in a field as a youth. He became a circuit-riding preacher in Wiltshire in 1782 and soon was all over England. He married Mary Cooke in 1788. Clarke served at such places as the Channel Islands, the Shetland Islands, and in London (c. 1805 on). He was president of the Methodist Conference three times, and also printed an Arabic Bible. His eight-volume *Commentary on the Holy Bible* (London, 1812–26) was the result of 40 years of labor. Clarke died of cholera/plague. When asked if he was trusting Christ as he died, he said, "I do! I do!" For a time he denied "the eternal Sonship" of Christ.

Walter Scott (1)

Aug. 15, 1771
Edinburgh, Scotland

Sept. 21, 1832
Abbotsford, Scotland

Poet and historical novelist. He was a life long invalid. Scott authored two series of over 20 historical novels, including *Ivanhoe*, which made him famous. His narrative poem, *The Lady of the Lake* was one of his best. Margaret Charlotte became his wife in 1797. After his marriage, he lived five months out of the year in Edinburgh and seven months in the country. He built a mansion in Abbotsford in 1812, living as a country gentleman. He was made a baronet (British heredity of honor, below a baron, above a knight) in 1820. He invented the term "freelance." His life could be divided as follows: years of preparation (1771–1802); years of narrative poems (1802–14); years of Waverly novels (1814–32). Scott suffered several paralytic strokes, and said as he died, "There is only one book—The Bible." His favorite Bible verse was John 9:24.

Richard Watson (2)

Feb. 22, 1781
Barton-upon-Humber, England

Jan. 8, 1833
London, England

Wesleyan Methodist theologian. Watson was with the Methodist New Connexion (1801–7), editor of a Liverpool newspaper (1807–12), and then re-entered the Wesleyan ministry in 1812. He was actively interested in the organization of their foreign missionary society, serving as one of its secretaries, 1816–30. Watson was active in the anti-slavery movement and published several books including *Christian Institutes* (1823), a masterpiece of Methodist (Arminian) theology.

Rowland Hill

Aug. 23, 1744
Hawkstone Park, England

April 11, 1833
London, England

Outstanding evangelist of the Church of England, a powerful and witty preacher. Hill was in sympathy with WHITEFIELD and Calvinistic Methodism. He was curate at Kingston in 1773. He visited India and Scotland, always attracting large crowds. His evangelism endeavors spanned ten years. Hill had a good inheritance, making it possible for him to build Surrey Chapel, London, in 1783 where he preached to large audiences until shortly before his death. He had 3,000 children in 13 Sunday schools. At one point he attacked WESLEY, which he later deeply regretted. His chief work was

Village Dialogues (1810). He died saying, "And when I'm to die, Receive me, I'll cry; For Jesus hath loved me, I cannot tell why."

William Wilberforce

Aug. 24, 1759
Hull, England

July 29, 1833
London, England

Politician, philanthrophist, and promoter of the abolition of slave trading. Wilberforce began his political career by founding the Proclamation Society to combat vice. He was converted (1784) and took up the abolition cause (1786), proposing his first motion for abolition of slave trade (1789), which did not carry until 1791. As a Parliament member for Hull (1780), Yorkshire (1784), and Bramber, Sussex, 1812–25, he aggressively pursued the passage of bills to end slavery. Wilberforce married Barbara Spooner. He helped found the Church Missionary Society (1799) and the British and Foreign Bible Society (1804). In 1807 an act of Parliament ended the slave trade. In 1823, he founded the Anti-Slavery Society. He wrote *Practical View of Christianity* (1797). He published *Appeal. . .on Behalf of Negro Slaves in the West Indies*, which moved for the abolition of slavery and the emancipation of slaves. In 1825, he retired from the House of Commons. He was able to curb the powerful East India Company and was instrumental in having its charter revoked, after his death, in 1859. He was a key figure of the Clapham sect (group of wealthy Anglican Evangelicals who lived in the Clapham area, northwest of London). One month after his death, slavery was abolished throughout the British Empire. His favorite Bible verses were Luke 18:13 and Galatians 6:9.

"Christianity condensed: admit, submit, commit, transmit"

Hannah More

Feb. 2, 1745
Stapleton, England

Sept. 7, 1833
Clifton, England

Writer and philanthropist. She organized numerous Sunday schools, wrote over 50 tracts, promoted the Bible Society, encouraged the ministry of missions, and supported the abolitionist cause. Hannah lived with her sisters at Wrington, ten miles from Bristol (1786), at Barley Wood (1802), and finally at Clifton (1828). Her cheap repository Tracts helped reach the working classes. She had millions of her tracts printed (beginning c. 1788) and was a powerful evangelical Anglican. She never married.

John McMillan

Nov. 11, 1752

Nov. 16, 1833

First Presbyterian pastor to serve a congregation west of the Allegheny Mountains. McMillan went to southwestern Pennsylvania in 1776 to Pigeon Creek Church, and fearlessly reorganized the congregation. He opened a "log cabin" or academy in Canonsburg in 1791, which grew to be one of the parent institutions of Washington/Jefferson College, Washington, PA.

Lorenzo Dow

Oct. 16, 1777
Coventry, Connecticut

Feb. 2, 1834
Washington, D.C.

Eccentric Methodist preacher who became an evangelist in 1798. Converted by the ministry of Hope Hull in 1791, he was "dropped" from his conference for going to England and Ireland, 1799 and 1805, to preach specifically to Catholics. From then on, Dow worked independently but maintained his Methodist doctrine. His marriage to Peggy Holcomb took place on Sept. 3, 1804. In an 1821 revival in Jacksonborough, GA, local rowdies forced Dow to close the meeting (throwing bricks and stones into the windows of the church). Dow went to a saloon and overturned a barrel of whiskey.

The next day he prayed for God to destroy the town. Within 20 years, fires, winds, and floods did just that. He had long hair and a beard, which caused him to be ridiculed as "Crazy Dow." He was a great advocate of camp meetings, and a catalyst in the formation of the primitive Methodist Church in England.

"Deathbed repentance is blowing smoke from a spent candle in Heaven's face."

Augustus W. Hare

Nov. 17, 1792
Rome, Italy

Feb. 18/19, 1834
Rome, Italy

Model country minister and pastor of a secluded country parish in Alton-Barnes, 1829–33, where he had a solid work after graduating from New College, Oxford. Hare moved to Italy for health reasons in 1833, where he died. Hare wrote *Memorials of a Quiet Life*. Along with his brother, Julius, he edited *Guesses at Truth* (1827) and published *Sermons to a Country Congregation* (2 vols., 1836).

William Carey

Aug. 17, 1761
Paulersbury, England

June 9, 1834
Serampore, India

"Father of Modern Missions" and missionary to India. Carey was a shoemaker 1775–89, school-teacher, and Baptist pastor. He was converted on February 10, 1779, at a prayer service, following a witness from John Warr, a fellow cobbler. He then became a Baptist pastor in Moulton (1786) and Leicester (1790). He married Dorothy Plackett in 1781 (died 1807 following a mental breakdown). He then married Charlotte Rumohr (1761–1821) in May, 1808 and Grace Hughes Forbes in 1822. His second wife was a lifelong invalid and a lady of means who had come to India for health reasons. On Oct. 2, 1792, he founded a Baptist Missionary Society in Kettering after giving a historic sermon ("Enquiry...") on Isaiah 54:2–3, five months earlier. Carey sailed to India on June 13, 1793, and served there for 40 years until his death. It was six years before he baptized his first convert in 1800. That same year he settled in Serampore, a Danish colony 13 miles north of Calcutta. Carey taught languages at Ft. William College in Calcutta, 1800 onward, and translated portions of Scriptures into 44 dialects. In 1812, the Serampore printing presses and manuscripts were destroyed by a fire. He established Serampore College (1818) and the Agricultural Society of India (1820). Through his efforts, the tradition of widow-burning was abolished in 1829. He died of repeated attacks of fever and other complications. Some of his last words were, "When I am gone, say nothing about Dr. Carey; speak about Dr. Carey's Saviour." Felix Carey (1786–1822) was his oldest son and he became the first missionary to Burma (Mynamar).

"Attempt great things for God, expect great things from God."

Robert Morrison

Jan. 5, 1782
Morpeth, England

Aug. 1, 1834
Canton, China

First Protestant missionary to China. Converted (1798), Morrison was a Presbyterian under the London Missionary Society who arrived in Canton (1807) and served for 25 years until his death. He married Mary Morton (1791–1821) on February 20, 1809, at Macao, which was the same day he was appointed translator to the East India Company (this gave him legal footing for remaining on Chinese soil). He divided his time with EIC and missionary work. Morrison and his assistant, WILLIAM MILNE, founded the Anglo-Chinese College at Malacca in 1818 and translated the Bible into Chinese in 1819 (published in 1823). The NT had been translated in 1814 after 1,813 days of work. He published a Chinese grammar (1814), and a Chinese dictionary (1821). Morrison also knew Hebrew, Latin, and Greek. He returned to England in 1823 with several thousand books. Morrison married Eliza Armstrong (1824) and returned to China (1826).

William Carvosso

March 11, 1750
Mousehole, England

Oct. 13, 1834

Methodist layman. He was converted at age 21. Carvosso said, "I emptied myself of self and sin, and filled myself with God." In 1774, he became a class reader (home Bible study leader) and served in this capacity for 60 years. Carvosso supported his wife and three children on a poor farm, which grew to be a fruitful garden. His visits, prayers, and exhortations were the means of hundreds of conversions.

Edward Irving

Aug. 4, 1792
Annan, Scotland

Dec. 7, 1834
Glasgow, Scotland

Leader in the Catholic Apostolic or Irvingite Church. Irving served as THOMAS CHALMER's assistant in Glasgow (1819–22) and won fame for his sermons at the Regent Square Church, London before veering into strange doctrines (1822–32). The original Caledonian Chapel in London was too small, so a new church was built in Regent Square in 1827. Deposed from Presbyterianism (Church of Scotland) in 1832, he majored on gifts, tongues, prophesies, and healings. Irving died of tuberculosis.

William McKendree

July 6, 1757
William City, Virginia

March 5, 1835
Gallatin, Tennessee

First American-born bishop of the Methodist Episcopal Church. After his 1787 conversion under the preaching of John Easter, McKendree became an evangelist the next year. He served in Virginia until 1796 and then he headquartered in Kentucky. In 1808 he was made bishop to succeed RICHARD WHATCOAT. McKendree was ASBURY's assistant during the last eight years of ASBURY's life. McKendree then took Methodism to the West. In 1828, he donated 480 acres in Lebanon, IL for Lebanon (McKendree, in 1830) College.

Thomas McCrie

Nov. 1772
Dunse, Scotland

Aug. 5, 1835
Edinburgh, Scotland

Presbyterian divine and historian. McCrie was an ordained minister of an anti-burgher church, Edinburgh, in 1796. After ten years, he parted company with the ministry over some civil subjects and united with others to form the Constitutional Presbytery. He pastored the West Richmond St. Church 1809–35. His great work was the *Life of JOHN KNOX* (2 vols., 1812). McCrie wrote numerous and valuable works on American history.

John Emory

April 11, 1789
Spainards Neck, Maryland

Dec. 16, 1835
Near Reistertown, Maryland

Methodist editor and publisher. After pastoring in the Philadelphia Conference, Emory became a book agent and editor in New York, 1824–32. He was bishop in the Methodist Church, 1832–35. He founded the *Methodist Quarterly Review* and headed The Methodist Book Concern. Emory married Caroline Sellers on October 12, 1813 (died: 1815) and Ann Wright on May 12, 1818. Emory died after being thrown from his carriage and was buried in Baltimore, MD.

John Lowell

May 11, 1799
Boston, Massachusetts

March 4, 1836
Bombay, India

Founder of the Lowell Institute, Boston, MA in 1839, and great philanthropist. He spent most of his life traveling. In 1816, he went to India as a merchant to the East Indies with his father's textile business. Lowell married Georgina Amory on April 6, 1825, and they had two children. Lowell left over $250,000 for the maintaining of free courses on religion, science, literature, and the arts at the institute.

William White
Father of the American Episcopal Church

April 4, 1748
Philadelphia, Pennsylvania

July 17, 1836
Philadelphia, Pennsylvania

Second presiding bishop of Protestant Episcopal Church (Episcopal Church in 1967), **1796–1836, and chaplain of the US Senate, 1790–1800.** White established the Episcopal Church independent of the Church of England. He was ordained in England in 1772, but returned to Philadelphia where he became assistant, then rector of Christ Church 1776–1836, and served as Congress chaplain, 1777–89. White was made bishop of Pennsylvania in England in 1787. Eight children came from his marriage to Mary Harrison in February, 1773.

John S. Smith

1750
Gloucester, England

Sept. 21, 1836
London, England

Organist and composer who gave us the music to "The Star Spangled Banner." Though greatly beloved as the American National Anthem (lyrics written by FRANCIS SCOTT KEY), it has always been hard to sing. The tune appeared in Smith's fifth collection of glees (1799), arranged for three voices, and entitled "Anacreon in Heaven." Reference to the Greek poet implies that the tune was known before his time.

Luther Rice

March 25, 1783
Northboro, Massachusetts

Sept. 25, 1836
Edgefield, South Carolina

Baptist missions enthusiast. He first helped form the American Board of Commissioners for Foreign Missions. He sailed with HALL and NOTT in 1812. Rice's Congregational ties were cut in 1813 after he became immersed via the Baptist ministry expanding in India the year before by WILLIAM WARD. Returning to America in 1813, he organized the American Baptist Home Missionary Society. He led the organizing of the First Baptist national convention in Philadelphia in 1814. Later known as the triennal convention, it was a federation of local missionary societies with Rice being the principal agent at that time. Henceforth he devoted his energies to developing Baptist missionary and educational enterprise. He also organized the American Baptist Publications Society. He issued the first Baptist weekly, *The Columbian Star* in 1822. At the time of his death the society had under its appointment more than 100 missionaries. He is buried at Prince Pleasant Church, Washington, D.C.

Charles Simeon

Sept. 24, 1759
Reading, England

Nov. 12/13, 1836
Cambridge, England

Church of England clergyman. Simeon was converted in 1779. In 1783, he became pastor of the Church of the Holy Trinity in Cambridge where he served for 54 years. He helped found the Church Missionary Society (1799) and also assisted in founding the British and Foreign Bible

Society (1804). His outline sketches of the Bible are in a 17-volume *Homiletics* (2,536 sermon outlines). He promoted an evangelical revival spirit and missions expansion in the Anglican community. His favorite Bible verse was Ephesians 3:18.

John Rippon

April 29, 1751
Tiverton, England

Dec. 17, 1836
London, England

Baptist pastor. He served 64 years as pastor of Carter Lane Church, London (1772–1836). This followed JOHN GILL's 52-year ministry there. Rippon published *Selection of Hymns from the Best Authors* (source of "How Firm a Foundation") in 1787. Rippon was editor and publisher of *Baptist Annual Register* (1790–1802).

Johann G. Nageli

May 26, 1773
Wetzikon, Switzerland

Dec. 26, 1836
Wetzikon, Switzerland

Wrote the music for "Blest Be the Tie that Binds," the famed JOHN FAWCETT hymn. Nageli established a music publishing firm in Zurtan and was founder and president of the Swiss Association for the Cultivation of Music. Being a close friend of Beethoven (1770–1827), Nageli published most of his music. He applied the Pestalozzian system of music learning. He also published works by BACH and HANDEL. Nageli was a composer of folk songs and choral music.

Elijah P. Lovejoy

Nov. 9, 1802
Albion, Maine

Nov. 7, 1837
Alton, Illinois

Presbyterian minister and abolitionist editor. He became a martyr. Lovejoy stirred feelings throughout the North against slavery. He was in St. Louis, 1833–36, and married Celia French on March 4, 1835. His bold, outspoken editorials in the *Alton Observer* (1836 onward) aroused mobs to wreck his presses three times. He died from gunshot wounds when his newspaper office was burned by a mob. This contributed to the sentiment in the North for the abolition of slavery.

Edward D. Griffin

Jan. 6, 1770
East Haddam, Connecticut

Nov. 8, 1837
Newark, New Jersey

President of Williams College, Williamstown, MA 1821–36 where he enlarged the curriculum and injected evangelical fervor. He saved it from financial disaster. He married Frances Huntington on May 17, 1796, and had two children. Griffin pastored in New Hartford, CT (1795–1801); worked at the First Presbyterian Church, Newark, NJ as an associate (1801–7), and served as pastor (1807–9). Park St. Church of Boston was his next pastorate (1811–14), followed by the Second Church, Newark (1815–21). He wrote from *Lectures in Park St. Church* (1813) to *The Doctrine of Divine Efficiency* (1833).

Joshua Marshman

April 20, 1768
Westbury Leigh, England

Dec. 5, 1837
Calcutta/Serampore, India

Baptist missionary to India. Before becoming a missionary, Marshman was a weaver by trade. Marshman married Hannah Shepherd in 1791 and had six children. In 1799 with WILLIAM WARD and others, he went to India to join missionary WILLIAM CAREY. They were soon known as the famed "Serampore Trio." Marshman taught, WARD printed, and CAREY translated and preached. In 1818, he published the first newspaper in a non-European language in the East, *Mirror of News*, in the Bengali dialect. In 1821, he published the monthly *Friend of Indians*, the first English magazine published there. In 1827, the Serampore Mission left the Baptist fold. Marshman was an able Orientalist, publishing a Chinese version of the Bible which he translated. His wife, Hannah, not only cared for her six children but also cared for CAREY's turbulent family, several missionary widows, and many orphans of both natives and missionaries.

Samuel Marsden

July 20, 1764
Horsforth, England

May 12, 1838
Windsor, Australia

Apostle of New Zealand. Marsden married Elizabeth Triston in 1793. In 1794 he went as a chaplain of the Church of England to a penal colony at Paramatta, Australia, establishing a farm to train convicts. Marsden also started schools and a seminary in New South Wales. Largely a failure in attempts to evangelize convicts and aboriginal people, his labors amongst Polynesian people of the South Sea Islands had significant results. Burdened for the Maoris people in New Zealand, Marsden and two laymen founded a mission in 1814 to help civilize and Christianize the nation. He made seven visits there, the last made in 1837 under the Church Missionary Society, when he was lame and almost blind.

Zachary MacAulay

1768

May 13, 1838

Philanthropist and abolitionist. He was the British governor of Sierra Leone, 1793–99. MacAulay was associated with WILLIAM WILBERFORCE for many years. He sought to abolish the British slave trade, and to halt slavery overseas. In 1823, he helped found the Anti-Slavery Society and London University. He edited the journal *The Christian Observer* (1802–16).

Robert Grant

1779
Bengal, India

July 9, 1838
Dalpoorie, India

Hymn writer of "O Worship the King" (music arranged by WILLIAM GARDINER, but originating from Franz Hayden). In 1785, Grant's family moved to London. He was an Anglican son of a Scottish businessman. In 1818, he was elected to Parliament, representing four towns. Grant helped Jews to gain their civil liberties by a bill he introduced in 1833. Grant was elected governor in Bombay in 1834 (the same year he was knighted). He was a popular and benevolent philanthropist who wrote twelve hymns.

Christmas Evans
The Welsh Bunyan

Dec. 25, 1766
Esgair-Waun (Ysgaerwen), Cardiganshire, Wales

July 19, 1838
Swansea, Wales

Famed Baptist evangelist who led his nation in revival 100 years before EVAN ROBERTS did the same. Evans lost an eye shortly after his conversion, when he was 17, from a senseless gang fight. His parents were poor and unable to care for him adequately. After his father died in 1775, he was raised by an often cruel relative. Leaving Presbyterianism, he joined the Baptist Church in 1788, being baptized in the river Duar. He was ordained in 1789. Katherine Jones became his wife in 1790. Evans's evangelism progressed throughout Wales from Lleyn (1789–92), to the Isle of Anglesey (1792–1826), to Tonyvelin (1826–32), and then to Caernarvon, (1832 on). Evans saw large numbers of converts in coal mines, churches, and open fields. Evans became known as a fiery preacher whose one-eyed, dramatic style drew great crowds. He mastered Hebrew, Greek, and Latin languages. Christmas Evans said as he died, "...I have never labored without blood in the vessel. Good bye! Drive on!"

Gideon Blackburn

Aug. 27, 1772
Augusta County, Virginia

Aug. 23, 1838
Carlinville, Illinois

Presbyterian clergyman, educator, and pioneer missionary to the Cherokee Indians. He married Grizzel Blackburn on Oct. 3, 1793. He pastored Presbyterian churches, Louisville, and Versailles, KY early on. He worked with Cherokee youth in Tennessee, 1804–10, and started several schools in Franklin, TN. Blackburn's preaching, teaching, and introduction of agricultural methods to the Indians was largely successful. Blackburn was president of Harpeth Academy, 1810–27. He was made president of Danville (VA) College (Centre College), 1827–30. He raised funds for his theological college, which opened as Blackburn Theological Seminary, Carlinville, IL in 1857.

Hugh J. Rose

June 9, 1795
Little Horsted, England

Dec. 22, 1838
Florence, Italy

Pre-Tractarian New Testament scholar. Rose was identified with a group of High Churchman known as the Clapton Sect, who functioned as an intimate religious family. The group had a diversity of goals with one being the spread of the Evangelical Message which they accomplished through the aggressive distribution of Tracts For the Times (series of 90 papers). Their efforts began the Church Missionary Society (1799) and the British and Foreign Bible Society (1804). Rose was a brilliant scholar at Cambridge and Durham. In 1832 he founded the *British Magazine* to restore the purity and spirituality of the English Church. A key meeting at Rose's Hadleigh Rectory in 1833 is considered the "official beginning" of the Tractarian Movement. Rose was vicar of Horsham (1822–30), rector of Hadley (1830–36), and principal of King's College, London (1836–38).

Wilbur Fisk

Aug. 31, 1792
Brattleboro, Vermont

Feb. 22, 1839
Middletown, Connecticut

Methodist minister and first president of Wesleyan University, Middletown, CT 1830–39. Fisk entered the Methodist Church ministry in 1818. He married Ruth Peck on June 9, 1823. Fisk was principal of the Wesleyan Academy in Wilbraham, CT from 1825–30. He raised the quality and standard of New England Methodism. He wrote *Travels in Europe* (1838). He was the first American Methodist theologian to receive recognition outside of his denomination. He wrote on missions and temperance and against Calvinism and universalism.

Johan O. Wallin

Oct. 15, 1779
Delecarlia (Dalarna), Sweden

June 30, 1839
Uppsala, Sweden

Lutheran hymnwriter, chruchman, and poet. In 1837, Wallin was made archbishop of Uppsala, after having held various pastoral charges at Solna, Stockholm (1812), and Vasteras (1816). He revised the Swedish Lutheran Church hymnbook. He compiled the popular Psalm Book in Sweden known as *Wallin's Psalm Book* (1819), which included 130 of his hymns. Wallin is known as "David's Harp of the North."

Hermann Olshausen

Aug. 21, 1796
Oldesloe, Germany

Sept. 4, 1839
Erlangen, Germany

Moderate Lutheran theologian and New Testament exegete. In 1820, Olshausen began teaching at Berlin. The following year, he became professor at Konigsberg, where he taught until 1834, when he was called to Erlangen in Bavaria. His great work was his *Commentary on the New Testament* (1830–40). Olshausen was an able scholar and devoted Christian who died of tuberculosis.

John Williams (1)

June 29, 1796
Tottenham, London, England

Nov. 20, 1839
Erromanga, New Hebrides Islands

Missionary martyr to the Pacific Islands who was sent there by the London Missionary Society in 1816. Williams was converted at age 18 at the City Road Tabernacle, married Mary Chauner in 1816, and arrived in the Society Islands on November 17, 1817. Williams was creative, scholarly (learned the local dialects), and industrious, building a sixty-foot boat to reach other island groups. He settled at Taiatea and in 1823 discovered the Island of Rarotonga where he later translated parts of the Bible into the native language. His voyages included the Herveys (Cook Isles), Samoa (1823–33). By 1834, no island of importance within 2,000 miles of Tahiti had not been visited. He was in England from 1834–38, returning with 16 new missionaries. . He was murdered and cannibalized in return for cruelties previously inflicted on natives by British soldiers. His wife retired to England in 1842 and died in 1852. Three out of eight of their children survived. His favorite Bible verse was John 8:36.

David Jones

1797
Neuaddwyd, Wales

1840
Mauritius

Missionary pioneer to Madagascar. Jones went with Thomas Bevan (and their wives) to Mauritius in 1818, then went on to pioneer the work in Madagascar with the London Missionary Society. Malagasy fever took his wife, baby, and the Bevan family of three, leaving David to minister alone. He helped the slave trade to be outlawed there in 1820. He left the country, 1830–40, then tried to return. In 1835, his missionary efforts were hindered when Christianity was labeled a forbidden religion. The seeds he sowed reaped a later harvest. He and David Griffiths engaged in translation so that the first Bible printed in an African language was published in 1835. In June, 1840, he sought redress from the queen and was held prisoner. Managing to escape, he fled to Mauritius, where he died shortly thereafter of fever.

Nathanael Emmons

April 20, 1746
East Haddam, Connecticut

Sept. 23, 1840
Franklin, Massachusetts

Congregationalist theologian and pastor in Franklin, MA 1773–1827, for 54 years. Emmon's house was a seminary where 87 young men were trained for the ministry. He founded the Massachusetts Missionary Society and was its president the first twelve years. Emmons married Deliverance French on April 6, 1775, Martha Williams on November 4, 1779, and Abigail M. Mill on September 28, 1831. He had no use for long trousers and wore knee breeches, a wig, and chewed tobacco. Six volumes of his works were published in 1842.

John Leland

May 14, 1754
Grafton, Massachusetts

Jan. 14, 1841
Cheshire, Massachusetts

Baptist evangelist and home missionary. He worked to disestablish the Episcopal Church in Virginia and the Congregational Church in Massachusetts. Leland married Sarah (Sallie) Divine on September 30, 1776, and they had nine children. Leland was converted at age 18, pastored small Baptist churches (such as in Culpepper County, VA, 1777–91), and lived in Cheshire, MA from 1791–1841, serving as an evangelist. In Virginia, he baptized 1,278 and preached over 3,000 sermons. Leland's influence was widespread. Article I of the Constitution was formed as a result of his letter to President GEORGE WASHINGTON. He advocated separation of church and state, the abolition of slavery, and traveled widely in his attempts to vindicate the civil and religious rights of all men. He helped elect James Madison to the Virginia Convention and also wrote 21 hymns. He wrote *Short Essays on Government* (1820).

George C. Cookman

Oct. 21, 1800
Hull, England

after March 11, 1841
at sea (Atlantic Ocean)

Eloquent Methodist preacher. He began his ministry in Philadelphia after coming to America in 1825. Cookman was the chaplain of the United States Senate in 1839. His farewell sermon at the Capitol was a wonderful display of oratorical power. Cookman set sail from New York for England on March 11, 1841, on the steamship *President* and was never heard of again.

George A. Baxter

July 22, 1771
Rockingham County, Virginia

April 24, 1841
Hampden-Sydney, Virginia

Dean of Hampden-Sydney (VA) Seminary (Union Theological Seminary, Richmond, VA in 1898), **1831–41.** Baxter began as a Presbyterian evangelist and also headed the New London Academy. He married Annie Fleming on January 17, 1798. In 1799, he began pastoring in Lexington and Monmouth, VA. He became president of Washington College in Virginia, 1813–29. Baxter had excellent teaching skills.

Abner Jones

April 28, 1772
Royalston, Massachusetts

May 29, 1841
Exeter, New Hampshire

New England Christian Church minister. Jones was against sectarian names and human creeds; so in 1801, he organized the Christian Church in Lyndon, VT. Jones married Damaris Pryor in 1796 and Nancy Clark on August 1, 1839. In due time, Jones was joined by JAMES O'KELLEY (a Methodist) and BARTON STONE (a Presbyterian) to form the Christian Church as a movement, also known as the Christian Connection. He made his living teaching school and practicing medicine.

Finis Ewing

July 10, 1773
Brevard County, Virginia

July 4, 1841
Lexington, Missouri

One of three co-founders (Samuel King and Samuel McAdow also) of the Cumberland Presbyterian Church in 1814. Ewing was converted at a frontier revival, in 1800 under JAMES McGREADY, having moved to Logan County, KY in 1795. Ewing rejected the rigid views of predestination, and in 1810 formed an independent work which gave the human will a greater place in conversion and led to the new denomination, after which he moved to New Lebanon, MO in 1820. Ewing married Peggy Davis in 1793. He pastored in Lexington the last five years of his life and published *A Series of Lectures on the Most Important Subjects of Divinity* (1827).

John Breckenridge

July 4, 1797
Cabell's Dale, Kentucky

Aug. 4, 1841
Cabell's Dale, Kentucky

Renowned Presbyterian pastor, educator, and missions enthusiast. Breckenridge married Margaret Miller in January, 1823 and Mary Babcock in 1840. Breckenridge pastored in Lexington, KY (1823–26), and Baltimore, MD (1826–31). He then moved to Philadelphia as secretary of the Board of Education 1831–36. He had a famous debate with Catholic prelate, John Hughes (1797–1864), which was published in 1836. This was followed by a teaching position at Princeton Seminary, 1836–38. Breckenridge then served as secretary of the Board of Foreign Missions, 1838–40. He was the brother of ROBERT BRECKENRIDGE.

Johann F. Herbart

May 4, 1776　　Aug. 14, 1841
Oldenburg, Germany　　　　　　　　　　　　　　　　　　　　　　　　　　　　　　　　　Gottingen, Germany

Psychologist, philosopher, and educator. He became interested in PESTALOZZI's methods. Herbart was professor at Gottingen (1805), at Konigsberg (1809), then again at Gottingen (1833). Herbart is considered the founder of modern pedagogics (science or art of teaching or education). He believed that educational methods and systems should be based on psychology and ethics. He taught the importance of literature and history.

William Balch

1775　　　1842

Congregational minister and the first US Navy chaplain. He received his commission from President John Adams (1735–1826) on October 30, 1799. Balch served on the USS *Congress* and the USS *Chesapeake*. There were prior chaplains with the Continental Navy (like his father), but William was the first to serve officially.

Thomas Arnold

June 13, 1795　　　　　　　　　　　　　　　　　　　　　　　　　　　　　　　　　　　　　　　June 12, 1842
East Cowles, Isle of Wight, England　　　　　　　　　　　　　　　　　　　　　　　　Rugby, England

Anglican teacher and beloved headmaster (famous for his influence) **of Rugby School, 1827–42**. A man of deep piety, Arnold was the father of poet and critic Matthew Arnold (1822–88). Arnold settled at Laleham in 1817 and helped young men prepare for universities. He became a priest (1828) and was made professor of modern history at Oxford (1841). His extensive education was based upon a strong religious foundation. He laid the foundation of the modern public school system in England with its emphasis on religious training, moral character, and public service. Arnold was the founder of the Broad Church Party within the Church of England, opposing the Oxford Movement. He wrote *Principles of Church Reform* (1824), *History of Rome* and *Fragment on the Church* (1844). Some of his last words were, "Thank God for giving me this pain! How thankful I am that my head is untouched."

"Religion is a man seeking God; Christianity is God seeking man."

John Ireland

Sept. 8, 1761　　Sept. 2, 1842
Ashburton, England　　　　　　　　　　　　　　　　　　　　　　　　　　　　　　　　　Westminster, England

Anglican minister, dean of Westminster Abbey in 1816, philanthropist, and vicar of Croyden, 1793–1816. Ireland was also rector of Islip at Oxfordshire and dean of the Order of Bath, 1816–35. Ireland had wealth and used it generously in funding scholarships at Oxford and prizes at Westminster School to further free education. Additionally, he left funds for Oxford Bible professorships.

William Hone

June 3, 1780　　Nov. 6, 1842
Bath, England　　　　　　　　　　　　　　　　　　　　　　　　　　　　　　　　　　　　Tottenham, England

Independent preacher, political satirist, writer, and book dealer. Hone entered the bookselling business when he was 20. He was tried for writing parodies on the litany, the Athanasian Creed, and the church catechism in 1817, but was acquitted in December, 1820, a great victory for the free press. Later in life he preached in Weigh

House Chapel, Eastcheap, London. His successful satire, *The Political House That Jack Built* (1819) went through 54 editions. Hone wrote the *Apocryphal New Testament* (1820, all material not in the New Testament).

Robert Haldane

Feb. 28, 1764
London, England

Dec. 12, 1842
Edinburgh, Scotland

Preacher, writer, and philanthropist. He was born into a Scottish family. After his 1793 conversion, he devoted his property and services to Christ. Within 15 years, he had distributed $350,000 for charitable purposes. Early on, Haldane was a Congregationalist, but about 1798, became a Baptist. During his lifetime, he educated 300 young men for the ministry through preaching in tabernacles and theological seminaries. He also lectured on Romans at Geneva University. From 1798–1819, he was active in Geneva and southern France. He wrote *Divine Revelation* (1816) and *Romans* (1835).

Sarah Martin

June 1791
Great Yarmouth, England

1843
Great Yarmouth, England

Philanthropist. Sarah was a dressmaker who became interested in the poor and criminal young people. From 1819 on, she visited the jails weekly, found work for discharged prisoners, and devoted her funds to helping others. She became poor herself and was assisted by a corporation in Yarmouth.

Francis S. Key

Aug. 1, 1779
Ripe's Creek, Maryland

Jan. 11, 1843
Baltimore, Maryland

Episcopalian lawyer who gave us the poem which became our national anthem, "The Star Spangled Banner" in 1931. Key was reared in a godly home. He married Mary Lloyd on Jan. 19, 1802, who gave him eleven children. On September 13–14, 1814, while detained on a British ship during the War of 1812, he witnessed the bombardment of Ft. McHenry (key to Baltimore defenses). The flag, still flying at dawn, inspired him to write the verses (music by JOHN S. SMITH). He was active in and a founder of the American Sunday School Union in 1824. Key was a vestryman at St. John's Church, Anapolis, MD, and later attended Christ Church, Washington, D.C. He was also the district attorney for Washington, D.C., 1833–41. He is buried in Frederick, MD. His favorite Bible verse was Psalm 143:8.

Alexander V. Griswold

April 22, 1766
Simsbury, Connecticut

Feb. 15, 1843
Boston, Massachusetts

Presiding bishop of Protestant Episcopal Church (Episcopal Church in 1967), 1836–43. Griswold married Elizabeth Mitchelson (1785) and Amelia Smith (1827), having a total of 14 children. Griswold began as a pastor in Plymouth, CT in 1795 and then served at St. Michael's Church, Bristol, RI from 1804–30. He was the first and only bishop of the Eastern Diocese, 1810–30. He then pastored St. Peter's Church, Salem MA, 1830–35. Griswold published *Prayers Adapted to Various Occasions* (1835), *The Reformation* (1843), and *Social Prayer Meetings* (1858).

Robert M. McCheyne

May 21, 1813
Edinburgh, Scotland

March 25, 1843
Dundee, Scotland

Church of Scotland minister. Like BRAINERD, living only a scant 29 years, McCheyne made an impact on his country. He was converted as a result of his 26-year-old brother's death. McCheyne served at St. Peter's Church, Dundee 1836–38. His 1,100 members loved him and considered him a holy young man. Ill health forced his resignation in 1838 after a two-year ministry. McCheyne went to Europe and Palestine on behalf of Jewish evangelism in 1839. Upon his return, he held successful crusades in Ireland and Scotland. He died of typhoid fever which he caught while visiting ill friends. He once wrote in his diary, "Live so as to be missed when dead." His *Memoirs*, which is highly regarded, was written by ANDREW BONAR. His last words were I Corinthians 15:58.

Noah Webster

Oct. 16, 1758　　　　　　　　　　　　　　　　　　　　　　　　　　　　　May 28, 1843
West Hartford, Connecticut　　　　　　　　　　　　　　　　　　New Haven, Connecticut

Lexicographer and writer. In 1808, Webster began his *An American Dictionary of the English Language,* which was completed in 1828. Webster worked for 38 years to produce the dictionary (1790–1828). It contained 70,000 words. He also prepared a spelling book, a grammar, and a reader for the schools. Webster also sought to correct mistakes in translation and grammar in the Bible. He married Rebecca Greenleaf on October 26, 1789 and later Martha Dana in 1830, and had eight children. Early on, he authored the *Blue-Backed Speller*, used for years in American schools. As he was dying, he quoted II Timothy 1:12.

Washington Allston

Nov. 5, 1779　　　　　　　　　　　　　　　　　　　　　　　　　　　　　　July 9, 1843
Waccamaw, South Carolina　　　　　　　　　　　　　　　　　Cambridge, Massachusetts

Painter who achieved great fame in Europe, uncommon for an American. Allston married Ann, a sister of W. E. Channing (1780–1842), in 1809. He lived in England, 1811–18, where he produced some of his best pictures. He returned to Boston in 1818, then moved to Cambridge where he lived in comparative seclusion. During his lifetime, he sold single pictures for thousands of dollars and had an order for one costing $25,000. Among his paintings are *Belshazzar's Feast* and *Dead Man Revived by Touching the Bones of Elisha*. He was also a gifted poet. When his mother died, he wrote, "She is now with her Saviour. There is no consolation for the bereaved like this. Nor, indeed, can there be any other to a believing Christian."

Bourne H. Draper

1775　　　　　　　　　　　　　　　　　　　　　　　　　　　　　　　　　　　Oct. 12, 1843
Cumnor, England　　　　　　　　　　　　　　　　　　　　　　　　Southampton, England

Hymn writer of such as "Ye Christian Heralds, God Proclaim." Draper began as a printer's apprentice at the Clarendon Press of Oxford. He joined the Baptist Church, was ordained in 1804, and began pastoring at Chipping-Norton Baptist Church. Draper later pastored at Southampton. He wrote 36 books and many hymns.

John Foster

Sept. 17, 1770　　　　　　　　　　　　　　　　　　　　　　　　　　　　　　Oct. 15, 1843
Halifax, England　　　　　　　　　　　　　　　　　　　　　　　　　　Stapleton, England

Essayist and clergyman. Foster was the pastor of several small Baptist churches in England and Ireland, 1792–1806. While at Downsend, he wrote *Essays* (1805) which won for him the reputation of being "one of the most profound and eloquent English writers." A throat disorder forced him to give up speaking and turn to writing 1806–17. Regaining his health, he again pastored at Downsend (1817–21) and lectured in Bristol (1821–25). His major work was *Essays on Decision of Character*. Foster pursued many literary projects, contributing 184 articles to the *Eclectic Review* (1806-39). *His Evils of Popular Ignorance* (1820) was also well known.

Albert B. Thorvaldsen
Bertel Thorwaldsen

Nov. 19, 1770
Copenhagen, Denmark

March 24, 1844
Copenhagen, Denmark

Danish sculptor. He lived in Rome, 1797–1838. Thorvaldsen became famous and received commissions from all over Europe. Most familiar of his sculptures is the *Lion of Lucerne* displayed in Switzerland. His greatest religious work was the group, *Christ and His Apostles*. Thorvaldsen's last work was an unfinished bust of LUTHER. In Rome he came under the influence of Antonio Canova (1757–1822), an Italian sculptor.

Asahel Grant

Aug. 17, 1807
Marshall, New York

April 24, 1844
Mosul, Turkey

Missionary (physician and explorer) **to the Nestorians in Persia** (near Constantinople) beginning in 1835, at a place called Urumiah with ABCFM. Prior to his missions interest, Grant practiced medicine in Utica, NY. He married Electa Loomis on Aug. 23, 1827 and in 1835 Judith Campbell (1814–39). His second wife and twin daughters died in 1839. Judith's educational work was continued by FIDELIA FISK. Grant gained the confidence of the Persian officials, which allowed him to be able to do much for the Persian people. This position convinced him to stay the last ten years of his life ministering in Persia. After the massacres of 1843 (Turks killing thousands of Nestorians), he settled in Mosul. Grant died in an epidemic among the refugees.

Henry Nott

1774
England

May 2, 1844
Tahiti

Missionary to Tahiti (Society Island of Polynesia). Nott was a bricklayer by trade. Thirty missionaries, six wives, and three children sailed on the *Duff* during the seven-month voyage, leaving in August, 1796. He was one of the first missionaries sent out by the newly organized London Missionary Society, arriving in Tahiti in 1797. In 1819, the treacherous King Pomare II was converted. Hundreds of villagers followed his example. Idols were destroyed and temples formerly used for pagan worship became Christian meeting-houses. When the king was baptized May 16, 1819, some 5,000 people witnessed the event. He had served 22 years without a convert. He became the principal Bible translator into Tahitian, which he completed while on furlough, 1836–38. Nott returned to England only twice during his 47-year ministry.

Asahel Nettleton

April 21, 1783
Killingworth, Connecticut

May 16, 1844
East Windsor, Connecticut

Congregational evangelist. Nettleton was converted in 1801 and later served at different failing churches. After they revived, he went to another such church, never asking for money for his services. He had an active ministry in Connecticut, Massachusetts, and New York 1812–22. Nettleton was a strong Calvinist who opposed the methods of FINNEY and others. In 1822, he had an attack of typhoid fever, from which he never fully recovered. In 1830–31, he held meetings in New York City. He never married. He published *Village Hymns* (1824). Nettleton spent his last decade at East Windsor Seminary (Hartford Theological Seminary) as a counselor to young ministers. In 1833, with other conservatives, he founded the Theological Institute of Connecticut in order to combat "new measures" revivalism (FINNEY) and "New Haven Theology" (Yale's NATHANIEL W. TAYLOR and LYMAN BEECHER).

Alexander Carson

1776
Annahone, Ireland

Aug. 24, 1844
Belfast, Ireland

Presbyterian turned Baptist evangelist in 1804. He was a pastor of a Presbyterian church in Tubbermore, Ireland, when he withdrew from the denomination. Most of Carson's congregation followed him as he preached in barns and fields. Later, a stone church was built for him in 1814. Carson accepted Baptist principles and shared them with others. His writings upon this subject have been widely read.

Oliver Holden

Sept. 18, 1765
Shirley, Massachusetts

Sept. 4, 1844
Charlestown (Boston), Massachusetts

Composed the most familiar music (of three tunes written) **for "All Hail the Power of Jesus Name"**, (1792) (lyrics by EDWARD PERRONET). At age 21, Holden moved to Charlestown (Boston) and labored as a carpenter to rebuild the town after its burning by the British. He married Nancy Rand on May 12, 1791, and they had six children. Holden was a Puritan pastor, a Mason, a music teacher, a realtor, and a politician.

David Nelson

Sept. 24, 1793
Jonesboro, Tennessee

Oct. 17, 1844
Oakland, Illinois

Presbyterian clergyman and physician. Nelson married Miss Deaderick in 1815. He served as a surgeon in the War of 1812. By 1830, he was founder and first president of Marion College, Palmyra, MO from 1831–35, which became a famous midwestern teacher's college. Nelson's strong anti-slavery sentiments forced his resignation. He later started a school at Oakland, IL for the training of ministers.

Barton W. Stone

Dec. 24, 1772
Port Tobacco, Maryland

Nov. 9, 1844
Hannibal, Missouri

Presbyterian minister who sought Christian unity. Stone was converted at age 19. He was in charge of three congregations in Bourbon County, KY from 1796–98. Elizabeth Campbell became his wife (July 2, 1801), and Celia Bowen (Oct. 31, 1811), producing eleven children. Stone renounced Calvinism in 1801 and was a key evangelist in the early 1800's in the "camp meeting revivals." Hearing of JAMES MCCREADY's work, he organized a similar meeting at Cane Ridge Camp Meeting in 1801. Upon leaving Presbyterianism (1804), he urged his followers to join with ALEXANDER CAMPBELL (whom he met in 1830) to form the Disciples of Christ (1832). Between these dates, he was organizing churches and evangelizing. He founded the *Christian Messenger* to promote these views.

Daniel Parker

April 6, 1781
Culpepper County, Virginia

Dec. 3, 1844
Elkhart, Texas

Founded the Two-Seed-in-the-Spirit Predestinarian Baptists. Parker based his views on Genesis 3:15. Converted in 1802, he pastored in Tennessee (1806–17) and Illinois (1817–33). He moved to Texas in 1834 causing much dissension among Baptists in the frontier. Parker opposed all forms of organized church work, including missionary, Bible, and temperance societies, as well as Sunday schools, colleges, theological seminaries, and instrumental music in churches. He extended his work throughout North Carolina, Tennessee, Kentucky, Illinois, Indiana, and Texas. Parker was an ultra-Calvinist predestinarian.

Thomas F. Buxton

April 1, 1786
Earl's Colne, England

Feb. 19, 1845
Overstrand, England

One of the first friends of the blacks in Africa. He married Hannah Gurney in 1807 (ELIZABETH FRY, prison reformer was a sister-in-law). Buxton was converted in 1813. He was brought up under both Anglican and Quaker influence of Josiah Pratt, secretary of the Church Missionary Society. In 1818, he became a Whig member of Parliament for Weymouth, which he represented until 1837. His goal was to gain emancipation for all slaves within the British dominions starting in 1821. Serious illness increased in later years. Three concerns were lifelong battles: reform of the penal code (reducing offenses which gave death penalties and prison conditions), the treatment of non-Western peoples under British rule, and slavery. DAVID LIVINGSTONE "put teeth" into Buxton's burdens.

Jason Lee

June 28, 1803
Near Stanstead, Quebec, Canada

March 12, 1845
Stanstead, Quebec, Canada

Pioneer Methodist missionary to the Oregon area. Converted in a Wesleyan Methodist revival in 1826, Lee went over the Oregon Trail (1834), near Pocatetto, Idaho, to fulfill the request of the Nez Perce and the Flathead Indians who desired to learn more about the white man's religion. He preached the first non-Catholic sermon west of the Rocky Mountains on July 27, 1834. Lee is credited for founding Salem, OR in 1834–35. He married Anna Pittman (September 24, 1803–June 26, 1838) on July 26, 1837, who died following childbirth, and Lucy Thompson in 1839 (died: 1842). From 1838–40, he visited Washington, D.C., reporting on Oregon. In 1842, he founded Oregon Institute (Willamette University) in Salem. He returned east in 1844. Stanstead was considered part of Vermont during his days. He is buried in Salem, OR.

August W. von Schlegel

Sept. 8, 1767
Hannover, Germany

May 12, 1845
Bonn, Germany

Literary critic, poet, and translator. Schlegel was the son of a Lutheran clergyman. He and his brother, Friedrich (1772–1829), a poet and author, founded the journal *Athenaeum* in 1798 which was the voice of German romanticism. Schlegel lectured on aesthetics at Jena, and literature and art at Berlin. He tutored the children of French writer Madame De Stael (1766–1817), 1803–17. In 1818 he became professor of church history at Bonn till death. He studied Oriental languages and literature, and was noted for his Shakespearian translations (17 plays published in ten volumes), 1797–1810. He was also a pioneer Sanskrit scholar.

Andrew Jackson

March 15, 1767
Waxhaw, South Carolina

June 8, 1845
near Nashville, Tennessee

Seventh president of the United States, 1829–37, defeating John Q. Adams. Jackson was the first president to ride on a train. Born in a log cabin, he was known as "Old Hickory." He married Rachel Robards in 1791 (died: Dec. 22, 1828). Tennessee joined the Union in 1796, and Jackson was its first representative to Congress. Jackson, a Democrat, had a brilliant career as a soldier in the War of 1812, defeating the Creek Indians (1814), and the British at New Orleans (1815). He was re-elected in 1833 by defeating Henry Clay 219–49. His administration, called the Jacksonian democracy, saw political parties adopt the convention system and the national debt paid in full for the last time. When he became president, he had 166 slaves. He was a champion of the farmer and laborer. Jackson was converted in 1839 through the witness of a Nashville Presbyterian pastor, Dr. Edgar. His home in Tennessee is called "The

Hermitage" As he died, he said, "My sufferings...are nothing in comparison with those of my Saviour, through whose death I look for everlasting life."

John Stauch

Jan. 25, 1762
York County, Pennsylvania

July 1845
Crawford County, Ohio

President of Ohio Synod (ALC, ELCA in 1988), 1818–1925, 1828–1929 and evangelist. Stauch was called to preach at age 19. He married Elizabeth Hogmyer in the summer of 1787. He took a church in Morgantown, PA and was soon solicited to preach for a few Germans in Fayette County, PA, 20 miles further west. After six years in the wilderness, he returned to Reading, PA where he was licensed to preach. He then went back to Salem, Morgantown, Redstone and Washington County, where he had ten preaching places in German Lutheran settlements. He covered this 100 miles by 160 miles every four weeks. Stauch's wife died in 1793 and he married Catherine Troutman in 1796. Soon he was going to Ohio, Kentucky and Virginia for some twelve years. In 1806, he moved to Columbiana County, OH. His 50 years of preaching included traveling 100,000 miles, preaching 10,000 sermons, confirming 1,516 people, and baptizing over 3,000 people. He married 481 couples and attended about the same number of funerals.

William Yates

Dec. 15, 1792
Loughborough, England

July 3, 1845
Red Sea

English Baptist missionary to Bengal, India, 1815. He was an able linguist with the Baptist Missionary Society. Yates prepared dictionaries, grammars, and manuals in Sanskrit, Bengali, Arabic, and Hindustani. Yates also translated all of the Bible into Bengali and much of it into Sanskrit, 1839 on. He lived mostly in Calcutta doing his linguistic and translation work. Failing health caused him to sail for England, but he died on the passage up the Red Sea.

Sarah Hall Boardman Judson

Nov. 4, 1803
Alstead, New Hampshire

Sept. 1, 1845
St. Helena

Second wife of missionary Adoniram Judson. Sarah married George Boardman on July 4, 1825 (died: 1831). She and ADONIRAM were married on April 10, 1834, and they returned to Maulmain, South Burma, where Judson had moved his headquarters in 1827. A school building and church were established there, where she was helping in some translation work, such as Bible selections, tracts, and part of *Pilgrim's Progress*. In 1845, her failing health motivated Judson to return to America. She died, however, during the voyage, off the coast of southern Africa. It was a great shock to children waiting for them in New York City when ADONIRAM arrived alone. One son, Adoniram Brown Judson (1837–1916), was a New York surgeon, whose papers on orthopedics appeared in American and European journals. Another son, Edward Judson (1844–1914), was pastor of the Berean Baptist Church, New York City 1881–1914. This congregation moved into the Judson Memorial Church in 1890. Of JUDSON's 13 children, Sarah bore him eight. She had a total of eleven children.

Elizabeth Gurney Fry

May 21, 1780
Norfolk, England

Oct. 12, 1845
Ramsgate, England

Quaker founder of modern prison reforms, who established an order of nursing sisters. Elizabeth was converted after hearing the testimony of a William Savery. In 1800, she became wife of Joseph Fry, a London merchant, and they had eleven children. She insisted on visiting the inmates in Newgate Prison in 1813 and was horrified at the conditions. She began her prison ministry in 1817. Her brother, JOSEPH GURNEY, assisted her in her efforts. She organized a ladies' committee to visit Newgate Prison and founded an association to help women prisoners (1821). Her travels and labors bore fruit throughout Europe, where prison reform was desired, beginning in France in 1839. In 1840, she formed the Protestant Sisters of Charity to care for and rehabilitate discharged prisoners. Some of her last words were, "My dear Lord, help and keep Thy servant." Her favorite Bible passage was Luke 7:36–50.

Michael S. Alexander

May 1799
Schonlanke, Prussia, Germany

Nov. 23, 1845
Belbeis, Egypt

First Anglican bishop in the Ottoman Empire, Jerusalem, 1841–45. He married Miss Levy in 1821. Alexander was born a strict orthodox Jew who moved to England at age 21 and, on June 22, 1825, was converted to Christianity, reading the New Testament and listening to B. B. Golding of Stonehouse. After his ordination in the Anglican Church he joined the London Jews' Society. He worked for the conversion of the Jews first in Danzig (Gdansk) Poland, (1827–30), and then in London (1830–41). He also taught Hebrew at King's College beginning in 1832. Alexander died on his way back to England while traveling on a pastoral missionary visit.

John C. Smith

Feb. 12, 1765
Sharon, Connecticut

Dec. 7, 1845
Litchfield County, Connecticut

President of American Bible Society, 1831–45, and the governor of Connecticut, 1813–17. Smith married Margaret Evertson on Oct. 29, 1786. He was admitted to the Connecticut bar in 1786; then was elected to the Connecticut House of Representatives, 1793, 1796–1800; serving as an ardent supporter of Federalism and Congregationalism. Smith remained in Connecticut politics, 1800–17. He was also the president of the ABCFM, 1826–41.

Charles T. Torrey

Nov. 21, 1813
Scituate, Massachusetts

May 9, 1846
Baltimore, Maryland

Abolitionist hero. He served Congregational pastorates in Princeton, NJ and Salem, MA. Torrey moved to Maryland, where he led efforts to spirit black slaves north via the Underground Railroad. May Ide became his wife on March 29, 1837. He was arrested and jailed for aiding runaway slaves in 1843. His poor treatment in prison brought on tuberculosis which killed him at age 33. He was honored by a public funeral in Boston.

Isaac McCoy

June 15, 1784
Fayette County, Pennsylvania

June 21, 1846
Louisville, Kentucky

Baptist missionary to the Indians. McCoy moved to Kentucky at the age of six with his family. He married Christina Rolke in 1803 and had 13 children. Ordained a Baptist, the triennial Convention appointed him to be a missionary among the Indians in Illinois and Indiana. This work would go on for 29 years. In 1822, he established the Carey Mission near Niles, MI. In 1826, he resigned from the Carey Mission in order to work for the creation of a territory in which the Indian tribes could be colonized. He made ten trips to Washington D. C. on horseback to encourage this concept. In 1842, he organized the American Indian Mission Association, which was absorbed into the Southern Baptist Convention Home Mission Board. McCoy suffered much during his years and is remembered as a pioneer in Indian evangelistic efforts outside of the northeast.

Elias Smith

June 17, 1769
Lyme, Connecticut

June 29, 1846

Baptist minister. He was an effective evangelist, traveling with Abner Jones for 40 years preaching, "Restoration." In 1808, Smith established the *Herald of Gospel Liberty*, first weekly religious newspaper in the US. He married Mary Burleigh on Jan. 7, 1793 and Rachel Thurber in 1814, producing several children. Smith advocated three tenets: 1) no head but Christ, 2) no confession, but the Bible, and 3) no denominational names.

David Abeel

June 12, 1804
New Brunswick, New Jersey

Sept. 4, 1846
Albany, New York

Missionary to China in 1830. Abeel's conversion changed his career from medical studies to the ministry. Being proficient in the Chinese language, he traveled in Siam (Burma), Indonesia, and Malaya. Remaining single throughout his life, Abeel promoted missions in Europe and America then returned to China in 1838. He inaugurated the Dutch Reformed Church Mission in Amoy in 1844. Ill health brought him home in 1845 and he eventually died of pulmonary tuberculosis. He was with ABCFM (1830–35) and the Dutch Reformed Church (1835–46). He wrote three books.

Thomas Clarkson

March 28, 1760
Wisbeach, England

Sept. 26, 1846
Playford Hall, England

Anti-slavery leader. Clarkson's involvement began when he won the prize in Cambridge in 1785 for an essay on slavery. The paper's circulation had a wide radius. Working with Wilberforce and others, beginning in 1788, he devoted his time to bringing about the emancipation of the slaves, which happened on March 25, 1807. In 1833, the Emancipation Act was decreed for British colonies. Clarkson also wrote *History of Abolition of the Slave Trade* (1808).

James Evans

Jan. 18, 1801
Hull, England

Nov. 23, 1846
England

Canadian missionary. His exploits make him one of the greatest pioneer workers ever for Christ. Evans was converted at a Methodist camp meeting. Coming to Canada in 1822, Evans became a teacher at L'Orignal, Lower Canada, and then at Rice Lake in Upper Canada. He married Mary Smith in 1822 and had one child. He was sent to the St. Clair Mission near Sarnia to work with the Ojibwa Indians (1834) and he worked in the Lake Superior regions (1838). In 1840, the Wesleyan Methodist Missionary Society designated him as general superintendent of a new mission in the northwestern territories (Hudson's Bay Company) at Norway House, in what is now southern Manitoba, located on northern Lake Winnipeg, where heathen Indian tribes converged to buy and sell. From traders, he secured thin sheets of lead. He made casts of the 36 Cree symbols he created with the melted lead and used them as type. For ink, he mixed soot and sturgeon oil together. For paper he used birch bark from trees. Inserting them in a jack screw used for packing bales of fur, he had an improvised printing press, until one was sent to him from England. He then pressed forth to the Arctic Circle, traveling up to 6,000 miles a year, sometimes through raging blizzards at 60 degrees below zero temperature, 90 miles a day with fierce wolf-dogs. In 1846, he was involved in the accidental death of Thomas Hassall, trusted teacher and interpreter. He never recovered from the incident and returned to England where he died of a heart attack.

Joseph J. Gurney

Aug. 2, 1788
Earlham Hall, England

Jan. 4, 1847
Earlham Hall, England

Eminent Quaker philanthropist and scholar. Gurney was interested in prison reform (started by his sister Elizabeth Gurney Fry). As of 1818, Gurney was a minister of the Society of Friends who labored to abolish the slave-trade and advocated temperance. He studied science, math, and literature as a hobby and was proficient in six languages. Stephen Grellet was responsible for Gurney's strong evangelical leanings. From 1837–40, he was in Canada, the United States addressing Congress (and President Van Buren), and the West Indies. In 1842, Gurney traveled to France to advance abolition of slavery in its colonies. He wrote several books.

Alexandre R. Vinet

June 17, 1797
Ouchy, Switzerland

May 4, 1847
Clarens, Switzerland

French-Swiss Reformed theologian, moralist, and literary critic. He was influential in establishing the Swiss Reformation. An almost fatal illness in 1823 turned Vinet's life to devotion to Christ. He became a defender of freedom of worship, advocated separation of Church and State, and believed that conscience, not dogma, was the foundation for faith. His views were expressed in his book of 1826. Vinet was a professor of French literature at Basel (1817–37), a theology professor at Lausanne (1837–45) and founded a Free Church in the Canton of Vaud in 1845. He wrote hymns and homiletics.

Thomas Chalmers

March 17, 1780
East Anstruther, Scotland

May 30, 1847
Morningside, near Edinburg, Scotland

Powerful preacher and Free Church founder. Chalmers was the leader of the Evangelical Party that seceded from the Church of Scotland in 1843. After he was licensed to preach on July 31, 1799, he pastored in Kilmeny, 1803–15, during which time he was converted in 1811. He then pastored in Glasgow at the parish of Tron (1815–18) and parish of St. John's (1818–23), then taught moral philosophy at St. Andrews (1823–28). He taught theology at the University of Edinburgh 1828–43. In 1843, Chalmers led 471 ministers out of the established church to cause one of the biggest splits in church history, known as the Disruption. Chalmers was the first moderator of the New Free Church of Scotland and principal and professor of the New Free Church College/Divinity School in Edinburgh, 1843–47. He wrote *Institutes of Theology* (pub. 1849). His favorite Bible verse was Acts 16:31.

"Worldliness desecrates the holy, Christianity consecrates the secular."

J. L. Felix Mendelssohn-Bartholdy

Feb. 3, 1809
Hamburg, Germany

Nov. 4, 1847
Leipzig, Germany

Composer, conductor, pianist, and famous musician who wrote the music for "Hark! the Herald Angels Sing." His father adopted the surname of his wife's Christian brother when they turned from Judaism to Lutheranism and moved the family to Berlin in 1811. He made his public debut as a pianist in October, 1818 at age nine and wrote five symphonies by the time he was twelve. He was a dedicated Lutheran who married Cecile Jeanrenaud on March 28, 1837; they had five children. She was a widow of a French Reformed pastor. Mendelssohn presented Bach's *St. Matthew's Passion* on March 11, 1829, for the first time since the composer's death which began a revival of Bach's legacy of choral music. Mendelssohn composed an enormous number of works which included symphonies, overtures, chamber music, concertos, organ and piano works (overture for Shakespeare's *A Midsummer Night's Dream* (1826), written when he was but age 17) vocal music, and two oratorios: *St. Paul* (1836) and *Elijah* (1846). He also helped found the Berlin Academy of Arts and was the co-founder in 1843 and director of the Leipzig Conservatory. Music to the famed Christmas carol came 100 years after CHARLES WESLEY wrote the lyrics. Other famous works include *Italian Symphony* and the *Reformation Symphony*. He wrote special music for JENNY LIND. In 1835, Mendelssohn settled in Leipzig. He died at age 37, possibly the result of overwork.

Henry F. Lyte

June 1, 1793
Ednam, Scotland

Nov. 20, 1847
Nice, France

Anglican hymnwriter. He gave us the comforting hymns, "Jesus, I My Cross Have Taken" (music by Mozart) and "Abide with Me," 1847 (music by WILLIAM MONK). It was not used until Lyte's farewell pastoral service at Lower Brixham where he had served for 24 years (1823–47). Early on, he was curate at Taghmon (1815–17) and at Marazion (1817–23). Suffering from asthma and tuberculosis, Lyte went to Nice, France, for relief, but died one month later. He wrote more than 80 hymns and paraphrased many Psalms.

Marcus Whitman

Sept. 4, 1802
Rushville, New York

Nov. 29, 1847
Waiilatpu, Oregon

Martyred Presbyterian missionary and physician. Whitman was in medical practice in Canada (1825–29) and in Wheeler, NY (1830–34). He founded the first Protestant church on the Pacific coast. Whitman is considered instrumental in securing the Oregon country for the United States. He married Narcissa Prentiss (born: 1808) on February 18, 1836; they had one daughter who drowned at age two. Just married, he ministered to the Cayuse Indians of Waiilatpu, near Walla Walla, WA in the spring of 1836. In winter, 1842–43, he made the 3,000-mile ride from Washington to the East Coast to save the Oregon missions by going to mission leaders in Boston and political leaders in Washington, DC. He, his wife, and twelve other persons were massacred by Cayuse Indians, who bitterly resented the invasion of the whites, fearful of losing their land. Five of the murderers were later hanged. Father Brouillet, Catholic priest, conducted the funeral with ten of the bodies in a common grave.

Dorothy A. Thrupp

June 20, 1779
Paddington, London, England

Dec. 14, 1847
St. Marylebone, London, England

Hymn writer. She gave us the beloved hymn "Savior Like a Shepherd Lead Us," 1836 (music by WILLIAM BRADBURY). Under the pseudonym, "Iota," Dorothy contributed many hymns to W. Carus Wilson's *Friendly Visitor and Children's Friend*. She was the editor of *Hymns for the Young* around 1830, in which all hymns were unsigned. In another collection her hymns were signed "DAT."

William Howley

1765
Ropley, England

1848

Archbishop of Canterbury, 1828–48. Howley was elected fellow of New College, Oxford, 1785–1804. He then became canon of Christ Church (1804–9), regius professor of divinity (1809–13), and bishop of London (1813–28). Several of his works were published.

Ashbel Green

July 6, 1762
Hanover, New Jersey

May 19, 1848
Philadelphia, Pennsylvania

Stated clerk of Presbyterian Church (USA in 1983) in the US of America, 1790–1803, and president of Princeton (NJ) College (University in 1898), **1818–22.** Green was also one of the Seminary founders. From 1785–1812, he was a professor of math and natural philosophy at

Princeton. He married Elizabeth Stockton (1785), Christina Anderson (1809), and Mary McCulloh (1815). He had one son. He pastored the Second Presbyterian Church, Philadelphia, PA from 1793–1812 after serving as assistant 1787–94. Greene was editor of the *Christian Advocate* (1822–34) as he returned to Philadelphia and authored several books, including *History of Presbyterian Missions* (1820). He was the chaplain to Congress, 1792–1800, and president of the Board of Directors of Princeton Theological Seminary, 1812–48. He was the first college president to include the study of the Bible in the curriculum.

Nathaniel Kendrick

April 22, 1777
Hanover, New Hampshire

Sept. 11, 1848
Hamilton, New York

First president of Hamilton (NY) Literary and Theological Institute, 1836–46, renamed Madison University (Colgate–Rochester (NY) Divinity School in 1928), **1846–48**. Kendrick was converted in a Baptist revival in 1797. He pastored in Middlebury, VT (1810–17); Eaton, NY (1817–22); Marrisville (1817–20); and then began teaching in 1822 at Hamilton. Kendrick authored *Trials and Encouragements of Christ's Faithful Ministers* (1824).

John Hunt

June 13, 1812
Balderton, England

Oct. 4, 1848
Viwa, Fiji Islands

Missionary to Fiji Islands. Hunt was converted at Swinderby, where he was a farm laborer. In 1838, he was ordained, married, and appointed by the Wesleyan Methodist Missionary Society of London to go to the islands. With the JAMES CALVERT family and one other couple, he arrived in Fiji in 1839. Hunt labored at Rewa at Samosamo, 1838–42 and from 1842–48 at Viwa. He helped in the conversion of many barbarous cannibals, translated the Bible into Fijian (NT published in 1853 and whole Bible published in 1884 after his death), and died at age 34 of dysentary.

Bernard Barton

Jan. 31, 1784
Carlisle, England

Feb. 19, 1849
Woodbridge, England

Known as the "Quaker Poet." Barton was Britain's counterpart to the American Quaker poet, JOHN GREENLEAF WHITTIER. After attending a Quaker school and serving a shopkeeper apprenticeship, Barton joined his brother in a corn and coal business at Woodbridge in Suffolk. His wife died a year after they were married. Barton lived in Liverpool for a short time, but returned to Woodbridge, and served as a clerk in a local bank for almost 40 years. From 1812–45, he published ten books of verse, many of which became hymns: "Walk in the Light" (music by Franz Hayden), "There Is a Life More Dear", and "We Journey Through a Vale of Tears," among others. Barton was a good friend of English essayist, Charles Lamb (1775–1834).

Mary Lyon

Feb. 28, 1797
Buckland, Massachusetts

March 5, 1849
South Hadley, Massachusetts

Educator. She opened a school with 80 pupils, in South Hadley, Nov. 8, 1837, called Mt. Holyoke Seminary (College in 1893), and was its president until her death. Mary was converted one Sunday on her way home from the Baptist church she attended. Early in her career, she taught, but in 1834 she left the classroom to raise funds for building an academy for girls. Mt. Holyoke became a training school for lady missionaries and Christian workers and teachers. She trained around 3,000 women and gave half of her $200 per year salary to missions and charities. Her philosophy was "study and teach nothing that cannot be made to help the world to Christ." She died following a bout with erysipelas (deep-red inflammation of the skin or mucus membranes).

Anne Bronte

Jan. 17, 1820
Thorton, England

May 28, 1849
Scarborough, England

Novelist and poet who wrote several hymns. Anne was the youngest of the three famous Bronte sisters. Her sisters, Emily and Charlotte were also well-known writers. In 1847, her poems were published under the pseudonym "Acton Bell." Anne also wrote *Agnes Grey* (1847) and *The Tenant of Wildfell Hall* (1848). One of her more famous hymns was "Spirit of Truth, Be Thou My Guide." She died of consumption at age 29.

James K. Polk

Nov. 2, 1795
Pineville, North Carolina

June 15, 1849
Nashville, Tennessee

Eleventh president of the United States, 1845–49. Polk was the first president to be associated with the Methodist Church. From 1821–25, he was in Tennessee politics. He married Sarah Childress on January 1, 1824. From 1825–39, he was a member of the United States Congress and governor of Tennessee, 1839–41. In the presidential election, Polk, a Democrat, defeated Henry Clay, a Whig, 170–105. He worshiped at the Foundry Methodist Church in Washington, but often attended First Presbyterian Church because of his wife's affiliation. He was baptized and received into the Methodist Church, South, by JOHN B. MCFERRIN shortly before he died.

William B. Tappan

Oct. 29, 1794
Beverly, Massachusetts

June 18, 1849
West Needham, Massachusetts

Congregational poet and hymn writer. Tappan hymns included "Tis Midnight, and on Olive's Brow" 1822 (music by WILLIAM BRADBURY). He was in the clock repair business in Philadelphia until 1822, when he became superintendent of the American Sunday School Union (serving for 27 years until his death). He traveled widely, establishing Sunday schools and holding revivals. He served in Cincinnati, Philadelphia, and Boston. He wrote and published poetry, 1819–49. Tappan died of cholera.

Lewis Mayer

March 26, 1783
Lancaster, Pennsylvania

Aug. 25, 1849
York, Pennsylvania

German Reformed pastor in Shepherdstown, VA (1808-21), and York, PA (1821-25). Mayer married Catharine Line on November 5, 1809, and they had four children. He later married Mary Gonder. Mayer conducted a German Reformed Seminary at both of his pastorate locations, later moving it to Mercersburg, PA in 1835. He retired in 1835 to write a history of the Reformed Church denomination.

Samuel Miller

Oct. 31, 1769
near Dover, Delaware

Jan. 7, 1850
Princeton, New Jersey

First professor of church history and government at Princeton Theological Seminary, 1813-50. Early in his career, he was the associate pastor of the First Presbyterian Church, NYC from 1793-1813. Miller was prominent in the discussions that led to the disruption of the Presbyterian Church in 1837. His opposition to New England theology helped nudge Princeton Seminary into old school Presbyterianism in the 1830s. He was a wise and efficient teacher. He wrote from *A Brief Retrospect of the 18th Century* (1803) to *Primitive and Apostolic Order of Christ Vindicated* (1840).

Edward H. Bickersteth Sr.

March 19, 1786
Kirkby, Lonsdale, Westmoreland, England

Feb. 28, 1850
Watton, Hertfordshire, England

Anglican clergyman, hymn writer, and co-founder of the Evangelical Alliance. Bickersteth was converted at age 19. He went to Africa in 1816, under the sponsorship of the Church Missionary Society, serving as a traveling secretary for this organization. From 1830, until his death 20 years later, he pastored in Watton. In 1846, Bickersteth helped to bring Christian leaders together for the Evangelical Alliance Conference held in London. The goal was to present a united Christian front in lieu of the political upheaval in Europe. They drew up a statement of faith emphasizing the unity of His "body of believers" as literally defined in the Bible as the "church of Christ." The Alliance grew to be a well-respected religious body that, in spite of some variant branching, continued into the 21st Century. His son, Bishop EDWARD H. BICKERSTETH JR., was also a prolific hymn writer. His *Help to Studying Scriptures* (1814) was also very popular, and was published in 21 editions. Edward Sr.'s hymnbook, *Christian Psalmody* (1833), contained over 700 hymns, and in seven years, had 59 editions printed. In addition, Bickersteth edited the 50-volume *Christian Family Library*. He said as he died, "I have no other ground of confidence than the blood of Jesus. Christ first, Christ all in all."

Adoniram Judson

Aug. 9, 1788
Malden, Massachusetts

April 12, 1850
Bay of Bengal

One of history's greatest missionaries. Judson went to Burma in 1813 as the first American Baptist missionary abroad. He was converted at age 24 when an unbelieving friend from Brown University, where he graduated in 1807, died in a hotel room next to his. He enrolled at Andover (MA) Seminary in 1808. He married ANN HASSELTINE on February 5, 1812, and immediately left for India with the NEWELLS, but was diverted to Burma in 1813. He soon left the American Board of Commissioners of Foreign Missions and helped start the American Baptist Missionary Union, by having LUTHER RICE return to the States to establish it. Judson ministered faithfully for six years until he saw his first convert in 1819 and the sprouting of an organized church. Because of the English/Burmese War, he was imprisoned for 17 months (1824-26) in unbelievably primitive conditions. After his wife ANN died (1826) he ministered in Amherst, Burma, and the seaport town of Maulman. The failing health of his second wife, SARAH BOARDMAN, whom he had married on April 10, 1834, motivated him to return to America (1845-47). She died during the stressful voyage in 1845. He later married EMILY CHUBBUCK on June 2, 1846. Judson translated the Bible into Burmese and compiled an English/Burmese dictionary in 1849. Seven of his ten children died very young. When asked if the prospects to evangelize the world were possible, he said, "As bright, Sir, as the promises of God." He died on a cruise he specifically took for health reasons and was buried at sea. As he died, he said, "...I feel so strong in Christ." His wife awaiting his return was shocked upon the docking of the ship to learn of this. He died leaving 100 national pastors and 7,000 church members. He had 13 children. His favorite Bible passages were Ephesians 3:17-18 and Matthew 2:2.

William Wordsworth

April 7, 1770
Cockermouth, England

April 23, 1850
Rydal Mount, England

Greatest poet of the English Romantic Movement since MILTON. Wordsworth's devotion to the Church of England was deep and sincere. He married Marie Anne Vallon, who gave him a daughter, Anne Caroline, in 1792. Later in 1802, he married Mary Hutchinson, who gave them daughter Dora (1804-47). He lived at Grasmere, 1799-1813. From 1813 on, he lived at Rydal Mount (where he is buried) with his sister, Dorothy, whose journals on his life are the main source of biographical material on the famed writer. Wordsworth always claimed that nature was his greatest inspiration. He lived on inherited income and is remembered for a famous line, "Plain living and high thinking are no more." "The Prelude," an autobiographical spiritual poem (1805) and one of his most famous works, was published after his death. He was poet laureate of England, 1843-50, even though he did not produce any poetry during these years.

William Walford

Jan. 9, 1773　　　　　　　　　　　　　　　　　　　　　　　　　　　　　　　　　　　　　June 22, 1850
Bath, England　　　　　　　　　　　　　　　　　　　　　　　　　　　　　　　　　　　Uxbridge, England

Writer of the great devotional hymn, "Sweet Hour of Prayer," (1850) (music by WILLIAM BRADBURY). Walford was a Congregational pastor at Stowmarket in Suffolk (1798-1800), at Great Yarmouth in Norfolk (1800-13), and at Uxbridge in Middlesex (1824–31 and 1833–48). Walford was a classical tutor at Homerton, 1814–31. He authored *The Manner of Prayer* (1836) and T*he Book of Psalms, a New Translation.*

Johann A. W. Neander

Jan. 17, 1789　　　　　　　　　　　　　　　　　　　　　　　　　　　　　　　　　　　　　July 14, 1850
Gottingen, Germany　　　　　　　　　　　　　　　　　　　　　　　　　　　　　　　　Berlin, Germany

Church historian of note. He was a Lutheran convert from Judaism in 1806. Neander became professor of church history, NT exegesis, Christian ethics, and systematic theology at Heidelberg (1812), and then Berlin (1813). His six-volume *General History of the Christian Religion and Church* (1825–52) treated Christianity as evidence of God at work in the world throughout history, not as a system of dogma to be defended. He exerted great personal influence in the church and had a big influence on the university students.

Henry B. Bascom

May 27, 1796　　　　　　　　　　　　　　　　　　　　　　　　　　　　　　　　　　　　　Sept. 8, 1850
Hancock, New York　　　　　　　　　　　　　　　　　　　　　　　　　　　　　　　Louisville, Kentucky

Most eloquent Methodist preacher of his day. Bascom sided with the South when the Methodist Episcopal Church split in 1844 over the slavery question. Bascom was converted in 1811, served as chaplain of the U.S. Congress (1824–26), president of Madison College, Uniontown, PA (1827–29), and was a professor of moral science at Augusta (KY) College (1832–42). Miss Van Antwerp became his wife on March 7, 1839, giving him two children. Bascom was elected president of Transylvania University, Lexington, KY 1842–49, and was elected a Methodist bishop in 1846. He was the most eloquent Methodist pulpit orator of his day.

Charles Meineke

May 1, 1782　　　　　　　　　　　　　　　　　　　　　　　　　　　　　　　　　　　　　　Nov. 6, 1850
Oldenburg, Germany　　　　　　　　　　　　　　　　　　　　　　　　　　　　　Baltimore, Maryland

Composed response music to "Glory Be to The Father," often called "The Doxology." HENRY GREATOREX composed a similar response. In 1810, Meineke left Germany for England. He then went to Baltimore, MD in 1820 where he was the organist at St. Paul's Episcopal Church, 1822–50. He published *Music for the Church, Containing Sixty-two Psalm and Hymn Tunes in Four Parts Together with Chants, Doxologies, and Responses* (1844).

John J. Audubon

April 26, 1785　　　　　　　　　　　　　　　　　　　　　　　　　　　　　　　　　　　　Jan. 27, 1851
Les Cayes, Santo Domingo (Haiti)　　　　　　　　　　　　　　　　　　　　　　　　New York, New York

Artist, naturalist, and leading ornithologist. Audubon is considered to be history's leading expert on birds. After studying drawing in France, he came to the U.S. (1803) and began by painting birds in the Philadelphia area (1804). Two sons were born from his marriage to Lucy

Bakewell in June, 1808. He then moved to Kentucky and by 1820, was making trips down the Mississippi and Ohio Rivers to observe birds. His *Birds of America* (1827–38), published in four volumes, had 1,065 life-sized drawings in full color. *Ornithological Biography* (1831–39) in five volumes, was also published in England. The National Audubon Society, started in 1905. Concerning his works, he said, "They are all exact copies of the works of God, who is the Great Architect and Perfect Artist." His father was a French sea captain and his mother a Creole servant girl.

James A. Haldane

July 14, 1768
Dundee, Scotland

Feb. 8, 1851
Edinburgh, Scotland

Scottish evangelist. Born two weeks after his father's death, Haldane lost his mother when he was six. Haldane was in the navy, 1785–94. Soon he was converted and preaching the gospel throughout Scotland. In 1797, he founded the Society for Propagating the Gospel at Home. He became the first Congregational minister in Scotland (1799) and installed a "tabernacle" in Leith Walk (1801), seating more than 3,000 where he would minister the next 50 years. Embracing Baptist principles as of 1808, like his brother ROBERT who built him his church, he sought to restore the life and condition of the apostolic church, which was developed in the next generation by the Christian Brethren.

Karl K. F. W. Lachmann

March 4, 1793
Brunswick, Germany

March 13, 1851
Berlin, Germany

Textual critic and philologist. Lachmann was the first expert to seek the restoration of the oldest attainable biblical text. He opened the way for other researchers such as TISCHENDORF and WESTCOTT-HORT, who built upon his reference foundation. Lachmann was professor of philosophy at Konigsberg (1818) and then at Berlin (1825) until his death. He is considered the founder of modern philological criticism and a true textual critic of the New Testament. His most important book was *Commentary on Lucretius* (1850). When he turned his attention to the New Testament text, he applied the same principles as in editing the Greek and Latin classics. He cast aside the Received Text and late manuscripts and reconstructed the text from the most ancient manuscripts, versions and Fathers.

Karl F. A. Gutzlaff

July 8, 1803
Pyritz, Pomerania (Germany)

Aug. 9, 1851
Hong Kong

Missionary to China and proficient sinologist (one who studies the Chinese language and culture). Converted in 1821, Gutzlaff went to Batavia (Jakarta) (1826), worked among the Chinese in Siam (Thailand) (1828), to Malacca and Singapore (1829), to Bangkok, Thailand (1830), and finally to China (1831), where he helped MORRISON with his Chinese associate, translate the Bible into Chinese. He was an agent of the Netherlands Missionary Society. In 1834, he was secretary to the British minister and also established the Chinese Union School to train native preachers in Hong Kong in 1844. He married Mary Nowell in 1830 (died: 1831) and Mary Wanstall in 1832. He made a trip to Europe (1844) after her death, then married Dorothy Gabriel (1850). He started the Chinese Evangelistic Society which HUDSON TAYLOR used as his mission society. In response to his appeal, the first Germans arrived in 1847. Gutzlaff wrote a few books about his work, including *China Opened* (2 vols., 1838). He had a wide range of influence on many people. He died of gout and the dropsy.

Stephen Olin

March 2, 1797
Leicester, Vermont

Aug. 16, 1851
Middlebury, Connecticut

Methodist preacher and educator. He was a professor at Franklin College, Athens, GA from 1826–34. Olin was president at Randolph Macon College in Ashland, VA (1834–37), and of Wesleyan University, Middletown, CT (1842–51). Olin was a preacher of great power and eloquence. He married Mary Ann Bostick on April 10, 1827 (died: in Naples, Italy, in 1839), and Julia Lynch on October 18, 1843. Bad health plagued him all his life. Olin also wrote several books.

John Philip

April 14, 1775
Kirkcaldy, Scotland

Aug. 27, 1851
Hankey, Cape Town, South Africa

British Congregational missionary to South Africa. Philip was converted in the Haldaul revival. He pastored Belmont Congregational Church, Aberdeen, Scotland, 1805–19. He married Jane Russ in 1809. In 1822, he began nearly 30 years of pastoral care at Union Church, Capetown, with 30 stations in South Africa under his supervision working under the London Missionary Society. He got civil rights for the colony inhabitants in 1828. Philip was both hated and loved because of his opposition to apartheid (racial segregation—political and economic discrimination). His grave is in a black graveyard in a black township.

Allen F. Gardiner

1794
Basildon, England

Sept. 1851
Picton Island, Chile, South America

Missionary to Tierra del Fuego (island archipelago off tip of South America divided by Chile and Argentina). Gardiner was converted in 1820 when on warship travels to Chile, Tahiti, and South Africa. When his wife died in 1834 (married eleven years), he went to Port Natal (province of Republic of South Africa, facing the Indian Ocean), where he married again in 1837, and worked among the Zulus the same year. He helped to found the town of Durban. He next ministered to the Indians of South America. From 1838–43 he traveled widely: Argentina, Chile, Australia, Dutch East Indies, South Africa, and Brazil. In 1844, he founded the Patagonian Missionary Society (South American Missionary Society) to bring the gospel to the aboriginal Indians of South Argentina. He helped missions in Bolivia, returned to Britain, and got only modest response for his burden. He and six others then went to Picton Island (Chile) off the Tierra del Fuego archipelago in the Patagonia Region in December, 1850. Their provisions never arrived, so they died of starvation. His last diary entry was September 6. A search party found the bodies on the beach in January, 1852. His favorite Bible verse was Ezekiel 18:31.

Thomas H. Gallaudet

Dec. 10, 1787
Philadelphia, Pennsylvania

Sept. 10, 1851
Hartford, Connecticut

Philanthropist, educator, and founder of the first school for the deaf in America in 1817, in Hartford, CT. Gallaudet was its principal until 1830, also setting up normal schools in the area, 1830–38. He had gone to Europe to study deaf education methods. He married Sophia Fowler on August 29, 1821, who gave him two sons. Gallaudet was chaplain at an insane asylum in Hartford, 1838–51. Gallaudet wrote from *Bible Stories for the Young* (1838) to *Plan of a Seminary for the Education of Instructors of Youth* (1851).

Archibald Alexander

April 17, 1772
near Lexington, Virginia

Oct. 22, 1851
Princeton, New Jersey

President of Hampden-Sydney (VA) College (Union Theological Seminary, Richmond, VA in 1898), **1796–1806, and first professor at Princeton.** This Presbyterian theologian and educator pastored the Pine St. Presbyterian Church in Philadelphia, PA, one of the largest congregations in the country, 1807–12. In 1812, he was appointed the first professor at Princeton Theological Seminary, teaching pastoral theology and polemics the rest of his life. Alexander was well known for his extemporaneous speaking. The first year, there were three students who met in his home. Before he died, however, over 1,800 candidates for the ministry studied under him. He died of dysentery. He said as he died, "...But though friends die, God liveth for ever..." His sons were JOSEPH and JAMES ALEXANDER.

Warren Flenniken

Jan. 9, 1805
Mecklenberg City, North Carolina

Oct. 31, 1851
Hopewell, South Carolina

Stated clerk of Associate Reformed Presbyterian Church, Greenville, SC 1834–46. He married Jane Pressley in November, 1832. Flenniken began his ministry in Hopewell and Union, SC from 1832–48, leaving the Union work in 1837 because of health reasons. He took an active part in temperance reform. As a theologian, he was thoroughly Calvinistic. His active preaching ministry concluded in April, 1847, when he had a severe attack of pneumonia.

Moses Stuart

March 26, 1780
Wilton, Connecticut

Jan. 4, 1852
Andover, Massachusetts

Congregational pastor and educator. Abigail Clark became his wife in 1806, giving him nine children. Stuart pastored the First Church of New Haven, CT, from 1806–10. From 1810–48, Stuart was professor of sacred literature at Andover (MA) Theological Seminary, where he attained great eminence as a teacher and author. He taught himself German and Hebrew. He opposed Unitarianism rigorously calling it "halfway house on road to infidelity." Among his 40 books, he did translations of Greek and Hebrew grammars. He wrote from *Hebrews* (1827) to *Exegetical Essays* (1867).

Elijah Hedding

June 7, 1780
White Plains, New York

April 9, 1852
Poughkeepsie, New York

Methodist bishop, 1824. Hedding was converted at age eight under BENJAMIN ABBOTT. He was ordained a deacon by Bishop WHATCOAT and an elder by Bishop ASBURY. Hedding first served in the Vermont cities of Plattsburg, Cambridge, and Bridgewater and also in Canada as an evangelist. Lucy Blish became his wife on January 10, 1810. Hedding opposed the extreme abolitionist Methodists of New England. He was instrumental in founding the first Methodist periodical in the United States, *Zion's Herald* in Boston in 1823. Hedding was president of General Biblical Institute (Boston University School of Theology), Concord, NH from 1847–52. In 1856, Hedding College in Abingdon, IL was named in his honor. He was confined to his home for the last 16 months with various afflictions, especially dropsy.

Friedrich W. A. Frobel

April 21, 1782
Oberweissbach, Germany

June 21, 1852
Marienthal, Germany

Lutheran educator who founded the kindergarten. He founded the Universal German Educational Institute at Greisheim in 1816. From 1831–37, Frobel taught in Switzerland. His first youngster (kindergarten) class was created in 1837 in Blankenburg, Germany. In 1840, he originated the name "kindergarten" (meaning child's garden). Although the concept of educating preschool children was banned for a while, its merits soon prevailed. Frobel's "kindergarten" was soon recognized as a priceless educational contribution. Frobel was further acclaimed for the gentle methods he employed in education. He started other kindergartens in his remaining years. He advocated that the work of the educator is primarily guidance.

Philander Chase

Dec. 14, 1775
Cornish, New Hampshire

Sept. 20, 1852
Robin's Nest, Illinois

Presiding bishop of Protestant Episcopal Church (Episcopal Church in 1967), **1844–52.** Chase married Mary Fay (age 16) in 1796 and Sophia Ingraham in July 1819, who gave him a total of four children. He was a home missionary in northern New York (1799–1805), New Orleans (1805–11), and Christ Church Hartford, CT (1811–17). He was the first Episcopal bishop of Ohio (1818–31), lived in Michigan (1831–35), and was president of Cincinnati College (1821–22). Chase founded and was first president of Kenyon College, Gambier, OH (1824–31), then was a bishop of the Illinois diocese (1835–52). In 1839, he established Jubilee College, Robin's Nest, which closed during the Civil War. Because he was a successful commercial farmer, he was able to sustain his pioneering work.

Philip Milledoler

Sept. 22, 1775
Rhinebeck, New York

Sept. 22, 1852
Staten Island, New York

President of Rutgers College and New Brunswick (NJ) Theological Seminary, 1825–41. Milledoler graduated from Columbia College in 1793 and became prominent in the Reformed Church. He married Susan Benson (March 29, 1796), and Margaret Steele on (Nov. 4, 1817), having a total of ten children. From 1800–13, Milledoler held important pastorates in New York City and Philadelphia and pastored at the Collegiate Reformed Church, New York City, 1813–52. Milledoler was one of the founders of the American Bible Society in 1816.

Samuel B. Wylie

May 21, 1773
Moylarg, Ireland

Oct. 13, 1852
Philadelphia, Pennsylvania

Professor and, in a sense, CEO of the antecedents of the Reformed Presbyterian Theological Seminary, Philadelphia (Pittsburgh in 1856), 1810–17, 1823–27. Wylie fought for Irish independence but left Ireland in 1798. Wylie married Margaret Watson on April 5, 1802; they had seven children. He became an instructor in grammar school before teaching Latin and Greek at the University of Pennsylvania in 1828. Wylie authored *The Two Sons of Oil* (1803) and *Memoir of Alexander McLeod* (1855).

Daniel Webster

Jan. 18, 1782
Salisbury, New Hampshire

Oct. 24, 1852
Marshfield, Massachusetts

Orator, statesman, and lawyer. Webster graduated from Dartmouth in 1801, married Grace Fletcher on May 29, 1808 (died: Jan 21, 1828), and Caroline LeRoy on Dec. 12, 1829. Webster was a member of the U.S. House of Representatives (1813–17 and 1823–27) and a U.S. Senator (1827–41 and 1845–50). He refused the vice presidency in 1841, but served as secretary of state, 1841–43 and 1850–52. Webster was known as the "defender of the Constitution." He was a member of the Christian Church and publicly expressed his love for the Bible. He, along with statesmen Henry Clay and

John Calhoun, overshadowed the presidents in American politics in the 1830s and 1840s. His last words were, "I still live." Webster was one of history's greatest orators. He never went to law school.
"What a man does for others, gives him immortality."

Samuel Lee

May 14, 1783
Longnor, England

Dec. 16, 1852
Barley, England

Oriental scholar who became professor of Arabic at the University of Cambridge in 1819. Lee was professor of Hebrew (1831–48), and until his death, was also pastoring at Barley (1838–52). Lee authored a Hebrew grammar (1830). He translated the Bible into Syriac, Malay, Persian, Hindustani, Coptic, and Arabic for the Bible Society. He was proficient in eight languages by age 25.

Asa Shinn

May 3, 1781
New Jersey

Feb. 11, 1853
Brattleboro, Vermont

President of Methodist Protestant Church (United Methodist Church in 1968), **1838–46.** Shinn was converted in 1799 at a Methodist service. `Shinn married Phebe Barnes in 1807 and later Mary Gibson, giving him a total of five children. He went with the Methodist Protestants in 1828 when a split came within Methodism which opened up early leadership responsibilities for him, as the MPC was organized in 1830. His *Essay on the Plan of Salvation* (1813) was the first systematic theology written by an American Methodist. A kick in the head by a horse led to his insanity, confined to an asylum from 1843 until his death ten years later.

Ernest L. Hazelius

Sept. 6, 1777
Neusaly, Prussia (Nowa Sol, Poland)

Feb. 20, 1853
Lexington, South Carolina

President of Lutheran Theological Southern Seminary, Lexington (Columbia in 1911), SC 1836–52. Hazelius came to America (1800) and married Hulda Cummings (1810). Hazelius taught Latin, Greek, and theology at a Moravian seminary in Nazareth, PA (1800–9); pastored in New Jersey (1809–15); taught at Hartwick (NY) Seminary (1815–30); and Gettysburg (PA) Seminary (1830–33). He wrote many books.

Anthony N. Groves

Feb 1, 1795
Newton, England

May 20, 1853
Bristol, England

Early leader in the Christian (Plymouth) Brethren movement and missionary to Baghdad and India. Groves was associated with JOHN N. DARBY at Trinity College, Dublin. He moved to Exeter (1816) and took a small church near there (1825). In 1829, he left for Baghdad, Mesopotamia (Iraq) with others (including JOHN KITTO), where his wife Mary died of the plague. He served from 1833–52 in Bombay, India, as a missionary, remarrying in 1835. He died at the home of his brother-in-law, GEORGE MULLER, a pioneer of simple, apostolic, missionary principles.

Frederick W. Robertson

Feb. 3, 1816
London, England

Aug. 15, 1853
Brighton, England

Gifted Anglican preacher and revivalist who was commonly known as "Robertson of Brighton." Robertson married Helen Denys in 1841. He pastored at Winchester (1840–42), at Christ Church, Cheltenham (1842–47), and then had a brilliant six-year ministry at Trinity Chapel, Brighton (1847–53). Robertson was a "preacher's preacher" who left a tremendous impact on his generation, especially reaching the working men. He had an unorthodox view on inspiration and atonement. He died of tuberculosis at age 37 after a year of illness.

Joseph M. Bimeler

c 1778
Wurttemberg, Germany

Aug. 27, 1853
Zoar, Ohio

German eccentric and communitarian leader. Bimeler came to Philadelphia on April 14, 1817, and bought a 5,500-acre tract of land along the Tuscarawas River in eastern Ohio. His sect was the "Kingdom of Zoar" (named after the city, Zoar, OH), a communal-type religious community which flourished. He married and also supervised the establishment of the community brewery, mill, and textile factory. Bimeler also served as the civil and religious leader of his sect, called the Separatists of Zoar, which survived until 1898.

James R. Willson

April 9, 1780
Elizabeth, Pennsylvania

Sept. 29, 1853
Coldenham, New York

Sole professor, and in a sense, CEO of the antecedents of the Reformed Presbyterian Theological Seminary (Pittsburgh in 1856), **1836–51.** In Willson's days, it was called the Coldenham (NY) Academy (1827–30 and 1833–38), Eastern Seminary of Coldenham (1838–40) which merged with Western Seminary to form Allegheny (PA) Seminary (1840). This seminary moved to Cincinnati in 1845 and Norwood, OH in 1849, where he taught until 1851. He married Jane Roberts in 1807. He was teacher in 1806 and principal at Bedford, PA (1809–15), and in Philadelphia (1815–17). He pastored churches at Newburgh and Coldenham, NY (1817–30) and in Albany, NY (1830–33). He was involved with the 1833 split in the RPC.

William Gardiner

March 15, 1770
Leicester, England

Nov. 16, 1853
Leicester, England

Composer of several hymns, including "Where Cross the Crowded Ways of Life" (lyrics by Frank North in 1905), **and "How Precious Is the Book Divine."** Gardiner was a successful hosiery manufacturer and active in many music festivals. On his frequent business trips to the Continent, he gathered materials for two collections of books. LOWELL MASON composed some of his melodies. Gardiner arranged "O Worship the King," 1815 (lyrics by ROBERT GRANT). He introduced the concept of adapting classic works for use as hymn tunes.

Ralph Wardlaw

Dec. 22, 1779
Dalkeith, Scotland

Dec. 17, 1853
Easterhouse, Scotland

Pastor and educator of the Scotch Independents who studied in connection with the Associate Secession Church. Wardlaw was, however, strongly in favor of independence from a state church, so he became a Congregationalist in 1800 and pastored in Glasgow. In 1811, he became professor of theology at the Glasgow Theological Academy, staying for many years. He wrote from *Atonement of Christ* (1830) to *On Miracles* (1852).

William Jay

May 8, 1769
Tisbury, England

Dec. 27, 1853
Bath, England

Congregational pastor at Argyle Chapel, Bath, 1791–1853. Jay attracted large congregations. JOHN FOSTER called him the "prince of preachers." Jay was simple, evangelical, and Biblical. His first work was *Duties of Husbands and Wives* (1801). He wrote *Evening and Morning Exercises* (1829–31), prayers, and meditations.

James Thomson

1788
Creetown, Scotland

1854

Pioneer Baptist explorer and evangelist to South America, 1818–26. Thomson roamed the cities and villages of Ecuador, Columbia, Argentina (1818–21), Chile (1821–22), and Peru (1822–29); valiantly distributing Scriptures and trying to establish Bible-study schools. Thomson was the first Latin American missionary introducing the Bible to South America. He pioneered public education. He was in Mexico (1827–30), Caribbean (1831–38), and Canada (1838–42). His wife died in Madrid in 1848. He went out under the British and Foreign Bible Society until 1849 when he went independent. He founded the Spanish Evangelization Society about the time of his death.

Thomas Campbell

Feb. 1, 1763
County Down, Ireland

Jan. 4, 1854
Bethany, Virginia (West Virginia)

Helped found the Restoration Movement with his son, ALEXANDER. Campbell was a Presbyterian minister of Irish origin who immigrated to America (1807) and founded the Christian Association, Washington County, PA, (1809). He was a minister of the Secession Church that broke away from the Church of Scotland. He conflicted with Presbyterianism over matters of Calvinist doctrine and the administration of the Lord's Supper. He and his son founded the Disciples of Christ in 1832. Campbell was an evangelist and schoolteacher. He resided with his son at Bethany and became blind just prior to his death.

Henry Kumler Sr.

Jan. 3, 1775
Lancaster County, Pennsylvania

Jan. 8, 1854
Butler County, Ohio

Bishop of Church of United Brethren in Christ (United Methodist Church in 1968), **1825–45.** Kumler married Susanna Wingert on September 5, 1797, and they had twelve children. He was ordained to the ministry in 1814 and was a circuit preacher in Pennsylvania (1814–15), Virginia (1816–19), and Ohio (1819–25). He was appointed presiding elder in 1817. Kumler was a farmer in Butler County, OH after 1819. He helped develop attitudes against secret societies, alcoholic beverages, higher education, and slavery. He established a printing house and published his denomination's first periodical, *Religious Telescope* (1841).

Jakob P. Mynster

Nov. 8, 1775
Copenhagen, Denmark

Jan. 30, 1854
Copenhagen, Denmark

Bishop and theologian. Early in Mynster's life, influenced by Immanuel Kant, he was converted. He became chaplain of Church of Our Lady in Copenhagen in 1812 after pastoring on the island of Zealand, 1802–12. Mynster gathered large congregations and won fame as a preacher. In 1828, he was the king's personal chaplain after pastoring in Copenhagen, 1812–28. He was court preacher from 1826–34. In 1834, he was made bishop of Zealand, which was the highest church office in Denmark. He opposed Kierkegaard (1813–55), a philosopher and theologian who was once his student, and Grundtvig because they both tolerated liberalism. He stood against revivalists as well as rationalists. He published numerous sermons.

James Montgomery

Nov. 4, 1771
Irvine, Scotland

April 30, 1854
Sheffield, England

Poet and Journalist. As a Moravian hymn writer, Montgomery wrote over 400 hymns including, "Angels from the Realms of Glory" 1816 (music by HENRY SMART), "The Lord Is My Shepherd," and "In the Hour of Trial" (music by SPENCER LANE). He settled in Sheffield in 1792 and became owner and editor of the *Iris* (1794–1825), a newspaper. Montgomery was several times imprisoned and fined for his publication of certain political articles. He opposed slavery and promoted the singing of hymns in Anglican worship and the cause of foreign missions. He lectured on poetry and literature. Montgomery received a royal pension, 1833 on. He was 43 years old when he became a Moravian. He wrote his first book of poems in 1806 and concluded with a hymnbook in 1853. He died in his sleep.

Robert Newton

April 8, 1780
Roxby, England

April 30, 1854
Easingwold, England

Methodist minister who gained a wide reputation as a pulpit orator. Newton was converted in 1798. He became a member of the British Conference in 1799, elected president of the group four times. In 1839, he was sent to America as a delegate to the conference there. His biography, *Life*, was written by another in 1855. A volume of his sermons was published in 1856.

Robert Donnell

April 1784
Guilford County, North Carolina

May 24, 1854
Athens, Alabama

Early leader of the Cumberland Presbyterian Church. In 1806, Donnell became an evangelist for the group and by 1811, was a leader, preaching mostly in Alabama till his death. Donnell was a founder of Cumberland University in Lebanon, Tennessee. He married Ann Smith (1818) and Clarissa Lindley (1832). Donnell kept Alabama as his home base from which to do his work, which spread to Tennessee and western Pennsylvania. He was the first president of the mission board of Cumberland Presbyterian Church.

Emily Chubbuck Judson

Aug. 22, 1817
Eaton, New York

June 1, 1854
Hamilton, New York

Third wife of ADONIRAM JUDSON. Emily was a Baptist who was well known in American literary circles as a writer of moralistic works and was one of the earliest U.S. advocates for higher educational opportunities for women. Emily married ADONIRAM JUDSON on June 2, 1846, and they had two children. She was an English teacher at Utica (NY) Female Seminary. They sailed to Burma in July, 1846. Their second child died ten days after ADONIRAM's death in 1850. Shortly thereafter, Emily, being in poor health herself, returned to the States and lived in Boston and then in Hamilton, NY in 1851. In addition to being a novelist and poet, Emily also wrote a hymn. She used the pen name Fanny Forester. Emily died of tuberculosis at age 36—the same age of ADONIRAM's first wife, Ann, when she passed on. She wrote from *How to Observe the Golden Rule* (1841) to *My Two Sisters* (1854).

Leonard Woods

June 19, 1774
Princeton, Massachusetts

Aug. 24, 1854
Andover, Massachusetts

Congregational educator who was elected professor of theology at Andover Seminary when it began in 1808. He held this position until his retirement in 1846. Woods defended Calvinism against Unitarianism. Woods aided in the founding of the American Tract Society. He married Abigail Wheeler on Oct. 8, 1799, who gave him eight children, and later the widow of Dr. Ansel Ives. He pastored at Newbury, MA from 1798–1808.

Jonathan M. Wainwright

Feb. 24, 1792
Liverpool, England

Sept. 21, 1854
New York, New York

Episcopal pastor who came to America in 1803 from Liverpool. Wainwright pastored at Christ Church in Hartford, CT in 1816, after serving as assistant pastor at Trinity Church in New York City from 1810–16. Wainwright also pastored at Grace Church in Boston (1821), at Trinity Church in Boston (1834), and at St. John's Chapel in New York City (1837). He became provisional bishop of New York in 1852.

John Kitto

Dec. 4, 1804
Plymouth, England

Nov. 25, 1854
Cannstatt, Germany

Early Plymouth Brethren leader, missionary researcher and writer. Kitto was a librarian in Plymouth. At age twelve, due to an accident, he became permanently deaf. He was converted in 1824. Kitto learned dentistry from Anthony Groves, who later paid his printing education by the Church Missionary Society. He went to Malta (island in Mediterranean), 1827–29, but his health failed. Kitto tutored Groves' children, 1829–33, during his tour to Baghdad, Mesopotamia (Iraq). With deafness curbing his activity, he returned to England in 1852, becoming an Independent. He concentrated his efforts in producing biblical works such as the *Pictorial Bible* (1835–38) among others. He founded and edited the *Journal of Sacred Literature* 1848–53. As he died, he said, "Pray God to take me soon."

Martin J. Routh

Sept. 18, 1755
S. Elmham, England

Dec. 22, 1854
Oxford, England

English patristic scholar and educator who was president of Magdalen College, Oxford 1791–1854. Routh was much respected and revered by the Tractarians. He was an orthodox Church of England partisan. He published the five-volume *Reliquiae Sacrae*. Routh did not marry until age 65 and died at age 94.

John Scudder

Sept. 3, 1793
Freehold, New Jersey

Jan. 13, 1855
Wynberg, South Africa

First medical missionary sent by an American Board (ABCFM). Scudder was ordained by the Dutch Reformed Church and was married to Harriet Waterbury in 1816. They had 13 children. Scudder went to Ceylon (Sri Lanka) and India, in 1819, where he founded the Arcot Mission. He preached in almost every large town in southeastern India. Scudder opened hospitals and schools, and established a mission at Madras (1836–42). He was in the U.S. (1842–46) for health reasons, returning to India (1846–54). Scudder would stand in the hot sun for eleven hours at a time preaching and distributing literature. Seven sons became missionaries to India. A total of 43 members of the Scudder family gave 1,100 years to missionary service including granddaughter, Ida Scudder, who opened the first medical school for women in Asia. On medical leave, he was stricken with a stroke and soon died. He is buried in Madras.

Julius C. Hare

Sept. 13, 1795
Valdagno, Italy

Jan. 23, 1855
Hurstmonceaux, England

Broadchurch theologian who was Anglican rector in Hurstmonceaux, 1832–55, later an archdeacon in Lewes (1840), and chaplain to Queen Victoria (1853). He married the sister of Frederick D. Maurice (Church of

England theologian, educator, 1805–72) in 1844. Hare was a Protestant champion of the Broad Church Party during the time of the Tractarian movement (purpose: to encourage the High Church party to gain control of the Church of England, begun at Oxford. Ninety *Tracts for the Times* were published at Oxford to remain aligned to historical rituals, sacraments, etc.) He opposed this. Hare collected a private library of 12,000 volumes. His first book was *Guesses at the Truth* (1827), which he edited with his brother, Augustus. *The Victory of Faith* (1840) and *The Contest with Rome* (1851) were among his works.

Klaus Harms

May 25, 1778
Fahrstedt, Germany

Feb. 1, 1855
Kiel, Germany

Lutheran preacher and theologian. He was converted via Scripture study at the University of Kiel by the time of his graduation in 1802. He was the university preacher and earnestly opposed the rationalism of his time. Harms was an evangelical leader who served as assistant pastor at Lunden/Holstein, 1806–16. He then transferred to Kiel where he spent the rest of his life preaching. He also was the archdeacon at St. Nicolai (1816), chief preacher at St. Nicolai (1835), and was made provost (1835). Besides his writings against rationalism, he also composed many hymns. He produced a three-volume work on pastoral theology, 1830–34. He opposed union attempts between Reformed and Lutheran churches. Harms lost his sight in 1849, forcing his retirement.

James Ramsey

March 23, 1771
Lancaster County, Pennsylvania

March 6, 1855
Frankfort Springs, Pennsylvania

President of Canonsburg (PA) (Pittsburgh Theological in 1959) **Seminary, 1821–41**. In 1821, Ramsey became professor of theology at Associate Seminary. He died in the home of his son-in-law, Dr. William M. McClure.

Thomas Kelly

July 13, 1769
Stradbally, Ireland

May 14, 1855
Dublin, Ireland

Hymnwriter of "Hark, Ten Thousand Harps and Voices" (music by Lowell Mason), **"Look, Ye Saints! The Sight is Glorious"** (music by William Monk), **"Crown the Savior"** (music by Henry Smart), **and many others**. Kelly prepared to be a lawyer. However, he was converted and ordained in the Irish Episcopal Church in 1792. His fervent evangelical preaching brought him into disfavor with the archbishop of London. Kelly left the established church, became Independent, and built several Christian chapels at Athy, Port Arungton, Wexford, Waterford, and elsewhere. He wrote 765 hymns.

Spencer H. Cone

April 30, 1785
Princeton, New Jersey

Aug. 28, 1855
New York, New York

Baptist pastor of note who was the chaplain of Congress, 1815–16. Sally Morrell became his wife on May 10, 1813. Cone pastored at Alexandria, VA (1816–23), at the Oliver Street Church, New York City (1823–41), and the First (Broome Street) Baptist Church, New York City (1841–55). Cone was president of the Baptist General Conference (1832–41), founder and president of the American/Foreign Bible Union (1837–50), and president of the American Bible Union (1850–55). He wrote *The Backslider* (1827).

Joseph Claybaugh

July 1, 1803
Frederick County, Maryland

Sept. 9, 1855
Oxford, Ohio (?)

President of Associate Reformed Church (Pittsburgh Theological in 1959) **Seminary, Oxford, OH 1839–55**. Claybaugh graduated from Washington (PA) and Jefferson College in 1822 and was principal of Chillicothe (OH) Academy 1825–27, then taught at ARCS.

Stephen Grellet

Nov. 2, 1773
Limoges, France

Nov. 16, 1855
Burlington, New Jersey

Quaker minister, missionary, evangelist, and philanthropist. Raised a Catholic, Grellet came to New York in 1795 as a disciple of Voltaire. The influence of John Penn (1729–95), the grandson of WILLIAM PENN, brought Grellet into Quaker circles. Moved by a WILLIAM PENN book and converted while hearing Deborah Derby, he joined the Friends in 1796. Grellet preached in Philadelphia's Yearly Meeting and had a profound impact on many. He moved to New York City in 1799 because of a yellow fever plague in Philadelphia. He traveled across the country, 1799–1807. Rebecca Collins became his wife on July 11, 1804, giving him one child. Over a ten-year period, Grellet preached in nearly every country in Europe, holding meetings in mines, hospitals, prisons, and asylums. His business ventures in NYC paid the bills. Grellet retired to Burlington in 1834. He wrote *Scripture Lessons for Schools* (1820). His prayer is one of the most famous ever. It began this way: "I expect to pass through this world but once. . . for I shall not pass this way again." His favorite Bible verse was Isaiah 57:15.

Josiah Conder

Sept. 17, 1789
London, England

Dec. 27, 1855
London, England

Congregational layman and hymn writer. Conder became proprietor of his father's bookstore in 1811. He owned and edited the *Eclectic Review*, and edited a non-conformist newspaper, *The Patriot*. Conder served as editor of the first hymnbook of the Congregational Union in 1836, which included 60 of his own hymns. He also edited the *Modern Traveler* (1825–29). Conder wrote the words for the hymn, "The Lord Is King." His *Hymns of Praise*, containing all his hymns and poems, was published in 1856.

Adolphe T. Monod

Jan. 21, 1802
Copenhagen, Denmark

April 6, 1856
Paris, France

French Reformed preacher who had three brothers in the ministry. Monod grew up in Geneva where his father pastored in the French Church. Contact with THOMAS ERSKINE led to his conversion. Monod founded a church in Naples in 1825, serving there until 1827, when he was called to Lyons, 1828–31. He taught in Montauban Seminary (1836–47) and then preached to great crowds at the Oratorie Reform Church, Paris (1847–56). Monod was the foremost pulpit orator of his time. One of his brothers was FREDERIC MONOD.

Robert A. Schumann

June 8, 1810
Zwickau, Germany

July 29, 1856
Endenich, Germany

Composer for such pieces as, "Lord, Speak to Me, that I May Speak" (words by F. R. HAVERGAL). After a hand injury, Schumann turned from piano playing to composing. He married Clara Wieck (1819–96) on Sept. 12, 1840; she was one of history's greatest pianists. They had eight children, five surviving. Schumann wrote symphonies, chamber music, piano compositions (*Papillons* and *Carnaval*), solos and orchestral works (*Spring Symphony* and *Rhenish Symphony*). His tendencies toward insanity increased; in 1854 he was committed to an asylum, where he died. His promotion of other able composers often saved them from obscurity.

James B. Finley

July 1, 1781
North Carolina

Sept. 6, 1856
Eaton/Cincinnati, Ohio

Outstanding Methodist evangelist. Finley married Hannah Strane on March 3, 1801. Converted on his way home from a camp meeting in Cane Ridge, KY in August, 1801, he had a remarkable ministry with great crowds that gathered at camp meetings. He basically served in western New York, Pennsylvania, and Ohio as district presiding elder, 1816–56. For six years he labored successfully as a missionary to the Indians of Upper Sandusky in northern Ohio on Lake Erie, 1821–27. He was an eight-time delegate to the General Conference and an author during his 45-year ministry.

Joseph Hoffman

March 19, 1780
Cumberland County, Pennsylvania

Nov. 8, 1856

Bishop of the Church of the United Brethren in Christ (United Methodist Church in 1968), **1821–56**. This itinerant preacher was ordained by PHILIP OTTERBEIN on October 2, 1813. Upon OTTERBEIN's death, Hoffman took charge of his congregation for nearly four years. In 1817, he moved to Fairfield County, Ohio. Apparently he retired from the office of bishop in the prime of his life, although he regarded himself as a bishop for life. Twice married, he was the father of eleven children. Five of his sons became ministers. Hoffman is buried in Lewisburg, Ohio.

Hugh Miller

Oct. 10, 1802
Cromarty, Scotland

Dec. 23, 1856
Portobello, Scotland

Geologist and first editor of Free Church newspaper, *The Witness*, **1840 on.** Miller's geological works, *The Old Red Sandstone* (1841), *Vestiges of the Natural History of Creation* (1844), and *Footprints of the Creator* (1849), helped to popularize the science of geology and defend Biblical revelation and creation. Miller's profession was stone masonry and bank accounting. In a fit of insanity, he took his own life near Edinburgh.

Eli Smith

Sept. 13, 1801
Northford, Connecticut

Jan. 11, 1857
Beirut, Syria (Lebanon)

Congregational missionary and scholar who translated nearly all the Bible into Arabic beginning in 1846. Smith went with the ABCFM to Malta (1826) and then to Syria (Lebanon), 1833. Smith traveled throughout the Mediterranean establishing Armenian and Nestorian missions in Asia Minor, Armenia, Georgia, and Persia. He married Sarah Huntington on July 21, 1833 (died: 1836), Maria Chapman on March 9, 1841 (died: 1841), and Hetty Butler on October 23, 1846, having a total of six children. He worked on a Bible translation into Arabic the last ten years of his life, making lengthy trips into Palestine, 1852 onward.

David T. Stoddard

Dec. 2, 1818
Northampton, Massachusetts

Jan. 22, 1857
Seir/Urumiah, Iran (Persia)

Congregational missionary to the Nestorians in Persia, 1843–48 and 1851–57. Stoddard directed a school for boys in Seir, Persia. He visited the states, 1848–51, and was very successful in gaining support for his work. He married Harriet Briggs (February 14, 1843) and later Sophia D. Hazen (Feb. 14, 1851). Stoddard wrote *Grammar of the Modern Syriac Language* (1853).

Walter H. Medhurst

April 29, 1796
London, England

Jan. 24, 1857
London, England

Missionary, linguist, and Oriental scholar with the London Missionary Society. Medhurst went to church as a missionary printer in 1816. He married Elizabeth Braun in 1817. Medhurst worked in Malaya, India, Borneo, Java, and on the Chinese coast, spending several years with Chinese immigrants in Java, Indonesia. He lived in Malacca, Penang, and Batavia, 1817–43. He headquartered in Shanghai, China, 1843–56. Medhurst completed translating the Bible into Chinese in 1853 and published the 20-volume *Chinese Repository* (1838–67). He died three days after his arrival in London from his Asian mission field.

William Colgate

Jan. 25, 1783
Kent, England

March 25, 1857
New York, New York

Baptist layman, soap manufacturer and philanthropist who came as a child to Baltimore, MD (1795), then moved to New York City (1804). The Colgate-Palmolive-Peet Co. begun in 1806 as a tallow business, grew to become one of the largest establishments in the world of its kind, partly because soap became one of the biggest sellers in the 1840s. Mary Gilbert became Colgate's wife in 1811, giving him three sons, who all carried on the "family" soap business. Colgate followed the business with intelligence and initiative. The company headquartered in Jersey City, NJ. He supported Madison (Colgate) University in Hamilton, NY. In 1838, he founded the Tabernacle Congregation, an independent work. He also founded the American and Foreign Bible Society.

Barnabas Shaw

April 12, 1788
Elioughton, England

June 21, 1857
Capetown, South Africa

Wesleyan missionary to South Africa who joined the Methodists and was employed as a local preacher. Shaw married Jane Butler in 1815. In 1816, he went to the field where he preached without government approval. He was also opposed by the Anglican and Dutch Reformed Church. Shaw then went 400 miles inland and established a thriving mission. This was at present-day Langsberg Mountains, on the border with Namibia. Shaw taught the people for 21 years, was an invalid in England for six years, 1837–43, and then returned to Africa for 14 more years of missionary service.

William J. Conybeare

Aug. 1, 1815
England

July 22, 1857
Weybridge, England

Church of England clergyman and biblical scholar. Conybeare was the first principal of Liverpool Collegiate Institute, 1842–48, where he was joined in 1845, by his friend, JOHN S. HOWSON. He became vicar of Axminster, Devon, 1848–54, resigning due to illness. In connection with HOWSON, Conybeare published *Life and Letters of St. Paul* (2 vols., 1850–52).

Henry Havelock

April 5, 1795
Bishop Wearmouth, England

Nov. 24, 1857
Lucknow, India

Christian soldier. Havelock entered the British army as a second lieutenant (1815) and went to India (1823). On this voyage, he had a strong spiritual experience. He served in the Burmese War (1824–26), was very heroic in the Afghan War (1838–42), and was appointed adjutant-general, 1854. He commanded a division in the Persian War, 1856–57. In the Sepoy Rebellion (revolt of Indian soldiers in British army against British rule in India, 1857) his military genius was displayed as

The Saints Go Marching In

the city of Lucknow, India, was retaken. As the battle ensued, Havelock developed severe dysentery, from which he died, as his troop of 1,000 men defeated India's 5,000 troop, led by Sahib. Havelock was a devout Baptist. As he died, some of his last words were, "Come, my son, and see how a Christian can die."

Daniel Baker

Aug. 17, 1791
Midway, Georgia

Dec. 10, 1857
Austin, Texas

Presbyterian pastor, educator, and evangelist who pastored numerous churches in Virginia (1816–22), Washington, DC (1822–28), Savannah, GA (1828–31), and Alabama (1831–40). Baker was a missionary evangelist to Texas in 1840, and pastored in Holly Springs, MS from 1841–48. He finally settled in Austin, TX, where he founded Daniel Baker College at Brownwood and became its first president, 1855–57. He married Elizabeth McRobert in 1816 and published *Revival Sermons*.

Charles Cook

May 31, 1787
London, England

Feb. 21, 1858
Paris, France

Founder of Methodism in France and Switzerland. Cook began his work in France in 1816 and conducted numerous evangelistic campaigns. Many small Methodist societies were formed—some joining the Reformed Church, some remaining independent. Cook founded the French Conference of Methodists in 1852.

Nathaniel W. Taylor

June 23, 1786
New Milford, Connecticut

March 10, 1858
New Haven, Connecticut

Congregational pastor, teacher, and theologian. He married Rebecca M. Hine on October 15, 1810, giving him at least one child. Taylor pastored the First Church, New Haven, CT (1812–1822), and then became professor of theology at Yale Divinity School (1822–58). Taylor's appeals to logic, rather than emotion, caused his opponents to found Hartford (CT) Seminary in 1834. His New Haven Theology was borrowed from Congregationalists and nineteenth-century moralism. His writings were published after his death.

John M. Peck

Oct. 31, 1789
Litchfield, Connecticut

March 14, 1858
Rock Spring, Illinois

Baptist home missions pioneer. Peck was converted in a revival at the Congregational Church, Litchfield, in 1807 and became a zealous and resourceful frontiersman. He married Sarah Paine on May 8, 1809, and had ten children. He moved to Greene County, TN in 1811, where he switched from Congregationalist to Baptist. He went to Missouri (1817–22), then to Illinois (1822–27). In 1827, he established Rock Springs Seminary (merged into Shurtleff College in Upper Alton, IL in 1835/36). The school was located in his hometown of Rock Springs, IL where he lived, 1822 on. His pleas led to the formation of the American Baptist Home Mission Society in 1832. A fire in 1852 destroyed thousands of his books. With hardly any education, Harvard University gave him an honorary degree in 1852. Peck's writings included *Guide for Emigrants* (1831) and *The Pioneer Preacher* (1855). He wrote five books.

Johannes E. Gossner

Dec. 14, 1773
Hausen, Germany

March 20, 1858
Augsburg/Berlin, Germany

Minister and founder of the Gossner Foreign Missionary Society. Converted by reading spiritual books (c. 1797), Gossner served in three parishes (1797–1804), then at Dirlewang (1804–11). From 1811–17, he was in literary work. The Catholic Church defrocked him in 1817 for his evangelical views in Munich. He pastored in St. Petersburg (Leningrad), Russia 1820–24. He joined the Lutheran Evangelical Church in 1826. From 1829–46, he pastored the Bethlehem Church (Bohemian Lutheran) in Berlin. In 1842, Gossner founded his society, which sent out 140 missionaries (mainly to North India). Only sixteen of them had a theological education. From 1846 on, he worked with a hospital which he founded in Berlin.

Johann G. B. Winer

April 13, 1789
Leipzig, Germany

May 12, 1858
Leipzig, Germany

Theologian and New Testament scholar who taught at Leipzig University, 1819–23. He was then called to Erlangen as an professor, returning to Leipzig, 1832–death. Winer prepared *Grammar of the Idioms of the New Testament*, a Chaldee language grammar, and a collection of background material for understanding Scripture (Bible Dictionary).

Bennett Tyler

July 10, 1783
Middlebury, Connecticut

May 14, 1858
South Windsor, Connecticut

First president of Theological Institute of Connecticut (Hartford Theological Seminary in 1879), **East Windsor Hill, 1834–57**. Tyler opposed the views (New Haven Theology) of NATHANIEL TAYLOR of Yale Divinity School, and soon he was president/professor of theology at the new, fledgling Hartford Seminary. Twelve children came from his marriage to Esther Stone on November 12, 1807. Tyler was president of Dartmouth University, Hanover, NH 1822–28. He also served as a Congregational pastor in South Britain, CT (1808–22), and Portland, ME (1828–34). He died suddenly at his daughter's home. He wrote three books.

Ebenezer Henderson

Nov. 17, 1784
Dunfermline, Scotland

May 16, 1858
Mortlake, England

Missionary and biblical scholar. From 1803–14, Henderson served in the East Indies, Denmark, Sweden, and Finland. He then went to Iceland (1814) and to Russia (1816). Henderson was president of the LMS Missionary College, Hoxton, England in 1826, and a professor of theology at Highbury College, England, (1830–50). He was familiar with a large number of languages. He was a contributor to the Bible Societies of Iceland, Scandinavia, and Russia. His works ranged from *Prophecies of Daniel* (1811) to *Translations of the Minor Prophets* (1845).

Jabez Bunting

May 13, 1779
Manchester, England

June 16, 1858
London, England

Wesleyan Methodist minister who became president of Wesleyan Theological College 1834–58, the first Methodist College in England. Entering the Methodist ministry in 1799, Bunting helped organize Methodism into a church, independent of the Church of England. For 18 years, he was a secretary of the Wesleyan Missionary Society and four times president of the Conference. Bunting had a beautiful spirit and wisdom from God. He lived in London from 1833 on, holding influential positions in the Wesleyan headquarters.

Jacob J. Janeway

Nov. 1774
New York, New York

June 27, 1858
New Brunswick, New Jersey

Stated Clerk of Presbyterian Church (USA in 1983) **in the US of America, 1807–17**. Martha G. Leiper became his wife, and they had seven children. Janeway was ordained in 1799, becoming an associate pastor

(1799–1816), and then pastor of the Second Church, Philadelphia, PA (1816–26). He then pastored the First Reformed Church and was vice president of Rutger's College, 1833–39, both in New Brunswick, NJ. Janeway wrote several books.

Eleazar Williams

c 1789
Caughnawaga, Quebec, Canada

Aug. 28, 1858
Hogansburg, New York

Episcopal missionary to Indians. Williams served for a time as a missionary among the Oneidas in upstate New York (1813) and translated the *Episcopal Prayer Book* into Iroquois, before heading a party of Oneida chiefs which trekked to Green Bay and founded an Indian nation (1821). He simplified the Mohawk language. Williams married Madeleine Jourdain on March 3, 1823, who gave him three children.

Henry W. Greatorex

Dec. 24, 1813
Burton-on-Trent, England

Sept. 10, 1858
Charleston, South Carolina

Musical composer of Gloria Patri-"Glory Be to the Father" (CHARLES MEINEKE composed a similar response), one of the most famous responsive choruses. Greatorex came to America in 1839 and served as an organist in Episcopal churches: at St. Paul's, Hartford, CT; Calvary, New York City; and in Charleston, SC. Greatorex compiled a collection of music which included 37 of his original hymn tunes. He died of yellow fever.

Isaac B. Woodbury

Oct. 23, 1819
Beverly, Massachusetts

Oct. 26, 1858
Charleston, South Carolina

Composer who arranged music for "Speed Away" (lyrics by FANNY CROSBY) and several other hymns. Woodbury taught for several years in Boston, moving to New York in 1849. There he directed music at Rutgers Street Church and later edited *The Musical Review* and *The Musical Pioneer*. He died at age 39, three days after arriving in Charleston, SC. Woodbury had six children. He also wrote a second tune to WATT's "When I Survey the Wondrous Cross."

Henry U. Onderdonk

March 16, 1789
New York, New York

Dec. 6, 1858
Philadelphia, Pennsylvania

Episcopal pastor and hymn compiler. He married Elizabeth Carter on April 15, 1811. Onderdonk pastored in Canandaigua, NY (1816–20); St. Ann's, Brooklyn, NY (1820–27); and in Philadelphia (1827–36). In 1836, he succeeded Bishop WHITE as bishop of Pennsylvania. Subject to a chronic intestinal disorder, he became addicted to brandy (liquor) in order to relieve his pain. He resigned in 1844 and was suspended from official ministry until 1856. Onderdonk was one of the compilers of 212 hymns found in the *Episcopal Prayer Book* (1827–71). He wrote several books and hymns. He was a leading member of the committee preparing the *American Prayer Book*.

James Carnahan

Nov. 15, 1775
Carlisle, Pennsylvania

March 3, 1859
Newark, New Jersey

President of Princeton (NJ) College (University in 1898), **1823–54**. Carnahan was the graduate with the highest honors in 1800 and later became a trustee at Princeton. Carnahan married Mary van Dyke and was licensed to preach by the Presbyterian Church of New Brunswick in 1804. He pastored at the United Church of Whitesborough, NJ and also in Utica, NY from 1804–14.

Samuel A. Worcester

Jan. 19, 1798
Massachusetts

April 20, 1859
Park Hill, Indian Territory (Oklahoma)

Congregational missionary to the Cherokee Indians. In 1827, he moved to New Echota, GA. For many years, the newspaper, *Worcester* he edited was the only one available in the Indian language. As a result, he became the target for anti-Indian hate programs in the South and was in a Georgia prison for two years, 1831–33. He married Ann Orr (July 19, 1825), and Erminia Nash (April 3, 1841), giving him one daughter. Forced out of Georgia, he settled in Arkansas, and then in Oklahoma, 1835–59, where at Park Hill Mission, he built houses, a church, a school, a printing office, and a book bindery. He started a Cherokee Bible Society and Temperance Society.

George W. Doane

May 27, 1799
Trenton, New Jersey

Apr. 27, 1859
Burlington, New Jersey

Episcopalian bishop, hymn writer, pastor and educator who wrote "Softly Now the Light of Day" (1824) and "Fling Out the Banner, Let it Float" (1848). Eliza Callahan became his wife in 1829, giving Doane two sons. He was professor at Washington (Trinity) College, Hartford, CT (1824–28), then assistant at Trinity Church, Boston, MA (1828–32). In 1832, he moved to Burlington, NJ after becoming bishop of the state. Doane established St. Mary's Hall Church School for Girls, of which he became rector (1837), also founding Burlington College for Men (1846). He published *Songs by the Way*.

James W. Alexander

March 13, 1804
Hopewell, Virginia

July 31, 1859
Sweet Briar Springs, Virginia (West Virginia)

Presbyterian pastor and educator. Early in his ministry, Alexander pastored in Charlottesville, VA (1827–29), and then at the First Presbyterian in Trenton, NJ (1829–32). He was a professor of rhetoric (1833–44), and of church history (1844–51), at Princeton. Alexander also pastored the Fifth Avenue Church (formerly Duane Street Church) in New York City, 1844–49 and 1851–59. He was known to have at least one child, a son. His literary works include *Thoughts on Family Worship* and *Breaking the Crucible and Other Translations*. He devoted much time to translating German and Latin hymns into English; some of these were BERNARD's "O, Sacred Head, Now Wounded" and "Jesus, How Sweet Thy Memory Is." One of his poems ends with these words: " ...for he who dies believing, dies safely—through Thy love." He died from dysentery, as did his father, ARCHIBALD ALEXANDER.

Karl Ritter

Aug. 7, 1779
Quedlingburg, Prussia (Germany)

Sept. 28, 1859
Berlin, Germany

Renowned Geographer. Ritter's physician father passed away in Karl's formative years. Initially Ritter was exposed to a Rousseau type thought base where conformity to natural laws and enlightenment were stressed. A wealthy banker took a keen interest in Ritter, hired him as tutor to his own brood, and became a financial patron to insure higher education opportunities to him. During this time of 1814–19, Ritter developed a keen interest in geography and drew up a manual on physical geography. In 1820, he became a history professor at the University of Berlin and remained there for the rest of his life. Ritter replaced the antiquated "dry bones and dust" approach to geographical study with an enthusiasm that proved contagious. Geography was presented as a mighty window into God's handywork. In order to support the value of Biblical works, he realized the need and produced *The Comparative Geography of Palestine and the Sinaitic Peninsula*. The four-volume set was translated into English (1866) and remains of great interest to Bible students.

Karl J. P. Spitta

Aug. 1, 1801
Hanover, Germany

Sept. 28, 1859
Burgdorf, Germany

Lutheran pastor (1828 on) and hymn writer. Spitta's Psalter und Harfe (Pirna, 1833) contained 61 hymns and was exceedingly popular. Early in life, 1824–25, while serving as a tutor to a private family, Spitta passed through a deep spiritual experience which prompted his hymn writing. His Huguenot family fled to Germany from the Roman Catholic persecutions occurring against Christians in France. He pastored at Wechold near Hoya in Hanover (1837–47), was Lutheran superintendent of Wittingen (1847–53), and chief pastor of Peine (1853–59). A few weeks after his pastoral appointment to Burgdorf, he suddenly died.

John A. James

June 6, 1785
Blandford, England

Oct. 1, 1859
Birmingham, England

Congregational pastor who pastored Carr's Lane Chapel in Birmingham, 1806–59. James was a preacher of unusual power and was an indefatigable pastor in his labors. His best book was *The Anxious Enquirer after Salvation Directed and Encouraged* (1834). James' writings number 17 volumes and were published, 1860–64. He was educated at the theological seminary at Gosport and was one of the promoters of the Evangelical Alliance.

Louis Spohr
"Ludwig Spohr"

April 5, 1784
Brunswick, Germany

Oct. 22, 1859
Kassel, Germany

Composer of hymns such as "All Things Bright and Beautiful." Spohr married Dorette Scheidler in 1806 (died: 1834) and Marianne Pfeiffer in 1836. His widest fame followed the production of his opera *Faust* at Prague on September 1, 1816. Spohr was a violinst of great reknown. His concerts throughout Europe and England were widely acclaimed. He wrote oratorios, operas, violin concertos, and chamber music. Spohr was established as court musician at Cassel in 1822. He visited London to conduct as late as 1853.

John Brown (2)

May 9, 1800
Torrington, Connecticut

Dec. 2, 1859
Charles Town, Virginia (West Virginia)

Radical Messianic abolitionist. Brown prepared for the Congregational ministry. He married Dianthe Lusk (1820) and Mary A. Day (1832), having a total of 20 children. Brown was in and out of several successful businesses. He was an anti-slave leader in Kansas, 1855–58. In 1856, he led a band of guerrillas in the Pottawatomie Massacre in which five proslave settlers were killed. With 21 followers, Brown attacked the US Arsenal at Harper's Ferry in Virginia (WV) on Oct. 16, 1859, in a plan to liberate Southern slaves through armed intervention. He was caught, tried, convicted of treason, and hanged. Brown was a man with many friends and many foes. He stated in a letter that he was a firm and humble believer in the religion of Jesus Christ. He is buried in John Brown Farm State Historic Site, Lake Placid, NY.

John Seybert

July 7, 1791
Manheim, Pennsylvania

Jan. 4, 1860
Bellevue, Ohio

Bishop of Evangelical Association, 1839–60. After the death of JACOB ALBRIGHT in 1808, the Church was without a bishop for 31 years. Then in 1839, Seybert was unanimously elected to this position. His whole life was one of utter simplicity and self-denial. He was converted in

1810 by Matthia Bentz. He became an evangelist in the NY circuit in 1820, traveling also in Pennsylvania and Ohio circuits. He was assigned to the Salem district, 1829–33, and did missionary work in northwestern cities of Pennsylvania in 1833. Seybert never married and he never took a vacation. He traveled by horse and buggy 175,000 miles (equal to seven times around the world at the equator). He preached 9,850 times, conducted thousands of prayer and class meetings, made 46,000 pastoral visits, and visited 10,000 sick and afflicted. His last entry in his diary on December 28, 1859 says, "One soul saved." He is buried in Flat Rock, Ohio.

Joseph A. Alexander

April 24, 1809
Philadelphia, Pennsylvania

Jan. 28, 1860
Princeton, New Jersey

Presbyterian scholar, linguist, educator, and author. Alexander was a teacher at Princeton Theological Seminary most of his life and an eminent Bible scholar. Born the son of ARCHIBALD ALEXANDER, he was professor of ancient languages and literature (1830–33), taught oriental and biblical literature (1834 on), apologetics and church history (1838–51), and biblical and church history (1851 on). He wrote several books including *Translation and Commentary of Psalms* (1850) to *Mark* (1858).

Henry Drummond (1)

Dec. 5, 1786
Grange, England

Feb. 20, 1860
Albury, England

Politician, writer, founder and "Apostle" of the Catholic Apostolic Church in 1827. Drummond was a banker (1810–13) and a member of Parliament from West Surrey (1847–60). In 1817, he met Robert Haldane and supported this Genevan clergyman against the Socinians. In 1826, about 50 people met in his Surrey home and studied biblical prophecy. Drummond soon became an apostle, evangelist, and prophet of this church. He wrote from *Social Duties and Christian Principles* (1830) to *Discourses on. . .the Church* (1858).

Friedrich W. K. Umbreit

April 11, 1795
Sonneborn, Germany

April 26, 1860
Heidelberg, Germany

Educator and theologian who accepted a professorship at Heidelberg in 1820. Umbreit spent his life devoted to the study of the Old Testament, preparing several well-known commentaries. It is said that Umbreit's work opened the eyes and hearts of many to the beauty of the Old Testament. He wrote commentaries on the following books of the Bible: Ecclesiastes, Song of Solomon, Job, Proverbs, most of the minor prophets and Romans.

Isaak Da Costa

Jan. 14, 1798
Amsterdam, Netherlands

April 28, 1860
Amsterdam, Netherlands

Poet and Reformed theologian who belonged to a family of wealthy Portuguese Jews. He was converted and baptized on October 20, 1822 in Leiden, Netherlands via WILLEM BILDERDIJK. He was married to Hanna Belmonte. Da Costa was a brilliant poet and apologist, especially in opposing the German Tubingen School. In 1839, he led in the formation of the Christian Reformed Church, along with ABRAHAM KUYPER. Da Costa taught at Amsterdam Seminary, which was founded by the Free Church of Scotland. Da Costa was identified with every movement of the time favorable to revival. He was co-founder of the Friends of Israel in 1846. He wrote *The Four Witnesses* (1851) and various historical and theological treatises.

John Winebrenner

March 25, 1797
Walkerville, Maryland

Sept. 12, 1860
Harrisburg, Pennsylvania

Founder of Church (Churches in 1903) **of God** (in North America in 1845) (General Conference), **Harrisburg, PA** (Findlay, OH), **1830**. Winebrenner married Charlotte Reutter (Oct.

10, 1822), and Mary Mitchell (November 2, 1837), who gave him at least six children. He began as a pastor in the German Reformed Church, Philadelphia (1817–20), and Harrisburg (1820–28). He was deposed from the Reformed Church, in 1828, because of his opposition to drinking, slavery, worldliness and his emphasis on evangelism. As a result, he started a new denomination and presided over it from 1845–48 and 1857–60. He wrote several books. A theological seminary in Findlay, OH is named after him.

John V. Hall

March 14, 1774
Diss, England

Sept. 22, 1860
Kentish Town, England

Bookseller and author. He was an earnest and eloquent advocate of total abstinence from liquor and other substances that are harmful to the body and to the soul. In 1804, Hall bought a bookseller's shop in Worcester and was converted. Leaving Worcester in 1814, he was a book dealer in Maidstone, 1814–50. Hall is best remembered as the author of the book entitled, *The Sinner's Friend* (1821). During his lifetime the book was published in 30 languages, with 30 million copies distributed. He was the father of CHRISTOPHER NEWMAN HALL, who was an author and Congregational clergyman in London.

George Croly

Aug. 17, 1780
Dublin, Ireland

Nov. 24, 1860
Holborn, London, England

Anglican poet, novelist, dramatist, historian, satirist, and clergyman who gave us the hymn, "Spirit of God, Descend Upon My Heart" (music by F. ATKINSON) among many others. At age 30, Croly went to London and devoted his life to literary endeavors, publishing his first book of poetry in 1817. He also wrote two widely read historical novels. Croly was a strong opponent of liberalism and served as pastor of St. Stephens in Walbrook, London, in 1835, drawing great crowds. He died suddenly while walking one day.

Lars L. Laestadius

1800
Arjeploug, Sweden

1861

Lutheran pastor and leader of the revival movement in Lapland, Scandinavia. After ordination in 1825, Laestadius became pastor of Sweden's northernmost parish, Karesuanto. His parishioners were Lapps and Finns living in Swedish Lapland. Severe illness and the death of his three-year-old son precipitated a religious crisis from which he emerged as a revivalist. The resulting revival spread through Swedish and Norwegian Lapland, but found its largest following in northern Finland. The last decade of his ministry was in the parish of Pajala. He wrote in Swedish, but preached in Finnish. Immigrants from northern Finland have brought his heritage to America, calling themselves Apostolic Lutherans.

Heman Humphrey

March 26, 1779
West Simsbury, Connecticut

April 3, 1861
Pittsfield, Massachusetts

President of Amherst (MA) College (started in 1821), **1823–45**. He married Sophia Porter on April 20, 1808. From 1817–23, Humphrey was a Congregational pastor in Pittsfield. Humphrey toured France in 1838. He wrote pamphlets against slavery and intemperance which enjoyed a wide circulation. Humphrey authored *Domestic Education* (1840), *Letters to a Son in the Ministry* (1742), and *Life of T. H. Ballaudt* (1857).

Walter Scott (2)

Oct. 31, 1796
Moffatt, Scotland

April 23, 1861
Mays Lick, Kentucky

Co-founder of the Disciples of Christ (c 1827), along with ALEXANDER (in US) and John Campbell. (in Ireland). Scott came to America in 1818. He became a follower of ALEXANDER CAMPBELL (The Campbellites) (1822), leaving the Baptists shortly (1827). Six children came from his successive marriages to Sarah Whitsett on Jan. 3, 1828, Annie B. Allen (1850), and Mrs. Eliza Sandige (1855). He published *The Evangelist*, and served as an evangelist, seeing about 1,000 converted annually for some 30 years. He was a key founder in the restoration movement's birth.

Ezra S. Ely

June 13, 1786
Lebanon, Connecticut

June 18, 1861
Philadelphia, Pennsylvania

Stated clerk of Presbyterian Church (USA in 1983) **in the US of America, 1825–36**. Converted at age 12, Ely pastored the Pine St. Church, Philadelphia, PA from 1817–34. He sought to expand into Missouri, 1834–44, but met with financial difficulty. Next, he pastored the First Presbyterian Church, Philadelphia 1844–51. Ely married Miss Carswell and then Miss Holmes. They gave him a total of six children. Ely suffered a stroke in 1851, which left him paralyzed.

Elijah C. Bridgman

April 22, 1801
Belchertown, Massachusetts

Nov. 2, 1861
Shanghai, China

First American Protestant missionary to China. Bridgman was sponsored by the American Board of Commissioners for Foreign Missions. He was joined by British missionary, ROBERT MORRISON, at Canton, China, in 1830. In 1832, he started a mission press and edited the *Chinese Repository*, 1832–47, and published it in English. In 1838, he assisted in developing one of the earliest medical programs under mission sponsorship. Eliza J. Gillett (1805–71) married him on June 28, 1845. Bridgman moved his ministry to Shanghai, China, in 1847, pastoring, translating, and supervising the publishing of a Bible.

Thomas S. Smith

Dec. 21, 1788
Martock, England

Dec. 10, 1861
Florence, Italy

Evangelically minded churchman who left his pastorate among the poverty stricken in order to study medicine. Smith devoted his life to improving conditions among slum dwellers. He helped to expose the evils of child labor, and helped to secure passage of the Factory Act, prohibiting children from being hired in British mines and mills. He began as a London physician (1820) and was appointed to the London Fever Hospital (1825). Smith spent much time investigating epidemics of cholera, yellow fever, and other contagious diseases. In 1830, he published his famed *Treatise on Fever*.

William Cunningham

Oct. 2, 1805
Hamilton, Scotland

Dec. 14, 1861
Edinburgh, Scotland

Free Church theologian. Cunningham was a powerful advocate of the 1843 disruption when the Free Church of Scotland was formed. He was also the founder of the Evangelical Alliance. In government, he was a Presbyterian; in doctrine, a strong Calvinist. Cunningham followed THOMAS CHALMERS as principal of Free Church/New College in Edinburgh, Scotland (1847), beginning to teach there (1843). He wrote several books and was a good friend of the Presbyterian theologian, CHARLES HODGE.

Samuel H. Turner

Jan. 23, 1790
Philadelphia, Pennsylvania

Dec. 21, 1861
New York, New York

Professor at General Theological Seminary, New York City of historic theology (1818 on) and of biblical learning (from 1821) until his death forty years later. Turner was ordained in the Episcopal Church and pastored, 1814–17. Turner married Mary Beach on May 23, 1826, and they had at least three children. He wrote commentaries on Hebrews (1852), Romans (1853), Ephesians (1856), and Galatians (1856).

Dorthea Trudel

1813
Mannendorf, Switzerland

1862

Prayer warrior and healer. Dorthea was converted at 22 years of age and, sometime later, entered into a deeper experience with God. Many people in her area testified of marvelous cures wrought by her prayers.

Thomas H. Horne

Oct. 20, 1780
London, England

Jan. 27, 1862
London, England

Biblical scholar and bibliographer. Horne was ordained in the Church of England in 1819. He was an assistant librarian at the British Museum, 1824–60. He was curate of Christ Church (1819–25), and assistant at Walbeck Chapel (1825–33), prebendary at St. Paul's Episcopal Church (1831), rector in (1833) of two London churches. In 1818, he published *Introduction to the Critical Study and Knowledge of the Holy Scriptures* (3 vols.).

Charles F. Mackenzie

April 10, 1825
Portmore, Scotland

Jan. 31, 1862
Malo Isle, British Central Africa (Angola)

Church of England missionary to central Africa. In 1855, Mackenzie went with Bishop John Colenso (1814–83) to Natal (eastern province of South Africa). He returned to England and aroused missions interest for this area. In 1861, he was consecrated as the first bishop from Universities' Missions to Africa. His newly commissioned diocese covered the area bordering on Lake Nyasa, which today represents the countries of Tanzania, Mozambique, and Nyasaland (Malawi) in east central Africa. Mackenzie died from a fever, while hurrying to meet LIVINGSTON. His canoe capsized, losing all his medicines. He died soon afterwards.

Andrew Reed

Nov. 27, 1787
London, England

Feb. 25, 1862
London, England

Hymn writer of "Holy Ghost, with Light Divine" (music by LOUIS GOTTSCHALK). Reed was an ardent philanthropist who was largely instrumental in founding the London Orphan Asylums and other homes for society's outcasts. Reed was ordained a Congregationalist. He married Eliza Holmes, also a hymn writer of note, in 1816. He pastored the New Road Chapel, London, for fifty years, 1811–61. Reed visited the U.S. in 1834–35 to study educational and religious systems. He composed 21 hymns.

William Meade

Nov. 11, 1789
near Millwood, Virginia

March 14, 1862
Richmond, Virginia

Third bishop of the Protestant Episcopal Church of Virginia. Meade entered the ministry in 1811. He married Mary Nelson (Jan. 31, 1810), and Thomasia Nelson (Dec. 2, 1820). He was an evangelical, missionary-minded, and curate/rector in Millwood, VA from 1813–23. He was the founder of the Protestant Episcopal Theological Seminary of Virginia in 1823. Meade served as bishop, 1841–62. After the Oxford Movement in the Anglican Church started, Meade helped restore interest in the separate Episcopalian movement of America. Meade wrote *Old Churches, Ministers, and Families of Virginia* (1857) and several other books.

Theodore Frelinghuysen

March 28, 1787
Millstone, New Jersey

April 12, 1862
New Brunswick, New Jersey

President of American Bible Society, 1846–62, and of Rutgers College and New Brunswick (NJ) Theological Seminary, 1850–62. NBTS separated from Rutgers in 1856, but same president was utilized until 1924. Frelinghuysen also served as attorney general of New Jersey (1817–29) and one term as a senator from New Jersey (1829–35). He was elected mayor of Newark, NJ (1835–39) and chancellor of University of NY, NYC (1839–50). Frelinghuysen married Charlotte Mercer in 1809 and Harriet Pumpelly on October 14, 1857. Known as the "Christian Statesman," he ran for vice-president with Henry Clay of the Whig Party in 1844. He also served as a lawyer.

George W. Bethune

March 18, 1805
New York, New York

April 28, 1862
Florence, Italy

Pastor and hymn writer, including "There is No Name So Sweet on Earth" (music by WILLIAM BRADBURY). Bethune married Mary Williams on Nov. 4, 1825. He was ordained in the Dutch Reformed Church, serving pastorates in Rinebeck, NY (1827–30); Utica, NY (1830–34); Philadelphia, PA (1834–49); Church on the Heights in Brooklyn Heights, NY (1850–59) and 21st Street Church, NYC from 1859–62. Bethune turned down chancellorships of several universities in favor of concentrating on his research and writings, which included, *The British Female Poets* (1848) and *The Fruits of the Spirit* (1849). Other hymns he wrote were: "Come, Let Us Sing Of Jesus," "O Jesus When I Think of Thee", and "When Time Seems Short and Death is Near." Bethune died suddenly of brain congestion in Italy.

Nathan Bangs

May 2, 1778
Stratford, Connecticut

May 3, 1862
New York, New York

Distinguished Methodist preacher, editor, and writer. From 1804–12, he was in Canada ministering on circuits from Niagara to Quebec. Bangs married Mary Bolton on April 23, 1806, who gave him one son. He headed the Methodist Book Concern 1820–28, then edited the *Christian Advocate*, 1828–32. Bangs founded the Methodist Missionary Society and served as its secretary (1836–41), after which he became president of Wesleyan University, Middleton, CT (1841–42). He then pastored in New York, 1842–52. Bangs wrote a four-volume *History of the Methodist Church* (1838–40) and also edited *Methodist Quarterly Review* (1832–36). He was a foe of Calvinistic election and predestination.

James H. Thornwell

Dec. 9, 1812
Marlboro District, South Carolina

Aug. 1, 1862
Charlotte, North Carolina

Renowned Presbyterian pastor and educator. Thornwell was converted in the early 1830s while serving as a schoolteacher. Thornwell married Nancy W. Witherspoon on Dec. 3, 1835. He pastored in Lancaster (1835–37); was professor of logic at South Carolina College (Univ.), Columbia, SC (1837–39); pastor in Columbia, SC (1839–41); professor of literature and apologetics at SCC (1841–51); president of the same (1852–55); pastor in Columbia; and professor of theology at Presbyterian Theological Seminary, Columbia, SC (1855–62). He also founded the *Southern Presbyterian Re-*

view. His collected writings were edited in four volumes. Thornwell is considered the leader of the Old School Branch of Presbyterianism, and led in the formation of the Presbyterian Church in the US in 1861. He was perhaps the most influential southern minister before the Civil War.

John B. Sumner (1)

1780
Kenilworth, England

Sept. 6, 1862

Archbishop of Canterbury, 1848–62. A Cambridge graduate, Sumner was ordained in 1803 and was bishop of Chester, 1828–48. He was an evangelical who opposed the Oxford movement and baptismal regeneration, but he voted for the Catholic Emancipation Bill in 1829. From 1820–28, he was canon in the cathedral of Durham.

William B. Johnson

June 13, 1782
John's Island, South Carolina

Oct. 2, 1862
Greenville, South Carolina

First president of Southern Baptist Convention, 1845–49. Eight children came from Johnson's marriage to Henrietta K. Hornby in 1803. He was converted at a Beaufort, SC revival. He pastored four churches 1806–52, all in South Carolina except from 1811–15, when he served in Savannah, GA. Johnson helped to found Furman University in Greenville, SC in 1825. He was also a founder of the American Baptist Missionary Society in 1841 (president 1841–44) and active in South Carolina circles.

Christian G. Barth

July 13, 1799
Stuttgart, Germany

Nov. 12, 1862
Calv, Germany

Missions enthusiast who pastored in Mottlingen, Germany, 1824–38. Barth retired to Calv (near Stuttgart), where he founded the Missionary Society of Wurtemberg Province. This missionary society came into active cooperation with missionary organizations all over the world. Barth wrote several books on practical Christianity and composed missionary hymns. He compiled a collection of Bible stories, *Stories for Christian Children* that sold one million copies.

Rudolf E. Stier

March 17, 1800
Fraustadt, Germany

Dec. 16, 1862
Eisleben, Germany

Lutheran commentator whose life was consumed with Bible study. Stier taught theology at the Mission School in Basel, 1824–29. He held pastorates at Frankenleben and Wichlinghausen, 1829–47. From 1850 until his death, he was superintendent at Schkeuditz and then at Eisleben. His 1843 *Words of the Lord Jesus* strongly supports inspiration. He wrote commentaries on *Ephesians* (1846), *Hebrews* (1862), and *James* (1860). He edited a *Polyglot Bible* with K. G. W. Theile (1864–55).

Lyman Beecher

Oct. 12, 1775
New Haven, Connecticut

Jan. 10, 1863
Brooklyn, New York

Pastor and first president of Lane Theological Seminary, Cincinnati, OH (affiliated with McCormick Theological Seminary, Chicago in 1931), **1832–50**. He pastored the Second Presbyterian Church there during the same time. Beecher was converted in 1795 while at Yale University, under the influence of TIMOTHY DWIGHT. Early in life, Beecher pastored the East Hampton Presbyterian Church, Long Island, NY (1799–1810); Congregational churches in Litchfield, CT (1810–26); and Hanover St. Congregational Church, Boston, MA (1826–32). He founded the American Bible Society in 1816. He married Roxana Foote on Sept. 19, 1799 (died: 1816); Harriet Porter in November, 1817;

and Lydia Jackson on July 7, 1835. He had 13 children including Henry W. and Harriet Beecher Stowe. Lyman Beecher was an ardent foe of slavery, dueling and drunkenness, strongly supporting temperance platforms. He edited the *Christian Union*. He was tried as a heretic for his moderate Calvinism in 1835. In the 1838 Presbyterian split, he stayed with the "New School."

Edward Robinson

April 10, 1794
Southington, Connecticut

Jan. 27, 1863
New York, New York

Bible scholar and professor of biblical literature at Union Theological Seminary, NYC 1837–63. Robinson married Eliza Kirkland on September 3, 1818, and Therese A. L. Von Sakob in 1828. He taught at Andover (MA) Theological Seminary from 1830–33. He was renowned for his geographical study trips to the Holy Land in 1838, 1852, and 1856. Some consider him the father of Biblical Geography. He wrote 15 books on the subject, starting with *Bible Researches in Palestine* (1841). His *Greek Harmony of the Gospels* was considered the best of his time. He was plagued with epilepsy from time to time.

Robert Baird

Oct. 6, 1798
near Uniontown, Pennsylvania

March 15, 1863
Yonkers, New York

Presbyterian evangelical leader and temperance advocate who was ordained following his Princeton Seminary training. Baird married Fermine DeBuisson on August 24, 1824. He directed Princeton Academy (1822–27), and was an agent for the American Sunday School Union (1829–34). Baird resided in Europe from 1835–43, ministering in Catholic countries. Upon his return to America, he became secretary of the Foreign Evangelical Society. Baird traveled extensively on behalf of the Sunday School movement, crossing the Atlantic Ocean 18 times. He wrote *Religion in America* (1843).

Thomas J. (Stonewall) Jackson

Jan. 21, 1824
Clarksburg, Virginia (West Virginia)

May 10, 1863
Fredericksburg, Virginia

Outstanding Christian general for the South in Civil War days, second only to Robert E. Lee. In 1846, Jackson graduated from West Point and immediately began participating in the Mexican War. He was converted in 1849 through the Presbyterian Church in Lexington, VA, and the pastor, Wilham White, while a professor in the military academy. He joined the church there in 1851. From 1851–61, he was an instructor at the Virginia Military Institute (VMI). He married Eleanor Junkin on Aug. 4, 1853 (died in childbirth Oct. 22, 1854), and Mary A. Morrison on July 16, 1857. Jackson was made a general in the Confederate army in 1861. As a result of the firm stand he and his brigade took at the First Battle of Bull Run, he earned the nickname, "Stonewall" Jackson. In 1862, he was the leader in the Peninsular Campaign, Valley Campaign, Second Battle of Bull Run, Antietam, Fredericksburg, and other skirmishes. He observed the Lord's Day and prayed often on the battlefield. During a successful Confederate campaign at Chancellorsville, VA, Jackson was accidentally mortally wounded by his own men on May 2, 1863. He succumbed eight days later at the age of 39 with pneumonia complications. He died at Guiney's Station. His last words were, "Let us go over the river and sit in the shade of the trees." He is buried in Lexington, VA.

Ralph Emerson

Aug. 18, 1787
Hollis, New Hampshire

May 20, 1863
Rockford, Illinois

President of Andover (MA) (Andover–Newton in 1931) **Theological Seminary, 1842–53**. Emerson married Eliza Rockwell on Nov. 27, 1817, and together they had several children. Emerson pastored Congregational churches at Norfolk, CT (1816–29); Andover, MA (1829–

53); Newburyport, MA (1853–58); and Rockford, IL (1858–63). He also lectured at the Chicago Theological Seminary, 1858–63.

John S. Pressly

Nov. 11, 1793
Abbeville County, South Carolina

June 1, 1863
near Generostite, North Carolina

First president of Clark and Erskine Theological Seminary, Due West, SC 1837–60 and a divinity professor. He taught school for a time and served two terms in the SC legislature before he began preaching. He founded the Academy at Due West (mid 1820s) which later developed into Erskine College and Seminary. The son of Samuel Pressly, John began pastoring at Ebenezer and Bethel in Jefferson County, GA in 1842. He married Martha J Strong (born: Jan. 18, 1820) on Sept. 29, 1842; they had no children. The work of the seminary was discontinued for a decade during the Civil War, 1860–69. It then reopened in 1869.

Francois S. L. Gaussen

Aug. 25, 1790
Geneva, Switzerland

June 18, 1863
Geneva, Switzerland

Evangelical preacher and Reformed theologian who was opposed by the established church. While studying theology in Geneva, Gaussen was converted. He helped to found the Evangelical Society of Geneva in 1831. Gaussen was also an evangelist in Italy and England and taught at Geneva. He helped found a Reformed theological school in 1834, defending the faith and teaching dogmatics. Early in his ministry, Gaussen pastored in Satigny, Switzerland, until his evangelical views prohibited his continuance.

Clement C. Moore

July 15, 1779
New York, New York

July 10, 1863
Newport, Rhode Island

Professor of Greek at General Theological Seminary, 1821–50. Moore first taught Hebrew and Greek, then Oriental and Greek literature. He married Catharine Taylor on November 20, 1813. Moore gave 60 lots in New York City in 1822 to provide a permanent home for General Theological Seminary. He authored a Hebrew lexicon. Moore also authored the famous Christmas poem "A Visit From Saint Nicholas" (" 'Twas the Night Before Christmas") December 23, 1823. He wrote it as a gift to his children. He was the son of an Episcopalian clergyman.

Samuel Houston

March 2, 1793
Lexington, Virginia

July 26, 1863
Huntsville, Texas

General, statesman, and president of the Republic of Texas, 1836–38, 1841–44. The city of Houston, TX was named after him. Houston married Eliza Allen on January 22, 1829 (separated after three months), Tiana Rogers (1830), and Margaret Lea (1840); he had eight children. Houston served as a soldier, lawyer, congressman, and governor of Tennessee, 1827–29, before going to Texas in 1833. Houston routed the Mexican forces out of Texas (April, 1836) with the victory over Santa Anna in the Battle of San Jacinto, helped annex Texas into the Union in 1845, and was the first senator from Texas, 1846–59. He served as governor of Texas from 1859–61, but was deposed when he supported the Union in the Civil War.

Thomas Raffles

May 17, 1788
London, England

Aug. 18, 1863
Liverpool, England

Eminent Congregational pastor. Raffles pastored in Hammetsmith, outside London, 1809–11. From 1812 until his death, he was pastor at Liverpool, England. Blackburn Academy was founded by Raffles to educate Independent ministers. The school moved to Manchester, becoming the Lancashire Independent College. Among his writings were several hymns which were widely used, such as, "Higher in Yonder Realms of Light."

Richard Whateley

Feb. 1, 1787
London, England

Oct. 1, 1863
Dublin, Ireland

Anglican archbishop of Dublin, 1831 on. Whateley was an educator, theologian, and social reformer. He deflated critics of Christianity, such as skeptic David Hume (1711–76). From 1825–31, he was professor of political economy at St. Alban Hall, Oxford. He was a liberal in religion and politics. He published 60 volumes of essays and sermons. Whateley published works in fields of logic and rhetoric. He was helped by the Broad Church Movement (Protestants opposing Oxford High Church Movement in England). He wrote *Elements of Logic* (1826) and *Elements of Rhetoric* (1828). He strongly opposed Calvinism.

Frederic J. J. G. Monod

May 17, 1794
Monnaz, Switzerland

Dec. 30, 1863
Paris, France

French evangelical pastor. Monod was the brother of ADOLPHE MONOD. While a student at Geneva, his faith was revived under the teaching of ROBERT HALDANE. Frederic served at the National Protestant Church of France in Paris from 1820–49, which was called the Oratorie. In 1824, he established and edited a magazine for the Evangelical French Protestants for 43 years. Monod helped found the Union of Evangelical Free Churches in France in 1849, and guided the development of this alliance.

Edward Hitchcock

May 24, 1793
Deerfield, Massachusetts

Feb. 27, 1864
Amherst, Massachusetts

Scientist and geologist. He married Orra White in 1821, and they had six children. From 1821–25, Hitchcock served as the pastor of the Congregational Church, Conway, MA. He was made professor of natural theology at Amherst College, 1825–45 and 1854–64. Hitchcock was president of Amherst from 1845–54 and became widely known for his geological researches. Hitchcock wrote on various subjects, his most noted *The Religion of Geology* (1851) being widely accepted. He believed in an old earth that was created by God.

Cesar H. A. Malan

July 7, 1787
Geneva, Switzerland

May 18, 1864
Vandoeuvres, Switzerland

Evangelist who, like FRANCOIS GAUSSEN, found pulpits closed to him. Malan gathered a following first in his house, then in a small chapel which he built himself on his own property, and where he preached for 43 years. He was ordained in the French Reformed Church in 1810, but was not converted until 1817. Malan married in Geneva in 1811. He traveled widely as an evangelist after 1830 to Germany, France, the Netherlands, and Scotland. Malan wrote more than 1,000 hymns and tunes, composing the music for "Take My Life, and Let It Be," 1874 (lyrics by F. R. HAVERGAL). He greatly influenced Protestant hymn singing in France and was responsible for CHARLOTTE ELLIOTT's conversion.

Albert Knapp

July 25, 1798
Tubingen, Germany

June 18, 1864
Stuttgart, Germany

Poet and hymn writer. In 1820, Knapp became vicar at Feuerbach, then at Gaisburg. His first poetical work *Christian Poems* was published in 1824. In 1835, he became pastor at St. Leonhard's Church in Stuttgart. Knapp wrote over 1,200 original hymns and poems. He also wrote *Treasury of Hymns for the Church and Home*. This was a collection of 3,590 hymns published in Stuttgart in 1837.

Fidelia Fiske

May 1, 1816
Shelburne, Massachusetts

July 26, 1864

First single woman missionary to Persia. Fidelia was converted at age 15, and joined the Congregational Church. Influenced by her uncle, PLINY FISK (Syrian missionary) and inspired by MARY LYON (a seminary teacher), she went to Urmia, Persia (Iran), in 1843. She opened a boarding school called Westovian Female Seminary with the American Board of Commissioners for Foreign Missions and its Nestorian Mission, at Oroomiah, starting with only six girls. After 15 years of labor in the field, illness forced her to return home. Her last years were spent volunteering time to Mt. Holyoke (MA) Female Seminary, where she had taught earlier. Research does not reveal why she added the "e" to the family name of "Fisk."

Theodor Fliedner

Jan. 21, 1800
Eppstein, Germany

Oct. 4, 1864
Kaiserswerth, Germany

Philanthropist, cleric, and founder of Lutheran deaconess institutions. Fliedner was orphaned at age 13. He married Friederike Muensier (1800–42), and, after her death, he married Karcline Berthean. Fliedner started an evangelical church at Kaiserswerth, 1821–49; and established the value of using deaconesses to assist him by caring for the sick and the spiritually destitute in 1836. Much of his effort was devoted to raising money for 37 of his mother houses. At the time of his death he had some 1,600 deaconesses involved in the ministry, and some had been full-time since 1849. In 1826, he founded the first German society for prison reform. Fliedner also organized the Prisoners' Society, a refuge for discharged women prisoners in 1833. He influenced the thinking of such as FLORENCE NIGHTINGALE.

Irah Chase

Oct. 5, 1793
Stratton, Vermont

Nov. 1, 1864
Newton Center, Massachusetts

First president of Newton (MA) (Andover-Newton in 1931) **Theological Seminary, 1825–45.** Chase married Harriet Savage (March 15, 1821), and Martha Raymond (Oct. 13, 1835). He had a total of nine children. Chase was ordained to the Baptist ministry in 1817 and taught at the Columbian College in Washington, D.C. from 1818–25. Raising the standards of education among the Baptists was one of his greatest concerns. His books range from *Remarks on the Book of Daniel* (1844) to *Baptism* (1851).

James D. Burns

Feb. 18, 1823
Edinburgh, Scotland

Nov. 27, 1864
Mentone, France

Hymn writer. Burns' works included, "Still With Thee, O Lord" (1857) and "Thou, Lord, Art Love, and Everywhere" (1858). He followed his theology teacher, THOMAS CHALMERS, into the Free Church of Scotland in 1843. Burns served at Dunblane, Scotland, until 1847, when his health necessitated his move to Madeira, an island in the North Atlantic, north of the Canary Island group. Upon his recovery, he pastored in Hampstead, England. Burns wrote 40 original hymns.

Karl Ullmann

March 15, 1796
Epfenbach, Germany

Jan. 12, 1865
(K)Carlsruhe, Germany

Evangelical theologian. Ullmann was professor at Heidelberg (1821–29), at Halle (1829–36), and then back to Heidelberg (1836–56). He opposed rationalism, favoring a union between Lutheran and Reformed Churches in Baden. He sought the influence of the Baden church in the support of Pietism. He also sought to improve the status of Lutheran clergy and unite Protestant factions. Ullman opposed *Life of Christ*, written by David Strauss (1808–74), a liberal German philosopher who viewed the Bible as mythical. It made Christ look more like a man than part of the Godhead.

Thomas C. Brownell

Oct. 19, 1779
Westport, Massachusetts

Jan. 13, 1865
Hartford, Connecticut

Presiding bishop of Protestant Episcopal Church (Episcopal Church in 1967), **1852–65**. Charlotte Dickinson became his wife on August 6, 1811. He was a bishop with the Connecticut diocese, 1819–65. Brownell was the first president of Washington (Trinity) College in Hartford, CT from 1823–31, and then chancellor until his death. Early in his career, he taught at Union College, Schenectady, NY. He wrote *The Family Prayer Book* (1823) and *Religion of Heart/Life* (1839).

Elisha P. Swift

Aug. 12, 1792
Williamston, Pennsylvania

April 3, 1865
Pittsburgh, Pennsylvania

Father of the Presbyterians' Foreign Mission Board, 1831, and co-founder in 1827, with Francis Herron, of Westminster Theological Seminary (Pittsburgh Theological Seminary). Swift was an evangelical educator. He pastored at the Second Presbyterian Church, Pittsburgh, 1819–31.

Abraham Lincoln

Feb. 12, 1809
Near Hodgenville, Kentucky

April 15, 1865
Washington, D.C.

Sixteenth President of the United States, 1861–65. The electoral votes were: Lincoln—180, three opponents—112 (1860); Lincoln—212, McClellan—21 (1864). A Republican, Lincoln was known as the Great Emancipator because he officially declared Negro slavery at an end with the Emancipation Proclamation in 1863. He guided the Union during the difficult days of the Civil War, which began one month after his inauguration and ended five days before his death. He had four sons from his marriage on November 4, 1842 to Mary Todd (December 13, 1818–July 16, 1882) . In 1834, he began political service in the Illinois Congress and then the US Congress in 1846. His career contained more defeats than victories. He became a lawyer in 1836. He is noted for the Lincoln-Douglas Senatorial Debates of 1858; however, he lost that Senate race. The famous Gettysburg Address was given on Nov. 19, 1863. His strong Quaker background influenced his consistent prayer life. He was shot by John Wilkes Booth (drunk) at Ford Theater in Washington, D.C. on April 14, 1865. In response to a friend who saw Lincoln reading the Bible shortly before he died, he said, "Yes, I am profitably engaged. Take all of this book on reason that you can, and the rest on faith, and you will, I am sure, live and die a happier and better man." His favorite Bible verses were Exodus 20:1–17 and Mark 3:25." Lincoln never went to law school or college. Charles Darwin was born on the same day as Lincoln. Lincoln was the son of a carpenter and martyred on Good Friday.

"With malice toward none, with charity for all."

Isaac Williams

Dec. 12, 1802
Aberystwith, Wales

May 1, 1865
Stinchcombe, England

Oxford-educated Anglican priest, poet, and theologian who was a member of the Tractarian Movement. Williams went to Trinity College, Oxford, in 1832. Williams contributed to *Lyra Apostolica* (1836) and the well known *Tract 80 Reserve in Communicating Religious Knowledge*. After losing the chair of poetry at Oxford in 1842, he retired to concentrate upon his own poetry. He was the curate at Bisley (1842–48) and at Stinchcombe (1848–65).

Lydia H. Huntley Sigourney

Sept. 1, 1791
Norwich, Connecticut

June 10, 1865
Hartford, Connecticut

Authoress, poet, and teacher. Lydia taught in Hartford and Norwich before her marriage to Charles Sigourney on June 16, 1819, from which they had two children. She began to write verse at age seven. The first book she wrote was *Moral Pieces in Prose and Verse* (1815), written for the girls at a school she and a friend had established at Hartford. Her writings, including many hymns and 67 books, featured morality and sentimental ideas.

Isaac Taylor

Aug. 17, 1787
Lavenham, England

June 28, 1865
Stanford Rivers, England

Author of several philosophical and religious books. He settled early in his life in Ongar, England. In 1818, Taylor was on the staff of *Eclectic Review*. He invented a copper-engraving process and spent most of his adult life in Stanford Rivers. He wrote *The Natural History of Enthusiasm* (1829), *The Natural History of Fanaticism* (1833), *The Physical Theory of Another Life* (1836), *The Restoration of Belief* (1855), *The Spirit of Hebrew Poetry* (1861), and many others. His books range from *Elements of Thought* (1823) to *Considerations on the Pentateuch* (1863).

Francis Wayland

March 11, 1796
New York, New York

Sept. 30, 1865
Providence, Rhode Island

Baptist preacher and educator. He married Lucy L. Lincoln (November 21, 1825), and Mrs. Hepsy S. Howard Sage (August 13, 1838), giving him a total of three children. Wayland tutored at Union college, Schenectady, NY (1817–21), and also pastored the FBC of Boston (1821–26). Wayland was best known for his presidency of Brown University, Providence, RI from 1827–55. From 1855–56, he pastored the FBC of Providence. His textbooks were widely used. In later years, he wrote and worked with prisoners. He became nationally known as a pioneer leader in education and an inspiring teacher. He wrote works ranging from *Elements of Moral Science* (1835) to *Thomas Chalmers* (1864).

Hugh Stowell

Dec. 3, 1799
Douglas, Isle of Man, England

Oct. 8, 1865
Pendleton, England

Prominent evangelical clergyman and hymn writer. Stowell wrote "From Every Stormy Wind that Blows" (music by THOMAS HASTINGS). After serving several curacies, he was appointed rector of Christ Church at Salford, England in 1831, remaining there until his death. Stowell had a large Sunday school and was an outstanding Church of England cleric. He wrote some 50 hymns.

William V. Wallace

March 11, 1812
Waterford, Ireland

Oct. 12, 1865
Chateau de Bages, France

Composer of the music for "Immortal Love, Forever Full" and "We May Not Climb the Heavenly Steeps" (lyrics of both by J. G. WHITTIER). Of Scotch descent, Wallace became an accomplished violinist. His marriage unfortunately ended in divorce. Wallace traveled widely to North and South America and France, after which he presented two operas in London: *Maritana* (1845) and *Matilda of Hungary* (1847). *Lurline* (1860) was another successful opera. One source has his birthdate as June 1.

George L. D. T. Harms

May 5, 1808
Walsrode, Germany

Nov. 5, 1865
Hermannsburg, Germany

Lutheran pastor, evangelist, and mission organizer. Harms was converted in 1830 while meditating on John 17:3. He then became a pastor in Hermannsburg. His community was wonderfully changed, and an unprecedented revival broke out in North Germany. In 1834, he founded a missionary society in Larenburg, which became a part of the North German Mission in 1836. In 1849, Harms founded the Hermannsburg Mission, a missionary training school, which served as a seminary as well as a mission agency. In 1854, he became the pastor and also established a missionary magazine. His preaching was simple and clear and very popular with the peasants (common people). He also opened new stations in South Africa for agricultural missionaries.

Benjamin Kurtz

Feb. 28, 1795
Harrisburg, Pennsylvania

Dec. 29, 1865
Philadelphia, Pennsylvania

One of the founders of the Gettysburg (PA) Theological Seminary (Susquehanna University in 1825) and editor of the *Lutheran Observer* (1833–61). Kurtz married Ann Barnett, Mary C. Baker, and Mary Calhoun, which resulted in a family of ten children. Kurtz pastored in Hagerstown, MD (1815–31); in Chambersburg, PA (1831–33); and in Baltimore, MD in 1833. He advocated the union of the German Lutheran and Reformed Churches. He wrote works ranging from *Infant Baptism* (1840) to *Lutheran Prayer Book* (1856). His book, *Why Are You a Lutheran?* (1843), was widely circulated.

Samuel R. Maitland

Jan. 7, 1792
London, England

Jan. 19, 1866
Gloucester, England

Church of England clergyman and historian. Maitland became curate of Christ Church, Glasgow, 1823–27. He was keenly interested in mission work among the Jews in Germany and Poland. Maitland was appointed the librarian and keeper of the Lambeth Manuscripts (Church of England's historical documents housed in Lambeth, London, headquarters for the work) and also served as librarian to the archbishop of Canterbury from 1838–48. He edited the *British Magazine* (1839–49), wrote several books, and had many diversified interests.

Eliphalet Nott

June 25, 1773
Ashford, Connecticut

Jan. 29, 1866
Schenectady, New York

President of Union College, Schenectady, NY 1804–66, serving 62 years at this post, graduating 4,000 students. Nott was a prominent Presbyterian and a leading temperance advocate. He married Sarah Benedict (July 4, 1796), Gertrude Tibbitts (Aug. 3, 1807), and Urainia Sheld (August 8, 1842). He pastored the First Presbyterian Church, Albany, NY from 1798–1804. He invented the stove as a means of heating and made a fortune from it.

Alexander Campbell

Sept. 12, 1786
Ballymena, Ireland

March 4, 1866
Bethany, Virginia (West Virginia)

Helped found the restoration movement, along with his father, THOMAS, resulting in the Disciples of Christ (Christian Church) and the Churches of Christ. Campbell came to America in 1809, and became a Baptist minister. Two years later, in 1811, he married Margaret Brown and began the new movement. He sought to end denominationalism after settling in the Virginia area (this region became the state of West Virginia in 1863). His following of 12,000 joined with Barton Stone's Christian Church of 10,000 in 1832 in Lexington, KY, after breaking with the Baptists in 1830 over the baptismal regeneration issue. Within a few years the DOC (CC) was officially founded, as a result, even though half of Stone's group was not part of the founding group. He founded Bethany College in 1840, serving as its president, 1840–60. He preached in Kentucky, Ohio, Indiana, West Virginia, and Tennessee. The DOC grew from 22,000 in 1832 to 350,000 in 1864. Campbell predicted Christ's return to be in 1866. He was the editor of *The Christian Baptist* (1823–30) and *The Millennial Harbinger* (1830–66).

"*Where Scriptures speak, we speak; where they're silent, we're silent.*"

John P. Crozer

Jan. 13, 1793
West Dale, Pennsylvania

March 11, 1866
Upland, Pennsylvania

Manufacturer and philanthropist. Crozer was a wealthy dealer in cotton goods who gave generously to churches and colleges. He married Sallie Knowles in 1825. He acquired a large fortune in manufacturing cotton and built a Baptist church in Upland, NY in 1852. He served as president of Pennsylvania Baptist Educational Society, 1855–66. In 1858, he built a $845,000 college building and endowed a professorship at Bucknell (PA) University. Crozer Theological Seminary, Chester, PA started in 1867, because of his investments. It closed in 1970, and became a part of Colgate-Rochester (NY) Seminary.

John Keble

April 25, 1792
Fairford, England

March 29, 1866
Bournemouth, England

Hymn writer and tractarian. Keble wrote the well-known hymn, "Sun of My Soul" (music by Ritter). He was more widely known as the Anglican cleric who sparked the "high church" wing of the Church of England. They sought to restore ancient traditions dropped by the reformers. He was a professor of poetry at Oxford, 1831–41. His Oxford Sermon, "National Apostasty," of July 14, 1833, ignited the Oxford Movement. He married in 1835. Keble was a vicar of Hursley, 1836–64, and wrote the *Christian Year* (1827). Keble College at Oxford University was opened in 1869. His favorite Bible verse was Isaiah 30:15.

Manuel Matamoros

Oct. 8, 1835
Lepe, Spain

July 31, 1866
Lausanne, Switzerland

Spanish Protestant whose life and sufferings aroused great interest in many countries. After hearing a sermon by a Pastor Ruet, Matamoros began to study Scripture, which resulted in his renouncing Catholicism. He served ministries in Granada, Seville, and Barcelona in 1860. He was soon jailed for his fervent Protestant activities. After banishment from Spain, he set up a school in Pau, France, before going to Lausanne in May, 1866.

John M. Neale

Jan. 24, 1818
London, England

Aug. 6, 1866
East Grinstead, England

Translated more hymns from Latin and Greek into English than anyone else in history (some are paraphrases rather than translations). Neale had a knowledge of 20 languages and authored books on a diversity of subjects, including church history and architecture. He was influenced by the Oxford High Church Movement. His ill health hindered steady participation in ministries. From 1846–66, he was warden of Sackville College, East Grinstead. He founded the Sisterhood of St. Margaret's.

Francis L. Hawks

June 10, 1798
New Bern, North Carolina

Sept. 27, 1866
New York, New York

Episcopal pastor and educator. He married Emily Kirby in 1823, and Olivia Trowbridge after Emily's death, having a total of eight children. Hawks pastored the following churches: St. Thomas, NYC (1831–43); Christ Church, New Orleans, LA 1844; Calvary Church, NYC (1849–62); Christ Church, Baltimore (1862–65); and Holy Savior, NYC (1865–66). Hawks was the first president of the University of Louisiana, Shreveport, 1844–49. Hawks was an eloquent preacher and wrote at least two books on his denomination.

Christian Metz

Dec. 30, 1794
Neuwied, Prussia (Germany)

July 27, 1867
Amana, Iowa

Leader of Amana Church Society. Beginning in 1817, Metz led a sect known as the Community of True Inspiration, which was an offspring of radical Lutheran Pietism, 1823–1842. To escape persecution, he established a communal colony in Buffalo, NY from 1842–54. Feeling the need for more land and separation from encroaching cities, a mass exodus of sect members joined a small enclave of the society (1855) set up by JOHANN ROCK (1745) in the rolling hills of southeastern Iowa. In the same year that community, calling itself the Ebenezer Society, was christened the Amana Colony and was incorporated as the Amana Society in 1859. Metz continued as its leader until his death.

James Edmeston

Sept. 10, 1791
Wapping, London, England

Jan. 7, 1867
Homerton, England

Hymnist, architect, surveyor, and devoted layman in the Church of England. Edmeston wrote the hymn, "Savior, Breathe an Evening Blessing" (music by GEORGE STEBBINS). He was fond of children, and many of his 2,000 hymns were written for use in Sunday school. He published songbooks in 1820 and 1846. He wrote twelve volumes, mostly poems and hymns. Edmeston was also a loyal supporter of the London Orphan Asylum. He served as warden in the Church of St. Barnabas.

William Goodell

Feb. 14, 1792
Templeton, Massachusetts

Feb. 18, 1867
Philadelphia, Pennsylvania

Congregational missionary to the Near East, 1831–65. At age 15, Goodell walked 60 miles to Phillips Academy in Andover, MA with his trunks on his back. Abigail Davis became his wife on Nov. 19, 1822, and gave him eight children. Appointed by the ABCFM, Goodell worked in Syria, 1823–28. When all missionaries were asked to leave Syria in 1828, he went to Malta. In

1831, he founded a new mission among the Armenians of Constantinople, Turkey, where he labored until 1865. He returned to Philadelphia in 1865. Goodell translated the Bible into Armeno-Turkish (published in 1873).

Joshua Soule

Aug. 1, 1781
Bristol, Maine

March 6, 1867
Nashville, Tennessee

Bishop in the Methodist Episcopal Church, 1824–67. Soule became an evangelist in New England, 1803–16. He married Sarah Allen on Sept. 18, 1803, and they had eleven children. He was one of the writers of a new constitution for Methodism in 1808, knowing Methodist law as no other. He became a pastor in New York (1820–22) and a representative to the Baltimore Conferences (1822–24). In 1824, after being made bishop, he was assigned to serve in the western and southern Methodist conferences. Upon the division of the church in 1845, he became the senior bishop of the Methodist Church South. He opposed Calvinism.

Ithamar Conkey

May 5, 1815
Shutesbury, Massachusetts

April 30, 1867
Elizabeth, New Jersey

Composer of music for "In the Cross of Christ I Glory" (lyrics by JOHN BOWRING). After serving as organist at Central Baptist Church, Norwich, CT, Conkey went to NYC in 1850, where he became a well-known bass singer. He participated in the choirs of Grace Church and Calvary Episcopal Church of NYC from 1850–61. From 1861 until his death, he sang at Madison Avenue Baptist Church, NYC.

Charles Philip Krauth

May 7, 1797
New Goshenhoppen, Pennsylvania

May 30, 1867
Gettysburg, Pennsylvania

Lutheran leader who was the first president of Pennsylvania (Gettysburg in 1921) **College, 1834–50**. Krauth married Catherine Heiskell on December 7, 1820, and then Harriet Brown in 1834, resulting in four children. He pastored at two Virginia churches (1819–27) and then in Philadelphia at St. Matthew's Lutheran Church (1827–33). He was a professor of biblical philology and church history at Gettysburg Seminary, 1850–67, and was the father of CHARLES PORTERFIELD KRAUTH.

Jeremiah B. Day

Aug. 3, 1773
New Preston, Connecticut

Aug. 22, 1867
New Haven, Connecticut

President of Yale College, 1817–22 (University in 1887), **and College and Divinity School, New Haven, CT 1822–46**, which was preceded by his teaching math and natural philosophy there beginning in 1803. Day followed TIMOTHY DWIGHT as president. He married Martha Sherman (January 14, 1805), and Olivia Jones (September 24, 1811). In 1817, he was ordained into the Congregational Church. Day's life was noted by his remarkable influence over young men. He also wrote a series of mathematical textbooks.

Michael Faraday

Sept. 22, 1791
Newington Butts, Surrey, England

Aug. 25, 1867
Hampton Court, England

Physicist and chemist who began as an assistant to Sir Humphrey Davy (renowned scientist and physicist, 1778–1829) at the Royal Institution (1813), later becoming its director (1825), and a professor of chemistry from 1833–67). Faraday married Sarah Barnard on June 12, 1821. He was a pioneer in developing electric current, discovering the principle of the electric motor and mechanical refrigeration, although he did not realize the practical value of either at this time. On October 28, 1831, he discovered generating electricity by means of magnetism. All commercial electricity would be generated from this principle. Faraday produced several technical textbooks and 158 published papers at the Royal Institution. His work, *On the Various Forces in Nature*, reveals his Christian approach to science. He once said, "... the thought of death…brings to the Christian the thought of Him who died, who rose again for the justification of those who believe in Him." He had a Sandemanian funeral. His favorite Bible verse was II Timothy 1:12. He is considered one of the ten most important scientists in history.

Johannes Muelhaeuser

Aug. 9, 1803
Notzingen, Germany

Sept. 15, 1867
Milwaukee, Wisconsin

Founder and first president of First Evangelical Lutheran Synod of Wisconsin (WELS in 1959), **1850–60**. Muehlhaeuser came to America in 1837 as the Langenberg Society's first missionary to America. He pastored in Rochester, NY for a time and then went to Milwaukee, WI where he pastored Grace Lutheran Church, 1849–67. He was known for his work among the poor, sick, and needy.

John M. Krebs

May 6, 1804
Hagerstown, Maryland

Sept. 30, 1867
New York, New York

Presbyterian minister of great prominence. Krebs graduated from Dickinson College, Carlisle, PA (1827), and Princeton (NJ) Theological Seminary (1830). He pastored the Rutgers Street Presbyterian Church, NYC and spent his ministry in that church, 1830–67. Krebs had no equal in the knowledge of church law and the history of Presbyterianism. He was chairman of the national Presbyterian Reunion Committee.

John Strachan

April 12, 1778
Aberdeen, Scotland

Nov. 1, 1867
Toronto, Ontario, Canada

First Anglican bishop of Toronto, 1839 on. Strachan came to Canada in 1799. He was the premier Church of England advocate in Canada and the rector of St. James' Church in Toronto, 1813–67. He built dozens of Canadian parishes, pressured the goverment to open public schools, founded King's College (University of Toronto) in 1821, and became its first president. He also helped found McGill University. He became archdeacon of York in 1825. In 1850, after the university became nondenominational, he helped establish Trinity College, Canada's most distinguished Epsicopal learning institution.

James Hamilton

Nov. 27, 1814
Paisley, Scotland

Nov. 24, 1867
London, England

Eloquent and eminent Presbyterian pastor. Hamilton pastored the National Scotch Church of Regent's Square, London, 1841–67. His fame as a pulpit orator spread, and he attracted large audiences. Hamilton authored several works, including *Life in Earnest* (1844), *Royal Preacher* (1851), and *The Prodigal Son*. He edited the *Presbyterian Messenger* (1849 on) and *Evangelical Christendom* (1864 on). He also wrote *Our Christian Classics* (4 vols., 1857–59).

Joseph Torrey

Feb. 2, 1797
Rowley, Massachusetts

Nov. 26, 1867
Burlington, Vermont

Congregational educator and theologian. Torrey pastored in Royalton, VT but gave most of his adult life to the University of Vermont. He began as professor of Greek and Latin (1827–42), then became instructor of intellectual and moral philosophy (1842–62). Finally, he served as president from 1862–66. He also translated NEANDER's *Church History* (1854), and wrote *A Theory of Art* (1874).

Karl O. Rosenius

1816

1868
Nysatra, Sweden

Founder of the Evangelical National Institution. Rosenius was a lay preacher in the Lutheran Church in Sweden. He prepared the way for the Free Church Movement in Sweden and was its leader from 1842 on. Two societies were later formed from his efforts, the National Evangelical Foundation and the Swedish Mission Covenant (Evangelical Covenant) Church. He edited the *Pietist* (1842–62).

William B. Bradbury

Oct. 6, 1816
York, Maine

Jan. 7, 1868
Montclair, New Jersey

Music teacher and publisher. Bradbury composed the music for some of the world's greatest hymns: "Just As I Am" (1849), "Sweet Hour of Prayer" (1859), "Jesus Loves Me" (1861), "My Hope is Built" (1863), "He Leadeth Me" (1864), "Savior Like a Shepherd Lead Us," "Even Me," "Praise Him All Ye Little Children," and "Holy Bible, Book Divine" (1858). Varied writers provided the lyrics. At age 17, he studied in Boston under LOWELL MASON and Sumner Hill at the Boston Academy. He served as the organist at FBC from 1841–47 and published 59 music collections (SS and choir books). He founded the Bradbury Piano Company (manufactured pianos) in 1854, and introduced music to the public schools in New York City by organizing free singing classes. His *Golden Series* (1861–67) of songs sold over three million copies. In 1863, Bradbury, along with GEORGE ROOT, founded the New York Normal Institute for the purpose of training music teachers.

William O'Brian

Feb. 6, 1778
Gunwen, England

Jan. 8, 1868

Methodist minister who founded the Bible Christian Church in Devonshire, England, in 1815, which was a split off from Methodism. O'Brian left the business world in 1814, for preaching in North Devonshire and Cornwall counties. His career in evangelism took him to the US in 1831. His Christian Church movement spread to Canada (1846), but was joined to the United Methodist Church (1907). He is buried in Brooklyn, NY.

John H. Hopkins

Jan. 30, 1792
Dublin, Ireland

Jan. 9, 1868
Rock Point, Vermont

First Episcopal bishop of Vermont in 1832. Hopkins married Melusina Muller on May 8, 1816. They had 13 children. He was ordained in 1823, pastoring Trinity Church in Pittsburgh, PA from 1824–27. Hopkins was a zealous high-churchman. He served at St. Paul's Church, Burlington (1832–56), and was involved in education (1856–68). He wrote *Vindication of Slavery* and the lyrics and music to the Christmas carol, "We Three Kings" (1862). *The Primitive Church* (1835) and *The Law of Ritualism* (1866) were written to defend Episcopalianism.

David Brewster

Dec. 11, 1781
Jedburgh, Scotland

Feb. 10, 1868
Allerby, Scotland

Physicist who discovered the polarization of light, invented the kaleidoscope in 1815, and mastered difficult problems of optics. In *More Worlds than One*, Brewster wrote "When our Saviour died, the influence of his death extended backward in the past, to millions who never heard his name, and forward in the future, to millions who will never hear it…It reaches to the remotest lands and affects every living race." Though licensed to preach by the Edinburh presbytery, Brewster felt his calling was to engage in scientific pursuits. He was principal of the united colleges of St. Leonard and St. Salvador at the University of St. Andrews, 1837–59. Brewster published his findings on light polarization by reflection and refraction in a series of papers in the "Philosophical Transactions" of the Royal Society of London (beginning, 1813). His books range from *Treatise of the Kaleidoscope* (1819) to *Memoirs of Sir Isaac Newton* (1855).

William C. Burns

April 1, 1815
Kilsyth, Duns, Scotland

April 4, 1868
Yingkou, China

Devoted missionary to China. Burns was converted through the preaching of a Mr. Bruce in January, 1832, during the raging cholera epidemic. He became an evangelist, laboring with great success in England, Ireland, and Canada, 1839–46. On June 9, 1847, he went to China to take charge of the missions of the English Presbyterian Church. As he identified with the people and their needs, his influence increased and soon he was preaching to great multitudes. Burns was an inspiration and help to young HUDSON TAYLOR. He planted good works in Pehchuia (Baichuan), Fukien (Fujian) and Peking (Beijing), dying in a remote area he had gone to visit because of its desperate need.

Robert B. C. Howell

March 10, 1801
Wayne County, North Carolina

April 5, 1868
Nashville, Tennessee

Second president of Southern Baptist Convention, 1851–57. Howell was raised an Episcopalian, but turned Baptist in 1821. Ten children came from his marriage on April 23, 1829 to Mary Ann Toy. Howell pastored at Cumberland Street Baptist Church, Norfolk, VA (1827–34); FBC, Nashville, TN (1834–50 and 1857–67); and the Second Baptist Church, Nashville (1850–57); when Nashville's population was 6,000. Howell helped found Southern Baptist Seminary, Greenville, SC in 1859. He became the editor of *The Baptist* in 1835. He authored at least three books, which included *The Terms of Sacramental Communion* (1841) and *The Way of Salvation* (1849).

Robert S. Hardy

July 1, 1803
Preston, England

April 16, 1868
Headlingly, England

Wesleyan missionary and Buddhist scholar. For 23 years Hardy was a missionary in Ceylon, 1825–48, and afterwards labored in England in several important circuits. He wrote many authoritative books on Buddhism in Ceylon and on Dali literature. His last work was *The Legends and Theories of the Buddhists compared with History and Science* (1866).

Frances B. Waters

Jan. 16, 1792
Somerset (Wicomico), Maryland

April 23, 1868
Baltimore, Maryland

President of Methodist Protestant Church (United Methodist Church in 1968), **1830–34, 1846–50, and 1862–66**. In 1818, Waters was made president of Washington College, Chestertown, MD, where he served for several years. It was at his suggestion that the Methodist Protestant Church name was adopted. He married Margaret Chairs (1818), and Elizabeth Chairs (1833).

William Brown

July 7, 1796
Cumberland County, Pennsylvania

May 11, 1868

Bishop of the Church of the United Brethren in Christ (United Methodist Church in 1968), **1833–68**. Brown was converted in 1812. He married Sarah Kock on September 27, 1819, and was ordained that same year. He opposed booze and petitioned that no member of the church be allowed to operate a distillery. Brown worked to develop the United Brethren Church on the western frontier. He is buried near Otterbein, IN.

George Junkin

Nov. 1, 1790
Kingston, Pennsylvania

May 20, 1868
Easton, Pennsylvania

President of Lafayette College, Easton, PA 1832–41, and of Miami University, Oxford, OH 1841–44, returning to serve as president of Lafayette, 1844–48. Two daughters came from his marriage to Julia Miller on June 1, 1819. He pastored in Milton, PA from 1819–30. Junkin was also president of Washington College (Washington & Lee University), Lexington, VA from 1848–61. At the outbreak of the Civil War in 1861, he returned to Philadelphia. Junkin was prominent in the Old School division of the Presbyterian Church. His works range from *The Vindication* (1836) to *Hebrews* (1873).

Billy Bray

June 1, 1794
Twelveheads, England

May 25, 1868
Twelveheads, England

Flaming Methodist evangelist. Bray's early life was given to drinking and smoking. At age 29, he was converted while reading JOHN BUNYAN's works. Bray began his evangelism in his hometown of Cornwall, and soon was preaching to fellow miners, often being ill-clad, hungry, and sleeping outdoors. His enthusiasm was unparalleled. He would run, clap, and shout "Glory!" The countryside was soon aflame with revival. He died in the same house in which he was born. His marriage date is unknown.

"I work for a great company...Father, Son, and Holy Ghost!"

James Buchanan

April 23, 1791
near Mercersburg, Pennsylvania

June 1, 1868
Lancaster, Pennsylvania

Fifteenth president of the United States, 1857–61, preceding ABRAHAM LINCOLN. Buchanan, a Democrat, defeated John Fremont by an electoral vote of 174–114. His faith in Christ was more apparent after he left the White House. He failed to prevent South Carolina from seceding from the Union, which triggered the Civil War. He was a moderate who was attacked from both sides. As the Southern states seceded, he said he had no constitutional power to use force against them. After passing the bar, he became a member of the U.S. House of Representatives at age 30 (1821–31), US minister to Russia (1832–34), US senator from Pennsylvania (1834–45), secretary of state (1844–49), and then U.S. minister to Great Britain (1853–56), after which he was elected president. In 1844, he wrote, "I am a believer..." Near the end of his life, he wrote, "...through the merits and atonement of His Son." He said as he died, "O Lord Almighty, as Thou wilt." He was the only bachelor President.

Robert Vaughan

Oct. 14, 1795
Near Welsh border, England

June 15, 1868
Torquay, England

Congregational minister and historian. Vaughan began pastoring in Worcester, England, in 1819. After moving to Kensington, London, he became professor of history at the University of London, 1834–43. In 1843, he was principal of Lancashire Independent College near Manchester. Vaughan founded the *British Quarterly Review* (1845). He pastored at Uxbridge near London (1857) and then at Torquay (1867).

William Allen

Jan. 2, 1784
Pittsfield, Massachusetts

July 16, 1868
Northampton, Massachusetts

Congregational pastor and educator. Allen graduated from Harvard in 1802. He pastored at First Congregational Church, Pittsfield, MA from 1810–17. He became president of both Dartmouth University, Hanover, NH (1817–19) and Bowdoin College, Brunswick, ME (1820–29). He married Maria Wheelock (Jan. 28, 1813), who gave him eight children, and then Sarah Breed (December 2, 1831). He compiled the *American Biographical and Historical Dictionary* (1809).

August F. C. Vilmar

Nov. 21, 1800
Solz, Germany

July 30, 1868
Marburg, Germany

Lutheran theologian who rigorously opposed rationalism with his *Theology of Facts*, defending the retention of the early Christian creeds. Vilmar compiled a hymnbook and wrote many theological works. He directed the high school at Marburg (1833–50), and was a professor of theology at Marburg University (1855–68). Vilmar also served as a government councellor at Kassel, 1850–55, and sought freedom of the church from the state. He exerted great influence in the education of the Hessian clergy.

Karl I. Nitzsch

Sept. 21, 1787
Borna, Germany

Aug. 21, 1868
Berlin, Germany

Lutheran founder of "Meditation Theology" (evangelical moderate). Nitzsch was a professor of systematic and practical theology at Bonn University (1822–47), then succeeded Philip Marheineke at Berlin University (1847–58), subsequently becoming the university preacher. Nitzsch was provost of St. Nicolai University in 1855 and is remembered as an active promoter of the Evangelical Union. His teaching was ethical rather than dogmatic. He defended the Prussian Union and was influenced by Schleiermacher (1768–1838).

Henry H. Milman

Feb. 10, 1791
London, England

Sept. 24, 1868
Sunninghill, near Ascot, England

Wrote lyrics for "Ride On! Ride on in Majesty" (1823) (music by JOHN DYKES), and twelve other hymns. In theology a liberal, Milman belonged to the Broad Church Party of the Anglican Church and wrote Church and Jewish histories from a critical viewpoint. His writings included poetry, translations, editions of other works, and original works. He was a professor of poetry at Oxford University (1821–31), and the vicar of St. Mary's, Reading (1835–45). He also served as canon at Westminster Abbey (1845–49), and dean of St. Paul's Church, London (1849–68). His great work was *A History of Latin Christianity Down to the Death* (died: 1455) *of Pope Nicholas* (1859).

Lorrin Andrews

April 29, 1795
East Windsor, Connecticut

Sept. 29, 1868
Honolulu, Hawaii

Congregational (ABCFM) missionary to the Hawaiian Islands, 1828–41. Mary Wilson became his wife in 1827. Andrews founded some of the islands' first schools including Lahainaluna Seminary in 1831. Andrews started the first island newspaper (1834), made the first translation of part of the Bible into Hawaiian, and published a dictionary (1865). He served as a judge, 1845–59, in various Hawaiian courts.

Friedrich W. Krummacher

Jan. 28, 1796
Mors, Germany

Dec. 10, 1868
Potsdam, Germany

Reformed preacher and writer. Krummacher was one of the most influential and eloquent preachers of his times. He began his ministry in Frankfurt-on-the-Main (1819), then went to Ruhrort (1823), to Gemarke (1825), and finally to Elberfield (1834). In 1847, he pastored the Trinity Church in Berlin. In 1853, he was court chaplain at Potsdam to the king of Prussia. Krummacher supported the Prussian Union and the Evangelical Alliance. He wrote *The Risen Redeemer*.

Henry Cooke

May 11, 1788
Maghera, Ireland

Dec. 13, 1868
Belfast, Ireland

Presbyterian pastor and educator who went to Belfast in 1829, staying there until his death. Cooke was professor of sacred rhetoric and president of the Assembly's College at Belfast in 1847. He was best known for his orthodoxy against Arianism in the Irish Church. Cooke wrote the hymn, "Jesus, Shepherd of the Sheep."

Cyrus Byington

March 11, 1793
Stockbridge, Massachusetts

Dec. 31, 1868
Belpre, Ohio

Missionary to American Indians. Byington was a Congregationalist who worked among the Choctaw Indians, compiling a grammar and a dictionary in the Choctaw language. From 1820–68, he specifically worked among Indian tribes based in Mississippi and accompanied them on their westward migration. In 1834, he settled at Eagletown, OK, where he organized seven churches and started Hannubree Seminary to enhance native leadership. He went to NYC in 1851, because of his health, but returned to his work among Choctaw people.

Charles Elliot

May 16, 1792
Greenconway, Ireland

Jan. 8, 1869
Mt. Pleasant, Iowa

President of and teacher at Iowa Wesleyan College, Mount Pleasant, IA 1856–61, 1863–66. This Methodist leader came to America in 1814. For a time Elliot engaged in mission work among the Wayandotte Indians in the region of the Upper Sandusky River (northern Ohio on the Lake Erie border). He was a professor at Madison College in Uniontown, PA from 1827–31. For many years, he edited different Methodist papers. Elliot wrote a history of the division of Methodism, called *The Great Secession* (1855).

Charlotte Alington Pye Barnard

Dec. 23, 1830
London, England

Jan. 30, 1869
Dover, England

Prolific ballad composer. At the age of eight, Charlotte declared that she would become a writer. By the age of 17, her writing had made her a young celebrity. The town fathers of Louth selected her to lay the cornerstone for the new railway station in 1847. In 1854, she married

Charles C. Barnard, parson of St. Olave's in nearby Ruckland. Her success as a composer led to her presentation at court in London in 1856. Charlotte was a student of William H. Holmes. Beginning in 1858, she published over 100 ballads under the pseudonym "Claribel." The best known is "Come Back to Erin." Charlotte also wrote and published two volumes of poetry. She composed the music for "Give of Your Best to the Master" (lyrics by Howard Grose) and "Jesus, Tender Shepherd, Hear Me." She died from typhoid fever at the age of 39.

Richard G. Pardee

Oct. 12, 1811
Sharon, Connecticut

Feb. 11, 1869
New York, New York

Widely known Sunday school worker. At age 17, Pardee went to live with an uncle in Seneca Falls, NY. It was while in this home that Richard surrendered to the Lord in 1831 and desired to became involved in the Sunday School ministry at the local church. He was greatly frustrated by the lack of quality Sunday School training material. He made several trips to ministries having successful Sunday School programs, including that of L. B. Tousley. He became an elder in the Presbyterian Church and moved to New York City in 1853. Pardee was active in the New York Sunday School Union, and served as an agent for them, 1853–63. Pardee wrote two books, *The Sunday School Worker* and *The Sunday School Index*. For the last six years of his life, he traveled to every state in the Union except California, promoting Sunday school endeavors.

Elizabeth Cecelia Clephane

June 18, 1830
Edinburgh, Scotland

Feb. 19, 1869
Melrose, Scotland

Writer of the hymns "Beneath the Cross of Jesus" (music by Frederick Maker) **and "The Ninety and Nine,"** both completed in 1868. The last poem was discovered by Ira Sankey in 1873, in a magazine, whereupon he added the music extemporaneously in a Moody revival meeting. Of delicate health herself, Elizabeth ministered to the sick and poor of Melrose, Scotland, and became known as "the Sunbeam." A member of the Presbyterian Free Church, she wrote eight hymns, which were published in *Family Treasury* (1872–74).

Jonas King

July 29, 1792
near Hawley, Massachusetts

May 22, 1869
Athens, Greece

Missionary to Greece and diplomat; ordained as a Congregationalist in 1819. King traveled in Egypt and Syria, 1822–25. He relinquished the professorship of languages at Amherst (MA) College (1828), married Annetta Mengous (1829), went to Greece as a missionary (1831), settling in Athens for the rest of his life. There he established a church and a school. His book *Mariolatry* (1844) was condemned by the Greek Synod. Between 1851–57, he was the US consular agent at Athens. He often conflicted with the Greek Orthodox Church, being tried at Athens (1852), and anathematized by the Synod of Athens (1863).

Ernest W. Hengstenberg

Oct. 20, 1802
Frondenburg, Germany

May 28, 1869
Berlin, Germany

Lutheran orthodox leader and theologian. While Hengstenberg was a tutor at Basel, family sorrow and ill health focused his attention on spiritual things, resulting in his conversion and study of the Bible. He joined the faculty of Berlin University (1824) and became a professor of theology (1828). Hengstenberg founded and edited the *Evangelical Church Journal* (1827–69). He strongly opposed the rationalism of his time and wrote extensively of it.

Samuel Nott

Sept. 11, 1788
Franklin, Connecticut

June 1, 1869
Hartford, Connecticut

Congregational (ABCFM) missionary to India. Nott, JUDSON, HALL, NEWELL, and RICE were all ordained shortly before sailing on their historical mission to India in 1812. He married Roxanna Peck. He left with HALL and RICE on the second embarkment, JUDSON and NEWELL preceding them. He reached Bombay, India (1813), but liver illness forced him to return to America (1815). He pastored in Galway, NY (1822–29) and in Wareham, MA (1829–49).

Samuel B. Wilson

March 17, 1783
Lincoln Co., North Carolina

Aug. 1, 1869
Farmville, Hampden-Sidney, Virginia

Dean of Hampden–Sydney (VA) Seminary (Union Theological Seminary, Richmond, VA in 1898), 1841–59. Ordained in 1806, Wilson pastored in Fredericksburg, VA, 1806–41. He taught theology along with his presidency.

Duncan Matheson

Nov. 22, 1824
Huntoly, Scotland

Sept. 16, 1869

Open-air evangelist. Matheson was converted upon hearing ANDREW BONAR preach. He began to teach fellow-workmen the things of Christ. The Duchess of Gordon, hearing of his zealous and successful labors, offered to employ him as a missionary at a salary of 40 pounds a year. He used much of this to purchase tracts and help relieve the poor. He went to the Crimea (Ukraine), and distributed 52,000 tracts, 622 Bibles, and 1,477 Testaments. In October (1857), he went to Whitehaven (1858), to Malvern (1859), Banffshire (1860), to Castle Rock and to Forder (1866). He was the editor of *Herald of Mercy*.

George Peabody

Feb. 18, 1795
South Danvers (Peabody), Massachusetts

Nov. 4, 1869
London, England

Well-known merchant and philanthropist. Peabody was a wholesale dry goods merchant in Baltimore, 1815–37, but settled as a banker in London in 1837, where he was instrumental in building tenements for the workingmen of London. He used his credit to support American credit abroad in the years following the panic of 1837. He founded and endowed (for $1,400,000) Peabody Institute, Baltimore, MD in 1857; Peabody (MA) Institute; Peabody Museum, Yale University; Peabody Museum, Harvard University; and the Peabody Education Fund to Advance Education in the South. He never married, so his five million dollars was left to relatives. His gifts totaled about 8.5 million dollars. He is buried in Peabody.

Hiram Bingham Sr.

Oct. 30, 1789
Bennington, Vermont

Nov. 11, 1869
New Haven, Connecticut

Congregational pastor and pioneer missionary to the Sandwich Islands (Hawaii), **1819**. Bingham built the first church in Honolulu in 1821, called Kawaiahao Church. He pastored, created a written language for those to whom he ministered, translated the Scriptures in 1839, became a trusted advisor to the Hawaiian King Kamehameha III and of the chiefs in their hostile relations with foreigners. He later pastored a black church in New Haven, CT. In 1847, he wrote extensively about his experiences on the Hawaiian Islands. Bingham married Sybil Moseley (1792–1848) on Oct. 11, 1819 (her health forced their return home in 1841), and Naomi Morse on August 24, 1854.

Louis M. Gottschalk

May 8, 1829
New Orleans, Louisiana

Dec. 18, 1869
Tijucas, Rio de Janeiro, Brazil

Composer of "Holy Ghost, with Light Divine" (lyrics by ANDREW REED). Gottschalk was recognized as the first American-born piano virtuoso and was sent to Paris at age 13 to study piano, where he made his piano debut in 1845. He toured Europe and met with great success, especially in Spain, returning to America in 1853. He wrote as many as 90 piano pieces. Such numbers as *The Dying Poet, La Mort*, and *The Last Hope*, were included in his concerts. He toured South America and died near Rio de Janeiro of yellow fever. He was reinterred to Greenwood Cemetery in New York City.

Justin Perkins

March 5, 1805
West Springfield (Holyoke), Massachusetts

Dec. 31, 1869
Chicoppee, Massachusetts

Missionary to Persia (Iran), 1833 on, (under ABCFM), working among the Nestorians (modern Christian body in Iran and Turkey, remnant of the fifth century followers of NESTORIUS). Perkins labored most of his life there. He married Charlotte Bass on July 21, 1833, who gave him seven children (several died in childhood). He headquartered at Urimia (Rezaiyeh), Persia, where he established a mission in 1835. Perkins translated the Bible and other books into the Nestorian dialect and the Bible into modern Syriac. He also wrote commentaries on Genesis and Daniel. Additionally, Perkins wrote *Missionary Life in Persia* (1861). Besides literary exploits (some 80 books), he was an evangelist and a musician.

Luigi de Sanctis

Dec. 31, 1808
Rome, Italy

Dec. 31, 1869
Florence, Italy

Italian evangelical preacher and theologian. Sanctis headed a parish in Rome, 1840–47. He left the Catholic Church in 1849, and married. In 1850, he went to Geneva, Switzerland to preach among the Italian political refugees, workingmen, and ex-priests. In 1853, he was ordained into the Waldensian ministry. Sanctis founded the Free Italian Church. He wrote a great deal against Catholicism.

John McClintock

Oct. 27, 1814
Philadelphia, Pennsylvania

March 4, 1870
Madison, New Jersey

Methodist scholar and preacher known for his ten-volume *Cylopedia of Biblical, Theological and Ecclesiastical Literature* (1867–81), which was written in collaboration with JAMES STRONG. McClintock began this great work in 1853, and three volumes appeared before his death. He married Caroline Wakeman in 1837, and Catherine Emory in October, 1851. McClintock also taught classical literature and mathematics at Dickinson College, Carlisle, PA (1836–48); pastored at St. Paul's Church, New York City (1857–60); pastored the American Chapel, Paris (1860–64); and was the first dean of Drew University Theological Seminary, Madison, NJ (1867–70). He was the editor of *The Methodist Quarterly Review*, 1848–56.

Edward Thomson

Oct. 12, 1810
Portsea, England

March 22, 1870
Wheeling, West Virginia

Methodist bishop, 1864–70. Thompson came to America in 1818, and made his home in Wooster, OH. He was converted by a circuit rider while practicing medicine in Ohio in 1830. Thomson was principal of Norwalk (OH) Seminary (1838–43); president of Ohio Wesleyan

University, Delaware (1843–60); and editor of the *New York Christian Advocate* (1860–64). He married Maria L. Bartley (July 4, 1837), and Annie E. Howe (May 9, 1866). Thomson also published three books. He died of pneumonia in a hotel.

Calvin Kingsley

Sept. 8, 1812
Annsville, New York

April 6, 1870
Beirut, Syria (Lebanon)

Methodist bishop, 1864–70. Kingsley married Delia Scudder in 1841. After graduating from Allegheny College, Meadville, PA, he became a math professor (1846–56), except for two years when he was pastoring. Kingsley was also editor of the *Western Christian Advocate*, 1856–64. In 1869, he visited India and China following a trip to Europe in 1867. He died of a heart ailment while on a missions trek to the Holy Land.

Emma Hart Willard-Yates

Feb. 23, 1787
Berlin, Connecticut

April 15, 1870
Troy, New York

Pioneer in women's education. Emma married Dr. John Willard (1759–1825) on August 10, 1809. In 1814, she opened a boarding school for girls in her home, which became the Troy Female Seminary in 1821, opening up higher education to women. Before her death, some 15,000 girls had studied there. She was a champion for women's education, a lofty patriot, and a committed Christian. She went to Europe in 1830. On September 17, 1838, she married Dr. Christian Yates. Emma also wrote several books and a volume of poems including "Rocked in the Cradle of the Deep." In 1895, the school was renamed Emma Willard School.

James Y. Simpson

June 7, 1811
Bathgate, Scotland

May 6, 1870
Edinburgh, Scotland

Obstetrician, physician, and professor of midwifery at Edinburgh University from 1839 on. Simpson was married in 1839, and was converted about the same time. Simpson is known for his introduction of chloroform in 1847, and of other anesthetics, especially for midwifery. Queen VICTORIA made him her personal physician in Scotland in 1846. He used chloroform in 1853, at the birth of Prince Leopold. Simpson was made a baronet in 1866, the first to be awarded to a Scottish physician.

Charles J. H. Dickens

Feb. 7, 1812
Landport, Isle of Portsea, England

June 9, 1870
Gadshill, England

Novelist of all-time literary favorites such as *Oliver Twist, A Tale of Two Cities,* and the immortal *A Christmas Carol* (1843). Dickens' imprisonment in 1824, for debt, was the story basis for *David Copperfield,* one of history's great novels. On April 2, 1836, he married Catherine Hograth, with whom he had a family of ten children, although they separated in 1858. Dickens' books, which attacked many of the evils of his time, stimulated social reform. His *Sketches by Boz* (1836) and *The Pickwick Papers* (1836–37) launched his career. Dickens said in his will, "I commit my soul to the mercy of God through our Lord and Savior Jesus Christ." He never graduated from grade school. His pen name was Boz. He suffered from insomnia and died of a paralytic stroke. He was buried at Westminster Abbey.

Lars P. Esbjorn

Oct. 16, 1808
Delsbo, Sweden

July 2, 1870
Ostervala, Sweden

Founder of the Swedish Lutheran Church in America. Ordained June 11, 1832, Esbjorn became known as an advocate of the temperance and revival movements. He pastored in Sweden, 1835–49. Coming to America, he organized the first Swedish-Lutheran churches of the Augustana Synod in Andover, Galesburg, and Moline, IL while pastoring at Andover, 1849–56. He was professor of theology at Illinois State University, Springfield, IL from 1856–60. Then, he founded and was first president of Augustana Seminary, Rock Island, IL from 1860–63. This school later became a part of the Lutheran School of Theology at Chicago. He married three times; Amalia Gyllen Borga, in 1836 (died 1852); Helen Magnusson, in 1853 (died same year); and Gustava Magnusson, in 1856. He had eleven children. He returned to Sweden in 1863, where he pastored in Ostervala till death.

Maria Dyer Taylor

1837
Penang, Malaya

July 23, 1870
Chinkiang (Zhenjiang)

China's first lady in missions. As wife of HUDSON TAYLOR, she was responsible, in many ways, for getting his great work started. In 1855, at age 18, she went to teach at the girls' school in Ningpo, China. Here she met HUDSON and they were married on January 20, 1858. She started a small primary school. When female CIM missionary recruits arrived at the field, it was Maria who was knowledgeable and able to train them in language, adapt them to Chinese culture and missionary work. All this, while giving birth to eight children. Of these children, two died at birth, and two in childhood. All four who did survive became China Inland Mission missionaries. Her last, born in 100-degree weather, survived for 13 days and Maria died three days later at age 33.

Andreas Irion

Nov. 17, 1823
Thuningen, Germany

July 23, 1870
Marthasville, Missouri

President of German Evangelical Preacher Seminary (Eden Theological Seminary, St. Louis, MO in 1883), **Marthasville, MO 1857–70**. In 1853, Andreas went to Marthasville, MO to teach at German Evangelical Seminary (Eden) founded in 1850. He lectured on new evangelical cathechism. He is buried in Marthasville, MO.

John T. Pressly

March 28, 1795
Abbeville, South Carolina

Aug. 13, 1870
Allegheny, Pennsylvania

President of Theological Seminary of United Presbyterian Church, Pittsburgh, PA 1831–33, removed and renamed, **Allegheny (PA)** (Pittsburgh in 1939) **Theological Seminary, 1833–70**. Pressly pastored the Associate Reformed Church, Allegheny, for nearly 40 years. He helped to form the United Presbyterian Church in 1858, in which he served. His father was DAVID PRESSLY. John taught theology at his seminaries.

David G. Farragut

July 5, 1801
Campbell's Station (near Knoxville) Tennessee

Aug. 14, 1870
Portsmouth, New Hampshire

Naval leader. The fleet Farragut commanded in the Civil War was the most powerful that had ever sailed up to that time for America. Farragut was adpoted at age seven by a naval commander and entered the navy at age nine as a midshipman. As commander of the Union Navy in the Civil

War, he blockaded the Gulf of Mexico, captured New Orleans, 1862; gained control of the Mississippi River up to Vicksburg, MS; and captured Mobile, AL in 1864. The merchants of New York presented him with $50,000 in government bonds, and on July 25, 1866, he was named admiral. In 1868, he was placed in charge of the European operations and visited most European ports and sovereigns. Despite his well-known "Damn the torpedoes" fighting words, his letters to family show a deep respect for the Lord, love of church, and realization that his times were in God's hands. He married Susan Marchant (September 24, 1823), and Virginia Loyall (December 26, 1843).

Robert E. Lee

Jan. 19, 1807
Stratford, Virginia

Oct. 12, 1870
Lexington, Virginia

Episcopalian patriot, hero, soldier, and general of the South. Lee married Mary A. Custis on June 30, 1831 and they had seven children. Lee served during the Mexican War (1846–48), was superintendent of West Point (1852–55), and lieutenant colonel of the Cavalry on the Texas frontier (1855–61). He commanded the troops to suppress JOHN BROWN's raid at Harper's Ferry (1859), and he resigned a commission in the US Army (1861). Jefferson Davis (1809–89), president of the Confederacy, promoted Lee from commander of the Northern Virginia forces to Commander-in-Chief of the Confederate Army in February, 1865. Lee surrendered to General Grant at Appomattox, VA (April 9, 1865), after being defeated earlier at Gettysburg (July 1–3, 1863). He also served as president of Washington (and Lee) College (University) in Lexington, VA from 1866–70. He was well-known for keeping the Lord's Day and calling for days of prayer and fasting. On September 28, 1870, he was stricken with apoplexy (stroke) and died shortly thereafter. He said, "In all my perplexities and distresses, the Bible has never failed to give me light and strength." His favorite Bible verse was Psalm 144:1.

John C. Jacobson

April 8, 1795
Burkhall, Denmark

Nov. 24, 1870
Bethlehem, Pennsylvania

President of Moravian Church in NA (North), Bethlehem, PA 1849–67. He went to Nazareth, PA and taught theology at Moravian Theological Seminary, 1820–26. Jacobson married Lisetta Schnall in 1826. Jacobson was a pastor in Bethania, NC (1826–34); and the principal at Salem Female Academy, Winston-Salem, NC (1834–44). He was made presiding officer of Provincial Elders Conference, Bethlehem, PA from 1849–67, and ordained bishop in 1854.

Albert Barnes

Dec. 1, 1798
Rome, New York

Dec. 24, 1870
Philadelphia, Pennsylvania

Presbyterian pastor and commentator whose 11-volume *Notes on the Old Testament* (1870) and *Notes on the New Testament* (1832–48) were widely used. From 1824–30, he ministered in Morristown, NJ. In an 1829 sermon, "The Way of Salvation," Barnes drew the fire of conservative Presbyterians. He was tried for heresy in 1830, but was acquitted in 1835, for his belief in an unlimited atonement (Christ died for everyone, not just the chosen). He still, however, denied the doctrine of original sin (man inherits this bondage from his birth). His trial was the cause of the split into the Calvinist Old School and New School Revivalist Presbyterians in America in 1837 (reunited in 1870, but difference of opinions still existed). Barnes also pastored the First Church, Philadelphia, PA from 1830–67. His wife's name was Abby Smith. He was an active abolitionist and a strong evangelical preacher. Barnes was an avid opponent of slavery and drinking. He was a Sunday School enthusiast.

Henry Alford

Oct. 7, 1810
London, England

Jan. 12, 1871
Canterbury, England

Dean of Canterbury, 1857 on. Alford wrote the hymns "Come Ye Thankful People, Come," 1844 (music by George Elvey), and "Ten Thousand Times Ten Thousand" (music by JOHN DYKES). He was honored as a poet, preacher, painter, musician, and scholar in the field of sacred literature. At age 16, he wrote in his Bible, "I do this day, in the presence of God and my own soul, re-new my covenant with God and solemnly determine henceforth to become His and to do His work as far as in me lies." He was ordained in 1833, became a vicar in Wymeswold (1835–53), and then served a large congregation at Quebec Chapel in Marylebone, London (1853–57). He greatly admired German higher criticism. Alford wrote his own epitaph, "The inn of a pilgrim traveling to Jerusalem." His greatest work was a four-volume edition of the *Expositor's Greek New Testament* (1841–61). Alford also compiled *Psalms and Hymns* (1844).

Thomas H. Skinner

March 7, 1791
Harvey's Neck, North Carolina

Feb. 1, 1871
New York, New York

Presbyterian pastor, preacher, and theologian. Skinner pastored the Fifth Presbyterian Church of Philadelphia, 1816–32. He was a professor at Andover (MA) Theological Seminary (1832–35), and then pastored at the New Mercer Street Church of New York City (1835–47). From 1848 onward, he was professor of rhetoric and theology at Union Theological Seminary of New York City. His first book was *Aids to Preaching and Hearing* (1839). He had several children.

James O. Andrew

May 3, 1794
Wilkes County, Georgia

March 2, 1871
Mobile, Alabama

Bishop in the Methodist Episcopal Church, 1832–66. From 1812–32, he served in Georgia and the Carolinas. In the 1844 Methodist conference, Andrew was asked to suspend his ministry because he was a slave owner. He led the southern ministers in the split that followed in May, 1845. In 1846, still a slave owner, he became the first Southern Methodist bishop. Four children came from his marriages to Ann McFarlane (1816), Mrs. Lenora Greenwood (1844) (died: 1854), and Mrs. Emily S. Childers (1854). He wrote *Family Government* (1847) and *Miscellaneous* (1855).

Robert C. Grier (1)

March 2, 1817
Mecklenburg County, North Carolina

March 30, 1871
Due West, South Carolina

President of Erskine College, Due West, SC 1847–59, 1865–71. Grier was licensed by the First Presbytery in April, 1839, then he received calls from Bethany and Pisgah churches. In August, 1840, he married Barbara Moffatt and by June, 1841, he was ordained and installed as pastor. He pastored until 1847, when he was made president of Erskine College. Grier had many gifts, and in 1858, became professor in the seminary. In 1860, he took the pastorate of the Due West Church. His wife, Barbara, died in 1896. They had eleven children.

Edward T. Taylor

Dec. 25, 1793
Richmond, Virginia

April 5, 1871
Boston, Massachusetts

Real-life model for "Father Mapple," in Henry Melville's *Moby Dick*. Converted in Boston at age 17 at an ELIJAH HEDDING revival, Taylor was a salty, uneducated ex-seaman. Deborah Millett became his wife on

October 12, 1819, and they had six children. He presided for over 40 years, 1830–71, as Methodist chaplain at Boston's Seaman's Bethel. He was one of the greatest preachers of his day and a friend of Ralph Waldo Emerson (1803–82).

Adrian VanVliet

March 28, 1809
Netherlands

May 9, 1871
Dubuque, Iowa

First president of German Presbyterian College and Seminary of Northwest (University of Dubuque Theological Seminary in 1920), **Dubuque, IA 1852–71**. This Presbyterian educator came to America in 1847. VanVliet married in New York, and came to Galena, IL in 1849, where his wife died. He pastored the German Evangelical Church (First German Presbyterian Church, 1854), Dubuque, IA from 1853 until his death. VanVliet started the college in his home.

Georges Darboy

Jan. 16, 1813
Fays-Billot, France

May 24, 1871
Paris, France

Catholic archbishop of Paris, 1863–71. From 1859–63, he was the bishop of Nancy. Darboy was a constant opponent of the Roman Catholic Church's doctrines. He supported Episcopal independence and, at the First Vatican Council from 1869–70, he opposed the defining of papal infallibility. When he sought to suppress the Jesuits (Catholic religious society), he was assassinated by Communards (French Communists), while blessing his executioners in the prison yard of La Roquette.

Milton Bird

Oct. 23, 1807
Barron Co, Kentucky

July 26, 1871
Princeton, Kentucky

State clerk of Cumberland Presbyterian Church, Memphis, TN 1850–72. Converted February 20, 1824, Bird was ordained in April, 1830. He moved to Pennsylvania and pastored Pleasant Hill Congregation in Washington County. Bird married Elizabeth A. Dunham on November 4, 1834. In 1840, he moved to Uniontown and became connected with Madison College as a professor, 1841–42. He pastored in Uniontown, then moved to Jeffersonville, IN in 1847, to take charge of the "Book Concern" in nearby Louisville, KY. In 1855, he moved to Princeton, KY where he pastored and was president of Old Cumberland College. He was in St. Louis in 1858 editing the *St. Louis Observer*, then returned to Caldwell County to pastor at the Bethlehem congregation. He died of severe congestion.

Nathan S. S. Beman

Nov. 26, 1785
New Lebanon, New York

Aug. 6, 1871
Carbondale, Illinois

Presbyterian pastor and educator. Beman ministered in Hancock County, GA from 1812–22. From 1823–63, he pastored the First Church, Troy, NY. He advocated revivals throughout the denomination, showed abolition fervor and became the leader of the New School (a division of Presbyterianism) in 1837. Beman was president of Rensselaer Polytechnic Institute, Troy, NY from 1845–65. He married twice. He attacked prelacy in the Episcopal and Catholic churches. Beman authored *Sermons on Atonement*.

John C. Patteson

April 1, 1827
Feniton Court, London, England

Sept. 20, 1871
Nukapu, Santa Cruz Islands, Melanesia

Missionary to Melanesia who was murdered (with two companions) by the natives of Nukapu, Santa Cruz Islands (administered by the Solomon Islands). Unscrupulous traders had kidnapped some natives initiating their hatred for white men. Patteson was an Anglican cleric who went to New Zealand in 1855. In 1861 he was made bishop of Melanesia. After 20 years at Mota (chief island), 760 of 800 natives were baptized. He had linguistic ability, wrote grammars, translated the Scriptures into several languages and spoke 23 dialects. His boat, *Southern Cross*, took him many places. His mission base was in New Zealand until 1867, when it was moved to Norfolk Island, which was closer and warmer. His favorite Bible passage was Isaiah 53.

Charlotte Elliott

March 18, 1789
Clapham, London, England

Sept. 22, 1871
Brighton, England

Gave the world the most widely used hymn ever, "Just As I Am" (1834). In 1821, a serious illness left Charlotte an invalid. In 1822, she met evangelist CEASAR MALAN and devoted her life to the Lord. They corresponded for 40 years. Elliott wrote her famous hymn at home, alone while family members were at a church function. She wrote some 150 hymns and was a member of the Church of England and a life-long resident of Brighton.

George Brown

Jan. 29, 1792
Washington County, Pennsylvania

Oct. 26, 1871
Springfield, Ohio

President of Methodist Protestant Church (United Methodist Church in 1968), **1858–66**. Brown was converted in a camp meeting held near Baltimore on August 13, 1813. He entered the Baltimore Conference in 1816 and served circuits for several years in Maryland, Virginia and Pennsylvania. In 1828, he withdrew from the parent church and joined the Associated Methodist Churches, which became the Methodist Protestant Church in 1830. In 1853, he compiled a new hymn book. Around 1854, he became president of Madison (PA) College. In 1860–61, he edited the *Western Methodist Protestant*, published at Springfield, OH.

Robert J. Breckenridge

March 8, 1800
Cabell's Dale, Kentucky

Nov. 27, 1871
Danville, Kentucky

Presbyterian pastor and theologian. Breckenridge practiced law in Kentucky (1823–31), pastored the Second Church, Baltimore, MD (1832–45); was president of Jefferson (PA) College (1845–47); pastored the First Church, Lexington, KY; served as superintendent of public instruction for the state of Kentucky (1847–53); and founded and taught theology at Danville (KY) Seminary (1853–69). Breckenridge represented Old School Presbyterianism and was opposed to the reunion of segmented religious factions. He wrote two books on *The Knowledge of God* (1858–59). He was the brother of JOHN BRECKENRIDGE.

Osmon C. Baker

July 30, 1812
Marlow, New Hampshire

Dec. 20, 1871
Concord, New Hampshire

President of Newbury (VT) Biblical Institute, 1841–44, and of General Biblical Institute, Concord, NH 1852–66. Both schools were forerunners of Boston University School of Theology in 1867. Baker married Mehitabel Perley in 1833. He was converted at age 15 and was ordained as a Methodist in 1829. Baker served as principal of the academy in Newbury, VT from 1838–44, organizing the theological society of Newbury Seminary in 1840. Baker was a professor at GBI 1847–50, becoming a Methodist bishop in 1852. A fatal stroke of paralysis came December 8, causing his death a few days later.

James B. Taylor

March 19, 1804
Barton-upon-Humber, England

Dec. 22, 1871
Richmond, Virginia

First president of Southern Baptist Convention Missions, 1845–71. Taylor married Mary S. Williams on Oct. 30, 1828; six children came from their union. He pastored the Second Baptist Church (1826–39) and Grace Baptist (1839–45), both located in Richmond, VA. He attended the first Baptist convention which became the influential Southern Baptist Convention. Taylor authored several biographical works and helped to organize Virginia Baptist Seminary.

Issachar J. Roberts

Feb. 17, 1802
Sumner County, Tennessee

Dec. 28, 1871
Upper Alton, Illinois

Baptist missionary to China and the Far East who helped the first Baptist mission program at Hong Kong in 1842, then going to Canton in 1844. Roberts moved to mainland China where he met the revolutionary Tien Wang (a young warlord). He served in China, 1837–66, under the Roberts Fund (established in 1836) for the China Mission Society. On January 4, 1830 he married and had at least two children. In 1849, he married again. He was Southern Baptist from 1846–52, then independent Baptist. He was in Shanghai from 1862–66, after which he returned to the States. He died of leprosy.

John Geddie

1815
Banff, Scotland

1872
near Melbourne, Australia

Canadian missionary to the New Hebrides Islands. Immigrating to Nova Scotia in 1816, he was converted at age twelve listening to a missionary speaker. He was ordained a Presbyterian and pastored in Cavendish, Prince Edward Island (Canadian province in the Gulf of St. Lawrence). He married Charlotte McDonald. Geddie arrived in the New Hebrides in 1840, where he served for 20 years on Aneityum Island. It is said of his ministry, "No Christians in 1848, no heathens in 1872." By 1854, some 2,000 had been converted, and the entire island was Christianized. He retired to Australia for health reasons, and died of influenza on a trip to Melbourne.

Robert Gray

1809
near Sunderland, England

1872

First Anglican bishop in 1847 and metropolitan archbishop in 1853 of Cape Town, South Africa. Gray received international recognition in 1863 when he excommunicated the liberal bishop, John Colenso of Natal, who had published a *Zulu Bible Dictionary*. This event became known as the Colenso Affair. As a result of this, he promoted the independence of the South African Church and added five sees. He traveled widely, promoted missions, enlisted recruits, and raised money. He is regarded as the father of Anglicanism in southern Africa.

Johann K. W. Loehe

Feb. 21, 1808
Furth, Germany

Jan. 2, 1872
Neuerdettelsau, Germany

Theologian and philanthropist. Loehe was deeply concerned about the welfare of his fellow countrymen emigrating to America. He established missionary training centers to train men for work among Germans in America. He pastored in Neuerdettelsau from 1837–72. He married Helene Andreae in 1837 (died: 1843). He never remarried. In 1846, he founded a seminary which trained American Lutheran pastors under the direction of WILHIEM SIHLER. Some of the missionaries he sent included the founders of the Lutheran Missouri (1841) and Iowa (1854) Synods. A persuasive preacher,

Loehe founded the Lutheran Society of German Home Missions (1849), and an institution of deaconesses (1853).

Henry F. Chorley

Dec. 15, 1808
Blackley Hurst, England

Feb. 16, 1872
London, England

Wrote the hymn, "God the Omnipotent." Chorley gave up his job in a merchant's office in Liverpool to become a musical journalist. He was with the *London Athenaeum*, beginning in 1830, serving as its musical editor for 35 years. Chorley was considered a journalist, novelist, dramatist, and poet, writing about music, literature, and art. He came from dedicated Quaker stock. His writings range from *Music and Manners in France/Germany* (1841) to *Duchess Endeanour* (1866).

Gustav F. Oehler

June 10, 1812
Ebingen, Germany

Feb. 19, 1872
Tubingen, Germany

Old Testament theologian. For several years, Oehler taught in the Missionary Institute at Basel and at the theological seminary in Tubingen. Oehler became a pastor and professor at Schonthal, Wurttemberg in 1840. He spoke up in behalf of confessional Lutheranism and further believed that several authors wrote the Pentateuch with two authors writing Isaiah. Oehler was at Breslau 1845–52 and back at Tubingen 1852 on.

Conrad Kocher

Dec. 16, 1786
Dietzingen, Germany

March 12, 1872
Stuttgart, Germany

Composer of the music for "As with Gladness Men of Old" (1838) and "For the Beauty of the Earth." Kocher studied piano and composition. Eventually, church choral music became his major interest. Kocher founded the School of Sacred Song in Stuttgart in 1821. He popularized four-part singing in the churches and wrote two operas.

Samuel F. B. Morse

April 27, 1791
Charlestown (Boston), Massachusetts

April 2, 1872
New York, New York

Inventor of the telegraph. Morse's communication line from Baltimore to Washington was completed May 24, 1844, with the immortal message, "What hath God wrought." The government spent $30,000 on the project. He married Lucretia Walker (September 29, 1818), and Sarah Griswold (August 9, 1848), resulting in a family of eight children. He oversaw the laying of the transatlantic cable, 1857–58 and invented the Morse Code, an audio/visual signal language of dots and dashes or long and short sounds. Morse was also a painter and sculptor. His father was JEDEDIAH MORSE. Samuel began telegraphic experiments at age 40, after a successful career as a portrait painter in Boston, Charleston, NC and NYC. He died of pneumonia. His favorite Bible verse was Numbers 23:23.

Thomas C. Upham

Jan. 30, 1799
Deerfield, New Hampshire

April 2, 1872
New York, New York

Congregational philosopher. From 1825–67, Upham was professor of mental and moral philosophy at Bowdoin College, Brunswick, ME. He and his wife, Phebe Lord, whom he married on May 18, 1825, had several adopted children. Upham advanced the colonization of blacks and supported the Temperance movement. He was an early advocate of international peace tribunals. In 1867, he retired to Kennebunkport, ME. He wrote some 60 books, was also a poet, and traveled to Europe, Egypt, and Palestine. His works range from *Constitution of the Congregational Church* (1829) to *The Absolute Religion* (1872).

Thomas Hastings

Oct. 15, 1784
Washington, Connecticut

May 15, 1872
New York, New York

Composer of music for "Rock of Ages," 1830 (lyrics by AUGUSTUS TOPLADY), **"From Every Stormy Wind That Blows"** (lyrics by Hugh Stowell), **"The Macedonian Cry"** (lyrics by SAMUEL STENNETT), **and "Majestic Sweetness,"and wrote lyrics for songs such as "Hail to the Brightness."** He married Mary Seymour on September 15, 1822. Hastings wrote some 600 hymns and composed more than 1,000 hymn tunes. He was a pure albino and was able to read a printed page upside down. He taught in several New York cities including Oneida County, Troy, Utica, and New York City, where he lived from 1832–72. Hastings led several choirs including Bleecker Street Presbyterian Church, and wrote several musical books, including *Dissertation on Musical Taste* (1822) and *History of Forty Choirs* (1854), a summary of his own musical experiences. He wrote works ranging from *Musica Sacra* (1816–22) to *Short Anthems* (1865). He edited the *Western Recorder* (1823–32) in Utica.

William Ellis

Aug. 29, 1794
London, England

June 9, 1872
Hoddesdon, England

Congregationalist missionary to the South Sea Islands, 1816–23. He was responsible for the first printing press there (Tahiti). Ellis then traveled to Hawaii where he aided in translating the Bible into the natives' tongues. He became the foreign secretary of the London Missionary Society in 1830; and from 1832–39, he was a traveling agent in England for the LMS. His second wife, Sarah Stickney (1812–72), whom he married in 1837, wrote *The Poetry of Life*. In 1852, 1853, 1856, and 1863, Ellis went to Madagascar to establish missions on the island. He published three books on this missionary-planting endeavor. In his later years, he pastored a Congregational Church in Hodderton.

Norman MacLeod

June 3, 1812
Campbelltown, Scotland

June 16, 1872
Glasgow, Scotland

Author and clergyman of the Church of Scotland who sought to improve the conditions of the working class. He pastored in Dalkeith (1843–51), at Barony Church, Glasgow (1851–57), then was chaplain to Queen VICTORIA (1857–60). He was a founder of the Evangelical Alliance (1847) and remained in the Presbyterian Church during the split (1843). He was a liberal theologian and a zealous missionary. He accomplished much in social and educational pursuits. MacLeod edited the *Edinburgh Christian Magazine* (1849–72) and *Good Words* (1860–72).

George W. Eaton

July 30, 1804
Henderson, Pennsylvania

Aug. 3, 1872
Hamilton, New York

President of Madison University (Colgate-Rochester (NY) Divinity School in 1928), **Hamilton, NY 1856–68.** Eaton began teaching at Georgetown (KY) College, 1831–33. At Madison, he was a professor of church history (1837–50), of biblical theology (1850–59), of doctrinal theology (1859–61), of homiletics and practical theology (1861–65), continuing to teach practical theology until 1871.

Lowell Mason

Jan. 8, 1792
Medfield, Massachusetts

Aug. 11, 1872
Orange, New Jersey

Musical composer and educator. At age 16, Mason was leading the village choir and directing singing schools. He lived in Savannah, GA (1812–27), then moved to Boston (1827–51), where he was responsible for getting music into the public schools, 1838 on. Four children came from his marriage to Abigail Gregory in 1817. He established the Boston Academy of Music in 1833. Early on, he traveled around the country holding conventions in various cities. Mason was also choir director at Bowdoin Street Church for 14 years. Mason left his huge music library to Yale University and resided in New York City from 1851 on, where he published hymnals and choral collections. He composed over 1,000 tunes and 500 arrangements. He composed music for: "Work for the Night Is Coming," "A Charge to Keep," "When I Survey the Wondrous Cross," "From Greenland's Icy Mountains" (1829), "My Faith Looks up to Thee" (1832), "There Is a Fountain" (1830), "Nearer My God to Thee," and "O, Could I Speak" (1856). His son, William (1829–1908), was a concert pianist.

Nikolai F. S. Grundtvig

Sept. 8, 1783
Udby, Denmark

Sept. 2, 1872
Copenhagen, Denmark

Bishop, preacher, hymn writer, and poet. Grundtvig led an evangelical theological movement that revitalized the Danish Lutheran Church. He was in Copenhagen (1808–14), majoring on translation work (1815–21). He pastored in Presto (1821–28), and studied the history of the world (1828–39). He opposed the liberal Soren Kierkegaard, and, from 1825 on, had a large following. In 1830, he visited England three times. Grundtvig was important in the establishing of public high schools. He brought savage attacks on liberalism. In 1839, he became chaplain (pastor) of the Church of Vartov Hospital (aged home) in Copenhagen, where he served until his death. He was made a bishop in 1861. He wrote hundreds of Danish hymns and left five volumes of poems and hymns. He held Christ to be above the Bible, seemingly an unusual position.

Peter Cartwright

Sept. 1, 1785
Amherst County, Virginia

Sept. 25, 1872
near Pleasant Plains, Illinois

Methodist circuit-riding evangelist and frontier preacher who blazed a trail for 70 years through Kentucky, Tennessee, Indiana, Ohio, and Illinois, from 1803 on. Cartwright's family migrated to Logan County, KY in 1743, where he was converted at a revival near there at Lane Ridge camp meeting, Russellville in 1801. Nine children came from his marriage to Frances Gaines on August 18, 1808. He left Kentucky because of his distaste for slavery and went to Pleasant Plains, IL in 1824 (same year elected representative), where he was a presiding elder for 40 years. Cartwright was re-elected, defeating a little-known lawyer (ABE LINCOLN) for the Illinois state legislature in 1832. He later ran against ABRAHAM LINCOLN for the U.S. House in 1846, but lost. Stories relate how he rebuked the actions of General JACKSON, beat up rowdies and broke up wild dances. His horseback exploits alone, braving bandits, Indian attacks, hostile backwoodsmen, and the wilderness have never been equaled. Throughout his ministry, he baptized more than 12,000 and preached more than 15,000 times.

Francis Vinton

Aug. 29, 1809
Providence, Rhode Island

Sept. 29, 1872
Brooklyn, New York

Episcopal cleric who was pastor at Trinity Church, New York City from 1859 on. Vinton married Maria Whipple (October 8, 1838) and Elizabeth M. Perry (November 3, 1841). In 1869, he became professor of church law and polity at General Theological Seminary, New York City. Vinton also was a soldier, engineer, and lawyer. He wrote *Lectures on the Evidences of Christianity* (1855).

Jeremiah W. Loguen

1813
Davidson County, Tennessee

Sept. 30, 1872
Saratoga Springs, New York

Methodist leader who escaped from slavery in Tennessee in 1834. Loguen married Caroline Storum in 1840; they lived in Syracuse, NY. He went to Canada and later to New York, running schools for Negro children. Loguen was active in the underground railroad in New York City, helping fugitive slaves to escape from the South and establish free lives in the North. He pastored the African Methodist Episcopal Zion Church in New York (1843–50) and was bishop of the same (1868–70).

Jean H. M. D'Aubigne

Aug. 8, 1794
Eaux-Vives (Geneva) Switzerland

Oct. 21, 1872
Geneva, Switzerland

Church historian and pastor of the French Protestant Church in Hamburg, Germany, 1819–24. After five years there, D'Aubigne went to Brussels, Belgium, as chaplain to King William I (ruled: 1815–40). Returning to Geneva in 1830, he helped in a new orthodox college founded by the Evangelical Society of Geneva and taught church history. He also visited Scotland and England briefly, although he spent the majority of his life in Geneva. D'Aubigne wrote *History of the Reformation* (5 vols., 1835–53).

John Bowring

Oct. 17, 1792
Exeter, England

Nov. 23, 1872
Exeter, England

Public official, linguist, and hymn writer of "In the Cross of Christ I Glory" (music by ITHAMAR CONKEY). It is hard to understand how a Unitarian could write a song like that, but, perhaps like EDMUND SEARS, Bowring was part of a conservative element in the movement. He was a member of Parliament for ten years. In 1849, he was appointed British consul at Hong Kong and chief superintendent of trade in China. He was governor of Hong Kong, 1854–56. He also visited Siam (Thailand) and the Philippines. He translated English and published poetry in many languages. He could speak twelve languages.

William Shaw

Dec. 8, 1798
Glasgow, Scotland

Dec. 4, 1872
London, England

Methodist missionary to South Africa. In 1820, Shaw went to Grahamstown, Cape Colony, as a chaplain to the British colonists who had settled on the tip of Africa. His missionary work among the Kaffir tribesmen began in 1823. Shaw married Ann Maw on December 31, 1817 (died: July 6, 1854) and then Mrs. Ogle on March 12, 1857. His missionary work grew to include several stations and over 5,000 people in 37 years of work. From 1823–30, he planted six missions in Ciskel and Transkel. Shaw tried to ease tensions between the English settlers and the Xhosa-speaking population during the bloody conflicts of 1834–52. He supervised the work north of the Orange River (1838), and focused on the Natal region (1842). He retired to England in 1856.

Joshua Leavitt

Sept. 8, 1794
Heath, Massachusetts

Jan. 16, 1873
Brooklyn, New York

Congregational pastor in Stratford, CT 1825–28. He married Sarah Williams in 1820. Leavitt served as secretary of the Seaman's Friend Society, 1828–31, and editor and proprietor of the *New York Evangelist* (1831–37). Leavitt was a renowned journalist, lecturer, and antislavery politician. He was also editor of the *Independent* (1848–73). Leavitt also edited *The Christian Lyre*, the first hymn book published in America that contained editorial notes on the hymns also.

Baptist W. Noel

July 16, 1798
Leightmont, Scotland

Jan. 19, 1873
Stanmore, England

Anglican priest with evangelical zeal. He pastored at St. John's Chapel in London, 1827–48. Noel helped found the Evangelical Alliance in Britain in 1846. When he left the Church of England, he became a Baptist pastor at John Street Chapel, London, 1849–68. Noel twice headed the English Baptist Union and led social causes in London. He published several hymns and books ranging from *A Plea to the Poor* (1841) to *Hymns About Jesus* (1868).

Matthew F. Maury

Jan. 14, 1806
Fredericksburg, Virginia

Feb. 1, 1873
Lexington, Virginia

One of the greatest meteorologists and hydrographers (science of mapping waters), Maury was a naval officer with an outstanding witness. Eight children came from his marriage to Ann Hall Herndon on July 15, 1834. Maury joined the Navy in 1825, became a commander, and was director of the U.S. Naval Observatory, Washington, D.C. from 1844–61. As a result of a stagecoach accident in 1839, he was lame for life. He began his career by surveying harbors and studying winds and currents. Maury developed wind and current charts of the Atlantic which cut sailing time and improved sea safety. Paths called "shiplanes" were first designed by him in 1854, but originated with the Bible (Psalm 8:8). His *Physical Geography of the Sea* (1855) was the first classic work of modern oceanography. Additionally, he wrote many works on geology and geography. Maury became a professing Christian in 1867, and joined the Episcopal Church, London.

Thomas Guthrie

July 12, 1803
Brechin, Scotland

Feb. 24, 1873
Brechin, Scotland

Preacher, editor, social reformer, and philanthropist. Guthrie was a bank manager, 1826–30. He was a Presbyterian pastor in Abirlot (1830–37) and at Old Greyfriars Church, Edinburgh (1837–40). He ministered to great crowds at St. John's Church, Edinburgh, 1840–64, which was erected 50 yards away from his former church and drew visitors from all over the world. Guthrie supported the Free Church that commenced at the disruption of the Presbyterian Church in 1843. In 1844, Guthrie became an intense temperance advocate. After 1847, he devoted his energies to "ragged schools" for the poor. He edited the *Sunday Magazine* (1864 on). His *Ezekiel* (1855) sold 50,000 copies. Guthrie's funeral in Edinburgh attracted 30,000 mourners.

Charles P. McIlvaine

Jan. 18, 1799
Burlington, New Jersey

March 13, 1873
Florence, Italy

President of Kenyon College, Gambier, OH 1832–40, and its Bexley Hall Theological Seminary [Colgate–Rochester (NY) Theological Seminary in 1968], **1841–69**. McIlvaine was also bishop of the Episcopal Church in the diocese of Ohio, 1832–73. Emily Coxe became his wife on Oct. 8, 1822. McIlvaine was an eloquent preacher and successful administrator. President LINCOLN sent him to England after the Trent Affair (the unlawful seizure of a British ship) to improve relations with the United States. McIlvaine lived in Clifton, OH from 1846 on, after living in Gambier, OH from 1843–46. He wrote *Evidences of Christianity* (1832). He died while on a vacation trip.

David Livingstone

March 19, 1813　　　　　　　　　　　　　　　　　　　　　　　　　　May 1, 1873
Blantyre, Scotland　　　　　　　　　　　　　　　　　　Ilala, Northern Rhodesia (Zambia)

Africa's beloved pioneer missionary and explorer. Livingston studied theology and medicine while he was working as a piecer in a cotton mill. He was converted at age 20 while reading Dick's *Philosophy of the Future State*. Livingstone was deeply challenged to examine central Africa and traveled some 30,000 miles through it. He first arrived in Africa in 1841, and married Mary Moffat (1821–April 27, 1862) in March, 1845, daughter of missionary, ROBERT MOFFAT. They were separated half of their 18 years of marriage. She died in his arms at Shuppnoa on the Zambezi. His ministry included the spreading of the gospel, healing the sick, recording African geography, helping to stop the Portuguese slave trade, and seeking the source of the Nile River. Early in his expedition, he was attacked and maimed by a lion. He is credited with discovering Lake Ngami (1849), the Zambezi River (1851), Victoria Falls (1855), and Lake Nyasa (1859). He originally served under the London Missionary Society (1841), then under the British government (1849), and finally under the Royal Geographical Society (1866). He wrote *Missionary Travels* (1857), a best seller. After being considered missing for some time, he was finally found by HENRY STANLEY in Ujiji in 1871. Just before his death, he said, "Build me a hut to die in. I am going home." He was found dead on his knees. The natives buried his heart in Africa, but his body was buried in Westminster Abbey on April 18, 1874. His favorite Bible verse was Matthew 28:20.

"Anywhere, provided it be forward!"
"Jesus was a missionary and a physician."
"Men are immortal till their work is done."

William H. McGuffey

Sept. 23, 1800　　　　　　　　　　　　　　　　　　　　　　　　　　May 4, 1873
near Claysville, Pennsylvania　　　　　　　　　　　　　　　　Charlottesville, Virginia

Educator who is remembered for his famous series of elementary readers, the *McGuffey Readers* (1836–57), of which 140 million copies were sold. McGuffey married Harriet Spinning (1827) and Laura Howard (1857), having a total of six children. McGuffey was professor of languages at Miami University, Oxford, OH (1826–36), president of Cincinnati College (1836–39), Ohio University in Athens (1839–43), and taught moral philosophy at the University of Virginia (1845–73). In his readers, he taught that morality was as important as reading. The forward to his reader said, "The Christian religion is the religion of our country." He was a Presbyterian.

Salmon P. Chase

Jan. 13, 1808　　　　　　　　　　　　　　　　　　　　　　　　　　May 7, 1873
Cornish, New Hampshire　　　　　　　　　　　　　　　　　　New York, New York

Chief justice of the Supreme Court, 1864–73. His law practice began in Cincinnati in 1829. Chase married Katherine Garniss (March 4, 1834), Eliza Smith (Sept. 26, 1839), and Sarah Ludlow (Nov. 6, 1846); he had a total of six children. In 1840, Chase branched into politics and served as governor of Ohio, 1856–60. Chase was secretary of the Treasury in LINCOLN's administration, 1861–64. On March 3, 1865, Congress authorized the famed words, that he submitted on American coins, "In God We Trust." Paralyzed in August, 1870 with a stroke, he was an invalid until his death. He was the nephew of PHILANDER CHASE and an Episcopalian. His likeness is portrayed on a $10,000 bill.

William H. Bishop

1793
Troy, New York/Maryland

May 20, 1873
Amez, Maryland

Bishop of African Methodist Episcopal Zion Church, 1852–73; senior bishop, 1853–68. Bishop was converted on January 9, 1830. He was licensed to preach in 1835, and joined the Troy (NY) conference on January 20, 1837. He was ordained as a deacon (1838), then as an elder (1840). He retired in 1868.

William R. Featherstone

July 23, 1846
Montreal, Quebec, Canada

May 20, 1873
Montreal, Quebec, Canada

Wrote the hymn "My Jesus, I Love Thee," (1863) (music by A.J. GORDON), when he was a teenager. Featherstone's family attended the Wesleyan Methodist Church, Montreal (St. James Methodist, United Church). Little is known about his life.

Thomas Beveridge

Oct. 9, 1796
Cambridge, New York

May 30, 1873
Xenia, Ohio

President of Xenia (OH) (Pittsburgh Theological in 1959) **Seminary, 1855–71.** Beveridge pastored in Ohio (1821–24), was an evangelist (1824–27), and pastored in Philadelphia (1828–35). From 1835–55, he was professor at Associate Theological Seminary, Canonsburg, PA. The seminary moved to Xenia, OH in 1855, and he continued to teach until 1871. He labored for years upon a new *Metrical Version of the Psalms*.

Heinrich A. W. Meyer

Jan. 10, 1800
Gotha, Germany

June 21, 1873
Hanover, Germany

Clergyman and Bible scholar who wrote a distinguished commentary on the New Testament, 1832–47. From 1821–48, Meyer engaged in pastoral duties in Osthausen, Meiningen, Harste, Hoya, and Neustadt/Hanover. He retired to Hanover (1848), and devoted the rest of his life to writing and revising his commentaries, completely retiring (1865) from his positions of superintendent and consistorial counselor.

Christopher Rush

Feb. 4, 1777
near New Bern, North Carolina

July 16, 1873
Philadelphia, Pennsylvania

Bishop of African Methodist Episcopal Zion Church, 1828–72; senior bishop, 1828–52. Rush was converted at age 16, and went to New York from his home state of North Carolina in 1798. He joined the AMEZC (1803) and was licensed to preach (1815). Rush served with JAMES VARICK (founder) in the early days of the movement but lost his eyesight in 1852. Better education for his race was one of Rush's major burdens.

Samuel Wilberforce

Sept. 7, 1805
Clapham, London, England

July 19, 1873
Abinger, England

Anglican bishop, originally representing Oxford, 1845–1869 and later Winchester, 1869–73. Wilberforce was the son of WILLIAM WILBERFORCE. He was rector of Brightstone, Isle of Wight, 1830–40. Samuel supported pastoral reforms and innovations, founded new churches and the first Anglican theological college at Cuddesdon in 1854. Wilberforce opposed liberalism and Darwinism, debated Thomas Huxley (evolutionary biologist, 1825–95), and was considered a powerful orator. He wrote extensively. A fall from a horse killed him.

Samuel S. Schmucker

Feb. 28, 1799
Hagerstown, Maryland

July 26, 1873
Gettysburg, Pennsylvania

First president of Lutheran Theological Seminary at Gettysburg (PA), 1826–1864. Schmucker was a Lutheran leader who participated in the founding of LTS from 1832–34, and also the college called Pennsylvania College (Gettysburg College). He married Elenora Geiger (February 28, 1821), Mary C. Steenbergen (October 12, 1825), and Esther M. Wagner (April 28, 1849), producing a total of 13 children. He also assisted in forming the Evangelical Alliance in 1845, with the goal for presenting a unified front for Christian denominations. Schmucker promoted relief to persecuted Protestant Christians through a national United Week of Prayer. He published more than 40 works. His evangelical views (against baptismal regeneration, consubstantiation, etc.) caused some Lutheran discomfort.

Gardiner Spring

Feb. 24, 1785
Newburyport, Massachusetts

Aug. 18, 1873
New York, New York

Presbyterian pastor of the famed Brick Church of New York City for 63 years, from August 8, 1810, until his death in 1873. Fifteen children came from his marriages to Susan Barney (May 25, 1806) and Abba G. Williams (August 14, 1861). Spring ardently pleaded for reunion in the Presbyterian Church and saw it before his death. He helped to found the American Bible Society (1816), the American Tract Society (1825), and the American Home Missionary Society (1826). Spring also wrote several books, including *The Power of the Pulpit*. His *Traits of Christian Character* (1813) was his first book.

John Todd

Oct. 9, 1800
Rutland, Vermont

Aug. 24, 1873
Pittsfield, Massachusetts

Congregational minister and author. Mary S. Brace became his wife on March 11, 1827, giving him nine children. Todd served in Groton, MA (1827–33), at EDWARD's Church in Northampton, MA (1833–36); at the First Church in Philadelphia, PA (1836–42); and at the First Church of Pittsfield, MA (1842–73). Todd wrote many widely circulated books.

Robert S. Candlish

March 23, 1806
Edinburgh, Scotland

Oct. 19, 1873
Edinburgh, Scotland

Pastor of the Free Church of Scotland after Thomas Chalmers' death. With CHALMERS, Candlish insisted on the independence of the Church from civil authorities and joined the 1843 Disruption, from which was formed the Free Church. He was one of the founders of the Evangelical Alliance in 1845. He pastored at St. George's Church, Edinburgh (1834–73), and was also principal of the New (Free Church) College (1862–73). He wrote several books.

Jacob Knapp

Dec. 7, 1799
New York

1874
Rockford, Illinois

Perhaps the first well-known Baptist evangelist. Knapp was converted at age 17, following the death of his mother, while praying in the woods. Another source tells of his conversion at Masonville (NY) Baptist Church in 1819. He left Episcopalianism and pastored in Springfield and in Watertown, NY. He went into evangelism in September, 1833, and held crusades throughout the Northeast. Fifteen hundred people were converted in his Albany, NY crusade.

Knapp also contributed his energies to the Temperance movement. He moved to Hamilton, NY in 1835, but later in life moved to Illinois. He saw divine intervention several times in his ministry and was greatly used in the Lord's work.

George Scott

1804 *1874*
Edinburgh, Scotland

Wesleyan Methodist minister and missionary. Scott became a Methodist in 1827. He was sent to Stockholm, Sweden, in 1830 as chaplain to a group of English laborers who were employed by a manufacturer. His preaching attracted large crowds, but he was opposed by local clergy and the press. Scott was forced out of the country in 1842, and CARL ROSENIUS took over his work. Scott spent the remainder of his life as a Wesleyan minister in England and Scotland.

William Sparrow

March 12, 1801 *Jan. 17, 1874*
Charlestown, Massachusetts Alexandria, Virginia

Dean of Virginia Theological Seminary, Alexandria, VA 1842–74. Sparrow married Frances Greenleaf on February 13, 1832 and had 10 children. He taught at Miami University, Oxford, OH (1824–25); was a founder of a theological seminary (Kenyon College) in Washington, Ohio (1825); and was vice-president of administration at Gambier (OH) Theological Seminary. He was ordained a priest in the Episcopal Church in 1826. At VTS he was also a teacher of theology, (1828–41). He was a leading figure in the low church evangelistic work and a delegate to various Episcopal diocesan conventions.

William Sandys

Oct. 29, 1792 *Feb. 18, 1874*
London, England London, England

Arranger of the music for the Christmas carol, "The First Noel." Sandys was a music researcher. He maintained a successful legal practice from 1816–1873, heading the law firm of Sandys and Knott at Gray's Inn Square in London. His pioneering work in the revival of interest in carols resulted in his publishing three works on the subject.

Thomas Binney

April 30, 1798 *Feb. 24, 1874*
Newcastle-on-Tyne, England Clapton, London, England

Congregational minister who worked to obtain reunion with the Church of England. In 1824, Binney began pastoring at Newport, Isle of Wight (an island in the English Channel). Here he wrote the hymn, "Eternal Light." He pastored at Weigh-House Chapel in London, 1829–69. He attacked the established church, saying in 1833, "The Church of England destroys more souls than it saves." Binney introduced anthems and the chanting of Psalms into worship. He wrote *Twenty-four Reasons for Dissenting* and *Is It Possible to Have the Best of Both Worlds?* (1853).

Francis Mason

April 2, 1799 *March 3, 1874*
York, England Rangoon, Burma (Myanmar)

Missionary to Burma who came to America in 1818 as a shoemaker from England. Mason married Lucinda Gill in 1825 (died: 1828); Helen M. Griggs on May 23, 1830 (died: 1896); and Ellen H. Bullard in 1847. In 1830, he went to Burma as a Baptist missionary. Mason succeeded GEORGE BOARDMAN in the work among the Karens and translated a number of books for use by these native tribespeople. At Toungoo, more than 6,000 converts were baptized and 126 churches began during a ten-year period. He also wrote *Story of a Working Man's Life* (1870).

Edward N. Kirk

Aug. 14, 1802 — *March 27, 1874*
New York, New York — Boston, Massachusetts

Pastor and evangelist. Kirk pastored at Fourth Presbyterian Church, Albany, NY (1829–40), receiving 1,000 new members during his pastorate; visited Europe (1837–39); was secretary of the Foreign Evangelical Society (1839–42); and then pastored the Mt. Vernon Congregational Church, Boston, MA (1842–71). His most famous convert (through a SS teacher) was D. L. MOODY in 1854. Kirk participated in evangelistic endeavors in many eastern cities. He wrote *Lectures on Parables*. He wrote from *Memoirs of Reverend John Chester* (1829) to *Lectures on Revivals* (1874). Kirk was almost blind in his later years.

Thomas DeWitt

Sept. 13, 1791 — *May 18, 1874*
Kingston, New York — New York, New York

Outstanding Dutch Reformed pastor who served at Hopewell and New Hackensack, NY, 1812–27. Dewitt then became one of the pastors of the Collegiate Church in New York City serving there 47 years until his death in 1874. He edited the *Christian Intelligencer* (1831–43). He had a marked influence in the life of New York City as a favorite pastor and preacher.

Karl R. Hagenbach

March 4, 1801 — *June 7, 1874*
Basel, Switzerland — Basel, Switzerland

German-Swiss Church historian and theologian. Hagenbach accepted a position at the University of Basel in 1823, where, for 51 years, he taught church history and dogma and helped lead the school into a more orthodox position. He was a powerful preacher and stressed the confessions of the Church. He was also president of the Swiss Protestant Relief Society. He endeavored to reconcile culture and Christianity, publishing many books.

Lydia Odell Baxter

Sept. 8, 1809 — *June 22, 1874*
Petersburg, New York — New York, New York

Writer of the hymn, "Take the Name of Jesus With You" (1871) (music by WILLIAM DOANE). Lydia was converted under the ministry of Eben Tucker, a Baptist missionary. She and her sister helped form a church in Petersburg, NY. After her marriage, she moved to New York City. Lydia was an invalid for most of her adult life, but her positive outlook made her home a gathering place for Christian workers. Other hymns of note that she wrote include "I'm Weary, I'm Fainting" and "The Master Is Coming." She published *Gems by the Wayside* (1855), a book of devotional poems.

Patrick Fairbairn

Jan. 28, 1805 — *Aug. 6, 1874*
Hallyburton, Scotland — Glasgow, Scotland

Presbyterian theologian and writer. Fairbairn's pastoral experience included the Orkney Islands, Northern Scotland (1830–36); Bridgeton, Glasgow (1836–40); and Salton, East Lothian (1840–43); where he left the established church to help form and lead the Free Church until 1853. In 1856, he became principal and professor of theology at the Free Church College in Glasgow. His works range from *The Typology of Scripture* (2 vols.) to *Pastoral Theology* (1875). He was a member of the Old Testament revision committee.

Thomas A. Morris

April 28, 1794
near Charleston, West Virginia

Sept. 2, 1874
Springfield, Ohio

Bishop in the Methodist Episcopal Church, 1836–74. Morris preached in Ohio, Kentucky, and Tennessee, 1816–34; then he became the first editor of the *Western Christian Advocate*. He married Abigail Scales (1814), and Lucy Merriwether (1844). He was considered a wise and able bishop. Health problems caused Morris to retire in 1868.

John E. Bode

Feb. 23, 1816
St. Pancras, London, England

Oct. 6, 1874
Castle Camps, England

Writer of hymn, "O Jesus, I Have Promised" (1868) (music by ARTHUR MANN). Bode tutored at Christ Church in Oxford, 1840–47 and served as an Anglican rector of Westwell, Oxfordshire in 1847 and of Castle Camps, Cambridgeshire (1860–74). He delivered the Bampton Lectures [Canon John Bampton of Salisbury (died: 1751) left in his will an endowment for an annual lectorship at St. Mary's Church, Oxford, to defend the Christian faith] at Oxford in 1855. He published three books of hymns and poems, his major writings being collections of original ballads.

Francois P. G. Guizot

Oct. 4, 1787
Nimes, France

Oct. 12, 1874
Val-Richer, France

Historian statesman. Guizot was Minister of Foreign Affairs, 1840–48 (until the abdication of Louis Philippe). Previously he was Minister of Public Instruction, 1832–36. He was raised in a Huguenot home, wrote largely on themes connected with religion, and was the leader of the Reformed Church in France. He taught history at the Sorbonne, 1812–30. Guizot was the premier of France, 1840–48, but was forced into retirement to his country estate in Normandy by the events of the February Revolution of 1848 (European explosion due to crop failures, widespread political repression, and emergence of nationalism). At his estate, he wrote for another 25 years. His first wife, Elisabeth Charlotte Pauline de Meulan (1773–1827), was an authoress, as was his second wife, Marguerite Andree Elisa Dillion (1804–33). He wrote the six-volume *History of the Revolution in England* (1826–56) and the six-volume *History of Civilization in Europe* (1829–32), which emphasized the role of the middle class. Guizot died a poor man. He had no patience with those who criticized religion or politics. Guizot said, "God and the religion of Christ are my guides…"

Phoebe Worrall Palmer

Dec. 18, 1807
New York, New York

Nov. 2, 1874
New York, New York

Lay evangelist and exponent of Christian holiness. Converted at an early age, Phoebe married a physician, Walter C. Palmer, on September 28, 1827. A revival in 1832, at Allen Street Methodist Church, helped in their "desire for holiness". She lost several children, one tragically. Phoebe claimed sanctification (an act by God to forever make something holy—moral progress does not "grow" into holiness) on July 26, 1837. She soon became a popular speaker. The Palmers went to Great Britain and Ireland for four years. She wrote ten books beginning with *The Way of Holiness* (1845). She opposed slavery and liquor and retained the support of much of her denomination. Her husband died in Ocean Grove, NJ on July 20, 1883. Although she never spoke in tongues, her emphasis on Pentecost and Spirit baptism helped pave the way for later Pentecostal and charismatic movements. She participated in over 300 camp meetings and revival campaigns. She wrote the lyrics for "The Cleansing Wave." Her favorite Bible verse was Joel 2:28.

Edward Mote

Jan. 21, 1797
London, England

Nov. 13, 1874
Horsham, England

Wrote the hymn "My Hope is Built on Nothing Less," also known as "The Solid Rock," (1834) (music by WILLIAM BRADBURY). Mote settled at Southwark, a London suburb, where he became a successful cabinet-maker and devoted churchman. He wrote more than 100 hymns that were published in his *Hymns of Praise*. In 1852, he began a 21-year pastorate at the Baptist church in Horsham, Sussex. He was the first to use the phrase "gospel hymn."

Konstantin L. F. von Tischendorf
"Lobegott Friedrich Konstantin von Tischendorf"

Jan. 18, 1815
Lengenfeld, Germany

Dec. 7, 1874
Leipzig, Germany

Biblical scholar and textual critic whose valuable contributions to biblical textual criticism included the search for manuscripts. In 1844, Tischendorf found a valuable Greek manuscript of the OT. On his third search, he made his most famous find, the Codex Sinaiticus at the Monastery of St. Catherine on Sinai on February 4, 1859. This is one of the oldest known manuscripts of the Greek Bible. He was a student of the original languages and texts of the Bible. From 1859 on, he was a professor at Leipzig University. He published many helpful contributions to NT studies.

Joseph P. Webster

March 22, 1819
Manchester, New York

Jan. 18, 1875
Elkhorn, Wisconsin

Composer of the music for the beloved hymn, "In the Sweet By and By" (lyrics by SANFORD BENNETT) and "I Believe Jesus Saves" (lyrics by WILLIAM MCDONALD). Webster spent a number of years in New York and Connecticut, teaching music and giving concerts. Webster was a talented musician, playing the flute, violin, and piano. Before the Civil War, he settled at Elkhorn, WI and met BENNETT. Webster produced over 1,000 compositions.

Jean F. Millet

Oct. 4, 1814
Gruchy, France

Jan. 20, 1875
Barbizon, France

Landscape and genre painter of the Barbizon School (group of French artists, mostly landscapists some who lived in Barbizon on the edge of a forest) who became known as the foremost religious painter of his time. Millet painted peasant life and nature scenes almost totally from memory. He married Pauline Ono in 1841 (died: 1844) and Catherine Lemaire in 1845. He moved to Barbizon in 1848. He was known for his drawings, pastels, and etchings. Some of his best works include *Man with the Hoe* (1863), *The Reapers*, *The Gleaners* (1857), *The Angelus*, and *The Potato Planters*.

John E. Gould

1822
Bangor, Maine

March 4, 1875
Algiers, Africa

Composer of "Jesus Savior, Pilot Me" (1871) (lyrics by EDWARD HOPPER), written the night before he left America, never to return. Early in his life, he had a music store in New York City, then went into the piano business in Philadelphia, PA. In September of 1874, Gould traveled to England, Europe, and Africa in search of a climate kind to his delicate health.

Robert Milligan

July 25, 1814
County Tyrone, Ireland

March 20, 1875
Lexington, Kentucky

First president of College of the Bible (Lexington Theological Seminary in 1965), **1864–75**. Milligan's parents immigrated to America when he was four, and settled in Trumbull County, OH. Milligan joined the Reformed Presbyterian Church at age 21. He opened a classical school in Flat Rock, KY in 1837. He married Ellen Russell in January, 1842, the same year that he was ordained by THOMAS CAMPBELL of the Disciples of Christ, whose teachings he had been pursuing. Feeble health began as early as 1842, when violent attacks of inflammatory rheumatism nearly proved fatal. In 1854, he served as a professor of mathematics at Bethany (VA) College. He was president of Kentucky University, Harrodsburg, KY which moved to Lexington and became the College of the Bible. Milligan wrote seven books and energetically taught young men up until his last illness.

John S. B. Monsell

March 2, 1811
St. Columb's, Ireland

April 9, 1875
Guildford, England

Writer of the hymn, "Fight the Good Fight With All Thy Might." Monsell served as an Anglican chaplain, chancellor, rector, and vicar at various dioceses in Ireland and in Egham, England, 1853–70. His final position commenced in 1870, at St. Nicholas Church, Guildford. Monsell wrote over 300 hymns and advocated fervent singing, even in church. He died after he was struck with falling masonry while he watched workmen repair his church in Guildford. His writings range from *Hymns and Poems* (1832) to *Simon the Cyrenian and Other Poems* (1876). He published eleven volumes of poetry.

Samuel P. Tregelles

Jan. 30, 1813
Falmouth, England

April 24, 1875
Plymouth, England

Outstanding Greek scholar of the New Testament. Tregelles was born a Quaker, but was an adherent of the Darbyite Plymouth Brethren (both the Quakers and the Brethren were against organized church worship) for a time before joining the Presbyterian Church. He was converted around 1835, by his cousin, BENJAMIN NEWTON. Tregelles wrote various publications dealing with his excellent critical edition of the New Testament, called the *Greek New Testament* (1857–72). He also translated Heinrich Gesenius' (1786–42) *Hebrew Grammar*.

William Arnot

Nov. 6, 1808
Scone, Scotland

June 3, 1875
Edinburgh, Scotland

Eminent preacher and author whose writings have had a wide circulation. Arnot was minister of St. Peter's Church in Glasgow (1838), joined Chalmers' Free Church movement (1843), and then ministered in Main Street, Glasgow (1850–63) and at the Free High Church in Edinburgh (1863–75). Arnot wrote biographies of James Halley (1842) and JAMES HAMILTON (1870). His most well-known books were *Illustrations of the Book of Proverbs* (1851–58) and *The Parables of Our Lord* (1864). He traveled to America three times.

John E. Giles

April 20, 1805
Dartmouth, England

June 24, 1875
London, England

Baptist pastor and hymn writer who wrote, "Thou Hast Said, Exalted Jesus." Giles was ordained in 1830 and pastored at Salter's Hall Chapel, London; at South Parade, Leeds, in Sheffield; at Rathmines, Dublin; and at Clapham Common, London. Giles was a strong defender of the Baptist faith. He visited Hamburg, Germany and Denmark on behalf of the Baptist cause.

Simeon B. Marsh

June 1, 1798
Sherburne, New York

July 14, 1875
Albany, New York

Composer of one tune for Wesley's "Jesus, Lover of My Soul." Marsh received great encouragement from THOMAS HASTINGS. For 30 years he conducted "singing schools" in the Albany presbytery, Amsterdam, NY. Marsh was a devoted Presbyterian layman. He edited the *Intelligencer* and the *Sherburne News* (1841) newspapers. He was also active in Sunday school work. His wife died in 1873.

Connop Thirlwall

Feb. 11, 1797
Stephney, London, England

July 27, 1875
Bath, England

Progressive Anglican bishop of St. David's, Wales. Thirlwall upset his peers in Parliament by voting to admit Jews to parliament and to disestablish the Anglican Church in Ireland; his was the sole vote. He was a competent biblical student, helping to revise the English translation of the Old Testament. He was cleric at Kirby Underdale, 1834–40. His most famous work was *History of Grace* (8 vols., 1835–44).

Hans Christian Andersen

April 2, 1805
Odense, Denmark

Aug. 4, 1875
Copenhagen, Denmark

Author, novelist, and poet. The son of a poor shoemaker, Andersen received an education through generous patrons. His father died in 1816. He ran away to Copenhagen at age 14, where he was accepted into the Royal Theater as an apprentice actor and singer. He wrote plays, novels, and travel books with Christian morals. Andersen won worldwide fame through his *Fairy Tales*, which were published in several volumes, 1835–77. Of his more than 150 stories, the most widely known are: "The Ugly Duckling," "The Red Shoes," "Thumbelina" (with a well-remembered refrain), "The Snow Queen," and "The Emperor's New Clothes." He wrote the carol, "Barn (Child) Jesus," ending with "… Hallelujah, Hallelujah, Child Jesus!" He never married.

Charles G. Finney

Aug. 29, 1792
Warren, Connecticut

Aug. 16, 1875
Oberlin, Ohio

One of the greatest revivalists/evangelists in history and president of Oberlin (OH) College, 1851–66. Finney joined a law office in Adams, NY (1818), after coming to NY (1794). He was converted on October 10, 1821, while walking in the woods. Finney immediately left the law business for the ministry and began preaching in small communities in upstate New York counties (Jefferson, Oneida, and St. Lawrence), 1824–27. Finney married Lydia Andrews in July, 1824 (died: 1847); Elizabeth F. Atkinson in 1848 (died: 1863); and Rebecca A. Rayl in 1864 (died: 1907). He held great crusades in Wilmington, DE; NYC; Boston, MA; Philadelphia, PA; Lancaster, NY; and Rochester, NY from 1827–32. His Rochester revival in 1830–31 saw 1,000 of the 10,000 population saved. He founded the *New York Evangelist* in 1830. Cholera and respiratory illnesses curtailed traveling, so he pastored the Second Free Presbyterian Church (1832–34) and the Congregational Broadway Tabernacle (1834–37). He pastored the Congregational Church, Oberlin, OH (1837–72), and was president of Oberlin College (1852–66), the first Christian college to accept black students on equal standing with whites. Finney also wrote *Lectures on Revival* (1835). His *Lectures on Systematic Theology* was published in 1846. More than 500,000 people were converted under his revival endeavors. He stated, "A revival is nothing else than a new beginning of obedience to God." His favorite Bible verse was Jeremiah 29:13.

Asa B. Everett

1828   *Sept. 1875*
Virginia   near Nashville, Tennessee

Composed the music for "Footprints of Jesus," "Who at My Door Is Standing" (lyrics by Mary Slade for both), and other hymns. Everett studied music extensively including four years in Leipzig, Germany. In connection with his brother, they formed the L. C. Everett Company of Richmond, VA (later Pennsylvania), which had more than 50 music teachers prior to the Civil War. Everett wrote numerous gospel songs and edited a number of hymn collections.

Walter F. Hook

March 13, 1798   *Oct. 20, 1875*
London/Worcester, England   Chichester, England

Anglican vicar in Leeds, England, 1837–59, when he was appointed dean of Chichester. During this 22-year period, Hook built 21 churches and was greatly active in executive religious affairs. He served at Moseley (1825-27), Birmingham (1827–28), and Coventry (1828–37). Hook wrote *A Church Dictionary* (8th volume completed in 1859), the eight-volume *An Ecclesiastical Biography* (1845–52), and the twelve-volume *Lives of the Archbishops of Canterbury* (1860–76), among others. He quarreled with Ed Pusey (1800–82) over ritualism at St. Saviour's, Leeds.

Horatio B. Hackett

Dec. 27, 1808   *Nov. 2, 1875*
Salisbury, Massachusetts   Rochester, New York

Outstanding professor of New Testament Greek at Rochester (NY) Theological Seminary, 1870 on. Prior to this, Hackett served as a professor of Latin at Brown University, Providence, RI (1835–39), and then taught biblical literature at Newton (MA) Theological Institution (1839–70). Hackett was recognized as one of the best American scholars ever. His works included *Commentary on the Acts* (1852) and *Illustrations from Scripture* (1855). Among his translations was the American edition of William Smith's *Bible Dictionary* (1868–70), which he edited with Ezra Abbot (1819–84).

Brownlow North

Jan. 6, 1810   *Nov. 9, 1875*
Chelsea, England   Tullichewan, Scotland

Evangelist from the Free Church of Scotland. In November of 1854, while visiting at Dallas Moors, North was converted and soon began to distribute tracts among the destitute in Elgin, Scotland. From 1856 until his death, North held revivals in leading cities in England and Scotland. He extended his ministry to Ireland in 1859.

John Wilson

Dec 11, 1804   *Dec. 1, 1875*
Lauder, Scotland   Bombay, India

Missionary to India with the Scottish Missionary Society. He married his first wife, Margaret Bayne, in 1828 (died: 1835). He remarried, and they had 20 good years of ministry. Wilson spent his life in Bombay, arriving in 1829, and as the head of the mission college there, he gained a commanding audience. His counsel was sought by British authorities, and his influence was felt in many directions. He helped establish Bombay University in 1857. Wilson mastered ten languages.

Priscilla L. Sellon

c 1821 — 1876

Founder of the first post-Reformation religious community in the Church of England. With E. B. Pusey's assistance, Priscilla's charity work among the destitute grew into the "Devonport Sisters of Mercy." Schools and orphanages were also founded. The sisters heroically nursed the sick in the cholera epidemic of 1848.

Meta S. Heusser

April 6, 1797 — Jan. 2, 1876
Hirzel, Switzerland — Hirzel, Switzerland

German hymn writer and song writer. Meta, the daughter of a Swiss pastor, spent her life at Hirzel, a beautiful village in sight of Mt. Rigi and Lake Lucerne of Switzerland. Her husband, Johann Heusser, was an eminent physician who placed the care of a large household and a demanding social schedule upon her. Meta wrote many songs and poems, which flowed from a heart close to God.

Edmund H. Sears

April 6, 1810 — Jan. 16, 1876
Sandisfield, Massachusetts — Weston, Massachusetts

Writer of the famed Christmas carol, "It Came Upon a Midnight Clear" (music by RICHARD WILLIS). Sears was not the typical Unitarian, for he wrote "Although I was educated in the Unitarian denomination, I believe and preach the Divinity of Christ." He graduated from Harvard Divinity School in 1837. He married Ellen Bacon on November 7, 1839, and they had four children. He pastored Unitarian churches in Wayland (1839–40), Lancaster (1840–47), and Weston, MA (1865–76). He was the editor of the *Monthly Religions Magazine* (1847–65). he famed hymn was first published on December 29, 1849 in *The Christian Register*. His most notable book was *The Fourth Gospel* (1872).

John B. Dykes

March 10, 1823 — Jan. 22, 1876
Kingston-Upon-Hall, England — Ticehurst, England

Composer of many hymns (about 300), including "Holy, Holy, Holy," 1861 (lyrics by REGINALD HEBER), "Lead Kindly Light," 1865 (lyrics by J. H. Newman), "Jesus the Very Thought of Thee," 1866 (lyrics by BERNARD OF CLAIRVAUX), "I Heard the Voice of Jesus Say" (lyrics by HORATIUS BONAR), and "The King of Love My Shepherd Is." At age ten, Dykes was the church organist at his grandfather's church. He ministered in Durham as precentor of Durham Cathedral, 1849–62, then served as the vicar of St. Oswald's in Durham (1862–76).

Henry B. Smith

Nov. 21, 1815 — Feb. 7, 1876
Portland, Maine — New York, New York

Eminent scholar and theologian. Smith was converted at a revival held at Bowdoin College, Brunswick, ME. On January 5, 1843, he married Elizabeth L. Allen and their union produced four children. Smith was a Congregational pastor of West Amesbury, MA from 1842–47, and then taught history and theology at Amherst College. In 1850, he joined the faculty of Union Theological Seminary of NYC, teaching church history (1850–55) and systematic theology (1855–74). He edited *The Presbyterian Review* (1862–71). He was a beloved leader of the New School of Presbyterianism, helping in its reunion of 1867. Smith also wrote several books, beginning with *The Relations of Faith and Philosophy* (1849). Some sources give the year 1877 as the year of his death.

James L. Breck

June 27, 1818
near Philadelphia, Pennsylvania

March 30, 1876
Benicia, California

Missionary and first dean of Nashotah House, 1842–50, also founder and first president of Seabury Divinity School, Fairbault, MN (Seabury-Western Theological Seminary, Evanston, IL), **1859–67**. Breck helped open the West to Episcopalianism, founding many churches, and effectively evangelizing the Indians. He moved to St. Paul, MN in 1850, working with the Chippewa Indians from 1855–59. He married Jane M. Mills on August 11, 1855, and Sarah Styles in 1864. He moved to Benicia, CA in 1867–76, working in schools he founded.

Samuel S. Wesley

Aug. 14, 1810
London, England

April 19, 1876
Gloucester, England

Greatest musical genius of the Wesley family (grandson to CHARLES WESLEY). Wesley served as organist at five parish churches and four cathedrals, including Hereford (1832–42), Exeter/Leeds (1842–49), Winchester (1850–65), and Gloucester (1865–death). In 1850, he was professor of organ at the Royal Academy of Music. Wesley sought to improve English cathedral music and was considered the outstanding organist of his time. He had six children. Wesley composed the music for the hymn, "The Church's One Foundation," plus 129 others.

Friedrich K. D. Wyneken

May 13, 1810
Verden, Germany

May 4, 1876
San Francisco, California

President of the Lutheran Church Missouri Synod, 1850–64. Home missionary development and organization was his ministry area. Wyneken came to America in 1838, and headed Lutheran home missions activities. He wrote *The Distress of the German Lutherans in North America*, which incited many noble men from Germany to migrate to the States. He was perhaps the first American pastor to condemn secret orders. He married Marie Buuck on August 31, 1841. They had 13 children. Wyneken died in the home of his son-in-law. His pastorates were in Baltimore (1850–59) and Cleveland (1864–75). He lived in Ft. Wayne, IN from 1859–64.

William B. Sprague

Oct. 16, 1795
Andover, Connecticut

May 7, 1876
Flushing, New York

Presbyterian pulpit orator who pastored the Second Presbyterian Church at Albany, NY from 1829–69. Sprague pastored the Congregational Church at West Springfield, MA from 1819–29. He spent the last seven years of his life in literary work, retiring to Flushing, Long Island. Sprague married Charlotte Eaton (Sept. 5, 1820); Mary Lathrop (Aug. 2, 1824); and Henrietta B. Lathrop (May 13, 1840), producing a total of ten children. He wrote the *American Pulpit Annals* in nine volumes (1857–69). He collected autographs, manuscripts, and pamphlets.

George Peck

Aug. 8, 1797
Middlefield, New York

May 20, 1876
Scranton, Pennsylvania

Methodist pastor who joined the Genesee (named after the western New York river with spectacular waterfalls) Conference in 1816. Peck was converted at age 15. He married May Myers on June 10, 1819, who gave him four children. Beginning in 1824, he filled the office of presiding elder for many years. Peck was principal of the Oneida (lake in central New York) Conference

Seminary (1835–40), editor of the *Methodist Journals* (1840–52), and then pastor in Pennsylvania (1852–73). Peck also wrote several books. He retired in 1873.

John Eadie

May 9, 1810
Alva, Scotland

June 3, 1876
Glasgow, Scotland

Pastor, professor, and commentator. From 1835–63, Eadie was pastor of the Cambridge Street Presbyterian Church of Glasgow. In 1863, he and several other church members left to form the new Lansdowne Church, serving until death. For 33 years, 1843–76, Eadie was a professor at the United Presbyterian Church Theological Seminary (United Secession Divinity Hall). His works range from *The Divine Lord* (1855) to *I Thessalonians* (pub. 1877). He was a New Testament scholar.

David Edwards

May 5, 1816
Denbigshire, Wales

June 6, 1876
Baltimore, Maryland

Bishop of the Church of the United Brethren in Christ (United Methodist Church in 1968), 1849–76. Edwards came to America in 1821, arriving in Baltimore. He married Lucretia Hibbard on December 10, 1839, and served as editor of *Religious Telescope* (1845–49), of *Unity Magazine* (1853–57), and *Sunday School Literature* (1854–57). He traveled widely, was a great prayer warrior and a forceful preacher. He helped establish Otterbein College, Westerville, OH.

Edmund W. Sehon

April 14, 1808
Hardy Co, Virginia

June 7, 1876
Bowling Green, Kentucky

Director of Methodist Church South (United Methodist Church in 1968) **Missions, 1850–68**. Sehon's parents helped train him for a law career, but the Lord changed his direction. He was married on September 4, 1833 to Carline McLane. He pastored in Kentucky, Tennessee, and St. Louis through 1850. After 1868, he continued to pastor in such places as Louisville and Bowling Green, KY. He died of heart trouble.

George D. Cummins

Dec. 11, 1822
near Smyrna, Delaware

June 26, 1876
Lutherville, Maryland

Reformed Episcopal Church founding bishop, 1873–76. Cummins was converted at a revival at Dickinson College, Carlisle, PA. He became a Methodist in 1841. He then became an Episcopalian rector in 1845. Alexandrine Balch became his wife on June 24, 1847. He served in several cities including Christ Church, Norfolk, VA (1847); St. James, Richmond, VA (1853); Trinity, Washington (1854); St. Peter's, Baltimore (1858); and Trinity, Chicago (1863). After 28 years, the emphasis on ritualism caused him to leave the Episcopal Church. On December 2, 1873, accompanied by eight clergy and twenty lay leaders, he organized the new Reformed Episcopal Church in New York City. He was the first bishop; upon his death at home, he was succeeded by CHARLES CHENEY.

George Smith (1)

March 26, 1840
Chelsea, London, England

Aug. 19, 1876
Aleppo, Turkey

Assyriologist (scholar of the history, language, and antiquities of ancient Assyria). Smith taught himself Oriental languages, and, in intervals of leisure, made a study of the Ninevite sculptures in the British Museum. His investigations attracted professional attention. Smith made three expeditions to Nineveh but was stricken with a fatal fever on his third trip. He deciphered the Chaldean account of the flood from Austen Layard's (1817–94) tablets (1872), and by excavations in Nineveh (1873), discovered missing fragments of the tablets revealing the duration of the Babylonian dynasties. Smith wrote many books on his work and was considered without equal in his field. He was stricken with fever at Ikisji and removed to the British consulate where he died.

Edmund S. Janes

April 27, 1807 *Sept. 18, 1876*
Sheffield, Massachusetts New York, New York

Bishop in the Methodist Episcopal Church, 1844–76. Janes pastored in New Jersey, Pennsylvania, and New York, 1830–44. He was elected financial secretary of the American Bible Society in 1840. Janes resigned to become a bishop in 1844 (last bishop to be elected by an undivided church), a position he held for 32 years. He was influential because of his wisdom, gentleness, and devotion. He passed away one month after his wife's death.

Edward F. Rimbault

June 13, 1816 *Sept. 26, 1876*
London, England London, England

Composer of the music for the hymn, "O Happy Day" (1854) (lyrics by PHILIP DODDRIDGE in 1735). Rimbault served as organist at several London churches including Swiss Church, Soho; St. Peter's Church, Vere Street; St. John's Wood Presbyterian; and St. Giles-in-the-Fields. He was a highly respected music scholar. He served as editor of the Motet Society and founded the Musical Antiquarian Society in 1840.

Johannes Rebmann

Jan. 16, 1820 *Oct. 4, 1876*
Gerlingen, Germany Kornthal, Germany

Missionary, linguist, and explorer in East Africa. Rebmann was appointed in 1846, by the Church Missionary Society to the East African Mission at Bombasa (southeast coast of Kenya) to assist JOHANN L. KRAPF. He married widowed teacher, Mrs. Tyler (died: 1866). Rebmann continued the work when KRAPF left and became the spiritual leader for tribes along the African coast. He served on the field for 29 years without a furlough, returning to Germany in 1875, blind and ill. He married another widow, Mrs. Flukh, just before he died. He translated Luke and John into Swahili.

John P. Durbin

Oct. 10, 1800 *Oct. 19, 1876*
near Paris, Kentucky Philadelphia, Pennsylvania

Methodist preacher. He was converted in 1811. He was an evangelist in Indiana and Ohio, 1818–25. Frances B. Cook became his wife on September 6, 1827. Durbin served as president of Dickinson College, Carlisle, PA from 1834–45. Durbin pastored in Philadelphia, PA from 1845–50. From 1850–72, he was secretary of the Missionary Society of the Methodist Episcopal Church. He wrote *Observations in Europe* (2 vols., 1844) and *Observations in the East* (2 vols., 1845) as a result of his travels for the mission board. Soon after being stricken with paralysis, he died.

Richard Fuller

April 22, 1804 *Oct. 20, 1876*
Beaufort, South Carolina Baltimore, Maryland

President of Southern Baptist Convention, 1859–61. He was the ninth child in his family and was converted in October, 1831, under evangelist DANIEL BAKER shortly after his marriage to Charlotte Bull in August. Fuller pastored in Beaufort, SC from 1832–47, where he had a spirited conflict with John England, Catholic bishop of Charleston, SC. He and 132 members of his church started Seventh Baptist Church, Baltimore, 1847–71, called Eutaw Place Baptist Church, 1871–76.

His church members in Baltimore were both Northern and Southern in their views; he sought to justify slavery by Scripture, debating FRANCIS WAYLAND of Brown University through the printed page. Fuller wrote several works, including *Baptists and Communion* (1849).

Melanchthon W. Jacobus

Sept. 19, 1816 — Oct. 28, 1876
Newark, New Jersey — Allegheny, Pennsylvania

Presbyterian pastor and educator. Jacobus was the pastor of the First Presbyterian Church in Brooklyn, NY (1839–50), and of the Central Presbyterian Church in Pittsburgh (1858–70). From 1851–76 he was a professor of Oriental and biblical literature at the Western Theological Seminary in Allegheny, PA. In 1848, Jacobus began publication of *Notes on the New Testament* (4 vols., 1849–59) and *Notes on the Book of Genesis* (2 vols., 1864–65).

James L. Nicholson

c 1828 — Nov. 6, 1876
Ireland — Washington, D.C.

Writer of the hymn, "Whiter Than Snow" (1872) (music by WILLIAM FISCHER). Nicholson came to America in the early 1850s and settled in Philadelphia (where he is buried). He was an active member of Wharton Street Methodist Episcopal Church. In 1871, Nicholson moved to Washington, where he worked as a clerk in the post office. He taught Sunday school, led in singing, and assisted in evangelism endeavors.

Albertus C. Van Raalte

Oct. 17, 1811 — Nov. 7, 1876
Wanneperveen, Netherlands — Holland, Michigan

Dutch Reformed Church leader, founder and first unofficial president of Hope College, Holland, MI 1851–65. He led until 1866, when the first official president (Phelps) was installed. As a young Dutch pastor, Van Raalte opposed the efforts by King William I (ruled: 1815–43) to bring the church under state control. Seven children came from his marriage to Christiana J. DeMoen on March 11, 1836. Van Raalte brought the Separatists (those who left the state church) to Michigan in 1847, initiating the Dutch religious influx to America. In 1850, some 13 churches formed the Reformed Church of America.

Simeon H. Calhoun

Aug. 15, 1804 — Dec. 14, 1876
Boston, Massachusetts — Buffalo, New York

Educational and evangelistic missionary to Syria, Greece, and Turkey. In his early years, Calhoun studied law. After his conversion (1831), while tutoring at Williams College (Williamstown, MA), he became an agent of the American Bible Society in Turkey and Greece (1837). In 1844, he was appointed a missionary under the ABCFM and subsequently under the Presbyterian Board to Syria. Calhoun served at the seminary at Abeih on the slopes in Lebanon. He married Emily Reynolds in 1846.

Philip P. Bliss

July 9, 1838 — Dec. 29, 1876
Rome, Pennsylvania — near Ashtabula, Ohio

Outstanding hymn writer. Bliss died at age 38, on his way to Chicago to join MOODY in meetings, when his train plunged through a trestle resulting in 92 deaths. It was a shocking and a premature loss to Christianity. His wife, Lucy J. Young, whom he married on June 1, 1859, died with him —both burned to death. Bliss was converted at age twelve. Early in his business career, he taught in Pennsylvania public schools, then became involved in the music business in Chicago with the Root and

Cady Company in 1865. He was music director and Sunday school superintendent for the First Congregational Church. Bliss became the music director for evangelist DANIEL WHITTLE in 1874. He wrote the lyrics and music to "Wonderful Words of Life," "Almost Persuaded," "Let the Lower Lights Be Burning," "Whosoever Will," "Hallelujah, What a Savior," "Hold the Fort," "Once for All," "The Light of the World," "Hallelujah, 'Tis Done," "Dare to Be a Daniel," and "Jesus Loves Even Me." He also wrote the words to "My Redeemer" and the music for "It Is Well With My Soul" (1876) and "I Gave Myself for Thee." He compiled several songbooks.

Sarah P. Haines Doremus

Aug. 3, 1802
New York, New York

Jan. 29, 1877
New York, New York

Founder and first president of the Woman's Union Missionary Society of America, 1861. Sarah married businessman, Thomas C. C. Doremus in 1821, and had nine children. She was a founder of the House and School of Industry (1850) and of a nursery and child's hospital (1854). Her work was the first of more than 40 female missionary agencies founded between 1860 and the turn of the century. In addition to foreign outreaches, Sarah was the first director of the Women's Prison Association. She was a tremendous humanitarian in helping the urban poor and downcast and was a worker in the Dutch Reformed Church. She was successful in enlisting the aid of other women in her causes.

Sir Henry W. Baker

May 27, 1820
Vauxhall, Surrey, England

Feb. 12, 1877
Monkland, Herefordshire, England

Baron and noted writer of over 33 hymns. Baker wrote "The King of Love My Shepherd Is" (paraphrase of Psalm 23) (music by s), "Sing Praise Ye the Lord", "Redeemed, Restored, Forgiven," and composed the music for "Art Thou Weary" (music by Stephen the Sabite). He was an Anglican vicar at Monkland, 1851–77. Baker was also editor-in-chief of the *Anglican Hymns Ancient and Modern* (1861), contributing many hymns, tunes and translations. More than any other person, Henry Baker influenced the singing of hymns in the Anglican community. Baker's dying words were from one of his hymns:

"Perverse and foolish oft I strayed,
But yet in love He sought me,
And on His shoulder gently laid,
And home, rejoicing, brought me."

John H. Stockton

April 19, 1813
New Hope, Pennsylvania

March 25, 1877
Philadelphia, Pennsylvania

Hymn writer and pastor. Stockton wrote the words and music for "Only Trust Him" (1874), and composed the music for "Glory to His Name" (lyrics by ELISHA HOFFMAN), and "The Great Physician" (lyrics by WILLIAM HUNTER). He was converted at a Methodist camp meeting at Paulsboro, NJ in the summer of 1832 and ordained shortly thereafter into the Methodist ministry. During his pastoring years, though in feeble health, Stockton devoted considerable time and energy to church music.

Alexander R. Reinagle

Aug. 21, 1799
Brighton, England

April 6, 1877
Kindlington, England

Musical writer and publisher. Reinagle composed music for "In Christ there is no East or West" (lyrics by JOHN OXENHAM). He was organist of St. Peter's-in-the-East, Oxford, England, 1822–53. *Psalm Tunes for the Voice and Pianoforte* was produced in 1830. He composed a considerable amount of music and published collections of hymn tunes in 1836 and 1840. Reinagle came from an extremely musical family.

William A. Muhlenberg

Sept. 16, 1796
Philadelphia, Pennsylvania

April 8, 1877
New York, New York

Episcopalian clergyman, poet, and philanthropist. As an infant, Muhlenberg was baptized a Lutheran, but as a young man, he joined the Episcopal Church. While a rector in Lancaster, PA from 1821–26, he wrote some of his best-known hymns. Muhlenberg also was the rector at a church in Flushing, Long Island, NY from 1826–46, and at the Free Church of the Holy Communion, New York City in 1846. He founded Fleesbury Institute, a boy's school (1828), and established St. Paul's College (1838). He founded the First Protestant sisterhood in the United States in 1852. He founded St. Luke's Hospital in New York City in 1858 and became its director. He never married. He was interested in greater liturgical freedom to evangelicals in the Episcopal Church.

William G. Brownlow

Aug. 29, 1805
Wythe County, Virginia

April 29, 1877
Knoxville, Tennessee

Methodist preacher, journalist, and governor of Tennessee. Orphaned at an early age, Brownlow eventually became a circuit-riding preacher in southern Appalachia. He often clashed with journalists, F. A. Ross, a Presbyterian, and J. R. GRAVES, a Baptist. In 1836, he married Eliza A. O'Brien. At the end of the Civil War, his staunch Unionism led to his appointment as governor of Tennessee, 1865–69. He edited the *Tennessee Whig* (1838–61), *Jonesboro Whig and Independent* (1839–49), and *Knoxville Whig*, (1849–61) then ended by confederate troops. His house in Knoxville was the last over which the Union flag was displayed. He was elected to the US Senate, serving to 1864–75. He opposed blacks voting and advocated a separate territory for them.

Lewis Tayler

March 27, 1802
Northumberland, New York

May 11, 1877
Albany, New York

Brilliant and profound scholar. Jane Keziah became his wife in 1833. In his early years, Tayler practiced law, then was called to be principal at Waterford, NY, followed by a professorship of Greek and Latin at the City University of New York City from 1838–50. In 1850, he accepted a professorship of Greek at Union College, Schenectady, NY. He authored several books on creation, science, and the Bible.

Friedrich A. G. Tholuck

March 30, 1799
Breslau, Prussia (Germany)

June 10, 1877
Halle, Prussia (Germany)

Theologian, evangelical professor at Halle University, 1826–77, for 51 years. Tholuck was converted through Baron von Kottwitz. He was briefly in Rome, 1827–29, as chaplain of the Prussian Embassy. He became the university's preacher (1835) and consistorial councilor (1867). Tholuck combined sanctity and scholarship in his preaching and teaching. He helped Halle turn from rationalism to evangelism. His Pietist leanings, his works and pastoral care marked him as an influential leader of his time. He wrote commentaries on John, Romans, and Hebrews.

Nathan L. Rice

Dec. 29, 1807
Garrard County, Kentucky

June 11, 1877
Chatham, Kentucky

Presbyterian clergyman and president of Westminster College, Fulton, MO 1869–74. Rice married Catherine P. Purch on October 3, 1832. He pastored in Bardstown, KY (1833–41); in Paris, KY (1841–44); Cincinnati, OH (1845–53); St. Louis (1853–57); Chicago (1857–61) and at 5th Avenue Presbyterian Church, NYC (1861–67). He was a professor of theology in Danville, KY from 1874–77. In 1843, Rice had his famous debate with ALEXANDER CAMPBELL (Disciples of Christ) on the subject of baptism. His life was devoted to pastoring, teaching, and editing, although he also debated JONATHAN BLANCHARD on slavery, E. Pingree on universal salvation, and J. B. Purcell on Romanism. His first book was *Romanism, the Enemy* (1851). He is buried in Fulton, MO.

Mary Carpenter

April 3, 1807
Exeter, England

June 14, 1877
Bristol, England

Philanthropist whose life was spent improving the criminal class. Mary organized reform schools for delinquent girls, founding Red Lodge in Bristol in 1829. She visited India four times from 1860–76 and the United States and Canada in 1873, in order to develop social improvement enterprises. Her biography was documented in *Life and Work* (1879).

Henry Rogers

Oct. 18, 1806
St. Albans, England

Aug. 20, 1877
Pennal Towers, North Wales

English essayist and writer. Early on, he pastored in Dorset (1829–32), lectured at Highbury College (1832–36), and taught at University College, London (1836–39). Rogers became professor of philosophy at the Independent College, Birmingham, 1839–58. In 1858, he served as principal of Manchester Independent College most of his remaining years. Rogers was an anti-tractarian and an anti-rationalist. He wrote *The Eclipse of Faith* (1852) and *The Superhuman Origin of the Bible Inferred from Itself*, plus some biographies.

William Hunter

May 26, 1811
near Ballymena, Ireland

Oct. 18, 1877
Cleveland, Ohio

Prolific hymn writer whose most noted work was "The Great Physician" (music by JOHN STOCKTON). Hunter's family came to America when he was six years old and settled in York, PA. He was ordained into the Methodist ministry and served in the Pittsburgh Conference. From 1844–52 and 1872–76, Hunter was editor of the *Christian Advocate*. He was a professor of Hebrew and Biblical literature at Allegheny (PA) College, 1855–70. Hunter wrote 125 hymns, forming three collections.

William E. Munsey

July 13, 1833
Bland County, Virginia

Oct. 23, 1877
Jonesboro, Tennessee

Pastor/evangelist of the Methodist Church, South. Munsey was converted at a camp meeting at age 17, and became a powerful preacher. On May 17, 1860, he married Virginia Blair. From 1858–69, Munsey ministered in Chattanooga, TN; Knoxville, TN; Abingdon, VA; Bristol, TN; Alexandria, VA; and Baltimore, MD. From 1869–75, he served in Jonesboro, TN and New Orleans, LA. His preaching on eternal death, a lost soul, and the resurrection was exceptional.

William H. Bathurst
Aug. 28, 1796
Clevedale (near Bristol), England

Nov. 25, 1877
Lydney Park, England

Hymnist who wrote, "O for a Faith that Will Not Shrink" (music by W. Havergal). Bathurst was rector of Barwick-in-Elmet, near Leeds, 1820–52. After struggling with the Anglican position on baptism and burial services as mandated in the *Book of Common Prayer,* Bathurst resigned his pastorate. In 1863, he became steward of his family estate and a representative for Bristol to Parliament. He authored *Hymns for Public and Private Use* (1830). Bathurst wrote in excess of 35 hymns, some of which were "O Lord Before Thy Mercy Seat, " "Holy Spirit from on High," and "O Give Thanks Unto the Lord."

George N. Allen
Sept. 7, 1812
Mansfield, Massachusetts

Dec. 9, 1877
Cincinnati, Ohio

Professor and founder of Oberlin Musical Association. Allen composed music for "Must Jesus Bear the Cross Alone" (THOMAS SHEPHERD wrote the first verse). Allen's musical education began through the public school system in Boston, MA under the instruction of LOWELL MASON. Allen had such a refined musical intellect that he became an instructor in the Science of Music while still a student at Oberlin (OH) College. In 1837, Allen established the Oberlin Musical Association, one of the first organizations of its type in America which was modeled after the trade guilds in Europe. After his graduation in 1838, he continued to teach music. By 1847, he added to his professorial schedule the subjects of geology and natural history, personal interests in which he greatly excelled. Allen taught at the college until his retirement in 1864. His work as a music educator laid the foundation for the Oberlin Conservatory of Music, which was established in 1865. He compiled the *Oberlin Social and Sabbath Hymn Book* (1844).

Chester G. Allen
1838

1878

Composed music for "Praise Him, Praise Him" (1869). Allen collaborated in compiling several collections of Sunday School songs, such as *Bright Jewels* (1869). He worked in New York with BRADBURY, DOANE, SHERWIN and CROSBY, who wrote the lyrics for the above.

James B. Mozley
Sept. 15, 1813
Gainsborough, England

Jan. 4, 1878
Oxford, England

Theologian and writer. From 1840–56, Mozley resided as a fellow of Magdalen College, after which he became vicar at Old Shoreham, Sussex. He was the Bampton lecturer in 1865, and is remembered for his lectures on the "Miracles." He was made a canon of Worcester in 1869 and a Regius professor [professors of Oxford and Cambridge whose chairs were founded by Henry VIII (ruled: 1509–47)] of divinity at Oxford from 1871–death. Mozley was an independent Anglican. He wrote works ranging from *The Influence of Ancient Oracles* (1836) to *Lectures and Other Theological Papers* (1883).

Alexander Duff
April 26, 1806
Auchnahyle, Moulin, Scotland

Feb. 12, 1878
Sidmouth, Edinburgh, Scotland

Outstanding Presbyterian missionary (first missionary of the Church of Scotland to India) who went to Calcutta, India, 1830–34, 1840–49, and 1857–64. Duff married, and later joined the Free Church in 1843. His English school grew into a missionary college, and Duff gained acceptance by the upper-class Hindus, traveling widely, and advising mission schools and governmental educational departments. In addition to Christian doctrine, he taught English, literature, and science. He visited the United States (1854) and South Africa (1863). In 1864, he retired for health reasons, but he remained active by teaching evangelistic theology at the New College in Edinburgh, 1867–78, and giving rousing challenges in support of missions. He founded the *Calcutta Review* (1844) and aided in establishing the University of Calcutta. He wrote *The India Mutiny* (1858) among others.

"We can give without loving, but not love without giving."

George G. Scott

July 13, 1811
Gawcott, England

March 27, 1878
London, England

Prominent church architect. Scott was a successful exponent of the Gothic revival style. In 1838, he designed his first church, St. Giles in Camberwell, London. Scott also worked on the Martyr's Memorial at Oxford in 1841. He restored cathedrals at Ely, Hereford, Salisbury, and Gloucester. In 1849, Scott was appointed architect to Westminster Abbey, and was later buried in the nave of this famous church. In 40 years, he built or started 500 churches, 39 cathedrals, and 25 universities/colleges. Scott wrote several books on the history of religious architecture, many published posthumously. He was the grandson of famed English clergyman, Thomas Scott.

George A. Selwyn

April 5, 1809
Church Row, England

April 11, 1878
Lichfield, England

Missionary and first Anglican bishop in New Zealand. Selwyn was appointed the first missionary bishop of New Zealand and Melanesia in 1841. He founded the Melanesian mission, using his own vessel, the *Southern Cross*. His heroic and inventive methods won him wide respect and influence on church growth. Selwyn enlisted several people to become missionaries, including JOHN PATTESON and CHARLES MCKENZIE. He returned to England (1867), and became a Lichfield bishop (1868). Selwyn College was established at Cambridge University in 1882, in his memory. His wife's name was Sarah.

William Whiting

Nov. 1, 1825
Kensington, London, England

May 3, 1878
Winchester, England

Wrote the hymns, "Eternal Father, Strong to Save" and "Now the Billows, Strong and Dark." For over 35 years, Whiting was a master of Winchester College Chorister's School, 1842–78. Whiting published *Rural Thoughts and Other Poems* (1851), and wrote other poetry as well as hymns.

Joseph Henry

Dec. 17, 1797
Albany, New York

May 13, 1878
Washington, D.C.

Secretary and chief executive of the Smithsonian Institute in Washington. He invented the electromagnet, 1827–31, several years before the days of the telegraph. He married Harriet Alexander in May, 1830. Henry was reared in the local First Presbyterian Church and began serving this post in December of 1846. The institution soon served the nation and the world by the discoveries that it made. He contributed nearly 100 articles and monographs on scientific subjects. He wrote, "…that the power and love of God are brought into relation with the weakness and sinfulness of man in the Lord Jesus Christ—of these great truths I have no doubt…Upon him [Christ] I'll rest my faith and hope." His funeral was attended by dignitaries from across the nation. The henry is a unit of electrical inductance.

The Saints Go Marching In

Knowles Shaw

Oct. 13, 1845
Venice, Ohio

June 7, 1878
McKinney, Texas

Evangelist and songwriter. Shaw wrote the hymn, "Bringing in the Sheaves" (music by GEORGE MINOR). He was converted in 1852, and after teaching school for a few years, began preaching. He became an evangelist and was known for his singing as well as his preaching. He saw some 11,400 converted in his 19 years of evangelism. In 1874, he served as pastor of the Christian Church, Chicago, IL. He lived in Rushville, IN. Shaw was killed when the train on which he was traveling derailed.

Adolph C. Preus

June 29, 1814

June 8, 1878
Trondhjem, Norway

President of Norwegian Synod (ALC, ELCA in 1988), **1853–62**. Preus came to America in 1850 and pastored in Koshkoning, WI from 1850–60. He married Engel Brun in 1850 (died: 1860) and Martha Adland in 1861 (died: 1900). He was one of three pastors who organized the NS in 1851. He organized two churches: Our Saviour's, in Chicago, 1860–63 and Coon Prairie, WI from 1863–72. He went to Norway in 1872 and pastored in Holt, Ostre Nedenes (1872–78) and was provost there (1874–78).

Charles Hodge

Dec. 27, 1797
Philadelphia, Pennsylvania

June 19, 1878
Princeton, New Jersey

Leading Presbyterian theologian who spent over 50 years lecturing in biblical studies at Princeton Seminary. Hodge taught 3,000 students there. Converted during a revival at Princeton while just a student from 1815–19, Hodge began teaching (1820) and continued until his death. He was an instructor (1820–22), professor of Oriental and Biblical Literature (1822–40), and of theology (1840–78). He married Sarah Bache in 1822, and had eight children. After her death, he married Mary Stockton in 1852. For over 40 years, he served as the editor of *Biblical Repertory* (Princeton Review) (1836–78). His main work was the three-volume *Systematic Theology* (1872–73). Hodge was an able defender of the Reformed faith. His son was ARCHIBALD HODGE. His commentary on Romans is outstanding.

Catherine Winkworth

Sept. 13, 1827
Holborn, London, England

July 1, 1878
Monnetier, France

Regarded as one of the best hymn translators from German. Catherine translated many hymns to the English language, including "Now Thank We All our God" (1858) and "Praise Ye the Lord, the Almighty." She settled in Clifton, England in 1862, and worked to promote higher education for women. She lived most of her life in Manchester. She was a devoted member of the Church of England. She authored *Lyra Germanica* (2 vols., 1855–58).

John D. Lang

Aug. 25, 1799
Greenock, Scotland

Aug. 8, 1878
Sydney, Australia

Remarkable political and spiritual leader in Australia. Lang was the first minister of the Church of Scotland in Australia. He edited several secular newspapers. He founded the Scots Church in Sydney in 1823, and many emigrants came to the new colonies through his efforts. Lang was in a position of political leadership, and many attended his graveside service.

Elizabeth Payson Prentiss

Oct. 26, 1818
Portland, Maine

Aug. 13, 1878
Dorset, Vermont

Presbyterian author (novelist and juvenile writer) who wrote the hymn, "More Love to Thee, O Christ" (music by WILLIAM DOANE), in 1869. Elizabeth was the daughter of EDWARD PAYSON. She married George L. Prentiss in April, 1845, and they had at least one child and moved to New Bedford, MA. He was a Congregationalist pastor who later taught at Union Theological Seminary, New York City. She wrote more than 20 books with wide sales, her most famous being, *Stepping Heavenward* (1869). She was sickly much of her life and died at her summer home.

Julius Muller

April 10, 1801
Breig, Silesia (Germany)

Sept. 27, 1878
Halle, Germany

Lutheran theologian. Muller taught theology and pedagogy at Gottingen University (1831–35), then taught dogmatics at Marburg University (1835–39). He opposed the rationalistic tendencies of the day and took a stand on the immutable Bible. From 1839–78, he taught theology at Halle. Muller authored *The Christian Doctrine of Sin* (1839). He was a defender of the Prussian Union.

John E. Vassar
Uncle John Vassar

Jan. 13, 1813
Poughkeepsie, New York

Dec. 6, 1878
Poughkeepsie, New York

One of the great personal soul winners and Christian workers of all time. Vassar was a former Poughkeepsie, NY brewery worker and was converted at LaFayette Street Church. He married Mary Lee in 1838 and joined the church on April 3, 1842. He was engaged in revival crusade works from 1850 on. His ministry was nationwide in army camps, to miners, Mormons, blacks, settlers, and mountaineers. Thousands were converted through "Uncle John." He worked with the American Tract Society and the Duchess County Baptist Association in New York. He organized Sunday Schools among the troops in the Civil War. His last words were "Farewell…Hallelujah."

Dorothy Wyndlow Pattison
Sister Dora

Jan. 16, 1832
Hauxwell, England

Dec. 24, 1878
Walsall, England

Social worker. Dorothy, a genteel English lady, left the comforts of her father's home to join the Church of England's "Sisterhood of the Good Samaritans." Her dedicated efforts soon earned her the familiar name of "Sister Dora." In 1865, she went to the Cottage Hospital at Walsall, where she labored with success. Illness overtook her in 1876, and she died of cancer.

Abraham B. Hasbrouck

Nov. 29, 1791
Kingston, New York

Feb. 23, 1879
Kingston, New York

President of Rutgers University and New Brunswick (NJ) Theological Seminary, 1841–50. Hasbrouck married Julia Ludlum on Sept. 12, 1819. He was admitted to the New York Bar in 1818 and became a member of the U.S. House of Representatives from New York, serving in the 19th Congress from 1825–27. In 1831, he became the president of the Ulster County (NY) Bank. He was also the first president of the Ulster Historical Society in 1859.

Howard Malcom

Jan. 19, 1799
Philadelphia, Pennsylvania

March 25, 1879
Philadelphia, Pennsylvania

President of Georgetown (KY) College, 1840–49. He married Lydia Shields (May 1, 1820) and Ruth Dyer (June 26, 1838), and they had five children. Malcom was a Baptist pastor in Hudson, NY (1820–26); Boston, MA (1827–35); and Philadelphia, PA (1849–51). Malcom was the founder of the American Tract Society and of the American Sunday School Union, 1826–27. He was also a representative of Baptist Missionary Society, 1835–38, traveling widely around the world. He served as the president of Bucknell University, Lewisburg (PA) from 1851–57, and Hahnemann Medical College, Philadelphia, 1874–79. He wrote *Nature and Extent of the Atonement* (1829) to *Travels in Southeastern Asia* (1839).

Edward R. Ames

May 20, 1806
near Amesville, Ohio

April 25, 1879
Baltimore, Maryland

Methodist Episcopal Church bishop, 1852–79. In 1830, Ames became an evangelist in the Indiana Conference. He was also the correspondence secretary of the Missionary Society for the South and the West in 1840. Ames also served as presiding elder from 1844–52. President LINCOLN consulted with him and gave him several special commissions. Ames strongly opposed slavery. He traveled over 25,000 miles for home missions. He said as he died, "When I can do no more work, I care not how soon I die. All right." His birthplace was named for his father.

Sarah J. Buell Hale

Oct. 24, 1788
Newport, New Hampshire

April 30, 1879
Philadelphia, Pennsylvania

Magazine editor whose persistent efforts made Thanksgiving Day a national holiday. Sarah finally persuaded President LINCOLN in 1863 to issue the official proclamation. Sarah married David Hale (died 1822) in October, 1813 and was left with five children. She lived in Boston (1828–41) and in Philadelphia (1841–79). She was active in world missions organizations. She was one of the first women magazine editors in America, editing *Ladies Magazine* (1828–37), Boston, MA and then *Godey's Lady's Book* (1837–77), Philadelphia, PA. One of her poems was "Mary's Lamb."

Samuel Gobat

Jan. 26, 1799
Cremines, Switzerland

May 11, 1879
Jerusalem, Palestine

Missionary to Abyssinia (Ethiopia). Gobat visited Paris and London (1823) to learn Arabic, Ethiopic, and Amharic, and was then sent by the London Missionary Society to the field (1826). Gobat ministered in Egypt and Syria but jumped at the opportunity to go to Abyssinia (Ethiopia) when it opened to missionaries, 1830–36. While he was there from 1830–39, he translated the Bible into Arabic. He married Maria Zellerin in 1833/34. From 1839–46, he was in Malta, printing it. In 1845, Gobat, a Lutheran up to this time, was ordained in the Anglican Church. In 1846, he became the bishop of Jerusalem and founded schools and hospitals throughout the nation. He left behind 37 Palestinian schools, with a combined enrollment of 1,400 students, and 12 churches.

William L. Garrison

Dec. 10, 1805
Newburyport, Massachusetts

May 24, 1879
New York, New York

Social reformer, journalist, abolitionist, and first advocate for freedom for slaves. On July 4, 1829, in Boston's Park St. Church, Garrison delivered his first public speech against slavery. He visited England (1833), founded the *Liberator* (1835), the foremost anti-slavery journal, and served as editor until 1865. Garrison married Helen Benson on September 4, 1834, and they had seven children. A riot against abolitionists in Boston on October 21, 1835, nearly ended his life. He burned the Constitution at Framingham, MA on July 4, 1854. Garrison was opposed to war, alcohol, debt imprisonment, and prostitution, and he advocated suffrage for women and Indians. When orthodox churches showed indifference, he turned to unorthodox groups, such as spiritualism. At his burial, Wendell Phillips said, "William Garrison was the noblest of Christians, a leader, brave, tireless, unselfish." He is buried in Boston.

Johannes A. A. Grabau

March 18, 1804
Ovenstedt, Germany

June 2, 1879
Buffalo, New York

President of Buffalo Synod (ALC, ELCA in 1988), **1845–79**, which originated in Milwaukee, WI. Grabau was a Lutheran pastor, editor, and teacher, who opposed the union of Lutheran and Reformed doctrine. He married Christine Burggraf on July 15, 1834, and they had three children. He was arrested for his beliefs (opposed the United Church of Prussia) as he served St. Andrew's Church, Erfurt, 1834–39. Grabau immigrated to America in 1839. He founded the Martin Luther Seminary, Buffalo, NY in 1840. He served the Trinity Lutheran Church, Buffalo, NY, for nearly 40 years, gaining 1,000 members. The Prussians formed the Buffalo Synod in 1845. In 1930, the Buffalo Synod merged with the Ohio and Iowa Synods to form the American Lutheran Church.

Frances R. Havergal

Dec. 14, 1836
Astley, England

June 3, 1879
Swansea, Caswall Bay, Wales

Hymn writer and one of history's most devoted women. Frances was converted at age 15 through the witness of Miss Cooke, who became her stepmother. She knew five languages—English, French, German, Italian and Latin, and read the Bible in its original languages, Greek and Hebrew. Frances sang, composed music, played the piano, was active in Sunday School, and helped the poor. She was often in poor health and was very frail. She wrote several hymns, including "True-Hearted" (STEBBINS), "I Gave My Life for Thee," 1858 (BLISS), "Like a River Glorious," 1874 (MOUNTAIN), "Take My Life, and Let It Be," 1874 (MALAN), "Lord, Speak to Me" (SCHUMANN), and "Who Is on the Lord's Side?" (REICHARDT). She contributed to *Good Words* and other English journals. Frances' writings ranged from *The Ministry of Song* (1870) to *Poetical Works* (pub. 1884). *Kept for the Master's Use* is her best known work. She died of peritonitis.

Henry T. Smart

Oct. 26, 1813
London, England

July 6, 1879
London, England

Composed music for "Lead on O King Eternal" (lyrics by ERNEST SHURTLEFF) **and "Angels from the Realms of Glory" (1867)** (lyrics by JAMES MONTGOMERY). Smart was an excellent organist of his time, serving at Blackburn, Lancashire; Regent Street, London; St. Luke's Church, Old Street, (1844–64); and at St. Pacras Church, London (1865–79). Smart totally lost his eyesight in 1865. He wrote many pieces of music and was an authority on organs.

Joseph Mullens

Sept. 2, 1820
London, England

July 10, 1879
Chacombe, German East Africa

Missionary and secretary of the London Missionary Society. Mullens labored as a missionary in India, 1843–58. From 1858–72, he remained active in the LMS in England. He visited America and Madagascar in 1873–74. On his way to Ujiji, he became ill and died. His mission's interest in Africa took place in his later years.

Daniel Drew

July 29, 1797
Carmel, New York

Sept. 18, 1879
New York, New York

Methodist capitalist. In early life, Drew was a cattle driver and dealer. He was subsequently prominent as a steamboat builder, but was most widely known from his connection with railroads and as a leading stock speculator on Wall Street. Drew married Roxana Mead in 1832. In midlife, he joined the Methodist Church. The failure of Kenyon, Cox, and Company, caused the loss of his great fortune, which at one time was about 15 million dollars. He suffered complete financial ruin as a result of the Depression of 1873, and went bankrupt in 1876. However, he founded Drew Theological Seminary at Madison, NJ; the Drew Ladies' Seminary; and built the Methodist Church, Carmel, besides aiding several other church enterprises. He was a relentless business manipulator of the stock market, but lived correctly and tried to do good with all that he possessed.

Joseph P. Thompson

Aug. 7, 1819
Philadelphia, Pennsylvania

Sept. 20, 1879
Berlin, Germany

Congregational pastor of Broadway Tabernacle of New York City 1845–71. Thompson pastored at Chapel Street Church, New Haven, CT from 1840–45. He married Lucy O. Bartlett on May 5, 1841. After her death, he married Elizabeth C. Gilman on October 25, 1853. They had six children. He exerted a wide influence as a preacher, writer, and advocate of philanthropic enterprises. Thompson was also an authority on Egyptology. He retired to Germany in 1871 for health reasons.

Jacob Abbott

Nov. 14, 1803
Hallowell, Maine

Oct. 31, 1879
Farmington, Maine

Popular writer for the young who, as an educator, taught for many years while devoting his life to literary work. Jacob Abbott was a professor at Amherst, MA (1825–29); established the Mt. Vernon Girls' School in Boston (1827–33); and pastored the Eliot Church in Roxbury (1834–35). Abbott married Harriet Vaughan on May 18, 1829, and, after her death, married Mary D. Woodbury in 1853. He was the father of well-known LYMAN ABBOTT. In 1839, he moved to Farmington and wrote extensively. Abbott was a Congregationalist. He co-authored 31 literary works and authored 180 other volumes, including the widely read *Rollo Books* (28 vols), and many other stories for children, 1834 on. His most well-known work was *The Young Christian* (1832).

Lovick Pierce

March 17, 1785
Halifax County, North Carolina

Nov. 9, 1879
Sparta, Georgia

Outstanding leader in the Methodist Church, South. Pierce was converted by a circuit riding preacher in 1804. He married Ann Foster on Sept. 28, 1809 and served as chaplain in the War of 1812. He withdrew from the conference after the war to practice medicine in Greensboro, GA until 1821. In 1822, he rejoined the Methodist Conference and served as a member of every General Conference until his death. He preached at least 11,000 times, 1824–79. His son, George Pierce (1811–84), was also a famed Southern Methodist preacher.

Charles F. Schaeffer

Sept. 3, 1807
Germantown, Pennsylvania

Nov. 23, 1879
Philadelphia, Pennsylvania

First president and professor at Lutheran Theological Seminary at Philadelphia, 1864–78. Schaeffer married Susanna Schumucker on Aug. 27, 1832; they had five children. He pastored in Carlisle, PA (1829–34); and Hagerstown, MD (1834–39); taught at Lancaster, OH (1840–43); Capital University in Columbus, OH (1843–45); Red Hook, NY (1845–51); Easton, PA (1851–55); and was professor of German at Pennsylvania College in Gettysburg (1855–64). He wrote commentaries on Matthew, and revised many German works.

Robert Jamieson

1802
Edinburgh, Scotland

1880

Presbyterian preacher who, along with A. R. FAUSSETT and DAVID BROWN, prepared the well-known *Commentary on the Bible*. Jamieson served seven years at Weststruther, then seven years at Currie St., Edinburgh. He sought to prevent the schism of 1843, but took the evangelical side when it happened. In 1844, he became the pastor of St. Paul's Free Church, Glasgow, serving there until his death.

Gilbert Haven

Sept. 19, 1821
Malden, Massachusetts

Jan. 3, 1880
Malden, Massachusetts

Bishop of the Methodist Church. Haven joined the New England Conference in 1851 and held prominent positions. He was converted during student days at Wesleyan Academy in Wilbraham, MA. He married Mary Ingraham in 1851 (died: 1860) and they had two children. He pastored in five locations (1851–61), lived in Europe (1861–62) and pastored at North Russell St. Church, Boston, MA (1863–67) and served as the editor of *Zion's Herald* (1867–72). Once he became bishop (1872), he headquartered in Atlanta, helped plant Methodism in Mexico (1873), and took a trip to Liberia (1876), where he contracted malaria, which eventually killed him. Haven was a friend of the black race and advocated civil rights. His writings range from *The Pilgrim's Wallet* (1866) to *Christus Consolator* (pub. 1893).

James Lenox

Aug. 19, 1800
New York, New York

Feb. 17, 1880
New York, New York

President of American Bible Society, 1864–71. Lenox, a philanthropist, was a partner in his father's real estate firm. He assembled one of the best collections of Bibles in America. He donated land for a Presbyterian hospital and a home for aged women, contributing over $12,000 to charities (mostly Presbyterian) in his lifetime. Lenox never married.

Jeremiah B. Jeter

July 18, 1802
Bedford County, Virginia

Feb. 18, 1880
Richmond, Virginia

Southern Baptist minister of great influence. Converted during a revival in 1821, Jeter married Margaret Waddy (October 5, 1826); Sarah A. Gaskins (December, 1828); Charlotte E. Warton (June, 1849); and Mary C. Dabbs (May 5, 1863). He spent most of his life in Richmond, VA, pastoring at FBC (1836–49) where 1,384 of the 1,717 members were black, at Second Baptist, St. Louis (1849–52), and at Grace St. Church, Richmond (1852–70). Jeter was the first president of the Foreign Mission Board of the SBC from 1845–49. Jeter was the editor of *Religious Herald* (1865–80) and refuted ALEXANDER CAMPBELL in his *Campbellism Examined* (1855).

Johann C. Blumhardt

July 16, 1805
Stuttgart, Germany

Feb. 25, 1880
Bad Boll, Germany

Evangelist whose preaching drew large crowds with miraculous healings. Blumhardt was a teacher at the missionary institution at Basel, 1830–38. He pastored in Mottlingen in Wurtemberg, 1838–52. He was the first healing evangelist of note. Blumhardt spent the latter part of his life, 1852 on, at Bad Boll, near Goppingen. There, he was instrumental in developing a center for missionary work and for victims of all kinds of illnesses. He purchased the royal watering place, and sufferers from all ranks of society and many countries flocked there to be cured.

Alfred Saker

July 21, 1814
Bourough Green, England

March 13, 1880
England

Founded Baptist Missionary Society in the Cameroons. Saker was converted at age 16, then in 1843, went to West Africa. He married Helen Jessup in 1840 and founded Bethel Station in Douala country (1845), with the baptism of his first convert (1849). Saker translated the New Testament into Douala (1862); then he completed the Old Testament translation (1868); with the complete Bible published (1872). In 1876, he retired to England in failing health, having labored for 32 years, opening the Cameroon mission field.

Alexander Raleigh

Jan. 3, 1817
Kirckchudright, Scotland

April 19, 1880
London, England

Independent minister and author who first ministered in Greenock, Scotland, (1844); then at Rotherham, England (1850–55); at Glasgow, Scotland (1855–59); and at London (1859–80). Raleigh was twice elected chairman of the Congregational Union. His chief works were *Quiet Resting Places* (1863), *The Story of Jonah*, *The Little Sanctuary and Other Meditations*, and *Thoughts for the Weary*. His last published work was *From Dawn to the Perfect Day* (1883).

William Hanby

April 18, 1808
Washington County, Pennsylvania

May 17, 1880
Westerville, Ohio

Bishop of the Church of United Brethren in Christ (United Methodist Church in 1968), 1845–80. Hanby served as editor and abolitionist. He was converted in the home of SAMUEL MILLER, whose daughter, Anne, he married in 1830. He became publishing agent for the denomination in 1837, in Circleville, OH and served as the pastor there from 1853 on. Hanby was editor of the *Religious Telescope* (c. 1840–45 and 1849–53).

Rufus Anderson

Aug. 17, 1796
North Yarmouth, Maine

May 30, 1880
Boston, Massachusetts

Corresponding secretary (CEO) of American Board of Commissioners for Foreign Missions (UCBWM in 1961), 1840–66. Anderson began as assistant secretary in 1826. He was successful as an administrator and wrote several volumes on mission work. He traveled the world, 1819–63, on various mission trips and gained a reputation as an outstanding missionary authority, as well as a devoted Congregationalist. He married Eliza Hill on January 8, 1827, and their union produced five children. Anderson wrote a five-volume reference work entitled *Missions History of the American Board* (1872).

Henry A. Boardman

Jan. 9, 1808
Troy, New York

June 15, 1880
Philadelphia, Pennsylvania

Famed Presbyterian pastor of the Tenth Presbyterian Church in Philadelphia, 1833–76, and pastor emeritus until his death. Boardman was a member of the board of directors of Princeton Seminary, 1835–80. His published works included *The Scriptural Doctrine of Original Sin* (1839), *The Bible in the Counting House* (1854), and *Sanctification Tried by the Word of God*.

Justus Doolittle

June 23, 1824
Rutland, New York

June 15, 1880
Clinton, New York

Presbyterian missionary to China, 1849–1869, 1872–73 who reached the cities of Foochow, Tientsin, and Shanghai. Doolittle wrote *The Social Life of the Chinese* (2 vols., 1816) and *Vocabulary and Handbook of the Chinese Languages* (2 vols.).

Samuel R. Brown

June 16, 1810
East Windsor, Connecticut

June 20, 1880
Monson, Massachusetts

Presbyterian missionary to China and Japan who also went to Macao (Portuguese island off China near Hong Kong) (1838) and then to Hong Kong (1843). Elizabeth Bartlett became his wife on October 10, 1838. Brown opened the first Protestant school in Canton, in 1847, then went back to New York, where he pastored and taught at Rome, (1848–51) and Elmira (1851–59). In 1859, he went to Japan for the Dutch Reformed Church pioneering education work there. He also helped establish the first Japanese Protestant congregation in Yokohama in 1872. The first Protestant seminary in Japan (Meiji Gakuin in Tokyo) began in his home in 1878. He pastored and translated until 1879. He wrote the first grammar of *Colloquial Japanese* (1863).

Barnas Sears

Nov. 19, 1802
Sandisfield, Masachusetts

July 6, 1880
Saratoga Springs, New York

President of Newton (MA) (Andover-Newton in 1931) **Theological Seminary, 1839–48** and professor of theology, 1836–on. Sears pastored a Baptist church in Hartford, CT (1829–31) and then became professor of ancient languages at the Theological Institute (Colgate University in 1890) Hamilton, NY from 1831–33. Five children came from his marriage to Elizabeth G. Carey on July 6, 1830. He helped form a German Baptist Church in Europe. He became president of Brown University, Providence, RI from 1855–67. He was general agent of the Peabody Educational Fund, 1867–80 and edited the *Christian Review* for the same years. He is buried in Brookline, MA.

William A. Hallock

June 2, 1794
Plainfield, Massachusetts

Oct. 2, 1880
New York, New York

First general secretary of American Tract Society, 1825–70. Hallock was editor of the *American Messenger* (1830–70) and prepared a large number of tracts for the press. He also edited the *Child's Paper* for 25 years. Fanny L. Lathrop became his first wife on September 1, 1829 and Mrs. Mary Lathrop was his second. His writings range from *A Memoir of Harlan Page* (1835) to *The Hallock Ancestry* (1866).

William Bruce

March 9, 1828
Scotland

Nov. 10, 1880
Xenia, Ohio

President of Xenia (OH) (Pittsburgh Theological in 1959) **Seminary, 1871–80.** Bruce graduated from Franklin College in 1850, studied theology at Canonsburg, was licensed in September 1853, by Richard Presbytery and ordained on April 26, 1855 by the Philadelphia Presbytery. He was professor of didactic theology at Xenia from October, 1874 until his death. He was moderator of the General Assembly of 1879.

Lucretia Coffin Mott

Jan. 3, 1793
Nantucket, Massachusetts

Nov. 11, 1880
near Philadelphia, Pennsylvania

Quaker, reformer, and founder of the Women's Rights Movement in America, 1848. Lucretia married James Mott on April 10, 1811, and they had six children. She became a minister in 1821 and, with Elizabeth Stanto, held a women's rights convention in 1848 at Seneca Falls, NY. This meeting put the women's rights issues clearly before the public. Her message spread rapidly through her writings and lecturing. Lucretia was also an active abolitionist and one who participated in universal peace issues. In 1833, she founded the American Anti-Slavery Society. In 1850, she turned her home into a refuge for runaway slaves. In 1869, she gave the dedicatory address at the founding of Swarthmore (PA) College.

William F. Lehmann

Oct. 16, 1820
Wurtemberg, Germany

Dec. 1, 1880
Columbus, Ohio

President of Capital University (Trinity Lutheran Seminary in 1978), **Columbus, OH 1857–88, and of Ohio Synod** (ALC, ELCA in 1988), **1854–60, 1878–80.** Lehmann was a Lutheran pastor, professor, and editor who came to America in 1824. When the Ohio Synod broke from the Missouri Synod, he became its leader. For 30 years, he pastored the Trinity Church, Columbus, OH after a smaller pastorate from 1840–46.

Henry (Harry) Moorhouse

Sept. 27, 1840
Manchester, England

Dec. 27, 1880
Manchester, England

Great evangelist. Moorhouse challenged D. L. MOODY to combine Bible study with his preaching. Upon his conversion at age 21, he began to distribute tracts and to actively win souls. His conversion was amazing. In a cheap Manchester rooming house, he was about to commit suicide when he heard someone read the story of the Prodigal Son. Three days later, he was led to Christ. He fervently preached in the streets and marketplaces. Moorhouse made four trips to America. On one such mission in 1868, he preached in MOODY's Chicago Church on John 3:16 each night for a week. Moorhouse's teaching/preaching style is said to have constructively changed D. L. MOODY's preaching.

Edward A. Washburn

April 16, 1819
Boston, Massachusetts

Feb. 2, 1881
New York, New York

Episcopal pastor of Calvary Church of New York City 1865–81. Washburn was an eminent scholar, writer, and preacher of great power. He married Frances Lindsey on June 16, 1853, and they had one daughter. Prior to settling in New York, Washburn pastored in Newburyport, MA; Hartford, CT; and at St. Mark's of Philadelphia. His writings began with *The Social Law of God* (1875) and ended with *The Beatitudes* (1884).

Johann H. Wichern

April 21, 1808
Hamburg, Germany

April 7, 1881
Hamburg, Germany

Founder of the Inner Mission, 1848, in Wittenberg at an Evangelical Church Congress sponsored by the German Evangelical church. Wichern's work was among the children who were forced to survive in the worst corners of the city. In November of 1833, he opened a correction center for juvenile offenders. Other associated facilities followed, such as a second institution in Berlin in 1858. He was commissioned by the Prussian Goverment to suggest penal improvements. Many church and state honors were bestowed upon him for his efforts to care for those who were victims of a very imperfect and treacherous German society.

William M. Punshon

May 29, 1824
Doncaster, England

April 14, 1881
London, England

Wesleyan Methodist minister. Punshon served from 1849–67 as pastor in New Castle-on-Tyne, Sheffield, Leeds, London, and Bristol. During the period of 1867–73, he presided over General Conferences in Canada, while pastoring the Metropolitan Church of Toronto. He also served as secretary of the Wesleyan Missionary Society, 1875–81, after returning to England in 1873.

Benjamin Disraeli

Dec. 21, 1804
London, England

April 19, 1881
Beaconsfield, London, England

Conservative prime minister and first Lord Beaconsfield, Disraeli was a renowned statesman and novelist. He was a member of Parliament from 1837–80, some 43 years. In 1839, he married Wyndham Lewis (died: 1872), the widow of a politican. He and WILLIAM GLADSTONE alternated as prime ministers, Disraeli serving in 1868 and from 1874–80. He annexed the Fiji Islands and the Transvall, waged war with the Afghans and Zulus, and had Queen VICTORIA crowned empress of India in 1876. He is the author of *Conigsby* (1844), *Sybil* (1855), and other novels. A baptized convert from Judaism on July 31, 1817, he did much to advocate the cause of Jewish evangelism. He wore evening dress when writing his books.

Stephen Paxson

Nov. 3, 1808
New Lisbon, Ohio

April 22, 1881
St. Louis, Missouri

American Sunday School Union missionary. Paxson was an Illinois farmer born with a speech impediment. At age 30, his daughter asked him to go to Sunday school to help win a prize. This led to his conversion. Soon he was traveling throughout the midwest teaching, counseling, preachin, and distributing literature, books, and Bibles. He kept a list of 83,000 children he helped to start attending Sunday school. He started Sunday schools in log cabins, tobacco barns, taverns, and dance halls. In 30 years of labor, he started 1,314 new Sunday Schools.

Joseph J. Clinton

Oct. 3, 1823
Philadelphia, Pennsylvania

May 24, 1881
Atlantic City, New Jersey

Bishop of African Methodist Episcopal Zion Church, 1856–81; senior bishop, 1868–81. Clinton was converted at age 15, and licensed to preach at age 17. Clinton became an evangelist (1843), and was ordained as an elder (known as bishop) (1856). Under his guidance, eleven annual conferences were organized. He supervised the work of many missionaries to the South. His wife, Letitia Sosco Clinton, passed away on September 23, 1893.

Rudolph H. Lotze

May 21, 1817
Bautzen, Germany

July 1, 1881
Berlin, Germany

Philosopher and educator, Lotze taught at Leipzig, 1842–44, then was professor of philosophy at the University of Gottingen in 1844, where he stayed for 37 years. He did go to Berlin, 1880–81 until just a few months before his death. He was considered one of the best equipped and most efficient leaders against modern materialism, having a firm faith in theism. His private philosophy entertained the concept of an ethical universe, a concept paralleling the golden rule. He believed in a personal God. "The ultimate substance is God, the good and personal of whom all beings are parts without losing their selfhood."

George S. Fisch

July 6, 1814
Nyon, Switzerland

July 3, 1881
Vallorbe, Switzerland

Theologian and evangelical church leader. Fisch succeeded ADOLPHE MONOD of the Free Church in Lyons, France in 1846. Fisch took a prominent part in the Synod of 1849, which formed the union of Evangelical Churches of France. In 1855, he was called to Paris as the colleague of EDWARD PRESSENSE. From 1863–81, he was president of the Synodical Commission of Free Churches.

John Cumming

Nov. 10, 1807
Fintray, Scotland

July 5, 18812
London, England

Scottish Church Leader. Cumming was a lifetime pastor of the National Scottish Church at Crowne Court in Covent Garden, London, 1833–81. Cumming gained a reputation as an expounder of prophecy and an opponent of Catholicism. He published many works on these subjects, from *Apocalyptic Sketches* (1841) to *Destiny of Nations* (1864).

George H. Borrow

July 5, 1803
East Dereham, England

July 26, 1881
Oultonbroad, England

Writer, linguist, traveler, and colporteur (peddler) of religious books. Borrow had a natural inclination for adventure and became familiar with the habits and language of the gypsies in England and Spain. From 1827–40, and again in 1844 and 1854, he wandered on foot in Europe and in the East, working at times for a newspaper. He worked for the British and Foreign Bible Societies (1833–40) to distribute books in Russia in 1833, Portugal and Spain (1835–40). In 1840, he married and settled in England to write. Borrow prepared the New Testament in the Chinese-Tarter language. He knew more than 20 languages, seven of which he was fluent in by the age of 16. His writings range from *The Zincali, On the Gypsies in Spain* (1841) to *Romany Rye* (1857).

Erastus O. Haven

Nov. 1, 1820
Boston, Massachusetts

Aug. 2, 1881
Salem, Oregon

Methodist bishop, 1880, and educator. Five children came from Haven's marriage to Mary F. Coles. He taught in Armenia (NY) Seminary, (1843–45); pastored in New York City (1848–52) and taught at the University of Michigan (1854–56). He also held positions as editor of *Zion's Herald* (1856–62), president of the University of Michigan (1863–69), president of Northwestern University (1869–72), and chancellor of Syracuse University (1874–80). Haven advocated that slave owners should not be church members. He wrote works ranging from *Young Man Advised* (1856) to *Textbook Rhetoric* (1869).

Sidney Lanier

Feb. 3, 1842
Macon, Georgia

Sept. 7, 1881
Lynn, North Carolina

Presbyterian poet who was called the "Voice of the South." Lanier was a Southerner at heart, who lived for many years in the North. He had the ability to communicate a positive view of the South (travelogs) in a manner that was acceptable to Northerners during the post-Civil War era. He was the balm of Gilead that was desperately needed to reach the generation traumatized by the Civil War. He served in the Confederate army and was captured by Union forces near the end of the conflict. In addition to creating moving poetry, Lanier wrote travelogs on the diversified flavor to be found in the South, 1861–65. He married Mary Day on Dec. 21, 1867 and had four sons. After a period of ill health and poverty, he settled in Baltimore in 1873, played in the Peabody Symphony Orchestra, and lectured in English literature at Johns Hopkins University. Lanier was also a hymn writer, with his most well-known work being "Into the Woods My Master Went" (1880). Lanier struggled for many years with impaired health, dying at the age of 39 from tuberculosis. Georgia's largest lake is named after him.

Stephen S. Foster

Nov. 17, 1809
Canterbury, New Hampshire

Sept. 8, 1881
Worcester, Massachusetts

Radical abolitionist who persistently interrupted worship services to flail the church for its lack of concern toward the slavery issue. These attacks provoked numerous mob scenes. Foster wrote *The Brotherhood of Thieves* (1843). He married Abigail Kelley on Dec. 31, 1845. He was a Dartmouth University graduate in 1838.

James A. Garfield
Twentieth President of the United States

Nov. 19, 1831
Orange, Ohio

Sept. 19, 1881
Elberon, New Jersey

20th president of the United States, 1881. Garfield was converted, March 4, 1850, at the age of 19. Lucretia Rudolph became his wife on November 11, 1858, and gave him five children. He was a major general in the Civil War for the Union army (1861–63), then became a lay preacher for Disciples of Christ in Ohio (1863–81), while serving as president of Hiram (OH) College (1863–80). He was also a U.S. Congressional Representative. Garfield was elected Republican president in 1881, defeating Winfield Hancock 214–155 in electoral votes, but he served only four months. He was shot on July 2 by Charles Guiteau (a disappointed office-seeker) in a railway station in Washington, D.C., and died shortly thereafter. He was a powerful speaker. Garfield said as he died, "God's will be done, Doctor. I am ready to go if my time has come." He was the first president to use a telephone and the first to openly confess he had been "born again." He was the last president to be born in a log cabin.

Stuart Robinson

Nov. 14, 1814
Strabane, Ireland

Oct. 5, 1881
Louisville, Kentucky

Clergyman and editor. Robinson came to America in 1818. In September, 1841, he married Mary Brigham, and they had eight children. He pastored Presbyterian churches in Kanawha Salines, VA (1842–47); Frankfort, KY (1847–52); Fayette St. (1852–53) and Central Presbyterian (1853–56), both of Baltimore. He was professor at the theological seminary, Danville, KY (1856–58) and pastored the Second Presbyterian Church, Louisville, KY (1858–81). He edited *The True Christian*. He was an old school Presbyterian, opposed to any reunion with the northern church.

Josiah G. Holland

July 24, 1819
Belchertown, Massachusetts

Oct. 12, 1881
New York, New York

Wrote the Christmas carol, "There's a Song in the Air" (music by KARL HARRINGTON). Initially, Holland practiced medicine for a short time in Springfield, MA. Next, he established a weekly newspaper. Three children came from his marriage to Elizabeth Chapin on October 7, 1845. Holland joined the editorial staff of the *Springfield Republican* (1850) in Massachusetts and communicated with his readers through his "Timothy Titcomb Letters." He also wrote poems and novels, selling some 350,000 copies. He helped found *Scribner's Monthly* (Century Magazine) and served as its editor, 1870–81.

Henry P. Tappan

April 18, 1805
Rhinebeck, New York

Nov. 15, 1881
Vevay, Switzerland

First president of the University of Michigan, 1852–63. He married Julia Livingston on April 17, 1828. They had five children. Tappan pastored at the Congregational Church, Pittsfield, MA (1828–32) and was professor of moral philosophy at the University of New York City (1832–38). The remaining years of his life were spent in Europe.

Johann L. Krapf

Jan. 17, 1810
Tubingen/Derendingen, Germany

Nov. 26, 1881
Kornthal, Germany

Lutheran missionary/explorer to Kenya. Krapf was sent to Abyssinia (Ethiopia) by the Church Missionary Society, where he served, 1838–44. He was in Abyssinia when expelled because of hostile Catholic opposition. He married in 1841, and he went to Mombasa, an island in British East Africa (Kenya), to begin a work among the Moslems, Swahelis and Wanika tribes in 1843. His goal was to build a chain of mission stations in East Africa. He had to bury his wife, Rosina Dietrich, and daughter there. Krapf translated the NT into Swahili. In 1853, Krapf discovered Mt. Kenya (17,058 ft.), the highest point on the African continent. He then returned to Europe (1855), because of poor health, although he visited Mombasa (1861) and Abyssinia (1867).

George E. Street

June 20, 1824
Woodford, England

Dec. 18, 1881
London, England

English architect, noted for his many churches in the Gothic revival style. Street's extensive travels through Europe influenced his commissions. He was diocese architect to York, Winchester, Oxford, and Ripon. Street also was a professor of architecture at the Royal Academy of London from 1871 on. Street also became president of the Royal Institute of British Archtitects in 1881.

Leonard Bacon Sr.

Feb. 19, 1802
Detroit, Michigan

Dec. 24, 1881
New Haven, Connecticut

Congregational pastor, reformer, educator, editor, hymn writer, and author. Bacon was the son of the missionary to the Indians, David Bacon. He married Lucy Johnson (July, 1825) and Catherine Terry (June, 1847). Bacon fathered 14 children. He pastored the First Church of New Haven, CT from 1825–66 (41 years). He was a theology instructor at Yale Theological Seminary (1866–81), also lecturing on church policy (187181). Bacon was an ardent anti-slavery advocate. He tried to serve as a peacemaker in the many theological debates within Congregationalism. In 1848, he was a founder of the *New York Independent* (1848) and co-editor until 1864. His key work was *The Genesis of New*

England Church (1874). Bacon's hymns include "O God, Beneath Thy Guiding Hand," "Though Now the Nations Sit Beneath," and "Wake the Song of Jubilee."

Mary B. C. Slade

1826
Fall River, Massachusetts

1882
Fall River, Massachusetts

Hymn writer who wrote "Footprints of Jesus," "Who at My Door Is Standing?" (music for both by AsA EVERETT), **"Tell It Again"** (music by RIGDON MCINTOSH). Mary was a schoolteacher and served for a time as assistant editor of the *New England Journal of Education*. She married a clergyman and spent her entire life in her hometown. She wrote a number of gospel song texts.

John S. Stone

Oct. 7, 1795
West Stockbridge, Massachusetts

Jan. 13, 1882
Cambridge, Massachusetts

First president of Episcopal Divinity School, Cambridge, MA 1867–76. Stone previously was a professor of theology at the school from 1862–67. His marriages to Sophie M. Adams (May 2, 1826) and Mary Kent (September 5, 1839) brought him eight children. Stone served as rector of St. Paul's of Boston, (1832–41); Christ Church of Brooklyn, NY (1842–52); and St. Paul's Church of Brookline, MA (1852–62). He wrote three books.

Enoch Pond

July 29, 1791
Wrentham, Massachusetts

Jan. 21, 1882
Bangor, Maine

First president of Bangor (ME) Theological Seminary, 1857–82. The school began in 1814, but had no president until Pond. Fourteen children came from his marriages to Wealthy A. Hawes (Aug. 28, 1814), Julia A. Maltby (May 17, 1825), and Ann (Mason) Pearson (July 9, 1839). He pastored a Congregational church, Auburn, MA from 1815–32, and was also a professor and writer. Pond taught theology at BTS (1832–56) and was professor of church history (1832–70). Pond wrote works ranging from *Christian Baptism* (1817) to *History of God's Church* (1871).

Adolphus E. Ryerson

March 24, 1803
Victoria, Ontario, Canada

Feb. 19, 1882
Toronto, Ontario, Canada

Methodist pastor, editor, educator, and administrator. Ryerson was converted in 1812. From 1841–47, Ryerson became the first president of Victoria University, Toronto. He served as superintendent of education for Canada West, Ontario (1844–76) and was instrumental in designing Ontario's school system (1874–79). He also was the first president of the Canadian Methodist Church from 1874–78. He edited *The Christian Guardian*, 1829–40. His huge funeral was at Metropolitan Church, Toronto.

Dora (Dorothy) Greenwell

Dec. 6, 1821
Greenwell Ford, England

March 29, 1882
Clifton, England

Writer especially known for her hymn "My Savior" (music by WILLIAM KIRKPATRICK). Dora lived in the English towns of Durham, London, Torquay, and Clifton. She was a noted poet and prose writer whose works were chiefly Christian in nature. Her writings included poetical volumes (1848–50), *Carmina Crusis* (1869), and *Songs of Salvation* (1873). Her prose creation was *The Patient of Hope* (1860).

Dante G. Rossetti

May 12, 1828
London, England

April 9, 1882
Berchington, England

Victorian poet and artist. Rossetti is credited with founding the Pre-Raphaelite Brotherhood of Artists in 1848. His winning personality created a magnetism, drawing others to him. His paintings were divided into three categories: small Biblical scenes presenting minute detail, the Dante theme in watercolor, and etherial expressions of the soul. He married Elizabeth (Lizzy) Siddal in May, 1860, a watercolor artist with rare instinct for color. They had a stillborn child in 1861, and Lizzy died two years later from tuberculosis. She was buried with a manuscript of poems by her husband. She, and his sister, CHRISTINA ROSSETTI, were his main subjects. Many of his topics were drawn from his father's themes (Gabriele Rossetti 1783–1854), an Italian poet and commentator on Dante, after whom the young Rossetti was named. His most famous works were "Beata Beatri" (1865) and "Dante's Dream"(c. late 1870s). His poetical works are a reflection of his devotion toward his wife. They are"House of Life" (1870's), "The Blessed Damozel", "The Ballads of Rose Mary," "The White Ship" and "The King's Tragedy". He struggled with a drug habit brought on by his wife's premature passing, criticism of his work, and insomnia. He withdrew from public life in his later years. Rossetti is credited with reviving Gothic art in England.

John N. Darby

Nov. 18, 1800
London, England

April 29, 1882
Bournemouth, England

Considered the founder of the Christian (Plymouth) Brethren denomination and lifelong evangelist. Darby took a dispensational viewpoint on the Scriptures. His movement stressed Bible study, godly living, and missionary zeal. He left the Church of England (1831), after having served as a parish priest in Dublin (1828) and another in Plymouth, England (1830). The goal of the Plymouth Brethren Society was to restore the simple Christian church practice, with every Christian serving as a minister. The popularity of the denomination was widely spread and helped initiate the fundamentalist movement. He stressed premillennial prophecy and ecclesiastical separatism. He also published many Bible study books. Darby made seven trips to the United States and Canada (1859–74) and translated the Bible into French (NT 1859; OT 1878–80). He never married. For many years he edited *The Christian Witness*.

Giuseppe Garibaldi

July 4, 1807
Nice, France

June 2, 1882
Island of Caprera, Italy

Italian patriot and soldier, Garibaldi became a noted general recognized as almost invincible on land and sea. He began fighting for unification of Italy in 1834. After political exile in Uruguay (1836–48) for aiding patriot forces and on Staten Island, NY (1849–54), where he worked as a candlemaker, he went to Italy. He was married three times, including to Anite de Silva who died in 1849. He joined Victor Emmanuel II of Sardinia and led the Red Shirts in a successful war of liberation against Austria in 1859 and 1866. He promoted and established the present constitutional kingdom in Italy. On delivering certain flags to the Hungarian Hussars in Naples, he said, "I am a Christian, and I speak to Christians. I love and venerate the religion of Christ because Christ came into the world to deliver humanity from slavery, for which God has not created it." He retired to his lonely farm in Capena, a barren island off Sardinia.

James A. Brown

Feb. 19, 1821
Lancaster County, Pennsylvania

June 19, 1882
Lancaster, Pennsylvania

President of Lutheran Theological Seminary at Gettysburg (PA), 1865–81. Brown was a Lutheran pastor, chaplain, professor, and editor. He held pastorates in Baltimore, Maryland; Zion, York, PA; and St. Matthew, Reading, PA. For a short period of time, he was a professor and then became president of Newberry (SC) College in 1860. He also served as president of the General Lutheran Synod (1866) and editor of the *Lutheran Quarterly* (1871). He was disabled by paralysis in 1879, and resigned.

John Zundel

Dec. 10, 1815
Erslingen, Germany

July 1882
Cannstadt, Germany

Composer of music for "Love Divine, All Loves Excelling" (1870) (lyrics by CHARLES WESLEY), along with many other hymns. Zundel was organist of St. Anne's Lutheran in St. Petersburg and bardmaster of the Imperial Horse Guards prior to this. He was one of the great organists of his time, playing at Beecher's Plymouth Congregational Church in Brooklyn (1850–80), after coming to America in 1847. He returned to Germany in 1880. He published several books and edited four music journals. His first book was *Instruction Book for the Melodeon* (a small reed organ) (1853).

Johannes Oosterzee
"Jan Jakob van Oosterzee"

April 17, 1817
Rotterdam, Netherlands

July 29, 1882
Wiesbaden, Germany

Dutch Reformed Evangelical Theologian. Oosterzee first pastored at Kemnes-Binnendijk (1840) and then in Rotterdam (1844). In 1862, he was called to Utrecht University as professor of theology. In connection with his teaching, he published many valuable works. Many of these works have been translated into English. Oosterzee contributed to JOHN LANGE's *Commentaries*. He wrote *Theology of the New Testament*.

Edward H. Palmer

Aug. 7, 1840
Cambridge, England

Aug. 11, 1882
Desert, Suez, Egypt

Orientalist. From 1867–70, Palmer made expeditions to the Sinai Peninsula. He became acquainted with the Bedouins, African and Arabian desert nomads. In 1871, he was made professor of Arabic at Cambridge, until the Sudan War. Palmer was sent to Egypt to negotiate with the Bedouins, but was captured and murdered along with two of his companions in the El Tur Desert (southern Sinai Peninsula). His books on the Bedouin way of life are some of the best in the field.

Henry Kumler, Jr.

Jan. 8, 1801
Myerstown, Pennsylvania

Aug. 19, 1882
Dayton, Ohio

Bishop of the Church of the United Brethren in Christ (United Methodist Church in 1968), 1841–82. Kumler was converted at age eleven, was ordained a deacon at age 21, and an elder at age 24. He married Christian Zeller on June 25, 1820. He served as an evangelist for his denomination, remaining a strong advocate of infant baptism, and opposing worldliness. The United Biblical (Theological) Seminary, Dayton, OH used Kumler as an agent to promote their institution.

Charles W. Fry

May 29, 1837
Salisbury, England

Aug. 23, 1882
Park Hall, England

Writer of the familiar hymn "The Lily of the Valley" (music by WILLIAM HAYS). Fry was converted at a local Wesleyan Chapel at age 17. He then went into the building business. When the Salvation Army came to Salisbury in 1878, Charles, who played the cornet, and his three sons, started the group's brass band. By popular demand, they were all soon involved in musical evangelism, leaving the business world behind in 1880. Thus began the Salvation Army band.

William H. Allen

March 27, 1808
Bradford, Maine

Aug. 29, 1882
Philadelphia, Pennsylvania

President of American Bible Society, 1872–80. Allen married Martha Richardson, Ellen Ronora, Mary F. Quincy, and Anna Gamwill. He was a professor of chemistry and natural history at Dickinson College, Carlisle, PA (1836–46) and at Girard College, Philadelphia, PA where he became president (1849–62 and 1867–82). He also served as president of Pennsylvania Agriculture College (Penn State University), State College (University Park), PA from 1865–67.

Johann J. Herzog

Sept. 12, 1805
Basel, Switzerland

Sept. 30, 1882
Erlangen, Germany

German Reformed theologian and church historian. Herzog was responsible for much of the original research and editing, 1854–68, of a mammoth 22-volume reference work, later revised as *The New Schaff-Herzog Encyclopedia of Religious Knowledge* (pub. in U.S., 1882–84). He taught church history in Lausanne, Switzerland (1835–47), and in the German towns of Halle (1847–54) and Erlangen (1854–77), prior to his retirement.

Robert Paine

Nov. 12, 1799
Person County, North Carolina

Oct. 19, 1882
Aberdeen, Mississippi

Bishop in the Methodist Episcopal Church, South, 1846–82. Prior to fulfilling his official positions, he was an evangelist, 1818–30. Paine was the first president of LaGrange College, Franklin (AL) County, 1830–46. Nine children came from his marriages to Susanna Beck in 1824, Amanda Shaw in 1837, and Mary Millwater in 1839 (died: January 3, 1904). In 1844, Paine prepared a peaceable plan of separation to the Methodist Church from his Episcopal ties. He preached in Confederate camps and secured chaplains for their army.

Oscar Ahnfelt

May 31, 1813
Gullarp, Sweden

Oct. 22, 1882
Karlshamn, Sweden

Sweden's spiritual troubadour (wandering singer). Ahnfelt was an evangelical Lutheran Pietist lay preacher, hymn writer, and guitarist who, under the influence of CARL ROSENIUS, began to travel as an evangelist using both music and preaching to minister to those assembled. He composed or arranged the music for all of fellow pietist LINA SANDELL–BERG's hymns, singing them throughout Scandinavia. She wrote that Ahnfelt had sung her songs into the hearts of the people. The state church opposed pietistic hymns and tried to silence Ahnfelt by forcing him to sing before King Karl (Charles) XV (reigned 1859–72). The king was so moved by Ahnfelt's music that he informed Ahnfelt that he could sing as much as he desired in both of his kingdoms, Sweden and Norway. He provided guitar and piano accompaniment for his composed hymns. His wife, Clara Stromberg, was also a songwriter. JENNY LIND, Pietist known as the Swedish Nightingale, provided financial assistance for his hymnbook and introduced his arrangements of the SANDELL hymns to America. Ahnfelt is well known for composing music for "Day by Day" (1865) and "The Sign of the Cross."

Titus Coan

Feb. 1, 1801
Killingsworth, Connecticut

Dec. 1, 1882
Hilo, Hawaii

Missionary to Hawaii, Coan began his missionary trek in 1822, when he sailed to Patagonia, a barren region of South America in Argentina and Chile between the Andes Mountains and the Atlantic Ocean. His main burden, however, was for the people of Hawaii, whom he served for almost 50 years (1835–82), with only a brief visit to the States (1871–72). Coan was fluent in the native dialects and preached with mighty power which resulted in great revivals. He received 7,382 into his church in the city of Hilo on Hawaii, the largest of the islands. By 1860, his church included 11,960 members. Coan was first married to Fiedlia Church on November 3, 1834 (died 1872), and then to Lydia Bingham in 1873. He was converted in a FINNEY revival in western New York.

Archibald C. Tait

Dec. 22, 1811
Edinburgh, Scotland

Dec. 3, 1882
London, England

Archbishop of Canterbury, 1868–82. He was headmaster of Rugby School (1842), then dean of Carlisle (1849) and Addington. In 1856, he was made bishop of London. Tait served during the uproar over disestablishing the Anglican Church in Ireland. He agreed to the withdrawal of Anglican rule there, after a personal appeal from Queen VICTORIA. As a result of this upheaval, Tait sponsored the Public Worship Regulation Act of 1874, which opposed the spread of the Oxford Movement. He wrote several books. He dealt carefully and fairly with new movements arising in his day, exercising a moderate influence on extremist views.

Jeremiah C. Lanphier

1809
Coxsackle, New York

c 1883

Layman Evangelist responsible for world evangelism endeavor. In 1842, Lanphier made a profession of faith at Broadway Tabernacle Church, while employed as a merchant in NYC. Lanphier organized a noon-hour prayer meeting for businessmen, 1857–62. It began on Sept. 23, 1857, and resulted in a worldwide revival unmatched in history. He also was on staff as a lay missionary at the Old North Dutch Church in New York City, which he joined in 1857 (located on Fulton and Williams Street.) Lanphier was a great man of prayer. He was still serving at the church at age 74. His death is unknown.

Charles Porterfield Krauth

March 17, 1823
Martinsburg, Virginia (West Virginia)

Jan. 2, 1883
Philadelphia, Pennsylvania

Lutheran pastor and educator. Krauth was the most influential and conservative Lutheran theologian of his time. From 1842–61, he pastored in Baltimore, MD; Shepherdstown, VA; Winchester, VA; and Pittsburgh, PA. His marriages were to Susan Reynolds (1844), and upon her death, Virginia Baker (1855). For many years, 1864–83, he was professor of theology at the Lutheran Seminary, Philadelphia, PA and was considered the most accomplished scholar there. Krauth also served as professor of philosophy at the University of Pennsylvania, beginning in 1868. He was the son of CHARLES PHILIP KRAUTH. He wrote *The Conservative Reformation and Its Theology* (1871).

P. Gustave Dore

Jan. 6, 1832
Strasbourg, France

Jan. 23, 1883
Paris, France

Artist and illustrator whose Bible engravings have no equal. In 1848, after study in Paris, Dore made his first series of sketches for a French journal and was soon regarded as the foremost illustrator in Europe. His illustrations have appeared in the world's great literary classics including Dante's *Inferno*, Cervantes's *Don Quixote*, Milton's *Paradise Lost*, and Tennyson's *Idylls of the King*. He was also a painter of note and a sculptor of two well-known works, one in Paris and one in San Francisco.

William E. Dodge

Sept. 4, 1805
Hartford, Connecticut

Feb. 9, 1883
New York, New York

Renowned merchant dealing in metals, lumbering, and coal-mining development. He married Melissa Phelps on June 24, 1828. Dodge was president of several insurance companies, a director in all the leading telegraph companies and a leading spirit in the building of several railroad companies. He owned thousands of acres of land, gave away millions to benevolent causes and honored the Lord's Day. In an 1872 address, he said, "Unless we get an idea of what it is to be lost, we cannot know what it is to be saved. Jesus Christ came to seek and to save the lost…A saved sinner myself, I can declare that God desires not the death of the wicked."

Jacob Erb

May 25, 1804
Manheim, Pennsylvania

April 29, 1883

Bishop of the Church of the United Brethren in Christ (United Methodist Church in 1968), **1837–83**. Erb was converted at age 16, and ordained at age 21 in 1825. He spoke fluent German as well as English. In 1825, Erb traveled 1,000 miles on foot to New York and Canada to establish churches. He baptized JOHN WINEBRENNER, founder of Church of God in North America on July 4, 1830. He pastored Old Otterbein Church in Baltimore, MD 1841–48, and also in York and Harrisburg, PA. Erb married Elizabeth Sherk. He is buried in Shiremanstown, PA.

Josiah Henson

June 15, 1789
near Port Tobacco, Maryland

May 5, 1883
Dresden, Ontario, Canada

Black slave, the real-life model for "Uncle Tom" in the famous novel, *Uncle Tom's Cabin* **(1852)**. Henson married a slave girl in 1811, and they had twelve children. Escaping from his Maryland owner in 1830, they traveled to Ontario. Henson became a Methodist pastor at Dresden. In 1849, he published his autobiography. He was the leader of the abolition movement in 1870, and made three trips to Britain for that cause. He remarried around 1870.

Jesse T. Peck

April 4, 1811
Middlefield, New York

May 17, 1883
Syracuse, New York

Methodist bishop, 1872 on. Peck married Persis Wing on Oct. 13, 1831. He was principal of Gouverneur (NY) Wesleyan Seminary (1837–41); of Troy Conference Seminary, Pultney, VA (1841–48); and president of Dickinson College, Carlisle, PA (1848–52). He pastored in Washington, DC (1852–54); New York (1856–58); San Francisco and Sacramento, CA (1858–66).

Peck pastored in Albany, NY from 1867–70. He helped to found Syracuse (NY) University, while he pastored there, 1870–72.

Eliza Agnew

Feb. 2, 1807
New York, New York

June 14, 1883
Manepay, Ceylon (Sri Lanka)

Missionary to Ceylon, which at that time was a British colony. In 1840, Eliza was the first single woman missionary to the area. She remained head of the Central Boarding School for girls at Oodooville nearly 40 continuous years, 1842–79. Miss Agnew was known as "the mother of 1,000 daughters." Former students living in all corners of the world prayed for her when she was stricken with paralysis. She sailed in 1839, under ABCFM, never to return to the United States.

Thomas R. Birks

Sept. 28, 1810
Staveley, England

July 19, 1883
Cambridge, England

Evangelical preacher and Church of England theologian. Birks was ordained in 1837, became rector at Kelshall in Hertfordshire (1844–66), and then accepted the pastorate of the Trinity Church of Cambridge (1866–77). In 1872, he was made professor of moral philosophy at Cambridge University. For 21 years, he was the honorary secretary of the Evangelical Alliance, a fellowship of conservative denominations. His 25 works covered Biblical, scientific, and prophetic subjects. In 1851, he also wrote *Memories of Rev. E. BICKERSTETH SR.*, his father-in-law. Several of Birks' more than 100 hymns appeared in the Psalters compiled by EDWARD BICKERSTETH SR. "The Heavens Declare Thy Glory", and "O Come, Let Us Sing to the Lord," were among Birks' more well-known creations.

Robert Moffat

Dec. 21, 1795
Ormiston, Scotland

Aug. 8, 1883
Leigh, England

Missionary to South Africa and Bible translator. One year, "Wee Bobby Moffat" was the only convert in his pastor's church. He left the girl he loved (Mary Smith) in 1816 to go to Africa, arriving January 13, 1817. She joined him in 1819, and they were married there on December 27. Moffat served much of his time in Kuruman, Bechuanaland, South Africa, under the London Missionary Society. Moffat also worked with the Bushmen and Hottentots. It was during his only furlough home to Scotland from 1839–43, that he inspired David Livingstone (who married Moffat's daughter Mary) to go to Africa. He was the first major pioneer missionary to Africa. For 49 years, he ministered there and translated the Bible into local dialects, especially Bechuana (Tswana), in 1857. His fourfold outreach was evangelization, exploration, literature, and civilization, emphasizing agriculture. He returned to England in 1870 because of failing health. There his wife died in 1871. One son, John S. Moffatt (1835–1918), carried on much of the work of his father. They had ten children, three died, and five became missionaries.

Stephen R. Riggs

March 23, 1812
Steubenfield, Ohio

Aug. 24, 1883
Beloit, Wisconsin

Presbyterian missionary to American Indians in the Dakotas, 1837–83. Riggs was sent by ABCFM to the Lac Qui Parle mission near Ft Snelling, MO in 1837. Nine children came from his marriages to Mary Longley on February 16, 1837 (died 1869), and Annie Ackley in 1872. He organized numerous mission schools in the West, and laboriously prepared some 50 textbooks, grammars, and dictionaries in their language. He established a mission at Traveree des Sioux in 1843, and built a boarding school for Dakota children at Hazelwood in 1854. He also translated the Bible into the Dakota Indian dialect in 1880. Riggs wrote *Forty Years Among the Sioux*

(1880) among many other books. He retired to Beloit, supervising the work of other missionaries and making frequent visits to the Dakota reservation.

Edwin F. Hatfield

Jan. 9, 1807
Elizabethtown, New Jersey

Sept. 22, 1883
Summit, New Jersey

Stated clerk of Presbyterian Church in the US of America (New School), 1846–70, and of Presbyterian Church in the USA (USA in 1983), **1870–1884**. Hatfield married Mary Taylor on April 27, 1837, and they had five children. He pastored the Seventh Church (1835–56) and North Church (1856–63), both in New York City. He was a special agent of the Union Theological Seminary from 1846–64 and 1870–73, in New York City, bequeathing his 6,000-volume library to it. He wrote the seminary's history in 1876. Hatfield also produced *Church Hymn Book* (1872).

Sojourner Truth

c 1790
Hurley (near Kingston), New York

Nov. 26, 1883
Battle Creek, Michigan

Famed black female evangelist. Sojourner's legal name was Isabella Baumfree Van Wagener. She was reared a slave, but was set free by Isaac Van Wagener in 1809. She bore five children to an older slave named Thomas, whom she was forced to marry. In 1827, she escaped and said she believed that God called her into full-time service. Beginning in 1841, she assumed the name Sojourner Truth, to fit that calling. She left New York on June 1, 1843 to begin her "crusade." President LINCOLN received her at the White House. She had great personal magnetism and supported the abolition of slavery and rights of women. She was six feet tall, a powerful speaker, and wore a satin banner across her chest which said "Proclaim liberty throughout the land unto all the inhabitants thereof."

Wendell Phillips

Nov. 29, 1811
Boston, Massachusetts

Feb. 2, 1884
Boston, Massachusetts

Orator and abolitionist. Phillips was converted under LYMAN BEECHER's ministry. His stand against slavery was strengthened when he witnessed the mob attack on WILLIAM GARRISON because of his antislavery position. He favored ending slavery even at the cost of dissolution of the Union. He married Ann T. Greene on October 12, 1837 and rose into prominence with his speech in Boston on December 8, 1837. During the last years of his life, Phillips devoted his energies to prison reform, women's rights, prohibition, and the treatment of Irish and American Indians. He was in much demand as a lecturer and was considered one of the finest speakers of his time.

Hans L. Martensen

Aug. 19, 1808
Flensburg, Denmark

Feb. 3, 1884
Copenhagen, Denmark

Lutheran theologian who worked in education before becoming a bishop of Zealand, a province of the southwest Netherlands in 1854. He held this position until his death. He became professor of theology at the University of Copenhagen (1838) and then a court preacher (1845). He was one of the truly great preachers of his day. Like JAKOB MYNSTER, his predecessor at Zealand, he did not agree with NIKOLAI GRUNDVIG's liberalism, breaking with him in 1863. He ignored Kierkegaard's attacks on him. In 1865, Martensen was made private chaplain to the King of Denmark and his family.

Samuel W. Williams

Sept. 22, 1812
Utica, New York

Feb. 16, 1884
New Haven, Connecticut

President of the American Bible Society, 1881–84, Congregational missionary, sinologist, and diplomat. In 1833, Williams went to Canton, China, as a printer with the ABCFM. He edited the *Chinese Repository*. In 1835, he moved to the Portuguese island of Macao, and while there, learned the Japanese language from sailors. He married Sarah Walworth on Nov. 25, 1847, and they had five children. Williams became secretary and interpreter of the U.S. legation at Peking, China (1855–75) being in the U.S,. 1860–62. In 1877, Williams became a professor of Chinese at Yale University in New Haven (CT) till his death. He wrote *The Middle East Kingdom* (2 vols. in 1883).

Johann F. Ahlfeld

Nov. 1, 1810
Mehringen, Germany

March 4, 1884
Leipzig, Germany

Eminent and eloquent Lutheran clergyman. Ahlfeld pastored in the German towns of Alseleben (1838) and at Halle (1847). From 1851 until his death, he pastored St. Nicholas' Church at Leipzig. His evangelical preaching attracted great crowds. Ahlfeld taught homiletics and pastoral theology at the Leipzig Theological Seminary and helped revise LUTHER's *Old Testament*. Many of his sermons were published.

John S. Inskip

August 10, 1816
Huntington, England

March 7, 1884
Ocean Grove, New Jersey

First president of National Camp meeting (Christian Holiness Partnership in 1997), **1867–84**. Inskip was a Methodist pastor, Civil War chaplain, author, and editor. He came to America at age five. He married Martha Foster on November 1, 1835. He was constantly in demand for revivals and camp meetings, going full–time into holiness revivalism in 1871 and assuming the editorship of *Christian Standard* (1876). He pastored several Methodist churches. The custom was for men and women to sit on opposite sides of the sanctuary. While at Springfield, OH he started families sitting together. In 1881-82, he took an extensive tour to England, India, and Australia, traveling 31,000 miles, conducting 500 services, and seeing 5,000 converted.

A. D. Clark

Dec. 23, 1813
Lancaster, Pennsylvania

April 12, 1884
Allegheny, Pennsylvania

President of Allegheny (PA) (Pittsburgh in 1959) **Theological Seminary, 1870–84**. Clark attended Franklin and Marshall College, Lancaster, PA from 1831–39, studied theology at Allegheny Seminary, licensed (April 30, 1844) and ordained (August 12, 1846) by Second Presbytery of Ohio. He became president of Franklin and Marshall College in 1845, then professor of Biblical literature at Allegheny Seminary, 1847–84. He spent the winters at the seminary and summers at the college until 1861. He was also pastor of Sixth Church, Allegheny.

Cyrus H. McCormick

Feb. 15, 1809
Walnut Grove, Virginia

May 13, 1884
Chicago, Illinois

Industrialist, inventor of farm machinery, and manufacturer. McCormick's reaping machine (July, 1831) revolutionized agriculture and, at the same time, brought him great wealth and worldwide fame at the young age of 22. He invented the first mechanical reaper in 1831 (patented in 1834), and built a factory in Chicago in 1847, to make farming equipment. In 1848, his patent was not renewed so a period of lawsuits against competition began. In 1851, he demonstrated the reaper at a London exhibition. In 1855, it won a Grand Medal of Honor in Paris. In 1857, he brought a Presbyterian exposition to Chicago. Nancy Fowler (1835–1923) became his wife on January 26, 1858, and they had seven children. McCormick was considered a pioneer in the business world. He gave $100,000 to establish the McCormick Theological Seminary in Chicago in 1859. His factory was destroyed in the Chicago Fire of 1871. He was an active, conservative Presbyterian layman. His wife later gave away eight million dollars to various Christian causes. His son, Cyrus H. McCormick (1859–1936) succeeded as president in 1884.

Silas J. Vail

Oct. 6, 1818
Brooklyn, New York

May 20, 1884
Brooklyn, New York

Composed the music for "Close to Thee" (1874), a FANNY CROSBY hymn. After working as a hatmaker in Danbury (CT), Vail entered the business world of New York City with music as a hobby. He composed a number of hymn tunes and was associated in editing a number of collections, one of which was *Songs of Grace and Glory* (1874) with WILLIAM F. SHERWIN.

Benjamin B. Smith

June 13, 1794
Bristol, Rhode Island

May 31, 1884
New York, New York

Presiding bishop of Protestant Episcopal Church (Episcopal Church in 1967), **1868–86**. During his tenure, Smith saw 52 bishops consecrated. He was ordained as a deacon (1817) and a priest (1818). He served in Marblehead, MA; Charlestown, VA; Shepherdston, VA; Middlebury, VT; Philadelphia, PA; and Lexington, KY from 1818–30. He was the bishop of Kentucky beginning on October 31, 1832.

John L. Dagg

Feb. 13, 1794
Middleburg, Virginia

June 11, 1884
Haynesville, Alabama

First recognized Southern Baptist systematic theologian. Raised in Presbyterian surroundings, Dagg turned Baptist after studying infant baptism. He was converted (1809) and ordained (1817), pastoring small churches in northern Virginia. He was married to Fannie H. Thorton on December 18, 1817, then to Mrs. Mary Young Davis in 1831. He then pastored the Fifth Avenue Baptist Church, Philadelphia, PA from 1825–34, when his voice gave him problems. He became president of the Haddington Institute, Philadelphia, PA from 1834–36. He then spent 1836–44 in Tuscaloosa, AL as president of the Alabama Female Athenaeum. He then was president of Mercer University, Penfield, GA from 1844–54, retiring from his teaching in 1856. He lived in Georgia for the next 15 years writing. His *Evidences of Christianity* was published in 1868. His first book was *Manual of Theology* (1857).

Matthew Simpson

June 21, 1811
Cadiz, Ohio

June 18, 1884
Philadelphia, Pennsylvania

President of Garrett Biblical Institute (GETS in 1974), **Evanston, IL, 1859–79**. Simpson was a prominent and influential Methodist bishop from 1852 onward. Ellen H. Verner became his wife on Nov. 3, 1835. From 1835–37, he was pastor of Liberty St. Church in Pittsburgh. He was the first president of Indiana Asbury (DePauw) University of Greencastle, in 1839–48. He taught at Allegheny College, Meadville, PA (1837–39). During the Civil War, Simpson was a friend and frequent adviser to President LINCOLN, delivering the eulogy at his funeral in Washington, D.C. and in Springfield, IL. LINCOLN had said he was the greatest orator he ever heard. When LINCOLN's successor, Andrew Johnson, ordered all seized property to be returned to the southern church, Simpson warmly supported Johnson's impeachment precedings which narrowly failed. He was editor of the *Western Christian Advocate* (1848–52).

Johann P. Lange

April 10, 1802
Sonnborn, Prussia (Germany)

July 8, 1884
Bonn, Germany

Reformed theologian, Bible scholar, and exegete. Lange pastored several United Evangelical churches (1825–41) including Duisburg (1832–41). He taught theology at the Universities of Zurich, Switzerland (1841–54) and of Marburg (1872–75). He was a consistorial counselor (1854–60). In 1875 he moved to Bonn, spending the rest of his life as a writer and a teacher of dogmatic theology at the University of Bonn. Lange also wrote some hymns. His 25-volume commentary is well-known, as well as his *Life of Jesus* (1844–47).

Isaac A. Dorner

June 20, 1809
Neuhausen, Germany

July 8, 1884
Wiesbaden, Germany

Lutheran theologian. Dorner was a professor of theology at Tubingen (1838), Kiel (1839), Konigsberg (1843), Bonn (1847), Gottingham (1853), and Berlin (1861–84). He wrote extensively to counter the extremists among German Biblical critics, especially F. C. Baur (1792–1860). He was a follower of the Evangelical Church of Prussia and strove for Christian unity. He wrote such works as the *Doctrine of the Person of Christ* (1859). He was influenced by Freidrich Schleiermacher (liberal theologian, 1768–1834). He was a leader in the movement for Christian unity.

Jeremiah (Jerry) McAuley

1839
Kerry County, Ireland

Sept. 18, 1884
New York, New York

Founder of the first rescue mission in America, the Water Street Mission (WSM). McAuley came to New York at age 13, became involved with the city's criminal element, and survived as a river thief. While serving time in Sing Sing Prison, 1857–64, on a false charge of highway robbery, he was converted (1862) by the witness of a female parish "missionary," and finally pardoned (1864). McAuley joined Methodism and, in October of 1872, founded "The Helping Hand Mission" at 316 Water St., NYC (renamed WSM in 1876). A new building was erected in 1876. In 1882, he founded the Cremorne Mission on W. 32nd St. He suffered and died from tuberculosis. As he died, he said, "It's all right up there." McAuley's funeral was the largest NYC had seen up to that date. His wife's name was Maria.

John L. Taylor

May 20, 1811
Warren, Connecticut

Sept. 23, 1884
Andover, Massachusetts

President of Andover (MA) (Andover–Newton in 1931) **Theological Seminary, 1868–77**, teaching there till 1879. Taylor graduated from Yale (1835), from Yale Seminary (1839), and was ordained on July 18, 1839. He pastored at South Church, Andover, MA (1839–52) and was treasurer/trustee of Phillips Academy and Seminary (1852–68). He was also president of Andover National Bank, 1873–80.

James E. Latimer

Oct. 7, 1826
Hartford, Connecticut

Nov. 27, 1884
Syracuse, New York

Dean of Boston (MA) University School of Theology, 1873–84. Latimer taught Latin and geology at Genesee Wesleyan Seminary (1849), then was principal of the NH Conference

The Saints Go Marching In

Seminary, Northfield, VT (1851). He also served as principal of Fort Plain (NY) Seminary (1854), was a teacher of languages in Elmira (NY) Female College (1859), pastor in New York: Elmira, Rochester, and Penn Yan, 1861–68, and joined BUST (1870) as a professor of theology.

William Palmer

Feb. 14, 1803 — Dublin, Ireland
1885 — London, England

Anglican who took an active part in the Oxford Movement with NEWMAN, Pusey (1800–82), KEBLE, ROSE and other sensitive young Englishmen. Palmer came under the influence of Oxford divinity professor, Charles Lloyd (1784–1829) and the Oxford Movement (emphasized apostolic succession, a return to celibate clergy, confessions, and other trappings associated with "high church" worship, although it staunchly opposed Roman Catholicism). These Tractarian leaders (so named for the *Tracts for the Times* which they aggressively distributed espousing the need for change within the Church of England) lamented the dropping of these practices. Tract No. 90, by J. H. Newman, (1801–90), which attempted to interpret MARTIN LUTHER's Thirty–Nine Articles for Reformation within a "catholic" premise, stirred up a fire of protest resulting in the closure of the "Tract Series." This desire to go back to "high church views" was a catalyst in further encouraging the needs for a reformation movement, away from both Catholics and dissenters.

William A. Scott

Jan. 31, 1813 — Rock Creek, Tennessee
Jan. 14, 1885 — San Francisco, California

First president of San Francisco (San Anselmo, CA in 1890) **Theological Seminary, 1871–85**. Ann Nicholson became his wife on January 19, 1836. Scott pastored Prebyterian churches in Tuscaloosa, AL (1840–42) and in New Orleans (1842–54), founded and pastored Calvary Church in San Francisco (1854–61), and served his last pastorate in NYC (1863–70). Scott sympathized with the South and the "Old School" views. He wrote *Daniel* (1854) to *The Christ of the Apostles' Creed* (1881).

Charles G. Gordon

Jan. 28, 1833 — Woolwich, England
Jan. 26, 1885 — Khartum, Nubia (Sudan)

General and national hero for exploits in China, 1860–64, and Africa, 1875–85. Gordon suppressed the Taiping Rebellion, which earned him the title, "Chinese Gordon." He fought in the Crimean War in 1855, in many parts of the British Empire. He developed his own mystical brand of Christianity, his conversion resulting from his father's death in 1865. In 1873, after several diplomatic missions, he was appointed governor of Equatorial Provinces of Central Africa by the khedive (turkish deputy) of Egypt. His authority extended to the Sudan. As the governor–general of Sudan, he sought to eliminate the slave trade. After ten months of putting up a heroic defense, Gordon and his troops were defeated at the fall of Khartoum (Sudan capital), where he was killed by Moslem rebels two days before additional troops arrived. He is considered to be a martyr. His favorite Bible verse was I John 4:15.

William C. Crane

March 17, 1816 — Richmond, Virginia
Feb. 27, 1885 — Independence, Texas

President of Baylor University, Independence (Waco in 1886), **TX 1864–85**, leading the school through the difficult years of the Civil War and Reconstruction. Crane was ordained in 1838 and pastored, 1839–51, beginning in Montgomery, AL. He served as president of Mississippi Female College (1851–57), Semple Broaddus (MS) College (1859–60), and Mount Lebanon (LA) College (1860–64).

Susan Bogert Warner

July 11, 1819
New York, New York

March 17, 1885
Highland Falls, New York

Hymn writer of "Jesus Bids Us Shine" (music by EDWIN EXCELL). Susan lived on Constitution Island, 1837–85. She wrote religious novels and children's stories. Her work, *The Wide, Wide World* (1850) was one of the most popular novels of the 19th Century, second only to *Uncle Tom's Cabin*. It portrayed the religious development of a 13-year-old orphan. She and her sister, Anna, ministered to cadets for years through Presbyterian Sunday School programs. Susan wrote under the name of Elizabeth Wetherell. Another well-known novel that she wrote was *Queechy* (1852), depicting the spiritual growth of a young girl.

Christopher Wordsworth

Oct. 30, 1807
Lambeth, England

March 20, 1885
Lincoln, England

Anglican bishop and hymn writer of "O Day of Rest and Gladness" (music arranged by LOWELL MASON). Wordsworth became the public orator of Cambridge and headmaster of Harrow School, 1836–44. He was a canon at Westminster in 1844 and a priest in Stanford-in-the-Vale from 1850-69. He served as bishop of Lincoln, 1869–85. Wordsworth wrote 127 hymns and was a nephew of the famed writer, William Wordsworth. He was a Greek scholar and wrote *A Commentary on the Entire Bible* (1856–70). He wrote *The Holy Year*. His writings range from *Athens and Attica* (1836) to *Public Appeals on Behalf of Christian Liberty* (2 vols., 1886).

William R. Williams

Oct. 14, 1804
New York, New York

April 1, 1885
New York, New York

Baptist pastor of Amity Church in NYC for 53 years, 1832 until his death. Williams graduated from Columbia College (University), NYC in 1822. Upon his conversion, he left his law practice to enter the ministry. Two sons came from his marriage to Mary S. Bowen in April, 1847. Williams founded Rochester (NY) Theological Seminary around 1850. His works range from *Miscellanies* (1850) to *Eras and Characters of History* (1882).

Henry A. Stern

April 11, 1820
Unterreichenbach, Germany

May 13, 1885

Anglican missionary of German Jewish origin who dedicated himself after his own baptism in 1840 in London, to reach the Jews. He worked among Jews and Moslems in Asia Minor and Persia (1844–55), then in Constantinople (1853–58), then Crimea and Arabia (1858–59). Stern traveled widely and worked principally in Abyssinia (Ethiopia) among the Falasha Jews, 1859–61. He was imprisoned and tortured in Addis Ababa, Ethiopia, 1863–67. He spent the last years of his life in London. His writings include *Dawn of Light in the East* (1854).

Victor M. Hugo

Feb. 26, 1802
Besancon, France

May 22, 1885
Paris, France

Poet, dramatist and novelist, authoring *The Hunchback of Notre Dame* and *Les Miserables*, (1862). Hugo was a man of faith, hope and charity; all plucked from his favorite verse, I Cor. 13:13. He believed in God and the Bible. He said, "Let there be a Bible in every hut…Sow the villages with the gospel…Jesus has something better to teach than Voltaire!" His most famous book featured the outcasts of Parisian society—a gypsy girl and a deformed bell ringer. In 1843, his daughter was killed in a boating accident, greatly affecting him. Although he was not known as a religious writer, several of his characters seem to operate in Jesus' name. Elected to the French assembly, he fled when Napoleon led a coup in 1851. He returned in 1870. At his death, he was hailed a national hero and his funeral procession lasted six hours. Hugo is considered France's premier poet. He is also considered France's greatest genius or greatest egotist, depending on whether you liked him or not!

Samuel I. Prime

Nov. 4, 1812
Ballston, New York

July 18, 1885
NYC/Manchester, Vermont

Presbyterian minister and educator. Prime married Elizabeth T. Kemeys (October 15, 1833), and Eloisa L. Williams (August 17, 1835). He pastored in the New York cities of Ballston Springs (1833–35) and Matteawan (1835–40). From 1840-85, he edited the *New York Observer*. He was active in the Evangelical Alliance, secretary to the American Bible Society in 1849, Prime also wrote for *Harper's Magazine* (1853–85). His books included *The Power of Prayer* (1859) and *Thoughts on Death of Children*. He edited *The Presbyterian* (1858).

William P. Mackay

May 13, 1839
Montrose, Scotland

Aug. 22, 1885
Portree, Scotland

Writer of the favorite hymn "Revive Us Again," (1863) (music by JOHN HUSBAND), which he revised in 1867. Mackay was educated at the University of Edinburgh and practiced medicine for a number of years, until he felt called to the ministry. In 1868, he became the pastor of the Prospect Street Presbyterian Church, Hull, England. Of the many hymns he wrote, 17 appeared in the *Praise Book* (1872), a popular church hymnbook.

Stephen H. Tyng

March 1, 1800
Newburyport, Massachusetts

Sept. 3, 1885
Irvington, New York

Eminent and eloquent Episcopal cleric. Tyng served in Georgetown, D.C. (1821–23); at Queen Anne Parish, MD (1823–29); at St. Paul's in Philadelphia (1829–33); at the Church of the Epiphany in Philadelphia (1833–45); and at St. George's in NYC (1845 until his retirement in 1878). Nine children came from his union with Anne Griswold on August 5, 1821 and Susan Mitchell in July, 1833. He wrote works ranging from *Law and the Gospels* (1832) to *Office and Duty of a Christian Pastor* (1874). He was a vigorous promoter of Sunday schools.

Anthony A. C. Shaftesbury
Lord Ashley—Anthony A. Cooper

April 28, 1801
London, England

Oct. 1, 1885
Folkestone, Kent, England

Philanthropist and reformer. Shaftesbury was known as Lord Ashley, although his real name was Anthony A. Cooper. He answered the call to help the poor. In 1826, he entered Parliament and proved to be an effective social and industrial reformer. Shaftesbury was called the "first philanthropist for lunatics" in 1827. He married Lady Emily Cowper in 1830 (died: 1872). Three years later, he had compassion on and took up the cause of the factory children, and in 1840, started a campaign to free boy chimney sweeps. He then fought to free children from mines (1842), and founded Ragged School Union (1844). He is credited with establishing the Mines (labor) Act (1842), Ten Hours (labor) Bill (1847), and the Factory (labor) Act (1874). He was elected commissioner of Public Health in 1848. Shaftesbury succeeded his father as the seventh Earl of Shaftesbury (1851), refused a cabinet post (1855), and accepted the position of "Bishopmaher" to Prime Minister Paloustar, 1855–56. Lord Ashley assumed an evangelical position with the Church of England, supporting MOODY and SANKEY in 1875. He was a true friend of the oppressed as evidenced as chairman of the Ragged School Union for 39 years. His national funeral was held at Westminster Abbey. His favorite Bible verses were Matthew 25:44–45.

Azel D. Cole

Dec. 1, 1818
Sterling, Connecticut

Oct. 15, 1885
Nashotah, Wisconsin

Dean of Nashotah (WI) House, 1850–85. Cole attended Brown University, 1835–38 and received a Doctor of Divinity from General Theological Seminary in 1841. He married Elizabeth Perry. He was an Episcopal rector of St. Luke's in Racine, WI in 1849. He was buried in the Nashotah Cemetery.

Wilhelm Sihler

Nov. 12, 1801
Bernstadt, Germany

Oct. 27, 1885
Fort Wayne, Indiana

First president of Concordia Theological Seminary, Ft. Wayne, IN 1846–61. Sihler was a Lutheran pioneer pastor, synodical leader, and organizer who was converted from rationalism to conservatism in Dresden, Germany. He began preaching in Pomeroy, OH in 1844. He withdrew from the Ohio Synod in 1845, because of its unionistic (loyal to U.S. at time of Civil War) position. Sihler is credited as being one of the founders of the Missouri Synod. He wrote hundreds of articles for various publications.

James Hannington

Sept. 3, 1847
Hurstpierpont, England

Oct. 29, 1885
Busoga, Lake Victoria, Uganda

Martyred missionary and first Anglican bishop of East Equatorial Africa (Southern Sudan, central Uganda and Kenya). Hannington was converted in 1874 by reading a book sent to him after being ordained. He married Blanche Hankin-Turvin in 1877. He was sent to Africa first by the Anglican Church Missionary Society, 1882–83, but an illness forced him to return early. On June 24, 1884, he began his second trip to Africa. Returning to Mombasa in 1885, he led a perilous expedition, was seized by the order of Chief Kebaka Mwanga (the Bugandan ruler at Busoga), and murdered eight days later by the superstitious native tribesmen of Uganda (along with 46 porters). Hannington had trudged from the East Coast of Africa to plant churches, but German imperialism ruling on the coast made Mwanga suspicious of his motives. His favorite Bible verse was Luke 9:62.

John F. Young

Oct. 30, 1820
Pittston, Maine

Nov. 15, 1885
New York City, New York

Translator of "Silent Night, Holy Night," from its original German to English. Young was an Episcopalian who served in Jacksonville and Tallahassee, FL (1845–48); in Texas, Mississippi, and Louisiana (1848–55); and then for twelve years in New York City. In 1867, Young became bishop of Florida. He was active in the development of the University of the South, Sewanee, TN.

John S. Howson

May 5, 1816
Giggleswick, England

Dec. 15, 1885
Bournemouth, England

NT scholar and dean of Chester, 1867–85. Earlier in his career, Howson was principal of Liverpool College from 1849–65, teaching there since 1845. He is best known as the joint author with WILLIAM CONYBEARE of *The Life and Epistles of St. Pau*l (1850–52). Howson was active in establishing the order of deaconesses in connection with the Anglican Church. He also wrote several other books on the Apostle Paul. His works range from *Deaconesses* (1862) to *Thoughts for Saints' Days* (published, 1883).

John B. Gough

Aug. 22, 1817
Sandgate, England

Feb. 18, 1886
Frankford, Pennsylvania

Famous temperance orator who came to America in 1829. After years as an alcoholic, 1834–42, Gough signed a total abstinence pledge in 1842 and became a convincing lecturer on temperance reform. He married Lucretia Fowler (Dec. 18, 1839), and Mary Whitcomb (Nov. 23, 1843). He gave some 5,000 speeches from 1843 until his death. Gough personally persuaded 215,179 people to sign the abstinence pledge. He died of a stroke. His favorite Bible verse was Hebrews 7:25.

Richard C. Trench

Sept. 9, 1807
Dublin, Ireland

March 28, 1886
London, England

Anglican archbishop of Dublin, 1864–84, and biblical scholar. In 1832, Trench married his cousin. As a writer, Trench stimulated interest in New Testament studies with his famed *Notes on the Parables* (1840) and *Notes on the Miracles* (1846). He also wrote poetry. His last book was *Poems* (1855). Trench was professor of divinity at King's College, London (1846–56), and dean of Westminster College (1856–62). He opposed the disestablishment of the Irish Church, but guided the Church with sanity and moderation. In 1875, he suffered a severe accident on a boat crossing to Ireland and never fully recovered.

"Thou camest not to thy place by accident."

Leopold von Ranke

Dec. 21, 1795
Wiehe, Germany

May 23, 1886
Berlin, Germany

Professor of history at the University of Berlin, 1825–71. In 1827, under the direction of the Prussian Government, von Ranke did research at Rome, Venice, and Vienna. He produced several works relating to Christian history, writing a total of 54 volumes. Von Ranke stressed scientific objectivity, relying on original sources for his material. His goal was to discover God in history.

John W. Nevin

Feb. 20, 1803
Strasburg, Pennsylvania

June 6, 1886
Lancaster, Pennsylvania

Theologian, scholar, and educator. Nevin and PHILIP SCHAFF created "Mercersburg Theology" (the balance of head and heart, objective and subjective). Seven children came from his marriage to Martha Jenkins in 1835. He was a Presbyterian who taught at Western Theological Seminary, Pittsburgh, PA from 1830–40. He then served on the staff and taught as sole professor at German Reformed Seminary, Mercersburg, PA from 1841–53, and joined the Reformed Church. He was also president of Marshall College, Mercersburg (1841–53) (merged with Franklin College in 1853 to form FMC), and of Franklin and Marshall College (University), Lancaster (1866–76), his church college. He emphasized tradition and the church and opposed revivalism excesses. He edited the *Mercersburg Review* (1849–52).

John L. Wilson

March 25, 1809
Salem, South Carolina

July 13, 1886
Salem, South Carolina

Director of Presbyterian Church (PC USA in 1983) **in the United States Missions, 1861–84**. Wilson was a missionary in Cape Palmas and Gabon, West Africa, 1834–52, with ABCFM. Jane Bayard became his wife on

May 21, 1834. He was secretary of Foreign Missions for the Presbyterian Church, NY (1853–61), and for the Southern Presbyterian Church, Columbia, SC (1861–85). His ministry included teaching the sick, founding schools, compiling grammars and dictionaries, and translating gospels. He was also instrumental in breaking up the slave trade in Africa. He edited *The Missionary* for some 20 years, 1866–86.

John Maclean

March 3, 1800
Princeton, New Jersey

Aug. 10, 1886
Princeton, New Jersey

President of Princeton (NJ) College (University in 1896), 1854–68. Maclean began teaching at Princeton in 1818 in the field of mathematics. He also founded the Alumni Association of Nassau Hall in 1826. Maclean was ordained as a Presbyterian in 1828. From 1829–54, he served as vice president. He was responsible for building the East College (1832), the West College (1836), and for establishing several scholarship funds for needy students. He authored two volumes of history about Princeton in 1877.

Joseph M. Scriven

Sept. 10, 1819
Seapatrick, Ireland

Aug. 10, 1886
Bewdley, Ontario, Canada

Hymn writer of one of history's favorite hymns, "What a Friend We Have in Jesus" (music by CHARLES CONVERSE). Scriven was a Congregationalist who migrated to Canada about 1844. He spent his life helping others in any way he could. He was influenced by the Plymouth Brethren. Twice Scriven tragically lost fiancés shortly before marriage; one drowned on the eve of their wedding in Ireland. Later in Canada, Eliza Roche died of an illness a few weeks prior to another planned wedding. Many years later, Scriven also drowned. His death, however, was surrounded by mysterious circumstances on Rice Lake in Ontario. He lived at Port Hope, Ontario.

Archibald A. Hodge

July 18, 1823
Princeton, New Jersey

Nov. 11, 1886
Princeton, New Jersey

Presbyterian theologian. Archibald was the son of CHARLES H. HODGE and lectured for 50 years at Princeton. Elizabeth Holliday became his wife (1847), and Margaret M. Woods his second wife (1862). Hodge was a missionary in India, 1847–50. He pastored at Lower West Nottingham, MD (1851–55); Fredericksburg, VA (1855–61); and Wilkes-Barre, PA (1861–64). Hodge next taught at Western Theological Seminary, Allegheny, PA (1864–77), and then theology at Princeton (1878 until his death), succeeding his father, about whom he wrote a biography, *The Life of Charles Hodge* (1880). He was a sound Bible expositor and strong orthodox leader. He wrote *Outlines of Theology* (1860) to *Popular Lectures on Theological Themes* (1887).

Jacob J. Glossbrenner

July 24, 1812
Hagerstown, Maryland

Jan. 7, 1887
Churchville, Virginia

Bishop of Church of the United Brethren in Christ (United Methodist Church in 1968), **1845–87**. Glossbrenner was converted at age 17 from Lutheranism. He served as an evangelist from 1831 on. He married Maria Shuey on February 14, 1833. Glossbrenner was a forceful preacher and an astute administrator who advocated advanced study for ministers and meaningful missionary programs. Despite his own anti-slavery sentiments, he stayed with the church "flock" in southern Virginia during the Civil War.

Rowland H. Prichard

Jan. 14, 1811
Graienyn, Wales

Jan. 25, 1887
Holywell, Wales

Hymn composer of "Our Great Savior" (lyrics by J. W. CHAPMAN) and **"Come, Thou Long-Expected Jesus"** (lyrics by CHARLES WESLEY). Prichard was a man of humble rank who spent most of his life in his hometown. At age 69, he became a loom tender's assistant at the Welsh Flannel Manufacturing Company at Holywell. Prichard was a well-known musician and led singing regularly at his church.

Henry W. Beecher

June 24, 1813
Litchfield, Connecticut

March 8, 1887
Brooklyn, New York

Famous editor and influential pastor of Plymouth Congregational Church. Henry was one of 13 children born to the famous preacher LYMAN BEECHER, and the brother of author HARRIET BEECHER STOWE. In 1825, the family moved to Boston. In 1828, the teenage Beecher was converted at a revival in Amherst, MA. Ten children came from Henry's marriage to Eunice Bullard (Aug 26, 1812–March 8, 1897) on Aug. 3, 1837. Beecher pastored a Presbyterian church in Lawrenceburg, IN (1838–39) and Second Presbyterian Church in Indianapolis, IN (1839–47). From Oct. 10, 1847, until his death 40 years later, Beecher pastored at the Plymouth Church in Brooklyn, where he preached to over 2,500 each week. His *Plymouth Collection of Hymns and Tunes* (1855), named after his church, was his major contribution to hymnology. He was an outspoken advocate of reform and had much political influence to support his anti–slavery position, women's suffrage, and support of the Union Army troops. Beecher was a powerful and convincing speaker with his sermons drawing national attention. He became editor of the *Congregational Independent* (1861–64), and later (1870–81) edited the *Christian Union* (*Outlook*). Beecher visited England to defend the Union Cause in 1863. In 1865, he gave an oration when the Union flag was once again raised at Fort Sumter, SC (site of first clash of the U.S. Civil War on April 12, 1861. In 1874, he was charged with adultery, but acquitted by civil jury in a 112-day 1875 trial and ecclesiastical tribunal. He withdrew from the Congregational Association in 1882. Beecher's work, *Revolution and Religion* (1885) was considered highly controversial along with his later-in-life views, which expressed a disbelief in a literal hell, rejection of Calvinism, and acceptance of evolutionary stages. He had a normal day on March 3, but that night fell into a coma for five days before expiring. He was one of the most popular lecturers and after-dinner speakers in America. His last words were, "Going out into life, that is dying, now comes the mystery." He is buried in Greenwood Cemetery, Brooklyn.

Archer T. Gurney

1820

March 21, 1887
Bath, England

Anglican hymn writer. Gurney's education was headed toward a law degree, but he changed course and entered the ministry. In 1849, he took Holy Orders of the Church of England and was curate for four years at Buckingham. In 1858, Gurney became chaplain at Court Church, Paris, France. In 1862, he contributed 147 of his hymns to *The English Book of Praise*. He also wrote poetry.

Ray Palmer

Nov. 12, 1808
Little Compton, Rhode Island

March 29, 1887
Newark, New Jersey

Hymn writer of the famed hymn, "My Faith Looks Up to Thee" (1830) (music by LOWELL MASON). Palmer left home at 13 because of poverty and took a job in a Boston dry goods store. He joined Park Street Congregational Church and married Ann M. Wand on Oct. 3, 1832. He became a Congregational cleric who, upon his ordination in 1835, began a 30-year pastoral career. He served 15 years at Central Church, Bath, ME and then 15 years at the First Church, Albany, NY. He was corresponding secretary of the American Congregational Union in NYC from 1866–78, which helped finance the construction of over 600 churches. Palmer's works range from *Spiritual Improvement* (1839) to *Voices of Hope and Gladness* (1880). His poetical works fill more than 350 pages. He also translated BERNARD's "Jesus, Thou Joy of Loving Hearts."

Ion G. N. Keith-Falconer

July 25, 1856 — May 1887
Edinburgh, Scotland — Aden, Arabia (Yemen)

Lay missionary to the Moslem World. Converted as a boy, Keith-Falconer became interested in cycling. At Cambridge University, he set a world record for a five-mile race—15 min., 11 sec. On Oct. 7, 1885, Ion and his wife went to Aden (capital of Yemen) on the southern corner of the Arabian Peninsula, representing the Free Church of Scotland. They founded the Sheikh Othman Hospital near Aden. Back on the continent, Keith-Falconer lectured on the Arabic language at Cambridge. He and his wife returned to the field, but fell victims to Aden national fever. He died at age 31. His great commission was to "call attention to Arabia."

Carl F. W. Walther

Oct. 25, 1811 — May 7, 1887
Langenschursdorf, Germany — St. Louis, Missouri

Theologian; founder of the Lutheran Church—Missouri Synod; its first president, 1847–50, 1864–78; and first president of Concordia Seminary, St. Louis, 1850–87 (which he helped found in 1839). The Concordia Theological Seminary, Ft. Wayne, IN merged into the St. Louis campus, 1861–75. Walther came to America in 1837, with 750 Lutherans, settling in Missouri and, more than any other individual, brought organization to the Lutheran Church in America. His marriage to Christiane Bunger on September21, 1841, gave him six children. From 1853–76, Walther wrote several books in the German language. He was a skilled organist.

John B. McFerrin

June 15, 1807 — May 10, 1887
Rutherford County, Tennessee

Secretary of Missions for the Methodist Church South, 1870–78. McFerrin was converted in 1820. He was a missionary and elder to the Cherokee Indians around Ft. Oglethorpe, GA in 1829, and was considered an authority on Tennessee Methodism. He pastored in Alabama and Tennessee, 1829–40. He had at least four children from his marriages to Almyra A. Probart (1833), and Cynthia T. McGavock (1855). He was a counselor to President JAMES POLK and preached the president's funeral in Nashville, TN in 1849. He edited the *Christian Advocate* (1840–58), was a book agent for his denomination (1858–66), secretary of Domestic Missions (1866–78) and book agent (1878–87). He is buried in Nashville.

Mark Hopkins

Feb. 4, 1802 — June 17, 1887
Stockbridge, Massachusetts — Williamstown, Massachusetts

Congregational theologian, moral philosopher, and educator. Hopkins was president of Williams College, Williamstown, MA (1836–72), following teaching philosophy and rhetoric there (1830–36). He was pastor of the Williams College Church for 47 years (1830–87), and also president of American Board of Commissioners for Foreign Missions (1857–87). He and his wife, Mary Hubbell, whom he married on December 25, 1832, had ten children. Hopkins taught 1,730 of the 1,760 graduates of Williams College and was considered one of the foremost teachers in the nation. He was the great-nephew of SAMUEL HOPKINS. President GARFIELD said, "The ideal college is a log with a student at one end and Mark Hopkins at the other." Among his published works were *Evidence of Christianity* (1846) and *Teachings and Counsels* (1884).

Thomas J. Comber

Nov. 7, 1852
Comberwell, London, England

June 27, 1887
Loango, French Congo (Congo)

Baptist missionary to the Congo. Comber was converted at age 16. In 1875, he was sent as a missionary to the Cameroons in West Africa. During his trek there, Comber met ALFRED SAKER (Baptist missionary), whose failing health was taking him back to England. Comber later met GEORGE GRENFELL and they ministered together in the Congo, Central Africa (between Cameroon and Zaire). Minnie, his bride of four months, died in June, 1879, of meningitis. Comber died eight years later at age 35 from a rampant fever, on board a ship en route to England. In 1886, his Congolese servant was the first Baptist Missionary Society convert to be baptized.

William McMaster

Dec. 24, 1811
County Tyrone, Ireland

Sept. 22, 1887
Toronto, Ontario, Canada

Canadian statesman and Baptist layman who left his estate to found Woodstock College in 1860. The theological department moved to Toronto (1881), then the whole institute became known as McMaster University (1887). The school began on evangelical truth but turned liberal. McMaster had come to Toronto in 1833, and got involved in a dry goods business. In 1867, he founded the Bank of Commerce, and within two decades of leadership, it became one of the largest banks in the country. He was a leader in Toronto's original Baptist congregation and erected a building on Jarvis Street in 1875.

George J. Webb

June 24, 1803
Wiltshire, England

Oct. 7, 1887
Orange, New Jersey

Composed the music for the famed hymn, "Stand Up for Jesus" (1830) (lyrics by GEORGE DUFFIELD). Webb came to Boston in 1830. For 40 years, he was organist of the Old South Church of Boston and active with LOWELL MASON in the musical affairs of the city. Six children came from his marriage to Carolin Merriam. Webb became widely known as a choral and orchestral conductor.

Jenny Lind Goldschmidt

Oct. 6, 1821
Stockholm, Sweden

Nov. 2, 1887
Malvern, England

Soprano soloist considered one of the greatest of her time both for vocal art and theatrical musical performances. Jenny first appeared on stage at age nine. Her Lutheran grandmother instilled an abiding faith in God in her young granddaughter. Jenny sang various opera roles in Stockholm (1838–44), Germany (1844–47), England (1847–49), and America (1850–52), having been brought over by P. T. Barnum. Jenny was converted on a gospel boat in New York City harbor where Olaf Hedstrom was preaching. Her acquaintance with Bishop Edward Stanley led to her determination to give up the stage as a career. She abandoned opera in 1849, for concert singing. When she came to the States, 30,000 people met her ship in New York City. The first concert ticket sold at auction for $225. Each concert included "I Know That My Redeemer Liveth." On Feb. 5, 1852, she married Otto Goldschmidt (born: 1829), her piano accompanist. Jenny became a British citizen in 1859. Her last public appearance in concert was in Dusseldorf, January 20, 1870, and as a singer in 1883. While in semi-retirement in England, she took active interest in the

Bach choir conducted by her husband and was a professor of voice at the Royal College of Music in 1883. She suffered a paralytic stroke shortly before death.

Edmund A. DeSchweinitz

March 20, 1825
Bethlehem, Pennsylvania

Dec. 18, 1887
Bethlehem, Pennsylvania

President of Moravian Church in NA (North) 1878–87, and of Moravian Theological Seminary, Bethlehem, PA 1867–84. DeSchweinitz married Lydia J. de Tschirschky (1850) and Isabel A. Boggs (1868) who gave him one child. He pastored the Moravian Church in Lebanon, PA (1851–53), at the First Church in Philadelphia, PA (1853–60) Lititz, PA (1860–64), and in Bethlehem, PA (1864–80). He was the first editor of his denomination's paper, the *Moravian* (1856–66). He wrote histories of the Moravian movement and was a strong supporter of its missionary endeavors.

Mary J. Kinnaird
Lady Kinnaird

1816

1888

Founder and director of Zenana Mission (Interserve in 1986) **1845–88, and YWCA co–founder.** The Society for Promoting Female Education in the East was set up in London by Lady Kinnaird in 1834, to provide teachers and funds for a work that had 22 schools centering in Calcutta. The Calcutta Normal School (for Christian Female Teachers) got her attention. It was opened March 1, 1852, the date the sponsoring mission was born, the Zenana Bible Mission. Although closely linked to the Church Missionary Society, she insisted the work be inter-denominational. Mary would become the co-founder (with Emma Robarts) of the YWCA in 1855. In 1855, she opened a home for FLORENCE NIGHTINGALE's nurses, returning from the Crimean War and working girls in London. Other homes were started in 1877 that she merged with the fledgling YWCA and directed that work in London. Mary was the wife of Hon. Arthur Kinnaird, a Scottish Liberal MP, and was a leading figure among British evangelical upperclass families in London. In 1880, the work was called Zenana Bible and Medical Mission. The Kinnaird College for Women was founded in 1913 in Lahore. In 1952, the name was changed to Bible and Medical Mission Fellowship and in 1986 to Interserve.

Peter Parker

June 18, 1804
Framington, Massachusetts

Jan. 10, 1888
Washington, D.C.

Medical missionary and diplomat. Parker was ordained Presbyterian and sent by the ABCFM to China in 1834. He arrived shortly before ROBERT MORRISON's death. He opened a hospital in Canton and founded a medical missionary society there in 1838. He treated more than 50,000 patients. Parker married Harriet C. Webster on March 29, 1841, and they had one son. Parker lived in Washington, D.C. from 1858–88, and was associated with the Smithsonian Institute and the American Evangelical Alliance. He is remembered as a primitive medical missionary that would have many follow in his footsteps.

Patrick H. Mell

July 19, 1814
Walthourville, Georgia

Jan. 26, 1888
Athens, Georgia

President of Southern Baptist Convention, 1863–71, 1880–88. Mell married Lurene H. Cooper (June 29, 1840), by whom he had nine children, and Elizabeth E. Cooper (December 24, 1861), by whom he had six. He was a professor of ancient languages at Mercer College (University), Macon, GA from 1841–55. Mell pastored in Greensboro, (1842–52); Bairdstown, (1852–62); and Antioch, GA (1862–88). He was active at the University of Georgia (1856–88), vice-chancellor (1860–72), and chancellor (1878–88). He was well known as a prince of parliamentarians, and served as the moderator of the Georgia Baptist Convention for 25 years.

Asa Gray

Nov. 18, 1810
Sauquoit, New York

Jan. 30, 1888
Cambridge, Massachusetts

Harvard Botanist known to millions of students. Gray was a prolific writer for scientific journals, author of many textbooks and professor of botany at Harvard, 1842–88. His *Manual of Botany* is still a standard reference book. He helped revise Carl Linnaeus' (Swedish Botanist) system of plant classification. In his *Natural Science and Religion*, he states, the "advent…of a divine Person, who, being made man, manifested the divine nature in union with the human; and that this manifestation constitutes Christianity. Having accepted the doctrine of incarnation, itself the crowning miracle, attendant miracles are not obstacles to belief." He combined outstanding scientific reputation with an evangelical Christian faith. He was a Congregationalist, and visited Europe in 1838. His works range from *Elements of Botany* (1836) to *Letters of Asa Gray* (1894).

James G. Small

1817
Edinburgh, Scotland

Feb. 11, 1888
Renfrew-on-the-Clyde, Scotland

Wrote the hymn, "I've Found a Friend" (1863) (music by George Stebbins). Small was ordained in the Free Church of Scotland (Presbyterian) in 1847; then he became the pastor of the Free Church of Bervie, near Montrose. He was greatly interested in hymnology and published *Hymns for Youthful Voices* (1859) and *Psalms and Sacred Songs* (1859).

John K. Mackenzie

Aug. 25, 1850
Yarmouth, England

April 1, 1888
Tient-Tsin, China

Medical missionary to China. Mackenzie was converted at a Moody crusade in Bristol in 1867. Impressed with the Moody ministry, he joined the Presbyterian Church at age 17 and became very active in missionary work. In 1875, he went to Hankow and worked in medical work for nearly four years. He married (1877), and then transferred to Tien-Tsin (1879). In 1880, he dedicated a hospital there. He contracted smallpox and died at age 38.

William F. Sherwin

March 14, 1826
Buckland, Massachusetts

April 14, 1888
Boston, Massachusetts

Wrote the lyrics and music for the hymn, "Sound the Battle Cry." He also composed the music for the hymns, "Break Thou the Bread of Life" (1877) and "Day Is Dying in the West" (lyrics by Mary Lathbury). Sherwin was a Baptist layman. He received his music training from Lowell Mason. He organized and directed several amateur choruses and served as the music director of the Chautauqua Assembly in New York.

Edward Hopper

Feb. 17, 1816
New York, New York

April 23, 1888
New York, New York

Wrote the hymn "Jesus, Savior, Pilot Me" (1871) (music by John Gould). Hopper was ordained as a Presbyterian and held pastorates for eleven years in Greenville, NY and Sag Harbor, Long Island, NY. Then, he returned to NYC to pastor the Church of the Sea and Land, a mission church for sailors for most of his remaining life. He died of a heart attack while writing a poem.

William Lincoln

1825
East London, England

April 25, 1888

Plymouth Brethren preacher and writer who was converted at age 17, by reading PHILIP DODDRIDGE's book, *Rise and Progress of Religion*. From 1849–59, he had a curacy at Southwark. Lincoln preached in the Anglican Church from 1859–62 at the Beresford Chapel in Walworth. He then broke from the state church and authored *Javelin of Phinehas*, which revealed the evils of the church/state union. Lincoln joined the United Brethren movement, preaching primarily on prophecy and apostasy.

Johann K. F. Keil

Feb. 26, 1807
Oelsritz/Lauterbach, Germany

May 5, 1888
Rodlitz, Saxony (Germany)

Lutheran scholar and exegete who joined the faculty of Dorpat (Estonia) University in 1833 as a teacher of OT and NT exegesis and Oriental languages. Keil remained at the school until his retirement 25 years later in 1858. He settled in Leipzig (1859), where he wrote and served the Lutheran Church, then moved to Rodlitz (1887). He wrote many evangelical works, including *Old Testament Commentary* with FRANZ DELITZSCH (1861–72). His *Introduction to the Old Testament* was his most valuable work.

George Duffield Jr.

Sept. 12, 1818
Carlisle, Pennsylvania

July 6, 1888
Bloomfield, New Jersey

Wrote the hymn "Stand Up, Stand Up for Jesus" (music by GEORGE WEBB and ADAM GEIBEL). Duffield was a Presbyterian pastor in Brooklyn, NY (1840–47); Bloomfield, NJ (1847–52); Philadelphia, PA (1852–61); Adrian, MI (1861–65); Galesburg, IL (1865–69); Saginaw, MI (1869–74); and was an evangelist in Ann Arbor, MI (1874–77) and Lansing, MI (1877–80). He retired to Bloomfield to live with his son.

Johannes H. A. Ebrard

Jan. 18, 1818
Erlangen, Germany

July 23, 1888
Erlangen, Germany

Reformed theologian and clergyman. Ebrard served as a professor of theology at Zurich (1844–47) and at Erlangen (1847–61). Ebrard also pastored the French Reformed Church of Erlangen, 1875–88. He was a prolific writer who used several pseudonymns. His works include *The Gospel History* and *Apologetics*.

John W. Burgon

Aug. 21, 1813
Smyrna, Turkey

Aug. 4, 1888
Chichester, England

Scholarly dean of Chester, who violently opposed the English Revised Version of the Bible in 1881, and the Westcott-Hort Greek text upon which it was based. Burgon wrote *The Revision Revised* (1883); however, he did not claim inspiration for the KJV text or perfection of any Greek text. Many KJV defenders have erroneously used him as their authority. He was vicar of St. Mary's, Oxford (1863) and dean of Chicester (1876).

Robert Young

Sept. 10, 1822
Edinburgh, Scotland

Oct. 14, 1888
Edinburgh, Scotland

Presbyterian layman and theologian of the Free Church. Young learned the trade of a printer, and from 1847–56, he engaged in bookselling and printing. In 1856, he went to India to head the Mission Press at Surat. He returned to Scotland in 1861 and conducted missionary conferences until 1874. His *Analytical Concordance* (1876–79) is very well known.

Horatio G. Spafford

Oct. 20, 1828
North Troy, New York

Oct. 16, 1888
Jerusalem, Palestine (Israel)

Wrote the hymn, "It Is Well With My Soul" (1873) (music by BLISS). This is considered to be the most dramatic hymn story on record. Spafford's three daughters drowned in the Atlantic Ocean, November 22, 1873, when two ships collided. Later, as he crossed the ocean to rejoin his rescued wife, Spafford wrote the hymn in the vicinity of the collision. He had already lost everything in the Chicago Fire in 1871. He was a faithful Presbyterian layman. His remaining days were spent developing children's homes, known as Spafford Homes.

Isaac Errett

Jan. 2, 1820
New York, New York

Dec. 19, 1888
Terrace Park (Cincinnati), Ohio

Disciples of Christ pastor in Pittsburgh, 1840–71. Errett married Harriet Reeder on October 18, 1841. He was associated with ALEXANDER CAMPBELL in editing *The Millennial Harbinger* and later the *Christian Standard* (1866–88). He delivered the funeral message for President JAMES GARFIELD in September, 1881. He was active in education and missions projects. His works range from *Christian Missions* (1875) to *Our Position* (1885).

James P. Boyce

Jan. 11, 1827
Charleston, South Carolina

Dec. 28, 1888
Pau, France

Educator and theologian, president of Southern Baptist Convention, 1872–79, 1888. Converted in the spring of 1846, under the preaching of RICHARD FULLER in Charleston, he pastored FBC, Columbia, SC and was a professor at Furman University, Greenville, SC from 1855–59. Lizzie L. Ficklen became his wife on December 20, 1858. Boyce also organized the Southern Baptist Theological Seminary, Greenville, SC (1859–61), serving as its chairman (1859–88) and its first president in 1888. He helped move the seminary to Louisville, KY in 1877. For health reasons, the last years of his life were spent in Europe, having battled gout for 17 years. He served as a Confederate chaplain and also in the SC legislature during the Civil War.

Alessandro Gavazzi

March 21, 1809
Bologna, Italy

Jan. 9, 1889
Rome, Italy

Patriot and reformer. Gavazzi was born of Catholic parents, but eventually went to England and renounced the Roman Church. He fled from Rome to London in 1849 and organized Italian Protestants in London. After returning to Italy, he became chaplain to Garibaldi's army in 1860. He spent years in Great Britain and America speaking about the evils of the papal system and authored several books on the subject. He was one of the organizers of the Free Italian Church (1870), founded officially (1875), and was professor of oratory in Rome Theological Seminary. His works range from *Memoirs* (1851) to *The Priest in Absolution* (1877).

David Trumbull

Nov. 1, 1819
Elizabeth, New Jersey

Feb. 4, 1889
Valparaiso, Chile

Congregational missionary who was the first permanent Protestant witness in South America. Trumbull arrived in Chile in 1845, and worked for 45 years under the Foreign Evangelical Society and the Seaman's Friend Society. He was key in getting religious toleration granted in 1865. His work was transferred to the Presbyterian

Mission Board in 1873. He was effective in jail ministries and in the hospital. He also ministered to servicemen and established a school for girls. He became a Chilean citizen in 1886.

Holland N. McTyeire

July 28, 1824
Barmwell County, South Carolina

Feb. 15, 1889
Nashville, Tennessee

Bishop of the Methodist Church, South, after 1866. McTyeire married Amelia Townsend on November 9, 1847. He pastored in Alabama, 1848–49, 1862, and 1866, and in Louisiana 1849–58. He was the founding president of Vanderbilt University, 1873–89, which later separated from Methodism in 1914. He helped to found The Colored (Cumberland) Methodist Church. McTyeire edited both the *New Orleans Christian Advocate* (1851–58) and the *Nashville Christian Advocate* (1858–66). He wrote a *History of Methodism* (1884).

William Thompson

Feb. 18, 1806
Goshen, Connecticut

Feb. 27, 1889
Hartford, Connecticut

President of Theological Institute of Connecticut, East Windsor Hill, CT 1857–79, (renamed and relocated), **Hartford (CT) Theological Seminary, 1879–88**. Thompson was ordained in 1833 as pastor of a church, North Bridgewater, MA. He married Eliza Butler in 1834 (died: 1879). In 1834, he became the third professor of the fledgling institute where he stayed until his death 54 years later. Thompson died from pneumonia.

William H. Monk

March 16, 1823
Brompton, London, England

March 1, 1889
Stoke Newington, London, England

Composed the music for "Abide With Me" (1861). After serving as an organist for six years at various London churches, Monk was appointed choir director at King's College, London, in 1847, and became the organist there two years later. In 1852, he became the organist at St. Matthias' Church, Stoke Newington, until his death. His work, *Hymns: Ancient and Modern*, is world renowned, including 50 of his own hymn tunes. He was professor at the National Training School for Music and at Bedford College, 1876 on.

Alfred Edersheim

March 7, 1825
Vienna, Austria

March 16, 1889
Menton, France

Prominent biblical scholar, minister of the Free Church in Old Aberdeen, Scotland, 1849–61, until health problems took him to St. Andrews Presbyterian in Torquay, 1861–75. Edersheim was also a missionary in Romania and England. Born of Jewish parents, he came under the influence of Scottish Presbyterian John Duncan, a chaplain to workers on a Danube River bridge, Budapest, Hungary. In 1842, he became a Christian. He went to New College in Edinburgh and became a missionary to Jews in Jassy, Romania, 1846–49. He was ordained as a Scotch Presbyterian (1846), but turned to the Church of England (1875). He then was vicar at Loders, 1876–82. His *Life and Time of Jesus the Messiah* was published from 1883–90 (2 vols.). He was an authority on Jewish culture and wrote much about it. He also lectured at Oxford.

Asa Mahan

Nov. 9, 1799   *April 4, 1889*
Vernon, New York   Eastbourne, England

First president of Oberlin (OH) College, 1835–50. Mahan was a renowned Congregational clergyman and educator. He married May Dix on May 9, 1828, and Mary E. Chase in 1866. He pastored in Pittsford, NY (1829–31); Cincinnati, OH (1831–39); Jackson, MI (1855–57); and Adrian, MI (1857–60). He was president of Cleveland (OH) University (1850–54), and of Adrian (MI) College (1860–71). In 1871, he joined the Wesleyan Methodists and retired to Eastbourne. His works range from *Doctrine of Christian Perfection* (1839) to *Critical History of Philosophy* (2 vols., 1883, NY).

Theodore D. Woolsey

Oct. 31, 1801   *July 1, 1889*
New York, New York   New Haven, Connecticut

President of Yale College and Divinity School (University in 1887), **New Haven, CT 1846–71**. Woolsey married Elizabeth Salisbury (September 5, 1833) and Sarah Pritchard (Sept. 6, 1854), giving him 13 children. He did extensive studying in Leipzig, Bonn, and Berlin. In 1831, he became Greek professor at Yale, and served in this capacity until he became president. He was a strong evangelical and had a strong mind. He wrote many books. Some claim he made the first systematic study of American politics, and his writings on international law are authoritative. He was the nephew of TIMOTHY DWIGHT SR.

Elvina M. Reynolds Hall-Myers

June 4, 1820   *July 18, 1889*
Alexandria, Virginia   Ocean Grove, New Jersey

Wrote the touching hymn "Jesus Paid It All" (music by JOHN GRAPE) written in a choir loft while the pastor was giving a lengthy prayer. Elvina first married Richard Hall, and after his death, married Rev. Thomas Myers of the Baltimore Conference of the Methodist Church in 1885. She attended Monument Street Methodist Church in Baltimore for 40 years.

James Boyce (1)

July 13, 1808   *July 29, 1889*
Sardis, North Carolina   Due West, South Carolina

Stated clerk of Associate Reformed Presbyterian Church, Greenville, SC 1848–79, and president of Erskine Theological Seminary, Due West, SC 1869–1889. Boyce married Mary Ann Bell (died: 1847, leaving four children), then Martha Witherspoon on Jan. 1, 1850. Early on, Boyce pastored the Brick Church and New Hope Church of Fairfield County, SC. In 1869, he began teaching at Erskine Seminary and continued until his death. He edited the *Christian Magazine of the Youth* (1843–51). He traveled much and had a heart of tenderness and love.

Horatius Bonar

Dec. 19, 1808   *July 31, 1889*
Edinburgh, Scotland   Edinburgh, Scotland

Presbyterian hymn writer, poet, and preacher. Bonar wrote some 600 hymns, including, "I Heard the Voice of Jesus Say," "I Was a Wandering Sheep," and "Hallelujah for the Cross" (1882). In the Church of Scotland, he led the North Parish, Kelso, 1837–43. He was active in founding the Free Church of Scotland in 1843, and continued pastoring in Kelso until 1866. Bonar then pastored Chalmers Memorial Grange and Free Church of Edinburgh, 1866–89. He was a friend of the MOODY/SANKEY ministry. His wife's name was Jane Lundie, and his brother was ANDREW BONAR. His writings range from *The Night of Weeping* (1846) to *Until the Daybreak and Other Hymns* (1890). He was a strong pre-millennialist.

George Z. Gray

July 14, 1838
New York, New York

Aug. 4, 1889
Sharon Springs, New York

President of Episcopal Divinity School, Cambridge, MA 1876–82. Grey married Kate Forrest in 1862. He served as rector of St. Paul's Church, Kinderhook, NY (1863–65), and Trinity Church, Bergen Point, NJ (1865–76). He was the warden of Racine (WI) College from 1882–89. He also authored books ranging from *Spiritual Doctrine of Recognition in the World to Come* (1875) to *The Church's Certain Faith* (1890).

Theodor Christlieb

March 7, 1833
Birkenfeld, Germany

Aug. 15, 1889
Bonn, Germany

Lutheran evangelical theologian who became pastor of the Islington German Church of London (1858–65), after pastoring in Friedrichaften (1865–68). Christlieb was appointed professor of practical theology and university preacher at Bonn (1868–89), influencing such men as Prince William (later emperor), his student (1877–80). He opposed the liberalism of his day and took part in the work of the Evangelical Alliance. He was the founder of the Evangelistic Union, a training school for evangelists, which later was removed to Barmen. He wrote *Medical Missions* (1889).

Reuben D. Robinson

1818
Clark, Indiana

Aug. 18, 1889
Indianapolis, Indiana

President of Fort Wayne (IN) College (Taylor University, Upland, IN in 1891), **1855–65, 1869–70, and 1872–77**. Robinson was a prominent Methodist layman, and was a presiding elder (district superintendent). He had blond hair, was 6 feet tall and weighed 225 pounds. He served as a trustee and professor of languages at the college prior to his presidency.

Thomas H. Vail

Oct. 21, 1812
Richmond, Virginia

Oct. 6, 1889
Bryn Mawr, Pennsylvania

Episcopal cleric who founded Bethany College, Topeka, KS and was its president. He served as rector of Christ's Church, Cambridge, MA (1837–39); St. John's Church, Essex, CT (1839–44); Christ's Church, Westerly, RI (1844–57); St. Thomas' Church, Taunton, MA (1857–63); and Trinity Church, Muscatine, IA (1863–64). Vail was also the first bishop of Kansas, 1864–89. He wrote *The Comprehensive Church* (1841).

Edwin Hatch

Sept. 4, 1835
Derby, England

Nov. 10, 1889
Oxford, England

Wrote hymns, including "Breathe on Me" (music by B.B. MCKINNEY) and **"Breathe on Me, Breath of God,"** (1878) (music by ROBERT JACKSON). Hatch was a Church of England professor of classics in Trinity College, Toronto, Ontario; a rector of a Quebec high school; fellow of McGill University in Montreal (1859–66); and vice-principal of St. Mary's Hall, Oxford (1867–85). He also served as rector of Pureligh, Essex in 1883; though residing in Oxford. Hatch delivered Bampton's Lectures, "Organizations of Early Churches" (1880) and the Hibbert Lectures (1888). It is said that he had unbounded energy and enough plans and dreams to fill a dozen lifetimes.

Eugene A. F. Bersier

Feb. 5, 1831
Morges, Switzerland

Nov. 19, 1889
Paris, France

French Free Reformed preacher and writer who worked for church unity and wrote on church history and liturgy. Bersier was called to preach while he was on an American tour in 1850. From 1855–77, he pastored three Free Churches in Paris. In 1877, this church joined the Reformed (established) Church of France. Bersier preached with great power, and he ranks as one of France's greatest preachers. He wrote *The Gospel in Paris Sermon* (1884).

Robert Browning

May 7, 1812
Camberwell, London, England

Dec. 12, 1889
Venice, Italy

English poet who wrote many biblical and Christian themes with deep insight. Browning emphasized the soul and the future life especially. His "Saul and Death in the Desert" is an example. In 1846, he married Elizabeth Barrett (March 6, 1806–June 30, 1861), who also excelled in poetry. They lived in Florence, Italy, until her death, at which time he returned to England. Elizabeth said as she died, "It is beautiful." His poem "Pauline" was published in 1833 when he was but 20, but he won his fame with *The Ring and the Book* (1868–69), a long, narrative poem about a Roman murder trial. Browning and TENNYSON were England's greatest poets; both were spiritual men.

"Trust God; see all, nor be afraid."

Joseph B. Lightfoot

April 13, 1828
Liverpool, England

Dec. 21, 1889
Bournemouth, England

Theologian, scholar, and textual critic. Lightfoot wrote many commentaries on the New Testament, as well as works on church fathers. These works won him great fame. He was a professor of divinity at Cambridge from 1861–71 and was fluent in seven languages. He was a member of the New Testament revision committee, 1870–80 (Revised Version of the New Testament). Lightfoot was canon of St. Paul's 1871–79, and became bishop of Durham in 1879, promoting church and social reform.

Ebenezer Dodge

April 21, 1819
Salem, Massachusetts

Jan. 5, 1890
Hamilton, New York

President of Madison University (Colgate-Rochester (NY), Divinity School in 1928), **Hamilton, NY 1868–90**. Dodge married Sarah A. Putnam (1846), and Eleanor F. Rogers (1863). He pastored a Baptist Church in New Hampton, NY from 1846–49; and then was a professor of Biblical Criticism at Theological Institute, Hamilton, NY. He later taught Evidences of Revealed Religion (1853–61) and Doctrinal Theology (1861–67) at Madison.

Joseph H. Neesima

Feb. 14, 1843
Yedo (Tokyo), Japan

Jan. 23, 1890
Oiso, Japan

Founder of Doshisha College, Kyoto, Japan. Neesima began his life as a devout Buddhist. He managed to come to America by hiding on a boat from Shanghai to Boston in 1864. Neesima attended Philipps Academy, Amherst (MA) College and Andover (MA) Theological Seminary, where he was converted. He returned to Japan with ABCFM in 1874 and founded the Christian College (University in 1883) in Kyoto with eight students. Neesima married on Jan. 3, 1876. Doshisha

English School is Japan's oldest private university and has over 30,000 students. Neesima was an evangelist and started his school with the primary goal to train pastors.

Alexander M. Mackay

Oct. 13, 1849
Rhymie, Scotland

Feb. 8, 1890
Nassa, Tanzania/Usambiro, Uganda

Missionary to Uganda with the Church Missionary Society in 1876. Upon arriving in East Africa, Mackay built a road to Lake Victoria in Nyanza, 230 miles inland. He and 200 workers reached Zanzibar despite many hazards, delays, and unforeseen difficulties. The Uganda Mission was established in 1878, in spite of opposition and persecution. Mackay was expelled in 1887, after he translated the gospel of Matthew into Ugandan and the Bible into the Swahili language. He became ill with malaria and died after four days of fever, shortly after meeting HENRY STANLEY.

Franz J. Delitzsch

Feb. 23, 1813
Leipzig, Germany

March 4, 1890
Leipzig, Germany

Lutheran Old Testament scholar, theologian, and Orientalist. Delitzsch advanced the understanding of the Jewish and rabbinical background in New Testament studies. He was of Jewish lineage, and a professor at Leipzig (1842), Rostock (1846), Erlangen (1850), and Leipzig, 1867–90. He translated the New Testament into Hebrew in 1877. He also wrote Old Testament commentaries (*Isaiah* was especially controversial) and opened a school to study rabbinical material. His writings are very helpful in understanding the original Hebrew text. In 1886, he founded a seminary at Leipzig to aid in missionary work to the Jews. His special field was exegesis. He wrote much post-Biblical Jewish literature.

Daniel R. Goodwin

April 12, 1811
North Berwick, Maine

March 15, 1890
Philadelphia, Pennsylvania

Dean of Philadelphia Divinity School (merged into Episcopal Divinity School, Cambridge, MA in 1974), **1868–83**. He first served as professor of modern languages at Bowdoin College, Brunswick, ME from 1835–53, and was librarian a good part of that time as well. Goodwin married Mary Merrick on Jan 2, 1838. He was ordained deacon (1847) and priest (1848) in the Episcopal Church. He was president of Trinity College, Hartford, CT (1853–60); provost at the University of PA (1860–68); and professor of systematic theology at PDS (1865–90). Goodwin was considered the most influential evangelical of his denomination during his time.

Lewis Davis

Feb. 14, 1814
Craig County, Virginia

March 23, 1890
Dayton, Ohio

Bishop of the Church of the United Brethren in Christ (United Methodist Church in 1968), **1853–90, and president of Union Biblical Seminary** (United Theological Seminary in 1954), **Dayton, OH 1871–83**. Davis pastored in Westerville, OH and was considered the father of higher education in the United Brethren churches. He married Rebecca Bartels and was the president of Otterbein University, Westerville, OH from 1850–57 and 1861–72.

Johann H. Kurtz

Dec. 13, 1809
Montjoie, Germany

April 26, 1890
Marburg, Germany

Conservative Lutheran exegete and Church historian. Kurtz became headmaster in religion at the Mitau, Latvia, gymnasium (1835), professor of church history (1849) and of OT from 1859–64 at Dorpat University. In 1871, he settled down at Marburg where he was engaged in literary pursuits for the rest of his life. He is best known for his *Bible History* (1847) and *History of the Christian Church* (1849). His works on the Old Testament made many concessions to modern higher criticism.

Thomas B. Freeman

Dec. 6, 1809
Twyford, England

Aug. 12, 1890
Accra, Gold Coast (Ghana)

Wesleyan Methodist missionary, son of a black father and white mother. Freeman offered himself to West Africa in 1837, arriving at the Gold Coast (Ghana) in January, 1838. He married his third wife, a local woman, in 1854. He made visits throughout the country and to Nigeria and the areas in between. From 1857–73, he supported himself with farming and working in government service in Ghana. Back in the ministry in 1873, he built a strong church and 35 schools. He retired in 1885. He was married three times, his first two wives dying within a few weeks after arriving in Africa.

Henry P. Liddon

Aug. 20, 1829
North Stoneham, England

Sept. 9, 1890
Weston-Super-Mare, England

Renowned Church of England preacher, orator and theologian. Liddon was an energetic supporter of the Oxford Movement. He served as vice-principal of Cuddesdon Theological College (1854–59), and of St. Edmunds Hall, Oxford (1859–64). He was prebendary of Salisbury Cathedral (1864) and the Bampton Lecturer (1866) on the subject of the divinity of Christ. As canon of St. Paul's Cathedral in London from 1870–death, he attracted great crowds and was known worldwide. He was most concerned with church unity and had a strong evangelical witness. He was a professor of exegesis at Oxford University, 1870–82 and took a trip abroad in 1885. In 1871, he denied the right of the Church of England to revise the Athanasian Creed, causing a severe controversy. His sermons attracted great crowds. He wrote on *Divinity of Our Lord and Savior Jesus Christ*.

Catherine Mumford Booth

Jan. 17, 1829
Ford, England

Oct. 4, 1890
Claxton, England

Wife of William Booth and the "Mother of the Salvation Army." Catherine was a sickly child of a devout mother and alcoholic father. She was educated at home, reading the entire Bible before age twelve. She received assurance of her salvation at age 16, met WILLIAM in 1851, and married him on June 16, 1855. Together they built the worldwide Salvation Army ministry, which grew to 25,000 officers in 91 countries. She was enthusiastically accepted as a gracious soft-spoken preacher whose words gained boldness from her knowledge of Scripture. Catherine first began to preach in January, 1860, and had successful missions in Margate (1867) and Portsmouth (1873). She dealt with much pain throughout her life, beginning with adolescent spinal curvature. She was stricken with cancer in 1888 and was ill for two years. She has been characterized as a "mother of eight, evangelist, breadwinner, confidante to her husband, theologian of Salvation doctrine, promoter of women's rights, and moral crusader." She said as she died, "The waters are rising, but so am I. I am not going under but over…go on living well, the dying will be right." Her writings range from *Papers on Practical Religion* (1879) to *Popular Christianity* (1887). Her favorite Bible verses were 2 Corinthians 12:9 and Ezekiel 37:19.

Austin Phelps

Jan. 7, 1820
West Brookfield, Massachusetts

Oct. 13, 1890
Bar Harbor, Maine

Congregational clergyman and author. Phelps pastored Pine St. Church, Boston, MA (1842–48), and taught at Andover (MA) Theological Seminary (1848–79). He married Elizabeth Stuart (September, 1842); Mary Stuart (April, 1854), and Mary A. Johnson (June, 1858). Phelps was a strong conservative and chairman of the faculty of the seminary, 1869–79.

Henry M. Dexter

Aug. 13, 1821
Plympton, Massachusetts

Nov. 13, 1890
New Bedford, Massachusetts

Congregationalist hymn translator of such as CLEMENT OF ALEXANDER's "Shepherd of Tender Youth" and others. Dexter married Emeline A. Palmer on Nov. 19, 1844. Dexter pastored at Manchester, NY (1844–49) and at Pine St. Church (Berkley Temple) in Boston, MA (1849–67). He was also the editor of *The Congregationalist* (1856–90). He was known as a historical scholar of denominations. He wrote from *The Voice of the Bible and the Verdict of Reason* (1858) to *The Congregationalism of the Last 300 Years* (1880).

William H. Campbell

Sept. 14, 1808
Baltimore, Maryland

Dec. 7, 1890
New Brunswick, New Jersey

President of Rutgers College and New Brunswick (NJ) Theological Seminary, 1863–88. Campbell married Katherine Schoonmaker in 1831 and served as Principal of Erasmus Hall, 1833–39. He pastored in East New York, NY (1839–41) and at the Third Reformed Church, Albany, NY (1841–48). Campbell was principal of Albany Academy (1848–51) and professor of Oriental literature at Rutgers (1851–63). He wrote two books.

Richard W. Church

April 25, 1815
Lisbon, Portugal

Dec. 9, 1890
Dover, England

Anglican dean of St. Paul's, 1871–90, and a liberal high churchman. He was in Italy from 1818–20, then went to Oxford in 1830. Church was a fellow of Oriel College, Oxford (1838–52), and later the rector of Whatley (1852–71). He worked to calm the outcry against his friends in the Tractarian movement. He wrote several biographies and *Oxford Movement, Twelve Years* (1833–45, published 1891).

Nathaniel Woodard

1811
England

1891
England

Anglican priest and educator. Woodard was ordained in 1842. He founded a series of schools which provided a middle–class public school education in an Anglican setting. The primary ones were St. Nicholas' at Lansing, St. John's at Hurstpierpoint and St. Saviour's at Ardingly. His ideas were outlined in the controversial *Plea for the Middle Classes* (1845). The Society of St. Nicholas, which Woodard founded, furthered his ideas. There were a total of 18 Woodard schools established throughout England.

Edward H. Plumptre

Aug. 6, 1821
London, England

Feb. 1, 1891
Wells, England

Anglican hymn writer who wrote, "Rejoice, Ye Pure in Heart" (1865) (music by ARTHUR MESSITER). Plumptre also won fame as a scholar, theologian, and preacher. He served as chaplain of King's College (1847–68), professor of pastoral theology (1853–63), professor of NT exegesis (1864–81), and dean of Wells (after 1881). His literary works include classics, history, theologyl, poetry, popular Bible exegesis, and biographies. He was on the committee appointed to revise the English version of the OT from 1869–74.

Tufve (Tuve) N. Hasselquist

March 2, 1816 — Hasslarod, Sweden
Feb. 4, 1891 — Galesburg, Illinois

President of Augustana Lutheran Church (LCA, ELCA in 1988), **1868–70; of Augustana College, 1863–66, and Seminary, Paxton, IL, 1866–75; and of the College and Seminary, Rock Island, IL** (Lutheran School of Theology, Chicago in 1964), 1875–1891. Hasselquist pastored in Sweden (1839–52) before he came to America and married Eva Cervin on May 24, 1852 (died: 1881). He pastored in Galesburg, IL (1852–63); Paxton, IL (1863–75); and Rock Island, IL (1875–91). He fought particularism (exclusive devotion to one's own interests) in his church.

James M. Pendelton

Nov. 20, 1811 — Spotsylvania County, Virginia
March 4, 1891 — Bowling Green, Kentucky

Baptist pastor, professor and journalist. His parents moved to Kentucky during his first year of school. Pendelton was converted at age 17 and ordained in Hopkinsville, KY in 1833. He pastored at Bethel, Hopkinsville (1833–37) and Bowling Green, KY (1837–57); was professor of theology at Union University. He married Catherine Garnett on March 13, 1838. He pastored then in Murfreesboro, TN (1857–62); Hamilton, OH (1862–65); and Upland, PA (1865–83), having a role in founding Crozer Theological Seminary. He was the first theologian to advocate Landmarkism {asserts an unbroken succession of Baptist churches since the New Testament}, first using the work in 1854. He and JAMES GRAVES pioneered this thinking. He edited the *Tennessee Baptist*. He wrote nine books; his best known book is *An Old Landmark Reset* (1856). His book, *Christian Doctrines* (1878), distinguishes him as a great Baptist theologian.

Howard Crosby

Feb. 27, 1826 — New York, New York
March 29, 1891 — New York, New York

Presbyterian pastor and educator. Crosby was a professor of Greek at the University of the City of New York (1851–59) and of Rutgers University (1859–63), along with being the president of New Brunswick (NJ) Theological Seminary, and pastor of the First Presbyterian Church of New Brunswick. He pastored the Fourth Ave. Church in New York Ciity (1863–91) and was chancellor of the University of the City of New York (1870–81). He married Margaret E. Givan, and they had one son. He was active in philanthropic and educational reforms, and wrote much on biblical subjects. His works ranged from *Lands of the Moslems* (1851) to *Will and Providence* (1890). He said on his deathbed, "My heart is resting sweetly with Jesus, and my hand is in His."

Josiah B. Grinnell

Dec. 22, 1821 — New Haven, Vermont
March 31, 1891 — Marshalltown, Iowa

Leading abolitionist in the pre-Civil War days, Grinnell was removed from his pulpit at the First Congregational Church, Washington, D.C. in 1851. As a speaker, he formed a strong anti-slavery style of oratory. Grinnell married Julia A. Chapin on February 5, 1852. It is rumored that he was the young man to whom Horace Greeley (1811–72) said, "Go West, young man, go West." He headed west to Iowa where he founded the town of Grinnell in 1854. He served as a trustee in the local college, 1854–84, resulting in the college being named for him. He was very active in politics and was a member of the U.S. House of Representatives, 1863–67.

Adolf A. Saphir

Sept. 26, 1831
Budapest, Hungary

April 3, 1891
London, England

Presbyterian clergyman and writer. Saphir and his family were converted from Judaism by a Jewish mission of the Church of Scotland. He studied in Berlin, Glasgow, Aberdeen, and Edinburgh. He became pastor of the English Presbyterian Church in South Shields (1856–61), at St. Mark's Presbyterian Church in Greenwich (1861–72), at Notting Hill in London, (1872–80), and at Belgrave Presbyterian Church in London (1881–88). For seven years, Saphir was incapacitated with bad health; he died of angina pectoris (coronary artery disease).

Edward D. Pressense

Jan. 7, 1824
Paris, France

April 8, 1891
Paris, France

Theologian and politician. Pressense pastored the Free Evangelical Congregation of the Taitbout, Paris, 1847–70. He was deputy to the National Assembly from the Department of the Seine, 1871–76 and was elected a life senator of France in 1883. Pressense continued to preach throughout France and Switzerland. He wrote books and edited a French journal, 1854–91.

Eduard G. E. Reuss
Edouard Guillaume/Wilhelm Eugen(e) Reuss

July 18, 1804
Strasburg, Germany

April 15, 1891
Strasburg, Germany

Biblical scholar and theologian. Reuss took orders in the French Protestant Church and returned to Strasburg in 1828, becoming an Alsatian scholar (Latin title for cleric from Alsace-Lorraine area of Germany). He held many positions of importance at the local Protestant seminary, where he taught for 60 years. He was the first dean after they were incorporated into the theological faculty of the newly formed German University of Strasbourg. His chief interest was biblical science. He edited CALVIN's works in 38 volumes and did a French translation and commentary of the Bible (16 vols.).

Thomas J. Conant

Dec. 13, 1802
Brandon, Vermont

April 30, 1891
Brooklyn, New York

Professor of Hebrew and biblical exegesis at Rochester (NY) Theological Seminary, 1851–90. This Baptist professor of languages also taught at Colby University 1827–1833, and at Hamilton Theological Institute (Colgate University in 1890) 1835–51. He was also in the service of the American Bible Union, 1857–75, editing their revisions of the New Testament. He married Hannah O. Chaplin on July 12, 1830; they had ten children.

A. Friedrich Craemer

May 26, 1812
Klein-Langheim, Germany

May 3, 1891
Springfield, Illinois

President of Concordia Theological Seminary, Springfield, IL (Ft. Wayne, IN in 1916), **1875–91.** Craemer was a Lutheran pioneer pastor, missionary, and professor. For several years, Craemer tutored noble families in Germany and England. He was ordained in 1845. He founded a mission colony at Franklin, MI from 1845–50. In 1950, he became president of Practical Seminary, Ft. Wayne, IN (20 students). In 1861, it combined with the Theological Seminary at St. Louis (he and C.F.W. WALTHER were the only faculty). In 1875, he went with Practical Seminary to Springfield, IL, where the name was changed to Concordia Theological Seminary. He taught 41 years, 1850–91, in the seminary.

Thomas V. French

Jan. 1, 1825
Burton-on-Trent, England

May 14, 1891
Muscat, Arabia

Anglican missionary sent by the Church Missionary Society to Agra, India. From 1850–63, French developed St. John's College in England, offering education to Moslem and Hindu children. In 1869, he developed St. John's Divinity School in Lahore to train pastors. A good scholar and preacher, he was appointed the first Anglican bishop of Lahore from 1877–87. He retired to Britain in 1887, but he soon responded to a call for evangelists to Arabia in 1891. Stricken by health problems, he died while on this missionary enterprise to Arabia, evangelizing in Muscat.

James Gilmour

June 12, 1843
Cathkin, Scotland

May 21, 1891
Tientsin, China

Congregational missionary to Mongolia. Gilmour was converted at age 19 at Glasgow University. He left for the field with London Missionary Society, 1870–82, and spent his summers with nomadic Mongols, seeking to become one of them. In the winters, he lived in Peking. Gilmour married Emily Pankard on December 8, 1874 (died: 1885). His patience, with little response, was a challenge to many. He labored 15 years before his first baptism. He became a lay doctor and worked with the Mongols until his death from typhoid fever.

Frederic H. A. Scrivener

Sept. 29, 1813
Bermondsey, London, England

Oct. 30, 1891
Hendon, England

Church of England headmaster of Falmouth School, 1846–56, and a New Testament textual scholar. Scrivener is remembered for his comprehensive study of New Testament manuscripts, which was published as *Plain Introduction to the Criticism of the New Testament* (1861). He also served as rector of St. Gerrans (1861), prebendary of Exeter, 1874–91, and vicar of Hendonz (1876). He edited a Greek text of the New Testament, the *English Revised* (1870–81), which defended the Received Text.

Samuel A. Crowther

c 1809
Ochugu, Nigeria

Dec. 31, 1891
Lagos, Nigeria

African missionary and first black bishop of the Church of England. Crowther was sold into slavery at age twelve but was rescued by the British in 1822. He was placed into an African mission school (1827), then went to England for further education and ordination (1843). He worked at Abeokuta, 1846–56, then founded the Niger Mission in 1857, leading it for 30 years. He started many schools and churches in Nigeria and participated in several expeditions, 1859–72. He became bishop, in 1864, of the Niger territories. Crowther also prepared schoolbooks and translated them into the Yoruban language. His wife's name was Susanna. He died of a stroke, in desolate circumstances, as his African staff had been dismissed, suspended, or transferred.

Spokane Garry

1811
Spokane, Washington

Jan. 13, 1892

American Indian chief and missionary. Garry was converted at an Indian school at Winnipeg, attending from 1825–32. He returned to his Spokane tribe to organize a congregation and open a school. He was instrumental in preventing many Indian brothers from joining Chief Joseph's insurrection in 1876–77, while he promoted peace and progress among the Northwest tribes. In 1887, he signed a treaty forfeiting his followers' lands to the U.S. government for compensation not received by the time of his death. He is buried in Greenwood Cemetery, Spokane.

Charles H. Spurgeon

June 19, 1834
Kelvedon, England

Jan. 31, 1892
Menton, France

Often called the "Prince of Preachers." Spurgeon was converted on January 6, 1850, in Artillery St. Primitive Methodist Chapel in Colchester, while visiting during a snowstorm. He heard a message on Isaiah 45:22. He was baptized soon after. He began to preach at age 16. Spurgeon pastored Waterbeach Baptist Church in Cambridgeshire (1852), then took a small church, New Park Street Church in London (1854). In a few years, it was the largest Baptist church in the world and a tourist spot, also. He married Susannah Thompson on January 8, 1856, who became an invalid at age 33. Moving from Exeter Hall, he began using Surrey Garden's Music Hall in 1856, which seated 10,000. His Metropolitan Tabernacle opened in 1861 (age 27), seating nearly 6,000 and was filled. He wrote many books, founded a pastor's college (1861) called Spurgeon's College, then an orphanage (1867), published many sermons, and opposed liberalism all his life. He edited *The Sword and the Trowel* and published *The Treasury of David* (1865), an exposition of the Psalms. In 1887, contending for the truth of the Bible, he left the Baptist Union during the Downgrade Controversy (Spurgeon leaving the Baptist Union because of liberal inroads). He last preached at the Tabernacle on June 7, 1891. During his tenure there, he added 14,692 members to his church, and by his death, the church had 5,307 members (many had moved, died, or discontinued). His wife died October 22, 1903.

Noah Porter

Dec. 14, 1811
Farmington, Connecticut

March 4, 1892
Farmington, Connecticut

President of Yale College and Divinity School (University in 1887), **New Haven, CT 1871–86.** Porter was a Congregational clergyman and educator. He married Mary Taylor on April 13, 1836. He pastored at New Milford, CT (1836–43) and Springfield, MA (1843–46). From 1846–92, he was a professor of metaphysics and philosophy at Yale. He was the principal editor (revised editions) of *Webster's Dictionary* (1890) and published works including *The Human Intellect* (1868) and *Elements of Moral Science* (1884). He preferred writing over teaching.

James Calvert

Jan. 3, 1813
Torquay/Pickering, England

March 8, 1892
Hastings, England

Appointed in 1838 as a powerful Wesleyan missionary to the Fiji Islands. Converted at age 18, while apprenticed to a printer, Calvert later printed many books himself. He married Mary Fouler in 1838. He labored basically in Lakeba, 1838–55 and 1860–64, and saw a marvelous transformation there. He served in Bromley, Kent (1867–72); then in Kimberley, South Africa (1872–81), ministering in the diamond fields. He returned to England (1881), where his wife, Mary, died (1882). In 1886–87, he revisited the Christianized Fiji Islands, once referred to as "Cannibal Islands," then toured Australia and America on behalf of the mission.

John Cairns

Aug. 23, 1818
Ayton Hill, Scotland

March 12, 1892
Edinburgh, Scotland

United Presbyterian divine who served at the Golden Square Church, Berwick-upon-Tweed, 1845–76. Cairns traveled throughout Europe and America, learned several languages, and spoke at special conferences. He became a professor at the United Presbyterian Theological College,

Edinburgh (1876), then became principal (1879). He never married but lived with his sister. Foremost, he was a pulpiteer, second a writer and was greatly missed at his passing.

David H. Agnew

Nov. 24, 1818
Noblesville (Christiana), Pennsylvania

March 22, 1892
Philadelphia, Pennsylvania

Anatomist and surgeon. Graduating from the University of Pennsylvania, he married Margaret Erwin in 1841. Agnew was connected with various medical colleges all of his life and attained worldwide fame. He was professor of surgery at the University of Pennsylvania, 1871–89. As an expert in gunshot wounds, he was the chief medical consultant in the attempt to save the life of President JAMES GARFIELD in 1881. He served the government as surgeon throughout the Civil War. In the most difficult and dangerous operations, he used either hand with equal ability. He devised and secured the manufacture of a great variety of helpful surgical appliances and was one of the first to adopt antiseptic surgery. In one of his last letters he wrote, "Christ to me is all, and my aspiration is for the immortality to come." To a minister that he did not charge payment, he wrote, "You owe me nothing. To your Master and my Own I owe all things,…but a little service rendered to Him who gave himself for me."

Jonathan Blanchard

Jan. 19, 1811
Rockingham, Vermont

May 14, 1892
Wheaton, Illinois

First president of Wheaton (IL) College, 1860–82 and a strong evangelical leader. Blanchard married Mary Bent in 1838, and they had 12 children, one of them becoming the next college president (CHARLES). He was ordained as a Presbyterian (1838), pastored the Sixth Presbyterian Church in Cincinnati, 1837–45 and attended an anti-slavery convention in London (1843), after becoming an ardent abolitionist (1834). He served as president of Knox College in Galesburg, IL from 1845–57 and founded and edited the *Christian Era* (1858). Blanchard was a founder of the North Central Association of Colleges, a strong foe of the Masonic order, and advocate of temperance. He founded *The Christian Cynosure* and The National Christian Association in 1868. He died at his daughter's home.

George R. Clarke

Feb. 22, 1827
Ostego County, New York

June 22, 1892

Co-founder (with his wife) and director of the Pacific Garden Mission, Chicago, IL 1877–92, the second rescue mission in America. Clarke was converted in 1846, and was admitted to the bar in 1853. Clarke then turned to real estate. He was active in the Civil War and also with the miners in Denver, CO. He married SARAH DUNN on January 23, 1873. In 1877, the Clarkes opened the mission, which is still in existence and flourishing today, relocating to 386 S. Clark St. in 1880.

John G. Whittier

Dec. 17, 1807
near Haverhill, Massachusetts

Sept. 7, 1892
Hampton Falls, New Hampshire

Quaker poet and anti-slavery crusader. Whittier was a master poet. Many of his poems became hymns, such as "Dear Lord and Father of Mankind," and "We May Not Climb the Heavenly Steps." His best-known poem was "Snowbound" (1866). He was the first to suggest the Republican Party. He had much opposition in New England because of his views. He was in the Massachusetts legislature in 1835. In 1836, he moved to Amesbury, north of Boston, where he spent most of his later years. Beginning in 1839, he was editor for WILLIAM LLOYD GARRISON for 20 years, becoming a strong abolitionist. He wrote editorials for the National Era from 1847–59. Other popular poems are "The Barefoot Boy" and "Barbara Fritchie". He never married and had many health problems.

Alfred Tennyson
Alfred, Lord Tennyson

Aug. 6, 1809
Somersby, England

Oct. 6, 1892
Aldworth, England

Victorian poet-laureate of England, 1850 until death, succeeding WORDSWORTH. Tennyson was the son of George C. Tennyson, the rector of Somersby, one of twelve children. He wrote a 6,000-word epic poem when he was twelve. His literary career began in 1830. He was married to Emily Sellwood on June 13, 1850. They had two children. His "In Memoriam" (1850) established him as a poet. He noted, "The peace of God came into my heart." Other popular poems were "Maud" (1855) and "Idylls of the King" (1859). His poem "Enoch Arden" (1864) was also well known. Tennyson was made a baron in 1884. "Crossing the Bar" was written shortly before his death.

William H. Miles

Dec. 26, 1828
Springfield, Kentucky

Nov. 14, 1892
Louisville, Kentucky

First bishop and senior bishop of Colored (Christian in 1956) **Methodist Episcopal Church, 1870–92**. Miles was born a slave and was owned by Mrs. Mary Miles, who later freed him. As was the custom at that time, he took the name of his "master." Miles joined the Methodist Church, South (1855, and was licensed to preach (1857). He was an eloquent speaker. He supported black colleges like Lane College, Jackson, TN and Paine Seminary, Augusta, GA.

Fenton J. A. Hort

April 23, 1828
Dublin, Ireland

Nov. 30, 1892
Cambridge, England

English theologian and biblical scholar. Hort joined BROOKE FOSS WESTCOTT in 1853 to produce the authoritative The New Testament in the Original Greek (1881). He helped translate the English Revised Version of the NT, beginning in 1870, published May 17, 1881. A few days previous (May 12) the first volume of The Westcott-Hort New Testament also appeared. Their work relied upon a relatively small group of unicals and versions, with a few later manuscripts having similar texts, the chief authority being the Vatican and Sinaitic manuscripts, the Boharic version and Origen. He was a vicar of St. Ippolyts near Hitchin, 1857–72; then moved to Cambridge University, where he served at Emmanuel College as lecturer, professor of divinity, and reader.

Andrew A. Bonar

Aug. 29, 1810
Edinburgh, Scotland

Dec. 31, 1892
Glasgow, Scotland

Presbyterian preacher and author, brother of HORATIUS BONAR. Bonar began his ministry in 1838 at Collace, and joined the Free Church when it began in 1843. He visited Palestine with his friend, R. M. MCCHEYNE, in 1839, and wrote about it later. He pastored the Finnieston Church in Glasgow, 1856–92. Bonar was involved with the evangelical and revival movements of MOODY and MCCHEYNE and was concerned with Jewish evangelism. He was a premillennialist and wrote various books, the last of which was *Christ and His Church in the Book of Psalms* (1859). His favorite Bible verse was John 1:16.

Phillips Brooks

Dec. 13, 1835
Boston, Massachusetts

Jan. 23, 1893
Boston, Massachusetts

Episcopalian bishop, songwriter, and preacher. Brooks is the author of the beloved Christmas carol "O Little Town of Bethlehem," 1865 (music by Lewis Redner), which was inspired by a Holy Land trip. His conversion and call to preach came during student days at Harvard. He pastored two churches in Philadelphia, Church of the Advent (1859–62) and Holy Trinity (1862–69), and served as rector of Trinity Episcopal Church in Boston (1869–93). In 1880, he preached in Westminster Abbey and before Queen Victoria in Windsor, England, the first American to preach to a member of the royal family. He never married and became bishop of Massachusetts in 1891. Brooks wrote several books and supported the rights of blacks. His works range from *Yale Lectures on Preaching* (1877) to *Essays to the Law of Growth* (1902). He died after a brief illness, possibly pneumonia. He was 6 feet 4 inches and 300 lbs.

Benjamin T. Roberts

July 25, 1823
Gowanda, New York

Feb. 27, 1893
Catharugus, New York

Founder of the Free Methodist Church, Pekin, NY, in 1860; its first general superintendent, 1860–93; and First President of Chili Seminary, North Chili, NY (Roberts Wesleyan College, Rochester, NY in 1945), **1866–79**. Roberts was converted at age 21 in 1844, at a revival meeting. He married Ellen Stowe on May 3, 1849, and they had seven children (including Benson Roberts). He purchased a farm, constructed a school, and held the mortgage for 20 years. His break up with Methodism in 1858 was because of his objection to affluency, the use of organs, and the wearing of gold and costly apparel. Also, he rejected pew renting, hence the name "Free" Methodists.

Lucy Larcom

March 5, 1824
Beverly, Massachusetts

April 17, 1893
Boston, Massachusetts

Hymn writer. At age seven, Lucy began to write poetry and was noticed by John G. Whittier. Lucy, her sisters, and mother (father died) moved to Lowell, MA and began to work in a clothing factory, 1835–46. She found time to study many subjects. She went on to teach in Looking Glass, IL and then went back to Massachusetts where she taught from 1854–62, at Wheaton Seminary (College), Norton, MA. She edited *Our Young Folks* (1865–74). Her last poem "The Unseen Friend" in 1892, expressed her faith. Her best-known hymn was "Draw Thou My Soul, O Christ."

Robert C. McAll

Dec. 17, 1821
Macclesfield, England

May 11, 1893
Paris, France

Congregationalist and founder of McAll Mission. McAll pastored churches in several cities. At age 50, he began evangelistic work in a communistic quarter of Belleville, a Paris suburb. In 1882, he started a mission. By 1888, it numbered 126 stations and reached as far as Algeria. His wife died on May 6, 1906. He wrote many tracts and wrote or translated 50 hymns.

Samuel Morris

1873
Ivory Coast

May 12, 1893
Fort Wayne, Indiana

Died at age 20, but impacted many people at Taylor University, Ft. Wayne, IN. Morris was born a poor, black, Kru boy in Africa, who was converted through the testimony of a missionary near Monrovia, Liberia. This was after he ran through the jungle following a "light" (Holy

Spirit). Asking where could he learn more, he was told to find Stephen Merritt in New York. The very first person that he asked after he got off the boat in NY knew Merritt and soon Morris was sitting at his feet. Morris went on to Taylor University and turned the school upside down with revival fervor before an illness (dropsy) took his life. "Angel in Ebony" was a film produced by Taylor University about his life. *Light in the Forest* is a book about him, also.

John Ellerton

Dec. 16, 1826
London, England

June 15, 1893
Torquay, England

Composer of 86 hymns (68 for special occasions), including "Savior, Again to Thy Dear Name" (music by EDWARD HOPKINS). Ellerton was an Anglican pastor at St. Nicholas' of Brighton where he wrote his first hymns for parish children. He became vicar of Crewe Green in Cheshire in 1850 and taught English and Bible history at the Mechanics' Institute. He was also rector of Hinsrock, Barnes and White Roding. He translated several hymns from Latin. In 1881, he published *Notes and Illustrations of Church Hymns*.

James R. Graves

April 10, 1820
Chester, Vermont

June 26, 1893
Memphis, Tennessee

Southern Baptist preacher, editor and publisher who led in the founding of the Landmark movement. With little formal education, Graves became a schoolteacher in Kingsville, OH (1840–42), and Jessamine County, KY (1842–43). He married Florence Spencer in 1845 and, upon her death, married twice more. Soon he was pastoring at Second Baptist Church in Nashville in 1845 and editing the *Tennessee Baptist* (1848). By 1859, it had a circulation of 13,000. He continued editing until 1889. In 1851, at his meeting in Cotton Grove, TN; he stated that Baptist-type churches enjoy an unbroken succession since the time of Christ. He was a keen debater and Bible student. His debates against Jacob Dietzhe, a Methodist, were classic. As an agitator and controversialist of the first magnitude, he kept the SBC in continual and often bitter controversy for over 30 years. He could keep congregations for up to 3 ½ hours with no sign of weariness on either side. He opposed any power beyond the local church. He began pastoring the FBC of Memphis in 1870, and on August 17, 1884, had a stroke while preaching there, making him an invalid the rest of his life. In 1889, his followers separated from the SBC and formed the American Baptist Association.

John Leyburn

April 25, 1814
Lexington, Virginia

July 13, 1893
Waynesboro, Virginia

Stated clerk of Presbyterian Church (USA in 1963) in the US (Old School), 1850–62. Leyburn was ordained, 1836 and pastored the Tabb St. Church, Petersburg, VA from 1840–49. He became secretary of the Board of Publication in Philadelphia in 1849, and later editor of the *Presbyterian*. Leyburn made a trip to the Holy Land and then worked with Presbyterian Publications.

W. P. Lockhart

Oct. 15, 1835
Kirkcaldy, England

Aug. 12, 1893
Ballater, England

Young men's evangelist. Lockhart was converted in Wales in 1855 while travelling with his cousin. One day while walking alone the words "It is finished" flashed across his mind and he was suddenly converted. He was baptized February 2, 1859 and became a member of Myrtle Street Baptist Church and got involved with the YMCA in his early days. He supported himself as a merchant, then as a manager, in the Liverpool Investment Building Society. He preached in parks, in halls, and Open Toxteth Tabernacle, which he pastored for 24 years. He preached in all parts of the British Isles, and, on occasions, in Spain.

G. E. C. Ferdinand Sievers

May 18, 1816
Lueneburg, Germany

Sept. 9, 1893
Frankenmuth, Michigan

First director of Lutheran Church-Missouri Synod Missions, 1850–93. Sievers immigrated to the USA in 1847. He married Karoline Koch on May 5, 1850; they had nine children. He pastored in Frankenmuth, MI; Amelith, MI; Saginaw, MI; Bay City, MI; Trinity Lutheran of Minneapolis, MN; Monitor, MI; Mount Pleasant, MI; and Beaver, MI.

Telfair Hodgson

March 14, 1840
Columbia, Virginia

Sept. 11, 1893
Sewanee, Tennessee

First dean of University of the South, Sewanee, TN, 1878–93. Hodgson graduated from Princeton and attended General Theological Seminary, NYC. He was ordained as a deacon and priest in the Episcopal Church and married Frances Potter on April 16, 1865. He was the rector of an Episcopal Church, Keyport, NJ (1865–69) and of Trinity Church, Hoboken, NJ (1873–78). He also served as dean of the theology department and taught history, homiletics, and pastoral theology.

Benjamin Jowett

April 15, 1817
Camberwell, London, England

Oct. 1, 1893
Headley Park, England

Greek scholar, clergyman, and excellent teacher. Jowett translated Greek classics into English. He was a Master (1870) and a professor of Greek (1885) at Balliol College, Oxford, his alma mater. He was vice-chancellor of Oxford, 1882–86, influenced by German philosophy, taking a liberal stance in theology. He wrote commentaries on the *Epistles of Paul* (1855) and *Essays and Reviews* (1860). He was tried in 1860 for views expressed in an essay "On the Inspiration of Scripture" in *Essays and Reviews* but was acquitted. His translation of *Plato's Dialogues* (1871) introduced Socrates and his circle to the English world. He was known as "The Great Tutor." As he died, he said, "Mine has been a happy life. I thank God for my life…".

Thomas E. Peck

Jan. 29, 1822
Columbia, South Carolina

Oct. 2, 1893
Hampden-Sydney, Virginia?

Dean of Hampden–Sydney (VA) Seminary (Union Theological Seminary, Richmond, VA), **1883–93.** Peck married Ellen C. Richardson on Oct. 28, 1852, and they had seven children. He pastored Second Presbyterian Church (1845–46), Broadway St. Church (1846–57), and Central Church (1857–60), all in Baltimore, MD. Before he became dean, he taught church history at HSS from 1860–83.

William Smith

Enfield, England

Oct. 7, 1893
London, England

English lexicographer and Biblical scholar. Smith became professor of Greek and Latin at New College, London, where he started writing on scholarly topics and editing Greek and

Latin classics. He was the editor of the *Quarterly Review* (1867–71). He also edited many dictionaries that were of great value to classical and Bible students.

John L. Nevius

March 4, 1829
near Ovid, New York

Oct. 19, 1893
Chefoo, Yantai, China

Presbyterian missionary to the Shantung area in China. In 1853, Nevius finished seminary, was ordained, married Helen Coan in June, was appointed and assigned to Ningpo. He was in Ningpo (1854–59), Hangchow in 1859, Japan (1859–61), Tungchow (1861–64), America (1864–69), and Chefoo (1871–93). He also made a trip to Korea in 1880. He strongly promoted indigenous missions. His "Nevius Method" was a plan for mission work that stressed Bible study and self-support.

Philip M. Schaff

Jan. 1, 1819
Chur, Switzerland

Oct. 20, 1893
New York, New York

Greatest church historian of all time. Schaff came to America in 1844, to teach at German Reformed Theological Seminary at Mercersburg, PA until 1865. He married Mary E. Schley in December, 1845; they had three children. He worked with the New York Sabbath Association, 1865–70, while living in New York City. He was a professor there at Union Theological Seminary, 1870–93. Schaff became a Presbyterian in the early 1870s. He was empowered to select and invite scholars to be on the American Committee of the English Revised Version in 1871. He wrote a three-volume *Creeds of Christendom* (1877) and co-edited the *Schaff-Herzog Encyclopedia of Religious Knowledge* (22 vols.). Then came his seven-volume *History of the Christian Church* (1882–92). He founded the American Society of Church History in 1888 and was active in the Evangelical Alliance. He edited 25 volumes of *A Commentary on the Holy Scriptures* (1865–80). He died of a brain hemorrhage.

Joseph C. Price

Feb. 10, 1854

Oct. 25, 1893
Elizabeth City, North Carolina

Founder and first president of Livingstone College (LC), Salisbury, NC 1881–93. A brilliant scholar, great gospel preacher, and world-famous orator, Price sought to educate the whole man: head, hands, and heart. He turned down other positions to give his life to the college. He went to London as a delegate to the Ecumenical Methodist Conference. He was so inspired by the people assembled there that he was persuaded to remain in England and speak on behalf of the fledgling LC that the conference had adopted. While in England, he raised $10,000 for its establishment and came home in 1882 to follow through.

Charles Scott

Dec. 18, 1822
New Windsor, New York

Oct. 31, 1893
Holland, Michigan

President of Hope College, Holland, MI 1881–93. Scott received his education from Rutgers (1844), and New Brunswick Theological Seminary (1851). He pastored at Shawangunk, NY from 1851–66. He received a degree from the University of New York in 1875. He became a professor at Hope (1866–77), served as vice president (1878–81), and acting president, 1881–85.

Daniel A. Payne

Feb. 24, 1811
Charleston, South Carolina

Nov. 2, 1893
Xenia, Ohio

Bishop of African Methodist Episcopal Church, 1852–93. Payne married Julia Ferris (1847), and after her death, Eliza J. Clark (1853). He was trained in Lutheran Seminary, Gettyburg, PA. He switched from Lutheranism to AMEC in 1841. He pastored (1837–50) then purchased Central State (Wilberforce) University, Xenia, OH in 1863, and served as its president (1863–76). He was in England, 1867–68. He promoted church literature societies, debated, traveled, and wrote. He educated the denomination that RICHARD ALLEN founded. One source says he died November 29 in Wilberforce, OH and another source says he died in Baltimore, December 2, 1893.

Peter I. Tchaikovsky

May 7, 1840
Kamsko-Votkinsk, Russia

Nov. 6, 1893
St. Petersburg (Leningrad), Russia

Widely known composer, Tchaikovsky lived on the subsidy of a wealthy widow he never met. In 1864, his overture to a play, *The Storm*, began his career. He was professor of harmony at Moscow Conservatory, 1866–78, a teacher, composer, and music critic. Tchaikovsky produced symphonic poems, concertos, symphonies, operas, chamber music, overtures, ballets, and anthems ("Praise Ye the Name of the Lord"). Tchaikovsky visited the U.S. in 1891. He conducted an orchestra at the dedication of Carnegie Hall in New York City. He died of cholera three days after he drank a glass of unboiled water, during an epidemic.

James Morison

Feb. 14, 1816
Barthgate, Scotland

Nov. 13, 1893
Glasgow, Scotland

Scottish Presbyterian pastor, evangelist, theologian, and founder of the Evangelical Union. Morison trained for the United Secession Church, but his preaching at Kilmarnock in 1840, that Christ died for all, caused him to be accused of teaching against the Westminster Confession. Expelled (1841), he founded the Evangelical Union with nearly 100 churches (1843). He moved to Glasgow to pastor at Dundas Street Church (1851–93) and was principal and professor at a theological hall that he established (1843–93) His writings range from the *Nature of the Atonement* (1841) to *Sheaves of Ministry* (1890). He edited *The Evangelical Expository* (quarterly magazine), 1854–67. After his death, the churches in the Evangelical Union united to form the Congregational Union of Scotland in 1897.

Walter Gowans

1868
Canada

Dec. 1, 1893
Ghirku, Nigeria

Cofounder of Sudan Interior Mission. He was inspired by his mother, Margaret Gowans, ROWLAND BINGHAM, and THOMAS KENT, to set out for the interior of West Africa, known then as the Sudan. He seems to have been the leader.

"Sixty million are at stake! Is it not worth risking even our lives for so many?"

George J. Elvey

March 27, 1816
Canterbury, England

Dec. 9, 1893
Windlesham, England

Composed music for "Crown Him with Many Crowns" (1868) (lyrics by Matthew Bridges), **"Come, Ye Thankful People, Come"** (lyrics by HENRY ALFORD), **and "Soldiers of Christ, Arise"** (lyrics by CHARLES WESLEY). Elvey was a skilled organist before age 17; and, at age 19, he was the organist at St. George's Chapel in Windsor, the church of the royal family. He served there for 47 years and was involved in many royal activities. He wrote "Festival March" for the wedding of Princess Louise and was knighted in 1871.

John J. Moore

c 1804
Berkeley County, West Virginia

Dec. 9, 1893
North Carolina

Bishop of African Methodist Episcopal Zion Church, 1868–93; senior bishop, 1888–93. Moore escaped slavery, and his family settled in Bedford County, PA. He was converted (1833), and joined the Methodist Conference (1839). He traveled as an evangelist in Pennsylvania and Ohio and started Zion Church in San Francisco. He died on a train from Greensboro to Salisbury, NC.

William Milligan

March 15, 1821
Edinburgh, Scotland

Dec. 11, 1893
Edinburgh, Scotland

Church of Scotland (CS) New Testament scholar. During the Disruption Controversy of 1843, Milligan adhered to the Established Church, yet holding liberal Broad Church views. He pastored at Cameron and Kilconqunar in Fifeshire from 1844–60, then became professor of Biblical criticism at the University of Aberdeen, serving there till his death. He helped in New Testament revision and was made principal clerk of the CS in 1886. His works range from *Resurrection of Our Lord* (1881) to *Resurrection of the Dead* (1894).

Martin Lauer

Jan. 18, 1824

Dec. 29, 1893
Pheinpfalz, Germany

Director of Evangelical Association Mission (United Methodist Church in 1968), **1879–93**. Lauer was editor of the *Christian Messenger* (1875–1879) and head administrator, 1879 till death. He was a lively participant in conference business meetings and always expressed support and interest in church endeavors. He challenged others, through his speeches, to consider publication ministries.

William D. Longstaff

Jan. 28, 1822
Sunderland, England

April 2, 1894
Sunderland, England

Wrote the hymn "Take Time to Be Holy" (1890) (music by GEORGE STEBBINS), after hearing a sermon on I Peter 1:16. Longstaff was the son of a wealthy shipowner and a close friend of Arthur A. Rees, who left the Anglican Church and established the Bethesda Free Chapel. He served as treasurer for the chapel and as head of maintenance for the building. He was a close friend of MOODY and SANKEY.

William M. Thomson

Dec. 31, 1806
Springfield (Springdale), Ohio

April 8, 1894
Denver, Colorado

Presbyterian missionary to Syria and Palestine, 1831–74. Thomson married Eliza H. Hanna (June 6, 1832) and Maria Abbot (Aug. 3, 1835); he had three children. Thomson opened the first boarding school for boys in the old Turkish Empire at Beirut in 1835 and wrote popular works on Biblical archaeology and geography, including *The Land and the Book* (1859). After 1876, he resided in New York City.

William A. Passavant

Oct. 9, 1821
Zelienople, Pennsylvania

June 3, 1894
Pittsburgh, Pennsylvania

Lutheran clergyman, home missionary, and philanthropist. In 1867, he was one of the founders of the General Council of the Evangelical Lutheran Church of North America. Passavant pastored the English Lutheran Church in Pittsburgh from 1845–53. His last 50 years were devoted to editorial work, home missionary movements, establishments of mercy institutions (hospitals, orphanages), the first Protestant hospital in Pittsburgh (1849), Thiel College, Greenville, PA (1870), and the Lutheran Theological Seminary, Chicago (1891). He married Eliza Walter on May 1, 1845, and they had five children. He edited the *Missionary* (1848–61) and founded and edited the *Workman* (1881–87).

Frank Bottome

May 26, 1823
Belper, England

June 29, 1894
Tavistock, England

Writer of the hymn "The Comforter Has Come" (1890), for which William Kirkpatrick wrote the music. Bottome entered the ministry of the Methodist Church in the USA in 1850. He married Margaret McRonald (December 29, 1827–November 14, 1906) in 1850. In 1872, he received an honorary Doctorate of Divinity from Dickinson College in Carlisle, PA. She became president of the International Order of the King's Daughters and Sons, a Bible study and self-improvement group, which she helped found in 1886. He wrote several hymns and published *Centenary Singer* (1869) and *Round Lake* (1872).

Herman A. Preus

June 16, 1825
Kristiansand, Norway

July 2, 1894
Lee, Illinois

President of Norwegian Synod (ALC, ELCA), **1862–94.** Preus was one of the organizers of this synod, its second president, a Lutheran pioneer pastor, and church official. He came to America and married Carolina Keyser in 1851. The headquarters for his group known as the Norwegian Lutheran Synod of America was in Wisconsin. He also sponsored black missions in 1877 and pastored in Spring Prairie, WI from 1851–94.

James Strong

Aug. 14, 1822
New York, New York

Aug. 7, 1894
Round Lake, New York

Author of famed concordance. Strong was a Methodist layman who taught exegetical theology at Drew Theological Seminary, Madison, NJ from 1868–93. He married Marcia A. Dustin on July 18, 1845 and had six children. In 1847, he moved from teaching in Poultney, VT to Flushing, NY where he became president of Flushing Railroad. From 1858–63, he was professor of Biblical literature and acting president of Troy (VT) University. He co-authored, with McClintock, the ten volume work, *Cyclopedia of Biblical Theology and Ecclesiastical Literature* (1867–86). He produced his famed *Exhaustive Concordance of the Bible* in 1890. He wrote several other books, 1852–91.

David Swing

Aug. 23, 1830
Cincinnati, Ohio

Oct. 3, 1894
Chicago, Illinois

Presbyterian clergyman renowned in the Chicago area. Swing was professor of languages at Miami (OH) University from 1852–64. He was converted in a Methodist revival meeting. He married Elizabeth Porter in 1855 and had two children. In 1866, he pastored at Westminster Presbyterian, a church which consolidated with North Church (1869), making it The New

Fourth Presbyterian Church of Chicago. He pastored the large congregation until 1874, when he was tried for heresy and acquitted, withdrawing from his denomination. He founded the Central Independent Church in 1875, which was held at Central Music Hall (3,000 attending) 1880 on, pastoring it until his death. He published his sermons.

James McCosh

April 1, 1811
Carskeoch, Scotland

Nov. 16, 1894
Princeton, New Jersey

President of Princeton (NJ) College (University in 1898), **1868–88**. McCosh pastored in Brechin, Scotland (1839–51), then he was professor of logic and metaphysics at Queen's College, Belfast (1851–68). He entered the Free Church of Scotland with many others in 1843. He married Isabella Guthrie on September 29, 1845 and had one son. He was a prolific writer and defended Presbyterian views well. He wrote *Christianity and Positivism* (1871), which attempted to reconcile science with religion. McCosh was one of the first theologians to defend evolution in his written works.

William G. T. Shedd

June 21, 1820
Acton, Massachusetts

Nov. 17, 1894
New York, New York

Presbyterian professor at Union Theological Seminary, NYC 1862–93. Shedd married Lucy A. Myers on October 7, 1845 and had four children. He began teaching at the University of Vermont (1845), at Auburn (NY) Presbyterian Theological Seminary (1853), and at Andover (MA) Theological Seminary, 1855–62. He pastored Brick Church of NYC in 1862. Shedd taught biblical literature (1863–74) and systematic theology (1874–90) at Union. He was an orthodox Calvinist theologian who wrote many books, including a three-volume *Dogmatic Theology* (1888–94). He opposed liberalism.

Alexander Young

June 4, 1815
Glasgow, Scotland

Dec. 5, 1894
Lordsburgh, California

President of Associate Reformed Church Seminary, Oxford, OH 1855–58, renamed **Monmouth** (Pittsburgh in 1999) **(IL) Theological Seminary of Northwest, 1858–74, and Allegheny (PA) Theological Seminary, 1887–91**, teaching there since 1876. An ordained Presbyterian, Young pastored in Monmouth, IL from 1859–71.

John Lord

Dec. 27, 1810
Portsmouth, New Hampshire

Dec. 15, 1894
Stamford, Connecticut

Historian and lecturer. Lord did some preaching for the Congregational Church in Massachusetts. He then turned to writing and lecturing and began to travel in 1840. He was in England, 1843–46. He married Mary Porter in May, 1846, and Louisa Tucker in 1864, and had two children. He settled at Stamford in 1854. Lord gave over 6,000 lectures on many subjects. He also wrote an eight-volume history series (lectures), *Beacon Lights of History* (1884–96).

Christina G. Rossetti

Dec. 5, 1830
London, England

Dec. 29, 1894
London, England

Anglican poet. Christina was the sister of artist, D. G. ROSSETTI. She never married, although she had been engaged to artist James Collinson, ending the relationship when he became a Roman Catholic. Christina wrote several hymns and carols and published her first book of poetry in 1862, *Goblin Market and Others*. Three collections of poems followed in 1866, 1875, and 1881; plus two other works, a *Book of Prayers for Every Day of the Year* (1874) and *Letter and Spirit of the Decalogue* (1883). Her works were often religious and melancholy.

John N. Waddell

April 2, 1812
Wilmington, South Carolina

Jan 9, 1895
Birmingham, Alabama

First state clerk of Presbyterian Church in U.S. (USA in 1983), **1861–65**. He married Martha Robertson (November 27, 1832), Mary Werden (August 24, 1854) and Harriet Snedecor (January 31, 1866). Waddell was a founder of the University of Mississippi, Oxford, MS and taught ancient languages there, 1848–57. He pastored the Presbyterian Church of Oxford during those same years. He taught at the Presbyterian Synodical College, LaGrange, TN, 1857–60 and was president of the same. Waddell was a chaplain in the Confederate army. He then was chancellor of the University of Mississippi, 1965–74; secretary of education of Southern Presbyterian Church, Memphis, TN, 1874–79 and chancellor of Southwestern Presbyterian University, Clarksville, TN 1879–88.

Adoniram J. Gordon

April 19, 1836
New Hampton, New Hampshire

Feb. 2, 1895
Boston, Massachusetts

Baptist minister, educator, author, and musician. Gordon composed the music for "My Jesus, I Love Thee" (FEATHERSTONE) and "In Tenderness He Sought Me" (WALTON). Converted at age 15, he married Maria Hale in 1863; they had eight children. He pastored in Jamaica Plain, MA (1863–69) and at Clarendon St. Baptist Church, Boston, MA (1869–95). He also founded the Boston Missionary Training School in 1889, which developed into Gordon College and Divinity School, serving as its first president until his death. He welcomed females and minorities into his training school and mission endeavors. He was a close friend to MOODY (the tent for his 1877 crusade being next door to Gordon's church). He was a leader in developing prophetic conferences. His last word was, "Victory!" as he lay on his deathbed. His tombstone is inscribed, "Until He Comes." He wrote works ranging from *New Vestry Hymn Book* (1872) to *Yet Speaking* (pub. 1897). He edited *Watchword* (1878–95). He authored many books, including *The Two-Fold Life* (1884) and *How Christ Came to Church* (1895).

Theodore D. Weld

Nov. 23, 1803
Hampton, Connecticut

Feb. 3, 1895
Hyde Park, Massachusetts

Revivalist, abolitionist, and temperance reformer. Weld was converted under the ministry of CHARLES FINNEY while attending Hamilton College, Clinton, NY. In 1827, he became an abolitionist and temperance lecturer. He was expelled at Lane Seminary in Cincinnati because of his anti-slavery stance, and some 32 "Lane rebels" departed for Oberlin College. He married Angelina Grimke (1805–1879), on May 14, 1838. After his voice gave out, he channeled his efforts into editing and writing. *Slavery As It Is* (1839) sold 100,000 in its first year. With disagreement arising over the issue of political action, he farmed in Belleville, NJ (1840–54); taught school in Perth Amboy, NJ (1854–63) and Lexington, MA (1864–67), retiring to Hyde Park in 1867. He lobbied in Congress for a time, especially with the radical faction of the Whig Party, with John Q. Adams (1767–1848).

William M. Taylor

Oct. 23, 1829
Kilmarnock, Scotland

Feb. 8, 1895
New York, New York

Congregational minister who served first at the Derby Road Church, Liverpool, England, for 16 years. He married Jessie Steedman on October 4, 1853; they had nine children. Taylor came to America in 1871 and pastored the Broadway Tabernacle of New York City from 1872–92. He suffered a stroke in 1893. His books range from *Life Truths* (1862) to *The Boy Jesus* (1893).

Frederick Douglass

Feb. 11, 1817　　　　　　　　　　　　　　　　　　　　　　　　　　　Feb. 20, 1895
Tuckahoe, Maryland　　　　　　　　　　　　　　　　　　　　　　　　Washington, D.C.

Abolitionist, writer, and orator. Douglass was the son of a black slave mother and white father. In 1832, Douglass was purchased by a Baltimore shipbuilder. He escaped from bondage in 1838, and fled to New Bedford, MA where he learned to read and write. He was saved, "…I gathered scattered pages of the Bible from the filthy street gutter and washed and dried them [so] that in moments of leisure I might get a word or two of wisdom from them." His anti-slavery speeches were very successful. He married Anna Murray in September, 1838, and Helen Pitts in 1884. In 1841, he changed his name from Bailey to Douglass. In 1845, he wrote his autobiography. He traveled to England from 1845–47 on a successful tour. In Rendleton, IN he was beaten by a white mob and left for dead. He campaigned hard for LINCOLN, and also edited an anti-slavery journal, *The North Star of Rochester* (1847–60). He was also minister to Haiti for the U.S. Government from 1889–91, and served on various presidential appointments for four US Presidents. Douglass also crusaded for temperance and women's rights. He said, "I love the pure, peaceable, and impartial Christianity of Christ."

Robert W. Dale

Dec. 1, 1829　　　　　　　　　　　　　　　　　　　　　　　　　　　March 15, 1895
London, England　　　　　　　　　　　　　　　　　　　　　　　　Birmingham, England

Congregational evangelical preacher and liberal politician. Dale was converted in 1843 and pastored Carr's Lane Congregational Church in Birmingham (1859–95), having served earlier as co-pastor there (1853–59). He held progressive opinions, which advocated the disestablishment of the Church of England. He was involved in seeking to improve education on the local level by being seated on the school board. He was chairman of the Congregational Union, 1868–1869, and visited Australia in 1887. A key work was *The Atonement* (1875). His works range from *Life and Letters of John A. James* (1861) to *Essays and Addresses* (1899) and also included *Discourses on Special Occasions* (1866).

John A. Broadus

Jan. 24, 1827　　　　　　　　　　　　　　　　　　　　　　　　　　　March 16, 1895
Culpepper County, Virginia　　　　　　　　　　　　　　　　　　　　Louisville, Kentucky

Southern Baptist scholar, professor, preacher, and president of Southern Baptist Theological Seminary (SBS) Louisville, KY 1889–95. Broadus was converted at age 16 in a revival at Mt. Poney Church, Culpepper. He was a school teacher in Clarke County, VA in 1844. He married Maria Harrison on November 14, 1850 (died: October 21, 1857), and Charlotte Sinclair on January 4, 1859, resulting in a family of six children. From 1852–63, he taught at the University of Virginia and/or pastored the Baptist church there in Charlottesville, VA. He actually helped found SBS, Greenville, SC in 1859, teaching Greek, NT, and homiletics until his death. Closing during the Civil War, it reopened in 1865, with seven students. He pastored in Cedar Grove and Williamston, SC, during the interim. He helped move it from Greenville, SC to Louisville, KY in 1877. His homiletic masterpiece, *On The Preparation and Delivery of Sermons* (1870), was a result of teaching one student in 1865. His Lectures on the *History of Preaching* (1876), *Jesus of Nazareth* (1890), and *Harmony of the Gospels,* were also notable.

Henry B. Ridgaway

Sept. 7, 1830
Talbot County, Maryland

March 30, 1895
Evanston, Illinois

President of Garrett Biblical Institute (GBI), Evanston, IL 1884–95. He married Rosamund Caldwell in 1855. From 1855–81, Ridgaway was a Methodist pastor in Virginia; Baltimore, MD; Portland, ME; New York; and Cincinnati, OH. He was a professor of historical theology at GBI from 1882–84 and also practical theology. He authored many books on biographies and Holy Land travels, such as *The Lord's Land* (1876).

Absalom B. Earle

1812
Charlton, New York

March 30, 1895
Newton, Massachusetts

Renowned Baptist evangelist who traveled 370,000 miles in America and Canada, held nearly 40,000 meetings, and saw 160,000 conversions in 58 years. Converted at age 18, Earle usually held union crusades with some 20 churches backing the meetings. He began preaching in 1830 and, as a result of his influence, 400 went into the ministry. His sermons include, "The Unpardonable Sin" (20,000 converts) and "The Joy of Salvation."

Philip Phillips

Aug. 13, 1834
Cassadaga, New York

June 25, 1895
Delaware, Ohio

Hymn writer and singing evangelist. Phillips traveled all over the English-speaking world giving concerts, singing at meetings and writing and composing hymns, such as "Home of the Soul," etc. He married Odlie M. Clarke on September 27, 1860. He changed from a Baptist to a Methodist in 1860. In 1866, he was the musical editor of *The Methodist Book Concern*. In 1868, he visited England, where he sang 200 nights for the SS Union. In 1872, he made a singing tour of the world. His H*allowed Songs* was used by MOODY/SANKEY as a teaching book for a time. His books include *Early Blossoms* (1860) and *Gem Solos* (1887). His *The American Sacred Songster* (1868) sold 1,100,000 copies.

Marcus M. Wells

Oct. 2, 1815
Otsego, New York

July 17, 1895
Hartwick, New York

Wrote the lyrics and music to "Holy Spirit, Faithful Guide." Wells was converted in a mission in Buffalo, NY, and spent most of his life near Hardwick, NY, where he farmed and made farm equipment. In October, 1858, while at work in his cornfield, the sentiment for this hymn inspired him. He finished it the next day, and it was published within a month in the *New York Musical Pioneer*.

George F. Root

Aug. 30, 1820
Sheffield, Massachusetts

Aug. 6, 1895
Bailey's Island, Maine

Musician and educator who composed the music for "Ring the Bells of Heaven," and "When He Cometh." Root also wrote the lyrics and music for "Why Do You Wait." He taught in Boston, 1839–44, then moved to NYC in 1844 and began a music-teaching ministry. He married Mary Woodman in August, 1845. In 1853, he founded, with WILLIAM BRADBURY, The New York Normal Institute to train music teachers. He moved to Chicago (1859), and developed the Root & Cady music firm, which was destroyed by fire (1871). Then he was affiliated with the John Church Company, Cincinnati, OH. However, he kept his residence in Chicago, acting as its agent with George F. Root and Sons. His songs numbered 200 and his compiled and published songbooks numbered 70.

Cecil Frances Humphreys Alexander

April 1818
Redcross, Ireland

Oct. 12, 1895
Londonberry, Northern Ireland

Hymn writer who ministered to the deaf and women. Cecil's hymn writing began while helping her godsons learn their catechism, writing "All Things Bright and Beautiful." In 1850, she married William Alexander (1824–1911), a bishop in Derry, Ireland, who became primate of the Church of Ireland in 1893. She wrote many of her 400 hymns for the children of her Sunday School class. Her *Hymns for Little Children* (1848), which was only 30 pages long, went through 100 editions. Cecil's hymns included "Jesus Call Us" (1852) (music by WILLIAM JUDE), "He Is Risen," "There Is a Green Hill Far Away," 1878 (music by GEORGE STEBBINS), and "Spirit of God, That Moved of Old."

Asahel C. Kendrick

Dec. 7, 1809
Poultney, Vermont

Oct. 21, 1895
Rochester, New York

Baptist educator and professor of Greek at Madison (Colgate) **University, Hamilton, NY 1832–50**. He married Ann Hopkins (1838), and Helen M. Hooker (1857). Kendrick taught at Rochester University (1850–95) and briefly at Rochester Theological Seminary (1865–68). He was a member of the American NT Revision Committee, 1872–80. He wrote B*iblical Commentary on the New Testament* (6 vols., 1856–58).

Cornelius V. A. VanDyck

Aug. 13, 1818
Kinderhook, New York

Nov. 13, 1895
Beirut, Syria (Lebanon)

Medical missionary to the Near East and Arabic scholar. VanDyck ministered in Syria from 1840 until his death. He married Julia Abbott on December 23, 1842; they had four children. He also completed an Arabic translation of the Bible begun by ELI SMITH and published it in 1865. He worked to revive Arabic literature and excelled in science, the medical field, math and astronomy. He managed *The Mission Press* (1857–80).

Samuel F. Smith

Oct. 21, 1808
Boston, Massachusetts

Nov. 16, 1895
Boston, Massachusetts

Baptist pastor who gave us "America" in 1831. Smith was but 24 years old and an Andover (MA) Seminary student when he wrote it. He married Mary Smith on September 16, 1834; they had six children. He taught modern languages at Waterville College (Colby University) (1834–42), and pastored in Newton, MA (1842–54), He knew 15 languages. He also edited the *Boston Christian Review* (1842–48). As editor of the publication *Baptist Missionary Union* (1854–69, 1875–76, 1880–82), he visited key mission stations in Europe and Asia. He died of a heart attack at a train station. He also wrote "The Morning Light Is Breaking" (music by GEORGE WEBB).

Sylvanus D. Phelps

May 15, 1816
Suffield, Connecticut

Nov. 23, 1895
New Haven, Connecticut

Baptist hymn writer of "Something for Thee" (music by ROBERT LOWRY). Phelps was pastor of FBC, New Haven, CT from 1846–74, during which time the church received 1,217 new members and had 615 baptisms. He moved to Providence, RI (1874) then to Hartford, CT (1876) in order to edit *Christian Secretary*. He was the father of WILLIAM L. PHELPS.

Daniel S. Warner

June 25, 1842　　　　　　　　　　　　　　　　　　　　　　　　　　　　　Dec. 12, 1895
Bristol (Marshallville), Ohio　　　　　　　　　　　　　　　　　Grand Junction, Michigan

First editor of *Gospel Trumpet* (Vital Christianity) and founder of Church of God, Anderson, IN 1881–95. Warner was converted at a schoolhouse revival in 1865. He was expelled from the Church of God in NA for his "entire sanctification" belief. He settled in Anderson, IN. He believed in foot washing and baptism by immersion.

John Miley

Dec. 25, 1813　　　　　　　　　　　　　　　　　　　　　　　　　　　　　　　Dec. 13, 1895
Hamilton, Ohio

Methodist theologian and minister who entered the ministry in 1838, serving in the circuits of Ohio and Washington Square Church in NYC until 1873. Miley taught at Wesley Female College, Cincinnati, OH from 1849–50. He became professor of theology at Drew Theological Seminary, Madison, NJ from 1873–95. He was held in high respect as a conservative theologian. He wrote *Atonement in Christ* (1879) and *Systematic Theology* (1892, 1894). He developed Methodist Arminian Theology opposing Calvinistic limited atonement.

Nathaniel G. Clark

Jan. 18, 1825　　　　　　　　　　　　　　　　　　　　　　　　　　　　　　　Jan. 3, 1896
　　　　　　　　　　　　　　　　　　　　　　　　　　　　　　　　　　　　Calais, Vermont

Corresponding Secretary (CEO) of American Board of Commissioners to Missions (UCBWM in 1961), **1866–94**. Clark married Mary Bowland on Aug. 16, 1854 (died: February 11, 1959) and Elizabeth Sargent on May 8, 1961. He was professor of English literature and Latin at Vermont University, Burlington, 1852–63, and then taught at Union College, Schenectady, NY from 1863–65. He published many books and died of rheumatism and heart disease. He was ordained on October 13, 1857 in Burlington, VT.

Samuel Sprecher

Dec. 28, 1810　　　　　　　　　　　　　　　　　　　　　　　　　　　　　　　Jan. 10, 1896
Williamsport, Maryland　　　　　　　　　　　　　　　　　　　　San Diego, California

President of Wittenberg University, Springfield, OH (Trinity Lutheran Seminary, Columbus, OH in 1978), **1849–74**. Sprecher was a Lutheran pastor, scholar and educator who was influenced by SAM SCHMUCKER. He served congregations in Harrisburg, PA; Martinsburg, VA; and Chambersburg, PA from 1836–49. He also was the professor of theology and philosophy (1874–80) and systematic theology (1880–84) at Wittenberg.

Atticus G. Haygood

Nov. 19, 1839　　　　　　　　　　　　　　　　　　　　　　　　　　　　　　　Jan. 19, 1896
Watkinsville, Georgia　　　　　　　　　　　　　　　　　　　　　　　Oxford, Georgia

Methodist Episcopal Church South bishop, editor, and educator. Haygood married Mary Yarbrough in June, 1859. He was the Sunday school secretary of the denomination (1870–75), president of Emory College, Oxford, GA (1875–84); and became an agent of the John F. Slater Fund (1884–90), which sought to encourage education for blacks in the South. He was elected bishop in 1882 but declined the post. He was a friend to the blacks and wrote books on the social problems. He edited the *Wesleyan Christian Advocate* (1878–82). He founded Paine Institute (College) Augusta, GA in 1883, with Cucius Holset, servicing Georgia and Florida Methodists. Haygood became a bishop in 1890 and lived in Los Angeles, CA from 1890–93, establishing churches on the West Coast. He lived his last three years as a semi-invalid. WARREN CANDLER was his successor at Emory.

Thomas A. Armitage

Aug. 2, 1819
Pontefract, England

Jan. 20, 1896
Yonkers, New York

Baptist historian and preacher who wrote the famous *A History of the Baptists and Preaching* (1887–90). Armitage was originally a Methodist until he came to America (1838) and changed his views on baptism (1839). He pastored the Washington Avenue Baptist Church in Albany, NY (1839–48), and Norfolk Street Baptist Church (Fifth Avenue Baptist Church, then Park Avenue Baptist) in New York City (1849–96). In 1850, he led in the formation of the American Bible Union and served as its second president.

Joseph Barnby

Aug. 12, 1838
York, England

Jan. 28, 1896
London, England

Composer, conductor and organist. Barnby wrote 46 anthems and 246 hymn tunes, including "When Morning Guilds the Sky" (1868) and "Now the Day is Over." He was a musical protégé, entering the choir of Yorkminster at age seven, and following in his father's footsteps as an organist by age twelve. He studied at the prestigious Royal Academy of Music in London in 1854. He was the organist and choirmaster at St. Andrew's in London (1863–71) and at St. Anne's in Soho (1871–76) and director of music at Eton College (1875–92). Lady Edith Mary Silverthorne became his wife in 1878, the same year he founded the London Musical Society. He was conductor of the Royal Albert Hall Choral Society (1886–96), conducting the rehearsals and concerts of the Royal Academy of Music (1886–88) and head of the Guildhall School of Music in London in 1892. Barnby was knighted in 1892. He conducted many performances of BACH and arranged copious renditions of sacred choral music. He also edited five hymnals, the most noted one being, *The Hymnary* (1872).

Talbot W. Chambers

Feb. 25, 1819
Carlisle, Pennsylvania

Feb. 3, 1896
New York, New York

Reformed pastor of the Second Church in Somerville, NY 1840–49, and of Collegiate Dutch Church in NYC 1849–96. Chambers married Louise Freylinghuysen on May 21, 1841; they had eleven children. He organized the Alliance of Reformed Churches, holding the Presbyterian System and served as president of the same, 1892–96. He authored several books ranging from *The Noon Prayer Meeting* (1858) to *A Companion to the Revised Old Testament* (1885).

Thaddeus C. Blake

March 17, 1825
near Petersburg, Tennessee

Feb. 9, 1896
near Nashville, Tennessee

Stated clerk of Cumberland Presbyterian Church, Memphis, TN 1883–1896. Blake married Nannie M. Johnson (Oct. 15, 1851), and Lizzie Means (Sept. 15, 1886). He wrote valuable books and edited excellent journals. He edited the *Banner of Peace* and the Cumberland Presbyterian church papers. In 1857, he was elected secretary of the board of missions. From 1874–78, he was agent, or manager of the publishing house. He was 6 feet 7 inches tall. He suffered from a chronic ailment caused by a severe fall in 1879. During his last week, a surgical operation was performed, but uremic poisoning took his life.

Hsi Shengmo

1837
Shansi (Shanxi), Province, China

Feb. 19, 1896

Outstanding pastor, evangelist and former Confucian scholar. After his education, Shengmo was a peacemaker, a solver of problems and quarrels among his humble villagers. His first wife passed away. At age 30, he married again and became an opium addict. In 1877, famine stalked the province of Shansi. Then he met missionary David Hill, who lived twelve miles away from him. Reading literature given him, he was converted in 1879. He wrote two tracts and about 60 hymns in his early Christian life. He started 45 refuge houses for opium users in four provinces. In 1886, HUDSON TAYLOR ordained him to pastor over a wide area. For the last five years of their lives, he and his wife lived apart so she could direct a needed work among women addicts. City after city was reached through evangelism endeavors. In his own home, he challenged 200 people about enlarging the work. On a visit to D. E. HOSTE (successor to HUDSON TAYLOR), he fell unconscious. He had developed a serious heart problem and six months later was taken to his heavenly home. Shengmo means "Demon Overcomer."

Charles W. Schaeffer

May 5, 1813
Hagerstown, Maryland

March 15, 1896
Germantown, Pennsylvania

President of Lutheran Theological Seminary (LTS) at Philadelphia, 1879–96. Schaeffer married Elizabeth Ashmead in 1837; they had four children. He pastored in Pennsylvania all his life: Barrow Hill, PA (1835–41); Zion's Church, Harrisburg (1841–49); and St. Michael's Church, Germantown (1849–75). He taught church history at LTS from 1864–96. He edited three periodicals, including *The Lutheran*. His first book was entitled, *Family Prayer* (1861).

Elizabeth Rundle Charles

Jan. 2, 1828
Tavistock, England

March 28, 1896
Hampstead Heath, London, England

High Church Anglican author who married Andrew P. Charles, a philanthropist in 1851 (died: June 4, 1868). Some of her poems were published in 1858–59. She was also a painter. They made their home among the poor in Hampstead. She also wrote the words to "Praise Ye the Triune God" (music by FREDERICH FLEMMING). She wrote around 50 books, her most famous being *The Chronicles of the Schonberg-Cotta Family* (1862), which was a historical romance about MARTIN LUTHER. She wrote simple hymns, intended primarily for children. Her works ended with *Lapsed But Not Lost* (1877). In 1885, she founded a home for incurables and called it Friedenheim.

Robert Lathan

Dec. 27, 1829
Fairfield County, South Carolina

June 15, 1896
Bradley, South Carolina

Stated Clerk of Associate Reformed Presbyterian Church, Greenville, SC 1880–90, living in Yorkville from 1859–84. Lathan graduated from Erskine College in 1855, then took seminary work. He married Fannie Barron on May 10, 1859. He pastored in Yorkville and Tirzah, SC from 1859–74. He taught at Erskine Theological Seminary, 1884–94, then took the pastorates of churches in Bradley and Cedar Springs, SC. He was ill for a year before he died. There are conflicting reports as to the cause of his death: Bright's disease, dropsy, tumor, etc.

Harriet Beecher Stowe

June 14, 1811
Litchfield, Connecticut

July 1, 1896
Hartford, Connecticut

Her fame rests upon the epic work, *Uncle Tom's Cabin*, **written and published, 1851–52**. This book sold 500,000 copies and was translated into 20 languages. It was a factor in causing the Civil War. In 1824, she moved to Hartford, CT to attend the local Female Seminary. She moved to Ancuwah in 1832. The daughter of LYMAN BEECHER and sister of HENRY WARD BEECHER, she married Calvin Stowe in Cincinnati on January 6, 1836 (died: 1886). They had seven children, including twin daughters born on September 29, 1850. They moved to Brunswick, ME, 1850, then moved to Andover, MA, where her husband taught in the Seminary, 1853–78. Harriet also wrote more than 40 volumes of prose, poems, and hymns including "Still, Still with Thee" (music by MENDELSSOHN). Late in life, she became an Episcopalian. She suffered a stroke in 1890. Her favorite Bible verses were Hebrews 12:22–24 and John 15:15.

Arthur C. Coxe

May 10, 1818
Mendham, New Jersey

July 20, 1896
Clifton Springs, New York

Episcopalian hymn writer of such as "O, Where Are Kings and Empires Now?" (1839). Coxe married Katherine Hyde on Sept. 21, 1841. He served in four churches: St. John's in Hartford, CT (1842–54); Grace Church in Baltimore, MD (1854–63); Calvary Church in New York, NY (1863–65); and St. Ann's in Morrisania, NY. He was made bishop of western New York in 1865, with his headquarters in Buffalo. He was a strong conservative and opposed the Catholic view of history and acceptance of every version of the Bible. His books range from *Christian Ballads* (1840) to *Holy Writ and Modern Thought* (1892).

John M. Stevenson

May 14, 1812
Washington County, Pennsylvania

Aug. 22, 1896
Hawthorne, New Jersey

General secretary of the American Tract Society, 1870–92. Stevenson was converted at age 20 while attending revival meetings in Ohio. In 1841, he was elected professor of Greek in Ohio University, but his heart was set on preaching. In 1842, he was ordained as a Presbyterian. He pastored in Troy, OH from 1842–45. He traveled for the ATS (1845–48), and pastored First Presbyterian Church, New Albany, IN (1848–56). He then became secretary to the ATS until 1870, and its leading executive thereafter.

Philip Phelps

July 12, 1826
Albany, New York

Sept. 4, 1896
Albany, New York

President of Hope College, Holland, MI 1866–1878. In 1850, Phelps entered the ministry as pastor of Greenborough Church, Westchester County, NY. He married Margaret Jordan in 1853 and had three children. In 1859, he accepted an appointment as principal of Hope Academy. He was responsible for founding the first English-speaking Reformed Church in Holland, Hope Church, and for establishing a theological department at the college, which later became Western Theological Seminary.

William G. Tomer

Oct. 5, 1833

Sept. 26, 1896
New Jersey

Composed the music for "God Be With You Till We Meet Again" (1883). During the Civil War, Tomer served in the 153rd Pennsylvania Infantry. After the war, he spent 20 years as a government employee in Washington, D.C. During this time, he served as music director at Grace Episcopal Church. He spent his last year of life as a New Jersey schoolteacher.

Edward W. Benson

July 14, 1829
Birmingham, England

Oct. 11, 1896
Hawarden, England

Hymnbook compiler and Archbishop of Canterbury, 1882–96. Benson first served at the Rugby School, Warwickshire, for which he produced the *Rugby School Hymnbook* (1856). From 1859–72, he was headmaster of the New Wellington College in Berkshire and compiled several editions of a hymnal for them entitled, *The Wellington College Chapel Hymn Book* (1860, 1863, and 1873). In 1877, he became the first bishop of Truro in Cornwall. He was also interested in relations with Eastern churches, with the exception of Rome. Benson wrote volumes of sermons. He translated several Latin and Greek hymns and wrote "O, Jesus Crowned with All Renown." He vigorously opposed the disestablishment of the Welsh Church in 1893. He was the first archbishop to be buried in the Cathedral since Reginald Pole in 1558.

Charles H. Mackintosh

Oct. 1820
Glennalure Barracks, Ireland

Nov. 2, 1896
Cheltenham, England

Plymouth Brethren preacher and Bible expositor. Mackintosh was converted at age 18 and greatly helped by J. N. DARBY. He opened a school in Westport (1844) and taught for nine years, then traveled to Dublin for a career in evangelism and journalism (1853). He was active in the revivals of 1859–60. He edited the monthly periodical *Things Old and New* and published the *Notes on Pentateuch* books with the familiar C.H.M. initials.

Frederick C. Atkinson

Aug. 21, 1841
Norwich, England

Nov. 30, 1896
East Dereham, England

Organist, choirmaster, and composer. Atkinson was a boy chorister at Norwich Cathedral from 1849–60. He served as an organist and choirmaster at St. Luke's Church in Manningham, Bradford, at Norwich Cathedral, 1881–85, and at St. Mary's Parish Church in Lewisham, after 1886. He composed several Anglican hymns and anthems, including the music for "Spirit of God, Descend Upon My Heart" (lyrics by GEORGE CROLY).

Peter C. Scott

March 7, 1867
Glasgow, Scotland

Dec. 8, 1896
Nzawi, Kenya, East Africa

Founder and first general director of Africa Inland Mission, 1895–96. Scott died as a young visionary who went to Africa and did not live to see age 30. He came to America in 1879, his family settling in Philadelphia. He had a fine singing voice, but also grew up with health problems. In November 1890, he went to Africa with SIMPSON's International Missionary Society. While in the Congo, he buried his brother John, who accompanied him, then left for England because of illness. He felt British East Africa would be a good place of service. In America, he shared his vision with A. T. PIERSON and the AIM was born. In August, 1895, eight went to Africa. They reached Nzawi, 250 miles from the coast, and established their first station. Within ten months, four stations were opened in Kenya with houses built of bricks. After 14 months in BEA, he was planning to return home but walking 2,600 miles took a toll on his health, and he soon died of black-water fever. His last words were, "I want the arm of the Lord of hosts around me." His last diary entry was, "Here I am, Lord, use me in life or in death."

Thomas B. Pollock

May 28, 1836
Strathallan, Isle Man, England

Dec. 15, 1896
Birmingham, England

Anglican pastor and hymn writer. Pollock was ordained in 1860, and was curate of St. Luke's, Staffordshire; St. Thomas', London; and St. Alban's, Birmingham. At the latter, he worked 30 years as an assistant to his brother, helping in education and welfare programs. He also wrote several hymns such as "Great Creator, Lord of All" (1876).

George L. Pilkington

1865
Dublin, Ireland

1897
Uganda, Africa

Missionary to Uganda with the Church Missionary Society. Pilkington arrived in 1890 but it was nearly a year before he finally reached Uganda where MACKAY had died a few months before. He saw a great revival there between 1893–94. Near the end of 1897, he was killed with his beloved Baganda soldiers in a skirmish during a Sudanese raid against the government. He translated the Bible into Lugandan. He had great linguistic ability.

Henry Drummond (2)

Aug. 17, 1851
Stirling, Scotland

March 11, 1897
Tunbridge Wells, England

Free Church of Scotland writer and evangelist who lectured and wrote on Christianity, natural history, and science. Raised as a Christian, Drummond pastored in Malta early in his ministry. He worked hard with his students and was associated with D. L. MOODY in evangelism and Bible teaching from 1873 on. He is most remembered for his powerful commentary on I Corinthians 13, *The Greatest Thing in the World*. He was also a professor of theology and lecturer in natural science at Free Church College, Edinburgh (1877–84) and in Glasgow, Scotland (1884–97), lecturing also in the US and Australia. He toured Africa in 1888. He believed in evolution. His works range from *Natural Law in the Spiritual World* (1883) to *The New Evangelism* (pub. 1899). He died after suffering two years of a crippling malignant illness. He never married.

James T. Ward

Aug. 21, 1820
Georgetown, D.C.

March 11, 1897
Westminster, Maryland

President of Westminster (MD) Theological Seminary (Wesley Theological Seminary, Washington, D.C. in 1955), **1886–97**. For 25 years, Ward pastored in Maryland, Washington, D.C., West Virginia and Philadelphia. He was also president of Western Maryland College, Westminster, 1866–86. He wrote *A Daily Manual for Bible Readers* (1894, Baltimore). He was active in the Methodist Protestant Church.

Johannes Brahms

May 7, 1833
Hamburg, Germany

April 3, 1897
Vienna, Austria

Composer and pianist who wrote in every musical area except opera. Brahms combined romanticism and classicism. He remained in Vienna after 1863, and was a close friend of ROBERT SCHUMANN and his family. He never married and was grounded in Lutheran church music, composing a few sacred motets. His compositions are usually given the highest praise by critics. His choral masterpiece is "A German Requiem" (1868), using words entirely from the German Bible. He wrote well-known symphonies (C Minor, D Major, E Major, E Minor) plus "The Academic Testeral Overture" and "Tragic Overture." His last compositions were a group of eleven organ preludes based on the Lutheran chorale.

James H. Brookes

Feb. 27, 1830
Pulaski, Tennessee

April 18, 1897
St. Louis, Missouri

Presbyterian pastor, author, and editor. Brookes married in 1854 and pastored Washington Avenue Church, Dayton, OH, until 1858; Second Presbyterian Church (1858–64), and Walnut Street Church, St. Louis, MO; which he organized with 149 former members of Second Presbyterian (1864–97). He was a Bible scholar and spoke at premillennial conferences in 1878 and 1880. He founded and edited *Truth or Testimony for Christ* (1875–97). C. I. SCOFIELD was greatly influenced by him. Brookes authored over 200 tracts and booklets and was a strong dispensational premillennialist.

Edward M. Goulburn

Feb. 11, 1818
Chelsea, England

May 3, 1897
Turnbridge Wells, England

Church of England divine who was a fellow of Merton College, Oxford, 1839–46. Goulburn was a tutor and dean from 1843–45. He then served in many positions: chaplain to the Oxford bishop (1847–49); curate of Holywell, Oxford (1844–50); headmaster of Rugby (1850–58); minister of Quebec Chapel, London (1858–59); vicar of St. John's in Paddington, London; chaplain to the Queen (1859–66); and finally dean of Norwich (1866–89). His works range from *The Doctrine of the Resurrection* (1851) to *JOHN W. BURGON* (2 vols., 1892).

Hermann M. Schaeffer

Aug. 22, 1839
Laoe, Lippe-Demold, Germany

May 11, 1897
Rochester, New York

President of German Baptist Deptartment of Rochester (NY) Divinity School (North American Baptist Seminary, Sioux Falls, SD in 1950), 1872–83. Schaeffer graduated from NABS in 1864 and was ordained on May 17, 1867. He was a pastor and author.

Clara H. Scott
Clara H. Jone—Mrs. Henry Scott

Dec. 3, 1841
Elk Grove, Illinois

June 21, 1897
Dubuque, Iowa

Wrote the lyrics and music for "Open My Eyes that I May See" (1895). Clara began teaching music in 1859 at the Ladies' Seminary at Lyons, IA. In 1861, she married Henry Clay Scott. She began her creative writing, contributing to various song collection but was tragically killed when thrown from a buggy by a runaway horse.

David Brown

Aug. 17, 1803
Aberdeen, Scotland

July 3, 1897
Aberdeen, Scotland

Free Church of Scotland minister. At the time of the disruption in 1843, Brown went with the Free Church, becoming a pastor at St. James in Glasgow. He taught at Free Church College in Aberdeen, Scotland, 1857–87, and was appointed its president in 1876. He was one of the founders of the Evangelical Alliance. He wrote several books and was a postmillennial believer. In later years, he became tolerant of liberalism. Along with A.R. FAUSETT and ROBERT JAMIESON, he helped produce a famous commentary series.

Emily E. Steele Elliott

July 22, 1836
Brighton, England

Aug. 3, 1897
London, England

Wrote the hymn "Thou Didst Leave Thy Throne" (1864) (music by TIM MATTHEWS). Emily was a niece of CHARLOTTE ELLIOTT and was active in missions work. Most of her hymns were used in her father's Anglican church in Brighton. She was the editor of *Church Missionary Juvenile Instructor* for six years and published over 70 of her hymns in *Chimes of Consecration* (1873) and *Chimes for Daily Service.*

William W. How

Dec. 13, 1823
Shrewsbury, England

Aug. 10, 1897
Leenane, Ireland

Bishop and hymn writer. How wrote several hymns, including "O Jesus, Thou Art Standing," and "O Word of God Incarnate." An Anglican, he was known as the "Poor Man's Bishop." He was the curate at Kidderminster and Holy Cross in Shrewsbury (1845–51), rector of Whittington (1851–79), rural dean of Oswestry (1853–79), chancellor of St. Asaph's Cathedral (1859–88). In 1879, he became the bishop of east London, a poverty-stricken area. In 1888, he became the bishop of Wakefield. He wrote over 60 hymns. His works range from *Daily Family Prayers* (1852) to *The Closed Door* (1898). He died while vacationing.

George M. Grossman

Oct. 18, 1823
Grossbieberau, Germany

Aug. 24, 1897
Waverly, Iowa

First president of Wartburg Theological Seminary in Dubuque, IA 1853–75, and president of Iowa Synod (ALC, ELCA in 1988), **1854–93**. Grossman married Nannie Steppes, then came to Saginaw, MI in 1852. After his involvement in the controversy with the Missouri Synod, he left for Dubuque, IA in 1853. He organized the German Lutheran Synod of Iowa with immigrants. He was the president of Wartburg Normal College in Waverly, IA, 1878–94.

Jane L. Borthwick

April 9, 1813
Edinburgh, Scotland

Sept. 7, 1897
Edinburgh, Scotland

Translated many German hymns into English, including "Be Still, My Soul," and "My Jesus, As Thou Wilt." Jane was second only to CATHERINE WINKWORTH in this area of translation. She and her sister Sarah, Mrs. E. J. Findlater (1823–1907), devoted themselves to this task. Jane translated 61 hymns, and Sarah translated 53. She was a Free Church of Scotland member and greatly supported home and foreign missions. She also wrote original hymns. Many of these hymns are published in *Thoughts For Thoughtful Hours.*

William A. Ogden

Oct. 10, 1841
Franklin County, Ohio

Oct. 14, 1897
Toledo, Ohio

Wrote the lyrics and music for "Look and Live," "Seeking the Lost," and "Where He Leads, I'll Follow." Odgen served in the Civil War for four years. After studying music under great teachers, he taught normal music schools and conducted musical conventions. From 1887 until death, he was music supervisor for Toledo's public school system.

Charles J. Vaughan

Aug. 6, 1816
Leicester, England

Oct. 15, 1897
Llandaff, Wales

Church of England clergyman and educator. Vaughan was the headmaster of Harrow, preparing hundreds of university graduates for the ministry from 1844–59. He became the vicar of Donaster (1860–69); master of the Temple (1869–94); also the dean of Llandaff, Wales (1879–91). He also founded the University College of Cardiff, Wales; becoming the president in 1894, at the age of 78. He wrote works ranging from *Romans* (1859) to *The School of Life* (1885), a total of some 40 volumes.

James Legge

Dec. 20, 1815
Huntly, Scotland

Nov. 29, 1897
Oxford, England

Congregational missionary and sinologist. Legge was sent by the London Missionary Society to Malacca as a missionary to the Chinese in 1839. He married Mary Morison (1816–1852) in 1839. She was a great missionary and educator, who died in childbirth. He translated *Chinese Classics* (1841, 28 vols.). When Hong Kong became a British colony in 1842, he moved to Hong Kong, developed a seminary there, and pastored the English-speaking Union Church from 1843–73. In 1873, he returned to England and taught Chinese language and literature at Oxford from 1875–97. In 1894, he was the first person (outside of the British royal family) to be depicted on a Hong Kong postage stamp.

John A. Wood

1828

C 1898

Holiness proponent and pastor. Converted at age ten, Wood surrendered his life to the Lord and prepared for the ministry. He pastored in North Attleboro, MA and married his wife, Mary, in February, 1850. They pastored in Vermont until 1857, when they went to the Court Street Church in Binghamton, NY, remaining until 1860. During the summer of 1858, at the district camp meeting, 80 members of his church, seeking holiness, experienced a special renewal. As a result, Wood wrote *A Perfect Love*, a classic in holiness circles. After this, he pastored in Waverly, NY; Wilkes-Barre: and Scranton, PA. In 1867, they started a camp meeting in Vineland, NJ for the special promotion of holiness. He preached far and wide, in 24 states and on every continent, spending the last 18 years of his life in California, preaching in 52 different churches.

Benjamin W. Newton

1805
Plymouth, England

1898
Tunbridge Wells, England

Plymouth Brethren leader in his early years. Newton taught from 1830–47 in Plymouth. In 1845, he and DARBY split over prophetic teachings (Newton opposed "secret rapture"). He left Plymouth in 1847, after his writings displeased some of his church members. He then pastored in Bayswater, London, where large congregations gathered to hear him. He continued his written ministry until well into his 90s and was a steady contributor to the *Christian Witness*. Although he was considered a remote individual, his high personal honor code conveyed his strong testimony. In later years he adopted Calvinistic views.

Robert L. Dabney

March 5, 1820
Louisa County, Virginia

Jan. 3, 1898
Victoria, Texas

Dean of Hampden-Sydney (VA) Seminary (Union Theological Seminary, Richmond, VA in 1898), **1859–83**. He married Lavinia Morrison on March 28, 1848, was ordained as a Presbyterian, and began teaching theology in 1853 at Hampden-Sydney. This Southern Presbyterian theologian also co-pastored the local college church, 1858–74. He served as a chaplain of Virginia in the Confederate army in the Civil War. In 1883, he moved to Austin, TX and taught philosophy at the University of Texas (1883–94), helping to start Austin Theological Seminary and teaching there (1884–95). He became infirm and totally blind in 1890, but continued lecturing until 1897. He was a Calvinist and his works range from *Memoir of Francis S. Sampson* (1855) to *Penal Character of the Atonement of Christ* (1898).

Henry G. Liddell

Feb. 6, 1811
Binchester, England

Jan. 18, 1898
Ascot, England

Dean of Christ Church and Greek lexicographer. Liddell tutored at Christ Church, Oxford, 1836–45, and prepared and published his Greek-English Lexicon in 1843 after nine years of work with Robert Scott. In 1846, he was appointed headmaster of Westminster School. He then became dean of Christ Church, 1855–92, during which time he was made chaplain to the queen in 1862. After 1891, he lived in retirement in Ascot. He authored *A History of Ancient Rome* (2 vols., 1855.).

Henry P. Smith

1825
England

Jan. 28, 1898
Bournemouth, England

Composed music for "O Master Let Me Walk with Thee" (lyrics by WASHINGTON GLADDEN). Smith was a Church of England cleric at Eversley, 1849–51, and a curate to liberal Charles Kingsley (1819–75). He also served as curate of St. Michael's Yorktown, Camberley, Surrey (1851–68) and as the vicar of Great Barton, Suffold (1868–82). He was a chaplain at Christ Church, Cannes, France (1882–95) and the canon of cathedral in Gibraltar (1892–98).

William F. Moulton

March 1, 1835
Leek, England

Feb. 5, 1898
Cambridge, England

Bible scholar. In 1858, Moulton entered the Wesleyan ministry, but wanted to teach more than preach, so he became a tutor for Richmond College. He was the youngest member of the New Testament Revision Committee, 1870–81. In 1874, he became the headmaster of the Leys School in Cambridge, remaining there until his death. He was a Greek scholar, a learned Hebraist and father of JAMES H. MOULTON.

Frances E. C. Willard

Sept. 28, 1839
Churchville, New York

Feb. 18, 1898
New York, New York

Temperance champion, Frances assumed the secretariate of the Women's Christian Temperance Union in 1874, and built the organization into a most influential movement at that time, being president of National WCTU (1879–98) and Worlds WCTU (1887–98). She taught esthetics (love of beauty) at Evanston College for Ladies in Illinois, 1871–74. She led women's meetings for D. L. MOODY in 1877, in Boston. She was converted at Northwestern Female College in Evanston, IL following a bout with typhoid fever. Frances helped found the Prohibition Party in 1884. Upon her death, Congress called her "the first woman of the nineteenth century." She averaged 400 lectures a year. Her legacy included establishing a temperance hospital, an office building in Chicago, a world-wide WCTU organization with memberships of two million, and 20 states that enacted women's suffrage to some degree. She was a Methodist who was refused ordination when she sought it, and was president of the National Council of Women in 1890. Her favorite Bible verse was Colossians 3:17.

George Müller

Sept. 27, 1805
Kroppenstadt, Prussia (Germany)

March 10, 1898
Bristol, England

History's man of faith. Müller was converted attending a home prayer meeting while at Halle University in 1825. He went to London (1829) to train as a missionary to the Jews and moved to a pastorate in Bristol (1832). He married Mary Groves on Oct. 7, 1830 (died: Feb. 6, 1870), and Susannah Sangar on November 30, 1871 (died: January 13, 1894). In 1834, he founded the Scripture Knowledge Institute, an umbrella for all his activities. In 1836, Müller opened an orphan home (26 orphans) in Bristol, which would by 1875 care for 2,100 children at a time. He was father to more than 10,000 orphans, helped 121,000 students, sent out 163 missionaries, received over 20,000 answers to prayer, printed 111 million tracts, and prayed in $5 million; never asking anyone but God for anything. Some of Müller's last years, 1875–92, were given to worldwide evangelism in 42 countries. He wrote five books and was a leader in the Christian (Plymouth) Brethren movement. His favorite Bible verse was Psalm 81:10.

Guido H. F. Verbeck

Jan. 23, 1830
Zeist, Netherlands

March 10, 1898
Tokyo, Japan

Reformed missionary to Japan, 1859, arriving there at a time when Christianity was outlawed. Verbeck joined the Moravians (1846), then came to America (1852). He married Maria Manion on April 18, 1859; they had seven children. As an instructor at Nagasaki, he won recognition and respect from Japanese authorities and in 1868, was asked to establish a Japanese educational system and supervise foreign teachers. This institution later became Imperial University in Tokyo. He was an advisor to the Japanese government until 1877. The ban against Christianity was lifted through his influence. In 1879, he returned to missionary activity.

William E. Gladstone

Dec. 29, 1809
Liverpool, England

May 19, 1898
Hawarden, Wales

Great Christian statesman: four times prime minister of Great Britain under Queen Victoria (1868–1884, 1880–85, 1886, 1892–94). Gladstone was a member of parliament almost continually, 1832–95. He married Catherine Glynne in July, 1839. Later, he married Anne Robertson. He was a liberal and opposed the imperialism of Disraeli, another Christian prime minister. He dominated political life with his intellect and oratory seeking to apply Christian principles to both domestic and foreign affairs. His greatness of intellect and earnest Christian character made him world-renowned. He was buried in Westminster Abbey, where his wife joined him upon her death on June 14, 1900. He was either adored or hated. He thought more like a clergyman than a politician. One of his books was titled *The Impregnable Rock of Scripture*. Gladstone once said, "All I am, all I have, all I hope for the future is indissolubly bound to my faith in Jesus Christ as God's Son." He disestablished the Irish/Anglican Church and supported the interest of Irish Catholic institutions. Illness forced him to stop work on March 6, 1898, as he grew steadily weaker.

Edward Bellamy

March 26, 1850
Chicopee Falls, Mass.

May 22, 1898
Chicopee Falls, Mass.

Economist, journalist, and author. Bellamy was the son of a Baptist minister. He married Emma Sanderson in 1882 and spent some years in Hawaii. He founded the *Springfield Daily News* (1877), and was best known for his novel, *Looking Backward* (1888), a socialist work. Later, he published *Equality* (1897), which dealt with social problems. He died of tuberculosis.

Sanford F. Bennett

June 21, 1836
Eden, New York

June 12, 1898
Richmond, Indiana

Doctor and hymn writer. Bennett wrote the famous hymn "In the Sweet By and By" (music by JOSEPH WEBSTER). He was converted in a Methodist revival. In the early 1850s, his poetry began appearing in the Illinois Gazette. He settled in Elkhorn, WI in 1860, and became the editor of *The Independent*, a weekly newspaper. After serving in the Civil War with the 40th Regiment of Wisconsin volunteers, he opened a drugstore in Elkhorn and studied medicine. He was a physician for 22 years. "In the Sweet By and By" was published in *The Signet Ring* (1867), a Sunday school hymnbook.

Otto E. L. Bismarck
Iron Chancellor

April 1, 1815
Schonhausen, Germany

July 30, 1898
Friedrichsruh, Germany

Premier of Prussia, 1862–71; its first chancellor; and the most noted German statesman of the nineteenth century. Bismarck served as ambassador to Russia (1859–62) and France (1862–76). He was made a count (1865) and a prince (1871). He said, "I, however, can only recognize as the will of God that which is contained in the Christian gospels." He also said, "I would to God that I had not other sins upon my soul, for which I can only hope for forgiveness in a confidence upon the blood of Christ." He married Johanna Von Puttkamer in July, 1847. By provoking a series of wars, he forged the divided German principalities into a united nation. He proclaimed William I emperor in 1871, but retained complete control of domestic and foreign policy. Upon the emperor's death in 1888, William II came to power. Bismarck was dismissed by William II (1890), although they were reconciled later (1894).

John Caird

Dec. 15, 1820
Greenock, Scotland

July 30, 1898
Greenock, Scotland

Church of Scotland preacher, philosopher (thought to be the reality), **and theologian**. Caird served as minister in the Church of Scotland, 1845–62: pastoring at Newton-on-Ayr (1845), Looty Yeste's, Edinburgh (1847), Errol (1849), and Park Church, Glasgow (1857). He was a professor of theology (1862–73) and principal (vice-chancellor) of Glasgow University (1873–93). Along with his brother, Edward, he followed the New Hegelian movement (followers of George Hegel, 1770–1831; German philosopher). His greatest sermon ever was "Religion in the Common Life", using Romans 12:11 as his text. He preached this sermon before Queen VICTORIA. His works range from *Introduction to the Philosophy of Religion* (1880) to The *Fundamental Ideas of Christianity* (2 vols., published 1899). *The Americana Encyclopedia* says he died in London.

George Ebers

March 1, 1837
Berlin, Germany

Aug. 7, 1898
Tutzing, Germany

Egyptologist and novelist. Ebers was professor of Egyptology at Jena and at Leipzig, 1870–89. During a visit to Egypt in 1873, he discovered the important sixteenth century BC medieval papyrus now known by his name. A facsimile edition with translation was published in 1875. He wrote archaeological works and several novels, intending to stimulate popular interest in Egyptology, and translated historic novels. He said in his *Story of My Life*, "Our mother did not fail to endeavor to inspire us with love for the Christ-child and the Saviour and to draw us near to him. Years of my own investigation and thought brought me to the same conviction which she had reached."

Alexander Crummel

March 3, 1819
New York, New York

Sept. 9, 1898
Point Pleasant, New Jersey

Episcopal minister and missionary to Liberia. Crummel was the son of an African-born slave. He became an influential Episcopal Church leader, becoming a priest in 1844. In 1848, he went to England, to raise funds for the abolitionist movement (opposition to slavery and slave trade). He served 20 years, 1853–72, as a missionary to Liberia; then in 1873, organized St. Luke's Church in Washington, D.C., serving until 1894. Several years after the death of his first wife, he married Jennie M. Simpson in 1880. He taught at Howard University, Washington, 1895–97; after which he began the American Negro Academy in New York City. He published several books, including *The English Language in Liberia* (1861) and his autobiography in 1894.

William C. Dix

June 14, 1837
Bristol, England

Sept. 9, 1898
Cheddar, England

Wrote the hymns "As with Gladness Men of Old" (1861) (music by CONRAD KOCHER) **and "What Child Is This?"** (1865). Dix was an Anglican that became the manager of a marine insurance company in Glasgow, Scotland. He was a student of both Ethiopian and Greek and translated a number of hymns from those languages into English. His own hymns were published in three languages. He had only a grammar school education.

John Hall

July 31, 1829
Ballygorman/Market Hill, Ireland

Sept. 17, 1898
Bangor, Ireland

Presbyterian leader who began to preach in 1849. For three years, Hall was a missionary in West Ireland. Hall married Emily B. Irwin in 1852, and they had four children. He became the pastor of the First Presbyterian Church at Armagh (1852–58) and at Mary's Abbey (Rutland Square Church), Dublin (1858–67). On November 3, 1867, he came to the Fifth Avenue Church, New York City where he served until death. He was elected chancellor of the University of New York, 1881–91. He was also an author.

Nathan Wardner

Oct. 25, 1833
Lewis, New York

Nov. 11, 1898
West Chazy, New York

President of Wesleyan Methodist Church in America (Wesleyan Church), **1875–90.** Wardner was a chaplain in the Union army during the Civil War. He also served as president of the Champlain Conference in 1861, 1873–74 and 1897–98. During his career, he served as Connectional editor, pastor, and evangelist. He married Christina Wheeler, then Lucinda E. Wheeler.

Robert R. McBurney

March 31, 1837
Castle Blayney, Ireland

Dec. 27, 1898
Clifton Springs, New York

Developer of the YMCA movement in America. McBurney came to America in 1854, built the first American YMCA building in New York City in 1869 and initiated most of the programs and leadership patterns the YMCA still uses. He never married. He led the noon prayer meetings at the Old Dutch Church during revival days in the late 1850s. He was the only paid officer of the YMCA in 1862. McBurney was a member of St. Paul's Methodist Church and was active in the Evangelical Alliance.

John Mackenzie

1835
Knockando, Scotland

1899
Port Elizabeth, South Africa

Missionary and statesman, converted at age 18. In 1858, Mackenzie was ordained to be a missionary to South Africa. He married Ellen Douglas the same year and went to Cape Town through the London Missionary Society. They ministered north of Cape Town in Matabele to the Bakololo tribes. In 1864, they settled at Shosong and began a ten-year ministry to the Bechuana/Tswana peoples. In 1876, they worked in Kuruman and saved Bechuanaland for the British. He was a propagandist of imperial expansion in Britain (1885–91) and a missionary at Hankey, Cape Colony (1891–99).

Cornelius G. MacPherson

Sept. 26, 1806
Halifax County, North Carolina

Jan. 8, 1899
Louisville, Kentucky

Stated clerk of Cumberland Presbyterian Church, Memphis, TN 1841–1850. McPherson served as pastor of the CPC at Huntsville, AL. He was the editor of *The Cumberland Presbyterian*, published at Nashville, and did various other literary work besides preaching regularly. He closed his career as a teacher at Memphis, where he owned and conducted the Memphis Female College for many years. He was an able preacher, teacher and journalist. He died as a result of the grippe (influenza).

Charles P. T. Chiniquy

July 30, 1809
Kamouraska, Quebec, Canada

Jan. 16, 1899
Montreal, Quebec, Canada

Presbyterian convert from Roman Catholicism who spent his lifetime opposing his former religion. Chiniquy was ordained a Catholic priest in 1833 and served in Quebec until 1846. In 1851, he started a Catholic colony in St. Anne, IL, with 7,500 French Canadians. In 1858, he left Catholicism, taking his congregation with him to join the Canadian Presbyterian Church, and pastored there until 1888. Today it is the First Presbyterian Church. He toured England and Australia in his crusades. Although his *Fifty Years in the Church of Rome* (1886) became very popular, he suffered severe physical abuse, because of his bitterly hostile attacks on Catholicism.

Charles S. Robinson

March 31, 1829
Bennington, Vermont

Feb. 1, 1899
New York, New York

Presbyterian clergyman and hymnologist. Robinson pastored in Troy, NY (1855–60); Brooklyn, NY (1865–68); then in Paris, France; and the 11th (Madison Avenue) Church, New York City (1870–87). He married Harriet R. Church in 1858. His works range from *Hymns of the Church* (1862) to *Simon Peter* (1889). He edited *Every Thursday* (1890–99), and compiled several hymnbooks.

John Williams (2)

Aug. 30, 1817
Old Deerfield, Massachusetts

Feb. 7, 1899
Middletown, Connecticut

Presiding bishop of Protestant Episcopal Church (Episcopal Church in 1967), **1889–99, and first president (dean) of Berkeley Divinity School, Middletown (New Haven), CT 1851–99.** Williams was also the rector of St. George's Church, Schenectady, NY (1842–48) and president of Trinity College, Hartford, CT (1848–52). He was a professor of theology at Berkeley from 1853–92. He became a bishop in 1865. He never married. His books range from *Ancient Hymns of Holy Church* (1845) to *Studies on the Book of Acts* (1888).

John R. Sweney

Dec. 31, 1837
West Chester, Pennsylvania

April 10, 1899
Chester, Pennsylvania

Composed music for many hymns, including "Fill Me Now" (Stokes), "Give Me Jesus," "My Savior, First of All," "Beulah Land," 1875 (Stytes), "Tell Me the Story of Jesus," 1880 (CROSBY), "More About Jesus," "There Is Sunshine in My Soul Today" (1887), "Tell Me the Story of Jesus" (CROSBY), "Holy, Holy Is What the Angels Sing" (OATMAN) and "Will There Be Any Stars in My Crown" (1897). Following the Civil War, Sweney was a professor of music at Penn Military Academy for 25 years. During that time, he also directed music at Bethany Presbyterian Church, Philadelphia.

Monier Williams
Sir Monier Williams

Nov. 12, 1819
Bombay, India

April 11, 1899
Cannes, France

British Sanscrit scholar. Monier Williams taught Oriental languages at Haileybury and Cheltenham and taught Sanscrit at Oxford from 1860–87. His main work at Oxford was founding the India Institute, 1875–96. He made three trips to India to develop the work and authored many books in Sanscrit, Hindustani, and other Indian languages.

Samuel H. Kellogg

Sept. 6, 1839
Quogue, Long Island, New York

May 3, 1899
Landour, India

Presbyterian scholar and missionary to India, 1866–76, mostly at the Theological School at Allahalad. Kellogg married Antoinette W. Hartwell on May 3, 1864 (died: 1876), and Sarah C. Macrum on May 20, 1879, giving him a total of eight children. He pastored Third Presbyterian, Pittsburgh, PA (1877–81); taught theology at Allegheny Theological Seminary (1877–85); and pastored at St. James Square Presbyterian Church, Toronto, Ontario (1886–92). In 1892, he returned to India to help revise the Hindi OT. Kellogg wrote seven books ranging from *A Grammar of the Hindu Language* (1876) to *Handbook of Comparative Religion* (1899). He died from a bicycle fall.

William G. Blaikie

Feb. 5, 1820
Aberdeen, Scotland

June 11, 1899
North Berwick, Scotland

Free Church of Scotland cleric who was in the established church ministry until 1842. Blaikie pastored at the Free Church in Edinburgh (1844–68) and was the professor of apologetics and pastoral theology at New College in Edinburgh (1868–97). He wrote works ranging from *Bible History* (1859) to *Heroes of Israel* (1894).

Samuel Harris

June 14, 1814
East Machias, Maine

June 25, 1899
Litchfield, Connecticut

Congregational pastor and theologian who served at East Machia (1834–41), Conway, MA (1841–51) and at Pittsfield, MA (1851–55). Harris married Deborah R. Dickinson (April 30, 1839), and Mary S. Fitch (Oct. 11, 1877). He was a professor of systematic theology at Bangor (ME) Theological Seminary (1855–67); professor and president of Bowdoin College (University) Brunswick, ME (1867–71); and professor of systematic theology at Yale (1871–95). His writings range from *Zaccheus* (1874) to *God, Creator and Lord of All* (2 vols., 1897).

Rigdon M. McIntosh

April 3, 1836
Maury County, Tennessee

July 2, 1899
Atlanta, Georgia

Choral director, teacher, composer, and editor. He composed music for "Tell It Again" (lyrics by MARY SLADE) and "On Jordan's Stormy Banks I Stand" (lyrics by SAMUEL STENNETT). McIntosh married Sallie McClasson, was converted through her influence, and joined the Methodist Church South. In the 186s, he began a 30-year relationship as music editor for MCS Publishing House. He led the music departments at Vanderbilt University, Nashville, TN (1875–77) and at Emory College, Oxford, GA (1877–95). Then, in 1895, he established his own publishing company.

Alexander B. Bruce

Jan. 30, 1831
Aberargie, Scotland

Aug. 7, 1899
Glasgow, Scotland

Free Church of Scotland theologian. Bruce held pastorates at Cardross (1859–68) and Brought Ferry (1868–75). He served as a professor of apologetics and NT exegesis at Free Church College, Glasgow, until his death. He produced many scholarly writings from T*he Training of the Twelve* (1871) to *Hebrews* (1899).

William Butler

Jan. 30, 1818
Dublin, Ireland

Aug. 18, 1899
Old Orchard, Maine

Methodist missionary. Butler came to America in 1850, and in 1856, while pastoring in Lynn, MA; Butler answered the call for Indian missions. He married Clementina Rowe (1820–1913) on November 23, 1854, after losing his two previous wives (the Lewis sisters). They had four children. He ministered in India, 1856–64, and 1883–84. He served in Mexico (1873–79), after pastoring (1865–69), and acting as secretary of the American and Foreign Christian Union, New York City (1869–73). In both countries, he was the first Methodist missionary there. He later wrote about the foreign fields in which he had worked.

William M. Grier

Feb. 11, 1843
York County, South Carolina

Sept. 3 1899
Due West, South Carolina

President of Erskine College, Due West, SC 1871–99. He was wounded in the Civil War at Williamsburg on May 5, 1862, taken prisoner, and finally returned home. Grier married Nannie McNorries on October 25, 1864. He became a minister in the Associate Reformed Presbyterian Church and taught for many years at Erskine. He taught such subjects as mental and moral philosophy, pastoral theology and homiletics in the seminary. He also edited the *Associate Reformed Presbyterian*. In 1864, he connected with the Second Presbytery. He was licensed (April, 1866) and settled as pastor at Oak Hill, AL (August, 1867). He succeeded his father as president of EC. He was just 28 years old when he said, "I am relying upon the Divine blessing and the cordial support of those who have elected me."

Charles H. Corey

Dec. 12, 1834
New Canaan, New Brunswick, Canada

Sept. 9, 1899
Richmond, Virginia (?)

President of Richmond (VA) Theological Seminary, 1868–1898. In 1899, the year of his death, the school merged with Wayland University to become Virginia Union University of Theology. It was started to provide training for black preachers. Shortly after being ordained a Baptist minister, Corey resigned his charge and served with the US Christian Commission to the end of the war in 1867. He then became principal of Augusta, GA Institute. He wrote *Reminiscences of 30 Years Labor among the Colored People of the South*.

James Ellor

1819
Droylsden, England

Sept. 27, 1899
Newburgh, New York

Composed music for one of the three tunes for "All Hail the Power of Jesus' Name" (1838). Ellor was a hatmaker in his hometown and, by age 18, he was leading the choir in the local Wesleyan Chapel. He worked with railroad construction for a while, then came to America in 1843. In America, he worked at a hatmaker's store and helped found a church in Bloomfield, NJ. He became nearly blind and died at the home of his son.

Horace L. Hastings

Nov. 26, 1831
Balnford, Massachusetts

Oct. 21, 1899

Minister and writer who began preaching at age 17 and wrote hymns at an early age. Hastings was widely sought as an evangelist. In 1866, he established and published the Christian, a monthly paper in which appeared many of his 450 hymns. His best-known hymn was "Shall We Meet Beyond the River?" He wrote against infidels.

Robert C. Lowry

March 12, 1826
Philadelphia, Pennsylvania

Nov. 25, 1899
Plainfield, New Jersey

Wrote the lyrics and music for "Shall We Gather at the River" (1864), "Nothing But the Blood," and "Christ Arose" (1874), and music for "Follow On," and "All the Way My Savior Leads Me," "I Need Thee Every Hour," "We're Marching to Zion," and "Something for Thee." Converted at age 17, Lowry pastored four churches in Pennsylvania and New York from 1854–75. He became music editor with the Bigelow-Main Publishing Company in 1868. He taught at Bucknell University and pastored in Lewisburg, PA (1869–75) and in Plainfield, NJ (1876–85). He was a Baptist. His songbook, *Pure Gold*, sold more than 1 million copies.

Augustus Rauschenbusch

Feb. 13, 1816
Altena, Germany

Dec. 5, 1899
Wandsbek/Hamburg, Germany

First president and teacher of German Baptist Department of Rochester (NY) Divinity School (North American Baptist Seminary, Sioux Falls (SD) in 1950), **1858–89**. Converted in Berlin, Rauschenbusch was a Lutheran pastor in Altena from 1840–46, after which he came to America and worked with the American Tract Society. He became a Baptist in 1851. He returned to Germany (1853–54) and married Caroline Rung, then pastored Pinoak Creek Baptist Church, Gasconade County, MO (1855–56). He authored doctrinal books and retired to Wandsbek, Germany.

Dwight L. Moody

Feb. 5, 1837
Northfield, Massachusetts

Dec. 22, 1899
East Northfield, Massachusetts

One of the greatest evangelists of all time. Moody was to the nineteenth century, what GEORGE WHITEFIELD was to the eighteenth century, and what Billy Graham was to the 20th Century. He traveled more than 1 million miles, spoke to more than 100 million people, and dealt personally with nearly 50,000 individuals, all before the days of rapid transportation and mass communication. "Baptized" as an infant in a Unitarian church, he became a Congregationalist and, with only an eighth-grade education behind him, worked on the farm to help his widowed mother. In 1854, he went to Boston, where he was converted as a result of his Sunday school teacher's witness (Ed Kimball) on April

26, 1855. He went to Chicago in 1856 to continue work as a shoe salesman and got active in building Sunday Schools in 1858. He married EMMA REVELL on August 28, 1862. He pastored the Illinois St. Church, 1863–66 (eventually Moody Church). He became president of Chicago YMCA, 1865. IRA SANKEY joined him (1870) to assist with music and songleading. Within a year, the great Chicago Fire destroyed his church, then meeting in Farwell Hall. They went to England and Scotland in 1871, holding huge crusades; conducted 85 meetings, ended up in London in April 1875. Moody and SANKEY, held large city-wide crusades in Brooklyn in 1875, preaching to 20,000 per day, sometimes admitting only non-church members by ticket. They also held crusades in 1876, in Philadelphia, New York, Chicago, and many other places. He established the Mount Herman School for Boys (1879), the Northfield School for Girls (1881), and the Chicago Evangelization Society (Moody Bible Institute) (1886). It opened in 1899. The 1893 World's Fair in Chicago was used as a great evangelistic endeavor. On one Sunday, 72,000 people were reached in 56 separate meeting locations. Stricken as he preached in Kansas City, MO he was taken by train to his home. As he died, he said, "I see earth receding; heaven is opening. God is calling me." His favorite Bible verse was John 3:16.

John Ruskin

Feb. 8, 1819
London, England

Jan. 20, 1900
Coniston, England

Writer, art critic, and social reformer who championed the Gothic revival supported in *The Seven Lamps of Architecture* (1849). Ruskin memorized large portions of Scripture. He married Effie Gray (1848), but the marriage was annulled in 1854. In 1869, he became professor of fine arts at Cambridge University. By his writings and the founding of the Guild of St. George in 1871, he promoted the dignity and moral destiny of men. He expressed his disturbance for the rapid growth of industrialism. He lived on a small income, after giving away his large fortune. He was engaged in a libel case against James M. Whistler over the question, "What is art?" Ruskin lost in the 1878 case, withdrew from Oxford professorship, and lived in seclusion the rest of his life. His other renowned works were *Modern Painters* (5 vols.) and *The Stones of Venice* (3 vols.).

Enoch L. Fancher

Jan. 10, 1817
Dutchess County, New York

Feb. 9, 1900
New York, New York

President of American Bible Society, 1885–1900. Fancher grew up on a farm. After entering the Methodist ministry and preaching in Lenox, MA until 1839, he turned his sights on law. Here, he obtained fame and wealth as an attorney and judge. However, he never strayed from his Christian commitment.

William H. Green

Jan. 27, 1825
Groveville, New Jersey

Feb. 10, 1900
Princeton, New Jersey

Presbyterian theologian and a professor of OT and Semitic studies at Princeton Seminary, 1851–96. From 1849–51, Green was pastor of Central Church of Philadelphia. He married Mary E. Colwell (June 26, 1852), and Elizabeth Hayes (April 28, 1858). He declined the presidency of Princeton in 1868, but served as chairman of the American Old Testament Revision Company and published several scholarly works from *Hebrew Grammar* (1861) to *General Introduction to the Old Testament* (2 vols., 1895–99). He held strong verbal inspiration of the Bible.

Conrad S. Fritschel

Dec. 2, 1833
Nuremburg, Germany

April 26, 1900
Dubuque, Iowa

President of Wartburg Theological Seminary, Dubuque, IA 1875-1900. The Seminary moved from Dubuque to St. Sebald, IA; then to Mendota, IL; and back to Dubuque. Fritschel came to America in 1853. He was ordained as a Lutheran in Hamburg, Germany, in 1854, and moved to Dubuque that same year. In 1854, he organized the Evangelical Lutheran Synod of Iowa in St. Sebald, Iowa. He married Margerthe Prottengeler on January 20, 1856 who gave him eleven children. He was a home missionary to Wisconsin, 1854–56, a pastor in Detroit, and a Wartburg faculty member, 1858 on, where he taught for 42 years. He traveled to Russia and Germany (1866, 1871, 1891). His brother, Gottfried (Dec.19, 1836–July 13, 1889), also taught at Wartburg. He was the father of MAX FRITSCHEL. He is buried in Mendota, IL.

Richard S. Willis

Feb. 10, 1819
Boston, Massachusetts

May 7, 1900
Detroit, Michigan

Composed the music for "It Came Upon the Midnight Clear" (lyrics by EDMUND SEARS) and also gave us the English translation of "Fairest Lord Jesus" from German. While in Europe, Willis became a friend of MENDELSSOHN. He was a music critic for several journals, 1848–64. He resided in Detroit after 1861. Early on, he was a vestryman at the Church of Transfiguration in NYC.

Olof Olsson

March 31, 1841
Vermland, Sweden

May 12, 1900
Rock Island, Illinois

President of Augustana College and Theological Seminary, Rock Island, IL (Lutheran School of Theology, Chicago), **1890–1900**. Olsson was ordained a Lutheran (1863), came to America (1869), pastored in Lindsborg, KS and became professor of theology at Augustana, 1876–88. He married Anna Johnson in 1864 (died: 1867). He also pastored in Woodhull, IL in 1890. His works range from *At the Cross* to *To Rome and Home*.

Edwards A. Park

Dec. 29, 1808
Providence, Rhode Island

June 4, 1900
Andover, Massachusetts

President of Andover (MA) (Andover-Newton in 1931) **Theological Seminary, 1853–1868**. Park was a Congregational theologian, educator, and editor. He pastored First Congregational Church, Braintree, MA (1831–36), and taught rhetoric and theology at Andover, (1836–81). He married Anne M. Edwards in September, 1836, the great-granddaughter of JONATHAN EDWARDS. He founded the *Bibliotheca Sacra* (1844) and was its editor (1851–84), serving on its staff for some 40 years. He wrote several scholarly works. He was perhaps the last great defender of the faith at Andover.

Richard S. Storrs

Aug. 21, 1821
Braintree, Massachusetts

June 5, 1900
Brooklyn, New York

Congregational pastor of the Church of the Pilgrims in Brooklyn for 54 years, 1846–1900. Storrs married Mary E. Jenks, on Oct. 1, 1845. He was one of the editors of the *Independent* (1848–61), and the president of the American Board of Commissioners for Foreign Missions (1887–97). He authored many works on history, missions, and the Bible. Early on, he studied law. He was known for his pulpit oratory.

John C. Ryle

May 10, 1816
Macclesfield, England

June 10, 1900
Liverpool, England

Low Church Anglican bishop of Liverpool, 1880–1900. Ryle was converted (1837), then spiritually awakened (1838), upon hearing Ephesians 2 read. He began preaching in Exbury, and then went to Winchester. He also ministered at Helmingham (1844–61), then at Stradbroke (1861–69). He lost wives, 1847 and 1860, both after only two years of marriage. Later in Liverpool, he met his third wife. He was a prominent evangelical and wrote many tracts and pamphlets on doctrine and books on practical subjects (2 million distributed), including *Expository Thoughts on Gospels* (7 vols.). He built 90 places of worship, staffed them with 136 ministers, and enthusiastically backed the MOODY/SANKEY meetings of 1883. His works range from *Biographical Lectures* (1854) to *Light from Old Times* (1891).

Cyrus Hamlin

Jan. 5, 1811
near Waterford, Maine

Aug. 8, 1900
Lexington, Massachusetts

Congregational missionary educator to Turkey. He married Henrietta Jackson in September, 1838. Hamlin founded the Bebek School and Seminary along the Bosporus River soon after his arrival in 1839. He directed Bebek Seminary, Constantinople, from 1840–60. Resigning from the American Board in 1860, he opened Robert College (University of the Bosphorus) in Istanbul, serving as president until 1873, and later moving it to Constantinople. Although opposed by many forces, his perseverance gained him much respect. Upon his return to America, Hamlin became professor of theology at Bangor (ME) Theological Seminary (1877–80), then was president of Middlebury (VT) College (1881–85). He returned to private life in Lexington, in 1885.

John H. Yates

Nov. 21, 1837
Batavia, New York

Sept. 5, 1900
Batavia, New York

Wrote the hymn, "Faith Is the Victory" (1891) (music by IRA SANKEY). Yates was engaged in the shoe business, then worked in a hardware firm for 15 years. He was licensed a Methodist, but ordained a Baptist, pastoring the West Bethany Free Will Baptist Church for seven years. His poetic ability attracted the attention of IRA SANKEY. He maintained his life long home in Batavia and, from 1886–96, edited a local paper.

Friedrich M. Muller
Max Muller

Dec. 6, 1823
Dessau, Germany

Oct. 28, 1900
Oxford, England

Orientalist and philologist. Muller specialized in Sanskrit (religious and literary language of India) and went to Paris and London to prepare an edition of the *Rig Veda*, publishing six volumes from 1849–74. He settled at Oxford in 1850, teaching comparative philology from 1868–75. After studying mythology and comparative religions, he concluded that all religions teach only two ways of salvation: salvation by works or salvation by grace through faith. He edited 51 volumes of *The Sacred Books of the East*. He was given many honors by governments and societies and was a voluminous writer. His last known works are *Chips from a German Workshop* and *Lectures on the Science of Language*. He said as he died, "I am so tired."

Frederic L. Godet

Oct. 25, 1812
Neuchatel, Switzerland

Oct. 29, 1900
Neuchatel, Switzerland

Reformed conservative theologian. Godet was the tutor of the crown-prince of Prussia from 1838–44. He pastored for 24 years, the last 15 being at Neuchatel (1851–66), having previously supplied pulpits for churches in Val-De-Ruy (1844–51). Godet was a professor of exegetical and critical theology in the state church there (1850–73), withdrawing to help found the Free Evangelical Church and teach at the new academy (1873–87). He retired in 1887. His *Commentary on the Gospel of John* (1886) was his best-known book.

Daniel Shuck

Jan. 16, 1827
Harrison County, Indiana

Nov. 2, 1900
California

Bishop of United Brethren in Christ (EUBC, United Methodist Church), 1861–1900. Reared in Harrison County, Indiana, Shuck served on evangelistic circuits in Indiana and Kentucky, 1844–58. He married Harriet B. Cannady on March 11, 1847. After ministering in Missouri, 1858–61, he opened up a work on the Pacific coast. He was the first president at San Joaquin Valley College in Woodbridge, CA in 1879.

Samuel J. Stone

April 25, 1839
Whitmore, England

Nov. 19, 1900
Charterhouse, England

Anglican pastor and hymnwriter of "The Church's One Foundation," 1866 (music by SAM WESLEY). Stone was the curate of Windsor, 1862–70. He then served 21 years at his father's parish, St. Paul's, in poverty-stricken Haggerston from 1870–90, having full pastorate in 1874. In 1890 he became rector of All-Hallows-on-the-Wall in London, serving there until his death. He also wrote seven books of verse.

Arthur S. Sullivan

May 13, 1842
Lambeth, London, England

Nov. 22, 1900
Westminster, London, England

Composed music for "Onward Christian Soldiers." Sullivan was best known for his collaboration with W. S. Gilbert in writing 14 comic operettas, the two most famous being *The Mikado* and *HMS Pinafore*, which were performed for the Savoy Operas. He was influenced by MENDELSSON and Schubert, trained in Leipzig, 1858–61, and became organist at St. Michael's Church in Chester Square in 1861. He was already famous at age 21. He met W. S. Gilbert in 1867. He wrote "The Lost Chord" and the grand opera *Ivanhoe* (1891). He was knighted in 1883. No one has surpassed him as music composer for operettas. Sullivan held several organist positions and taught at the Royal Academy.

Willibald Beyschlag

Sept. 5, 1823
Frankfort, Germany

Nov. 25, 1900
Halle, Germany

Evangelical church leader, journalist, and theologian. Beyschlag fought for a broadminded Christianity. He was a minister at Koblenz from 1850–56, then in 1856–60, he was vicar at Trier (Treves). In 1860, he was a professor of practical theology at Halle. After 1870, he helped draw up a new constitution for the Prussian Church, and supported the rights of laity and the autonomy of the church. He questioned the traditional confessions, which had done so little to renew the spiritual life of the church in his day. As a mediating theologian, he formed a middle party in the church, mediating between confessionals and liberals.

George W. Northrup

Oct. 15, 1826
Antwerp, New York

Dec. 30, 1900
Chicago, Illinois

First dean of Baptist Union Theological Seminary (University of Chicago Divinity School in 1892), **Morgan Park, IL 1867–92**. Northrup was professor of systematic theology and department head there from 1892 on, and taught church history at the seminary there 1896–97. He was ordained a Baptist minister in Rochester in 1857.

Thomas Newberry

1811
England

1901

Editor of the Englishman's Bible. Newberry spent a 25-year period in diligent study of the Bible in the original Hebrew and Greek. His major work is often called the Newberry Bible. He wrote articles and books such as *Notes on the Temple, Notes on the Tabernacle*, and *Parables of Our Lord*.

Philip D. Armour

May 16, 1832
Stockbridge, New York

Jan. 6, 1901
Chicago, Illinois

Meat-packing executive, president of Armour and Company of Chicago, 1875–1901. Armour was first a miner in California, 1852–56. He began in the wholesale grocery commission business in Milwaukee, 1856–63; became head of the pork-packing firm of Armour, Plankinton, and Company, transferred to Chicago in 1870, and reorganized under the name of Armour and Company. Armour introduced on-premise slaughtering and utilization of animal waste and was one of the first to use refrigerator cars to transport meat cross-country and to make canned meat products. He founded the Armour Mission at a cost of $250,000 and made 2 million dollars by guessing correctly that the Civil War would end before others thought it would. When Union victories depressed the market, ruined traders were forced to pay him $40 a barrel for pork that he could buy for $18. Armour had a son of the same name (1893–January 18, 1958).

Hiram R. Revels

Sept. 1, 1822
Fayetteville, North Carolina

Jan. 16, 1901
Aberdeen, Mississippi

Educator, African Methodist Episcopal pastor and first black senator. Revels pastored in Indiana, Baltimore (MD), Kentucky, Kansas, and Tennessee (1845–53), prior to serving as an evangelist (1854–61). During the Civil War, he was chaplain to a Union black regiment, 1864–65, He pastored in Natchez, MS 1866–69, finally joining the Methodist Episcopal Church in 1868. In the post-Civil War period, he was the first Negro elected to the U.S. Senate 1870–71. Two children came from his marriage to Phoebe Bass. Revels was president of Alcorn College, Lorman, MS from 1871–83. Holly Springs (MS) was the location of his last pastorate (1875–80), after which he was a presiding elder in Mississippi Methodism (1884–1901).

Elias Riggs

Nov. 19, 1810
New Providence, New Jersey

Jan. 17, 1901
Scurati, Turkey

Missionary to the Near East and Bible translator who spent 63 years in Turkey, 1838–1901, specifically in Smyrna (1838–53) and Constantinople (1853–1901). He married Martha J. Dalzel in 1832 and they shared a lifetime of labor together. Riggs spent 1832–38 in Greece. As an ordained Presbyterian, he translated the Bible into Armenian, Bulgarian, and Turkish. He wrote or translated 478 hymns into Bulgarian. He mastered 12 languages (Semitic languages and Greek) and used 21 (seven ancient, 14 modern). His family (descendants and spouses) accounted for more than 4,000 years of missionary service in five generations.

Robert Graham

1822
Jan. 20, 1901
Lexington, Kentucky

President of College of the Bible (Lexington Theological Seminary in 1965), **1875–95**. Graham's parents emigrated to Pittsburgh when he was nine years old. Following his graduation from Bethany College in 1847, he rode horseback to Fayetteville, AR, where he established the Christian Church and founded Arkansas College (University of Arkansas). During the Civil War, he pastored the Walnut Street Christian Church, Cincinnati (1862–64); then he moved to California to pastor Santa Rosa Christian Church (1864–66). From 1869–75, he was president of Hocker Female College (Hamilton College, Clinton, NY). While president of CB, he taught English literature, homiletics and mental and moral philosophy.

Queen Victoria V

May 24, 1819
Kensington, London, England
Jan. 22, 1901
Osborne, Isle of Wight, England

England's (United Kingdom of Great Britain and Ireland) longest reigning monarch, 1837–1901 (63 years, 7 months, 2 days). Victoria's maiden name was Victoria Guelph. She and prime minister WILLIAM GLADSTONE (both Christians) brought England to world leadership. She, however, preferred BENJAMIN DISRAELI as prime minister. She said, "I believe in the finished work of Christ for me." Victoria married Prince Albert on February 10, 1840 (died: December 14, 1861, of typhoid fever), and they had nine children. Under her leadership, industry, imperialism, and morality prospered. She spoke German and French, played the piano, sang, and danced. She was only 5 feet tall.

Edward J. Hopkins

June 30, 1818
Westminster (London), England
Feb. 4, 1901
London, England

Composer of "Savior, Again Thy Dear Name We Raise." Beginning in 1843, Hopkins was the organist at Temple Church, London, for 55 years. In addition to composing service music, anthems, hymns, and chants, he was highly respected as a hymnal editor. He was also the music editor for the *Congregational Church Hymnal*.

Jonathan Weaver

Feb. 23, 1824
Carroll County, Ohio
Feb. 6, 1901
Dayton, Ohio

Bishop of Church of the United Brethren in Christ, Dayton, OH 1865–89. He married Keziah L. Robb on February 24, 1847 (died: November 14, 1852), and Mary E. Forsythe in 1853. Converted at a camp meeting at age 17, Weaver pastored (1847–52), was presiding elder (1852–57), and general agent for Otterbein University, Westerville, OH (1857–65) before becoming an Ohio bishop. He wrote such works as *Discourses on the Resurrection* (1871) to *Christian Theology* (1900).

Daniel W. Whittle

Nov. 22, 1840
Chicopee Falls, Massachusetts

March 4, 1901
Northfield, Massachusetts

Evangelist and hymn writer. Included in the 200 hymns Whittle wrote were "I Know Whom I Have Believed," "There Shall Be Showers of Blessings" (1883), "The Banner of the Cross," "Christ Liveth in Me," "Why Not Now" (1891), "Moment By Moment" (1893), and arranged "Have You Any Room for Jesus" (1878). He was wounded while a major in the Civil War. He resigned from the Elgin Watch Company in 1873 for evangelism. An alias he used was "El Nathan." P. P. BLISS and JAMES MCGRANAHAN were his song leaders.

William Arthur

Feb. 3, 1819
Kells, Ireland

March 9, 1901
Cannes, France

Wesleyan missionary and clergyman. Raised a Presbyterian, Arthur joined the Wesleyans at age twelve. He went to India in 1839, but his health caused his return in 1841. He served as secretary of the Wesleyan Mission Society (1851–68) and as honorary secretary (1871–88); he was also the first principal of Belfast Methodist College (1868–71). *Mission to Mysore* (1847) and *Religion Without God* (1885) were among his works.

Benjamin Harrison

Aug. 20, 1833
North Bend, Ohio

March 13, 1901
Indianapolis, Indiana

Twenty-third president of the United States, 1889–93. Harrison was a colonel in the Civil War, 1862–65, and prayed for his boys by name in a cold Nashville camp. He was a lawyer while seeking political offices in 1867–81, losing the Indiana governorship in 1876. He was known as a prominent debater. He was elected Republican senator, 1881–87. Harrison is remembered for winning the 1888 election in the Electoral College, 233–168, despite the fact that Grover Cleveland received 95,713 more popular votes. A staunch Republican, his policies were in keeping with the party line. The Bering Sea difficulties were adjusted by arbitration, the Pan American Congress was held, the McKinley law was passed, and six new states were added to the Union during his tenure. Cleveland defeated him the second time around in 1892, 276–145. He returned to the law field in his post-presidential days. He had a great interest in foreign missions after his term expired. He married Mary Scott Lord Dimmick (April 30, 1858–January 5, 1948; niece of his first wife). He was a Presbyterian.

Charlotte M. Yonge

Aug. 11, 1823
Otterbourne, England

March 24, 1901
Otterbourne, England

Novelist who dedicated her life and talents to the Lord. Charlotte taught Sunday School for all her adult life in Otterbourne, which must surely be a record. She edited *The Monthly Packet* (1851–99), a magazine for girls. She is best known for her support of the Oxford Movement through her novels, beginning with *The Heir of Redclyffe* (1853). She published some 160 works.

John Jasper

July 4, 1812
Williamsburg, Virginia

March 28, 1901
Richmond, Virginia

One of the greatest black preachers of all time, from 1839 on. Converted July 25, 1839, he became a famous funeral preacher. He was born a slave but was set free from slavery in 1865. Jasper pastored the Sixth Mount Zion Baptist Church, Richmond, VA from 1865 on. His third wife died in 1874, and his fourth wife survived him. In 1878, he preached the sensational sermon, "The Sun Do Move," which was preached over 250 times after that time. He preached to thousands each week, including segregated whites in the audience. He was married four times. His first wife divorced him; his second, Candus Jordan, bore him several children. When she was unfaithful, he divorced her. He said as he died, "I have finished my work. I am waiting at the river, looking across for further orders."

John Stainer

June 6, 1840
Southwark, London, England

April 1, 1901
Verona, Italy

Organist and composer of sacred music. Stainer composed over 150 hymn tunes including "God so Loved the World," many anthems and oratorios, and several cantatas; including the well-known "Crucifixion" (1887). At age seven, he was chorister in St. Paul's Cathedral. From 1863–72, he was an Oxford University organist. He served as organist of St. Paul's Cathedral (1872–88) followed by teaching music at Oxford University (1889–99). Stainer was knighted by Queen VICTORIA in 1888, the year his eyesight failed.

James Chalmers

Aug. 4, 1841
Ardrishaig, Scotland

April 8, 1901
Rish Point, Goaribari Island, New Guinea

Martyred Congregational missionary to the southwest Pacific Islands. He was converted in November, 1859, at a revival at Inverary, convicted by Rev. 22:17. Chalmers married his first wife (1865), and then married a Mrs. Harrison (1888). He went to Rarotonga in the Cook Islands (1867), then to Papua, New Guinea (1877), where he labored for 24 years. He established a training center at Port Moresby and saw many areas transformed. He served with the London Missionary Society and wrote at least three books about his work from 1885–95. He was well respected by many, including Robert L. Stevenson (novelist, 1850–94), whom he met in Samoa in 1890. He often courted danger, by going unarmed among savage tribes who had never before seen a white man. He, Oliver Tomkins, and twelve native Christians were massacred, beheaded, and cannibalized by savages during a journey to explore new territory. His favorite Bible verse was Revelation 22:17.

John J. Esher

Dec. 11, 1823
Baldenheim, Germany

April 16, 1901
Alsatia, France

Bishop of Evangelical Association (United Methodist Church in 1968), **1863–1901**. Esher came to America in 1830, and was converted in Warren, PA under JOHN SEYBERT. From 1836–45, he pastored in Des Plaines and Northfield IL. He served as a home missionary in Illinois and Iowa, 1845–63, cracking the ice more than once on the Mississippi River. He helped establish North Central College and Evangelical Theological Seminary, Naperville, IL, and visited Japan three times. He organized the first conference of the EA in Europe in 1865. He was a preacher and theologian who wrote the German book, *Systematic Theology*.

Rufus C. Burleson

Aug. 7, 1823
Funt River, Alabama

May 14, 1901
Waco, Texas

President of Baylor University, 1851–61, 1886–97. He pastored at FBC of Houston, TX 1848–51. Burleson married Georgiana Jenkins on January 3, 1853. During his time, he preached in every town in Texas, excluding railroad stations. Baylor University, associated with the Baptist Convention, moved in 1886, from Independence, TX, to Waco. He baptized SAM HOUSTON, military and political leader of the Texan Territory. He assisted in establishing a railroad system in Texas, and served as a pioneer of co-education in the South.

Maltbie D. Babcock

Aug. 3, 1858
Syracuse, New York

May 18, 1901
Naples, Italy

Pastor, extremely talented in music and athletics. Babcock was one of those individuals blessed with a myriad of talents and abilities. He enjoyed sports, music, and the outdoors. He was a superior student at Syracuse University and Auburn Theological Seminary. He played several instruments, directed the glee club and school orchestra, was a competitive athlete, performed impersonations, was a gifted artist, and a quality craftsman. Many believed Babcock could have become a professional musician if he had not been called into the ministry. He married Catherine E. Tallman on October 4, 1882. Ordained a Presbyterian, he pastored in Lockport, NY (1882–87); Brown Memorial Church, Baltimore, MD (1887–99); and the Brick Street Church, New York City (1899–1901). After pastoring for only 18 months in New York City, he went on a trip to the Holy Land, where he was stricken with the brucellosis fever (bacterial infection) that took his life. He committed suicide by cutting arteries of his wrist and drinking corrosive sublimate as a result of acute melancholia. Although he did not publish anything during his lifetime, after his untimely death, his wife collected and published many of his writings and poems, one of which was the now famous hymn, "This Is My Father's World" (music by FRANKLIN SHEPHERD).

George L. Mackay

March 21, 1844
Zerra, Ontario, Canada

June 2, 1901
Tamsui, Formosa (Taiwan)

Missionary to northern Formosa. Mackay went to Formosa in 1871 as an appointee by the Presbyterian Church in Canada. After only five months of training, he was able to preach his first sermon in Chinese. He headquartered at Tamsui (Damshui) and married a Chinese wife, Tui Chang Mia (Minnie). He trained native workers, promoted indigenous missions, and established 60 churches with 2,000 members. His death was a result of throat cancer. His story is told in *From Far Formosa* (1896).

William R. Nicholson

Jan. 8, 1822
Greene County, Mississippi

June 7, 1901
Philadelphia, Pennsylvania

First dean of Reformed Episcopal Seminary, 1886–1901. Nicholson married Jane Shaw (November 27, 1845), and later married Katharine Stanley (October 18, 1866). In 1874, he joined the RE Church and was rector of Second Reformed Episcopal Church, Philadelphia. He served as rector in New Orleans, LA; Cincinnati, OH; Boston, MA; and Newark, NJ. He was ordained a bishop on February 24, 1876. He wrote several books, beginning with *Blessedness of Heaven*.

John L. Dyer

March 16, 1812
Madison County, Ohio

June 10, 1901
University Park, Colorado

Methodist home missionary who went to Colorado in 1861. In 1864, Dyer carried mail and food over Mosquito Pass on skis each week during the winter and preached three times a week, earning the title "The Snowshoe Evangelist." He married Harriet Foster on Deember 4, 1833 (died: July 14, 1847), and Lucinda Rankin on November 7, 1870.

Ralph E. Hudson

July 9, 1843
Napoleon, Ohio

June 14, 1901
Cleveland, Ohio

Composed music for "Satisfied," "Blessed Be The Name" (1888), and "At the Cross" (1885), and wrote the lyrics for "I'll Live for Him," and the lyrics and music for "A Glorious Church." Hudson married Mary Smith on March 4, 1863. He taught at Mt. Vernon College, Alliance, OH from 1864–69. Although primarily a Methodist evangelist, he was also an active singer and a music publisher in Alliance.

Franklin W. Fisk

Feb. 16, 1820
Hopkinton, New Hampshire

July 4, 1901
Chicago, Illinois

First president of Chicago (IL) Theological Seminary, 1888–1900. Fisk taught at Beloit (WI) College, 1854–59. From April 28, 1859, he was connected with the CTS, a professor there from the beginning of the seminary. His education was at Yale College (University). He traveled extensively in Germany, Arabia, Egypt, Greece, and Palestine, 1871–72. It has been said of him that he had good sense and sound judgement, was a man of quick and tender sympathy, loyal to friends and firmly committed to Christ. Hoping to find better health in California, he made a trip there with his wife, but his condition worsened. Returning home, he was bedridden for two months before his passing. He was buried in Lake Geneva, WI where for many years they had a summer home.

Brooke F. Westcott

Jan. 12, 1825
Birmingham, England

July 27, 1901
Durham, England

Anglican New Testament scholar, prelate, theologian and church historian. Westcott toiled with F. J. A. HORT for 28 years to produce *The New Testament in the Original Greek* (1881). He taught at Harrow School (1852–69) and was divinity professor at Cambridge (1870–90), when he was made bishop of Durham (1890–1901). He was the motivating power behind the Cambridge Mission to Delhi in 1876. He became canon of Westminster in 1883. He identified with coal miners to resolve a bitter strike in 1892. Four of his seven sons were missionaries to India; one, Foss Westcott,(1863–1949) was outstanding. Westcott died at Auckland Castle, palace of the local bishops.

James Walch

June 21, 1837
Edgerton, England

Aug. 30, 1901
Llandudno, Wales

Composed music for "O Zion Haste." For most of his life, Walch served as an organist in English churches, including Duke's Alley Congregational in Bolton, 1851–57, Walmsley Church (1857), Bridge St. Wesleyan Chapel (1858), St. George's Parish in Bolton (1863), and in Barrow-in-Furness (1877), where he also maintained a music business.

Isabella Thoburn

March 29, 1840
St. Clairsville, Ohio

Sept. 1, 1901
Lucknow, India

Missionary and educator in India, and first missionary of the Women's Foreign Missionary Society of the Methodist Church, 1869. She served in India for 32 years, founding a school for girls at Lucknow (first Christian college for women in Asia) in April, 1870. The school was later called Isabella Thoburn College and is now associated with Lucknow University. She was also engaged in evangelism and Sunday School work. She was the sister to JAMES THOBURN, and went to India with CLARA SWAIN. She never married and died of cholera. Isabella returned to the U.S. from 1880–81 and 1886–91, due to health reasons.

William McDonald

March 1, 1820 *Sept. 11, 1901*
Belmont, Maine Monrovia, California

President of the National Camp Meeting (Christian Holiness Partnership in 1997), **1884–94**. McDonald was a pastor, evangelist, author, editor, and songwriter who wrote the hymns "I Am Coming to the Cross" (music by WILLIAM FISCHER), and "I Believe Jesus Saves" (music by JOSEPH WEBSTER). He became preacher in the local Methodist Church in 1839. He edited *Advocate of Christian Holiness* (1870–83). He pastored in Maine, Wisconsin, Massachusetts, Rhode Island, and New York (26 places in 61 years). India and England were a part of his missions tour. He was stricken with poor health in 1894.

William McKinley

Jan. 29, 1843 *Sept. 14, 1901*
Niles, Ohio Buffalo, New York

Twenty-fifth President of the United States, 1897–1901. McKinley was converted in a revival meeting at age ten and became a life-long Methodist. He was active in the Union cause, from 1861–64, serving in several battles. Ida Saxton became his wife in 1871, and they made their home in Canton, OH. He began his career as a lawyer (1867–77), served in the U.S. Congress (1877–91), and then was elected governor of Ohio (1892–96). In both presidential elections, he defeated WILLIAM JENNINGS BRYAN in electoral votes, 271–176 and 292–155. During McKinley's Republican administration, America obtained the Philippines and Hawaiian Islands, and won the Spanish-American War in 1898. He often entertained guests at the White House with Sunday-evening "hymn sings." His faith is seen through his statement, "My belief embraces the divinity of Christ and a recognition of Christianity as the mightiest factor in the world's civilization." He was shot on September 6, 1901, at the Music Hall of the Pan-American Exposition in Buffalo (NY), soon after being elected to his second term. He died eight days later. His assailant was an anarchist, Leon Czolgosz. Some of his last words were, "Nearer, my God, to Thee, Nearer to Thee. It is the Lord's way. Good bye all." His likeness is on a $500 bill.

Henry B. Whipple

Feb. 15, 1823 *Sept. 16, 1901*
Adams, New York Fairbault, Minnesota

President of Seabury Divinity School (Seabury-Western Theology Seminary, Evanston, IL in 1933), **Fairbault, MN 1860–1901**. Whipple was ordained a deacon (1849) and priest (1850) in the Episcopal Church. He was rector of Zion Church of Rome, NY (1850–57); of Church of Communion, Chicago, IL (1857–59); then was made bishop of Minnesota until his death. The first Protestant service in Cuba, 1871, was conducted by Whipple. He was married twice and worked extensively among the American Indians.

George T. Purves

Sept. 27, 1852 *Sept. 24, 1901*
Philadelphia, Pennsylvania New York, New York

Presbyterian pastor in Wayne, PA 1877–80, Baltimore, MD 1880–86 and served at the First Presbyterian Church, Pittsburgh, PA (1886–92). He then was professor of New Testament literature and exegesis at Princeton Theological Seminary (1892–1900). In 1900, he pastored the Fifth Avenue Church, New York City. He wrote *The Apostolic Age* (1900) and books of sermons.

Joseph H. Thayer

Nov. 7, 1828
Boston, Massachusetts

Nov. 26, 1901
Cambridge, Massachusetts

Congregational pastor and Greek textual critic, who prepared the monumental *Greek-English Lexicon of the New Testament*. Thayer pastored in Salem, MA (1859–64), was a professor of sacred literature at Andover Theological Seminary (1864–82), and a professor of New Testament criticism and interpretation at Harvard (1884–1901). He helped found the American School of Oriental Research in Jerusalem, and did some translation work.

Martin C. Knapp

March 27, 1853

Dec. 7, 1901
Southern Michigan

One of the founders of the Pilgrim Holiness Church and also founder of God's Bible School in Cincinnati, OH. Knapp was converted at age 19 through Lucy J. Glenn, whom he would marry in 1876. While pastoring in Michigan, he published his first book, *Christ Crowned Within* and was forced to auction off his furniture to finance this venture. He started editing a holiness periodical, *The Revivalist*, on September 5, 1892 and moved to Cincinnati. In September, 1897, the International Holiness Union and Prayer League was organized in Knapp's home. This grew into the PHC which eventually helped form the Wesleyan Church. In 1900, he purchased a two-acre tract, and founded GBS. He died of typhoid fever at age 48.

Johann M. F. Heinrich Hofmann

1824
Darmstadt, Germany

1902

Painter who practiced in various German cities before settling in Dresden in 1862 as professor in the Academy. Hofmann's best paintings were of religious subjects including *Christ in the Temple, Christ Taken Prisoner*, and *Christ in Gethsemane*. His works were engraved and photographed extensively.

George C. Needham

1840
Ireland

1902

Evangelist and Bible teacher. In 1861, he experienced a revival in the southern part of Ireland. He attended SPURGEON's college and later published the first authorized biography of SPURGEON. With H. GRATTAN GUINNESS, he made an evangelistic tour of Ireland, finding and encouraging many small groups of believers' meeting in difficult places. Once in the States, he spearheaded a Bible "conference" of sorts in New York City (1868), Philadelphia (1869), St. Louis (1870) and Galt, Ontario (1871). The meetings resumed in 1875, and the famous Niagara Bible Conference was developed. Needham was widely known for his role as secretary of the prophetic conferences of 1878 and 1886. From 1879–81, he pastored the church MOODY founded in Chicago.

Joseph Packard

Dec. 23, 1812
Wiscasset, Maine

1902

Dean of Virginia Theological Seminary, Alexandria, VA 1874–95. He was ordained an Episcopal priest in 1837, served as a professor at Bristol (PA) College (1834–36), then had a long-time relationship at VTS (1836–95) where he was professor of sacred literature, serving 15 years as dean. He married Rosina Jones in January, 1838. He was a member of the American Committee for Revision of the Bible, 1872–85.

James Robertson

April 24, 1839
Dull, Scotland

Jan. 4, 1902
Toronto, Ontario, Canada

Canadian Presbyterian pastor-missionary who was the real-life model for the character, the "sky pilot," in RALPH CONNOR's stories. Robertson came to Ontario with his family in 1855. He directed Presbyterian missions in the vast wilderness of the Canadian Northwest with firmness, love, and humor, 1881–1902. From four congregations, he influenced the start of 140 churches, as well as 226 mission programs serving over 1,000 communities. He pastored in Norwich, Ontario (1869–74) and at Knox Church, Winnipeg (1874–81); also lecturing at Manitoba College (1877–81). He was moderator of the Presbyterian Church of Canada in 1895.

Andrew B. Davidson

Dec. 1831
Kirkhill, Scotland

Jan. 26, 1902
Edinburgh, Scotland

United Free Church of Scotland scholar. Davidson was ordained in 1863, and became professor of Hebrew and Old Testament exegesis and Oriental languages at New College, Edinburgh, the same year. Davidson served there for the rest of his life. Remaining unmaried, he was considered the foremost British Bible scholar of his day. His literary work was small in quantity, but large in quality. He is best remembered for his *Introductory Hebrew Grammar* (1874). His writings spanned the years 1861–1903. His *Commentary on Job* was regarded by some as the first scientific commentary on the OT in the English language. His favorite Bible verse was I Timothy 2:5.

C. Newman Hall

May 22, 1816
Maidstone, England

Feb. 18, 1902
London, England

Congregational pastor of Albion Church in Hull, 1842–1854, and Surrey Chapel in London, 1854–1876. His tract, "Come to Jesus" (1846), had a circulation of three million in 40 languages. In 1876, Hall's congregation went with him to Lambeth and changed the name to Christ Church, where he ministered until 1892. "My Friends, Follow Jesus" was a tract generating 250,000 copies. He was known as the "Dissenter's Bishop." He wrote from *It is I* (1848) to *Autobiography* (1898).

James H. Fairchild

Nov. 25, 1817
Stockbridge, Massachusetts

March 19, 1902
Oberlin, Ohio

President of Oberlin (OH) College, 1866–89, 1896–98. Fairchild married Mary Kellogg on November 29, 1841, and after being ordained the same year, he spent the rest of his life at Oberlin. He began as a tutor (1838–42), was a professor of languages (1842–47), math (1847–58), and moral philosophy and theology (1858–66). He traveled to Europe, Asia, and Africa from 1879–81. He wrote such books as *Moral Philosophy* (1869), *Woman's Right to the Ballot* (1870), and *Elements of Theology* (1892). He was an outstanding administrator.

George W. Warren

Aug. 17, 1828
Albany, New York

March 17, 1902
New York, New York

Composed music for "God of Our Fathers" (lyrics by DANIEL ROBERTS). Although musical in his youth, Warren engaged for a while in Albany business. He was an outstanding organist, playing at St. Peter's Episcopal Church, Albany (1846–58); St. Paul's Church of Albany (1858–60); Holy Trinity Church, Brooklyn (1860–70); and St. Thomas' Church, New York City (1870–1900).

Henry A. Tupper

Feb. 29, 1828 — Charleston, South Carolina
March 27, 1902 — Richmond, Virginia

Executive secretary of Southern Baptist Convention Missions, 1872–93. Tupper married Nancy Boyce on November 1, 1849. He was ordained in 1850, pastored in Granitesville, SC (1850–53) and then in Washington, GA (1853–72). During the Civil War, he served as chaplain of the 9th Georgia regiment of the Confederates. He wrote three books.

Thomas D. Talmage

Jan. 7, 1832 — Gatesville/Boundbrook, New Jersey
April 12, 1902 — Washington, D.C.

Perhaps the greatest preacher in history, pastoring the Brooklyn (NY) Tabernacle, 1870–94. He served at the Central Presbyterian Church (1869–70), when a new church was erected (1870) called the Brooklyn Tabernacle. Talmage, a Presbyterian, was converted at age 18 and pastored the Dutch Reformed Church in Belleville, NJ (1856–59); in Syracuse, NY (1859–62); then at Second Reformed Church, Philadelphia (1862–69). He married Mary Avery in 1856 (drowned: June 9, 1862), Susan Wittenmore on May 7, 1863 (died: Aug. 5, 1895), and Mrs. Charles Collier on Jan. 26, 1898. His church was destroyed by fire three times (December 22, 1872; October 13, 1889; May 13, 1894), the last time came after his farewell message. The last two churches seated over 5,000. He was at the First Presbyterian Church, Washington, D.C. from 1895–99. His sermons were printed in some 3,600 newspapers reaching 20 million readers weekly. He won thousands to Christ. Talmage was stricken with a cerebral hemorrhage in Mexico in March, and returned home by train. His sermons are classics. He edited various Christian journals from 1873 on, including *The Christian Herald*, (1890–1902), and wrote many books. He is buried in Greenwood Cemetery in Brooklyn.

William Taylor

May 2, 1821 — Rockbridge County, Virginia
May 18, 1902 — Palo Alto, California

Methodist Bishop, from 1882 on, and one of the greatest evangelists and missionaries in the movement's history. Taylor married Annie Kimberlin in 1846. After his conversion in 1841 at a Methodist camp meeting, he traveled extensively as an evangelist (1842–49), a missionary in California (1849–56), an evangelist in the East and Canada (1856–61), a missionary to England and Australia (1862–66), Africa (1866–70), India (1870–75), Chile and Peru (1877–84), and then back to Africa (1884–96). He was with MOODY in England in 1875. Taylor University of Upland, IN was named after him in 1890. He was active in the National Holiness Association. He wrote many books.

Gjermund Hoyme

Oct. 8, 1847 — Valdres, Norway
June 9, 1902 — Eau Claire, Wisconsin

President of United Norwegian Lutheran Church (ALC, ELCA in 1988), **1890–1902.** He came to America (1851), and was ordained a Lutheran (1873). Hoyme married Ida O. L. Olsen in 1874 (died: 1905). After pastoring in Duluth, MN and Menominee, WI (1874–76); he pastored the largest NLC in America at Eau Claire, WI (1876–1902). He authored *In Moments of Peace*. He was president of the Norwegian-Danish Conference, 1886–90.

Henry G. Appenzeller

Feb. 6, 1858
Souderton, Pennsylvania

June 11, 1902
West Coast, Korea

Pioneer Methodist missionary to Korea. Appenzeller married Ella Dodge on December 17, 1884, went to Korea in 1885 and, in 1887, founded Chong Dong First Methodist Church (Bethel Chapel), Seoul, with Korean leadership. He served as pastor until his death. His daughter, Alice, was the first white child ever born in Korea. He translated the Bible into Korean, opened a bookstore in 1894, wrote many tracts, and published the *Korean Christian Advocate*. Appenzeller encouraged a liberal arts approach to theological education. Korean culture and religion were valued by him. He died when a boat, the *Kumagawa*, taking him to a Bible translation meeting in Mokpo, collided with a Japanese vessel, the *Kisawaga*, off the western coast in a fog. He died at 44, losing his life in an attempt to save his Korean translation assistant and a Korean child entrusted to his care.

Eugene A. Hoffman

March 31, 1829
New York, New York

June 17, 1902
New York, New York

President of General Theological Seminary, New York City 1879–1902. Hoffman was ordained to the Episcopal ministry (1851) and married Mary Crooke in 1852. He enjoyed many years of pastoring at Grace Church, Elizabethport, NY (1851–53); Christ Church, Elizabeth, NY (1853–63); St. Mary's, in Burlington, NJ (1863–64); Grace Church, Brooklyn Heights, NY (1864–69); and at St. Mark's, Philadelphia, PA (1869–79).

Thaddeus C. Reade

March 29, 1846
Steuben County, New York

July 25, 1902

President of Taylor University, Upland, IN 1891–1902. The school moved from Ft. Wayne to Upland during his days in 1893. Reade was converted at age 13 and was licensed to preach at age 15. He met Ella Dodge at Ohio Wesleyan College and married her. They began their work together at the Fairfield Union Academy: he as principal, she as teacher. In 1872, he was at Defiance, OH as a member of the Central Ohio Methodist Conference. Mrs. Reade prayed and sang on the streets in front of saloons. She caught a severe cold from exposure and died. Reade then pastored in Sidney, OH where he met a widow, Mrs. Laura Kirkley, whom he married. She outlived him by a couple of years. He served in such places as Fostoria and Zanesville before going to Taylor.

James J. J. Tissot

Oct. 15, 1836
Nantes, France

Aug. 8, 1902
Chenecey-Bullion, France

Illustrator and painter who opened a studio in London in 1870. Tissot was popular in Paris for his brilliant paintings of fashionable women. After studying in London from 1859–69, he then switched to religious scenes. He did 365 watercolor pictures and 150 pen-and-ink sketches of Christ in Palestine, 1884–94. At the time of his death, he was painting Old Testament illustrations, 1893–96, having completed 372 watercolors.

Joseph Angus

Jan. 16, 1816
Bolam, England

Aug. 28, 1902
Hampstead, London, England

President of Regents Park College, 1849–93. Angus, Baptist educator, also pastored New Park Street Church in London, 1838–42, then became secretary of the Baptist Missionary Society. His *Bible Handbook* (1854) had a wide circulation. He became president of the Baptist Union in 1865.

Christoph E. Luthardt

March 22, 1823
Maroldsweisach, Germany

Sept. 21, 1902
Leipzig, Germany

Lutheran theologian. Luthardt taught at Munich (1847–51) and Erlangen (1851–54), was professor at Marburg (1854–56), and a professor of systematic theology and New Testament exegesis at Leipzig, (1856–1902). He had a great reputation as a pulpit orator and university lecturer. His confessional Lutheranism was developed at Erlangen University with FRANZ DELITZSCH promoting JOHANN HOFMANN's (theologian, 1810–77) views. He helped found the General Evangelical-Lutheran Conference in 1868, and was president of the Leipzig Mission Society.

William J. Reid

Aug. 17, 1834
S. Argyle, New York

Sept. 22, 1902
Pittsburgh, Pennsylvania

Stated clerk of United Presbyterian Church (PC USA in 1983) **of North America, 1875–1902.** Reid graduated from Union College in 1855, then Monmouth (IL) College. Mary Bowen became his wife on Oct. 29, 1862. He pastored the First United Presbyterian Church, Pittsburgh, 1862 on. He also edited the *United Presbyterian* (1867 on) and was the corresponding secretary of the United Presbyterian Board of Home Missions, 1868–72.

George Rawlinson

Nov. 23, 1812
Chadlington, England

Oct. 6, 1902
Canterbury, England

Historian and Orientalist. From 1861–89, Rawlinson was Camden professor of ancient history at Oxford. He was canon of Canterbury in 1872, and rector of All Hallow's Church, London, 1888–1902. He wrote commentaries on various OT books and several books of church history. He used his archaeological knowledge to defend orthodox Christianity. His works range from *The Historical Evidences of the Truth of the Scripture Records* (1859) to *Kings of Israel and Judah* (1890).

Aaron R. Wolfe

Sept. 6, 1821
Mendham, New Jersey

Oct. 6, 1902
Montclair, New Jersey

Presbyterian educator and hymn writer. Wolfe conducted a woman's school in Tallahassee, FL from 1852–55 and founded the Hillside Seminary for young ladies in Montclair in 1859. He served as the principal until his retirement in 1872. In 1858, he contributed eight hymns to *Church Melodies*, including "A Parting Hymn We Sing" and "Complete in Thee" (music by T. J. Bittikofer).

William O. Cushing

Dec. 31, 1823
Hingham Center, Maryland

Oct. 19, 1902
Lisbon, New York

Writer of 300 hymns. Some of Cushing's most outstanding hymns were: "Ring the Bells of Heaven," "Follow On" (1880), "Hiding in Thee," "Under His Wings" (1896), "When He Cometh," and "There'll Be No Dark Valley" (1896). For more than 20 years he pastored Christian Churches in Searsburg, Auburn, Brooklyn, Buffalo, and Sparta, NY. His wife died in 1870, at which time ill health forced his retirement from the active ministry.

Walter Reed

Sept. 13, 1851
Belroi, Virginia

Nov. 22, 1902
Washington, D.C.

American army surgeon. He married Amelia Laurence in 1876. Reed was professor of bacteriology at the Army Medical College in Washington, D.C, after 15 years of frontier service as curator of the army. He was commissioned in 1900, to investigate the cause of yellow fever. Epidemics of typhoid were occurring among the troops during the Spanish-American War (waged in 1898 by the U.S. to free Cuba and other Caribbean islands from Spanish tyranny and blockades). Reed identified the mosquito as the carrier and recommended its extermination. His protocols banished the often fatal disease from Havana, Cuba, where it had prevailed for three centuries. A military hospital in Washington, D.C. is named in his honor. He continued to specialize in tracking the cause and progress of epidemic diseases. He worked with a medical museum from 1893 on and became known as one of the leading bacteriologists in America. His father was a Methodist preacher.

Joseph Parker

April 9, 1830
Hexham-on-Tyne, England

Nov. 28, 1902
London, England

One of London's greatest preachers. He married Ann Nesbitt in 1851. He pastored the Banbury Congregational Church (1853–58) and the Cavendish St. Congregational Church, Manchester (1858–69). From 1869–1902, Parker was the Congregational pastor of the Poultry Chapel, which grew to occupy the City Temple, built in 1874. He visited the U.S. five times. Twice he was chairman of the Congregational Union of England and Wales. He traveled widely on lecture tours and wrote the 25-volume *People's Bible* (1885–95), his chief work. His works range from *Ecce Deus* (1868) to *Pulpit Bible* (1901).

Henry S. Cutler

Oct. 13, 1824
Boston, Massachusetts

Dec. 5, 1902
Boston, Massachusetts

Composed music for "The Son of God Goes Forth to War" (lyrics by REGINALD HEBER). Cutler visited Europe in 1844, and became interested in cathedral choirs. In 1846, he was made organist at Grace Church of Boston and later at the Church of the Advent, where he had the first robed choir in the US. From 1858–65, he was the organist at Trinity Church in New York City and several other churches in the East. He received a Doctor of Music degree from Columbia University in 1864. He edited and published the *Trinity Psalter* (1864) and *Trinity Anthems* (1865). Cutler retired in 1885.

Richard F. Weymouth

Dec. 26, 1822
Plymouth Dock (Devonpor, England

Dec. 27, 1902
Brentwood, England

Baptist philologist and New Testament scholar who edited the Weymouth New Testament. In 1869, Weymouth was appointed headmaster of a boys' school at Mill Hill, London, 1869–86. He was in Acton, 1886–91, then went to Brentwood, after founding a boys' school. His New Testament was not published until 1903, after his death. He produced the *Resultant Greek Testament* and the classic *New Testament in Modern Speech*, an idiomatic translation.

Joseph R. Wilson

Feb. 28, 1822
Steubenville, Ohio

Jan. 21, 1903
Princeton, New Jersey

Stated Clerk of Presbyterian Church (USA in 1983) **in US, 1865–98**. Wilson taught at Hampden-Sydney (VA) College (1851–55), at The Presbyterian Theological Seminary of Columbia, SC (1870–74), and at Southwestern Presbyterian University of Clarksville, TN (1885–92). He pastored at Staunton, VA (1855–58); at Augusta, GA (1859–70); and at FBC of Wilmington, NC (1874–85). He was the father of future President WOODROW WILSON.

Joseph Parry

May 21, 1841
Cyfarthfa, Wales

Feb. 17, 1903
Cartref, Wales

Composed a tune for WESLEY's immortal, "Jesus, Lover of My Soul" although the two other melodies are more accepted. Parry conducted a private music school in Danville, PA from 1871–73. He then returned to Wales, where he was professor of music at the Welsh University College at Aberystwyth, 1873–79. He also taught at the University College at Cardiff from 1888 until his death.

Frederic W. Farrar

Aug. 7, 1831
Bombay, India

March 22, 1903
London, Canterbury, England

Influential Church of England churchman who was an educator at Harrow (1856–71), and Marlborough (1871–76), rector of St. Margaret's, canon of Westminster at London College (1876), and archdeacon of the same (1883). Farrar preached Charles Darwin's funeral in 1882. He was chaplain of the House of Commons from 1890–95. From 1895–1903, he was dean of Canterbury. He wrote both theological works and fiction. His *Life of Christ* (2 vols., 1874) is widely read in many languages, as was his *Life of St. Paul* (2 vols., 1879). He was involved in both social and philanthropic causes. He wrote the well-known *Mercy and Judgment* (1881). His works range from *Seekers after God* (1868) to *The Life of Lives* (1900). He denied eternal punishment in his book, *Eternal Hope*. He wrote while standing up.

William H. Milburn

Sept. 26, 1823
Philadelphia, Pennsylvania

April 10, 1903
Santa Barbara, California

Chaplain of the U.S. Senate, 1893–1903. At age five, Milburn had an accident which damaged his eyes, and by age 30, he was totally blind. He married on Aug. 13, 1846. He served as the House of Representatives chaplain, 1845, 1853, and 1885–93 and as the Senate chaplain in 1893. Milburn, a Methodist, pastored from 1845–53, then devoted many years to lecturing and traveling 1.5 million miles. He wrote four books.

George D. Boardman Jr.

Aug. 18, 1828
Tavoy, Burma

April 28, 1903
Atlantic City, New Jersey

Baptist minister, son of missionary, GEORGE BOARDMAN Sr. Ella W. Covell became his wife on Aug. 14, 1855. Boardman pastored, most notably, the First Baptist Church of Philadelphia (1864–94); after pastoring in Rochester, NY (1856–64). He was a liberal preacher and one of the principal promoters of the Parliament of Religions. His most important production was *Title of Wednesday Evening Lectures*, 981 lectures on a complete exegesis of the Bible. His other works include *Studies in the Creative Week* (1877) as his first major work and *Our Risen King's Forty Days* (1902) as his last.

Randolph S. Foster

Feb. 22, 1820
Williamsburg, Ohio

May 1, 1903
Newton Center, Massachusetts

Methodist bishop in 1872. Foster entered the ministry in 1837. He married Sarah Miley in July, 1840 (died: 1871). After laboring in Ohio until 1850, Foster was transferred to the New York Conference. He became president of Northwestern University (1857–60), returned to the pastorate in NYC (1860–68), and served as president of Drew Seminary (1870–72), after teaching there (1868–70). He visited Methodist home mission fields around the country. He authored several books beginning with *Objections to Calvinism* (1849).

John F. Hurst

Aug. 17, 1834
near Salem, Maryland

May 4, 1903
Washington, D. C.

Methodist clerk, church historian, and bishop in 1880. From 1858–66, Hurst pastored in Newark, NJ. He was professor of theology in the Mission Institute of the Methodist Episcopal Church for the training of German ministers, first at Bremen, at Frankfurt, 1866–71. He taught historical theology at Drew Theological Seminary (1870–80), was president of the same (1873–80). In 1891, he was chancellor of the American University, Washington, D.C., which he helped found. He wrote *History of Rationalism* to the *Literature of Theology*. A key work was *A History of the Christian Church* (2 vols, 1897–1900).

Henry Blodget

July 13, 1825
Bucksport, Maine

May 23, 1903
Bridgeport, Connecticut

Congregational missionary under the American Board of Commissioners for Foreign Missions. Blodget was a missionary to China, 1854–94. He helped translate the New Testament into the colloquial Mandarin of Peking, where he lived from 1864 on.

Joseph A. Beebe

June 25, 1832
Fayetteville, North Carolina

June 6, 1903
North Carolina

Bishop of Colored (Christian in 1956) **Methodist Episcopal Church, 1873–1903; senior bishop, 1892–1903.** One of 17 children, Beebe was born a slave and learned the trade of a shoemaker. Both his father and his grandfather were preachers. He was converted (1851), and later married Cornelia Bockrum (1858). He was ordained in the Methodist Church South as a deacon (1865) and then as an elder (1866). The CMEC was founded in 1870–71, and Beebe was made the presiding elder and soon a bishop.

Carolina Sandell Berg
Mrs. C. Berg

Oct. 3, 1832
Froderyd, Sweden

July 27, 1903
Stockholm, Sweden

Lutheran hymn writer who wrote "Day By Day" (1865) (music by OSCAR ANNFELT) and **"Children of the Heavenly Father," among her 650 hymns.** Carolina was called the "FANNY CROSBY" of Sweden. Her husband of 1867, was Stockholm merchant C. O. Berg. At age twelve, she was healed of a childhood paralysis, and at age 26, she lost her father to the sea. In 1953, 10,000 people gathered in the parsonage yard of Froderyd for the dedication of a bronze statue of her.

Spencer Lane

April 7, 1843
Tilton, New Hampshire

Aug. 10, 1903
Readville, Virginia

Composed music for "In the Hour of Trial" (lyrics by JAMES MONTGOMERY). Lane served three years with the Union army in the Civil War. After teaching music in NYC, he went to Woonsocket, RI where he established a music store. For 13 years, he served as the organist at St. James Episcopal Church. He later served in Monson, MA; Richmond, VA; and at All-Saints Church, Baltimore, MD as choirmaster and organist.

Alvah Hovey

March 5, 1820
Greene, New York

Sept. 6, 1903
Newton Centre, Massachusetts

President of Newton (MA) (Andover-Newton in 1931) **Theological Seminary, 1868–98**. He was ordained a Baptist minister, pastored in New Gloucester, NH from 1848–49. Hovey had been connected with the institution since 1849. He was the assistant teacher of Hebrew (1849–55), professor of church history (1853–55), and professor of theology and Christian ethics (1855–1900). He married Augusta Rice on September 24, 1852. Hovey wrote many books, from ISAAC BACKUS (1858) to BARNAS SEARS (1903).

Thomas M. Clark

July 4, 1812
Newburyport, Massachusetts

Sept. 7, 1903
Middletown, Connecticut

Presiding bishop of Protestant Episcopal Church (Episcopal Church in 1967), **1899–1903**. He left the Presbyterian Church in 1836, for the Episcopal Church. Clark began his ministry as rector of Grace Church, Boston (1836–43); then St. Andrew, Philadelphia, PA (1844–47); Trinity Church, Boston (1847–51); and Christ Church, Hartford, CT (1851–54). He authored *Formation of Character* and *The Efficient Sunday School Teacher* among others.

Godfrey Thring

March 25, 1823
Alford, England

Sept. 13, 1903
Shamley Green, England

Church of England hymnbook editor and hymn writer. Thring was ordained into the Church of England in 1846. He held several curacies (pastorates), and in 1858, he succeeded his father as rector of Alford. He became prebendary of East Harptree at Wells Cathedral, 1876–93. His publications included a Church of England hymn book. He added a verse to "Crown Him with Many Crowns" (1874), which was written by Matthew Bridges (1800–94) (music by GEORGE ELVEY). He wrote many hymns with some 25 published.

Samuel A. Ward

Dec. 28, 1847
Newark, New Jersey

Sept. 28, 1903
Newark, New Jersey

Composed music for "America the Beautiful" (1882), long before the lyrics were written by KATHERINE BATES. Ward established a successful retail music store and was active in the musical life of Newark. He married Virginia Ward (no relation) in 1871. In 1880, he succeeded HENRY CUTLER as organist at Grace Episcopal Church, Newark. He founded the Orpheus Club of Newark in 1889, directing it until 1900.

Emma Revell Moody

July 5, 1843
London (?), England

Oct. 10, 1903
Northfield, Massachusetts

Wife of the famed evangelist, D. L. MOODY. Emma's family emigrated to Chicago in 1849, when she was just seven. After graduating from high school, she taught briefly, then married D. L. MOODY on August 28, 1862. She escaped the Great Chicago Fire in 1871. She served with her husband in his evangelistic campaigns and Sunday school work, doing much of his correspondence.

Henry C. Trumbull

June 8, 1830
Stonington, Connecticut

Dec. 8, 1903
Philadelphia, Pennsylvania

Congregational clergyman (ordained 1862) and editor who in 1872 was issued a call to establish the International Uniform Sunday School Lessons. He worked for the railroads, 1851–58. Trumbull was moved by a challenge from CHARLES FINNEY in 1852. He married Alice C. Gallaudet in 1854 (died: 1891). He was an army chaplain and a prisoner of the Confederates in the Civil War, then secretary of the New England Department of the American Sunday School Union, 1865–71. In 1875, he became editor of the *Sunday School Times*, published in Philadelphia. He wrote 33 books on a variety of subjects from *Friendship, the Master Passion* (1891) to *Old Time Student Volunteers* (1902).

Daniel (Dion) DeMarbelle

July 4, 1818

Dec. 18, 1903

Wrote lyrics and music for "When They Ring Those Golden Bells" (1887). DeMarbelle toured America as a musician and actor with an opera company. He was the first clown for the Bailey Circus. He started his own circus but lost everything in a Canadian fire. After he wrote his song, his royalties were stolen, and he lived in poverty in Elgin, IL.

Francois Coillard

1834
Asnieres-Les-Bourges, France

1904
Africa

Pioneer missionary to Barotseland (west Northern Rhodesia), Africa. In 1857, at age 23, Coillard was ordained in Paris by the Paris Evangelical Mission, sailed to Basutoland in the Republic of South Africa and was stationed at Leribe. He went to Barotseland, Rhodesia and Nupraland, 1878–79. He married a Scottish lady, Christina Mackintosh (1829–91), who was a faithful missionary companion for 30 years. He worked among the Barotses until his death. He took his first furlough in 23 years, 1880–82, raising support for a Barotse mission, which he founded in 1886.

George Salmon

Sept. 25, 1819
Cork, Ireland

Jan. 22, 1904
Dublin, Ireland

Theologian, writer, and mathematician who was educated at Trinity College, Dublin. Salmon was at Dublin University (1845–88), also serving as regius professor of divinity (1866–88). He became provost at Trinity College in 1888. He wrote *Cautions for the Times, Introduction to the New Testament* (1885), and some textbooks on math. From 1871 on, he was chancellor of St. Patrick's Cathedral in Dublin.

George A. Minor

Dec. 7, 1845
Richmond, Virginia

Jan. 29, 1904
Richmond, Virginia

Composed music for "Bringing in the Sheaves." Minor served in the Confederate army during the Civil War. For several years he taught music and conducted singing schools and music conventions. He married Jennie B. Pope on November 10, 1886, and was a member of First Baptist Church, Richmond. He also manufactured pianos and organs.

Edwin Hodder

Dec. 13, 1837
Staines, England

March 1, 1904
Henfield, England

Wrote the hymn "Thy Word is Like a Garden, Lord." Hodder went to New Zealand at age 19 with a group of idealistic pioneers in the interest of sociology. He entered the English Civil Service (1861), serving until his retirement (1897). His *New Sunday School Hymn Book* (1862) contained 23 of his own hymns. He also wrote *The Life of a Century* (1900).

Robert Machray

May 17, 1831
Aberdeen, Scotland

March 9, 1904
Winnipeg, Manitoba, Canada

First primate of the Anglican Church in Canada, 1893–1904. Machray was ordained a deacon (1855), and a priest (1856), of Ely Cathedral. He was dean of Sidney Sussex College, Cambridge, England (1859–65); was consecrated a bishop in 1865; served as Lord Bishop in Rupert's Land (Manitoba) (1865–93); and was prelate of St. Michael and St. George, 1893 on, which was in connection with his high post. He helped the church in Canada to become independent from missionary status to England. From a scattered handful of Anglican clergy, he saw the Anglican Church grow to more than 200 clergy serving in nine Episcopal sees.

Egbert C. Smyth

Aug. 24, 1829
Brunswick, Maine

April 12, 1904
Andover, Massachusetts

President of Andover (MA) (Andover-Newton) **Theological Seminary, 1877–96.** Smythe married Elizabeth Dwight on August 12, 1857. He was a professor of rhetoric at Bowdoin, Brunswick, ME (1854–56), and then at Andover (1856–90), also teaching church history. He was the co-founder and editor of the *Andover Review* (1886–92). He authored several books, including *Three Discourses on Religious History of Bowdoin* (1858) to *Influence of* JONATHAN EDWARDS (1901). The seminary creed did not bind him in doctrine; hence, he turned the seminary towards liberalism.

Emmanuel V. Gerhart

June 13, 1817
Freeburg, Pennsylvania

May 6, 1904
Lancaster, Pennsylvania

First president of Lancaster (PA) Theological Seminary, 1868–1904. The school was in Mercersburg, PA, 1868–71. Gerhart was ordained to German Reformed ministry in August, 1842. He married Eliza Rikenbaugh in 1843 (died: 1864); Mary Hunter in August, 1865 (died: 1866) and Lucia Cobb on December 29, 1875. He served as the president of Heidelberg College, Tiffin, OH, and professor in the Reformed Seminary, Tiffin, OH from 1851–55. He also served as the first president of Franklin and Marshall College, Lancaster, PA from 1855–66, then became the professor of systematic and practical theology at LTS in 1868. He pastored in Gettysburg, PA from 1863–69. Moving to Lancaster in 1871, he taught classes up until the week of his death. He wrote *History of Christian Religion* (2 vols., 1891).

Henry M. Stanley
John Rowlands

Jan. 28, 1841
near Denbigh, Wales

May 10, 1904
London, England

Explorer and journalist who, on behalf of the *New York Herald*, in 1869, was sent to Africa to find a renowned missing explorer. Upon finding him in the Central African bush (Ujiji on Lake Tanganyika) Stanley casually inquired, "DAVID LIVINGSTONE, I presume?" on November 10,

1871. He never graduated from grade school. Stanley was on his own at a young age, working his way to America as a cabin boy from Liverpool to New Orleans, where he was employed and adopted by a merchant named Stanley, whose name he assumed. He fought on both sides of the Civil War. He was converted by LIVINGSTONE's life. He picked up LIVINGSTONE's torch and charted over two million square miles of Africa, exploring off and on, 1874–88. He helped Belgium open up the Congo, and assisted missionary work in Uganda in 1875. He married Dorothy Tennant on July 12, 1890. He wrote *In Harvest Africa* (2 vols., 1890) among others.

Joseph A. Seiss

March 18, 1823
Graceham, Maryland

June 20, 1904
Philadelphia, Pennsylvania

Lutheran minister and a most eloquent preacher who held pastorates at Martinsburg, VA (WV) (1843–47); Cumberland, MD (1847–52); Lombard St. Lutheran in Baltimore, MD (1852–58); and St. Johns and Holy Communion in Philadelphia (1858–1904). He was reared a Moravian but joined the Lutherans in 1839. In 1843, he married Elizabeth Barnitz. He had strong premillennialist beliefs and was known for his volumes on *Revelation* (1865). He was chairman of the board of Lutheran Theological Seminary in Philadelphia from 1865 until his death. He died while tending to his duties as president of the board of directors of LTS. He wrote from *Hebrews* (1846) to *Recent Sermons* (1904). Seiss edited *The Lutheran* and was an editor of the *Prophetic Times*, 1863–75.

Frederick D. Huntington

May 28, 1819
Hadley, Massachusetts

July 11, 1904
Hadley, Massachusetts

Protestant Episcopal bishop. Huntington started out as a Unitarian but was converted to orthodoxy and became the first PE bishop of central New York in 1869. He was the pastor of the South Congregational (Unitarian) Church in Boston, 1842–45. He married Hannah Sargent in 1843. From 1845–59, he served as editor of the *Monthly Religious Magazine*. He was a preacher at Harvard College in 1855. He accepted the Trinity, Deity, and redemptive work of Christ, and the doctrine of apostolic succession, which caused his resignation from Harvard in 1860. He became the first rector of Emmanuel Episcopal Church in Boston, 1861–69. In 1869, as bishop, he relocated to Syracuse, NY. He continued to apply Christian principles to social problems, and in this respect, was a forerunner of the Social Gospel movement. He wrote works ranging from *Sermons for the People* (1856) to *Personal Religion in Women* (1900).

George C. Lorimer

June 4, 1838
Edinburgh, Scotland

Sept. 7, 1904
Aix-Les Bains, France

Baptist pastor. He came to the US as an actor in 1855, joined the Baptist church while his company was playing in Louisville, KY and left the stage to study at Georgetown (KY) College. Lorimer pastored Walnut Street Church, Louisville, KY; Paducah, KY (1860–68); FBC, Albany, NY (1968–70); Tremont Temple, Boston, MA (1870–79 and 1891–1901); in Chicago (1879–90); and Madison Avenue Baptist, NYC (1902–04). He opposed liberalism. His works range from *Under the Evergreens* (1872) to *The Modern Crisis in Religion* (1904).

Frederick Whitfield

Jan. 7, 1829
Threapwood, England

Sept. 13, 1904
Croydon, London, England

Wrote the beloved gospel song, "O How I Love Jesus." Whitfield was ordained in the Church of England and served churches in Otley, Kirby-Ravensworth, Greenwich, Bexley, and Hastings. He wrote some 30 books of verse and prose, including *Sacred Poems and Prose* (1861 and 1864), which contained 26 hymns.

William T. Sleeper

Feb. 9, 1819
Danbury, New Hampshire

Sept. 24, 1904
Wellesley, Massachusetts

Wrote the well-known hymns, "Ye Must Be Born Again" and "Jesus, I Come" (music to both by GEORGE STEBBINS). Ordained to the Congregationalist ministry, Sleeper served in home mission work in Worcester, MA and later in Maine, where he helped establish three churches. He was pastor of Summer Street Congregational Church in Worcester, MA for over 30 years.

John J. S. Perowne

March 13, 1823
Burdwan, India

Nov. 6, 1904
Southwick, England

Church of England bishop. Perowne served in numerous positions throughout his lengthy career, including vice-principal of St. David's College, Lampeter (1862–72), prebendary of St. Andrew's and canon of Llandaff Cathedral (1869–78), dean of Peterborough (1878–90), and bishop of Worcester (1890–1901). He was a member of the OT Company of Bible Revisers, 1870–74 and was general editor of the *Cambridge Bible for Schools* (Cambridge, 1877), including his own commentaries on five of the Minor Prophets. He was the son of a missionary to India. His brother, EDWARD, also served the Church of England.

Jeremiah E. Rankin

Jan. 2, 1828
Thorton, New Hampshire

Nov. 28, 1904
Cleveland, Ohio

Wrote the immortal hymn, "God Be With You 'Til We Meet Again," 1883 (music by WILLIAM TOMER) **and "Tell It to Jesus"** (music by EDMUND LORENZ). Rankin was ordained a Congregational minister (1855) and served churches in New York, Vermont, Massachusetts, Washington, D.C., and New Jersey, returning to Washington (1889) to become president of Howard University until 1903. He compiled several gospel songbooks.

Thomas D. Bernard

Nov. 11, 1815
Clifton, England

Dec. 7, 1904
Wimborne, England

Church of England clergyman. Bernard was ordained a deacon (1840) and a priest (1841). He held several clerical positions in different churches until 1895. He preached at Oxford in 1855, 1862, and 1882. He was the Bampton lecturer in 1864. He published lectures under the title, *Progress of Doctrine in the New Testament*.

James P. Eagle

Aug. 10, 1837
Maury County, Tennessee

Dec. 20, 1904
Little Rock, Arkansas

Southern Baptist president, 1902–04, and Arkansas governor, 1889–1893. Eagle married Mary Kavanaugh Oldham, and was badly wounded in the Civil War. He served several terms in the state legislature and was the Speaker of the House in 1885. He was elected governor of Arkansas and also served as the president of the Arkansas Baptist Convention, 1880–1904. Following his governorship 1889–93, he returned to farming (cotton plantation) and preaching and helping small Baptist congregations.

Ada R. Gibbs

1865
England

1905
England

Composed music for "Channels Only" (lyrics by Mary Maxwell). Ada spent her life in England and was evidently active in the Keswick movement. She married William J. Gibbs and was involved in the Bible Conference movement, which emphasized deeper living. She published *24 Gems of Sacred Songs* (1900). Her son was a director of Marshall, Morgan, and Scott Publishers.

Edward J. Gray

July 27, 1832
Centre County, Pennsylvania

Jan. 20, 1905
Baltimore, Maryland

President of Williamsport (PA) Dickinson Seminary (Lycoming College), **1874–1905**. He had Methodist roots and graduated from the school he led for so many years in 1858. Early on, Gray served a succession of pastorates with distinction. An eloquent preacher, he led the school for 31 years. He was often referred to as a preacher for preachers. He was elected to five General Conferences between 1888–1904.

Albert H. Schauffler

Sept. 4, 1837
Constantinople, Turkey

Feb. 15, 1905
Cleveland, Ohio

Missionary. He was the son of Congregational missionaries. Schauffler was ordained in 1865, and served in Constantinople, Turkey, until 1870. He worked in Prague, Austria (1872–74); then he served in Brunn, Moravia (1874–81). His affliction forced him to return to America, where he devoted his life to home mission work among Slavic people, opening Bohemian, Slovak, and Polish missions in many places.

Lewis "Lew" Wallace

April 10, 1827
Brookville, Indiana

Feb. 15, 1905
Crawfordsville, Indiana

Lawyer, diplomat, soldier and author. Wallace is best remembered as the author of *Ben Hur* (1880) and other novels, including *The Fair God* (1873) and *The Prince of India* (1893). He married Susan A. Elston in 1852. He served the Union cause in the Civil War (1861–65), practiced law in Crawfordsville (1865–78), was the governor of New Mexico territory (1878–81), and was the minister to Turkey (1881–85). He was president of the court that convicted the Confederate commandment of Andersonville Prison (cruel prisoner of war camp for Union prisoners). He was never a member of any church. *Ben Hur* sold 300,000 copies in ten years and was translated into many languages. His favorite Bible verse was Matthew 2:1.

William E. McLaren

Dec. 13, 1831
Geneva, New York

Feb. 19, 1905
New York, New York

Founder (1881) and first president of Western Theological Seminary (Seabury-Western Theological Seminary, Evanston, IL in 1933), **Chicago, IL 1885–1905**. McLaren began as a Presbyterian, 1860–72, after which he was ordained as an Episcopalian deacon (1872) and as a priest (1873). He was the rector in Cleveland, OH in 1883. He also founded the Waterman Hall, a school for girls in Sycamore, IL in 1885. He also summoned the first diocesan retreat held by the Episcopal Church in this country. He is the author of several books, ranging from *Catholic Dogma: Antidote of Doubt* (1883) to *The Essence of Prayer* (1901).

James R. Murray
March 17, 1841
Andover, Massachusetts

March 10, 1905
Cincinnati, Ohio

Composed the music for "Away in a Manger." After serving in the Union army during the Civil War, Murray was employed by Root and Cady of Chicago. He also served as the editor of the *Song Messenger*. He taught music at Andover Theological Seminary (1871–81), then became associated with the John Church Company of Cincinnati (1881–1905). He composed many gospel songs.

John B. Calkin
March 16, 1827
London, England

April 15, 1905
Islington, London, England

Composed the music for "I Heard the Bells on Christmas Day" (lyrics by HENRY LONGFELLOW) **and "Fling Out the Banner"** (lyrics by GEORGE DOANE). In 1847, Calkin began as the organist at St. Columbia College near Dublin. He then returned to London six years later and held various positions as organist and choirmaster, including a position at Woburn Chapel. In 1889, he was appointed professor at the Guildhall School of Music.

Heinrich C. Schwan
April 5, 1819
Horneberg, Germany

May 29, 1905
Cleveland, Ohio

President of Lutheran Church-Missouri Synod, 1878–99. Schwan was a pastor, missionary and church official. He was ordained in 1843, and then became a missionary to Brazil. He married Emma Blume on April 4, 1849 in Rio de Janeiro, Brazil. He came to America in 1850. He served as pastor in Black Jack, MO (1850–51) and Zion Church, Cleveland, OH (1851–99) and was a synodical officer (1852–78). He popularized the use of Christmas trees in American church services.

J. Hudson Taylor
May 21, 1832
Barnsley, England

June 3, 1905
Changsha, China

Founder and first general director of China Inland Mission (Overseas Missionary Fellowship), **1865–1902.** Taylor was one of the giant missionaries along with LIVINGSTONE, CAREY and JUDSON. He was converted at age 17 in 1849 while his mother was praying for him in a distant city. Arriving in Shanghai, March 1, 1854 at age 21, he traveled extensively and courageously throughout China. He adopted native dress in 1855. He returned to England in 1860. His Lammermuir party (first CIM party of 16 men) arrived in Shanghai in 1866. He sent out a prayer request and appeal to double the CIM missionary force, to 70 recruits (1881), then asked for 100 (1886). The 1890s saw great increases in the CIM force, and by 1895, they had the largest missionary body in China. The Boxer Rebellion in 1900, which killed so many, prompted Taylor to return out of retirement in Switzerland to China. The uprising in northern China was the result of a secret society, the Harmonious and Righteous Fists, who set out to destroy all foreign influences in China. Members of this society were trained in the art of Kung-fu, which became known to Westerners as "boxing" in an attempt to describe this martial art. Taylor married MARIA DYER (1837–70) on January 20, 1858 (died: July 23, 1870), then Jane Faulding (1843–1904) in 1871. He started 205 mission stations, encouraged 840 missionaries to the field, and saw 125,000 converts. His favorite Bible verses were John 19:30 and Mark 11:22.

Samuel G. Green

Dec. 20, 1822
Falmouth, England

Sept. 15, 1905
London, England

English Baptist minister. He pastored at High Wycombe (1844–47) and at Taunton (1847–51). Green was a classical tutor (1851–63) and president of Horton College (Rawdon) in Bradford, England (1863–76). He became the book editor of the Religious Tract Society, London, in 1876; and later served as secretary before retiring in 1899. He authored many books on the Bible, church history, and theology. Green's most popular work was *Handbook to Grammar of the Greek New Testament* (1870). His writings range from *Addresses to Children* (1849) to *Handbook of Church History* (1904).

George MacDonald

Dec. 10, 1824
Huntly, Scotland

Sept. 18, 1905
Ashtead, England

Novelist, poet, and writer of Christian allegories. In 1851, he published his first collection of poems and also married Louisa Powell that same year. MacDonald became a Congregationalist minister at Trinity Chapel, Arundel, from 1850–53, where he was ordained. The deacons lowered his salary, because his theology was suspected of having a heretical tinge, philosophical and ascetic, causing his resignation in 1853. His view left some hope for the heathen to find redemption, which caused his deacons to oppose him. Because of this, he devoted himself to teaching, preaching, and full-time writing in various places. He moved to Manchester, then later to London. His first book was *Within and Without* (1855), a dramatic poem. C. S. Lewis said he owed much to him, because of the quality of cheerful goodness in his works. He spent part of 1881–1905 in India because of poor health. Tuberculosis took his life, as well as that of his parents and four of his children. He wrote 52 works, including 25 novels, and is remembered for his children's books, especially *At the Back of the North Wind* (1871) and *The Princess and the Goblin* (1872). MacDonald also authored "Phantast" (1858), a poem which established his reputation, *Diary of an Old Soul* (1880), and *The Elect Lady* (1888). He also wrote *The Miracles of Our Lord* (1886).

Thomas J. Barnardo

July 4, 1845
Dublin, Ireland

Sept. 19, 1905
Surbiton (near London), England

Evangelist, philanthropist, and founder of Dr. Barnardo's Home in 1899 for needy children. Barnardo was converted in 1862 during a revival. He went to London during the cholera epidemic in 1866, enrolled as a medical student, and began evangelism endeavors in Stepney, East London. He opened his child care center (1867), then opened the East London Juvenile Mission (1868). His motto was, "No destitute child ever refused admission." He opened his first home for destitute boys on Stepney Causeway (1870), and the Girls Village Home in Barkingside (1876). During that time, he married Syrie Elmslie in 1873. In 1887, an office opened in Toronto. He founded the Young Helpers League in 1891. At the time of his death, 112 homes were operating, helping 59,384 children. He also helped 20,000 emigrate to Canada, materially assisting another 250,000. The "Barnardo Homes" trained the children in the faith of their parents.

Charles J. Ellicott

April 25, 1819
Whitwell, England

Oct. 15, 1905
Birchington-on-sea, England

Anglican bishop and Bible commentator. Ellicott served as a professor of divinity at King's College, London, 1858–61, and also as the rector of Pilton until 1858. He was a dean at Exeter in 1861, then served as bishop of Bristol and Gloucester, 1863–97, continuing at Gloucester until his death. He helped establish Gloucester

Theological College in 1904. For eleven years, he was chairman of the committee of scholars engaged in the translation of the English Revised Version (1881). He wrote several commentaries, including The Complete Bible Commentary for English Readers (7 vols., pub. 1897). His works range from The History of the Sabbath (1844) to Sermons at Gloucester (1905).

George Williams

Oct. 11, 1821
Dulverton, England

Nov. 6, 1905
Torquay, England

Founder of the YMCA (Young Men's Christian Association). Converted by Pastor Evan Jones in 1837, at a Congregational meeting, Williams was zealous for the Lord at age 16. He married Helen Hitchcock in 1841. At 23 years of age, on June 6, 1844, he established the YMCA. His idea was to have a place where Christianity could be spread by reaching the neglected youth of London's shops and churches. The ministry spread into Boston and Montreal in 1851 and had 5,000 worldwide branches, including 2,000 in the U.S. He was the treasurer of YMCA, 1863–83 and president 1886 on. Williams was knighted by Queen VICTORIA in 1894. His funeral was at St. Paul's Cathedral in London.

Stephen M. Merrill

Sept. 16, 1825
Mount Pleasant, Ohio

Nov. 12, 1905
Keyport, New Jersey

Methodist bishop. Merrill entered the ministry (1864) and was ordained as a bishop (1872), serving in St. Paul, MN (1872–80); and in Chicago, IL (1880–1904). He married Anna Bellmire on July 18, 1848, who survived him by only a few days. He was second only to JOSHUA SOULE in his knowledge of Methodist law. He became the editor of The Western Christian Advocate (1868) and authored twelve books including: Christian Baptism (1876), New Testament Idea of Hell (1878), Second Coming of Christ (1879), Aspects of Christian Experience (1882), and Organic Union of American Methodism (1892).

Mary Anne Pepper Kidder

March 16, 1820
Boston, Massachusetts

Nov. 25, 1905
Chelsea, Massachusetts

Baptist songwriter of 1,000 hymns. She spent her entire life in Massachusetts. Her two best known hymns are "Is My Name Written There?" (music by F. Davis) and "Did You Think to Pray?" (music by Perkins). She also wrote "We Shall Sleep, But Not Forever." She was blinded as a teenager, but fortunately, her sight was restored after a few years. She belonged to the Methodist Church.

James Stewart

Feb. 14, 1831
Edinburgh, Scotland

Dec. 21, 1905
Lovedale, South Africa

Missionary and educator in South Africa from 1861 until his death. Stewart went to the field as an assistant to DAVID LIVINGSTONE and dedicated his life to healing and educating Africans. He married in 1866. In 1867, he founded the Lovedale Institute near Capetown, where he was serving as principal when he passed away. It was the first industrial educational missionary enterprise in Africa. Stewart was the first person to train missionaries as medical assistants and was compassionate to the natives. He also helped pioneer missions in Malawi and Kenya.

Edward H. Perowne

1826

1906
Burdwan, India

Evangelical Church of England clerk. Son of a missionary, Perowne served as curate of Maddermarket, Norfolk. He was a fellow, tutor, and later, master of Corpus Cristi College. He also served as the bishop of St. Asaph, vice-chancellor of Cambridge University, honorary chaplain to Queen VICTORIA and examining chaplain to the Worcester bishop. He never married. His brother, JOHN, was a Church of England bishop.

W. Spencer Walton

1850
London, England

1906

Wrote the hymn "In Tenderness He Sought Me." As a teenager, Walton made sea voyages to the Far East and Africa for health purposes. He worked as an evangelist from 1872–82. He went to South Africa, where he opened the nondenominational Cape General Mission in 1889. The mission later merged to form the South Africa General Mission in 1894. Walton was associated with Pastor A. J. GORDON, who wrote the music to his hymn.

Paton J. Gloag

May 17, 1823
Perth, Scotland

Jan. 9, 1906
Edinburgh, Scotland

Presbyterian clergyman, exegete, and theologian. Gloag held pastorates at Dunning, Pershire, Blantyre, Lanarkshire, and Galashiels in Selkirshire, 1840–90. He served as the moderator of the General Assembly of the Church of Scotland in 1889. He also taught at the University of Aberdeen, 1896–99 and wrote several books.

John C. Keener

Feb. 7, 1819
Baltimore, Maryland

Jan. 19, 1906
New Orleans, Louisiana

Bishop of the Methodist Episcopal Church South, 1870–1906. Keener was a Baltimore businessman before entering the ministry in 1841. He pastored in Alabama (1841–48) and in New Orleans (1848–65). He served as editor of *New Orleans Christian Advocate* (1866–70). He founded a mission in Mexico in 1873, and wrote several books, ranging from *The Post Oak Circuit* (1857) to *Garden of Eden and the Flood* (1900).

Jemima Thompson Luke

Aug. 19, 1813
Islington, London, England

Feb. 2, 1906
Newport, Isle of Wight, England

Congregationalist hymn writer of "I Think When I Read that Sweet Story of Old." Jemima had a serious illness which prevented her from being a missionary. She married Samuel Luke, a Congregational pastor, in 1843 (died: 1868). After her marriage, she began her literary career. In 1868, she retired to the Isle of Wight. She edited both the *Missionary Repository* (1841–45) and a children's magazine.

Milton Valentine

Jan. 1, 1825
Uniontown, Maryland

Feb. 7, 1906
Gettysburg, Pennsylvania

Theologian, educator, and president of Lutheran Theological Seminary, Gettysburg, PA 1884–1903. Valentine married Margaret Galt on Dec. 18, 1855. He pastored in Winchester, VA (1852–54); and Reading, PA, 1859–66; then became a professor of church history and polity at LTS, (1866–68). He was president of Gettysburg (PA) College, 1868–84. He also taught systematic theology while president of the school, 1884–1903. He served as editor of *Lutheran Quarterly* (1871–76, 1880–85, and 1898–1906). He authored several books ranging from *Natural Theology* (1885) to *Christian Theology* (1906), which makes concessions to evolutionism, Puritanism, and Reformed theology.

Sam H. Hadley

Aug. 27, 1842
Malta, Ohio

Feb. 9, 1906
New York, New York

Beloved superintendent of the McAuley Water Street Mission of New York City 1886–1906. The Holy Spirit transformed a dying drunkard into a prince among mission workers. Hadley married on July 23, 1874, and in July, 1875, his 19-year-old bride died. In 1879, he remarried, but alcohol nearly destroyed him. Like MEL TROTTER, he was a chronic drinker and felt he was dying. He was a forger of checks, a liar, and a gambler. So he stumbled into the mission that he would later direct. He heard JERRY McAULEY tell about Christ and was gloriously converted on April 23, 1882. Now all was changed, and upon JERRY McAULEY's death in 1884, it was Hadley that would head the work. On his death bed he murmured, "What will become of my poor bums?" J. WILBUR CHAPMAN was so touched with his life that he wrote his biography.

Susan B. Anthony

Feb. 15, 1820
South Adams, Massachusetts

March 13, 1906
Rochester, New York

Quaker social reformer and advocate of women's rights. Susan was reared in a Quaker family. She advocated equal pay for women teachers, higher education for women, and temperance for men. She attended a meeting of Elizabeth C. Stanton's in 1851, which encouraged her feminist interests. They joined forces to lead the women's suffrage movement, which finally triumphed in 1928. She began the first woman's state temperance society in America in 1852. She fought against slavery in 1857 and pushed for co-education. In 1868, she and others published *The Revelation*. In 1869, she founded the National Woman's Suffrage Association, (merged in 1890 to form the National American WSA), which she led until 1900. In 1872, she cast her ballot, and, although indicted for illegal voting, she was never fined. In 1899, she made her last public appearance of note in London. She never married. She is buried in Mount Hope Cemetery, Rochester.

William Kelly

1820/1821
Ireland

March 27, 1906
Exeter, England

Brethren writer. Kelly was converted at age 20 and joined the work led by JOHN N. DARBY. He edited DARBY's writings (3 vols., 1867–83). He was a prolific writer and gifted lecturer, who opposed all biblical criticism. He edited the *Bible Treasury* for 50 years (1856–1906). His personal library housed over 15,000 books. He was known as a scholar and keen textual critic as well as a controversialist. For 30 years, he lived in Overnsey, Channel Islands, but in later years lived in Blackheath, London. He led a moderate wing of independent Brethren.

John C. Geikie

Oct. 26, 1824
Edinburgh, Scotland

April 1, 1906
Bournemouth, England

English cleric and writer. Geikie was ordained a Presbyterian in 1848. He pastored in Halifax, Canada (1851–54); Toronto, Canada (1854–60); Sunderland, England (1860–67); and London, England (1867–73). He became an Anglican in 1860 and served as a curate at St. Peter's, Dulwich (1876–79); rector of Christ's Church, Neuilly, Paris (1879–81); vicar of St. Mary's Church, Barnstable (1883–89); and vicar of St. Martin-of-Palace, Norwich (1889–90). He wrote *The Life and Words of Christ* (2 vols., 1877). His writings range from *Life in the Woods* (1864) to *The Vicar and His Friends* (1901).

Edward H. Bickersteth, Jr.

Jan. 25, 1825
Isington, London, England

May 16, 1906
London, England

Poet and bishop. Bickersteth wrote the hymn "Peace, Perfect Peace" (1875) (music by GEORGE CALDBECK). He was an Anglican who served successively, beginning in 1848, at Banningham, Norfolk, and Christ Church in Tubbridge, Wells. He was also dean of Gloucester. He married Rosa Bignold on Feb. 24, 1848. He served as vicar of Christ Church in Hampstead, London (1855–85) and as bishop of Exeter (1885–1900). He was the eldest son of Evangelical clergyman, EDWARD BICKERSTETH Sr. He authored twelve books, three hymnals, and many pieces of poetry. Of the over 30 hymns he wrote, some of the most memorable are "Stand, Soldier of the Cross" and "O Brothers, Lift Up Your Voices."

Stephen A. Repass

Nov. 25, 1838
Wytheville, Virginia

June 2, 1906
Allentown, Pennsylvania

President of Lutheran Theological Southern Seminary Salem, VA (Columbia, SC), **1872–84**. Repass pastored at Salem, VA (1869–72); Staunton, VA (1884–85); and Allentown, PA (1885–1906). He served in the army during the Civil War. He was also president of General Synod South (1871–72), a member of the Common Service Commission, president of Muhlenberg College Board, Allentown, PA (1886–1906) and editor of the *Church Messenger*.

William L. Pressly

May 3, 1837
near Due West, South Carolina

June 8, 1906
Due West, South Carolina

President of Erskine Theological Seminary, Due West, SC 1889–1906. William was the son of Erskine College's founder, E. E. Pressly, who served from 1839–47 as its first president. Francis E. Wideman became his wife on December 23, 1858, they had nine children. In 1862, he was ordained and began his pastoral ministry in Generostee and Concord, both in Anderson County, SC. He was called to the ARP Church in Due West in 1871, serving from 1872–1889. This position already established him at Erskine, and it was a relatively easy transition from pastor to seminary president.

Ann Preston

1810
Ballamacally, Ireland

June 21, 1906
Toronto, Ontario, Canada

"Holy Ann" is best known for her answers to prayer. Ann was convicted of her need for salvation at a Methodist meeting, where she was converted. She worked for a Christian family, the Reids. When they moved to America, she came with them. She always prayed two hours each day. She outlived the Reids and then lived with a friend in Toronto, attending the St. Berkeley Methodist Church. She got amazing answers to prayer (water out of a dry well, etc.) She died of a stroke.

George Grenfell

Aug. 21, 1849
Sancreed, England

July 1, 1906
Basoko, Congo (Belgian Congo)

Baptist Missionary and explorer in the African Cameroons, 1874–78. Grenfell was converted at age ten while attending a Baptist Sunday school. He married Mary Haules in 1876, but lost her after eleven months. After her death, he married his Jamaican housekeeper, Rose Esgenleyn in 1878. He opened mission stations up the Congo River as far as Stanley Pool, 1878–81. He surveyed and chartered much of the Congo basin and various tributaries. He established various mission stations from 1881–84. He surveyed the Congo River up to the Equator with his river steamer, the *Peace* (1884), and after traveling 15,000 miles, his findings were published by the Royal Geographic Society in 1886. After 1889, his base was Balboa. In 1893, he became commissioner of the Congo state. By 1896, he had a string of mission stations, some of which were in Musuko, Civi, Isangila, and Manyanga. His last important exploration was along the Aruwimi River, 1900–2. Condemning official atrocities caused him to be treated with disfavor. He violently protested to Leopold of Belgium against his maladministration. He died of African fever.

George Matheson

March 27, 1842
Glasgow, Scotland

Aug. 28, 1906
North Berwick, Scotland

Minister and hymn writer. Matheson wrote the famous and beloved hymn "O Love That Will Not Let Me Go" in five minutes, on June 6, 1882. He had exceedingly poor vision and was nearly blind at age 18, which caused him to cancel his engagement; he never married. He pastored at Clydeside Church, Innellan (1868–86) and at St. Bernard's Parish Church, Edinburgh (1886–99), when ill health forced retirement. He helped the Clydeside Church grow to 2,000 members. He was a Presbyterian with great ability.

Samuel I. Schereschewsky

May 6, 1831
Tanroggen, Lithuania

Sept. 15, 1906
Tokyo, Japan

Episcopal missionary and bishop who came to America in 1854. Schereschewsky was converted by reading the NT and studied in a Presbyterian Seminary from 1855–58. He joined the Episcopal Church in 1858. He was ordained a priest in 1860 and went to Shanghai, 1860–63; Peking, China; 1863–75; and back to Shanghai, 1877–83, 1895–97. He translated the Bible into Mandarin while in the U.S. from 1886–95. He married in 1868. He was paralyzed by disease in 1883, and spent 1897–1906 in literary work in Japan.

Friedrich W. Baedeker

Aug. 3, 1823
Witten, Germany

Oct. 9, 1906

Pioneer international evangelist. Baedeker traveled widely, preaching in Austrian castles; to Greeks, Jews, and Turks in Smyrna; to socialists in Munich; to Zurich students in Finnish; and in Russian universities. He married Auguste Jocobi in 1851, who lived only three months more. In 1859, he became a naturalized British citizen. In 1862, he married Harriet Ormsby, a widowed mother. He was converted under the preaching of LORD RADSTOCK WALDEGRAVE in a Brethren meeting in 1866 at Weston-Super-Mare. After ten years of Bible study and preaching at home in Westphalia, Germany, he toured throughout Germany (1874), and then in Russia (1875), preaching the gospel. He finally settled in St. Petersburg (Leningrad) in 1877. He was introduced by LORD RADSTOCK WALDEGRAVE to evangelical nobility. He visited prison camps throughout Russia, from the Caucasus to Siberia, distributing Bibles and preaching, 1887–1903. In 1887, he helped with Baroness Mathilde Von Wrede prison ministries in Finland. He died of pneumonia, saying several times, "I am going to see the King in His beauty."

Samuel (Sam) P. Jones

Oct. 16, 1847
Oak Bowery, Alabama

Oct. 15, 1906
near Perry, Arkansas

Second only to D. L. MOODY as an evangelist in his generation. Jones moved with his family to Cartersville, GA in 1858. He fought in the Civil War and married Laura McElwain on November 24, 1868. His law practice was ruined by alcohol, until he was converted in August,

1872, through his dying father's plea. He became an evangelist for the North Georgia Conference from 1872–80, and for the Methodist Episcopal Church South. From 1880–92, he was a financial agent of North Georgia Orphanage. In 1884, Jones extended his preaching beyond Georgia. His colorful, powerful preaching launched him into wide-scale evangelism endeavors in Memphis, TALMAGE's church in Brooklyn, Nashville, and many other places. He became one of the most powerful public speakers of his generation, holding large city wide crusades. He saw over 500,000 converted. He died on a train after collapsing. Jones wrote at least four books of his stories and/or sermons. He was laid in state at the capital rotunda in Atlanta upon his death.

Anne Ross Cousin

April 27, 1824
Hull, England

Dec. 6, 1906
Edinburgh, Scotland

Musician, author, and linguist, Anne is best remembered for writing the hymn, "The Sands of Time Are Sinking," which some say was D. L. MOODY's favorite hymn. Inspired by the writings of SAMUEL RUTHERFORD, she created a poetic tapestry of 19 verses, which was later condensed into her famous hymn, also called "Immanuel's Land" or "Rutherford's Hymn." It was published in *The Christian Treasury* in 1857. She composed and published 107 more poems and hymns. In 1847, she married William Cousin, a minister in Chelsea, London. They ministered in three cities in Scotland, serving in the Scottish Free Church (Presbyterian).

Robert Rainy

Jan. 1, 1826
Glasgow, Scotland

Dec. 22, 1906
Melbourne, Australia

Church of Scotland clergyman, orator, author, and educator. Rainy was professor of church history (1862–1900), and the principal of New College of Edinburgh (1874–1906) and professor of church history (1862–1900). He led the delicate negotiations leading to the union of the Free Church and the United Presbyterian Church in Scotland in 1900 and served as the first moderator of the new united body. He pastored at the Free High Church in Edinburgh, 1854–62.

John G. Paton

May 24, 1824
Kirkmamhoe, Scotland

Jan. 28, 1907
Canterbury/Melbourne, Australia

United Presbyterian missionary to the New Hebrides Islands (Vanuatu). Paton was converted as a child because of his father's godly witness. He served as a home missionary in Glasgow, Scotland, 1847–57, then went to the field on the island of Tanna in 1858. There, death struck his wife, Mary Ann Robson (died: Feb. 12, 1859), and his infant son (died: March 20, 1859). From 1866–81, he worked on the island of Aniwa before moving to Melbourne, Australia. He spent considerable time in Australia, Canada, and Britain, recruiting funds and personnel. He then returned to the New Hebrides Islands with his second wife, Margaret Whitecross, whom he married in 1864 (died: May 16, 1905). His mission ships were all known as *Dayspring*, losing his last in 1896. By 1899, 25 out of 30 islands in the group had missionaries due to Paton's zeal. On the field, he was divinely protected many times. His son, Frances (1870–1938), continued his work. He preached his last sermon in December, 1906. His favorite Bible verse was Matt. 28:20.

Eric B. Hulbert

July 16, 1841
Chicago, Illinois

Feb. 17, 1907
Chicago, Illinois

Dean of University of Chicago Divinity School, 1892–1907. Hulbert married Ettie E. Spencer in 1869. He became the professor of church history at Baptist University Theological Seminary in Chicago, 1882–92, then became president (the school's name changed in 1892). He pastored in Manchester, VT (1865–68); Chicago, IL (1868–69); St. Paul, MN (1869–71); San Francisco, CA (1871–76); and at Fourth Baptist, Chicago, IL (1876–82). He was on the staff of the *American Journal of Theology and Biblical World*.

John Dickson

June 15, 1820   Feb. 22, 1907
Chambersburg, Pennsylvania   Chambersburg, Pennsylvania

Bishop of Church of the United Brethren in Christ, Dayton, OH 1869–89. Dickson was converted and joined the church in 1843. He married May J. Adair (November 14, 1848) and was ordained (January 26, 1850), in York, PA. He was a builder of churches and helped many people, refusing numerous offices of the denomination. He was an able, expository preacher and a concise writer, retiring in 1893. He is buried in Chambersburg, PA.

Fredrik K. Nielsen

Oct. 30, 1846   March 24, 1907
Aalborg, Denmark   Aarhus, Denmark

Bishop, theologia, and church historian. Nielsen was considered the greatest in this field from Scandinavian countries. His advice was constantly sought. He was a catechist (teacher) at Our Savior's Church, Copenhagen, in 1873. He then became a professor of church history at Copenhagen University, 1877–1900. He served as the bishop of Aalborg (1900–5) and Aarhus (1905–7).

Georg Sverdrup Sr.

Dec. 16, 1848   May 3, 1907
Balestrand, Norway   Minneapolis, Minnesota

President of Augsburg Theological Seminary (merged into Lutheran Theological Seminary in 1963), **Minneapolis, MN 1876–1907**. Sverdrup was a Lutheran clergyman and educator. He married Katherine Heiberg (1874) and Elise S. Heiberg (1890). He came to America in 1874, and began to teach theology at ATS. He also served as the secretary of the Lutheran Board of Missions from 1876–1907. He helped found the Norwegian Lutheran (Free) Church, and served as president from 1894–97.

John Watson

Nov. 3, 1850   May 6, 1907
Manningtree, England   Mount Pleasant, Iowa

Presbyterian minister at Sefton Park Presbyterian Church, Liverpool, 1880–1905. He served two pastorates in Logiealmond (1875–77) and Free St. Matthews Church, Glasgow (1877–80), where he married Jane Ferguson. Watson also wrote under the pen name of "Ian Maclaren," publishing a series of popular "kailyard" fictional pieces sentimentalizing Scottish country life, beginning in 1894. He became ill and died on a third tour of America.

Johannes Deindoerfer

July 28, 1828   May 14, 1907
Nuremburg, Germany   Waverly, Ohio

President of Iowa Synod (ALC, ELCA in 1988), **1893–1904**. Deindoerfer was a Lutheran pastor, synodical organizer, official, editor, and author. He was ordained in Hamburg, Germany, in 1851. He served as a pastor in Michigan, Iowa, Wisconsin, and Ohio, 1851–89. He separated from the Missouri Synod and was the founder of the Iowa Synod in 1854, serving as vice-president from 1854–93. He also edited *Kirchenblatt* (1878–1904).

George W. Coleman

Oct. 10, 1830
Perry, New York

July 3, 1907
Gainesville, New York

General superintendent of Free Methodist Church, 1886–1903. He lived in Gainesville, NY, was converted as a youth, and was ordained in 1863. Coleman married Laura Warren on November 25, 1868. He served pastorates in the Genesee Conferences (1865–86), then transferred to the Wisconsin Conference (1886–1903). He was a man of unquestioned integrity and intense convictions.

Annie L. Walker Coghill

1836
Kiddermore, England

July 7, 1907
Bath, England

Wrote the hymn "Work, for the Night Is Coming" (1860) (music by LOWELL MASON), which was first published in 1868. Annie moved to Canada, where her father was a civil engineer. During this time, she and her sisters conducted a private school for girls, 1857–63. She then returned to England and became a governess and book reviewer. She married Harry Coghill in 1883 and they made their home near Hastings, England.

James McGranahan

July 4, 1840
near Adamsville, Pennsylvania

July 9, 1907
Kinsman, Ohio

Composed many outstanding hymns, including "Bringing Back the King," "Christ Returneth" (1878), "Sometime We'll Understand," "There Shall be Showers of Blessings" (1883), "I Know in Whom I Have Believed," "Christ Receiveth Sinful Men" (1883), "I Will Sing of My Redeemer" (1887), "The Banner of the Cross" (1889), "Verily, Verily," "Hallelujah for the Cross," and "Christ Liveth in Me." He wrote the lyrics and music to "Go Ye into All the World." McGranahan married Addie Vickery in 1863. After serving as a music teacher for a number of years, he replaced BLISS as the music director for the DAN WHITTLE crusades, 1877–87. He had a wonderful tenor voice, and a commanding personality, and was a pioneer in the use of men's choirs. His ministry ceased because of bad health.

William S. Hays

July 19, 1837
Louisville, Kentucky

July 23, 1907
Louisville, Kentucky

Wrote the music for the hymn, "The Lily of the Valley" (lyrics by CHARLES FRY). Hays was imprisoned by Union forces in New Orleans for writing songs sympathetic to the Confederacy. He worked on steamboats for several years, then joined the staff of the *Louisville Courier-Journal* (1868–98). During his lifetime, he wrote 300 songs. His most loved was "Mollie Darling," which sold one million copies. Hays was well known in Louisville, KY. He was married.

Robert S. Maclay

Feb. 7, 1824
Concord, Pennsylvania

Aug. 18, 1907
San Fernando, California

Pioneering Methodist mission leader in the Far East. Maclay worked in Foochow, China, 1846–72, then moved to Japan in 1872, where he opened the first Methodist mission. He married Henrietta Sperry (July 10, 1850), and Sarah Barr (June 6, 1882). He transferred his operations to Korea in 1884 to develop Methodist missions. He returned to the U.S. in 1888. He founded the Anglo-Chinese College in Foochow (1881), an Anglo-Japanese college in Tokyo (1883), and the Philander

Smith Biblical Institute in Tokyo (1884). He became dean of the Maclay College of Theology in San Fernando, CA (University of Southern California College of Religion, Los Angeles) in 1888.

John S. Norris

Dec. 4, 1844
West Cowles, Isle of Wight, England

Sept. 23, 1907
Chicago, Illinois

Composed music for "Where He Leads Me, I Will Follow" (lyrics by E. W. Blandy). During the period of 1868–78, Norris served Methodist churches in Canada, New York, and Wisconsin. He married Elizabeth Hurd in Canada in 1870. He became a Congregationalist and pastored in Wisconsin from 1878–82. He also held pastorates at several places in Iowa from 1882–1901, then moved to Chicago. He wrote over 100 hymns.

William B. Bodine

1840
Trenton, New Jersey

Sept. 28, 1907
Mount Pocono, Pennsylvania

Dean of Bexley Hall at Kenyon College (Colgate-Rochester (NY) Divinity School in 1968), **Gambier, OH 1876–85**. Bodine attended Princeton College. He was consecrated as an Episcopalian deacon (1864) and as a priest (1865). He pastored at Memorial Church in Baltimore, MD (1865–69); Christ Church in Brooklyn, NY (1871–76); and the Church of the Savior in Philadelphia, PA (1892–1907).

George C. Hugg

May 23, 1848
near Haddonfield, New Jersey

Oct. 13, 1907
Philadelphia, Pennsylvania

Composed music for "No, Not One" (lyrics by JOHNSON OATMAN). At age 12, Hugg was the director of the choir at the Presbyterian Church in Berlin, NJ. He moved to Philadelphia, PA and served both Tabernacle Presbyterian Church and Broad and Arch Methodist Church as their choirmaster. In later years, he was active in Harper Memorial Presbyterian Church for over 16 years. He composed music and published many collections of songs for Sunday school.

Daniel C. Roberts

Nov. 5, 1841
Bridgehampton, New York

Oct. 31, 1907
Concord, New Hampshire

Episcopalian hymn writer who wrote "God of Our Fathers," 1876 (music by George Warren). This song was published in 1894. After serving in Vermont and Massachusetts, Roberts became a vicar of St. Paul's Church, Concord, NH in 1878 where he served for 30 years. He was the president of the New Hampshire State Historical Society for several years.

Horatio R. Palmer

April 26, 1834
Sherburne, New York

Nov. 15, 1907
Yonkers, New York

Wrote the words and music for "Yield Not to Temptation" (1868), and composed music for "Come, Sinner, Come" (lyrics by W. E. Witter) **and "Master, the Tempest Is Raging," (1874)** (lyrics by MARY ANN BAKER). Palmer married Lucia Chapman in 1855. Then in 1857, he began leading the music department of Baptist Academy, Rushford, NY. After the Civil War, he settled in Chicago, IL, and served as editor of the *Concordia*. He also worked as the dean of summer school of music in Chatauqua, NY from 1877–91.

Priscilla J. Owens

July 21, 1829
Baltimore, Maryland

Dec. 5, 1907
Baltimore, Maryland

Wrote the powerful and beloved hymn "Jesus Saves" (1868) and "We Have an Anchor," 1882 (music by WILLIAM KIRKPATRICK for both). Priscilla was a public school teacher for 49 years in her hometown. She was a member of the Union Square Methodist Church and interested in Sunday school. Her literary efforts, both prose and poetical, appeared in many religious periodicals.

William T. Thomson
Lord Kelvin of Largs

June 26, 1824
Belfast, Ireland

Dec. 17, 1907
Netherhall, Scotland

Mathematician, physicist, and inventor. Known as Lord/Baron Kelvin, his real name was William Thomson. He entered Glasgow University at the age of ten and was matriculated one month later. Kelvin served as a professor of natural philosophy at Glasgow University, Scotland, 1846–99. He was in the Church of England. He was considered a leading physical scientist in his day and was involved in designing and laying the first transatlantic cable in 1858. He produced several inventions, including a ship's compass, which was largely free from the magnetic influence of the ship's iron. As a pioneer in thermodynamics (science of relationship between heat and mechanical work), he is best known for formulating the "Kelvin scale" of absolute temperature. He vigorously defended Christianity. He became chancellor of GU in 1904.

Edward G. Andrews

Aug. 7, 1825
New Hartford, New York

Dec. 31, 1907
Brooklyn, New York

Bishop of Methodist Episcopal Church, 1872–1904. He began his Methodist ministry in 1848. He served a pastorate in central New York for six years, and then became the principal of Cazenovia (NY) Seminary, 1854–62. He returned to the pastorate in Stamford, CT (1862–64); and Brooklyn, NY (1864–72). Andrews headquartered in Des Moines, IA (1877–80); Washington, D.C. (1880–88); and New York City (1888–1904). He traveled on behalf of missions to Europe and India (1876–77), Mexico (1881), Japan, Korea, and China (1889–90). He was a brilliant preacher, sound in doctrine, yet receptive to current trends. He is buried in Syracuse, NY.

Frank F. Ellinwood

June 20, 1826
Clinton, New York

1908
Cornwall, Connecticut (?)

Director of Presbyterian Church USA Missions, 1871–85. Ellinwood married Rowana Hurd on June 26, 1853, and after her death, married Laura Hurd on April 15, 1867. He pastored Second Presbyterian in Belvidere, NJ (1853–54), and Central Presbyterian in Rochester, NY (1854–65). He joined the staff of the Presbyterian Church in 1866. In his later years, he taught comparative religions at the University of New York City (1886–1904). He lived in Cornwall, CT. He wrote *Oriental Religions and Christianity* (1892) and *Questions and Phases of Modern Missions* (1899).

Adolf Hoenecke

Feb. 25, 1835
Brandenburg, Germany

Jan. 3, 1908
Wauwatosa, Wisconsin

President of Wisconsin Lutheran Seminary, Watertown, WI 1866–70; St. Louis, MO 1870–78; Milwaukee, WI 1878–92; and Wauwatosa (Nequon in 1929), **WI 1892–1908.** Hoenecke was a Lutheran pastor, professor, and synod organizer. He spent his elderly years in Switzerland, coming to America in 1863. He served as the founder of the Lutheran Wisconsin Synod, Watertown, WI, from 1866–70, and 1878–1908. From 1876–90, he also pastored at St. Matthew's, Milwaukee, WI, and also led a church in Missouri. His education made him the spiritual leader of the Wisconsin Synod until his death. For many years, he was the editor of *Gemeindeblatt* and founded the *Theologische Quartalschrift* in 1903. His life's work, *Dogmatik*, was published after his death. He was a strong, conservative leader and great expounder of the gospel.

George E. Merrill

Dec. 19, 1846 — *Jan. 11, 1908*
Charlestown, Massachusetts — Hamilton, New York

President of Colgate Theological Seminary [Colgate-Rochester (NY) Divinity School in 1928], **Hamilton, NY 1899–1908**. Merrill pastored Baptist churches in Springfield, MA (1872–77); Salem, MA (1877–85); Colorado Springs, CO (1885–87); and Immanuel Church, Newton, MA (1890–99). He authored several books, including *Crusaders and Captives* (1890) to a commentary, *Song of Solomon* (1905).

Jacob Chamberlain

April 13, 1835 — *March 2, 1908*
Sharon, Connecticut — Madanapalle, India

Dutch Reformed medical missionary to India. He married Charlotte Birge on Sept. 7, 1859. Chamberlain went to India (1859) and founded the Aricot Mission in Madras after arriving on April 12, 1860; then served at Palamanair (1860–63) and Madanapalle (1863–1901), establishing hospitals in both localities. He had 30,000 patients during his first ten years in India. He translated church literature into local dialects and also chaired the translation committee of the Bible into Telugu in 1873, serving on the American Bible committee for revision of the Telugu Bible, 1873–94. He founded a theological seminary at Madanapalle in 1887, which was reputed to be the first theological seminary on the mission field, and served as its principal, 1891–1902. He became the first moderator of the synod of South India in 1902. On one of his tours he contracted a jungle fever that weakened his health and by 1907 he was too weak to continue his ministry. His works range from *The Bible Tested* (1878) to *The Kingdom in India* (1908).

Charles H. Fowler

Aug. 11, 1837 — *March 20, 1908*
Burford (Clarendon), Ontario, Canada — New York, New York

Methodist missionary, educator, and bishop in 1884. From 1862–73, Fowler occupied pastorates in Chicago. He married Myra Hitchcock in 1868. He was the president of Northwestern University, 1873–76. He also served as editor of *Christian Advocate* (1876–80) and was the secretary of the Methodist Missionary Society (1880–84). He served in San Francisco, CA (1884–92); Minneapolis, MN (1892–96); Buffalo, NY (1896–1904); and New York City (1904–8). In 1887, he was one of the founders of Nebraska Wesleyan University, Lincoln, NE. During a world tour in 1888, he visited China, founded universities in Nanking and Peking, and opened the first Methodist church in Russia in the city of St. Petersburg (Leningrad). His writings range from *Fallacies of Colenso Reviewed* (1861) to *Patriotic Ovations* (pub. 1910).

Charles C. Hall

Sept. 3, 1852 — *March 25, 1908*
New York, New York — New York, New York

President of Union Theological Seminary, NYC 1897–1908. Hall married Jeanine S. Boyd on August 2, 1877. He pastored the Presbyterian church, Newburgh, NY (1875–77), and the First Church, Brooklyn, NY (1877–98). He ministered in India and the Far East (1902–3 and 1906–7), and wrote several books, including *Into His Marvelous Light* (1892) to *The Witness of the Oriental Consciousness to Jesus Christ* (1908).

Edward Abbott

July 15, 1841
Farmington, Maine

April 5, 1908
Boston, Massachusetts

Editor, clergyman, and writer in the American religious press. The son of Jacob Abbott, Edward Abbott pastored the Pilgrim Congregational Church in Cambridge, MA from 1865–69. He switched to Episcopalianism in 1879. He became the rector of St. James Church in Cambridge, MA from 1879–1906. He edited *The Congregationalist* (1869–78) and *Literary World* (1878–88 and 1895–1903). His writings range from *Baby's Things* (1871) to Phillips Brooks (1900).

Morgan Dix

Nov. 1, 1827
New York, New York

April 29, 1908
New York, New York

Episcopalian pastor and author. Ordained a deacon (1852) and a priest (1853), Dix assisted at St. Mark's in Philadelphia (1853) and at Trinity Church in NYC (1855), later becoming pastor there (1862). He published many books, including *The Gospel and Philosophy* (1886) and *Seven Deadly Sins* (1888). His writings range from *The Manual of the Christian Life* (1864) to *History of the Parish of Trinity Church, New York City* (4 vols., 1898–1906).

Phoebe Palmer Knapp

March 9, 1839
New York, New York

July 10, 1908
Poland Springs, Maine

Composed the music for 500 gospel tunes, including "Blessed Assurance" (1873). Phoebe had a large pipe organ in her elegant apartment in New York City's Hotel Savoy. She played a new melody for Fanny Crosby and then asked her to supply lyrics for it. In a few minutes, they had completed this great hymn. At age 16, she married Joseph F. Knapp, founder of the Metropolitan Life Insurance Company. They attended John Street Methodist Church in New York City. He died in 1891, leaving her an annual income of $50,000. She also wrote the music for "The Cleansing Wave," 1875 (lyrics by Phoebe Palmer).

Charles Bigg

Sept. 12, 1840
Manchester, England

July 15, 1908
Oxford, England

Church of England classical scholar, theologian, and historian. Bigg served as classical master in Cheltenham College (1866–71) and headmaster of Brighton College (1871–81). He also ministered as rector of Fenny Compton Church in Leamington (1887–1901), and was honorary canon of Worcester (1889–1901). In 1901, he began teaching church history at Oxford University. He authored *The Origins of Christianity* (1909), as well as his Bampton lecture of 1886, *The Christian Platonists of Alexandria*.

Henry C. Potter

May 25, 1834
Schenectady, New York

July 21, 1908
Cooperstown, New York

Episcopal bishop of New York. Potter laid the cornerstone for the massive Cathedral of St. John the Divine, NYC in 1892. He created a sensation on April 30, 1899, when he attacked the corruption of New York's infamous Tammany Hall administration in a great service at St. Paul's Chapel, New York. He was frequently called on by the city to arbitrate union disputes. He became rector at St. John's Church, Troy, NY (1859–66); at Grace Church, NY (1868–83); and became a bishop in 1886. In 1885, he inaugurated the Advent Mission, revival retreats for clergy and laymen. His writings range from *Sisterhoods and Deaconnesse*s (1871) to *Reminiscences of Bishops* (1906).

Winfield S. Weeden

March 29, 1847
Middleport, Ohio

July 31, 1908
Bisby Lake, New York

Composed music for "I Surrender All" (1896), "My Mother's Prayer," and "Sunlight," (1897) (all lyrics by JUDSON VAN DEVENTER). Weeden taught singing schools and later entered evangelistic work. He had a fine solo voice and was a talented song leader at various conventions. He compiled several collections of songs. He retired to New York City, where he owned a small hotel in lower Manhattan.

Fredrik Franson

July 17, 1852
Nora/Pershyttan, Sweden

Aug. 2, 1908
Idaho Springs, Colorado

Missionary-statesman, and first director of TEAM, 1890–1908. TEAM was known then as the Scandinavian Alliance Mission. Franson came to Nebraska in 1869. Then, in 1872, he moved to Chicago, where a prolonged illness and Romans 10:8 resulted in his conversion. In 1880, he started five churches in Colorado and Nebraska. Ordained on January 20, 1881, he became an evangelist. He traveled in Europe from 1881–90, and was imprisoned several times. He was a member of the Moody Church all his life and was a great soul winner and a man of faith, prayer, and piety. Many revivals in Europe are traced back to the prayers and preaching of Franson, as well as in other mission fields, 1901–8. He contributed to the founding of the Baptist General Conference, the Evangelical Covenant of America, the Evangelical Free Church of America, and several mission organizations. TEAM currently supports the work of 892 missionaries in 22 fields.

Ira D. Sankey

Aug. 28, 1840
Edinburgh, Pennsylvania

Aug. 13, 1908
Brooklyn, New York

Well-known Christian music personality. Sankey was converted in 1856 at a revival in the local King's Chapel Church. He moved to Newcastle in 1857, where he was active in the First Methodist Church. He married Fanny Edwards on September 9, 1863. He met MOODY at a YMCA convention meeting in Indianapolis, IN in 1870, and went to Chicago to assist MOODY there. He served as the music director and soloist in the MOODY crusades (1873–99), one of which was a highlighted tour of Great Britain (1873–75). Other crusades included Chicago, Boston, San Francisco, Baltimore, and St. Louis, 1875–81. His sight left him in 1903, but through this time he continued to write music. Sankey composed music for several great hymns, including "There'll Be No Dark Valley," "Trusting Jesus," "The Ninety and Nine," "I am Praying for You" (1874), "Grace, 'Tis a Charming Sound" (1875), "Faith is the Victory," "Hiding in Thee" (1877), "Shelter in the Time of Storm" (1888), "When the Mists Have Rolled Away" (1887), and "Under His Wings" (1896). He sold 50 million copies of his *Gospel Hymns and Sacred Songs*. The royalties from his six best-selling editions of *Gospel Hymns* were sent to finance MOODY's northern schools as well as several other Christian projects. He was a Methodist, and continued to be active with MOODY in crusades and Northfield activities. In 1898–99, he embarked on a 30-stop tour in Great Britain presenting "Sacred Song and Story." He died in his sleep.

Lewis H. Redner

Dec. 15, 1830
Philadelphia, Pennsylvania

Aug. 29, 1908
Atlantic City, New Jersey

Composed music for BROOKS' "O Little Town of Bethlehem." The music came to him in a dream on Christmas Eve in 1868. Redner was a wealthy real estate broker in Philadelphia, PA and served as the organist in four churches in that city. He also served as organist and superintendent of Sunday school at Holy Trinity Episcopal Church for 19 years. He saw the church grow from 36 to over 1,000. He never married and lived with his sister. He died after three days of illness.

Walter C. Smith

Dec. 5, 1824
Aberdeen, Scotland

Sept. 20, 1908
Kinbuck, Scotland

Wrote the hymn "Immortal, Invisible, God Only Wise." Smith was an ordained minister in the native Free Church of Scotland. He pastored at Chadwell Street, Illington, London (1850–57); Roxburgh Free Church, Glasgow, Scotland (1857–76); and the Free Church of Edinburgh, where he remained until his retirement (1876–94). He served as a moderator in 1893. He pastored for 44 years of his life.

Calvin W. Mateer

Jan. 9, 1836
near Mechanicsburg, Pennsylvania

Sept. 28, 1908
Tsingtau, China

Presbyterian missionary to China. Mateer went to the field in 1863, and spent most of his life there. He established a boys' school (1864), which developed into Shantung Christian College (1878). This was the first Christian College in China. He served as president of the college until 1895. He married Julia Brown on December 23, 1862 (died: 1898); and Ada Haven on September 23, 1900; in Chefoo, China. He was a master of language, a teacher, a mechanic, and an electrician. He worked on a translation of the Bible into Mandarin in 1907. He died of dysentery.

Daniel C. Gilman

July 6, 1831
Norwich, Connecticut

Oct. 13, 1908
Norwich, Connecticut

President of American Bible Society, 1903–08. From 1855–72, Gilman was a fundraiser, organizer, and professor at Yale Univerity's Sheffield Scientific School. He became the first president of the University of California (1872–75); then president of Johns Hopkins University, Baltimore, MD (1875–1901); and of Carnegie Hall (1901–4). He married Mary Ketcham in 1861 (died: 1869) and then Elizabeth Woolsey in 1877. He wrote several books ranging from *Life of James Monroe* (1883) to *Launching of a University* (1906).

Hiram Bingham Jr.

Aug. 16, 1831
Honolulu, Hawaii

Oct. 25, 1908
Baltimore, Maryland

Congregational (ABCFM) missionary to Micronesia. Bingham married Minerva C. Brewster on November 18, 1856. They went to the Gilbert Islands in 1857, and labored there until 1875 (except an 1865 furlough) at Abaiang. He lived in Honolulu after 1875 because of health reasons. They published a Bible in Gilbertese in 1890, as well as commentaries, hymn tunes, *Grammar* (1861), and a dictionary (1907). Bingham's father, HIRAM BINGHAM SR., was also a Pacific missionary. He wrote several commentaries in Gilbertese.

Philip Von Rohr

Feb. 13, 1843
Buffalo, New York

Dec. 22, 1908

President of Evangelical Lutheran Synod of Wisconsin (WELS in 1959), **1889–1908**. Rohr pastored in Winona, MN 1866–1908; where his church became the largest church in the state. He left the Buffalo Synod to form a separate body (1866) and was the last president of this entity, with its peaceful demise (1875). He joined the Wisconsin synod in 1877.

Joseph Spiers

1837

1909

Co-founder of Children's Special Service (Scripture) Union in 1879. Spiers was a leading voice along with TOM BISHOP until about 1900. In 1867, he took a group from his north London Sunday School to a special children's service at St. John Baptist Chapel in the West End. Payson Hammond was conducting a unique children's service that inspired Spiers. He immediatly started a children's meeting in his home on Sunday and, after one year, expanded it to St. Jude's Church, Mildmay, in the East End. He had 300 children coming after one year. He and THOMAS BISHOP joined forces, and soon he was able to resign his job and devote the next 40 years of his life to CSS. In 1880, they started using cards that were titled "Commitment to Read the Bible Daily." By 1885, they were simply called "The Scripture Union." This grew to a world-wide ministry, and by 1889, 500,000 members were reading the Scriptures daily in 28 languages.

Egerton R. Young

April 7, 1840
Smith's Falls/Crosby, Canada

1909
Bradford, Ontario, Canada

Methodist minister and missionary. Young was sent to a mission station called Norway House, Manitoba. There he served among the Indians for five years, 1868–73. He then ministered at Beren's River mission station for three years. He returned to Ontario and served as a missionary evangelist, 1876–88, later touring, speaking, and writing on the work with the Methodist Indian Missions, 1888 on. He was married. His writings range from *By Canoe and Dog-Train* (1890) to *Battle of the Bears* (1907).

Selah Merrill

May 2, 1837
Canton Center, Connecticut

Jan. 22, 1909
Andover, Massachusetts

Congregational archaeologist. Merrill was a chaplain in the Civil War (1864–65), studied in Germany (1868–70), traveled in the Holy Land with the American Palestine Exploration Society (1875–77) and the U.S. Consul to Jerusalem, 1882–86, 1891–94, and 1898–1905. During those years, he made discoveries that settled the location of the second wall of the city. The site of Calvary depended on this finding. He wrote several books including *East of the Jordan* (1881–83) to *Ancient Jerusalem* (1906).

Henry G. Weston

Sept. 11, 1820
Lynn, Massachusetts

Feb. 6, 1909
Upland, Pennsylvania

First president of Crozier Theological Seminary [Colgate-Rochester (NY) Divinity School in 1970], **Chester, PA 1868–1909**. Weston married Endamile VanMeter in 1845. He was ordained a Baptist. He held several pastorates; including Washington and Richland, IL (1843–46); Peoria, IL (1846–59); and Oliver Street, New

York City (1859–68). He edited the *Baptist Quarterly* (1869–77). He also authored several books, including *The Communion Lectures* (1867) to *Matthew* (1900).

Theodore L. Cuyler

Jan. 10, 1822
Aurora, New York

Feb. 26, 1909
Brooklyn, New York

Author and clergyman who ministered at Lafayette Avenue Presbyterian Church, Brooklyn, NY 1860–90. Cuyler pastored in Ohio (1846–49) and at Third Presbyterian, Trenton, NJ (1849–53). Although his work was overshadowed by BEECHER and TALMAGE, this trio had three great Brooklyn churches simultaneously. He married Annie Mathiot in 1853. He was the leader in the revival of 1858 while pastoring at Market St. Reformed Church in NYC from 1853–60. His last years were spent in literary and reformed work. His 22 written works range from *Pointed Papers for the Christian Life* (1878) to *Our Christmastides* (1904).

Daniel March

July 21, 1816
Millbury, Massachusetts

March 2, 1909
Woburn, Massachusetts

Pastor. March was a Congregationalist and ordained in 1845. He served in Cheshire, CT (1845–48); Nashua, NH (1848–54); Philadelphia, PA (1861–76); and in Woburn, MA (1855–61 and 1876–93). His Philadelphia pastorate was Presbyterian. He was interested in missionary endeavors around the world. He married Jane P. Gilson (1841), and Anna B. LaConte (1878). His writings range from *Religion for Heart and Home* (1858) to *Morning Light in Many Lands* (1891).

William W. Rand

Dec. 8, 1816
Gorham, Maine

March 3, 1909
New York, New York

General secretary of American Tract Society, 1892–1902. Upon graduating from Bangor Theological Seminary (1840), Rand became a Reformed Church minister (1841). He lived in New York City, then pastored in northern New York, 1841–48. He was an editor for ATS (1848), and began secretarial work (1862), editing all books, tracts, and periodicals. He authored *Bible Dictionary* (1860–77). He was publishing secretary from 1872 on. On the afternoon preceeding his death, he corrected proofs of a Spanish Sunday school paper. He had poetic gifts and was a linguist.

Marianne Hearn

Dec. 17, 1834
Farmingham, England

March 16, 1909
Barmouth, Wales

Wrote the hymn "Just As I Am, Thine Own to Be." Marianne was an active member of College Street Baptist Church in Northampton and taught a large Bible class for young women. She was on the editorial staff of several papers and often wrote under the pen name of "Marianne Faringham." Her literary works total 20 volumes.

Charles H. H. Wright

March 9, 1836
Dublin, Ireland

March 22, 1909
London, England

Anglican clergyman. Wright was curate of Middleton-Tyas (1859–63), chaplain of English church in Dresden (1863–68), and of Holy Trinity, Boulogne-Sur-Mer (1868–73); incumbent of St. Mary's, Dublin (1874–85); and of Bethesda Church, Dublin (1885–91); vicar of St. John's, Liverpool (1891–98); Bampton lecturer at Oxford (1878); Donnellan lecturer at Dublin (1880); and was the annual, famous Grimfield lecturer on the

Septuagint at Oxford (1893–97). He wrote many pamphlets against Catholicism and was a strong evangelical. His writings range from *Grammar of the Modern Irish Language* (1855) to *Light from Egyptian Papyri* (1908).

Anders S. Nielsen

April 6, 1832
Saaby, Denmark

March 26, 1909
Withee, Wisconsin

President of Danish Evangelical Lutheran Church (LCA, ELCA in 1988), **1879–83, 1885–87 and 1891–94.** Nielsen immigrated to the USA in 1871. His wife's name was Johanna. He was ordained on November 17, 1871, having been a lay preacher in Denmark. He pastored in Cedar Falls and Fredsville, IA (1872–79); at Trinity Church, Chicago, IL (1879–93); and Withee, WI (1893–1903). He was one of the four founders of the DELC.

Marcus Dods

April 11, 1834
Belford, England

April 1909
Edinburgh, Scotland

Free Church of Scotland clergyman and Biblical scholar. Dods was ordained in 1864 and began his ministry at Renfield Free Church in Glasgow. He remained there until he began teaching NT theology at New College, Edinburgh, in 1889, where he popularized modern biblical scholarship. In 1891, he was acquitted of heresy charges brought against him. In 1907, he was principal of his own college. He did accept higher criticism, which leaned the Scottish Presbyterians toward liberalism. His works range from *The Prayer That Teaches to Pray* (1863) to *The Bible's Origin and Nature* (1905). He edited LANGE's *Life of Christ* and *The Works of* AUGUSTINE. He wrote commentaries on *Genesis* and *I Corinthians* in *Exposition's Bible*.

Sheldon Jackson
"Apostle to Alaska"

May 18, 1834
Minaville, New York

May 2, 1909
Asheville, North Carolina

Presbyterian frontier missionary pioneer in Alaska. Jackson married Mary Voorhees on May 18, 1858. From 1859–69, he was a home missionary in Wisconsin and Minnesota. In 1869, he became the missionary superintendent in six Rocky Mountain states which were dominated by Mormons. He went there in 1870, opening several schools and churches. He first went to Alaska in 1877, as a government employee, to open schools for whites, Indians, and Eskimos. He then became superintendent of missions in Sitka, Alaska, to evangelize the people living in those vast, remote, frozen stretches of the North. He was there from 1884–1907. He died following surgery. In 1892, he introduced reindeer into Alaska.

Erastus Johnson

April 20, 1826
Lincoln, Maine

June 16, 1909
Waltham, Massachusetts

Wrote the hymn "Rock That Is Higher Than I" (1873) (music by WILLIAM FISCHER). Johnson, in poor health after his Bangor (ME) Theological Seminary studies, took a sea voyage to California and moved there. He lived in the West for 20 years, spending eight years as a California rancher and eleven years farming in Washington State. He then returned to the East and worked in the oil industry for 20 years, retiring to Waltham, MA.

Will L. Thompson

Nov. 7, 1847
East Liverpool, Ohio

Sept. 20, 1909
New York, New York

Wrote the lyrics and music for several beloved hymns, including "Softly and Tenderly" (1899), "Jesus is All the World to Me" (1904) "There's a Great Day Coming," and "Lead Me Gently Home, Father." *Who's Who* gives Beaver Co, PA as Thompson's birthplace and music biography collections gives East Liverpool, OH. He established a successful publishing firm in East Liverpool and Chicago. He married Elizabeth Johnson on April 23, 1891. He visited dying MOODY, who praised his songs.

George E. Post

Dec. 17, 1838
New York, New York

Sept. 29, 1909
Beirut, Lebanon

Presbyterian medical missionary in Lebanon, 1863–1909. Post married Sarah Reed on September 17, 1863 and went to Tripoli, Lebanon. He became a well-known teacher, physician, botanist, and linguist in the Middle East. He served from 1869–1909 on the faculty of the Syrian Protestant College (American University) as professor of surgery. He also wrote many books on Syria, Palestine, medicine, and various topics.

Dudley Buck

March 10, 1839
Hartford, Connecticut

Oct. 6, 1909
West Orange, New Jersey

Composer, organist, and music teacher. Buck was the organist at North Congregational Church, Hartford, CT while teaching and composing, 1862–75. He also served at St. James Episcopal Church, Chicago, IL; St. Paul's Church, Boston, MA; and the Music Hall Association, Boston, MA. He pastored at Holy Trinity Church, Brooklyn, NY from 1875–1903. He wrote many music books, anthems, cantatas, and church organ music.

Henry C. Lea

Sept. 19, 1825
Philadelphia, Pennsylvania

Oct. 24, 1909
Philadelphia, Pennsylvania

Publisher and church historian, active in public affairs, interested in good government, and church history. Lea married his cousin, Anna Jardon, on May 27, 1850. He worked in the publishing business (Lea and Blanchard, Philadelphia), 1843–47 and 1860–80. He developed a large collection of books and manuscripts and donated them to the University of Pennsylvania. He also acquired millions of dollars in real estate. His retirement in 1880 was because of poor health, and allowed him to study and write *The Rest of the Night*. He wrote the four-volume *History of the Inquisition of Spain* (1906), but his greatest work was *History of the Inquisition in the Middle Ages* (3 vols., 1888).

William A. Alexander

Jan. 19, 1857
Kosciusko, Mississippi

Nov. 15, 1909
Memphis, Tennessee

Stated clerk of Presbyterian Church in U.S. (USA in 1983), **1898–1909**. Alexander pastored in MS: Lexington, Yazoo City (1879–84), and Canton (1884–92). He married Ora Reid on Oct. 15, 1890. He became the professor of biblical languages and literature at Southwestern Presbyterian University in Clarksville, TN, 1892–1909. He died in a train station on the way from Clarksville to Yazoo City for the Mississippi Synod annual meeting.

Charles N. Crittendon

Feb. 20, 1833
Henderson, New York

Nov. 16, 1909
San Francisco, California

Businessman, evangelist, and philanthropist, Crittendon moved to New York and established a pharmaceutical company, 1861–82. In 1882, he was converted when his four-year-old daughter, Florence, died. He felt a need to evangelize the slums, so opened a mission and home for women. In 1890, he launched his welfare and evangelism program. His chain of mission homes for homeless women, known as the Florence Crittendon homes, numbered 75 by his death.

George P. Fisher

Aug. 10, 1827
Wrentham, Massachusetts

Dec. 20, 1909
Litchfield, Connecticut

Congregational clergyman and historian with a lifetime ministry at Yale University. Fisher served as college pastor and professor of divinity (1854–61), college preacher (1861–64), professor of church history for 40 years (1861–1901), and dean (1895–1901). He was the president of the American Historical Association in 1898. He authored several books ranging from *Supernatural Origin of Christianity* (1865) to *EDWARDS on the Trinity* (1903). He leaned towards liberalism but stressed that church historians were to be impartial and accurate in their findings.

Samuel O. G. Clough (Cluff)

1837
Dublin, Ireland

1910
Timahoe, Ireland

Wrote the hymn "I Am Praying for You" (1860). Clough was ordained as a minister in the Church of Ireland and became a pastor in Torquay, Ireland. He published a series of songs under the title, *Tomogue Leaflets*. He graduated from Trinity College in 1862. In 1874, he became associated with the Plymouth Brethren. His family name is sometimes spelled "Cluff."

Andrew R. Fausset

Oct. 13, 1821
Silverhill, Ireland

1910

Church of England clergyman belonging to the Evangelical School movement. Fausset served a church position in Durham (1847–59), then became rector of St. Cuthbert in York, England (1859–1910). He served as the canon of York after 1885. He helped in writing famed commentaries on the team of JAMIESON, Fausset, and BROWN. His writings range from *Scripture and the Prayer Book in Harmony* (1854) to *Study of the Book of Common Prayer* (1894).

Robert Flint

March 14, 1838
Dumfries, Scotland

1910

Presbyterian philosopher and theologian who was active in the Church of Scotland. Flint was employed in lay mission work for a number of years, then licensed to preach in 1858. He served as parish minister in Aberdeen and Kilconquhar, 1859–64. He then taught at St. Andrews (1864–76) and was professor of divinity at the University of Edinburgh (1876–1903). His writings range from *Christ's Kingdom on Earth* (1865) to *On Theological Biblical and Other Subjects* (1905).

Wayland Hoyt

Feb. 18, 1838
Cleveland, Ohio

1910
Philadelphia, Pennsylvania (?)

Baptist pastor, scholar, and author. He married Maud Mansfield in 1864. Hoyt served in Pittsfield, MA (1863); at 9th St., Cincinnati, OH (1864–67); at Strong Place, Brooklyn, NY (1868–81); in Philadelphia, PA (1882–89 and 1896–1905); and in Minneapolis, MN (1890–96). After 1896, he taught at the Theological Seminary of Temple College, Philadelphia, PA. He authored several books ranging from *Hints and Helps in the Christian Life* (1880) to *Teaching of Jesus* (1907).

Timothy R. Matthews

Nov. 4, 1826
Colmworth, England

Jan. 5, 1910
Tetney, England

Composed the music for "Thou Didst Leave Thy Throne." Matthews tutored at Windsor and had a lifelong friendship with George Elvey, who studied organ under him. He held the curator position at St. Mary's, Nottingham (1859), then was rector at North Coates until his retirement (1907). He compiled more than 100 hymn tunes and edited several hymn collections.

James Boyce (2)

Jan. 25, 1860
Gaston, County, North Carolina

Jan. 27, 1910
Due West, South Carolina?

Stated clerk of Associate Reformed Presbyterian Church, Greenville, SC 1891–1909. Boyce married Jennie Thompson on October 17, 1883. He pastored in Louisville, KY (1882–97) and Huntersville, NC (1897–99). He served as president of Due West (SC) Female College (Women's College of Due West), 1899–1910. He worked as the editorial associate of the Reformed Presbyterian (1896) and assistant clerk of the ARC (1897).

George B. Addicks

Sept. 9, 1854
Hampton, Illinois

Jan. 31, 1910
Warrenton, Missouri

President of German Seminary, Central Wesleyan College, Warrenton, MO (Northeast State Teachers College, Kirksville, MO), 1895–1910. Addicks was ordained a Methodist in 1878. He married Mary W. Wellemeyer on June 26, 1884. He also taught practical theology and philosophy at the school, 1890–1910.

Harriet E. Peck Buell

Nov. 2, 1834
Cazenovia, New York

Feb. 6, 1910
Washington, D.C.

Wrote the touching hymn "A Child of the King" (1876) (music by JOHN SUMNER). Harriet was a regular contributor to *Northern Christian Advocate* in Syracuse, NY for 50 years. She made her home in Manlius, NY and was an active member of the Methodist Church. In 1898, she moved to Washington, DC, but maintained a summer home in Thousand Island Park, NY.

Cornelius H. Wedel

May 12, 1860
Margenau, Germany

March 28, 1910
Newton, Kansas

First president of Bethel College, North Newton, KS 1893–1910. Wedel was also a minister and historian. His family migrated to Goessel, KS in 1879, where he taught school, 1879–80. At age 18, he was baptized. In 1890, he was ordained in the Mennonite Church and taught school for three years at Halstead, KS. He married Susanna Richert on March 30, 1891. In

1896 and 1898, he made extensive trips to Germany, the Netherlands, Switzerland, and Russia for research in the denomination's history. He taught Bible, church history, Mennonite history, and German literature. He also pastored the Bethel College Mennonite Church, 1897–1910.

Enoch Eby

Nov. 15, 1828
Juanita County, Pennsylvania

April 26, 1910
Leni, Illinois

Moderator of Church of the Brethren for eleven years between 1878–1895. In 1847, Eby married Hettie Howe (died: 1861) and, in 1864, Annie Gilfillen. He had nine children. In 1855, he moved to Illinois where he frequently assisted organizing new congregations. He helped found the Domestic and Foreign Mission Board (1880), serving as chairman/president from 1880–85 and 1893–99. He was an effective public speaker.

Henry H. Jessup

April 19, 1832
Montrose, Pennsylvania

April 28, 1910
Beirut, Lebanon

Missionary to Syria and Lebanon, who first served in Tripoli from 1856–60, then was sent to Beirut. In 1870, Jessup transferred from the American Board of Commissioners for Foreign Missions to the Presbyterian Board of Foreign Missions. He became a professor at Syria Theological Seminary in Beirut. He married Carolina Bush (July 7, 1833–July 2, 1864) on Oct. 7, 1857; Harriet Dodge (born: Aug. 8, 1836) on Oct. 1, 1868; and later, Theodosia Lockwood in August, 1884. He lived in Tripoli, Abeih, and Beirut. He edited the *Arabic Journal* and wrote books about Mid-East missions, from *The Woman of the Arabs* (1873) to *53 Years in Syria* (2 vols., 1910).

Emil Schurer

May 2, 1844
Germany

April 30, 1910

New Testament scholar in Biblical studies, especially Judaism. Schurer is also famous for his monumental five-volume work *A History of the Jewish People in the Time of Jesus Christ* (1890–91). He taught at Leipzig (1869–78), Giessen (1878–90), Kiel (1890–95), and Gottingen (1895–1910).

Alexander MacLaren

Feb. 11, 1826
Glasgow, Scotland

May 5, 1910
Edinburgh, Scotland

First president of Baptist World Alliance, 1905, and Baptist pastor at Union Chapel in Manchester, England, 1858–1903. MacLaren was converted at age 14, and may have been the greatest expository preacher ever, excluding G. CAMPBELL MORGAN. His crowds were second only to SPURGEON's. His church seated 2,000. He read a chapter of the Bible in Greek and Hebrew each day. He married his cousin, Marion MacLaren, in 1856. He ministered at Portland Chapel in Southampton from 1846–58. His published sermons, preached in Manchester from 1864–73 (21 vols.) are still used. In 1883, he went to Australia for a preaching mission. He moved back to Scotland in 1909. He also published *Pulpit Prayers* (1909).

Anna L. Waring

April 19, 1823
Plas-Y-Velin, Wales

May 10, 1910
Clifton, England

Wrote several hymns, including "In Heavenly Love Abiding" and "Jesus, Lord of Heaven Alone." Anna was an Anglican with a gentle spirit and a merry, quiet humor. She learned Hebrew and read the Hebrew Psaltery daily. She started writing hymns in her teen years. She supported the Discharged Prisoners' Aid Society and often visited Bristol prisons.

Henry G. Guinness, Sr.

Aug. 11, 1835
Montpelier House, Ireland

June 21, 1910
Bath, Ireland

Evangelist, writer and head of East London Institute for Missions (Regions Beyond Missionary Union in 1899), **1873–1887.** He also founded the Livingston Inland Mission, 1880 in the Congo and other missions in South America and Sudan. Guinness was a foreign missions promoter. Having been converted in 1853 through his brother's witness, he became an evangelist in 1857, beginning in Wales. While traveling as a missionary evangelist from 1857–72, he married Fanny Fitzgerald on October 2, 1860 (died: November 3, 1898). In 1872, he established Harley House, London (missions college). Its first missionaries were sent out in 1875. From 1873–87, he headed the ELIM. During this time, he started a missions magazine (1878) and lost two daughters to diphtheria (1879). When he finished up with ELIM (1887), he wrote his first book. In 1899, he united various missionary enterprises under RBMU, supporting 100 missionaries and sending out 1,000 more. Guinness married Grace Hurditch in 1903 and toured the world for missions, 1903–7, before retiring in Bath. He was a student of prophecy and a gifted devotional speaker.

Florence Nightingale
Lady with the Lamp

May 12, 1820
Florence, Italy

Aug. 13, 1910
London, England

Founder of modern nursing. Florence felt the call of God to develop this field. In 1851, she trained with the Protestant deaconesses at Kaiserwerth, Germany. In 1853, she headed a Hospital for invalid gentlewomen in London. Then in 1854, she, with 38 nurses, went to the Crimean War zone in Scutari (Uskvdar) Turkey to organize the care of wounded English soldiers. She assisted there, coping with unbelievable conditions. Her focus on sanitation and the necessity for a disciplined, organized staff changed nursing practices. She founded a school at the St. Thomas and Wings College Hospitals in London upon her return in 1856. She wrote the first nursing textbook, *Notes on Nursing* (1860) and made nursing a respectable career. She continued to advise on health care in the American Civil War (1861–65) and the Franco-Prussian War (1870–71). She was an invalid the last twenty years of her life. She was an Anglican and never married. Her favorite Bible verse was Matthew 17:4.

Cornelius E. Crispell

March 14, 1820
Marbletown, New York

Aug. 29, 1910
Gardiner, New York

President of Faculty (CEO) of Western Theological Seminary, Holland, MI 1869–79. Crispell pastored at Piermouth, NY (1857–63); was a professor at Rutgers College, New Brunswick, NJ (1863–66); and Hope College (1866–77). He then pastored in Spring Valley, NY, 1879–1905.

W. Holman Hunt

April 2, 1827
London, England

Sept. 7, 1910
London, England

Painter of Christian themes and famous for his *The Light of the World* (Revelation 3:20: Jesus knocking on the door), 1851–54, which has been placed in Keble College, Oxford. Hunt also painted *Christ Among the Doctors, Nazareth,* and *Our Savior Entering the Temple.* He initiated the Pre-Raphaelite Brotherhood in 1848 (artists attempting to paint realistically rather than adhering to the dogmatic rules of art as defined by Raphael). He went to Palestine in 1854 and 1875 to study local color for his paintings. A stay in Italy brought forth works illustrating John Keats' poems. The writer, JOHN RUSKIN, supported him as he traveled in Europe. He is buried in St. Paul's Cathedral, London.

William Raws

Oct. 7, 1854
Melbourne, Australia

Sept. 18, 1910
Keswick Grove, New Jersey

First director of America's Keswick Conventions, Whiting, NJ 1897–1910. Raws moved to northern England as a teen, religious but unsaved. He married in 1879, but became an alcholic for about ten years. His mother and wife died during that time. When he came to the states and was converted, he began witnessing in the Germantown, PA, area. He remarried, started a mission, and purchased 880 acres near Whiting, NJ to establish Keswick Colony. The term "Keswick" means conventions. Initially they represented a gathering of Christians from a Reformed background, mainly evangelical Anglicans, who gathered to share the power of prayer. During the MOODY/SANKEY revivals, they became annual summer gatherings of evangelicals with an emphasis on reverent Bible study, an enthusiasm for foreign missions, and a purpose to encourage "practical holiness."

Heinrich J. Holtzmann

June 17, 1832
Karlsruhe, Germany

Oct. 4, 1910
Baden-Baden, Germany

Gifted biblical scholar who was a professor of NT exegesis at Strasbourg, 1874–1904. In NT studies Holtzmann introduced the idea that Mark was the oldest of the Synoptic Gospels and traced the sources of the present Gospel accounts. His scholarship and conclusions were reflected in his exegetical studies, 1863–1910. He wrote extensively and pastored at Baden (1854–57), taught NT exegesis at Heidelberg (1858–74), and at Strasbourg (1874–1904). He wrote many German books.

John E. Clough

1836
Frewsbury, New York

Nov. 23, 1910
Rochester, New York

Baptist missionary to India. As a converted skeptic, Clough went to India in 1865 with his wife and son. In 1866, he took up residence with the Telugus, living in Ongole. This became the center of his work, ministering among the outcast Madigas in some 400 villages. His ministry started with only eight converts, but soon there were thousands. He labored to help in time of famine, 1876–78. In 1878, under his direction, 3,536 converts were baptized in three days. That same year, 9,966 members were added to the church, making 13,000 baptized members. By 1883, his ministry had 21,000 members; and by retirement in 1901, after 40 years of work, he had 55,000 converts. He and his first wife, Harriet Sunderland, ministered until 1893 when she died. He then married Emma Rauschenbush (1859–1940), retired in 1905, and stayed in India until 1910.

Robert Murray

Dec. 25, 1832
Earlstown, Nova Scotia, Canada

Dec. 10, 1910
Halifax, Nova Scotia, Canada

Presbyterian hymn writer and one of the most influential ministers in the Maritime Provinces. Because of his literary skill, Murray was appointed editor of *Presbyterian Witness* and served in that position for more than 50 years. He wrote several hymns, including "From Ocean unto Ocean."

Ulrik V. Koren

Dec. 22, 1826
Bergen, Norway

Dec. 19, 1910
Decorah, Iowa

President of Norwegian Synod (ALC, ECLA in 1988), **1894–1910.** Koren married Elsie E. Hysing on Aug. 18, 1853. He then came to America and began pastoring at Washington Prairie from 1853–1910. He became a member of the Church Council of Norwegian Synod in 1861, and was vice president of the Iowa district, 1876–94. He procured the campus for Luther College, Decorah, IA, teaching there, 1874–75.

Clara A. Swain

July 18, 1834
Elmira, New York

Dec. 25, 1910
Castile, New York

First woman missionary doctor and Methodist pioneer missionary, who, in 1869, went to Bareilly, India, with ISABELLA THOBURN. Clara worked for 14 years (1870–84), going back to America for health reasons (1876–79), after opening the first women's hospital in Asia in 1872. She was said to be the first woman physician sent by a missionary society to a non-Christian world. She was in Khetri State from 1885–95, a physician in the palace of the Rajah (Rani Saheba). A Mogul ruler, impressed by her dedication, gave her 40 acres of land, including a palatial residence. She continued her work in India then returned again to America in 1896, retiring in Castile. She returned to India, 1906–8.

Gustav A. Warneck

March 6, 1834
Naumberg, Germany

Dec. 26, 1910
Halle, Germany

Lutheran historian of missions. He founded a mission journal in 1874. Warneck served many years as a pastor at Raitzsch, Dommitsch, Rothenschirmbach (1875–96), then became a professor of missions at the University of Halle (1896–1908). In 1879, he founded and became the first president of the Saxon Provincial Missionary Conference, which began holding regular missions conferences in churches. He also served as the secretary of the Committee of German Missions, 1885–1901. After retiring in 1896, he was made honorary professor of missions at Halle. He wrote much on mission topics and is considered by some to be the founder of modern missiology.

James C. Hepburn

March 13, 1815
Milton, Pennsylvania

1911
East Orange, New Jersey (?)

Presbyterian medical missionary to the East, Hepburn went to Singapore (1841–43) and to Amoy, China (1843–46). He married Clara Leete in October, 1840 (died: 1906). From 1846–59, he practiced medicine in New York City because of his wife's poor health. He went to Yokohama, Japan (1859), and stayed there until his retirement (1892). He was an educator, a physician, and a surgeon. He wrote the *Japanese and English Dictionary* (1867). He also had a key role in translating the Bible into Japanese.

Samuel A. Ort

Nov. 11, 1843
Lewistown, Pennsylvania

Jan. 6, 1911
Springfield, Ohio

President of Wittenberg College, Springfield, OH (Trinity Lutheran Seminary, Columbus, OH), **1882–1900**. Ort married Ann E. Senteny on September 23, 1875. He was ordained a Lutheran in 1865 and pastored in Louisville, KY (1874–78), and NYC (1878–80). He served as a professor of theology at Wittenberg, 1880–1910. He was also the president of the General Synod in 1887. He was an orator of note and an inspiring teacher.

Charles J. Little

Sept. 21, 1840
Philadelphia, Pennsylvania

March 11, 1911

President of Garret Biblical Institute (GETS in 1974), **Evanston, IL 1895–1911**, and professor of theology there, 1891–1911. Little married Anna M. Schultze in Berlin, Germany on December 3, 1872. He was ordained a Methodist in 1862, then held pastorates in Newark, DE (1862–63), and in Philadelphia area churches (1863–74). He was a professor of philosophy and history at Dickinson College (1874–85), of logic and history at Syracuse University (1885–91), and of theology at GBI (1891–1911).

Joseph Y. Peek

Feb. 27, 1843
Schenectady, New York

March 17, 1911
Brooklyn, New York

Composed music for "I Would Be True" (lyrics by HOWARD WALTER). Peek was a carpenter, farmer, and druggist's clerk prior to serving with the Union forces in the Civil War. From 1881–1904, he worked as a florist. He was a Methodist lay preacher who ministered in many places. He was ordained on January 22, 1911, less than two months before his death. He played the piano, banjo, and violin.

Thomas S. Hastings

Aug. 28, 1827
Utica, New York

April 2, 1911
New York, New York

President of Union Theological Seminary, NYC 1887–97. Hastings married Fanny de Groot on July 1, 1852, and was ordained as a Presbyterian the same year. He held pastorates in Mendham, NJ (1852–56) and West Church, NY (1856–82). Then he became professor of sacred rhetoric and pastoral theology at Union (1882–1904) and a lecturer on pastoral theology (1904–11). He was the son of the famed hymn writer, THOMAS HASTINGS.

Hannah H. Whitall Smith

Feb. 7, 1832
Philadelphia, Pennsylvania

May 1, 1911
Iffley, England

Quaker (until 1859), philanthropist and author, who wrote many devotional works, the most famous was *The Christian's Secret of a Happy Life* (1875) with over two million copies sold. Hannah married Robert P. Smith in 1851; they had five children. They were both converted in 1858 under Plymouth Brethren influence, which she joined. In 1867, she received the "second blessing." She conducted Bible classes in her Philadelphia home. They went to England (1873–74), then came back to America (1875–95), returning to England again, 1895. She authored *God of All Comfort* (1901) and was a pioneer in the English Keswick movement. The Keswick Convention, founded in 1874, was a result of their meetings. Hannah was active in women suffrage and temperance causes, a founder of the WCTU in 1874. Unfortunately, one of her daughters married atheist philosopher, Bertrand Russell. She died in the home of her bachelor son, Logan.

Arabella C. (Katherine) Hankey

1834
Clapham, England

May 9, 1911
London, England

Wrote the lyrics to the gospel songs "Tell Me the Old, Old Story" and "I Love to Tell the Story." Both were written in 1866. Arabella taught in Sunday school and organized a Bible study among working girls. She made a trip to South Africa to bring home her invalid brother. Royalties from her publications were given to missions. Her 100 hymns include her 55-stanza poem on the life of Christ. She spent her last years in a hospital visitation ministry.

Arthur T. (A. T.) Pierson

March 6, 1837
New York, New York

June 3, 1911
Brooklyn, New York

Great pastor and Bible expositor. Pierson married Sarah Benedict on July 12, 1860. He pastored a Presbyterian Church, Waterford, NY (1863–69); Fort Street Presbyterian Church, Detroit, MI (1869–82); and Bethany Tabernacle, Philadelphia, PA (1883–89). He edited *Missionary Review of the World* (1888 on). He became a Baptist in 1891. In 1892, he was called to succeed CHARLES SPURGEON at London's Tabernacle. He served until 1893, after which he lectured at MBI. From 1893–1901, he was president of Gordon College and Divinity School in Boston. Pierson was baptized by immersion in 1896, which severed former ties. He lectured in Exeter Hall, London, 1904–7. He often spoke at MOODY's Northfield Conferences and The Student Volunteer Movement, which began in 1886 after a young man responded to a message about being a missionary. Pierson Bible College in Seoul, Korea was founded in his honor. He died upon returning from an Orient trip. He authored 14 books, his writings ranging from *The Crisis in Missions* (1886) to *Godly Self-Control* (1909).

Carry Moore Gloyd Nation

Nov. 25, 1846
Garrard County, Kentucky

June 9, 1911
Leavenworth, Kansas

Saloon-smashing prohibition fanatic. Converted at age ten, Carry helped rally crusades to curb alcoholism. She was embittered by a miserable first marriage to an alcoholic (Charles Gloyd on Nov. 21, 1867), who died soon after their marriage. She married Rev. David Nation in 1877. By 1899, she was active in crusading against saloons. She walked into the Hotel Casey Ballroom in Wichita, KA in 1901, with a swinging hatchet, destroying liquor supplies and saloon property. Her husband divorced her that same year for desertion. In 1908, she lectured in Britain. She was six feet tall and a very heavy woman. She was imprisoned 30 different times and shot at. She built a home for drunkard's wives in Kansas City. She also opposed corsets, short skirts, and smoking.

Francis Paget

Mar. 20, 1851
London, England

Aug. 2, 1911
London, England

Scholar and pastor. Paget was a high churchman who came from a simple background— a boy that rread his Bible daily at a public school. From 1869–77, he divided his time between Christ Church College, Oxford, and vacationing in London. He married Helen Church on March 28, 1883 and pastored at Bromsgrove, 1883–85. Paget was made canon of Christ Church, 1892–1900, the year his wife died. He was appointed bishop of Oxford (May 1901), serving until illness curtailed his activities (June 1910). From 1885–92, he was professor of pastoral theology at Oxford.

Daniel K. Flickinger

May 25, 1824
Seven Mile, Ohio

Aug. 29, 1911
Columbus, Ohio

Director of Church of the United Brethren in Christ Missions, Huntington, IN 1857–85, 1897–1905. Flickinger married Mary Lintner on February 25, 1847 (died 1851), then Catherine Glossbrenner on July 9, 1853 (died: August, 1854). He later married Susan Woolsey on Oct. 30, 1855. He was a foreign missionary bishop, 1885–1911, and during that time made twelve missionary tours to Africa, five to Germany, and then wrote extensively on the subject of missions, *The Church's Marching Orders, Our Missionary Work,* and *55 Years of Ministerial Life* (1907). He lived in Hamilton, IN.

John W. McGarvey

March 1, 1829
Hopkinsville, Kentucky

Oct. 6, 1911
Lexington, Kentucky

President of College of the Bible (Lexington Theological Seminary in 1965), **1895–1911**. McGarvey married Ottie Hix on March 23, 1853. He was ordained into the Disciples of Christ (1852) and pastored in Fayette, MO (1851–53); Dover, MO (1853–62); and Lexington, KY (1862–74). He also served as professor of sacred history at College of the Bible, 1864–1911, and worked with religious newspapers for 50 years. He wrote from *Commentary on Acts* (1863) to *Authorship of Deuteronomy* (1932).

Flora Hamilton Cassel

Aug. 21, 1852
Otterville, Illinois

Nov. 17, 1911
Denver, Colorado

Composed music for "The King's Business" and "Loyalty to Christ" (lyrics of both by her husband, ELIJAH). Flora's father was a Baptist pastor. In 1873, she became the head of the music department at Shurtleff College, Upper Alton, IL. There she married Dr. E. Taylor Cassel. She died tragically when her long skirt wrapped around the buggy step and frightened horses dragged her to death.

Howard Osgood

Jan. 4, 1831
Plaquemine Parish, Louisiana

Nov. 28, 1911
Rochester, New York (?)

Baptist pastor and educator. Osgood married Caroline Lawrence on April 14 1853 (died: 1898). Osgood pastored in Flushing, NY (1856–58); and in New York City (1860–65). He also served as a professor at Crozier Seminary, Chester, PA (1868–74); and of Rochester (NY) Theological Seminary (1875–1900). He translated the introductions of Exodus, Leviticus, and Numbers in the LANGE *Commentary*.

Elmore Harris

1854
Brantford, Ontario, Canada

Dec. 19, 1911
India

First president of Toronto Bible College (Ontario, BC), **1896–1906**. Converted at age 16, Harris founded and pastored the Walmer Road Baptist Church, Toronto, in 1889. In May 1894, he met with eleven others and founded a school. He resigned the pastorate to become the president of the school. While on a missions trip to India, he became ill with smallpox and died. He also helped found the Toronto Baptist College (McMaster University).

Griffith John

Dec. 14, 1831
Swansea, Wales

1912
England

Congregational missionary. In 1901, under his leadership, several stations were established in the province of Hunan. Although he began to preach at age 14, John was actually ordained in 1855, then he married and went to Shanghai, China, as a missionary, 1855–61 with the London Missionary Society. After this, they moved to Hankow, 1861–1906, becoming the first Protestant missionary in central China. John traveled to the far west of China in 1868. Then in 1870, they voyaged to England. His wife died en route. John married again in 1874, (died: 1880). He co-founded the first Protestant mission in inland China with Robert Wilson. John translated the NT into two Chinese dialects, Mandarin and Wen-li. He returned to England in January, 1912.

Dewitt C. Huntington

April 27, 1830
Townsend, Vermont

Feb. 8, 1912

Wrote the hymn "O Think of the Home Over There." Huntington was ordained to the Methodist ministry in 1853. Huntington held pastorates in Rochester, Syracuse, and Alion (NY); Bradford, PA; and Lincoln, NE. Huntington married Mary E. Moore on May 24, 1853 (died 1866), then married Francis H. Davis on October 27, 1868. He also served as the chancellor of

Nebraska Wesleyan University, Lincoln, NE from 1898–1908. Tullis O'Kane, who wrote the music for his hymn, died two days after Huntington.

Andrew M. Fairbairn

Nov. 4, 1838
Inverkeithing, Scotland

Feb. 9, 1912
London, England

Congregational theologian and scholar, Fairbairn pastored in Bathgate, Scotland (1861), and Aberdeen (1872). Fairbairn also served as the principal of Airdale Congregational Theological College in Bradford, England, in 1877; then Mansfield College in Oxford, England 1886–1909. Fairbairn authored several books, from *Philosophy of Religion and History* (1876) to *Philosophy of the Christian Religion* (1902). A gifted teacher, liberal in doctrine, he was well-known for his learned essays in *Contemporary Review*.

Charles Loyson
Pere Hyacinthe

March 10, 1827
Orleans, France

Feb. 9, 1912
Paris, France

Founder of the Christian Catholic Church of Switzerland in 1873, a break-away sector similar to the Old Catholic Church. Loyson was a French Carmelite priest and an eloquent preacher. He was excommunicated in 1869 for his dubious orthodoxy and stinging criticisms of Vatican methods, protesting against papal infallibility. He married (1872), then pastored in Geneva (1873) and in Paris (1879), before returning to Switzerland (1901).

Tullis C. O'Kane

March 10, 1830
Fairfield County, Ohio

Feb. 10, 1912
Delaware, Ohio

Composed music for "O Think of the Home Over There." The author of the hymn, Dewitt Huntington, died two days earlier. After tutoring math at Ohio Wesleyan University, O'Kane became a public school principal in Cincinnati, OH in 1857. In 1867, he moved to Delaware, OH and traveled for an organ company. Soon his Sunday School collections were published.

John Hyde
"Praying Hyde"

Nov. 9, 1865
Carrolton, Illinois

Feb. 17, 1912
Clifton Springs, New York

Presbyterian missionary to India remembered as a renowned prayer warrior. Hyde was known as the man that never sleeps but prays (up to 36 hours at a time). It was not uncommon for Hyde to spend a month basically in prayer. He was a missionary to India in 1893, sent by a Presbyterian board upon graduation from McCormick Theological Seminary, Chicago. In 1902, he had his first furlough. In his lifetime, he saw much revival sweep throughout the Pun Jabbi mission, one of his answers to prayer. He won people daily to Christ and established the annual Sialkot Conference for Christian workers in 1904. In 1910, he organized Feoszepore (moga) training school for village workers. Hyde died of a brain tumor (sarcoma). On his deathbed he said, "Shout the victory of Jesus Christ." He was the son of a Presbyterian pastor and never married.

Albert L. Peace

Jan. 26, 1844
Huddersfield, England

March 14, 1912
Liverpool, England

Composed music for Matheson's immortal hymn, "O Love That Wilt Not Let Me Go" (1885). Peace became the organist at Glasgow Cathederal (1879–97), then went to St. George's

Hall in Liverpool, England, and served as organist there (1897–1912). Peace was a prominent organist and often played at the opening services of newly installed organs. He edited several collections of hymns for the Church of Scotland.

Henry Varley

Oct. 25, 1835
Tattershall, England

March 30, 1912
Brighton, England

Evangelist who said to MOODY on his first visit to England, "The world has yet to see what the Lord can do with a man that is wholly consecrated to Christ." In 1868, he gave up his private business and became a missionary/evangelist around the world. Varley was converted at age 16. He built the West London Free Tabernacle which seated 1,700. Varley resigned his pastorate in 1882.

Isaac K. Funk

Sept. 10, 1839
Clifton, Ohio

April 4, 1912
Montclair, New Jersey

Lutheran pastor and editor. He entered the ministry in 1861. Funk married Eliza Thompson in 1864. Funk pastored at St. Matthews Evangelical Lutheran Church in Brooklyn, NY from 1865–72. He also served as the associate editor of the *Christian Radical*, Pittsburgh, PA (1872–73); of the *Metropolitan Pulpit*, New York City (1873–76); the *Homiletic Review* (1878); and the *Literary Digest* (1890). He founded the firm of Funk and Wagnalls with Adam Wagnalls in 1878, and was an earnest prohibitionist. In 1901, he began the publication of the *Jewish Encyclopedia*. He wrote three books.

John Harper

May 29, 1872
Houston, Scotland

April 14, 1912
Atlantic Ocean

Hero of the *Titanic*. Harper was converted at age 13, on March 28, 1886. From 1897–1910, he pastored in Govan, a suburb of Glasgow, where the church grew from 25 to nearly 500. That church was renamed the Harper Memorial Baptist Church. In 1905, his health broke and his wife died in 1906. Yet he was always bright and joyful. In 1910, he became pastor of Walworth Road Church, London. In 1911, he conducted the best meetings at Chicago's Moody Memorial Church since Moody's ministry and was invited back for three months of ministry. En route, the night before the *Titanic* sank, he was seen on the deck seeking to lead a young man to Christ. That night, when 1,522 drowned and 712 were saved, it was Harper who ordered men to do their best for the women and children and look out for others. For 50 minutes of terror, with many crying for help, John Harper asked many, "Are you saved?" One, who was rescued clinging to a board, was saved both ways. Later he testified in Hamilton, Ontario, that he was Harper's last convert, before Harper himself drowned.

Willis J. Beecher

April 29, 1838
Hampden, Ohio

May 10, 1912
Auburn, New York

Presbyterian OT scholar, educator, and pastor. Beecher pastored in Ovid, NY (1864–65); was a professor at Knox College in Galesburg, IL (1865–69); and pastored at the First Church of Christ in Galesburg (1869–71). Beecher also was a professor of Hebrew at Auburn Theological Seminary, 1871–1908. He married Sara M. Bolter on June 14, 1865. In 1893, he began to prepare the OT Sunday School Lessons for the *Sunday School Times*. He wrote from *Farmer Tompkins and His Bibles* (1874) to *Reasonable Biblical Criticism* (1911).

James R. Miller

March 20, 1840
Harshaville, Pennsylvania

July 2, 1912
Philadelphia, Pennsylvania

Presbyterian clergyman and author. Miller pastored in New Wilmington, PA (1867–69); at Bethany Church, Philadelphia, PA (1869–78); at Broadway Church, Rock Island, IL (1878–80); at Holland Memorial Church, Philadelphia (1880–98); and St. Paul's Church, Philadelphia, (1900 on). He married Louise E. King on June 22, 1870. Miller was editorial superintendent of the Presidential Board of Publication, Philadelphia, 1887–1912. Miller wrote more than 60 books. His writings ranged from *Week Day Religion* (1880) to *Devotional Hours with the Bible* (8 vols., 1909–13), which sold more than two million copies.

William M. Durham

1873
Kentucky

July 7, 1912
Los Angeles, California

Pentecostal leader. Durham was associated with Baptists, 1891–98, then went to Minnesota and embraced Holiness teaching. Converted in 1898, he pastored a small mission in Chicago (North Avenue) and went to Los Angeles to attend the Azusa Street Mission revival. On March 2, 1907, he experienced Spirit baptism. Upon returning to Chicago, he made his North Avenue Mission an important local Pentecostal center and issued a monthly magazine, *The Pentecostal Testament*. Durham was responsible for forging a non-Wesleyan view of sanctification as an option for Pentecostals. His views, for the most part, were the foundation for the Assemblies of God. He moved to Los Angeles in 1910, clashed with WILLIAM SEYMOUR, and started his own mission. He died of pneumonia shortly thereafter.

Jonathan Haralson

Oct. 18, 1830
Lowndes County, Alabama

July 11, 1912
Montgomery, Alabama

President of Southern Baptist Convention, 1898–99. Haralson was converted at age 14. A layman, he married Mattie E. Thompson (April 9, 1859), and Lida J. McFaddin (May 20, 1869). He was president of the Alabama State Baptist Convention 1874–92. He practiced law in Selma, AL becoming judge of the city court there (1876–92), then of the Supreme Court of Alabama (1892–1910). He lived in Selma, AL most of his life.

Nicholas M. Steffens

March 13, 1839
Emden, Germany

July 24, 1912
Holland, Michigan

President of faculty (CEO) of Western Theological Seminary, Holland, MI 1884–95. Steffens married Jane Graham in 1863 and came to America in 1872. He held pastorates in Silver Creek, IL (1872–76); Zeeland, MI (1878–82); and Holland, MI (1883–84). He was on the faculty of Dubuque Theological Seminary, (1895–98), then pastored in Orange City, IA (1898–1900). He then returned to Western Theological Seminary 1903–12, as a professor. He married Jane Graham in 1863.

Samuel M. Jackson

June 19, 1851
New York, New York

Aug. 2, 1912
Washington, Connecticut

Presbyterian clergyman, editor, educator, and philanthropist. Jackson was ordained in 1876. He then pastored a church in Norwood, NJ from 1876–80; after which he engaged in philanthropic, educational, and literary works. From 1885–1912, he was connected with the Charity Organization Society. He served as a professor of church history at New York University, 1895–

1912. He was a devoted associate of historian PHILIP SCHAFF. Jackson worked on many scholarly dictionaries and encyclopedias and was the editor-in-chief of *The New SCHAFF-HERZOG Encyclopedia of Religious Knowledge* (12 vols., 1907–11). He never married.

William G. Fischer

Oct. 14, 1835
Baltimore, Maryland

Aug. 12, 1912
Philadelphia, Pennsylvania

Composed music for "I Love to Tell the Story" (1869), "I Am Coming to the Cross," "The Rock That Is Higher Than I," "Whiter Than Snow" (1873), and other hymns. Fischer studied music at night while learning the bookbinding trade at J. B. Lippincott's in Philadelphia. Through the store, he became widely known as a music teacher and a choral conductor. Fischer was a professor of music at Girard College, Philadelphia, PA from 1858–68, then resigned to enter the piano business with J. E. GOULD. He also led singing at revivals.

William Booth

April 10, 1829
Nottingham, England

Aug. 20, 1912
London, England

Evangelist, founder and first general of Salvation Army, 1865–1912. Booth was converted in a Methodist chapel in 1844. At age 20, on a visit to London, he was recorded having said, "What a city to save!" Booth moved there as a pawnbroker, then pastored there 1851–61. He became a Methodist preacher in Spalding (1852) but resigned from the Methodist New Connection (1861), which he had joined (1854). Booth married CATHERINE MUMFORD on June 16, 1855 (died: 1890). In 1865 he took over the work known as the Christian Mission in London's East End. This organization ministered to the poor, and became the Salvation Army in 1878. They came to America in March, 1880 to expand the ministry. Rapid growth also brought violent opposition, 1880–85. By 1884, some 600 preachers from the Salvation Army were jailed because of preaching in the open air. His social service programs began in 1887. Officers were appointed similar to military positions. Booth authored *In Darkest England* (1890) among others. He became a great evangelist, and his seven children helped him in the work. His parting words to his son were, "I'm leaving you a bonnie handful." At his funeral, 40,000 attended, and 150,000 people filed by his coffin. Booth had preached 60,000 sermons and had 16,000 officers in his Salvation Army organization throughout 58 countries. Booth's eight children, born within a 12-year period are as follows: WILLIAM BRAMWELL (1856–1929), BALLINGTON (1857–1940), Catherine (1858–1955), Emma Moss (1860–1903), Herbert Howard (1862–1926), Marion Billups (1864–1937: retarded from convulsive attacks at birth), EVANGELINE CORY (1865–1950: first woman general), Lucy Milward (1867–1953), and a ninth adopted child, George.

James Harper

1823
Antrim, Ireland

Nov. 6, 1912
Xenia, Ohio

President of Xenia (OH) (Pittsburgh Theological Seminary in 1959) **Seminary, 1881–99.** Harper graduated from Royal Belfast College and Seminary and was licensed by the Belfast Presbytery in 1849. He was ordained on Oct 31, 1850 by the Associate Presbytery of Albany and became the moderator of the General Assembly in 1868. He pastored Fourth Avenue Presbyterian in New York City, 1850–68. He was a professor at Newberry Seminary (1867–78) and at Xenia Seminary (1878–99).

Conrad von Orelli

Jan. 25, 1846
Zurich, Switzerland
Nov. 7, 1912

Author of many scholarly works. Orelli was chaplain at the Zurich orphan asylum, 1869–71, then privatdocent (teacher paid by students) at the University of Basel (1871), and associate professor (1881). His writings in German began in 1871. Orelli served as president of the international Congress of Religions at Basel in 1907. He wrote the *OT Prophecy of the Consummation of God's Kingdom*.

Susan Lincoln T. Mills

Nov. 18, 1826
Enosburg, Vermont
Dec. 12, 1912
Oakland, California

Missionary and educator. Susan married Cyrus T. Mills in 1848 (died: 1884) and accompanied him on his mission assignment to Ceylon in 1854. She served in Ceylon (1854–60) and Hawaii (1860–64) with her husband until 1865; at that time they returned to America to take the leadership of a faltering girls' school in Benicio, CA. The school developed into Mills College, Oakland, CA in 1871.

Charlotte (Lottie) Moon

Dec. 12, 1840
Viewmont, Virginia
Dec. 24, 1912
Kobe, Japan

Southern Baptist Church's most dedicated and famous missionary. Lottie worked in Tengchow and P'ingtu, China, for nearly 40 years. She was converted under JOHN BROADUS in December, 1858. Lottie taught in Virginia, Kentucky, and Georgia 1863–72. She dedicated herself to go to China in 1873. She traveled to Tengchow (Qingdao). She went on furlough, 1876–77 and had a romantic friendship with C. H. Toy but remained unmarried. In 1883, she closed her Tengchow school to concentrate on evangelism. She began her work in P'ingtu in 1885. She was instrumental in instigating the first Christmas offerings in 1888 after she wrote a letter pleading for help. This provided three additional missionaries. The first offering was nearly $3,000 in 1888. In 1993, it was $82 million. The Lottie Moon Christmas offering for Foreign Missions was named in 1918 and since then has raised millions of dollars annually. She furloughed (1891) and during the Boxer Rebellion (1900) fled to Japan. She died on a ship in the harbor of Kobe, Japan, from starvation, during a great famine, which she suffered by choice with her Chinese friends. A faithful nurse sought to bring her back to America to no avail after her sympathy fast began. She literally made world missions important to Southern Baptists.

Christopher E. Nestle

May 1, 1851
Stuttgart, Germany
March 9, 1913
Stuttgart, Germany

Biblical scholar, Lutheran orientalist, Semetic scholar, and pastor. Nestle worked most of his life on the preparation of the most authentic Greek text of the New Testament. He held professorships at Ulm, 1883–90 and 1893–98; Tubingen, 1890–93; and at Maulbronn, 1898 on. Nestle published the first edition of his *Greek New Testament* in 1898 and revised it constantly until his death. He wrote *An Introduction to the Greek New Testament*.

Harriet Ross Tubman
Araminta Tubman

c 1821
Dorchester County, Maryland
March 10, 1913
Auburn, New York

Leading Abolitionist. Harriet married John Tubman in 1843, but he refused to attempt to escape. Harriet escaped from slavery in 1849; determined to have liberty or death. She helped over 300 slaves escape via the underground railroad. She was called the "Moses of her people." Harriet was a nurse and a spy for the Union forces in South Carolina during the Civil War. In 1863, she assisted the Union Army in freeing over 750 slaves in one raid. She made 19 perilous trips into the Deep South guiding hundreds of slaves to a new life. At one time there was a $40,000 reward for her capture. She settled in Auburn, NY in 1857. In her later years, she used a small pension of $20 a month to assist a home for aged blacks. Tubman was buried in Ohio with full military honors. She could neither read nor write. Her favorite Bible verse was Exodus 15:1.

William J. Northen

July 9, 1835
Jones County, Georgia

March 25, 1913
Atlanta, Georgia

President of the Southern Baptist Convention, 1899–1901, and governor of Georgia, 1890–94. Northen married Mattie M. Neel on Dec. 19, 1860. He served as the principal of Mt. Zion Academy (1857–74), was elected to the Georgia House of Representatives, 1877–78 and 1880–81, and to the Senate (1884–85) as a Democrat. He was very active in the American Tract Society, Sunday School Union, the American Bible Society, and in his church, Ponce de Leon Baptist Church, Atlanta, GA. Northen was president of the Georgia Baptist Convention, 1896–1910.

John P. (J.P.) Morgan

April 17, 1837
Hartford, Connecticut

March 31, 1913
Rome, Italy

American financier and industrial organizer, the son of an international banker. Morgan got into banking in 1861. He married Amelia Sturges in 1861 (died: 1862) and Frances L. Tracy in 1865. In 1871, the firm of Drexel and Morgan was formed. His father, Junius, died in 1890 and Anthony Drexel (banker; born: 1826) died in 1893; hence in 1895, J.P. Morgan and Company was founded. Morgan organized the first billion-dollar corporation, U.S. Steel, in 1901, after buying Andrew Carnegie's interests. He also consolidated International Harvester. He did both investment and commerical banking. A domineering man, he met his match in TEDDY ROOSEVELT. When ROOSEVELT left for Africa, Morgan quipped that he hoped "the first lion he meets does his duty." During the 1907 financial panic, Morgan decided to support the stock market, easing the situation. In his will, he states that Jesus Christ was his senior partner in all his enterprises.

William W. Borden

Nov. 1, 1887
Chicago, Illinois

April 9, 1913
Cairo, Egypt

China Inland Mission missionary to the Muslims. Borden was converted at Moody Church via R. A. TORREY at age seven. He attended Yale University (1906–9) and Princeton Theological Seminary (1909–12). Borden was very wealthy, having inherited $1 million at age 21. He planned to go to northwest China to work with Muslims and so traveled to Cairo for a study of Arabic and Islamic culture. In the 14 weeks in Cairo before his sudden death, he organized a city-wide canvas with literature. He died of cerebral spinal meningitis at age 25. He left $1 million to Christian causes. His "No Reserve! No Retreat! No Regrets!" statement is legendary. The book, *Borden of Yale*, has made a great impact. He was unmarried. Memorial services were held all over the world for him.

"No Reserve! No Retreat! No Regrets!"

William C. Doane

March 2, 1832
Boston, Massachusetts

May 17, 1913
Albany, New York

Episcopalian hymn writer of many songs, such as "Ancient of Days" (music by Albert Jeffries). Doane married Sarah K. Condit on November 7, 1853 and was ordained in 1856. He served as a rector at St. Mary's Church, Burlington, NJ (1859–63); in Hartford, CT (1863–67); in Albany, NY (1867–69); and bishop of Albany, NY in 1869; where he established All Saints' Cathedral. Doane also taught at Burlington (NJ) College (1854–60), at Trinity College (1863–67), and was the chancellor of the University of New York, in Albany (1902–09). He was an author also.

Johannes Bading

Nov. 24, 1824
Rixdorf, Germany

May 24, 1913
Milwaukee, Wisconsin

President of first Evangelical Lutheran Synod of Wisconsin (WELS in 1959), **1860–89** (except 1864–67). He was sent to Wisconsin by the Langenberg Society in 1853. He pastored in Calumet, Theresa, Watertown, and at St. John's, Milwaukee, all in Wisconsin. He resided at Northwestern College in Watertown for many years. He then traveled to Germany and Russia to raise funds for the school, 1863–64. Bading also served as president of the Northwestern trustees for many years, 1865–1912. He was president of the Synodical Conference, 1882–1912.

John Binney

Feb. 23, 1844
Philadelphia, Pennsylvania

June 12, 1913
Middletown, Connecticut

President (dean) of Berkeley Divinity School, Middletown (New Haven in 1928), **CT 1899–1908**. Binney married Charlotte Bush on May 20, 1869. He was ordained as a deacon (1868) and then as a priest of the Episcopal Church (1869). Binney began teaching Hebrew and OT literature at BDS (1874), adding NT interpretation (1882). He lived in Middletown, CT.

Samuel A. Barnett

Feb. 8, 1844
Bristol, England

June 17, 1913
Hove, England

Church of England priest and social reformer who devoted himself for 21 years to the cultural improvement of East London. Barnett married Henrietta Weston (May 4, 1851–June 10, 1936) in 1873. He was a vicar of St. Jude's in London (1873–93), canon of Bristol Cathedral in 1893, first warden of Toynbee Hall (1884–1906), and canon of Westminster Abbey (1906–13). He founded the first "University Settlement" in London's East End, which brought students to live in the inner city. Barnett used social reforming ideas to win the working class back to the church. He wrote from *Practical Socialism* (1888) to *Vision and Service* (1917).

Arne E. Boyum

April 7, 1833
Balestrand, Norway

July 29, 1913
Rushford, Minnesota

President of Hague Synod (ALC, ELCA in 1988), 1876–87. Boyum came to America in 1853 and pastored for almost 40 years in Arendal, MN (1858–96), being pastor emeritus (1906–13). He married Anne I. Tuphellen in 1859.

Edward M. Bounds

Aug 15, 1835
Shelbyville, Missouri

Aug. 24, 1913
Washington, Georgia

Methodist minister and writer best known for his books on prayer. For years Bounds reserved 4:00–7:00 each morning for prayer. He preached for the Methodist Episcopal Church in the South and pastored in Monticello, MO; Nashville, TN; Selma, AL; and St. Louis, MO, after which he turned to special evangelistic work in the church. His St. Louis ministry began at St. Paul's Methodist in 1875 and later, at First Methodist, in the same city. He married Emma Barnett (1876), and after her death, married her cousin, Harriet Barnett (1887). During this time, he edited the *SL Advocate* for eight years. He spent most of his time writing while he lived in Washington, GA from 1896–1913. Bounds was an old-time Methodist, a prisoner during the Civil War, accused of loyalty to the Confederacy. Bounds helped edit the *Christian Advocate* in Nashville, 1892–96. His *Complete Works on Prayer* is a classic. His *Power Through Prayer* (1907) was his most widely circulated book.

James Orr

April 1, 1844
Glasgow, Scotland

Sept. 6, 1913

Theologian who entered the ministry in 1871. Orr pastored the East Bank United Presbyterian Church, Harwich, Scotland, 1874–91. He also served as a professor of church history at the United Presbyterian Theological College (1891–1900), and taught apologetics and theology at Glasgow College of the United Free Church (1900–13). Orr helped unite the Presbyterian and Free Churches in 1900. He wrote books ranging from *The Christian View* (1893) to *Revelation and Inspiration* (1910). He was one of a small number of British theologians invited to participate in the Fundamentals project, 1909–15. He was in America often. He wrote books such as *The Virgin Birth*, etc. He edited the five-volume *The International Standard Bible Encyclopedia* (published in 1915).

Daniel C. Greene

Feb. 11, 1843
Roxbury, Massachusetts

Sept. 15, 1913
Tokyo, Japan (?)

Congregationalist missionary to Japan, 1869–1913. Greene helped to translate the Bible into Japanese. After living in Kobe (1870–74) and Yokahama (1874–80), he went to Kyoto (1881–87), where he was acting professor of OT at Doshisha Kyoto. From 1890–1913, he resided in Tokyo. He wrote extensively. He married Mary J. Forbes in 1869.

Robert Tomlinson

1842
Ireland

Sept. 18, 1913
Cedarvale, British Columbia, Canada

Missionary to the Nishga Indians in British Columbia. He was one of the first Englishmen to work at the headwaters of the Skeena River. Tomlinson joined the Church Missionary Society in Ireland after medical training at Trinity College and arrived at Metlakatla in 1867. He served on the Nass River for eleven years with Robert Doolan and they established the mission at Kincolith. In 1883, he moved to Metlakatla, where WILLIAM DUNCAN had established his village. When DUNCAN was forced to leave in 1887, Tomlinson resigned from the missionary society and returned to the Skeena River. He established a non-sectarian mission, Meanskinisht, at Cedarvale. He rejoined DUNCAN at New Metlakatla, 1908–12.

Joshua W. Hering

March 8, 1833
Beaver Dam, Maryland

Sept. 23, 1913
Westminster, Maryland (?)

President of Methodist Protestant Church (United Methodist Church in 1968), **1891–1900**. Hering married Margaret Trumbol in 1855 (died: 1883) and Catharine Armacast in 1888. He was in the medical field from 1855–67. Then he was elected cashier of the Union National Bank, Westminster, a position he held till his death. He was one of the founders of Western Maryland College (McDaniel College), Westminster, MD, serving for over 40 years, their treasurer or chairman of the Board of Trustees. In 1895 and 1897, he was elected state senator.

Mary A. Lathbury

Aug. 10, 1841
Manchester, New York

Oct. 20, 1913
East Orange, New Jersey

Wrote the hymns "Break Thou the Bread of Life" (1877) and "Day Is Dying in the West" (music for both by WILLIAM SHERWIN). Mary was the daughter of a Methodist pastor and an artist by profession. She taught drawing and painting at Newbury (VT) Academy and also in New York City. She associated with bishop JOHN VINCENT, who founded the Chautauqua movement and also the "Look-Up Legion," a youth movement. She never married.

Herrick Johnson

Sept. 22, 1832
Kaughnewaga, New York

Nov. 20, 1913
St. Louis, Missouri (?)

Presbyterian educator and clergyman. Johnson married Catherine Hardenbergh on Sept. 6, 1860 (died: 1907). Johnson was the pastor of the Third Church, Troy, NY (1860–62); the Third Church, Pittsburgh, PA (1862–68); and the First Church, Philadelphia, PA (1868–74). He was a professor of homiletics and pastoral theology at Auburn Theological Seminary (1874–80), and at McCormick Theological Seminary (1880–1906). He wrote from *Christianity's Challenge* (1880) to *The Ideal Ministry* (1908).

Granville A. W. Waldegrave (Lord Radstock)

April 10, 1833

Dec. 8, 1913
Paris, France

English lord who was an ambassador for Christ in many countries of the world. He inherited his title in 1857. After college, an illness almost took Radstock's life, which led to his conversion. In 1858, he married Susan Calcraft. He could have become a diplomat, but instead, began to give speeches at dinner engagements. He made seven trips to India, constantly developing ways to infiltrate the country with the gospel. In East London, he started Immigrant Homes, where 70,000 would receive physical and spiritual help. In Weston-Super-Mare, England, Radstock led FREDERICK BAEDEKER to Christ in 1866. While in Paris, France, whose aristocracy had rejected him, he met the aristocracy of Russia, who invited him to St. Petersburg (Leningrad). He spent 10-15 hours a day witnessing door-to-door. Visits to Scandinavian countries produced great results. Divine healing and the crucified life were additional insights he taught and experienced. His wife died in 1892.

John T. McFarland

Jan. 2, 1851
Mount Vernon, Indiana

Dec. 22, 1913
Maplewood, New Jersey

Wrote the third stanza of "Away in a Manger." McFarland was active in the Methodist Church. McFarland married Mary Burt on Aug. 19, 1873. He held pastorates in Iowa, Illinois (1880–96); Brooklyn, NY (1897–99); and in Topeka, KS (1899–1905). He was president of Iowa Wesleyan College, Mt. Pleasant (1884–91); then became the editor of *Sunday School Publications for Methodism* (1909). He authored several books.

Andrew B. Shelly

Sept. 23, 1834
Bucks County, Pennsylvania

Dec. 26, 1913
Philadelphia, Pennsylvania

President of General Conference Mennonite Church (Mennonite Church USA in 2002), **Newton, KS 1869–96.** Shelly married Fannie Weinberger in 1868. He pastored in Bucks County, 1870–74. During the next 30 years, he was a dominant personality in his church's life. He was secretary of the mission board, 1889–1911. He died while visiting with friends. Shelly's funeral was held at his Quakertown, PA home on Jan. 1, 1914.

Lizzie S. Tourjee Estabrook

Sept. 9, 1858 — Newport, Rhode Island
Dec. 28, 1913 — Auburndale, Massachusetts

Composed music for "There's a Wideness in God's Mercy" (lyrics by Frederick Faber). Lizzie was the daughter of Dr. Eben Tourgee, founder of New England Conservatory of Music. She attended college at Wellesley (MA) from 1877–78. She married Franklin Estabrook (Boston industrialist) in 1883; they had two sons. She was also a music teacher and organist at Centenary Methodist Church in Auburndale. Lizzie died of myocarditis (inflamation of the middle muscular layer of the heart wall).

Thomas Crosby

1840 — Pickering, England
Jan. 13, 1914

Canadian Methodist missionary to the Indians on the Pacific Coast, who greatly inspired OSWALD J. SMITH. Crosby came to Canada (1856) and began teaching in the Indian school at Nanaimo, BC (1863). He married Emma Douse in 1874 and moved to Port Simpson, BC. For 50 years he ministered to the Indian tribes off the Pacific Coast, by walking or canoeing, summer and winter, especially in British Columbia. Crosby was the first Methodist to include medical work in Canadian missions. He retired in 1907.

John K. McLean

March 31, 1834 — Jackson, New York
Feb. 16, 1914 — Berkeley, California (?)

First president of Pacific School of Religion, Berkeley, CA 1894–1911. He was board chairman for PSR from 1880–94. McLean married Sarah Hawley on June 26, 1861; he was also ordained as a Congregationalist that same year. McLean pastored in Connecticut (1861–62); Massachusetts (1863–67); Springfield, IL (1867–72); and at First Church, Oakland, CA (1872–95). He also served as president of the California Oriental Mission and as president of the State Board of Corrections, 1906–14.

Samuel R. Driver

Oct. 2, 1846 — Southampton, England
Feb. 26, 1914 — Oxford, England

Church of England Hebrew scholar and canon at Christ Church College, Oxford, 1883–1914. Samuel succeeded Ed Pusey (1800–82) and did careful textual and critical studies for most of the OT writings and served on their OT Revision Committee, 1876–84. Samuel also worked at New College as a fellow (1870–83) and was a tutor (1875–83). His works were from *A Treatise on the Uses of the Tenses in Hebrew* (1874) to *Genesis and Exodus* (1911).

William G. Moorehead

March 19, 1836 — Rix Mills, Ohio
March 1, 1914 — Pittsburgh, Pennsylvania

President of Xenia (OH) (Pittsburgh Theological Seminary in 1959) Seminary, 1899–1913. Moorehead was a United Presbyterian minister and scholar. He served as a missionary of the American and Foreign Union in Italy, 1862–69. He also pastored at First Church, Xenia, OH 1870–75; and at Third Church, Xenia. He became a New Testament literature and exegesis professor, 1873–99, at Xenia Seminary. He was also one of the editors of the *Scofield Reference Bible*. He was a prominent premillenialist who spoke frequently at Bible institutes and Bible conferences. He was married.

Thomas A. Bowman (1)

July 15, 1817
Berwick, Pennsylvania

March 3, 1914
Orange, New Jersey

Bishop of Methodist Episcopal Church, 1872–1914. Bowman married Matilda Hartman in 1842. He organized Dickinson Seminary (Lycoming College), Williamsport, PA from 1848–58. He also served as president and professor at Asbury University (DePaul University) (1858–84) and president (1884–99). He was chaplain of the U.S. Senate, 1864–65, and visited Methodist conferences in Europe, India, China, Japan, and Mexico. He was buried in Greencastle, IN where he lived most of his life.

Lille M. N. Stevens

March 1, 1844
Dover, Maine

April 6, 1914

President of National Women's Christian Temperance Union, 1894–1914. She follows FRANCIS WILLARD in this position. She married Michael Stevens, a merchant, in 1867. In 1874, she started her NWCTU work in Maine. She was elected president of the World's WCTU in 1898 as well. She lived in Portland, Maine.

Frederick S. Arnot

Sept. 12, 1858
Glasgow, Scotland

May 1914
Johannesburg, Union of South Africa

Plymouth Brethren missionary explorer to Central Africa. In 1881, Arnot went to South Africa via Christian Brethren and then proceeded from Durban to the upper Zambezi region in 1885, encountering many narrow escapes from death along the way. He worked amongst the Barotse, 1882–84. He was in Angola (1884) and in Northern Rhodesia (Zambia) (1888). Arnot married on one of his furloughs. He worked in America for the South African General Mission. He was the greatest African explorer since the days of LIVINGSTONE and STANLEY, discovering the source of the Zambezi River. At the time of his death, 61 missionaries were working at 16 stations in five areas of Central Africa.

Charles S. Horne

April 15, 1865
Cuckfield, England

May 2, 1914
Toronto, Ontario, Canada

Congregationalist minister of Allen St. Congregational Church, Kensington (1889–1903) and of WHITEFIELD's Chapel in Tottenham Court Road (1903–14). Horne was a liberal member of the House of Commons and the only clergyman in the House who, at the same time, held a pastorate, 1910–14. He saw the need for unity between religion and politics. He died suddenly while on a trip.

Alfred R. Tucker

April 1, 1849
Woolwich/Windermere, England

June 15, 1914
London, England

Anglican missionary, 1891–1911, and bishop, 1898–1911, to Uganda. In 1900, Tucker was consecrated third bishop of Eastern Equatorial Africa. He succeeded HANNINGTON and Parker, who served in Uganda, 1890–98. He arrived December 25, 1890 having walked 900 miles to the interior. When he arrived, there were 200 Christians, and in his 21 years of service, he saw that number grow to 100,000. Tucker served as canon of Durham, 1911–14. He was responsible for Uganda coming under the British crown. His wife Josephine Sim, (because of ill health), remarried in England during his 18 years in Africa. He died suddenly attending a meeting of a Committee on Faith and Order.

August L. Storm

Oct. 23, 1862
Motala, Sweden

July 1, 1914
Stockholm, Sweden

Wrote the hymn "Thanks to God" (music by JOHN HULTMAN) Storm spent most of his life in Stockholm where he attended school and worked as an office clerk. He was converted under the ministry of the Salvation Army and later joined the corps. He served as a finance secretary at the SA headquarters in 1892. Storm was a powerful preacher. He was crippled in 1899 from a back disorder.

Robert Jackson

1842
Oldham, England

July 12, 1914
Oldham, England

Teacher, composer, conductor, and organist. Jackson composed the music for "Breathe on Me, Breath of God" (1878). He began his organ career at St. Mark's Grosvenor Square in London. In 1868, he succeeded his father as the organist at St. Peter's Church in Oldham. His father was the organist there for 48 years; Robert served 46 years (combined service, 94 years). For many years he was a member of the Halle Symphony Orchestra at Birmingham.

Milton S. Terry

Feb. 22, 1840
Coeymans, New York

July 13, 1914
Los Angeles, California

Methodist minister, theologian and educator, pastored in several New York churches (1862–1879), and was presiding elder of New York City (1879–83). He married Francis Atchinson on May 15, 1864. Terry then was the professor of Hebrew and Old Testament exegesis and doctrine at Garret Biblical Institute of Evanston, IL 1884 on. In 1887, he was at the University of Berlin lectures absorbing German critical approach to Scripture. He was a major force in moving Methodism into a mostly liberal Protestant camp. He preached a Sunday evening sermon the day before his death. Terry wrote several books, from *Biblical Hermeneutics* (1883) to *The Shinto Cult* (1910).

Henry W. Wilbur

May 15, 1851
Easton, New York

Sept. 5, 1914
Saratoga Springs, New York

First General Secretary of Friends General Conference, 1905–14. Wilbur married Eliza Sowle on October 21, 1880. He began editorial work in 1875. Wilbur was the editor of *Vineland Independent* (1876–84) and *New York Voice* (1896–98). He became a minister with the Religious Society of Friends. He died suddenly while presiding at a Friends General Conference. His writings ranged from *A Study in Doctrine and Discipline* to *Development of the Spiritual Perceptions* (1914).

James O. McClurkan

Nov. 13, 1861
Yellow Creek, Tennessee

Sept. 17, 1914
Nashville, Tennessee

Founder and first president of the Trevecca Nazarene College, Nashville, TN 1901–1913. During a special evangelistic revival in the Cumberland Presbyterian Church near Dickson, TN, McClurkan was converted at age 13. The Tennessee Cumberland Church Presbytery licensed him to preach on Sundays while teaching school during the week at the Yellow Creek community. He married Martha Rye on Nov. 15, 1882 (she lived to be over 100 years old). He pastored briefly at Cumberland Presbyterian Church, Decatur, TX in 1886. In the late 1880's he moved to California to pastor in Visalia and Salem. He later pastored in San Jose where he heard holiness and sanctification preaching. On Nov.

5, 1901, the Bible Training School opened. In 1907, McClurkan and P. F. BRESEE, exchanged letters laying the groundwork for a union, not occurring until after McClurkan's death. In 1910, he named the school, Trevecca, after a Welsh school which trained ministers for pastorates, springing from the Wesleyan revivals in Britain. New property was available and on the day the school was to open on the new campus, he died.

Benajah H. Carroll

Dec. 27, 1843
near Carrollton, Mississippi

Nov. 11, 1914
Fort Worth, Texas

Founder and first president of Southwestern Baptist Theological Seminary, 1901–14. The school began as a seminary of Baylor University in 1905, changed names in 1908, and then changed locations to Fort Worth in 1910. Carroll was converted in 1865, after being a skeptic, when he attended a Methodist camp meeting and was challenged by John 7:17. He married Ellen Bell on Dec. 28, 1866, and Hallie Harrison in 1899 and had a family of ten children. He pastored in Burleson County, TX (1866–70); and also at FBC, Waco, TX (1871–99). He then became a professor and dean of the Bible department at Baylor University 1902–14. He taught Bible and theology there from 1872 on. Carroll authored 33 published books, including a 13-volume set, *An Introduction of the Bible*. He was 6'4" tall and had a beard to his waist.

Edward Kremser

April 10, 1838
Vienna, Austria

Nov. 27, 1914
Vienna, Austria

Composed the music for "We Gather Together" (1877) and other hymns. In 1869, Kremser became the chorus master for the Vienna Mannergesangverein and also conducted other choral groups. He composed numerous vocals, men's choruses, and other instrumental works.

Thomas M. Lindsay

Dec. 6, 1843
Lesmahagow, Scotland

Dec. 6, 1914

Church historian who abandoned his career as a university teacher to study for the ministry. In 1872, Lindsay was elected to the chair of church history at the Free Church of Scotland's Theological College in Glasgow, remaining there until his death. He also served as principal (1902–14) and convener of the Foreign Missions Committee of the Free Church of Scotland (1886–1900). He was very active in helping the needy and was a great missions supporter. His writings included *Luther and the German Reformation* and *A History of the Reformation in Europe* (2 vols., 1906–7.)

Robert J. Willingham

May 15, 1854
Beaufort District, South Carolina

Dec. 20, 1914
Richmond, Virginia

Executive secretary of Southern Baptist Convention Missions, 1893–1914. Willingham married Corneille Bacon on Sept. 8, 1874. He was ordained (1878), then held pastorates in Talbotton, GA (1870–82); Barnesville, GA (1882–87); FBC, Chattanooga, TN (1887–91); and FBC, Memphis, TN (1891–93). Willingham visited many mission fields. The missions giving increased from $100,000 to $600,000 during his tenure. He was quite ill from 1908 until his death.

Chester D. Hartranft

Oct. 15, 1839
Frederick Township, Pennsylvania

Dec. 30, 1914
Wolfenbuttel, Germany

President of Hartford (CT) Theological Seminary, 1888–1903. Hartranft was a Congregationalist who pastored the Dutch Reformed Church in South Bushwick, NY (1864–66), and in New Brunswick, NJ (1866–78). In 1878, as a result of switching to Congregationalism, he became a professor of biblical and church history at Hartford, prior to his presidency. Hartranft married Annie F. Berg in 1864 and later Ida T. Berg on November 22, 1911. He conducted the Oratorio Society for ten years and engaged in literary work in Germany after 1903.

Ferrar Fenton

December 4, 1832   c 1915
Waltham, England

Layman who produced a Bible, translated from the original Hebrew and Greek. Fenton was a student until age 28. Financial reverses then compelled him to become an operator in a factory, where he soon became a manager. He amassed a fortune as the promoter of the De Beers Company for the development of the South African diamond mines, after the panic of 1882. A great believer in Bible inerrancy, he considered "higher criticism" as either a wild delusion or deliberate swindle. Fenton wrote many books, but his chief work is his *Bible in Modern English with Critical Notes* (London, 1903), which he spent 50 years researching.

Vernon J. Charlesworth

April 28, 1839   Jan. 5, 1915
Barking, England   London, England

Wrote the hymn "A Shelter in the Time of Storm" (1885). IRA SANKEY (who wrote the music) found the poem in a paper that Charlesworth edited. *The Postman* was a favorite journal for fisherman. He was also the co-pastor with NEWMAN HALL at Old Surrey Chapel in 1864 and was educated at Homerton College. Charlesworth was a clergyman and headmaster of SPURGEON's Stockwell Orphanage, 1869.

Revere F. Weidner

Nov. 22, 1851   Jan. 5, 1915
Center Valley, Pennsylvania   Tangerine, Florida

First president of Chicago Lutheran Theological Seminary, Maywood, IL (Lutheran School of Theology, Chicago in 1964), 1891–1915. Weidner also taught dogmatics and Hebrew exegesis. He married Emma Jones on July 10, 1873. Weidner served a series of Lutheran pastorates in Phillipsburg, PA (1873–78) and taught English and logic at Muhlenberg and at St. Luke's Philadelphia, PA (1878–82). He had a teaching career at Augustana College and Seminary at Rock Island, IL (1882–91); also he was a professor of dogmatic theology in Rock Island and Chicago (1891–94). He wrote several books, including *LUTHER's Small Catechism* (1880) to *Christology* (1913).

Mary M. Slessor
"White Queen of Okoyung"

Dec. 2, 1848   Jan. 15, 1915
Gilcomston (suburb of Aberdeen), Scotland   Itu, Nigeria

United Presbyterian missionary to eastern Nigeria. Mary's family moved to Dundee in 1859. As a young girl, she began to work in Dundee Mills in 1862 to support her drunken father and impoverished family. Converted as a teenager, she offered her services to a foreign missions board and received instruction at Edinburgh. She sailed for Calabar in 1876 and pioneered missions programs. Mary went where few men dared to go in eastern Nigeria. In 1880, she took charge of a mission at Old Town in Calabar and began a work at Creektown in Okoyung. In 1885, tribal abuses, including human sacrifice, came to an end. She arbitrated disputes, fought poverty, and organized an African court. She heard of the death of both her mother and sister in 1886. She continued alone in 1888 to work among the Okoyung as vice-council for them. Mary adopted native dress and lifestyles, and took in African children as her own. After a church service, January 1915, she fainted. Lingering for a few days, her last words were "O God, release me."

Elizabeth V. Duncan Dawson-Baker

c 1849   Jan. 18, 1915

Faith healer and educator. The daughter of a Methodist minister, Elizabeth was inspired at a temperance lecture to dedicate her life to Christian work. Her first marriage to W. A. Dawson ended in divorce because of abuse. Her second husband, C.W. Baker (doctor), also separated from her. Ellizabeth and her four sisters opened the Elim Faith Mission in Rochester, NY in 1895. She went to India in 1898 and met PANDITA RAMABAI. Elizabeth also founded Elim Tabernacle, Faith Home, and Bible Training School, all located in New York. In 1907 she changed her denomination to identify with the Pentecostals. In 1924, her surviving sisters closed the ministries.

Anna B. Warner

Aug. 31, 1820   Jan. 22, 1915
Long Island, New York   Highland Falls, Constitution Island, New York

She wrote the beloved children's song "Jesus Loves Me" (1859) and "Praise Him, All Ye Little Children" (music of both by WILLIAM BRADBURY). Anna's song is sung by millions. She often wrote under the pseudonym of Amy Lothrop. She wrote several novels, books on nature and hymn compilations. Anna lived near West Point and conducted Bible classes for cadets. She was a Presbyterian and was buried with military honors. Her sister was SUSAN B. WARNER.

Matthias Loy

March 17, 1828   Jan. 26, 1915
near Harrisburg, Pennsylvania   Columbus, Ohio

President of Capital University (Trinity Lutheran Seminary in 1988), **Columbus, OH 1881–90, and of Ohio Synod** (ALC and ELCA in 1988), **1868–78, 1880–96**. Loy was ordained as a Lutheran in 1840. He married Mary Willey on Dec. 25, 1853. Loy pastored in Delaware, OH (1849–65), then began to teach theology at Capital (1865–1904). He edited the *Lutheran Standard* (1864–91) and wrote several books, from *The Doctrine of Justification* (1869) to *Sermon on the Mount* (1909).

Frances J. Crosby
Fanny Crosby

March 24, 1820   Feb. 12, 1915
Southeast, New York   Bridgeport, Connecticut

Greatest hymn writer in the history of the Christian church. Fanny was blinded at six weeks old by a country doctor's mistake. Her father died in the year of her birth, and in 1821, her mother moved to North Salem, NY. In 1830, at the age of ten, she could recite much Scripture. She attended the blind school in New York City as a pupil (1835–58) and teacher (1847–58). Crosby was converted Nov. 20, 1850 at John St. Methodist Church (Broadway Tabernacle) in New York City, where she was a lifelong member. Her first publication was *The Blind Girl and Other Poems* (1844), which included her first hymns. She also appeared before a joint session of Congress that same year. Fanny married Alexander Van Alstyne, a blind musician who played the piano and coronet, March 5, 1858 (died: 1902). Since her name was so well known, she rarely used his name. Her hymns were written from 1864 on. Meeting WILLIAM BRADBURY was a door opener for her talents. Fanny wrote "Blessed Assurance", "Rescue the Perishing," "Safe in the Arms of Jesus," "Saved by Grace," "To God Be the Glory," "Praise Him," "Pass Me Not," "He Hideth My Soul," "I Am Thine, O Lord," "Near the Cross," "The Cleansing Wave," "Close to Thee," "Redeemed," "All the Way My Savior Leads Me," "Jesus Is Calling," "Be Thou Exalted," "Give Me Jesus," "My Savior First of All," "Savior More Than Life to Me," "Tell Me the Story of Jesus," "Though Your Sins Be as Scarlet," 'Tis the Blessed Hour of Prayer," "To the Work," "Will Jesus Find Us Watching," "Never Give Up," and over 7,000 more. She asked for only $2.00 per hymn and lived a frugal life, a far cry from the commercialism of this time. She could write little more than her name, so her husband, a friend Caroline Writer; or her secretary, Eva C. Cleaveland, transcribed for her. Fanny wrote her last hymn, "In the Morn of Zion's Glory," February 11, 1915, to comfort a neighbor's family who lost a child. She died the next day. Her favorite Bible verse was I John 3:2.

Amanda B. Smith

Jan. 23, 1837
Long Green, Maryland

Feb. 15, 1915
Sebring, Florida

Ex-slave who became an outstanding missionary/evangelist. Converted in a Methodist Church, Smith was assured of her salvation in 1856, whereupon she was called into evangelistic work. Her first husband (Calvin Devine, married September, 1854) was killed in the Civil War. She married her second husband, James Smith, in 1863. He died in 1869, along with her youngest child. That same year, she began preaching in camp meetings in Nebraska, moving on to Salem, NJ where she saw great revival. She left for Europe (1876) beginning with the Keswick Conference in England (1878–79), traveling on to India (1879–81), West Africa (1882–90) and back to England before returning home to preach along the Eastern seaboard (1890). She lived in Harvey, IL in 1892, and started the Amanda Smith Orphan's Home, 1899–1912. She then retired to Sebring.

Thomas K. Cheyne

Sept. 18, 1841
London, England

Feb. 16, 1915
Oxford, England

Old Testament scholar and professor of interpretation of Scripture at Oxford, 1885–1908, and canon of Rochester, 1885–1908. Cheyne was a fellow at Balliol College, Oxford, from 1868–82. He insisted on a broad and comprehensive study of the Bible in light of literal, historical, and scientific considerations. He taught on the interpretation of Holy Scriptures and authored several commentaries on prophetic books. His writings ranged from *Isaiah* (1868) to *Traditions and Beliefs of Ancient Israel* (1907). He was also the co-editor of the *Encyclopaedia Biblica* (4 vols., 1899–1903). Some considered him a radical critic because of his exposition and criticism of Old Testament books.

Rudolph Dubs

May 31, 1837
near Worms, Germany

March 31, 1915
Harrisburg, Pennsylvania

Bishop of Evangelical Association, 1875–1902, 1914–15, and of United Evangelical (United Methodist Church in 1968) **Church, 1906–13**. Dubs came to America in 1852. Converted in 1854, he served as a pioneer missionary pastor in the Midwest. He also served as a presiding elder, editor of a German magazine from 1902 on, scholar, theologian, forceful speaker, and skilled executive.

John G. Princell

Sept. 18, 1845
Tolg, Sweden

May 1, 1915
Chicago, Illinois

President and teacher of Trinity Evangelical Theological Seminary, 1904–14. Princell was the unofficial founder of the Evangelical Free Church. He arrived in America, May 21, 1856 and eventually settled in Princeton, IL. He was converted at age 17, in the spring of 1862. Princell was ordained by the German Lutheran Ministerial Council of Pennsylvania and served at the Gustavus Adolphus Lutheran Church in NYC, 1872–79. In 1879, he was excluded from the Augustana

Synod because of his loyalty to the Scriptures, as taught by his friend, PAUL WALDENSTROM (communion for believers only, historic belief in the atonement, etc.) In 1880, he went to Ansgar College, Knoxville, Ill serving as president until 1884, when the school closed. He pastored at Temple Church, Minneapolis (1894–96) and in Franconia, MN (1896–1902). In 1901, he and others formed the Swedish Bible Institute of Chicago. The school operated out of Twelfth Avenue Church through 1914. Pneumonia took his life.

Henry M. Turner

Feb. 1, 1834
Newberry, South Carolina

May 8, 1915
Windsor, Ontario, Canada

Bishop of African Methodist Episcopal Church, 1880–1915; first senior bishop, 1900–15. Turner married Eliza A. Peacher (August 31, 1856); Marsha DeWitt in August, 1893; Harriet Wayman (Aug. 16, 1900); and Laura P. Lemon (Dec. 3, 1907). He was the first black chaplain to serve in the Civil War. Turner pastored in Baltimore and Washington, D.C from 1858–63; was in the Georgia legislature in 1868; served as postmaster in Macon, GA (1869) as a customs inspector; and served in the U.S. secret service. He traveled to Africa four times in the 1890s to strengthen AME work. He founded the *Voice of Missions* (1892).

William M. Groton

Nov. 28, 1850
Waldoboro, Maine

May 25, 1915
Philadelphia, Pennsylvania

Dean of Philadelphia Divinity School (merged into Episcopal Theological School, Cambridge, MA in 1974), **1900–15**. Groton was ordained a deacon (1876) and a priest (1877) in the Episcopal Church. He served as rector of St. Anne's Church, S. Lincoln, MA (1876–78); Trinity Church of St. Stephen, NB, Canada (1878–81); and Christ Church, Westerly, RI (1881–98). He married Hannah Babcock on January 21, 1883, then taught at PDS in 1898.

Henry (Harry) G. Guinness Jr.

Oct. 2, 1861
Toronto, Ontario, Canada

May 25, 1915
London, England

Head of the East London Institute for Missions, 1887–98, and of Regions Beyond Missionary Union (merged into World Team in 1995), **1898–1914**, succeeding his father. Guinness married Annie Reed on March 11, 1887; they eventually had ten children. In 1891, they visited the Congo, working there with the Congo and Balolo Mission (Regions Beyond Missionary Union in 1899). This was started by his father. The Belgians challenged him with the exploitation of the natives. Guinness later returned to the Congo in 1910. He died from a virus back in England after three unsuccessful operations.

Erik Ekman

Jan. 8, 1842

Aug. 18, 1915
Stromsbro (near Gavle), Sweden

President of Mission (Evangelical in 1937) **Covenant Church Board of Foreign Missions, 1885–1904**. Ekman was active in a revival movement in Sweden. He was also active in the Swedish Mission Covenant, from August 2, 1872, when it was organized, until 1904, when he was asked to resign because he advocated universalism. He accepted a position as director of a life insurance company. He was well known as a member of the Swedish Riksdag, publisher, author, and schoolman in Kristinchamn.

Gerrit J. Kollen

Aug. 9, 1843
Netherlands

Sept. 5, 1915
Holland, Michigan

President of Hope College, Holland, MI 1893–1911. Kollen came to America (1851) and married Mary Van Raalte (1879). His wife was the daughter of ALBERTUS C. VAN RAALTE (founder of Hope). Kollen went to Hope College as an assistant professor of math and natural philosophy from 1871–78. He then became professor of applied math and political economy from 1878–93 prior to his presidency.

Samuel Pollard

April 20, 1864
Camelford, England

Sept. 15, 1915
Stone Gateway, China

Missionary to the Miao in Southwest China. Converted at age eleven, Pollard sailed under Bible Christian Church auspices in 1887. He went to Chaotung, Yunnan Province, 1500 miles up the Yangtze River. In 1890, he married a young lady from the China Inland Mission. Pollard ministered to the independent aboriginal people. He then went to Nosuland centering in Shikmenkan, across the Kujeichow provincial border where Miao tribes were converted, and several thousand became Christians. He died from typhoid.

Edith L. Cavell

Dec. 4, 1865
Swardeston, England

Oct. 12, 1915
Brussels, Belgium

Nurse who was shot by a German firing squad in World War I. Edith served in London hospitals until 1906. In 1907, she became matron of Depages Clinic in Brussels. Beginning Aug. 20, 1914, while she was serving there, German troops occupied the city of Brussels. Edith attended to both Allies and Germans. She also assisted in the escape of hundreds of Allied soldiers who would have been killed by the Germans. She herself was arrested on August 5 and tried October 7–8. She was a wonderful, spiritual lady. Before she died, she stated: "Standing as I do, in view of God and eternity…I realize that patriotism is not enough. I must have no hatred or bitterness against anyone."

Martin G. Hanson

July 11, 1859
Kenyon, Minnesota

Oct. 14, 1915
Fairbaut, Minnesota

President of Hague Synod (ALC, ELCA in 1988), **1899–1904, 1910–15**. Hanson married Caroline Runcie on October 20, 1886. He was ordained to the Norwegian Lutheran Ministry in 1884. Hanson pastored Immanuel Church, St. Paul, MN (1884–92); Trinity Church, Grand Forks, ND (1892–98); and was president of Red Wing Evangelical Seminary, 1898 onward. He lived in Red Wing, MN.

Jacob Conzett

Jan. 17, 1834
Schiers, Switzerland

Oct. 24, 1915
Cincinnati, Ohio (?)

President of German Prsebyterian College and Seminary (University of Dubuque Theological Seminary in 1920), **Dubuque, IA 1871–81**. Conzett's family came to America in 1846, settling in Galena, IL, and then Dubuque. He became the fourth student of ADRIAN VAN VLIET and eventually took a small German congregation in Dyersville, IA, on July 5, 1859. He married Cornelia Taas in 1861 (died: December 6, 1901, after having given birth to eight children). Because of his impatience with those who could not meet his standards, the student enrollment dwindled to two before he resigned in 1881. He then pastored various German Presbyterian churches, the last one being Fairmont Presbyterian, Cincinnati, OH in 1891.

John T. Grape

May 6, 1835
Baltimore, Maryland

Nov. 2, 1915
Baltimore, Maryland

Composed the music for "Jesus Paid It All" (lyrics by ELVINA HALL). Grape was a successful coal merchant in Baltimore. For many years, he was active in Sunday school and directed the choir at Monument St. Methodist Church; then he ministered as choir director at Harford Avenue Methodist Church. Grape wrote several hymn tunes.

Phineas F. Bresee

Dec. 31, 1838
Franklin, New York

Nov. 13, 1915
Los Angeles, California

Founder of the Church of the Nazarene and general superintendent, 1907–1915, and first president of Pacific Bible College, 1901–10, renamed **Nazarene University, Los Angeles, 1910–11,** (Point Loma Nazarene University, San Diego, CA in 1998). Converted in a Methodist meeting (1856), Bresee moved to Iowa (1857). He married Maria Hibbard in 1860 at the Methodist Church in Davenport, NY. They had six children. He pastored a total of 37 years, in Iowa (1858–83) and then two Methodist churches in Southern California, (1883–95). He organized the movement in October, 1895, in Los Angeles, CA. In 1907, they merged with an East Coast group and became the Pentecostal Church of the Nazarene. In 1908, they merged with the Holiness Church of Christ, strong in the South. In 1919, the name reverted to CN. Bresee emphasized doctrines of holiness and sanctification as taught by WESLEY.

Booker T. Washington

April 5, 1856
Hale's Ford, Virginia

Nov. 14, 1915
Tuskegee, Alabama

Educator, lecturer, writer and founder of Tuskegee (AL) Institute (son of a mulatto slave and a white man). After the emancipation, Washington's family moved to Malden, WV and joined a Baptist church there. He then went to the Hampton (VA) Normal and Agricultural Institute, 1872–75. He taught there after graduation; then he went to Tuskegee, AL to organize Tuskegee Institute, a trade and professional school for black youth in 1881. He married Maggie Murray on Oct. 12, 1893. Washington made a speech on education, in Sept. 18, 1895, at the Atlanta Exposition, which made him famous; replacing FREDERICK DOUGLASS as chief spokesman for his race. He was respected among royalty and presidents. When he died of a heart attack, Washington had a legacy of 100 buildings, 1,500 students, 200 faculty members, and an endowment of $2 million at Tuskegee Institute. His books range from *Future of the American Negro* (1899) to *The Man Fartherest Down* (1912). His *Up from Slavery* (1901) was well received, translated into at least 15 languages.

William H. Doane

Feb. 3, 1832
Preston, Connecticut

Dec. 24, 1915
South Orange, New Jersey

Composed the music for some of our greatest hymns, including "Though Your Sins Be As Scarlet," "'Tis the Blessed Hour of Prayer," "To the Work," "Will Jesus Find Us Watching," "Pass Me Not," "Safe in the Arms of Jesus," "Near the Cross," "Rescue the Perishing," "To God, Be the Glory," "I Am Thine, O Lord," "Savior More Than Life to Me," "Tell Me the Old, Old, Story," "More Love to Thee," and "Take the Name of Jesus With You." The first eleven mentioned were FANNY CROSBY hymns. Others he collaborated with were CATHERINE HANKEY, ELIZABETH PRENTISS, and LYDIA

BAXTER. Doane moved to Cincinnati at age 29 and was president of a woodworking machinery factory there, J. A. Fay and Company. He was very active in the ministry of Mt. Auburn Baptist Church and married Fanny Treat on November 2, 1857. Beginning in 1862, following a severe illness, Doane published 40 songbooks, including the *Baptist Hymnal,* and composed 2,300 songs. Doane was a prime collaborator with FANNY CROSBY. He received more than 70 patents for machinery that he developed. He was wealthy and gave away large sums of money to various causes. *Encyclopedia Americana* says he died in Cincinnati.

Gaston B. Cashwell

c 1860/1862 — 1916
Dunn, North Carolina

Leader of Pentecostalism in the South. In 1903, Cashwell joined the newly formed Pentecostal Holiness Church, leaving the Methodist Church. Cashwell was an evangelist to both blacks and whites. In November, 1906, he went to Los Angeles, CA to Azusa Street Mission where WILLIAM SEYMOUR and other Christian leaders prayed for his ministry. Cashwell took the Pentecostal message to Holiness churches in Dunn, NC which became a miniature Azusa Street ministry. He engaged in a preaching tour from 1907–9, and A. J. TOMLINSON was one of his converts. In 1909, he left his Pentecostal Holiness Church, evidently disappointed at not being elected to head the PHC. He then conducted revivals in the South, mostly in independent churches.

William H. DeHart

March 21, 1837 — Feb. 14, 1916
New Brunswick, New Jersey — Plainfield, New Jersey

First stated clerk of Reformed Church in America, 1896–1914. DeHart married Janette Rich on May 12, 1870. DeHart was ordained in 1868 and held pastorates in Churchville, PA (1868–71); New York City (1871–77); Jamaica, NY (1877–87); Bethlehem, NY (1887–88); and the Third Church in Raritan, NY (1888–1911). He retired in Plainfield, NJ.

Eric Norelius

Oct. 26, 1833 — March 15, 1916
Hassela, Sweden — Vasa, Minnesota

President of Augustana Lutheran Church (LCA, ELCA in 1988), **1874–81, 1889–1911.** Norelius came to America in 1850. He was ordained in the Swedish Lutheran Church and pastored in Altica, IN from 1855–60. He served as pastor at Red Vasa, Spring Garden and Goodhue, all in Minnesota, 1860–1915. Norelius founded St. Ausgar Academy (Gustavus Adolphus College) in St. Peter, MN in 1865. He authored *History of the First Swedish Lutheran Congregation in America* (2 vols., 1890, 1916).

George A. Schulte

Nov. 30, 1838 — March 19, 1916
Neustadt-Goedens, Hannover, Germany — Newark, New Jersey

Director of North American Baptist Missions, 1892–1916. Schulte came to America in 1850–51 and settled with his family in Buffalo, NY; there he was converted and baptized. He graduated from Rochester Seminary in 1863. He pastored the Second Baptist Church in Buffalo (1863–70), followed by 21 years at the FBC of New York City (1872–92). He did much to unify the missionary work of the German churches.

Josiah Strong

Jan. 19, 1847
Naperville, Illinois

April 28, 1916
New York, New York

Congregational minister with a passion for social activist concerns. Strong married Alice Bisbee on August 29, 1871, pastored in Cheyenne, WY (1871–73) and was a professor at Western Reserve College (1873–76). He pastored in Sandusky, OH (1876–81), served as secretary of home missions (1881–84) and pastored Central Congregational, Cincinnati, OH (1884–86). He served as secretary of the Evangelical Alliance, 1886–1898. He resigned the Alliance to found and lead the League for Social Service, 1898–1902. In 1902, it became the American Institute for Social Service. Strong coined the slogan, "Safety First" and he edited *Social Progress*. He began a monthly publication *The Gospel of the Kingdom,* in 1908 and lived in South America, 1909–10. His writings range from *Our Country* (1885) to *Our World* (1915).

B. Fay Mills

June 4, 1857
Rahway, New Jersey

May 1, 1916
Grand Rapids, Michigan

Outstanding evangelist, although he lapsed from 1897 to 1915. Mills was ordained as a Congregationalist in 1878. He married Mary Russell on Oct. 31, 1879. He pastored in Cannon Falls, MN; Fourth Presbyterian, Albany (Greenwich), NY (1878–84); and Rutland, VT from 1884–86. He was an evangelist, 1886–97, and thousands were converted at his crusades. His "district campaigns" began in Cleveland in 1891; then in St. Paul, Columbus, and other major cities. It is believed that it was he who introduced the decision card. He saw 200,000 converts in twelve years. In 1893, he began to preach the social gospel philosophy and became a Unitarian pastor in Oakland, CA from 1899–1903. He was in Los Angeles (1904–11) and took time to visit China, Japan, and the Philippines (1907–8), founding religious and ethical organizations. He went to Chicago, 1911–14. Mills later realized his error and recommitted his life to Christ. He began crusades again in 1915 going to Decatur, IL; Toledo, OH; and Beloit, WI. *He wrote Power from on High* (1890) to *The New Revelation* (1908).

Timothy Dwight (2)

Nov. 16, 1828
Norwich, Connecticut

May 26, 1916
New Haven, Connecticut

Congregational president of Yale University, 1886–99. Dwight tutored at Yale College for several years, 1851–55. Following his education at Yale, Dwight studied at Bonn and Berlin (1856–58), and became a professor of sacred literature (N.T. Greek) in Yale Divinity School (1858–86). He married Jane Wakeman on December 31, 1866, and was the grandson of TIMOTHY DWIGHT (1). The Yale Divinity School was started under his administration in 1888.

Arthur H. Messiter

April 12, 1834
Frome, England

July 2, 1916
New York, New York

Composed the music for "Rejoice, Ye Pure in Heart" (lyrics by EDWARD PLUMPTRE). He came to America in 1863 and began his ministry as an organist in Poultney, VT then in Philadelphia, PA. In 1866, he became the organist at Trinity Church in NYC, serving there for 31 years. His male choirs served as models in the Episcopalian churches. Messiter married Margaret Gaddis in October, 1871.

Daniel Bliss

Aug. 17, 1823
Georgia, Vermont

July 28, 1916
Beirut, Syria (Lebanon)

Congregational (ABCFM) missionary and educator to Syria, 1855–1916. Bliss married Abby Wood on Nov. 23, 1855, and they had two sons. Bliss was a pioneer educator, president of Syrian Protestant College, 1864–1902 and founder of the influential American College in Beirut, Syria (Lebanon) in 1920. He wrote two philosophy books in Arabic. Early on, he served in Abeih and Su al-Gharb, managing schools, traveling, and preaching.

Harry Monroe

Jan. 17, 1853
Exeter, New Hampshire

July 31, 1916
Chicago, Illinois

Director of the Pacific Garden Mission, Chicago, IL 1892–1912, succeeding the founder, GEORGE CLARKE. In his early years, Monroe was an alcoholic, became associated with a counterfeiter, and was eventually arrested in Detroit, MI. Monroe left the Detroit area and went to Chicago where he was converted at the PGM. He served as a song leader, soloist, and assistant at the mission for twelve years.

Samuel R. Smith

Sept. 16, 1853
Hershey, Pennsylvania

Sept. 12, 1916
Lebanon, Pennsylvania

General Secretary of Brethren in Christ Church, Grantham, PA 1899, 1901–10, and first president of Messiah College, 1909–1916. Smith married Elizabeth Light and they had ten children. In his early days, he taught school and engaged in the manufacture of pastry goods. He was a member of the Brethren in Christ Church, was ordained (1906), and became a bishop (1913).

Horace G. Underwood

July 10, 1859
London, England

Oct. 12, 1916
Atlantic City, New Jersey

Pioneer Presbyterian missionary to Korea. Underwood came to America in 1872. Underwood's father developed the Underwood Typewriter Service. Horace was ordained to the Reformed Church, but was sent by the Presbyterian Board to Korea in 1885. Then in 1886, he opened an orphanage. In 1889, Underwood organized the Sai Mun An Church. Underwood married Lillias S. Horton, the Queen's physician, on March 13, 1889. He taught at the Presbyterian Theological Seminary, Pyeng Yang, Korea and at New York University from 1907 on. He wrote several books ranging from *English-Korean Dictionary* (1884) to *Introduction to the Korean Spoken Language* (1915).

Carl A. Björk

July 29, 1837
Jonkoping, Sweden

Oct. 16, 1916
Chicago, Illinois

President of Mission Covenant (Evangelical Covenant in 1937) **Church, 1885–1910.** Björk was trained to be a cobbler. He served in his country's armed forces, 1856–64. By 1863 the Rosenian revival was at full tide in the area, and he was converted. In 1864, he left for America. He became a natural leader among the Mission Covenant friends. He married Johanna C. Boman in 1866 (died: 1876) and then Augusta Peterson in 1898. The office of president became his on February 17, 1895. He leaned heavily on secretarial assistance in his administration.

Charles E. Cheney

Feb. 12, 1836
Canandaigua, New York

Nov. 15, 1916
Chicago, Illinois

Helped found the Reformed Episcopal Church in 1873 and served as a second bishop in the same church, 1876, 1887–89. Cheney was ordained a priest in the Protestant Episcopal Church in 1858. Cheney married Clara Griswold on April 25, 1860, and was rector of Christ Episcopal Church in Chicago from 1860 till his death. Cheney signed the "Chicago Protest" against the "unprotestantising" of the church which helped start the Tractarian Movement. He succeeded GEORGE CUMMINGS as the leader in 1876. His writings include *28 Sermons* (1880) to *A Belated Plantagenet* (1914).

William A. P. Martin

April 10, 1827
Livonia, Indiana

Dec. 18, 1916
Peking, China

Presbyterian missionary and educator to China. Martin married Jane Vansant in 1849 (died: 1893). He went to China in 1850 and was a missionary to Ninzpo, 1850–59. From 1863–68, he founded and established Presbyterian missions in Peking. From 1869–94, he was president of Tungnen Kuan government school. Martin served as president of Imperial University (1898–1900) and professor of international law at the University of Wuchang (1902–05). He was an advisor in international law to the Chinese government.

Henry D. M. Spence-Jones

Jan. 14, 1836
London, England

1917

Congregational clergyman and church historian. Jones held a number of educational and church positions, 1865–1917. He was a professor at St. David's College, Lampeter, Wales (1865–70); rector of St. Mary's de crypt with all Saints and St. Owen, Gloucester (1870–77); principal of Gloucester Theological Seminary (1875–77); vicar and rural dean of St. Pancras, London (1877–86); and dean of Gloucester, 1886 on. Jones also edited the *Pulpit Commentary*.

Andrew Murray

May 9, 1828
Graff-Reiner, South Africa

Jan. 18, 1917
Wellington, South Africa

Founder and first director of South Africa General Mission (Africa Evangelical Fellowship in 1965 which in 1998, merged into SIM), **1889–1913**. Converted in 1845 while studying in Utrecht, Netherlands, Murray was a Dutch Reformed minister who wrote *With Christ in the School of Prayer*, a classic book on prayer. Murray married Emma Rutherford of Cape Town, Africa on July 2, 1856 (died January 2, 1905). His ministry began in Bloemfontein (1848–60) and continued in Worcester (1860–64); Cape Town (1864–71); and then Wellington (1871–1906). Murray was also active in different evangelism endeavors. His work, *Abide in Christ*, was very famous. He founded the Huguenot Seminary and the Mission-training Institute in 1877. He opened up new fields in Bechuanaland, Ntaserland, and Mahonaland. Murray's last words were, "God is worthy of trust." His father, Andrew Murry Sr. (1794–1866), was a Scottish pioneer minister and evangelical leader of South Africa.

Louisa M. R. Stead-Wodehouse

c 1850
Dover, England

Jan. 18, 1917
Penkridge, South Rhodesia (Zimbabwe)

Wrote the hymn, "Tis So Sweet to Trust in Jesus" (music by WM. KIRKPATRICK) upon the death of her husband. Louisa was converted at age nine, and came to America in 1871. In 1875, she married Mr. Stead, who died while trying to rescue a drowning child. Then Louisa went to Africa, where she married Robert Wodehouse. They returned to America in 1895 when he served as a Methodist pastor. In 1901, she returned to Southern Rhodesia, Africa.

Samuel C. Edsall

March 4, 1860
Dixon, Illinois

Feb. 17, 1917
Rochester, Minnesota

President of Seabury Divinity School (Seabury-Western Theological Seminary, Evanston, IL in 1933), **Faribault, MN 1901–17**. Edsall married Grace Harmon on April 11, 1883 (died: 1913). Edsall was ordained in the Episcopal Church and founded the St. Peter's Mission in Chicago, IL in 1887. He served as a reader (1877–88); then rector of St. Peter's Church, Chicago, IL (1889–99); missionary bishop of North Dakota (1899–1901); and bishop of Minnesota (1901–17). He wrote *Prayer Book Preparation for Confirmation* (1898).

Folliott S. Pierpont

Oct. 7, 1835
Bath, England

March 10, 1917
Newport, England

Anglican hymn writer of "For the Beauty of the Earth" (1864) (music by Conrad Kocher). He began as classical master at Somersetchire College and then became an independent writer. Pierpont lived at Babbicombe, Devonshire, and other places, doing occasional teaching. He wrote a number of hymns and published several volumes of verse.

Milton Wright

Nov. 17, 1828
Rush County, Indiana

April 4, 1917
Dayton, Ohio

Bishop of Church of the United Brethren in Christ, 1877–81, 1885–1905, located at Dayton, OH 1877–92, Huntington, IN 1892 on. His minority groups were known as the Old Constitution (radicals) that split from the New Constitution (liberals) in 1889. Wright married Susan C. Koerner on November 24, 1859 (died 1889). They were the parents of the famed airplane inventors, Orville and Wilbur Wright. Converted at age 14, Wright was a missionary to Oregon (1857–59); then he returned to Indiana to teach theology at Hartsville College (1859–69). He also edited the *Religious Telescope* (1869–73).

James H. Moulton

Oct. 11, 1863
Richmond, England

April 7, 1917
Mediterranean Sea

Methodist theologian, Greek and Iranian scholar. Moulton assisted his father, William F. Moulton, at the Leys School, 1886–1902. He then became a tutor at Wesleyan College, Didsbury (1902–17) and was a professor of Hellenistic Greek and of Indo-European philology at Manchester University (1908–17). Moulton was traveling from India through the Mediterranean Sea when his ship was torpedoed and sunk. His writing includes *An Introduction to the Study of NT Greek* (1895) to *The Christian Religion in the Study and Street* (pub. 1919).

Henry B. Swete

March 14, 1835
Bristol, England

May 10, 1917
Hitchin, England

Anglican biblical and patristic scholar. Swete was the curate at three places, 1858–72. He served as pastor and as divinity lecturer at the University of Cambridge, 1875–77. Swete was also the rector of Ashdon, Essex (1877–90) and the professor of pastoral theology at King's College in London (1882–90). Then, 1890–1915, he served as professor of divinity at Cambridge University. Swete never married. His writings included *England vs. Rome* (1868) to *The Parables of the Kingdom* (1920). He also authored *Old Tesament in Greek According to the Septuagint*.

Rudolph Sohm

Oct. 29, 1841
Rostock, Germany

May 16, 1917

Jurist and church historian. Sohm taught law at Gottingen (1866–70), Freiburg (1870–72), Strassburg (1872–87) and at Leipzig in 1887. Sohm held the view that the church is spiritual and that the law is secular. From those ideas, the canon of law in Catholicism (abandonment of the primitive ideal of the church) was developed. He wrote on church history, church and state, and church polity.

James Denney

Feb. 5, 1856
Paisley, Scotland

June 12, 1917

Pastor and theologian. He pastored the Broughty Ferry Free Church, 1886–97, then became a professor of New Testament languages, literature, and systematic theology at the United Free Church of Scotland College from 1897–1915. Denney wrote several commentaries on New Testament writings. Denney is known for his work on the atonement and for his book, *The Death of Christ* (1903). His books ranged from *Thessalonians* (1892) to *The Way Everlasting* (1911). He tried to adjust Christian doctrines to materialistic views.

William D. Hyde

Sept. 23, 1858
Winchendon, Massachusetts

June 29, 1917
Brunswick, Maine (?)

President of Bowdoin College, Brunswick, ME 1885–1917, and Congregational hymn writer. Hyde married Prudence Phillips on November 6, 1883. He became a pastor in Paterson, NJ in 1883, then served as a professor of philosophy at Bowdoin. He was called the "boy president" at 27 years old. Hyde wrote on education, ethics, practical idealism, and theology, and served as university preacher at several institutions. He wrote works ranging from *Practical Ethics* (1892) to *The Five Great Philosophies of Life* (1911).

Paul P. Waldenstrom

July 20, 1838
Lulea, Sweden

July 14, 1917
Ludingo, Sweden

Theologian and churchman, founder of the reform movement in Sweden known as the Mission Covenant in 1878. Today, this denomination is known as the Evangelical Covenant Church in America. Waldenstrom was a maverick Lutheran who resigned from the state church and helped found the Free Church movement in Sweden. Waldenstrom was active in revival movements. He also held pastorates, editorial positions, and was a respected theologian. He worked for the Evangelical National Association in 1882.

Hosea W. Jones

Sept. 16, 1846
Delaware, Ohio

July 16, 1917
Gambier, Ohio

Dean of Bexley Hall at Kenyon College [Colgate–Rochester (NY) Divinity School in 1968] **Gambier, OH 1891–1917**. Jones was ordained as a deacon (1870) and as a priest (1871) by Bishop Bedell. Jones led several general conferences and pastored from 1870–85. Jones was a professor of church history (1885–1917) and was the dean of the seminary (1901–17). He authored *Notes on Prayer Book* (1895).

Ernest W. Shurtleff

April 4, 1862
Boston, Massachusetts

Aug. 24, 1917
Paris, France

Congregational hymn writer of "Lead On, O King Eternal" (1887) (music by HENRY SMART). Shurtleff served pastorates in Ventura, CA (1889–90); Plymouth, MA (1891–98); and First Congregational, Minneapolis, (1898–1905). He married Helen Cramer on July 20, 1899. Shurtleff then went to Paris in 1905 to direct student activities at the Academy in Latin Quarters. Shurtleff did relief work during World War I. His books include *Poems* (1883) to *Heaven in Easter* (1896).

Oswald Chambers

June 24, 1874
Aberdeen, Scotland

Nov. 15, 1917
Zeiton, Egypt

Bible teacher and evangelical mystic. The son of a Baptist pastor, Chambers was converted as a result of CHARLES SPURGEON's preaching. From 1906–7, he toured the world, preaching among Methodist and Pentecostal Holiness groups. He married Gertrude Hobbs in 1910 (died: 1966), then served as the principal of Bible-training College at Clampham Common, London, 1911–15. From 1915–17, Chambers was the superintendent of the YMCA huts in Egypt, a ministry among military personnel in desert camps. He died while working with a YMCA chaplain among troops. He had misdiagnosed appendicitis, which resulted in peritonitis. His *My Utmost for His Highest* (1927) is a well-known devotional book, used by multitudes, including President George W. Bush. His favorite Bible verse was Luke 11:13.

Robert Anderson

1841
Dublin, Ireland

1918

Lay theologian, barrister, writer, and Bible teacher. Anderson wrote the hymn "Safe in Jehovah's Keeping" (music by DANIEL TOWNER). He was converted at age 19 through the preaching of John Hall at his own church in Dublin. In 1868, he became an advisor on the Irish affairs committee to the home office in matters related to political crime. He served as the head of criminal Investigation at Scotland Yard, 1888–1901. He was, perhaps, the best-known Presbyterian layman evangelist of his time, as well as a dispensational Bible teacher. He was especially versed in apologetics and prophecy. He authored several books, ranging from *The Gospel and Its Ministry* (1876) to *Misunderstood Texts of the New Testament* (1916). He had two sermons on *The Fundamentals* (1910–15).

William B. Carpenter

March 26, 1841
Liverpool, England

1918

Anglican priest and prolific writer. Carpenter was a curate of three small churches (1864–70), then vicar of St. James, Holloway (1870–79), and Christ Church, Lancaster Gate (1879–84). Carpenter won the admiration of Queen VICTORIA, who appointed him the chaplain to the bishop of London (1879–84), after which Carpenter was appointed the bishop of Ripon in 1884. He was responsible for the founding of Ripon College, Oxford, England. His works ranged from *Thoughts on Prayer* (1871) to *Witness to the Influence of Christ* (1905).

Charles Wagner

Jan. 3, 1852
Wibersviller, Germany

1918

Cleric and moral essayist. Wagner left Germany (1876) and the Lutheran Church for France to unite with the liberal wing of the French Protestant Church in Remiremont, 1876–82 and then in Paris (1882). Wagner opened a Sunday School and did pastoral work and preaching. He took much interest in working with classics. He founded several popular university extension courses under the auspices of the Society for Promotion of Morality. He authored titles from *Youth* (1893), which attacked degenerate tendencies in life and literature, to *Home of the Soul* (1909). He also wrote *The Simple Life* in 1903.

Annie Sherwood Hawks

May 28, 1835
Hoosick, New York

Jan. 3, 1918
Bennington, Vermont

Baptist hymn writer of "I Need Thee Every Hour" (1872). Annie lived in Brooklyn and was a member of the Hanson Place Church. Her pastor, Robert Lowry, encouraged her in hymn writing and added the music to this hymn. In 1859, Annie married Charles H. Hawks, and they had three children. He died in 1888. Annie wrote most of her 400 poems, 1868–76. She retired in Bennington, VT at the home of her daughter.

Sarah Dunn Clarke

Nov. 13, 1835
Cayuga County, New York

Jan. 19, 1918

Co-founder and "mother" of the Pacific Garden Mission of Chicago. She was converted on a train platform in Scranton, PA when a friend asked her to give her heart to God. After having taught school in New York and Iowa, Sarah started a mission at State and 23rd Street in 1869. Sarah met Colonel GEORGE R. CLARKE, a realtor, and they were married on January 23, 1873. In 1877, George left the business world and helped Sarah continue the mission on south State Street. One of her converts was BILLY SUNDAY. Her husband died in 1892. She continued the work, never missing a meeting for 27 years. After being injured in an accident in 1912, she was forced into retirement.

George T. Caldbeck

1852
Waterford, Ireland

Jan. 29, 1918
Epsom, England

Composed music for "Peace, Perfect Peace" (lyrics by EDWARD BICKERSTETH). Caldbeck received training at the National Model School in Waterford and at Islington Theological College. Ill health prevented Caldbeck from his missionary aspirations. Instead, he became an Irish schoolmaster and evangelist. In 1888, he moved to London to become an independent evangelist.

John B. Sumner (2)

March 25, 1838
Lime Hill, Pennsylvania

May 9, 1918
Binghamton, New York

Composed music for "A Child of the King" (1877) (lyrics by HARRIET BUELL). Sumner pastored Methodist churches in Wyalusing, PA and Kirkwood and Binghamton, NY. Sumner was a music singing instructor. He saw Miss Buell's poem for "A Child of the King" in a magazine and put it to music. He was a gifted tenor. With two other music ministers, he put together a conference trio, which often sang at Chautauqua meetings. He and his wife, Alma, gave singing lessons with a three-foot music book and a melodeon.

Ludwig I. Nommensen

Feb. 6, 1834
Nordstrand (Schleswig), Island (Germany)

May 23, 1918

Missionary to Sumatra. Nommensen gave 56 years of tireless work in Sumatra (an island in Indonesia) helping the Batak Church come into existence. It became one of the largest churches in Southeast Asia. In 1861, Nommensen sailed to Sumatra on Christmas Eve to begin missionary service with the Rhenish Missionary Society. In 1865, he baptized his first converts in the Silindung Valley. In 1866, he married Katoline Gutbrodt (died: 1887). He translated the New Testament into Batak (1878) and penetrated the remote Toba Lake region (1886). He remarried (1892), but she died (1909). A son was murdered in Sumatra in 1901. Nommensen was still active during the fiftieth anniversary of the Batak Church in 1911. Upon his death there were 180,000 members of the Batak Church Ministry in over 500 churches. By 1993, there were 2 ½ million members.

Washington Gladden

Feb. 11, 1836
Pottsgrove, Pennsylvania

July 2, 1918
Columbus, Ohio

Liberal theologian and social gospel exponent. Gladden wrote the hymn "O Master, Let Me Walk with Thee," 1912 (music by HENRY SMART). Gladden married Jennie Cohoon on Dec. 5, 1860 (died: 1909). After his ordination in 1860, he pastored at First Congregational Methodist Church, Brooklyn (1860–61); in Morrisana, NY (1861–66); North Adams, MA (1866–71); and North Congregational Church, Springfield, MA (1874–82). Gladden became the editor of *The Independent* in 1871. He pastored at First Congregational Church, Columbus, OH from 1882–1914 with great success. He applied Christian principles to problems of industry, commerce, and politics. He was moderator of the National Council of Congregational Churches 1904–7. In 1905, he opposed a large money gift offered by the Standard Oil Company to the Congregational Church Foreign Mission Board, calling it "tainted money." He wrote 38 books and called for Christians to build the kingdom of God based on social justice, popularizing the social gospel. His books ranged from *Plain Thoughts on the Art of Living* (1868) to *Live and Learn* (1914). Gladden and LYMAN ABBOTT promoted higher criticism (study of Bible with the object of facts of authorship and dates of composition).

Joseph H. Gilmore

April 29, 1834
Boston, Massachusetts

July 23, 1918
Rochester, New York

Wrote the well-known hymn, "He Leadeth Me" (1863) (music by WILLIAM BRADBURY), while a visiting speaker in Philadelphia. Gilmore married May Parkhurst (May 10, 1861) and Lucy Brown (September 21, 1865). Gilmore was ordained a Baptist in 1862. His father was the governor of New Hampshire, 1863–64. Gilmore became a pastor briefly, 1865–67, at the Second Church of Rochester, NY. He was a professor of Hebrew, logic, rhetoric, and English literature at the University of Rochester, NY from 1867–1911. He edited the *Concord* (NH) *Monitor* (1864–65). He wrote *Familiar Chats About Books and Reading* (1892).

Walter Rauschenbusch

Oct. 4, 1861
Rochester, New York

July 25, 1918
Rochester, New York

Baptist theologian who had a liberal view on the basic tenents of the faith. Rauschenbusch was educated in Westphalia (conservative pietistic school of Reformed tradition) and then at Rochester Theological Seminary. He became the pastor of a small congregation, Second German Baptist Church of German immigrants on the west side of New York City in 1886–97. He labored for eleven years, knowing that social needs had to be addressed as well. In 1891, his hearing began to diminish. He and eight other Baptists formed the "Brotherhood of the Kingdom" in 1892. He married Pauline Rother on April 12, 1893. Rauschenbusch left New York City to teach NT in the German department of Rochester (NY) Seminary (1897–1901), then church history in the English division (1903–18). His *Christianity and* *the Social Crisis* (1907) made him a leader in social gospel activities. He wrote many other books, his most well known, *A Theology of the Social Gospel* (1917). He died from cancer.

Howard E. Smith

July 6, 1864

Aug. 13, 1918
Norwalk, Connecticut

Composed music for "Love Lifted Me" (lyrics by JAMES ROWE). Smith was an active musician throughout his life and served many years as a church organist in Connecticut. Smith composed a number of hymn tunes, but not much other information is known about him.

William P. DuBose

April 11, 1836
Winnsboro, South Carolina

Aug. 18, 1918
Sewanee, Tennessee

Dean of the University of the South, Sewanee, TN 1894–1908. DuBose was wounded twice and captured in 1862 during the Civil War. He married Anne Peronneau on April 30, 1863 (died 1873), and then Maria L. Yeager on December 18, 1878 (died 1887). Dubose was ordained into the Episcopal Church and served as rector of St. John's in Winnsboro, SC (1866–68) and Trinity Church in Abbeville, SC (1868–71). He began teaching both OT and NT language and interpretation in 1871, as well as becoming U.S. chaplain. Some feel he was America's greatest Episcopal theologian. His books range from *The Soteriology of the New Testament* (1892) to *Turning Points in my Life* (1912).

William Duncan

April 3, 1832
Bishop Burton, England

Aug. 30, 1918
Metlakatla, Alaska

Pioneer missionary to Alaska under the auspices of the Church Missionary Society of the Anglican Church. Duncan was a dry goods clerk who had a zeal for God. He arrived at Fort Simpson (near Prince Rupert), BC, in 1857. He began work with the Tsimpshian Indians and saw remarkable results. A meeting with President Grover Cleveland saw the Indians granted official refuge on any American island close to their home. One such island was Metlakatla, where Duncan led them in 1862. He has been chronicled, extolled, criticized, eulogized, cursed, and adulated.

Isaac Clark

June 30, 1833
Canterbury, Connecticut

Sept. 2, 1918

Dean of Howard University School of Divinity, Washington, DC 1901–16. Clark married Sophie T. Hastings on January 1, 1862. Ordained as a Presbyterian, he pastored in Elmira, NY (1861–68); First Congregational Church, Aurora, IL (1868–72); Elm Place Church, Brooklyn, NY (1872–74); Rondout, NY (1874–82); and Edwards Congregational Church, Northampton, MA (1882–1910). He began his ministry at Howard as professor of theology, homiletic, and English exegesis, 1891–1901.

William S. Pitts

Aug. 18, 1830
Orleans County, New York

Sept. 25, 1918
Brooklyn, New York

Wrote the lyrics and music of "The Church in the Wildwood" in honor of the "little brown church" two miles northeast of Nashau, IA which he helped organize, encouraging Pastor J. K. Nutting to build the church (1857). It was dedicated (1864). The song was first sung by him at that church in 1864. Pitts practiced medicine for 40 years near Fredericksburg, IA from 1866–1906.

James A. Grier
May 8, 1846
Waltz's Mills, Pennsylvania

Oct. 6, 1918
Bellevue, Pennsylvania

President of Allegheny (PA) (Pittsburgh in 1959) **Theological Seminary, 1891–1909.** Grier married Ada Bruen on July 15, 1874. He was ordained as a United Presbyterian in 1874. Grier held pastorates at Locust Hill, PA (1874–83) and Monroe, PA (1883–86). He also served as professor of systematic theology at Allegheny, 1886–1909. Grier authored *Secret Societies* (1880) and *Pastoral Homilies* (1909).

Charles C. Converse
Oct. 7, 1832
Warren, Massachusetts

Oct. 18, 1918
Highwood, New Jersey

Composed music for Joseph Scriven's famous hymn, "What a Friend We Have in Jesus." Converse also wrote compositions for symphonies, overtures, string quartets, oratorios, and other hymn tunes. He moved to Germany, 1855–59, and after his return to America, he received his law degree in 1861. He practiced law in Erie, PA. Converse married Eliza J. Lewis on January 14, 1858. He wrote under the pseudonym of "Karl Reden" at times.

Agnes Weston
March 28, 1840
London, England

Oct. 23, 1918
Devonport, England

"The Sailor's Friend" was converted at age 17. Weston began working among the poor, sick, alcoholics, soldiers, and sailors. In 1874, she opened the Royal Sailor's Rest at Devonport. This mission became a center for evangelistic work, Bible classes, reading, gathering of families and much more. She sent tracts to every ship touching port in the United Kingdom. A monthly letter to sailors for ship distribution had 60,000 circulation at her death. Her life long associate was Sophi Wintz (1847–1929). They were both accorded a full naval funeral.

James W. Hood
May 30, 1831
Kennett Township, Pennsylvania

Oct. 30, 1918
Fayetteville, North Carolina

Bishop of African Methodist Episcopal Zion Church, 1872–1918; senior bishop, 1893–1916. Hood married Hannah L. Ralph on October 4, 1852 (died: April 15, 1855); Sophia Nugent in May, 1858 (died: September 13, 1875); and Katie McKoy on June 6, 1877. He was a missionary to Nova Scotia (1860) and then to freemen within the Union lines in North Carolina (1863). President Theodore Roosevelt consulted him in Negro matters. Hood's books range from *The Negro in the Christian Pulpit (*1884) to *The Second Book of Sermons* (1908). He oversaw the establishment of Zion Wesley Institute (Livingstone College) in Sallisbury, NC. The seminary founded there, Hood Theological Seminary, was named in his honor.

Howard A. Walter
Aug. 19, 1883
New Britain, Connecticut

Nov. 11, 1918
Lahore, India

Wrote the hymn "I Would Be True" (1906) (music by Joseph Peek). Walter was a Congregationalist and taught English at Waseda University in Tokyo, Japan. He married Marguerite B. Darlington on November 21, 1910. In 1913, he joined the YMCA staff for India and Ceylon. There, Walter worked with Mohammedan students in Lahore, India. He worked also in evangelism endeavors. He died of a heart attack at age 35 during an influenza epidemic. His books ranged from *My Creed and Other Poems* (1912) to T*he Fact and Meaning of Islam* (1918).

Augustus Schultze

Feb. 3, 1840
Nowawes, Germany

Nov. 12, 1918
Bethlehem, Pennsylvania

President of Moravian Theological Seminary, Bethlehem, PA 1885–1918. He taught at the French Academy in Lausanne, Switzerland (1861–62); and at Moravian College, Niesky, teaching classics (1862–70). Schultze married Adde E. Peter on July 5, 1876. Schultze was one of three governing men in the Moravian Church, 1881–93. He edited the German Moravian hymn book and magazine and wrote *History of the Widow's Society of Bethlehem* (1880) to *Systematic Christian Doctrine and Theology* (1909).

Heinrich Voth

Feb. 19, 1851
Taurida, Russia

Nov. 26, 1918
Vanderhuf, British Columbia, Canada

Mennonite leader. He married Sarah Kornelsen on June 12, 1873. He was converted while teaching at a Mennonite village school at Klippenfeld for two years. In 1876, his family emigrated to America to a farm near Bingham Lake, MN. At first he led the Sunday School, then entered the ministry. He was ordained as an elder in 1885 after which he pastored the Bingham Lake MB Church for many years. He traveled as an evangelist and held meetings in all MB churches. Voth served as moderator of the General Conference for 14 years, (1901–15) and chairman of Mennonite Brethren Board of Foreign Missions (1909–18).

Charles C. Case

June 6, 1843
Linesville, Pennsylvania

Dec. 1, 1918
Oberlin, Ohio

Composed music for "Why Not Now?" (1891) (music by DAN WHITTLE), a beautiful invitation song. Case lived most of his life in Gustavus, OH and was under the influence of the singing schools there. Case led the music at the Chautauqua Lake (NY) conferences for twelve years and was the choir director at Moody Church, Chicago for three years. He married Annie Williams on April 23, 1866. Case authored *The Choice* (1875) to *Choice Songs* (1903).

J. Wilbur Chapman

June 17, 1859
Richmond, Indiana

Dec. 25, 1918
Jamaica, Long Island, New York

Widely sought Presbyterian hymn writer ("One Day"), evangelist, and pastor in Ohio and Indiana. After his conversion at a Sunday school service, Chapman married Irene Steddon on May 10, 1882 (died: 1886); Agnes Strain on November 4, 1888 (died: 1907); and Mabel Moulton on Aug. 30, 1910. He pastored the Dutch Reformed Church in Albany, NY from 1885–90; the Bethany Presbyterian Church, Philadelphia, PA from 1890–93 and 1896–99; one of the country's largest churches at that time. He worked with MOODY in the 1893 World's Fair campaign, which began his evangelism interests. He also mentored BILLY SUNDAY. He then pastored the First Presbyterian Church, NYC from 1899–1902. From 1903–18, Chapman headed the evangelism department of the Presbyterian Church. Together with CHARLES ALEXANDER he held "Saturation Evangelism" crusades in major cities. The Philadelphia (1908), Boston (1909), and Chicago (1910) crusades were the greatest. Chapman compiled song books and wrote the great song, "One Day", in 1910 (music by CHARLES MARSH). This could perhaps be the greatest gospel song ever written. He also wrote "'Tis Jesus" and "Our Great Saviour" (music of both by Rowland Pritchard) He died after emergency gall bladder surgery. He was the first director of the Winona Lake (IN) Bible Conference. His more than 30 books range from *Ivory Palaces of the King* (1893) to *When Home Is Heaven* (1917).

Joseph S. Exell

May 29, 1849
Melksham, England

c 1919

Church of England clergyman who was curate of Eston-super-Mare, Somersetshire, 1881–84. Exell also served as vicar of Townstall, St. Savior, Somertshire, 1884–90; and rector of Stoke Fleming, Darmouth, Devonshire after 1890. He compiled the *Biblical Illustrator*, which covered all the books in the Bible, and wrote several other reference works.

John N. Figgis

1866

1919

Anglican theologian, apologist, and historian whose original thinking and writing on the relationship between church and state sounded the alarm as to the dangers in religion and human freedom from the all-competent modern state. Figgis was a parish priest (1892–1902), and vicar of Marnhull (1902–7). He had a middle-age conversion, and became an evangelist. He wrote *The Divine Right of Kings* (1892).

Lewis Hartsough

Aug. 31, 1828
Ithaca, New York

Jan. 1, 1919
Mount Vernon, Iowa

Wrote the lyrics and music for "I Am Coming, Lord." Hartsough married Isabella Cornish on July 21, 1852, and was ordained a Methodist in 1853. He served churches in the Oneida (NY) Conference for 15 years. He was appointed the first superintendent of Utah Missions, and moved to Salt Lake City in 1869, where he became "the Father of Methodism" in Utah. From 1871–73, he saw two great revivals in Epworth, IA and also traveled over 400,000 miles in home mission endeavors. Hartsough was transferred to the Dakotas during 1874–95. Hartsough retired to Mount Vernon, IA in 1895.

Theodore Roosevelt

Oct. 27, 1858
New York, New York

Jan. 6, 1919
Oyster Bay, New York

Twenty-sixth President of the United States, 1901–09, succeeding the assassinated McKinley. Roosevelt's 1904 popular majority was one of the largest ever with the electoral vote being 336–140 over Alton Parker. He married Alice Lee on October 27, 1880, (died: 1884) and Edith Carow (April 16, 1861–September 30, 1948) on December 2, 1886. His "Rough Riders" were established in Cuba during the Spanish-American War. He became governor of New York (1899) and vice-president (1901). He was the first president to ride in an automobile (August 22, 1902 in Hartford, CT) and also the first to visit a foreign country while in office. As Republican president, Roosevelt enforced the Sherman Anti-trust Act and began construction of the Panama Canal. In November, 1906, he visited Panama and Puerto Rico. He took several hunting trips to Africa, 1909–10 and explored Brazil in 1914. Roosevelt held Christian values. He wrote several books. His last words were, "Please put out the lights."

Johann K. Nikander

Sept. 3, 1855
Lammi, Finland

Jan. 13, 1919
Hancock, Michigan

President of Finnish Evangelical Lutheran Church (LCA, ELCA in 1988), **1890–98, 1902–19, and first president of Suomi College and Theological Seminary, Hancock MI 1896–1918** (Lutheran School of Theology, Chicago in 1964). Nikander was ordained in 1879 then came to

America in 1884. Nikander pastored churches in Michigan, 1885–97, and married Sanna K. Rajala on July 27, 1902. He authored *Finnish Bible History* in 1906.

Jacob S. Gubelmann

Nov. 26, 1836
Berne, Switzerland

Feb. 10, 1919
Rochester, New York

President of German Baptist Department of Rochester (NY) Divinity School (North American Baptist Seminary, Sioux Falls, SD), **1884–1915**. He also was a professor of theology and homiletics for some of these years. Gubelmann was ordained in Louisville, KY on January 13, 1861 He pastored the German Baptist Church, Louisville, KY (1860–62); St. Louis, MO (1862–68); and in Philadelphia (1868–84). He was a professor of theology and homiletics at the Rochester school from 1884–94. He wrote books on Bible inspiration and the Holy Spirit.

David B. Willson

Sept. 27, 1842
Philadelphia, Pennsylvania

Feb. 13, 1919
Pittsburgh, Pennsylvania

Professor and CEO of Reformed Presbyterian Theological Seminary, Pittsburgh, PA 1875–1916. He was ordained in 1870. Willson pastored in Allegheny, PA from 1870–75, and began teaching Biblical literature and child evangelism at the seminary in 1875. He also edited the *Reformed Presbyterian and Convenanter*, 1874–95. Willson married Martha J. Grier (August 21, 1873) and Mary R. Galbraith (August 14, 1883).

Adolf F. Schauffler

Nov. 7, 1845
Constantinople, Turkey

Feb. 18, 1919
New York, New York (?)

Presbyterian clergyman and home missionary, son of missionaries. Schauffler pastored the Olivet Church of New York City from 1872–87. He married Julia Baker in August, 1884. He was also the superintendent of the New York City Missionary and Tract Society, 1887–1902 and president of the New York City Mission after 1902. He was very active in Sunday School work. Schauffler wrote books on youth-related subjects.

Julia H. Johnston

Jan. 21, 1849
Salineville, Ohio

March 6, 1919
Peoria, Illinois

Wrote over 500 hymns, including "He Ransomed Me" and "Grace Greater Than All Our Sins" (music by DANIEL TOWNER). Julia's father pastored the FPC in Peoria, IL, 1856–64. For 41 years, she was the superintendent of the Sunday School department there. For 20 years, she was the president of the local Presbyterian Missionary Society. She wrote for David C. Cook Publishers. Julia never married.

Frederick W. Stellhorn

Oct. 2, 1841
Hanover, Germany

March 17, 1919
Columbus, Ohio

President of Capital University, 1899–1910, and dean of Evangelical Lutheran Theological (Trinity Lutheran in 1978) **Seminary, Columbus, OH 1908–19**. Stellhorn married Christiana Buenger on January 3, 1866, (died: 1899) and Louise Darst on July 10, 1901. He pastored in St. Louis, MO (1865–67); and in DeKalb Co., IN (1867–69). He then served as a professor at Northwestern University, Watertown, WI (1870–74); and at Concordia College, Ft. Wayne, IN (1874–81). He taught theology and German at Capital University, 1881–1919. He wrote several books.

James W. Bashford

May 29, 1849
Fayette, Wisconsin

March 18, 1919
Pasadena, California

Methodist pastor, educator, and missionary bishop to China. Bashford married Jane Field on Sept. 24, 1878. He held pastorates in Jamaica Plain, MA (1878–80); Auburndale, MA (1881–84), Portland, ME (1884–87), and Buffalo, NY (1887–89). He then became president of Ohio Wesleyan University, Delaware, OH from 1889–1904. Bashford became a bishop in 1904. At age 55, he went to Shanghai, China, and served for eleven years, fulfilling a college goal. In 1907, he organized a China Centennial Thank Offering which raised $600,000. In 1912, he urged President Taft to recognize the new Chinese Republic. Bashford wrote books on China missions and believed that evolution and higher criticism were compatible with Christianity. He wrote works ranging from *Outline of Science of Religion* (1891) to *The Oregon Missions* (1918).

Edward P. Hart

June 6, 1835
Middlesex, Vermont

March 20, 1919
Alameda, California

General superintendent of Free Methodist Church, 1874–1908. Hart was converted in 1859 and married Martha C. Bishop on Aug. 9, 1860. He was ordained in October, 1860. Hart lived in Alameda, CA most of his life. As an evangelist in Michigan, he established a movement there and helped found Spring Arbor Seminary in 1871. Hart was an administrator, a wise officer, and a superior preacher. Failing health in 1908 caused his resignation.

Timothy Richard

Oct. 10, 1845
Flaldybrenin, Wales

April 17, 1919
London, England

Missionary to China. Richard was converted in a revival in 1859. He was ordained and sailed to North China under the Baptist Missionary Society in 1869. Richard worked in Chefco, 1870–75, then moved to Ch'ingcow, 200 miles inland. He greatly assisted the people during the famine days of 1876–79. Richard directed the Christian Literature Society in 1891, leaving BMS. He then pursued his literary and educational work, aimed at the high class citizenry. Due to illness, he retired in 1915.

George H. Jones

Aug. 14, 1867
Mohawk, New York

May 10, 1919
Miami, Florida

Methodist missionary to Korea, 1887, stationed at Seoul. He studied the Korean language, literature, history, and beliefs. Jones married Margaret Bengel on May 10, 1893. Jones founded 44 congregations and brought over 2,800 Koreans into the Christ Church in Chemuloc, 1893–1903. While in the States (1903–7), he helped translate the Bible into Korean and served as the president of Biblical Institute and Union Theological Seminary (1907–11). He served as editorial secretary to the Board of Foreign Missions, 1913 on, also lecturing at Boston University.

Henry J. Heinz

Oct. 11, 1844
Pittsburg, Pennsylvania

May 14, 1919
Pittsburgh, Pennsylvania (?)

Founder of the Heinz plants, known for its catchy "57 varieties", and Sunday School enthusiast. While growing up in Sharpsburg, PA Heinz helped his mother's big garden grow. By the time he was twelve, the garden plot was 3 ½ acres, and a career selling vegetables was on its way. The company eventually produced 126 products, and by 1867, was doing $100 million dollars a year business in 26 plants. He married Sarah Young on September 23, 1869 (died 1894). He spent 64 years promoting the Sunday School concept wherever he went. One could readily see "pickles was a sideline" and the work of the gospel was the main business of his life. Heinz had tickets in his pocket to go to a New York City Sunday School gathering when he died of pneumonia. In his will, he left over $500,000 to Sunday School work. Heinz was a Presbyterian, but also gave to many worthy Methodist causes.

George Hodges (1)

Oct. 6, 1856
Rome, New York

May 27, 1919
Boston, Massachusetts

President of Episcopal Divinity School, Cambridge, MA 1894–1919. Hodges was ordained as a deacon (1881), and then as a priest (1882) of the Episcopalian church. He served as the assistant rector (1881–89) and rector of Calvary Church, Pittsburgh, PA (1889–94). He was president of the South End House Association. He was one of the first to be known as one who preached a "social gospel." He authored several books ranging from *The Episcopal Church* (1889) to *Religion in a World at War* (1917).

John H. Sammis

July 6, 1846
Brooklyn, New York

June 12, 1919
Los Angeles, California

Wrote the familiar gospel song "Trust and Obey" (1887) (music by DANIEL TOWNER). Sammis moved from Brooklyn to Logansport, IN where he became a successful businessman. He also worked for several years as a YMCA worker. He attended McCormick and Lane Seminaries. Sammis was ordained in 1880, then pastored in Michigan, Minnesota, and Indiana. He taught at BIOLA until his death.

Wilhelm Becher

April 15, 1850
Graben, Germany

June 13, 1919
St. Louis, Missouri

President of Eden Theological Seminary, St. Louis, MO 1902–19. Becher was ordained in Baden, German, in 1871 before coming to the U.S. After receiving extensive German education, he pastored in Nebraska and Missouri, then became professor at Eden, 1883–1919. He is buried in St. Louis.

Frank E. Graeff

Dec. 19, 1860
Tamaqua, Pennsylvania

July 29, 1919
Ocean Grove, New Jersey

Wrote the great comforting hymn "Does Jesus Care?" (1901) (music by LINCOLN HALL). Graeff was a minister in the Philadelphia Conference of the Methodist Church from 1890 on. He was known as the "Sunshine Minister." He wrote more than 200 hymns, scores of poems, and the book *The Minister's Twins*. In 1900, in deep despair on his knees, he shouted, "I know He cares. I know my Savior cares." He was devoted to little children.

Charles J. Fowler

Feb. 6, 1845
Bristol, New Hampshire

Sept. 30, 1919
St. Johnsbury, Vermont (?)

President of the National Camp Meeting 1894–1899, renamed National Association of Holiness (Christian Holiness Partnership in 1997), **1899–1919**. Under Fowler's leadership, membership topped 1,000 and a missionary arm was developed World Gospel Mission. He was converted at a winter revival renamed in 1869 under H.F. Durant's preaching. He too, soon began holding revivals, having a great one in Littleton, NH. He married Emily P. Sinclair on February 12, 1874 (died:

1939). In 1883, he joined the New Hampshire Conference of the Methodist Episcopal Church and served various pastorates in New Hampshire and Massachusetts. He rose to leadership in the ranks of the Holiness movement and started preaching at the national camp meetings in 1890 in Decatur, IL. He was an editor and writer. His last book was *Chair Talks on Perfection*.

Daniel B. Towner

March 5, 1850
Rome, Pennsylvania

Oct. 13, 1919
Longwood, Missouri

Composed music for some of our greatest hymns, including "At Calvary" (NEWELL), "Trust and Obey" (SAMMIS), "Grace Greater Than All Our Sins" (J. JOHNSTON), "Saved by the Blood" (Henderson), "My Anchor Holds" (W.C. Martin), "Ship Ahoy" (Cartwright), Nor Silver Nor Gold" "Anywhere With Jesus" (JESSE BROWN), "Safe in Jehovah's Keeping" (ANDERSON), "The Road Leads Home," and "Only a Sinner" (both by GRAY). Towner married Mary McGonigle on Dec. 26, 1870. Towner was the music director of Methodist churches in Binghamton, NY (1870–82); Cincinnati, OH (1887–84); and Covington, KY (1884–85). In 1893, he became head of the music department of Chicago Bible Institute (MBI). He died while leading music in a crusade. He has been credited with composing more than 2,000 songs. He edited many music books. He wrote MBI's "Christian Fellowship Song."

Lansing Burrows

April 10, 1843
Philadelphia, Pennsylvania

Oct. 17, 1919
Americus, Georgia

President of Southern Baptist Convention, 1914–16. Burrows was converted in May, 1858. He fought in the Civil War and was imprisoned. He was ordained and married Lullie Rochester in 1867 (died: 1901). He pastored in Stanford, KY in 1867; Lexington, MO (1867–69); Bordentown, NJ (1870–76); Newark, NJ (1876–79); Lexington, KY (1879–83); Augusta, GA (1883–99); at FBC, Nashville, TN (1899–1909); and in Americus, GA (1909–16).

Albert B. Simpson

Dec. 15, 1844
Bay view, Cavendish, PEI, Canada

Oct. 29, 1919
Nyack, New York

Founder and first president of Christian and Missionary Alliance, 1887–1919; its missions program, 1887–98; and of Nyack (NY) College, 1882–1919, which he began as a missionary training college. By 1950, some 300 missionaries had been sent out from the school. Simpson was converted while reading a tract in 1858, *Marshall's Gospel Mystery of Sanctification*. He married Margaret Henry on September 12, 1865, in Toronto. Simpson pastored Knox Church in Hamilton, Ontario (1865–74); Walnut Street Presbyterian in Louisville, KY (1874–80); then at the fashionable Thirteenth Presbyterian Church in NYC (1880–82). He resigned that pastorate in 1882 to begin a storefront work, seeking souls. His Alliance Gospel Tabernacle became one of New York's largest churches. Here, Simpson was a missions enthusiast, editor, hymn writer, and author. He organized the Christian Alliance (1887) and International Missionary Alliance (1889), which merged (1897). He edited *The Alliance Weekly* (1887–1919) and wrote 16 volumes on the Bible itself. He wrote about 70 other books, from *The Gospel of Healing* (1884) to *Christ's Life* (1911). He also edited *The Word, The Work and The World*, a weekly publication. He wrote the hymns "Launch Out" (music by RUSSELL CARTER), "Regions Beyond" (music by his wife), "What Will You Do With Jesus?" (Stocks), "A Missionary Cry" and "Yesterday, Today and Forever" (music for both by J.H. Burke). In May, 1919, he suffered a stroke the night following an ordination service. On October 28, while sitting on his front porch praying for his missionaries, he went into a coma and died the next day.

George G. Findlay

Jan. 3, 1849
Welshpool, Wales

Nov. 2, 1919

Methodist educator and biblical scholar. Findlay served as an assistant tutor at Headingley College (1870–74), and a classical tutor at Richmond Theological College, (1874–81). He then became a classical tutor in NT exegesis and classics at Headlingley Theological Institute, 1881–1917. Findlay spent most of his life teaching theology to students; he also authored several commentaries and other books, ranging from *Epistles of Paul* (1892) to *Fellowship in the Life Eternal* (1909).

Nicholas J. Holmes

Sept. 9, 1847
near Spartenburg, South Carolina

Dec. 17, 1919
Greenville, South Carolina

Founder and first president of Holmes College of the Bible, Greenville, SC 1898–1919. Holmes was converted in 1863 in a meeting conducted by his father and W P. Jacobs. He married Lucy Simpson on September 29, 1876. He was a lawyer for about 14 years prior to entering the ministry. In 1893, while pastoring Second Presbyterian Church in Greenville, Holmes purchased a few acres on Paris Mountain and built a cottage for use during the summer. In 1895, he was sanctified and entered the Holiness ministry. In 1898, he purchased the Altamont Hotel property and made plans to open a school with the motto, "Live for Others." He and his wife invited some other like-thinking men to join him for a ten-day Bible study. The resulting school was moved from Paris Mountain to Greenville in 1914.

Manie Payne Ferguson

1850
Oarlow, Ireland

c 1920

Wrote the hymn "Blessed Quietness" (1902) (music by W.S. Marshall). Manie, with her husband, founded a number of "Peniel" Missions on the West Coast. She was committed to the Wesleyan theological emphasis. She published her hymns in *Echos from Beulah*. Manie led HALDOR LILLENAS to the Lord. Her death date is unknown.

Tom Bishop

1840

1920

Co-founder, along with JOSEPH SPIERS, and general secretary of the Children's Special Service Mission (Scripture Union), 1900–1920. Payson Hammond's meeting, at John St. Baptist Chapel, London, inspired Bishop as it had SPIERS, in 1867. Bishop was a young civil servant and he began a childrens emphasis at Surrey Chapel, south of the Thames. He and JOSEPH SPIERS joined forces in April, 1868, and soon the concept of CSSM was formed. Bishop was a writer and organist, Spiers a magnetic preacher. Bishop supervised the work from his home until November, 1878, and then he opened a small office in London. In April, 1879, an organization known as Children's Scripture Union was launched.

Finis E. Yoakum

1851

1920

Faith leader and social reformer. Yoakum gave up a medical career and founded the Pisgah Home Movement. He married his wife, Mary, in 1873. In 1874, he was wounded in a severe accident but made a good recovery through prayer. In Southern California, he devoted much of his time to healing meetings. He edited the periodical, *Pisgah*. Yoakum died of a heart attack.

Johannes Schaller

Dec. 10, 1859
St. Louis, Missouri

Feb. 7, 1920
Wauwatosa, Wisconsin

President of Wisconsin Lutheran Seminary, Wauwatosa, WI (Mequonin in 1929), **1908–20**. Schaller married Emma Mumm on September 19, 1882. He pastored in Little Rock, AR (1881–85); and Cape Girardeau, MO (1885–89). He was a professor at New Ulm (MN) Seminary (1889–93) and became president there (1893–1908). This was a seminary school for teachers. Schaller authored *Book of Books* and *Biblical Christology* (1918).

James M. Buckley

Dec. 16, 1836
Rahway, New Jersey

Feb. 8, 1920
Morristown, New Jersey

Methodist, pastor, and editor. He entered the ministry in 1858. Buckley pastored in New Hampshire (1859–63); Detroit, MI (1863–66); Brooklyn, NY (1866–69, 1872–75 and 1878–80); and Stamford, CT (1869–72 and 1875–78). After serving in these various churches, he became the editor of *The New York Christian Advocate* (1880–1912), Methodist's largest circulating periodical at that time. Buckley also ministered as president of Methodist Hospital in Brooklyn, NY from 1882–1916. His writings range from *Appeals to Men of Sense…*(1869) to *History of the Methodist Episcopal Church* (1912). His most popular was a travelogue, *Travels in Three Continents* (1894).

Wilson T. Hogue

March 6, 1852
Lyndon, New York

Feb. 13, 1920
Springfield, Illinois

Bishop of Free Methodist Church, 1903–19, and founder and first president of Greenville (IL) College, 1892–1904. He entered the ministry in 1873. Hogue married Emma L. Jones on December 29, 1874. Outside of B.T. ROBERTS, the founder, Hogue was the outstanding personality of Free Methodists and by far its greatest pulpiteer. His greatest accomplishment was the expansion of the publishing program of the church. A stroke incapacitated him from 1918–20. He was able to complete his two-volume history of the Free Methodist Church in 1918. Hogue was the editor of *The Free Methodist* (1894–1913) and *The Earnest Christian* (1908–11). He also authored several books, from *Hymns That Are Immortal* (1906) to *The Holy Spirit—A Study* (1916). He died of pneumonia.

George S. Fisher

Nov. 10, 1855
near Cass Lake, Minnesota

March 22, 1920
Guayaquil, Ecuador

President of Gospel Missionary Union (Avant Ministries in 2004), **Kansas City, MO 1892–1920**. Fisher was born of missionary parents. His organization was originally called World's Gospel Mission. On May 14, 1890, he married Fannie Early, later the same day they sailed from New York City to the Sudan. Fisher was secretary of the Kansas YMCA prior to his mission ministry, resigning in 1892. He opened Ecuador to missions in 1896 and French Sudan (Mali) in 1913 to help start a missions work there. He died after contracting typhoid fever, while on a field trip.

Francis N. Peloubet

Dec. 2, 1831
New York, New York

March 27, 1920
Auburndale, Massachusetts

Congregational minister and Sunday School writer. Peloubet pastored four Massachusetts churches: Cape-Ann/Lanesville (1857–60), Oakham (1860–66), Attleboro (1866–71), and Natick (1872–83). He married Mary Thaxter on April 28, 1859. He is best remembered as the author of 44 annual volumes of *Select Notes on the*

International Sunday School Lessons (1875–1920), with some 2 million copies sold. Peloubet and JOHN VINCENT revolutionized the Sunday School movement. In 1884, he went into full-time writing, moving to Auburndale in 1890. He also wrote *Suggestive Illustrations in the NT* (3 vols., 1898–99) to *Oriental Light* (1914). He is best known for his research work, *Peloubet's Bible Dictionary*. His works filled the growing need for Biblical instruction in Sunday School.

Reinhold Pieper

March 2, 1850
Carnwitz, Pomerania (Poland)

April 3, 1920
Riverton, Illinois

President of Concordia Theological Seminary, Springfield, IL (Fort Wayne, IN in 1976), **1891–1914**. Pieper pastored in Wrightstown and Manitowoc, WI. While president at Concordia, Pieper also taught exegetics, homiletics, and church history. He also pastored at Chatham and Riverton, IL until his death. He knew Lutheran theology and taught it well.

Abraham Schellenberg

Aug 29, 1845
Halbstadt, Russia

April 11, 1920
Buhler, Kansas

First general secretary of Mennonite Brethren Mission Services, Hillsboro, KS 1881–1902. In 1864 he was converted. He married Katharina Lohrenz on February 25, 1868, and had seven children. He was minister in his home church (1869) at Ruckenau and elder (1875). He traveled as an evangelist, 1875–1879. The family came to America and Moundridge, KS in 1879. After migrating from Russia, Schellenberg served for 30 years as the pastor of the Mennonite Brethren Church, Buhler, KS. He was elected moderator 18 times, 1880–1900. He was a missions enthusiast. After his wife died, he married Suzanna Flaming on February 17, 1885. Twelve more children were born. In 1907, he moved to Escondida, CA where he pastored a MB church until 1915. He then retired to his Kansas farm.

Eliza E. Hewitt

June 28, 1851
Philadelphia, Pennsylvania

April 24, 1920
Philadelphia, Pennsylvania

Wrote many gospel songs, including "More about Jesus," "There is Sunshine in my Soul Today," "Will There Be Any Stars" (SWENEY), "Give Me Thy Heart," "Stepping in the Light," "Singing I Go" (KIRKPATRICK), "Come Unto Me" (WARD MILHAM), "Since the Fullness of His Love Came In," "Drifting" (music for both by B D. ACKLEY), "Let the Joy Overflow" (music by Jackson), "When We All Get to Heaven" (EMILY WILSON), and "Shall I Turn Back?" Eliza was a public school teacher for many years, but spinal trouble confined her to bed. She was an active member of the Olivet Presbyterian Church in Philadelphia. When she moved to another section of town, she attended the Calvin Presbyterian Church. Eliza never married.

Handley C. G. Moule

Dec. 23, 1841
Dorchester, England

May 8, 1920
Cambridge, England

First principal of the New Evangelical Theological College, Ridley Hall, Cambridge, 1881–89, and professor of divinity, 1899–1901. Moule became the leading light in English evangelicalism. He served as the bishop of Durham from 1901–20 and often spoke at Keswick and church congresses. He was a solid, spiritual, scholarly churchman; his hymns, poems, and books were widely circulated. One such book was *Outlines of Christian Doctrine*. His works range from *Poems from Subjects Connected with Acts* (1869) to *Auckland Castle* (1918).

John H. Vincent

Feb. 23, 1832
Tuscaloosa, Alabama

May 9, 1920
Chicago, Illinois

Methodist bishop, 1888–1904, and originator of uniform Sunday School lessons 1872, also the founder of the Chautauqua conferences in western New York State in 1874. He pastored in New Jersey (1852–56) and in Joliet, IL (1857–64), and became pastor of Trinity Church, Chicago in 1864. Vincent married Elizabeth Dusenbury on November 10, 1858. Vincent held the first Sunday School Institute in America in 1861. He was on the staff of the Methodist SS Union, 1866, and editor of its publications, 1868–88. He produced the first standard Sunday School curriculum, writing *The Sunday School Teacher*, a monthly manual with lesson ideas. His bishoprics included Buffalo, NY; Topeka, KS (1888–1901); and Zurich, Switzerland (1901–4). He retired in 1904. He wrote several books.

Henry L. Gilmour

Jan. 19, 1836
Londonberry, Ireland

May 20, 1920
Delair, New Jersey

Wrote the lyrics to "Haven of Rest" (music by George D. Moore) **and composed music for the hymn, "He Brought Me Out"** (lyrics by H. J. ZELLEY). Gilmour came to America at age 16 and married Letitia P. Howard in 1858. He was a Confederate prisoner in the Civil War. In 1869, Gilmour moved to Wenonah, NJ, where he organized a Methodist church in his home in 1885. He served the church for some 25 years as its music director.

William H. Roberts

Jan. 31, 1844
Holyhead, Wales

June 26, 1920
Wayne, Pennsylvania

Stated clerk of Presbyterian Church (USA in 1983) **in the U.S., 1884–1920**. Roberts married Sarah E. McLean on June 11, 1867. He was ordained in 1873, and pastored in Cranford, NJ from 1873–77. Roberts then served as librarian at Princeton Theological Seminary (1878–86), professor of theology at Lane Seminary (1886–93), and pastor at Fourth Presbyterian, Trenton, NJ (1895–1900). He was on numerous committees for his denomination.

Lucius H. Holsey

July 3, 1842
near Columbus, Georgia

Aug. 3, 1920
Atlanta, Georgia

Bishop of Colored (Christian in 1956) **Methodist Episcopal Church, 1873–1920; senior bishop, 1903–1920**. Holsey married Harriet Turner on November 8, 1863. He was ordained by the Methodist Church in the South in 1869, then pastored in Georgia until 1873. Holsey and ATTICUS HAYGOOD founded Paine College, Augusta, GA. He authored *Church Manual* and *Church Hymnal* (1892), to *Little Gems* (1905). He also edited the *Gospel Trumpet*.

George F. Pentecost

Sept. 23, 1842
Albion, Illinois

Aug. 7, 1920
Philadelphia, Pennsylvania (?)

Pastor and evangelist. Pentecost was converted at Georgetown (KY) College about 1861. He married Ada Webber on Oct. 6, 1863 and held pastorates from 1864–69 at Greencastle, IN; Evansville, IN; and Covington, KY. Following this, he pastored at Hanson Place, Brooklyn, NY (1868–71); Warren Avenue, Boston, MA (1871–80); and Tompkin Avenue Congregational, Brooklyn (1880–87). He also began working with MOODY in Scotland (1887–88), and ministered to English-speaking Brahmins in India (1889–91). Pentecost pastored the Marlebone Church, London (1891–97); and First Presbyterian Church, Yonkers, NY (1897–1902). He then served as an evangelist for several years, finishing his ministry at Bethany Presbyterian in Philadelphia, 1914–20. He wrote a ten-volume commentary, *Bible Studies* (1880–89).

William Sanday

Aug. 1, 1843
Holme Pierrepont, England

Sept. 16, 1920

New Testament scholar and theologian. Sanday, through his books, was a pioneer in biblical criticism, introducing it to English students and the Anglican world. He served in several positions at Hatfield Hall in Durham (1866–76), then became principal (1876–83). He was a professor at the University of Oxford (1883–95), and professor of divinity and canon of Christ Church, Oxford, in 1895. Sanday wrote many books, ranging from *The Study of the NT* (1883) to *The Position of Liberal Theology* (1920). He was also professor of exegesis in Exeter.

Henry A. Buttz

April 18, 1835
Middle Smithfield, Pennsylvania

Oct. 6, 1920
Madison, New Jersey

President of Drew University Theological School, Madison, NJ, 1880–1912. Buttz married Emily Hoagland on April 11, 1860, and they had two daughters. He entered into the Methodist ministry and pastored several churches in New Jersey and New York, 1858–69. From 1867 on, he taught NT Greek at Drew. Buttz authored *Epistle of Romans in Greek*. He attended various Methodist conferences and was a member of the General Conference, 1884–1912. He was basically a Greek exegesis teacher, influencing some 3,000 Methodist ministers. Buttz is buried in Madison, NJ.

Charles M. Alexander

Oct. 24, 1867
Meadow, Tennessee

Oct. 13, 1920
Birmingham, England

One of the best directors of evangelistic crusade singing. Alexander was converted at age 13 as a result of a revival meeting at Cloyd's Creek Church in 1881. His father's death in 1890 caused him to go into full-time service. In 1893, Alexander worked with D. L. MOODY in revival meetings during The Chicago World's Fair. He was a song-leader, soloist, and personal worker for Milan Williams (1894–1901); R. A. TORREY (1902–06); and J. WILBUR CHAPMAN (1908–18). His warmth, lively singing, joy, and soulwinning were a great help to those men. He helped TORREY in his round-the-world ministry. Piano accompaniment for his solos replaced the SANKEY organ era. Alexander married HELEN CADBURY, heiress to the Cadbury chocolate fortune, on July 14, 1904. At their wedding feast in Liverpool (England) 2,100 poor were fed and a 2,500-voice choir sang. Charles assisted her with the Pocket Testament League, which she had begun when only 13. The day after participating in a wedding, he died of a heart attack.

Ellen Huntington Gates

1835
Torrington, Connecticut

Oct. 23, 1920
Torrington, Connecticut

Wrote several hymns, including "The Home of the Soul," "I Will Sing You a Song," "Eternity," "The Prodigal Child," and "Slumber Song." PHILIP PHILLIPS wrote the music for the first two songs mentioned. Ellen also wrote the words for "Your Mission," which greatly impressed President LINCOLN. Most of her verses, she wrote for *Harpers*, such as "The Body is the Soul." Ellen also authored books, including *Treasures of Kurium* (1897) and *The Dark: To the Unborn Peoples* (1910). She married Isaac E. Gates.

Daniel M. Stearns

June 2, 1844
Pictou, Nova Scotia, Canada

Nov. 6, 1920
Philadelphia, Pennsylvania

Founder and first president of D.M. Stearns Missionary Foundation, Inc., North Wales, PA 1892–1920, and dynamic missionary-minded pastor. Early on, Stearns was pastor of Grace Reformed Episcopal Church, Scranton, PA from 1886–95, then he went to the Reformed Episcopal Church, Scranton, PA, and served it till death. By 1893, nearly two million dollars a year was going to missions. An outstanding Bible teacher, he held some 20 weekly or biweekly classes in nearby cities. He published a monthly, *Kingdom Tidings*. By 1913, he was giving six times to missions over church expenses, a foretaste of the O. J. SMITH era, a generation later. During his 28 years there, $1,237,677.83 went to missions.

Abraham Kuyper

Oct. 29, 1837
Massluis, Netherlands

Nov. 8, 1920
Hague, Netherlands

Calvinist theologian and prime minister of the Netherlands, 1901–05. Kuyper was converted by the witness of a poor peasant girl, Pietje Baltus. He was a theologian and statesman who founded and led the Anti-Revolutionary Party (making Calvinists a strong political force). Kuyper became a strict Calvinist. Kuyper pastored in Brest (1863–68), Utrecht (1868–70), Amsterdam (1870–74), and served in Parliament, 1874–80 and 1908–20 and was a professor of theology at Free University in Amsterdam, 1880–1901. He led an exodus of 100,000 people from the Reformed Church and founded the Free University of Amsterdam (1880), where he taught for many years and the Reformed Free Church (1886). Kuyper fought hard against liberal theology. He edited a daily political newspaper, *De Standard*, 1872–1919. He wrote several books, ranging from *Calvinism* (1899) to *The Revelation of John* (1935). His *Encyclopedia of Theology* is most outstanding. His favorite Bible verse was I Corinthians 1:27.

Solomon C. Dickey

June 24, 1858
Columbus, Indiana

Dec. 23, 1920
Winona Lake, Indiana (?)

Presbyterian pastor. He graduated from Wabash (IN) College in 1881. He became an ordained Presbyterian minister in 1882 and married Lizzie Reid on June 1 of that same year. Dickey pastored in Auburn, NE (1882–86); Monticello, IN (1886–89); and Peru, IN (1889–94). Dickey was secretary of home missions for Indiana, 1894–96, and founded the Winona Lake (IN) Bible Conference in 1895. This would become the premier conference grounds and home of evangelist, BILLY SUNDAY. Dickey served as its director and general secretary for many years.

Alexander Whyte

Jan. 13, 1837
Kirriemuir, Scotland

Jan. 6, 1921

Free Church of Scotland clergyman and pulpit orator at Edinburgh's prestigious Free St. George's Church, 1870–1916. Whyte's church was the largest and most influential in the denomination. He married Elizabeth Barbur in 1881. In 1898, he was elected moderator of the General Assembly of the Free Church of Scotland. He served as principal and professor of New Testament at New College, Edinburg, from 1909–18. He produced widely read sermonic writings. His writings range from *Commentary on the Shorter Catechism* (1892) to *THOMAS SHEPERD* (1909). Whyte was the "Last of the Puritans." He died in his sleep.

Edgar P. Stites

March 22, 1836
Cape May, New Jersey

Feb. 7, 1921
Cape May, New Jersey

Wrote many hymns, including "Trusting Jesus," 1876 (music by IRA SANKEY) **and "Beulah Land," 1875** (music by JOHN SWENEY). For more than 60 years, Stites was a member of First Methodist Church of Cape May, NJ. He did some preaching among Methodists. He frequently used the pseudonym "Edgar Page" for his hymns. He served in the Civil War and then as a missionary to the Dakotas for a short time.

Benjamin B. Warfield

Nov. 5, 1851
Lexington, Kentucky

Feb. 17, 1921
Princeton, New Jersey

Presbyterian theologian and educator. Warfield graduated from the College of New Jersey (Princeton University) (1871), then from PTS (1876). Warfield married Anne Kinkead on Aug. 3, 1876 (died 1918). He taught at Western Theological Seminary, Allegheny, PA from 1878–87. In 1881, a publisher favored the article "Inspiration," which he co-authored with A.A. HODGE. He went to Princeton Theological Seminary serving as professor of theology, 1887–1921 and as president, 1902–03 and 1913–14. He edited *The Presbyterian and Reformed Review*. He was a great defender of the inspiration of Scripture, of CALVIN's *Institutes* and "The Westminster Confession." His works range from *Introduction to the Textual Criticism of the New Testament* (1886) to *Counterfeit Miracles* (1918). He died before more liberal theology dominated the faculty, forcing his successor, J. G. MACHEN, to leave Princeton.

Jesse Brown Pounds

Aug. 31, 1861
Hiram, Ohio

March 3, 1921

Wrote several hymns, including "The Way of the Cross Leads Home" (1887) (GABRIEL), "I Know That My Redeemer Liveth" (J. FILLMORE), "The Touch of His Hand on Mine" (Henry Morton), and "Beautiful Isle of Somewhere," 1897 (music by Ferris). Jesse wrote for over 30 years for JAMES H. FILLMORE. In 1897, she married Rev. John E. Pounds, pastor of Central Christian Church, Indianapolis, IN. Her published works include nine books, 50 cantata librettos, and over 40 gospel song texts.

Frank W. Gunsaulus

Jan. 1, 1856
Chesterville, Ohio

March 19, 1921
Chicago, Illinois

Methodist and Congregationalist pastor. Gunsaulus married Anna Long on Sept. 20, 1875. He began his ministry on the Methodist circuit based in Harrisburg, OH. He pastored Congregational churches in Columbus, OH (1879–81); Newtonville, MA (1881–85); Baltimore, MD (1885–87); Plymouth Church, Brooklyn, NY (1887–99); and Central Church, Chicago (1899–1919). He also served as the president of the Armour Institute of Technology from 1893–1921, with PHILIP D. ARMOUR, a meat packer, being one of his members. He wrote works ranging from *Metamorphoses of a Creed* (1879) to *MARTIN LUTHER and the Morning Hour in Europe* (1917).

John W. Beardslee Sr.

Nov. 13, 1837
Sandusky, Ohio

March 31, 1921
New Brunswick, New Jersey

First president of Western Theological Seminary, Holland, MI 1895–1919, beginning as a professor there in 1888. Beardslee pastored in Constantine, MI (1864–84), and at the North Reformed Church in West Troy, NY (1884–88). From 1919–21, he lectured at NBTS. He specialized in Biblical languages, literature, and exegesis.

George F. Wright

Jan. 22, 1838
Whitehall, New York

April 20, 1921
Oberlin, Ohio (?)

Congregational clergyman and geologist. Wright served pastorates at Bakersfield, VT (1862–72) and Andover, MA (1872–81). He developed an interest in geology which attracted worldwide attention, showing the harmony of science and religion. He traveled in Siberia and Greenland. Wright married Huldah Day on August 28, 1862 (died: 1899). He then married Florence Bedford on September 22, 1904. He taught NT language, literary word, harmony of science and revelation, at Oberlin (OH) Theological Seminary, 1881–1907. His 16 books range from *Logic of Christian Evidence* (1880) to *Story of My Life and Work* (1916). He edited *The Bibliotheca Sacra* (1884–1921).

Robert H. Nassau

Oct. 11, 1835
Montgomery Square, Pennsylvania

May 6, 1921
Ambler, Pennsylvania

Presbyterian medical missionary to West Africa. Nassau distinguished himself as an able linguist and observer of the African scene. He began work in Africa on July 2, 1861, on Corisco Island off the coast of present day Equatorial Guinea and also at Benito on the mainland. He continued this work until 1870. He married Mary Latta in September, 1862 (died: 1870), then Mary B. Foster on October 10, 1881 (died 1884). From 1870–1906, he served at missions on the Ogowe River, Palimbila, Kangwe and Batanga. Nassau resigned in 1906 after 45 years as an explorer, translator, ethnologist, and scientist. He lived the last years of his life in Ambler, PA after serving churches in Florida. He wrote C*rowned in Palamand* (1874) to *History of the West Africa Mission* (1919).

Edwin O. Excell

Dec. 13, 1851
Uniontown, Ohio

June 10, 1921
Louisville, Kentucky

Wrote the words and music of "Since I Have Been Redeemed" (1884), "I Am Happy in Him," and "Grace Enough for Me." Excell also composed the music for many hymns including "Count Your Blessings" (1897) (OATMAN), "Let Him In" (1891), "All for Jesus" (music for both by JONATHAN ATCHINSON), "I'll Be a Sunbeam," "He Died for Me" (JOHN NEWTON) "Jesus Bids Us Shine" (SUSAN WARREN) and "I Do, Don't You?" (M. Miller). He was converted while leading the music in a Methodist church revival in East Brody, PA, shortly after marrying Eliza Jane Bell on June 6, 1871. He moved to Chicago in 1883 and composed more than 2,000 gospel songs and published 90 songbooks with his publishing company. Excell served as a song leader for SAM JONES for 20 years. He died during a city wide crusade while assisting GYPSY SMITH.

James B. Gambrell

Aug. 21, 1841
Anderson, South Carolina

June 10, 1921
Dallas, Texas

President of Southern Baptist Convention, 1917–20. Gambrell married Mary T. Corbell on January 13, 1864. He was ordained in 1867 and held pastorates at West Point, Oxford, and Clinton, MS until 1877. He was the president of Mercer University (1893–96), superintendent of missions in Texas (1896–1910), and served as the secretary of the Texas Convention (1914–20). He also served as a professor at Southwestern Baptist Theological Seminary. Gambrell was the editor of *Baptist Record* (1877–92) and *Baptist Standard* (1910–14). He died a few months after returning from a visit with European Baptists.

Cyrus I. Scofield

Aug. 19, 1843
near Clinton, Michigan

July 24, 1921
Douglaston, Long Island, New York

Bible scholar who produced the famous *Scofield Reference Bible*, completed (1909) and published (1911). Scofield's mother died at his birth. Scofield began as a career lawyer before his conversion in 1879 in St. Louis, MO, at age 36, through the witness of Thomas McPheeters, a YMCA worker. He left a promising law career in Kansas because of alcohol abuse and returned to St. Louis, leaving behind Leontine Cerre (divorced in 1883) and two daughters. He married Hettie Van Wert on July 14, 1884. He pastored First Congregational (Scofield Memorial) Church in Dallas, TX from 1882–95 and 1902–5. Under this ministry, the church grew from 14 to over 800. Between these years in Texas, Scofield pastored in Northfield, MA from 1895–1902. D. L. MOODY attended this church. Thus, as MOODY's pastor, Scofield had the honor of conducting his funeral in 1899. Scofield was the first president of Central American Mission (1890–1919) and the first president of Philadelphia School (College in 1958) of the Bible (1914–21). Scofield's first book was *Rightly Dividing the Word of Truth* (1882). Scofield's dipensational, premillennial Bible was edited with financial assistance from prominent businessmen, some of which had questionable religious ties. A new edition of his famed Bible was issued and used until 1967, when a *Revised Scofield Bible* was published.

Benjamin C. Conner

Jan. 5, 1850
Marion, Maryland

Aug. 18, 1921
Williamsport, Pennsylvania

President of Williamson (PA) Dickinson Seminary (Lycoming College), 1912–21. He married Bettie S. Tyler on August 16, 1877. Conner became a member of the Central Pennsylvania Methodist Annual Conference in 1878 and served there all his life. He began as a teacher of Natural Sciences at the Seminary, 1876–79. His pastorates were in Sinnemahoning, PA in 1880; Grace Church, Williamsport (1881–83); Harrisburg (1884–86; York (1887–91); Mulberry St., Williamsport (1892–94); Bloomsburg (1895–99); Ridge Avenue, Harrisburg (1900–2); and Altoona (1903–05). Conner served as superintendent for the Altoona District from 1906–11. He was 63 years old when he began his presidency. He is buried in Wildwood Cemetery, Williamsport.

Judson Swift

Aug. 19, 1921
New York, New York

General secretary of American Tract Society, 1908–21. Swift pastored for 25 years among such as the church at Irvington-on-Hudson, at Adrian (MI) College, and Grace Presbyterian Church in Oswego, NY. In 1894, he joined the ATS as field secretary for the Middle Atlantic States. Presidents THEODORE ROOSEVELT and WOODROW WILSON were his friends. He was an able and forceful preacher, a clear writer, an excellent executive and an advocate of Christian literature. He died after an illness of several months.

Alexander Beers

March 4, 1862
Bloomfield, Iowa

Sept. 12, 1921
Portland, Oregon

First president of Seattle (WA) Pacific College (University in 1977), **1893–1916**. It was called Seattle Seminary until 1915, then SPC. Beers was converted at age 19 at a revival meeting held by the Ashcraft brothers in the White Schoolhouse in Gresham, OR. He married Adelaide L. Newton in 1889 (died: July 6, 1940). He pastored Free Methodist churches in Seattle for most of 1893–1907. Beers pastored in Portland, OR from 1916–19. His funeral was held in the Methodist church in Gresham, OR.

Walter R. Lambuth

Nov. 10, 1854
Shanghai, China

Sept. 26, 1921
Yokohama, Japan

Director of Methodist Church South (United Methodist Church in 1968) **Missions, 1894–1910, and bishop 1900 on**. Lambuth married Daisy Kelley on August 2, 1877. He was a medical missionary in China (1877–86) and in Japan (1886–91). After returning to the U.S. in 1891, he served as field secretary, 1892–94. Lambuth founded two hospitals in China and a college in Japan. He edited *Review of Mission* for ten years. He spent time in Brazil, Africa (1910), the Congo (1911), Europe (1913), Siberia (1916–18), and Manchuria (1921). Lambuth College, Jackson, TN was named in his honor. His ashes were buried next to his mother's in Shanghai.

William J. Kirkpatrick

Feb. 27, 1838
Duncannon, Pennsylvania

Sept. 29, 1921
Philadelphia, Pennsylvania

Musical composer and publisher. Kirkpatrick wrote the words and music for "Lord, I'm Coming Home" and "Saved to the Uttermost." He composed the music for "He Hideth My Soul," "Redeemed" (CROSBY), "We Have an Anchor" and "Jesus Saves" (OWENS), "'Tis So Sweet to Trust in Jesus" (STEAD), "Lead Me to Calvary" (HUSSEY), "The Comforter Has Come" (BOTTOME), "My Saviour" (GREENWELL), "You May Have the Joy Bells" (Ruark), "My Faith Has Found a Resting Place" (Edmonds), "O to Be Like Thee" (CHISHOLM), "'Tis Burning In My Soul" (White), "Singing I Go," "Give Me Thy Heart" and "Stepping in the Light" (HEWITT), "Meet Me There" (H. E. Blair), and "When Love Shines In" (BRECK). He moved to Philadelphia in 1855, became a member of Wharton Street Methodist, and worked as a furniture dealer (1862–78) and directed music at Grace Methodist Church (1886–97). He married S. J. Doak in 1861 (died: 1878), Sarah Bourne on October 12, 1893 (died: 1915) and Mrs. L. E. Sweney on January 17, 1917. He compiled some 100 songbooks.

Benjamin Winget

Jan. 27, 1845
Huron, New York

Oct. 29, 1921
St. Petersburg, Florida

Director of Free Methodist World Missions, 1895–1915. Winget married Mary Spencer on Sept. 28, 1868 (died: April 5, 1884), and Ida Collins on August 5, 1885. He pastored many churches briefly throughout the state of New York beginning in the Albany area (1865) and ending in the Rochester area (1895). He also visited the leading missionary fields of the world.

Peter T. Forsyth

May 12, 1848
Aberdeen, Scotland

Nov. 11, 1921
Hampstead, England

English Congregationalist theologian, writer, and teacher. In 1901, he became principal of Hackney Theological College in Hamstead, London, and served there until his death. He fused evangelical orthodoxy with intellectual qualities of modern scholarship to produce the books and sermons of his time. He emphasized the crucifixion and resurrection. He served five pastorates: Shipley (1876–79), Hackney (1880–85), Manchester (1885–89), Leicester (1889–94), and Cambridge (1894–1901). His most famous work was *The Person and Place of Jesus Christ* (1909). His books range from *Positive Preaching and the Modern Mind* (1907) to *This Life and the Next* (1918).

Augustus H. Strong

Aug. 3, 1836
Rochester, New York

Nov. 29, 1921
Rochester, New York

President of (and professor of Biblical theology) Rochester (NY) Theological Seminary (Colgate-Rochester Divinity School in 1928), **1872–1912**. Strong was converted in April, 1856, at home on spring break from Yale. Strong pastored FBC in Haverhill, MA (1861–65) and FBC in Cleveland, OH (1865–72). He married Harriet Savage on November 6, 1861 (died: 1914), and Marguerite Jones on January 1, 1916. He was the key theologian (1885–1910) at Rochester, a conservative, but tolerant, which prepared the way for the liberal swing of the school. He wrote seven theological textbooks, his three-volume *Outline of Systematic Theology* of 1886 was his classic. He was active in the Northern Baptist Convention, accommodating such as WALTER RAUSCHENBUSH. He made a world tour of Baptist Missions, 1916–17. His *A Tour of the Missions* (1918) was his last book.

John L. Puckett

Jan. 22, 1847
Howard County, Indiana

c 1922

President of Christian Congregation, 1892–1921. Puckett worked on the farm and in a blacksmith shop in Richland County, WI. He was in active duty during the Civil War and was wounded. Puckett received medical training and practiced in Cassville, IN where he also pastored the Christian Church for ten years. Puckett married Mary Golding (born: 1849) in 1866.

Mary Ann(a) Baker

Sept. 16, 1831

c 1922

Hymn writer and temperance advocate. Raised in Chicago, Mary Ann lost her parents and brother to tuberculosis, leaving her to care for her bedridden sister. She constantly struggled with bitterness and feelings of rebellion for the grief and challenges in her life. In 1874, DR. HORATIO R. PALMER, who wrote the music, requested her to write a song/poem to express her losses. The hymn she produced was, "Master, the Tempest Is Raging" (1875). Mary Ann was a strong Baptist and also active with the Women's Christian Temperance Union.

William F. Yocum

July 20, 1840
Salem, Ohio

c 1922
Florida

President of Fort Wayne (IN) College (Taylor University, Upland, IN, in 1893), **1877–88**. He was ordained as a Methodist in 1880. Yocum married Sarah Hanchette on November 17, 1868. He served as a professor at Lawrence University, Appleton, WS from 1868–76. Yocum was then called to Fort Wayne College. After service there, he became president of Florida Agriculture College, Tallahassee, FL from 1892–93 and 1896–1900. He was also a professor at the University of Florida, Gainesville, 1901–5, and active in Florida education thereafter.

James Iverach

June 1, 1839
Caithness, Scotland

1922

Theologian who was ordained in 1869 and held pastorates at West Calder, Edinburgh (1869–74), and at Ferryhill, Aberdeen (1874–87). Iverach was also a professor of apologetics and dogmatics in the United Free Presbyterian Church College, Aberdeen (1887–1907); became principal there (1905–07); and professor of NT language and literature after 1907. His writings range from *Life of Moses* (1881) to *Other Side of Greatness and Other Sermons* (1906).

Edward P. Jones

Feb. 21, 1872
Cayuga, Mississippi

1922
Evanston, Illinois (?)

President of National Baptist Convention of America, 1915–22. Jones married Harriet Wynn on November 19, 1896. He was ordained as a Baptist in 1894. Jones pastored at Mount Heroden Church, Vicksburg, MS (1902–18) and at Mount Zion Church, Evanston, IL (1918–22). During his administration, Jones purchased the National Theological Seminary and Training School in Nashville, TN. He was active in Republican politics in Mississippi.

Luther T. Townsend

Sept. 27, 1838
Orono, Maine

1922
Brookline, Massachusetts (?)

Methodist clergyman and writer, who entered the ministry in 1864. Townsend married Laura C. Huckins on September 27, 1865. For four years, he pastored in three Massachusetts churches, then became professor of Hebrew, Chaldee, New Testament Greek, historical theology, practical theology and sacred rhetoric at Boston University School of Theology from 1867–93. In his later years, he devoted his time to writing. His works range from *Credo* (1869) to *Riddle of Inspiration* (1921).

Andrew Young

1869
Crossdykes, Scotland

1922

Missionary surgeon. Young went as a layman to the Congo in 1890–96. Health problems brought him home. Following medical training in Glasgow, he went to China under the Baptist Mission Society in 1905. Young served in China for 17 years. He married during his first year there. Young excelled as a surgeon as well as a preacher and administrator.

William Henry Collison

Nov. 12, 1847
County Armagh, Ireland

Jan. 23, 1922
Kincolith, British Columbia, Canada

First missionary to the Haida Indians in the Queen Charlotte Islands, British Columbia. Collison was the first to preach to the Haida and Nishga Indians in their own languages. After serving as a schoolteacher in Cork, he arrived at Metlakatla in 1873, with his wife, Marion Goodwin, an experienced nurse, who became the first white woman to live in Metlakatla. After working there with WILLIAM DUNCAN, the couple established the first permanent mission to the Haida at Masset on the Queen Charlotte Islands. Collison was ordained in 1879. In 1880, he traveled up the Skeena River to open a mission church at Hazelton. In 1884, he transferred to the mission village of Kincolith on the Nass River. There he supervised the erection of a new church in 1891. Two years later, this building burned and Collison spent the winter of 1895–96 in Ireland raising money for another church, which still stands. He worked among the Nishga until his death, serving 49 years in missions altogether. His autobiography, *In the Wake of the War Canoe*, was published in 1915.

James S. Moffatt

July 17, 1860
Wheeling, Arkansas

Jan. 25, 1922
Columbia, South Carolina

President of Erskine College, Due West, SC 1907–21. Moffatt married Jennie M. Grier on Nov. 22, 1886. He was ordained to the Associate Reformed Presbyerian ministry the same year. He pastored in Charlotte, NC (1886–87) and Chester, SC (1887–1907). He attended the Western Missouri Presbyterian of the UP Church, Mulberry, MO, and later graduated from Allegheny (PA) UP Seminary.

David H. Bauslin

Jan. 21, 1854
Winchester, Virginia

March 3, 1922
Bucyrus, Ohio

First dean of Hamma Divinity School (Trinity Lutheran Seminary in Columbus, OH in 1928), **Springfield, OH 1911–22**. Bauslin was ordained as a Lutheran (1878) and pastored four Ohio churches: in Tippecanoe City (1878–81), Bucyrus (1881–89), Springfield (1889–93), and Canton (1893–96). He married Elizabeth Clark on June 5, 1897. Bauslin served as a professor of theology at HDS from 1896–1922. He was active in the organization of the United Lutheran Church. He edited *Lutheran World* (1901–2); his first book was entitled *Is the Ministry an Attractive Vocation?* (1901).

Williston Walker

July 1, 1860
Portland, Maine

March 9, 1922
New Haven, Connecticut (?)

Congregational churchman and church historian. He married Alice Mather on June 1, 1886. Walker authored many standard works on church history subjects beginning in 1883. Walker taught church history at Hartford (CT) Theological Seminary (1889–1901); then was a professor at Yale University (1901–22). His last writing was *A History of the Christian Church* (1918), his most famous work.

Lucy Rider Meyer

Sept. 1, 1849
New Haven, Vermont

March 16, 1922
Chicago, Illinois

Founder and first president of Chicago Training School for City, Home, and Foreign Missions, 1885–1917 (merged with Garret Theological Seminary, Evanston, IL in 1934). Lucy was converted in a Methodist revival at age 13. She founded the deaconess order of the Methodist Church in 1880. Her goal was to train women for Christian service. She married Josiah S. Meyer on May 23, 1885. Her husband worked closely with her at the school. Lucy taught Bible, social services and missions at the school. She wrote the lyrics and music for "He Was Not Willing." Her school was the first American "deaconess" training center for single female students attending CTS, who wanted to do social and medical work among Chicago's poor. She wrote *Children's Meetings and How to Conduct Them* (1884). By the time of her retirement in 1917, more than 40 philanthropic organizations could be traced to her influence.

Pandita S. Ramabai

April 23, 1858
Karnataka/Gunganal, India

April 5, 1922
Mutki, India

Converted Hindu reformer, born into the highest caste in southern India but grew up in poverty in a poor Brahman family. By 1870, Pandita had memorized thousands of Hindu scriptures, and eventually learned four languages. In 1876–77, her father, mother, and sister all died of starvation. Pandita married a lawyer in 1880 (died: 1881 of cholera) who was beneath her caste and was rejected by reform-minded Hindus. Their daughter was born also in 1880 (died: 1921). In 1882, Pandita moved to Puni and began a work for widowed women. She went to England in 1883 for further education, and it was there that she was converted and baptized on Sept. 29, 1883. In 1886, she traveled to America to raise funds for high caste Hindu girls, especially child widows. In 1887, she formed the Ramabai Association in Boston. She returned to India in 1889 to open Sarada Sadan (Home of Wisdom), which provided and tended for widowed women. Pandita started a farm in 1896 at Poona during a severe famine to care for over 300 people. This farm helped support the school and orphanage (built 1900) called Mutki Sadan

Mission (Place of Salvation). She also supervised a new Marathi translation of the Bible. Pandita wrote *The High-Caste Hindu Woman* (1887).

Nicholas Castle

Oct. 4, 1837
Bristol, Indiana

April 18, 1922
Philomath, Oregon (?)

Bishop of the United Brethren in Christ (EUB, UMC), **1877–1922**. He entered the ministry in 1857 and became a traveling pastor and presiding elder in Indiana and Michigan. Castle married Catherine Hummor on June 14, 1860 (died: 1879) and Ellen Livingood in 1881. Castle authored several books including *The Witness of the Holy Spirit* and *The Exalted Life*. He is buried in Philomath, OR.

William H. Jude

September 1851
Westleton, England

Aug. 8, 1922
London, England

Composed music for "Jesus Calls Us" (1887) (lyrics by CECIL ALEXANDER) **and "Just the Same"** (lyrics by Addie) He also wrote a second tune to SABINE BARING-GOULD's "Onward Christian Soldiers." Jude began his ministry as an organist at Blue Coat Hospital in Liverpool; in 1889, he became the organist at Stretford Town Hall near Manchester. Jude was a popular lecturer and recitalist and traveled throughout Great Britain and Australia. He wrote the operetta, *Innocents Abroad*.

Austin Scott

Aug. 10, 1848
Maumee, Ohio

Aug. 16, 1922
New Brunswick, New Jersey (?)

President of Rutgers University and New Brunswick (NJ) Theological Seminary, 1891–1906. He was secretary to George Bancroft, a historian. Scott taught German at the University of Michigan, and helped arrange materials for the history of the U.S. Constitution, 1875–82, while teaching history at John Hopkins College. Scott married Ann Stearns on February 21, 1882. Scott went to Rutgers in 1883 as a professor of history, economics and law. After his presidency, he stayed at Rutgers and taught political science, 1906–22.

Marvin R. Vincent

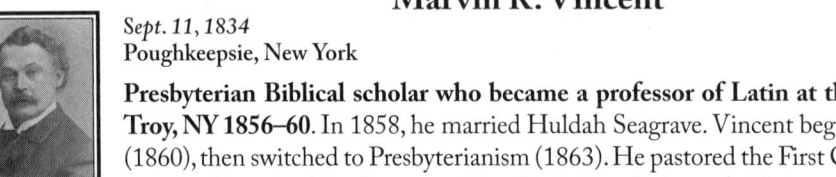

Sept. 11, 1834
Poughkeepsie, New York

Aug. 18, 1922

Presbyterian Biblical scholar who became a professor of Latin at the Methodist University, Troy, NY 1856–60. In 1858, he married Huldah Seagrave. Vincent began his Methodist ministry (1860), then switched to Presbyterianism (1863). He pastored the First Church of Troy (1863–73); and the Church of the Covenant, New York City, (1873–88). He became a professor of the New Testament at Union Theological Seminary in 1885. His works range from *Translation of BENGEL's Gnomon of the New Testament* (1860–62) to *The Gospel of Luke* (1902). He published *Word Studies in the New Testament*.

Elias C. Morris

May 7, 1855
Springplace, Georgia

Sept. 5, 1922
Helena, Arkansas

First president of National Baptist Convention of America, 1893–1921. He was ordained as a Baptist in 1879, and pastored the Centennial Baptist Church, Helena, AR beginning in June of the same year. He was also on the founding board of the Arkansas Baptist College, Little Rock, in 1884, serving as president the first two years. Morris married Fannie Austin on November 27, 1884. He was active in FCC, BWA, the Masons, and was an Odd Fellow member. He survived many challenges and led the NBC movement into a unified body.

Samuel Fallows

Dec. 13, 1835
Pendleton, England

Sept. 5, 1922
Chicago, Illinios

Presiding bishop of Reformed Episcopal Church, 1835, 1877–79, 1889–94, 1897–1900, and 1902–22. Fallows' family came to Wisconsin in 1848. He married Lucy B. Huntington on April 9, 1860 (died: 1916). He was vice president of Galesville University, 1859–61, then served active service in the Civil War, 1861 and 1865. He was in the Methodist ministry, 1859–74, then became rector of St. Paul's RE Church, Chicago, 1876 on. Fallows was president of Illinois Wesleyan, Bloomington (1874–75), then president of the board of managers of the Illinois State Reformatory (1891–1912). In 1919, he became the president of the Chicago School for Home Nursing.

Johnson Oatman

April 21, 1856
Medford, New Jersey

Sept. 25, 1922
Norman, Oklahoma

Noted hymn writer. He began his song writing in 1892. Oatman wrote some of our greatest hymns, including "No Not One" (1895) (HUGG), "Count Your Blessings" (1897) (EXCELL), "Higher Ground" (1898) (GABRIEL), "He Included Me" (SEWELL), "Tell It Wherever You Go," "Sweeter Than All," "The Last Mile of the Way" (all by William Marks), "Holy, Holy Is What the Angels Say" (SWENEY), "I'll Be a Friend to Jesus" (Dennis), and "Jesus Took My Burden" (B. M. Lillenas). He was ordained a Methodist but never pastored, working in mercantile business and life insurance. He wrote over 3,000 hymns and received only $1 for most of his poems. PHIL KERR states he died in Mt. Holly, NJ in 1926.

William J. Seymour

May 2, 1870
Centerville, Louisiana

Sept. 28, 1922
Los Angeles, California

Pentecostal minister and evangelist. Seymour molded Pentecostalism into a national movement. He was a former Holiness preacher and pupil of CHAS. F. PARHAM. Smallpox left him scarred and blind in one eye. After work as a hotel waiter in Houston while attending PARHAM's classes, he moved to Los Angeles. Seymour established the Apostolic Faith Gospel Mission at 312 Azusa Street. His introduction to the "speaking in tongues" phenomena and the San Fancisco earthquake (both occuring in April, 1906) fed his pentecostal spirit. As a result, from 1906–9, The Apostolic Faith Gospel Mission was the center of Pentecostal fervor and pilgrimages. This was considered the birthplace of Pentecostalism, and it spread rapidly. Seymour married Jenny Moore on May 13, 1908. Seymour conducted services at Azusa Street until he died.

James Hastings

March 26, 1852
Huntly, Scotland

Oct. 15, 1922
Aberdeen, Scotland

Presbyterian theologian and editor of several religious dictionaries and an encyclopedia, considered to be standard reference books. They included *Dictionary of the Bible* (5 vols., 1894–1904) and *Encyclopedia of Religion and Ethics* (12 vols., 1908–22). In 1889, Hastings founded and was editor of the *Expository Times* (1890–1921). This biblical scholar also pastored three churches from 1884–1911, the first two being of the Free Church denomination. He pastored St. Cyrus Church in Montrose (United Free Church) from 1901–11. In 1911, he returned to Aberdeen to write. He edited over 32 volumes.

Gottleib Heinmiller

Oct. 15, 1853
Albany, New York

Oct. 15, 1922
Cleveland, Ohio

Director of Evangelical Association Missions (Methodist), **1901–14 and bishop of EA 1915–22**. With his parents, Heinmiller moved to Iowa at age 15 and was converted at 17. Heinmiller married Mary Hamm on March 29, 1877 (died: January, 1878), Louise Mueller in 1880 (died: 1909), and Emma Kaechele. For health reasons, Heinmiller went to Germany in 1878, where he served several pastorates in Strasbourg and Dresden, and headed an Evangelical Seminary in Reutlingen, 1885–91. He edited a German language paper of his denomination, 1891–1915, while living in Cleveland, OH. He visited South America in 1906, Japan and China in 1916–17.

Frank D. Altman

Aug. 7, 1855
Richmond, Indiana

Oct. 20, 1922
Lincoln, Nebraska

President of Western Theological Seminary (Lutheran School of Theology, Chicago, in 1967), **Atchinson, KS 1895–1910**. Altman was ordained in 1882, then married Josephine E. Smith on Dec. 6, 1883. He pastored in Tippecanoe City, OH (three years); in Emporia, KS (five years); in Kansas City, MO (five years); Bendena, KS; and Dixon, IL. He was a member of the board of trustees of Midland College, Fremont, NE for 22 years and served as president for 17 years. From 1910–19, he pastored St. Paul's Church, Dixon, IL.

Lyman Abbott

Dec. 18, 1835
Roxbury, Massachusetts

Oct. 22, 1922
Cornwall-on-Hudson, New York

Liberal Congregational editor, writer, and pastor who succeeded HENRY W. BEECHER **at Plymouth Church, Brooklyn, NY 1887–99**. Abbott was converted at age 18 after hearing BEECHER preach. Abbot, and his family lived in Farmington, ME from 1838–43. His widowed father then moved the family to New York City where Abbott graduated from New York City University in 1853. He married Abby F. Hamlin on October 14, 1857 (died: 1907). In 1859, his interest changed from law to the ministry. Early in his ministry, he pastored in Terre Haute, IN (1860–65), and at the New England Church, New York City (1866–69). He was editor of *The Illustrated Christian Weekly* (1870–76), and of *Christian Union* (1876–81), which was renamed *Outlook* (1881–93) while he was editor. From 1899 on, he was writing full-time. His practical treaties emphasized social reform. Abbott's published works range from *The Results of Emancipation in the U.S.* (1867) and *Jesus of Nazareth* (1869), to *What Christianity Means to Me* (1921). Abbott sought to reconcile evangelical-liberal tendencies but later succumbed to such as the acceptance of evolution. He wrote a *Dictionary of Christian Knowledge*.

James M. Thoburn

March 7, 1836
St. Clairsville, Ohio

Nov. 28, 1922
Meadville, Pennsylvania

Methodist bishop to India who was the brother of ISABELLA THOBURN. Thoburn pioneered much missionary work in India, serving from 1859–1908: Naini Tal (1859–70), Lucknow (1870–88), Calcutta (1888–96), and Bombay (1896–1908). In 1861, he married Sarah Downey (died in 1862 after she gave birth to a son). He began a work in Burma (1879), and in Singapore (1885). He retired to Meadville, PA from 1908–22. In 1880, he married Anna Jones (died: 1902). Thoburn was an evangelist throughout India and the Philippines and authored several works on his missions experiences. When the Philippines opened in 1898, he was first on the field.

John Wanamaker

July 11, 1838
Philadelphia, Pennsylvania

Dec. 12, 1922
Philadelphia, Pennsylvania

Merchant and philanthropist who used his wealth for Christian causes, such as CROWELL and LETOURNEAU did. Wanamaker's clothing business became the largest department store in the world. He began as an errand boy in a retail store at $1.50 per week. He was converted in 1856 at First Independent Church. In 1858, Wanamaker became the first salaried secretary of the YMCA, and organized the Bethany Presbyterian Church with 27 people. He married Mary B. Brown in 1860 and founded his firm in 1861 in Philadelphia. In 1865, Wanamaker funded the building of Bethany Presbyterian, dedicating it in 1868. He was the Sunday School superintendent there for 50 years. In 1871, he purchased the *Sunday School Times*. Bethany College began holding classes in the Sunday school building. They eventually had over 6,000 attending in 1897. He was a great help to MOODY's crusade in Philadelphia in 1875–76. Wanamaker opened Grand Depot (forerunner to the department store) in 1876. In 1888, he organized the first Penney Savings Bank in the basement of the Sunday school. He was the postmaster general from 1889–93. He sent relief ships to Belgium in 1914. He pioneered modern newspaper advertisements and created Christian and Easter commercial ads.

Robert B. Girdlestone

Oct. 3, 1836
Sedgely England

1923

Church of England cleric, superintendent of the translation department of British and Foreign Bible Society, 1866–1876. Girdlestone worked as the principal of Wycliffe Hall in Oxford (1877–89), and was minister of St. John's, Downshire Hill, Hampstead (1889–1901). He served on various committees connected with the Church Missionary Society and the Society for the Promotion of Christian Knowledge. His works range from *Anatomy of Skepticism* (1863) to *Monotheism* (1907).

Hammer W. Webb-Peploe

Oct. 1, 1837
Woebley, England

1923

Church of England cleric. Webb-Peploe served as curate at Woebley Union from 1863–76. He also served as vicar of King's Pyon with Birley (1866–76); vicar of St. Paul's, Onslow Square, London (1876–93); and prebendary of St. Paul's Cathedral, London, 1893 on. He was one of the founders of the Keswick movement (Deeper Life or Victorious Life Movement). Spiritual experiences were emphasized more than Bible exposition or doctrine. Webb-Peploe was active in many interdenominational movements of evangelical content and was a select preacher at Cambridge University. He wrote works ranging from *I Follow After* (1894) to *The Beautiful Name* (1910).

Theodore H. Dahl

April 2, 1845
Baastad, Norway

Jan. 18, 1923
Minneapolis, Minnesota

President of United Norwegian Lutheran Church (ALC, ELCA in 1988), **1902–17.** Dahl married Rebekke Gjertson on Dec. 27, 1867. Ordained a Lutheran, he pastored at Litchfield, MN (1868–73); Green Bay, WI (1873–81); and Staughton, WI (1881–1902). He served as chairman of the Board of Regents of the UNLC Seminary in Anthony Park, MN and also at St. Olaf College, Northfield, MN. He was decorated by King Haakon VII of Norway.

Khama III

1835   *Feb. 21, 1923*
Mashu, Bechuanaland   Serowe, Bechuanaland

Chief of the Bamangwato tribe of northern Bechuanaland (present-day Botswana in central South Africa). Khama attended a mission school and became a Christian in 1862. He married Elizabeth Mmabesse (died: December 16,1889) in 1866, Gasekette Gaseitsiwe (died: 1891.) in 1890, Sefakwanb (divorced: 1899) in 1895 and Sembone Mmakgosi (1878– Sept. 11, 1937) in 1899. He was persecuted for his beliefs by his heathen father. In 1875, Khama became the tribesman chief of the Ngwato and ruled at Shoshang with justice, equity, and Christian principles. Khama remained loyal to Christ and to the tribe by combining Christian ideals with traditions. Khama met LIVINGSTONE in Africa. His tribal territory was set aside as a native reservation in 1895, the year he visited England. He ruled his people until his death. He was associated with the London Missionary Society.

Robert S. Mac Arthur

July 31, 1841   *Feb. 23, 1923*
Dalesville, Quebec, Canada   New York, New York (?)

President of Baptist World Alliance, 1911–23. Mac Arthur married Mary Fox on August 4, 1870, the same year of his ordination. He was converted at age 13. He pastored Calvary Baptist Church, New York City from 1870–1911, building a congregation of over 5,000 members. He lectured often on foreign travel. Mac Arthur authored several books, including *Calvary Pulpit*, *Christ and Him Crucified* (1889), to *What Think Ye of Christ?* (1921).

Mary Ann Thomson

Dec. 5, 1834   *March 11, 1923*
London, England   Philadelphia, Pennsylvania

Wrote the hymn "O Zion, Haste" (music by JAMES WALCH). Mary Ann spent her early years in England, then came to America and became the wife of John Thomson. Her husband was the first librarian of the Public Library of Philadelphia. For many years, she was a member of the church of the Annunciation of Philadelphia where her husband was the accounting warden. Mary Ann published many poems and hymns.

Thomas Bowman (2)

May 28, 1836   *March 19, 1923*
Leigh Gap, Pennsylvania   Allentown, Pennsylvania (?)

Bishop of Evangelical Association (United Methodist Church in 1968), **1875–1915, and the Evangelical Church, 1922–23**. Bowman was converted in 1854. He married Dianna Young on April 26, 1856. He pastored many churches in eastern Pennsylvania (1859–75) and was a presiding elder (1870–75) in the EA. Bowman served as the principal of Union Biblical Institute (Evangelical Theological Seminary) from Naperville, IL, 1896–1911, and was president of publications there for 20 years. He also attended many world conferences. His writings range from *Historical Review* (1890) to *The Great Salvation* (1909). He was considered a great pulpiteer.

Daniel S. Tuttle

Jan. 26, 1837   *April 17, 1923*
Windham, New York   St. Louis, Missouri

Presiding Bishop of Protestant Episcopal Church (Episcopal Church in 1967), **1903–23**. Tuttle was the rector of Zion Church in Morris, NY from 1862–67. He married Harriet Foote on Sept. 12, 1865; they had two children. In his lifetime, he participated in the consecration of 89 other bishops. He rode west with early "sodbusters," and in 1867, became the bishop of the New American frontier, including all of what is now Montana, Utah and Idaho. Tuttle served in St. Louis, MO from 1886–1923.

William R. Nicoll

Oct. 10, 1851
Lumsden, Scotland

May 4, 1923

Journalist, cleric, theologian, and editor. Nicoll was the son of a Free Church of Scotland minister. Nicoll pastored at Dufftown (1874–77) and Kelso (1877–85). He served as editor of *Expositor* (1885–1923) and founded the *British Weekly* (1886–1923). He helped mold progressive thinking in the British Isles for many years. He published *Bookman* (1891), and edited the *Expositor's Greek Testament* (1897–1900). His writings range from *Calls to Christ* (1877) to *Princes of the Church* (1921).

Eudorus B. Bell

June 27, 1866
Lake Butler, Florida

June 15, 1923
Springfield, Missouri

Founder of Assemblies of God and first chairman (general superintendent), **1914, 1920–23**. Bell was a former Baptist pastor turned Pentecostal. He pastored Baptist churches for 17 years, the last of which was located in north Fort Worth, TX. He heard about WILLIAM DURHAM's North Avenue Mission in Chicago and, after eleven months, received the "Pentecostal Experience" on July 18, 1908. He married Katie Kimbrough in 1909. He held camp meetings in Texas, Arkansas, and Missouri. His first Pentecostal pastorate was in Malvern, AR where he published *Word and Witness*. This paper issued the "call" to Hot Springs, AR (December, 1913), where the AG was organized (April, 1914). He edited the *Pentecostal Evangel* (1914–16). J. ROSWELL FLOWER said he was the "sweetest, safest and sanest" man he had met in Pentecostal circles. He served as a pastor in Findley, OH (1917–18), and general secretary (1919–20) of the new movement.

Lyman Stewart

July 22, 1840
Cherry Tree, Pennsylvania

Sept. 28, 1923
Los Angeles, California

President and general manager of Union Oil Company, 1894–1905, and chairman of the board after 1905. He married Sarah A. Burrows in 1867. In the early part of his life, Stewart was active in the Immanuel Presbyterian Church. He had moved to California in 1882 where the oil industry was just emerging. He was a founder of Hardison and Stewart Oil Company in 1883, which merged with three other companies to form Union Oil Company 1889–90, centered around oil fields in Santa Paula, CA. He became president of Union Oil Company, (1898), but lost control of the company (1916) when a court ordered its reorganization. Stewart was a founder of Biola University in 1908 and prime mover in getting world reknown evangelist, R. A. TORREY, to come to Los Angeles, where he founded and pastored, Church of the Open Door, 1915–24. With his brother, Milton (1838–1923), Stewart financed the publication of *The Fundamentals*, 1910–15, with A.C. DIXON, Louis Meyer and R. A. TORREY being the general editors. It is thought that the word "fundamentalism" came into common usage after these volumes were produced.

John Clifford

Oct. 16, 1836
Sawley, England

Nov. 20, 1923
London, England

President of Baptist World Alliance, 1905–11. Clifford was a Baptist minister and social reformer. Converted at age 14, his congregation in Paddington, London, became so large that a chapel at Westbourne Park was built, and he pastored there, 1858–1910. He became a champion of the working class by rescuing BALFOUR's Educational Act and defending the Baptist

Union against SPURGEON's heresy charges. He wrote works ranging from *George Mostyn* (1874) to *The Ultimate Problems of Christianity* (1906).

Thomas H. Law

Aug. 26, 1838
Hartsville, South Carolina

Dec. 14, 1923
Spartianburg, South Carolina (?)

Stated clerk of Presbyterian Church in US (USA in 1983), **1910–22, and a stated clerk of SC Synod, 1875–1923**. Law married Anna Adger on March 16, 1884. He pastored in Florence, SC (1862–65), and in Spartanburg, SC (1869–84). He was also an evangelist in Charleston, SC (1867–69) and a field secretary for the American Bible Society (1887–1901).

John H. Jowett

Aug. 25, 1864
near Halifax, England

Dec. 19, 1923
near Croyden, England

Widely known Congregational preacher and pastor. Jowett married Lizzie Winpenny in 1891. He served at St. James Congregational Church in Newcastle (1889–95), and at Carr Lane Congregational Church, Birmingham (1895–1911). Then, he came to America and pastored at Fifth Avenue Presbyterian Church, New York City from 1911–18. Jowett returned to London in 1918, and served at Westminster Chapel, 1918–22. He was a great evangelical expository preacher. His books include *From Strength to Strength* (1898) to *The Whole Army of God* (1916). Jowett authored *The Passion for Souls, Silver Lining,* and *The High Calling* (1909).

Sabine Baring-Gould

Jan. 28, 1834
Exeter, England

Jan. 2, 1924
Lew Trenchard, Devonshire, England

Hymn writer and brilliant scholar. Baring-Gould wrote the favorite hymn, "Onward Christian Soldiers" (music by ARTHUR SULLIVAN). In 1864, he also wrote "Now The Day is Over" (music by JOSEPH BARNBY) for a neighboring Sunday school rally. At the age of 30, he entered his first pastorate as curate of Horbury Bridge, 1864–67. This pastorate was followed by service in Dalton and East Mersea, 1867–81, before becoming rector of Lew-Trenchard, 1881. Baring-Gould, who spoke six languages, had one of the most brilliant, eclectic minds of Victorian England. In addition to being an acclaimed author, he was an archaeologist, architect, artist and teacher. He completed over 30 novels on diversified topics covering history, theology, and travel, while employing literary styles of biography, poetry, and fiction, completing over 30 novels. Baring-Gould also pioneered a collection of folk songs. It is recorded that at one point he had more books under his name than any other author in the British Museum Library. His primary research tome was the 16-volume *Lives of the Saints* (1872–77). His family estate in Lew Trenchard was preserved and is now serving in the early twenty-first century as a hotel.

W. H. Griffith Thomas

Jan. 2, 1861
Oswestry, England

Jan. 2, 1924
Philadelphia, Pennsylvania

Minister, educator, scholar and evangelist in the Anglican Church. Thomas was converted on March 23, 1878 at age 17. He served as rector in 1885, then as vicar of St. Paul's, London, 1896–1905. He married Alice Monk in 1898. He moved to Oxford University and taught at Wycliffe Hall (1905–10), and at Wycliffe College (part of the University of Toronto), Toronto (1910–19). He later moved to Philadelphia while traveling widely in Bible conference work. He wrote 21 books and helped L. S. CHAFER found Dallas Seminary. He opposed Catholicism, high church Anglicanism, Protestant legalism, German biblical criticism, and WARFIELD's view of Keswick. His books were from *Methods of Bible Study* (1903) to *The Apostle John* (1923).

Henry Wace

Dec. 10, 1836
London, England

Jan. 9, 1924

Church of England cleric. Wace served as curate of St. Luke's, London (1861–63); curate of St. James (1863–69); lecturer of Grosvernor Chapel (1870–72); chaplain of Lincoln's Inn, London (1872–80); preacher in London (1880–96); rector of St. Michael's, Cornhill (1896–1903); and dean of Canterbury (1903–24). His books range from *Christianity and Morality* (1876) to *Story of the Resurrection* (1923).

Clarence Larkin

Oct. 28, 1850
Chester, Pennsylvania

Jan. 24, 1924

Outstanding student and scholar especially in the field of prophecy. Larkin's charts and books such as *Rightly Dividing the Word* show remarkable insights. He was converted through the YMCA at age 19. He worked as a bank clerk and received a degree in mechanical engineering in 1873. He was an Episcopalian, but at age 32, he left the Episcopal Church. He was a Baptist pastor in Kennett Square, PA (1889–98) and in Fox Chase, PA (1898–1919). His prize work, *Dispensational Truth*, was first published in 1918. This popular work caused him to devote himself to writing for the rest of his life. He also wrote *Revelation* (1919) and *Daniel* (1929).

T. Woodrow Wilson

Dec. 28, 1856
Staunton, Virginia

Feb. 3, 1924
Washington, D.C.

28th President of the United States, 1913–21, during the troublesome days of WWI (elected 1912, 1916). He graduated from the College of New Jersey (Princeton University) in 1879 and took his graduate studies at Johns Hopkins University, 1883–85. Wilson married Ellen Axson on June 24, 1885 (died: August 6, 1914), and Edith Galt (October 15, 1872–December 28, 1961) on December 18, 1915. Wilson's first book is entitled *Congressional Government* (1885). He served as professor of political science at Princeton University (1890–1902), and as president (1902–10). He became governor of New Jersey, 1910–12. This Democrat defeated ROOSEVELT and Taft (1912), 435–88 and Charles Hughes (1916) 277–254, in the electoral college. In April, 1917, he led the U.S. into WWI, which ended in November, 1918. His strong Christian faith helped him through the Treaty of Versailles, 1918–19 to end the war and create the League of Nations. He said "The Bible is the Word of Life". His administration passed women's suffrage, child labor laws, and established the Federal Reserve System. He suffered a stroke on September 25, 1919, in Pueblo, CO, after which he retired to Washington, D.C. He wrote many books. His likeness is on a $100,000 bill. He wore a size 12.5 shoe. His favorite Bible verse was Ecclesiastes 11:4.

Charles L. Thompson

Aug. 18, 1839
Allentown, Pennsylvania

April 14, 1924
New York, New York (?)

Home missionary statesman. Thompson served as a Presbyterian pastor at Janesville, WI (1862–67); First Church, Cincinnati, OH (1867–72); Fifth Church, Chicago (1872–77); Third Church, Pittsburgh, PA (1877–81); Second Church, Kansas City, MO (1881–88); and Madison Avenue Church, New York City (1888–98). He also served as secretary of Home Missions of the Presbyterian Church, 1898–1914. He wrote on America's great heritage, *History of American Revivals* (1877) and *The Soul of America* (1919).

Churchill H. Cutting

Sept. 12, 1842
Southbridge, Massachusetts

April 23, 1924
New York, New York

President of American Bible Society, 1919–24. Cutting married Mary Dutton on May 5, 1864 (died: 1909). He was manager of the ABS (1882–1916) and vice-president (1916–19). He also directed the American Baptist Foreign Missionary Union, 1893–1911. In politics, he was a Republican. Cutting, a prominent Baptist layman, was a merchant most of his life.

Granville S. Hall

Feb. 1, 1846
Ashfield, Massachusetts

April 24, 1924
Worcester, Massachusetts

Psychologist, philosopher, and educator whose studies in European universities have given his theology a skeptical bent. Hall taught philosophy and psychology at Antioch College, Yellow Springs, OH (1872–76); English at Harvard (1876–77) and Williams College, Williamstown, MA (1878–81); and psychology and pedagogy at Johns Hopkins University, Baltimore (1881–88), where he founded one of the first psychology laboratories. He edited psychology magazines from 1887 on. In 1889, Hall went to Clark University, Worcester, MA, to serve as president and professor of psychology until 1919. In 1891, he became the first president of the American Psychological Association. He wrote works ranging from *Aspects of German Culture* (1881) to *Life and Confessions of a Psychologist* (1923). His most influential book was *Adolescence* (1904).

Marion Lawrance

Oct. 2, 1850
Winchester, Ohio

May 1, 1924
Portland, Oregon

Promoter of organized Sunday school activities. In 1873, he moved to Toledo, OH where he spent 34 years as Sunday school superintendent at Washington Street Congregational Church. Lawrance married Flora Gaines on October 15, 1874. His ministry developed into the model Sunday School for the entire country. He traveled up to 35,000 miles annually and delivered 500 addresses. He wrote nine books and once spoke to 1,200 SS children in a Coptic SS in Cairo, Egypt. When Lawrance inquired how such a great SS began there, he was told, "By someone who read your book." He headed the Ohio SS Association for ten years, then led the International SS Association until 1922. His books ranged from *How to Conduct a Sunday School* (1905) to *The Sunday School Organized for Service* (1914).

William F. Nichols

June 9, 1849
Lloyd, New York

June 5, 1924
San Francisco, California

First president of Church Divinity School of the Pacific, Berkley, CA 1893–1923. Nichols married Clara Quintard on May 18, 1876, and was ordained to the Episcopal Church. He served as rector of Grace Church, Newington, CT (1873–77); Christ Church, Hartford (1877–87); and St. James Church, Hartford, CT (1887–90). In 1893, Nichols became the bishop of California and founded CDSP. He wrote *On the Trial of Your Faith* (1895) to *Some World-Circuit Saunterings* (1913).

Edward A. Larrabee

March 31, 1852
Chicago, Illinois

June 13, 1924
Chicago, Illinois

Dean of Nashotah (WI) House, 1909–21. Larrabee was ordained as an Episcopalian and served at St. John's Church, Quincy, IL (1876–79); at St. Paul's, Springfield, IL (1879–84); and at the Church of the Ascension (1884–1909). He authored *Sacramental Teaching of the Lord's Prayer* (1888), *The Temple of His Body* (1905), and *The Calls of the Conqueror* (1907).

August F. Ernst

June 25, 1841
Hanover, Germany

Aug. 8, 1924
Watertown, Wisconsin (?)

President of the Joint Synod of Minnesota and Michigan (WELS in 1959), **1892–1901**. Ernst came to America in 1863. He was a Lutheran pastor from 1864–68 in Brooklyn and at First Church, Albany, NY. Ernst taught at Northwestern College, Waterford, WI from 1869 on and became president, 1870–1919. He married Agnes Hartwick on January 6, 1887. He was active in politics in 1896, when Wisconsin turned into a Democratic state.

Richard G. Moulton

May 5, 1849
Preston, England

Aug. 15, 1924
England

Educator and literary critic. Moulton was a lecturer in literature at Cambridge University (1874–90), and a professor of literature at the University of Chicago (1892–1919). He married Alice Cole on Aug. 13, 1896. Moulton retired in 1919 and returned to England. He specialized in Shakespeare and Biblical literature. Moulton authored *The Modern Reader's Bible* (25 vols., 1895–1907). His books range from SHAKESPEARE *as a Dramatic Artist* (1885) to *The Whole Bible at a Single View* (1918).

Angus Crawford

June 5, 1850
Cobourg, Ontario, Canada

Sept. 8, 1924
Washington, D.C.

Dean of Virginia Theological Seminary, Alexandria, VA 1898–1916. Crawford was ordained an Episcopal deacon (1876) and a priest (1877). He married Susan Brown in 1880. He was Protestant Episcopal rector of Mt. Holly, NJ from 1876–87. He became professor of Hebrew and OT literature, 1887 on.

Anthony J. Showalter

May 1, 1858
Rockingham County, Virginia

Sept. 15, 1924
Chattanooga, Tennessee

Composed music for the great hymn, "Leaning on the Everlasting Arms" (1887) (lyrics by ELISHA HOFFMAN). Showalter married Calile Walser (November, 1881) and Eleanor Dorsey (June, 1912). He moved to Dalton, Georgia, in 1884, and founded his own publishing company. He was an elder in the First Presbyterian Church of Dalton and served as their music director for many years. Showalter conducted singing schools throughout the South.

Maria B. Woodworth-Etter

July 22, 1844
Lisbon, Ohio

Sept. 16, 1924
Indianapolis, Indiana

One of the first popular woman evangelists. Maria was converted at age 13 at a revival at the local Christian (Disciples of Christ) Church. She was with the Winebrennerian Churches of God, 1884–1912, then with the Pentecostals, 1912 on. In 1885, she began to stress faith healing, and the crowds came, some 25,000 at Alexandria, IN. Her conversions ran about 500 per week, and by 1889, she had an 8,000-seat tent. Maria married P. H. Woodworth (died: 1892), and they had six children; five died of illness. In 1902, she married Samuel Etter. She was the forerunner of AIMEE SEMPLE MCPHERSON and KATHRYN KUHLMAN. Her meetings were Pentecostal style, except for speaking in tongues.

Charles E. Cowman

March 13, 1868
near Toulon, Illinois

Sept. 25, 1924
Los Angeles, California

Founder and first president of Oriental Missionary Society, 1901–24. Cowman had a vision for world evangelism. He married Lettie Burd on June 8, 1889. He was converted in Grace Methodist Church in Chicago in January, 1894, via evangelist HENRY OSTROM. On September 3, 1894, at Moody Church, A. B. SIMPSON challenged them to missionary service. They headed to Japan without any support on February 1, 1901. The Cowmans originated the first blanket coverage of a nation in mission history. Within five years (1912–17), every Japanese home (9 million) had received gospel literature at a cost of $100,000. Ill health forced him to leave Japan on November 3, 1917, and a heart attack in September, 1918, worsened his condition. OMS is in the tradition of Wesleyan Arminian theology. His funeral was at Trinity Methodist Church.

Frank Weston

Sept. 13, 1871
London, England

Nov. 2, 1924
Tanzania

Anglican bishop of Zanzibar, 1908–24, who developed a great empathy for the African people. Weston was principal of St. Andrew's Training College in Kiungani, 1901–8. He was involved in the Kikuyu Dispute of 1913 (sought to unite all Protestant churches of East Africa). He also worked for and inspired the drive for Christian Unity at the Lambeth Conference of 1920; he succeeded in Kenya. He wrote *The One Christ* (1907), his best book. He was a fine orator and upholder of African knights.

Charles C. Luther

May 17, 1847
Worcester, Massachusetts

Nov. 4, 1924
Farmingdale, Long Island, New York

Wrote hymn "Must I Go and Empty Handed" (1878) (music by GEORGE STEBBINS). Luther was a journalist and lay evangelist. He was ordained by the FBC in Worcester in 1886. In 1889, he moved to Mansfield, PA where he became an evangelist. Luther then pastored the FBC in Bridgeport, CT from 1891–93. Later, he worked on many evangelistic outreaches under the Baptist Mission Board of New Jersey. Throughout his life, Luther wrote more than 25 hymns.

C. S. Hanley

1925

Director of World Faith Missionary Association (Evangelical Church Alliance, Bradley, IL in 1928), **1887–1925**. Hanley founded the WFMA in Shenandoah, IA in 1887. By his death there were nearly 400 members across the country. His wife, Minnie, recalled, "Few have caught the vision, which my husband had to bring Christian leadership into harmonious relation to each other."

Masahisa Uemura

1857

1925
Japan

Presbyterian pastor and theologian. Uemura was baptized in 1873. He was born a Shintoist and became ordained in 1879. He started the first YMCA in Japan and helped to translate the Old Testament into Japanese. Uemura made many preaching tours throughout Southern Japan. In 1905, he started Japan Theological Seminary and pastored Fukimachi (Fujimicho) Church in Tokyo for over 30 years. He was a long time promoter of the Church of Christ in Japan. He died of a heart attack. His daughter succeeded him at the church.

George J. Kunz

1863
Pennsylvania

Jan. 6, 1925
Kalamazoo, Michigan

President of National Association of Holiness (Christian Holiness Partnership in 1997), **1921–25**, Methodist pastor and evangelist. Kunz was converted in a revival meeting in a Methodist Church in Doon, Ontario, in 1883. He married Hattie Sizer in 1886. He was appointed as conference evangelist for the Troy Annual Conference (1900), which he had joined (1890). While speaking with the pastor of the host church at a regional National Holiness Association Convention, he fell to the floor and died of a heart attack. He was buried in Syracuse, NY where he lived.

Newman Smythe

June 25, 1843
Brunswick, Maine

Jan. 6, 1925

Congregational pastor at Harrison St. Chapel (Pilgrim Church) in Providence, RI (1867–80); First Church, Bangor, ME (1870–75); First Presbyterian Church, Quincy, IL (1876–82); and First Church, New Haven, CT (1882–1907). Smythe married Anna Ayer on June 20, 1871 and authored ten books including *The Religious Feeling, A Study for Faith* (1877) and *Story of Church Unity* (1924). He was a leading liberal of his time. He labored in vain to unite the Congregational and Episcopal churches.

Joseph D. Wilson

July 9, 1840
New York, New York

Jan. 21, 1925
Philadelphia, Pennsylvania

Dean of Reformed Episcopal Seminary, 1903–24. Wilson was ordained deacon (1866) and priest (1867). He married Catharine H. Offley on January 14, 1869 (died: 1873), and Sara Merrill on November 4, 1879. He was rector of Calvary Church, Pittsburgh (1867–74); of Christ Church, Peoria, IL (1874–79); St. John's, Chicago (1879–89); and Immanuel Church, St. Louis (1889–90). He live in Idaho (1890–95) and served as rector of the Church of Our Lord, Victoria, British Columbia (1895–1901). He came to RES as a professor of history in 1901.

Joseph Rowntree

May 24, 1836
England

Feb. 24, 1925

Quaker philanthropist and social reformer. Rowntree founded a very successful cocoa manufacturing business that was carried on by his son, Benjamin (1871–1954). Rowntree pioneered better working conditions, higher wages, and pensions for old age. He founded the model village of New Earswich, promoted adult education and fought intolerance. He wrote to improve social consciousness. *The Temperance Problem and Social Reform* (7th ed., 1900) and *The Taxation of the Liquor Trade* (1909) were among the works he co-authored.

Sun Yat Sen

1866
near Macao, China

March 12, 1925
Peking, China

Chinese statesman who was the principal founder of the Chinese Republic in 1911. In exile from 1895–1911, Sun Yat Sen lived in Hawaii, the USA, England, and Japan. He returned after the Manchu Dynasty had been overthrown by a revolution, and was made provisional president of the new republic. In 1912, he resigned but retained great influence. The antidemocratic policies of the militarist Yuan and his successors were repugnant to Sun, who finally formed a separate government in Canton in 1921 and 1923. He continued to struggle against the militarists in the north until his death, which occurred in the midst of unification negotiations. As a Christian, he promoted nationalism, democracy, and the people's livelihood. He cooperated with Chinese Communists during his first years of struggle against the northern warlords. His wife, Ch'ing-ling Soong (1891-May 29, 1981) was the sister of MADAME CHIANG KAI SHEK. After his death from cancer, rival warlords dominated the country.

Amzi C. Dixon

July 6, 1854
near Shelby, North Carolina

June 14, 1925
Baltimore, Maryland

Baptist pastor, writer, and evangelist. Dixon was baptized at age twelve, along with 97 others in a revival led by his father. Dixon began his pastoral ministry in Chapel Hill, NC (1876–80); in Asheville, NC (1880–82); at Immanuel Baptist Church, Baltimore, MD (1882–90); and at Hanson Place Baptist Church, Brooklyn, NY (1890–1901). Here, he often rented the Brooklyn Opera House for Sunday afternoon evangelistic meetings. He went on to pastor at Ruggles St. Baptist Church, Roxbury (Boston) (1901–06), while acting as president of Gordon College and Divinity School (1903–5). He married Mary Falson on July 1, 1880 (died: 1922) and HELEN CADBURY ALEXANDER, the widow of CHARLES ALEXANDER in 1924. He followed R. A. TORREY at Chicago Avenue Church (Moody Church), 1906–11. Dixon pastored at Metropolitan Tabernacle, London, England (1911–19), and finally at University Park Baptist Church, Baltimore, MD (1921–25). His written works range from *The True and the False* (1890) to *Higher Critic Myths and Moths* (1921). He was the first executive secretary and editor of *Fundamentals* (1910–15). He died of a heart attack.

William J. Bryan

March 18, 1860
Salem, Illinois

July 26, 1925
Dayton, Tennessee

Anti-evolutionary leader, famous Democratic politician and Presbyterian layman. Bryan was converted at age 14 in a revival meeting in Salem at the Cumberland Presbyterian Church. He married Mary Baird (June 17, 1861–January 21, 1930) on October 1, 1884. He served as a congressman for Nebraska, 1891–95. He was an idol of the Populist movement of the 1890s, and an outstanding Christian defender of the faith. Bryan practiced law in Illinois and Nebraska, 1883–91, and was a Chautauqua lecturer. He ran unsuccessfully three times for the U.S. presidency in 1896, 1900, and 1908. Bryan served as secretary of state under President WOODROW WILSON. Bryan is most remembered for his defense of Biblical creation at the Scopes Trial against Clarence Darrow in Dayton, TN in 1925. Although he won the case, he died in his sleep five days after the trial ended. He wrote the book, *The Bible and Its Enemies* (1921), and other books based on the defense of biblical themes. His works range from *The First Battle* (1897) to *In His Image* (1922). Bryan College in Dayton, TN was named in his honor. He was an elder in the Presbyterian Church in Lincoln, NE.

Solomon J. Gamertsfelder

Oct. 10, 1851
near Warsaw, Ohio

Aug. 6, 1925
Dearborn, Michigan

First president of Evangelical Theological Seminary (GETS in 1974), **Naperville, IL 1909–20**. Gamertsfelder was ordained in the Evangelical Association in 1881. He married the editor of *Church Woman*, Emma Spreng (December 15, 1859–July 6, 1952), on May 30, 1883. He pastored in Cleveland, OH (1879–80); Napoleon, OH (1881–83); West Salem, OH (1883–85); and Circleville, OH (1885–87). He also served as editor of *The Evangelical Messenger* (1887–95), then as a professor of systematic theology at ETS (1895–1925). He wrote *A Bible Study on Prayer* (1907) and *Systematic Theology* (1921).

James C. R. Ewing

June 23, 1854
Rural Valley, Pennsylvania

Aug. 20, 1925
Princeton, New Jersey

Presbyterian missionary educator in India for 43 years, 1879–1923. Ewing married Jane Sherrard on June 24, 1879. He was in Mainpuri (1879–83) and Sah Haranpur (1883–88). He headed the Forman Christian College in Lahore, India, from 1888–1918. He was also dean of the faculty (1890–1907) and its vice-chancellor (1910–17). He was an expert linguist and published the first *Greek-Hindustani New Testament Dictionary* and hymnal. Later in life, Ewing was knighted and honored by the emperor. He lectured at Princeton Theological Seminary the last three years of his life.

John W. Work Jr.

Aug. 6, 1872
Nashville, Tennessee

Sept. 7, 1925
Nashville, Tennessee

Wrote the gospel song, "Go Tell It on the Mountain" (1907). Work and his brother, Frederick, were leaders in collecting, arranging, and promoting Negro spirituals. Work returned to his alma mater, Fisk University, Nashville, to teach Latin and Greek. In 1923, Work became president of Roger Williams University of Nashville. He published *Folk Songs of the American Negro* (1907).

Chauncey Goodrich

June 4, 1836
Hinsdale, Massachusetts

Sept. 29, 1925
near Peking, China

Congregational missionary to China for 60 years, 1865–1925. Moving to Peking, 1873–1911, he taught astronomy and Christian evidences in North China College. He married Sarah Boardman Clap on May 13, 1880. Goodrich taught in Gordon Missionary Theological Seminary, Tungchow, in 1905. Goodrich headed the team which translated the Bible into Mandarin Chinese in 1918. Goodrich also composed many Chinese hymns and wrote *A Character Study of Mandarin Colloquial* (10,400 characters). He chaired the translation committee of a *Common Speech Mandarin Bible*, which appeared in 1919.

Hubert P. Main

Aug. 17, 1839
Ridgefield, Connecticut

Oct. 27, 1925
Newark, New Jersey

Composer and editor. Main married Louise DeGroff on Sept. 18, 1865. He accepted a position in 1867 with the William B. Bradbury Company (Main and Biglow) in New York, that focused on compiling, editing, proofreading, etc. The company was eventually purchased by Hope Publishers. Main was very knowledgeable on music copyrights. He wrote from *The Victory* (1870) to *Songs of Liberty* (1919), and claimed to have composed 1,000 hymns.

Russell H. Conwell

Feb. 15, 1843
South Worthington, Massachusetts

Dec. 6, 1925
Philadelphia, Pennsylvania

Baptist lawyer, publisher, writer, educator, and clergyman. Conwell was converted while recovering from a Civil War wound. He married Jennie Hayden in 1865 (died: 1872), and remarried to Sarah Sanborn in 1874. He practiced law in Boston, 1870–79. Conwell pastored Grace Baptist Church, 1881–91, renamed Baptist Temple of Philadelphia in 1891 until his death. He was the founder and president of Temple University (begun in the basement of the church), 1888–1925. His sermon, "Acres of Diamonds," was preached over 6,000 times. His book of the same title, 1888, made him famous and wealthy. By 1893, the church had over 3,000 members. His books range from

Why the Chinese Emigrate (1874) to *Borrowed Axes* (1923). He was a forerunner of such as BRUCE BARTON, NORMAN V. PEALE, and Robert Schuler.

James Wood

Nov. 12, 1839
Mount Kisco, New York

Dec. 19, 1925
Mount Kisco, New York

President of American Bible Society, 1911–19. Wood was a humanitarian engaged in various enterprises to help the underprivileged. He married Emily Morris on June 6, 1866. He was manager of Haverford (PA) College, 1885 on, trustee of Bryn Mawr (PA) College (1887–1918) and president of the board of managers of the NY State Reformatory for Women (1900–18). Wood was active in the Society of Friends denomination.

Charles A. Blanchard

Nov. 8, 1848
Galesburg, Illinois

Dec. 20, 1925
Wheaton, Illinois

President of Wheaton (IL) College, 1882–1925, succeeding his father, JONATHAN BLANCHARD, having taught at the school since 1872. Blanchard married Ella Milligan on October 26, 1873 (died: 1884); Jennie Carouthers on June 20, 1886 (died: 1894); and Dr. Frances Carouthers on February 18, 1896. He pastored the College Church of Christ in Wheaton (1878–83) and Chicago Avenue Church (Moody Church) Chicago (1883–85). Blanchard fought against secret societies such as Masons, Lodges, etc. He authored *Modern Secret Societies* (1903). He served as president of the Chicago Hebrew Mission, 1913–26. He was a Congregationalist who led Wheaton to uphold sound doctrine and high academics. Blanchard's greatest work was *Getting Things from God* (1915). He wrote *Educational Papers* (1883) to *Visions and Voices* (1926).

Alfred Plummer

Feb. 17, 1841
Heworth, England

1926

Church of England theologian and historian. Plummer was a teacher at Trinity College, Oxford, 1865–75. One of his last pupils was Johann Dollinger (1799–1890; German Catholic historian), whose works he translated. Plummer was master of University College, Durham, 1875–1902. He wrote several books on church history, plus several commentaries including *Expositor's Bible and Pulpit Commentary*.

Edward H. Glenny

Nov. 3, 1852
Bifrons, Barking, England

Jan. 7, 1926
London, England (?)

Director of North Africa Mission (Arab World Ministries, Upper Darby, PA in 1952), **1883–1924**. Glenny was a business entrepreneur, writer, preacher, and supervisor of several Gospel Halls in London. He was converted under GEORGE MULLER around age 13. He married Miss Horne on September 4, 1877 at Bristol. Glenny helped found NAM on November 5, 1881 in Algeria with H.G. GUINNESS and George Pearse. In 1883, he returned to Barking, London, and set up a new headquarters. He began a deputation work around the country, trained new recruits, and made occasional visits to the field. He was incapacitated, however, because of health after 1902.

John A. Singmaster

Aug. 31, 1852
Macungie, Pennsylvania

Feb. 27, 1926
Gettysburg, Pennsylvania

President of Lutheran Theological Seminary at Gettsburg (PA), 1903–26. Singmaster married Caroline Hoopes on November 1, 1877. He pastored in Schuykill Haven, PA (1876–82); Macungie, PA (1882–86); Brooklyn, NY (1887–90); and Allentown, PA (1890–1900). Singmaster went to the seminary in 1900 as theology professor. He also wrote the Sunday School lessons for the *Lutheran Observer* for 20 years and edited the *Lutheran Quarterly* (1905–26).

Benjamin F. Lee

Sept. 18, 1841
Bridgeton, New Jersey

March 12, 1926
Wilberforce, Ohio

Bishop of African Methodist Episcopal Church, 1892–1926; senior bishop, 1915–26. Converted in 1865 at Wilberforce University, Lee later served as a theological professor (1873–75) and president (1875–84) there. Lee married Mary Ashe on December 30, 1872. He edited *The Christian Recorder* (1884–92). His voluntary retirement in 1924 was a first in the movement.

Philip M. Watters

Sept. 3, 1860
Brooklyn, New York

March 29, 1926
New York, New York (?)

Dean of Gammon Theological Seminary (Interdenominational Theological Center in 1959), **Atlanta, GA 1914–25**. Watters married Hyla Stowell on September 3, 1885. He pastored Central Valley, NY (1885–87); Warwick, RI (1888–90); Dobb's Ferry, NY (1890–94); Washington St. Church, Poughkeepsie, NY (1895–96); Grace Church, New York City (1897–1900); St. James' Church, Kingston, NY (1901–4); and Washington Square Church, New York City (1911–13). Watters was a Methodist, Mason and Republican.

Walter B. Hinson

1862
England

April 8, 1926

Pastor and founder of Portland (OR) Bible Institute (Western Conservative Baptist Seminary that opened after his death in 1927). Hinson came to America in 1883 and was ordained Baptist. He married Ethelwynne Wadsworth in 1898. He pastored in Montreal, Quebec; San Diego, CA; and then moved to Portland where he pastored the White Temple, then conducting his ministry at East Side Baptist Church from 1909 on. The thriving church was renamed the Hinson Memorial Baptist Church after his death. He authored several books.

George R. Stuart

Dec. 14, 1857
Talbott, Tennessee

May 11, 1926
Birmingham, Alabama

Widely known pastor and evangelist. Stuart married Zollie Sullins on September 6, 1882, and they had five children. Converted at age 14 in a revival meeting, he was ordained Methodist and pastored in Cleveland, TN, (1883–84); Centenery Church, Chattanooga, TN, (1890–91); Knoxville, TN, (1912–16); and First Church, Birmingham, AL (1916–26). Stuart was also an evangelist for the Methodist Church across the South, 1892–1907. He wrote from *Book of Sermons, Stories and Parables* (1907) to *What Every Methodist Should Know* (1923).

Daniel Crawford

Dec. 7, 1870
Gourock, Scotland

June 3, 1926
Luanzo, Zambia

Missionary to the "Long Grass of Central Africa." Crawford had a meager education. He was converted on May 15, 1887, through a Sunday school teacher and became associated with the Plymouth Brethren. Landing on the coast of Africa on May 9, 1889, he and F.S. ARNOT served on the border of North Rhodesia and the Belgian Congo in Katanga (Shaba, Zaire) (1889–95) and Luanzo (1895–1926). Crawford married Grace Tisley in September, 1896, at Blantyre, Nyasaland. He took his only furlough in 1911 to write his book, *Thinking Black,* and to plead the cause of African missions in Europe and the U.S. He translated the Bible into Luba, finishing in January, 1926. On May 29, 1926, he scratched his hand on a rough board on a shelf by his bed. As a result, infection and gangrene set in, causing his death.

Walter W. Moore

June 14, 1857
Charlotte, North Carolina

June 14, 1926
Richmond, Virginia

President of Union Theological Seminary, Richmond, VA 1904–26. Moore married Loula Fries on May 18, 1886. He was ordained as a Presbyterian in 1881 and served as an evangelist to western New York, 1881–82. He became a pastor in Millersburg, KY (1882–83), and was a professor of Hebrew language and literature at Union Theological Seminary (1883–1912). Moore's writings range from *A Year in Europe* (1904) to *A Real Boy Scout* (1920).

Edward I. Bosworth

Jan. 10, 1861
Dundee, Illinois

July 1, 1926
Oberlin, Ohio

President of Oberlin (OH) Theological Seminary, 1903–23. Bosworth married Bertha McClure on October 1, 1891, and they had four children. He was ordained a Congregationalist in 1886 and pastored in Mt. Vernon, OH from 1886–87. Bosworth taught Bible at Oberlin (1887–90), and New Testament languages and literature (1892–1927). He lectured in Japan (1907) and in Turkey (1911). His writings range from *Studying the Acts and Epistles* (1898) to *Life and Teaching of Jesus* (1924).

Conrad H. L. Schuette

June 17, 1843
Hanover, Germany

Aug. 11, 1926
Columbus, Ohio

President of Ohio Synod (ALC, ELCA in 1988), 1896–1924. In 1865, Schuette married V.M. Wirth and was ordained Lutheran. He pastored St. Mark's Church in Delaware, OH (1865–73), and taught math at Capital University, Columbus, OH (1873–80), becoming president (1890–94). Schuette taught theology and Christian ethics at Evangelical Lutheran Seminary, a divison of CU (1880–95) and was president of the National Lutheran Council (1923–24).

Henry E. Nichol

Dec. 10, 1862
Hull, England

Aug. 30, 1926
Skirlaugh, England

Wrote lyrics and music of "We've A Story to Tell to the Nations" (1896). Nichol abandoned his intended career as a civil engineer to study music at Oxford University in 1888. He wrote many melodies, mostly for Sunday school anniversary services. Nichol wrote under the pseudonym "Colin Sterne."

Edwin A. Abbott

Dec. 20, 1838
London, England

Oct. 13, 1926
London, England

Anglican schoolmaster, writer, scholar, and headmaster of the City of London School, 1865–89. Abbott devoted himself to theological study and writings aimed at the general public. *Philomythus* (1891) is a superb psychological treatment of theological rationalizing. He wrote biographies and books on textual criticism and several religious romances.

David N. Beach

Nov. 30, 1848
South Orange, New Jersey

Oct. 18, 1926
Southington, Connecticut

President of Bangor (ME) Theological Seminary, 1903–21. Beach was ordained a Congregationalist in 1876. He pastored in Rhode Island, Massachusetts, Minnesota, and Colorado, 1876–1902. During his ministry, he eliminated many saloons from Cambridge, MA. He married Lillian Tappan on December 31, 1878 (died: 1902); Dora Freeman on December 18, 1903 (died: 1915); and Ellen U. Walkley on October 20, 1916. He also wrote several books, 1886–1917.

David Baron

1855
Suwalki, Poland

October 28, 1926

One of the founders of the Hebrew Christian Messianic Testimony, 1893. Baron was an Orthodox Jew. He entered a rabbinical college at the age of ten and became a distinguished scholar. As a youth, he was troubled about payment for his sins. At age 22, he met Mr. Koenig in Hull, and was invited to a gospel meeting at the Mildmay Mission. It took him twelve months to overcome his prejudices and become a Christian. He spent 1879–87 at Harley College under HENRY E. GUINNESS, preparing for missionary work. From 1881–93, he worked full-time with Mildmay in Scotland. Together with an Orthodox Jew, Charles Schonberger, he founded the HCMT in 1893. In 1901, the Testimony was able to open its own premises. Soon, branch missions were opened in different parts of the world.

Charles S. Nash

Feb. 18, 1856
Granby, Massachusetts

Nov. 22, 1926
Berkley, California

President of Pacific School of Religion, Berkeley, CA 1911–20. Nash was ordained a Congregationalist in 1884 and served as pastor of the First Church, East Hartford, CT from 1884–90. Nash married Marie L. Henry on May 15, 1889. He served as professor of homiletics and pastoral theology at Hartford (CT) Theological Seminary, 1891–1911, and was active in several clubs.

David J. Burrell

Aug. 1, 1844
Mount Pleasant, Pennsylvania

Dec. 5, 1926
Madison, New Jersey (?)

Pastor of Reformed and Presbyterian Churches. Burrell married Clara de Forest on October 18, 1871. He pastored at Westminster Presbyterian, Chicago (1872–76); Second Presbyterian, Dubuque, IA (1876–87); Westminister Presbyterian, Minneapolis, MN (1887–91); and the Marble Collegiate Reformed Church, New York City (1891–1903). Burrell also taught at Princeton from 1903 on. His writings range from *The Religions of the World* (1888) to *The Laughter of God* (1918). His sermon, "The Knowledge of God," is in *The Fundamentals* (1910–15).

Sarah Doudney

Jan. 15, 1841
Portsea, England

Dec. 15, 1926
Headington, England

Wrote the hymn, "The Christian Goodnight" (music by IRA SANKEY). Sarah revealed an unusual literary ability at a very early age. She wrote the "Lessons of the Water-Mill" at age 15 and published a number of novels in her lifetime. She also contributed numerous articles to the *Sunday Magazine*. Sarah spent most of her life in quiet seclusion in Cobham.

Frederick C. Klein

May 17, 1857
Washington, D.C.

Dec. 28, 1926
Berwyn, Maryland

Director of Methodist Protestant (United Methodist in 1939) **Church Missions, 1908–26.** Klein was ordained in 1880. He married Mary Patton on August 16, 1883. He traveled to Japan in 1883 and then returned to the States to pastor the First Church, Pittsburgh, PA from 1893–94. Klein also pastored the Trinity Church, Allegheny, PA (1894–95); in Laurel, DE (1895–1901); First Church, Newark, NJ (1901–5); and Mt. Royal Avenue Church, Baltimore, MD (1905–08). He was a Democrat and a Mason.

Frederick A. Graves

1856
Williamstown, Massachusetts

Jan. 1927
Zion City, Illinois

Pentecostal songwriter. Graves gave us the lyrics and music for "Honey in the Rock" (1895). He was orphaned at age nine, and discovered he had epilepsy at age 14. Converted in childhood, he joined the Congregational Church. Graves went to hear a healing evangelist, Alexander Dowie, in Minneapolis, MN and received permanent healing. He moved his family to Zion City, IL where he stayed the rest of his life. He was ordained at age 62 in the Assemblies of God. Nearly 1,000 attended his funeral.

Frederick C. Maker

1844
Bristol, England

Jan. 1, 1927
Bristol, England

Composed music for "Beneath the Cross of Jesus" 1881 (lyrics by Elizabeth Clephane), **and "Dear Lord and Father of Mankind," 1887** (lyrics by J. G. Whittier). Maker wrote a number of hymn tunes in 1881, contributing several to the *Bristol Tune Book*. He spent his entire life in Bristol serving as the organist for the following churches: Milk St. Methodist Free Church, Clifton Downs Congregational Church, and Redland Park Congregational Church, 1882–1910. For 20 years, he was a visiting professor of music at Clifton College.

George E. Horr

Jan. 19, 1856
Boston, Massachusetts

Jan. 22, 1927
Belmont, Massachusetts

President of Newton (MA) (Andover-Newton in 1931) **Theological Seminary, 1908–25.** Horr was ordained a Baptist in 1879. He pastored the FBC, Tarrytown, NY (1879–84) and the FBC, Charlestown, MA (1884–91). He married Evelyn Sacchi on March 16, 1886. Horr was editor-in-chief of *The Watchman* (1891–1903) and professor of history at Newton in 1903, until shortly before his death. He wrote *The Baptist Heritage* (1923).

James Stalker

Feb. 21, 1848
Creiff, Scotland

Feb. 5, 1927

Free Church of Scotland minister, scholar, writer, and professor. Stalker's first book *The Life of Jesus Christ* (1879) is considered one of the great books of all time. He pastored: St. Brycedales, Kirkcaldy, (1874–87) and St. Matthew's, Glasgow (1887–1902). Stalker then taught church history at United Free Church College, Aberdeen, 1902–26. He also frequently lectured in America. His last book was *The Ethics of Jesus* (1909).

Solomon Ginsburg

June 8, 1867
Suwacki, Poland

March 31, 1927
Sao Paulo, Brazil

Baptist missionary to Brazil for 33 years, 1894–1927. With Erik Alfred Nelson, Ginsburg founded the first Baptist church in the Amazon Valley. He was converted from Judaism by a Jewish missionary in London. After graduating from Harley College, London, he went to Brazil. He soon was baptized and ordained by Southern Baptists. He wrote *A Wandering Jew in Brazil*, an autobiography. He was buried in the Protestants' Cemetery in Sao Paulo, Brazil.

Frederick A. Blom

May 21, 1867
near Enkoping, Sweden

May 24, 1927
Uddevalla, Sweden

Wrote the hymn, "He the Pearly Gates Will Open" (music by ELSIE AHLWEN). Blom came to America in the early 1900s. He pastored a Mission Covenant church until he resigned in 1915. Blom was backslidden and became a member of the Socialist Party. After his renewal, he pastored a Swedish Congregational church in Titusville, PA before returning to Sweden in 1921 to pastor in Sater, Dalarna, Rattvik, and a Baptist church in Uddevalla.

Francis E. Clark

Sept. 12, 1851
Aylmer, Quebec, Canada

May 25, 1927
Newton, Massachusetts

Founder of the Christian Endeavor Society, February 2, 1881, one of the greatest youth movements of all time. On October 3, 1876, Clark married Harriet Abbott; they had five children. He pastored Williston Congregational Church in Portland, ME (1876–83) and Phillips Congregational Church in South Boston (1883–87), after which he went full-time into CE work. By then, there were 7,000 societies in existence. Clark was president of CE Int. (1887–1925), and World's (1895–1927). The World Christian Endeavor Society began in 1895 with the motto, "For Christ and the Church." He traveled for 44 years, which included five world tours. In 1926, he presided at a London gathering from 40 nations. His works range from *The Children and the Church* (1882) to *Memories of Many Men in Many Lands* (1922). He wrote 37 books on youth ministry. Cerebral hemorrhage and uremic poisoning contributed to his death.

John B. Bury

Oct. 16, 1861
Monaghan, Ireland

June 1, 1927
Rome, Italy

Historian and librarian. Bury was a student at Trinity College, Dublin (1885), and became a professor of modern history (1893) and Greek (1898). Bury taught history at Cambridge University, 1902–27. He is best known for his work on the history of the Byzantine Empire and for studies and research on the Roman Empire. Bury was a learned and accomplished scholar who was plagued with illness the last 17 years of his life. His writings range from *A History of the Late Roman Empire* (1889) to *The Idea of Progress* (1920).

Charles E. Prior

Jan. 27, 1956
Moosup, Connecticut

June 27, 1927
Bridgeport, Connecticut

Wrote stanzas two and three of "I'll Go Where You Want Me to Go" (Mary Brown wrote the first verse and CARRIE ROUNSEFELL, the music). Prior moved to Jewett City, where he became a bank official and organist at the local Congregational church. Later, he held a position in the Security Company of Hartford, CT and was music director of the Baptist church in Hartford. Prior published several collections of Sunday school books.

David C. Cook

Aug. 28, 1850
East Worcester, New York

July 29, 1927
Elgin, Illinois

Founder and first president of David C. Cook Publishing Company (Cook Communications, Colorado Springs, CO), **Elgin, IL 1875–1927**. At the age of 14, he joined the Methodist Church. He started by organizing Sunday Schools for the underprivileged. Cook married Marguerite Mural in 1875, the same year he began his publishing ventures in Lakeview (Chicago). He was a pioneer in his field. He moved the DCPC to Elgin, IL in 1882. Cook produced 43 books, with circulation passing 4.5 million.

James E. K. Aggrey

Oct. 18, 1875
Anamabu, Gold Coast (Ghana)

July 30, 1927
New York, New York

Educator, orator, and missionary. Converted at age 14, Aggrey received his education at Livingstone College, Salisbury, NC (1898–1902), where he taught English literature (1902–20) after graduating. Aggrey married Rose Douglass in November, 1905. They had four children during the time they labored for benefits of rural blacks. He declined the college presidency in order to return to Africa in 1924. He helped to establish the Prince of Wales College at Achimota, Gold Coast in 1924 after traveling the African continent, 1920–23. He preached as an evangelist throughout West Africa, while studying for his Ph.D. He died of meningitis on a visit to America to write his doctoral dissertation. He was the seventeenth son of an important chiefdom counselor.

George A. Funkhouser

June 7, 1841
Mount Jackson, Virginia

July 30, 1927
Dayton, Ohio

President of Union Biblical Seminary (United Theological Seminary in 1954), **Dayton, OH 1885–1907**. He participated in the siege of Vicksburg, was wounded, and taken prisoner during the Civil War. Funkhouser was ordained as a United Brethren in 1870. Funkhouser married Susan Kumler on Oct. 26, 1871. He founded UBS in 1871 and taught Greek exegesis for the next 40 years. The school's name was changed to Bonebreak Theological Seminary in 1909. He declined the position of bishop in 1893.

George W. McDaniel

Nov. 30, 1875
Grimes County, Texas

Aug. 12, 1927
Richmond, Virginia

President of Southern Baptist Convention, 1924–26. McDaniel was converted at Narasota (TX) Baptist Church in 1892. He married Martha Scarborough on March 20, 1898. His pastorates included: Temple, TX (1900–02); Gaston Ave. Church, Dallas, TX (1902–4); and FBC, Richmond, VA (1904–27). McDaniel was a Democrat. His writings include *Our Boys in France, The People Called Baptists, The Churches of the New Testament, A Memorial Wreath, Seeing the Best*, and *The Supernatural Jesus*. He was a strong creationist in the era of evolution debate.

Jesse Jones Penn-Lewis

Feb. 28, 1861
Neath, Wales

Aug. 15, 1927
London, England

Outstanding woman who blessed everyone she saw. Raised in a Calvinistic Methodist connection church, Jesse was reading the Bible at age four. At age 19, she married Mr. Penn-Lewis. She was converted on January 1, 1882, and her husband soon followed after her example. Jesse began to work at the YWCA in Richmond, although she became ill for almost all of 1889. In

1896, she and her husband moved to Leicester for a business advance. Soon she was asked to come to a YWCA Conference in Stockholm, Sweden. She began to write profusely, her *War on the Saints* (1912) being a classic. In the fall of 1896, she was in St. Petersburg (Leningrad), Russia. Then for two to three years, it was Switzerland, Scandinavian countries, Canada, U.S, India, and back to Russia She basically talked about the crucified life. EVAN ROBERTS had a physical breakdown after his WelshRevival and the Penn-Lewis' gave him their home in which to recuperate.

Eldon G. Burritt

Sept. 9, 1868
Hilton, New York

Aug. 26, 1927
Clifton Springs, New York

President of Greenville (IL) College, 1908–27. Burritt married Carrie A. Turrell on August 31, 1895. He started his ministry by serving as principal of a preparatory school for boys in Rochester, NY (1891–93); professor of Greek at Greenville (1893–99); principal at Wesington Springs (SD) Seminary (1900–02); principal at Evansville (WI) Seminary (1902–05); and vice-president at Greenville (1905–08). Burritt wrote *The Pupil and How to Teach Him* (1911).

Carl F. W. Gausewitz

Aug. 29, 1861
Maple Grove (Reedsville), Wisconsin

Sept. 4, 1927
Milwaukee, Wisconsin

President of Joint Synod of Minnesota and Michigan (WELS in 1959), **1904–07, 1913–17**. Upon finishing his Lutheran education, Gausewitz pastored in Zion, WI from 1882–85. He married Anna Booth on June 26, 1884. From 1885–1906, he pastored St. John Lutheran in St. Paul, MN. During part of that time, he was president of the Minnesota Synod, 1894–1906. From 1906–27, he pastored Grace Lutheran Church, Milwaukee. Not only did he serve as a pastor and administrator, but he developed a *Small Catechism* which was bilingual, finishing it in 1917. *The Small Catechism* had a profound impact on thousands of children in Lutheran elementary schools, Sunday schools, and confirmation classes. He was president of the Synodical Conference, 1912–27. He was in the church preparing for a communion service when he died suddenly.

Wilford L. Robbins

Aug. 7, 1859
Boston, Massachusetts

Sept. 5, 1927
Bethel, Maine (?)

President of General Theological Seminary, New York City, 1903–16. Robbins never married and was ordained into the Episcopal Church as a deacon (1884) then a priest (1885). Robbins began his service as rector of Church of Our Redeemer, Lexington, MA (1885–87) and as dean of All Saints' Cathedral, Albany, NY (1887–1903). He authored *An Essay Toward Faith* (1900) and *A Christian Apologetic* (1902).

Frederick Zucker

Sept. 2, 1842
Breitenau, Bavaria (Germany)

Sept. 13, 1927
Fort Wayne, Indiana

Director of Lutheran Church Missouri Synod Missions, 1894–1911. Zucker married Marie Kremmer in 1874. He began as a missionary of the Leipzig Mission Society in India (1870–76); pastored in Brooklyn, NY (1876–79); taught at Concordia College, Fort Wayne, IN (1881–1921) and served as president of the same (1879–81). Zucker lived out his years as the librarian of Concordia.

John G. Govan

Jan. 19, 1861
Glasgow, Scotland

Oct. 3. 1927
Perth, Scotland

Rural evangelist. In 1884, Govan heard friends testify to "the blessing of a clean heart" they had received at Keswick. He gave up his business in 1885, entering a ministry in the rural areas of Scotland. From that time on, his life was prayer meetings, visitation evangelism and preaching. He married Annie Martin in 1894. She too was burdened for souls and was also a gifted soloist. Influenced by D. L. MOODY and WILLIAM BOOTH, Govan conducted evangelistic work in the poorest, vice-ridden areas of Glasgow. From 1896–1912, they headquartered in Rothesay, and then moved to Edinburgh, extending their work to Ireland. Govan preached at the annual convention of Faith Mission and the following morning suffered a stroke, was unconscious for three days, and died.

Eugene R. Hendrix

May 17, 1847
Fayette, Missouri

Nov. 11, 1927
Kansas City, Missouri

Bishop in the Methodist Episcopal Church South, 1886–1927, and first president of Federal Council of Churches (NCC in 1950), **1908–12**. He pastored in Leavenworth, KA (1869–70); Macon, MO (1870–72); St. Joseph, St. Louis, MO (1872–76); and Glasgow, MO (1876–77). He was the president of Central College, Fayette, MO from 1878–86. Hendrix married Annie Scarritt on June 20, 1872, and they had four children. Central Collegiate Institute in Altrus, AR changed its name to Hendrix College in 1889 to honor him. His writings range from *Around the World* (1877) to *If I Had Not Come* (1916).

Ellen M. Stone

July 24, 1846
Roxbury, Massachusetts

Dec. 13, 1927
Chelsea, Massachusetts

Congregational missionary teacher to Turkey who made headlines in 1901, when she was kidnapped, Sept 3, by bandits in Macedonia. Ellen was finally released from six months of captivity after American churches paid the $65,000 ransom. She wrote and lectured about her experiences. Stone never married; she went to Bulgaria as a missionary (1878) then on to Turkey (1898).

Edward P. Field

1855
India

1928

Founder of Cogee Open Air Mission, 1892 (New South Wales Prayer Band, Open Air Campaigners in 1922), **in Sydney, Australia**. After his education in England, Field emigrated to Sydney in 1876. He studied law, was called to the bar in 1884, and became prosperous and well known. In 1890, he was diagnosed with throat cancer. This brought about his conversion. He soon began to do hospital visitation and open-air preaching. Many were converted. He gathered together a band of 28 helpers and a movement was formed.

George H. Morrison

Oct. 2, 1866
Glasgow, Scotland

1928

Scotland's most famous preacher of his time. Morrison pastored the Wellington United Free Church, Glasgow. Graduating from the Free Church College, Glasgow, he became ALEXANDER WHYTE's associate at Free St. George's, Edinburgh, for one year. He then pastored at Thurso; after four years, he moved to Dundee and then moved to his life's work in Wellington (c. 1902). He made over 1,000 calls a year in his community. His strength was in his knowledge of the Bible, and the needs of his people.

Anthony S. Shelly

Feb. 28, 1853
Milford Town, Pennsylvania

Jan. 5, 1928
Germantown, Pennsylvania

President of General Conference Mennonite Church (USA in 2002), **Newton, KS 1896–1902, 1905–11, and 1917–20**. Shelly married Percilla Stauffer in 1875. He taught school from 1875–84 and then headed the English department of the Mennonite Preparatory School of Halstead, KS. In 1888, he returned to Pennsylvania and became an evangelist. From 1890–1915, he pastored Herford Mennonite Church of Bally, PA. He died of a heart attack.

Charles P. Sabatier

Aug. 3, 1858
St. Michel-de-Chabrillonoux, France

March 4, 1928
Strasbourg, Germany

Calvinist pastor and historian who pastored at St. Nicholas in Strasbourg, 1885–89. Sabatier became interested in FRANCIS OF ASSISI and wrote much about him and the Franciscans. Sabatier was expelled from Germany in 1889 because he refused to become a German citizen. In France, he pastored St. Cierge-la-Serre, Ardeche, 1889–94. When health caused his retirement, he turned to writing and historical studies.

James F. Love

July 14, 1859
Elizabeth City, North Carolina

May 3, 1928
Richmond, Virginia

President of Southern Baptist Convention Missions, 1915–28. Love married Caroline Gregory on Aug. 14, 1894. He pastored in Rayboro and Rocky Mount, NC; Wadesboro, NC; Suffolk, VA; and at FBC, Baltimore, MD. He led the SBCM during WWI, in inflation, and Depression times which caused a million-dollar deficit. Throughout his ministry, Love visited many mission fields and urged loyalty to Baptist principles and policy.

David S. Warner

Oct. 29, 1857
Livingston County, New York

May 13, 1928
Spring Arbor, Michigan

President of Spring Arbor (MI) Seminary, 1893–1905. Warner was converted at a revival. He was a professor of math and science at the seminary (1879–83) and also taught at Gerry (NY) Seminary (1883–87). Warner was principal of AM Chesebrough (Roberts Wesleyan, North Chili, NY in 1945) Seminary, 1906–8, and editor of *Methodist Sunday School Lessons* (1908–19). He served as a bishop in the Free Methodist Church, 1919–27. He made several trips to Palestine and Egypt. He was a gifted writer, scholar, teacher, and preacher.

Edmund L. Stanley

April 7, 1847
Hendricks County, Indiana

May 21, 1928
Wichita, Kansas

First president of Friends University, Wichita, KS 1898–1918. Stanley married Martha E. Davis on Sept. 2, 1871. He was superintendent of schools, Lawrence, KS (1880–95), then the Kansas state superintendent of public instruction (1895–97). In 1901, he saw the first five students graduate from Friends University. In the Kansas Yearly Meeting, he served as Clerk for 39 years. In May, 1928, he was seriously hurt when hit by a car in downtown Wichita, dying shortly thereafter.

William H. T. Gairdner

1873
Ardossan, Scotland

May 22, 1928
Cairo, Egypt

Anglican missionary and Arabic scholar. Gairdner traveled to Cairo with the Church Missionary Society in 1898 to study Arabic and Islam. He reorganized the Arabic Anglican church and pioneered the translating of Christian literature into Arabic. Gairdner was also a gifted musician and hymn writer. He collected nearly 300 Eastern tunes for use in Christian worship. He was at Cairo most of 1899–1928. In 1910, he attended the Edinburgh World Missionary Conference.

Eber Teter

Jan. 28, 1846
Boxley, Indiana

June 29, 1928
Sheridan, Indiana (?)

President of Wesleyan Methodist Church in America (Wesleyan Church in 1968), **1899–1927, and director of Wesleyan World Missions, 1901–19**. Teter married Elizabeth Howard on November 3, 1872. Converted as a child, he pastored in Indiana and Tennessee and was president of the Indiana Conference, 1887–1901. Teter also traveled as an evangelist, fought in the Civil War and was an active prohibitionist.

Warren H. Landon

July 8, 1851
Alburgh, Vermont

July 14, 1928
San Anselmo, California (?)

President of San Francisco Theological Seminary, San Anselmo, CA 1909–28. Landon married Florence E. Phelps on January 22, 1880 and was ordained as a Presbyterian the same year. Landon pastored in Palmyra, NY (1879–86) and at Calvary Presbyterian Church, Portland, OR (1887–92). He also taught theology at SFTS from 1892–1913, and apologetics and missions, 1913 on.

Henry C. Sheldon

March 12, 1845
Martinsburg, New York

Aug. 4, 1928
West Newton, Massachusetts (?)

Methodist theologian and church historian. Sheldon served as pastor at St. Johnsbury, VT (1871–72) and Brunswick, ME (1872–74). He married Louise McLellan on September 16, 1873. He taught historical theology at Boston University, 1875–95, and was the professor of systematic theology, until 1921. Sheldon's books range from *History of Christian Doctrine* (2 vols., 1886) to *The Essentials of Christianity* (1922).

Truman G. Brownson

April 2, 1851
Afton, New York

Aug. 7, 1928
Charlottesville, Virginia

President of California College (merged into Berkeley Baptist Divinity School in 1910, American Baptist Seminary of the West in 1977), **1896–1907**. Brownson graduated from Colgate University and then pastored in Three Rivers, MI from 1879–82. He pastored in Albany, OR from 1884–87. Brownson served as president of McMinnville (OR) College, 1887–96. He taught at Benedict College, Columbia, SC from 1918–26. His wife was Franc Hayden. He died from a blood clot on the brain.

Alexander Marshall

Dec. 13, 1846
Stranraer, England

Aug. 9, 1928

Evangelist. Marshall was converted after he moved to Glasgow. One night he went to hear Gordon Forlong who was preaching in a circus tent. This prompted his desire to be an evangelist. He worked in a drapery warehouse to provide for his needs. He was a big help to the MOODY-SANKEY meetings in Glasgow in 1874. He left for Canada in late 1879, and soon was preaching also in the United States, West Indies, Iceland, New Zealand, Russia, and other places of the world. Tens of thousands of his booklets *God's Way of Salvation,* were printed. He was a tireless tract distributor. He edited the *Herald of Salvation* for many years.

Russell K. Carter

Nov. 18, 1849
Baltimore, Maryland

Aug. 23, 1928
Catonsville, Maryland

Wrote words and music to "Standing on the Promises," 1886 (lyrics by A. B. SIMPSON). Carter also composed the music for "Launch Out." He was an instructor at Penn Military Academy, Chester, MD from 1869–72; professor of chemistry and sciences (1872); and professor of engineering and mathematics (1891). In 1887, Carter was ordained into the Methodist ministry and was active in the Holiness movement through camp meeting activities. In the years before his death, he practiced medicine in Baltimore.

Reuben A. Torrey

Jan. 28, 1856
Hoboken, New Jersey

Oct. 26, 1928
Biltmore, North Carolina

First President of Moody Bible Institute, 1889–1908; Bible Institute of Los Angeles (CA), 1912–24; and founder and first director of Montrose (PA) Bible Conference, 1908–28. Torrey did many things well. He served as pastor, educator, evangelist, and author, having few equals in these fields. He was converted at Yale University in 1875 and pastored the Congregational Church, Garrettsville, OH from 1872–82. Torrey married Clara Smith on October 22, 1879. He also pastored the Open Door Church (1883–86), and Peoples Church (1886–89), both in Minneapolis. In 1889, he became associated with D. L. MOODY. He pastored Moody Church, Chicago (1894–1902), and Church of the Open Door, Los Angeles, CA (1915–24), which he helped organize. He was a world evangelist (1902–5), evangelist in the U.S. and Canada (1906–11), then went back to Great Britain in 1911. In Australia, he saw 20,000 converted, with his tour ending with a five-month London crusade. Music director CHARLES ALEXANDER assisted him from 1901 on. He saw over 100,000 people converted. His forty books are considered Christian classics and range from *How I Bring Men to Christ* (1893) to *Lectures on the First Epistle of John* (pub. 1929). He died at his home where he retired in 1924, and is buried on the grounds of MBC.

Flavius J. Lee

July 18, 1875
Cleveland, Tennessee

Oct. 28, 1928
Cleveland, Tennessee

General Overseer of Church of God, Cleveland, TN 1923–28. Lee originally worked at Hardwick Stove Company. He first married Nora Milian and, upon her death, married again. He became general overseer when the assembly ousted AMBROSE J. TOMLINSON in a major split. He was known as a man of prayer and was highly regarded for his piety, modesty, and humility. Lee died due to asthma and a heart infection, while seeking healing only from the Lord.

Louis Haeberle

May 26, 1838
Faurndau, Germany

Nov. 15, 1928
St. Louis, Missouri

President of German Evangelical Preacher Seminary, Marthasville, MO 1879–83 (renamed and relocated), **and Eden Theological Seminary, St. Louis MO 1883–1902.** Haeberle served as pastor of St. John's Evangelical Church, St. Louis, for 17 years. He also founded the Emmaus Epileptic Home in Marthasville, MO.

Edgar Y. Mullins

Jan. 5, 1860
Franklin County, Mississippi

Nov. 23, 1928
Louisville, Kentucky

President of Southern Baptist Convention, 1921–23; Southern Baptist Theological Seminary, Louisville, KY 1899–1928; and Baptist World Alliance, 1923–28. Mullins moved with his family to Corsicana, TX at age eight. He was converted on October 30, 1880, in a revival meeting in Dallas (William E. Penn, tent evangelist) and was baptized the same year. At SBTS, the enrollment went from 256 to 501 under his leadership. Mullins married Isla Hawley on June 2, 1886. He pastored in Harrodsburgh, KY (1885–88); Lee Street Baptist Church, Baltimore, MD (1888–95); and FBC, Newton, MA (1896–99). He also wrote several books. His main interest was in apologetics which was evident in his first book. His works range from *Why Is Christianity True?* (1905) to *Christianity at the Crossroads* (1924).

Walter A. Sellew

Feb. 27, 1844
Gowanda, New York

Jan. 16, 1929
Jamestown, New Jersey

Bishop of Free Methodist Church, 1898–1929. Converted in his senior year at Dartmouth (1869), he was ordained (1872) and pastored in Tonawanda, NY; Rochester, NY; Spring Arbor, MI; Dunkirk, NY; Gerry, NY; Albany, NY; and Buffalo, NY from 1872–86. Sellew married Jennie Peters on June 4, 1873 (died: 1895) and Rebecca Muse on March 31, 1897. Sellew also made missionary tours of denomination stations in Japan in 1906, 1910, and 1926.

Frederick B. Meyer

April 8, 1847
London, England

Jan. 28, 1929
London, England

Outstanding pastor and president of Regions Beyond Missionary Union (RBMU), 1888–1921. Converted at age seven, Meyer was a beloved and well-known Baptist clergyman. He pastored at the following churches: Duke St. Baptist, Richmond (1868–69); assistant at Pembroke Chapel, Liverpool (1869–72); and Priory St. Baptist Chapel, York (1872–74). This is where he met MOODY in 1873, and actually launched MOODY's revival ministry in England by hosting him when MOODY's other contacts failed. Meyer then ministered at Victoria Road Baptist Church, Leicester (1874–78); at Melbourne Hall, Leicester (1878–88); Regent's Park Chapel, London (1888–92 and 1909–15); and Christ Church, Lambeth (London) (1892–1907 and 1915–20). He toured America 13 times beginning in 1891 and touched many lives including J. W. CHAPMAN. Meyer was an evangelist for the Federation of Free Churches (1905) and became president of the Baptist Union (1906). His books ranged from *Elijah and the Secret of His Power* (1887) to *A Winter in South Africa* (1908). He married Jane Jones in 1871, who died only six weeks before he did. His tracts had a circulation of five million. He preached over 15,000 sermons. His last words were, "Read me something from the Bible, something brave and triumphant."

Newell D. Hillis

Sept. 2, 1858
Magnolia, Iowa

Feb. 25, 1929
Brenxville, New York

Presbyterian pastor and author. Hillis married Annie Patrick (1862–November 1, 1930) on April 14, 1887. He pastored in Peoria (1886–90) and Evanston, IL (1890–94). Hillis succeeded DAVID SWING at Central Church, Chicago, IL (1894–1899); then succeeded LYMAN ABBOTT at Plymouth Congregational Church, Brooklyn (1899–1924); resigning after suffering a cerebral hemorrhage. He was president of Plymouth Institute from 1914–29. Hillis resigned from the Presbyterian denomination before the Presbyterian leaders could begin a heresy trial (because of liberalism) against him. He wrote about 25 books ranging from *A Man's Value to Society* (1896) to *The Better American Lectures* (1921). His 1,000 sermons were printed in Chicago and Brooklyn newspapers for 75 years.

Geoffrey A. Studdert-Kennedy

June 27, 1883
Leeds, England

March 8, 1929
Liverpool, England

Anglican priest who is best known as the military padre of WW I. Studdert-Kennedy was known to soldiers as "Woodbine Willie." He was curate in Rugby and Reeds, 1908–14. He served as vicar of St. Paul's, Worcester (1914–21), then rector of St. Edmund, Lombard Street, London (1922–29). Studdert-Kennedy continued preaching, writing hymns, and publishing books throughout his life. He won the Military Cross for bravery as chaplain in 1917, and died of the flu. He wrote works ranging from *Rough Rhymes* (1918) to *The Word and the Work* (1925).

Peter S. Vig

Nov. 7, 1854
Egtved, Denmark

March 21, 1929
Blair, Nebraska

President of Trinity Theological Seminary (merged into Wartburg Theological Seminary, Dubuque, IA in 1961), **Blair, NE 1896–99, 1909–26**. Vig was a Lutheran pastor, educator, and church official who came to America in 1879 for work and study. Vig returned to Europe briefly when he attended the Missionary Institute of Copenhagen. He taught in a Danish high school in Elkhart, IA from 1884–85 and was ordained in Neenah, WI in 1885. He pastored a Danish Lutheran Church, Jacksonville, IA from 1885–87 before becoming a professor in the Seminary at West Denmark, WI. He pasored in Luck, WI (1887–92), then was a professor at a seminary at Elkhart, IA (1894–96), and pastored there (1899–1902).

Charles H. Brent

April 9, 1862
Newcastle, Ontario, Canada

March 27, 1929
Lausanne, Switzerland

Episcopalian bishop and pioneer in the twentieth Century ecumenical movement. Brent served as pastor and associate in Boston (1891–1901), bishop of the Philippines (1901–17), where ill health terminated his stay; bishop of Western New York (1919–26) and in Europe (1926–28). He was also the chief initiator of the World Conference on Faith and Order, which met in Lausanne, Switzerland, 1927. His writings range from *With God in the World* (1899) to *Adventures in Prayer* (pub., 1932).

Katherine L. Bates

Aug. 12, 1859
Falmouth, Massachusetts

Katharine Lee Bates

March 28, 1929
Wellesley, Massachusetts

Writer of the patriotic hymn, "America the Beautiful" (music by SAMUEL WARD). Bates composed this widely used hymn (1893), while on a trip through the Colorado Rockies, and then rewrote it in its present form (1904). She attended Wellesley College in 1879, and six years later, taught there, eventually heading the English department. Her father was a Congregational minister. She never married. Bates' books range from *English Religious Drama* (1893) to *America the Dream* (1930). Other hymns of note are "Dear God, Our Father" and "Our Fathers, in the Years Grown Dim."

Sadhu S. Singh

Sept. 3, 1889
Rampur, India

after April 18, 1929
Tibet (Nepal)

Evangelist born in a high-caste Sikh family. Singh became a Christian in 1903 at age 15, while attending an American Presbyterian mission school, and was baptized at Simla on Sept. 3, 1905. He began to preach after his family cast him out of their home in 1904. At age 16, Singh donned the saffron robe of the "holy man," and for the rest of his life traveled as a sadhu (monk) from village to village preaching the gospel. In 1907, he began a work in a leprosy hospital at Sabathu. Singh also made trips to Afghanistan and Tibet, starting in 1908. In 1909, he founded St. John's Divinity College in Lahore to train people for the ministry. In 1911, he handed back his preacher's license and returned to the Sadhu's life. In 1912, he traveled through North India and the Buddhist states. In 1918–22, he preached in Asia, Europe, America, and Australia. He returned back from Tibet in 1923. He wrote *With or Without Christ* (1925–27). He was never heard from again after his trip to Tibet which began April 18, 1929.

R. P. Mackay

1847
Woodstock, Ontario, Canada

May 27, 1929
Woodstock, Ontario, Canada

President of Toronto Bible College (Ontario Bible College), **1912–29**. He was vice president in 1898, when the first building was erected. From 1912, when the institution was re-organized until his death, Mackay also served as chairman of the Board of Governors. He had an active prayer life, and was an inspiration to many. Just a week before his death, he presided over a board meeting which planned the dedication of a new building at the school on Spadina Road.

Thomas H. Lewis

Dec. 11, 1852
Dover, Delaware

June 14, 1929
Washington, D.C. (?)

President of Methodist Protestant Church (United Methodist Church in 1968), **1908–12, 1920–28**. Lewis married Mary Ward on December 11, 1877, and they had six children. He pastored in Cumberland, (1875–77), and Baltimore, MD (1878–82). Lewis organized and served as president of Westminster (MD) Theological Seminary (Wesley Seminary) (1882–86), and he was president of Western Maryland College, Westminster (1886–1920). He moved to Washington, D.C. in 1920. Lewis' books range from *The Good Life* (1905) to *The Minister and His Own Soul* (1926).

W. Bramwell Booth

March 8, 1856
Halifax, England

June 16, 1929
Hadley Wood, England

General of Salvation Army, 1912–29. Bramwell was the eldest son and successor to WILLIAM BOOTH. Booth was largely responsible for the development of the Salvation Army. He was converted at age seven at a meeting conducted by his parents at Walsall. Booth served as an evangelist, 1875–80. He began as chief-of-staff in 1880 and, once he became general, he extended the army's youth services and focused on missions. Bramwell married Florence Soper (1861–June 10, 1957), a physician's daughter, in 1882. She was a worker in the army beginning 1880, organizing Women's Social Work (1883), and orchestrating rescue work among the poor (1912). Booth's last words were "Jesus, Jesus, Jesus."

Charles F. Parham

June 4, 1873
Muscatine, Iowa

June 29, 1929
Baxter Springs, Kansas

Early leader in the modern Pentecostal movement, and founder of Bethel College, Topeka, KS. Parham was converted at age 13. He was influenced by the Holiness movement, and his work, *Latter Rain*, was a predecessor to modern-day Pentecostalism. He left Methodism in 1895 to become an independent Holiness preacher and evangelist. He married Sarah Thistlewaite (1896), and they opened a healing home, called Bethel, in Topeka, KS (1898). In Houston, TX in 1905, he opened a Bible school. Among the students was WILLIAM J. SEYMOUR, a Holiness teacher who took Parham's teaching to Azusa Street in Los Angeles. Charges of sexual misconduct, dropped in 1905, and espousal of British Israelism led to his declining influence. He went to Baxter Springs in 1911 and developed the Apostolic Faith Church.

Frederick G. Booth-Tucker

March 21, 1853
Monghyr, India

July 17, 1929
London, England

Active in Salvation Army, along with wife, Emma Moss Booth-Tucker. Frederick was converted in 1875 at a MOODY crusade. He married Louisa Bode in 1877 (died: 1887). Having training as an attorney and member of the Indian Civil Service, he opened the SA's work in India in 1882. Frederick married Emma Moss Booth (fourth child of WILLIAM BOOTH) on April 10, 1888, and changed their name, at William's insistence, to Booth-Tucker. Born January 8, 1860, Emma had managed the BOOTH family affairs on behalf of her parents. She was considered an able speaker, and had trained women cadets in London from 1880–88. Together, they first served in India (1888–91), then returned to England (1891–96), before serving as joint commanders in the United States (1896–1903). Emma was killed in a train wreck near Dean Lake, IA on October 28, 1903. Frederick returned to England and married Mary (Minnie) Reid (1864–1934) in 1906. He served in India again and in Ceylon, 1907–19. He retired in 1926. He wrote *In Darkest India and the Way Out* (1891) to *Monograph of Salvation Army* (1900).

Leila Naylor Morris

April 15, 1862
Pennsville, Ohio

July 23, 1929
Auburn, Ohio

Hymn writer who wrote lyrics and music for "Let Jesus Come into Your Heart" (1898), "What If It Were Today?", "The Fight Is On," "The Conflict of the Ages," "Wonderful Story of Love," "The Stranger of Galilee," "At the Battle's Front," "Nothing Satisfies but Jesus," "Sweet Will of God," "Nearer, Still Nearer," and "Sweeter as the Years Go By." Converted at age ten, Leila was a lifelong Methodist, active in Holiness camp meetings and developed her poetic ability early. She opened a millinery shop in McConnelsville, OH and married Charles H. Morris in 1881. In 1913, her eyesight began to fail, and soon she was blind. Her greatest works were written during this time. Leila wrote over 1,000 hymns. In 1928, they moved in with their daughter, Mrs. W. R. Lunk.

Henry Ernst

May 17, 1842
Anspach, Germany

Aug. 9, 1929
St. Paul, Minnesota

First president of Luther Seminary (merged into Wartburg Theological Seminary, Dubuque, IA in 1932), **Afton and St. Paul, MN, 1885–1927**. Ernst married Albertine Krahn on February 23, 1868. He entered the Lutheran ministry in 1865 and was associated with the Missouri Synod until 1881, and then the Ohio Synod, 1881–84. Ernst lived in St. Paul, MN, after pastoring in Wisconsin, Illinois, and Indiana. He also served 44 years as professor and dean of the theology department along with the presidency at Luther Seminary.

Arthur S. Peake

Nov. 24, 1865
Leek, England

Aug. 19, 1929
Manchester, England

Methodist Biblical scholar. Peake authored several biblical works, including *The Problems of Suffering in the Old Testament* (1904). He is most remembered for his *Commentary on the Bible* (1919). He edited the *Holborn Review* (1919–29) and headed the Theological Institute at Manchester (Hartley Primitive Methodist College), 1892–1904. When the University of Manchester decided to set up a divinity school in 1904, Peake defined the program and was appointed Rylands professor of biblical criticism and exegesis, 1904–29. He had considered ordination into the Church of England, but chose to remain a Methodist layman. In doing so, through his dedication to theological education, he is credited with raising the standard of ministry in the Methodist Church.

Gottleib B. Christiansen

Oct. 27, 1851
Denmark

Sept. 27, 1929
Brush, Colorado

President of United Danish Evangelical Church (ELCA in 1988), **1896–1921**. Christiansen married Jensine Larsen on June 25, 1881 (died: November 21, 1941). He pastored in Council Bluffs, IA (1881–1885); Albert Lea and Owatonna, MN (1886–90, 96–97); Blair, NE (1890–96); Omaha, NE (1897–1904) and Audubon, IA (1904–1922). Christiansen retired to Ebeneezer Mercy Institute, Brush, CO from 1922–1929. He was also president of Trinity Seminary, Blair, NE from 1890–96. He wrote *Recollections of our Church Work* 1877 to 1927.

Harold Begbie

1871
Fornham St. Martin, England

Oct. 8, 1929
Ringwood Hants, London, England

Author and journalist who retired to his farm but later returned to journalism. Begbie wrote novels, children's stories, and biographical studies. The contents focused on movements that bettered society and Christianity. In total, Begbie authored nearly 50 books, including *Broken Earthware* (1909), *Twice Born Men, Other Sheep* (1911), *Life Changers, On Buchmanism, Life of WILLIAM BOOTH* (1920), *Broken Lights,* and *Life Changers* (1927). He visited the U.S. and Russia during WWI. His writings range from *The Political Struwelpeter* series (1899–1901) to *Black Rent* (1928).

Bernard Angel

1860
Bucharest, Romania

Oct. 20, 1929

Evangelist to the Jews who established a Hebrew-Christian mission in New York City. Angel spoke seven languages and could read in ten. He attended a rabbi school in Germany, went to Paris for a newspaper position, then came to America. While he was in America, he heard the gospel and was converted. Angel started his witness to the Jews in 1895. Communists attended his mission many times (Leon Trotsky came once). His wife's name was Gertrude, and their daughter, Ruth, took over the work after Angel's death.

Rudolf Kittel

March 28, 1853
Eningen, Germany

Oct. 20, 1929
Leipzig, Germany

Lutheran theologian, Old Testament scholar, philologist, and pastor. Kittel compiled the best possible Hebrew text of the Old Testament. His masterpiece *Biblia Hebraica* is considered the most reliable biblical text in

Hebrew. Kittel pastored (1876–79), lectured at Tubingen (1879–81), taught at Stuttgart (1881–88), taught Old Tesstament exegesis at the University of Breslav (1888–97) and at the University of Leipzig (1898–1929). Kittel wrote works ranging from *The Scientific Study of the Old Testament* (1910) to *Great Men and Movements in Israel* (1929). His son was GERHARD KITTEL.

John R. Straton

April 6, 1875
Evansville, Indiana

Oct. 29, 1929
Clifton Springs/Warwick, New York

Pastor of Calvary Baptist Church, New York City, 1918–29. Straton married Georgia Hillyer on November 2, 1903. He was converted under a SBC evangelist, James Hawthorne. He taught at Baylor University (1903–5); pastored Second Baptist of Chicago (1905–07); Emmanuel Church, Baltimore, MD (1908–13); and FBC, Norfolk, VA (1913–17). Straton won awards for oratory and writing against the sin of drunkenness. He attacked the city's theaters in 1922. He debated J. Emerson Fosdick in 1925 in the famous New York clash against liberalism. He withdrew from the Northern Baptist Convention in 1926. He edited *The Calvary Pulpit* and *Faith Fundamentalism*. He was an ardent foe of Al Smith during the 1928 presidential campaign. He died on the day of the stock market crash, which left his church in debt, hindering his successors for many years. His books ranged from *The Salvation of Society* to *The Fakes and Fancies of the Evolutionists* (1925)

Arthur H. Mann

May 16, 1850
Norwich, England

Nov. 19, 1929
Cambridge, England

Composed music for "O, Jesus, I Have Promised" (lyrics by JOHN BODE). Mann served as an organist in several different places from 1870–75. In 1875, he went to King's College, Cambridge, where he served as organist until his death some 54 years later. Mann was a noted authority on HANDEL, a skillful trainer of boys' choirs, and wrote numerous hymn tunes, anthems, and organ arrangements.

Elisha A. Hoffman

May 7, 1839
Orwigsburg, Pennsylvania

Nov. 25, 1929
Chicago, Illinois

Presbyterian pastor and hymn writer; wrote the lyrics and music for "Give Him the Glory," "Is Your All on the Altar," "Are You Washed in the Blood?", "I Must Tell Jesus," "Is It Not Wonderful," "Is Thy Heart Right With God?" "What a Wonderful Savior," the lyrics for "Glory to His Name," (music by JOHN STOCKTON) and "Leaning on the Everlasting Arms," (music by ANTHONY SHOWALTER), among 2,000 songs. Hoffman was connected with the Evangelical Association for many years, then he pastored First Church, Benton Harbor, MI for 33 years.

Edward Nemeschy

Oct. 18, 1861
Buffalo, New York

Dec. 4, 1929
Niagara Falls, New York

President of Buffalo Synod (ALC, ELCA in 1988), **1913–22**. Nemeschy received his training at Martin Luther Seminary, Buffalo, NY. Nemeschy served Lutheran congregations in Altamont, IL (1884–1900) and St. Paul's, Niagara Falls, NY (1900–29). He married Lydia Wendt in 1885, and they had five children. He preached his last sermon on December 1, 1929 and died three days later. The funeral was at St. Paul's.

William F. Warren

March 13, 1833
Williamsburg, Massachusetts

Dec. 6, 1929
Brookline, Massachusetts

First dean of Boston (MA) University School of Theology, 1867–73, 1885–91, and 1903–11. Warren was ordained a Methodist in 1855, and pastored in Wilbraham and Boston, MA from 1854–61. He married Harriet Merrick on April 14, 1861. Warren was professor of systematic theology in Mission Institute, Bremen, Germany, 1861–66. In 1867, the Methodist Biblical Institute relocated to Boston as the above-mentioned school. Then he was president of Boston University, 1873–1903, and professor until 1923. Warren became a liberal and taught evolution, influencing Methodism to depart from its spiritual roots. Warren's books range from *The True Key to Ancient Cosmology* (1882) to *The Universe via MILTON* (1915).

Edward S. Ufford

Feb. 10, 1851
Neward, New Jersey

Dec. 8, 1929
Union, Maine

Wrote the lyrics and music to "Throw Out the Lifeline," 1890 (GEORGE STEBBINS arranged the music). Ufford held several Baptist pastorates beginning at FBC, East Auburn, ME in 1879; then Alna, ME and Canton, Dedham, Hingham, Winchendon, and Willimansett, MA. The inspiration for his famed song came after witnessing coast guard units throwing life-lines to wrecked ships near Boston. Ufford also compiled Christian songbooks.

John E. Wood

May 21, 1867
near Glasgow, Kentucky

Dec. 15, 1929
Danville, Kentucky (?)

President of National Baptist Convention of America, 1925–29. Wood was converted at age twelve. He married Ella B. Redd on February 19, 1891. He was pastor at FBC, Danville, KY in 1898. He pastored and taught school at Munfordville, Woodsonville, Bardstown, and Elizabethtown, KY in his early days. For more than 26 years, he edited and published a weekly newspaper, *The Torch Light*. In addition, he was moderator of the General Association of Kentucky Baptists for nine years.

William M. Clow

1853
Glasgow, Scotland

1930
Glasgow, Scotland

Presbyterian preacher who served in five different churches, 1881–1911. Clow became a teacher of divinity (1911) and later principal of United Free Church College, Glasgow, (1921). His best writings include *The Cross in Christian Experience* (1908), *The Secret of the Lord*, *The Day of the Lord*, *The Evangel of the Strait Gate*, and *Five Portraits of Jesus*.

Wilifrid B. Grubb

1865
Liberton, Scotland

1930

Anglican missionary to Paraguay. At age 19, Grubb applied to South American Missionary Society; at age 21, he went to Keppel Island in the West Falklands. In 1889, Grubb began a pioneer work among the Indians of Paraguayan Chaco. It was several years before the Indians had confidence in him, and he saw his first convert. They called him "Peacemaker of the Indians." For 20 years, from 1889–1909, he traveled by horse 15 miles a day exploring remote areas of Argentina and Bolivia. In 1898, he married May Bridges. He returned to England in 1911, in poor health.

Alfred T. Schofield

1846
Lancashire, England

c 1930

London physician who was converted at age 15. Schofield became the first person to receive the Nobel Peace Prize in medicine and obstetrics. He received his M.D. degree with honor from Brussels University. Schofield was not only a successful physician but also a member of various medical staffs and societies. He wrote several books including *Faith Healing*, *The Knowledge of God*, *Christian Sanity*, *The Divine In Man*, and *The Life that Pleases God*.

Mark Guy Pearse

Jan. 3, 1842
Camborne, England

Jan. 1, 1930
London, England

World famous Wesleyan preacher. Pearse entered the Wesleyan ministry in 1863. Worldwide preaching tours and many books on Cornish and religious themes gained him an international reputation. He held pastorates in Leeds, Ipswich, Bristol, and other places. He became mission director at St. James Hall in connection with the West London Mission, 1889–1904. His books include *The Gentleness of Jesus*, *Sermons for Children*, *Simon Jaspar*, *Cornish Stories*, *His Mark*, *Praise*, *Rob Rat*, and *Orthodox Devil*.

Stanley White

May 2, 1862
Richmond, St. Isle, New York

Jan. 21, 1930
New Brunswick, New Jersey (?)

Director of Presbyterian Church USA Missions, 1907–25. White married Henrietta Kneass on May 20, 1891, and they had six children. He pastored Hillside Church, Orange, NJ from 1888–1907. White became chaplain of Rutgers University after 1926. His travels include Central America, Syria, Egypt, India, China, Korea, Japan, and Russia.

Franklin L. Sheppard

Aug. 7, 1852
Philadelphia, Pennsylvania

Feb. 15, 1930
Germantown, Pennsylvania

Composed the music for "This Is My Father's World," 1901 (MALTIE BABCOCK). In 1875, Sheppard moved to Baltimore to take charge of his father's foundry firm. He was a member of Zion Protestant Episcopal Church, Baltimore, where he served as organist and vestryman. Later, Sheppard was music director of Second Presbyterian Church of Baltimore. He went on to be president of the Presbyterian Board of Publications.

Benson H. Roberts

Oct. 9, 1853
Brockport, New York

March 2, 1930
Cantonsville, Maryland

President of A.M. Chesebrough Seminary, N. Chili, NY (Roberts Wesleyan College, Rochester, NY in 1945), **1883–1906**. The school was called Chili Seminary, 1883–85. Roberts married Emma J. Sellew in 1877. Roberts was superintendent of the Christian Home for Girls, Pittsburgh, PA (1907–11); a preacher at Berea (KY) College and pastor of Union Church there (1911–19). He was the son of BENJAMIN ROBERTS. The preaching credentials, taken from his father, were returned to Benson in 1910. He also pastored the Presbyterian Church, Relay, MD in 1922. Roberts was active in the ecumenical movement.

Martin G. Brumbaugh

April 14, 1862
Huntingdon County, Pennsylvania

March 14, 1930
Pinehurst, North Carolina

Educator and governor of Pennsylvania, 1915–19. Brumbaugh was ordained by German Baptist Brethren. He married Anna Konigmacher in 1884 and Flora Parks on January 29, 1916. Brumbaugh's educational work began as president of Juanita College, Huntington, PA (1895–1906 and 1924–30) and then as professor of pedagogy at the University of Pennsylvania (1895–1900 and 1902–06). He also served as superintendent of schools in Philadelphia, PA from 1906–15. Brumbaugh's books include *History of Brethren* to *Story of ROOSEVELT* (1922).

Arthur J. Balfour

July 25, 1848
Whittingehame, Scotland

March 19, 1930
near Woking, England

British statesman and philosopher. After Balfour was appointed as a conservative member of Parliament in 1874, he served as the prime minister of England (1902–5), and foreign secretary for the government (1916–19). In 1917, Balfour produced the Declaration which committed Great Britain to secure a national home for the Jewish people in Palestine. Theologically, he defended Christian theism. Balfour continued the political legacy of WILLIAM GLADSTONE. His writings range from *Defense of Philosophic Doubt* (1879) to *Theism and Thought* (1923).

George W. Carter

Jan. 4, 1867
Rosario, Argentina

March 19, 1930
New York, New York (?)

President of New York (International in 1978) Bible Society, 1907–30. Carter married Urainia M. Smith on December 12, 1896 (died: 1915), and Miriam Abba Pope on June 28, 1922. He was ordained a Methodist in 1893, and pastored St. Paul's Church, Hartford, CT (1895–98); West Haven Church, New Haven, CT (1898–99); and in Sea Cliff, NY (1899–1907). He joined the Reformed Church in America in 1911. He authored *The Faith of the Presidents*.

Kanzo Uchimura

March 18, 1861
Edo (Tokyo)/Satama, Japan

March 28, 1930

Independent leader in Japan who was converted as a college freshman at Sapporo Agricultural College by the witness of students. In 1881, he founded and headed the independent Japanese church, which was a large group of unbaptized believers. Uchimura attended Amherst (MA) College, 1884–88, then returned to Japan. He wrote against the sins of the government and the nation in general from his "pulpit" of a Tokyo Journal. In 1926, Uchimura founded the *Japan Christian Intelligencer*. Uchimura also edited *The Bible Study*, a 22-volume Bible commentary.

Charles W. Abel

Sept. 25, 1862
London, England

April 10, 1930
Woolrich, England

Missionary to the Papuans. Abel was converted at age eleven during a MOODY crusade. He attended Cheshunt College, Cambridge, for medical training after spending several years in New Zealand. He then went to New Guinea with the London Missionary Society on October 23, 1890. In 1890, Abel began to work with the savage Papuans on Kwato Island in New Guinea. He married Beatrice Moxon (1869–1939) in November, 1892, in Australia. In 1917, he resigned from LMS and formed the Kwato Extension Association. Abel survived the Papuans but died following a car collision in England. His ashes were returned to Kwato.

Randall T. Davidson

April 7, 1848
Edinburgh, Scotland

May 25, 1930
London, England

Archbishop of Canterbury, 1903–28. Davidson was curate of Dartford (1874–77), then chaplain to ARCHIBALD TAIT (1877–82) and to EDWARD BENSON (1882–83). Davidson was also dean of Windsor (1883), bishop of Rochester (1891), and bishop of Winchester (1895). He succeeded FREDERICK TEMPLE in 1903, to the Anglicans' highest post. His tenure as archbishop was during an especially difficult time in English history, but he won the trust of Queen VICTORIA because of his moderation. After retirement, Davidson was made Baton of Lambeth. He wrote *Life of Archbishop TAIT* (1891) to *Occasions* (1925).

George Smith (2)

London, England

June 2, 1930
Victoria, B.C., Canada

President of Evangelical Union of South America, NA Section (Avant Ministries in 2004), **1911–28**. This movement merged into Gospel Missionary Union in 1975. Smith was a missionary in Argentina in 1887. Back in England in 1902, he joined Regions Beyond Missionary Union, the predecessor to EUSA. Smith moved to Toronto to develop EUSA.

Elijah T. Cassel

Nov. 27, 1849
Indiana

July 3, 1930
South Gate, California

Wrote the hymns "Loyalty to Christ" and "The King's Business" (music for both by his wife, FLORA). Cassel, an active Baptist layman, practiced medicine in Hastings, NE. Cassel entered the ministry at age 60 and pastored Bethel Baptist Church, Denver, CO (1911–17), and FBC, Ft. Morgan, CO (1919–21). His wife, FLORA, was killed in Denver. Cassel remarried in 1917. In 1922, he moved to Huntington Park, CA and remained active at FBC there.

Jesse L. Hurlbut

Feb. 15, 1843
New York, New York

Aug. 2, 1930
Newark, New Jersey

Methodist layman known for his 30 books on Bible study, Bible history, and Sunday School work. Hurlbut is especially known for his *Hurlbut's Story of the Bible* (1901), with 5 million copies in print. He married Mary M. Chase on March 5, 1867 (died: 1913). Hurlbut pastored churches in New York (1865–79), was the agent of the Methodist Sunday School Union (1879–84), and was the editor and secretary of the Sunday School Union and Tract Society (1888–1900). He pastored in Morristown, NJ (1900–4); and in Orange, NJ (1904–6). He was district superintendent of the Newark district from 1909–14. Hurlbut was also one of the founders of the Epworth League. His books range from *American History* (1880) to *The Story of Chautauqua* (1921).

Lyman E. Davis

Dec. 28, 1854
Perrysburg, Ohio

Aug. 13, 1930
Baltimore, Maryland

President of Methodist Protestant Church (United Methodist Church in 1968), **1912–20**. Davis married Ella Wood on October 23, 1877. He began pastoring in 1878 and served churches in Tarrytown, Rochville Center, Middletown, Albany, and Saratoga, all in New York, and Grace Church of Pittsburgh, PA. From 1913 until his death, he was basically editor of the *Methodist Recorder* in Pittsburgh. He was a member of the Executive Committee of the Federal Council of Churches of Christ in America and of the National Reform Association.

Karl Kumm

Oct. 19, 1874
Hanover, Germany

Aug. 22, 1930
Pacific Beach, California (?)

Founder of Sudan United Mission (Action Partners) **in 1904**, comprised of 22 denominations. Kumm founded missions, hospitals, and schools. He joined the German army, but only for a year. On a visit to friends in London in 1895, he wandered one day into a mission hall in the East End where he heard EDWARD GLENNY speak of the work with the North Africa Mission. He attended Harley College and came under the influence of HENRY G. GUINNESS SR., whose daughter, Lucy (1865–1906), he married in February, 1900 in Cairo, Egypt. Kumm went to work with Moslems in Egypt under the auspices of NAM in 1899. In 1902 he went to Libya to gain knowledge of the Hausa language. In July, 1904, a team of four, led by Kumm, entered Sudan. He was the first white man to traverse the north central African divide between the Shari River (from northwest corner of Nigeria through Chad) and the Nile River (segmenting S. to N, the eastern third of Sudan). In 1906, he presented his missionary scope to groups in the US. Around August of that year, his wife died. His second marriage was to Frances G. Cato of Australia in 1911. From 1907–24, Kumm founded branches of SUM in many other countries, with his last visit to Africa being in 1923. Poor health influenced his decision to resign in 1925. He was an Episcopalian and lived out his days in Pacific Beach, CA from 1925 on.

William A. Spooner

July 22, 1844
London, England

Aug. 29, 1930
Oxford, England

Hilarious Anglican cleric, educator at Oxford's New College from 1867 to 1924. Spooner confused several generations of students with his transposition of sounds and syllables, which came to be known as "Spoonerisms." For example, he might say, "Is the bean dizzy?" instead of "Is the dean busy?" or "for a blushing crow" instead of "for a crushing blow."

John C. Bowman

Aug. 15, 1849
Chambersburg, Pennsylvania

Sept. 11, 1930
Coatesville, Pennsylvania

President of Lancaster (PA) Theological Seminary, 1908–20. Bowman was ordained to the Reformed Church ministry in 1875, then pastored in Shepherdstown, WV (1875–82), and Hanover, PA (1882–90). He married Amelia Davis on January 8, 1878. He went to LTS in 1891, and taught New Testament exegesis until 1904, then practical theology, 1904–20. Bowman died after an accident near Honeybrook, PA.

Carrie Parker Rounsefell

March 1, 1861
Merrimack, New Hampshire

Sept. 18, 1930
Durham, Maine

Composed music for "I'll Go Where You Want Me to Go" (lyrics by Mary Brown and CHARLES PRIOR). Carrie moved from Merrimack to Manchester, NH when only a child. She married William E. Rounsefell and traveled as a singing evangelist, always using a small autoharp to accompany her singing. During her later years, Carrie was a member of the Church of God. In 1928, she moved to Durham.

Louis F. Benson

July 22, 1855
Philadelphia, Pennsylvania

Oct. 10, 1930
Philadelphia, Pennsylvania

Presbyterian lawyer, pastor, editor, and hymnologist. Benson briefly practiced law from 1877–84 before entering Princeton (PA) Theological Seminary, where his father was a trustee. Benson married Caroline Warren on June 1, 1887. He then began pastoring the Church of the Redeemer, Germantown, PA from 1888–94. Benson resigned in order to edit a series of hymnals for the General Assembly of the Presbyterian Church, USA: *The Presbyterian Hymnal* (1895), *The Congregational Hymnal* (1896), and *The Chapel Hymnal* (1898). He owned one of the largest libraries on hymnology in the country (9,000 volumes). His hymns include "The Light of God is Falling," "O Sing a Song of Bethlehem," and "O, Thou Whose Feet Have Climbed Life's Hill." Examples of his work are: *Studies of Familiar Hymns* (1903), *The English Hymn: Its Development and Use in Worship*, and *The Hymnody of the Christian Church* (1927–30).

Robert D. Wilson

Feb. 4, 1856
Indiana, Pennsylvania

Oct. 11, 1930
Princeton, New Jersey (?)

Perhaps the most brilliant mind in church history. Wilson could speak over 20 languages; he was a learned linguist, Presbyterian cleric, and OT scholar. Wilson married Ellen Howard on June 20, 1889. He taught OT at Western (Pittsburgh) Theological Seminary (1880–1900), OT and semitic philosophy at Princeton Theological Seminary (1900–29), and Westminster Seminary (1929–30). He was a Presbyterian philologist and theologian who was a professor and co-founder, with GRESHAM MACHEN of the Westminster Theological Seminary in 1929. Wilson was a great defender of the faith. His writings range from *Elements of Syriac Grammar* (1890) to *Scientific Old Testament Criticism* (1923). He produced Hebrew textbooks as well.

Edwin C. Dargan

Nov. 17, 1852
Springville, South Carolina

Oct. 26, 1930
Chicago, Illinois

President of Southern Baptist Convention, 1911–13. Dargan married Lucy Graves on June 12, 1878; they had five children. He pastored three churches in Virginia (1877–81); FBC, Petersbury, VA (1881–87); Dixon, CA (1887–88); Citadel Square Church, Charleston, SC (1888–92); Kentucky churches (1892–94 and 1906–07); and FBC, Macon, GA (1907–17). Dargan was an editor of the Sunday School Board of SBC from 1917–27. From 1892–1907, Dargan taught homiletics at Southern Baptist Theological Seminary in Louisville, KY. His works range from *Colossians* (1890) to *The Bible Our Heritage* (1924).

George Whelpton

May 17, 1847
Redbourne, England

Nov. 25, 1930
Oxford, Ohio

Composed music for "Hear My Prayer, Oh Lord." Whelpton came to America at age four and enlisted in the Civil War at age 13. He became a choral director in Buffalo, NY from 1903–25. Whelpton also joined the editorial staff of Century Publishing Company, New York City from 1903–16, where he compiled *Hymns of Worship and Service* and *The Church Hymnal*. He also worked for A. S. Barnes Company, 1916–25.

J. Lincoln Hall

Nov. 4, 1866
Philadelphia, Pennsylvania

Nov. 29, 1930
Philadelphia, Pennsylvania

Composed music for "I Belong to the King," 1896 (lyrics by IDA SMITH), "Does Jesus Care?" 1901 (lyrics by FRANK GRAEFF), and "He is Mine," 1912 (music by C. AUSTIN MILES). Hall wrote lyrics and music to "Some Day, I Shall Be Like Him." Hall used the pseudonym, Maurice A. Clifton. He was a prominent song leader, composer, and music publisher from Philadelphia. Hall wrote music for many cantatas, oratorios, anthems, and hundreds of gospel songs. He was associated with Hall-Mack Publishing Company in Philadelphia.

William E. Barton

June 28, 1861
Sublette, Illinois

Dec. 7, 1930

Congregational clergyman and author. Barton married Esther Bushnell on July 23, 1885 (died: November 7, 1925); and they had six children. He held several pastorates in Tennessee and Ohio; he then pastored at Shawmut Church, Boston, MA (1893–99) and First Church of Oak Park, IL (1899–1924). At Chicago (IL) Theological Seminary, he lectured on applied practical theology (1905–09) and on ecclesiastical law (1911–24). Barton's books range from *Life of the Hills of Kentucky* (1889) to LINCOLN *at Gettysburg* (1930). He died of pneumonia. His homes were in Oak Park, IL and Foxboro, MA.

Ada R. Habershon

Jan. 8, 1861
England

c 1931

Wrote the hymns "He Will Hold Me Fast" (music by ROBERT HARKNESS), **"Shine Just Where You Are"** (music by HENRY BARRACLOUGH), **and "Will the Circle Be Unbroken"** (music by CHARLES GABRIEL). Ada possessed unusual ability as a writer and speaker, and gained much fame as a lecturer. She was a great help in the MOODY 1884 London crusade. Ada first wrote hymns from a sickbed in 1901. When CHARLES ALEXANDER requested her song-poems in 1905, she gave him over 200.

Emma Mott Whittemore

1850
New York, New York

Jan. 1, 1931
New York, New York

Rescue mission founder of Doors of Hope. Emma and her businessman husband, Marcus Whittemore, were converted at New York City's Water Street Mission. In 1890, she established the first Door of Hope (home for fallen and unfortunate women) in New York City. She was part of the CMA movement, where A. B. SIMPSON encouraged and helped her. By the time of her death, 97 homes were in operation. She was first president of the International Union of Gospel Missions, 1914–18. She engaged in evangelistic endeavors and promoted her work till her death. She was the female counterpart to the rescue mission ministry work of MEL TROTTER. Most of the young women converts were prostitutes. She may have "saved more fallen women than any other individual."

Robert H. Charles

Aug. 6, 1855
Cookstown, Ireland

Jan. 30, 1931

Anglican theologian and biblical scholar. Charles served in curates at Whitechapel and Kensington (1883–89), then lectured in London (1889–98). He was also a professor of Greek at Trinity College, Dublin (1898–1906); a Grinfeld lecturer at Oxford (1906–13), and a general editor of the *Apocrypha* and *Pseudepigrapha of the Old Testament* (1913). Charles was a guest lecturer at many universities throughout the United Kingdom. His later days were spent as canon (1913–31) and archdeacon of Westminster Abbey (1919–31). His theological strength was Jewish eschatalogy and apocalyptics. His books range from *Forgiveness and Other Sermons* (1886) to *Commentary on Daniel* (1929). He was a great authority on the Apocrypha.

Edward Rondthaler

July 24, 1842
Schoeneck, Pennsylvania

Jan. 31, 1931
Winston-Salem, North Carolina

President of Moravian Church in NA (South), **Salem 1890 –1913, Winston-Salem, NC 1913–29**. Rondthaler married Mary Jacobson on October 1, 1867. He pastored Moravian churches in Brooklyn, NY (1865–73); at First Church, Philadelphia, PA (1874–77); and at

Central Church, Winston-Salem, NC (1877–1908). He was ordained a bishop on April 22, 1891. Rondthaler was president of Woman's College in the South, Salem, NC from 1884–87. He was active in world Moravian affairs. He wrote *50 years of "Annual Papers on World Events"* (1928).

John W. Baer

March 2, 1861
Rochester, Minnesota

Feb. 8, 1931
Pasadena, California (?)

General secretary of Christian Endeavor (World), 1900–08, and (Int) 1890–1902. Baer was a banker, involved in journalism in Cedar Rapids, IA from 1879–81, and was also in the grain and coal business in Minneapolis, MN in 1881. He married Lora VanDusen on July 22, 1884. He served as the president of Occidental College, Los Angeles, CA from 1906–16, and as the moderator of the Presbyterian Church in 1919.

Ozora S. Davis

July 30, 1866
Wheelock, Vermont

March 15, 1931
near Kansas City, Missouri

President of Chicago (IL) Theological Seminary, 1909–29. Davis was a Congregationalist and hymnwriter. He married Grace Tinker on November 17, 1896. He served in churches in Vermont, Massachusetts, and Connecticut until 1908. In 1927, Davis was the moderator for the National Council of Congregationalist Churches. After his presidency ended, he taught theology. His books range from *Pilgrim Faith* (1913) to *Church and Community Occasions* (1929). He died on a train from California going east, presumably, to Chicago.

Kankarayan T. Paul

March 24, 1876
Salem, India

April 11, 1931
Salem, India

Leader of YMCA in India. Bishops AZARIAH and Paul were the leaders who organized the National Missionary Society of India in 1905. In 1912, Paul became the general secretary of the YMCA of India, Burma, and Ceylon (Sri Lanka). He traveled widely in America and Great Britain and served as president of the All-India Christian Conference. In his latter days, he got involved in Indian political activities. He became national general secretary of the YMCA in 1916. His last words were: "I have done my duty to my God and my country. I die in peace."

Garfield T. Haywood

July 15, 1880
Greencastle, Indiana

April 12, 1931
Indianapolis, Indiana

First presiding bishop of Pentecostal Assemblies of the World, Indianapolis, IN 1915–32. Haywood moved with his parents to Indianapolis where he spent the rest of his life. He developed cartoonist talents early in life. He was a pastor, songwriter, and an executive. On Feb 11, 1902, he married Ida Howard. Another pastor turned his Indianapolis church over to Haywood in late 1908. Three years later, in 1911, he helped form the Pentecostal Assemblies of the World, leading it until he died. He was active in the early founding of the Assemblies of God in 1914. It was in 1915, when he took the leadership with a new doctrine—baptizing in Jesus' name only—which he followed the rest of his life. He wrote the hymn, "Jesus, the Son of God" (music arranged by Rosa Johnson). In 1924, his Apostolic Faith Temple was renamed Christ Temple, as it relocated to a 1,200-seat building. That year, many of the white members left to form the United Pentecostal Church.

David F. McGill

March 22, 1857
West Alexander, Pennsylvania

April 26, 1931
Belleville, Pennsylvaina

Stated clerk of United Presbyterian Church (PC USA in 1983) **of North America, 1903–30**. McGill married Hattie Weddle on June 12, 1884. He pastored Sixth Church, Allegheny, PA (1885–1911) and in Ben Avon, PA (1911–15). He was also a professor of church history and government at Pittsburgh Theological Seminary, 1915 on. From 1891–1914, McGill served as editor of the *United Presbyterian*. He was active in Reformed Presbyterian activities.

Samuel P. Brooks

Dec. 4, 1863
Milledgeville, Georgia

May 14, 1931
Waco, Texas

President of Baylor University, Waco, TX 1902–31, transforming it from a small college to a full university status. Brooks married Mattie Sims on Dec. 24, 1895. He lectured on educational subjects and was also the corresponding secretary of the Texas Baptist Educational Commission. Brooks organized the Texas State Peace Congress in 1907, and was the Grand Orator of Northwest Masonic Grand Lodge of Texas, 1908–22. From 1914–17, Brooks was president of the Baptist Convention of Texas. He defended his university when evolution and liberalism crept in, making him a target of J. FRANK NORRIS.

George F. Moore

Oct. 15, 1851
West Chester, Pennsylvania

May 16, 1931
Cambridge, Massachusetts

Presbyterian pastor, educator, and author. Moore was an Old Testament scholar with a remarkable knowledge of rabbinical source literature. Moore married Mary Hanford on April 25, 1878 (died: 1924). He pastored in Zanesville, OH from 1878–83. Moore taught OT at Andover (MA) Theological Seminary (1883–1902) and history of religions at Harvard (1904–21). He is best known for his work, *Judaism in the First Century of the Christian Era* (3 vols., 1927–30). Early on, he wrote *The Literature of the Old Testament* (1913). He also wrote a two-volume *History of Religions* (1913–19). He was editor of *The Harvard Theological Review* (1913–24).

Edwin W. Stephens

Jan. 21, 1849
Columbia, Missouri

May 22, 1931
Columbia, Missouri

President of Southern Baptist Convention, 1905–07. Stephens married Laura Moss on September 26, 1871. He served as editor and publisher of *Columbia* (MO) *Herald* (1870–1905). Stephens was also president of E. W. Stephens Publishing Company in Columbia, 1905–15, and president of Central Baptist Publishing Company of St. Louis. Stephens also served as chairman of the commission to build the state capital in Missouri. He was a deacon at FBC in Columbia. He wrote *Around the World*.

Francis A. O. Pieper

June 27, 1852
Carwitz, Germany

June 3, 1931
St. Louis, Missouri

President of Concordia Seminary, St. Louis, MO 1887–1931, and of Lutheran Church Missouri Synod, 1899–1911. Pieper married Minnie Koehn on Jan. 2, 1877. He pastored in Manitowoc, WI (1875–78), and was professor of theology at CS (1878–87). Pieper also served as editor of *Lehre* and *Wehre* and wrote both German and English books, 1880–1931. Under his leadership, the seminary grew to over 500 students and the denomination to over 1 million adherents. His three-volume *Christian Dogmatics* (1917–24) published in German is his legacy. He opposed all doctrinal compromise. Most of his books were written in German.

Nathan Soderholm

Jan. 15, 1866
Trono, Sweden

July 12, 1931
Uppsala, Sweden

Lutheran archbishop of Uppsala, 1914 on, leader in the ecumenical movement, theologian, historian, gifted thinker, and author. In 1890, Soderholm attended a D. L. MOODY Northfield Student Conference and was challenged with a vision of church unity. Soderholm was a minister of the Swedish Church in Paris, 1894–1901. He taught comparative religion at Uppsala University, 1901–12, then two years as professor of theology at Leipzig. In 1914, he became chancellor of the University of Uppsala. Soderholm labored to bring the Christian Conference on Life and Work to Stockholm in 1925. He was a pacifist. In 1930, he received the Nobel Peace Prize. He wrote from *Christian Fellowship* (1923) to *The Nature of Revelation* (1933).

Eric G. Hjerpe

March 2, 1853
Hillringberg, Sweden

July 16, 1931
Chicago, Illinois

President of Mission (Evangelical in 1937) **Covenant Church, Chicago, IL 1910–27**. He was converted in 1874. It was in 1879 that he emigrated to America, coming to Lake City, MN. He married Josephine Peterson in 1881. Hjerpe pastored in Galesburg, IL (1885–87); New Britain, CT (1888–1900); Jamestown, NY (1901–05); and in Bethany Covenant, Chicago, IL (1906–1909). During his tenure, a Sunday School department was established as well as *The Covenant Companion*, and a new constitution that passed in 1923. He lost two children during this time: a son, Fridolph (1917), and a daughter, Lillian (1920).

Charles T. Studd

Dec. 2, 1860
Spratton, England

July 16, 1931
Ibambi/Imbi, Belgian Congo (Congo)

Gifted missionary, first director of Heart of Africa Mission, 1912–18, renamed Worldwide Evangelization Crusade, 1919–31. Studd was converted at age 18 as a result of a home visit witness. He became an outstanding cricket player, 1883–85. As one of the Cambridge Seven, he went to China in 1885. While he was there, in 1887, he inherited approximately $125,000.00, which he gave away to Christian work. He married Priscilla Stewart in March, 1888 (died: 1929). Leaving China in 1894 because of health problems, he toured U.S. universities from 1896–97 in speaking engagements. Studd inspired the formation of the Student Volunteer Movement. They went to Oolacamund, India (1900–6), and then he went on to Niangara, Belgian Congo (1910–31). They set up an independent work, having been turned away by mission boards because of his health. They were separated, while Priscilla ran their mission out of London and he labored in Africa. She made one brief visit to Africa in those 20 years.

Hans G. Stub

Feb. 23, 1849
Muskego, Wisconsin

Aug. 1, 1931
St. Paul, Minnesota

President of Norwegian Synod, 1910–17, which merged with UNLC to form Norwegian Lutheran Church in America (ALC, ELCA in 1988), **1917–25**. Stub married Didrikke Ottesen on Aug. 11, 1876 (died: 1879); Valborn Hovind on July 31, 1884 (died: 1901); and Anna Skabo on Aug. 8, 1906. Stub was a professor at Luther Seminary in Madison, WI (1878–85) and Robbinsdale, MN (1885–96); and at Luther College in Decorah, IA (1896–1900). He pastored as well.

The Saints Go Marching In

E. Lyman Hood

Aug. 18, 1858
Ravenna, Ohio

Aug. 14, 1931

President of Atlanta (GA) Divinity School, 1905–19. Hood married Jessie Raymond on January 28, 1886 (died 1922), then Margaret Evans on October 5, 1925. He also served as the superintendent of Congregationalist Missions and schools in the Southwest, 1888–94. He pastored in River Edge, NJ from 1919–24, and was professor at Honolulu Theological Seminary, 1924 on. Hood authored books on history and education including *Pedagogy in the Middle Ages* (1898) to *Christ in the Church and in Literature* (1911).

William C. Dewitt

Oct. 31, 1860
Tiskilwa, Illinois

Sept. 25, 1931
Pasadena, California

Dean (until 1926), then president of Western Theological Seminary, Chicago, 1905–23, Evanston, IL (Seabury-Western Theological Seminary, Evanston, IL in 1933), **1923–28**. Dewitt married Martha Cossitt on July 20, 1886. He was ordained into the Episcopal Church and served as rector of Grace Church, Freeport, IL (1886–88), and of St. Andrew's Church, Chicago, IL (1889–1906). He was also the deputy (appointed to act for another) to three general conventions of the denomination. Dewitt lived mostly in Evanston.

Fleming H. Revell

Dec. 11, 1849
Chicago, Illinois

Oct. 11, 1931
Yonkers, New York

Publisher and president of F. H. Revell Company, 1890–1931. Revell left school at the age of nine to go to work, later entering the publishing business in 1869. His sister, EMMA, married D. L. MOODY. In 1882, he married Josephine Barbour. He specialized in the publication of works by MOODY and his evangelical colleagues. Revell moved from Chicago to New York in 1906. He was also associated with the New York Life Insurance Company, and was a trustee of several Christian companies. He was a Presbyterian. He wrote *Manual of Instruction for Confirmation Classes* (1900) and *Decently and in Order* (1914).

Albert B. Marshall

July 10, 1849
Bryan, Pennsylvania

Oct. 29, 1931
Bellevue, Nebraska (?)

President of Omaha (NE) Theological Seminary, 1910–20. Marshall married Jane E. Hervey (Sept. 1, 1875), and Mary E. Hallock (June 12, 1915). He was ordained a Presbyterian in 1874. He pastored in Morris, IL (1875–78); in Lisbon, OH (1879–87); the First Church, E. Liverpool, OH (1887–94); the Central Church, Des Moines, IA (1894–1903); the First Church, Minneapolis, MN (1903–10); in Clarinda, IA (1920–25); and in Bellevue, NE (1926 to date unknown)..

Ida Kahn

Dec. 6, 1873
Kiukiang, China

Nov. 9, 1931
Shanghai, China

Physician and surgeon who was adopted from a Methodist Mission. In 1892, Ida and Mary Stone came to America. Kahn finished medical school at the University of Michigan and then returned to Kiukiang. Together, they opened Danforth Hospital in 1900. In 1903, Kahn moved to Nanchang, where she was the only trained physician for the population of 300,000. In 1910–11, she traveled to Germany and to England.

William McKibbin

May 24, 1850
Pittsburgh, Pennsylvania

Dec. 20, 1931
Cincinnati, Ohio

President (and theology professor) **of Lane Theological Seminary, Cincinnati, OH** (affiliated with McCormick Theological Seminary, Chicago in 1931), 1904–25. McKibbin was ordained a Presbyterian in 1873. McKibbin married Nancy Patterson on Sept. 10, 1874. He pastored Seventh Church, Pittsburgh, PA (1873–74); Central Church, St. Paul, MN (1874–79); Second Church, Pittsburgh, PA (1880–88); and First Church of Walnut Hills, Cincinnati, OH (1888–1904). He died at his home.

Knud C. Bodholt

Feb. 9, 1855
Tyrstrup, Denmark

Dec. 23, 1931
Racine, Wisconsin

President of Danish Evangelical Lutheran Church (LCA, ELCA in 1988), **1894–95, 1903–11, and 1918–20**. Bodholt emigrated to America (1870) and was ordained (1882). He married Jensine Kreiberg in 1882 (died: 1883), then married Julie Smith in 1884 (died 1933). Bodholt pastored in Marquette, NE (1882–87); in Omaha, NE (1887–94); in Manistee and Big Rapids, MI (1895–1900); in Marinette, WI, and Menominee, MI (1900–05); in Dwight, IL (1905–09); and in Racine, WI (1909–21).

Melvil Dewey

Dec. 10, 1851
Adams Center, New York

Dec. 26, 1931
Hylands County, Florida

Pioneer librarian who devised the decimal system for classifying and cataloging books in 1876. The Dewey decimal system is now used universally. Dewey debated between library or missionary work, but went to Boston in 1876 to help organize the American Library Association. He headed the library at Columbia University, New York City (1883–88), and served as director of the NY State Library in Albany (1888–1906). In 1895, he founded a cooperative residential club in Lake Placid, NY. Dewey married Annie Godfrey (October 10, 1878), and Emily Beal (May 28, 1924).

Peter C. Lutkin

March 27, 1858
Thompsonville, Wisconsin

Dec. 27, 1931
Evanston, Illinois

Episcopalian organist and hymnologist who founded the American Guild of Organists. Lutkin composed the music for "The Lord Bless You and Keep You." He first served in the ministry as a choir boy under Canon Knowles (1869), then as the organist of St. James' Church, Chicago (1872). Lutkin married Nancy Carman on October 27, 1885. In 1891, Lutkin began teaching at the music school of Northwestern University, Evanston, IL. He became the dean of the School of Music, 1897–1928. He established an a cappella choir, which remained at the top of its field for many years. He conducted the annual North Shore Festival in Evanston, 1909–30. He died while working on a new hymnal with CHARLES M. STUART.

Annie H. Barker

1844

Jan. 1932

Wrote the hymn, "When the Mists Have Rolled Away" (music by IRA SANKEY). She was a resident in a county home: penniless, alone, friendless, and forgotten. One night, Annie heard a voice on the radio say, "We wish to dedicate this song to its author, wherever she may be." It was her hymn about heaven. Afterward, she said, "I'm so tired, help me to bed"…and she died that night and went home to heaven.

Robert S. Williams

Oct. 27, 1856
Caddo Parrish, Louisiana

Jan. 13, 1932
Augusta, Georgia

Bishop of Colored (Christian in 1956) **Methodist Episcopal Church, 1894–1932; senior bishop, 1920–32**. Williams joined the Christian Methodist Episcopal Church (1876) and was ordained deacon (1881), and elder (1883). He served churches in Texas, Washington, D.C., South Carolina, and Georgia. Williams was also a delegate to the third ecumenical Methodist Conference in London in 1901, and wrote a book of sermons.

Charles Gore

Jan. 22, 1853
Wimbledon, England

Jan. 17, 1932
London, England

Anglican theologian, bishop, and leader of the liberal school of thought in the Anglo-Catholic movement. Gore was a brilliant scholar. He taught at Trinity College, Oxford; was vice-principal of Cuddesdon College (1883–93); librarian of Pusey House, Oxford (1884–93); canon of Westminster (1894–1902); bishop of Worcester (1902); of Birmingham (1905); and of Oxford (1911–19). He then retired in London. He led the high church into modernism. His books range from *Leo the Great* (1880) to *Reflections on the Litany* (1932).

James G. K. McClure

Nov. 24, 1848
Albany, New York

Jan. 18, 1932
Lake Forest, Illinois

First president of McCormick Theological Seminary, Chicago, IL 1905–28. He was ordained a Presbyterian in 1874, and pastored in New Scotland, NY from 1874–79. McClure married Annie P. Dixon on November 19, 1879 and they had five children. He traveled to Europe and the Holy Land (1879–80); pastored in Lake Forest, IL (1881–1915); and was president of Lake Forest College (1897–1901). His books ranged from *Possibilities* (1896) to *History of the Presbyterian Theological Seminary* in Chicago (1929).

Albert H. Stilwell

April 8, 1855
Binghamton, New York

Jan. 26, 1932
Seattle, Washington

President of Spring Arbor (MI) Seminary, 1883–93. He served as the second principal at only 28 years old. When Stilwell left Spring Arbor, the school had four faculty members, a graduating class of seven, campus value of $10,000, and an annual budget of $1,200. He was also president at the Chili (Roberts Wesleyan) Seminary, 1879–83. He married Mary Lena Matthewson on August 19, 1885. In 1897, he was president of the Mt. Vernon (IL) Collegiate Institute. He taught in Crab Orchard, IL in 1898. From 1899–1902, he became principal of Evansville (IN) Seminary. He then served at Seattle Seminary for 14 years, 1902–16. Stilwell was an early Free Methodist leader.

Charles M. Stuart

Aug. 20, 1853
Glasgow, Scotland

Jan. 26, 1932
Evanston, Illinois (?)

President of Garrett Biblical Institute (GETS in 1974), **Evanston, IL 1912–24**. Stuart married Emma Littlefield on October 10, 1883. He was ordained Methodist in 1880, and pastored River Forest, IL (1880–83); Fort St. Church, Detroit (1883–85); and was professor of sacred rhetoric at Garrett (1896–1909). Stuart also served as assistant editor of *Northwestern Christian*

Advocate (1886–96). His books began with D*escriptive Text of Photogravures of Holy Land (1890)* and ended with *Studies of* CHARLES J. LITTLE (1916).

John W. Hughes

May 16, 1852
Eagle Creek, Kentucky

Feb. 22, 1932
Wilmore, Kentucky

Founder and first president of Asbury College, Wilmore, KY 1890–1905. Hughes was converted on Dec 26, 1868. He married Mary Wallingford on July 28, 1880. He spent twelve years in the pastorate, and one year in evangelism before being called of God to establish Asbury College. Hughes pastored the Methodist Church, Carlisle, KY from 1887–89, then went into evangelism. His motto was: "Free salvation for all men and full salvation from all sin."

Thomas C. Horton

Aug. 3, 1848
Cincinnati, Ohio

Feb. 27, 1932
Los Angeles, California

Minister and cofounder of Bible Institute of Los Angeles (BIOLA). Horton was a successful businessman by age 27. He married Anna Kingsbury on May 15, 1872 (died: 1920), then Harriet Ransom on March 16, 1922. He served as YMCA secretary in Indianapolis in 1876 and later, the same position in St. Paul, MN, and Dallas, TX from 1904–6. He worked out of Hope Presbyterian Church in St. Paul as an evangelist. He was associate pastor to A. T. PIERSON at Bethany Presbyterian, Philadelphia, PA (1885–89), and pastored First Congregational Church of Dallas (1900–3). In 1906, while serving at Immanuel Presbyterian Church, Los Angeles, he founded the Fisherman's Club. It was in 1908 that he founded BIOLA, with the help of LYMAN STUART. He was the associate pastor of the Church of the Open Door, 1915–24 and editor of the *King's Business* (1910–25).

Charles R. Hemphill

April 18, 1852
Chester, South Carolina

March 9, 1932
Louisville, Kentucky

First president of Presbyterian Theological Seminary of Kentucky, 1901–17, renamed **Louisville (KY) Presbyterian Theological Seminary, 1917–20.** Hemphill married Emma L. Muller on September 1, 1875 (died: 1920). He was ordained a Presbyterian and taught at Columbia Theological Seminary, 1874–78. He was a professor of Greek and Latin at Southwest Presbyterian University (1879–82); professor of biblical literature at Columbia Seminary (1882–85); and pastor of Second Church of Louisville, KY (1885–99). Beginning in 1893 till near his death, Hemphill taught at LPTS.

John Hughes

Nov. 22, 1873
Dowlais, Wales

May 14, 1932
Llantwit Farde, Wales

Composed music for "Guide Me, O Thou Great Jehovah" (lyrics by WILLIAM WILLIAMS). At age twelve, Hughes moved to Llantwit Farde, where he stayed the rest of his life. Hughes became a clerk and an official in the traffic department of Great Western Railway. He was a lifelong member of Salem Baptist Church, serving as deacon and precentor. Hughes composed many marches, anthems, and hymn tunes with lyrics by WILLIAMS.

Henry Lockwood

Jan. 4, 1869
Albany, New York

June 10, 1932
Englewood, New Jersey

Stated Clerk of Reformed Church in America, 1914–32. Lockwood married Bertha Booraem on June 20, 1894 (died: 1924). He pastored Knox and Second Berne Churches in Albany County, NY (1894–1901); East Millstone, NJ (1901–25); and Hudson Avenue Church, Englewood, NJ (1925 to date unknown). Lockwood was the permanent clerk, 1907–14, prior to his high-post position.

George B. Stewart

Feb. 28, 1854
Columbus, Ohio

June 23, 1932
Auburn, New York

President of Auburn (NY) Theological Seminary (moved to Union TS campus in 1939), **1899–1926**. Stewart married Mary Thompson on June 18, 1879, (died: 1903) and then Ella Hart on December 7, 1914. Stewart was ordained a Presbyterian in 1879. He pastored Calvary Church, Auburn, OH (1878–84) and Market Square Church, Harrisburg, PA (1884–99). He taught practical theology at Auburn as well as being its president. Stewart authored several books, ranging from *Centennial Memorial* (1894) to *Efficiency Tests for Pastors and Churches* (1915).

Henry E. Jacobs

Nov. 10, 1844
Gettysburg, Pennsylvania

July 7, 1932
Philadelphia, Pennsylvania

Dean, 1894–1920 and president of Lutheran Theological Seminary at Philadelphia, 1920–27. Jacobs was principal of Thiel College, Greenville, PA from 1868–70. He also worked at Gettysburg College (1870–83), teaching Latin and history (1870–80), the classics (1880–81) and Greek (1881–83). Jacobs married Laura Downing on July 3, 1872, and they had five children. In 1883, he became professor of systematic theology at LTS. Jacobs translated various theological works from German and contributed to theological periodicals. He was also involved in many Lutheran conferences. He edited *The Lutheran Review* (1881–96) and *The Lutheran Commentary* (13 vols., 1895–99), writing many books on Lutheran history. His works range from *The Lutheran Movement in England* (1891) to Lincoln's *Gettysburg World Message* (1920).

Earl Cranston

June 27, 1840
Athens, Ohio

Aug. 19, 1932
near New Richmond, Ohio

Bishop in the Methodist Episcopal Church, 1896–1932. Cranston married Martha Behan (Oct. 7, 1861), Laura Martin in 1874, and Lucie M. Parker (November 5, 1905). He pastored in Ohio (Marietta, 1867; Portsmouth, 1868–69; Columbus, 1870); then Winona, MN (1871); Jacksonville, IL (1872–74); Evansville, IN (1874–75); Cincinnati, OH (1875–78); and Denver, CO (1878–80). Cranston also worked as a publishing agent of the church from 1884–96 and was in charge of outreach to Mexico in 1903. From 1904–16, he was bishop of Washington, D.C., then spent the rest of his life speaking for Methodist unity.

Arthur H. Smith

July 18, 1845
Vernon, Connecticut

Aug. 31, 1932
Claremont, California

Congregational missionary. Smith married Emma Dickinson on September 8, 1871. They went to China (1872) under the ABCFM (1880). The Smiths moved on to Shantung, 1880–90 to evangelize and write a series of books. His first book was *Proverbs and Common Sayings of Chinese* (1888). Smith was actually in Peking during the Boxer siege in 1900. After 1906, Smith was a missionary evangelist. He retired to Claremont in 1926.

Annie J. Flint

Dec. 24, 1866
Vineland, New Jersey

Sept. 8, 1932
Clifton Springs, New York

Bedridden invalid for 40 years, outstanding poet, and songwriter. Flint wrote the hymns "He Giveth More Grace" and "What God Hath Promised." She was afflicted by crippling arthritis as a young adult, and entered the sanitarium in Clifton Springs, NY. She was unable to walk at age 30. Annie lived in this home directed by Mrs. E. J. Comstock from 1906 on. From her bed, she wrote songs, poems, leaflets, books, and greeting cards which circled the globe.

Morris D. Landis

Feb. 20, 1866
Lyonsville, Pennsylvania

Sept. 11, 1932
near Harrisburg, Pennsylvania

First presiding bishop of United Christian Church, Cleona, PA 1913–32. Landis was raised in the United Christian Church, Palmyra, PA. He married Nellie Weltmer (died: May 17, 1931) and they had one daughter. He was ordained in 1905. He pastored various congregations in that part of the country. His Biblical preaching and administrative leadership was well appreciated. He was bi-vocational, and in partnership with his father Jacob, his brother David, and later, his brother-in-law, Cyrus Zimmerman in the J Landis Shoe Company of Palmyra, PA. He was in charge of the annual Cleona camp meeting of the church. He died from a heart attack in an ambulance en route to the Harrisburg hospital coming from the Hershey hospital.

Charles H. Gabriel

Aug. 18, 1856
Wilton, Iowa

Sept. 15, 1932
Los Angeles, California

One of the greatest composers of gospel music in history. He was associated with some 8,000 gospel songs. Gabriel, who never took a music lesson, sometimes used the pseudonym, "Charlotte G. Homer." He settled in Chicago in 1895. From 1912, he was associated with Rodeheaver Publishing Company (edited 35 songbooks) and sang noted songs with his duet partner, EDWIN O. EXCELL. Gabriel wrote the words and music of "More Like the Master," "The Awakening Chorus," "Some Bright Morning," "O, It Is Wonderful," "O That Will Be Glory," "He Lifted Me," "My Savior's Love," "Pentecostal Power," "Send the Light," "Sail On," "Jesus, Blessed Jesus," "Where the Gates Swing Outward Never," "I Want You to Know Him," and "He Is So Precious to Me." He composed music for "Higher Ground" (OATMAN), "His Eye Is on the Sparrow" (ED MARTIN), "Since Jesus Came into My Heart" (McDANIEL), "The Way of the Cross Leads Home" (POUNDS), "Just When I Need Him Most" (POOLE), "I Need Jesus" (WEBSTER), "I'll Go Where You Want Me to Go" (ROUNSEFELL), "As a Volunteer" (W. S. Brown), "Brighten the Corner" (OGDEN), "All Hail, Emmanuel" (VAN SICKLE), "Help Somebody Today," and "There Is Glory in My Soul" (Grace Davis). According to PHIL KERR, Gabriel died in Berkeley, CA.

Samuel Chadwick

Sept. 16, 1860
Burney, England

Oct. 16, 1932

Wesleyan evangelist and educator. Converted at age ten, Chadwick began to preach at age 16 and was a lay evangelist at age 21. He entered the Wesleyan ministry (1883), became the editor of the *Joyful News* (1905), then was principal of Cliff College (1913). Chadwick was president of the Wesleyan conference in 1918. He encouraged lay evangelism and holiness.

Palmer Hartsough

May 7, 1844
Redford, Michigan

Oct. 24, 1932
Plymouth, Michigan

Wrote the hymn, "I Am Resolved" (music by JAMES FILLMORE). Hartsough moved to Plymouth, MI in 1856 and began teaching singing in schools throughout Michigan, Illinois, Iowa, Ohio, Kentucky, and Tennessee for the next ten years. He settled in Rock Island, IL and opened a music studio. In 1893, Hartsough was associated with Fillmore Publishing, Cincinnati, OH until 1903. He was ordained a Baptist in 1906 and pastored in Ontario, MI, 1914–27. Hartsough never married.

Francis L. Patton

Jan. 22, 1843
Warwick, Bermuda

Nov. 25, 1932
Warwick, Bermuda

President of Princeton (NJ) College, 1888–98; University, 1898–1902; and first president of Theological Seminary, 1902–13. Patton married Rosa Stevenson on October 10, 1865, and was ordained a Presbyterian the same year. He pastored at the 84th Street Presbyterian Church, New York (1865–67); in Nyack, NY (1867–70) and at Jefferson Park Presbyterian Church, Chicago, IL (1874–81). He taught at McCormick Theological Seminary (1872–81), and became professor at Princeton, (1881–88). His most memorable book was *Fundamental Christianity* (1926).

Horace N. Allen

April 23, 1858
Delaware, Ohio

Dec. 11, 1932
Toledo, Ohio

Presbyterian missionary, diplomat, and first resident Protestant missionary in Korea. Allen went to China as a medical missionary and then to Korea in 1884. While he was in Korea, he was appointed court physician. He immediately established a hospital under government control. From 1888 until his death, he remained involved in U.S./Korean relations and wrote several books on Korea. He served as U.S. Minister and consul general in Korea, 1890–1905. Allen married Frances Messenger. He settled in Toledo, OH in 1905, where he practiced medicine.

Rik Fields

1933

General Superintendent of Pentecostal Church of God (Inc. in 1978), **Chicago, IL 1926–27, Ottumwa, IA 1927–31** (Joplin, MO, in 1951). Fields was the first to serve in this position for any significant span of time. In 1920, he was arrested and jailed in West Plains, MO for praying for a young man's healing. The charges were dismissed. His title was changed from chairman to moderator in 1929. Bad health caused his resignation.

Walter Lock

July 14, 1846
Dorchester, England

1933

Warden of Keble College, 1897–1911. Lock was ordained a deacon (1872) and a priest (1873) in the Anglican Church. From 1870–97, he was a tutor and assistant warden at Keble College, Oxford. In addition, he served as professor of exegesis at the University of Oxford (1895–1919), canon of Christ Church and professor of divinity (1919–27). His most well-known book was *The Bible and Christian Life* (1905).

Andrew G. Voight

Jan 22, 1859
Philadelphia, Pennsylvania

Jan. 2, 1933
Columbia, South Carolina

President of Lutheran Theological Southern Seminary, Newberry, SC 1891–98; Mt. Pleasant, SC 1898–1911; Columbia, SC 1911–33. Voight married Clara Eisenhardt on Jan. 10, 1884. His pastorates included Mt. Holly, NJ, (1883–85) and Willmington, NC (1898–1903). Voight also taught Bible at Newberry College in South Carolina, (1885–89); and was president at Thiel College, Greenville, PA (1889–91) and taught theology at LTSS, then known as Southern Theological Seminary (1892–98). He also served as president of United Synod Lutheran Church, South (1906–16).

Calvin Coolidge

July 4, 1872
Plymouth, Vermont

Jan. 5, 1933
Northampton, Massachusetts

Thirtieth president of the United States, 1923–29. Coolidge became president after the death of Warren G. Harding (1865–1923). He was elected to a full term in 1924 defeating two candidates, 382–149. Coolidge married Grace Goodhue (January 3, 1879–July 8, 1957) on October 4, 1905. His political career started in Massachusetts as a state senator (1912–15), lieutenant governor (1916–18), and Republican governor (1919–21). In 1919, he called the state militia to halt the Boston police strike. He became vice–president (1920) and was moderator of the National Council of Congregational Churches (1923). Coolidge's domestic philosophy included supporting big business. He joined Washington's First Congregational Church, and said, "I think the Church must preach a new birth, a change of heart, a change of living. America was born in a revival of religion." He died of a heart attack.

Cornelius M. Steffens

Sept. 28, 1866
Veldhuizen, Germany

Jan. 15, 1933
Cook County, Illinois (?)

President of German Presbyterian College and Seminary of the Northwest, Dubuque, IA 1907–20, renamed University of Dubuque (IA) Theological Seminary, 1920–23. Steffens came to America in 1870. He was ordained in 1895 (presumably Presbyterian). He married Anna Meulendyke on April 29, 1898. Steffens pastored in Rochester, NY (1895–98), and Little Falls, NJ (1898–1900). He was greatly interested in the Americanization of foreign speaking people in U.S. Steffens was successful at his endeavors and wrote a book on fund-raising in 1930.

William W. Webb

Nov. 20, 1857
Germantown, Pennsylvania

Jan. 15, 1933
Milwaukee, Wisconsin

Dean of Nashotah (WI) House, 1897–1906. Webb became a deacon (1885) and priest (1886) of the Episcopal Church. He also served as an assistant in Middletown, CT and Philadelphia, PA from 1885–89. He was rector of St. Elizabeth, Philadelphia (1889–92); professor of theology at Nashotah (1892–97); and canon of All Saints' Cathedral in Milwaukee, WI (1892–1906). Webb was made bishop of Milwaukee in 1906. He never married. Webb wrote three books.

Samuel D. Chown

April 11, 1853
Kingston, Ontario, Canada

Jan. 30, 1933
Toronto, Canada

Prominent Methodist clergyman who was instrumental in bringing about the union of the Methodist Congregationalists and Presbyterians in Canada in 1925, to form the United Church of Canada. Chown pastored in small areas (1879–91), in Montreal in 1893. and in three large Toronto churches (1894–1902). In 1910, he was made General Superintendent of Canadian Methodism as a result of having dealt well with social problems, 1902–10.

Archibald H. Sayce

Sept. 25, 1845
Shirehampton, England

Feb. 4, 1933

Archaeologist and philosopher. Sayce was ordained into the Episcopal Church a deacon (1870) and a priest (1871). He served as deputy professor of comparative philology (1876–90) and as professor of Assyriology at Oxford (1891–1919). From 1879–1908, he spent winters on a houseboat on the Nile River. Sayce's scholarly activity covered Assyriology, oriental history, Biblical criticism, the Hittites, Jewish people, archaeology and philology. His works range from *Assyrian Grammar* (1872) to *Assyrian Papyri* (1906).

Frank K. Sanders

June 5, 1861
Batticotta, Ceylon (Sri Lanka)

Feb. 20, 1933
Rockport, Massachusetts

Bible scholar and educator. Sanders married Edith Blackman on June 27, 1888. He taught Biblical literature at Yale University (1891–1901), Bible history and archaeology, as well as serving as dean of Yale Divinity School (1901–5). He served as secretary of the Congregational Sunday school and Publishing Society (1905–8), president of Washburn (KS) College (1908–14), and director of the Board of Missionary Preparation (1914–27). He wrote from *The Teacher's Life of Christ* (1907) to *Old Testament History* (1921).

Harlan P. Beach

April 4, 1854
South Orange, New Jersey

March 4, 1933
Winter Park, Florida

Congregational missionary and professor of missions. Beach married Lucy L. Ward on June 29, 1883, and was ordained the same year. The Beachs went to China as missionaries for seven years, 1883–90. He then promoted the work of Student Volunteer Movement as their educational secretary, 1895–1906. Educationally, Beach taught missions at Yale Divinity School (1906–21) and lectured on missions at Drew Seminary (1921–28). Poor health brought on retirement in 1928. He wrote many books ranging from *The Cross in the Land of the Trident* (1895) to *World Missionary Atlas* (1925).

Amos R. Wells

Dec. 23, 1862
Glens Falls, New York

March 6, 1933
Auburndale, Massachusetts (?)

Educator and author, editor of *Peloubet's Notes* for Sunday School lessons, 1901–33. Wells also was a professor of Greek and geology at Antioch College, Yellow Springs, OH from 1883–92. While at Antioch, Wells became the editorial secretary of Christian Endeavor and managing editor of *CE World* until his death. Wells married Ana McNair in 1894. He wrote more than 100 volumes of stories, helps, and devotional books from *Sunday School Problems* (1895) to *Bible Sayings* (1931)

Berryman Green

July 25, 1864
Charlotte County, Virginia

March 10, 1933
Riverside, California

Dean of Virginia Theological Seminary, Alexandria, VA 1916–31. Green married Cornelia D. Bouldin on July 1, 1891, the same year he was ordained Episcopal priest. He was rector of the South Farnham Parish, VA (1891–93); St. James Church, Leesburg, VA (1893–96); and Christ Church, Alexandria, VA (1896–1902). He then returned to his alma mater as professor of English, Bible, and homiletics (1902), before becoming dean (1916).

Theodor Zahn

Oct. 10, 1838
Mors, Germany

March 15, 1933
Erlangen, Germany

New Testament scholar who held professorships at five different German universities. Zahn is noted for the accuracy of his work. He did pioneer work on the New Testament Canon, edited a New Testament commentary, and wrote many other books. Zahn was a conservative teacher of NT at Neustrelitz (1861–65); and the Universities of Gottingen (1865–77); Keil (1877–78); Erlanger (1878–88, 1892–1909); and Leipzig (1888–92). He was the leader in opposing the radicalism of Adolph Harnack (1851–1930).

Byron H. DeMent

May 17, 1863
Silver Springs, Tennessee

March 17, 1933
New Orleans, Louisiana

First president of Baptist Bible Institute [New Orleans (LA) Baptist Theological Seminary in 1946], 1918–27. DeMent was ordained as a Missionary Baptist in 1886, and married Maggie Nicholas on January 3, 1893. He pastored in Lexington, VA (1893–96); at Walnut St. Church, Louisville, KY (1900–3); the FBC, Waco, TX (1904–6); was a professor at Southern Baptist Theological Seminary (1906–14); and pastor of FBC, Greenwood, SC (1914–17). DeMent continued to teach New Testament and doctrines at NOBTS after his tenure of presidency ended.

Edwin F. Hyde

June 23, 1842
New York, New York

March 30, 1933
New York, New York

President of American Bible Society, 1924–30. A well-known banker, Hyde served in the Civil War in 1862, married Marie E. Brown on Nov. 18, 1868, then practiced law, 1863–86. For 33 years, 1886–1919, he was a vice-president and trustee of the Central Trust (Central Union Trust) Company and president of the Philharmonic Society of New York City for 13 years. He was treasurer of Princeton Theological Seminary, 1898–1924, a member of the Reformed Church, and a lifelong Republican in politics. He was a member of the Marble Collegiate (Dutch Reformed Church) of New York City.

Johanna Veenstra

April 19, 1894
Paterson, New Jersey

April 9, 1933
Lupwe, Nigeria

Missionary to Nigeria. She worked as a city missionary in Grand Rapids, MI 1914–17. Veenstra went with the Sudan United Mission to Nigeria arriving in Lagos on January 20, 1920. She worked in a remote area in the northern part of the country. Veenstra studied the Hausa language in Donga, then made Lupwe her permanent home in 1921. She attempted to reach the Kutteb people. Her exploits put new life into the Christian Reformed missions program, her denomination. She founded a boarding school and clinic, working tirelessly with a congregation that was known for demon worship, child marriages, and polygamy. In December, 1932, with her body demanding rest, the nagging pain in her side was diagnosed as appendicitis. Shortly after a "successful" operation, she uttered her last words…at age 39. "I'm not sorry. It is all in the will of God. I could not have chosen anything better than to go like this. I'm unworthy, only a sinner saved by grace…thrown into the presence of the Lord Jesus, victor over death!"

Henry J. Van Dyke

Nov. 10, 1852
Germantown, Pennsylvania

April 10, 1933
Princeton, New Jersey

Presbyterian hymn writer of "Joyful, Joyful, We Adore Thee," 1907 (music by Ludwig Beethoven) and author of *The Other Wise Man* (1896). He married Ellen Reid on December 13, 1881. He pastored United Congregational Church, Newport, RI (1879–85) and Brick Presbyterian Church, New York City (1883–1900). He served as a professor of English literature at Princeton, University, 1900–13 and 1919–23. In 1906, he was chairman of the committee that produced *The Book of Common Worship of the Presbyterian Church*. Van Dyke was active politically as U.S. Minister to the Netherlands and Luxembourg (1913–17), then served as a chaplain in the US Navy (1917–19). He was confidante of President WOODROW WILSON. Van Dyke also authored books on many topics from *The Reality of Religion* (1884) to *Gratitude* (1930). He believed in evolution.

John McNeill

July 7, 1854 — *April 19, 1933*
Houston, Scotland — Frinton-On-Sea, Scotland

Presbyterian Evangelist and pastor who was known and loved by much of the Christian world. Both Moody and Spurgeon appreciated McNeill. Because of his fervent evangelism and crowd appeal, he served churches no longer than four years, rescuing one church after another going from poor crowds to capacity crowds in a few months. As a youth, he was converted at Inverkip through a letter from Peter Douglas, a local Free Church pastor. His brief pastorates included McCrie-Roxburgh Church, Edinburgh (1885–89), and Regent Square, London (1889–91). Around July 8, 1891, his first wife died, leaving him with four small children. Sixteen years of evangelism endeavors followed, 1892–1908. He then served short term pastorates at Christ Church, London; St. George's, Liverpool; St. Cooke's, Toronto; and Central, Denver. He helped the English YMCA during WWI years. He went back to his pastoring routine in South Highland; Birmingham, AL; Ft. Washington, NY (1920–24); and the Church of the Open Door, Los Angeles (1926–28). He died in a nursing home. He arranged the music for Edwin Orr's "Cleanse Me."

Burton R. Jones

Dec. 3, 1845 — *April 20, 1933*
York, New York — Pasadena, California

Bishop of Free Methodist Church, 1894–1919. Jones was converted in a sweeping revival at the Free Methodist Church, Greigsville, NY at age 20. He served as a district elder in Michigan and Ohio conferences for 14 years. Jones also taught at Spring Arbor (MI) Seminary, 1886–88 and was editor of the *Free Methodist*, Chicago (1890–94). He married Helen Hart on July 16, 1895.

Joel A. Wright

Sept. 5, 1853 — *May 14, 1933*
Chelmsford, Massachusetts — Boston, Massachusetts

Founder and director of First Fruits Harvesters Association (New England Fellowship of Evangelicals in 1932), **1898–1924.** He married Mary Goodwin in 1874. Wright was converted at age 26. He served as pastor of Freewill Baptist churches in several New Hampshire and Vermont towns and was later affiliated with the Free Methodists. He felt interdenominational work could strengthen churches and send missionaries everywhere. On May 20, 1897, he formed the First Fruit Harvesters Association in Warren, NH, and directed it until he retired in 1924. On August 30, 1903, he dedicated some of his property to become the Rumney (NH) campground.

Seth C. Rees

Aug. 6, 1854 — *May 22, 1933*
Westfield, Indiana — Pasadena, California

Evangelist and General Superintendent of Pilgrim Holiness Church (Wesleyan Church in 1968), **1897–1905, 1926–33, and director of Pilgrim Holiness World Missions, 1898–1905.** Rees was converted at age 14. He is the father of Paul Rees. He married Hulda Johnson in December, 1876 (died: 1898) and Frida J. Stromberg in November, 1889. His pastorates included: Friends Churches Smithfield, IN (1884–88); Raisin Valley, MI (1888–89); and Portsmouth, RI. Rees also started twelve rescue homes. He founded the Pilgrim Church of California in 1917. Others like himself (disaffected Nazarenes) joined him. The Holiness Union, that he had formed with Martin W. Knapp (1897), merged with them (1922) and the new name PHC was given.

Melvin G. Kyle

May 7, 1858
near Cadiz, Ohio

May 25, 1933
Pittsburgh, Pennsylvania

President of Xenia (OH) (Pittsburgh in 1959) **Theological Seminary, Xenia, OH 1914–20, St. Louis, MO 1920–30, and archaeologist**. Kyle became a minister in 1886. He was a renowned United Presbyterian clergyman and archaeologist. For years, he presided over the Board of Foreign Missions. He began to teach biblical theology and archaeology at XTS from 1908–22 and was editor of the *Bibliotheca Sacra* (1921) and of the *Sunday School Times* (1911–33). Kyle became interested in archaeology during a visit to Egypt, resulting in his exploration at Sodom and Gomorrah, 1924, and at Kirjath-Siepher, 1926–28. Kyle documented his work in books. He wrote many scholarly works, especially dealing with Old Testament criticism and archaeology.

William J. McGlothin

Nov. 29, 1867
near Gallatin, Tennessee

May 28, 1933
Gastonia, North Carolina

President of Southern Baptist Convention, 1930–32. He was ordained in 1891, taught at Bardstown (KY) Institute (1889–91), tutored in Hebrew and Old Testament (1893–94), and taught in other areas at Southern Baptist Thelogical Seminary (1894–1919). He headed the correspondence school, 1915–19. McGlothin married May Williams on June 8, 1907 (died: 1926), and they had five children. On December 28, 1929, he married Mary Bates. McGlothin was the president of Furman University, Greenville, SC 1919–37. He wrote from *A Guide to the Study of Church History* (1908) to *History of Furman University* (1926).

Albert H. Newman

Aug. 25, 1852
Edgefield, South Carolina

June 4, 1933
Austin, Texas

Baptist church historian and educator. Newman taught at Rochester (NY) Theological Seminary (1877–81); at McMaster University, Toronto (1881–1901); Baylor University, (1901–09 and 1913–20); Southwestern Baptist Seminary (1909–13); and at Mercer University, Macon, GA (1921–29). Newman married Mary Ware on July 15, 1873. He was also the church history editor for the new *Schaff-Herzog Encyclopedia*. He was a born linguist and was able to read in twelve languages. He wrote *Manual of Church History* (1903), a standard textbook for many.

Louis A. Banks

Nov. 12, 1855
Corvallis, Oregon

June 17, 1933
Roseburg, Oregon

Methodist pastor, writer, evangelist, and supporter of the temperance movement. He married Mary Millhoven in 1877 (died: 1883); Jesse Ainsworth on January 6, 1884 (died: 1919); and Florence Akien on July 21, 1920. Banks held pastorates in Portland, OR; Vancouver and Seattle, WA; Boise City, ID; Cincinnati and Cleveland, OH; St. John's, Brooklyn, NY; and First Methodist Churches of Boston, New York City, and Denver. He held large union crusades, 1911–13. He was an evangelist for the American Anti-saloon League and also for the World Prohibition Movement, 1913–33. His numerous books range from *The People's Christ* (1891) to *Sermons for Reviving* (1928).

James Mountain

July 16, 1844
Leeds, England

June 27, 1933
Tunbridge Wells, England

Composed music for "Like a River Glorious," 1876 (lyrics by F. R. HAVERGAL), **"Jesus, I Am Resting" (1876), and "I Am His and He is Mine" (1876)**. Mountain was influenced by a MOODY/SANKEY visit to England in the early 1870s. He traveled as an evangelist in England (1874–82) and went on a world tour (1882–89). Mountain pastored at Tunbridge Wells, 1889–97. He then became a Baptist and founded St. John's Free Church there, staying until his death.

Charles A. Tindley

July 7, 1851
Berlin, Maryland

July 26, 1933
Philadelphia, Pennsylvania

Outstanding pastor and hymn writer. Tindley pastored Calvary Methodist Church of Philadelphia from 1902 until his death. At one time, Tindley had over 12,000 members and led the largest Methodist church in the world (7,109 members at the time of his death). In 1924, a larger building was built and the name was changed to Tindley Temple Methodist Church. He often preached a famous sermon, "Heaven's Christmas Tree." He wrote the lyrics and music for beloved gospel songs, "Stand by Me," "Leave It There," "We'll Understand It Better By and By," and "Nothing Between." Tindley married Daisy Henry and, upon her death, Jenny Colton in 1927. He had six children.

Adam Geibel

Sept. 15, 1855
Baden, Germany

Aug. 3, 1933
Philadelphia, Pennsylvania

Composed music for "Someday He'll Make It Plain to Me," "Satisfied," and the second tune to "Stand Up for Jesus." Geibel came to America as a child having lost his eyesight at nine days old due to improper medication for an eye infection. He became a proficient organist, conductor, and composer while he lived in Philadelphia. Geibel married Kate Rinck on November 24, 1881 (died: 1906). He was a Presbyterian layman who formed Geibel Music Company, which later became Rodeheaver-Hall-Mack Company.

John White

Jan. 6, 1866
Dearham/Roe Farm, England

Aug. 7, 1933
Kingsmead Close, England

Wesleyan Methodist missionary to Southern Rhodesia, 1894–1931. White was converted at age 16 and offered to go as a lay evangelist to Australia. Instead, he entered Didsbury College in 1888 for training. White did go to Africa, where he worked with the Mashosna people for 40 years. From 1892–94 he was at Klerxsdorf in Transvaal, South Africa. From 1894 on, he was with the Mashonaland Mission in Zimbabwe. In 1898, he founded the Nenguwo (Waddilove) training center. He served as chairman and general superintendent, 1901–26. White was greatly respected and loved by the people. With the help of a native evangelist, White translated the New Testament into the Shona language in 1907.

Charles H. Parkhurst

April 17, 1842
Framingham, Massachusetts

Sept. 8, 1933
Atlantic City, New Jersey

Presbyterian pastor at Madison Square Church (merged with First Presbyterian in 1881), **New York City 1880–1918.** Parkhurst graduated from Amherst, MA (1866) and was a principal of the high-school there (1867). He studied theology at Halle (1869–70) and at Leipzig (1872–73); was a professor at Williston Seminary, Easthampton, MA (1870–71); and was pastor of the Congregational Church, Lenox, MA (1874–80). He became president in 1891 of the Society for Prevention of Crime. His outspoken preaching against the corruption in City Hall touched off the Lezow Investigation, which uncovered evidence of collusion between crime rings and police. Parkhurst married Ellen Bodman (November 23, 1870) and Eleanor Marx (April 18, 1927). His writings were from *Forms of the Latin Verb Illustrated by the Sanskrit* (1870) to *My 40 Years in New York* (1923), his autobiography.

Issac M. Haldeman

Feb. 13, 1845
Concordville, Pennsylvania

Sept. 27, 1933
New York, New York

Pastored the First Baptist Church, New York City 1884–1933. Haldeman was a powerful preacher. He married Edda Quinby on October 3, 1883. His early pastorates included Brandywine, PA (1871–75), and Wilmington, DE (1875–84). Haldeman authored four books on the second coming of Christ and nine editions of *How to Study the Bible* (1912). His most popular book was *The Tabernacle, Priesthood, and Offerings*. He was known as "the Dispensational Pastor" and was an opponent of liberal tendencies, contending with such men as H.E. Fosdick and WALTER RAUSCHENBUSCH. He was a strong, premillennial, conservative voice in the Northern Baptist Convention, which was veering to the left theologically. He wrote several books.

Inanzo O. Nitobe

1863
Morioka, Iwate, Japan

Oct. 15, 1933
Victoria, British Columbia, Canada

Christian statesman who had ambition to promote understanding between Japan and America. Nitobe returned to Japan with a Philadelphia Quaker bride. He taught at Sapporo College, then at Kyoto Imperial University, and finally at First National College, Tokyo, in 1906. Nitobe later served as president of National Imperial College, 1906–13, and at Tokyo Women's Christian College, 1918 on. He was known as the "Father of Japanese liberalism." From 1919–26 he served as under secretary general of the League of Nations.

James Rowe

Jan. 1, 1865
Devonshire, England

Nov. 10, 1933
Wells, Vermont

Gospel songwriter. He wrote lyrics for "I Would Be Like Jesus" (1911), "I Walk with the King," "Love Lifted Me" (1912), and "I Am So Glad Salvation's Free" (c. 1912). After working for the Irish government for four years, Rowe came to America in 1890 at age 24 and settled in Albany, NY, where he married Blanche Clapper. After working on the railroad and being superintendent of the Hudson River Humane Society, Rowe spent the rest of his life in literary pursuits. He was associated with various publishing enterprises (Waco, TX; Chattanooga, TN; and Lawrenceburg, TN) and lived out his days in Wells, VT, with his daughter.

Marcus D. Buell

Jan. 1, 1851
Wayland, New York

Nov. 24, 1933
Winter Park, Florida

Dean of Boston (MA) University School of Theology, 1889–1904. Buell married Edith V. Houghton on December 13, 1875 (died: 1931). He entered the Methodist ministry in Rochester, NY (1875–79), then pastored in Brooklyn and Hartford, CT (1879–83). He then went to Boston University where he taught New Testament Greek and exegesis, 1884–1922, also serving as dean emeritus. Buell's first book was *Greek Studies in Mark* (1890).

J. Stuart Holden

1874

1934

Evangelist and man of prayer. Holden was known around the world. He was vicar of St. Paul's, London, which was known as an evangelistic center. For 25 years, Holden crossed the Atlantic Ocean nearly every summer to preach in Northfield, MA, and New York churches on Sundays. He was booked to sail on the *Titanic*, but his wife fell ill before his departure and he cancelled the trip. He said " 'Go ye' is as much a part of Christ's Gospel as 'Come unto Me.' You are not even a Christian until you have honestly faced your responsibility in regard to the carrying of the Gospel to the ends of the earth. What is your part in that great task?" He also said, "God has called us to co-operate with Him in making the Gospel known to our generation." He edited the *Home Messenger Magazine* and authored many books.

Leander W. Munhall

June 7, 1843
Zanesville, Ohio

Jan. 7, 1934
Philadelphia, Pennsylvania (?)

Methodist evangelist and writer. Munhall edited the *Methodist*. He lived most of his life in Germantown, PA. He was a great witness for Christ and continued Wesleyan doctrines, such as sanctification. Munhall took part in 33 battles during the Civil War, 1862–65. He married Mary Thomas on September 21, 1871. He began his evangelism career in 1874, which stretched for 50 years, seeing 200,000 converts, traveling 1,250,000 miles.

Henrietta E. Soltau

Dec. 8, 1843
Devon, England

Feb. 5, 1934
London, England

Missionary administrator in China. Henrietta became HUDSON TAYLOR's key assistant in charge of women's work for the China Inland Mission. From 1875–89, she directed a home for missionary children. In 1889, she became the head of a home for the preparation of female candidates. Headquartering in London over a 27 year period, she trained 547 women en–route to China. Henrietta was able to get away for one year to go to China herself, visiting 44 of these missionaries and covering 6,000 miles in 1897. WWI put a stop to her training work in 1916.

John A. Davis

Aug. 7, 1871
Afton, New York

March 17, 1934
Bible School Park, New York

President of Practical Bible Training School, 1917–34. Davis was converted in an evangelistic crusade at FBC, Afton, NY. After graduating from MBI in 1893, he became an evangelist. He then pastored the Hallstead (PA) Baptist Church, 1893–99, before going back into evangelism. He married Etta Carr on June 19, 1894. While in a meeting in Hazelton, PA on April 5, 1900, God spoke to him about starting a Bible school, which opened in Lestershire (Robinson City, NY later that year. In 1910, they obtained 33 acres and expanded into the former White City Amusement Park.

Carrie Ellis Breck

Jan. 22, 1855
Walden Vermont

March 27, 1934
Portland, Oregon

Wrote lyrics for these hymns: "When Love Shines In" (1874) (music by WILLIAM KIRKPATRICK), **"Face to Face" (1898), "Nailed to the Cross" (1899), "Shall I Crucify"** (GRANT TULLAR, music to previous three) **and "Help Somebody Today" (1904)**. After childhood, Breck crossed the country to Portland were she attended a Presbyterian church. As the wife of Frank Breck, she was a devoted housewife and mother of five daughters. She created lyric inspiration as she did housework around the home, writing more than 2,000 poems before her death.

David McKinney

May 20, 1860
Philadelphia, Pennsylvania

April 26, 1934
Cincinnati, Ohio

First president of Cedarville (OH) College, 1896–1915. McKinney was ordained to the Reformed Presbyterian ministry in 1884 and married Carrie Chapin on June 3, 1891. He pastored in Elgin, IL (1884–86); at the First Reformed Presbyterian, Cincinnati, OH (1888–1914); and at the First Presbyterian, Cincinnati, OH (1914–26). McKinney also helped bring social and municipal reform to Cincinnati.

Robert Laws

May 28, 1851
Aberdeen, Scotland

Aug. 6, 1934
London, England

Free United Presbyterian Church medical missionary to Malawi in 1875. Laws opened the first school in Nyasaland. He joined the Livingstonia Mission in 1875. He was educated largely by self-instruction. Laws was a skilled physician and theologian. He founded over 700 schools in Nyasaland and also built a 48-foot steamboat which he sailed up the Zambesi River, dismantled, carried overland, and reassembled on Lake Nyasa, 300 miles upstream. He headed the work at Livingstonia, 1894–1927, after which he retired from his 52-year ministry. By 1914, the work he began had 49 missionaries, over 9,000 communicants, and 57,479 students. He had at least 60,000 native converts.

Archibald T. Robertson

Nov. 6, 1863
Chatham, Virginia

Sept. 24, 1934
Louisville, Kentucky

Perhaps the greatest Greek authority of all time. Converted at age 13, Robertson was a NT professor at Southern Baptist Theological Seminary, Louisville, KY from 1888 on. He married Ella Broadus on November 27, 1894, daughter of his beloved mentor. Robertson's two most notable works are *Harmony of the Gospels* (1922) and *Syllabus of New Testament Greek Syntax* (1903). He taught Greek to over 6,000 students. His 1,454-page *Greek Grammar* (1914) was the greatest in the field. Robertson produced 44 scholarly works on Greek and New Testament studies. His last book was *Passing on the Torch* (1934). He was a founder of the Baptist World Alliance and helped write its constitution.

A. Paget Wilkes

Jan. 19, 1871
Titchwell, England

Oct. 5, 1934
Winchester, England

Church of England missionary to Japan. Wilkes was converted under F. B. Morris' visit to Ipswich in 1892. He went to Japan in 1897 under the auspices of the Church Missionary Society to work with B.F. BUXTON. He married Gertrude Barthord in 1897 and started a Bible school. He also co-founded the Japan Evangelistic Band in 1902 and dedicated his whole life to missionary work. Wilkes' centered his work in Kobe, Japan, where he emphasized prayer, Holy Spirit guidance, and sanctification. He died of a heart attack.

James M. Hubbert

June 15, 1850
Cassville, Missouri

Oct. 6, 1934
New Brunswick, New Jersey

Stated Clerk of Cumberland Presbyterian Church, Memphis, TN 1896–1906. Hubbert married Minnie Brewster on January 16, 1882. He pastored in Lincoln, IL (1879–87); at First Church, Nashville, TN (1888–93); and in Lebanon, TN (1894–1901). Hubbert served as dean of Cumberland Theological Seminary, Marshall, MO, and professor of homiletics at Missouri Valley College, Marshall, MO from 1902–6. Hubbert was the assistant stated clerk for the General Assembly of the Presbyterian Church USA from 1907–21. He died in an automobile accident.

Elmer B. Bryan

April 23, 1865
VanWert, Ohio

Oct. 15, 1934
Detroit, Michigan

President of Colgate Theological Seminary [Colgate-Rochester (NY) Divinity School in 1928], **Hamilton, NY 1909–21**. Bryan married Margaret L. Scott on June 28, 1889. A Baptist, he began his ministry working in high school educational activities (1882–92) and in educational work in the Philippine Islands (1901–3). Bryan was president of Franklin (IN) College (1905–9) and Ohio University (1921–34). He lived out his days in Athens, OH and died at Ford Hospital.

Helen Barrett Montgomery

July 31, 1861
Kingsville, Ohio

Oct. 18, 1934
Summit, New Jersey

Baptist philanthropist that willed $500,000 to 86 churches, colleges, hospitals, and missions. Daughter of a Baptist pastor, Montgomery taught Bible classes in Philadelphia and Rochester, NY, areas from 1887–1927. She married businessman William A. Montgomery (1854–1930) on September 6, 1887. She was licensed to preach in 1892. Her husband became successful in the automobile industry. She was president of the Northern Baptist Convention (1921) and a delegate to the Baptist World Alliance (1923). She translated the New Testament (from original Greek) in 1924, the *Centenary Translation*. As a lecturer and writer, she was in great demand among seminaries and churches. All her life she promoted world missions. She wrote *Western Women in Eastern Lands* (1910), selling over 100,000 copies.

Frederick F. Richter

Oct. 24, 1852
Riesa, Germany

Oct. 18, 1934
Clinton, Iowa

President of Iowa Synod (ALC, ELCA in 1988), **1904–26**. Richter was a Lutheran pastor, professor, and synod president who came to America in 1872. He pastored at Mendoneta, IL from 1876–94 and was president of the seminary there. Richter was president of Clinton College (Wartburg College), Dubuque, IA from 1894–1902. From 1901–26, he edited the Iowa Synod's weekly paper. He united Lutherans in Australia. He retired in 1926 because of ill health. Richter also took a leading part in the 1930 merger of the Buffalo, Iowa, and Ohio Synods.

Walter S. Athearn

July 25, 1872
Marengo, Iowa

Nov. 13, 1934
St. Louis, Missouri

Disciples of Christ leader in religious education. Athearn taught pedagogy at Drake University in Des Moines, IA (1900–4); was dean of Highland Park Normal College in Illinois (1906–9); professor of religious education at Drake University (1909–16); and professor at Boston University (1916–29); followed by the presidency of Butler University in Indianapolis (1931–34). He married Florence Royalty on June 15, 1894 (died: June 8, 1917) and Frances Smith on September 14, 1929. He wrote at least ten books from *The Church School* (1914), to *The Minister and the Teacher* (1932).

George F. Taylor

Aug. 10, 1881
Magnolia, North Carolina

Nov. 16, 1934
Franklin Springs, Georgia

First president of Franklin Springs (GA) Bible Institute (Emmanuel College in 1939), **1919–26, 1929–31, and General Superintendent of Pentecostal Holiness Church** (International in 1975), **1913–17**. Taylor left the Methodist Church South in 1903, for the Holiness movement (Pentecostal Holiness Church after 1908). His tongues experiences gave credibility to the Pentecostal movement. Taylor also edited the *Pentecostal Holiness Advocate*, 1917–25 and 1929–34. In his latter years, he was a faculty member at Emmanuel College. His wife's name was Ella.

Sylvanus C. Breyfogel

July 20, 1851
Reading, Pennsylvania

Nov. 24, 1934
Reading, Pennsylvania

Bishop of Evangelical Association, 1891–1922 and of Evangelical Church (United Methodist Church in 1968) **1923–34, and president of Schuylkill Seminary** (renamed Evangelical School of Theology), **Reading, PA** (United Theological Seminary in Dayton, OH) **1927–34**. He married Kate Boas on May 8, 1877 (died: August 1, 1928), and had six children. Breyfogel preached extensively and participated in missionary tours to China, Japan, and Russia. He was active in the FCC. He wrote *Evangelical Landmarks* among others.

George Milligan

April 2, 1860
Kilconquhar, Scotland

Nov. 25, 1934
Glasgow, Scotland

New Testament scholar. Milligan was the minister at St. Matthew's, Morningside (1883–94); Caputh, Perthshire (1894–1910); and professor of divinity and biblical criticism at Glasgow University (1910–32). He was the moderator of the General Assembly of the Church of Scotland (1923) and the first chairman of the Scottish Sunday School Union for Christian education (1926). He wrote works ranging from *History of the English Bible* (1895) to *The New Testament in Its Transmission* (1932). His writings include *The Vocabulary of the Greek Testament* (1914–29).

Betty Scott Stam

Feb. 22, 1906
Albion, Michigan

Dec. 8, 1934
Miaosheo, China

Beheaded with her husband by Communists. The martyrdoms stunned the Christian world. Betty's father, a Presbyterian pastor, took the family to China when she was six months old. She returned to the States and attended Wilson College and Moody Bible Institute in Chicago. Betty left for China in the fall of 1931, married John Stam on October 25, 1933, and gave birth to baby Helen on September 11, 1934. She was arrested at Tsingteh, China, and killed soon after.

John C. Stam

Jan. 8, 1907
Patterson, New Jersey

Dec. 8, 1934
Miaosheo, China

Beheaded with his wife by Communists. Stam was converted via a blind evangelist at his father's Star of Hope Mission on May 28, 1922. Stam entered Moody Bible Institute in 1929, where he met his future wife, BETTY SCOTT, and graduated one year later. He went to China in September, 1932 and married there on October 25, 1933. He first served at Tsingteh (Jingde), then Wuhu, and was arrested when he went back to Tsingteh for services. The China Inland Mission couple was beheaded two days later. Their baby daughter, Helen, was spared as a result of a Chinese Christian prisoner who was killed as a substitute for her life. A Chinese pastor cared for baby Helen until she was put into a mission home. Their martyrdom stirred interest in missions as the deaths of WILLIAM BORDEN and JIM ELLIOT.

Francis Y. Pressly

Jan. 18, 1853
Due West, South Carolina

Dec. 18, 1934
Due West, South Carolina

President of Erskine Theological Seminary, Due West, SC 1906–33. He married Louise Reid on October 10, 1877. He was a missionary in Louisville, KY (1876–80); pastor at Mt. Zion,

MO (1874–76 and 1880–86); Starkville, MS (1886–90); and Abbeville, SC (1890–94). From 1893 on, he was professor of Greek and German in Erskine College. Pressly was president of Erskine College, 1899–1907. Declining health led to his retirement in 1933.

Adelaide A. Pollard

Nov. 27, 1862
Bloomfield, Iowa

Dec. 20, 1934
New York, New York

Wrote the well-known hymn, "Have Thine Own Way, Lord," 1902 (music by GEORGE STEBBINS). Adelaide went to Chicago, where she taught in several girls' schools in the 1880s. She took an interest in Alexander Dowie's work and claimed healing of diabetes. She taught for eight years at the Nyack Missionary Training School. Pollard went to Africa prior to WWI, to Scotland during the war years, and then came back to New York. She was a devout Presbyterian.

Oliver W. Van Osdel

1846

1935

Discerning fundamental Baptist, active in the WCFA, BBU, and GARB. Van Osdel pastored Baptist churches in Aledo, IL; Rock Island, IL; Ottawa, KS; Galesburg, IL; Spokane, WA; and Wealthy Street Baptist of Grand Rapids, MI in 1895 and 1909–34. He led this church out of the NBC in 1909 and organized the Michigan Orthodox Baptist Association.

Fermin L. Hoskins

June 8, 1865
Scio, Oregon

Feb. 18, 1935
Myrtle, Idaho

Bishop of United Brethren in Christ, Huntington, IN 1905–33. He was converted and joined the UBC at Huntsville, WA at age 19. Hoskins married Minnie Simonton on December 18, 1892. Hoskins taught in public schools of Washington, Oregon and Idaho, and served as principal of Washington Seminary, Huntsville, WA. He was ordained into the United Brethren Church in 1895. Then, he served as the president of Central College, Huntington, IN in 1911 and also Edwards College of Albion, WA for a short time. Hoskins lived briefly in Myrtle, ID. He died of lung cancer and was buried in Albion, WA.

Josiah S. Caldwell

Aug. 2, 1862
Charlotte, North Carolina

April 7, 1935
Philadelphia, Pennsylvania

Bishop of African Methodist Episcopal Zion Church 1904–34, senior bishop, 1922–34. Caldwell married Ella Melchor in January, 1881. He entered the AMEZC ministry in 1890, pastoring in Elizabeth City, NC; Petersburg, VA; New York, NY; and in Philadelphia, PA until 1904. He also served as financial secretary of AMEZC, 1900–4. Caldwell was a delegate to ecumenical conferences in London (1901), in Toronto (1911), and again in London (1921). He wrote *Book of Sermons* (1908).

Dyson Hague

1857
Toronto, Ontario, Canada

May 6, 1935
(Cambridge) Ontario, Canada

Fundamentalist Anglican minister. Early on, he was rector at St. Paul's, Brockville, Ontario and at St. Paul's, Halifax, Nova Scotia. He taught at Wycliffe College, Toronto, 1897–1901 and pastored after 1901. Hague was a leader of Canadian fundamentalism prior to the T.T. SHIELDS era. He was rector of a number of Anglican churches, including St. James Cathedral, Toronto. He published several books on the English reformation and contributed to *The Fundamentals* (1910–15).

Thomas E. Lawrence
Lawrence of Arabia

Aug. 15, 1888
Tremadoc, Wales

May 19, 1935
Bovington Camp, England

Soldier and author, hardly remembered for his work as a biblical archaeologist. Lawrence grew up in an evangelical household. In 1909, this scholar walked more than 1,100 miles in broiling heat, through what is now Syria, Lebanon, and Israel, to study crusader castles for an honors thesis at Oxford University. In 1910, he was foreman on a dig in Jerablus, Syria, which once was the eastern capital of the ancient Hittite Empire. As war loomed, he joined British intelligence in Cairo at the outbreak of WWI, and in January, 1917, was sent as a military advisor to Prince Feisal during the Arab revolt against Turkish rule. From 1922, he was connected with the air force. He died in a motorcycle accident from skull injuries. He wrote a few books.

Jane Addams

Sept. 6, 1860
Cedarville, Illinois

May 21, 1935
Chicago, Illinois

Famous social reformer, founder of Hull House in Chicago's West side, 1889. Jane was a devout Presbyterian (had Quaker father) who worked for the poor, the immigrants, and the minority groups in her neighborhood; along with Ellen Gates Starr. She won the Nobel Peace Prize in 1931. Near the end of her life, she regretted that Hull House was not more closely related to the church. She was also a suffragist and peace activist. She never married. Some of her books include *Democracy and Social Ethics* (1902) to *The Excellent Becomes Permanent* (1932).

Joseph Stump

Oct. 6, 1866
Marietta, Ohio

May 24, 1935
Minneapolis, Minnesota

First president of Northwestern Lutheran (Luther-Northwestern in 1982) **Theological Seminary, Fargo, ND 1920–27, Minneapolis, MN 1927–35**. Stump married Alice A. Cooper on June 18, 1891. They had seven children. Stump was ordained Lutheran (1887) and pastored at several locations: Great Bend, PA (1887–89); Ephrata, PA (1889–92); and Grace Church Phillipsburg, NJ (1892–1915). He was also professor of theology at Chicago Lutheran Theological Seminary of Maywood, IL from 1915–20. His writings range from *Life of MELANCHTHON* (1897) to *The Christian Faith* (1932).

Levi Mumaw

Nov. 6, 1879
near Winesburg, Ohio

June 4, 1935
Scottdale, Pennsylvania

Director of Mennonite Central Committee, Akron, OH 1920–35. Mumaw married Fannie Shoemaker on June 9, 1903 (died: 1921) and Alice Hershey in 1923. In 1910, he was called to Scottdale to serve as treasurer of the Mennonite Publishing House. Soon they asked him to be the secretary as well, which two positions he held till death. By virtue of positions held, he served on the executive committees of the Mennonite Publication Board and the Mennonite Board of Missions and Charities. Mumaw was a good song leader, not only in local congregations, but in area-wide revivals. He took care of all business matters in the publication of *Church Hymnal* (1927). He died of acute Bright's disease.

John D. Leslie

June 1, 1860
Statesville, North Carolina

June 11, 1935
Dallas, Texas

Stated clerk of Presbyterian Church in US (USA in 1983), **1922–35**. Leslie married Gertrude Mattison in 1885 (died: 1896), Alma LeGrand in 1899 (died: 1909), and Ella Ragland in 1913. He was ordained in 1883. He pastored in Mississippi and Texas until 1921. From 1886–1922, he was a stated clerk in several locations. His books included *The Second Coming of Christ* (1904) to *Presbyterian Law and Procedures* (1930). He had a heart attack on June 6th at a dinner, dying shortly thereafter.

Aaron M. Hills

Feb. 4, 1848
Niles, Michigan

Sept. 11, 1935
Pasadena, California

Founding president of Texas Holiness University (became Bethany [OK] Nazarene in 1920), **Greenville, TX 1899–1906; of Olivet Nazarene College, Kankakee, IL 1909–10; and Oklahoma Holiness University, Bethany, OK 1912–13**. He was also a Congregationalist pastor and evangelist and an early-day Nazarene theologian and educator. He was a graduate of Oberlin (OH) College and Yale Divinity School.

John G. Lake

March 18, 1870
St. Mary's, Ontario, Canada

Sept. 16, 1935
Seattle, Washington

Faith healer, missionary, and pastor. Lake was ordained to the Methodist ministry at age 21, but chose a business career. He was with Dowie's Christian Catholic church, 1901–6, Zion, IL, and then became a Pentecostal. After a number of healings in his family, he felt led to go to South Africa in 1907. He took his wife and seven children to start the Apostolic Faith Mission there. His wife died in December, 1912, while he was away on an expedition into the Kalahari Desert. He returned to the States (1912), married Florence Switzer (1913) and settled in Spokane, WA, founding the Apostolic Church. In the next few years he reportedly saw thousands of healings. He moved to Portland, OR, in May, 1920, and started another work. One of his converts there was GORDON J. LINDSAY. He died of a stroke.

James M. Gray

May 11, 1851
New York, New York

Sept. 21, 1935
Chicago, Illinois

President of Moody Bible Institute, Chicago, 1904–34 (called "Dean" from 1901–24), **and hymn writer**. Gray wrote lyrics for many hymns; "Nor Silver Nor Gold" (1900), "Only a Sinner" (1905), "Bringing Back the King," "What Did He Do?" and "Christian Fellowship Song." He was raised in a Christian home. However, in 1873, he read in WILLIAM ARNOT's book *Laws from Heaven* that "A soul not won to Jesus is lost," which brought about his conversion. He was rector of the First Reformed Episcopal Church of Boston, 1880–92. Influenced by A. J. GORDON in 1893; he taught summer sessions at Northfield Conference in Massachusetts and traveled in conferences, 1894–1904. Gray was a theologian, Bible teacher, Sunday school promoter, evangelist, author, and administrator, who led in expansion efforts for Moody Bible Institute. He was also one of seven editors for the *SCOFIELD Reference Bible* (1909). He edited *Moody Monthly* (1907–35). His works range from *Synthetic Bible Studies* (1900) to *Steps on the Ladder of Faith* (1931). He frequently was supply preacher at Moody Church. Gray was stricken with a heart attack on September 15, 1935, and died in Passavant Hospital.

Joshua Levering

Sept. 12, 1845
Baltimore, Maryland

Oct. 5, 1935
Baltimore, Maryland

President of Southern Baptist Convention, 1908–10. Levering married Martha W. Keyser (November, 1870), Margaret Keyser (sister of his first wife) in 1892, and Helen Woods (April, 1901), resulting in a family of seven children. After working for several years, he became a partner with his father importing coffee in the mid-1860s. Levering served as president of the board of the Southern Baptist Theological Seminary, Louisville, KY from 1895–1935. In 1896, he was the prohibition candidate for the U.S. presidency.

Amos D. Wenger

Nov. 25, 1867
Edom, Virginia

Oct. 5, 1935
Harrisonburg, Virginia

President of Eastern Mennonite College and Seminary, Harrisonburg, VA 1922–38. Wenger married Mary Hostetter on July 1, 1897 (died: 1898), and Anna Lehman on September 27, 1900; he had eight children. He pastored in Missouri (1894–95); Iowa in 1896; Millersville, PA (1897–1908); and Fentress, VA (1908–22). Wenger also pastored in Harrisonburg during his presidency. He was handicapped and died suddenly in his home.

Henry C. Vedder

Feb. 26, 1853
De Ruyter, New York

Oct. 13, 1935
Chester, Pennsylvania

Baptist clergyman, educator, and church historian. He married Minnie M. Lingham in 1877. Vedder was a member of the editorial staff of *The Examiner* (1876–92), the leading Baptist newspaper in New York. He was also the editor of the *Baptist Quarterly Review* (1885–92), then editor again of *The Examiner* (1892–94), in Chester, PA and professor of church history at Crozer Theological Seminary, 1894–1926. Fundamentalists, however, sought to have him removed from Crozer, believing he helped the school go modernistic. He wrote 15 books ranging from *Baptists and the Liberty of Conscience* (1883) to *Short History of Baptist Missions* (1927).

John W. Hurse

July 10, 1866
Colyerville, Tennessee

Oct. 14, 1935
Kansas City, Missouri

President of National Baptist Convention of America, 1929–33. Hurse united with the church at age 15. In 1886, he moved to Kansas City, MO. He worked at various jobs including coachman, asphalt worker, and packing-house worker. In 1898, he entered the ministry. With limited education, Hurse preached on the street corners in the sinful and deprived sections of the city. He married Janie Frye in the early 1900s, and upon her death, married Lula Butler, a well-known gospel singer. He pastored Pilgrim Baptist Church, and thereafter, founded and pastored St. Stephen's Baptist Church, Kansas City, MO, from 1903–35.

Reinhold Seeberg

April 5, 1859
Livonia/Porrafer, Germany

Oct. 23, 1935

Lutheran theologian. Seeberg taught at Dorpat (Tartu) and Estonia for five years, was professor of church history and New Testament exegesis (1889–94), professor of theology at the University of Erlangen (1894–98), and professor of theology at the University of Berlin (1898–1935). Seeberg was also president of the Christian Social Alliance until 1893. He wrote on social life and the church. He wrote *History of Dogma*.

William A. (Billy) Sunday

Nov. 19, 1862
near Ames, Iowa

Nov. 6, 1935
Chicago, Illinois

Evangelist who held large city-wide crusades in the 1910s, preaching 1895-1935. Sunday was reared in an orphanage in Glenwood and Davenport with his brother, Ed, 1874-76. He moved to Nevada, IA graduating from high school in 1876. In 1883, Sunday was discovered by "Pop" Anson of the Chicago White Socks. He played major league baseball for Chicago (1883–88), Pittsburgh, and Philadelphia (1888–91), with a reputation for base stealing. He was converted at age 23 in 1886, at the Pacific Garden Mission in Chicago. He married Helen Thompson on September 5, 1888, and they had four children. His ministry began as a YMCA staffer and progressed to being an associate of J. W. CHAPMAN, 1893–95. Sunday held his first crusade in Garner, IA in 1896. He was ordained by Chicago Presbyterians in 1903. His 1917 Boston crusade was his second largest with 63,484 converts. His 1917 New York crusade had 98,267 converts and was the highlight of his life. He was instrumental in bringing in prohibition. His sermon, "Get on the Water Wagon" was a classic. Home for the Sunday family was Winona Lake, IN since 1910 where HOMER RODEHEAVER, his song leader, also lived. He semi-retired in 1930. His 300 crusades reached 80 million people with some one million conversions. In 1933, he suffered the first of three heart attacks. His funeral was at Moody Church with HARRY IRONSIDE presiding and preaching. For years a large Billy Sunday Tabernacle seating thousands was the main attraction at Winona Lake Bible Conference. His favorite Bible verses were Psalms 34:9–10. He is buried in Forest Park, IL. Of three authentic reference works we have date of birth listed as November 18, 1862; November 19, 1862; and November 19, 1863.

William E. Blackstone (2)

Oct. 6, 1841
Adams, New York

Nov. 7, 1935
Pasadena, California (?)

Founder and first president of Chicago Hebrew Mission (AMF Int. in 1993), **1887–91**. He married Sarah Smith in June 5,1866 (died: 1908). Blackstone was a Methodist evangelist, author, and friend of the Jews, who settled in Oak Park, IL in 1870, where he became a successful businessman. Converted at age eleven at a Methodist church revival, he went into full-time work in 1878. In 1890, Blackstone headed the first conference between Jews and Christians in Chicago. He wrote the widely circulated book, *Jesus is Coming in 1908*, often seen with only his initials on it. He was committed to helping Jews return to Palestine. He went to China publishing and distributing Bibles for five years, 1909–14. Back in America, he administered the Milton Stewart fund for the distribution of Christian literature around the world.

James H. Breasted

Aug. 27, 1865
Rockford, Illinois

Dec. 2, 1935
New York, New York

Historian and archaeologist. He married Francis Hart on October 22, 1894. At the University of Chicago, Breasted taught Egyptology, Semitic languages, and Oriental history, 1905–33. He was director of Haskell Oriental Museum (1901–31) and the Oriental Institute in Chicago (1919–35). Breasted led numerous research projects in the Near East. *Who Was Who in America* (Volume I) has almost a whole column on his exploits. His writings range from *Erman's Egyptian Grammar* (1894) to *The Dawn of Conscience* (1933).

Walter S. Martin

1862
Rowley, Massachusetts

Dec. 16, 1935
Atlanta, Georgia

Composed music for "God Will Take Care of You," lyrics by his wife, Civilla. Originally a Baptist, Martin pastored the FBC, Troy, PA. He changed, in 1916, to the Disciples of Christ. He was a professor at Atlantic Christian College, Wilson, NC. He married Civilla Durfee Holden of Nova Scotia, and they wrote many songs together such as "The Old-Fashioned Way" and "The Blood Will Never Lose Its Power." In 1919, Martin moved to Atlanta where he was headquartered for his Bible conferences and evangelistic crusades. He helped begin the Practical Bible Institute, Johnson City, NY.

Frank M. North

Dec. 3, 1850
New York, New York

Dec. 17, 1935
Madison, New Jersey

President of Federal Council of Churches (NCC in 1950), 1916–20, **and hymn writer of "Where Cross the Crowded Ways of Life" (1905)**. North married Fannie Stewart on May 27, 1874 (died: 1878), and Louise McCoy on December 23, 1885. After being ordained a Methodist in 1872, he served churches in New York (1873–86) and Middletown, CT (1887–91). North was editor of the *Christian City* (1892–1912). He helped draft the "Social Creed of the Churches" for the FCC in 1908. He served as executive secretary (1912–24) and secretary of United Methodist Church Missions (1924–28). He retired in 1928.

Henry A. Klein

Feb. 17, 1869
Spring, Texas

Dec. 21, 1935
Gathine, Kentucky

President of Concordia Theological Seminary, Springfield, IL (Ft. Wayne, IN in 1976), **1922–35**. Klein married Minnie Schoor on July 19, 1894. He was ordained an evangelist in Lutheran Church Missions in 1892, pastored in Chattanooga, TN (1892–1902), and was a missionary to Brazil (1902–7). His other pastoral positions included Wittenberg, WI (1907–10); St. Joseph, MO (1910–15); and Collinsville, IL (1915–22). Klein wrote *Sermons for the Home*. He was killed in an automobile accident. His wife died a few hours later. They were on their way to Florida for a vacation.

J. Walter Malone

Aug. 11, 1857
Clermont County, Ohio

Dec. 30, 1935
Cleveland, Ohio

First General Superintendent of Ohio Yearly Meeting (Evangelical Friends Church - Eastern Region in 1971), **1889–1904, and founder and first president of Cleveland (OH) Bible College** (Malone College, Canton, OH in 1957), 1892–1918. Malone began the college with six students. He married Emma Brown (1859–1924) on Jan. 19, 1886. For 25 years, he served as founder and pastor of the First Friends Church, Cleveland. His railroad and oil enterprises helped him to be a large benefactor to the underprivileged (meals, job training, and founding the local rescue mission). He also authored a 12-volume correspondence course on the New Testament. He founded a mission work in India (1892) and one in Africa (1901).

Cleveland K. Benedict

March 24, 1864
Marietta, Georgia

Jan. 9, 1936
Cleveland, Ohio

Dean of University of the South, Sewanee, TN 1910–22. Benedict married Olivia Proctor on April 24, 1895. He was ordained in the Episcopal Church as a deacon (1890) and as a priest (1892). Benedict pastored in

Steubenville, OH (1890–92) and in Glendale, OH (1892–1910). He was also a trustee of Kenyon College, Gambier, OH from 1896–1910, and a member of Phi Beta Kappa and Beta Theta Pi. Later in life, he lived in Cincinnati.

Edgar Mahon
Jan. 10, 1936

Founder and first director of Mahon Mission, 1900–36, a great work in South Africa. Mahon's parents joined those flocking to the newly discovered gold mines in the Johannesburg region. The Salvation Army was there, and Edgar was devoted to them and to Christ. At the Salvation Army Training School, he met Joey Buchler. In 1891, he was assigned to the Fort Salisbury, Rhodesia area. Returning to his headquarters, he married Joey. In Mashonalan his lungs went bad and he contracted tuberculosis, but was divinely healed. They moved to the Orange Free State. In 1904, a church was established, connected with the Grace Missionary Church of Zion, IL. They spent five years at Kalkoenkrantz. Savages became saints, and crowds up to 8,000 gathered to hear his message. In Natal, many more were saved and healed. The gospel spread to the mountains of Basutoland. Mahon died soon after an annual Christmas conference with 1,000 natives attending.

Gustaf A. Brandelle

March 19, 1861
Andover, Illinois

Jan. 16, 1936
Rock Island, Illinois

President of Augustana Lutheran Church (LCA, ECLA in 1988), **1918–35**. Brandelle was ordained Lutheran in 1884 and married Lydia Appell on March 18, 1886. Brandelle pastored in Denver, CO (1884–1918) and then at Grace Church, Rock Island, IL (1918–23). For eight years he was president of the National Lutheran Council and a board member of Evangelical Lutheran Augustana Synod Missions. Brandelle was also editor of the *Augustana Journal* (1897–1906).

J. Rudyard Kipling

Dec. 30, 1865
Bombay, India

Jan. 18, 1936
London, England

Anglican poet who wrote the hymn "God of Our Fathers, Known of Old" (1897), which became known as "The Recessional" and written to commemorate Queen VICTORIA's Diamond Jubilee. Kipling began his journalistic career in India, 1882–89, then married Caroline Balestier (Dec. 31, 1865–Dec. 19, 1939) on Jan. 10, 1892. He lived in Vermont, 1892–97, where he wrote *Captains Courageous* (1897) and *The Jungle Book* (1894–95). From 1899 until his death, he purchased the manor house of Bateman's Burwash in Sussex County, where he lived the rest of his life. He won the Nobel Prize in 1907. His only son was killed in WWI in 1915. Kipling was buried in Westminster Abbey, London. He never attended college. He had insomnia. When unable to sleep, he would wander through his house and garden.

George V
(George Frederick Ernest Albert)

June 3, 1865
London, England

Jan. 20, 1936
Norfolk, England

King of Great Britain and Northern Ireland and Emperor of India, 1910–36. He was the grandson of Queen VICTORIA, married Princess Victoria Mary (1867–1952) on July 6, 1893, and bore the title of the Prince of Wales, 1901–10. He had six children. George V was officially crowned king on June 22, 1911. He reigned during World War I, the Irish insurrection, the first

Labour Party government, world wide economic depression and the rise of totalitarianism. He died at Sandringham House. Nearly 500,000 viewed his body and 3 million thronged the streets.

Jay T. Stocking

April 19, 1870
Lisbon, New York

Jan. 27, 1936
Newton Centre, Mass.

Congregational pastor and hymn writer. Stocking taught English at a preparatory school in New Jersey (1895–98), was ordained in 1901, and studied at the University of Berlin (1902–3). He married Grace Porter on October 21, 1903. He held pastorates in Vermont, Washington D.C., New Jersey, and Missouri, 1903–35, prior to his final service in Newton Center, Massachusetts. Stocking also authored children's stories. He wrote *The Dearest Spot on Earth* (1908) to *The Child In the Congregation* (1929).

Charles E. Hurlburt

June 11, 1862
Dubuque, Iowa

Jan. 28, 1936
Los Angeles, California

General director of Africa Inland Misson, 1878–1926. Hurlburt married Alta Houghton in 1887, and they had five children. He had a Baptist background and was involved in many enterprises. He left YMCA secretaryships in Pennsylvania to go to Africa. Hurlburt helped found the AIM (1895) and helped form the IFMA (1917). He pioneered in East Africa—Kenya (1901), Tanzania, Congo (1909), Uganda, and French Equatorial Africa (1925). Hurlburt helped to plan President THEODORE ROOSEVELT's African hunting expedition in 1909. In 1925, he founded the Unevangelized Africa Mission. He died from a heart attack.

Henry B. Parks

July 4, 1859
Campbell County, Georgia

Feb. 1936
Oakland, California

Bishop of African Methodist Episcopal Church, 1908–36; senior bishop, 1926–36; and director of its missions department, 1896–1908. Parks was educated at Atlanta University and rose to be director of AMEC Missions (Connectional Missionary Secretary), joining the Bethel AMEC in Atlanta. He served as a bishop in the South, mainly Alabama and Tennessee. After 1911, his area of responsibility focused on the western states, establishing a home base in the Oakland, CA area. Parks was an eloquent and impressive preacher.

Joseph S. Shoemaker

Feb. 1, 1854
Philadelphia, Pennsylvania

Feb. 6, 1936
Dakota, Illinois

First president of Mennonite Board of Missions (Mennonite Church USA Missions in 2002), **Elkhart, IN 1906–21.** Shoemaker married Elizabeth Brubaker on December 6, 1877; they had nine children. He was a member of the Mennonite Board of Education (1903–20), moderator of the Mennonite Council (1905–9), and the president of the Mennonite Board of Publications (1908–33). Shoemaker was widely used as an evangelist, and he was beloved by leaders in the Mennonite denomination.

James H. Fillmore

June 1, 1849
Cincinnati, Ohio

Feb. 8, 1936
Cincinnati, Ohio

Composed music for "I Am Resolved" (lyrics by PALMER HARTSOUGH), **"I Know That My Redeemer Liveth"** (lyrics by JESSIE POUNDS) **and "The Beautiful Garden of Prayer"** (lyrics by Scholl). With a Christian church background, Fillmore took over his father's singing school engagements at age 16 to support his family after his father died. Fillmore learned the printing trade and music typesetting. Along with his brothers, he established the Fillmore Music House of Cincinnati. He also published many collections of songs and the monthly *Musical Messenger*.

Leonard G. Broughton

1864
Wake County, North Carolina

Feb. 22, 1936
Atlanta, Georgia

Founded and pastored the Tabernacle Baptist Church, 1897–1913, and the Baptist Tabernacle 1929–31, both in Atlanta. Broughton was ordained in 1893, followed by his marriage to Roxana Barnes. He founded the Tabernacle Baptist Infirmary (1903), which became Georgia Baptist Hospital (1913). His pastoring positions were at Christ Church, London, England (1913–18); FBC in Knoxville, TN (1918–21); Grove Avenue Baptist, Richmond, VA (1921–26); and FBC, Jacksonville, FL (1926–29). Later in life, he engaged in Bible conferences and evangelism endeavors. Broughton's first book was *Old Wine and New Bottles* (1904) and his last *Spirit–Lit Eyes* (1933).

William D. MacKenzie

July 16, 1859
Fauresmith, South Africa

March 29, 1936
Germiston, South Africa

President of Hartford (CT) Theological Seminary, 1903–30. MacKenzie married Alice Crowther on April 27, 1883 (died: 1926). He was ordained as a Congregationalist in 1882 and was professor of theology at Chicago Theological Seminary, 1895–1903 and also at Hartford during his presidency. He wrote many books ranging from *Ethics of Gambling* (1893) to *Man's Consciousness of Immortality* (1933).

Charles M. Meserve

July 15, 1850

April 20, 1936
North Abington, Massachusetts

President of Shaw University Divinity School, Raleigh, NC 1894–1919. Meserve married Abbie Whittier (November 19, 1878) and Julia Philbrick (May 16, 1900). He was principal of high schools in Rockland, MA (1877–85) and Springfield, MA (1885–89). From 1889–94, he was superintendent of Haskell Institute, a US Indian Industrial Training School in Lawrence, KS. He frequently gave addresses on the Black and Indian problems. He was a Baptist and a Republican.

Edmund H. H. Allenby

April 23, 1861
Brackenhurst, England

May 14, 1936
London, England

Major general, conqueror of Jerusalem, December 9, 1917, leading victorious troops into the city, defeating Turkey. Allenby won Palestine by searching through I Samuel 13. He followed Jonathan's plan of attack, causing the Turks to flee Jericho in disorder (as did the Philistines) on February 14, 1918. Allenby held the titles of first viscount and British field marshal. He actively served in various wars from 1884 on and married in 1896. From 1919–25, he was the high commissioner in Egypt. Isaiah 31:5 was fulfilled as two planes caused the frightened Turks to flee.

Samuel L. Brengle

June 1, 1860
Fredericksburg, Indiana

May 20, 1936
Scarsdale, New York

Worldwide evangelist, working with the Salvation Army. Brengle was converted in a little Methodist chapel in Olney, IL on December 24, 1872. He began to do Sunday school work and sang in the church choir. Graduating from DePaul University, he became a Methodist minister in four locations. He took further training at Boston Theological Seminary, where MOODY's crusade strengthened him. Brengle was sanctified on January 9, 1885, and met WILLIAM BOOTH in late 1885 at a meeting in Tremont Temple. He married Elizabeth Swift on May 19, 1887 (died: April 4, 1915), then went to London to train with the SA. Back in America, he headed various SA corps, but evangelism was in his bones. He preached far and wide in America (1897–1904), in many foreign countries (1905–10), then back in America (1911–15). From 1919–31, he was the principal of the SA training school in New York City. He authored eight books. A heart attack at his son's home on May 18, 1936, ushered him into heaven soon thereafter. His funeral was at the Centennial Memorial Temple of New York City.

Percy Dearmer

Feb. 27, 1867
Kilburn, England

May 29, 1936
Westminster, London, England

Anglican hymnologist, scholar, and writer who popularized and adapted medieval church music for use in worship. After four rectorships (1891–1901), Dearmer served as the vicar of St. Mary the Virgin in Primrose Hill, London (1901–15), applying the ideals he set out in *The Parson's Handbook* (1899). Dearmer married Mabel White (1891) and Mary Knowles (1916). He was a YMCA lecturer during WWI (1914–18), a professor of Church Art at King's College in London (1919–36), canon of Westminster (1931–36), and a chaplain, His works range from *Religious Pamphlets* (1898) to *Christianity and the Crisis* (1933).

John A. Morehead

Feb. 4, 1867
Pulaski County, Virginia

June 1, 1936
Salem, Virginia

Director of National Lutheran Council (in USA in 1967), **1923–30, and first president of Lutheran World Convention** (Federation in 1947), **1923–35**. Morehead married Nellie Fisher on October 6, 1892, and was ordained the same year. His areas of service included pastorship at the First English Church, Richmond, VA (1894–98); president and professor of sytematic theology at Southern Lutheran Theological Seminary (1898–1903); president of Roanoke College, Salem, VA (1903–20); and president of the United Synod of the South (1910–14). Morehead strove energetically for Lutheran unity. His most quoted words were, "We want to help each other." His compassion, resourcefulness, and tireless service won him respect and affection from many, including President HERBERT HOOVER.

Hugh R. Mackintosh

Oct. 31, 1870
Paisley, Scotland

June 3, 1936
Stornoway, Scotland

Beloved professor of systematic theology at New College, Edinburgh, 1904–36, then dogmatics at the University of Edinburgh when NC united with UE in 1935. Mackintosh emphasized the forgiveness mediated through the gospel in his widely read books, from his first, *The Doctrine of the Person of Jesus Christ* (pub. 1912) to his last, *The Highway of God* (pub. 1931). After Mackintosh was ordained in the Free Church of Scotland, he pastored at Tayport (1897–1901) and at Aberdeen (1901–4). He was a liberal evangelical.

Wilbur F. Tillet

Aug. 25, 1854
Henderson, North Carolina

June 4, 1936
Nashville, Tennessee

Dean of Vanderbilt Divinity School, Nashville, TN 1886–1916. Tillet was ordained a Methodist (1883), pastored in Danville, VA (1880–82) and then began the Vanderbilt association. He became professor of systematic theology there, 1882–1919 and professor of doctrine, 1919 on. Tillet married Kate Schoolfield on Nov. 15, 1888 (died: 1889) and Laura McCloud on Jan.

25, 1894 (died: 1935). His writings range from *Our Hymns and Their Authors* (1889) to *Providence, Prayer, and Power* (1926). Tillet helped select hymns for hymnals and wrote hymns such as, "O Son of God Incarnate."

John M. VanderMuelen

April 12, 1870
Milwaukee, Wisconsin

June 7, 1936
Louisville, Kentucky

President of Louisville (KY) Presbyterian Theological Seminary, 1920–30. VanderMuelen's Reformed Church pastorates in Michigan were at Kalamazoo (1896–99) and Grand Rapids (1899–1901). He was superintendent of home missions in Oklahoma (1901–3) and professor at Hope College (1903–9). Mary Veneklasen became his wife on June 15, 1905. Other pastorates were at Grace Reformed Church of New York City (1909–12); at Second Presbyterian of Louisville, KY (1913–17); and at First Presbyterian of Oak Park, IL (1917–20).

Olof Hedeen

June 19, 1860
Undersaker, Sweden

June 15, 1936
Traverse City, Michigan

Missions secretary (president) **of the Baptist General Conference, 1920–30**. He came to America in 1883. Hedeen married Wilhelmina Estrom in 1883 (died: 1893), Hanna Carlson in 1896 (died: 1926), and Hanna Frodell in 1930. He pastored the Evangelical Lutheran Church, Manchester, NH (1885–90); a Swedish Baptist Church, Brooklyn, NY (1890–96); and finally the Englewood Swedish Baptist Church, Chicago (1914–21). He was a professor of theology (Swedish Department) at the University of Chicago, 1896–1914, known as the Morgan Park Theological Seminary.

Florence L. Reed Crawford

Sept. 1, 1872
Coos County, Oregon

June 20, 1936
Portland, Oregon

Founder and first general overseer of Apostolic Faith Mission of Portland, OR 1907–37. Florence was married to Frank M. Crawford, a building contractor, in 1890 and had two children. She separated from him after 16 years of marriage. Converted early at a dance party, she attended the Azusa Street revival in Los Angeles in 1906. She then began evangelizing in Washington, Minnesota and Canada. Her headquarters moved to Portland, OR in 1907, having two auditoriums accommodating more than 3,000 people. Her teachings were strict Holiness doctrine and practice. Fringe teachings on female leadership and separation from other groups caused a split in 1919, out of which came the Open Bible Standard Churches.

Samuel D. Gordon

Aug. 12, 1859
Philadelphia, Pennsylvania

June 26, 1936
Winston-Salem, North Carolina

Devotional lecturer and writer. Gordon became assistant secretary of Philadelphia's YMCA 1884, and state secretary of the Ohio YMCA, 1886–95. He began preaching in Bible conferences and missionary conventions in 1895. He married Mary Kilgroe on June 5, 1902. Gordon supported the Keswick ministry in England, speaking at conventions in 1909 and 1932. He wrote 24 devotional books, from *Quiet Talks on Power* (1901) to *Quiet Talks about the Old Book* (1937). His best seller was *Quiet Talks on Prayer* (1904).

Heinrich Coerper

March 3, 1863
Meisenheim, Germany

July 8, 1936
Dingligen, Germany

Founder and first director of the Liebenzell Mission, 1899–1936. After his conversion, Coerper sought to serve the Lord. He was pastor of the Chapel Church, Heidelberg, 1880–94. He then ministered in Essen and Strassbourg, coming to help Pastor Roeschman of Hamburg in 1899. When the pastor died in 1901, Coerper was ready to extend the vision, and under his leadership, overseas ministries greatly expanded. Property in the Black Forest of Liebenzell became available. Coerper was convinced that home and foreign missions worked together. In 1933, he suffered his first stroke that would eventually take him. By 1936, there were 88 missionaries in China. The Liebenzell work started as a branch of the China Inland Mission. He died while visiting his children.

Samuel P. Cadman

Dec. 18, 1864
Wellington, England

July 12, 1936
Plattsburg, New York

Congregational minister, liberal theologian, author, and president of Federal Council of Churches (NCC in 1950), **1924–28.** Cadman joined the Wesleyan Methodist Church, in Lawley, upon his conversion (1880) and preached his first sermon (1881). After marrying Lillian Wooding (1889), he moved to New York (1890), which began his 46-year ministry. Cadman pastored in Millbrook (1890–93), Yonkers (1893–95), Central Methodist (Metropolitan Temple) (1895–1901), and then Central Congregational Church, Brooklyn (1901–36), all in the greater New York City area. He was active in home missions, was a chaplain (1916), and began a radio ministry (1923). He was the first radio minister for FCC on NBC, 1928–36. According to a poll in 1925, he was one of America's greatest preachers. His 13 books include *Charles Darwin and Other English Thinkers* (1931) and *The Pursuit of Happiness* (1935), his last. His first book was *William Owen* (1912). He held honorary doctorates from nine universities.

James L. Barton

Sept. 23, 1855
Charlotte, Vermont

July 21, 1936
Brookline, Massachusetts

Corresponding secretary (CEO) of American Board of Commissioners for Foreign Missions (UCBWM in 1961), **1906–36.** Barton married Flora Holmes on June 3, 1885, and was ordained a Congregationalist the same year. He was a missionary in Harpoot, Turkey (1885–92), and a professor at the Mission Theological Seminary (1888–92). His wife's ill health prevented continuing residence in Turkey. He traveled widely after becoming affiliated with the ABCFM in 1894. He retired in 1927. Barton wrote from *The Missionary and His Critics* (1906) to *Near East Relief* (1930).

Arthur S. Lloyd

May 3, 1857
Alexandria County, Virginia

July 22, 1936
Darien, Connecticut

Director of Episcopal Church Missions, 1900–19. Lloyd married Lizzie Blackford June 30, 1889 (died: March 1932). He received education from six schools of higher learning, was a deacon (1880) and a priest of the Episcopal Church (1881). He served at St. Luke's Church in Norfolk, VA from 1885–1900. Lloyd then became a bishop of the NY diocese, May 13, 1921. He lived in New York City but died during a visit to his daughter's home.

Richard C. H. Lenski

Sept. 14, 1864
Greifenberg, Prussia (Germany)

Aug. 14, 1936
Columbus, Ohio

Dean of Evangelical Lutheran Theological (Trinity Lutheran in 1978) **Seminary, Columbus, OH 1919–35**, teaching there, 1911 on, in the fields of exegesis, dogmatics, and homiletics. Emigrating to America (1873), Lenski was ordained (1887). He then married Marietta Young on February 1, 1888 (died: 1923), and Helen Gruner on May 12, 1924. He pastored in Baltimore, MD, and Trenton, Springfield, and Anna (all in Ohio), until 1911. Lenski remained associated with Capital University, Columbus, OH from 1911 on. His works are from *Biblische Frauenbilder* (1895) to *Romans* (1936). He did a mammoth commentary on the Greek New Testament (11 vols., 1931–38).

Frank Bartleman

December 14, 1871
near Carversville, Pennsylvania

Aug. 23, 1936
Los Angeles, California

Pentecostal evangelist and author. Bartleman was converted on October 15, 1893 at Grace Baptist in Philadelphia (RUSSELL CONWELL's church), then attended Moody Bible Institute. He married Anna Land on May 2, 1900. In Los Angeles, he met WILLIAM J. SEYMOUR. He was soon involved in the Azusa Street revival, 1906–8. Bartleman became an evangelist and in 43 years wrote over 550 articles, 100 tracts and six books. He strove for unity among the Pentecostals. Theologically, he was always looking for the latest work of God. He opposed all forms of militarism, including the purchase of war bonds, the existence of Boy Scouts, and argued for a neutral pacifism in WWI. He wrote from *My Story* (1909) to *The Deity of Christ* (1926).

Lewis E. Jones

Feb. 8, 1865
Yates City, Illinois

Sept. 1, 1936
Santa Barbara, California

Wrote words and music to well-known gospel songs. Jones wrote "There Is Power in the Blood" (1899), "I've Anchored in Jesus" (1901), and "Lean on His Arms." He served as physical director of the YMCA in Davenport, IA; general secretary in Fort Worth, TX; and in Santa Barbara, CA 1915–25. Hymn writing was a hobby for him. He sometimes used the pseudonyms Lewis Edgar, Edgar Lewis, and Mary Slater. His schooling was completed at Moody Bible Institute.

Fred B. Smith

Dec. 24, 1865
Lone Tree, Iowa

Sept. 4, 1936
White Plains, New York (?)

Evangelist. He married Minnie Colvin (June 2, 1886) and Lillian Eberenz (October 13, 1917). From 1898–1913, Smith worked with the YMCA, visiting the U.S. Army in Cuba in 1898 and traveling across America, 1899–1901, on their behalf. Smith was international secretary in 1910 and prominent in the Man and Religion Forward Movement, which resulted in the establishment of more than 1,500 new branches of the YMCA. After WWI, he became an ardent advocate of international peace. Smith also wrote from *Men Wanted* (1911) to *Must We Have War?* (1929).

Jonathan Goforth

Feb. 10, 1859
near Thorndale, Ontario, Canada

Oct. 8, 1936
Wallaceburg, Ontario, Canada

Renowned Presbyterian missionary to China. Goforth was converted as a result of an invitation by Lachlan Cameron. He was a pastor in Ontario in 1877. After study at Knox College, he was ordained a Presbyterian in 1886. He married ROSALIND BELL-SMITH on October 25, 1887, and they went to Honan Province, China together to open a station in Changte known as the North Honaw (Henan) Mission in 1888. Goforth saw the need of reaching both the poor and the rich. He barely escaped the Boxer Rebellion in 1900 (he was left for dead), went home to Canada to recuperate, then went back to China. Goforth sent out 50 converts as evangelists, baptizing as many as 4,000 soldiers a year. In 1907, he saw a great revival in Korea. From 1925–33, he labored in Manchuria, as the Changte work was taken over by the United Church of Canada (much to his displeasure), into which the Canadian Presbyterian Church merged in 1925. Goforth became blind in March of 1933, leaving China in 1934 and returning to Canada. He wrote *By My Spirit* (1912), and his wife wrote his biography. On the day before he died, he preached on "How the Spirit's fire swept Korea." He died in his sleep. His funeral was at Knox Presbyterian Church, Toronto, Ontario.

Ezra S. Tipple

Jan. 23, 1861
Camden, New York

Oct. 17, 1936
New York, New York

President of Drew University Theological School, Madison, NJ 1912–28. Tipple entered the Methodist ministry in 1887, pastored at St. Luke's (1887–92); Grace Church (1892–97 and 1904–5); and St. James' Church all in New York City (1897–1901). Edna White became his wife on June 24, 1897. Tipple was professor of theology at Drew from 1905 on. His books ranged from *Heart of Asbury's Journal* (1905) to *The Wendels* (1936).

Lizzie De Armond

1847

Oct 26, 1936

Songwriter. Data on her is sketchy, but Lizzie joined the Swarthmore (PA) Presbyterian Church November 26, 1895, and was secretary of the Ladies Aid 1890–1906 when her son died in 1901. Lizzie taught in various Sunday school departments, 1919–31. She wrote the words to "If Your Heart Keeps Right," "Mother's Prayers Have Followed Me," (music by B. D. Ackley for both) "The End of the Road" (1920) (music by Elton Roth) and "Good Night and Good Morning" (c. 1922). Her song, "Good Night and Good Morning", written after losing her daughter, was sung at Billy Sunday's funeral, and hers as well, by Homer Rodeheaver who wrote the music.

Wilbur P. Thirkield

Sept. 25, 1854
Franklin, Ohio

Nov. 7, 1936
Brooklyn, New York

Dean of Gammon Theological Seminary (Interdenominational Theological Center in 1954), **Atlanta, GA 1883–99.** Mary Haven became Thirkield's wife on Oct. 27, 1881. He entered the Methodist ministry (1878), becoming bishop (1912). Thirkield secured assistance in several areas; endowment, equipment of $600,000, and serving as general secretary of Freedman's Aid, 1900–6. He was then president of Howard University, Washington, D.C., 1906–12, which grew from 936 to 1,409 under his leadership. He wrote several books.

Samuel E. Hill

July 9, 1868
Hardwick, Vermont

Nov. 9, 1936
Beloit, Wisconsin

First president of Gideons, 1899–1902. Hill was in the Central Hotel, Boscobel, WI with John Nicholson and W. J. Knights on September 14, 1898, having devotions together when this movement was born. Hill was converted at age 16 in Belle Plaine, IA. He married Frances DeGore in 1898, moved to Beloit, and became very active in the First Presbyterian Church. Hill's profession was the paint/glass business.

The Saints Go Marching In

Philip W. Crannell

Dec. 26, 1861
Albany, New York

Dec. 2, 1936
Denver, Colorado

First president of Central Baptist Theological Seminary, Kansas City, KS 1903–26. Crannell was converted and called to the ministry on Dec. 31, 1882. He married Fannie Grout on April 2, 1884. Ordained as a Baptist in 1888, he pastored in several areas: Baldwinsville, NY (1888–94); FBC in Corning, NY (1894–1900); and FBC of Topeka, KS (1900–4), becoming involved with the Kansas City Seminary (CBTS). He died of intestinal cancer in a Presbyterian hospital. His last words were, "Underneath are the everlasting arms." His books ranged from *The Lesson Analyzed* (1910) to *Seams in Glory* (1926).

Peter P. Bilhorn

July 22, 1865
Mendota, Illinois

Dec. 13, 1936
Los Angeles, California

Singer, publisher, and composer. Bilhorn composed over 2,000 gospel songs, the lyrics and music for "Sweet Peace, the Gift of God's Love" and "The Best Friend Is Jesus," and the music for "I Will Sing the Wondrous Story" (1886) (lyrics by FRANCIS ROWLEY) and "Living Where the Healing Waters Flow" (lyrics by IDA OGDEN). Peter and his brother had a successful business in Chicago, the Eureka Wagon and Carriage Works. After he was converted in 1883 at Moody Church, Chicago, under the preaching of GEORGE PENTECOST, he focused his efforts on work for the Lord. Bilhorn studied music under GEORGE ROOT and GEORGE STEBBINS. Bilhorn became a noted evangelist as well as a singer. In 1900, he conducted a 4,000 strong choir in London and was invited by Queen VICTORIA to sing in Buckingham Palace. He assisted evangelist BILLY SUNDAY as the song leader for his revivals participating prior to 1908, when HOMER RODEHEAVER became the primary musical director for the campaigns. To meet the musical needs of evangelists, he invented a folding pump organ and founded the Bilhorn Organ Company in Chicago.

James H. Snowden

Oct. 18, 1852
Hookstown, Pennsylvania

Dec. 19, 1936
Pittsburgh, Pennsylvania (?)

Presbyterian scholar, preacher, and journalist. Snowden married Mary Ross on August 1, 1878. Early on, he pastored in Huron, OH (1879–83); at First Presbyterian Church in Sharon, PA (1883–86); and the Second Church of Washington, PA (1886–1911). Snowden taught at Pittsburgh's Western Theological Seminary, 1911–29. As an editor for over 38 years, he was instrumental in protecting denominational stability during this era of theological turmoil. His works included *Psychology of Religion* (1917) to *Discovery of God* (1932).

William W. Rugh

Oct. 15, 1867
Salem, Pennsylvania

Dec. 31, 1936
Philadelphia, Pennsylvania

Founder and first president of Bible Institute of Pennsylvania (Philadelphia College of the Bible in 1958), **1913–36.** Converted at age twelve, Rugh began an itinerant Bible-teaching ministry in the Allentown area and later in Williamsport, PA. Rugh started a weekly Bible teaching circuit walking 60 miles a week from town to town with his literature in tow. He directed the Inland South America Ministry Union. He opened a school, July 8, 1913, making it a point to know and love all of his students. Rugh is buried in Williamsport, PA. He authored several books.

Wellesley C. Bailey

April 28, 1846
Thornbury House, Abbeyleix, Ireland

1937

Leader of the first concentrated effort to minister to victims of leprosy. Bailey was converted at age 20, on the eve of his departure for Australia to make a fortune as a gold prospector. Failing, he returned home. Soon after, he sailed to India, in 1869, where his brother was an army officer. While there, he was touched by the needs of poor people, and applied to the American Presbyterian Mission to teach at their school in Ambala. Bailey's life changed after visiting a leper asylum. These lepers needed the gospel but also good food, clothing, and medical care. Through this new ministry, he soon had converts. In 1871, he married Alice Grahame (died: 1924). They returned to Ireland (1873), raised some money, joined the Church of Scotland Missionary Society, and returned to Chamba, India (1875), where they opened a small leper asylum. In 1879, he moved to Wazirabad where he started a new work. Soon calls came from other places. He went back to Edinburgh, where he started his Mission to Lepers in India. Returning to India, 1886–87, the work expanded. Calls came from Burma and Hanchow, China, as well as other countries. His last tour was 1913–14. Soon there were seven stations in China. He resigned in 1917.

J. Gresham Machen

July 28, 1881
Baltimore, Maryland

Jan. 1, 1937
Bismark, North Dakota

Conservative apologist and theologian. Machen was one of the most brilliant and heroic fundamentalists of all time. In 1901, he graduated from Johns Hopkins University, first in his class. He became a Princeton graduate (1905) and was ordained (1914). He taught NT literature and exegesis at Princeton Theological Seminary, 1906–29, but felt compelled to leave when liberal tendencies developed. Machen founded, became president, and taught at Westminster Theological Seminary, 1929–37. He founded the Independent Board for Foreign Missions (1933) and was tried by Presbyterian authorities for disobedience (1935). In 1936, he was expelled from the Presbyterian denomination and helped found the Presbyterian Church of America (Orthodox Presbyterian Church in 1937). His books range from *The Origin of Paul's Religion* (1921) to *What Is Christianity?* (pub., 1950). Important apologetic books include *Christianity and Liberalism* (1923), *What Is Faith?* (1925), *Christian Faith in the Modern World* (1936), and *Christian View of Man* (1937). He was a well-known Greek New Testament scholar. He never married and died of pneumonia on a trip.

Clellan A. Bowman

Aug. 29, 1861
Dauphin, Pennsylvania

Jan. 6, 1937
Coral Gables, Florida (?)

President of Schuylkill (PA) (United Theological Seminary, Dayton, OH in 1954) **Seminary, 1901–10**. Bowman married Caroline B. Krimmel on June 25, 1902. He was an educational missionary to Oregon for the Evangelical Church prior to 1895. Since then, he has been involved with the development of Albright College Institute, Myerstown, PA, and its consolidation with Central Pennsylvania College, New Berlin, PA, in 1902, to form Albright College. He was an early president and then served again in 1923–29. He was a Republican and a Mason.

Clarence A. Barbour

April 21, 1867
Hartford, Connecticut

Jan. 16, 1937
Providence, Rhode Island

President of Rochester (NY) Theological Seminary (Colgate-Rochester Divinity School in 1928), **1915–29**. Barbour married Florence Newell on July 28, 1891, and was ordained a Baptist the same year. Barbour pastored Lake Avenue Church of Rochester, NY (1891–1909), was Associate Secretary of the International Committee of the YMCA (1909–15), and was president of the Northern Baptist Convention (1916–17). His books included *Fellowship Hymns* (1910) and *Service Song Book* (1917). In 1929, he became president of Brown University.

Arcturus Z. Conrad

Nov. 26, 1855
Shiloh, Indiana

Jan. 22, 1937
Boston, Massachusetts

Strong evangelical Congregational pastor, writer, and leader who pastored Ainalie Street Church, Brooklyn, NY (1885–90); Old South (First) Congregational, Worcester, MA (1890–1902); and Park Street Church of Boston (1906–37). Conrad married Harriet Adams on August 26, 1885, and Jean Livingston on November 9, 1932 (died: 1937). He retired to Cambridge, MA. He wrote *Flashes from My Forge* (1900) to *You Must Go Right On* (1931).

John MacNeill

July 7, 1874
Paisley, Scotland

Feb. 10, 1937
Hamilton, Ontario, Canada (?)

President of Baptist World Alliance, 1928–33. He was at the FBC in Winnipeg, Manitoba 1899–06. MacNeill pastored Walmer Road Baptist Church, Toronto, 1906–30. His favorite sermon was "Shattering the Nest," first preached in London in 1914. MacNeill authored *World Power and Many Mansions*. His later years, 1930–37 were spent as the principal and theology professor at McMaster University in Hamilton, Ontario. He died of a heart attack.

John T. Axton

July 28, 1870
Salt Lake City, Utah

Feb. 20, 1937
Washington, D.C. (?)

Congregational minister and first U.S. Army Chief of Chaplains, 1920–28. Axton served in the Philippines and on the Mexican border, receiving many decorations in WWI. He married Jane Bean on August 28, 1891. Axton officiated at the interment of the Unknown Soldier at Arlington Cemetery. He was a Republican and a Mason.

Hampton H. Sewell

Jan. 7, 1874
Near Atlanta, Georgia

March 11, 1937
Temple, Georgia

Composed music for "He Included Me" (lyrics by JOHNSON OATMAN). After several years as a merchant and a farmer, Sewell became an evangelistic singer, beginning his work with Charles Dunaway in 1909. For more than 25 years, he was engaged in evangelism throughout the South. Sewell wrote about 500 songs and published three collections. He also wrote, "He's Everything to Me."

Adolf G. Deissman

Nov. 7, 1866
Langenscheid, Germany

April 5, 1937

Lutheran New Testament scholar and ecumenist. Deissman clearly established that the Greek of the New Testament was the language of everyday life at that time. This discovery was a major factor in leading to the movement of modern speech translations of the Bible. He taught NT exegesis in Heidelberg (1897–1908) and Berlin (1908–34). Deissman served at WCC gatherings at Stockholm (1925) and at Lausanne (1927). His best-known works were *Light from the Ancient East* and *Paul*. He showed the value of papyri for NT Greek.

James S. Luckey

Aug. 1, 1867
Short Tract, New York

April 7, 1937
Houghton, New York

President of Houghton (NY) College, 1894–96, 1908–37, serving when it changed from a seminary to a college in 1923. They saw the enrollment grow from 159 to 417 during his tenure. Luckey married Edith Bedell on June 28, 1894. He was the principal of Union School, Millerton, NY from 1898–1902. He was an instructor at Oberlin (OH) College, 1905–7, a Wesleyan Methodist and Republican.

William F. McDowell

Feb. 4, 1858
Millersburg, Ohio

April 26, 1937
Washington, D.C.

Methodist bishop beginning in 1904. McDowell was an influential leader and great preacher. He and Clotilda Lyon married on September 20, 1882 (died: 1930). He held Ohio pastorships at Lodi (1882–83), Oberlin (1883–85), and Tiffin (1885–90). McDowell was chancellor of the University of Denver (1890–99), corresponding secretary of the Board of Education (1899–1904), bishop in Chicago (1904–16), and bishop in Washington, D.C. (1916–34). His spiritual life gave him power in the pulpit, weeping at times, swaying student audiences. He wrote from *In the School of Christ* (1910) to *Lectures on Christian Biography* (1933). He preached in Morgantown, NC and traveled back home the day before he died.

Carl C. Hein

Aug. 31, 1868
Weisbaden, Germany

April 30, 1937
Columbus, Ohio

President of Ohio Synod (one of three synods to merge in 1930 to form ALC), **1924–30, and of American Lutheran Church** (ELCA in 1988), **1931–37**. After he came to America in 1873, Hein married Anna M. Froemke on October 22, 1889. He pastored in Marion, WI (1888–91); Salem Church, Detroit, MI (1891–1902); and Trinity Church, Columbus, OH (1902–25). In 1933, he became president of the National Lutheran Council and attended many world conventions.

Lauress J. Birney

Sept. 11, 1871
Dennison, Ohio

May 10, 1937
Pasadena, California

Dean of Boston (MA) University School of Theology, 1911–20. Birney married Laura Close on Sept. 8, 1895. He pastored in Walpole, MA (1899–1901); Park Ave. Church, Park, MA (1902–05); Newton Center, MA (1906–8); and Maid Center, MA (1908–11). He also served as a trustee for Boston University, 1909–11. Birney became a Methodist bishop in 1920.

Mabel Johnston Camp

Nov. 25, 1871
Chanute, Kansas

May 25, 1937
Chicago, Illinois

Wrote lyrics and music of "Jesus, Savior," "He Is Coming Again" (1913) and composed music for "That Beautiful Name" (lyrics by Jean Perry). Mabel was the daughter of a banker and she had a beautiful contralto voice and was also an accomplished pianist. Mabel married a young lawyer, Norman H. Camp in 1896, whose testimony won her to Christ. She was, at one time, a member of Moody Church, Chicago and greatly supported her husband's evangelistic teaching ministry. Mabel had many health problems.

Clara Tear Williams

Sept. 22, 1858
Painesville, Ohio

July 1, 1937
Houghton, New York

Wrote lyrics for "Satisfied" (music by RALPH HUDSON), a truly beautiful hymn. From 1882–90, Clara traveled with Mary DePew in evangelism for Methodist and Wesleyan Methodist churches. She married W. H. Williams, a lay preacher in 1895. They lived in Canton and Massillion, OH, Philadelphia, and then retired to Houghton, NY. She had a great influence on young George Beverly Shea, who later blessed millions with his singing.

Nathan E. Wood

June 6, 1849
Forrestville, New York

July 8, 1937
Arlington, Massachusetts

President of Newton (MA) (Andover-Newton in 1931) **Theological Seminary, 1899–1908, and Gordon College, 1908–10.** Wood married Alice Boise on June 27, 1873, and was ordained a Baptist in 1875. He pastored Baptist churches in Chicago (Centennial, 1875–77 and Memorial, 1884–87); was principal of an Academy, Beaver Dam, WI (1877–84); pastored Strong Place, Brooklyn (1887–92); at Brookline, MA (1892–94); at FBC, Boston (1894–99); and at FBC, Arlington, MA (1909–19), while teaching part-time at Gordon. He wrote from *History of First Baptist Church of Boston* (1899) to *Man and Sin* (1927).

Burnett H. Streeter

Nov. 17, 1874
Croydon, England

Sept. 10, 1937
Basel, Switzerland

Anglican priest, theologian and Biblical scholar, remembered for the results of his study of the Synoptic problem. Streeter was a fellow and dean of Pembroke College at Oxford (1899–1905), fellow of Queen's College at Oxford (1905–33), and provost there (1933–37). His most important work was *The Four Gospels* (1924). In a series of publications, he dealt with many different modern problems from a Christian viewpoint. His writings range from *The Spirit* (1919) to *The Buddha and the Christ* (1932). He and his wife were killed in an airplane crash.

Charles E. Jefferson

Aug. 29, 1860
Cambridge, Ohio

Sept. 12, 1937
Fitzwilliam Depot, New Hampshire

Congregational pastor of the famed Broadway Tabernacle, New York City 1898–1937, where an eight-story church was erected in 1908. Belle Patterson became his bride on Aug. 10, 1887. He pastored the Central Church, Chelsea, MA 1887–98. He was known as one of the greatest and most influential preachers of his day. Jefferson was highly educated at Ohio Wesleyan, Delaware and Boston (MA) University. He emphasized the deity of Christ and the authority of the Bible. Jefferson's writings range from *Quiet Hints to Growing Preachers in My Study* (1891) to *Like a Trumpet* (1934).

James H. McConkey

Feb. 15, 1858
Wrightsville, Pennsylvania

Sept. 30, 1937
Washington, Pennsylvania

Writer and prayer warrior. McConkey headed the Silver Publishing Company. His best-known book is *Three-fold Secret of the Holy Spirit* (1897). He came to Pittsburgh (1914) and started his company (1916). His publishing efforts produced 90 tons of free devotional literature sent throughout the world in 18 languages. He allegedly spent hours in daily prayer. Louise H. McCraw wrote McConkey's biography.

Josiah P. Landis

Oct. 27, 1843
Brickerville, Pennsylvania

Oct. 17, 1937
Dayton, Ohio

President of Union Biblical Seminary, 1907–09, renamed Bonebreak Theological Seminary (United Theological Seminary in 1954), **Dayton, OH 1910–21**. Landis was ordained as a United Brethren minister in 1871 and married Addie Kumier on June 6, 1872. Landis' Ohio pastorships were in Dayton (1871–74), in Miltonville (1874–77), and in Germantown (1877–80). He was a professor of Hebrew exegesis and Old Testament theology at UBS from 1880–1909.

Charles W. Gordon
Ralph Conner

Sept. 13, 1860
Glengarry County, Ontario, Canada

Oct. 31, 1937
Winnipeg, Manitoba, Canada

Presbyterian teacher, minister, missionary, and writer. Gordon became a missionary in Banff, Alberta (1890–93), followed by a pastorship at St. Stephen's Church, Winnipeg, Manitoba (1894–1924). During WWI, he was a chaplain with the Canadian forces overseas. Gordon played an important part in merging denominations into the United Church of Canada in 1925. He wrote 26 novels under a pseudonym, Ralph Conner, the best-known novels being *The Sky Pilot* (1899) and *The Man from Glengarry* (1901). His first book was *Behind the Marshes* (1897). He believed only godly men could build a great nation. He was a social gospel activist.

Hugh R. L. "Dick" Sheppard

Sept. 2, 1880
Windsor, England

Oct. 31, 1937
London, England

Immensely popular vicar of St. Martin-in-the-Fields, London, who made his parish church the most lively and well-known in the British Empire, 1914–1926. From 1907–11, Sheppard was at Oxford House in London. He married Alison Lennox in 1915. Sheppard was an enthusiast for church reform, broadcasting, and pacifism. Sheppard served as dean of Canterbury (1929–31) and canon of St. Paul's Cathedral (1934–37). Illness plagued him often, and 100,000 paid their respects to the family viewing his body after he died. He wrote *Two Days Before* (1924) and *The Impatience of a Parson* (1927).

George Sverdrup Jr.

Aug. 3, 1879
Minneapolis, Minnesota

Nov. 11, 1937
Minneapolis, Minnesota

President of Augsburg Theological Seminary (merged into Luther Theological Seminary in 1963), **Minneapolis, MN 1911–33**. Sverdrup was instructor at Syrian Protestant College in Beirut (1906–7); professor of math at Augsburg College at Minneapolis, MN (1907–8); and professor of Old Testament at Augsburg Seminary, 1908 onward. Iljalma Stenvig became his wife on August 17, 1909.

Elias Cottrell

Jan. 31, 1853
Holly Springs, Mississippi

Dec. 5, 1937
Holly Springs, Mississippi

Bishop of Colored (Christian in 1956) **Methodist Episcopal Church, 1894–1937; senior bishop, 1932–37**. Cottrell married Catherine Davis on January 1, 1880. Early in his ministry, he pastored in Tennessee and Mississippi. Cottrell was a member of the General Conference (1882–94), book agent (1882–86), educational commissioner (1890–94), and fraternal messenger of the General Conference in Omaha, 1892. At Mississippi Industrial College of Holly Springs, he was the general manager and treasurer.

Isaac Lane

March 3, 1834
Jackson, Tennessee

Dec. 6, 1937
Jackson, Tennessee

Bishop of the Colored (Christian in 1956) **Methodist Episcopal Church, 1873–1937**. Lane was born a slave and had no formal education. He married Francis Ann Boyce in 1854 (died: 1896) and Mary Smith in 1897. Lane served as the presiding elder of Jackson district (1866–70) and then pastored at Liberty Church (leading church in the area) (1870–77). He founded Lane Institute (renamed Lane College in 1896) (1885) and Theological School (1888) and was president of their trustees until 1917. Much of the school was destroyed by fire in 1904. He was the trustee of the property and the publishing house. He died of a stroke in his home at age 103. Following ELIAS COTTRELL's death, Lane was the second bishop of CMEC to die within 24 hours of another.

Leopold Cohn

1862
Berezna, Hungary

Dec. 19, 1937
Brooklyn, New York

First president of the Williamsburg Mission to the Jews, 1911–24 (renamed), **and of the American Board of Missions to the Jews** (Chosen People Ministries in 1988), **1924–37**. Both of Cohn's parents died when he was seven years old. He became an orthodox rabbi and married Rose Hoffman in 1880 (died: April 4, 1908). They came to America in March, 1882, and he was converted as he read Malachi 3:1 ("Behold, He has already come.") Cohn was baptized at Bushwick Baptist Church and settled in Brooklyn, NY. He rented a vacant store and started services. In 1898, he began a magazine entitled *Chosen People*. In 1904, he moved to the Williamsburg area of Brooklyn, which had a large Jewish population of 50,000. In 1920, he founded the bilingual *Shepherd of Israel*. Cohn was a member of the Marcy Avenue Baptist Church. He died of pneumonia after suffering a ruptured stomach ulcer.

Cyrus S. Nusbaum

July 27, 1861
Middlebury, Indiana

Dec. 27, 1937
Wichita, Kansas

Wrote lyrics and music to "His Way with Thee" (1898). Nusbaum was ordained a Methodist and married Harriett E. Erwin in 1886; pastored in Kansas until 1895. He then pastored in Ottawa, KS (1897–1903); was presiding elder of Independent District (1903–7); and then pastored in Parsons, KS (1908–14). Nusbaum became conference evangelist in 1914 and a U.S. Army captain in WWI.

J. Taylor Smith

1861 (?)
England

late 1937
at sea

Curate, bishop of Sierra Leone, and chaplain-general to the military. Smith traveled in Great Britain and around the world. He was converted at the age of eleven after meditating on John 14:14. Later, he heard a message on Jeremiah 1:4, 8 which challenged him to Christian service. Working with the Church Missionary Society, he turned down Calcutta and Uganda calls, but felt impressed to go to Sierra Leone. He went in February, 1891. He was made bishop in 1897. From 1914–18, he was serving British troops out of the war office in London, presumably. In 1924, he became president of Scripture Gift Mission. In 1925, he became chaplain-general which took him many places throughout the empire. In 1937, he spoke at Moody Centennial meetings throughout the States. He died on board the ship *Orion* en route from the Far East back home and was buried at sea.

John W. Kliewer

June 8, 1869
Berdichiev, Poland

Feb. 9, 1938
Newton, Kansas

President of Bethel College, North Newton, KS 1911–20, 1925–32. Kliewer came to America in 1874 with his parents. He was ordained as a Mennonite in 1901; married Emma Ruth on October 30, 1902, (died: 1935); pastored in Wadsworth, OH (1901–3); and in Berne, IN (1903–11). He served as secretary of the Mennonite movement (1902–8), and was the president of the Foreign Mission Board (1910–35). He made a trip around the world, 1920–21, to inspect mission fields. Kliewer was vice-president of FCC (1913–16) and pastored the Bethel College Church (1932–35). He suffered a stroke on October 16, 1932.

Engret M. Broen

Oct. 7, 1863
Tufsingdalen, Norway

Feb. 24, 1938
Oslo, Norway

First president of Lutheran Brethren Seminary, Fergus Falls, MN 1903–38. Broen married Juilana Roton (died: 1933), whereupon he married Elizabeth Roton in August, 1934. He was an evangelist and Bible teacher. He wrote for several periodicals, composed a few songs, was a tenor soloist and played the guitar. He died of pneumonia on a world wide missions trip.

Robert P. Wilder

Aug. 2, 1863
Kolhapur, India

March 27, 1938
Oslo, Norway

Founder of the Student Volunteer Movement. Wilder supervised two generations of great international conventions of college-age Christians. The movement was born in 1886 at Mt. Hermon under D. L. Moody bearing the slogan "Evangelization of the World in this Generation." Wilder married Helene Olsson on September 7, 1892. He served in India (1892–1902); had a student ministry in Europe (1902–16); returned to the US and worked with the YMCA (1916–19); was general secretary of the SVM (1919–27); and then went to Egypt (1927–33), afterward returning to Norway. His writings range from *Among India's Students* (1899) to *The Great Commission* (1936). Wilder's father, Royal G. Wilder (1816–87), was a missionary to India. Grace E. Wilder (1861–1911), his sister, was an SVM promoter and missionary to India.

Charles M. Jacobs

Dec. 5, 1875
Gettysburg, Pennsylvania

March 30, 1938
Philadelphia, Pennsylvania

President of the Lutheran Theological Seminary at Philadelphia, 1927–38. Jacobs married Abigail Shearer on October 5, 1905. After being ordained (1899), he pastored at St. Peter's, North Wales, PA (1899–1904); then Christ Church, Allentown, PA (1904–13); becoming a professor of Church history at LTS (1913–38). His books included *The Way* (1922) and *Helps on the Road* (1933). Jacobs was the co-editor of Luther's works in English (6 vols., 1915–32).

Charles L. Wells

June 23, 1858
Boston, Massachusetts

April 18, 1938
Sewanee, Georgia

Dean of University of the South, Sewanee, TN 1922–38. Wells was ordained in the Episcopal Church serving as rector of Hingham, ME (1882–84); and then at Christ Church of Gardiner, ME (1884–88); professor at Seabury Divinity School of Minneapolis (1888–92); professor of history at the University of Minnesota (1894–99); and dean of Christ Church of New Orleans

(1899–1909). Marie Goddard became his wife on January 28, 1886. He was rector of Christ Church, Macon, GA from 1915–16 and began to teach church history at University of the South in 1916.

Hugh L. Elderdice

July 24, 1860
Carlisle, Pennsylvania

May 12, 1938
Westminister, Maryland

President of Westminster (MD) Theological Seminary (Wesley Theological Seminary, Washington, DC in 1955), **1897–1932**. Elderdice was ordained in 1885 and served in churches in Baltimore and Pocomoke City, MD for twelve years. During his tenure, the seminary expanded. More campus buildings and faculty residences were built. Elderdice was professor of homiletics after his retirement.

Hiram F. Reynolds

May 12, 1854
Lyons, Illinois

July 13, 1938
Wollaston, Massachusetts

General Superintendent of Church of the Nazarene (and its antecedent), **1907–32, and first director of its world missions, 1906–16, 1926–28**. Converted at a Methodist church (1876), Reynolds identified with the Wesleyan Methodists (1879), the same year he married Stella Byerd. He joined the Association of Pentecostal Churches of America in 1895. This group merged with PHINEAS F. BRESEE's Pentecostal Church of the Nazarene in 1907 (after 1919, Church of the Nazarene). He played a formative role in the development of the CN and vigorously supported its mission enterprises.

Paul D. Rader

Aug. 26, 1879
Denver, Colorado

July 19, 1938
Hollywood, California

Great pastor, evangelist and president of the Christian and Missionary Alliance, 1919–24. Rader's conversion came at age nine under his Methodist father's ministry. He married his wife, Mary Caughran, in Tacoma, WA, while coaching football there at the College of Puget Sound around 1905. He pastored Congregational churches in Boston and Portland, ME (1906–08), was backslidden and in business with an oil company (1908–11) before rededicating his life. Rader was an associate of the CMA tabernacle in Pittsburgh (1912–15); and pastored Moody Church, Chicago (1915–21). While he was president of CMA, missionary numbers doubled from 250 to 500. Next, Rader headed the Chicago Gospel Tabernacle, 1922–29, which became the evangelistic center of the Midwest. He was on the air for 14 continuous hours on Sundays in 1923, the first major evangelistic use of radio. He established the Maranatha Bible and Missionary Conference in Muskegon, MI in 1926. He toured the world twice, in 1929 and 1931. Rader started tabernacles in Los Angeles (1931–33), Toronto, Minneapolis, Asbury Park, NJ and in Fort Wayne, IN, where he pastored (1935–36). He moved to Los Angeles in 1937. Rader wrote the lyrics and music of "Only Believe," "Old Time Power" (1921) and "I've Found the Way" (1928). Rader's converts included CHARLES FULLER and future U.S. President, RICHARD NIXON. He also was remembered as an "old-time boxer." He died of carcinoma (cancerous tumor). His funeral was at Hollywood Presbyterian Church and was buried at Forest Lawn Cemetery.

Gustav A. Julicher

Jan. 26, 1857
Falkenberg, Germany

Aug. 2, 1938
Marburg, Germany

New Testament scholar. In 1887, Julicher taught NT history and church history at the University of Berlin, followed by teaching theology at the University of Marburg, 1888–1923. Julicher was on the committee of the Church Fathers of the Royal Prussian Academy of Berlin. He was considered a liberal theologian and historical critic. His principal writings were *Parables of Jesus* (2 vols., 1888–89), and *Introduction to the New Testament* (1894).

Thorton C. Whaling

June 5, 1858
Radford, Virginia

Sept. 12, 1938
Columbia, South Carolina

President of Columbia Theological Seminary, Decatur, GA 1911–21. Whaling married Lucy Muller on December 20, 1883 and was ordained a Presbyterian one month earlier. He pastored in Cheraw, SC (1883–90); Birmingham, AL (1890–92); Lexington, VA (1896–1905); and First Presbyterian, Dallas, TX (1905–10). Whaling served as professor of theology and apologetics at Louisville (KY) Presbyterian Seminary, 1921–29. He was a lecturer and evangelist after 1930.

James O. Fraser

Aug. 26, 1886
London, England

Sept. 25, 1938
Paoshan, China

CIM Missionary to China. Despite great promise as a musician, Fraser followed the call of God to the remotest parts of inland China in 1908, where the Burma road crosses the mountainous borderland. Fraser labored there with the despised, neglected "Children of the Ranges," the numerous Aboriginal tribes, and the Lisu people, who were a Tileto-Burmese minority living in the high mountains along the borders of China and Burma (Myanmar). By 1919, 60,000 believers had been baptized. He married Roxie Dymond on October 24, 1929. He died of malignant malaria.

Graham Taylor

May 2, 1851
Schenectady, New York

Sept. 26, 1938
Ravinia, Illinois

Sociologist who was ordained in the Dutch Reformed Church. Taylor married Leah Demarest in 1873 (died: 1918), and then Isabella McClintock in November, 1921 (died: 1926). He pastored in Hopewell, NY (1873–80), and at the Fourth Congregational Church, Hartford, CT (1880–92). He became professor of social economics at the Chicago Theological Seminary (1892), and founded the Chicago Commons Social Settlements (1894). Taylor was president of the Chicago School of Civics/Philanthropy, 1903–20. He wrote from *Religion in Social Action* (1913) to *Chicago Commons Through 40 Years* (1936). Through his teaching and writing, he promoted the social gospel (emphasis more on humanitarian needs than spiritual needs).

Monroe Vayhinger

May 28, 1855
Delaware, Indiana

Nov. 1, 1938
Upland, Indiana (?)

President of Taylor University, Upland, IN 1908–21. Vayhinger was ordained a Methodist in 1885. He married Culla Johnson on March 28, 1889. He was professor of math and Bible at Moores Hill (IN) College (1883–90), and professor of philosophy (1894–1904). He served a pastorate at Madison, IN (1904–6) and then at Hartsville, IN (1906–8). Vayhinger served as an evangelist as well. He taught Bible at the Missionary Banks Bible School of Indianapolis.

Samuel J. Mosher

Oct. 30, 1884
Starke County, Ohio

Nov. 8, 1938
Mount Pleasant, Ohio

General superintendent of Ohio Yearly Meeting (Evangelical Friends Church—Eastern Region in 1971), **1920–29**. Mosher was a spiritual leader, pastor, and evangelist. He was a great lover of people and of the Ohio Yearly Meeting for which he carried a deep and wholesome concern.

Annie W. Armstrong

July 11, 1850
Baltimore, Maryland

Annie W. Armstrong

Dec. 20, 1938
Baltimore, Maryland

Leader among Southern Baptists, who helped advance home and foreign mission programs. Converted at age 19, Annie taught an infant class at Eutaw Place Baptist Church in Baltimore. Unmarried, Armstrong was in Richmond, VA, in 1888 when she led the way in forming the Women's Missionary Union. She wrote letters by hand to all the societies, asking them to contribute to the first Christmas offering, which resulted in $2,833.49 for LOTTIE MOON in China in 1888. From 1888–1906, she shaped its direction as corresponding secretary. As of 1934 she was and is honored through an annual Annie Armstrong Offering for home missions. She was independently wealthy allowing her to volunteer much of her time. She was bedridden her last two years.

James M. Black

Aug. 19, 1856
South Hill, New York

Dec. 21, 1938
Williamsport, Pennsylvania

Voluminous hymn writer. Black wrote the lyrics and music for the famed hymn "When the Roll Is Called Up Yonder," (1892) and composed music for "Look to the Lamb of God," "I Remember Calvary," and "Where Jesus Is, Tis Heaven." He was educated in singing and organ playing, taught voice at several schools, and wrote over 1,500 songs. Daniel Towner, head of the music department at Moody Bible Institute, Chicago, IL was influential in launching Black's musical career. Black edited more than a dozen gospel songbooks. In 1905, he participated on the joint commission for the Methodist hymnal. Black was an active member of the Pine Street Methodist Church, Williamsport, PA from 1904–38, serving as their song leader and a Sunday School teacher. His 1894 "Songs of the Soul" sold 400,000 copies.

Ching-Yi Cheng

1881
Beijing, China

1939

Pastor and ecumenist who had six narrow escapes during the Boxer Rebellion (anti-foreigner movement in northern China, resulting in the killing of thousands of Christians and over 200 missionaries) in 1900. Cheng engaged in New Testament translation work and then was pastor of an independent work in Peking, 1908 on. Cheng actively supported unity for the Christian church and for China. He attended world missionary conferences in 1910 (gave a key address), 1919, 1928, and 1938. Cheng was the first moderator for the Church of Christ General Assembly in 1927. He shifted responsibility from foreign missions to the Chinese church.

John B. Frazier

1870

1939

Southern Methodist who was the first Chief of Chaplains in the U.S. Navy, November 5, 1917. At that time there were five other senior chaplains on duty, but Frazier's ability and judgment of human nature made him the most logical choice.

George W. Taft

July 17, 1865
Salem, Michigan

Jan. 21, 1939
De Land, Florida

President of Northern Baptist Theological Seminary, Chicago (Lombard), **1918–32**. Taft married Mary Boyden on June 26, 1889 (died: 1890) and then Jessie Humpstone on November 14, 1892. Taft served as a missionary professor and evangelist to Japan (1889–97); a field worker for the Baptist Foreign Missionary Society (1897–1902); a pastor at Pittsburgh and Norman, OK, at Hastings, NE (1902–13); and president at Grand Island (NE) College (1913–16).

Thomas Newlin

Dec. 28, 1855
New London, Indiana

Jan. 25, 1939
Whittier, California

President of Pacific College (George Fox University in 1949), **1891–1900**. Newlin married Olive Wilson on July 10, 1884. He was principal of Spiceland Academy (1886–91), vice-president of Wilmington (OH) College (1900–2), dean of Guilford (NC) College (1902–7), president of Whittier (CA) College (1907–15), and president of Guilford College (1915–17). Newlin belonged to the Friends (Quaker) Church.

Lewis G. Jordan

c 1854
Meridian, Mississippi

Feb. 25, 1939
Philadelphia, Pennsylvania

Director of National Baptist Convention USA Missions, 1896–1921. Born on a farm, Jordan survived slavery without a mother's love or a father's protection. He received his education in Nashville and pastored in Mississippi and Waco, Texas. He was pastoring the Union Baptist Church, Philadelphia, PA, when he was elected to the missions post, which caused a move to Louisville, KY. The LOTT CARY Foreign Mission Convention was formed in 1898. He began to publish the *Mission Herald*, which reached a circulation of 8,000 by 1901. He started his assignment without a missionary on the field or a dollar in the treasury. He helped 200 Africans get trained in Baptist schools in the US. He made four missionary trips to Africa and six to Europe. In 1901, he organized the Women's Connection Auxiliary. His visit to South Africa in 1904 was very successful. Jordan resigned his position with NBC because of ill health.

Charles A. Stoll

Oct. 28, 1872
Brookfield, Wisconsin

April 5, 1939
McPherson, Kansas

President of Central Christian College, McPherson, KS 1923–39. He attended Greenville (IL) College, 1900–04. Stoll married Emma Baldwin on August 26, 1903. He was ordained a Free Methodist in 1905. He was dean of Central Academy and College (1915–18), and acting president (1919–23). During WWI he was educational secretary of YMCA and lecturer.

William M. Ramsay

March 15, 1851
Glasgow, Scotland

April 20, 1939
Borunemouth, England

Archaeologist, known for his research into the history of the Christian church. Ramsay served first at the University of Aberdeen (1866–71); Oxford (1872–76); professor of Classical Art/Archaeology at Oxford (1880–86). From 1886–1911, he was the professor of humanity at Aberdeen University then traveled and lectured in the US on occasions. In the course of his studies, he traveled extensively in Turkey, making a special observation of the geography and topography of Asia Minor, 1889–91, 1898, and 1901–5. Ramsay was a special lecturer at prestigious universities in England and the US. His books range from *The Historical Geography of Asia Minor* (1890) to *Asianic Elements in Greek Civilization* (1927). He also published the following works: *St. Paul, the Traveler and Roman Citizen* (1895), *Historical Commentary on Galatians* (1899), *Letters to the Seven Churches in Asia* (1904), *Cities of St. Paul* (1907), *Luke the Physician* (1908), and *Trustworthiness of the NT* (1915). Ramsay was knighted.

Howard B. Grose

Sept. 5, 1851
Millerton, New York

May 19, 1939

Wrote lyrics for "Give of Your Best to the Master" (lyrics by CHARLOTTE BARNARD). Grose married Caroline Bristol on August 13, 1877. He pastored at FBC, Poughkeepsie, NY (1883–87) and at FBC, Pittsburgh, PA (1888–90). He was president of the University of South Dakota, Vermillion, 1890–92, followed by other educational positions. Grose served as Missions editor, 1910–33 for the American Baptist Home Mission Society. He also wrote his first book, *Aliens or Americans* (1906) and last, *George Edwin Horr, A Biography* (1928).

Thomas T. (T. T.) Martin

April 26, 1862
Smith County, Mississippi

May 23, 1939
Jackson, Mississippi

Southern Baptist tent evangelist who held crusades throughout the South, 1900–39. Martin married Ivy Manning on June 1, 1905. He was a Southern Baptist pastor in Glenview, KY (1890–91 and 1895–96); Canon City, CO (1891–93); Leadville, CO (1894–95); Beattyville, KY (1896–97); and Cripple Creek, KY (1897–1900). He preached to miners in the open air. Martin wrote five books, including *Gems from the Sick Room* (1897) to *The Communist Party* (1932). His favorite sermon was "Going to Hell in Droves." Martin organized teams of gospel singers and evangelists known as the Blue Mountain Evangelists. His circus tents seated about 700. He attacked liberalism in the SBC but stayed in the movement. He was buried in Gloster, MS.

Gustav B. Kimmel

April 22, 1874
Dayton, Ohio

July 14, 1939
Naperville, Illinois (?)

President of Evangelical Theological Seminary (GETS in 1974), **Naperville, IL 1919–39**. Kimmel married Esther C. Breyfogel on May 19, 1904. He was ordained in the Evangelical Church in 1900 and began pastoring in Indianapolis (1900–8) and in Dayton (1908–13). He was professor of theology from 1913 on at GETS and lived in Naperville, IL.

John W. Welch

Nov. 13, 1859
Seneca, New York

July 14, 1939
Springfield, Missouri

Chairman (general superintendent) **of Assemblies of God, 1915–20, 1923–25, and first president of Central Bible College, Springfield, MO 1922–25, 1931–39**. Welch married on January 25, 1879. He spent many years as an organizer for the American Sunday School Union and as an evangelist for the CMA, which ordained him in 1899. Welch was influenced by Pentecostal Evangelist Cox in Muskogee, OK. His pastorates were in St. Galena, KS; Essex, MO; and Modesto, CA.

Judson W. Van Deventer

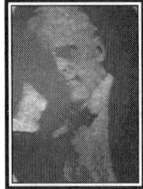

Dec. 5, 1855
near Dundee, Michigan

July 17, 1939
Temple Terrace (near Tampa), Florida

Wrote lyrics for the touching and popular invitation hymns, "I Surrender All" (1896), **"My Mother's Prayers," and also "Sunlight,"** 1897 (music by WINFIELD WEEDEN). In 1885, Van Deventer toured Europe, visiting art galleries and studying art. Van Deventer was supervisor of art in a Sharon, PA high school and was active in his Methodist church, singing in the choir. He gradually gained in popularity as an evangelist; assisted by singer, W. S. WEEDEN. Van Deventer also wrote the lyrics and music for "A Heart Like Thine," "Sweeping This Way," and "We Shall Shine as the Stars."

George B. Kulp

July 23, 1845
Philadelphia, Pennsylvania

July 21, 1939
Battle Creek, Michigan

General superintendent of Pilgrim Church (Wesleyan Church in 1968) **and director of PC World Missions, 1905–21**. Kulp married Annie Rodenberger on March 6, 1869. He pastored Methodist churches in Pennsylvania (1872–82) and Michigan (1882–98). He built a church in Battle Creek, MI, in 1900. Kulp saw the membership of the International Apostolic Holiness Union grow from 70 to 400 churches.

Waldo S. Pratt

Nov. 10, 1857
Philadelphia, Pennsylvania

July 29, 1939
Hartford, Connecticut

Music educator at Hartford (CT) Theological Seminary, 1882–1917. Pratt served as professor of music and hymnology. He married Mary Smyly, July 5, 1887 (died: 1935). He lectured at the Institute of Musical Art, New York City, 1905–20. For several years, he was organist of Asylum Hill Congregational Church of Hartford and conductor of the Hosmer Hall Choral Union there. Pratt's first book was *Musical Ministries in the Church* (1901). His *History of Music* (1907) was a long, standard text. His last work was *The Music of the French Psalter* (1939).

William B. Bagby

Nov. 5, 1855
Coryelle County, Texas

Aug. 5, 1939
Porto Alegre, Brazil

Great Pioneer Southern Baptist missionary to Brazil. Bagby was converted under the preaching of RUFUS BURLESON. Anne Luther became his wife on October 23, 1880. Hearing a missions challenge, they boarded a boat for South America on January 12, 1881. They were in Salvador (1882–84) then Rio de Janeiro (1884–1900). They organized the FBC of Rio de Janeiro with four members in 1884. In 1891, he went to Campos and Sao Paulo (1900–29), then later to Port Alegre (1930–39). His wife died in 1942 in Recife on her way to the US. Of their nine children, four died, and five became missionaries to South America. Bagby left behind 694 churches and 53,000 Baptists. He was a Democrat and a Mason.

Joseph R. Stevenson

March 1, 1866
Ligonier, Pennsylvania

Aug. 13, 1939
Princeton, New Jersey

President of Princeton (NJ) Theological Seminary, 1914–36, during the days of turmoil (MACHEN split of 1929). After being ordained a Presbyterian in 1890, he pastored at Sedalia, MO (1890–94); was a professor of church history at McCormick Theological Seminary (1894–1902); married Florence Day on May 16, 1899; pastored at Fifth Avenue Church, New York City (1902–9) and at Brown Presbyterian Memorial Church, Baltimore, MD (1909–14). The conflict at Princeton saw total reorganization in 1929, replacing retiring conservatives with more liberal instructors.

Tryphena C. Rounds

March 22, 1843
Peoria, Illinois

Aug. 28, 1939
Augusta, Georgia

President of Chicago Hebrew Mission (AMF Int. in 1993), **1897–1918**. Tryphena married George Rounds, October 8, 1863 (died: 1894) . For a while, she was secretary to FRANCIS WILLARD, founder of WCTU. After serving CHM faithfully for many years, she went with companion Anna Utley to Augusta, GA where she taught Bible classes for 20 years.

William E. Biederwolf

Sept. 29, 1867
Monticello, Indiana

Sept. 10, 1939
Palm Beach, Florida

Presbyterian evangelist and educator. Biederwolf was converted at age 20 at a Monticello Presbyterian church revival with Frank Palmer as the pastor. Early in his life, he served as a chaplain in the Spanish-American War. He married Ida Casad on April 16, 1896, then pastored at Broadway Church, Logansport, IN, from 1898–1900. He entered lifetime evangelistic work, assisting J. WILBUR CHAPMAN (1900–6), and then he went on his own (1906–24). He founded the Family Altar League (1909) and also raised funds for a leper home in Korea, which he visited (1920). His greatest crusade was in Oil City, PA 1914. Thousands came to hear him. He was director of the Winona Lake (IN) Bible Conference (1922–39) and School of Theology (1923–33) during the BILLY SUNDAY era. Biederwolf pastored the Royal Poinciana Chapel (a wealthy congregation) in Palm Beach, FL 1929–39. He wrote from *A Help to the Study of the Holy Spirit* (1903) to *The Wonderful Christ* (1937). His *Millennium Bible* (1924) was a profound book.

Milton G. Evans

Dec. 7, 1862
near Ebensberg, Pennsylvania

Sept. 17, 1939
Clifford, Pennsylvania

President of Crozer Theological Seminary [Colgate-Rochester (NY) Divinity School in 1970], **Chester, PA 1909–34.** He was a teacher at Keystone Academy in Factoryville, PA from 1883–87. Evans married Josephine Rivenburg on June 24, 1890. He then went to Crozer in 1890 as an instructor in Hebrew, 1890–95. He was a professor of biblical theology (1895–1907), of Christian theology (1907–9), and of comparative theology (1907–9). He made his home in Chester, PA.

Ira M. Price

April 29, 1856
Welsh Hills, Ohio

Sept. 18, 1939
Chicago, Illinois

Baptist Orientalist and Semitic scholar. Price married Jennie Rhodes on June 13, 1882 (died: 1905), and then Elizabeth McDowell on August 21, 1919. He served several short language professorships at various schools before being made a full professor of Semitic languages and literature at the University of Chicago, 1900–25, where he had taught, beginning in 1892. He taught at Baptist Union Theological Seminary, 1882–92.

Herbert Buffum

Nov. 13, 1879
Lafayette, Illinois

Oct. 9, 1939
Los Angeles, California

Evangelist and prolific songwriter (lyrics and music) of thousands of songs such as: "When I Take My Vacation in Heaven," "The Loveliness of Christ," "The Old-Fashioned Meeting," "I'm Going Higher Some Day," and "He Keeps on Loving Us Still" (music by LILLENAS). Moving to California with his family, Buffum was converted at age 18. He began as a pastor in the Nazarene Church, Salt Lake City, UT. Then he traveled as an evangelist—preaching, singing, playing the piano, and composing songs publicly from audience requests. He wrote the famed "My Sheep Know My Voice" at age 18 and "It Takes the Storm Clouds to Form the Rainbow" upon his mother's death.

Frederick Pfotenhauer

April 22, 1859
Celle, Germany

Oct. 19, 1939
Chicago, Illinois

President of the Lutheran Church—Missouri Synod, 1911–35. He was ordained in 1880, and pastored in Odessa, MN. Pfotenhauer married Helene Brauer on Oct. 10, 1882, who gave him eleven children. He was a traveling missionary in Minnesota and the territories of Dakota and Montana (1880–87); followed by pastorships at Lewiston, MN (1887–94); and then at Hamburg, MN (1894–1911). He lived in Chicago in later years.

Oswald E. Brown

Dec. 8, 1861
Canton, Missouri

Oct. 22, 1939
Nashville, Tennessee

Dean of Vanderbilt Divinity School, Nashville, TN 1920–32. Brown married Anna Muse on August 21, 1890. He was a missionary to China with the Methodist Church South, 1890–92. He then began a lifelong professorship of church history at Vanderbilt, 1892–1937. Brown's writings range from *Life and Letters of Laura Haygood* (1894) to *Church History after 45 Years* (1937).

Samuel A. Moffett

Jan. 25, 1864
Madison, Indiana

Oct. 24, 1939
Monrovia, California

Pioneer Presbyterian missionary to Northern Korea. Influenced by the YMCA, D. L. MOODY, and Student Volunteer Mission, Moffett sailed for Korea in 1889, arriving January 25, 1890. He moved to Pyongyang in 1893, and became the first Protestant missionary to take up residence in inland Korea. By 1895, he had purchased 110 acres inside the city, which became the theological and medical center of Presbyterian labors in Korea. He married Mary Fish on June 1, 1899 (died: 1912), and Lucia Fish on June 30, 1915. Four Presbyterian churches started in 1907. His 46 years of labor there were spent co-founding Union Christian College (Soong Jun University) and founding the Presbyterian Theological Seminary in 1901 with two students in his home. He was forced out of Korea in 1936 by the Japanese. The huge Presbyterian work in Korea today owes its roots to Moffett. One son, Samuel H. Moffett (born 1916), carried on a great work in Korea also.

Silas W. Bond

Jan. 13, 1864
Nora, Illinois

Dec. 3, 1939
Santa Paula, California

President of Houghton (NY) College, 1896–1908. Bond was the first to pursue turning the seminary into a college. He was converted at age 17. Bond married Hattie West on August 11, 1896 (died: February 1, 1928), and Jesse Ward in 1932. He founded Miltonvale (KS) Wesleyan College in 1909, and served as its president until 1916. He was in business from 1916–22. He left Kansas in 1931, and moved to California. He died after five days of heart trouble.

Frank C. Thompson

1858
Elmira, New York

1940
California

Compiler of the Thompson Chain Reference Bible. Thompson had two daughters by his wife, Laura. He was a licensed Methodist preacher in 1879 and associate pastor at Asbury Methodist Church, Rochester, NY from 1911–23. While pastoring in Genesee County, New York, he saw the need for a sequential (consecutive, consequent, successive) Biblical reference, and produced the first edition in 1908. In 1914, B. B. Kirkbridge took over the Bible sales. The reference book was revised in 1929 and 1934 with over 6 million copies sold.

Max C. E. Fritschel

Feb. 21, 1868
St. Sebald, Iowa

Jan. 1, 1940
Dubuque, Iowa

President of Wartburg Theological Seminary, Dubuque, IA 1905–32. Fritschel began to teach at Wartburg (1891) and then became a professor (1893). He was a leading theologian of the Iowa Synod and a son of CONRAD FRITSCHEL. He married Henrietta Hillemann in 1895.

The Saints Go Marching In

It was during his administration that a new seminary was erected. Fritschel struggled with a heart ailment for four years before his death. Fritschel's memorial service was at St. John's Lutheran Church in Dubuque with EMMANUEL POPPEN preaching.

William B. Anderson

Dec. 7, 1868
Monmouth, Illinois

Jan. 6, 1940
Philadelphia, Pennsylvania (?)

Director of United Presbyterian Church (PC USA in 1983) **of North America Missions, 1916–38.** After being ordained in 1897, Anderson went to India as a missionary (until c. 1900). Mary Heidelbaugh became his wife on June 30, 1897 (died: 1928). He was Associate Secretary of the Board of Foreign Missions, UPCNA from 1909–10 and 1914–16. His books included *Bible Lessons for Bible Teachers* (1901) to *A Watered Garden* (1919).

Carl G. Boberg

Aug. 16, 1859
Monsteras, Sweden

Jan. 7, 1940
Kalmar, Sweden

Wrote lyrics for the famed song, "How Great Thou Art" (1885), although it was not made famous until the Billy Graham New York City Crusade of 1957. This hymn passed from Swedish to German, to Russian, and then into English. Boberg was converted at age 19 and, soon after, began to preach and write hymns. He edited *Witness of the Truth* (1890–1916) and was a member of the Swedish Parliament, 1911–24. Both of his wives passed away early, leaving him a widower for much of his life.

Samuel K. Mosiman

Dec. 17, 1867
Middletown, Ohio

Jan. 24, 1940
Bluffton, Ohio

President of Bluffton (OH) College, 1910–35. Mosiman married Amalia S. Krehbiel on July 10, 1902 (died: 1905), and Emille S. Hamm on August 12, 1909. He was superintendent of the Mennonite Indian Mission School, Cantonment, OK from 1897–1902; teacher of Greek and philosophy at Lebanon, OH in 1908; and then became president at Bluffton. He was active in Mennonite and Federal Council of Churches activities.

Mark A. Matthews

Sept. 24, 1867
Calhoun, Georgia

Feb. 5, 1940
Seattle, Washington

Great evangelical Presbyterian pastor. Matthews pastored the First Church, Seattle, WA from 1901–40. Great crowds came to hear the gospel from this premier northwest church with 110 elders, 65 deacons, 13 assistants, 26 branch churches, and 9,000 members. Matthews was converted at age 13. Matthews also pastored in Calhoun, GA (1888–93); Dalton, GA (1893–96); and Jackson, TN (1896–1901). He married Grace Jones of Wales on August 24, 1904. He was a strong fundamentalist but did not believe in hellfire. He collapsed in his study on the day of his death and, while being carried to an ambulance said, "Sir, I still have my boots on."

Rufus H. McDaniel

Jan. 29, 1850
near Ripley, Ohio

Feb. 13, 1940
Dayton, Ohio

Wrote lyrics for the great gospel song, "Since Jesus Came into My Heart," 1914 (music by CHARLES GABRIEL). McDaniel was ordained in the Christian Church in 1873 and soon thereafter married Margaret Dragoo. He served in several pastorates in the Southern Ohio Conference of Christian Churches, including Cincinnati, but retired in Dayton. "I Have Been Born Again" (music by CHARLES GABRIEL JR.) was among the more than 100 hymns he wrote.

Charles E. Markham

April 23, 1852　　　　　　　　　　　　　　　　　　　　　　　　　　　　　　　　March 7, 1940
Oregon City, Oregon　　　　　　　　　　　　　　　　　Westerleigh, Stanton Island, New York

One of the great poets of his generation who considered himself to be nondenominational, although he had a Methodist affiliation. Markham's marriage with Annie Cox lasted from 1875–84. After their divorce, he married Cavaline Bailey in 1887. They also separated and he then married Anna Murphy (December 29, 1859–April 16, 1938) in 1898. Markham was a teacher, principal, and superintendent in Oakland, CA, from 1890–99; after which he moved to New York, where he devoted himself to lecturing and writing. He was also a hymn writer. His first work was *The Man with the Hoe and Other Poems* (1899). This famed poem was translated into 40 languages, earning him $250,000.

Julius Richter

Feb. 19, 1862　　　　　　　　　　　　　　　　　　　　　　　　　　　　　　　　　March 28, 1940
Germany

Lutheran missionary, historian, and leader. Richter pastored for 25 years. He was professor of missions at the University of Berlin, 1920–30. After WARNECK's death in 1910, Richter became joint editor of WARNECK's German missionary magazine. In addition, Richter wrote some 30 different books on missions and related subjects.

T. Albert Moore

June 29, 1860　　　　　　　　　　　　　　　　　　　　　　　　　　　　　　　　March 31, 1940
Acton, Ontario, Canada　　　　　　　　　　　　　　　　　　　　　　Toronto, Ontario, Canada

First secretary of the United Church of Canada, 1925–36. In 1879, Moore entered the Methodist ministry. Moore pastored churches in nine places, 1884–1903. From 1910–25, he was secretary of the Board of Temperance and Moral Reform of the Methodist Church (Board of Evangelism and Social Services). He married Mary Newton and later Annie Forster. Moore was also an evangelist and survived a heart attack in 1938.

Charles F. Andrews

Feb. 12, 1871　　　　　　　　　　　　　　　　　　　　　　　　　　　　　　　　　April 5, 1940
Birmingham, England　　　　　　　　　　　　　　　　　　　　　　　　　　　　Calcutta, India

Anglican until 1914, then an independent missionary to India, 1904–40; named by Indian friends "Christ's Faithful Apostle." Andrews was a close friend of Gandhi, who named him "Friend of the People." He never married. He was converted while having his personal devotions. Andrews went to Delhi in 1904 to teach at St. Stephen's College, after which he settled at Santiniketan, 100 miles from Calcutta. When he went to South Africa to help Indian laborers in 1913, he met Gandhi. Andrews used hymns, architecture, and art as new ways to present the gospel. He identified himself with Indian causes and the goals of India's leaders. He represented Indians abroad (Fiji, Kenya, British Guiana) as well. He wrote three works on Gandhi, plus *Christ in the Silence* (1933) to *The Inner Life* (1939). His autobiography is *What I Owe to Christ* (1932).

Samuel H. Chester

Jan. 17, 1851　　　　　　　　　　　　　　　　　　　　　　　　　　　　　　　　　April 27, 1940
Mt. Holly, Arkansas　　　　　　　　　　　　　　　　　　　　　　　Montreat, North Carolina

Director of Presbyterian Church (PC USA in 1983) **in the United States Missions, 1895–1912**, and secretary of foreign correspondence, 1912–27. Susan W. Willard became Chester's wife on April 15, 1884. He pastored at Castanea Grove, NC (1875–82); at Hawfields and Cross Roads Churches, TN (1883–88); in Franklin, TN (1888–91); and in Nashville, TN (1891–92). Chester was a Democrat and a Mason. He retired to Montreat, NC.

Charles P. Meeker

April 28, 1871
Philadelphia, Pennsylvania

May 15, 1940

President of Chicago Hebrew Mission (AMF Int. in 1993), **1923–40**. Meeker was converted at age 20. Meeker married Amy Drew on September 1, 1900. He was the pastor of Ewing Street Congregational Church, Chicago, 1899–1910. He was an evangelist for Moody Bible Institute (1910–15) and was head of their practical Christian work (1915–23). He was also involved with the South China Boat Mission and with the Ceylon and India General Missions.

Leonard L. Legters

July 8, 1873
Clymer, New York

May 18, 1940
Porterville, California

Pioneer with CAMERON TOWNSEND in the work of Wycliffe Bible Translators, which started (1933) in Keswick, NJ, resulting in the completion of the first linguistics course in Sulphur Springs, AR (1934). Legters married Maud Adkission in 1906 and became a missionary to the Indians in Oklahoma, 1906–10. He pastored in South Carolina (1915–24) and then was field secretary for Latin America (1924–30). He was of Reformed-Presbyterian persuasion and suffered a severe coronary thrombosis May 12, the opening day of a Bible conference at a Baptist church, and died at the local hospital.

Robert R. Moton

Aug. 26, 1867
Amelia County, Virginia

May 31, 1940
Capahosic/York River, Virginia

Educator. Moton graduated from Hampton (VA) Institute and then taught there, 1890–1915. He married Elizabeth Harris on June 7, 1905 (died: 1906) and Jennie Booth on July 1, 1908, resulting in a family of five children. In 1915, he succeeded BOOKER T. WASHINGTON as president of the famed Tuskegee (AL) Institute, leading it until 1935. Moton was a Republican, a Baptist, and a Mason. He wrote *Racial Good Will* (1916), *Finding a Way Out* (1920), and *What the Negro Thinks* (1929).

Elwood Worcester

May 16, 1862
Massillon, Ohio

July 19, 1940
Kennebunkport, Maine

One of the first to recognize help for emotional disorders with pastoral counseling. Worcester served as chaplain and professor of philosophy at Lehigh University, Bethlehem, PA (1890–96); as Episcopal rector at St. Stephen's, Philadelphia (1896–1904); and at Emmanuel Church, Boston (1904–29). His program attracted the attention of many psychiatrists. Worcester married Blanche Rulison on August 7, 1894. His writings included the co-authorship of *Religion and Medicine* (1908) to *Making Life Better* (1933). His Emmanuel movement gave birth to the field of pastoral counseling as well as spawning spiritual healing organizations within the Episcopal Church.

Virgil O. Stamps

Sept. 18, 1892
Upshur County, Texas

Aug. 19, 1940
Dallas, Texas

Father of Southern gospel music. Stamps wrote his first song, "Man Behind the Plow," at age 22. He had a powerful bass voice, organized quartets, composed gospel songs, and began publishing in 1924 through his V. O. Stamps Music Company in Jacksonville, Texas. In 1926, J. R. BAXTER joined the firm and in 1928, they had a new office in Dallas with their own printing press. Radio usage began in 1936. His Stamps-Baxter Music Company became one of the world's largest. Stamps' "all-night singing jubilees" (8 p.m.–7 a.m.) packed the largest sports arenas, such as Dallas, in 1938. His Stamps Quartet were pioneers in southern-style music. Stamps composed the music for "When the Saints Go Marching In" (lyrics by Presley) in 1937. He began *Gospel Music News,* which circulated 50,000 at his death. He was a Methodist that made southern gospel music "big-time."

Charles E. Burton

March 19, 1869
Poweshlek County, Iowa

Aug. 27, 1940
George's Mills, New Hampshire

General secretary (CEO) of Congregational Christian Churches (United Church of Christ in 1957), **1931–38**. Burton married Cora King on October 17, 1898. He pastored Puritan Church in Chicago, IL (1895–99); at the Lyndale Church of Minneapolis, MN (1899–1909); and at Euclid Avenue Church, Cleveland, OH (1911–14). Burton was also secretary of the Home Mission Society, 1914–21. He was a leader in the merger of the Congregational and Christian Churches which transpired in 1931. His books include *Finding a Religion to Live By* and *National Council Digest*.

Labayan G. Aglipay

May 8, 1860
Philippine Islands

Sept. 1, 1940
Manila, Philippine Islands

Founder and first bishop of the Independent Catholic Church of the Philippines in 1902, which gained more than 1 million followers. In 1898, Aglipay accepted a post as military chaplain of the Revolutionary army, resulting in his excommunication by the Catholics because of involvement in the insurrection against the Spanish. He was made vicar general by the Philippine patriot, Aguinaldo. Aglipay ran for president in 1935 but lost to Manuel Quezon.

Melvin E. Trotter
Mel Trotter

May 16, 1870
Orangeville, Illinois

Sept. 11, 1940
Holland, Michigan

"Mr. Rescue Mission," who did more for that cause than any other. Lottie Fisher became his wife on April 23, 1891 (separated: 1920s). Trotter became a helpless alcoholic; and on his way to commit suicide in Lake Michigan, he was converted at the Pacific Garden Mission in Chicago on January 19, 1897. After giving his testimony in Grand Rapids, MI, he stayed and built one of the largest rescue mission ministries in the nation, 1900–40. He was ordained in Grand Rapids in 1905 and served as interim manager of Pacific Garden Mission, Chicago, 1912–18. During World War I, he preached at army bases for 20 months and saw 15,000 conversions. He was also a yearly speaker at Northfield Bible Conference in Northfield, MA (1900–31), and traveled as an evangelist in the US and Great Britain (1921–40). Trotter used HOMER HAMMONTREE as his song leader and GEORGE BECKWITH as his pianist. Trotter was able to start many missions with the new converts after BILLY SUNDAY's crusades. Trotter sent converts out to open up 66 other missions across America. He wrote *The Double Cure* (1920). He is buried in Graceland Mausoleum in Grand Rapids.

Gustaf A. Andreen

March 13, 1864
Porter, Indiana

Oct. 1, 1940
Chicago, Illinois

President of Augustana College and Theological Seminary, Rock Island, IL (Lutheran School of Theology, Chicago in 1964), **1901–34**. Andreen married Mary Strand on August 7, 1890. He served as instructor at Augustana (1883–84), professor of languages at Bethany College of Lindsborg, Kansas (1886–93), instructor of German (1894–1900); then of Scandinavian languages (1900–1) at Yale. He wrote many books, ranging from a 1900 Swedish title to *History of Augustana College* (1935).

Ballington Booth

July 28, 1859
Brighouse, England

Oct. 5, 1940
Blue Point, Long Island, New York

Founder and first general of Volunteers of America, 1896–1940, and was general of Salvation Army (USA), 1887–96, until he split with his father, WILLIAM BOOTH, over the Salvation Army's authoritarian international hierarchy. Volunteers of America had similar objectives but had a more democratic organization and spearheaded prison evangelism. Maud Charlesworth became his wife on September 16, 1886. Early on, he led the development of the Salvation Army in Australia, 1884–87. Booth wrote the lyrics and music of "The Cross Is Not Greater" and authored *From Ocean to Ocean*. He was also ordained a presbyter in the Evangelical Church in Chicago in 1896. VOA was incorporated on November 6, 1896.

Wilfred T. Grenfell

Feb. 28, 1865
Parkgate, England

Oct. 9, 1940
Charlotte, Vermont

One of history's most dedicated missionaries. Grenfell ministered to 2,000 whites and 5,000 Eskimos in Labrador. He was converted at a MOODY crusade in 1885 in London. He began his 40-year ministry in Labrador (1892) after joining the Royal National Mission to Fisherman (1889). He served as an evangelist and a skilled physician, founding five hospitals, seven nursing clinics, three orphanages, cooperative stores, local industries, fox farms, schools, and recreational facilities. He operated medical ships also. Grenfell escaped death several times in harrowing ventures to remote communities. He married Anne MacClanahan (November 11, 1885–December 9, 1938) on November 18, 1907. His writings range from *Harvest of the Sea* (1905) to *The Romance of Labrador* (1934). His 24 books include two autobiographies written in 1922 and 1932. Ill health forced his retirement in 1935 to Vermont.

George F. Woodson

May 20, 1861
Pittsburgh, Pennsylvania

1941
Wilberforce, Ohio

President of Payne Theological Seminary, Wilberforce, OH 1902–37. Woodson married Laura Smith on August 10, 1898. His wife was born in Cincinnati. He had four children. He was ordained in the African Methodist Episcopal Church. He pastored in the Bermuda Islands, 1888–90 and in the New Jersey Conference until 1895. In 1895, he became associated with PTS. He was on the board of directors of PTS (1897–1938) and a trustee at Wilberforce University (1902–36). He taught systematic theology at Payne and also pastored in Wilberforce, OH, from 1920–22.

Charles G. Trumbull

Feb. 20, 1872
Hartford, Connecticut

Jan. 13, 1941
Pasadena, California

Editor, associated with his father, HENRY TRUMBULL, in the *Sunday School Times*, 1893. Trumbull was a learned Presbyterian. Aline VanOrden became his wife on November 18, 1897. In 1903, he became editor, vice president, secretary, and director of the *Sunday School Times* Company till his death. He established Keswick Grove (NJ) summer conferences in 1924. Trumbull wrote for newspapers in Toronto and Philadelphia. His eight books include *Pilgrimage to Jerusalem* (1904) to *Prophecy's Light on Today* (1937).

Thomas R. Kelly

June 4, 1893
near Chillicothe, Ohio

Jan. 17, 1941
Haverford, Pennsylvania

Philosopher and author. Kelly married Lael M. Macy. He worked with German prisoners in England (1917–18) and (1924–25), he was guiding the activities of the Quaker community in Berlin. He taught philosophy at Haverford (PA) College, 1936–41. His essay, "Holy Obedience" states that "suffering for others is a pathway to God." On the morning of his death, he told his wife, "Today will be the greatest day of my life." He had just accepted an invitation to meet with Harper and Brothers about a small book on devotional practice. That evening, while drying dinner dishes, he slumped to the floor with a massive coronary, which took his life. These devotional addresses were published later as *A Testament of Devotion*.

Eugene M. Bartlett

Dec. 24, 1885
Waynesville, Missouri

Jan. 21, 1941
Siloam Springs, Arkansas

Wrote and composed the popular gospel song, "Victory in Jesus (1939)." In 1914, he entered full-time music ministry, traveling to churches and singing conventions. He married Joan Tatum in 1916. Bartlett was president of the Hartford (AR) Music Company 1918–35, publishing songbooks and editing *Herald of Song*, a music magazine. Later he was affiliated with the Stamps-Baxter Music Company, Dallas, TX. and the JAMES D. VAUGHN Music Company, Lawrenceburg, TN. He was widely known as a gospel singer and singing school teacher throughout Arkansas, Oklahoma, Texas, Alabama, and Tennessee. He also wrote, "I Heard My Mother Call My Name in Prayer," and "Everybody Will Be Happy Over There." Bartlett was a member of FBC in Hartford and very active in SBC circles. He wrote and composed "Set My Soul Afire."

John Oxenham

Nov. 12, 1852
Manchester, England

Jan. 24, 1941
London, England

Congregationalist poet and hymn writer who wrote lyrics for "In Christ There Is No East or West" (music by ALEXANDER REINAGLE). For several years, Oxenham was engaged in business with his father, a wholesale merchant. During this time, he traveled in Europe and America. His real name was William Arthur Dunkerley, but his chosen pseudonym proved successful. Oxenham was a deacon of Ealing Congregational Church and taught a Bible class. He wrote 40 novels and several books of poetry and prose.

Enos H. Hess

April 14, 1872
New Danville, Pennsylvania

Jan. 26, 1941
Grantham, Pennsylvania

President of Messiah College, Grantham, PA, 1922–34. Hess loved both farming and education. He was converted May 20, 1894, and ordained in the Brethren in Christ in 1897. Barbara Hostetter was his first wife in 1900 and Elizabeth Cassel his second. Hess farmed from 1901–8 and began to teach in 1910, staying on the faculty at Messiah College until his death. He helped subsidize his livelihood by farming and assisted the college through their financial challenges.

Lewis Glenn

Dec. 14, 1874
Switzerland County, Indiana

Feb. 2, 1941
Intercession City, Florida

First president of Evangelistic Faith Missions, Bedford, IN 1905–41. In 1905, Glenn sailed for Egypt and began a faith ministry. Severe trials tested his faith: being stoned in Alexandria, the death of two of his children, and the death of his wife in 1939. Glenn had a heart attack in a car after a preaching engagement. For the next 40 years, his son, VICTOR, carried on his missionary commitments.

James D. Vaughan

Dec. 14, 1864
Giles County, Tennessee

Feb. 9, 1941
Lawrenceburg, Tennessee

Composed 500 gospel songs including "I Dreamed I Searched Heaven for You" and "If I Could Hear My Mother Pray Again." In 1910, he published a songbook for male quartets, which allowed him to start a school of music in 1911. Vaughan Phonograph Records followed in 1921. Vaughan was a former mayor of Lawrenceburg, TN, from 1923–27, who established the first radio station in Tennessee, WOAN, in 1921. In 1939, his music schools broke all previous records. More than 27 million copies of the Vaughan Hymnbooks (50 different titles) have been distributed. He had 16 quartets traveling across the country selling them. He was a Nazarene whose quartet arrangements were sung widely. More than 7,000 attended his funeral at Nazarene Tabernacle.

David S. Schaff

Oct. 17, 1852
Mercersburg, Pennsylvania

March 2, 1941
New York, New York (?)

A distinguished church historian like his father, PHILIP SCHAFF. His wives were Lue Haynes (1877–81) and Ella Andrews. Schaff pastored in the First Presbyterian Church in Kansas City, MO (1883–89); in Jacksonville, IL (1889–97); and was a church history professor at Lane Theological Seminary, Cincinnati (1897–1903). David taught at Western Theological Seminary, Pittsburgh, PA from 1903–25. He lectured at Union Theological Seminary in New York City from 1925–29. Schaff's books range from *Commentary on Acts* (1882) to *The Reformation and Its Influence* (1917).

Louis F. W. Lesemann

April 1, 1869
Hoyleton, Illinois

April 22, 1941
Terre Haute, Indiana

President of Chicago Training School (merged with Garrett Theological Seminary, Evanston, IL in 1934), **1918–34**. Ordained as a Methodist in 1896, Lesemann began pastoring in St. Charles, MO (1892–93) and in the following Illinois cities (1893–1912): Rock Island, Dolton, Clyde, South Englewood, Morgan Park, at Trinity in Chicago, and La Grange. He married his second wife, Olive Horne, in 1933. While on a trip from his Evanston home, he had a sudden heart attack and died.

James G. Frazer

Jan. 1, 1854
Glasgow, Scotland

May 8, 1941
Cambridge, England

Anthropologist and folklore classical scholar. Frazer was professor of social anthropology at the University of Liverpool, 1907–32. He was instrumental in founding the *Cambridge Review* (1889). His works are of great importance in the study of anthropology, myths, and religion. He produced the twelve-volume *The Golden Bough* (1890–1912), which was a study of magic and religion. He also wrote the three-volume *Folklore in the Old Testament* (1918). He wrote from *Totemism* (1887) to *Totemiga* (1939).

Frank G. Coffin

June 14, 1874
Marshall County, Iowa

June 9, 1941
Iowa City, Iowa

President of American Christian Church (United Church of Christ in 1957), **1919–31**. Coffin married Lula Klump on November 15, 1894. He pastored in Iowa (1891–1905); Dayton, Ohio (1905–11); and Albany, New York (1911–19). He was president of Palmer College, 1919–28. Coffin pastored the Congregational Christian Federated Church, Columbus, OH, from 1928 on. He wrote *The Church Facing the Future* (1922). He was a Mason.

Evelyn Underhill Moore

Dec. 6, 1875
Wolverhampton, England

June 15, 1941
Hampstead, England

Mystical writer. Author of 33 books, Underhill was the first woman to be a lecturer at Oxford University in 1922. Mysticism indicates a warm and immediate feeling of God's Spirit. She prayed for an hour each day. The mysticism she taught was not from Eastern religions, or monastic, as in Catholicism, but a spiritual union with Christ. She married Hubert S. Moore in 1907, when she was 32, remaining an Anglican, the faith of her husband. She was sought after for retreat leader, and visited the poor in London three times a week. In 1939, she became a pacifist. Her most renowned book is *Worship* (1936), although her first book *Mysticism* (1911) launched her career.

William P. Ladd

May 13, 1870
Lancaster, New Hampshire

July 1, 1941
New Haven, Connecticut (?)

President (dean) of Berkeley Divinity School, Middletown, CT 1917–28, New Haven, CT 1928–41. He was ordained a deacon (1897) and an Episcopal priest (1898). Ladd then served as rector in St. Barnabas Church, Berlin, NH from 1897–1902. He taught church history at Berkeley in 1904. Ladd married Ailsie Taylor of London in June 1916. He also lectured on church history at Hartford (CT) Theological Seminary, 1921–25. Ladd became president of the American Theological Society in 1929. He was a long time Episcopalian.

Lynwood W. Kyles

May 3, 1874
Ivy Depot, Virginia

July 8, 1941
Winston-Salem, North Carolina (?)

Bishop of African Methodist Episcopal Zion Church, 1916–41; senior bishop, 1934–41. Kyles married Jenny Smith (1897), Louella Bryan on December 18, 1908, and Josephine Humbles (1926). He entered the AMEZC ministry in 1896, and served as editor and general manager of AMEZC Review (1908–16). Kyles was elected bishop on May 16, 1916. He also served as a delegate to the fourth Ecumenical Conference in London, 1921. He lived in Winston-Salem, NC and pastored for many years. Some give him a July 19th death date.

Jacob Howe

April 22, 1855
Port Elgin, Ontario, Canada

July 10, 1941
Royal Oak, Michigan

Director of the United Brethren in Christ Missions, Huntington, IN 1905–36. Howe married Elsie Bowie on October 18, 1880 (died: Nov. 1935). His home missions activity in the Niagara (Canada) circuit, 1893–1905, was impressive. Howe left Canada in 1905, residing in

Huntington, IN for 31 years before retiring to the home of his daughter. He also traveled to Africa in 1913 and to other fields later.

Paul T. Barth

Oct. 19, 1872
Atlanta, Georgia

Aug. 25, 1941
Atlanta, Georgia

First president of Beulah Heights Bible College, Atlanta, GA, 1918–42, and General Overseer of the Pentecostal Church of Christ (International Pentecostal Church of Christ in 1976), **1921–39**. As a young man of 19, Barth went to Marietta, OH where he learned the piano business in a factory. He eventually returned to Atlanta, married his wife, Hattie, and associated with the CMA. When he took a Pentecostal church in 1916, he left the piano business so he could labor fulltime. In 1914, the Beulah Heights Campground was founded. In June, 1937, he suffered a nervous breakdown and became an invalid from that time on.

Robert J. Craig

1872
Ontario, Canada

Sept. 1, 1941
Minneapolis, Minnesota

First president of Glad Tidings Bible Institute, San Francisco, CA (Bethany College of Scotts Valley, CA in 1950), **1919–41**. Converted as a youth, Craig was a Methodist minister during the 1906 San Francisco earthquake. His first wife died in 1902, and he then married Mary McCulloch in 1909 (died: May 1943). After a Pentecostal experience, his Glad Tidings Temple (pastor 1913–41) and Bible school mushroomed, becoming the hub of West Coast Pentecostalism. Craig edited *Glad Tidings Magazine* (1921–39). He died while attending the Assemblies of God General Council meeting.

Henry C. Early

May 11, 1855
Augusta County, Virginia

Sept. 1, 1941
Harrisonburg, Virginia

Moderator of Church of the Brethren seven years during 1904–19. Early married Mary Showalter in 1876, having eleven children (five died in infancy) He then married Emma Martin in 1922. Early pastored in Mill Creek, VA from 1884–1921, and was an evangelist and policy maker. From 1901–24 he served on the Brethren mission board. Early had a personal annual correspondence of 1,500 letters during these years.

Warren A. Candler

Aug. 23, 1857
near Villa Rica, Georgia

Sept. 25, 1941
Atlanta, Georgia

Bishop in the Methodist Episcopal Church South, 1898–1939, and in the Methodist Church, 1939–41. Candler married Nettie Cartwright on November 21, 1877, while pastoring in Georgia, 1875–86. He was president of Emory College (1888–98), and chancellor of Emory University (1914–21). He was a key figure in moving Emory in 1914 from Oxford to Atlanta, GA. He wrote many books ranging from *History of Sunday Schools* (1880) to *Young J. Allen, the Man Who Seeded China* (1931). He opposed the union of the Methodist Church. He was also the assistant editor of *The Christian Advocate* (1939), issued from Nashville. The Candler School of Theology is named after him. Candler is buried in Oxford, GA.

George Allan

Jan. 31, 1871
East Taeiri, New Zealand

Oct. 26, 1941
La Paz, Bolivia

First director of Bolivian Indian Mission (Andes Evangelical Mission in 1966, which merged into SIM in 1981), **1907–41**. Allan married Mary A. S. Stirling on October 20, 1898. His daughter, Margarita Hudspith, remained 44 years in Bolivia. He left New Zealand (1899) and arrived in Uruguay (1900). He gave nearly 40 years to Bolivian evangelization with the Quichua Indians as his main target, 1903 on. From 1909, their base was San Pedro. With a native Bolivian, Crisologo Barron, they translated the New Testament and Psalms into the Quichua language. By 1990, 45,000 members of the Union of Evangelical Churches were worshipping in over 600 churches. The story of his efforts is told in *Ripening Fruit*. He died of heart failure.

Jacob C. Kunzmann

Dec. 31, 1852
Baushclott, Germany

Oct. 31, 1941
Seattle, Washington

President of Pacific (Lutheran in 1952) **Theological Seminary Seattle, WA** (Berkeley, CA closed in 1932 and reopened in 1952), **1919–32**. Kunzmann was educated at Thiel, Greenville, PA (1875) and in Philadelphia (1878). He was ordained by the Pittsburgh Synod in June, 1878. That same year, he married Anna Mathay on June 20th, and they had six children. He pastored in Greensburg, PA (1881–92) and Pittsburgh, PA (1892–99). He was the superintendent of English Missions General Council of the Lutheran Church, 1899–1918.

Frederick J. F. Jackson

Aug. 10, 1855
Ipswich, England

Dec. 1, 1941
Englewood, New Jersey

Anglican theologian and church historian. Jackson was the curate of Ottershaw (1879–81); of St. Charles, Cambridge (1882–84); and of St. Botolph, Cambridge (1884–90). He was a tutor in 1882 and dean, 1895–1916 at Jesus College, Cambridge. He married Anna M. Everett in October 1895 (died: 1931) and Clara Fawcett in 1932. Jackson was a professor in Christian institutions such as Union Theological Seminary in New York City from 1916–34. Jackson's writings range from *History of the Christian Church* (1891) to *History of Church Historians* (1939).

L. Franklin Gruber

May 13, 1870
near Reading, Pennsylvania

Dec. 5, 1941
Maywood, Illinois

President of Chicago Lutheran Theological Seminary (Lutheran School of Theology, Chicago in 1964), **Maywood, IL 1926–41**. Gruber was ordained in 1901 and married Amelia Hoehn on October 7, 1902. He pastored at the Church of Holy Communion, Utica, NY (1902–8); at St. Mark's Church, Minneapolis, MN (1908–14); and at the Church of the Reformation, St. Paul, MN (1914–27). Gruber was also a professor of theology and author of several books.

Paul S. Leinbach

Sept. 21, 1874
Womelsdorf, Pennsylvania

Dec. 7, 1941
Philadelphia, Pennsylvania (?)

President of Associated Church Press, 1925–35. Leinbach married Belle Martin on May 26, 1898 (died: 1908), and Helen DeLong on August 2, 1910. He was ordained in the Reformed Church (1898) and served a pastorate (1917). He then worked as the editor of the *Reformed Church Messenger* (1917–41). In his later years, he was active in the Evangelical and Reformed Church circles. He was a Republican and a Mason.

Henry Ostrom

Sept. 19, 1862
Bellville, Ontario, Canada

Dec. 20, 1941
Chicago, Illinois

Hymn writer of the great song, "Is It the Crowning Day?" (music by CHARLES MARSH). A Methodist pastor, Ostrom was widely used as an evangelist, preaching in factories, mines, theatres, and colleges. He lived in Chicago and was on the extension staff of Moody Bible Institute from 1921 on. He used the alias, G. W. Whitcomb, for his hymn-writing signature. His works included *Out of the Cain Life* (1896), *Replete Religion, The Dearest Psalm, Greatness* (1904), *Crisis in Church Work* (1908), and *The Law of Prayer* (1910).

Cortland Myers

June 3, 1864
Kingston, New York

Dec. 26, 1941
Los Angeles, California (?)

Strong Baptist fundamentalist. Myers married Jennie Williams on July 8, 1890. He pastored First Baptist Church of Syracuse, NY (1890–93); First Baptist (later Baptist Temple) of Brooklyn (1893–1909); Tremont Temple, Boston (1909–21); and Immanuel Baptist, Pasadena, CA from 1921 on. He was known for his outspoken criticism of liberalism. Myers was active in the World's Christian Fundamentalist Association and signed the call for the preconvention meeting on Baptist fundamentals in Buffalo, NY in 1920, speaking on "Things not Shaken." His writings range from *Making a Life* (1899) to *The Fact of a Future Life* (1931).

Enoch E. Byrum

Oct. 13, 1861
near Union City, Indiana

Jan. 5, 1942
Anderson, Indiana

Editor of Gospel Trumpet (Vital Christianity) **and leader of Church of God, Anderson, IN 1896–1916.** Ordained in 1892, he toured the world in 1904, examining ancient manuscripts of the Bible. Byrum married Lucena Beardslee on October 1, 1908. He wrote extensively; his first work was *The Boy's Companion* (1890) and the last *How We Got Our Bible* (1905).

Andrew C. Zenos

Aug. 13, 1855
Constantinople, Turkey

Jan. 25, 1942
Chicago, Illinois

Presbyterian theologian. Zenos married Ruth Schlager on October 11, 1882. He pastored at Brandt, PA (1881–83); was professor of Greek at Lake Forest (IL) University (1883–88); taught New Testament exegesis at Hartford (CT) Theological Seminary (1888–91); was professor of church history at McCormick Theological Seminary, Chicago (1891–94); and was professor of Biblical theology there (1894–1932). His writings range from *Elements of Higher Criticism* (1895) to *Presbyterianism in America* (1937).

George A. Smith

Oct. 19, 1856
Calcutta, India

March 3, 1942
Balerno, Scotland

Scottish Biblical scholar and preacher, who helped establish higher criticism of the Old Testament. After traveling in Egypt and Syria, Smith pastored Queen's Cross Free Church in Aberdeen, Scotland, 1882–92. He was then appointed professor of Old Testament languages, literature, and theology at the United Free Church College of Glasgow (1892–1909) and was principal of Aberdeen University (1909–35). His books ranged from *Book of Isaiah* (2 vols., 1888–90) to *Jeremiah* (1923).

Henry J. Zelley

March 15, 1859
Mount Holly, New Jersey

March 16, 1942
Trenton, New Jersey

Writer of the lyrics for "Heavenly Sunlight" (1899) (music by GEORGE COOK) **and "He Brought Me Out"** (music by H. L. GILMOUR). Zelley served more than 50 years as a Methodist minister in New Jersey, ministering at 19 churches before retiring in 1929. More than 1,500 hymns came from his pen. Zelley attended Pennington (NJ) Seminary and Taylor University, Upland, IN.

Henry C. Morrison

March 10, 1857
Bedford, Kentucky

March 24, 1942
Elizabethton, Tennessee

Evangelist, founder and first president of Asbury Theological Seminary, 1923–42, and president of Asbury College, Wilmore, KY 1910–25, 1933–40. Converted at age 13, via a revival meeting in a Methodist South service in Glasgow, KY, Morrison was ordained a Methodist. Early on, he pastored in the following Kentucky towns: Bedford, Stamford, Covington, and Highland. Morrison was an outstanding evangelist who held over 1,200 revivals with thousands of converts, 1890–1910. He married Laura Bain on June 20, 1888 (died: November 29, 1893); Geneva Pedlar on April 9, 1895 (died: March 23, 1914); and Bettie Whitehead on February 17, 1916 (died: 1945). He was president of Pentecostal Publishing Company and edited the *Pentecostal Herald* (1890–1925). He wrote 25 books. The Holiness churches were replacing Methodism as the key supporter of Asbury in the last half of the twentieth century. He traveled 500,000 miles and preached 15,000 times. The day before he died from a weakened heart caused by asthma, he preached on "How to Win Sinners to Christ" at a revival.

Annie S. Murphy

March 30, 1942
Burbank, California

Writer of lyrics and music to "Constantly Abiding" (1908). Annie was married to Will K. Murphy, who had a successful pottery business in Ohio. She used her wealth and influence for God, singing and speaking in different places. Around 1929, her husband died, stripping her of her wealth. Having lost all her earthly possessions in the Depression years, she lived with relatives in Burbank, CA. PHIL KERR visited her shortly before her death.

Walter C. Woodward

Nov. 28, 1878
near Mooresville, Indiana

April 14, 1942
Richmond, Indiana

General secretary of Friends United Meeting, Richmond, IN 1919–42. Woodward married Catherine Hartman on September 18, 1912. He taught at Pacific College, Forest Grove, OR (1906–7) and at Earlham College, Richmond (1910–15). He was editor of *The American Friends* from 1917 on. His writings were from *History of Political Parties in Oregon* (1913) to *Timothy Nicholson, Master Quaker* (1927.)

John D. Jones

April 13, 1865
Ruthin, Wales

April 19, 1942

Beloved pastor in Bournemouth, England, 1898–37. In 1889, Jones began his ministry at Newland Church in England and was married in July of that same year. After ten years, he began his lifetime work in 1898, at Richmond Hill Congregational Church (1,100 members), Bournemouth. He ministered there until retiring, June 6, 1937. In 1899, he first visited the US and met MOODY shortly before the latter's death. In July, 1917, his wife died, and in 1923, his only son died in

Gold Coast, Africa. In September, 1933, he remarried. He wrote *If a Man Die* the year following his first wife's death. He retired to Wales in 1937. His tombstone in Bournemouth reads, "John Daniel Jones, Preacher of the Gospel. Simply to Thy Cross I Cling."

Zebarney T. Phillips

May 1, 1875
Springfield, Ohio

May 10, 1942
Washington, D.C

Chaplain of the U.S. Senate, 1927–42. Phillips married Sallie Winston, in September, 1906. He was ordained a priest in the Protestant Episcopal Church in 1900. He was rector of Church of Our Savior, Cincinnati (1901–02); of Trinity Church, Chicago (1902–9); at Oxford, England (1909–11); of St. Peter's Church, St. Louis (1912–22); of Church of the Saviour, Philadelphia (1922–24); of Epiphany Church, Washington D.C. (1924–41); then dean of Washington Cathedral, 1941 on.

Samuel P. Matheson

Sept. 20, 1852
Kildonan, Manitoba, Canada

May 19, 1942
Winnipeg, Manitoba, Canada

Primate of the Anglican Church of Canada, 1909–30. He was consecrated a bishop in 1903 at the Holy Trinity Church, Winnipeg. In 1905, Matheson became lord archbishop and metropolitan of Rupert's Land (territory of the Hudson's Bay Company, northern Canada, which was later Manitoba). He was ordained a deacon (1875) and a priest (1876) of St. John's Cathedral in Winnipeg, Manitoba, of which he later became a canon, 1882–1902. At the same time, Matheson was a professor of theology at St. John's College, 1882–1906.

Rosalind Bell-Smith Goforth

May 6, 1864
London, England

May 31, 1942
Toronto, Ontario, Canada (?)

Missionary leader, wife of Jonathan Goforth. Rosalind came to Montreal, Quebec, in 1867 and was converted at age twelve. In 1885, she graduated from the Toronto School of Art and began preparing to leave for London for more studies. On a scenic boat trip to Niagara Falls, she met "a city missionary," who was wearing shabby clothes but "had a wonderful challenge in his eyes." They were married on October 25, 1887, and soon sailed to China. They labored in Honan, where they trained hundreds of Chinese pastors and evangelists. In 1900, both barely escaped during the Boxer Rebellion. They went to Korea (1907) and Manchuria (1925). Five of their eleven children died in infancy or early childhood. She wrote *Goforth of China* (1937).

Emily Divine Wilson

May 24, 1865
Philadelphia, Pennsylvania

June 23, 1942
Philadelphia, Pennsylvania

Writer of lyrics and music for "I Will Pilot Thee," and composed music for "When We All Get to Heaven," 1898 (music by Eliza Hewitt). Emily lived in Philadelphia all her life and married John G. Wilson in 1887. He was a Methodist pastor of Wharton Memorial Church at the time of his death on August 2, 1933. She was musical and had dramatic art ability.

George A. Barton

Nov. 12, 1859
Farnham, Quebec, Canada

June 28, 1942
Weston, Massachusetts

Biblical and Semitics scholar. Barton was a minister of the Society of Friends, 1879–1918, before he was ordained an Episcopalian. He married Caroline Danforth on June 26, 1884 (died: May 30, 1930), and Katherine Hagy on June 6, 1931. He was professor of Semitic languages and biblical literature at Bryn Mawr (PA) College (1891–1922); professor of Semitic languages and history of religions at the University of Pennsylvania (1922–32); and professor of New Testament literature and language at Divinity School of the Protestant Episcopal Church in Philadelphia, PA (1921–37). Barton's writings range from *The Religious Use of the Bible* (1900) to *The Apostolic Age and the New Testament* (1936).

Edmund S. Lorenz

July 13, 1854
North Lawrence, Ohio

July 10, 1942
Dayton, Ohio

Composer, publisher of the music for many hymns such as, "Tell It to Jesus," 1888 (lyrics by J. RANKIN), **"The Name of Jesus," 1901** (lyrics by W. C. Martin), **and "I Want My Life to Tell for Jesus."** Lorenz was a preacher, editor, composer, and author. He and Florence Kumler married on October 1, 1878. He pastored a United Brethren church, Dalton, OH (1884–86) and then served two years as a president of Lebanon Valley College, Annville, PA (1886–88). Lorenz launched Lorenz Publishing Company in Dayton in 1890, which later grew into a big business.

Marcus O. Bockman

Jan. 9, 1849
Langesund, Norway

July 21, 1942
Minneapolis, Minnesota

President of the United Norwegian Lutheran Seminary in Minneapolis, 1890–1902, St. Paul, MN 1902–17 (as a result of a merger with the Hague Seminary of Red Wing, MN in 1917), **and of Luther** (Luther-Northwestern in 1982) **Seminary, St. Paul, 1917–30.** In 1875, Bockman came to America and married Leonharda Holby in 1875 (died: 1888) and then Inga Holby in 1896 (died: 1937). Bockman pastored near Kenyon, MN (1875–86); was professor of theology at St. Olaf College in Northfield, MN (1886–90); and pastored at St. Anthony Park, MN (1902–15). His death resulted from infection of a broken hip from a fall.

W. M. Flinders Petrie

June 3, 1853
Charlton, Kent, England

July 28, 1942
Jerusalem, Palestine

World authority on archaeology, with strong credentials as an Egyptologist. Petrie's interest began (1874) and was brought to fruition (1880) when he began excavations of the utmost importance in Egypt. The excavating extended until 1924 and uncovered many valuable historical records. Petrie was a deeply religious man, whose excavations in Palestine, 1926–38 were motivated by a desire to expand the knowledge of biblically recorded events. Petrie authored over 75 volumes, beginning in 1880 with *Stonehenge*. He became professor of Egyptology at University College, London, 1892–1933. He followed in the footsteps of his maternal grandfather, Mathew Flinders, famed explorer in Australia.

Muallah M. Sa'eed

June 1, 1863
Iran

July 29, 1942

A Kurdish doctor, outstanding Moslem convert to Christianity. Very few Mohammedans are converted and have a vast outreach to their own people. Here is one. Muallah was an Islamic teacher and priest from the caucasian Kurdish tribe. The more Muallah taught the Koran, the more its errors were revealed to him. At age 18, while comparing the Koran to the Bible, he was converted. He was banished from his home with his brother seeking to kill him. He studied in England, became an outstanding physician, and continued to witness wherever he went. Years later, he was invited to be court physician by the Shah of Iran.

Johannes A. Hultman

July 6, 1861
Hjartlanda, Sweden

Aug. 7, 1942
Glendale, California

Composed music for "Thanks to God" (lyrics by August Storm). Hultman came to America in 1869. He first pastored in Fridhem, NE, and then served as music director at Douglas Park Covenant Church in Chicago, 1879–81. Next, he traveled as an evangelist, pastoring, and sharing his musical abilities. Hultman was known as "The Sunshine Singer." After pastoring at the Salem Square Church in Worcester, MA, he moved back to Sweden in 1909.

Leslie M. Anglin

Feb. 23, 1882
Stewart County, Georgia

Sept. 5, 1942
Taian, China

Founder and first president of Home of Onesiphorus (Kids Alive Int. in 1983), **1916–27**. Anglin married his wife, Ava (July 28, 1884 – Sept. 28, 1952) on July 18, 1904. They went to China as missionaries in November, 1910. In 1916, he started the ministry with a widow and five children. He returned to America in 1937 and brought with him Samuel Hsiao. Upon returning to China after his furlough, he was imprisoned due to WWII conflicts. He died in a concentration camp.

Wilson Carlile

Jan. 14, 1847
Brixton, London, England

Sept. 26, 1942
Woking, England

Layman who founded the Church Army, after a career in business. A business failure in 1873 led to his conversion and pastoring. Carlile was ordained by the Anglican Church in 1880, at age 33, to pastor a Kensington parish. In 1882, he founded and led the Church Army to work in the slums, do open-air evangelism, and train lay preachers until his death 60 years later. He was rector of St. Mary-at-Hill, London, 1892–1926. He wrote from *The Church and Conversion* (1882) to *Baptism of Fire* (1907).

George O. Webster

April 25, 1866
Washington County, New York

Oct. 1, 1942
Essex, New York

Writer of the lyrics for "I Need Jesus," (music by Charles Gabriel) **and "Love Led Him to Calvary."** Webster was the son of a Baptist preacher and was converted at age 21. He was ordained a Baptist and served in Vermont and Indiana before going to Essex, where he pastored the Federated church for the last 18 years of his life. In 1923, at age 47, he rededicated his life with the thought, "How much I need Jesus." He wrote some 2,000 hymns. I. H. Meredith conducted his funeral.

John H. W. Cook

June 20, 1873
Wandiligong, Victoria, Australia

Oct. 3, 1942
Toronto, Ontario, Canada

General secretary of Evangelical Union of South America (NA section, Avant Ministries in 2004), **1928–42**, which merged to become part of the Gospel Missionary Union in 1975. Cook went to Argentina in 1899. His fiance, Miss Perry (1876–1970), arrived in 1901 and they were married in January. Cook served there until 1928, during which time he started an orphanage in Tres Arroyos. They then went to Toronto to head the work in 1929.

Wilbur G. Voliva

March 10, 1870
near Newton, Indiana

Oct. 11, 1942
Chicago, Illinois

General overseer of the Christian Catholic (Christ Community in 1995) **Church, Zion, IL, 1907–42.** Voliva was associated for four years with the Christian Church and was ordained through the Christian Connection (New Light) in 1889. Mollie Steele became his wife on August11, 1892. He held pastorates in Indiana, Illinois, New York, Maine, and Ohio, 1889–99. He also was overseer in Australia, 1901–06. Upon John Dowie's death in 1907 (the movement's founder), Voliva inherited the leadership of the CCC.

Samuel A. Bill

1863
Belfast, Northern Ireland

Oct. 18, 1942
Iuro, Nigeria

Missionary to Nigeria. The Qua Iboe Church is a thriving, indigenous African Church in southeast Nigeria because of Bill, who without backing of a mission or money, went alone in 1887 to face life among an unknown tribe in a vast area of dense forest, swamps, and treacherous rivers. Ten years earlier, MARY SLESSOR had come to Calabar. Bill went inland up the Qua Iboe River to the village of Ibuno, where he slowly began to share the gospel to the animists. He worked among the Efik-speaking people, in spite of weekly bouts of fever. Soon 100 were attending a weekly meeting. A friend joined him in 1888. In 1890 he returned to Belfast to marry Grace Kerr, bringing her back to Ibuno. They built a church housing the 300 members. He is buried with his wife, Gracie, on the bank of the Qua Iboe River. A hospital was opened at Etinan in tribute to this man and his vision.

Andrew C. Craft

1871
Georgia

October 18, 1942
Toccoa, Georgia

General moderator of Pentecostal Fire–Baptized Holiness Church, LaGrange, GA 1918–38. Craft was converted in early August, 1883, in an old log Methodist church near the banks of the Savannah River. His wife, Susan, lived 1874–1968. From about 1901–11 he was in evangelistic and mission work in the town of Toccoa, GA. In October, 1911, he founded the Toccoa Orphanage which cared for some 1,500 children in its first 30 years. He was the General State Secretary for the PHC from 1911–14. In 1942 they turned the work over to the state.

Peter C. Nelson

Jan. 28, 1868
Elehoise, Denmark

Oct. 24, 1942
Fort Worth, Texas

First president of Southwestern Assemblies of God College, Enid, OK 1927–42. Nelson came to America in 1872 and married Myrtle Garmong on June 16, 1893. He was converted around age 20 in Harlan, IA, via a visiting minister. Nelson became a Baptist pastor, evangelist, and YMCA worker in the 1910s. From 1920–27, he served as a Pentecostal evangelist. In 1927, Nelson went to Enid, OK, where he founded a church, opened Southwestern Bible School, and became affiliated with the Assembly of God movement. A year after his death, the school was moved to Waxahachie, TX.

Reuben A. (Bud) Robinson

Jan. 27, 1860
White County, Tennessee

Nov. 2, 1942
Pasadena, California

Nazarene evangelist, a colorful and well-known personality. Robinson was an evangelist of great magnitude. In private, he often stuttered but never when he preached. Robinson was converted on August 1, 1880, via a Methodist evangelist at a Texas camp meeting near Peniel. He married Sallie Harper on January 10, 1893. From 1895 until his death, he was an evangelist. Robinson saw over 100,000 people saved, preached over 33,000 sermons, and gave over $85,000 to Christian education. On September 8, 1942, he became ill and was confined to his home until his death.

Cecil A. Dye

May 1, 1909   c late 1942
Fort Wayne, Indiana   Bolivia

Martyr. Dye was one of five missionaries martyred in the jungles of Bolivia by the Ayores, a native tribe never before contacted by white people. The others who shared the same fate were his brother Bob Dye, George Hosbach, Dave Bacon, and Eldon Hunter. In 1937, Cecil Dye felt led to start a church in Saginaw, MI. It began September 18 of that year. In early 1938, he left the Chrysler Corporation to be full-time. By September, 1939, a new building was built and the name of the church changed from Fifth Ave. Baptist to Saginaw Bible Tabernacle. January of 1940 saw the birth of a youth outreach called the Cloud Club. From this club, in 1942, eight young men, including the pastor, and two young women felt God's call to Bolivia. Meanwhile, the church had grown from six to 352. These missionaries left New Orleans in November, 1942, and hoped to reach the Ayores. The five men left Santa Cruz (or Robore) never to be seen again. One widow, Jean Dye (Bob's wife), wrote the book, *God Planted Five Seeds*. Cecil's wife was Dorothy. Later, she married Larry Johnson of New Tribes Mission. Three of the killers later accepted Christ and in 1983, the New Testament was available in the Ayore language. His martyrdom gave birth to New Tribes Mission.

Roland V. Bingham

Dec. 19, 1872   Dec. 8, 1942
East Grinstead, England   Toronto, Ontario, Canada

First director of Sudan Interior Mission (SIM Int.), 1893–1942. Bingham was converted at age 15 at a Salvation Army meeting in his hometown and came to Canada in 1889, burdened for Africa. Bingham joined the Salvation Army in 1890. In 1892, he dedicated his life to missions via A. J. GORDON's ministry. He was ordained a Baptist. With no support, Bingham sailed on Nov. 4, 1893 to Lagos, Nigeria, with WALTER GOWANS and Tom Kent, both of whom died in 1894. Bingham returned to America in 1896 and married Helen Blair on May 24, 1898 (died: Nov. 1960). In 1898, he organized a mission council (SIM Board) to recruit candidates. He went back to Africa briefly in 1900 (second failed attempt to open Sudan) and again in 1914. In 1901, the first mission station opened in Patigi, Nigeria. From 1922–28, Bingham went around the world sharing his burden for Africa with others. He also founded Evangelical Publishers (1912) and Canadian Keswick Bible Conference (1924). By his death, SIM had 400 missionaries. He was long-time editor of the *Evangelical Christian* (1904–42). He wrote an account of his work and was stricken a few days later, lapsing into a coma on December 4. His funeral was at Cooke's Presbyterian Church.

E. Howard Cadle

Aug. 25, 1884   Dec. 20, 1942
Fredricksburg, Indiana   Indianapolis, Indiana

Pastor of the largest church in America of his era, Cadle Tabernacle, Indianapolis, IN. On Christmas Day, 1908, Cadle married Ola Collier. He was converted on March 14, 1914, in the home of his parents, leaving behind a life of alcoholism, gambling, and racketeering. Soon after leaving the temptations of the street, he went into the car business, shoe repair business and was very successful. Cadle invited GYPSY SMITH to Indianapolis for a crusade in 1919. Soon he built a 10,000-seat tabernacle in 1921, with a 1,400-seat choir loft to be used for revival and evangelism. He dedicated these in honor of his praying mother. In a dispute, he lost the tabernacle in 1923, but bought it back from the bank in

1931. His radio program, *The Nation's Family Prayer Period*, moved to WLW, Cincinnati, in 1932. It became the first daily religious broadcast on radio and was widely listened to nationally. Some 600 small churches in rural Appalachia considered him their pastor. His tabernacle was razed in 1968. He died of Bright's disease (class of water-soluble, proteins in the urine, and heightened blood pressure; a disease named after Richard Bright, 1789–1898 an English physician.)

Edgar J. Helms

Jan. 19, 1863
Malone, New York

Dec. 23, 1942
Watertown, Massachusetts (?)

Founder of Goodwill Industries, 1919. This is a nationwide and international employment center for handicapped people that sells about anything. Helms also founded the Hull Street Mission in Boston (1892), was superintendent of the Boston City Missionary Society, 1893–95 and professor of evangelism at Boston University School for Theology (1916). He married Eugenia Preston on June 12, 1892 (died: 1899). He then married Grace Preston on August 11, 1901. He was part of the New England Conference of Methodists from 1895–1942. Helms lived in Boston. Goodwill Industries was a home missions project of the Methodist Church. His favorite Bible verse was John 6:12.

George W. Carver

Jan. 4, 1860
near Diamond Grove, Missouri

Jan. 5, 1943
Tuskegee, Alabama

Educator and scientist of great proportions. Carver was born into slavery and orphaned before he could walk. Plagued by prejudice and ill health, he became one of the most remarkable human beings who ever lived…a benefactor of all mankind. He was converted as a teenager through the Seymour family, which he stayed with in Olathe, KS. In 1891, he studied piano and art at Simpson College (IA). In 1896, he journeyed from Iowa State (with a masters degree in agriculture and bacterial botany) to join BOOKER T. WASHINGTON at Tuskegee Institute (AL), staying 47 years. He produced over 300 new uses for the peanut and over 100 for the sweet potato and soybean. He used flour, milk, and peanuts for over 500 different dyes. Early on, he toured as a pianist to raise funds for the institute and later, his paintings received world-wide praise. He was the friend of three presidents. In 1921, he spoke before the U.S. House of Representatives regarding a tariff on peanuts. He had an enduring faith in God, was an ardent Presbyterian and never married. When lauded for his contribution to his race, he said, "I am only God's helper…I am certain He has not had in mind any particular race, but the needs of all humanity." Responding to racial slurs, his axiom: "Fighting hatred back at ignorance is an exercise in uselessness." His favorite Bible verses were Proverbs 3:5, 6 and Philippians 4:13.

Howard A. Kelly

Feb. 20, 1858
Camden, New Jersey

Jan. 12, 1943
Baltimore, Maryland

Episcopalian surgeon and gynecologist who joined the medical staff of Johns Hopkins Hospital, Baltimore, MD, from 1889–1919. Kelly was given nine children by his wife Laetitia Bredlow, whom he married on June 27, 1889. He founded the Howard A. Kelly Hospital, Baltimore, in 1892. Kelly pioneered medical research in using radium to treat cancer. He wrote over 500 scientific articles on his medical findings and about his Christian faith, which began early in a Christian home.

Albert W. Beaven

Oct. 21, 1882
Moscow, Idaho

Jan. 24, 1943
Rochester, New York

President of Federal Council of Churches (NCC in 1950), **1932–34; of Association of Theological Schools, 1940–42; and of Colgate-Rochester (NY) Divinity School, 1929–43**. In 1908, he was ordained a Baptist.

Beaven pastored Lake Avenue Baptist Church, Rochester, NY from 1909–29. Beaven married Grace Haddow on June 23, 1909 (died: April 15, 1938) and Marion Barbour on May 27, 1939. His writings range from *Living Together* (1926) to *Remaking Life* (1940).

Mary Reed

Dec. 4, 1854
Lowell, Ohio

April 1943
Chandag Heights, India

Missionary to the lepers at Chandag, India. Mary was converted at age 16. She arrived in India in 1885, commissioned by the Methodist Episcopal Church Missionary Society. As she began to teach and evangelize Hindu women, her health failed her. In 1890, her leprosy forced her to take a furlough. By a miracle, her leprosy was arrested, making it possible for her to minister to lepers in India for a total of 52 years, from 1891 on. She worked exclusively in the hills of eastern Kumaun. In 1898, she severed her ties with Womens Foreign Missionary Society to work full-time with lepers. By then, 67 of her 85 lepers in the colony were Christians. Mary died from an accident due to her failing eyesight.

David W. Myland

1858
Canada (near Cleveland, Ohio)

April 8, 1943
Columbus, Ohio

Pentecostal minister, evangelis, and educator. Myland grew up in Cleveland, OH, and was associated with Methodism. Having experienced healing, he joined the CMA in 1890. In 1912, when CMA parted with the Pentecostal movement, Myland stayed with the latter. He founded the Ebenezer Bible Institute, Chicago (1915–18), and then taught at Beulah Heights Bible Institute, Atlanta, GA (1918–20). Over the next 23 years, he pastored churches in Pennsylvania, Michigan, and Ohio. He produced a hymnbook including some of his own hymns. The Latter Rain theology, central to early Pentecostalism was responsible for a short-lived movement in the late 1940s. Myland owes at least some of its success to his 1910 book on the subject.

Thomas W. Currie

Jan. 23, 1879
Durango, Texas

April 22, 1943
Tempe, Texas

President of Austin (TX) Presbyterian Theological Seminary, 1922–43. Currie married Jeanette Roe on August 26, 1913. He began to teach Bible at Austin in 1911, and once he became president, also taught church history. Currie was active in YMCA work during WWI. He was also a Mason and was involved in many ecumenical endeavors. Currie pastored Highland Park Presbyterian Church of Dallas, 1932–37, perhaps on a seasonal basis. He developed Bible extension courses for the University of Texas. He wrote *Studies in the Psalms*.

Allen E. Cross

Dec. 30, 1864
Manchester, New Hampshire

April 23, 1943
Manchester, New Hampshire

Congregational hymn writer and pastor. Ordained on December 29, 1892, Cross served the following churches in Massachusetts: Cliftondale (1891–96); Park Church, Springfield (1896–1901); was associate at Old South Church, Boston (1901–11); and then pastored at Milford (1914–25). He wrote two books and 17 hymns, which included "Jesus, Kneel Beside Me" and "America, the Shouts of War Shall Cease."

William Aberhart

Dec. 30, 1878
near Seaforth, Ontario, Canada

May 23, 1943
Vancouver, British Columbia, Canada

Canadian political leader and Baptist lay preacher. Aberhart married in 1902. He was a teacher (1906–14) and a high school principal (1915–35) at Crescent Heights High School in Calgary, AL. His Bible class at Westbourne Baptist Church evolved into Calgary Prophetic Bible Conference in 1918. His CP Bible Institute opened in 1925. He began a popular radio evangelistic ministry in 1926 called *The Radio Sunday School*, which was an outgrowth of his weekly classes that filled the Grand Theater. Aberhart was a strong dispensationalist and formed the Social Credit Party of Alberta, leading it to a resounding victory in the provincial elections of 1935. He became the premier of Alberta that year, and its attorney general in 1937. He was re-elected in 1940, and after his death, his most able pupil, ERNEST MANNING, carried on his Christian political leadership in Alberta. His main goal was to assist the recovery of the farmers.

Terrot R. Glover

July 23, 1869
Bristol, England

May 26, 1943
Cambridge, England

Baptist scholar. Glover married a lady named Alice in 1897. He was a professor of Latin at Queen's University, Kingston, Canada (1896–1901); classic lecturer at St. John's College (1901–11); ancient history lecturer (1911–39); public orator at the University of Cambridge (1920–39); and a guest professor at the University of California in 1923. Glover served as president of Baptist Union of Great Britain and Ireland in 1924. His writings focused on the classical era and the events of early Christianity. His writings range from *Studies in Vercek* (1904) to *Cambridge Retrospect* (1943).

Juregen L. Neve

June 7, 1865
Schleswig, Germany

Aug. 12, 1943
Springfield, Ohio

Lutheran theologian and Church historian. Neve married Martha Flemming (August 23, 1895) and Charlotte Mangelsdorf (Aug. 31, 1935). He served as professor of church history at Chicago Theological Seminary (1887–92); Western Theological Seminary, Atchinson, KS (1898–1909); and at Hamma Divinity School, Springfield, OH (1909–43), where he taught doctrinal history. His writings range from *Free Church vs. State Church* (1900) to *History of Christian Thought* (1943).

William A. Matthews

April 6, 1868
Rowley Regis, England

Aug. 18, 1943
Los Angeles, California

Founder and first president of Los Angeles Baptist College (Northwest Baptist Seminary, Tacoma, WA, in 1974), **1927–43**. Matthews served the first twelve years without remuneration. The school met in Calvary Baptist Church for many years. Matthews married Della Burton in Alton, IL on June 22, 1892. He was ordained a Baptist in 1891 and pastored in St. Louis and in several Illinois towns, including Carbondale, Cambridge, Paw Paw, Aurora, and at Tabernacle Church, Chicago, until 1911. Matthews was president of Ewing College, 1911–13, and pastored in Dinuba and Los Angeles, CA, until 1927.

William Paton

Nov. 13, 1886
London, England

Aug. 21, 1943
Kendal, England

Presbyterian minister and writer. Paton was converted in 1905. In 1911, he became secretary to the Student Christian Movement. He was in India, 1916–19. He became secretary of The International Missionary Council. He married Grace MacDonald (1911) who became a Catholic (1936). Paton's 1916 paperback, *Jesus Christ and* *the World's Religions,* sold over 50,000 copies. Paton was general secretary of the National Christian Council of India, Burma, and Ceylon, 1922–27. Paton authored several works on missions and edited the *International Review of Missions* for 16 years. He played a vital role in the formation of the WCC.

William L. Phelps

Jan. 2, 1865
New Haven, Connecticut

Aug. 21, 1943
New Haven, Connecticut

University professor at Yale and author. Phelps married Annabel Hubbard on December 21, 1892 (died: 1939). He began his lifelong association with Yale University in 1892, teaching English literature. He was a full professor, 1901–33, and received many honors for his scholarship. His writings range from *The Beginnings of the English Romantic Movement* (1893) to *The Children's Anthology* (1941). He was the son of SYLVANUS D. PHELPS.

Simone Weil

Feb. 3, 1909
Paris, France

Aug. 24, 1943
Ashford, England

Brilliant French Jewess, who, by choice, lived close to the impoverished laborers, sharing their work and life. She became profoundly Christian and close to Roman Catholicism, though never officially embracing that allegiance. Her *Waiting for God* reveals her mystical faith. Simone opposed the Spanish Civil War in 1936 and worked for the French Free government in London in 1942, refusing to eat more than the official ration in occupied France. Ravaged by pleurisy, she lived out her days in a sanitarium, where she died at age 34.

Charles D. Tillman

March 20, 1861
Tallassee, Alabama

Sept. 2, 1943
Atlanta, Georgia

Composer. Tillman composed the music for "Life's Railway to Heaven" (Abby), "My Mother's Bible" (Williams), "When I Get to the End of the Way" (Cole), and "Ready." He worked as a house painter, traveling salesman, and sang first tenor in a quartet. In 1887, he began his career as an evangelistic singer, and shortly thereafter, established a publishing company in Atlanta. In 1891, in Lexington, SC, he loaned a tent to a black revival meeting where "Old Time Religion," a song which he later published, was first heard.

Charles E. Byrer

July 10, 1870
Middlebranch, Ohio

Sept. 27, 1943
Columbus, Ohio

Dean of Bexley Hall Theological Seminary at Kenyon College [Colgate-Rochester (NY) Divinity School in 1968], **Gambier, OH 1926–40**. Byrer married Rose A. Bower on June 24, 1897. He was ordained as a deacon (1900) and a priest (1901) in the Episcopal Church. Byrer pastored in Cambridge, OH (1900–02); Mechanicsburg, OH (1902–5); at Church of the Good Shepherd, Columbus, OH (1905–10); and at Christ Church, Springfield, OH (1910–22). He served as a professor of church history at Kenyon, 1922–26.

Ambrose J. Tomlinson

Sept. 22, 1865
Westfield, Indiana

Oct. 2, 1943
Cleveland, Tennessee

Founder and first overseer of Church of God (and COG of Prophecy, Cleveland, TN), **1903–43, out of which several denominations developed**. On April 24, 1889, Tomlinson married Mary J. Taylor. Also converted in 1889, Tomlinson became a widely used Pentecostal evangelist who was called "Mr. Church of God." The name of the Church of God first appeared in 1907 when Tomlinson was moderating at a convention. He served as the group's overseer and missions head, 1900–43, establishing its headquarters in Cleveland, TN, in 1909. During this era, he also served as president of Lee College, 1918–22 which he founded in Cleveland, TN, also. Ambrose traveled extensively as an evangelist, starting many new churches. In 1923, a split (over giving Tomlinson unilateral authority) occurred in the Cleveland-based Church of God (which legally became the Church of God of Prophecy in 1952). Tomlinson fought for unity among his followers. His son, HOMER, carried on in the leadership of the original Church of God ministry. F. J. LEE became overseer of the split in 1923 (CG–Cleveland) and MILTON TOMLINSON, another son headed the CG of Prophecy in 1943.

Daniel Kauffman

June 20, 1865
Juniata, Pennsylvania

Jan. 6, 1944
near Parnell, Iowa

One of the great leaders of the Mennonite Church for some 40 years. Kauffman married in 1887 to Ota Bowlin (died: 1890). He was converted in 1890 under the preaching of J. S. Coffman. He became a bishop in 1896. He was a prime mover in the organization of the Mennonite General Conference, and served as its first moderator at age 33. In 1902, he married Mary C. Shank (1879–1968) and lived in Missouri, mostly at Bersailles, until 1909, when he moved to Scottdale, PA. His natural gift as a speaker, teacher, writer, and leader made him a dominant figure in the movement. At one time, he was a member of 22 committees and boards. Kauffman was president of Goshen (IN) College, 1922–23. He was the editor of the *Gospel Herald* (1908–43). His books range from *Manual of Bible Doctrine* (1898) to *The Devotional Side of Life* (1942). His closing months were spent in the Iowa home of his daughter.

Joseph E. Ramseyer

Feb. 7, 1869
New Hamburg, Ontario, Canada

Jan. 25, 1944
Fort Wayne, Indiana

Founder and first president of Ft. Wayne (IN) Bible College (Summit Christian College in 1990, Taylor University), **1912–44, and the Missionary Church Association, 1900–44**. Ramseyer was converted in 1885. In 1896, he was baptized by immersion at a CMA conference and excommunicated from the Defenseless Mennonites for following unacceptable holiness doctrines. He married Katherine Zeller on October 27, 1896 (died: July 31, 1899). He founded both of the above institutions in 1898, uniting people of vision from both the Defenseless Mennonites and the CMA. Ramseyer married Macy Garth on May 15, 1902. He had no children.

Cleland B. McAfee

Sept. 25, 1866
Ashley, Missouri

Feb. 4, 1944
Jaffrey, New Hampshire

Wrote lyrics and music for "Near to the Heart of God" (1901). McAfee married Harriet Brown on August 10, 1892. He was ordained a Presbyterian, taught at Park College, and pastored the College Church, Parkville, MO from 1891–1901. He pastored Forty-first Street (First) Church, Chicago, IL (1901–4), and then Lafayette Avenue Church, Brooklyn (1904–12). McAfee was professor of systematic theology at McCormick Theological Seminary (1912–30) and secretary of the Presbyterian Board of Foreign Missions (1930–36). Upon retiring to New Hampshire, he remained active by lecturing, preaching, teaching, and writing. He wrote several books.

Ernest C. Wareing

May 29, 1872
Volga, Indiana

Feb. 4, 1944
Chattanooga, Tennessee (?)

First president of Associated Church Press, 1919–24. Wareing married Mary Matlock on May 7, 1896. He was ordained into the Methodist ministry in 1901, and pastored in Indiana at Plainfield (1901–3), Williamsport (1903–8), Plymouth (1908–10), and Brazil (1910–12). He was the editor of the *Western Christian Advocate of Cincinnati* (1916–32). He pastored in Ft. Wayne, IN (1932–33) and Chattanooga, TN (1933–36). He was involved in many Methodist organizations and conferences. Wareing wrote works ranging from *Knights of the White Shield* (1906) to *The Other Shepherd*. He retired in Chattanooga.

John T. Manson

Aug. 30, 1861
New Haven, Connecticut

Feb. 21, 1944
New Haven, Connecticut

President of American Bible Society, 1934–44. Manson married Mrs. Frank Benedict on January 15, 1908 (died: July 4, 1919) and then Mrs. Frank Trowbridge on April 29, 1922. Manson was director of Niagara Alkali Company, Equitable Life Assurance Society of the U.S., and the Security Insurance Company. Manson retired in New Haven, CT, his hometown. He was a Presbyterian, a Republican, and a Mason.

John A. Ingham

Jan. 13, 1868
Meridian, New York

March 20, 1944
Leonia, New Jersey

Stated Clerk of Reformed Church in America, 1932–43. Ingham married Mary Stebbins on September 28, 1892. Ingham was ordained as a Presbyterian in 1892. His pastoring posts included Irvington-on-Hudson, NY (1894–1910) and the Second Reformed Church, New Brunswick, NJ (1910–20). He served on the denominational staff, 1920–32. Ingham lived in Leonia, NJ, had three children, and belonged to two fraternities.

Herbert L. Willett

May 5, 1864
Ionia, Michigan

March 27, 1944
Winter Park, Florida

Founder and first dean of Disciples Divinity House, Chicago, IL 1894–1921. Willett married Emma Price on January 4, 1888. He was ordained into the Disciples (Christian) Church in 1890. He pastored in Dayton, OH (1887–93) and was an instructor of Bible in Ann Arbor, MI (1893–94). Along with his leadership, he taught such subjects as Semitic languages, Oriental languages, and literature at the University of Chicago. He pastored the Memorial Church of Christ, Chicago, 1908–20; and Union Church, Kenilworth, IL from 1927 on. His books range from *Life and Teachings of Jesus* (1898) to *The Jew Through the Centuries* (1931).

A. B. T. Moore

May 1944

President of Gideons, 1909–17 and secretary, 1917–32. Moore led the Gideons through a period of great growth. He resigned in July, 1932 when overhead expenses had to be reduced because of the depression. Moore continued to edit the *Gideon* from Minneapolis, MN. He was from Cedar Rapids, IA and was a Presbyterian.

Richard Davidson

March 29, 1876
Ayr, Ontario, Canada

May 24, 1944
Toronto, Ontario, Canada

President of Emmanuel College of Victoria University, Toronto, 1932–43. Davidson was professor of Old Testament Studies, beginning 1928 and a member of the United Church of Canada. Edith Northwood became his wife on June 20, 1906. Davidson was associated with the ecumenical movement and the World Council of Churches. He was an associate professor at University College of Toronto (1906–10), and a professor at Knox College of Toronto (1910–28).

W. Renwick McChesney

July 7, 1871
near Wampun, Pennsylvania

June 13, 1944
Zenia, Ohio

President of Cedarville (OH) College, 1915–40. McChesney began teaching at Franklin College, Columbus, OH (1890) and then transferred to Cedarville (1894). He married Martha Morton on July 17, 1895 (died April 25, 1939), and Mary Turner on June 5, 1943. He was dean of the Reformed Presbyterian Seminary at Cedarville College. McChesney was also a widely used lecturer and was a Republican.

James Moffatt

July 4, 1870
Glasgow, Scotland

June 27, 1944
New York, New York

Presbyterian New Testament scholar, write, and Bible translator. On September 29, 1896, Moffat married Mary Reith. Moffatt held two pastorates in United Free churches: at Dundonald (1896–1907) and Broughty Ferry (1907–12). He served on the faculties of Mansfield College, Oxford (1911–15); the United Free Church College, Glasgow (1915–27); and the Union Theological Seminary, New York (1927–38) as professor of church history. He translated the New Testament (1913) and the Old Testament (1924), both from their original languages. Moffatt also edited a 17-volume *Commentary of the New Testament* (1928–49). *The Moffatt Bible* appeared in 1935. He wrote from *The Historical New Testament* (1901) to *The Books of the Prophets* (1939).

George W. Truett

May 6, 1867
Hayesville, North Carolina

July 7, 1944
Dallas, Texas

President of Southern Baptist Convention, 1927–29 and Baptist World Alliance, 1934–39. Truett was a renowned Southern Baptist Convention personality. In 1886, he was converted at a revival at Clay County in North Carolina and moved to Texas with his family in 1889. As a student at Baylor University, Waco, TX, Truett was credited with the fund-raising activities, from 1890–94, that contributed greatly to wiping out the University's debt of $92,000. He helped build the Cooperative Program. He married Josephine Jenkins on June 28, 1894. He pastored the great First Baptist Church of Dallas from 1897 until his death (47 years later), and watched the membership grow from 715 to 7,804. Over the years Truett took 19,531 members into his church. One source said 18,124 additions and 5,337 baptisms were recorded. *A Quest for Souls* was one of his major works. He preached in many world centers and left 14 volumes of his sermons.

William F. Anderson

April 22, 1860
Morgantown, Virginia (now West Virginia)

July 22, 1944
Kensico, New York

Bishop in the Methodist Episcopal Church, 1908–39 and in the Methodist Church, 1939–44. Anderson married Jennie Ketcham on June 9, 1887, and they had seven children. He pastored the Mott Avenue Church in New York City (1887–89). He pastored in Kingston, NY (1890–94); Washington Square, NY (1895–98); and Ossing, NY (1899–1904). He was the resident bishop of Chattanooga (1908–12), Cincinnati (1912–24), and Boston (1924–32). He also taught at Florida Southern College, Lakeland, 1937–41. Anderson made five trips abroad. He wrote two books. Funeral services were held in Christ Church, New York City.

Alfred G. Garr

July 23, 1873
Danville, Kentucky

July 23, 1944
Charlotte, North Carolina

Pentecostal missionary, evangelist, and pastor. While pastoring a small California church, Garr was the first white pastor to testify of his tongues experience on June 16, 1906. This occurred at the Azusa Street Mission. From 1906–11, he and his wife, Lillian Anderson (died: 1916), had a good ministry in India, Japan, and China. Garr later married Hanna Erickson in 1919 and traveled as an evangelist, 1919–30. He pastored in Charlotte, NC at the Garr Auditorium, 1930–44.

Wilbert W. White

Jan. 16, 1863
Ashland, Ohio

Aug. 12, 1944
New York City, New York

First president of Biblical Seminary of New York (New York Theological Seminary in 1969), **1900–40.** He married Ella Henderson on March 31, 1885, and was ordained in the Presbyterian Church that same year. White taught Old Testament Theology at Xenia (OH) Seminary (1890–95) and at Moody Bible Institute (1895–97). White wrote many books ranging from *Twelve Minor Prophets* (1894) to *How to Study* (1930).

John Sung

Sept. 27, 1901
Hong Chek, Hinghwa, China

Aug. 18, 1944
near Peking (Beijing), China

China's greatest evangelist, 1927–42. Converted in 1909 during the Hinghwa Revival, Sung came to the U.S. (1920) and graduated from Ohio Wesleyan University, Delaware, OH (1923). In 1926, he received his Ph.D. from Ohio State University, Columbus and entered Union Theological Seminary, NYC. His reaction to liberal theology there was so intense that he was confined to a mental hospital for six months. He returned to China in 1927. For three years, he served in his home area and then spent three years with the Bethel Band in Shanghai. Sung went to almost every province in China revitalizing the church. He had thousands of converts. Sung was seriously ill when he returned to Shanghai in January, 1940, retiring in 1942 because of bad health, suffering from cancer and tuberculosis. He was a Methodist.

Egbert W. Smith

Jan. 15, 1862
Greensboro, North Carolina

Aug. 25, 1944
Greensboro, North Carolina

Director of Presbyterian Church (PC USA in 1983) **in the United States Missions, 1912–32.** Mary Wallace became Smith's wife on April 15, 1891. He was involved in evangelism for the North Carolina Synod (1890–93); pastored the First Church of Greensboro, NC (1893–1905); and pastored the Second Church of Louisville, KY (1906–11). His writing ranged from *The Creed of Presbyterians* (1901) to *Christ and Latin America* (1935).

James H. Cannon Jr.

Nov. 13, 1864
Salisbury, Maryland

Sept. 6, 1944
Chicago, Illinois

Colorful and outspoken Methodist church bishop and temperance advocate, 1918–38. Cannon married Laural Bennett on August 1, 1888, who gave him nine children (died: 1928) and then Helen McCallum on July 15, 1930. He was active in the Anti–Saloon League (superintendent in Virginia), 1910–20 and helped promote the prohibition amendment in the U.S. Constitution. He was director of Lake Junaluska (NC) Conference (1911–19) and president of Blackstone (VA) Female Institute (1914–18). Cannon directed the work of missions in Mexico, Cuba, Brazil, and the Belgian Congo, 1918–34. Cannon's zealous views led him to oppose Alfred E. Smith in the 1928 elections. He claimed he did not shave for 25 years because of his hectic schedule. He visited Europe ten times.

Aimme Kennedy Semple McPherson

Oct. 9, 1890
near Ingersoll, Ontario, Canada

Sept. 27, 1944
Oakland, California

Founder and first president of Church of the Foursquare Gospel, 1923–44, and of Life Bible College, 1924–44. Aimme was converted at age 17, via a Pentecostal revival conducted by Robert Semple, whom she later married on August 12, 1908. He died of malaria on August 19, 1910, in Hong Kong, where they went as missionaries after her conversion. Next, Harold McPherson became her husband on October 24, 1911, whom she divorced in 1921 (died: 1968), and finally she wed David Hutton on September 13, 1931, divorcing in 1935. She began as an evangelist (1915) in Ontario and then moved to Los Angeles (1918). She pioneered a Christian radio station (1924) and established a network of stations (1932). Aimme was a sensational and successful revivalist who organized and built the 5,000-seat Angelus Temple in Los Angeles, where she headquartered, 1923–44. It grew to 66,000 members, baptizing more than 40,000. In 1926, she disappeared for 36 days until found in the desert in Mexico near Douglas, AZ. She claimed she was kidnapped. She claimed the gifts of healing and tongues. She collapsed and died suddenly in a hotel room after taking an overdose of sleeping tablets, ruled to be accidental, perhaps causing a heart attack. Her writings ranged from *The Bridal Call* (1915) to *This Is That*.

Joseph S. Flipper

Feb. 22, 1859
Atlanta, Georgia

Oct. 10, 1944
Atlanta, Georgia

Bishop of African Methodist Episcopal Church, 1908–44; senior bishop, 1936–44. Flipper was ordained in 1880 and lived in Atlanta, GA. He married Amanda Slater, on February 24, 1880 (died: December 24, 1918), then married Susie Erwin on April 14, 1922. Flipper pastored in Georgia, was dean of Turner Theological Seminary (1903–4), and president of Morris Brown College (1904–8), both in Atlanta. He was against wearing robes in services and having women preachers. Flipper traveled widely, preaching throughout the South.

Robert L. Moyer

Jan. 17, 1886
Montgomery, Pennsylvania

Oct. 16, 1944
Minneapolis, Minnesota

Dedicated associate of WILLIAM B. RILEY in FBC and school affairs in Minneapolis, 1927 on, succeeding RILEY in 1942, serving until his death in 1944. Moyer was converted May 13, 1912, in evangelistic meetings near Williamsport, PA. The text of the message was John 3:14. His first wife's name was Flora Rock, whom he married on August 4, 1915, and his second wife's name was Effie. He was an evangelist (1915–20), and then pastor of the First United Brethren Church in Minneapolis (1920–27). He was appointed dean of Northwestern Bible School in 1927. He died of nephritis (kidney disease). Moyer's first book was *Christ in Isaiah 53* (1936).

Henry P. Crowell

Jan. 27, 1855
Cleveland, Ohio

Oct. 23, 1944
Chicago, Illinois

Outstanding Presbyterian manufacturer and philanthropist who was responsible for much of the growth of Moody Bible Institute in Chicago. The famed campus building, Crowell Hall, was named in his behalf. Crowell was converted at age nine after his pastor, Dr. Hawks, spoke to him after the funeral of his father, Luther. He was influenced by MOODY's visit to Cleveland, 1873. He moved to North Dakota in 1878, where he farmed until 1881. He married Lillie Wick on June 29, 1882 (died: January 10, 1885) and then Susan Coleman on July 10, 1888. Crowell's business headquarters were at Ravenna, OH where he was president of Quaker Mill (1881–91), of American Cereal (1891–1944) and Quaker Oats (1922–42). He served at the same time as Moody Bible Institute's Chairman of the Board, 1902–45. He finally left the Presbyterian Church 1943, because of its liberal tendencies. He died as he sat down in a train seat on his way home. His biography entitled, *Breakfast Table Autocrat*, was written by R.E. DAY.

William Temple

Oct. 15, 1881
Exeter, England

Oct. 26, 1944
Westgate-on-Sea, Canterbury, England

Archbishop of Canterbury, 1942–44, and son of FREDERICK TEMPLE. Temple became prominent in English life through his interest in social work, economics, politics, and theology. He crusaded against slums, usury, dishonesty and greed in business. He was headmaster at Repton School (1910–14), rector of St. James, Picadilly, London (1914–18), and canon of Westminster (1919–21). He married Frances Anson in 1916. He later became bishop of Manchester (1921–29) and archbishop of York (1929–42). Temple laid the groundwork for the World Council of Churches. An ardent advocate of social reform and of international cooperation, Temple organized the interdenominational Conference on Christian Politics, Economics and Citizenship in Birmingham in 1924. In 1925 he became chairman of the Archbishops' Commission on Doctrine in the Church of England. He presided over the Malvern Conference on the application of Chrisitan principles to social reconstruction in 1941. He wrote from *The Faith and Modern Thought* (1915) to *The Church Looks Forward* (1944). He placed much importance on Jesus Christ and the need to proclaim Him.

Daniel W. Fooks

Feb. 13, 1874
near Paducah, Kentucky

Dec. 12, 1944
Paducah, Kentucky

Stated clerk of Cumberland Presbyterian Church, Memphis, TN 1915–44. Fooks married Maggie Rudolph on May 2, 1894, and was ordained in 1900. He pastored at First Church, Paducah, KY, in 1909, and First CPC, Nashville, TN, from 1915–24. In 1924, he made a survey of China for the denomination's Women's Board of Missions. Fooks was a superintendent of transportation, a financial agent, and secretary/treasurer of the Board of Trustees of the General Assembly of CPC. As stated clerk he traveled all over the bounds of the Church again and again, being in more homes and more CP Churches that any other minister in any period of the Church's history. He wrote many deeds and wills.

Tsurin P. Kanamori

1857
Kumamato, Japan

1945

Evangelist to Formosa, Korea, and Japan. In 1876, Kanamori and 40 youths formed the Kumamoto Band which founded the Congregational churches of Japan. Kanamori pastored a Congregational church in Okayama Province and taught theology at Doshisha College. In 1891, he became a liberal for 20 years. The death of his wife, after giving him nine children, caused him to return to the evangelical cause. He is best known for his three-hour sermon, "God, Sin, and Salvation." His evangelism efforts brought 50,000 conversions to Christ. *The Christian Belief* was his well-known booklet.

Robert (Ralph) E. Neighbor

August, 1872
Michigan

1945

Noted Bible teacher, missionary to Brazil under the Southern Baptists, and founder of a number of large churches. Neighbor pastored East Macon (GA) Baptist (1896–1901); Marue Baptist, Doublin, GA (1901–02); FBC Americus, GA (1902–06); FBC, Salisbury, NC (1906–08); Southside Baptist, Spartanburg, SC (1908–11); Tabernacle Baptist, Augusta, GA (1914–16); FBC, Elyria, Ohio (1919–25); Rader (Chicago Gospel) Tabernacle (1926–27); and Mount Pleasant Baptist in Vancouver, British Columbia (1930–31). In 1931, he went into Bible conference teaching and missionary endeavors. In Brazil, Neighbor went into the interior where white men had never gone. He translated the Scriptures, took the first printing press to Brazil, and printed the first Brazilian Bibles. He also ministered in the British Isles, Israel, and India. He wrote 99 books, three of which were poetry and two of songs. Titles were such as *The New Daily Devotional Volume*. As a pastor, he was known for his large prayer meeting attendances.

Vedanayagam S. Azariah

Aug. 17, 1874
Vellalanvilai, India

Jan. 1, 1945
Dornakal, India

First bishop of the Anglican Church in India. Starting in 1903, it was called the Indian Missionary Society of Tinnevelly. Azariah was married in 1898 to Ambu Samuel and had six children. He formed the National Missionary Society in 1905. Ordained a deacon (1909), he was appointed a bishop (1912). At Dornakal, as a bishop of the Church of England, he had six clergy and 8,000 Christians under him. Azariah then formed an independent ministry with a church body of over 100,000 members by 1930. The Cathedral of Dornakal was dedicated in his honor in 1939. After 33 years of work, he left a Christian community of over 400,000. He wrote books in Tamil, including *Christian Giving*.

Henry W. Frost

Jan. 7, 1858
Detroit, Michigan

Jan. 8, 1945
Morristown, New Jersey

First president of IFMA, 1917–27, which he founded. Frost married Abbie Ellinwood on September 12, 1883 and they had seven children. He was in the oil production business in Attica, NY from 1880–88, and ordained a Presbyterian in 1904. He was active in the work of the China Inland Mission, serving as its secretary (1889–93), and as its home director (1893–1919) in Philadelphia. He spoke at many Bible conferences. Frost's works range from *Heart Songs* (1917) to *Little Sermons from the Pentateuch* (1928).

John W. Goodwin

March 13, 1869
North Berwick, Maine

Jan. 26, 1945
Pasadena, California

General Superintendent of Church of the Nazarene, 1916–40. Goodwin married Bertha Billings on November 28, 1888. He was originally ordained in the Advent Christian Church on April 6, 1893; then pastored various churches, 1893–1905; joining the Nazarenes in 1905. He pastored in Pasadena, CA (1905–7); was district superintendent for the Nazarenes in Southern Caifornia (1908–11); pastored in Oakland, CA (1913–14); and then in San Diego, CA in 1915.

John F. Childs

Sept. 24, 1892
Middleton, Georgia

Feb. 16, 1945
Bethesda, Maryland

President of Central (SC) Wesleyan (Southern Wesleyan in 1994) **College, 1927–28, 1932–45**. Childs was a prominent member of the Wesleyan Methodist Church all of his life. He married Ethel Newton on August 22, 1926, and became a professor of Latin and Greek at CWC the same year, acting as president and treasurer in 1927. Childs died at age 52 at the National Naval Medical Center, following several months of declining health.

Eric Liddell

Jan. 16, 1902
Tientsin, China

Feb. 21, 1945
Wiesien, China

Possibly the most well-known Christian athlete of his time. Liddell was a Rugby football player, an Olympic champion, and world record-breaker in track. His story was made into a widely seen movie called *Chariots of Fire* (1981). He was born of missionary parents. Liddell went to Scotland at age five and was educated there. In 1923, he joined the Glasgow students' Evangelistic Union. In the 1924 Olympics in Paris he refused to run his normal 100-m. race because it was scheduled on Sunday. Instead he ran the 400-m. race and won the gold medal with a new world record of 47.6 seconds. Through the London Missionary Service, he left Scotland and went to Tsientsin, China, as a teacher, in 1925, at the Anglo-Chinese Christian College. On furlough in 1931, he was ordained a Congregationalist. Florence MacKenzie (1911–84) became his wife on March 27, 1934. In 1937, he left Tientsin for Siaochang to do rural work. When the oppression began in China in 1941, Liddell sent his family to safety in Canada. He and 1,800 others were interned by the Japanese in March 1943, in Weisien Internment Camp. He died there of a brain tumor and severe influenza.

Alfred E. Garvie

Aug. 28/29, 1861
Zyrardow, Poland

March 7, 1945

English Congregational minister and educator. Garvie held pastorates at Macduff (1893–95) and at Montrose (1895–1903). He was a professor at Hackney College and New College, London, 1903–07. He became principal of the latter (1907), and was principal of both (1924). Garvie embraced Lutheran theology. He was somewhat liberal and active in ecumenical endeavors. He wrote from *The Ethics of Temperance* (1895) to *Religious Education* (1906).

Henry W. Lohrenz

Feb. 2, 1878
Harvey County, Kansas

March 16, 1945
Hillsboro, Kansas

Founder and first president of Tabor College, Hillsboro, KS 1908–31 and General Secretary of Mennonite Brethren Missions Services, Hillsboro, KS 1919–36. Lohrenz began preaching in Ebenfeld, KS on January 6, 1904. During the Christmas holidays of 1906, Lohrenz sent his senior ring to Anna Friesen who later became his wife. His last years were spent teaching at the Corn Academy and Bible School, 1935–44. He was the first Mennonite to shape principles and policies giving unity and direction to the entire missionary operation.

David Lloyd-George

Jan. 17, 1863　　　　　　　　　　　　　　　　　　　　　　　　　　　　　　　　　March 26, 1945
Chorlton, Manchester, England　　　　　　　　　　　　　　　　　　　　　　　Llanystumdwy, Wales

British statesman and liberal member of Parliament for 54 years, beginning in 1890. Lloyd-George helped secure the passage of unemployment and sickness insurance legislation. He was Prime Minister of Britain, 1916–22, and played a principal role in the formulation of the Treaty of Versailles in 1919, which ended World War I and formed the League of Nations. He married Margaret Owen (c. 1863–January 20, 1941) in 1888 and Frances Stephenson, who was his secretary of 30 years, in 1943. He was a member of the Disciples/Church of Christ denomination, others say Baptist. He encouraged the disestablishment of the Church of England.

Harry Strachan

June 27, 1872　　　　　　　　　　　　　　　　　　　　　　　　　　　　　　　　　March 28, 1945
Fergus, Ontario, Canada　　　　　　　　　　　　　　　　　　　　　　　　　　San Jose, Costa Rica

First president of Latin American Mission, 1921–45. Strachan married Susan Beamish (1864–1950) on June 15, 1903. He was converted when the gospel was presented to him on the street. He joined the Free Church. Through the Evangelical Union of South America, he served in Argentina, 1903–18, doing pastoral missionary work in Tandil (190 miles south of Buenos Aires). He formed the LAM organization to reach the needs of Latin America. After his death, his wife, Susan, directed the mission, 1945–50, until she passed away. His dreams were further carried out by his son, KENNETH, which included the formation of a radio ministry to Latin America in 1948.

Dietrich Bonhoeffer

Feb. 4, 1906　　　　　　　　　　　　　　　　　　　　　　　　　　　　　　　　　　April 9, 1945
Breslau, Germany　　　　　　　　　　　　　　　　　　　　　　　　　　　　Flossenburg, Germany

Lutheran martyr who was a pastor and theologian—brilliant in thought and person. Bonhoeffer was a student pastor in Barcelona (1928–29), studied in the US (1930–31), and criticized Hitler's abusive dictatorship in 1933. He served at a German church in London (1933–35), then headed a seminary for the Confessing Church in Finkenwalde, Germany (1935–37). Authorities banned Bonhoeffer from preaching in 1940 because he was involved in the resistance movement against Hitler. He was arrested by Hitler's agents in Berlin on April 5, 1943, for his outspoken opposition to German tyranny and for helping smuggle a number of Jews into Switzerland. He was hung immediately after conducting a Sunday worship service for prisoners. While he was preaching, Allied armies were approaching a few miles away. He was engaged to be married at the time of his death. His writings included *The Cost of Discipleship* (1937), *Life Together* (1939), and *Way to Freedom* (1936). His favorite Bible verse was Matthew 16:24.

Lee R. Scarborough

July 4, 1870　　　　　　　　　　　　　　　　　　　　　　　　　　　　　　　　　　April 10, 1945
Colfax, Louisiana　　　　　　　　　　　　　　　　　　　　　　　　　　　　　　Amarillo, Texas

President of Southern Baptist Convention, 1938–40, and of Southwestern Baptist Theological Seminary, Fort Worth, TX 1914–42. Scarborough was converted at age 17. May (Neppie) Warren became his wife on February 4, 1900. Scarborough pastored FBC in Cameron, TX (1896–1901), and then the FBC in Abilene, TX (1901–8). He taught evangelism at SBTS (1908–14), and directed the $75-million campaign for the SBC (1919–23). He also helped develop the cooperative program. He wrote 14 books beginning with *Recruits for World Conquests* (1914), but his most reknowned work was *With Christ after the Lost* (1919). Men such as HYMAN APPELMAN and JOHN RICE caught much of his fire for soul-winning. His last book was *After the Resurrection—What?* (1942).

J. Louis Guthrie

May 20, 1877
Seymour, Iowa

April 17, 1945
Little Rock, Arkansas

First president of Missionary Baptist Seminary, Little Rock, AR 1934–45. Guthrie taught in the public schools of Iowa, Missouri, Oklahoma, and Arkansas. He taught at Union University, Jackson, TN (1911–13) then was president of Laneview (TN) College (1913–1915). He taught at Oklahoma Baptist University, Shawnee, OK (1915–25) then was president of Caledonia (AR) Baptist Academy (1926–28). While in Shawnee, he helped the North Church sponsor missionary and educational work on an independent basis. He had an avid interest in Biblical languages.

Lewis S. Mudge

Aug. 24, 1868
Yonkers, New York

April 29, 1945
Philadelphia, Pennsylvania

Stated clerk of Presbyterian Church (USA in 1983) **in the USA, 1921–38**. Mudge married Carolina Paxton on February 11, 1896 (died: September 22, 1922) and then Anne Bolton on December 17, 1925. Mudge pastored at First Church, Beverly, NJ (1895–99); First Church, Trenton (1899–1907); First Church, Lancaster, PA (1908–14); and Pine Street Church, Harrisburg, PA (1914–21). He was a representative to many Presbyterian ecumenical conferences.

H. Wheeler Robinson

Feb. 7, 1872
Northampton, England

May 12, 1945
Oxford, England

Baptist Old Testament scholar and theologian. Robinson was baptized March 28, 1888, upon his conversion. He married Alice Ashford and took a pastorate in Pitlookry, England (1900–3) and at St. Michaels Baptist Church, Coventry (1903–6). He was professor of philosophy of religion at Rawdon Baptist College, Leeds, 1906–13, then pastored during the war years. He was the principal of Regent's Park College, London 1920–42. Robinson was a speaker's lecturer at Oxford and president of the Baptist Historical Society. He was considered England's leader in OT studies. His interest in OT theology was reflected in his many books, which were from *The Christian Doctrine of Man* (1911) to *Inspiration and Revelation in the Old Testament* (1946).

G. Campbell Morgan

Dec. 9, 1863
Tetbury, England

May 16, 1945
London, England

Great expository preacher, perhaps the greatest ever. Morgan was a Congregational minister who studied only the Bible for seven years. He preached his first sermon at age 13. He was a master in Jewish Collegiate School in Birmingham, 1883–88. He married Annie Morgan on August 20, 1888, who gave him seven children. He pastored the Stone Church, Staffordshire (1888–92); the Rugeley Church, Birmingham (1892–97); and the New Court Chapel, London (1897–1904). Morgan was also a speaker for the Northfield (MA) Bible Conference, 1901–4. MOODY wanted him as a regular Northfield (MA) Conference speaker as early as 1897. His most important work was done as pastor of Westminster Chapel in London, 1904–17 and 1933–45, where a dead, poorly-attended congregation resurrected into a large, lively ministry. He was the president of Cheshunt College, Cambridge 1911–14. Morgan traveled in America and Canada, 1917–32, speaking to great crowds with numerous conversions. During this time, he pastored the

Tabernacle Presbyterian Church, Philadelphia, 1929–32. He wrote 60 books, his first being *Discipleship* (1897), and his last, *Luke* (1931). His *The Crises of the Christ* (1903) is outstanding. His commentaries on books of the Bible are among the best. His biography, *Man of the Word*, was written by his daughter-in-law. *Ripley's Believe It or Not* (10th series) states Morgan memorized the entire Bible.

Robert A. Jaffray

Dec. 16, 1873
Toronto, Ontario, Canada

July 29, 1945
Nakassar, Celebes Islands, Indonesia

Outstanding Christian Missionary and Alliance missionary to the Netherlands East Indies (Indonesia). Jaffray was converted at age 16 at the St. James Presbyterian Church, Toronto, via his Sunday School teacher, Annie Gowan. Total surrender came under the preaching of A. B. SIMPSON. After being appointed a missionary to China in 1897, he served in Kwangai, South China. He married Minnie Donner on August 7, 1900. In 1916, Jaffray opened the CMA mission work in the French colony of Annam (later Vietnam). In 1928, Jaffray started work among the Dyack headhunters in Borneo and sent Chinese missionaries to serve there. Soon 15,000 people were converted. From 1931–42, he was in Nakassar, Celebes, Indonesia, where he was arrested. During World War II, the Japanese put him in an internment camp, where he later died on a filthy prison cot at Parc-Park two weeks before the war ended and prisoners freed. Some of his last words were, "Let us keep our eyes steadily upon the goal…Even so, come, Lord Jesus."

James V. Quamina

April 28, 1879
Plymouth, Tobago

Aug. 4, 1945
Trinidad

Founder and first director of Fundamental Baptist Mission of Trinidad and Tobago, 1912–45. Quamina was raised as a Moravian, and taught at Richmond Street Anglican School in Trinidad for a time. He studied in Antigua, and while visiting the island of Tortola, he married Inez Smith in 1900. At Mico College in Antigua, he read 50 sermons by T D. TALMAGE, and was converted. He joined a Gospel Mission Team (1909) and began to pastor in Port-of-Spain, Trinidad (1910). He left the Apostolic Holiness Church and settled on biblical doctrines in 1912 without any support or recognition. By 1921, he had 120 converts and went to America to be ordained a Baptist. From 1921 until his death, he expanded the work and a steadfastness developed, winning many to Christ. He died from the affects of high blood pressure.

Austin K. DeBlois

Dec. 17, 1866
Wolfville, Nova Scotia, Canada

Aug. 10, 1945
Philadelphia, Pennsylvania

President of Eastern Baptist College and Theological Seminary, Wynnewood, PA 1926–36. DeBlois married Erminie Day on June 25, 1890. He was president of Shurtleff College, Alton, IL (1894–99); pastored at FBC, Elgin, IL (1899–1902); at FBC, Chicago, IL (1902–11); and FBC, Boston, MA (1911–26). From 1900–1, he traveled in Europe and Africa. DeBlois wrote many books ranging from *Bible Study in American College*s (1899) to *Christian Religious Education* (1939).

Max I. Reich

March 17, 1867
Berlin, Germany

Aug. 11, 1945
George School, Pennsylvania (?)

Director of International Hebrew Christianity Alliance, 1921–26, 1935–38. Reich married Esther Lorenzen on September 5, 1888. The Reichs came to the USA in 1915. He was one of the founders of the HCA in America. He helped found the International arm of the movement in

1927. For years he was a teacher of Jewish evangelism at Moody Bible Institute. He wrote many books ranging from *Life and Letters of J. G. McVicar* to *Jubilee* and other poems.

Orville B. Ulery

Dec. 24, 1880
North Hampton, Ohio

Aug. 13, 1945
Springfield, Ohio

General secretary of Brethren in Christ Church, Grantham, PA 1928–43. Ulery was converted at age 20. He married Effie Wingert on March 10, 1895. He was long time co-pastor of Beulah Chapel in Springfield, OH (1910–14) and bishop of Clark County, OH (1914–45). From 1924–27, he was editor of *Evangelical Visitor*, a BIC denominational paper. He was closely associated with the publishing work of the BIC, and was also recognized as an evangelist and Bible teacher.

John M. Birch

May 28, 1918
Landaur, India

Aug. 25, 1945
Hwangkao, China

Missionary to China. In 1940, Birch went to China under World Baptist Missionary Fellowship. Birch was converted at age seven at West Baptist Tabernacle, Vineland, NJ. At Mercer University, Macon, GA, he rebelled against the compromise of worldliness and liberalism. He was a captain in the U.S. Army in China as an intelligence officer. While he was in China, Birch found General Doolittle (aviator who was shot down over China in WWII) and his raiders and led them to safety. Birch was murdered by the Chinese Communists after the war was over, bayonetted in a ditch near Hsuchow where he bled to death. He was an outspoken patriot in whose honor an organization of right-wing, anticommunist zealots was founded by Robert Welch in 1958. It was called the John Birch Society.

Harper G. Smythe

March 16, 1873
New York, New York

Aug. 25, 1945
Cleveland, Ohio

Writer of lyrics and music for "Make Me a Channel of Blessing" (1903). Smythe served as song leader for MAUD B. BOOTH and J. WILBUR CHAPMAN. In 1913, he went to Cleveland as music director of the Euclid Avenue Baptist Church and became very involved in the city's musical growth. He was the song leader for the Republican Convention in 1924. He wrote *Let's Adventure into Personality* in 1941. Smythe suffered a stroke while song leading.

Harry E. Stillwell

Nov. 1866
Cheapside, Ontario, Canada

Sept. 6, 1945

General Secretary of the Canadian Baptist Overseas Mission Board, Maritimes (1911–18), and the Ontario and Quebec Boards (1918–38). Stillwell was a part of the first graduating class of McMaster University in 1894. After marrying Ettie Timpany on September 15, 1895, he went to India. His wife died on the mission field in 1912. Stillwell later married Bessie Churchhill and after her death, Mrs. J. G. Brown became his third wife. In 1921 he visited the mission field of Bolivia.

Iva Durham Vennard

Dec. 27, 1871
Prarie City, Illinois

Sept. 12, 1945
Chicago, Illinois

President of Chicago (IL) Evangelistic College (Vennard College, University Park, IA in 1959), **1910–45.** In 1889, Iva won a vocal contest at the University of Normal in Illinois. Soon afterward, she was singing, testifying, and preaching revivals with great success. At Lima, NY, in February, 1896, she almost lost her life in a dorm fire at the Genesee Wesleyan Seminary. She was a deaconess of the Methodist Episcopal Church. She opened Epworth Evangelistic Institute in St. Louis, February, 1903. Iva married Thomas Vennard, a successful architect and mason contractor, on June 8, 1904, in Bloomington, IL. She resigned from the institute in 1910 and moved to Chicago where she opened the Chicago Evangelistic College. She played a leading role in the founding of World Gospel Mission in 1910. Iva was active in the National Holiness Association. She took a world trip preaching and resting, 1920–21. Iva's husband died suddenly on October 13, 1930. Coupled with the Depression years, 1930–33 was a time of great reliance on the Lord. Gastric pneumonia accompanied by intestinal pain and nausea resulted in surgery in July, 1943. Iva never fully recovered. Harry Jessop, her successor, conducted her funeral with about 600 in attendance.

George C. Stebbins

Feb. 26, 1846
East Carlton, New York

Oct. 6, 1945
Catskill, Brooklyn, New York

Grand old man of gospel music who lived just seven months shy of 100 years. Stebbins knew Christian leaders over three generations. Elma Miller became his wife in 1868. He directed music at FBC in Chicago, 1870–74. Stebbins went to Boston in 1874 as music director of Clarendon St. Baptist (A. J. GORDON), 1874–76 and then served at Tremont Temple, 1876 on. He was associated with MOODY, PENTECOST, WHITTLE, and many others as musical director and singer, 1876–1901. From 1880 on, he was the conductor of music at the annual Northfield (MA) conferences. Stebbins composed music for 1,600 hymns including "Have Thine Own Way, Lord" (POLLARD), "Must I Go and Empty-Handed" (C. LUTHER), "Saved By Grace" (CROSBY), "Jesus Is Calling" (CROSBY), "Ye Must be Born Again" (SLEEPER), "Jesus I Come" (SLEEPER), "True Hearted" (HAVERGAL), "Take Time to Be Holy" (LONGSTAFF), "Throw Out the Lifeline" (UFFORD), "There Is a Green Hill Far Away" (ALEXANDER), "In the Secret of His Presence" (Ellen Gorek), and "I've Found a Friend." Later in life, he left the Baptists to become a Methodist. Several editions of *Gospel Hymns* sold over 10 million copies with $397,388 going to Northfield (MA) School Trust Fund.

Frederick H. Knubel

May 22, 1870
New York, New York

Oct. 16, 1945
New Rochelle, New York

President of United Lutheran Church in America (LCA, ELCA in 1988), **1918–44**. Knubel married Christine Ritscher (June 26, 1895), and Jeannie L. Christ (July 11, 1925). He was the founder and pastor of the Church of Atonement, New York City from 1896–1923. Knubel was a member and officer of several Lutheran and inter-denominational works while being active in American Bible and tract societies. He was one of the founders of The National Lutheran Council in 1918.

Cosmo G. Lang

Oct. 31, 1864
Aberdeen, Scotland

Dec. 5, 1945
Kew, England

Archbishop of Canterbury, 1928–42. Lang was of Scottish Presbyterian parentage. After studying for the bar, he was ordained an Anglican in 1890. Next he worked as a curate in a Leeds parish until 1893. Lang returned to Oxford as the dean of divinity and fellow at Magdalen College, 1893–96. From 1896–1901, he was a vicar of Portsea and a prison chaplain. He was also bishop of Stepney (1901–8) and at the same time, canon of St. Paul's Cathedral in London, then served in York for 20 years (1908–28). Lang was a close friend of KING GEORGE VI and was involved in Edward VIII's abdication in 1936 to marry American divorcé Wallis Warfield Simpson. Lang wrote from *Miracles of Jesus* (1900) to *Principles of Religious Education* (1906). He died on his way to a railroad station.

Arno C. Gaebelein

Aug. 27, 1861
Greiz, Germany

Dec. 25, 1945
Mt. Vernon, New York

Author and Bible teacher who specialized in prophecy, conferences, and writing, 1899–1945. Gaebelein edited *Our Hope* (1894–1945). The paper demised in 1958. He came to America (1879) at age 18 and was ordained as a Methodist (1885). He held pastorates in Baltimore (1882–84); New York City (1884–87); and Hoboken, NJ (1887–91). Gaebelein married Emma Grimm on April 9, 1885 (died: November 21, 1938). By 1891, he was a full time missionary to the Jews. He soon found himself directing the Hope of Israel Mission, New York City from 1894–99. In 1899, he left Methodism because of liberal tendencies. He spoke at many Bible conferences and wrote about 50 books ranging from *Harmony of the Prophetic Word* (1905) to *Half a Century* (1950). He was a leading figure in the growth of fundamentalism and dispensationalism in America.

Barclay F. Buxton

1860

1946

Cofounder of the Japan Evangelistic Band in 1903, along with PAGET WILKES. Buxton was converted under D. L. MOODY at the Cambridge Mission Society in November, 1882. Ordained into the Church of England in 1885, he sailed for Japan in October, 1890, under the CMS. He centered at Matsuye, West Coast of Honshu Island, and by 1892 several churches were started. In 1897, he was joined by the WILKES'. Their new mission was first called One by One Band of Japan. Buxton was chairman of the council to oversee the mission.

John R. Clements

Nov. 28, 1868
Newry, Ireland

Jan. 9, 1946
Johnson City, New York

First president of Practical Bible Training School, 1900–17. His family emigrated to America when he was two, came to Binghamton, NY in 1886, then he went into various business ventures. He was converted under MOODY's preaching at the First Presbyterian Church, Binghamton, NY, and remained a member of that church until his death over 50 years later. Clements was an active member for 40 years (1894–1934) and served as president of the New York Christian State Endeavor (1910–16). Clements wrote the lyrics for "No Night There" (1897) and "Jesus Leads"; plus he wrote over 3,000 other song-poems.

David J. Nyall

Jan. 19, 1863
Vall, Sweden

Feb. 6, 1946
Minneapolis, Minnesota

First president of North Park Theological Seminary and College, 1892–1905, 1912–24. Nyall came to the US in 1886. He pastored in Sioux City, IA, from 1887–88. He then served on the faculty of the Swedish department of Chicago Theological Seminary (1888–90), then at the Skogsbergh Covenant School (1890–93). He served as president of Walden College, McPherson, Kansas (1905–8); editor of *Minneapolis Veckoblad* (1908–9), Minneapolis; and professor of Scandinavian languages and literature at the University of Washington, Seattle (1910–12). After resigning as president of NPC in 1924, he continued to teach there. He married Lovisa Skogsbergh (1857–August 20, 1940). He was knighted by the King of Sweden in 1929, and authored more than 30 books.

Albert J. Ramaker

Oct. 3, 1860
Milwaukee, Wisconsin

Feb. 12, 1946
Rochester, New York

President of German Baptist Deptartment of Rochester (NY) renamed Colgate-Rochester, 1915–28, and Divinity School (North America Baptist Seminary, Sioux Falls, SD in 1950), 1928–34. Ramaker married Minna Winkler on November 24, 1886. He pastored in Cleveland, OH, 1886–89. He was an instructor in German at Rochester (1889–90) and professor of church history, Pauline Epistles, and Book of Acts (1890–1935). He wrote books in German and in English, which included *Our Missions in Germany and Central Europe* and *Anabaptist Hymns and Writers*.

Robert H. Coleman

Nov. 1, 1869
Bardstown, Kentucky

Feb. 13, 1946
Dallas, Texas

Independent publisher of hymnals and gospel songbooks for more than three decades. Coleman supplied many hymnals to be used by Baptist churches, especially the Southern Baptists, publishing some 32 different hymnals. Coleman was an associate of GEORGE TRUETT beginning in 1903 (except during the years of 1909–15, when Coleman was the business manager for the *Baptist Standard* publication). Although he never wrote any hymns personally, he was devoted to music and led the singing for many Southern Baptist Convention annual meetings. He sold his publishing business to the SBSS Board in 1944.

Charles M. Sheldon

Feb. 26, 1857
Wellsville, New York

Feb. 24, 1946
Topeka, Kansas

Congregational pastor and writer of the novel, *In His Steps* (1896) which sold over 6 million copies in many languages. It questioned what Jesus would do in any situation if he were living on earth today. He edited *The Christian Herald* and pastored early in Waterbury, VT from 1886–88. On May 20, 1891, he married Mary Merriam. In 1900, Sheldon edited *Daily Capital,* a Topeka newspaper, for one week. He chronicled the news events that might surround Jesus' earthly life in the twentieth century. Circulation jumped from 30,000 to 370,000 for the week. He was also founder of the Central Congregational Church of Topeka, pastoring 1889–1912 and 1915–19, while still writing 33 other books. He edited *The Christian Herald* (1920–25). His 50 books range from *Richard Bruce* (1891) to *The Scrapbook* (1942). One source of data says his famed book sold 28 million copies, seventh all-time in history.

C. Austin Miles

Jan. 7, 1868
Lakehurst, New Jersey

March 10, 1946
Pitman, New Jersey

Writer of the lyrics and music of the beloved hymn "In the Garden," written in March, 1912, after he read John 20. He also wrote "Win Them One by One," "A New Name in Glory," "If Jesus Goes with Me," and "Dwelling in Beulah Land" and composed the music for "Still Sweeter Every Day" (lyrics by W. C. MARTIN), "But This I Know" (lyrics by Clarence Kohlmann), "Submission" (lyrics by Connan), and "He Is Mine" (lyrics by J.L. HALL). Leaving the pharmacy business in June, 1898, Miles began working with Hall-Mack, becoming editor and manager in 1905. He continued on in an editorial capacity when the company merged with Rodeheaver (1935) and stayed until the company moved from Philadelphia to Winona Lake, IN (1942). He married Bertha Haagan.

William H. Matthews

July 23, 1868
McHenry, Illinois

March 11, 1946
Clearwater, Florida

General secretary of American Tract Society, 1922–44. Matthews married Eva Chandler on July 9, 1895. Ordained a Presbyterian in 1898, he served the following churches: Marengo, IL (1898–1901); Central Church, Chicago (1901–6); First Church, Grand Forks, ND (1907–17); and Greenwich Church, NYC (1918–22). He contributed to many Christian periodicals on the life and works of JOHN BUNYAN, the place of Christian literature in modern life, and home mission work in the Northwest. He recorded *Pilgrim's Progress* as a talking book for the blind in 1935 and made several trips to England and Scotland.

Roy T. Williams

Feb. 13, 1883
Many, Louisiana

March 24, 1946
Tuscumbia, Missouri

General superintendent of Church of the Nazarene, 1916–46. Williams married Eunice Harvey in 1906. Williams was a teacher at Peniel College, Greenville, TX (1907–11, and became president (1911–13). From 1913–15, he was an active evangelist. *The Perfect Man, Temptation, Glimpses Abroad, Sanctification,* and *Attitudes and Relations* were all written by him. Prior to his death from a cerebral hemorrhage, he lived in Kansas City, MO. The song, "My Ivory Palace Home," was written in dedication to him.

William H. Goler

Jan. 1, 1846
Halifax, Nova Scotia, Canada

April 16, 1946
Winston-Salem, North Carolina

President of Livingtone College, 1894–1916, and first president of Hood Theological Seminary, Salisbury, NC 1903–12. Goler served as an apprentice to a bricklayer and plasterer from age 15 to 21, working in Boston until 1874. He pastored St. Matthew's AME Church, Greensboro, NC, from 1881–84. He married Emma Unthank on April 26, 1888. He became an instructor at LC (1884), the new dean (1893), with the title changing to president (1894).

Samuel P. Spreng

Feb. 11, 1853
near Woosier, Ohio

April 19, 1946
Naperville, Illinois

Bishop of Evangelical Association, 1907–22, and of Evangelical Church (United Methodist Church in 1968), **1923–46**. Spreng married Margaret Beck on September 18, 1878. He pastored in five Ohio cities (1875–83), was made presiding elder (1883–87) and pastored Madison Avenue Mission, Cleveland (1887–1907). He was editor of the *Evangelical Messenger* (1887–1907) as well. He went on a missionary tour to China and Japan, 1908–9 and crossed the Atlantic Ocean 14 times in missions endeavors. He wrote many books ranging from *Life of JOHN SEYBERT* (1884) to *What Evangelicals Believe* (1929).

Joseph H. King

Aug. 11, 1869
(Rockmill Township) Anderson County, South Carolina

April 23, 1946
Anderson, South Carolina

General Superintendent of Pentecostal Holiness Church (International in 1975), **1917–45, and first director of PHC Missions, 1913–37**. King was converted on August 11, 1885, at Allen's Campground in Franklin County, GA. He married Willie King in 1890 and Blanche Moore on June 1, 1920, living for many years in Franklin Springs, GA. King left Methodism and embraced

Pentecostalism (1908) and became a bishop (1937). His Fire-Baptized Holiness Association, 1900–11 was the forerunner of the Pentecostal Holiness Church in a merger in 1911. He took a trip around the world, 1911–13. At the time of his death, his denomination was responsible for the founding of 700 churches with over 26,000 members. He preached as an evangelist for 54 years. King's writings included *From Passover to Pentecost* (1911) and *Twelve Select Sermons*.

Edward D. Carpenter

June 3, 1859
Sandy Creek, New York

May 3, 1946
Sandy Creek, New York

President of the Wesleyan Church in America (Wesleyan Church in 1968), **1927–39**. Carpenter entered the ministry as a pastor in the Syracuse Conference. Carpenter also pastored the Lisbon Center Church (1899–1910) and the Glen Falls Church (1914–20). He lived and served in New York State all his life, retiring to Syracuse, 1940–46.

Dixon E. Hoste

July 23, 1861
Brighton/Aldershot, England

May 11, 1946
Newington Green, England

General director of the China Inland Mission (Overseas Missionary Fellowship), **1902–35**. Hoste was converted during a MOODY/SANKEY crusade of 1882 in Brighton, England. He married Gertrude Broomhall on Sept. 5, 1893. Hoste worked for 11 years in Shansi, North China, prior to his directorship appointment in 1902. He continued what J. HUDSON TAYLOR started. From 1896–1902, he was superintendent of the CIM work in Honan (Henan) Province. During World War II, he was interned in Shanghai as a prisoner of the Japanese, 1941–45.

Philip E. Howard Sr.

April 1, 1870
Lynn, Massachusetts

June 22, 1946
Moorestown, New Jersey

Publisher of the *Sunday School Times* for many years. Howard had been involved with the company since 1891. He married Annie Trumbull on October 27, 1891 (died: April 11, 1943). Howard wrote many books including the biography of his wife's father, HENRY C. TRUMBULL (1905), and wrote the biography of his son, CHARLES TRUMBULL (1944). He was an editor and part owner of the *Sunday School Times*. His son was PHILIP HOWARD JR., a Presbyterian.

John L. Nuelsen

Jan. 19, 1867
Zurich, Switzerland

June 26, 1946
Cincinnati, Ohio

Bishop in the Methodist Episcopal Church, 1908–39, and in the Methodist Church, 1939–46. Nuelsen married Luella Stroter on September 8, 1896. Nuelsen was professor at St. Paul's College, Sedalia, MO (1890–92); at Central Wesleyan Seminary, Warrenton, MO (1894–99); and at Nast Theological Seminary, Berea, OH (1899–1908). From 1912 on, Nuelsen headed Methodism in Europe, headquartered at Zurich. He wrote books in German and English.

Alma Birdell White

June 16, 1862
Kinnicunik, Kentucky

June 26, 1946
Zarepath, New Jersey

Founder of Pentecostal Union, 1901–17 renamed Pillar of Fire Church, Zarepath, NJ 1917–46. Alma was converted as a teenager in a revival with William Godbey. She married a Colorado Methodist pastor, Kent White, on December 21, 1887. She had moved there in 1882 to become a pioneer schoolteacher. Her emphasis on holiness, her habit of organizing missions and camp meetings, and her preaching at revivals brought her into constant conflict with other bishops. Alma incorporated her movement at Zarepath, and through it, founded six schools, 1908–25. In 1909, her husband left her when she refused to accept "speaking in tongues." She wrote 35 books from *Looking Back from Beulah* (1902) to *Everlasting Life* (1946). She also purchased two radio stations. Alma was a strong anti-Catholic.

Howard H. Russell

Oct. 21, 1855
Stillwater, Minnesota

June 30, 1946
Westerville, Ohio

Attorney-turned-preacher Russell was a devoted Congregationalist who married Lillian Davis on August 17, 1880 (died: 1939). He pastored in North Amherst and Berea, OH (1885–88); Tabernacle Congregational Church, Kansas City (1888–91), and Armour Mission, Chicago (1891–93). He is noted for founding the Anti-Saloon League in Ohio and for promoting his prohibition program, the National Anti-Saloon League of America, into 36 states, 1893–1937. He paraded through leading cities on a horse-drawn water wagon. He first organized this in Ohio, having attended school in Oberlin.

Curtis L. Laws

July 14, 1868
Aldie, Virginia

July 7, 1946
New York, New York

Baptist editor of the *Watchman Examiner* (1913–40). Laws was ordained a Baptist in 1892. He married Grace Burnett (April 25, 1894), and Susan Tyler (Feb. 14, 1922). He pastored the First Baptist Church, Baltimore, MD (1893–1908) and the Greene Avenue Baptist Church, Brooklyn (1908–13). His editorial office was in NYC, and his conservative pen greatly aided his generation. Laws first used the word "fundamentalist" in 1920 after attending a pre-convention rally in Buffalo, NY. He helped organize Eastern Baptist Theological Seminary in Philadelphia and Association of Baptists for World Evangelism. He was a strong conservative in the NBC which was going liberal. He retired in 1938 and returned to Baltimore.

Carrie Judd Montgomery

April 8, 1858
Buffalo, New York

July 26, 1946
Oakland, California

Minister-teacher, writer, editor, director of faith homes, and social worker, whose ministry of 65 years was truly amazing. Carrie worked and associated with the Episcopal Church, and the Holiness healing movement. Reared in an Episcopal home, she was converted at age eleven. Her *Prayer of Faith* in 1880, told of a remarkable healing she had experienced. In 1881, she founded *Triumphs of Faith*, a magazine she would edit for 65 years. It bridged the Holiness/Pentecostal movements and stressed healing, social work, and missions. She moved to Oakland, CA, on May 14, 1890, and married a wealthy businessman (mining business), George S. Montgomery. She organized a CMA Church in 1890, as well as the People's Mission. They established the Home of Peace in 1893 and ran an orphanage, 1895–1908, which was then given to the Salvation Army. They made missionary trips and welcomed missionaries to stay at the HOP. They became very active in the Salvation Army activities there. She was a charter member of the General Council of the Assemblies of God in 1918. She pastored The Beulah Heights Chapel in Oakland in later years. Her last book was her autobiography, *Under His Wings* (1936).

Otho Winger

Oct. 23, 1877
Marion, Indiana

Aug. 13, 1946
Wabash, Indiana

Moderator of the Church of the Brethren six times during 1921–1934. Ida Miller became Winger's wife in 1902. He was professor of church history and philosophy at Manchester College, N. Manchester, IN (1907–11) and its president (1911–14). He lived in North Manchester, where he authored his many books, which include from *Life of Elder R. H. Miller* (1909) to *The Frances Slocum Trail* (1943).

John R. Sampey

Sept. 27, 1863
Fort Deposit, Alabama

Aug. 18, 1946
Louisville, Kentucky

President of Southern Baptist Convention, 1936–38, and Southern Baptist Theological Seminary, Louisville, KY 1929–42. Converted at age 14, Sampey spent his lifetime at the Southern Baptist Theological Seminary beginning as an instructor in 1885. Sampey first married Annie Renfroe on September 16, 1886 (died: 1925) and then Ellen Wood on May 16, 1926. His teaching specialty was Old Testament interpretation. His books ranged from *The First Thirty Years of the Southern Baptist Theological Seminary* (1890) to *Memoirs of John R. Sampey* (1946). He was on the Sunday School committee of SBC for 45 years. He was one of the founders of the Baptist World Alliance and he took several preaching tours to Brazil.

Kirsopp Lake

April 7, 1872
Southampton, England

Nov. 10, 1946
S. Pasadena, California

Anglican biblical scholar who taught history at Harvard University, 1914–38. Lake served curacies at Lumley (1895–97) and at the University of Leyden in the Netherlands (1904–13). He participated in a series of archaeological expeditions to the Middle East, 1930–39, and wrote several books, including the five-volume *Beginning of Christianity*. Lake married Helen Forman and later Silvia Tipple. His writing began with *Text of the New Testament* (1898), and ended with *An Introduction to the New Testament* (1937). He cast doubt on the empty tomb in a 1907 book. His best book was *The Earlier Epistles of St. Paul* (1913).

Walter D. Kallenbach

July 20, 1905
Everett, Massachusetts

Nov. 16, 1946
Canonsburg, Pennsylvania

Brilliant blind evangelist. Kallenbach lost his sight in a hunting accident on January 4, 1927 at the age of 22. He was converted in a hospital in Virginia in 1927 as he mused over Matt. 6:24. Shelburne Wyly became his wife on May 19, 1932. Kallenbach was the only blind man to earn two doctorate degrees and to memorize the whole New Testament. He won many honors, was a member of numerous prestigious clubs and organizations, and wrote several books. He had 25 operations, seven on his brain. Kallenbach's evangelistic ministry began in 1935, but came to an untimely end when he was killed by an automobile on a remote highway. He wrote a series of books *That Men May Know* (1938), *Believe* (1939), *Live* (1939), *See* (1940).

Arthur C. Headlam

Aug. 2, 1862
Whorlton, England

1947

Anglican bishop, theologian, and educator. Headlam disliked the division in separate party factions in the Church of England and tried to mediate between them. He was one of the most influential bishops of his time. He was a fellow of All Saint's College, Oxford (1885–96); chaplain (1888–96); and theological lecturer in Ariel and Queen's Colleges (1888–93); and Trinity College (1895–96); rector of Welwyn (1896–1903); principal of King's College in London (1903–18); professor of dogmatic theology there (1903–17); professor of divinity at Oxford (1918–23); and bishop of Gloucester (1923–45). Headlam married Evelyn Wingfield in 1900 (died: 1924). He was a theological lecturer at New College and Oridel College, Oxford since 1924. He wrote from *Ecclesiastical Sites in Isavria* (1893) to *The Fourth Gospel as History* (published, 1948).

Carl G. Wallenius

Dec. 28, 1865
Stockholm, Sweden

Jan. 14, 1947
Evanston, Illinois (?)

President of Swedish Theological Seminary (Kendall College, Evanston, IL), **1909–18, 1924–31**. Wallenius married Hilda Johnson on October 25, 1894. He was professor of theology and Swedish at the Seminary, 1889–1906. Next he pastored the Bethany Methodist Church, Chicago, IL, president of Wesley Academy and Theological Seminary of Evanston, 1924–31, then Emmanuel Methodist of Evanston, after 1931.

James H. Rushbrooke

July 29, 1870
London, England

Feb. 1, 1947
Bristol, England

President of Baptist World Alliance, 1939–47, and first general secretary, 1928–39. Rushbrooke married Dorothea G. Weber on June 16, 1902. The couple was interned in Germany during WWI. Rushbrooke pastored in Nottingham (1897–99); in Derby (1901–6); at Archway Road Baptist, Highgate, North London; and Jampstead Garden Suburban Church (a United Free Church) (1906–20). He organized Baptist World congresses in Toronto (1928), Berlin (1934), and Atlanta (1939). He wrote several books and worked tirelessly for religious freedom. He edited the *Peacemaker* (1908–14) and *Goodwill* (1915–20). The headquarters of BWA moved from London to Washington in 1940.

Grace Livingstone Hill-Lutz

April 16, 1865
Wellsville, New York

Feb. 23, 1947
Swarthmore, Pennsylvania

Novelist and poet who produced a series of character-building romantic novels loved by teenagers and adults alike. The daughter of a Presbyterian minister, Grace married Reverend Thomas Hill on December 8, 1892 (died: 1899); they had two daughters. She later married Flavius J. Lutz and established her home in Swarthmore, PA. His irrational behavior climaxed by his walking out of the home. Her writing career stretched from *A Chautaugua Idyl* (1887) to *All Through the Night* (1945). Her daughter later completed some of her mother's transcripts and outlines. Grace was a dedicated Presbyterian. One of her most widely read novels was *The Enchanted Barn* (1918), as was *The Witness* (1937). She wrote 80 novels with four million in circulation in America alone. She also wrote under the name of Marcia MacDonald. She died at her home from an infection after an appendectomy.

Francis L. H. Pott

Feb. 22, 1864
New York, New York

March 7, 1947
Shanghai, China

Episcopal missionary and educator to China, 1886 on. Susan Wong became his wife (August 23, 1888) and Emily G. Cooper (June 12, 1919). Pott was an evangelist who later became president of St. John's University in Shanghai, serving there for 50 years, 1891–1941. His writings were from *The Outbreak in China* (1900) to *Short History of Shanghai* (1928). He retired to the United States.

Smith Wigglesworth

June 10, 1859
Menston, England

March 12, 1947
Wakefield, England

Evangelist who was noted for his faith and answers to prayer. Wigglesworth was hardly known outside his hometown until age 48, when he had a Pentecostal experience. Prior to this, he was a plumber with limited education who claimed he never read anything but the Bible. As an evangelist, he stressed salvation, divine healing, and baptism by the Holy Spirit. His wife's name was Polly. There are six books in print about his ministry.

James D. Perry

Oct. 3, 1871
Germantown, Pennsylvania

March 20, 1947
Summerville, South Carolina

Presiding bishop of Protestant Episcopal Church (Episcopal Church in 1967), **1930–37**. Perry married Edith Weir on January 2, 1908. Perry was rector at Christ Church, Fitchburg, MA (1897–1904); St. Paul's Church, New Haven, CT (1904–11); bishop of Rhode Island, beginning June 6, 1911; a senior Red Cross chaplain during WWI (1918–19); and an overseer at Harvard University (1937–43). In 1933, he went on a five-month fact-finding trip to the Orient for Episcopal missions.

Robert H. Glover

Oct. 17, 1871
Leeds, Quebec, Canada

March 23, 1947
Philadelphia, Pennsylvania

President of IFMA, 1927-35, 1938-39. This missionary educator and statesman married Caroline Prentice (March 14, 1876-January 27, 1953) on November 20, 1902, in Worester, MA. Glover was a missionary to China with the CMA from 1894-1913. He was foreign secretary of Christian Missionary Alliance, 1913-20. Glover was the director of missionary course at Moody Bible Institute (1921-26), and home director of China Inland Mission (1930-43). He saw 500 new missionaries join the ranks and 100 mission stations added. Glover wrote *The Progress of World-Wide Missions* (1924). He retired in Germantown, PA in 1943.

Henry Ford

July 30, 1863
Greenfield, Michigan

April 7, 1947
Dearborn, Michigan

Premier automobile manufacturer who produced the Model T Ford (1909), the assembly line concept (1913), and the Model A (1927). Ford married Clara Bryant on April 11, 1888, and they had one son, Edsel. Two German engineers actually invented the automobile and Ford mass-produced them. Was organizer and president of Ford Motor Co., 1903-19 and 1943-45 which produced 36 million automobiles and trucks, 1903-50. In June, 1941, he signed contracts with a labor board. After his son, Edsel's death, he presided again, 1943-45. He eventually employed over 100,000 workers. Ford banned smoking in his plant and often talked of his love for the Bible. He said: "All I know of truth, honesty, and idealism, I have learned from the Bible. If I had my way, a chapter of the Bible would be read every morning in every school." He was worth 2 billion dollars when he retired for good. He wrote three books. He distributed $40 million between 1908–47, quite an accomplishment for a high school dropout.

Derwyn T. Owen

July 29, 1876
Twickenham, England

April 9, 1947
Toronto, Ontario, Canada

Primate of the Anglican Church of Canada (and archbishop of Toronto), **1934–47**. Owen married Nora Jellett on April 20, 1904, and they had five children. He was curate at St. James Cathedral, Toronto (1902–8); rector of Holy Trinity Church (1910–14); rector and dean at Christ Church Cathedral, Hamilton, Ontario (1914–25); bishop of Niagara (1925–32); and archbishop of Toronto (1932–34). Owen was the first president of the Canadian Council of Churches in 1944. He died of a heart attack.

John W. Phelps

Dec. 13, 1870
State Center, Iowa

April 20, 1947
Anderson, Indiana

President of Church of God Missionary Board, Anderson, IN 1912–27. Phelps married Eureka Hillman on November 22, 1895. He was originally a Methodist, switching to the Church of God in 1905. Phelps taught at the Kansas City College of Business, 1906–11. He was hired by the Gospel Trumpet Company (Warner Press), after which he became involved in missions and resumed his education career teaching public speaking at Anderson College. He died shortly after having a major stroke.

Millard L. Robinson

July 28, 1880
Westfield, Massachusetts

April 23, 1947

President of New York (International in 1978) **Bible Society, 1930–46.** Entering the Methodist ministry in 1906, Robinson married Marion Bean on October 6, 1906 (died: January 26, 1911) and Edna W. Stitt on February 5, 1914. He was pastor at First Church, Manchester, NH (1906–07); director of the YMCA, Philadelphia, PA in 1908; associate pastor of Hanson Place Church, New York City (1909–10); and pastor of 17th Street and 11th Street Churches (1910–14). Robinson then became general secretary of the New York City Society of his denomination, 1914–30. He was a Mason and a member of several clubs in the New York City area.

Frederick G. Smith

Nov. 12, 1880
Lacota, Michigan

April 24, 1947
Anderson, Indiana

Editor of *Gospel Trumpet (Vital Christianity)* and leader of Church of God, Anderson, IN 1917–30. Smith was ordained in 1900 and married Birdie Mitchell on March 30, 1902. He served as a missionary to Syria and the Near East, 1912–14. Smith authored several books, including *The Revelation Explained* (1908) to *Prophetic Lectures on Daniel and the Revelation* (1941).

Ludwig E. Fuerbringer

March 29, 1864
Frankenmuth, Michigan

May 6, 1947
St. Louis, Missouri

President of Concordia Seminary, St. Louis, MO, 1931–43. He pastored in his hometown of Frankenmuth, 1885–93. Fuerbringer was a Lutheran theologian and married Anna Zucker on Nov. 5, 1896. He taught at Concordia, 1893–1907. Fuerbringer was president of the Lutheran Synodical Conference, 1927–44. He was the editor of the ten-volume *Men and Missions* (1924–33) and also edited the German bi-weekly *Der Lutheraner* for 45 years. His writings range from *Letters of C.F. Walther* (1915) to *Persons and Events* (1947). His funeral was at Holy Cross Lutheran Church in St. Louis.

Warren J. Moulton

Aug. 30, 1865
Sandwich, New Hampshire

May 7, 1947
Bangor, Maine

President of Bangor (ME) Theological Seminary, 1921–33. Moulton married Helen W. Shute on June 21, 1900. He was ordained a Congregationalist in 1899, then traveled to Palestine and the Middle East, 1902–3. When he returned, he began to work for Bangor Seminary and was active in many educational and civic activities in Maine. Moulton often contributed articles to scholarly works and was active in Oriental research activities.

John W. Robinson

Jan. 6, 1866
Moulton, Iowa

May 30, 1947
Naini Tal, India

Bishop in Methodist Episcopal Church, 1912–39, and in the Methodist Church, 1939–47. Robinson married Elizabeth Fisher on August 27, 1891. He was ordained (1890) and then transferred (1892) to the North India Conference, where he spent 20 years at Lucknow pastoring an English-speaking work. He was elected a missionary bishop in 1912, spending his lifetime in the area of Lucknow (northeast India near Nepal).

William (Will) H. Houghton

June 28, 1887
South Boston, Massachusetts

June 14, 1947
Los Angeles, California

President of Moody Bible Institute, Chicago, 1934–47. Houghton was converted in 1901 at age 14 in an evangelistic meeting in Lynn, MA. He became R. A. TORREY's song leader, 1910–15. He married Adelaid Franks in June, 1914 (died: 1916) and then Elizabeth Andrews on December 14, 1918. His early pastorates were in Canton, PA (1915–17); New Bethlehem, PA (1918–22); and FBC, Norristown, PA (1922–24). He pastored at the Baptist Tabernacle, Atlanta, GA (1925–30), and at Calvary Baptist, New York City (1930–34), doubling the membership of both places. Houghton also began Moody Institute of Science in 1938. He wrote the lyrics for "By Life or By Death" (music by GEORGE SCHULER), "Songs in the Night" (music by J. T. Noe), "The Christian Goes Right On," "Love the World Through Me," and "Lead Me to Some Soul Today" (music by WENDELL LOVELESS for the last three). His book, *Back to the Bible* (1940), was very effective. Under his leadership, the *Moody Monthly* grew from 35,000 to 75,000 subscribers (students from 898 to 1,420). Having had coronary problems, he had a heart attack in a locked room of a hotel. Rushed to a hospital, he soon died. His funeral was at Moody Church, Chicago, although they were members at North Shore Baptist.

David N. Claudon

March 30, 1867
Livingston County, Illinois

July 7, 1947
Valparaiso, Indiana

First director of Congo Inland Mission (Africa Inter-Mennonite Mission in 1972), **Elkhart, IN 1912–26**. Raised in the Salem Mennonite Church, Gridley, IL, Claudon became a Christian while very young. In time, he would become an outstanding layman-teacher, merchant, banker, editor, SS superintendent, deacon, song leader, and president of the local board of education. On March 1, 1891, he married Kathryn Egly (October 4, 1867–September 1, 1956), and they had seven children. He helped organize a children's home in Flanagan, IL and an old people's home in Meadows, IL. He ran a lumberyard in Meadows to support himself. His missions tasks included expediting missionaries to the field (processing candidates, obtaining passports) and looking after all the official business (correspondence and shipping) from his home. He and seven others were the original board members of the CIM. They moved to Valparaiso in 1927. He accidentally scalded himself in a bathtub and died from severe burns six weeks later.

Henry C. Thiessen

Oct. 20, 1883
Henderson, Nebraska

July 25, 1947
Los Angeles, California

Baptist pastor and educator. Thiessen was converted at age 15 through the preaching of J. H. Pankratz. He took an interest in Christian work immediately. All this happened in a Mennonite Brethren Church, however he later became a Baptist. He married Anna Bullar on March 23, 1903. He pastored in Pandora, OH (1909–16); was professor at Ft. Wayne (IN) Bible College

(1916–23); Northern Baptist Seminary (1925–28); Evangelical University, Jersey City, NJ (1929–31); Dallas Seminary (1931–35); and Wheaton (IL) College (1935–46). He was a balanced Bible student and writer. In 1946, he became president of Los Angeles Baptist Seminary and died soon thereafter, asthma attacks being a prime problem.

James B. Chapman

Aug. 30, 1884
Yale, Illinois

July 30, 1947
Indian Lake/Vicksburg, Michigan

General superintendent of Church of the Nazarene, 1928–47. Chapman was converted at a Holiness camp meeting in Oklahoma at age 14. He preached 238 times the first year after his call to preach, when he was still a teenager. Chapman married Maud Frederick on February 18, 1903 (died: 1940) and then Louise Robinson in June, 1942. He served as an evangelist (1900–5) and then pastored in Duvant, OK (1905–8) and in Vilonia, AR (1908–10). He was later president of Peniel College, Greenville, TX from 1912–18. In 1918 he returned to Bethany, OK to pastor and travel. Chapman was also editor of *Herald of Holiness* (1922–28). As a missionary and an evangelist, he traveled some 30,000 miles in his lifetime. Chapman supervised missions in China, Japan, Latin America, and Africa, 1931–40. He encouraged the founding of the Nazarene Theological Seminary, Kansas City, MO.

Rodney (Gypsy) Smith

March 31, 1860
Wanstead (near London), England

Aug. 4, 1947
at sea (Atlantic Ocean)

Evangelist whose ministry circled the globe. Although he had a Methodist background, Smith was interdenominational in scope. He preached in barns, meadows, warehouses, tents, churches, and halls on five continents. His singing was always a special treat. He was a gypsy who was converted at a revival meeting on Nov. 15, 1876 as a child. His first wife was Anne Pennock, whom he married on Dec. 17, 1879 (died: 1937). He became associated with the Salvation Army until 1882, when he began his evangelism endeavors. Gypsy came to America as an unknown evangelist in 1889 and had 400 converts at his first revival in Brooklyn. His 1892 services in Edinburgh grew into the Gypsy Gospel Wagon Mission. From 1897–1912, he became a special missionary of the National Free Church Council, during which two worldwide tours were made. He ministered to British troops in France, 1914–18. Gypsy Smith wrote the lyrics for "Jesus Revealed in Me" and "Not Dreaming." When he was 78 he married Mary A. Shaw on June 2, 1938 (she was age 27). He died of a heart attack on the *Queen Mary* while coming to America on another trip (some say 50 trips were made). His writings range from *As Jesus Passed By* (1905) to *The Beauty of Jesus* (1932).

John W. Wood

Aug. 4, 1866
New York, New York

Aug. 7, 1947
New York, New York

Director of Episcopal Church Missions, 1919–40. He also served as the general secretary of the Brotherhood of St. Andrew 1890–1900. Wood married Harriet Drom in 1891 (died: 1931) and Regina Lustgarten in 1939. He was a vestryman of St. Peter's Church of New York City and a Republican. In a series of overseas trips, Wood visited Episcopal mission fields abroad.

William Pearce

Oct. 15, 1862
Hayle, England

Sept. 2, 1947
Rochester, New York

Bishop of Free Methodist Church, 1908–47. Pearce came to America in 1884 and eventually established a pastorate in the California area, 1889–96. Pearce married Alma Knoll on May 14, 1889 (died: October 3, 1908); Sarah Dickson on July 21, 1915 (died: September 14, 1917); and

Mabel Kline on June 8, 1922. In 1927, he visited Japan. Pearce wrote *Our Incarnate Lord*. He lived for many years in Rochester, NY and served for 16 years as board chairman of the Free Methodist Publishing House.

Nicholas N. Hiebert

July 29, 1874
Litchfelde, Ukraine

Sept. 14, 1947
Hillsboro, Kansas

General secretary of the Mennonite Brethren Mission Services, Hillsboro, KS, 1902–19. Hiebert married Susan Wiebe in May, 1899 (died: January 1, 1963). Their home church was in Bingham Lake, MN. They went to India in 1899, returning 18 months later because of illness. Hiebert then worked to promote the cause of missions and evangelism in churches. He served as secretary of the mission board (1901–36), Bible teacher, evangelist, writer (1901–47), and pastor in Mountain Lake, MN (1918–30).

Walter Taylor

Oct. 16, 1865
Pittsburgh, Pennsylvania

Oct. 23, 1947
St. Petersburg, Florida

Director of Pacific Garden Mission, Chicago, IL 1918–36. Taylor was converted on February 21, 1896, after the death of his first wife. He then left the business world, going into YMCA work which led him to enroll at Moody Bible Institute. Ethel Robinson became his wife in 1898. Taylor would preach and Ma Taylor would play the piano and pray; they were loved by many. From 1902–18, he was director of the Old Brewery Mission in Montreal, Quebec. While superintendent of the Pacific Garden Mission in Chicago, Taylor wrote several gospel choruses, which included "For Me, For Me."

Henry Beets

Jan. 5, 1869
Koedyk, Netherlands

Oct. 29, 1947
Grand Rapids, Michigan

"Mr. Christian Reformed Church" who was his denomination's first stated clerk, 1902–42, and their first director of World Missions, 1920–39. Clara Poel became his wife on Sept. 11, 1895 (died: 1946). Beets pastored in Sioux City, IA (1895–99); at LaGrave Ave. Church (1899–1915); and Burton Heights Church (1915–20); both located in Grand Rapids, MI. He edited *The Banner* (1904–29), a Reformed Church paper, and the *Reformed Review* (1915–40). Beets also wrote Dutch and English books. His writings were from *Toiling and Trusting* (1890) to *Fifty Years of CR Mission Work* (1940).

Robert E. Speer

Sept. 10, 1867
Huntingdon, Pennsylvania

Nov. 23, 1947
Bryn Mawr, Pennsylvania

President of Federal Council of Churches (NCC in 1950), **1920–24**. Speer was a much respected Presbyterian mission board executive, serving, 1891–1937 as secretary of the Board for Foreign Missions for the Presbyterian Church, USA. Speer was also an active administrator in the Student Volunteer Movement. He married Emma Bailey on April 20, 1893. He made his first tour (1896) and helped organize the World Missionary Conference in Edinburgh (1910). He downplayed the fundamentalist-modernist controversy, telling both sides missionary activity was too great to exhaust energy in theological wrangles. He spent three years in South America. His 69 books began with *The Gospel of Luke* (1892) and ended with *Jesus and Our Human Problems* (1946).

William B. Riley

March 22, 1861
Greene County, Indiana

Dec. 5, 1947
Golden Valley, Minnesota

First president of Northwestern Schools, Minneapolis, MN, 1902–47 (Bible School 1902, Seminary 1935, and College 1944) **and president of World's Christian Fundamentalist Association, 1919–29**. Riley married Lillian Howard on December 31, 1890 (died: August 10, 1931), and Marie Acomb (1887–1971) on September 1, 1933, giving him a total of six children. Converted in a revival in August 1875, he pastored in New Albany, IN (1887–88); Lafayette, IN (1888–90); Bloomington, IL (1890–93); and Calvary Baptist, Chicago, IL (1893–97). He stayed in the Northern (American) Baptist Convention until his deathbed, being the most influential voice in slowing down the organization's liberal tendencies. He pastored at FBC, Minneapolis (1897–1942), growing from 585 to 3,550, and also was president of the World's Christian Fundamentalist Association, (1919–29). Riley was responsible for establishing Billy Graham's Minneapolis headquarters and leading the Minnesota State Baptist Convention to take an independent stance. They left the NBC in 1948. He often debated evolutionists. He published many books, including a 40-volume *Bible of the Expositor* and the *Evangelist*. His books ranged from *The Greater Doctrines of Scripture* (1893) to *The Preacher and His Preaching* (1947). Billy Graham conducted his funeral.

John McNaugher

Dec. 30, 1857
Allegheny, Pennsylvania

Dec. 12, 1947
Pittsburgh, Pennsylvania

President of Allegheny (PA) Theological Seminary, 1909–12, renamed Pittsburgh (PA) Theological Seminary, 1912–1930 (merged with Xenia in 1930), **and Pittsburgh-Xenia Theological Seminary, 1930–42**. The merger of two seminaries, PXTS with Western Theological Seminary in 1959 created Pittsburgh Theological Seminary. Beginning in 1887, McNaugher was a professor of New Testament literature and exegesis. He married Ella Wilson on April 26, 1888. His first book was *The United Presbyterian Church—Its History and Mission* (1899), and his last *Yesterday, Today, and Forever* (1947).

Edward J. Higgins

Nov. 26, 1864
Highbridge, England

Dec. 14, 1947
Plainsfield, New Jersey

General of Salvation Army, 1929–1934. Higgins married Catherine Price of Wales in 1888 (died: 1952). He then came to America in 1894, serving as secretary to Emma Booth-Tucker and EVANGELINE CORY BOOTH, both daughters of WILLIAM BOOTH. Higgins returned to London in 1905 and served at the headquarters as chief of staff to WILLIAM BRAMWELL BOOTH 1919–29. EVANGELINE BOOTH replaced Higgins in 1934. From 1935–45, Higgins lived in Sebring, FL. One of Higgins's seven children married ALBERT ORSBORN (sixth general of the SA).

Alfred N. Whitehead

Feb. 15, 1861
Ramsgate, England

Dec. 30, 1947
Cambridge, Massachusetts

Mathematician, logician, and philosopher. Whitehead lectured in math at Trinity College, Cambridge (1885–1911) and at the University of London (1911–1914). During this time, Evelyn Wade became his wife on December 16, 1890. He later served as professor of mathematics at the Imperial College of Science and Technology in London (1914–24) then as professor of philosophy at Harvard University (1924–36), where he helped reconcile metaphysics with science. Whitehead's writings included *Treatise on Universal Algebra* (1898) to *Modes of Thought* (1938). He and his pupil, Bertrand Russell, wrote *Principia Mathematica* (3 vols., 1910–13). He wrote *Religion in the Making* (1926).

George H. Cook

c 1878   *1948*

Composer of "Heavenly Sunlight," 1899 (lyrics by HENRY ZELLEY). Cook was converted at age 14, having been influenced by Negro evangelist, AMANDA SMITH. His ministry included preaching, singing, directing choirs, organizing bands and orchestras, and training gospel singers. Cook retired in Ocean Grove, NJ.

Charles R. Watson

July 17, 1873   *Jan. 10, 1948*
Cairo, Egypt   Bryn Mawr, Pennsylvania

Director of United Presbyterian Church (PC USA in 1983) **of North America Missions, 1902–16**. Watson taught school from 1894–97. He was ordained on July 26, 1900, and then pastored the First Church, St. Louis, MO from 1900–2. He married Maria Elizabeth Powell on November 20, 1902. Watson visited Middle Eastern mission fields, 1903–4. He was president at the American University of Cairo, Egypt 1914–45 and is credited with writing several books.

L. Glenn Lewis

April 6, 1873   *Feb. 11, 1948*
Elgin, Pennsylvania   Santa Cruz, California

First president of Central Christian College, McPherson, KS 1914–23. Lewis was converted at age 22 and married Alice E. Black in 1897 (died: August 5, 1947). He pastored in many places: Bradley Town, PA; Galion, OH; Pomeroy, OH; Zanesville, OH; Cleveland, OH; and Jackson, MI. He was the district superintendent in the California Conference for four years. He founded Central Academy in 1914. Lewis was the denomination's educational secretary, 1919–32. Later, he pastored at Central Church, Chicago; First Church, Los Angeles; and in West Hollywood, CA. He traveled widely with one complete world tour. As a Free Methodist pastor, he erected or remodeled nine Free Methodist churches and six parsonages.

Ralph H. Long

Dec. 3, 1882   *Feb. 19, 1948*
Loudonville, Ohio   New York, New York

Executive director of the National Lutheran Council (in USA in 1967), **1930–48**. Sarah Bachman became Long's wife on June 10, 1909. He pastored at Newton Falls Church, Warren, OH (1909–13); at Zion Church, Coraopolis, PA (1913–21); and at St. Paul's Lutheran Church, Pittsburg, PA (1921–27). He was stewardship secretary of the Evangelical Lutheran Joint Synod of Ohio, 1927–30. Long lived in Rockville Centre, NY.

Civilla Durfee Martin

Aug. 21, 1866   *March 9, 1948*
Jordan, Nova Scotia, Canada   Atlanta, Georgia

Writer of lyrics for "God Will Take Care of You," 1904 (music by her husband, WALTER) and **"His Eye Is on the Sparrow," 1905** (music by CHARLES GABRIEL). Civilla married WALTER S. MARTIN. In 1916 they changed from Baptist to the Disciples of Christ denomination. Her musical talents were most helpful in the evangelistic campaigns of her husband. They co-wrote a number of other hymns, including "The Old-Fashioned Way." She also wrote "Accepted in the Beloved" (music by W. P. LOVELESS).

William T. N. Schwarze

Jan. 2, 1875
Chaska, Minnesota

March 14, 1948
Bethlehem, Pennsylvania

President of Moravian Theological Seminary, Bethlehem, PA, 1928–43. He was ordained Moravian in 1896. He pastored in Alberta, Canada (1896–1900), then at a Seminary in Anitgua (1900–3). Schwarze married Ethel Greider on July 19, 1905. He served as a professor of philosophy and church history at Moravian College, 1903–48. He wrote on Moravian historical subjects. He was very active in civic affairs in Bethlehem, PA.

George L. Carpenter

June 20, 1872
Newcastle, Australia

April 9, 1948
Sydney, Australia

General of Salvation Army, 1939–46. Carpenter joined the Salvation Army (1891), first serving in Australia for 18 years, then moving to England (1911) to serve for 16 years at the international headquarters. He worked in the editorial department and as secretary for their literary affairs. He married Minnie Rowell in 1899 (died: 1960). Carpenter was second in command of the Salvation Army in Australia (1927–33), which he followed by service in eastern South America (1933–37), and then to head up the work in Canada (1937–39). His works included *Keep the Trumpets Sounding* and *Banners and Adventures*.

Niels P. Gravengaard

April 17, 1864
Hemmet, Denmark

April 21, 1948
Des Moines, Iowa

President of Danish Evangelical Lutheran Church (LCA, ELCA in 1988), **1911–18, 1920–22.** Gravengaard immigrated to the USA in 1888 attending Lutheran seminaries in West Denmark, WI, and Philadelphia. He married Anna Rasmussen on August 17, 1892 (died: 1959). Ordained, June 12, 1892, he pastored in Sioux City, IA (1892–94); Oak Hill and Atlantic-Avoca, IA (1894–1900); Cedar Falls and Waterloo, IA (1900–9); Kronberg, NE (1909–20); St. John's, Des Moines, IA (1920–27); and Los Angeles, CA (1927–35). Gravengaard was the first (temporary) president of Grand View College, Des Moines, IA, from 1895–97. He authored *A Christmas Gift* (1920).

Beresford J. Kidd

Jan. 1, 1864
Birmingham, England

May 15, 1948

Anglican Church historian who was ordained into the Church of England in 1887. Kidd married his wife, Agnes, in 1894. He served as assistant curate of St. Philip and St. James churches in Oxford (1887–1900); as vicar of St. Paul's, Oxford (1904–20); as chaplain and lecturer of theology at Pembroke College, Oxford; as warden of Keble College, Oxford (1920–39); and as a professor at the Theology School of Oxford. He wrote several books from *The Thirty-nine Articles* (1899) to *The Primacy of the Roman See* (1936).

Christopher J. Balfe
"Lucky Baldwin"

Dec. 28, 1871
New York, New York

May 23, 1948
Williams Bay, Wisconsin

Well-known prison chaplain. This criminal left his life of sin behind when he was converted on November 25, 1908, at McAuley Water Street Mission in New York City. Shortly thereafter, he was attending Moody Bible Institute in Chicago, IL and helping "Mother" SARAH CLARKE with jail work. From 1910 til death, Balfe served as chaplain at Bridewell Prison in Cook County,

IL, seeing over 12,000 converts. On June 5, 1912, he married Anna Bolte. He died of cornary thrombosis at home.

Luther B. Bridgers

Feb. 14, 1884
Margaretsville, North Carolina

May 27, 1948
Atlanta, Georgia

Methodist minister who wrote the words and music to "He Keeps Me Singing," one of our most beloved hymns. Bridgers began preaching in Methodist churches while he was still a student at Asbury. In 1910, Bridgers suffered the tragic loss of his wife and three sons in a house fire (father-in-law's house) in Harrodsburg, KY. Verse four of the hymn is especially pertinent to his loss. He married Aline Winburn in 1914, traveled as an evangelist, 1914–32, then pastored in Georgia and North Carolina.

Rufus M. Jones

Jan. 25, 1863
South China, Maine

June 16, 1948
Haverford, Pennsylvania

Quaker theologian, whose interpretations of Christianity were considered liberal by many. However, Jones' influence in his denomination and at Haverford College was substantial. He married Sarah Countant (July 3, 1888) and Elizabeth Bartram Cadbury (March 11, 1902). In 1893, he joined the faculty at Haverford College and became the editor of *The American Friend*. He soon became a lecturer of national fame, speaking in many American colleges. For more than 40 years, he taught psychology, philosophy, ethics, Bible, and the development of Christian thought. He wrote 56 books and hundreds of articles, editorials, and pamphlets. In his writings, he interpreted the life of mystic relationship with Christ which he felt could be practically lived in the modern world. His books were from *Life of Eli and Sybil Jones* (1889) to *A Call to What Is Vital* (1948).

Benjamin Davidson

Sept. 14, 1860
Thurso, Scotland

June 23, 1948
Elyria, Ohio

Founder and first director of Ceylon and India General Mission, 1893–1921, (merged in 1968 to become International Christian Fellowship, which in 1989 merged into SIM), **and first director of India Mission** (Christar in 1999), **1930–48** (name changed to International Missions in 1954 upon its entrance into Pakistan). He married Alice Bell on July 12, 1903 (died: April 19, 1957). Davidson was a veteran missionary to India. He was known for his warm Christian spirit and deep faith. He worked with the Telugu-speaking people of Hyderabad State and saw many converts. Early on, he was a tea company agent in Ceylon (Sri Lanka).

Gustav Edwards

1874
Sweden

June 27, 1948
Turlock, California

President of Trinity Evangelical Theological Seminary, 1915–38, 1940–45. Edwards was an evangelist for three years in Sweden before he went to China for six years as a missionary. He trained in Chicago, 1910–12, and served as pastor of Lake View Free Church, Evanston Free Church and Elim Free Church of Chicago, 1912–26. In 1916, he was called by the Swedish Evangelical Free Church of America to take charge of its schoolwork. In 1926, the church obtained property in Chicago and opened the Free Church Academy and Bible Institute. They became affiliated with MBI until 1927. Edwards was instructor and dean until 1944.

Henry B. Hemmeter

Dec. 24, 1869   *July 2, 1948*
Baltimore, Maryland   Elyria, Ohio

President of Concordia Theological Seminary, Springfield, IL (Fort Wayne, IN, in 1976), **1936–45**. Hemmeter married Anna Heitmueller on April 4, 1893. He pastored Our Savior Lutheran Church, Baltimore, MD (1892–95); St. Andrew's Lutheran, Pittsburgh, PA (1895–1902); Trinity Lutheran, Pittsburgh, PA (1905–8); Bethlehem Lutheran, St. Louis, MO (1908–14); St. Matthew's, Rochester, NY (1918–28); and was president of Concordia College, Conover, NC from 1914–18 and 1928–36. He wrote two books.

Andrew P. Stirrett

Sept. 30, 1865   *July 9, 1948*
Camlachie, Ontario, Canada   Jos, Nigeria

One of Africa's great missionaries, the "White Doctor," to the Hausas of central Sudan and Nigeria. Stirrett preached 20,000 times and reached 1.5 million people with the gospel. Between 1902–48, he spent only five years away from the field. He provided Hausa Bibles in 1932. Stirrett never married. Doug Percy tells the story of Stirrett in *Stirrett of the Sudan*.

Gerhard Kittel

Sept. 23, 1888   *July 11, 1948*
Breslau, Germany   Tübingen, Germany

Biblical scholar. Kittel was an instructor at Kiel (1913); at Leipzig (1917); professor of NT in Greifswald (1921–26); and in Tübingen (1926–45). His main interest was the Jewish background of the New Testament. He believed this element prevailed over the Greek element in the New Testament writings. The Allies imprisoned Kittel in 1945 for his book *The Jewish Question*. He wrote several books.

John M. Moore

Jan. 27, 1867   *July 30, 1948*
Morgantown, Kentucky   Dallas, Texas

Methodist Church South leader. Moore married Bessie Harris on March 25, 1901. Moore was a Methodist bishop, 1918–38. He was one of the three men that negotiated the historic merger in 1939. He served as a bishop in Brazil (1918–22) and in several southern stateside areas until 1938; and was active in ecumenical endeavors. He wrote lyrics and music to "Burdens Are Lifted At Calvary." He pastored in St. Louis, MO (1895–98); San Antonio, TX (1898–1902); Dallas, TX (1902–6); and St. Louis, MO (1909–10). Moore was secretary of home missions (1910–18).

Maude Charlesworth Booth

Sept. 13, 1865   *Aug. 26, 1948*
Limpsfield, England   Great Neck, Long Island, New York

Co-general with husband of Salvation Army (USA) 1887–96, and general of the Volunteers of America, 1940–48. Maude married BALLINGTON BOOTH on September 16, 1886. They traveled to America in 1887, and she faithfully helped her husband and the new movement develop in March, 1896. She was active in prison work and a founder of the PTA. During WWI, she traveled with the YMCA. She founded the Volunteers Prison League in 1897. Booth's best-known works were *Branded* (1897) and *Twilight Fairy Tales* (1906). DAN POLING conducted her funeral at New York City's Marble Collegiate Church.

Yu Hsiang Feng

Sept. 26, 1882
Ching-hsien, China

Sept. 4, 1948
Black Sea

Chinese general, baptized by Liu Fang in the Methodist Church after his conversion at a JOHN R. MOTT service, 1912. About half of Feng's 30,000 troops became baptized Christians. In 1924, Feng became commander-in-chief of the People's Armies. Feng married Li Te Ch'uan in 1926. He joined CHIANG KAI SHEK's Nationalist Army in 1927. Then he commanded the People's Allied Anti-Japanese Army after the invasion of 1937. He broke with CHIANG KAI SHEK. He was a loyal Christian and military man. Feng died in a fire aboard the ship *Pobeda*, a Russian vessel, on the Black Sea on his way to a conference.

Harold D. Dieter

Oct. 26, 1904
Fullerton, Pennsylvania

Sept. 6, 1948
Allentown, Pennsylvania

President of Beulah Park Bible School, 1932–34, renamed Allentown (PA) Bible Institute (United Wesleyan College in 1972), **1934–48**. Dieter married Laura Easterday (1923) and was ordained in the Pilgrim Holiness Church (1926). He received his education at BPBS.

Alfred T. Howard

March 12, 1868
Schoolcraft, Michigan

Nov. 12, 1948
Dayton, Ohio

Bishop of United Brethren in Christ, 1913–46; of United Evangelical Brethren in Christ (United Methodist Church in 1968), **1946–68; and president of Bonebreak Theological Seminary** (United Theological Seminary in 1954), **Dayton, OH 1921–29, 1933–38**. He was ordained as a United Brethren in 1894 and married May Stevenson on June 14, 1894. Howard was also superintendent of missions to Japan (1898–1912) and general superintendent of foreign work (1913–21).

Anna M. Jarvis

May 1, 1864
Grafton/Webster, West Virginia

Nov. 24, 1948
Westchester, Pennsylvania

Founder of Mother's Day. Moving to Philadelphia in 1903, Anna began work in an insurance company. In 1907, she invited several of her friends over the second Sunday in May to commemorate her mother's death, May 9, 1905. An idea was born and local Christian merchant, John Wanamaker, encouraged her. She wrote the Sunday school at Andrews Methodist Church, Grafton, WV, where her mother had taught for over 20 years, and carried out the first planned Mother's Day program there on May 10, 1908. In 1910, Governor W. Glasscock of West Virgina issued the first Mother's Day proclamation. In 1914, President WOODROW WILSON signed a resolution confirming the observance. She lived to see 43 other nations adopt this practice.

Frederick Brand

Sept. 9, 1863
Eden, New York

Jan. 1, 1949
St. Louis, Missouri

Director of Lutheran Church—Missouri Synod Missions, 1921–48. Brand was ordained Lutheran on Sept. 19, 1886. He married Emma Thieme on Nov. 15, 1887. Brand pastored in Braddock, PA (1886–93); St. Paul's, Pittsburgh, PA (1893–1903); and Trinity Church, Springfield, IL (1903–20). He was vice-president of the LCMS, 1917–29. From 1921–22, Brand visited the mission fields of India and China (China again in 1926). He wrote *Our Task in China* (1922). He died of a heart attack.

Joseph D. Williams

March 27, 1870
Bakerstown, Pennsylvania

Jan. 23, 1949
Jacksonville, Florida

First president of St. Paul (MN) Bible Institute (Crown College in 1992), **1916–25 and president of Simpson College, San Francisco, CA 1934–45**. Williams taught at Nyack (NY) College, 1895–1901, and was ordained in the Christian and Missionary Alliance in 1898. He married Harriet LeNeve on April 22, 1908. He pastored in Brooklyn (1895–1909), Indianapolis (1910–12), and St. Paul (1915–23). He did some education work in Ft. Wayne, IN and in the Phillippine Islands. He lived out his days in Atlanta.

Peter Marshall

May 27, 1902
Coatbridge, Scotland

Jan. 25, 1949
Washington, D.C.

Chaplain of the U.S. Senate for only two years, 1947–49, but made a lasting impact for Christ. Politicians came early to the senate so as not to miss his opening prayers. The writings of his wife, *Prayers of Peter Marshall* (1954), gave him worldwide recognition. Marshall came to America in 1927 and married Sarah Catherine Wood on November 4, 1936. He was ordained a Presbyterian and pastored in Covington, AL (1931–33); at Westminster Church, Atlanta, GA (1933–37); and the New York Avenue Church (1,800 members), Washington, D.C. (1937–45). He became a U.S. citizen in 1938. Marshall died of a heart attack. Several of his sermons appear in *Mr. Jones, Meet the Master* (1949). His life story was told in *A Man Called Peter*, written by his wife.

Lucy McGill Waterbury-Peabody

March 2, 1861
Belmont, Kansas

Feb. 25, 1949
Beverly, Massachusetts

Founder and first president of Association of Baptists for World Evangelism, 1927–35. Peabody married Norman Waterbury on August 18, 1881 (died: 1886) and Henry Peabody on June 16, 1906 (died: 1908), who left her a considerable estate. She taught deaf people in Rochester, NY and in Madras, India, among the Telugus, 1881–86. Peabody was editor of *Women's Baptist Foreign Mission Society World Friendship* (1887–1906), and founded Children's World Friendship and was later editor of their magazine. She later worked with IDA SCUDDER. She became director of Women's Christian College in Madras, then Women's Christian College of Vellore, and the Shanghai, China Medical College. She was a member of the International Council for Missions, 1913–26. She served on many NBC (ABC) boards. ABWE was born in 1927, when liberalism came to the Philippines. She lived in Georgetown, MA, in her later life and was buried in Pittsford, NY. She worked closely with HELEN MONTGOMERY.

Bernard B. Sutcliffe

Nov. 6, 1872
Halifax, Nova Scotia, Canada

Aug. 3, 1949
Portland, Oregon

First president of Multnomah School of the Bible, Portland, OR, 1936–43. Sutcliffe was converted on a train on June 1, 1901, after being witnessed to. He married Emma Anderson on June 1, 1906. He pastored the Presbyterian church of St. Joseph, MO, from 1906–16. Sutcliffe was also on the MBI staff, 1916–22, and later pastored in Tacoma, WA. He was confined to his bed the last year of his life.

Gerhardus Vos

March 14, 1862
Heerenveen, Netherlands

Aug. 13, 1949
Grand Rapids, Michigan

Presbyterian clergyman, author, and theologian. Vos taught at Holland Christian Reformed Church Seminary (Calvin Theological Seminary), 1888–93. He became the first professor of Biblical theology at Princeton (NJ) Seminary, 1893–1932. Vos was ordained Presbyterian in 1894. On September 7, 1894, Vos married Catherine Smith. His books range from *Mosaic Origin of Pentecostal Codes* (1886) to *Biblical Theology* (1948). His books, *The Teaching of Jesus* (1915) and *Pauline Theology* (1930) were two important works. He is buried in Roaring Branch, PA.

Edwin G. Zorn

Dec. 10, 1892
Chicago, Illinois

Aug. 21, 1949
Chicago, Illinois

Executive Secretary of Independent Fundamental Churches of America, 1939–49. Zorn married Alice Maurer on October 23, 1915, and they had four children. He was a member of the engineering department for the B & O Railroad (1911–13), and with Industrial Publications, Inc. (1914–31). He was a secretary of CBMC of Chicago, 1931–38. Independent Fundamental Churches of America was greatly benefited by his administrative leadership.

Ruth A. Paxson

Nov. 19, 1875
Manchester, Iowa

Oct. 1, 1949
Westfield, Massachusetts

Great Bible teacher, author, and conference speaker. Paxson never married. She first served in YMCA work. As a member of Moody Church she went to China in 1911 and served 25 years. Paxson and Edith Davis (died: 1943) traveled in Bible Conference ministries. Paxson's book, *Life on the Highest Plane*, is outstanding.

William T. Manning

May 12, 1866
Northhampton, England

Nov. 18, 1949
New York, New York

Episcopalian bishop of New York, 1921–46. Manning made the headlines for his controversial opinions opposing remarriage after divorce and urging the firing of Bertrand Russell from his New York teaching post for supporting adultery and atheism. Manning married Florence Antwerp in 1895. He served as rector at churches in Landsdowne, PA (1896–98); Christ's Church, Nashville, TN (1898–1903); before going to New York City to be vicar of St. Agnes Chapel of Trinity parish (1903–8), and rector of Trinity Church (1908–21), the wealthiest religious congregation in the country. Manning raised millions of dollars for St. John's Cathedral in 1940 (which began in 1892) but was not yet completed at the time of his death. He retired at the end of 1946.

Daniel W. Kurtz

Oct. 9, 1879
Hartville, Ohio

Nov. 22, 1949
LaVerne, California

College and seminary president. Kurtz married Ethel Wheeler on September 7, 1909. He was ordained a bishop in 1914. He was president of McPherson (KS) College (1914–27) and of Bethany Biblical Seminary, Oakbrook, IL (Richmond, IN, in 1994) (1932–37). He was four times the moderator for the Church of the Brethren, 1926–36. He pastored First Church, Long Beach, CA from 1927–32. Kurtz's books range from *Fundamental Doctrines of the Faith* (1911) to *The Gospel of Jesus* (1936).

William C. Poole

April 14, 1875
Easton, Maryland

Dec. 24, 1949
Lewes, Delaware

Wrote lyrics for "Count Me" (music by HALDOR LILLENAS), **"Just When I Need Him Most"** (music by CHARLES GABRIEL), **"Sunrise," "I Shall See the King," "In the Garden With Jesus"** (music of all three by B.D. ACKLEY). Poole was converted at age eleven. He grew up on a family farm and was educated at Washington College, Chestertown, MD. In 1900, he was ordained into the Methodist ministry and served various pastorates for 35 years in the Wilmington (DE) Conference. It was CHARLES GABRIEL who inspired him to write song texts.

William O. E. Oesterley

July 13, 1866
Calcutta, India

1950

Church of England theologian. Oesterley was an examiner in Hebrew and Greek Testament for the University of London, 1909–23. Oesterley was a professor of Old Testament history at King's College, University of London, 1926–36. Then he was appointed chaplain to the bishop of London and the prebendary of St. Paul's Cathedral. He was a prolific author and was editor of *Church and Supporter* (1897 on).

Seth Sykes

1950

Wrote lyrics and music to the beloved chorus with his wife, "Thank You Lord for Saving My Soul." He also wrote the choruses: "Love, Wonderful Love," and "Running Over." Seth composed only the music for "Calvary Love" (C. Watkins) and "Give Me Calvary Love" (Williams). He lived in the United Kingdom. His wife, Bessie (born: 1905), helped in the songwriting ventures. Bessie wrote lyrics and music to "Love, Wonderful Love" and "I Took a Plunge in the Crimson Flood."

John C. Broomfield

July 4, 1872
Eyemouth, Scotland

Jan. 8, 1950
St. Louis, Missouri

President of Methodist Protestant Conference (United Methodist Church in 1968), **1928–36**. Broomfield married Moselle Donaldson on October 6, 1898. He pastored MP churches: First Church, Uniontown, PA (1896–98); Fourth Church, Pittsburgh, PA (1898–1905); and MP Temple, Fairmont, WV (1905–24 and 1937–39). He became the traveling president of the Pittsburgh Conference, 1924–28. At the United Methodist union of 1939, he was consecrated bishop of the Missouri area. He surveyed educational, medical, and evangelistic work of churches in Japan, China, and India.

Walter A. Maier

Oct. 4, 1893
Boston, Massachusetts

Jan. 11, 1950
St. Louis, Missouri

Lutheran scholar and "Lutheran Hour" radio preacher. Maier was the greatest evangelistic voice in the history of the Lutheran Church. Prior to his marriage to Hulda Eickhoff on June 14, 1924 (died: December 27, 1986 in Ft. Wayne, IN), he did evangelistic work among German war prisoners brought to U.S. refugee camps on the East Coast, 1917–19. Maier had many outreaches running concurrently in his life. He edited *The Walther League Messenger* (1920–45), while teaching Old Testament exegesis and Semitic languages at Concordia Theological Seminary in St. Louis, MO from 1922–50, and preaching his daily radio Bible message. He helped pioneer Christian radio as early as 1924, at Concordia.

Maier founded *The Lutheran Hour*, a 30-minute radio program broadcast over 1,200 stations, in 36 different languages, in 55 countries, reaching 20 million people. He directed and preached this program first through Columbia Broadcasting (1930–35) and then on the Mutual Network (1935–50). Maier received as many as 10,000 letters a day, with 70 people processing them. He was supported solely through his college salary. The radio evangelistic outreach was his ministry. Maier's radio messages/sermons appeared in 20 books, from *The Lutheran Hour* (1931) to *1,000 Radio Voices for Christ* (1949). His 600-page book on marriage, *For Better, Not for Worse*, was a classic. He held crusades entitled, "Bringing Christ to the Nations." He missed his first broadcast in 20 years because of illness on January 1, 1950 and died from a series of heart attacks.

Samuel W. Latimer

Oct. 1, 1872
Newnan, Georgia

Jan. 14, 1950
Cleveland, Tennessee

General overseer of Church of God, Cleveland, TN 1928–35. Latimer was married on October 29, 1893 to Margaret Wright (died: January 17, 1952). They had ten children. He was the first pastor of the church in Spring Place, GA. In 1924, he became the pastor of the North Cleveland Church of God in Cleveland, TN. He was the editor and publisher for the Church of God Publishing House, 1926–28 and 1935 on. He then pastored in Rome and in Dalton, GA.

Joseph F. Newton

July 21, 1880
Decatur, Texas

Jan. 24, 1950
Merion, Pennsylvania

Pastor in various affiliations. Newton's early pastorate was at FBC, Paris, TX, from 1897–98, when he left the SBC. He served as an associate in a non-sectarian church in St. Louis, 1898–1900. Newton married Jennie Deatherage on June 14, 1900. He then pastored at People's Church, Dixon, IL (1901–8) and Little Brick Church, Cedar Rapids, IA (1908–16). He was a Universalist, 1903–25. His book, *The Builders*, 1914, was widely read in Masonic circles. Newton served as pastor at City Temple, London (1916–19) and Church of the Divine Paternity, NYC (1919–25). Becoming an Episcopalian in 1925, he pastored three churches in Philadelphia: Memorial Church of St. Paul (1925–30); St. James (1930–38); and St. Luke and Epiphany (1938–50). He authored 30 books, from *David Swing* (1909), to *Life Victorious* (1946). He died of a heart attack.

Clairborne M. Hill

Nov. 16, 1857
Suisun, California

Jan. 27, 1950
Los Angeles, California

President of Berkeley (CA) Baptist Divinity School (American Baptist Seminary of the West in 1977), **1904–37**. Hill married Anna Pengra on December 21, 1884, and was ordained a Baptist the same year. Hill pastored in Eugene, OR (1884–90); was superintendent of home missions for Oregon American Baptists (1890–93); and pastored 10th Avenue Church, Oakland, CA (1893–1904).

Orin E. Tiffany

March 27, 1868
Havana, Minneapolis

Feb. 1, 1950
Wheaton, Illinois (?)

President of Seattle (WA) Pacific College (University in 1977), **1916–26**. Tiffany married Grace English on August 17, 1897 (died: 1922) and Kathrine MacDonald on June 16, 1925. He headed the history department of Greenville (IL) College (1896–1903); taught history at Western Maryland College, Westminster (1905–15); taught at Whitworth College, Spokane, WA (1926–29); and headed the history and social science department of Wheaton (IL) College (1929–44).

The Saints Go Marching In

Daniel T. Muse

March 15, 1882
Booneville, Mississippi

Feb. 4, 1950
Oklahoma City, Oklahoma

General superintendent of Pentecostal Holiness Church (International in 1975), **1937–50**. Muse was converted January 18, 1913, via James Campbell, and sanctified shortly thereafter. He faithfully served his church in every capacity from janitor to senior bishop. This includes pastor, conference superintendent, general secretary, and chairman of the General Board/Conference for nearly eight years. His wife's name was Adelaide, whom he married on October 7, 1906. He headed the PHC Missions program, 1937–45 and 1949–50.

Niels C. Carlsen

June 1, 1884
Hjoerring, Denmark

Feb. 6, 1950
Blair, Nebraska

President of United Danish Evangelical Lutheran Church, 1925–45 (full-time since 1930), **renamed United Evangelical Lutheran Church** (ALC, ELCA in 1988), **1945–50**. Carlsen married Martha Neve on June 15, 1910; and they had ten children. He also pastored at Superior, WI and Duluth, MN from 1910–30. In 1948, Carlsen began negotiations, which led to the organization of the ALC. He died of a heart attack.

Edwin H. Hughes

Dec. 7, 1866
Moundsville, West Virginia

Feb. 12, 1950
Washington, D.C.

Bishop in the Methodist Episcopal Church, 1908–39, and in the Methodist Church, 1939–48. Hughes married Isabel Ebbert on June 8, 1892 (died: 1938) and they had eight children. Hughes pastored at Newton Center, MA (1892–96); Malden, MA (1896–1903); and was president of DePauw University, Greencastle, IN (1903–8). In 1908, he moved to San Francisco to begin bishop responsibilities. He was president of Boston University (1923) and chancellor of the American University of Washington, D.C. (1933). He was one of three famous leaders of 1939 involved in the reunion of the Methodist Church. His speech, "The Methodists Are One People," was spoken to a group of 14,000 as three Methodist groups merged together in Kansas City, MO to form the Methodist Church in 1939. He wrote several books. He wrote from *Thanksgiving Sermons* (1909) to *I Was Made a Minister* (1943).

Rees Howells

Oct. 10, 1879
Brynammon, Wales

Feb. 13, 1950
Llandrindad Wells, Wales

Welsh miner and spiritual giant as told in the book, *Rees Howells: Intercessor,* by NORMAN GRUBB. His father earned 35 cents a day to support his family of eleven children. Howell started work in the mines at age twelve, leaving for America to seek his fortune in 1888. He was converted in a Methodist church in Connellsville, PA, via a converted Jew, Maurice Reuben. He married Elizabeth Jones on December 21, 1910. Howell returned to Wales, resuming work in the coal mines, only to leave again to lead a mighty revival in Africa. He founded the Bible College of Wales at age 40. He had a very bad heart attack February 8, and his last words were "Victory—Hallelujah!"

Ira B. Wilson

Sept. 6, 1880
Bedford, Iowa

April 3, 1950
Los Angeles, California

Wrote lyrics for the hymn, "Make Me a Blessing" (1904) (music by GEORGE SCHULER). Wilson was trained at Moody Bible Institute about 1902. In 1905, he went to Lorenz Publishing Company of Dayton, OH as an editor and composer. Wilson's seasonal choir cantatas sold more than 1.5 million copies. He made his home in Los Angeles after 1930. Sometimes Wilson used the pseudonym Fred B. Holton.

August Marahrens

Oct. 11, 1875
Hanover, Germany

May 3, 1950
Kloster Loccum, Germany

President of the Lutheran World Convention (Federation in 1997), **1935–45**. Marahrens was a Lutheran pastor and bishop. He pastored in Hanover (1905–09); was director of the Erichsburg Theological Seminary (1909–20); was bishop of the Lutheran Territorial Church, Hanover (1924–47); and was abbot at Loccum (1928–50). He was considered an evangelical pastor's pastor, and was involved in legal means to defend the church during the troubled 1930s.

Walter E. Musgrave

Sept. 7, 1880
near Stockport, Ohio

May 6, 1950
Huntington, Indiana

Bishop of United Brethren in Christ, Huntington, IN 1925–59. Musgrave married Anna Yarnell on February 6, 1904. Converted at age 19, he pastored in Ohio (1902–15); was the superintendent of Scioto District for the Church of United Brethren (1915–20); and executive secretary of Otterbein Forward Movement (1920–25). Musgrave was president of the Missionary Society, 1933 on. He wrote a history of the United Brethren in 1945. Musgrave was a Republican who lived most of his life in Huntington.

Grant C. Tullar

Aug 5, 1869
Bolton, Connecticut

May 20, 1950
Ocean Grove, New Jersey

Composed music for "Face to Face" (1898), "Nailed to the Cross," "Shall I Crucify My Savior?" (music of all three by Carrie Breck). He also wrote "Our Best" (music by S.C. Kirk) and "Oh, It is Wonderful" (music by Rosemans). Tullar was converted at a Methodist camp meeting near Waterbury, CT at age 19, and was ordained a Methodist. He became an evangelist, then a musical evangelist for George A. Hilton for ten years. In 1893, Tullar and Issac Meredith founded Tullar-Meredith Publishing Company of New York. He was married in 1897.

William Evans

Jan. 1, 1870
Liverpool, England

May 21, 1950
Los Angeles, California

Foremost Bible teacher of his time and author of over 40 volumes. Evans came to the United States (1889) and was the first graduate of Moody Bible Institute (1892). He pastored in Goshen, IN (1895–97) and in Wheaton, IL (1897–1900). He married Laura Torgerson on June 25, 1902. Evans was the director and teacher of Moody Bible Institute's Bible curriculum (1901–5) and associate dean and teacher at Bible Institute of Los Angeles (1915–18). He was ordained as a Presbyterian then served as a Bible conference evangelist, 1918–50. He produced the ten-volume *Through the Bible*, along with his twelve other books, from *The Book of Books* (1902) to *From the Upper Room to the Empty Tomb* (1934).

Leo H. Lehmann

Dec. 6, 1895
Kingstown, Ireland

June 19, 1950
Brooklyn, New York

Director of Christ's Mission (merged into International Teams in 1984), **1940–51**, during its influential time of providing a haven for ex-Catholic priests. Lehmann was a Roman Catholic priest in 1929 before he made his break to join the Reformed Church. His wife's name was Margaret, and they had two sons. Lehman edited *The Converted Catholic Magazine* and wrote *Souls of a Priest* and various other booklets on Catholicism.

Hugh T. Kerr

Feb. 11, 1871
Elora, Ontario, Canada

June 27, 1950
Pittsburgh, Pennsylvania

Presbyterian clergyman, 1897–1945. Kerr married Olive M. Boggs on June 12, 1901. He pastored Oakland Church, Pittsburgh, PA (1897–1901); First Church, Hutchison, KS (1901–7); Fullerton Avenue Church, Chicago (1907–13); and his longest pastorate at Shadyside Church, Pittsburgh, PA (1913–45). Kerr was one of the first radio preachers in America, 1922–42. He wrote more than 20 books from *Book of Family Devotion* (1910) to *The Christian Sacraments* (1944).

Florence Allshorn

Dec. 19, 1887
Sheffield, England

July 3, 1950
England

Missionary and educator of missionaries. Raised in Sheffield, Florence worked on the cathedral staff. She encouraged factory girls and Sunday school teachers alike. In 1920, she was accepted by the Church Missionary Society for service in Uganda. She was a born educator, and at Iganga, had a wonderful school. She read I Corinthians 13 every day for a year to help her really love "her people." She returned to England in 1924 with a bad lung. The CMS asked her to help in a training college for female missionaries, which she did until 1940. She then founded St. Julian's Community, in Sussex, which was a place for those who needed fellowship and a new start. In 1950, the community moved to Coolham, to larger quarters. She had Hodgkin's disease, and after weeks of painful illness, she died.

Richmond A. Montgomery

July 16, 1870
Hendricks County, Indiana

July 16, 1950
Jonesville, Michigan

President of Lane Theological Seminary, 1926–50 (affiliated with McCormick Theological Seminary, Chicago, in 1931). He was president at the time of the move from Cincinnati to Chicago. Montgomery was ordained as a Presbyterian in 1896 and married Mary F. Allbanda in May, 1897 (died: July 20, 1940). He held pastorates from (1896–1917); including ministries in Duluth, MN (1899–1904); Xenia, OH (1904–9); and Ottumwa, IA (1909–14). Montgomery served as president of Parsons College, Fairfield, IA (1917–22) and of Centre College, Danvillle, KY (1922–26).

Evangeline C. Booth

Dec. 25, 1865
London, England

July 17, 1950
Hartsdale, New York

General of Salvation Army, 1934–39, and the USA division, 1904–34. As the daughter of WILLIAM BOOTH, she remained single her whole life. Evangeline was converted at age ten as a result of seeing a picture of Jesus on the cross, and her parents praying with her. Early in her career, she was appointed Captain of the Great Western Hall (London) when there was great opposition. She courageously faced fierce riots. From Parliament she obtained the repeal of by-laws forbidding the SA to hold open-air meetings. Booth organized a Salvation Army work in Klondike, AK, during the gold rush of 1898, having served as the Canadian director, 1896–1904. She was an able public speaker, giving her first speech at age 15. Booth won many honors and awards and wrote some Salvation Army songs and books: *The War Romance of the Salvation Army* with GRACE L. HILL (1919), *Love Is All* (1925), *Towards a Better World* (1928) and *Woman* (1930). She died of arteriosclerosis (thickening of the blood vessell walls).

Francis D. Gamewell

Aug. 31, 1857
Camden, South Carolina

Aug. 7, 1950
Clifton Springs, New York

Methodist educational missionary to China beginning in 1881. Gamewell married Mary Porter (1804–November 27, 1906) on June 29, 1882, and Mary Ninde (1858–August 26, 1947) on May 12, 1909. He was professor of chemistry and physics at Peking University, 1889–1900. Gamewell served as chief-of-staff at the British embassy during the Boxer Rebellion siege of Peking in 1900 and is credited with saving the lives of 3,500 people inside barricades. He was the field secretary of the Methodist Board of Missions, 1901–8.

William B. Pugh

Jan. 20, 1889
Utica, New York

Sept. 14, 1950
near Thermopolis, Wyoming

Stated clerk of Presbyterian Church (USA in 1983) **in the USA, 1938–50.** Pugh married Emma Schaperkotter and was ordained in 1915. He pastored Beacon Street Church, Philadelphia, PA (1915–28), and First Church, Chester, PA (1929–38). Pugh was involved in many denominational and ecumenical activities with the FCC and WCC. He was also chaplain in WWI and lived in Wallingford, PA. He is buried in Arlington (MD) National Cemetery.

William L. Pettingill

Aug. 27, 1866
Central Square, New York

Sept. 15, 1950
New York, New York

Baptist pastor and an editor of the *Scofield Reference Bible*. He married Harriet Lockhart in 1890 and Etta Dodge on January 15, 1936. Pettingill was a pastor at North Baptist, Wilmington, DE (1903–13); was dean of Philadelphia School of the Bible (1914–28), which he cofounded with C. I. SCOFIELD; and pastor at FBC, New York City (1948–50). Pettingill wrote many commentaries. He promoted dispensational premillennialism, was a popular speaker at Bible and prophetic conferences, and was known as a strong fundamentalist leader. His books range from *Israel* (1905) to *Nearing the End* (1948). He is buried in Wilmington, DE.

Louis S. Bauman

Nov. 13, 1875
Nora Springs, Iowa

Nov. 8, 1950
Washington, D.C.

Pastor, evangelist, and first director of Grace Brethren Missions, 1907–46. Bauman was the key individual in the early days of the Grace Brethren churches. He was ordained on August 4, 1894 by the Brethren Church. He married Mary Wakeman on April 28, 1898 (died: 1909), and Retta Stover on April 8, 1912. Bauman pastored in Morrill, KA (1894–95); Auburn and Cornell, IL (1895–97) and Mexico and Roann, IN (1897–1900). He then pastored the First Church in Philadelphia, PA (1900–10); Sunnyside, WA (1911–13); First Church in Long Beach, CA (1913–48) which started as a result of his revival meetings in the area; and Grace Brethren in Washington, D.C. (1948–50). Bauman helped establish Ashland (OH) Seminary, then supported Grace Theological Seminary's establishment in 1937 at Winona Lake, IN. He wrote much on prophecy (e.g., *Light from the Bible Prophecy*, 1940), and was a conference speaker of note.

Paul W. Fleming

Oct. 15, 1910
Los Angeles, California

Nov. 21, 1950
Mount Moran, Wyoming

Chairman, founder, and first president of New Tribes Mission, 1942–50. Fleming pioneered a faith movement that struggled for recognition, but resulted in a worldwide program with headquarters in Sanford, FL. Fleming was converted at the Church of the Open Door and influenced to missions and evangelism by PAUL RADER. He married Cherrill Harter on June 13, 1936, and in 1937 he went to British Malaya to reach the Sakai tribe. He returned home in 1940 with cerebral malaria. In 1942, he recruited CECIL DYE to go to Bolivia. The death of DYE's mission team in 1942 gave birth to New Tribes Mission. He started the magazine *Brown Gold* (1943). Fleming died tragically at age 40 in a Grand Teton Mountains airplane crash with 20 others (twelve missionaries, eight children). The airplane was a C-47 converted for passenger transportation and was on its way to South America. By the mid-1990s, New Tribes Mission had 2,000 missionaries in 21 countries among 200 tribal groups.

Charles R. Brown

Oct. 1, 1862
Bethany, West Virginia

Nov. 28, 1950
New Haven, Connecticut

Dean of Yale University Divinity School, New Haven, CT 1911–28, and Congregational minister. Converted in the fall of 1885 at Trement Temple in Boston at a WILLIAM BOOTH night of prayer, Brown switched from Methodism to Congregationalism in 1892. He pastored at the Wesley Chapel Methodist Church, Cincinnati, OH (1889–92); at Winthrop Congregational Church, Boston, MA (1892–96); and at First Congregational Church, Oakland, CA (1896–1911). He married Alice Tufts on September 23, 1896. Brown was known as a liberal preacher and teacher, a Republican and a Mason. In 1924, he was named one of the 25 most influential preachers in America. He retired in 1928. His writings range from *Two Parables* (1898) to *Dreams Come True* (1944). He greatly influenced theological liberalism. For eleven years he pastored the University Church while at Yale.

B. B. Crimm

March 14, 1886
Beith, Texas

Dec. 1, 1950
Marshall, Texas

Widely known as the "Cowboy Evangelist." Crimm was a star athlete at Howard Payne College, Brownwood, TX. He preached in 25 states and brought over 140,000 into church membership. Of this number, 600 became ministers. Graduating from HPC in 1912, he spent three years at Baylor University, Waco, TX. During his first three years of Christian service, he pastored Baptist churches in Rowena, Valley View, and Eden (all in Texas), in his early days. Crimm acquired his own tent and equipment and became an evangelist, living in Marshall. He died in an automobile accident. He was thrown from the car, driven by pastor H.A. Fisk. The car failed to make a curve on slippery asphalt. He had been holding a revival at Cuero and was making an overnight visit to his home.

Olav M. Jonswold

June 17, 1881
Flekkefjord, Norway

Jan. 4, 1951
Milwaukee, Wisconsin

President of Evangelical Free Church Association (Evangelical Free Church of America in 1950), **1926–33, 1935–43.** Jonswold came to America in 1903 and married Gardia Mathiansen on November 6, 1909. He served as pastor of Norske Church, Boston, MA (1910–18); Second Norwegian Free Church, Brooklyn, NY (1918–32); and Salem Evangelical Free Church, Chicago, IL (1934–49).

Henry (Harry) A. Ironside

Oct. 14, 1876
Toronto, Ontario, Canada

Jan. 15, 1951
Cambridge, New Zealand

Pastor of Moody Church, 1930–48, and renowned Bible teacher. Ironside was converted alone in his room at age 13, while reading Proverbs 1:24–32. He began preaching at 14. The family moved to California, where he worked with the Salvation Army, and then the Plymouth Brethren

Society. With no formal education or ordination, he traveled across the country as a Bible conference speaker from 1896–1929. Ironside organized the Western Book and Tract Company in Oakland, CA, in 1914. He then moved to Texas and taught at the Evangelical (Dallas) Theological College, 1924–30. Even after his call to the pastorate at Moody Church in Chicago, Ironside continued 40 weeks a year on the road—always returning to preach at Moody on Sunday. He married Helen Schofield on January 5, 1898 (died: May 1, 1948) and then Ann Hightower on October 9, 1949 (died: March 8, 1978). He wrote the beautiful lyrics for "Overshadowed" (music by GEORGE SCHULER) and authored some 80 books, pamphlets, and commentaries. These range from *Notes on Daniel* (1911) to *Notes on Ezekiel* (1949). In 1935, Ironside preached the funeral sermon for Evangelist BILLY SUNDAY. Although blind during his final years, he continued to travel, dying on a preaching trip in New Zealand. He was buried there. Ironside was probably the greatest Bible teacher of his generation.

Amy B. Carmichael

Dec. 16, 1867
Millisle, Northern Ireland

Jan. 18, 1951
Dohnavur, India

Missionary to India and founder of the Dohnavur Fellowship in 1926. Carmichael came to Christ at age 16 while attending a Wesleyan Methodist boarding school at Harrogate. She was called to missions on January 13, 1892, as she pondered the words, "Go ye…" In November, 1895, she arrived in Tinnevelly, South India, after a brief time in Japan, 1893–94 for the Church of England and stayed for 55 years until her death. In 1901, she settled in Dohnavur. Amy formed the Dohnavur Fellowship, in 1925, with the purpose of rescuing children from the corruption of temple prostitute service. Her society became independent in 1927. At first, Carmichael ministered only to the needs of young girls, but later to young boys as well. After a fall in 1931, she became an invalid. Although she had serious arthritis, she wrote 35 books, inspiring devotional material, and poetry still quoted today, including *If* (1938). She never married. Her favorite Bible verse was Jude 24.

Thomas L. Aaron

Aug. 4, 1897
Good Hope, Georgia

Jan. 20, 1951
Franklin Springs, Georgia

President of Franklin Springs (GA) Bible Institute, 1933–39, renamed Emmanuel College, 1939–51. Aaron was converted in a tent meeting at age 16 and was married to Francis Huggins in 1923. He later pastored in Georgia, Alabama, Oklahoma, and Washington D.C. Reopening a school in 1933 after it was temporarily shut down during the Depression, he led it into a college status. Despite a devastating fire on March 21, 1946, the ministry grew. He suffered a heart attack on August 18, 1949 from which he never recovered.

Ethel Robinson Taylor

c 1868

Jan. 20, 1951
St. Petersburg, Florida

Wrote lyrics and music to "Calvary Covers It All." Ethel is better known as "Ma Taylor." She married WALTER TAYLOR in 1898. She and her husband were superintendents of the Pacific Garden Mission, Chicago, 1919–36. Before her conversion, Ethel was in the entertainment field. One night at the altar, she led WALTER MACDONALD to Christ. She said to him, "Calvary covers it all," and a song was born. She wrote several choruses also.

Howard C. Fulton

1891   *Jan. 21, 1951*
     Chicago, Illinois

Active in GARB circles, and pastor of Belden Avenue Baptist Church (Crossroads Baptist) **in Chicago, 1931–51.** He pastored in Franksville and Norfold, WI, and Grand Rapids, MI, in his early days. When the GARB was organized in 1932, he was the host pastor. His church became a key church in Chicago in the 1930s. During his ministry there, 1,841 accepted Christ and joined the church. The events of his death were bizarre. He dropped dead in the pulpit at 11:55 a.m. before 350 of his parishioners as he was finishing his sermon, "The Touch of God." The church treasurer, Henry F. Weiler, dropped dead of a heart attack a few minutes later, precipitated by seeing his pastor die.

J. Taylor Hamilton

April 30, 1859   *Jan. 29, 1951*
Antigua, West Indies   Bethlehem, Pennsylvania

President of Moravian Theological Seminary, Bethlehem, PA 1918–28, and bishop in the Moravian Church, 1905–28. He became a teacher at Nazareth Hall Military Academy (1877–81) and pastor of Second Moravian Church in Philadelphia, PA (1881–86). Hamilton married Cecilia E. Black on June 7, 1886 (died: 1944). He taught Greek, church history and practical theology at MTS from 1886–1903, and also authored several books on Moravian historical topics ranging from *History of the Moravian Church in America* (1895) to *Twenty Years of Pioneer Missions in Nyassaland* (1912).

Evan J. Roberts

July 8, 1878   *Jan. 29, 1951*
Lougher, Wales   Cardiff, Wales

Wales saw revival twice in history, once with CHRISTMAS EVANS, and a hundred years later with Roberts, 1904–6. In his mid-twenties, Roberts preached to, prayed for, and saw some 165,000 converted and a nation turned upside down spiritually. It started in his home church, Moriah, in Lougher. Roberts never married. He lived out his years in obscurity in Leicester, England, teaching a small Bible class. He returned to Wales in 1925.

Ralph E. Diffendorfer

Aug. 15, 1879   *Jan. 31, 1951*
Hayesville, Ohio   Madison, New Jersey

General secretary of United Methodist Church Missions, 1924–49 (through the 1939 merger). For most of his life, Diffendorfer was connected with the home and foreign missionary program of his denomination. He married Edna Saylor on November 4, 1903. His books range from *Junior Studies in the Life of Christ* (1903) to *Church and Missions in Japan* (1941). He was often called a "missionary statesman," highly respected by all.

Lloyd C. Douglas

Aug. 27, 1877   *Feb. 13, 1951*
Columbia City, Indiana   Los Angeles, California

Ordained as a Lutheran minister and novelist known for his book, *The Robe* (1942), which sold over 2 million copies. He married Bessie Porch on April 7, 1904 (died: December 30, 1944). Douglas pastored in North Manchester, IN (1903–5); Lancaster, OH (1905–8); Washington, D.C. (1908–11); Ann Arbor, MI (1915–21); Akron, OH (1921–26); Los Angeles, CA (1926–29); and at the St. James United Church, Montreal, Quebec (1929–33). The last four churches were Congregational congregations. Another popular book of his was *The Big Fisherman* (1948). He did not start writing novels until he was past 50 years of age, his first being *Magnificent Obsession* (1929). His first nonfiction book was *Wanted—A Congregation* (1920).

N. Alvin Jepson

Feb. 19, 1888
Plainfield, Iowa

Feb. 19, 1951
Seattle, Washington

President of Christian Nationals Evangelism Commission (Partners International), **1943–51**. He was converted at age twelve while working in the fields. In 1920, he became a Seattle chiropractor and chairman of CBMC. Jepson married Margaret Wheaton on June 30, 1922. He soon started China Native Evangelistic Crusade (early name). Jepson was a member of First Presbyterian Church. He was an extremely large man, weighing 310 pounds. He died of a lymph gland infection. For more than 25 years, he read the whole book of Romans every morning before 6:00 a.m.

Elizabeth M. Jenkins

April 29, 1853
Mount Pleasant, Ohio

March 26, 1951
California

General superintendent of Ohio Yearly Meeting (Evangelical Friends Church—Eastern Region in 1971) **Missions, 1895–1913**. Elizabeth's mother, Sara (1818–1902), was the founder and first director of the EFM from 1884–1895. She was a member of Mt. Pleasant Friends Church, and an elder, 1896 on. Elizabeth took a trip to visit India and China, 1906–8. She was known as "Miss Lilly," beloved by all who knew her.

Basil J. Mathews

Aug. 28, 1879
Oxford, England

March 29, 1951
Oxford, England

Methodist educator and writer. Mathews married Anne Passmore in 1905 (died: 1939) and Winifred Wilson in 1940. He was on the literary staff of *Christian World* (1904–10); was editorial secretary of London Missionary Society (1910–19); and was literature secretary of World's Committee of the YMCA, Geneva, Switzerland (1924–29). Mathews taught Christian World Relations at Andover-Newton Theological Seminary (1931–44), at Boston University, and at Union College, University of British Columbia, Canada (1944–49). Mathews wrote more than 40 books from *The Splendid Quest* (1911) to *Booker T. Washington* (1948).

Charles H. Phillips

Jan. 17, 1858
Milledgeville, Georgia

April 12, 1951
Cleveland, Ohio

Bishop of Colored (Christian in 1956) **Methodist Episcopal Church, 1902–48; senior bishop, 1937–46**. Phillips was converted on December 26, 1874. He married Lucy Tappan on Dec. 16, 1880 (died: 1913) and Ella Cheeks on Aug. 28, 1918. He was the president of Lane College, Jackson, TN (1883–84); pastor of Chapel CMC, Memphis, TN (1885–87); Israel Memorial Church, Washington, D.C. (1887–91); and in Louisville, KY (1891–93). Phillips also was editor of *Christian Index* (1894–1902). He made three trips to Europe. Phillips brought credibility to the once scorned denomination.

Benjamin G. Shaw

Aug. 26, 1878
Pope, Mississippi

April 14, 1951
Salisbury, North Carolina

Bishop of African Methodist Episcopal Zion Church, 1924–51; senior bishop, 1944–51. Shaw started pastoring in 1898. He pastored in Greenwood, and Sharkey Circuit, MS; Payne Chapel, Little Rock, AR; St. John's Chapel, New Alabany, IN; Hood Temple, Evansville, IN; and then at the Washington Metropolitan Church in St. Louis, 1910–20. There, he led the congregation in obtaining a huge building. Shaw was the first director of evangelism for the denomination, 1920–24. He is buried in Birmingham, AL.

Ben M. Bogard

March 9, 1868
Elizabethtown, Kentucky

May 29, 1951
Little Rock, Arkansas

A key leader in the American Baptist Association, author and pastor. Bogard pastored in Princeton, KY (1892–94); Charleston, MO (1894–1901); Searcy, AR (1902–7); Texarkana, TX (1907–14); Itasca, TX (1914–18); and Antioch Baptist, Little Rock, AR (1921–45). He led in forming the Arkansas State Association of Missionary Baptists, and Sheridan Baptist College. He was also on the Sunday School committee of the ABA. Bogard was dean of Missionary Baptist Seminary, Little Rock, AR, from 1943–45 and represented Baptist causes in 235 public debates. He married Lynn O. Meacham, and they had two children.

Galen B. Royer

Sept. 8, 1862
Lewisburg, Pennsylvania

June 4, 1951
Near Huntingdon, Pennsylvania

Secretary of Church of the Brethren Missions, Elgin, IL 1902–18. Royer was a pastor, teacher and administrator. He studied business in Mt. Morris, IL from 1883–93, and at Valparaiso where he assisted his father in the administration of the college, and taught music and commericial courses. He married Anna Miller in 1885. He suceeded his brother-in-law as secretary of what later became the General Mission Board. He traveled to Europe and Asia in 1907, 1910, and 1913–14 to inspect Brethren missions. After his retirement, he taught missions at Juniata (PA) College, 1918–24. From 1924–36, he pastored in Pittsburgh and Johnstown, PA. He wrote a series of biographies of biblical characters for his children, and several books on Brethren missions, histor, and leaders.

Harrison S. Elliott

Dec. 13, 1882
St. Clairsville, Ohio

June 27, 1951
New York, New York

Methodist theologian and educator. Elliott was secretary of the International Committee of the YMCA (1910–22), then instructor of pedagogy at Drew Theological Seminary (1911–23). He became professor of theology and head of the religious education department at Union Theological Seminary, New York City from 1925–50. Elliott married Grace Loucks on June 24, 1927. His books range from *Student Standards of Action* (1914) and *Can Religious Education Be Christian?* (1940).

Samuel Goudie

Aug. 11, 1866
Hespeler, Ontario, Canada

July 2, 1951
Stouffville, Ontario, Canada

President of United Missionary Society, Elkhart, IN 1922–37. He married Eliza J. Smith on March 20, 1889. Goudie was converted at age 17 and ordained at the Ontario Conference in 1891. He spent 28 years as district superintendent of Ontario, 1905–33. He served as the chairman of the board of the United Missionary Church, 1912–43. He also pastored for 26 years.

Ida Reed Smith

Nov. 30, 1865
Philippi, West Virginia

July 9, 1951
Philippi, West Virginia

Wrote lyrics for, "I Belong to the King," (music by Lincoln Hall) **and "Only a Touch"** (music by B. D. Ackley). Smith lived her lifetime in the Philippi area, having a burden for caring for younger family members and her father's farm. Her father died and her mother was an invalid. Ida, too, became an invalid and lived near poverty.

Nevin C. Harner

Feb. 5, 1901
Near Berlin, Pennsylvania

July 24, 1951
Lancaster, Pennsylvania

Executive secretary of Association of Theological Schools, 1950–51. Harner was ordained to the Reformed Church in 1924 and married Flora Morton on August 2, 1926. He taught religious education at Evangelical and Reformed Theological Seminary, 1929–45 and 1947–51. Harner also served as dean 1943–45. He was president of Heidelberg College, Seneca, OH 1945–47. He wrote works ranging from *The Educational Work of the Church* (1939) to *I Believe: A Christian Faith* (1950).

William Kuhn

Dec. 9, 1869
Philadelphia, Pennsylvania

July 24, 1951
Oak Park, Illinois

Director of North American Baptist Missions, 1916–46. Kuhn served his denomination well in missions, youth, and executive responsibilities. He was converted December 31, 1887. Kuhn pastored Second German Baptist (Pilgrim Church), Philadelphia, PA from 1897–1913. His wife's name was Ida. Kuhn died after a six-week illness and a major operation.

Richard H. Crossfield

Oct. 22, 1868
Lawrenceburg, Kentucky

July 30, 1951
Birmingham, Alabama

President of College of the Bible [Lexington (KY) Theological Seminary in 1965], **1912–21**. Crossfield married Annie Terry on February 5, 1895. He pastored in Glasgow, KY (1892–95); Gwensboro, KY (1896–1908); First Christian Church in Norfolk, VA (1924–27); and Birmingham, AL (1927–37). He was president of Transylvania College, Lexington from 1918–21 and 1938–41, and of William Woods College, Fulton, MO from 1921–24.

James J. D. Hall
Bishop of Wall Street

Sept. 18, 1864
Greenville, Alabama

Sept. 6, 1951
New York, New York (?)

Hall had one of the most unique evangelistic outreaches of anyone in his generation, perhaps in the twentieth century—a telephone evangelist. Ordained Episcopalian, he became a chaplain of the Alabama state prison (1904–8), then was superintendent of Galilee Mission, Philadelphia, PA (1908–19). Years later, following work with city missions, he was in New York City. From 1928–37, he preached on the street in clerical garb to hundreds of hurrying financiers. His main ministry started Dec. 29, 1939, when someone called him and said, "Sorry, I got the wrong number." Hall retorted, "No, you haven't" and witnessed to the man. Before the days end, 15 other callers called and soon Circle 6-6483 became the most important number in the city. He had a high of 600 calls per day, averaging 2,000 a week and 70,000 a year. "Daddy" Hall in his spare time put up posters and signs all over the area, pointing people to Christ.

Elbert Russell

Aug. 29, 1871
Friendship, Tennessee

Sept. 21, 1951
St. Petersburg, Florida

Dean of Duke University Divinity School, Durham, NC 1928–41. Russell married Lieuetta Cox on August 14, 1895. He taught Bible and history at Earlham College, Richmond, IN (1895–1915) and was director of Woolman School, Swarthmore, PA (1917–24). At Duke, he was professor of Biblical interpretation, 1926–45. Russell's books ranged from *The Parables of Jesus* (1909) to *The History of Quakerism* (1942).

John P. Koehler

Jan. 17, 1859
Manitowoc, Wisconsin

Sept. 30, 1951
Neillsville, Wisconsin

President of Wisconsin Lutheran Seminary, Wauwatosa, WI 1920–29, relocated to **Mequon, WI 1929–30**. Koehler married Amalia Rohlfing on January 4, 1882 (died: 1938), and they had ten children. He pastored at Two Rivers, WI (1882–88), and served as inspector and professor at Northwestern College, Watertown, WI (1888–1900). He then began his ministry at WLS, in 1900, as a professor of NT exegesis, hermeneutics, liturgics, and music. He was a historian and the author of several books.

Sylvester C. Michelfelder

Oct. 27, 1889
New Washington, Ohio

Sept. 30, 1951
Chicago, Illinois

General Secretary of Lutheran World Convention, 1945–47, renamed Lutheran World Federation, 1947–51. Michelfelder married Florence Kibler on June 24, 1914. Ordained Lutheran in 1914, he pastored in Willard, OH (1913–21), and in Pittsburgh, PA (1921–26). He was superintendent of the International Mission Society in Pittsburgh (1926–31), then pastored in Toledo, OH (1931–45). He was secretary of the board of publications of the American Lutheran Church 1941–45. He wrote *Life Adjustments* (1940) and *So You Are Thinking* (1946). He is buried in New Washington, OH.

James A. Kelso

June 6, 1873
Rawal Pindi, India

Nov. 3, 1951
Pittsburgh, Pennsylvania

President of Western Theological Seminary, Allegheny, PA 1909–12, Pittsburgh, 1912–44. Kelso married Wilhemina Wise on June 29, 1898, and was ordained a Presbyterian the same year. He went to Western to teach Hebrew (1897), and then became a professor of OT literature (1901). Kelso's first book had a German title (1901), and his last was *The Hebrew Prophet and His Message* (1922).

Cornelius H. Suckau

Jan. 23, 1881
Newton, Kansas

Nov. 12, 1951
Omaha, Nebraska

First president of Grace College of the Bible, 1943–50. Suckau married Lulu Johnson on June 24, 1909. They did pioneer missionary work in Korba, India, under the General Conference Mennonite Church until 1928. Suckau had a heart condition since 1921, but he lived 30 years longer. He pastored the 1,000-member First Mennonite Church of Berne, IN from 1928–43. He had his telephone installed too low to answer standing up. He answered every call on his knees.

Elton M. Roth

Nov. 27, 1891
Berne, Indiana

Dec. 31, 1951
Glendale, California

Wrote lyrics and music for a great gospel hymn, "In My Heart There Rings a Melody" and "How Can I Help But Love Him." Roth was converted at age twelve in a revival meeting. He met his wife, Emma Scherer, at Ft. Wayne (Summit) Bible Institute. Roth started his ministry as an evangelist, then taught for six years at Nyack (NY) College. He moved to Los Angeles in 1930 where he taught, wrote, and directed choirs at BIOLA Baptist Theological College and City College. Elton was a soloist who traveled in many concert tours. He wrote some 100 hymns.

Robert M. Honeyman

1863   1952

Director of Montrose (PA) Bible Conference, 1928–39. Honeyman was director of the YMCA in Norristown, PA until 1914. In 1916, he was elected the executive secretary of MBC. He extended his influence by holding evangelistic meetings carried on, largely, in rural areas and in small towns. He built excellent relations between the village and the conference. By 1925, they could accommodate 200 guests. Half of Honeyman's 50-year ministry was given to making the Montrose Bible Conference into a major Christian retreat in the East.

Pat M. Neff

Nov. 26, 1871   Jan. 20, 1952
McGregor, Texas   Waco, Texas

President of Southern Baptist Convention, 1944–46, and Baylor University, Waco, TX 1932–47. During his leadership, the school doubled and became debt free. Neff married Myrtle Mainer on May 31, 1899. He practiced law in Waco, TX (1897–1921), and was governor of Texas (1921–25). Neff was involved with much of the political life of Texas. He was also a member of Rotary, Masons, and the FBC of Waco.

George VI of England
Albert Frederick Arthur George

Dec. 14, 1895   Feb. 6, 1952
Sandringham, England   Sandringham, England

King of Great Britain and Ireland, 1936–52, and emperor of India, 1936–48. He gained the throne May 12, 1936, after the abdication of his brother, Edward VIII. George witnessed WWII, the decline of the empire, establishment of the welfare state, and the devaluation of the British pound. On April 26, 1923, George married Elizabeth Bowles-Lyon (August 4, 1900–March 30, 2002). She was crowned queen consort and became a great asset to the monarchy through her calm spirit, friendly wit, gracely manner, and keen mind. Beginning in the summer of 1951, when her husband was stricken with ill health, she stepped in to fulfill the duties of the sovereign. Elizabeth, who later became known as the "Queen Mother" after her husband's death, traveled extensively on behalf of the crown. In early 2002, at over 101 years of age, Elizabeth was still making public appearances. George VI was the first British monarch to visit America, coming to the World's Fair in New York City. During this trip, while visiting U.S. President, Franklin D. Roosevelt in Washington DC, on June 9, 1939, King George and Queen Elizabeth enjoyed a concert, including a medley of patriotic songs performed by Chief Whitefeather, at the request of the U.S. Indian Bureau. The Indian Chief closed his program with the song, "I'd Rather Have Jesus." When he finished, he asked the Queen, knowing her to be a religious woman, "Your majesty, I would respectfully ask you: Do you know Jesus as your own personal Saviour?" She replied, "The Lord Jesus is the possessor of my heart; and my husband (King George VI) is also a believer." He died of a coronary thrombosis and was succeeded by his daughter Elizabeth II.

Francis H. Rowley

Dec. 14, 1854   Feb. 14, 1952
Hilton, New York   Boston, Massachusetts

Wrote lyrics of the great song, "I Will Sing the Wondrous Story," 1886 (music by PETER BILHORN). Rowley married Ida Babcock on June 11, 1878 (died: December, 1940). He was ordained a Baptist and pastored in Titusville, PA (1879–84); N. Adams, MA (1884–92); Oak Park, IL (1892–96); Fall River, MA (1896–1900); and FBC, Boston, MA (1900–10). From 1910–45, Rowley was president of Massachusetts Society for Prevention of Cruelty to Animals.

Harold Needham

Dec. 18, 1885
Glendora, California (?)

March 11, 1952
Vista, California

Founder and first president of Southern California Bible School (Vanguard University in 1976), **1920–39, and College, Costa Mesa, CA 1939–44**. Harold and his wife, Huldah, met at Nyack Institute. Needham began work as an associate pastor at Bethel Mission (Church) in 1918 in Los Angeles. Believing a need existed for a Pentecostal Bible School, they began classes in a donated home. On a missions trip to India, Huldah took sick and died on January 22, 1921, at age 32. He returned home to become president of the newly started school. In 1927, he was able to move from a large home to some property in Pasadena. Three graduates were BROGER, Bowman, and Roberts who started Far East Broadcasting Company. In 1940, the ownership of the school was transferred to the Assemblies of God.

George W. Garlock

Feb. 22, 1877
near Bradford, Pennsylvania

March 14, 1952
Buffalo, New York

President of A.M. Chesebrough Seminary North Chili, NY (Roberts Wesleyan College, Rochester, NY in 1945), **1921–30**. Converted as a child, Garlock began his ministry in a Presbyterian church in Jacksonburg, WV. He married Amanda Miller in 1898. Ordained into the Free Methodist ministry in 1907, he pastored FM pulpits in West Greece, NY; Brockport, IL; and Hillsboro, IL. In WWI, he was YMCA secretary and chaplain in England and Russia. In WWII, he was personnel director with the Rochester Signal Works.

Herbert A. Smith

Oct. 17, 1874
Naperville, Illinois

March 17, 1952
Newton, Massachusetts

Congregational hymnologist. Smith taught hymnology and church music at Chicago Theological Seminary and Divinity School (1901–16), and at Boston University (1917–44). He directed music at Chautauqua, NY 1921–28 (evidently summers). Smith is the founder of the New England Choir Directors Guild. He edited and compiled eight hymnbooks and was a pioneer in the field of church music in mainline denominations. He edited *The Hymnal for American Youth* (1919) to *The New Church Hymnal* (1937).

Harry Rimmer

Sept. 9, 1890
San Francisco, California

March 19, 1952
Pacific Palisades, California

Brilliant fundamentalist and defender of the faith whose preaching and writing ministry encouraged thousands. He was converted in 1912. Rimmer spent six months researching and six months preaching each year. He married Mignon Brandon on February 13, 1914, and was ordained to the Friends Church the same year. He became a Presbyterian in 1919. In 1920, he started the Research Science Bureau, Inc., in Denver, CO, through which he scientifically proved the inspiration of Scripture. He was president of Research Science Bureau, 1920–52, and wrote 29 books. Rimmer pastored First Presbyterian Church, Duluth, MN from 1934–40. He wrote *Harmony of Science and Scripture* (1936), *Dead Men Tell Tales* and *Christianity, and Modern Crisis* (1914). He died of cancer. The Rimmer Memorial Hospital in Quito, Ecuador, stands in honor of his fund-raising activity on behalf of Indian health care.

Samuel M. Zwemer

April 12, 1867
Vriesland, Michigan

April 2, 1952
Rochester, New York

Greatest missionary authority on the Moslem world. Zwemer responded as a college student in 1886. He was the 13th of 15 children. In 1890, he was ordained by the Reformed Church in America. He went to the Arabian Peninsula (1891–1905, 1910–12), the US (1905–10), then Cairo, Egypt (1912–29) with the Nile Mission. He married Amy Wilkes on May 18, 1896 (died: 1937), and Margaret Clarke in 1940 (died: 1950). In 1904, they had two daughters who died in July within eight days of each other. Zwemer served on the Princeton faculty for ten years and edited *Moslem World* for 36 years. He founded the Arabian Mission of the Dutch Reformed Church. Zwemer wrote many books on the Moslems. He saw relatively few Moslems converted, but he created a great interest in reaching them. Zwemer died of a heart attack following a lecture.

Stafford Cripps

April 24, 1889
High Wycombe, England

April 21, 1952
Zurich, Switzerland

English political leader. Cripps married Isobel Swithinbank on July 11, 1911. He was called to the bar (1913), and was made solicitor general (1930). He was ambassador to Moscow, Russia, 1940–42. Cripps was the leader of the House of Commons in 1940, president of the Board of Trade (1945–47), and chancellor of the exchequer (1947–50). His books included *Cripps on Commenseration*, *God in Our Work*, and *Towards Christian Democracy* (1946). He retired from public life on October 20, 1950 because of ill health, going to a sanitorium in Zurich. Cripps belonged to the Plymouth Brethren Church.

A. Mildred Cable

Feb. 21, 1878
Guildford, England

April 30, 1952
London/Dorset, England

Author and pioneer missionary to China. In 1901 Mildred sailed to China and began a lifelong partnership with Evangeline and Francesca French. She first settled at Howchow in Shansi Province, and concentrated on education work with women. In 1913, with her two companions, they set out "to visit" every city of the Kansu Province situated beyond the Great Wall. They reached them all in eight months after 1,500 miles of travel. This was where no Western single woman had ever traveled. Several times they covered the northwest area from inner Mongolia to Tibet, and from the Kansu Province to Sinkiang, headquartering in Suchow, the "City of Criminals." In August, 1936, all foreigners were ordered to leave the area. Following her retirement, Mildred visited Australia, New Zealand, India, and South America. Her several books tell of her travels and ministry.

Charles B. Williams

Jan. 15, 1869
Shiloh, North Carolina

May 4, 1952
Lakeland, Florida

Made a famous translation of the New Testament in 1937, utilizing Greek verbs. Williams was ordained Baptist in 1890. He married Alice Owen on January 2, 1899 (died January 23, 1925). From 1890–1905, he lived in North Chester, PA; Texarkana, TX; Stephenville, TX; Brucetown, TN; and Shiloh, NC. He became professor of Greek at Southwestern Baptist Theological Seminary, 1905–19. Williams was president of Howard University, Birmingham, AL (1919–21); taught NT at Mercer University, Macon, GA (1921–25); and taught Greek and ethics at Union University, Jackson, TN (1925–32). He married Lucille Bruner (Dec. 26, 1925) and Edith Stallings (Aug. 26, 1934). He wrote many books.

Walter T. Conner
Jan. 19, 1877
Center (later Rowell), Arkansas

May 26, 1952
Forth Worth, Texas

Baptist theologian. Conner was converted in 1894 in a Methodist meeting after the family had moved to Texas. He pastored in Tuscola, TX (1898–99); at Caps, TX (1899–1900); then continued in several small Baptist pastorates until 1908. Conner's education at Baylor also occupied these years. He married Blanche Horne of Albany, TX on June 4, 1907. He taught at Southwestern Theological Seminary, 1910–49. He taught systematic theology, English NT, Biblical Theology, and Greek NT exegesis. Conner wrote *A System of Christian Doctrine* (1924) and *The Cross in the New Testament* (1954).

Robert E. Winsett
Jan. 15, 1876
Bledsoe County, Tennessee

June 26, 1952
Dayton, Tennessee

Popular songwriter and publisher in the early days of the Pentecostal movement. Winsett composed lyrics and music to over 1,000 songs, including "Jesus Is Coming Soon," while founding the Winsett Music Company of Dayton, TN. He played the piano, guitar, mandolin, violin and sang. Winsett also taught music for 42 years. He married Birdie Harris on January 15, 1908 (died: 1927) and Ruth Shelton on May 28, 1930.

Norman H. Camp
June 25, 1867
Bement, Illinois

July 9, 1952
Chicago, Illinois

Bible teacher and evangelist. Camp married MABEL JOHNSTON in 1896. While practicing law in downtown Chicago, he attended a Bible class taught by WILLIAM R. NEWELL and was converted. His famous tract, "The Way of Life Made Plain," was written in 1900 and 16 million copies have been distributed in 16 languages. He was associated with Moody Bible Institute, 1917–52 and was the editorial secretary in the colportage division of Moody Press. Camp was a member of Edgewater Presbyterian Church.

Robert C. McQuilken
Feb. 16, 1886
Philadelphia, Pennsylvania

July 15, 1952
Asheville, North Carolina

First president of Columbia (SC) Bible College (University in 1994), **1923–52, Evangelical Teacher Training Association, 1930–43**. He was converted in the United Presbyterian Church. McQuilken married Marguerite Lambie on September 10, 1912. He was associate editor of *Sunday School Times* in Philadelphia (1912–17) and a Bible conference teacher (1917–22) who supported Presbyterian beliefs. He was one of the initiators of the Victorious Life Conferences, 1913–23. McQuilken founded the BL Conference Center (1928), as well as Ben Lippen School, Asheville, NC (1940). He withdrew from the Southern Presbyterian Church in 1951 and founded the Independent Evangelical Churches Fellowship. His books ranged from *Victorious Life Studies* (1918) to *Law and Grace* (1958).

Arthur W. Pink
April 1, 1886
Nottingham, England

July 15, 1952
Stornoway, Scotland

Great Bible teacher. Pink claimed to be interdenominational but leaned toward Plymouth Brethren. He attended Moody Bible Institute and pastored in Silver Mines, CO, before marrying Vera Russell about 1903 (died: August 17, 1962). In 1924, Pink moved to Philadelphia, started writing, and began holding Bible classes in homes. His *Studies in the Scriptures* had 32 volumes. He then returned to England.

Monroe E. Dodd

Sept. 8, 1878
Brazil, Tennessee

Aug. 6, 1952
Long Beach, California

President of Southern Baptist Convention, 1934–35. Dodd married Emma Savage on October 10, 1904. He pastored in Fulton, KY (1904–08); FBC, Paducah, KY (1908–11); Walnut St., Louisville, KY (1911–12); and FBC, Shreveport, LA (1912–50), where he received 15,000 members into his church. He took preaching trips to South America and the southwest Pacific. Dodd was very influential in starting the Baptist Bible Institute (New Orleans Baptist Theological Seminary in 1918) and in launching the Cooperative Program of the SBC. In 1927, he founded Dodd College (later merged with Centenary College, Shreveport, LA). He raised millions of dollars for Baptist causes and baptized 7,000 converts. His written works ranged from *Jesus Is Coming* (1917) to *The New Testament Three Sixteens* (1936).

Rufus D. Bowman

Jan. 23, 1899
Dayton, Virginia

Aug. 19, 1952
Emporia, Kansas

President of Bethany Theological Seminary Oak Brook, IL (Richmond, IN, in 1994), **1937–52**. Bowman married Eva Craun on June 16, 1925. He was ordained into the Church of the Brethren in 1926; pastored in Roanoke, VA (1926–29); was secretary of the Board of Christian Education, Elgin, IL (1929–34); and pastored in Washington, D.C. (1934–37). He also taught practical theology while serving as president at BTS.

J. Frank Norris

Sept. 18, 1877
Dadeville, Alabama

Aug. 20, 1952
Keystone Heights, Florida

Father of the independent Baptist movement, president of World Baptist Fellowship, 1935–1952. Norris was the most fearless, powerful preacher of his generation. A Methodist, Norris was converted at a revival conducted by J. A. Oswalt at age 13. He was a student at Baylor University (1898–1902), married Lillian Gaddy on May 5, 1902, then held a brief pastorate at McKinney Avenue Baptist Church in Dallas (1905–8) which grew from 100 to 1,000. Norris edited the *Baptist Standard* (1907–9). He pastored FBC, Ft. Worth, TX (1909–52), with 10,000 members and Temple Baptist Church, Detroit, MI (1935–51), with 8,000 members at the same time, traveling by air between the two cities. His assistants, ENTZMINGER and VICK, were a big help. He opposed liberalism in the SBC, the liquor crowd, and evolutionists. He was expelled from the SBC in 1924. Norris edited *Searchlight* (1917–27) and the *Fundamentalist* (1927 on). He started World Baptist Fellowship (1935) and Bible Baptist Seminary, Fort Worth, TX (1939). In self–defense, he shot and killed a businessman, D. E. Chipps, on July 17, 1926, who entered his study threatening to kill him. Norris died of a heart attack while at a youth rally.

Lewis S. Chafer

Feb. 27, 1871
Rock Creek, Ohio

Aug. 22, 1952
Seattle, Washington

Founder and first president of Evangelical Theological College, 1924–36, renamed **Dallas (TX) Theological Seminary, 1936–52**. Chafer married Ella Case on April 22, 1896 (died: 1944). He moved to Northfield, MA in 1901 where he met C. I. SCOFIELD who influenced him. Chafer, ordained a Congregationalist (1900), changed to Presbyterianism (1907). In 1915, he moved to New York City. He served as an evangelist (1900–14) and Bible conference speaker (1914–24), then pastored at Scofield Memorial Church, Dallas (1923–27). Throughout his life, he was active with Central American Mission. Chafer's books ranged from *Satan* (1909) to an eight-volume *Systematic Theology* (1948), a subject he taught until his death. Chafer died while ministering. His book, *True Evangelism* (1911) was opposed by some. He was a dispensationalist and a premillennialist. He edited *Bibliotheca Sacra* (1940–52).

Frederick G. Kenyon

Jan. 15, 1863
London, England

Aug. 23, 1952
Godstone, England

Archaeologist, Greek manuscript writer, and philosophist who was a firm believer in the Bible. Kenyon was educated at New College in Oxford. He joined the staff (librarian) of the British Museum in 1889 and directed there, 1909–35 until his retirement. Kenyon was a foremost Bible scholar, working with Greek papyri and NT manuscripts. He published classical texts such as *Our Bible and the Ancient Manuscripts* (1895). Kenyon's goal was to show that science is in agreement with the Scriptures. He was the president of the British School of Archaeology in Jerusalem, 1920–52. He wrote from *Classical Texts from Papyri* (1891) to *The Bible and Modern Scholarship* (1948).

Baylus B. McKinney

July 22, 1886
Helfin, Louisiana

Sept. 7, 1952
Bryson City, North Carolina

Southern Baptist's greatest hymn writer, with 600 published songs. McKinney wrote the lyrics and music to "Neath the Old Olive Tree," "The Nail Scarred Hand," "Satisfied with Jesus," "He Lives on High," "Back to Bethel," and "Wherever He Leads I'll Go," some 149 in all, and 115 tunes for other hymn writers, such as "Breathe on Me." McKinney married Leila Routh on June 11, 1918 (died: March 1, 1985, in San Antonio, TX). He was the music editor for the Dallas firm headed by ROBERT H. COLEMAN, 1918–35. He started out as an evangelist, taught music at Southwestern Baptist Theological Seminary (1925–35) also becoming an associate pastor at Travis Avenue Baptist, Ft. Worth, TX (1932–35). He was the music director of the Baptist Sunday School Board in Nashville (1935–41), and secretary of the Church Music Department (1941–52). He died from injuries due to an automobile accident, five days after it occurred.

Charles M. Fillmore

July 15, 1860
Paris, Illinois

Sept. 19, 1952
Indianapolis, Indiana

Wrote lyrics and music of "Tell Mother I'll Be There," one of the most convicting songs ever written. In 1896, President MCKINLEY left by train to be with his dying mother and wired the physician Fillmore's immortal words, "Tell Mother I'll Be There." Fillmore spent several years as a schoolteacher, then became a Disciples of Christ pastor in Indiana, Utah, and Ohio, pastoring in Indianapolis, 1907–39.

George G. Bartlett

June 3, 1872
Sharon Springs, New York

Oct. 7, 1952
Philadelphia, Pennsylvania (?)

President of Philadelphia Divinity School (merged into Episcopal Divinity School, Cambridge, MA in 1974), **1915–37**. He was ordained a deacon (1898) and priest (1900) into the Episcopal Church. Bartlett married Cecilia Neall on May 9, 1905. He was rector of the Memorial Church of St. Paul, Overbook, PA (1902–8); dean of Cathedral of Our Merciful Savior, Fairbault, MN (1908–11); and rector of Church of Our Savior, Jenkintown, PA (1911–15).

Henry D. Campbell

1864   Oct. 14, 1952

General Secretary of Africa Inland Mission, 1926–41, and president of IFMA, 1937–38. Campbell went to the Belgian Congo under CMA from 1892–1916. He was an associate pastor at Moody Church, 1919–24. Campbell continued to edit *Inland Africa* up until his final illness, a stroke one year before his death. In his early days in the Congo, he was associated with PETER C. SCOTT, the mission's founder. He wrote *Congo Chattel*.

Louis J. Sieck

March 11, 1884   October 14, 1952
Erie, Pennsylvania   St. Louis, Missouri

President of Concordia Seminary, St. Louis, MO, 1943–53. He was ordained Lutheran on September 11, 1904. Sieck married Ottilie Obermeyer on September 21, 1905. Sieck pastored Zion Church in St. Louis, 1914–43. He was also active in the leadership of radio station KFUO of Clayton, MO. Sieck was president of Lutheran Publicity Organization for 21 years and of St. Louis Pastoral Conference for 24 years. He was an administrator who preached Christ-centered sermons.

Ernest O. Sellers

Oct. 29, 1869   Oct. 19, 1952
Hastings, Michigan   Eola, Louisiana

Composed music for "Thy Word Have I Hid in My Heart" and "Wonderful, Wonderful Jesus" (lyrics by ANNA RUSSELL). He began musical singing with Evangelist FRED SMITH in 1896. He was converted at the Lansing (MI) YMCA. Sellers also taught music at Moody Bible Institute, 1908–19. From 1919 until his retirement in 1945, Sellers was the music director of Baptist Bible Institute (New Orleans Baptist Theological Seminary in 1946).

Ambrose B. Crumpler

1863   Oct. 23, 1952
Near Clinton, North Carolina   Clinton, North Carolina

Holiness evangelist, pastor, and church leader of Holiness Church of North Carolina, 1898–1908. In the late 1880s Crumpler moved to Missouri where he was converted. In 1896, he returned to NC to establish the Holiness message. Working with the Methodist Episcopal Church South, he held revivals in churches and tents. Attacks on worldliness, tobacco users, and bishops led to his founding a Holiness Church in 1898 in Goldsboro, NC. As a result, he broke with the Methodists. Furthermore, he was violating a troublesome rule forbidding holding meetings in the vicinity of a Methodist work without the permission of the pastor. His *Holiness Advocate* (1900–8) taught holiness, healing and right conduct. The Pentecostal phenomena swept away his following (1907), and he openly opposed those (1908), such as GASTON CASHWELL, who taught that tongues was the only initial evidence of the baptism. He returned to the Methodist Church and became active in the prohibition movement, practicing law in Clinton. His movement merged with the Fire-Baptized Holiness Association in 1911 to form the Pentecostal Holiness Church.

Arthur A. Glen

June 15, 1891   Oct. 23, 1952
Cooper, Michigan   Pontiac, Michigan

First Director of Hiawatha (Continental in 1984) **Baptist Missions, Escanaba, MI** (Grand Rapids in 1977), **1942–52.** Glen's father was killed in a hunting accident when he was five months old. He was converted in Bristol, MI, while Baptists were holding gospel meetings in the town hall. He married Florence Ballinger, and was ordained in 1926 after pastoring in Prescott and Twining, MI. From 1929–33, they were in home missions work. The First Baptist Church of Pontiac supported him during the lean years 1933–37. They resigned because of liberalism and in 1937 formed the Blessed Hope Bible Conference at Piatt Lake. This began what was known as Hiawatha Land Independent Baptist Missions. The small logging towns of upper Michigan were his burden. He was killed in an auto accident en route to a Hiawatha Land Council meeting at FBC, Pontiac.

William M. Danner

June 22, 1863
Mercer County, Illinois

Nov. 14, 1952
Washington, D.C.

First general secretary of American Leprosy Mission (ALM Int.), **Greenville, SC 1911–37**. Reared on an Iowa farm, he was active in YMCA activities in Iowa (1890–94), Louisville, KY (1894–1906), and Denver, CO (1906–7). He was with the Kellogg Company in Boston, MA from 1907–11. When he began with ALM, the budget was $15,000 a year and when he retired, it ran almost $500,000 annually. In 1919 he was helping the YMCA in New York City. He was widely acclaimed as being primarily responsible for the establishment of the federal leprosarium in Carville, LA later known as the U.S. Public Health Hospital. This was in 1921. After the death of his first wife, Lois Rutledge in 1943, he married Laura Townshend. He lived the last seven years of his life in Washington.

Horace E. Thompson

Oct. 18, 1865
Limerick, Maine

Dec. 1, 1952
Chelsea, Massachusetts

President of New England School of Theology (Berkshire Christian College, Lenox, MA in 1958), **Brookline, MA 1910–20**. Thompson married Nellie Thompson (1889) and Lulu Webster (1929). He was ordained Advent Christian in 1896 and pastored in Fall River, MA (1896–1904); Buffalo, NY (1905–08); Taunton, MA (1908–14); and Boston, MA (1935 on). Thompson's first book was *Pleasure and Profit in Bible Study*.

Allen Emery Sr.

March 17, 1875
Watertown, Massachusetts

Dec. 18, 1952
Weymouth Heights, Massachusetts

Director of Vision New England, 1914–51. Emery was led to Christ as a young man by Samuel Sayford and was a dedicated layman in the wool business. He married Elsie Doris Conant. He led Boston's Union Rescue Mission, served on the boards of Wheaton and Gordon Colleges and was a deacon in his church. In 1916, he was full-time chairman of the Billy Sunday Boston crusade for a year. He was treasurer of the Emery-Conant Company, Inc., wool merchants of Boston, MA.

Robert L. Stuart

Sept. 12, 1883
Basham, Virginia

c 1953
Wichita, Kansas (?)

President of Taylor University, Upland, IN 1931–45. Stuart was ordained Methodist in 1906. He married Josie Conner on March 24, 1908. He served pastorates in Iowa: in Whiting, Paulina, Akron, Humboldt, Spencer, and Newton (until 1928); then in El Dorado, KS (1928–31); and in Wesley Methodist Church of Wichita, KS, thereafter.

Charles D. Bonsak

March 11, 1870
Westminster, Maryland

Feb. 5, 1953
Elgin, Illinois

Secretary of Church of the Brethren Missions, Elgin IL 1922–41. Bonsak married Ida Trostle on December 16, 1891 and was ordained in the Church of the Brethren in 1895. He pastored the Church of the Brethren, Washington, D.C. (1906–9); taught Bible at Blue Ridge College, New Windsork, MD (Maryland Collegiate Institute, Union Bridge, MD) (1909–12); and then president (1913–15). Bonsak directed the Forward Movement in the denomination, beginning in 1920, when he moved to Elgin, IL.

James L. Kraft

Dec. 11, 1874
Stevensville, Ontario, Canada

Feb. 16, 1953
Chicago, Illinois

Developer and founder of the Kraft Cheese products, an outstanding Baptist layman. He was raised as one of eleven children in a devout Mennonite home. He settled in Chicago in 1905. Kraft married Pauline Platt on June 2, 1909. He became identified with the cheese business by starting an organized corporation in 1909 known as Kraft Foods Corporation. He lived in Evanston, IL. and was the Sunday school superintendent of North Shore Baptist for 40 years. He is buried in Evanston.

Frederick M. Lehman

Aug. 7, 1868
Mecklenbergh, Germany

Feb. 20, 1953
Pasadena, California

Wrote lyrics and music to a famous song, "The Love of God," also "No Disappointment in Heaven" and "The Royal Telephone." Lehman came to America in 1872, and was converted at age eleven. He married Emma Dermyer in 1891. Lehman served as a Nazarene pastor in Iowa, Indiana, and at the First Church in Kansas City, MO. Lehman went to Pasadena, CA in 1914 as a writer, editor, and publisher. The third stanza of his widely used song was found on a prison wall.

Hugh Black

March 26, 1868
Rothesay, Scotland

April 6, 1953
Upper Montclair, New Jersey

Preacher and professor. He pastored in Paisley, Scotland 1891–1906. Black married Edith Kerr on June 28, 1898. He spent the last ten years at St. George's United Free Church in Edinburgh as ALEXANDER WHYTE's associate. Black came to America in 1906 and was a professor of homiletics and practical theology at Union Theological Seminary in New York City from 1906–38. In 1941 he became chairman of a British War Relief society. Black was known as a great preacher, and his books range from *The Dream of Youth* (1894) to *Christ or Caesar* (1938).

Edmonson J. M. Nutter

Nov. 3, 1879
Bradford, England

April 6, 1953
New York, New York

President of Nashotah (WI) House, 1925–47. Nutter came to America in 1905. He was ordained a deacon (1910) and priest (1911) in the Episcopal Church. Nutter was a curate at Grace Church, Chicago, IL (1911–14); rector at St. John's Church, Chicago, IL (1914–18); and rector of Church of the Messiah, Detroit, MI (1918–25). His final days were spent teaching pastoral theology at Nashotah House.

A. Stuart McNairn

Jan. 18, 1873
Edinburgh, Scotland

April 13, 1953
London, England

First general secretary of Evangelical Union of South America (British Section), **1911–52**. The Evangelical Union of South America began by the union of several small missions working in South America. McNairn was converted in his late teen years. He married Beatrice Allison in 1904. They were stationed in Cuzco, Peru, 1904–11, returning to Britain because of his wife's health. He majored in emphasizing evangelism and church planting. McNairn died of cerebral thrombosis in a hospital.

Harlan P. Douglass

Jan. 4, 1871
Osage, Iowa

April 14, 1953
Montclair, New Jersey

Congregational Christian minister who was research director in New York for social and religious activities, 1919–35. Douglass pastored in Manson, IA; Ames, IA; and Springfield, MO, from 1894–1906. Douglass married Rena Sherman on June 25, 1895. For eleven years, he was with the American Missionary Association. He was also editor of *Christendom* (1938–48). His books range from *Christian Reconstruction in the South* (1909) to *Decade in Church Unity* (1948).

Wilbur K. Thomas

Dec. 21, 1882
Amboy, Indiana

April 15, 1953
Monterey, Massachusetts

Director of American Friends Service Committee, Philadelphia, PA 1918–29. He married Elizabeth Folger on August 16, 1905. From 1930–46 he was executive director of the Carl Schurz Memorial Foundation. He was president of the Pennsylvania Forestry Association, 1939–47 and pastored the Congregational Church in Otis, MA in 1947.

Arthur W. McKee

Oct. 15, 1890
Worcester, Massachusetts

June 7, 1953
Winona Lake, Indiana

Song leader and gospel soloist, manager of Cedar Lake (IN) Bible Conference, 1930–38, and Winona Lake (IN) Bible Conference, 1938–53. McKee composed music to such hymns as "Such Love as God's" and "To Eternity." He was converted in 1910 while still a student at Colby Academy, Waterville, ME, during a revival meeting with John Blair. He was an All-American guard for Dartmouth's basketball team. He married Ethel Nelson, a chorus and music composer, on June 2, 1914. He was PAUL RADER's music director at Moody Church, 1916–20, and then served at the Church of the Open Door in Los Angeles. He then traveled with GYPSY SMITH from 1929–34. A series of heart attacks claimed his life in his sleep.

Adam Clayton Powell Sr.

May 5, 1865
Soak Creek, Virginia

June 12, 1953
New York, New York

Pastor who built the largest black congregation in the world—the Abyssinian Baptist Church, New York City. It boasted over 15,000 members. As one of 17 children, Powell was born in a one-bedroom log cabin. He married Mattie Fletcher Schafer in 1889. While at Yale University, 1893–1908, he pastored the Immanual Baptist Church, New Haven, CT. In 1908, he took over the 1,600 member New York City congregation with nearly $150,000 in debt. Within 15 years, they dedicated a new building in 1921. Powell crusaded against vice and prostitution. He retired in 1937 turning over the leadership to his son Adam C. Powell Jr. whose flamboyant personality kept the church going. Unfortunately, young

Powell's corrupt ways cast shadows over the ministry, causing a surge of violence in the civil rights movement. Further corruption surfaced during his Congressional years, resulting in his expulsion from Congress. Adam Sr. wrote several books upon retirement.

Ernest I. Pugmire

March 4, 1888
Kansas City, Missouri

June 24, 1953
New York, New York

General of Salvation Army (USA), 1944–53. Pugmire married Grace Vickers on September 14, 1911. He enjoyed a colorful career with the Salvation Army starting in the finance department in Toronto, Ontario, 1907–15. He served in the same post in Winnipeg, Manitoba, 1915–19. He traveled to Peking, China (1919–20), and Tokyo, Japan (1920–25). Pugmire was chief secretary (1925–31) and financial secretary (1931–33) in Chicago. He was also territorial commander of various states, 1935–44. He is buried in Atlanta.

Jakob D. Du Toit

Feb. 21, 1877
Paarl, South Africa

July 1, 1953
Pretoria, South Africa

Afrikaans biblical scholar, pastor, and poet. Du Toit compiled a famous Afrikaans Psalter and translated the Bible into the Afrikaans language. His dedication to Calvinism and his patriotism were revealed through his many poetic works.

G. Alfred Lundmark

June 19, 1901
St. Joseph, Missouri

July 10, 1953
Paris, France

President of Home of Onesiphorus (Kids Alive, Int. in 1983), **1927–53**. Lundmark married Florence Johnson on June 14, 1924. When the Anglins came to America, he and his wife started the first office in a tiny room in their basement. After a trip to China (1931), they incorporated the business (1932). He died in a hotel room en route to the Middle East and Hong Kong.

Charles W. Tobey

July 22, 1880
Roxbury, Massachusetts

July 24, 1953
Bethesda, Maryland

Congressman from New Hampshire who possessed Biblical values. Tobey was a one-term president of the NH Baptist State Convention. He married Francella Lovett (June 4, 1902), and Loretta Rabenhorst (May 26, 1948). Tobey was a member of the NH House of Representatives (speaker 1919–20); NH Senate (1925–26); and NH governor (1929–30). He went to Washington as a member of the House (1933–39), and as a member of the Senate (1939–51). He pled for honesty in government often using Biblical quotations. He was a Republican and a Mason.

Henry Hepburn

Nov. 3, 1872
Hopkins, Missouri

Aug. 1, 1953
Winona Lake, Indiana

Presbyterian pastor of Buena Memorial Church, Chicago, December 15, 1908, until his death. Hepburn married Isabelle Speer on May 6, 1902 (died: March 1, 1937), and was ordained on June 5, 1902. His earlier pastorates included First Church, Monett, MO (1902–05) and First Church, Aurora, IL (1905–8). Hepburn was also a Mason. Students in Chicago that attended his church included WILBUR SMITH and OSWALD SMITH.

Francis J. McConnell

Aug. 18, 1871
Trinway, Ohio

Aug. 18, 1953
Lucasville, Ohio

Bishop in the Methodist Episcopal Church, 1912–39; the Methodist Church, 1939–44; and president of the Federal Council of Churches (NCC in 1950), **1928–32**. McConnell married Eva Thomas (July 23, 1871–February 19, 1968) on March 11, 1897. He pastored four churches in Massachusetts 1894–1903 including Ipswich and Cambridge following graduation from Boston University. He then pastored the New York Avenue Church, Brooklyn, NY from 1903–9. McConnell was president of DePaul University (1909–12). He served as bishop in Denver (1912–20), Pittsburgh (1920–28) and New York City (1928–44). His 24 books ranged from *The Divine Immanence* (1906) to *By the Way* (1952), an autobiography. His most reknowned work was *Is God Limited?* (1924). He died on his 82nd birthday.

Albert C. Knudson

Jan. 23, 1873
Grandmeadow, Minnesota

Aug. 28, 1953
Cambridge, Massachusetts

Dean of Boston (MA) University School of Theology, 1926–38, and Methodist OT scholar, theologian and philosopher. Knudson married Mathilde Johnson on July 7, 1899 (died December 13, 1948). He taught at Iliff School of Theology (1898–1900); at Baker University, Baldwin, KS (1900–02); and at Allegheny College, Meadville, PA (1902–06). Knudson was also professor of Hebrew and OT exegesis (1906–21) and of systematic theology (1921–43) at Boston University. He defended the art of higher criticism. He wrote many books, including *The OT Problem* (1908) to *Basic Issues in Christian Thought* (1950). His most famous work was *The Religious Teaching of the OT* (1918).

Henry H. Tweedy

Aug. 5, 1868
Binghamton, New York

Sept. 11, 1953
Brattlebury, Vermont

Congregational pastor, educator and hymn writer. Tweedy married Grace Landfield on August 12, 1902. He pastored Plymouth Church, Utica, NY (1898–1902); South Church, Bridgeport, CT (1902–09); and was professor of theology at Yale Divinity School (1909–37). He edited and compiled a number of hymnbooks, and wrote several hymns.

G. Arvid Hagstrom

Sept. 8, 1867
Sundsvall, Sweden

Sept. 16, 1953
St. Paul, Minnesota

First missions secretary (president) of Baptist General Conference, 1907–09, 1930–33, and first president of Bethel College and Theological Seminary, St. Paul, MN 1914–41. Hagstrom was the key individual in founding the Baptist General Conference. He married Caroline Anderson on June 1, 1892 (died: February 6, 1933) and Ebba Brundin on July 26, 1934. From 1907–9 he traveled 58,085 miles; visited 828 churches, schools, homes; preached 986 sermons and replied to 9,384 communications. Hagstrom pastored the First Swedish Baptist Church, St. Paul, MN, from 1909–13. He wrote some historical biographies.

Robert E. McAlister

1880
Cobden, Ontario, Canada

Sept. 25, 1953
Toronto, Canada

Director of Pentecostal Assemblies of Canada Missions, 1917–33, and secretary–treasurer of the same, 1919–32. McAlister was reared a Presbyterian and became an evangelist in western Canada. He returned from an Azusa Street meeting in Los Angeles in 1906 as a Pentecostal.

McAlister established churches in Westmeath and Ottawa, Ontario. He pastored London (ON) Gospel Temple, 1920–39, after helping charter POAC in 1919. He was the first general secretary-treasurer of the POAC from 1919–37. McAlister edited the *Pentecostal Testimony* (1920–37), which he founded. Early on he was an architect of the non-Trinitarian Oneness Theology within modern Pentecostalism.

Frank V. C. Cloak

Feb. 14, 1876
Philadelphia, Pennsylvania

Oct. 2, 1953
Philadelphia, Pennsylvania

Presiding bishop of Reformed Episcopal Church, 1937–57. He married Harriet A. White on July 6, 1899 (died: June, 1946). He was rector of St. John's Church, Chillicothe, IL (1899–1904); Church of the Redeemer, Detroit, (1904–7); the Emmanuel Church, Philadelphia (1907–26); and Christ Memorial Church, Philadelphia (1926 on). He taught in Philadelphia high schools, 1912–25. He became bishop on November 9, 1931.

Ganz P. Raud

Sept. 25, 1882
Estonia

Oct. 3, 1953
Paris, France

General director of European Christian Union, 1904–22 renamed Bible Christian Union, 1922–53 (which merged into the Evangelical Alliance Mission in 1993). He spent more than 50 years in preaching and Bible teaching in Europe. Raud's father was an Estonian preacher. After an all-night prayer meeting on January 1, 1904, he began his life's work. He worked in England until 1915, and after WWI broke out, he came to America, establishing his headquarters in Brooklyn, NY. By 1927, some 81 missionaries ran 132 gospel halls, with the largest proportion being Russian. Eastern Europe became the focus until WWII, after which Western Europe gained attention. Raud was found in his hotel bedroom with his head resting on an open Bible at Psalm 143, perhaps praying, when a heart attack claimed him.

Joseph H. Cohn

March 27, 1884
Austria-Hungary

Oct. 5, 1953
New York, New York

President of American Board of Missions to the Jews (Chosen People Ministries in 1988), **1937–53.** Cohn's father, LEOPOLD, a former rabbi, was largely responsible for his conversion at age seven. He joined his father in the work of ABMJ in 1907. He was ordained a Baptist and became the general secretary of the work in 1911. Cohn married Josephine Stone in May, 1916, although they later separated. Cohn was instrumental in translating the New Testament into Yiddish. He had a radio broadcast called *The Chosen People*, and led the ministry into a worldwide outreach. A split of board members in 1944–45 started a new ministry, the American Association for Jewish Evangelism. He was found dead in the Beacon Hotel near the mission headquarters. He wrote several books.

Malla P. Moe

Sept. 12, 1863
Hafslow, Norway

Oct. 16, 1953
Bethel, Swaziland, Union of South Africa

One of history's great missionaries, headquartered in Swaziland. Malla was converted at age 15 when her dying aunt said, "Meet me in heaven." Shortly thereafter, she gave her heart to the Lord. Following the death of her parents, she came to America in 1884 and was influenced by FRED FRANSON. Moe went to Africa in May, 1892, and established Bethel Mission in 1896. She enjoyed only two furloughs (1902–6, 1916–22) in 61 years of service (none in the last 30 years). Moe lived very simply and frugally and traveled by foot and donkey while developing twelve mission stations. In 1927, she began a ministry of evangelism, at age 65, with her "gospel wagon." Africa seldom had any better missionary.

She was an evangelist, church planter, teacher and preacher. She served under the Scandinavian Alliance Mission (TEAM). She died from pneumonia (surrounded by African friends) only a month and four days after her 90th birthday.

Carl P. Højbjerg

June 12, 1873
Holstebro, Denmark

Oct. 28, 1953
Denmark

President of Grand View College and Seminary (Lutheran School of Theology, Chicago in 1964), **Des Moines, IA 1915–26**. Højbjerg married Hilda Boving on July 16, 1903. He immigrated to teach at Grandview, 1904–07. He was president of Nebraska Folk School and pastor, 1907–12. Højbjerg served pastorates in Denmark, 1912–14. He was the president of Dancbod Folk School (1926–31), pastored in Nysted, NE (1931–36), then returned to Denmark to pastor in Ringe (1937–43). He lived in Holte in his last days.

Delavan L. Pierson

Oct. 27, 1867
Waterford, New York

Nov. 5, 1953
Clifton, New Jersey

Religious editor. He married Emma Dougherty on Februry 13, 1895 (died: 1937). Pierson was managing editor of *Missionary Review of the World* (1891–1911), then became editor-in-chief. He also edited *Northfield Echoes* (1894–1904) and wrote for the *Sunday School Times* (after 1907). Pierson's books ranged from *For Each New Day* (1896) to *Why Believe It?* (1928). He was the son of the great preacher, ARTHUR T. PIERSON. In a research mystery, *Who Was Who in America* (vol. 1) has him dying on July 11, 1938. Our source is a *Sunday School Times* article.

Karl P. Harrington

June 13, 1861
Somersworth, New Hampshire

Nov. 14, 1953
Middleton, Connecticut

Composed the music for "There's a Song in the Air" (lyrics by JOSIAH HOLLAND). Harrington married Jennie Canfield on November 25, 1886. He was a well-known Latin teacher at the University of North Carolina, Chapel Hill (1891–99); University of Maine, Orono (1899–1905); and Wesleyan University, Middleton, CT (1889–91 and 1905–29). He served in various Methodist churches as an organist and choir director. His books range from *Helps…Study…Latin* (1888) to *Richard Alsop* (1939).

Gerhard B. F. Hallock

Jan. 28, 1856
Holiday's Cove, West Virginia

Dec. 6, 1953
Rochester, New York

Presbyterian clergyman and author. Until 1890, Hallock pastored in Scottsville, NY, from 1885–89; then he became co-pastor of Brick Presbyterian Church, Rochester, NY (one of the largest churches in the denomination). He married Anna Cobb on May 8, 1888. Hallock authored many books, including *Upward Steps* (1899) and *2,100 More Choice Sermons for Children* (1940s). He specialized in sermon collections.

Gordon A. Sisco

April 12, 1891
Coaticook, Quebec, Canada

Dec. 16, 1953
Toronto, Ontario, Canada

Secretary of United Church of Canada, 1938–52. Sisco married Edith Bothwell, on August 16, 1916. He was ordained in the Methodist Church the same year. Sisco was active in affairs of the United Church of Canada, and the Inter-Congregational Council. He also served as executive in

World Presbyterian Alliance, Methodist Ecumenical Conference, and the Canadian Council of Churches. He pastored various churches, 1916–38. Sisco lived in Toronto.

James H. Hunter

Dec. 30, 1890
Ayrshire, Scotland

1954

Outstanding journalist. Hunter came to Canada in 1913 and was with the *Toronto Globe* for ten years. From 1929 on, he edited *Evangelical Christian* out of Toronto. He married Margaret Diggins on June 7, 1940. His first novel, *Mystery of Mar Saba*, is quite well known. Hunter's 1951 novel, *Thine is the Kingdom,* won Zondervan's first prize for fiction. His *Flame of Fire* is the biography of ROLAND BINGHAM.

Jack Troup

1896

1954
Spokane, Washington

Superintendent of Gospel Union, Fifeshire, Scotland, 1928–30, and of Tent Hall, Glasgow, 193245. Troup came to America under MBI auspices, 1938–39. He was an evangelist in England and Ireland, 1945–49. He worked with J. FRANK NORRIS for six months in 1950 in Ft. Worth, then went back to England in 1951. Troup came to Canada and returned to the U.S. in 1953. He died while preaching.

Samuel A. Fulton

Nov. 13, 1877
Clay County, Illinois

Jan. 2, 1954
West Allis, Wisconsin

President of Gideons, 1921–29, 1932–35. Fulton married Luella McChesney on September 19, 1906 (died: March, 1952), and Gladys Schwartz on December 2, 1952. He was a traveling salesman for Iowa Soap Company (1903–10), was involved in the retail department store business (1910–13), and established the Fulton Company of Marshalltown, IA in 1913. He served on the Gideon cabinet for 29 years and was a member of the United Presbyterian Church of North America. Fulton was a Republican who lived out his days in Wauwatosa, WI.

Cary G. Taylor

June 12, 1871
Russiaville, Indiana

Jan. 24, 1954
New London, Indiana

President of Bible Holiness Seminary (John Wesley College in 1970, closed in 1980), **Owosso, MI 1913–24**. His wife's name was Ella. Taylor held pastorates in Indiana, Illinois, and Kentucky. He was president of Kingswood Holiness College (1924–27) and of Frankfort Pilgrim College (1927–47). Taylor developed orphanages in Illinois and Indiana, and maintained a rescue mission in Indianapolis.

Randall A. Carter

Jan. 1, 1867
Fort Valley, Georgia

Feb. 6, 1954
Chicago, Illinois

Bishop of Colored (Christian in 1956) **Methodist Episcopal Church, 1914–54; senior bishop, 1946–54**. Carter married Janie Hooks on April 22, 1891. He pastored in Georgia, 1892–94, then became the presiding elder, 1894–98 and 1903–14. Carter was a Mason and Republican who lived in Chicago. His books range from *Morning Meditations and Other Selections* (1917) to *Gathered Fragments* (1939).

David V. Jemison

April 21, 1875
Marion, Alabama

Feb. 20, 1954
Selma, Alabama (?)

First president of National Baptist Convention in the USA, 1940–53. Jemison married Henrietta Phillips on June 18, 1902, and they had six children. He pastored the Tabernacle Baptist Church, Salem, AL, 1903–29 and 1938–45; and in St. Louis St. Baptist Church, Mobile, AL from 1929–35. Jemison was a Democrat and a Mason. His books included *The Deplorable Condition of the Church* to *The Minister and His Message* (1935). He was a strong civil rights activist.

Keith L. Brooks

Feb. 23, 1887
Norwich, New York

Feb. 23, 1954
Los Angeles, California

President of American Prophetic League, 1938–54. Brooks was exceptional in his prophetic knowledge and edited *The Prophecy Monthly* since 1930. Brooks married Laura A. Woodman on June 20, 1930. He was converted under Evangelist JOHN A. DAVIS. Brooks was ordained as a Baptist and taught at Practical Bible Institute (1914–17) and the Bible Institute of Los Angeles (1917–28), as well as directing its correspondence school. He edited *The King's Business* (1921–28). Brooks' books included *The Summarized Bible* and many booklets and charts on prophecy. He died two weeks after suffering a stroke.

Franklin N. Parker

May 20, 1867
New Orleans, Louisiana

March 1, 1954
Atlanta, Georgia

Dean of Candler School of Theology, Atlanta, GA 1919–36. Parker married Minnie Jones on December 20, 1899. Converted at age 17, he pastored several Methodist churches in Louisiana, 1886–1902. He taught Bible literature at Trinity College, Durham, NC (1911–15) and systematic theology at Emory University (1915–42). Parker declined an election to become a Methodist bishop in May, 1918.

Orlando H. Milligan

Sept. 11, 1873
East Brady, Pennsylvania

March 17, 1954
Alquippa, Pennsylvania

Stated clerk of United Presbyterian Church (PC USA in 1983) **of North America, 1931–53.** Milligan married Ivy Moore on September 7, 1898. He pastored in Cedarville, OH (1903–8) and the Avalon Church, Pittsburgh, PA (1909–48). Milligan was the clerk of the Allegheny Presbytery, 1911–47. He lived in Alquippa, PA, and edited the *United Presbyterian Digest* (1942 on).

Perry Hayden

Feb. 9, 1901

March 18, 1954

Quaker miller of Tecumseh, MI, who received much publicity for his unique project. Raised an Episcopalian, he became a Christian at age 19. Hayden married Elizabeth Comfort. He planted one cubic inch of wheat on September 26, 1940. Six years later, his project resulted in a crop of 72,110 bushels, worth $150,000, which was used to feed the starving people of Europe. He was the president of Quaker Flour Mills and called his project "Dynamic Kernels."

Christian N. Hostetter Sr.

May 15, 1868
Mount Joy, Pennsylvania

April 4, 1954
Washington Borough, Pennsylvania

General Secretary of Brethren in Christ Church, Grantham, PA 1917–21, 1923–27; director of Brethren in Christ Missions, 1910–19; and president of Messiah College, 1916–22. Hostetter married Ella Neff on October 27, 1891, and they had six children. He was converted at age 30 and was known as a man of conviction, though tolerant in spirit. Hostetter discontinued growing tobacco on his farm. He was chairman of the Mission board, 1919–44, and served as an evangelist, while donating his time as college president.

Thomas A. Lambie

Feb. 8, 1885
Pittsburgh, Pennsylvania

April 14, 1954
Jerusalem, Palestine

Missionary doctor to Africa. When Lambie was eleven, he was deeply influenced by a dream that confirmed his faith. He married Charlotte Clancy/Clave on April 20, 1909 (died: 1946), and after her death, Irma Schneck on Oct. 1, 1947. He served as a Presbyterian medical missionary to Egypt, Khartoum, and southern Sudan (1907–18). He pioneered in West Abyssinia (Ethiopia) (1919) and in Addis Ababa (1922). Lambie built seven hospitals in the Middle East, including a large hospital for HAILE SELASSIE. He joined SIM in 1927. He opened 15 missionary stations and was field director, 1939 onward. During the Italian occupation of Ethiopia, 1935–41, Lambie served as executive director of the Ethiopian Red Cross. He died in the home of the warden of the Garden Tomb while preparing an Easter sunrise service message. He named six post-resurrection appearances and said, "Seven" (completion) and went to heaven. He is buried in Pittsburgh.

Horace F. Martin

April 1, 1876
Corning, Missouri

April 15, 1954
Seattle, Washington

President of Western Theological Seminary (Lutheran School of Theology, Chicago in 1967), **Fremont, NE 1925–39**. CLTS was part of Midland College at the time of his involvement. He was the superintendent of schools in Nebraska, 1900–3, then was ordained as a Lutheran in 1905. Martin married Martha C. Kastberg on July 12, 1910. He pastored Grace Church, Muscatine, IA (1905–8); First Church, Iowa City, IA (1908–12); Trinity Church, Abilene, KS (1914–16); and Matthews Church, North Liberty, IA (1916–17).

Gustav E. Bergemann

Aug. 9, 1862
Hustisford, Wisconsin

May 13, 1954
Fond Du Lac, Wisconsin (?)

President of First Evangelical Lutheran Synod of Wisconsin 1908–17, renamed Evangelical Lutheran Joint Synod of Wisconsin and other states, 1917–33 (WELS in 1959). Bergemann married Emma Anger on October 31, 1887. He pastored Trinity Church, Bay City, MI (1887–92); St. Paul's Church, Tomah, WI (1892–99); and St. Peter's Church, Fond du Lac, WI (1899 on). He was a member of Indian Missions Board, 1903–17.

Willard L. Sperry

April 5, 1882
Peabody, Massachusetts

May 15, 1954
Boston, Massachusetts

Dean of Harvard Divinity School, Cambridge, MA 1922–53. Sperry married Muriel Bennett on December 15, 1908, and the same year, was ordained into Congregational ministry. He pastored the Central Church of Boston (1914–22), and also served as professor of theology at Andover (MA) Theological Seminary (1917–25). Sperry's writings range from *Disciplines of Liberty* (1921) to *The Ethical Basis of Medical Practice* (1951). He is buried in Cambridge, MA.

William O. Carver

April 10, 1868
Wilson County, Tennessee

May 24, 1954
Louisville, Kentucky

Southern Baptist pastor, professor, missiologist and one of the first to teach missions exclusively. Carver married Alice Shepard on Dec. 29, 1897. Carver pastored New Salem Church, Deatsville, KY 1896–1907. Carver taught New Testament interpretation at Southern Baptist Theological Seminary (1896–1923), and comparative religion and missions at the same seminary (1899–1943). In 1907 he helped found the Women's Missionary Union Training School at SBTS. Carver served as managing editor of *Review and Expositor* (1919–42). A famous book of his was *Centennial History of New Salem Baptist Church* (1903). It was renamed, Carver School of Missions and Social Work in 1953. His books range from *Missions and The Plan of the Ages* (1909) to *The Glory of God in the Christian Calling* (1949).

Arthur J. Gossip

1873
Glasgow, Scotland

May 27, 1954
Glasgow, Scotland

Well-known pastor in Scotland. Gossip graduated from the University of Edinburgh in 1899 and began pastoring St. Columbia's Church in Liverpool the same year. He pastored West United Free Church in Farfar (1901–10); then St. Matthew's United Free Church of Glasgow (1910–21); and the Beechgrove Church of Aberdeen (1921–28). Following his wife's death in 1927, he preached his famous sermon, "But When Life Tumbles In, What Then?" He became professor of practical theology and Christian ethics at Trinity College in Glasgow, serving until 1945. In 1939 Trinity College became part of Glasgow University.

William P. Merrill

Jan. 10, 1867
Orange, New Jersey

June 19, 1954
New York, New York

Wrote the hymn "Rise Up, O Men of God" (music by AARON WILLIAMS). Converted at age eleven, Merrill was ordained into the Presbyterian ministry in 1890 and married Clara Helmer on September 15, 1896. Merrill pastored Trinity Church, Philadelphia (1890–95); Sixth St. Church, Chicago, 1895–1911; and Brick St. Church, New York City (1911–36). His books ranged from *Faith Building* (1895) to *We See Jesus* (1934). He was liberal in theology.

John T. Stone

Sept. 7, 1868
Stowe, Massachusetts

June 27, 1954
Chicago, Illinois

President of McCormick Theological Seminary, Chicago, IL 1928–40. Stone pastored in Utica, NY; Courtland, NY; and Baltimore, MD from 1894–1909. Stone was widely known as pastor of Fourth Presbyterian Church of Chicago, 1909–30, which grew from 500 to 3,000 members. He was president of the Chicago Bible Society and director of the Chicago Sunday Evening Club. He married Bessie Parsons (November 28, 1895) and Marie Briggs (June 22, 1932). He chaplained during World War I and wrote many books, including *Winning Men* (1946).

R. W. Blackwood & Bill Lyles

Oct. 23, 1921 (Blackwood, top picture)
Dec. 7, 1920 (Lyles, bottom picture)
Ackerman, Mississippi (Blackwood)
Catoosa County, Georgia (Lyles)

June 30, 1954

Clanton, Alabama

Members of the Blackwood Brothers Quartet, probably the most famous quartet in history. These two men were tragically killed in a plane crash on this date. The original quartet, starting in 1934, was made up of Roy, 34; Doyle, 20, and James, 16, three brothers, plus R.W. (13), son of Roy. They enjoyed overnight success, winning talent contests and singing over the radio. They stayed together through 1942, when various other members came on the scene—Bill Lyles sang bass from 1947–54. The Blackwood Brothers and George Beverly Shea pioneered in the recording field, recording with RCA Victor. The Blackwoods were regulars on Arthur Godfrey's TV show. On the day of the tragedy, they sang at the Chilton County Beach Festival. R. W. (pilot), went up for a test flight in the afternoon. Bill Lyles (co-pilot), and a local fan, John Ogburn, 18, went along. After several landing failures, with sudden wind shifts, they stalled and crashed before hundreds of "fans."

Emma F. Eaton

June 29, 1869
Canton, Ohio

July 24, 1954
Bangalore, South India

First president of International Gospel League, Pasadena, CA, 1906–49. Eaton was a missionary to India with the Church of the Nazarene. Emma developed cancer and was forced to return to the States. Then, by faith, she returned to India and started the India Gospel League. Emma was assisted by her husband, daughter, and the Harold Platt family. She trained, encouraged, and supported many national workers, evangelists, teachers, and Christian women.

James E. McConnell

Jan. 12, 1892
Atlanta, Georgia

July 24, 1954
Newport Beach, California

Wrote lyrics and music of "Whosoever Meaneth Me." For many years, McConnell served as choir director, pianist, and singer in evangelistic meetings conducted by his Baptist father. In 1922, he began a successful radio career, known as *Hymn Ties*, which was carried by NBC. This show featured him singing familiar hymns of all churches. McConnell helped pioneer religious television in his latter years.

Albert C. Wieand

Jan. 17, 1871
Wadsworth, Ohio

July 24, 1954
Pomona, California

Founder and first president of Bethany Theological Seminary, Oak Brook, IL (Richmond, IN, in 1994), **1905–32**. There he served as professor of biblical literature, 1932–46. Wieand married Katherine Broadwater on June 16, 1909. He also wrote many books from *Analytic Outline Diagram of the Life of Christ* (1914) to *The Gospel of Prayer* (1953).

Graham Frank

March 19, 1873
Cynthiana, Kentucky

Aug. 21, 1954
Dallas, Texas

First executive secretary (president in 1968) **of Christian Church** (Disciples of Christ), **1913–46**. Frank married Emma Lucas on March 9, 1899. He pastored in Nicholasville, KY (1897–99); Philadelphia (1900–03); Liberty, MD (1904–17); and Central Christian Church, Dallas, TX (1917–42). Frank was active in denominational activities and was a Mason.

Edgar P. Ellyson

Aug. 4, 1869
Damascus, Ohio

Aug. 24, 1954
Kansas City, Missouri

Minister, theologian, and a founder of the Church of the Nazarene. He was converted at age eight. He married Emily Soule on June 19, 1893 (died: 1943). Ellyson was president of Christian Workers Training School, La Grand, IA from 1898–1906. A Quaker minister in Marshalltown, IA, he accepted a call to be president of Peniel College, Greenville, TX, serving 1907–11. His long-standing sympathies with the Holiness movement and his work at the college led him to the conference at Pilot Point, TX, where the Nazarene Church was born in 1908. He was elected a general superintendent and spent 1908–11 as such. Then Ellyson was president of (Point Loma in 1998) Nazarene University, Los Angeles (San Diego in 1973) 1911–13, and president of Bresee College, Hutchinson, KS, from 1921–23. He became editor of the denomination's Sunday School publications in 1923. His *Theological Compendium* (1908) was the first systematic theology book produced by the American Holiness Movement.

Frederick D. Kerschener

Aug. 28, 1875
Clear Spring, Maryland

Aug. 24, 1954
Indianapolis, Indiana

First president of School of Religion (Christian Theological Seminary in 1958), **Indianapolis, IN 1924–44.** Kerschener married Pearl Archer on August 25, 1909 (died: September 13, 1912), and Elise Martin on June 15, 1915. He was president of Milligan College, TN (1908–11) and Texas Christian University, Ft. Worth (1911–15). He was a professor of Christian doctrine at Drake University, Des Moines, IA, 1920–24. Kerschener wrote a variety of books, ranging from *Religion of Christ* (1912) to *Stars* (1940).

Clarence H. Benson

Aug. 13, 1879
Minneapolis, Minnesota

Sept. 16, 1954
Maitland, Florida

General secretary of the Evangelical Teacher Training Association, 1930–52, which he helped to found. He was known as "Mr. Christian Education." He married Rena Clark in August, 1908. Benson was ordained to the Presbyterian ministry and held pastorates in New York and Pennsylvania (1908–19), and the Union Church in Kobe, Japan (1919–22). Benson taught at Moody Bible Institute, 1922–42 and headed the Christian Education Department from 1924 on. Benson developed textbooks entitled *All Graded Bible Services* (1925–33), cofounded Scripture Press in 1934 to publish them, and wrote *The Sunday School in Action*. He helped found the National Sunday School Association and its *Uniform Bible Lessons* series.

Joseph L. Peacock

June 15, 1873
Paisley, Scotland

Sept. 24, 1954
Raleigh, North Carolina (?)

President of Shaw University Divinity School, Raleigh, NC, 1920–31. Peacock married Edna Arnold on June 26, 1901 (died: June 10, 1927). Ordained a Baptist in 1900, he pastored in Norwood, RI (1899–1901); 1st Church, Goffstown, NH (1901–3); Calvary Church, Westerly, RI (1903–8) and was librarian at Westerly Public Library (1908–1919). After leaving Shaw, he pastored at Tarboro, NC (1932–40) and Saxton's River, VT (1940–43). He served numerous civic and religious organizations. He was buried in Westerly, RI.

Urban V. W. Darlington

Aug. 3, 1870
Graefenberg, Kentucky

Oct. 1, 1954
Huntington, West Virginia (?)

Bishop in the Methodist Episcopal Church South, 1918–39, and in the Methodist Church, 1939–49. Darlington served in Europe and in several conferences of the South. He married Lyda Clark, and later, Virginia Bourne on February 12, 1913. He pastored in Washington, KY (1896–1900); Covington, KY (1900–5); Parkersburg, WV (1905–08); and Huntington, WV (1909–13). He was president of Morris Harvey College, Barboursville, WV, from 1917–18, which later moved to Charleston. Darlington is buried in Frankfort, KY.

Marguerite T. Doane

Nov. 13, 1868
Cincinnati, Ohio

Oct. 17, 1954
South Orange, New Jersey

First director of Society for Foreign Mission Welfare (Overseas Ministries Study Center in 1967), **Ventnor, NJ 1922–54**. Marguerite and her sister, Ida (died: 1942) purchased a brown clapboard cottage in Ventnor, and remodeled it into four apartments for use as furlough housing for missionaries. Some 8,000 missionary adults and 4,000 children, from more than 150 North American agencies had furlough housing needs met from 1922–82 by the apartments. The modest beginning grew until there were 40 apartments in 1964, covering an entire block. Marguerite helped LUCY PEABODY establish the Association of Baptists for World Evangelism in 1927, when liberalism threatened their missionary work in the Philippines.

Anna B. Russell

April 21, 1862
Pine Valley, New York

Oct. 29, 1954
Corning, New York

Wrote the hymn, "Wonderful, Wonderful Jesus" (music by ERNEST SELLERS). Anna spent most of her life in Corning, NY, where she was an active member of the First Methodist Church. She lived with her sister, Cora C. Russell, and they both wrote a number of hymns.

Albert M. Johnson

July 9, 1882
Willshire, Ohio

Nov. 18, 1954
Huntington, Indiana

Bishop of the United Brethren in Christ, Huntington, IN 1929–51. Johnson was licensed (1900) and ordained into the Church of the United Brethren in Christ (1904). He married Ollie M. Stetler on April 2, 1909. He pastored in Rockford, OH; Celina, OH; Zanesville, IN; Warren, IN; and Van Wert, OH. He was a successful evangelist as well.

Lelwellyn L. Berry

Feb. 26, 1876
Hampton, Virginia

Nov. 23, 1954
New York New York

Director of African Methodist Episcopal Church Missions, 1934–54. Berry pastored successfully at St. James AME Church, Winston-Salem, NC; Emmanuel AME Church, Portsmouth, VA (grew to 1,500 members) and St. John's AME Church, Norfolk, VA. Berry married Beulah Harris in 1900. He traveled around the world on behalf of his board far more than any other in his office.

Edward H. Roberts

Aug. 1, 1895
Middle Granville, New York

Dec. 13, 1954
Princeton, New Jersey

President of Association of Theological Schools, 1952–54, and executive secretary of the same, 1938–42. Roberts married Esther Hill on December 22, 1928. He was a Presbyterian and was connected with Princeton Theological Seminary most of his life. Roberts served as a professor of systematic theology (1930–37), of homiletics (1937–53), as dean of students (1937–45), and as dean (1945–54).

Albert W. Palmer

May 18, 1879
Kansas City, Missouri

Dec. 16, 1954
Altadena, California

President of Chicago (IL) Theological Seminary, 1930–46. Palmer married Sara Wedd on June 6, 1904. Ordained a Congregationalist in 1904, he pastored at Plymouth Church, Oakland, CA (1907–17); Central Union of Honolulu (1917–24); First Church of Oak Park, IL (1924–30); and was a lecturer of religion at the University of Southern California (1949–51). Palmer wrote many books from *Drift Toward Religion* (1914) to *How Religion Helps* (1948). He was an affirmed liberal. He is buried in Los Angeles, CA.

Mary Stone

Dec. 12, 1872
Kiukiang, China

Dec. 29, 1954
Pasadena, California

Chinese Methodist educator. Mary was the first girl in her area to grow up with unbound feet. She received an American education with a friend, Ida Kahn. She edited the book *Gospel of the Kingdom* after 1908. In 1918 Mary organized the League for Social Service and became a leader in the Social Gospel Movement. Stone founded Bethel Mission in Shanghai, in 1920, which graduated more than 2,500 nurses by the time of her death.

John R. Mott

May 25, 1865
Livingston Manor, New York

Jan. 31, 1955
Orlando, Florida

Methodist layman, remarkable leader, and administrator in missions and ecumenism. Mott was converted by J.E.K. Studd at Cornell University at a revival meeting in 1879. He married Leila White on November 26, 1891 (died: early 1950s). He was student secretary of the international committee of the YMCA (1888–1915) and general secretary of the American YMCA (1915–31). He helped found the Student Volunteer Movement (1888–1920) and served as president of World's Student Christian Federation (1895–1920) and its chairman (1920–28). Mott presided at the famed World Missionary Conference in Edinburgh in 1910 of which he was chairman. Mott founded the International Missionary Council in 1921 and was active in the international ecumenical movement, 1910–48, although he remained committed to evangelism and missions. In a sense he was the father of the WCC having been a leader in each of the movements that led up to its formation. He served as honorary president of the Amsterdam (1948) and Evanston (IL) gatherings (1954). In 1946 he was a cowinner of the Nobel Peace Prize. His books ranged from *World's Conquest* (1897) to *The Larger Evangelism* (1944). He wrote *The Evangelization of the World in This Generation* (1900). He is buried in the Episcopal Cathedral Church (St. Peter and St. Paul) Washington D.C.

Thoro Harris

March 31, 1873
Washington, D.C.

March 27, 1955
Eureka Springs, Arkansas

Composer and publisher. Harris wrote the lyrics and music to many hymns such as "All That Thrills My Soul Is Jesus" (1931), "He's Coming Soon" (1944), "Don't Turn Him Away," "Grumblers," and "Give Me Oil in My Lamp." He began composing hymns as a teenager, and had his first hymnal published in Boston in 1902. In 1903, he moved to Chicago, where he worked with many of the great musical leaders of that time. He wrote the famous children's chorus "Jesus Loves the Little Children," in 1921. He spent the rest of his life, from 1932 on, in Eureka Springs, AR.

Thomas T. Shields

Nov. 1, 1873
Bristol, England

April 4, 1955
Toronto, Ontario, Canada

"Mr. Fundamentalism of Canada" and president of the Union of Regular Baptist Churches of Ontario and Quebec (Evangelical Baptist Churches of Canada), **1927–29, 1937–48**. He was converted in his youth. Shields came to Canada in 1888. He married Elizabeth Kitchen in 1899 (died: 1932). He then married Leota Griffin in 1934. Shields pastored Ontario churches, 1894–1910: these were Florence (1894–95), Patton (1895–97), Delhi (1897–1900), Wentworth St., Hamilton (1900–4), and Adelaide St., Toronto (1904–10). Shields pastored at Jarvis Street Church of Toronto for 45 years, 1910–1955. After 300 members left him in 1921, he founded *The Gospel Witness*, a weekly magazine in 1922 that went to 30,000 homes in 60 countries. He was president of Baptist Bible Union, 1923–30. He organized the Toronto Baptist Seminary in 1927, the year he was expelled from the Baptist Convention of Ontario and Quebec for exposing liberalism at McMaster University. He wrote from *Christ in the Old Testament* (1923) to *How to Receive Eternal Life* (1951).

William A. Fountain

Oct. 29, 1870
Elberton, Georgia

April 23, 1955
Atlanta, Georgia

Bishop of African Methodist Episcopal Church, 1920–52; senior bishop, 1944–52. The eldest of 18 children, Fountain married Jessie Williams on June 29, 1893 (died: September, 1898), and then Julia Allen on October 24, 1899. He pastored various Georgia churches, 1892–1911, and was the district supervisor of several areas. Fountain was president of Morris Brown University, Atlanta, GA, 1911–20, the largest educational institution of the denomination. He went blind in 1951.

Clinton N. Howard

July 28, 1868
Pottsville, Pennsylvania

April 25, 1955
Washington, D.C.

Bible and temperance lecturer and crusader for prohibition and peace. He crusaded for things others ignored. Howard married Angeline Kellar on May 1, 1888. He was the chairman of the World Peace Committee, 1920–24, representing 41 nations. Howard was the general superintendent of the International Reform Federation of Washington, D.C. He worked as the editor of *Progress*, and as the chairman of the National United Community Enforcement, 1924–36. His most famous sermon was "Pearls of Paradise," in which he described the 208 names of Christ. WILLIAM J. BRYAN said, "I have never heard his equal."

William J. Schieffelin

April 14, 1866
New York, New York

April 29, 1955
New York, New York (?)

President of American Leprosy Mission (ALM Int.), **Greenville, SC 1906–48**. Schieffelin was a research scholar in chemistry. However his leprosy work was his main mission in life. He married Louise Shepard on February 5, 1891. In 1906, the New York Committee of the "Mission to Lepers in India and the East" met in his home. In 1908, he was elected chairman of the committee, and in 1920, president of the corporation, retiring in 1948. He became the unfailing friend of leprosy patients throughout the world. He has been on boards of Citizens Union, American Bible Society, Tuskegee Institute, and Hampton Institute. He fought for good government in New York City for over 60 years.

Edward Mott

Dec. 9, 1866
Morean, New York

May 3, 1955
Portland, Oregon

General superintendent of Ohio Yearly Meeting (Evangelical Friends Church—Eastern Region in 1970), **1904–14, and president of Portland Bible Institute** (merged into Seattle (WA) Pacific College in 1967), **1922–33**. Mott married Ada Miller in 1887. Mott acted as the presiding clerk of the Ohio Yearly Meeting, 1903–19. He taught at Cleveland Bible Institute, 1904–19. He was the presiding clerk of Oregon Yearly Meeting of Friends, 1924–44. He wrote several books, including, *The Christ of the Eternities*.

Winifred R. Cox

Dec. 9, 1879
Randolph County, North Carolina

May 14, 1955
Thomasville, North Carolina

First president of Apostolic Holiness University (John Wesley College, High Point, NC, in 1959), **1905–25, 1928–31**. The school was first called Greensboro (NC) Bible and Literary School. Cox was an evangelist for the Church of the Nazarene for 25 years. He married Elma Upperman on August 30, 1910. Converted at age 20, he was general superintendent of Pilgrim Holiness Church, 1922–26. Cox founded a church and a Bible and Literary School in Greensboro, NC. The school grew from six to 200 students. After the school closed in 1931, he felt led to found People's Bible College in 1932, which for four years occupied the same building the former school had. He taught there, 1932–55. He also pastored PHC in High Point, NC, and Glenwood Friends Church. He was conducting a revival at the Peoples Methodist Church, in Thomasville, when taken to a hospital where he died.

Mary McLeod Bethune

July 10, 1875
Mayesville, South Carolina

May 18, 1955
Daytona Beach, Florida

Founder and first president of Daytona Normal and Industrial School for Girls, 1904–23, and Bethune-Cookman College, 1923–41 (after it merged with Cookman Institue in 1923), **Daytona Beach, FL 1904–47**. She married Albertus Bethune in May, 1898. Mary graduated from Moody Bible Institute in 1895. Bethune's goal was to provide education for the black railroad laborers' children. She founded her school on October 3, 1904 with $1.50, her four-year-old son, and five girls who paid $.50 a week tuition to be educated on old crates, boxes in odd rooms in an old house by the city dump. By 1923, there were 600 students, 32 faculty members, and an $800,000 campus free of debt. Bethune was also founding president of the Central Life Insurance Company. She chaired the Florida State Teacher's Association, and as a devoted Methodist, the United Council of Church Women. Bethune was a director of the

Division of Negro Affairs of the National Youth administration, 1935–44, and a special advisor to President Franklin D. Roosevelt on problems of U.S. minorities.

Jim H. Green

June 21, 1882
Todd, North Carolina

May 23, 1955
Greensboro, North Carolina

President of People's Bible College (John Wesley College, High Point, NC, in 1959), **Greensboro, NC 1932–52**. He pastored in North Carolina (1905–18), then traveled as an evangelist (1918–23). He pastored the Lighthouse Mission, 1929–31. Green then felt led to start a Bible School in Greensboro. The school moved from Greensboro to High Point in 1978. He was the founder of several camp meetings and the People's Methodist Church (which later merged with the Evangelical Methodist Church). Green married Minnie M. Grogan, and they had seven children. He died of a heart attack.

Christine A. Gibson

Jan. 3, 1879
Georgetown, British Guiana (Guyana)

May 30, 1955
Providence, Rhode Island

Founder and first president of Zion Bible Institute, East Providence (Barrington in 1985), **RI, 1924–55**. Christine began to work with native Indians at Anna Regina in her home country. In 1904, she came to Faith Home, a missionary rest home in East Providence. In 1910, she married Reuben A. Gibson and for 14 years they worked together until Reuben died of Bright's disease in May, 1924. In November, 1924, she opened the institute with three students. It was a miracle school, showing how God provided through a mini-GEORGE MUELLER type faith and prayer ministry.

George W. Richards

April 26, 1869
Farmington, Pennsylvania

June 11, 1955
Lancaster, Pennsylvania

President of Lancaster (PA) Theological Seminary, 1920–39 and of Evangelical and Reformed Church (United Church of Christ in 1957), **1934–38**. Richards married Mary Mosser on November 19, 1890, and was soon ordained to the Reformed Church. He pastored Salem Church, Allentown, PA (1890–99), then was a professor of church history at LTS (1899–1939). He wrote many books from *Historical and Doctrinal Studies on the Heidelberg Catechism* (1913) to *Creative Controversies in Christianity* (1938). Richards translated many of Karl Barth's sermons into English.

Lewis W. Sturk

Feb. 1, 1895
Bad Axe, Michigan

June 13, 1955
Defiance, Ohio

General superintendent of Pilgrim Holiness Church (Wesleyan Church in 1968), **1946–53**. Sturk was one of the first students at Owosso (MI) Bible College. Sturk married Mae Taylor, and they had five children. He pastored in Ellsworth, MI, (1921–26); First Pilgrim Holiness Church in Flint, MI (1926–37); First Pilgrim Holiness Church in Cincinnati, OH (1937–43); and served as the Superintendent of the Ohio district (1943–46). He died of a heart attack.

J. Irvin Overholtzer

July 20, 1877
Banta, California

Aug. 5, 1955
Pacific Palisades, California

Founder and first director of Child Evangelism Fellowship, Pacific Palisades, CA (Warrenton, MO in 1976), **1937–52**. Overholtzer had a Church of the Brethren background. He married in 1897 and was involved in business for many years. He became burdened for children, beginning in 1934 (age 57). He founded CEF in PAUL ROOD's office at BIOLA, Los Angeles, CA. Since then, millions of children have attended "Good News Clubs" around the world. In May, 1937, he incorporated CEF in Illinois and in 1942 the magazine, *Child Evangelism*, was started. He died of a heart attack.

J. Wilmot Mahood

Aug. 22, 1864
Huron County, Ontario, Canada

Aug. 7, 1955
Ford Dodge, Iowa

Founder and first president of London Bible College (Ontario Bible College), **1935–44**. From 1877–99, Mahood pastored in Iowa. In his younger years, Mahood was a Methodist evangelist and worked with J. WILBUR CHAPMAN. He married May Rundle on October 11, 1887. Then in 1928, he began leading the extension staff of MBI. He founded London Bible College in 1935 with classes two nights a week in the London Gospel Tabernacle. He was a widely known author beginning with *The Art of Soul Winning* (1901) to *A Study in Christian Certainties* (1938).

Grace Woodman Haight

Sept. 22, 1863
Springfield, Massachusetts

Aug. 9, 1955
Greenville, South Carolina

Independent missionary in China for 30 years, and then a boat missionary on the Nile River. Haight was an associate editor of the *Southern Missionary*. At 70, she became a professor in missions and hymnology at Bob Jones College (University in 1947), 1930–55. Haight authored many poems and children's books. She died in the campus hospital.

Joachim Wach

Jan. 25, 1898
Chemnitz, Germany

Aug. 27, 1955
Locarno, Switzerland

Theologian who specialized in modern science and liberal thought. He lectured at Leipzig (1924–1935); at Brown University, Providence, RI (1935–46); then in Chicago, IL (1945–55). In his works, which include Sociology of Religion (1944), he explored religious experiences as well as the social aspect of religion. His books vary from a German work (1924) to *Types of Religious Experiences* (1951). He was an Episcopalian and unmarried.

Daniel N. Buntain

Nov. 18, 1888
Prince Edward Island, Canada

Sept. 8, 1955
Edmonton, Alberta, Canada

General superintendent of Pentecostal Assemblies of Canada, 1937–44. Buntain pastored a Methodist Church in Winnipeg, Manitoba, 1919–25. In 1928, he joined the ranks of Pentecostalism and pastored a Wesleyan Church in Indiana. Then he was the president of Manitoba Pentecostal Assemblies of Canada. Buntain pastored the Central Pentecostal Tabernacle (1945) and founded Northwest Bible College in Edmonton, Alberta (1947).

Arthur G. Ball

July 8, 1884
Charlevoix, Michigan

Sept. 23, 1955
Guatemala City, Guatemala

Lay leader of World Gospel Crusades. Ball was a Southern Californian builder and contractor who gave his life to church, Sunday school, youth, Mexican, and Japanese missions. He married Mabel Hencensim (October 15, 1907) and Eula Mudd (May 4, 1954). Ball and his wife were converted in 1912 in a Free Methodist Church in Los Angeles. At age 61, God called him to be a self-supported missionary builder in South America. He went to Medelin, Colombia, to supervise the building of Manantiales Bible School. Ball originated and distributed small, globe, kitchen table banks to raise funds for missions. Each day a family would put coins into the bank before their meal. He died of a heart attack.

Mamie White Colvin

June 12, 1883
Westview, Ohio

Oct. 30, 1955
Clearwater, Florida

Crusader for the temperance movement. Colvin was converted in a Quaker revival meeting in Westfield, IN. During her lifetime, she won every possible temperance award through her oratorical efforts, beginning at Wheaton College. She married D. Leigh Colvin on September 19, 1906. He was national president of the Inter-Collegiate Prohibition Association and a judge of the contest where she was giving a speech on "their" favorite topic. She won the contest and his heart. From 1944–53, she was the national leader of the WCTU, leading 400,000 women, and editing the *Union Signal*. She died in the pulpit as she prepared to address the congregation of the First Methodist Church. She was buried in Westfield, IN. Her husband, David, ran for president of the United States in 1936 on the Prohibition ticket. He was born January 28, 1880 in Charleston, Ohio and died September 7, 1959.

Lloyd C. Kelley

April 13, 1874
Mount Sterling, Alabama

Dec. 10, 1955
Madison, Indiana

Founder and first president of Clear Creek Baptist Bible College, Pineville, KY, 1926–54. He was ordained (1899) and married Nancy Newland (1907). Kelley held pastorates in Birmingham, AL; three churches in Kentucky; Orlinda, TN (1907–14); and at FBC, Campbellsville, KY (1914–20). Kelley also pastored the FBC, Pineville, KY, from 1920–42, where he started his school. Originally, he called it Clear Creek Mountain Preacher's School.

Edwin M. Poteat

Nov. 20, 1892
New Haven, Connecticut

Dec. 17, 1955
Raleigh, North Carolina

Baptist pastor and educator. Poteat married Wilda Hardman on June 17, 1917. He was a missionary to China (1917–29); pastor at Pullen Memorial, Raleigh, NC (1929–37 and 1948–55); and at Euclid Avenue Baptist, Cleveland (1937–44). Poteat was the president of Colgate-Rochester Divinity School, 1944–48. His writings ranged from *Coming to Terms with the Universe* (1931) to *Jesus' Belief in Man* (1956).

Homer A. Rodeheaver

Oct. 4, 1880
Union Furnace, Ohio

Dec. 18, 1955
Winona Lake, Indiana

Musical director for the BILLY SUNDAY evangelistic crusades, 1909–31. Rodeheaver led the singing, sang solos, and played the trombone. He composed music for "Then Jesus Came" and "You Must Open the Door." He made recordings, 1913–42. He went on a world tour with WILLIAM BIEDERWOLF, 1923–24. His Rodeheaver Publishers of Sacred Music (1910–35) and Rodeheaver-Hall-Mack Company (Chicago, Philadelphia, 1935–41; Winona Lake, 1941 on), became the world's largest gospel music publishers. In 1942, he became the music director of Bob Jones University, with an auditorium later bearing his name. He never married. He was president of Rodeheaver-Hall-Mack Company, Winona Lake, IN, where he lived at Rainbow Point, (bought in 1912), with his sister, Ruth R. Thomas. As a Methodist, he was involved in a boy's ranch in Palatka, FL, in his later years.

Charles P. Jones

Jan. 9, 1878
Hamilton, Missouri

Dec. 20, 1955
Kansas City, Missouri

Wrote the lyrics and music to "Come Unto Me" and "Deeper and Deeper." Jones married Myrtle Moling on February 2, 1898 (died: March, 1945), and Clara McConnell on April 24, 1946. He was a Baptist pastor of churches in Missouri (1896–1913), the general superintendent of Kansas City Baptist Union (1914–25) and head of the Kansas City Baptist Association (1925–45). He was a Democrat and a Mason.

Edward P. Gates

June 21, 1886
Fulton, Kansas

1956
Belmont, Massachussetts

General secretary of Christian Endeavor (World), 1920–29, and Christian Endeavor (Int.), 1919–29. He became field secretary of Illinois, 1911–20. Gates married Estella Jorgensen of Chicago, IL on January 10, 1914, and they had one son. Gates was the advisor in American and foreign travel beginning January 1, 1931. He was a Baptist and a Mason who lived in Belmont, MA.

William H. Jordan

March 18, 1866
Vinton, Iowa

1956
Omaha, Nebraska

First president of Omaha (NE) Bible Institute (Faith Baptist Bible College in 1967), **1924–42**. Jordan married Phoebe Martin on June 5, 1894, and was ordained as a Presbyterian just two weeks later. He pastored in three Iowa centers and in Jerseyville, IL from 1906–12. He served as an evangelist (1912–16); then pastored in Shenandoah, IA (1916–21); Omaha, NE (1921–24); and Bethany Presbyterian Church in 1935. The school began in the facilities of the Third Presbyterian Church where he pastored.

Stanley B. Vandersall

Nov. 2, 1886
East Liberty, Ohio

c 1956
West Roxbury, Massachusetts

General secretary of Christian Endeavor (World), 1929–31, 1934–49. Vandersall was ordained in the Evangelical Church, 1908. He married Leah Talbott on June 30, 1914. Vandersall pastored in Canton and Lorain, OH (1906–09); Methodist Church, Sparrowsbury, NY (1909–12); and was on staff of the Ohio CE movement (1919–29). Vandersall held various positions in the movement including editor, 1937–46. He was also active in the Lord's Day League of New England. He wrote *Christian Endeavor Essentials* (1938).

P. James (Jim) Elliot

Oct. 8, 1927
Portland, Oregon

Jan. 8, 1956
Curaray Beach, Ecuador

One of the five Auca Indian martyrs. Raised in a Plymouth Brethren home, he was saved at age six. Elliot was at Wheaton (IL) College 1945–49, and began a courtship with Betty Howard in 1946. In 1947, he spent the summer in Mexico where his Auca interest began. In 1952, Elliot went to Ecuador with Pete Fleming, building Shandia Mission Station in the jungle and working in it, 1952–53, when a flood destroyed it. Elliot married Betty on October 8, 1953, and from 1953–55, they worked among the Quichua Indians. Along with his colleagues; NATE SAINT, Ed McCully, Roger Youderian, and Pete Fleming, Elliot strove to make contact with the mysterious Auca Indian tribe. They were speared to death just two days after an exciting face-to-face contact with the Aucas. Elliot's story and that of his colleagues was written by his wife, Elisabeth (Betty), in *Through Gates of Splendor* and *Shadow of the Almighty*. His favorite Bible verse was Isaiah 42:16.

"*...He is no fool who gives what he cannot keep to gain what he cannot lose.*"

Nate Saint

Aug. 30, 1923
Huntingdon Valley, Pennsylvania

Jan. 8, 1956
Curaray Beach, Ecuador

One of five Auca Indian martyrs. Nate was converted at age 13 and served for three years in the U.S. Army Air Corps during WWII. Saint was the pilot of the Piper Cruiser that landed on "Palm Beach" in a daring plan to contact the Stone Age Auca Indians. Wooden spear wielding Aucas came to the beach and killed the missionaries. Nate was married to Marjorie Farris on February 14, 1948, who later married ABE VANDERPUY. Saint went to Ecuador in 1948 with Missionary Aviation Fellowship, opening a base at Shell Mera. He invented a number of safety features in missionary aviation circles. For twelve weeks, they had contact with the Aucas prior to their martyrdom. His watch stopped at 3:12 p.m. His sister, RACHEL SAINT, and Betty Elliot, widow of JIM, finally reached the Aucas.

Carey S. Thomas

Feb. 7, 1883
Pezanse, England

Jan. 10, 1956
Denver, Colorado

Baptist pastor and educator. Thomas pastored Baptist churches in Milburn, NJ (1909–18); Belmont Avenue, Philadelphia (1918–25); and FBC of Altoona, PA (1925–50). He taught earlier at Philadelphia School of the Bible and spoke at many Bible conferences. He was president of Conservative Baptist Theological Seminary, Denver, CO, from 1950–56. He suffered from leukemia, left his office December 31, 1955, to go to the hospital and then nine days later went to heaven.

Arnold J. Grunigen

1902

Jan. 18, 1956
Palo Alto, California

President of Christian Businessmen's Committee, 1950–52. Grunigen was a born salesman, beginning at age twelve, never graduating from high school. He grew up in a Christian home (his father often preached on street corners) and began as an account executive with Weeden and Company Investments. He married Susan Weber on August 5, 1924 (died: October 13, 1975). They had two children. Grunigen was the governor of the National Association of Security, a member of the Security Exchange Commission, and was associated with J. Barth and Company at the time of his death. He was a longtime board member of Mt. Hermon Bible Conference and an elder in the Calvary Presbyterian Church, San Francisco, CA. He died of brain cancer.

Ernest B. Gordon

March 2, 1867
Boston, Massachusetts

Feb. 10, 1956
Brewster, Cape Cod, Massachusetts

Excellent linguist and able student of the causes and nature of apostasy. The son of A. J. GORDON, Ernest contributed to the *Sunday School Times* for 30 years, wrote a column, "Religious Survey" (1922–56), and authored 22 books. His best-known books are *The Leaven of the Sadducees* and *A Book of Protestant Saints*. Gordon lived in Francestown, NH.

Paul W. Rood

Aug. 1, 1889
Barnum, Minnesota

Feb. 22, 1956
La Canola, California

President of World's Christian Fundamentalist Association, 1929–49, succeeding WILLIAM B. RILEY. Rood married Neva Nystrom on June 25, 1913. He was ordained in Mission (Evangelical) Covenant Church and pastored the Swedish (First Covenant) Tabernacle, Seattle, WA (1915–22); Beulah (First Covenant) Tabernacle, Turlock, CA (1922–33); and Lake View Covenant, Chicago (1933–35). He was president of BIOLA University, 1935–38. Rood wrote many books and served as an evangelist.

John E. Park

March 7, 1879
Belfast, Northern Ireland

March 4, 1956
Cambridge, Maine

Congregationalist pastor, educator, and hymn writer. Park married Grace Burtt on April 28, 1906. Park served as pastor of Second Congregational Church, Newton, MA (1907–26), and as president of Wheaton College, Norton, MA (1926–44). He wrote many books, ranging from *The Keen Joy of Living* (1907) to *Exodus* (Int. Bible Series) (1949). He wrote a number of hymns, including "We Would See Jesus."

John S. Stamm

March 23, 1878
near Alida, Kansas

March 5, 1956
Kansas City, Missouri

Bishop of Evangelical Church (UMC in 1968), **1926–50; president of Federal Council of Churches** (NCC in 1950), **1948–50; and president of Evangelical School of Theology,** (United Theological Seminary, Dayton, OH in 1954), **Reading, PA 1934–41.** He entered the Evangelical Church ministry in 1899. He married Priscilla Wahl (February 2, 1884–December 19, 1965) on March 19, 1912. Stamm pastored in Bloomington and Glasgow, MO, and Manhattan, Downers Grove, and Oak Park, IL until 1919. Stamm was a professor of theology at Evangelical Theological Seminary, Naperville, IL, 1919–27. He also served as the general secretary of evangelism for the Evangelical Church, 1927–34. As bishop, he served eight years in Kansas City, MO, and 16 years in Harrisburg, PA. He wrote *Evangelism and Christian Experience* (1930).

William M. Scott

Feb. 10, 1882
Charlotte, North Carolina

March 10, 1956
Tampa, Florida

President of National Primitive Baptist Convention, 1934–51, 1952–56. Scott married Lula Davidson of Charlotte, NC. He pastored at Shiloh Primitive Baptist Church, Pensacola, FL, until 1923. He then served at New Salem Primitive Baptist Church in Tampa, FL, until his death. In Tampa, he performed 803 marriages, 510 funerals, saw 1,900 converted, and built a new church building in 1951.

Edgar D. Jones

Dec. 5, 1876
Hearne, Texas

March 26, 1956
Detroit, Michigan

President of the Federal Council of Churches (NCC in 1950), **1936–38.** Jones was ordained into the Disciples of Christ in 1901. He married Francis Willis on January 23, 1902. He pastored in Kentucky (1901–3); in Cleveland, OH (1903–6); at the First Church, Bloomington, IL (1906–20); Central Church, Detroit, MI (1920–26); and Central Woodward Church, Detroit

(1927–47). He retired in 1947 and settled in Pleasant Hill, MI. Jones wrote many books, ranging from *The Inner Circle* (1914) to *Sermons I Love to Preach* (1953).

Albert J. Levengood

Oct. 2, 1886
Clark, Ohio

March 30, 1956
Dayton, Tennessee

Founder and first director of Tennessee Mountain Mission, Dayton, TN, 1938–56. Levengood was converted at a Sunday School, when brought by a neighbor. He married Ella Martin on Sept. 19, 1916. He pastored a Reformed church in Walnut Creek, OH; Warren, PA; Indianapolis, IN; Louisville, KY; St. Louis, MO; and New Bedford, OH. He was burdened for mountain people and started SS classes, home Bible studies, and Bible lessons in public schools. He excelled in Bible prophecy, taught at Bryan College, Dayton, TN, for eight years and directed their Christian service program. He died of cancer.

William R. Newell

May 22, 1868
Savannah, Ohio

April 1, 1956
Deland, Florida

Bible teacher and writer of the beloved hymn, "At Calvary" (1895). In 1879, at MOODY's suggestion, Newell began to conduct interdenominational Bible classes in Chicago, Detroit, Toronto, St. Louis, London, Cairo, etc. That same year, he became the assistant superintendent and teacher at Moody Bible Institute. Newell married Mellicent Woodworth on June 9, 1896. He wrote many books, including *Old Testament Studies* (1905), *Romans* (1920s), *Revelation* (1930s), and *Hebrews* (1940s). He identified with the Plymouth Brethren. Newell, the student, gave DANIEL TOWNER, the teacher, his famous lyrics between classes at Moody Bible Institute. Before the day was over, TOWNER had the melody written.

Ragner A. Arlander

Feb. 18, 1876
Stockholm, Sweden

April 6, 1956
Minneapolis, MN

Missions secretary (president) of Baptist General Conference, 1935–45. Arlander came to America in 1891 and moved to Cadillac, MI, in 1893. He was converted under the ministry of his uncle, Lons Arlander. He was ordained (May 12, 1899), and married Emily Anderson (May 23, 1900). He pastored in Chicago, IL (1899–1901); was an evangelist (1901–03); pastored in Valley, NE (1903–5); Evanston, IL (1905–9); Big Springs, SD (1909–20); and at Elim Baptist in Minneapolis, MN (1920–35), during the Depression years. His funeral was at Elim Baptist, where he was a member for 35 years.

Charles H. Marsh

April 8, 1886
Magnolia, Iowa

April 12, 1956
La Jolla, California

Composed music for OSTROM's "Is It the Crowning Day?", CROSBY's "The Lights of Home," "I'll Sing It Today" (lyrics by B. Hopkins) **and CHAPMAN's great hymn, "One Day."** Marsh taught at BIOLA University (1915–19) and at the University of Redlands (CA) (1919–26). He was the organist and choirmaster of First Presbyterian Church, Ft. Wayne, IN (1928–32); at FBC, Gainesville, FL (1932–35); and at St. James-by-the-Sea Episcopal Church, La Jolla, CA (1936–56). Marsh produced solo arrangements, instrumental works, anthems, and more.

John W. Long

Nov. 3, 1882
Sussex County, Delaware

May 5, 1956
Pennsylvania

President of Dickinson Seminary, Williamsport, PA 1921–29, with a Junior College added, 1929–48, and Lycoming College, 1948–55. Before becoming president, Long held a series of pastorates in the Central Methodist Pennsylvania Conference, the last at St. Paul's Church, State College, PA. In 1948, his school became a four-year, degree-granting college, now known as Lycoming. He married Mildred Lewis.

Dawson E. Trotman

March 5, 1906
Bisbee, Arizona

June 18, 1956
Schroon Lake, New York

Founder, 1933, and first director of Navigators, 1943–56. Trotman became a Christian in 1926 in Lomita, CA after memorizing several verses of Scripture in a contest at church. Suddenly, John 1:12 and 5:24 made a difference. He withdrew from the Presbyterian Church in 1931. He began a Bible study in his home in 1933. It was later called Navigators in 1934. He was the father of "follow-up," the principle of nurturing the convert and helping him grow. He developed the follow-up program for the Billy Graham crusades, beginning in Shreveport, LA, in 1951. In 1953, the movement moved to a 970-acre estate in Glen Eire, Colorado. His book *Born to Reproduce* is a classic. He drowned, tragically, at Schroon Lake, possibly of a heart attack, in JACK WYRTZEN's presence. He was attempting to rescue a girl who fell while water skiing. His wife, Lila Clayton (married in 1932), and associate, LORNE SANNY (died: 2005), continued the movement.

William H. S. Demarest

May 12, 1863
Hudson, New York

June 23, 1956
New Brunswick, New Jersey

President of Rutgers University and New Brunswick (NJ) Theological Seminary, 1906–22, and of NBTS, 1925–35, the seminary having its own president, 1925 on. Demarest never married. He was ordained in the Reformed Church in America and pastored in Walden, NY (1888–97); Catskill, NY (1897–1901); and was a professor of church history at NBTS (1901–24). He wrote several books ranging from *History of the Reformed Church* (1893) to *On the Constitution of the RCA* (1928).

Edward A. Steiner

Nov. 1, 1866
Czechoslovakia

June 30, 1956
Claremont, California

Congregational minister and sociologist. Steiner was born of Jewish parentage. He married Sara Levy on August 31, 1891 (died: January 7, 1940) and Clara Perry on October 25, 1941. He was ordained Congregational in 1891. Steiner pastored in Minnesota and Ohio, 1891–99. He was also a professor of sociology at Grinnell (IA) College, 1903–41, where he is buried. He wrote many books, from *Tolstoy, the Man* (1903) to *The Eternal Hunger* (1925).

Glenn Clark

March 13, 1882
Des Moines, Iowa

Aug. 16, 1956
Minneapolis, Minnesota

College professor and founder in 1930 of "The Camps Farthest Out" to develop spiritual athletes. He married Louise Miles in 1907. He taught in Des Moines, IA, and Aledo, IL from 1905–12. He taught a Bible class at the local Plymouth Congregational Church. He was a professor of English and athletic coach at Macalester College, St. Paul, MN, from 1912–40. Clark edited *Clear Horizons Magazine* in 1940. He authored over 50 books on prayer and Christian living including, *Sincere Desire, What Would Jesus Do?* and *I Will Lift Up My Eyes*.

John K. Benton

May 24, 1896
Banks, Alabama

Aug. 21, 1956
Nashville, Tennessee

Dean of Vanderbilt Divinity School, Nashville, TN 1939–56, and president of Association of Theological Schools, 1950–52. He served as a pilot in WWI from 1917–19. Benton married Lois Cooper on August 6, 1934. He was a professor at Birmingham-Southern (AL) College (1926–29), Drew University (1931–37), and Duke University (1938–39). Benton was ordained as a Methodist. Benton wrote *Christianity and Mental Hygiene* (1937).

William T. Gaston

Feb. 18, 1886
Denver, Arkansas

Aug. 26, 1956
Santa Cruz, Calfornia

First general superintendent of the Assemblies of God, 1925–29. Gaston married Artie Mattox on July 4, 1906. He was ordained (1910), and one of the 300 who helped bring the Assemblies of God into existence (1914). He pastored the Central Assembly in Springfield, MO from 1920–25; and was active as an evangelist, walking throughout Arkansas preaching. Gaston was the president of Central Bible College, Springfield, MO (1926–29); pastor in San Diego and North Hollywood, CA (1929–35); at Bethel Temple, Sacramento, CA (1935–44); and was the superintendent of the Northern California/Nevada district (1944–56). He died of a heart attack.

Mont E. Hawkins

Jan. 3, 1880
Pearson, Michigan

Sept. 12, 1956
Mishawaka, Indiana

President of Baptist Mid-Missions, Cleveland, OH 1927–43. Hawkins was saved at age 28, leading his father to Christ just before he died that same year. Hawkins married around 1913; his wife's maiden name was Porter. He pastored the FBC of Mishawaka, IN (1920–36); after serving at North Chester, MI (1912–14); Manistee, MI (1914–15); and at FBC, Hastings, MI (1916–20). He was a Bible expositor and missions enthusiast sending at least 50 young people into Christian service from his Mishawaka pastorate.

Walter Grossmann

Aug. 3, 1907
Irving, Alberta, Canada

Sept. 16, 1956
Shafter, California

Bishop of the Reformed Church in the United States, 1935–56. Being influenced by his minister father, Grossmann was ordained in 1933 and married Dorothy Mueller the same year. W. J. Krieger and Grossmann were the two leaders who led people out of the Evangelical and Reformed Church in 1934 when they merged to become the United Church of Christ. Seventeen churches formed the RCUS as conservative Reformed churches. He pastored in Hosmer, SD (1933–52), then in Shafter, CA (1953–56). Grossmann's two sons entered the ministry. His death was due to a heart attack.

Walter L. Lingle

Oct. 3, 1868
Rowan County, North Carolina

Sept. 19, 1956
Mooresville, North Carolina

First president of Presbyterian School of Christian Education (Union Theological Sminary in 1995), **Richmond, VA 1916–22, 1923–29.** Lingle was ordained as a Presbyterian in 1897. He married Alice Dupuy on January 2, 1900, and served pastorates in Dalton, GA (1989–02); Rock Hill, SC (1902–7); and First Church, Atlanta, GA (1907–11). Lingle was a professor of Hebrew and Sunday School work at McCormick Theological Seminary (1911–14). He taught church history and missions at Union Theological Seminary, 1914–24. Lingle was president of Davidson (NC) College, 1929–41. He is buried in Davidson.

Ruth Rouse

Sept. 17, 1872
Clapham Park, London, England

Sept. 29, 1956

Missionary, evangelist, and pioneer, reaching students in countless universities and colleges around the world. Ruth was converted about age 17 through a layman leading seaside services. She was a member of SPURGEON's church, 1879–92, but joined the Church of England upon the pastor's death. She made her first trip abroad in 1897 to all the Scandinavian countries. From 1897–99, she was in North America as a Student Volunteer secretary and visited at least 100 universities and colleges. Ruth was in India, 1899–1901, when bad health forced her home. From 1925–39, she was educational secretary of the Missionary Council of the National Assembly of the Church of England. JOHN MOTT asked her to be the traveling secretary for the World's Student Christian Federation, which she did for 19 years, traveling to 65 countries. In her last years, Ruth worked with the archives of WSCF and JOHN MOTT. She never married.

Charles E. Matthews

March 23, 1887
Gasconade County, Missouri

Oct. 5, 1956
Marshall, Texas

Secretary of evangelism of the Home Mission Board of SBC for nearly ten years. Matthews supervised many evangelism endeavors throughout the denomination. He was converted at age 27 at FBC, Fort Worth, TX and ordained in 1921. He pastored the Travis Avenue Baptist Church, Fort Worth, 1922–46, which grew from 200 to 6,034 members. He wrote many books.

Hattie M. Sexton Barth

July 20, 1876
Indianapolis, Indiana

Oct. 31, 1956
Atlanta, Georgia

President of Beulah Heights Bible College, Atlanta, GA 1942–56. The school was founded by her husband, Paul, who died in 1941. She was a cofounder along with her mother's help, Elizabeth Sexton. Hattie pastored the Barth Memorial Church, Atlanta, GA and died after a heart attack. She was editor of the *Bridegroom's Messenger*, perhaps the oldest Pentecostal publication. She was a woman preacher respected by everyone who heard her.

Green L. Prince

Aug. 15, 1870
Princeville, Texas

Nov. 29, 1956
Galveston, Texas

President of National Baptist Convention of America, 1933–56. Prince entered the Christian ministry after 29 years as a schoolteacher. He married Laura, who died February 20, 1939, and then Gertrude Johnson in June, 1940. In 1944, he became the president of Mary Allen College, Crockett, TX. Prince pastored in San Antonio, TX; Muskogee, OK; St. Joseph, MO (for 10 years); Denver, CO; and in Galveston, TX (for 23 years).

George T. Stephens

Feb. 24, 1884
Waubuno, Lambton, Ontario, Canada

Dec. 4, 1956
Greensboro, North Carolina

Evangelist. Stephens was converted as a 17-year-old, falling on his knees during a walk along Lake Ontario. He had just attended a chapel in Toronto. Mother Stephens, only 42, died soon afterward, having assurance her son was saved. He pastored briefly in Spokane, WA, then married Dessie May Seller (1884–1926) with JAMES GRAY officiating. They went to Spokane for a nine-month crusade in a wooden tabernacle. He preached in it for six weeks, then tore it down, and moved to another section of the city. This was done five times there. A great seven-week crusade was held in High Point, NC, in 1925. During World War II, he ministered in many camps where over 29,000 professed faith in Christ. After 47 years of traveling across the country, they settled in Greensboro in 1953.

Edith M. Brown

March 24, 1864
White Haven, England

Dec. 6, 1956
Srinagar, Vashmir, India

Founder and first director of Christian Medical College, Ludhiana, India, 1895–1951. Edith came to India on November 9, 1891. In October 1894, she opened up this work with four students, a borrowed hospital, some school rooms, and 50 pounds. In her lifetime, she saw to it that both undergraduate and most graduate courses were available in medicine, dentistry, nursing, and other allied paramedical areas. The main hospital had 740 beds. In 1909, non-Christian students were first admitted. In 1915, it was recognized by the government as a medical school. After retiring, she lived on a houseboat in Kashmir. Her final prayer was "Lord, do with me what ye will; only use me in the service of others." She never married.

Jack Coe

1918
Oklahoma City, Oklahoma

Dec. 16, 1956
Dallas, Texas

Pentecostal healing evangelist. While in the army during World War II, Coe was miraculously healed. He was ordained by an Assembly of God church (1944) and began large healing campaigns (1947). In 1950, he started *Herald of Healing* magazine, with an eventual 250,000 circulation. Coe was expelled from the Assembly of God Church for his extreme independence and practices in 1953. He then established his Dallas Revival Center in 1954. In February, 1956, he was arrested for practicing medicine without a license but was released on a $5,000 bond in Miami, FL. The case was dismissed after a two-day trial. He continued his work but shifted his priorities to missions and a children's home. In December, 1956, he came down with bulbar polio and died. He left a widow, Juanita.

Claude A. Roane

July 12, 1877
Goucester County, Virginia

Dec. 19, 1956
Alliance, Ohio

General superintendent of Ohio Yearly Meeting (Evangelical Friends Church—Eastern Region in 1971), **1930–51, and its mission program, 1927–43.** Roane was a pastor, evangelist, and executive. He served on the missionary board, 1912–57. From 1930–51, he led evangelistic and pastoral work, with church extension being one of his main concerns. He was an energetic preacher and diligent administrator. Roane pastored Friends church in Newport News, VA (7 years); Portsmouth, VA (11 years); Alliance, OH (6 years); and Highland Avenue, Columbus, OH (2 years).

Alice E. Walls

June 10, 1887

c 1957
Walwingham, Ontario, Canada

Editor of *The Missionary Tidings*. Walls was the first woman ever ordained by any church in Canada. She was converted at age eleven. She later joined the Free Methodist Church on August 18, 1918, in Ridgeway, ON. She served as a pastor, 1910–21, and then a teacher at Lorne Park College, 1924–42. When she was made editor of *The Missionary Tidings*, she moved to the U.S. and the Winona Lake, IN headquarters of the Free Methodist Publishing House

Lewis J. Sherrill

April 18, 1892
Haskell, Texas

Jan. 29/30, 1957
New York, New York

President of Association of Theological Schools, 1938–40, and the first executive secretary of the same, 1936–38. He and LUTHER WEIGEL were co-leaders in the development of ATS from 1918-36. Sherrill married Helen Hardwicke on May 12, 1921, and was ordained Presbyterian the same year. He pastored the First Presbyterian Church, Covington, TN, from 1921–25. He was a professor of religious education at Louisville Theological Seminary, (1925–1950); dean, (1930–1950); and professor of theology at Union Theological Seminary (1950–57). He wrote many books, from *Presbyterian Parochial Schools, 1846–70* (1932) to *The Gift of Power* (1955).

William A. Knight

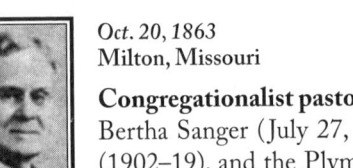

Oct. 20, 1863
Milton, Missouri

Feb. 11, 1957
Framington, Massachusetts

Congregationalist pastor and hymn writer. Knight married Maude Russell (Nov. 30, 1886) and Bertha Sanger (July 27, 1931). . He pastored the Brighton Community Church, Boston, MA (1902–19), and the Plymouth Church, Framington, MA (1919–34). His first book, *The Song of Our Syrian Guest* (1904) was a large seller. His last book was *A Crisis in Morningdale* (1947).

John E. Brown Sr.

April 2, 1879
near Oskaloosa, Iowa

Feb. 12, 1957
Leucadia, California

Evangelist, founder, and first president of John Brown University, Siloam Springs, AR, 1919–48. Brown was converted through the ministry of the Salvation Army at age 17 on May 15, 1896/97. Brown married Juanita Arrington on December 19, 1899. He became president of Scarritt Collegiate Institute, Nashville, TN from 1901–3, and editor of *Worldwide Revival*. He directed summer conferences in Siloam Springs, AR, from 1913–40. He founded his famed school for young men, started several radio stations, authored over 40 volumes, and was a widely used evangelist and speaker. He was interested in the head, heart, and hand of youth. A second JBU was started later in Pacific Beach, CA. His son, John Jr., continued the work. He died as a result of a fall in his home. His school was first known as Southwestern Collegiate Institute changing to John E. Brown College in 1920.

Everett C. Herrick

June 13, 1876
Livermore, Maine

Feb. 13, 1957
Newton Centre, Massachusetts

President of the Newton (MA) Theological Seminary, 1926–31, and first president of the merged Andover-Newton Theological Seminary, Newton Centre, MA 1931–46. Herrick married Sarah Hall on October 19, 1904. He pastored at FBC, Charleston, MA (1901–14); FBC, Fall River, MA (1914–26); and served as president of the Massachusetts Baptist Convention (1923–24).

Clarence E. Macartney

Sept. 18, 1879
Northwood, Ohio

Feb. 19, 1957
Beaver Falls, Pennsylvania

One of the great Presbyterian pastors of all time. Macartney never married. He pastored the First Church, Patterson, NJ (1905–14); the Arch St. Church, Philadelphia, PA (1914–27); and the First Church, Pittsburgh, PA (1927–53). He authored 57 books during the period, 1913–57, and lectured at many colleges, conferences, and seminars. His autobiography, *The Making of a Minister*, is one of his best. He stayed within the denomination to maintain a conservative witness and did not leave his denomination as did J. GRESHAM MACHEN and others.

Helen Thompson Sunday
"Ma Sunday"—Mrs. Billy Sunday

June 25, 1868
Dundee, Illinois

Feb. 20, 1957
Phoenix, Arizona

Wife of the famed evangelist, BILLY SUNDAY. She lived for years at Winona Lake, IN, Bible Conference center. She was the unofficial hostess after her husband's death, always welcomed on the platform of the Billy Sunday tabernacle. Helen married BILLY SUNDAY on September 5, 1888. From 1908 on, she was general manager of her husband's campaigns, including finances, and the hiring and firing of staff. She was active in the work of Youth for Christ and spoke at some of Billy Graham's crusades. She was the mother of four children. She had a heart attack in 1948. Helen died of cancer of the liver and a heart ailment at the home of Paul Hanes, her grandson. She is buried in Chicago.

William F. Arndt

Dec. 1, 1880
Mayville, Wisconsin

Feb. 25, 1957
Cambridge, England

Missouri Lutheran NT scholar and theologian who served as professor of New Testament and classical philology at Concordia Theological Seminary, St. Louis, MO 1921–51. Arndt pastored earlier in Bluff City, TN (1903–5); St. Joseph, MO (1905–10); and Brooklyn, NY (1910–12). He taught Latin, Greek, and Hebrew at St. Paul's College at Concordia, MO, from 1912–21. He married Emma Vetter on July 23, 1907 (died: June 18, 1933). His greatest work was the translation and adaptation of F.W. Gingrich's *Lexicon of the Greek New Testament* (1957). At his death, he was helping the Evangelical Lutheran Church establish a Seminary in conjunction with Cambridge University. His writings ranged from *Does the Bible Contradict Itself?* (1926) to *Greek-English Lexicon of the NT* (with F. W. Gingrich) (1957). He died on a train between Cambridge and London.

Isobel S. Miller Kuhn

Dec. 17, 1901
Toronto, Ontario, Canada

March 20, 1957
Wheaton, Illinois (?)

Outstanding missionary to southwest China with China Inland Mission (Overseas Christian Fellowship), **1928–1957**. Isobel was raised in an earnest Presbyterian home. In college, she came across a statement from DANTE, "In His will is our peace," which prompted her conversion. In 1924, she applied to the CIM. Attending MBI, she finally sailed for China on October 11, 1928. Isobel married John Kuhn on November 4, 1929. They served in Chengchiang (1929–30) and Tali (1930–34), both in Yunnan. In 1942, there were serious disappointments and hardships while the political climate was changing. They wound up supervising churches along the Burma Road. After a furlough to America, she went back to China (1947) until being forced out by the Communists (1950). She worked with the Lisu tribe, (1934–44, 47–50), and in Thailand (1951–54). Her book, *In the Arena*, traces her life and ministry, 1924–57. *Nests Above the Abyss* (1947) recounts incidents in her life especially with certain Chinese people she met from the Lisu tribe, with which they worked. Isobel returned to the U.S. in 1954 where she underwent major surgery for breast cancer. This was a disease she fought for three years, while writing books in her Wheaton, IL home. A few of her eight books sold over 100,000 copies.

Peter W. Philpott

Nov. 25, 1865
Iona, Ontario, Canada

April 2, 1957
Toronto, Ontario, Canada

Pastor of Moody Church, 1922–29. Philpott was converted at a Salvation Army street meeting in 1883. He married Jessie Menzies on July 22, 1887 (died: 1955). He joined the Salvation

Army (1884–94), was an evangelist (1894–96), then pastored an independent church (Philpott Tabernacle) in Hamilton, Ontario (1896–1922), seeing it grow from 35 to 1,700 members. When he pastored at Moody, he erected their present facilities through a mammoth $1 million building program. He pastored at the Church of the Open Door, Los Angeles, CA from 1929–34, then moved back to Canada. Philpott was a noted Bible preacher and teacher, preaching a total of 22,000 times.

Ivan V. Neprash

1883

April 13, 1957
New York, New York

Founder and first director of Russian Missionary Service (Slavic Missionary Service), **1933–57**. Neprash was converted at age 20 while teaching in a German Mennonite settlement in the Ukraine. He came to the U.S. in 1918 and became a pastor, Bible school teacher, and editor of the *Sower of Truth* magazine. Because of his efforts, 15,000 Ukrainian and Russian NT's were printed in Moscow and Kharkov in 1927. His wife was Margaret Isaakov Neprash. During his tenure, more than 5 million tracts in Slavic languages were printed and distributed; several Christian books were written and published. He lived in Philadelphia but, upon completing a preaching assignment in New York City, died while waiting for a train at Penn Station.

Ezra C. Gillentine

Feb. 27, 1886
Dorsey, Mississippi

May 4, 1957
Hattiesburg, Mississippi

Editor-in-chief of American Baptist Association Publications, Texarkana, TX 1941–55, the top post in the movement, which selects their presidents annually. Gillentine married Verda Voyles (June 10, 1913), and was ordained June 10, 1916. He held pastorates in Oklahoma (1920–25 and 1938–41); Alabama (1928–31); and Mississippi (1932–38). Gillentine was the president or moderator of the Yellow Creek Baptist State Association of Alabama, in Mississippi, and Oklahoma. He served for the Baptist General Assembly and the Liberty Baptist Association. Gillentine was an evangelist and president of the ABA from 1938–40.

Louis Berkhof

Oct. 13, 1873
Emmen, Netherlands

May 18, 1957
Grand Rapids, Michigan

First president of Calvin Theological Seminary, Grand Rapids, MI 1931–44. Berkhof came to the U.S. in 1881. In 1893, he made a public profession of faith. Berkhof married Reka Dykhouse on September 16, 1900 (died: 1928), and Dena Heyns on July 11, 1933. He pastored in Allendale, Michigan (1900–2) and in Grand Rapids, MI (1904–6). In 1905, he began writing theological books in Dutch and English. Berkhof became a well-known Christian Reformed theologian. He was called to Calvin in 1906 and spent three decades teaching systematic theology to almost every Christian Reformed pastor of his time. He was professor of Biblical Theology (1906–14), New Testament (1914–20), and Systematic Theology (1926–44). His *Systematic Theology* (1941) sold over 100,000 copies in five languages. His last book was *The Second Coming of Christ* (1953).

Otto E. Kriege

Nov. 20, 1865
Belleville, Illinois

June 11, 1957

President of German Seminary, Central Wesleyan College, Warrenton, MO (Northeast State Teachers College, Kirksville, MO), 1910–25. Kriege married Emma R. Frick on September 16, 1890 (died: 1947), and was ordained a Methodist that same year. He pastored in Arlington, NE from 1890–93 and in Missouri. He taught psychology and ethics (1899–1910), and later became president of New Orleans (LA) University (1915–35). He wrote *History of West German Conference* (1907), *History of Methodism* (1909), and *A Century of Service* (1940).

Martha Snell Nicholson

1886
Fullerton, Nebraska

June 27, 1957
Willmington, California

Great poet of the mid–twentieth century. Martha took the mantle of ANNE J. FLINT, another lifelong invalid. She was converted as a child and became afflicted with tuberculosis, ankylosed (growing together) spine, angina, Parkinson's disease and cancer. Arthritis crippled her first, reducing her to 4' 8" and 80 pounds. Martha's husband died in 1948. They had no children. She suffered immensely, 1928–57, but her wonderful 900 poems have been distributed in over a million leaflets.

William M. Runyan

Jan. 21, 1870
Marion, New York

July 29, 1957
Pittsburg, Kansas

Writer of many wonderful hymns including composing music for "Great Is Thy Faithfulness," (lyrics by THOMAS CHISHOLM). Some of Runyan's lyrics and music include "He Is So Real to Me," "The Savior for Me," and "Sanctuary." He also wrote lyrics for "Jesus, Name I Love," "He Came to Me One Day," "In the Hollow of His Hand," "Oh, What Love!" "Jesus, Oh, What a Name," and "Assurance March," with music from various friends. Runyan was ordained as a Methodist in 1891 and held various pastorates in Kansas for twelve years. He became an evangelist in 1903, associating with John Brown University. From 1925–48, he worked with Moody Bible Institute and Hope Publishing Company. Runyan married Lena Knapp.

Basil Malof

July 28, 1883
Talsen, Latvia

Aug. 15, 1957
Berkeley, California

Born Nicholas Fetler, great Russian pastor and evangelist. Today Global Baptist Mission, Asheville, NC carries on the work that he led, 1944–57. Malof was converted at age 15. A Baptist, he went to SPURGEON's Pastors School in London, returned to Russia in 1901, and started a dozen gospel halls in St. Petersburg (Leningrad). He also built a 2,000-seat Gospel Tabernacle. Malof was arrested during a service in his church and sentenced to Siberian exile. This was changed to banishment abroad. He married Barbara Kovalevsky in 1913. In the spring of 1915, he, his wife, and six-month old son arrived in New York City. They would eventually have twelve children, who formed a family orchestra led by "bandmaster" James (Jackey). Malof went back to Europe and started a Russian Bible Institute in Berlin, 1920–27. In 1927, he dedicated a 2,000-seat Salvation Temple in Riga, Latvia, which became his headquarters until 1939. Malof returned to the States, providentially, two months before the war broke out in Europe. He started a Russian Bible Institute in Philadelphia, which trained some 100 Russian evangelists and missionaries. Malof founded the Russian Bible Society. He returned to Europe with his first party of 23 missionaries, and established ministries in nine countries.

I. G. Martin

April 18, 1862
Kirksville, Missouri

Aug. 23, 1957
Pasadena, California

Wrote the lyrics and music of "The Eastern Gate" and the music for "My Sheep Know My Voice" (lyrics by HERB BUFFUM). The former was written in 1905, prompted by a remark from PHINEAS BRESEE. Martin was in vaudeville working as an actor and singer until he surrendered to preach in Milwaukee at a crusade where PETER BILHORN led the singing. Martin was a singing evangelist who was sponsored by the Epworth League. He was active in Nazarene circles. He traveled for years as a preacher, teacher, and hymn writer.

Frank A. McElwain

Dec. 14, 1875
Warsaw, New York

Sept. 19, 1957
Lexington, North Carolina

President of Seabury Divinity School, Faribault, MN, 1918–32, and Seabury-Western Theological Seminary, Evanston, IL 1938–44 (merged in 1933). McElwain married Helen DeMuth (November 17, 1903) and Mabel Lofstrom (July 28, 1920). He was ordained in an Episcopal church and pastored in Missouri, 1902–05. He began his ministry at Seabury as a teacher in 1905, was a warden (1907–12), and then professor of theology (1933–38). He is buried in Faribault, MN.

Johann J. Sibelius
Jean Sibelius

Dec. 8, 1865
Tavastehus, Finland

Sept. 20, 1957
Traeskaendael, Finland

Composed music for "Be Still My Soul." The lyrics were written by KATHARINA SCHLEGEL 220 years earlier. Sibelius married Aino Jarnef in 1892. Sibelius was a famed composer that had a great love for nature and folklore. In 1893, he was appointed professor of composition at Helsingfors Conservatory. In 1897, he received the state annuity (yearly pension) that allowed him to concentrate on composition. He wrote seven symphonies, 1899–1924. In 1904, he moved to Jarvenpaa. One of his most popular pieces was *Finlandia* (1899).

Carl C. Harwood Sr.

May 27, 1898
Pattonsburg, Missouri

Sept. 22, 1957
Denver, Colorado

Founder and first president of Western Bible Institute (Colorado Christian University in 1985), **Denver, CO 1948–57.** Harwood was converted in his early 20s under RICHARD S. BEAL in Tucson, AZ. He married Mildred Anderson about 1923. They attended Denver Bible Institute and did colportage work while pastoring in Jackson Hole, WY. Other pastorates followed in Springfield, CO; Somerton, AZ; and the FBC in El Centrito, CA, from 1928–34. Harwood went into evangelism and served the staff of the Fuller Evangelistic Association. He did child evangelism work for the Pacific Northwest out of Yakima, WA. Going to Denver, Harwood not only founded and presided, but taught ministerial students many practical subjects. Concurrently during those years, he pastored the Webster Evangelistic Center (Central Bible Church). He was a severe diabetic, which led to heart trouble. His son, Carl Jr., succeeded him.

Harry D. Clarke

Jan. 28, 1888
Cardiff, Wales

Oct. 14, 1957
Lexington, Kentucky

Evangelist who wrote the lyrics and music for popular choruses such as "God Has Blotted Them Out," "Let Go and Let God," "Into My Heart," "Fishers of Men," and "He Careth for You." Clarke came to America to go to Moody Bible Institute, where he was in charge of practical work after 1919. He was BILLY SUNDAY's song leader when RODEHEAVER was absent and led the music for HARRY VOM BRUCH and JOHN R. RICE. As a Baptist minister, he built tabernacles in Watertown and Sioux City, IA. Clarke was married twice. He also wrote "He Touched Me."

Hughell E. W. Fosbroke

April 5, 1875
Netherton, England

Oct. 19, 1957
Winchester Center, Connecticut (?)

President of General Theological Seminary, New York City, 1917–47. Fosbroke came to America in 1890. He taught at Nashotah (WI) House, 1900–2, became a deacon and a priest in the Episcopal Church in 1900, and married Blanche Peter on June 12, 1901. He taught at Episcopal Theological Divinity School, Cambridge, MA, 1901–16. His classes included Hebrew, OT, and history. He lived in Winchester Center, CT.

George W. Sanville

March 21, 1879
Chester, Pennsylvania

Oct. 24, 1957
Philadelphia, Pennsylvania

Dean of hymnbook compilers. Sanville was converted in a Methodist revival. In 1898, he compiled his first songbook. Sanville married Harriet Simkins on June 3, 1904. In 1906, he began managing Praise Publishing Company. He was the manager of the Rodeheaver Hall-Mack Company, 1912 until his death. Sanville was responsible for 35 to 50 million hymnals. He also wrote a hymn history book, *Forty Gospel Hymn Stories*.

Gerald B. Winrod

March 7, 1900
Wichita, Kansas

Nov. 11, 1957
Wichita, Kansas

Editor of *The Defender* (100,000 circulation). Winrod was a controversial religious and political figure. He was converted at a camp meeting and launched a tirade against liberalism, evolution, and communism. Winrod started the Defenders of the Faith, 1925, in Salina (Wichita), KS, a missionary endeavor. In April, 1926, he started his magazine. He was sympathetic with the Nazis because of his extreme racism, which included a theory of a Jewish conspiracy for the evils of the world.

Kirby Page

Aug. 7, 1890
Tyler County, Texas

Dec. 16, 1957
La Habra, California

Social evangelist and author. Page was a Disciple of Christ minister with a passion for pacifism and social reform. Page married Mary Folse on September 2, 1914. Page pastored in Iowa (1912–15); Chicago, IL (1915–16); and New York City (1918–21). He left the pastorate to work for the YMCA in France during WWI. He traveled and lectured for American Friends Service Committees and Fellowship for Reconciliation, because he opposed war and capitalism. He also opposed Marxism and Communism. After 1921, he was a freelance lecturer and political activist. His first book was entitled *Something More* (1920) and his last *The Light Is Still Shining in the Darkness* (1946). He believed that teaching must lead to a nonviolent, cooperative, social order. He is buried in Pasadena, CA.

Dorothy L. Sayers

June 13, 1893
Oxford, England

Dec. 18, 1957
London, England

Scholar and writer whose fame rests mainly on her stories of mystery and detection. Her first major work was *Whose Body* (1923). An Anglican, she turned to theological writing. Dorothy married Athreton Fleming in 1926 (died: 1950). She edited plays for BBC radio, including *The Man Born to Be a King* (1941–1942). She wrote a drama for the Canterbury Cathedral Festival, *The Zeal of Thy House*, in 1937. She wrote from *Cloud of Witnesses* (1927) to *New Sayers Omnibus* (1956). *The Mind of the Maker* (1941) was outstanding.

Edwin W. Smith

Sept. 7, 1876
Aliwal North, South Africa

Dec. 23, 1957

Missionary, anthropologist, and linguist to South Africa. Smith carried on his father's work, for 17 years, from the Primitive Methodist Church. Smith served as a visiting professor to many American schools. In 1898, he returned to Basutoland (Lesotho). In 1902, he began working in Northern Rhodesia (Zambia), until 1915, among the Baila-Batanga people. He worked with the British and Foreign Bible Society, 1916–39. In 1927, he helped found the Industrial African Institute. He then worked with the Phelps-Stokes Foundation in African research.

George A. Chambers

Oct. 8, 1879
near Lindsay, Ontario, Canada

Dec. 17, 1957
Kitchener, Ontario, Canada

First general superintendent of Pentecostal Assemblies of Canada, 1919–34. He was converted in his late teens in Toronto. Chambers married Ide Williamson on September 9, 1902. At the Hebden Mission in Toronto, he came in contact with Pentecostalism. He began his ministry in the New Mennonite Brethren in Christ. In 1906, they were impressed with the Azusa Street Mission in Los Angeles. Chambers served several pastorates in Ontario: Vineland, Ottawa, Arnprior, Peterborough, and Kitchener. He wrote an autobiography at the end of his life. Chambers died of a heart attack.

Perry B. Fitzwater

Sept. 8, 1871
Mathias, West Virginia

Dec. 29, 1957
Evanston, Illinois

One of the grand old men of the Moody Bible Institute. Fitzwater married Addie Kaylor in July, 1898. He was dean of Bible departments in Manchester (IN) and Lavern (CA) colleges, 1905–13. Fitzwater taught homiletics at MBI (1913–54) and was in charge of the pastors' courses (1934–54). Fitzwater was a Presbyterian. He was killed by an automobile, while crossing a street near his home. His books ranged from *The Church and Modern Problems* (1916) to *Preaching and Teaching the New Testament* (1957). He wrote Sunday School lessons published in about 2,600 newspapers in America.

Albert Hughes

June 17, 1888
Bradford, England

1958

Author, Bible teacher, and conference speaker, of Toronto, Ontario. In his early twenties, Hughes was converted in a Baptist Church in England. He pastored the High Park Baptist Church of Toronto in the 1930s. He married Margaret Grove on June 28, 1933. In 1937, he founded the Church of the Crusaders, pastoring until 1949. In 1944, he founded the Muskoka (ON) Bible Conference, heading it until 1963. He edited *The Challenger* for many years and wrote many books. *Saul Becomes Paul* was widely acclaimed by WILBUR SMITH, book authority.

Blanche Kerr Brock

Feb. 3, 1888
Green Forks, Indiana

Jan. 3, 1958
Winona Lake, Indiana

With her husband, VIRGIL, singing team, and gospel hymn composer, known as the "Singing Brocks." They were married on September 24, 1914, after meeting at Earlham College, Richmond, IN. She composed the music for his "If You Could Know," "Beyond the Sunset" (1936), "Resting in His Love," "Sing and Smile and Pray," and "He's a Wonderful Savior to Me." They traveled in evangelism and lived at Winona Lake, IN. Their monument (erected May 30, 1958) has "Beyond the Sunset" lyrics chiseled into it. She died of cancer. Much like the MARTINS and Gaithers, they were a great husband–wife songwriting team.

Erick A. Halleen

Nov. 3, 1874
Angermanland, Sweden

Jan. 12, 1958
Los Angeles, California

President of Free Church of America, 1922–50, and Evangelical Free Church of America (a merger in 1950 with Evangelical Free Church Association created EFCA), **1950–51**. Halleen married Emma Flink on June 4, 1896. He was ordained into the EFCA in 1895 and pastored in Milaca, MN (1896–99); Holcomb, NE (1899–1904); Minneapolis, MN (1904–17); and Rockford, MN (1918–27).

Henry S. Kimura

April 7, 1874
Gosen, Japan

Jan. 14, 1958
Tokyo, Japan

Congregational evangelist considered to be the MOODY or SUNDAY of Japan. Kimura studied at MBI from 1900–1. Kimura married Kamri Sakazaki on September 4, 1902. Upon returning to Japan, he conducted extensive revivals and campaigns in cities throughout the nation, as well as in Manchuria, Korea, Hawaii, and islands in the South Pacific.

John C. O'Hair

Dec. 13, 1876
Little Rock, Arkansas

Jan. 14, 1958
Chicago, Illinois

Founder and first director of Grace Gospel Fellowship, 1939–58, which rejects water baptism for today. O'Hair married on July 11, 1901 while on furlough from Mexico City. He was secretary to the U.S. ambassador. O'Hair began pastoring North Shore Congregational, Chicago, July 17, 1923, and began a radio ministry the next year. This church became the leading church of the new movement. O'Hair wrote many books and booklets. CORNELIUS STAM continued the movement in the next generation.

Frank C. Phillips

Aug. 6, 1911
Estevan, Saskatchewan, Canada

Jan. 17, 1958
Englewood, California

Director of Portland (OR) Youth for Christ, and former executive director of World Vision. Phillips was an oustanding organizer and executive. He married Velma on July 18, 1934. He spent three years in China. Converted under T. T. SHIELDS, he launched Portland YFC on March 24, 1945 and directed it until 1956. The rallies had 2,000 attendees weekly. In 1950, he became BOB PIERCE's associate in World Vision.

William E. Fuller Sr.

Jan. 29, 1875
Mountville, South Carolina

Jan. 20, 1958
Atlanta, Georgia

Founder and first bishop of Colored Fire-Baptized Holiness Church of God, Atlanta, GA, 1908–26, renamed FBHCG of America, 1926–28. He was converted in 1892 and joined New Hope Methodist Church in Mountville, SC. Fuller was raised and ordained in an African Methodist Episcopal Church. He joined the fledgling new movement (Fire-Baptized Holiness Association) in Anderson, SC in 1898. In 1908 he separated from that movement (because of segregation trends) and started CFBHC in Greer, SC. He married his first wife in 1897 (died: 1905), then Emma Wright in 1910.

Soon 50 churches were started, and he became an evangelist, a man of vision, and a leader of a dedicated following. His son, William E. Jr., succeeded him and continued the leadership into the twenty-first century.

Frederick D. Leete

Oct. 1, 1866
Avon, New York

Feb. 16, 1958
St. Petersburg, Florida

Bishop in the Methodist Episcopal Church, 1912–39, and the Methodist Church, 1939–58. Leete was converted at age 13 in a revival conducted by his father. He married Jeanette Fuller on July 28, 1891 and Zoe Morrison in 1953. He pastored in New York (1888–1906) and at Central Church, Detroit, MI (1906–12). Leete served in Atlanta, GA (1912–20); Indianapolis, IN (1920–28); and Omaha, NE (1928–36). He wrote books ranging from *Every Day Evangelism* (1909) to *Adventures of a Traveling Preacher* (1952). He is buried in Syracuse, NY.

Albertus J. Rooks

Jan. 17, 1896
near Zeeland, Michigan

Feb. 24, 1958
Grand Rapids, Michigan

First president of Calvin College, Grand Rapids, MI, 1902–19, 1925–28. After education at Hope College, Holland, MI and the University of Michigan, he was appointed to Calvin's faculty, 1894–1900. He was professor in the literary department as well, 1900–19. Rooks was made dean of the faculty (1919), a position he held until retirement (1942).

Joseph A. Davis

March 4, 1879
Detroit, Michigan

March 4, 1958
Summit, New Jersey

President of IFMA, 1936–37, and first director of South America Indian Mission, 1914–39, renamed South America Mission, 1939–58, Lake Worth, FL. Davis married Mable Kleis on July 24, 1909. With his wife and three children, he went to South America to reach savage Indian tribes and start a mission, serving in Argentina and Paraguay, 1914–19. Upon his return to America, Davis helped in the administration of the mission. It grew to 125 missionaries in five countries. The present name of the mission was adopted in 1939.

William Tapper

Jan. 16, 1905
Evanston, Illinois

March 20, 1958
Chicago, Illinois

Executive secretary (president) of Baptist General Conference, 1953–58. He received his degree from Bethel Seminary in 1931. His title was Executive Secretary of the Board of Trustees bridging the gap from Missions Secretary TURNWALL to General Secretary DAHLQUIST. He married Eva Nelson on June 9, 1931, and pastored from 1928–43 and 1949–53. He was the first director of Bible school and youth work for BGC from 1943–49.

Peter MacFarlane

April 12, 1884
Northcote, Minnesota

April 3, 1958
St. Paul, Minnesota

Presbyterian superintendent of St. Paul's rescue gospel mission. MacFarlane was a well-known leader of rescue mission work. He expanded the missions, beginning in 1909, from no property to being one of the nation's largest missions with a boys' club and camp work. He organized other missions elsewhere. MacFarlane was an evangelist and helped underprivileged children. He married Nelle Nelson on October 24, 1934.

Nyles G. Huffman

Sept. 27, 1918
Colby, Kansas

April 5, 1958
San Felipe de Progreso, Mexico

Founder and first president of Airmail from God Mission (Trans-World Missions in 1979), **1949–58** until his death in a plane crash in Mexico. Huffman was converted at Riverside (CA) Union Church (D.V. Alderman, pastor), while attending junior college. He married his wife, Bernice, on Aug. 23, 1941. He was in the Air Force and stationed in Washington, 1942–45. Huffman began a radio ministry and began dropping gospel tracts in Mexico. He had 2,000 people enrolled in his Bible courses, including six native Mexican evangelists. Nyles Jr. was born one month after his father was killed.

Doris Coffin Aldrich

Dec. 19, 1906
Seattle, Washington

May 9, 1958
Portland, Oregon

Beloved women's writer. Doris had a column named "Out of the Mixing Bowl" in *Moody Monthly* for many years. She was converted at age nine by a friend and neighbor, Mrs. Otis Whipple. She married Will Aldrich, who was the president of Multnomah Bible College in Portland, on June 24, 1937. While Doris was mothering nine young children (ages 8–19), she was killed in an automobile accident.

Robert G. McCutchan

Sept. 13, 1877
Mount Ayr, Iowa

May 15, 1958
Claremont, California

Outstanding Methodist educator, church musician, and hymnologist who wrote the music for "Let All the World in Every Corner Sing" (lyrics by GEORGE HERBERT). McCutchan married Carrie Sharp on November 23, 1904 (died: July 20, 1941) and Helen Cowles, December 11, 1944. He was the dean of the School of Music at DePaul University, Greencastle, IN, from 1911–37, and was a guest lecturer and music editor of hymnals. He retired to Claremont in 1937. He wrote several books from *Better Music in Our Churches* (1925) to *Hymn Tune Names* (1957). His 1937 work, *Our Hymnody*, was the first important hymnal handbook in America. He is buried in Greencastle, IN.

Leonard A. Stidley

Dec. 14, 1898
Fort Madison, Iowa

May 29, 1958
Oberlin, Ohio

President of Oberlin (OH) Theological Seminary, 1948–56, and of American Association of Schools of Religious Education, 1955–57. Stidley married Constance Hill on August 29, 1923. He was ordained Methodist in 1929. He pastored the Church of All Nations and Neighborhood House, New York City from 1931–37. He began teaching theology at Oberlin in 1937. One of his books is *Religious Education* (1946).

Samuel Higginbottom

Oct. 27, 1874
Manchester, England

June 11, 1958
Port Washington, New York

Agricultural missionary. Higginbottom came to America in 1894 and married Jane Cody on October 28, 1904. He went as a Presbyterian missionary to India, 1903–45. Higginbottom was active on behalf of lepers and the blind and received many awards. He organized an Agricultural Institute at Allahabad in 1919 to improve crop production in India. He retired to Babson Park, FL in 1945. Upon his retirement, Higginbottom founded and directed the Christian service Training Center, Inc., at Babson

Park, FL. His books range from *The Gospel and the Plow* (1921) to *Sam Higginbottom, Farmer* (1949), his autobiography. Higginbottom was not interested in evangelism, believing good works would spread Christianity.

Edward S. Ames

April 21, 1870   *June 29, 1958*
Eau Clair, Wisconsin   Chicago, Illinois

Dean of Disciples Divinity House, Chicago, IL 1927–45. Ames married Mabel Van Meter on July 6, 1893. He was a professor in the field of philosophy at DDH from 1895–1927. Ames pastored the University Church of the Disciples of Christ, Chicago 1900–40. His books were from *Psychology of Religious Experience* (1910) to *American Philosophies of Religion* (1936). He was a licensed theologian who also taught at Butler University, Indianapolis, and Chicago University.

William O. Mendenhall

May 10, 1879   *July 5, 1958*
Ridge Farm, Illinois   Westfield, New Jersey

Presiding clerk of Friends United Meetings, 1927–35; president of Friends University, Wichita, KS 1918–34; and of Whittier (CA) College, 1934–43. Mendenhall married Lucy Osgood on June 22, 1907. He was a professor of mathematics at Earlham College, Richmond, VA from 1907–13. After 1943, he began ministering with the Society of Friends with special assignments to American Friends Service Committee.

Arthur R. Clippinger

Sept. 3, 1878   *July 18, 1958*
Lurgan, Pennsylvania   Dayton, Ohio

Bishop of Church of United Brethren in Christ, 1921–46; Evangelical United Brethren in Christ (United Methodist Church in 1968), **1946–58; and senior bishop, 1946–51**. Clippinger married Ellen Mills on October 16, 1907. He pastored Congregational Churches in New Cumberland, PA (1905–07); in Connecticut (1907–10); at Euclid Avenue United Brethren Church, Dayton, OH (1910–18); and served as conference superintendent (1918–21).

Paul H. Buehring

July 5, 1880   *Aug. 16, 1958*
Elkhorn, Wisconsin   Columbus, Ohio

Dean of Evangelical Lutheran Theological (Trinity Lutheran in 1978) **Seminary, Columbus, OH 1936–46**. Buehring remained unmarried and pastored Zion Lutheran Church, St. Mary's, OH (1905–11), then was principal of Hebron (NE) Academy (1911–19). Buehring was professor of theology at ELTS from 1919–36. In addition, he edited *Mission Studies*, beginning in 1931, and wrote *The Spirit of the American Lutheran Church* (1940).

James McGinley

July 15, 1901   *Aug. 22, 1958*
Baller, Scotland   Portland, Oregon

Beloved Bible conference speaker at such places as MBI Founder's Week and other leading conferences. McGinley first went to Canada, then he pastored the Baptist Temple in Brooklyn in the 1950's. He later became an evangelist and conference speaker. His anecdotes and good humor were well known. McGinley died, of a cerebral hemorrhage, in a hotel room.

Ralph Vaughan-Williams

Oct. 12, 1872
Down Ampney, England

Aug. 26, 1958
Down Ampney, England

One of the best known English composers of the twentieth century. From 1904, he displayed a keen interest in English folk songs. He collected them and used them in orchestral rhapsodies. Vaughan-Williams served as the musical editor for *The English Hymnal* in 1906. After army service in WWI, he became professor of composition at the Royal College of Music, London, and conductor of the London Bach Choir, 1920–28. His numerous compositions include nine symphonies, several operas, incidental music for plays, along with hymns and other religious music.

Harry T. Stock

Nov. 10, 1891
Springfield, Illinois

Aug. 30, 1958
West Medford, Massachusetts

Congregational educator and hymn writer. Stock married Grace Frame on July 24, 1917. He started as an instructor at Chicago Theological Seminary (1917–22); worked with the denomination's Education Society (1922–38); and was general secretary of Christian Education for Congregational and Christian Churches. Stock wrote many books from *Christian Life Problems* (1927) to *Christian Education in Our Church* (1944).

Bentley D. Ackley

Sept. 27, 1872
Spring Hill, Pennsylvania

Sept. 3, 1958
Winona Lake, Indiana

Composer of the famed ACKLEY brothers. As a boy, he learned to play the melodeon piano, coronet, clarinet, and piccolo; playing in his father's 14-piece band. He served as an organist in churches in New York City and Brooklyn 1888–1907. Ackley was the pianist and secretary for the BILLY SUNDAY–HOMER RODEHEAVER evangelistic team, 1907–15. He composed music for some 3,500 hymns with many providing lyrics including: "In the Service of the King," "Till the Whole World Knows," "Amazed," "You Cannot Hide from God" (A. H. ACKLEY), "Sunrise," "In the Garden with Jesus," "I Shall See the King" (POOLE), "I Would Be Like Jesus," "I Walk with the King" (ROWE), "God Understands," "Joy in Serving Jesus," "The Glory of His Presence," "Have I Grieved Thy Holy Spirit?" "He Rose Triumphantly," "He Loved Me in Spite of My Sin" (O. J. SMITH), "If Your Heart Keeps Right" (DEARMAND), "Since the Fullness of His Love Came In," "Drifting" (HEWITT), "Transformed" (Burroughs), "Jesus," "Jesus Will" (OGDEN), "It is Different Now" (CHISHOLM) and "Because of Him" (BENNER). He worked for the RODEHEAVER Company in Winona Lake, IN, in later years. Meeting O. J. SMITH in 1930 was a great occasion for both brothers, resulting in the production of many great songs.

Jennie E. Hussey

Feb. 8, 1874
Henniker, New Hampshire

Sept. 5, 1958
Concord, New Hampshire

Wrote the hymn "Lead Me to Calvary," 1921 (music by WILLIAM KIRKPATRICK). Jennie was seriously afflicted with hardship and suffering. She first published a verse when she was 13 years old. She cared for her invalid sister most of her adult life. This sister prompted many of her hymns. Jennie was a lifelong Quaker and lived out her days at the Home for the Aged in Concord.

Louis Entizminger

June 28, 1878
Blythewood, South Carolina

Sept. 24, 1958
Nederland, Texas

First president of Arlington (TX) Baptist College, 1939–47. Entizminger married Ada Frier on December 28, 1903. Entizminger was an associate of J. FRANK NORRIS at FBC, Fort Worth, TX, from 1913–18. He helped build their Sunday school from 249 to 5,000, through visitation and building large classes. From 1918–22, he pastored in Lakeland, FL, and at FBC, New Orleans, LA. Entizminger was involved in Sunday school work and evangelism, 1922–31. He then pastored in San Antonio and in Norris, TX. He authored a few books and a Sunday School record system.

George K. A. Bell

Feb. 4, 1883
Norwich, Hayling Island, England

Oct. 3, 1958
Canterbury, England

Anglican bishop and ecumenist. Bell was ordained in the Church of England in 1907. From 1914–24, he was chaplain to the Archbishop of Canterbury, RANDALL DAVIDSON. During that time, he married Henrietta Livingstone on January 8, 1918. Bell was the dean of Canterbury (1924–29), and served as the bishop of Chichester (1929–58). He was greatly interested in the ecumenical movement. Bell presided as the first chairman of the WCC Central Committee, 1948–54. He was moderator of WCC in Amsterdam (1948), and became honorary president in Evanston (1954). Bell supported the Confessing Church of Germany during its struggles with Hitler. His writings range from *The Life of Randall Davidson* (1955) to *The Kingship of Christ* (1954). He wrote four series of *Documents on Christian Unity* (1924, 1930, 1948, 1958). His last sermon was on Luke 17:10 in a Lutheran church in Odense, Denmark.

George Bennard

Feb. 4, 1873
Youngstown, Ohio

Oct. 10, 1958
Reed City, Michigan

Writer and composer of the great hymn, "The Old Rugged Cross." Bennard was converted at a Salvation Army meeting in Lucas, IA, at age 16. He felt called to be a gospel minister, but the untimely death of his father left George responsible for supporting his mother and four sisters. With educational funds lacking, he gained his theological knowledge through association with other ministers and his own personal reading and study. The family moved to Illinois where he met his first wife, Armainta Behler, whom he married on February 25, 1895. Believing deeply in the outreach of the Salvation Army, both he and his wife were involved in this ministry. In 1910, he joined the Methodist Episcopal Church and spent many years traveling as an evangelist throughout the United States and Canada. After the death of his first wife, he married Hannah Dahlstrom. In 1913, during a revival in Albion, MI, Bennard wrote the famous hymn, "The Old Rugged Cross," to which he gained the copyright that same year. He wrote many other hymns including: "Speak, My Lord," "Tell Me His Name Again," "Have Thy Way, Lord," and "A Mighty Revival." He died in a local hospital in Reed City, six miles from his farm. For many years before his death, there was a twelve-foot-high wooden cross in the center of town bearing the words, "The Old Rugged Cross—Home of Living Author, Rev. Geo. Bennard."

Jacob Heemstra

Jan. 2, 1888
Orange City, Iowa

Oct. 23, 1958
Orange City, Iowa

First president of Northwestern College, Orange City, IA 1928–51. Heemstra received his education at Hope College (1910) and Western Theological Seminary, Holland, MI (in 1914). He was licensed by the Reformed Church in 1914, and pastored the Trinity Reformed Church,

Chicago, 1914–18. Heemstra served as a professor at Central College, Pella, IA from 1918–28. His wife's name was Hannah, and they had four sons.

George L. Robinson

Aug. 19, 1864
West Hebron, New York

Dec. 17, 1958
Chicago, Illinois

Presbyterian educator, theologian, and archaeologist. Robinson married Jessie Harvey (March 27, 1894) and Lilian Mueller (January 1, 1920). He pastored in Boston, taught at Knox College, Toronto and Protestant College of Beirut, Syria, prior to 1898. He was professor of Old Testament Literature and exegesis at McCormick Theological Seminary, Chicago, 1899–1939. He wrote *Leaders of Israel* (1906) to *The Short Story of a Long Life* (1957).

Robert S. Swanson

Dec. 25, 1890
New York, New York

Dec. 25, 1958
Glen Head Island, New York

President of Christian Businessmen's Committee, 1949. Swanson was born and died on Christmas day. He was the general manager and treasurer of S. B. Thomas, Inc., Wholesale Bakers of New York City, and a member of First Presbyterian Church of Flushing, NY. He was active in Pocket Testament League, CBMC, Gideons, Word of Life Fellowship, etc. Swanson died while playing with his grandchild.

William G. Scroggie

March 3, 1877
Malvern, England

Dec. 28, 1958

Bible teacher, pastor and author. Scroggie married Florence Hudson (1900) and Joan Hooker (1941). Scroggie pastored at Sunderband (1903–10), Charlotte Chapel in Edinburgh (1913–33), and Metropolitan Tabernacle in London (1938–44). Scroggie's home and church were destroyed by the bombing of World War II. Though one of nine children, he went to college to prepare for the ministry. He also traveled extensively abroad, 1933–37. Scroggie wrote many expository studies and books on Christian living, such as *The Land and Life of Rest* (1950) and *The Unfolding Drama of Redemption* (2 vols., 1957).

William W. Sweet

Feb. 15, 1881
Baldwin, Kansas

Jan. 3, 1959
Dallas, Texas

Methodist minister, educator and historian. Sweet married Louise Neill on May 18, 1906. He was professor of history at Ohio Wesleyan University, Delaware, OH (1911–13) and DePauw University, Greencastle, IN (1913–27); professor of American church history at the University of Chicago (1927–46); Garrett Biblical Institute (1946–48); the Perkins School of Theology, and Southern Methodist University (1948–58). He wrote 27 books, from *The Methodist Episcopal Church and the Civil War* (1912) to *Religion in American Culture, 1740–1865* (1952). His most notable work was his book, *The Story of Religion in America* (1930).

Richard A. Forrest

July 14, 1881
Wilmington, Delaware

Jan. 13, 1959
Toccoa Falls, Georgia

Founder and first president of Toccoa Falls Institute (College), **1911–57, and president of Evangelical Teacher Training Association, 1943–50**. Forrest was converted at age 17 and joined the Presbyterian church. Forrest married Evelyn Drennen on December 24, 1901. He pastored a mission church in Orlando, FL, and a CMA church in Atlanta, GA. The school was born when Forrest was able to buy a 58-room, 100-acre hotel complex, which was listed at $25,000, for a mere $10 down in 1911.

Eivind Berggrav

Oct. 25, 1884
Stavanger, Norway

Jan. 14, 1959
Oslo, Norway

President of World Council of Churches, 1950–59, and first president of United Bible Societies, 1949–57. Berggrav was a bishop, author, and resistance leader during WWII. He was headmaster of a folk school (1909–19), minister at Hurdal (1919–25), and chaplain at Oslo Prison (1925–28). He also served as bishop of Tromso (1929–37) and bishop of Oslo (1937–50). From 1909–59, Berggrav edited a theological review. He helped to unite Norway in 1940, then was imprisoned by the Germans from 1942–45. During his lifetime, Berggrav wrote around 30 books, from *The Prisoner's Soul and Our Own* (1932) to *Man and State* (1951).

Andrew H. Argue

1868
Ottawa Valley, Ontario, Canada

Jan. 24, 1959
Toronto, Ontario, Canada

Pioneer Pentecostal evangelist and key figure in the Pentecostal Assemblies of Canada in the 1910s. Converted as a young man, Argue was a successful and prosperous realtor in Winnipeg. After he came under the influence of a number of Holiness preachers, he went to Chicago in 1907 to investigate revival reports. At a service conducted by WILLIAM DURHAM, he had the "tongues" experience. He soon became a lay preacher with the Holiness Movement Church and had a part in the founding of Calvary Temple, Winnipeg. It soon became one of Canada's largest Pentecostal churches. Argue published the *Apostolic Messenger*, conducted *Clater Revival Broadcast*, held revivals, established churches, and evangelized Indians. His children continue his legacy and outreach.

John W. Hatch

March 2, 1864
Presque Island, Maine

Jan. 26, 1959
St. Petersburg, Florida

President of Montpelier (VT) Seminary (Vermont College), **1913–34.** Hatch pastored in Maine at the following: Kingman (1894–97), Easton (1898–99), Winterport (1900–3), and Belfast (1904–6). He married Isabelle Flye on October 26, 1896 (died: October 10, 1915), then married Nellie Worth on October 5, 1919. He was district superintendent, 1907–12, in East Maine Methodist Conference. After his presidency, he remained in the Vermont Conference until 1941, then was with the Maine Conference, 1941–44. He is buried in Orono, Maine.

William E. Pietsch

Aug. 8, 1886
Brooklyn, New York

Feb. 2, 1959
Long Beach, California

President of Independent Fundamental Churches of America, 1935–37, and executive secretary of the same, 1933–35. Pietsch pastored the Calvary Gospel Center, Grand Rapids, MI. He founded and directed the Alaska Evangelization Society in 1935. Pietsch had a broadcast that went throughout the Midwest. He began this radio ministry in 1942 in Kalamazoo, MI, then moved it to Waterloo, IA, from 1945–61. His wife, Mildred, was a singer, and his son, Timothy, was a famed missionary to Japan. CHARLES FULLER, who was ordained alongside Pietsch, performed his funeral.

Orman L. Shelton

March 1, 1895
Kingman City, Kansas

March 3, 1959
Indianapolis, Indiana

President of School of Religion (Christian Theological Seminary, the name change came at the end of his leadership), **Indianapolis, IN, 1944–58**. Shelton married Ruby Stratten on August 13, 1913. He pastored First Christian, Denison, TX (1928–32); Ponca City, OK (1932–38); Wichita Falls, TX (1938–41); and Independence Blvd. Christian Church, Kansas City, MO (1941–44). Shelton was involved in many denominational (Disciples of Christ) activities.

Lester (Les) Barnett

Nov. 12, 1909
Eldorado, Illinois

March 6, 1959
Hollywood, California

Organist and converted Hollywood personality. In 1936, Barnett moved to Hollywood to work with David Rose, Walter O'Keefe, and Martha Raye among others. In April 1947, he was converted at a revival in Springfield, MO. Barnett traveled with Evangelist JACK SHULER. In 1950, he married his wife, Kathryn. For the rest of his life, he worked with PHIL KERR and other evangelists. Barnett participated in the Manila, Philippine, crusade with BOB PIERCE in 1957.

Henry Schultze

July 18, 1893
Prarie City, Iowa

March 6, 1959
Grand Rapids, Michigan

President of Calvin College, Grand Rapids, MI 1940–51. Schultze was highly educated, attending school at: Calvin, Princeton, Yale, and the University of Chicago. He was professor at Grundy College, Grundy Center, IA from 1920–24. He pastored the Sherman St. Christian Reformed Church in Grand Rapids, 1924–26. He became a professor at Calvin Theological Seminary before and after his leadership at the college, serving 1926–40 and 1951–56.

Gustaf F. Johnson

Dec. 27, 1873
Nassjo, Sweden

March 11, 1959
Minneapolis, Minnesota

Great pastor-evangelist of the Evangelical Covenant Church. At the age of nine, the family moved to America settling in Texas. At about age twelve, Johnson received salvation at an evangelistic meeting. At age 16, he delivered his first sermon on Psalm 84. At age 18, he went to Japan under TEAM until ill health brought him home in 1894. Refused at a Bible school because he had no money and was sick, the Holy Spirit became his teacher. Johnson pastored in East Chain, MN, for a year. He married Huldah Nyquist in 1896 (died: July 21, 1956). He pastored in Holdrege, NE from 1898–1900. From 1901–14, he pastored the Rockford (IL) Free Church, which grew from 147 to 720 and a Sunday school of over 1,200. From 1914–39, he pastored the Swedish Tabernacle (First Covenant Church) of Minneapolis. Johnson pastored the Park Avenue Covenant Church in Minneapolis, 1939–52.

Theodore L. Lewis

Feb. 15, 1903
Springfield, Missouri

March 12, 1959
Hamilton, Massachusetts

President of Gordon College and Divinity School, Wenham, MA 1944–59. He married Mattie Barclay on December 5, 1925. Lewis pastored Harrison Street Church, Oak Park, IL (1929–41), and FBC, Hammond, IN (1942–44). He taught theology at Northern Baptist Theological Seminary, Chicago, 1941–44. Lewis was a member of NAE, Evangelical Society, and Phi Alpha Chi. He retired to Hamilton, MA.

The Saints Go Marching In

Harold L. Lundquist

Nov. 1, 1894
Minneapolis, Minnesota

March 17, 1959
Chicago, Illinois

Executive director of Evangelical Child and Family Agency, Chicago, 1952–56. He was also active in the Chicago area as an educator and Presbyterian pastor. Lundquist married Beatrice Anderson on September 12, 1922. He served at Moody Bible Institute in various capacities (1924–47), including being a professor of Bible (1941–47). Lundquist pastored the First Evangelical Free Church, Chicago, 1947–52. He wrote from *Can America Be Saved?* (1939) to *Out of the Question Box* (1958).

Aaron Matthews Sr.

1879
Santos, Florida

April, 1959
Yahala Lake, Florida

Founder and first bishop of Church of God by Faith, Gainesville, FL, 1914–59. Growing up around Ocala, FL, Matthews came to Bostic, FL, at age 19. He started railroading on the Atlantic Coast Line as section hand, then became a cook and started firing engines. In 1904, he married Nancy Scippio and moved to Jacksonville. Matthews was converted in an AME church. He heard a man preaching holiness in the street in 1913 and knew it was right for him. Matthews and his brother-in-law would team up and go about preaching and healing the sick. Soon, a movement was started.

Ralph W. Riley

Jan. 12, 1900
Valdosta, Georgia

April 5, 1959
Newark, New Jersey

President of American Baptist College and Theological Seminary, Nashville, TN, 1944–56. Riley pastored in Live Oak, FL (1924–25); Atlanta, GA (1928–32); Rome, GA (1933–37); Montgomery, AL (1939–44); and Hopewell Baptist, Newark, NJ (1956–59). During his tenure as college president, the school saw its greatest growth with several buildings added.

Ernest I. Reveal
"Pappy" Reveal

April 15, 1880
Charleston, West Virginia

April 8, 1959
Evansville, Indiana

Famed Presbyterian rescue mission worker in Evansville, IN. Reveal said he wasted many years in wayward living. He was the oldest of twelve children and was converted on January 24, 1904. He married Edna Wiltrout on August 17, 1910 (died: January 14, 1977, at age 92), and they had two children. He went to Evansville, and in 1917 established a rescue mission. MEL TROTTER recommended him there. He would serve there until his death. Reveal's annual Bible conference was a big event to the community. In 1929, Camp Reveal began. His Evansville mission became one of the nation's largest and most effective missions in the country.

Reverdy C. Ransom

Jan. 4, 1861
Flushing, Ohio

April 22, 1959
Wilberforce, Ohio

One of the African Methodist Episcopal Church's greatest personalities. Ransom was converted in 1881, and held pastorates in Allegheny, PA; Springfield and Cleveland, OH; Illinois; Charles St. AME Church, Boston, MA, 1905–12, and New York. He was editor of *The AME Review* (1912–24) in New York City. He was a bishop, 1924–52, and a key proponent of the Social gospel. Ransom delivered the invocation at the 1940 Democratic National Convention. He founded the

"Niagara Movement" (forerunner of the NAACP). He married Emma Conner in 1887 (died: 1943), and then married to Myrtle Reaf 1944–59.

Frank W. Boreham

March 3, 1871
Tunbridge Wells, England

May 18, 1959
Melbourne, Australia

Known more by his sermonic writings than for his pulpit preaching. Boreham averaged one book a year, from his first book, *The Whisper of God* (1891) to *The Last Milestone* (pub., 1971). A teen injury at work left him lame for the rest of his life. He moved to London as a clerk and preached his first sermon in 1891. Although born an Anglican, he was baptized in London Baptist Church in 1892. In 1896, he married, and they had five children. After two years at Spurgeon's College, he went to Mosgiel, New Zealand, where he pastored a Baptist church till 1906. He pastored the Baptist Tabernacle of Hobart, Tasmania (1906–16) and then the Armadale Baptist Church (1916–28), close to Melbourne. He left the pastorate to spend full-time in travel, lecturing, and preaching. In 1937, he began noonday services in Scots Church, Melbourne. He delivered his final sermon in 1956. Boreham wrote 80 books. He was the last student to be personally approved by SPURGEON for his college. He wrote a five-volume series *Life Verses* depicting biographical data on Christian leaders.

John F. Dulles

Feb. 25, 1888
Washington, D.C.

May 24, 1959
Washington, D.C.

Famed secretary of state, 1953–59, and an active liberal Presbyterian layman. Dulles married Janet Avery on June 26, 1912. He practiced law with Sullivan and Cromwell in New York, 1911–49. Acceptance of an assignment in 1917, by President WOODROW WILSON to Central America, began his public service career. In 1921, he became closely associated with the FCC. Dulles was the negotiator of the Japanese Treaty of 1951, and was involved in many international political activities throughout the EISENHOWER years. Previously, Dulles had served in diplomatic posts under Presidents WILSON, Roosevelt, and TRUMAN. As Secretary of State, he traveled 550,000 miles to all parts of the world. Dulles resigned from his career on April 15, 1959, with incurable cancer.

Druie A. (Scotchie) McCall

Aug. 8, 1895
Star, Mississippi

June 16, 1959
Chicago, Illinois

Executive secretary and director of evangelism for some 1,500 Southern Baptist churches in Mississippi, 1939–50. McCall married Margie Parks on February 12, 1917. He pastored the Lynn (MS) Baptist Church and then the Griffin Memorial Church, Jackson, MS, from 1925–34. This was followed by the First Baptist Church, Philadelphia, MS from 1934–39. Under his main ministry in the SBC, the Brotherhood, music, and BSU departments were added, all state denominational indebtedness was paid off, and a building in front of the State Capitol was purchased, both in 1945. He pastored the Tabernacle Baptist Church, Chicago, IL, from 1950–52 and became the revival promotion director for the *Sword of the Lord*.

Edward D. Dimnent

Aug. 14, 1876
Chicago, Illinois

July 4, 1959
Holland, Michigan

President of Hope College, Holland, MI 1918–31. Dimnent never married. He graduated from Hope in 1896. He began as a professor of Greek in 1898 and was the professor of economics and business administration after 1930. Hope Memorial Chapel was later named Dimnent Memorial Chapel by the Board of Trustees on August 14, 1969.

Charles T. Leber

Nov. 11, 1898
Baltimore, Maryland

July 30, 1959
São Paulo, Brazil

Director of Presbyterian Church USA Missions, 1936–59. Leber married Elizabeth Heath on May 12, 1923. He pastored Forest Park Church, Baltimore, MD (1924–28); and Green Ridge Church, Scranton, PA (1928–36). From 1936–55, he made several missionary trips to most major nations in the world. Leber was a vice president of NCC and authored three books. More than any other single American, he moved missions into the ecumenical age. In 1958, he got the name of the Presbyterian board changed to Commission on Ecumenical Mission and Relations.

Henry S. G. Tucker

July 16, 1874
Warsaw, Virginia

Aug. 8, 1959
Richmond, Virginia

Presiding bishop of Protestant Episcopal Church (Episcopal Church in 1967), **1938–46, and of Federal Council of Churches** (NCC in 1950), **1942–44**. He married Mary Warnock on April 18, 1911. He went to Japan as a missionary in 1889; served as president of St. Paul's College, Tokyo (1903–12); and bishop of Kyoto (1912–23). He was professor of theology at The Union Theological Seminary, Richmond, VA, from 1923–27. Tucker became Bishop of Virginia, 1927–44. His books range from *Reconciliation through Christ* (1910) to *Explaining the Silent Shore of Memory* (1951).

John L. Stauffer

Nov. 13, 1888
Spring City, Pennsylvania

Aug. 15, 1959
Harrisonburg, Virginia

President of Eastern Mennonite College and Seminary, Harrisonburg, VA 1935–48. Stauffer married Lydia Kolb on August 3, 1910. He was ordained in 1911 and pastored in Altoona, PA until 1918, when he joined the faculty of Eastern in the Bible department. He was a bishop in 1934 and a strong leader among Virginia Mennonites. After 1948, he was active in Bible conference work.

Haldor Lillenas

Nov. 19, 1885
Stord Island, Norway

Aug. 18, 1959
Aspen, Colorado

Wrote the lyrics and music for more than 4,000 hymns. They include "Wonderful Grace of Jesus" (1918) "Wonderful Peace," "My Wonderful Lord," "The Theme of My Song," "The Peace That Jesus Gives," "It Fills and It Thrills," "The Calvary Road," "Jesus Will Walk with Me," "How Can I Be Lonely," "Don't Turn Him Away," "I Know a Name," "The Bible Stands," the music for "Jesus Has Lifted Me," "Count Me" (W. C. POOLE), "It Is Glory Just to Walk with Him" (CHRISTIANSEN), "My Ivory Palace Home," and "Lord, Send Me There" (lyrics of both by Herrell). Early on, Lillenas was a chemist. He was converted in Astoria, OR at age 20, at a street corner meeting, conducted by the Peniel Mission of Portland, OR. He married Bertha Mae in 1910 (March 3, 1889 – April 13, 1945), and Lola Kellogg. Lillenas traveled as an evangelist, 1914–16. He pastored in Pomona, CA; Auburn, IL; Peniel, TX; Redlands, CA; and Indianapolis, IN. Lillenas organized his Lillenas Publishing Company in Indianapolis (1924), which was later purchased by the Nazarene Publishing Company in Kansas City, MO (1930). His wife, Bertha Mae, wrote the lyrics and music for "Jesus Is Always There," "Victory Is Nigh," and the music for "Jesus Took My Burden" (lyrics by OATMAN).

Noel Lyons

June 12, 1901
Blue Knob, Arizona

Oct. 21, 1959
Los Angeles, California

President of Greater Europe Missions, 1950–59. On February 2, 1930, Lyons was converted in the First Presbyterian Church, Hollywood, CA. He managed the Forest Home Conference Grounds in California. He sold his mansion to movie star, Jackie Cooper, and went to work for the Putnam Dye Company, Quincy, IL. He then headed up MBI's Extension Department, 1942–47. Working with YFC opened his eyes to Europe's need, and he helped Bob Evans start Greater Europe Mission. Lyons directed the home office while Evans directed the field activities. Surgery on December 5, 1958, detected advanced cancer, which eventually took his life.

William (Billy) P. Nicholson

April 3, 1876
near Bangor, Northern Ireland

Oct. 29, 1959
Southern Ireland

Evangelist reared by a sea captain. Nicholson was almost destroyed in a storm around Cape Horn, an experience that instilled a spiritual interest in him. He was saved upon his return home, May 22, 1899. Nicholson attended school in Glasgow, Scotland, and began to hold services in small villages. He became an evangelist of the Landarkshire Christian Union in 1903. He assisted J. WILBUR CHAPMAN in Australia in 1909, and then held great crusades in Northern Ireland (Ulster), 1910–26, in which thousands were converted. He was ordained a Presbyterian in 1914. Nicholson journeyed around the world ten times. PERCY CRAWFORD was converted during his meeting in Los Angeles. Nicholson wanted to return to Ireland for his final years, but unfortunately, on his way there in 1959, he had a heart attack during the voyage. Nicholson was put ashore in the south of Ireland and died in a hospital there. He once said in a sermon, "John did no miracle: but all things that John spake of this Man were true. And many believed on Him there. … I would covet no greater eulogy in this life or over my corpse when dead." That passage (John 10:41–42) was engraved on his tombstone.

Frank C. Huston

Sept. 12, 1871
Orange, Indiana

Nov. 11, 1959
Jacksonville, Florida

Wrote lyrics and music to "It Pays to Serve Jesus." Huston spent time briefly as a public schoolteacher. He became a singing evangelist who enjoyed a long and successful ministry with the Disciples of Christ. For 17 years, he served as national officer of various patriotic organizations, including commander-in-chief of Sons of Union Veterans. Beginning in 1898, he composed over 400 poems with several of these transitioning to hymns.

Titus Lowe

Dec. 17, 1877
Bilston, England

Nov. 27, 1959
Indianapolis, Indiana

Bishop in the Methodist Episcopal Church, 1924–39, and in the Methodist Church, 1939–59. Lowe married Anna Creed on October 18, 1901 (died: April 4, 1911), Edith Egloff on January 6, 1913, and Ellen Stoy in 1957. After immigrating to the United States at age 14, he pastored in Braddock, PA (1900–3); Calcutta, India (1903–8); South Fork, PA (1908–9); Cedar Falls, IA (1909–13); and Omaha, NE (1913–21). Lowe also served as bishop of Singapore (1924–28); Portland, OR (1928–39) and Indianapolis, IN (1939–48). He directed the "Crusade for Christ" campaign that collected $25,000,000 for the reconstruction of Methodist churches, schools, and hospitals, which were damaged or destroyed during WWII.

Clarence A. Mummart

July 14, 1874
Welsh Run, Pennsylvania

Dec. 2, 1959
Hagerstown, Maryland

President of Huntington (IN) College, 1912–15, 1925–32. Mummart married Lillie Zimmerman on March 10, 1896. After making a confession of faith at age 15 in temporary Lutheran settings, he was ordained by the United Brethren in 1901. He pastored for 31 years in Pennsylvania, Indiana, Ohio, and Michigan. Beginning in 1933, he pastored at Otterbein United Brethren Church, Greencastle, PA. Mummart was the bishop of a United Brethren Church, 1921–25 and 1937–41, and a member of the General Conference six times.

Wallace E. Rollins

Jan. 26, 1870
Marshall, North Carolina

Dec. 14, 1959
Sweet Briar, Virginia (?)

Dean of Virginia Theological Seminary, Alexandria, VA 1931–40. Rollins was ordained priest of the Episcopal Church in 1898. He married Helen Collins (October 14, 1903) and Marion J. Benedict (September 3, 1946). He became rector of Emmanuel Church, Covington, VA (1897–1904); of St. Thomas Church, Christiansburg, VA (1906–08); chaplain at Sweet Briar (VA) College (1908–13); then went to VTS as professor of church history in 1913. He was highly respected. The Wallace E. Rollins Professorship of Religion at Sweet Briar (VA) College was established in his honor in 1957. He wrote *Jesus and His Ministry* (1954) with his wife.

Thomas Moseley

March 18, 1886
Birmingham, England

Dec. 17, 1959
Glendale, California

President of Nyack (NY) College, 1940–58, and Accrediting Association of Bible Colleges, 1951–52. Moseley was converted (1909) and came to Nyack (1913). He sailed for China in 1915 as a missionary and married Eva Palmquist on November 17, 1917 in China. Moseley returned to America for more schooling in 1927, and then went back to China, 1931–40, before heading his alma mater.

Benjamin A. Baur

1890

1960

Songwriter and pastor in Rochester, NY. Baur wrote the lyrics and music for several wonderful choruses such as, "Wonderful Jesus," "It is the Lord," "What the World Needs is Jesus," "Jesus Saves," "I Love Thee," and "I've Found a Friend". His music was his personal gift to God.

Arthur A. Luther

1892
Fairview Town, Pennsylvania

1960

Wrote lyrics and music "Jesus Never Fails" and numerous choruses. Luther went into evangelism for the United Brethren Church, preaching, leading the singing, and playing the piano. He married Irena Lehnies. Later, Luther became field secretary of the Christian Church, and pastored First Congregational, North Collins, NY. He also served as mission superintendent at Williamsport, PA, and helped with social service work in Lancaster, PA.

Edward B. Paisley

April 2, 1890
Gurdon, Arkansas

c 1960
Richmond, Virginia

President of Presbyterian School of Christian Education (Union Theological Seminary, Richmond, VA, in 1995), **1933–43**. Paisley married Alston Thomas Pickney on June 16, 1920. He pastored churches in Bartlett, McAllen, and Laredo, TX (1916–25); Bethany Congregation, Bridgeport, CT (1925–27); and began teaching at the above school in 1928. The school was then known as General Assemblies Training School for Lay Workers.

Reuben E. Nelson

April 12, 1905
Lake Elizabeth, Minnesota

Jan. 6, 1960
New York, New York

First general secretary of America Baptist Convention (AB Churches in the USA in 1972), **1950–59**. Nelson married Edith Peterson on September 6, 1933. He pastored the First Swedish Baptist Church, Brockton, MA, from 1931–34. Nelson was on the staff of Bethel College, St. Paul, MN (1934–37), and became professor (1937–39). He was executive secretary of the Minnesota Baptist Convention (1939–43) and of the Detroit Baptist Convention (1943–45). He helped on the staff of American Baptist Convention (1945–50) and the Baptist World Alliance Executive Committee (1950–59). His funeral was at Central Baptist Church, St. Paul, MN.

James E. Bennet

April 28, 1875
Port Jervis, New York

Jan. 11, 1960
Brooklyn, New York

Outstanding Christian lawyer from New York City. Bennet, converted at age six, was affiliated with First Bible Presbyterian Church of New York City and active in many major Christian organizations. At age 17 he was a reporter for a country daily newspaper and was teaching school at age 19. At age 22, he studied law, and at 26 was admitted to the New York bar. Bennet headed various corporations and had 1,000 employees working for him at one time. He married Elizabeth Morris.

Jesse R. (Pap) Baxter

Dec. 8, 1887
Lebanon, Alabama

Jan. 21, 1960

Wrote lyrics for "After the Sunrise," "What Love," and the lyrics and music for "Farther Along," along with W. B. Stevens and others. Baxter wrote thousands of gospel songs. He formed the Baxter Quartet and married Clarice Howard (1898–1972) on June 23, 1918. He formed a partnership with V. O. STAMPS in 1926 to form Stamps-Baxter Music Company with offices moving to Dallas in 1928. Their school of music trained several generations of young people. Baxter was a member and the choir director of a Methodist church, serving on several boards within the church. He popularized gospel music around the country through the publication of "shape-note" songbooks and by sponsoring numerous quartets on the radio. His wife headed the company upon his death.

Clarence W. Hatch

Feb. 13, 1903
Gordon, Nebraska

Jan. 29, 1960
Anderson, Indiana

Executive Secretary of Church of God, Anderson, IN 1955–60. Hatch pastored in Forrest, IL from 1924–27. He married Mildred Sutt in 1925. He then pastored in Salem, OR (1929–32) and Woodburn, OR (1933–37). He became executive secretary of Associated Budgets of the Church of God (1938), renamed World Service of the Church of God (1941). In 1940, he instituted

The Saints Go Marching In

Christ's World Service Day which became an annual occasion in the COG. Hatch set up the Board of Pensions of COG (1949) and was elected as first full time executive secretary of the executive council of the COG (1959). He died of a massive heart attack. Hatch is affectionately remembered as "Mr. Stewardship."

Henry W. DuBose

May 18, 1884
Spring Hill, Tennessee

Feb. 11, 1960
Richmond, Virginia (?)

President of Presbyterian School of Christian Education (Union Theological Seminary, Richmond, VA in 1995), **1944–54, and American Association of Schools of Religious Education, 1951–53**. DuBose married Marie Webb on April 14, 1915. Ordained as a Presbyterian in 1910, he pastored in Versailles, Kentucky; Mobile, Alabama, and Danville, Virginia until 1922. DuBose also pastored First Church, Spartanburg, SC (1923–37); Highland Park, Dallas, TX (1937–42); and Trinity Presbyterian, Montgomery, AL (1942–44).

William M. Strong

March 3, 1877
Brooklyn, New York

Feb. 20, 1960
Temuco, Chile

Founder and general director of Soldiers and Gospel Mission of South America (Gospel Mission of South America in 1963), **1923–59**. Strong was converted at age 35. Strong married Jessie Tomkins on April 2, 1903. He was the head of his own insurance company until God spoke to him. He worked among the armed forces of Chile at age 45 with his wife and two teens. Both children eventually served in Chile for over 50 years. Strong died while passing out a tract on a railroad platform.

Thomas O. Chisholm

July 29, 1866
near Franklin, Kentucky

Feb. 29, 1960
Ocean Grove, New Jersey

Methodist hymn writer of great gospel songs. He wrote lyrics to "Great Is Thy Faithfulness" (WILLIAM RUNYAN) "Living for Jesus," (HAROLD LOWDEN) "Trust in the Lord" (W.P. LOVELESS) "The Mercies of God" (Thomas), "He Was Wounded for Our Transgressions," "They Are Buried in the Deep Deep Sea" (DUNLOP), "Oh, to be Like Thee" (KIRKPATRICK), "It is Different Now" (B.D. ACKLEY) and "My Trusting Heart Rejoices" (Goesskle). Chisholm wrote over 1,200 poems throughout his lifetime. He was converted after hearing H. C. MORRISON preach in 1893. Chisholm married Catherine Vandervere in 1903, and pastored in Winona Lake, IN from 1909–16. Chisholm spent the rest of his life as an insurance agent in Vineland, NJ, from 1916–53. He died in a Methodist home.

Charles W. Butler

May 13, 1873
Caro, Michigan

April 17, 1960
Gresham, Oregon

President of Cleveland (OH) Bible College (Malone College, Canton, OH in 1957), **1921–36; New John Fletcher College, 1936–42, renamed Kletzing College, University Park, IA 1942–46; and of National Association of Holiness** (Christian Holiness Partnership in 1997), **1928–42**. Butler was converted at age 15 while praying in his room. He married Catherine Cronkright on September 1, 1892 (died: 1918) and Selma Schilling on September 12, 1921. He was ordained a Methodist in 1896 and pastored in the Detroit Conference, 1891–1908. Butler was an evangelist, 1908–11 and 1946–60. Preaching in Holiness camp meetings was his specialty. He became ill while preaching at a revival in Gresham, and died of acute hepatitis shortly thereafter.

Leticia Burd Cowman

March 3, 1870
Thayer, Iowa

April 17, 1960
Los Angeles, California

President of Oriental Missionary Society, 1928–49, and grand "Old" lady of the gospel. Leticia married CHARLES COWMAN on June 18, 1889 (died: September 25, 1924), and they went to Japan in 1901. She was converted at Grace Methodist in Chicago in December, 1893. She became a world traveler, lecturer, writer, and source of inspiration. Her devotional classics include Streams in the Desert (1925) and Springs in the Valley. *The Vision Lives* is her biography written by Ben Pearson. She died on Easter Sunday. Her *Streams in the Desert* have sold over six million copies in more than twelve languages.

Toyohiko Kagawa

July 10, 1888
Kobe, Japan

April 23, 1960
Tokyo, Japan

Christian social reformer and leader of labor movements that bettered millions. After his conversion from Buddhism at age 15 (baptized June 14, 1904) and being disinherited by his family, Kagawa studied at Princeton Theological Seminary, 1914–16 and returned to Japan in 1917. He toiled in the slums from 1919–34, devoting himself to serving the poor and helpless. Kagawa sought peace amongst a warlike culture and founded the first labor union (Friends of Jesus) (1921), Anti-War League (1928), and Kingdom of God Movement (1930). He was imprisoned, 1921–22 and 1940, for leading a nationwide evangelical movement and also because of pacifist views. Kagawa was an evangelist and poet and wrote more than 180 books, including *The Psychology of Poverty*. He felt a Christian economic life would reform the world. He conducted evangelistic tours on four continents and saw 225,000 converted because of his love for the poor. Because of Kagawa's work, the government closed slum areas of major cities. His works ranged from *Before the Dawn* (1925) to *Behold the Man* (1941).

Harry Trust

Jan. 11, 1883
Ivybridge, England

May 2, 1960
Pittsfield, Massachusetts

President of Bangor (ME) Theological Seminary, 1933–52. Trust was ordained a Congregationalist (September 18, 1913), and married Lillian Knowleon (January 3, 1917). He pastored in Winthrop, ME (1914–17); Biddeford, ME (1917–21); Springfield, OH (1921–26); and Mansfield, OH (1926–33). He was active in community affairs and in his denomination.

Charles R. Erdman

July 20, 1866
Fayetteville, New York

May 9, 1960
Princeton, New Jersey

Presbyterian Professor of practical theology at Princeton Seminary, 1906–36. Erdman influenced many young ministerial students and was the last of the conservative leadership there, staying on, even though MACHEN and R. D. WILSON left. He married Estelle Pardee on June 1, 1892. He pastored Overbrook (PA) Church (1892–97); First Church, Germantown, PA (1897–1906); and First Presbyterian, Princeton, NJ (1924–34). He was president of the board of Foreign Missions for his denomination, 1928–40. Erdman's writings were numerous beginning with *Coming to the Communion* (1912). His expositions of the books of the Bible were extensive, beginning with *Mark* (1916) and ending with *Revelation* (1936). Erdman wrote 35 books and was a popular preacher in the Bible Conference movement.

Thorvald O. Burnvedt

May 29, 1888
Kragero, Norway

May 12, 1960
Minneapolis, Minnesota

President of Lutheran Free Church (ALC, ELCA in 1988), **1930–58**. Burnvedt came to America in 1903 and married Anna Tollefson on August 24, 1921. He pastored Lutheran Churches in Tacoma, WA (1915–18); Brooklyn, NY (1919–20); and Minneapolis, MN (1920–30). He taught at Lutheran Bible Institute and Augsburg Theological Seminary, 1922–29. Burnvedt co-edited *The Concordia Hymnal* and the devotional *Life and Light*.

Robert E. Jones

Feb. 19, 1872
Greensboro, North Carolina

May 18, 1960
New Orleans, Louisiana

Bishop in the Methodist Episcopal Church, 1920–39, and in the Methodist Church, 1939–60. Jones was converted at age 16. He married Valena MacArthur on February 4, 1901 (died: 1920). He later married H. Elizabeth Brown. He pastored four churches in North Carolina and was the editor of the *Southwestern Christian Advocate* (1904–20). Jones was the first black, along with Matthew Clair, to be elected a Methodist bishop. He promoted the establishment of the Gulfside Assembly, Waveland, MS, an important center for black Methodists. Jones was bishop of the New Orleans area.

William E. Sangster

June 5, 1900
London, England

May 24, 1960
London, England

Methodist pastor and evangelism enthusiast who entered the Wesleyan ministry in 1922. Sangster pastored in Liverpool, Leeds and Scarborough. Sangster married his wife, Margaret, in August, 1926. From 1939–55, he pastored the Westminster Central Hall of London, drawing large crowds. From 1950–58, he was president of the Methodist Conference of Great Britain. In 1955, Sangster was in charge of the Home Mission Department and was involved in many other evangelism endeavors. His books range from *Why Jesus Never Wrote a Book* (1932) to *Give God a Chance* (1959). He died of muscular dystrophy.

Ida S. Scudder

Dec. 9, 1870
Ranipur, India

May 24, 1960
Vellore, Kodiakanal, India

Outstanding medical missionary to India, the third generation of a great missionary family. In 1894, Ida received her call. At the time, she was in India on a short-term commitment—primarily to be near her dying mother. There were three separate knocks on her door—men seeking a woman doctor to minister to their wives in childbirth. Although her father was a trained physician, they refused his services and allowed their wives to die rather than be assisted by a male practitioner. Ida was a helpless bystander. She returned to America, secured her medical training and returned to India in 1900, establishing a hospital that first year. Her goals included combating the fear of and apathy toward medical care, giving gynecological care, and fighting plagues. She organized hospitals, clinics, nursing schools, and medical education at Vellore. She did her first surgery in 1902. By 1906, she was treating 40,000 people annually. Scudder opened the first medical college for women in Asia in 1918: The Christian Medical College. She directed the greatly expanded Shell Hospital in Vellore (1923), which she had established (1900). She was supported in her efforts by a great fund–raising campaign in America. Her medical complex became one of the largest in Asia, and by 1947 was also accepting male students. By 1950, it was affiliated with Madras University and considered one of the outstanding interdenominational Christian institutions in Asia.

Benjamin F. Hitchcock

Aug. 10, 1886
Indianapolis Indiana

June 18, 1960
Kalamazoo, Michigan

Founder and first director of Rural Bible Mission, Plainwell, MI 1935–55. At age 18, Hitchcock was converted at a Free Methodist Church in Indianapolis. He married Alice Lutgen on June 19, 1912 (died: May 1, 1918) and then Ethel Messler on July 31, 1919. He pastored a FMC in Mishawaka, IN. Self-taught, he pastored several small churches in Michigan, which included The FMC in Temperance, and several Methodist Protestant Churches such as Marcellus (1919–21); Leonard (1921–29); Flint (1929–31); and Assyria (1932–35). As a chalk artist, Hitchcock soon was in evangelism throughout southern Michigan. He visited one room schools in the daytime and found 75 percent of the children attended no church. This was in the early 1930s and during depression time. It was an all out effort to provide spiritual help. Finally, he had a heart attack, retired to Florida, and returned to Michigan where he died.

Mark D. Ormston

Dec. 17, 1890
St. John's, Michigan

June 23, 1960
Jackson, Michigan

Bishop of Free Methodist Church, 1936–58. Ormston married Minnie Dresselhaus on August 14, 1912. Converted at age 15, Ormston pastored in eastern Michigan (1916–27), was conference Sunday school secretary (1919–27), and superintendent of Eastern Michigan Conference (1927–35). Ormston was active in Spring Arbor (MI) Conference as chairman of the Commission on Missions. During his tenure, he was able to eliminate all debt of the organization. Ormston was an able administrator and spirit-filled preacher.

Alfred H. Ackley

Jan. 21, 1887
Spring Hill, Pennsylvania

July 3, 1960
Whittier, California

Hymn writer of the famed ACKLEY brothers. Alfred wrote the lyrics and music to "He Lives," "God's Tomorrow," "Take Up Thy Cross," "Heartaches," "It Is Morning in My Heart," "Jesus Is the Joy of Living," "Wonderful," "When the World Forgets," "When God Is Near," "When I am with Him," "Dearer Than All," "Only Shadows," and "The End of the Road." He wrote the lyrics to "Till the Whole World Knows," "In the Service of the King," "Amazed," "You Cannot Hide from God," with his brother, B.D. ACKLEY adding the music. His most famous hymn, "He Lives," was written in 1932 after hearing a radio preacher deny the resurrection. He was responsible for writing some 1,500 songs. After graduating from Westminster (MD) Theological Seminary, Ackley was ordained in 1914. He pastored Presbyterian churches in Elmhurst and Wilkes-Barre, PA, and in Escondido, CA. Ackley participated in BILLY SUNDAY's evangelistic services and was associated with the RODEHEAVER music company. JOHN BROWN University in Siloam Springs, AR awarded him an honorary Doctor of Sacred Music degree. He was an accomplished cellist. Ackley was married twice; his first wife's name was Helen.

Fred F. Brown

Nov. 27, 1882
Glenville, North Carolina

Aug. 9, 1960
Knoxville, Tennessee

President of Southern Baptist Convention, 1933. Ordained a Baptist in 1913, Brown married Nona Dover on April 12, 1914, and they had five children. Brown pastored in Harrodsburg and Frankfort, KY; at FBC, Sherman, TX (1916–21); and at FBC, Knoxville, TN (1921–46). Brown wrote *This Is My Church* (1929). He was a special chaplain in WWI at the request of President WILSON. He was very active in his denomination.

Norman B. Harrison

Dec. 14, 1874
Caldwell, New Jersey

Aug. 9, 1960
Minneapolis, Minnesota

Presbyterian pastor, teacher, writer, and evangelist. Harrison was ordained (May 21, 1898) and married Emma B. Smith (June 8, 1899). After pastoring in various places, he went to University Church, Seattle, WA (1911–21), then was an evangelist in the Pacific Northwest (1921–24). Harrison pastored Memorial Church, St. Louis, MO (1924–29), and Oliver Church, Minneapolis, MN (1929–39). At the end of his life, he traveled as an evangelist. Many of his book titles begin with the word "His," *His Power, His Love, His Coming, His Bequest*, etc.

Ralph S. Cushman

Nov. 12, 1879
Poultney, Vermont

Aug. 10, 1960
Herkimer, New York

Methodist leader, poet, and author. Cushman was a leader in the Temperance movement. He married Maude Hammond on August 20, 1902. He pastored in Bryantville, MA (1902–4); Acushnet, MA (1904–6); Danielson, CT (1906–11); Fall River, MA (1911–15); and Geneva, NY (1915–17). He also pastored the Asbury Church in Rochester, NY (1920–32); was elected bishop in 1931; served in Denver, CO (1932–39); and St. Paul, MN (1939–52). Cushman wrote many books including *Studies in Stewardship* (1917) to *The Prayers of Jesus* (1954). He was widely known for his poetry about the Christian Life.

Frank P. Ekings

Dec. 16, 1877
Paterson, New Jersey

Aug. 20, 1960
Altadena, California

First president of Evangelical Baptist Missions, Kokomo, IN 1928–45. Ekings married Anna Fairhurst (1883–1968) on November 25, 1908. He was active in the Madison Ave. Baptist Church, Paterson, NJ. As a layman, Ekings practiced medicine in Paterson, 1904–48, then he retired and moved to Altadena, CA. He was active at the Lake Ave. Congregational Church, Pasadena, CA and was a volunteer chaplain at the Los Angeles County Jail. At the jail, he led over 5,000 to Christ.

Phil T. Kerr

Sept. 1, 1906
Los Angeles, California

Aug. 31, 1960
Leguna, California

Proficient writer and composer of gospel music (3,000 choruses, 200 hymns). Kerr was converted at age six following a family devotion time. Kerr married Iris Wyatt on November 9, 1927. The son of missionary parents, he spent his earlier years working with Christian Endeavor, publishing gospel music, managing a Christian radio station, conducting evangelistic campaigns, and training young people in musical evangelism. He directed Monday Night Musicals at Pasadena (CA) Auditorium beginning in March, 1945. This ministry allowed new converts an open door for exposure. His songs included "His to Command," "The Lover of My Soul," "Melody Divine," "Over in Glory," "His Love Sent Him to the Cross," "I'm Trusting in Jesus Today," "Where He Leads Me," "Breaking Through the Clouds," "Broadcasting for Jesus," and "Why Should I Care."

Merrill T. MacPherson

July 18, 1891
Reynoldsville, Pennsylvania

Sept. 6, 1960
Weyburn, Saskatchewan, Canada

Former Presbyterian, later IFCA leader. MacPherson began his ministry as an evangelistic singer (1916–18), then became Presbyterian pastor at Ashton and Franklin Grove, IL (1921–23). He married Ruth Johnston on May 11, 1921. MacPherson pastored at Spencer Memorial, Brooklyn,

1924–26. He was radio evangelist, a pastor, 1930–36, when he left his denomination. In 1936, MacPherson founded the Church of the Open Door, Philadelphia (Fort Washington, PA). He was the president of the IFCA from 1944–46. Poor health caused his retirement in 1948. He wrote the chorus, lyrics, and music of "Coming Soon," and the music for "Just Fall in Love with Jesus," lyrics by Ruth Withun. He was stricken with a cerebral hemorrhage while on vacation in Canada and died within a couple weeks. He is buried in Roselyn, PA.

Percy B. Crawford

Oct. 20, 1902
Minnedosa, Manitoba, Canada

Oct. 31, 1960
Trenton, New Jersey

Broadcaster, youth evangelist, and first president of King's College, Belmer, NJ 1938–41; Newcastle, DE 1941–55; Briarcliff Manor, NY 1955–60, which he founded in 1938 in Briarcliff Manor, NY. Crawford was the greatest youth evangelist of his time along with JACK WYRTZEN. He was converted on September 23, 1923 in the Church of the Open Door in Los Angeles, with WILLIAM P. NICHOLSON preaching. He attended BIOLA (1923–25), and Wheaton (IL) College, (1927–29). Then in 1931, he launched Saturday night youth rallies in Philadelphia. His radio program, which started in 1931, was entitled *Young People's Church of the Air* and was heard on 450 stations. Crawford married RUTH DUVALL, a tremendous pianist, on September 18, 1933 (died: October 28, 1986). Crawford directed Pinebrook Bible Conference in Stroudsburg, PA in 1938 and edited *Pinebrook Gospel Songbook Series*. In 1945, he spoke to 75,000 at the YFC rally at Soldier's Field, Chicago. Crawford had a television ministry entitled *Youth on the March*, 1949–58 and wrote several gospel choruses, "One Grand Day" and "Hanging There for Me" (music by W.P. LOVELESS). He suffered a heart attack (Oct. 29) en route to a meeting in Lancaster, PA, while entering a restaurant. Billy Graham spoke to 2,500 at his Philadelphia funeral. Graham and WYRTZEN considered him their evangelism mentor. He is buried at Pinebrook.

Donald G. Barnhouse

March 28, 1895
Watsonville, California

Nov. 5, 1960
Philadelphia, Pennsylvania

Presbyterian pioneer radio preacher, pastor, journalist, and author. Barnhouse was the second well-known Pennsylvanian to die within a week (see PERCY CRAWFORD). Tom Haney of Christian Endeavor led Barnhouse to Christ as a teen. Barnhouse was with the Belgian Gospel Mission (1919–25), after which he pastored Grace Presbyterian Church in Philadelphia, PA (1925–27). Barnhouse pastored the 10th Avenue Church of Philadelphia from 1927 until his death. He married Ruth Tiffany in 1922 (died: 1944) and Margaret Bell in June, 1954. He had a radio ministry called *Bible Study Hour* from 1928 onward. He was the editor and founder of *Revelation Magazine* (1931–49), which was later called *Eternity* (1950–60). Barnhouse was a strong ultra-Calvinist, but enthusiastic in getting out gospel literature to the ends of the earth. He was the founder of the Alliance of Confessing Evangelical Ministries. His writings range from *His Own Received Him Not* (1933) to *God's Grace* (1959). From 1940 onward, Barnhouse spent six months every year at Bible Conferences until he died of a brain tumor. He is buried in Doylestown, PA.

Halford E. Luccock

March 11, 1885
Pittsburgh, Pennsylvania

Nov. 5, 1960
Hamden, Connecticut

Professor of homiletics at Yale Divinity School, 1928–53. From 1909–16, Luccock pastored in New York and Connecticut, during which time he married Mary Whitehead on June 17, 1914. He served in a ministry in Windsor, CT (19110–12); taught at Hartford (CT) Theological Seminary (1912–14); pastored at St. Andrew's, East Haven, CT (1914–16); taught and was registrar at Drew Theological Seminary, Madison, NJ (1916–18). Luccock was the editorial secretary of the Methodist

Board for Foreign Missions, 1918–24, and was editor of the *Christian Advocate* (1924–28). He wrote 26 books and was the "Simeon Stylites" columnist for the *Christian Century* (1949–61). His works ranged from *Fares, Please!* (1916) to *In the Minister's Workshop* (1944). He died in his sleep from cancer.

William W. Hamilton

Dec. 9, 1868　　　　　　　　　　　　　　　　　　　　　　　　　　　　　　　　Nov. 19, 1960
Hopkinsville, Kentucky　　　　　　　　　　　　　　　　　　　　　　　New Orleans, Louisiana

President of Southern Baptist Convention, 1941–42, and of Baptist Bible Institute (New Orleans (LA) Baptist Theological Seminary in 1946), **1928–42**. Hamilton married Zula Doyle on May 31, 1893, and pastored 1893–1906. He became an evangelist, 1906–09 and 1918–22. Hamilton pastored at Lynchburg, VA (1909–18), and at St. Charles Avenue Church, New Orleans, LA (1922–28 and 1942–47). When he took office at BBI, $353,000 in bonds were in default because of the Great Depression. Hamilton's faith, integrity, and influence held the school together. He wrote many books, from *Helping Hand* (1908) to *Helping Hand Reissued* (1948).

Charles L. Pyatt

Feb. 25, 1886　　　　　　　　　　　　　　　　　　　　　　　　　　　　　　　　Nov. 19, 1960
Jacksonville, Illinois　　　　　　　　　　　　　　　　　　　　　　　　　Lexington, Kentucky

Executive secretary of Association of Theological Schools, 1946–50. Pyatt married Grace Strawn on September 6, 1910 (died: September, 1936), and was secretary of AEF in France, 1917–19. Pyatt pastored in Indianapolis, 1919–20, and was ordained a Christian Church (Disciples of Christ) minister. In 1920, he started at the College of the Bible (Lexington Theological Seminary in 1965) as professor of OT. He later served as chairman of the faculty, 1928–38 and became the dean after 1938.

James G. Dale

June 21, 1870　　　　　　　　　　　　　　　　　　　　　　　　　　　　　　　　Dec. 5, 1960
Oak Hill, Alabama　　　　　　　　　　　　　　　　　　　　　　　Tamazunchale, SLP, Mexico

Founder and first director of Mexican Indian Mission (merged into Unevangelized Fields Mission in 1971), **1930–59**. Dale went to Mexico in 1899 to be director of a college and seminary in Rio Verde. His wife-to-be, Catherine Neel, went to Mexico as a medical missionary in 1898. They were married (1901) and remained in Rio Verde until the revolution (1913), when they had to leave the country and return to America from 1913–19. They returned to Mexico in 1919 and worked in Tampico. In 1929, they began a new work among the Aztec Indians in Tamazunchale with a hospital and a Bible school. Their son, John, joined them, and the Mexican Indian Mission was formed to reach six Indian tribes with 20 missionaries. Mrs. Dale passed away May 28, 1941.

John C. Thomas

Sept. 6, 1891　　　　　　　　　　　　　　　　　　　　　　　　　　　　　　　　Dec. 13, 1960
Meyersdale, Pennsylvania　　　　　　　　　　　　　　　　　　　　　Apple Valley, California

Baritone singer. Thomas married Dorothy Kaehler on March 5, 1924. In the 40 years between 1913 and 1953 his rich baritone voice was heard in musical comedy and opera, on the radio, and from the concert stage. His first formal recital was in 1918. His operatic debut was in Washington D.C. in *"Aida"*. He continued training in Europe, working with Vienna opera companies. After 1920, he appeared in operas in Chicago, Philadelphia, and San Francisco. He made his debut in February, 1923 in *La Traviata*. In the spring of 1933, he was signed by the Metropolitan Opera Company. He appeared regularly with the MOC until 1945901. He continued his concerts and once in Chicago sang before 100,000 people. He made several Christian albums under the International Sacred label. From the time he reached a studio and approached the microphone, he spent some 30 minutes in prayer.

C. C. Adams

Dec. 12, 1884
Huntington, Tennessee

c 1961
Philadelphia, Pennsylvania

Director of National Baptist Convention USA Missions, 1941–61. Adams was pastor of the New Bethlehem Baptist Church, Philadelphia, PA. He served earlier churches in North and South Carolina and Tennessee. Some of his accomplishments as mission head included the Carrie Dyer Maternity Hospital in Monrovia, Liberia, and the expansion of the foreign mission enterprise in Nigeria. He raised $100,000 for missions in 1943 and $2 million between 1944 and 1954. He made trips to Africa in 1945 and 1947.

William G. Nyman

Dec. 29, 1884
Chicago, Illinois

Jan. 10, 1961
Glendale, California

Stabilizer of Wycliffe Bible Translators in its early days. Nyman married Etta Ahlstrand on June 4, 1912. He was converted in 1915 after hearing a message, "Born Again." He was a key official in a large Chicago lumber mill. In 1930, the Nyman's moved to California where he represented Wheaton College on the West Coast. In February, 1939, he was stricken with a serious heart ailment that kept him bedfast. He opened his home to missionaries. The CAMERON TOWNSENDs were among those that would be nursed back to health there. They decided to headquarter the fledgling Wycliffe organization there in Glendale. From 1942–55, he was both secretary and treasurer for the organization. Serving without salary, he kept the home department down to 7 percent of the total budget. On December 13, 1960, he suffered a massive heart attack.

Edwin G. Baker

Dec. 3, 1885
Toronto, Ontario, Canada

Jan. 24, 1961
Toronto, Ontario, Canada

President of Toronto Bible College, 1929–51. Baker married Gina MacNaughton in September, 1913. He began his business career with Moore Corp. LTD, Toronto (1909), and later was the chairman of the board (1945). Baker headed Canadian Life Insurance Company beginning in 1951. He was a corporate executive and very busy, yet, he led a young college into maturity.

Emmanuel F. Poppen

Oct. 14, 1874
New Dundee, Ontario, Canada

Feb. 13, 1961
Columbus, Ohio

President of American Lutheran Church (ELCA in 1988), **1938–50**. Poppen married Anna Trebel on August 4, 1897. He pastored the following churches in Ohio: Versailles (1895–97), St. Mary's (1897–1905), Sidney (1905–15), and Grove City (1915–30). Poppen was president of Ohio District ALC from 1931–37, and a delegate at various conventions. He edited hymnals and was active in his denomination.

Edward J. Parker

Aug. 2, 1869
Elgin, Illinois

Feb. 16, 1961
Asbury Park, New Jersey

General of Salvation Army (USA), 1934–43. Parker married Eva Thompson on January 11, 1893. He was in the Salvation Army all his life. He began as executive secretary for the New England states (1895–98), then director of printing/publishing (1898–1903), men's social services secretary (1903–27) and executive officer for Eastern states (1927–30). Parker lived most of his life in Belmar, NJ. He is buried in Valhalla, NY.

Alfred C. Snead

Aug. 16, 1884
Ellisburg, Pennsylvania

March 4, 1961
Orlando, Florida

President of Christian and Missionary Alliance Overseas Missions, 1921–56, and first president of EFMA, 1945–46, 1955–57. Snead pastored in Cresskill, NY, in 1907 and was missionary to India and assistant treasurer of the mission, 1907–09. He married Mary Kinding on June 8, 1909. Snead taught at Wilson Academy of Nyack, NY (1911–12), and at Nyack College (1918–30). His first book was *The Eternal Christ* (1937).

James H. Franklin

May 13, 1872
Pamplin, Virginia

March 23, 1961
Richmond, Virginia

President of Crozer Theological Seminary (Colgate-Rochester (NY) Divinity School in 1970), **Chester, PA 1934–43, and secretary of American Baptist Foreign Mission Society** (ABC in the USA Int. Ministries in 1972), **1912–34.** Franklin married Augusta Terry on November 15, 1900. He was ordained as a Baptist in 1896 and pastored in Leadville, CO (1898–1901); Cripple Creek, CO (1901–4); and FBC, Colorado Springs, CO (1906–12). Franklin presided over the Northern Baptist Convention, 1935–36. He wrote three books.

Nathan R. Wood

Aug. 13, 1874
Wyocena, Wisconsin

March 26, 1961
Portland, Oregon

Dean/president of Gordon College and Divinity Schoo, Wenham, MA 1910–44. Wood married Isabel Bliss on June 14, 1900. He pastored in West Medford Baptist, MA from 1901–11, and became a professor at Gordon in 1908. The CEO of the College was called dean from 1910–19 and president after 1919. From 1944 on, Wood was an interim pastor and conference speaker. His writings ranged from *The Witness of Sin* (1905) to *Seven Lamps of Fire* (1942).

Robert Harkness

March 2, 1880
Bendigo, Australia

May 8, 1961
London, England

Greatest gospel pianist of his era, Harkness joined the TORREY/ALEXANDER team (until 1908) in Australia in 1902. Alexander led him to the Lord. He composed music for some 2,000 songs: "Such Love," "He Will Hold Me Fast" (lyrics by ADA HABERSOHN), "In Jesus," "When I See My Saviour," "No One Knows But Jesus," and the lyrics and music of "No Longer Lonely," "Only Believe and Live," "Shadows," "When the Shadows Flee Away," "Sometime," "Thine, Lord," "Travelling Home," "Wondrous Peace," "Get God's Sunshine," "Are We Down-Hearted?" and "Why Should He Love Me So?" Throughout his life, Harkness made six worldwide tours. He lived in London and Pasadena, CA. His wife died in 1959.

Frank J. Neuberg

Dec. 31, 1908
Prague, Czechoslovakia

May 9, 1961
Chicago, Illinois

President of Evangelical Theological Society, 1953. Neuberg was raised as a Hebrew Christian and served in the Czech army before the days of Hitler. He never married. He taught at National Bible Institute (1943–45); at Baptist Bible Seminary (1945–47); at Johns Hopkins University (1948–49); at Wheaton (IL) College (1950–57); and at North Park Theological Seminary (1957–61). Neuberg's teaching specialty was Hebrew and Old Testament. He died of a heart attack.

Issac N. McCash

June 5, 1861
Cumberland County, Illinois

May 20, 1961
Columbia, Missouri

President of Phillips University, Tulsa, OK 1916–38. McCash married Marietta Tandy on October 5, 1886 and was ordained in the Disciples of Christ ministry in 1890. He pastored the University Church, Des Moines, IA from 1893–1904. McCash worked with the Anti-Saloon League of Iowa (1904–07), and the American Christian Missionary Society (1909–13). He was president of Spokane (WA) University, 1913–16. McCash was active in the Masons. His name is in the Oklahoma Hall of Fame and his bust in the Historical Society. He lived in Enid, Oklahoma. He wrote *Ten Plagues of Modern Egypt* in 1903.

Lawrence B. Saint

Jan. 29, 1885
Sharpsburg, Pennsylvania

June 15, 1961
Huntington Valley, Pennsylvania

Artist of stained glass. Saint was converted under the ministry of J. WILBUR CHAPMAN. He drew his inspiration from travels in Europe, viewing historic cathedral windows. Saint's work can be found in various academies, museums, libraries, and churches in America. He married Katherine Proctor on June 10, 1910. He designed and painted Bryn Athyn (PA) Cathedral, 1917–28. From 1928–35, he directed the stained glass department of the Washington Cathedral and Mt. Saint Alban Church of Washington, D.C. He used 9,000 pieces of glass to tell the story of the "Last Judgment." His "Shepherd Psalm" covers 330 square feet and took 15 months to make. It is in the Church of the Open Door in Philadelphia. He was a Baptist. He was the father of NATE, RACHEL, and PHIL SAINT.

Robert C. Lawson

May 5, 1883
New Iberia, Louisiana

July 2, 1961
New York, New York

Founder and bishop of the Church of Our Lord Jesus Christ of Apostolic Faith, 1919–61, a large Pentecostal denomination. Lawson began with a promising career as a singer. Around 1913, he became sick with tuberculosis. Lawson was converted attending a church in Indianapolis, and was healed completely. Lawson met his wife, Carrie Fields, in Leavenworth, KS, on an evangelistic trip. He married in 1914. He established churches in St. Louis, San Antonio, and Columbus, Ohio, 1914–19. Lawson moved to New York City and, in July, 1919, began services on the street, organizing the Refuge Church of Christ in 1923. In 1923, he took his first of 37 trips to the Holy Land. In 1926, he established the Church of Christ Bible Institute. He opened the R.C. Lawson Institute in Southern Pines, NC in 1931. He founded funeral homes, a day care center, a bookstore, a record store, and a publishing company for his *Contender for the Faith*. In 1935, he expanded the work into the Caribbean. His wife died in August, 1948. In 1950, he took a trip around the world and married Evelyn Burke in 1951. In 1957, there was a split, and those that left founded the Bible Way Church of Our Lord Jesus Christ World Wide.

Michael J. Mintern

July 28, 1880
Victoria, Australia

July 11, 1961
Ellison Bay, Wisconsin

General Overseer of Christian Catholic (Christ Community in 1995) **Church, Zion, IL 1942–59.** Mintern went to Zion, IL (May, 1906) and married May Butler (December, 1907). After her death, he married Iris Laytham on January 19, 1958. Mintern worked with WILBUR VOLIVA in the editorial department of weekly publications. He pastored the Shiloh Tabernacle, Chicago, IL, in the 1920s and 1930s. He developed a church home for seniors, a church youth camp, and a worldwide missions program at the tabernacle. Mintern resigned 15 days after a tragic fire destroyed the Zion facilities on April 11, 1959.

O. J. Read

c 1900

July 22, 1961
Fort Worth, Texas

President of Christian Congregation, 1921–61. Read pastored First Congregational Church, Ft. Worth, TX. Read later pastored the Christian Congregational Church, Fort Worth, TX with an address of 4005 Howard Street.

Einar Ekberg

July 29, 1905
Malmo, Sweden

Aug. 5, 1961
Sodertalje, Sweden

One of the finest gospel singers of his time. Ekberg's first recording was in New York in 1925. He made over 500 recordings in his lifetime. Ekberg married Gunborg in 1927, and they had four daughters: Brigit, Gun, Margit, and Annette. He was the soloist in the Philadelphia Church in Stockholm for 25 years. He wrote numerous songs and traveled and sang all over the world. Ekberg moved to America in 1948.

Frank N. D. Buchman

June 4, 1878
Pennsburg, Pennsylvania

Aug. 7, 1961
Freudenstadt, Germany

Founder and head of the Moral Re-Armament movement, 1938–61. As a Lutheran minister (ordained in 1902), Buchman worked in a parish in Philadelphia, but he resigned in disillusionment. He had a spiritual awakening at Keswick, England, in 1908. He was YMCA secretary at Penn State College (1909–15), and lectured in personal evangelism at Hartford (CT) Seminary (1916–21). He took up evangelical work among students and traveled widely. His movement took shape at Oxford University in 1921. He was indifferent to doctrine and did not confess the fundamentals of the Christian faith. Its purpose was to create a moral and spiritual change that would prevent war. In 1929–38, the movement was called the Oxford Group. The name (MR) developed in London in 1938. After WWII, Buchman visited many countries and established missions and training assemblies. He established Moral Re-Armament headquarters in Mackinaw Island, MI (1942), and held a world assembly in Caux, Switzerland (1946). He wrote *Moral Rearmism* (1938) to *The World Rebuilt* (1951). Buchman died of a heart attack. His last words were, "The world must be governed by men governed by God. Why not let God run the whole world?" His four absolutes were purity, honesty, unselfishness, and love. He never married.

H. Orton Wiley

Nov. 15, 1877
Marquette, Nebraska

Aug. 22, 1961
Pasadena, California

First president of Northwest Nazarene College (Univ. in 2000), **Nampa, ID 1916–26, and president of Nazarene University 1913–16,** renamed **Pasadena College** (Point Loma Nazarene University, San Diego, CA in 1998), **Los Angeles, 1926–29, 1933–49.** Wiley married Alice House on November 8, 1902. He pastored Berkeley (CA) Nazarene Church, 1905–9. He was secretary of General Board of Education of his denomination since 1915, and edited the denominational paper. He published a three-volume work *Christian Theology* (1941), a standard text for Arminian Holiness adherents. He edited *The Herald of Holiness* (1928–36).

Norman S. Townsend

Feb. 2, 1917　　　　　　　　　　　　　　　　　　　　　　　Sept. 8, 1961
Tuxedo Park, New York　　　　　　　　　　　　　　Wolfeboro, New Hampshire

Sunday School leader. Townsend was converted on November 12, 1937 under Rich Elvee's ministry. He married Ruth Truessale on June 18, 1941. He pastored Quidesset Baptist Church, North Kingstown, RI from 1944–58, and soon this church became the largest in the state (from 68 to 1,051 in Sunday School). Townsend was the Scripture Press representative in the East, 1958–61. Townsend made three evangelistic trips to Europe in 1950, 1955 and 1960. He died of a heart attack.

Dag Hammarskjöld

July 29, 1905　　　　　　　　　　　　　　　　　　　　　　　Sept. 17, 1961
Jonkoping, Sweden　　　　　　　　　　　　　　near Ndola, Northern Rhodesia

Statesman and second secretary general of the United Nations, 1953–61. Hammarskjöld was secretary of the Bank of Sweden in 1935 and its chairman, 1941–48. From 1936–45, he was Sweden's undersecretary of finance. He entered the foreign office in 1946 as a financial expert. In 1951, he became foreign minister. Finally, he succeeded Trygve Lie, April 10, 1953, in the U.N. post. He was against France and England in the 1956 Suez Crisis, and against Russia's aggression toward Hungary the same year. The emergence of the Republic of the Congo in July, 1960, caused numerous problems for him to solve. His father was a Christian prime minister of Sweden. Dag once served as secretary of the Swedish Christian Youth Movement, and was considered a distinguished Lutheran layman. He never married. His public utterances showed great faith in God. He spoke at the dedication of the Meditation Room at the United Nations. On his fatal flight to Ndola, he had the book, *The Imitation of Christ*, by THOMAS Á KEMPIS with him. He died in a plane crash while attempting a Congo cease-fire. He was posthumously awarded the Nobel Peace Prize for 1961. He is buried in Upsala, Sweden.

Alfred Haapanen

Oct. 19, 1874　　　　　　　　　　　　　　　　　　　　　　　Sept. 24, 1961
Karvia, Finland　　　　　　　　　　　　　　　　　　　Houghton, Michigan

President of Finnish Evangelical Lutheran Church (LCA, ELCA in 1988), **1922–50**. Haapanen married Alma Granqvist on May 26, 1908. He was ordained as a Finnish Evangelical Lutheran in 1906 and his pastorates include Fairport Harbor, OH (1907–13); Ironwood, MI (1913–19); and Hancock, MI (1919–24).

George M. Blackett

Aug. 12, 1891　　　　　　　　　　　　　　　　　　　　　　　Oct. 9, 1961
London, England　　　　　　　　　　　　　　　Calgary, Alberta, Canada

President of Canadian Bible College, Regina, Saskatchewan, Canada, 1941–54. Blackett was led to the Lord by his mother at age 13. He attended Toronto Bible College and pastored in Owen Sound, Ontario, until 1931. He pastored churches in Toronto and Winnipeg. He married Lucy Ivory on June 19, 1918. He was associated with the CMA. Blackett died of cancer.

George A. Miller

July 8, 1868　　　　　　　　　　　　　　　　　　　　　　　Oct. 12, 1961
Mendon, Illinois　　　　　　　　　　　　　　　　　　Oakland, California

Bishop in the Methodist Episcopal Church, 1924–30, and in the Methodist Church, 1939–61. Miller married Margaret Ross in 1895 (died: Oct. 20, 1955). He pastored in the following cities in California: Hanford (1896–1900); Fresno (1900–04); San Francisco (1908–09 and 1914–16); and San Jose (1909–14). He went to South America and became a bishop in Mexico City; Buenos Aires, Argentina; and Santiago, Chile, 1924–34. Miller pastored in LaFayette, CA, in 1934. He wrote his autobiography *Growing Up* at age 91. He crossed the Andes 56 times and traveled 200,000 miles by sea.

Mordecai F. Ham

April 2, 1877
Scottsville, Kentucky

Nov. 1, 1961
Pewee Valley, Kentucky

Evangelist for over 50 years of his life. The devotional habits of his boyhood home led to his conversion around age eight. Ham married Bessie Simmons on July 1, 1900 (died: December 4, 1905) and Annie Smith on June 3, 1908 (he was 31; she was 15). He went into evangelism in 1902, holding crusades and fighting against liquor, evolution, and communism. W. J. Ramsey was Ham's associate, 1912–45. Ham pastored briefly at FBC, Oklahoma City, 1927–29. He was preaching the night Billy Graham and GRADY WILSON were saved in Charlotte, NC in 1934. Some one million converts resulted from his evangelism endeavors, which included area-wide tent campaigns and radio work. He often sought out the most well-known sinners in town during his crusades for personal evangelism encounters. He published *The Old Kentucky Home Revivalist*.

Helen H. Lemmel

Nov. 14, 1864
Wardle, England

Nov. 1, 1961
Seattle, Washington

Wrote lyrics and music to "Turn Your Eyes upon Jesus" (1918). In all, Helen wrote over 500 poems and hymns. She wrote *Story of the Bible* for children. Helen came to America in 1873. She had a brilliant voice, singing in concerts and churches. Helen traveled widely and taught voice at MBI and BIOLA. She was a member of Ballard Avenue Baptist Church, Seattle, WA, from 1904. She also wrote, "His Banner over Us."

Charles H. Mason

Sept. 9, 1866
Bartlett, Tennessee

Nov. 18, 1961
Detroit, Michigan

Founder and first bishop of Church of God in Christ, Memphis, TN 1907–61. Often referred to as COGIC, this group became one of the largest black denominations in America. Mason was converted in 1880. He and CHARLES P. JONES founded Church of God in Christ in 1894. Mason married Alice Saxton (died: 1903), Lelia Washington in 1903 (died: 1936), and Elsie Washington in 1943. In 1906, he received the signs of speaking in tongues. This caused a split with C P. JONES, and his movement was born. Mason lived in Memphis, TN. He was popular with white Pentecostals.

Ole K. Hallesby

Aug. 5, 1879
Aremark, Norway

Nov. 22, 1961
Oslo, Norway

Lutheran theologian and writer. Converted in 1902, Hallesby served as professor of theology at the Free Faculty of Theology Seminary, 1909–51. He became a champion of Lutheran orthodoxy in Norway. Hallesby was arrested in 1943 and imprisoned until the end of the war, opposing German occupation of Norway, 1940–45. He wrote many devotional books that have been translated into various languages. Throughout his life, he opposed liberal churchmen. Hallesby wrote 67 books, including *Christian Dogmatics* (1920) and *Christian Ethics* (1928). His most famous work was *Prayer* (1931), with more than 50 printings.

Gordon C. Davis

June 29, 1896
Hallstead, Pennsylvania

Dec. 7, 1961
Bible School Park, New York

President of Practical Bible Training School, 1934–61. Upon the death of his father, John Davis, Gordon assumed the leadership. He was the school's registrar, treasurer, and superintendent of men. Davis personally gave separate speech and vocal lessons to each senior student. He married Hazel Bowden on June 16, 1920. Davis was superintendent of the school, 1925–34. He delivered the school from indebtedness on May 25, 1944. He died from a lung tumor.

Lillian H. Trasher

Sept. 27, 1887
Jacksonville, Florida

Dec. 17, 1961
Assiout, Egypt

Missionary to Egypt. Lillian was converted from Catholicism as a teen. Lillian worked in a North Carolina orphanage. In 1910, she broke off her wedding engagement ten days before, and went to Egypt. She never married. Trasher started an orphanage in Assiout, 230 miles south of Cairo. She joined the Assemblies of God in 1919. Her work continued to develop until 1954. She had over 1,200 in her "family." A Moslem official once said, "God will take her to paradise."

Arlo A. Brown

April 15, 1883
Sunbeam, Illinois

Dec. 19, 1961
Wilmington, Delaware

Dean of Drew University Theological Seminary, Madison, NJ 1929–34 and first president of Association of Theological Schools, 1936–38. Brown married Grace Lindale on February 14, 1914. He served in various positions, 1907–14. He was superintendent of teacher training for the Board of Sunday Schools of the Methodist Church (1914–21), and was president of the University of Chattanooga (1921–29). Brown was president of Drew University, 1929–48, but in 1934, a separate leader for the dean position was created. Brown's writings range from *Studies in Christian Living* (1914) to *Youth and Christian Living* (1929). He was buried in Chestertown, MD.

Kenneth S. Wuest

Dec. 16, 1893
Chicago, Illinois

Dec. 27, 1961
Oak Park, Illinois

One of the great Greek teachers of all time, his classes stimulated students (including this editor) at Moody Bible Institute, 1929–58. He taught Bible and authored 20 books. Wuest married Jeanett on December 26, 1924. He was converted in a German Methodist Church in Chicago. He attended Wheaton Bible Church in Illinois. Wuest died from a malignant tumor.

Campbell B. Smith

1900
Eganville, Ontario, Canada

Dec. 30, 1961
Napanee, Ontario, Canada

General superintendent of Pentecostal Assemblies of Canada, 1945–1952. Smith was converted to the Pentecostal movement (1924), and attended Pentecostal Bible College (1926). He was ordained in 1928 and married Beulah Argue in July, 1928. Smith pastored in Saskatchewan, Ontario and British Columbia. He was twice president of Eastern Pentecostal Bible College, 1940–44 and 1958–61. Smith died in an automobile crash.

Hiram A. Boaz

Dec. 18, 1866
Murray, Kentucky

Jan. 2, 1962
Dallas, Texas

Bishop in the Methodist Episcopal Church, South, 1922–39, and in the Methodist Church, 1939–62. Boaz married Carrie Browne on October 2, 1894. He pastored in Georgetown, Ft. Worth, Abilene, and Dublin (all in Texas), 1889–1902. From 1902–11 and 1913–18, he was president of Polytechnic College (Texas Women's College in 1913), Fort Worth. In 1920, he became the president of South Methodist University, then served as bishop in Japan, Korea, Liberia, China, Arkansas, Oklahoma, and Texas.

Edgar J. Goodspeed

Oct. 23, 1871
Quincy, Illinois

Jan. 13, 1962
Los Angeles, California

Baptist NT educator, known for a complete translation of the Bible. From 1898–1900, Goodspeed traveled to Europe and the Middle East. He was active in collating the NT Greek manuscripts in America, 1898–1907. He married Elfelda Bond on December 3, 1901. He was associated with the University of Chicago (1900–37) and was the chairman of the NT department (1923–37). His translation was known as *Goodspeed's Complete Bible* (1939), preceded by his popular New Testament in 1923. Goodspeed taught at the University of California, Los Angeles, 1938–43. He wrote many works during the last 20 years of his life, including *Papyri from the Cairo Museum* (1902) to *Matthew* (1953).

George Jeffreys

Feb. 28, 1889
Nantyffylon, Wales

Jan. 26, 1962
Clapham, England

Founder and leader of Elim Foursquare Gospel Alliance (Elim Pentecostal Church). Jeffreys was converted on November 20, 1904, at Shiloh Chapel. In 1915, he formed the Elim Evangelistic band in Monaghan. Jeffreys was an evangelist, 1925–34, and saw great results. He worked widely in Switzerland, the Netherlands, Sweden, and France. In 1940, he founded the Bible-Pattern Church Fellowship.

Elmer F. McCarty

Feb. 28, 1875
Coopersville, Michigan

Feb. 3, 1962
Seattle, Washington

Director of Wesleyan Methodist Church in America (Wesleyan Church in 1968) **World Missions, 1923–43.** McCarty was converted at age 17 and served WMC for 67 years. He married Susan Casler in 1907 (died: 1936), then Margaret Randall in 1941. He served as pastor and Michigan conference president. He was also a missionary to Sierra Leone, West Africa, for four years.

F. Townley Lord

Oct. 27, 1893
Burnley, England

Feb. 9, 1962
Greenville, South Carolina

President of Baptist World Alliance, 1950–55. Lord married Sarah Entwisle on June 16, 1917. He pastored English churches (1916–30) and at Bloomsbury Central Baptist, London (1930–58). He was a professor of religion at Furman University, Greenville, SC, from 1958–62. A film, *Generous Spirit* brought him most of his recognition. Lord served as the editor of the *Baptist Times* (1941–56) in London and authored several books ranging from *Man and His Character* (1926) to *You Can Master Life* (1955).

Clyde H. Dennis

Nov. 29, 1912
Fort Dodge, Iowa

Feb. 14, 1962
Los Angeles, California

Founder and first president of Good News Publishers, Westchester, IL 1937–62. Converted at age 18 at a Plymouth Brethren Bible Conference in Centerville, IA, Dennis stood as a pioneer in the development of colorful gospel tracts. His company circled the globe with tracts. Dennis married Muriel Benson on June 12, 1937. One day in Minneapolis, he bought enough paper to make 40,000 tracts for $20. In three months, the tracts were all distributed. Dennis moved to Evanston, IL in 1940 and, using his bedroom as his office, started the Tract Club of America. They moved to California in 1953 because of health reasons.

Arthur J. Bowen

May 16, 1871
Swansea, Wales

Feb. 16, 1962
Brooklyn, New York

Secretary of South Africa General Mission (Africa Evangelical Fellowship in 1963, which merged into SIM in 1998), **1913–48, and president of IFMA, 1939–43.** Bowen sailed for Africa in 1892, but ill health forced him to return to Britain. He married Jessie Gibbs on March 20, 1897. He ministered in the Congo until 1903, then from 1903–13 pastored in Chatham, London, and Ontario. Bowen also worked closely with OSWALD J. SMITH.

J. Arthur Hamlett

April 10, 1882
near Henderson, Tennessee

Feb. 17, 1962
Kansas City, Missouri

Bishop of Colored (Christian in 1956) **Methodist Episcopal Church, 1922–62**; senior bishop, 1954–58, the name changing under his leadership. Hamlett pastored in West Tennessee and Kansas City, MO. He married Lena A. Hercey in 1904 and founded Phillips School of Theology at Lane College (Interdenominational Theological Seminary in 1959). He attended the Annual Conference, 1906–14, and edited the *Christian Index* (1914–22).

Lida S. Leech

May 12, 1873
Mayville, New Jersey

March 4, 1962
Long Beach, California

Wrote about 500 gospel songs, including "Someday He'll Make It Plain to Me" (music by ADAM GEIBEL). Lida wrote the lyrics and music to "God's Way Is the Best Way," and "One Moment in Heaven." During her childhood, she lived in the Cape May and Court House, NJ. Lida was the organist at Bethany Methodist Church in Camden, NJ. She traveled widely as a pianist at evangelistic meetings. She moved to Hollywood, CA, in 1944 with her husband.

William T. Milliken

Jan. 4, 1871
Cargill, Ontario, Canada

March 13, 1962
Portland, Oregon

President of Western Conservative Baptist Seminary, Portland, OR 1930–45. Milliken came to the United States in 1896 and married Emily Mosher on May 4, 1896 (died: February 4, 1942). He pastored in Mapleton, St. Paul, and Park Rapids, MN; Fort Collins, CO; Detroit, MI; and Oregon City and Salem, OR, from 1896–1923. Milliken served as the director of religious education for the Oregon Baptist Convention (1922–29) and pastored the Grace Church, Portland, OR (1931–46).

George K. Harris

Feb. 17, 1887
Winona, Minnesota

March 14, 1962
Toronto, Ontario, Canada

Baptist missionary to China. Harris graduated from MBI in 1916 and went to the field the same year to work with China Inland Mission. For 34 years, he worked in Sining, Tsinghai. In 1950, he went to Thailand where he worked with the Malay people. Harris retired in 1960, after 45 years of work with Moslems. He buried two children in northwest China and his wife in Thailand. He wrote *How to Lead Moslems to Christ* (1946).

William Y. Bell

Feb. 23, 1887
Memphis, Tennessee

April 10, 1962
South Boston, Virginia

Bishop of Colored (Christian in 1956) **Methodist Episcopal Church, 1938–62: senior bishop, 1958–62.** He was ordained deacon (1912) and elder (1915). Bell married Annabelle Compton (1913) and later Ruby Hall (1948). Following World War II, he was the dynamic pastor of the Williams Institutional Church in Harlem. He lived in South Boston, VA.

Henry B. Washburn

Dec. 2, 1869
Worcester, Massachusetts

April 25, 1962
Cambridge, Massachusetts

President of Episcopal Divinity School, Cambridge, MA 1920–40. Washburn was ordained deacon (1894) and priest (1896). He was rector at St. Mark's Church in Worcester, MA from 1898–1908. Washburn married Edith Colgate on May 20, 1908 (died: July 29, 1952). He became professor of church history at EDS, 1908–40. Washburn was the executive secretary of the Army and Navy Commission of his denomination, 1941–46. He authored several books.

Loyal H. Larimer

Oct. 27, 1869
New Cumberland, Ohio

April 26, 1962
Wilmington, Delaware

Dean of Hamma Divinity School (Trinity Lutheran Seminary, Columbus, OH in 1978), **Springfield, OH 1924–40.** Larimer began preaching in Shanesville, OH in 1879. He married May Rees on August 14, 1902 (died: 1920). Larimer served at Hamma Divinity School as a professor of OT languages and literature (1908–22), and served as a professor of homiletics and practical theology (1923–45). He lived most of his life in Springfield, OH.

John W. Beardslee, Jr.

July 11, 1879
Constantine, Michigan

May 10, 1962
New Brunswick, New Jersey (?)

President of New Brunswick (NJ) Theological Seminary, 1935–47. He was ordained into the Reformed Church in 1910. Beardslee married Francis Davis on August 8, 1912. He was a professor at Hope College (1905–13); at Western Theological Seminary, Holland, MI (1913–17); a professor at New Brunswick teaching Greek and New Testament exegesis (1917–49) and was the dean in charge of New Testament (1949–53).

Meredith G. Standley

1877
Cincinnati, Ohio

May 13, 1962
Miami, Florida

President of God's Bible School, Cincinnati, OH 1911–49. Standley was an early evangelist with the Pilgrim Holiness Church. He married Bessie Queen in 1902. He was the editor of *God's Revivalist* (1902–50). Through the years, Standley and his wife worked with several local rescue missions and a home for unwed mothers. He left the school under a cloud (1950) with hints of financial irregularities over the use of mission funds (1906) and then again in the 1940s, when large amounts of funds raised by the school's supporters could not be accounted for. He wrote his defense and autobiography in *My Life as I Have Lived It for God and Others*. He continued to preach in Pilgrim Holiness churches in his later life. Standley's wife died in Miami on April 11, 1960.

James C. Moore

May 2, 1988
Draketown, Georgia

June 1, 1962
Ashburn, Georgia

Wrote the lyrics and music to "Where We'll Never Grow Old." He was ordained into the Baptist ministry and was a pastor in six Georgia towns and Hawthorne, FL. Moore served for two years as president of the Southwest Singing Convention. He wrote over 500 gospel songs.

Noah E. Byers

July 26, 1873
Sterling, Illinois

June 15, 1962
Decatur, Georgia

First president of Goshen (IN) College, 1903–13. He was the principal, 1895–1903, before becoming the president of GC. Byers married Emma LaFevre in 1898 (died: 1946), then married Edna Hanley. Byers was on the board of directors as the chairman of Elkhart (IN) Institute, 1898–1903, which began as a private and commercial school. He served as the president of Bluffton (OH) College, 1913–38. Byers was a pioneer in Mennonite education endeavers.

Helmut R. Niebuhr

Sept. 3, 1894
Wright City, Missouri

July 5, 1962
Greenfield, Massachusetts

Evangelical and Reformed (United Church of Christ) **theologian and pastor**. Niebuhr examined theological matters in the light of sociology, history, and psychology. He married Florence Mittendorff on June 9, 1920. He pastored in St. Louis (1916–18), served at Eden Seminary (1919–22 and 1927–31), and was president of Elmhurst (IL) College (1924–27). Niebuhr was a professor of Christian social ethics and theology at Yale Divinity School, 1931–62. His writings range from *Social Sources of Denominationalism* (1929) to *The Responsible Self* (1963). Other writing included: *The Meaning of Revelation* (1941), *Radical Monotheism, Christ and Culture* (1951) and *Western Culture* (1960).

Samuel H. Gapp

March 28, 1873
Egg Harbor City, New Jersey

Aug. 9, 1962
Bethlehem, Pennsylvania

President of Moravian Church in NA (North), 1930–46. He was ordained in the Moravian Church, became a deacon (1894), presbyter (1900), and bishop (1942). Gapp pastored at St. Charles, MN; Elizabeth, NJ; and Emmaus, PA from 1899–1905. Gapp married Rosina Vogt, on September 5, 1900 (died: May 27, 1961). He taught at Moravian College (1905–18); pastored the Bethlehem Church (1918–25) and headed Moravian Missions (1925–46).

Clarence Bouma

Nov. 30, 1891
Harlingen, Netherlands

Aug. 12, 1962
Grand Rapids, Michigan

First president of Evangelical Theological Society, 1949–50. Bouma married Tessie Luidens on September 29, 1918, and was ordained in the Christian Reformed Church in 1923. He pastored in Passaic, NJ from 1923–24, then went to Calvin Theological Seminary (1924), and began to teach ethics and apologetics (1926). He was associated with the school most of his life.

The Saints Go Marching In

Odiloon Van Steenberghe

1890   Aug. 25, 1962

Codirector (with JOHN C. WINSTON) **of Belgian Gospel Mission, 1936–59**, which merged into Greater Europe Mission in 1971. He married Victorine Modave on January 29, 1910. The Lord protected him during heavy fighting in WWI in 1914. By years' end, he knew he was converted. During the 1920s, he held evangelistic crusades, distributed Scriptures, and traveled much in his country, which was void of Christianity. By 1934, there were 100 workers scattered in 66 provinces. After the founder, Ralph Norton, passed on, the mantle fell on Van Steenberghe. World War II turmoil and the death of his wife October 3, 1954, were additional trials. He died of a heart attack on a train station platform.

Safara A. Witmar

Jan. 31, 1899   Sept. 11, 1962
Grabill, Indiana   Fort Wayne, Indiana

President of Fort Wayne (IN) Bible College (Summit Christian College in 1990, Taylor University), **1945–57; of Accrediting Association of Bible Colleges, 1952–53; and its executive secretary, 1953–62**. Witmar married Edith McLean on February 28, 1924. He was ordained by the Missionary Church Association. Witmar taught at FWBC (1924–32), and served as a dean (1935–43). While he was the dean, the college expanded and was accredited by the North Central Association. He was an Air Force chaplain, 1943–45.

Robbins W. Barstow

Feb. 18, 1890   Sept. 17, 1962
Glastonbury, Connecticut   Stamford, Connecticut

President of Hartford (CT) Theological Seminary, 1930–44. Barstow married Dorothy Rogers on October 13, 1916. He was ordained as a Congregationalist in 1916, pastored at Woodstock, VT (1917–19); Concord, NH (1920–23); and at the First Church, Madison, WI (1924–30). Barstow was on the staff of the Church World Service (1944–50), of NCC (1951–52) and was the director of Overseas Union Church (1953–59). He wrote *Getting Acquainted with God* (1928).

Charles E. Maddry

April 10, 1876   Sept. 17, 1962
Chapel Hill, North Carolina   Chapel Hill, North Carolina

Executive secretary of Southern Baptist Convention Missions, 1933–44. When Maddry became secretary, the board was more than $1 million in debt. When he left, there was no indebtedness for the first time since its founding in 1845. He was ordained in 1902 and married Emma Parker on May 2, 1906. He pastored in Kentucky, North Carolina, and Texas until 1920, then served as the corresponding secretary at the NC State Convention (1921–26) and as general secretary of the denomination (1926–32). He also pastored the FBC, Hillsboro, NC (1951–57). He wrote several books from *Day Dawn in Yorubolland* (1939) to *Charles E. Maddry*, an autobiography. He died following a heart attack, which occurred August 30, 1962. He is buried in Richmond, VA.

Harold S. Bender

July 18, 1897   Sept. 21, 1962
Elkhart, Indiana   Chicago, Illinois

First dean of Goshen (IN) Biblical Seminary (Associated Biblical Mennonite Seminary, Elkhart, IN in 1990), **1945–62**. Bender married Elizabeth Horsch on May 9, 1923 (died: 1988). He began to teach at Goshen College (1924), and became dean (1931), before going to the seminary. In

1927, he founded the Mennonite Historical Society, and became editor of the *Mennonite Quarterly Review*. Bender was president of the Mennonite World Conference, 1952–62, and the general editor of the *Mennonite Encyclopedia* (1955–59). He was reared in a Christian home and had two daughters. Bender died of cancer.

Clyde J. Kennedy

July 2, 1907
Halifax, Nova Scotia, Canada

Sept. 22, 1962
Mooreston, New Jersey

President of American Council of Christian Churches, 1959–61. Kennedy pastored at Calvary Bible Presbyterian Church, Glendale, CA (1939–57, and in Tacoma, WA (1957–60). Ordained as a Bible Presbyterian, he was the president of Shelton College from 1960 until his death. His wife's name was Dorothy. On May 17, 1962, a tumor was found on his brain, and he died shortly thereafter.

John T. Brenner

July 11, 1874
Hutisford, Wisconsin

Sept. 30, 1962
Bay City, Michigan

President of Evangelical Lutheran Joint Synod of Wisconsin and other states (WELS in 1959), **1933–53**. Brenner was a pastor in Milwaukee, WI, and served on various Wisconsin Synod boards. He possessed an unswerving devotion to the truth. He shaped the fiscal policies the WELS still holds today. When he was elected president, the synod was deeply in debt, and the depression was in full swing. Under his leadership, the synod pulled itself out of debt and adopted a "balanced budget" policy (don't-borrow-to-pay-the-coal-bill principle).

Stephen J. Corey

April 29, 1873
Rolla, Missouri

Oct. 11, 1962
Carmichael, California

President of College of the Bible [Lexington (KY) Theological Seminary in 1965], **1938–45, 1948–49, and of United Christian Missionary Society** (Christian Churches/Disciples of Christ/Missions), **1930–38**. Corey married Edith Webster on October 1, 1901. He pastored in Rochester, NY (1898–1903) and also served in missions executive posts (1903–30). He wrote several books related to missions, 1910–38, from *Missions in the Sunday School* (1910) to *The Wilder Range of World Missions* (1937).

Harold C. Etter

Dec. 28, 1895
Windsor, Ontario, Canada

Oct. 19, 1962
Near Chehalis, Washington

Founder and first Director of International Christian Leprosy Mission, 1943–62. Etter went to Peking, China in 1924. During his furlough, he served as high school principal for five years while working among Japanese residents in British Columbia. He married Jean Teebels (November 30, 1899–June 26, 1978) on January 1, 1930 in Penticton, BC. Etter was associated with Christian leprosy work for 38 years, which he founded in September, 1943. He was traveling from Portland, OR to Vancouver, BC, when he stepped out of his car (perhaps out of gas) and was struck by oncoming traffic and killed instantly.

Isaac H. Meredith
March 21, 1872 *Nov. 2, 1962*
Norristown, Pennsylvania Orlando, Florida

Composed music for "Beautiful Words of Jesus" (lyrics by ELIZA HEWITT). At 19, Meredith was challenged to write sacred music at Ocean Grove Assembly in New Jersey. He began his career as a soloist. He established his own Muller-Meredith publishing firm in New York City in 1893. He was the music director for many Methodist and Baptist churches. At times he was the song leader for BILLY SUNDAY and GYPSY SMITH. Meredith composed over 4,000 songs in his lifetime.

Henry B. Trimble
Dec. 26, 1885 *Nov. 13, 1962*
Hot Springs, Virginia Atlanta, Georgia

Dean of Candler School of Theology, Atlanta, GA 1936–53. Trimble was also their professor of homiletics, 1931–37. He married Martie Cargille in 1914. Trimble pastored Methodist churches in Haber Springs, AK (1910–11); Clarendon, AK (1911–12); Hot Springs, AK (1914–55); Fort Smith, AK (1915–17); Pine Bluff, AK (1918–22); Nashville, TN (1922–28); and Ashville, NC (1928–31). He wrote several books, ranging from *Stewardship* (1928) to *Every Creature* (1940).

Abraham B. Machlin
Dec. 24, 1891 *Nov. 16, 1962*
Mogilew, White Russia (Belarus) Winona Lake, Indiana

President of American Association for Jewish Evangelism (Friends of Israel in 2000), **1952–62, and Jewish evangelist**. He came to America in 1915, after fleeing Siberia (3,500 miles: 790 of them on a sled in winter). Machlin married Edna Hackstedt on February 13, 1920 (died: July 27, 1960). He was converted at LEOPOLD COHN's Williamsburg Mission in Brooklyn and directed the Buffalo (NY) Hebrew Christian Mission, 1920–44. In 1944, the AAJE was founded in Chicago, and he became its leader. He was also the editor of *Salvation* and traveled, speaking in prophecy conferences.

Bill J. Carle
1905 *Nov. 17, 1962*
near Milwaukee, Wisconsin St. Louis, Missouri

One of the great soloists of his day. Carle sang in a Lutheran Church in Columbus, WI, as a child. He learned to sing in five languages, performing in many places ranging from the Chicago Symphony to the NYC stage. He sang three times at the White House and also for KING GEORGE VI. Carle married Ethel Brocke (Dixie). Roy McKeown of Los Angeles YFC led him to Christ on April 21, 1951. Carle was very active in Youth for Christ and Christian recordings. He died of a heart attack.

Ned B. Stonehouse
March 19, 1902 *Nov. 18, 1962*
Grand Rapids, Michigan Philadelphia, Pennsylvania

President of Evangelical Theological Seminary, 1957. Stonehouse married Winigrace Bylsma on September 1, 1927 (died: March, 1958) and Margaret S. Robinson on May 30, 1959. He was an instructor at Westminster Theological Seminary of Philadelphia, 1929–62. He was dean of the faculty at WTS, 1955–62. He was prominent in the Orthodox Presbyterian Church, 1936 on. He was also the editor of *International Commentary on the New Testament* (9 vols., 1951–62) and several other books, from *The Witness of Matthew and Mark* to *Christ* (1944) to *Paul* (1957). He is buried in Grand Rapids, MI.

Helena P. M. Wilhelmina

Aug. 31, 1880 — The Hague, Netherlands
Nov. 28, 1962 — Apeldoorn, Netherlands

Queen of the Netherlands for 50 years, Sept. 6, 1898–1948. Her full name was Helena Pauline Maria Wilhelmina. She married Heinrich Ernst on Feb. 7, 1901 (died: July 3, 1934). Her credits include the establishment of the World Court at The Hague, the revision of education laws, social legislation, and self-government to the East Indies. She was in exile in England in WWII. Her daughter, Juliana, succeeded Wilhelmina upon her abdication. She is buried in Dolft, Netherlands.

Jack Shuler

July 12, 1918 — Prairie, Texas
Dec. 9, 1962 — Sherman Oaks, California

Powerful evangelist of his day. He held many large crusades throughout the nation, 1946–60. Shuler was the son of BOB SHULER. Don DeVos and Herb Hoover were his songleaders for the crusades. During his early years, he pursued a film career. He was converted in Cleveland, TN as a Bob Jones University student. Since 1946, Shuler held citywide crusades with crowds up to 18,000. He died of a lung disease.

Norman A. Madson

Nov. 16, 1886 — Manitowoc, Wisconsin
Dec. 10, 1962 — Mankato, Minnesota

First president of Bethany Lutheran Theological Seminary, Mankato, MN 1946–57. Madson married Elsie Haaskenson on August 31, 1918, and they had seven children. He pastored in Bode, IA, 1920–25; Chicago, IL; and Hibbing and Princeton, MN. Madson was a chaplain in WWI. He was the president of the Norwegian Synod of the American Evangelical Lutheran Church (Evangelical Lutheran Synod), 1934 and 1941–46. He wrote several books from *At Bethlehem's Manger* (1935) to *The Word that Can Never Die* (1966). He was the eleventh of 14 children.

Henry J. Kuiper

Dec. 22, 1885 — Grand Rapids, Michigan
Dec. 12, 1962 — Grand Rapids, Michigan

President of Evangelical Press Association, 1950–52. Kuiper married Cornelia Freyling. He was ordained in Luctor, KA; pastored in Holland, MI (1910–13); Chicago, IL (1913–19); Broadway Avenue Reformed Church (1919–29); and Neland Avenue Christian Reformed Church (1929–44), the last two located in Grand Rapids, MI. Kuiper was the editor of the *Banner* for many years. He began as their part-time editor (1929), and became full-time in 1944.

H. Lee Burtchin

Aug. 15, 1893 — Lima, Ohio
Dec. 28, 1962 — Lima, Ohio

President of Christian Union, Chilicothe, OH 1938–53. Burtchin was licensed in the Christian Union, September 2, 1917. He pastored Christian Union Churches about six years, then served several Methodist churches until 1930, before returning to the Christian Union. His pastorates were mostly in Ohio, with some in Indiana and Missouri. He married Grace Barber on March 18, 1917 (died: January 4, 1930), Ruth Bowsher on October 12, 1933 (died: February 6, 1957), and Doris Stull on May 18, 1958 (died: September 4, 1985). He died of a stroke in a local hospital.

Robert S. Kerr

Sept. 11, 1896
Ada, Oklahoma

Jan. 1, 1963
Washington, D.C.

Governor of Oklahoma, 1943–1947, and U.S. Senator, 1948–63. Kerr married Reba Shelton on Dec. 5, 1919 (died: February 12, 1924) and Grayce Breen on December 26, 1925. He was heavily involved in the Oklahoma oil industry, 1926–43. Kerr had great influence in the 87th Congress. He was a Democrat, a Missionary Baptist, a Mason, and a spiritual political leader. Born in a log cabin, he became a millionaire when oil was discovered on his property. He gave nearly $1 million to Oklahoma Baptist University. Kerr died of a heart attack while talking to his physician.

Arthur J. Brown

Dec. 3, 1856
Holliston, Massachusetts

Jan. 11, 1963
New York, New York

Presbyterian clergyman and mission executive. Brown is one of the oldest men included in this compilation, having died at age 106. Brown married Jennie Thomas on July 10, 1883 (died Dec. 24, 1945). He pastored from 1883–95 in Ripon, WI; Oak Park, IL; and Portland, OR. He was a clergyman and author and was involved as a secretary with Presbyterian Church Missions, 1895–1929. His writings range from *Reports from Visits to Missions* (1902) to *Centenarian Memoirs* (1956). *The Foreign Missionary* (1907) was his best of 16 books. Brown was a leader and participant in numerous ecumenical endeavors.

Roland Q. Leavell

Dec. 21, 1891
Oxford, Mississippi

Jan. 15, 1963
Chattanooga, Tennessee

President of New Orleans (LA) Baptist Theological Seminary, 1946–58. Leavell married Lilian Yarborough on June 26, 1923. He pastored at First Baptist Church, Oxford, MS (1919–23); in Picayan, MS (1925–27); in Gainesville, GA (1927–37); and in Tampa, FL (1942–46). He served as superintendent of Evangelism Home Mission Board of the Southern Baptist Convention, 1937–42. Leavell toured many mission fields. NOBTS relocated to new facilities in 1953. His 15 books range from *Are You an Ashamed Workman?* (1932) to *The Christian Business* (1964). He died while he was conducting a series of studies in the Gospel of Matthew at the FBC in Chattanooga.

C. Harold Lowden

Oct. 12, 1883
Burlington, New Jersey

Feb. 27, 1963
Collinswood, New Jersey

Hymn writer who gave us the music for "Living for Jesus" (lyrics by T. O. CHISHOLM) **and "Christ Is Not a Disappointment"** (lyrics by C.W. Waggoner). Lowden wrote the lyrics and music for "I've Found Real Joy," "Walking with Jesus," and "Proclaim It Wherever You Go." He began writing songs at twelve years of age and played the violin. Twelve years later, he served as the musical editor for the Evangelical and Reformed Church Board, establishing his own business in Camden, NJ. For eight years, he taught music at the Bible Institute of Pennsylvania in Philadelphia. Lowden served as minister of music for the Linden Baptist Church, Camden, NJ, for 28 years. He retired in 1961.

Sherwood Eddy

Jan. 19, 1871
Leavenworth, Kansas

March 3, 1963
Jacksonville, Illinois

Evangelical YMCA executive. Eddy went to India where he was national secretary (1896–1911), and YMCA secretary for all of Asia (1911–31). Early on, he was primarily an evangelist to students in Asia, working with JOHN MOTT and ROBERT E. SPEER, traveling widely, 1907–48. During WWI days, he was in Europe as a secretary with British and American armies. From 1926–46, he conducted seminars on European leadership. His student-orientation work was in social reform, which caused some to consider him liberal and a contributor to the decline of the spiritual life in the YMCA. His many books range from *India Awakening* (1911) to *Why I Believe* (1957). Later in life, he gave social religion more time, making himself ambassador for personal and social salvation. He wrote over 30 books, and was influenced to social religion through the writings of WALTER RAUSCHENBUSH and REINHOLD NIEBUHR. He married Maude Arden in 1898 (died: 1945) and Louise Gates in 1946.

Garfield B. Oxnam

Aug. 14, 1891
Sonora, California

March 12, 1963
White Plains, New York

Controversial Methodist bishop, 1936 on, serving as president of Federal Council of Churches (NCC in 1950), 1944–46, and World Council of Churches, 1948–54. Oxnam married Ruth Fisher on August 19, 1914. He pastored the Church of All Nations, Los Angeles, CA from 1919–27. Oxnam became president of DePaul University, Greencastle, IN 1928–36. As bishop, he served in Omaha, NE (1936–39); Boston, MA (1939–44); New York (1944–52); and Washington (1952–63). In 1953, his support for social justice movements brought him before a House Committee from Congress where he was falsely accused of being a Communist. He retired in 1960 afflicted with Parkinson's disease. He is buried in Cambridge, MA. He wrote books from *The Mexican in Los Angeles* (1920) to *A Testimony of Faith* (1958).

Henrietta C. Mears

Oct. 23, 1890
Fargo, North Dakota

March 18, 1963
Beverly Hills, California

Outstanding leader in Christian education and founder and first president of Gospel Light Publications, Ventura, CA 1933–49. Upon graduation from the University of Minnesota in 1913, Mears began to teach high school chemistry. She was the chief executive and teacher of the college department at the First Presbyterian Church, Hollywood, CA, from 1928–63. Mears built their Sunday School and youth ministries to one of the largest in the country with 6,500 students. In less than three years, the Sunday School grew from 1,450 to 5,000 in 1930. Of these, 500 would later go into Christian work. Mears was converted at age seven via the FBC, Minneapolis, MN, and Pastor WILLIAM RILEY. Later, while teaching Sunday School at this church, her class of 18-year-old girls grew from 5 to 500. She founded Forest Home Christian Conference Center (1938) and Hollywood Christian Group (1949). Mears greatly influenced BILL BRIGHT, RICHARD HALVORSON, and LOUIS H. EVANS JR. She cofounded the National Sunday School Association in 1946. Mears received an honorary doctorate from Bob Jones University in 1949. In 1961 she founded Gospel Literature International (GLINT). Mears never married. She lived with the BRIGHTS from 1951 until she died of a heart attack in her sleep.

George Hodges (2)

July 8, 1905
Hilliard, Florida

April 8, 1963
Jacksonville, Florida

One of the great Baptist Bible Fellowship pastors of his generation. Hodges' life would end in a bizarre scenario of murder. He married Maude Blountses on June 25, 1925. In 1927, he was led to Christ by a lay preacher, Henry Durden. In 1928, he surrendered to preach and pastored in Folkston, Homeland, and Lake Park, GA, until 1936. In 1936, he began his Jacksonville ministry at Glenwood Baptist Church. By 1938, the crowds packed the place. When the church refused to build, he went ten miles away and started the Beaver Street Church in 1939, with 34 members. The work grew so that additional buildings were built in 1946, 1951, and 1958. Attendance was reaching 2,500 and soon there were 5,000 members. In 1953, his 15-year-old, Elizabeth, was killed in a car accident. He was president of BBF, 1957–59. All eight of his children were in the Lord's work. One Monday morning, he was found dead from gunshot wounds in the church parking lot. A woman in the area pled insanity, and was placed into an asylum. She died a few months later. Three thousand people attended the funeral, with the procession stretching ten miles.

Roy L. Smith

Jan. 28, 1887
Nickerson, Kansas

April 20, 1963

Methodist writer, preacher, editor, and publisher. Although Smith grew up in a poor home, twelve universities gave him honorary degrees. He married Mabel Conley on April 6, 1908, and pastored from 1908–21 in Kansas, Illinois, Minnesota, and California. He pastored First Church of Los Angeles, 1932–40 (world's largest Methodist church). He wrote over 40 books and served as the editor of *Christian Advocate* (1940–48). Smith died on the way to a preaching assignment. He wrote *New Lights for Old Lamps* (1953) among others.

Julia Cady Cory

Nov. 9, 1882
New York, New York

May 1, 1963
Englewood, New Jersey

Hymn writer of such as "We Praise Thee, O God, Our Redeemer." Julia married Robert H. Cory in 1911. Converted after hearing devotions at a Valentine's party on Feb. 14, 1920, she attended Brick Presbyterian Church of NYC. At age eight, she began to write hymns, writing her most famous hymn before age 20 at the request of an organist for a Thanksgiving song. She was a well-known architect in NYC and an active church member.

Aiden W. Tozer

April 21, 1897
La Jose, Pennsylvania

May 13, 1963
Toronto, Ontario, Canada

Spiritual giant of the Christian and Missionary Alliance Church. Tozer was converted in 1915 listening to a street preacher in Akron, OH. He was reared on a farm and always found time to read. He began witnessing and studying the Bible immediately after his salvation. Tozer married Ada Pfautz on April 26, 1918; they had seven children. He pastored in Morgantown, WV; Toledo, OH; Indianapolis, IN (1920–28); Southside Alliance Church, Chicago (1928–59); and The Avenue Road Church in Toronto, Ontario (1959–63). He served as the editor of *The Alliance Witness* (1950–63). Some of his 30 books were translated into 15 languages. His books range from *Wingspread* (1943) to *The Knowledge of the Holy* (1961). *The Pursuit of God* (1948) was a classic. He died of a sudden heart attack.

Joseph B. Walton

May 29, 1885
Ercildoun, Pennsylvania

May 24, 1963
Swarthmore, Pennsylvania

General secretary of Friends General Conference, Philadelphia, 1915–51. He taught at Friends School in Wilmington, DE (1905–06) and Philadelphia, (1906–07). Walton married Louis Haviland on August 17, 1910. Walton served as financial secretary for New York Friends meetings (1907–10); financial secretary, Charity Orthodox Society, NYC (1910–11); and graduate secretary of Student YMCA, New York City (1911–14).

Thomas J. Bach

May 22, 1881
Flaunskjold, Denmark

June 12, 1963
Yucaipa, California

Director of TEAM, 1928–46. Bach was converted at age 18 through a tract he received in Copenhagen, where he was studying engineering. Bach married Anna Anderson on November 25, 1905; they had five children. He was a missionary to Venezuela under Scandinavian Alliance Mission (TEAM) 1905–26. Bach traveled to different countries for many years as the mission's representative before taking on its leadership. He took a brief vacation, flying to California on June 8. Suffering from hiccups, he dropped dead on the lawn while returning to his guest apartment. Bach was a member of the Evangelical Covenant Church.

William J. Trent

Dec. 30, 1873
Charlotte, North Carolina

June 12, 1963
Salisbury, North Carolina (?)

President of Livingstone College, Salisbury, NC 1925–57. He served in the Spanish American War, 1898, then was president of the Greenville (TN) Secondary School, 1899–1900. Trent married Annabelle Mitchell on April 3, 1904 (died: 1907), Maggie Tate on June 20, 1909 (died: June 1, 1934), Hattie Covington on December 22, 1935 (died: 1952), and Cleota Collins on June 19, 1953. Trent served as general secretary of the YMCA, Ashville, NC (1900–11), and was executive secretary of YMCA, Atlanta, GA (1911–25).

Otto E. Dick

March 16, 1901
Elwood, Indiana

July 1, 1963
Rochester, Minnesota

President of Oregon (IL) Bible College (Atlanta in 1991), **1949–63.** Dick specialized in English and educational administration work. He taught school and served in school administration in Indiana for over 20 years. Dick was a member of the Church of God, Hillisburg, IN. In 1946, he resigned as principal of Circleville (OH) High School to move to Oregon, IL, where he became an instructor at Oregon Bible College. In 1948, he became registrar and the following year superintendent (president) of the school. Dick died after undergoing open-heart surgery. His wife's name was Blanche.

Hakon Jorgensen

Oct. 12, 1881
Nyborremoeh, Denmark

July 16, 1963
Seattle, Washington

President of Danish Evangelical Lutheran Church (LCA, ELCA in 1988), **1926–36.** Jorgensen came to America in 1897 and married Theresa Grumstrup on October 29, 1908 (died: 1959). Jorgensen pastored in Oakhill, IA (1908–10); Tyler, MN (1910–14); Heiland, SD (1914–21); the Nain Lutheran Church, Newell, IA (1921–48); and Cordova, NE (1948–57). He died in a Seattle retirement home, but was buried in Newell.

John Carlsen

Sept. 29, 1899
Tromso, Norway

July 18, 1963
Minneapolis, Minnesota

First director of World Mission Prayer League, 1938–46, and Global Gospel Fellowship 1953–63. Carlsen was a mighty prayer warrior and one of the great Lutherans of his generation. Carlsen went to Bolivia in 1938 and directed the mission part of the time from Bolivia and other times from the home base. In 1947, he became an evangelist for the Evangelical Lutheran

Church. Through GGF, Carlsen continued a radio ministry, which he began in 1949. He established Indian outreaches in Arizona and Minneapolis, MN. He had several heart attacks leading to his death.

Arnold T. Ohrn

Jan. 22, 1889
Raymond, Wisconsin

July 31, 1963
Berkeley, California

General secretary of Baptist World Alliance, 1948–60. Ohrn married Elin Carlsson on June 21, 1919. He served as a professor at Norwegian Baptist Theological Seminary, Oslo (1918–41) and president (1946–48). He was the foreign missions secretary (1927–46), president (1932–48), and general secretary of the Baptist Union (1941–46). Ohrn worked with the underground church during WWII from 1941–46. He wrote *The Gospel* and the *Sermon on the Mount* (1939). He was a visitor with three other ministers to the Union of Socialist Republics in 1955. He is buried in Oslo, Norway.

Jesse M. Bader

April 15, 1886
Bader, Illinois

Aug. 19, 1963
New York, New York

Ecumenist and general secretary of the World Convention of Christian Churches of Christ (Disciples), 1930–63. Bader married Golda Elam on August 31, 1910, and pastored in Atchison, KS from 1911–18. He served as the secretary of Evangelism for the Disciples of Christ (1920–31), of FCC (1932–50), and NCC (1951–53). He was very active in WCC activities. Bader authored Evangelism in a Changing America (1957). Billy Graham credits him for encouraging him into ecumenical evangelism.

Ralph T. Davis

Feb. 11, 1895
East Orange, New Jersey

Aug. 19, 1963
Clermont, Florida

General Secretary of Africa Inland Mission, 1941–56, and president of IFMA, 1943–46, 1947–48, 1950–52, and 1956–59. Davis married Ellan Ortlieb on August 20, 1919. Raised in a Christian home, he served as a missionary to Africa under AIM from 1921–35, ministering in the Congo and French Republic of Africa. Davis assumed administrative duties with AIM, Brooklyn, NY 1936–41. Davis was frequently called on for counseling by other mission boards and was in constant demand as a missions speaker. He flew over 100,000 miles during his mission trips. He was active in mission leadership positions until 1962, serving as international general secretary, IGS, 1855–62. Davis died in his home of heart disease.

May Whittle Moody

March 20, 1870
Chicago, Illinois

Aug. 20, 1963
East Northfield, Massachusetts

Composed the music for "Moment by Moment" (1893) and "The Story of Jesus Can Never Grow Old" (lyrics of both by her father). May was the daughter of evangelist DAN WHITTLE and married Will Moody (son of D.L. MOODY) on Aug. 29, 1894. They had six children (two died in infancy). She lived in Northfield, MA where Will had charge of the schools. May had a beautiful voice and sang for both her father's and for D.L. MOODY's meetings.

Colby D. Hall

Dec. 29, 1875
Madisonville, Kentucky

Aug. 26, 1963
Fort Worth, Texas

First dean of Brite College of the Bible (Brite Divinity School in 1963), **1914–47**, a division of Texas Christian University, Ft. Worth, TX. Hall married Beatrice Tomlinson on Aug. 19, 1909. Ordained to the Disciples of Christ (1898), he was a pastor in Hillsboro, TX (1904–6); was educational secretary of TCU (1906–9); pastor in Waco, TX (1909–12); and professor of English

Bible at TCU (1912). He was dean of the University, 1920–43. He saw TCU grow from 13 students at Thorp Spring, to what it is today. His writings ranged from *A History of TCU* (1947) to *New Light Christians* (1959).

Guy W. Playfair

Sept. 12, 1882
Baldur, Manitoba, Canada

Sept. 10, 1963
Toronto, Ontario, Canada

Director of Sudan Interior Mission (SIM, Int.), 1943–57. Playfair was converted in a Methodist camp meeting. He was a well-known athlete (bicyclist, mile runner). He was a member of Moody Church and went to Africa in 1911 to develop a work in Nigeria. He became the field director for SIM in 1917, and saw that work grow dramatically. Playfair married Elizabeth Christie on April 12, 1916 (died at Jos, Nigeria), and Joyce Nethercott on October 20, 1926.

Walter R. MacDonald

Jan. 30, 1904
Gravenhurst, Ontario, Canada

Oct. 1, 1963
Westminster, Maryland

Evangelist known as "Happy Mac." MacDonald was on stage with Eddie Cantor who said, "Mac has the fastest feet in the world." He was master of ceremonies for Fred Waring's Pennsylvanians. His wife divorced him one month after their marriage, and from that time on, he remained single. He was led to the Lord by MA TAYLOR at Pacific Garden Mission on May 29, 1925, while in Chicago between engagements. When MacDonald discussed his multiple sins, MA TAYLOR simply said, "Calvary Covers It All," which she developed into a great gospel song. He saw over 20,000 people converted, including 15 preachers, during his evangelistic ministry, 1925–61. Complications from diabetes set in after he was stricken in a Baltimore meeting, Sunday, September 29, 1963.

Eugene B. Hawk

Sept. 6, 1881
Blountsville, Tennessee

Oct. 12, 1963
Dallas, Texas

President of Perkins School of Theology (SMU), Dallas, TX 1933–51. Hawk married Dora Patterson on April 9, 1912 (died: December 8, 1918) and Amanda Hawkins July 27, 1920. He was ordained a Methodist in 1911 and pastored in Fort Worth, TX (1916–20); Temple, TX (1920–22); Fort Worth, TX (1925–31); and Louisville, KY (1931–33). Hawk taught homiletics and ministerial efficiency at Perkins. He died suddenly.

Samuel M. Shoemaker

Dec. 27, 1893
Baltimore, Maryland

Oct. 30, 1963
Burnside, Maryland

Episcopal rector who emphasized one-to-one personal evangelism. Shoemaker was converted while with the YMCA in China, 1917–19. He served at Calvary Episcopal Church in New York City (1924–52) and Calvary Episcopal Church in Pittsburgh, PA (1952–62), where he reached the gold club crowd. Shoemaker helped laymen found Alcoholics Anonymous. He married Helen Smith on April 26, 1930. From 1932–41, he was active in the Moral Re-armament Movement. He is buried in Garrison, MD. He wrote 38 books including *Realizing Religion* (1921) to *Beginning Your Ministry* (1963). His most renowned was *Religion That Works* (1928).

Ernest M. Wadsworth

June 25, 1877
England

Nov. 14, 1963
Wheaton, Illinois

Director of Great Commission Prayer League from 1929 on. Wadsworth was known for his prayer life and community affairs activities. He pastored the Riverside Baptist Church in Buffalo,

NY from 1911–1930. He married Ella in 1895 (died: December 20, 1957). He then married Lillian Powers in 1958. Wadsworth visited the Holy Land in 1958. He broke his hip in 1961, after that, his health deteriorated rapidly. He was active in helping to found CBMC.

Clive S. Lewis

Nov. 29, 1898
near Belfast, Northern Ireland

Nov. 22, 1963
Oxford, England

Novelist, poet, and apologist. Lewis was one of the most popular authors in history. He was wounded in France in WWI in 1918. He was a gifted and talented fellow and professor in English literature at Magdalen College, Oxford (1924–55), and Cambridge (1954–63). He was elected to the Chair of Medieval and Renaissance English at Cambridge in 1954. Lewis was converted from paganism in 1931, and returned to the Church of England. He married Joy D. Gresham (1915–July 13, 1960), an American Jewish Christian convert in April, 1956, when she was ill with cancer. He wrote popular satires on profound subjects. *The Problem of Pain* (1940), *Screwtape Letters* (1942), and *Mere Christianity* (1952) are widely known. His *The Chronicles of Narnia* (1950–56) is a series of stories for children. Lewis wrote on apologetics. His 40 books have sold an estimated 40 million copies. His first book was *Spirits in Bondage* (1919) published under the pseudonym, Clive Hamilton. Other works include *Surprised by Joy* (1955) and *A Grief Observed* (1961), his last published under the pseudonym N. W. Clerk. Unbelievers have been converted and Christians' lives straightened through his writings. Lewis died from heart and kidney failure on the day of President Kennedy's assassination. He is buried in the graveyard of the Holy Trinity Church in Headington Quarry, Oxford. A few of his beliefs and practices were rather unorthodox for protestant Christianity. His favorite Bible verse was Exodus 3:14.

John Aberly

Sept. 18, 1867
Albrightsville, Pennsylvania

Dec. 21, 1963
Gettysburg, Pennsylvania

President of Lutheran Theological Seminary at Gettysburg (PA), 1926–40. Aberly married Alice Strauss on August 3, 1889 (died: August 1, 1904). He was a missionary in India (1890–1923) and a professor of missions and theology at Lutheran Theological Seminary, Maywood, IL (1923–26). Aberly wrote several books including *Bible Biographies* (1910) to *An Outline of Mission History* (1945).

Henry G. Brubaker

Nov. 7, 1896
Rheems, Pennsylvania

Dec. 22, 1963
Upland, California

General secretary of Brethren in Christ Church, Grantham, PA 1944–63. Brubaker was converted at age 17, at a revival meeting at Messiah Bible School, Grantham, PA. He married Anna Niesley on August 14, 1928. Brubaker was president of Beulah/Upland College 1933–39 and 1949–54. From 1954–57, he was bishop for the Pacific/CA District. Right after his marriage, he began a continuous relationship with Upland College. His duties included serving as dean of men, business manager, teaching in different departments, and serving as president. Brubaker served the community with ten years of service to the Upland Planning Commission, and also taught some at Azusa College and Los Angeles Baptist Seminary.

Philip E. Howard Jr.

Jan. 25, 1898
Philadelphia, Pennsylvania

Dec. 25, 1963
Vero Beach, Florida

Associated with the *Sunday School Times*, **1927–61**, continuing in the tradition of his father, PHILIP E. HOWARD, SR. Howard was converted at age twelve as a result of his parents' influence, and joined the Presbyterian Church in Swathmore, PA. On June 14, 1922, Howard married Katherine

Gillingham, and they had six children. One of their children, Elisabeth, later married JIM ELLIOT. Howard served in Belgium, 1922–27. He then joined the *Sunday School Times* staff and became editor in 1946. Howard was a noted Republican. He died suddenly in his home. *Sunday School Times* ceased publication in 1967.

Samuel Hsaio

Dec. 25, 1909
Hopei Province, China

Feb. 5, 1964
Chicago, Illinois

Home of Onesiphorus (Kids Alive) **leader** who was rescued from certain starvation as a twelve-year-old Chinese boy in 1921 by LESLIE M. ANGLIN. Later at the home, Hsaio became an evangelist, married, and had six children. He eventually translated for General Marshall of the U.S. Army. Hsaio spent most of his adult life presenting the work and the needs of the Home throughout America.

Allan A. Swift

Dec. 29, 1885
London, England

Feb. 13, 1964
Toronto, Ontario, Canada

President of Eastern Bible Institute (Valley Forge Christian College, Phoenixville, PA, in 1976), **Aldenville, PA 1938–49**. Swift migrated to Canada and was converted in 1906 in a Methodist Church in Stratford, Ontario. From 1920–29, he served as a missionary to China. His wife's name was Carrie. He spent much of his life pastoring the Trinity Pentecostal Church of Elizabeth, NJ, from 1929–37, 1949–61.

Robert R. Brown

Oct. 19, 1885
Dagus Mines, Pennsylvania

Feb. 20, 1964
Omaha, Nebraska

Pastored the Christian Missionary Alliance Church, called Omaha Gospel Tabernacle, beginning in 1923. Brown was converted in a revival meeting in Helvetia, PA at age 18. He married Mary Smith on January 1, 1912 (died: February 15, 1963). His radio program *Church of the Air* was the first religious broadcast, having begun April 8, 1923, on station WOW and continuing until his death in 1964. He wrote the music to the chorus "Rolled Away," and conducted many crusades and conferences, traveling around the world. He was a tireless servant of Christ. Early in his ministry, Brown pastored for ten years in Beaver Falls, PA, and in Chicago. He founded a Bible Conference Center at Okoboji Lakes, IA, in 1935.

Andrew E. Mitchell

March 10, 1877
Elora, Ontario, Canada

March 16, 1964
Pasadena, California

First president of Go Ye Fellowship, Los Angeles, C, 1944–64. Mitchell married Sadie Bryant in 1902 (died March, 1919). He then married Jennie Clay on May 12, 1920, whose ministry was also widely used. They had six children, including two sons, HUBERT and BRYANT. Mitchell came to the States at age 18. He was ordained in the Open Bible Standard Church. Mitchell was an artist, a musician, and was active in street and jail ministries. The cause of his death was melanoma.

William M. Smith (1)

Feb. 28, 1872
near McKean, Pennsylvania

April 2, 1964
Westfield, Indiana

Founder and superintendent (CEO) of Union Bible College, Westfield, IN 1911–64. Smith was converted as a small child, just shy of four years old, as result of his mother's loving rebuke. He married Ida Miller (September 23, 1862–January 7, 1920) on October 16, 1893, and they began their ministry in Cleveland, OH. They then pastored Friends Churches in Marion and Carthage, IN. He married Annie H. Worth on June 13, 1922. Smith wrote many books and booklets and was a well-known Bible expositor and writer. His funeral was April 5, at the First Friends Church in Westfield.

Douglas MacArthur

Jan. 26, 1880
near Little Rock, Arkansas

April 5, 1964
Washington, D.C.

Army General dismissed by President TRUMAN in 1951 in Tokyo in an unpopular decision. MacArthur graduated from the United States Military Academy in 1903. He was ranked first of 95 in his graduating class. In WWI, he served in France. In 1935, he was a military advisor to the Philippine government. He was the supreme Allied commander of the Far East forces, 1941–51, in WWII, and was responsible for the Japanese defeat. MacArthur's April 19th speech in Congress was climaxed by "Old soldiers never die; they just fade away." His first marriage was to Henrietta Brooks and lasted from 1922–29, after which he married Jean Fairchild in 1937 (died: Jan. 22, 2000). MacArthur loved the Bible. He said, "Our hope and faith rests upon the cross and the flag." He is buried in Norfolk, VA. His favorite Bible verse was Luke 11:2.

Elrod D. Head

Nov. 15, 1892
Sparta, Louisiana

April 13, 1964
San Angelo, Texas

President of Southwestern Baptist Theological Seminary, Fort Worth, TX 1942–53. Head was ordained on May 14, 1913. Head married Gladys Thorton in 1916 (died: 1921) and Effie McDaniel on May 10, 1924. He pastored in Valley Mills, TX (1916–33) and Whitney, TX (1932–42). His first book was *The Indian Renaissance*. He taught at Baylor University, 1920–32.

Thomas Wyatt

Jasper County, Iowa

April 19, 1964
Montebello, California

Evangelist and radio minister. Wyatt was reared in Jasper County, IA. He began a midwestern healing ministry that attracted *Look Magazine* (Nov. 23, 1937). In 1937, he moved to Portland, OR and started the *Wings of Healing* radio ministry. Wyatt established Bethesda World Training Center in 1953. He moved to Los Angeles in 1959. A heart attack December 9, 1962, took his life.

Harry Holt

April 6, 1905
Neligh, Nebraska

April 27, 1964
Ilsan, Korea

Founder and president of Holt Ministries, an adoption of orphans ministry, 1956–64. The ministry was based in Eugene, OR, resulting in 3,000 adoptions. Holt was raised in the Plymouth Brethren Church, then became a Baptist. He married his cousin, Bertha Holt, on December 31, 1927. They lived in Creswell, OR and had 14 children, including eight adopted orphans. Holt was a farmer, then entered into the logging and sawmill business. He died of a heart attack at his orphanage, ten miles north of Seoul. The orphanage had 700 beds and served as a processing station for adoption purposes. "Grandma" Holt continued the work into the 1990s.

Ina Duley Ogdon

April 3, 1872
Rossville, Illinois

May 1964
West Toledo, Ohio (?)

Hymn writer. She wrote "Brighten the Corner" (CHARLES GABRIEL), "You Must Open the Door" (HOMER RODEHEAVER), "Jesus," "Hark, I Hear My Name," "Jesus Will" (all three by B.D. ACKLEY), "Living Where the Healing waters Flow" (BILHORN) and "Pause for a Moment of Prayer" (music by

Waugh). Ina married James Ogdon on September 2, 1896. Ina passed up an opportunity to travel widely, singing in the Chatanqua circuit, in order to care for her family and sick father. Her song, "Brighten the Corner," traveled around the world in her place. She began writing in 1899, which resulted in several hundred poems, texts for hymns, stories, and articles. She was a Republican and member of the Disciples of Christ. Some of her books include *A Keepsake from the Old House* and *My Dakota Book*.

Ebenezer G. Vine

Aug. 23, 1884
London, England

May 10, 1964
Philadelphia, Pennsylvania

General director of Regions Beyond Missionary Union (merged into World Team in 1995), **1939–45, 1947–51**. Vine married Elizabeth Hawes in 1907 (died: 1935). In 1945, he went to the Bihar field and became field director for 18 difficult months following World War II. In 1948, he built up a Council for RBMU in the U.S. and worked for 16 years establishing the North American headquarters, 1948–64. Vine was responsible for works in Borneo and West New Guinea. He was stricken with a heart attack in the pulpit, hospitalized two weeks, and died.

Harry L. Reed

Dec. 15, 1867
Port Byron, New York

May 23, 1964
Salisbury, Connecticut (?)

President of Auburn (NY) Theological Seminary (moved to Union TS campus in 1939), **1926–36**. Reed was ordained a Congregationalist in 1897. He pastored First Congregational Church, Albany, OR, from 1897–1903. He married Elsie M. Otheman on May 18, 1905. Reed was professor of NT languages and criticism at Auburn, 1909–39.

Harry R. Smith

Feb. 17, 1900
Philadelphia, Pennsylvania

May 28, 1964
San Francisco, California

President of Christian Business Men's Committee, 1959. Smith was vice president of Bank of America. He came to Los Angeles (1920), then was transferred to San Francisco (1926). Smith was converted after hearing R. A. TORREY preach at the Church of the Open Door. He married Orpha Bower on February 20, 1926 (died: June 6, 1946), and Margory Herman on September 20, 1952.

Harold C. Mason

Nov. 9, 1888
Kunkle, Ohio

June 2, 1964
Winona Lake, Indiana (?)

Bishop of United Brethren Church, 1921–25, and president of Huntington (IN) College, 1932–39. Mason married Alta McFate on Dec. 25, 1909. He pastored in Blissfield, MI (1913–18); Montpelier, OH (1918–21); and was professor of philosophy and dean at Adrian (MI) College (1925–29). He taught at Winona Lake (IN) School of Theology (1939–43), at Northern Baptist Theological Seminary (1943–48), and at Asbury Theological Seminary (1948–61). He wrote *The Teaching Task of the Local Church* (1960).

Ira D. Warner

Sept. 14, 1886
Clayton, Ohio

July 1, 1964
Upland, California

Bishop of Church of the United Brethren in Christ, 1929–46; Evangelical United Brethren Church (United Methodist Church in 1968), **1946–64; senior bishop, 1951–54**. Warner married Edna Landis on June 28, 1911 (died: July 8, 1934). He pastored in Chattanooga, TN (1911–13); Dayton, TN (1913–17); and Canton, OH (1923–29). He married Ada Visick on June 6, 1937. His first book was *Effective Church Education in Sunday School* (1931), his last, *Spiritual Priorities for Church School Leaders* (1944). He is buried in Whittier, CA.

John R. Mulder

Nov. 28, 1893
Holland, Michigan

July 3, 1964
Grand Rapids, Michigan

President of Western Theological Seminary, Holland, MI 1942–60. Mulder was ordained as a Reformed minister in 1921, and married Jeanette Schoon on May 25 of the same year. He was a professor of philosophy and Bible at Central College, Pella, IA (1921–24) and was pastor of Bethany Church, Chicago, IL (1924–28). He began his career at Western in 1928 as a theology professor.

Harland J. O'Dell

June 18, 1914
Bedford, Michigan

July 3, 1964
Canton, Ohio

President of ACC, 1955–58. Odell was the pastor of the Canton (OH) Gospel Center 1939–64. He helped form the International Council of Churches, Amsterdam (1948); the ICC, Geneva, Switzerland (1950), and the Latin American Alliance, São Paulo, Brazil (1951). Odell was the guide of the ICC tour of Israel. In 1960, he traveled around the world. He died of a kidney condition. O'Dell gave his last message from his hospital bed, June 14, on "Preparation for Dying."

James G. Gilkey

Sept. 28, 1889
Watertown, Massachusetts

July 14, 1964
Weekapaugh, Rhode Island

Congregational educator, pastor, and hymn writer. He married Calma Howe on June 7, 1916. Gilkey pastored the South Church, Springfield, MA, from 1917–23. He was a professor of biblical literature at Amherst (MA) Theological Seminary, 1923–30. He returned to the South Church and remained for 38 years. He wrote the hymn "Outside the Holy City" (1915) and the book, *A Faith to Affirm* (1940).

Alvin C. York

Dec. 13, 1887
Pall Mall, Tennessee

Sept. 2, 1964
Nashville, Tennessee

One of the most decorated heroes of World War I. While growing up, York was known as a hell-raiser and a "nuisance" to the community, as he frequented bars. In 1914, he radically altered his life. After one of his best friends was killed in a bar fight, York attended a prayer meeting and was converted. He became a member of the Church of Christ in Christian Union, where he taught Sunday school classes and led the choir. His church preached a strict moral code which forbade drinking, dancing, movies, swimming, swearing, popular literature, and moral injunctions against violence and war. In 1917, York received a draft notice. Following his church's teachings, he wrote on the back, "Don't want to fight" and sent it back to the local draft board. His case was denied at both the local and state levels. While in basic training, he distinguished himself as an expert marksman. This confused his trainers as he repeatedly spoke of his objection to war. He was called before his company commander, George Buxton. For several weeks, the two spoke openly about Alvin's convictions and soon Buxton convinced Alvin that God sometimes ordains war as moral and necessary. Finally, Alvin agreed to teach others how to shoot, but not kill others himself. York married Gracie Williams on June 7, 1919, and they eventually had seven children. On October 8, 1919, in the Argonne-Meuse in France, he single-handedly destroyed several machine gun nests, taking under his control 132 captives in the process and killing 28 Germans. When he reported afterwards to his brigade commander, the general said, "Well, York, I hear you have captured the whole…German army." York replied, "I only have one hundred and thirty two." When asked why he decided to kill, he said it was because he saved more lives by taking out the machine guns than if he hadn't killed at all. He carried a New Testament all through the fighting and often witnessed to others. He was given honors that included the French Croix de Guerre, the Congressional Medal of Honor, and over 50 other medals. York settled on a farm in Tennessee. In 1954, he suffered a cerebral hemorrhage that would leave him bedridden for the remainder of his life. He was buried with full military honors in the Pall Mall, TN cemetery, with over 8,000 attending his funeral. A movie, *Sergeant York,* was made in 1941, depicting his heroic acts.

Hampton T. Medford

Jan. 29, 1885
Marion, North Carolina

Sept. 14, 1964
Washington, D.C.

Director of African Methodist Episcopal Zion Church Missions, 1928–48. Medford was ordained deacon (1907), elder (1910), and consecrated bishop on May 16, 1948. His pastorates included Cherryville Circuit, NC; China Grove, NC; Cleveland Circuit, NC; Moore's Chapel, Salisbury, NC; Grace Church, Charlotte, NC; Jacob Street Tabernacle, Louisville, KY; Loguen Temple, Knoxville, TN; and John Wesley Church, Washington, D.C. He served in Africa during the first quadrennial in the episcopacy.

William G. S. Dobbie
Old Dob Dob

July 12, 1879
Madras, India (Chennai)

Oct. 3, 1964
Kensington, London, England

Defender of Malta. Dobbie was converted at age 14, kneeling at his bedside during Christmas break. He served in the South African Border War, 1901–2, and married Sybil Orde-Browne in 1904. In WWI, he issued the order for the occupation of Germany. In WWII, Malta was the most bombed spot in the world, but was England's lifeline between Gibraltar and Africa. It withstood 2,300 bombings, with just four planes and 16 anti-aircraft guns.

Herbert C. Hoover

Aug. 10, 1874
West Branch, Iowa

Oct. 20, 1964
New York, New York

31st President of the United States, 1929–1933, preceding Franklin D. Roosevelt. Hoover married Lou Henry (1874–January 7, 1944) on February 10, 1899. He defeated Al Smith, 444–87 for the presidency. The "Great Depression" hit in October, 1929, when the stock market crashed. In 1932, he lost to F. D. Roosevelt, 472–59, basically because of the Depression. He had Quaker church affiliations and was involved with many humanitarian activities, with relief and food prior to and following his presidency in the TRUMAN era. He once stated: "The whole inspiration of our civilization springs from the teachings of Christ and the lessons of the prophets. To read the Bible for these fundamentals is a necessity of American life." Hoover addressed seven Republican national conventions, concluding in Chicago in 1960. One of his books was *Individualism* (1922). His funeral was held in West Branch, IA.

George L. Edstrom

May 15, 1906
Chicago, Illinois

Nov. 2, 1964
Minneapolis, Minnesota

Soloist who worked out of Minneapolis for many years. Edstrom was ordained a Baptist in 1938, after his Moody Bible Institute training and was a key tenor soloist at Moody Church. He pastored at FBC, Rochester, MN from 1935–48, traveled with evangelist PAUL ROOD and served as a radio pastor for Northwestern Bible School. In later years, he was the office manager for the Billy Graham headquarters in Minneapolis.

John P. C. Meyer

Feb. 27, 1873
Zittau, Wisconsin

Nov. 10, 1964
Mequon, Wisconsin

President of Wisconsin Lutheran Seminary, Mequon, WI 1937–54. Meyer taught there for 44 years, 1920–64. He married Lydia Reinke on November 26, 1903. In his early years of ministry, he served a parish in Beaver Dam and Oconomowoc, WI. He was president of Dr. Martin Luther College, New Elim, WI until 1973. Meyer preached at St. Marcus Church, Milwaukee, WI, just one day before entering the hospital where he died.

Harry S. Mason

Oct. 17, 1881
Gloversville, New York

Nov. 15, 1964
Torrington, Connecticut

Composed the music for "Are Ye Able" (lyrics by EARL MARLAT). For 25 years, Mason served on the faculty of Auburn (NY) Theological Seminary, teaching fine arts and religion. He was an Episcopalian, but most of his 54 years as a church organist were spent in Presbyterian churches. His longest ministry lasted for 27 years, at the Second Presbyterian Church, Auburn, NY.

Karl E. Mattson

Oct. 9, 1905
Warren, Minnesota

Nov. 15, 1964
Rock Island, Illinois

President of Augustana Theological Seminary, Rock Island, IL 1948–62 (Lutheran School of Theology, Chicago, in 1964). Mattson was ordained a Lutheran in 1930 and married Eva Bergendoff on July 30, 1932. He pastored the First Lutheran Church, East Orange, NJ (1930–39); and Bethesda Lutheran, New Haven, NJ (1939–45). Mattson was president of LST from 1962–64. He was the editor of the *Bible Study Quarterly* of the International Council Lessons. He was a lecturer and the director of Upsala College, East Orange, NJ. He wrote *The Glory of Common Tasks* (1952).

Albert M. Malotte

May 19, 1895
Philadelphia, Pennsylvania

Nov. 16, 1964
Los Angeles, California

Composer of the beautiful "Lord's Prayer" musical setting. Malotte was a boy soprano at St. James Episcopal Church, Philadelphia, PA, later uniting with the Presbyterians. He became one of the world's greatest concert organists. In 1927, he settled in North Hollywood, CA, and became music arranger for Walt Disney. He devoted most of his life to composing and teaching. Malotte wrote musical scenes for the following motion pictures: *The Enchanted Forest* (1945), *The Lady and the Tramp* (1955), and *The Big Fisherman* (1959). His wife's name was Marguerite. He suffered a cerebral hemorrhage in 1962.

Paul Carlson

March 31, 1928
Culver City, California

Nov. 24, 1964
Stanleyville, Belgian Congo

Missionary martyr in the Congo. Raised in a Christian home, Carlson was interested in missions as a teen. After his marriage to Lois Lindblaw on September 16, 1950, they went to the Congo in 1961, and served as Evangelical Covenant medical missionaries. Beginning in 1962 in remote Wasolo, they saw 200 patients a day. The U.S. Air Force dropped 600 Belgian paratroopers in Stanleyville to rescue white hostages (of which he was one) held captive by Simba rebel soldiers (Congolese rebels). Some 80 white hostages were slain by the rebels during the coup. He tried to scale a wall to safety, but was shot six times and killed. Mrs. Carlson last saw her husband September 9, 1964.

Oscar E. Sanden

July 20, 1901
Oslo, Norway

Dec. 20, 1964
Stillwell, Minnesota

Evangelist and pastor, authority on the relationship of science and the Bible. Sanden was educated in the United States. He married Carolyn Peterson on September 4, 1931. He began his ministry in Baton Rogue, LA, in 1923. He pastored the Florida St. Presbyterian Church (1923–30); and Alamo Heights Presbyterian Church, San Antonio, TX (1936–42). During his ministry, he held over 100 crusades. His first book was *Travels of a Viking* (1938).

Arthur S. Rogers

March 11, 1869
Newberry, South Carolina

Dec. 23, 1964
Rock Hill, South Carolina

Stated Clerk of Associate Reformed Presbyterian Church, Greenville, SC, 1910–39. Rogers was ordained Associate Reformed Presbyterian in 1896. He was founder and pastor of a church in Rock Hill, SC, from 1896–1948. He married Millie Lynn on October 3, 1906 (died: May 25, 1925), and Janie Garrison on November 5, 1930.

David L. Cooper

August 31, 1886
Nashville, Tennessee

1965

Founder of the Biblical Research Society of Los Angeles. Cooper was converted on an Easter Sunday night, 1905. On June 12, 1912, he married Florence Pepper and soon enrolled at Southern Baptist Seminary in Louisville. He pastored in Waterford, KY, from 1912–20 but felt a call to reach Jewish people in 1923. In 1924, he enrolled at the University of Chicago Divinity School for intensive study in Semitic languages. In 1926, Cooper headed the Jewish department of BIOLA. The department was closed in 1930 so he started his own organization. Although Cooper is not Jewish, his burden was undeniable as millions of his books were freely given to Jews around the world. His life story is in the book *A Modern Gideon and Mrs. Gideon*. A leading rabbi was quoted as saying that Cooper did more to reach Jews for Christ than any other man of his time.

John Linton

1888
Scotland

1965
Pontiac, Michigan

Baptist evangelist, 1938–56, 1960–65. Linton ran away when he was 13, resulting in his conversion. He immigrated to Canada, where he responded to his call to preach in Hamilton, Ontario. He attended Gordon Bible College in Boston, then entered the pastorate. Linton pastored in Reston, Manitoba (1915–16); Toronto (1916–20); Montreal (1920–25); High Park Baptist Church, Toronto (1925–34); New York City (1936–38); and Windsor Ontario (1957–60). He went into conference speaking and evangelism, taking his crusades to the States and Canada. Linton died in the pulpit while conducting a service. Many of his sermons were published in the *Sword of the Lord*.

Walter M. Montaño
The Monk Who Lived Again

c 1965

Director of Christ's Mission (merged into International Teams in 1984), **1950–60**. On January 3, 1927, the unhappy monk escaped from the Dominican Monastery. Soon he was preaching Christ in the largest auditoriums of South America and some of Latin America's most exclusive universities. Montaño came from a politically prominent family of Bolivia. He received his doctorate of philosophy from San Marcos University, Lima, Peru. Montaño was a former friar of the Dominican Order and a priest in the Catholic church. His book, *Behind the Purple Curtain*, tells his story.

Richard E. Day

June 1, 1882   *Jan. 4, 1965*
Terre Haute, Indiana   Alhambra, California (?)

Outstanding author of Christian classic books. His contribution to Christian biographies was not excelled in his time—*So Pilgrim Rang the Bells* (JOHN BUNYAN), *Rhapsody in Black* (JOHN JASPER), *Bush Aglow* (D. L. MOODY), *Shadow of the Broad Brim* (CHARLES SPURGEON), *Flagellant on Horseback* (DAVID BRAINERD), etc. Day was ordained a Baptist minister in 1906 and married Jessie Myers on May 16, 1908. Upon her death, he married Irene W. McAulay on June 18, 1951. He pastored in California (1906–24), in Sunnyvale, Napa, San Diego, and Riverside; in Phoenix, Arizona (1924–31) and Hamilton Square Baptist Church, San Francisco, (1931–40). After 1940, he became an evangelist and pulpit supplier, active in the Northern Baptist Convention. He wrote *The Next Great Awakening* (1920) to *Revivals* (1957).

Morley R. Hall

Aug. 18, 1893   *Jan. 26, 1965*
Courtland, Ontario, Canada   Toronto, Ontario, Canada

Secretary of Baptist Churches of Ontario and Quebec in 1946; of Independent Churches of Canada in 1952; and of the Fellowship of Evangelical Baptists in 1953, 1957–64. Hall was converted at age eleven. He attended Toronto Bible College and was interested in home missions. So, he served in such places as Timmins, Ontario, 1922–30. He went to Calgary, Alberta, in 1930, starting a school and Westbourne Baptist Church. Hall pastored at West Side Baptist Church, Hamilton, Ontario, 1948–53. He was the first secretary of the Home Missions board in 1961.

Homer A. Hammontree

March 3, 1884   *Feb. 2, 1965*
Greenback, Tennessee   Maryville, Tennessee

Soloist and song leader for MEL TROTTER's evangelistic endeavors, 1916–35. Hammontree directed the music department of the Moody Bible Institute, 1936–42. He traveled with SUNDAY and RODEHEAVER, using his musical talents, and ministered in many army camps during WWI and WWII. He was never married. "Ham" was a superb songleader and gracious gentleman. He composed a few hymns, including "Under the Blood" (lyrics by Waley) and "Fill All My Vision" (lyrics by A. B. CHRISTIANSEN). He left the Chicago area in 1958 for Tennessee.

Charles O. Baptista
Mr. Gospel Films

Sept. 25, 1894   *Feb. 9, 1965*
San Crustabal, Venezuela   Elmhurst, Illinois

President, founder, and director of the first Christian film company, Baptista Film Mission, Chicago (1942–47), Wheaton, IL (1947–65). The company originated in his home. Baptista combined mechanical skill, dramatic art, and a passion for souls. Baptista came to America as a Catholic in 1909, and later was converted at Buena Memorial Presbyterian Church in Chicago. His work was originally called the Scriptures Visualized Institute. He died of a heart attack, survived by his wife Virginia.

Harry D. Loes

Oct. 20, 1892
Kalamazoo, Michigan

Feb. 9, 1965
Chicago, Illinois

Writer of great gospel choruses, such as "Everybody Ought to Love Jesus," "Every Moment of the Day," "Hallelujah, I'm Saved," "Life Begins," and "From the Bottom of My Heart." Loes composed the music for "Blessed Redeemer," "Love Found a Way" (lyrics for both by A.B. CHRISTIANSEN), "I Owe Everything to Jesus" (lyrics by BARNETT) and both lyrics and music to "All Things in Jesus," and "Twas Jesus' Blood." He began to write under the teaching of DANIEL TOWNER. Many of his songs came from the result of hearing PAUL RADER preach. Loes was an evangelist for twelve years. He served as music director at FBC, Okmulgee, OK, and at FBC, Muskogee, OK, from 1927–39. He joined the music faculty at Moody Bible Institute in 1939, serving there for most of his remaining years. One of his students was JOHN W. PETERSON. Loes wrote some 1,500 hymn texts and 3,000 hymn tunes.

R. Kenneth Strachan

June 1, 1910
Tandil/Buenos Aries, Argentina

Feb. 24, 1965
Pasadena, California

President of Latin American Mission, 1950–65, following in the footsteps of his father, HARRY, the mission board's founder. Strachan joined the mission in 1936. He served as a missionary in Guatemala and other Central American countries. Strachan married Elizabeth Walker on December 27, 1940, and they had six children. Strachan introduced "Evangelism in Depth" crusades, taking one country per year, beginning in Nicaragua in 1960. He was a greatly respected missions leader. He died from cancer (Hodgkin's disease).

Kaneo Oda

Oct. 6, 1901
Osaka, Japan

Feb. 28, 1965
Osaka, Japan

Bishop of Free Methodist Church, 1946–62. Oda was converted at age twelve under the ministry of Teikichi Kawabe. He married Soda on March 4, 1927. He was appointed a missionary to China by Japan FMC, 1939–46, and built a thriving congregation in Peking. Oda was a conference supervisor, professor, college president, evangelist, interpreter, and translator. He encouraged world wide Free Methodist activities. Oda was very active in Japan Youth for Christ.

Charles F. McKoy

July 24, 1878
Bangor, Maine

March 12, 1965
Calcutta, India

An amazing retiree's story of faith and fortitude. At age twelve, McKoy was converted at Columbia Street Baptist Church, Bangor. He pastored FBC, Eton, MA (1905–11); at FBC, Long Branch, NJ (1913–19); at Green Avenue Baptist, Brooklyn (1920–33); and at Wightman Baptist, Oyster Bay, NY (1934–49). Still unmarried at age 71 in 1949—with no money, a Bishop Pillai challenged him to be a missionary. He went to India, Hong Kong, and Japan, on six world preaching tours. He met a number of heads of state personally. He preached in 53 countries and saw 28,000 converts. He traveled by camel, donkey, pushcart, rickshaw, bicycle, and old cars. BOB PIERCE promoted his ministry. The book, *The Real McKoy*, is a classic.

Clarence E. Pickett

Oct. 19, 1884
Cissna Park, Illinois

March 17, 1965
Boise, Idaho

Director of American Friends Service Committee, Philadelphia, PA, 1929–50. Pickett married Lilly Peckham on June 25, 1913. He was ordained to the Society of Friends in 1913; pastored in Toronto, Ontario (1913–17); Ooskaloosa, IA (1917–19); was secretary of the Young Friends Organization of America (1919–22); and professor of Biblical literature at Earlham College, Richmond, IN (1923–29). He was a co-winner of a 1947 Nobel Peace Prize. Pickett was honorary secretary of AFSC from 1950–55, then executive secretary emeritus, and served on several commissions and organizations. He wrote *For More Than Bread* (1953). He is buried in Media, PA.

Amos A. Stagg

Aug. 16, 1862
West Orange, New Jersey

March 17, 1965
Stockton, California

"Grand old man" of the University of Chicago, football coach, and professor, 1892–1933. In 1889, he was named to the first All–American football team. He pioneered the forward pass and T–formation. Stagg married Stella Robertson on September 10, 1894 (died: 1964). He went to the College of Pacific as a football coach (1933–46) from age 71 to 84. He had a 115–74 and twelve ties record with the Western Conference, and won seven championships. He won many awards including "The All-Time Christian Coach." Stagg's influence was awesome in sports circles. His lifetime coaching record was 309–200 and 35 ties. He lived to be 102 years old.

Jasper C. Massee

Nov. 22, 1871
Marshallville, Georgia

March 27, 1965
Atlanta, Georgia

Baptist pastor. Massee was the youngest of 13 children. Massee married Sallie Steward in 1893 (died: 1895), then married Mary Oliver on June 30, 1896 (died: 1932), after which he married Edna Blair on August 25, 1935. He pastored in Kissimmee, FL (1893–96); Orlando, FL (1897–99); Lancaster, KY (1899–1901); Mansfield, OH (1901–3); Raleigh, NC (1903–8); Chattanooga, TN (1908–13); Dayton, OH (1913–19); Brooklyn, NY (1920–22); and at Tremont Temple, Boston, MA (1922–29), which grew to 4,000 members. From 1920–26, he was the spokesman for fundamentalists in the Northern Baptist Convention. He then went into evangelism and conference speaking, 1929–38. He taught homiletics at Eastern Baptist Theological Seminary, 1938–41. Massee wrote 23 books throughout his ministry and eventually retired in Atlanta, GA.

Gordon S. Seagrave
Burma Surgeon

March 18, 1897
Rangoon, Burma

March 28, 1965
Namhkam, Burma

Gruff-talking, gentle-hearted Baptist medical missionary. Seagrave married Marion Morse on September 11, 1920. Beginning in 1922, under American Baptist FMS, he served 40 years in Burma, opening hospitals, ministering, and serving 5,000 patients a year. Seagrave won a chestful of medals and lifelong gratitude from hundreds of Allied troops. He performed battlefront surgery during World War II. His first book was *Burma Surgeon* (1943). He also wrote *My Hospital in the Hills* (1955), his last among others. His hospital was among the Karens at Namhkam, in the Shaw states bordering on China. In 1950, he was in prison ten months for aiding rebellious tribesmen.

Jesse H. Arnup

July 18, 1881
Norfolk, Ontario, Canada

April 4, 1965
Toronto, Ontario, Canada

Secretary of the United Church of Canada Missions, 1925–52. Arnup was ordained in 1910 and a member of St. Clair Avenue United Church, Toronto, for nearly 50 years. He married Ella Leeson on June 30, 1910, and they had six children. He served in Home Missions in Saskatchewan (1904–6), as the secretary of the Laymen's Missionary Movement in the Methodist Church (1910–12), field secretary of the Methodist Missionary Society (1912–13), assistant secretary of foreign missions in the Methodist Church (1913–26), and moderator of the United Church of Canada in 1944.

Mack C. Ehlert

Feb. 14, 1898
Denmark

April 5, 1965
Edinburg, Texas

Founder and first president of Rio Grande Bible Institute, Edinburg, TX 1946–65. Ehlert was converted while working on a dairy farm in Minnesota at age 17. He was ordained as a Baptist and served as an evangelist and preacher. From 1936–46, he made trips to the Rio Grande Valley, sleeping in a tent. There, God gave him a vision of a Spanish-English Bible School, which he finally established. He died of a heart attack.

Clifton L. Fowler

Aug. 7, 1882
Kirksville, Missouri

April 10, 1965
Coral Gables, Florida

First president of Denver (CO) Bible Institute (Colorado Christian University in 1985), **1914–37**. Fowler was converted at age 18 in St. Louis, MO by a personal witness on the street. He was ordained as a Baptist in 1905, and pastored until 1913. He married Angie Anderson on May 22, 1912. Fowler opened DBI on October 26, 1914 with two students. During his Denver days, he pastored the Church of the Open Bible (Berean Fundamental Church), 1922–40. He also edited *Grace and Truth* (1928–48). He founded Berean Missionary Society in 1934. He married Rose Encinas on October 22, 1959. He wrote *Fundamental Facts of the Faith* (1936).

Russell I. Humberd

Nov. 3, 1893
La Place, Illinois

May 5, 1965
Flora, Indiana

Well-known pastor and author. Humberd married Anna Marie on July 6, 1915, and they had seven children. He received assurance of salvation while ministering at Lost Creek, KY. After graduating from MBI, he took a church in Michigan, then pastored in Pennsylvania for 13 years, teaching at Altoona (PA) Bible Institute at the same time. He moved later to Akron, OH, then back to Flora, IN. His radio broadcast reached 25 states. Many of his sermons were published in the *Sword of the Lord*. He wrote 13 books, including *Humberd's Bible Charts* and *The Book of Revelation*. Humberd spoke in 112 Christian colleges and Bible schools throughout his ministry. His Humberd Press sent booklets and tracts around the world. He identified with the Grace Brethren Church.

Theodore E. McCulley

Nov. 23, 1900
Givin, Iowa

May 6, 1965
Wheaton, Illinois

President of Christian Business men's Committee, 1954–55, and executive director, 1956–65. In January, 1917, he was converted because of the witness at a Saturday night youth club held in a home. McCulley worked for a bakery in Des Moines, IA, in 1922. He worked at Carpenter Baking Company in Milwaukee, WI (1939), and was promoted to vice president and manager (1941). The company had 150 employees and a $2 million annual income. His son, Ed McCulley, was one of the five missionaries killed by Auca Indians in 1956.

William S. Hottell

Jan. 3, 1878
Coopersburg, Pennsylvania

May 15, 1965
Howell, Michigan

Writer and pastor. Hottell was converted at age twelve under the ministry of Adam Gehret, Mennonite Brethren in Christ Church, Coopersburg, PA. He married May High on July 11, 1902. The "home study" Sunday School Lessons began in his Allentown, PA pastorate in 1912. Hottell compiled the *International Sunday School Lessons* published by Union Gospel Press of Cleveland, OH, from 1914–59. He pastored several growing churches in eastern Pennsylvania until 1920. He was in Bible conference work, 1920–44, along with pastoring in Altoona, PA; Hamilton, Ontario; Detroit, MI; and Hazel Park, IL. He also served as president of Denver Bible Institute (Colorado Christian University in 1985) 1942–44. Hottell was ordained as a Baptist, but pastored IFCA churches.

Henry H. Halley

April 10, 1874
White Sulpher, Kentucky

May 23, 1965
Chicago, Illinois

Author of the famed *Halley's Handbook of the Bible*. In 1898, Halley was ordained into the Disciples of Christ Church. He married Madge Gilles in 1899 and served as a pastor in Kalamazoo, MI, for eight years. Halley was inspired to write his handbook in 1922 in Indiana when someone took notes on his lectures. A 16-page leaflet of suggested Bible verses to memorize, printed in 1924, was the beginning. Many copies of his handbook have been sold, making Bible study easier for countless Christians. Sales have passed 5 million, with 90 printings and 25 editions, plus publication in more than a dozen foreign countries. For many years, he gave Bible recitals in thirty-five states, sharing statements about the historic setting of Bible books. His funeral services were conducted at Chicago's North Shore Baptist Church.

Guy L. Vannah

Sept. 5, 1887
Mount Vernon, Maine

May 27, 1965
Port Clyde, Maine

President of New England School of Theology (Berkshire Christian College, Lenox, MA, in 1958), **Brookline, MA 1920–50**. Vannah began teaching at Berkshire in 1914, part time, for $150 per year. He was ordained on April 22, 1915. He married Irma Marshall on October 17, 1916. He pastored in North Carver, MA, in 1915; West Wareham, MA, from 1920–23 and Melrose, MA from 1929 on. He also held pastorates in Boone, NC; East Norfolk, CT; Goodwin's Mills and Friendship, ME.

Walter O. Lewis

Feb. 22, 1877
Stanberry, Missouri

May 28, 1965
Washington, D.C.

General secretary of Baptist World Alliance, 1939–48. Lewis married Maggie Rogers on September 8, 1903, (died: April 1904) and Jessie Thompson on September 26, 1907. He served as a pastor in Missouri (1897–1910) and then taught at William Jewell College, Liberty, Mo (1910–22). During WWI, he went back to Europe as a missionary in 1918. He also ministered as the European representative of American Baptist Foreign Missionary Society from 1922–39 and became known as "Mr. Relief." He spoke several languages. Lewis helped move the BWA headquarters from London to Washington, D.C. in 1940.

Raymond R. Crawford

Dec. 7, 1891
Menefee Valley, California

June 3, 1965
Portland, Oregon

General overseer of Apostolic Faith Mission of Portland, OR 1937–65, succeeding his mother, Florence, who founded the mission. Converted Oct. 23, 1908, his motto became "saved to serve," so he helped his mother for 26 years. Crawford was one of the first evangelists to use airplanes to travel. In 1920, he became the first pilot in America to use a plane for Christian work. Crawford married Freda Lind on Dec. 4, 1920 (died: 1941), and Edna Hazel on Aug. 28, 1942 (died: Dec. 6, 1986, age 90).

Syngman Rhee

April 26, 1875
Hwanghai, Korea

July 19, 1965
Honolulu, Hawaii

President of Korea, 1948–60, and outstanding Methodist leader. Rhee was converted in 1897, when he was arrested and imprisoned for opposing the monarchy. He lived in political exile, 1910–45, in Hawaii, after serving as a missionary teacher in Korea in 1910. He was the president of the Korean Provisional Government established at Shanghai, 1919–41, waging constant battle with the Japanese-controlled country. Rhee married Francesca Donner on October 8, 1934. During his leadership, no liquor was ever served. He fled to Hawaii again when a popular uprising forced him from office, April 27, 1960. His government was toppled by a civilian revolt, triggered by charges of vote fraud. He was a constant Bible reader and wrote several books, including *Spirit of Independence* and *Japan Inside Out*. He was a much loved man; and when he died, one million people crowded the streets for his funeral, which was held at Chung Dong Methodist Church, Seoul, July 27, 1965.

Carl E. Lund-Quist

Sept. 19, 1908
Lindsborg, Kansas

Aug. 26, 1965
Minneapolis, Minnesota

General secretary of Lutheran World Federation, 1951–60. Lund-Quist was ordained as a Lutheran in 1936. He held a pastorate at the Concordia Lutheran Church, Chicago (1936–41) and was a student pastor at the University of Minnesota (1941–46). He served on the staff of the National Lutheran Council (1946–51) and was also the vice-chairman of the World's Student Christian Federation (1956–65). He is buried in Fremont, NE.

Charles E. Gremmels

Aug. 9, 1877
New York, New York

Aug. 28, 1965
New York, New York

Outstanding businessman of New York City. Gremmels was born on the fourth floor of a tenement house on the east side. At twelve, he quit school and went to work, and at age 14, he attended a mission service in the Bowery of New York City. As Mother Byrd presented the gospel, he responded at testimony time, saying, "I believe!" Gremmels married Helen Salzmann on June 10, 1903 (died: June 1957). After 20 years in a broker's office, he became involved in real estate and became the president/director of Providential Reality/Investment Company in NYC. He was an Episcopalian. Gremmels spoke monthly at the Bowery Mission, and from time to time brought converts needing employment home.

Albert Schweitzer

Jan. 14, 1875
Kayserburg, Germany

Sept. 4, 1965
Lambarene, Gabon

Theologian, philosopher, mission doctor, and organist in Gabon. Schweitzer's book, *The Quest of the Historical Jesus* (1906), established him as a theologian the year he decided to be a mission doctor. He was never connected to a particular missionary society. In 1913, he left for Lambarene (then in French Equatorial Africa) and became its missionary surgeon. He founded a hospital there with 365 beds and a leper colony. Schweitzer married Helen Bresslau on June 18, 1912, and was imprisoned during World War I in France as a German civilian prisoner of war. He won the Nobel Peace Prize in 1952. Schweitzer wavered between theism and pantheism and was greatly concerned about ethics. He would be the most well-known liberal missionary of the century. He did not believe in the deity of Christ. He was the son of a Lutheran clergyman. His conviction that "small people" need simple healing resulted in his refusal to make necessary improvements despite available funds. His works range from *Paul and His Interpreters* (1912) to *Out of My Life and Thought* (1949).

Robert P. Shuler

Aug. 4, 1880
Grayson County, Virginia

Sept. 11, 1965
Cambria, California

Methodist evangelist and pastor, father of evangelists JACK and Phil Shuler. Shuler married Nelie Reeves on October 4, 1905. He pastored in Virginia, Louisiana, and Tennessee (1902–6); then in Texas, (1906–20). He then went to Trinity Methodist in Los Angeles, 1920–53, ministering to 5,000 members. He ran for the Senate in 1932 as a Prohibitionist and received over 500,000 votes. He was a great Fundamentalist leader. Many of his sermons were published in *The Sword of the Lord* as well as three of his books including *Some Dogs I Have Known*, by the SL Publishers. He edited *The Methodist Challenge*. He owned a radio station, KGEF, through which he fought corruption and depravity.

Peter H. Eldersveld

Jan. 19, 1911
Kalamazoo, Michigan

Oct. 14, 1965
Chicago, Illinois

Pioneer radio preacher for *Back to God Hour* sponsored by the Christian Reformed Church, 1943–65, heard on over 300 stations. Eldersveld married Harriet Kuiper on July 7, 1937, and they had three children. Eldersveld was ordained in 1938 and pastored in Iowa and Chicago, 1938–46. He spoke in many meetings across the nation and produced books from his radio programs.

Irwin K. Curry

Oct. 14, 1882
near Hershey, Pennsylvania

Oct. 25, 1965
Hershey, Pennsylvania

Presiding Bishop of United Christian Church, Cleona, PA 1932–65. Curry grew up in a Christian home, attended various churches, and married Ann O'Neal on January 4, 1908. They had ten children. He worked on a farm until 1939 and was part owner of a feed mill. He became associated with the United Christian Church and became its chief spokesman, evangelist, encourager, all of which he did well, along with his business. He died of tuberculosis.

Paul W. H. Frederick

March 7, 1873
Washington, Pennsylvania

Nov. 1, 1965
Fremont, Nebraska

First president of Pacific (Lutheran in 1952) Theological Seminary, Portland, OR 1910–14, Seattle, WA 1914–19 (closing in 1932 and re-opening in Berkeley, CA in 1952), professor, 1914–19, and dean, 1918–31. Frederick married Gertrude Klieves on May 10, 1898 (died: June 20, 1959) and organized the First Lutheran Church, San Bernardino, CA, in 1903. He pastored at Trinity Lutheran Church, Pasadena, CA from 1907–11. Frederick served at Western Seminary (College), Fremont, NE, from 1931–53, where he taught Bible and theology. A fall in 1963 fractured his hip and caused a steady decline in his health.

Clarence Erickson

Jan. 31, 1894
Kenyon, Minnesota

Nov. 11, 1965
Glendale, California

Successor of Paul Rader at the Chicago Gospel Tabernacle, 1931–53, and director of "Heaven and Home Hour," 1933–65. Erickson served in WWI in Pedro, CA. He began preaching in 1920. Erickson married on Aug. 28, 1923. He traveled as an evangelist until 1931. His son-in-law, Russ Killman, continued his radio program *The Heaven and Home Hour*. Erickson hosted large conferences and led a great outreach on Chicago's north side.

Everett F. Swanson

Dec. 13, 1913
Sycamore, Illinois

Nov. 15, 1965
Oak Park, Illinois

Founder and first president of Compassion International, 1952–65. Swanson was a Baptist General Conference evangelist, 1932–38 and 1951–61. He married Miriam Edwards on December 16, 1934. He pastored in Mt. Vernon, WA (1938–44) and Central Avenue Baptist, Chicago, IL (1944–51). He saw the need in Korea in 1951 and sought help, organizing Compassion. His work has grown into a large Christian humanitarian ministry.

C. Oscar Johnson

Sept. 22, 1886
Coal Creek, Tennessee

Nov. 24, 1965
Oakland, California

President of Baptist World Alliance, 1947–52. Johnson married Rose Long on Sepember 6, 1910. He pastored in Newport Beach, CA (1910–11); Los Angeles, CA (1911–15); Campbellsburg, KY (1915–20); and Tacoma, WA (1920–31). He also pastored the Third Baptist Church, St. Louis, MO from 1931–58, where he took in 11,000 members. He was comfortable in both conventions: president of the Northern Baptist Convention, 1932–3, and later vice-president of the Southern Baptist Convention. Johnson served as an instructor at Berkeley (CA) Divinity School, 1958–60.

Henry C. Crowell

April 13, 1897
Chicago, Illinois

Nov. 25, 1965
Winnetka, Illinois (?)

Investment executive at Moody Bible Institute. Crowell was the son of the famed Quaker Oats executive, Henry Parsons Crowell. He married Perry Kimball on June 24, 1920, and served as the assistant to the business manager at MBI (1923–26), assistant to the president (1926–39), and executive vice president (1939–65). He lived in Winnetka, IL, and became a MBI trustee, beginning February, 1936.

Coulson Shepherd

Aug. 7, 1891
Mount Vernon, New York

Dec. 5, 1965
Patchogue, New York

Baptist Jewish evangelist, 1965, founder and director of "Message to Israel," a mission and radio ministry to Jews in 1937. Shepherd married Edith Howell on July 9, 1914. He was raised Methodist, but, through the witness of Thomas P. Kelley in 1919, he was converted. He was ordained in 1922 and pastored in Crum Lynne, PA (1921–1925); FBC of Patchogue, NY (1926–1933); and FBC, Atlantic City, NJ (1933–1940s). He authored several books and tracts.

Martin R. DeHaan

March 23, 1891
Zeeland, Michigan

Dec. 13, 1965
Grand Rapids, Michigan

Bible teacher, founder and director of *Radio Bible Class* (named in 1941), **1938–65**, a worldwide radio ministry that he directed until he died. DeHaan started with just one station in Detroit and soon had a nationwide audience of some 600 stations. His son, RICHARD, continued his ministry after his death. DeHaan married Priscilla Venhuizen on June 25, 1914. He was a medical doctor in his early years and was converted at age 30 in October, 1921, facing death (reaction to medicine he had been given) in a hospital in Grand Rapids. DeHaan left Calvary Reformed Church in 1929 to start the independent Calvary Undenominational Church in Grand Rapids, MI from 1929–38. He had heart attacks in 1938 and 1946. He was one of the leading Bible teachers in America, authoring 25 books and many booklets, plus editing the devotional, *Our Daily Bread*. In July 1965, he was in a serious automobile collision, from which he never really recovered. He refused to solicit funds on the air or through the mail. His books include, *The Chemistry of the Blood* and *Answers to Bible Questions*.

Henry F. Schuh

May 30, 1890
Tacoma, Washington

Dec. 21, 1965
Columbus, Ohio

President of American Lutheran Church (ELCA in 1988), **1951–60**. Schuh was ordained on July 4, 1915. He married Amelia Koerner on July 11, 1916. They had three children. He pastored in Ashland, OH (1915–16) and Toledo, OH (1916–30). He directed stewardship finances with ALC from 1930–50. He was a delegate to many overseas conventions and conferences.

John A. Morrison

Feb. 6, 1893
near St. James, Missouri

Dec. 23, 1965
Anderson, Indiana

President of Anderson (IN) College and Theological Seminary, 1919–58, during which time the school grew from 50 to 1,251 and the faculty from 5 to 50. Morrison married Eunice Drennen on September 25, 1912. He was ordained into the Church of God in Anderson in 1916. He pastored in Delt, CO from 1917–19. He then served as a professor at Anderson College and wrote several books, including *Deacon of Dobbinsville* (1921) and *As I Was Thinking*. He died of a heart attack, and his funeral was at Park Place Church of God, where he was a member for 46 years.

William M. Branham

April 6, 1909
near Berksville, Kentucky

Dec. 24, 1965
Amarillo, Texas

Great Pentecostal healing and deliverance evangelist. He was converted in 1928. Branham began his ministry as an Independent Baptist. In 1933, he preached to 3,000 in a tent revival in Jeffersonville, IN with many converted. He married Hope Brumbech in December, 1934. His wife and baby died in 1937 in the Ohio River flood. After their death, he traveled on the Pentecostal circuit filling many auditoriums with needy people. He later married Meda Broy. In 1946, he said an angel appeared to him in a cave and gave him healing power and discernment. Branham's ministry peaked in the years, 1946–55. He had huge meetings through 1955, second only to Oral Roberts. In 1948 he began *The Voice of Healing* magazine. He toured Europe and Africa in the early 1950s. The IRS filed suit against him in 1955 for tax evasion. Around 1960, his support waned as he began to emphasize non-conventional doctrines and philosophies. He implied he might be the messenger of Malachi 4:5. Branham was killed in an automobile accident. He was not buried until Easter, 1966, because his wife was unable to decide where to bury him.

Eugene R. Kellersburger

Aug. 6, 1888
Cypress Mills, Texas

Jan. 10, 1966
New York, New York (?)

General secretary of American Leprosy Mission, NYC 1941–1953. Kellersburger married Edna Bosche (died: 1923) and Julia Skinner on Feb. 3, 1930 (died: 1986). He was a Presbyterian medical missionary to the Belgian Congo, 1916–40, ministering to people with tropical diseases, specfically leprosy, and won several honors. At his Bibanga hospital, he treated over 10,000 cases of African sleeping sickness. He founded the Bibanga Agricultural Leprosy Colony. His second wife authored nine books.

John A. Aasgard

April 5, 1876
Albert Lea, Minnesota

Jan. 13, 1966
Cokato, Minnesota

President of Norwegian Lutheran Church in America, 1925–46, renamed **Evangelical Lutheran Church** (ALC, ELCA in 1988), **1946–54.** Aasgard was ordained a Lutheran in 1901, then pastored in DeForest, WI from 1901–11. He married Ragnhild Hoyme on April 7, 1902. Aasgard served as the editor of the *Lutheran Journal* (1908–11) and as the president of Concordia College, Moorhead, MN from 1911–25.

Joe Getz

Nov. 20, 1889
Morton, Illinois

Feb. 15, 1966
Morton, Illinois

First leader of the Apostolic Christian Churches of America, Peoria, IL, 1956–66. Basically, he pastored in Morton most of his life. The title was not president but could have been secretary. Current officials feel he was the leading light during this time. This was an evangelical Baptist movement prior to 1918.His wife was Elizabeth Altordfer.

Walter N. Roberts

Aug. 17, 1898
Lewisburg, Ohio

Feb. 20, 1966
Dayton, Ohio

President of Bonebreak Theological Seminary, 1938–54; United Theological Seminary, 1954–65, both of Dayton, OH; of American Association of Theological Schools, 1956–59; and executive secretary of the same, 1954–56. Bonebreak merged with Evangelical School of Theology, Reading, PA to create UTS. Roberts married Marjorie Miller on August 22, 1922 (died: 1971). He was ordained into the ministry in August, 1924, and served as a missionary to the Phillipines, 1925–30. He also pastored in Dayton, OH, from 1932–38. He died within a few hours following his return from a 4 ½ month missions trip. He wrote *The Filipino Church* (1936).

Talmage Payne

Sept. 20, 1896
Salt Lake City, Utah

March, 1966
East Point, Georgia

First president of Carver Bible Institute and College, Atlanta, GA, 1943–63. Payne spent his childhood around Seattle, WA. While working in Alaska, he missed a train that crashed and killed everyone. He felt destined to accomplish something for God, so he attended MBI and graduated in 1924. His wife, Grace, was born June 6, 1898, in Rochester, NY. They served in China, 1925–41. They went separately to China with CIM and were married there in 1928. They began to work with the Lisu people that JAMES FRAZER had pioneered. Some 630 families became Christians. Mrs. Payne died January 2, 1993 in Marietta, GA.

Frank R. Birch

Aug. 23, 1893   *March 26, 1966*
Solon, Michigan

Director of Wesleyan Methodist Church in America (Wesleyan Church in 1968) **World Missions, 1942–59, and president of EFMA, 1950–52**. Birch was converted at age 17, and married Zola Kinneson in 1915 (died: 1950). He went to Sierra Leone, West Africa, to serve, 1919–39. In his later years, he directed Wesleyan homes in Brooksville, FL.

Andrew W. Blackwood

Aug. 5, 1882   *March 28, 1966*
Clay Center, Kansas   *Andrew W. Blackwood*   Lakeland, Florida (?)

Outstanding pastor, educator, and author with the United Presbyterian Church. Blackwood married Carolyn Phillips on April 6, 1910. He pastored in Pittsburgh, PA; Columbia, SC; and Columbus, OH from 1908–25. He taught Bible and English at Louisville (KY) Presbyterian Seminary (1925–30); was a professor of homiletics at Princeton Theological Seminary (1930–50); and a professor of theology at Temple University (1950–58). Blackwood was a prolific writer of at least 22 books widely used by pastors, from *The Fine Art of Preaching* (1937) to *Evangelical Sermons for Special Days* (1961).

William B. Eerdmans

Nov. 4, 1882   *April 12, 1966*
Bolsward, Netherlands   Grand Rapids, Michigan

Founder and first president of Eerdmans Publishing Company, Grand Rapids, MI 1910–66. Eerdman came to America in 1901 and married Paula Install on August 31, 1911. In 1910, he founded a business that has grown into a major publishing house, focusing on theological books advocating Reformed/Calvinistic doctrine. Eerdman also founded the Calvin Foundation in Grand Rapids, MI, in 1950.

Fred Hoskins

Jan. 8, 1906   *April 20, 1966*
Allenville, Illinois   Garden City, New York

General secretary (CEO) of Congregational Christian Churches, 1956–57, and co-president of United Church of Christ, 1957–61. Hoskins married Alice Gardner on September 15, 1927 and was ordained a Disciples of Christ minister the same year. He was the director of religious education in two churches, 1926–37. He then pastored the United Congregational Church, Bridgeport, CT (1937–46); Plymouth Congregational Church, Des Moines, IA (1946–50); and First Congregational Church, Oak Park, IL (1950–56). He was professor at Chicago Theological Seminary (1961–64), and pastored the Community Church, Garden City, NY (1964–66).

Berlin M. Nottage

1899   *May 1966*
Bahama Islands, Caribbean   Detroit, Michigan

Outstanding pastor and conference speaker. Nottage received his formal education at government schools and moved to New York in 1909 to begin his ministry. In 1932, Nottage went to Detroit where his ministry at Bethany Tabernacle eventually reached out to the rest of the country, Canada, the Bahamas, Bermuda, and Jamaica. He had a weekly radio program and spoke at many Bible conferences across the land.

Eugene C. Routh

Nov. 26, 1874
Legrange, Texas

May 12, 1966
Dallas, Texas

Wrote the hymns "I Know the Bible Is True" (music by B. B. McKinney) **and "Speak to My Heart."** Routh married Mary Wroe on December 20, 1897 (died: June 21, 1925, and Alice Routh on July 7, 1926. Routh was ordained a Baptist in 1901. He wrote several books from *Life Story of J.B. Gambrell* (1929) to *According to the Scriptures* (1955). He was the editor of several journals, including *South-Texas Baptist* (1907–1912) and *The Commission* (1943–48).

Archie K. Bracken

Sept. 13, 1884
Inman, Tennessee

June 15, 1966
Pasadena, California

President of Bethany Nazarene College (Southern Nazarene University in 1986), **1920–28, 1930–42**. Bracken married Gertrude Humble on June 8, 1903 (died: 1904 giving birth to a baby boy who also died). He then married Mattie Green on Auust 27, 1908. He taught rural schools in Texas (1909–14); taught at Southeastern Nazarene College, Donaldson, GA (1917–18); and was president of Peniel College, Greenville, TX (1918–19). He later became the dean at Olivet Nazarene College, Kankakee, IL.

Roy L. Laurin

July 16, 1898
Chicago, Illinois

June 22, 1966
Pasadena, California

Christian leader in Southern California for 35 years, pastoring the San Gabriel Union Church for ten years. Laurin also pastored for 13 years at Eagle Rock (CA) Baptist Church. He then resigned pastoring and began his writing and radio ministry. He spoke at many Bible conferences and traveled to Hawaii, Central and South America and Europe. He wrote several books, including *Meet Yourself in the Bible*, a devotional exposition of seven NT books.

Bernard D. Zondervan

Oct. 8, 1910
Harrison, South Dakota

July 3, 1966
Grand Rapids, Michigan (?)

One of two famous brothers who started Zondervan Publishing Company in the bedroom of their home in Grandville, MI, in 1931. The Zondervans started the company as young men. Zondervan married Wilma Plas on June 8, 1933. He served as the Sunday School superintendent in his Christian Reformed Church. His son also shared his name. Both he and his son died of cancer.

Harvey H. Springer

Jan. 18, 1907
Tecumseh, Oklahoma

July 8, 1966
Denver, Colorado

Evangelist and pastor of FBC, Englewood, CO. Springer was converted at a revival meeting at Capitol Baptist Church, Oklahoma City, OK. He was a graduate of Practical Bible Training College of Johnson City, NY. Fourteen months later, in 1936, he was called to FBC where he pastored 30 years. Springer stood 6'5" tall and had a voice like a foghorn. One of his revival meetings in Englewood, CO, reaped over 900 conversions. He edited *Western Voice* and founded the Independent Bible Baptist Mission. He was known for his saying "Well, glory!" He was kicked by a horse during a rodeo at his Silver State Youth Camp, 25 miles southwest of Denver, and died nearly 13 hours later. His wife Evalena Shaffer, an exceptional pianist, died February 5, 1977.

Donald Gee

May 20, 1891
London, England

July 20, 1966
London, England

Chairman of Pentecostal World Fellowship, 1955–58. Gee was converted (1905) in a Congregational Church, London, via Methodist Seth Joshua, and married (1913). In 1920, he began pastoring in Leith, Scotland. Then he pastored a Pentecostal Church in Edinburgh until 1932. In 1928, he took a six-month tour of Australia, opening up a worldwide conference and evangelism ministry for the next 23 years. From 1951–64, he was the principal of the Bible College of Assemblies of God in Kenley, England. His second marriage was to Jean Combs on October 3, 1964. He was the editor of *Pentecost*, but his best known book is *Concerning Spiritual Gifts*. He died of heart failure.

Arthur B. Langlie

July 25, 1900
Lanesboro, Minnesota

July 24, 1966
Seattle, Washington (?)

Governor of Washington, 1941–45, 1949–57. Langlie had a strong testimony for Christ. He married Evelyn Baker on September 15, 1928. His career began as a local lawyer (1926–35), then as mayor of Seattle (1938–41). He served in active duty in the Navy during WWII and won numerous awards for his leadership and patriotism. He was a Republican and a Presbyterian.

Vincent Joy

June 22, 1914
Baldwin, Long Island, New York

Aug. 31, 1966
Anchorage, Alaska

Director of Central Alaska Missions (merged with Far Eastern Gospel Crusade in 1971, renamed SEND in 1981), **1937–66.** Joy married Beckie Coffee on August 25, 1934 (died: 1984). In 1937, the mission was incorporated. They ministered in an Indian village in Copper Center. By 1957, there were 22 missionaries and a hospital. Later a Bible school, radio station, and periodical developed.

Tom Speer

March 10, 1891
Fayetteville, Georgia

Sept. 6, 1966
Nashville, Tennessee

"Dad" Speer, head of the amazing musical Speer family that blessed audiences with gospel music for decades. Speer grew up in Cullman County, AL. He wrote many songs, sang at every opportunity, and taught in many music schools. One of his students was Mosie Lister. He married Lena Brock (1900–67) in 1920. In 1921, he and his wife organized the Speer Quartet and began to travel in singing conventions. His theme song was "Won't We Be So Happy." He also wrote "I Never Shall Forget the Day."

Granville H. Montgomery

May 27, 1903
Merrimac, Virginia

September 30, 1966
Kansas City, Missouri

Pastor, superintendent, evangelist, and editor in the Pentecostal Holiness Church. Montgomery was converted in 1918, and pastored both in the South and the East. He was the editor of the *PHC Advocate* (1937–49). He also managed the PHC publishing house and was the superintendent of evangelism. From 1952–61, Montgomery wrote most of Oral Roberts' books and edited his publications. He edited the *Christian Challenge* (1961–63). Montgomery was also an editor and president of Defenders, Inc., 1963–66. Three of his seven children were born deaf.

Robert J. G. McKnight

July 9, 1878
Slippery Rock, Pennsylvania

Oct. 4, 1966
Pittsburgh, Pennsylvania

First president of Reformed Presbyterian Theological Seminary, Pittsburgh, PA 1916–53. McKnight married Grace Patterson on September 20, 1905. He was ordained as a Reformed Presbyterian in 1903 and pastored in Wilkinsburg, PA from 1906–16. He then went to RPTS in 1916 as a teacher of Bible literature. He was also the president of Keystone Driller Company and Laydee Land Company, both in Beaver Falls, PA.

Smiley Blanton

May 7, 1882
Unionville, Tennessee

Oct. 30, 1966
New York, New York (?)

Psychiatrist who, with NORMAN V. PEALE, started the Blanton-Peale Institute of Religion and Psychiatry, New York City in 1937. Smiley married Margaret Gray on October 18, 1910. He was instructor of speech at Cornell (NY) University (1907–11), then at the University of Wisconsin, (1914–24). He directed the Minneapolis Child Guidance Clinic (1924–27), was professor of Child Study at Vassar University (1927–31), then served again at Cornell University as an associate professor of clinical psychiatry (1933–38). He practiced medicine in NYC off and on from 1931 on. In 1943, Vanderbilt University utilized his talents. As a Christian, he and Dr. Peale helped scores of people with their emotional problems. He wrote several books including *The Healing Power of Poetry* (1960). He is buried in Nashville, TN.

Albert S. Reitz

Jan. 20, 1879
Lyons, Kansas

Nov. 1, 1966
Inglewood, California

Pastor and songwriter. He wrote the lyrics and music to "Teach Me to Pray, Lord," "Twas a Glad Day When Jesus Found Me," "The Shepherd of Love," and "Oh, Wonderful Love." Reitz traveled for seven years with Evangelist HENRY OSTROM. He was ordained a Baptist. He held pastorates at FBC, Berlin, WI (1918–21); Rosehill Baptist, Los Angeles; and Fairview Baptist, Inglewood, CA (1926–52). His wife's name was Elsie. He wrote over 100 hymns from 1911–66.

Harry L. Bowlby

Jan. 26, 1874
near Asbury, New Jersey

Nov. 17, 1966
Bloomfield, New Jersey

Executive director of Lord's Day Alliance, New York City (Atlanta in 1970), **1913–54**. Ordained in 1904, Bowlby pastored at First Presbyterian Church, Altoona, PA from 1905–13. Bowlby married Bertha H. Watson on November 6, 1909. In both world wars, he was a visiting speaker to military camps and forts. He belonged to many historical and cultural societies. Bowlby was a Republican and a Mason. He lived in Poughkeepsie, NY.

James A. Jones

Oct. 3, 1911
Laurinburg, North Carolina

Nov. 17, 1966
Richmond, Virginia

President of Union Theological Seminary, Richmond, VA, 1955–56 and of Association of Theological Schools, 1960–62. Jones married Mary Boyd on June 20, 1934, and was ordained a Presbyterian in 1935. He pastored in Henderson, NC (1935–39), and in Charlotte, NC (1939–55). Jones served as the chairman of the Board of World Missions in his denomination, 1964–66. He belonged to several clubs in the Richmond area. He wrote *The Holy Spirit* and *Today* (1950).

Charles F. Weigle

Nov. 20, 1871
Lafayette, Indiana

Dec. 3, 1966
Chattanooga, Tennessee

Wrote the lyrics and music for "No One Ever Cared for Me Like Jesus" in 1932, "Ever in Thee, O Lord," "Down Deep in the Sea," and wrote lyrics to "I Have Found a Hiding Place," "A Little Nearer Home," "I Sing of Thee," "Christ Is More to Me Than Ever," and "Wondrous Grace Hath Blessed My Soul" (music of all by G. B. Muller). Weigle was converted at a Methodist revival meeting in Lafayette at age twelve. He married Mollie Ratch in 1892. He headquartered in Sebring, FL, from 1915-51. He was an outstanding evangelist, but his wife would not follow his dedication and left him around 1927. She died in 1932. That is when he wrote his classic song, "No One Ever Cared For Me Like Jesus." He continued as an evangelist and singer. He became a Baptist in 1933, having previously been in the Friends (Quaker) Movement. He married his second wife, Carrie Hitt (died: March 1, 1962). Weigle then lived out his days at Tennessee Temple University, Chattanooga, TN. He wrote some 400 other songs.

Joseph (Joe) H. Hankins

1889
Arkansas

1967

Great evangelist who, as a youth, was known as a weeping prophet. Hankins was converted at his bedside via his mother reading John 3:16. He pastored in Pine Bluff, AR; Bells, TN (1925–26); Whitewright, TX (1926–29); and Childress, TX (1929–35). Then he went to the FBC, Little Rock, AR, from 1937–42. At FBC he saw 2,943 join, an average of 227 baptisms per year, and the Sunday School grow from 257 to 1,400 members. He went into full-time evangelism in 1942, holding many large crusades.

Thomas Tiplady

Jan. 1, 1882
Wensleydale, England

Jan. 7, 1967

Methodist hymn writer. Tiplady's ministry began as he inaugurated the Guild Hall services at Portsmouth, England. In 1919, he preached and lectured in 43 states in the US in five months. He has many hymns in church hymnals including "Beyond the Wheeling Words of Light," and "O Men of God, Go Forth to Win."

Ivan L. Holt

Jan. 9, 1886
DeWitt, Arkansas

Jan. 12, 1967
Atlanta, Georgia

President of Federal Council of Churches (NCC in 1950), **1934–36, and longtime Methodist bishop, 1938–56.** Holt married Leland Burks on June 6, 1906 (died: 1948), Mrs. Starr Carithers in 1950 (died: 1958), and Modena Rudiswell on April 15, 1960. He pastored in St. Louis, MO (1909–11); Cape Girardeau, MO (1911–15); taught at Southern Methodist University (1915–18); and pastored at St. John's Methodist Church, St. Louis, MO (1918–38). His bishop locale included Dallas (1940–44) and Missouri (1944–56). He was president of the World Methodist Council in 1951. He wrote a few books beginning with *The Return of Spring to a Man's Soul* (1934). He is buried in St. Louis.

Paul H. Roth

Dec. 21, 1880
Utica, New York

Jan. 13, 1967
Minneapolis, Minnesota

President of Northwestern Lutheran (Luther-Northwestern in 1982) **Theological Seminary, Minneapolis, MN 1935–50.** He pastored in Beloit, WI (1906–13); and at St. John's Church, Maywood, IL (1913–17). Roth married Sara Landers on April 22, 1914 (died: 1925), and Marie

Dahl on August 16, 1926. He began at NLTS (at Fargo, North Dakota, until 1927) as a professor of history in 1920. He wrote many tracts and articles.

Harry M. Shuman

July 18, 1875
Mineral Point, Pennsylvania

January 17, 1967
Deland, Florida

President of Christian and Missionary Alliance, 1925–54, and of Nyack (NY) College, 1926–40. Shuman married Ada Baker in 1903 (died: 1949). He then married Helen Watson on May 6, 1954. He pastored in Washington, PA and Wilmington, DE from 1909–17. He also served as the Superintendent of Central District (six states), 1917–25. He edited *The Alliance Witness* (1930–50). He was a Spirit-filled man of faith.

Otto F. K. Dibelius

May 15, 1880
Berlin, Germany

Jan. 31, 1967
Berlin, Germany

President of the World Council of Churches, 1954–61. Dibelius married Armgard Wilmanns on November 13, 1907 (died: December 2, 1952). He pastored (1907–25), was superintendent (1925–33) in East Prussia, was removed by the Nazis in 1933 from any official church position, and was jailed seven times. Dibelius was a Lutheran bishop of Berlin, of the East German province of Brandenburg (1945–66), and was the head of the German Evangelical Church Conference (1949–61), which he helped found by bringing all denominations into one. He was a supporter of the Confessing Church and an outspoken opposer of Nazism and Communism. Dibelius was barred from East Germany after the war. He wrote three books.

Albert W. T. Orsborn

Sept. 4, 1886
Maidstone, England

Feb. 4, 1967
Boscombe, England

General of Salvation Army, 1946–54. Orsborn was converted at age 15 at one of his father's evangelistic meetings in London's east end (Walthanstow). He married Evalina Barker in 1909 (died: 1942) and Evelyn Berry in 1944 (died: 1945). Orsborn then married Phyllis Taylor on August 2, 1947. He led a work in New Zealand (1933–36), in Scotland, and in Ireland (1936–40), and was a British commander (1940–46). In January 1947, he received a Royal summons to Buckingham Palace, for an audience with King GEORGE VI, a great supporter of the work of the Salvation Army. He attended the wedding of Princess Elizabeth and Prince Phillip (1947) and the Coronation of Queen Elizabeth II (1953). Orsborn was the first Salvation Army general to give a world radio broadcast and the first to be seen on television. He was an able and talented poet, composing over 200 songs and choruses and writing many inspirational verses. He traveled widely as a speaker. He wrote *The House of My Pilgrimage*.

Roger W. Babson

July 6, 1875
Gloucester, Massachusetts

March 5, 1967
Lake Wales, Florida

Economist and business analyst. Babson was founder of the Business Statistics Organization of Babson Institute, Wellesley Hills, MA, and with his wife, founded Webber College, Babson Park, FL, and Midwest Institute, Eureka, KA. Reared as a Congregationalist, Babson testified of his faith in Christ in public encounters. On March 29, 1900, he married Grace Knight (died: 1956) and after her death, married Nona Dougherty on June 1, 1959 (died: 1963). Known as a financial genius, he began to tithe as a youth and never ceased as prosperity came his way. In a business success leaflet that he sent to his clients, he included the Ten Commandments and the "New Commandment" of Jesus. He was a prohibition candidate for U.S. president in 1940. He wrote several books.

Thomas A. Melton

Sept. 5, 1893
Gaston City, North Carolina

March 11, 1967
Charlotte, North Carolina

General superintendent of Pentecostal Holiness Church (International in 1975), **1946–53**. Before his teen years, Melton worked twelve hours a day in a cotton mill. At age 15 he was converted in a tent revival. At Holmes Bible College he met Emma Young, whom he married on June 11, 1919. His pastorates from 1923 to early 1940s were in Winston-Salem, NC; Danville, VA; Marion, NC; Durham, NC; Hurt, VA; and Leaksville, NC. He also directed the PHC missions program, 1950–61. From 1953–61, he resumed pastoring. His last message was March 8th at PHC in Charlotte, NC, on Psalm 73.

Henry H. Bagger

Nov. 12, 1893
Brooklyn, New York

March 14, 1967
Philadelphia, Pennsylvania

President of Lutheran Theological Seminary at Philadelphia, 1952–62. Bagger married Margaret Finck on August 20, 1920. He pastored in Morgantown, WV (1919–21) and Butler, PA (1921–30). He was also the president of Pittsburgh Synod of Evangelical Lutheran Churches (1930–40), after which he pastored the Holy Trinity Church, Lancaster, PA (1940–52). Bagger was involved in various Lutheran causes. He is buried in Butler, PA.

George T. B. Davis

July 4, 1873
near Staunton, Illinois

March 21, 1967

Responsible for distributing New Testaments by the millions to China, Latin America, the Philippines, and to the Jewish people. Davis was led to Christ by his parents, his father being a pastor, when he was eight years old. He went to England in 1904 and helped with revival journalism for the TORREY crusades. He was a Presbyterian evangelist and also worked with PTL from 1912–24. Davis's ministry was headquartered in Philadelphia and was called Million Testaments Campaign. Davis married Rose Fox on November 20, 1934 (died: March 23, 1981). He wrote several books, from *D. L. MOODY* (1899) to *When the Fire Fell* (1945).

Edward J. Carnell

June 28, 1919
Antigo, Wisconsin

April 25, 1967
Oakland, California

Controversial theologian, educator, and president of Fuller Theological Seminary, 1954–59. After Carnell married Shirley Rowe on January 1, 1944, he was ordained a Baptist, taught at Gordon College and Divinity School, 1945–48, then at Fuller as a professor of apologetics and theology. After 1959, he taught ethics and philosophy of religion. His writings include *An Introduction to Christian Apologetics* (1948), the controversial *The Case for Orthodox Theology* (1957), and *The Case for Biblical Christianity* (1969). He wrote nine books in all. This intellectual awakening caused Fuller Seminary to be suspect as to leaving its founding principles. Carnell was an important link between the liberal and conservative movements and was largely responsible for articulating the contemporary New Evangelical [a term first used by HAROLD OCKENGA in 1948, popularized by theologians, led by Fuller Seminary. In essence, some northern fundamentalists felt that fundamentalism needed to be purged of sectarian, combative, anti-intellectual and anti-cultural traits. Fundamentalists saw the movement as compromising in music, standards, ecumenical evangelism (liberals joining evangelicals in sponsorship) and weak in defending biblical absolutes] position. He died of a barbiturate overdose while attending a conference. He is buried in Whittier, CA.

J. Friedrich Heiler

Jan. 30, 1892
Munich, Germany

April 28, 1967
Munich, Germany

Writer and scholar of history and religion, a leader in Christian unity enterprises. Heiler was influenced by NATHAN SODERHOLM and converted from Catholicism to Lutheranism in 1919. Heiler was a professor of comparative religions in Marburg, 1922 on. He organized the German High Church movement in 1929 and introduced an evangelical form of monasticism. His most important book was an analysis on prayer, *Das Gebet* (1918) (*Prayer* in English, 1923). He also wrote *Form and Essence of Religion* (1961).

Petrus O. I. Bersell

May 6, 1882
Rock Island, Illinois

May 1, 1967
Minneapolis, Minnesota

President of Augustan Lutheran Church (LCA, ELCA in 1988), **1935–51**. Bersell married Emilia Bergh on August 20, 1908 (died: December 1958). He pastored in Chicago Heights, IL (1906–11); at the Grace Lutheran Church, Chicago, IL (1911–13); and in Ottumwa, IA (1913–35). He edited *The Lutheran Brotherhood Bond* (1930–67). He was also president of National Lutheran Council (1941–45) and the chairman of Lutheran Service Commission (1941–64).

Leon Rosenberg

Feb. 15, 1875

May 17, 1967

Long time director of the American-European Bethel Mission, Inc., Los Angeles, CA. Rosenberg was born into an orthodox Jewish family, and his study of prophecy caused his conversion. He began an active ministry in 1899. During his ministry, he suffered the restraints of Czarism, cruelties of Communism, and horrors of Nazism. Rosenberg married his wife Fanny in 1899. He ministered in Odessa, Russia, 1899–1922 under the British Mildmay Mission. He then went to Frankfurt, German, which had a large Jewish population. In 1927, he went to Lodz, Poland. After WWII, he changed the name from the Bethel Mission of Eastern Europe to AEBM, 1945, expanding to Israel and America, with headquarters in Los Angeles.

Algoth Ohlson

July 28, 1880
Brevik, Sweden

June 23, 1967
Oakland, California (?)

President of North Park Theological Seminary and College, Chicago, IL 1924–49. He immigrated to the United States in 1900. He married Ruth Carlson on September 6, 1911 and was ordained to Mission (Evangelical) Covenant Church in 1915. He pastored in Lowell, MA (1915–18) and in Chicago (1918–24). He was decorated Knight of the North Star by the King of Sweden in 1947. He retired to Oakland, CA.

Bruce Barton

Aug. 5, 1886
Robbins, Tennessee

July 5, 1967
New York, New York

Journalist, advertising executive, author, and congressman. Two books made him famous: *The Man Nobody Knows* (1925) and *The Book Nobody Knows* (1926). He grew up in Oak Park, IL, where his father was a Congregationalist minister. Barton moved to New York City in 1909 and then married Esther Randall on Oct. 2, 1913 (died: Nov. 20, 1951). He was the editor of *Every*

Week (1914–18) and an honorary member of the Board of Batten, Barton, Durstine, and Osborn, a firm he started in 1918. He worked for several years in an advertisement agency in NYC and also served as a member of the House of Representatives from New York. He originated the saying, "A man may be down, but he's never out." A faithful Congregationalist, he remained in advertising till he had a stroke in 1957. His funeral was at Central Presbyterian Church in NYC. He wrote *The Resurrection of the Soul* (1912) to *He Upset the World* (1932).

George W. Wailes

Aug. 22, 1866
Salisbury, Maryland

July 12, 1967
Philadelphia, Pennsylvania

Dean of Reformed Episcopal Seminary, 1936–59. He was ordained a Presbyterian minister in 1897. Wailes married Lucretia M. Franklin on October 8, 1902 (died: August 8, 1918). He pastored Scots Church, Philadelphia (1897–1908) and was professor of English Bible and Greek at Ursinus College, Collegeville, PA (1908–19). He taught exegetical theology at RES (1919–26), then was professor of Biblical language and English Bible at Temple University (1926–49), overlapping with his RES leadership, which he continued until age 93.

Maud Cary

Nov. 19, 1877
Little Falls, Minnesota

July 15, 1967
Liberty, Missouri

Undoubtedly Morocco's greatest missionary. In 1901, Maud sailed with four other Gospel Missionary Union missionaries to begin 50 years of service to this country just south of Spain. She studied Arabic and Berber. After 23 years, with very little results, she returned home for her first furlough. Back in Morocco at age 47, Maud finally began to see some fruit. WWII took its toll, but with more missionaries coming in 1948, things improved further. A Bible institute opened (1951); and, with her retirement (1955), a Bible correspondence course was developed with 30,000 Moslems enrolling. It was not a great revival she saw, but in a most difficult area she simply stayed with the vision until a solid work developed. The doors closed in 1967 to all foreign missionaries. She died at the "Odd Fellow's Home" in Missouri at age 89.

Sherman L. Greene

June 16, 1886
Vicksburg, Mississippi

July 25, 1967
Atlanta, Georgia

Bishop of African Methodist Episcopal Church, 1928–67; senior bishop, 1953–67. Greene was converted at age ten in a rural camp meeting by Elder Brookins. He held pastorates in Little Rock, AR; in Shreveport and New Orleans, LA; and was a presiding elder in Mississippi, 1906–19. Greene served as the president of Shorter College in Little Rock, AR from 1918–24. Greene married Pinkie Spencer on June 21, 1905 (died: September 1961), then married Callie Logan on May 28, 1962. He was a highly respected man in his denomination, a born leader, who headquartered his work in Atlanta.

Arthur Stace

Feb. 5, 1885
Sydney, Australia

July 30, 1967
Sydney, Australia

Extraordinary witness. Stace was a thin, little man, no more than 5 feet, three inches tall. He was uneducated and could barely write his name. Yet, for 37 years this incredible person would rise at 5 a.m. each morning to walk the streets of Sydney and its suburbs, secretly writing with chalk on the pavements just one word...*Eternity*. In this way, day after day, he preached his sermon, estimated at over 500,000 times, to the busy crowds of shoppers and workers. He averaged writing it 50 times a day and was usually home by 10 a.m. His message even appeared in Melbourne, 1,000 miles away. Occasionally, the message would change to "*Obey God,*" but it soon returned to the original word. After 24 years of this mysterious message appearing everywhere, his pastor at Burton Street Baptist Church asked him in 1956, "Are you *Mr. Eternity*?" Back came the answer, "Guilty, your honor!" Stace was raised in a dysfunctional family. At the age of 14, he moved into a coal mine and served his first jail time at age 15. After serving in WWI, 1914–18, he became a drifter, feeding out of rubbish bins. On August 6, 1930, he wandered into a needy men's meeting and heard the gospel. Afterwards, in University Park, he cried out to God to save him. In November, 1932, he heard evangelist JOHN RIDLEY speaking on Isaiah 57:15, stressing the word "eternity." He was thereafter compelled to bring this message to the world the only way he felt he could.

Samuel D. Press

May 24, 1875
Cambria, Wisconsin

Aug. 14, 1967
St. Louis, Missouri

President of Eden Theological Seminary, St. Louis, MO, 1918–41. Press married Elise Scheef on January 15, 1907. He was ordained to the ministry of the Evangelical Synod of North America in 1896. He pastored several churches in Texas till 1908 (Marlin, Gay Hill, back to Marlin, Houston). He was professor of theology at Eden, 1908–19. He lived in Webster Groves, MO.

Armin G. Weng

Oct. 9, 1897
Oshkosh, Wisconsin

Aug. 29, 1967
Rockford, Illinois

President of Chicago Lutheran Theological Seminary (Lutheran School of Theology-Chicago in 1964), **Maywood, IL, 1941–1942, 1948–1964.** Weng married Helga Westerberg on June 21, 1924 (died: 1946), and Marjory Ruth on September 6, 1947 (died: August, 1964). He pastored at First English Lutheran, Bridgeport, CT (1922–27); Immanuel Lutheran, Philadelphia, PA (1927–30); Holy Trinity, Elgin, IL (1930–37). He also served as president of the Illinois Synod, 1937–48. He was the editor of *Gleaner*, (1938–67).

T. Christie Innes

June 29, 1909
Aberdeen, Scotland

Sept. 15, 1967
Pittsburgh, Pennsylvania (?)

Strong Presbyterian pastor. Innes married Anna Grant and Dorothy Liddle. He came to the US in 1944 after he pastored in Toronto, 1939–44. Then he served as the general secretary of American Tract Society, 1944–48. He pastored at Calvary Presbyterian, San Francisco, CA (1948–53); Collingwood Presbyterian of Toledo, OH (1953–60); and Eastminster Presbyterian of Pittsburgh (1960–67). He wrote four books, from *Thrilling Voices from the Past* (1936) to *Battle Tested Religion* (1944).

V. Raymond Edman

May 9, 1900
Chicago Heights, Illinois

Sept. 22, 1967
Wheaton, Illinois

President of Wheaton (IL) College, 1940–64, during some of the school's greatest days. Edman was converted as a high school senior in an evangelistic meeting in Chicago Heights, IL in June 1918, with evangelist I. E. Honeywell. He married Edith Olson on June 18, 1924, who was a missionary educator to the Quechua Indians in Ecuador (1923–28), and pastored the Gospel Tabernacle (CMA) in Worcester, MA (1929–35). Health problems brought him home from the mission field, so he taught history and political science at Wheaton College, 1936–40, and also succeeded A.W. TOZER as editor of the *Alliance Weekly*. During his presidency at Wheaton, 14 major buildings were constructed. He was a close friend of JOHN R. RICE and the *Sword of the Lord*. During chapel, while he was preaching to 1,800 students, he had a heart attack, slumped to the floor, and went immediately to heaven. His sermon was called "The Presence of the King." Billy Graham conducted the funeral. Edman wrote 19 books, from *Swords and Plowshares* (1947) to *Then and There* (1964). Edman's life verse was Nahum 1:7.

Nye J. Langmade

March 10, 1892
Brainerd, Minnesota

Oct. 4, 1967
Salina, Kansas

President of Independent Fundamental Churches of America, 1940–42, executive secretary of the same, 1950–55, and first president of Midwest Bible College (merged to become Calvary Bible College, Kansas City, MO in 1962), **1938–54**. Langmade married Lillibelle Clayson on April 8, 1913. Before he went into the ministry, he opened a chain of grocery stores, 1914–22. His pastorates were Wadena (MN) Bible (1922–25); Duluth (MN) Gospel Center (1926–28); Midway Tabernacle, Boone, IA (1929–32), Salma Bible Church (1932–46); and Gospel Center, St. Louis, MO (1946–52). He was stricken with fever one day after producing his 12,718th consecutive radio broadcast of "Bit of Cheer and Sunshine," started in 1932.

Arthur T. Morgan

Aug. 27, 1901
Lufkin, Texas

Oct. 18, 1967
Tulsa, Oklahoma

General superintendent of United Pentecostal Church, Hazelwood, MO 1951–67. Morgan grew up in Louisiana and was ordained into the Pentecostal Assemblies of the World in 1929. He pastored in Louisiana and Texas, served as the superintendent of the South Central District of the Pentecostal Church (1944–45), then as secretary/treasurer of the Texas district of UPC (1945–51). He died suddenly of a heart attack.

Arthur Petrie

1888
London, England

Nov. 4, 1967
Seattle, Washington

Christian and Missionary Alliance missionary and pastor. At the time of his death, he was a professor at the Seattle (WA) Bible Training School of the Philadelphia Church, serving there, 1957 on. He died of wounds he suffered in a fall on October 22, 1967, resulting in severe head injuries. Petrie wrote many books and pamphlets during his life and often had prize-winning sermons published in the *Sword of the Lord*. His wife's name was Dorothy.

J. Whitcomb Brougher

Jan. 7, 1870
Vernon, Indiana

Nov. 10, 1967
Glendale, California (?)

Strong fundamentalist who (like WILLIAM RILEY) **stayed in the Northern Baptist Convention**. He pastored the FBC of Paterson, NJ (1894–99); the FBC of Chattanooga, TN (1899–1904); White Temple, Portland, OR (1904–10); Temple Baptist, Los Angeles (1910–26); FBC of Oakland, CA (1926–30); Tremont Temple, Boston (1930–35); and associate pastor, FBC Glendale, CA (1935–45). He was president of the American Publication Society, 1913–17, and of NBC in 1926. He married Corinna S. Morse, on July 28, 1891 (died: 1939) and Margaret T. Wood in 1945.

J. Kenneth Pfohl

Aug. 13, 1874
Winston-Salem, North Carolina

Nov. 27, 1967
Winston-Salem, North Carolina

President of Moravian Church in NA (South), Winston-Salem, NC 1929–53. Pfohl married Bessie Whittington on Aug. 21, 1901 (died: Nov. 23, 1971). He was principal at Clemmons (NC) School (1900–03), pastored at Christ Church (1903–08), and at Home Church (1908–34), both in Winston-Salem, NC. He was consecrated a bishop of the Moravian Church in 1931. He was active in many Moravian activities such as trustee of Moravian College and Seminary and of Salem College. Pfohl wrote *The Moravian Church* (1926). He was made pastor of Salem Congregation in 1931 and actually led two churches (see above) till 1934. He then resigned the Home Church, pastoring at Salem till 1962, and compiled each year's "Things Worthy of Remembrance" into the volume *Memorabilia of Salem Congregation*, 1931–61.

Henry H. Savage

July 23, 1887
Blair, Nebraska

Dec. 3, 1967
Muskegon, Michigan

President of National Association of Evangelicals, 1954–55. Savage married Bessie Jenson on Dec. 25, 1912. He had three wonderful missionary children, Bob, Jim and Helen. He was a lifelong pastor of the FBC of Pontiac, MI from 1924–61, broadcasting his Sunday a.m. service starting in 1926. He was also the chairman and co-founder of Maranatha Bible Conference of Muskegon, MI. He wrote from *Facts* (1930) to *Finalities* (1959). He was active in Conservative Baptist circles.

Dick H. Walters

Dec. 11, 1907
Borculo, Michigan

Dec. 11, 1967
Grand Rapids, Michigan

President of Reformed Bible College, Grand Rapids, MI 1943–67. Walters helped guide the college through its early years. The college had only been in existence four years when he became president.

Leland S. Brubaker

March 6, 1899
Merced, California

Dec. 29, 1967
Lavern, California

Secretary of Church of the Brethren Missions, Elgin, IL 1942–57. He married Marie Woody in 1921, and they served as missionaries in Shansi, China, 1924–27. From 1928–36, he pastored in Covina, CA. He then spent four years as national director of the Brethren Young People's Department, 1936–40. His interest in missions was apparent, with trips to Europe, 1934–35, and in 1938, and to Japan in 1940. During the war years, he helped formulate Brethren relief policy. From 1957–64, when he retired, he was director of the Family Service Association in Elgin, IL.

John H. Paul

Sept. 23, 1877
Rapides Parish, Louisiana

Dec. 31, 1967
Ft. Wayne, Indiana

President of Taylor University, Upland, IN, 1922–31. Paul married Effie Eichardson on September 22, 1898, and Corey Stephens in 1946. He pastored rural Methodist churches in Texas and Mississippi until 1903. He was the editor of *Pentecostal Herald* (1904–8) and professor of philosophy at Meridan (MS) College, 1909–13. Paul was also vice president of Asbury College, Wilmore, KY (1916–22) and president of John Fletcher College, Oscaloosa, IA (1934–37). He wrote from *Silver Keys* (1907) to *Life and Times of Bishop William Taylor* (1927).

Aaron J. Kligerman

April 14, 1891
Novogard/Bolinsk, Russia

1968

Evangelist to the Jews. Kligerman was editor of *The American Hebrew Christian* (1934–66). In 1909, Aaron was given a NT in Odessa and was dealt with by Leon Rosenberg. His first marriage was to Jean K. Kac of Baltimore and then to Mimi L. Proctor, Jan. 21, 1951. One source says he married Dora Schinleck in 1911. Charles Mutchnick preached at the Chicago Hebrew Mission, resulting in Kligerman's conversion in 1912. He became a Hebrew Christian minister. Extensive schooling for Kligerman followed at MBI and the University of Dubuque (IA) Theological Seminary. From 1923–48, he worked among the Jews in Baltimore. Ordained a Presbyterian, he went to NYC with the board of National Missions, USA, to acquaint the Christian world with the need to reach Jewish people. He was elected president of the Hebrew Christian Alliance, with headquarters in London. He wrote *Messianic Prophecies in the Old Testament*.

Fredrich Tritton

1887
England

1968

First president of Friends World Committee, Philadelphia, PA 1938–46, 1948–50. Tritton was from England and had little formal education, yet he had an unusual ability to learn languages. He taught himself French, Spanish, and German. He did agricultural work during WWI as a conscientious objector. In 1920 he joined the Society of Friends and was made assistant secretary of the Friends Council for International Service. After attending the World Conference of Friends at Swarthmore, PA, he became aware of the "Quaker world." He lived here and was at home with his American "brothers" but remained a European.

Robert P. Daniel

Nov. 2, 1902
Ettrick, Virginia

Jan. 7, 1968
Petersburg, Virginia (?)

President of Shaw University Divinity School, Raleigh, NC 1936–50. He married Blanche Taylor on Sept. 11, 1929. He was a professor at Shaw University, 1926–36. Daniel was ordained to the Baptist ministry in 1940. In 1950, he became president of Virginia State College in Petersburg, VA. He was active in many religious and political activities, and also active in the Masons.

Bob Jones Sr.

Oct. 30, 1883
Shipperville, Alabama

Jan. 16, 1968
Greenville, South Carolina

Founder and first president of Bob Jones University, 1927–47. Jones was saved at age eleven, became a Sunday School superintendent by age 13, and was ordained at age 15. He married Bernice Sheffield on October 24, 1905 (she died less than a year later in August, 1906), and then Mary Stollenwerck on June 17, 1908. Jones was one of the most effective evangelists of his generation, holding crusades in every state and in 30 countries, beginning in 1920, preaching 12,000 times to 15 million people. He started BJU because of the great demand for Christian education. The school began in Panama City, FL, in 1926. It then moved to Cleveland, TN (1933) and finally reached university status with its establishment in Greenville, SC (1947). At his death, the school had 4,000 students and a value of $50 million. His biography is *Builder of Bridges* by R. R. Johnson.

"Do right [even] if the stars fall."

Fred F. Bosworth

Jan. 17, 1877
Utua, Nebraska

Jan. 21, 1968
Miami, Florida

Early Pentecostal leader, pastor, and healing evangelist. Bosworth was converted at a revival at the First Methodist Church of Omaha, NE. In September 1906, he accepted the Pentecostal message in Zion City, IL. He went to Denver, CO, in 1910, then to Dallas, TX, to pastor a church that rose to prominence as a revival center. In 1918, Bosworth left the Assemblies of God and joined the CMA. He held large crusades and healing campaigns, 1919–48. He welcomed blacks, which caused criticism. The last six years of his life, Bosworth worked for missions in Africa. He married Estella Hayde. His daughter, Lanore, married MERRILL DUNLOP.

Daniel A. Poling

Nov. 30, 1884
Portland, Oregon

Feb. 7, 1968
Philadelphia, Pennsylvania

President of Christian Endeavor (World), 1927–62 and (Int.), 1925–49, 1954–55. Poling married Susan VanderSall on September 25, 1906 (died: July 1918), and Lillian Heingartner on August 11, 1919, giving him a total of eight children. He pastored at Marble Collegiate Reformed Church, New York City (1923–30) and Baptist Temple, Philadelphia, PA (1936–48). He was editor of *Christian Herald* (1925–65). In the 1920's, he had a weekly radio program over NBC network. His son, Clarke, was one of the four chaplains drowned on the USS Dorchester in WWII on February 3, 1943. He worked with Temple University in 1948 and its Chapel of the Four Chaplains. He lost a mayoral race in Philadelphia in 1951. He wrote from *Mothers of Men* (1914) to *He Came from Galilee* (1965). His autobiography was *Mine Eyes Have Seen the Glory* (1959).

Edward J. Young

Nov. 29, 1907
San Francisco, California

Feb. 14, 1968
Huntingdon Valley, Pennsylvania

Instructor of Old Testament at Westminster Theological Seminary, Philadelphia, PA 1936–68 and professor from 1946 on. Young married Lillian Riggs on July 25, 1935 and was ordained Presbyterian the same year. He taught at Winona Lake (IN) Summer School of Theology, 1950–68. He wrote twelve books, from *The Prophecy of Daniel* (1949) to *Genesis Three* (1966). His three-volume *Commentary on Isaiah* (1965–72) is widely known. He spoke Russian, Arabic, Hebrew, and other Semitic languages. He is buried in Plymouth Meeting, PA.

Robert C. Grier (2)

Oct. 12, 1889
Due West, South Carolina

Feb. 18, 1968
Greenville, South Carolina

President of Erskine College, Due West, SC 1921–54. Grier married Gladys Patrick on November 17, 1915. Upon his ordination with the Associate Reformed Presbyterian Church in 1914, he pastored in Louisville, KY (1914–18), and in Columbia, SC (1918–21). He then gave the rest of his life to activities at Erskine College, where his father (WILLIAM GRIER), and his grandfather, (ROBERT C. GRIER) had served as presidents before him. Robert Grier Jr. led the school with finesse and initiated a development plan for its continued growth.

Horace G. Smith

March 28, 1881
Ransom, Illinois

Feb. 20, 1968
St. Petersburg, Florida

President of Garrett Biblical Institute (GETS in 1974), Evanston, IL 1932–53. Smith married Edith Gotsuch on September 1, 1909. He pastored in Glencoe, IL (1912–17); Evanston, IL (1917–24); and Wilmette, IL (1926–32). He led Garrett through the Depression and helped it gain financial stability again. He saw the name change from Biblical Institute to Theological Seminary. He wrote two books at the end of his leadership days.

John W. Behnken

March 19, 1884
Cypress, Texas

Feb. 23, 1968
Hollywood, Florida

President of Lutheran Church-Missouri Synod, 1935–62. Behnken married Gertrude Geisler on August 13, 1909 (died: July 27, 1910). He then married Hilda Grassmuck on April 22, 1914, and they had eight children. He pastored Trinity Lutheran Church, Houston, TX from 1908–35, and served as vice president of the denomination, 1929–35. He authored *Noonday Sermons* (1926) and *Mercies Manifold* (1951).

Roger M. Hickman

Nov. 28, 1888
South West, Missouri

Feb. 25, 1968
Lakeland, Florida

Composed music for Oswald Smith's great song "Saved, Saved." At age 16, Hickman moved to Independence, MO, and was converted at age 20. He met his wife at MBI and they served as evangelists until she died in 1942. He later was on staff at churches in Louisiana and Florida. He worked as a music director at Baptist Bible Institute in Lakeland, FL, from 1949–53, and wrote over 100 gospel songs.

Ferdinand Q. Blanchard

July 23, 1876
Jersey City, New Jersey

March 4, 1968
Cleveland, Ohio

Clergyman and hymn writer. Ordained a Congregationalist, Blanchard pastored at Southington, CT (1901–4); East Orange, NJ (1904–15); and at Euclid Avenue Congregational Church, Cleveland, OH, 1915 to retirement. He married Ethel West, June 19, 1901. He was moderator of the Congregational Christian Churches for the term ending in 1944. Blanchard wrote the hymns, "O Child of Lowly Manger Birth" (1906) and "Before the Cross of Jesus" (1928).

Charles E. Fuller

April 25, 1887
Los Angeles, California

March 19, 1968
Los Angeles/Pasadena, California

Director of a most effective evangelistic radio ministry, *The Old-Fashioned Revival Hour*, beginning in Los Angeles in 1934. Fuller reached millions of listeners weekly from his Pasadena-based radio broadcast for nearly 40 years. He married Grace Payton on October 21, 1911 (died: June 11, 1966) and graduated from Pomona (CA) College. He owned an orange orchard at the time of his conversion, which occurred in the backseat of a car following a Paul Rader crusade at the Church of the Open Door, Los Angeles, CA, July 30, 1916. In 1919, he entered BIOLA. He pastored Calvary Baptist Church of Placentia, CA, from 1925–32. The radio ministry began in 1930 on one station (evening services of his church) but soon grew to reach the entire U.S. by 1937 via mutual radio network. Gospel Broadcasting Association was launched in 1933. It reached ten million listeners in 1939, and the world in 1942. By 1944, it was the most popular religious broadcast in America. Broadcasts were recorded live (CBS) from the Municipal Auditorium, Long Beach, CA, where thousands attended until July 12, 1958. It is estimated that two million were converted through the years, one being Jerry Falwell. His theme song arrangement of the "Heavenly Sunshine" chorus was sung around the world. He founded Fuller Theological Seminary, Pasadena, CA, in 1947 with Harold Ockenga. Fuller's funeral was conducted at the Lake Avenue Congregational Church. He was buried at Forrest Lawn Cemetery.

Samuel H. Miller

Feb. 3, 1900
Philadelphia, Pennsylvania

March 20, 1968
Cambridge, Massachusetts

Dean of Harvard Divinity School, Cambridge, MA, 1959–68. Miller married Myra Studley (1918) and was ordained as a Baptist (1923). He pastored the Calvary Church in Belmar, NJ (1923–28); in Arlington, NJ (1928–30); at FBC, Clifton, NJ (1930–35); and at Old Cambridge Baptist Church (1935–59). He also taught philosophy of religion at Andover-Newton Theological School, Newton Center, MA from 1951–58. Miller was a strong ecumenist courting Jews and Catholics. He died of a heart attack. His writings ranged from *The Life of the Soul* (1951) to *Religion in a Technical Age* (1968).

Martin L. King Jr.

Jan. 15, 1929
Atlanta, Georgia

April 4, 1968
Memphis, Tennessee

Black Baptist minister who led the nonviolent civil rights movement from the mid-1950s. Born Michael Luther King Jr., he later had his name changed to Martin. He was educated at Crozer Theological Seminary, Chester, PA. King married Coretta Scott on June 17, 1953 and they had four children. He pastored at Dexter Avenue Baptist Church in Montgomery, AL from 1954–60. He organized opposition to bus segregation in Montgomery in 1956, which began his civil rights leadership (boycott by 50,000 blacks). He became the dominant leader against racial segregation, and helped found Southern Christian Leadership Conference in 1957. He co-pastored Ebenezar Baptist Church in Atlanta with his father, 1960–68. King led 250,000 people in a march on Washington, D.C. on August 28, 1963. At that time, he gave his famous "I Have a Dream" and "We Shall Overcome" speeches. King won the Nobel Peace Prize in 1964, as the youngest ever to receive the honor. That same year, the Civil Rights Act was passed. He led a campaign for voting rights in 1965. King was assassinated by gunfire while in Memphis organizing a demonstration on behalf of the local sanitation workers. James Earl Ray was the alleged assassin. Since 1986, the United States has honored King's memory with a national holiday. He wrote at least four books. Some suggested that he had Communist associations, although he dispelled these concerns with his sermon, "Why a Christian Cannot Be a Communist." He wrote books ranging from *Stride Toward Freedom* (1958) to *Why We Can't Wait* (1964). His favorite Bible verse was Exodus 9:1.

Norman J. Baugher

Aug. 4, 1917
York County, Pennsylvania

April 20, 1968
Elgin, Illinois

General Secretary of Church of the Brethren, Elgin, IL, 1952–68. Baugher married his wife, Ruth Crist, on June 1, 1940. He pastored in Maryland, Pennsylvania, New York, Indiana, and in Long Beach, CA, from 1945–52. He was the recording secretary of NCC (1957–60), vice president of NCC (1964–66), chairman of planning and program (1966–68), and was involved in various antipoverty programs. He made several trips overseas and was very active in WCC and NCC activities.

Raymond T. Richey

Sept. 4, 1893
near Atwood, Illinois

April 22, 1968
Houston, Texas

World-famous healing evangelist. In 1911, Richey's eyes were healed after a boyhood injury. He worked at a tabernacle near an army camp in Houston, TX, during WWI. He held many tent meetings with the troops. At that time, he contracted tuberculosis and was again healed in 1919. In 1920, he began healing crusades. In one of his crusades in Tulsa, OK, in 1923, over 11,000 were converted. He pastored at Evangelist Temple, Houston, TX, from 1927–62. The funeral was there on April 25th.

Warner Sallman

April 30, 1892
Chicago, Illinois

May 27, 1968

Artist of "Head of Christ," one of the most famous Christian art pieces ever produced. There are over 165 million copies circulating the world. Sallman was converted at Waveland Congregational Church in Chicago, at a CHAPMAN revival. He married Ruth Anderson on May 31, 1916. They were active in the Mission (Evangelical) Covenant Church. He then became a commercial artist. In February 1924, did the charcoal drawing which became an oil painting of the *Head of Christ*.

Tommie Titcombe

Sept. 17, 1881
Swindon, England

May 29, 1968
Toronto, Ontario, Canada

Missionary among the Yagba people of Nigeria, 1908–30. Titcombe's life is an amazing story of someone going to live among primitive people and seeing a large and healthy church established. He was converted to Christ at a railway mission in 1902. The following year, he went to Canada. In 1906, he heard a missionary challenge about Nigeria. Pastor PHILPOTT and the Gospel Tabernacle in Hamilton, OH, supported him as he sailed for Nigeria under SIM, in 1908. Settling in Egbe, Titcombe's first baptism totals 83 men and 16 women in 1912. A new church is built in 1915, and on November 22 of that year he married Ethel McIntosh. By 1916, 1,513 were attending services at 14 outstations. In 1921, a new church is dedicated and 19 outstations were listed with 2,025 members. By 1925, a 40-bed maternity hospital was completed and 27 young men go to Bible school from Egbe. In August, 1930, his illness causes him to leave the field. In 1951, Titcombe College is established in Egbe. His wife, Ethel, died in Toronto on February 18, 1970.

Victor E. Cory

July 30, 1893
North Baltimore, Ohio

June 2, 1968
Wheaton, Illinois

Founder of Scripture Press Publishing Company, 1932, located in the western suburbs of Chicago, IL. Cory married Bernice Tucker on June 16, 1922, and they had four sons. Converted following a spiritual Valentine's Day party, February 14, 1920, he served as the general manager of Moody Press, 1927–32. Cory was also active in several Chicagoland Christian activities such as the Pacific Garden Mission, National Sunday School Association, Chicago Sunday School Association and the Great Commission Prayer League.

Franklin C. Fry

Aug. 30, 1900
Bethlehem, Pennsylvania

June 6, 1968
New Rochele, New York

Lutheran ecumenist; president of the United Lutheran Church in America, 1944–62 (one of the four denominations that merged in 1962); **of Lutheran Church in America** (ECLA in 1988), **1962–68; and of Lutheran World Federation, 1957–62.** Fry married Hilda Drewes on May 17, 1927. He pastored in Yonkers, NY (1925–29) and at Trinity Lutheran Church, Akron, OH (1929–44). He was the secretary of evangelism in the ULC from 1930–38, the moderator of WCC at Evanston (1954) and at New Delhi (1961). He was very active in the Lutheran World Council and led the Lutheran drift to the left. He was a founder of the Lutheran World Federation in 1947 and headed Lutheran World Relief, 1945–68. He received 32 honorary degrees.

Joseph Blinco

May 6, 1912
Whitehaven, England

June 9, 1968
San Bernardino, California

Evangelist with the Billy Graham Association, 1955–66. Blinco was a Cumberland miner's son born into poverty. He was converted in 1928. He married Ethelwynn B. Crawford. Blinco pastored in England, 1951–55. He preached for 35 years and also served as a soloist for many crusades with Chris LaChona. He was the general director of the Forest (CA) Home Conference Center, 1966–68. GRADY WILSON conducted his funeral with over 450 people attending.

Jack Holcomb

1921
Waco, Texas

July 13, 1968
Dallas, Texas

One of the most effective soloists in his generation. Hearing Holcomb sing was a memorable experience. His amazing, breaking tenor voice (hit high C easily) created an emotional response, as he sung in crusades with various evangelists, such as JACK SHULER. Born into a poor family, he became provider for them at a young age. He worked his way through college, and soon was singing across the land. His grave went unmarked for 35 years.

Samuel E. Duncan

April 27, 1904
Madisonville, Kentucky

July 10, 1968
Salisbury, North Carolina

President of Livingstone College, Salisbury, NC, 1957–68. Duncan married Ida Hauser on May 16, 1933. He served as science teacher and athletic coach at Washington High School, Reidsville, NC (1927–30, 38–46) and was principal at Dunbar High School, E. Spencer, NC (1931–37). He was active in many civic and church-related organizations, including president of North Carolina Council of Churches in 1967.

Harry O. Anderson

Feb. 2, 1892
Oakland, California

July 16, 1968

Outstanding evangelist in Northern Baptist Convention circles. He graduated from William Jewell College and Gordon College, leaving in 1915. From 1920 on, he was an evangelist and author. Anderson married Mildred Price on June 29, 1926. He was vice president of Northern Baptist Seminary in 1937 and was an evangelist for *Christian Life Magazine* for a number of years.

Caleb D. Pettaway

Dec. 18, 1886
Ferriday, Louisiana

Aug. 20, 1968
Little Rock, Arkansas

President of National Baptist Convention of America, 1957–67. Pettaway married Jennie Vagner (June 12, 1918), and was ordained (March 25, 1920). He pastored various churches in Arkansas, including Shiloh Baptist in Little Rock, 1927–46. Upon the death of his first wife, he married Cleola Hampton on June 5, 1952. He was the founder and president of United Friends of America.

Douglas Horton

July 27, 1891
Brooklyn, New York

Aug. 21, 1968
Berlin, New Hampshire

General secretary (CEO) of Congregational Christian Churches (United Church of Christ in 1957), **1938–55**. He was the architect of the merger of the Congregational Christian Church and the Evangelical and Reformed Churches in 1957 to produce the United Church of Christ. Horton married Carol Williams on May 9, 1916 (died: 1944). Then he married Mildred McAfee on August 10, 1945. He pastored in Middletown, CT (1916–23); Brooklyn, MA (1925–30) and the United Church of Hyde Park in 1931. He lectured at Union Theological Seminary, New York City from 1943–55. He was a liberal who helped organize the NCC in 1950. He served as the president and dean of Harvard Divinity School, 1955–59. The student body almost doubled during this time. He gave the first appearance of KARL BARTH into English with his translation of *The Word of God* and the *Word of Man* (1928). He wrote 14 books from *Out into Life* (1925) to *Toward an Undivided Church* (1967). He is buried in Randolph, NH.

Arthur C. Lichtenberger
Jan. 8, 1900   *Sept. 3, 1968*
Oshkosh, Wisconsin   Bethel, Vermont

Presiding bishop of Protestant Episcopal Church (Episcopal Church in 1967), **1958–64**. Lichtenberger married Florence Tate on February 8, 1924. He served in WWI. Briefly he was a missionary in China, teaching in Wauchang, until a Communist uprising in 1927 caused him to leave. He then was rector of Grace Church, Cincinnati, OH (1928–33); of St. Paul's, Brookline, MA (1933–41); and dean of Trinity Cathedral Seminary, New York City (1948–50). From 1950–58, he was Bishop Coadjutor of the Diocese of Missouri. In late 1961, he was the first head of a non-Roman American Church to meet formally with a pope of the Roman Catholic Church. His courtesy call on Pope John III was while he was en route to New Delhi, India. He retired in Cambridge, MA. In 1963, Lichtenberger was afflicted with Parkinson's syndrome. His ashes are interred at Chapel of Christ Church in St. Louis, MO.

David H. Johnson
Oct. 23, 1893   *Sept. 26, 1968*
Chicago, Illinois   Wheaton, Illinois

Director of TEAM, 1946–61. Johnson was well-known and effective as a missionary executive, seeing missionaries increase from 225 to 820. He also wrote the lyrics and music of "Lord, Lay Some Soul upon My Heart." He was converted at Moody Church about 1908 and attended MBI and North Park College. Johnson married Edna Swansberg on Nov. 14, 1925. He was an evangelist for ten years. He then accepted a pastorate at Lakeview Mission Covenant Church, Chicago, IL from 1936–46.

Betty A. Olsen
Oct. 22, 1934   *Sept. 26, 1968*
Bouake, Ivory Coast   North Vietnam

Missionary martyred in Vietnam. Raised in Africa as a daughter of missionaries, Betty was sent away eight months a year for schooling, beginning at age eight. This separation greatly saddened her and was intensified by her mother's death from cancer, when Betty was 17. She eventually enrolled at Nyack College and identified with the CMA missions program for her own future. She went back to Africa, but working with her father and stepmother created some tension, so she returned to work as a nurse in Chicago. Bill Gothard had some input in her life, expanding his program based on his counsel to her. She arrived in (South) Vietnam, and on January 30, 1968, she and others were at Banmethuot when the Communists came in. Five missionaries were killed; she and Hank Blood were taken prisoner. They were forced to walk 13 hours a day and survived on meager rice rations. She had severe dysentery and died following eight brutal months of torment by the Viet Cong. She was a nurse at a leprosarium when captured.

Alva J. McClain
April 11, 1888   *Nov. 11, 1968*
Aurelia, Iowa   Waterloo, Iowa

Founder and first president of Grace Theological Seminary and College, Akron, OH, 1937–39, Winona Lake, IN 1939–62. Grace College was established in 1948. McClain was converted under evangelist Louis S. Bennett. He married Josephine Gingrich on June 7, 1911. He was ordained into the Brethren Church in 1917, then pastored First Church, Philadelphia, PA from 1918–23. He also taught at Philadelphia School of the Bible (1919–23); at Ashland (OH) College and Seminary (1925–27); at BIOLA (1927–29); and at Ashland Theological Seminary as a professor of theology and apologetics (1930–37), after which he was dismissed because of his fundamentalist views. He was a strong dispensational premillennialist. He retired in 1962.

Doss N. Jackson

July 14, 1895
Balch, Arkansas

Nov. 29, 1968
Oklahoma City, Oklahoma

First editor-in-chief of American Baptist Association Publications, Texarkana, TX 1925–41, and news service director of North American Baptist Association (Baptist Missionary Association of America in 1969), **Little Rock, AR 1954–1968**. Jackson was converted at a revival on Aug. 29, 1913 near Newport, AR and married Erma Gilbert on Nov. 9, 1918. He served as the president, 1935–37, of ABA enlarging the scope of influence for the movement. In 1950, the NABA split away from the ABA. His position was the top executive post in the denomination that selects presidents annually.

Homer A. Tomlinson

Oct. 25, 1892
Westfield, Indiana

Dec. 4, 1968
Queens Village, New York

Overseer of the Church of God, 1943–69. Upon the death of his father, A. J. Tomlinson, in 1943, Homer took over the leadership of the ministry and its missions program, 1943–68. Tomlinson married Marie Wunch on November 22, 1919. He was involved in various areas of his father's movement, 1916–28. Together they founded Lee College of Cleveland, TN. He also served as the New York State CG overseer, 1923–43. Homer left a successful advertising business to keep a New York church, that had rejected his father's aggressive views, in the fold. He authored several books, including *Home Study Bible Lessons* (20 vols., 1919) to *The Shout of a King* (1968). When his brother, Milton, took over leadership of the spin-off, Church of God of Prophecy, in 1943 (Cleveland, TN), Homer built separate headquarters for the main Church of God movement. Homer Tomlinson ran for president of the United States in 1954.

Karl Barth

May 10, 1886
Basel, Switzerland

Dec. 9, 1968
Basel, Switzerland

Founder of neo-orthodoxy, reformed theologian, one of the most influential men of modern times. Barth began pastoring a Reformed Church in Geneva, 1909–11, where he also wrote his commentary. He then pastored at Safenwil, Switzerland, 1911–21, during which time he married Nelly Hoffmann on March 26, 1913. They had five children. He joined the Social Democratic Party in 1915. He held the chair of theology at Gottingen (1921–25), Munster (1925–30), and Bonn (1930–35) universities. He was a professor of theology at Bonn until the Nazis expelled him in 1935, at which time he taught theology at Basel, 1935–62. He spoke at the Amsterdam WCC founding (1948) visited America (1962) and Rome (1966). However, he turned away from liberal theology to restore belief in the fundamental dogmas of Christianity. He taught neo-orthodoxy (reaction against liberal theology; however, it denies verbal inspiration, saying that the Bible contains the Word of God, and gives some biblical phrases liberal meanings). He drafted the *Barmen Declaration* (1934), and his *Church Dogmatics* (1932–36), which was first published in 1936 while he was at Bonn. It grew to twelve volumes by his retirement in 1967. His exhaustive works include a commentary on *Romans* (1919) (which expressed his idea of the radical transcendence of God) to *Witness to the World* (1986).

Kenneth S. LaTourette

Aug. 8, 1884
Oregon City, Oregon

Dec. 26, 1968
Oregon City, Oregon

Church and Oriental historian. LaTourette made a Christian commitment at age twelve. He taught in China, 1910–12, but returned home for health reasons. He then taught at Denison University, Granville, OH 1916–21. He became associated with Yale University in 1921, serving as chairman of the department of religion (1938–46), director of graduate studies at the Divinity School (1946–53), and Sterling professor of missions and Oriental history (1950–53), emeritus from 1953 on. Latourette never married. He had American Baptist Convention affiliations. Among his more than 80 works were *The History of Christian Missions in China* (1929), *The Chinese: Their History and Culture* (2 vols. 1934: 3rd ed. 1946), *The History of the Expansion of Christianity* (7 vols. 1937–45), *A History of Japan* (1947), and *Christianity in a Revolutionary Age* (5 vols., 1958–62). When visiting his sister, he was struck by a car and killed in front of his family home.

William F. McConn

Sept. 4, 1888
Colony, Kansas

Feb. 3, 1969
Largo, Florida

President of Marion (IN) College (Indiana Wesleyan University in 1988), **1932–60**. McConn was converted at age 13 in a tent meeting and married Viva Ebling on June 12, 1919 (died: 1953). He was ordained a Wesleyan Methodist in 1924. He served as president of Miltonvale (KS) Wesleyan College from 1924–32. From 1960 on, he pastored in Lakeland and Merritt Island, FL.

Thomas E. Paul

April 11, 1906
Shamokin, Pennsylvania

Feb. 27, 1969
Reading, Pennsylvania

First director of Evangelical Congregational Church Missions, 1948–69. Paul was converted in his youth. Paul taught high school (1926–30), then pastored most of his life (1930–69), four churches in Pennsylvania, 1930–48, in conjunction with his missionary leadership. He lived in Shillington, PA, during his mission leadership days, also serving as head of the Northeast India General Mission for a decade. His wife, Marion, was a faithful companion. He had surgery, but his disease could not be stopped, so he died after nine weeks in the hospital.

Helen Cadbury Alexander-Dixon

Jan. 10, 1877
Birmingham, England

March 1, 1969
Birmingham, England

Founder and first director of Pocket Testament League, 1908–41. Helen was heiress to the Cadbury chocolate fortune. Helen wrote verses three and four of "Anywhere with Jesus" at age 13, to add to Jesse Pounds' verses one and two and TOWNER's music. Her father, a Quaker industrialist, gave her a Testament to carry to school in 1893. Helen became the wife of CHARLES M. ALEXANDER on July 14, 1904 (died: October 13, 1920). She then married AMZI C. DIXON in 1924 and incorporated PTL, September 12, 1928, in Birmingham. Her writings include *A Romance of Preaching*.

Albert Bretschneider

Feb. 6, 1883
Cleveland, Ohio

March 20, 1969
Rochester, New York

President of German Baptist Deptartment of Colgate-Rochester (NY) Divinity School, 1934–40, and German Baptist Seminary, Rochester, (North American Baptist Seminary in Sioux Falls, SD in 1950), **1940–44**. Bretschneider married Emma Sutter in 1912 and was ordained the same year. He pastored in Evansville, IN (1912–13), and at Clinton Hill Baptist Church, Newark, NJ (1916–25). Bretschneider served as the general secretary of young people and Sunday School work of NAB conference, 1926–28. He then taught English and Greek at NABS (1928–34), church history and NT (1934–52), and was dean (1934–40). He was associate pastor at Grace Baptist, Union City, NJ (1952–53) and interim at Agdon Baptist Church, Spencerport, NY (1953–56).

Paul E. Scherer

June 22, 1892
Mt. Holly Springs, Pennsylvania

March 26, 1969
Columbus, Ohio

Lutheran pastor and educator. Following graduation from Lutheran Theological Seminary in Philadelphia, Scherer was ordained in 1916. On September 4, 1919, he married Lillie Fry Benbow and, in 1920, began a 25-year ministry at Holy Trinity Lutheran Church in New York City. He started a public radio ministry in 1932. He became a professor of homiletics at Union Theological Seminary in New York City (1945–60) and a visiting professor of homiletics at Princeton (NJ) Theological Seminary (1961–68). His books range from *When God Hides* (1934) to *The Word God Sent* (1965). From 1945–57, he also worked as an associate editor of *The Interpreter's Bible*.

Dwight D. Eisenhower

Oct. 14, 1890
Denison, Texas

March 28, 1969
Washington, D.C.

Thirty-fourth president of the United States, 1953–61. A soldier and statesman, Eisenhower was an inspiration in war and peace. Early on, he was affiliated with the River Brethren, a pacifist group meeting in homes. He began his military career in 1915. He became a member of the Presbyterian church and married Mamie Geneva Doud on July 1, 1916 (November 14, 1896–Novovember 1, 1979). Eisenhower was the Allied Commander in North Africa in 1942 and Commanding General of the Allied Forces in December 1943, directing crucial landings in Sicily, Italy, and Normandy. By 1944, he was a general. He also served as Chief of Staff of the US Army (1945–48), president of Columbia University (1948–50), and supreme commander of NATO forces (1950–52). He was the second president to join a church while in office, the National Presbyterian Church in Washington on February 1, 1953. On April 5, 1953, he inaugurated the first Presidential Prayer Breakfast. He suffered a stroke in 1955 and was briefly incapacitated. In 1956, he signed an act making "In God We Trust" the national motto and established the practice of opening cabinet meetings with silent prayer. On his deathbed, Billy Graham aided him in the matter of assurance of salvation. He is buried in Abilene, KS.

"The utterances of God as recorded in the Bible are ever the need of mankind."

Grace Noll Crowell

Oct. 31, 1877
Inland, Iowa

March 31, 1969
Dallas, Texas

Prolific Methodist verse writer. Converted during a revival meeting at age 16, she married Norman H. Crowell on September 4, 1901. In 1906, Grace began to write, eventually publishing some 37 books and 5,000 poems. She was the American Mother of the Year in 1938. One of her last books was *Let the Sun Shine In* (published 1970). Her poetry is devotional, biblical, and inspiring. Crowell's work has appeared in scores of journals (i.e., *Saturday Evening Post*, etc.).

Thaddeus F. Gullixson

Sept. 4, 1882
Bode, Iowa

April 2, 1969
Casper, Wyoming

President of Luther Theological (Lutheran-Northwestern in 1982) **Seminary, St. Paul, MN, 1930–54.** Gullixson was the youngest of ten children and married Bessie Friers on October 21, 1908 (died: 1961). He pastored in Pierre, SD (1907–11) and at First Lutheran in Minot, ND (1911–30). He was also a professor of theology at the St. Paul based Seminary. Gullixson was vice president of the Evangelical Lutheran Church (1925–48) and president of the American Lutheran Conference (1934–38). He was one of the eight men appointed by President TRUMAN to the Commission on Naturalization and Immigration, reporting on their investigation in 1952. He was known for his spirit of openness and humility.

Herbert Welch

Nov. 7, 1862
New York, New York

April 4, 1969
New York, New York

Bishop in the Methodist Episcopal Church, 1916–39; in the Methodist Church, 1939–67; and in the United Methodist Church, 1968–69. Welch married Adelaide McGee on June 3, 1890 (died: 1958). Welch pastored from (1890–1905). He was president of Ohio Wesleyan University, Delaware (1905–16); bishop of Japan and Korea (1916–28); bishop of Pittsburgh (1928–32); Shanghai (1932–36); Boston (1938–39); and chairman of the Methodist Committee for Overseas Relief (1940–48). Welch lived to age 106.

Walter R. Bowie

Oct. 8, 1882
Richmond, Virginia

April 23, 1969
Alexandria, Virginia

Episcopalian educator, hymn writer, and pastor. Bowie married Jean Laverack on Sept. 29, 1909. He served as rector in Greenwood, VA (1908–11); at St. Paul's, Richmond, VA (1911–23); and Grace Church, New York City (1923–29). He was a professor of practical theology (1939–50) and professor of homiletics (1950–55) at Union Theological Seminary, Richmond, VA. He was also a lecturer at Seabury-Western Divinity School, Evanston, IL, from 1955–69. Bowie's books range from *The Children's Year* (1916) to *Learning to Live* (1969). He was an advocate of the social gospel and modern theology. He was active on the American Standard Bible Committee and was also an associate editor for the *Interpreter's Bible* (1955).

Abraham Vereide

Oct. 7, 1886
Vereide, Norway

May 1969

Active layman responsible for getting the presidential prayer breakfasts started in Washington, D.C. in 1953. Vereide married Mattie Hansen on Aug. 25, 1910. He served as pastor in Wisconsin, Washington, Oregon, and Massachusetts, 1910–35. The concept of the prayer breakfasts began in the 1930s when Vereide was spiritually counseling President Franklin Roosevelt. The Lord gradually revealed to him that his life's work was to guide political leaders, at all levels of government, to a prayer reliance on the Lord's guidance. It mushroomed into governor and local political prayer breakfasts across the country.

Albert F. Gray

March 18, 1886
St. Thomas, North Dakota

May 2, 1969
Portland, Oregon

First president of Warner Pacific College, Portland, OR 1937–57. Gray married Rosa Brannon on June 17, 1909. He was an evangelist (1905–15); pastor in Clarkston, WA (1915–20); principal of Pacific Bible Institute (later Warner Pacific) (1920–23); pastor in Walla Walla, WA (1923–24); in Yakima, WA (1925–26); in Anderson, IN (1926–33); and in Seattle, WA (1933–38). He wrote from *Menace or Modernism?* (1926) to *Times and Tides on the Western Shore* (1966), an autobiography.

Erwin M. Strom

April 24, 1891
Benson, Minnesota

May 3, 1969
Fergus Falls, Minnesota

President of Lutheran Brethren Seminary, Fergus Falls, MN 1938–49. Strom was converted at age 17 in Tioga, ND. He married Bertha Hanson. He pastored in Eau Claire, WI from 1927–32, before teaching at Lutheran Bible School in Grand Forks, ND (later Fergus Falls). It became the above mentioned seminary in 1935. After his presidency there, he continued to teach until a stroke incapacitated him.

Paul R. Jackson

May 16, 1903
Flandreau, South Dakota

May 15, 1969
Chicago, Illinois

President of the Baptist Bible Seminary, Johnson City, NY (Clark's Summit, PA in 1967) **1949–60, and National Representative of GARB, 1960–69**. He was converted at age 15 under Bible teaching in Wibaux, MT. He married Stella Chappell on November 16, 1926, then pastored rural churches in North Dakota (1926–29); in Strathmore, CA (1929–34); at FBC in Cerres, CA (1934–45); and as an interim pastor at Wealthy Street Baptist Church in Grand Rapids, MI (1945–46). He was a council member of GARB from 1944–60. As president of the Baptist Bible College, school assets grew from $50,000 to $1 million during his leadership. His son, Mark, continued his active service in the GARB ministries.

Joseph H. Oldham

Oct. 20, 1874
Bombay, India

May 16, 1969
St. Leonards-on-Sea, England

Key Anglican ecumenical leader who served as honorary president of World Council of Churches gatherings in New Delhi, India, 1961, and in Uppsala, Sweden, 1968. Oldham was the secretary of the student Christian movement (1896–97); the YMCA (1897–1900); the World Missionary Conference (1908–10) and the International Missionary Council (1921–38), which he was instrumental in founding. Oldham was the organizing secretary of the Edinburgh World Missionary Conference held in 1910. He helped launch the WCC, served as secretary to the Council on Christian Life and was on the Christian Frontier Council, 1942–45. His work emphasis showed a strong dedication to African missionary endeavors. He edited the *International Review of Missions* (1912–27) and wrote a few books. He was honorary president of the WCC in 1948.

Frederick C. Fowler

Dec. 2, 1901
Denver, Colorado

May 24, 1969
Newland, North Carolina

President of National Association of Evangelicals, 1950–51. He married Anna Bucher on March 14, 1928. Ordained a Presbyterian in 1927, Fowler pastored in Marietta, PA (1927–30); Mt. Union, PA (1930–36); at Knoxville Presbyterian Church, Pittsburgh, PA (1936–44, 46–54); and at First Presbyterian Church, Duluth, MN (1954–68). He served as a chaplain in WWII in the Far East, 1944–46. Fowler had a well-known reputation as a pastor. He was found dead in bed. He is buried in Knoxville, TN.

Walter L. Wilson

May 27, 1881
Aurora, Indiana

May 24, 1969
Kansas City, Missouri

Renowned soul-winner and first president of Kansas City Bible College (merged to become Calvary Bible College, Kansas City, MO in 1962), **1932–34, 1938–55**. Wilson was one of the greatest personal soul winners in history. He was saved in 1896 at a tent meeting. He began a medical career in 1904, and then went into the tent business, 1912–28. Wilson pastored the Central Bible Hall (Church) in Kansas City, 1920–60. He married Marion Baker on January 6, 1904 (died: August 6, 1962) and then Ruth Selden on January 10, 1964. His radio ministry began in 1924. He was a regular attendant at the Plymouth Brethren Church. He could take any conversation, especially among his medical patients, and turn it into a soul-winning opportunity with many converted as a result.

Robert G. LeTourneau

Nov. 30, 1888
Richford, Vermont

June 1, 1969
Longview, Texas

Inventor of earth moving equipment; founder and first president of LeTourneau College, Longview, TX 1947–61; and president of Christian Businessmen's Committee, 1941–48. LeTourneau quit school in the eighth grade to work in a foundry. He was converted at age 16 at his bedside after an encounter with an evangelist. He moved to San Francisco in 1906. LeTourneau eloped with 16-year-old Evelyn Peterson on August 29, 1917. He ran a garage (1917–29), then founded his own company, heading it (1929–69). His infant son died in 1919. He built the first plant in Stockton, CA, in 1921. In 1926, he constructed the Oakland Stockton highway while inventing a rooter and a bulldozer. In 1933, he applied rubber tire technology to heavy machinery. In 1935, he built a factory in Peoria and established a Christian foundation. From 1941–45, LeTourneau supplied 70 percent of earth moving machinery for the Allies in WWII. In 1946–47, he built a plant in Longview, TX. He founded and built Tournata, Liberia (1952) and Tournavista, Peru (1954). From 1955–68 he continued to develop advances in heavy machinery. His machinery was used worldwide to clear and build roads, plus other huge land moving projects. LeTourneau gave the Lord 90 percent of his funds. He affiliated himself with the Christian and Missionary Alliance. *Mover of Men and Mountains* is his autobiography.

Sydnor L. Stealey

March 7, 1897
Martinsburg, West Virginia

July 24, 1969
Raleigh, North Carolina

First president of Southeastern Baptist Theological Seminary, Wake Forest, NC 1951–63. Stealey married Jessie Wheeler on October 16, 1920. Stealey served in the army in World War I then taught in a high school (1920–22), and later taught at the college level (1922–24). He pastored in Missouri, Kentucky, Indiana, Virginia, and North Carolina, 1925–42. He taught church history at the Southern Baptist Seminary, 1942–51. He edited *A Baptist Treasury* (1958). His first authored book was *Epistemology* (study of the nature of knowledge) in 1932.

George A. Long

Nov. 29, 1884
Greenville, Pennsylvania

Aug. 7, 1969
Akron, Ohio

President of the Pittsburgh-Xenia (Pittsburgh in 1959) **Theological Seminary, 1942–53.** Long was ordained by the Allegheny Presbytery on June 5, 1912; pastored at the Second Presbyterian Church in Allegheny, PA (1912–21); and in Homewood, PA (1921–42). Wilson was the moderator of the Presbyterian General Assembly in 1955. He was trained at Westminster College, New Wilmington, PA (1909), and at PTS (1912).

C. Hoyt Watson

Dec. 12, 1888
Eudora, Kansas

Aug. 17, 1969
Seattle, Washington

President of the Seattle (WA) Pacific College (University in 1977), **1926–59.** Watson married Elsie Waters on June 15, 1910. He taught at the University of Kansas, 1918–23, and then at the University of Washington for one year. Watson also pastored churches in Kansas and Washington. During his 33 years as president at Seattle Pacific, the School of Missions, department of education, and teacher training were developed. He wrote *Deshazar* (1950).

Edmund C. Reim

Feb. 12, 1892
New Elm, Minnesota

August 22, 1969
Eau Claire, Wisconsin

President of Immanuel Lutheran College and Seminary, Eau Claire, WI 1959–67, and Wisconsin Lutheran Seminary, Mequon, WI 1954–57. Reim began his ministry in Kenosha, WI, at St. Luke's Lutheran Church in 1914. He married Selma Schaller in 1915. He pastored at St. Paul's and St. John's of Calvary, WI, and Trinity Lutheran, Neenah, WI. He was professor at Wisconsin Lutheran Seminary of Mequon, WI, from 1940–57. From 1959–69, he was active in establishing and teaching in the seminary department of Immanuel Lutheran College. When the Church of the Lutheran Confession was organized, he served in many capacities, not only at the school, but also as editor of the *Theological Journal*, and essayist at conventions and pastoral conferences. Reim led in the withdrawal from the Wisconsin Synod and the Evangelical Lutheran Synod to form the CLC.

Christian E. Rediger

Dec. 31, 1887
near Flanagan, Illinois

Aug. 24, 1969
Bloomington, Illinois

Director of Congo Inland Mission (Africa Inter-Mennonite Mission in 1972), **Elkhart, IN 1936–50.** Rediger married Bena Oyer on May 11, 1908. During his years with the mission (March 9, 1908–April 10, 1962), Rediger traveled widely abroad and at home. During his tenure, mission stations went from 105 to 316. He also served on the staffs of Bluffton (OH) and Marian (IN) colleges. Rediger was ordained in 1919 with the Evangelical Mennonite Conference and pastored with them for ten years.

Henry E. Grube

July 3, 1909
Mobile, Alabama

Aug. 28, 1969
Mobile, Alabama

Founder and pastor of Mobile Gospel Tabernacle, 1942–69, which changed its name to Greystone Bible Church. Grube was converted while a student at Bob Jones University on February 1, 1929. Ordained a Baptist, he served as an evangelist, 1931–41. On Jan. 22, 1934, he married Eldora Miller. Grube organized Greystone Christian School in 1947, and helped start 20 Christian day schools. Grube ministered at People's Church, Toronto, one week a year for 25 years. He had a wide ministry helping such as the MEL TROTTER Mission in Grand Rapids, the Gospel Center in St. Louis, and speaking in major conferences across the land. He died of a heart attack.

Elmer Becker

May 30, 1899
Waterloo County, Ontario, Canada

Aug. 28, 1969
Huntington, Indiana

President of Huntington (IN) College, 1941–65. Becker came to the US to attend school at Huntington. He married Inez Schad on December 22, 1923 and was ordained with the United Brethren in Christ in 1930. Becker pastored three churches in the Niagara Circuit area (1924–31), and then a church at Kitchener, Ontario (1931–37). He was general secretary of church education (1937–40) and general secretary of education for the UBC (1940–69). His first book was *The Evangelism of Youth* (1937).

Elmer G. Anderson

Jan. 28, 1886
Chicago, Illinois

Sept. 14, 1969
Pasadena, California

Director of Church of the Nazarene World Missions, 1916–25, and president of the International Gospel League, Pasadena, CA 1949–69. He was a good friend of the Eatons (founders of IGL) and helped them get to the mission field in India. Upon Emma Eaton's death, Anderson became president of IGL. He married Ruby Duckett in 1914, while he was treasurer of the General Board of Foreign Missions. From 1933–49, he was financial secretary of Eastern Nazarene College, Wolliston, MA. His funeral was in the Pasadena Church of the Nazarene.

Josef Nordenhaug

Aug. 2, 1903
Oslo, Norway

Sept. 18, 1969
Arlington, Virginia

General secretary of Baptist World Alliance, 1960–69. Nordenhaug came to America in 1928. He married Helen Rampp on August 7, 1934. He pastored in Prestonburg, KY (1933–36), in Vinton, VA (1936–41), and in Lynchburg, VA (1941–48). He edited the *Commission* (1948–50). Nordenhaug was president of the Baptist Theological Seminary in Ruschlikon, Switzerland, 1950–60.

Floyd H. Lacy

July 27, 1890
Sutton, West Virginia

Sept. 25, 1969
Duarte, California

Leader of great black gospel singing group, the Cleveland Colored Quintet, five men from Cleveland who traveled around the country, 1922–47, ministering to full-capacity auditoriums. Lacy was the high tenor. The quartet was from a CMA background and widely known. Lacy married Lillie Calendar (died: 1963) and then Pearl Madison on September 8, 1964. Others in the group were A. E. Talbot (died: 1947), J. W. Parker, H. D. Hodges, and S. R. Jones.

James C. Baker

June 2, 1879
Sheldon, Illinois

Sept. 26, 1969
Claremont, California

Bishop in the Methodist Episcopal Church, 1928–39; in the Methodist Church, 1939–67; and in the United Methodist Church, 1968–69. He married Lena Benson on June 12, 1901. Baker was professor of Greek at Wesleyan College, Cameron, MO from 1898–1902. He pastored in Ashland, MA (1903–05), in McLean, IL (1905–07), and at Trinity Church in Urbana, IL (1907–28). As bishop, he went to Japan, Korea, Manchuria (China) (1928–32), San Francisco (1932–48) and Los Angeles, CA (1948–52). Baker organized the Wesley Foundation and helped develop the campus ministry of his denomination across the land while at Urbana.

Joe E. Rose

Aug. 9, 1892
Grand Rapids, Michigan

Sept. 30, 1969
Waynesville, North Carolina

Well-known gospel singer with a wide radio ministry, *Hymns of All Churches* **broadcast, reaching millions, 1934–45.** Rose grew up attending the MEL TROTTER Rescue Mission, Grand Rapids, MI. He became an elder in a Presbyterian church in Chicago. Later he worked in the Chautauqua Movement, served in WWI as a navy aviator, studied voice, then went into business and broadcasting. Upon retiring, he went to Waynesville, NC, and joined the Presbyterian Church where Pastor Calvin Thielman's preaching convicted him. After his conversion, he continued his singing in many meetings, albums, programs, and films. He married Wilsie Smathers.

James E. Hoffman

July 24, 1893
Allegan, Michigan

Oct. 17, 1969
Hasbrouck Heights, New Jersey

Stated clerk of Reformed Church in America, 1943–61. He was ordained in 1920. Hoffman married Catherine Hekhuis on June 17, 1920. Hoffman pastored the First Reformed Church, Hasbrouck Heights, NJ, from 1920–44. He was a member of the executive board and on the Board of Directors of Religion in American Life. Hoffman was also involved with the National Council of Churches.

Ellsworth V. Steele

Feb. 19, 1908
Ratherum, Idaho

Oct. 20, 1969
San Jose, California

Founder and first president of World Mission Fellowship, Oregon City, O, 1946–69. He and his wife, Vida McDonald (born: June 14, 1908), married in 1927, were saved through a Christian radio program in Alberta. Steele was selling life insurance prior to salvation, but went to Bible college soon after. After graduating in 1941, they went to the Congo with WEC to care for children whose parents had leprosy. But they never arrived. The ship on which they were traveling was sunk by the Germans off the shore of South Africa. They were made prisoners of war, with Vida being released in a year and Ellsworth remaining a prisoner until 1945. Seeing the many orphans in Europe, they felt burdened to start World Missions to Children (European Christian Orphanage). They also started New Hope School in Oregon. After her husband's death of heart trouble, in 1969, Vida went on to work as a WEC missionary in Gambia at age 70, and in Brazil at 79. She died in October, 2000 at age 92 due to congestive heart failure.

Willard G. Cram

Dec. 11, 1875
Doudton, Kentucky

Oct. 29, 1969
Nashville, Tennessee

Director of Missions of United Methodist Church South Missions, 1926–39. Cram married Rosella Hogan on June 6, 1900, and they went as missionaries to Korea, 1902–17. He was active in the Centenary Revival (over 100 years) under the Board of Missions in Korea (1920–22) and was the director of the Centenary movement (1922–26). Cram actively participated in Methodist missions all his life, retiring from Korea in 1944 to Nashville, TN.

Frank G. Clement

June 2, 1920
Dickson, Tennessee

Nov. 4, 1969
Brentwood, Tennessee (?)

Elected governor of Tennessee at age 33, one of the youngest ever, 1953–59, 1963–66. Clement, a Methodist, had an outstanding Christian testimony. He married Lucille Christianson on Jan. 6, 1940. Clement entered law practice in Tennessee in 1941, served with the FBI (1941–43), and the Tennessee Utilities Commission (1946–50). He was the keynote speaker at the Democratic Convention in Chicago in 1956. Clement returned to practice law in 1967–69. He is buried in Dickson.

Albert D. Helser

July 10, 1897
Thornville, Ohio

Dec. 20, 1969
Winfield, Illinois

Director of Sudan Interior Mission, 1957–62, and missionary to Nigeria. Helser's parents and pastor, E. B. Bagwell, were responsible for his conversion. He married Lola Bechtel on August 15, 1922, serving with the Student Volunteer Movement, 1919–22. He was ordained into the Church of the Brethren in 1922 and went to Nigeria the same year. Helser served in the city of Garkida until 1936. Then he went to Kano (state in Nigeria) until 1957. He had 35 years of effective work in Africa. Helser wrote many books including *Life of Christ* (translated into Bura in 1925) to *Africa's Bible* (1951). Bura is a Nigerian ethnic group. He is buried in Thornville.

James N. Bedford

1907 — *1970*
Houghton, New York

President of London (Ontario) Bible Institute (Tyndale College), **1945–54**. Bedford graduated from MBI in 1932. Further schooling was at North Park College, Houghton College, and Eastern Baptist Theological Seminary. He pastored Baptist churches in Springfield, PA (1937–39) and Corning, NY (1939–44). In 1954, he took the pastorate of Beulah Baptist Church in Detroit. His later years were spent in Bible conferences, working out of the Moody Bible Institute.

Frederic I. Drexler

1878 — *1970*

Founder and first president of California Baptist Theological Seminary (American Baptist Seminary of the West in 1974), **Los Angeles** (Covina in 1951), **CA, 1944–c. 1955**. Following ministries in North Dakota and Michigan, the Drexler family moved to California in 1911 where Frederic pastored in northern California. He was deeply concerned with the availability of Baptist theological education in the West. He constantly stressed biblical studies and evangelism. He established the Drexler Lectures in 1955.

Anton Marco

c 1910 — *c 1970*

Outstanding opera singer, converted in 1950. During WWII, Marco served with the USO in Europe, entertaining wounded soldiers. In 1950, he became the leading baritone for the San Carlos Opera Company, then his wife was converted. He began to attend the FBC, Hackensack, NJ, and under Joseph Stowell's witnessing, was led to the Lord in his home, September 1950. He made his last operatic appearance Nov 12, 1950. He began to sing for Word of Life, and JACK WYRTZEN's encouragement helped him through the transition to Christian songs. He spent a year with Latin America Mission. He traveled with Larry McGill in evangelistic work.

Gladys Aylward

Feb. 1, 1902 — *Jan. 3, 1970*
near London, England — Taipei, Formosa (Taiwan, China)

Missionary to China. Told by others that she was unqualified for missionary work, Gladys worked with prisoners, lepers, and the evangelization of the Chinese people. She was converted in her twenties after counseling with a pastor's wife. On October 15, 1930 (at age 33) she left Liverpool, England on a train trip across Europe, Russia, and Asia, but finally reached Yangcheng, China. She learned the Chinese language, began caring for wounded soldiers and children in need, and became a Chinese citizen in 1936. Gladys was caring for over 100 children when the Japanese attacked. In 1940 she fled with them 240 miles southwest over rivers and mountains to Sian, capitol of Shensi. After recovering from illness, she continued her work among lepers. She was in England, 1947–55, again in recovery from an illness she contracted in China. She then went to Formosa to open an orphanage. A motion picture, *Inn of the Sixth Happiness* was made of her work in 1959. A severe flu took her life. Earlier on her last day, she spoke to a gathering of soldiers' wives. Over 1,000 friends attended her funeral.

George S. Milner

Sept. 30, 1879
Gardner, Illinois

Jan. 2, 1970
Cleveland, Ohio

President of Baptist Mid-Missions, Cleveland, OH, 1945–59. Milner was converted in 1890 and began a 75-year ministry with Cedar Hill Baptist Church, Cleveland, OH. He developed two Ohio camps and was the president of the Baptist Home of Ohio for 19 years. Milner was active both in civic and in business circles in Cleveland. His Milner Electric Company was a very successful endeavor.

Juan E. Gattinoni

June 24, 1878
Italy

Jan. 7, 1970
Buenos Aires, Argentina

Bishop in the Methodist Episcopal Church, 1932–39; in the Methodist Church, 1939–67; and in the United Methodist Church, 1967–70. Gattinoni was born into a Catholic family who moved to Argentina, where he was converted around age 15. He married Minnie E. Rayson, then pastored the Central Church of Montevideo (capital of Uruguay), 1911–21, and finally the Central Church of Buenos Aires in Argentina till retirement in 1944. He taught at Union Theological Seminary, New York City, after 1944.

Teacher G. Eggers

Oct. 15, 1888
Farrar, Missouri

Jan. 17, 1970
Inglewood, California

Director of International Lutheran Laymen's League, St. Louis, MO, 1930–50. Eggers graduated from Concordia Teacher's College, Seward, NE in 1910. He taught at Zion School in Delmont, SD (1910–16), then served as teacher and principal at Emmaus School in Fort Wayne, IN (1916–30).

Raymond J. Wade

May 29, 1875
La Grange, Indiana

Jan. 24, 1970
St. Petersburg, Florida

Bishop in the Methodist Episcopal Church, 1928–39; in the Methodist Church, 1939–67; and in the United Methodist Church, 1967–70. Wade married Ella Yarian on December 4, 1904 (died: 1909), and Myrtle Mudge on Aug. 6, 1913 (died: March 3, 1969). Wade pastored in northern Indiana (1894–1915) and was secretary of the General Conference (1920–28). As bishop, he served in Sweden (1928–39) and Detroit (1940–48).

Daniel Burke

Dec. 5, 1873
New Berlin, New York

Jan. 26, 1970
Summit, New York

President of American Bible Society, 1944–62. Burke was an outstanding Methodist layman. Burke was admitted to the bar in New York (1896) and opened his own law office (1899). He married Kate Bundy on August 20, 1901 (died: 1945) and Charlotte Adams on January 6, 1951. His office became Burke and Burke in 1928, with which he was associated until his death. He was a member of the Wall Street Club and was involved in many local business endeavors. The annual budget of ABS went from $913,000 to over $5 million during his days as president. The translations of Scripture went from 104 to 308 languages.

Henry H. Ness

Aug. 6, 1894
Oslo, Norway

Jan. 29, 1970
Seattle, Washington

First president of Northwest Bible Institute (College) **of Assemblies of God, Kirkland, WA 1934–49.** Ness immigrated to Minneapolis, MN, worked for Standard Oil Company, and served in WWI. He was converted and served as a pastor in Brainerd, MN; Fargo, ND; and Hollywood Temple in Seattle, WA. He also began a school with church support. He later pastored in Oakland and Hayward, CA, before returning to Seattle, WA. The Los Angeles Baptist Theological Seminary gave him an honorary doctorate.

Gale Ritz

March 25, 1895
Henry County, Ohio

Feb. 14, 1970
Findlay, Ohio

President of Winebrenner Theological Seminary, Findlay, OH 1949–63. Ritz was also professor of OT there. He married Harriette Smith in December, 1947. He was a member of the Hancock County Ministerial Association, Society of Biblical Literature, International Religious Education Association, and Academy of Religion. He also was a part of the Findlay Rotary Club, Symposium Masonic Lodge, and the Zion Church of God near Hamler, OH. Ritz died of a heart attack.

Viljo K. Nikander

Aug. 3, 1903
Hancock, Michigan

March 18, 1970
Staten Island, New York

President of Suomi College and Theological Seminary (Lutheran School of Theology, Chicago, in 1964), **Hancock, MI 1937–47.** Nikander's father, JOHANN, was the first president of the school. He was ordained in Duluth, MN, on June 4, 1925. He pastored the Finnish Lutheran Church, Allston, MA from 1933–35, while getting his Ph.D. from Harvard. He married Sylvia Engstrom on October 10, 1935. After he served at Suomi, he was dean of the philosophy department of Wagner College, Staten Island, NY from 1947–70.

Thomas B. (Tom) Rees

c 1911/1912
Blackburn, England

April 1970

Evangelist, second only to ERIC HUTCHINGS in evangelism throughout England, in his generation. Converted in his teens, Rees immediately became active in evangelism. He joined the Church Pastoral Aid Society in arranging camps for London slum boys. He then conducted many united missions in northern Ireland, where thousands were converted. After WWII, he conducted 54 mass rallies in Royal Albert Hall in London and held campaigns in major British cities. He also went to America more than 50 times for campaigns, conferences, and retreats.

Lela G. McConnell

June 1, 1884
Honey Brook, Pennsylvania

April 7, 1970
VanCleve, Kentucky

Founder and first president and of Kentucky Mountain Holiness Association, 1924–70, and of Kentucky Mountain Bible Institute, VanCleve, KY 1931–70. McDonnell never married, but she was a mother to thousands. She was converted at age 13 and sanctified at age 20. That year, 1904, she joined the National Holiness Association. In her early years of ministry, she served as a missionary to Canada. Sickness forced her to a warmer climate in Kentucky, where she served for over 40 years. In 1924, McConnell began the Kentucky Holiness Association with the promise of Joshua 17:18. Soon a Bible school was in operation that sent out 400 Christian workers to 28 countries of the world. Her staff increased to 100, and 82 buildings have been built, including churches, schools, a radio station, and a farm. She was a Methodist all her life. At the time of her death, she was the longest participating member of the National Holiness Association. As she died, she said, "The gates are opening. I'm coming, Jesus."

James W. Storer

Dec. 1, 1884　　　　　　　　　　　　　　　　　　　　　　　　　April 12, 1970
Burlington, Kansas　　　　　　　　　　　　　　　　　　　Nashville, Tennessee

President of the Southern Baptist Convention, 1954–55. Nora Wilbanks became Storer's wife on Dec. 31, 1912. He pastored in Oklahoma (1913–15); Ripley, TN (1915–18); Paris, TN (1918–21); Greenwood, MS (1921–25); Richmond, VA (1925–31); and FBC of Tulsa, OK (1931–56). His books included *Truth Enters Lowly Doors* (1937) to *The Preacher: His Belief and Behavior* (1953).

Addison C. Raws

Jan. 21, 1893　　　　　　　　　　　　　　　　　　　　　　　　April 24, 1970
Philadelphia, Pennsylvania　　　　　　　　　　　　　　Toms River, New Jersey

Director of America's Keswick Conventions, Whiting, NJ (for 60 years), **1910–70.** Raws took over the work at age 17 when his father died. He took courses at Rutgers, New Brunswick, NJ, in his early days. He married Emma Conner in 1917, and they had four children, including a son, WILLIAM, who succeeded him. Raws saw the Victorious Life Conferences make Keswick their permanent headquarters in 1924.

George E. Epp

June 15, 1885　　　　　　　　　　　　　　　　　　　　　　　　May 7, 1970
Sheboygan, Wisconsin　　　　　　　　　　　　　　　　　Naperville, Illinois

Bishop of Evangelical Church, 1930–46; of Evangelical United Brethren Church, 1946–68; and in the United Methodist Church, 1968–70. Epp married Cora Runkel on September 3, 1907. He pastored at several locations in Wisconsin: Menomonee Falls (1906–07), Prairie de Chien (1907–11), Milwaukee (1911–16), and Racine (1916–19). He was executive secretary/treasurer of the Board of Missions, 1919–30, and president after 1934, supporting over 1,000 missionaries. He visited both Europe and the Orient.

William Turnwall

Aug. 31, 1893　　　　　　　　　　　　　　　　　　　　　　　　May 16, 1970
Daggett, Michigan　　　　　　　　　　　　　　　　　　Minneapolis, Minnesota

Missions secretary (president) **of Baptist General Conference, 1946–53.** Antionette Skooglun became Turnwall's wife on July 5, 1922 (died: February 20, 1956). In 1922, he was ordained at Gowrie, IA and served as a missionary/evangelist to Iowa, 1922–24. He pastored in Forest City, IA (1924–27); in Denver, CO (1927–31); in Evanston, IL (1931–39); and at Temple Baptist Church, Duluth, MN (1939–45). After 1963, he served as an interim pastor where needed.

Marion H. Reynolds Sr.

June 9, 1898　　　　　　　　　　　　　　　　　　　　　　　　May 27, 1970
Greely, Kansas　　　　　　　　　　　　　　　　　　　Los Angeles, California

Director of Fundamental Evangelistic Association, Los Angeles, 1928–70. This fundamentalist leader also founded Big Bear Lake (CA) Bible Conference (1927) and the Fundamental Bible Institute in Los Angeles (1936). Reynolds pastored Grace Fundamental Church of Los Angeles. His son, MARION H. REYNOLDS JR., served on the church staff and carried on the work at the Bible Institute. Reynolds died of a heart attack while attending a midweek prayer meeting.

Asa A. Allen

March 27, 1911
Sulpher Rock, Arkansas

June 11, 1970
San Francisco, California

Pentecostal healing revivalist. Asa was converted in 1934, in a "tongue-speaking" Methodist church revival. His wife's name was Lexia, whom he divorced in 1967. He was licensed by the Assemblies of God (1936), although they terminated his service (1956) because of his arrest (1955) for drunk driving. In 1951, he bought his own revival tent and established headquarters in Dallas, TX. Two years later, he had his own radio program, and by 1954, he had started his *Miracle Magazine*. When JACK COE died (1956), Allen was alone in the faith-healing field. He began Miracle Revival Fellowship (an association of several hundred independent congregations) (1956) and Miracle Valley (a spiritual community which became his headquarters), which consisted of over 2,500 acres near Bisbee, Arizona (1958). Allen died in a motel room of sclerosis of the liver while his team was conducting a meeting in West Virginia. Don Stewart, his associate since 1958, carried on the work, relocating in Phoenix.

Frank C. Laubach

Sept. 2, 1884
Benton, Pennsylvania

June 11, 1970
Syracuse, New York

Literacy missionary who taught some 100 million people in 35 countries to read. Effa Seely became Laubach's wife on May 15, 1912. He was a missionary evangelist to the Philippines in 1915, serving there until 1929. In 1929, he began his linguistic work among the Moro tribe on the island of Mindanao. In 1935, his "Each One, Teach One" motto went to other countries. Until 1953, he traveled around the world and spread the gospel. His reading primers were translated into 311 languages in 103 countries. Laubach was a Congregationalist and a Mason. He wrote 56 books including *Why There Are Vagrants* (1915) to *Toward World Literacy* (1960). The Laubach Literacy Fund was in New York City (1955–63) and then relocated to Syracuse, NY (1963 on).

"Lead America!...Win the world for liberty and Christ."

Daniel T. Niles

May 4, 1908
Jaffna, Ceylon (Sri Lanka)

July 17, 1970
Vellore, India

President of World Council of Churches, 1968–75. In 1927, Niles entered the Christian ministry. He studied at United Theological College at Bangalore, South India, 1929–33. Ordained (1936) as a Methodist evangelist, he became the general secretary of the National Christian Council of Ceylon (1941). He delivered the keynote addresses at the Inaugural Assembly of the WCC in Amsterdam in 1948. Niles pastored in Point Pedro (1946–50), and in Maradand (1950–53), both in Ceylon. He became the executive secretary of the Department of Evangelism for WCC in 1953. Also in 1953, he became the superintendent minister of St. Peter's Church in Jaffna and principal of Jaffna Central College. Later, he was general secretary of the East Asia Christian Conference and a prolific author. Niles wrote 45 hymns. He spoke at the WCC conclaves at Evanston (1954) and Uppsala (1968). He was committed to ecumenism and evangelism. He died of cancer.

J. Roswell Flower

June 17, 1888
Belleville, Ontario, Canada

July 23, 1970
Springfield, Missouri

First executive director of Assembly of God Foreign Missions, 1919–25. Flower married Alice Reynolds (born 1890) on June 1, 1911. He moved to Zion City, IL, in 1902, then to Indianapolis, IN, where the family was in a CMA church. He accepted Pentecostal doctrine in 1907. They joined others in 1914 to organize the Assemblies of God. His *Christian Evangel* became the forerunner of the *Pentecostal Evangel*. Flower was general secretary and editor of the denomination's publications (1914–59). He lived in St. Louis (1915–17) and Springfield, MO (1917–25). He pastored in Scranton, PA (1926–30); was district superintendent (1930–36); and general secretary and treasurer (1936–59) of the denomination. He received an honorary degree from Bob Jones University in 1946. Flower was a member of the City Council in Springfield, MO, from 1953–61. Flower gave 57 years of service to the Assembly of God ministry. He helped start the World Pentecostal Fellowship.

Robert L. Powell

Jan. 22, 1888
Lowell, Mississippi

July 30, 1970
Tacoma, Washington

GARB Council member for 20 years, chairman for four years. Powell was ordained a Baptist in 1911 and married Altha Talbot on September 4, 1919. He pastored in Mississippi, Louisiana, and Texas (six churches), 1912–31. He then went to his longest work, Temple Baptist Church, Tacoma, WA, from 1934–62. Powell served his country as a chaplain during WWI and was active in missions and educational enterprises.

Mark Fakkema

Jan. 12, 1890
Holland, Michigan

Aug. 1970
Chicago, Illinois

Executive director of the National Association of Christian Schools, 1947–60. Loving the Lord from his early youth, Fakkema transferred his love into promoting Christian education for the Reformed Church. He married Gretta VanHakken on October 4, 1916. Fakkema taught at Chicago's Christian High School (1918–26) and then served establishing Reformed Christian schools in the National Union of Christian Schools (1926–47). When he left to join NACS in 1947, he had set up 120 schools for the program. Fakkema was the manager of Christian School Service, Inc. ,1960–70.

Ivan Q. Spencer

Nov. 28, 1888
Allegheny Foothills, Pennsylvania

Aug. 17, 1970
Rochester, New York

Founder and first president of Elim Bible Institute, 1924–49, and founder of Elim Fellowship, 1933–49, both of Lima, NY. Spencer married Minnie Back on April 30, 1913. For a while he farmed and then served as an evangelist. He joined the Assembly of God fellowship in 1920 as an evangelist. Spencer pastored in Hornell, NY from 1920–24, whereupon he left the Assemblies of God and opened up EBI in Endwell, NY. He moved EBI to several locations, finally settling at Lima, NY, in 1951.

Frederick B. Harris

April 10, 1883
Worcester, England

Aug. 18, 1970
Washington, D.C.

Chaplain of the US Senate, 1942–46, 1949–69. Harris was ordained a Methodist in 1912 and married Helen Streeter on June 4, 1914. He pastored in Trenton, NJ (1912–14); Long Branch, NJ (1914–18); Grace Methodist, New York City (1919–24); and at Foundry Methodist, Washington, D.C. (1924–55). Harris was a special ambassador to Korea in 1956. His books included *The Blossoming Bough* and *Footprints on the Sand*. He conducted the funerals of President HERBERT HOOVER, Senator Robert A. Taft, and General DOUGLAS MACARTHUR. He is buried in Rockville, MD.

Napoleon B. Vandall

Dec. 28, 1896   *Aug. 23, 1970*
Creston, West Virginia   Akron, Ohio

Wrote lyrics and music of "After," "My Home Sweet Home," "Just One Glimpse," and "My Sins Are Gone." Vandall was converted at a Methodist camp meeting in Sebring, OH, in 1920. His ministry included the evangelistic field, preaching, and singing. His home was in Akron, OH, where he had a radio ministry for 20 years, starting in 1940. The song "After" was written as a result of his son's serious automobile accident. Mrs. Vandall died on February 27, 1973.

Judson A. Rudd

Nov. 28, 1902   *Oct. 6, 1970*
Belpre, Kansas   Chattanooga, Tennessee

President of Bryan College, Dayton, TN 1936–55. Rudd married Lucile Searcy on Sept. 7, 1927. He was an instructor of commerce and business administration at the University of Alabama, 1927–30. He then went to Bryan where he taught math (1931–56), was treasurer (1932–40), and professor of business, 1956 on. Rudd was a Baptist. He suffered a stroke ten days prior to his death.

William T. Patterson

April 30, 1884   *Oct. 12, 1970*
Glasgow, Scotland   Cincinnati, Ohio

President of Lane Theological Seminary (affiliated with McCormick Theological Seminary, Chicago, in 1931), **1950–70.** Patterson came to the U.S. (1910) and was ordained a Presbyterian (1913). He married Wanda Carey on December 3, 1913. He pastored in Norwood, OH (1920–47) and Batavia, OH (1947–57). Patterson served with the YMCA and the American Expedition Forces in WWI. He was involved with many civic and denominational activities, and was also a Republican and a Mason.

John Wargelin

Sept. 30, 1881   *Dec. 1, 1970*
Kyro, Finland   Livonia, Michigan

President of Suomi College and Theological Seminary (Lutheran School of Theology, Chicago in 1964), **Hancock, MI 1919–27, 1930–37.** Wargelin immigrated (1890) and was ordained (1906). He married Marie Hoikka on January 6, 1908. He pastored Finnish Lutheran Churches in Sault Ste Marie, Republic, and Negaunee, MI; Waukegan, IL; and Eveleth, Duluth, and Minneapolis, MN. He was also president of the Finnish Evangelical Lutheran Church (Suomi Synod), 1950–55.

Jasper A. Huffman

Feb. 28, 1880   *Dec. 7, 1970*
Elkhart County, Indiana   Winona Lake, Indiana

President of Winona Lake (IN) Summer School of Theology, 1939–54, educator, and author. Huffman married Elizabeth Lambert on May 5, 1901 (died: 1949) and Olive Sando on January 1, 1951 (died: 1969). Converted at age eleven through a revival (preacher: Andrew Good) in a schoolhouse in Elkhart County, he was ordained into the Missionary Church in 1904. Huffman served as dean of Taylor (IN) University's School of Religion (1936–45), and dean of Winona Lake (IN) Summer School of Theology (1926–39). In 1954, he was appointed dean of Bethel College, Mishawaka, IN. He began his editorship of *Higley Sunday School Lessons* (1937). Huffman wrote *Redemption Completed* (1904) to *Profile of a Modern Pentecostal Movement* (1968).

James C. (Jim) Rayburn

July 21, 1909
Marshalltown, Iowa

Dec. 17, 1970
Colorado Springs, Colorado

Founder and first director of Young Life, 1941–64, which was an exciting evangelistic concept to reach high school students for Christ. James and his wife, Maxine, began this work as "home missionaries" to New Mexico, 1933–36. As a Presbyterian minister, he was frustrated at not having a means to reach youth. His Young Life Ministries became the vehicle. Rayburn incorporated the ministry in 1941 in Texas and took the concept of reaching and training key high school leaders and athletes to have an impact on others across the country. He started *Young Life* magazine in 1944. The headquarters were established at Star Ranch, Colorado Springs, CO, in 1946–47.

Marc Boegner

Feb. 21, 1881
Epinal, France

Dec. 18, 1970
Strasbourg, France

President of World Council of Churches, 1948–54. For many years, Boegner was the leading French Protestant leader. He married, became professor of theology at Missionary College of Paris (1911–18), and then accepted the pastorate of the Reformed Church of Passy in Paris (1918–70). Boegner served as president of the Federation of Protestants in France (1929–61) and president of the National Council of Reformed Church in France (1938–50). He wrote many French books, and one English book, *Jesus Christ*.

Alfred Valdez

1916

1971

President of Full Gospel Fellowship of Churches and Ministers, 1963–66, 1968–70. Valdez's first sermon was preached in Melbourne, Australia at the age of eight years. After graduating from Glad Tidings Bible School (Bethany College in 1950), he began to serve as a pastor and evangelist. His pastorate of note was the Milwaukee (WI) Evangelistic Temple for 16 years. As an evangelist, he conducted meetings in 72 foreign countries and many major cities of South America. An illness took him suddenly.

Fred Bruffett

Oct. 4, 1883
Carthage, Missouri

Jan. 11, 1971
Kansas City, Missouri

Founder and first chairman of Association of Fundamental Ministers and Churches, Kansas City, MO 1931–69. Converted in his teen years in a schoolhouse revival meeting in Carthage, Bruffett married Hallie Northangel on May 3, 1907. He traveled to Kansas City in 1919 and stayed the rest of his life. He was founder and pastor of the Gospel Tabernacle of the First Church of God (1952–53) and of People's Church (1953–65). The AFM is a fellowship, not a denomination. It is nondenominational and has members from various backgrounds.

John L. Brasher

July 20, 1868
Clear Creek, Alabama

Jan. 25, 1971
Attalla, Alabama

President of Central Holiness University, 1917–24, renamed John Fletcher College, 1924–26 (Vennard College in 1951), **University Park, IA**. Brasher was principal of the John Snead High School for 14 years. He held meetings in 36 states and 25 counties in Alabama. He continued preaching into his nineties. He was the founder of the Brasher Springs Camp Meeting in 1940. Brasher preached to a large congregation there on his 100th birthday.

Ralph M. Riggs

June 16, 1895
Coal Creek, Tennessee

Jan. 31, 1971
Santa Cruz, California

General superintendent of Assemblies of God, 1953–59. Riggs served as pastor, missionary, educator, author, and administrator. He attended the Assembly of God formation at Hot Springs, AR in 1914, and pastored in Syracuse, 1916–19. While a missionary to South Africa (until 1925), he met and married Lillian Merian. Next he pastored the Central Church, Springfield, MO (1931–39). He was district superintendent of the southern Missouri district (1939–43) and assistant general secretary (1944–52). He taught at Bethany (WV) Bible College (1959–68).

James C. (JC) Penney

Sept. 16, 1875
Hamilton, Missouri

Feb. 12, 1971
New York, New York

Founder in 1902 of JC Penney Company, which grew to more than 2,000 retail stores, 1,700 in the US. Penny married Berta Hess on August 24, 1899 (died: 1910); Mary Kimball July 29, 1919 (died: 1923); and then Caroline Autenreith on August 10, 1926. In 1902, Penney opened his first store in Kemmerer, WY. Five years later, he launched the "Golden Rule Chain" and introduced profit sharing. In 1913, he incorporated it as the JC Penney Company. The next year, he moved his headquarters from Salt Lake City to New York City. Penney was president of his company until 1917, chairman of the board (1917–58), and honorary chairman (1958–71). In 1929, JC Penney was worth $40 million, but went broke the next year with the stock market collapse. He rebuilt the company after his spiritual renewal. In 1951, corporate sales went past $1 billion. At his death, he had 1,660 outlets with over $4 billion sales. He worked three days a week keeping five secretaries busy. His writings included *50 Years with the Golden Rule* and his autobiography, *J.C. Penney*. He died of a heart attack. His favorite Bible verse was Luke 6:31.

Robert Laidlaw

Sept. 8, 1885
Dalry, Scotland

March 12, 1971
Auckland, New Zealand

Evangelistic tract author. In 1886, Laidlaw's family relocated to Dunedin, New Zealand. He accepted Christ in 1902. In 1907, he moved to Auckland. In 1909, he commenced a mail-order business under the name of "Laidlaw Leeds." In 1913, Laidlaw authored *The Reason Why*. Outside of salvation tracts by FORD PORTER and BILL BRIGHT, this may be the most effective evangelistic tract ever written. Translated into 30 languages, with over 20 million distributed, it is believed thousands have come to Christ through this evangelistic tool. It is a 46-page booklet in which he shares his own testimony. He married Lilian Watson in San Francisco in 1915. In 1918, his company name was changed to Farmers' Union Trading Company. From 1939–44, he was co-field director of the Soldiers' and Airmen's Association.

Wyand Wichers

Feb. 15, 1886
Zeeland, Michigan

March 28, 1971
Kalamazoo, Michigan

President of Hope College, Holland, MI 1931–45. Wichers became an instructor at Hope (1909–13) and then a professor (1913–25). Wichers joined the Order of Orange-Bassau in 1936. He served as president of the General Synod of the Reformed Church, 1937–38. He was also a banker at Holland, MI, before becoming vice president of Western Michigan University, Kalamazoo, 1945–58. In 1968 he wrote *A Century of Hope*. His wife's name was Alyda.

William B. Lipphard

Oct. 29, 1886
Evansville, Indiana

April 14, 1971
Yonkers, New York

Executive director of Associated Church Press, 1951–61. Lipphard married Helen Dickinson on October 15, 1914. He was active in the American Baptist Convention, serving in the Foreign Missions Society in various staff positions, 1913–71. He was editor of their *Missions* magazine (1932–52). Lipphard was a delegate to many congresses and conventions around the world and wrote extensively. He is buried in Rochester, NY. He wrote from *The Ministry of Healing* (1920) to *Disillusioned World* (1967).

Thomas W. Graham

Oct. 12, 1882
Carlsbad, Ontario, Canada

June 4, 1971
Greenwich, Connecticut

President of Oberlin (OH) Theological Seminary, 1923–48. Graham came to America in 1904. He married Kate Fullerton on June 16, 1910 (died: January, 1958), and Beatrice Smith on October 1, 1959. He was ordained as a Presbyterian, pastored in Minneapolis, MN (1912–20), was professor of homiletics at Oberlin (OH) College (1923–48); counselor of religious work at the YMCA, New York City (1948–59); and was on staff at the First Church, Greenwich, CT (1959–71). He is buried in Oberlin.

Earle G. Griffith

April 26, 1895
Bethesda, Ohio

June 10, 1971
Anderson, South Carolina

President of Baptist Bible Seminary, Johnson City, NY (Clarks Summit, PA in 1967), **1936–45**. Griffith pastored several churches including Emmanuel Baptist, Toledo, OH; Bethel Baptist, Erie, PA; and FBC, Johnson City, NY. He was executive vice president of Piedmont Bible College until his retirement. Griffiths married Effie Ward on May 2, 1917. He was on the Council of the GARB. He died while on a visit to his son.

Lynn H. Hough

Sept. 10, 1877
Cadiz, Ohio

July 14, 1971
New York, New York

Dean of Drew University Theological School, Madison, NJ, 1934–47. Hough was a Methodist clergyman and educator who pastored various Methodist churches in New Jersey, New York City, Brooklyn, and Baltimore, MD from 1898–1914. By 1906, he was a prolific author and active in many clubs in the New York City area. He then became professor of theology at Garrett Biblical Institute (1914–19); president of Northwestern University (1919–20); pastor of Central Methodist in Detroit (1920–28); and pastor of the American Presbyterian Church in Montreal (1928–30). He was professor of homiletics as he began his work at Drew in 1930. He married Blanch Horton on October 13, 1936. He was a Mason. He wrote from 1906 to *The Living Church* (1959). *The Dignity of Man* was a key book.

Clarence A. Nelson

Sept. 8, 1900
St. Paul, Minnesota

July 21, 1971
Minneapolis, Minnesota

President of North Park Theological Seminary and College, Chicago, 1950–59, and Evangelical Covenant Church, Chicago, 1959–67. Nelson was converted at age 15. Blanche Nordell became his wife on October 27, 1926. He was ordained in the Evangelical Covenant Church in 1927, pastored in Evanston, MN (1926–29), and at the Salem Covenant Church, Minneapolis, MN (1929–45). He was president of Minnehaha Academy, Minneapolis, MN (1943–50), and of Covenant

Palms, Miami, FL (1967–69). He was interim president of the Covenant Church in Excelsior, MN, at the time of his death from a stroke.

William V. S. Tubman

Nov. 29, 1895
Harper, Liberia

July 23, 1971
London, England

Liberian politician and president, 1944–71. Tubman received a Christian education and was a teacher and lawyer in his early days. In 1923, he became Senator. In 1928, Tubman was a lay minister with the Methodist Church. He married Antoinette Padmore on September 17, 1948. In 1954, Tubman was at the dedication of ELWA Radio Ministry in Monrovia. Tubman encouraged other nations besides America to share in Liberia's development. Under his leadership, his people became involved by voting and paying taxes. His budget rose from $750,000 in 1944 to $30 million in 1960. He died following an extensive surgical procedure.

David Tsutada

March 6, 1906
Singapore

July 25, 1971

Outstanding Japanese evangelical leader and pastor. In 1919, Tsutada received "David" as his Christian name. He was converted in London on March 5, 1928. He returned to Japan on February 1, 1930. Tsutada married Esther Monuko Tobiyama on April 1, 1931. On June 24, 1942, he was imprisoned. After the war, he began the work of the Immanuel General Mission on October 21, 1945. He contributed to the birth of the Japan Protestant Federation (1948) and founded the Immanuel Bible Training College (1949). In 1953 he was vice chairman of the World Congress of YFC, held in Tokyo. In 1954, he was the chairman of the prayer committee for the Billy Graham meetings in Tokyo. When Graham returned in 1967, he was executive chairman for the crusade.

Russell H. Stafford

April 4, 1890
Wauwatosa, Wisconsin

July 31, 1971
Hartford, Connecticut

President of Hartford (CT) Theological Seminary, 1945–58. He was ordained Congregationalist in 1914. Stafford married Lillian Mae Crist on April 23, 1921. Stafford pastored the Open Door Congregationalist Church in Minneapolis (1915–19); First Congregational Church in Minneapolis (1919–23); Pilgrim Congregational Church in St. Louis (1923–27); and the Old South Church in Boston (1927–45). He served as the moderator of the International Congregational Council, 1958–71. He wrote from *Finding God* (1923) to *We Would See Jesus* (1947).

Albert G. Johnson

Jan. 4, 1887
Liverpool, England

Aug. 27, 1971
Portland, Oregon

President of Western Conversative Baptist Seminary, Portland, OR 1956–65. Johnson married Mary Johnson on February 23, 1910 and came to America in 1913. He pastored at Albany Park Baptist Church, Chicago, IL (1918–24); at Temple Baptist Church, Detroit, MI (1924–34); and Hinson Memorial Baptist, Portland, OR (1934–55). More than 3,500 new members were taken in. He was active in the Conservative Baptist movement and was president of CBFMS, 1951–56.

Charles E. Brown

Dec. 30, 1883
Elizabethtown, Illinois

Sept. 16, 1971
Anderson, Illinois

Editor of *Gospel Trumpet (Vital Christianity)* and leader of the Church of God, Anderson, IN, 1931–51. Brown was ordained in the Church of God on August 21, 1903. He married Carrie Becker on October 1, 1907. He pastored in Philadelphia, PA (1912–14); Detroit, MI (1915–26); and Chicago, IL (1928–30). Brown was also secretary of the Church of God Foreign Mission Board, 1927–29. His first book was *The Hope of His Coming*.

William F. Albright

May 24, 1891
Coquimbo, Chile

Sept. 19, 1971
Baltimore, Maryland

Methodist biblical archaeologist and the first person to confirm the accuracy of the Dead Sea Scrolls after their discovery in 1947. In 1919, Albright took a trip to Palestine, working in Jordan and Arabia. He directed the American School of Oriental Research in Jerusalem, 1921–29 and 1933–36, and edited their *Bulletin* (1931–68). Ruth Norton became his wife on August 31, 1921. He excavated many biblical sites, 1922–34. Albright was professor of Semitic languages at Johns Hopkins University of Baltimore, MD, from 1929–58. Albright's research enabled him to prove the accuracy of many important biblical dates. His works included *From the Stone Age to Christianity* (1940–46), *The Archaeology of Palestine* (1949) and *Yahweh and the Gods of Canaan* (1968).

Ralph J. Danhof

July 28, 1900
Chicago, Illinois

Oct. 13, 1971
Grand Rapids, Michigan

Stated clerk of Christian Reformed Church, 1945–70. Danhof married Margaret VanDellen on September 22, 1926 and she gave him four children. Danhof was ordained to the ministry of CRC in 1929. He pastored in Pella, IA (1929–34); Holland, MI (1934–45); and Neland Avenue CRC of Grand Rapids, MI (1945–71), where he remained for the rest of his life.

William Culbertson

Nov. 18, 1905
Philadelphia, Pennsylvania

Nov. 16, 1971
Chicago, Illinois

President of Moody Bible Institute, Chicago, 1948–70, and Accrediting Association of Bible Colleges, 1953–55. Culbertson was ordained in the Reformed Episcopal Church in 1927 and married Catharine Gantz on March 16, 1929. Culbertson was a rector of Grace Church, Collingdale, PA (1927–30); of St. John's-by-the-Sea, Ventnor, NJ (1930–33); and at the Church of the Atonement in Germantown, PA (1933–42). He was made a bishop in 1937. Culbertson was dean of education at MBI from 1942–48 and also edited *Moody Monthly* (1947–71).

J. Howard Pew

Jan. 27, 1882
Bradford, Pennsylvania

Nov. 27, 1971
Ardmore, Pennsylvania

Industrialist layman and philanthropist. Pew married Helen Thompson on January 3, 1907 (died: 1963). He went to work for the family-owned Sun Oil Company as an engineer and served as president, 1912–47. He then became board chairman of Sun Oil Company, director of Sun Ship Building and Dry Dock Company, and director of the Philadelphia National Bank. He was a heavy supporter of Grove City (PA) College, where he served as president of the board of trustees. Pew supported all kinds of causes from CARL MCINTIRE's ICC to *Christianity Today*. He lived in Admore, PA. His funeral service at Ardmore Presbyterian Church had Billy Graham assisting Pastor William Faulds.

Leonard J. Franz

Nov. 1, 1895
Inman, Kansas

Jan. 12, 1972
Hillsboro, Kansas

President of Tabor College, Hillsboro, KS 1951–52, 1953–54, and 1956–62. Franz married Helen Reimer on May 20, 1920. He was converted while attending Tabor, recuperating from an accident. He served 14 years as chairman of the Mennonite Brethren Conference Board of Publications. Franz was also superintendent of Hillsboro Public Schools, 1925–43. He was professor of history and government at Tabor until 1970. In September 1971, he suffered a heart attack at his daughter's home in Boston.

Ben Gordon

Jan. 23, 1900
Grand Rapids, Michigan

Jan. 22, 1972
Boca Raton, Florida

Director of Gull Lake Bible Conference (Ministries), **Hickory Corners, MI, 1941–61**. Gordon was a successful businessman from Grand Rapids, MI, who developed the Gordon Food business. He married the daughter of Issac VanWestenberge, his predecessor at Gull Lake. He died of a heart attack by his boat dock on a vacation.

Frank Houghton

Aug. 24, 1894
Stafford, England

Jan. 25, 1972
Pembury, England

General Director of China Inland Mission (Overseas Missionary Fellowship), **1941–51**. Houghton headed the work in war-torn China in 1920 until forced out. He married Dorothy Cassels on July 12, 1923. He served in the CIM office in London (1928–36) and then went back to China (1937–48). Houghton wrote *China Calling* in 1936. Houghton was vicar of St. Mark's in Leamington, England, 1953–60, and was rector of St. Peter's Prayton, Banbury, England, 1960 on.

Mahalia Jackson (Hackenhull-Galloway)

Oct. 26, 1911
New Orleans, Louisiana

Jan. 27, 1972
Evergreen Park, Illinois

Famous singer. Mahalia lived in Chicago, IL 1927–72, and sang for five American presidents. She began singing at the age of four in the children's choir at Plymouth Rock Baptist Church in New Orleans, LA. Her singing career started as soloist for Salem Baptist Church. She sang in storefront churches, revival tents, and ballrooms early on. She refused fabulous offers to sing in nightclubs. Her first gospel record appeared in 1934. Jackson married Isaac Hackenhull in 1936 (divorced in 1961) and Sigmond Galloway on July 2, 1964; it lasted three years. She appeared in Carnegie Hall on October 4, 1950. Jackson made the record, "Move On Up a Little Higher" (1954) which sold 2 million copies and revolutionized the gospel-singing field. She had eight songs that sold 1 million copies. She entertained personal greetings from Queen Elizabeth II and Winston Churchill and gave a performance for the king and queen of Denmark. Her tour included the 1958 Newport Jazz Festival, joining Duke Ellington in his gospel interlude, "Black, Brown, and Beige." She sang at the John F. Kennedy inauguration in 1961 and later at the famous MARTIN L. KING speech at Lincoln Memorial, Washington, in 1963. She died of a heart attack.

James R. Hull

Nov. 17, 1907
State College, Mississippi

Feb. 6, 1972

Outstanding layman and businessman from NYC. Hull was saved at age seven at an evangelistic meeting. He married Rosalie Paschal on Dec. 31, 1932. He worked with Mutual Life Insurance Company, 1928–72. Hull began in a sales office in Meridian, MS, and worked his way up to executive vice president (1950–59), president (1959–67), and chairman of the board (1967–72). As a Presbyterian layman, he was the crusade chairman for the famous Billy Graham Crusade in NYC in 1957.

Abner R. Reddin

Feb. 8, 1918
Forcyde, Arkansas

Feb. 12, 1972
Conway, Arkansas

President of Central Baptist College, Conway, AR, 1954–66. Reddin was converted at age 17. He pastored several churches, mostly in Arkansas (Bearden, Ashdown, etc.), and established the missions program for the state. Reddin married Lizzie B. Leslie in 1942. He was a part-time pastor in Arkansas, 1945–51 for the Baptist Missionary Association of America. During his leadership at Central College, enrollment grew from 30 to 250. The initial debt of the college was reduced in 1957. Reddin also served as president of Southwestern Baptist College, Laurel, MS, from 1969–71.

Paul W. Thomas

Sept. 28, 1894
Stockton, California

March 1, 1972
Baywood Park, California

Director of Pilgrim Holiness Church World Missions, 1930–46, and General Superintendent of PHC (Wesleyan Methodist Church in 1968), **1962–66**. Thomas was converted on Jan. 14, 1912 in Colorado Springs, CO. He married Alice Howard on June 12, 1918 (died: October, 1943) and Kathryn Bufkim on March 21, 1945. He became president of Colorado Springs Bible Training School, 1919–30. Thomas and Walter Surbrook led PHC through a reorganizational shuffle in 1930.

Chester E. Hardy

Sept. 2, 1882
Alexander City, Alabama

March 4, 1972
Alexander City, Alabama

President of Trevecca Nazarene College, Nashville, TN 1915–19, 1921–25, and 1928–37. While not serving as president, Hardy was almost always connected with the college as a teacher or serving on the Board of Trustees. He showed signs of becoming an outstanding physician, having graduated second in his medical class at the University of Tennessee, but yielded instead to a pastoral call. He married Mary Crain in August, 1907. He pastored First Nazarene Churches in Los Angeles and Nashville and was a frequent speaker at camp meetings and conventions all over the country. In 1907, Hardy entered the education field as president of Missouri Holiness College, DeSart, MO. Utilizing his medical background, he became a professor in the science department at Trevecca, 1908–14. Hardy led the school from a Pentecostal Mission affiliation to a merger with the Church of the Nazarene.

Irvin W. Musser

Sept. 9, 1881
Mt. Joy, Pennsylvania

March 12, 1972
Harrisburg, Pennsylvania

Director of Brethren in Christ World Missions, Grantham, PA 1919–49. Musser was converted at age twelve in a revival at a local church. He married Naomi Zercher on November 19, 1903, and they had four children. He was ordained on January 30, 1915, and served as district secretary, 1915–35. In 1938, he was made a bishop over Lancaster and York Counties in Pennsylvania. Musser also served as president of Messiah Children's Home, 1940–60.

Eugene C. Scott

July 24, 1889
Columbus, Mississippi

March 19, 1972
Atlanta, Georgia

Stated clerk of Presbyterian Church in U.S. (USA in 1983), **1935–59**. Emma Foust became Scott's wife on June 28, 1916. He pastored at Aberdeen, MS (1916–18); Gadsen, AL (1918–21); and Ensley, AL (1923–26). Scott assisted the stated clerk of the presbytery and served as treasurer, 1926–35. He resided in Dallas, TX (1935–50) and in Atlanta, GA (1950–59). Scott was a Mason. He is buried in Westview Cemetery.

Herbert G. Tovey

May 6, 1888
Melbourne, Australia

March 20, 1972
Escondido, California

"Mr. Music" of Bible Institute of Los Angeles, who wrote "A Passion for Souls" (music by Foss Fellers) **and "God's Matchless Grace"** (music by ART McKEE). Tovey left his native Australia in 1912 to attend Moody Bible Institute. He married in 1915, but his wife died in 1940, then later married Eva Sacherson on December 25, 1942. In 1919, he joined the music faculty of BIOLA. Tovey served there until 1953. Next, he pastored the First Baptist Church of Montebello, CA. Tovey wrote many gospel choruses.

James A. Deweerd

May 23, 1916
Olivet, Illinois

March 28, 1972
Pennville, Indiana (?)

World War II hero, editor, and early TV evangelist. In WWII, Deweerd was a chaplain (captain) in northern France, 1943–45, earning awards for bravery, including the Purple Heart. He became an evangelist, and lecturer from 1937–72. He edited *The Christian Witness* (1947–57) and was president of Kletzing (Vennard) College, 1949–51. He conducted a daily radio broadcast and weekly telecast on WLW, Cincinnati, 1952–57, which was a carry over from the old Cadle Tabernacle, which he pastored in Indianapolis. He married Mildred J. Geyer on June 5, 1963. He lived out his days in Pennville, IN, writing. His writings ranged from *The Realities of Christian Experience* (1940) to *What Is Worthwhile* (1970).

Erling Eidem

April 23, 1880
Goteborg, Sweden

April 1972

President of World Council of Churches, 1948–50. Elisabeth Elklund became his wife in 1909. Eidem was Archbishop of Uppsala, Sweden, from 1931 on. He was lecturer at the University of Lund (1913–24). Eidem was rector at Gardstanga (1924–28), taught at the University of Uppsala in 1926, and at the University of Lund (1927–28). He wrote several Swedish books.

Olivier Beguin

Jan. 2, 1914

April 1, 1972
Switzerland

General secretary of United Bible Societies, 1949–72. Beguin was first involved in Bible Society activities while working in Geneva on behalf of prisoners of war in Europe during WWII. He made his home in London, but traveled widely. His fluency in French, German, and English (his gifts of understanding across frontiers and his unfailing openness to people) were used to expand his labors. He married Agnes Mansfeld. He went into a hospital in October, 1971, but his illness grew steadily worse.

Martha Louise Moenich von Blomberg

March 1, 1896
Hamburg, Germany

April 6, 1972
Exeter, New Hampshire

Baroness and missions enthusiast. Martha's travels took her to over 125 countries where she conferred with leaders on Christian problems, lecturing in key meetings, and meeting many ranks and races of people. She traveled more than a million miles working with more than 100 missionary societies and churches. Martha was converted in 1904, via a German Emanuel Baptist Church. She felt the call to become a world missionary. Her travels began in 1922 upon graduation from Nyack Bible College. She went to Shanghai, China and worked ten years in the rescue of social slaves. Then she went to Korea and Japan, conducting meetings for Christian workers. She was a prisoner in Germany during WWI. She was in the jungles of Brazil (1937), Russia (1939), Mexico (1942), and Afghanistan (1945). She joined the Moody Church in Chicago in 1942. She went from country to country, into palaces or huts. On November 6, 1959, she married Baron Richard Fritz von Blomberg.

Jacob Stam

Sept. 18, 1899
Hawthorne, New Jersey

April 19, 1972
Miaocheo, China

President of D. M. Stearns Missionary Foundation, North Wales, PA, 1949–72. This outstanding lawyer was the brother of JOHN STAM, martyred missionary to China. In 1915, he was the amateur shorthand champion for the New York district. Stam had law offices in New York City (1915–22), then set up a general practice in Paterson, NJ as a legal counselor (1922–28). Stam married Dena Bowman on April 6, 1923 (died: Nov. 1965). In 1950, he presented a case before the US Supreme Court. He served on many boards of Christian organizations.

J. Edgar Hoover

Jan. 1, 1895
Washington, D.C.

May 2, 1972
Washington, D.C.

Director of the FBI, 1924–1972. Hoover was a Presbyterian, a Mason, and a great booster of Sunday schools. His favorite Bible verse was Micah 6:8. He once said, "The criminal is the product of spiritual starvation." Hoover never married. He began his career as a messenger in the Library of Congress. He entered the Department of Justice in 1917 and soon had the top position when he was only 29 years old. With the advent of WWII, the FBI agents increased from 600 to 5,000. His office captured or killed criminals and hunted down Communists. Hoover was often attacked by the media. His books included *Persons in Hiding* (1938), *Masters of Deceit* (1958), and *J. E. Hoover on Communism* (1969). He said: "For me, Jesus is a living necessity" and "To trust in the Lord with all thine heart is the only path to happiness, success, and true fulfillment."

Herman F. Swartz

May 12, 1871
Carlisle, Pennsylvania

May 10, 1972
Santa Barbara, California

President of Pacific School of Religion, Berkeley, CA 1922–38. Swartz was ordained a Congregationalist in 1898. He married Omega Kinsell (January 1, 1901) and later Edna M. Lindsay (June 27, 1917). He pastored in Mansfield, MA (1898–1901); Webster Groves and St. Louis, MO (1907–10); and Santa Barbara, CA (1943–46). Swartz also was superintendent of the City Missionary Society, Cleveland, OH (1901–07); secretary of the Congregational Home Missionary Society (1911–18); instructor in pastoral care at Hartford (CT) Theological Seminary (1917–21); and general secretary of the Congregational World Movement (1920–22). As president of PSR, he had to do difficult fund-raising (Depression years) and worked very hard to enlist students. He taught homiletics and social ethics.

William O. Carrington

1880
Georgetown, British Guiana

May 21, 1972
Long Island, New York

President of Hood Theological Seminary, Salisbury, NC 1910–20. Carrington was equally known for his pastoral leadership at the First AME Zion Church, Brooklyn, NY, 1936–64. He saw the church grow from 2,000 members to 5,600. He served as instructor in the School of Religion, Howard University, Washington, DC from 1920–24 and 1932–36. Carrington was also the editor of the *AME Zion Quarterly Review* (1924–32). He and his wife, Pearl, had four children.

Van V. Eddings

April 6, 1890
Ashland, Oregon

May 26, 1972
Whittier, California

General director of Orinoco River Mission of Venezuela, 1920–60 (merged into TEAM in 1980). Eddings was converted in 1908 in Los Angeles via T.C. HORTON. After attending BIOLA University in Los Angeles, he went to Venezuela in 1914 and married Gara Van Loenen (born: February 6, 1892) on November 26, 1914. During his ministry, around 50 missionaries came to Venezuela and a Bible institute was established in Las Delicias in 1939. Eddings ministered, 1936–61 in Cuidad, Bolivar and in the state of Bolivar (eastern part) on the banks of the Orinoco River in Venezuela. He retired from Venezuela in 1964.

Duncan Campbell

Feb. 13, 1898
Scotland

May 28, 1972
Lausanne, Switzerland

Revivalist. Campbell was converted in 1913 as he attended a prayer meeting directed by his father at the Faith Mission. In 1917, he was a machine gunner for the British forces in WWI. After training at the Faith Bible College in Edinburgh, he began a ministry in evangelism. He was married in 1925. Campbell pastored on the island of Skye, 1923–49, then re-entered evangelism with great results. In 1949, a revival swept the island of Lewis/Harris in the Outer Hebrides. For five weeks in Barvas, he conducted four services daily (7 and 10 p.m., 1 and 3 a.m.). In April, 1958, he became the principal of the Faith Mission Bible College in Edinburgh. In 1967, he ministered across Canada. His last message was delivered in Lausanne on I Corinthians 9:26. He had a heart attack and died four days later. One comment on his ministry: "You never hear Campbell preach without going home praying."

Watchman Nee

Nov. 4, 1903
Swatow, China

June 1, 1972
Anhwei Province, China

Pastor and evangelist who suffered in a Chinese prison for many years. Nee was the founder of the Little Flock Movement. He left a legacy of devotional material and biblical works. Nee was converted in 1920 at a Dora Yu revival meeting while still in college. By 1932, he and his Plymouth Brethren groups spread to Shanghai and farther north. He visited England and America in 1933. He married Charity Chang on October 19, 1934. She died in 1971 after a fall from a stool in her home causing broken ribs and internal injuries. By 1948, his business ventures moved into his Little Flock Church. He was arrested in 1952. Nee was still serving a 20-year prison sentence imposed by the Communists for his evangelization when he died of a heart attack. He used his time in prison, as BUNYAN did, to write. Nee wrote *The Normal Christian Life* and *The Spiritual Man* (1928).

Jack P. Schofield

July 17, 1882
Beulah, Kansas

June 2, 1972
Poplar Bluff, Missouri

Wrote lyrics and music for the familiar evangelistic song, "Saved," which was inspired by a sermon by Mordecai Ham on the "Cities of Refuge." Schofield was an evangelistic singer with Ham, T. T. Martin, and others. About 1918, he became associated with the Home Mission Board of the Southern Baptist Convention. In 1931, he retired from evangelism and entered the real estate business in Ft. Scott, KS. He later moved to Poplar Bluff, MO.

Hardy C. Powers

June 7, 1900
Oglesby, Texas

June 10, 1972
Bethany, Oklahoma

General superintendent of Church of the Nazarene, 1944–68. Powers married Ruby King on February 22, 1922. He pastored Nazarene churches in California (1926–31) and in Iowa (1931–36). He was also chairman of the board of general superintendents, 1949–59, and supervised the work in foreign countries, having a dedicated interest in missions.

J. Gordon Holdcraft

Aug. 31, 1878
Chicago, Illinois

June 30, 1972
Philadelphia, Pennsylvania

Director of Independent Board for Presbyterian Foreign Missions, 1940–52, and president of the same, 1950–72. Holdcraft was converted in 1890 in his Chicago home after reading passages from the Bible. He was ordained as a Presbyterian in May 1908 and married Nellie Cowan October 12, 1909 (died: March 16, 1976). Holdcraft transferred to Bible Presbyterianism, 1940, after serving in Korea, 1909–40, under the Presbyterian Church USA. He was active in Korean evangelism and Presbyterian advancement. He wrote *Into All the World* and wrote for ACC and ICC causes.

Irvine J. Harrison

Dec. 5, 1909
Mild May, Ontario, Canada

July 5, 1972
Athens, Greece

President of Southern California Bible College (Vanguard University in 1976), **Costa Mesa, CA 1944–56.** Harrison came from Canada in 1943. He had served as a pastor and district officer in the Assemblies of God. The utilization of Ralph Carmichael's musical ministry further enhanced the school. In 1948, a huge move was made from the out-grown Pasadena property to a new location, Santa Ana. It was an abandoned army air base now part of the newly developed Costa Mesa properties. He oversaw a merger of a small San Diego school, Berean Bible Institute, into SCBC in 1949. The school opened on September 11, 1950 on the new 128 acres. Financial problems abounded and student enrollment dropped despite his heroic attempts. However, it was a graduate of SCBC, Louis Richards, who went to Korea, that led Paul Cho, future great pastor in Seoul, to Christ.

Hallie G. Gantz

May 13, 1910
near Durham, Oklahoma

July 21, 1972
Enid, Oklahoma

President of Phillips University, Tulsa, OK, 1961–72. Gantz was the first alumnus to become the school's president. His wife, Sylvia Baker, whom he married on Nov. 7, 1933, also attended Phillips. He pastored in Ft. Worth, TX (1933–36); near New Haven, CT (1936–38); Lubbock, TX (1938–48); and the First Christian Church in Tulsa (1948–61). He was active in the Kiwanis Club and the Masons, and served on the board of trustees of United Christian Missionary Society. He died of a heart attack.

Clovis G. Chappell

Jan. 8, 1882
Flatwood, Tennessee

Aug. 18, 1972
Waverly, Tennessee

Southern Methodist clergyman, who filled Methodist pulpits throughout the South, and author. Chappell was converted while attending Webb School, Bell Buckle, TN. Cecile Hart became his wife on April 15, 1908. He pastored in many different places (1908–32), then pastored at First Methodist Church, Birmingham, AL (1932–36); St. Luke's Methodist Church, Oklahoma City, OK (1936–41); Galloway Memorial Methodist, Jackson, MS (1941–45); and First Methodist, Charlotte, NC (1945–49). From 1949 on, Chappell filled pulpits at Bible conferences and other preaching assignments across America. His many books ranged from *The Village Tragedy* (1921) to *Surprises of the Bible* (1967). His funeral was held at First Methodist Church, Waverly.

Ruth Caye Jones

1902
Wilmerding, Pennsylvania

Aug. 18, 1972
Erie, Pennsylvania

Wrote tremendous duet, "In Times Like These." Ruth taught herself to play both the piano and organ. She married Bert Jones and they had an evangelism ministry primarily, but not exclusively, in Methodist churches. In 1948, they began a radio ministry, a weekly family devotional which was broadcast directly from their home, in Erie. They had five children, with three sons being ordained preachers.

Dallas F. Billington

Jan. 23, 1903
Kirksey, Kentucky

Aug. 26, 1972
Akron, Ohio

Pastor of the Baptist Temple, Akron, OH. In 1934, Billington started his church with 13 people and a $1.18 offering in a rented schoolroom, and it grew into 16,000 members. The first auditorium was built (1937) and a second auditorium was built (1949), which seated 2,800. The work grew so large that it averaged 6,500 in Sunday School, the largest in the country in the early 1960s. In September, 1924, Billington was converted at a revival, in Paducah, KY with Evangelist Howard Williams. He married Nell Stokes on June 14, 1926. Billington originally was in the tire business; but soon after moving to Akron from Paducah, KY, in 1925, God called him to pastor. He was a Wesleyan Methodist early in his ministry. He died of a heart attack. B. R. LAKIN conducted his funeral with 6,000 attending. His son, Charles, continued the ministry.

Geoffrey F. Fisher

May 5, 1887
Nuneaton, England

Sept. 14, 1972
Sherborne, England

Archbishop of Canterbury, 1945–61, and president of World Council of Churches, 1948–54. Fisher married Rosamond Forman on April 12, 1917, and they had six sons. He was headmaster of Repton School (1914–32); served as bishop of Chester (1932–39); and then Bishop of London (1939–45). During the war years in London, he housed 300 homeless people in Lambeth Palace. Fisher met with Pope John XXIII (December 1960), becoming the first archbishop of Canterbury to visit the Vatican in Rome since the Reformation. He also visited Jerusalem and Constantinople.

Rutherford L. Decker

May 27, 1904
Wellsburg, New York

Sept. 21, 1972
Smithville, Missouri

President of National Association of Evangelicals, 1946–47. Decker married Gladys Jarnagin on Dec. 5, 1923. He pastored, 1922–43, in Laveta, Denver, Fort Morgan, and Collins, CO, plus also in Laramie, WY. He became pastor of Temple (Covenant) Baptist Church, Kansas City, MO from 1943–64. Decker was the first chairman of World Fellowship of Evangelicals and Prohibition Party nominee for President of the United States in 1960. He died, following a stroke, in Independence, MO during an interim pastorate. His residence was Liberty, MO.

Kittie L. Suffield

Sept. 16, 1884

Oct. 23, 1972
Pasadina, California

Nazarene songwriter. Kittie wanted to be a concert artist from the time she was a young child. Her ambitions changed after her conversion at age 19. She gave up concert ambitions and began evangelistic work, traveling with evangelist Mae Taylor who wrote "Meeting in the Air." Kittie wrote the lyrics and music to "God Is Still on the Throne" in 1929 after heavy trials. She also wrote "Little Is Much When God Is In It." Suffield was a talented musician, both as a coloratura (lyric soprano with high range, runs, trills) soprano and a pianist. During one trip, Suffield was on a train that became stuck in a heavy snowstorm. A man named Fred Suffield took a lantern and guided the train passengers to his house. She later wrote Fred a thank-you letter for his kindness. The correspondence continued and eventually they were married. They became traveling evangelists out of the Los Angeles area, working a few times with George Beverly Shea.

Worthy A. Spring

July 22, 1896
Millersburg, Ohio

Oct. 26, 1972
Milbury, Ohio

President of Cleveland (OH) Bible College (Malone College, Canton, OH in 1957), **1936–48**. Spring and his wife, Etta Hall, whom he married on May 29, 1924, worked hard to build this college. In 1924, he was ordained in the United Brethren Church and pastored three churches in Ohio: the Emmanuel Church in Cleveland (1926–28 and 1937–41); in Zanesville (1928–34); and in Akron (1934–36). He was found dead the day after his wife's funeral; she died October 23, 1972.

Melvin G. Larson

April 13, 1916
Minneapolis, Minnesota

Oct. 29, 1972
Minneapolis, Minnesota

President of Evangelical Press Association, 1958–60. Larson was converted on March 12, 1939, while singing in the church choir, where the pastor's message convicted him. At the time, he was a student at the University of Minnesota. He was one of the great Christian journalists of his generation. He married Carolyn Alfors on May 6, 1944 (died: 1984). He edited *Youth for Christ Magazine* (1948–57) during YFC's greatest days. He then became editor of his denomination's (EFC) journal, the *Evangelical Beacon* (1957–72). He authored 23 books.

Theodore W. Anderson

July 4, 1889
Salina, Kansas

Nov. 26, 1972
Chicago, Illinois

President of Mission Covenant Church, 1933–37, renamed **Evangelical Covenant Church, Chicago, 1937–59**. Anderson was converted at home as a child. He attended school at North Park College and at the University of Chicago. He married Evelynn Johnson on August 30, 1916. He was president of Minnehaha Academy, Minneapolis, 1913–33. In 1947, Augustana College/Seminary gave him an honorary doctorate. In 1952, he was honored by the King of Sweden, Gustav VI, receiving the Order of the North Star.

Raymond S. Haupert

March 9, 1902 — Dec. 15, 1972
Watertown, Wisconsin — Bethlehem, Pennsylvania

President of Moravian Theological Seminary, Bethlehem, PA, 1944–69. Haupert was ordained a Moravian in 1924, and that same year he began teaching at MTS as a professor of biblical literature and languages. He married Estelle McCanless on July 30, 1932. He was involved in banking 1969–71. Haupert authored *The Lacish Letters* (1938) to *Pioneers in Moravian Education* (1954).

Carroll M. Wright

July 6, 1887 — Dec. 16, 1972
Baltimore, Maryland — Green Cove Springs, Florida

General secretary of Christian Endeavor (Int.), 1934–47. Wright married Martha A. Webb on November 8, 1910 (died: 1970) and Gertrude C. Patriquin on October 29, 1970. He was an accountant in the field of banking and finance, 1905–19, and began work with CE in 1920, in the department of travel. He served as director of public relations for the Christian Herald Association, 1947–57, and was director of Christian Herald's Memorial Home Community, 1957 on. He retired to Green Cove Springs, FL. He was a Congregationalist and a Mason.

Harry S. Truman

May 8, 1884 — Dec. 26, 1972
Lamar, Missouri — Kansas City, Missouri

Thirty-third president of the United States, 1945–53. On June 28, 1919, Truman married Elizabeth Wallace (1885–October 18, 1982, 97 years old) and established a men's clothing store in Kansas City. This statesman was the son of a farmer and served as the Jackson County judge (1922), before being elected to the U.S. Senate from Missouri (1934). He became vice president in January, 1945. Upon Franklin Roosevelt's death in April, 1945, he became the Democratic president. In 1948, he upset Thomas Dewey, 303–18, on the electoral vote count. Strom Thurmond and Henry A. Wallace siphoned necessary votes away from Dewey. He authorized deployment of the atomic bomb and assisted European recovery after WWII through the Marshall Plan. Truman removed General DOUGLAS MACARTHUR on April 11, 1951, which was a major bombshell, from the Far East command during his tenure in the White House. He is remembered for his vigor and integrity. Truman was a Baptist. He is buried in Independence, MO. He never went to high school, was an excellent poker player, and was left-handed.

"The buck stops here."

Tommy Hicks

1909 — 1973

Missionary evangelist and faith healer. Hicks was successful in overseas evangelism in the 1950s. His most well-known meeting was in 1954 in Argentina at the Hurricane Football Stadium, where over 110,000 people attended; the two-month crusade netted over 300,000 decisions, including the vice president of Argentina. The crusade lasted two months with three million attending. He wrote several books on his experiences.

Oswald T. Allis

Sept. 9, 1880
Wallingford, Pennsylvania

Jan. 12, 1973
Wayne/Bryn Mawr, Pennsylvania

Presbyterian Old Testament scholar, clergyman, and educator. Allis was an instructor of Old Testament at Princeton Seminary (1910–22), and assistant professor there (1922–29) in the field of Semitic studies. He married Ruth Robinson on Sept. 21, 1927. In 1929, when the major split took place at Princeton, he left with R. D. WILSON, CORNELIUS VANTIL, and J. GRESHAM MACHEN to become a faculty member of the newly formed Westminster Seminary, 1930–36, continuing to teach Old Testament. He had been an editor of the *Princeton Theological Review* (1918–29), and later a contributing editor of *Christianity Today* (1938–73). Besides his Old Testament expertise, he was a defender of Reformed theology, including amillennialism. A great conservative scholar, he authored nine books. His most important books were *The Five Books of Moses* (1943), *Prophecy and the Church* (1945), and *The Unity of Isaiah* (1950). *Basic Christian Doctrines* (1965) was his last.

Joseph McCaba

Jan. 1, 1900
Paterson, New Jersey

Jan. 22, 1973
Ft. Lauderdale, Florida

General director of Evangelical Baptist Missions, Kokomo, IN 1945–64. McCaba was converted as the result of the witness of fellow workers at a dye-house. He became a missionary in Niger (French Sudan) for 20 years. He reduced the Djerma language to writing and translated the NT to give them the Word of God. McCaba was known as "the teacher that laughs" by the natives, the name later became the title of his autobiography. He was an outstanding diplomat and was decorated by the president of Niger.

E. Stanley Jones

Jan. 3, 1884
Clarksville, Maryland

Jan. 26, 1973
Barceilly, Italy

Outstanding Methodist missionary to India. Jones was converted in 1901 and married Mabel Lossing on February 11, 1911. He was an evangelist to the high castes of India for 66 years (1907–73) pastor of the English Church, Lucknow (1907–10); district missionary of the United Provinces (1911–17), working out of Sitapur, to the poor, as well as the educated (1917–54). In 1914, he contracted a serious illness. Jones was elevated to a bishop in 1928, but he resigned within 24 hours so he could continue his missionary work, saying, "I am called to be an evangelist and a missionary." He founded two Christian Ashrams (religious retreat) at Sal Tal in 1929 and Lucknow. For years, he spent six months at a time in India, then six months in America. His evangelism spread throughout six continents. Jones authored 29 books, including *The Way* (1948), to his spiritual biography *A Song of Ascents* (1968), *The Christ of the Indian Road* (1925), which sold 700,000 copies in 20 languages, and *The Christ of Every Road* (1939). His books passed 3.5 million sales. His last book was *The Unshakeable Kingdom and the Unchanging Person* (1972). Jones' emphasis on peace, racial brotherhood and social justice gave him a "liberal" reputation, perhaps unfairly. He died at Clara Swain Hospital. He stated "I came to Christ bankrupt…He took me, forgave me…by grace was I saved…the gift of God".

Paul Myers
First Mate Bob

May 31, 1896
Camden, Michigan

Jan. 28, 1973
Tustin, California

Host of the "Haven of Rest" radio broadcast which greeted listeners with "Ahoy there, shipmates!" and the clanging of a bell. His first wife died soon after the birth of a daughter. He married Thelma Stovall in 1920, and they had four children. She was saved July 24, 1924. It was the clanging of a bell on a foggy morning on the waterfront of San Diego that brought Myers out of a drunken stupor. He telegraphed his family, "Thank Him for the answer." He said yes to Christ as he said good-bye to skid row. He began his broadcasts 30 days after his conversion on February 15, 1934, by reading a Gideon Bible in a San Diego rooming house. Myers and the crew of the Good Ship Grace blessed multitudes during his near 40-year ministry, retiring in 1971. He died of pneumonia.

Merle L. Davis

March 12, 1893
Richmond, Indiana

Feb. 3, 1973
Richmond, Indiana

Director of Friends United World Ministries, Richmond, IN, 1936–54. His official title during his 1936–54 ministry was administrative secretary of the American Friends Board of Missions of the Five Years Meeting. Davis married Margaret Farlow. He served as principal of the Friends School, Holguin, Cuba, 1919–24. From 1955–65, he served as pastor of the Salem Friends Meeting, Liberty, IN, and also managed a bookstore in Richmond after leaving the Five Years Meeting office.

Peter K. Regier

June 4, 1891
Moundridge, Kansas

Feb. 19, 1973
Newton, Kansas

Executive secretary of General Conference Mennonite Church (Mennonite Church USA in 2002), **Newton, KS 1950–60.** Rediger married Marie Stauffer on August 17, 1921. He served as pastor in Wayland and Noble, IA (1922–24); West Zion Mennonite Church, Moundridge, KS (1927–41); and in Reedley, CA (1943–50). After his leadership position in the denomination, he pastored three more Mennonite churches, 1960–69.

Paul S. Allen

July 12, 1898
Laingsburg, Michigan

March 1, 1973

President of Simpson College, San Francisco, CA, 1951–63. In 1955, the college moved from Seattle, WA. Allen was converted at age ten at his father's church in St. Louis, MO, under Evangelist J. D. WILLIAMS. He married Lucy Derr on March 19, 1926, and they had three children. He was a missionary to Palestine and Iran under the Christian and Missionary Alliance board, 1921–35. Allen pastored at Bryan and Cleveland, OH (1936–41) and was district superintendent of the CMA for several states (1941–51).

Pearl Sydenstricker Buck-Walsh

June 26, 1892
Hillsboro, West Virginia

March 6, 1973
Danby, Vermont

Missionary-teacher, 1921–31, in Chinese universities and author of the best-selling book, *The Good Earth* **(1931),** which eventually was translated into three languages. Pearl's parents were Presbyterian missionaries to China where Pearl spent almost half of her life. She married John Buck, an agricultural missionary, on May 13, 1917. She later divorced and then married Richard Walsh on June 11, 1935 (died: May, 1960). She resigned from the Presbyterian Board of Foreign Missions in 1933 due to conservatives demanding her dismissal because of her emphasis on social service. Pearl wrote many books, including *East Wind—West Wind* (1930) to *The Good Deed and Other Stories of Asia* (1970). She won the Pulitzer Prize for *The Good Earth* (stories of her parents) (1931) and the Nobel Prize (1938) for her biographical literature.

Robert J. McCracken

March 28, 1904
Motherwell, Scotland

March 7, 1973
near Bangkok, Thailand

Pastor of the noted liberal Riverside Church, New York City 1946–67, succeeding H. E. Fosdick. McCracken pastored the Marshall Street Baptist Church of Edinburg, 1928–32. McCracken married Maude Ibbotson on March 6, 1929 (died: 1969) and Sally Koch in June, 1972. In 1932, he became pastor of Dennistown Baptist Church of Glasgow and began to teach theology at the Baptist Theological School of Scotland. In 1938, he went to Canada and joined the faculty of McMaster University, Hamilton, Ontario. He taught theology and philosophy of religion, becoming head of the Department of Religion, 1944–46. In 1954, in the midst of his Riverside responsibilities, he joined the faculty of Union Theological Seminary. He retired in 1967, after having written four books while at Riverside. He died at sea on a world cruise, March 8, local time.

Kent S. Knutson

Aug. 7, 1924
Goldfield, Iowa

March 12, 1973
Minneapolis, Minnesota

President of the American Lutheran Church (ELCA in 1988), **1970–73**. Knutson married Norma Arneson on September 5, 1951. He was the pastor of Our Savior Lutheran, Staten Island, NY, from 1954–58. He was head of the systematic theology department at Luther Seminary, St. Paul, MN (1958–68) and president of Wartburg Theological Seminary, Dubuque, IA (1968–70). He was stricken with a rare, terminal brain disorder that affects the central nervous system, known as Creutzfeldt-Jakob Disease (CJD). The onset of the disease symptoms began after a mid-1972 trip around the world that took him to Lutheran churches in the Far East and India.

Howard T. Mills

Sept. 13, 1887
Applegate, Michigan

March 16, 1973
Owosso, Michigan

President of Bible Holiness Seminary (John Wesleyan College in 1970, closed in 1980), **1933–47**. Mills was converted in "the Crusaders' Campaign" in the Methodist Church in 1907. He was a teacher for several years 1905–33 in the Sanilac County Public School. Mills married Anna Walker in 1909 (died: 1954) and Lillian Benedict in 1955. He was ordained in 1934 and then became the secretary of education in the Pilgrim Holiness Church.

Gordon J. Lindsay

June 18, 1906
Zion City, Illinois

April 1, 1973
Dallas, Texas

Founder and first president of Voice of Healing, 1948–67, renamed Christ for the Nations, Dallas, TX 1967–73, and president of Full Gospel Fellowship of Churches and Ministers, 1967–68, 1970–73. The name changed because worldwide ministries evolved. Lindsay was converted in 1925 in Portland, OR at a CHARLES PARHAM revival. He married Freda Schimpf on November 14, 1937, who was converted in his Oregon City, OR, revival. He pastored in Tacoma, WA; Pillirop, MT (1937–44); and Ashland, OR (1944–47). He started *Voice of Healing* magazine with headquarters in Shreveport, LA 1948–52. In 1952 he moved to Dallas, TX. He published the *Voice of Healing* (1948–67) which eventually was called *Christ for the Nations* (1968–73) He started a worldwide Native Church crusade (1962) (full gospel fellowship of ministers and churches) and opened a Bible school (1970) (CFTN Institute). Lindsay died while on the platform at a school chapel service. His wife and son, Dennis, carried on his work. He wrote over 250 books and pamphlets.

J. Christy Wilson

July 22, 1891
Columbus, Nebraska

April 8, 1973
Duarte, California

Presbyterian missionary to Iran. Wilson married Fern Wilson (no relation) on April 7, 1917. He went as an evangelistic missionary, 1919–40, to Tabriz in Azerbaijan in northwestern Iran under the Presbyterian Board of Foreign Missions. He also went to Russia and other countries of the Middle East. He authored several books in Persian including a textbook on the art, archaeology, and architecture of Iran. In 1939, he returned to the US and became associate professor of ecumenics (unity, church union) at Princeton Theological Seminary, 1940–62. He also directed the field work of ministerial students and wrote *Ministers in Training* (1957). He became visitation pastor at First Church, Princeton (1962–63) and the same at First Church, Monrovia, CA (1965–70), during which time he also taught missions courses at Fuller Theological Seminary. His son, J. Christy Wilson Jr. (1922–February 8, 1999) was born in Iran and died in Duarte, CA. He was a missionary to Afghanistan for 23 years, then became the professor of world missions at Gordon-Conwell Theological Seminary from 1975 on.

Peter E. Schellenberg

April 20, 1898
Buhler, Kansas

April 9, 1973
Bluffton, Ohio

President of Tabor College, Hillsboro, KS, 1942–51. Schellenberg served as a professor of psychology at Bethel College, North Newton, KS from 1931–41. He continued his association at Tabor until 1954. Thereafter, he taught and was dean at Bethel College, Reedley (CA) College, and Bluffton (OH) College. This well-known Mennonite educator died unexpectedly in his home.

Bernice Tucker Cory

June 26, 1899
Chicago, Illinois

April 21, 1973
Wheaton, Illinois

Cofounded Scripture Press Publications with her husband. Bernice married VICTOR CORY on June 16, 1922, and they had four sons. With Victor, she began writing Sunday school lessons in 1932. Bernice became editor-in-chief of the company and supervised the Sunday school materials and biblical study courses used by 70 denominations in 78 countries. The Corys were members of Wheaton Bible Church.

Casper C. Warren

May 28, 1896
Sampson County, North Carolina

May 20, 1973
Charlotte, North Carolina

President of Southern Baptist Convention, 1956–57. Warren married May Stickland (August 26, 1925) and Sibyl Townsend (January 19, 1962). He served in World War I. He pastored Lexington Avenue Baptist, Danville, KY (1928–38); Immanuel Baptist, Little Rock, AR (1938–43); and FBC, Charlotte, NC (1943–58). Warren directed the 30,000 movement of SBC from 1956–64, which had a goal of starting 30,000 preaching points.

Paul Zimmerman

Aug. 29, 1906
Ravenna, Michigan

May 31, 1973
Chattanooga, Tennessee

Founder and first director of Cedine Bible Mission, Spring City, TN 1946–66. Zimmerman was converted on November 15, 1928 in a revival in Salem, MI. He married Ruth Baker on June 30, 1934. With his wife, they worked with a rural mission organization and noticed the lack of evangelism amongst the Blacks. He began to minister to them and after 39 children memorized

200 verses, he sought for a camp. It was when they rented eight acres that Camp Cedine came into being. In 1950, a 100-acre farm was bought with $2,000 borrowed money. After being trained at MBI and Wheaton College, he did church planting in Yorkville, MI, and also in Kentucky. Zimmerman died of prostate cancer.

James D. Murch

Oct. 23, 1892
New Vienna, Ohio

June 16, 1973
Cincinnati, Ohio

First president of Evangelical Press Association, 1949–50, and chairman of National Religious Broadcasters, 1956–57. Murch married Olive Cameron on August 25, 1915. He was ordained into the Disciples of Christ in 1915. Murch edited *Lookout* (1918–25) and *Restoration Herald* (1925–34). He served as a professor of church history at Cincinnati Bible Seminary, 1925–37. Murch was instrumental in starting the school and served as its president, 1928–35. He worked with Standard Publishing Company, 1935–45 and wrote 16 books. He was the editor of *Action Magazine* (1945–58) in the early days of the National Association of Evangelicals. He was the managing editor of *Christianity Today* (1958–61). His works range from *Successful Prayer Meetings* (1930) to *Adventuring for Christ* (1973). He became a leader of the independents (Christian Churches and Churches of Christ) who separated from the Disciples of Christ in 1968.

J. Elwin Wright

July 9, 1890
Corinth, Vermont

June 29, 1973
Tunjunga, California

Cofounder and first general director of National Association of Evangelicals, 1942–48, and Director of New England Fellowship of Evangelicals, 1929–50, succeeding his father, Joel. He was greatly burdened about the need for unity among evangelicals. NEFE was called Firstfruits Harvester's Association, 1929–32. Wright married Florence Dunkling on July 8, 1911. He was Presbyterian. Wright was a delegate at various conferences of church leaders in 51 countries, 1946–56. He was co-secretary of a Commission for World Evangelical Fellowship (1951–59) and honorary secretary (1959–73). He wrote the *Old-Fashioned Revival Hour* (1939) and *Manna in the Morning* (1943).

J. Paul Taylor

April 1, 1895
Mount Vernon, Illinois

July 2, 1973
Woodstock, Illinois

Bishop of Free Methodist Church, 1947–64. Taylor married Lillian Ambrose on August 8, 1917. He served in the Central Illinois and Genesee Conferences of the Free Methodists for 50 years. He pastored, served as an evangelist, and was superintendent for seven years. Taylor authored several works, including *The Music of Pentecost*; *Holiness, The Finished Foundation*; and *Godly Heritage*.

Joseph M. Dawson

June 21, 1879
Maypearl, Texas

July 6, 1973
Corsicana, Texas

Southern Baptist Convention minister, executive, and advocate of civil liberty. Dawson married Willie Turner on June 3, 1908 (died: April 18, 1963). He was converted in a revival in a Baptist Church in Italy, TX, in 1892 and pastored in Hillsboro, TX (1908–12); Temple, TX (1912–15); and at FBC, Waco, TX (1915–1946). He was the first executive director of Baptist Joint Committee on Public Affairs, 1946–53. At the founding of the United Nations, he arrived with 100,000 signatures and called for religious liberty to be in the charter of the UN. Dawson founded Protestants and Other Americans United for Separation of Church and State and served as temporary executive director, 1947–48. When it comes to social justice, free society, civil rights, world preaching, religious liberty, and public morality, no one was a better advocate than Dawson. He wrote twelve books. They range from *The Light that Grows* (1924) to *Jose Navarro* (cofounder of Texas, 1964).

Edward V. Rickenbacker
Eddie Rickenbacker

Oct. 8, 1890
Columbus, Ohio

July 23, 1973
Zurich, Switzerland

Famous aviator. Rickenbacker married Adelaide Durant on September 16, 1922. He was known as an auto racer and won many races. In WWI, he led with 26 combat victories—the most decorated American pilot of the war. In WWII, he again won many honors for combat excellency. In October, 1942, he was rescued with six others after 24 days at sea on rubber rafts. The crew would have died if Eddie, the oldest person on the raft, had not encouraged them to "keep the faith" and "believe in their rescue." Rickenbacker was president of Eastern Airlines, 1955–59. Under his leadership, an airline made the first profits in aviation history. He wrote three books. Rickenbacker said, "I pray every night of my life to be given the strength and power to continue my efforts to inspire others." He wrote *Fighting the Flying Circus* (1919), *Seven Came Through* (1943), and *Rickenbacker, An Autobiography* (1967).

L. Nelson Bell

July 30, 1894
Longsdale, Virginia

Aug. 2, 1973
Montreat, North Carolina

Famed Presbyterian medical missionary to China and cofounder of *Christianity Today* in 1955, serving as its executive director, 1955–73. Bell was converted at age eleven in an evangelistic service in January, 1906, at the First Presbyterian Church, Waynesboro, VA. He married Virginia Leftwich on June 30, 1916; their daughter, Ruth, married Billy Graham. He became the chief surgeon at Tsingkiangpu (Huaiyin) Hospital from 1916–41. He cared for over 150,000 patients. Next, he practiced surgery in Asheville, NC, from 1941–56, retiring afterwards because of a recurring cardiac condition. In 1955–56, he and Billy Graham founded *Christianity Today*. Bell's biography is titled *A Foreign Devil in China*. In 1941, he cofounded the *Southern Presbyterian Journal* (*Presbyterian Journal* in 1979) and worked as associate editor, 1941–73. He died in his sleep at home a few hours after addressing a missions conference.

Walter R. Williams

March 10, 1884
Mount Victory, Ohio

August 7, 1973
Lakeland, Florida

General superintendent of Ohio Yearly Meeting (Evangelical Friends Church—Eastern Region in 1971), **1951–57, and its mission program, 1943–54**. Williams went as a missionary to China, 1909–27. He was an instructor at Malone College, Canton, OH for eight years. He was the general superintendent of Ohio Yearly Meeting 1951–57, and pastored twelve years at Damascus and Cleveland's First Friends Church. Williams' books include *Ohio Friends in the Land of Sinim* and *The Rich Heritage of Quakerism*. He married Myrtle Hosack.

Clinton H. Churchill

1888

August 26, 1973

Chairman of National Religious Broadcasters, 1945–47, and founder and pastor of the Churchill Tabernacle in Buffalo, NY, in 1925 until it closed in the early 1950s. Churchill was of a Methodist background and formerly a businessman, converted under BILLY SUNDAY in 1917. He pastored North Delaware Methodist, Buffalo (1917–21), and then traveled as an evangelist

(1921–22). He founded the radio station WKBW (Well–Known Bible Witness) in 1926 and broadcast over it for years. After the church closed, the buildings were used for secular radio and TV ministries.

Alexander B. Mackey

April 16, 1897
Highway, Kentucky

Sept. 3, 1973
Nashville, Tennessee

President of Trevecca Nazarene College, Nashville, TN 1937–63. In his early years, he taught in rural schools in several places: Clinton County, KY (1915–20); Albany High School, Albany, KY (1921); and Cumberland County, KY (1922–23). Mackey also served in WWI. He was also superintendent of Buena Vista High School, Cythiana, KY, from 1924–25. Mackey went to Trevecca in 1925, and remained there for the next 42 years. He held almost every position possible, from janitor to president. He was the high school principal (1926–29) and then dean of the college (1929–36) before becoming its president. He raised the college out of the indebtedness of the depression, building seven major buildings and purchased a new campus in Highway, Kentucky. Mackey had the privilege of awarding his mother her college degree when she was 72 years old. He married Lyla Thrasher on February 15, 1935.

Timothy S. K. Dzao

Nov. 20, 1908
Changai, China

Sept. 17, 1973
Hong Kong, China

Outstanding Chinese evangelist, founder and president of Ling Liang Worldwide Evangelistic Mission, 1942 on. Converted in 1925, Dzao was baptized as a Methodist. In the 1930s, he was packing in nearly 2,000 people every week in his Changai services. He traveled throughout the Orient in crusades. He was married July 9, 1932, to Tang Lin An. Dzao wrote *A Bible Treasury* (27 vols. in Chinese). When he could no longer preach in China, he moved from Hong Kong to Indonesia, where he established churches and schools. He founded Gamaliel University of Djakarta, Indonesia, in 1954.

Albert E. Day

Nov. 18, 1884
Euphemia, Ohio

Oct. 12, 1973
Front Royal, Virginia

Influential Methodist clergyman who was chosen as one of the six leading preachers in America in 1940 in a Christian Century poll. Day married Emma Reader on September 28, 1904. His first pastorates were in Bellefontaine, Cincinnati, Delaware, and Canton, OH (1904–25) and at Christ Church, Pittsburgh, PA (1925–32). He then went to Mount Vernon Place in Baltimore, MD, from 1932–37 and 1947–57. He also pastored at First Methodist of Pasadena, CA from 1937–45. Day wrote many books, from *Present Perils in Religion* (1928) to *An Autobiography of Prayer* (1952). He retired to Front Royal, VA.

Louis W. Goebel

June 8, 1884
Carlinville, Illinois

Oct. 22, 1973
Webster Groves, Missouri

President of Evangelical and Reformed Church (United Church of Christ in 1957), **1938–53.** Goebel was ordained into the Evangelical Synod of North America on April 7, 1907. He married Edith Roesche on June 26, 1912; they had three children. Goebel held pastorates in Bellevue, KY (1907–11), and at First Evangelical Church, Chicago, IL (1911–38). He also served as vicepresident of Evangelical and Reformed Church, 1934–38. Goebel was involved with WCC events and lived in Webster Groves, MO. He wrote a book called *I Believe.*

George S. Schuler
April 18, 1882   Oct. 30, 1973
New York, New York   Sarasota, Florida

Composed music for "Make Me a Blessing" (1909) (lyrics by IRA WILSON) **and "Overshadowed"** (lyrics by HARRY IRONSIDE). For 40 years, 1914–54, Schuler served as a member of the music faculty of MBI. He married his second wife, Anne Helmerich, in the mid–1910s. Schuler composed many gospel songs, and published a number of collections of piano and organ music. After 1951, he served on the editorial staff of the Rodeheaver Company. He wrote the music to "By Life or By Death," "Cling to the Promises," "He's Looking on You," "In the Hollow of His Hand," and "My Hope Is In Thee."

Lester A. Welliver
Feb. 2, 1896   Nov. 13, 1973
Stockton, Pennsylvania   Gaithersburg, Maryland

President of Westminster (MD) Theological Seminary (Wesley Theological Seminary, Washington, DC in 1955), **1943–55**. Welliver was ordained Methodist in 1918. He married Eleanor Yeaworth on October 2, 1923. He Welliver pastored in Altoona, PA (1922–24); Bellwood, PA (1924–28); Lewisburg, PA (1928–33); Clearfield, PA (1933–36); Williamsport, PA (1942–43); and Stevens Memorial in Harrisburg, PA (1961–65).

William T. Phillips
June 27, 1893   Nov. 30, 1973
Birmingham, Alabama   Mobile, Alabama

Founder and senior bishop of Apostolic Overcoming Holy Church of God, Birmingham AL, 1916–73. In 1911, Phillips married Viola Sherman. He was converted in a Methodist church and sanctified in a Holiness church in Birmingham, AL in 1912. Phillips led his church for over half a century, 1916–73. He also owned the Phillips Printing Company and *People's Mouthpiece* magazine. He wrote *The End of the Age*.

Edward C. Swanson
1884   Nov. 30, 1973
New York Mills, Minnesota   Rancho Cordova, California

President of St. Paul (MN) Bible Institute (Crown College in 1992), **1926–35**. Swanson married Sigrid Osterberg in 1911 and they had five children. They served in pastorates, Indian missions and evangelistic ministries in the Northwestern District. He pastored in Battle Lake, MN, from 1919–25. The St. Paul campus was acquired during his tenure as president. It was under his leadership that the present building and grounds were acquired in 1935. In 1938, he moved to California where he pastored in Santa Rosa and Santa Monica. He retired in 1948 but continued to supply various churches. Funeral services were held in the CMA church in Santa Rosa.

Arthur H. Graves
June 19, 1902   Dec. 25, 1973
Chicago, Illinois   Lakeland, Florida

President of Southeastern College of Assembies of God, Lakeland, FL 1947–55, 1965–68. Graves married Ethlyn Griffin on May 10, 1927. He began his ministry in Texas with pastorates in Houston and Dallas. In 1934–35, he was the dean of men at Central Bible College, Springfield, MO. In 1949, he became the first full-time president of SCAG. Graves pastored in Norfolk, VA in 1935 and at Free Gospel Church, Flushing, NY, from 1955–65.

Ralph Freed

Oct. 1, 1892
Budapest, Hungary

Dec. 29, 1973
Monte Carlo, Monaco

General Director of Trans-World Radio, 1954–73. Freed's son, DR. PAUL E. FREED (founder and president), began the work in 1951. The first station, in Tangier, Morocco (known as the Voice of the Tangier) needed a manager, so the 62 year-old, along with his wife, Mildred, went to the field a second time, after having served for 21 years as CMA missionaries in the Middle East. The first broadcast was aired in February, 1954, over a 2,500-watt transmitter. Mildred died on November 22, 1957. In 1959, Trans-World Radio moved to Monte Carlo, Monaco. Ralph remarried in 1960 and together (Ralph and Nora Freed) served in Monte Carlo until his death.

David G. Moses

Jan. 22, 1902
Namakal, India

1974
India (?)

President of World Council of Churches, 1961–68. Moses married Dora Timothy on May 27, 1927 (died: April, 1954), and Helen Mathew on August 19, 1960. He served as a professor of philosophy at Hislop College, Nagpur, India (1926–42), and was principal there (1942–72). He was also the chairman of International Missionary Council, 1955–60. Moses was ordained as a Presbyterian in 1961. He lived in Nagpur, India. He took an active part in negotiations, which led to the union of five denominations in the Church of North India in 1970. He was active in the United Church of Northern India and Pakistan.

Noel Smith

Aug. 7, 1900
Greenvale, Tennessee

Jan. 12, 1974
Springfield, Missouri

Founding editor of the *Baptist Bible Tribune* and its editor, 1950–74. Smith despised what he felt was the phony writing, preaching and music of his time. He was ordained in 1928 and pastored SBC churches, 1934–47, following 15 years with Southern Express Company. He left the SBC in 1947, citing failure to face issues. He edited *The Fundamentalist* (1947–50), and then he helped start the Baptist Bible Fellowship. Smith was a member of the High Street Baptist Church of Springfield, MO. He was a discerning student of religious events. He was working on the *Tribune* the night he died.

Charles B. Foelsch

March 31, 1891
Ottumwa, Iowa

Jan. 20, 1974
New York, New York (?)

President of Pacific Lutheran Theological Seminary, Berkeley, CA 1952–61. Foelsch married Pauline Gray on May 4, 1920. He pastored in Wilkinsburg, PA (1920–27); Charleston, SC (1927–34); Sunbury, PA (1934–40); and Washington, D.C. (1940–42). He then became president of Chicago Lutheran Theological Seminary, 1942–47. After his term there, he returned to pastor at Holy Trinity Church, NYC (1947–52); later, he pastored the Christ the King Church, Chicago, IL (1961–63); and Christ Church, NYC (1966–74). He wrote *A Mighty Fortress* (1924) and *His Word for My Way* (1962).

Kenneth Cummings

Sept. 14, 1918
Sparta, Michigan

Jan. 26, 1974
Tacoma, Washington

Outstanding song leader, musican, youth enthusiast and faithful preacher. Cummings was the first tenor in the America Back to God quartet, 1939–42. He married Wanda Halstead, a chalk-talk artist, on July 1, 1941, and they went to England and Europe for Youth for Christ (1949–52).

Then they served with Conservative Baptist Foreign Missionary Society in Portugal (1953–59). After 1959, he was their Pacific Northwest representative. He died of a heart attack.

C. I. Armstrong

Feb. 23, 1846
Feb. 8, 1974
Atlanta, Georgia

President of National Association of Holiness (Christian Holiness Partnership in 1997), **1942–46**. He pastored at Bradford and Houghton for eleven and nine years, respectively. He was the first Wesleyan missionary to the Onondaga Indians, near Syracuse. He was in the field of evangelism off and on throughout his life. He also took two world mission tours. He was active in the NAE, National Holiness Association (name of the above 1950–70), and served on the boards of Houghton College and Asbury Theological Seminary. He died after a brief illness.

Fred Donnelson

Nov. 16, 1897
Missouri Valley, Iowa
Feb. 9, 1974
Springfield, Missouri

First director of Baptist Bible Fellowship Missions, Springfield, MO, 1950–68. Donnelson was converted in a BILLY SUNDAY crusade meeting in Marshalltown, IA, at age twelve. He and his wife, Effie Robb, married on September 25, 1920. He pastored at a Baptist church in Lake Zurich, IL in 1921; Messiah Baptist, Chicago, IL (1922–30); and at FBC, Plainfield, IL (1930–33). He was a missionary to China, 1933–49, where he established the Shanghai Baptist Tabernacle and also a Bible college. He also served in the Chekiang Province, 1933–38. After his retirement in 1968, he moved to San Diego, CA. He was in a coma five weeks before death, never recovering from surgery in November, 1973. The funeral was conducted at High St. Baptist Church in Springfield, MO.

J. Arthur Heck

Nov. 24, 1892
Reading, Pennsylvania
Feb. 11, 1974
near Lebanon, Ohio

President of Evangelical School of Theology, Reading, PA (United Theological Seminary, Dayton, OH in 1954), **1941–54**. Heck was converted in October, 1904. He married Martha Glick on June 28, 1916 and was ordained into the Evangelical Church the same year. Heck held pastorates in Pennsylvania (1913–24), then was an instructor of Bible and philosophy at Schuylkill College, Reading, PA (1924–29). He also taught at EST (1923–34) and served as the general secretary of Christian education for EC (1934–41).

Paul J. Lindell

Aug. 13, 1915
Kikungshan, China
March 1, 1974
Minneapolis, Minnesota

Director of World Missionary Prayer League, Minneapolis, MN 1946–74, a Lutheran organization headquartered in Minneapolis. Born of missionary parents, Lindell was schooled in China until he was ready for college, at which time he came to the States. He attended Augsburg College and Gustavus Adolphus College. He began his ministry at Bible camps, retreats, church mission conventions, high school assemblies, and travels to various mission fields. He married Margaret Sovik on August 23, 1940, and they joined the staff of WMPL. Lindell traveled to Asia and Europe in 1957. Toward the end of his life, he influenced 100 individuals from 54 different occupations to go to fields in Latin America, Central Asia, and East Africa. On March 7, 1969, he was told he had cancer, but he crowded in five more years of leadership. His funeral was at his home church, the Evangelical Lutheran Church in Minnehaha Falls, MN.

Herman D. Mitzner

Oct. 1, 1893
Aqusta, Wisconsin

March 7, 1974
Los Angeles, California

Secretary of International Church of Foursquare Missions International, 1950–65. Mitzner was converted at age twelve in a revival meeting in Friends Church, Marion, OR. He married Lela Bond on September 7, 1919 (died: October 23, 1935) and then Nita Becker on February 20, 1939. After graduating from Life Bible College, he was associated with Angelus Temple headquarters. Mitzner traveled as an evangelist, district supervisor, and had a lifetime of missionary activity.

William W. Boyce

Nov. 12, 1888
Gastonia, North Carolina

April 20, 1974
Greenwood, South Carolina

President of Erskine Theological Sminary, Due West, SC, 1941–59. Boyce made profession of faith at York (county in SC) ARP Church where his father pastored. He became pastor of the First ARP Church in Charlotte, NC. After a brief year in Mexico, he served for ten years as pastor in Salem, TN; Ebenezer, VA; Unity Church in Lancaster County, SC; and Mooresville, NC from 1913–23. He married Lucile L. Faulkner on June 29, 1916 (died of a fall in 1940). He pastored Sardis ARP Church, Charlotte, NC (1924–30), and the First ARP Church in the same city (1930–39). Losing his wife as he began his Erskine ministry was difficult, but he served nobly, continuing as a part-time professor until 1966.

Elmer G. Deal

June 2, 1899
Orland, Indiana

April 14, 1974
Bradenton, Florida

Director of Rural Bible Mission, Plainwell, MI 1955–1969. Deal grew up on a farm during the Depression in Bronson, MI, delivering groceries and other menial jobs. He was active in Bronson Baptist Church, south of Coldwater. He married Susie Gibbs in 1919. He found and fixed an abandoned school bus, using it to bring children to church near Quincy, MI. Deal helped B. F. HITCHCOCK develop a ministry amongst rural children. In 1941, the family moved to Gull Lake, MI, and from then on it was Bible schools, Sunday Schools, revival, and gospel presentations. One of his converts was PHILIP ARMSTRONG, a famed missionary leader. He retired to Florida, helped in a Bible church there, had surgery, and died shortly thereafter on Easter from a heart attack.

Liston Pope

Sept. 6, 1909
Thomasville, North Carolina

April 15, 1974
Trondheim, Norway

Dean of Yale University Divinity School, New Haven, CT, 1949–62. Pope married Bonnie Purvis on February 3, 1934, and then Gerd Thoresen. He was ordained a Congregationalist in 1935. Pope pastored Humphrey St. Congregational Church, New Haven, CT, from 1935–38. He then joined Yale as a professor of social ethics, 1938–73 and was a guest lecturer at many clubs and activities in WCC. He edited the *Social Action* (1942–48) and wrote *Mill Hands and Preachers* (1942) and *The Kingdom Beyond Caste* (1957).

Tim Spencer

July 13, 1908
Webb City, Missouri

April 26, 1974
Apple Valley, California

Wrote the lyrics for "Christ Is a Wonderful Savior" and "Room Full of Roses." Spencer joined ROY ROGERS and Bob Boland in 1933 founding the famous Western singing group: the Sons of the Pioneers. In 1934, Spencer married Velma Blanton. He was converted in December, 1948,

The Saints Go Marching In

at First Presbyterian Church of Hollywood. He began a Hollywood Christian group and formed the Manna Music Company. He wrote the lyrics and music for "It's Your Life."

Harold C. Slade

1903
Oxford, Nova Scotia, Canada

May 16, 1974

Voice of Fundamentalism in Canada. Slade pastored in Timmonse, Ontario, from 1929–47 and came to Jarvis Street Baptist as associate pastor in 1947. Slade was successor to T. T. SHIELDS' work in Toronto, 1955–1974. He became president of Toronto Baptist Seminary and edited the *The Gospel Witness*. He associated with CARL MCINTIRE in the ICC and spoke at many of their conferences. Slade was general secretary of the Union of Regular Baptists, 1941–47. He was one of the organizers of the Fundamental Baptist Congress and chairman of five of them. He was stricken with two coronary attacks.

Samuel J. Bradford

Feb. 14, 1903
St. Anne, Missouri

May 21, 1974
Lebanon, Missouri

Founder and president of Denver (CO) Baptist Bible College (Faith Baptist Bible College, Ankeny, IA in 1986), **1952–61**. Bradford married Dorothy Hale on January 2, 1928. He was a leader in the formation of the Conservative Baptist Association. Bradford pastored at Beth Eden Baptist Church, which had 1100 members, 1936–61. He also founded Camp Eden (opened in 1944 on 150 acres) and Eden Manor retirement center (opened in 1962 for over 100 families). During the last years of his life, he was an Independent Baptist. He was killed in a tractor accident on his farm.

Sankey L. Blanton

Sept. 5, 1898
Ellenboro, North Carolina

June 11, 1974
Wilmington, North Carolina

President of Crozer Theological Seminary [Colgate-Rochester (NY) Divinity School in 1970], **Chester, PA 1950–62**. Blanton served as pastor of churches in New Haven, CT, and Wilmington, NC. Prior to the presidency of Crozer Seminary, he was a dean of the School of Religion at Wake Forest College, Winston-Salem, NC.

Sanford Fleming

May 2, 1888
Adelaide, Australia

June 14, 1974

President of Berkeley (CA) Baptist Divinity School (American Baptist Seminary of the West in 1977), **1937–57, and of Association of Theological Schools, 1944–46**. Fleming married Clarice Crossing on August 23, 1915. He pastored in New Haven, CT (1914–17); Adelaide, Australia (1920–22); and San Francisco, CA (1922–25). He then became a professor of church history and religious education in 1926 at Berkeley. Fleming's books range from *Children and Puritanism* (1933) to *Where Jesus Walked* (1952). He also authored the seminary's history, *The Making of Ministers*.

Henry D. Zimmerman

March 30, 1894
Oberowisheim, Germany

June, 21 1974
Yackerstown, New Jersey

Founder and first director of the American branch of Liebenzell Mission, Schooley's Mountain, NJ, 1941–62. From 1924–33, Zimmerman and his wife were in China. In 1939, they came to America to visit mission friends. WWII prevented their return to China. They were able, with a few friends, to start the Liebenzell Mission in the US. They called it Mission Home Eben-Ezer, Inc. The name was changed in 1951 to Liebenzell Mission. They returned to Germany 1951–52. God miraculously worked, as mission homes were obtained and laborers sent in.

Arthur J. Moore

Dec. 26, 1888
Waycross, Georgia

June 30, 1974
Atlanta, Georgia

Methodist bishop and evangelist. Moore married Mattie McDonald on April 26, 1906 (died: 1964). Converted at age 21, he was ordained in 1914 into the Methodist Church South. Moore pastored at Travis Park Church, San Antonio, TX (1920–26), and served at FMC, Birmingham, AL (1926–30). In 1930, he became a bishop, serving in the Pacific Coast area till 1934 and then as an overseas bishop, 1934–40. He rekindled a missionary spirit and cleared the board of a $17 million debt in 1937. Moore was also the president of the Board of Missions, 1940–60, and was very active in World Methodism. Moore authored several books, from *The Sound of Trumpets* (1934) an autobiography, to *Bishop to All People* (1973).

George R. Warner

July 28, 1900
Oakesdale, Washington

July 1, 1974
Glendora, California

General secretary of World Gospel Mission, Marion, IN, 1934–53; president, 1953–68 and president of EFMA, 1946–48. During Warner's tenure, the mission grew from 33 to over 200; and from 2 to 15 fields. He was converted in a revival at Alderdale, WA. Warner went to China as a missionary, 1924–31. He married Bertha Bartlett on November 2, 1926. On the field, they escaped death many times. Warner visited 64 countries, and edited *Call to Prayer*. He was a member of the Evangelical Methodist Church.

Tony Fontaine

1927

July 2, 1974
Canoga Park, California

Outstanding soloist who produced "Cold, Cold Heart," which sold over 1 million copies (1952—Mercury Records). Fontaine was converted as the result of a terrible automobile accident on September 3, 1957. He was a recording, television, radio, and stage star, appearing at many top nightclubs and television programs. He recorded over 30 albums. Fontaine married Kerry Vaughn. Gospel Films featured a film of his life.

Frederick C. Grant

Feb. 2, 1891
Beloit, Wisconsin

July 11, 1974
New York, New York

President of Western Theological Seminary, 1928–33, and of Seabury-Western Theological Seminary, both of Evanston, IL, 1933–38, after a merger occurred in 1933. Grant was ordained as an Episcopalian deacon (1912) and as a priest (1913). He married Helen Hardie on June 24, 1913. He was a rector in Dekalb, Dixon, Evanston, and Chicago, IL (1913–24), and served as a professor of biblical theology at Union Theological Seminary, New York City (1938–59). Grant was a liberal, ecumenical Anglican. His works range from *The Economic Background of the Gospels* (1926) to *Dictionary of the Bible* (1963). He edited the *Anglican Theological Review* (1924–55).

Percy L. Urban

June 3, 1886
Philadelphia, Pennsylvania

Aug. 16, 1974
New Haven, Connecticut

President (dean) of Berkeley Divinity School, New Haven, CT 1947–57. Urban was ordained Episcopalian in 1914. He married Mary Hodge on June 10, 1922. Early on, he taught philosophy at St. John's University in Shanghai, China. He joined the Berkeley staff in 1923 lecturing theology (1923–35), associate professor

(1935–41), and professor of systematic theology (1941–47). Urban was rector at St. John's Church, New Haven, CT, from 1924–41. He was honorable canon of Christ Church Cathedral, Hartford, CT, from 1950–74.

Georgia E. Harkness

April 21, 1891
Harkness, New York

Aug. 21, 1974
Claremont, California

Methodist author and educator. Harkness grew up in a town named after her grandfather and was converted at age 14 at a revival meeting. She taught on the faculty of Elmira (NY) College (1922–37); Mount Holyoke College, South Hadley, MA (1937–39); Garrett Biblical Institute (Garrett-Evangelical Theological Seminary) (1939–50); and was professor of applied theology at Pacific School of Religion, Berkeley, CA (1950–74). She traveled to Europe (1924); Madras, India (1938); Amsterdam (1948), and Lund, Sweden (1952). Harkness never married. Harkness was ordained in 1926 and was recognized as a theological scholar. Her hymn "Hope of the World" was used for the WCC (Evanston) Conclave. She wrote 36 books, from *The Church and the Immigrant* (1921) to *Biblical Backgrounds to the Middle East Conflict* (pub., 1976). She retired in 1961 in Claremont. She was a well-known female theologian. She is buried in Harkness, NY.

Elmer D. Henson

Aug. 7, 1901
Colony, Oklahoma

Aug. 26, 1974
Ft. Worth, Texas

Dean of Bright College of the Bible, 1955–63, renamed Bright Divinity School, 1963–71, a division of Texas Christian University, Ft. Worth, TX. Henson married Eva May Kemp on August 7, 1926. He pastored Christian churches in Van Alstyne, TX (1927–29); Garland, TX (1929–32); Commerce, TX (1932–37); San Angelo, TX (1937–45); and Bethany Christian, Houston, TX (1945–55), with the church growing from 389 to 1,000 members. He was involved in many organizations relating to his denomination.

P. Lewi Pethrus

March 11, 1884
Vastra Tunheim, Sweden

Sept. 1974
Stockholm, Sweden

Pastor, missions promoter, and international Pentecostal leader. Pethrus was baptized a Baptist in 1889. In 1907, he switched from Baptist to Pentecostalism. He married Lydia Danielsson in April, 1913 (died December 30, 1966). He held a pastorate at the Filadelfia Church in Stockholm, 1911–58. From 1911–12, he began a mission and a publishing house. He then established a Bible school in 1915. In 1955, he hosted the World Pentecostal Conference. His church grew to be the largest Pentecostal church in the world before 1975.

William W. Breckbill

Feb. 4, 1907
Danville, Pennsylvania

Sept. 2, 1974
Williamsburg, Pennsylvania

President of American Coucil of Christian Churches, 1950–53. Breckbill married Anna Hixson on April 12, 1934. He was converted after twelve years in the ministry at a Keswick (NJ) Victorious Christian Life Conference where ROBERT MCQUILKEN preached. Breckbill became the pastor of the First Evangelical Methodist Church, Altoona, PA, in 1945. He was also the founder and general superintendent of the Evangelical Methodist Church, Memphis, TN, in 1946. He traveled widely, preaching throughout all the states and in many countries around the world. In 1952, a split in the EMC caused him to found the EMC in America.

James H. Straughn

June 1, 1877
Centerville, Maryland

Sept. 9, 1974

Methodist bishop, 1939–48, with a long history in the Methodist Protestant Church prior to the 1939 merger. Staughn was one of three men that negotiated the historical reunion of Methodist entities to form the United Methodist Church. Straughn was ordained in 1903, and married Clara Morgan on June 1, 1904. He pastored in Washington, D.C. (1901–4); Lynchburg, VA (1904–6); Laurel, DE (1912–19); and Baltimore, MD (1910–12, 1920, 1932–36); and Washington, D.C. (1923–26). He also served as president of West Lafayette (OH) College, 1906–1910. He wrote *Inside Methodist Union* (1955). He is buried in Maryland.

Ernest C. Colwell

Jan. 19, 1901
Hallstead, Pennsylvania

Sept. 12, 1974
Orlando, Florida

Dean of the University of Chicago Divinity School, 1938–45; first president of Claremont (CA) School of Theology, 1957–68; and president of Association of Theological Schools, 1958–60. Colwell was an instructor of English and Bible at Emory University, Atlanta, GA, from 1924–28, during which time he married Annette Carter on May 7, 1925. He also taught NT in UCDS from 1930–44. He served as the president of the University of Chicago (1945–51), dean of the faculty, and was a professor of NT and vice president at Emory University (1951–57). From 1971–74, he was a visiting professor of Greek, Stetson University, Deland, FL. A life long Methodist, his books included from *The Greek of the Fourth Gospel* (1931) to *New or Old?* (1970). He is buried in DeLand, FL.

Clayton A. Risley

Dec. 16, 1915
Chouteau County, Montana

Oct. 11, 1974
Chicago, Illinois

Known as "Mr. Sunday School." Risley married June Root on October 9, 1942. He pastored Hillyard Baptist Church, Spokane, WA, from 1943–52, which grew into one of the largest Sunday schools in the state. Risley also served as executive secretary of the National Sunday School Association, 1952–63. In 1965, he was appointed secretary of the Christian Education of the World Evangelical Fellowship. He was tragically shot to death in an apparent robbery attempt outside his Chicago, IL office.

Joseph P. Free

Oct. 1, 1911
Cleveland, Ohio

Oct. 12, 1974
Freehaven Park Rapids, Minnesota

Outstanding archaeologist who taught at Wheaton (IL) College, 1935–67. Free was converted as a child and married Ruby Aldrich on Aug. 20, 1935. He excavated at Dibon in Arab Palestine, 1951–52, and at Dothan, 1953–60, 1962, and 1964. Free was an authority on archaeology as is evident by his column in the *Sunday School Times* (1942–64). He also authored *Archaeology and Bible History* (1969).

Victor Buksbazen

Oct. 22, 1903
Warsaw, Poland

Oct. 22, 1974
Galveston, Texas

Founder and first director of Friends of Israel, 1938–73. Born into an orthodox Jewish family, he first heard the gospel from his father; then one night, reading the gospel of Matthew by flickering candlelight, he found Christ. He studied at the University of Warsaw, then took a teaching post there. This was followed by the holocaust of war, the anti-Semitic horrors, and years of missionary work in Poland and England. He and his wife, Lydia Sitenhof, emigrated from England in December, 1940. He founded Friends of Israel in Philadelphia. He died in his sleep at a friend's house.

Stephen G. Spottswood

July 18, 1897
Boston, Massachusetts

Dec. 1, 1974
Washington, D.C.

US religious and civil rights leader, bishop, 1932–72. Spottswood was ordained in the African Methodist Episcopal Zion Church after graduating in 1919 from the Gordon College of Theology in Boston. He married Viola Hooker on June 10, 1919 (died: October 1953), and Mottie Elliott on December 15, 1969. He then joined the NAACP and commenced a two-fold career as civil rights activist and pastor of churches in Maine, Connecticut, North Carolina, Indiana, and New York. From 1936–1952, he was pastor of the John Wesley National A.M.E. Zion Church in the nation's capital. In 1955, he was elected to the board of directors of the NAACP and in 1961 became board chairman.

John R. Gilpin

May 8, 1905
Walton, Kentucky

Dec. 7, 1974
Ashland, Kentucky

Longtime editor of the *Baptist Examiner*, 1928–74. Gilpin was a strong Calvinist-Baptist voicepiece. He pastored in Independence and Walton, KY; then Rossmaine Baptist, Cincinnati, OH (1928–29); followed by FBC, Russell, KY (1929–54). He was most well known for his last pastorate, Calvary Baptist, Ashland, KY. Through his influence, many churches were organized in northeastern KY. Many of his sermons, tracts, and booklets were published. He married Helen Aylor.

J. Herschell Griffin

June 30, 1896
near Lula, Georgia

Dec. 8, 1974

General moderator of Pentecostal Fire-Baptized Holiness Church, LaGrange, GA 1938–49, 1953–57. Griffin was converted on August 13, 1913, in Yonah, Georgia. Four years later, he began to preach in Nicholson, GA. In 1921, he became pastor there. He also was the general superintendent of the Home and Foreign Mission Board of the denomination, 1926–28 and 1939–47. In 1930, he married Nola Gosnell (born 1909). He served several terms as the South Carolina State Moderator.

Donald R. Falkenberg

July 3, 1894
Grand Valley, Pennsylvania

Dec. 13, 1974
Kissimmee, Florida

Founder and first president of Bible Meditation League (Bible Literature International in 1967), **Columbus, OH 1923–1964**. Falkenberg married Leah Priest on December 24, 1916. He was ordained United Brethren in 1932. He was an evangelist and had a radio ministry called *Missionary Radio*, 1965 on. His first book was *The Beauties of Galatians* (1926).

Charles B. Widmeyer

July 19, 1884
Berkley Springs, West Virginia

Dec. 14, 1974
Pasadena, California

Nazarene hymn writer and president of Bethany (OK) Nazarene College (Southern Nazarene University), **1914–20**. Widmeyer wrote the lyrics and music to "Come and Dine." Widmeyer married Madue Logue on June 5, 1907; his second wife was Dorothy. He pastored in San Diego, CA, from 1920–21. He then went to Pasadena (CA) College as president, 1923–26, serving as professor of religious education after his term of presidency. He traveled to various countries.

Jackie L. Burris

Nov. 21, 1905
Los Angeles, California

c 1975

One of the great evangelists of his generation, Burris and his wife held area-wide crusades. Burris accepted Christ at Angeles Temple under AIMEE SEMPLE MCPHERSON in August, 1923, at age 17, a gang member, having never gone to a church before. Burris married Pauline on April 17, 1927. He became a Baptist as his ministry expanded. Revivals he began would run every night for six to eight weeks and twice on Sunday. In 1930, they gave their last $10 to a contractor to draw plans for a tabernacle in Youngstown, OH, and an 18-month revival broke out: services every night and three times on Sunday. Each service was packed, and over 1,000 were converted. In 1936, he took his first of three trips around the world. Burris held crusades in tents, some of which seated 5,000, and filled some of the largest auditoriums in the country.

Einer Waermo

March 13, 1901
Sweden

c 1975

Tenor soloist. Waermo sang early on in light opera. Soon he was singing in Finland and Norway as well as his own country. In 1927, he sang with the Stockholm Symphony Orchestra, on the radio, and at fashionable dinners. He was impressed with the change in the life of a recently converted friend and went to church with him. He stopped in a beautiful snow-covered park, and beneath a cold winter sky, decided for Christ. He went with evangelist Frank Mangs on a series of campaigns. Soon he came to America and was singing in churches and camp meetings. He met Constance Reed (of Sweden) and they married. Once, on a train, he sang "I Found a Friend" and four people were saved. He lived in Los Angeles, traveling back to Sweden three times. He attended the Immanuel Christian Assembly. He sang in the Hollywood Bowl and made several recordings.

Ernest E. Miller

Sept. 16, 1893
Middlebury, Indiana

Jan. 11, 1975
Goshen, Indiana

President of Goshen (IN) College, 1940–54. Miller married Ruth Blosser on June 20, 1918. They did relief work in the Near East (1919–20), served as missionaries to India (1921–37), and he was the principal of Dhamtari Christian Academy, Dhamtari, CP, India (1930–37). Miller was active in various Mennonite activities, including education and publications.

Charles C. Donaghue

Aug. 23, 1889
Thornfield, Missouri

Jan. 16, 1975
Richmond, Missouri

President of Christian Union, Chilicothe, OH, 1953–62. Born into a pastor's home, Donaghue became a barber in Tryon, OK. He married Alma Loomis in 1911 (died: 1968). He pastored in Milo, IA (1932–41), and then in places such as Excelsior Springs, MO, and Henesy, OK (1941–53). He retired to Polo, MO, where he did a lot of Bible teaching in the area. He also had a lovely singing voice, which blessed many people. Donaghue was a quiet man, loving and kind, but firm. He had three daughters and one son. He died of heart failure.

Fred C. Kuehner

May 12, 1912
Philadelphia, Pennsylvania

Jan. 30, 1975
Philadelphia, Pennsylvania

Dean of Reformed Episcopal Seminary, 1959–75. Kuehner graduated from RES in 1939. His ministry included teaching at Westminster Theological Seminary, pastoring the Reconciliation

Church, Philadelphia, and also pastoring at St. Mark's Church of Jenkintown. His wife was Eleanore Deichen. He came to RES in 1951 as chairman of the Biblical languages and within a decade was made dean. He was also assistant editor of Sunday school material for the American Sunday School Union, and with others, worked on the translation of the NIV for the American Bible Society.

Henry P. VanDusen

Dec. 11, 1897
Philadelphia, Pennsylvania

Feb. 13, 1975
Belle Meade, New Jersey

President of Auburn Theological Seminary, and Union Theological Seminary (same facilities), **New York City 1945–63 and of Association of Theological Schools, 1942–1944**. VanDusen married Elizabeth Bartholomew on June 19, 1931, after being ordained in 1924. His ministry began as an instructor at Union in 1926, teaching systematic theology there, 1936–63. He authored several books from *In Quest of Life's Meaning* (1926) to *Dag Hammarskjold* (1967). He helped found the journal, *Christianity and Crisis* (1941). He and his wife committed suicide rather than suffer from disabling conditions.

Charles V. Fairbairn

Nov. 22, 1890
Ventor, Ontario, Canada

Feb. 20, 1975
McPherson, Kansas

Bishop of Free Methodist Church, 1939–61. Fairbairn married Lena Vannest on July 21, 1915. He pastored in the Methodist Church of Canada, 1913–18, and then joined the Free Methodist Church in 1918. He served as pastor and superintendent in East Ontario and Kansas, as well as a conference evangelist. Fairbairn authored *What We Believe* and *I Call to Remembrance*.

Miner B. Stearns

April 10, 1902

Feb. 23, 1975

President of Global Gospel Broadcasts (Global Outreach Mission in 1974), **1954–74**. Stearns was one of five men on the forming committee of the World Conference of Missionary Radio, founded in 1954. He and the other five men directed WCMR until 1965 when a part time executive director was hired. The name was changed to International Christian Broadcasters in 1964 because it worked with both radio and television. Stearns once said, "No errorless system has yet been developed in spite of the resource of truth to be found in an infallible Bible."

Sanford C. Yoder

Dec. 5, 1879
Iowa City, Iowa

Feb. 23, 1975
Goshen, Indiana

President of Goshen (IN) College, 1923–40, and of Mennonite Church Board of Missions (Mennonite Church USA Missions in 2002), **Elkhart, IN, 1921–44**. Yoder was converted in 1902 and became a well-known Mennonite leader. He married Emma Stutsman on September 23, 1903. He pastored a church in Kalona, IA, from 1913–21. He then taught in the Bible Department of Goshen (IN) College, 1944–52. He made several trips to foreign countries and was considered a statesman and leader.

Levi T. Pennington

Aug. 29, 1875
Amo, Indiana

March 17, 1975
Newberg, Oregon

President of Pacific College (George Fox University in 1949), **1911–41**. Pennington's 30-year tenure there is believed to be the longest ever for any Oregon college president. Pennington married Bertha Waters on June 1, 1898 (died: June 28, 1903), and Florence Kidd on February 28, 1905. He pastored Friends churches in Indiana, 1904–11 and was a widely known public speaker.

Pennington was still active as a traveling lecturer at age 93. His biography is *Portrait of a Quaker: Levi T. Pennington, 1875–1975: A Critical Biography* by Donald McNichols (1980)

Chiang Kai-Shek

Oct. 31, 1887
Fenghua, China

April 5, 1975
Taipei, Taiwan

General statesman and president of the Republic of China, 1928–75. Kai-Shek met Dr. Sun Yat-Sen in Japan in 1906 and joined his party. After his son's death (1925), he became general of the Southern Army in Peking, China (1928). Chiang married his second wife, May-ling Soong (MADAME CHIANG KAI-SHEK) on December 1, 1927. He and his wife were Methodists and very dedicated Christians. Kai-Shek was converted on October 23, 1930, when he was trapped by the enemy. He helped found the Republic of China. He fled the mainland of China in 1949 and established Chinese leadership (13 million people) in Formosa (Taiwan), after years of warfare with the Japanese and Communists. His own quote declared, "I have been a constant reader of the Bible." His conversion from Buddhism to Methodism was because he felt the Bible revealed God's plan for China.

William J. Walls

May 8, 1885
Rutherford, North Carolina

April 23, 1975
Yonkers, New York

Bishop of African Methodist Episcopal Zion Church, 1924–75; senior bishop, 1951–75. He was an evangelist, 1898–1905. He then pastored in Lincolnton and Sausbuel (NC) (1905–13), and Broadway Temple in Louisville, KY (1913–20). Walls also edited *Star of Zion* (1920–24) and authored *J.C. Price, Educator and Race Leader* to *Reality of the Black Church*. Walls married Dorothy Jordon on December 6, 1956.

William B. Blakemore

July 22, 1912
Perth, Australia

May 2, 1975
Dallas, Texas

Dean of Disciples Divinity House, Chicago, IL 1946–75. Blakemore was ordained in the Disciples of Christ in 1941. He married E. Josephine Gilstrap on June 2, 1942. He gave many years of service to the University of Chicago as a professor of practical theology (1948–72) and professor of ecumenical Christianity (1971–75). Blakemore attended many ecumenical conventions and wrote articles on the subject. He was very active in his Chicago church/educational activities. He wrote six books.

John Murray

Oct. 14, 1898
Bonar Bridge, Scotland

May 8, 1975
Badbea, Scotland

Outstanding Scotch theologian. Murray was struck by shrapnel during the last German offensive and permanently lost sight in his right eye in July, 1918. He enrolled in Princeton (1924) and, upon graduation, returned to Scotland (1927). In 1930, he returned to the States and the new Westminster Theological Seminary, Philadelphia. He spent the greater part of the rest of his life, 1930–66, as professor of systematic theology. He was ordained in 1937 at the Orthodox Presbyterian Church which MACHEN had founded. He married a longtime friend, Valerie Knowlton, in 1966, when he was close to 70 years old. He returned to Scotland in 1966, pastored the Free Church at Ardgay, two miles from his home during his last years. In 1974, cancer was discovered. He wrote several books.

Charles E. Cowen

Sept. 24, 1904
Fordland, Missouri

May 10, 1975
Anglewood, Colorado

President of Kansas City College and Bible School, Overland Park, KS, 1954–69. Converted in his late teens, Cowen gave 50 years of ministry to the Bible Holiness Movement. He married Helen J. Carrier on May 23, 1928. He established the local Church of God (Holiness) of Columbia, MO, and served there for more than 20 years. He also pastored the Overland Park Church of God (Holiness) for nine years. In 1969, they moved to Littleton, CO, where he pastored the Church of God (Holiness) and founded the Rocky Mountain Christian School.

Alexander L. Glegg

July 1, 1882
London, England

June, 1975

Lay evangelist. Glegg trained as an electrical engineer at London University, but his great love was evangelism. Converted at Keswick Convention as a young man, he soon was involved in mission work in Wandsworth, and for nearly 50 years was responsible for the ministry at Down Lodge Hall. Glegg spoke at many campaigns and conventions, and thousands were won to Christ. He conducted many meetings in Albert Hall in the 1940s. Part of his counsel to young evangelists was to play golf. Billy Graham acknowledged a great debt to Glegg. His published works went around the world. Such publications include *Life with a Capital L* and *Four Score and More*.

Mabel Francis

July 26, 1880
New Hampshire

June 7, 1975
Ft. Meyers, Florida

Missionary in Japan, 59 years. Francis began teaching school at age 15 and left for Japan in 1909, via the Christian & Missionary Alliance. She served as an evangelist and church planter, starting 20 C&MA churches. She was known as the American woman, always smiling, who rode a bicycle. Francis was awarded Japan's highest civilian honor and was invited to speak at official functions. During WWII, she lived in a Catholic monastery for safekeeping. She retired to the States in 1966 at age 86.

Milton T. Wells

Nov. 14, 1901
Riverhead, New York

June 30, 1975
Springfield, Vermont

President of Eastern Bible Institute (Valley Forge Christian College, Phoenixville, PA, in 1976), **Green Lane, PA 1949–60**. Wells ministered throughout the Northeast in various congregations. His wife died November 22, 1970.

Paul E. Little

Dec. 30, 1928
Philadelphia, Pennsylvania

July 9, 1975
Ontario, Canada

One of the most active Inter-Varsity personalities. Little had a Plymouth Brethren Assemblies background. In 1950, he joined IV staff in Illinois and, for the next 25 years, served in various capacities as international students director, NYC (1954–57); regional director in Dallas, TX (1957–60); evangelism national director (1960–67); and assistant to the president (1967–75). Little also taught evangelism, 1964–75 at Trinity Evangelical Divinity School, Deerfield, IL and shared his ministry with midwestern churches in 1970. During his career, Little spoke in over 200 college campuses on four continents. His books have been printed in over 20 languages. He married Marie Huttenlock in 1953. He was killed in an automobile accident. He wrote *Know What You Believe* (1967), *Know Why You Believe*, and *How to Give Away Your Faith*.

James A. Stewart

Feb. 12, 1910
Dumbaraton, Scotland

July 11, 1975
Asheville, North Carolina

First director of European Evangelistic Crusades, Buffalo, NY (Global Outreach Mission in 1970s), **1943–52**. Stewart was known as a boy preacher from ages 14-23. He was involved in various evangelistic outreaches in Great Britain, 1928–33. The call then came to Latvia (1934) where he had great services, to Poland (1935), Czechoslovakia (1936), to Hungary, 1937–38, where he married Maude Cobb on March 23, 1938. He got involved in Scripture evangelism, 1938–47, getting Bibles out in many places. He went to Poland in 1939. In 1940, he came to America and gave birth to the EEC. He returned to Europe (1945–46), to Norway in 1947 and radio evangelism (1949–50). He went to Scandinavia (1953) and back to Scotland (1954). He started the Russian Bible Society in 1957. An ear operation in 1971 started a deterioration of his health.

Paul P. Petticord

June 22, 1907
Lost Springs, Kansas

July 18, 1975
Portland, Oregon

First president of Western Evangelical Seminary (George Fox University in 1996), **near Milwaukee, OR 1944–75, and president of National Association of Evangelicals, 1956–57**. Petticord married Grace Spaulding on June 7, 1930. He was ordained in the Evangelical United Brethren Church in 1931. Petticord pastored in Covallis, OR (1930–34); Yakima, WA (1935–41); and Salem, OR (1941–42). He was involved with the Christian Holiness Association and the Oriental Missionary Society.

Hugh C. Benner

April 4, 1899
Marion, Ohio

Aug. 2, 1975
Leawood, Kansas

General Superintendent of Church of the Nazarene, 1952–68, and first president of Nazarene Theological Seminary, 1945–52. Benner married Audrey Carroll on July 19, 1923, and was ordained the same year. Benner served as professor at Eastern Nazarene College, Wollaston, MA (1921–25), and at Pasadena (CA) College (1925–30). He held pastorates in Santa Monica, CA (1931–36), and Spokane, WA (1936–45). His first book was *Tithing, Divine Challenge*.

Cornelius P. Haggard

Sept. 11, 1911
Pomona, California

Aug. 16, 1975
Arcadia, California

President of Pacific Bible College (Azusa Pacific University in 1981), **1939–75, and Accrediting Association of Bible Colleges, 1957–59**. Haggard was converted at age 16, praying in his room following a Sunday morning service. Haggard pastored South Los Angeles Community Church, 1933–40. He married Emma Gilbert on June 29, 1939. He was a member of the Evangelical Methodist Church. He made three missionary trips on behalf of the school and missions.

Tom M. Olson

Feb. 23, 1888
Chicago, Illinois

Aug. 17, 1975

Promoter and supplier of gospel tracts that touched the world. Olson married in 1929. From age 21, he and his wife, Marie Letourneau, spent a lifetime producing tracts, which were distributed by the millions free of charge across the United States and the world in many foreign languages. Olson worked with IRWIN MOON at the "Sermons from Science" exhibit at the San Francisco World's Fair, 1939–40. This began a regular column in R. G. LETOURNEAU's *Now* publication,

1939–75. As a young man, he ministered in Iowa, Indiana, and Illinois, walking thousands of miles distributing literature. Along with CLYDE DENNIS and FORD PORTER, this trio of tract enthusiasts have brought the gospel by printed leaflets to untold millions.

Thomas W. Jones

Dec. 8, 1889
Plymouth, Pennsylvania

Aug. 24, 1975
Wilkes-Barre, Pennsylvania

Director of Primitive Methodist Church Missions, 1935–58. Jones ministered seven years in Guatemala and 48 years in his home field. His pastorates were: Carnegie, St. Clair, Nanticoke Plains, Parsons, and North Tiverton, RI. His wife's name was Hannah. He often invited student pastors to his church where he would give them private lessons in public speaking or in common sense practices. His funeral was held at the First Primitive Methodist Church of Wilkes-Barre.

Haille Selassie
The Conquering Lion

July 23, 1892
near Harar, Ethiopia

Aug. 27, 1975
Addis Ababa, Ethiopia

Emperor of Ethiopia, 1930–74. Selassie married Wolzero Menen (1891–Feb. 15, 1962) on July 30, 1911 who was only 4' 4" inches tall. He was only 5' 4" tall. He became emperor on Nov. 2, 1930 at the age of 38 and was a very progressive leader. Slave trading was abolished in his reign. The Italian armies forced him to flee, 1936–41, but he was restored in 1941 and began reconstruction and rehabilitation. Selassie welcomed evangelical causes, such as World Gospel Crusades, Moody Film Ministry, etc. He shared his faith with Sudan Interior Mission leaders. On Sept. 12, 1974, he was deposed, accused by the armed forces of having exploited public funds. Selassie was a great encouragement to Christian missions in Africa.

Cordas C. Burnett

Feb. 6, 1917
Mounds, Illinois

Aug. 27, 1975
London, Springfield, Missouri

President of Bethany College, Santa Cruz (Scotts Valley), **CA 1959–71**. Burnett was converted on Thanksgiving Day, 1933, at a youth rally in Springfield, IL under the ministry of E.H. Chamberlain. He was supposed to play football at that time, but an injury prevented him. Burnett married Dorothy Talley on June 3, 1937. He later became an Assembly of God minister and held pastorates in South Bend, IN (1940–45); Chicago, IL (1945–48); and Cincinnati, OH (1952–54). He also taught at Central Bible Institute, Springfield, MO (1948–52) and was vice president of the same (1954–58). Burnett was involved in NAE and YFC activities.

Gaylord M. Couchman

Sept. 11, 1906
Popejoy, Iowa

Aug. 30, 1975
Brainerd, Minnesota

President of University of Dubuque (IA) Theological Seminary, 1953–75. Couchman married Esther Dunkerton on July 29, 1935. He was ordained as a Presbyterian in 1934. He pastored in Grimes, IA (1934–35); Lake City, IA (1936–39); Boone, IA (1939–43); and Westminster Presbyterian Church in Dubuque, IA (1943–53). He was the director of church relations at Dubuque Theological Seminary, 1968–71. In 1971, Couchman served as mayor of Dubuque.

Dale D. Welch

April 19, 1896
Strawberry Point, Iowa

Sept. 8, 1975
Dubuque, Iowa

President of University of Dubuque (IA) Theological Seminary, 1936–47. Welch married Margaret Aitchinson on June 25, 1920. He began teaching at Dubuque in 1922. He was ordained in 1923. He was president of Alma (MI) College in Michigan (1947–50), and of Hastings (NE) College (1952–57). He was a Republican, a Mason, and a Rotarian. He was the second former DTS president to die within ten days of each other.

G. Beachamp Vick
Mr. Baptist Bible Fellowship

Feb. 5, 1901
Russellville, Kentucky

Sept. 29, 1975
Springfield, Missouri

President of Arlington (TX) Baptist College, 1948–50, and first president of Baptist Bible College, Springfield, MO, 1950–75. Vick married Eloise Baker in 1919. He served at FBC, Fort Worth, TX 1921–30, on J. FRANK NORRIS' staff. Vick did evangelistic work, 1928–36, with Wade House. He went to Temple Baptist Church of Detroit, building the Sunday School under Norris's direction, 1936–48. He then pastored there, 1948–75, as J. F. NORRIS' prodigy. On September 5, 1954, the new church on Grand River Boulevard was dedicated, seating 5,000. At this time the Sunday School of 4,120 was the nation's largest. The membership grew to 14,000 under Vick as the sole pastor, 350 members went into full-time work. He led 119 other pastors in founding the Baptist Bible Fellowship in 1950 and inspired its world mission outreach. Vick was an able preacher, administrator, friend to thousands, and evangelist. He led two large ministries concurrently, one in Springfield, MO (college of 2,400 students) and the other in Detroit, MI (church of 14,000). He died of a heart attack in his college office.

Riley B. Montgomery

July 19, 1895
Boone Mill, Virginia

Oct. 16, 1975
Lexington, KY

President of College of the Bible (Lexington Theological Seminary in 1965), **1949–64.** Montgomery married Lucy Walker on September 16, 1922. He was ordained by the Disciples of Christ in 1916 and then pastored, 1919–23. Montgomery also taught at McCormick Theological Seminary of Chicago (1931–33) and was president of Campbell Institute Bules Creek, NC (1933–35). He served as president of Lynchburg (VA) College (1936–49), having served on staff there (1923–26 and 1934–36).

Paul Beckwith

May 12, 1905
Durand, Michigan

Nov. 4, 1975
Birmingham, Alabama

Pianist, who began as a teenager playing the piano at BILLY SUNDAY crusades. Beckwith teamed up with MEL TROTTER and HOMER HAMMONTREE in many crusades. He also worked with HOMER RODEHEAVER in his early days of ministry. Beckwith then went to Dallas, TX, and worked with Inter-Varsity until 1952, then with the staff of Southeastern Bible College, Birmingham, 1970–75. He never married. He loved to write hymns. In a coma for some time, he suddenly said audibly, "Jesus, I'm coming!" as he died.

Ezra A. Shank

Nov. 17, 1902
Broadway, Virginia

Nov. 13, 1975
Harrisonburg, Virginia

Executive secretary of South Africa General Mission, 1948–63, renamed **Africa Evangelical Fellowship** (which merged into SIM in 1998), **1963–67, and president of IFMA, 1952–54**. He married Blanche Layman on June 12, 1924. Shank was a home missionary in Canton, OH from 1926–30, then went to Ethiopia as a missionary until he was expelled in 1936. In Ethiopia, his mission grew from 95 missionaries to 265. Shank returned to the States and joined a Baptist church in Brooklyn, NY.

Norman L. Trott

Sept. 25, 1901
Baltimore, Maryland

Nov. 16, 1975
Gaithersberg, Maryland

President of Wesley Theological Seminary, Washington, D.C. 1955–67. He served in the U.S. Army in 1918. Trott married Lillian Durfee on September 2, 1930. He was ordained Methodist in 1935, and held pastorates in Arburus, MD (1926–33); Baltimore, MD (1933–39); Brunswick, MD (1939–47); and Hagerstown, MD (1947–50). Trott also served as district superintendent of Baltimore, 1950–55, and was very active in world affairs of the Methodist Church. He wrote from *What Church People Think* (1937) and *Teenagers Tell* (1948).

John Smart

Dec. 9, 1906
Scotland

Nov. 18, 1975
Oak Park, Illinois

President of Emmaus Bible School, Chicago, IL (Dubuque, IA, in 1984), **1965–75**. Smart was four years old when his family immigrated to Victoria, British Columbia. He was converted in his late teens in Alberta, Canada. He began his ministry as a missionary to the West Indies in 1932. On June 18, 1938, he married Fay Surgenor and they settled in Toronto. From 1951–65 the Smarts ministered out of Plainfield, NJ.

Byang Kato

June, 1936
Sabzuro, Nigeria

December 19, 1975
Mombassa, Kenya

Evangelical theologian. Kato was converted at age eleven through a missionary, and enrolled in a Sudan Interior Mission school a year later. He married Jummai in January, 1957. In 1958, he began a teaching and counseling ministry. He continued his education in Nigeria, England, and America, graduating in 1973 from Dallas Theological Seminary. In 1974, he was appointed secretary of the World Evangelical Fellowship Executive Committee. That year, he gave two papers at the Lausanne Congress on World Evangelism. He was attacked from the WCC-related All Africa Council of Churches. He traveled to such places as South Africa and Alaska. Kato was married and had three children. His drowning off the coast of Mombassa brought shock waves to evangelicals all through Africa…similar to the impact of the DAWSON TROTMAN drowning in America, almost two decades earlier.

Leslie D. Weatherhead

Oct. 14, 1893
London, England

Jan. 3, 1976
Bexhill, England

Pastor of the City Temple, London, 1936–60. Weatherhead served early on as a pastor of the English Methodist Church of Madras, India, 1919–22. He ministered at Oxford Road Methodist in Manchester, 1922–25. He pastored at Brunswick Methodist Church in Leeds, 1926–36. In 1955, he was elected president of the Methodist Conference. While in India, he married the daughter of a missionary. He wrote at least 35 books including *The Transforming Friendship* (1928) to *Psychology, Religion, and Healing* (1951).

Glenn Griffith

Aug. 17, 1894
Augusta, Kansas

Jan. 12, 1976
San Antonio, Texas

First president of Wesleyan Holiness Association of Churches, 1959–76. Griffith was converted and called to preach in 1912. He then served in WWI. In 1925, he joined the Church of the Nazarene, prior to becoming a well-known, full-time evangelist in Holiness circles. He was also CN district superintendent in Idaho and Oregon (1937–45) and in Colorado (1946–51). Sensing worldliness in CN, he left the denomination in 1955 and held an eight-week tent meeting near Nampa, ID, resulting in the formation of the Bible Missionary Union Church. In 1959, he left that organization over the issues of divorce and remarriage. He then formed the Wesleyan Holiness Association of Churches. He is remembered as a fiery revivalistic preacher.

Henry G. Perry

New York, New York

Jan. 12, 1976
Oradell, New Jersey

General secretary of American Tract Society, 1947–63. Having majored in economics and finance, Perry spent the first 22 years of his business career in the investment banking business on Wall Street. In 1942, he joined the executive staff of United Service to China as comptroller, and during the next five years transmitted more than 40 million dollars to China for Christian colleges, orphanages, and general rehabilitation work. More than 207 million tracts were transmitted during his administration. He saw a new headquarters building erected in Oradell, NJ, in 1962.

John M. Price

Nov. 21, 1884
Fair Dealing, Kentucky

Jan. 12, 1976
Fort Worth, Texas

First president of American Association of Schools of Religious Education, 1947–51. Price was converted in a revival meeting on August 11, 1899. Price married Mabel Falk on July 11, 1916. His lifelong work was teaching at Southwestern Baptist Seminary, Fort Worth, TX, from 1915–56. He organized the religious education department, traveled to over 40 countries, and wrote seven books, including *The Unfolding Life* (1963).

Chester A. Tulga

Feb. 17, 1886

Jan. 22, 1976
Albuquerque, New Mexico

Secretary of the Conservative Baptist Association of America, 1947–59. Coming from the American Baptist Associations, Tulga wrote many books, beginning with *The Case*. He was a Baptist pastor for 25 years in such places as LaGrange, Oh; Galeton, PA; Miles, OH; North Platte, NE; Brookings, SD; and Norwood Park in Chicago. He taught at Eastern Baptist Institute of Somerset, KY, for two years. From 1945–56, he served as research secretary for the Conservative Baptist Fellowship, documenting compromise in the movement. This was climaxed by his *The Foreign Mission Controversy in the Northern Baptist Convention*. He then affiliated with the GARB and later the American Baptist Association. He retired in Chicago, IL. Tulga died of cancer.

Louis L. Talbot

Oct. 19, 1889
Sydney, Australia

Jan. 22, 1976
Mission Vejo, California

President of Bible Institute of Los Angeles, CA, 1938–52. Talbot came to America and attended MBI where he was converted under the preaching of JOHN HARPER. Talbot married Lucille Hogue on December 27, 1916 (died: 1960), while pastoring a Congregational Church in Davis, TX. He then married Carol Terry in 1964. Following graduation from McComick Theological Seminary in 1917, he pastored at Madison St. Congregational Church in Oak Park, IL. He was a Presbyterian pastor in Keokuk, IA (1921–25); Oliver Presbyterian, Minneapolis, MN (1925–29); and Philpott Tabernacle, Hamilton, Ontario (1929–32). After several pastorates, he took the Church of the Open Door, 1932–48 and began his BIOLA position as well in Los Angeles. The church grew from 1,200 to 3,500; the school grew from 300 to 1,000. They paid off a $1 million debt. He was present for the ground-breaking ceremonies (1957) for the new campus, having suggested the move (1953).

Elmer E. Flack

Oct. 3, 1894
Mendon, Illinois

Feb. 16, 1976
St. Paul, Minnesota

Dean of Hamma Divinity School (Trinity Lutheran Seminary, Columbus, OH in 1978), **Springfield, OH 1940–60**. Flack married Erna Dorow on June 18, 1916. He was ordained as a Lutheran on October 31, 1918, after which he held a pastorate at the Church of the Advent, Chicago, IL, from 1918–23. He then became a professor of OT language and literature at Hamma (1923–36), professor of theology (1936–40), and secretary of the faculty (1923–40). He wrote *The Revelation of John* (1936).

Kathryn Kuhlman

May 9, 1907
Concordia, Missouri

Feb. 20, 1976
Tulsa, Oklahoma

Evangelist and charismatic faith healer. Kathryn was converted in 1921 in the local Methodist Church, which had a Baptist evangelist. Kuhlman was ordained into the Evangelical Church Alliance. She had Baptist roots. She began to preach in Boise, ID, in 1928, and married evangelist Burroughs A. Waltrip on October 18, 1938. They divorced in 1948. Her faith healing and Holy Spirit baptism began in 1946. Beginning July 4, 1948, she headquartered and preached in Pittsburgh (1950–75), while holding crusades elsewhere, weekly services in Youngstown, OH and monthly services in Los Angeles (1965–73). Thousands claim to have been healed under her radio and television ministry. She authored several books, which sold millions of copies, including *I Believe in Miracles* (1962) to *From Medicine to Miracles* (1978). Kathryn died of pulmonary hypertension, following open heart surgery. She is interred in Glendale, CA.

Allen S. Meck

Nov. 1, 1886
Meckville, Pennsylvania

Feb. 27, 1976
Lancaster, Pennsylvania

President of Lancaster (PA) Theological Seminary, 1947–57. Meck married Olivia Hahn on May 23, 1911, and was ordained into the Reformed Church July 2 of the same year. He pastored in Ephrata, PA (1911–16); Easton, PA (1916–31); and Trinity First Church, York, PA (1931–47). Meck preached in over 3,100 churches. He was the secretary of evangelism in the Evangelical and Reformed Church, 1938–76.

Frank D. Gifford

June 22, 1891
Elizabeth, New Jersey

March, 7, 1976
Hempstead, New York (?)

Dean of Philadelphia Divinity School (merged into Episcopal Divinity School, Cambridge, MA, in 1974), **1946–59**. Gifford married Hazel Frey on May 30, 1917. He was ordained an Episcopalian in 1917. He was minister of Trinity Church in Woodbridge, NJ (1913–16); Holy Trinity Cathedral, Tokyo, Japan (1916–18); Grace Chapel, New York City (1918–20); Emmanuel Church, Norwich, NY (1920–23); and St. Thomas Church, Mamaroneck, NY (1923–46). He was also professor of pastoral theology as well as dean at PDS from 1946 on. Gifford's first book was *Building the King's Highway* (1942).

Rufus D. Reisdorph

Sept. 27, 1896
Leola, South Dakota

March 8, 1976
Grand Island, New York

General superintendent of Wesleyan Methodist Church, 1959–63. Reisdorph married Ruby Levans on October 25, 1927, following his ordination in June. He served as president of Dakota Conference, WMC, 1928–40; Sunday School secretary and editor of the denomination, 1940–43 and 1947–59. Reisdorph wrote many Sunday School papers and quarterlies. He was the president of Miltonvale (KS) College, 1946–48. He preached the night before he died.

Bernard L. Montgomery

Nov. 17, 1887
Kennington, England

March 24, 1976
Alton, England

WWII hero famous for his campaign as the commander of the British Eighth Army in Africa, which routed the Germans under Erwin Rommel at El Alamein and secured Northern Africa for the Allies in 1942. Montgomery's troops were known as the Desert Rats. Montgomery married Betty Carver in 1927 (died: 1937). He participated in the Normandy campaign as the field commander, and after the war, he was the deputy supreme commander of NATO forces, 1951–58. He was a man of prayer and considered an outstanding Christian general. He died in his sleep. His funeral was at St. George's Chapel, Windsor.

Jesse H. Baird

April 27, 1889
Clintonville, Pennsylvania

April 3, 1976
Oakland, California

President of San Francisco Theological Seminary, San Anselmo, CA, 1937–57. Baird married Susanna Bragstad on July 4, 1917. He was ordained as a Presbyterian in 1916. Baird pastored in Idaho; Ohio; FPC, Boise, ID (1920–26); FPC, Pomona, CA (1926–28); FPC, Salt Lake City, UT (1928–31); and FPC, Oakland, CA (1931–37). He also authored several books.

Gerald L. K. Smith

1897
Pardeeville, Wisconsin

April 15, 1976
Glendale, California

Founder of the Christian Nationalist Crusade. Smith was an ardent anti-Communist and known for his opposition to President Franklin D. Roosevelt over the radio. He delivered his anti-Communist views in a monthly magazine called *The Cross and the Flag*. He also lectured and wrote for some 200 small newspapers. A supporter of Governor Huey Long for president, Smith cradled the dying man in his arms when he was shot and delivered his graveyard oration. Smith died of pneumonia and burial was in Eureka Springs, AR. He was succeeded by his widow, Elana F. Smith.

Karl D. Hummel

March 23, 1898
Los Angeles, California

May 15, 1976
Dallas, Texas

President of Central American Mission, Dallas, TX, 1924–51. Hummel was the first missionary to fill the head post. Raised in a gospel-preaching Methodist church, he received assurance of salvation under R. A. TORREY at the Church of the Open Door. Hummel married Guelph McQuinn on January 19, 1920. He began a missions hospital in Honduras and served in Guatemala and Nicaragua, 1919–24, in missionary evangelism.

Wilbur M. Smith

June 9, 1894
Chicago, Illinois

May 20, 1976
San Marino, California

Probably the most brilliant evangelical scholar since J. GRESHAM MACHEN. Smith was a professor of Bible at MBI (1938–47), Fuller Seminary (1947–63), and Trinity Evangelical Seminary (1963–71). Smith married Mary Ostrosky on August 27, 1917. He was an authority on books, and an outstanding Bible teacher. His messages and writings were filled with prophecy and history, not available elsewhere. He was ordained Presbyterian and served several churches (1918–37): Orlean City, MD (1918–22); Baltimore, MD (1922–27); Covington, VA (1927–30); and in Coatesville, PA (1931–37). His "In the Study" column in *Moody Monthly* was classic. He edited Peloubet's notes on the International Sunday School Lessons, 1934–70. His writings range from *Some Much Needed Books* (1934) to the *Minister in His Study* (1973), an autobiography. His some 60 books were led by *Therefore Stand* (1945). His library of 25,000 books may have been the largest privately owned in the country.

Waldo E. Harder

March 3, 1918
Newton, Kansas

May 28, 1976
Durham, Kansas (?)

President of Grace Bible Institute (University), **Omaha, NE, 1961–71,** during his tenure, enrollment rose from 321 to 556, with a radio station and student center being established. In his early ministry, Harder worked with Hopi Indians in Arizona 1943–45. He went to the Berean Academy in Ebing, KS, from 1945–51 and served as a missionary to Zaire, 1952–61. He pastored the Central Heights Mennonite Church, Durham, KS, until shortly before his death from congestive heart failure.

Mitsuo Fuchida

Dec. 3, 1902
Kashiwara-shi, Japan

May 30, 1976
Kashiwara, Japan

Leader of the 360-plane attack on Pearl Harbor, HI, Dec. 7, 1941, and the only pilot to live through the war. The attack resulted in America losing 18 vessels, 165 aircraft, and 2,403 lives. Fuchida was an "ace" pilot with over 10,000 flying hours to his credit in the Imperial Japanese Navy. Fuchida married Haruko on Jan. 7, 1933. He was converted April 14, 1950, at a PTL street meeting via GLEN WAGNER and a Jacob DeShazer tract. After his conversion, he became an evangelist in Japan until 1958 when he moved to Berkeley, CA, and had a worldwide witness. He died of diabetes complications.

Earl B. Marlatt

May 24, 1892
Columbus, Indiana

June 13, 1976
Winchester, Indiana

Methodist clergyman and author who wrote the hymn "Are Ye Able" (music by HENRY MASON). Marlatt became a professor of philosophy of literature and religious education at Boston University in 1925 and was dean of Boston (MA) University School of Theology, 1938–45. He then was a professor of philosophy of religion at SMU, 1946–57. He wrote several hymns and books ranging from *Chapel Windows* (1924) to *Lands Away* (1944).

Willis J. King

Oct. 1, 1886
Rose Hill, Texas

June 17, 1976
New Orleans, Louisiana

Dean of Gammon Theological Seminary (Interdenominational Theological Center in 1959), **Atlanta, GA, 1932–44**. King entered the Methodist ministry in 1908, holding pastorates in Greenville, TX; Boston, MA; Galveston, TX; and Houston, TX. He married Permella Kelly on June 4, 1913 (died: February 1943), and Emma Arnold on June 28, 1944. King then began teaching OT and Christian sociology at GTS from 1918–30. He was elected bishop in 1944 and assigned to Liberia, Louisiana, and then Mississippi. King was chosen delegate to the Conference on Life and Work (1937), to the Missionary Convocation, Leopoldville, Belgian Congo (1946), and to the World Methodist Council (1961). He was decorated with the Order Star of African Redemption and the Knight Commander Order of Pioneers (Liberia). In 1975, he was honored as the oldest living United Methodist bishop when the Council of Bishops met in New Orleans. He retired to New Orleans, LA, and wrote several books. He wrote *The Negro in American Life* (1926).

Jimmy Stroud

June 17, 1915
Lee, Florida

June 17, 1976
Memphis, Tennessee

Director of Memphis (TN) Union Mission. This mission was far more than just a ministry to homeless people. There was the radio/TV ministry, the headquarters of YFC, plus the traditional nightly chapel services, clothing give-away, counseling, beds, and meals. There was also a home, hospital, jail visitation program, Calvary Colony—which was a rehabilitation work among alcoholics on Mud Island—and a Beale Street Rescue Mission for Blacks. Stroud was converted in 1935 in Charleston, WV, and worked with Pat Withrow for nine years in missions. He was a Baptist. His radio/TV program was called *Above the Clouds*. Stroud reached thousands with the gospel message with many facets of outreach. June 17 was an amazing day for him: born, died, married his wife, Dortha Bailey, on June 17, 1941, and opened the Memphis Union Mission, June 17, 1945.

Harry L. Turner

Aug. 31, 1886
Campbellford, Ontario, Canada

June 19, 1976
St. Petersburg, Florida

President of Christian and Missionary Alliance, 1954–60. Turner had a long and fruitful ministry. He served nine years as a missionary in Argentina, was a Bible conference speaker and evangelist throughout North America, an interim pastor in Gospel Tabernacle in New York City, pastor of Delta Tabernacle, Hamilton, Ontario, Canada, director of the theology department and dean at St. Paul (MN) Bible College, and vice president of the CMA. In February of 1908, he was converted, healed of a serious illness, and called to the ministry at the same time. After 1960, he joined the faculty of Simpson College in San Francisco. He went to the Philippines (1962) where he taught at Ebenezer Bible College until retirement (1968). He preached in 37 different denominations and in over 900 churches, as well as in England, South America, India, Near and Far East and in Congo.

Charles F. Pfeiffer

March 23, 1919
Philadelphia, Pennsylvania

July, 1976

Outstanding Old Testament scholar of Bible history and archaeology. Pfeiffer married Lucille on August 28, 1940. He pastored (1944–55), then taught at MBI, his alma mater (1955–59). Pfieffer was a professor of OT, Semitics, Assyriology, and Egyptology at Gordon Divinity School, 1959–64. Pfeiffer served as co-editor of the famed *Wycliffe Bible Commentary*. He was a Reformed Presbyterian who taught at Eastern Michigan College, Ypsilanti, in later years. He also taught at King's College, Briarcliffe Manor, NY.

John H. Walker

March 6, 1900
Delhi, Louisiana

July 12, 1976
Cleveland, Tennessee

General overseer of Church of God, Cleveland, TN, 1935–44 and president of Lee College, 1930–35, 1944–45. He served as associate pastor in two Louisiana churches, 1919–25. Walker marrried Blanche Jenkerson on October 14, 1926. He taught at Church of God Bible Training School (1927–30) and was their general superintendent of education (1930–35). Walker also served as the director of Church of God World Missions, 1948–52.

Abdel R. Wentz

Oct. 8, 1883
Black Rock, Pennsylvania

July 19, 1976
Oehnsparu, Pennsylvania

President of Lutheran Theological Seminary at Gettysburg (PA), 1940–51. Wentz married Mary Kuhlman on August 15, 1917. He was a professor of history at Gettysburg College (1909–16) and of church history for 40 years, (1916–56). Wentz authored several books on history and was active in the Lutheran World Federation. He also served on a 14-man committee to form the WCC. His writings are from *The Beginnings of the German Element in York County* (1916) to *A New Strategy for Theological Education* (1937).

Lucy Turner Iske

Dec. 13, 1909
Anchorville, Michigan

July 23, 1976
Mt. Clemens, Michigan

Director of Anchor Bay Evangelistic Association, Maryville, IL, 1945–63. Lucy married Harold Iske in June, 1936. They met at Angeles Temple, Los Angeles and were married by AIMEE S. MCPHERSON. Shortly thereafter they founded and co-pastored the Bethel Temple Church, New Baltimore, MI. The Anchor Bay Bible Institute was started there and they were both teachers in it. She had an aggressive missionary vision and was responsible for students and others going out to many different countries. They moved to California in 1964 where she later died of congestive heart failure.

Oliver B. Greene

Feb. 14, 1916
Greenville, South Carolina

July 26, 1976
Greenville, South Carolina

Baptist evangelist from the southeast. Greene was converted at age 19, through the prayers of his family and through a sermon on Romans 3:23, in a country church outside Greenville. Greene married Aileen Collins on September10, 1939. From 1939–66, he conducted tent revivals with over 200,000 conversions. He also started the radio program *The Gospel Hour* in 1939, which was heard on 180 stations at the time of his death. He wrote 26 commentaries, 33 books, and some 100 tracts. He also visited many mission fields. His funeral was at Tabernacle Baptist, Greenville, SC.

Gould Wickey

Sept. 25, 1891
Eschol, Pennsylvania

Aug. 7, 1976
Chevy Chase, Maryland

Executive secretary of Association of Theological Schools, 1942–46. Wickey was ordained Lutheran in 1916, and married Ethel Basehoar on August 29, 1917. He pastored briefly and was a professor of philosophy at Concordia College, Moorheard, MN, from 1920–26. He was president of Carthage (IL) College (1926–29), and executive secretary of the board of education of United Lutheran Church (1929–59).

Bonnie L. Cox

May 1, 1899
Walton County, Georgia

Aug. 11, 1976
Griffith, Georgia

General superintendent of Christian Holiness Church, Griffith, GA 1946–60. Both parents passed away before Cox was one year old. He married Elizabeth Bramblett on July 23, 1916. Saved as a teenager, he pastored from 1924–46 in Edgefield, SC; Augusta, GA; and Piedmont, AL. Cox attended the dedication of the headquarters building of CHC. His last ministry was at the White County (GA) Youth Camp the week of July 4th. As a pastor, evangelist, teacher, and writer, he was highly esteemed in his movement.

Fred F. Goodsell

Sept. 21, 1880
Montevideo, Minnesota

Aug. 13, 1976
Auburndale, Massachusetts

Executive vice president (CEO) of American Board of Commissioners for Foreign Missions (UCBWM in 1961), **1930–49**. Goodsell married Lulu Service on June 29, 1905. He was ordained as a Congregationalist in 1905 and went as a missionary for ABCFM to Turkey the same year. He became involved in the YMCA war service in Russia, Romania, and Siberia (1916–19); then he returned to Turkey (1919–29). Goodsell authored *Inductive Turkish Lessons* (1926).

Bob Hughes

Aug. 8, 1932
Center, Texas

Aug. 21, 1976
Dallas, Texas

Outstanding missionary to the Philippines. Hughes served in the air force in the Philippines and was converted there by the witness of missionary, Joe Vella. Back home, he attended Baptist Bible College, where he met Helen Johnson, whom he would marry in 1954. He held a student pastorate in Springdale, AR. In 1956, they went to Cebu City in the Philippines. Their Bible Baptist Church had about 6,000 in attendance when they dedicated a new building in 1973. He also started a Bible college and through both ministries, 18,000 people were hearing the gospel each week. In 1974, he launched a campaign to distribute one million Bibles in the native languages. Hughes returned to the states for cancer treatment in 1975. In early 1976, weak in body, he spoke for ten minutes to 5,000 at JACK HYLES' pastor's school in Hammond, IN. One of the young couples responding to that memorable address was Rick and Becky Martin, who are now doing an amazing work in the Philippines also. He died at only 44, leaving a mighty mark on Independent Baptist Missions.

Luther A. Weigle

Sept. 11, 1880
Littlestown, Pennsylvania

Sept. 2, 1976
New Haven, Connecticut

Dean of Yale University Divinity School, New Haven, CT 1928–49, and president of Federal Council of Churches (NCC in 1950), **1940–42**. Weigle was ordained Lutheran and pastored at Bridgeport, CT, from 1903–4. He married Clara Boxrud on June 15, 1909. He then served as professor of philosophy at Carleton College, Northfield, MN (1905–16) and was dean there (1910–15). Weigle then went to Yale as a professor of Christian nurturing (1916–24), and of religious education (1924–49). He and LEWIS SHERILL were co-leaders in the development of Association of Theological Schools, 1918–36. He wrote a well-received book, *The Pupil and the Teacher* (1916). His last book was *Genesis Octapla* (1965).

Russell J. Meade

Feb. 23, 1923　　　　　　　　　　　　　　　　　　　　　　　　　　　　　　Sept. 10, 1976
Strafton, Colorado　　　　　　　　　　　　　　　　　　　　　　　　　　Chicago, Illinois

President and founder of Chicago (IL) Bible (Christian) Life College, 1954–76. Meade began his ministry in the Foursquare denomination upon graduating from LIFE Bible College. Leaving the denomination, he came to Chicago in 1954 and assumed the leadership of the Chicago Bible College, which had begun in the Philadelphia Church in Chicago, which he also pastored for nine years. He incorporated the college and secured separate facilities. It continues today as Christian Life College in Mt. Prospect, IL. He was also president of Full Gospel Fellowship of Churches and Ministers, Int., a position he held at his death. His wife's name was Ella. His son-in-law, Daryl R. Merrill, continued the ministry at CLC. Meade died at Presbyterian-St Luke's Hospital following open-heart surgery.

John G. Ridley

Sept. 8, 1896　　　　　　　　　　　　　　　　　　　　　　　　　　　　　　Sept. 26, 1976
Sydney, Australia　　　　　　　　　　　　　　　　　　　　　　　　　　Sydney, Australia

Evangelist throughout Australia. Ridley was converted in 1915 through the preaching at Burton Street Baptist Tabernacle, Sydney. He was in active service in WWI and seriously wounded, then, upon recovery, began evangelism endeavors in 1925. Ridley married Dorothy Chapman on August 18, 1926. From 1949 on, he had many enterprises going on under Ambassadors for Christ. He was a prolific writer of books, booklets, and tracts.

Joseph L. Gingrich

Feb. 7, 1894　　　　　　　　　　　　　　　　　　　　　　　　　　　　　　　Oct. 22, 1976
McAlisterville, Pennsylvania

Conference secretary of National Fellowship of Brethren Churches, 1929–52. He was converted in 1919. Gingrich married Beatrice Smith on the same day he graduated from Ashland College, June 3, 1920. He was pastor in Masontown, PA (1920–26); Johnstown, PA (1926–36); Long Beach, CA (1936–40); Allentown, PA (1940–44); Conemauth, PA (1944–48); Sterling, OH (1948–55); and Leamersville, PA (1955–59). He was also moderator of the National Conference of FGBC in 1954.

Robert V. Moss

March 3, 1922　　　　　　　　　　　　　　　　　　　　　　　　　　　　　Oct. 25, 1976
Wilson, North Carolina　　　　　　　　　　　　　　　　　　　　　Montclair, New Jersey

President of Lancaster (PA) Theological Seminary, 1967–69; of United Church of Christ 1969–76; and of Association of Theological Schools, 1969–72. Moss married Junia Keppel on June 20, 1946, and was ordained into the United Church of Christ in 1946. He taught at Franklin Marshall College (1946–50) and began as a professor of New Testament at Lancaster (1951–57). He authored three books, 1955–58. He was an outspoken advocate of liberal programs and causes.

Oscar C. Markham

Oct. 27, 1900　　　　　　　　　　　　　　　　　　　　　　　　　　　　　　Oct. 27, 1976
Pulaski, Tennessee　　　　　　　　　　　　　　　　　　　　　　　　　Dover, Tennessee

President of Mid-Continent Baptist Bible College, Mayfield, KY 1957–76. Markham married Bonnie Paysinger on March 8, 1925. After her death, he married Annie C. Parrish on February 15, 1957. He was ordained on August 25, 1929, in Pulaski, TN, and served pastorates in both Tennessee and Kentucky. From 1949–57, he was a teacher, dean, and registrar at MCBBC.

Harry Denman

Sept. 26, 1893
Birmingham, Alabama

Nov. 8, 1976
Birmingham, Alabama

Methodist leader in evangelism. Denman never married. He was in the coal and iron business, 1904–15. He served as the secretary of the Birmingham Sunday School Association (1915–19) and was manager of First Methodist Church of Birmingham (1919–38). Denman was the executive secretary of the Board of Evangelism of the Methodist Church, preaching and teaching 1939–64. He began the Foundation for Evangelism and was known for his personal austerity and eloquence.

Gordon Palmer

June 2, 1888
Coveney, England

Nov. 15, 1976
Los Angeles, California

President of Eastern Baptist College and Theological Seminary, Wynnewood, PA 1936–48. Palmer came to America in 1909. He married Mila Treat on September 9, 1919. He held pastorates in Winters, CA (1909–14); Azusa, CA (1914–15); Mumford, NY (1916–17); Mason, MI (1917–18); South Park Church, Los Angeles, CA (1919–28); and FBC, Pomona, CA (1928–36). His first book was *The Gospel According to Easter* (1938).

G. Ford Porter

Feb. 5, 1893
Ottawa County, Michigan

Nov. 20, 1976
Indianapolis, Indiana

Author of the most famous tract in history, "God's Simple Plan of Salvation," which has a circulation of over 550 million, **and founder and first president of Indiana** (Heritage in 1985) **Baptist College, Indianapolis, IN 1956–66.** He married Ida Hunton (Nov. 26, 1888–July 23, 1982) on Sept. 1, 1921. Porter held a pastorate at FBC, Princeton, IN from 1926–40, where the tract was born. Porter wrote the tract on May 19, 1933. He then moved to Indianapolis, IN, to pastor at Berean Missionary Baptist (1940–47) then at Lifegate Baptist (formerly Berean Gospel Temple) (1947–76). He founded Berean Gospel Distributors Inc. After his death, his son, Robert F. Porter, carried on his ministry.

William J. Burgess

Sept. 7, 1897
Whittington, Arkansas

Dec. 4, 1976
Little Rock, Arkansas

Director of Baptist Missionary Association of America Missions, Little Rock, AR, 1951–69. Burgess was active in the BMA all his life as a pastor, educator, and evangelist. Burgess married Dova Collie (born: August 17, 1897) on May 25, 1916. He pastored two churches in Arkansas for 16 years each: Temple Baptist Church in Little Rock and Springfield Baptist Church in Greenbrier. During his tenure at BMAAM, the missions offering grew from $38,000 to $634,000 plus. He also published numerous works, especially in the field of prophecy.

Everett A. Keaton

July 3, 1889
Oto County, Nebraska

Dec. 13, 1976
Pompano Beach, Florida

Moderator of Churches of Christ in Christian Union, Circleville, OH, 1921–51. Keaton attended God's Bible School. He served the High Street Church in Chillicothe, OH, for 24 years from 1918–42. His combination of zeal and stability marked his years as moderator. He pastored the North Columbus Church, 1942–48. He helped found the Mount of Praise Bible School (Circleville Bible College in 1954), and was its president, 1948–52. He took an active part in establishing the Advocate Publishing House, and was editor of the *Church of Christ Advocate* until health forced his resignation from many duties in 1952. He had preached 115 revivals with 5,666 responses to the gospel among other activities. He retired to Pompano Beach, FL.

Samuel M. Cavert

Sept. 9, 1888 *Dec. 21, 1976*
Charlton, New York Bronxville, New York

General secretary of Federal Council of Churches, 1921–50, renamed **National Council of Churches, 1950–54, and secretary of World Council of Churches, 1954–1957**. Cavert grew up in a Christian home. He was secretary of the YMCA in NY (1910–12), and a professor at Union Seminary in New York City (1915–16). He was ordained as a Presbyterian in 1915. He married Ruth Miller on November 14, 1918 (died February 10, 1920 following childbirth). He then married Ruth Twila Lytton on June 28, 1927. Cavert was active as a chaplain in WWI. He authored ten books from *Securing Christian Leaders for Tomorrow* (1926) to *Church Co-operation and Unity in America* (1970). He also edited *The Pulpit Digest*. He was a conservative who tolerated liberalism. Cavert suggested the name, World Council of Churches. He was a leader in the ecumenical movement.

W. Herschel Ford

Nov. 21, 1900 *Jan. 1, 1977*
Monroe, Georgia

Southern Baptist pastor and author. Ford married Maybelle Archibald (October 15, 1919) and was ordained (November 19, 1922). Ford held pastorates in Andrews, NC (1926–29); at FBC, Hendersonville (NC 1932–34); at Broadway Church, Knoxville, TN (1934–39); at Southside Baptist Church, Jacksonville, FL in 1939 and then later in Texas. His first book was *Principles of the Christian Religion* (1930). He wrote many books on Bible exposition.

Johannes (Hans) E. R. Lilje

Aug. 20, 1899 *Jan. 6, 1977*
Hanover, Germany Hanover, Germany

President of World Council of Churches, 1968–75; of World Lutheran Federation, 1952–57 (helped found WLF in 1947), **and general secretary of the Lutheran World Convention** (Federation in 1947), **1937–45**. After imprisonment in WWII in 1944, Lilje served as president of the central committee for Inner Missions of the Evangelical Church of Germany (1946–77) and as a Lutheran bishop (1947–77). He authored German and English books, 1946–64, and sought to challenge evangelical Christians with contemporary issues.

Orie O. Miller

July 7, 1892 *Jan. 10, 1977*
Middlebury, Indiana Lititz, Pennsylvania

Director of Mennonite Central Committee, Akron, OH 1935–58. Miller was converted at age 13 at evangelistic meetings in his home church. He married Susan Wolf on Aug. 26, 1915 (died: February 14, 1958), and then married Elta Sensenig on January 9, 1960. Miller worked with Miller Hess and Company, Akron, PA, from 1916–70. He served as president (1954–62), and as chairman of their board (1962–70). He helped in several Mennonite relief programs and projects, going to Russia in 1920 with food and supplies and helping to launch the Mennonite Central Committee. He is buried in Ephrata, PA.

Paul Hutchens

April 7, 1902
Thorton, Indiana

Jan. 23, 1977

Writer of Christian novels. Hutchens wrote choruses, including "On the Cross for Me." He authored the well-known series *The Sugar Creek Gang* for juniors and the novels, *Romance of Fire, Cup of Cold Water,* and *Yesterday Rain.* Hutchens married Jane Freerks on December 20, 1924. He was a young evangelist and ordained a Baptist in 1925. Early in his life, 1929, he developed tuberculosis, so he began his writing career in the Santa Clara, CA sanitorium. Hutchens then moved to Waterloo, IA, from 1943–55 and then to Cascade, CO. He ministered to everyone he met.

Alfred A. Kunz

May 21, 1893
Brooklyn, New York

Feb. 1, 1977
Fort Myers, Florida

Director of Pocket Testament League, 1941–63. Kunz turned PTL into a mighty force, sending teams to army camps during WWII to distribute the NT. He married Florence Palmer on May 7, 1917. He worked with the YMCA until 1926, then served as an evangelist and was involved with camp work in the 1930s. In 1938, Kunz came on the PTL board and soon had a worldwide ministry. He was Plymouth Brethren.

James O. Buswell

Jan. 16, 1895
Burlington, Wisconsin

Feb. 3, 1977
Quarryville, Pennsylvania

President of Wheaton (IL) College, 1926–40. Buswell was dismissed for his fundamentalist Presbyterianism which caused misunderstandings. Buswell was a founder of the ACC and also of the Bible Presbyterian Church USA, along with MCINTYRE and MACRAE. He was taught the gospel at a very early age and believed in Christ from then on. Buswell married Helen Spaulding on May 20, 1918. He pastored in Minnesota, at a Presbyterian church, Milwaukee, WI (1919–22); and at a Reformed church, Brooklyn, NY (1922–26). He was ordained as a Presbyterian and served as a professor of theology and apologetics at Faith Theological Seminary, Wilmington, DE, from 1940–47. He served as the president of National Bible Institute (Shelton College), Ringwood, NJ (1941–56), and teacher and dean of Covenant College and Theological Seminary, St. Louis, MO (1956–70). He broke with CARL MCINTYRE in 1956. He wrote a two-volume *A Systematic Theology* (1962–63). His first book was *Problems in the Prayer Life* (1928).

L. Gilbert (Gil) Dodds

June 23, 1918
Norcatur/Reiger, Kansas

Feb. 3, 1977
St. Charles, Illinois

Brethren minister who held the world record for the indoor mile run for many years. Converted at age 13, Dodds had a strong Christian testimony and spoke at YFC meetings, Word of Life crusades, and church functions. His wife was Irma Seeger. From 1943–48 he won 21 straight races for the indoor mile. He never raced on Sunday, and Philippians 4:13 was his trademark. Dodds won the Sullivan Award (athlete of the year) in 1943. Dodds set the record with 4.06.4 time (March 18, 1944) at Chicago Stadium, and again broke the record with 4.05.3 time at Madison Square Gardens (January 31, 1948). In 1958, he became a track coach at Wheaton College. Dodds claimed the Evangel Brethren Church, Ashland, OH, as his church. In the 1960s, Dodds was a guidance counselor at Naperville (IL) High School. He died of a brain tumor.

Gordon H. Smith

Dec. 16, 1902
Buenos Aires, Argentina

Feb. 13, 1977
Deland, Florida

One of the great missionaries of our time, serving with CMA in Cambodia and Vietnam, 1928–55. Smith married Laure Ivory on June 12, 1928. On the field, they did translation work, built churches, treated lepers (4,500 people), and escaped numerous brushes with death. They flew a light plane for their ministry, 1946–53. Then in 1958, Smith was associated with World Wide Evangelization Crusade.

Janani Luwum

1922
Acholi, Uganda

Feb. 17, 1977
Kaupala, Uganda

Archbishop of Uganda and martyr. Luwum was born into the Acholi tribe whose homeland was in northern Uganda. He was converted in January 1948, as a result of hearing evangelist Yusto Otunno. Attending a missionary-led training college, he began to preach in the open air. He took further training in England, 1958–59 and 1962–65. In 1969, he was made bishop over the Langi and Acholi people. The Anglican Church was very weak in the north so he visited every parish, worked with agricultural centers, leprosy works, and raised support for homeless girls. In January 1971, disaster came as General Amin seized control of the government. Prominent Christian leaders were murdered. In 1972, 58 European missionaries were expelled. In 1974, Luwum was made archbishop of the whole country. Attempts to meet with Amin failed. Finally Amin called for Luwum privately for a conference. Evidence afterwards indicates he was asked to sign a false confession that he had plotted to overthrow the dictator. When he refused, he was tortured and executed (shot). He was an Anglican. In 1981, a guerrilla force invaded Uganda and deposed Amin.

William R. White

Dec. 2, 1892
Brownsboro, Texas

March 4, 1977
Waco, Texas

President of Baylor University, Waco, TX, 1948–61. White married Edna Woods on Jan. 17, 1916 (died: Dec. 16, 1948). He then married Catherine Tarwater on June 20, 1950 (died: Sept. 14, 1970). White then married Ioda Mohr on Aug. 28, 1971. He held pastorates in Fort Worth (1931–35), Oklahoma City (1935–40), and Austin, TX (1940–48). He also served as president of Hardin-Simmons University, Abilene, TX (1940–43); and editorial secretary of the Sunday School Board, SBC (1943–45). His first book was *The Royal Road to Life* (1938), and his last *A Manifesto of Faith* (1967).

William S. Nelson

Oct. 15, 1895
Paris, Kentucky

March 26, 1977
Hyattsville, Maryland

Dean of Howard University School of Divinity, Washington, D.C. 1940–49. Nelson was highly educated, attending universities in Europe as well as in the States. He married Blanche Wright on May 5, 1926. He was an instructor of religion and philosophy at Howard, 1924–26 and then served in executive positions until 1931. He was president of Shaw University, Raleigh, NC (1931–36), and of Dillard University, New Orleans, LA (1936–40). He lectured in universities in India, 1947–48. Nelson was the dean of Howard University (1948–61) and professor of Christian theology (1961–64). He was the founder and editor of *Journal of Religious Thought*. Nelson was a Baptist and contributed numerous articles to journals. He is interred in Lincoln Memorial Cemetery, Suitland, MD.

William E. Ashbrook

March 19, 1896
Washington, Pennsylvania

April 5, 1977
Columbus, Ohio

Fundamentalist pastor and writer. Ashbrook married Gertrude Shane on September 20, 1921 (died: December 24, 1987). He pastored the Liberty UP in Hubbard, OH (1922–28); the Neil Avenue UP (1928–32); and the Glen Echo UP (1932–40); both in Columbus, OH. Highly educated, Ashbrook pastored in the United Presbyterian Church until he withdrew in 1940 citing the inroads of modernism and the infiltration of the FCC. He then founded the Calvary Bible Church of Columbus which he pastored until his retirement in 1972. He published *The New Neutralism* in 1958. For years he was associated with the IFCA, but led several churches in Ohio to withdraw and helped form the Ohio Bible Fellowship in 1968 after a five-year feud. He was one of the strongest opponents of New Evangelicalism.

George Fisk

Sept. 17, 1905
Binghamton, New York

April 16, 1977
Charlottesville, Virginia

Father of missionary aviation, a great pioneer in modern missions. Fisk's dream of reaching the lost in Borneo was the stimulus for the birth of six major mission aviation programs. He sensed God's call to Borneo (1913) and sailed there with his wife Anna (1929). In 1932, while on a difficult journey deep in the jungle, he noticed how the hornbills soared with ease overhead, covering in just minutes the distance they had struggled through in hours. By 1935, he had his pilot's license and soon was soaring over the jungle in mission work. Leaving Borneo on the eve of WWII, he met with three US Navy pilots in 1943 to plan Christian Airmen's Missionary Fellowship (Missionary Aviation Fellowship). This started a ripple effect and shortly Sudan Interior Mission, JAARS (Wycliffe Program), CMA, MBI, and Presbyterian mission aviation efforts were "taking off."

Kenneth R. Maurer

Oct. 21, 1918
Pitman, Pennsylvania

April 28, 1977
Myerstown, Pennsylvania

First president of Evangelical School of Theology, Myerstown, PA 1953–70. Maurer was pastor of the Lawn Evangelical Congregational Church, Myerstown, PA, and professor of Church history at EST as well as dean. He also served as pastor at St. John's, Allentown, PA, and in Frackville, Myerstown, and Mt. Culmen, PA.

Charles D. Fulton

Sept. 5, 1892
Kobe, Japan

May 27, 1977

Director of Presbyterian Church (PC USA in 1983) **in the United States Missions, 1932–61**. Fulton was ordained as a Presbyterian on July 25, 1915, and held a pastorate in New Jersey, 1916–17. He married Nancy Ravenel on October 10, 1917. Fulton then went to Japan as a missionary, 1917–25. After his return to the States, he was appointed field secretary and served on the executive committee of Foreign Missions of the Presbyterian Church, 1925–31. Fulton authored *Star in the East* (1938) and *Now Is the Time* (1944).

Milton G. Baker

Jan. 13, 1919
Cortland, New York

June 6, 1977
Wheaton, Illinois

Foreign secretary of Conservative Baptist Foreign Missions Society, 1952–77, and president of EFMA, 1961–63, 1972–74. Baker was converted in Cortland (NY) Baptist Church at age ten, where his father was a deacon. He married Beatrice Camp on June 26, 1940. Baker held a pastorate at the Dover (NH) Baptist Church, 1945–52. As missions leader, he supervised the activities of CBA's over 450 missionaries and made trips to Africa, South America, and the Near East.

Alfred R. Jackson

Nov. 5, 1909
Williamsport, Pennsylvania

June 13, 1977

President of Christian Business Men's Committee, 1961. Jackson was an attorney at law in the city of Williamsport. He practiced law since his graduation from the University of Pennsylvania Law School. He was the first assistant district attorney for four years and also served as president of the Lycoming County Bar Association. He was a Presbyterian elder and Sunday school teacher. Jackson also served as president of the board of trustees of Stony Brook School, Long Island, NY.

Wernher von Braun

March 23, 1912
Wirsitz, Germany (now Wyrzisk, Poland)

June 16, 1977
Alexandria, Virginia

German-American engineer, rocket expert, and top space scientist. From 1937 to 1945, von Braun directed German rocket research and developed the V-2 liquid-fuel rocket of WWII. He began experimental work with rockets under the sponsorship of the German Rocket Society (1930), and the German Army then employed him (1932). In March, 1945, he went to Bavaria and surrendered to the US Army. He came to the US (1945) and became an American citizen (1955). He married Maria Von Quistorp on March 1, 1947. He first worked in White Sands Proving Grounds, NM, and then in Ft. Bliss, TX. In 1950, he was assigned to Redstone Arsenal, near Huntsville, AL, where he headed the Redstone guided-missile program and developed rocket engines that led to manned flights (especially the Apollo Moon flights). Van Braun was the director of NASA and the US guided missile program. He wrote *First Men to the Moon* (1960). Von Braun often spoke about his belief in the Bible, the Creator, and God.

Lloyd L. Ramseyer

Nov. 5, 1899
Normal, Illinois

June 24, 1977
New Webster, Indiana

President of Bluffton (OH) College, 1938–65. Ramseyer married Ferne Yoder on June 4, 1927. He taught high school in Heyworth, IL, from 1924–27, and was principal there until 1936. He worked at Ohio State University, 1936–38, and was very active in Mennonite activities as well as education activities in Columbus, OH, besides his accomplishments at Bluffton.

Scott T. Clark

Dec. 9, 1883
Concordia, Kansas

Aug. 27, 1977
Newberg, Oregon

First president of Friends Bible (Barclay in 1990) **College, Haviland, KS 1917–35.** Clark married Elsie Grace Coppack on September 1, 1910 (died: 1970). He was president of a Bible school in Colorado Springs, 1936–40. Clark was a dedicated teacher of Christ and education and a very effective pastor in Virginia, California, Oregon, and Idaho, 1942–61. He taught Greek at George Fox College while pastoring in Chehalem Center, OR (1952–58). He read the NT in Greek yearly and wrote *The Dynamics of the Gospel* (1972). The last ten years of his life, he attended Piedmont Friends Church in Portland, OR. He is buried in Greenleaf, ID, where he retired until 1967.

Benjamin J. Smith

Dec. 27, 1899
Barnesville, Georgia

Aug. 29, 1977
Chicago, Illinois

Bishop of Colored (Christian in 1956) **Methodist Episcopal Church, 1954–74; senior bishop, 1970–74.** Smith married Hermion Jackson on March 3, 1928. He pastored New Hope Church, Evanston, IL (1924–28); Williams Institutional Church, New York City (1928–29); Jubilee Temple, Chicago (1929–30) and Jamison Temple, Kansas City, MO (1930–35). He was general secretary of the board of religious education of the denomination, 1935–54, and became a bishop in 1954. He was active in World Council of Churches activities. He lived in Memphis in later years.

Ethel Waters

Oct. 31, 1896
Chester, Pennsylvania

Sept. 1, 1977
Chatsworth, California

Soloist, who was converted out of show business, vaudeville singer, dramatic film/TV actress, and Broadway star. Ethel was reared a Catholic. She was married at age thirteen to Merritt Purnsley (age 23). The marriage only lasted one year. She was converted the same year through evangelist R. J. Williams at a revival in Chester in 1908 in a Methodist church, but remained backslidden for 40 years. At age 21, Ethel was the first woman to sing "St. Louis Blues" professionally in a theater in Baltimore. She got her big break singing at the Plantation Club in New York City in 1923. She was first known as Baby Star and later became known as Sweet Mama Stringbean. Her film career began in 1929. In 1938, Waters gave a concert recital in Carnegie Hall. In 1957, at the Billy Graham crusade in New York she dedicated her life to the Lord and sang "His Eye Is on the Sparrow," because, she said, her "precious Jesus always had His eye on this little sparrow." She appeared in many subsequent crusades. She acted in the Christian film, *The Heart is a Rebel.* Her last words were "I love you" to Julie Harris, her assistant since 1952. Cancer, heart trouble and diabetes all took their toll on the 350-pound Ethel, and in her 80th year, she went to heaven.

Robert E. Nicholas

Nov. 14, 1882
Ontario, Canada

Sept. 5, 1977
Maywood, Illinois

Philanthropic contributor to Wheaton (IL) College. Nicholas came to the Chicago area at age 19 and entered the hardware business which expanded into the home furnishing and appliance industry. In 1914, as a 32-year-old successful businessman, his sister called him from Saskatchewan—urging him to come to the revival being held in their little village church. It was here that he dedicated his all to the Lord. He was a board member at Wheaton beginning in 1932 and served in various capacities such as vice-chairman, budget committee, investment committee, and finance committee member. He was a financial consultant and real estate developer from nearby Oak Park. He was a trustee, 1932–70. Nicholas donated the funds for the R. E. Nicholas Library whose cornerstone was laid in 1951. For 48 years, his time, talent, and finances helped to develop Wheaton College. He was perhaps the most influential layperson connected with the college. Nicholas was also a trustee of Moody Bible Institute, and director of the Oak Park Trust and Savings Bank. His wife, Mabel, died in 1991. He also developed the Oak Park Mall. Nicholas published his autobiography in 1961, *Life Has Been Good.*

Clement E. Hershey

Oct. 1912

Sept. 8, 1977
Fresno, California

Radio Bible teacher, musician, composer, and evangelist. Hershey was leader of a dance band, but started dating a Christian girl. Listening to evangelist PAUL RADER one night, he was converted. He pastored a large church in Marion, OH, continued his work as an evangelist, and had a radio ministry. He wrote the chorus, "I'm in Love with Jesus." Hershey traveled through 50 states and in 34 countries presenting the gospel. He directed a Bible teaching radio broadcast, *Bible Basics*, and presented a Bible course, "Basic Bible Truths." He was president and director of the Alaska Evangelization Society and went on many speaking trips there. He attended the world congress of the ICC in Geneva (1950) and in Amsterdam (1962).

Sam F. Pannabecker

April 15, 1896
Petoskey, Michigan

Sept. 14, 1977
Elkhart, Indiana

President of Mennonite Biblical Seminary, Chicago (Associated Mennonite Biblical Seminary, Elkhart, IN, in 1990), **1948–58**. Pannabecker married Sylvia Tschantz on August 3, 1921. After teaching science at Bluffton (OH) College (1918–23), he went to China as a missionary and educator (1923–41). He was unable to continue missionary service because of the revolution and unrest. As he left office, the school moved to Elkhart, and he continued as dean (1958–64), registrar (1964–69), and archivist (1969–77). Pannabecker authored three major publications dealing with the history of his denomination.

Joseph S. Otteson

April 27, 1893
Wolverton, Minnesota

Sept. 17, 1977
Pikeville, Kentucky

Founder and first president of Southland Evangelistic Center, 1942–46, renamed Southland Bible Institute, Wolfpit, KY 1946–61 (relocated to Ashland, KY, in 1975), because of a devastating fire at the original campus. Otteson's parents had emigrated from Norway. He left the farm for Moody Bible Institute and graduated from there in 1917. He went with Scandinavian Alliance Missions (TEAM) to India shortly thereafter marrying Esther Seeland in 1921. After 21 years of ministry there, he was invited by home missionaries in eastern Kentucky to establish a training center for mountain youth. Otteson had a radio broadcast, the *Bible Truth Hour*, 1948–77. He served as the first president of the National Home Missions Fellowship (Association of North American Missions). Otteson died in a tragic car accident.

Paul Gupta

Feb. 20, 1920
Andhra Pradesh, India

Nov. 13, 1977
Chennai (Madras), India

Founder and first president of HBI Global Partners, 1950–77. Although a brilliant student, Gupta failed in school; although a devoted son, he stole from his father; although a devout Hindu and named for a god, he lived a life of debauchery before his conversion. Gupta was raised a Hindu, but Hinduism offered him nothing. He was gloriously led to Christ by a missionary conducting a street meeting. His birth name was Nagaruru Vankateswami and, upon his conversion, he was given the name Paul. He was influenced by BAKT SINGH. He married Devi Raju on May 2, 1946. Gupta was trained in the ministry at BIOLA University, and ordained on November 25, 1950. He organized the Hindustan Bible Institute in 1952 in Madras, and by 1957, they had good facilities.

Albert E. Brumley

Oct. 29, 1905
Spiro, Oklahoma

Nov. 15, 1977
Powell, Missouri

President of Brumley-Hartford Enterprises, 1926–43, of Albert Brumley and Sons, 1943–77; music publisher and composer. From 1932–66 he was also a staff writer for Hartford (which he later bought), then Stamps-Baxter Music Companies. Brumley wrote the lyrics and music to "I'll

Fly Away," "I'll Meet You in the Morning," "Turn Your Radio On," and "This World Is Not My Home." "I'll Fly Away" was inspired in 1929, while picking cotton on a farm. Brumley married Goldie Schell on August 30, 1931. He was also a member of the Nashville Songwriters Gospel Music Association and the Country Hall of Fame. He was a Church of Christ member and composed over 600 songs. His business centered in Powell, MO.

Glenn Wagner

April 8, 1907
Washington, Illinois

Dec. 5, 1977
Ft. Myers. Florida

Outstanding football player who became educator and evangelist. In Wagner's early years, he attended the University of Illinois, where he excelled in football. He married Lucretia Bond on October 1, 1931. He was also president of Washington Bible College, Lanham, MD, from 1940–45. During those years, Wagner was very active with Pocket Testament League in the distribution of Scripture in army camps. Throughout his life, he served in various evangelistic endeavors.

Wilfred Kitching

Aug. 22, 1893
London, England

Dec. 15, 1977
Bexhall-on-sea, England

General of Salvation Army, 1954–63. Kitching was commissioned as an officer in 1914 and served for 30 years in various capacities, including service in Australia and Sweden (1946–51) and as head of evangelism activities (1951–54). Kitching married Kathleen Bristow on November 12, 1929. He was musically talented and composed many songs. His father was WILLIAM BOOTH's secretary. He wrote *Soldier of Salvation* (1967) and his autobiography, *A Goodly Heritage* (1967).

R. Gordon Spaugh

June 15, 1904
Winston-Salem, North Carolina

Dec. 24, 1977
Winston-Salem, North Carolina

President of Moravian Church in NA (South), Winston-Salem, NC 1953–68. Spaugh gave 26 years of pastoral service to Home Church, Salem, 1928–54. He married Katherine Riggan. In 1967, he was faced with many social upheavals which had their effect on the church. There were the petty rifts and financial difficulties. It was felt an era closed with his retirement. He was called to the Unity Synod in Czechoslovakia. While there, he suffered a stroke.

Henry C. Wingblade

Dec. 16, 1883
Aterville, Kansas

Dec. 30, 1977
St. Paul, Minnesota

President of Bethel College and Theological Seminary, St. Paul, MN 1941–54. After his graduation from Washburn College, Topeka, KS, in 1910, Wingblade began teaching English at Bethel Academy. He then worked his way up to the presidency of the college. During his reign as president, the college went from 123 to 500 students, the seminary from 52 to 174 students, and five new buildings were added. After his work at the school, Wingblade pastored at Trinity Baptist, New York City (1953–61), and Village Creek Baptist, Lansing, IA (1961–72). Wingblade died of cancer.

Roy G. Ross

June 25, 1898
Forest, Illinois

Jan. 8, 1978
Pompano Beach, Florida

General Secretary of National Council of Churches, 1954–63. Ross was ordained Disciples of Christ in 1920. He held pastorates in Carrollton, IL; North Cornwall, CT, and Milwaukee, WI, until 1925. He then was the national director and youth director in Washington, D.C. from 1926–28.

Ross married Elizabeth Greene on August 27, 1929. He also served as executive secretary of United Christian Missionary Society (1928–36) and general secretary of Council of Religious Education (1936–50).

Joseph D. Graber

Oct. 18, 1900
Noble, Iowa

Jan. 25, 1978
Goshen, Indiana

President of Mennonite Board of Missions (Mennonite Church USA Missions in 2002), **Elkhart, IN 1944–59**. Graber married Minnie Swartzendruber on June 28, 1925. He served in India, 1925–42. He was a prolific author on missions and exerted wide influence in his field. Graber taught missions at Goshen (IN) Biblical Seminary, 1955–63.

Merlin G. Smith

Aug. 26, 1894
Delta, Ohio

Feb. 2, 1978
Gerry, New York

President of Spring Arbor (MI) Seminary, 1926–33, of A. M. Chesebrough Seminary, North Chili, NY, 1933–45, renamed and relocated, Roberts Wesleyan College, Rochester, NY 1933–57. Smith married Emma Young on September 12, 1916. He was head of the Department of Mathematics, Physics and Astronomy at Greenville (IL) College, 1919–26. Smith was well-known in Free Methodist circles.

Paul F. Beachum

Sept. 18, 1888
Oconee County, South Carolina

Feb. 13, 1978
Greenville, South Carolina

General director of Pentecostal Holiness Church Missions, 1925–46, and president of Holmes Bible College, Greenville, SC 1919–78. Beachum married Sarah Lane on March 22, 1911. He also pastored Holmes Memorial Church, Greenville, SC, from 1919–78. Leadership of 60 years at one place is surely a record seldom matched. In 1946, he went to South Africa to inspect the work of his denomination and to plan a new Bible college.

Archer E. Anderson

Dec. 30, 1899
Elizabeth, New Jersey

Feb. 22, 1978
Helena, Montana

Pastor of First Presbyterian Church, Duluth, MN 1939–54. Anderson married Lillian Kissling on November 5, 1925 (died: May 4, 1982). He worked with Central American Missions in Guatemala, 1922–30. Anderson was ordained as a Presbyterian on October 18, 1931, and held pastorates in Texas (1931–35), Narberth, PA (1935–39), and later in New Mexico and Montana. Anderson also taught at Philadelphia School of the Bible.

George D. Strohm

June 17, 1898
Pittsburgh, Pennsylvania

Feb. 28, 1978
Goshen, Indiana

President of St. Paul (MN) Bible Institute (Crown College in 1992), **1943–59**. Strom was converted on September 30, 1917, in Dorseyville, PA at the CMA Church. He married Hazel Hodil on June 18, 1919, (died: December 1, 1975). The couple ministered in Saville, PA, (1923–25), China (1925–27), and the Philippines (1927–31). Illness curtailed his mission field activity and he became dean at SPBI (1932–40), then Nyack (NY) College (1940–43) in the same capacity. He was known for his missionary films and slides and was a gifted organizer, promoter, and developer. His World Missions Night at the Minneapolis Auditorium drew crowds up to 10,000 in a tremendous missionary evening program. He retired to Syracuse, IN, in 1965, and pastored the nearby Concord United Methodist Church.

Thomas MacDonald

May 22, 1890
Brooklyn, New York

March 10, 1978
Quarryville, Pennsylvania

General director of Bible Christian Union, 1953–66. After marrying Fannie Davis on October 10, 1914, MacDonald came under the ministry of G. P. Raud in 1916, as an engineer of great promise. In 1923, he made his first visit to believers in what was then known as White Russia (Belorussia) and Poland. He traveled widely in Eastern Europe between WWI and WWII and also in Western Europe after 1945. He succeeded the founder, G.P. Raud, in 1953 to head the mission. MacDonald inaugurated a Biennial European Workers' Conference to encourage the 112 missionaries serving in eleven countries.

Virgil P. Brock

Jan. 6, 1887
near Celina, Ohio

March 12, 1978
Leslie, Michigan

With his wife, Blanche, a singing evangelistic team and gospel hymn writers. Converted at age 16 in a revival meeting, Brock and his wife, Blanche, whom he married on September 24, 1914, traveled as evangelists and were known as the "Singing Brocks." They traveled for the Quakers throughout Indiana, 1922–36, then became independent after that. An outstanding hymn writing team, Brock wrote some 500 songs. In later years, he led the singing for the Sutera twins' campaigns. His last days were spent at Youth Haven Ranch in Rives Junction, MI. His hymns include "Beyond the Sunset," "Resting in His Love," "If You Could Know," "Sing and Smile and Pray," and "He's a Wonderful Savior to Me." His wife wrote the music to all. Brock had a Quaker background. He was an evangelist for 40 years to every state in America. Their famed grave monument in Winona Lake, IN, has the words to "Beyond the Sunset" engraved upon it.

C. Adrian Heaton

April 13, 1914
Bellevue, Michigan

March 26, 1978
Pacific Palisades, California

President of California Baptist Theological Seminary, Covina, CA 1959–74 which merged into BBDS in 1974; **and simultaneously president of Berkeley (CA) Baptist Divinity School** (American Baptist Seminary of the West in 1977), **1968–75; and of American Association of Schools of Religious Education, 1953–55.** Heaton was led to Christ by his father, a Baptist minister, in Lansing, MI, in 1920. Heaton married Ada Grooms on September 13, 1938. He served on the faculty of Northern Baptist Seminary (1940–47); was on the staff of MBI (1943–47); and was a professor of Christian Education at Eastern Baptist Seminary, Philadelphia, PA (1947–59). A massive cardiac arrest on December 14, 1970 resulted in his being hospitalized for eight months.

Eugene S. Briggs

Feb. 1, 1890
Howard County, Missouri

April 25, 1978
Edmond, Oklahoma

President of Phillips University, Tulsa, OK, 1938–61. Briggs married Mary Gentry on August 19, 1914. Prior to 1938, he served as president of Christian College, Columbia, MO; Missouri State Department of Education, and the State Teachers College, Durant, OK. When Briggs arrived at Phillips, the school was suffering from the Depression. With planned foresight toward the school's potential, he embarked on a growth plan to meet the demands of the day. His remarkable building program included the Enid Building, Clay Hall, Earl Butts Dorm, Science Building, Student Center, Fine Arts Building, and the Marshall Building, among the total of 15 new buildings and wing additions. Briggs was known as the builder president, because so many construction projects were carried on during his administration. The school also doubled its enrollment. He was an insurance executive for many years.

Herbert J. Taylor

April 18, 1893
Pickford, Michigan

May 1, 1978
Park Ridge, Illinois

Manufacturing company executive of Chicago as president of Club Aluminum Company, 1933–52, and chairman of the Board, 1952–68. Taylor married Gloria Forbrich on June 21, 1919, and later, Ramona Lockhart. He began in the real estate business in Pauls Valley, OK, from 1919–24. He then moved to Barrington, IL, to work at Jewel Tea Company, 1924–33, as an assistant to the president. He authored *The Four Way Test* adopted by Rotary International of which he was president, 1954–55. Taylor was Methodist and served as the Billy Graham Chicago Crusade chairman in 1962.

Basil W. Miller

Feb. 26, 1897
Laconia, Indiana

May 7, 1978
Pasadena, California

First director of World Wide Missions, Pasadena, CA 1957–78. Miller was converted at age 12 via Evangelist David Hill in Oklahoma City where the family had moved. He married Esther Kirk on August 16, 1921. Miller was a Nazarene journalist and writer for both juveniles and adults. He pastored in Chicago, IL; Pittsburgh, PA; New York, NY; and Pasadena, CA. He was a member of the faculty of Pasadena (CA) College. Miller wrote several biographies and history books, as well.

William Rice
Bill Rice

Aug. 25, 1912
Dundee, Texas

May 29, 1978
Murfreesboro, Tennessee

Evangelist and founder of the Bill Rice Ranch (summer camp/conference and deaf ministry), **Murfreesboro, 1953.** Rice was orphaned as a teenager. He worked for three years, 1938–41, on the MBI evangelistic staff, then had a nationwide ministry of his own, starting in 1941. He pastored in Gainesville, TX (1935–37), and Dubuque, IA (1939–41). He and his wife, Cathy Widner, were married in 1936 and they had a deaf daughter. They founded the 1,500-acre ranch where he was the "cowboy" director. Rice edited the *Branding Iron*. He assisted his brother, JOHN RICE, in editing the *Sword of the Lord*. Rice was incapacitated his last two years and died in his bed at home from a stroke. His son, Bill Rice III, carried on the ministry.

Glenn Schunk

Feb. 3, 1918
Freeport, Illinois

June 6, 1978
South Bend, Indiana

Widely used evangelist. Schunk was converted from Catholicism in 1943. He graduated from Bob Jones University in 1950 where he worked on the school radio station, WMUU, writing and acting in radio plays and having parts in two of the University films. Schunk resigned all positions in February, 1956 to enter full-time evangelism as an Independent Baptist. He held crusades across the country. He was a good friend of Pillsbury Baptist Bible College.

Luther W. Youngdahl

May 29, 1896
Minneapolis, Minnesota

June 21, 1978
Washington, D.C.

Governor of Minnesota, 1947–51. Youngdahl married Irene E. Engdahl on June 23, 1923. He served in WWI. He was assistant city attorney in Minneapolis, MN (1921–23); then practiced law with Judge Tifft (1923–30); was a municipal court judge (1930–36); district court judge

(1936–42) and then associate justice with the Minnesota Supreme Court (1942-46). He was a federal judge for the U.S. District Court of D.C. (1951-66) and a senior judge (1966-78). Youngdahl was a dedicated Lutheran and spoke at many Christian functions. He is buried in Arlington National Cemetery.

Walter F. Barfoot

Oct. 17, 1893
Collingwood, Ontario, Canada

June 28, 1978
Kerrisdale, British Columbia, Canada

Primate of the Anglican Church of Canada, 1951-58. Barfoot was active in WWI, 1916-19, in France, serving as a captain. He was a tutor and professor of apologetics at the University of Emmanuel College in Saskatoon, Saskatchewan, 1926–34. He also served as canon of St. John's Cathedral in Winnipeg, Manitoba (1934–41), and bishop of Edmonton, Alberta (1941–51). He spent his retirement in California and British Columbia. His funeral was at St. Mary's Church in Kerrisdale.

Robert G. Lee

Nov. 11, 1886
Fort Mill, South Carolina

July 20, 1978
Memphis, Tennessee

President of Southern Baptist Convention, 1949–51, and pastor of Bellevue Baptist Church, Memphis, TN 1927–60. Born in a log cabin, Lee was baptized on August 5, 1898, in the Fort Mill Baptist Church, following his conversion in a July revival meeting. Lee married Bula Gentry on November 28, 1913. He pastored in Edgefield, SC (1919–21); at FBC, New Orleans, LA (1921–25) and at Citadel Square Baptist Church, Charleston, SC (1925–57). His 32-year ministry at Bellevue had a membership growth from 1,739 to 9,469. Lee baptized 7,649 converts and received 24,071 new members. One of Lee's greatest sermons was "Pay-day, Some Day." He preached that sermon 1,275 times, resulting in some 10,000 conversions. He was known for his great pulpit oratory. He authored 50 books from *Feet to Fathoms* (1926) to *If I Were a Jew* (1977).

Myron F. Boyd

July 19, 1909
Shelbyville, Illinois

July 31, 1978
St. Louis, Missouri

Bishop of Free Methodist Church, 1964–76; chairman of National Religious Broadcasters, 1954–56; president of National Association of Evangelicals, 1972–73; and National Holiness Association, 1954–58, 1968–71, renamed Christian Holiness Association (Christian Holiness Partnership in 1997), **1971–72**. Boyd married Ruth Putnam on June 28, 1932. He was converted as a teen in Greenville, IL. He pastored in Florida and British Columbia, 1932–48. Boyd was the speaker on the *Light and Life Hour*, a worldwide radio program, 1945–65. He wrote *To Tell the World* (1964).

Robert T. Ketcham

July 22, 1889
Nelson, Pennsylvania

Aug. 21, 1978
Chicago, Illinois

National representative for GARB, 1948–60, and president of ACC, 1944–47. Ketcham was converted on February 16, 1910 at the Galeton (PA) Baptist Church. He married Clara Hasker on November 4, 1912 (died: 1920), and Mary Smart on June 1, 1922. He had limited eyesight since 1913, suffering from conical cornea, so he remained near blindness (90 per cent) throughout his ministry. Ketcham held pastorates at Baptist churches in Roulette, PA (1912–15); Brookville, PA (1915–19); Butler, PA (1919–23) and Niles, OH (1923–27). He withdrew from the Northern Baptist Convention in 1928, then continued pastoring in Elyria, OH (1928–32); Central Baptist in Gary, IN (1932–39), and Walnut Street. Baptist in Waterloo, IA (1939–48). The church in Gary, IN had 900 additions under his pastorship. He wrote several books and was a founder of the GARB in 1932. He edited the *Baptist Bulletin* (1938–55). He was a national consultant for the GARB, 1960–66. Ketcham had seen 13,000 converts and 598 people into Christian work from his different pastorates. He had a major heart attack in May, 1959, and two major strokes on December 9, 1976 and June 30, 1978. His funeral was at the Belden Avenue Baptist Church in Chicago.

William H. Neff

Dec. 4, 1902 — *Aug. 25, 1978*
McKeesport, Pennsylvania — Greensboro, North Carolina

General superintendent of Pilgrim Holiness Church (Wesleyan Church in 1968), **1955–66**. Neff was ordained in 1927 by the Ohio district of Pilgrim Holiness. Neff pastored in Winchester, OH; Radford, VA; Pasadena, CA; and Battle Creek, MI. He was the district superintendent of the California-Arizona area (1935–45) and of North Carolina (1949–54). Neff served his church as an evangelist both in America and abroad. His wife's name was Jean.

Robert W. (Bob) Pierce

Oct. 8, 1914 — *Sept. 6, 1978*
Fort Dodge, Iowa — Duarte, California

Founder and first president of World Vision, 1950–67, and of Samaritan's Purse, 1970–78. Pierce's work was unparalleled in compassion for suffering humanity. He traveled by airplane often to a needy area, taking pictures of earthquakes, famines, and wars, bringing his pictures back to the states to raise finances for aid. He married Lorraine Johnson on November 24, 1936. He was ordained a Baptist in 1940, after several years in Nazarene circles. He also founded Worldwide Pictures at Duarte, CA. He directed Seattle YFC and took trips to China, 1947 and 1949. Pierce also held crusades in Tokyo, Manila, etc. In Korea, 1950, he saw a starving child, lying at the door of a Lutheran orphanage—there was no room for her. When he protested, the director placed the little girl in his arms and said, "What are you going to do about it?" He "adopted" her for $10 a month, went home, and World Vision was born. By 1965, over 65,000 children in 20 countries were being supported this way. He spent 1968–69 in a Swiss hospital, completely exhausted. He died of leukemia (diagnosed in 1973) after complete "burn out" in the City of Hope Hospital. Seldom has there lived a man who could better challenge an audience to involvement on behalf of those "who no one cares about."

"I have seen what breaks the heart of God."

Eppling Reinhartz

June 21, 1901 — *Sept. 14, 1978*
East Liverpool, Ohio — White Rock, South Carolina

President of Lutheran Theological Southern Seminary, Columbia, SC 1961–70. Reinhartz was ordained a Lutheran in 1929, and married Isabella Martin on June 27, 1930. He succeeded his father as pastor of St. John's Evangelical Lutheran, E. Liverpool, OH (1930–38), and served on the staff of the United Lutheran Church (1938–45) as general secretary, statistician, archivist, and necrologist (1947–60).

Robert W. Frank

Sept. 17, 1890 — *Sept. 23, 1978*
Greencastle, Indiana — Denver, Colorado

President of McCormick Theological Seminary, Chicago, IL 1947–56. Frank married Grace Haun (June 17, 1913) and Edna Kolls (August 9, 1921). He was ordained as a Presbyterian on April 18, 1916. Frank pastored at Marengo, IL (1917–19), and Harvard, IL (1919–20). He went to Presbyterian Theological Seminary in 1920 to teach sociology, religious education, philosophy of religion, and Christian ethics.

W. Shelburne Brown

Jan. 13, 1918
Olivet, Illinois

Oct. 3, 1978
San Diego, California

President of Pasadena (CA) College, 1964–73, renamed and relocated, Point Loma (Nazarene University in 1998) **College, San Diego, CA 1973–78**. Brown was married to Lois Jarzyna on March 25, 1940. He pastored in Carson City, NV; Banning, CA, and Alhambra, CA, from 1942–52. He also served as superintendent of the Los Angeles District of the Church of the Nazarene, 1952–64. During his tenure as college president, the student body increased from 1,201 to 1,905. Through his vision and leadership, the college was moved from Pasadena to San Diego. He died following a ten-month illness caused by a malignant tumor on the optic nerve.

Harold K. Sheets

March 29, 1903
Detroit, Kansas

Oct. 8, 1978

General superintendent of Wesleyan Methodist Church in America (Wesleyan Church in 1968), **1959–68**. Sheets married Miriam Niesley in 1927 and had three daughters. He pastored in Pasadena, CA (1931–34); Ottawa, KS (1934–36); was a Kansas Missionary (1936–38) and pastored First WMC, Enid, OK (1938–45). He was head of the denomination's youth ministries (1945–55) and general home missions secretary (1955–59).

Anders Nygren

Nov. 18, 1890
Gothenburg, Sweden

Oct. 20, 1978
Lund, Sweden

President of Lutheran World Federation, 1947–52. Nygren was eight years in parish ministry joining the faculty of Lund University, 1924–48, as professor of systematic theology. He was considered Sweden's greatest theologian of his time. He was bishop of Lund, 1949–58.

Royal Brougham

Sept. 17, 1894
St. Louis, Missouri

Oct. 30, 1978
Seattle, Washington

Sports reporter in Seattle, for 40 years, who had an outstanding testimony. Brougham married Alice Swanson on April 14, 1915. He became a reporter for the *Post-Intelligence* in Seattle, WA. He was promoted to managing editor (1911) and to associate editor (1925). Brougham funded a foundation and belonged to Sigma Delta Chi and Rotary Clubs.

James L. Fowle

Oct. 14, 1897
Washington, North Carolina

Nov. 13, 1978
Chattanooga, Tennessee

President of Chattanooga (TN) Bible Institute, 1935–78. Fowle married Katherine Ferguson on January 26, 1925 (died: May 1950). He pastored the Central Presbyterian Church, St. Louis, MO, from 1923–28, and was a leader in the BILLY SUNDAY campaign there during this time. He pastored the First Presbyterian Church, Chattanooga, TN, for nearly 40 years, 1928–66. Along with Lee Roberson, Fowle was a prominent Chattanooga Christian and civic leader, with a scholarly approach to Scripture. He was active in many community programs. Ben Haden paid him high compliments at a dinner in his honor for the impact he had on Haden's life.

Paul B. Peterson

Feb. 11, 1895
Chicago, Illinois

Dec. 8, 1978
Pasadena, California

Director of Eastern European Mission (Eurovision in 1985, then merged with Slavic Gospel Association in 1989), **1927–78**. Peterson ministered in ten European nations in radio, literature, and relief work. He married Signe Anderson on June 2, 1922. He spent his life helping Russians and Eastern Europeans, starting work with the Russian Missionary Society in 1922 and serving in Poland and Latvia, 1924–26. He co-founded the EEM with Herbert Schmidt and C. W. Swanson. Peterson moved from Chicago, IL, to Pasadena, CA, in 1952.

Cecil B. Day

Dec. 10, 1934
Savannah, Georgia

Dec. 15, 1978
Atlanta, Georgia

One of the most successful Christian businessman ever. Son of a Baptist minister, Day's father died when he was 15. He married Uldine Smith on July 16, 1953. He graduated from Georgia Tech in 1958 and went into real estate. Soon he owned a million dollars worth of land and income property. In 1969, he sold his holdings for 14 million dollars, the largest single real estate transaction in Georgia history at that time. He built his first motel on Tybee Island, connected by a bridge to Savannah. He refused to sell or house alcoholic beverages on his sites. With employees building inns, Day spent three years visiting three banks a day. In eight years, he had 301 motels with 42,000 rooms. Founder of the Days Inn motel chain, his wife sold the company for $639 million to the Reliance Capital Group in 1984. He was active in Dunwoody (GA) Baptist Church. Bone cancer would take his life while in his prime at age 44.

Clifford E. Barbour

Jan. 26, 1895
Pittsburgh, Pennsylvania

Jan. 10, 1979
Maryville, Tennessee

President of Western Theological Seminary, 1951–59, and of Pittsburgh (PA) Theological Seminary, 1959–62 (as Pittsburgh-Xenia Seminary merged with WTS in 1959). Barbour married Laura Taber (June 28, 1922) and Alice Patton (August 2, 1950). He was ordained and pastored at a Presbyterian Church in Knoxville, TN from 1928–51. He also served as dean of the Religion School at the University of Tennessee, 1933–51. He wrote two books in 1930: *Sin and the New Psychology* and *Young People's Department of Graded Material*.

Everett J. Fulton

Oct. 6, 1893
Ottawa, Ohio

Jan. 17, 1979
Jamesville, Wisconsin

Open Bible Church leader; chairman of Pentecostal Fellowship of North America, 1954–56; president of Eugene (OR) Bible College, and pastor of Lighthouse Temple, Eugene, OR 1934–47 (pastored there again 1956–60). He married Pauline Smyly on June 16, 1921, and pastored in such places as Martinez, CA; Dayton, OH, and Portland, OR, from 1926–79. Fulton served as president of Open Bible Standard Churches (1947–53), and of Open Bible College, Des Moines, IA (merged into EBC in 1986) (1960–65). He remained in good health until 15 hours before his death when breathing difficulties hospitalized him.

Mark Peachey

Oct. 23, 1916
Salisbury, Pennsylvania

Feb. 6, 1979
Louisville, Kentucky

First president of Conservative Mennonite Board of Missions/Charities, Irwin, OH 1954–68. Peachey married Fannie Beitzel on December 22, 1939. He lived on a farm, 1939–57, in Rosedale, OH, and was active in the United Bethel Mennonite Church, Plain City, OH. Peachey later lived in Harrisonberg, WV, and Louisville, KY. He was president of the Mennonite Fellowship, 1975–79. He died of leukemia.

Arthur M. Rogers

Feb. 12, 1911
Rock Hill, South Carolina

Feb. 18, 1979
Anderson, North Carolina

Stated clerk of Associate Reformed Presbyterian Church, Greenville, SC 1954–71. Converted at age twelve, Rogers helped in an Atlanta, GA, church (1933) then in a White Oak, SC, church (1934). From 1935–43, he ministered in Memphis, TN. Rogers married Katherine Whiteside on June 20, 1941. He moved to Barstow, FL (1943), then to Chester, SC (1950). He later pastored at Young Memorial, Anderson, SC. He died after a brief illness.

Edward C. Fendt

Feb. 17, 1904
Michigan City, Indiana

March 14, 1979
Columbus, Ohio

Dean of Evangelical Lutheran (Trinity Lutheran in 1978) Theological Seminary, Columbus, OH, 1946–59, and president, 1959–71. Fendt was also an instructor of Bible at Capital University, 1929–36, and professor of theology in 1936. He compiled *What Lutherans Are Thinking*.

Alfred W. Ruscoe

Dec. 20, 1897
Birmingham, England

March 14, 1979
Fort Washington, Pennsylvania

Secretary of World-Wide Evangelization Crusade of North America, 1936–60. Ruscoe was converted in a foxhole during WWI in France in 1917. Ruscoe was a missionary in the Congo and Nigeria, 1920–29. From 1933–35, he toured throughout Africa. He later went to Canada and founded the branch of WEC in North America in 1936. Ruscoe married Ellen Hellesen on November 11, 1941. Ruscoe was a member of the Reformed Episcopalian Church.

Lloyd R. Day

Oct. 12, 1905

March 21, 1979
Indianapolis, Indiana

President of God's Bible School, Cincinnati, OH 1950–62. Day attended school at GBS and the University of Cincinnati. He taught in the high school there until 1938. He became the principal, 1938–50. He commenced his leadership at GBS with a 1 million-dollar indebtedness which he greatly reduced. He inaugurated the Alumni Association and put staff and faculty in the Social Security program. After eating a noon meal with his wife, Dixie, transplanting flowers, he died suddenly of a heart attack.

Axel B. Ost

June 2, 1888
Darlarna, Sweden

April 7, 1979
Salem, Oregon

First general director of Christian Fellowship Union, McAllen, TX 1945–66. Ost came with his family at age ten to America. While attending North Park College and the University of

Chicago, he met Martha Lundell, whom he married on May 28, 1912. His eighth child was JOHN OST. From 1912–20, he pastored and then became an evangelist under the Evangelical Covenant Church. In 1927, he began to write in the *Mission Friend*. Later he traveled as an independent evangelist. Often he drove for days hauling a tent, and when he arrived in a town, he would set the tent up and preach the same night. Ost and his wife had nine children. In 1943, he visited Cuba, the Dominican Republic and Haiti, and in 1944, he visited Mexico. Ost built his first church in Texas in 1945. By 1948, the work had reached into Mexico. A gifted linguist, Ost taught himself Spanish in the midnight hours. He was 56 when he began this outreach work. He won hundreds to Christ and was loved by all who knew him.

Charles B. Booth

Dec. 26, 1887
Brooklyn, New York

April 15, 1979
San Diego, California

General of Volunteers of America, 1948–58. Booth married Naomi Bailey in January, 1913 (died: 1925), and Betsy I. Ross on September 8, 1927. He held general secretary positions in the movement across the nation. Charles was the son of BALLINGTON BOOTH. In addition to Booth's prison ministry, he was an involved Mason. He lived in LaMesa, CA.

Hiram S. Scates

Aug. 25, 1907
McKenzie, Tennessee

April 17, 1979
Memphis, Tennessee

Stated clerk of Cumberland Presbyterian Church, Memphis, TN 1955–75. Scates taught in public schools in Tennessee, Arkansas, Missouri, and Texas, 1925–48. He was ordained to the Cumberland Presbyterian Church in 1931. Scates married Erma Johnson on November 25, 1932. He pastored in Calico Park, AR (1936–40); Marshall, MO (1940–42); Dallas (1944–50); Fresno, CA (1950–54), and Memphis, TN (1954–55).

Wilbour E. Saunders

Sept. 20, 1894
Warwick, Rhode Island

May 12, 1979
Webster, New York

President of Colgate-Rochester (NY) Divinity School, 1949–60. Saunders married Mildred Paige on September 22, 1919 (died: 1950), and Esther Gosnell on January 2, 1952. Saunders was ordained Baptist. He held several pastorates, including FBC of Rahway, NY (1923–27); Marchy Ave., Brooklyn, NY (1927–32) and FBC of Rochester, NY (1966–68). He served in education positions, 1933–48. Saunders lived in Webster, NY.

Oscar J. Naumann

June 24, 1909
Wood Lake, Minnesota

June 19, 1979
Milwaukee, Wisconsin

President of Evangelical Lutheran Joint Synod of Wisconsin and other states, 1953–59, renamed Wisconsin Evangelical Lutheran Synod, 1959–79. Naumann married Dorothy Schwarz on September 5, 1936 and they had seven children. He pastored in Toledo, OH (1936–40); served as professor at Dr. Martin Luther College, New Ulm, NM (1940–46) and pastored in St. John's Lutheran Church, St. Paul, Minnesota (1946–59).

J. Barton Payne

Sept. 12, 1922
San Francisco, California

June 30, 1979
Mount Fuji, Japan

Executive secretary of American Association of Christian Schools, 1946–50; secretary of Evangelical Theological Society, 1955–61; and president of the same, 1966. Payne was ordained Evangelical Free and Reformed Presbyterian. He was a professor of OT at Bob Jones

University, Wheaton Graduate School, Trinity Evangelical Divinity School, and Covenant Theological School. He was involved in several archaeological expeditions in Palestine. Payne also worked on the NIV Bible. He died in a fall while mountain climbing, following a sabbatical spent lecturing throughout Asia and teaching Bible with his wife, Dorothy, in India.

Nathan L. Bailey

Oct. 5, 1909
Wilmington, Delaware

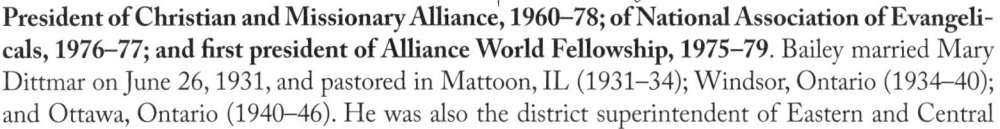

July 10, 1979
near Nottingham, England

President of Christian and Missionary Alliance, 1960–78; of National Association of Evangelicals, 1976–77; and first president of Alliance World Fellowship, 1975–79. Bailey married Mary Dittmar on June 26, 1931, and pastored in Mattoon, IL (1931–34); Windsor, Ontario (1934–40); and Ottawa, Ontario (1940–46). He was also the district superintendent of Eastern and Central Canada (1946–60) and their national vice president (1954–60). From 1963–76, he was president of World Relief Commission. He died following an automobile accident between Nottingham and Ashby at 4:45 p.m. Two heart attacks followed as doctors worked over his crushed chest. He died at 7:30 p.m. He is buried in Nyack, NY.

Leslie R. Marston

Sept. 24, 1894
Maple Ridge, Michigan

July 14, 1979
Warsaw, Indiana

Bishop of Free Methodist Church, 1935–64; president of Greenville (IL) College, 1927–36; and of National Association of Evangelicals, 1944–46. Marston married Lila Thompson on August 16, 1921. He began teaching at Greenville in 1920, then became dean, 1921–26. Marston also served as chairman of the World Relief Commission, 1950–59. He retired in 1964, having never served as a pastor, which is unusual for a FM bishop. Marston authored several books from *Emotions of Young Children* (1925) to *Living Witness* (1960).

John G. Diefenbaker

Sept. 18, 1895
Neustadt, Ontario, Canada

Aug. 16, 1979
Ottawa, Ontario, Canada

Prime minister of Canada, 1957–63, and leader of the opposition, 1963–67. Diefenbaker was a Baptist and a Mason. Diefenbaker married Edna Brower on June 29, 1929 (died: 1951), and Olive Palmer in 1953 (died: December, 1976). He became a lawyer in Saskatchewan (1919), then in British Columbia (1951), in Alberta (1954) and in Upper Canada (1959). He practiced in Prince Albert, Saskatchewan, 1922–57. Diefenbaker also served in the House of Commons, 1950–64, opposed Britain's entry into the European Common Market and refused to equip missiles with nuclear warheads. From 1957–79, he was a member of the Queen's Privy Council of Canada and of the Imperial Privy Council. He wrote *One Canada* (1977). He launched the development of Canada's vast Arctic lands.

William (Billy) R. McCarrell

Feb. 8, 1886
Chicago, Illinois

Aug. 25, 1979
New Port Richey, Florida

Founder, president of Independent Fundamental Churches of America, 1933–35, 1946–49, and executive secretary of the same, 1933, 1935–40. McCarrell was converted in 1904. He was ordained as a Congregationalist on June 14, 1905. McCarrell pastored the Cicero (IL) Bible Church, 1913–60 and directed the building of an auditorium, which was built in 1929 to seat 1,500 and married Minnie Mense on October 14. He was known as "God's Big Fisherman" because of his soul-winning efforts. He founded the Fisherman's Club, which won 64,927 people to Christ, in its first 18 years, then spread to 81 different cities. He was a founder of the Bible Church movement and also taught personal evangelism at MBI. McCarrell was a trustee of Wheaton (IL) College and Pacific Garden Mission. He and the IFCA left the ICC in 1953, after eleven years of participation.

Arthur S. DeMoss

Oct. 26, 1925　　　　　　　　　　　　　　　　　　　　　　　　　　　　　　　　Sept. 1, 1979
Albany, New York　　　　　　　　　　　　　　　　　　　　　　　　Philadelphia, Pennsylvania

Soul winner and president of National Liberty Corporation of Valley Forge, PA, a mail-order health insurance company. DeMoss, according to *Fortune Magazine*, gave nearly half his salary to Christian causes. He was converted on October 13, 1950 under the preaching of HYMAN APPELMAN in an Albany, NY, crusade. DeMoss married Nancy Sossomon on November 30, 1957. He died of a heart attack while playing tennis with his son. At his funeral, 300 stood up indicating that they had come to Christ through his witnessing. His foundation continued, under his wife's leadership.

Paul C. Empie

Feb. 10, 1909　　　　　　　　　　　　　　　　　　　　　　　　　　　　　　　　Sept. 1, 1979
St. Johnsville, New York　　　　　　　　　　　　　　　　　　　　　　Zionville, Pennsylvania

Executive director of National Lutheran Council (in USA in 1967), **1948–66**. Empie married Katharine Smith on December 27, 1930. He organized a mission church in Philadelphia, pastoring there until 1937. Empie was the superintendent of the Lutheran Home for Orphans and Aged in Germantown, PA (1937–41); secretary of Benevolence of Pennsylvania ministerium of the United Lutheran Church (1941–44); and the assistant national director (1944–48). Empie also served on the staff of the USA national commission World Lutheran Federation, 1967–72.

Winnie Bonner

Nov. 14, 1919　　　　　　　　　　　　　　　　　　　　　　　　　　　　　　　　Sept. 3, 1979
Sylhet, East Pakistan　　　　　　　　　　　　　　　　　　　　　　　　　　　　　India

Indian leader in Youth for Christ. Winnie was converted in 1942 in her last year of college alone on a hilltop. At the first YFC rally in Calcutta, India, she dedicated her life to the Lord and became YFC's secretary in 1947. In 1949, she became an evangelist. Bonner preached in all the prisons in Japan in 1953. She also started Bible clubs in Delhi and Hyderabad in 1959. In 1976, she went to England to work with Asians but returned to India for rest and treatment for health problems. Bonner was a powerful speaker with a tender heart.

Gayle F. Lewis

Nov. 14, 1898　　　　　　　　　　　　　　　　　　　　　　　　　　　　　　　　Sept. 7, 1979
Elgin, Pennsylvania　　　　　　　　　　　　　　　　　　　　　　　　Springfield, Missouri

Chairman of Pentecostal Fellowship of North America, 1956–59, and general superintendent of Assemblies of God, 1952–53. Lewis was converted at age 16 and later married Mary Stevenson on May 31, 1917. Lewis was ordained in 1923 and pastored Assembly of God churches in Ohio: Austinburgh (1921–24), Conneaut (1924–27), and Canton (1927–30). He was the superintendent of Central District, 1930–45, traveling to 55 countries to preach the gospel. He also served as general superintendent of the denomination, 1945–66.

Milo C. Ross

Jan. 17, 1911　　　　　　　　　　　　　　　　　　　　　　　　　　　　　　　　Sept. 13, 1979
Salem, Oregon　　　　　　　　　　　　　　　　　　　　　　　　　　　　Medford, Oregon

President of George Fox College (University), **Newberg, OR, 1954–71**. During his years as a Friends pastor, Ross and his first wife Helen, started churches in Talent and Medford, OR. He also pastored in Rosedal, OR; Greenleaf, IL; and Seattle, WA. For seven years, he was minister for *Quaker Hour,* a radio program of the Friends Church, started in 1953. During his tenure at GFU, the enrollment more than doubled and six new buildings were constructed. His second wife, Alice, joined him in a tour of 24 nations, 1967–68. He pastored the Reedwood Friends Church, Portland, commencing in 1970.

Bessie Traber

March 1, 1889
Perry, New York

Sept. 15, 1979
Abington, Pennsylvania

First general director of the Bible Club Movement, Upper Darby, PA, 1936–62. Bessie was educated at Vassar and the University of Pennsylvania. Traber spent three and a half years in the Philippine Islands, where children's clubs began. She then went to Philadelphia, where she had her first meeting in October, 1936, and eight boys were saved on that occasion. Her associate was Bernice Jordan.

Allen R. Blegen

July 12, 1905
Decorah, Iowa

Sept. 21, 1979
Wheaton, Illinois

Outstanding Lutheran radio evangelist and pastor. He married Francis Parker on June 22, 1927. Blegen pastored in Lisbon, IL, 1930–37, converted by reading his Bible and heeding his pastor at confirmation. He trained in Minneapolis and then went to Elgin, I, in 1937, where he began his lifelong ministry. Blegen was an evangelical spokesman for the American Lutheran Church. He founded and led the Lutheran Bible Institute, Chicago (1939–50), and directed Elgin Youth for Christ (1948–55). In 1955, he pastored the Immanuel Lutheran Church of Chicago. His newsletter was *The Work Alone*. His broadcast for years was *The Lutheran Gospel Hour*. Outside of WALTER MAIER, he may have been the leading evangelical Lutheran spokesman of his generation.

John Zoller

Oct. 17, 1889
Rodney, Ontario, Canada

Sept. 27, 1979
Shelby, Michigan

Early radio evangelist of "America Back to God" and pastor of the Zoller Gospel Tabernacle in Detroit. Zoller married Ora Irwin on November 21, 1919 (died: 1984). He had intended to be a doctor, but an evangelistic series in Sebewaing, MI, brought him to Christ and changed his goals. He worked with the CMA among the Indians in New Mexico from about 1924–30. He then pastored a Wesleyan Methodist Church in Detroit in the early 1930s. Zoller started the radio program, *America Back to God* on WJR in Detroit around 1934, and continued until his death. Ezra Mistele (Coal & Coke Company), became an early sponsor while Douglas Hine helped with music and business. From 1934–38, he helped out at a Baptist church. He then founded the ZGT and for nearly 20 years, 1938–57, he pastored and broadcast the services. On April 15, 1938, he held a Good Friday service at Olympia Stadium that drew some 13,000 with hundreds converted. The church (tabernacle) was started June 12, 1938. It had 800 members in its first couple of years. Soon, thousands attended his church and he had a mailing list of 60,000. ABTG featured radio, printed literature, prayer groups, and mass meetings. In the late 1950s, Zoller moved to Stony Lake, MI (mailing address in New Era), where a staff of six kept his broadcast on some 38 stations with printed materials going out. He held evangelistic crusades across the country. After he left the pastorate, his ministry was known as "Christ for Everyone." Zoller died in a hospital from a heart attack.

Noel O. Perkin

Jan. 15, 1893
London, England

Oct. 3, 1979
Springfield, Missouri

Executive director of Assembly of God Foreign Missions, 1927–59, and president of EFMA, 1959–61. Perkins went to Canada and was a banker in Toronto. He then served in Argentina, 1918–21, as an independent missionary. He married Ora Blanchard on August 16, 1922. Perkins served two pastorates in western New York, 1922–26. His 32-year leadership took the fledgling Assembly of God work and made it into a leader in world evangelism.

C. Gordon Brownville

Jan. 28, 1898
Quincy, Massachusetts

Oct. 10, 1979
Delray Beach, Florida

Pastor of Tremont Temple in Boston, MA, 1935–1945, 1961–66. Brownville married Elizabeth Miller on November 7, 1921 (died: 1985), and was ordained a Baptist on March 29, 1928. Brownville pastored in Philadelphia, PA (1928–30); at FBC, Asbury Park, NJ (1930–35); at 10th Ave. Baptist, Los Angeles, CA (1947–52); in Binghamton, NY, and in Richmond, VA (1954–61). His first book was *Romance of the Future* (1938).

Tsu-Chen Chao

Feb. 14, 1888
Deqing, Zhejian, Chekiang Province, China

Nov. 21, 1979
Beijing, China

President of World Council of Churches, 1948–51, theologian and educator. After studying at Vanderbilt University, Chao returned to China to teach in Sochow University, 1917–25. He then became a professor of philosophy at Yenching University in Peking (1926), becoming dean (1928) until the early 1950s when removed. Chao was a delegate in the International Missionary Council in Jerusalem (1928) and in Madras (1938). He was ordained an Anglican and was opposed by Communist students in 1952, possibly suffering from the Cultural Revolution. He lived for many years in Peking. Some reports indicate he lost his faith before his death.

Glenn A. Reece

Oct. 26, 1902
Stanton Co., Kansas

Nov. 28, 1979
Wilmington, Ohio

General secretary of Friends United Meeting, Richmond, IN 1957–67. Raised in Quaker teaching, Reece married Velma Leonard on December 21, 1924. He pastored Friends United Churches, 1930–44 in Alva, OK; Glen Elder, K, and Central City, NE. He then went to Plainfield, IN, where he was superintendent of Western Yearly Meeting, 1944–57. After his leadership role, he pastored in Sabina, OH, from 1967–68 and New Vienna, OH, where he died of cancer.

Charles L. Taylor

Jan. 27, 1901
Hartford, Connecticut

Dec. 12, 1979
Nellsley Hills, Massachusetts

President of Episcopal Divinity School, Cambridge, MA 1944–56; of American Association of Theological Schools, 1954–56; and executive secretary of the same, 1956–66. Taylor married Hannah Chamberlin on June 14, 1924 (died: 1972), and Margaret Bennett on May 4, 1974; they had seven children. He was a professor of Old Testament at EDS from 1925–56. Taylor pastored at St. Gabriel's Episcopal Church in Marion, MA, from 1931–44.

Marion C. Patterson

Dec. 29, 1899
near Jamestown, New York

Dec. 13, 1979

President of Practical Bible Training School, 1961–70. Patterson had been vice president since 1929. He married Mary A. Nestor in 1924 (died: June 16, 1974). He was not the preacher that his predecessors were (JOHN and GORDON DAVIS), but delighted in the business end of the school. It was largely through Patterson's financial genius that the mortgage was paid off on the 33 acres where the school moved in 1910. With this accomplishment, the Lord guided Patterson in funding a building project to replace the dilapidated facilities that came with the property (previously the White City Amusement Park). Patterson was instrumental in raising huge sums of money for the school.

Richard H. Wilmer

April 13, 1918
Ancon, Panama

c 1980

President (dean) of Berkeley Divinity School, New Haven, CT 1957–1969. Wilmer married Elizabeth Green (June 6, 1942) and Sarah King (August 2, 1969). He was ordained in the Episcopal Church in 1942. He served St. John's Church, Mt. Ranier, MD (1942–45); was a navy chaplain (1945–46); was chaplain and professor of Bible at University of the South, Sewanee, TN (1948–53), and ministered to Yale University students in New Haven, CT (1953–57). From 1970–80, he was professor of religious studies at the University of Pittsburgh. He authored *The Doctrine of the Church in the English Reformation* (1952).

Elizabeth Davis George

1879
Texas

1980

Church planter-missionary to Liberia and founder of the Elizabeth Davis Native Interior Mission. Rejected by Texas Baptist leaders because she was black, George obtained backing from the National Baptist Convention and arrived in Liberia in 1914. In 1919, a British businessman proposed marriage, which she accepted. His support was her means to stay in Africa. She served as an evangelist and church planter for more than half a century and founded the Bible Industrial Academy. Her husband died in 1939. She then became independent, relying on small contributions given through Elizabeth Davis George Clubs. By the 1960s, the Elizabeth George Baptist Association had 27 churches. When she reached her 90s, she turned the work over to the Liberians and retired to Austin, Texas.

Herbert B. Shaw

Feb. 9, 1908
Wilmington, North Carolina

Jan. 3, 1980
Indianapolis, Indiana

Bishop of African Methodist Episcopal Zion Church, 1953–80; senior bishop, 1975–80. Shaw entered the ministry in November, 1927, serving as associate pastor of Union Wesley Church, Washington, D.C. He married Ardelle Shaw on September 1, 1931. Shaw served as pastor at Bowen's Chapel, St. Andrews, and Price Memorial, all in NC, from 1929–37. From 1937–43, he was a presiding elder of the Wilmington area. Shaw then served as secretary-treasurer of the Department of Home Missions, and Pension and Ministerial Relief, 1943–52, until elected bishop on May 18, 1952. He was an able business executive, industrious and cautious, and an evangelist. He served on many commissions and attended various conferences connected with the NCC and WCC. Shaw was a Mason and visited Russia in 1962. He died at the Board of Bishops Winter Meeting. He is interred in Wilmington.

Arthur D. Katterjohn

Dec. 8, 1929
Chicago, Illinois

Jan. 8, 1980
Wheaton, Illinois

One of the great band directors of his time. Katterjohn's band career began in 1952 in Saline, MI, schools. He directed the Wheaton College Band from 1968 until his death and led their orchestra until 1978. He was the president of the College Band Directors National Association. He was a member of Wheaton Bible Church and died after a five-year battle with cancer.

Ernest A. Payne

Feb. 19, 1902
London, England

Jan. 14, 1980
Pitsford, England

President of World Council of Churches, 1968-75. Payne married Winifred Davies on October 28, 1930. Ordained a Baptist, he pastored Bugbrooke Baptist Church (1928–32); then was on the headquarters staff of the Baptist Missionary Society (1932–40); senior tutor at Regent's Park College (1940–51); and general secretary of Baptist Union of Great Britain and Ireland (1951–67). He was vice president of the Baptist World Alliance, 1965–70. He wrote from *The Free Church Tradition in the Life of England* (1944) to *Violence, Non–violence and Human Rights* (1971).

Theodore Elsner

Dec. 20, 1898
Brooklyn, New York

Jan. 15, 1980
Philadelphia, Pennsylvania

Chairman of National Religious Broadcasters, 1948–52. He married Miriam Gregory on April 29, 1916. Elsner himself was on radio for 40 years in the Philadelphia area in connection with his 36–year ministry at Calvary Memorial Church, 1938–74. He was an encouragement to Billy Graham during the early days of his *Hour of Decision* broadcast. His daughter, Millie Dienert, is a well-known speaker for women.

Cyril E. Homer

March 12, 1914
Gloucestershire, England

Jan. 19, 1980
near Wilcox, Arizona

President of Southeastern College of Assemblies of God, Lakeland, FL 1955–58, 1970–79. Homer moved to Wales as a youth and then came to America in 1929 at age 15. He met his wife, Ruth Greven, at Central Bible Institute, Springfield, MO, and married her on September 9, 1937. His pastoral ministry included New Philadelphia, Massillon, Dayton, OH; Georgia, Florida, and Minnesota. He was in heavy demand as a speaker for conventions and camps. In his second tour of duty at SC, enrollment went from 592 to over 1,200. The Homers were going from Lakeland to their retirement home in California. Mrs. Homer was driving in the desert 50 miles from Wilcox when he had a cardiac arrest in the car.

Guy E. King

April 24, 1905
Blanchard, Michigan

Jan. 20, 1980
Grand Rapids, Michigan

Director of Hiawatha Baptist (Continental in 1984) **Missions, Escanaba** (Grand Rapids in 1977), **MI 1952–73.** King's father died when he was age ten, and soon the mother moved to Grand Rapids. He married his wife, Marian, in February, 1927. He was converted after going to church with a friend. He worked at F. W. Woolworth and attended the Baptist Bible Institute (College) in Grand Rapids. They became missionaries with HBM and went to Watersmeet, MI, from 1946–52.

Part of the ministry was to Indians at a nearby reservation. The Kings moved to Escanaba, the location of the office, upon his taking the directorship.

George A. Butterick

March 23, 1892
Seaham Harbour, England

Jan. 23, 1980
Louisville, Kentucky

President of Federal Council of Churches (NCC in 1950), **1938–40**. Butterick was a well-known leader in the liberal wing of Christianity in the twentieth century. He married Agnes Gardner on June 27, 1916. He pastored at First Congregational, Quincy, IL (1915–18); First Congregational Church, Rutland, VT (1919–21); First Presbyterian Church, Buffalo, NY (1921–27); and then had a famous tenure at the Madison Avenue Presbyterian Church, New York City (1927–54). He was also a lecturer at Union Theological Seminary in that city, 1937–54. He was a professor of preaching at Garrett Theological Seminary, Northwestern University (1961–70); a visiting lecturer at Vanderbilt University Divinity School, Nashville and at Southern Baptist Theological Seminary, Louisville, KY (1972–80). His books range from *The Parables* (1925) to *The Power of Prayer Today* (1970). His liberalism was evidenced by his editorship of the 12-volume *Interpreter's Bible* (1952). He lived in Louisville, KY. He is buried in Charlevoix, MI.

Clemens H. Zeidler

Jan. 11, 1911
Milwaukee, Wisconsin

Feb. 2, 1980
Minneapolis, Minnesota

President of Northwestern Lutheran (Luther-Northwestern in 1982) **Theological Seminary, Minneapolis, MN 1956–76**. Zeidler pastored the Trinity English Lutheran Church of Appleton, WI, from 1940–54. Once president of NLTS, it grew from the second smallest to the second largest of the Lutheran Church in America seminaries. His wife's name was Pearl. His funeral was at Transfiguration Lutheran Church in Minneapolis.

Edmund G. Kaufman

Dec. 26, 1891
Moundridge, Kansas

Feb. 14, 1980
Newton, Kansas

President of Bethel College, North Newton, KS, 1932–52. In 1917 he was ordained to the Mennonite ministry. Kaufman married Hazel Dester on June 10, 1917 (died: 1948), Anna Baumgartner in 1950 (died: 1961), and Edna Ramseyer in 1965. He was an educational missionary to China at Kai Chow, Hopei, 1917–27. He served at Bluffton (OH) College, 1929–31 and then joined the school as a professor of sociology. Kaufman left the Bethel staff (1964) and traveled to India (1967). He authored seven books including *Basic Christian Convictions*.

Gerald H. Kennedy

Aug. 30, 1907
Benzonia, Michigan

Feb. 17, 1980
Laguna Hills, California

Well-known Methodist bishop, 1948 on, serving the Los Angeles area, 1952 on. Kennedy was the youngest man (age 40) ever elected bishop in Methodism. Kennedy married Mary Leeper on June 2, 1928, then pastored the First Congregational Church, Collingwood, CT (1932–36); Calvary, San Jose, CA (1936–40); FMC, Palo Alto, CA (1940–42); and St. Paul's, Lincoln, NE (1942–48). Kennedy also served as a bishop in Portland, OR (1948–52), and in Los Angeles (1952–72). From 1969–73, he pastored at FMC, Pasadena, CA. No other bishop ever carried a dual position, so this brought criticism. He authored 17 books, from *His Word through Preaching* (1947) to *My Third Readers Notebook* (1974). Kennedy did not believe in eternal punishment. He is buried in Hollywood Hills, CA.

Theodore F. Adams

Sept. 26, 1898
Palmyra, New York

Feb. 27, 1980
Richmond, Virginia

President of Baptist World Alliance, 1955–60. Adams was vice president of the same, 1947–50. He was the first American clergyman to administer communion to Soviet churchgoers after the Communist takeover in 1917. Adams married Esther Jillson on February 26, 1925. He pastored at Cleveland Heights (OH) Baptist Church (1924–27); at Ashland Avenue Baptist Church, Toledo, OH (1927–36) and at FBC, Richmond, VA (1936–68), where he was pastor-emeritus till his death. He also taught a preaching course at Southeastern Baptist Theological Seminary, Wake Forest, NC from 1968–78. Adams preached on the radio for 22 years and later on television. He also authored four books from *Making Your Marriage Succeed* (1953) to *Baptists around the World* (1967).

Herbert M. Griffin

May 13, 1895
Owatonna, Minnesota

March 9, 1980
Lancaster, Pennsylvania

President of IFMA, 1954–56, and veteran missionary with China Inland Mission (Overseas Missionary Fellowship). Griffin married Frances MacMillian in 1917 (died: July 24, 1965). He was a Baptist missionary in China, 1922–40; half of the time he spent as secretary of the China Council. He was Home Director of CIM, 1943–60. Griffin retired to Waterloo, IA.

Verne D. Roberts

Aug. 28, 1888
New Hampshire

March 11, 1980
St. Petersburg, Florida

Director of Bolivian Indian Mission (Andes Evangelical Mission in 1966, merged into SIM in 1981), **1941–56**. He went from MBI, then to Bolivia in 1921. Roberts married Mary in 1922 (died: 1952), and they had no children. He ministered in Aiquile until 1935 when he moved to Cochabamba. In his later years, he returned to Bolivia in 1956 and remained there until ten days prior to his death.

Jesse Owens
James Cleveland Owens

Sept. 12, 1913
Danville, Alabama

March 31, 1980
Tuscon, Arizona

One of the world's great athletes who won four gold medals in 1936 Olympics in Berlin. These medals were for the 100-meter run, 200-meter run, broad jump, and as a member of the relay team. At age five, Owens almost bled to death after surgery done by his mother in his home to remove a lump on his chest, but God answered prayer. His family walked nine miles to church. The Owens family moved north to Cleveland, OH, where in high school, he became a track star. Then, it was the Olympics in Berlin, much to the dismay of Hitler. Owens married Ruth Solomon in 1931. He was with the office of civilian defense, Philadelphia (1940–42), director of black personnel at Ford Motor Company (1942–46). A crisis came May 18, 1945, when Owens had surgery to correct paralysis (waist down). He then worked with Leo Rose Sporting Goods Company (1946–52), and was secretary of the Illinois Youth Commission (1952–55). Owens briefly led an orchestra and acted in films. He lived out his days in Chicago and was an active Baptist. From the 1936 triumphs, there were reversals: bankruptcy and paralysis, until his faith was firmly re-established in the God of his youth. Owing income tax money was another setback, but he persevered and, with the help of God, finished as one of the most honest, hard-working, decent men of his century.

Howard D. Higgins

Aug. 23, 1903
New York, New York

April 6, 1980
Southhampton, Pennsylvania

Presiding Bishop of Reformed Episcopal Church, 1957–75. He was ordained a Presbyterian of REC in 1925. Higgins married Ethel Scott on September 23, 1944. He was the rector of First REC, New York City, 1928–54. Higgins was a professor at the REC Seminary, Philadelphia, 1930–72. He edited the *Episcopal Recorder* and lived in Pipersville, PA. He taught such subjects as theology, church history, and apologetics. Higgins was a bishop in the New York and Philadelphia Synod, 1942–72. He is buried in Bala-Cynwyd, PA.

William R. Tolbert

May 13, 1913
Bensonville, Liberia

April 12, 1980
Monrovia, Liberia

President of Baptist World Alliance, 1965–70, and president of Liberia, July 23, 1971–80, till his assassination. Tolbert married Victoria David in 1936; they had eight children. Tolbert also pastored Zion Praise Baptist Church, Bensonville, Liberia, for 12 years. His political career began in 1943. Around 1951, he became vice president of the country, serving quietly in the shadow of President TUBMAN. He died as a result of assassination.

Alden D. Kelley

Feb. 22, 1903
Brooklyn, New York

April 18, 1980
Gambier, Ohio

President of Seabury-Western Theological Seminary, Evanston, IL 1944–56. Kelley married Edna B. West on September 6, 1930, and was ordained the same year. Kelley served as a chaplain at St. Francis House (Episcopal student center), Madison, WI, from 1931–39. He was the secretary for the college work of the Episcopal Church, 1939–44. Kelley was also the president of the Anglican Theological Review.

Charles E. Butterfield

May 16, 1900
Everett, Washington

April 27, 1980
Bellevue, Washington

President of Northwest College of Assemblies of God, Kirkland, WA 1949–66. Butterfield dropped out of high school and worked in a lumber mill. He became a Christian at a Baptist church in Everett, WA. Butterfield married Edith Demarest on September 27, 1926; they had nine children. He went to Albany, OR, and started the First Assembly of God Church. He then pastored at Bethany Temple, Everett, 1926–49. During his ministry, he preached in 59 countries.

John C. Jernigan

Sept. 21, 1900
Sparta, Illinois

May 5, 1980
Cleveland, Tennessee (buried)

General overseer of Church of God, Cleveland, TN 1944–48; president of Lee College, Cleveland, TN 1951–52; and first chairman of Pentecostal Fellowship of North America, 1948–50. Converted in 1921, Jernigan held pastorates in Tennessee, Texas, and Illinois before being assigned to the state overseership in 1926. His autobiography is *From the Gambling Den to the Pulpit* (1977).

Henry K. Sherrill

Nov. 6, 1890
Brooklyn, New York

May 11, 1980
Boxford, Massachusetts

Presiding bishop of Protestant Episcopal Church (Episcopal Church, 1967), **1947–58; first president of National Council of Churches, 1950–52, and president of World Coucil of Churches, 1954–61**. He was a chaplain in World War I from 1917–19. Sherrill married Barbara Harris on September 6, 1921. Sherrill served in the Church of Our Savior in Brooklyn (1919–23), was rector of Trinity Church in Boston (1923–30); bishop of Massachusetts (1930–47) and was president of Yale University Council (1960–65). His books included *William Lawrence* (1943) to *Among Friends* (1962), his autobiography. He was an excellent orator.

Millar Burrows

Oct. 26, 1889
Cincinnati, Ohio

April 29, 1980
Winter Park, Florida

Scholar, teacher, writer, and minister. Burrows contributed much to the Christian scholarly world. He couldn't remember a time when he was not intensely conscious of being a dedicated disciple of Christ. He married Irene Gladding on July 6, 1915. Ordained into the Presbyterian Church, he pastored in Wallace, TX, from 1915–19. He was college pastor and professor of Biblical literature at Tusculum College, Greenville, TN (1920–23), and Brown University (1925–34), where he taught the same and also history of religions. At Yale Divinity School, he was professor of Biblical Theology, 1934–58. Burrows was director of the American School of Oriental Research, 1931–32 and 1947–48 (Jerusalem and Baghdad). He wrote *The Dead Sea Scrolls* (1955) and *More Light on the Dead Sea Scrolls* (1956) and was a contributor to *The Interpreter's Dictionary of the Bible*. His first book was *Outline of Biblical Theology* (1946). He was a Congregationalist and retired in Winter Park, FL.

G. Douglas Young

Sept. 2, 1910

May 20/21, 1980

First president of Jerusalem University College, 1957–78. Early on, Young pastored in Philadelphia and was principal of Kingston (Nova Scotia) Academy. He then taught at Faith Theological Seminary, and in 1948 became professor of Semitic Languages and dean of the seminary at Northwestern Schools, Minneapolis. He then was dean and professor of Old Testament literature at Trinity Evangelical Divinity School, Deerfield, IL, from 1957–62. In 1958, he founded the Institute of Holy Land Studies in Jerusalem (Jerusalem University College). His burden was to develop students intellectually and spiritually by providing graduate and undergraduate levels of instruction and also developing cultural understanding of the modern Middle East. He was also involved with "Bridges for Peace," a movement to build Jewish-Christian relations. His books range from *A Grammar of the Hebrew Language* (1951) to the famed *Young's Bible Dictionary* (published 1984).

Oliver R. Harms

Dec. 11, 1901
Cole Camp, Missouri

June 3, 1980
Houston, Texas

President of the Lutheran Church—Missouri Synod, 1962–69. Harms married Bertha Serrien on June 20, 1926. He pastored the Trinity Lutheran Church, Eden, TX (1926–35), and Trinity Lutheran of Houston, TX (1935–39). Some Texas administration work followed with a call to be first vice president of the same (1941–48) and president (1948–50). He was a director of the denomination (1950–56), fourth vice president (1956–59) and first vice president (1959–62).

Christian N. Hostetter Jr.

Jan. 22, 1899
Washington Borough, Pennsylvania

June 29, 1980
Mechanicsburg, Pennsylvania

President of Messiah College, Grantham, PA 1934–60. Hostetter married Anna Lane on Nov. 9, 1922. He served as an evangelist and pastored a BIC congregation at Reiffton, PA, from 1922–34. Hostetter was secretary of the Board of Home Missions of the Brethren in Christ Church, 1925–46 and 1947–52. He was also bishop of this same group (1937–57) and moderator at the Annual Conference (1941, '48, '52, '55). Hostetter served as Mennonite Central committeeman (1948–67) and chairman (1953–67). He especially loved farming and flowers.

Percy S. Brewster

Sept. 20, 1908
London, England

July 1, 1980
London, England

President of Pentecostal World Fellowship, 1970–73. Brewster was an evangelist and opened over 46 new Pentecostal churches in Great Britain. Converted under the ministry of GEORGE JEFFREYS, he was the pastor of City Temple in Cardiff, Wales, 1939–74, and also served as the editor of the *World Pentecost Magazine*. His wife's name was Doris. Brewster served as president and general secretary of the Elim Pentecostal Churches. He died of a brain tumor.

Henry J. Long

Jan. 18, 1897
Cashion, Oklahoma

July 4, 1980
Davison, Michigan

President of Greenville (IL) College, 1936–62. Long was converted in November, 1913, at a Free Methodist Church revival in Cashion, OK, and married Lena Watson on September 3, 1919 (died: October 4, 1980). He served in WWI in 1918. He became a professor of chemistry at Greenville, 1927–36. Beginning in 1962, he was on staff at Los Angeles Pacific College. He died the day after they moved from Greenville to be near their daughter.

Harry F. Baughman

Jan. 23, 1892
Everett, Pennsylvania

July 11, 1980
Bala Cynwyn, Pennsylvania

President of Lutheran Theological Seminary at Gettysburg (PA), 1951–62. Baughman married Joretha Liller on October 17, 1916. He pastored Trinity Lutheran Church, Keyser, WV (1913–18); St. Stephen's Lutheran Church, Pittsburgh, PA (1918–25); and Trinity Lutheran Church, Germantown, PA (1925–41). Baughman went to the Seminary in 1941 to teach homiletics. His books include *One Having Authority* (1935) to *Epistle to Philippians*.

Bertha T. Shooks-Jensen

March 16, 1907
East Liverpool, Ohio

Aug. 1, 1980
Grand Rapids, Michigan

Director of *Children's Bible Hour*, Grand Rapids, MI 1949–72. "Aunt Bertha" was known by thousands of children. She married Ernest B. Shooks on September 4, 1929. He died at age 34. She then married William Jensen. Under her direction, the broadcast went from five stations to 287. She worked at the Canton (OH) Gospel Center, 1940–47.

Henry M. Shires
Jan. 28, 1913   *Aug. 2, 1980*
Bernardsville, New Jersey   Los Altos, California

President of Church Divinity School of the Pacific, Berkeley, CA, 1936–50. He was ordained an Episcopalian in 1937. Shires married Loie Judkins on June 29, 1941. Shires also served as rector at San Leandro, CA (1940–42); Alameda, CA (1942–51); Los Altos, CA (1952–54); and was professor of NT at Episcopal Theological School, Cambridge, MA (1954–76). He later lived in Los Altos, CA. He wrote *The Eschatology of Paul* (1966) and *Finding the Old Testament in the New* (1974).

Vincent Brushwyler
July 28, 1903   *Aug. 16, 1980*
Newark, New Jersey   San Jose, California

First director of Conservative Baptist Foreign Missionary Society (CB Int.), **Wheaton, IL 1943–64, and president of EFMA, 1948–50, 1952–54**. Brushwyler was converted on January 19, 1919, in Good Samaritan Rescue Mission, Newark, NJ, where Walter Tibbetts was the speaker. Brushwyler married Nan Kjelstad on September 5, 1931. He pastored the Evangel Baptist Church in Newark, NJ, from 1931–42. The missions money grew from $1,000 to $40,000 annually. Starting with no missionaries, they eventually had 418. He also pastored at FBC, Muscatine, IA (1942–44), and FBC, Glen Ellyn, IL (1964–69).

W. Maxey Jarman
May 10, 1904   *Sept. 8, 1980*
Nashville, Tennessee   Nashville, Tennessee

Baptist layman who started a shoe empire. Jarman married Sarah Anderson on October 10, 1928, and was secretary/treasurer of the shoe company (1925–32), president (1932–47), chairman (1947–69) and chairman of the executive/finance committee (1969–73). The company name was changed to GENESCO in 1959. Jarman was MBI trustee for several years and SBC vice president in 1950. He wrote two books.

Merrill F. Unger
July 16, 1909   *Oct. 14, 1980*
Baltimore, Maryland   Severna Park, Maryland

Chairman of Old Testament department of Dallas Theological Seminary, 1948–67. Unger received his education at John Hopkins University and Dallas Seminary. He was a member of Reinhart Bible Church, Dallas. He pastored at West Ferry Church, Buffalo, NY (1934–40); in Dallas, TX (1943–44), and in Baltimore, MD (1944–47). He married Elsie Dawson on September 9, 1949. Unger wrote 25 books including: *Biblical Demonology* (1952) and *Archaeology and the Old Testament* (1954). His most famous works are *Unger's Bible Dictionary* (1957) and *Bible Handbook* (1966).

Samuel G. Ziegler
Oct. 14, 1884   *Oct. 30, 1980*
Hanover, Pennsylvania   Lebanon, Ohio

Director of Evangelical United Brethren (Methodist Church in 1968) **Missions, 1921–46**. Ziegler married Georgia Redding on October 10, 1911 (died: 1974); he was ordained United Brethren the same year. He held pastorates, Duncannon, PA (1909–11); Otterbein Memorial Church, Baltimore, MD (1914–17), and St. Paul's Church, Hagerstown, MD (1917–21). He lived in Dayton and authored three books, 1924–30. After 1946, he was an associate secretary for the denomination's mission board.

George A. Lang

Jan. 1, 1901
Detroit, Michigan

Nov. 9, 1980
Sioux Falls, South Dakota

President of North American Baptist Seminary, Rochester, NY, 1944–50, Sioux Falls, SD 1950–59. He married on August 30, 1927. Lang pastored in many locations such as: FBC, Lorraine, KS (1926–34), Calvary Baptist, Tacoma, WA (1934–38), and Ebenezer Baptist, Detroit, MI (1938–44). It was during his leadership the school was moved from Rochester, NY, to Sioux Falls, SD. He continued on the faculty for eight years into the new administration. He was professor of pastoral theology.

Myrtle Nordin Huarte

Feb. 26, 1900
Lake Lillian, Minnesota

Nov. 24, 1980
Richfield, Minnesota

Founder and first director of Latin American Lutheran Mission, Laredo, TX, 1936–60. Myrtle grew up teaching Sunday School and VBS. She went to Colombia as a missionary but poor health hastened her return in 1929. Another stint was attempted there, 1936–37, with the same results. From the 1940s, she pioneered a work in Mexico and married Porfirio Huarta, a native Mexican of Spanish descent. She lived in Texas for a time in the early 1970s, went home to Minnesota where she was admitted to a nursing home in 1976. She was an evangelical Lutheran teacher, evangelist, pioneer missionary, and developed a great work.

Bertram W. Doyle

July 3, 1897
Lowndesboro, Alabama

Nov. 29, 1980
Gary, Indiana

Bishop of Colored (Christian in 1956) **Methodist Episcopal Church, 1950–70; senior bishop, 1962–70.** Doyle married Mansy Stewart on August 12, 1918. Doyle either taught or was a dean at various colleges, 1921–27 and was ordained in 1925. He taught at Fisk University, Nashville, 1927–37, was the secretary of education of CMEC, and was a delegate to the World Conference in Oslo (1961) and London (1966).

Willis G. Haymaker

April 6, 1895
Shippenburg, Pennsylvania

Dec. 12, 1980
Lenoir, North Carolina

Ministry in evangelism spanning 60 years. Haymaker married Dorothy Taylor on July 27, 1921. After helping with campaigns with such as BOB JONES SR. (1940–45), JOHN R. RICE (1945–49). He became the advance crusade director for the Billy Graham team, 1949–70. Haymaker was involved in tabernacle preparation and also in the development of the prayer program. He was a ruling elder of First Presbyterian Church, Lenoir, NC, where he moved to in 1931.

Harland Sanders
Colonel Sanders

Sept. 9, 1890
Henryville, Indiana

Dec. 16, 1980
Louisville, Kentucky

Founder of the Kentucky Fried Chicken business and a convert at age 75, via Evangel Tabernacle, Louisville, KY. Sanders married Claudia Ledington on November 17, 1948. He had three children from a previous marriage. He started in business operating a gas station, then a restaurant (Sander's Cafe), Corbin, KY, from 1929–56. He developed a "secret recipe" with eleven herbs. He then approached restaurants, saying, "Just try my chicken." That was all he needed. He flew 250,000 miles a year. He began the fried chicken franchise operations in 1956 and kept it until 1964, when he sold it for 2 million dollars. The business, that has kept his name, kept growing—it sold again in 1971 for 285 million. Thirty years later, there were over 10,000 outlets around the world. The "Colonel" is buried in Cave Hill Cemetery, Louisville. Early on, he worked for an insurance company.

John R. Rice
Mr. Fundamentalism

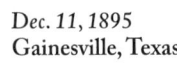

Dec. 11, 1895
Gainesville, Texas

Dec. 29, 1980
Murfreesboro, Tennessee

Long time editor of the *Sword of the Lord* (1934–80), with a circulation up to 300,000. Rice was an evangelist and a prolific writer (124 books). He was converted at age nine. He married Lloys Cooke on September 27, 1921, and they had six daughters. Early on, he taught at Wayland (TX) Baptist College, 1921–22, and served in Texas churches, evangelizing the area. Rice pastored Galilean Baptist, Dallas, TX, from 1932–39 (8,000 converts). He moved to Wheaton, IL, in 1939, where his publishing ministry increased. Rice held city-wide crusades in the 1940s with many denominations participating, in such places as Cleveland, TN; Buffalo, NY, and Springfield, MO. He was an authority on soul winning and prayer and started a radio broadcast in 1959 called *Voice of Revival*. He had 35–60 million books and pamphlets in circulation, which have won at least 24,000 souls to Christ. He moved to Murfreesboro in 1963. His *What Must I Do to Be Saved* booklet has 40 million copies in 40 languages. His conflict with Billy Graham over "ecumenical evangelism" lost him considerable support. However he was a wise and consistent fundamentalist that appreciated good men from various persuasions, one of the last of the old-time fundamentalist leaders who practiced this. Rice also wrote the lyrics and music of several quality gospel songs including "Jesus Is Coming," "Let the Sun Shine Again," "O Bring Your Loved Ones," and "So Little Time." He suffered a brain hemorrhage on December 17, slipped into a coma, and passed away twelve days later. The funeral service was held at Franklin Road Baptist Church. His *Rice Reference Bible* came out a couple of months after his death.

George A. Palmer

Feb. 14, 1895
Philadelphia, Pennsylvania

Jan. 11, 1981
Elkton, Maryland

Founder of Morning Cheer Ministries and member of the National Religious Broadcasters Hall of Fame. Palmer married Rachel Ann Stowe in June 1919. His radio ministry began in 1932 with the song "Jesus Never Fails." This daily morning program was characterized by a family-oriented format. In 1942, he began a ministry to servicemen near Fort Dix (Wrightstown, NJ) and in downtown Philadelphia. Palmer, for years, had the *Morning Cheer* broadcast in the Philadelphia area. His Morning Cheer Ministries emphasized family and evangelistic outreach. He founded Sandy Cove Bible Conference Center in 1946. The MC Bible (at Sandy Cove) Conference also began that year. Christian camping programs were added in 1951. A ranch for teens came in 1956 and a Boys' Christian Home in India in 1960.

Joseph C. Kearney

June 9, 1892
Toronto, Ontario, Canada

Jan. 21, 1981
Summerville, South Carolina

President of Cummins Memorial Theological Seminary, Summerville, SC, 1930–58. Kearney came to the USA in 1919 and married Anna Gibson on March 9, 1925. He came to CMTS in 1923 and served as dean and professor of theology. He was ordained bishop in 1930 after having been superintendent of home missions for the Reformed Episcopal Church, 1923–30. In 1951, he became the presiding bishop of the denomination. At CMTS, he was the first official president, following other pioneers who developed the school.

Russell V. DeLong

Aug. 24, 1901
Dover, New Hampshire

Jan. 29, 1981
St. Petersburg, Florida

President of Northwest Nazarene College (University in 2000), **Nampa, ID 1928–32, 1935–42**. Converted at age 16 and ordained on April 20, 1925, he pastored in Walham, MA, from 1924–26. He married Doris Gale on September 10, 1926. At the college, he was also professor of philosophy and theology. He was dean at Nazarene Theological Seminary in Kansas City (1945–53) and was a speaker on the *Showers of Blessing* radio broadcast (1945–61). DeLong was an evangelist, 1953–57, holding 61 city-wide crusades, visiting 63 countries, and writing 32 books. DeLong also served as president of Pasadena (CA) College, 1957–61. He died of cirrhosis of the liver.

Robert Parsons

Jan. 7, 1905
Apollo, Pennsylvania

Feb. 7, 1981
Chicago, Illinois

Parsons spent his lifetime associated with Moody's radio station, WMBI, Chicago. Parsons was a program director for many years. Shortly after high school he had his own dance clubs, bands, etc. Parsons played saxaphone and clarinet. Converted, he attended MBI and, during his four-year stint there, almost died with a ruptured appendix. He worked for $10 a week and lost two sons during those days. His wife, Lucille, was a great help to him. Parsons started volunteering at a radio station and soon became the program manager. He composed the popular "Singing of His Love," and "Heaven in My Heart" (lyrics by Ida Gurney). His duties included vocal and instrumental soloist, director of several choral groups, and speaker on devotional periods. He led singing, conducted the choir, and taught Sunday School at Galilee Baptist Church (merged with New Life Community). He had a leg amputated shortly before his death.

D. Martyn Lloyd-Jones

Dec. 20, 1899
Cardiff, Wales

March 1, 1981
Ealing, England

Famed pastor of Westminster Chapel in London, 1943–68, where he served as G. Campbell Morgan's assistant, 1938–43. He joined Calvinistic Methodist Chapel, Llangeitito, Wales, in 1914. Lloyd-Jones began his career as a doctor (medical degree) in 1921. Lloyd-Jones was converted, 1923–24. and became a member of the Royal College of Physicians (of England) in 1925. He decided to enter the ministry in 1926. On January 9, 1927, he married Dr. Bethany Phillips, and was ordained in Whitefield's Tabernacle on October 26, 1927. He also pastored a Presbyterian church in Port Talbot, Wales, 1927–38. Lloyd-Jones became an outstanding English evangelical leader and his books made a great impact. His Friday night Bible classes in London drew 1,500 attendees. He was an expository preacher, believed prayer could bring revival, and influenced many preachers. In 1939, he wrote his first book, *Why Does God Allow War?* In 1959, he published *Revival* and a two-volume *Sermon the Mount*. He published *Sermons on Romans* (1970) and *Ephesians* (1972). His *Spiritual Depression* (1965) was an outstanding book. An illness in March, 1968, ended his ministry at WC and an illness in 1980 stopped all preaching.

Everett L. Cattell

Sept. 16, 1905
Kensington, Ohio

March 2, 1981
Columbus, Ohio

President of Malone College, Canton, OH, 1960–72. Cattell was converted at his bedside at age 13 after hearing evangelistic preaching in the Friends church. Cattell married Catherine DeVol on August 31, 1927. He was a missionary in India for 20 years, 1936–57. He was a key leader in the founding of the Yeotmal Biblical Seminary in India and served as first chairman of its board of directors. He also served as general superintendent of the Ohio Yearly Meeting, 1957–60, and did some writing. He died of heart failure.

Chester Bitterman

Nov. 30, 1952
Lancaster, Pennsylvania

March 7, 1981
Bogota, Colombia

Wycliffe translator and martyr. Bitterman was shot and killed and left bound and gagged, draped in a rebel flag, in a stolen bus parked in a residential area. Bitterman, the Wycliffe Bible translator, was killed 48 days after he was kidnapped by members of the M-19 guerrilla movement. Bitterman was 28 years old, the father of two children, and husband of Brenda Gardner of Glen Burnie, MD. He resided in Lancaster, PA, and earlier went to Columbia Bible College. He arrived at Colombia in 1979. He was making arrangements to go to Caryona-speaking Indians when illness sent Chester to Bogota for gall bladder surgery. On January 19, the mission compound was struck by hooded terrorists who later demanded all members of the Summer Institute of Linguistics leave Colombia. Bitterman witnessed to them and played chess with them, before his martyrdom. Bitterman was accused of being a CIA agent. His burial was 300 miles southeast of Bogota (outpost of Loma Linda), headquarters for the Summer Institute of Linguistics.

Merrill E. Nicholls

August 27, 1903
Highland Park, Michigan

March 12, 1981
Los Angeles, California (?)

Chairman of Pentecostal Fellowship of North America, 1979–81. Nicholls was also active in the Foursquare denomination, pastoring for 26 years, 1933–59. He was married 46 years to his wife, Vinita Wallin, whom he married on August 29, 1935. From 1951–59, he taught at Life College, Los Angeles, and was district supervisor and chairman of Mount Vernon (OH) Bible College, 1959–74. From 1974–81, he served as the Foursquare General Supervisor. Nicholls became vice president of the denomination, 1980–81. He died following a massive stroke.

A. Brant Reed

Nov. 29, 1913
near St. Louis, Missouri

March 14, 1981
Summit, New Jersey

First director of High School Evangelism Fellowship (Touch the World in 1999), **Bergenfield, NJ, 1938–82**. Reed grew up in Plymouth Brethren circles and was greatly nurtured by such as PERCY CRAWFORD and JACK WYRTZEN. Early on, he developed the Elizabeth (NY) Prayer Fellowship. He married May Nelson on June 12, 1943. Reed died of encephalitis and a high fever.

E. Schuyler English

Oct. 12, 1899
New York, New York

March 16, 1981
Philadelphia, Pennsylvania

Evangelical scholar, founder and first president of Pilgrim Fellowship, 1943–81, and president of Philadelphia School of the Bible, 1936–39, teaching there 1935–47. English married Eva Schultz on March 2, 1937 (died: August 22, 1956) and Ruth Kephart on July 4, 1959. He was with the Curtis Publishing Company (1922–31), president of American Bible Conference Association, Inc. (1930–47); managing editor of *Revelation* (*Eternity*) (1931–39); faculty of PSB (1935–47); and editor of *Our Hope* (1946–58) and *The Pilgrim* (1944–81). English was the chairman of *The New Scofield Reference Bible* committee. In the years before his death, he lived in Merian, PA. He died of a heart attack. He wrote from *Studies in Matthew* (1935) to *Studies in Hebrews* (1954). He is buried in Gladwyne, PA.

Helen Steiner Rice

May 19, 1900
Lorain, Ohio

April 23, 1981
Wyoming, Ohio

Perhaps history's most prolific poet. She once estimated that she wrote some 2 million poems. Go into any gift store, stop at any card rack, and you will see the poems from Rice. Her banker/husband shot himself to death during the stock market collapse of 1929. Following her husband's tragic death, she joined Gibson Greeting Cards in Cincinnati, in 1931, for whom she worked for the next half century. Whatever the occasion, there was a verse from her heart and pen. Until the 1950s, her poems were relatively few in the religious and inspirational vent, because of company restrictions. But then, with her flourishing success, she began an ever–widening influence. Her fame skyrocketed when she wrote "The Priceless Gift of Christmas" which was read on *The Lawrence Welk Show* in 1960. For the rest of her life, she wrote such as "A Child's Faith," "When I Must Leave You," and "The End of the Road Is but a Bend in the Road." She said, "I only put to rhyme the truths God placed on my heart."

Ron Ormond

May 11, 1981

Produced nine Christian films after being converted out of the Hollywood environment. Ormond worked there for many years writing or directing more than 60 feature-length movies. He commanded 67 units of the Civil Air patrol in southern California. He did a year-long stint with Lowell Thomas's *High Adventure* TV program. Ormond moved his family to Nashville. After two near fatal accidents in his private plane, he surrendered to Christ and so the Christian world had another producer (*The Burning Hell*, *The Grim Reaper*, *The Land where Jesus Walked*). Cancer, a heart attack, and a second operation hastened his death. His wife June and son Tim carried on the work for a while. He was a member of Franklin Road Baptist Church, Murfreesboro, TN, and his funeral was in Nashville.

Zachery T. Johnson

June 18, 1897
Athens, Georgia

May 30, 1981
Lakeland, Florida

President of Asbury College, Wilmore, KY, 1940–65. Johnson married Sadie Mershon on September 11, 1916. Johnson served as head of the history department at State Teachers College, Hattiesburg, MS (1929–34) and as vice president of AC (1935–40). While he was at Asbury, he paid off their $400,000 debt and acquired a $700,000 endowment. He was a widely sought speaker at retreats, conferences, and camp meetings.

William T. Watson

May 21, 1901
south of Luberton, North Carolina

June 5, 1981
Clearwater, Florida

Founder and first president of Trinity College, St. Petersburg, FL, 1932–81. Watson was converted at age 14 and attended Toccoa Falls Bible Institute, graduating in 1922. He married Lucy Roberts and went to Florida in 1924 to organize the Gospel Tabernacle in St. Petersburg, FL. He served as pastor there until 1951. Watson also founded the Florida Bible Institute in 1932. Billy Graham attended and graduated from Trinity College before going to Wheaton College. In 1951, the school moved to Bellair, FL, and the name changed to Trinity College. In 1962, the school moved to Dunedin and then on to New Port Richey, FL, in 1987. Watson's Gospel Tabernacle seated 4,000 and the great evangelists of his generation such as BILLY SUNDAY, GYPSY SMITH, R. A. TORREY, W. B. RILEY, etc., preached there. Watson died following a ten-month bout with cancer.

John L. Patten

May 5, 1908
Stewartville, Minnesota

June 18, 1981
Des Moines, Iowa

President of Omaha (NE) Bible Institute (Faith Baptist Bible College in 1967), **1947–65**. Under his leadership, the name changed to Omaha Baptist Bible Institute (1952–60) and Omaha Baptist Bible College (1960–65). Patten was converted in a Baptist deacon's home in 1924 then went to Northwestern Bible School. Patten married Hazel Carpenter on September 7, 1932. Patten pastored for 18 years and taught classes at the Omaha school, 1945–75. He also wrote three books.

Karl S. Paulo

March 31, 1913
Akron, Ohio

June 22, 1981
Abingdon, Virginia

President of Kentucky Bible Institute and Kentucky Mountain Holiness Association, Van Cleve, KY, 1970–81. This Methodist leader, Paulo, succeeded founder LELA MCCONNELL. He graduated from the school (1936) and began to teach there (1949). Paulo married Bessie Seldomridge on June 1, 1940. From 1941–49, he taught in a Mt. Carmel high school. Paulo ministered in trips to Bolivia and Japan. He died of a heart attack.

William A. Chapman

March 13, 1902
Chicago, Illinois

July 3, 1981
Grant Park, Illinois

Founder and first president of World Home Bible League (Bible League), **South Holland, IL 1938–49**. He was raised on a small farm in the "Chicagoland" area. Chapman and his wife, Elizabeth (married on July 31, 1925), canvassed homes in Walkerton, IN looking for Bible-less homes. The rest of his story is given in the book, *Story without End*, as millions of Bibles have gone to every section of the globe. He stayed on as chairman of the board until 1956 when his co-worker BILL ACKERMAN took over the work. Since 1969, they have put Bibles in every home in over 70 countries throughout the world. He died in a tractor accident on his farm. Funeral services were held at Thorn Creek Reformed Church in Lansing, IL. His wife died October 7, 1999, at age 97 in S. Holland, IL.

Ivan H. Hagedorn

Feb. 9, 1897
Westfield, Pennsylvania

July 20, 1981
East Lansdowne, Pennsylvania

Evangelical Lutheran Church pastor who was ordained in 1921. Hagedorn married Ingehar Dowling on March 21, 1921, and pastored St. Paul's Church, Collingswood, NJ 1921–32 and Bethel Church, Philadelphia, 1932 on. He contributed sermons to such publications as *Sword of the Lord* and *Homiletic Digest*.

Benjamin R. Lacy

July 30, 1886
Raleigh, North Carolina

Aug. 3, 1981
High Point, North Carolina

President of Union Theological Seminary, Richmond, VA 1926–55. He started as a home missionary in Wake County, NC from 1914–17, and served as chaplain and captain in World War I. Lacy married Emma White on April 19, 1919. He pastored Central Presbyterian, Atlanta, GA, from 1919–26, pastored College Church and was the chaplain of Hampden-Sydney College after 1956. Lacy wrote *Revivals in the Midst of the Years* (1943).

Morrow Coffey Graham

Feb. 23, 1892
Steele Creek, North Carolina

Aug. 14, 1981
Charlotte, North Carolina

Mother of Billy Graham who lived in Charlotte, NC. Morrow was married to W. Franklin Graham (died: 1962), and they had three other children besides Billy: Catherine McElroy, Jean (Mrs. Leighton) Ford, and Melvin. For many years she was a piano teacher and a Sunday school teacher. She was also an effective writer. At age 87, she wrote 537 letters in that year alone. She was a member of Calvary Church.

Ebenezer Gettys

Sept. 26, 1895
Tirzah, South Carolina

Aug. 30, 1981
Due West, South Carolina

Secretary of Associated Reformed Presbyterian Church Missions (World Witness), **1940–76**. Gettys served in WWI, 1917–19, and married Mary M. Millen on August 26, 1924. They went to India (Pakistan) as missionaries, 1924–39. He pastored in South Carolina (1940–43), and then served as director of Religious Education of the denomination (1943–53). From 1950–55, Gettys was editor of the *Associate Reformed Presbyterian*. He wrote two books and served several churches as supply pastor.

William E. Kuhnle

Sept. 3, 1910
Detroit, Michigan

Sept. 6, 1981
Milwaukee, Wisconsin

GARB Council member for 18 years and long-time pastor of Garfield Baptist Church, Milwaukee, WI, beginning in 1941. Kuhnle had TB of the spine since age five. He graduated from MBI in 1935 and was an associate in Waterloo, IA, from 1937–41. He married Edna Stephenson on February 11, 1937. He was a great blessing as he used his handicap to inspire others. He retired in 1976 and wrote several choruses, including "Wouldn't It Be Wonderful!"

Philip E. Armstrong

Oct. 1, 1919
Bronson, Michigan

Sept. 13, 1981
near Glenallen, Alaska

Director of Far Eastern Gospel Crusade (SEND), **1950–80, and president of IFMA, 1970–73**. Due to the influence of his Sunday School teacher, ELMER DEAL, Armstrong was converted at age 16 while reading a tract in his room. Armstrong was a soldier in WWII in the Philippines, 1942–45, and married Bobbie Payne on January 12, 1946. Armstrong caught a vision of winning souls and became an ordained Baptist in 1943. He helped found FEGC in 1947. His mission focused on the Philippines, Japan, and Taiwan. He was killed in an airplane crash when his missionary plane ran out of fuel on a trip from Petersburg to Glenallen. Four others perished in the crash at sea. The four-hour trip was at 3 ½ hours when the unexpected trouble came.

Joseph C. MacAulay

July 4, 1900
Belfast, Ireland

Sept. 13, 1981
New York, New York

President of London (ON) Bible College, 1960–66. MacAulay was converted at age nine in Alloa, Scotland, via the ministry of B. McColl Barbour at a boys' Bible club meeting. MacAulay emigrated to Canada in 1920 and became the pastor of the Dufferin Baptist Church, Toronto. He married Helen Duncombe on May 27, 1925. He pastored in Toronto until 1921, Cleveland, OH (1922–26); Quebec City (1926–29); Sault Ste. Marie, Ontario (1929–39), and the Wheaton (IL) Bible

The Saints Go Marching In

Church (1939–51). He taught theology, evangelism, and Bible at MBI (1951–60) and also taught at New York School of the Bible (1971–81). MacAulay wrote 25 hymn texts and 20 hymn tunes.

Arthur K. White

March 15, 1889　　　　　　　　　　　　　　　　　　　　　　　　　　　　Sept. 14, 1981
Denver, Colorado　　　　　　　　　　　　　　　　　　　　　　　Zarephath, New Jersey

President of Pillar of Fire, Zarephath, NJ 1946–80. White succeeded his mother, Alma White, who was the founder of the movement. He married Kathleen Staats on September 6 1915 (died: April, 1973) and Bertha Hollander on July 5, 1974. White became bishop in 1932 and assisted in the development of the educational and radio ministries phase of his denomination, spending some of his time in Denver, CO. His books were from *Your Home, Your College* (1922) to *Some More White Family History* (1980). He led in the development in Alma White College, Zarephath, NJ; Belleview Christian College, Westminster, CO, and radio stations in Denver, Cincinnati, and Zarephath.

E. C. Hadley

Dec. 10, 1894　　　　　　　　　　　　　　　　　　　　　　　　　　　　Sept. 15, 1981
Watseka, Illinois　　　　　　　　　　　　　　　　　　　　　　　　　Danville, Illinois

Founder and first director of Grace and Truth Publishers, Danville, IL 1931–1976. Hadley was converted at a Quaker church during his childhood. He was active in Plymouth Brethren circles all his life and was a missionary in Mali Republic under Gospel Missionary Union for six years beginning in 1920. He started Grace and Truth Publishers in 1931 and served as an itinerant preacher until about 1975. His wife died in 1971. He died of a stroke.

Louis H. Evans Sr.

May 31, 1897　　　　　　　　　　　　　　　　　　　　　　　　　　　　　Sept. 21, 1981
Goshen, Indiana　　　　　　　　　　　　　　　　　　　　　　　Pasadena, California

Presbyterian pastor of famed First Presbyterian Church, Hollywood, CA 1941–53. Evans married Marie Egly on December 22, 1921. Evans pastored FPC, Westhope, ND (1922–25); Calvary PC, Wilmington, CA (1925–28); FPC, Pomona, CA (1928–31); and Third PC, Pittsburgh, PA (1931–41). Evans was minister-at-large for the denomination, 1953–62. His son, Louis, pastored in Washington, D.C. and later, La Jolla, California. Evans wrote frequently on the topic of marriage and authored at least six books.

L. Brooks Hays

Aug. 9, 1898　　　　　　　　　　　　　　　　　　　　　　　　　　　　　　Oct. 11, 1981
Russellville, Arkansas　　　　　　　　　　　　　　　　　　　Chevy Chase, Maryland

President of Southern Baptist Convention, 1957–58. Hays married Marion Prather on February 2, 1922. He was a Baptist deacon in Russellville, KY (1923–28); a lawyer (1928–34) in Little Rock, AR; a Sunday School teacher and superintendent at Second Baptist Church; then a congressman. Hays went to Washington in 1942 and served until 1958 in the House of Representatives. He brought Governor Faubus and President EISENHOWER together for the 1957 desegregation of a Little Rock high school. He was defeated by a write-in segregationist in 1958. Hays served various appointments under Presidents EISENHOWER (1959–61), Kennedy (1961–63), and Johnson (1963–64). He was a vice president of the NCC in 1969 and published several books including his autobiography, *Politics Is My Parish* (1981).

Elton Crowell

Dec. 31, 1912
Pleasant Lake, Indiana

Oct. 13, 1981
Meadow Vista, California

Evangelist and violinist for many years. Crowell spoke to crowds of five to 10,000 in crusades held in churches, tents, auditoriums, and fairgrounds. He conducted more than 700 crusades and traveled over 2 million miles. His outreach included Canada, Latin America, Europe, Africa, and the Holy Lands. Crowell married Edith Harris on April 12, 1934, and she helped in the meetings, singing, and/or playing the organ. They lived in Michigan for a while, then moved to California.

Ernest S. Williams

Jan. 7, 1885
San Bernardino, California

Oct. 25, 1981
Springfield, Missouri

General superintendent of Assemblies of God, 1929–49, and president of Central Bible College, Springfield, MO 1929–31, 1939–48. Williams was converted on November 13, 1904. He began his ministry in a mission in San Francisco in 1907. He married Laura Jacobsen on November 17, 1911. He pastored several places (1907–20); then Highway Tabernacle, Philadelphia (1920–30). Williams wrote *Notes on Theology*.

Frank Masserano Sr.

June 28, 1914
Memphis, Tennessee

Oct. 26, 1981
Memphis, Tennessee

President of International Ministerial Fellowship, Fridley, MN, 1958–81. This is a fellowship of independent Pentecostal ministers. Masserano was converted at about age 14 by Italian Pentecostal farmers who migrated to the Memphis area. He married Iris Viehe on January 1, 1936, who was already an evangelist. They co-pastored the Bethel Assembly Church, Memphis, TN, for 45 years. With two others, L. L. Kirkman and George Stigletts, they formed the above mentioned fellowship. Once a year they would have a Thanksgiving convention in Memphis. He died of a heart attack.

Charles C. Parlin

July 22, 1898
Wausau, Wisconsin

Nov. 15, 1981
Englewood, New Jersey

President of World Council of Churches, 1961–68. He was admitted to the New York State Bar in 1923 and was a practicing lawyer for many years. He also served in WWI. Parlin married Miriam Boyd on October 11, 1924, (died: October, 1972) and Kaye Chiange in February, 1976. Parlin was an effective layman in many areas. In 1944, he led the General Conference which called for prayer, seeking a victory in WWII. He was president of the World Methodist Council, 1970–71.

Reuben E. Larson

June 13, 1897
Bancock, Iowa

Nov. 17, 1981
Orange City, Florida

Cofounder with CLARENCE JONES and co-director of HCJB World Radio Missionary Fellowship, 1931–47. Larson was converted in a revival at age 16 in his home church. He married Grace Richardson on December 28, 1921, was an evangelist with CMA (1917–24) and became a missionary to Brazil (1926–32). He met CLARENCE JONES, where they began a radio ministry together (HCJB) in Quito, Ecuador, serving there until 1972. He was a member of FBC, Pontiac, MI.

Raymond O. Corvin

Aug. 25, 1915
Ada, Oklahoma

Nov. 21, 1981
Oklahoma City, Oklahoma

Founder and first president of Southwestern College of Christian Ministries, Oklahoma City (Bethany), OK 1946–59. Corvin was one of the most brilliant men of our times—with six earned degrees. He was converted in 1932 as a young man under Ellis Roberts and was a boyhood friend of his son, Oral Roberts. He married Eula Staton on December 16, 1939. Corvin pastored Pentecostal Holiness Churches in Columbia, SC, and Norman, OK, from 1939–46. At the encouragement of PHC officials, his school was launched. From 1959–62, he continued to help at SCCM as well as help develop curriculum for Oral Roberts University. From 1962–68, he was the dean of the graduate school of theology at ORU. All through this time, he was constantly studying and writing, his *Crusaders Bible Studies* sold over 150,000 copies. Corvin was president of International Bible Seminaries, 1969–74. From 1974–81, he developed Modular Education, Inc., which allowed him more time to continue to develop his 90-plus Bible courses, including four volumes on the end times. He died of a heart attack.

Burton Opper

Nov. 1, 1883
near Lakeside, Ohio

Nov. 24, 1981
Pompton Plains, New Jersey

Director of India Mission (Christar in 1999), **Reading, PA, 1940–54**. He was director also in 1955, the year the mission changed its name to International Missions. Opper first went to India in 1916 and called his work the India Mission. He married Hazel Newlin (died: 1972), whom he met at Taylor University, January 1, 1919. He knew Telugu (to reach Hindus) and Urdu (to reach Muslims). His parish was a little village, Hindapur, 63 miles from Bangalore. Opper had a small church and boys' boarding home of some 60 students. He retired from active missionary service in 1968. At age 95, he was still going strong.

Gideon B. Williamson

Nov. 26, 1898
New Florence, Missouri

Dec. 30, 1981
Mesa, Arizona

General Superintendent of Church of the Nazarene, 1946–68, and president of Eastern Nazarene College, Wollaston, MA 1936–45. He pastored in Farmington, IA (1921–27), Austin Church, Chicago (1927–31) and First Church, East Cleveland, OH (1931–36). Williamson married Audrey Johnston on June 6, 1931.

Lily O'Hanlon

1904

1982

Cofounder of International Nepal Fellowship. Following a time of prayer and fasting while on furlough in Ireland, Lily (Pat) O'Hannon of the Ludhiana Medical College in Punjab, and Hilda Steele (1907–1992) of the Zenana Bible Medical Mission, determined to bring a medical work together with hopes of reaching Nepalis with the gospel. The work was called Nepali Evangelistic Band. They opened a dispensary in 1936 at Nautanwa, four miles south of the border of Nepal (some 1,000 exiles lived there). They were allowed to enter Nepal in November, 1952, and settled in Pokhara. O'Hanlon was allowed to build a leprosarium (1959), with a permanent building erected (1966).

Elmer Wagler

May 7, 1899
Peoria (?), Illinois

Jan. 4, 1982
Clearwater, Florida

Founder and first director of Southern Highland Evangel, 1932–52. Raised in a Christian home, Wagler was still lost and finally saved at the Pacific Garden Mission, Chicago, at age 25. He had a speech impediment, sought a speech therapist, considered suicide, was converted, and attended MBI. He married Margarite Ogden on July 1, 1928 (died: 1972) and they began work on isolated creeks on mule back. They went from country school to country school, taught Sunday schools, planted churches, moving every two-three years in Kentucky and West Virginia. They started Camp Evangel, Biggs, KY. From 1952–67, they started Rest Haven, a new work in Miami, FL, where 1,000 missionaries a year could stay as they went in and out of the country. They swapped cars and helped missionaries in many ways. He married Ruth Swanson in 1973. He died in his sister's home.

J. Hubert Cook

Feb. 10, 1909
Buenos Aires, Argentina

April 11, 1982
Wheaton, Illinois

General secretary of Evangelical Union of South America (NA Section, Avant Ministries in 2004) **1942–75, merged into Gospel Missionary Union, 1975–76, and president of IFMA, 1959–62**. Cook was converted as a small boy in special services in Argentina. He moved to Canada (1929), then went to Brazil (1937), married his wife Elna on November 20, 1937, and in 1942 became the general secretary of EUSA, 1942–61. Under his leadership, the mission grew from 30 to 140 missionaries. He attended Dallas Theological Seminary.

Frederick W. Schroeder

June 24, 1896
Peotone, Illinois

April 16, 1982
Elmhurst, Illinois

President of Eden Theological Seminary, St. Louis, MO 1941–62. Schroeder married Laura Uhlhorn on May 21, 1919. He pastored Tabor Evangelical Church, Chicago, from 1918–41. He was the moderator of the Evangelical and Reformed Synod (1950) and a delegate to the WCC Convention (1954). He wrote *Preaching the Word with Authority* (1954).

Richard G. Flexon

June 18, 1895
Downer, New Jersey

April 19, 1982
Salisbury, Maryland

General superintendent of Pilgrim Holiness Church (Wesleyan Church), **1958–62, and director of PHC World Missions, 1946–58**. Flexon's mother died when he was just six, the same year he was converted under his father's ministry. Flexon married Emma Hunter on June 16, 1915. He pastored at McKeesport, PA, and Shacklesford, VA (1915–19), where he also served as president of Beulah Holiness Academy (1919–29). He was the president of Central Pilgrim College, Bartlesville, OK, from 1962–64. As a powerful evangelist, he spent his senior years raising funds for God's Bible School in Cincinnati, OH. Some 150,000 responded to his altar calls.

David J. Fant

Jan. 27, 1897
Atlanta, Georgia

April 23, 1982

President of New York (International in 1978) **Bible Society, 1946–63**. Fant married Sara Willis on August 19, 1920. He was ordained a Baptist minister on June 1, 1921. He pastored the First Congregational Church, Woodhaven, NY (1921–27); directed the Long Island Evangelistic Association (1927–29); pastored the Bel-lerose Baptist Church, Brooklyn, NY (1934–37) and the Gospel Tabernacle, New York City from 1940 on. Fant was involved with CMA from time to time and wrote, *The Advance of Rome on America* and *All about the Sunday School*.

W. Cameron Townsend

July 9, 1896
Riverside County, California

April 23, 1982
Waxham, North Carolina

Founder and first director of Wycliffe Bible Translators, 1935–71. Townsend was a missions pioneer like CAREY and LIVINGSTONE. He was a Bible-distributing missionary to Guatemala, 1917–32. It all started when a native asked him, "If your God is so smart, how come he doesn't know our language?" He spent ten years getting the NT into their language. This started the movement involving hundreds of missionaries that has resulted in the translation of portions of the Bible into 1,000 different languages. Townsend married Elvira Malmstrom on July 9, 1919 (died: December 24, 1944), and later, Elaine Mielke on April 4, 1946. He began his work at Keswick, NJ (1933), starting his linguistic courses in Sulpher Springs, AR (1934), the first three-month Bible translator school. Two years later, his Summer Institute of Linguistics was incorporated in Mexico, which later moved to the University of Oklahoma campus. In 1963, WBT workers totaled more than 1,100. In 1985, WBT had 6,000 members working with 1,000 language groups. Townsend published his translation of *The New Testament in Cavchivel* (1931).

Calvin G. Carter

Sept. 18, 1892
Tolar, Texas

May 30, 1982
Glen Rose, Texas

President of Hispanic Baptist Theological Seminary, San Antonio, TX 1949–60. Carter was converted in the summer of 1905. He was ordained a Baptist on May 2, 1917, at FBC, Ft. Worth. After service in WWI, he pastored in Dewar, OK. Carter married Amelia S. Harris on May 11, 1919 (died: February, 1971), and Gladys Hardy on March 25, 1972. They served for about a year in Brazil, 1926–27 until health derailed them. After a pastorate in Timpson, TX, from 1934–35, he then took the FBC, Raymondville, with the understanding that they were to have a Mexican mission. Soon he was working with the El Paso Baptist Association. Carter moved to Corpus Christi, then San Antonio, always burdened to continue his work with Mexicans. He conducted funerals at the rate of one per week. He died from complications from the shingles.

Fred Hornshuh

Jan. 13, 1884
Oregon City, Oregon

June 17, 1982
Portland, Oregon

Founder and first general chairman of Bible Standard Missions Conference (Open Bible Standard Church in 1935), **1919–30.** In 1935, BSM became a part of Open Bible Evangelistic Association (OB Standard Churches). Hornshuh was converted in 1907. He married Beulah Calkins on May 4, 1910. He helped found Bible Standard Conferences (1917), the Bible Standard Mission (1919), and the Lighthouse Temple, Eugene, OR. He preached a tent revival meeting in Eugene, OR, in 1925. He also founded Eugene (OR) Bible College, serving as president until 1930. He pastored in Klamath Falls, OR (1930–37); Tacoma, WA (1937–44); and Portland, OR (1944–51). Hornshuh also served as the editor of *Bible Standard Magazine* (*Overcomer*), 1919 on.

Eugene L. Clark

March 13, 1925
Maxwell, Nebraska

June 29, 1982
Lincoln, Nebraska

Music director of *Back to the Bible* radio ministry, 1950–63. Clark wrote lyrics and music of "Nothing Is Impossible." Upon graduating from MBI, he joined *Back to the Bible*, Lincoln, NE. Clark married Ferne Vincent on August 1, 1955. He wrote three cantatas, more than 100 gospel choruses, and produced 20 records. Crippling arthritis and later blindness in 1978 confined him to his bed, 1963–82.

Reuben H. Mueller

June 2, 1897
St. Paul, Minnesota

July 5, 1982
Franklin, Indiana

Senior bishop of Evangelical United Brethren (United Methodist Church in 1968) **Church, 1954–68, and president of National Council of Churches, 1963–66**. Mueller married Magdalene Staffacher on December 26, 1919. Mueller served pastorates in Minnesota and South Bend and Indianapolis, IN, before becoming a district supervisor in 1937. He was the executive secretary of the Board of Christian Education in 1943. He also served as bishop (1954) of the United Methodist Church (1968).

Oren H. Baker

June 10, 1894
Alderson, West Virginia

July 11, 1982

Executive secretary of Association of Theological Schools, 1952–54. Baker was ordained as a Baptist in 1919 and married Margaret Benedict on September 8, 1923. Baker pastored at FBC, Morgantown, WV (1922–28); pastored at Parsells Avenue Baptist Church, Rochester, NY; taught Applied Christianity and Pastoral Counseling at Colgate-Rochester Theological Seminary, 1935–45; and then was appointed its dean in 1945. Baker also served in France during WWI.

Charles H. Stevens

Jan. 10, 1892
Johnson City, North Carolina

July 16, 1982
Winston-Salem, North Carolina

First president of Piedmont Bible College, Winston–Salem, NC 1945–63, 1964–70. At age 19, Stevens finally had the assurance of his salvation. He pastored in North Fork, KY (1919–23), Cliffside (NC) Baptist Church (1923–25) and Salem Baptist Church, Winston-Salem, NC (1925–28). Stevens married Grace Weaver in the summer of 1927. He then pastored the First Baptist Church, Bessemer, AL (1928–34), returning to the WS church (Salem), 1934–72. That church voted to supply RALPH FREED's salary (which made it possible for Freed's son, PAUL, to start Trans-World Radio). He was also moderator of Southwide Baptist Fellowship, 1964–65, and hosted the same in 1959.

Conrad Lund

Jan. 5, 1922
Plentywood, Montana

July 17, 1982

President of Lutheran Bible Institute of Seattle (Trinity Lutheran College), **1971–81**. He married Ann Sponheim in 1948. Lund pastored at Calvary of Golden Valley, Minneapolis, MN (1947–50) and at Multiple Parish, Poplar, MT (1950–52). He served as a chaplain in the US Air Force, 1952–54. Lund also pastored at Mount Zion, Edmonton, Alberta (1954–57) and St. Paul of Shorewood, Seattle, WA (1961–71). He was president of Camrose Lutheran College, 1957–61.

Smith J. Jones

June 21, 1929
Winchester, Kentucky

July 18, 1982
Durham, North Carolina

President of Iliff School of Theology, Denver, CO 1969–81. Under Jones's leadership, the student number increased from 110 to 375. From 1948–61, Jones was in Nashville working a variety of positions with the Methodist Board of Education. From 1961–66, he was on the faculty of Garrett Theological Seminary. From 1966–69, he pastored the Gobin Memorial UM Church in Greencastle, IN, on the campus of DePauw University. He married Bonnie Schuldt. Jones had been dean at Duke University for only 18 months when a sudden heart attack took his life. His *Your God Is Too Small* (1952) was widely acclaimed.

John B. Phillips

Sept. 16, 1906

July 21, 1982

Author of *The New Testament in Modern English* (1958). Phillips was the vicar at Church of the Good Shepherd, Lee (1940–44); at St. John's, Redhill in 1945, prebendary at Chechester Cathedral (1957–60) and canon at Salisbury Cathedral (1964–69). He was also the author of many widely known books, from *Letters to Young Churches* (1947) to *Peter's Portrait of Jesus* (1976).

Keith Green

Oct. 21, 1953
Sheep's Head Bay, New York

July 28, 1982
Lindale, Texas

Young contemporary musical artist whose outreach ministries were called Last Day ministries, from 1977 on. Green was converted in 1973 and married his wife, Melody, on December 25, 1973. In 1975, they left the world's music and started serving the Lord. Green held concerts regularly until a plane crash took his life along with 11 others. Taking off from the Lindale ranch, an accident occurred: the pilot, Don Burmeister, the Smalleys and their six children, and Green and his two children were killed. Green's wife, Melody, renamed their Last Day Ministries to Youth With a Mission in 1991. She continued with the ministry until 1996, which is the year she married her second husband, Andrew Sievright.

Wynn T. Stairs

Jan. 4, 1901
Temperance Vale, New Brunswick, Canada

Aug. 13, 1982
Saint Stephens, New Brunswick, Canada

Director of the United Pentecostal Church Int. Missions, Hazelwood, MO 1945–62. Stairs was converted in October, 1920. He held pastorates in St. Stephens (1917–46) and married Margaret Delano on October 10, 1934. He made missionary trips to many sections of the world, a vision which began while he was working at a saw mill in 1924. In his later years, he returned to St. Stephens.

Milton H. Otto

Dec. 6, 1914
Cherokee, Iowa

Aug. 20, 1982
Mankato, Minnesota

President of Bethany Lutheran Theological Seminary, Mankato, MN 1957–76, and also of Evangelical Lutheran Synod, 1954–57. Otto served as vicar at Princeton, MN; taught at Eau Clair, WI; pastored in Cottonwood, MN, and Lawler, IA. He retired from his teaching in 1980 because of poor health, having seen 50 men graduate from the seminary in the service of the ELS. His wife's name was Marjorie. His funeral was conducted at Mt. Olive Lutheran Church, Mankato, MN.

G. Archer Weniger

April 12, 1915

Sept. 6, 1982

Fundamentalist leader. Weniger was the founder and editor of *The Blue Print*, a weekly newspaper opposing liberalism, new evangelicalism, and compromise. For many years, he pastored the Foothill Blvd. Baptist Church, Oakland (moved to Castor Valley), CA. He helped found Lucerne Christian Conference and taught at San Francisco Baptist Seminary.

A. Eric Hutchings

May 9, 1910
Warrington, England

Sept. 21, 1982

Evangelist whose crowds were England's largest in his generation, except for the Billy Graham crusades. Hutchings married his wife, Mary, on October 26, 1935. Brought up in a Christian home, he was converted in his early teens. Before his ministry days, he worked in the legal department of an insurance company. Hutchings began getting active in Youth for Christ and arranged Billy Graham's first service on British soil. He began his evangelism endeavors in 1952 in Hastings. Hutchings' largest crusade was in Birmingham in 1960 (five weeks, with over 100,000 attending). His ministry was known as the Hour of Revival.

John S. Wimbish

June 19, 1915
Macon, Georgia

Sept. 25, 1982

Well-known Baptist pastor. Wimbish was a salesman for the National Cash Register Company when he was called into the ministry in 1939. He graduated from MBI in 1943, then he went to Mercer University in Macon, GA. He pastored the Avondale Baptist Church there, 1943–46. He became pastor of FBC, Edgefield, SC (1946–50); at Calvary Baptist Church, New York City (1950–58); then at Seminole Heights (FL) Baptist (1958–68). He also held three other pastorates, 1968–77, before retiring to Valrico, FL.

George E. Ladd

July 31, 1911
Alberta, Canada

Oct. 10, 1982 (?)
Pasadena, California (?)

Theologian, who spent a lifetime studying and teaching. Ladd was converted at age 19 in Spearsmont, ME (where his doctor father had moved the family) in a small Methodist church with a lady pastor. He married Winifred P. Webber on July 11, 1933. He pastored the FBC of Gilford, NH (1933–36) and of Montpelier, VT (1936–42). Ladd pastored Blaney Memorial Church in Boston, MA, from 1942–45. From 1946–50, he was an instructor in Greek and New Testament at Gordon College, his alma mater. He then spent the rest of his life teaching Biblical Theology at Fuller Theological Seminary, 1950 on. His advocacy for a critical, yet loyal, approach to Holy Scripture was influential. He was a member of Temple Baptist Church, Los Angeles, CA.

Lester Roloff

June 28, 1914
Dawson, Texas

Nov. 2, 1982
Normangee, Texas

Pastor, evangelist (40 years), and children's home director. Roloff married Marie Brady on August 10, 1936. He will always be remembered for his confrontation with the state of Texas over the issue of licensing his facilities in the 1970s. His People's Church, Corpus Christi, TX (28 years as pastor), branched into a radio ministry (*Family Altar Program*) on 90 stations and gave assistance to troubled young people through a series of five homes he had built. He was killed in an airplane crash with four staff members en route to a Kansas City, MO, meeting. A huge funeral of 4,500 was held at the coliseum in Corpus Christi where he had lived since 1944.

Johannes H. V. Knudson

Oct. 10, 1902
Nysted, Nebraska

Nov. 14, 1982
Des Moines, Iowa

President of Grand View College and Seminary (Lutheran School of Theology, Chicago, IL, in 1964), **Des Moines, IA 1942–53**. Knudson married Ellen K. Paulsen on July 19, 1934. He taught at GVS, Des Moines, IA (1927–35), then pastored in Askov, MN (1935–39) and in Hartford, CT (1939–42). Knudson was also professor and dean of the Graduate School of Lutheran School of Theology, Maywood, IL, from 1954–82.

Frank C. Torrey

Nov. 16, 1894
Osceola Mills, Pennsylvania

Dec. 10, 1982
Boca Raton, Florida

President of IFMA, 1946–47. He was a pastor and also involved in Bible Conference outreach. Initially, Torrey was a professor at the Philadelphia School of the Bible, 1924–25. He then pastored FBC of Cherry Creek, NY (1927); the Merrit Park Gospel Church of Creeskill, PA (1927–31) and the Calvary Baptist Church of Altoona, PA (1931–37). After pastoring three different churches in ten years, Torrey found his "home" pastorate at the Calvary Independent Church of Lancaster (PA), where he served for 26 years from 1937–1963. He was in Bible Conference work, 1963–70, and was widely used in these endeavors.

Richard A. Foster

Oct. 5, 1900
Monsell, Missouri

Dec. 14, 1982
Green Forest, Arkansas

First director of United Missionary Fellowship (Biblical Ministries Worldwide in 1987), **Lawrenceville, GA 1950–65**. He married Reah Craig (January 15, 1922) and Mary A. Buckland (June 26, 1943). Foster taught in Lawrenceville, GA, and Phoenix, AZ in a Bible college; pastored in Riverside and Sacramento, CA, at Bible churches; also directing the Pioneer Bible Mission in that area. He was the assistant minister at Carmichael Bible Church, Sacramento, CA from 1965–72. Later, he returned to Caseville, MO, and Green Forest, AR, to pastor. He died of cancer in a rest home.

Samuel H. Shane

June 29, 1903
McDonald, Pennsylvania

Dec. 17, 1982

Stated clerk of the United Presbyterian Church (PC USA in 1983) **of North America, 1954–58**, when that denomination merged in 1958 with the Presbyterian Church in the US of America to form the United Presbyterian Church in the USA. He married Sarah L. Rohrer. He pastored the Second UPC, Indiana County, PA (1928–36); was associate pastor of First UPC, Indiana, PA (1936–37); and stated supply of the Plum Creek UPC, Indiana County, PA (1930–37). From 1937–44, he pastored the Second UPC, Washington, PA. Shane was manager-treasurer of the Board of Christian Education of the UPC of North America, 1945–58. He lived in Glenside, PA.

Walter V. Grant

1913
Arkansas

1983

Healing evangelist and author, he was a successful businessman before becoming an Assemblies of God minister in 1945. Grant launched his first campaign (1949) although poor health stopped him (1956). He became vice president of the Voice of Healing organization and a consultant to many healing evangelists. Writing was one of his strengths. He started the *Voice of Deliverance* (1962) and by 1973 had two million circulation. He authored some 600 books and, except for GORDON LINDSAY, was the most important writer on healing. His son, W. V. Grant Jr., carried on a similar ministry.

George M. Alexander

May 15, 1914
Jacksonville, Florida

Jan. 9, 1983
Columbia, South Carolina

Dean of University of the South, Sewanee, TN 1956–74. Alexander married Mary Bedell on May 25, 1935. He pastored three churches in Florida (1939–48), and also Trinity Church in Columbia, SC (1949–55). He served as secretary of the Episcopal diocese in Florida, 1941–48. Alexander also lectured at St. Augustine's College in Canterbury, England, in 1960. He authored the *Handbook of Biblical Personalities*.

Lillian Levescente Dickson

Jan. 29, 1901
Prior Lake, Minnesota

Jan. 14, 1983
Taipei, Formosa (Taiwan)

Outstanding missionary and president of Mustard Seed, 1948–83. Lillian and her husband, Jim Dickson (February 23, 1900–June 15, 1967), composed one of the greatest missionary teams ever. Lillian and Jim were married on May 16, 1927. From 1927–40 and 1946–69, they spread the gospel in Formosa in an unparalleled fashion. During WWII, from 1940–46, they served in British Guiana (Guyana). BOB PIERCE considered her the greatest missionary he ever knew. Her life's story was so intense and powerful that it appeared in *Reader's Digest* in July, 1962. Lillian was a friend to the lepers and tuberculars, a mother to the orphaned and distressed, a teacher of the Aborigines, counselor to native children in prison, helping hand to blind and deaf, Angel of Mercy to those in her bamboo clinics, and an accordionist at the outdoor meetings. Formosans called her "the littlest lady with the biggest heart." Jim was the principal of the Taiwan Theological College for over 30 years. She wrote *These My People*, 1958.

Frank E. Gaebelein

March 31, 1899
Mount Vernon, New York

Jan. 19, 1983
Arlington, Virginia

Educator, founder and headmaster of Stony Brook School, Long Island, NY, 1921–63. Gaebelein was the son of A. C. GAEBELEIN and married Dorothy Medd on December 8, 1923 (died: November 1980). He organized SBS and it became the model of early Christian high schools. Gaebelein was a visiting faculty lecturer and Bible Conference speaker in many churches. In 1963 he became co–editor of *Christianity Today* magazine, later the general editor of the *Expositor's Bible Commentary* (1972–83) series and played a key part in the development of the NIV version of the Bible. He also authored 15 books, ranging from *Down through the Ages* (1924) to *From Day to Day* (1975).

Howard H. Clark

April 23, 1903
Fort MacLeod, Alberta, Canada

Jan. 21, 1983
Toronto, Ontario, Canada

Primate of Anglican Church of Canada, 1959–70. Clark was ordained in 1932 and two years later, married Anna Wilson. He led the Christ Church Cathedral in Ottowa, Ontario (1945–54), then served as a bishop in Edmonton, Alberta (1954–59), after which he lived in Winnipeg, Manitoba (1959–67). He was slowed down by a stroke in 1972. He then moved to Toronto and became the chancellor of Trinity College, 1972–82.

Horace F. Dean

Feb. 27, 1897
Waxahachie, Texas

Jan. 30, 1983
Media, Pennsylvania

Founder and director of Christ for America, 1943–61. Dean was converted in 1915, when he was challenged by John 5:25. He married Jean Osborne on June 28, 1921. After he saw evangelist Hyman Appelman reap 2,000 converts from a crusade in Philadelphia, PA in 1942, he started preaching evangelistic campaigns, himself, throughout the nation, directing 450 area–wide crusades. Thousands were converted through his ministry. He influenced 35 men to go into evangelism. He conducted many visitation seminars, was a member of Grace Chapel in Havertown, PA, and wrote many books.

Efird B. Keisler

Dec. 13, 1897
Gilbert, South Carolina

Jan. 30, 1983
Saluda, South Carolina

President of Central Lutheran Theological Seminary (Lutheran School of Theology, Chicago in 1967), Fremont, NE 1949–1964. Keisler was married to Mabel Sease, ordained in 1923 and served as a missionary in the southeast, 1923–27. He pastored at St. John's Lutheran Church, Spartanburg, SC (1927–31) and at Redeemer Lutheran Church, Newberry, SC (1931–46). Keisler also served as a professor at Western Theological Seminary, Fremont, Nebraska (1947–49) and as pastor of St. John's Lutheran Church, Clinton, SC (1964–69).

G. Christian Weiss

Nov. 19, 1910
Stillwater, Minnesota

Jan. 31, 1983
Bella Vista, Arkansas

President of Gospel Missionary Union, 1939–51, and first director of *Back to the Bible* (radio broadcast, Lincoln, NE) **Missionary Agency, 1952–78**. Weiss was converted in Pine River, MN. He pastored a Baptist Church in Grove City, MN, from 1929–32. He married Olga Holmberg on July 8, 1930 (died: January, 1960) and Evelyn Whitfield in 1961. He also served as a missionary in Minnesota (1932–35); and in Morocco (1936–40). He traveled during his ministry to 100 countries. He wrote much, including *On Being a Real Christian* printed in 25 languages.

Harold R. Heininger

Aug. 13, 1895
Lima, Ohio

Feb. 3, 1983
Lebanon, Ohio

President of Evangelical Theological Seminary (GETS in 1974), **Naperville, IL 1939–55**. He was a soldier in WWI and began teaching at ETS in 1923. Heininger also served as a bishop of the Evangelical United Brethren, 1954–83. He served in the northwest area until he retired in 1969. He spent his later years in Naperville, IL.

Paul M. Levengood

Dec. 26, 1917
Walnut Creek, Ohio

Feb. 21, 1983
Dayton, Kentucky

Director of Tennessee Mountain Mission, 1956–82. Leavengood married Lillia Hummel in the early 1940s. He helped his parents develop TMM and its outreach, developing the camp work, and pastoring several spots in rural Tennessee. He was a diligent, people person, serving faithfully in the hills of Tennessee. He had a heart attack and stroke. His younger brother carried on his work.

Fred M. Barlow

March 1, 1921
Marlington, West Virginia

Feb. 22, 1983
Lakeland, Florida

Greatest Sunday School authority since the CLAYTON RISLEY days. Barlow was converted when Albert Rudolph, a layperson, knocked on his door and invited him to Sunday School and church in Akron, OH. He held many Sunday School conferences, speaking in numerous colleges and seminaries. Barlow married Meathyl Forte, and they had four children. He held pastorates in New York, Ohio, and Michigan, 1943–59. In 1959 he was elected National Sunday School Consultant for Regular Baptist Press and the GARB. He died of cancer.

R. Dennis Heard

Nov. 10, 1918
Coal Hill, Arkansas

Feb. 26, 1983
Joplin, Missouri

President of Pentecostal Church of God (Inc. in 1978) **of America, Inc., Joplin, MO 1953–75.** Heard was converted on December 27, 1937, in a Los Angeles Pentecostal Assembly. Heard married Edith Shaffer on December 5, 1939. He was the divisional officer of the Pentecostal Young People's Association in Los Angeles, 1938–42. He also served as editor of *PYPA Witness* (1942–46) and was national PYPA president, 1946–49. He also pastored in Bakersfield, CA, (1942–46 and 1949–53), and at First Community Church, Joplin, MO (1978–83), where he lived his last 30 years. He traveled to 34 countries.

Catherine Wood Marshall LeSourd

Sept. 27, 1914
Johnson City, Tennessee

March 18, 1983
Boyton Beach, Florida

Inspired author of many popular books, including *Mr. Jones, Meet the Master* (1949), *A Man Called Peter* (1951), *Beyond Ourselves* (1961), and *Christy* (1967). Catherine was asked to speak at many churches and writing seminars. Catherine married Peter Marshall on November 4, 1936 (died: Jan. 25, 1949–former chaplain of the U.S. Senate). Her book about his life, *A Man Called Peter* (1951), was made into a movie in 1955, and later *Christy* (1967) also was made into a movie. Her books, *Chosen Books*, established in 1952, sold very well. Catherine married Leonard LeSourd on November 14, 1959 (died: February, 1996).

Raymond F. Hamilton

Feb. 24, 1905
Muscatine, Iowa

March 23, 1983
Albuquerque, New Mexico

President of ACC, 1961–63, 1972, and GARB Council Member, 1934–62. Hamilton was converted by the witness of a friend and pastor in October, 1921. Hamilton married Katherine Thomas on June 22, 1924, and they had three children. He began as an assistant pastor, then later became pastor at Central Baptist Church, Gary, IN (1933–39); Pana, IL (1939–45); Calvary Baptist, Quincy, IL (1945–47); Burholme Baptist, Philadelphia, PA (1947–51); Belden Avenue Baptist Church, Chicago, IL (1951–63); and Temple Baptist, Portsmouth, OH (1969–83). Hamilton also served as the American secretary of ICC from 1963–83.

Henry Bast

May 6, 1906
Zaltdrummel, Netherlands

March 29, 1983
Grand Rapids, Michigan

Radio evangelist for *Temple Time*, sponsored by the Reformed Church of America from 1952 on. Bast pastored the Richmond Reformed Church, Grand Rapids, MI, from 1933–39, then was college pastor and professor of Bible at Hope College, Holland, MI until 1944. Bast was married to Sara Gerding (1933–39), Henrietta Gerding (1940–56) and Agnes Banderly (April 23, 1956–until death). He pastored at Bethany Reformed Church in Grand Rapids, 1944–56 and 1963–72. He was professor at Western Theological Seminary, Holland, MI from 1956–60.

C. Stacey Woods

Sept. 10, 1909
Sydney/Bendigo, Australia

April 10, 1983
Lausanne, Switzerland

First president of Inter-Varsity, 1940–60. Woods came to America in 1930 to complete his education at Wheaton (IL) College and Dallas (TX) Theological Seminary. He developed Inter-Varsity in Canada, 1934–52, and started Inter-Varsity in the States at the Univ. of Michigan in 1939. Woods married Yvonne Ritchie in 1939. In 1941, Woods founded *His* magazine and edited it, 1950–52. He moved to Lausanne, Switzerland in 1961 to expedite his general secretaryship of the International Fellowship of Evangelical Students, 1947–71. He and BILL BRIGHT were leaders in the expansion of the college student movements more than anyone else in their generation. He wrote *The Growth of a Work of God* (1978).

Corrie Ten Boom

April 15, 1892
Amsterdam, Netherlands

April 15, 1983
Placentia, California

Renowned WWII survivor and writer of many books, including *The Hiding Place* (1971), which developed into a widely used film in 1975. Raised in a godly home, she was a watchmaker, 1911-1944 in Haarlem, Netherlands. A raid on her family's watch shops by the Gestapo on February 28, 1944 placed her in Ravensbruck death camp. Corrie spent time in this Nazi concentration camp for hiding Jewish refugees in her home. She was released on January 1, 1945. She made a post-war visit there in 1947. Her heroic actions in World War II prompted speaking engagements, so she traveled around the world for her last 25 years, speaking in 60 countries. Ten Boom made her final visit to the Netherlands in 1976, then retired to California to Shalom House. Chuck Smith conducted her funeral, April 22. She is buried in Santa Ana, CA. Her favorite Bible verse was Psalm 91:1.

Gaines M. Cook

April 3, 1897
Leroy, Illinois

April 19, 1983
Black Mountain, North Carolina

Executive secretary (president in 1968) of Christian Church (Disciples of Christ), 1946–64. Cook married Edith Rose on September 15, 1921. Ordained in Washington, D.C. in 1917, he pastored in Tallula, IL (1920–21); Fisher's Island, NY (1921–25) and Centennial Church, Bloomington, IL (1925–28). Cook also served as the Director of the Ohio Christian Missionary Society (1928–31) and as the state secretary of Ohio Christian Churches (1931–46). He represented the Disciples of Christ at three WCC assemblies, 1948, 1954 and 1961.

Harry J. Hager

May 16, 1899
Grand Rapids, Michigan

May 14, 1983
Holland, Michigan

Pastor of Bethany Reformed Church in Chicago, IL 1929–75. This church had 3,000 members, making it the largest in the denomination. Hager was ordained in 1920 and pastored a Presbyterian church in Volga, SC (1920–21) and Forest Grove, MI (1924–26). Hager married Jeanette VanderWerp on August 12, 1924. He was a professor of Bible and college pastor at Hope College in Holland, MI from 1926–29. He held many revival crusades and went to Europe eleven times. He was a good friend of JOHN R. RICE.

Charles W. Koller

March 11, 1896
Waco, Texas

May 19, 1983
Melrose Park, Illinois

President of Northern Baptist Theological Seminary, Chicago (Lombard), IL, 1939–61. Koller was ordained as a Baptist in 1922 and was a student pastor while attending Southwestern Baptist Theological Seminary. He married Selma Steinhaus on September 9, 1924. He pastored at Clinton Hill Baptist Church, Newark, NJ, from 1927–38. He was the Director of the Chicago Bible Society in 1938. He was a member of the General Council of the Northern Baptist Convention since 1941. Warren Wiersbe credited his communication skills to Koller.

Hyman J. Appelman

Jan. 7, 1902
Moghiliev, Russia

Hyman Appelman

May 28, 1983
Kansas City, Missouri

Converted Jewish evangelist with a worldwide ministry, 1942–83. Appelman came to America in 1914 and practiced law in Chicago, 1921–25. He was converted in the pastor's study of a Christian church in Denver, CO, on March 19, 1925. He then served in the U.S. medical division of the army, 1925–30. Appelman married Verna Cook on September 4, 1930. They had two children. He pastored in Oklahoma and Texas, 1930–34, He was an evangelist for the Texas SBC from 1934–42. Soon he was holding large meetings as an independent evangelist. His 1940 (Philadelphia) and 1942 (Detroit) crusades sparked a comeback to city wide revivals, which had been dormant since the BILLY SUNDAY days. He traveled 40 weeks out of the year and probably preached more revival services than any man in history. His books numbered around 40. Many have said that he was the greatest preacher they ever heard.

John A. Mackay

May 17, 1889
Inverness, Scotland

June 9, 1983
Princeton/Hightstown, New Jersey

President of Princeton (NJ) Theological Seminary, 1936–59; of Association of Theological Schools, 1948–50; and of World Alliance of Reformed Churches, 1954–59. Mackay married Jane Wells on August 16, 1916. He was principal of a college in Peru (1916–25), writer and evangelist for South American Federation of YMCA's (1925–32), and secretary for the Presbyterian Board of Foreign Missions (1932–36). His *Preface to Christian Theology* (1941) began his ecumenical theology emphasis. He was the editor of *Theology Today* (1944–51). In 1960, he became a professor at American University, Waington, DC. His books range from *The Other Spanish Christ* (1932) to *Redidade Idolatria* (1970), writing in both Spanish and English.

Charles P. Taft

Sept. 20, 1897
Cincinnati, Ohio

June 24, 1983
Cincinnati, Ohio

President of Federal Council of Churches (NCC in 1950), **1946–48**. Taft married Eleanor Chase on October 6, 1917 (died: 1961). Taft was a Cincinnati lawyer. He passed the Ohio bar in 1922. He served as a member of the City Council (1938–42, 1948–51, 1955–57) and as the mayor of Cincinnati (1955–57). He wrote several books including: *City Management: the Cincinnati Experiment* (1933) and *Democracy in Politics and Economics* (1950). He was an Episcopalian and the son of President William H. Taft.

Wilfred O. H. Garman

Aug. 15, 1899
Philadelphia, Pennsylvania

July 2, 1983
Pittsburgh, Pennsylvania

Founder and first president of Associated Gospel Churches, 1958–79, and president of ACC, 1947–50. Garman married Josephine Hill on June 26, 1931. He was ordained in the United Presbyterian Church (1925) but became independent (1939). He pastored in Altoona, PA (1929–39), and at the Callende Memorial Church, Wilkinsburg, PA (1939–73). His AGC ministry helped fundamentalists get into the chaplaincy. He also held a pastorate in Monroeville, PA, after 1974.

Fred R. Brock Jr.

July 25, 1910
Flint, Michigan

July 5, 1983
Bothell, Washington

President of Western Baptist Bible College, El Cerrito, CA (Salem, OR, in 1978), **1964–73**. The oldest of seven children, Brock was converted at age eight. After graduating from MBI in 1932, he married Dorothie Tuttle and had four sons. Early pastorates were in Breckenridge, CO; Strathmore, CA, and Petaluma, CA. He was a missionary for four years to the Navajo Indians in Arizona. In 1946, Brock began a long association with the college as a part-time instructor.

Harold J. Doan

June 1, 1924
Wyoming, Michigan

July 28, 1983
Los Angeles, California (?)

President of Church of God General Conference, Morrow, GA 1954–68. Doan married Jean Lindsay Koontz on April 12, 1944. He served as pastor of the Church of God in Chicago until 1953. He then served as pastor of the Morning Star Church of God in South Bend, IN, from 1953–55. In 1955, he moved to Oregon, IL, to serve as editor of the *Restitution Herald* and executive director of the Church of God, General Conference. He was a part-time instructor at Oregon Bible College. They moved to Los Angeles and pastored Valley Church of God until the time of his death. He was also in the advertising business with his brother, Michael. He died four days after a massive heart attack.

Roy Keith

Jan. 20, 1907
Halltown, Missouri

July 31, 1983
Springfield, Missouri

Dominant leader in the early days of the Fundamental Methodist Church, Springfield, MO, 1944–71. Raised in a Christian home in Plano, MO, Keith was converted in his early twenties via a woman preacher. He married Lora Williams on June 13, 1929 (died: 1994). He worked on a farm and was associated with the Methodist Protestant Church for a while. He pastored small churches in southwestern Missouri, John's Chapel of Ash Grove, MO, being a dominant one as he led that work at several different intervals. He helped organize a number of churches in the area. He pastored in Aurora, MO from 1964–76. In later years, he was supply pastor, held revivals, and conducted funerals. He died of cancer and on his deathbed he said, "So much to do."

Henry Barraclough

Dec. 14, 1891
Windhill, Yorkshire, England

Aug. 17, 1983
Philadelphia, Pennsylvania

Wrote the lyrics and music to "Ivory Palaces" (1918), a beautiful hymn, which he was inspired to write after hearing J. WILBUR CHAPMAN speak on Psalm 45:8. In 1914, Barraclough joined the CHAPMAN/CHARLES ALEXANDER evangelistic team as a pianist in England. He followed them on tour to America and remained there, serving in WWII. From 1919–61 he served the General Assembly of Presbyterian churches in America. He was first their secretary and later worked as manager on the administration department staff. Barraclough's love of music began with organ and piano lessons when he was only five and carried him on to write 20 hymn texts and 120 hymn tunes.

Alfred Carleton

March 26, 1903
Albany, New York

Aug. 22, 1983
Columbus, Ohio

Executive vice president (CEO) of American Board of Commissioners for Foreign Missions, 1954–64, renamed United Church Board for World Missions, 1961–70. Carleton married Mary Cashmore on February 1, 1929. He was a teacher in Turkey (1924–27) and Syria (1930–53), serving as president of Aleppo College, Syria (1937–54). Carleton was a member of the general board of the NCC. He also served as trustee at Andover-Newton Theological Seminary, Newton Center, MA. He lived in White Plains, NY.

Carlyle Scott

Mar. 1, 1910
Montgomery County, Indiana

Aug. 25, 1983
Indianapolis, Indiana

Evangelist for over 50 years from Crawfordsville, IN. During his crusades, Scott witnessed over 70,000 coming forward during the invitations, and at least 163 men dedicating their lives to the ministry. Scott's wife was named Gertrude.

Paul F. Bauman

June 12, 1908
Genoa City, Wisconsin

Sept. 7, 1983
Genoa City, Wisconsin

First director of Rural American Missionary Society, 1960–72. Bauman was saved as a teenager in Genoa City. Early on, he worked in insurance, marrying Nellie Rowe (1908–1983) on August 21, 1933. In the 1930s, Bauman began starting and building up churches in Tennessee. During the 1940s, he was in the Millington (Memphis area), TN, Naval Air Base working in the military. He pastored in Connorsville, IN and Henry, IL, and ran a bookstore in each place. He started the Tennessee Mountain Mission, Dayton, TN, 1952-53, working in schools and developing the Cumberland Camp. Bauman worked in Kermit, WV, as the RAMS developed, then moved to Beckley, WV. He died of heart failure after a very aggressive ministry to the forgotten people of Appalachia.

Ruth Carter Stapleton

Aug. 7, 1929
Archery, Georgia

Sept. 26, 1983
Hope Mills, North Carolina

Baptist healing evangelist who was thrust into prominence as President Jimmy Carter's sister in 1976 during the presidential campaign. Converted in 1950, she inspired spiritual interest in her brother's life. During the 1950s, Ruth suffered severe mental depression. Following this, she began to promote holistic health through complete "inner healing," a combination of in-depth psychology and faith healing. Stapleton opened a 35-acre retreat center called "Holovita" (whole life). She witnessed to many celebrities, including Larry Flynt. She died of cancer of the pancreas after a five-month battle. She wrote *The Gift of Inner Healing* (1976) and *The Experience of Inner Healing* (1977).

Maynard Force

July 17, 1904 — Two Harbors, Minnesota
Oct. 1, 1983 — Los Angeles, California

First president of California Lutheran Bible Institute, 1950–77. Force was a Bible teacher and evangelist from the time of his student days and into retirement. He was widely used in his circles. On August 23, 1923, he had a deep spiritual experience that led him to a decision to serve the Lord. Ordained by the Augustana Lutheran church in 1931, he pastored Calvary Lutheran Church, Moline, IL until 1940. During this time, he married Edna Benson (died: November 12, 1978). He was co-pastor at Trinity Lutheran, Minnehaha Falls, MN from 1940–48, then was called to teach at the Lutheran Bible Institute in Minneapolis. He went to California and founded CLBI, heading it for 26 years. After his retirement, he was a Bible teacher at Hope Lutheran Church in Minneapolis, MN, for six years. He last preached on May 27, 1983.

Edward M. Blaiklock

July 6, 1903 — Birmingham, England
Oct. 26, 1983 — Auckland, New Zealand

Baptist apologist and classics professor. Blaiklock came with his family, in 1909, to New Zealand. He taught classics in biblical and ancient history at Auckland University for 42 years and was professor of classics for 20 years before retiring in 1968. In 1921, Blaiklock accompanied two friends to an evangelical meeting for young men conducted in the Auckland Baptist Tabernacle and was strongly attracted by the message he heard. As he wrote later, "I went home and thought. The next morning I was a Christian." He married Kathleen Minnie Mitchell on November 13, 1928 (died February 8, 1978) and they had two sons. He frequently led tours to important archaeological sites in Bible lands. He was a leading layman of the Baptist Union of New Zealand and its president in 1970. Blaiklock was an apologist for the Christian faith, both in newspapers and on the radio. He edited the *Zondervan Pictorial Bible Atlas* (1969) and his other writings range from *Acts* (1959) to *Archaeology of the NT* (1970). He died of cancer.

Frank E. Mann

May 21, 1898 — Sidney, Indiana
Oct. 26, 1983 — Warrington, Missouri

Director of Child Evangelism Fellowship Grand Rapids, MI (Warrenton, MO, in 1976), **1966–71**. He married Elva Crowe on June 4, 1924. Mann was converted in a Brethren Church in Minneapolis in 1927. He was an auto parts buyer in Minneapolis, then became a chiropractor in 1936. Mann moved to Kansas around 1936 and became involved in CE work. He was soon the director for Kansas, then director of North Carolina area activities, before coming to head the International office. He died of a liver disease.

George D. Fleming

Jan. 21, 1890 — Ionia County, Michigan
Oct. 29, 1983 — Ft. Wayne, Indiana

Director of the United Brethren in Christ Missions, Huntington, IN 1936–61. Fleming married Daisy Griff on December 24, 1911 (died: August 25, 1976). He was a missionary in Sierra

Leone, 1909–32. After 1961, he served in churches in Michigan and Ontario. During the last year of his life, Fleming preached 13 times in Jamaica within a two-week period. He died in a hospital.

Julian C. McPheeters

July 6, 1889
Oxley, Missouri

Oct. 31, 1983
Lexington, Kentucky

President of Asbury Theological Seminary, Wilmore, KY 1942–62. McPheeters married Ethel Chilton on January 28, 1914. He was an evangelist (1912–17), then pastored Methodist churches in Missouri (1919–21), Montana (1921–23), Tucson, AZ (1923–30), and California. He was the pastor at Glide Memorial Methodist, San Francisco, CA, from 1930–48 and worked as the editor of the *Herald* (1942–62). McPheeters saw Asbury grow from 60 to 250 students. He wrote eleven books from *Sons of God* (1929) to *Faith for Men in Arms* (1913).

Arthur B. Cunningham

March 17, 1928
Hastings, Michigan

Nov. 10, 1983
Tuscon, Arizona

Director of Hiawatha (Continental in 1984) **Baptist Mission, Escanaba, MI, 1973–77, relocated in Grand Rapids, MI, 1977–83.** Converted at age 13 at Assyria Gospel Church, Cunningham attended Moody Bible Institute and married Edith Hyma in November, 1948. They lived in Mt. Pleasant, MI, and worked in children's work. He then became pastor of Dover (MI) Baptist Church; of Bible Baptist Church, Marlette, MI (1958–62); White Lake Baptist, Montague, MI (1962–67) and Maplelawn Baptist, Grand Rapids, MI (1967–73). He was preaching in Tucson, AZ, where he died of a massive stroke (cerebral hemorrhage).

Lester Place

Oct. 24, 1912
Valley Forge, Pennsylvania

Nov. 10, 1983
Lancaster, Pennsylvania

Evangelist, known for his "Musical Places" ministry. Place married Grace Haldeman on Sept. 26, 1936. He graduated from MBI in 1944 and they worked with PERCY CRAWFORD for a time. They then began their own ministry. Without children, they were able to travel full-time and see the ministry grow. They used marimbas, musical bells, saxophone, piano, octave chimes, and a steel guitar. They were members of Limerick (PA) Chapel. He died with a sudden heart attack while ministering in a restaurant to a church group.

James A. Duffecy

Oct. 9, 1912
Sydney, Australia

Nov. 17, 1983
Toronto, Ontario, Canada

First International Director of Open-Air Campaigners, 1965–83. Duffecy was converted at age twelve via Open-Air at Coogee Beach and worked twelve years for the *Sydney Sun*. Duffecy married Joyce Mayhew on Oct. 3, 1936. He joined the Open Air staff in 1940. He was soon field director, and then opened a work in New Zealand (1954) and in Canada (1956). He moved to the States in 1957.

William E. Hill

July 29, 1907
Atlanta, Georgia (?)

Hopewell, Virginia

Founder and first director of Presbyterian Evangelistic Fellowship, Decatur, GA 1958–74. Hill made a profound impact upon Presbyterianism in the twentieth century: lover of youth, pastor, community reformer, powerful preacher, Christian educator, author, church statesman and one of the founding fathers of the Presbyterian Church in America. In 1958, he left his pastorate at West End Presbyterian Church in Hopewell, VA, to concentrate on evangelism. He started holding crusades in the United States and for ten years was booked constantly. In 1965, a second evangelist joined him. In 1969, the first PEF Evangelism Conference was held in Montreat, NC. PCA Mission to the World became a part of this as it was born in 1970. It started the PCA in December, 1973.

W. Elwyn Davies

Aug. 24, 1917
Bryn Siriol, Wales

Dec. 13, 1983
Hamilton, Ontario, Canada

General director of Bible Christian Union, 1973–83, and president of IFMA, 1979–83. For 37 years, Davies served as a missionary and missionary leader for BCU. He grew up under the influence of the Welsh revival and married Pamela M. Hepworth on August 14, 1941. During WWII, he served as a British intelligence agent and chaplain. After the war, they served as BCU missionaries in Holland before moving to Canada to develop and direct the work of BCU. In September, 1982, he was forced to retire as he was in the middle of a two-year bout with cancer.

Eugene R. Bertermann

Sept. 2, 1914
Bittern Lake, Alberta, Canada

Dec. 29, 1983
Akron, Ohio

Executive director of Far East Broadcasting Company, 1971–78, and chairman of National Religious Broadcasters, 1957–75. Bertermann married Ruth Hoffman in 1937. From 1935–59, he traveled the world on behalf of the *Lutheran Hour* radio ministry. He was executive director of the Far East Broadcasting Company, 1971–78, and in 1979 became associated director of Luthern Bible Translators, Orange, CA. Bertermann died while visiting his son.

David C. K. Watson

1933

1984
York, England

Anglican priest and author. Watson served as curate at St. Mark's Church, Gillingham, Kent, England, 1959–65. He then moved to York to do student work. He led over 60 university mission teams. From 1974 onward, he led many festivals worldwide using singers, dancers, and musicians incorporated into acts of worship. One of his books, *Fear No Evil*, describes his battle with cancer.

Jacob Gartenhaus

Jan. 15, 1896
Bukowsko, Austria

Jan. 3, 1984
Chattanooga, Tennessee

Founder and president of International Board of Jewish Missions, Inc., Chattanooga, TN 1949–84. Gartenhaus came to America as an Orthodox Jew. Upon his conversion in 1916, he was beaten severely. From 1921–49, he directed Jewish Missions for the SBC Home Missions Board. He graduated from MBI and Southern Baptist Theological Seminary, Louisville, KY, and was a prolific writer of books, tracts, and articles. He became one of the most respected Christian Jews of all time, and was very effective in witnessing to both Jew and Gentile. Gartenhaus married Lilian Brown on June 1, 1922. His funeral was held at Highland Park Baptist Church, Chattanooga, TN.

William F. Ball

Aug. 3, 1908
Mount Pleasant, South Carolina

Jan. 6, 1984
Miami, Florida

Bishop of African Methodist Episcopal Church, 1956–84; senior bishop, 1976–84. Ball was converted on June 30, 1921, in Grant Memorial AME Church, Jacksonville, FL. Educated at Edward Waters College, Jacksonville, FL and Wilberforce (OH) University, Ball was ordained deacon (1926) and elder (1928). He married Agnes Marie Moton in 1927. He pastored in Florida, Tennessee, and Kentucky. He helped the St. Paul Church in Chattanooga retire its debt in 1938 and added 1,250 members to the Grand AME Church in Jacksonville. While pastoring the Bethel Church in Miami he added 1,000 members in five years.

John C. Smith

1904 *Jan. 15, 1984*

Director of Presbyterian Church Missions, 1959–73. Smith was also one of the six concurrent presidents of the WCC from 1968–75. He was involved in particular with missions directed toward third world countries.

James B. Crichton

July 24, 1922 *Jan. 30, 1984*
Alhambra, California Memphis, Tennessee

President of Mid-South Bible College, Memphis, TN (renamed Crichton College upon his death), **1953–84**. Crichton attended John Brown University and Dallas Seminary. He came to Mid-South as a teacher in 1952. He was married to Margaret Gillis on June 13, 1953. He traveled widely in speaking engagements and had a radio program, *Pause for Power*. He wrote several newspaper articles. Crichton was active in the First Evangelical Church of Memphis and early on was a Methodist missionary.

Leslie E. Maxwell

July 2, 1895 *Feb. 4, 1984*
Salina, Kansas Three Hills, Alberta, Canada

President of Prairie Bible Institute, 1922–72. Maxwell continued teaching there until 1981. He was converted at age 21 in his own room in Kansas City, MO. Maxwell founded the Three Hills School, Alberta, in a farmhouse with eight students. The school grew to own over 100 buildings with 1,000 students on the 130-acre campus. He also pastored the Prairie Tabernacle beginning in 1922. Maxwell married Pearl Plummer on April 12, 1925, and they had seven children. He edited the *Prairie Overcomer* and also had a radio broadcast. Maxwell wrote four books, including *Born Crucified* (1945), which was a classic, and *Crowded to Christ*. Close to 2,000 missionaries went out during his tenure.

Roland H. Bainton

March 30, 1894 *Feb. 13, 1984*
Ikeston, England Roland H. Bainton New Haven, Connecticut

Congregational Church historian and author. Bainton traveled to Vancouver, BC (1898) and to America (1902). He taught church history at Yale, 1920–62, with his Reformation scholarship being his strongest area. He married Ruth Woodruff, a Quaker, on June 8, 1921 (died: 1966), and they had five children. Bainton was a pacifist. His most famous written work was *Here I Stand: A Life of Martin Luther* (1950), which sold 1.2 million copies. His writings range from *Debtors to God* (1930) to *History and Hope* (1978). Much of his writing was during his last two decades of retirement. *The Church of Our Fathers* (1941), a Sunday School text, is another of his classics.

Martin Niemöeller

Jan. 14, 1892 *March 6, 1984*
Lippstadt, Germany Wiesbaden, Germany

President of World Council of Churches, 1961–68. Niemöeller began training for the Imperial German Navy as a cadet at Kiel, assuming the command of a U-boat in 1916. He married Else Bremer on April 20, 1919 (died: August, 1961). In 1920, he helped organize the Academic Defense

Corps. In 1923, he was appointed director of Protestant Home Missions (Inner Missions Society) for the province of Westphalia. On June 29, 1924, he was ordained in a Prussian church after studying theology at Munster University. He resigned his missions post to pastor at St. Anne's Lutheran Church in Dahlem, a suburb of Berlin, 1931–37. He formed the Pastor's Emergency League (1933) and met with Hitler, resulting in the Barmen Theological Declaration (1934). Niemöeller was arrested on July 1, 1937, and imprisoned for seven months in Moabit. He was tried for treason, but was finally acquitted and freed. Niemöeller was re-arrested in 1938, sent to Sachsenhausen concentration camp, and transferred to Dachau concentration camp in 1941. In 1945, he was sent to the Austrian Tyrol (region or province), reportedly scheduled for death, when he was released by the Americans. He was elected vice president of the Evangelical Church. He visited Moscow (1946) and the US (1955). In August, 1961, he was injured in an automobile accident that killed his wife. His favorite Bible verses were Romans 14:7–8.

Bascom (B. R.) Lakin

June 5, 1901
Wayne County, West Virginia

March 15, 1984
Lynchburg, Virginia

Great Baptist evangelist who had a great sense of humor and love for souls (100,000 conversions) over his 50 years of preaching. Lakin was converted in a revival meeting at age 18 in the church at the forks of Big Hurricane Creek with J. C. Simpkins presiding. Lakin traveled to early meetings in Kentucky and West Virginia on a mule. He pastored Euclid Avenue Baptist, Bristol, CT (1937–39). In 1939 he became an associate of Howard Cadle, Indianapolis, IN, and became his successor (pastor and radio) at Cadle Tabernacle (1941–52) before entering the evangelistic field. Lakin married Violet Crabtree. He worked out of Jerry Falwell's ministries in Lynchburg, VA, in his later days. His funeral was held at Thomas Road Baptist Church.

James H. Hutchins

Dec. 2, 1888
Rockwell, Iowa

March 24, 1984
Pasadena, California

Pastor of Lake Avenue Congregational Church, Pasadena, CA 1921–59. This small church grew to over 1,800 and eventually missionary giving exceeded the operating budget. The Lake Avenue Church erected a new auditorium in 1951. Hutchins was converted as a boy under the ministry of Charles M. Sheldon, pastor of Central Congregational Church, Topeka, KS. He married Mary Stephens on June 15, 1916. His first pastorate was the First Congregational Church, Springfield, OH, from 1918–21. He was active in many evangelical causes.

Melvin H. Snyder

Jan. 1, 1912
Evansville, Indiana

April 4, 1984
Marion, Indiana

General Superintendent of Pilgrim Holiness Church, 1958–68, renamed Wesleyan Church, 1968–80. Snyder married Eloise Brown on July 30, 1933. He was ordained to PHC in 1938. Snyder served as an evangelist (1930–35), then pastored in Marion, IN (1935–42). He was active in the merger of PHC and Wesleyan Methodist Church in 1968. He was active in the Holiness movement. He also composed some songs.

Victor V. Glenn

Nov. 11, 1913
Fayoum, Egypt

April 9, 1984
Bloomington, Indiana

President of Evangelistic Faith Missions, Bedford, IN, 1941–82. Born of missionary parents, Glenn was able to continue the ministry his father, Victor, started in eight countries. Glenn married Jennie Elliott (October 25, 1910–May 25, 1988) on November 9, 1936. He pastored the

Faith Mission Church, Bedford, IN, for some years. He began a radio ministry in 1951 that at one time was on 100 stations.

John R. Richey

April 8, 1899
Kentucky

April 9, 1984
Hemet, California

First president of Open Bible College [Eugene (OR) Bible College in 1986], **Des Moines, IA 1930–39**. John and his wife, Louise Hansen, whom he married on April 26, 1925, helped establish Pentecostalism in the Des Moines area. In 1932, over 32 ministers left the Foursquare movement and began the Open Bible Evangelical Association. He was the first chairman of the Open Bible Standard Church, 1935–38.

Harold Voekel

Feb. 14, 1898
Philadelphia, Pennsylvania

April 13, 1984
Duarte, California

Veteran Presbyterian missionary to Korea. Voekel was trained at MBI and went to Korea in 1920. He married Gertrude Swallen. Voekel was involved in one of the greatest revivals in history. When the Korean War started in 1950, he became the chaplain for the South Korean troops. He ministered to 150,000 prisoners of war; of those POW's over 130 went on to seminaries. He worked closely with World Vision and BOB PIERCE.

Joseph A. Synan

Feb. 18, 1905
Pocohontas, Virginia

April 18, 1984
Hopewell, Virginia

General superintendent of Pentecostal Holiness Church (International in 1975), **1946–69, and chairman of Pentecostal Fellowship of North America, 1950–52, 1963–65**. Synan was converted at age 16. He married Minnis Perdue on August 12, 1926. He pastored in numerous churches, 1924–34, in the Tidewater, VA, area. He also served as superintendent of the East Virginia conference (1934–41) and was the assistant general superintendent (1941–45). He wrote several books, including *The Good Minister of Jesus Christ* (1951) and *The Trinity of God* (1980). His son, Harold V. Synan, (born: 1934) was a historian and bishop in his denomination.

Ramsay Pollard

Feb. 15, 1903
Cleburne, Texas

April 20, 1984
Memphis, Tennessee

President of Southern Baptist Convention, 1960–61. Early in his ministry, he pastored in Texas, including the FBC, Fort Worth, TX. He pastored for many years at the Broadway Baptist Church, Knoxville, TN (3,600 members), 1939–60. Pollard was the pastor of Belleville Baptist Church, Memphis, TN, following R.G. LEE, 1960–72. His wife, the former Della Pickle, died in January, 1980.

Alton F. Liddick

Sept. 25, 1905
Philadelphia, Pennsylvania

May 1, 1984
Brooksville, Florida

Director of Wesleyan Methodist Church in America Missions (Wesleyan Church Missions in 1968), **1959–68**. Liddick was converted at age eight at a BILLY SUNDAY revival. He married Ruth Sension on July 1, 1933, and went to India, 1934–41. He was Conference president of India (1945–51) and served on the staff of Houghton College (1951–54). Liddick also served as assistant secretary for world missions, 1954–59. He played several musical instruments.

Paul Erb

April 26, 1894
Newton, Kansas

May 7, 1984
Mount Pleasant, Pennsylvania

Mennonite educator and journalist. Erb was converted at age eleven in an evangelistic meeting, married Alta Eby on May 27, 1917, and was ordained as a Mennonite in 1919. He was an English instructor at Hesston (KS) College (1917–40), dean (1933–40), professor of English at Goshen (IN) College (1941–45), and editor of *Gospel Herald* (1944–62) in Scottsdale, PA. Erb was the executive secretary of the Mennonite Church, 1953–61, and was involved in many Mennonite education and missionary causes. His *Alpha and Omega* (1955) helped in the debate over eschatology. He wrote three other books.

Francis A. Schaeffer

Jan. 30, 1912
Germantown, Pennsylvania

May 15, 1984
Rochester, Minnesota

Outstanding philosopher. Schaeffer was converted in 1930, at age 18, after reading the Bible for six months and attending a tent meeting, conducted by ANTHONY ZEOLI. His L'Abri (the Shelter) Christian Fellowship in Huemoz, Switzerland, was a spiritual oasis for many young people. Schaeffer married Edith Seville (born: November 3, 1914) on July 6, 1935, and immediately entered Westminster Theological Seminary, Philadelphia. He was the first minister in the Bible Presbyterian Church. In 1937, he was involved in founding Faith Theological Seminary. He pastored in Chester, PA (1941–43) and St. Louis, MO (1943–48). He went to Lausanne, Switzerland, as a missionary in 1947 with the Independent Board for Presbyterian Foreign Missions. A spiritual crisis resulted in renewal (1951), and he founded his LCF retreat (1955). There were beginnings of L'Abri in England (1958), then it came to America (1979). He moved to Rochester in 1972. Schaeffer's books range from *Escape from Reason* and *The God Who Is There* (1968) to *How Should We Then Live?* (1976). He wrote 24 books, selling over 3 million copies in at least 20 languages. The book *A Christian Manifesto* (1980) sold 300,000 copies. He combined mystical and philosophical ideas in his lectures and writings with Biblical truths. He died of cancer at home. His favorite Bible verses were Isaiah 2:2–3.

Bernard M. Christensen

Oct. 21, 1901
Porterfield, Wisconsin

July 11, 1984
St. Paul, Minnesota

President of Augsburg Theological Seminary (merged into Luther Theological Seminary in 1963), **Minneapolis, MN, 1937–62**. In 1930, he went to Augsburg and became a professor of philosophy and theology. Christensen married Lily Grace Gundersen on August 6, 1935. He edited the *Lutheran Messenger* (1931–34), was a professor of theology at LTS from 1963–84, where he remained active in community affairs.

James O. Phillips

June 16, 1929
Paducah, Kentucky

July 13, 1984
Ypsilanti, Michigan

First president of Faithway Baptist College, Ypsilanti, MI 1974–84. Phillips was saved at a church service in Paducah, KY. He attended Bob Jones Univ. and married Carol Porter in August, 1950. He went into business (accounting), but then was called to preach while in Rogers, AR. He pastored in the Ozarks while selling his business. He became assistant pastor in Vinita, OK and Flint, MI, then pastored the Rawsonville (MI) Community Church in Ypsilanti/Township, the name changing to Faithway Baptist Church in 1963. He pastored there, 1963–84 with membership going from 60 to 1,300. Phillips started an academy, institute (1969), and college (1974). He died of cancer at only 55 years of age.

Kenneth E. Geiger

Sept. 22, 1916
Pandora, Ohio

July 20, 1984
en route to Ilorin, Nigeria

General secretary of United Missionary Church, 1955–69, renamed Missionary Church, 1969–81, and president of National Holiness Association (Christian Holiness Partnership in 1997), **1960–64**. Raised in the General Conference Mennonite Church, Geiger was converted at age 15. In 1938, he began pastoring Chapel Hill Missionary Church, Union, MI. In 1939, he married Miriam Condon. He pastored the Brenneman Memorial Missionary Church in Goshen, IN (1943–51), then was district superintendent in Indiana (1951–56) for the mission. Geiger lost his life in an automobile accident en route to the Nigerian Conference of the United Missionary Church of Africa in Ilorin. Also perishing in the same accident was Gene Ponchant, general secretary of Missionary Church Missions (World Partners), 1974–84. Ponchant was born November 9, 1926 in Cincinnati, married Carol Sipp on June 29, 1950 and was a missionary in Sierre Leone, Africa, 1952–67.

Frank H. Woyke

Jan. 18, 1905
Grieshenow, Russia

Aug. 1, 1984
Southbury, Connetticut

First executive secretary of North American Baptist General Conference, 1946–68. Woyke came to America in 1908, and was converted at age 14. He attended every Baptist World Congress, beginning with Berlin in 1934. Woyke married Christine Jacopian in 1937. He taught at German Baptist Seminary, Rochester, NY (NABS in Sioux Falls, SD in 1950), 1936–43. He became the associate secretary for Baptist World Alliance in 1968, responsible for world relief and study programs.

John W. Dickhaut

Feb. 11, 1913
Mount Vernon, Indiana

Aug. 19, 1984
Columbus, Ohio

First president of Methodist Theological School, Delaware, OH 1959–81. Dickhaut joined the Ohio Conference in 1937 and served a number of pastorates there. He married Margaret Sapp on June 30, 1939. He became area superintendent of Dayton, OH (1954–55); of Columbus, OH (1955–57), and was a member of the Board of Education of the Ohio Conference (1960–84).

L. D. Foreman

March 8, 1913
Sebastian County, Arkansas

Aug. 24, 1984
Malaita, Solomon Islands

President of Missionary Baptist Seminary, Little Rock, AR, 1946–66. Foreman was converted under the ministry of MORDECAI HAM. He entered the first class of the Baptist Bible School (new MBS), where he stayed as student, teacher, and president for 35 years. He helped start Texas Baptist Institute, California Baptist Institute, and Gulf Coast Baptist Institute. For 50 years he was a preacher, pastor, evangelist, lecturer, educator, editor, and author. His most well-known book was *Bible in Eight Ages*. He pastored Woodhaven Baptist Church, Little Rock, beginning in 1966 when he returned from a world tour. He won over 2,000 to Christ. He died as he was about to administer baptism. He walked to a rock, sat down, laid back and was ushered into the Lord's presence.

Christiana Tsai

Feb. 12, 1890
Nanking, China

Aug. 25, 1984
Lancaster County, Pennsylvania

Blind Chinese evangelist and author. Converted out of a Buddhist home as a result of Mary Leaman's witness, Tsai served in a Chinese government girl's school, where many found Christ.

From 1916–31, she held evangelistic meetings, by faith, throughout more than half the provinces of China. In 1931, she was stricken with a malignant malaria of the bone marrow, making it impossible for her to move or speak for eight months and unable to open her eyes for one and a half years. Blind and confined to a bed from 1931, Tsai continued to have a ministry throughout the world through her book, *Queen of the Dark Chamber*, translated into 16 languages plus English Braille. As a result of her book, many Chinese soldiers and officers found Christ. Her friend, Mary Leaman, helped her escape Communism in China in 1949, taking her to "Leaman's Paradise," a homestead in Pennsylvania. She wrote and witnessed from her bedside until death.

William C. Martin

July 28, 1893
Randolph, Tennessee

Aug. 30, 1984
Little Rock, Arkansas

President of National Council of Churches, 1952–54. Martin married Sally Beene on July 1, 1918. He held pastorates in Houston, TX (1921–25), Port Arthur, TX (1925–28), Little Rock, AR (1928–31), and at First Methodist, Dallas, TX (1931–38). Martin was a Methodist Bishop, beginning on May 3, 1938, serving in Kansas and Nebraska (1939–48) and in Dallas/Ft. Worth, TX (1948–64). He was president of the Methodist Church Council of Bishops in 1953. He was also on the faculty of Perkins School of Theology, Dallas, TX from 1964–68. He wrote *To Fulfill This Ministry* (1949) and *Proclaiming the Good News* (1954).

Anthony Zeoli

Sept. 1, 1898

Sept. 9, 1984
Popano Beach, Florida

Active in evangelism and Bible conference ministry since 1925. His broadcast was called the *Radio Bible Hour* in Philadelphia, beginning in 1940. Zeoli spent six of his first 22 years in prison before hearing the gospel and becoming a Christian. He committed so much Scripture to memory that he became known as "The Walking Bible." His story was made into a movie, *Free Forever*. He wrote 15 books.

Leroy M. Lowell

Aug. 10, 1894
Cortland, New York

Sept. 9, 1984
Spring Arbor, Michigan

President of Spring Arbor (MI) Seminary, 1935–45, 1955–57, and professor of Bible and theology, 1928–35. Lowell was the pastor of Free Methodist churches in California, Kansas, and Michigan. He edited the denominational youth papers (1941–56), and served as first speaker on *Light and Life Hour*, which he founded (1944–51). Lowell was married to his wife, Helen (born: August 7, 1897), for 68 years. He lived near Lakeland, FL, after retiring. Lowell authored *Building the House Beautiful*.

Charles E. Boren

Jan. 23, 1909
Anna, Illinois

Sept. 13, 1984

Evangelist who was converted out of riotous living in Chicago, IL; Cicero, IL; and Detroit, MI. Boren's life was spared twice (rendered unconscious on train tracks; policemen's bullets missing him). Boren was converted on March 27, 1932, at Beulah Baptist Church in Detroit, MI. After graduating from MBI, he became an evangelist living in Winona Lake, IN. Many hardened sinners were converted in his crusades.

Herbert J. Gezork

June 15, 1900
Insterburg, Germany

Oct. 21, 1984
Vero Beach, Florida

President of Andover-Newton Theological Seminary, Newton-Centre, MA, 1950–65. Gezork pastored at FBC, Berlin, Germany (1925–28) in pre-Hitler climate, and was general secretary of German Baptist Youth Movement (1930–34). Coming to America in 1936, he was a professor of religion at Furman University, Greenville, SC from 1937–38. He married Ellen Markus on May 22, 1937. He was an associate professor of biblical history at Wellesley (MA) College, 1939–43. After he served at Wellesley, he went to Andover-Newton as a professor of social ethics, 1943–50. Gezork taught at Harvard (1965–68) and directed the Department of Religion at Chautauqua (NY) Institution (1968–72). He is interred at Newton Centre, MA.

Theodore A. Hegre

March 17, 1908
Woodville, Wisconsin

Oct. 27, 1984
Singapore

First director of Bethany Fellowship, Minneapolis, MN 1945–1980, and Bethany Fellowship Missions, 1963–82. Hegre married Lucile Conley on October 1, 1935, was ordained (1944) after becoming the pastor of Bethany Missionary Church in Minneapolis, MN (1943). He also served as president of the Bethany Fellowship Training Center 1948–80. He wrote several books from *The Cross and Sanctification* (1960) to *Creative Faith* (1980). He died of a heart attack.

Herbert Lockyer Sr.

Sept. 10, 1886
Plumstead, England

Nov. 30, 1984
Colorado Springs, Colorado

Preacher, traveler, and author. Lockyer was converted at age 18, as a result of hearing a born-again actor's testimony. Lockyer married Lily Fory on May 11, 1912 (died: 1978). He preached for 25 years in Scotland then came to America, 1936–57. He was under the auspices of MBI, very well received, and held many Bible conferences. He wrote 50 books, including the series *All of the Bible: Men, Prayers, Kings/Queens, Promises, Miracles, Parables, and Doctrines*. He also edited the *Christian Digest*. He retired to Bromley, England, where he is buried. He died in his son's home surrounded by his books.

Ben M. Herbster

Aug. 26, 1904
Prospect, Ohio

Dec. 16, 1984
Dayton, Ohio

President of United Church of Christ, 1961–69. Herbster married Elizabeth Beam on June 25, 1929. He was ordained to the Reformed Church in 1929 and held pastorates at Corinth Blvd. Reformed Church, Dayton, OH (1929–31) and Zion United Church of Christ, Norwood, OH (1931–61). He was very active in WCC and was a member of the Reformed World Alliance, International Congregational Council, and the Masons. He died of complications following surgery.

Joy F. C. Ridderhof

March 30, 1903
Minneapolis, Minnesota

Dec. 19, 1984
Stanton, California

Founder and first director of Gospel Recordings, Los Angeles, CA 1939–78. Ridderhof was converted through a woman evangelist holding revival services. She was a missionary to Honduras, 1933–37, until illness brought her home. She put the gospel on records with a portable recording device for non-readers, which she invented. She began this ministry in 1938 and requests poured in from everywhere in the world. More than 3,200 languages used her ministry. A ton of records was shipped out each week. She never married.

Audrey Wetherall Johnson

December 1, 1907
Leicester, England

Dec. 22, 1984
Carmel, California

Founder of the Bible Study Fellowship, an interdenominational, world wide ministry with about 800 classes studying the Bible in depth. In 1936, Audrey sailed to China under the China Inland Mission, and was assigned the following year to Yu-Kiang in Kiangsi Province. In 1939, Audrey began a work in Lin Ming Kwan, Hopeh Province. She was interned by the Japanese during WWII (1942), then returned to England following the war (1945). Returning to China, she served on the faculty of China Bible Seminary in Shanghai in 1947. The following year, she was under house arrest by the Communists who forced her to leave the country in 1950. In 1952, five women in San Bernardino, CA, asked for a Bible study. In 1958, BSF was incorporated in Oakland, CA, and grew to almost 3,000 classes with 100,000 members. Cancer struck her in 1979 forcing retirement. In 1980, BSF headquarters moved to San Antonio, TX. Johnson published her autobiography, *Created for Commitment* (1982).

W. Douglas Roe

July 21, 1906
Camden, New Jersey

Dec. 29, 1984
Montrose, Pennsylvania

Founder of the Montrose Broadcasting Corporation, president for 30 years and director of Montrose (PA) Bible Conference, 1940–65. He married Natalie Moore on Dec. 29, 1931. Roe served as president of the Philadelphia School of the Bible, 1944–49. The radio ministry blessed thousands in Pennsylvania and New York when WPEL began broadcasting on May 30, 1953.

Avis M. Burgeson Christiansen

Oct. 11, 1895
Chicago, Illinois

Jan. 14, 1985
Niles, Illinois

One of the most prolific hymn writers ever, 1920–66. Converted as a child through the influence of Christians around her, Avis married Ernest Christiansen on November 29, 1917 (died: December 1964). She had two daughters. She and her husband were members of Moody Church, with her husband serving as an executive at MBI for more than 30 years. She joined in 1915, when PAUL RADER was pastor. Her hymns include "Up Calvary's Mountain," "Love Found a Way," "Blessed Redeemer" (LOES), "Precious Hiding Place," "Only Glory By and By," "Precious Melody," "Lost in His Love," "In the Shadow of the Cross," "Deep Down in My Heart," "Trusting Thee More" (LOVELESS), "Only One Life" (DUNLOP), "Jesus Has Lifted Me," "It Is Glory Just to Walk with Him" (LILLENAS), "Only Jesus," "Blessed Calvary" (LATHAM), "I Know I'll See Jesus Some Day" (S. Lawrence), "Grace Abounded More" (PETERSON), "My Hope Is in Thee" (SCHULER), "Believe on the Lord Jesus Christ" (CLARK), and "Calvary Love" (R. HUGHES). Avis died of a stroke.

Lance B. Latham

March 21, 1894
Dentonville, Pennsylvania

Jan. 15, 1985
Chicago, Illinois

Composer, pianist, and founder of the Awana Clubs. Latham composed music for "Only Jesus," "When You Get the Love Jesus in Your Heart" (lyrics by Howard Jones) and "Blessed Calvary" (lyrics by AVIS CHRISTIANSEN). He married Virginia Highfield on October 14, 1924. He took over the youth work of Chicago Tabernacle under PAUL RADER. Latham began pastoring North Side Gospel Tabernacle, Chicago, IL, in 1933 and led it for half a century. Camp Michawana was founded in

1939 and Camp Awana in 1946. In 1950, he founded the Awana Clubs (Scripture-based, church-sponsored clubs for boys and girls, ages three through 16, modeled after other scouting groups). He was one of the great pianists of his generation. "Doc" Latham was a great blessing to many. In 1978, Latham conducted his 57th year of summer camp work at Camp Awana in Wisconsin. He also helped start New Tribes Mission. The Awana Clubs had spread to 52 countries by the time of his death. DAVE BREESE preached his funeral message.

Harold J. Ockenga

July 6, 1905
Chicago, Illinois

Feb. 8, 1985
Hamilton, Massachusetts

Pastor of Park Street Congregational Church, Boston, MA 1936–69; first president of Fuller Theological Seminary, 1947–54, 1959–63; of Gordon-Conwell Theological Seminary, 1969–79; of Gordon College and Divinity School, 1969–76; and first president of National Association of Evangelicals, 1942–43. Ockenga married Audrey Williamson on August 6, 1935 (died: spring, 1988). He was ordained a Presbyterian in 1931 and pastored at Breeze Point Church, Pittsburgh, PA, from 1931–36. Ockenga is credited with coining the term "New (Neo) Evangelicals (ism)." His books include *These Religious Affections* (1937) and *Faith in a Troubled World* (1972). He set an example of strong national leadership amongst evangelicals. He was chairman of the board of *Christianity Today,* 1956–81. He was honored as Clergyman of the Year in 1982. He died of cancer.

Andrew Gih

Jan. 10, 1901
Shanghai, China

Feb. 13, 1985
Los Angeles, California

Chinese evangelist and founder and first director of Evangelize China Fellowship, 1947–81. Gih was converted while a student in Mission School. He graduated from Bethel Seminary in Shanghai in 1925. On January 10, 1928, he married Dorcas Chang. Three times in his life, they lost all their belongings. They lost a school, an orphanage, a seminary, and three churches to Chinese Communists. In 1928, he saw 1,000 converted in one meeting in Hinghwa, Fukien. He joined the Bethel World-Wide Evangelistic Band, 1931–33. He saw wonderful revival all over China, 1928–35. From 1938–45, he rescued 1,000 orphans. He saw the work expand to Taiwan, Hong Kong, Macao, Singapore, Malaya, Indonesia, and Thailand, 1949–65. Gih preached in more than 30 universities in China. Under his leadership, ECF established 375 churches and chapels, seven schools, and two seminaries in seven countries.

Fred P. Corson

April 11, 1896
Millville, New Jersey

Feb. 16, 1985
Cornwall, Pennsylvania

Methodist bishop, 1944–68. Corson was ordained in 1920. He married Frances Beaman on March 22, 1922, was a member of many clubs and was involved in many denominational and ecumenical activities. Corson pastored in Jackson Heights, NY, and New York City (1919–24); West Haven, CT (1924–26); Pt. Washington, NY (1926–28); and Simpson Church in Brooklyn (1928–30). He served as president of Dickinson College, Carlisle, PA, from 1934–44 and wrote the first book on its history. Corson was the chaplain of the Republican and Democratic conventions in 1948 and 1952. He also served as vice president of World Methodist Council (1956–61), and president (1961–66). He wrote several books from *The Pattern of a Church* (1946) to *Steps to Christian Unity* (1964).

Jaroy Weber

Dec. 27, 1921
Shirley, Louisiana

Feb. 19, 1985
Dallas, Texas

President of Southern Baptist Convention, 1975–76. Weber was converted in 1928. He became a pastor at age 16 at the Baptist Church in Little Cypress, TX, just after graduating from high school in Shirley, LA. After one year there, he went to Orange, TX (1939–49); then to FBC of West Monroe, LA (1949); Beaumont, TX, and the FBC of Lubbock, TX when he became president of SBC. He married Nettie Wiggins on February 17, 1939. Weber described himself as a "conservative who cares."

John L. Yost

March 9, 1893
Gastonia, North Carolina

March 6, 1985
White Rock, South Carolina

President of Lutheran Theological Southern Seminary, Columbia, SC, 1945–60. Yost graduated from LTSS and was the oldest living alumnus at time of his death. He married Eva L. Dunning on May 24, 1917. He served churches in Tennessee and North Carolina (1917–29) followed by Redeemer Lutheran, Atlanta, GA (1929–45). During his tenure, the faculty doubled and the campus enlarged with new buildings worth several million dollars.

Zeno C. Tharp

Oct. 26, 1896
Traverse City, Michigan

March 7, 1985
Greenville, South Carolina

General overseer of Church of God, Cleveland, TN 1952–56, and president of Lee College. Cleveland, TN 1935–44. Tharp was converted at a campground in Durant, FL, in 1907. He married Annie Caruthers on January 18, 1914. He attended Lee College (1921–23), then later served at a church in Greenville, SC, that became the largest church in the denomination with 1,000 in Sunday School (1927–35). As president at Lee, he helped the school grow from 100 to 600 students.

Merrill C. Tenney

April 16, 1904
Chelsea, Massachusetts

March 18, 1985
Winfield, Illinois

President of Evangelical Theological Society, 1951. Tenney was an oustanding educator from Wheaton College. He was ordained Baptist in 1928. Tenney married Helen Jaderquist on September 5, 1930. Tenney was a member of the faculty of Gordon College, 1930–1943, also teaching Greek and New Testament in 1938. He went to Wheaton in 1944 and was a professor of Bible and theology. He became the dean of Wheaton's graduate school, 1947–71, and taught until he retired in 1977. He wrote from *Resurrection Realities* (1945) to *The Bible Almanac* (1980). His *Zondervan Pictorial Encyclopedia of the Bible* (4 vols., 1975) is a classic.

Gordon H. Clark

Aug. 31, 1902
Philadelphia, Pennsylvania

April 9, 1985
Westcliffe, Colorado

Calvinist philosopher and president of Evangelical Theological Society, 1965. Clark married Ruth Schmidt on March 27, 1929 (died: July 28, 1977), then taught philosophy at the University of Pennsylvania (1924–36) and at Wheaton College (1936–44). He began teaching at Butler University, Indianapolis, IN, in 1945 where he chaired the philosophy department until 1973. After withdrawing from the Orthodox Presbyterian Church in 1949, Clark referred to his conversion experience as an "unimportant psychological happening insisting on verbal revelation rather than subjective experience." From 1974–84, he taught at Covenant College, Lookout Mountain, TN. He was an evangelical intellectual and a strong Calvinist, serving in the Reformed Presbyterian Church. He wrote more than 20 books and commentaries, from *A Christian Philosophy of Education* (1946) to *The Biblical Doctrine of Man* (1984). He died of a liver condition.

Charles D. Kirkpatrick

April 16, 1921
Rockford, Illinois

April 12, 1985
Fort Wayne, Indiana

Director of Free Methodist World Missions, 1964–1985, and president of EFMA, 1974–1976. Kirkpatrick married Ivanella Bendorf in 1947. He served pastorates in Wisconsin and Oregon (1943–49), was in the Northwest Conference (1949–56), and was superintendent of Pacific Northwest Conference (1956–64). He was a member of the Board of Administration of the Methodists, 1960–64.

Baker J. Cauthern

Dec. 20, 1909
Huntsville, Texas

April 15, 1985
Richmond, Virginia

President of Southern Baptist Convention Missions, 1954–79. Under Cauthern's leadership, the board grew from 908 missionaries to 3,008 and mission giving went from $6.7 million (1954) to $76.7 million (1979). Cauthern married Eloise Glass on May 20, 1934, while pastoring at the Polytechnic Baptist Church, Fort Worth, TX, from 1933–39. He also served as professor of missions at Southwestern Theological Seminary, Fort Worth (1935–39). He served in China (1939–45) and was secretary of the Orient (1945–53). He taught at Golden Gate Baptist Theological Seminary, Mill Valley, CA (1980–84). He died of an apparent stroke.

Daniel K. Ost

Feb. 13, 1926
Elim, Alaska

April 21, 1985
Baker, Louisiana

Founder and first president of Missionary Revival Crusade, 1976–85. Ost was an outstanding missionary, evangelist and educator, specializing in the field of Mexico. Ost married Ruby Waltner on September 27, 1945. Converted (1941), he went to the field of Mexico (1967), later settling in Mexico City (1976), where he founded five churches where thousands eventually attended. He also founded the Calvary (Calvario) Ministerial Bible Institute, Monterrey, Mexico, in 1955 which produced over 400 pastors.

William C. Standridge

Dec. 4, 1898
Sweetwater, Tennessee

May 15, 1985
Howell, Michigan

Founder and director of Independent Faith Missions, Greensboro, NC 1950–64. Standridge was saved in a Methodist Church in Flint, MI. He married Eliza Daly on June 24, 1925. He ran a grocery store, then pastored in Birch Run, MI, in a Methodist Protestant Church until 1939. He founded the Dexter-Joy Bible Fellowship Church in Detroit that went through many changes. In 1944, it was renamed Baptist and moved to Warren Ave. (Warren Baptist Church). It was called Bethlehem Baptist in the 1960s. He went to Amsterdam, Netherlands, in 1948 at the founding of the ICC. He traveled to Italy and became burdened for that country. Through the years, his mission developed from that burden. He pastored the Inter-State Baptist Church in Memphis, TN, for six years in the 1970s. He came back to Michigan, was stricken with leukemia, and possibly died of an infection.

Paul J. Emery

April 2, 1909
Akron, Ohio

June 18, 1985
Allentown, Pennsylvania

President of Northeast Bible Institute (Valley Forge Christian College, Phoenixville, PA, in 1976), **Green Lane, PA 1963–72**. Emery married Dorothy on June 28, 1930. He influenced and assisted THOMAS ZIMMERMAN in the beginning of his ministry and pastored in Benton Harbor, MI (1936–41); Warren, OH (1941–47); Dayton, OH (1947–57); and Allentown, PA (1980–84). He was very active in the Assemblies of God activities all of his life.

Stanley S. Kresge

June 11, 1900
Detroit, Michigan

June 30, 1985
Pontiac, Michigan

Methodist businessman from the Detroit area. Kresge married Dorothy McVittie on October 2, 1923. He worked with his family's store chain (Kresge—Woolworth 5 & 10—Kmart), 1923–77. He served in various positions in the main office (1930–45), and eventually became the CEO (1950–85). Kresge was the president of the Kresge Foundation of Troy, MI, from 1952–66. He assisted in many Christian causes and served at his home church, Metropolitan Methodist. This was formerly North Woodward Methodist where he was greatly influenced by the 30-year ministry of Merton S. Rice and BILLY SUNDAY's 1916 Detroit Crusade. Galatians 2:20 was one of his favorite verses.

Willem A. Visser't Hooft

Sept. 20, 1900
Haarlem, Netherlands

July 4, 1985
Geneva, Switzerland

Honorary president of World Council of Churches assembled in Sweden (1968); Nairobi, Kenya (1975); and Vancouver, Canada (1983). Visser't Hooft was a giant in the ecumenical movement with WCC increasing from 135 to 300 denominations. He married Henrietta Boddaert on September 16, 1924. He also served as secretary of the World YMCA (1924–31); general secretary of the World's Student Christian Federation (1931–38); and edited *The Student World* (1928–38). He was the first general secretary of WCC from 1948–66. His books were from *Social Gospel in America* (1928) to *World Council of Churches* (1982). He was influenced by JOHN MOTT and KARL BARTH. He was involved with the Netherlands Reformed Church. He wrote *Has the Ecumenical Movement a Future?*

James C. Sams

Feb. 10, 1909
Cochran, Georgia

July 10, 1985
Jacksonville, Florida

President of National Baptist Convention of America, 1967–85. Sams married Cordelia Fleming on September 29, 1930. Ordained a Baptist, Sams pastored in Lakeland, FL (1935–58) and Jacksonville, FL (1958-85). He was also president of the Progressive Baptist Convention of Florida for 37 years, and first vice president of NBC from 1961-67. He was also a trustee of Edward Waters College, Jacksonville, FL.

Kenneth O. White

Aug. 29, 1910
London, England

July 12, 1985
Tucson, Arizona

President of Southern Baptist Convention, 1964. White married Pearl Woodworth on July 14, 1926. He pastored FBC in Santa Monica, CA (1926–30); New Salem Church, Gainesville, FL (1934–36); Kirkwood Church, Atlanta, GA (1936–44); Metropolitan Baptist Church, Washington, D.C. (1944–49); First Baptist Church, Little Rock, AR (1949–53); and FBC, Houston, TX (1953–65).

James D. Grey

Dec. 18, 1906
Princeton, Kentucky

July 26, 1985
New Orleans, Louisiana

President of Southern Baptist Convention, 1952–53. Grey was converted at age twelve at a revival at Second (Immanuel) Baptist Church in Paducah, KY, under J. W. T. Givens preaching. Grey married Lillian Tooke on September 16, 1927. He was ordained in 1935 and held pastorates in Vikery, TX (1929–31); Tabernacle Baptist Church, Ennis, TX (1931–34); FBC, Denton, TX (1934–37), and FBC, New Orleans, LA (1937–85). In New Orleans, the church grew from 1,546 to 4,000 members, with a $26,000 to $420,000 annual budget. A new edifice was built in 1954.

Howard Skinner

March 25, 1906
Otsego, Michigan

July 26, 1985
Phoenix, Arizona

Founder of Maranatha Bible Conference, Muskegon, MI, with HENRY SAVAGE. Skinner's father was a Methodist pastor. He married Ada Rupp on June 11, 1929; they met at Taylor University. They both were gifted concert pianists, and he was a bass soloist. They presented "Music and Art" concerts with chalk artist, Karl Steele. Their team traveled throughout the Midwest. He arranged the music for a couple of choruses.

Eugene C. Blake

Nov. 7, 1906
St. Louis, Missouri

July 31, 1985
Stamford, Connecticut

Ecumenical leader and stated clerk of the Presbyterian Church in the USA, 1951–58, and of the United Presbyterian Church (PC USA in 1983) **in USA, 1958–66; president of National Council of Churches, 1954–57; and general secretary of World Council of Churches, 1966–72**. Blake pastored at Nicholas Collegiate, New York City (1932–35), First Church, Albany, NY (1935–40), and Pasadena (CA) Presbyterian Church (1940–51). He married Valeina Gillespie (Sept. 12, 1929) and Jean Hoyt (June 14, 1974). In 1960, he preached in Bishop Pike's Episcopalian (Grace Cathedral) Church in San Francisco and called for Protestant unity. This led to the formation of Consultation on Church Union (COCU). He led many Protestants in the march on Washington in 1963, led by M. L. KING. Blake was also active in civil rights activities. He led in the production of a new confession of faith for the UPC USA in 1967, a modern expression of the old social gospel. He retired to Stamford in 1972. He wrote three books. His last was *The Church in the Next Decade* (1966).

Alfred Ewald

July 6, 1901
North Tonawanda, New York

Aug. 4, 1985
St. Paul, Minnesota

President of Wartburg Theological Seminary, Dubuque, IA 1957–65. He married Luella Kappler in 1931. He was pastor of Hope Lutheran, St. Paul, MN (1923–50) and president of the Minnesota District ALC (1950–57).

Ernest E. Long

July 26, 1901
Brighton, England

Aug. 11, 1985
Toronto, Ontario, Canada (?)

Secretary of United Church of Canada, 1955–72. Long came to America (1910) and was ordained (1926). He married Dorothy Toye (born: June 10, 1901) on August 18, 1931. Long pastored in Ontario: at Tillsonburg (1927–33); Barrie (1933–40); Kirkland Lek (1940–43); Lake Fairmont-St. Giles in Montreal, Quebec (1943–

53), and Humbercrest Church, Toronto, Ontario (1953–55). He was active with World Methodist Council and the World Alliance of Reformed Presbyterian Churches.

Bernard M. Loomer

March 5, 1912
Belmont, Massachusetts

Aug. 15, 1985

Dean of University of Chicago Divinity School, 1945–54. Loomer was an insurance adjuster and loan investigator, 1934–35. He married Elizabeth Janz on September 3, 1937. He was a part time instructor at the UCDS from 1940–41. Loomer became a full-time instructor (1941) and assistant professor of ethics and dean of students (1943). After this, he became the assistant dean, 1944–45, before he headed the work. Loomer was also an associate professor of philosophy and religion, 1948–54, becoming the professor, 1954 on.

Irwin J. Lubbers

Nov. 15, 1895
Cedar Grove, Wisconsin

Sept. 8, 1985
Grand Rapids, Michigan

President of Hope College, Holland, MI 1945–63. Lubbers married Margaret VanDonselaar on January 1, 1923. He was a professor of English at Hope College (1923–29); Carroll College, Waukesha, WI (1930–34) and was president of Central College, Pella, IA (1934–45). Lubbers almost died in an automobile accident in 1947. Although he never deviated from the faith of a covenant child, that incident made his Christian commitment stronger. He was very active in the Reformed Church.

Dorlan H. Queener

Oct. 31, 1913
Elk Valley, Tennessee

Oct. 4, 1985
Cleveland, Tennessee

Director of the Church of God of Prophecy World Missions, Cleveland, TN, 1946–63. Queener was one of the great preachers of the denomination. He married Rosa Brunner on November 24, 1934 (died: March 1969) and Nina Reagan on October 11, 1970. In 1938 he became state overseer for Oklahoma. During his leadership, countries developed for evangelism and missions were developed and outreach went from 14 to 55 countries and from 12,399 overseas followers to 51,679.

Paul F. Elliott

March 26, 1904
Mason, Michigan

Oct. 7, 1985
Brooksville, Florida

President of National Holiness Association (Christian Holiness Partnership in 1997), **1950–54, and of Owosso (MI) College, 1960–66**. Elliott married Dorcas Backus on August 5, 1925. He was a business manager for the Bible Holiness Seminary, Owosso, MI. During the Depression, he picked pears for $2 a day and served pastorates in Ventura, CA; Dover, PA, and McKeesport, PA, 1937–43. In 1946, he was the general secretary of the Sunday school and youth programs for the Pilgrim Holiness Church and was general superintendent of the church, 1966–68. In 1970, they moved to Brooksville where he assisted in founding a retirement center, Wesleyan Villages, and held the presidency until his death. He led the mid-winter camp meetings there.

Theodore H. Epp

Jan. 27, 1907
Oraibi, Arizona

Oct. 13, 1985
Lincoln, Nebraska

Founder and first director of worldwide radio ministries known as *Back to the Bible*, Lincoln, NE 1939–84. Epp was converted on August 10, 1927, and married Matilda Schmidt on August 10, 1930. He was a Mennonite pastor in Goltry, OK (1932–36); church planter (1936–38); and pastor in Kingman, KS (1938–39). They went to Lincoln in 1939, where he developed a radio broadcast: the first program aired on May 1, 1939. He produced *Good News Broadcaster* (1942–85), developed a missions program (1952) and a correspondence school (1960) and touched the world with his radio and literature (some 70 books). His radio ministry grew to 600 stations with ten overseas offices. He died of heart failure.

Nicholas B. H. Bhengu

Sept. 5, 1909
Eshowe, Zuzuland, Africa

Oct. 16, 1985

Greatest African evangelist of all time. Bhengu trained at the Bible School in Dumisa, Natal, South Africa. He entered evangelism in 1938 and conducted "Back to God Crusades." In 1950, he held a crusade in East London, South Africa, that attracted 40,000 in the morning and 50,000 in the evening lasting for six months. By 1959, Bhengu had established 50 churches with 15,000 members. Later crusades in Zimbabwe and Mozambique were greatly blessed. Seventeen hundred churches, 450 preachers, and 250,000 members were his legacy at the time of his death. After many of his crusades, the crime rate dropped by one-third. He died of cancer, with over 20,000 attending his funeral.

James E. Wagner

May 16, 1900
Royer, Pennsylvania

Oct. 20, 1985
Wyncote, Pennsylvania

President of Evangelical and Reformed, 1953–57, and co-president of the United Church of Christ, 1957–61. Wagner married Ruth Felty on October 30, 1923. He pastored North Street Church of God, Harrisburg, PA (1922–31) and St. Peter's Evangelical and Reformed Church of Lancaster, PA (1931–52). Wagner was an instructor in Bible and Religion at Franklin and Marshall Academy, Lancaster, 1935–42. He was also a member of General Council of E&R from 1938–50.

Charles W. Keysor

July 14, 1925
Pittsburgh, Pennsylvania

Oct. 22, 1985
Clearwater, Florida

Founder and first director of Good News (evangelical caucus in the Methodist Church), **Wilmore, KY, 1967–85**. Keysor married Ingeborg Wickstrom on December 27, 1947. He was converted at the Billy Graham crusade in July, 1959, in Wheaton, IL, after having been employed in Christian circles. Keysor wrote an article describing the beliefs of Methodist evangelicals (1966) and transferred his church membership to the Evangelical Covenant Church (1968). In 1977, he founded the Forum for Scriptural Christianity in the Methodist Church, which soon was known as the Good News movement. He began to teach journalism at Asbury College (1981); then they moved to Clearwater, where he pastored another Evangelical Covenant church (1983). He died of cancer.

William W. Ayer

Nov. 7, 1892
Shediac, New Brunswick, Canada

Nov. 18, 1985
St. Petersburg, Florida

Pastor of Calvary Baptist Church, New York City, 1936–49, and first chairman of National Religious Broadcasters, 1944–1945. Ayer's conversion took place as a result of a 1916 BILLY SUNDAY revival meeting in Boston, accepting Christ at his bedside in Somerville. He married Lucille Woodward on May 1, 1919 (died: 1967), and Barbara Scofield on August 1, 1968. He pastored in Mason City and Atlanta, IL (1920–22); Valparaiso (1922–27); Central Baptist Church, Gary, IN (1927–32) and Philpott Tabernacle, Hamilton, Ontario (1932–36). His radio ministry, covering 41 years, was called *Marching Truth*. His New York church grew from 400 to 1,600 members with some 5,000 conversions. In 1947, he was considered the third most important citizen in NYC (behind Cardinal Spellman and Eleanor Roosevelt). Ayer was a widely used conference speaker and evangelist (especially in England and South America his last 35 years). He was still writing and speaking when he died of a heart attack.

Clifford Lewis

March 27, 1909
Red Level, Alabama

Nov. 19, 1985
Kansas City, Missouri

President of Kansas City Bible College (which, in 1961, merged to become Calvary Bible College), **1956–59**. Lewis was an evangelist of great magnitude and a radio preacher for 54 years. His broadcast was called *Christ for Everyone*. He was the founder/pastor of Grace Baptist Church, Kansas City. He married Helen Kline on August 12, 1940, and later Mabel Johnson. Throughout his ministry, he went to over 100 countries. He wrote several books and edited *Faith Magazine*. He taught briefly at two seminaries.

David Bronstein

July 13, 1919
Newark, New Jersey

Dec. 10, 1985
Clearwater, Florida

Secretary for the International Hebrew Christian Alliance, 1962–85. Bronstein married Mary Hall on October 30, 1943. He took a Presbyterian pastorate in Lyons, NE, from 1943–45. He was an associate pastor of First Hebrew Christian Church, Chicago, IL (1945–58), then went to Jones Memorial Center (Presbyterian), Chicago Heights, IL (1958–62), working in urban renewal. He was the nephew of Jacob Peltz, IHCA president, 1965–67. Bronstein had heart attacks for 15 years before dying of kidney failure.

Anne Baxter

May 7, 1923
Michigan City, Indiana

Dec. 12, 1985
New York, New York

Actress. Baxter appeared in several movies, maintaining a Christian testimony. Anne's first play was *Seen But Not Heard*. In 1936, her first motion picture was produced. *The Razor's Edge* (1946) earned her an academy award as best supporting actress. Baxter married John Hodiak on July 7, 1946. She gave up her career to marry an Australian cattle rancher, Randolph Galt, on Feb. 18, 1960. She later married David Klee on Jan. 30, 1977. She also performed in *All About Eve*, (another Oscar nomination) and *The Ten Commandments*. In 1983, she began acting on the television series *Hotel*. Baxter collapsed on Dec. 4, 1985, while walking down Madison Ave., dying of a cerebral hemorrhage. She was a Presbyterian. She lived in Easton, CT.

Kenneth R. Adams

Oct. 11, 1914
London, England

Dec. 18, 1985
Abington, Pennsylvania

Firstgeneral director of Christian Literature Crusade, Ft. Washington, PA, 1941–74. This ministry, founded in Colchester, England, in 1941, grew to managing 70 book centers in 40 countries and employing 250 workers. Converted at age eight, Adams married Bessie Miners on September 14, 1938, then came to America in 1947. Adams inaugurated the journal *Floodtide*. He was also a member of Faith Community Church in Roslyn, PA. He died in a local hospital.

William E. Reed

March 13, 1915
Boydsville, Arkansas

Dec. 25, 1985
Indianapolis, Indiana

Executive secretary of Church of God, Anderson, IN 1971–80. Reed married Naomi McAdoo on April 3, 1937. He served his denomination as pastor, evangelist, writer and executive. Reed held pastorates in Piggott, AR (1937–39); Lutesville, MO (1939–40); East Prairie, MO

(1941–45), and Anderson, IN (1945–50). He preached in every state and several countries and was the executive secretary of the Board of Church Extension and Home Missions of CG from 1950–71. He authored several books, including *Winning Others to Christ* (1953) and *A Story to Tell*. He died following a brief illness.

Lois Crawford

Oct. 2, 1892
Boone, Iowa

Jan. 8, 1986
Boone, Iowa

Pioneer Christian radio executive, founder of many thriving Christian ministries. Crawford was affiliated with her father in the work of the Boone Biblical Ministries, succeeding him as president upon his death in 1936, and serving until her death, 50 years later. She pioneered the Christian radio station KFGQ ("Keep Faithful, Go Quickly") as radio announcer and manager. This Christian radio station was the first, west of the Mississippi River. It began in 1927 with ten watts of power, and grew to 5,000 watts over a period of time. Crawford was the first woman in the US to obtain a First Class Radio Telephone License in 1927. In her spare time, she conducted services in nearby mining camps and settlements. She started a two-year Bible school, Christian day school (K-12), a children's home, old people's homes, Camp Decision, and a Christian bookstore. Crawford also edited a monthly magazine, *Times of Refreshing*. She never married.

Millard E. Collins

Nov. 17, 1893
Hutchinson, Kansas

Jan. 23, 1986
Arlington, Texas

President of Southwestern Assemblies of God College, Waxahachie, TX 1947–59. Collins was converted in a Methodist revival in Thomas, OK, at age 19. He served in WWI from 1917–21. Returning home, he married Nellie Price. From 1926–32, he was superintendent of four public school systems in Oklahoma and helped five rural churches in the Christian Church. In Archer City, TX, Collins was active with the Pentecostal movement, helping to establish the Shield of Faith Bible Institute in Ft. Worth, TX, from 1934–40. He helped conserve or establish five Assembly of God churches in Texas.

Oswald J. Smith

Nov. 8, 1889
Odessa, Ontario, Canada

Jan. 25, 1986
Toronto, Ontario, Canada

Missionary statesman. Smith was converted in a TORREY crusade in Toronto, on January 18, 1906. He married Daisy Billings (March 13, 1890–November 1, 1972) on September 12, 1916. His early days found him pastoring in Chicago, IL (1914–15); Toronto (1915–19, 1920–21, 1922–26) in three different churches; Gospel Tabernacle of Los Angeles (1927–28) and the Cosmopolitan Tabernacle of Toronto (1928–30). His main ministry headquarters was at People's Church in Toronto, 1930–1959, purchasing the Central Methodist Church in 1930. From 1920–50, he preached in crusades all over the world (53 countries); raised over 23 million dollars at his annual missions conventions; and authored 35 books in 128 languages that have sold over 1 million copies. He wrote 1,200 hymns, poems, and gospel songs including "There Is Joy in Serving Jesus," "God Understands," "The Glory of His Presence," "He Loved Me in Spite of My Sin," "He Rose Triumphantly," "Have I Grieved Thy Holy Spirit?" (B.D. ACKLEY), "Then Jesus Came" (RODEHEAVER), "Saved" (HICKMAN), "The Song of the Soul Set Free" (A.H. ACKLEY), "Safely Anchored" (SCHULER), "I'm Singing for My Lord" (REDD HARPER), and the lyrics and music for "Deeper and Deeper." Seldom has there ever been a man that has excelled in so many phases of ministry.

Curt Emmons

July 19, 1894
Kenton, Ohio

Feb. 2, 1986
St. Petersburg, Florida

Evangelist who, with his family, held crusades for over 28 years. Emmons and his family traveled by trailer, using 14 musical instruments, a film library, and equipment for a children's hour preceding the evening services. They held many city wide crusades. Emmons headquartered at Winona Lake, IN. He was an MBI graduate.

Frederick Coutts

Sept. 21, 1899
Kirkcaldy, Scotland

Feb. 6, 1986
London, England

General of Salvation Army, 1963–69. Coutts married Bessie Lee in 1925 (died: 1967) and Olive Gatrell in 1970. Coutts spent his early life in Scotland and served in WWI. From 1920–35, he was in charge of evangelistic centers in Great Britain. He served in the International Headquarters in London in literary work (1935–53), was the principal of the training school (1953–57) and worked in Sidney, Australia (1957–63).

Eugene L. Smith

April 13, 1912
Rockwell City, Iowa

Feb. 20, 1986

General secretary of United Methodist Church Missions, 1949–64, heading 1,100 missionaries in 47 countries. At age 16, at a summer conference of the YMCA, Smith made a committment to Christ. During college, Smith found the Lord very close in a crisis involving the closing of the International House, which the small campus had started. He married Idalene Gullege on July 12, 1939 (died: 1983) and Elaine Cooke in 1984. Early pastorates were in Roswell, NJ (1938–44); Emory Church, Jersey City, NJ (1944–47) and St. Mark's Church, Brooklyn (1947–49). In 1964, he became the executive secretary in the US for the WCC. His ashes are interred at Rockaway Valley (NJ) United Methodist Church.

Benjamin S. Weiss

Dec. 12, 1890
Denison, Iowa

Feb. 20, 1986
Pasadena, California

Educator, personal worker, and strong influence for God and good in Southern California. Weiss was converted at age eleven in Defiance, IA. He was a member of Evangelical United Brethren Church. He served as the Rolian High School principal/vice principal in Los Angeles, CA, for 26 years until 1955. His wife died in 1949. Weiss was chairman of counselling for the first Billy Graham crusade in Los Angeles in 1949; he also worked for later Graham crusades in the city. He was a Sunday school supertintendent for 31 years.

George D. Armerding

Oct. 17, 1899
Jersey City, New Jersey

G̲e̲o̲r̲g̲e̲ D̲e̲w̲e̲y̲ A̲r̲m̲e̲r̲d̲i̲n̲g̲

Feb. 28, 1986
Santa Cruz, California

President of Christian Business Men's Committee, 1963. Armerding came to Christ in his teens through the preaching of his brother, Carl, at a conference near Bethlehem, PA, on July 4, 1916. On August 22, 1925, he married Helen Warren. He became associated with the Mojonnier Brothers Company (a manufacturer of food processing equipment) in October, 1930. After some years in the Chicago area, he was transferred to the West Coast, residing near Oakland, CA. He co-authored *Dairy Plant Management*. He was a member of a Plymouth Brethren Church.

Henry H. Mayes

Feb. 18, 1898
10 miles south of Tazewell, Tennessee

March 3, 1986
Middlesboro, Kentucky

Of all the unusual exploits done for Christ, the editor wonders if this isn't the most unique. Mayes was a miner at Fork Ridge (TN) Coal Company for 43 years. He married Lillie Minton (June 7, 1903–May 15, 1986) on May 2, 1917. He made signs and hauled them all over the United States, erecting them on major highways. He did this for 68 years, 1918–86. The signs were wooden slats at first, but concrete signs replaced them in about 1940. These signs were 12 feet tall and weighed about 1,400 pounds. Mayes was but 138 pounds and worked unbelievably hard with the help of a couple of others. The signs, mostly in the shape of crosses, stated things like: "Prepare to Meet God," "Jesus Is Coming Soon," and "Get Right with God." He moved to Middlesboro, KY in 1946. Mayes made his last sign trip in 1975. He was also responsible for sending out 56,000 pint-size bottles with "Prepare to Meet God" in them in 14 languages; they were thrown into oceans, lakes, and rivers. His exhibits can be found at the Museum of Appalachia in Norris, Tennessee. For a while, Mayes attended the Church of God, but died nondenominational.

Buford A. Norris

Feb. 12, 1909
Newton, Kansas

March 4, 1986
Albuquerque, New Mexico

President of Christian Theological Seminary, Indianapolis, IN 1959–74. Norris married Shirley Underwood on July 14, 1933. He was ordained to the Disciples of Christ ministry in 1933. He pastored in Milford, KS (1933–35); at Second Christian Church, Washington, PA (1935–39) and at First Christian Church, Pampa, TX (1939–48). He went to Butler University School of Religion to head the preaching department (1950–54), when he became the assistant dean (1954–59). He was active in many Disciple's activities as well as community affairs in Indianapolis, IN.

Helmut Thielicke

Dec. 4, 1908
Wuppertal, Germany

March 5, 1986
Hamburg, Germany

Theologian, educator, and preacher, called to professorship at Heidelberg, 1936–40. Thielicke married Marie-Luise Herrmann in 1941. From 1940–45, he was highly restricted because of his criticism of the Nazis. He entered the army (1940) and was ordained (1941), becoming a pastor in Ravensburg. In 1942, he pastored the St. Mark Church in Stuttgart. He became the head of the logical office of the Wurttemberg Church in 1943 and began his service at the University of Tubingen, serving as professor of systematic theology (1945–51), and rector (1951–54). He then began his work at the University of Hamburg. He was dean of the faculty and professor of systematic theology (1954–60), when he became rector of the same (1960–74). His reputation in America rests on the volume of sermons translated into English. His ethics and systematic theology show him to be strong in the historic Christian faith.

Russell D. Barnard

July 20, 1898
Delphi, Indiana

March 10, 1986
Winona Lake, Indiana

Director of Grace Brethren Missions, 1944–66. Barnard developed 100 missionaries in seven fields into a thriving force. Barnard married Fern Hartzler on June 6, 1923. He was converted at age 14 in a revival meeting in his home church, the First Brethren Church, Flora, IN. He pastored at the First Brethren Church, Mansfield, OH (1923–29); the First Brethren Church, Dayton, OH (1929–44); and the First Brethren Church, San Diego, CA (1944–46). From 1964–76, he spoke at many missions conferences.

Robert Benson

Aug. 26, 1930
Nashville, Tennessee

March 22, 1986
Nashville, Tennessee

Nazarene pastor and publisher. He married Peggy Siler on September 4, 1951. Early on, Benson pastored in Florida, Missouri, California, and Tennessee. He joined his father in Nashville to develop the John T. Benson Publishing Company. After he began writing, he became a much sought-after speaker and from 1979, he traveled, wrote, and spoke. He was friend and counsellor to many in Christian work. He fought cancer for twelve years before dying. He wrote such as *He Speaks Softly, Laughter in the Walls, Come Share the Being,* and *Something's Going on Here*.

Frank B. Stanger

Aug. 31, 1914
Cedarville, New Jersey

April 17, 1986
Lexington, Kentucky

President of Asbury Theological Seminary, Wilmore, KY, 1962–82. Stanger graduated from Asbury College (1934) and from the Seminary (1935). He married Mardelle Amstutz on June 2, 1937. Stanger pastored the First Church of Collingswood, NY, from 1951–59. He then became the executive vice president of Asbury. He wrote several books including, *The Pauline Doctrine of Conscience* (1940) and *A Workman That Needeth Not to Be Ashamed* (1958).

Clarence W. Jones

Dec. 15, 1900
Sherrard, Illinois

April 29, 1986
Largo, Florida

Cofounder with Reuben Larson and co-director of HCJB World Radio Missionary Fellowship, 1931–47, and president, 1950–51, 1953–61. Jones was converted under PAUL RADER at Moody Church on October 27, 1918. He married Katherine Welty on August 2, 1924 (died: Oct. 7, 1993), and they had four children. He pioneered missionary radio along with REUBEN LARSON. Jones moved to Quito, Ecuador, in 1930, and on Dec. 25, 1931, HCJB ("Heralding Christ Jesus' Blessings") began broadcasting. He wrote several gospel choruses and was a trombonist. Jones also originated the Awana youth program that LANCE LATHAM made famous at the RADER Tabernacle in 1950. Retiring in 1961, he promoted Christian radio until his death. He moved to Largo in 1970. He was the first inductee in 1975 to the NRB Hall of Fame.

Kenneth L. Bazar

March 16, 1930
Longview, Texas

April 30, 1986
Houston, Texas

Editor-in-chief of American Baptist Association Publications, Texarkana, TX, 1980–86, the top post in the movement, which selects their presidents annually. Bazar was saved as a teenager and was one of the youngest students ever to enroll in Baptist Missionary Seminary, Little Rock, AR. He married Mary York on October 2, 1952, and pastored in Waco, TX; Monticello and Ft. Smith, AR, until 1960, then was assistant editor of the *ABA* (1961–69) while also pastoring in Hope, AR. He pastored at Unity Baptist, Little Rock (1972–77), then went to the missions office of ABA (1978–80). Residing in Texarkana, he was diagnosed with bone marrow cancer in 1984, which took his life. His wife died six weeks later.

Theodore C. Mercer

Sept. 3, 1920
Spring City, Tennessee

May 4, 1986
Chattanooga, Tennessee

President of Bryan College, Dayton, TN 1957–86. Mercer had announced his retirement plans for the end of the 1986 academic year, but a sudden heart attack preceded this plan by one month. He had earlier served as public relations officer at Muskingum College, New Concord, OH and as registrar, dean of men and assistant to the president at Bob Jones University. He was a member of FBC, Dayton, TN, where he taught the men's Bible class for over 25 years. He was active in many civic, community, and professional services, much of it connected with Rhea County, TN. His wife was the former Alice Moore. His son, David, received his second degree from Bryan College at its commencement, six days after his father's death.

Irwin A. Moon

Nov. 30, 1907
Grand Junction, Colorado

May 7, 1986
Placentia, California

Founder, in 1945, and longtime director of Moody Institute of Science. Moon was the producer and host of the award-winning Moody science film series, including "The God of Creation" and "The God of the Atom." He produced 39 films, with a staff of 27 workers. Early on after his conversion, he pastored Montecito Park Union Church, Los Angeles, 1929–37. He joined MBI in 1938 and preached on military bases with his "Sermons from Science" (1941–45). Moon's wife's name was Margaret; they had four children. He died following a stroke.

Louis D. Newton

April 27, 1892
Screven County, Georgia

June 3, 1986
Atlanta, Georgia

President of Southern Baptist Convention, 1947–48. Newton married Julia Carstarphen on April 30, 1915. He was a professor at Mercer University, Macon, GA (1913–17), served as editor of *Christian Index* (1920–29), and held a pastorate at Druid Hills Baptist, Atlanta, GA (1929–68). He authored four books and was named Clergyman of the Year by Religious Heritage Association members in 1953. Newton was a journalist, very active in the SBC, and a gifted speaker.

Mary Carter-Crowley

April 1, 1915
Slater, Missouri

June 18, 1986
Dallas, Texas

Founder of Home Interiors, and one of the most successful Christian businesswomen of the twentieth century. She initially started Home Interiors in the buildings of the First Baptist Church of Dallas, where she taught Sunday school. Crowley initiated the concept of "in-home parties," where women could view attractive decorations for their homes and at the same time receive a message of inspiration from the displayer for the evening. In 1935, Mary Carter started in Dallas with a $100 loan as a single mother with two small children. In 1957, Mary obtained a loan for $6,000 from a Dallas bank; and by 1975, the company was grossing $70 million annually. In 1986, the sales topped $500 million with 13,500 distributors nationally and 45,000 distributors worldwide. Mary was the first woman to be on the Billy Graham Board of Directors. She married David M. Crowley. She died of cancer. You can find evidence of Mary's business in multiplied thousands of homes across the US.

V. Carney Hargroves

Sept. 4, 1900
Nansemond County, Virginia

June 25, 1986
Gwynedd, Pennsylvania

President of Baptist World Alliance, 1970–75. Hargroves married Marcissa Daniel on December 1, 1928. He also served in China as a teacher, then, upon returning to the U.S., he pastored in Princeton, NJ (1925–27) and in Richmond, VA (1927–32). In 1932, he became the pastor of the Second Baptist Church, Germantown, PA serving until the 1970s. Hargroves was president of ABC (1954) and the first president of the NAB fellowship (1966). His ancestors in Virginia have lived on the same property since 1667.

Elza Moss

Sept. 7, 1915
Sissonville, West Virginia

July 10, 1986
Sissonville, West Virginia

President of Primitive Advent Christian Church, Sissonville, WV 1967–86. Moss was converted at age 14 in an Advent schoolhouse-church in his locality. He married Garnet Berry on September 4, 1937 (died: August 20, 1996). He was in construction, especially in the field of welding, all of his life. About 1953, Moss was ordained and began to pastor small churches (up to as many as four at one time). He also held revivals, one went six weeks with some 72 conversions. Many looked to him for leadership, because he was a tremendous example of "tent-making" to pay for the ministry. Kidney cancer spread to bone cancer, which ended his life.

Howard C. Estep

Dec. 3, 1916
Hernden, West Virginia

July 15, 1986
Yorba Linda/Colton, California

Evangelist, Bible teacher. and director of World Prophetic Ministry, Colton, CA. Estep was converted while on board a naval destroyer ship around 1939. He began his ministry as an evangelist to East Coast towns. He married Marian Ashmun on October 31, 1940, and came to California in 1949. He founded *The King is Coming* TV program and also a radio program with news especially relating to Bible prophecy. Estep wrote many articles and booklets on prophetic subjects and spoke in many conferences.

Joseph T. Bayly

April 5, 1920
Germantown, Pennsylvania

July 16, 1986
Rochester, Minnesota

President of Evangelical Press Association, 1960–62. Bayly was converted in his childhood via home and church. He married May DeWalt on December 18, 1943, and they had seven children. He was associated with Inter-Varsity, 1944–60, then with David C. Cook Publishing Company, 1963 on. Although he had a strong Presbyterian background, he gravitated to an interdenominational church. He authored nearly a dozen books, as well as working as a magazine editor of *His* magazine (1952–60) and writing a column for *Eternity* magazine for 25 years. One of his books is *The Gospel Blimp* (1960). Bayly lost three sons under the age of 20. He died of complications after heart surgery.

Bernard H. Phaup

July 17, 1912
Farmville, Virginia

July 18, 1986
Charlotte, North Carolina

General Superintendent of Wesleyan Methodist Church in America, 1959–68, renamed Wesleyan Church, 1968–73. Phaup married Dorothy Foster on October 16, 1935. He served as a pastor in Redford, VA (1932–35); Charlotte, NC (1935–38, 1948–53 and 1981–86); Alvasta, VA (1938–41); High Point, NC (1941–46), and Thomasville, NC (1973–81). He died in the parsonage of St. Paul Wesleyan Church where he was the pastor.

Daniel E. Beauchamp

July 20, 1910
near Eastman, Georgia

July 16, 1986
Commerce, Georgia

General Moderator of the Pentecostal Fire Baptized Holiness Church, LaGrange, GA 1957–77. Beauchamp was one of twelve children. On October 31, 1931 he married Inez Dunlap. In November, 1937, he attended a revival at the Holiness Church at Five Points in Thomaston, GA, where he was converted. He pastored the church in Thomaston, GA, from 1941–44, at which time he was transferred to Rome, GA. He was there until he went to the Galilee Church in Madison County. He pastored in Nicholson (1950), Athens (1954), and Commerce (1964), all in Georgia. He was general secretary of Foreign Mission Board (1959–57) and general superintendent of the same (1977–79).

Milton B. Lindberg

March 24, 1894
Grove City, Minnesota

July 19, 1986
St. Petersburg, Florida

President of Chicago Hebrew Mission, 1940–53, renamed American Messianic Fellowship (AMF Int. in 1993), **1953–61**. Lindberg was converted on January 13, 1906, in a special children's meeting in his father's church. Lindberg married Beth McKinney on June 21, 1921. They served as missionaries in Lebanon and Jerusalem, 1925–29. He was then on staff of Biblical Research Society, 1930–38. His books had a circulation of over 250,000. Lindberg was an outstanding evangelist to the Jews.

Maurice Stevens

May 5, 1921
Portsmouth, Ohio

July 21, 1986
Lexington, Kentucky

Founder and first president of Go Int., Wilmore, KY, 1968–86. Stephens was converted at a Methodist youth gathering at age 21. He married Bev Harmon on August 16, 1947. He pastored three years at Ravenna, KY (1951–54) and other churches in the eastern USA (1954–68). He was always interested in evangelism and missionary work and took teams overseas. As a Methodist evangelical, Stevens headquartered the work in Wilmore, KY. He had three children. Contracting malaria while in Africa hastened his death.

Leonard W. Heroo

May 22, 1916
Nantucket, Massachusetts

August 2, 1986
Providence, Rhode Island

President of Zion Bible Institute, East Providence (Barrington in 1985), **RI, 1960–83**. Heroo graduated from ZBI in 1936. Soon he was teaching there; in 1960, he became the president of the school as well as pastor of Zion Gospel Temple. He married Edna Azevedo in 1957. He spoke at the 5th World Conference of Pentecostal Churches in Toronto in 1958. Ill health forced him to retire from his positions in 1983. Those that heard him preach say that he was a preacher of preachers that kept audiences spellbound.

James Forrester

May 15, 1909
Edinburgh, Scotland

Aug. 5, 1986
Newport News, Virginia

President of Gordon College and Divinity School, 1960–68, and of Westmont College, Santa Barbara, CA 1948–50. Forrester was converted at age 18 in Canada. He married Melba Walsh on November 10, 1939. Forrester began his ministry with Canadian Inter-Varsity (1937–39), was a chaplain in WWII, also teaching at Whitworth (CA) College (1939–42). He held pastorates at Calvary Baptist, Anaheim, CA (1942–47) and in Los Angeles, CA (1950–57).

Ralph J. Montanus

Dec. 18, 1919
New York, New York

Aug. 9, 1986
Boca Raton, Florida

Blind radio evangelist. Montanus was converted in 1936 after hearing an evangelist in the Salvation Army Corps in Astoria, NY. Montanus married Beatrice Butler on March 25, 1940, and they had five children. He and his wife sang lovely duets together. He was born blind in one eye and the other faulty eye went blind in 1942. He founded the Gospel Association of the Blind in 1948. Montanus was ordained into the Conservative Baptist movement and pastored at Bethany Baptist in Jamaica, NY, for a time. He conducted a weekly radio broadcast.

J. McDowell Richards

Nov. 6, 1902
Statesville, North Carolina

Aug. 10, 1986
Summerville, South Carolina

President of Columbia Theological Seminary, Decatur, GA, 1932–71. Richards went to Columbia as a professor of practical theology. During his tenure, the student body grew from 56 to over 200; and, in later years, women and blacks were admitted. Richards, the son and grandson of Presbyterian ministers, was ordained Presbyterian also in 1928. He pastored in the north Georgia mountains, 1928–32, and married Mary Knight on Dec. 31, 1929. He studied at Oxford, held several advanced degrees, and was one of the first southerners to be named a Rhodes scholar. Richards was a Democrat and lived most of his life in Summerville, SC. He was involved in numerous denominational activities. In 1957, he framed the "Atlanta Manifesto," a document signed by area ministers that contributed to improved race relations in this pivotal southern capital city. He wrote *Change and the Changeless* (1972). He is buried in Liberty Hill, SC.

Vance H. Havner

Oct. 17, 1901
Hickory, North Carolina

Aug. 12, 1986
Greensboro, North Carolina

Colorful Bible conference speaker since 1940. Havner was converted at an early age at a revival at Corinth Baptist Church, Jugtown, NC. Havner was ordained as a "boy preacher" of 16 years and traveled to over 1,000 crusades as an evangelist. Havner blessed thousands with his preaching. He had a dry wit and humor that complimented the great truths in his messages. He preached in many major conferences and churches. Havner also pastored at Salem Baptist Church, Weeksville, NC (1924–34), off and on, and at FBC, Charleston, SC (1934–40). He married Sara Allred in December 1940 (died: 1973). Havner authored 38 books in all. He died in his sleep. Billy Graham conducted his funeral.

Herbert S. Mekeel

Feb. 14, 1903
Dayton, Ohio

Aug. 24, 1986
Schenectady, New York

President of National Association of Evangelicals, 1958–59. Mekeel never married. He was ordained in 1935 and served on the staff of churches in Edmonton, Alberta and in Ottawa, Ontario. Mekeel pastored the First Presbyterian Church, Schenectady, NY from 1937–79. Mekeel was president and trustee of Albany (NY) Bible Institute, 1946–60. He was a resourceful scholar.

Cynthia Clark Wedel

Aug. 26, 1908
Dearborn, Michigan

Aug. 24, 1986
Alexandria, Virginia

President of National Council of Churches, 1969–72, and of WCC, 1975–83. Cynthia married Theodore Wedel on May 4, 1939 (died: July 19, 1970). She was involved in the work of the Episcopal Church (1931–39) and was a teacher in the National Cathedral School for girls in Washington, D.C. (1939–48). Wedel was a member of the National Council of the Episcopal Church, 1955–62. She also served as the assistant and associate general secretary of NCC from 1962–69. Wedel authored several books, including *Citizenship, Our Christian Concern* (1952) and *Faith or Fear* (1974). She pressed for women's ordination. She died of cancer.

Edwin T. Dahlberg

Dec. 27, 1892
Fergus Falls, Minnesota

Sept. 6, 1986
Phoenix, Arizona

President of National Council of Churches, 1957–60. Converted at a Swedish Baptist church revival in Fergus Falls at the age of ten, he became a pacifist in 1917 and was ordained the next year. From then on, he considered himself to be an evangelical liberal. Dahlberg married Emilie Loeffler on August 27, 1918. Dahlberg pastored the FBC in Potsdam, NY (1918–21); Maple St. Church in Buffalo, NY (1921–31); FBC in St. Paul, MN (1931–39); FBC in Syracuse, NY (1939–50); and Delmar Baptist Church in St. Louis, MO (1950–62), staying as pastor emeritus until his death. He was president of the ABC (1946–48) and was active in the WCC (1948–54). He wrote Y*outh and the Homes of Tomorrow* and *This Is the Rim of East Asia*.

Ruth Duvall Crawford-Porter

May 2, 1916
Collingswood, New Jersey

Oct. 28, 1986
Stroudsburg, Pennsylvania

Considered by many to be one of the greatest pianists ever, especially as an accompanist. She grew up in an evangelical Methodist home. Ruth wrote the music to many gospel choruses. She married Percy Crawford on September 18, 1933 (died: October 31, 1960). From 1933–60, she played the piano and sang for family, friends, and rallies and molded her four sons into a famed quartet which made the Pinebrook Bible Conference and radio ministry come alive. She continued her *Pinebrook Praises* radio program until 1965. She also excelled on the organ and harp. Crawford compiled 17 hymnals, trained seven quartets, orchestrated arrangements, and led several choral groups. Ruth married Robert Porter, a chiropractor, in March 1966 (died of cancer). She also died of cancer.

Owen Cooper

April 19, 1908
Vicksburg, Mississippi

Nov. 12, 1986
Jackson, Mississippi

President of Southern Baptist Convention, 1973–74. Cooper was a layman and served as a chemical company executive for many years. He married Elizabeth Thompson on September 2, 1938. He taught vocational agriculture (1930–35), was assistant director of Mississippi Planning Commission, (1936–40) and executive director of Mississippi Farm Bureau Federation (1940–48). Cooper was executive vice president of Mississippi Chemical Company, Yazoo City, MS (1948–60) and president of the same (1960–72). He also served as a vice president of the Baptist World Alliance.

Louis P. Lehman

Sept. 12, 1914
Chicago, Illinois

Dec. 24, 1986
Grand Rapids, Michigan

Orator and preacher. Lehman powerfully preached and sang. He wrote the famed chorus "God Bless Our Boys" during WWII. He was converted in a Sunday School class at Moody Church when he was six years old and began to preach at age nine. He established the Franklin (PA) Gospel Tabernacle at age 15. Lehman married Edna Davis on January 15, 1941, and they had two daughters. He hosted a daily radio program, *Bit of Heaven*, for 40 years on some 80 stations. He pastored in Portland, OR (1945–52); at Calvary Church, Grand Rapids, MI (1952–64); at a Mennonite Brethren Church, Bakersfield, CA (1967–84); then back to CC, Grand Rapids, in 1984. He died suddenly of natural causes during a Christmas Eve play he wrote with 2,500 people in attendance. He dropped over on the platform at 11:10 p.m. Lehman also wrote lyrics and music to, "I'm Going to Occupy" and "Whatever He Wants for Me."

Boris Bessmertny
c 1925   *1987*

Young French evangelist who spoke four languages. Bessmertny was in charge of French Youth for Christ activities in the late 1940s. He held over 42 city wide crusades and hosted the 1949 World Congress of Evangelism at Cannes, France. He edited the French *Jeunesse Pour Christ*.

Finis J. Dake
1902   *1987*
Iberia, Missouri

Editor of the famous *Dake's Annotated Bible*, 1961–63. Dake was ordained into the Assembly of God and pastored at Christian Assembly, Zion, IL from 1932–37. He left the Assembly of God denomination and joined the Church of God in Cleveland, TN, then later became an Independent. Dake's Bible soon replaced SCOFIELD's popularity throughout the Pentecostal movement. Dake was a "holiness" preacher so well known for memorizing large amounts of Scripture and being able to quote it without error that he gained the title "the walking Bible." During his eighty-four years he started a Bible school and held numerous evangelistic meetings and lectures. Dake also hosted a radio broadcast two times a day for 13 years, answering any question about the Bible. The Bible was first published in Lawrenceville, GA, in 1961. His wife's name was Dorothy.

David J. Du Plessis
Mr. Pentecost

Feb. 7, 1905   *Feb. 2, 1987*
Piquetbergh, Twenty-four Rivers, South Africa   Pasadena, California

Du Plessis was a great evangelical, ecumenical, and charismatic movement leader. Du Plessis was converted in 1916 after the family moved to Basutoland (Lesotho). Known as "boy preacher" at the young age of 15, he was ordained in 1930 by the Apostolic Faith Mission. Du Plessis married Anna Jacobs on August 13, 1927 and they had seven children. From 1947–58, he was organizing secretary of the World Pentecost Fellowship in Basel, Switzerland. In 1949, he came to the United States. He taught at Lee College, Cleveland, TN (1949–52), and pastored in Stamford, CT (1952–56). He joined the Assemblies of God denomination in 1955. He was not always accepted by his colleagues, because of his work with WCC (attending all assemblies beginning with Evanston II in 1954) and fraternizing with Catholics. They revoked his credentials (1962) then restored them (1980). He attended the Second Vatican Council in 1964 as an observer. He encouraged the charismatic movement in all churches. Du Plessis spent his later years at Fuller Theological Seminary. Pope John Paul II honored him in 1983. Du Plessis died of cancer.

Heber O. Van Gilder
March 25, 1897   *Feb. 6, 1987*
Fairmount, West Virginia   Blanchester, Ohio

President of Western Baptist Bible College, Oakland, CA 1948–56, relocated to El Cerrito, CA 1956–64 (Salem, OR in 1978), **and first National Representative of GARB, 1944–48.** Van Gilder married Belle Lynch Harris in June, 1918, and then Lois Peters. He pastored FBC, Perkasie, PA (1921–22); FBC, Lebanon, OH (1922–25); Central Baptist Church, Columbus, OH (1925–32); Temple Baptist Church, Portsmouth, OH (1932–44); and FBC, Los Gatos, CA (1964–70). Western Baptist Church that he pastored was in Oakland, CA (1948–56) and in El Cerrito, CA (1956–64). Van Gilder also helped organize the GARB and the Baptist Bible Union.

Eugene A. Erny

July 10, 1899
Racine, Wisconsin

Feb. 14, 1987
Greenwood, Indiana

President of Oriental Missionary Society, 1949–62, and of EFMA, 1954–55, 1957–59. Erny spent nine years in Peking, China, 1929–38, and eleven years in Allahabad, India, before coming back to the States in 1949 to head the organization of 200 missionaries, 1,000 pastors, and 800 churches.

Henry J. Heydt

May 1904
Hoboken, New Jersey

Feb. 22, 1987
Florida

First president of Lancaster (PA) Bible College, 1933–53. The school was first known as the Lancaster School of the Bible. Heydt was committed to a "biblically grounded and scholastically efficient institution." With scarce resources and limited space he saw the school through the difficult Depression years.

Peter Trutza

June 5, 1910
Curtici, Romania

March 3, 1987
Hollywood, Florida

Founder and first president of Romanian Missionary Society, Wheaton, IL 1968–80. In Romania, Trutza was professor and president of the Baptist Theological Seminary in Bucharest (1932–41), while pastoring the FBC (1939–41). In 1937, he married Miss Earl Hester. He came to the States and pastored Romanian Baptist Churches in Detroit and Gary, IN, from 1941–52. Trutza became a US citizen in 1947. From 1956–67 he served as professor of missions at Northern Baptist Theological Seminary. He traveled to over 40 countries in preaching endeavors. He suffered a stroke in church on Sunday, March 1st, never regained consciousness, and died two days later.

Samuel C. Patterson

July 16, 1916
Fort Morgan, Colorado

March 12, 1987
Pensacola Beach, Florida

First President of Reformed Theological Seminary, Jackson, MS 1975–78. Patterson was not declared president until 1975, but he was the driving force in founding the school in 1967, serving as chairman of the board of trustees until 1975 and on the faculty. He presided over the extension campus in Orlando, FL as well, 1975–78. He served as a naval reserve chaplain to the marines in WWII. He pastored the Leland (MS) Presbyterian Church (1946–50), and was president of French Camp (MS) Academy (1950–67). He was a well-known evangelist in the South. Patterson died of a heart attack while camping.

Elam J. Daniels

Nov. 1, 1908
Obrien, Florida

March 13, 1987
Orlando, Florida

One of the greatest evangelists of the SBC who held large, area-wide crusades. Daniels pastored for 16 years in Tampa, Eagle Lake, Winter Garden, and Fort Pierce, FL, and in Fairfield, AL. He began his evangelism endeavors in 1947. In five years of ministry 1979–84, he held many overseas crusades and saw 1 million converted. Daniels edited a family magazine and wrote many books. Some feel he preached to more people in history than anyone else, except for Billy Graham.

Carl Armerding

June 16, 1889
Jersey City, New Jersey

March 28, 1987
Hayward, California

Missionary, pastor, educator, author, and artist. Armerding was converted at age 15 through Plymouth Brethren evangelist, George Mackenzie. He married Eva Mae Taylor on June 27, 1917 (died: 1964). After brief missionary service in Honduras and the Bahamas (1912–14), he moved to New Mexico (1917–27). Here he was active in reaching Indians and preaching in Brethren Assemblies. From 1927–43, he preached in Canada, USA, New Zealand, Palestine, and Europe. In his later years, he was a Bible conference speaker and in great demand. Armerding was fluent in the Spanish language and traveled often to Central America encouraging the Christians there. He taught at MBI (1946–47), Dallas Seminary (1947–48) and at Wheaton (IL) College (1948–62). He is buried in Elmhurst, Illinois.

Cornelius Van Til

May 3, 1895
Grootegast, Netherlands

April 17, 1987
Erherheim, Pennsylvania

Theologian, scholar, and unofficial CEO (president) at Westminster Theological Seminary, Philadelphia, PA 1925–65. Although never actually called president, he was the leading voice of WTS until Ed Clowney was made the first president in 1965. Van Til came to America in 1905, married Rena Klooster on September 5, 1925 (died: January 11, 1978). Van Til was ordained in Christian Reformed Church in 1927, then pastored briefly at the Spring Lake (MI) Christian Reformed Church, 1927–28. He began his valuable teaching ministry as professor of apologetics at Princeton Theological Seminary, 1928–29. When the MACHEN-led split occurred at Princeton, he went with the "refiners" to Westminster Theological Seminary, Philadelphia, where he taught, 1929–72, giving valuable time to the seminary. He taught apologetics and wrote 20 books and articles from *The New Modernism* (1946), which analyzes Barthianism, to *The God of Hope* (1978). His most famous book was *The Defense of the Faith* (1955). He mentored CARL HENRY and FRANCIS SCHAEFFER.

Roy H. Wead

May 17, 1916
Fort Rice, North Dakota

April 19, 1987
Springfield, Missouri

President of Trinity Bible College, Ellendale, ND 1958–82. Wead was an Assemblies of God pastor and denominational official with strong ties in the salvation/healing emphasis. He served as superintendent of the Indiana district with WILLIAM BRANHAM as his assistant. Wead pastored in South Bend, IN. He saw renewal in some areas of the Catholic Church. Roy married Rosa Short on January 4, 1940.

J. Edwin Orr

Jan. 15, 1912
Belfast, Ireland

April 22, 1987
Asheville, North Carolina

Authority on revivals and evangelizing techniques. Orr was converted on his ninth birthday through the witness of his mother in Belfast. He became and evangelist in 1933. Orr married Ivy Carlson on January 15, 1937. He was ordained a Baptist on January 15, 1940. Orr served in WWII as an air force chaplain, 1943–46. In 1949 he moved to Southern California. He was a professor of World Missions at Fuller Theological Seminary, 1976–87. He traveled to 140 countries. In later years, his ministry was known as Mission to the Academic Community. He wrote several songs, including "Cleanse Me" (music arranged by JOHN MCNEILL). He died from a heart attack while preaching.

Donald D. Luttrell

March 23, 1924
Oakland City, Indiana

May 22, 1987
San Juan, Puerto Rico

Director of Calvary Baptist Mission, 1955–67, renamed **Calvary Evangelistic Mission, 1967–87, San Juan, Puerto Rico, 1955–67**. Luttrell married Ruth Tidik in 1946 and was ordained as a Baptist in 1950. Luttrell began his ministry working with Youth for Christ. He was a repected missionary "bush pilot," 1952 on, in Vieques, Puerto Rico. His radio station WIVV went on the air in 1955. He died of diabetes and poor blood circulation.

Frank H. Caldwell

Jan. 26, 1902
Corinth, Mississippi

May 25, 1987
Charlotte, North Carolina

President of Louisville (KY) Presbyterian Theological Seminary, 1936–64. Caldwell was ordained as a Presbyterian in 1925 and pastored until 1930 in Bradsfordsville, KY, and McComb, MS. Caldwell married Fannie Wells on September 14, 1926. He became professor of homiletics at LPTS in 1930 and served as executive director of the Presbyterian Foundation, Inc., 1964–71.

William K. Harrison

Sept. 7, 1895
Washington, D.C.

May 25, 1987
Bryn Mawr, Pennsylvania

Army leader whose testimony was shared with many in private and public places. A 1917 graduate of the US Military Academy, Harrison was a second lieutenant in the cavalry in WWI in 1917. During WWII, he accompanied the Thirtieth Infantry Division overseas to England and the continent and was the most highly decorated soldier in his division. In 1946, he was in charge of reparations, economic, and industrial affairs in Japan. After 1951, he was chief of staff of the Far East and United Nations Command. He also served as senior delegate of the United Nations Command Truce Team at the time the Korean Armistice was signed on July 27, 1953. In 1954, Harrison spoke to a group of children and told them to put their trust in God and "follow the teachings of Jesus Christ. I still study not only military subjects but what I consider the most important subject, the Bible." He then served as lieutenant-general and as Commander-in-Chief of the Caribbean Command 1954–57. He retired March 1, 1957 after 40 years of service. His medals include a Distinguished Service Cross, the Distinguished Service Medal, the Legion of Merit, the Silver Star, the Bronze Star with one Oak Leaf Cluster, and the Purple Heart. After retiring, he served as chairman of the board of Dallas Theological Seminary and also became the director of the Evangelical Welfare Agency of Chicago, 1957–59, before retiring to Florida. Harrison's wives were Eva Toole (1896–1976) and Forrest King.

Frank Carlson

Jan. 23, 1893
near Concordia, Kansas

May 30, 1987
Concordia, Kansas

Republican representative, senator and governor. Carlson married Alice Frederickson on August 26, 1919. Carlson won 13 out of 13 elections 1928–62. He was very active in Christian work, especially Youth for Christ. He served six terms as a member of the House of Representatives (1928–47), was the governor of Kansas (1947–51), and US Senator (1951–62). He was a Baptist and a Mason.

The Saints Go Marching In

Paul Friedrich

Sept. 2, 1901
St. Charles, Missouri

June 26, 1987
St. Louis, Missouri

Director of International Lutheran Laymen's League, St. Louis, MO, 1951–67. Friedrich had a lifetime association with the Lutheran Church Missouri Synod. He was associated for 17 years with the Cranbrook Institutions in Bloomfield, MI. He married Marguerite Rieder on March 27, 1926, and later married Marjorie. He was active in the Lutheran Television Productions of *This is the Life*. The ILLL had more than 120,000 members.

Dean G. McKee

July 28, 1904
Stockport, Iowa

July 19, 1987
Decatur, Georgia

President of Biblical Seminary of New York (New York Theological Seminary in 1969), **1946–60**. McKee married Mildred Schwartz on August 30, 1928 (died: October, 1970), and Adele Dieckmann on November 14, 1972. Ordained a Presbyterian, he worked in religious education in a New York City Reformed Church 1928–31. He began his work at BS (1931) as a professor of church history and Greek, became dean (1941), and president (1946). He finished his career as professor of English Bible at Columbia Theological Seminary, Decatur, GA (1961–74). McKee died following a bout with stomach cancer for a year.

Peter Deyneka Sr.

July 12, 1898
Storlolemya, Russia

July 26, 1987
Wheaton, Illinois

First president of Russian Gospel Association (Slavic Gospel Association), **1934–74**. Deyneka came to America in 1914 and was converted on January 18, 1920, under PAUL RADER at Moody Church. Deyneka married Vera Demidovich on May 23, 1926. Known as "Peter Dynamite" for his strong preaching, Deyneka's autobiography is entitled *Twice-Born Russian*. He preached in Russia five different trips and edited the *Gospel Messenger*. Deyneka pioneered Russian broadcasting (1941) from HCJB Quito, founded Russian Bible Institute (1942) in Toronto, and Transferring Institute, Argentina (1950) to train Slavic youth. He was a member of Moody Church in Chicago.

Harold S. Laird

Aug. 8, 1891
Newcastle, Pennsylvania

Aug. 25, 1987
Quarryville, Pennsylvania

President of the Independent Board for Presbyterian Foreign Missions, 1936–50. Laird married Velma McKinney on June 21, 1917 (died: 1958), and Betty McConnell in 1960. He was ordained as a Presbyterian in May, 1917. Laird held pastorates at Arlington Church, Baltimore, MD (1917–18); Henry Memorial Church, Philadelphia, PA (1919–25); FPC, Lewiston, PA (1925–29); Collingswood, NJ (1929–33); Central Church, Wilmington, DE (1933–36) and the First Independent Church, Wilmington, DE (1936–52). After 1952 he remained in Bible conference work, then helped organize the Faith Theological Seminary, which met for a time in his church.

John W. Bradbury

July 23, (?)

Sept. 1987
Massachusetts

Editor of the *Watchman Examiner*, 1938–64. Bradbury was a Baptist pastor in Kansas City, MO; Lancaster, PA; Bales Baptist Church, Chicago, IL; and Wadsworth Avenue Baptist Church, New York City from 1929–36. He was associated with C. L. LAWS, editor of the *Watchman Examiner*

(1934–37) whom he succeeded. He was sound, opposed all separatist movements, and served the Fundamentalist Fellowship and the Foreign Mission Board of the NBC. He was a trustee of Gordon College and of Northern Baptist Theological Seminary. Bradbury was a well-known Bible expositor and served two years in World War I in France.

Donald P. Shidler

Feb. 7, 1903
Lanark, Illinois

Sept. 3, 1987
Kansas City, Missouri

President of Gospel Missionary Union (Avant Ministries in 2004), **Kansas City, MO, 1952–69**. During Shidler's leadership, the ministry expanded to Panama, British Honduras, Bahama Islands, Mexico, Canada, and Alaska. In 1966, the outreach in Europe was in ten countries. Shidler continued to write and travel out of the mission office after 1968. He married his wife, Christine, on October 7, 1922.

Ray T. Pedigo

Aug. 22, 1912
Bridgeport, Oklahoma

Sept. 5, 1987
Tulsa, Oklahoma

Director of Missions to Japan, Campbell, CA, 1959–85. Pedigo started his missionary work in Japan and started boat, radio, and church ministries to reach the masses. He later developed boat and radio ministries in the Philippines, and was acquainted with many Filipino pastors there. Pedigo trained at Southern California Bible (Vanguard in 1976) College, Costa Mesa, CA, and he arrived in Japan in September, 1952. He played a Hawaiian guitar. His radio broadcast, *The Voice of Life* aired over a 50,000-watt station in Tokyo that went forth for 20 years. He owned a giant printing press where orders for 1 million tracts were served. MTJ ministered in hospitals, prisons, leper colonies, isolated villages, etc. Then it was to the Philippines for more of the same. His wife, Lita, was with him when he died.

Harry T. Hardwick

Nov. 9, 1914
near York, Pennsylvania

Sept. 13, 1987
Longview, Texas

President of St. Paul (MN) Bible Institute (Crown College in 1992), **1959–68**. Raised on a farm, Hardwick came to know the Lord through Alonzo Horn, whose daughter, Edith, he married on December 24, 1934. They were married 53 years. After graduating from Nyack (NY) College, Hardwick served CMA churches in Portsmouth, VA, and Upper Darby, PA. He taught at Nyack (1954–59) and after his leadership at SPBI served as president of LeTourneau College, Longview, TX (1968–75). Hardwick was the chancellor of the same, 1975–85. Five major campus buildings were constructed then. His life verse was I Chronicles 29:11, and he was known for his "knowledge puffs up, but love builds up" relationship with his staff. He was a beloved leader and wise counselor and administrator. Hardwick died of congestive heart failure.

J. Stratton Shufelt

Aug. 8, 1910
Yorkville, Illinois

Sept. 19, 1987
Muskegon, Michigan

Soloist and songleader for many evangelists. He was converted at age 10. Shufelt married Marjory Isel on June 15, 1937. Shufelt was a licensed evangelist with CMA. Shufelt was music director for A.W. Tozer in Chicago (1935–38) and was the minister of music and youth at Moody Church (1938–47). He was active in YFC, 1946–57. He directed crusades for most all major evangelists of his time and directed music at Maranatha Bible Conference in the summer. He died of cancer.

Hallie L. Chesser

Sept. 15, 1898
Williston, Florida

Sept. 30, 1987
Tampa, Florida

General overseer of Church of God, Cleveland, TN 1948–52. Raised on a farm, Chesser was 21 years old when he was converted and shortly thereafter called into the ministry. He married Ethel Lowry on October 3, 1932. He pastored in Florida off and on (1928–60), the longest tenure being in Clearwater (1933–39 and 1956–60). He was on the executive committee of the NAE from 1950–53 and helped draw up the constitution of the Pentecostal Fellowship of North America. Prior to his leadership role, he was assistant General Overseer (1944–48) and following, was general secretary and treasurer (1952–54).

Wendell P. Loveless

Feb. 2, 1892
Wheaton, Illinois

Oct. 3, 1987
Honolulu, Hawaii

Beloved composer of many hymns, including "Precious Hiding Place" (1928), "Only Glory By and By," "Precious Melody," "Deep Down in My Heart," "In the Shadow of the Cross" (A.B. CHRISTIANSEN), "He Came to Me One Day," "Jesus, Oh, What a Name!" "Oh, What Love!" "The Assurance March" (WILLIAM RUNYAN), "Lead Me to Some Soul Today" (WILL HOUGHTON), "Songs in the Night" (Graves), and the famous chorus "Sweeter Than the Day Before" (1936) (Robert Loveless). He also wrote the words and music to many songs and choruses including "All Because of Calvary," "I Love to Hear His Voice," "Altogether Lovely," "I Have Christ in My Heart," "I Haven't Words to Tell," "Til You Know Jesus," "There's Joy in Following Jesus," "Glory to God," "V Is for Victory," and the song, "Nearer and Dearer to Me." Loveless married Velma Stone on November 8, 1920. He was converted in 1924 as a result of reading his Bible and soon became a Bible teacher and pioneer of Christian radio. They attended Wheaton Bible Church. While he directed the WMBI radio station in Chicago from 1926–47, his staff grew from 2 to 160. He had a Bible conference ministry (1947–52), pastored Wheaton Evangelical Free Church (1952–57); Community Church, Boca Raton, FL (1957–61); was director of KAIM, Honolulu, HI (1961–66) and was on staff of First Chinese Church of Christ there after 1966. His last word was "Jesus."

Alfred M. Landon

Sept. 9, 1887
West Middlesex, Pennsylvania

Oct. 12, 1987
Topeka, Kansas

Governor and presidential candidate, he was an active Methodist layman. Landon married Margaret Fleming (January 9, 1915) and Theo Cobb (January 15, 1930). In 1932, he was elected governor of Kansas, residing in Topeka. In 1936, Landon was the Republican candidate for president who lost in a landslide to the popular Franklin D. Roosevelt's second-term victory, 523-8 in the electoral college. He served in the US Army in WWI. He was active in the Methodist Church, chairman of the important committee on Publishing Interests in the Kansas Conference, and helped in the uniting of the publishing works of the three Methodist Churches at their merger in 1939.

Lawrence Rose

Nov. 2, 1901
Monterey, Mexico

Oct. 17, 1987
Kent, Connecticut

President of General Theological Seminary, New York City 1947–66. Rose undertook a ministry in churches in Deer Lodge and Phillipsburg, MT, in 1928. In 1934, he became chaplain of the American Congregation at Holy Trinity Church, Tokyo, Japan. He returned to the US in 1941; became dean at Berkeley Divinity School, New Haven, CT (1942–47), and directed the

Christian Research Foundation (1958–63). He had an illness for several months and was survived by his wife of 55 years, Caroline B. A. Rose, and three daughters.

Everett S. Graffam

April 19, 1915
New Britain, Connecticut

Oct. 20, 1987
Ft. Myers, Florida

President of Buffalo Bible Institute (NY) [merged into Houghton College (NY) in 1968], **1954–61, and of World Relief Corporation, 1967–78**. Graffam had a business background, working at Club Aluminum of Chicago and Britain, CT; at Gridely Machine Company; and at Home Life Insurance of New York City. He ministered via radio in the East and was very active in Youth for Christ and Word of Life. He died in his home following a stroke.

Grady B. Wilson

Aug. 28, 1919
Charlotte, North Carolina

Oct. 30, 1987
Charlotte, North Carolina

Billy Graham's boyhood friend and associate since 1947. Wilson was a good evangelist and also read Scripture on the "Hour of Decision" radio broadcasts for many years. His great wit kept the Graham team jovial through the years. He was converted on the same night as Graham via MORDECAI HAM in September, 1934. Wilson married Wilma Hardie on June 5, 1943. He pastored Friendship Baptist, Charleston, SC, for seven years and in three other South Carolina cities. He died of a heart attack.

Orlando Costas

1942

Nov. 5, 1987
Ponce, Puerto Rico

Latin American evangelical missiologist. Costas was converted at a Billy Graham crusade meeting at Madison Square Gardens, New York City, in 1957. After graduating from Bob Jones University and Garrett Evangelical Seminary, Costas pastored Baptist churches in Yauco, PR, and Milwaukee, WS. He moved to Costa Rica in 1970. In 1973, he created the Latin American Center for Pastoral Studies in San Jose. He taught in six continents. In 1980, Costas became professor of missiology at Eastern Baptist Theological Seminary in Philadelphia. Later, he was dean and professor of missions at Andover Newton Theological School near Boston. His wife's name was Rose. His outstanding book was *Christ Outside the Gate*. He died of cancer at 45.

Leon Mauer

Dec. 22, 1914
Terre Haute, Indiana

Nov. 19, 1987
Livonia, New York

Evangelist and president of Indiana (Heritage in 1985) **Baptist College, Indianapolis, IN, 1966–72**. He also taught at Indiana State University. From 1972–87, Mauer was an evangelist and preached in many places and crusades. He wrote *Soul Winning; Challenge of the Hour*. A funeral service was held November 23 at his home church, Bible Baptist Church in Terre Haute, Indiana.

Robert C. Savage

April 30, 1914
Barron, Wisconsin

Nov. 27, 1987
Muskegon, Michigan

Veteran missionary of World Radio Missionary Fellowship at Quito, Ecuador. He pastored FBC, Romeo, MI and FBC, Washington, MI. He married Wilda Johnson on September 16, 1938. He went to Columbia in 1942 with TEAM. In 1944, he went to Quito, Ecuador and was vice president of YFC in Latin America, 1947–54. From 1954–66, he was vice president of WRMF. Savage served there as program director, U.S. director, and various other positions. He was the son of Baptist pastor HENRY SAVAGE. He compiled eight songbooks in Spanish and wrote many songs and choruses. His wife, Wilda, wrote lyrics and music to a great missionary song, "Lord, Send Me." He pastored Daulton Baptist Church, Muskegon, MI 1969–77.

Andrew J. Foster

June 27, 1925
Ensley, Alabama

Dec. 3, 1987
Senyl, Ruwanda

Founder and first director of Christian Ministry for the Deaf, Detroit, MI, 1956–87. Foster overcame physical, spiritual, educational, and racial barriers to become the premier Black leader in reaching his race's deaf population. In 1942, he moved to Michigan. He zoomed through college, earning three degrees in five years. Doors of most mission boards were closed to Blacks, so he founded the Christian Mission for Deaf Africans. He reached West Africa in 1957. He opened up deaf schools in Ghana and Nigeria. In 1961, he married Berta Zuther of Germany. During his 30 years of service, 31 schools and two centers for the deaf were established in 13 African countries, along with about the same number of Sunday Schools and churches. He went to be with the Lord in an airplane accident.

Melvin I. Burkholder

Feb. 3, 1907
Shippensburg, Pennsylvania

Dec. 29, 1987
Huntington, Indiana

First president of Huntington (IN) College Graduate School Christian Ministries, 1942–72. The school was the seminary program of Huntington College. Burkholder married Edith Holtry on October 1, 1931. He pastored in Pennsylvania, Maryland, Virginia, Ohio, and Indiana. In his later years, he served as chaplain at the local hospital for ten years. His funeral was held at College Park United Brethren Church, where he once pastored.

Peter P. Maravich
Pistol Pete

June 22, 1948
Aliquippa, Pennsylvania

Jan. 5, 1988
Pasadena, California

Great basketball player. Maravich's wife's name was Jackie. During his All-American career at LSU (graduating in 1970), he was the College Player-of-the-Year in 1970. His 44 points per game remains a college record. Maravich played with the Atlanta Hawks (1970–74); New Orleans Jazz (1974–80); and Boston Celtics in 1980. Maravich was in the NBA All-Star game in 1973, '74, '77 and was inducted into the Hall of Fame in 1987. He was converted in November, 1982 in his home in Metairie, LA. He died of a heart attack during a pickup game with James Dobson and others. Reportedly, his last words before collapsing were, "I feel great!" The movie *The Pistol* was made about him.

Samuel N. Morris

March 6, 1900
Paducha, Texas

Jan. 13, 1988

Baptist Evangelist and primary enemy of the liquor industry after Evangelist BILLY SUNDAY's death. Morris was converted June 23, 1918, at a revival conducted by J. D. Fuller in a schoolhouse in Red River County, TX. Morris pastored in Weatherford, TX, started a broadcast in 1928, and also pastored in Stamford, TX. He taught Bible at Hardin-Simmon University and ministered in San Antonio, TX. Morris married Louise Martin in 1932. For years he fought the liquor industry on radio stations in America and Mexico with his *Voice of Temperance* program beaming, in 1936, from Del Rio, TX, across the Mexican border. He wrote 16 publications.

David O. Fuller

Nov. 20, 1903
Brooklyn, New York

Feb. 2, 1988
Grand Rapids, Michigan

Pastor and GARB Council member for 27 years, longer than anyone else in the history of the movement. Fuller was converted in a tent revival in Asheville, NC in 1917, which was conducted by CHAPMAN and ALEXANDER. He married Virginia Emery on September 9, 1931. They never owned a television set. Fuller pastored at Chelsea Baptist Church, Atlantic City, NJ (1929–34), and at Wealthy St. Baptist Church, Grand Rapids, MI (1934–74). He helped found the *Children's Bible Hour* in 1942, was a very strong preacher, and a trustee of Wheaton (IL) College for 40 years. He also headed the Which Bible? Society (1974–88). His defense of the King James Version of the Bible is well known. He was heading to a Sunday School class when he suddenly became ill and was rushed to a hospital, where his heart stopped. He baptized this editor.

Alphaeus H. Zulu

June 29, 1905
Nqutu, South Africa

Feb. 28, 1988
Ulundi, South Africa

President of the World Council of Churches, 1968–75. He married Adelaide Magnaza on January 3, 1929 and upon her death, Lillian Mkhize on February 23, 1985. Zulu was appointed assistant curate at St. Faith's Mission in Durham (1940–60), assistant bishop of St. John's diocese in the Transkei (1960–66), then became bishop of Zululand (1966–70). He was a member of the African National Congress (ANC), 1942–60, but left the group in 1975 as he accepted the national chairmanship of the Inkhatha Freedom Party that was an arm of the nonviolent movement that would help the freedom of South Africa. This led to much rejection and criticism. He refused to condone any form of violence. Zulu was ordained an Anglican priest in 1942. He traveled much, 1958–84.

Glenn V. Cunningham

Aug. 4, 1909
Elkhart, Kansas

March 10, 1988
Menifee, Arkansas

World record holder for the mile run in the 1930s. Winner of a silver medal in the 1,500 meters in the 1936 Berlin Olympics, he was considered one of the first great indoor runners despite the fact that his legs had been so badly burned from a gasoline explosion in childhood that he was expected never to walk again. After nearly a year of exercise, he learned to walk again, and in his words, "by the grace of God, I learned to run again." During WWII, he was in the Navy and established new physical training programs at both the Great Lakes and San Diego training stations. He lived on a ranch in Kansas and held summer camps and activities for handicapped children. Cunningham was named the greatest track performer in the history of Madison Square Garden in 1979.

Walter L. Surbrook

March 4, 1891
Croswell, Michigan

March 20, 1988
Kernerville, North Carolina

General superintendent of Pilgrim Holiness Church (Wesleyan Church in 1968), **1933–46, and president of Owosso John Wesley College, 1948–55**. Surbrook was converted at age 22. He was ordained in the Pilgrim Holiness Church. He was a teacher, (1922, 1924–30); and the first president of Kingswood (KY) Holiness College (1927–30). He married Jessie Bingham on April 8, 1932. Surbrook was president of Pilgrim Bible College, Kernersville, NC, from 1946–48. He was in evangelism (1955–

59) and pastored the Trinity (NC) Wesleyan Church (1959–63). He was back at PBC from 1963–71 as dean of theology and a teacher. Surbrook's first book was *Awakening Messages and Stirring Experiences* (1930).

Gerhard Claas

Aug. 31, 1928
Wetter, Germany

March 21, 1988
Lodi, California

General secretary of Baptist World Alliance, 1980-88. Claas married Irmgard Saffran on July 29, 1954. He was converted in 1942; pastored FBC, Dusseldorf (1953-58); served as youth secretary of German Baptist Union in Hamburg (1958-64); pastored the Onckon Baptist Church in Hamburg (1965-67); and served as general secretary of the same (1967-76). He was also the associate secretary of BWA from 1976-80, and worked with the Evangelical Free Church. Claas died in an automobile crash near Lodi. His funeral was held at a Baptist Church in Volmarstein, Germany, where he was converted, baptized, married, and where he often preached. More than 1,000 people attended his funeral.

Daniel I. VanderPool

Sept. 6, 1891
Pollock, Missouri

March 21, 1988
Chandler, Arizona

General Superintendent of Church of the Nazarene, 1949-64. VanderPool was converted in a Free Methodist church on March 27, 1909, and began preaching in schoolhouses. He became a Nazarene in 1913. VanderPool was seriously ill in 1915. Shortly thereafter, he preached a six week revival and started a church with 42 members. From 1916-23, VanderPool headquartered out of Colorado (small churches and evangelism). He pastored (1918-37) in such places as Denver, CO (1924-28); Pasadena, CA (1929-34); and Walla Walla, WA (1934-37). From 1937-49, he was district superintendent of the Northwest District.

Edwin J. Pudney

March 3, 1897
England?

March 29, 1988
Boca Raton, Florida

First president of Unevangelized Fields Mission (UFM Int. in 1980), **Philadelphia, PA** (Bala Cynwyd, PA in 1980), **1931-61, and president of IFMA, 1948-50**. Pudney married Lilian Patton on March 21, 1921 (died: April 21, 1982), and a woman named Dorothy after his first wife died. From 1923-31, they went to the Belgian Congo and worked with Heart of Africa Mission (WEC). In March 1931, Unevangelized Fields Mission was formed as a spin-off of the above with missionaries in Congo and Brazil. The Pudneys moved to Toronto to bring the mission to NA. In 1941, they moved to Lancaster, PA, and extended the vision. They moved to Bala Cynwyd, PA (1954), and headed UFM until retirement (1961).

Arthur M. Ramsey

Nov. 14, 1904
Cambridge, England

April 23, 1988
Oxford, England

Archbishop of Canterbury, 1961-74, and president of WCC, 1961-68. He was subwarden at Lincoln Theological College (1930-36); canon of Durham Cathedral; and professor at University of Durham (1940-50). Ramsey married Joan Hamilton on April 8, 1942. He also served as a bishop of Durham (1952-56) and archbishop of York (1956-61). Ramsey made the first official visit in 400 years as an Anglican head to see Pope Paul VI in Rome in 1966. He retired on his 70th birthday in 1974. His writings ranged from *The Gospel and the Catholic Church* (1936) to *God, Christ, and the World* (1969).

Fred Jordan

Aug. 7, 1909
Thurber, Texas

April 24, 1988
Los Angeles, California

Apostle of the highway, Jordan would hitchhike everywhere using it as a tool to win people to Christ. He was converted at age 21, and pastored the First Baptist Church, Southgate (suburb of LA), 1934-41. The church grew from 156 to 1,400 and the Sunday School from 62 to 868. His unique evangelism started in 1941 when he was pastoring a Baptist church. Jordan then resigned and founded the American Soul Clinic in Southern California which specialized in house-to-house visitation and witnessing. One summer between Los Angeles and San Francisco, averaging more than 400 miles a day for several weeks, he won more than 500 motorists to Christ. His first hitchhiking convert became a full-time missionary to Mexicans in the San Antonio area.

Wallace E. Johnson
The Praying Millionaire

Jan. 5, 1901
Edinburgh, Mississippi

April 27, 1988
Memphis, Tennessee

Headed the Holiday Inn chain. Johnson married Alma McCool on August 10, 1924. Johnson was founder and chairman of his building company, the Wallace Johnson Enterprises, in Memphis, 1941-88. He was an active Baptist layman as well as the cofounder and vice-chairman of Holiday Inn, 1953-88, establishing his headquarters in Memphis, TN. He traveled many miles in fund-raising for meetings, promoting such organizations as Campus Crusade.

Vesphew (Vep) B. Ellis

March 11, 1917
Oneonta, Alabama

April 30, 1988

Ellis published over 500 songs and wrote lyrics and music for many others, including "Do You Know My Jesus," "Let Me Touch Him," and "My God Can Do Anything." Ellis played the keyboard, strings, and bass. Ellis was a minister for the Church of God in Cleveland, TN, for 49 years. He also pastored at Harvest Temple Church of God, Largo, FL. His wife's name was Pat. Ellis served as a music director and helped the Oral Roberts' crusades for six years.

Walter Staten

Dec. 25, 1928
Portsmouth, Ohio

May 12, 1988
Huntington, West Virginia

First president of Tri-State Bible College, South Point, OH 1970–88. Staten was saved as a child and became a real Bible student while quite young. He married Borma Smith on May 18, 1957. He pastored a Bible church in Clintonville, WI (1957–61), and Fond Du Lac, WI (1961–69). He taught classes as well. He attended Dallas Theological Seminary and Piedmont Bible College. He emphasized expository preaching and said "give the people something to believe." He had a massive stroke at TBS suddenly and died in a hospital.

Festo Kivengere

Nov. 1, 1919
Uganda

May 18, 1988
Nairobi, Kenya

Anglican bishop from Uganda, Africa, barred from his native land by Idi Amin in 1977. Kivengere was converted in 1939 in a great East African revival. He was a powerful evangelist, traveling and preaching all over the world. Kivengere's wife's name was Mera. He worked as an educator (1941–60), evangelist (1962–64), attended Pittsburg Theological Seminary (1964–67), joined

African Enterprise in 1971, and was bishop of Kigezl, Uganda (1972–77). Kivengere worked as a translator for Billy Graham in East Africa. He fled into Rwanda (1977) but returned (1979). In 1982, when thousands of refugees were expelled from their homes, he organized assistance for them although it was dangerous and unpopular to do so. He died of leukemia in a local hospital.

John E. Douglas

March 8, 1903
Walto County, West Virginia

May 30, 1988
Dallas, Texas

First president of World Missionary Evangelism, Inc., Dallas, TX, 1957–88. Douglas was converted under the preaching of A. A. ALLEN. He married Edith Richardson on August 20, 1924. WME sponsors mission farms, treatment of lepers, training schools for the handicapped, food for hunger centers, native ministers, and hundreds of churches in 17 countries. Douglas returned from India with seven orphans to begin the work. This has since grown to 200 orphanage centers which care for thousands of children around the world. He died of a heart attack.

Clyde W. Taylor

Nov. 7, 1904
Fort Smith, Arkansas

June 3, 1988
Arnold, Maryland

Leading figure in National Association of Evangelicals history, general director, 1948–54, and executive secretary of EFMA, 1945–74. Taylor was a CMA missionary to Peru (1925–27), to Columbia (1931–41), then pastored Central Baptist, Quincy, MA (1941–44). Taylor married Ruth Marstaller on June 7, 1930. He served as secretary of NAE's Office of Public Affairs (1944–63). He was general secretary of World Evangelical Fellowship, 1970–74. Taylor was a longtime lobbyist in Washington, D.C. for Christian causes. He traveled to 92 countries of the world in 40 years. He died in his home.

Charles E. S. Kraemer

April 25, 1909
Bonham, Texas

June 23, 1988
Charlotte, North Carolina

President of General Assembly Training School for Lay Workers, 1954–59, renamed Presbyterian School of Christian Education (Union Theological Seminary in 1995), **Richmond, VA, 1954–74.** Kraemer married Beryl Birdsong on September 9, 1932, in Greenville, TX. Ordained Presbyterian in 1934, he pastored in Hawesville, KY (1934–36); Kansas City, MO (1936–41); Leland, MS (1941–45); and the First Presbyterian Church of Charlotte, NC (1945–54). He was a visiting professor of religion in Brazil (1958), Mexico (1961), Taiwan (1964), Russia (1969), and Britain (1969).

Josiah M. Kibira

Aug. 28, 1925
Kashenye, Tanzania

July 18, 1988
Bukoba, Tanzania

President of Lutheran World Federation, 1977–84. Kibira was converted on March 21, 1947. He married Martha Jeremiah on November 25, 1951; they had nine children. He was a schoolteacher (1950–57), then a bishop of the Evangelical Lutheran Church of Tanzania for the diocese of his home district (1964–77), traveling the world on behalf of his work.

Cleo W. Buxton

Nov. 4, 1919
Haslett, Michigan

July 28, 1988
Lakewood, Colorado

General secretary of Officer's Christian Union, 1952–72, a ministry amongst the military, with headquarters in Englewood, CO. Buxton was a hero in WWI, highly decorated. He married his wife, Louisa, August 3, 1946, and after graduating from Princeton Seminary in 1950, he was ordained a Baptist minister. He taught ROTC at Knox College, Galesburg, IL, and then became the first full-time staff member of OCU. During his 20 years as leader, the *Command Magazine* was created with other expansions. Spring Canyon, CO, was developed for a Christian retreat center. His life touched thousands. He died in his sleep and funeral services were held at Our Savior's Lutheran Reformed Church, Lakewood, CO, on August 3.

Frank Shultz

May 15, 1895
Shipshewana, Indiana

July 30, 1988
Jackson, Michigan

Founder and first president of Galilean Baptist Missions, Grand Rapids, MI (Baptist Church Planters, Ellyria, OH in 1985), **1950–62**. Once converted, Shultz married Ruth Jones in 1930 and upon her death he married Minnie Hammond (October 24, 1898–June 20, 1982) in 1932. He started various Sunday schools including one near Grand Rapids, called Cook SS. This one started on March 19, 1936 when they held a class for 14 children at Cook School. In 1947, he sold his business, and with the support of 14 churches, began their outreach ministry. In 1951, it was incorporated as GBM. Eventually he started 21 churches, including the large Good News Church of Grand Rapids. He started churches in stores, schools, and halls or any other available space. Shultz did not really begin until age 50, and in the following 30 years he started 220 churches. At age 88, Shultz married Vivian Clark and she died six months after his passing.

Charles H. Strickland

Oct. 21, 1916
Cincinnati, Ohio

Aug. 9, 1988
Olathe, Kansas

General Superintendent of Church of the Nazarene, 1972–88. Strickland pastored in Moultrie, GA (1937–38); Waycross, GA (1938–39); Atlanta, GA (1939–42) and Dallas, TX (1946–48). He was responsible for the Nazarene work among Europeans in South Africa 1948–65, including teaching there at the Nazarene Bible College in Florida, South Africa. From 1967–72, he was president of the Nazarene Bible College, Colorado Springs, CO. He and his wife had four sons.

Bartlett Peterson

Oct. 29, 1908
Boston, Massachusetts

Sept. 7, 1988
Springfield, Missouri

First full-time president of Central Bible College, Springfield, MO, 1948–58. Peterson completed a degree in law but chose to continue in the ministry. From 1940–43, he was Minnesota District Secretary. He taught at North Central Bible College, Minneapolis, MN (1940–48), while serving as Minnesota district superintendent (1943–48). He was elected to the office of general secretary of the denomination (1959), serving until his retirement (1975). He was involved in radio ministry for 27 years, both in planning and participation. From 1975–88, he preached and taught across the nation and overseas. His wife's name was Lee.

Alfred L. Patterson
Mr. Missionary Baptist

Nov. 2, 1903
Mabank, Texas

Sept. 13, 1988
Longview, Texas

Secretary/treasurer (CEO) of American Baptist Association Missionary Committee, Texarkana, TX, 1952–73. Patterson was converted in 1912 near Alma, TX. He married Vera Richardson on September 22, 1929. He came to Texarkana in 1938. Patterson was an auditor/accountant (1938–44); a business manager (1944–52); and helped with ABA Sunday School committee. Patterson was a member of Unity Baptist Church and was frugal, plain spoken, and well received.

Bernard Confer

Aug. 27, 1914
Rebersberg, Pennsylvania

Sept. 17, 1988
Teaneck, New Jersey

First director of Lutheran World Relief, Baltimore, MD, 1946–81. Confer joined LWR (1946), was appointed administrative secretary (1948), and the executive director (1953). He led the organization in the aid to Europeans after WWII to develop work among needy peoples of Asia, Africa, and Latin America. He served with the U.S. Army in WWII in Korea. Confer married Hallie R. Baker. He was a member of St. Paul's Lutheran Church in Teaneck, NJ. He was on various boards serving as trustee, consultant, honorary chairman, and other positions.

C. J. Rediger

Nov. 20, 1902
Livingston County, Indiana

Oct. 10, 1988
Lincoln, Illinois

Founder and first director of Rural Home Missionary Association, Morton, IL, 1942–58. Rediger was converted at age 13 in the Evangelical Mennonite Church near Gridley, IL. He married Mirtle Pohle. It was his burden and concept that churches should be started in small towns and villages across America. Starting in the early 1940s, living in Morton, IL, with no income to speak of, he took off, and asked the Lord to guide him. He stopped in Lyford, IN (population 200), and years later, after starting the Lyford Bible Church, it averaged 135 in attendance. The story was repeated hundreds of times. He ran a bookstore in Carthage, IL, until 1974. He was a member of the IFCA.

Anthony A. Hoekema

July 26, 1913
Drachten, Netherlands

Oct. 17, 1988
Frederick, Maryland

Theologian. Hoekema was ordained in 1944 in the Christian Reformed Church. He pastored 12th St. CR Church, Grand Rapids, MI (1944–50); Bethel CR Church, Paterson, NJ (1950–54) and Alger Park CR Church, Grand Rapids, MI (1954–56). He began teaching at Calvin Theological Seminary (1955), taught Bible at Calvin College, 1956–58, and was professor of systematic theology at the seminary until his retirement (1978).

Milo A. Rediger

July 26, 1913
Pioneer, Ohio

Oct. 18, 1988
Indianapolis, Indiana

President of Taylor University, Upland, IN 1965–75, 1979–81. Rediger was a scholar, teacher, and adminstrator. He was academic dean, 1945–50, 52–65, professor of philosophy (1943), and vice president (1954). He was at Taylor a lifetime except as a teaching fellow at NY University (1941–43), and dean of the College at the University of Dubuque (1950–52). At Taylor, the enrollment tripled and nine major building projects were undertaken during his tenure. His wife's name was Velma. She wrote his biography entitled, *My Poem, My Song*, his pilgrimage from a shy farm boy to university president. The Milo A. Rediger Chapel/Auditorium is named in his honor.

Maurice Heinrich

June 14, 1916
Los Angeles, California

October 23, 1988
Victorville, California

Founder and first director of Handclasp Int., Crest Park, C, 1970–85. Heinrich was a delinquent as a youth, but was converted in a Pentecostal church in California at age 23. He married Lois Depp in 1941. As a machinist, his trade helped lead his interests in using his talents to help others. After WWII service, he attended a Four Square Church in Santa Anna, TX, and participated in their mission program by taking food into Mexico on weekend trips. Soon Heinrich was assisting in the distribution of medicine, seeds, and other commodities. After a trip to Pakistan, he fell ill to kidney failure, which caused his death.

George Havens

Sept. 17, 1920
Santa Anna, Texas

Oct. 26, 1988
Dallas, Texas

World's smallest cowboy. Although Havens was only 4'11" tall and weighed only 125 pounds, his voice, testimony, and guitar touched many lives. From 1939–50, he worked as a stuntman in Hollywood movies. (He was only 4'2" tall and 82 pounds then). Havens was converted as a result of STUART HAMBLEN's conversion and the witness of businessman Kline Debowe. Following his conversion in 1950, he started Cowboy Camp Meetings in 1966 with his wife Lucy, whom he married in 1956. These ten-day sessions were held every June in Santa Anna, TX. Havens died of rare nonsmoker's lung cancer.

Bryce B. Augsburger

May 15, 1922
Berne, Indiana

Oct. 29, 1988
Joliet, Illinois

President of Denver (CO) Baptist Bible College (Faith Baptist Bible College in Ankeny, IA in 1986), **1966–79**. Augsburger was active in various Baptist groups. He pastored FBC in Galveston, MI (1947–49); at Livernois Ave. Baptist Church in Detroit, MI (1950–58), and at Marquette Manor Baptist Church in Chicago, IL (1958–66). He made his home in Romeoville, IL, and died in a hospital nearby.

Tressie V. Myers

May 28, 1903
near Kinross, Iowa

Oct. 29, 1988
Keokuk, Iowa

Director of Nurses Christian Fellowship, 1950–68. Tressie's mother died when she was 15 and she took over the home duties to help her two older brothers and two younger sisters. She began her teaching career in public schools in Iowa and Illinois. She graduated from nursing school in Chicago in 1938 and eventually became head nurse and instructor at Michael Reese Hospital. A small group of students asked her to become the faculty advisor for their Bible study group. That was the beginning of her association with NCF. She inspired dozens of nurses to go overseas as missionaries. Tressie retired and worked diligently at the First Baptist Church of Keokuk, IA. She had Parkinson's disease and died of cardiac and pulmonary arrest.

Thomas B. McDormand

March 15, 1904
Bear River, Nova Scotia

Nov. 5, 1988
Amherst, Nova Scotia, Canada

Secretary of the United Baptist Convention of Atlantic Provinces, 1967–70, and of the Ontario/Quebec Provinces, 1950–56. McDormand married Irene H. Webb on Oct. 26, 1931. He was ordained as a Baptist in 1929 and pastored in Nova Scotia, 1929–38. McDormand served as the editor for the *Baptist Publications of Canada* (1942–48) and was also the president of Eastern Baptist College and Seminary of Philadelphia, PA from 1961–67. His autobiography is *A Diversified Ministry* (1987).

Colin W. Bell

April 10, 1903
Liverpool, England

Nov. 8, 1988
Kent's Store, Virginia

Director of American Friends Service Committee, Philadelphia, PA 1959–68. He was a buyer, then personnel director of British Home Stores, LTD, London, 1928–42. Bell married Elaine Conyers on September 28, 1946. He was chairman of Friends Ambulance Unity, Chungking,

China (1943–46); director of Asian Activities of AFSC, Philadelphia (1946–49); director of Friends International Center, Geneva, Switzerland (1950–55), and associate director of AFSC, Philadelphia (1955–59).

Charles Leaming

Dec. 16, 1903
Woodward, Iowa

Nov. 8, 1988
St. Petersburg, Florida

President of St. Petersburg (FL) Bible Institute (Logos Christian College and Seminary in 2001), **1947–80**. Leaming's conversion came at a prayer meeting in his uncle's home. He started in the insurance field until a revival meeting at Des Moines Gospel Tabernacle rekindled his desire to become an evangelist. In 1930, he gave his first sermon on radio in Cedar Rapids, IA, and was on the radio for over 50 years. In 1946, he came to St. Petersburg, FL, and began a lifetime of pastoring, broadcasting, and teaching to the entire area. He pastored the Faith Temple, 1947 on. Leaming was one of the founders of the National Religious Broadcasters and helped start several Open Bible Churches.

Harlan Popov

March 7, 1907
Krasno, Gradishte, Bulgaria

Nov. 13, 1988
Glendale, California

Founder and first president of Evangelism to Communist Lands (Door of Hope Int.), **Pasadena, CA 1972–79**. Popov had an incredible testimony because of 13 years in a Communist prison, 1952–65 in the Gulag Archipelago Islands. He had been the pastor of the largest Protestant church in Bulgaria. Popov founded the mission in order to help others under bondage. He married Ruth Pernevi.

J. Vernon McGee

June 17, 1904
Hillsboro, Texas

Dec. 1, 1988
Atascadero, California

Bible teacher to the world on his *Through the Bible* broadcast, 1967 on. McGee was a radio preacher for 40 years. His program later went global in 40 languages, going through the entire Bible every five years. He pastored in Presbyterian churches in Decatur, GA; Nashville, TN (1933–41) and Cleburne, TX (1941–49). His earlier radio program, *The Open Bible Hour* began in 1941. He then pastored the Church of the Open Door in Los Angeles, 1949–70, which had 4,000 members and supported 106 missionaries. He saw the midweek service grow from 20 to 3,000 and authored more than 100 books, including *Defining the Bible*. His radio ministry continues after his death. "He, being dead, yet speaketh" (Hebrews 11:4) is literally true here.

Ray Hart

Feb. 9, 1941
Kinston, North Carolina

Dec. 3, 1988
Ephrata, Pennsylvania

One of the great soloists of his time. Hart sang in the Metropolitan Opera in New York City and traveled and studied in five foreign countries. His wife's name was Barbara. He dedicated his life to the Lord while sitting in an NBC office and was soon singing at the Pastor's School, Hammond, IN (Pastor JACK HYLES), and assisting CURTIS HUTSON in crusades, beginning in 1977. One night after singing at Liberty Baptist Church, he had an epileptic seizure. He was found dead the next morning in his room.

B. Raymond Charles

Aug. 19, 1918
near Salunga, Pennsylvania

Dec. 5, 1988
Lancaster, Pennsylvania

President of Eastern Mennonite Charities, Salunga, PA 1956–80. Charles also served as chairman of the board, 1956–66. Ordained in 1941, he married Anna L. Bucher on July 15, 1942. He was ordained bishop on July 11, 1964, in the Mennonite church. Charles lost his left eye in August 1971 because of a tumor. In 1983 he was diagnosed as having cancer of the liver. He died in the same home he lived in since age six. He was a farmer when not active in Christian work, which included pastoring Chestnut Hill Mennonite Church and teaching Bible at Lancaster Mennonite High School.

Walter Carlson

Nov. 21, 1918
Spokane, Washington

Dec. 27, 1988
Sawyer, Michigan

Radio voice known to multitudes listening to WMBI, Chicago, 1942–88. Carlson was saved at age 19 following a visit to a Mission (Evangelical) Covenant Church the family attended in Spokane. He married Norma Martin on June 29, 1946, and they had seven children. He did news, special events, interviews, and was the most dominant voice in Christian radio for decades. He died of liver cancer.

Dorothy Clark Haskin

March 19, 1905
Boston, Massachusetts

1989

Most prolific female writer of her generation. Her 55 books and 5,000 published articles appeared everywhere. At age four, she became a toe dancer and child actress. For the next 18 years, she danced and acted on the stage and on the screen. On February 13, 1931, she married Roy Haskin. Her eventually invalid husband died in July, 1959. Through the First Presbyterian Church of Hollywood, CA, she was converted in the fall of 1932. She went to BIOLA and began her writing career in 1940. Her first article was "Ringing Doorbells for Christ" for the *Sunday School Times*. Twenty-one of her submitted twenty-three articles were published that first year. In September, 1959, she joined World Vision as missions research department manager. As a result, she visited 26 countries besides traveling all over America. Her first book was *Practical Primer on Prayer* for Moody Press. It sold 57,000 copies.

Richard Woike

May 18, 1905
New York, New York

Jan. 5, 1989
Mountain View, California

President of Christian Business Men's Committee, 1956. Woike was a Presbyterian layman, active in both the New York (1957) and Southern California (1963) Billy Graham crusades, serving as chairman of the executive committee of the latter. He was converted at age ten, and at 16 was challenged by PAUL RADER at Ocean Grove, NJ, to reaffirm his faith and dedicate his life to the Lord. Living in Hartford, CT, he worked with an insurance firm. He moved to New York to become co-owner of a small automobile mutual insurance company. In three years, he bought out his partner and became owner and president at age 32. It went from $100,000 in assets to $7 million. Woike was widely used as a teacher of the Men's Bible Class at FBC, Hackensack, NJ. He led ANTON MARCO, former opera soloist, to Christ.

George J. Poole

Jan. 4, 1918 — Minneapolis, Minnesota
Jan. 22, 1989 — Hollywood, Florida

One of HCJB's most active missionaries. Poole married Margaret Carne on September 9, 1942. Poole left for Quito, Ecuador, in 1947. His program, *Morning in the Mountains* was broadcast around the world. His 35 years of ministry on the field overlapped with some 20 years as U.S. director and office manager. Early on in life, Poole directed Youth For Christ in Ft. Wayne, IN. He died of cancer.

Frederick A. Schiotz

June 15, 1901 — Chicago, Illinois
Feb. 25, 1989 — Minneapolis, Minnesota

President of Evangelical Lutheran Church (one of the three to merge in 1960 forming ALC), **1954–60; president of American Lutheran Church, 1960–70** (ELCA in 1988); **and of Lutheran World Federation, 1963–70.** Schiotz married Dagny Aasen on August 23, 1928. He pastored at Zion Lutheran, Duluth, MN (1930–32); Trinity Lutheran, Moorehead, MN (1932–38) and in Brooklyn, NY (1945–48). He was the executive secretary of the student services commission of ALC from 1938–45. Schiotz also served on the staff of the National Lutheran Council, 1948–54.

James A. Millard

April 8, 1912 — Bristol, Tennessee
March 4, 1989 — Fairhope, Alabama

Stated clerk of Presbyterian Church in US (USA in 1983), **1959–72.** Millard married Sunshine Hopper on June 12, 1937. He was ordained as a Presbyterian in 1935 and served pastorates in Virginia, Louisiana, and Arkansas, 1935–62. He was a professor of church polity and an administrator at Presbyterian Theological Seminary, Austin, TX (1952–55), and professor of homiletics (1956–59). Millard also served as treasurer of the denomination while he was clerk. He lived in Atlanta, GA.

C. Stuart Hamblen

Oct. 20, 1908 — Kellyville, Texas
March 8, 1989 — Santa Monica, California

Hollywood entertainer, converted at the Billy Graham Los Angeles, CA, Crusade in 1949. He also wrote lyrics and music to "Until Then," "How Big Is God," "This Ole House" (Song of the Year, 1955), "They That Wait Upon the Lord," "Is He Satisfied?" "He Bought My Soul at Calvary," and "Known Only to Him." Hamblen married Veeva (Suzy) Daniels on April 24, 1933. He was raised in a Methodist parsonage and ignored the Lord until October 31, 1949, when he was converted in his hotel room after 21 years in an acting/singing career (acted as a villain in 28 western movies). He was convicted at the BG crusade the night before, and called Graham asking him to come to his room early in the morning. At the rendezvous, Hamblen said to the Lord, "You are hearing a new voice" and was converted. Later, a friend said to him, "You're a new man!" Stuart replied, "It is no secret what God can do" and a number one hit song was born. He ran for president in 1952 on the Prohibition Party and received 72,881 votes, more than any Prohibition candidate had ever received. In 1971, he began his popular KLAC Sunday morning network radio program, *The Cowboy Church of the Air* which ran for more than a decade. Hamblen died following an operation for a brain tumor and his funeral service was conducted by Billy Graham at Hollywood Presbyterian Church, where he was a member. He died of brain cancer.

*"When you see me fall asleep, say amen but don't you weep.
I've got so many million years that I can't count them."*

Alan Redpath

Jan. 9, 1907
Newcastle-upon-Tyne, England

March 16, 1989
Birmingham, England

Pastor of Moody Church, Chicago, IL, 1953–62. In 1936, Redpath left a business career to join the National Young Life Campaign in Britain as an evangelist, and then became pastor of the Duke Street Baptist Church near London, 1940–53. While at Moody Church, he founded the Mid-America Keswick Convention in 1954. Under his leadership, blacks were allowed to be members for the first time. In 1962, he became pastor of Scotland's largest Baptist church, Charlotte Chapel, Edinburgh. He retired from that position in 1966 due to health problems. He then traveled extensively as an international speaker for the English Keswick Convention and other missionary societies. He authored six books, from *Victorious Christian Living* (1955) to *Captive to Conquest* (1978).

Donald W. Basham

Sept. 17, 1926
Wichita Falls, Texas

March 27, 1989
California

Bible teacher, editor, and author. Both Basham and his wife, Alice Roling, were converted after they were married in 1949. He was ordained a Disciples of Christ minister in 1955. Basham pastored churches in Washington, D.C. (1936–61); Toronto, Ontario (1961–64), and Sharon, PA (1964–67). After his first book, *Face Up with a Miracle*, was published, he left the pastorate and moved to Fort Lauderdale in 1967 to begin teaching and writing. He was the editor of *New Wine Magazine* (1975–87) and wrote the book *Deliver Us from Evil* (c 1972) while working in Christian Youth Ministries. Basham lived in Fort Lauderdale, FL, until 1978; in Mobile, AL, 1978–86 and then in Elyria, OH. He had 1 1/2 years of illness before a fatal heart attack.

C. Reuben Lindquist

Jan. 8, 1902
Elgin, Illinois

April 1, 1989
St. Louis, Missouri

Director of Berean Mission, Inc., St. Louis, MO 1945–72. He was somewhat involved in the leadership of BM, 1940–45, but not full-time until 1945. Lindquist was converted as a lad of twelve in a country schoolhouse in western Nebraska in response to an invitation from Revelation 3:20. He married Georgiena Hamond on July 20, 1953. He was an evangelist in the 1930s. He served as the president of Denver Bible Institute, 1937–42 and was very active in conference speaking and trips to mission fields. Lindquist pastored at St. Louis Gospel Center, 1943–45. Lindquist was a member of Brentwood (MO) Bible Church.

Edmund F. Wagner

Jan. 12, 1898
New York, New York

April 6, 1989
Mt. Vernon, New York

President of the American Bible Society, 1967–1985. Wagner married Mildred Borgstede on October 15, 1919. Wagner, a devout Lutheran, was an outstanding banker and real estate broker. He was partners with the Joseph Milner Company (1922–38); with E. F. Wager & Company (1938–42); president of General Realty and Utilities Corp. (1944–58) and president of Seamen's Bank for Savings, New York City (1958–65).

Arthur R. Mckay

Feb. 16, 1918
Waterbury, Connecticut

April 15, 1989
Alexandria, Virginia

President of McCormick Theological Seminary, Chicago, IL, 1957-70 and of Association of Theological Schools, 1968–70. Mckay taught at Russell Sage College, Troy NY, (1942–47). Mckay married Ann Usher on July 3, 1943. He was ordained as a Presbyterian in 1944 and then pastored in Merrick, NY (1944–47), and in Binghamton, NY 1952-57. He was vice president of Lane Theological Seminary (McCormick affiliate), 1957–89.

Harry M. Lintz

Sept. 4, 1900
Greenville, Tennessee

April 22, 1989
Prescott, Arizona

Baptist evangelist from 1937 until retirement. Lintz was on the extension staff of MBI, 1928–37, as an evangelist and conference speaker. He grew up in rural Tennessee and was converted at age 13 in a revival near Cedar Creek (population 25). He won many medals and honors in high school, pastored in Greenville, TN (1924–28) and Lake Charles, LA (1937–41), then went into evangelism, which was climaxed by speaking to 55,000 at an Easter sunrise service in Soldier's Field in Chicago in the early 1940s. He called his work the Victory Crusade Evangelistic Association after 1937. He married Esther J. Olsen on January 5, 1939 (died: August 1, 1964), and Mildred Anderson on December 7, 1968. In later life, he belonged to the First Baptist Church, Prescott.

Theodore W. Willingham

Jan. 20, 1898
Sebree, Kentucky

April 29, 1989
Kansas City, Missouri

President of Olivet Nazarene College, Kankakee, IL 1926–37. Willingham married Mary Cusick on October 21, 1915, and they had four children. He was ordained Nazarene in 1920. Willingham pastored in Danville, IL (1919–23), and was treasurer and financial secretary of the college (1923–26). He became an evangelist, 1938–40, and district superintendent of the Missouri area after 1940.

W. Marvin Sheffield

Nov. 28, 1904
Coleman, Texas

May 12, 1989
Abilene, Texas

First president of Congregational Methodist Church, Florence, MO, 1941–61, This evangelist and pastor became the editor of the *Messenger* in 1937, serving as the editor-in-chief until 1980. He led in the opening of the Congregational Methodist Bible School in February, 1944, and became a teacher 1945–53. He later resumed his teaching duties in 1960 while the school was in Tehuacana, TX, and served as the head of the Department of Biblical Literature until 1972. He decided at this time not to move with the school to Florence, MS but to reside in Brownwood, TX, until his death. He was married 63 years to Margaret and was one of the CMC's greatest leaders. He died about four hours after an automobile accident.

R. T. Perritt

May 26, 1926
Winnsboro, Texas

May 15, 1989
Clinton, Oklahoma

President of Oklahoma Missionary Baptist College, Marlow, OK, 1963–89. Raised in a Christian home, Perritt was saved at age 13. He married Betty Powell on November 23, 1944. He pastored in Sherman, TX (1949–51), and Fort Worth, TX (1951–56). He then went to Cavanaugh MB Church, Ft. Smith, AR where he pastored, 1956–59. Then came the move to Marlow, OK, where he pastored the Fifth St. MB Church, 1959–80, taking on the college leadership also. From 1980 until his death, he pastored in Ardmore, OK (1980–83) and the Broadway Ave. MB Church, Clinton (1983–89). He was serving both the pastorate and the college until his death of cancer.

R. Curtis Smith

Feb. 3, 1915
Cameron, Texas

May 17, 1989
Olathe, Kansas

First president of Mid-America Nazarene College, Olathe, KS, 1966–85. After getting his education at Bethany College, Oklahoma City, OK, and Boston University, Smith married Marge Camfield on February 7, 1937. He pastored in Greenville, Dallas, and Corpus Christi, TX from 1937–50. He was assistant to president Roy Cantrell at Bethany College, 1950–65. He was challenged to start a new college in order to take some of the load off Bethany and became a fund-raiser, speaking across the country and in churches and camps. When MANC opened in a cornfield, there were 263 students, and some 2,000 when he left it 20 years later. The property value rose from $279,341 to $15,332,563 during this time. He preached the funerals of both parents of James Dobson, renowned leader of *Focus on the Family*. He had a series of little strokes, then a multiple stroke took his life.

John H. Satterwhite

Jan. 1, 1913
Newberry, South Carolina

May 23, 1989

President of Hood Theological Semianary, Salisbury, NC 1938–53. Highly educated, Satterwhite served as instructor of religion and philosophy at Livingstone College, Salisbury, NC. He was appointed dean of Hood Theological Seminary and served as professor of theology there, 1940–56. He married Lucille C. Mills on September 24, 1942. Satterwhite became the first black professor on the faculty of Wesley Theological Seminary, Washington, D.C., teaching there, 1958–72. Satterwhite also served as pastor of Trinity AME Zion Church, Washington, D.C., from 1956–72 and was editor of the *AME Zion Quarterly Review* (1980–89). He returned to Hood, serving as dean of Institute for Black Ministries, 1972–74.

Henry C. Ball

Feb. 18, 1896
Brooklyn, Iowa

May 27, 1989
San Antonio, Texas

Founder and first president of Latin America Bible Institute, San Antonio, TX, 1926–40. Ball was converted in 1910 in a little Methodist church in Kingsville, TX. He married Sunshine Marshall on June 20, 1918 (died: August 16, 1993). He started and pastored the El Templo Christiano Church in San Antonio, 1918–36, then moved to a ranch in 1936 in Saspanmco, TX. He was the first superintendent of the Latin America District for Assemblies of God, 1918–54. His school was moved to El Paso, TX, in 1941. Upon leaving the school, he was a missionary in Chile, 1941–43. He then traveled widely for AG missions on special assignments, 1943–54. From 1954–61, he was engaged in publishing and editorial ventures. His *Himnos De Gloria* hymnbook was published into several million copies. From 1961–85, he was back in San Antonio where he founded and pastored the El Salvador Church. He broke his hip in November, 1988, and never recovered properly.

Corwin C. Roach

Aug. 14, 1904
Cleveland, Ohio

May 28, 1989

Dean of Bexley Hall Theological Seminary at Kenyon College, Gambier, OH, [Colgate-Rochester (NY) Divinity School in 1968], **1941–58.** Roach was ordained a deacon (1927) and a priest (1928) into the Episcopal Church. He married Agnes B. Spencer on June 30, 1930. He also became a professor of Hebrew and Old Testament at the divinity school in 1930. Roach was the local priest at Harcourt Parish and instructor in Bible at KC, Gambier, OH, from 1935–38. He also taught philosophy and history at North Dakota State University, Fargo, 1960–77.

D. Mark Buntain

Jan. 26, 1923
Winnipeg, Manitoba, Canada

June 3, 1989
Calcutta, India

Pentecostal missionary to India. Buntain married Hulda Munroe (born: 1926) in 1944 and began as pastor in Saskatchewan. He then became an evangelist to several countries. He started the Calcutta Mission of Mercy upon going to India in 1953. Buntain pastored the Assembly of God Church there, which had 4,000 members, representing six different languages. His mission complex fed 22,000 daily, had a hospital, nursing school, six village clinics, a hostel for destitute youths, twelve schools instructing 6,000 children, and a staff of 1,000 nationals. Upon his death, his wife continued the work.

Cy Nelson

April 17, 1909
Bridgeport, Connecticut

June 4, 1989
Los Angeles, California

President of Gospel Light Publications, Ventura, CA 1949–80, and of Gospel Literature Int. (GLINT), Ontario, CA 1963–86. Raised in a Christian and Missionary Alliance Church, Nelson moved to California with his parents at about age twelve and joined the First Presbyterian Church, Hollywood. He married Margaret Greig on September 17, 1938. Nelson soon became a confidante of HENRIETTA MEARS and helped develop many of her visions. He directed Mt. Hermon (CA) Bible Conference, 1939–49. His ability as a pianist also enhanced his career. Soon he was directing Gospel Light Publishing Company (and its subsidiary GLINT), working at Forest Home Conference, and developing Sunday school conferences in several places. Nelson was bitten by a brown recluse spider about a year before he died. His health quickly deteriorated, and heart trouble soon took its toll.

John B. Bentley

Feb. 9, 1896
Hampton, Virginia

June 12, 1989
Hampton, Virginia

Director of Episcopal Church Missions, 1948–64. Bentley began his ministry in Alaska by pastoring at Anvik, 1921–25. He married Elvira Carr on May 28, 1921. He was ordained deacon (1922) and priest (1929) in the Episcopal Church. He was suffragan bishop of Alaska (1931–42), and bishop of Alaska (1942–48), where he traveled great distances on dogsled. He served in WWI, his highest rank being captain.

Walter R. Martin

Sept. 10, 1928
New York, New York

June 26, 1989
San Capistrano, California

Founder and first director of Christian Research Institute, 1965–89. Martin was ordained as a Baptist in 1951 and was considered the foremost cult authority in the world. He worked for Zondervan Publishing, 1955–65, before starting his Christian Research Institute. The institute began in Wayne, NJ, then moved to Irvine, and San Capistrano, California. He wrote many books and articles for major magazines. He died of a heart attack. His major work was *The Kingdom of the Cults* (1965).

Harold B. Pretlove

June 24, 1903
Brooklyn, New York

July 17, 1989
Greenville, South Carolina

President of American Board of Missions to the Jews (Chosen People Ministries in 1988), **1954–71.** Pretlove was the opposite of his predecessor, JOSEPH COHN. He was a Gentile and had no formal training in the Scriptures, yet God used him to successfully fill the need. Pretlove married Mary Dezendorf on June 24, 1925 (died: 1954) and Leona McCoy on July 3, 1956. Pretlove was an executive with Dugan Brothers Bakery which was operated by a Christian family, 1926–54. He was active in New York Bible Society (1946–50) and president (1950–54). He was ordained as an independent Baptist.

Homer C. Hoeksema

Jan. 30, 1923
Grand Rapids, Michigan

July 17, 1989
Grand Rapids, Michigan

First president of the Theological School of Protestant Reformed Church, Grandville, MI 1964–88. Homer was the son of cofounder Herman Hoeksema, who along with HENRY DANHOF and George Ophoff, founded the PRC in 1924. This was a split from the Christian Reformed Church over the issue of "common grace." He pastored the Protestant Reformed Church of Boone, IA (1949–55), then the same in South Holland, IL (1955–59). Hoeksema married Gertrude Jonker. He was professor of the school when it started in the basement of the First Protestant Reformed Church in Grand Rapids, until it moved to a newer complex in Grandville, MI, in 1959. He worked in Tasmania the last year of his life, and died of cancer.

Florent D. Toirac

May 14, 1913
Palmarejo, Cuba

July 27, 1989
Ft. Wayne, Indiana

Director of Spanish World Gospel Mission, Winona Lake, IN, 1959–89. Toirac was one of 12 children witnessed to and won by a missionary in Cuba. In 1938, he began his service as a missionary himself to Haiti. Toirac married Dorothy Lee on December 27, 1942. He went to the States in 1950 and then served in France, 1953–57. In 1958, on his way to Spain, he became burdened for radio evangelism to the Spanish-speaking world. In 30 years, Toirac's radio work grew to 175 stations in 21 countries.

Elver C. Thomas

Dec. 13, 1920
near Lake City, Florida

Sept. 22, 1989
Cleveland, Tennessee

Chairman of Pentecostal Fellowship of North America, 1984–86, and general overseer of Church of God, Cleveland, TN 1982–86. Thomas pastored in Otis, FL (1940–41); North Carolina (1942–47); and Charlotte, NC (1952–54). From 1947–52, he was denominational Sunday School and Youth Director of North Carolina. He founded or established the following: North Carolina Bible School (East Coast Bible College), Pathway Book Stores, Pathway Mutual Insurance Company and Pathway Press. He married Alice Douglas. At the time of his death, he was chairman of the Church of God Home for Children Benevolence Board in Sevierville, TN. His funeral was at the North Cleveland Church of God.

Raymond J. Davis

Nov. 22, 1910
Grand Rapids, Michigan

Oct. 2, 1989
Sebring, Florida

Director of Sudan Interior Missions, 1962–75, and president of IFMA, 1967–70. Converted at age 14 at Berean Baptist Church in Grand Rapids under Pastor Howard Keithly's preaching on John 6:37, Davis went as a missionary to Ethiopia (1934–37) and Nigeria (1938–59). Davis married Evelyn Carr on February 1, 1939. He later served as field director for all East Africa, 1954–89, directing the work of over 1,300 missionaries. Davis wrote the book *Swords in the Desert*.

Carl J. Lawrenz

March 30, 1908
Lomira, Wisconsin

Oct. 14, 1989
Lomira, Wisconsin

President of Wisconsin Lutheran Seminary, Mequon, WI, 1957–78. Lawrenz married Irene Zabel in 1939. He first served at the St. Paul's Church of North Fond du Lac, WI (1932–44); then he was a professor of OT and education at WLS (1944–82). He played an important role in the training of over 1,200 preachers. Lawrenz retired in Lomira, WI, and died after a lingering cancer affliction.

Victor A. Ballantyne

March 31, 1916
Dallas, Texas

Oct. 16, 1989
Salem, Washington

First general superintendent of Evangelical Church of North America, Minneapolis, MN, 1971–82. Upon graduation from Western Evangelical Seminary, Ballantyne served his first church at Unionvale and Hopewell, OH, from 1937–41. He married Alta K. Warren on July 22, 1941. He then pastored in Monmouth, OR (1941–43); Willamette Blvd., Portland, OR (1943–50); and in Yakima, WA (1950–55). Other ministries followed at First Church in Seattle (1955–58) and the same in Eugene (1958–61). He was Conference Superintendent (1961–70) while residing in Milwaukie, OR. He moved to the headquarters in Minneapolis, MN, in 1971, when appointed general superintendent. Ballantyne was chairman of the board of World Gospel Mission, 1976–88. He was an accompanist for the Gospel Gleemen for more than 30 years.

Frank J. Lindquist

Nov. 26, 1899
McKeesport, Pennsylvania

Oct. 24, 1989
Minneapolis, Minnesota

Founder and first president of North Central Bible College (University in 2000), **Minneapolis, MN, 1932–61**. He began with 26 students and at the time of his death there were 1,174. He was ordained in the Assemblies of God in November, 1920. Lindquist pastored in Brainerd, MN (1921–22); Minot, ND, in 1923; and Minneapolis Gospel Tabernacle (1924–67). Lindquist married Irene Gunhus on February 22, 1928. He traveled extensively in Europe, the Middle East, and the Holy Land. Lindquist's first book was *Truth about the Trinity*.

Sloan S. Hodges

May 15, 1913
near Hodges, South Carolina

Oct. 30, 1989
Upper Marlboro, Maryland

Executive secretary of Progressive National Baptist Convention, 1970–79. Hodges married Martha Treece on June 24, 1943. Hodges pastored at FBC, Toronto, Ontario (1944–46); Thankful Baptist, Johnson City, TN (1946–50); Pilgrim Baptist, Hamilton, OH (1950–65); and Sardis Baptist, Cleveland, OH (1965–70). He traveled throughout the country and in many overseas ventures. He also served as an interim pastor, 1980–84 in Columbus, OH, and Fredericksburg, VA.

Gene E. Bartlett

April 18, 1910
Elkins, West Virginia

Nov. 3, 1989
Rochester, New York

President of Colgate-Rochester (NY) Divinity School, 1960–70. Bartlett was ordained a Baptist in 1934 and married Jean Kenyon on June 30, 1937. He pastored in Syracuse, NY (1937–42); Columbia, MO (1942–47); Evanston, IL (1947–53); at FBC, Los Angeles, CA (1953–60); and at FBC, Newton Centre, MA (1970–80). Bartlett was a member of University Christian Mission of the NCC from 1942–52, and a missionary preacher to Korea and Japan in 1954. He died of a heart attack.

Lloys Cooke Rice

Dec. 20, 1894
Hood City, Texas

Nov. 10, 1989
Murfreesboro, Tennessee

Wife of famed evangelist, JOHN R. RICE, and mother of six wonderful daughters. Lloys and JOHN RICE were married on Sept. 27, 1932. From 1932–40, she lived in Dallas, TX, where her husband pastored and started the *Sword of the Lord*. She managed the Sword bookstore and sold advertising. In her senior days, she traveled to women's conferences, sharing her mature wisdom. Mrs. Rice was a member of Franklin Road Baptist Church, Murfreesboro, TN. She had six daughters and 32 great grandchildren. On Nov. 5, she was hospitalized with a heart condition and died there a few days later.

Robert C. VanKampen

July 5, 1910
Chicago, Illinois

Nov. 20, 1989

Outstanding businessman who was converted at age 17. That same year, 1927, VanKampen began working for Hitchcock Publishing Company, and by the age of 29 was president and general manager. VanKampen Press became a subsidiary of Hitchcock Press, which assisted small publishers. VanKampen married Dorothy Ruisch on September 15, 1933. He was the board chairman at Western Springs Baptist Church in Illinois, that invited Billy Graham to be pastor in 1943. He was NAE's "layman of the year" in 1966. He made his home in Wheaton, IL, and Boca Raton, FL.

Del Fehsenfeld Jr.

May 17, 1947
McComb, Mississippi

Nov. 21, 1989
Niles, Michigan

Founder and first director of Life Action Ministries (an organization of "God and Country" musical teams that promote revival efforts in churches across the country), **Buchanan, MI, 1971–89**. Five young people and two married couples seeking revival helped him. It grew to a staff of over 100, sending gospel teams across the country.

Richard S. Beal

Dec. 10, 1887
Denver, Colorado

Nov. 25, 1989

Pastored FBC of Tucson, AZ, for 50 years, 1918–69. He was converted at his mother's knee around age eight. Beal married Mona Lelia Ballfinch on March 20, 1914 (died: c 1973). He pastored three churches in Missouri (1909–14), then pastored in Victor, CO (1914–18). Beal's Tucson church grew from 200 to over 3,000 and started 12 other churches. He was a leader in the formation of the Conservative Baptist Association. He also wrote ten volumes of sermons, *Rivers in the Desert* (1943). Beal preached his last sermon at age 95 and lived to be almost 102 years old.

Walter Hoving

Dec. 2, 1897
Stockholm, Sweden

Nov. 27, 1989
Newport, Rhode Island

Chairman of Tiffany's, an elegant jewelry store on Fifth Avenue, New York City 1955–80. Hoving produced the "Try God" pin and other Christian jewelry, the proceeds going to the Walter Hoving House for drug-addicted girls in Garrison, NY. He started his business career with the Macy Company in 1924. Hoving married Mary Field (November 4, 1924), Pauline Rogers (April 30, 1937) and Jane Langley (September 30, 1977). He was an Episcopalian.

James O. Patterson

July 21, 1912
Derma, Mississippi

Dec. 29, 1989
Memphis, Tennessee

Bishop of Church of God in Christ, Memphis, TN, 1967–89. Patterson succeeded the founder, C. H. MASON, after a seven-year crisis period in the movement. Under his leadership, the movement surpassed all other Pentecostal churches. Patterson married Deborah Mason, the founder's daughter on July 4, 1934 (died: June, 1985). The 1982 membership of 3,709,661 had grown ten times larger than at Bishop Mason's death. Patterson pastored the Pentecostal Temple, Memphis, TN, for many years. He married Mary Peat in April, 1989, eight months before he died. James was the father of GILBERT PATTERSON.

Clarence J. Pike

Dec. 3, 1900
Atlanta, Georgia

1990
Wilmore, Kentucky

President of Cascade College, Portland, OR, 1933–56, merged into Seattle (WA) Pacific College in 1967. Pike married Vivian E. Miller on October 1, 1925 (died: February, 1950) and Mildred M. Shafer, June 27, 1951. Ordained as a Methodist in 1923, he pastored in Springfield, OR, 1928–31 and became a faculty member of Cascade in 1931.

Tahib Simatupang

Jan. 20, 1920
Sidikalang, Sumatra, Indonesia

Jan. 1, 1990

President of the World Council of Churches, 1975–83. After Indonesia's proclamation of independence in 1945, Simatupang was involved in organizing the war to defend his country and later, in the peace negotiations with the Netherlands. He was chief of staff of the armed forces. He became president of the Christian Conference of Asia, 1973–84. He authored numerous books and articles on political, military, and ecumenical concerns in Indonesia.

Stuart G. Norris

July 16, 1901
Royalton, Ohio

Jan. 4, 1990
St. Paul, Minnesota

First president of Apostolic Bible Institute, St. Paul, MN, 1937–89. Norris was married in 1923 to Jessie Dunn, after both had become Pentecostal. He worked with the National Cash Register Company, and began to preach in Columbus, OH. Moving to New York City, to find work during the Great Depression, he founded a church. After two years, he went to St. Paul, MN, where he resurrected the Midway Tabernacle. There, he started the school which he would lead for 52 years. Connected with the United Pentecostal Church, Hazelwood, MO, the ABI has 4,000 alumni all over the world sharing the gospel. He died of congestive heart failure.

Robert G. Rayburn

Jan. 14, 1915
Newton, Kansas

Jan. 5, 1990
St. Louis, Missouri

First president of Covenant College, 1955–65, and Covenant Theological Seminary, St. Louis, MO 1955–76. The college moved to Lookout Mountain, GA, following his death. Rayburn married LaVerne Swanson on January 27, 1944. He was a soldier in WWII from 1944–47. After the war, he pastored the College Church, Wheaton, IL from 1947–50. He was a chaplain in the Korean War. From 1951–55, Rayburn also served as president of Highland College, Pasadena, CA. He was a member of the Reformed Presbyterian Church and pastored in Bellevue, NE; Gainesville, TX, and Hazelwood, MO.

Gordon Fraser

Jan. 12, 1990

First president of Indian Bible School, Flagstaff, AZ, 1958–70. Fraser was the founder of Southwestern School of Missions. He and his wife Thelma became active in rural Sunday school work in Washington and developed a growing interest in spiritual needs for tribes in the area. They learned of Dr. HARRY IRONSIDE's prayer for a Bible School for Indian people. In 1959, they moved to Flagstaff, AZ, and began teaching four Indian men around the kitchen table. The next year they purchased the first building for the beginning of the Indian Bible School.

Samuel Young

Sept. 8, 1901
Glasgow, Scotland

Jan. 25, 1990
Shawnee Mission, Overland Park, Kansas

General superintendent of Church of the Nazarene, 1948–72. Young came to the U.S. in 1916 and settled in Cleveland, OH. His first positions in the church were pastorates in Ohio, Maine, and Massachusetts, 1931–34. He was superintendent of the New England District of the church, 1934–40. Then came the association with Eastern Nazarene College, Quincy, MS, as college pastor (1940–45) and president of the same (1945–48). He came to the Kansas City area in 1954. Young visited several mission fields in the North and South American areas. His wife's name was Arlene.

Gray M. Blandy

Jan. 10, 1922
Newton, Massachusetts

Feb. 10, 1990
Clearwater, Florida

First president of Episcopal Seminary of the Southwest, Austin, TX, 1951–66. Blandy married Anne Dudley on July 15, 1939. He held various staff and educational positions in Cambridge, MA (1937–40); Troy, NY (1940–44); Houston, TX (1944–46), and Pasadena, TX (1946–47). Blandy also directed Episcopal College work at the University of Texas, 1947–52.

James I. McCord

Nov. 24, 1919
Rusk, Texas

Feb. 19, 1990
Princeton, New Jersey

President of Princeton (NJ) Theological Seminary, 1959–83, and of American Association of Theological Schools, 1978–80. Early in his ministry, McCord pastored Presbyterian churches in Manchester, NH, and Austin, TX. He married Hazel Thompson on August 29, 1939. He was a dean and professor of theology at Austin (TX) Presbyterian Theological Seminary, 1941–59. After 1983, he served as president of the United Board for Higher Christian Education in Asia and was founder and chancellor of Center for Theological Inquiry of Princeton, 1983–89. McCord received 22 honorary degrees from seven countries. He died of Parkinson's disease.

James A. Cross

Dec. 12, 1911
Crawfordsville, Florida

March 10, 1990
Lake City, Florida

General overseer of Church of God, Cleveland, TN, 1958–63; president of Lee College, Cleveland, TN 1966–70; and chairman of Pentecostal Fellowship of North America, 1961–63. Cross married Nellie McClure on Sept. 24, 1934, and pastored in Sanford, FL (1934–35); Semmions, SD in 1936; Lake Worth, FL (1938–40); Manatee, FL (1940–1943); Tampa, FL (1943–44); and Chattanooga, TN (1945–50). He was overseer in Nebraska (1937–38), Pennsylvania (1951–52), South Carolina (1953–54) and assistant overseer of the denomination (1954–58). He authored *Glorious Gospel* (1956) and *Healing in the Church* (1962).

David C. Cook III

June 11, 1912
Elgin, Illinois

April 6, 1990
Elgin, Illinois

President of David C. Cook Publishing Company, Elgin, IL (Cook Communications, Colorado Springs, CO), **1934–84**. Cook grew up in Mesa, Arizona. In March, 1932, his father died suddenly of pneumonia. He stepped into his father's place in the family business at age 22. The company became a leader in Sunday School materials for years, publishing all kinds of studies and helps. He married Anna Lawrence on October 3, 1937 and Nancy Nagle on Nov. 11, 1983. In 1944, he founded the David C. Cook Foundation, which led into a missions outreach. Cook was a Methodist. He was a major factor in the growth of his company, continuing the heritage of grandfather and father. He wrote *Walk in High Places* (1964).

Ralph D. Abernathy

March 11, 1926
Linden, Alabama

April 17, 1990
Atlanta, Georgia

American Baptist minister and civil rights activist who succeeded MARTIN LUTHER KING as leader of the Southern Christian Leadership Council, 1968–77, which they cofounded in 1957. Abernathy married Juanita Jones on August 31, 1952. He pastored at FBC, Montgomery, AL (1951–61), and at West Hunter Street Baptist, Atlanta, GA (1961–83). Abernathy's autobiography, *And the Walls Came Tumbling Down* (1989), was censured by the Civil Rights Movement for his attacks on M.L. KING, (whose body he held as KING died from an assassin's bullet).

Rhett C. Mullinax

Oct. 27, 1901
Central, South Carolina

April 23, 1990
Elon College, North Carolina

President of Central (SC) Wesleyan (Southern Wesleyan in 1994) **College, 1948–68**. Mullinax was active in Wesleyan Methodist circles and married his wife, Helen, on December 24, 1929; they had five children. He taught at William & Mary College, Central, SC (1925–28); pastored Carlisle Church in Spartanburg, SC (1929–43); and was president of the South Carolina Conference (1943–48). Mullinax served as a high school principal and as a registrar and dean of theology at CWC.

John G. Mitchell

April 7, 1900
South Shields, England

May 17, 1990
Portland, Oregon

Passion of an evangelist, heart of a pastor, the simplicity of a teacher. Mitchell was converted in Calgary, Alberta, in 1916, while he was working as a toolmaker. Mitchell pastored the Central Bible Church in Portland, OR, for 37 years, and taught at Multnomah School of the Bible for 20 years, which he founded in 1936. He was a Bible teacher on the *Know Your Bible Hour* for four decades. His wife's name was Mary.

Millard J. Berquist

Jan. 29, 1902
Kansas City, Kansas

May 22, 1990
Overland Park, Kansas

First president of Midwestern Baptist Theological Seminary, Kansas City, MO 1957–73. Berquist was the first president of the SBC seminary. Previously, he had pastored Riverside Baptist, Jacksonville, FL, and FBC, Tampa, FL, for 15 years. During his seminary tenure, 1,500 students from 40 states and 16 countries would attend. Upon his retirement, he served interim pastorates in Missouri and Florida. He also taught at Carson-Newman College, Jefferson City, TN, for a time. His wife's name was Gladys. Berquist died after a five-month bout with cancer.

Franklin O. Nelson

Nov. 30, 1909
Minneapolis, Minnesota

June 19, 1990
Minneapolis, Minnesota

Director of Baptist General Conference Global Missions, 1959–75. Nelson was converted at age ten at Bethlehem Baptist Church. He married Phileda Ogren on June 7, 1939. He pastored Minnehaha Baptist (1935–39), and Edgewater Baptist (1954–58), both in Minneapolis, MN. Nelson served in Burma, (1939–42 and 1945–51) and in Addis Abab, Ethiopia (1975–76). He was deputation chairman for BGCM, 1942–45 and 1951–54. He began having small strokes in 1986.

Byron L. Osborne

March 27, 1894
Greensboro, North Carolina

June 20, 1990
North Canton, Ohio

President of Cleveland (OH) Bible College, 1951–57, renamed and relocated Malone College, Canton, OH 1951–60. Osborne taught there for 40 years, 1920–60. He was the reading clerk of the Ohio Yearly Meeting, 1921–51. Osborne edited the *Evangelical Friend*, 1935–47. He also served as superintendent of Cleveland Quarterly Meeting those same years. Osborne wrote *Homer Cox: The Man and His Message*.

James S. Stewart

July 21, 1896
Dundee, Scotland

July 1, 1990

Scholar, professor, author, preacher, with far-reaching impact. Stewart pastored in Scotland at Auchterarder (1924–28); Beechgrove Church in Aberdeen (1928–35); and North Morningside Church of Edinburgh (1935–47). In 1931, he married Rosamund Anne Barron (died: 1986) and they had two sons. From 1947–66, he was professor of NT language, literature, and theology at New College at the University of Edinburgh, Scotland. In 1952, he was appointed as a chaplain to the queen. In 1963, he was moderator of the General Assembly of the Church of Scotland. He encouraged the Billy Graham crusades in Scotland when numbers of his Church of Scotland colleagues did not.

Fred Garland

June 2, 1906
Roanoke, Virginia

July 6, 1990
West Palm Beach, Florida

Beloved, old-time evangelist who preached and promoted revival for half a century. Living the wild, teen life, Garland headed to Washington, D.C., then New York City. He became involved in heroin, shoplifting, and was finally imprisoned. By the time he was paroled on September 29, 1936, his left lung had developed tuberculosis. With inevitable surgery, a promise of five years to live, and $16 in his pocket, he found a friend in CHARLES STEVENS and became his associate. Garland was finally soundly converted, after which he traveled far and wide, 1940 on. His first wife was Carolyn Gergen. Later he married Elizabeth Boone on March 18, 1949. Garland was active with the Int. Board for Jewish Evangelism in later years. He also encouraged many young evangelists.

Donald A. McGavran

Dec. 15, 1897
Damoh, India

July 10, 1990
Altadena, California

Church growth leader and renowned head of the School of Missions at Fuller Theological Seminary, 1965–80. He was saved at age 14 and baptized in the First Christian Church, Tulsa, OK. He married Mary E. Howard (March 12, 1898–April 5, 1990) on August 29, 1922. Mc-

Gavran served as a missionary in India, 1923–56, under the United Christian Missionary Society (Christian Church-Disciples of Christ). In 1954, as he traveled across Africa, he saw the challenge of rapid church growth, and it became his conviction that "It is God's will that His Church grow, that His lost children be found." He wrote his conclusions in his book, *The Bridges of God* (1955). He became professor of Missions in Indianapolis, IN (1956–60); was director of Institute of Church Growth at Northwest Christian College, Eugene, OR (1961–65); then was dean at Fuller Theological Seminary (1965–71); beoming senior professor 1971–78. He wrote many books on church growth and was considered an authority on that subject. His wife's name was Mary. His favorite Bible verse was Acts 5:14. He died of cancer.

Donald R. Heiges

June 25, 1910
Biglerville, Pennsylvania

Aug. 10, 1990
Gettysburg, Pennsylvania

President of Lutheran Theological Seminary at Gettysburg (PA), 1962–76, and Philadelphia, 1964–70. Heiges married Mary Kump on June 1, 1935. Ordained in 1935, he was a member of the faculty and chaplain at Gettysburg, PA, College, 1934–44. In 1944, Heiges was called into work for the United Lutheran Church and served as student pastor and counselor at Columbia University, New York City, 1945–50. From 1950–58, he was the executive secretary of college/university work for the National Council. He also served as dean of Chicago Lutheran Seminary, 1958–62. He wrote *The Christian Calling* (1958).

William B. Berntsen

Oct. 6, 1915
Chicago, Illinois

Aug. 16, 1990
St. Paul, Minnesota

President of Northwestern Schools, Minneapolis, MN, 1965–67, and Roseville, MN, 1972–84. The school was closed, 1967–72. In 1970, it moved from a four-acre plot to 100 acres. Two hundred freshmen enrolled in 1972, and at the time of his death, the school had 1,000 students. He married Beryl Catshall on October 5, 1942. Berntsen was the music and Christian education director in a number of churches: at Burton Ave. Baptist, Waterloo, IA, from 1938–42; at Scofield Memorial Baptist, Dallas, TX; at Jefferson Park Bible, Chicago, IL; and at FBC, Denton, TX. W. B. RILEY invited him to Northwestern in 1946. He was chairman of the music department until 1965. He died of amyloidosis (conversion of starch into sugar).

Joseph H. Jackson

Sept. 11, 1900
Jenestown, Mississippi

Aug. 18, 1990
Chicago, Illinois

President of National Baptist Convention in the USA, 1953–82. He was ordained a Baptist (1922), and married Maude Alexander (1926). He pastored at Bethel Church, Omaha, NE (1926–30) and at Monumental Church, Philadelphia, PA (1934–41). He was the executive secretary for the mission board, 1934–41. Jackson pastored Mt. Olivet Baptist Church, Chicago, IL from 1942–90. Despite several challenges and defections (Gardner Taylor, M.L KING and followers), Jackson's denomination grew from 4.5 million to 8 million under his leadership.

A. Ray Cartlidge

Sept. 26, 1906
Cincinnati, Ohio

Sept. 7, 1990
Frankfort, Michigan

President of Lane Theological Seminary (affiliated with McCormick Theological Seminary, Chicago, in 1931), **1979–90**. Cartlidge married Mary Ann Caldwell in 1928. He pastored in Presbyterian churches in Ohio, Illinois, and Pennsylvania, 1933–71. He served at FPC in Champaign, IL (1939–54); and at the Church of the

Covenant in Erie, PA (1954–71). Cartlidge also worked as an interim pastor for four churches, 1971–80. He spent his winters in Fort Myers, FL, and the summers in Frankfort, MI.

Frederick F. Bruce

Oct. 12, 1910
Elgin, Scotland

Sept. 11, 1990
Buxton, England

Great evangelical scholar of his time. Bruce's books and Bible commentaries were well received. He married his wife, Betty, in 1936. He taught Greek and New Testament at the University of Edinburgh (1935–38), Leeds (1938–47), biblical history and literature at Sheffield (1947–59), and biblical criticism and exegesis at Manchester (1959–78). Bruce was also the editor of *Evangelical Quarterly* (1949–80). He was a popular speaker, especially in Plymouth Brethren circles. His writings ranged from *The New Testament* (1943) to *Colossians*, *Philemon*, and *Ephesians* (1984). He wrote *Second Thoughts on the Dead Sea Scrolls* (1956). Bruce died of cancer.

J. Sutherland Logan

July 18, 1913
Clydebank, Scotland

Sept. 14, 1990
Philadelphia, Pennsylvania

President of Chicago (IL) Evangelistic College, 1958–59, relocated and renamed Vennard College, University Park, IA 1959–68. Logan began preaching as a boy of 13. His early ministry was with the Salvation Army and London City Mission. For 20 years he ministered in England, including being chaplain for six years to the household of King GEORGE VI and Queen Elizabeth, as well as to the street gangs of London. He came to America in 1949 and engaged in a preaching tour to every state. He served with the Church of the Nazarene and the Evangelical Methodist Church. He moved to Brandon, FL, in 1972 as pastor and teacher of a ministry to drug addicts. In 1980, he moved to Vineland, NJ, and joined the Wesleyan Church a year later.

W. Jack Hudson

March 3, 1922
Greenville, South Carolina

Oct. 5, 1990
Charlotte, North Carolina

Longtime pastor of Northside Baptist Church, Charlotte, NC 1955–90. This church had a large Christian day school, a radio ministry, and beautiful facilities. Hudson also served as moderator of the Southwide Baptist Fellowship, 1963–64 and 1971–72, hosting it seven times.

Fred D. Jarvis

Jan. 27, 1914
Cleaton, Kentucky

Oct. 16, 1990
San Juan, Texas

Founder and first president of New Life League, Phoenix, AZ 1954–83. Jarvis was an outstanding missionary to the Orient, poignant writer (*The Crime of the Century*) and efficient communicator for the forgotten peoples of the world. On September 15, 1930, Jarvis (age 16), attended a street meeting in Chicago led by TORREY JOHNSON and was converted. He married Clara Musil on June 5, 1937. He pastored First Baptist Church, Buda, IL (1936–38), and headed other ministries concluding with evangelism endeavors (1943–46). In 1946, he went to China with TEAM. Expelled in 1949, he went to Japan. He started Missionary Equipment Service and NLL ("Serving Those who Serve"). Tents, sound trucks, visual aides, and literature were made available to missionaries and native pastors. He also had a broadcast on 67 stations to seven countries.

Ariel C. Ainsworth

Sept. 19, 1903
Norwalk, Connecticut

Nov. 4, 1990
Lenoir, North Carolina

President of Berkshire Christian College, Lenox, MA, 1957–68. He served as a part-time pastor in Waterbury, CT, and as a part-time teacher until 1951, after which he taught full-time. During Ainsworth's tenure in 1958, the school's name was changed from New England School of Theology and a new 60-acre campus was obtained in Brookline, MA. Ainsworth also served a pastorate at the Advent Christian Church in Daluda, SC in the later years of his ministry.

Carl K. Becker

Jan. 31, 1894
Manheim, Pennsylvania

Nov. 7, 1990
Myerstown, Pennsylvania

His 1,100-acre leprosy village in Oicha, Belgian Congo (Zaire), was one of the wonders of 20th century missions. Becker was converted as a result of a catechism class in a German Reformed Church. He began practicing medicine in Boyertown, PA, and also married his wife, Marie Bodey, on September 26, 1922. Receiving an urgent call from the Africa Inland Mission, Becker sailed for Africa in 1928, leaving a $10,000+ year job for an income of $720 annually and going to a primitive outpost he knew nothing about. He first located at Katwa, calling their home a "mud mansion." Then they briefly were at Aba, and in 1934 went to Oicha in the dense Ituri forest to work among the Pygmies and other forest tribes—a most unlikely place for a mission hospital. Within two years, he was treating 200 patients every day. Weekends were devoted to evangelism endeavors. Lepers became his burden and by the early 1950s he was treating 4,000 resident patients at his 1,100-acre "village." He was performing 3,000 operations and delivering 500 babies annually. In 1964, a rebellion by Simba guerrillas almost took his life, so he fled at age 70. He later returned, rebuilt the work, and finally returned to the U.S. at age 83 in 1977. He was considered as important a medical missionary as ALBERT SCHWEITZER, and considerably more evangelical. He was associated with the Evangelical Congregational Church.

Malcolm Muggeridge

May 24, 1903
Sanderstead, England

Nov. 14, 1990

Editor, writer, journalist, and social critic. Muggeridge married Katherine Dobbs in September, 1927. A foreign correspondent for the *Manchester Guardian* in the 1930s, Muggeridge became a military spy in Africa during World War II, an avocation he spoke disparagingly of. He became a popular television personality in the 1950s and '60s. Muggeridge's outspoken and opinionated views on just about everything both bemused and dismayed his media audience, leading to a ban on his BBC broadcasts after a perceived slight to the royal family. A onetime Socialist and agnostic, he became a born-again Christian in his old age, writing several books on religion including *Jesus Rediscovered* (1969). His writings ranged from *Three Flats* (1931) to *Conversion: A Spiritual Journey* (1988).

Eugene Jordan

Aug. 31, 1920
Birmingham, Alabama

Dec. 5, 1990
St. Paul, Minnesota

Talented and productive missionary. Jordan was witnessed to and converted while traveling with a dance band during college days. He was undoubtedly one of the greatest marimba players ever. People sat spellbound at his performances. Jordan married Ruth Stam on December 11, 1927, and served on the staff of MBI for several years before going to HCJB in Quito, Ecuador, in 1951 for a lifetime of missionary service. He went on a team with Don DeVos and Spencer DeYoung to the

Netherlands in the late 1940s. Jordan was a member of Ruhama Baptist Church, Birmingham, AL. He died of a brain tumor.

Harry V. Richardson

June 27, 1901
Jacksonville, Florida

Dec. 13, 1990
Atlanta, Georgia

Dean of Gammon Theological Seminary, 1948–59, and first president of Interdenominational Theological Seminary, Atlanta, GA 1959–68. Raised an Episcopalian, Richardson married Selma T. White in 1927. He graduated from Harvard University in 1932, pastoring an AME Chapel at Narragansett Pier, RI, during those days. From 1933–46, he was chaplain of Tuskegee Institute. He then supervised a staff of 27, directing the Program for Better Trained Rural Ministry until 1948. He was affectionately known as the "Quiet Crusader." After 1968, he was called back three times as interim president to keep the school (ITS) established.

Harry G. Saulnier

Aug. 19, 1902
New York, New York

Dec. 22, 1990
Lombard, Illinois

Director of Pacific Garden Mission, Chicago, IL 1940–86. "Hallelujah Harry" was one of the great mission men of all time. Saulnier married Gene Tucker on June 30, 1928. On March 1, 1940, he left his Commonwealth Edison Company job to work for the Pacific Garden Mission. Under Saulnier's leadership the Servicemen's Center began (1942), and the "Unshackled" radio program began (1950). Over 10,000 people made decisions for Christ annually at the mission.

James P. Dees

Dec. 30, 1915
Greenville, North Carolina

Dec. 25, 1990
Statesville, North Carolina

Director of Anglican Orthodox Church, 1963–90, including its missionary arm and founder and first president of Cranmer Seminary, Statesville, NC 1971–90. Dees founded this denomination on November 15, 1963, upon resigning from the Episcopal Church citing its emphasis on the Social Gospel. His was a movement to get the Anglican community back to the faith of their Reformers and to the 1928 *Book of Common Prayer*. Bob Jones University granted him an honorary degree in 1965. The movement spread across the country and into many foreign countries. Dees also pastored the Trinity Episcopal Church in Statesville. He was a genuine patriot and student of national and world affairs.

Wandaro Dabaro

c 1910
district of Humbo, Wolaitta, Ethiopia

1991

Evangelist of Ethiopia. This former Satan worshipper became a great evangelist in southern Ethiopia during a time of tremendous persecution. Dabaro's father was the witch doctor on Mount Humbo, among the Wolayto people. The first missionaries reached these people in 1928. Wandaro first heard the gospel (1930), was converted, and baptized (1933). The Italians seized Addis Ababa on May 5, 1936, and the emperor fled. The next year all missionaries were expelled, leaving only 48 believers in the country. The Italians were defeated in 1941 and the missionaries returned the following year to find 10,000 Christians and 100 churches—much of it a result of Dabaro's leadership. By 1943, the number had grown to 15,000. Wandaro had suffered much (torture, threats, etc.). The church again was persecuted under the Communist regime, 1974–91.

Thomas F. Zimmerman

March 26, 1912
Indianapolis, Indiana

Jan. 2, 1991
Springfield, Missouri

Perhaps the greatest leader of the Assemblies of God movement. His family had been Methodist, but joined a Pentecostal church in 1917 after his mother was healed of tuberculosis after being prayed over. Zimmerman married Elizabeth Price on June 17, 1933. He pastored in Harrisburg, IN (1934–35); South Bend, IN (1936–39); Granite City, IL (1939–43); Springfield, MO, (1943–47); and served as chairman of the National Religious Broadcasters (1954–56), which he helped found in 1944. He was the general superintendent of Assemblies of God (1959–85); president of the National Association of Evangelicals (1960–61); chairman of Pentecostal Fellowship of North America (1968–70); chairman of Pentecostal World Fellowship (1964–70 and 1973–89); and first president of Assemblies of God Theological Seminary (1972–85). He retired in 1985.

James L. Cleveland

Dec. 5, 1931
Chicago, Illinois

Feb. 9, 1991
Culver City, California

Gospel singer, composer, and Baptist minister. Cleveland taught nine-year-old Aretha Franklin to sing; years later, he produced her Grammy Award-winning album, *Amazing Grace*. He acted in the film, *Save the Children* (1951). Cleveland began a pastorate in Los Angeles in 1961 at New Greater Harvest Baptist and then Cornerstone Institutional Baptist. He was a singer with various groups, some of which he founded on his own. Cleveland recorded over a dozen "gold" albums and a total of 46 albums, won three Grammy Awards, and became the first gospel artist to receive a star on Hollywood's "Walk of Fame." Cleveland composed "Everything Will Be All Right" and "Peace, Be Still," among hundreds of gospel songs. In 1968, he founded the Gospel Music Workshop of America whose annual conventions attracted thousands of church musicians. He died of respiratory problems.

Herman N. Baker

April 8, 1911
Grand Rapids, Michigan

Feb. 10, 1991
Stewart, Florida

Founder and first president of Baker Book House, Grand Rapids, MI 1939–67. The Baker family traveled to the Netherlands early in his life but returned to America in 1925. Baker married Angeline Sterkenburg in 1931 and was active in the Christian Reformed Church. In 1939, he opened a bookstore in Grand Rapids, MI, with his collection of books. In 1940, he published the first book, *More Than Conquerors*, by William Henricksen. By 1959, BBH had published 147 titles, and in 1966 they moved their facilities to suburban Ada, MI. By 1969, they had published 747 titles. He died while on vacation.

Sante U. Barbieri

Aug. 2, 1902
Due Ville, Italy

Feb. 15, 1991

President of World Council of Churches, 1954–61, and a Methodist bishop. Barbieri married Odette Oliveria on October 4, 1924. He was converted in Fundo, Brazil, at age 21, and ordained a Methodist in 1925. Barbieri taught (1925–34), and was president of Methodist Seminary in Porto Alegre, Brazil (1934–39). He served as a professor and sat on the board of directors of Union Theological Seminary of Buenos Aires, 1940–49, pastoring until 1947. Barbieri became a naturalized citizen of Argentina in 1956. He was known as an author, traveler, and an ecumenist.

John P. "Jack" Odell

June 17, 1915
Chicago, Illinois

Feb. 15, 1991
Reedsburg, Wisonsin

Familiar radio voice for nearly 40 years of the Pacific Garden Mission's *Unshackled* radio program, touching many lives. Odell was an announcer for WCFL in Chicago, IL, as well as a cab driver. Odell was converted in his car, pulling off the road to pray. EUGENIA PRICE asked him to direct *Unshackled* in 1952. He announced, directed, and wrote for the program until 1990. He was a member of the Church of God.

Gareth B. Miller

April 12, 1928
Criglersville, Virginia

Feb. 16, 1991
Rivervale, New Jersey

Founder and president of Farms International, Inc., Knife River, MN, 1961–91. The Millers lived in New York City in later years attending the Bergen Baptist Church (SBC), Waldwick, NJ. He became an outspoken advocate for morality in public affairs. His vision for Farms did not stress charity, but cooperation; not acquisition, but stewardship. A rheumatic heart kept him from an agricultural mission in Burma, yet he became an international missionary through his world interests. He was a man of the soil and studied Scripture with a farmer's insight.

Carl H. Lundquist

Nov. 16, 1916
Elgin, Illinois

Feb. 27, 1991
St. Paul, Minnesota

President of Bethel College and Theological Seminary, St. Paul, MN 1954–82; of National Association of Evangelicals, 1978–79; and of Christian College Consortium, 1983–91. Lundquist attended Bethel, 1939–42, and after his graduation, married Nancy Zimmerman, Sept. 15, 1942, who gave him four children. Lundquist pastored Elim Baptist Church, Chicago, Il (1943–53). He also was chairman of Fellowship of Evangelical Seminary presidents in its early days. He died of cancer.

Robert A. Cook

June 7, 1912
Santa Clara, California

March 11, 1991
New York, New York

President of Youth for Christ, 1948–57; of National Association of Evangelicals, 1962–63; of King's College, Briarcliffe Manor, NY 1962–85; and chairman of National Religious Broadcasters, 1985–88. Cook was converted at age six at a CMA church in Cleveland, OH, under Pastor R. E. Nelson. Cook became one of his generation's greatest Christian leaders. He married Coreen Nilsen on September 24, 1935 (born: April 12, 1914), and pastored Midwest Bible Church in the early 1940s. Moving on to head four great organizations, Cook proved to be a great spiritual motivator, a tremendous preacher, and one of the most talented platform personalities of his time. He died of leukemia.

Walter Elmo McAlister

Dec. 13, 1897
Manitoba, Canada

March 17, 1991
Toronto, Ontario, Canada

General superintendent of Pentecostal Assemblies Canada, 1952–62; chairman of Pentecostal Fellowship of North America, 1959–61; and Pentecostal World Fellowship, 1958–61. McAlister never attended formal Bible college, but was a devout student of the Bible, and known as a "boy-preacher". He was ordained in 1919, and established churches: Parkside in Saskatchewan, Stone in Toronto, Broadway in Vancouver. He was a strong administrator and hosted the World Pentecostal Conference in Toronto in 1958. He was the father of JACK MCALISTER.

Duane A. Reahm

Sept. 15, 1917
Sunfield, Michigan

March 19, 1991
Huntington, Indiana

Bishop of the United Brethren in Christ, 1969–81, and director of its missions, 1961–69, 1973–81. Reahm married Leona Welker on July 6, 1940. He pastored in Kalamazoo, MI; Ft. Wayne, IN; Wilshire, OH; and Banner Street United Brethren, Grand Rapids, MI. He traveled around the world on behalf of missions several times. He was kind to this editor's mother who lived close to his church in Grand Rapids and attended often.

Chester G. Stanley

Sept. 15, 1900
Beloit, Ohio

March 26, 1991
Alliance, Ohio

General Superintendent of Ohio Yearly Meeting (Evangelical Friends Church, Eastern Region in 1971), **1960–68 and its missions program, 1951–56, 1958–60.** Stanley held pastorates in Deerfield, OH; Byhalia, OH; Hughesville, PA; Alliance, OH; Newport News, VA, and Highland Ave. Friends, Columbus, OH. He married Evangeline Mosher.

Percy Ray

May 21, 1910
Chalybeate, Mississippi

April 11, 1991
Myrtle, Mississippi

Evangelist, builder of 40 churches, Home Mission Board missionary of the Southern Baptist Convention, and pastor. Ray was converted at age 21 in Jackson, TN, while at Union University, through the prodding of a godly professor (I. N. Penick) and the prayers of Joe Odle. He pastored at Tiplersville (MI) Baptist Church beginning in 1930. On March 27, 1932, he made public profession of his faith in his church. One of his greatest accomplishments was the leading of Myrtle Baptist Church (1935 on), where he was the pastor for more than 50 years, and the building of Camp Zion. The purpose of the camp, which was started in 1948, was to "call America back to God." Ertus Pirkle, in his biography of Ray (*A Ray for God*), tells stories of amazing incidents of soul winning, preaching exploits, and the influence he had on so many people. Ray never married.

Hilding Halvarson

July 11, 1910
Preston, Washington

May 1, 1991
Hemet, California

Outstanding song leader, director of choirs, and soloist. Halvarson married Gertrude Wasell on June 4, 1932. Halvarson was a businessman in Seattle, WA, serving as president of the Bank and Office Company. He became involved as a lay worker in evangelistic endeavors, before going into full-time ministry in 1960. He was a song leader for Evangelist MERVE ROSELL and others. For 25 years, Halvarson ministered at Bibletown in Boca Raton, FL.

Eugene V. Stime

February 14, 1910

May 5, 1991

President of Lutheran Bible Institute of Seattle (Trinity Lutheran College), **1945–70.** He married Ruth Sletvold in 1938 (died: 1963) and Altrude Langhaug in 1965. He pastored in Prince Albert, Saskatchewan (1939–1940) before joining the faculty of LBI (1940–45). Later pastorates included First Lutheran of Richmond Beach, Seattle, WA (1970–1976); Bethel Lutheran, Seattle, WA (1976–87); and Central Lutheran, Everett, WA (1987–91).

Lennard Darbee

April 14, 1911
Mountain Home, Idaho

May 7, 1991
Seattle, Washington

Baptist turned Pentecostal evangelist. Darbee was converted at FBC in Tacoma, WA, at age 19, and attended Baylor University, Waco, TX, from 1932–35. He also pastored two churches in Tacoma, WA: Gatewood (1935–43), and Galilee (1943–46), before going into evangelism in 1946. He married his first wife, Nancy, in 1935 (died: 1967) and then Ruth in 1970. Darbee was influenced by the theology of William Freeman in Chicago in 1950. In 1964, Darbee started his "Rays of Faith" broadcast. His funeral was held at Bethel Temple in Seattle, WA.

Charles W. Anderson

Oct. 31, 1912
Camden, New Jersey

Charles William Anderson

May 15, 1991
Boca Raton, Florida

Founder and first president of Northeastern Collegiate Bible Institute, Essex Falls, NJ, 1950–80, which ceased to exist about a year before his death. Anderson was converted in high school by the witness of a friend who took him to church where he heard the gospel. For two years he was a Baptist pastor at National Park, NY. He pastored at Wissinoming Baptist Church in Philadelphia, PA, for five years, and at Brookdale Baptist in Bloomfield, NJ, from 1939–91. By 1955, Sunday school enrollment had gone from 174 to 1,300, and missions giving increased from $1,500 to $70,000 annually. He was with PTL in Japan (1950), in Africa (1955), and also served CBFMS.

Everett Smith

Sept. 11, 1892
Seattle, Washington

May 18, 1991
Santa Barbara, California

President of American Bible Society, 1962–67. In 1937, Smith became fiscal agent for the twelve district Federal Home Loan Banks. These banks were created by Congress in 1932, largely savings and loan associations. He sold more than 14 billion dollars of the obligations of the banks, the proceeds of which were advanced to the 4,850 member institutions primarily for the purpose of making loans to finance homes. In 1943 he was treasurer of the Retirement Fund of the Federal Home Loan Bank System. In 1961 he became a partner in the New York City firm of Chase Quincey and Company, dealers in US Government securities. He attended Hitchock Presbyterian Church in Scarsdale, NY. During his presidency of ABS, the annual Scripture circulation worldwide more than doubled.

Paul S. Rees

Sept. 4, 1900
Providence, Rhode Island

May 20, 1991
Boca Raton, Florida

President of National Association of Evangelicals, 1952–53. Rees was ordained by the Mission (Evangelical) Covenant Church in 1921. He pastored Pilgrim Tabernacle in Pasadena, CA (1920–23), Holiness Tabernacle in Detroit, after which he pastored the 1,500-member First Covenant, Minneapolis, MN (1938–58). He married Edith Brown on June 3, 1926. Rees ministered to pastors in Graham crusades, 1954–59. He began associating with World Vision, 1958–75 as vice president, directing pastors' conferences, eventually in 38 nations. He wrote from *Seth Cook Rees* (1934) to *Don't Sleep through the Revolution* (1969). He edited *World Vision Magazine* (1964–72). He was an evangelical statesman of the first degree and the son of SETH REES. He died of heart failure.

James N. Jeffrey

Jan. 22, 1929
Lampasas, Texas

May 30, 1991
Kansas City, Missouri

President of Fellowship of Christian Athletes, Kansas City, MO 1964–72. His wife was Francis Jeffrey. He was an outstanding football player at Baylor University, Waco, TX, in the insurance business in Fort Worth, TX (1951–63), and in Kansas City, MO (1972–74). Jeffrey was a member and deacon of Leawood Baptist Church, having moved from Texas to Overland Park, KS in 1963. He directed development at Baptist Memorial Hospital (1979–83) and worked for the Red Cross (1983–87).

W. Stanley Mooneyham

Jan. 14, 1926
Houston, Mississippi

June 3, 1991
Los Angeles, California

President of World Vision, Monrovia, CA 1969–82; of Evangelical Press Association, 1964–65; and Executive Secretary of National Association of Free Will Baptist, 1953–59. Mooneyham was converted at age 20 in Shawnee, OK, in 1946 at a service where a college student spoke. Mooneyham married LaVerda Green (December 13, 1946) and Nancy Callaway (June 1, 1984). In his early years of ministry, Mooneyham pastored in Tecumseh, OK (1948–49, and in Sulphur, OK (1949–52). He was editor of *Action Magazine* (NAE) (1959–64). He worked with the Billy Graham Association, 1964–69, planning the 1966 World Congress on Evangelism in Berlin, Germany. Mooneyham became an international consultant, 1984–91. At the time of his death, he was the pastor of Community Presbyterian Church, Palm Desert, CA. He died of kidney failure. He wrote from *China, the Puzzle* (1972) to *Dancing on the Straight and Narrow* (1989).

Owen H. Alderfer

June 7, 1923
Upland, California

June 4, 1991
Mechanicsburg, Pennsylvania

General Secretary of Brethren in Christ Church, Grantham, PA, 1964–73. He married Ardis Winter on June 15, 1945. Upon his ordination in 1946, Alderfer's first major work was pastoring BIC Church in Springfield, OH from 1951–55. He then served as professor of religion, Upland (CA) College (1955–65); professor of Church History, Ashland (OH) Theological Seminary, 1965–80; and professor of religion, Messiah College, Granthan, PA (1980–84); and bishop of BIC Church, West Milton, OH (1984–90). Alderfer edited the *Ashland* (OH) *Theological Bulletin* (1969–79) and wrote *Called to Obedience* (1974). His home was in Mechanicsburg, PA.

John C. Winston

Oct. 9, 1896
Redlands, California

June 4, 1991
Moorestown, New Jersey

Codirector (with ODILLON VAN STEENBERGHE) of Belgian Gospel Mission, 1936–59, which merged into Greater Europe Mission in 1971. Winston married Grace Williams on August 15, 1920. At BIOLA, Winston met Ralph Norton and learned of the work in Belgium. He went to Belgium in 1922. Winston stayed through the German occupation until 1940 and shipped tons of clothes to Belgium, 1940–45. Winston also served as a CMA elder in his closing years.

Donald McKnight

Oct. 18, 1924
Street, Maryland

June 25, 1991
Abingdon, Maryland

President of American Council of Christian Churches, 1982–84, and its executive director, 1988–91. McKnight was converted in a Methodist revival but left the movement when liberalism took over. He pastored the Evangelical Methodist Church in Dublin, MD, and was the general superintendent of the Evangelical Methodist Church of America. He married Jane Thompson on July 31, 1949. McKnight passed away at a cottage prayer meeting in the home of an EMC member.

Smallwood Williams

Oct. 17, 1907
Lynchburg, Virginia

June 28, 1991
Washington, D.C.

Founder and first presiding bishop of Bible Way Churches of Our Lord Jesus Christ, 1957–91. Williams pastored the headquarters church, Washington, D.C., since 1927. Williams married Verna L. Rapley on May 16, 1927; they had four children. The movement is Pentecostal in nature with about 300 churches and 300,000 members. It is kin to Church of Our Lord Jesus Christ of the Apostolic Faith.

Marion G. Bradwell

March 5, 1911
Bainridge, Georgia

July 9, 1991
Quitman, Georgia

Executive director of Lord's Day Alliance, New York City, 1965–70, relocated Atlanta, GA 1970–75 and Presbyterian pastor. Bradwell married Kathryn Smoot on August 17, 1937. He pastored Central Presbyterian, Athens, GA (1940–42); Reynolda Presbyterian, Winston-Salem, NC (1942–49); First Presbyterian, Waycross, GA (1949–53); and First Presbyterian, a division of Covenant Presbyterian, Albany, GA (1953–65). During his leadership of LDA, the magazine was changed from *The Leader* to *Sunday* and the movement grew to include 14 denominations. During this time, Bradwell traveled to 47 states. The later years of his life found him serving as associate or interim pastor in several Georgia churches. He died of a heart attack.

Mingdao Wang

1900
Peking, China

July 28, 1991
Shanghai, China

Influential preacher in the Chinese Church. Wang grew up in a very poor family. His father committed suicide before he was born. He was converted at age 14. In 1918, he contracted a severe sickness, which forced him to give up political ambitions and dedicate his life to Christian ministry. At age 20, he took a job as a teacher 100 miles from home, where he made a definite decision for Christ as a result of a fellow teacher's witness. Wang preached his first sermon in 1921, the year the Chinese Communist Party was founded. He married Debra Liu in August, 1928. After she died, he later remarried. He then started his own church in a home in Peking and finally his Christian Tabernacle building was opened in August1, 1937 about the time the Japanese Army marched into the city. Surviving the Japanese threats, the Communists came in 1949 when his church was running about 570 members. In 1950, he refused to sign a "Christian Manifesto," and from then on, was frequently at odds with China's Three-Self Patriotic Movement. In August, 1955, he preached for the last time in his church. He was imprisoned until January, 1980 (separated for 23 years from his second wife who was also arrested), for his religious beliefs. His second wife, Liu Qing Wun, died in Changai, at age 83, in spring, 1992.

D. Sidney Correll

May 12, 1907
Fullerton, California

Aug. 5, 1991
Roanoke, Virginia

First president of United World Missions, Dayton, OH, 1946–72, and of Correll Missionary Ministries, Charlotte, NC 1978–91. Correll was converted under AIMEE SEMPLE MCPHERSON at Angeles Temple. He married his wife, Helen, on June 19, 1925. In the midst of the Great Depression, he built the Christian Tabernacle in Dayton, OH, without debt, and pastored there

1933–38. He was president of International Ministerial Association, 1937–80, which he founded. He was a foremost evangelical leader of his time, making his headquarters in St. Petersburg, FL, from 1960–78. In 1978, he moved to Charlotte, NC, and incorporated CMM. He was active in Foursquare activities as well.

James B. Irwin

March 17, 1930
Pittsburgh, Pennsylvania

Aug. 8, 1991
Glenwood Springs, Colorado

Lunar Astronaut. He married Mary Ellen Monroe on Sept. 4, 1959 and they had five children. Irwin walked on the moon July 30, 1971, and was the first to die of the twelve astronauts who were part of the lunar mission. He viewed his Apollo 15 moon journey in July–August, 1971, as a spiritual experience which led him to found the Flight Foundation, an evangelistic mission in 1972. Irwin led six expeditions to Turkey in search of Noah's Ark. Irwin was a Baptist. He died of a heart attack. He wrote from *To Rule the Night* (1973) to *Destination Moon* (1989). He is buried in Arlington (VA) National Cemetery.

Edward (Eddie) Midura

Feb. 22, 1916
Chicago, Illinois

Aug. 11, 1991
Harwood Heights, Illinois

Youth for Christ Evangelist, encourager of God's servants. Midura was converted from a Jehovah Witness background in 1935. He married Alice Bakk on October 14, 1939. His ministry included trips to Finland, Sweden, and Poland. Midura also helped several Chicago churches move and helped to develop sound black leadership. Midura was a member of the Bethany Baptist Church, Harwood Heights, IL. His tombstone sums up his life: "Encourager." He was stricken on the sidewalk in front of his house on the way to Sunday School. He had just told his wife, "It's time to go."

Vaughn Shoemaker

Aug. 11, 1902
Chicago, Illinois

Aug. 18, 1991
Carol Stream, Illinois

Great cartoonist and painter of our time. Shoemaker was the chief cartoonist for the *Chicago Daily News*, (1924–1952); the *New York Herald Tribune* (1956–1961, and *Chicago Today* (1961–1991). Shoemaker married Eveyln Arnold on July 3, 1926. He won many awards for his work and became a famous lecturer and author of cartoon collections. He won two Pulitzer Prizes in 1938 and 1947. Shoemaker was the creator of the taxpayer character. He created the renowned cartoon character, John Q. Public. He is buried in Elmhurst, IL.

Orlando Waltner

Dec. 1, 1914
Marion, South Dakota

Aug. 30, 1991
Newton, Kansas

General secretary of General Conference Mennonite Church (Mennonite Church USA in 2002), **Newton, KS, 1962–69**. On June 9, 1939, Waltner married Vernelle Schroeder. They were missionaries to India for 17 years, 1939–56. Waltner was director of the denomination's missionary program, 1958–60. For some time, he was an associate pastor in Goessel, KS, and in later years was chaplain in a retirement home.

Jackson Snyder

Nov. 23, 1931
Findlay, Ohio

Aug. 31, 1991
Zeeland, Michigan

First president of Mission Possible, Ft. Worth, FL 1976–91. Snyder married Betty Bunts in the early 1950s. He was a building contractor, she a model. Fifteen years into their marriage, both were converted through the influence of the First Assembly of God Church in Findlay. A returned missionary relative also greatly influenced the spiritual awakening of the family. Snyder began to minister to Indians in Canada, was a nursing home administrator, then ended up in Haiti. There he built a church and began to raise funds for the Lord's work there, enlarging his outreach to the Dominican Republic also. He was involved in the Christian Hope Temple of Findlay, an independent Pentecostal church. He also worked with Int. Child Care, 1975–79. He suffered from heart trouble for 18 years, and while visiting his son, died.

W. Lynn Corbett

Sept. 27, 1927 *Sept. 3, 1991*

Longtime Southern Methodist leader. His pastoral assignments included several charges in the South Carolina circuit. He was instrumental in the formation of Southern Methodist College and served as its administrator. He also helped establish the First Southern Methodist Church of Orangeburg, SC, and later pastored in Eutawville, SC.

Allen W. Graves

Jan. 20, 1915 *Sept. 4, 1991*
Rector, Arkansas Louisville, Kentucky

Last president of American Association of Schools of Religious Education, 1961–66. He married Helen Cannon on June 1, 1937. Graves pastored SBC churches in Chicago, IL, and Kentucky (1935–41), Florida (1943–45), Virginia (1945–50), and Oklahoma (1951–55). Graves was longtime dean of religious education at Southern Baptist Theological Seminary (1955–69 and 1976–80), senior professor (1980–86) and dean emeritus (1986–91).

Homer F. Britton

Nov. 21, 1909 *Sept. 15, 1991*
Fort Madison, Iowa Covington, Kentucky

Widely used musician and evangelist, music director for the HYMAN APPELMAN crusades, 1943–50. Britton's solos and trombone music added much to the crusades. He was converted on October 26, 1932, at FBC, Ft. Madison, IA under the leadership of Pastor Joseph Fleming. He married his wife, Thelma, on March 15, 1933 (died: February 1, 1947), and then Linda Lowrie on December 8, 1948. Britton conducted revival meetings in churches and tents across America for 40 years, 1950–90. His headquarters were in Chattanooga, TN, until 1989, when he moved to Decatur, AL. He wrote many gospel choruses throughout his lifetime.

Martin H. Woudstra

July 23, 1922 *Oct. 3, 1991*
Bergum, Netherlands Kentwood, Michigan

President of Evangelical Theological Society, 1979. Woudstra was highly educated in Amsterdam, Hamburg, Germany, and Westminster Theological Seminary among other places. He was ordained November 8, 1953. He pastored Third Christian Reformed, Edmonton, Alberta (1953–55) and then began a lifelong teaching ministry at Calvin Theological Seminary, Grand Rapids, MI (1955–79) when he retired.

Lyle C. Anderson

March 25, 1903 *Oct. 4, 1991*
Randolph, New York Newfane, New York

Founder and first general director of American Mission for Opening Churches, Inc., Olcott, NY, 1943–79. Anderson founded AMOC in Niagara Falls, directing it until his retirement. He was married to Ruth Einfeldt on August 8, 1930 (died: February 20, 1962) and Pearl L. Farley on October 8, 1963 (died: September 7, 1986). He helped organize the Niagara Bible Conference in Olcott, NY, in 1936. Early on, he pastored the Ridge Road Union Church, Lockport, NY, 1935–40, after graduation from Moody Bible Institute. In 1940, he and his family moved to the Adirondack Mountains to reopen four churches. He also directed the Sacandaga Bible Conference in Broadalbin, NY, for several years. He conducted services where he lived at the Newfane Health Facility, 1986–91.

Ernest Ford
Tennessee Ernie Ford

Feb. 13, 1919　　　　　　　　　　　　　　　　　　　　　　　　　　　　　　　　　　　　　　　Oct. 17, 1991
Bristol, Tennessee　　　　　　　　　　　　　　　　　　　　　　　　　　　　　　　　　　　　Reston, Virginia

Recording artist and TV entertainer. He married Betty Heminger on September 18, 1942 (died: February, 1989). Tennessee Ernie Ford sold over 20 million copies of his famous album *Sixteen Tons* (1955). Ford also had an evening television variety show on NBC (1956–61) and a day-time show on ABC (1962–65). He produced over 80 albums. He also toured England and the Soviet Union and was awarded the Congressional Medal of Freedom in 1984. For years, Ford operated a 540-acre ranch north of San Francisco. He fell ill after attending a state dinner at the White House and died from a chronic liver disease.

Dennis F. Bennett

Oct. 28, 1917　　　　　　　　　　　　　　　　　　Nov. 1, 1991
Ponders End, England　　　　　　　　　　　　　　　　　　　　　　　　　　　　　　　　Edmonds, Washington

Episcopal clergyman identified with the charismatic renewal beginnings. Bennett moved to America in 1927. In 1959, he announced to his St. Mark's Episcopal congregation in VanNuys, CA, that he accepted speaking in tongues. He served there (1953–60) and then at St. Luke's Episcopal Church in Seattle, WA (1960–81). This church was ready to close but instead, grew to 1,000 under his leadership. Bennett's wife, Elberta, died in 1963; then he married Rita Reed (born: 1934) on October 15, 1966. He was found slumped over his computer, dead from a heart attack.

Houston Ward

Feb. 15, 1895　　　　　　　　　　　　　　　　　　　　　　　　　　　　　　　　　　　　　　Nov. 14, 1991
Alexander City, Alabama　　　　　　　　　　　　　　　　　　　　　　　　　　　　　　　Cantonment, Florida

President and bishop of Apostolic Faith Mission Church of God, Cantonment, FL, 1963–91. Ward was a mechanic for 50 years. Early on, he pastored in Youngstown, OH. His first wife, Sarah, died in February, 1973, his second wife was Julia. He built the AFMCG headquarters in Cantonment. He was a diabetic, which contributed to his death.

Don F. McKechnie

Oct. 28, 1914　　　　　　　　　　　　　　　　　　　　　　　　　　　　　　　　　　　　　　Nov. 16, 1991
Ontario, Canada　　　　　　　　　　　　　　　　　　　　　　　　　　　　　　　　　Ottawa, Ontario, Canada

President of Christian Business Men's Committee, 1958. At age 13, he was converted at the Gospel Tabernacle in Ottawa, under the ministry of Dr. W. E. Powers. McKechnie was an outstanding Canadian businessman and a senior partner in McKechnie, Boles, and Company, a corporation born in 1939 to simplify income tax forms. He earned the title of "financial doctor." In 1939, he began his accounting practice, earned his CPA degree, and soon had several branch offices. He married Berrty Beardsley on October 28, 1939. In 1944, McKechnie directed YFC. In 1945, he was chairman of Child Evangelism, traveling widely giving his testimony. He was active in the Christian Missionary and Alliance Church and was president of a children's home in Farm Point, Quebec. One day, McKechnie sat down in his office chair and died.

Joseph R. Brookshire

July 29, 1918
Perryville, Kentucky

Nov. 16, 1991
Lexington, Kentucky

Outstanding Methodist evangelist who conducted crusades for 40 years in 33 states and 23 foreign countries, preaching in over 1,100 revivals. Brookshire's wife was Marjorie Benefield. He was also a well-known soloist. His evangelistic fervor was used by many denominations; thousands were converted at his crusades. He died of malignant melanoma.

Alfred P. Klausler

Feb. 22, 1910
Hankinson, North Dakota

Dec. 1, 1991
Cicero, Illinois

Executive director of Associated Church Press, 1961–74. Klausler was a well-known Lutheran journalist and cleric. He married Signe Fox on June 28, 1934 (died: March 1990), was ordained the same year, then pastored Our Savior's Lutheran Church in Glendive, MT from 1934–42. Klausler was the executive secretary of the department of communications for the Walther League, 1946–66. He taught at Valparaiso (IN) University, 1950–52. Later, he was religion editor for *Westinghouse Broadcasting* (1969–79), and editor-at-large for the *Christian Century* (1974–91). Klausler lived in Cicero, IL, and wrote extensively.

Obed W. Stuckey

Dec. 19, 1898
Chicago, Illinois

Dec. 6, 1991
Vero Beach, Florida

Evangelist for many years. Stuckey received his education from MBI and Fort Wayne Bible Institute (Summitt College). He married Laura on August 6, 1919 (died: 1957), and then Ruth became his wife on November 1, 1958. Stuckey was on the staff of Detroit Rescue Mission, (1922–1933), then became an evangelist (1933–1980). He played the musical "saw." He worked out of the Detroit area. Stuckey retired to Vero Beach, FL in 1980.

Eric C. Rust

June 6, 1910
Gravesend, England

Dec. 14, 1991
Louisville, Kentucky

Well-known Southern Baptist theologian and professor at Southern Baptist Theological Seminary. Rust joined the faculty there in 1953 as professor of Christian apologetics. He then specialized in Christian philosophy, in 1958–79 as emeritus professor. He married Helen M. Ken in 1936. Early on, Rust pastored three Baptist churches in England, then taught at Rawdon Baptist College at the University of Leeds, England, 1946–52. Much of his speaking and writing addressed the relationship between science and the Christian faith. He authored 14 books.

Annie S. Bernsten

1911
Oslo, Norway

1992
Horton, Norway

Missionary to China, whose faith and work were immense. In Annie's earlier years, she was a leader in her Karl Marx youth club in the small town of Horton. While attending nursing school, she became a Christian. She went to China in 1938 with China Inland Mission, where she worked at the Shanghsien and Lungchuchai mission in Shensi Province until 1951. One day in June, 1941, they arrived in a small mountain village where drought had ravaged the natives for weeks. She refused to take her straw hat off as a salute to idols. Threatened to be killed if rain did not come by midnight, she prayed, and rain came at 11:30 p.m. Annie met GLADYS AYLWAARD who encouraged her. From 1953–55, she worked at the Rennie's Mill refugee camp. In 1955, she founded the Hope of Heaven rehabilitation center. Thousands of refugees from mainland China have been treated there. She received the distinguished "Member of the British Empire" honor for her tireless labors.

Lewis T. Corlett

Feb. 8, 1896
Homestead, Pennsylvania

Jan. 1, 1992
Duarte, California

President of Northwest Nazarene College (University in 2000), **Nampa, ID, 1942–52, and of Nazarene Theological Seminary, Kansas City, MO, 1952–66**. Corlett was converted at a Methodist church altar in Homestead, PA. His brother helped Corlett form the Methodist denomination's youth program. Corlett married Mary Elba Simpson on Sept. 12, 1919 (died: 1976), and pastored in Los Angeles, CA (1920–24); Billings, MT (1924–26); Grand Junction, CO (1926–27); Dover, NJ (1927–28) and Dallas, TX (1928–34). After his pastorates, he served on the faculty of Peniel College (Southern Nazarene University) Bethany, OK, from 1934–42. He later taught at Pasadena (CA) College, 1966–73.

Dale Moody

Jan. 27, 1915
Jones County, Texas

Jan. 22, 1992
Louisville, Kentucky

Outstanding Baptist theologian. Moody was converted at age twelve as he was riding his horse through the woods. He taught Christian theology at Southern Baptist Theological Seminary, Louisville, for decades, ending in 1983 under a cloud. He had written *The Word of Truth* and taught that the NT teaches the possibility of apostasy, which did not sit well there. He was a member of the WCC Faith and Order Commission for eight years in the 1960s. In 1969–70, Moody was the second Protestant and first Baptist to teach at the Gregorian University in Rome. Although a conservative, he felt he should be open to other groups. He led two Holy Land trips and was a prolific guest speaker.

Stephen W. Paine

Oct. 28, 1908
Grand Rapids, Michigan

Feb. 9, 1992
West Seneca, New York

President of Houghton (NY) College, 1937–72; of National Association of Evangelicals, 1948–49; and of Evangelical Theological Society, 1967. Paine was converted through talks with his father in Urbandale, MI, prior to 1917. He married Helen Paul on August 17, 1934, and they had five children. Paine started teaching at Houghton in 1934. In the summer of 1942, he surrendered completely to the Lord, who continued to use him in many capacities. A tragic period came with the loss of his 19-year-old daughter to spinal and bulbar polio in 1955. She was stricken as she was just starting her sophomore year at college at Houghton in 1953. He wrote several books from *Toward the Mark: Studies in Philippians* (1953) to *Beginning Greek* (1960–61). He is buried in Houghton, NY.

James A. (Jim) Savage

June 18, 1916
River Falls, Wisconsin

Feb. 10, 1992
Edinburg, Texas

Veteran missionary to South America. Savage went to Venezuela shortly after his marriage to June Hart on July 8, 1941. He served under TEAM in 1941, then was loaned to YFC from 1953–66, and headed their work in South America. Savage was headquartered the last six years of his mission work in Lima, Peru. He returned to TEAM and helped organize a seminary in Venezuela, 1967–75. Health problems then brought him home to the States.

Redd Harper

Sept. 29, 1903
Nocona, Texas

Feb. 16, 1992
Los Angeles, California

Converted cowboy, singer, and Christian actor. Harper entertained for several years in the Hollywood scene as a trumpet player, comedian, and radio singer. He was with the Jimmy Grier Orchestra for some time. He married his wife, Laura, on April 30, 1941. It was May 20, 1950, at a meeting of the Hollywood Christian Group in HENRIETTA MEARS' home, that he accepted Christ. He soon became the star of Billy Graham films, *Mr. Texas* and *Oil Town USA*. Harper wrote many songs and hymns and shared his testimony all across USA and Canada as well as Great Britain. He wrote lyrics and music for "Each Step of the Way," "My Testimony Song," "Lord, Keep Your Mighty Hand on Me," and also the music for some of O. J. SMITH's songs including, "Come with Your Heartache," "I'm Singing for My Lord," "My Heart Would Sing of Jesus" and "Safe with the Savior." In 1956 he began his own evangelistic ministry which took him on many missionary journeys.

Jamie Buckingham

March 28, 1932
Vero Beach, Florida

Feb. 17, 1992
Melbourne, Florida

Pastor, columnist, and author who was a renowned leader in charismatic circles. Buckingham pastored Baptist churches for ten years, then through a Full Gospel Businessmen's Convention in Washington, D.C., he switched doctrines. In 1967, he founded the Tabernacle Church, Melbourne, FL, which grew to 4,000. Buckingham wrote 38 books, including *Power for Living* with over 30 million readers. He was also the editor of *Ministries Today*. He died of cancer.

John S. Bonnell

Jan. 10, 1893
Prince Edward Island, Canada

Feb. 23, 1992
New York, New York

Leading liberal Presbyterian pastor of Fifth Avenue Presbyterian Church, New York City, 1935–63. Bonnell married Bessie Carruthers in June, 1923. He pastored in St. John, Nova Scotia (1923–29) and in Winnipeg, Manitoba (1929–35). He was a lecturer at Princeton Theological Seminary (1938–60) and president of New York Theological Seminary (1966–68). After his 1963 retirement from the pastorate, he was a tireless traveler speaking in many parts of the world. He authored numerous books from *What Are You Living For?* (1950) to *Presidential Profiles* (1971). His 27–year pastorate resulted in the Fifth Avenue Church's growth from 700 to 2,500 members.

Errol T. Elliott

Nov. 10, 1894
Carthage, Missouri

March 3, 1992
Indianapolis, Indiana

General secretary of Friends United Meeting, Richmond, IN, 1944–57. Elliott married Ruby M. Kelly on December 25, 1916. He was a pastor in Wichita, KS, and Boulder, CO (1926–30); field secretary for the Meetings of Friends (1930–36); pastor at First Friends Church, Indianapolis, IN (1936–42 and 1957–65); and president of William Penn College, Oskaloosa, IA (1942–44). From 1965–92, he was research associate at Earlham School of Religion, Indianapolis, IN.

Ford R. Philpot

July 16, 1917
Manchester, Kentucky

March 9, 1992
Lexington, Kentucky

Widely recognized evangelist of his time. Philpot served in the Marines, attended Asbury Theological Seminary, married his wife, Virginia, and entered a life of evangelistic endeavors. He was a United Methodist, yet people from many denominations participated in his more than 600 crusades. In 1959, Philpot produced the first religious television program in color, *The Story*.

Harold W. Reed

July 14, 1909
Haigler, Nebraska

March 18, 1992
Northridge, California

President of Olivet Nazarene College, Kankakee, IL 1949–75. Reed was converted at age 15, following an initial committment at age seven. He married Maybel Ripper on June 19, 1933. He pastored in Loveland, CO (1933–34); Junction City, KS (1934–36) and Newton, KS (1944–48). He was also president of Bresee College, Hutchinson, KS (1936–40). From 1975 on, he directed the Reed Institute of Leadership. Reed's memorial folder summed it up well: minister, scholar, educator, administrator, builder, world traveler, author, lover of people, friend to all.

Muriwhenua (Muri) Thompson

1930
Mamaranui, New Zealand

March 29, 1992

Maori tribes prophet and evangelist, one of New Zealand's great evangelical leaders. Born with a hole in his heart, Thompson was often sick. He came to Auckland (1946), and joined the Open Air Campaigners (1954). From 1956–57, he was in North America with OAC. In 1958, he conducted his first crusade in Kaikohe, followed by crusades throughout New Zealand. In 1963, he married Ena Hansen. In 1970, he ministered in the Solomon Islands. He spoke at Jesus marches in New Zealand in 1972. In 1974, he had major heart surgery. In 1975–91, he was with the Waitangi celebrations. The Treaty of Waitangi in the Bay of Islands in 1840 guaranteed the Maori people their rights to land, to means of livelihood, and preservation of their culture. His ministry would parallel that of an evangelist to the Indians of North America.

Wendell Zimmerman

April 29, 1916
Altrus, Oklahoma

March 29, 1992
Jacksonville, Florida

Editor of the *Baptist Bible Tribune* (1974–83), and one of the founders of Baptist Bible Fellowship, and key pastor in the movement. Zimmerman married Virginia Whitehead on February 6, 1938. He pastored the Kansas City (MO) Baptist Temple, 1943–68, following a small Arkansas pastorate. He organized the Jacksonville (FL) Baptist Temple which he led from 1968, to about 1982, when he and a large group of the membership felt they should relocate. They formed the Bible Baptist Temple, which he served until 1987 when his health began to fail. He had diabetic problems. That church was renamed the Sun Coast Baptist Church. He returned as a guest speaker and was sitting on the platform singing "We've a Story to Tell to the Nations" when he bowed his head and died.

Leonhard Steiner

Jan. 12, 1903
London, England

March 30, 1992
Basel, Switzerland

First chairman of Pentecostal World Fellowship, 1947–55. Steiner was active in Swiss Pentecostalism all his life. In 1945, he became the editor of *Promises of the Father*, pastored in Basel, and became the missions secretary. He led the first Pentecostal World Conference in Zurich in 1947. Steiner taught new birth/Spirit Baptism. He was also ecumenically involved in consultations with WCC representatives.

Charles P. (Chuck) Thomas

Sept. 28, 1923
Barterville, Kentucky

April 1, 1992
Springboro, Ohio

Director of Project Partner, 1964–84. Raised in a Christian home, Thomas committed his life to Christ on the battlefield in Germany during WWII. He married Donna Stanley on June 12, 1947. They finished school together in Anderson, IN, and then went to Wichita, KS where, after a brief associate pastorship, he pastored the Pawnee Ave. Church of God (AI) from 1952–77. He was a real innovator, starting with a trip to Mexico, obtaining a 40-passenger airplane, and piloting a part of his congregation over there. He would take some 6,000 people overseas for short-term activities such as building churches, clinics, disaster relief, etc. Many times they were threatened by third world situations. He also had a medical ship—a 47-foot yacht. They moved to Middletown, OH (1979), and expanded into Asia. Thomas had heart problems (1983) and turned the ministry over to his wife. He was healed in 1987, went to China, then succumbed to stomach cancer five years later.

Joseph D. Quillian

January 30, 1917
Buford, Georgia

April 3, 1992
Chewelah, Washington

President of Perkins School of Theology (SMU), Dallas, TX, 1960–81, and of Association of Theological Schools, 1972–74. Quillian married Elizabeth Sampson on December 15, 1944. He pastored Hillsboro Circuit, TN (1938–41); Nashville, TN (1941–42); Stamford, CT (1946–50); and was president of Martin College, Pulaski, TN (1950–54). He went to Perkins in 1954 as professor of worship and preaching.

J. Palmer Muntz

March 20, 1897
Buffalo, New York

April 29, 1992
Quarryville, Pennsylvania

Director of the Winona Lake Bible Conference, 1939–58. Muntz married Laura Wedekindt on December 19, 1922. He succeeded WILLIAM BIEDERWOLF at WLBC, extending a one-week conference to six weeks, plus conferences dedicated to the subjects of prophecy and the Jews. He helped the local Buffalo Hebrew-Christian Mission immensely. He was a Baptist pastor in Chaffee, NY (1922–24), and then at Cazenovia Baptist Church, Buffalo, NY (1924–63). Muntz was also active in various Conservative Baptist Association of America activities. He retired to King of Prussia, PA.

F. Carlton Booth

April 4, 1904
Essex Junction, Vermont

May 20, 1992
Pasadena, California

Multi-talented individual greatly used of God. Booth was converted at age 15 at a revival meeting at a Free Methodist Church in Seattle. For 14 years, Booth served as the song leader and soloist for WYRTZEN and CLAYTON in the Word of Life Ministries. He also led the singing for a few Graham and SUNDAY crusades. He married Ruth Elkins on August 30, 1927. He taught evangelism and music at South Pacific College (1926–29), at Providence Bible Insitute (1930–55) and was a professor of evangelism at Fuller Theological Seminary (1955–70). He was a faithful soul winner and served as secretary-treasurer of World Vision for 35 years.

Wilbur S. Konkel

Sept. 4, 1912
Boston, Colorado

May 24, 1992
Westminster, Colorado

Director of Pillar of Fire Missions, Westminster, CO, 1960–92. Konkel spent more than 25 years evangelizing in Europe, especially in England, where he was headmaster at the Pillar of Fire

College in North London. He married Elsie Morgan in 1942 (died: 1972) and Arlene Kline in 1973. Konkel pastored in Oakland, CA, from 1955–59. He divided time between the USA and England until 1960 when he went to Africa, establishing missions in several countries. By the time of his death, POF activities were in eight countries of the world. He wrote seven books, six were strictly hymn-story books—a subject he enjoyed. He became a bishop of the POF church in 1967.

Manuel Arenas

1932
Zapotitlan, Puebla, Mexico

May 27, 1992
Xicotepec De Juarez, Mexico

First president of Latin American Indian Ministries, Orange, CA, 1972–92. This work began as the Totonac Bible Center, Inc. This gifted Totonac Indian was the principal translator for Herman Aschmann. Arenas obtained a good education in the U.S. and Germany and returned to Mexico to establish a Bible school in La Union, Puebla, in 1968. He tried to expand his vision to all the tribal groups of Mexico and organized three different consultations of Christian leaders from other tribes. He died of cancer.

Carl Q. Lee

Jan. 19, 1907
Minot, North Dakota

June 3, 1992
Zion, Illinois

General overseer of Christian Catholic (Christ Community in 1995) **Church, Zion, IL 1959–76.** Upon graduation from eighth grade in 1918, Lee went to Zion, IL, to live with an uncle and aunt, after his mother died. He was converted (1921), then answered the call to the ministry (1930). On November 23, 1932, he married Gertrude Kuecler. He served 17 years as assistant to MICHAEL MINTERN, his predecessor. A new facility was dedicated in 1967.

Ruby Tibbits Tooze

Dec. 21, 1901
Trumansville, New York

June 6, 1992
Silverton, Oregon

President of National Women's Christian Temperance Union, 1959–74. She married Fred J. Tooze on September 17, 1931. Her promotion of the "Hour of Social Freedom" was the highlight of her administration. Over 100 television stations granted public service time to advertise the WCTU non-alcoholic beverage recipe book, resulting in thousands of requests. On the 50th anniversary of prohibition, January 16, 1970, she was on the front page of the *Wall Street Journal*. At the 100th national convention August 28–September 4, 1979 in Cleveland, OH she gave a wonderful final address as president. Her favorite jingle was, "My name's Tooze, it rhymes with booze, and I'm agin' it!"

Norman J. Clayton

Jan. 22, 1903
Brooklyn, New York

June 9, 1992
Pauling, New York

Songwriter (lyrics and music) and organist. Converted as a child (age six) in South Brooklyn Gospel Church, Clayton was the greatest Christian songwriter in the last half of the 20th century, excepting perhaps JOHN PETERSON and Bill Gaither. He married Martha Whistendahl in 1925. From 1942–57, he was the organist for Word of Life. It was JACK WYRTZEN, CARLTON BOOTH, and Clayton who inspired large audiences in New York City. He penned gospel songs such as "Jesus Alone," "Now I Belong to Jesus," "For All My Sins," "Some Sweet Day," "Jesus Is All You Need," "Faithful Forever," "If We Could See Beyond Today," "We Shall See His Lovely Face," "Since Christ the Savior Came," "Jesus Satisfies," "My Hope Is in the Lord," "One Glad and Glorious Day," and "Absolutely Free!" Clayton published some 30 songbooks from 1945–59, then tranferred the publishing and copyrights to the RODEHEAVER Company in 1959. In 1960, he moved to Canterport, NY. He was a Baptist church organist for 50 years.

David A. Cavin

May 18, 1918
Isabel, Kansas

June 30, 1992
Strafford, Missouri

President of Baptist Bible Fellowship, Springfield, MO 1955–57, 1977–80. Cavin was converted in 1932 during a tent revival with evangelist George Dotson. On June 7, 1936, he married Helen Maxine Miller. With no formal training of any kind, he began pastoring the Bible Baptist Church in El Reno, OK, in 1939. With 29 people, he built a great work until 1950 with a high of 665. From 1950–64, he pastored the Castleberry Baptist Church of Fort Worth, TX, which grew from 143 to 1,265. He was also widely used as an evangelist. The High Street Baptist Church of Springfield, MO, was his next ministry from 1964–86, with a membership of 5,000 when he resigned.

F. Paul Stocker

Dec. 19, 1899
Port Washington, Ohio

July 10, 1992
Bethlehem, Pennsylvania

President of Provincial Elders Conference of Moravian Church in NA (North), Bethlehem, PA 1946–56, 1960–66. Stocker married Evelyn Doster (1924) and Pauline Leibert (1959). He pastored the Third Moravian Church, NYC (1923–26); First Church, Indianapolis (1928–31); then back to the NYC charge (1931–33). After this, he went to the College Hall Church of Bethlehem, PA, from 1933–36. Stocker served in WWI and was involved in numerous Moravian and World Council of Churches activities.

Gilbert L. Guffin

Aug. 5, 1906
Marietta, Georgia

July 12, 1992
Marietta, Georgia

President of Eastern Baptist College and Theological Seminary, Wynnewood, PA 1950–61. Ordained in 1927, this effective cleric and educator began as a high school principal in Marietta, GA (1930–33), serving pastorates also (1927–33). Guffin pastored the FBC in Merchantville, NJ (1935–42); then in Jasper, AL (1942–47). He was chairman of the extension division of Howard College (Sanford University, Birmingham, AL), 1947–49. He made several tours in 45 countries and wrote extensively from, *How to Run a Church* (1948) to *The Bible* Vol. 1 (1973) and Vol. 2 (1974).

"Life is a trust given to each of us, a trust to be administered with accountability to the Giver."

Alvin N. Rogness

May 6, 1906
Astoria, South Dakota

July 12, 1992
Park Rapids, Minnesota

President of Luther Theological Seminary (Luther Northwestern in 1982), **St. Paul, MN 1954–74.** In 1934, Rogness was ordained and also married Nora Preus, who gave him five children. Early on, he pastored in Duluth, MN; Ames and Mason City, IA, and Sioux Falls, SD. In 1963, Augsburg Seminary, Minneapolis, merged with LTS. Under his leadership at LTS, property expanded from eight to 45 acres, making it possible for Northwestern Seminary of Minneapolis to relocate there in 1976 in a major merger. During his tenure, the enrollment grew from 458 to 773 students and the faculty from 17 to 39, making it the largest Lutheran Seminary in North America. He died of a heart attack while vacationing in Park Rapids.

Nelson C. "Bud" Hinkson

March 4, 1934
Eugene, Oregon

August 10, 1992
Starnberg, Germany

Foreign missions student minister. Hinkson made his decision for Christ at the University of Oregon, where he attended, 1952–56. He was in the U.S. army in Germany 1957–58. In 1961, he joined Campus Crusade and married Shirley Milligan. In 1967, he held an evangelistic blitz at the University of California, Berkeley, with the University Ambassador Team. Hinkson recruited leadership for Africa in 1972 and was called by God to Eastern Europe and the Soviet Union. From 1974–92, he found open doors in the Soviet Union and all other countries of Eastern Europe. He started the first Institute of Biblical Studies in the Soviet Union in 1991 and taught Biblical Bible Study Methods to more than 400 students in Russia. Hinkson established numerous indigenous ministries of evangelism and discipleship across Europe and Africa. He died in a bicycle accident.

Bernard Ramm

Aug. 1, 1916
Butte, Montana

Aug. 11, 1992
Laguna Hills, California

Educator who was best known for drawing evangelical theology into dialogue with science and culture. Ramm wrote 18 books and over 100 articles and reviews for journals and magazines. He concentrated on Christian apologetics, the Bible and science, and scriptural authority. Ramm was converted at age 17 through the witness of his brother at a summer camp. He began his academic career in 1943 at the Los Angeles Baptist Theological Seminary and moved on to teaching philosophy and apologetics at BIOLA. He taught at California Baptist Seminary of the West (American BTS) (1959–74 and 1979–86), and at Eastern Baptist Theological Seminary (1974–77). Ramm was influential in the founding of the American Scientific Affiliation. He wrote *The Christian View of Science and the Scripture* (1954).

Maxwell R. Gaulke

Aug. 10, 1910
Houston, Texas

Aug. 16, 1992
Houston, Texas

President of South Texas Bible Institute, Houston, TX 1953–66, and Gulf Coast Bible College (Mid-America Bible College, Oklahoma City, OK in 1985), **1966–75**. Gaulke founded the above school and was president for 22 years. He was converted at Anderson (IN) College campus in the office of a teacher, Amy Lopez, in 1931. He married Isabelle Lowe on Aug. 26, 1933. Gaulke pastored in Duluth, Montevideo and St. Paul Park, MN, from 1934–40. He then pastored at the First Church of God, Chicago (1940–47) before going to Houston and the First Church of God (1947–75). He took the step of faith to start a Bible school which gained full membership in the AABC in 1968.

Rómulo Sauñe

Jan. 17, 1953
Chakiqpampa, Peru

Sept. 5, 1992
Peru

Martyr, preacher, and Bible translator. For years Sauñe worked with missionaries from Wycliffe Bible Translators and the Presbyterian Church to translate the entire Bible for his Quechua people. He grew up near Ayacucho, a small shepherd village. He married Donna Jackson on August 13, 1977. In 1978, he graduated from Latin America Bible Institute and the following year returned to Peru from the US. His labors saw the Aycuho Quechua New Testament completed and dedicated (1982) and then the entire Bible (1987). He received the World Evangelical Fellowship Religious Liberty Award in Manila, June 23, 1992, just 2 1/2 months before his martyrdom. Returning home from a visit to the grave of his grandfather (murdered two years earlier), he and some 20 others were shot and killed as they encountered a roadblock.

Walter F. Bruce

Dec. 23, 1911
Pleasant Hill, Pennsylvania

Sept. 11, 1992
Pearl, Mississippi

President of Congregational Methodist Church, Florence, MS, 1961–65, and its world missions program, 1966–81, and president of Wesley College, Florence, MS 1944–53, 1960–62. Raised in a Congregational Methodist atmosphere, Bruce taught Sunday School, lit lamps, and trimmed wicks for the country church. Preachers like him were called cornfield preachers because they were basically farmers. He married Lois Lister on August 6, 1940. They were students at God's Bible School in Cincinnati. His wife was a nurse for 35 years. He moved to Texas and pastored two part-time works (Commerce and Bonham, TX). They later moved to Lubbock, TX; Tehuazana, TX; Mt. Pleasant, TX (1953–57); and Houston (1957–60). He moved to Florence, MS, in 1972. Bruce pastored a country church near Laurel, MS, from 1981–92. He died four days after a stroke. His funeral was very large.

Fred P. Brown

Aug. 23, 1909
Birmingham, Alabama

Sept. 16, 1992
Chattanooga, Tennessee

Baptist evangelist. For over 60 years, Brown worked out of the Highland Park Baptist Church, Chattanooga, TN. He was converted at age seven after hearing a sermon on hell at a Presbyterian revival. At age 19, God called him to be an evangelist. He graduated from BJU in 1933. He was a strong Bible preacher and teacher. He won many to Christ. His wife, Donella, was active in the music program of his home church and died March 24, 1983, from cancer. He suffered a stroke on July 9, 1992 and never spoke again, passing away in a nursing home.

Bartholomew G. La Vastida

Dec. 24, 1887
Cuba

Sept. 30, 1992
Cuba

Cofounder (ELMER V. THOMPSON) and director of West Indies Mission (World Team in 1967), **1938–67** La Vastida was converted in 1909 by the witness of a Christian family in Troy, NY, while studying to be an engineer. He went back to Cuba as a radio preacher, evangelist. La Vastida married Elsie Lines in 1918 (died: August, 1930), and Fefita LaVastida on July 20, 1939 (died: January 24, 1991 at age 85). He had won her to the Lord when she was 15. He founded and became president of New Pines Seminary, created in 1923 for disadvantaged children. He pastored Presbyterian churches in Cuba, 1921–25 and 1928–34. He was an evangelist, 1925–28. By 1945, his school had 120 students. He was president of the Evangelical Association of Cuba, with 75 workers serving 100 churches (7,000 believers). He lived to age 104.

Joseph M. Kitagawa

March 8, 1915
Osaka, Japan

Oct. 7, 1992
Chicago, Illinois

Dean of University of Chicago Divinity School, 1970–80. Kitagawa came to the U.S. in 1941 and was soon put into a detention camp, 1941–45. He married Evelyn Rose on July 22, 1946. He became a member of the faculty of the University of Chicago in 1951 upon his graduation. Kitagawa became associate professor of the history of religions (1959–64), and then the professor. He was president of the American Society for the Study of Religions in 1960. He died of pneumonia after a stroke. He wrote from *Religions in the East* (1969) to *Religious Studies* (1991).

C. Ray Stedman

Oct. 5, 1917
Temvik, North Dakota

Oct. 7 1992
Grants Pass, Oregon

Founder and pastor of the Peninsula Bible Church, Palo Alto, CA, 1950–89. Stedman was converted in a Methodist tent revival meeting in Montana. He served in the U.S. Navy in WWII. He then married Elaine Smith on October 22, 1945. He was known for his community leadership. His church spawned several other new works. He authored 30 books, his most known were *Body Life*, *What On Earth's Going to Happen?* and *Authentic Christianity*. His "Evangelism through Church Renewal" lecture was widely used. He died three months after being diagnosed with kidney cancer.

Rudy Atwood

Dec. 16, 1912
Marion, Illinois

Oct. 16, 1992
Hollywood, California

World-renowned Christian pianist, probably the greatest since ROBERT HARKNESS. Atwood's rendition of "Heavenly Sunlight" was unsurpassed. It was the theme song for the *Old Fashioned Revival Hour* with CHARLES E. FULLER. Atwood served there, 1933–68. He also worked with a quartet from the Country Church of Hollywood, CA, which he pastored, 1933–38. In his later years, he held concerts in many halls and auditoriums, working out of Oak Forest (IL) Baptist Temple. He had a heart attack in a meeting while playing "When They Ring Those Golden Bells for You and Me" and died four days later.

Walter L. "Red" Barber

Feb. 17, 1908
Columbus, Mississippi

Oct. 22, 1992
Tallahassee, Florida

Baseball's beloved announcer, an outstanding Episcopalian layman, who was licensed as a lay preacher. He married Lylah Scarborough on March 28, 1931. Barber was converted in the fall of 1942 at an Episcopalian service. Although he was going through the ritual, he said it was very meaningful to him. Vin Scully said, "[Barber] was the finest baseball announcer who ever lived." He began broadcasting in Cincinnati (1934–39), then went to the Brooklyn Dodgers (1939-54), and then he joined the New York Yankees (1954-66). His reporting highlights included the first televised game (1939) and Jackie Robinson's entrance into baseball (1947). After an ulcer hemorrhage nearly killed him in 1948, his faith deepened, and he began preaching. He helped raise ½ million dollars for St. Barnabas House, New York City, a home for troubled teenagers and unmarried mothers. In 1972, he retired to Tallahassee.

Stan O. Ross

March 30, 1911
near Forest City, Minnesota

Oct. 24, 1992
Litchfield, Minnesota

President of Church of God General Conference, Morrow, GA 1968–80, and its missions program, 1961–69, 1972–74. Ross married Elna (Peggy) Ruhn on December 15, 1939. He was converted on November 10, 1940, and became involved in the Litchfield (MN) Church of God for many years. In 1961, he moved to Oregon, IL (at age 50), and served the General Conference in a variety of ways, superintendent of missions, college instructor, and office manager. From 1980–90, he was back home pastoring the Church of God in Litchfield. He was a blessing to many around the world.

J. Oswald Sanders

Oct. 17, 1902
Invercargill, New Zealand

Oct. 24, 1992
New Zealand

General director of Overseas Missionary Fellowship (formerly China Inland Mission), **1952–69**. A Baptist, Sanders was converted on March 11, 1911, under the preaching of John Q. Henry. He married Edith Dobson on December 19, 1931 (died: 1966) and Mary Miller in 1968 (died: 1972). He was the principal of New Zealand Bible Institute, Auckland, NZ (1933–45) and preached in Australia, representing CIM (1945–52). He directed the movement during the turbulent years of restructuring following the exodus from China. Under his leadership, the mission expanded from China to eight other countries. He retired in 1969, yet worldwide preaching and writing occupied him until his death. He wrote over 40 books, including *Spiritual Leadership* and *In Pursuit of Purity*, which have sold over 2 million copies in 23 different languages.

Charles M. Cooper

Jan. 7, 1909
Lima, Ohio

Oct. 28, 1992
Oakland, California

President of Pacific Lutheran Theological Seminary, Berkeley, CA 1961–73. Cooper was ordained to the Lutheran ministry in 1933, and married Alta Peterson on May 29, 1934. He was an instructor of OT at Lutheran Theological Seminary, Philadelphia (1936–41); assistant professor (1941–45); and professor (1945–53).

C. Dorr Demaray

Oct. 21, 1901
Nashville, Michigan

Oct. 31, 1992
Seattle, Washington

Free Methodist educator, pastor, evangelist, president of Seattle (WA) Pacific College (University in 1977), **1959–68, and president of Azusa (CA) College, 1941–48**, after some 17 years there. On August 26, 1925, Demaray married L. Grace Care and began teaching speech and English at Azusa College in 1930. He was ordained in 1941 to the Free Methodist ministry. When he moved to Seattle, WA, he pastored the First Free Methodist Church, 1948–59. In 1952, he raised $100,000 for a new sanctuary in one day. Upon retirement, Demaray carried many education assignments overseas for the General Missionary Board of the FMC.

Russell T. Hitt

Aug. 16, 1905
Toledo, Ohio

Nov. 4, 1992
Lancaster, Pennsylvania

Editor of *Eternity Magazine* (1953–89) and president of Evangelical Press Association, 1956–57. Hitt was one of the best-known journalists of his generation. After graduating from the University of Michigan in 1926, he served at various newspapers. He was brought up in a Plymouth Brethren home and made a public commitment to Christ on January 1, 1933, at Church of the Open Door, Los Angeles, CA, having come to Christ through the ministry of John Grimason, retired PB preacher. He married Lillian Schwartzel on December 3, 1938. Hitt was director of public relations at MBI (1938–47) and worked for *Christian Life Magazine*, National SS Association, and was a management consultant to various organizations (1948–53). He was an elder in the Presbyterian Church. His *Jungle Pilot* and *Cannibal Valley* books were collections of exciting missionary stories. He led Evangelical Ministries until he retired in 1975.

Albert J. Page

Nov. 5, 1920
Hertfordshire, England

Nov. 7, 1992
Chattanooga, Tennessee

Christian Business Men's Committee leader, 1966–92. He was on the executive staff since 1980, following his retirement, from 40 years with IBM. Page's last position was assistant to the president for special projects. Previously, he had served as national director of administration. Page was the diligent director of the National Convention, working behind the scenes overseeing multitudes of details. He had served two terms on the CBMC board, including one year as chairman, while he was at IBM. His wife's name was Joyce and they were married for 49 years. He officiated for high school, college, and professional football for 38 years. Page died suddenly while working in his front yard.

Elisha P. Murchison

June 18, 1907
Fort Worth, Texas

Nov. 18, 1992
Atlanta, Georgia

Bishop of Colored (Christian in 1956) **Methodist Episcopal Church, 1954–92; senior bishop, 1974–82.** Murchison married Imogene Ford on August 15, 1930. He entered the ministry in

1920 and pastored in Georgia, Texas, Massachusetts, and Illinois. He taught at Texas College, Tyler, TX, from 1932–35 and edited the *Christian Index* (1946–54), the voice of his denomination. Murchison represented his denomination at the formation of the WCC in Amsterdam and did missionary work in Africa.

John Brondsema

Oct. 17, 1920
Colton, South Dakota

Dec. 8, 1992
Grand Rapids, Michigan

First director of Faith, Bible and Tract League (Tract League), **Grand Rapids, MI, 1941–81**. Brondsema's father, Samuel, was a pastor in Canada; Muskegon, MI; and South Dakota. John started as a Christian schoolteacher, married Margaret Lachnite on January 31, and became a member of Alpine Ave. Christian Reformed Church in Grand Rapids. He started printing a few tracts, but the demand caused him to go full-time in the work in the late 1960s, selling tracts in America, later printing in some foreign countries and making them available free of charge. Heart problems led to his death.

Howard G. Hageman

April 19, 1921
Lynn, Massachusetts

Dec. 20, 1992
New Baltimore, New York

President of New Brunswick (NJ) Theological Seminary, 1973–85. Hageman married Carol Wenneis on September 15, 1945. He pastored at the North Reform Dutch Church, Newark, NJ, from 1945–73. He lectured in South Africa in 1956. He lecured at NBTS from 1961–73. He is interred in Brooklyn, NY. His writings were from *Lily among the Thorns* (1952) to *Posthumous Translation of Pulpit and Table* (1996). His biography is *Remembrance and Hope*.

Paul H. White

Feb. 26, 1910
Bowral, New South Wales, Australia

Dec. 21, 1992
Lindfield, New South Wales, Australia

Missionary doctor to Africa and author of the *Jungle Doctor* series of books. White married Beatrice Bellingham on August 11, 1936. The Whites worked in Tanganyika with the Church Missionary Society, 1937–41, where he was medical superintendent in the hospitals. He was physician to a million Africans and superintendent of seven hospitals in over a 11,000-mile area. He helped bring nearly 800 babies a year into the world. He was forced to retire early because of malaria and asthmatic attacks. Back in Australia, he wrote books, conducted broadcasts, and traveled throughout the continent sharing missionary evangelism. The *Jungle Doctor* books (22 books in the series) were geared to help doctors, nurses, and students in the art of personal evangelism. His *Jungle Doctor* radio programs had a wide following, 1942–1984.

James P. Wesberry

April 16, 1906
Bishopsville, South Carolina

Dec. 25, 1992
Atlanta, Georgia

Executive director of Lord's Day Alliance, Atlanta, GA, 1975–92. Wesberry was the first Baptist to hold the position after nine decades of Presbyterians. In 1988, the LDA celebrated its 100th anniversary. Wesberry was pastor of Morningside Baptist Church, Atlanta, 1944–75. He had an active career among the Southern Baptists, serving as president of the Georgia Baptist Convention, pastor of the SB Pastors Conference, and from 1970–91, was recording secretary of the Georgia Baptist Convention. He was also acting chaplain of the US House of Representatives during the 81st Congress. He married Ruby Perry on September 5, 1929 (died: December, 1941); Mary Latimer on June 1, 1943 (died: September 7, 1982), and Alice Spratlin on October 15, 1983. He wrote from *Prayers in Congress* (1949) to *The Lord's Day* (1986).

John L. Peters

Oct. 6, 1907
Vanburen, Arkansas

Dec. 26, 1992
Aurora, Colorado

Founder and first president of World Neighbors, Oklahoma City, OK, 1951–75. Peters saw the devastating effects of constant hunger, poverty, and disease in Asia during WWII. As an army chaplain during the war, a teenaged soldier bled to death in his arms. There he made a vow to God to help move the world to peace. In April, 1951, Peters preached an impromptu, heartfelt sermon at St. Luke's United Methodist Church in Oklahoma City, OK. He challenged the congregation to "answer the needs of the disinherited, the exploited, the poverty-stricken of soul and body" around the world. His headquarters was first in Columbus, OH, then moved to Oklahoma City in 1961. He started a program that began in India and spread to more than 45 countries, helping more than 25 million people. It became a model for grassroots, community self-help organizations. His wife's name was Maxine. He died from leukemia.

Howard W. Ferrin

Oct. 29, 1898
Auburn, New York

Jan. 12, 1993
E. Providence, Rhode Island

President of Barrington (RI) (Gordon in 1985) **College, 1925–64**. Ferrin was a widely known educator and Bible conference speaker. An MBI graduate of 1919, he had become a Christian at a conference as a high school freshman. He married Florence Cheney on December 31, 1921 (died: 1935), LANCE LATHAM being his best man. He then married Evelyn Fuller on June 1, 1936. He pastored in Providence, RI, from 1936–43, having begun a Bible school there in 1929 with 45 students. The location and the name changed in 1951 from Providence Bible Institute to become Barrington College. He died after a lengthy illness.

R. H. Edwin Espy

Dec. 30, 1908
Portland, Oregon

Jan. 17, 1993
Philadelphia, Pennsylvania

General secretary of the National Council of Churches, 1963–73, and leader in the ecumenical movement. Espy married Cleo Mitchell on September 21, 1944. He was the general secretary of the Student Volunteer Movement (1940–43); executive secretary of the National Student Council of YMCA (1943–55); and associate general secretary of the NCC (1958–63). Espy attended the first three World Convention Assemblies of the WCC: Amsterdam (1948), Evanston (1954) and New Delhi (1961). He wrote *The Religion of College Teachers* (1951) and had Baptist ties.

Franklin A. Broman

March 21, 1899
Duluth, Minnesota

Jan. 21, 1993
Carol Stream, Illinois

Longtime dean of men at Moody Bible Institute, 1937–65. Broman was a graduate of the University of Minnesota in 1922, the year he decided to leave business pursuits for God's service. Ordained a Presbyterian, Broman served as pastor in Austin, MN; Philadelphia, PA, and Minneapolis, MN. He married Martha McKerhan in 1927 and, upon her death, Millicent Guy on March 19, 1989.

Thomas A. Dorsey

July 1, 1899
Villa Rica, Georgia

Jan. 23, 1993
Chicago, Illinois

Dorsey blended his religious music (250 songs) with the blues and became one of the great songwriters of his time. Incidents in Chicago in 1921 and 1926 drew him into Christian music.

The Saints Go Marching In

Dorsey's best-known song was "Precious Lord, Take My Hand," which was translated into more than 50 languages. This song was prompted by a 1932 tragedy when his wife died during childbirth and the baby died the next day. He then married Kathryn Masoley. Dorsey was the director of the choir at Ebenezar/Pilgrim Baptist Church in Chicago for over 35 years, 1931 on. He also wrote "Peace in the Valley," "Just a Closer Walk with Thee" (music by John Hallett), and "I'm Going to Walk Right In." Most of the time, he wrote both lyrics and music. He died of Alzheimer's disease, after his retirement in 1983.

Anthony T. Rossi

Sept. 13, 1900
Messina, Italy

Jan. 24, 1993
Bradenton, Florida

Founder and first president of Bible Alliance Mission (Aurora Mission in 1999), **Bradenton, FL, 1978-92**. Rossi arrived in the U.S. in 1921. Knowing no English, Rossi worked as a machinist's assistant, in a grocery store, a farm, a cafeteria, and then a large restaurant. After reading the Bible in the New York Public Library, he was converted. He went to Florida in 1941 and joined the Methodist Church in Bradenton. In 1947, he founded Tropicana Products, Inc., which, under his leadership, became the largest fresh-chilled orange juice company in the world. He was married to Florence Stark who died on April 21, 1951. In 1978, he established the Aurora Foundation that has funded Christian educational institutions, missions, and many other charities. He also became an evangelist.

Phil Saint

Oct. 19, 1912
Jenkintown, Pennsylvania

Feb. 1993

Missionary to Argentina for 35 years. Phil was another of the famed children of stained glass artist, LAWRENCE SAINT. His brother, NATE, would die at the bloody hands of the Auca Indians. His sister, RACHEL, went into the jungle of the killers to win them for God, and Phil baptized the last of the killers to accept Christ. He was converted as a child and married Ruth Brooker on October 18, 1941. Influenced by PERCY CRAWFORD, he committed his life to Christ under ALBERT HUGHES' encouragement. Saint developed his unique gift as a chalk artist, traveling in evangelistic endeavors. During WWII, he was with the Pocket Testament League throughout Japan. Then came the call to the West Indies and eventually to Argentina, where he had amazing results in Buenos Aires. He ventured into the "tongues movement" and kept his background in evangelical causes, touching many lives. He died in a tractor accident.

Louis Van Ess

Feb. 20, 1915
Grand Rapids, Michigan

Feb. 12, 1993
Grand Rapids, Michigan

First director of Christian Reformed World Relief Committee, 1962–77. Van Ess' goal was business administration after graduating from Calvin College and the University of Michigan. He worked for years in the furniture industry and was part-time instructor in accounting at Calvin College. In 1962, he left the furniture business to devote time to CR missions programs. After working in Harlem, New York, and Rehoboth, NM, Van Ess became convinced of the need for a relief organization in the church. In essence, he was the founder of this entity. His desire was to show the poor how to improve their own destiny.

Ellwood A. Voller

June 12, 1916
Bay City, Missouri

Feb. 20, 1993
Spring Harbor, Michigan

President of Roberts Weslyan College, Rochester, NY, 1957–68 and Spring Arbor (MI) Seminary, 1968–79. A reknowned Free Methodist layman, Voller served in many civic and church functions. Known as "Woody"

Voller, he served in WWII, then got involved at Michigan State University as assistant dean of students, up until his 1957 call to Roberts. Upon retiring from college administration, he was manager of a gold mining company in Colorado as well as an Angora Goat Company.

James H. "Jim" Smith

Aug. 9, 1935
Charleston, West Virginia

Feb. 22, 1993
Dallas, Texas

Executive director of the Family Life Counseling Center, Highland Park Presbyterian Church, Dallas, TX. Smith excelled as a counselor, speaker, author, and teacher. He married Janet Morrison on June 5, 1958. He directed YFC in Wichita, KS (1959–71) and in Detroit, MI (1971–74). In 1974, he went to Dallas, TX, to direct Child Evangelism activities, which led to the founding of the Family Life Center in 1979. He wrote *Learning to Live with the One You Love*. He died of cancer.

Roy S. Nicholson

July 12, 1903
Walhalla, South Carolina

March 2, 1993
High Point, North Carolina

President of Wesleyan Methodist Church in America (Wesleyan Church in 1968), **1947–59, the only full-time president in WMC history**. A group of general superintendents led the denomination after 1959. Nicholson married Ethel Macy on June 26, 1924 (died: December, 1985), and Winifred Bisbing of Cedar Falls, IA, in October, 1986. Ordained in 1925, he pastored WM churches in East Radford, VA (1925–26); Long Shoals, NC (1926–30); Kannapolis, NC (1930–35); and later in Brooksville, FL (1969–74). He was the Sunday school secretary and editor (1935–39), then vice president of the denomination (1939–47). He was professor of Bible at Central (SC) Wesleyan College, 1959–68. His writings were from *Wesleyan Methodism in the South* (1933) to *True Holiness* (1985). In later years, he lived in High Point, NC.

Sherman E. Johnson

March 7, 1908
Hutchinson, Kansas

March 24, 1993
Berkeley, California

President of Church Divinity School of the Pacific, Berkeley, CA 1951–1971. Johnson married Jean Rogers on June 10, 1935. Ordained an Episcopalian in 1933, he pastored Trinity Church, Belvidere, IL; tutored at Seabury-Western Theological Seminary (1933–36); was professor of NT at Nashotah House (1936–40), and professor of the same at Episcopal Theological Seminary, Cambridge, MA (1941–50). His first book was *The Septuagint Translators of Amos* (1936).

Marian Anderson (Fisher)

Feb. 27, 1902
Philadelphia, Pennsylvania

April 8, 1993
Portland, Oregon

Black contralto who had no equal in her time. Anderson received her musical training in the States and abroad, growing up singing in Union Baptist Church, Philadelphia. After making her debut in 1924, she gave several hundred widely acclaimed concerts in Europe, 1929 and 1933–35, before she was recognized properly in the States at a New York City recital (December 30, 1935). She was the first African American to sing with the Metropolitan Opera Company. By 1941 she was one of America's top concert artists. Anderson sang at the Lincoln Memorial on Easter Sunday morning, 1943, to over 75,000 people. She married Orpheus H. Fisher on July 24, 1943, and lived in Danbury, CT. She appeared in 1955 in Verdi's *The Masked Ball*.

Arthur C. McGiffert Jr.

Nov. 27, 1892
Cincinnati, Ohio

April 9, 1993
Clearmont, California

President of Chicago (IL) Theological Seminary, 1946–58. McGiffert married Elisabeth Eliot on May 29, 1917. He was ordained in the Congregational Church in 1917 and pastored All Souls Church, Lowell, MA, from 1920–26. He then was professor of Christian theology at CTS (1926–39), before taking the presidency of Pacific School of Religion, Berkeley, CA (1939–46). McGiffert wrote from *Jonathan Edwards* (1932) to *Young Emerson Speaks* (1938). He retired at Mount Desert, Maine.

Marlyn Northfelt

Dec. 16, 1915
Minneapolis, Minnesota

April 10, 1993
Sarasota, Florida

President of Garrett Theological Seminary, 1970–74, renamed Garrett Evangelical Theological Seminary, Evanston, IL 1974–80, as result of merging with ETS. Northfelt married Dorothy Underwood on October 11, 1938. He was ordained to the Methodist ministry in 1945. Northfelt pastored in Yorkville, IL (1943–51); Lake Bluff, IL (1951–61); and was district superintendent of the Northern Illinois Conference, Chicago (1965–70). He was active in community affairs in his Sarasota, FL, retirement days.

William P. Fenn

Aug. 31, 1902
New Rochelle, New York

April 21, 1993
Doylestown, Pennsylvania

General secretary of United Board for Christian Higher Education in Asia, New York City, 1958–70. Fenn spent his early years in Asia where his parents were missionaries with the Presbyterian Board of Foreign Missions. He taught English at the North China American School in Tunghsien, China, 1923–26. From 1928–30, he was an associate professor of English at Berea (KY) College. He returned to China as head of the Department of Foreign Languages at the University of Nanking, 1932 and 1938, then joined the university in exile in Chengtu, Szechwan while enduring the war with Japan. In 1942, he was director of the UB's China Office. From 1947–58, he served as associate and executive secretary in the UB ministries. Fenn went throughout China "by postal truck…rail…riverboat…wheelbarrow, chair, or plain shank's mare…," seeking out the exiled China colleges. He married Frances L. Cocks on August 21, 1929 (died: 1964), and Priscilla H. Neff in 1967 (died: 1984).

Peter (Pat) J. Zondervan

April 2, 1909
Paterson, New Jersey

May 6, 1993
Boca Raton, Florida

Cofounder of the most successful Christian publishing company ever, and president of the Gideon's, 1956–58. Zondervan and his brother, BERNIE (who preceded him in death), founded the work in their bedroom in Grandville, MI, in 1932. He married Mary Swier on May 24, 1934. His list of ministries includes: Singspiration Music; a Christian radio station in Holland, MI; Christian Business Men's Committee; Winona Lake (IN) Assembly; Maranatha Bible Conference, Muskegon, MI, etc., via board membership, chairmanship, and financial interests. The city of Grand Rapids, MI, honored him with a P. J. Zondervan Day in December, 1973. Zondervan Publishing employed 1,400 at his death.

C. Elijah Autrey

Sept. 17, 1904
Columbia, Mississippi

May 8, 1993
Pensacola, Florida

Director of Evangelism for the Home Mission Board of the Southern Baptist Convention, 1960 on. Autrey's voice was most effective in evangelism for nearly half a century. He was converted in a revival in a small rural church near Winnfield, LA. He married Mae Bradford on January 31, 1925. He pastored Tullos (LA) Baptist Church, (1929–35); Temple Baptist of Ruston, LA (1935–38); FBC of Union City, TN (1938–41) and FBC of West Monroe, LA (1941–48), where he took in 1,300 members. He was secretary of evangelism for Louisiana (1948–51), then moved to Dallas to be associate to C. E. MATTHEWS in the Division of Evangelism of the HMB (1952–55). At Southwestern Theological Seminary, 1955–60, Autrey was professor of evangelism. He preached several two-week meetings in various places with attendance as high as 10,000 at a single meeting. His first book, *Basic Evangelism* (1959), has been translated into several languages. He traveled widely around the world in evangelism endeavors.

William H. Bentley

June 13, 1923
Chicago, Illinois

May 16, 1993
Chicago, Illinois

Cofounder and first director of National Black Evangelical Association, 1963–93. Bentley was converted at age 19 while stationed with the army in Colorado. Bentley was the first black Master of Divinity graduate at Fuller Theological Seminary in 1959. His group was formed in 1963 as the National Negro Evangelical Association, and by his death, it had 500 members. He pastored at Calvary Bible Church in Chicago's west side for 20 years. In 1951, he married Theo Jones (died: 1964), then Ruth Lewis on January 22, 1971. He was president of the NBEA (1970–76), and board chairman (1976–82). Bentley was president of the United Pentecostal Council of the Assemblies of God, Inc. Cambridge, MA from 1981–89. He taught black history and theology at several well-known colleges and seminaries. Bentley was associate pastor at Zion Temple Pentecostal Church, Chicago, 1984–93. He died of a heart attack as he was preaching on "The Love of God" at Progressive Beulah Pentecostal Church in Chicago. His last words were, "I see angels flying around."

Al Metsker

July 29, 1921
near Toronto, Kansas

May 26, 1993
Kansas City, Missouri

One of the century's great youth leaders, Metsker led a model program of youth rallies and Bible clubs in Kansas City, MO, 1943–87, interrupted briefly by a three-way bypass heart surgery in 1976. At age 18, Metsker came to Kansas City, and attended Central Bible Church, where Pastor Walter Wilson led him to the Lord on Easter Sunday, 1940. On June 19, 1943, he conducted his first Youth For Christ rally. He married Vidy Hughes one week later on June 26, 1943. Saturday night rallies, with 2,000 in attendance, continued for 45 years. The High School Bible Club movement started in 1945 and the Bible quiz program in 1946. More than 250,000 were converted during this span. He was active in YFC most of his days but worked with Youth Evangelism Association in later years.

Robert E. Cushman

Dec. 26, 1913
Fall River, Massachusetts

June 9, 1993
Rockport, Maine

Dean of Duke University Divinity School, Durham, NC, 1958–71. Cushman married Barbara Edgecomb on September 12, 1936. He was the son of Bishop RALPH CUSHMAN. He had two pastorates: in South Meridian, CT, from 1936–40; and Hamilton, NY, in 1941. He became an instructor in theology at Yale (1942–43); professor of religion at University of Oregon (1943–45) and professor of systematic theology at Duke University Divinity School (1945–58). He was a delegate to the WCC in London, Sweden (1952); Montreal, Quebec (1963) and an observer at the Second Vatican Council, 1963–65. He wrote widely. He stayed at Duke as research professor (1971–79) and lecturer in residence (1980–84). He was very active in Methodist church endeavors.

John R. Mumaw

March 12, 1904
Wayne County, Ohio

June 20, 1993
Harrisonburg, Virginia

President of Eastern Mennonite College and Seminary, Harrisonburg, VA, 1948–65. Mumaw came to Harrisonburg and EMS in 1920, and except for two years when he taught school in Ohio, he remained in Harrisonburg until his death. He became a faculty member in 1927, teaching English and Bible courses, later serving as dean of men and then campus pastor. On May 30, 1928, he married Evelyn King. When he became president, the school achieved accreditation and its enrollment more than doubled. Mumaw was also a pastor at various times, including 20 years at Lindale Mennonite Church near Harrisonburg and as founding pastor of the Dayton (VA) Mennonite Church. He did evangelism work and was a leader in the Virginia Mennonite Conference.

Bruce Dunn

Jan. 14, 1919
Toronto, Ontario, Canada

July 15, 1993
Champaign/Urbana, Illinois

Pastor of Grace Presbyterian Church, Peoria, IL, for 40 years. Dunn conducted the *Grace Worship Hour* broadcast beginning on radio (1951) and on television (1974). He died of a heart attack.

Demos Shakarian

July 21, 1913
Downey, California

July 23, 1993
Downey, California

Founder and first director of Full Gospel Men's Business Fellowship, 1952–93. This powerful group rivaled and eventually surpassed the non-Charismatic Christian Business Men's Committee. Shakarian was a highly successful dairy farmer and businessman brought up in the Armenian Pentecostal Church. Growing up in Los Angeles, he received healing for a hearing defect at age 13. In 1933, he married Rose Gabrellian. He began to organize gospel meetings. In 1945, over 20,000 came to the Hollywood Bowl. He then headed a 16-day campaign with Oral Roberts in 1951. In December, 1951, he held his first businessmen's breakfast with 18 attending. In January, 1952, it was incorporated. In October, 1954, the first national convention drew 600 men. In 1956, Canada joined ranks and soon it spread around the world. In 1965, a world convention was hosted in London. He was president till 1993, surviving a coup in 1989. He died of heart failure.

J. Mauldin Lesesne

Sept. 25, 1899
Kingstree, South Carolina

July 28, 1993
Due West, South Carolina

President of Erskine College, Due West, SC, 1954–66. Lesesne married Henrietta Fennell on November 13, 1935. He taught history at Rock Hill and Greenville, SC, high schools, 1921–40. Next, he headed the history department at Erskine College, 1940–54, before becoming president. Lesesne was a Presbyterian.

Paul B. Henry

July 9, 1942
Chicago, Illinois

July 31, 1993
Grand Rapids, Michigan

House of Representatives highly respected evangelical member. Henry was elected to his fifth congressional term in 1992, just 13 days after a three-inch malignant tumor was removed from his brain during emergency surgery. In an emotional moment, he was sworn in from a wheelchair during the January 5th, Washington D.C. Capitol ceremony, which was his last appearance on Capitol Hill. He was the son of theologian, CARL F. H. HENRY. Henry married Karen Borthistle on August 28, 1965. He was a professor at Calvin College, 1970–78, and long-time member of LaGrave Ave. Christian Reformed Church, Grand Rapids, MI. Before going to Washington, D.C. in 1985, he was in Michigan politics in Lansing, MI, from 1979–85. His book, *Christian Social Ethics*, revealed the importance of relating Christian faith to the political order. He died of brain cancer.

David Nettleton

Aug. 24, 1918
Philadelphia, Pennsylvania

Aug. 3, 1993
Lakeland, Florida

President of Faith Baptist Bible College, Ankeny, IA 1967–80 and GARB council member for 24 years. He headed Omaha (NE) Baptist Bible College, 1965–67, and led in the transfer from Omaha in 1967. Nettleton and his wife were both converted by witnessing students from Juniata College, Huntingdon, PA. On October 4, 1941, he married Ruth Ann Davis. He pastored the Peters Creek Baptist Church, Library, PA (1943–45), and then directed Pittsburgh Youth for Christ (1945–47). Then it was a series of pastorates—Endicott, NY (1947–53); Grace Baptist Church, Springfield, MA (1953–63); and Grandview Baptist, Des Moines, IA (1963–65). Following his educational ministry, Nettleton went back to pastoring, Parsippany, NJ (1980–85), and Fellowship Baptist, Lakeland, FL (1985–93). From 1988 on, he was chairman of the GARB council. He became ill with cancer in February, 1993, which claimed his life later in the year.

Vern Schild

Nov. 13, 1902
Siuox County, Iowa

August 4, 1993
Waterloo, Iowa

Founder and first director of Self Help, Waverly, IA, 1959–85. Schild married Marjorie Vosseller on December 11, 1932. In the early 1940s, he built a small machine out of used parts to load lime trucks. In 1943, he started manufacturing small, highly mobile machines for small contractors. The company grew to 650 employees. In 1963, this Schild-Bantam Company was merged into the Koehring Company of Milwaukee. Because of his own business success, Schild saw the need for small, inexpensive farm machinery for use in third world countries. Tractors and other equipment were donated to people in more than 50 countries. He was active in the Trinity United Methodist Church of Waverly.

Cornelius Keur

May 12, 1913
Muskegon, Michigan

Aug. 17, 1993
Phoenix, Arizona

Radio manager of station KAIM in Hawaii for many years. Keur had an unusual and varied career. He was converted in Muskegon, Feb. 27, 1927, at a meeting where Casey VanderJagt spoke. After graduating from MBI, Keur spent time in the Navy (1943–45), then returned to the WMBI staff and provided music in YFC endeavors (1945–48). He went to Hawaii in 1948, directing its YFC ministry until 1953. On April 16, 1950 he married Ferne Pennington (born: April 29, 1917)

He then established the radio ministry in 1953 (AM in 1956) and directed it for many years. Later they became a part of the Billy Graham Association. He wrote the music for "Satisfied with Jesus" and "Wonderful Savior."

Neil MacAulay

Sept. 22, 1919
Detroit, Michigan

Aug. 21, 1993
Chattanooga, Tennessee

Director of New Life Ministries, Chattanooga, TN. Neil and his wife, Pat, spent a half century getting the gospel out all over the world in 40 countries as well as 50 states. Neil was an evangelist and trumpeter, and Pat played the piano and organ, cowbells, accordion, and vibraharp. Their ministry was well received with huge responses in India. He married Pat Woodard on August 24, 1945. In early years, they traveled with evangelist JACKIE BURRIS. They lived in Boca Raton, FL (1955–54) directing much of the music at the Bible Conferences there (1957–70). They moved to Chattanooga in 1984. Their daughter, Darlene, married radio/TV host John Ankerberg. MacAulay died of Parkinson's disease, a week after breaking his hip.

Edward L. R. Elson

Dec. 23, 1906
Monongahela, Pennsylvania

Aug. 25, 1993
Washington, D.C.

Chaplain of the U.S. Senate, 1969–81. Elson pastored National Presbyterian Church, Washington, D.C., and baptized President EISENHOWER. He married Frances Sandys on May 22, 1929 (died: December, 1933) and Helen Chittick on February 8, 1937. Ordained a Presbyterian in 1930, Elson pastored the First Presbyterian Church of La Jolla, CA (1931–41); the National Presbyterian Church, Washington, D.C. (1946–73); and served as pastor emeritus, 1973 on. His writings range from *One Moment with God* (1951) to *Wide Was His Parish* (1986). Elson belonged to many clubs and received numerous honors. He died in the local Presbyterian hospital of heart failure and complications from Parkinson's disease. His sketch in *Who Was Who in America* (vol. 11, p. 84) is very lengthy.

Herbert R. Tyler

Dec. 20, 1914
Portland, Oregon

Aug. 30, 1993
Eureka, California

Evangelist. Tyler was converted at home on September 12, 1926 at the age of eleven. Six years in the armed forces coupled with time spent working in logging and construction camps of the great Northwest gave him a diversified background and unique insights. He married Cathy Barnes on July 15, 1939. He was active in many areas: evangelist, world traveler, humorist, high school assembly speaker, pastor 1945–62, and youth evangelist. He was heavily involved with Youth For Christ, and the rest of his life in evangelism. Tyler preached in 33 countries and 49 states, at times utilizing radio and TV to spread his message.

Charles E. Strauser

June 4, 1917
Luzerne, Pennsylvania

Aug. 31, 1993
West Chester, Pennsylvania

First director of Full Gospel Assemblies Int., Parkersburg, PA, 1962–93. Strauser served as a pastor with the Assemblies of God in churches in Pennsylvania and North Carolina. He pastored the Full Gospel Church, Coatesville, PA, from 1952–62. Strauser authored various Biblical studies now included within the curriculum of Full Gospel Bible Institute, Coatesville, PA. The organization which he founded serves ministers, church ministries, and congregations in 27 countries. In 1983, FGC moved to the Full Gospel Ministries complex in Parkesburg, PA, where he served as pastor until his death.

Winfield F. Ruelke
Uncle Win

Dec. 18, 1908
Winfield, Long Island, New York

Sept. 10, 1993
Nanticoke, Pennsylvania

Founder and first director of Children's Bible Fellowship, Carmel, NY, 1942–85. Win's ministry provided materials, training, and programs for Good News clubs, Hobby clubs, Bible clubs, street tracts and ministry, beach story time, Sunday school conferences, teacher training and workshops, and children's correspondence courses. He married May (Marion) Torge on October 10, 1936. In 1939, Ruelke began major camping programs, beginning at Lakeside Bible Conference, Holmes, NY, for children and youth. Later, property was purchased in Kent Cliffs, NY. A radio ministry began on December 5, 1943, known as *Uncle Win's Bible Hour*. In 1953, Pocket Testament League asked Ruelke to spearhead youth programs across the world. He visited more than 50 countries sharing his faith, vision, and expertise, meeting the physical and spiritual needs of children and youth. Hopetown School was born in 1956.

Ivan E. Olsen

May 19, 1914
Virginia, Minnesota

Sept. 21, 1993
North Platte, Nebraska

Founder and first president of Berean Fundamental Churches, 1932–53. Olsen was led to Christ by Evangelist Dick Zet. Following school at Denver Bible Institute, he spent his summers in northwest Colorado as an itinerant preacher in 13 villages. At his ordination in Denver in June, 1936, he testified that he had been called by God to establish Berean Fundamental Churches. Soon 16 Berean churches were started within a 150 mile radius of North Platte and a small denomination began. He married Alice Gustafson on November 11, 1937. Olsen pastored the North Platte Berean Church, 1936–79, and founded the Maranatha Bible Camp in 1938, directing it for 51 years.

Muriel Benson Dennis

April 27, 1914
Minneapolis, Minnesota

Sept. 30, 1993
Wheaton, Illinois

President of Good News Publishers/Crossway Books, Westchester, IL, 1962–85. When Muriel's husband died on February 14, 1962, she kept the vision for 25 years, and increased the ministry, Good News Publishing and Press/Crossway Books, in an ever-widening outreach. She married CLYDE DENNIS on June 12, 1937, and he became the "Father of the Modern Tract." They moved to California in 1953, where her husband died. Muriel returned from California to Westchester, IL. In 1979, Cornerstone Books (Crossway Books became a division), featured FRANCIS SCHAEFFER's *Christian Manifesto*. Lane Dennis, their son, became president in 1987. Muriel lived twelve days after a main artery to her heart ruptured.

William T. Snyder

Dec. 4, 1917
Altoona, Pennsylvania

Oct. 2, 1993
Ephrata, Pennsylvania

Director of Mennonite Central Committee, Akron, OH, 1958–82. Snyder entered MCC service in 1943 as a civilian public service volunteer and was assigned to Luray, VA. He married Lucille M. Steiner in 1944. In 1945, he became director of MCC's Aid Section, which brought 14,000 refugees from Europe to the Americas. During his tenure as director, workers with MCC grew from 497 to 850. They had three children. He attended Bethel Mennonite Church, Lancaster, PA.

Wilmos Csehy

Feb. 10, 1914
Phillipsburg, New Jersey

Oct. 5, 1993
Muncy, Pennsylvania

Greatly used violinist, who began to study at age three. Csehy was converted at age ten. He used a violin made in 1772 in Milan, Italy. He and his wife, Gladys, held concerts across the country, adding a series of gifted female soloists to their team. Gladys was a pianist and played the bells. They started a music camp and school in Muncy, PA, training hundreds. They were featured at numerous evangelical crusades and conferences and arranged the music for "Give Me Oil in My Lamp."

Arie R. Brouwer

July 14, 1935
Inwood, Iowa

Oct. 7, 1993
Teaneck, New Jersey

General Secretary of National Council of Churches, 1985–89, and stated clerk of Reformed Church in America, 1977–83. Brouwer led the NCC during a time of reorganization and downsizing due to financial problems. Brouwer married Harriet Korver on August 16, 1955, and was ordained to the Reformed Church ministry in 1959. He pastored in Michigan (1959–63); New Jersey (1963–68); was secretary to a couple denominational organizations (1968–83), including executive secretary of the denomination (1970–77). He was active in NCC and WCC activities, working out of his NYC office.

Howard Sugden

April 4, 1907
Kingston, Michigan

Oct. 14, 1993
Lansing, Michigan

Outstanding pastor and Bible conference speaker. Sugden was converted as an older teenager in a revival in Mayville, MI, conducted by evangelist B. H. Kady. He attended Johnson Bible School and Winona Lake (IN) Seminary where he met his wife, Lucille Miller, whom he married on December 21, 1928. Sixty years of pastoring followed: Peru(MI) Baptist (1929–34); Ganson St. Baptist, Jackson, MI (1934–51); London, Ontario, (1951–54); and then at South Baptist, Lansing, MI (1954–89). He died of complications of Parkinson's disease four years after retirement. He often spoke at such places as Moody Founder's Week Conferences, and was widely acclaimed beyond his local influence.

Homer Hummel

June 12, 1928
Quincy, Illinois

Oct. 19, 1993
Los Angeles, California

Director of Airmail from God (Trans World Missions in 1979), **1958–78.** Hummel graduated from high school at age 15 and from the University of Southern California at age 18. He married Eilene Huffman on April 9, 1949. His wife's brother, NYLES HUFFMAN, had started Airmail from God, and Hummel kept it going. The name of this mission changed to Trans World Missions, and he obtained the services of JOHN and Linnie OLSON to promote the work by radio. His life was divided into two busy segments. First, he was teacher of math and music at Fairfax High School in LA, for 40 years, 1948–88. Second, he took over the reins of the mission organization, administrating in the afternoons. Hummel also served as minister of music at Angelus Temple, 1953–72. Diabetes and a stroke finally took his life.

Lloyd W. Dahlquist

April 6, 1906
Wheaton, Minnesota

Oct. 24, 1993
Carol Stream, Illnois

General Secretary (president) of Baptist General Conference, 1959–69. Dahlquist was converted at age ten in a Tabernacle service in Duluth, MN. He married Ruth Ostrom on August 27, 1930. After graduation from Bethel Theological Seminary in 1928, he pastored BCC churches in

Clinton Falls and Little Falls, MN (1931–35); Montclair, NJ (1935–40), and Waukegan, IL (1940–42), prior to 3 ½ years service as army air corps chaplain during WWII. He pastored at Northwest Baptist Church, Chicago, IL (1946–59) and later at Calvary Baptist Church, Evanston, IL (1969–76).

W. Warren Filkin

Sept. 17, 1907
Kansas City, Missouri

Nov. 3, 1993
Wheaton, Illinois

Educator and conference speaker whose ministry as a **gospel magician** gave him an extended outreach in many meetings. Filkin was led to Christ as a junior in high school by a student that WALTER WILSON had won to the Lord a year before. On September 8, 1933, he married Marian Quick (died: 1981) and Esther Wyzenbeek on August 17, 1982. Early on, he helped in missions, county farms, and hospitals in the Kansas area, served on the faculty of MBI (1942–48), was professor of Christian education at Northern Baptist Seminary (1948–68) and at Trinity Evangelical Seminary (1968–74), when he became associate pastor to Warren Wiersbe at Moody Church (1974–81). He is featured in a gospel film production, *Quicker than the Eye*. Filkin had five children and was a member at FBC, Wheaton, IL. He died shortly after suffering a massive stroke.

Wesley Olsen

Jan. 23, 1925
Brooklyn, New York

Nov. 13, 1993
Phoenix, Arizona

President of Southwestern Baptist Bible College, Phoenix, AZ, 1983–93, and Accrediting Association of Bible Colleges, 1986–88. Raised in a Christian home, Olsen began pastoring at Christ Baptist, Brooklyn, NY, from 1946–51. On September 30, 1950, he married Elaine Nasshan. He then pastored Hillside (NJ) Baptist, 1951–58, while serving part-time at Northeastern Bible College. He was vice president of the same (CHARLES ANDERSON was president), 1958–79, and also active in Brookdale Baptist Church, Bloomfield, NJ. He had open heart surgery, but continued his educational leadership as academic dean and vice president of Lancaster (PA) Bible College, 1979–81. While at SBBC, his wife taught as well. His teaching efforts were in theology and Bible doctrines. He was an interim pastor in Sedona, AZ, from 1991–93. His death came as a result of prostate cancer.

Harold E. Westerhoff

Sept. 14, 1915
Hawthorne, New Jersey

Dec. 5, 1993
Wayne, New Jersey

General secretary of Christian Endeavor (World), 1954–66, and (Int.), 1956–66. Westerhoff was decorated with a Bronze Star for action in WWII. He was in various business enterprises most of his life, such as office comptroller for the Eclipse-Pioneer Division of the Bendix Aviation Corporation. He was in the forefront, fighting the liquor industry and opposing Communism.

Norman P. Grubb

Aug. 2, 1895
London, England

Dec. 15, 1993
Ft. Washington, Pennsylvania

Director of Worldwide Evangelization Crusade, 1931–63. Grubb was one of the most respected leaders in missions of his time. On November 24, 1919, he married Pauline Studd (died: 1981), the daughter of the famed C.T. STUDD, and they had three children. He was wounded as an officer in the British Army in WWI. At 19, he was converted in his room after an army major witnessed to him. The couple ministered in Belgian Congo (Zaire), 1919–27, and returned to London shortly before STUDD's death. In 1931, adverse circumstances had brought the mission to a place of almost total collapse. Grubb's 30 workers remained. The total income for one month was $250. Friends advised him to close the work, but he refused to quit. Slowly but surely, by faith, it grew to 1,000 workers in 40 countries of the world. This was a modern missionary miracle.

Adam W. Miller

Dec. 30, 1896
Baltimore, Maryland

Dec. 22, 1993
Anderson, Indiana

President of Church of God Missionary Board, Anderson, IN 1933–47, and dean of Anderson School of Theology, 1953–62. Confirmed as a Lutheran, Miller began to attend the Church of God in Anderson, IN, and was ordained into their ministry in 1918. He pastored the Church of God, Washington, D.C. (1919) and in Baltimore (1920). He married Grace Young in 1921 and from 1922–27, they served in Japan. Miller then pastored in Federalsburg, MA, from 1927–33. He became a professor of the Bible at Anderson (IN) College (1945), going full time (1948). He was also chairman of the Missionary Board, 1951–67. The chapel of Anderson University School of Theology was named in his honor. He wrote the books, *Introduction to the New Testament* (1942) and *Introduction to the Old Testament* (1976).

Norman V. Peale

May 31, 1898
Bowersville, Ohio

Dec. 24, 1993
Pauley, New York

Pastor of the Marble Collegiate Church, New York City, 1932-93. Peale had a powerful following through his writings, specifically *Guideposts Magazine*, with 1½ million circulation. Graduating from Boston University, he became pastor of Kings Highway Methodist, Brooklyn (1924-27), and of University Methodist Church, Syracuse, NY (1927-32). His New York City church grew from 200 to 4,000. He married Ruth Stafford on June 20, 1930. He and SMILEY BLANTON co-founded the BLANTON-Peale Institute of Religion and Psychiatry, New York City, in 1937. Peale's most renowned book was *The Power of Positive Thinking* (1952). His books feature humor, humility, and humanity, and encourage positive thinking—a forerunner of Robert Shuler's ministry a generation later. For years, his sermons and booklets went to 300,000 in 50 states and 106 foreign countries each month. The *Art of Living* was a radio broadcast he had for 40 years. He was elected president of the Reformed Church in America in 1969. He wrote from *A Guide for Confident Living* (1948) to *Positive Thinking Every Day* (1993).

Ira Stanphill

Feb. 14, 1914
Bellview, New Mexico

Dec. 30, 1993
Overland Park, Kansas

Inspirational songwriter. Stanphill distinguished himself as a young man becoming a singing evangelist in the Assemblies of God. He was converted at age twelve at a church service. From 1930-34, he sang on a daily radio program, over KGGF in Coffeeville, KS. In 1946 he entered full-time evangelism. He formed his own company, Hymn Time, in 1938, which was sold to ZONDERVAN in 1967. He pastored Rockwood Park Assembly of God, Fort Worth, TX, in 1966. His wives names were Zelma, killed in an automobile accident, and Gloria. He eventually preached and sang the gospel in all sections of the country and in 40 nations. He wrote and composed some 400 songs, including "Mansion over the Hilltop," "Room at the Cross for You," "Supper Time," "Follow Me," "I Know Who Holds Tomorrow," "Happiness Is the Lord," "God Has His Way in It All," "He Washed My Eyes with Tears," "Inside Those Pearly Gates," "Jesus and Me," "Unworthy," "We'll Talk It Over," "You Can Have a Song," "Thirty Pieces of Silver," and the chorus "God Can Do Anything But Fail."

Richard V. Moore

Nov. 20, 1906
Quincy, Florida

Jan. 2, 1994
Daytona Beach, Florida

President of Bethune-Cookman College, Daytona Beach, FL, 1947–75. Moore began his career at Pinellas High School, Clearwater, FL (1932–34); then was principal of Union Academy, Tarpon Springs, FL (1934–37); of Rosenwald High School, Panama City, FL (1937–44); BOOKER T. WASHINGTON High School, Pensacola, FL (1944–45); and state supervisor of Negro secondary schools (1945–47). Moore was very active in Methodist circles all his life. He brought international recognition to BCC for its contribution to higher education.

Samuel H. Sutherland

Sept. 4, 1900
Santa Rosa, California

Jan. 21, 1994
Carol Stream, Illinois

President of Bible Institute of Los Angeles (CA), 1952–70, and first president of Accrediting Association of Bible Colleges, 1947–51, 1964–67. Sutherland was a Presbyterian pastor at Grace Presbyterian Church in Hollywood, CA (1927–37, and Calvary Presbyterian there (1938–41). He became dean at BIOLA 1942–52, working under LOUIS TALBOT. Besides the AABC he was active in the IFCA.

Ed Darling

Sept. 30, 1914
Battle Creek, Michigan

Jan. 29, 1994
Detroit, Michigan

Director of Voice of Christian Youth (VCY), Detroit, 1941–59, this rally and club program became one of the largest Youth For Christ ministries in the world. Darling worked for Kelvinator Corporation prior to this, marrying Virginia Richards October 12, 1940. From 1959–61, he directed the Christian Supper Club, known as the Crossroads, a combination restaurant and Christian entertainment center. He was then in public relations for the Institute of Technology till 1984, after which he helped Al Kuhnle in Young River Ministries. He died following a second massive stroke.

James McLeish

Dec. 18, 1921
Clydebank, Scotland

Jan. 29, 1994
Kissimmee, Florida

President of Inter-Varsity, 1981–85. McLeish came to Canada in his youth and was converted at the People's Church, Montreal, under the preaching of evangelist JOHN LINTON in his mid-20's. He married Roberta McCarntey on October 4, 1946. Leaving the business world, he went to Inter-Varsity in 1952 and stayed a lifetime. He went from accounting to comptroller to vice president and then to president. His talents were in business systems and in the management of funds. After a brief time of retirement, he suffered congenital heart failure.

Walter H. Judd

Sept. 25, 1898
Rising City, Nebraska

Feb. 13, 1994
Mitchelville, Maryland

Represented Minnesota in the House of Representatives, 1943–63. Judd served in WWI (1918–19) and then became a Congregational Church medical missionary in China (1925–38). He served in Fukion (Fujian) Province (1926–31) and in Fenchow (Fenzhou) Province (1934–37). He married Miriam Barber on March 13, 1932. He lectured on foreign policy throughout the states (1938–40), warning of the potential Japanese aggression in over 1,400 speeches, and served as a doctor

The Saints Go Marching In

and surgeon in Minneapolis (1941–42). He gave the keynote address at the Republican Convention in 1960. He vigorously defended the Chinese Nationalist Church. He died of cancer.

Stephen D. Herron Jr.

June 19, 1917
West Blockton, Alabama

Feb. 25, 1994
Charlotte, North Carolina

First president of Hobe Sound (FL) Bible College, 1960–85. Hobe Sound Christian Academy came into being in 1961 under his leadership. Herron was conference president of the Wesleyan Methodist Churches of Alabama and served pastorates in Alabama, South Carolina, Tennessee, and Florida. Herron served as an evangelist and Bible teacher for many camp meetings. He edited a number of periodicals and wrote numerous articles and tracts. His funeral was held at the Bible Methodist Church, Pell City, AL.

Robert O. Schmidt

June 6, 1918
Wilmore, Kentucky

March 4, 1994
Arlington, Texas

Director of World Baptist Fellowship Missions, Arlington, TX 1962–84. Schmidt married Nadine Heide on August 14, 1941. His father was a Methodist preacher, but he was saved in 1944, at age 25, at a Baptist revival in Anthony, KS. He pastored four churches, 1947–54 (three in Kansas and one in Ft. Collins, Colorado). At the last church, he was challenged to go to the mission field by G. CHRISTIAN WEISS. They spent 1954–62 in France, starting a church and laboring in a difficult area. His 22 years in leadership of WBFM saw the mission personnel grow from twelve families to 82 familes. He had a heart attack in 1978 and his health was never good thereafter. After his tenure as director, he went to New Zealand for six months to work in missions.

Earl K. Oldham

April 16, 1920
Hereford, Texas

March 9, 1994
Grand Prairie, Texas

President of Arlington (TX) Baptist College, 1953–80. Oldham was a leader in the World Baptist Fellowship and a key figure in the continuing ministry of J. FRANK NORRIS. He pastored Calvary Baptist Church, Grand Prairie, TX, from 1945–90. He was responsible for several buildings at ABC in the days of its expansion. He wrote the book *Sail On*, a history of WBF. He is buried in Arlington, TX.

William W. Gothard Sr.

Oct. 17, 1905
Chicago, Illinois

March 17, 1994
LaGrange, Illinois

Executive director of Gideons, 1950–55. Gothard was converted listening to Billy Graham on the radio. He married Carmen Torres (November 15, 1908–January 19, 2000) on May 14, 1931, at Brookfield (IL) Methodist Church. They were both saved around 1943. Their home soon became the center of several Christian ministries: Pioneer Girls, Hi-Crusader Bible Clubs, Ambassador Sunday School Classes, and Campus Teams (Institute in Basic Youth Conflicts). They had six children. His son, Bill Gothard Jr., leads one of the largest Christian ministries in the world, Institute for Basic Life Principles in Oakbrook, IL. Gothard Sr. also served as executive director of Chicago Christian Businessmen's Committee (1955–60); board chairperson of Chicago's Pacific Garden Mission; and director of Chicago's Child Evangelism (1960–65). Soon thereafter, Gothard Sr. joined his son's ministry as a comptroller and watched God do amazing things without asking for funds.

J. Floyd Williams

October 12, 1924
Greenville, North Carolina

March 27, 1994
Greenville, North Carolina

General superintendent of Pentecostal Holiness Church, 1969–75, renamed International PHC, 1975–81; president of National Association of Evangelicals, 1980–81; and chairman of Pentecostal Fellowship of North America, 1976–78. In 1943, Williams married Bonnie Ashburn. Their 19 years of pastoral ministry began as pastor of Emmanuel Church, Raleigh, NC. He led in the relocation of the headquarters of IPHC from Franklin Springs, GA, to Oklahoma City, OK. He served as one of four assistant general superintendents, 1962–69, and was world missions director for his denomination, 1965–69.

John H. Kromminga

Aug. 25, 1918
Grundy Center, Iowa

March 31, 1994
Grand Rapids, Michigan

President of Calvin Theological Seminary, Grand Rapids, MI, 1956–83. Kromminga married Claire Otten (June 17, 1919–February 2, 1995), and they had three children. After graduating from Calvin, he pastored Christian Reformed Churches in Newton, NJ (1943–46); Des Plaines, IL (1946–49), and in Grand Haven, MI (1949–52). In 1952, he became professor of historical theology at CTS. As president, he guided the seminary through several needful changes, expanding the curriculum and the admission of women students. He taught in Reformed seminaries around the world. Upon retiring, he served as president of International Theological Seminary, Los Angeles, 1985–90. He served on many synodical committees and wrote many books. Kromminga died of cancer.

Elliott Stedelbauer

April 14, 1910
Molesworth, Ontario, Canada

April 9, 1994
Toronto, Ontario, Canada

President of Christian Business Men's Committee, 1966. Stedelbauer was converted at age eleven. He attended People's Church in Toronto. On May 23, 1931, he married Isobel Parker. Stedelbauer became a Canadian executive with wide influence, being also on the board of Youth For Christ. He worked for his father and got into leadership as president and owner of Stedelbauer Motors, Ltd. It was a Pontiac and Buick dealership which also included Vauxhall and GMC trucks. He was the seventh highest retail salesman in all GM sales organizations in Canada during his active sales days. He died from complications following a stroke.

Richard M. Nixon

Jan. 9, 1913
Yorba Linda, California

April 22, 1994
New York, New York

Thirty-seventh president of the United States (1969–August 9, 1974), the only president to resign from office. Nixon made a profession of faith in a PAUL RADER revival meeting as a teenager in a Quaker church, testifying of this in Christian Endeavor meetings. He held Sunday services in the White House. He married Pat Ryan (March 16, 1912–June 22, 1993) on June 21, 1940. They had two daughters, Tricia and Julie (who married David Eisenhower, grandson of the former president). After graduating from Whittier (CA) College, Nixon engaged in the practice of law until 1942, then served in the U.S. Navy, 1942–46, in WWII. From 1946–52, he was in Congress (House of Representatives, 12th Congressional district from California). The son of a storekeeper, Nixon gained a reputation in Congress as a fervid, anti-Communist, attacking "Left Wing views" and alleged Communist associations of his political opponents. He became widely known as a member of the House Committee on Un-American Activities. From 1952–60, he served as vice president under DWIGHT EISENHOWER, becoming one of the most active vice presidents in modern U.S. history—traveling extensively on behalf of the U.S. and filling in for the president during his several bouts of serious ill health. In 1960, he ran for the presidency but lost to John F. Kennedy in a very close contest, but won the election for president in 1968 and 1972. Nixon, a Republican, defeated Hubert Humphrey and George Wallace in 1968 and George McGovern in 1972 in a 520–17 electoral landslide. He made several overseas trips during this time and is credited with being one of the most astute presidents in foreign affairs. The U.S. began a dialogue with China as a result of his efforts. The Watergate scandal (named after Nixon staffers were caught breaking into Democratic Party offices in the Watergate Hotel in D.C.) proved his undoing. The error came in his denying knowledge of the act, and he was forced to resign and retire to private life less than two years after being re-elected. Nixon's speech and forced resignation were a shock to evangelicals. In 1985, Nixon became the first former president to voluntarily give up lifetime Secret Service protection, saving the American taxpayers $3 million a year. He wrote ten books, including *Six Crises* (1962); his memoirs; and his last, *Beyond Peace* (1994). He is buried on the grounds of the Nixon Library in Yorba Linda, CA, at the side of his wife.

Roy Just

Sept. 28, 1921
Reedley, California

April 25, 1994
Fresno, California

President of Tabor College, Hillsboro, KS, 1963–80. Known for his vision and optimism, Just began his career at Tabor, after his schooling, teaching sociology, 1950–55. He then taught sociology and philosophy at Fresno City College, 1955–63. During his administration at Tabor, he saw several academic and physical improvements. He inherited a campus expansion project and by 1970, the college community had invested nearly $2 million in new facilities, including a library, gymnasium, student center, cafeteria, and several residence halls. He served, 1980–85, as president of Columbia Bible College, Clearbrook, BC. He later moved to Fresno where he taught sociology at Fresno Pacific College, 1985–92. He was active in missionary activities. His wife's name was Evelyn. In February, 1994, he was diagnosed with pancreatic cancer. His funeral was at Bethany Mennonite Brethren Church in Fresno.

Maurice (Morry) Carlson

Dec. 29, 1914
Muskegon, Michigan

May 1, 1994
Tucson, Arizona

Ranch director for troubled children, administrator, saxophonist, and friend to hundreds of boys and girls. Carlson served his generation well with his wife, Dorothy Paulson. He worked with the *Children's Bible Hour* and with Muskegon YFC, when a Mrs. Hilton donated some property to him for a youth Bible camp and the rest is history. He was the founder of Youth Haven Ranches, first in Muskegon, then in Rivers Junction, MI, and in Picacho, AZ. These camps started many on the road to heaven. In later years, he was a walking miracle having cancer, vascular disease, diabetes, high blood pressure, and heart trouble. He had 15 major operations, 27 blood transfusions, a body full of artificial arteries, and was on the verge of having his legs amputated. He just kept going. He was converted by the witness of his family and responded in a Sunday night service. He was an excellent saxophonist.

Glen E. Seaborg

May 12, 1915
Joliet, Illinois

May 10, 1994
Champaign, Illinois

Executive director of Evangelical Church Alliance, Bradley, IL, 1949–91. Seaborg was converted at the Old Gospel Tabernacle in Joliet in 1933. On Sept 16, 1939, he married Beatrice Revels. In WWII he was a flight instructor for the navy. After the war he became active in the GT, later called Faith Bible Church. Seaborg worked at Phillips Petroleum Company until 1949.

Then came the 40-year association with ECA, with his wife serving as office administrator during this time. In recent years, they were members of First Social Brethren Church of Bradley, IL.

Richard Champion

March 25, 1931
Elkhart, Indiana

May 14, 1994
Springfield, Missouri

Longtime Assembly of God journalist and president of Evangelical Press Association, 1975–77. Champion married Norma Jean Black on October 3, 1953. He pastored in Macomb, IL, from 1953–55. From 1955–57, he was advertising and circulation manager for the *Pentecostal Evangel*. He was editor of the *CA Herald* and *CA Guide* (1958–64), becoming editor in 1984 upon Robert Cunningham's retirement. He taught journalism at Central Bible College since 1961 and was in demand as a speaker for writing seminars across the nation.

Clay Cooper

May 25, 1911
Manzanola, Colorado

May 22, 1994
Spokane, Washington

Missions enthusiast. Cooper's life was full of evangelism endeavors. He was promoting the World Wide Monthly Tracts Club (1947) and soon called it the Kids Tract Club (1948). In 1953, he made an extended tour of Africa and also Indochina, representing *The Sword of the Lord* as a correspondent. Cooper spent several of his last years in nursing homes and living out his days in his hometown of Spokane, WA.

Thomas Skinner

June 6, 1942
New York, New York

June 17, 1994
Norfolk, Virginia

Outstanding black evangelist, director of Tom Skinner Associates until he died. He was also engaged in civil rights activities. He married Vivian Sutton and after a divorce, Barbara Williams. Skinner was a leader of the Harlem Lord's gang, when he was converted while listening to a radio preacher in 1956. He soon was street preaching in 1959, ordained by the National Baptists. He began his career in the mid-1960s with evangelistic crusades in New York City's Harlem, where he grew up. He started a radio broadcast (1964) and organized his TS Crusades, Inc. (1966). From 1985 on, he worked with poor inner-city youth in Newark, NJ. John Perkins maintains that no one has done more to build bridges between black and white evangelicals than Skinner. Many black evangelical leaders feel he paved the way for them. He was chaplain for the Washington Redskins football team in the 1970s–80s. In 1992 he moved to Tracey's Landing, MD, where he started the Skinner Farm Leadership Institute. He died of lymphatic leukemia. His autobiography is *Black and Free* (1968).

William L. Wooley

March 6, 1925
Crystal Springs, Mississippi

June 20, 1994
Kansas City, Missouri

Director of International Union of Gospel Missions (Association of Gospel Rescue Missions in 2000), **Kansas City, MO 1974–89**. Wooley was converted at age 12 in Birmingham, AL. He married Madeleine Weir on August 13, 1950 (died: June 2001). Her death came as a result of a heart attack at the office of AGRM where she worked. They did home missions work in the Kentucky mountains in 1952. CMA rejected his application to be a missionary, so he pastored a CMA Church in Anniston, AL from 1957–58. One day, in frustration, he took a drive determined to find the will of God and ended up at a rescue mission in Montgomery, AL. His wife was praying at home. They found their calling: Wooley directed a mission in Pensacola, FL (1958–63); was executive-director of Alcoholic Rehab Center in

Albany, GA (1964–74), and then for the headquarters work. Wooley enlarged the scope and credibility of rescue mission work, traveling to many countries including England and Russia, seeing mission goals fulfilled there as well. He died of kidney failure.

John G. Olson

Oct. 13, 1918
New Auburn, Wisconsin

July 6, 1994
Los Angeles, California

Director of Trans World Missions, 1978–94. Raised on a farm in a Christian home, Olson married Linnie Claypool on July 6, 1944. In a bizarre twist of destiny, he died suddenly on their 50th wedding anniversary. Formerly active with Air Mail for God during the NYLES HUFFMAN era, the name change in 1979 found him running the home office and conducting a radio broadcast that promoted indigenous churches, orphanages and other missionary enterprises. His broadcast was well received, singing duets with his wife, challenging others to world evangelism. He became a familiar voice on the Christian airwaves.

J. Monroe (Monk) Parker

June 23, 1909
Thomasville, Alabama

July 17, 1994
Decatur, Alabama

Evangelist, educator, and president of Baptist World Mission, Decatur, AL 1969–84. Parker was a widely used evangelist and veteran educator. He was converted at age 19. He went to Bob Jones College (University) and traveled for five years as an evangelist. He returned to BJU to assume staff positions and became an assistant to DR. BOB. In 1949, he re-entered full-time evangelism, interspersed with a Decatur, AL, pastorate. He was then president of Pillsbury Baptist Bible College, Owatonna, MN, from 1958–65. The student body grew 20 percent each year that he was there. Parker conducted revival meetings throughout most of his life. His wife's name was Ruby. He died of congestive heart failure. Some 450 attended his funeral.

Byron S. Lamson

June 4, 1901
Boone, Iowa

July 19, 1994
Milwaukee, Wisconsin

Director of Free Methodist World Missions, 1944–64. Lamson was converted around age eight at a decision day service at the Free Methodist Church, Phoenix, AZ. On September 8, 1925, he married Freda Burritt (who later died). He then married Betty Kline on July 30, 1965. Prior to his main endeavor, he pastored at the FM Church, Riverside, CA (1924–27); was president of LA Pacific College (1930–39); pastored the FM Church, Evanston, IL, and also in Greenville, IL (1924–44). From 1964–70, he was editor of the *Free Methodist*. During his tenure, the number of missionaries went from 67 to 210, mission fields from 14 to 23, and mission church attendance from 9,000 to 50,000. He raised the $1 million a year budget one year in advance of spending it. Lamson traveled around the world, and assisted in baptizing thousands of new Christians in Africa, Asia, and Latin America.

Hafford H. Overbey

Jan. 16, 1902
Murray, Kentucky

July 28, 1994
Lexington, Kentucky

Founder and first executive secretary of Baptist Faith Missions, Warren, MI 1942–78, Lexington, KY, 1978–81. Overbey grew up at FBC, Wheaton, IL. BFM actually began in 1923. His missions interest grew by trying to raise support for a veteran missionary, Joseph Brandon of Brazil. In 1944, he and his family moved to Detroit, where he took the pastorate of Harmony Baptist Church.

The church went through name and location changes and, after 35 years, he left it as Twelve-Ryan Baptist Church, Warren, MI. BFM was incorporated in 1945 to promote and distribute financial support for missionaries.

Andrew W. Hughes

May 10, 1912
Cloquet, Minnesota

July 29, 1994

President of Christian Business Men's Committe 1962. Hughes was a member of the Fifth Avenue Presbyterian Church in New York City. He was active in athletics and business but he was converted after being challenged by Matthew 16:26. He married Gladys E. Fredrickson on October 7, 1933. Hughes was the treasurer of the Rheem Manufacturing Company in New York and director of R.G. LeTourneau Inc., of Longview, TX. He joined the Rheem Company in 1943 as production engineer and held a number of executive positions in sales, engineering, accounting, and plant management. He was comptroller, 1956–62. Hughes was an elder and Sunday School teacher, an active Gideon, and worked with CBMC in such diverse places as Los Angeles, Hibbing, MN, Baltimore, Newark, NJ, as well as in NYC.

Lucas C. "Luke" Huber

March 5, 1950
Lafayette, Indiana

Aug. 4, 1994
Lago Grande Lake, Brazil

Founder and first director of Project Amazon, Morton, IL, 1976–94. Huber was a man of tremendous vision, anticipating getting the gospel out through 100,000 churches along the Amazon. He and his wife, the former Christian Bunney, went there from southern Brazil in 1976. He found some 17 million people in river villages without the gospel. When he died, he had nearly completed the River New Testament Project. It was for those having difficulty reading and understanding the Bible. He and a companion, Lloyd Niles of Canada, in flight, banked and descended to make one last pass by the PAZ boat, anchored away from the shore. The plane suddenly went into a dive and crashed into the water. He died on impact, his companion surviving.

George W. Cornell

July 24, 1920
Weatherford, Oklahoma

Aug. 10, 1994
New York, New York

Religious editor for the Associated Press for 43 years. Cornell married Jo Ann Reeves on April 1, 1944. He began his career as a reporter for the *Reporter Daily Oklahoman*, Oklahoma City, OK (1943–44), then was newsman for the Associated Press, New York City (1947–51). He served in the army, 1944–47. When Cornell first began specializing in religious coverage in 1951, his columns were the first on the subject carried on a regular basis by a newswire service. A "journalist without peer" was what Billy Graham called him. Cornell's writings range from *They Knew Jesus* (1957) to *The Untamed God* (1975). He was an Episcopalian.

Jacob A. O. Preus

Jan. 8, 1920
St. Paul, Minnesota

Aug. 13, 1994
Burnsville, Missouri

President of Lutheran Church—Missouri Synod, 1969–81. Preus guided this denomination during its most turbulent years. He tried to halt theological liberalism and defend the authority of the Bible. Some 100,000 left the denomination, but he prevailed. He married Delpha Holleque on June 12, 1943. Ordained in the Evangelical Lutheran Synod in 1945, he pastored the South St. Church, St. Paul, MN (1945–46), and a Lutheran church in Luverne, MN (1950–56). He was professor at Bethany College, Mankato, MN (1947–50 and 1956–58); at Concordia Seminary, Springfield, IL (1958–69); and was president of the same (1962–69). In 1974, Preus suspended President John Titjen and 43 (of 47) faculty members of Concordia Theological Seminary of St. Louis over doctrinal irregularities. He became a teacher there after 1981. He died from a heart attack.

Paul Anderson

Oct. 17, 1932
Toccoa, Georgia

Aug. 15, 1994
Vidalia, Georgia

Billed as the "World's Strongest Man," Anderson set many records in weight lifting. At the 1956 Olympics in Melbourne, Australia, Anderson won the gold medal. He was very sick, however, a few days before the event and called upon the Lord to heal him. He dates his conversion from there. He married Glenda Garland on September 1, 1959, and the couple started the Pennsylvania Home for Troubled Youth (young men from ages 16–21). The home continues into the twenty-first century. He spoke, testified, and exhibited at reformatories, youth rallies, and churches of all kinds. A reoccurence of kidney problems (which plagued him in his youth), commonly known as Bright's disease finally took his life after 13½ years of illness.

Harold B. Kuhn

Aug. 21, 1911
Belleville, Kansas

Aug. 26, 1994
Lexington, Kentucky

President of Evangelical Theological Society, 1955. As a member of the Ohio Yearly Meeting, Kuhn served as a Friends' minister in Rescue, VA (1934–36) and at a Methodist Church in Beacon, IA (1938–39). He then served at Allen's Neck Friends Meeting, Dartmouth, MA (1939–41) and Waldo Congregational Church, Brockton, MA (1941–44). He was professor of philosophy and religion at Asbury Theological Seminary, 1944–82. After World War II, he and his wife did extensive relief work in East Germany and Poland. His wife, Anna, taught German at Asbury College, 1962–65 and 1971–78. He was founder and editor of the *Asbury Seminarian* (1946–78).

Charles F. Baker

Oct. 24, 1905
Dallas, Texas

Sept. 11, 1994
Escondido, California

President of Milwaukee (WI) Bible College, 1945–60, renamed and relocated **Grace Bible College, Grand Rapids, MI 1960–65**. Baker was raised in a Christian home and married Teresa Bettes (died: 1982) and Ruth Lohman on October 19, 1985. He retired and later developed difficulty with his feet. Early on, he attended Wheaton (IL) College. He helped J. C. O'HAIR with his radio ministry. Baker wrote many articles and books such as *Dispensational Theology, Truth, Understanding the Gospel,* and *Acts.* His only child, a son, died early in life.

Dale S. Crowley

May 14, 1899
Indian Territory, Oklahoma

Sept. 27, 1994
Clearwater, Florida

Radio voice for 70 years. He first broadcasted in Fort Worth, TX, in 1924. Converted as a teen, Crowley first found work on a railroad, then moved into radio. After he married, he took a pastorate in Southern California. In 1936, they moved to Washington, D.C., where his program, *Right Start for the Day* began (1940) and continued on WDDC almost until the time of his death. It featured Bible quizzes. Crowley also edited the paper, *Capital Voice.* He was an old-time, fundamentalist Baptist. His address, P.O. Box 1, Washington D.C., was so coveted, that a U.S. president tried to get it, but failed. He was stricken with subdural hematoma in 1992.

Carl Heinmiller

1892
Cleveland, Ohio

Oct. 15, 1994
Seattle, Washington

Director of Evangelical United Brethren Church (Methodist Church in 1968) **Missions, 1947–62**. Heinmiller married Winifred Johnson in 1917 (died: 1964), Loise Maurer in 1967 (died: 1980), and Ruth Densmore in 1984. The United Brethren movement later merged into the United Methodist Church. Heinmiller began his ministry as a pastor in Seattle (1927–33) and Portland (1933–35), then was a conference superintendent in the Oregon-Washington Conference of the Evangelical Church. In 1934, he was promoted to executive secretary of the Missionary Society of the Evangelical Church and later taught at American University of San Germán in Puerto Rico.

Arch H. Yetter

Aug. 16, 1903
Payton, Colorado

Oct. 29, 1994
Denver, Colorado

President of Rockmont College (Colorado Christian University in 1985), **Longmont, CO, 1954–63**. Yetter was converted at a meeting conducted by CLIFTON FOWLER. He married Daisy Burgess on June 9, 1928. He pastored in Fairplains, CO from 1929–34, often working in the mines to augment his income. He held tent meetings in mountain villages, played the saxophone, and was known as the "kid preacher." He pastored at Holly Hills Bible Church, Pomona, CA (1934–38) and then at Berean Fundamental Church in Denver, CO (1938–42). He began to teach at Denver Bible School 1942–54. From 1947–54, he started and pastored the Ashgrove United Church. Along with CARL HARWOOD, he started the Western Bible School. Yetter pastored the Northwest Evangelical Free Church, Arvada, CO, 1938–42. He retired at age 85 and died of a heart attack.

Marlin E. Miller

Nov. 29, 1938
Iowa City, Iowa

Nov. 3, 1994
Elkhart, Indiana

President of Goshen (IN) Biblical Seminary, 1974–90, and first president of Associated Mennonite Biblical Seminary, Elkhart, IN, 1990–94. GBS and Mennonite Biblical Seminary, Elkhart, merged in 1990 to form AMBS. Miller married Ruthann Gardner on June 12, 1960. The couple went to Europe in 1961 for further study. They had a ministry in Paris, France, 1968–74, ministering to African students. He died suddenly of a heart attack, while exercising in his home.

Rachel B. Saint

Jan. 2, 1914
Jenkentown, Pennsylvania

Nov. 11, 1994
Quito, Ecuador

Missionary and Bible translator. Rachel lived with the Aucas, her brother's (NATE SAINT) killers, and communicated the gospel to them. From 1937–49, she worked with recovering alcoholics at Keswick Colony of Mercy in New Jersey. She took her linguistic training in 1948 with Wycliffe Bible translators and went to Peru to work with the Piro Indians, and then the headhunting Shapras. Burdened for the Aucas in Ecuador, she arrived in February, 1955, and began to tackle this difficult language with some help from Dayuma. The following year, the Christian world was stunned by the murders of the five missionaries in Ecuador. In 1958, Rachel Saint and Elisabeth Elliot made a historic trip to the Aucas and lived two months with them. In 1965, the Gospel of Mark was finally available in the Auca language. She died of cancer and is buried in Tonampare, the village of the Huorani (Auca) tribe where she had been a missionary for nearly 40 years.

Leonard Ravenhill

June 18, 1907
Leeds, England

Nov. 27, 1994
Lindale, Texas

Revivalist and author of many books on revival. Ravenhill was converted at age 14, greatly affected by reading the life of DAVID BRAINERD. He joined a Wesleyan Methodist Church and around age 19 made unconditional surrender to Christ. He joined a party called The Holiness Trekkers, who walked the length and breadth of England, street preaching and holding gospel crusades. Ravenhill married his wife, Martha, on Sept. 30, 1939. He pastored in the Calvary Holiness Movement and came to the US in 1950. In 1951, he had to jump from a fourth story window to escape death in a Chicago hotel fire. In a hospital for three months, he was flown home to England on a stretcher. Returning in 1953 for more conference work, the family finally settled at Bethany Fellowship in Minneapolis where he became editor of *Dayspring*. He wrote several books. His *Why Revival Tarries* was a best seller.

Jesse Hendley

Oct. 11, 1907
Montgomery, Alabama

Nov. 30, 1994
Atlanta, Georgia

Pastor of a great SBC church in East Point, GA with membership of over 2,300. For more than 50 years, Hendley directed the "Radio Evangelistic Hour." He was a tremendously used evangelist in the 1940's and 1950's and a remarkable Greek scholar. In 1945, Hendley held a crusade in an Atlanta baseball stadium speaking to a crowd of 7,500, with hundreds being saved. He was a frequent speaker at *Sword of the Lord* Conventions.

Elmer B. Smick

July 10, 1921
Baltimore, Maryland

Dec. 7, 1994
South Hamilton, Massachusetts

Minister, educator, and president of Evangelical Theological Society, 1988. Smick married Jane Harrison on Aug 19, 1944. Ordained to the Presbyterian Church in America in 1947, he pastored the Evangelical Presbyterian Church, Trenton, NJ from 1947–56. He then became professor of OT Languages at Covenant Theol. Sem., St. Louis (1956–71); and of Old Testament at Gordon Conwell Theol, Sem., Hamilton, MA (1971–91). He was one of the editors of the NIV from 1968–76 and wrote *Archaelogy of the Jordan Valley* (1973). He lived in South Hamilton, MA. He died after an extended illness.

Bernard J. Haan

April 24, 1917
Sully, Iowa

Dec. 8, 1994
Sioux Center, Iowa

First president of Dordt College, Sioux City, IA 1957–1982. Haan married Deborah Harkema on July 21, 1942. He pastored the German Valley Christian Reformed Church in Sioux Center, IA from 1945–63. He was on radio for 25 years with his "Observations with Rev. B.J. Haan." Attendance at Dordt grew from 35 to 1,156 under his leadership. He died of congestive heart failure.

Walter H. Clark

July 15, 1902
Westfield, New Jersey

Dec. 15, 1994
Cape Elizabeth, Maine

President of American Association of Schools of Religious Education, 1957–1961. Clark was identified with Hartford Seminary Foundation as professor of the psychology of religion, 1962–69. He was dean of the School of Religious Education at HSF. He taught at the now-defunct Berkshire Christian College, Lenox (MA) school for 19 years, then was on the faculty of Bowdoin, Brunswick, MA and Middlebury (VT) Colleges until going to Hartford.

D. Elton Trueblood

Dec. 12, 1900
Pleasantville, Iowa

Dec. 20, 1994
Lansdale, Pennsylvania

Famed Quaker (Friends) theologian. Trueblood married Pauline Goodenow (Aug. 24, 1925) and Virginia Zuttermeister (Aug. 5, 1956). He was professor and chaplain, Stanford University, 1936–45. Trueblood then became professor of philosophy at Earlham College, Richmond, IN from 1946–66. He published his first of 37 books in 1936, *The Essence of Spiritual Religion* which called for the removal of rigid distinctions between clergy and laity. For Trueblood, every Christian was a minister. He also wrote *The Company of the Committed* (1961). He wrote his autobiography in 1974, *While It is Day*.

Frank R. Brown

June 24, 1902
New York, New York

Dec. 24, 1994
Salisbury, North Carolina

President of Hood Theological Seminary, Salisbury, NC 1953–1973. Brown was an elder in the AME Zion Church. Before the war, he pastored the Union Zion Church at New Britain, CT. His wife was Fletcher Jones. He saw the campus develop from dirt streets and about 50 men students, shortly after WW II, to a respected institution with a seminary graduating 40 ministers a year.

R. Willard Dunn

Oct. 26, 1911
Hillsborough, North Carolina

Dec. 25, 1994
Lexington, North Carolina

Founder and first president of Salem (OH) Bible College, 1956–73. As Dunn completed his presidency, the school was renamed Allegheny Wesleyan College. He married Ruby Bartley on April 15, 1935 (died: May 6, 1999). They were in the ladies' clothing business in Mebane, NC, for five years and then were converted through Wesleyan evangelist, Harold Lowman. Dunn pastored Wesleyan Methodist churches in Hillsdale, PA (1946–51) and Canton, OH (1951–56). After his days at Salem, he was business manager for God's Bible School, Cincinnati, for about ten years.

Frances A. Ibiam

Nov. 29, 1906
Unwana, Nigeria

1995

Medical missionary, statesman, and president of World Council of Churches, 1961–1968. Ibiam began a long association with Church of Scotland Mission in Calabar, Nigeria, in 1936. He married Eduora O. Saseghon on April 12, 1939, while he founded a hospital at Abriba, 1938–45. Ibiam served as governor of Eastern Nigeria at Enugu (1960–76), and was the president of All-African Christian Conference (1963–76). He was a Presbyterian and active in student movements. After a war ended in 1970, Ibiam remained in Nigeria, working toward reconstruction and relief.

J. Robert Ashcroft

Dec. 18, 1911
Philadelphia, Pennsylvania

Jan. 5, 1995
Springfield, Missouri

President of Evangel College, Springfield, MO 1958–1974. Ashcroft was converted as a child and began an evangelistic ministry as a teenager. On Sept. 18, 1935, he married Grace P. Larson and later pastored the Gospel Tabernacle in West Hartford, CT from 1945–47. He headed the Assemblies of God educational department nationally (1953–58) and was president of CBI (1958–63). He also served full time at Evangel while the enrollment tripled and seven buildings were erected. He later was president of Valley Forge Christian College, Phoenixville, PA (1982–84) and Berean College in Springfield, PA (1985–89). In 1987, he married his second wife, Mabel. His son is the well-known, one-time governor and senator from Missouri, John Ashcroft. John latter became attorney general in president George W. Bush's first term administration. J. Robert passed away one day after attending his son's swearing-in ceremony in Washington, DC.

Robert T. Fauth

Jan. 19, 1916
Westside, Iowa

Jan. 23, 1995
St. Louis, Missouri

President of Eden Theological Seminary, St. Louis, MO 1962–1981. Fauth was ordained Evangelical and Reformed in June, 1940. He pastored in Waverly at Tripoli, IA, (1940–48); Bethel Church, Detroit (1948–56); and Peace Memorial, Chicago (1956–62). He later served as interim president at Lancaster (PA) Theological Seminary.

Carl M. Gullerud

May 6, 1908
Tracey, Minnesota

Feb. 4, 1995
Eau Clair, Wisconsin

President of Immanuel Lutheran College and Seminary, Eau Clair, WI 1967–1984. He was married to Ruth Rodning, and upon her death, married Martha Brudvig on Aug. 16, 1950 for 44 years. He pastored in Brookings and Volga, South Dakota, (1932–41); Mt. Olive Lutheran, Mankato, MN (1941–59); and Salem Lutheran, Eagle Lake, MN (1942–62); the last two simultaneously. Much of this was in the Norwegian Synod, which he served as vice president (1946–50) and president (1950–54). He also edited the *Lutheran Sentinel*. He was professor of theology at ILS (1959–84) and president of the IL College, Eau Clair, WI (1962–78) as well. His memorial service was held at Messiah Lutheran Church, Eau Claire, WI.

Terrell C. Sanders

Feb. 28, 1927
Jennings, Florida

Feb. 4, 1995
Tortilla Flat, Arizona

President of Nazarene Theological Seminary, Kansas City, MO 1981–1992. Sanders was a student pastor in Roma, GA (1949–53), then attended NTS (1953–56). He pastored 1956–66. He was then district superintendent in North Carolina (1966–75) and Ohio (1975–81). Sanders wife was Edrell Whitman. In 1987, he visted China, Hong Kong, and Formosa. He died suddenly on Superstition Moutain in an automobile accident. The small pickup truck he was driving broke through the guard rail on Highway 88 and plunged 1,000 feet into a ravine about 35 miles east of Phoenix. He was in the midst of a revival meeting at the East Valley Church of the Nazarene in the Phoenix area.

Paul H. Eller

Jan. 27, 1905
Chadwick, Illinois

Feb. 17, 1995
Carefree, Arizona

President of Evangelical Theological Seminary (GETS in 1974), **Naperville, IL 1955–1967.** Eller was ordained into the Evangelical United Brethren Church in 1929, and went to the Evangelical Thelogical Seminary, Naperville, IL in 1930 as professor of church history. He married Nancy Heina on Aug. 20, 1935. He was dean of the school, 1952–55 and active in many WCC activities.

Henry J. Evenhouse

Dec. 28, 1910
Chicago, Illinois

March 2, 1995
Grand Rapids, Michigan

Director of Christian Reformed Missions, 1952–1976. Ordained in 1938, Evenhouse pastored CR churches as follows: Fourth, Paterson, NJ (1939–44); Burton Heights, Grand Rapids, MI (1944–1951) and First in Denver, CO (1951). His mission work with the denomination was first described as Director of Indian and Foreign Missions (1952–64), then Director of Foreign Missions (1964–1976).

Curtis Hutson

July 10, 1934
Decatur, Georgia

March 5, 1995
Murfreesboro, Tennessee

***Sword of the Lord* editor (successor to JOHN R. RICE), 1980–95**. Hutson was a Spirit-filled preacher, greatly used in conferences and pulpits across the country. He married Barbara (Gerri) Crawford on November 21, 1952 (born: August 22, 1934), and they had four children. Answering the call to preach, he ministered in a small church and augmented his income carrying mail. He attended a Sword of the Lord Conference in Atlanta and heard JACK HYLES speak on soul winning. It was life-changing. He went back to his Forrest Hills Church in Decatur, GA, and saw it grow from 40 to 7,900 during his 20-year ministry, 1956–77. From 1977–80, he held large crusades across the land with as many as 1,502 conversions in an eight-day crusade. With the mantle of the *Sword of the Lord* editorship upon him, Hutson continued to hold great conferences. Diagnosed with bone cancer in 1992, he continued writing (11 million circulation—books, tracts, booklets) and preaching (SOTL conferences in Chattanooga, TN; Greenville, SC; and Walkertown, NC) until his death at home.

Louis H. Ford

May 23, 1914
Clarksdale, Mississippi

March 31, 1995
Chicago, Illinois

Bishop of Church of God in Christ, Memphis, TN, 1990–95. which became the largest African-American Pentecostal denomination with 8.5 million followers. He married Margaret Little in 1933. For 60 years, 1934–95, Ford pastored the St. Paul COGIC, which started as a result of his street preaching. Ford was the assistant preaching bishop of the denomination, 1976–90. He died of pneumonia.

William M. Smith (2)

Dec. 18, 1915
Stockton, Alabama

April 12, 1995
Mobile, Alabama

Bishop of African Methodist Episcopal Zion Church, 1960–1992; senior bishop, 1980–92. Smith married Ida Anderson on Jan. 19, 1935, was ordained deacon (1937) and elder (1939). Many of Smith's pastorates were in Alabama, including St. Thomas, Perdita; Zion, Atmore; Zion Star and Zion Fountain, Brewton; Ebenezer, Montgomery; and Big Zion, Mobile. He pastored in Buffalo in 1960. Smith always labored in civic and community affairs along with his ministry. He was also assigned to nine mission conferences, including South American and Virgin Islands.

Burl Ives

June 14, 1909
Hunt, Illinois

April 15, 1995
Anacontes, Washington

Folk singer and guitarist. At the age of four, Ives earned 25¢ singing at an old soldiers' picnic. At Eastern State Teachers College in Charleston, IL, he paid for his meals by singing to the accompaniment of his banjo and guitar. In 1929, he embarked on an extended trip hitchhiking, riding freight trains and singing from Canada to Mexico, in 46 states. Later for several months, he traveled with J. FRANK NORRIS's evangelistic teams. In 1937, he went to New York City where he worked as a busboy and sang in churches. His acting career began in Carmel, NY, in 1938. He started his radio career in 1940 with a program called *The Wayfarin' Stranger*. In 1942–43, he was in Irving Berlin's soldier's show, *This Is the Army*. He recorded numerous albums of Christian songs. His simple folk-type music blessed many. He married Dorothy Koster in April 1971, and they lived in Anacontes, WA. He participated in many films from *Smokey* (1946) to *Earthbound* (1981).

Milton A. Tomlinson

Oct. 19, 1906
Cleveland, Tennessee

April 26, 1995
Cleveland, Tennessee

General overseer of Church of God of Prophecy, Cleveland, TN, 1943–90. The younger son of COG founder, AMBROSE TOMLINSON, Milton took over this branch of the ministry. He was converted in 1926 at the Assembly Tabernacle, and on Sept. 18, 1928, he married Ina Mae Turner. She, however, was not converted until March 11, 1952, the year that his COG ministry became officially known as Church of God of Prophecy. He was a lifelong resident of Cleveland, except for a one-year pastorate in Kentucky. Milton took the movement from 32,000 members in 20 nations to 260,000 members in 90 nations. He led the group to a new building in 1972 and the $1.5 million mortgage was retired in only four years. He was the long time editor of the *White Wing Messenger*, president of the Bible Training Institute of Lee College in Cleveland, and founder of the Tomlinson Home for Children. He wrote *Basic Bible Beliefs*.

Paul B. Smith

June 1, 1921
Toronto, Ontario, Canada

April 30, 1995
Toronto, Ontario, Canada

Pastor of People's Church, Toronto, son of renowned OSWALD J. SMITH. He married Anita Lawson on June 8, 1946. Smith pastored the famed church 1959–94, the church his father started in 1928. He wrote the music for the chorus, "Jesus Is My Savior," which his father wrote. He was an evangelist (1948–52), then became an associate pastor at the People's Church (1952–58). He led the church from a downtown auditorium seating 1600 to suburban Willowdale and a new building seating 2,500. He wrote such books as *Church Aflame*, *After Midnight*, *Naked Truth*, *World Conquest*, *Headline Pulpit*, *Perilous Times*, and *Other Gospels*.

S. George Coulter

May 16, 1912
Maher Aveely, North Ireland

May 11, 1995
Kansas City, Missouri

Director of world missions, 1960–64, and General Superintendent of Church of the Nazarene, 1964–80. Coulter's family moved to Canada when he was eleven years old. He was converted at age 13. He pastored in Alberta, Canada (1933–36); Denair, CA, (1936–41); Stockton, CA (1941–45); and Medford, OR (1945–48). He was then district superintendent for Northern California (1948–60) and secretary for foreign missions at CN headquarters (1960–64). His wife's name was Irene. He died in St. Joseph's Hospital.

W. Robert Hess

Oct. 24, 1922
Hughesville, Pennsylvania

May 16, 1995
North Canton, Ohio

General Superintendent of Evangelical Friends Church-Eastern Region, 1983–89, and of its missions program, 1972–77, and of the EFM, 1978–80. He was a missionary to India under Ohio Yearly Meeting of Friends for three terms, 1952–68. Hess was professor of philosophy and history at Malone College, Canton, OH, from 1968–83. Hess traveled around the world speaking in many conferences, retreats, and churches. He married Esther Garner.

Richard E. Morton

Sept. 2, 1908
Luck, Wisconsin

May 19, 1995
Lodi, California

President of Trinity Theological Seminary (merged into Wartburg Theological Seminary, Dubuque, IA, in 1961), **Blair, NE 1946–56**. Morton married Mildred E. Johnson on June 9, 1934. He wrote *God Invites Me* (1943). He pastored the First English Lutheran, Poy Sippi, WI

(1934–39) and at Ebenezer, Chicago, IL (1939–44). He was president of Dana College and Trinity Seminary, Blair, NE from 1944–46. He began pastoring at St. Paul Lutheran in Lodi, California in 1956.

Ralph Earle

Jan. 27, 1907
Dighton, Massachusetts

May 23, 1995
Chandler, Arizona

President of Evangelical Theological Society, 1962. Earle felt called to the ministry as a child. He married Mabel Mosher on August 25, 1932. He was converted in Westfield, IN, while he attended a private Friends academy. Both he and his wife were reared in the Friends church. Earle was professor of biblical literature at Eastern Nazarene College, Wollaston, MD, from 1933–45 and of NT at Nazarene Theological Seminary, Kansas City, MO from 1945 on. He pastored Nazarene churches in Woonsocket, RI (1934–43) and Everett, MA (1943–45). He made several trips abroad, which often resulted in speaking 250 times a year in revivals, conferences, camp meetings, and ministers' conferences. He died eleven days after suffering a stroke.

Robert J. Billings

Sept. 3, 1926
Massena, New York

May 28, 1995
Haines City, Florida

Christian school movement leader. Billings began his service as a missionary to the British West Indies in 1948, establishing three churches. He married Charlotte Ford on June 28, 1946, and had two sons, after which he pastored in Kingsport, TN, Shellytown, TX, and Mt. Vernon, IN. He wrote *A Guide to the Christian School* in the 1960s. Working with JACK HYLES in the First Baptist Church of Hammond school system, he became the first president of Hyles-Anderson College, 1973–75. He was a Republican candidate for Congress (1976), founded the National Christian Coalition (1978), and served as executive director of Moral Majority (1979). From 1981–86, he served as special assistant to the secretary of education in the REAGAN administration. In 1990, he organized a program to get Bibles into Russia. Billings' funeral services were held in Rome, PA, and Haines City, FL, where he worked with the Landmark Baptist Church since 1989.

Abner V. McCall

June 8, 1915
Perrin, Texas

June 11, 1995
Waco, Texas

President of Baylor University, Waco, TX, 1961–81. McCall arrived at Baylor at age 18, during the Depression in 1933, with $40, a work-scholarship, and a dream to be a lawyer. He married Frances Bortle in 1940 (died: 1969). It is felt that McCall did more for this school than any other leader. During his tenure, the school reached all-time peaks in enrollment, campus and building expansion, academic stature, national reputation, and capital assets. This brought him into high-profile activities in political, social, and denominational matters. He did not neglect his Baptist church, serving as a deacon for decades and a Sunday school teacher for 34 years.

Charles J. Woodbridge

Jan. 24, 1902
Chiakiang, China

July 1995
Honolulu, Hawaii

Fundamental Presbyterian minister, missionary, educator, and president of Evangelical Theological Society, 1952. Born of missionary parents, Woodbridge later served as a missionary in French Cameroon, West Africa. He was converted at age 16 at Mount Hermon School, Northfield, MA. At Princeton (NJ) University, he was an all-American soccer player for several years. He married Ruth Dunning (March 4, 1930) and later Doreen Shaw of England (December 28, 1963). He was the first director of the Independent Board for Presbyterian Foreign Missions, 1934–37. He pastored churches in Flushing, NY; Salisbury, NC (1937–45), and Savannah, GA (1945–50). Woodbridge taught at Fuller Seminary, Pasadena, CA (1950–53), and worked on the staff of Word of Life (1958–64). In 1964, he became independent as a conference speaker and teacher and visited over 80 countries. He wrote numerous books.

Arno Q. Weniger

Oct. 12, 1907
Lime Springs, Iowa

July 1, 1995
Lucerne, California

Founder and first president of San Francisco (CA) Baptist Seminary (Baptist College and Seminary of the West in 1987), **1958–76**. He married Mabel Holtz. Baptist pastor and educator, Weniger pastored at FBC of Pipestone, MN (1928–30); FBC of Bend, OR (1930–32); Pleasant Baptist of Vancouver, British Columbia (1932–36); Calvary Baptist of Salem, OR (1936–41) and Hamilton Square Baptist of San Francisco, CA (1941–76). He became a Christian at age ten and was ordained by the FBC of Bisbee, AZ. Weniger was a leader in fundamental Baptist circles. He cofounded the Lucerne (CA) Christian Conference Center and directed it, 1966–91. He died of a heart attack.

Stuart L. Anderson

Jan. 24, 1912
Elmore, Ohio

July 22, 1995
Long Beach, California

President of Pacific School of Religion, Berkeley, CA, 1950–71. Anderson married Razella Klepper on September 25, 1935. Ordained Congregationalist, he pastored the First Church, Argo, IL (1935–36); in Glendale, CA (1938–43) and Long Beach, CA (1943–50). He also was professor of homiletics during his time as president at PSR, and served as president emeritus, 1977–95. He wrote *A Faith to Live By* (1959).

Green T. Bustin

July 22, 1903
Scott County, Mississippi

July 22, 1995
Ocala, Florida

First director of Evangelical Bible Mission, Summerville, FL 1940–63. Bustin came to the Lord in his teens on December 12, 1921. He married Laura Cox in 1925/26 (died: 1948) and Alma Blatt in September, 1949. He was engaged in evangelism, then pastored Pilgrim Holiness Churches in Jonesboro, AR; Lake Charles and Alexandria, LA, getting encouragement from SETH REES. Bustin made a missionary trip around the world. He started Christ's Ambassadors, wrote books, and had specific ministries in Philippine Islands, Australia, Jamaica, and Europe. At age 90, he went to Belize and stayed for two years. He celebrated his 92nd birthday quietly and died later that day.

Henry L. Eddleman

April 4, 1911
Morgantown, Mississippi

July 28, 1995
Louisville, Kentucky

President of New Orleans (LA) Baptist Theological Seminary, 1959–70, and first president of Criswell College, Dallas, TX, 1972–75. Eddleman married Sarah Fox on September 7, 1937. Ordained a Baptist in 1931, Eddleman did educational and religious work in Palestine, 1935–41. He joined the faculty of NOBTS in 1941 teaching Old Testament Hebrew, 1941–42. He pastored the Parkland Church, Louisville, KY (1942–52), also teaching Old Testament Hebrew at Southern Baptist Seminary, Louisville (1950–54). He was president of Georgetown (KY) College, 1954–59. His first book was *To Make Men Free* (1954). He was a leading Southern Baptist educator.

Austin Watson

March 19, 1915
Uriel, Mississippi

July 28, 1995
Jackson, Mississippi

President of Congregational Methodist Church, Florence, MS, 1965–87. Watson was converted in the summer of 1926 under Bona Fleming and ordained on December 7, 1941. For the next 54 years, he pastored seven churches, preached 400 plus camp and revival meetings and served CMC as president. He was also secretary and a member of the board of directors of Wesley College, Florence, MS. In 1937, he married Mary Kate Peoples. He pastored churches in Laurel, Magee, and Foxworth, MS, until 1956, with the Methodist Protestant Church. Then he entered the CMC and organized the First CMC in Jackson, MS, which grew from 30 to 500. Postponing retirement, he pastored the CMC, Elkhart, TX from 1985–95, after he intended to retire. He died of cancer.

Charles L. Feinberg

June 12, 1909
Pittsburgh, Pennsylvania

Aug. 22, 1995
Walnut Creek, California area

Founder and first president of Talbot Theological Seminary, Los Angeles, CA, 1952–76. Feinberg was trained for 13 years to be a Jewish rabbi when he was converted at the University of Pittsburgh, through a Hebrew Christian friend, John Solomon. He was married in the home of Lewis Chafer to Ann Fraiman (born in Russia 1911–12, died: 1992) on May 14, 1935, the same date he received his Ph.D. in archaeology and Old Testament from John Hopkins University, Baltimore, MD. He taught at Dallas Theological Seminary (1935–48) and then at BIOLA (1948–52), before starting the seminary. He pastored two Presbyterian churches in the Dallas/Fort Worth area, 1936–41. In a time when evangelicals were not stressing academics, he was. He was known as an outstanding Old Testament teacher, having written some 13 books.

Delbert Flora

June 27, 1901
Nappanne, Indiana

Aug. 31, 1995
Ashland, Ohio

First dean of Ashland (OH) Theological Seminary, 1953–63. In early years, Flora homesteaded in Saskatchewan with his grandfather. He married Romayne K. Keyes on September 2, 1929 (died: 1997). He was a pastor, 1931–46, of a Brethren Church in Elkhart, IN. He taught at Ashland College (1946–51) and continued to teach at the seminary (1963–74), having some health problems thereafter.

Joseph W. Tkach Sr.

March 16, 1927
Chicago, Illinois

Sept. 23, 1995
Pasadena, California

Director of Worldwide Church of God, Pasadena, CA, 1986–95. Tkach married Elaine Apostolos on March 31, 1951. He joined the WCG in 1958 when he was living in Chicago. He moved to Pasadena in 1966 to work for the church. Tkach succeeded founder Herbert W. Armstrong and moved the group toward mainstream orthodoxy. His son, Joseph W. Tkach Jr., succeeded him. Joseph and his son led the WCOG through a doctrinal shift by embracing mainstream Christian concepts of the Trinity; emphasizing salvation through the grace of God alone; and lifting requirements that members tithe, observe the Sabbath, and believe in British-Israelism. This reformation from the top down, reforming an entire church body, was without parallel in church history. Tkach literally took a cult and changed it into a mainstream Christian denomination. A sermon on Christmas Eve in 1988 gave public credence to these changes. Tkach died following a four-month battle with bone cancer.

Leonard Hanes

March 31, 1915
Marshalltown, Iowa

Sept. 25, 1995
McAllen, Texas

President of Rio Grande Bible Institute, Edinburg, TX, 1968–81. Hanes was converted at age 25 through the witness of a fellow worker at a wheat company. He graduated from BIOLA and married Helen Regier on June 12, 1944. From 1947–55, he served with his wife in Colombia, under the Evangelical Union of South America (merged with Gospel Missionary Union in 1975, now AVANT). Health reasons brought them to Rio Grande Bible Institute in 1955 where he was academic dean and registrar until 1968. He was director of Radio Esperanza out of RGBI, 1983–88, and worked at the station. A massive stroke took his life.

Harold B. Sightler

May 15, 1914
St. George, South Carolina

Sept. 27, 1995
Greenville, South Carolina

Well-known pastor of Tabernacle Baptist Church, Greenville, SC. Sightler pastored from 1952 until his death 43 years later. Sightler saw the church grow from 168 to over 2,500 members. He was converted at age 12 at East Park Baptist in Greenville in 1926. He married Helen G. Vaughn on May 11, 1935. In 1940, he surrendered to preach and entered evangelism endeavors. In 1943, he started the *Bright Spot Hour* radio broadcast on area stations at a cost of $24 per week. It grew to reach five continents at a cost of $25,000 per month. On June 13, 1951, a fatal automobile accident took the life of his oldest daughter. Early on, he pastored in Mauldin, SC (1943–48) and Pelham (SC) Baptist (1948–52). The TBC ministry grew to include a day school, children's home, Bible institute, Bible college and ministry to widows. They also supported some 400 missionaries. The buildings were old, classic, but well maintained. He discouraged putting money into buildings when it could be used to build lives through missionaries. Visitors exclaimed that it was definitely a "spirit-filled church," as the congregation was free to express their enthusiasm in many unconventional ways. From 1948–84, he preached an average of 40 revivals per year.

Herman G. Braunlin

Oct. 16, 1904
Paterson, New Jersey

Oct. 5, 1995
Ridgewood, New Jersey

Beloved pastor of the Hawthorne (NJ) Gospel Church for 61 years. Braunlin began in 1925 with a Sunday afternoon Bible study and soon a Sunday school was added. In 1928, a tent was erected and the Summer Bible Conference began. On March 7, 1934, he left his business career in New York City and assumed the pastorship. He served until his retirement in 1986. Braunlin was president of the IFCA from 1949–52. His wife, Lydia Caliandro Braunlin died in 1986. Some 2,000 were a part of his church, including George Sweeting. Humble, spiritual, Bible teacher, and able administrator, he touched many lives.

Gilbert H. Johnson

March 19, 1904
Brooklyn, New York

Oct. 10, 1995
Ft. Myers, Florida

President of Evangelical Theological Society, 1959. Johnson began pastoring in 1925 in Dallas, TX; Morristown and Dover, NJ; Owen, Ontario; and Brockton, MA. Active in Christian and Missionary Alliance circles, he taught at Nyack College, 1940–60, pastoring the First Alliance Church of New York City for three years. From 1960–71, he was secretary of education for the denomination. The Johnson's moved to Shell Point Village in Ft. Myers, FL, in 1972. His wife died suddenly on November 15, 1994 after 68 years of marriage.

Hubert Mitchell

Nov. 7, 1907
Denver, Colorado

Oct. 27, 1995
Alhambra, California

President of Go Ye Fellowship, Los Angeles, CA, 1966–93. Mitchell was a legend in missions activity in his generation. His father, A. E. MITCHELL (founder of GYF) led him to the Lord by the workshop bench in his home at age 11. In 1934, Hubert was on his way to Sumatra. Hacking his way into the interior through 50 miles of dense, humid jungle, he found he was unable to explain "nailed to the cross" to the natives—they had never seen a nail. Opening a can of Japanese oranges, he found a nail in the bottom! Later, his young wife, mother of four, died as the Japanese soldiers were advancing upon them. Fifteen missionaries caught the last boat to America. They were aboard for 90 days in submarine-infested waters. He became the first YFC director in Los Angeles and married Rachel Edwardson from Norway. From 1946–51, he directed YFC in India, before coming to the YFCI office to head the worldwide activities until 1955. Chicago was a burden on his heart. Early on, Mitchell was pianist for the PAUL RADER campaign, the night the young RICHARD NIXON responded for salvation. He wrote the music for "He Giveth More Grace" (lyrics by ANNIE J. FLINT). He succeeded his father in Go Ye Fellowship, which has missionaries on seven fields. Jack Hayford conducted his funeral.

Merrimon Cuninggim

May 12, 1911
Nashville, Tennessee

Nov. 2, 1995
Cockersville, Maryland

President of Perkins School of Theology (SMU), Dallas, TX, 1951–60. He married Annie Daniel on June 10, 1939, and they had three children. Cuninggim served in several capacities prior to this: director of religious activities at Duke (1936–38); professor of religion at Emory (VA) and Henry College (1941–42); at Denison University, Granville, OH (1942–44), chaplain USNR on the battleship *Tennessee* (1944–46); and professor of religion at Pomona College, Claremont, OR (1946–51). Following his Perkins leadership, he was executive director of Danforth Foundation, St. Louis, 1960–66 and then became president of the same. His books range from *The College Seeks Religion* (1947) to *The Protestant Stake in Higher Education* (1961).

Robert D. Preus

Oct. 16, 1924
St. Paul, Minnesota

Nov. 4, 1995
Minneapolis, Minnesota

President of Concordia Theological Seminary, Springfield, IL 1974–76, relocated to Ft. Wayne, IN 1976–89. He married Donna Rockman on May 29, 1948. A lifelong Lutheran pastor and educator, Preus pastored in Mayville, ND, and Fisher, MN (1947–49); Harvard St. Lutheran Church, Cambridge, MA (1952–55); Mt. Olive Lutheran Church; Cross Lake Lutheran Church; and Clearwater Lutheran Church, Trail, MN (1955–57). He authored *The Inspiration of the Scriptures* (1955). He fought for three years in both secular and Lutheran Church—Missouri Synod courts to be reinstated as president after he was "honorably retired." He died of a heart attack.

Fred Cunningham

Feb. 5, 1921
Crane, Missouri

Nov. 18, 1995
Springfield, Missouri

Leader in the Fundamental Methodist Church, Springfield, MO c.1964–1984. Converted in an Assembly of God church in Aurora, MO, Cunningham pastored some 50 years at John's Chapel, Ash Grove, MO; in Monet, MO (20 years); Crane, MO (8 years); Aurora, MO (4 years); and Springfield, MO (3 years), among others. He married Leona Hamby on Nov. 11, 1939. Cunningham also held numerous revivals as an evangelist. He was a diabetic and died of congestive heart failure.

Richard C. Halverson

Feb. 4, 1916
Pingree, North Dakota

Nov. 28, 1995
Arlington, Virginia

Pastor of Fourth Presbyterian Church, Bethesda, MD (Washington, D.C. area), **1958–81, and chaplain of the U.S. Senate, 1981–95.** Halverson went to Hollywood, CA in 1935, seeking a career in motion pictures, and visited the Vermont Avenue Presbyterian Church. The pastor, David Cowie, led him to the Lord in his automobile outside the church. On Feb. 6, 1943, he married Doris G. Seaton, and they had three children. After pastoring the FPC, Coalinga, CA (1944–47), he was minister of leadership education at FPC, Hollywood, where hundreds of young people gave their lives to Christ (1947–58). Halverson made eleven trips to the Orient and served on boards and other capacities, for such as Campus Crusade, World Vision, and Navigators. He died in Arlington Hospital of congestive heart failure.

Herschel H. Hobbs

Oct. 24, 1907
Talladega Springs, Alabama

Nov. 28, 1995
Oklahoma City, Oklahoma

President of Southern Baptist Convention, 1961–63. He was converted at age 12 in Montevallo, AL. He married Zula Jackson on April 10, 1927 (died: 1984). Early Baptist pastorates were from 1929–49. Hobbs pastored the FBC, Oklahoma City, OK, from 1949–72, and was a preacher on the *International Baptist Hour.* In 1963, he chaired a committee that crafted the statement known as the Baptist Faith and Message. He died of a heart attack. Hobbs wrote at least 133 books.

Abraham E. Janzen

Nov. 22, 1892
Wasileuka, Ukraine

Dec. 2, 1995
Hillsboro, Kansas (?)

General secretary of Mennonite Brethren Mission Services, Hillsboro, KS, 1945–60. Janzen remained with the mission until 1975 as a historical researcher. He started teaching at Tabor College in 1916 and married Zola Lantz on Dec. 24, 1917. He taught at Friends (Barclay in 1990) University (1931–35) and returned to Tabor College as president (1935–42). During his mission leadership, the fields expanded from six to 16 and missionaries from 241 to 279. He wrote several books.

Julio C. Ruibal

1953
Sucre, Bolivia

Dec. 13, 1995
Cali, Columbia

Prominent Bolivian evangelist who was murdered by gunmen as he left a meeting of Protestant pastors. Ruibal was converted in the States while studying medicine and discipled by KATHERINE KUHLMAN. He returned to Bolivia in 1972 at the age of 19. Within weeks, he was preaching to packed crowds in the La Paz soccer stadium. At age 22, he founded the Neo-Pentecostal Movement (charismatic movement outside of Pentecostal circles) in Bolivia and was holding healing services in outdoor stadiums. After moving to Colombia from Bolivia in 1977, he opened a health clinic and founded the Christian Center in Cali. His wife's name was Ruth. His ministry so impressed the president, Hugh Banzer Suarez, that he loaned the young evangelist his presidential jet to travel to meetings.

Nita Barrow

Nov. 15, 1916
Barbados

Dec. 18, 1995
Barbados

President of the World Council of Churches, 1983–91. Barrow was the director of the WCC Christian Medical Commission, 1975–81. Her responsibilities included advising church-affiliated health institutions throughout the world on all developments in health care. She served as president of the YWCA and of the International Council for Adult Education. She was permanent representative and ambassador of Barbados at the United Nations and later, governor-general of Barbados. She was the first foreign official to visit Nelson Mandela in jail, which helped to convince South African authorities to free him.

John S. Groenfeldt

Aug. 20, 1917
Sturgeon Bay, Wisconsin

Dec. 20, 1995
Watertown, Wisconsin

President of Provincial Elders Conference of Moravian Church in NA (North), Bethlehem, PA, 1962–82. Groenfeldt was a pastor, educator, and administrator. He pastored in Bethlehem, PA, from 1942–47. He became the first full-time general secretary of the Board of Christian Education and Evangelism for this entity, 1947–66. He also became the editor of *The Moravian* in 1947. Groenfeldt was involved in NCC and WCC functions. He and his wife, Eva, retired in 1982. His funeral was held at the Moravian Church in Sturgeon Bay, WI.

Audrey Wagner Mieir

May 12, 1916

1996
Leechburg, Pennsylvania

Musician, composer and humanitarian. Mieir was converted at age six at Pastor Walter Smith's invitation. She started piano lessons at age ten, was church pianist at 13, and taught piano while attending Life Bible College. She married Charles Mieir in 1936. She played the piano for the *Foursquare Gospel Radio Broadcast*, 1937–45. From 1946–58 she organized a number of choirs. At age 33, God gave her a son, Michael. She formed 50 musical groups and the popular PHIL KERR Monday night musicals in the Pasadena Civic Auditorium. Her 150-voice Harmony Chorus was a musical revolution. Her Mieir Choir Clinics spread her compositions and style worldwide. Audrey ministered in many churches. For years, she was choir director of Bethel Union Church, Duarte, CA. She wrote the lyrics and music for "I'll Never Be Lonely Again" (1957), and "His Name Is Wonderful" (1959).

Garland Franklin

Sept. 16, 1904
Pine Top, Kentucky

Jan. 7, 1996
Kissimmee, Florida

First president of Scripture Memory Mountain Mission, Emmalena, KY, 1932–59. Franklin's parents died at an early age so he moved in with relatives in Michigan. He married Ellebore Sullivan in 1925. He graduated from Wheaton (IL) College in 1931. Franklin returned to his native Hyden in eastern Kentucky in 1932 to minister among the children of the mountain people. The ministry relocated to Emmalena, KY, in 1934. In 1936 SMMM was incorporated. SMMM grew to a staff of 40 and property of 440 acres having a modern camp facility.

James F. Durkin

Nov. 12, 1925
Chicago, Illinois

Jan. 12, 1996
Eureka, California

Founder and first director of Gospel Outreach, Eureka, CA, 1971–91. Durkin had an amazing ministry. He came to the Hoopa area in 1946 for the U.S. Forest Service. He owned the Sequoia Realty in Eureka, 1966–71, when he closed the business to become a minister for Gospel Outreach at his Lighthouse Ranch, which housed as many as 150 at one time. It began in 1970 as a ministry and communal home for wandering "Jesus freaks." The church was started in a storefront and ended up as the large Church of the Highlands whose 850 seats were packed for his funeral. Gospel Outreach had grown into an international organization with 60 churches and overseas missions on four continents.

Gerrit C. Berkouwer

June 8, 1903
Amsterdam, Netherlands

Jan. 25, 1996

Theologian and writer. Berkouwer's first main work was *Faith and Revelation in Recent German Theology* (1932). In 1937, he wrote KARL BARTH, expressing fear that BARTH's view ultimately led to nominalism. In 1938, he published *The Problem of Scripture Criticism*. In 1945, he assumed the chair of dogmatics at the Free University. He also pastored in the northern province of Friesland and later in a suburb of Amsterdam. His *Studies in Dogmatics* was 14 volumes of theology, which was published, 1952–76. Volume eight, *Man the Image of God*, was outstanding.

G. Allen Fleece

Dec. 2, 1909
Louisville, Kentucky

Feb. 2, 1996
Clinton, South Carolina

President of Columbia (SC) Bible College (University in 1994), **1952–68.** Upon the death of R. C. McQUILKIN, Fleece became the president. Fleece was ordained into the Presbyterian Church in 1934, marrying Isabell Berry on June 30, 1934. They had three children. He pastored First Presbyterian Church, Covington, GA (1934–35) and Central Presbyterian Church, Chattanooga, TN (1936–37). He was on the faculty of CBC (1938–43), of MBI (1944–45), and back to CBC (1946–47). He then pastored at the Westminster Presbyterian Church, Chattanooga, TN (1948–51), and back to CBC the third time (1951–52).

Helen Duff Baugh

Feb. 19, 1903
County Fermanagh, Ireland

Feb. 7, 1996
Kansas City, Missouri

Founder of Christian Business and Professional Women (Stonecroft Ministries), **Kansas City, MO 1930s-96.** Emigrating to America, Helen's family was scheduled to sail on the *Titanic* but switched ships at the last moment. As a young woman, she and her sisters formed the Duff Sisters Gospel Trio. On January 23, 1929, she married Elwood Baugh in San Jose, CA. There, she organized 24 prayer groups. After her banker husband witnessed to a female employee, they invited several employees to a dinner, and Helen shared the gospel. That was the beginning of the nondenominational, prayer-based CBPW clubs, local outreach groups which hold monthly dinner meetings. After her husband's death in 1941, she traveled, starting more groups. In 1948, MARY E. CLARK joined Helen as an associate in ministry. They founded Christian Women's Clubs, 1948–49. By the time of her death, 83 countries of the world were benefiting from her ministries.

Ernest C. Manning

Sept. 20, 1908
Carnduff, Saskatchewan, Canada

Feb. 19, 1996
Calgary, Alberta, Canada

Premier of Alberta, Canada, in 1943 at only age 34. Manning served as premier of Alberta longer than any other person, 1943–68. In 1927, listening to the radio station CFCN of Calgary, he heard a sermon by WILLIAM ABERHART. He was reassured of his salvation and felt the call of God to a life of active Christian service. He was the first graduate of the local Prophetic Bible Institute. In 1935, with ABERHART as premier, Manning joined the government as provincial secretary and shortly was minister of the Trade and Industry Departments. He married Muriel Aileen Preston on April 14, 1936 and they had two children. He was a warm friend to CBMC, Gideons, and YFC movements. His Social Credit Party was strongly defeated after 18 months following his retirement. He wrote *Political Realignment: A Challenge to Thoughtful Canadians* (1967).

Loyce C. Carver

Dec. 13, 1918
Decaturville, Tennessee

March 10, 1996
Portland, Oregon

General overseer of Apostolic Faith Mission, Portland, OR, 1965–93. Carver was converted in 1937 at a camp in Merril, OR. He began preaching in 1943, after his marriage to Mary Frymire on Dec. 14, 1940 (died: Sept. 15, 2000). He pastored in Dallas, TX (1948–49); San Francisco, CA (1949–52); Los Angeles, CA (1952–56), and Medford, OR (1956–65). He died of cancer.

Alfred Martin

June 23, 1916
Kahoka, Missouri

March 14, 1996
Dallas, Texas

President of Accrediting Association of Bible Colleges, 1979–80, and long-time educator at Moody Bible Institute. Converted as a child, Martin married Dorothy McKay on October 9, 1945. He pastored a Presbyterian church, Pine City, MN (1945–48), then began a lengthy ministry at MBI (1949–80), where he served as teacher, head of the evening school, dean of faculty, vice-president, and dean of education. Regrouping to the Dallas area, he taught at the Dallas Bible College (1981–85) and the Southern Bible Institute (1985–93). He died of Parkinson's disease.

Jack W. Murray

Oct. 6, 1913
Laurium, Michigan

March 20, 1996
Sellersville, Pennsylvania

Bible teacher, director of the Harvey Cedars (NJ) Bible Conference, 1941–51; pastor of the Church of the Open Door (of Philadelphia), Fort Washington, 1951–59; and founder of Bible Evangelism Organization, Inc., in 1960. Murray married Eleanor Stephens, daughter of evangelist GEORGE STEPHENS. He was president of Shelton College, Cape May, NJ, from 1955–60. He also helped found Clearwater (FL) Christian College and Biblical Theological Seminary in Hatfield, NJ. He often preached for JACK WYRTZEN. His wife wrote "Jesus Christ Is the Way" and lyrics and music for "Behold, He Comes."

Robert S. Denny

July 23, 1914
Somerset, Kentucky

April 5, 1996
Orlando, Florida

General Secretary of Baptist World Alliance, 1969–80. Denny married Mary Webb in August, 1939 (died: January 1959) and Jane Bean on December 19, 1959. He was the Baptist student director at LSU (1939–41); director of religious affairs at Baylor University, Waco, TX (1941–45); associate department student work, Baptist Sunday School Board, Nashville, TN (1945–56); and associate secretary of BWA (1956–69).

Jack Wyrtzen

April 22, 1913
Brooklyn, New York

April 17, 1996
Glen Falls, New York

Founder and director of Word of Life, 1940–90. Wyrtzen was the premier youth leader of his generation, a soul winner, and an effective speaker. He was converted in October, 1932, through the witness of George Schilling in a camp. On December 3, 1933, he walked away from his dance band and began witnessing everywhere. He married Margie Smith (May 10, 1912–January 1, 1984) on April 18, 1936. They had five children, including Don, an outstanding musician. The WOL broadcasts began October 25, 1941 with 250 attending the broadcast rally. Mushrooming growth produced his first Madison Square Gardens Rally on April 1, 1944, with 20,000 attending and 10,000 turned away. In 1946, he purchased property at Schroon Lake, NY, with camps opening in 1947 and headquarters moving from New York

City. On June 19, 1948, at an anniversary rally at Yankee Stadium, some 1100 were saved. The first overseas camp was started in Brazil (1958) with Bible clubs starting there (1959), and a Bible institute (1971). Soon he was traveling the world, inspiring youth and camp ministries everywhere. In the 1980's, they developed a second camp and conference center in Hudson, FL. His Word of Life Institute has put a one-year Bible curriculum into thousands of young lives. Upon Marge's death in 1984, he married Joan Steiner on May 6, 1986. He wrote the chorus, "Yesterday, Today, and Tomorrow" (music by son, Don Wyrtzen).

Harold B. Stalley

May 18, 1910
Bangalore, India

April 24, 1996
Leicester, England

Director of Arab World Ministries, Upper Darby, PA, 1951–75. He came during the time of the name change from North Africa Mission in 1952. Born of missionary parents, Stalley pastored in England. There, he was challenged to reach the Muslim world, especially through a book by missionary Lilias Trotter. He and his wife, Jess, arrived in Algeria in 1934 with the Algiers Mission Band. All went well until World War II, when he was under house arrest for 18 months while living in Tlemcen, Algeria. He was erroneously thought to be a British spy as the Germans had temporary control of the area as France fell. Liberated by the Americans who had landed in Oran in November 1943, he then worked with the Red Cross for a year, winning many to Christ. He later pastored in Bury-St. Edmunds, England.

Eric Wickberg

June 6, 1904
Gavle, Sweden

April 26, 1996
Stockholm, Sweden

General of Salvation Army, 1969–74. Wickberg spent his boyhood in Germany, and his youth in Switzerland. He became assistant in command in Switzerland (1948) and the same position in Sweden (1953). In 1957, he was the director of the work in Germany. In 1961, he returned to London as chief of the staff. He often read the NT in original Greek. He participated in the dedication of the Salvation Army Residence for Senior Citizens in NYC in February, 1969. He married Margarete Dietrich (1932) and Elvor Lindberg (1977). He wrote *The Charge—My Way of Preaching* and his autobiography, *God's Conscript*.

Lester F. Sumrall

Feb. 15, 1913
New Orleans, Louisiana

April 28, 1996
South Bend, Indiana

Pentecostal missionary statesman and director/chairman of Lester Sumrall Ministries, South Bend, IN, 1957–96. Sumrall was healed of tuberculosis at age 17 and soon became an evangelist. Sumrall married Louise Layman on Sept. 30, 1944. From 1947–65 he pastored the Calvary Assembly of God (Bethel) Church in South Bend, IN. He built a church in Manilla (1952) and one in Hong Kong (1959). He worked mainly out of his church, Christian Center Cathedral of Praise, South Bend, which he founded and pastored, 1965–96. Sumrall was the founder and owner of ten TV stations, 1972–96. He was also the founder and president of World Harvest Bible College, South Bend (1975–96), and the president of Indiana Christian University there (1989–96). He was the founder of the global Feed the Hungry, 1987–96. He wrote 130 teaching guides and books and published the *World Harvest Magazine*.

Herman Gockel

Oct. 11, 1906
Cleveland, Ohio

May 1, 1996
Cupertino, California

Member of National Religious Broadcasters Hall of Fame. In 1939, Gockel began working with the International Lutheran Laymen's League of St. Louis. He also wrote numerous books, one, *What Jesus Means to Me* (1948) selling over 400,000 copies. Early on, he pastored in Illinois and Indiana and headed advertising at Concordia Publishing House, St. Louis. His wife's name was Mildred. Gockel was the editor of *The Lutheran Church—Missouri Synod* magazine and headed the denomination's debut of the television program, *This Is the Life* in 1952. For 20 years, he supervised the writing and production of more than 500 episodes of the telecast. This program pioneered the syndicated religious drama.

Eugenia Price

June 22, 1916
Charleston, West Virginia

May 28, 1996
St. Simone, Georgia

Outstanding writer, radio and communication expert. Eugenia entered Northwestern Dental School, Chicago, IL (1936), and began her career as a radio writer and producer (1939). An old friend from Calvary Episcopal Church, Pittsburgh, PA, became the means of her conversion in 1949. She then closed out Eugenia Price Productions. In 1950, she began her Christian radio work with *A Visit with Genie*. Then from 1950–56 she wrote, produced and directed the famed *Unshackled* program of Pacific Garden Mission. In 1953, she wrote her first book, *Discoveries Made from Living My New Life*. In 1955, she wrote her autobiography, *The Burden Is Light*. In 1965, she released her first novel *The Beloved Invader*. In 1978, she received the Governor's Award in the Arts for Literature. Her some 35 books have sold 15 million copies in 17 languages. Much of her collection of papers, letters, and manuscripts are in the archives at Boston (MA) University.

Karl A. Olsson

June 10, 1913
Renton, Washington

June 2, 1996
Columbia, Maryland

President of North Park Theological Seminary and College, Chicago, IL, 1959–70. Olsson married Dorothy Carlson on Sept. 14, 1935. Ordained to the Evangelical Covenant Church in 1942, he pastored in Minneapolis and Chicago (1933–38); was instructor at NP College and Seminary (1938–40); and at the University of Chicago (1940–42 and 1945–48). Olsson also served as a chaplain in the army in WWII from 1942–45 and 1950–52. He then returned to NPTS where he was professor of church history, 1948–50, 52–59. His writings began with *Things Common and Preferred* (1959).

David A. Hubbard

April 8, 1928
Stockton, California

June 7, 1996
Santa Barbara, California

President of and professor at Fuller Theological Seminary, 1963–93, and president of American Association of Theological Schools, 1976–78. Hubbard was a Conservative Baptist educator who led Fuller Seminary, Pasadena, CA, in a different direction from that of the founding father's (CHARLES FULLER) moorings. He married Ruth Doyal on Aug 12, 1949. He was ordained in the Conservative Baptist Church in 1952. He was also professor at Westmont College, Santa Barbara, CA from 1957–63. Hubbard became a well-known conference speaker, university lecturer, and author, and spoke on *The Joyful Sound* for a while, which succeeded the *Old Fashioned Revival Hour*. Many changes took place at Fuller Seminary during his 30-year tenure, which were welcomed by some and frowned upon by others. His writings were from *Is God Dead?* (1961) to *Ecclesiastes, Song of Solomon* (1991). He died of a heart attack.

Annie R. Jiagge

Oct. 7, 1918

June 12, 1996
Ghana Accra, Ghana

President of the World Council of Churches, 1975–83. Jiagge came into the ecumenical movement with her involvement in the YWCA. She was the appeals court judge and then the first woman on the Supreme Court bench in Ghana. She was a member of the Evangelical Presbyterian Church. She spoke at the Kottayam world conference of Christian youth in 1952. In 1967, she represented the WCC at the Catholic laity conference in Rome and from 1984 onwards, was the moderator of the Commission on the Program to Combat Racism. She was also a committee member of the Christian Council of Ghana. Her husband's name was Frederick. Jiagge died after a long illness.

Bernard M. Loftin

March 5, 1915   *June 16, 1996*
De Ridder, California   Shreveport, Louisiana

President of Bible Missionary Institute, Rock Island, IL, 1968–83. Loftin was converted in a brush arbor meeting in Pleasant Hill, LA as a teenager. He married Nyla (Yvonne) Carnes on October 11, 1939. He then pastored several places in Louisiana, Illinois, and Oklahoma for the Church of the Nazarene. In 1956, Loftin switched his allegiance to the Bible Missionary Church. He taught at their college, 1962–64, then pastored in Duncan, OK, before returning as president. Following his tenure at the school, he was district moderator (1983–85), then went back to teaching at BMI (1985–92). He developed a slow-growing cancer, which eventually caused a heart attack.

C. Morse Ward

March 20, 1909   *July 12, 1996*
Toronto, Ontario, Canada   Modesto, California

Host of the Assemblies of God radio broadcast *Revivaltime*, 1953–78. Ward's family moved to Springfield, MO, when he was a teenager. On December 25, 1929, he married Dorothy Hymes. Up to 1945, they lived in Eastern Canada in a pastorate and later, evangelistic ministry. In 1945–55, he went to pastor the Full Gospel Tabernacle in Bakersfield, CA. He used radio very effectively there, and he was the unanimous choice to launch the nationwide Assemblies of God *Revivaltime* broadcast. For 25 years (1,300 weekly broadcasts), he spoke to some 12 million each week from Springfield. He also became president of Bethany College, Scotts Valley, CA, from 1973–78. He authored 23 volumes of radio sermons among other writings.

Floyd Ankerberg

Dec. 29, 1917   *Aug. 16, 1996*
Jacksonville, Florida   Arlington Heights, Illinois

Evangelist and missions enthusiast. Floyd's father, Joe, was a soul winner, street preacher, and spiritual patriarch. Ankerberg carried on in the highest tradition, and his son, John, continues on with an effective television program. He married Elaine Erickson on April 6, 1945, and she carried on Floyd's work after his death. He pastored for six years; and in the days of YFC's greatest outreach, he was Eastern regional director and an evangelist holding many crusades, 1947–57. He then directed Greater Chicago Sunday School Association, 1958–62, but with evangelism burning in his soul, re-entered that field until he died. In the latter years, great crowds gathered in many sections of the world. India, Haiti, and Romania were some of his favorite preaching targets. In 1985, he was found to have cancer and was told he had three months to live. After this discovery, he founded 300 churches in India, provided monthly support for 235 of them, and started a Christian orphanage in Romania.

Roy M. Pearson

March 10, 1914   *Aug. 31, 1996*
Somerville, Massachusetts   New London, New Hampshire

President of Andover-Newton Theological Seminary, Newton Center, MA, 1965–79. Ordained to the Congregational ministry in 1938, Pearson held pastorates in Swanzey, NH (1938–40); Amherst, MA (1940–47); and in Lexington, MA (1947–54). He held a number of offices with the Congregational Christian Churches and authored some nine books. He spent several summers as a volunteer pastor with the Maine Seacoast Missionary Society and preached and lectured in Europe as well. After his retirement, he was interim pastor in several places and a member of FBC of New London. He married Barbara Cerello on September 1, 1990. Life ended tragically for the 82-year-old Pearson and his wife, as he missed a stop sign and collided with another car. He was killed there and his wife died shortly thereafter in the hospital. His writings range from *Here's Faith for You* (1953) to *Prayers for All Occasions* (1990).

Alfred Jensen

Jan. 6, 1893
Des Moines, Iowa

Sept. 1, 1996
Brenderup, Denmark

President of the Danish Evangelical Lutheran Church, 1936–54, renamed American Evangelical Lutheran Church (LCA, ELCA in 1988), **1954–60**. Jensen came to America in 1911. He was ordained on November 28, 1920, and then pastored in Cordova, NE (1920–23 and 1930–32); Tyler, MN (1923–30); and Kimballtown, IA (1932–42). He married Nilda Schmidt on January 4, 1922, and they had four children. He later married Vera E. Hellfritzes in 1955.

Arthur S. Flemming

June 12, 1905
Kingston, New York

Sept. 7, 1996
Alexandria, Virginia

President of the National Council of Churches, 1966–69. Flemming married Bernice Moler on December 14, 1934. He was a member of the U.S. Civil Service Commission, 1939–48. He was a Methodist. He was president of Ohio Wesleyan College, Delaware, OH from 1948–53 and 1957–58. For 20 years, he served in various federal government official positions. He headed up the Office of Defense mobilization, and the Office of Production Management during WWII days. He had served as Secretary of Health, Education, and Welfare in the cabinets of President DWIGHT EISENHOWER, 1958–61. He was also president of the University of Oregon, Eugene, OR (1964–68) and of Macalester College, St. Paul, Minnesota (1968–71). Flemming was the second layman to be named to the NCC post since its inception in 1950.

Paul J. Levin

Oct. 13, 1914
Rock Island, Illinois

Sept. 7, 1996
Normal, Illinois

Baptist evangelist and distributor of gospel literature. Levin's mother led him to Christ when he was five. By age 17, he was in evangelism endeavors. Levin started in evangelism in 1934 with a blind gospel singer, Bob Findley (born: Cedar Rapids, IA, on August 19, 1903). Paul and Bob's duets are legendary with guitar and mandolin accompaniment. They traveled 40 years together. He married Dorothy Hayslip on March 17, 1936 (died: October, 1994). He wrote some 37 tracts and started Bible Tracts, Inc., which published over 455 million tracts in 94 languages by 1938. It was incorporated in May, 1955. He ministered on 30 radio stations with a daily broadcast. In 1995, a doctor told him he had cancer which had spread to his spine and ribs. He never recovered. Levin's last sermon was July 7, 1996, in Lincoln, IL, and his funeral was at Calvary Baptist Church, Normal, IL. He wrote *Pre–Wedding Days* (1935) and *One Step at a Time* (1976).

Richard V. Clearwaters

June 28, 1900
Wilmot, Kansas

Sept. 30, 1996
Minneapolis, Minnesota

Pastor of Fourth Baptist Church, 1940–82; founder and first president of Central Baptist Theological Seminary, 1956–82 (both in Minneapolis, MN); **and founder of Pillsbury Baptist Bible College, Owanatoona, MN 1957–58**. Both schools were part of the Conservative Baptist Association, in those days. After the accidental death of his youngest brother (age 11), Clearwaters was converted on December 10, 1921, at the Moran Methodist Church of Spokane, WA. He was called to preach while hearing his mother sing "The Ninety and Nine" in her kitchen. On April 17, 1935, he married Florence L. Welch (died: 1989). He pastored in Manhattan, IL (1926–29); Lawton, MI; and Bethel Baptist, Kalamazoo, MI (1935–39). In 1943, he was one of the founders of the CB Foreign Mission Society. Clearwaters was professor at Northwestern Schools and dean of their seminary for five years, 1951–56. In 1956, NS reorganized and dropped the seminary and Bible school, so he organized CBTS with 32 students, and a year later, PBBC with 110 students.

J. Edward Smith

Oct. 24, 1910
Philadelphia, Pennsylvania

Oct. 15, 1996
Sarasota, Florida

Director of Pocket Testament League, 1963–78. Under Smith's leadership, the agency became capable of sustaining a number of concurrent evangelistic campaigns in many parts of the world. He followed ALFRED KUNZ in this position. His wife's name was Charlotte. PTL expanded into 32 countries under his leadership. In 1976, he saw that the special bicentennial Gospel of John was sent to each member of Congress. He left an executive position in the Insurance Company of North America to accept the PTL position.

Charles W. Carter

May 14, 1905
Southport, Indiana

Oct. 21, 1996
Marian, Indiana

Wesleyan theologian. Carter was converted in an area-wide evangelistic crusade in Brookings, SD in 1923. In 1928, he and his wife, Elizabeth, went to Sierra Leone for three years with the Wesleyan Methodists. Following further education, they returned, 1934–35, and he presided at the Clarke Memorial Biblical Seminary. Back in the US, he taught such subjects as missions, Bible, and philosophy at Marion (IN) College, 1946–57. From 1959–71, Carter did the same at Taylor University, Upland, IN. From 1972–74, he taught in Taiwan, then back at Marion College (Indiana Wesleyan University) in 1988.

Oscar H. Hirt

Aug. 29, 1921
Philadelphia, Pennsylvania

Nov. 7, 1996
Collingswood, New Jersey

General director of Bible Club Movement, Upper Darby, PA 1965–95. From 1939–85, Hirt worked for O. H. Hirt, Inc., a Center City (NJ) photography and movie supply business founded by his father in 1912. He sold the business (1985) and it soon closed (1992). He was married to Jane Barron for 52 years. He also served on the BCM board before being named general director in 1965. When he arrived in 1965, there were fewer than 100 missionaries evangelizing through Bible study groups and clubs and teacher training. When he retired, there were more than 700 missionaries in 45 countries. He was a member of the Haddon Heights (NJ) Baptist Church.

Andrew Telford

April 12, 1895
Burlington, Ontario, Canada

Nov. 21, 1996
Boca Raton, Florida

Outstanding pastor and Bible conference speaker. Telford was converted at age 22 at his bedside after listening to Ebenezer Hooper preach. He served in WWI in France. He then served as a missionary with the Plymouth Brethren in Bolivia and Argentina, 1920–24, after marrying Mae Clifford (1900–64) on a July 30th in the early 1920s. Telford pastored in Three Rivers, MI (1924–32), then the Metropolitan Bible Church of Ottawa, Ontario (1932–43). He pastored the Berachah Church of Philadelphia, 1943–66. The church moved to a nearby suburb, Cheltenham, in 1959. Upon his wife's death, he married Henrietta Protst in 1966, who died about three years after his passing. Telford taught for 21 years at the Philadelphia College of the Bible, Washington Bible College, and Berean College in Allentown, PA. From 1966–92 he traveled in Bible conferences across the country, driving his own car up to age 97 and living in Boca Raton, FL. He attended MBI and was their oldest alumni for many years. He wrote 17 books on Bible study subjects.

Gordon Michalson

Aug. 22, 1911
Waverly, Minnesota

Nov. 28, 1996
San Diego, California

President of Claremont (CA) School of Theology, 1968–77. Michalson's pastorates in Methodist churches were in Kimball and Norwood, MN (1935–38) and in New Jersey, including East Orange (1939–42), Summit (1945–46), Montclair (1948–52), and Westfield (1952–58). He served in the US Navy, 1942–45. From 1958–60, Michalson was professor of historical theology at Garrett Theological Seminary, Evanston, IL. At Claremont, he saw the completion of three major building projects. He was president of MacMurray College, Jacksonville, IL, from 1960–68.

Paul E. Freed

Aug. 29, 1918
Detroit, Michigan

Dec. 1, 1996
Cary, North Carolina

Founder and first president of Trans-World Radio, Chatham, NJ, 1956–90, Cary, NC 1990–94, one of the most outstanding worldwide evangelistic thrusts in history. Freed's parents, RALPH AND MILDRED, were missionaries to the Arabs in the Middle East for 30 years. Freed married Betty Seawell (born: October 2, 1923) on October 17, 1945, and they had five children. While directing the Greensboro (NC) YFC (1946–50), he made six survey trips to Europe (1947–52), primarily Spain and Morocco. He was ordained a Southern Baptist in 1949 and served as an evangelist (1950–52). On February 11, 1952, he founded *Voice of Tangier*. On February 22, 1954, his father spoke the first words on a small transmitter of 2,500 watts in Tangier, Morocco. In December 1959, the station was transferred to Monte Carlo, Monaco, and incorporated under TWR. Soon more studios were born: Bonaire, Netherlands Antilles, (1964); Brazil and South Africa (1974); Sri Lanka (1978); Uruguay (1981); and radio stations in Albania (1990–93). Also there are transmitters in Cyprus and Guam. He traveled to 160 nations, and upon his retirement in 1993, the work had grown to 11 transmitters, with the gospel going out in 120 languages by the time of his death.

Milton B. Engebretson

Dec. 23, 1920
Grand Forks, North Dakota

Dec. 10, 1996
Northbrook, Illinois

President of Evangelical Covenant Church, Chicago, IL 1967–86. Engebretson married Esther Hollenbeck on December 12, 1945. Ordained in the ECC in 1956, he pastored Stotler Mission Covenant Church, Osage City, KS (1951–52); MCC, Manakato, MN (1954–57); Elim Covenant Church, Minneapolis, MN (1957–62); and was executive secretary of the denomination in Chicago, IL (1962–67). He died of cancer.

Wiley A. Welsh

June 23, 1917
Ft. Worth, Texas

Dec. 12, 1996
Dallas, Texas

President of Lexington (KY) Theological Seminary, 1965–74. Welsh was ordained ino the ministry of the Christian Church in 1935. He married Jennie Neal on August 7, 1938 (died: February, 1963) and Billie R. Cain on November 26, 1964. He was professor of NT at Brite Divinity School (1941–42, 1945–49) and pastored in Texas churches (1949–52). From 1974 on, he was president of the Christian Board of Publications, St. Louis, MO.

Timothy L. Smith

April 13, 1924
Central, South Carolina

Jan. 20, 1997
West Palm Beach, Florida

Pioneer for evangelicals in secular universities, a true historian of religion. Smith's articles appeared in nearly every historical journal. He married Anne Wright on June 26, 1944. He won acclaim for his 1957 book, *Revivalism and Social Reform*. He also wrote a history of the Nazarene Church entitled *Called unto Holiness*. He was professor of history and education at Johns Hopkins University, Baltimore, MD, for many years. He was a leading authority on the history of European immigration to the United States and the history of American education. Before his JH post, he pastored Nazarene churches in Cliftondale, MA (1944–48); Portland, MA (1948–49); and Boulder, CO (1957–58). He also taught at Eastern Nazarene College (1949–56); East Texas State College (1958–61); and the University of Minnesota (1961–68).

Paul Mininger

Jan. 24, 1908
Marshallville, Ohio

Jan. 23, 1997
Goshen, Indiana

President of Goshen (IN) College, 1954–71. Mininger had extensive education at Goshen College, Kansas City Baptist Seminary, Eastern Baptist Seminary, and the University of Pennsylvania. He was a public schoolteacher in Missouri and Kansas 1926–31. He then did mission work in Kansas and Pennsylvania, 1931–36. Mininger married Mary Ellen Erb on June 25, 1933. They had three children. Prior to his college leadership he pastored the North Goshen (IN) Mennonite Church, 1938–54. He passed away at the Greencroft Health Care facilities.

Frederick W. Whittaker

Jan. 26, 1913
New Haven, Connecticut

Jan. 23, 1997
Sarasota, Florida

President of Bangor (ME) Theological Seminary, 1952–78, and Association of Theological Schools, 1974–76. Whittaker married Shirley Johns on September 14, 1940. He was ordained in the Congregational Christian Church in 1944. He pastored in Robbinston and Red Beach, ME (1940–42); Yarmouth, ME (1943–44) and Shelton, CT (1944–48). He taught church history at BTS from 1948–52. He was active in the United Church of Christ. His funeral was at the First Congregational United Church of Christ in Sarasota.

Wes Auger

Nov. 23, 1919
Richmond Hill, Long Island, New York

Jan. 25, 1997
Greenville, South Carolina

Evangelist and gospel musician. Auger spent nearly a lifetime in crusades and church planting. He was converted as a teenager at PERCY CRAWFORD's Pinebrook Bible Conference. He married his wife, Dorothy, in November of 1939. For twelve years, he pastored the Calvary Baptist Church of Pompano Beach, FL in the 1960s. He had a standing tirade against Communism and wrote such books as *The Great Conspiracy*. He lived and worked out of Greenville, SC, for the last 30 years, where he died of a heart attack.

James A. Keiller

Aug. 27, 1906
Inverkeithing, Scotland

Jan. 25, 1997
Atlanta, Georgia

President of Beulah Heights Bible College, Atlanta, GA, 1958–74. Keiller's family came to America in 1908, settling in Kenosha, WI. He was converted there at age 14. He married Grace Modder (November 25, 1901–October 5, 1995) on June 10, 1931, and they had two sons. Keiller pastored in Kenosha, WI (1926–28); Beloit, WI (1928–34); Rapid City, SD (1936–38); Macon, GA (1946–49); Newton, IA (1951–56); Midland, MI (1956–58); and Atlanta, GA, 1958 on. He was ordained by the National and International Pentecostal Missionary Union (International Pentecostal Church of Christ). In this denomination, he served as general secretary, vice chairman, and general chairman. He attended MBI for a short time.

Vernon R. Wiebe

Nov. 7, 1926
Corn, Oklahoma

Jan. 28, 1997
Hillsboro, Kansas (?)

General secretary of Mennonite Brethren Mission Services, Hillsboro, KS, 1968–82, and president of EFMA, 1979–81. From 1952–65, Wiebe served Tabor College in a variety of capacities including dean of students, athletic director, and fund-raiser. His wife's name was Rubena. He was pastor of the Edmond (OK) MB Church, 1965–68. Wiebe accepted the mission's position and traveled around the world visiting, encouraging, and mentoring MB missionaries. He founded the Kansas 500 Mennonite Men's Chorus in 1969. Wiebe was interim president of Tabor College, Hillsboro, 1987–88. He died of lymphoma, which he had since November, 1995. His memorial service was in the MB Church in Hillsboro, KS.

Robert Blodgett

June 16, 1927
Kansas City, Missouri

Feb. 20, 1997
Brownsville, Texas

Founder and director of Mexican Border Missions, Brownsville, TX, 1960–97. Blodgett was converted in Kansas City. He married Dorothy Randall on July 3, 1954. Blodgett was in evangelism, then pastored in Mt. Moriah, MO. Headquartering in Brownsville, he expanded his evangelism and church planting burdens, and soon had 14 churches, up to 300 miles away. He had several outreaches, including a major one in San Luis Potosi. Heart trouble and surgery took its toll. Within a year, he died.

Alfred O. Fuerbringer

Aug. 11, 1903
St. Louis, Missouri

Feb. 26, 1997
Norman, Oklahoma

President of Concordia Seminary, St Louis, MO 1953–69. Fuerbringer's father (LUDWIG) served in the same position, 1931–43. Fuerbringer married Carolyn Kuhlman on June 1, 1934, and they had four children. Ordained Lutheran (1927), he pastored denominational churches as follows: Trinity of Norman, OK (1927–34); Trinity of Okmulgee, OK (1934–37) and St. Paul's, Leavenworth, KS (1937–41). He also served as president of Concordia Teacher's College, Seward, NE, 1941–53, and represented his denomination, Lutheran Church—Missouri Synod, in many capacities, both in the U.S. and abroad. From 1974–83, he was professor, coordinator of matching funds of Christ Seminary, Seminex, St. Louis. He suffered from lupus the last years of his long life.

Paul E. Kauffman
April 3, 1920   *March 3, 1997*

President of Asian Outreach, Int., 1966–97. Kauffman spent the first 17 years of his life in China and Korea with his missionary parents. He initiated a new Bible translation in the anticipation of the day when China would open up, which it has, and Chinese scholars and students are now using it. He developed many national leaders. With a burden to reach Asians for Christ, Kauffman and his wife, Janet, arrived in Hong Kong in 1960. In a one-room, one-desk office he began his ministry in 1966. Thirty years later, it had a network that involved dedicated Christian workers from 20 nationalities in 27 offices and ministry centers.

Rufus Jones
Jan. 19, 1915   *March 8, 1997*
Stewart, Tennessee   Lodi, California

President of Conservative Baptist Home Missionary Society (Mission to the Americas), **Wheaton, IL 1950–80, and of National Association of Evangelicals, 1966–67.** He married, March 10, 1936. Jones led the mission into urban ministry and campus ministry. He had a special burden for African-Americans. Jones was diagnosed with cancer in 1967 and given a few months to live. However, he lived for 30 additional years. The disease came back (1993), went into remission, and then came back to stay (1996). He also served as president of the International College and Graduate School of Theology in Honolulu.

Max R. Kronquest
March 26, 1910   *March 10, 1997*
Bertrand, Nebraska   Anchorage, Alaska

Director of Missionary Gospel Fellowship, Turlock, CA 1949–74. Kronquest was converted in 1929 through the influence of First Baptist Church, North Platte, NE. He went to Denver (CO) Bible Institute and married Vanita Hecht on April 3, 1933. He was afflicted with polio and rheumatic fever a good part of his life. He did evangelism in CCC Camps, and pastored in Brady, NE; Butte, NE; Lainsburg, MI, and Santa Fe, NM. Soon he was visiting prisons and working among migrant farm workers. He had a broadcast that reached into Mexico. Kronquest was visitation pastor at Grace Baptist, Santa Anna, CA, in later years. He also did volunteer work for Wycliffe Translators and Child Evangelism. He moved to Palmer, AK, to be near his son, where he had a stroke which caused his death.

Harold J. Barrett
Jan. 27, 1911   *March 20, 1997*
Lancaster, Pennsylvania   Wilkesboro, Pennsylvania

Director of Primitive Methodist Church Missions, 1958–86. Barrett married Margaret Charlton on September 5, 1936. He served as pastor of several churches in Wisconsin from 1938 on. He then served the Mt. Carmel (PA) PM Church for 25 years, 1952–77. He also served nine years as a missionary in Guatemala. He died after a lingering illness.

Earle Schultz
June 17, 1924   *April 9, 1997*
Trenton, Maryland   Glen Ellyn, Illinois

Youth for Christ leader for 50 years, he served in many capacities. Schultz was converted by a fellow soldier during his army air force service at Williams Air Force Base in Arizona in 1944. He married Barbara Frush on August 20, 1950 (born: April 22, 1924). Schultz's YFC ministry, with some overlapping, was directing the Hampstead, MD, rally (22 years); VP, Eastern Region (1959–72); Overseas Director (1972–74); Area Director, NA (1974–84); starting YFC in Mexico, Guatemala, and Panama, Military Representative (at least six years); and VP World Outreach Office (at least three years). He edited a video of *The History of Youth for Christ*, completed by WENDY COLLINS, when cancer was discovered in 1995.

Elizabeth (Betty) Greene

June 24, 1920
Seattle (Evergreen Point), Washington

April 10, 1997
Bellevue, Washington

Founder of missionary aviation as a tool for gospel outreach. Betty did the most to get this specialized service in motion. She was the first full-time staff worker and the first pilot for Missionary Aviation Fellowship. She was a Presbyterian and worked unselfishly in the denomination for 30 years. Betty was in the air force during WWII, flying radar missions and later was assigned to developmental projects that included flying B-7 bombers in high-altitude equipment tests. She began taking flying lessons at age 16. She and Jim Truxton, a navy pilot, who also had developed ideas about missionary aviation, teamed up with Grady Parrott and started Christian Missionary Airmen's Fellowship (MAF). The first service they attempted found her flying a plane down to Mexico in 1946 to Wycliffe people. Betty then helped in Peru, Nigeria, East Africa, and spent her last two years of service in Irian Jaya, 1960–62. NATE SAINT said that she "was a pilot of such caliber that local airline and military pilots regarded her with great respect." She was the first woman to fly over the Andes in a single-engine airplane. She retired in 1982.

Newton C. Conant

Nov. 18, 1900
Philadelphia, Pennsylvania

April 26, 1997
Rydal Park, Pennsylvania

Key leader in the Bible Protestant Church (Fellowship of Fundamental Bible Churches in 1985), **Penns Grove, NJ**. Conant went as a young man to Camden, NJ, and began the Bible Protestant Church without any money. It grew to 400 members during his 40-year ministry there. His wife's name was Edna. He wrote several books, his most well-known being *Changed by Beholding Him*. Al Odom of Harvey Cedars (NJ) Bible Conference said he was the greatest Christian he ever knew and that his love for Christ was unsurpassed. From 1970–75, he was in Africa. He served as a chaplain at Biblical Seminary, Hatfield, PA, from 1981–91. At age 93, he went to Moscow to train Christian leaders for the former Soviet Union at St. James Bible College there.

James M. Beddow

June 5, 1911
Chelby County, Montana

April 28, 1997
Independence, Kansas

President of Fire-Baptized Holiness Church (Bible Holiness Church in 1995), **Independence, KS, 1958–77**. Beddow lived in the Independence, KS, area. He married Elizabeth Sheahan on September 27, 1931 (died: May 10, 1943), Ruby Raney on October 11, 1946 (died: September 30, 1985) and Vera Wallingford on December 4, 1986. He was converted in January, 1937 and ordained at an Independence camp meeting in 1940. Beddow pastored BHC in Middletown, MO; Kansas City, MO; Fredonia, KS; Bowling Green, MO; Oswego, KS, and Altamont, KS.

Oliver W. Hasselblad

Feb. 7, 1909
Beresford, South Dakota

May 3, 1997
Redlands, California

General Secretary of American Leprosy Mission (ALM Int.), **Greenville, SC, 1959–74**. Early on, Hasselblad was an American Baptist medical missionary in Jorhat, India, 1938–59, working with leprosy patients. In India, his facility grew from 25 beds to 225 beds. After his retirement from ALM, he continued to work with lepers in Jamaica and the Hawaiian Islands. His wife's name was Norma. Hasselblad was a deacon in the Riverside Church, New York City, under the ministry of ROBERT MCCRACKEN. He died of lymphoid sarcoma (cancer) in a retirement center. He lived in Redlands the last 12 years of his life.

Ralph I. Yarnell

March 4, 1915
Snowshoe, Pennsylvania

May 9, 1997
Haines City, Florida

First general secretary of American Council of Christian Churches, 1958–64. Yarnell married Hilda Herbert on March 4, 1939. He serviced Evangelical United Brethren Churches in Ohio, 1944–49. He then founded the Grace Gospel Church in Marietta, OH, and was ordained on Aug.ust31, 1949. In 1958, Yarnell moved to Montclair, NJ, to become the general secretary of ACC with offices in New York City. He traveled to five continents and 30 countries and spoke in every state except Hawaii. In 1962, he returned to Marietta where again he pastored the same church whose name was changed to Grace Baptist Church. He then moved to Devola, OH. He helped to establish 23 Christian schools throughout Ohio. Yarnell was president of Independent Faith Mission for 23 years, headquartered in Greensboro, NC. He retired to Haines City, FL, in 1991.

William R. Cannon

April 5, 1916
Chattanooga, Tennessee

May 11, 1997
Atlanta, Georgia

Methodist bishop and dean of Candler School of Theology, Atlanta, GA, 1953–68. Ordained a Methodist in 1940, Cannon pastored in Oxford, GA (1942–43), and then went to CST as professor of church history and historical theology (1943–68). He then served as bishop in Raleigh, NC (1968–72 and 1980–84); Richmond, VA (1970–72), and back in Atlanta (1972–80). He gave the inauguration prayer for President Jimmy Carter in 1977. Cannon's writings were from *A Faith for These Times* (1944) to *The Book of Acts* (1989). He was one of the leading Methodist leaders of his generation.

"*The principles by which I have tried to live are complete devotion to Jesus Christ, loyalty to His church (United Methodist), daily Bible reading and prayer, service to others, and concern for the betterment of humanity.*"

Edward (Eddie) W. Martin

Nov. 25, 1915
Philadelphia, Pennsylvania

May 17, 1997
Lancaster, Pennsylvania

Evangelist. Martin was one of the most successful evangelists of his generation. With a Southern Baptist base, he reached out to people of many persuasions. Martin's family was converted by a woman passing out gospel tracts who came to their door. Now "Mother Martin" left tracts out for rebellious teenager, Eddie, and soon he too was converted. Martin was in the rock wool industry and, for a while, owned nearly 40 suits. He was called to preach as an evangelist. In the early 1940s, he led a gospel team for PTL and saw much spiritual fruit. Soon he was filling huge tents with thousands attending. He published *The Law of Harvest*. He spent considerable time in El Salvador. Martin worked with 1,250 pastors in 1,500 crusades and revivals. He often spent from 4:00 to 7:00 p.m. in personal visitation and soul winning. For 50 years, he traveled the country, headquarting from Lancaster, PA. He died of cancer.

Paul C. Hartford

Oct. 11, 1914
Portland, Oregon

May 19, 1997
St. Petersburg, Florida

Pioneer pilot. Hartford was one of the early Christian leaders to use an airplane for ministry. Converted at age eight, he was a trumpeter for AIMEE SEMPLE MCPHERSON at age 16. He married Dorothy Green on December 24, 1935 (died: December 10, 1995). He went to Cuba briefly as a missionary, then took a church in Pontiac, MI, from 1941–44 and enrolled in a flying course. He bought a plane and worked with a Wycliffe missionary for two months. Soon he obtained 300 acres of former pasture in Warsaw, IN, and with four planes, was training pilots how to fly. He formed Victory Sky Pilots. As Youth For Christ was spreading world wide, they assigned the Caribbean to him and he began the movement, island by island. He was the first to fly a single-engine plane over the Andes Mountains. He rebuilt his own engines whenever there was a need. Many years later he was vice president and pilot for World Opportunities, Los Angeles. In later years he opened a Christian counseling center in St. Petersburg, FL. He was a preacher, song leader and multi-talented in Christian outreaches. He died of complications of diabetes.

Samuel D. Proctor

July 13, 1921
Norfolk, Virginia

May 22, 1997
Mt. Vernon, Iowa

Respected preacher and educator, pastor of Abyssinian Baptist Church, Harlem, NY, 1972–89. Proctor married Bessie Tate on September 23, 1944. After helping to found the Peace Corps, where he gave leadership to the African division, he served as president of Virginia Union College, Richmond, VA (1955–60, and North Carolina A&T State, Greensboro, NC (1960–64). He retired as professor at Rutgers University, New Brunswick, NJ. Proctor continued to serve as distinguished professor at various places and became a mentor to MARTIN L. KING Jr. He wrote several books. He died of a heart attack while speaking at Cornell University, Ithaca, NY. At his funeral, Jesse Jackson said, "I have spent all of my adult life trying to make Dr. Proctor proud of me."

Lehmann Strauss

Nov. 29, 1911
Lancaster, Pennsylvania

June 5, 1997
Tampa, Florida

Pastor and Bible conference speaker. Strauss was led to Christ at age 16. He was married at age 20 in 1931 to Elsie Hannah (died: September 1989). In February, 1994, he married Diane Vaughan. Strauss was an independent Baptist pastor at Calvary Baptist Church of Bristol, PA, from 1939–58, during which time the membership increased to eight times the original number. Since 1945, he was a guest teacher of Old Testament history at Philadelphia Bible Institute (his alma mater). From 1958–63, he pastored the large Highland Park Baptist Church in Detroit. Then with many open doors, Strauss launched into a Bible conference ministry throughout the USA, Europe, and South Africa the last 34 years of his life. Radio began in the late 1960s via the *BIOLA Hour* and in the 1970s he developed his own *Bible Study Time* which continued after his death. With complications from a heart and blood disease taking its toll, he preached his last sermon back at Calvary Baptist on June 1, 1997. The 1 hour and 10 minute message was on "The making of a Christian Pastor," four days before his death. He was struck en route to Word of Life in Hudson, FL, and rushed to a Tampa hospital, where he died.

B. Myron Cedarholm

June 20, 1915
St. Paul, Minnesota

June 6, 1997
Dundedin, Florida

Founder and first president of Maranatha Baptist Bible College, Watertown, WI, 1968–83, and general director of Conservative Baptist Association of America, 1949–65. Cedarholm was led to the Lord by his parents and baptized at the age of seven. He married Thelma Melford (born: August 3, 1915) on September 6, 1941. He pastored the Lehigh Ave. Baptist Church of Philadelphia (1943–47), then worked with the Conservative Baptist Association of America (1947–49) as field director. He became president of Pillsbury Baptist College of Owatonna, MN, from 1965–68. Some 800 attended his funeral in Watertown, WI. His father, Anto Cedarholm, was a well-known gospel singer and evangelist, having association with such as TORREY and RILEY.

Witness Lee

1905
Shantung Province, China

June 9, 1997
Anaheim, California

Founder of Living Stream Ministry, Anaheim, CA. Lee worked with Watchman Nee in China before moving to the U.S. in 1962. He was a pastor and evangelist in China, 1934–49; then he went to Taiwan. Several evangelical books and ministries alleged that Lee and his "local church" movement were "cultic." Lee successfully sued Spiritual Counterfeits Project for libel in connection with the publication of *The God-Men*. In 1983, he settled out of court with Thomas Nelson Publishers, which ceased distribution of *The Mind Benders*.

Hattie A. Hackett Metcalf

June 13, 1907
Hood River, Oregon

June 12, 1997
Portland, Oregon

Director of International Christian Leprosy Mission, 1972–88. Metcalf worked with children, gave piano lessons, and showed interest in the disabled in early years. She married Gaylord Metcalf in 1929 (died: 1977). He was an artist and painter. Once accepting the responsibility of the above described work, she did it all; bookkeeper, fund raising and administrative work. Key in her tenure was the hospital in India and foster home in Manila. Through the years, Metcalf was active at the Family Baptist Church of Tigart, OR. They had one child, Charles, who died at age twelve in a sledding accident. Metcalf got a serious infection which took her life one day shy of her 90th birthday.

Harold van Broekhoven

Feb. 10, 1913
East Rutherford, New Jersey

June 30, 1997
Grand Rapids, Michigan

Director of Outreach, Int., Grand Rapids, MI, 1966–85. Broekhoven was raised in a Christian Reformed home, found the Lord early in life, then went to Wheaton (IL) College and Dallas Theological Seminary. He married Lorraine Chafer on September 20, 1938. The couple served under Central America Mission in Nicaragua (1941–43) and in Guatemala (1943–56). Here they were engaged in various outreaches, including the founding of TGNA (Telling Good News Abroad). They were goodwill ambassadors for World Radio Fellowship (HCJB conglomerate), 1945–65, traveling to the Middle East, Africa and Europe in endeavors to found and expand additional outlets. In 1965, Broekhoven founded Outreach whose three-fold ministry included publishing translations into Spanish and other languages, raising funds and establishing medical clinics, and radio outreach, developing the Institute of Theological Studies. Over 20 established seminaries have accessed material from them. This world traveler was teaching in India just a few months before his death, from pancreatic cancer.

Dezso Abraham

Sept. 15, 1920
Old, Hungary

July 10, 1997
Hamilton, New Jersey

Bishop of Hungarian Reformed Church in America, Poughkeepsie, NY, 1968–89. Abraham was a scholarship student at Princeton Seminary. He was raised in a Christian home in Roebling, NJ. He completed his studies at the Reformed Theological Seminary, Budapest, Hungary in 1942. Soon he was an associate in the 12,000 member Calvin Square Church of Budapest. In 1945, he became secretary of the Hungarian YMCA. In 1947–48, he studied at the Princeton Theological Seminary. Abraham pastored in Roebling, NJ, from 1948–54, during which time he married Margaret Szinyeri on January 14, 1951. He pastored in Perth Amboy, NJ (1954–74); Allen Park, MI (1974–89) and Bordentown, NJ (1989–97). He returned many times to Hungary. He met with President Jimmy Carter (1978) and with President RONALD REAGAN (1984). He had a heart attack and surgery for cancer.

John E. Hines

Oct. 3, 1910
Seneca, South Carolina

July 19, 1997
Austin, Texas

Presiding Bishop of Protestant Episcopal Church, 1965–67, renamed Episcopal Church, 1967–74. Hines married Helen Orwig on April 22, 1935. He was ordained Episcopalian in 1933; became curate of the Church of St. Michael and St. George, St. Louis, MO (1933–35); rector of Trinity Episcopal Church, Hannibal, MO (1935–37); St. Paul's Episcopal Church, Augusta, GA (1937–41) and Christ Episcopal Church, Houston, TX (1941–45). He was consecrated bishop, coadjutor of the diocese of Texas on October 18, 1945 and bishop of Texas, 1955–65. As the presiding bishop in the movement, he worked out of the New York City headquarters. Hines took a moderate stand on the issues of his time, race relations, revision of the prayer book, and ordination of women.

Kenneth C. Robb

Aug. 2, 1920
Butler, Pennsylvania

July 25, 1997
Rimer, Minnesota

President of Practical Bible Training School, 1971–80. Robb graduated from PBTS in 1942 and married Esther Gathany in the fall of that year. He pastored the Hunt (NY) Baptist Church, 1944–46, then the FBC, Riverdale, MD, for 17 years. He returned to PBTS where he became a member of the faculty (1963), adding the responsibilities of campus pastor (1966). A new gymnasium was named after him in the year he left.

John P. Strand

Oct. 7, 1916
Carpio, North Dakota

July 25, 1997
Remer, Minnesota

First president of Association of Free Lutheran Congregations, Minneapolis, MN, 1962–78. Strand married Mildred Thorsgard in 1945. He pastored Lutheran churches in Grafton and Vang, ND (1944–52) and in Tioga, ND (1952–64). The AFLC rejected a merger into The American Lutheran Church in 1962. He was dean of AFLTS (1964–66) and of AFLBS (1966–68). He also pastored in Medicine Lake, MN (1964–65) and St. Paul's Lutheran, Fargo, ND (1975–82). He retired to Remer.

S. Maxwell Coder

March 25, 1902
Straight, Pennsylvania

July 28, 1997
Carol Stream, Illinois

Vice president and head of education at Moody Bible Institute, 1947–69. On February 20, 1932, Coder married Elizabeth Dieterle. He was ordained into the Presbyterian Church in 1938. He pastored in the Grace Church, Camden, NJ (1935–38); Chelsea Church, Atlantic City, NJ (1938–43); and Evangel Church, Philadelphia, PA. In 1945, he joined the faculty at MBI and, as a dean, led MBI in many innovations during the CULBERTSON years. In 1951, the school changed to the two-semester plan and became accredited by the AABC and a womens dorm was built. He wrote two dozen books from *Youth Triumphant* (3-volume correspondence course) (1946) to *The Final Chapter* (1989).

Dwight R. Malsbary

May 22, 1899
California

July 28, 1997
DMZ line, South Korea

Missionary, patriot, reformation champion who had nearly 50 years of service in Korea before he was killed in a taxi accident. Both Malsbary and his wife graduated from the Sherwood Music School. They went to Korea for eleven years under the Presbyterian (USA) Board of Foreign Missions as music teachers. They were also active in evangelism endeavors. They eventually withdrew from this relationship and served under Independent Board for Foreign Missions, 1946 on. As the ICC took shape and churches of South Korea separated from the WCC, Malsbary handled all the details from about 1959 on. Malsbary helped develop a Bible institute in Pusan, taught in a seminary, and wrote Sunday school lessons and commentaries. Later, they moved north of Pusan, helping to start 25 churches and a seminary in Seoul. A few days after his funeral, his wife received "The Order of Civil Merit," the highest award given to a civilian from the office of the president of Korea.

Charles F. K. Nagel

Aug. 9, 1907
Philadelphia, Pennsylvania

Aug. 17, 1997
Philadelphia, Pennsylvania

President of D.M. STEARNS Missionary Foundation, North Wales, PA 1972–97. Raised in a Christian home, Nagel married Mildred Reitinger on April 5, 1934 (died: 1996). He was a banker all of his life at Provident Trust Company (Provident National Bank), ending as senior vice president. He was active all his life at the Reformed Episcopal Church of the Atonement, Germantown, PA. He was a member of the board of Reformed Episcopal Seminary for 52 years and the Philadelphia School of the Bible (Philadelphia Biblical University) for 50 years. He was hit by a car and seriously injured and died six months later.

Marion H. Reynolds Jr.

April 19, 1919
Los Angeles, California

Sept. 3, 1997
Los Angeles, California

Director of Fundamental Evangelistic Association, 1970–97; president of American Council of Christian Churches, 1966–68; and pastor of Grace Fundamental Church, Los Angeles. Along with his father, Marion Sr., Reynolds helped start the Fundamental Bible Institute in 1936. He wrote over 70 booklets and edited a fundamentalist journal for many years. He married Frances Chapman on November 4, 1938. Early on he was employed by Texaco, but accepted God's call into the ministry. He joined his father as a staff member at Grace Fundamental Church, Los Angeles. Upon the death of his father in 1970, the work was turned over to him. Soon they moved from LA to Los Osos, CA. He died after a brief illness.

Rich Mullins

Oct. 21, 1955
Richmond, Indiana

Sept. 19, 1997
near Lostant, Illinois

Contemporary Christian singer, Mullins wrote more than 90 songs, his most famous, "Awesome God," which became an instant praise and worship standard in 1988. From 1988 on, Mullins worked with Compassion Int., concentrating the last three years of his life on teaching music to Native American students on a Navajo reservation. Some of his songs are "Hold Me Jesus," "My One Thing," "While the Nations Rage," as well as "Sing Your Praise to the Lord." Mullins was en route to a benefit concert in Wichita, Kansas, where he lived, when his jeep went out of control on Interstate 39. He was thrown out of the vehicle onto the pavement, then run over by a tractor-trailer truck. Since 1986, he recorded nine records. His biography is *Rich Mullins: An Arrow Pointing Toward Heaven* (2000).

John F. McMahon

Sept. 16, 1910
Buffalo, New York

Sept. 23, 1997
Louisville, Kentucky

General of Volunteers of America, 1958–80. McMahon was the first such leader not related to BALLINGTON and MAUD BOOTH, the founders of VOA. During his tenure, VOA launched its national housing division to serve low to moderate income families, the handicapped, the elderly, and the disadvantaged. He grew up in the movement and in 1941 he was in charge of the work in Milwaukee, WI. In 1948, he was called to VOA headquarters in New York as the national field secretary serving until 1958. His wife died in 1977.

Allen A. MacRae

Feb. 11, 1902
Calumet, Michigan

Sept. 27, 1997
Coryville, Pennsylvania

First president of Faith Theological Seminary, Wilmington, DE (Elkins Park, PA), **1937–71; first president of Biblical Theological Seminary, Hatfield, PA 1971–82, which he helped found; and president of Evangelical Theological Society, 1960.** MacRae was saved as a result of a Christian home but later, in BIOLA, he settled the question once and for all. When MACHEN and ROBERT D. WILSON broke with Princeton in 1929, MacRae was beseeched to come and teach in the new Philadelphia school, Westminster Theological Seminary, specializing in Old Testament courses. MacRae knew eleven languages. When the Bible Presbyterian Church broke from the PCA in 1937, he joined CARL MCINTIRE in the forming of FTS in the Laird Harris building in Wilmington, DE. He married Grace Sanderson in 1944 and rescued some marooned aviators in the Grand Canyon on his honeymoon. He was an influential Presbyterian scholar and educator.

Harold W. Erickson

Sept. 18, 1903
St. Paul, Minnesota

Oct. 6, 1997
Rockford, Illinois

Well-known pastor of First Evangelical Free Church, Rockford, IL 1952–70. Converted at age 17, Erickson attended North Park College and Seminary, Chicago, graduating in 1924. His first two pastorates were in Little Falls and Cloquet, MN. He saw some 75 souls saved in two years. Erickson married Sarah Ledin on September 10, 1930 (died December 19, 1986). He pastored the First Covenant Church, Chicago, 1930–32. From 1933–43, he pastored the First Covenant Church in Portland, OR. From 1943–52, Erickson pastored Calvary Memorial Church, Racine, WI and the First Covenant Church, Oakland, CA. After leaving the Rockford charge, he served at the English Fellowship Church, Quito, Eucador. After this, he taught at Trinity Western College in British Columbia and served four interim pastorates: Rockford; Minneapolis; Pompano Beach, FL, and Deerfield, IL.

Harold K. Graves

March 25, 1912
Sale Creek, Tennessee

Oct. 21, 1997
Marin County, California

President of Golden Gate Theological Seminary, Berkeley, CA, 1952–59, Mill Valley, CA 1959–87. Graves married Frieda M. Kommer on September 29, 1933, and they had two children. He pastored in Hempridge, KY (1935–36); Buffalo Lick, KY, in 1936; FBC, Jeffersonville, IN (1936–41); FBC, Chickasha, OK (1941–45) and FBC, Bartlesville, OK (1945–52). He traveled widely to many sections of the world and was active in the Oklahoma Baptist Convention, 1941–52. His hobbies were bowling and photography. It was during his leadership at GGTS in 1959 that the school moved from Berkeley to 126 acres in Marin County at Mill Stream.

Charles E. Boddie

June 13, 1911
New Rochelle, New York

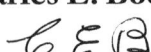

Oct. 27, 1997
Rochester, New York

President of American Baptist College and Theological Seminary, Nashville, TN 1963–80. Boddie also served as interim pastor of Berean Baptist in Nashville and was chaplain at Fisk University, Nashville, TN, following a pastorate at Mt. Olivet, New Rochelle, NY, from 1943–56. He also pastored in Elmira, NY, and Huntingdon, WV. From 1956–63, Boddie was active in American Baptist Foreign Mission Society, inspecting mission stations around the world. He married Lavina, and upon her death, Mabel Bell Crooks in 1970, who died November 8, 1997 in Nashville, TN, two weeks after Charles died.

Raymond E. Benson

July 28, 1913
Pasadena, California

Nov. 1, 1997
Portland, Oregon

Founder and first president of Medical Ambassadors Institute, Modesto, CA, 1974–88. Benson committed his life to the Lord around age 16 via the First Church of the Nazarene in Chicago. He soon was involved at the Chicago Gospel Tabernacle and the ministry of PAUL RADER. He married Louisa Hatfield on June 14, 1940. Already having his MD, he was granted a fellowship at Mayo Clinic serving as a junior surgeon in Rochester, MN from 1940–45. Benson then spent 1945–75 in Billings, MT. During this time, he began as an associate in a clinic and later established his own clinic with four surgeons working with him. About 1963, DICK HILLIS came to Billings and soon Benson was on overseas ventures with Overseas Crusades. This climaxed in Vietnam, 1973–75, where they lived, leaving one week before Saigon fell. Moving to Modesto, he founded the above mission's outreach ministry. Benson was on dialysis the last six and one-half years of his life. He broke his hip and died of congestive heart failure.

James Zirkle

July 19, 1942
Akron, Ohio

Nov. 1, 1997
western Guatemala

Founder and first president of Living Water Teaching, Caddo Mills, TX, 1979–97. Zirkle was converted as a teen at the Wintergreen Ledges Church of God in Akron. He was married to Marion Kays on November 7, 1964. For some time, he was employed in Akron at Goodyear Tire and also in construction work. They went to Guatemala as missionaries in 1979, about the same time his brother opened a work in Broken Arrow, OK, called Living Water Tabernacle. Work expanded to other Central American countries. A plane carrying short-term mission volunteers crashed into a mountain killing Zirkle, 57, and his son, James II, 30, one of the pilots, and nine others. Seven were injured. They were returning from a medical outreach in Playa Grande. Rain from Hurricane Mitch may have contributed to the crash. His wife continued the work.

Jack Cornelius

Aug. 17, 1922
Anniston, Alabama

Nov. 3, 1997
Foley, Alabama

Businessman who devoted much of his later years promoting and taking care of JOHN R. RICE. Cornelius was converted in 1974 reading the *Sword of the Lord*, and was married to Sue Wear on Dec. 19, 1975. He then retired from his business interests to serve the Lord. His business background included Corneilus and Sons Farms of Homestead, a partner in Lawrence Oil Company, and vice president of Atlantic Fertilizer Chemical Company.

After retiring, he and his wife moved to Birmingham, AL, where he spent a great amount of time helping Shades Mountain Independent Church. After his conversion, he led some 125 people per year to Christ. For over six months after RICE had a major heart attack, Cornelius traveled with him and was his assistant in every possible personal way. He then cofounded Titus, an outreach ministry. Cornelius moved to Ellijay, GA, in 1981. His death followed a long illness complicated by a blood ailment.

Ted DeMoss

Dec. 5, 1925
Albany, New York

Nov. 3, 1997
Chattanooga, Tennessee

President and executive secretary of Christian Business Men's Committee, 1977–90. DeMoss was converted at age twelve while visiting a cousin in Chicago. He married Edith Futch on August 29, 1947. DeMoss was a pilot in WWII, which gave him a love for flying and for years after, he traveled about 100,000 miles a year to meetings and conventions in Christian endeavors. Early on, he worked in Cluett Enterprises (Arrow Shirts) in Troy, NY. He then joined his cousin, ART DeMoss, in the insurance business, moving to Chattanooga about 1951. He was a soul winner, a teacher of discipleship and conducted numerous Bible classes while working with CBMC. He traveled around the world three times visiting some 70 countries. It is thought he died of a clogged artery.

Frank W. Smith

May 2, 1909
Redding, California

Nov. 3, 1997
Des Moines, Iowa

President of Open (Eugene (OR) in 1986) **Bible College, 1939–53; General Chairman of Open Bible Standard Churches, 1938–47, 1976–79,** (both in Des Moines, IA); **and chairman of Pentecostal Fellowship of North America, 1982–83.** Smith married Rose Jolly on June 22, 1930 (died of cancer on May 27, 1944). On August 15, 1945, he married Marie Christensen. He pastored in Hollywood, CA (1931–34); Fort Des Moines (IA) Open Bible Church (1934–38) and the First Church of the Open Bible in Des Moines (1939–76). He taught various Bible courses at Open Bible College, Des Moines, over a 20-year period. He wrote *Pentecostal Positive* (1975).

Warren W. Ost

June 24, 1926
Mankato, Minnesota

Nov. 6, 1997
New York, New York

Founder and first director of Christian Ministry in the National Parks, Boston, MA, 1952–96. Every year more than 250 college and seminary students work in 45 national parks, forests, and recreation areas, serving as Christian witnesses and interpreters of God's miraculous creation for more than 1 million visitors and employees. The burden started when, as a seminarian, he was working concessions in 1945 at Yellowstone Park, WY. For nearly 45 years, he traveled up to 35,000 miles each summer from Texas to Alaska. Ost worked to develop a program that deepened spiritual relationships among student staff employees and park visitors. On December 27, 1951, Ost was ordained into the Presbyterian Church (USA) ministry. He served on the staff of the NCC, 1952–72, when a reorganization of the NCC prompted this new movement. His wife of 43 years, Nancy Nesbitt, was his constant companion. He married her on May 15, 1954.

H. Ray Stewart

Sept. 21, 1917
Taylors, North Carolina

Nov. 9, 1997

First president of Pacific Coast Bible College, Sacramento, C, 1979–91. Stewart was converted on April 20, 1938, at Holmes Memorial Church in Greenville, SC. He began pastoring in South Carolina but expanded to Tryon, NC; Chilliwack, BC; National Church, Washington, D.C.;

Orlando, FL; Tulsa and Durant, OK; Atlanta, GA; and Tallahassee, FL. For ten years he served as dean and instructor at Holmes Bible College, Greenville, SC. His wife was Della Grace.

Donald M. Wagner

May 29, 1911
Nevis, Minnesota

Nov. 11, 1997
Tahlequah, Oklahoma

Founder and first president of Oak Hills (MN) Bible College, 1946–62. Wagner was a member of the First Baptist Church, Minneapolis, which continued to support him in his ministry until his death. His first pastorate was at the First Presbyterian Church, Long Prairie, MN. He married Agnes Knutson on September 11, 1934 (died October 3, 1997). After pastoring the First Baptist Church, Park Rapids, MN, for six years, he began an interest in rural ministries. This became a part of Oak Hills' ministry. In the fall of 1946, the Oak Hills Christian Training School opened its doors to 14 students. He was an instructor there until his retirement in 1976. He also directed the Oak Hills Family Bible Conferences in the summer for many years. He died at the Go Ye Medical Center.

Bob Jones Jr.

Oct. 19, 1911
Montgomery, Alabama

Nov. 12, 1997
Greenville, South Carolina

President of Bob Jones University, Greenville SC 1947-71. Jones continued the fundamental direction of the school carved out by his father, BOB JONES SR. He was converted at age five listening to his father's preaching in Aurora, IL. He was in the role of acting president upon his completion of college, from 1932 on, while his father was busy traveling. He married Fannie M. Holmes on June 1, 1938, in Cleveland, TN. They had three children with the eldest son, Bob Jones III, carrying on the family legacy by assuming the presidency in 1971. From the Bible, Jones learned the nature of man and from Shakespeare, the twists of human character—becoming an authority on both. Jones edited *Faith for the Family* (1973-86) and wrote seven books. He founded Unusual Films (appearing in several films himself) and the BJU Gallery of Sacred Art, the largest collection of religious art in the Western Hemisphere. On September 29, 1997, he was advised of the cancer that would take him six weeks later.

John Wimber

Feb. 25, 1934
Kirksville, Missouri

Nov. 17, 1997
Yorba Linda, California

Founder of Vineyard Ministries, Anaheim, CA, and president of Vineyard Ministries International. Early on, Wimber was successful in the music industry. He was converted in 1963. He was then ordained by the California Yearly Meeting of Friends, serving as co-pastor of the Yorba Linda Friends Church, 1970–75. In 1975, he joined C. Peter Wagner, of the Fuller Evangelistic Association and, as a church growth consultant, worked with hundreds of churches of all denominations. He left Fuller in 1977 to establish the Anaheim Vineyard. His "signs and wonders" ministry effected many and his church grew to 5,000. Soon some 500 churches were affiliated with his work. He taught "The Meticulous and Church Growth" course at FTS, 1982–85, which became very popular, and controversial.

Raymond Hoekstra

March 19, 1913
Niles, Michigan

Nov. 20, 1997
Dallas, Texas

Founder and first director of International Prison Ministry, Dallas, TX, 1970–98. "Chaplain Ray" had an amazing outreach to prisoners. He was converted in a tent campaign in the Los Angeles area. A former convict, Ron Bales, became a good friend of his and they traveled together in revivals. Hoekstra preached revivals in churches, witnessed on beaches and wherever he went. He built a large church in Indianapolis. In 1972, he married Leola Lindsey, who had traveled in evangelism with her husband, J. C. Bishop, until his death. The couple plunged into the prison work and it grew in such a way that they received up to 200 letters a day from prisoners, asking for free literature, Bibles, and books. Hoekstra's wife carried on as the director upon his death, brought on by exhaustion. His converts are legendary. Their stories are in his books.

Jim Vaus

Feb. 17, 1919
Los Angeles, California

Dec. 1, 1997
Headwater, Virginia

Director of Youth Development, Inc. Vaus married Alice Park on Oct. 23, 1947. Former gangster, wire tapper, and ex-convict, he was converted in the 1949 Billy Graham crusade in Los Angeles. He formerly had worked for Mickey Cohen, LA area mob leader. He moved to New York City to work with troubled youth. He worked in the Hell Gate area with street gangs. Vaus did things in East Harlem that city agencies and federal government had a difficult time matching: establishing youth camps, school, crisis center, ranch for runaways, etc. In 1970, he moved to San Diego, CA, where the burden was the same, but with more affluent troubled youth, instead of inner-city youth. His goal was "develop vital godliness and moral consciousness in youth." Vaus had a radio broadcast, *Reality,* and developed a national youth crisis hotline that received 300,000 calls a year. That part of the ministry remained in San Diego, while he and his son moved to Virginia to establish Headwaters Lodge, which he supervised during his last few years. He had many health problems, starting with polio early on, diabetes, Parkinson's, and congestive heart failure.

R. Bryant Mitchell

March 3, 1905
Los Angeles, California

Dec. 2, 1997
Eugene, Oregon

General chairman of Open Bible Standard Churches, Des Moines, IA, 1953–67, and chairman of Pentecostal Fellowship of North America, 1968. He also led the missions department of OBSC, 1941–47 and 1967–73. Mitchell was converted under his father's (A. E. MITCHELL) ministry at the age of 13 in Los Angeles. On June 6, 1929, he married Lola Lee Raney (died 1969). He pastored in Muscatine and Des Moines, IA, from 1930–35.) He left the Foursquare movement, and with 32 other ministers in 1932, helped form the Open Bible Evangelistic Association. From 1935–53, he was dean and instructor in the Open Bible College of Des Moines. He helped pioneer the missionary program of the denomination. He visited many areas of the world, including a 250-mile mule trip over the Andes Mountains into the heart of Columbia. He was a youth camp speaker in five states for some 25 years. Brother of HUBERT MITCHELL, the two sparked enough missionary enthusiasm as any two brothers in history. In 1970, he married Lucille Jenkins.

Joy Mackay

July 27, 1918
Philadelphia, Pennsylvania

Dec. 6, 1997
Philadelphia, Pennsylvania

Director of Pioneer Girls (Pioneer Clubs), **Wheaton, IL 1951–60**. Joy learned about Pioneer Girls in 1948 and started a club in the Philadelphia area in a housing development. She became a field representative in 1949 and was responsible for the work on the East Coast. In 1953, she led the movement into a new headquarters building in Chicago and was the key person in developing the financial base of Pioneer Girls. Joy was known for her sense of humor. After 1960, she took three trips to Europe and became a volunteer hospital chaplain, as she herself began to cope with Parkinson's disease and cancer.

Conrad J. I. Bergendorf

Dec. 3, 1895
Shickley, Nebraska

Dec. 23, 1997
Rock Island, Illinois

President of Augustana College and Theological Seminary, Rock Island, IL, 1935–48 (Lutheran School of Theology, Chicago, in 1964); **of Augustana College, 1948–62** (as the school divided into two categories); **and of Association of Theological Schools, 1946–48**. He married Gertrude Carlson on June 28, 1922 (died: 1979), and they had three children. After pastoring the Salem Lutheran Church of Chicago (1921–31), Bergendorf became dean and professor of systematic theology at ATS (1931–35). He was president of Augustana Swedish Institute, 1940–67 and served on several commissions of the WCC and Lutheran World Federation. His books range from *Olaxus Petri* (1928) to *The Church of Lutheran Reformation* (1967). Bergendorf edited the *Augustana Quarterly* (1929–48) and the *Lutheran Quarterly* (1949–52). His funeral was at St. John Lutheran Church, Rock Island, IL.

Roy H. Cantrell

Nov. 4, 1904
Kansas City, Missouri

Dec. 25, 1997
Bethany, Oklahoma

President of Bethany (OK) Nazarene College (Southern Nazarene College in 1986), **1947–72**. Cantrell was converted while attending Pasadena (CA) College as a freshman. He was professor (1927–29) and dean of men (1928–29) at Eastern Nazarene College, Wollaston, MA. He married Evelyn Mikkelson on June 19, 1929. He pastored Nazarene churches in Syracuse, NY (1929–34); and Notingham, NY (1934–39); then was district superintendent of the Ontario district for the denomination (1939–42), of Minnesota district (1942–46) and Kansas district (1946–48).

Georgi P. Vins

1928
Blagoveshchensk, Russia

Jan. 11, 1998

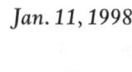

Leader of the Reform Baptists in the Soviet Union. His arrest and imprisonment in Russia caused considerable objections by people around the world. In 1961, Vins was one of the leaders of the RB movement which split from the recognized Baptist church that was a puppet of the government. In May, 1966, 500 members joined a demonstration in Moscow which put him into a labor camp for three years. He was released in May, 1969, only to be re-arrested in Kiev in 1974 and charged with vagrancy. On January 31, 1975, he was sentenced to five years imprisonment. On April 27, 1979, he was released, stripped of his citizenship and deported to the U.S. in an exchange for a spy release. He met President Carter two days later. His wife's name was Nadeshda. They had five children. He served as general secretary of the Council of Evangelical Baptist Churches, an organization of 2,000 persecuted congregations in the former Soviet Union. He founded Russian Gospel Ministries, Int., in Elkhart, IN. He died after being diagnosed with an inoperable malignant brain tumor in the fall of 1997.

Harold Lindsell

Dec. 22, 1913
New York, New York

Jan. 15, 1998
Lake Forest, California

Editor of *Christianity Today* (1969–78), and president of Evangelical Theological Society, 1971. He was converted in 1925. Lindsell was one of the original handpicked professors Charles Fuller chose for his faculty at Fuller Theological seminary. He is best known for his stand on inerrancy with his two books, *The Battle for the Bible* (1976), and *The Bible in the Balance* (1979). He was a Southern Baptist. He married Marion Bolinder on June 12, 1943. From 1944–47, he was associated with Nothern Baptist Seminary in various capacities. Then he went to Fuller Theological Seminary in 1947 as dean of the faculty and professor of missions, serving until 1964. From 1964–67, he was associate editor of *Christianity Today*. In later years, he was professor of apologetics at the Simon Greenleaf School of Law, 1983–89. His writings range from *Abundantly Above* (1944) to *New Harper Study Bible* (1991). Lindsell retired to Laguna Hills, CA. He was a longtime advisor to Billy Graham. He died after a long illness.

Alexander Haraszti

1920
Soltvadkert, Hungary

Jan. 16, 1998

Christian diplomat, surgeon and linguist. Haraszti was instrumental in securing invitations for Billy Graham to preach in several Eastern European countries in the 1970s and 1980s. Many feel his efforts began the unraveling of Communism there. He knew the tedious art of negotiation without compromising his Christian convictions. He was a surgeon who also had a Ph.D. in linguistics. Ordained as a Baptist, Haraszti was professor at a theological seminary in Budapest. In 1956, he translated Graham's book *Peace with God* into Hungarian. He served as a medical doctor in Ghana, Tanzania, and the Gaza Strip. He worked with the government and church elders in Hungary, Poland, East Germany, Czechoslovakia, and the Soviet Union arranging Graham's meetings. He spoke eight languages and was Graham's interpreter in the Hungary crusade where 35,000 responded to the invitation.

Clyde Landrum

1909
Lost Creek, Kentucky

Jan. 25, 1998
Winona Lake, Indiana

Conference secretary of Fellowship of Grace Brethren Churches, 1951–82. Landrum was baptized at Lost Creek, KY, Brethren Church, in 1917. He married Ruby Larson. He taught in elementary schools in KY, 1931–40. He also pastored in Pennsylvania, Indiana, and Kentucky. He served as assistant to the executive secretary of the Foreign Missionary Society, 1955–66, and was editor of the *Brethren Missionary Herald*, 1966–90.

J. E. Leslie Newbigin

Dec. 8, 1909
New Castle-upon-Tyne, England

Jan. 30, 1998
London, England

Bishop, theologian, and ecumenical statesman. Newbigin came to Christ through the British Student Christian Movement. In 1936, he was ordained by the Church of Scotland for work in India. He was a village evangelist (1936–47) and bishop of the church of South India in Madurai (1947–59). From 1961–65, he worked with the WCC serving for the Commission on World Mission and Evangelism. He returned to India as bishop in Madras until 1974. Back in England, he sought to reach pagan Britain. He was devoted to the mission and unity of the church. His autobiography is *Unfinished Agenda*.

Vaughn Chapman

March 14, 1921
Seattle, Washington

Feb. 2, 1998
Lynwood, Washington

Founder and director of Missionary Dentists, Seattle, WA (merged into Global Outreach Mission, Buffalo, NY in 1998), **1949–98**. Raised in a Christian home, Chapman moved to Evanston, IL, and studied dentistry at the University of Illinois. He married Mildred Fyfe on December 28, 1949, and headquartered in Seattle where he had a dental office. He made frequent mission trips, often with other dentists, and developed an office in Quito, Ecuador. He saw to it that dental equipment reached many missionary stations of the world and encouraged Christian dentists to volunteer time overseas instead of taking the traditional Hawaii vacation. He had numerous strokes and internal bleeding which led to his death.

Duane K. Tomhave

Aug. 4, 1936
Montevideo, Minnesota

Feb. 17, 1998
Milwaukee, Wisconsin

President of Wisconsin Evangelical Lutheran Synod Missions, 1984–98. He married Janice Hanson in 1960. Tomhave pastored the Emmaus Lutheran Church, Phoenix, AZ (1961–69) and then St. Thomas Lutheran, Phoenix (1965–67), overlapping each other. He was pastor at St. Paul Lutheran, Saginaw, MI (1969–79), and then pastored the Reformation Lutheran Church, Genesee Depot, WS (1979–84). While heading the denomination's world missions program, he made some 30 overseas trips and established eight new fields of service.

Chester A. Kirkendall

June 3, 1914
Searcy, Arkansas

Feb. 20, 1998
Jackson, Tennessee

Bishop of Christian Methodist Episcopal Church, 1970–86; senior bishop, 1982–86. Kirkendall married Alice Singleton on June 3, 1940 (died: 1995). He was president of Lane College, Jackson, TN, from 1950–70. In 1982, he saw the need for a new headquarters for the denomination and took the lead in locating property and drawing up plans. The headquarters were moved from Jackson to Memphis. In 1983, his vision became impaired and his influence began to wane. Kirkendall eventually became blind. In earlier years, he wrote Sunday school literature for the denomination in the Christian Education department.

John M. Allin

April 22, 1921
Helena, Arkansas

March 6, 1998
Jackson, Mississippi

Presiding bishop of Episcopal Church, 1974–85. Allin was ordained priest in 1945 and served the St. Peter's Church in Conway, AR, from 1945–50. Allin married Frances Kelly on October 18, 1949. He became curate of St. Andrews Church, New Orleans, LA (1950–51); rector of Grace Church, Monroe, LA (1952–58); rector and president of All Saints Junior College, Vicksburg, MS (1958–61); bishop coadjutor Diocese of Mississippi at the PE Church, Jackson, MS (1961–66); and bishop of the same (1966–73). He was chancellor of the University of the South (1973–79), and considered Jackson, MS, his home. Upon leaving the highest post, Allin was chaplain of Christ Memorial Chapel in Hobe Sound, FL (1986–94), and of St. Ann's Summer Chapel in Kennebunkport, ME (1991–97). During his tenure, he had to face a most divisive issue, the ordination of a woman, which he opposed but permitted. Several hundred thousand members left the denomination while he presided.

Lloyd (Roy) L. Aldrich

Sept. 1, 1899
Green Bay, Wisconsin

March 18, 1998
New Port Richey, Florida

First president of Detroit Bible College (Willim Tyndale Bible College), **1943–67.** Aldrich was converted in a Salvation Army meeting at the Masonic Temple in Seattle, WA. He was the first graduate of Dallas Theological Seminary in 1927, and at age 21, married Frances P. Long on June 11, 1928. They enjoyed 49 years of marriage. Upon his first wife's death, he married Constance Crawkey. They were married 13 years. Aldrich's ministry began at the Exposition Park Presbyterian Church, Detroit, MI (1928–30), after which he served at the Central Presbyterian Church, Detroit (1930–45). Starting a small school, he was able to see DBC grow to over 650 students. His brother, Willard, was president at Multnomah Bible College in Portland, OR. Aldrich died from heart failure after breaking a hip falling in the hospital.

Painummoottill J. Thomas

April 15, 1915
Kerala State, India

March 24, 1998
Tiruvella, India

India's man of compassion, he was a father to 10,000 children, trained over 3,000 missionaries and planted over 300 churches. Thomas also started India's first Bible college for women. SADHU S. SINGH dedicated him to the Lord when he was six. In 1944, he married Aleyamma Kurien, and then set out again as a barefoot preacher. He trained at Sydney (Australia) Bible Institute and Wheaton (IL) College. In 1952, he returned to India for his lifes work. He began a Bible institute in his home in Tiruvella and named his work, "Sharon Fellowship." Thomas's school had no starting time, closing time, exams or degrees. A woman's institute was added and a five-story building was completed in 1988 for both schools. During the last years of his life, he was afflicted with a deadly skin disease.

Morris Rockness

May 28, 1911
Tacoma, Washington

April 6, 1998
Brewster (Cape Cod), Maryland

President of IFMA, 1965–67, active in China Inland Mission/Overseas Gospel Fellowship all his life. With Norwegian roots, Rockness was converted at age 17 via the Evangelical Free Church of Tacoma, WA. Attending Prairie Bible Institute, he went to Henan, China, in 1937, where he met his wife. His first marriage was to Grace Weir, 1939–63, when she died. They escaped over the "hump" in the mid-1940s, returned to the U.S., and attended the University of Washington. Rockness was back in Shanghai, 1946–51, went to Singapore in 1952 and then back to the States as associate home director of CIM/OMF. On May 28, 1966, he married Ann McGowan. They went to Singapore (1968–71), then back to the States as regional director (1972–78). He developed Alzheimer's disease. A serious fall precipitated a blood clot which took his life.

Richard Winchell

Nov. 2, 1928
Columbus, Ohio

April 13, 1998
Stuart, Florida

Director of TEAM, 1975–94, and president of IFMA, 1983–85. Winchell was a well-known and respected mission leader of his generation. Married to Marjorie Lundquist on December 26, 1949, he began his missions career as a missionary to South Africa, 1950–68. In South Africa, he pioneered a church-planting ministry and founded Word of Life Publishers, publishing gospel books and literature in four languages. He was associate general director under VERNON MORTENSON, 1966–75. Winchell spoke in conferences and schools across the country. He had a long battle with cancer. They had just moved to Stuart when he suddenly passed away.

C. Russell Archer

Dec. 6, 1918
Sarahsville, Ohio

April 29, 1998
Dayton, Ohio

President of Open Bible College, Des Moines, IA 1953–60 and Dayton (OH) Bible College, 1976–86. He began preaching in San Francisco in 1935. He was ordained in 1940. Archer married Lavone A. Surls on January 18, 1941. He pastored in Des Moines (1943–53) and also (1960–76) at Faith Temple in the same city. From 1977–98, he served as Eastern Region Superintendent for the Open Bible Standard Churches. His funeral was held on May 2 at the First Church of the Open Bible, Dayton.

Hanna U. Zimmer Kroeger

October 5, 1913
Attabey, Turkey

May 7, 1998
Boulder, Colorado

Herbalist, alternative health researcher, and faith healer. Hanna was the youngest of six children who, at a very young age, learned to speak German, French, English and a variety of Turkish dialects. Her mother taught her the power of healing through the love of Jesus. Villagers would line up outside of their "mission home" to receive herbal poultices, get wounds dressed and broken spirits mended. At the age of 16, Hanna became an interpreter for Dr. Clark, an American missionary doctor. She next served under Dr. Brauchele at the Naturopathic Hospital in Dresden. She developed her hands-on-healing protocols: energetic techniques and measuring of vibrational waves. In 1938, she married Rudolf Otto Erich Kroeger, a mechanical engineer. During WWII he spent five years in a Russian concentration camp while Hanna raised their five children. The family emigrated to America (1953) and developed the Peaceful Meadow Retreat near Boulder, CO (1961). She began writing books (over 45) and giving seminars. Kroeger opened the first health food store in America. She died a year after her husband and was buried at the Chapel of Miracles they had created in the Colorado mountains.

Bernard Palmer

Nov. 21, 1914
Central City, Nebraska

May 7, 1998
Holdrege, Nebraska

Author of 165 books, most of them published by Moody Press. While studying law one night at age 19, Palmer paced the floor and settled his relationship with Christ. In 1941, he wrote his first novel, *Parson John*. He then produced the *Danny Orlis Story* for the *Back to the Bible* radio broadcast, which resulted in several books. Perhaps his most well known book is *My Son, My Son*, which accounts for the waywardness, but eventual conversion, of his own son just a few weeks before his death. Early on he was foreman and part owner of the Palmer Brother's Granite Company in Holdrege. They founded the Palmer's State Camp Carmel, a family vacation spot in northern Saskatchewan, in 1952. He was on the board of the Evangelical Free Church, Minneapolis, MN.

Ethel Macmamee Barrett

Dec. 28, 1913
upstate New York

May 10, 1998
Peoria, Arizona

Speaker, storyteller and author, Barrett left a great mark on her generation. Ethel authored more than 30 books totalling over 3 million in print. She had more than 30 recordings, including her best-selling **Stories to Grow On** series. Her husband died long before her. Gospel Light Publishers launched their Regal Books product line with her book, *Sometimes I Feel Like a Blob*. Her favorite book was *Holy War*. But it was her books for children that endeared her to many. Barrett was a gifted speaker at women's conferences, state/national conventions, and Christian educational seminars. Her gift of telling Bible stories was her trademark.

Wade H. Horton

Sept. 13, 1908
Lancaster County, South Carolina

May 15, 1998
Cleveland, Tennessee

General Overseer of Church of God, Cleveland, TN 1962–66, 1974–76. Horton married Ruby Gaines in 1931. He pastored (1933–52), all in North or South Carolina, except Washington, D.C. (1941–43). From 1952–58, he was foreign mission field representative. From 1966–74, he was in executive positions with the denomination. Horton pastored in Woodruff, SC, from 1978–84. He wrote several books including an eight-volume *Sound Scriptural Outline* series.

Edward F. Stevens

Sept. 7, 1940
Newcastle, Wyoming

May 21, 1998
Portland, Oregon

President of George Fox University, Newberg, OR, 1983–97. Stevens led the school from 549 to 2,225, adding 18 new undergraduate majors, nine graduate programs, and a merger with Western Evangelical Seminary in 1996. It then changed to university status. He married Linda Loewenstein on June 3, 1962. They had two daughters. From 1967–71, he was head basketball coach at Augustana College, Sioux Falls, SD. He served in various capacities at Sioux Falls (SD) College (University of Sioux Falls), 1975–83. He suffered a severe stroke on June 7, 1997, and began treatment for a brain tumor. He died in a convalescent center.

Julian A. Bandy

Dec. 29, 1905
Kissimmee, Florida

June 5, 1998
Ft. Myers, Florida

President of Toccoa Falls (GA) College, 1959–74, a school he once attended. Bandy married Eunice Bascom on December 4, 1933. Other marriages were to Leila Bascom and Deloris Burns. He pastored the Asheville (NC) Gospel Tabernacle (1933–48) and the Gospel Tabernacle Church of New York City (1948–52), among other Christian and Missionary Alliance Churches. He was assistant to President R. A. Forrest (1952–59), then succeeded his mentor, the founder. He was an excellent preacher and speaker.

Russell Dennis Sr.

Sept. 20, 1932
Indianapolis, Indiana

June 6, 1998
Greenwood, Indiana

President of Heritage Baptist College, Indianapolis, IN 1985–98. Dennis was converted at age 15 at a youth revival at Taylor University. He married Jean Crankshaw on December 28, 1957, meanwhile spending 13 years at Bob Jones University as a student, student teacher, staff, and finally getting his Ph.D. from 1953–66. He briefly assisted FORD PORTER in Indianapolis, then pastored in Sandusky, OH (1968–79), starting Heritage Baptist College and serving as its president (1980–85). He then brought the college to Indianapolis, merging it with Indianapolis Baptist College and headed the new ministry under the name Heritage. Dennis occasionally served as interim pastor during his latter years. He collapsed with heart failure May 29 and died shortly thereafter.

Harold M. Schmul

Jan. 26, 1921
Erie, Pennsylvania

June 26, 1998
Salem, Ohio

President of Interchurch Holiness Convention, Bedford, IN 1952–97. He was also pastor of Conservative Holiness Church, editor of the *Convention Herald*, 40 years, a leader in the movement. Schmul was the highly esteemed founder of the IHC, a grand "old man of old-time holiness." He was converted at age 14 at the Wesleyan Methodist Church of Falconer, NY. He married Lois Pauline. He pastored Wesleyan Methodist churches in North Springfield, PA (1941–45); Meadville, PA (1945–49) and Rochester, PA (1954–61). He served as an evangelist 1949–54. In 1951, he and evangelist, Robb French, founded their movement in order to counter worldliness and centralized power in the denomination. He started Schmul Publishing Company in 1953. Schmul pastored the Pilgrim Church, Salem, OH, from 1962–82 and 1986–95, where his funeral was held, June 30, 1998.

Roy Rogers
Leonard Slye

Nov. 5, 1911
Cincinnati, Ohio

July 6, 1998
Apple Valley, California

King of the cowboys from the 1930s to the 1960s who packed six-shooters to subdue the forces of evil. Rogers' musical talent will be remembered with his singing group, the Sons of the Pioneers. He married Arlene Wilkinson in 1936 (died: November, 1946). His TV show co-starred his second wife, DALE EVANS, (whom he married in 1947) and his horse, Trigger. He was one of the few that maintained decency and humility even though he was at the head of his profession. His conversion, evident in his performances in word and deed, was prompted by his wife, DALE, and her commitment to Christ.

Fred Bock

March 31, 1939
Great Neck, New York

July 31, 1998
Tarzanah, California

Church music composer and choral director. Bock was music director at First Presbyterian Church, Hollywood, CA. At age 24, he founded the music publishing division of Word, Inc. Bock composed or arranged more than 400 music pieces. After spending 1963–70 with Word, he started Gentry Publications, an educational music company, publishing music for school and concert use. He then started the Fred Bock Music Company, publishing church music for choir, organ, piano, and instruments. Before his 18 years of service at Hollywood (CA) Presbyterian Church as minister of music, he served as the minister of music at Bel Air Presbyterian Church in Los Angeles, CA, for 14 years. He passed away with complications from surgery.

G. Hunter Norwood

Feb. 4, 1918
Selma, Alabama

Aug. 3, 1998
Lake Worth, Florida

Director of Southern American Mission, Lake Worth, FL, 1958–83. Moving to Chattanooga with his parents, a team of students from Columbia Bible College drew Norwood's attention to spiritual matters as they visited Central Presbyterian Church. His pastor ALLEN FLEECE encouraged him and soon both were at CBC (pastor and student). He married Edith Blackburn on January 6, 1942. They went to Colombia under the South American Indian Mission, arriving on December 24, 1942. They went to Peru, 1952–57, and soon he was supervising the work in Bolivia and Brazil as well. When the founder (DR. DAVIS) died, the Norwoods came to Lake Worth, FL, to head the work. In later years, he taught an adult Sunday school class in North Palm Beach (FL) Presbyterian Church for five years. In 1996 a degenerative nerve disease confined him to a wheelchair and bed. He had six daughters.

R. W. Cunningham

Jan. 20, 1902

Aug. 6, 1998
Institute, West Virginia

President of Nazarene Training Bible College, 1955–70, a school which prepared African-American ministers for the pastorate. Cunningham pastored churches in Ohio before going to Institute, WV, where he pastored, 1949–70. In 1970, the school merged with Nazarene Bible College, Colorado Springs, CO. He was elected director of the NBC extension program in 1986, with such classes conducted at the First Church of the Nazarene in South Charleston, WV. His wife's name was Annette.

Loyed R. Simmons

May 3, 1910
Paducah, Kentucky

Aug. 10, 1998
Riverside, California

President of California Baptist College, Riverside, CA, 1958–69. Simmons married Queenie Gregg on May 20, 1936. He pastored Baptist churches in Zeigler, IL (1939–41); McLeansboro, IL (1942–43); Evans Avenue, Ft. Worth, TX (1944–51); Highland, Dallas (1952); First SBC, Tuscon, AZ (1953–55) and was the president of Grand Canyon College, Phoenix, AZ (1955–58).

Henry C. Schilling

July 9, 1902
New Bethlehem, Pennsylvania

Aug. 17, 1998
Brookville, Pennsylvania

Founder and first president of Transylvania Bible School (Biblical Life Institute in 2001), **Freeport, PA, 1938–92.** Schilling was converted in his mother's kitchen, aided by a coal miner. After 15 years as a Methodist pastor, he founded TBS as a training school for ministers and missionaries. He taught Greek, philosophy, and church history. Schilling was an evangelist and camp meeting preacher. He was president of White Pine Holiness Camp, Arbovale, WV, from 1968–82. He was also the founding editor of *The Fountain*, which began in the basement of the Methodist church in West Middlesex, PA. He took five world mission trips.

John W. Duggar

July 1, 1912
Plummerville, Arkansas

Aug. 20/22, 1998
Little Rock, Arkansas

President of Baptist Missionary Association Theological Seminary, Jacksonville, TX, 1973–83. Duggar was converted in his early teens in a Conway, AR, revival meeting. He married Eloise M. Boyd on February 20, 1938. The couple went to Brazil in 1939 but later returned for health reasons. Duggar pastored BMA churches in Sulphur Springs, TX (1941–43); Boguluasa, LA (1943–45); Port Arthur, TX (1945–50); Laurel, MI (1950–55); Lovett, TX (1955–61); Carthage, TX (1961–66); and then became director of the denomination's home missionary department (1966–73). He wrote a history of the denomination. They retired in Little Rock where he died of a stroke and heart failure.

Blake Farmer

August 6, 1925
Lynchburg, Texas

Sept. 28, 1998
Ennis, Texas

President of Southwestern Assembly of God College, Waxahachie, TX, 1964–78. Farmer was dean of students, teacher, and other administrative duties prior to this time. He was converted as a teen. Farmer married Ramona Freeman on May 2, 1948. He pioneered and built an Assembly of God Church in Jacinto City (east Houston), TX, from 1952–58. As president of SAGC, he led in several building programs, a multi-purpose building, new dorms, a cafeteria, etc. After his service there, the administration building was named honoring his memory. He was dean of Victoria (TX) Junior College and dean of students for some time after leaving SAGC. His teaching field was educational psychology which he taught throughout his career. He was a veteran of the navy in WWII. He retired to a farm in Ennis where he died of pancreatic cancer.

David J. Beam

Sept. 24, 1932
Morristown, New Jersey

Oct. 15, 1998
Monroeville, Pennsylvania

President of Free Gospel Bible Institute, Export, PA, 1961–98. Beam was converted at a Presbyterian church and soon became a preacher at street meetings as a teenager. He pastored the Free Gospel Church, Youngstown, OH from 1952–68, then married Claire Wilmerton on September 20, 1969. Beam taught and preached widely, had a daily radio broadcast, *Echoes of Faith,* on three stations. He would be considered an old-line Pentecostal preacher whose emphasis was holiness. Beam fought leukemia for six years before finally succumbing to the disease.

Elmer V. Thompson

Aug. 4, 1901
Kiowa, Colorado

Oct. 20, 1998
Columbia, South Carolina

Cofounder (BARTH LA VASTIDA) and director of West Indies Mission (World Team in 1967), **1936–67**. Thompson was converted at age eleven via an evangelist in an NBC church in Kiowa. His younger brother's death from flu epidemic in 1918 challenged him to Christian service. Thompson married Grace Evelyn McElheram on September 10, 1928 (died: 1997). His missions career spanned more than 60 years including being a missionary to Cuba, some ten years in Jamaica, where they had a Bible college, and later developing a prayer ministry for the mission. In Cuba, he founded the Cuba Bible Institute in 1928. In Haiti, another Bible institute opened (1938) and the work then expanded to the Dominican Republic (1939). He left Cuba to work out of the WIM office in Homer City, PA, from 1950–63, which they had obtained in 1945.

Fred B. Stair

March 7, 1918
Knoxville, Tennessee

Nov. 13, 1998
Charlotte, North Carolina

President of Union Theological Seminary, Richmond, VA, 1967–81. Stair married Martha Osborne on December 19, 1942. He pastored the First Presbyterian Church, Hickory, NC (1953–59) and the Central Presbyterian Church, Atlanta, GA (1959–67). During his tenure at UTS, the seminary restructured its curriculum and expanded continuing education programs. Following retirement, Stair served as executive director of the Presbyterian Church Foundation in Charlotte, NC. Funeral services were held at First Presbyterian Church, Charlotte.

Henry N. Hostetter

Oct. 8, 1902
Lancaster County, Pennsylvania

Nov. 14, 1998
Mechanicsburg, Pennsylvania

President of Brethren in Christ World Missions, Grantham, PA, 1951–68. Hostetter was converted at age eleven and baptized in the Susquehanna River. He married Beulah Hess on January 19, 1924. He was a member of a pastoral team of Manor-Pequea District, PA (1942–49), and served as bishop of that district (1942–57), pastoring the Manor BIC Church, Lancaster, PA, three different times (1949–74). Hostetter lived on the family farm in Manor Township until 1983. His travels took him around the world several times. He published his autobiography, *Reflections on My Heritage* (1995).

Prem Pradham

June 6, 1924
Ilam, Nepal

Nov. 15, 1998
Jutpani, Nepal

God's man for Nepal. Pradham was a cripple who sounded God's word throughout the Himalaya mountain regions. Serving in the British Air Force in WWII, he was shot down in the Middle East. Wounded in the leg by ground fire while parachuting, he barely escaped amputation, but was lame for life. As a soldier of Nepali ancestry in the Indian Army, he heard the gospel in northern India at a street meeting in 1951 and was converted. In 1954, he went to his own country of Nepal as an evangelist. In 1960, he was sentenced to six years in prison for baptizing converts. Between 1960–75, he spent ten years in a total of 14 different prisons, where he led many to Christ. In 1971, he started a school in Kathmandu. The following year he was sentenced to 54 years in prison. Bob Finley/Christian Aid Mission raised the ransom money needed to release him. In 1980, he began another school on his farm in Sarlai District. In 1986, the King of Nepal awarded Prem with the Social Service Medal of Honor for his humanitarian and educational work. In 1994, a third school was started across the border in India. Today hundreds of churches and some 500,000 believers in Nepal can trace at least part of their spiritual roots to this lame soldier of Christ.

John (J. D.) Sumner

Nov. 19, 1924 — Lakeland, Florida
Nov. 16, 1998 — Myrtle Beach, South Carolina

The greatest gospel bass singer of all time. Once you heard him, you would agree. *Guinness Book of Records* has him listed as the lowest bass singer in the world. He sang with the Sunshine Boys, 1943–54. When the Blackwood Brothers Quartet had that fatal airplane accident in 1954, it was Sumner who replaced Bill Lyles and served with the BBQ from 1954–65. In 1964, he bought the STAMPS Quartet Music Company from Frank Stamps. After that, he became the keystone of the STAMPS Quartet, and also sang with the Masters V, 1980–88. He and the STAMPS Quartet were backing soloists for Elvis Presley, 1972–77. He sang at Presley's funeral. Sumner was instrumental in founding the Gospel Music Association. He died of a heart attack while on tour. Twelve hundred attended the funeral at Christ Church, Nashville, TN. He composed over 700 songs, including "The Old Country Church."

Howard Higashi

Feb. 28, 1937 — Hawaii
Nov. 27, 1998

Songwriter and college witness. Higashi was born a third-generation Hawaiian of Japanese Buddhist ancestry. He married Lily Agena in 1965. He heard the gospel in 1968, moved to Los Angeles and this resulted in his conversion. The Higashis spent the rest of their lives going from campus to campus, shepherding others, writing spiritual songs, and ministering. They were instrumental in reaching hundreds of college students and many of their relatives with the gospel. He wrote "Where Is He, My Jesus?"

Doyle (Buddy) Harrison

Sept. 21, 1939 — Highland, Texas
Nov. 28, 1998 — Tulsa, Oklahoma

Founder and first president of Faith Christian Fellowship International, Tulsa, OK 1978–98. This was a fellowship of 300 churches in the USA and about 1,000 overseas. Harrison was an entrepreneur and a very successful businessman. He married Patsy Hagin on October 25, 1958. He was the business manager for the Ken Hagin Ministries, Borken Arrow, OK from 1966–76. Harrison founded the Harrison House Publishers, Tulsa, OK, in 1975 with three employees and a debt of $1,500. Twenty-five years later, he had 200 employees and had sold 100 million books from some 190 different author's contributions. He represented Network Christian Ministries, New Orleans, from 1985 on. He was an avid coin and stamp collector and wrote the book *Count It All Joy*.

Carl Holwerda

July 14, 1930 — Grand Rapids, Michigan
Dec. 29, 1998 — Grand Rapids, Michigan

Bible teacher, evangelist, and founder of Churches Unlimited. Holwerda was a blessing far beyond his humble roots. Afflicted with polio early on, his familiar limp and humor made him a beloved friend to all he met. After his Moody education, he was active in Youth For Christ, directing the Kalamazoo, MI rally with success until 1954. He married Marilyn Harrington on September 26, 1952. He pastored Baptist churches in Delhi, IL (1959–64); Joliet, IL (1964–68); and then at the Lake Center

Bible Church, Portage, IL (1968–84). After 25 years of pastoring, Holwerda launched out with his Churches Unlimited, Inc., to an itinerant ministry that took him throughout the central and eastern states. He died of cancer.

Costa Deir

Oct. 24, 1921
Ramlahi, Palestine

Dec. 30, 1998
Lima, New York

Director of Elim Fellowship World Missions, Lima, NY, 1965–83 and first president of International Leadership Seminars, 1973–98. Deir was reared in a Greek Orthodox Church but was converted in Palestine via a missionary. He emmigrated to the US in 1957, marrying Ruth Purdy in July, 1957. He traveled to Elim Fellowship (Lima, NY); was put on staff; pastored in Herimer, NY; then headed the missions program, taking numerous trips to such places as Africa and Central and South America. He became known for teaching leaders on the field, calling it International Leadership Seminars, Inc. He also taught at Elim Bible Institute. Deir had open heart surgery in 1957, but died with cancer.

Frank Fortunato

Nov. 28, 1906
Reggio Calabria, Italy

Jan. 20, 1999
Philadelphia, Pennsylvania

General overseer of Christian Church of North America, Transfer, PA 1954–75. Fortunato grew up Catholic. As a refugee family, they came to America and settled in western Pennsylvania. He became involved in illegal activity, working for the Mafia in New York City. He became a boxer. Losing several bouts and responding to the prayers of a mother, he began to attend an Italian Christian Church in New Castle, PA, in the early 30s. He started witnessing upon conversion and got involved with the Italian Pentecostal Fellowship of Churches, memorizing Scripture in a big way. He pastored churches in east Pennsylvania (Philadelphia) and west Pennsylvania (Erie, Beaver Falls). His last 25 years found him on mission trips to Europe, Australia, South America, as well as interim pastorates.

Almus M. Thorp

April 1, 1912
Manchester, New Hampshire

Jan. 20, 1999
Rochester, New York

Dean of Bexley Hall Theological Seminary at Kenyon College, Gambier, OH (Colgate-Rochester (NY) Divinity School in 1968), **1959–68.** Thorp married Merrill Kimball on June 15, 1938. He was curate and rector in Columbus, OH, 1937–1959. He "retired" to serve as interim rector of Christ Church, Pittsford, NY, and associate priest at St. Paul's Church in Rochester. Bexley Hall was originally at Kenyon College in Gambier, OH, but in 1968 Thorp oversaw the move to Rochester, NY, when it merged into Colgate-Rochester Seminary. He was director of the Episcopal Church's Board for Theological Education 1969–77. He was diagnosed with a cancerous, inoperable growth in his chest which made eating almost impossible. He is considered one of the leading Episcopalians of his time.

John Osteen

Aug. 21, 1921
Paris, Texas

Jan. 23, 1999
Houston, Texas

Pastor of the Lakewood Baptist Church, Houston, TX, later called Lakewood Church. He founded it in a dusty feed store on Mother's Day, 1959, with about 150 members. It grew to thousands with a world mission emphasis to 111 nations. Television carried their ministry around the world for 16 years, reaching millions. Osteen wrote some 30 books. Osteen began preaching at age 17. He was ordained as a Southern Baptist, and pastored churches in Hamlin, Baytown, and Houston, TX. In 1958, while pastoring at Hibbard Memorial Baptist Church in Houston, he received the Pentecostal experience (baptism of the Holy Ghost). A healing ministry soon followed. He died unexpectedly. His son, Joel, succeeded him, and in 2005, it was the largest church in America with 24,000 in attendance weekly.

John I. Page

Oct. 2, 1930
Ft. Scott, Kansas

Jan. 28, 1999
Ft. Scott, Kansas

President of Kansas City College and Bible School, Overland Park, KS, 1980–89. Page married Virginia Witt on August 1, 1951; pastored the Church of God (Holiness), Stockton, MO (1952–58); and in Ft. Scott, KS (1959–80). He was active in many secular and political causes, and president of the Bourbon County Police Chaplaincy, Ft. Scott (1965–80). He made his home in Prairie Village, KS.

Frank Veninga

June 8, 1913
Grosswolde, Germany

Jan. 28, 1999
Minneapolis, Minnesota

President of North American Baptist Seminary, Sioux Falls, SD, 1959–70, 1981–82. Veninga emigrated with his family to the US in 1925. The family became active in the German Baptist community and their home church, Evergreen Baptist in Brooklyn. He worked for the Sinclair Refining company, Manhattan, NY for seven years and married Otila A. Mauch on September 1, 1940 (died: 1993). He pastored Bethany Baptist, Milwaukee; State Park Baptist, Peoria, IL; FBC, Aplington, IA; and Temple Baptist Church, Pittsburgh, 1940–58. His sermon, "This Nation Under God," won him the 1949 Freedom's Foundation Award. From 1970–79, he was executive vice president of Eastern Baptist Theological Seminary, Philadelphia, PA. He returned to NABS and served as interim president, 1981–82.

G. Ray Carlson

Feb. 17, 1918
Crosby, North Dakota

Jan. 29, 1999
Springfield, Missouri

General superintendent of Assemblies of God, 1986–93, and chairman of Pentecostal Fellowship of North America, 1986–88. Worldwide AG adherents grew from 10 to 15 million during his tenure. Carlson was converted to Christ under the ministry of evangelist Blanche Britton in 1925. He married Mae Steffler on October 7, 1938. He first pastored in Thief River Falls, MN, from 1940–48. From 1948–61, he was district superintendent of AG in Minnesota. Carlson later was president of North Central Bible College (University in 2000), Minneapolis, MN, from 1961–69. He then was assistant superintendent of AG under , 1969–86. As head of the AG during a stormy period (fall-out from the PTL and Jimmy Swaggart scandals), he brought comfort and assurance to the movement. His writings range from *Romans* (1962) to *Prayer and the Christian's Devotional Life* (1980).

George E. Hedberg

June 3, 1910
Bay City, Michigan

Feb. 12, 1999
Rockford, Illinois

President of Home of Onesiphorous (Kids Alive Int. in 1983), **1954–83.** Hedberg married Astrid Soneson on November 26, 1932. For many years he was employed in banking, accounting, and insurance. He was active in several Christian organizations. He lived in Rockford, IL, since 1985 and was active in the Evangelical Free Church. Helping needy children and orphans, he was a blessing to thousands as he headed this work for 30 years. He was founder and director of Fairhaven Christian Retirement Center, Rockford; Rainbow Lake (MI) Bible Camp; and Pikeville (KY) Bible Institute.

Walter Gomez

March 13, 1916
Indiahoma, Oklahoma

Feb. 17, 1999
McAllen, Texas

Founder and director of Mexican Mission Ministries, Pharr, TX (merged into Global Outreach Mission, Buffalo, NY, in 1998), **1954–87**. Gomez grew up with the Comanche Indians and soon was conversing in five languages: English, Spanish, Comanche, and high and low German that his mother learned as a child. He was converted at age twelve. He married Lois Rawlings (Jan. 3, 1917–Nov. 26, 1999) on Nov. 14, 1936. They attended Northwestern Bible College in Minneapolis, then went to Mexico in the mid 1940s and started a Bible training center in 1955, after incorporating Mexican Mission Ministries. Soon things were flourishing at the Walter Gomez Evangelical Center in Pachuca and Hidalgo, Mexico (seminary, conference headquarters, dorms, auditorium). Cancer surfaced in 1992, but he carried on for several years.

Robert E. Naylor

Jan. 24, 1909
Hartshorne, Oklahoma

Feb. 21, 1999
Fort Worth, Texas

President of Southwestern Baptist Theological Seminary, Fort Worth, TX, 1958–78. Naylor entered the seminary in 1928 and then married Goldia Dalton on August 29, 1930 in Fort Worth, TX. Early on he pastored in several locations: Nashville, AR (1932–35); Malvern, AR (1935–37); Arkadelphia, AR (1937–44); Enid, OK (1944–47); and FBC Columbia, SC (1947–52). He then became pastor of Travis Avenue Baptist Church (1952–58). During his tenure at SBTS, five major building projects were begun or completed which expanded the seminary. Enrollment topped 4,100 students, making it the largest seminary in the world. Everybody spoke of his love for the Bible and his ability to preach. About 1,700 attended his funeral at Travis Avenue Baptist Church. Pastor Coggin said, "He was a great, great teacher. Nothing overshadowed this." President Hemphill said, "He may have been one of the greatest expositors of his generation."

Kenneth Tuinstra

June 11, 1932
Grandville, Michigan

Feb. 24, 1999
Ashland, Kentucky

President of Southland Bible Institute, Ashland, KY 1977–89. Tuinstra was raised in a Christian home, his father, George Tuinstra, being a minister. He married Janet DeSmith on August 15, 1952. He then pastored several Bible churches in Michigan, including one in Coopersville, MI until 1969. From 1969–72, the family served in Zambia, Africa. He then began teaching at SBI in 1972 before becoming president. Following his presidency, he traveled briefly. Stricken with several bloodclots, his remaining years were spent in a recliner where he did such things as write correspondence courses for Youth Haven Bible Camp. He died of kidney failure.

W. Frank Harrington

May 13, 1935
Kingstree, South Carolina

March 3, 1999
Atlanta, Georgia

Pastor of the largest Presbyterian Church (USA) in the country, he was pastor of the 11,000 member Peachtree Presbyterian Church in Atlanta for 27 years. When Harrington arrived in 1971, the annual budget was $306,000. His last year, it was $9.4 million. He baptized 1,000 adults and performed about 1,000 weddings. Membership at Peachtree grew from 2,400 to 11,882 during his tenure. He was co-chairman of the 1994 Billy Graham crusade there and also presided over an Atlanta memorial service for Jon Benet Ramsey, the little murdered beauty queen whose parents were Presbyterians. He first pastored in Hinesville, GA, then Fairview Church, North Augusta, SC, from 1965–71. His wife's name was Sara. Harrington died of a respiratory infection.

Delbert P. Vaughn

June 7, 1926
Dombe, Oklahoma

March 12, 1999
Houston, Texas

President of Houston (TX) Graduate School of Theology, 1983-97. Vaughn was a Friends (Quaker) theologian and professor, and pastored churches in Tonganoxie, KS; Fowler, KS; Pasadena, CA; Friendswood, TX; Texas City, TX; and Northshore, TX, before founding the Graduate School. With the backing of the Texas Area Friends Churches, he founded the school which was originally housed in the Institute of Religion building of Texas Medical Center in Houston. Early on, he taught at Friends (Barclay) University, Wichita, KS (six years), and Southwestern Business College (dean for four years). He wrote *Baptism with the Holy Spirit in the Writings of the Church Fathers*.

J. Brock Speer

Dec. 28, 1920
Double Springs, Alabama

March 29, 1999
Nashville, Tennessee

Patriarch of the legendary Speer family, Brock was the link between his parents and children in the amazing family singing group. His father, Tom, formed the singing group in 1921. His family moved to Nashville in 1946. After he matured, Brock was singing bass vocals for the family. His career spanned the horse and buggy, Model T Fords, to a customized bus. They traveled about 10,000 miles annually. He married Faye Ihrig on August 31, 1948 and had three children. He was a graduate of Trevecca Nazarene College, Nashville, TN in 1950. Brock sang the bass part for 63 of his 78 years. The group retired in 1998. They recorded with at least six record companies. Over 1,000 attended his funeral on April 1, 1999, at the First Nazarene Church of Nashville. He died in Baptist Hospital following a battle with Alzheimer's disease.

Cassie Bernall

Nov. 6, 1981
Littleton, Colorado

April 20, 1999
Littleton, Colorado

Teen martyr. Cassie's life had a great impact on her generation. A 17-year-old high school junior, Cassie was one of twelve students murdered in the Columbine High School massacre. As an early teen, Cassie considered suicide, being engrossed in the occult. Then Christ came into her life and all that goes with it—carrying a Bible to school and joining the vibrant West Bowles Community Church. Her murderers, Eric Harris and Dylan Klebold, came into the school on April 20th and gunned her down in the library, after asking her if she believed in God. Under a table, clutching her Bible, she said, "Yes, I believe in God." She was shot instantly. Another Christian, Rachel Scott, was also killed. Valeen Schnurr also said "Yes" to the question, and although she suffered nine bullets and shrapnel wounds, she lived. The memorial service of 70,000 heard Cassie and twelve others praised by Vice President Gore and Franklin Graham. Her mother, Misty, wrote her biography, *She Said Yes—The Unlikely Martyrdom of Cassie Bernall* (2001).

J. Oscar Wells

Oct. 2, 1916
Wellington, Texas

April 28, 1999

Longtime evangelist, Wells had a large following. Wells was converted at age nine at a J. H. Hankins revival meeting. He was one of three members in the first graduating class (1939) of the old Fundamental Baptist Bible Institute (Arlington Baptist College) of Fort Worth. Another of the graduates was John Birch, whom he accompanied to China until they were expelled. Since then, he conducted hundreds of meetings around the country, basically in independent and Southern Baptist Churches. His daughter was astronaut Shannon Lucid, who set a record for the longest time any American was in space in 1996. In China, he was unofficial chaplain to Chiang Kai Shek. Wells died after cancer surgery.

Marjorie Scoville Stiles

July 27, 1933
Pasadena, California

May 3, 1999
San Clemente, California

Musical gospel team with her sister Marileen. With multiple musical talents, these young ladies ministered for 18 years together in more than 3,000 programs in the 40s and 50s. They played a dozen instruments well; they held meetings featuring the marimba, vibra-harp, piano, and organ in rallies, banquets and crusades. Both girls married: Marjorie to Bob Stiles, leaving to serve as missionaries with Far East Broadcasting Company for many years in Okinawa, Philippines and the FEBC home office. They had three daughters. Marjorie battled cancer for years. It finally spread to her liver.

Robert E. Reeves

March 21, 1928
Wilkinson, Indiana

May 9, 1999
Columbus, Indiana

Executive director of Fellowship of Associates of Medical Evangelism, 1972–98. Reeves was raised in a Christian home, marrying Rosella Heifner on August 4, 1950. He then pastored in Brunswick, MO (1950–52); the Butler Christian Church, Morristown, IN (1952–61); and the Christian Church, Fairfield, IL (1961–67). Reeves then moved to Terre Haute, IN, where he pastored the Maplewood Christian Church. After hearing missionary doctors to Africa, Reeves became a pioneer in medical evangelism. He moved his family to Columbus, IN, in 1975. He died of gall bladder cancer.

Leo M. Thorton

April 13, 1922
Dayton, Oregon

May 14, 1999
Milwaukie, Oregon

President of Western Evangelical Seminary (George Fox University in 1996), **near Milwaukie, OR, 1976–87**. Ordained in the Free Methodist Church, he served primarily in the Evangelical United Brethren (Evangelical Church). He pastored in Battle Ground, WA, and Portland and Eugene, OR. He served three terms as a Republican member of the Oregon House of Representatives, 1968–74. He was president of National Holiness Association (Christian Holiness Partnership), 1980–82. Thorton was also a well known trombone player.

Louis Kaplan

Aug. 29, 1915
New York, New York

May 19, 1999
Phoenix, Arizona

Director of "Jewish Voice" Ministries, 1967–1998. Raised by Jewish parents, Kaplan came to know the Lord in Pahokee, FL on March 25, 1935, at a Nazarene revival. He received his Pentecostal experience (May 28, 1936) and preached the first time (October 22, 1937) in South Norwalk, CT. He held his first citywide healing campaign with Wilbur Ogilvie in September, 1949 in St. Nicholas Boxing Arena, New York City, with 40 churches cooperating. Kaplan was ordained by the Assemblies of God in 1956, and was a traveling evangelist in some 3,000 churches before starting "Jewish Voice" broadcasts in January, 1967. He died after suffering the effects of a severe stroke for over 21 months.

Oscar Moore

Feb. 24, 1909
near Hammon, Oklahoma

June 30, 1999
Bixby, Oklahoma

General superintendent of the Pentecostal Holiness Church (International in 1975), **1953–57**. Moore was sanctified in a revival meeting in April, 1924. He married Anna O. Moore on June, 1926. He served as general secretary of the PHC, 1941–53. During their retirement, they lived in Bixby, OK. He was an administrator of the Oral Roberts Evangelistic Association, 1960–69.

Robert W. Benton

Aug. 28, 1931
Guthrie County, Iowa

July 2, 1999
near Longmont, Colorado

President of Grace Bible Institute (University) **Omaha, NE, 1971–84; Arizona College of the Bible, 1989–96; and Accrediting Association of Bible Colleges, 1982–84**. Benton married Beryl Anderson on August 20, 1955. Ordained Baptist, he pastored at Community Church, Martensdale, IA (1959–64); Community Church, Tippecanoe, IN (1964–67); before joining the faculty of GBI in 1967. Benton was president of Northeastern Bible College, Essex Falls, NJ (1984–87) and director of development at Northwestern College, St. Paul, MN (1988–89).

J. Russell Killman

March 8, 1921
Chicago, Illinois

July 9, 1999
Hume Lake, California

Director of "Heaven and Home Hour," 1965–85. Killman was a radio speaker, evangelist, Bible teacher, world traveler, musician, and missionary. His personal preaching appearances also included tenor and cornet solos. He was converted at the Chicago Gospel Tabernacle in 1930 and traveled for seven years with LANCE LATHAM in the White Shirt Brigade across America. He married Claire Erickson in 1946 (died: January 1982) and Virginia Otto on November 20, 1982. He ministered in Taiwan, became a cinematographer for BIOLA with eight film credits, and was missionary in Hong Kong, 1954–58. He traveled widely in behalf of missions, at least five trips to South Africa. Killman died after a fall from the roof of his cottage.

Henry H. Budd

April 15, 1931
Prongua, Saskatchewan, Canada

July 19, 1999
Calgary, Alberta, Canada

President of Briercrest Bible Institute, Caronport, Saskatchewan, 1977–90. Converted in 1942 at a camp meeting, Budd and his wife, Evelyn Sawatsay (married 1953), served in Nigeria with SIM from 1955–65. He was then appointed as Dean of Faculty in 1967 at BBI. He continued teaching until 1999, when he retired on June 19, to Calgary.

Kenzy K. Savage

March 17, 1912
Alvord, Texas

July 28, 1999
Alberquerque, New Mexico

President of Latin American Bible Institute, San Antonio, TX, 1945–50, 1952–60. Savage was raised in a Christian home. He was converted in a revival in his father's Assemblies of God Church. He married Esther Dodson on May 8, 1930. He traveled in evangelism for many years and taught Spanish at Southwestern Assembly of God Bible Institute, Ft. Worth, TX, from 1939–43. While president of LABI, he taught Spanish and Bible. Upon leaving LABI, he was a supporter of the Spanish work for the Assemblies of God for the Central American Latin District, which included many western states. He continued as an evangelist until he retired. A heart attack, precipitated by chronic leukemia, caused his death. His autobiography is *The Spirit Bade Me Go*.

George M. Wilson

Oct. 19, 1913
Church's Ferry, North Dakota

Aug. 24, 1999
Minneapolis, Minnesota

First executive director of Billy Graham Evangelistic Association, Minneapolis, MN 1950–87, and one of the great leaders of the Youth for Christ Movement. Wilson married Helen Bjorck on Sept. 3, 1940. He was the owner and manager of Wilson Press, NW Book and Bible

House, Minneapolis, and business manager of Northwestern Schools, 1940–50. During the 1940s he directed Youth for Christ in Minneapolis, bringing great crowds together every Saturday night. He was also president of World Wide Publishers, Minneapolis, 1970–88. He has one of the longest sketches in *Who's Who in Religion* on page 564, describing all of his awards and accomplishments. Billy Graham preached, but George Wilson ran the organization. Wilson was the first board chairman of the Evangelical Council for Financial Accountability.

John C. Bennett

Jan. 25, 1952
Sacramento, California

Aug. 25, 1999
Indianapolis, Indiana

President of Advancing Churches in Missions Commitment (ACMC), Atlanta, GA, 1981–86, and the chief executive officer of Overseas Council for Theological Education and Mission, Indianapolis, IN 1995–98. Bennett provided general supervision to the work of the organization in the U.S. and coordinated program services to its 89 partner institutions and projects in 50 non-Western countries. He and his wife, Gail, were members of First Presbyterian Church, Southport, IN. He suffered a massive heart attack at age 47 and died in a local hospital.

Robert L. Gray

Dec. 3, 1927
Wilkinsburg, Pennsylvania

Aug. 26, 1999
Hinsdale, Illinois

President of Independent Fundamental Churches of America, 1972–75, 1978–81. Gray married Ruth McCarrell on April 7, 1951. He pastored the Westchester (IL) Bible Church from 1953 till his last days. Ordained in the IFCA in 1958, he served also as trustee or board member to the Ozark (AR) Bible Institute, Illinois Bible Church Mission, Light Bearers Association, and Open Air Campaigners. He was the son-in-law to the founder of the IFCA, WILLIAM MCCARRELL. He died after a lengthy illness from a heart attack.

Olin T. Binkley

Aug. 4, 1908
Harmony, North Carolina

Aug. 27, 1999
Wake Forest, North Carolina

President of Southeastern Baptist Theological Seminary, Wake Forest, NC, 1963–74 and of Association of Theological Schools, 1964–66. On July 24, 1933, Binkley married Pauline Eichmann after being ordained a Baptist minister in 1928. He pastored Chapel Hill (NC) Baptist Church, 1933–38. He headed the Department of Religion at Wake Forest College, Winston-Salem, NC, from 1938–44; then went to Southern Baptist Seminary, Louisville, KY. In 1946–52, Binkley began a long association with SBTS as professor of Christian sociology and ethics, then became dean in 1958. He was also an author.

Murrell F. Coughran

July 9, 1908
Tahoka, Texas

Aug. 28, 1999
Saunas, California

General superintendent of Pentecostal Church of God (Inc. in 1978) **of America, Inc., Kansas City, MO, 1949–51, Joplin, MO 1951–53, and its mission director, 1933–44.** Coughran was converted at Brush Arbor Camp Meeting in Dudley, TX, when he was eight years old. He married his wife, Margaret, in 1928. They went to India, 1932–34, when failing health caused them to return. He pastored in Fresno, CA, and soon became associated with the PCGA. In 1940, he became district superintendent of the California/Arizona District, soon taking the northern California responsibility when the districts divided, serving until 1969. He founded the Pentecostal Bible Institute, in 1946, on the Gilroy Campground. In 1953, he spoke at the World Pentecostal Conference, London; pastored at Seaside (1953–56);

at Calvary Temple, Campbell, CA (1956–61); and then served as central California superintendent (1961–63). He also built the Oak Park Community Church, Salinas, CA, and pastored there, 1964–78.

Kenneth H. Pearsall

June 15, 1918
Cynnbrook, New York

August 29, 1999
Nampa, Idaho

President of Northwest Nazarene College (University in 2000), **Nampa, ID, 1973–83.** Pearsall married Ruth Friend in 1944, and upon her death in 1952, married her sister, Ruby Friend, on July 18, 1953. Early on, he pastored three churches in New York and was field representative for Eastern Nazarene College, Wollaston, MA, until 1953. Pearsall also pastored the First Nazarene Church, Akron, Ohio (1953–58) and the First Church of Yakima, WA (1958–62). He was district superintendent of up-State New York (1962–68), then of the New England District (1968–73). Upon leaving New York City, he traveled in education endeavors in Korea and South Africa. Pearsall continued to hold revivals and missions conferences through 1991 when heart problems limited him from 1992 on.

Clyde W. Meadows

Jan. 3, 1901
Pamplin, Virginia

Sept. 9, 1999
Columbus, Ohio

President of Christian Endeavor (World) 1962–74, (Int.) 1959–63, and general secretary (World), 1967–174. Meadows may have been the most important man in the Christian Endeavor movement, save the founder. He married Mabel Mumma on Aug. 13, 1924 (died: Nov. 30, 1979), then Phyllis Rike on Nov. 21, 1980. He was converted during a revival meeting at Rocks Baptist Church near Hicksburg, VA. He was ordained in the United Brethren Church in 1927, and then pastored King Street Church, Chambersburg, PA, from 1928–61. Meadows then served as a UB bishop for the Eastern area, USA and Canada (1961–69), working with the Pennsylvania State SS Association (1969–80). He wrote several books beginning with *Why We Choose Christ*. Meadows edited the *United Brethren Hymnal*.

Don W. Holter

March 24, 1905
Lincoln, Kansas

Sept. 12, 1999
Prairie Village, Kansas

Founder and first president of St. Paul School of Theology, Kansas City, MO, 1958–71. Holter married Isabelle Elliott on June 20, 1931. Ordained as a Methodist in 1934, he served as a missionary in Manila, Philippine Islands, from 1935–45. He was president of Union Theological Seminary, Manila, 1940–45. He was a prisoner of war from 1942–45 with his family at the Santo Thomas Internment Camp. After the war, he pastored the Hamline Methodist Church, St. Paul, MN (1946–49), then served as professor at Garrett Theological Seminary, Evanston, IL (1949–58). From 1972–76, he was bishop, serving the Nebraska area. He wrote books on Methodism's history in Kansas and Nebraska.

S. Bruce Willson

July 27, 1910
Guezna, Turkey

Sept. 12, 1999
Pittsburgh, Pennsylvania

President of Reformed Presbyterian Theological Seminary, Pittsburgh, PA 1953–76. Willson married Doris G. Owens (Feb. 19, 1912–Nov. 9, 1988) on July 23, 1936. Ordained in 1936, he pastored the Reformed Presbyterian Church, Youngstown, Ohio (1936–41), then in Bloomington, Indiana (1941–48), followed by ministry in Greeley, Colorado (1948–53). While president of RPTS, he also taught church history and practical theology. He retired to Clarinda, IA, in 1980 and served as a supply pastor where needed. He later returned to Pittsburgh to a Reformed Presbyterian retirement home.

Bernard E. Underwood

Oct. 26, 1925
Bluefield, West Virginia

Sept. 22, 1999
Royston, Georgia

General superintendent of International Pentecostal Holiness Church, 1989–97; its mission director, 1969–73 (PHC) and 1977–89 (IPHC); and chairman of Pentecostal Fellowship of North America, 1994–95. Underwood was ordained in 1944 in the PHC. He worked in the youth department of the denomination out of Kingsport, TN (1946–53), was Christian educational director for the Virginia conference (1951–60), assistant superintendent (1958–64), and superintendent of the Virginia conference (1964–69) working out of Roanoke. His first book was *Gifts of the Spirit* (1967), and his last *16 NT Principles for World Evangelization* (1988). He married Esther Parramore on December 22, 1947. He founded the Chosen Union Christian College (Yonseiuhn) in Seoul.

Jerald C. Brauer

Sept. 16, 1921
Fond du Lac, Wisconsin

Sept. 26, 1999
Chicago, Illinois

Dean of University of Chicago Divinity School, 1960–70. Brauer married Muriel I. Nelson on March 18, 1945. He was ordained Lutheran in 1951. From 1955–60, he was Dean of the University's Federated Theological Faculty, which embraced three neighboring theological schools as well as the University's Divinity School. He was a leading scholar of Puritanism. Brauer also co-edited the quarterly journal *Church History* for more than 30 years. His last book was *John Nuveen: A Life of Service* (1997). His first book was *Protestantism in America* (1953)

William P. Brink

Sept. 21, 1916
Chicago, Illinois

Sept. 28, 1999
Grand Rapids, Michigan

Stated clerk of Christian Reformed Church, 1970–82. Brink married Alta Ibershof on July 25, 1941, and was ordained the same year. His pastorates included Goshen, IN (1941–44); at Archer Ave., Chicago, IL (1944–48); at Creston, Grand Rapids, MI (1948–53); at Bethany, Holland, MI (1953–64) and at Second, Fremont, MI (1964–70). Brink was also president of Young Calvinist Federation of NA, 1958–70. He wrote *Learning Doctrine from the Bible* (1965).

David H. L. Mauck

Aug. 14, 1918
Paradise, Kansas

Oct. 10, 1999
El Dorado Springs, Missouri

First director of Church of God Holiness World Missions, Overland Park, KS 1964–1983. Raised in a Christian home, Mauck felt the call to missions upon leaving high school. He married Lucille Baker in 1941, and they spent four years in Jamaica in the 1940's starting a school among other things. For many years, they went from country to country encouraging and helping start mission programs. Previous leadership had been held by board members since 1922.

Payne Stewart

Jan. 30, 1957
Springfield, Missouri

Oct. 25, 1999
Mina/Edmunds, South Dakota

One of the top golfers of his time, who met death in a most bizarre plane crash. Stewart married Tracey and had two children. His many victories included the PGA Championship in 1989, and the U.S. Open in 1991 and 1999. He was a member of the U.S. Ryder Cup team in 1987, '89, '91, '93, and the World Cup Team in 1987 and 1990. A Lear jet carrying Stewart and four others left Orlando, FL, headed for Dallas. Evidently the plane lost cabin pressure and continued on autopilot. The plane cruised 1,400 miles straight northward until it ran out of fuel four hours later, crashing into farmland. Payne's funeral was held at First Baptist Church, Orlando, with pastor James Henry proclaiming Christ in the nationwide telecast of that service.

Robert D. VanKampen

1939

Oct. 29, 1999
Chicago, Illinois

Antique Bible collector and multimillionaire investor, he founded the VanKampen Mutual Funds, creating a Scriptorium of ancient manuscripts in Grand Haven, MI, now relocated in Florida. Holdings include the book of Daniel from the 1455 Gutenberg Bible, Hebrew Torah scrolls, and papyrus/clay tablets dating back to 2000 BC. VanKampen wrote several books on eschataology, including *The Rapture Question Answered*, *The Fourth Reich*, and *The Sign*. He died of a viral heart condition.

Raymond F. Carter

Sept. 17, 1909
Cleveland, Oklahoma

Nov. 4, 1999
Tulsa, Oklahoma

President of Full Gospel Grace Fellowship, Tulsa, OK 1954–84. Carter married Virgil Gibbons on June 11, 1933. While plowing a field with a team of horses, he suddenly stopped, knelt, and gave his heart to Christ. He felt called to serve as a pastor and evangelist. He pastored in Solomon, AZ (1948–51), and Weston, MO (1952–67), then moved to Tulsa. His health began to fail in 1980.

Harold W. Boon

July 19, 1910
New Castle, Pennsylvania

Nov. 24, 1999
Decatur, Florida

President of Nyack (NY) College, 1958–75, and Accrediting Association of Bible Colleges, 1960–64. Boon was active in the CMA all his life. He met Hazel Fox at Nyack College in 1931 and married her. He pastored a CMA Church in Greenville, PA. During the 1940s he served as a US Navy chaplain. Boon served Nyack College for 35 years as a faculty member, registrar, academic dean, 1940–58, and president for 17 years. After retiring in 1975, the Boons moved to Florida where he was active in the Ormond Beach Alliance Church. His wife of 61 years survived him.

Jarl Wahlstrom

Sept. 7, 1918
Helsinki, Finland

Dec. 3, 1999
Helsinki, Finland

General of Salvation Army, 1981–86. Wahlstrom became a Salvation Army officer in August of 1939. During WWII, he became a military chaplain and married Maire Nyberg in 1944. He was very musical, playing the cornet, piano, mandolin, and guitar. Wahlstrom led the Salvation Army ministry in Canada and Bermuda (1972–76), and in Finland (1976–81). He spoke English, German, Finnish, and Swedish. In 1985, he led an International Youth Congress of 5,000 delegates to Berlin.

Theodore (Ted) M. Paulson

Oct. 3, 1917
Provost, Alberta, Canada

Dec. 5, 1999
Ponoko, Alberta, Canada

President of World Missions Fellowship, Oregon City, OR, 1961–77. Paulson was converted via a C. Oscar Lowrey radio broadcast and went to Prairie Bible Institute, Three Hills, Alberta, with $5 in his pocket. He married Margaret McDougall on August 16, 1946. He then taught Bible at Two Rivers Bible Institute for five years and art at New Brunswick Bible Institute, Carlea, NB, for four years. They served in Japan, 1952–62. Paulson returned to Kelona, BC, serving in various capacities from 1979–93. They retired in Wetaskinan, Alberta, where he was active in a Baptist church, 1993–99.

Carl E. Bates

Sept. 5, 1914
near Liberty, Mississippi

Dec. 21, 1999
Horse Shoe, North Carolina

President of Southern Baptist Convention, 1970–97. Bates was converted in the Hotel De Soto, New Orleans, on August 28, 1935. He married Myra Gray on November 15, 1939. He also pastored at Central Baptist Church, Winchester, KY (1941–43), and FBC, Leesburg, FL (1943–47). He was also president of the Baptist General Convention of Texas and the Baptist State Convention of North Carolina. Prior to that he was pastor of FBC of Texarkana, TX (1947–50), FBC, Amarillo, TX (1950–59), and FBC, Charlotte, NC (1959–80). He taught five years as professor of preaching and pastoral ministries at Southern Baptist Seminary, Louisville, KY.

J. Sidlow Baxter

Feb. 25, 1903
Sydney, Australia

Dec. 28, 1999
Santa Barbara, California

Outstanding Bible teacher and author, Baxter went to England early on. He was converted in meetings near Manchester about age 16. He was married to Ethel Smith for nearly 50 years when she died in 1978. He pastored Charlotte Chapel, Edinburgh 1935–53, then came to America. He engaged in Bible Conference and itinerant evangelism for the rest of his life, residing in Santa Barbara, CA. On April 29, 1979, he married Isabella Hall. He was an outstanding pianist and was used in this capacity many times. A prolific author of many books, his most well-known was *Explore the Book*.

Colin W. Williams

Aug. 17, 1921
Ballarat, Australia

Jan. 4, 2000
Orleans, Massachusetts

Dean of Yale Divinity School, New Haven, CT 1966–79. Born in a Methodist parsonage, Williams married Phyllis L. Miller on September 10, 1949. He was a leading ecumenist in Australia in the 1950s as one of a group who prepared the way for the later development of the Uniting Church. He was involved in the social issues of his time, the voter registration among African-Americans in the South in the 1960s and the anti-Vietnam protests in the early 1970s. He returned to Australia several times. He served the NCC, 1963–66. In the early 1990s, he was stricken with cancer and then Parkinson's disease.

Robert C. Cunningham

Dec. 23, 1914
Peterborough, Ontario, Canada

Jan. 7, 2000
Springfield, Missouri

Longtime Assembly of God journalist and president of Evangelical Press Association, 1962–64. In 1937, Cunningham became a member of the editorial staff at Gospel Publishing House. He also served as a supply pastor for various churches in the Springfield, MO, area. He married Helen M. Platte, and became editor of the *Pentecostal Evangel* in 1943, working there again as editor of the same, 1949–84. Ordained in 1945, Cunningham pastored in Ozark, MO (1943–47), and did missionary work in Lome, Togo (1985–86). He helped organize the International Press Association in 1970. He was one of the most respected Assembly of God personalities of his generation.

Richard L. Corsini

May 20, 1903

c. Jan. 9, 2000
Beaver Falls, PA

First director of Christian Church of North America Missions, Transfer, PA 1927–68. Corsini married Anna Somjak on January 21, 1924. He was converted (1926), called to the ministry (1928), and ordained on May 31, 1941, in Pittsburgh. Corsini pastored the Christian Church there briefly then helped in Midland and Coraopolis, PA. In 1930, he became engaged in home missions work in Fairmont, WV. Then in nearby Clarksburg, WV, he started a work which he pastored, 1930–51. Because of his interest in missions, he traveled to many countries, especially to Europe. Although missions was a part of the CCNA early on, he incorporated the society in 1948. In 1953, he became the first full-time missions director with an office in Pittsburgh. He had an intinerant ministry in his later days, preaching in many churches.

David M. Stowe

March 30, 1919
Council Bluffs, Iowa

Jan. 10, 2000
Englewood/Tenefly, New Jersey

Executive vice president (CEO) of United Church Board for World Ministries, 1970–85. Stowe married Virginia Ware on November 25, 1943. Ordained as a Congregationalist in 1943, he was a missionary and university professor in Peking, China (1947–50), and associate minister at the Congregational Church, Berkeley, CA (1951–53). He served as chairman of the religion department of Carleton College, Northfield, MN (1953–56) then was educational secretary of the UCBWM (1956–62). Stowe taught theology in Beirut (1962–63) and was associate general secretary of UCBWM (1965–70). As head of UCBWM, he developed the policy that no missionary would serve overseas without being invited by the indigenous church. He was also involved in the struggle against apartheid in South Africa. He wrote three books.

Eric S. Fife

April 24, 1921
London, England

Jan. 19, 2000
Bradenton, Florida

Director of Inter-Varsity's Student Foreign Missions Fellowship, 1958–68. Fife became a Christian at age 15 at a boys' brigade camp meeting. From 1937–39, he spoke at youth meetings and street meetings in London. In 1940 he proclaimed the gospel in air-raid shelters in that same city. From 1941–46, he was holding meetings while serving in the Royal Air Force in North Africa. Fife married Joan Edith on August 17, 1946 and pastored in Winchester, England, 1947–54. He came to the US to work with the North Africa Mission (Arab World Ministries) and in 1958. He joined with IV for missionary challenge emphasis on the more than 800 campuses involved. He traveled to more than 40 countries of the world and died from a cold, which accelerated his asthma.

Tom Landry

Sept. 11, 1924
Mission, Texas

Feb. 12, 2000
Dallas, Texas

One of the great coaches in NFL history, along with Vince Lombardi. In 1941, Landry was co-captain, MVP, and All-State on the Mission High School football team that finished 12-0. In 1942, he enrolled at the University of Texas (Austin) on a football scholarship. From 1943–45, he was in the army air corps as a co-pilot in WWII and discharged after 30 bombing missions over Europe. In 1948, he became captain of the Texas football team. He married Alicia Wiggs on January 28, 1949. Upon getting his BA from the University of Texas, he became a player with the Brooklyn/New York Yankees. In 1950, joined the NY Giants after AAFC-NFL merger. In 1954, he became player-coach with the NY Giants as all-pro defensive back. He attended a men's Bible study which led to his conversion soon after, in 1959. He gave his testimony at Billy Graham crusades. In 1960 Landry became the youngest coach in the league when he started with the Dallas Cowboys. He was awarded a ten-year contract (1964), and won Coach of the Year for the first time (1966). His team won the Super Bowl in '72 and '78, and he won his 200th game in 1981. In 1986 he had his first losing season in 21 years. In 1989, he was fired by the new Cowboys' owner after 29 seasons. He had won 270 games, more than anyone in history, save George Halas and Don Shula. In 1990, he was elected to the Pro Football Hall of Fame. His funeral was at the University Methodist Church where he attended for many years.

Charles M. Schulz

Nov. 26, 1922
Minneapolis, Minnesota

Feb. 12, 2000
Santa Rosa, California

Famous cartoonist. Schulz's *Peanuts* presentations on the comic pages for 50 years endeared him to millions. Schulz was raised Lutheran, but in later life he switched to the Church of God, Anderson, IN. He told readers of *Decision Magazine* in 1963, "I cannot fail to be thrilled every time I read the things that Jesus said, and I am more and more convinced of the necessity of following him." Through his comic strip, he preached a little, but didn't proselytize. The strip began October 2, 1950. It eventually reached 2,600 newspapers in 75 countries, spawning 1,400 books that sold 300 million copies. He retired just over a month before his death.

Thomas A. Langford

Feb. 22, 1929
Winston-Salem, North Carolina

Feb. 13, 2000
Durham, North Carolina

Dean of Duke University Divinity School, Durham, NC, 1971–82. Langford married Ann M. Daniel on December 27, 1951. He was ordained to the Methodist ministry in 1952. He joined the Duke faculty early on as professor of religion, 1956–70, and professor of systematic theology, 1971 on. He was a representative of the World Methodist Council in theological discussions with the Catholic Church and the Lutheran World Federation, 1975 on. Later, Langford was vice provost for academic affairs (1984–90), provost (1991–94), and a trustee of Duke endowment (1992–97). His books ranged from *In Search of Foundations* (1969) to *Theology in the Wesleyan Tradition* (1983).

M. Jack Suggs

June 5, 1924
Electra, Texas

Feb. 27, 2000
Fort Worth, Texas

Dean of Brite Divinity School, 1976–89, a division of Texas Christian University, Fort Worth, Texas. During Suggs tenure, he saw growth of students from 20 to 230. He married Ruth Barge on November 13, 1943. Suggs was ordained in the Christian Church, also known as the Disciples of Christ, in 1948. He pastored the First Christian Church in Gladewater, TX (1948–50) and in Wendell, NC (1950–52). Suggs began his teaching at BDS in 1952. He wrote a few books beginning with *The Layman Reads His Bible* (1957) to *Wisdom, Christology, and Law in Matthew's Gospel* (1970). He belonged to many clubs and organizations.

Priscilla C. Patten Benham

Jan. 30, 1950
Berkeley, California

March 6, 2000
Oakland, California

President of Patten University, Oakland, CA, 1983–2000. Priscilla's mother, Bebe Patten, founded Patten College, Christian Cathedral, and Patten Academy. Priscilla was a twin daughter of Dr. Bebe and C. Thomas Patten. Her twin sister Rebecca was also involved in this ministry in a strong way. Priscilla taught NT at PC since 1975. On March 30, 1986, she married her musician husband, Don Benham. Priscilla was a well-known violinist. She founded and directed the 60-voice Patten (Academy) Youth Choir (1973), as well as the 65-member Cathedral Chorale (1975). She died following a long illness.

Walter B. Knight

March 17, 2000

Author of preaching aid books. In early years, Knight was a news correspondent. He married Alice Neighbour in 1930. In 1936 Knight began writing for various Union Gospel Press publications. He was in Cleveland, OH, 1957–69 with them. The Knights then moved to Austin, TX. He was a chaplain in the army during WWII. Knight pastored for 55 years. He wrote *3,000 Illustrations for Christian Service* when he was 50. *Master Book of New Illustrations* is another key book. He was also a good preacher. He authored eight books of illustrations.

Waldo Yeager

July 19, 1908
Eden, Ohio

April 1, 2000
Toledo, Ohio

President of Christian Business Men's Committee, 1953, 1957, and 1960. In 1929, Yeager's father died. He had to support the family by working on a road crew and selling eggs from house to house. In August, 1935, he married Olive Fuller (died: September, 1997). He started the Cortland Produce Company with a friend. Soon, he was sole owner and the business began to boom. This freed him to speak, work with his church, the Christian Fellowship of Toledo, Child Evangelism, Youth for Christ, etc., and represent CBMC in many ways. He sold the business in 1966 and semi-retired, but kept these many outreaches going, staying in the Toledo area. Death was of natural causes following a cold.

Shadrach M. Lockridge

March 7, 1913
near Bremond, Texas

April 4, 2000
San Diego, California

First president of National Missionary Baptists of America, 1988–93 and pastor of Calvary Baptist Church, San Diego, CA, for more than 40 years. Lockridge preached in crusades, revivals, religious rallies, and evangelistic conferences around the world. In 1941, he married Virgil M. Thomas. He pastored Fourth Ward Baptist, Ennis, TX (1941–42); Antioch Baptist, Mexia, TX (1942–49) and Greater Mt. Zion Baptist Church, Dallas, TX (1949–52). From August 1952 until 1993, he took a struggling church with $25,000 assets to more than $1 million. He wrote *The Challenge of the Church* (1968), *Holy Fires*, and *The Lordship of Christ*. He traveled extensively with Billy Graham preaching all over the world. His wife died in October, 2000.

Kyung Chik Han

Dec. 29, 1902
Pyong Yang, Korea

April 19, 2000
Seoul, Korea

Korea's beloved pastor of the twentieth century. What BAKHT SINGH was to India, HOJI HONDA to Japan, so Han was so Korea. He was a beloved Christian leader in a time of much persecution and martyrdom (1950s), which led to the building of some of the largest churches in history, during the 1970s and 80s. Converted at age 14 through a Korean evangelist, he married Chan Bin Kim in the early 1920s. Han was in the U.S. from 1925–31. He pastored the Second Presbyterian Church of Sinju in North Korea, 1933–42, when he came under Japanese scrutiny and was forbidden to preach. He founded an orphanage and old people's home there. Fleeing south (1945), he founded the Young Nak Presbyterian Church of Seoul, with about 20 refugees, and taught in the Han Kook Theological Seminary, 1945–50. In 1950, during the Korean War, the Communists took his new church building away—they had only had three services in it. After the war, Han continued his pastorate there, and his church grew to 4,574 baptized members with a Sunday school of over 5,000. He taught in the Presbyterian Theological Seminary (1951–59), and was president of Union

Christian College in Korea (1954–58). The book, *New Day Dawning*, describes his work. Since then, there have been several super churches in Korea, one led by Paul Cho with over 200,000 members (the largest in the world). However, the pioneer and encourager during days of suffering, bringing revival, was Han.

William S. "Bill" Dillon

Dec. 3, 1907
Steamboat Springs, Colorado

May 6, 2000
Schaumburg, Illinois

Songwriter and rescue mission director. Dillon spent his childhood in western Nebraska. His minister father led him to Christ at age ten. While ministering in Ft. Wayne, IN, he met Mildred Leightner and they married on September 17, 1932. She wrote and arranged hundreds of pieces of music including "Safe Am I" and "I Wish You Knew My Jesus." Dillon took over the Sunshine Gospel Mission, Chicago, in 1941 and directed it until 1970. Also, in 1943, he was one of the founders of New Tribes Mission. He had a tireless schedule of prayer groups and Bible study classes at his River Grove home. Dillon attended Bethel Community Church. He died in Friendship Village Retirement Home after a long ministry to thousands of inner-city poor and homeless people. He also authored a dozen books and trained scores of missionaries. His son, Bill Jr., continues his work and vision.

F. Donald Coggan

Oct. 9, 1909
London, England

May 17, 2000
Winchester, England

Archbishop of Canterbury, 1974–80. Coggan married Jean Strain on October 17, 1935, the same year he was ordained into the priesthood. They had two daughters. He lectured at Manchester University (1931–34), was curate of St. Mary's Islington (1934–37), professor of NT at Wycliffe College, Toronto (1937–44); principal of London College of Divinity (1944–56); bishop of Bradford (1956–61); and bishop of York (1961–74). As archbishop, Coggan's organizational expertise greatly influenced the structure of the Church of England. In 1967, he became president of the United Bible Society. His writings range from *A People's Heritage* (1944) to *Psalms* (*The People's Bible Commentary*, 1999). He was chairman of the committee that provided the New English Bible (1970) and its revision (1989).

P. Vernon Mortenson

May 28, 1912
Spokane, Washington

May 18, 2000
Seattle, Washington

Director of TEAM, 1961–75, and president of IFMA, 1962–65. Mortenson worked in a bank in Spokane (1929–34) then went to MBI (1934–37). He married Frances L. Pihlstrom on Nov. 6, 1938. They went to China and worked in church planting, 1939–45. From 1948–61, he worked in TEAM's office as assistant to the general director, David Johnson. During his tenure as president, he began the Missionary Orientation Class for Candidates and wrote a missionary handbook published in 1948. He produced audio-visual materials and wrote many articles and books. He made 28 overseas trips and saw the mission grow to 1,000 missionaries in 23 fields. He was consulting director, 1975–93.

E. Dewitt Baker

Jan. 13, 1919
Hillsdale, Michigan

May 21, 2000
Huntington, Indiana

President of Huntington (IN) College, 1965–79. Baker married Evelyn Middaugh on Aug. 16, 1942. He was a public school teacher (1940–41), then served as a pilot for the navy (1941–45). He then was a high school principal (1945–49), before serving as a missionary in Sierra Leonne, West Africa (1949–65). Baker was very active in his United Brethren in Christ denomination.

James M. Boice

July 7, 1938
Pittsburgh, Pennsylvania

June 15, 2000
Philadelphia, Pennsylvania

As pastor of 10th Presbyterian Church, Philadelphia, PA, he was a leading voice for the Presbyterian Church in America. Boice wrote or contributed to more than 60 books regarding the Bible or theology. He came to 10th Presbyterian Church in 1968, and in 32 years, the membership grew from 350 to 1,200. He was chairman of the International Council of Biblical Inerrancy. For years he had a radio ministry via the *Bible Study Hour*. He married Linda MacAmera. He led Evangelical Ministries and The Alliance of Confessing Evangelical Ministries for over a quarter of a century. Boice was diagnosed with liver cancer in the spring and died eight weeks later. R. C. Sproul said at his memorial service: "Here we had a valiant warrior for the church militant in our age."

B. Clayton Bell

Dec. 11, 1932
Tsingkaing, China

July 5, 2000
Montreat, North Carolina

Son of L. Nelson Bell, and Presbyterian pastor in Dallas. Clayton spent his first nine years in China, returning to the States in 1941. Bell served as pastor in Camden, Birmingham, and Dothan, AL, and Rome, GA, before going to Highland Park Presbyterian Church in Dallas, TX, in 1973. It was one of the largest congregations in the PCUSA. After the 1983 Presbyterian reunion, a sharp debate ensued as to whether the church should remain in the PCUSA, which he favored. He lost a larger percentage of members and had a heart attack. He retired in January 2000, after regaining some momentum at the church. He led in various Presbyterian renewal movements. He preached at Montreat the Sunday before his death, and was stricken with a heart attack shortly thereafter. His wife's name was Peggy.

William E. Currie

Nov. 9, 1927
near Windsor, Ontario, Canada

July 10, 2000
Munster, Indiana

President of American Messianic Fellowship (AMF Int. in 1993), **1974–89**. Currie met his wife, Swantina Zylstra, at Houghton (NY) College and pastored early on in Mt. Morris, NY. Coming to western Michigan, he pastored a couple of churches and taught at Grand Rapids School of the Bible and Music, 1954–59. He then pastored the well-known Cicero (IL) Bible Church (1959), before moving to Highland, IN (1971). Currie was a board member of AMFI for 40 years. From 1989 on, he was an evangelist and Bible teacher, representing AMFI as well. Currie also made annual trips to Israel. He died of a heart attack.

Robert A. K. Runcie

Oct. 2, 1921
Crosby, England

July 11, 2000
St. Albanseng, England

Archbishop of Canterbury, 1979–91. In 1950, Runcie was ordained a deacon (1950) and a priest (1951). He took up the curacy at Gosforth. He returned to Wescott House (1952), of which he became vice-principal, before becoming dean of Trinity Hall, Cambridge (1956) and principal of the theological college at Cuddesdon (1960). He became bishop of St. Albans, 1970–79, and hosted Pope John Paul II at Canterbury in May, 1982. However, his commitment to ordination of women in 1987 strained this relationship. In 1982, in a service for the dead in the Falklands War, he prayed for the Argentinian, as well as the British, soldiers who had lost their lives. His report, *Faith in the City* (1985), was regarded as ultra left-wing. He returned to live in St. Albans upon his retirement.

John T. Dean

August 23, 1930
Patterson, New Jersey

July 16, 2000
Jenison, Michigan

President of Grace Bible College, Grand Rapids, MI, 1965–85. Dean was converted in his early teens and married Helen Tweedy on November 21, 1952. He pastored in Michigan: at Belmont, Muskegon, and Byron Center. He was highly educated at Long Beach (CA) State University and he received his Ph.D. from Michigan State University, Lansing. Dean was a licensed clinical psychologist and pastoral counselor. Before becoming president of GBC, he served as teacher, dea, and vice president. He died of prostate cancer.

Bernard Holm

Nov. 20, 1906
Temple, Texas

July 21, 2000
San Antonio, Texas

President of Wartburg Theological Seminary, Dubuque, IA 1948–57. Holm began his Lutheran pastoring at Trinity Church, Shumway, IL (1930–31), then served on the faculty of Wartburg College (1931–35), when it was at Clinton, Iowa. He was on the faculty of the University of Maryland, College Park, MD (1941–44), then pastored at St. Matthews, Washington, D.C. (1944–48). He continued on the faculty at WTS after his days as president.

Clyde E. Van Valin

Nov. 24, 1929
Windham, New York

July 22, 2000
Wilmore, Kentucky

Bishop of Free Methodist Church, 1976–91. Valin married Beatrice Roushey on August 25, 1950. He pastored the Free Methodist Church in Allentown, PA, (1954–58), was eastern regional director for the denomination's youth program (1958–60) (working out of Winona Lake, IN), and was chaplain and director of the John Wesley Seminary Foundation, Wilmore, KY (1960–74) while pastoring the Wilmore FM Church (1961–76). He wrote *Transforming Grace and Tithing* (1990).

George A. Miles

April 28, 1904
Wayland, Michigan

July 30, 2000
Mitchellville, Maryland

President of Washington Bible Institute, Lanham, MD, 1938–40 and 1945–84, which in 1954, became Washington Bible College. Miles was converted in January, 1931. From 1932–45, he was a Bible teacher in the DC area. He was also president of the American Home Bible Institute from 1937–38, one of three schools which merged in 1938 to form the present institution. He was a structural engineer with the federal government until his appointment as full-time president of WBI in 1945. Miles also founded Capital Bible Seminary in 1958, which became a part of WBC. The school was moved to Lanham, MD, in 1969. Miles authored numerous Bible study courses and pamphlets on prophecy, in addition to traveling extensively to participate in Bible conference ministries. He married Ruth Crawford on October 22, 1938 (died: 1980) and then LaDelle in 1985. Miles served with the Pocket Testament League in the Orient and Africa. He was a member of the Barcroft Community Bible Church, Arlington, VA.

James T. Jeremiah

June 11, 1914
Corning, New York

August 7, 2000
Kettering, Ohio

President of Cedarville (OH) College, 1953–78, and GARB council member for 21 years. He was converted via a Sunday School teacher in Johnson City who got him interested in playing basketball at church. Early pastorates included service in Pomona, NY; Emmanuel Baptist, Toledo,

OH, and Emmanuel Baptist, Dayton, OH, prior to the Cedarville ministry. After 1978, he was chancellor with an office, but spoke at camps, senior citizen functions, and had a daily radio broadcast, *Senior Advantage*. His first wife, Ruby, died in 1991. He married Ethel Jones Rayburn on March 28, 1994. He had an aorta valve replaced and died immediately after surgery, his last words being "I love you so much." He wrote a book on heaven.

John (Jack) O. Percy

Jan. 2, 1908
Toronto, Ontario, Canada

Aug. 20, 2000
Sebring, Florida

First executivesecretary of IFMA, 1956–62. Percy moved countless people to tears and personal commitments to the mission fields with his 5,000 sermons and challenges. Conducting Bible and missionary conferences, he was truly a goodwill ambassador for world evangelism. Percy was converted at age 20. He was a longtime member of the IFCA. After 60 years of marriage, Mary died in early 1995 and Percy married Marilyn Bausch, July 29, 1995. He moved to the SIM retirement facility in November, 1998. He had prostate cancer for about twelve years before it settled in his bones, causing his death.

Herman A. Hoyt

March 12, 1909
Greenfield, Iowa

Aug. 29, 2000
Lancaster, Pennsylvania

President of Grace Theological Seminary and College, Winona Lake, IN, 1962–76. Hoyt married Harriet Fitz on August 30, 1930 (died: 1995). Hoyt taught New Testament and Greek at Ashland (OH) Theological Seminary (1935–37) and the same at Grace Theological Seminary, Winona Lake, IN (1937–62). He was very active in the Grace Brethren movement. Starting in the 1950s, he was in demand as a Bible teacher and spoke at conferences across the nation, specializing in eschatology and prophecy. He wrote from *This Do in Remembrance of Me* (1947) to *The End Times* (1969). He was a member of various evangelical boards.

Lester Myers

June 5, 1911
Concon, Oregon

Sept. 1, 2000
Mount View, California

Founder and first director of City Team Ministries, San Jose, CA 1957–83. This is really the work of San Jose Rescue Mission. It was December 24, 1954—Myers was dropped off at the Fresno (CA) Rescue Mission homeless and soaking wet. Drinking and gambling had cost him two marriages and several businesses. Here in Fresno, he was ordained a Baptist preacher and met and married Pauline Baker, who was running a shelter for women. With $465 in their pockets, they went to San Jose and started a ministry there in 1957. It began as a small soup kitchen and shelter for men, and became a full-service agency for needy people in nine U.S. cities and seven foreign countries. He died from complications of two strokes.

Bakht Singh

1904
Joya, Punjab, Pakistan

Sept. 16, 2000
Hyswerabad, India

Outstanding leader from India who spent a lifetime in evangelism and outreach efforts to reach his people. Singh was reared in the Sikh religion. In 1926, he attended the London Engineering College. In 1929, in a Winnipeg, Manitoba, YMCA, someone witnessed to him, "Christ in the heart…brings happiness." On February 4, 1932, he was baptized in Broadway West Baptist Church, Vancouver, BC. He arrived back in Bombay on April 6, 1933, not as an engineer, but as a preacher. His wife left him. Throughout South India, he went preaching until 1942, shaking Madras like no one else. Starting in 1942, he planted more than 6,000 indigenous churches and fellowships throughout India. His influence was felt in about 10,000 churches, which were planted in India, Pakistan, Sri Lanka, Australia, and the U.S. His

Bible training center, known as the Hebron Assembly, continues to equip hundreds of people for sharing their faith. He died of Parkinson's disease. An estimated 600,000 people from around the world attended memorial services to mourn Singh's death. He spoke four languages: Punjabi, Urdu, Hindi, and English.

Guy C. Johnson

Dec. 24, 1899
Vinton County, Ohio

Sept. 17, 2000
Worthington, Ohio

General Superintendent of Churches of Christ in Christian Union, Circleville, OH, 1944–60. Johnson traveled over 1 million miles, preaching nearly 5,000 times resulting in nearly 4,000 decisions during his denominational leadership. He saw over 100 churches join the movement, 54 of which he organized himself. He was converted on February 20, 1915 at Liberty Hull (OH) UB Church. He married Zelma Seitz, pastored Reeb Ave. (Grace Memorial) CCCU from 1929–44, and other churches in Ohio and Indiana. He was president of Circleville (OH) Bible College, 1952–53. His second wife, Claudia James, also preceded him in death. From 1960–64, he served as director of the denomination's missionary program. He visited the West Indies four times, crossed the Texas-Mexican border, Africa, and New Guinea. In 1973, he became district superintendent of the newly formed mideast district. He was one of the few in this book to live past 100 years of age.

Ernest D. Pickering

Dec. 14, 1928
St. Petersburg, Florida

Oct. 16, 2000
Clark Summit, Pennsylvania

Fundamentalist Baptist leader, Pickering had a varied and long career as the national executive secretary of IFCA, 1957–59. He married Ariel Thomas on August 16 1952 and pastored in New Kensington, PA, until 1957. He was pastor of Woodcrest Baptist Church, Fridley, MN; dean of Central Baptist Theological Seminary, Minneapolis, MN (1959–65); pastor of Bible Baptist Church, Kokomo, IN (1965–69); dean of Baptist Bible College, Clarks Summit, PA (1969–70); and president of the same (1970–78). He also pastored at Emmanuel Baptist Church, Toledo, OH (1978–85), and was president of Northwest Baptist Seminary, Tacoma, WA (1985–87). Moving on, Pickering then pastored Fourth Baptist Church, Minneapolis; and was president of Central Baptist Theological Seminary, Minneapolis (1988–93), before working with Baptist World Mission of Decatur, AL (1996–2000). Pickering was a foe of "new evangelicalism," writing such as *Biblical Separation*. In November, 1996, he lost his eyesight as a result of radiation treatments he received after cancer surgery to remove a malignant tumor from his frontal sinuses.

Sidney Langford

May 1, 1912
Philadelphia, Pennsylvania

Oct. 21, 2000
Glen Rock, New Jersey

General Secretary of Africa Inland Mission, 1956–77. Langford was ordained in 1934 by the Conservative Baptist Association. He married Jennie Long on January 22, 1938 in Aru Mission station in the Congo. For 59 years, he served with AIM. The first 21 years, he worked in Zaire and Sudan, 1935–56. After being director of AIM, he became a minister-at-large, 1977–87.

"My heart's desire is to show the compassion of Christ for the multitudes."

Howard P. Courtney

Dec. 20, 1911
Frederick, Oklahoma

Oct. 29, 2000
Glendale, California

Chairman of Pentecostal Fellowship of North America, 1952–54 and 1966–67; of World Pentecostal Fellowship, 1961–64; and Foursquare missions director, 1944–50. After graduating from Life Bible College, Courtney married Vaneda Harper on March 21, 1932. Converted in a Foursquare Church Christmas program at age 14, he pioneered churches in Wisconsin and Indiana, then worked with Dr. Jefferies in the large Portland, OR, church. He pastored in Riverside, CA 1936–39 and was district superintendent for the movement, eventually heading the missions program. Courtney was co-pastor of Angelus Temple (1950–53), pastor (1977–81), and served as vice president of the denomination for 30 years (1950–80). His last days were served as a guest speaker in many churches. He died of pneumonia and congestive heart failure.

Ralph W. Neighbor

July 21, 1906

Nov. 5, 2000
Salisbury, North Carolina

Pastor and evangelist. Son of R.E. NEIGHBOR, he became a Christian at age six at his father's knee. He married Ruth Zimmerman on June 29, 1929. He pastored Baptist Churches in Paw Paw, MI (1929–30); Northumberland, PA (1931–36) and Elyria, OH (1936–41). He directed the LeTourneau Center in Rockefeller Center, NYC, 1941–44. He then pastored the Gospel Temple of Fort Wayne, IN, from 1943–48. His radio experience began with PAUL RADER in Chicago in 1924 and was utilized especially in his last pastorate which brought him mail from 45 states and ten foreign countries. In 1950, he founded and pastored the Church of the Open Door of Elyria, OH. He was a unique gospel whistler. He often flew his own plane to various engagements.

Voyle H. Lewis

Oct. 16, 1912
Howell, Nebraska

Nov. 10, 2000
Olate, Kansas

General superintendent of Church of the Nazarene, 1960–85. Lewis pastored Nazarene churches in Norman, OK; Burlington, IA; and Houston, TX. He then served as an evangelist (1939–46) and was superintendent of the Houston District (1946–55). Lewis was then the first secretary of evangelism at CN headquarters, 1956–60. He wrote *The Church...Winning Souls*. His wife's maiden name was Esther Lambert.

Leonard S. Oliver

Aug. 22, 1914
Tampa, Florida

Nov. 22, 2000

President of Nazarene Bible College, Colorado Springs, CO, 1972–85. Oliver pastored the Nazarene Church, Twin Falls, ID (1943–46); was a teaching fellow at University of Nebraska (1947–49); was professor of theology and Christian Education at Bethany (OK) Nazarene College (1952–53); pastored the Nazarene Church, Enid, OK (1950–57); and was superintendent of the Alabama District (1957–64) and of the Illinois District (1964–72).

Allan E. Lewis

April 4, 1921
Angola, Africa

Nov. 30, 2000
Sebring, Florida

President of Baptist Mid-Missions, Cleveland, OH, 1959–83. Born of missionary parents, Lewis eventually moved to Philadelphia, then Kitchener, Ontario. He married LeAnn Nelson on July 18, 1943, then went to MBI, and afterwards took the pastorates of Randolph St. Baptist, Charleston, WV (1944–48), and Nottingham Ave. Baptist, Cleveland, OH (1948–60). As first full-time president of BMM, he saw 13 new fields open including an outreach to North America with 300 home missionaries. Missionary growth went from 669 to 1,161 under his leadership. In later years, he lived a half year in Sebring, FL and the other half in Euclid, OH. He visited many mission fields of the world. A ruptured aneurism caused cardiac arrest to take his life.

Wendy Collins

Sept. 21, 1927
Haileyville, Oklahoma

Dec. 19, 2000
Muskegon, Michigan

YFC enthusiast. Upon marrying Norma Buchsuehrer on July 20, 1949, Collins directed Milwaukee (WI) YFC from 1949–50. He spent 1951 in Scandinavia with a gospel team. He then served as director for the Montana/Wyoming YFC program (1952–54) and then moved to YFC Int. (1955–69), in public relations among other duties. From 1969–77, he was director of development for Gospel Films, Muskegon, MI, then worked with FRANCIS SCHAEFFER (Crestwood Agency) (1977–83), and Bibles for India (1983–85). From 1986–93, he was with World Home Bible League, South Holland, IL. His last major work was the completing of the YFCI video, *A Step Ahead of Time*, which he completed when the creator, EARLE SCHULTZ, passed away. He had problems with vertigo and numerous heart conditions which took his life.

Peter Deyneka Jr.

Sept. 13, 1931
Chicago, Illinois

Dec. 23, 2000
Wheaton, Illinois

Director of Slavic Gospel Association, 1975–91, and Peter Deyneka Russian Ministries, Wheaton, IL, 1991–2000. Deyneka, the son of PETER DEYNEKA SR., carried on the work that his father started. He served as a missionary to Ecuador and Argentina (1961–63); US Army chaplain and missionary in Seoul, Korea (1963–65); became assistant director of the Slavic Gospel Association (1966–74); married Anita Marson on June 14, 1968, and became the general director (1974–90). While in Argentina he directed the Russian Bible Institute. A shift in policies led to the forming of his own ministry in 1990. Deyneka had a six-month struggle with lymphoma.

Kenneth L. Pike

June 9, 1912
Woodstock, Connecticut

Dec. 31, 2000
Dallas, Texas

Internationally known linguist and Bible translator. Rejected by China Inland Mission for missionary service because of his nervous disposition and "difficulty with languages," Pike lived to receive ten honorary doctorates and 15 Nobel Peace Prize nominations for his work with tribal groups. In 1935, the Pioneer Mission Agency (Wycliffe Bible Translators) asked him to attend their camp and then go to Mexico to study the language of a tribe. In 1951, he completed translating their New Testament. He met Evelyn Griset and married her on October 20, 1938. Pike became the best teacher WBT had, returning to Arkansas each year to teach in the Summer Institute of Linguistics. He became their president. They met in Dallas, TX, from 1942–79. He also taught linguistics part-time at the University of Michigan, Ann Arbor, MI, 1948–77. In 1980 (50 years after being rejected for work in China), he was lecturing on linguistics at the Institute of Foreign Languages in Beijing. His first book, *Phonetics* (1943), was revolutionary in that field. His research into aboriginal languages took him on trips to Mexico, Guatemala, Ecuador, Peru, Ghana, Nigeria, Philippines, Nepal, and Irian Jaira. Pike died of septicemia, a toxic blood condition.

Chad (Chuck) Donnally

April 4, 1929
Pond Gap, West Virginia

Jan. 6, 2001
Greenacres, Florida

Founder and first president of Evangelical Bible Seminary, Greenacres, FL, 1975–2001. When he was twelve years old, Donnally was "the National Champion Fiddler." By age 16, he taught in a one-room schoolhouse. Converted at age 19, he was ordained into the ministry shortly thereafter. He attended Clarksville (TN) School of Theology. Donnally pastored many churches and finally became the founder and president of Evangelical Bible School, Greenacres Christian Academy, and the Evangelical Bible Seminary, all in the Lake Worth, FL, area.

Tillman Habegger

Jan. 14, 1906
Berne, Indiana

Jan. 18, 2001
Ft. Wayne, Indiana

President of the Missionary Church Association, 1958–68. Habegger was a key figure in getting the Missionary Church Association and the United Missionary Church to merge in 1969, producing "The Missionary Church." Habegger was converted at age 8 through the ministry of evangelist Edgar Clause. He surrendered for Christian service in meetings conducted by Luke and PAUL RADER. Evelyn Luginbill became his wife in 1930. His second wife, Marguerite, also preceded him in death. During the Depression years, he pastored at Eastlawn Church in Detroit, MI (1930–38) and then in Cleveland, OH (1938–47). Next, Habegger accepted a pastorate in Phoenix, AZ, from 1947–52. He served as superintendent of the Western District of MCA (1952–56) and then as its home secretary (1956–58). In his later years, Habegger taught Sunday school for the First Missionary Church of Ft. Wayne. He died at Riverbend Health Care Center at age 96.

Jack F. Hyles

Sept. 25, 1926
Italy, Texas

Feb. 6, 2001
Chicago, Illinois

Baptist preacher, soul winner, and church builder. Hyles was one of the most unique pastors of the 20th century. He built the First Baptist Church of Hammond (IN) into the largest church in America in his generation. He was reared in poverty and converted in August, 1937, in Dallas (TX). Hyles surrendered to preach on December 31, 1944 and married Beverly Slaughter on October 24, 1945. They had four children. Hyles pastored in Bogota, TX (1948); Marshall, TX (1949); Henderson, TX (1952); and then built up the Miller Road Baptist Church in Garland, TX from 44 to 4,128 members, 1952–59. In 1959, he went to FBC, Hammond. The church burned in 1964—the year the annual Pastors' School started. In 1972, the Baptist City complex of 29 acres (Hammond Baptist Elementary and High Schools) started. In 1974, with financial assistance from Christian businessman, Russell Anderson, Hyles-Anderson College moved to 76 wooded acres, increasing to an enrollment around 2,000. The 200 buses brought in from 7,000 to 15,000 people each Sunday, making respective trips for Sunday schools A, B, C, and D, using the same facilities three and four times each Sunday. Because of this, church attendance (including ministry extensions) regularly exceeded 20,000. Hyles preached across the country every Monday and Tuesday. He was a close confidant of *Sword of the Lord* founder, JOHN R. RICE. Many of Hyles' sermons were classics: such as "Stay in Crete," "Duty," and "Fresh Oil." Soul winning and separation were his strongest themes. Hyles Publications sold millions of the over 50 books he authored. First Baptist Church of Hammond was renowned for its yearly Pastor Schools, Youth Conferences and Women's Spectaculars. Jack Hyles died from complications following heart surgery at the University of Illinois Hospital. Some 7,500 out-of-towners attended the Friday evening memorial service, with an equal amount present the following morning for the "home crowd" tribute. Hyles was an icon in his time with thousands of pastors stirred to soul winning by his example and challenge. Following his death, Jack Schaap, the husband of his youngest daughter, Cindy, accepted the pastorship of FBC in Hammond.

Walter Meyer

Feb. 7, 1913
Eureka, Illinois

Feb. 6, 2001
Madison, Wisconsin

First president of Apostolic Christian Church (Nazarene) Richmond, VA, 1953–73. This was a split off Apostolic Christian Churches of America. Reared in a Christian home, Meyer married Wilma Pflederer on May 23, 1937 (died: 1951), and Joy Pflederer on May 3, 1953. He pastored

ACC Church, Tremont, IL, all his life, encouraged other pastors, and led the movement into a vigorous foreign missions program. He made several trips overseas. Meyer would be considered what old-timers called an exhorter, always challenging his associates on to the next level of Christian activity. Complications from a fall hastened his death.

Dale Evans Rogers

Oct. 31, 1912
Uvalde, Texas

Feb. 7, 2001
Apple Valley, California

"Queen of the Cowgirls." Dale was the wife of Roy Rogers, loved not only by her large family, but by millions who watched the duo in person, or in movies. She was converted at age ten in a revival in Osceol, AR. The first movie they made together was *Cowboy and the Senorita* in 1944. In 1947, they married. Since then, they appeared in 35 movies. When the movie westerns faded in the early 1950s, they began a television career, the *Roy Rogers Show,* running from (1951–57), and ending with the *Happy Trails Theatre* (1986–96). In 1951, she wrote "Happy Trails," which became their theme song. They recorded more than 400 songs. She wrote more than 20 books, including the popular *Angel Unaware*. Although married previously, her marriage to Roy was legendary. She was active in Christian evangelism projects all her life. She died of congestive heart failure at her home, following a heart attack (1992) and a stroke (1996). Her birth name was Frances O. Smith.

Rousas J. Rushdoony

1917

Feb. 8, 2001

Founder of the Chalcedon Institute and a key figure in the Christian Reconstructionist Movement. Rushdoony is regarded as a founder of the Christian homeschooling movement and an intellectual catalyst of the Christian right. His most influential book is *The Institutes of Biblical Law.*

David R. Swanson

1927

Feb. 11, 2001

Cofounder and director of Baseball Chapel. Swanson established weekly chapel services and Bible study groups with all Major League Baseball and National Football League teams, 1972–95, until he suffered a stroke. He also owned and operated WLIX, a Christian music radio station broadcasting throughout Long Island, New York City, and southern Connecticut.

Rufus Coffey

Nov. 15, 1926
Alto, Virginia

Feb. 12, 2001
Marston Mills, Massachusetts

Executive secretary of National Association of Free Will Baptists, 1967–79. Coffey married Maude J. Felder. Coffey served as the South Carolina State Association clerk and the foreign mission board director of missions education, 1962–67. He pastored the Denny Memorial Southern Methodist Church, Timmonsville, SC (1949–51); First Southern Methodist, Nashville, TN (1951–54), First Free Will Baptist, Darlington, SC (1954–57) and Florence, SC (1957–62). He returned to the pastorate in 1979. His funeral was at the Bowman (SC) Southern Methodist Church (his wife's home church). Coffey seldom preached a sermon without weeping.

Richard Wurmbrand

March 24, 1909
Bucharest, Romania

Feb. 17, 2001
Torrance, California

Founder and first director of *Voice of the Martyrs*, 1967–93. Richard and Sabrina Wurmbrand, Romanian pastor and wife, risked their lives to witness for Christ and endured terrible suffering under Communist rule. Brought up in a Jewish Orthodox family, Wurmbrand was an atheist. At a tuberculosis sanatorium, an old carpenter gave him a Bible and introduced him to Christ. Soon he was converted and baptized in Bucharest. In World War II, he was in and out of prison under Nazi occupation, trying to help Jewish orphans, Romanian Protestants, and gypsies. Once the Russians came in 1944, he had to "go underground" with his church. From 1948–56, he was interrogated and subjected to terrible forms of torture. Wurmbrand was in prison once again 1959–64. The Norwegian Israel Mission paid the Romanian government for Wurmbrand's release. They came to America to begin Christian Mission to the Communist world. On May 14, 1990, the couple returned to Romania after 25 years' absence, to a warm welcome.

Robert Hardgrave

Feb. 18, 2001
Hereford, Arizona

President of Indian Bible College, Flagstaff, AZ, 1971–84. Hardgrave and his wife Zillah began their work at the conservative Baptist Navajo Children's Home, Cottonwood, AZ in 1951. He served as pastor of the First American Indian Church of Los Angeles, and assistant to the chaplain for the county jail in Flagstaff, AZ, in addition to his work at IBC. He served in WWII under General George Patton. Hardgrave won many awards for combat bravery. He was married for 68 years.

Harvey Klapstein

Oct. 22, 1917
Edmonton, Alberta, Canada

Feb. 19, 2001
Lodi, California

President of Eugene (OR) Bible College, 1951–65. Klapstein's family moved to Lodi, CA in 1919. A love for music soon surfaced with his playing violin and cello. Having a wonderful singing voice, Klapstein was also widely used as a song leader, including a few times for Billy Graham. Joining the Bethel Open Bible Church caused him to surrender his life to the Lord. He married Alys Lucas on August 31, 1940. They pastored in Chilaquin, OR; Martinez, CA, and Des Moines, IA 1944–48. He was assistant dean of Open Bible College. In 1948, he led a large revival endeavor in Jamaica. Klapstein directed Youth for Christ in Eugene, 1949. He pastored 1972–87 in Largo, FL, Baldwin Park, and San Jose, CA.

Jesse H. Ziegler

Jan. 7, 1913
Limerick, Pennsylvania

March 7, 2001
Dayton, Ohio (?)

Executive secretary of Association of Theological Schools, 1966–80. Ziegler was ordained in the Church of the Brethren in 1931. He pastored in University Park, Maryland, 1935–41, marrying Harriet E. Curry on August 22, 1939. He taught at Bethany Theological Seminary (1941–59) and was associate director of ATS (1959–66). Ziegler became professor of religion and health at the United Theological Seminary, Dayton, Ohio, from 1981 on. He wrote *From the Broken Cup* (1942) to *ATS Through Two Decades* (1984). He lived out his days in Dayton, OH.

Armin Gesswein

Nov. 28, 1907 — Corning, Missouri
March 10, 2001 — San Juan Capistrano, California

Active in evangelism and revival efforts; noted for prayer ministry, promoting prayer seminars, meetings, and conferences. Gesswein was converted from hearing a Chicago preacher on the radio say, "You need to open your heart and receive Christ." After graduating from Concordia Seminary, St. Louis, he pastored in Long Island (1931–37) then went to Norway and saw a great awakening (1937–38). Gesswein married Reidun Gabrielsen on August 6, 1938. Except for three years teaching at Gordon College and Divinity School, Boston, MA, he traveled as an evangelist and conference speaker. He founded and directed Revival Prayer Fellowship in 1940. Prayer amongst Los Angeles pastors climaxed in 1949 with the Billy Graham crusade, participating in other crusades until 1969. He was later connect to CMA church activities.

Handley A. Hickey

May 5, 1913 — Galveston, Texas
March 11, 2001 — Galveston, Texas

President of Payne Theological Seminary, Wilberforce, OH, 1968–77. In 1950, Hickey married Argua Townsend. He taught four years at Payne in the fields of philosophy and ethics. He pastored the following African Methodist Churches: Bethel, Michigan City, IN; Saunders Memorial and Allen Temple, Detroit; Holy Trinity, Wilberforce, OH, and Bethel, Muncie, IN.

Merle (Mel) Johnson

Feb. 19, 1918 — Grand Rapids, Michigan
March 16, 2001 — St. Paul, Minnesota

Specialist in youth evangelism for over 50 years. Mel's radio voice challenged young people for the Lord, beginning with *Tips for Teens*, from 1953 on; with the format changing in 1978 to *Young Life America, Young World* and related names. Johnson began his ministry at the MEL TROTTER Mission, Grand Rapids, MI as youth director (1940–43), taking on the name, Mel, in honor of his mentor. He married Janet Leary on November 15, 1941. From 1943–49, he was the first director of the fledgling, but popular, *Children's Bible Hour.* He was in evangelism (1945–49), pastored Crusader's Church, Toronto (1949–52), directed Chicagoland YFC (1952–55), Minneapolis YFC (1955–61), and was vice president and spokesman for YFCI (1961–63). After that, he was in crusades and endeavors for youth around the country. In later years, he helped local Christian radio stations raise over $150,000,000 for their local needs in "Sharathons." He was Chairman of the Board of Northwestern College, Minneapolis 1978–97. He is especially appreciated by this editor (Ed Reese) because Mel was the human instrument that led him to Christ in March, 1941.

Alvin L. Barry

Aug. 4, 1931 — Woodbine, Iowa
March 23, 2001 — Orlando, Florida

President of Lutheran Church—Missouri Synod, 1992–2001. He married Jean Helm on August 24, 1952. Barry was ordained in 1956 and served as a pastor in a Wisconsin Synod congregation, Pilgrim Lutheran, Minneapolis, 1956–60, when he transferred to the Missouri Synod. He pastored at St. John and Peace Lutheran, Claremont, MN (1960–62) and Trinity Lutheran, Trimont, MN (1962–67). He then pastored in Fort Dodge, IA (1967–75); St. Louis, MO (1975–77), and Cedar Rapids, IA (1977–82). He died of kidney and liver failure.

Jack Sonneveldt

Dec. 19, 1916
Grand Rapids, Michigan

March 24, 2001
Muskegon, Michigan

First president of Gospel Films, Muskegon, MI, 1950–64. Sonneveldt was a western Michigan businessman, involved in many things. When he had a stroke eleven years before he died, he was chairman of nine boards. Raised in a Christian home, he was converted at age 14 at Berean Church. He married Dorothy Danielson in April, 1939 (died of cancer in 1962). His father owned a bakery supply store. Jack and other sons carried on the business, developing into the restaurant supply business of the Sonneveldt company. Being a businessman was secondary, as he founded the Grace Youth camps and was on boards of YFCI, CBMC, Missions for India, etc. He married Carol Brock, June 22, 1963. He was a good song leader and baritone horn player. He served the Navy in WWII. He died of congestive heart failure.

O. Ralph Isbill

Jan. 9, 1917
Burlington, Washington

March 29, 2001
Lodi, California

Director of Open Bible Standard Churches Missions, DesMoines, IA, 1947–67. He married Lulubelle Lowe on March 30, 1937. In 1940, Isbill and his wife were appointed missionaries to Sumatra. They returned during WWII dodging German submarines on the high seas. He was pastor of West Des Moines Open Bible Church while teaching at Open Bible College and serving on the missions board. He was the first full-time missions secretary in 1947. He made a great emphasis on indigenous missions. From 1967–80, he was the secretary-treasurer for Open Bible Churches.

James H. Germany

Feb. 9, 1914
Union, Mississippi

April 1, 2001
Covington, Indiana

Founder and first president of Bay Ridge Christian College, Kendleton, TX, 1960–82. Born in a cabin, he went on to Anderson (IN) College and then pastored Churches of God in Union, MS, and Muncie, IN before founding BRCC, a bi-vocational and predominantly black college, whose motto was "Where Youth Learn to Live and Lead." Actually the college started in Union, Mississippi in 1952, but moved because of racial hostility, relocating in 1960. Upon the death of his first wife, Janetta Marie, he married Treva Prather in 1993, then served as a supply pastor and was active in the Stringtown Church of God, living in Covington, IN.

John E. Riley

Jan. 23, 1909
Haverhill, Massachusetts

April 17, 2001
Nampa, Indiana

President of Northwest Nazarene College (University in 2000), **Nampa, ID, 1952–73.** Riley grew up in the Salvation Army and was influenced in his home by the Nazarene religion. He married Dorcas Parr on June 1, 1932. He pastored in New Haven, CT; Portland, ME, and Toronto, Ontario from 1932–44. The he went to Nampa ID, and pastored the College Church, 1944–52 while teaching at the college. He built the church of 960 members out of a handful of students, beginning on campus. While president, he taught theology. Later in life, he traveled, taught, and was an educational consultant overseas. He wrote the history of the college *From Sage Brush to Ivy* (1988). He read five books a week throughout his retirement days. He suffered a stroke and died eight days later. His wife died four months later on August 17, 2001.

Leon H. Sullivan

Oct. 16, 1922
Charleston, West Virginia

April 24, 2001
Scottsdale, Arizona

American Baptist pastor of Zion Baptist Church of Philadelphia, 1950–88, and leading spokesman for economic justice and social accountability. Sullivan married Grace Banks in August, 1945, received several honorary degrees, and was involved with several cultural and humanitarian endeavors in Philadelphia. He was founder of the African American Summit for business and government leaders. In addition, he founded the Opportunities Industrialization Centers in 1964 and the National Progress Association for Economic Development. He created the Sullivan Principles, which played a significant part in opposing apartheid in South Africa in 1977.

E. Brandt Gustavson

June 2, 1936
Rockford, Illinois

May 14, 2001

President, 1982–85, and executive secretary of National Association of Religious Broadcasters, 1990–2001. He married Mary Jane Gustafson on November 21, 1964. He managed the MBI station in Cleveland, OH from 1960–67. Prior to coming to NRB, Gustavson led the Moody Bible Institute (WMBI) Radio Ministry, 1968–86. He was vice president of development at MBI from 1974–76. From 1986–90, Gustavson was executive vice president of Trans World Radio, Chatham, NJ. His expertise in Christian radio was seldom matched in the history of this tool of evangelism. His favorite Bible verse was Nahum 1:7 He turned NRB around following the Christian broadcasting scandals of the 1980s which damaged its image and finances. He also was president of Evangelical Christian Publishers Association. He was diagnosed with terminal cancer of the liver and pancreas just two months before his death.

Jonathan Thigpen

Dec. 17, 1951
Nashville, Tennessee

May 20, 2001
Wheaton, Illinois

President of Evangelical Training Association, 1992–2001. Thigpen accepted Christ at age five at his mother's knee. He married Yvonne Howard on August 18, 1973. Concerned with young people, he opened a coffeehouse near Vanderbilt University. He attended Free Will Baptist College in Nashville. He served for three years in the Church Training Service Department of the Free Will Baptists. From 1984–90, he taught Christian Education at FWBC. He then served the Lord at Randall House Publications, 1990–92. In the prime of his life, on October 1, 1996, a doctor told him he had ALS (Lou Gehrig's Disease), and three to five years to live.

Charles S. Rooks

Oct. 19, 1924
Beaufort, North Carolina

May 20, 2001
Perrysburg, Ohio

President of Chicago (IL) Theological Seminary, 1974–84, Rooks was the first African-American to head this school. He was a leader in the United Church of Christ and in the African-American Christian community. Rooks married Adrienne Martinez on August 4, 1946 (died: February, 1999), and Elaine Hunter on August 1, 2000. Rooks pastored Shans Village Church, Orangeburg, NY (1951–53), and Lincoln Memorial Congregational Temple, Washington, D.C. (1960–63). He was then associate director and executive director for the Fund for Theological Education, Princeton, NJ, 1960–67. From 1984, he was executive vice president of the United Church Board for Homeland Ministries, New York City. His first book was *Rainbows and Reality* (1984) and his last, *Revolution in Zion* (1990).

Thomas (T.W.) Wilson

June 30, 1918
Charlotte, North Carolina

May 24, 2001
Black Mountain, North Carolina

Lifelong friend and associate of Billy Graham. T.W. (Thomas Walter) and his brother, Grady Wilson, were converted in the same Mordecai Ham revival meeting as Billy Graham in 1934. T.W. knelt in a field after fleeing the tent where the others were praying. Ordained a Baptist in 1939, he married Mary H. Sellers in 1942. He pastored churches in Alabama and Georgia and served as a vice president for Youth For Christ. He was also vice president of Northwestern Schools, 1948–51. From 1952–56, T.W. held revivals on his own before becoming executive assistant and associate evangelist with Billy Graham. He was a personal assistant on nearly all of Graham's overseas trips starting in 1962. One of his last crusades was in Bartlesville, OK, from October 8–11, 1995. He suffered a stroke in 1999, dying two years later. He was having lunch with his wife, Mary Helen, when he was stricken with a heart attack, and died at an urgent care center nearby.

Gerald D. Kellar

Oct. 14, 1916
Springfield, Arkansas

May 28, 2001
Harker Heights, Texas

First president of North American (Baptist Missionary Association in 1970) **Theological Seminary, Jacksonville, TX, 1956–67**. Kellar pastored churches in Texas, Kansas, and Mississippi, following his ordination in 1937. His wife's name was Mary Lou. Kellar was instrumental in the organization of the BMA of America in 1950 and served as its first president. He was the president of three other educational institutions as well: Jacksonville (TX) College (1944–56); Central Baptist College, Conway, AR (1967–70, and Southeastern Baptist College, Laurel, MS (1991–96).

Frank Stagg

Oct. 20, 1911
near Eunice, Louisiana

June 2, 2001
Lewisville, Kentucky

Southern Baptist theologian, he taught at New Orleans (LA) Baptist Theological Seminary, 1945–86, and Southern Baptist Seminary, Louisville, KY 1965–81. Stagg's specialty was New Testament. He married Evelyn Owen on August 19, 1935. He pastored the FBC, DeRidder, LA 1940–45. While at NOBTS, he wrote *The Book of Acts: The Early Struggle for an Unhindered Gospel*, which had the patterns of racial injustice in mind. Bigoted slander came his way. However, he was considered a pioneer in race relations in the South. At Southern, he edited the *Review and Expositor* (1964–71,73–75) and was often in conferences and other preaching endeavors. He retired to Bay St. Louis, MS.

Byran F. Archibald

May 8, 1912
Brockton, Massachusetts

June 17, 2001
Alhambra, California

President of Northern Baptist Theological Seminary, Oak Brook, IL, 1965–74. Archibald married Jane Walter on December 27, 1937, and was ordained by the Northern (American) Baptist Church in 1938. He pastored in Brockton, MA (1938–45); Springfield, MA (1945–56); Chevy Chase, MD (1956–63), and Haddonfield, NJ (1963–65). Once coming to NBTS, he lived in Oak Brook, IL. Early on, he did post-graduate work at Boston University (1944–52). From 1974–77, he served the Ohio Baptist Convention, after which he retired to his home in Craigville, MA for ten years. During this time he held several interim pastorates. In 1986, the Archibalds moved to Atherton Baptist Homes in Alhambra, CA. His funeral was at the First Baptist church there.

Ray P. Pannamaker

June 27, 1913
Elkton, Michigan

June 10, 2001
Elkart, Indiana

President of Bethel College, Mishawaka, IN 1959–74. When Pannamaker started at Bethel, the college had 329 students and 28 faculty members. He would finally bestow 1,201 degrees to graduates. As president, he was instrumental in acquiring 27 acres for the Bethel campus, oversaw three major construction projects, and implemented Bethel's intercollegiate athletic program. On June 16, 1935, he married Dorothy May Hygema (died: June 6, 2002). He was ordained by the United Missionary Church in 1938. He pastored in Detroit (1935–37); Yale, MI (1937–40); Calvary MBC Church, Detroit (1940–46), and in Nappanee, IN (1946–49). From 1950–55, he pastored the Brenneman Memorial Church in Goshen. From 1955–59, he was the first business manager of Bethel College and taught there. From 1974–79, he was director of services at GMC headquarters.

W. Edward Marquart

Oct. 6, 1909
Madison, South Dakota

June 29, 2001
Madison, South Dakota

First director of Red Sea Mission Team, Saratoga, CA, 1951–74. Marquart married Esther Viola Spaulding in 1936 (died: 1974). They moved to Big Whitefish Lake, MN in 1937, where they built and operated a summer resort, Beacon Heights, until 1971. During winter months, he taught in Duluth, MN, Brainerd (MN) Junior College, University of Minnesota, and Phoenix Christian High School. He pastored two churches while in Minnesota. During WWII, he was technical assistant in the Pentagon and consultant for radar installations around the world. He retired from teaching in 1964 to devote full time to the Red Sea Mission Team in and around Ethiopia. In 1976, he married Mabel Phelps Olum.

Richard Schilke

April 25, 1912
Janis Zewice, Poland

June 30, 2001
Berwyn, Illinois

Director of North American Baptist Missions, 1951–79. Schilke's family immigrated to North America in 1920. Following education at NABS in Rochester, he was ordained in 1939. In 1941, both his wife and child died during a difficult birth. He would later marry Kathryn. He spent ten years working in German-speaking Baptist churches in Canada and Anaheim, CA, from 1949–50. He led the growth of missions and eventually the denomination had 150 missionaries helping in evangelism, education, and medical needs in several fields. On May 13, 2001, there was a fire at his home in Oak Park, IL, which resulted in his subsequent death by smoke inhalation.

Reuben Speaks

Jan. 8, 1920
Lake Providence, Louisiana

July 3, 2001
Salisbury, North Carolina

Bishop of African Methodist Episcopal Zion Church, 1972–2001; senior bishop, 1992–96. Speaks married Janie Griffin on August 31, 1947 and pastored numerous AMEZC Churches, including Wallace Chapel, Summit, NJ (1948–1950); Varick in Philadelphia (1950–56); St Mark, Durham, NC (1956–64) and 1st Church in Brooklyn, NY (1964–72). As bishop, he served in Roosevelt, NY (1972–82); Wilmington, NC (1982–88), and Salisbury, NC (1988 on). His books ranged from *Higher Catechism for Ministers and Laymen* (1966) to *Prelude to Pentecost, A Theology of the Holy Spirit* (1985). He served World Methodism and World Council of Churches in various capacities and gave direction to the denomination's work in Africa.

James Singleton

Aug. 30, 1927
Key West, Florida

July 13, 2001
Mesa, Arizona

First president of International Baptist College, Tempe, AZ, 1982–95. Singleton was raised in a Brethren Chapel, where his grandfather led him to the Lord when he was age 12. After graduating from Bob Jones University, he married Mary Westfall on August 20, 1949. They were in a Methodist church in Fries, VA. Soon he was involved in Southern Baptist circles and pastored 1949–69 in Fries, VA; Henderson, NC; Atlanta, GA; Chattanooga, TN; Signal Mountain, TN; Shelbyville, TN; Vermilion, OH, and Albion, MI. The family moved to Tempe, AZ, in 1969 where he founded the Independent Tri-City Baptist Church, pastoring it till 1999. Soon an academy and college were added. He died of complications from cancer of the stomach.

John L. Knight

Nov. 2, 1915
Beverly, New Jersey

July 21, 2001
Tempe, Arizona

President of Wesley Theological Seminary, Washington, D.C. 1967–82. Knight pastored Lake Shore Park Methodist Church, Lynn, MA, from 1940–42. During his pastorate there, he married Alice Kingston on August 9, 1941. He then pastored at Bellview (TN) Methodist, 1942–43. Knight was also a professor and assistant to the president at Willamette University, Salem, OR (1943–46); president of Nebraska Wesleyan University, Lincoln (1946–49); pastor of Trinity Methodist Church, Columbus, OH (1954–61) and of First Methodist Church, Syracuse, NY (1961–67). He was also president of Baldwin–Wallace College, Berea, OH, from 1949–54.

Hart R. Armstrong

May 11, 1912
St. Louis, Missouri

July 29, 2001
Wichita, Kansas

Director of Christian Communications, Wichita, KS, and president of Evangelical Press Association, 1952–54. Armstrong spent his life preaching, serving as a missionary, writing and publishing more than 50 books, much of them dealing with prophecy. He married Iona R. Mehl on February 21, 1932. He was a missionary in Sumatra, Indonesia (1939), until forced evacuation (1942). He was a pioneer to many leading Pentecostals, crusade director for Oral Roberts' tent meetings, formulating mailings for KATHRYN KUHLMAN, after studying under AIMEE SEMPLE McPHERSON. In 1967, Armstrong moved to Wichita to become the editor and president of *The Defender*, a monthly magazine of 135,000 circulation. The group maintained houses for the elderly in six cities. He wrote from *To Those Who Are Left* (1950) to *Redemption: So Great Salvation* (1999). He died of cancer.

Gordon E. Sears

May 26, 1922
Hyannis, Massachusetts

July 31, 2001
Kalamazoo, Michigan

Pastor, song leader, and piano tuner for over 50 years. Sears married Mary Ruth Ficks on June 25, 1952, in Sunbury, PA. They had eight children. He was a U.S. World War II Navy veteran. He traveled with such musical notables as RUDY ATWOOD and Harold DeCou. He was one of the last great old-time song leaders and, from 1973–1988, he and his family criss crossed the nation. Four sons and a daughter played musical instruments. When contemporary music began to take over much of the Christian world, his books and articles warned people of its dangers. He worked with Youth for Christ in Canada, and then served with his pastor brother, Vic Sears, in Mishawaka, IN (Twin City Baptist Church) for several years. He pastored Trinity Baptist, Muskegon, MI, for four years prior to 1973. He was given a lovely farmhouse in southern Michigan where he, his wife, and single daughter lived. His funeral was August 3 at Grace Baptist Church, Angola, IN.

Robert B. Crawford

June 21, 1913
Birmingham, Alabama

Aug. 9, 2001
Nashville, Tennessee

First executive secretary of National Association of Free Will Baptists, 1944–48. Crawford married Rachel E. Gibbs. He pastored Sulpher Springs, Samantha, AL (1934–40); Oaklawn, Thomasville, TN (1940–43); First Church, Greenville, NC (1948–50, 1953–64); Bryan (TX) First, Bryan, TX (1950–53); Trinity Church, Greenville, NC (1964–68); First Church, Chipley, FL (1968–72), Ashland City, TN (1972–73), then Auburndale, FL (1974–76). He then served as public relations assistant at Free Will Baptist College, Nashville, TN. for 20 years. He was a soul winner, an encourager and a man of prayer.

Alfred B. Smith

Nov. 8, 1916
Midland Park, New Jersey

Aug. 9, 2001
Greenville, South Carolina

"Dean of Gospel Music." Smith was a composer, gospel soloist, song leader, lecturer, authority on church music, recording artist, and publisher. He was converted via HERMAN BRAUNLIN's preaching. While at Wheaton (IL) College, Smith was a song leader for a gospel team, Billy Graham being the evangelist. In 1941, he published his first chorus book, *Singspiration*, which became a best seller. This led to others in the series, plus a new series of *Favorites*, plus *Action*, a series for children. His compositions for "Be Thou Exalted" (CROSBY), "For God so Loved the World" and such works as "Surely Goodness and Mercy," "My Father Planned It All," and the lyrics and music for "I Have Never Lost the Wonder of It All," became very popular. Smith's wife, Catherine, whom he had married in 1946, died from a prolonged illness in 1960. Nancy Wilber became his wife in 1966, the year he sold *Singspirations* to Zondervan. Smith's solos were loved by many. He was one of those who held to conservative music when many other musicians drifted into more worldly, contemporary productions. He moved from Montrose, PA to Greenville, SC in 1984.

J. Leonard Bell

May 5, 1914
Holbrook, Nebraska

Aug. 25, 2001
Lynwood, California

Founder and first director of World Missions Far Corners, Inc., Long Beach, CA, 1958–2001. Bell was converted (1933) and married his wife, Mildred (1934). They went to Mexico as missionaries, 1947–53. He and Charles Turner started the work which has reached into 24 countries on five continents. It grew until they had 40 missionaries and several hundred national workers.

E. F. Folden

March 24, 1915
Hope, Minnesota

Aug. 28, 2001
Fargo, North Dakota

Founder and first president of STEER, Inc., Bismark, ND, 1957–72. Folden and his brother began planting and pastoring numerous churches in southern Minnesota and North Dakota. Feeling "Every Christian is a Missionary," he began a program of raising cattle to support missions. The death of his daughter, Lauri Jean, inspired him to enlarge on this idea and STEER, Inc. was incorporated in Park River, ND. The concept was for money to be donated by a businessman or youth group to buy a steer. The care and feed would be donated by a farmer or rancher. Upon its sale, the original price would be reinvested in another steer and the process repeated. Resulting profits, given to missions, have grown to nearly a million dollars a year.

Robert M. Brown

May 28, 1920
Carthage, Illinois

Sept. 4, 2001
Palo Alto, California

Presbyterian, theologian, writer, and activist, Brown was a proponent of liberation theology and cofounder of Clergy and Laity Concerned about Vietnam. He authored 28 books, including *The Sunday-School Primer*, *The Bible Speaks to You*, and a biography of a holocaust survivor, Elie Wiesel. He was arrested as a freedom rider during the 1960s civil rights movement and protested the US weapons policy. He married Sydney T. Brown on June 21, 1944. After ordination in the same year, he began as assistant chaplain at Amherst (MA) College, 1946–48. He was a professor of religion at Macalester College, St. Paul, MN (1951–53), and Union Theological Seminary, New York City (1953–62). He was professor of religion at Stanford (CA) University (1962–76), then professor of theology and ethics at Pacific School of Religion, Berkeley, CA (1979–85). His books range from *P. T. Forsyth: Prophet for Today* (1952) to *Dark the Night, Wild the Sea* (1998). He was general editor of the *Layman's Theological Library*, 1956–58.

Todd Beamer

Nov. 24, 1968
Flint, Michigan

Sept. 11, 2001
near Shanksville, Pennsylvania

Leader of heroic passengers aboard hijacked United Airlines Flight 93 airliner that crashed near Pittsburgh during the infamous 9/11 terrorist attacks on America. Due to the heroic actions of Frank and the other passengers and crew members, the highjackers were forced to crash the plane into a field instead of their intended Washington DC target (likely the U.S. Capitol). Beamer grew up in a Christian home and was baptized on profession of faith in the Christian Church, Swart's Creek, MI, in October, 1977. He attended Fresno (CA) State University, Wheaton (IL) College, and DuPaul University in Chicago, working for Johnson's Computer and Wilson Sporting Goods during the last two affiliations. He married Lisa Brosious in May, 1994. He was a Sunday School teacher. He then worked with Oracle Corporation, a salesman for computers, and was on his way from Newark to San Francisco for an important sales meeting with someone flying in from Tokyo. Prior to the group-wide effort to overtake the highjackers, Beamer was heard on the phone reciting the Lord's Prayer, then said, "Jesus, help me." He then prayed Psalm 23 and said, "Are you guys ready? Let's Roll!" "Let's Roll" became the rallying cry for the U.S. during the war against Al Qaida terrorists and the Taliban regime in Afghanistan.

Merve Rosell

June 18, 1912
St. Paul, Minnesota

Sept. 11, 2001
Peoria, Arizona

President of Global Concern, 1951–86, and evangelist. Rosell was converted at age nine at Bethesda Evangelical Free Church in Minneapolis, MN. He conducted church crusades, 1935–45, and then launched out into citywide crusades. He married Violette Weagant on August 29, 1936. Rosell was an effective, dedicated, Bible teaching evangelist that held huge crusades in the middle of the 20th century. Also, as an excellent musician, he produced several recordings and wrote several choruses including "Above the Clouds" and "My Captain of Salvation." Rosell was active in church evangelism and city wide crusades, preaching in some 50 countries of the world. His Kansas City Crusade had 250,000 attend in 22 days. His Des Moines, IA, crusade in Aug.–Sept., 1950, had 20,000 attending in three tents at the State Capitol, with 30,000 kneeling on the Capitol steps, praying for revival. CHARLES FULLER was guest speaker. His team consisted of HILDING HALVERSON, song leader; soloist, HOWARD SKINNER; chalk artist, Karl Steele; coordinator, Cy Jackson. He merged his work with World Opportunities (Roy McKeown director) in latter years. A heart-related illness took Rosell on the day 3,000 lost their lives in New York City.

James E. Franks

Nov. 30, 1918
Coopersville, Michigan

Sept. 12, 2001
Muskegon, Michigan

Humanitarian, Franks was in the floral business in early years. He married Shirley Stark on November 10, 1942 and they had six children, adopting three additional Korean children. He assisted major relief organizations for more than 50 years. In 1953, he began as director of the Midwest branch of World Vision, Inc. He was known for his work among orphans, refugees, at POW camps, and hospitals. He founded International Aid of Spring Lake in 1980, when World Vision consolidated its operations in California. A coup pushed him out of his presidency, hence in 1991, he cofounded Concern Int., which, in addition to providing medical supplies for needy people, paired doctors, engineers, and technicians with hospitals and other agencies needing expert assistance. He was the cofounder of the Vacationland Hymn Sings of the First Reformed Church, Grand Haven, Michigan. Franks was a member of Fruitport (MI) Christian Reformed Church. He battled infections and other serious health problems before dying in Mercy Hospital, Muskegon.

Raymond Van Der Veer

May 20, 1924
Bloomsfield, Connecticut

Sept. 14, 2001
St. Petersburg, Florida

Director of Cedar Lane Missionary Homes, Laurel Springs, NJ, 1973–89, a marvelous concept, started in 1950, to provide a place for missionaries home on furlough. Van Der Veer's cousin took him to church and, as a young boy of about 12, he became a Christian. He was in the air force in WWII. Attending school in Philadelphia, he then married Pearl Mondell, on June 1, 1946. They moved to Virginia where he pastored, 1946–50, then on to Claymount, DE, where he pastored some 20 years until the early 1970s, when he became the second director of CLMH. The Van Der Veers moved to St. Petersburg in 1989, where he eventually died of cancer of the throat.

Charles U. Harris

May 2, 1914
Raleigh, North Carolina

Sept. 16, 2001
Delaplane, Virginia

Dean of Seabury-Western Theological Seminary, Evanston, IL 1957–72. Harris married Janet Carlile on June 17, 1940 (died: January, 2000). Ordained in the Episcopal Church, deacon, (1938), priest (1939), he became rector of Trinity Church, Roslyn, NY (1940–46), and Trinity Church, Highland Park, IL, (1946–57). Harris was president and trustee of the Episcopal School of Theology in the Claremont, CA, cluster of higher education institutions. He helped launch the Joint Archaeological Expedition to Tell el Hesi, 1971–77. He was a participating member of several clubs and organizations. He is buried in Centreville, MD.

Ernest W. Oliver

Aug. 20, 1911
London, England

Sept. 20, 2001
St. Albans, England

General director of Regions Beyond Missionary Union (merged into World Team in 1995), **1961–76.** While at All Nations Bible College in England, God spoke to Oliver about going to India. He landed in Bombay on Nov. 11, 1935. Three years later, he married Margaret Honeywood on Oct. 26, 1938. He was a brilliant linguist and became a first class interpreter in the Hindi language for the Indian army. In 1937–38, he was able to enter Nepal. In 1941 (with the dawning of WWII), he served in Iraq and Iran as leader of an Indian Division. He was promoted to major. In 1947, he took the reins of the RBMU field in India. He opened the work in Nepal in 1954. From 1966–83, the Mission allowed him to work part-time with Britain's Evangelical Missionary Alliance. In 1970, he brought together three independent missionary training institutions to form the All Nations Christian College, which he chaired until 1980.

Kenneth J. Johnston

Nov. 14, 1912
San Francisco, California

Sept. 23, 2001
Tucson, Arizona

President of New Tribes Mission, Sanford, FL, 1959–87. Johnston married Lilly May, who passed on Dec. 31, 1995. He was pastoring in Santa Ana when he heard PAUL FLEMING preach on Missions. Ken resigned and joined New Tribes Mission in 1943. He started the first missions training center. After 1987, he continued his travel to many foreign countries encouraging missionaries and others. Suffering a massive stroke, he died 24 hours later. A memorial service was held September 29 at the NT Mission Aviation building in McNeal with his longtime friend, Mel Wyma, officiating.

Alden A. Gannett

Aug. 11, 1921
Geneva, New York

Sept. 23, 2001
Birmingham, Alabama

President of Southeastern Bible College, Birmingham, AL, 1960–69, 1972–81, interrupted by three years working with Unevangelized Fields Mission. He was chancellor of the same, 1981–85. The school grew from 80 to 350 students. He married his wife, Georgetta Salsgiver on May 27, 1944. They had 57 years together. He taught at Dallas (TX) Bible College, 1948–52 and also was pastor of Reinhart Bible Church in Dallas. He was president of London (ON) Bible College (1954–57) and taught Bible at Dallas Seminary (1957–60).

Joseph S. McCullough

March 29, 1911
Philadelphia, Pennsylvania

Oct. 13, 2001
Whiting, New Jersey

Director of Bolivian Indian Mission, 1956–66, renamed Andes Evangelical Mission (merged into SIM in 1981), **1966–74**. McCullough set sail for Bolivia in 1937. He married Elisabeth Dugan (December 25, 1911–April 5, 2004) in 1939. They labored among the Quechua Indians. From 1941–56, he represented the mission as Home Director and also pastored Hydegood Park Baptist Church in Plainfield, NJ. He helped bring Evangelism in Depth to Bolivia in 1965. From 1980–88, he pastored in the Ocean County Evangelical Free Church in Lakehurst, NJ. When he became the leader of BIM, there were about 200 churches. This grew to over 1,000 churches.

Paul M. Robinson

Jan. 26, 1914
Denver, Colorado

Oct. 26, 2001
Sebring, Florida

President of Bethany Theological Seminary, Oak Brook, IL (Richmond, IN. in 1994), **1953–75**. Robinson married Mary E. Howe on June 29, 1938 (died: April, 2000). Ordained in the Church of the Brethren, he pastored denominational churches in Ambler, PA (1936–40) and Hagerstown, MD (1939–53). He was president of the Greater Chicago Federation of Churches, 1957–60, midway through his leadership at Bethany. He wrote *Call the Witnesses* (1974). He was involved in various ecumenical projects as well as in the NCC. He pastored the Crest Manor Church, South Bend, IN, 1975–82. Midway through his leadership at Bethany he traveled to more than 100 countries of the world and retired to Sebring in 1989.

Raymond R. Peters

Dec. 28, 1905
Wirtz, Virginia

Nov. 2, 2001
North Manchester, Indiana

General secretary of Church of the Brethren, Elgin, IL 1947–152. Peters married Kathryn Eller on June 20, 1930. He pastored in Virginia, Kansas, and Ohio and concluded his ministry at the Manchester (IN) Church of the Brethren. He held several key posts in the denomination. He was national Youth Director and Director of Christian Education prior to 1947. He was chairman of the General board following his days as general secretary. He was moderator of the Annual Conference in 1967. He traveled to the Netherlands and Russia as well as visiting with the pope in the Vatican. His autobiography was *From Foothills to Mountaintops*.

Russell Myers

May 22, 1917
Winchester, Indiana

Nov. 4, 2001
Lakeland, Florida

General Superintendant of Ohio Yearly Meeting, 1968–71, renamed Evangelical Friends Church—Eastern Region, 1971–83. Myers married Marjorie Vought on June 13, 1940. They were together 62 years. Myers pastored in Byhalia–Somersville, Ohio, (1940–45); Alliance, Ohio, (1945–53); Canton, Ohio (1953–60); and Bell, California (1960–65). While in Alliance and Canton, he had a radio ministry. He was a trustee of Cleveland Bible College (1948–57), and Malone College, Canton, OH (1957–60). He traveled extensively around the world, visiting Friend's Missions, 1958–77. From 1965–68, he was executive secretary of the Board of Missions and Church Extension of the California Yearly Meeting of Friends. In 1983, he took the pastorate of Morningside Friends Church.

J. Harold Smith

June 14, 1910
Woodruff, South Carolina

Nov. 13, 2001
Knoxville, Tennessee

Great evangelist of his generation, he was also a radio minister, author, and pastor of churches in South Carolina, North Carolina, Tennessee, and Arkansas. In 1935, Smith established the worldwide *Radio Bible Hour*, Inc., and the *Our Good Neighbor* publication, headquartered in Newport, TN. He wrote 13 books. During his ministry, more than 1 million people made decisions for Christ, with hundreds of commitments to ministry. He was married to Myrtice Rhodes for 63 years. He is known for a most famous sermon, called "God's Three Deadlines." He was affiliated with the SBC, but his ministry spread far beyond those boundaries. His funeral was held at Brushy Creek Baptist Church in Easley, South Carolina.

Woodrow G. Drum

Sept. 11, 1903
Newton, North Carolina

Nov. 13, 2001
Nashua, New Hampshire

President of Emmanuel College, Franklin Springs, GA 1951–69. Drum was converted at age 20 at Franklin Springs Institute. He married Louise Sisk. He became principal of the high school there in 1935. Full accreditation was granted by the Southern Association of Colleges and Schools in 1967 under his leadership.

Don Lonie

Nov. 8, 1919
Pontiac, Michigan

Nov. 14, 2001
Knoxville, Tennessee

Great high school assembly speaker, invading the hearts of young people with the Christian message. He spoke in nearly 4,000 high schools, 1940–85. Lonie was converted through his Sunday School as a child. He married Betty Mistelle on September 20, 1947. Attending Moody and Wheaton, he was out on weekends in evangelism. Soon, his sincere, yet humorous way of sharing character and Christ was making a hit with teens across the country. Wherever he went in Bible Conferences, crusades, rallies, there was always a booking in the local high school. He became so effective that he was on the payroll of the School Assembly Service, a secular organization that valued his contribution. He made a few overseas trips as well, speaking at army bases, etc., a big success at such as Clark Air Force Field in the Philippines. Living in Farmington, MI, most of his life, he moved to Knoxville in 1985 to be close to family and his friend, Don Hoke, at Cedar Crest Presbyterian Church. Three long-play albums of his "chats" sold thousands of copies, such as *Don Lonie Talks With Teenagers*. He continued to speak in summer conferences and youth camps for another ten years. He had two bypass surgeries, and pneumonia, which took his life.

Lorton Heusel

May 19, 1926
Clay County Nebraska

Dec. 4, 2001
San Bernardino, California

General secretary of Friends United Meeting, Richmond, IN, 1967–78. Heusel was a Quaker pastor for more than 40 years. He began his ministry in 1949 at the Sugar Plain Friends Meeting near Thorntown, IN. He also served in Vermillion Grove, IL; Chicago; Wilmington, OH; and Indianapolis, IN. He married Joyce Ginzel on June 3, 1950. He made a round the world missions trip in the 1970s. On July 5, 1977, his wife was killed in a car-truck collision at a rural Nebraska intersection. Thirteen years later, he married Magaline Hoops, a missionary in Africa for some 30 years. In 1996, he served as interim pastor at First Friends Meeting in Whittier, CA.

Lester Pipkin

March 29, 1918
Omaha, Nebraska

Dec. 7, 2001
Bradley, West Virginia

Founder and first president of Appalachian Bible College, Bradley, WV, 1950–82. Pipkin was converted March 14, 1933, when evangelist PAUL HUTCHENS witnessed to him. He married Gretchen Hartz on August 15, 1939 (died: August 18, 1994), and Pat Mlekodaj on November 11, 1995. Early on, he was pastor of Calvary Memorial Church, Nervure, MN; dean of Education at Southland Bible Institute, Pikeville, KY; and instructor in Bible at Oak Hills Christian Training School in Bemidji, MN. He and his family came to Whitesville/Pettus, WV, in 1950 where, with another couple, Appalachian Bible Institute was established with seven students. In 1956, they moved to Bradley with 40 students. In 1961, everyone, from cooks to president, received $110 per month salary. Through the years, he also served as interim pastor in the area to at least four churches. He was a member of Faith Baptist Church of Prosperity, WV, and active in the IFCA movement. He died in the Alzheimer's unit of Pinecrest Hospital. His final words were, "I want to go home." The nurse said, "home to heaven?" He said, "yes."

Hovie F. Lister

Sept. 17, 1926
Greenville, SC

Dec. 28, 2001

Gospel musician. As a music publisher, record label executive, performer, and promoter, Hovie Lister was instrumental in helping to expand the Southern Gospel Music industry and popularize this musical art form around the world. As a young man, Hovie toured as pianist with famed evangelist MORDECAI HAM before attending the Stamps-Baxter School of Music. After honing his skills with the Homeland Harmony Quartet, the LeFevre Trio and the Rangers, Hovie formed the Statesmen Quartet in 1948. Under his direction, the Statesmen became one of the preeminent Southern Gospel groups in America with a national television program, film appearances, and hundreds of sold-out personal appearances to their credit. Their showmanship, which centered on a highly animated performance style, inspired countless musicians and set a high standard for other Southern Gospel groups to follow. He composed many songs, such as "When I Come to the End of the Road." His most popular recorded song is probably "Thanks to Calvary."

Jose Soren

June 21, 1908
Rio de Janeiro, Brazil

Jan. 2, 2002
Rio de Janeiro, Brazil

President of Baptist World Alliance, 1960–65. Soren was baptized at the age of eight in the FBC of Rio de Janeiro, pastored by his father. He studied at Rio Baptist College and the Baptist Seminary in Rio, then at Southern Baptist Theological Seminary in Louisville, KY. He began as pastor of the First Baptist Church of Rio in 1935. As a military chaplain with Brazilian forces in Italy during WWII, he was cited for bravery and highly decorated. He was a longtime teacher of theology at South Brazil Baptist Seminary, Rio. In 1955, he was the preacher of the BWA Congress sermon in London. Soren was head of the Executive Committee of the Brazilian Baptist Convention since the committee was organized.

J. Randolph Taylor

Jan. 12, 1929
Taichow, China

Jan. 4, 2002
Buck Mountain, North Carolina

President of San Francisco Theological Seminary, 1975–84, Taylor married Arline Johnson on June 1, 1951. Ordained a Presbyterian in 1954, he pastored the Church of Pilgrims, Washington, D.C. 1956–67; Central Presbyterian Church, Atlanta, GA, 1967–76; and the Myers Park Presbyterian Church, Charlotte, NC, 1976–85. He wrote *God Loves Like That* (1962).

Wallie (W.A.) Criswell

Dec. 19, 1909
Eldorado, Oklahoma

Jan. 10, 2002
Dallas, Texas

President of the Southern Baptist Convention 1968–70, and pastor of First Baptist Church, Dallas, TX, 1944 until death. Criswell is considered the father of modern conservatism in the SBC. Young Wallie was converted in a Texline, TX, church in 1919, under evangelist John Hicks. While attending Baylor University, he pastored small churches; and during his years at Southern Baptist Theological Seminary, Louisville, KY, he served a part-time position in Mt. Washington, where he met pianist Betty Harris, whom he married in 1935. He pastored the FBC, Chickasha, OK (1937–41) and the FBC of Muskogee, OK (1941–44). When Criswell took the FBC, Dallas, TX, after GEORGE TRUETT's death in 1944, there were 7,800 members. The annual budget grew from $250,000 to more than $10,000,000. Billy Graham was a member of his church. He authored the *Criswell Study Bible,* among other books—54 in all, including *Why I Preach That the Bible Is Literally True* (1969). He founded Criswell College and encouraged an emphasis on biblical preaching. He passed away at the home of his "son" in the Lord, Jack Pogue. His last words were, "I love you, son."

Edward R. Dayton

April 21, 1924
New York

Jan. 19, 2002
Seal Beach, California

Founder and first director of Missions Advanced Research and Communication Center (MARC), Monrovia, CA, 1966–90. Ted Engstrom invited Dayton to join the staff at World Vision to explore the use of technology in promoting the gospel around the globe. Dayton was a pioneer in exploring what has become known as the "unreached peoples" program with colleagues at Fuller Seminary and the US Center for World Mission. MARC began in the mid 1960s under his direction until his retirement in 1991. He was the vice president of World Vision and directed the program for the second Lausanne, Switzerland, Conference on World Evangelization in 1989. His wife, Marge, preceded him in death. He died from a stroke.

Watson Goodman

Jan. 22, 1920
near Milford, Ohio

Jan. 28, 2002
Goshen, Indiana

Founder and first president of World Missionary Press, New Paris, IN 1961–87. Watson was converted in December of 1937 while listening to his brother, WOODROW GOODMAN preach. He married Rose Stair on August 30, 1943 (died: February 2006). Goodman pastored in Milford, DE, before going to South Africa where they served for 16 years. Here a burden to give free Scripture booklets to the masses developed. So, in 1961, the worldwide ministry of publishing Scripture booklets began in Winona Lake, IN. It grew to a large facility in New Paris, where 260 volunteers and 38 paid staff produced 4 million booklets each month. Like GEORGE MUELLER's literature ministry, God provided the finances. Four hundred eighty million Scripture booklets and New Testaments went to 179 countries during his tenure. They were provided free. By January of 2000, over 300 language groups were reached. In February, 2001, WMP reached one billion portions in 219 nations. A memorial service was held February 1.

James W. Blackwood

Aug. 4, 1919
Ackerman, Mississippi

Feb. 3, 2002
Memphis, Tennessee (?)

Longest surviving member of the original Blackwood Brothers Quartet, James was often used as a gospel soloist as well. He married Miriam LeGrantham on April 4, 1939. James was 16 when the quartet first performed in 1934. This quartet worked out of Shenandoah, Iowa, via radio, returning to Memphis in 1950. He was the lead singer, in the 1940s, up until 1969 (except for 1948–50) and the featured soloist from 1970–81. Member of an Assembly of God Church, he lived in Memphis, TN. Recipient of nine Grammy Awards, he was beloved by the music industry. At age 34, he saw tragedy strike when two of the quartet members perished in a plane crash in Clanton, Alabama. James literally ran into the flaming wreckage to try and rescue his brother, R. W. JAKE HESS violently pulled him away from the flames that engulfed the plane. In later years, he was featured in many concerts, "sings," and other Christian endeavors and was the lead singer of the Master's V.

Samuel F. Wolgemuth

Sept. 24, 1914
Mt. Joy, Pennsylvania

Feb. 5, 2002
Arlington Heights, Illinois

President of Youth for Christ, 1965–73, and director of its overseas ministry, 1956–63. Wolgemuth, son of the pastor, was converted at age nine at an evangelistic service at the Brethren in Christ Church in Mt. Pleasant, VA. On June 22, 1938, he married Grace Dourte and sold farm implement machinery and auto parts around Waynesboro, PA, while pastoring the Fairview Ave. BC Church, 1939–52. Challenged at Winona Lake YFC conclaves, he went to Japan in 1952 to direct YFC. From 1956–65, he lived in Wheaton, IL, directing the worldwide ministry of YFC before becoming the president of the organization. He made eight missionary tours around the world, ministering in some 70 countries. Progressive suprarenal (gland connected with the kidney) palsy put him in a wheelchair in September, 2001, and he died a few months later.

Marga Buhrig

Oct. 17, 1915
Berlin, Germany

Feb. 13, 2002
Binningen, Switzerland

President of the World Council of Churches, 1983–91. Buhrig was engaged in ecumenical women's work in Switzerland and Germany, starting in 1946. From 1954 on, she worked in the worldwide ecumenical movement through the WCC Department for Co-operation of Men and Women in Church. She was director of Bolden Protestant Academy, near Zurich, 1971–81. She also served for a time as European secretary for women's work in the World Alliance of Reformed Churches.

George Weaver

March 12, 1927
McCloud, California

Feb. 15, 2002
Cincinnati, Ohio

President of Winebrenner Theological Seminary, Findlay, OH, 1977–88. Weaver married Bette Young who died in January, 2001. Previously, he pastored at various United Brethren Churches and served as bishop of the United Brethren Church, 1969–77. His funeral was at White Oak Christian Church in Cincinnati, Ohio, February 20, 2002.

Edgar Hoenecke

Aug. 5, 1903
Milwaukee, Wisconsin

Feb. 17, 2002
San Diego, California

Founder and first Director of Wisconsin Evangelical Lutheran Synod World Missions, 1955–78. From 1945–56, Hoenecke pastored the St. Peter Lutheran Church in Plymouth, MI. It was in 1955 that he embarked on a fierce mission through deserts and forest trails into the heart of Africa. He laid the groundwork for a missionary base in Zambia and spent several memorable hours with ALBERT SCHWEITZER in Lambarene, Gabon. In 1962, he carried his missionary work to San Diego County. For the next 16 years, he established WELS churches in several California cities. He celebrated his 75th wedding anniversary with his wife, Meta Bung, whom he married on July 10, 1926, and died of natural causes at Alvardo Hospital Medical Center at age 98. His memorial service was on March 17 at St. John Evangelical Lutheran Church, Wawatosa, WI.

John W. Alexander

April 7, 1918
Greenville, Illinois

Feb. 18, 2002
Madison, Wisconsin

President of Inter Varsity, 1965–81. During Alexander's tenure, the US branch of IV grew from 130 staff and 9,000 students to 674 and 31,000 on 825 college campuses. Prior to 1965, he was the chairman of the geography department at the University of Wisconsin in Madison. He wrote *Managing Your Work*, to help his staff plan their work better and *Fire in My Bones*, a book on Scripture memory. Alexander brought stability to the movement. His wife's name was Betty. Alexander died following surgery for pancreatic cancer.

J. H. Levang

Feb. 6, 1912
Fertile Township, Iowa

Feb. 20, 2002
Fergus Falls, Minnesota

President of Lutheran Brethren Seminary, Fergus Falls, MN, 1957–72. Levang married Silence D. Seglem. He pastored Lutheran churches in Aitkin, MN (1939–43); Brooklyn, NW (1943–45); Huxley, IA (1945–46); Calvary Lutheran Church, Chicago (1946–53); West Union, IA (1953–56); and Pasadena, CA (1956–57). From 1976–93, he was visitation pastor at Bethel Lutheran Church, Fergus Falls. He authored *The Church of the Lutheran Brethren*.

Don Odle

May 12, 1920
Muncie, Indiana

March 7, 2002
Muncie, Indiana

Basketball coach at Taylor University for 32 seasons, 1947–79, where he won 468 games, second most in the school's history. The Don J. Odle Gymnasium, built in his honor in 1975, saw him coach his final four seasons. He was a Taylor graduate in 1942. He also coached football, baseball, and golf there. He is most remembered for his Asian trips, giving the gospel at half times via his basketball teams. These trips to the Far East were initiated by an invitation from MADAME CHIANG KAI SHEK to coach the Chinese Nationalist basketball team for the 1960 Summer Olympics in Rome. Odle's "Venture for Victory" teams, made up of Christian American all-star college basketball players, played from 1952–64 in countries such as Japan, South Korea, and Vietnam. His twelve teams won 600 and lost 12. Over 60,000 children have attended his camp over ensuing years. He married his wife, Bonnie, on July 8, 1944. They attended Westminster Presbyterian Church in Muncie. He died after a long illness.

Mary E. Clark

May 12, 1905
Nottingham, England

March 9, 2002
Kansas City, Missouri

Leader in the Christian Business and Professional Women (Stonecroft Ministries), **Kansas City, MO, 1948–97**. As a young career woman, Clark committed her life to following Jesus. She spent the next 15 years as a missionary in rural Maine. In 1948, she joined Helen Duff Baugh as an associate in ministry and became a member of the National Board for Christian Business & Professional Women of America. Together, these two women established the many outreaches of what is now known as Stonecroft Ministries. Today, Stonecroft Ministries is a leading international ministry whose main purpose is to share the gospel of Jesus Christ with women.

Carl A. McIntire

May 17, 1906
Ypsilanti, Michigan

March 19, 2002
Collingswood, New Jersey

Mr. Fundamentalism, first president of American Council of Christian Churches, 1941–44, and president of Faith Theological Seminary, Elkins Park, PA, 1971–2001. McIntire began his crusading while a student at Princeton Theological Seminary in 1928. When MACHEN and R. D. WILSON withdrew from Princeton in 1929 and organized Westminster Seminary in Philadelphia, McIntire was one of the students who left with them. He married Fairy Davis on May 27, 1931 (died: 1933) and Alice Goss on July 15, 1935. In 1933, he went to Collingwood, NJ, to pastor a church of 1,000 members with $250,000 worth of property. He was 27 years old when he was suspended from the ministry by the Presbytery. He lost the property to the denomination, so on March 27, 1937, he set up a tent several blocks distant and 1,200 members marched there with him, leaving 75 behind. In 1937, he and others founded the Bible Presbyterian Church, started Faith Seminary, and began to edit the weekly *Christian Beacon*. In 1941, he founded the American Council of Christian Churches, and in 1948, the International Council of Christian Churches in Amsterdam, Netherlands, to counteract the founding of the World Council of Christian Churches. In 1955, McIntire launched his *20th Century Reformation Hour* radio broadcast. He sought to combat the influence of Soviet–US relations. In 1963, he expanded into Cape May, NJ, with the purchase of a hotel, the Christian Admiral. In 1971, he acquired property in Cape Canaveral, FL. In 1973 when the FCC cancelled his radio program, he went offshore in international waters and on September 19, announced "This is Radio FREE America, 1160 on your dial." In 1975, he was expelled by force from Kenya at the 9th World Congress of the ICC. Numerous conflicts with his determination to lead at all costs, led to the sizing down of his movements and projects. Hated and loved, he was one of a kind.

Edwin W. Kortz

Nov. 6, 1910
Easton, Pennsylvania

March 25, 2002
Nazareth, Pennsylvania

President of Moravian Church Missions, Bethlehem, PA 1956–75. Kortz was ordained by the Moravian church in 1935 and married Margaret E. Schwarze on July 30, 1937. He pastored parishes in Virginia, Ohio and Pennsylvania from 1934–39. He went to the Moravian Theological Seminary, Bethlehem, PA as professor of practical theology, 1949–56 and 1974–88. He was consecrated a bishop in 1966. Kortz became a chaplain of the Moravian Hall Square Retirement Company, Nazareth, PA from 1988 on. He wrote his first book, *My Bible Tells Me What to Believe* (1947) and his last *A Manual for the American Provinces of the Moravian Church* (1988).

Eugene Graham

July 7, 1931
near Moline, Illinois

May 25, 2002
Ypsilanti, Michigan

President of Faithway Baptist College, Ypsilanti, MI 1985–2000. (The school closed in 2003). Graham was converted in October, 1950 in Florida while serving in the navy. He married Lois Heykoop on June 1, 1957. He pastored Kingsport (TN) Baptist Temple; Calvary Baptist Church, MacIntire, GA; Bethel Baptist Church, Union Point, GA; Bible Baptist Church, Mariette, MI; Faith Baptist Church, Port Hope, ON, Canada, and Faithway Baptist Church, Ypsilanti, MI, where his funeral service was held on May, 29.

Arnold B. Come

March 9, 1918
Lansing, Michigan

May 26, 2002
Green Brae, California (?)

President of San Francisco (CA) Theological Seminary, 1967–82. Come married Elizabeth McClure on September 9, 1942. He pastored a Presbyterian Church in Philadelphia 1942–45. He taught philosophy and religion at Centre College (Danville) of Kentucky 1946–52 and then taught systematic theology at SFTS 1952–67. His works were from *Human Spirit, Holy Spirit* (1959) to *Reluctant Revolution* (1965).

Koji Honda

March 31, 1912
Kobe, Japan

April 6, 2002
Tokyo, Japan

Japan's greatest evangelist. Honda preached to over 1 million people in 40 years' time. He also wrote many books. Honda shined shoes, sold Bibles, and attended Bible school. He then started a church, Chuo Kyokai, in Kobe, where his parents found Christ. FRED JARVIS, Eddie Karnes, and Kenny Joseph prayed him into evangelism; and when he did start, it was nonstop. John Maekawa was his associate evangelist for many years. Children's crusades were held 5–6 p.m. with the main meeting starting at 7 in the city's largest auditorium, going for eight to ten nights. At one of his last crusades in Vietnam, he preached in Japanese, Joseph translated into English, someone else into Vietnamese and some 600 responded to trust Christ. He had seven children. Many called him Japan's Billy Graham to which Graham quipped, "I am America's Honda!"

Keith Kiser

Nov. 14, 1947
Lafayette, Tennessee

April 11, 2002
Powell, Tennessee

Pastor and Bible teacher. Kiser was converted in Cleveland, OH, in December, 1956. On May 3, 1969, he married Charlene Hogan and pastored at FBC, Evansville, TN from 1971–77. He worked with Baptist Mid-Missions from 1978–1986, ministering in Andover, England, and Kilwinning, Scotland. Kiser taught at Oklahoma City Baptist College, 1986–89. From 1989 till death, Kiser taught Bible Doctrine, Bible Survey, and Greek, at the Crown College, Powell, TN. During his last decade, he took on many responsibilities at Temple Baptist Church, Powell, TN, and coached high school girl's basketball. Energetic and enthusiastic, Kiser was "everlastingly at it," perhaps the reason for the sudden heart attack which took his life. It was a blood clot due to complications of knee surgery. In the casket, the Bible on his chest, Keith had a finger pointing to II Kings 22:8: "I've found the Book," a sermon and song that God had given him.

Harold F. Freeman

March 1, 1918
Swink, Colorado

April 11, 2002
Raytown, Missouri

National Executive Director of Independent Fundamental Churches of America, 1981–87. Freeman was convicted of his spiritual need on a dance floor, while hearing the song, "Shadrach, Meshach and Abednego" on the jukebox. He was converted on a back pew of church after hearing the message, "Who killed Christ?" He married Esther Lynn. After schooling, he pastored Grace Baptist Church, St. Louis, MO (1948–56); Salina (KS) Bible Church (1956–64); and Vallejo (CA) Bible Church (1964–77). Moving to the Chicago area, he was editor-in-chief of *The Voice*. From 1988– 92, he was in administration at Calvary Bible College, Kansas City, MO. He returned to his Vallejo pastorate (1992–96) and became associate pastor at Pleasant Grove (Kansas City Area) Bible Church (1998–2002).

Roy Gustafson

May 8, 1914
North Easton, Massachusetts

April 12, 2002
Raleigh, North Carolina

Longtime Billy Graham associate evangelist. Gustafson enlarged the scope of BGEA's international ministry and led more than 150 trips to the Middle East. Graham stated, "He was instrumental in sharing the gospel with thousands around the world, especially through teaching in the land of the Bible." His first trip to the Holy Land was in May, 1955.

Bill Dowell

July 8, 1914
Red Bank, Texas

May 2, 2002
Springfield, Missouri

First president of Baptist Bible Fellowship, Springfield, MO, 1950–52, 1962–63. Dowell was the youngest of ten children and converted early on. He first pastored Northside Baptist Church, Merkel, TX, in 1934, where he married his wife, Nola Callahan, on September 2, 1934. He later pastored FBC, Corcoran, CA; First Missionary Baptist Church, La Habra, CA; FBC, Linwood, CA, and Southgate Fundamental Baptist Church up to 1941. From 1941–63, Dowell pastored High Street Church, Springfield, MO, where he influenced many including Jerry Falwell, who was a member there and a student in BBF college, where Dowell taught. From 1963–68, he was pastor of Jacksonville (FL) Baptist Temple. He was executive vice president of BBC (1968–75) and upon the death of G. B. Vick, was president of the college (1975–83). He also pastored the Baptist Temple of Springfield, 1974–88.

Dave W. Breese

Oct. 14, 1926
Chicago, Illinois

May 3, 2002
Hillsboro, Kansas

Dynamic preacher, widely used author and president of Christian Destiny, 1968–2002. Breese was converted in Chicago at a Bible Club meeting via Mrs. Lance Latham. He attended Northern Baptist Theological Seminary and married Carol Flaming on March 7, 1953, after serving the Lord as YFC director in Vermillion County, IL, and Gary, Indiana. They directed YFC in Grand Rapids (1953–60) and Chicago (1960–67). Opportunities opened for him to speak in evangelism crusades,

Bible conferences, and on college campuses. He was involved in publications and moved his headquarters from Wheaton, IL, to Hillsboro, KS in 1984. Since 1987, he conducted *The King is Coming* TV program (World Prophetic Ministry) and shared pulpits with leading teachers in prophecy conferences. A stroke in 2000 incapacitated him, until it finally took his life. Dave Breese was large in body and in soul.

James C. Hoggard

Aug. 9, 1916
Jersey City, New Jersey

May 5, 2002
Maryland

Director of African Methodist Episcopal Zion Church Missions, 1952–72. Hoggard entered the New York Conference in June, 1939 and married Eva Santion on December 10, 1949. He pastored St. Francis Church, Mt. Kisco, NY; the Institutional Church, Yonkers, NY; and Little Rock Church in Charlotte, NC, 1951–52. He became bishop in 1972, after 20 years as editor of the *Missionary Seer* as part of his responsibilities in the mission's leadership. In latter years he lived in Indianapolis. "From childhood, I have tried to live and let live; to love God and serve him and to love my neighbor as I would love myself."

Torrey M. Johnson

March 15, 1909
Chicago, Illinois

May 15, 2002
Wheaton, Illinois

Unofficial founder and first president of Youth for Christ, 1944–48 and director of Boca Raton (FL) Bible Conference, 1967–82. Johnson was converted while a student at Wheaton College on January 16, 1927. He was active in athletics and debate and upon graduation married Evelyn Nelson on October 30, 1930, having been ordained as a Baptist earlier that year, May 24. He was in evangelism throughout Wisconsin and Michigan, 1931–33. In October, 1933, Johnson became pastor of Midwest Bible Church in Chicago, where he stayed until 1953. He also taught Greek at Northern Baptist Seminary, 1936–40. He started with nine men in the Depression years. It grew into a large center of evangelism, growing from 26 to 1,000. Torrey was the dynamo God used to begin Chicagoland YFC on April 27, 1944 in Orchestra Hall. At the first national convention in 1945, he was elected president of YFC. In 1948, he turned the reins over to his brother-in-law, BOB COOK, but not before it was a healthy organization in many cities and countries of the world. From 1950–67, he was engaged in evangelism across the world holding large area-wide crusades. He conducted a number of citywide crusades, including Oakland, CA. Retiring back in Wheaton, he gave his energies to the development of a senior citizen complex, Windsor Park Manor. The great YFC movement owes much to this energetic visionary. His wife died two days after his passing, so a double funeral was held.

Wilbur A. Holman

Aug. 13, 1911
Lawson, Missouri

May 22, 2002
Enid, Oklahoma

President of Christian Union, Chillicothe, OH, 1962–71. Holman was converted in 1925 at the age of 14. He married Cordie Piburn on January 16, 1934 (died: July 21, 1982), and preached his first sermon August 13, 1939. Cordie helped him operate a restaurant in Urbana, IL when he came down with tuberculosis. He was in a sanitarium, 1935–38. He preached in many of the denominational churches representing the college and/or council and helped found the Tri-State Camp in 1947. Following his presidency, Holman was academic dean of the Christian Union Bible College, 1982–87. He married Alice Graber on November 24, 1986.

Paul Lindstrom

Nov. 6, 1939
Park Ridge, Illinois

May 22, 2002
Prospect Heights, Illinois

Founder of the Christian Liberty Academy and a pioneer of the Christian homeschooling movement, headquartered in Arlington Heights in 1984. CLA was founded in 1968, growing from 50 to 900 students. There were also branch schools in Sudan and Cape Town, South Africa. Lindstrom married in 1961. He helped found the Church of Christian Liberty in March, 1965, in Mount Prospect, moving the church to Des Plaines, then Prospect Heights. He started his homeschooling program in 1972. He crusaded against abortion, the United Nations, and persecution of Christians abroad. Some 35,000 students were studying by correspondence at the time of his death, with tens of thousands of graduates. He died from sclerosing cholangitis, an autoimmune disease. It results in liver failure. Cancer findings prevented him from liver transplant.

Paul Tassell

July 20, 1934
Toledo, Ohio

June 3, 2002
Winter Haven, Florida

National Representative of GARB, 1979–96. Tassell provided sound leadership in this movement when it was going through tough times. He was converted (August, 1941) and preached his first sermon (September 1949) at a youth rally. While at Bob Jones University, he pastored Second Baptist Church, Elberton, Georgia, 1954–58. On August 4, 1956, he married his wife, Doris. He pastored Bethany Baptist Church, Galesburg, IL (1958–65); Campus Baptist Church, Ames, Iowa (1965–70) and Grandview Park Baptist Church, Des Moines, Iowa (1973–1979). In his later years, he battled Parkinson's disease.

"Scholarship without spirituality becomes skepticism."

Merrill C. Dunlop

May 9, 1905
Chicago, Illinois

June 15, 2002
Oak Park, Illinois

Beloved songwriter and outstanding pianist. Dunlop served the Lord musically for some 80 years. He was converted at age 13 in the old Moody Tabernacle. At age 15, he began to play piano at Calvary Church and by age 16, he was PAUL RADER's pianist at Moody Church. In 1925 he followed RADER to the North Side Tabernacle where for years, RADER, LANCE LATHAM, CLARENCE JONES, and Dunlop led an evangelistic thrust that brought thousands to Christ. He married Lanore Bosworth on September 11, 1932. He, like many other dedicated, talented people, got involved in the world program of Youth For Christ, and was on teams with Wally White and BOB COOK, traveling all over South America and in an around-the-world evangelistic endeavor. He wrote many songs and compiled several songbooks. He also traveled with evangelist JIMMIE JOHNSON and song leader CLYDE TAYLOR. His best known hymn was "My Sins Are Blotted Out," written while crossing the Atlantic Ocean in 1927. He also wrote the lyrics and music for "Only One Life," "I Believe the Answer's on the Way," "He Was Wounded for Our Transgressions," "All Day Long," "Because He Loved Me So," "Contentment in His Love" and "O, Won't that Be Joy, Joy?" In 1988, he became the organist for Judson Baptist Church in Oak Park. His piano expertise continued until 95 years of age.

Kenneth S. Kantzer

March 29, 1917
Detroit, Michigan

June 20, 2002
Victoria, British Columbia, Canada

Dean of Trinity Evangelical School, 1963–91; president of Evangelical Theological Society, 1968; and editor of *Christianity Today* (1978–82). Kantzer was a brilliant theologian who postponed his scholarly and writing aspirations to strengthen key evangelical institutions. He taught theology at Wheaton (IL) College, 1946–63, and later taught at Gordon College and Gordon Theological Seminary. In 1963, the senior class gave Kantzer enough money to take a year off for writing, but he returned the gift and became dean at Trinity, which needed a strong leader. He stayed there until retirement. His wife's name was Ruth. He died of a stroke following surgery.

Arnold Brown

Dec. 13, 1913
London, England

June 26, 2002
Toronto, Ontario, Canada

General of Salvation Army, 1987–91. As a boy, Brown immigrated to Belleville, Ontario, and entered the Salvation Army in 1935. He married Jean Barclay in 1939. For 22 years, he headed a corp (church). Then he served in the editorial department at territorial headquarters for ten years, becoming assistant editor of the *War Cry*. He produced a TV series known as *The Living Word*. In 1965, Brown made a great contribution in the SA's advertising and public relations for the centenary year. He was chief of staff (1969–74), then commander for Canada and Bermuda (1974–77). His autobiography is called *The Gate and the Light*. His funeral service was held in the Yorkminster Park Baptist Church on July 3.

Linton C. Johnson

Feb. 3, 1914
Alma, Georgia

June 26, 2002
Norfolk, Virginia

Founder and first president of Free Will Baptist Bible College, Nashville, TN 1942–44, 1947–79. Johnson went forward at age 14 to "join the church," but at age 17, under the ministry of I. K. Blackwelder, he received assurance of salvation. He pastored the Pine Level Church, 1934–36. He married Ruth Masser on March 30, 1940, and became the pastor of four churches in a Georgia circuit. In 1942, he was asked to head a new Bible school. Johnson emphasized teaching on assurance of salvation which he felt was a bit weak in his movement. The school helped shape the course of the denomination for a new day. He was a man of great vision.

Doug MacCorkle

Dec. 5, 1915
Boston, Massachusetts

July 8, 2002
Lancaster, Pennsylvania

President of Philadelphia College of the Bible, 1963–77, and Accrediting Association of Bible Colleges, 1973–78. MacCorkle was an energetic and enthusiastic leader. Before his Dallas Seminary training, he earned his degree in commercial art. Coming to PCB in 1963, he brightened it up, changing the paint from battleship gray to lively colors. He was responsible for the school becoming the first regionally accredited Bible college in the nation and also for making Bible college students eligible for federal aid programs. He was a great Bible teacher and influenced many students. He and his wife, Jeanette, a musician, organized a new music program at the school. As the school moved from downtown to suburbia, he stepped aside and W. Sherrill Babb replaced him. He retired to Cocoa Beach, FL, His funeral was held in Calvary Church, Lancaster, PA.

Richard De Haan

Feb. 21, 1923
Zeeland, Michigan

July 16, 2002
Grand Rapids, Michigan

Director of "Radio Bible Class," 1965–80, DeHaan continued this broadcast when founder, his father, M. R. DEHAAN, passed away. A third generation, Martin, his son, took over in 1985. During Richard's tenure, the radio and television broadcasts reached millions and his TV program, *Day of Discovery*, was one of the top in the religious field in the 1970s and 1980s. He served on the board of the Evangelical Council for Financial Accountability after leaving RBC. Parkinson's disease afflicted him for about ten years, resulting in nursing home care. He was known for his writings in the *Our Daily Bread* devotional guide.

Jared F. Gerig

June 29, 1907
Grabill, Allen County, Indiana

July 26, 2002
Glendale, Arizona

President of Fort Wayne (IN) Bible Institute (Summit Christian College in 1990, Taylor University), **1958–71; Accrediting Association of Bible Colleges, 1970–73; and of National Association of Evangelicals, 1964–65**. Gerig married Mildred G. Eicher on December 22, 1928. Ordained in the Missionary Church in 1931, he pastored their churches in Indiana, Ohio, and Arizona, 1929–45. He was dean of FWBI (1945–50), then at Azusa (CA) Pacific College (1950–52). He was president of the Missionary Church with headquarters in Fort Wayne, IN, 1952–58. Gerig was on numerous boards and a visiting professor to Jerusalem in 1964. He pastored the Missionary Church in Van Nuys, CA, in 1974. From 1977–87, he pastored Grace Bible Church in Sun City, AZ. Following hip surgery, Gerig died with pneumonia after 74 years of marriage.

Maynard Mathewson

Oct. 20, 1939
Harlansburg, Pennsylvania

Aug. 13, 2002
Lincoln, Illinois

Director of Rural Home Missionary Association, Morton, IL 1965–85. Mathewson devoted his entire adult life (40 years) to rural ministry. In the summer of 1958, while traveling with his parents, the family could not find a church to attend in southeast or northwest Wyoming which gave him a burden for rural areas. He ministered in Michigan, Pennsylvania, and Oregon in RHMA with his wife, Ruth. After this, they served churches in Montana for 15 years and then in Illinois for three years at Calvary Bible Church in Lacon, IL.

Dennis M. Aldridge

1916
Gallatin County, Illinois

Sept. 2, 2002
Pineville, KY

President of Clear Creek Baptist Bible College, Pineville, KY, 1954–82. Aldridge grew up in Eldorado, IL. Early on, he was professor of missions at CCBC, 1946–54, and after his retirement, he and his wife went to Zambia to teach at the Southern Baptist Seminary there. He devoted a lifetime of service to mountain missions and foreign missions, as well as pastoring numerous churches in the mountains of Kentucky and Tennessee. His wife, Kathleen, died October 1, 2000. On November 3, 2001, at age 84, he married former campus nurse, Evelyn Mottram, age 81.

Robert Hammond

March 1, 1914
Hong Kong, China

Sept. 2, 2002
Pasadena, California

Director of *Voice of China and Asia*, 1946–2002. Hammond's father was killed in a train wreck in China, derailed by Chinese bandits. Coming back to the States, his mother, Hattie, married Charles Storey. Hammond married Helen Reiton on June 16, 1939. Finishing his education at Pasadena (CA) College, he realized he could reach more people in one day by radio than in years of meetings, so he started *Voice of China* broadcasts. In July, 1946 their son, Eric, was killed as he crossed the street. This began an outpouring of gifts to build the first orphanage. Eight million dollars worth of relief clothing, quilts, blankets, food, medicines, and vitamins were given to thousands of hungry and destitute people. Soon Korea, Taiwan, Hong Kong, India, and the Philippines were also receiving help through Hammond's efforts.

Tom Johnstone

Jan. 28, 1903
Featherstone Park Village, England

Sept. 5, 2002
Toronto, Ontario, Canada

General superintendent of Pentecostal Assemblies of Canada, 1963–68. Johnstone came to Canada in 1911 (South Wellington, Vancouver, BC). His family began attending Pentecostal services in Nanaimo, BC, and he was converted at 19, in 1923. He was ordained by the fledgling PAOC. He pastored churches across Canada, was a district superintendent, president of Eastern Pentecostal Bible College (Master's College), 1944–50 and Western Pentecostal Bible College (Summit College).

Walter J. Dick

Nov. 1, 1918
Mt. Lake, Minnesota

Sept. 16, 2002
Quakertown, Pennsylvania

Director of Montrose (PA) Bible Conference, 1965–84. Dick grew up in a General Conference Mennonite background. A serious illness as a teen brought him into a real hunger to know God. As a student at Moody Bible Institute, he was saved at his bedside. He married Adella Fast on June 12, 1943. Dick then pastored the 2nd Mennonite Church, Philadelphia, PA (1943–49); the Richfield (PA) Mennonite Church (1949–60) and then taught and pastored at Grace Bible College, Omaha, NE (1960–64). He directed the famed Bible conference during some of its greatest days. He pastored at East Swamp Mennonite Church, Quakertown, PA, from 1984–91, where he remained the rest of his life. Prostate cancer developed into bone (spine) cancer which took his life. He had two daughters.

Kenneth L. Teegarden

Dec. 22, 1921
Cushing, Oklahoma

Sept. 22, 2002
Fort Worth, Texas

President of Christian Church (Disciples of Christ), **1973–85.** Teegarden married Wanda J. Strong on May 28, 1944. Early on, he pastored in Chandler, OH (1944–47); Texas City, TX (1947–48); Vernon, TX (1949–55), and Fort Smith, AK (1955–58). In 1947, he was pastoring in Texas City, when an explosion aboard a French freighter devastated the city. He was best known for his work as an administrative secretary of a commission in 1968 to restructure the church, which included drafting a 100-word identity statement defining the principles of the denomination. Upon leaving this office in 1985, Teegarden became professor at Brite Divinity School at Texas Christian University until 1989. He wrote *We Call Ourselves Disciples* (1975). He died of pneumonia, following a cerebral hemorrhage in May. His funeral was held at the University Christian Church.

Louis Palermo

Feb. 14, 1915
Melrose Park, Illinois

Sept. 26, 2002
Minneapolis, Minnesota

Singing evangelists around the world for over 50 years, the Palermo brothers blessed untold multitudes—Louis with his accordion and PHIL with his guitar. They grew up in a Catholic church. Their uncle was converted and, six years later, many in his family found the Lord. Louis and PHIL belonged to "The Midnight Brigade," a Gospel team which went to taverns on Chicago's north side, branching out to various cities. Both brothers married Swedish girls and began a lifelong association with Youth For Christ in 1947. Their first major ministry was in Italy. Louis married Jeanne Skogman. Since then, they have criss crossed America and went to several countries around the world: Japan, Brazil, Ecuador, and Sweden. Mora, MN, became home for Louis. In later years, PHIL moved to California, but their musical legacy lives on.

Samuel E. Boyle

Sept. 24, 1905
Beaver Falls, Pennsylvania

Sept. 30, 2002
Pittsburgh, Pennsylvania

Founder and first director of Reformation Translation Fellowship, Bloomington, IN 1950–96. Boyle grew up in Topeka, KS, and was converted at age 18. In 1934, he married Grace Bell, sailing to South China that same year with the Reformed Presbyterian Church of North America. They stayed until 1941. Grace died during childbirth in May of 1943. He then married Grace Robb in September of 1945. RTF began with *Christian Reformed Faith Monthly* in Chinese. In 1950, they moved to Kobe, Japan. They came to the States in 1961, where he directed the Christian Amendment Movement of the RPC until they returned to minister in Japan. They retired to Orlando, FL, then moved to Shawnee, KS, where Grace died in 1987. In 1992, at age 86, Sam married Orlena Lynn, who had spent 41 years in Kobe. They moved to the RPC Retirement Home in Pittsburgh. A memorial service was held October 2.

Wally S. Beebe

Feb. 27, 1934
Columbus, Ohio

Oct. 2, 2002
Atlanta, Georgia

Affectionately known as "Mr. Bus," Beebe, for over 30 years crusaded for church buses to bring children into Sunday school. Multitalented, brilliant and hardworking, Beebe was converted on Jan. 22, 1953, as a result of a tract. Beebe married Winnie Prairie on June 11, 1955. They served one term in the Bahamas, then directed Kankakee (IL) YFC in 1960, moving on to assist Bob Gray at the Baptist Tabernacle in Jacksonville, FL, from 1963–68. He pastored the FBC, Ruskin FL from 1971–73 and 1975–81, interrupted by a brief time helping JACK HYLES and the FBC of Hammond as their bus director. From 1982 on, the couple lived in Stockbridge, GA. He was an effective evangelist and directed an annual Bus Conference for years. He was editor of the *Church Bus News* for 31 years, up to the time of his death from a series of health problems and congestive heart failure which took his life after a few days in the hospital.

Louis Goldberg

Jan. 28, 1923
Los Angeles, California

Oct. 23, 2002
Charlotte, North Carolina

President of Evangelical Theological Society, 1983. Raised in an orthodox Jewish home, Goldberg married Carie Berman, on July 14, 1944. Working at Automatic Electric Company in Chicago, a fellow worker from Moody Church witnessed to him and he was converted in 1948. He got considerable education and pastored at Maranatha Baptist Church, Chicago, for six years, then Dairy Dale Baptist Church of Cedar Rapids, IA, for three years. He began a lifelong ministry at Moody Bible Institute, teaching there 1965–93. From 1968–2000, he spent every summer except one in Israel. His wife died in 1991. Goldberg was Scholar in Residence for Jews for Jesus, 1994–2000. When his health failed, he lived with his daughter in Charlotte. Goldberg died of pneumonia. His funeral was at Emmanuel Bible Church in Berwyn, IL.

Kash Amburgey

March 18, 1922
Lerose, Kentucky

Oct. 23, 2002
Mason/Cincinnati, Ohio

Pastor, salesman, and Holy Land tour host. Kash sold Bibles early on, was an evangelist and then became pastor of Bible Church of God, Lebanon, OH 1950–92. He began using radio, January 20, 1950, and one year later, the owner of the station asked him to sell various products every day, which he did for years. His last radio sermon was on September 29, 2002. It was his Holy Land Tours that made him famous. He conducted 78 tours there, going himself 81 times, accompanied by his wife 64 times. If you drove through Ohio, Indiana, or Kentucky with your car radio on, there is a good chance you have heard "Kash" trying to promote or sell something. He was affiliated with the Church of God, Cleveland, TN. Since he married Mary Lou Gilbreth on March 18, 1949, he resided in South Lebanon, OH, where he was stricken with a fatal heart attack, arriving at a Cincinnati hospital already expired.

Cornelius R. Stam

May 27, 1908
Paterson, New Jersey

Oct. 24, 2002
Carol Steam, Illinois

Founder and "Father" of the Berean Bible Society, a ministry of "grace" which rejects water baptism for this dispensation. Stam, O'HAIR, and CHARLES F. BAKER developed the movement known today as the Bereans. Stam was highly respected and came out of a very orthodox and well-known family in Christian circles. He was converted in 1922 after hearing a sermon by T. Houston. Influenced by J. C. O'HAIR, Cornelius began to embrace the apostleship and message of Paul in his early days. The martyrdom of his older brother, JOHN STAM, and John's wife BETTY, consumed his message for some time. He then pastored the Preakness (NJ) Community Church, which gave birth to the Berean Bible Society and its magazine, the *Berean Searchlight*, in 1940. In 1945, Stam moved to Milwaukee to help establish the Milwaukee Bible Institute. In 1953, the movement relocated to Chicago. Upon the death of J. C. O'HAIR in 1958, Stam pastored the famed North Shore Church of Chicago for two years, 1971–73. His wife, Henrietta, died in 1971. He then married Ruth Wahlstrom (died: September: 1998). He authored some 30 books on numerous Biblical subjects, his most well known, *Things that Differ*. He retired in 1993 to the Windsor Park Manor in Carol Stream, IL.

Charles W. Ewing

June 1, 1912
Vermont, Illinois

Oct. 27, 2002
Royal Oak, Michigan

President of Evangelical Church Alliance, Bradley, IL 1961–93. As a young adult, Ewing sang with his three brothers in a gospel quartet. He served in WWII for 32 months in the European Theater. After the war, Ewing pastored at least ten churches in Chicago, St. Louis, Omaha, Dayton, and lastly, Campbell Memorial United Methodist Church in Ferndale, MI. He had an extensive radio ministry on 52 stations and was active in the Temperance League of Illinois and the Prohibition Party. He was the first to lead in prayer in the U.S. Senate's new prayer chapel in Washington, D.C., in the 1970s. He was married 52 years to his wife, Helen Mae. His funeral was at the First United Methodist Church of Royal Oak, MI on October 31.

J. Philip Hogan

Dec. 4, 1915
Olathe, Colorado

Oct. 27, 2002
Springfield, Missouri

Executive director of Assemblies of God Foreign Missions, 1959–89, president of EFMA, 1968–70, 1976–78 and 1983–85. Hogan helped start four new ministries under this umbrella: Global University, Center for Ministry to Muslims, International Media Ministries, and Healthcare Ministries. During his tenure, the denomination's missions program grew from 753 missionaries in 69 countries to 1,464 missionaries in 120 countries, making it the tenth largest U.S. Protestant missions agency. Hogan was converted as a child during a revival meeting conducted by two women evangelists. He married Virginia Lewis on December 28, 1937. Starting out as an evangelist, he later pastored in Springfield, MO; Painesville, OH; and Detroit, MI. He went to China in 1947 and then to Taiwan, coming home in 1950. He pastored briefly in Florence, SC. He then became a field representative for the promotions department of AGFM. He was the founding chairman of the World Assemblies of God Fellowship and the keynote speaker at the organization's first congress on October 26, 1994. Under his 30 years of leadership, the budget was annually increased from $6,734,780 to $76,679,376 and the number of overseas churches went from 13,975 to 110,608.

Dwight Loder

July 8, 1914
Waverly, Nebraska

Nov. 9, 2002
Worthington, Ohio

President of Garrett Theological Seminary (GETS in 1974), **Evanston, IL, 1955–64**. Loder married Mildred E. Shay on September 17, 1939. He pastored in North Towanda, PA (1939–41), and Blossburg, PA (1941–1947). He served on the staff of Hennepin Avenue Methodist Church, Minneapolis, MN (1947–1950), becoming pastor (1950–55). Upon leaving Seabury, he became a Methodist bishop for the Michigan area. He lectured in many denominational settings, was a delegate to several conferences, and served as trustee of Albion College and Adrian College, both in Michigan.

Glenn L. Archer

March 29, 1906
Logan, Kansas

Nov. 15, 2002

Director of Protestants and Other Americans United for separation of church and state (POAU), 1948–76. Archer was converted at age 13 in a Wesleyan revival and affiliated with that church thereafter. He married Ruth Ford on June 16, 1928. He was a superintendent of schools in Densmore and Alemena, KS from 1927–39. Archer was assistant to the governor of Kansas, 1939–42. He succeeded Joseph Dawson as head of POAU. He led the fight against any kind of public aid for parochial schools and said that US Catholic cardinals, that voted for a pope, should be forced to forfeit their citizenship to the US. He died of Alzheimer's disease.

L. Venchael Booth

Jan. 7, 1919
Covington County, Mississippi

Nov. 16, 2002
Memphis, Tennessee

Primary founder of the Progressive National Baptist Convention, the first executive secretary, 1964–69, and its president, 1972–74. The 2.5 million-member denomination grew to the second largest black Baptist group in America. This group became the denominational home for leading civil rights activists, Martin Luther King, Jr., and Jessie Jackson. After Baptist ordination in 1941, he married Georgia J. Morris on June 3, 1942, pastored in Warrenton, VA (1942–1943) and Gary, IN (1944–1952). Booth pastored the Zion Baptist Church of Cincinnati, OH, 1952–84. His death came four days after the city of Cincinnati named the intersection across from the church, the L. Venchael Booth Corner. Booth is considered a key Black Christian leader in his generation.

Howard Goodman

1921
Alabama

Nov. 30, 2002

Unique singer and pianist. Goodman was born in poverty-stricken coal-mining hills. After working as an evangelist during the 1930s–1940s, he formed his family's singing groups with various combinations of his brothers and sisters. He married Vestal Freeman in 1949 and soon the family became known as the Happy Goodman Family. A new cast, with other family members providing instrumentation, captured Southern Gospel Music fans in the 1960s. They recorded numerous hit songs and received various awards. He had a most soulful lead voice and distinctive piano-playing style which saw him throwing his hands up and down on the ivories. He and his family established Life Temple Church in Madisonville, KY.

John R. Dellenback

Nov. 6, 1918
Chicago, Illinois

Dec. 7, 2002
Medford, Oregon

President of Christian College Consortium, 1976–83, and Council for Christian Colleges and Universities, 1980–85. It was called the Christian College Consortium, 1977–83. Dellenback married Mary J. Benedict on September 10, 1948. He was a partner in law in Medford (1952–66), member of the Oregon House of Representatives (1960–66), in Congress (House of Representatives) (1967–75), and director of the Peace Corps (1975–77). He was active in the United Presbyterian Church, served on the board of World Vision and was a staunch Republican. He died of viral pneumonia.

John Walvoord

May 10, 1910
Sheboygan, Wisconsin

Dec. 21, 2002
Dallas, Texas

President of Dallas (TX) Theological Seminary, 1952–86, and Evangelical Theological Society, 1954. In 1932, while Walvoord was getting his education at Wheaton College, he did rural and small-town missionary work in Nebraska and South Dakota during the summer. He married Geraldine Lundgren on June 28, 1939. They were married 63 years. Walvoord was not only a pioneering educator, but also a leading evangelical scholar on the subject of Bible prophecy. He also served as a distinguished author, renowned theologian, and religious broadcaster in addition to his role as president and chancellor of DTS. During his tenure there, the enrollment of the seminary went from 250 to 1,700 students, the campus tripled in size, and Dallas became widely known for its evangelical, dispensational, and premillennial emphasis. He authored 30 books, including *Armageddon, Oil, and the Middle East Crisis*, which sold 2 million copies in 16 languages. He wrote the lyrics, and Don Wyrtzen wrote the music to "Love Was When."

Robert F. Rice

March 18, 1921
Sioux City, Iowa

Dec. 26, 2002
Tulsa, Oklahoma

Founder and first director of Literacy and Evangelism International, Tulsa, OK, 1967–95. After graduating from Princeton, Rice married Alice Venable in 1946. They went to Korea as Presbyterian missionaries, arriving six weeks before the Korean War began. Bringing in over 700 homeless boys from the streets of Korea, they set up an orphanage for them. In 1965, they returned to the States and Rice taught missions at Oral Roberts University, Tulsa, OK. In 1967, he founded LEI with a vision to teach the illiterate half of the world to read by developing Bible–content literacy primers. He also instructed missionaries and local Christians how to use them to teach reading and writing. There are over 10,000 house churches in India started by people who became Christians as they learned to read using these primers. These primers were developed in 155 languages.

Lee Roy Shelton

Aug. 22, 1923
Morrow, Louisiana

Jan. 16, 2003
Pensacola, Florida

Pastor of Mt. Zion Bible Church, Pensacola, FL, 1978–02. Worldwide ministries developed out of the church he founded, despite the fact that he never asked for money. They included printing and distributing tracts, booklets, and books through Mt. Zion Publications and Chapel Library. Christian correspondence courses were written and distributed worldwide and a prison outreach developed nation wide. In early days, he pastored the FBC of Algiers in New Orleans, LA, then Mt. Zion Bible Church, Litchefield, MN, 1970–78. Thousands of souls were touched by his zealous evangelistic endeavors.

W. Thomas Younger

April 3, 1928
Gary, Indiana

Jan. 21, 2003
Salem, Oregon

President of Western Baptist College, El Cerrito, CA 1973–1978, relocated to Salem, OR, 1978–82. During his tenure, Younger helped the school evolve from a Bible ollege to a liberal arts college offering more diverse degrees. He was a pastor for 23 years in Indiana before going to the college. After the college days, he pastored in Walnut Creek, CA, and Auburn, IN. His wife's name was Davina. He resigned in 1982 after suffering a heart attack. He struggled with this condition the rest of his life.

Vernon Mclelland

July 4, 1929
Vancouver, British Columbia

Jan. 29, 2003
Rancho Mirage, California

Musician, author/journalist and associate of leaders in the Pentecostal movement. Mclelland was converted as a child of seven at the Broadway Tabernacle in Vancouver. Leaving Central Bible College, he became editor of the youth magazine of the Assemblies of God, then of *Youth for Christ* magazine. He married Lois Bender in 1954. He was associate to Charles Blair in Denver, CO, at the Calvary Temple (1957–67), then worked with World Literature Crusade (1969–79). During this time, he married his second wife, Mary Cawston Wagginer, whose missionary pilot husband had been killed in Africa. He helped in the Lausanne Conference of World Evangelism in 1974. During the Jim Bakker era, Mclelland was vice president of missions for PTL, 1979–87. He traveled as a consultant, musician, and speaker, 1987–94. The last decade of his life, he served as an accomplished violinist in the Benny Hinn crusades across America. After a Tampa, FL crusade, he was suddenly stricken at home with a cerebral hemorrhage and died, ten minutes later, in the arms of his neighbor, Tim LaHaye. He wrote 25 books, the last, a monumental tribute to Billy Graham with testimonials compiled from across the world. He was a member of Garr Memorial Church, Costa Mesa, CA.

Jerome Hines

Nov. 8, 1921
Hollywood, California

Feb. 4, 2003
New York, New York

Opera singer, whose Christian faith had an unusual outreach. Hines began his career with the Civic Light Opera Company of Los Angeles in 1940. From 1946 on, he was the leading bass of the Metropolitan Opera Company. He recorded for the top record companies and sang in many parts of the world. Hine's conversion came in 1952, alone with a Gideon Bible in a New York City hotel room. He married Lucia Evangelista on July 23, 1952, and began singing for the Lord as opportunities afforded. He was greatly motivated by George Bev Shea's singing. He sang at the White House at the request of President John Kennedy. His favorite opera was *Faust* because it carried a true Christian message. He and his family attended the Christian and Missionary Alliance Church in South Orange, New Jersey. Perhaps his greatest day professionally came October 23, 1962, when President Kennedy announced the American blockade of Cuba. That night was his final performance of *Boris Godunov* in the Bolshoi Theater in Moscow. Premier Khrushchev attended and applauded enthusiastically afterward, whereupon Hines came to his box and bowed. For a moment perhaps he helped ease the tensions between the two countries. He wrote *This Is My Story, This Is My Song* (1968).

David Morken

June 2, 1910
Audubon, Minnesota

Feb. 21, 2003
Lodi, California

Missionary statesman. Morken moved with his family to Los Angeles in 1922, and at age 16, he was converted. He attended LIFE College and began to preach and sing throughout southern California. He married Helen Mitchell and began to pastor in Lodi, CA. The Morkens and the HUBERT MITCHELL's went to Sumatra in 1929. They fled from the invading Japanese army in 1942. During the war years, he worked with YFC in Los Angeles. After the war, he returned to Asia: (China, Japan, and Hong Kong). Fleeing from China in 1950 was thrilling indeed under an adventure in God's protection as the Communists marched into Shanghai. He worked for Youth for Christ in the Orient for several years, and then became minister-at-large for World Vision. In 1972 (age 62), he went to Kabul, Afghanistan to pastor the only church limited to non-Afghan people. Twice he stood between soldiers, demolition crews and the building they were ordered to destroy, singing "All Hail the Power of Jesus' Name." Helen died in 1983. On Nov. 2, 1985, he married Wilma Christianson. He lived out his days in Lodi, were his memorial service was held at the Temple Baptist Church.

E. V. Hill

Nov. 11, 1933
Columbus, Texas

Feb. 24, 2003
Los Angeles, California

Prominent civil rights leader and pastor of Mount Zion Missionary Baptist Church in Los Angeles for more than 42 years. Hill's congregation became a focus of political and social activism that, according to the *Los Angeles Times*, "drew presidents and preachers alike." Unlike most African-American leaders, he was a political conservative who supported RONALD REAGAN and JERRY FALWELL. He helped form the Southern Christian Conference with MARTIN LUTHER KING JR and prayed the inaugural prayer for RICHARD NIXON's second term in 1972. Hill was a leader in the National Baptist Convention and a member of the Billy Graham Evangelistic Board since 1973. He spoke at the Graham-sponsored Conference of Evangelists in 1983 and 1986 in Amsterdam. His first wife, Jane Edna Hill, preceded him in death in October, 1987, and he was survived by his second wife, LaDean Hill, whom he married on May 8, 1992. He was a significant personality in the clergy of his generation and died after a bout with pneumonia.

"A strong church is a Bible-regulated church, a Christ-centered church and a prayer-powered church."

M. Virgil Ingraham

Oct. 30, 1916
Merrill, Oregon

Feb. 26, 2003
Ashland, Ohio

Director of Brethren Church Missions, Ashland OH, 1963–84. During Ingraham's tenure, missions expanded to India, Colombia, Malaysia, and Mexico. He married Alice N. Larson on June 14, 1941. From 1940–56, he served in the business world in accounting and administration, pastoring the Brethren Church in Stockton, CA some of that time. From 1956–63, he pastored the First Brethren Church, Nappanee, IN. He continued to speak in missionary conferences upon his retirement. Ingraham made ten round-the-world mission trips and attended the World Congress of Evangelism in Lausanne, Switzerland in 1974. He attended the Park Street Brethren Church in Ashland, OH, where his funeral was held.

Jack Dain

Oct. 13, 1912
England

March 3, 2003

General secretary of Zenana Bible and Medical Mission, 1948–52, renamed Bible and Medical Mission Missionary Fellowship (Interserve in 1986), **1952–58**. He was the international president, 1978–86. This missionary statesman was a former Anglican bishop of the Sydney,

Australia, diocese. He was the honorary co-secretary (with John Stott) of the World Evangelical Fellowship (Alliance) at its founding in 1951. He was federal secretary for the Church Missionary Society of Australia, 1959–65. He was key to Billy Graham's crusades in Sydney in 1968 and 1979. He helped organize the 1974 International Conference on World Evangelization, convincing Billy Graham to include a commitment to social responsibilities along with evangelism. Graham said, "He was one of the greatest Christians I ever knew and one of the best counselors I ever had." He died of complications related to a blood disease.

Robert J. Wells

Winnipeg, Manitoba, Canada

March 7, 2003
Fullerton, California

Evangelist, pastor, and co-worker with JOHN R. RICE for many years. He pastored the Burton Ave Baptist Church, Waterloo, Iowa, 1937–39. Wells succeeded JOHN RICE as pastor of Galilean Baptist Church, Dallas, Texas, 1939–44, moving a tent from section to section in the city every ten weeks because the church had burned to the ground. He was also Associate Editor of the *Sword of the Lord*, 1944–1956. During this time, he held evangelistic meetings and led great conferences on revival. His major work was the pastorate of the Central Baptist Church of Orange County, CA (beginning with a tent in Anaheim, CA), 1956–86. The church grew to over 4,000 members. Heritage Christian Schools, and several other churches and schools were started out of this home base. After a serious stroke in 1986, he retired to Palm Desert, California, curtailing his revival endeavors.

R. E. Harlow

March 15, 1908
Toronto, Ontario, Canada

March 10, 2003
Port Colburne, Ontario, Canada

Founder and first president of Emmaus Bible School, Toronto, ON (Dubuque, IA in 1984), **1941–52**. As a result of his love for missions, his books and correspondence courses now reach worldwide. He became a Christian on November 20, 1920 at twelve years of age. He married Ella M. Burritt (born: May 19, 1908) on March 9, 1935. The young couple went to the Congo as Missionaries on May 10, 1935, serving until 1941. Emmaus (day school) actually began in Toronto (1945), with 85 students, then move to Chicago (1953). The school was a correspondence course, 1941–45. His first correspondence course was *The Servant of Christ* (pub., 1955). His wife, Margaret, died in Yonkers, NY, from cancer in her right lung. He then married Gertrude Koppel on July 13, 1964. Everyday Publications printed his Bible courses in many languages. He suffered a heart attack on October 23, 1989. He was a beloved leader in the Plymouth Brethren movement. His biography is entitled *No Time to Quit*.

Abe C. Van Der Puy

Oct. 11, 1919
Sheybogan, Wisconsin

April 3, 2003
Keystone Heights, Florida

President of HCJB World Radio Missionary Fellowship, 1962–82, and chairman of National Religious Broadcasters, 1975–78. This veteran missionary to Ecuador gave 57 years to the ministry of HCJB in Quito, Ecuador. He arrived in Quito in 1945 where he operated a "gospel sound truck." His first wife, Dolores Hicks, died of cancer in 1965 after 22 years of marriage. In 1966, he married Marge Saint, widow of NATE SAINT. He helped form the HCJB World Radio's North American Ministries. The World Radio Network grew from one station in 1978 to 23 FM outlets, mostly along the US-Mexican border. Upon his return to the states, he broadcast a segment on *Back to the Bible*, 1979–91. He was president of WRN, 1983–97. He died from complications of hepatitis.

Paul N. Ellis

Sept. 30, 1912
Birds, Illinois

April 4, 2003
Indianapolis, Indiana

Bishop of Free Methodist Church, 1964–79. Ellis was converted at age 15 and married Delores Wells on August 5, 1935, and later, Naomi Diddle. He pastored at Marshfield, IN (1934–35); Marsh Hill (1935–38), Olney, IL; Mount Zion (1938–42); Urbana, IL (1942–48); Broadview, Toronto, ON (1948–54); West Morris Street (1954–63); and then was superintendent of the Wabash Conference, leading to his election as bishop. After retirement, he pastored in Lakeland, FL. He was a wide reader, earnest preacher, and wise administrator. His funeral was at John Wesley Free Methodist Church in Indianapolis.

James H. Costen

Oct. 5, 1931
Omaha, Nebraska

April 11, 2003
Atlanta, Georgia

President of Interdenominational Theological Center, Atlanta, GA, 1983–97, and of Association of Theological Schools, 1994–96. Costen first pastored at Mt. Pisgah Presbyterian Church, Rocky Mount, NY, then went on to found the Church of the Master in Atlanta, GA, in 1965. This was one of the first inter-racial congregations in Atlanta. From 1969–83, he was administrative dean of John C. Smith Seminary, newly relocated at ITC. In 1982, he was moderator of the General Assembly of the United Presbyterian Church, USA. Upon retirement, he became director of development for the Presbyterian Church of East Africa, expanding educational opportunities. Costen was married 50 years to his wife, Melva. He died of surgical complications.

William H. Taylor

June 29, 1914
Atlanta, Georgia

April 19, 2003
Savannah, Georgia

President of Central American Mission, Dallas, TX, 1959–74. Taylor and his wife, Stella, spent some 66 years ministering for CAM. They began their ministry in Costa Rica and made a great impact there. He became the second field director of the mission in the mid-1950s. One of his great contributions was the planning and relocation of CAM's home office to spacious property and beautiful buildings. He was instrumental in the founding of the Central American Theological Seminary in Guatemala. He was also involved in developing Ediciones Las Americas, CAM's Spanish language publishing house in Puebla, Mexico. Upon leaving the mission leadership in 1974, the couple went to Spain and ministered there developing the Royal Pines Ministry Conference and camp ministry. He was Warren Wiersbe's first pastor prior to going to Costa Rica.

Damon C. Dodd

Feb. 14, 1916
Flat River, Missouri

April 27, 2003
Norman Park, Georgia

Executive secretary of National Association of Free Will Baptists, 1949–53. Dodd served as a researcher, writer, evangelist, church planter, and educator for 70 years. He was converted in 1932 at age 16. He began pastoring in Missouri at age 21. He and his wife, Sylvia, moved to Nashville in 1942. They were missionaries to Cuba, 1945–48. When Sylvia died, after 58 years of marriage, he married Ola Maude Mercer. He spent 40 years ministering in Georgia and is well known for his book, *The Free Will Baptist Story* (1956).

Carl J. (Kelly) Bihl

Nov. 29, 1916
East Chicago, Indiana

May 1, 2003
Long Beach, California

President of Youth for Christ, 1963–65, and multi-talented evangelist, children's worker, magician, saxophone soloist, tenor soloist, and song leader. He was converted at age nine. Upon graduating from MBI, Kelly spent five years in the late 1940s with the *Children's Bible Hour* in Grand Rapids, MI, where he was known as "Uncle Bill" to thousands of kids. He was director of music at Calvary Church there. In 1948, he moved to Toledo, OH, to direct Youth For Christ. He also directed Child Evangelism and the high school Bible club program. In 1952, he went into full time evangelism with YFC. Bihl was the radio voice of John Brown University for 20 years, 1970–90. He died of complications from cancer. His funeral was on May 7, 2003, at the Seacoast Grace Brethren Church of Cypress, CA.

Dan Harrison

April 17, 1941
Hetsuo, China

May 19, 2003
Madison, Wisconsin

President of EFMA, 1995–97, and director of Inter-Varsity's SMFM, 1988–2003. He served as director of Urbana (IL) Mission Conventions in 1990, 1993 and 1996. Prior to 1987, he was a missions administrator for Wycliff Bible Translators. After 1997, he was director of Middle East Media. Thousands of students participated as missionaries through Inter-Varsity's global projects. His wife's name was Shelby. A funeral service was held at Christ Presbyterian Church in Madison, WI.

Paul T. Lauby

May 27, 1924

May 20, 2003

General Secretary of United Board for Christian Higher Education in Asia, 1970–89. Lauby was ordained in the United Church of Christ. He pastored several California churches while completing his graduate studies from Berkeley Divinity School and the University of Southern California. He and his wife, Edna, served as missionary educators at Silliman University in the Philippines, 1954–70. UBCHEA was supporting seven colleges in Asia, when he arrived. By his retirement, it was working with nearly 100 institutions in nine countries. In his latter days, he pastored in Newtown, PA.

F. Benjamin Davis

May 19, 1912
Indianapolis, Indiana

June 6, 2003
Indianapolis, Indiana

President of Central Baptist Theological Seminary, Indianapolis, IN, 1956–2003. During World War II, Davis served as a US Army Chaplain. Davis was an organizer, leader, and teacher. He pastored at Glenco Baptist Church, Indianapolis; Bethany Chapel Baptist, Ottawa, KS; Ninth St. Baptist Church, Lawrence, KS; and Mount Zion Baptist Church, Seattle, WA, 1942–54. He married Ruth Lomax on June 5, 1954 (died: November 30, 1990). It was on August 22,1954 he began a lifelong ministry at New Bethel Missionary Baptist Church in Indianapolis which lasted nearly 50 years. He was active as member and leader in many local and national positions of various groups. He was instrumental in developing the Haitian Baptist Mission. Known as "The Sage," he would often say, "There is no excuse for a dumb Christian." Leaders from around the country paid tribute at memorial services on June 13–14 held at his church, which is a part of the National Missionary Baptist Convention of America.

Lynn G. Gordon

April 8, 1912
Waxahatchie, Texas

June 14, 2003
Melbourne, Florida

General Secretary of Independent Board for Presbyterian Foreign Missions, Philadelphia, PA, 1968–82. Gordon was president of the board, 1972–95. Gordon married Marine Ford on May 26, 1935. His first church was in Fawn Grove, PA. He pastored in Gainesville, TX, from 1940–42. He served in WWII, 1942 until the end of the war, then attended Faith Theological Seminary, graduating in 1949. During the Korean War, he was a chaplain in Korea. He was president of the associated missions of the ICC, 1960–2003. Through the years, he helped organize 15 Bible Presbyterian churches. His wife survived him after 68 years of marriage. They retired to Florida in 1992. He wrote *The World's Greatest Truths*.

Larry Burkett

March 3, 1939
Winter Park, Florida

July 4, 2003
Gainesville, Georgia

Financial advisor to the Christian world; president of Christian Financial Concepts, 1976–2000, and co-director (Howard Dayton) **of Crown Ministries, 2000–3**. A former electrical engineer, Burkett inspired millions to apply biblical principles to financial management. As an unsaved businessman, he was converted under the ministry of Peter Lord in Florida. He married his wife, Judy Morgan, in 1958. He thereafter began to develop Christian principles, especially in the area of finances. He founded Christian Financial Concepts in 1976. It grew to 130 employees before it merged with Crown Financial Ministries in 2000. Burkett hosted three syndicated programs that aired on more than 1,000 radio stations. He also wrote more than 70 books. He is credited with helping create the finance sections in Christian bookstores. His final release, *Nothing to Fear*, stemmed from a protracted battle with kidney cancer. In 1989, he suffered a heart attack and in 1995 was diagnosed with cancer. He actually died of heart failure, with the cancer still in remission. He attended Blackshear Baptist Church in Gainesville, GA. His funeral was conducted July 11, 2003, at the Church of the Apostles in Atlanta.

Paul Brand

July 17, 1914
Southwest India

July 8, 2003
Seattle, Washington

Missionary surgeon, credited with a breakthrough in research and treatment of leprosy. His medical achievements and writings earned him international acclaim. Born of missionary parents, Brand met Margaret Berry, at London University and married her on May 29, 1943. The two surgeons returned to Vellore, India, in 1946, to teach at the Christian Medical College and Hospital. There, he pioneered surgical work with those suffering from the bacterial infection known as Hansen's Disease. He was the first to use re-constructive surgery to correct leprous deformities in the hands and feet. Brand was chief of rehabilitation at the US Public Health Services National Leprosarium at Carrville, LA from 1966–86. He wrote seven books, 100 scientific papers, and died from complications related to a subdural hematoma, following a fall.

William A. Mierop

June 26, 1912
Paterson, New Jersey

July 15, 2003
Quarryville, Pensylvania

President of Bible Institute of Pennsylvania, 1944–51, renamed Philadelphia Bible Institute, 1951–56 (Philadelphia College of the Bible in 1958), **and Accrediting Association of Bible Colleges, 1955–57**. These two schools existed separately in Philadelphia for 37 years until a merger on July 1, 1951. He began teaching in 1942, served a number of pastorates in New Jersey and Pennsylvania, and founded the annual Ocean City (NJ) Summer Bible Conference. He authored several volumes, including *Christ in the Levitical Offerings* and *A Twelve-Point Missions Program for the Local Church*. He married Marion Coxson (died: 1983), and then Aileen Kitner (died: 2002).

Bill Bright

Oct. 19, 1921
Coweta, Oklahoma

July 19, 2003
Orlando, Florida

Founder and director of Campus Crusade, perhaps the greatest visionary in Christian history. One goal consumed him: "The gospel to every living creature." He married Vonette Zachery on December 30, 1948. They had two sons. He started Campus Crusade in 1951 to reach the students of UCLA. Upon his death, there were outreaches in 191 nations with 26,000 employees and 225,000 trained volunteers in 60 ministries. His booklet, *The Four Spiritual Laws*, has been printed in 200 languages and distributed to 2 1/2 billion people. His *Jesus* film has been translated into more than 800 languages and seen by some 5 billion people in 234 countries. He began his ministry in Arrowhead Springs, CA, and in the mid-1990s moved the entire operation to Orlando, FL. In 2000, he was diagnosed with a lung disease known as pulmonary fibrosis, which eventually claimed his life. His favorite Bible verses were Acts 22:8, 10.

John D. Jess

July 12, 1913
Aurora, Illinois

July 23, 2003
Albuquerque, New Mexico

Radio evangelist of *Chapel of the Air*, 1939–76 and Bible teacher for over a half century. Early on, he served Al Capone as a bootleg liquor driver in Chicago, before he was gloriously converted. He was a young pastor in Moweaqua, IL, when he launched his *Chapel of the Air*, in nearby Decatur. Later, he moved to Quincy, IL, and started the Quincy Gospel Center. That church became Calvary Baptist Church, then moved on to Wheaton, IL, continuing his broadcast from that city for many years. He was survived by his wife whom he married in 1934.

Chester I. Miller

March 17, 1917
Lawrence County, Ohio

July 24, 2003
London, Ohio

General Overseer of Pentecostal Church of Christ, 1954–76 (which merged with Pentecostal Assemblies in 1976), **renamed International Pentecostal Church of Christ, London, OH, 1976–82**. Miller went to Brazil as a missionary in 1941 for his denomination. He married Rachel H. Yarborough on December 11, 1945 in Recife, Brazil. They returned to the USA in 1954 to the leadership post of the denomination. He married Annie Trent Frew (1983) upon the death of his first wife (1981). He also taught theology at Beulah Heights Bible College in Atlanta, Georgia.

Arnold T. Olson

Feb. 23, 1910
Minneapolis, Minnesota

July 25, 2003
Edina, Minnesota

President of Evangelical Free Church of America, 1951–76, and of National Association of Evangelicals, 1968–69. He was president of the Evangelical Free Church Association, 1943–46 and 1948–50 which merged in 1950 to form EFCA. He married Della E. Knudsen on November 9, 1930. Early pastorates included Houston, MN (1930–33); West Orange, NJ (1933); Staten Island, NY (1933–37), and Minneapolis, MN, (1937–52). He served as a chaplain, 1943–45, and was decorated with a Bronze Star. His first book was *The Peacemakers* (1956). He authored nine books and died in a hospice after a short illness.

James (Jimmy) T. Johnson

February 8, 1912
Montgomery, Alabama

August 7, 2003
High Rock, North Carolina

Well-known evangelist. Johnson blazed a trail across America, preaching for over 50 years in crusades large and small. His associates were Ed Lyman, soloist and song leader, and MERRILL DUNLOP, pianist. He was married December 22, 1944 to Virginia Cole. He was converted at age 17 in a campaign in his home church. His crusades were interdenominational, with a blend of his education at Bob Jones University and Wheaton College giving him the foundation for his life. For years he worked out of Fuquay Springs (Fuquay-Varina), NC, but the last 18 years of his life were in High Rock, where he pastored for a year. He hosted over 40 Holy Land tours to the Middle East.

Lester A. Crose

July 29, 1912
Santa Cruz, California

Aug. 11, 2003
Moorsville, Indiana

President of Church of God Missionary Board, Anderson, IN, 1954–75. Crose grew up in California, Japan, and Lebanon. He was ordained in Beirut in 1938. With his wife, Ruthie Hamon, whom he married in Barbados, 1934, he served in Lebanon (1945–50) and in Egypt (1950–52). As head of the denomination's mission activities, he traveled to many parts of the world. He was professor of missions at Anderson (IN) University, 1976–78. He wrote *Passport for a Reformation*.

Carl Goltz

Sept. 9, 1923
Fall City, Nebraska

Aug. 19, 2003
North Platte, Nebraska

President of Berean Fellowship of Churches, 1953–82. Goltz was converted at age 18, reading his Bible and attending a Presbyterian Church in Weed, California. He served in WWII from 1942–45. He married Doris Kemp on September 25, 1945. After graduating from MBI, he pastored the Berean Church, Torrington, WY (1950–56); then in Scotts Bluff, NE (1956–82); and then in North Platte, NE (1982–2002). He died of respiratory arrest complicated by pneumonia.

James D. Douglas

1922

Aug. 20, 2003
Scotland

Author, historian, Douglas edited and contributed to some of the most significant Biblical and church historical reference works in the last half of the twentieth century. These included *The New Bible Dictionary* (1961), *The New International Dictionary of the Christian Church*, *Dictionary of 20th Century Christian Biography*, and the *Expositors Bible Commentary* series. He was editor-at-large for *Christianity Today*. He died of a heart attack.

Wilbur E. Nelson

Sept. 25, 1910
Brighton, Colorado

Aug. 22, 2003
Laguna Woods, California

Founder of *The Morning Chapel Hour*, a nationally syndicated radio ministry. Nelson founded the radio ministry, March 25, 1944, a 15-minute broadcast heard one day a week and on one station. Soon it was *The Morning Chapel Hour*, a ½ hour daily program across the USA. Two resulting outreaches were the Evangelical Children's Home in Hong Kong, and a 2,000-seat auditorium at Isabelle Christian School in Pusan, Korea. He had a wonderful tenor voice that for years was heard singing his theme song, "It Is Morning." Wilbur died after five weeks of hospitalization for a variety of ailments.

His son, Norman, also a gifted vocalist, continues the ministries, now called *Compassion Radio*. He wrote the chorus "Christ Will Keep You Smiling" and composed the music for "Sooner or Later" (lyrics by Lulu Koch).

Donald J. Wolfram

Nov. 13, 1919
Zarephath, New Jersey

Aug. 25, 2003
Denver, Colorado

President of Pillar of Fire, 1982–2001, and director of Missions Program, 1992–2000. Wolfram married Phyllis Hoffman in 1948 (died: 1985). He taught extensively in Pillar of Fire high schools and colleges. He also was dean at Belleview Christian College, Westminster. Wolfram had a longtime radio ministry on KPOF Christian radio. He made dozens of missionary trips all over the world and recorded a daily missions program, *Go and Tell* for over 25 years. He loved music and could play nearly every band and orchestra instrument. He died after a brief bout with pancreatic cancer.

J. Ray Knighton

June 1, 1992
Chicago, Illinois

Aug. 30, 2003
Brunswick, Georgia

Founder and first director of MAP (Medical Assistance Program), **Brunswick, GA 1954–80.** This Christian health ministry served millions of people around the world. He was married 59 years to his wife, Beth, whom he married on October 13, 1943. He was the first director of Christian Medical and Dental Society, 1951–64. In 1954, a truck with eleven tons of soon-to-be-discarded pharmaceuticals pulled up outside his Chicago office. A drug company had heard of his interest in such a shipment. MAP was born—matching up excess pharmaceuticals with physicians in impoverished countries. When he died of congestive heart failure, the organization was providing nearly $150 million in essential medicine and medical supplies each year to hospitals, clinics and refugee centers serving some of the world's poorest communities. He received numerous awards and honors.

Johnny Cash

Feb. 26, 1932
Kingsland, Arkansas

Sept. 12, 2003
Nashville, Tennessee

Composer, recording artist, and TV personality, Cash was an icon of country music. Even though he struggled with a drug problem in his earlier days, he often sang at Billy Graham crusades and reaffirmed his Christian faith. He served in the US Air Force. He became an overnight success in 1956 with his song "I Walk the Line." His inspiration was his wife, June Carter (June 23, 1929-May 15, 2003), whom he married on March 1, 1968. She left him a son, John. He was a Baptist. He had four children from a previous marriage, 1954-66 to Vivian Liberto. He wrote his autobiography (*Man in Black*) and appeared in several films, including *North and South* (1985), *Stagecoach* (1986) and *Johnny Cash Is Coming to Town* (1987). He also co-wrote the film, *The Gospel Road*. Known as "The Man in Black," he recorded some 1,500 songs on 500 albums, selling some 53 million of them. He died from complications of diabetes.

Arthur W. Wilson

May 26, 1912
Aurora, Colorado

Sept. 6, 2003
Wichita, Kansas

President of Baptist Bible Fellowship, Springfield, MO 1959–62, 1965–67. Wilson was one of the most colorful preachers of the last half of the 20th century. Innovation, initiative, and intrigue characterized his citywide crusades, church-plants, evangelistic meetings, and sermons. He was known as "The Kansas Cyclone." Wilson was converted in December, 1931, after hearing evangelist Ira L. Deal. He married Rowena Totten on June 25, 1933. His mother and sister were saved hearing him preach at his ordination in 1937. He soon was preaching all through Colorado, planting and reorganizing churches. In September, 1938, he held a tent revival in Wichita, KS, resulting in the organization of the Fundamental Baptist Church (Wichita Baptist Tabernacle). On the first official Sunday service, 576 were present and 279 became charter members. A new building was dedicated on May 14, 1939, with 1,441 attending. His wife died in 1944 from a ruptured appendix. On September 17, 1945, he married Elaine E. Sweet. He helped reorganize or establish 23 churches in Kansas. In May, 1969, he became a full-time evangelist.

Kenneth E. Hagin

Aug. 20, 1917
McKinney, Texas

Sept. 19, 2003
Tulsa, Oklahoma

Founder of the Word of Faith movement, formerly with the Assemblies of God as a healing evangelist. Hagin was converted on April 22, 1933, and healed from a lingering disease. He began pastoring in Texas, attaining the Pentecostal experience in 1937. From 1949–63, he was an evangelist, working out of his home in Garland, TX, until 1966 when he moved to Tulsa, OK. There he started his Rhema Training Center in the suburb of Broken Arrow in 1974. Many charismatic leaders consider him a spiritual father as his message emphasized healing and faith. His "name it and claim it" theology came under question by some. Hagin formed the Rhema Ministerial Association International, which served 1,400 churches. His best-selling book, *The Believer's Authority*, sold one million copies. His 125 titles have 53 million copies in circulation. He pastored 8,000 members at his Rhema Bible Church. Some 23,000 graduated from his Rhema Bible Schools with campuses in 13 nations. His *Word of Faith* magazine had 250,000 in circulation. Hagin died in a cardiac care center, survived by his wife, Oretha, and son, Kenneth Jr., who continues the work. Eight thousand attended his funeral.

Derek V. Prince

Aug. 14, 1915
Bangalore, India

Sept. 24, 2003
Jerusalem, Israel

Charismatic Bible teacher and author, director of Derek Prince Ministries, 1963–2003. He lived in Israel, off and on from the 1940's. His daily radio program *Today with Derek Prince* reached half the world in nine languages. He wrote some 45 books on various subjects including God's destiny for Israel. His *The Spirit-Filled Believer's Handbook* was translated into more than 60 languages. In 1941, he became a Christian studying the Bible, while serving in the British Army. In 1945, he married Lydia Christensen, a Danish missionary, 26 years his senior. They immigrated to the U.S. in 1963 and pastored in Seattle. He helped found Intercessors for America in 1973 and led the Shepherding movement until 1983. His wife died in 1975, and in 1978, he married Ruth Baker. She died in 1988. He died of heart failure.

Joseph R. Shultz

May 9, 1927
Berlin, Pennsylvania

Sept. 24, 2003
Ashland, Ohio

President of Ashland (OH) Theological Seminary, 1963–82, and Ashland University, 1979–92. Shultz was a key leader in the Brethren movement. Early on, he pastored in Williamstown, OH (1948–52) and in Washington, D.C. (1956–1962). On June 17, 1950, he married Doris Hart. When he became dean of the Seminary, in 1979, there were only 22 students. When he left in 1992 there were 374. The library grew from 5,000 to 45,000 books. The university grew from 1,859 to 4,961 during his leadership there.

P. J. Titus

May 6, 1935
Vadasserikara, India

Sept. 25, 2003
Vizagn, India

Founder and president of Christ for India, 1981–2003. Titus was converted in 1955. In 1959, he married his wife, Mary. Feeling the need for more education, he came to New York with his high school diploma and eight dollars. He was burdened for his own people, and returned to India in 1982, starting the New Testament Church of India. Believing also in social welfare and education, he started Church on the Rock Theological Seminary, Nava Jeevan Public School in English, and the New Life Children's Home. He started with 30 students at COTR in 1983 and 20 years later, in 2002, there were 306 students. In 2001, over 16,000 new believers were baptized. His health declined, being a diabetic for 28 years and suffering cardiac disease. In March, 2003, he began kidney dialysis as both of his kidneys ceased functioning. His funeral took place at the COTR campus.

Phil Palermo

Aug. 23, 1918
Melrose Park, Illinois

Sept. 27, 2003
Lake Forest, Illinois

Musical evangelist, Phil and his brother, Louis (Louie) PALERMO toured the world for nearly 50 years. With Phil on the guitar, Louis on the accordion, they played and sang gospel songs to all nationalities. Phil married Edith Fjellman on January 30, 1943. His first musical ministry was with a group called "The Midnight Brigade." They sang and played gospel songs in Chicago's taverns and bars. Their first major trips with Youth for Christ began with a trip to Italy in 1947, where they ministered for six months. In 1967, they went on the first of six trips to Vietnam. One night they substituted for Bob Hope. In later years, upon their retirement in Irvine, CA, Phil held services for the Country Manor retirement home in Orange and at the Lake Avenue Congregational Church in Pasadena. He died of a heart attack accompanied by kidney failure one year and one day after his brother, Louis, died.

Alan D. Fiers

Dec. 17, 1906
Kankakee, Illinois

Sept. 28, 2003
Jacksonville, Florida

Executive secretary, 1964–68 (title changed) **and first president of Christian Church** (Disciples of Christ), **1964–73.** He married Elizabeth Kunz on June 14, 1931. Ordained in 1929 in the Disciples of Christ Church, he pastored in Shadyside, OH (1929–31); Hamilton, OH (1931–34); Newark, OH (1934–45); and Cleveland, OH (1945–51). He then became president of the Board of Missions and Education, 1951–64. He wrote *This Is Missions* (1953) and *Prayer and the Great Decisions of Life* (1960). It was significant that he created a formal, though voluntary, denominational body, something that ALEXANDER CAMPBELL tried to do in 1849 but failed. It was a representative assembly from a hodgepodge of congregations, national/international agencies, and state organizations. He lived out his days in Indianapolis and died at age 96, one of the 20th century's most revered men in the movement.

William Ackerman

April 24, 1919
Fair Lawn, New Jersey

Sept. 30, 2003
Prescott, Arizona

Director of World Home Bible League (Bible League), **1951–85, and first executive secretary of Evangelical Press Association, 1956–58.** Directing WHBL for 38 years, he expanded it into an international ministry. Scriptures were published in new languages and programs were started in new places such as Turkey, Korea, Nigeria, China, Cuba, and Egypt among others. He traveled widely in promotion and developed numerous fund-raising strategies. He was married 62 years to his wife Gertrude. He was buried in Prescott, AZ.

Willys K. Braun

Aug. 9, 1917
St. Louis, Missouri

Sept. 30, 2003
Wilmore, Kentucky

Founder and first director of Evangelism Resources, Wilmore, KY, 1976–98. Braun was converted as a teenage soldier and married Thelma Stillor on Sept. 6, 1941. After studies at Nyack College, he pastored. Then the young couple went to the Congo where they ministered 1945–74. Training nationals led him to 26 countries in Africa, extending beyond their CMA affiliation. In 1980, they returned to Africa and established the International Center of Evangelism in Leopoldville (Kinshasa). Some 700 have graduated from there. Schools soon began in India and other places for this nine-month course. He was on his way to India at age 86 when a cardiac arrest took his life a few hours before his flight.

Virgil Arrowhead

July 20, 1917
Manistique, Michigan

Oct. 2003
Mountain Home, Arkansas

National representative of New Testament Association of Independent Baptist Churches, 1974–89. Arrowhead was converted in a local Baptist church in 1935 under Pastor Arthur Glenn. He married Allison Selway on September 14, 1943. He was the founding pastor of Calvary Baptist Church, Lamar, CO (1956–66); pastored FBC of Hibbing, MN (1967–71); and Faith Baptist Church, Duluth, MN (1971–74).

David L. Stitt

Oct. 5, 1912
Ft. Worth, Texas

Oct. 3, 2003
Black Mountain, North Carolina

President of Austin (TX) Presbyterian Theological Seminary, 1945–71. During his leadership there, the student body grew from 18 to 150. He hired Rachel Henderlite, the first woman ordained in the former PCUS, as the first female professor. Early on, he pastored the Westminster Presbyterian Church, St. Louis, MO, from 1938–45. In 1940, he married Jane Dupuy (died: December 26, 2001). Upon leaving the academic post, he became pastor of Bellaire Presbyterian Church in Houston. The couple had six children. Later, he lost his eyesight, then died of heart failure.

Gail Terrell

Dec. 25, 1943
Dayton, Ohio

Oct. 10, 2003
Cincinnati, Ohio

President of Temple Baptist College, Cincinnati, OH, 1972–85. Terrell married Evelyn Ervin on July 29, 1967. He worked ten years in the chemical industry followed by 31 years of teaching at Cincinnati Baptist College, TBC, and Landmark Christian School, 1985–2001. He pastored Grace Baptist Church, Hamilton, OH, 1986–2003. He co-founded TBC with Chester Ratliff in Springdale, OH in 1972. The school is basically a commuter college. He died at University Hospital. A funeral service was held October 14 at Landmark Baptist Church, Cincinnati, with 3,000 attending.

Lawrence L. Rhoads

May 12, 1922
Cambridge, Ohio

Oct. 16, 2003
West Union, Ohio

President of Christian Union, Chillicothe, OH, 1971–86. Rhoads was converted in 1948 at age 26 and became the second graduate of the Christian Union Bible College. He was ordained August 14, 1957. He pastored seven different Christian Union Churches in Ohio: Wamsley, Byington,

Liberty Hill, Pennisten Chapel, Zion (Van Wert), West Union (20 years), and Otway (20 years), for a total of 56 years. He started the investment foundation of the denomination with a check of $1,000 in 1960. Its net worth in 2002 was over $250,000 dollars. He served five terms as general council president, 1971–1985.

Madame Chiang Kai Shek

March 3 or 5, 1897/1898
Shanghai, China

Oct. 23, 2003
New York, New York

First lady of China for some time with a remarkable Christian testimony for a century. Born Mei-Ling Soong, the third daughter of a prominent Methodist businessman and lay preacher. At eight years of age, she went to study in the States. Graduating from Wellesley, (MA) College in 1917, she returned to Shanghai. On December 1, 1927, she married General CHIANG KAI SHEK. Both of them took stands for Christ. She was a prominent anti-Communist spokeswoman during the 1950s and appealed for missionaries to evangelize Taiwan. She was known for her ruthless political savvy and for her Christian witness. Her sister had married Dr. Sun Yat-sen, and, upon his death, the mantle of the presidency of China fell on CHIANG KAI SHEK. With the Communist takeover of China in the late 1940s, the Kai Sheks moved to Taiwan (Formosa) and directed the events of Free China until his death in 1975. She retired to Long Island, NY. She was a Methodist. The marriage was childless. She died at the age of 105 or 106.

Larry Ward

Dec. 14, 1924
Sidney, New York

Oct. 25, 2003
Physon, Arizona

Founder and president of Food for the Hungry, Phoenix, AZ, 1971–82, and executive secretary of Evangelical Press Association, 1958–65. Ward has also served as managing editor for *Christian Life, World Vision Magazine, Baptist Bulletin,* and *Christianity Today*. His humanitarian service started when he was vice president and overseas director for World Vision, helping to build it to the largest Christian humanitarian religious organization in the world. Among the 70 countries he traveled to, Ward's greatest love was for Vietnam. He made 125 separate trips there between 1958 and 1998. Out of this burden, Food for the Hungry was born. Under his leadership, this organization grew to 2,000 field staff workers in 37 countries of the world. Ward was saved at a youth camp as a child. He was married to his first wife, Lorraine, for 52 years and, upon her death, married his second wife, June. He was finally bedridden with a variety of ailments.

Walter H. Smythe

Oct. 26, 1912
Springfield, Massachusetts

Nov. 1, 2003
Corono Del Mar, California (?)

Administrator in Youth for Christ and the Billy Graham Evangelistic endeavors. Smyth married Ethel R. Harbach in 1948. He was an associate of PERCY CRAWFORD for seven years before directing Philadelphia YFC, 1942–50. From 1950–87, he was with the Billy Graham Evangelistic Association. He directed BG Evangelistic Films, Washington, DC, 1951–57. He was a key figure in the international ministries as well as in North America from 1965 on. Smyth chaired the Amsterdam '83 and Amsterdam '86 International Conferences of Itinerant Evangelists. Smyth was an elder at Coral Ridge Presbyterian Church, Ft. Lauderdale, FL in latter years. A memorial service was held at Pacific View Memorial Chapel in Corono Del Mar on November 6th.

Bertist Rouse

Nov. 2, 1936
Plateau, Alabama

Nov. 18, 2003
Semmes, Alabama

Pioneer and first president of International Gospel Outreach, 1973–2003. Married to Anna Merle, Rouse pastored for 13 years in Methodist churches, then became an evangelist for the

Mississippi Conference for eight years. In 1973, he changed the name of his organization from Bertist Rouse Evangelistic Ministry, Inc., to the above, as he began sending missionaries overseas. He eventually had ministries in 32 countries. Bertist and Anna Merle considered themselves servants to those (missionaries) on the front lines. He wrote *The Little Foxes* and *International Christianity*.

Robert P. Rasmussen

May 4, 1955
Grand Rapids, Minnesota

Nov. 4, 2003
near Dillon, Montana

President of International Messengers, 1984–2001. He was a pastor of Evangelical Free churches in Fargo, ND, and Brooklyn Park in Minneapolis. Later, while living in Bemidji, MN, he got a vision for his work and established IM, with headquarters in Clear Lake, IA. He eventually moved to Libby, MT, where he established a training center for his work. He traveled to dozens of countries and locally was active at Faith Bible Church, Libby. He died in a bizarre incident. On his first elk-hunt, he bagged his first elk. During the night, heavy snowfall blocked the exhaust pipe for the camper heater where he was sleeping. He died of carbon monoxide poisoning.

Carl F. H. Henry

Jan. 22, 1913
New York, New York

Dec. 7, 2003
Watertown, Wisconsin

Theologian, journalist, evangelical leader, the first editor of *Christianity Today* (1956–68), and president of Evangelical Theological Society, 1969. Henry's life goal was to present biblical Christianity as intellectually credible and historically correct. J. I. Packer said of him, "he tore away great holes" in the liberal views that held sway over Protestantism. Gene Bedford led him to Christ at age 20. He was ordained in the American Baptist Convention. Henry married Helga Bender on August 17, 1940. His first book was *A Doorway to Heaven* (1941) which was a history of the Pacific Garden Mission. He began his ministry as a professor at Northern Baptist Theological Seminary (1942–47), then at Fuller Theological Seminary, Pasadena, CA, as the first acting dean (1947–56). In 1955, Billy Graham asked him to be the first editor of a new magazine which would showcase evangelical thought and *Christianity Today* was born. Henry lectured for World Vision, 1974–87. During this time, he wrote many works. He taught at Trinity Evangelical Divinity School, 1974 and 1987–91. In 1992, the Henrys left Virginia for Watertown, WI. Union University founded the Carl F. H. Henry Center for Christian Leadership in 1997. His *Uneasy Conscience of Modern Fundamentalism* (1947) was his first major work, and his last was *Horizons of Science* (1978). He completed a six-volume work, *God, Revelation, and Authority* (1983). Many volumes followed.

"To know God as the ultimate Who's Who, nurtures gratitude for all the days of one's years, including creation life, regenerate life, and resurrection life to come."

Robert Murfin

June 25, 1921
Greenfield, Indiana

Dec. 16, 2003
Summerlin, Nevada

Executive director of Evangelical Child and Family Agency, Wheaton, IL, 1963–72, and radio host. Murfin was one of those congenial personalities that made everyone feel good when they were with him. He attributes his salvation to his grandmother's influence upon his life. He was alumnus of the year at his alma mater, Moody Bible Institute, during one of the annual recognitions. He served in the navy in WWII, then married Jessie Johnson, whom he met at MBI evening school. He served as youth pastor at Moody Church, then pastored briefly in Los Angeles; three years in Hudsonville, MI; Christian Fellowship Church, Hammond, IN (1957–63); and at Bethel Community Church, Chicago (1973–89). For years, he hosted a popular program on radio station WMBI in Chicago called *Morning Clock*, filled with interviews, wit and history, 1971–93. In fact, one year he won as a write-in candidate for a secular radio contest called "Who Makes Your Morning." In 2000, the Murfins moved to Nevada where Bob died of cancer complications.

E. Wayne Wall

Aug. 10, 1936
Langley, South Carolina

Dec. 21, 2003
Lexington, South Carolina

Assistant editor of *The Biblical Evangelist* and pastor of Whiteford Church, Lexington, SC. Wall was highly educated, studying in five major schools of higher learning. He succeeded as an author, songwriter, poet, speaker, editor, and writer. He was married to Virginia Roberta for 46 years. He started the Metropolitan Baptist Tabernacle in Columbia, SC, in an old fruit stand. It moved to the suburbs and changed its name to Whiteford Church and Schools. He had the first church bus ministry in Columbia and hosted a radio, later television, program. Agreeing in philosophies with Robert Sumner, he was asked to take an active roll in the *Biblical Evangelist*.

Rueben H. Huenemann

Jan. 15, 1909
Waukon, Iowa

Dec. 23, 2003
Portland, Oregon

First president of United Theological Seminary, New Brighton, MN, 1960–70. The Huenemann family moved to Wisconsin in 1913. They moved to South Dakota in June, 1927, where he was a rural schoolteacher in Hutchinson County, 1927–29. He took schooling at Luther College, Decorah, Iowa and also at Mission House Seminary. He married Clara E. James on August 19, 1936 (died: August 17, 1999). Huenemann pastored Salem Reformed Church, St. Louis, MO (1938–44); Zion Evangelical and Reformed Church, Lodi, CA (1944–54); and Faith United Church of Christ (1954–60). From 1976–86, he served as interim minister in several churches in Minnesota, Washington, California, Nebraska, Oregon, Idaho, Mississippi, and Florida. From 1981–89, he represented the United Church of Christ at "Kirchentag" (Hamburg, Hannover, Dusseldorf, Leipzig) He preached his last sermon at Moreland Union Manor in Portland on March 18, 2001.

Vestal Goodman

Dec. 13, 1929
Fyffe, Alabama

Dec. 27, 2003

Gospel singer, Vestal Goodman became a Southern Gospel legend. Reared in the rich gospel music tradition around Sand Mountain, AL, she married HOWARD GOODMAN in 1949 and started the Singing Goodman Family. Fans across America best knew her through the group's subsequent appearances on the *Gospel Singing Jubilee* and on the PTL television network. Distinguished by her strong, powerful voice, Vestal reached the top of the Southern Gospel Music industry. With the Happy Goodman's popular rise in the mid-1980s, she remained the "Queen of Gospel Music" in the minds of many for the remainder of the twentieth century. "Rock of Ages" was a musical treat for everyone. Her funeral was January 1 at Christ Church, Nashville.

W. Jake Hess

Dec. 24, 1927
Linestone County, Alabama

Jan. 4, 2004
Opelika, Alabama

Gospel singer. Jake Hess started singing gospel music with a family group, the Hess Brothers, when he was just five years old. After singing with several other local groups, he accepted his first professional position, at the age of 16, with the legendary John Daniel Quartet. He served brief stints in the late 1940s with the Sunny South Quartet and the Melody Masters. In December, 1948, Jake joined the Statesmen and, over the next few years, cemented his place in Southern Gospel Music as a premier lead vocalist. Late in 1963, he left the Statesmen to form the Imperials. Forced to retire four years later (1968) due to persistent health problems, Jake sang on—forming his own family group, The Sound of Youth, and, in the early 1980s, filled a spot as one of the original Masters V. Hess sang at Elvis Presley's funeral in 1977, as he had at country legend, Hank Williams' funeral in 1953. Through the end of the century, Jake continued as one of Southern Gospel's most-distinctive stylists and best-loved personalities. Popular songs recorded: "Faith Unlocks the Door," "What a Wonderful World," "Faith," "I Believe in a Mansion in the Sky." Presley greatly admired Hess. A resident of Columbus, GA, since 1993, he suffered a heart attack on December 16, 2003. His funeral service was held January 7 at Morningside Baptist Church.

Jonathan Chao

Aug. 22, 1938
Chunggu, China

Jan. 12, 2004
West Covina, California

Founder and first director of China Ministries, Int., Pasadena, CA 1987–2004. He was director of the Christianity and China Research Center and a strong defender of China's house-church movement. He came to America in 1958. Chao married Rebecca Cheng in 1965. He counseled key national leaders. He had a four-month battle with lymphoma.

Darius S. Madden

Sept. 11, 1921
Athens, Texas

Jan. 16, 2004
Texarkana, Texas

Secretary/treasurer (CEO) of American Baptist Missionary Committee, Texarkana, 1980–1995. Madden pastored in Texas, Arkansas, Louisiana, and California. He pastored the Grace Missionary Baptist Church in Anaheim, CA 1966–80. He also taught at the California Missionary Baptist Institute there. He was active in WWII and part of the Allied landing force at Anzio Beach, Italy on January 22, 1944. He was a member of County Avenue Baptist Church in Texarkana and was married to his wife, Dorothy Sue, on Feruary. 18, 1946, for 59 years.

Charles V. Weber

Oct. 29, 1906
Rolla, Missouri

Jan. 21, 2004
San Diego, California

Executive secretary of Church of God, Anderson, IN 1960–71. Weber began his CG ministry in several pastorates: Creswell, OR (1925); Cottage Grove, OR (1926–27); Athens, OH (1928–1930); Moundsville, WV (1930–33); Oak Hill, WV (1933–35) and Pomona, CA (1935–41). He was an evangelist, 1941–44. Later pastorates included Bethany Church, Detroit (1944–48); Decatur, IL (1950) and San Diego, CA (1957–60). He and his wife, Roberta, were married on March 31, 1955 and held stewardship conferences across the nation for a short time. He edited the monthly *Abundant Life* magazine for 13 years. From 1948–60, he was an associate of C. W. Hatch, his predecessor. He retired to Fallbrook, CA, and his funeral was held at the Oceanside (CA) Community Church.

Bruce D. Cummons

July 25, 1924
Parkersburg, West Virginia

Jan. 24, 2004
Massillon, Ohio

Founder and pastor of Massillon Baptist Temple, he served over 40 years, also starting a Christian school and College. The church, founded Nov. 19, 1950, grew to 4,000 members with 1,200 in Sunday School. Early on, Cummons attended Bible Baptist Seminary of Fort Worth, TX, and was trained under J. FRANK NORRIS and LOUIS ENTZMINGER. He authored over 35 books and booklets and was editor of the *Baptist Reporter*. Cummons conducted over 250 revival meetings and, for 20 years, hosted the *Grace and Peace Hour* radio broadcast on some 45 stations. He and his wife, Wanda, were married for 56 years.

Bebe H. Patten

Sept. 3, 1913
Waverly, Tennessee

Jan. 25, 2004
Oakland, California

Founder and first president of Patten College (University), **Oakland, CA, 1944–82, and evangelist**. Patten preached in 38 states, 1931 to 1944. She founded Christian Evangelical Churches of America, Inc. (1944), Christian Cathedral (1944), and Patten Academy of Christian Education (1945). She conducted a highly successful crusade in Oakland, California during which she was inspired to build an institute for the training of evangelists and Christian workers. She founded the Oakland Bible Institute, which became Patten College and then Patten University. She taught there until just seven months before she passed away. She also pastored Christian Cathedral from its founding until her final few months.

Oran H. Griffith

Nov. 24, 1914
Gary, Texas

Jan. 28, 2004
Laneville, Texas

Editor-in-chief of American Baptist Association Publications Texarkana, TX 1955–80, the top post in the movement which selects their presidents annually. Griffith was saved at Mt. Bethel MBC in Gary, TX, in 1928. He married Alice M. Bradbury on Jan. 13, 1935. From 1936–48, he pastored small rural churches in Panola and Rusk counties. In 1948, he took his first full time pastorate at White Oak, TX, where he stayed till 1955. Griffith also pastored the Lowell St. Baptist Church in Texarkana until 1985. He returned to Laneville, TX, in 1985, to retire where he had graduated from high school years before.

Nora Lam

May 26, 1909
Shanghai, China

Feb. 2, 2004
San Jose, California

Chinese evangelist, who pioneered missionary ministry for women. Lam fled her native Shanghai as a refugee in 1958. She is best known for her book *China Cry*, which chronicles her suffering under Communist persecution. This was later turned into a movie. She immigrated to the US in 1966. Her ministries included distributing Bibles, saving orphaned babies, and helping persecuted believers. She had five children, two of whom are adopted. She died in a nursing home, following a stroke six months earlier.

G. Arthur Woolsey

Dec. 1, 1913
New Albany, Pennsylvania

Feb. 8, 2004
Sebring, Florida (?)

President of Baptist Bible College and Seminary, Johnson City, NY, 1960–67 and Clark Summit, PA 1967–70. Woolsey was converted at a revival meeting in his early teens. He pastored three small churches in Pennsylvania (1934–36): the Broad Acres Community (Central Baptist) Church, Binghamton, NY (1936–44); FBC, North Tonawanda, NY (1945–52); Walnut Street Baptist, Waterloo, IA (1952–59); and Brown Street Baptist, Alton, IL (1959–60). In 1970, he felt burdened to start a Baptist school in Florida. Soon Spurgeon Baptist Bible College, Mulberry, FL was developed (merged into Piedmont Bible College in 2002). He was married for over 50 years till his wife, Eldora, died in 1992. In 1995, he married his second wife, Dorothy. He died of pneumonia.

Dolphus Price

July 17, 1919
Falkville, Alabama

Feb. 10, 2004
Pinehurst, North Carolina

Evangelist. Early on, he pastored and held some revivals, 1938–50. After being challenged at a *Sword of the Lord* conference in 1950, he went into evangelistic work and held crusades throughout the country, 1950–81. An early crusade was in Decatur, AL, with 119 conversions. He was one of the founders of Baptist International Missions Inc. When diagnosed with cancer, he pastored Bensalem Baptist Church, Philadelphia, 1981–86. He resigned January 23, 1986, and re-entered the evangelistic field until poor health curtailed his activities.

Claude R. Rickman

Nov. 10, 1917
Transylvania County, North Carolina

Feb. 13, 2004
Seneca, South Carolina

President of Southern Wesleyan University, Central, SC 1968–79. Rickman served in the U.S. Navy in WWII and retired after 25 years of active and reserve duty as a Lt. Commander. He was married 62 years to his wife, the former Evelyn Tucker, whom he married on January 1, 1942. He pastored in Gastonia, NC 1948–50. He was involved in many facets of the Wesleyan Church of America, highlighted by his 42 years of service to SWU. He was professor, academic dean, alumni director and special assistant to the president when not serving as president. In 1968, he insisted on allowing a black student from Africa to enroll, making it the first private college in the state to admit a black. He died after an illness of nearly three years. Funeral services were held February 16 at First Wesleyan Church in Central, SC.

William E. Crumes

March 8, 1914
Louisville, Kentucky

March 7, 2004
Cincinnati, Ohio

Bishop of the Church of the Living God, Cincinnati, OH 1979–2003. Crumes married Dorothy Marshall on May 21, 1934. Early on, he was a licensed barber. Living in Louisville, KY, he moved to Cincinnati in 1948 to pastor upon being ordained. In 1958 he became a bishop. He was general secretary (1950–62) and vice-chief bishop (1962–79). He was responsible for a new national headquarters building of the Church of the Living God.

Johnny Hope

May 7, 1918
Paul's Valley, Oklahoma

Mar. 29, 2004
Oklahoma City, Oklahoma

Singer, organize, and efficient YFC director. Hope spent his youth with his family in the oil fields of northeast Oklahoma. He began his music career with guitar playing and singing vocals. He joined Steve Pringle, evangelist, and assisted in various revivals. Hope married Evelyn Hankins. He directed Youth for Christ in Oklahoma City, OK; Elkhart, IN; and finally Oakland, CA. He was later associated with Oral Roberts' ministry and then that of Rex Humbard. He and his second wife, Wilma, lived out their days in Oklahoma City.

Dale Oldham

March 30, 1903
Ripley, Oklahoma

April 2, 2004
Anderson, Indiana

Church of God (Anderson, IN) pastor and radio minister. Oldham was converted at age 16 in a friend's garage in Indianapolis, IN. He married Pauline E. Brown on August 26, 1924. From 1925–45, he pastored in Cynthiana, KY; Akron, IN; Lima and Dayton, OH. Oldham pastored the Park Place Church of God, Anderson, IN, from 1945–62. For more than 20 years, he was the radio minister of the *Christian Brotherhood Hour*, a special network program that was broadcast weekly around the world. In later years, he served as an evangelist working out of Eustis, FL. He authored a number of books, including *Living Close to God* and *Give Me Tomorrow*. He was the president of Gospel Trumpet Company (now Warner Press), 1947–58. He was the father of Doug Oldham, a popular soloist. He wrote the lyrics for "Something Worth Living For" (music by Bill Gaither).

Daniel C. Bultema

April 17, 1918
Muskegan, Michigan

April 16, 2004
Grand Rapids, Michigan

Executive Director of Grace Mission (Ministry International in 1984), **1967–84**, the missionary arm of Grace Gospel Fellowship. He married Margaret Timmer on May 8, 1941 (died: August 2006). Bultema left the business world in Muskegon, MI, and went to Milwaukee to train at Grace College, serving as assistant pastor at Fundamental Bible Church also. He pastored several churches, including Berean Bible Church, Holland, MI. Bultema worked with Gospel Films, and then began his ministry at Grace Mission in 1967. He saw the merger of Bethesda Mission and Grace Mission to form Grace Ministries International. He continued to serve in the office of this work until two weeks before his death of congestive heart failure.

Richard E. Blanchard

1925
Chungking, China

April 19, 2004
Swannanoa, North Carolina

Gospel songwriter, pastor, Blanchard wrote the lyrics and music for "Fill My Cup Lord." Born to Methodist missionary parents, the family returned to the States where he grew up in Indiana and North Carolina. He married Anne Carlton in 1947. Transferring to the Florida Conference in 1950 (from Georgia), he had 40 years of ministry at the following congregations: First Methodist, Orlando; Wesley Trinity Methodist, Miami; Palma Ceia Methodist Temple; First Methodist, Jacksonville; Riviera Beach Methodist, Community Methodist, Holiday, and Conway Methodist, Orlando. The Palma Ceia congregation had 3,000 members. He visited every home in the church during his first year. He wrote numerous gospel songs and traveled in over 75 countries. His health began to decline and they moved to be near their children.

William H. Weiben

March 2, 1919
Miller, South Dakota

April 19, 2004
Dubuque, Iowa

President of Wartburg Theological Seminary, Dubuque, IA, 1971–83. Weiben married Ilah Anderson on May 30, 1943. Pastorates followed in Trinity Lutheran Church, Bryan, OH (1943–50) and St. Paul's Lutheran Church, Waverly, IA (1953–58). From 1950–53, he was chaplain in the U.S. Air Force, serving one year in Korea. Weiben began to teach at the seminary in 1960. He taught systematic theology part-time at Wartburg in his latter years.

Jack Hamilton

June 17, 1919
Kansas City, Montana

April 25, 2004
Camarillo, California

Pioneer leader of Youth for Christ high school Bible Club movement. Hamilton received assurance of his salvation in Central Bible Church, Kansas City, at age 19. He married Mary Jean Weir on April 17, 1942, in Seattle while in military service. He began to work with Al Metsker in Kansas City YFC (1943–48), then went to the Detroit program (1948–50). YFC high school Bible Clubs started across the country because of his leadership, 1948–60, as he worked out of the YFCI headquarters in Wheaton, IL. Nationwide Bible quizzing developed under his leadership. One year alone, 100,000 teens were studying the Book of John. From 1960–69, he directed San Fernando, California, YFC. He worked briefly with Dick Ross and Dick Benware on selected projects, then became southern regional director of YFC, 1978–85, living in Miami and then Rome, GA. Health problems forced their final move to Camarillo in 1996, where he worked in his own church, Trinity Presbyterian, until his death.

Dick Darr

Jan. 21, 1926
Akron, Ohio

April 26, 2004
Akron, Ohio

President of Gospel Missionary Union (Avant Ministries in 2004), **Kansas City, MO, 1978–91**. Darr married Anne Koehl on October 12, 1946. He served, 1954–59, with United World Mission, then came to Gospel Missionary Union on November 5, 1959. He served in Mali (1959–67), then three years as East Coast representative of GMU (1967-70), returning to Mali until 1972. From 1972-78, he was vice president of administrative affairs. When he took office as president, the mission had just merged with the Evangelical Union of South America. He helped strengthen home-end administration. Seven hundred thirty-five churches comprised the supporting family when he took office. It had reached more than 1,200 when he retired.

Gleason Archer

May 22, 1916
Norwell, Massachusetts

April 27, 2004
Sterling, Kansas

Outstanding scholar, apologist and author. He married Virginia Atkinson on May 11, 1939 (died: August 26, 1962) and Sandra Larson on March 21, 1964. He was ordained in the Presbyterian Church in the U.S. in 1945, and transferred to the Evangelical Free Church in 1966. He was professor of biblical languages, Fuller Seminary, Pasadena, CA, 1948-65. He taught OT and Semetics at Trinity Evangelical Divinity School, 1965-86, 89-91. He spoke many languages. He wrote the *Encyclopedia of Biblical Difficulties* and *A Survey of Old Testament Literature Introduction*. He was a member of the steering committee of the International Council on Biblical Inerrancy. He was considered the intellectual father of the inerrancy movement. Funeral services were held May 3 at North Suburban Evangelical Free Church, Deerfield, IL.

J. Grady Parrott

Nov. 29, 1908
northern Virginia

May 2, 2004

President of Mission Aviation Fellowship, 1947–67. In 1942, Parrott joined the US Army Air Corps as an advanced flight instructor. He helped train British RAF pilots at Falcon Field outside of Phoenix, AZ. In 1945, he contacted a new organization called Christian Airmen's Missionary Fellowship, which was led by Jim Truxton and **Betty Greene**. With the name change, he molded MAF into a world-wide movement. At the time of his death, MAF had 62 airplanes in 16 countries, flying 3.2 million miles annually, supporting 600 Christian and humanitarian organizations. Their two largest programs were in Indonesia. His wife of 70 years died December 24, 2003. Parrott died shortly thereafter of pneumonia.

Lowell C. Wendt

Nov. 11, 1917
Colorado

May 11, 2004
Seattle, Washington

President of Independent Fundamental Churches of America, 1960–63, 1969–72. Wendt was converted as a young boy, attended BIOLA, married Marie Gunther in 1943, and began pastoral ministry at Montecito Park Union Church. Their pastoral ministry stretched 47 years at such places as Lake City Community Church, Hope Union Church, Reinhardt Bible Church, and Alderwood Community Church, where a memorial service was held.

John A. Huffman

Feb. 12, 1912
Dayton, Ohio

May 22, 2004
Carol Stream, Illinois

President of Winona Lake (IN) School of Theology, 1953–70. Huffman was the son of JASPER A. HUFFMAN whom he followed as president. He was married in 1935 to Dorothy Bricker. Huffman directed Boston, MA, YFC, 1944–54. He served on various church staffs as interim, assistant, associate, counseling, and visitation pastor from 1971 into the 1990s. He was the last living member of the NAE's founding committee and was the founding editor of their *Action* magazine. He conducted a daily radio program, 1939–51, in Boston reaching the entire New England area.

Stanley W. Chambers

July 20, 1915
Columbus, Ohio

June 2, 2004
Dexter, Missouri

General superintendent of United Pentecostal Church, Hazelwood, MO 1968–78. He married Catherine Strepka on September 7, 1940. Chambers pastored in Haselton, PA (1943–45), then was general secretary-treasurer of the UPC, St. Louis (1945–67). The denomination moved to Hazelwood in 1970 under his leadership.

Ronald Reagan

Feb. 6, 1911
Tampico, Illinois

June 5, 2004
Los Angeles, California

40th president of the United States, 1980–88. Reagan defeated Jimmy Carter, 489-49 in electoral college votes in 1980 and Walter Mondale, 535-13, in 1984, becoming one of the most popular presidents ever. His early contributions were in the entertainment industry as a sports announcer, motion picture and TV actor. His first film was in 1937. He married Jane Wyman on January 25, 1940 (divorced in 1948) and Nancy Davis on March 4, 1952. He hosted the TV series, *Death Valley Days*. (1962–66) and then served as governor of California (1967–74). Numerous honors came to him from many sources, especially in the area of patriotism. He was a member of Bel Air (CA) Presbyterian Church. Highlights of Reagan's presidency include the destruction of the Berlin Wall and the final thawing of the cold war with Russia as communism disintegrated. His Christian moral foundation influenced his tough stands. His strong leadership was marked by ease in taking the heat of controversy, wisdom in delegating, maintaining his humor, and being a great communicator. Reagan had a lasting impact on the world's economic future by changing tax policies, taming inflation and promoting free trade policies, although budget deficits grew. It was quite a jump from movie stardom to free-world leadership, but he made it most successfully.

Walter G. Muelder

March 1, 1907
Boody, Illinois

June 12, 2004
Boston, Massachusetts

Dean of Boston (MA) University School of Theology, 1945–72. As dean, his reputation as the pioneer of social ethics attracted respected scholars and leaders of world religions to join the faculty and broaden the school's instruction in world religion and philosophy. He doubled the size of the faculty. During Muelder's tenure, the school moved from its isolated location of Beacon Hill to its Commonwealth Avenue site. He made training more accessible to African-American church leaders. He led in nonviolence and civil rights activities. He was a Methodist pastor, educator, philosopher, and a social activist. He was an inspiration to MARTIN LUTHER KING. Albert Einstein publicly praised Muelder's "Idea of a Responsible Society." He married Martha Grotewohl on June 28, 1934. They were together for 63 years. They often held Friday night social gatherings for his students. After retirement, he taught a year at Berea (KY) College where he had started his teaching career in 1934. He died of a heart attack.

Walter H. J. Lang

Nov. 3, 1913
Omaha, Nebraska

July 10, 2004
Seattle, Washington

Founder and president of Creation Moments, Zimmerman (Foley), MN, 1960–80. He married Valeria Wessler in August, 1940 (died: January, 1999) Lang was ordained in April, 1940, as pastor of St. Paul Lutheran Church, Denton, TX. He pastored the black mission congregations of Holy Cross and Mt. Calvary in Houston, TX. In 1950, Lang pastored in Winslow, NE; then at Mt. Calvary, Denver, CO, and finally, at Grace Lutheran, Caldwell, ID. At this time, he felt led to leave pastoring and begin a full-time ministry in Creationism. Lang began the *Bible Science Newsletter* and traveled all over the US and in 26 countries spreading the Word through creation science. In many ways, he fathered the Creationism movement. The headquarters moved to Minneapolis in 1978. He and his wife began a ministry called Genesis Institute. They moved to Seattle in 1997. A funeral service was held there at the Lutheran Church of the Atonement on July 13.

James D. Glasse

Jan. 8, 1924
Prosser, Washington

July 11, 2004
Orind, California

President of Lancaster (PA) Theological Seminary, 1970–82. Glasse was ordained into the United Presbyterian Church (USA) in 1950. He began his career in North Carolina (1950–52) and Tennessee (1956–57). Glasse was on staff at Yale Divinity School, 1953–56. He then became a faculty member of Vanderbilt University, Nashville, TN, 1956–70, as professor of practical theology. Upon leaving Lancaster, he was interim pastor in Wilmington, DE; Pittsburgh, PA; Baltimore, MD; and Fairfax, VA. His first wife was Joan Steele Rowe. He later married Cherrie Poe Chichester in 1992. He wrote four books.

Francis W. J. W. Peck

Feb. 21, 1923
Kansas City, Kansas

July 20, 2004
Sapulpa, Oklahoma

President of Full Gospel Grace Fellowship, Tulsa, OK, 1984–2004. Graduating from Grace and Glory College, Kansas City (Mountain Grove), MO, Peck served as pastor in Oklahoma, Texas, and Pennsylvania for 28 years. He married Virginia Berryhill on May 27, 1944. Returning to Oklahoma in 1981, he taught in Grace Fellowship College, Broken Arrow, OK, and pastored the Bristow (OK) Gospel Tabernacle.

James W. Crumpton

May 17, 1918
Pelzer, South Carolina

July 22, 2004
Dallas, Texas

President of Maranatha Baptist Mission, Inc., Natchez, MS 1971–99. Crumpton was a farm boy, converted on August 14, 1935. He married Jennie L. Moore, on June 2, 1940 and began his pastoral ministry at West Side Baptist Church, Natchez, MS in 1941. In 1961, he and Mel Rutter started MBM. Rutter directed it the first ten years. For many years, Crumpton had a radio broadcast, *The Radio Revival Hour*. He also edited the *Maranatha* publication. Health caused retirement in 1999.

Richard A. LeTourneau

Jan. 3, 1925
Stockton, California

Aug. 3, 2004
Longview, Texas

President of LeTourneau College, Longview, TX, 1961–68, 1975–85. Richard was the son of Christian businessman, R. G. LE TOURNEAU, and became the president of his family's earth-moving machinery company, R. G. LeTourneau, Inc. He was an author and educator at LC.

The enrollment rose from 435 to over 1,000 under his leadership. In 1966, he took over the presidency of the company, later guiding the sale of the $70 million heavy equipment and off-shore jack-up rig manufacturer to Marathon Manufacturing Company. His family donated great sums of money to worthy causes around the world.

Charles E. Hummel

Aug. 8, 1923   *Aug. 16, 2004*

President of Barrington (RI) (Gordon in 1985) **College, 1965–75**. Hummel graduated from Yale University in 1944 with a degree in chemical engineering and a month later went into service in World War II. He had a lifelong interest in the relationship between science and religion and wrote two books. Many advances developed in his ten-year presidency as social and sports opportunities evolved. The Music Department received accreditation from the National Association of Schools of Music in 1969. The rest of his career was working for Inter-Varsity, where he served as interim director in the early 1960s and retired in 1988 as director of faculty ministries. He was a board member of the Episcopal Renewal Ministries. He wrote a booklet, *Tyranny of the Urgent*, that sold 1.2 million copies.

J. Irwin Miller

May 26, 1909   *Aug. 16, 2004*
Columbus, Indiana   New York, New York

President of National Council of Churches, 1960–63, the first layperson to hold the position. He married Xenia R. Simons on February 5, 1943. He worked with the Cummins Engine Company of Columbus, beginning as vice-president and general manager (1934–42), executive vice-president (1944–47), president (1947–51), and board chairman thereafter. Under his leadership, the company developed into 25,000 employees in 131 countries and $6 billion in annual sales. He was president of Irwin-Union Bank and Trust Company, 1947–54. Combating poverty and racism was especially important to him. In 1963 under his leadership, the NCC founded the Commission on Religion and Race. ML KING called him "the most socially responsible businessman in the country."

David W. Wiman

Aug. 31, 1910   *Aug. 16, 2004*
Oblong, Illinois   Paducah, Kentucky

Stated clerk of Cumberland Presbyterian Church, Memphis, TN 1945–54. Wiman was ordained August 26, 1932 and pastored in Illinois, Kentucky, and Tennessee, 1932–38. He served with the former Board of Tithing and Budget of the denomination (1938–44). He married Helen Bright on May 27, 1941, and pastored a church in Chattanooga, TN; the Morning Sun Church, Arlington, TN; the East Side Church, Memphis, TN; Margaret Hank Cumberland Presbyterian Church, Paducah, KY (nine years); and the Sturgis (KY) Cumberland Presbyterian Church (nearly 5 years). He was a Mason for 63 years. He wrote *History of the Colored Cumberland Presbyterian Church*, 1936.

Stephen Olford

March 29, 1918   *Aug. 29, 2004*
Zambia   Memphis, Tennessee

Bible teacher, founder and head of Encounter Ministries, Memphis, TN, 1970–96. Raised by missionary parents in Angola, Olford came to Christ early. During World War II, he launched Young Peoples Christian Fellowship in Newport, South Wales. After the war, he was involved in evangelism and preaching throughout the UK. He pastored the Duke Street Baptist Church, Richmond, England, 1953–59. Then came the call to Calvary Baptist Church, NYC, which he served, 1959–73.

He started a TV and radio program called *Encounter* and moved to Memphis in 1985 to develop a training program to encourage and equip preachers and teachers of God's Word. Olford led a powerful, Christ-centered ministry featuring exposition of Scripture. He served as a mentor and model to thousands of Christian workers, authoring numerous books and preaching resources.

Marion DeVelder

Jan. 28, 1912
Boyden, Iowa

Sept. 2, 2004
Holland, Michigan (?)

Stated clerk of General Synod, 1961–68, and first General Secretary of Reformed Church in America, 1968–77. He married Edith Wandscheer on August 15, 1935. DeVelder pastored for many years in Churchville, PA; Grand Rapids, MI and at Hope Church, Holland, MI, for nearly 20 years, where his memorial service was held. He was an ecumenical pioneer for the RCA building strong links to the WCC and other groups seeking unity of the church. A memorial service was held in Holland, MI, on September 8.

Joe V. Hotchkiss

Aug. 25, 1926
Niles, Ohio

Sept. 4, 2004
Westerville, OH

Executive director of International Council of Community Churches, 1966–81. He was the first and only layperson to serve as executive director. Hotchkiss served in WWII. He was chaplain to the Ohio House of Representatives, and the Ohio Senate. He was a former NFL official. His wife, the former Lillian Schifler, preceded him in death. A memorial service was held September 12 at the Gahanna (OH) Community Church.

Woodrow G. Goodman

Aug. 21, 1918
Olive Hill, Kentucky

Sept. 5, 2004
Upland, California

Founder and first president of Bethel College, Mishawaka, IN, 1947–59; president of Marion (IN) College 1960–76. Goodman graduated from Marion College (Indiana Wesleyan University) in 1939. . He married Marie Everest (born January 14, 1915) of Elkhart, IN September 30, 1939. She died within a month of her husband. He pastored Mennonite Brethren in Christ churches (Missionary Church) in northern Indiana and southern Michigan. He was one of four to incorporate World Missionary Press, which published 50 million scripture booklets annually. His brother, WATSON GOODMAN, directed that work. From 1976–83, he worked for Friends University, Wichita, KS as Institutional Research and Planning Associate. He moved to California in 1983, continuing to work part-time for Friends University until 1988.

Eddy S. Cline

May 21, 1933
Muncie, Indiana

Sept. 16, 2004
Muncie, Indiana

Director of CSI (Christian Service International), Muncie, IN 1978–2001. Cline married Shirley Pomeroy on Nov. 27, 1952. From 1962–1978, he pastored three Friends churches. After his CSI retirement, he worked at Farmland IN Friends Church as Senior Adult Minister. His funeral services were held there on Sept. 19. He had a long battle with liver cancer which took his life.

Harold R. Henninger

May 4, 1924
Doylestown, Ohio

October 25, 2004
Canton, Ohio

Longtime pastor of the Canton (OH) Baptist Temple, 1943–2004. Henninger was converted at age 15 under the preaching of DALLAS BILLINGTON at the Akron (OH) Baptist Temple. He served in the US Army in 1943 and married Carmine Sims on April 2, 1943. Upon going to Canton, he followed the usual type of outreach known to many Baptists as door-to-door visitation. The first service in 1943 grew to thousands. It became the fifth largest church in America by 1947. In 1963 the church moved to a new location on Whipple Avenue. A great missionary program developed which took him to many countries of the world. Lying in a hospital bed, recovering from a heart attack in November, 1964, he turned on the radio after reading Hebrews 11 and heard a report mentioning the Football Hall of Fame in his city. He decided to duplicate it with a Christian Hall of Fame which opened April 12, 1964. Today there are 104 paintings engraved on the corridor walls of the church. His life verse was Joshua 1:9.

Ted A. Lane

May 13, 1913
Duluth, Minnesota

Nov. 7, 2004
San Diego, California

Director of Assemblies of God Int. Fellowship, San Diego, CA 1986–2004. Lane was converted at age 15 at a Salvation Army meeting. At 21, he married Mildred and moved to Hibbing, MN. In 1940, he became a staff member at the Philadelphia Church, DeKalb, IL until 1951, when he moved back to Duluth to found the Calvary Temple Church. In 1964, Lane moved to San Diego to start a printing and publishing complex known as Master Productions. His wife died in January, 2003. Lane felt churches should be independent with no denominational headquarters. This distanced him from most Assembly of God leaders. A memorial service was held February 2–3, 2005, in San Diego.

Louis L. King

Nov. 30, 1915
Hurffville, New Jersey

Nov. 11, 2004
Ft. Myers, Florida

President of EFMA, 1963–64, and of Christian Missionary and Alliance, 1978–87 and its missions director, 1956–78. He was a leading missionary statesman in the movement. King was converted at a camp meeting at age 14. He married Esther L. Martz on April 14, 1939. He pastored churches in New York, Illinois, and Nebraska before going to India as a missionary from 1946–53. He often traveled 100,000 miles a year in behalf of world missions.

Billy J. Hargis

Aug. 3, 1925
Texarkana, Texas

Nov. 27, 2004
Tulsa, Oklahoma

Evangelist and anti-Communist fighter. Hargis was ordained by the Disciples of Christ in 1943. In 1950, he started his Christian Crusade and was one of the first evangelists to capitalize in television usage. He was married for 52 years to his wife, Betty Jane Secrest, whom he married on Dec. 21, 1951. From 1953–57, he floated a million hydrogen balloons carrying Scriptures, launched from West Germany into Communist countries. Overflowing with words and big ideas, he trumpeted them forth over 500 radio and 250 television stations, in films, books, gospel records, and from the pulpit in campaigns from the Holy Land to Los Angeles. His strong over-emphasis against Communism put him at odds with both secular and religious leaders. When the Disciples of Christ dropped him in 1966, he started the Church of the Christian Crusade, the American Christian College, and the David Livingston Missionary Foundation. His Christian Crusade had a $2 billion budget in 1972, solicited from his 250,000 mailing list. The college closed in 1977.

Rodney Sawatsky

Dec. 5, 1943
Manitoba, Canada

Nov. 27, 2004
Waterloo, Ontario, Canada

President of Messiah College, 1994–2004. He married Lorna Ewert in 1964. He was educated in both Canadian and American schools. Sawatsky served as president of Conrad Grebel College, Waterloo, Ontario, 1989–94, following other roles at the college. His key interests were religion, history and higher education. He died of a cancerous brain tumor. Funeral services were held December 1 at First United Church, Waterloo.

Mary Lee Daugherty

Sept. 16, 1934
Bluefield, West Virginia

Dec. 4, 2004
South Charleston, West Virginia

Founder and first director of Appalachian Ministries Educational Resource Center, Berea, KY 1985– 99. Daugherty's career began as a laywoman with the Presbyterian Church of Brazil. She taught at Morris Harvey College, 1967–83. She was a guest lecturer at Harvard Divinity School, 1977–79. Her AMERC was a consortium of 88 theological institutions from 52 denominations to train clergy and lay leaders for ministry in the Appalachian region. A memorial service was held December 12, at First Presbyterian Church, Charleston, WV.

Jay Van Andel

June 3, 1924
Grand Rapids, Michigan

Dec. 7, 2004
Grand Rapids, Michigan

Cofounder, with Richard DeVos, of the Amway Corporation in 1959. Early on, he was engaged in aviation, restaurant, and mail order businesses. He served in the Air Force, 1943–1946. VanAndel married Betty Hoekstra on August 16, 1952. She died in January 2004. The Amway story became one of the great American enterprises. It started in the basement of a home and became one of the largest businesses in his generation, providing a variety of products to consumers. DeVos became president and VanAndel, chairman of the board. In just ten years, by 1969, there were 100,000 distributors. He was active in his Christian Reformed Church in Grand Rapids. His Van Andel Institute handled his charitable giving.

Billy Murray

April 8, 1930
Nash County, North Carolina

Dec. 8, 2004
Charlotte, North Carolina

General overseer of Church of God of Prophecy, Cleveland, TN 1990–2000. Murray accepted Christ as a child and married Orna Lee Hensley on August 13, 1949. He pastored in Selma, Leaksville and Bethany, NC, then in Greenville, SC, in 1966. He served as Overseer of Tennessee (1972–77) then became assistant editor of the *White Wing Messenger*, (1977–89). During his tenure, the CGP expanded from 90 countries to over 120 and membership grew from 261,641 to 546,600. It is felt that he influenced the denomination into a more harvest-oriented direction.

"Christ is the message; the church is the messenger."

Edmund Robb

Sept. 14, 1926
Marshall, Texas

Dec. 15, 2004
Marshall, Texas

Methodist church evangelist and director of a foundation for theological education, Woodlands, TX 1978–92. Robb founded the Institute on Religion and Democracy in 1981. DIANNE KNIPPERS, the president, said Robb stood for the renewal of mainline churches and was against the spread of Soviet totalitarianism around the world. He served in the U.S. Navy in WWII. Ordained as a Methodist, he pastored and served as an evangelist for 50 years. He wrote *Betrayal of the Church*.

Roy L. Honeycutt

Oct. 30, 1926
Grenada, Mississippi

Dec. 21, 2004
Louisville, Kentucky

President of Southern Baptist Theological Seminary, Louisville, KY, 1982–93. Honeycutt married June Williams on August 31, 1948. Prior to joining SBTS, he pastored Scobey (MS) Baptist Church, Underwood (IN) Baptist Church, New Palm Baptist Church, Bardstown, KY and FBC, Princeton. He served as deacon of the School of Theology at the seminary (1975–80), was provost there (1976–82), and chancellor of the seminary from 1994 until the time of his death.

Marion D. Barnes

May 20, 1913
Junction City, Alabama

Dec. 22, 2004

President of Covenant College, Lookout Mountain, GA, 1965–78. Barnes married Vera Oltz (June 20, 1942). He began his career teaching physical and inorganic chemistry at the university level. He then worked as a research chemist at El Dorado, AR, and as a research administrator in St. Louis, MO. For five years, he served as chairman of the board of trustees of Covenant College and Seminary leading its relocation from St. Louis to Lookout Mountain in 1969. During his tenure, the campus property extended to hundreds of acres. He was active at Lookout Mountain Presbyterian Church. Beginning in 1984, he helped develop Daystar University, a Christian school in Kenya, into a university with thousands attending.

William H. Hinson

1936

Dec. 26, 2004

Conservative Methodist pastor. Hinson was the long ime pastor of the First Methodist Church, Houston, TX, until his retirement in 2001. He was one of the founders of the denomination's Confessing Movement, which represents 675,000 conservatives in Methodism. He served as its president until his death from complications of the massive stroke he suffered on November 28.

Reggie White

Dec. 19, 1961
Chattanooga, Tennessee

Dec. 26, 2004
Cornelius, South Carolina

Outstanding professional football player. White was the top NFL defensive player. He was the all-time leader in sacks for years, with 198, until Bruce Smith surpassed that record. He played 15 years with Philadelphia, Green Bay, and Carolina (1985–2000). He was elected to the Pro Bowl a record 13 consecutive times (1986–98). After eight years with Philadelphia, he signed as a free agent with Green Bay in 1993 for $17 million over four years. He worked tirelessly in the off-seasons with inner-city youth. He was outspoken about his Christian views, denouncing homosexuality, and was accused of using ethnic stereotypes. He was an associate pastor and prime investor in the Inner City Church of Knoxville, TN which burned on January 8, 1996. White suffered from a respiratory ailment for several years that affected his sleep. He died unexpectedly.

James L. Sullivan

March 12, 1910
Silver Creek, Mississippi

Dec. 27, 2004
Nashville, Tennessee

President of Southern Baptist Convention, 1976. Sullivan's greatest contribution, however, was as president of the Sunday School board (Lifeway Christian Resources), 1953–75. He gave wise leadership during the civil rights struggles of the 1950's and '60's, leading in the production of materials promoting the biblical view of human worth regardless of race. Beginning in 1932, he pastored churches in Kentucky (1932–38), Tennessee (1938–40, 46–50), Mississippi (1940–46), and Texas (1950–53). He married Velma Scott on October 22, 1935 (died: 1993). He wrote several books, beginning with *Your Life and Your Church* (1950). His memorial service was held at FBC, Nashville.

Stuart E. Lease

April 21, 1930
Jacobus, Pennsylvania

Dec. 28, 2004
Lakeland, Florida

President of Lancaster (PA) Bible College, 1961–79. Upon graduating from LBC in 1951, Lease pastored in North Eaton, Brockton, and Watertown, MA. He returned to LBC as dean in 1956. When he took the presidency in 1961, there were two buildings, less than 100 students, only six full-time faculty members and a library of 2,000 books. When he resigned, 17 years later, there were 36 acres, 15 buildings, more than 400 students, 20 full-time faculty, 34 full-time and eleven part-time staff and a library of 25,000 volumes. The name was changed from Lancaster School of the Bible to Lancaster Bible College in 1973. From 1980–83, he pastored the Faith Calvary Church in Lancaster. He also pastored the Faith Bible Chapel, Cochranville, PA, 1994–97, whereupon he moved to Florida. He was married to Barbara R. Rudisill for 55 years. His funeral was at Grace Baptist, Lancaster on January 8, 2005.

Philip Crouch

Dec. 6, 1916
Perry, Iowa

Jan. 20, 2005
Springfield, Missouri

President of Central Bible College, Springfield, MO 1963–80. He graduated from CBC in 1937 and was a missionary in Egypt, 1937–57. He then became a faculty member, 1957–63 of CBC. Crouch was responsible for the building of five buildings and left the college debt free. Total graduates under his leadership numbered 2,653. His subsequent ministry was station manager of Trinity Broadcasting Network, 1980–2002.

Decatur W. Nichols

Oct. 15, 1900
Charleston, SC

Jan. 24, 2005
Huntington Station, New York

Bishop of African Methodist Episcopal Church, 1940–76; senior bishop, 1969–76. Nichols lived to 104 years of age and was revered by all who knew him. He was ordained in Plainfield, NJ, in 1925. He began as pastor of Emmanuel Mission, New York City, with 18 members and an offering of $4.50. Emmanuel AMEC continued to grow, especially after a revival conducted by his father in 1927. He married Sarah K. Bailey in 1937. In 1940, he became the youngest bishop to ever be elected—and he would live to be the oldest as well. He was in Alabama (1940–48), then it was Philadelphia (1948–56), then came leadership in Florida (1956–64). He faced numerous financial challenges he was able to meet. He served in many capacities for years.

John H. Jacobson

Nov. 6, 1933
Evanston, Illinois

Feb. 8, 2005
Holland, Michigan

President of Hope College, Holland, MI 1987–99. During Jacobson's presidency at least five major building projects were finalized. Early on, he taught philosophy at Hamilton (NY) College and at Florida Presbyterian (Eckerd) College, St. Petersburg, FL. He then was active at Empire State College, State University of NY, Saratoga Springs, NY for many years. He was married to

Jeanne McKee for 50 years and he died of complications following a stroke. A memorial service was held at Siesta Key Chapel, Sarasota, FL on February 16.

Floyd B. Cherry

April 15, 1916
Dothan, Alabama

Feb. 22, 2005
Smithfield, North Carolina

Founder and first president of Carolina Bible Institute, Pine Level, NC 1975–90. Cherry was ordained in 1933 at age 17 with BOB JONES SR. preaching his ordination sermon. He married Edith Day on May 5, 1938. Cherry pastored in Alabama, Florida, and Georgia until moving to Durham, NC, in 1949. As pastor of Daniel's Chapel Free Will Baptist Church, near Wilson, NC, he taught adult classes starting CBI. After 1990, he pastored in Johnston County, NC.

Arthur H. Lewis

Aug. 25, 1923
Kalamazoo, Michigan

March 8, 2005
St. Paul, Minnesota

President of Evangelical Theological Society, 1973. Lewis was converted at age seven at Gull Lake (MI) Bible Conference. He was in the army air corps in WWII, flying 34 combat missions. He married his wife, Helen, whom he met at Wheaton College. He was a missionary to Portugal, author, and professor at Bethel University, Minneapolis, MN. He was also a translator of the New International Version of the Bible. He suffered a stroke during a trip to Iowa that left him partially paralyzed.

Nathaniel A. Urshan

Aug. 29, 1920
St. Paul, Minnesota

March 11, 2005
Indianapolis, Indiana

General superintendent of United Pentecostal Church International, Hazelwood, MO, 1978–2002. Urshan saw the "Oneness" Pentecostal denomination grow from 300,000 members to more than 4 million during his tenure. Beginning as a minor league baseball player, he suffered a near fatal bout with tuberculosis. Urshan then entered the ministry. He married Jean Habig on October 1, 1941. They were married for 63 years. He was the pastor of Calvary Tabernacle, Indianapolis, IN, 1949–78. The funeral was at Calvary Tabernacle on March 17.

Edward P. Clowney

July 30, 1917
Philadelphia, Pennsylvania

March 20, 2005
Charlottesville, Virginia

President of Westminster Theological Seminary, 1965–82, the first acting president of the school. He married Jean G. Wright on August 30, 1941. He pastored Orthodox Presbyterian churches in New Jersey, Illinois and Connecticut. He began work at Westminster, teaching practical theology, 1952–63. He wrote ten books including, *Preaching and Biblical Theology, Preaching Christ in All of Scripture, The Unfolding Ministry, Called to the Ministry* and *The Doctrine of the Church*. He was the anonymous author of *Christianity Today's*, "Eutichus" humor column in the 1950s. He died following a short illness.

Loren Sanny

Nov. 22, 1920

March 28, 2005
Colorado Springs, Colorado

Director of Navigators, 1956–1986. Sanny succeeded DAWSON TROTMAN when Daws suddenly drowned. He joined Navigators on Sept. 1, 1941, as a full-time staff member. For 15 years, he worked side by side with Trotman, including seven years "on loan" to the Billy Graham team developing follow-up materials and training counselors. He became a Christian, in 1938, while a student at Modesto (CA) Junior College. In 1943, he married Lucy Brooks. The ministry grew rapidly under his leadership with Navigators staff reaching 1,000 in 1973 and in 50 countries by 1982. From 1986–93, he was chairman of the board. He came down with pneumonia which took his life. He also had pancreatic cancer.

George Younce

Feb. 22, 1930
Patterson, North Carolina

April 11, 2005
Stow, Ohio

One of the great singers of his era (1964–99), Younce was the backbone of the Cathedral Quartet which became one of the most popular and influential gospel singing groups of all time. His father borrowed money to send him to the Stamps-Baxter School of Music in Dallas. His role as lead singer changed to that of bass singer, second only to J. D. SUMNER. He traveled five years with the Blue Ridge Quartet, and married Clara in 1955. In 1964, he joined three others at Rex Humbard's Cathedral of Tomorrow in Akron, OH and the Cathedral Quartet was born. His partners were Glen Payne, Bobby Clark, and Dan Coker. They began traveling full time, winning 70 Singing News Fan Awards over the next 35 years. He suffered a heart attack in 1987, but the quartet continued on until Payne's death in 1999. He and his son-in-law, Ernie Haase, founded the Signature Sound Quartet and made appearances on the Gaither Homecoming stage and videos. His funeral was April 19 at the Akron Baptist Temple, although he was a member of the Stow Alliance Fellowship Church.

Dianne Knippers

1952
Arlington, Virginia

April 18, 2005

President of the Institute for Religion and Democracy, 1993–2005, a conservative "think tank" in Washington, D.C. She married Edward Knippers. Knippers was an outspoken critic of liberalism, moving within mainline Protestant churches, especially the Episcopal Church. She was an advocate of persecuted Christians around the world. She died from complications of colon cancer.

Joe Mason

Oct. 24, 1910
Texhoma, Texas

April 23, 2005
Sun City, Arizona

Founder and first president of Prison Mission Association, Port Orchard, WA, 1955–91. He was converted through the Oxford Movement in California by a blind man. He was in the navy WWII. His first wife Helen Sutton died in 1971. He then married Ada Giebelhaus on March 25, 1972. PMA was founded in Weatherford, TX, in 1955. Later it relocated to Albuquerque, NM, Phoenix, AZ, then Riverside, CA. In the early 1970s the ministry expanded to several overseas countries. Upon Mason's retirement in 1991, the headquarters were moved to Port Orchard. This work is basically a literature and correspondence course ministry. In later years he suffered dementia and Alzheimers. A memorial service was held May 1, at Grace Bible Church, Glendale, AZ, his church in later years. His life verse was Acts 20:24.

Arthur M. Climenhaga

February 21, 1916
Granthem, Pennsylvania

April 25, 2005
Black Water Falls, West Virginia

Executive Director of the National Association of Evangelicals, 1964–67, and president of Messiah College, 1960–64. As a 23-year-old young man he became president of Upland (CA) College, 1939–44. He went to the mission field as a bishop of the Brethren in Christ Church in Zambia and Zimbabwe, 1951–1960. He served BICC in the Pacific-Midwest Conferences, 1967–1972. He then became vice president and dean of Western Evangelical Seminary, Portland, OR (1972–

1978), then was director of Academic Affairs, Ashland (OH) Theological Seminary (1978–82). He died while hiking with his wife. They resided at Messiah Village in Granthem.

Jacob Chelli

Jan. 20, 1934
Hubli, India

April 29, 2005
Greenville, South Carolina

Indian evangelist and educator. Chelli was responsible for getting 593 churches started. He saw 3,500 graduate from his school. He was converted out of a Hindu family in 1954. He and his wife had ten children. In 1969, he became president of Berean Baptist Bible College and Seminary until death. He spoke in many places around the world in mission conferences and as an evangelist. He also founded the Hebron Biblical Baptist Church in Hubli.

John Dunkin

April 9, 1920
Hamilton, Ontario, Canada

June 4, 2005

President of Los Angeles Baptist (Masters) **College 1959–85**. He married Jane Holmby (Dec. 28, 1940). He was responsible for the moving of the college from downtown Los Angeles to the Santa Clarita Valley in 1961. John MacArthur followed him as president, and was mentored by Dunkin.

Kenneth N. Taylor

May 8, 1917
Portland, Oregon

June 10, 2005
Wheaton, Illinois

Editor of the *Living Bible* and founder of Tyndale House Publishers. Taylor married Margaret West on September 13, 1940. He directed Moody Press, 1948–63. He began writing his "living scriptures" as a devotional help for his children. His family's dining room was the first company office. Then came *Living Letters* (paraphrased the Epistles) in 1962. No one accepted his work, so he decided to put it out (2,000 copies) himself and, by then, Tyndale House was born to care for his publishing ventures. His work was greatly enhanced after Billy Graham promoted it on television. He was president until 1984 and board chairman thereafter. He founded Living Bibles, Int., in 1968. His *Living Bible*, released in 1974, was compiled to help people wanting a simpler rendition of the Scriptures. It has sold over 40 million copies. It took him 16 years to produce this paraphrased copy of the Bible. He had ten children. Funeral services were at Wheaton College, June 15.

Jack MacArthur

March 30, 1914
Calgary, Alberta, Canada

June 15, 2005
Oregon

Pastor and radio preacher on *Voice of Calvary* for 63 years. It all began when MacArthur was a young preacher just a few years out of seminary. He married Irene Dockendorf on June 25, 1937 (died: January 14, 1999). As pastor of Eagle Rock Baptist Church, near Los Angeles, he felt the call to extend his ministry on the airwaves, beginning on June 28, 1942. In 1943, he pastored at Fountain Avenue Baptist Church, Hollywood, CA, and helped establish the Hollywood Christian Group. Roy Rogers and his wife Dale Evans came to Christ under his preaching. MacArthur than pastored FBC, Downey, CA. He then planted the Harry MacArthur Bible Church in memory of his father in Glendale. Later the church was renamed Calvary Bible Church upon moving to Burbank, 1954–69, with John MacArthur, his son, serving as associate pastor. When John took the pastorate at Grace Community Church, Sun Valley, CA, MacArthur moved to the FBC of Eugene, OR, where he served 1969–77. His interest was in biblical exposition, history, and apologetics. There is a memorial section at Master's Seminary, where he had some influence the last 20 years. His memorial service was held June 28.

Ian North

May 26, 1929
Hong Kong, China

June 18, 2005
Sydney, Australia

Founder and first president of Ambassadors for Christ, Int., 1972–91. North spent his earlier years in New Zealand and Australia. While studying at Hawkesbury Agricultural College, he was converted, soon receiving a call to missionary work. After graduating from Baptist Theological College of Victoria, Australia, in 1954, he and his wife, Dorothy, came to the United States. In 1957, he met Akbar Haqq and worked with him in India. In 1964, he joined AFCI and continued to work in India until 1971. After stepping down as director, he continued preaching in many places. In 1995, he moved back to Australia, where he ministered until the final weeks of his life.

Samuel T. Hemberger

July 9, 1921
Atlantic City, New Jersey

June 27, 2005
Aurora, Illinois

President of Conservative Congregational Christian Conference, St. Paul, MN, 1967–73, 1977–80. He married his wife, Anna Kettenring on August 28, 1945. He pastored in Tremont Larger Parish and Portland, both in Maine, and Union Congregational Church, Tuckahoe, NY early on. He pastored later in life at First Presbyterian Church, Aurora, IL (1982–90), and was an associate at Union Congregational Church, North Aurora, IL (1993–2001). He had heart disease for many years. A memorial service was held at First Christian Church, Aurora.

John M. Gillespie

March 10, 1917
Fresno, California

July 15, 2005
Anchorage, Alaska

Founder and first president of Arctic (Interac) Missions, 1951–86. Gillespie was converted at a Christian Endeavor Convention at age 14. He married Nadine Simmons on May 9, 1941. They soon headed for Valdez, Alaska, and served among the Athabaskan Indians in the interior of Alaska. In 1947 he founded the Victory Bible Conference grounds and camp, directing it until 1968. Gillespie also pastored Church of the Open Door in Anchorage, 1946–57 which grew from 50 to 400. He started AM in 1951 to help organize the independent missionaries. In 1958 a home office was started in Portland, OR. The work expanded into Canada in 1967 and grew to over 170 missionaries. Then from 1988–96 he was general director of World Missions Fellowship, Oregon City, OR.

Ellsworth Culver

April 14, 1927
Seattle, Washington

Aug. 15, 2005

First president of the Mercy Corps, Portland, OR 1979–93. Culver grew up in China and later assisted DICK HILLIS in the work of Orient Crusades, with headquarters in Formosa. When Dan O'Neill founded the Mercy Corps, Culver worked tirelessly building it into an internationally respected humanitarian organization. He helped expand the work into Africa, Asia and the Balkans. For the last ten years of his life, he worked to build bridges of understanding with North Korea by facilitating food aid, agricultural resources, and opportunities for dialogue. He tried to bring understanding and hope to people around the world.

Roger Schutz

May 12, 1915
Providence, Switzerland

Aug. 16, 2005
Taize, France

Ecumenical youth and monastic leader of Taize. Raised in a Reformed church, his father, the pastor, Roger dreamed of a community dedicated to helping those in need. In 1940, he bought a house in Taize, France. As a result of hiding Jewish refugees, he had to flee Switzerland, 1942–44. Returning to Taize, he cared for children and prisoners of war. In 1949, Schutz and others committed to a life of celibacy. In 1952, he wrote his *Rule of Taize*. His Church of Reconciliation was dedicated in 1962. Some 40,000 youth attended his first Council of Youth in 1974. He traveled world wide in the 1980s and in 1988, he dispatched one million copies of the New Testament to Russia. In 1990, he brought 80,000 young adults together in Prague, Czechoslovakia. Schutz was murdered in his 90th year, knifed to death by a woman attending an evening prayer service.

Allan Yuan

1914
Anhui Province, China

Aug. 16, 2005
Beijing, China

House church leader and prisoner for 22 years. He was converted in his parents' Peking home. Yuan was one of eleven preachers, including WATCHMAN NEE and MINGDAO WANG, who refused to join the Three Self Patriotic Movement after Mao Tse-tung's communist rule began in 1949. Yuan was arrested on April 19, 1958 because of his "counter-revolutionary" faith and sentenced to life in prison. However, he was released in 1979. As recently as 2003, he was continuing to baptize about 300 new converts a year. He died in a Beijing hospital and his son, Yuan Fu Sung, continues to lead his church. David Aikman's book, *Jesus in Beijing*, features Yuan's house-church leadership.

Charles L. Allen

June 24, 1915
Newborn, Georgia

August 30, 2005
Houston, Texas

Pastor of First Methodist Church, Houston, TX 1960–83, the largest Methodist Church in the world. (over 13,000 members). Allen was one of the great Methodist pastors of the 20th century. He married Leila Haynes on June 19, 1934. He started pastoring in Georgia from 1934–48, moving on to the capital in Atlanta, from 1948–60. Allen's Sunday morning services were televised from 1949–83 and he was a featured columnist with the *Houston Chronicle*. He preached on all five continents and in all 50 states. Allen authored 52 books, selling more than eight million copies, from *God's Psychiatry* (1953) to *The Beatitudes* (1967).

Oswald C. J. Hoffman

Dec. 6, 1913
Nebraska

Sept. 8, 2005
Snyder, Nebraska St. Louis Missouri

Lutheran Hour preacher, 1955–88. Hoffman followed the founder, WALTER MAIER, on this famous radio broadcast and had a 33-year ministry that touched millions. He married Marcia Linnell on June 29, 1940 and was director of public relations for the LCMS, 1948–63. He represented the Lutheran Church, Missouri Synod, at the Second Vatican Council and served as North American chairman for the 1974 World Congress on Evangelization in Lausanne, Switzerland. He served on the board of *Christianity Today*, 1981–2000. Hoffman's writings ranged from *The Passion Journal* (1950) to *There Is Hope* (1985). He died after a brief illness.

Ted Place

May 7, 1924
Passaic, New Jersey

Sept. 30, 2005
Homestead, Florida

Popular preacher and veteran Youth for Christ personality. Place married Pat Schlenker on August 23, 1947. They served in Detroit, 1947–58, as associate pastor and assisting ED DARLING at Voice of Christian Youth Rallies. He and his wife directed the children's program (Kids Klub) at the annual Winona Lake (IN) YFC Conferences in early July. He spoke at many rallies across the country. From 1958–68 he directed Miami (FL) YFC. Later he developed Ted Place Ministries which included family and marriage counseling, citywide Bible studies, personality seminars and radio/TV ministries for the last 25 years of his life. His final days were difficult until he finally died of pneumonia. A funeral service was held for him at Christ Fellowship Church, Perrine, FL, on October 15.

Joseph W. Coughlin

May 23, 1919
Hampton, Virginia

Oct. 2, 2005
Calhoun, Georgia

Founder of Christian Service Brigade (CSB). Coughlin taught at Houston College, Covenant College, and Gordon-Conwell Theological Seminary. He also served as a missionary in Costa Rica. CSB, a discipleship ministry for boys, began with a Sunday school class he taught during his sophomore year at Wheaton College in 1937.

Robert H. Thompson

Aug. 16, 1925
Oklahoma City, Oklahoma

Oct. 21, 2005
Oklahoma City, Oklahoma

President of Oak Hills Bible College, Bemidji, MN, 1970–82. Thompson married Roberta Joye Martin on June 1, 1945. Before coming to Bemidji from Oklahoma in 1948, he served in the navy in WWII, and earned a degree at William Jewell College, Liberty, MO. He joined the Oak Hills staff in 1950, teaching Bible and philosophy. In 1963, he was made head of the missions ministries. He moved back to Oklahoma City in 1982. He died of a massive heart attack.

Ira Eshelman

March 14, 1917
Lancaster, Pennsylvania

Nov. 2, 2005
West Palm Beach, Florida

Founder and first president of Boca Raton (FL) Bible Conference, 1949–67, best known for his ministry to professional athletes, serving for many years as chaplain of the National Football League, founding their pre-game chapel services. Eshelman served as World's Fair Parson in New York City (1964), producing sacred concerts at the RCA Pavilion. He founded Sports World Ministries to help professional athletes share their faith with the next generation. His married Viola Anderson on September 17, 1941.

F. Grace Wallace

Aug. 10, 1918
Beaumont, California

Nov. 2, 2005
Grants Pass, Oregon

Director of Nurses Christian Fellowship, 1968–84. After leading a Navigator ministry to servicemen and nurses in San Francisco, Wallace went to Dallas to work with the Red Cross. She then taught nursing at Cornell University, Ithaca, NY, and became involved with NCF. She was associate director, 1965–68. She worked on the East Coast, 1984–91, among nurses and students. Wallace moved to Merlin, OR, in 1991 where she shared a home with her sister. She was a member of the Shan Creek Community Bible Church there. A graveside service was held November 12.

Edward L. Frederick

Sept. 13, 1911
Amherst, Ohio

Nov. 4, 2005
Arroyo Grande, California

General Director of International Missions (Christar in 1999), **1955–71**. He was converted in a church service in his hometown. Frederick had spent 13 years in India as a missionary, during his 1939–55 mission ministry overseas, where he met his first wife, Olive, from England (died: January 15, 1989). The name of the mission was originally the Indian Mission. He moved the headquarters back to the States and under his tenure, nine more fields opened. The mission merged with the South China Boat Mission, following the name change in 1953 to IM. Muslim and Buddhist evangelism were added to the Hindu ministry. He married Marian Loucks on January 7, 1990. They ministered in a mobile park in Arroyo Grande for many years. From 1971–75 he was West Coast representative of the mission. He had cancer, dementia, and Parkinson's disease.

Roger J. Voskuyl

May 16, 1910
Cedar Grove, Wisconsin

Nov. 9, 2005
Santa Barbara, California

President of Westmont College, Santa Barbara, CA, 1950–68. Early on, Voskuyl, a graduate of Hope College, earned his doctorate in chemistry from Harvard, worked on the Manhattan Project during WWII. He married Gertrude Schaap on August 13, 1935 (died:1985), and later Margaret Jacobsen. He began teaching at Wheaton (IL) College in 1938 and became dean of the faculty in 1945. He served as acting president, 1947–48. At Westmont, the college gained accreditation in 1958, added eight major buildings, and increased enrollment from 218 to 700. Assets increased in value from $500,000 in 1950 to $10 million in 1968. Gifts increased from $103,000 to $1 million. His memorial service was held November 21, at El Montecito (CA) Presbyterian Church.

Dick Van Halsema

July 19, 1922
East Paris Michigan

Nov. 12, 2005
East Paris Michigan

President of Reformed Bible Institute (Kuyper College) **Grand Rapids, MI 1966–87**. Van Halsema preached his first sermon as a 21 year old soldier in a worship service on a WWII troop ship headed for Japanese controlled New Guinea in 1944. He married Thea J. Bouma on March 19, 1948. He served as pastor of three churches, including one in Monsay, NY, 1949–56 and Central Ave. Christian Reformed Church, Holland MI 1963–66. He was the CRC's first home missionary and first minister of evangelism 1958–65. He began editing *Missionary Monthly* in 1964 and was it's main writer, photographer, and manager for 36 years. He also trained missionaries in Mexico and the Middle East. He played the organ. His love for music was evident by composing/compiling a songbook of favorite Psalm tunes. He was stricken with Parkinson's disease. Rev. Jacob Eppinga, who delivered his eulogy at the memorial service November 19 at Calvin CRC said, "I never had a meeting with him without Dick saying 'Let's pray'."

Adrian P. Rogers

Sept. 12, 1931
West Palm Beach, Florida

Nov. 15, 2005
Memphis, Tennessee

President of the Southern Baptist Convention, 1979, 1986–87, and renowned pastor. Rogers was pastor of the 28,000-member Bellevue Baptist Church in Memphis, TN from 1973 to March, 2005, when he retired. Membership grew from 9,000 to 29,000. He was considered a key figure in the conservative takeover of the SBC, which had been drifting left for several years. He married Joyce Gentry on September 2, 1951. He pastored three churches in Florida and one in Mississippi,

1951–72, coming to Bellevue from FBC, Merritt Island, FL, 1964–72. he conducted crusades in Taiwan, South Korea, Israel, Russia, Romania, and Central and South America. He was hospitalized early in the month of November with pneumonia and colon cancer. Rogers was considered one of the great preachers of his generation. His *Love Worth Finding* broadcast aired on 2,000 radio stations.

W. Dale Cryderman

July 4, 1916
Detroit, Michigan

Nov. 16, 2005
Spring Arbor, Michigan

Bishop of Free Methodist Church, 1969–84. He married Dorothy Gates on October 19, 1935. Converted soon after, Cryderman felt God's call into the ministry. Cryderman began his ministry as pastor at the Free Methodist Church, Albion, MI, in 1940. In 1950, he was working with Youth for Christ in Japan. He served as superintendent of the Southern Michigan Conference, 1956–69. His wife died shortly before him in September. A serious fall contributed to his death five days later.

Charles W. Spicer

Oct. 14, 1930
Baltimore, Maryland

Dec. 13, 2005
Greenwood, Indiana

Founder and first president of Overseas Council for Theological Education and Missions, Indianapolis, IN 1974–95. During his leadership, approximately $85 million was raised to underwrite thousands of student scholarships and 71 major building projects. Spicer served with OMS International, Greenwood, IN, in various leadership roles. He visited 195 countries and traveled millions of miles in behalf of his ministry. His wife of 52 years, Phyllis, died in January 2005. He was active at Southport Presbyterian Church of Indianapolis.

Richard (Dick) Hillis

Feb. 13, 1913
Victoria, British Columbia, Canada

Dec. 14, 2005
Ripon, California

Missions leader with China Inland Mission, Youth for Christ and founder of Overseas Crusades (OC Ministries) **and first president, 1951–71**. Dick and his twin brother, Don (missionary to India), were converted while at BIOLA, at the Church of the Open Door under the ministry PETER PHILPOTT. In 1933, he departed to China as the youngest missionary candidate ever accepted by CIM (age 20). In 1936, he married Margaret Humphrey on April 8, 1938 (died: April 15, 1981). They served in Honan, China, 1936–41 and 1947–50, and were under house arrest the last 18 months. He went to Formosa in 1951 and founded this new work. In the great missionary leadership roles of the 1940's–60's, when Youth for Christ led in a great worldwide revival, there were five powerful leaders who impacted Asia: DAWSON TROTMAN, DAVID MORKEN, HUBERT MITCHELL, BOB PIERCE, and Dick Hillis, who was the last to die. Hillis founded Overseas Crusades in Taiwan in 1951 because YFC lacked the finances to support such a work. Hillis organized gospel teams to preach the gospel in every village, reaching the northern half of Taiwan. From 1951–55, there were 10,000 decisions a month that were followed up. In 1962, he and his family returned to the US to give leadership to OC, which eventually had 425 missionaries impacting 65 countries. On April 2, 1982, he married Ruth Kopperud, who died September, 2005. In 1983, OC began a radio broadcast into China via FEBC. Dick's memorial service was held in Woodmen Valley Chapel, Colorado Springs, CO, on Jan. 17, 2006. His brother, Don, died a couple months later.

"Let Christ be the Lord and I His servant. Every heart with Christ—a missionary, every heart without Christ-a mission field."

David Engelhard

Aug. 23, 1941
Grand Rapids, Michigan

Dec. 22, 2005
Grand Rapids, Michigan

General secretary emeritus of the Christian Reformed Church, 1994–2005. Engelhard was professor of OT and Hebrew at Calvin Theological Seminary for 24 years. He was married to Jeanne Stuit for 43 years. A three hour surgery, Feb. 24 removed a malignant brain tumor. He died of brain cancer after a ten-month battle. His funeral was Dec. 28, at Shawnee Park CRC.

Delmar L. Browning

June 4, 1928
Yuma, Colorado

Jan. 5, 2006
Marietta, Georgia

Founder and first president of Kingsway Christian College, Des Moines, IA 1968–2001. Browning married Amy Vinzant on May 25, 1947. Ordained (1957), he pastored two churches in Wisconsin: Mather (1958–63) and Needah (1963–65). In 1965, they moved to Des Moines where he pastored the Echos of Calvary Church (Kingsway Cathedral) until 1993. He founded Kingsway International Missions in 1966. He was founder of Kingsway Fellowship International, 1968–2000, a Pentecostal organization. He retired in 2000 to Atlanta. Funeral services were held Jan. 9 at First Church of the Open Bible, Des Moines.

Selwyn Hughes

1929

Jan. 9, 2006

Founder of Crusade for World Revival. An ordained Assembly of God minister, Hughes was also well known for his *Every Day with Jesus* daily devotionals, which are distributed in 130 nations. His funeral was January 17 in England. He had a long battle with cancer.

Jack McAlister

Feb. 2, 1924
Windsor, Ontario, Canada

Jan. 12, 2006
Ventura, California

Founder and first president of World Literature Crusade, Studio City, CA, 1946–80 (now Every Home Crusade). His concept was to evangelize the world by placing a piece of gospel literature in every home in a nation. Having material printed overseas and working through nationals, with ties to 415 mission agencies, resulted in over 50 million spiritual responses returned to national offices. An example of the program is India, which was covered in 14 years. He conducted a weekly radio broadcast and a series of five-hour television specials. He traveled to 66 countries of the world and was closely associated with OSWALD J. SMITH. He was the son of Pentecostal leader, Walter McAlister, and grew up in Toronto. He married Hazel Swanson on May 12, 1945 (died: April 16, 2002). From 1980 until his death, he directed and founded World's Prayer Network, a prayer ministry for missionary projects. He entered a retirement home in Ventura in the fall of 2005. His funeral was at Church on the Way in Van Nuys, CA. WLC has reached 194 nations.

Henry P. Hildebrand

Nov. 16, 1911
Stonefield, Russia

Feb. 7, 2006
Abbotsford, British Columbia, Canada

Founder and President of Briercrest (Sask) Bible Institute, 1935–46, (renamed and moved), **and Caronport, Sask 1946–77.** He married Inger Soeyland on August 12, 1937. Hildebrand immigrated to Canada with his family in 1925 to escape the growing Communist tyranny in Ukraine. In 1935, he came to Briercrest to lead the Briercrest Gospel Assembly. A Christian high school was also started in 1946 once the move was made to Caronport. He wrote at least eight books.

William T. Greig II

April 16, 1924
Minneapolis, Minnesota

Feb. 15, 2006
Ventura, California

President of Gospel Light Publishers, Ventura, CA, 1980–98. Greig became a Christian as a child. He married Doris Walters on November 22, 1951 (died: December 20, 1994) In 2001, he founded the not-for-profit Gospel Light Worldwide. He worked in Christian publishing endeavors for over 55 years.

Mark R. Moore

Sept. 30, 1916
Vilonia, Arkansas

Feb. 15, 2006
Kansas City, Kansas

President of Trevecca Nazarene University, Nashville, TN, 1968–79. Moore was a chaplain in the US army, 1944–46, and a prisoner of war. During his tenure at TNU, four residents' halls were added to the campus, faculty office building was renovated, seeing the annual budget grew from $1.1 million to $3.7 million and they purchased surrounding land. Full-time faculty grew from 40 to 49. His wife's name was Clarice. In 1979, he became executive secretary of the Department of Education for the Church of the Nazarene. He died after a long bout with cancer.

John Broger

Oct. 30, 1913
Nashville, Tennessee

Feb. 19, 2006
Palm Desert, California

Cofounder with Bob Bowman of Far East Broadcasting Company, and president, 1945–59. He married Dorothy M. Smeltzer in 1941. A third co-ounder was William J. Roberts. Broger was in commercial radio on the East Coast prior to his conversion. He left Florida for California where he met Bowman and, prior to the US involvement in WWII, they discussed the possibilities of reaching Asia via radio. On Dec. 20, 1945, the Far East Broadcasting Company was incorporated. Broger got the first radio license that was ever granted by the Philippine government. Leaving in 1959, he turned the leadership over to Bowman, who headed it until 1992. Broger joined the US Defense Department and for nearly 25 years worked in the Pentagon as director of information, until his death was imminent.

Anthony Burger

June 5, 1961
Cleveland, Tennessee

Feb. 22, 2006
Caribbean Sea

An outstanding pianist. After suffering third-degree burns on his hands as a baby, Burger began playing the piano at the age of three and, at age five, entered the Cadek Conservatory of Music in Chattanooga, TN. His career began as pianist for the Kingsmen, beginning in January, 1979, when he was 17. For a decade, he became a vital ingredient in the Gaither Homecoming Concerts and videos, along-side his own solo performances. Burger died suddenly from a heart attack during a performance on a cruise ship with the Gaither Homecoming team. He was survived by his wife, LuAnn, and three children. Memorial services were held February 28 and March 1 at Christ Church in Nashville, TN and also in Cleveland, TN on March 3. *The Best of Anthony Burger* was released on CD and DVD on April 21, 2006.

Henry M. Morris

Dec. 6, 1918
Dallas, Texas

Feb. 25, 2006
La Mesa, California

Founder of the Institute for Creation Research, Santee, CA, 1970. Considered the father of modern Creationism, Morris was a hydraulic engineer and professor before developing his critique of evolution, as published in his book, *The Genesis Flood* (1961). He wrote more than 60 books. His life pursuit was to demonstrate the validity of the Bible in every area, including science. He taught at Rice University, University of Minnesota, University of Louisiana, and Virginia Tech. His book, *The Bible and Modern Science* (1951), started the modern creationist movement. He also founded Christian Heritage College in San Diego. He married Mary Louise Beach on January 24, 1940. They had 66 years together. He died after his third stroke. A memorial service was held March 2.

James E. Andrews

Dec. 29, 1928
Whittenburg, Texas

March 7, 2006
Decatur, Georgia

Stated clerk of The Presbyterian Church in the United States (1973–83) and of The Presbyterian Church (USA) (1983–96). Andrews married Sarah Elizabeth Crouch on September 16, 1962. Ordained a Presbyterian in 1956, his major early work was director of public relations and assistant to the president, JAMES McCORD, of Princeton (NJ) Theological Seminary, 1960–71. He was a primary architect for the 1983 reunion of two former denominations. He was struck and killed by an automobile while walking near his home. Services were held on March 12 at Oakhurst Presbyterian Church, Decatur.

Ken Anderson

Dec. 23, 1917
Rembrandt, Iowa

March 12, 2006
Winona Lake, Indiana

Christian film producer. Anderson was considered a leader and pioneer in using films as an outreach tool. He was converted at Moody Church under DR. IRONSIDE's message. He married Doris Jones on Nov. 16, 1938 and began work in the Evangelical Free Church. He began to write and was an established author by 1945 when he was made editor of the *YFC Magazine*. He went with BOB PIERCE to China in 1948. Then he launched Gospel Films in 1949, which eventually released more than 200 evangelistic movies—including such as *Pilgrim's Progress*. When a close vote replaced him as director in 1960, he moved from Muskegon, MI to Winona Lake, IN, and started Ken Anderson Films. Here, he continued filmmaking. He traveled widely around the world giving him ideas for motion picture scripts and books. He was also a voluminous author, with articles appearing in dozens of journals. In 1991, InterComm was established to continue his vision. A memorial service was held in Winona Lake on March 18.

Sanford Haugen

April 13, 1926
Crary, North Dakota

March 21, 2006
Laredo, Texas

President of Latin American Lutheran Mission, Laredo, TX 1960–90. When his friends were killed in a serious automobile accident Haugen was prompted to give his life to Christ. In 1947, while working as a volunteer at the LALM in its infancy in San Antonio, TX, he met and married Florence, also a volunteer. They moved to Laredo, where he learned Spanish, and then to Minnesota and North Dakota where for many years, during the summers, he served as advocate, translator and pastor for the migrant workers there. They retired to Zapata, TX, in 1991 and Alzheimer's began to take it's toll on him. He was dearly loved by the Evangelical Lutheran Church of Mexico. His funeral service was held March 25th at the local Bethel Lutheran Church.

Frederick A. Caserta

Sept. 4, 1940
Buffalo, New York

April 9, 2006
Buffalo, New York

Founder and first president of Kingdom Bound Ministries, Williamsville (near Buffalo) **NY, 1986–2006**. Caserta was a secular rock promoter during the 1960s and 1970s, running Starstruck Productions, servicing clubs and high schools in western New York. In 1984, he was converted.

His first KB Christian music festival was held in October, 1987 with 6,000 attending on a snowy weekend. The annual festival attendance grew and in 2005 topped 63,000 people. He was able to share the gospel with over 1 million people. He was well known in the contemporary Christian music industry, working with Rebecca St. James, the Newsboys, and others. His wife's name was Cindy.

William W. Matthews

Dec. 5, 1912
Jacksonville, Florida

April 12, 2006
Birmingham, Alabama

Bishop of Church of God by Faith, Gainesville, FL 1959–84, son of the founder, AARON MATTHEWS. Without any formal education, William became a Christian and later was filled with the Holy Spirit in 1929. He married Katie Mae on October 11, 1937 and pastored in Belleview, Lake Alfred and Ocala, FL. His most memorable pastorate was in Ozark, AL, from 1945 until the late 60s. He resided in Birmingham, AL from 1997 on.

Don Dehart

Feb. 3, 1935
Shelby County, Indiana

April 15, 2006
Palm Harbor, Florida

Founder and first president of For Haiti with Love, Palm Harbor, FL 1982–2004. He worked in heavy construction in early years, serving as a traveling preacher on weekends. His wife, Eva Gardner, whom he married November 10, 1973 continued the work upon his death. Dehart had no tolerance for procrastination, whether it was feeding the hungry or mending the hurt, burnt-out and wounded. His compassion touched the lives of thousands. He died of cancer and a memorial service was held April 24 at First Presbyterian Church, Dunedin, FL.

William P. Thompson

Sep. 14, 1918
Beloit, Wisconsin

April 27, 2006
Chicago, Illinois

Stated clerk of the United Presbyterian Church in the USA, 1966–83. Thompson was the first president of the World Alliance of Reformed Churches (1970–77), and one of the presidents of the National Council of Churches in Christ (1975–78). Thompson's leadership led the Presbyterian Church through the civil rights struggles of the 1960s, the anti-Vietnam War movement and the battles for women's rights. He was basically a lawyer, spending most of his legal career in Wichita, KS. He married Mary Alice Wood on January 23, 1949, and was involved in numerous clubs and organizations. He worked with JIM ANDREWS to bring the 1983 merger of two Presbyterian denominations to form the present day Presbyterian Church (USA). Funeral services were held May 13 at the First Presbyterian Church, LaGrange, IL. Reports say he died in a suburban Chicago hospital.

Jeffery Bond

Oct. 12, 1954
Wiggins, Mississippi

May 8, 2006
Laurel, Mississippi

President of Southeastern Baptist College, Laurel, MS, 1996–2006. Bond pastored in Arkansas and Mississippi, and was on the faculty of SBC for 26 years. His wife's name was Emma. He died after a long battle with cancer. Funeral services were held for him on May 11 at Paramount Baptist Church, Perkinston, MS, where 200 gathered to hear his former pastor, George Reddin, among others, eulogize him.

John Ost

Sept. 12, 1931
Minneapolis, Minnesota

May 8, 2006
McAllen, Texas

President of Christian Fellowship Union, McAllen, TX 1966–86. His father was A. B. OST. John made a complete surrender to Christ at Taylor University, Upland, IN, in 1950 and went to McAllen to minister with CFU. In 1951, he went to the University of Mexico to learn Spanish. Ost married Clara Riveness on November 8, 1959. For 20 years prior to his leadership of CFU, and 20 years following, he pastored the McAllen Iglesia Biblica Church. He pioneered work in Mexico, establishing eight churches there. He also engaged in preaching trips to Argentina, Paraguay, Brazil, Spain, and the Ukraine. He was known to spend a couple hours each day in the Bible and prayer.

Neely D. McCarter

Oct. 4, 1929
Gastonia, North Carolina

May 10, 2006
Xian, China

President of Pacific School of Religion, Berkeley, CA 197991. McCarter married Jean Maxwell on May 28, 1954. His wife was born in Brazil of missionary parents. He taught Christian Education at Columbia Theological Seminary, Decatur, GA (1961–66) and at UTS (1966–73). He served as dean at Union Theological Seminary, Richmond, VA, from 1973–79. As president of PSR, he raised the school's endowment from $9 million to nearly $22 million-more money than the school had raised in its previous 124 years. He greatly improved campus buildings. McCarter was known for his wit, warmth, and wisdom. His last book was *The President's Educator* (1996). He was touring in China when he died.

Glen A. Lehman

Sept. 23, 1907
Abilene, Kansas

May 13, 2006
Grand Rapids, Michigan

Executive Secretary of Independent Fundamental Church of America 1959–72. A name change was made from executive secretary to national executive director upon his retirement. Lehman was converted March 5, 1933, in meetings at the Community Church of Grandview, IA, under the ministry of Victor A. Clocksin. He married Geraldine Moorhead on October 31, 1935. Graduating from Moody Bible Institute in 1940, he pastored from 1936–59 in Chicago, IL; Dubuque, IA; Waterloo, IA and Pekin,. IL. Lehman helped found 13 different Christian organizations. He also edited *The Voice* while heading the IFCA. His wife died in 1995, whereupon he married Juanita (Lehman), continuing on as elder statesman of the IFCA in his senior years.

Reuben H. Redal

Nov. 7, 1920
Souris, North Dakota

May 17, 2006
Tacoma, Washington

Founder and first president of Faith Evangelical Lutheran Seminary, Tacoma, WA, 1969–2004. He also pastored Central Lutheran Church, Tacoma 1952–2006 (54 years). Redal met his wife, Eleanor, while on tour with the St. Olaf College (Northfield, MN) gospel quartet. He was best known for his unwavering stand on biblical inerrancy and also helped found Lutheran Alert-National in 1965.

James C. West

Jan. 28, 1940
Berkley County, South Carolina

May 28, 2006
Summerville, South Carolina

President of Cummins Memorial Theological Seminary, Summerville, SC, 1987–2004. West was converted at an early age. He married Miriam Brown on December 23, 1967. He was a fourth-generation Reformed Episcopal cleric. West was rector of St. John's Church, Charleston, SC, 1976–98. He also taught at CMTS and was active in the wider Anglican Communion.

Leo Janz

June 12, 1919
Main Centre, Saskatchewan, Canada

June 8, 2006
Abbotsford, BC, Canada

Founder of the Janz team in 1954, which offered the gospel to war-torn Germany. As evangelist and member of the Janz Team Quartet, Leo worked with his brothers and others who assisted. The team has continued through the years to minister in Europe, as well as North and South America. Janz was married for over 60 years to his wife, Lydia. They retired to Abbotsford in their later years. Funeral services were held at Seven Oaks Alliance Church in Abbotsford.

Theodore (Ted) W. Engstrom

March 1, 1916
Cleveland, Ohio

July 14, 2006
Bradbury, California

Beloved Christian leader, president of Youth For Christ, 1957–63 and World Vision 1982–87. Engstrom was converted as a freshman at Taylor University in 1935. He was an executive's executive on the board of more Christian organizations than anyone in modern times. James Dobson said Ted missed only two Focus on the Family board meetings in 25 years. Author of 36 books and friend to just about everyone in Christendom during his life, Engstrom was BOB COOK's executive director in YFCI before becoming president (1951–57). His roots were in Grand Rapids, MI, where he worked for Zondervan (1940–51) and directed Grand Rapids YFC. He married Dorothy Weaver on November 3, 1939. She preceded him in death in January, 2005. He was active at Lake Avenue Congregational Church, Pasadena, CA, since 1972 and was executive vice-president of World Vision, 1963–80.

Finally, he was one of this author's most cherished friends. He gave me my first chance to preach as a 15-year-old at the youth meeting of the Mission Covenant (Evangelical) Church in Grand Rapids. He was the first leader to know of my love for biographies and answered 2-3 hours of questions at Maranatha Bible Conference in Muskegon, MI, over 50 years ago. When thinking of a forward for this book, I could consider no one else but Dr. Ted.

Leon Morris

March 15, 1914
Lithgow, Australia

July 24, 2006
Melbourne, Australia

New Testament scholar. Morris received his Ph.D. at the University of Cambridge in England on the subject which became his first major book, *The Apostolic Preaching of the Cross*. He served as warden of Tyndale House, 1960–64; principal of Ridley College in Melbourne, where they named a library after him. He was also visiting professor of New Testament at Trinity Evangelical Divinity School, Deerfield, IL. Morris published several theological works and commentaries on the Bible, notably *The Atonement: Its Meaning and Significance*, *New Testament Theology*, and *The Gospel According to John*.

David A. Seamands

Feb. 6, 1922
Vikarabad, India

July 28, 2006
Wilmore, Kentucky

United Methodist missionary and author of *Healing for Damaged Emotions*. Seamands married Helen Davis, June 2, 1942. They served as missionaries in India, 1946–62. From 1962–84, he was pastor of the United Methodist Church of Wilmore, KY. Seamands was professor of Pastoral Ministries at Asbury Theological Seminary, 1984–92, influencing many students. He was a leader in the evangelical renewal movements within the United Methodists. He was also a pioneer in the field of Christian counseling. His famous book has sold over a million copies, and has been translated into over 30 languages. His funeral was conducted August 1 in the church he pastored for 22 years.

James E. Annand

May 23, 1929
Glendale, California

Sept. 1, 2006
Charlestown, Rhode Island

Dean of Berkley Divinity School, New Haven, CT, 1982–1991. Annand married Connie Cousins, on Aug. 22, 1953. He was ordained Episcopalian in 1954. He was vicar at a church in Monterey Park, CA, 1956–58; rector at Christ Church, Westerly, RI, 1958–69; St. Paul's Church, Greenwich, CT, 1969–74; and then, interim rector at churches in Connecticut and Rhode Island, 1975–80. Annand then became a lecturer at BDS, 1981–82. He was generous, warm-hearted, ebullient, a realist with a wonderful sense of humor.

John W. Peterson

Nov. 1, 1921
Lindsborg, Kansas

Sept. 20, 2006
Scottsdale, Arizona

Most prolific evangelical song-writer of his generation. Peterson wrote 1,000 plus songs, including, "Heaven Came Down," "It Took A Miracle," "Over The Sunset Mountain," "Jesus Led Me All The Way," "So Send I You," "Springs of Living Water," "Jesus Is Coming Again," "Surely Goodness and Mercy," etc. Peterson also wrote 35 cantatas and musicals, including "No Greater Love," "Love Transcending," "Down From His Glory," and "Night Of Miracles." He married Marie Addie on Feb. 11, 1944. Their daughters' trio was well known for many years (Sandra, Candace, Pamela). Peterson served as a pilot in the US Air Force, 1942–45. Flying over the Burma "hump," inspired his song, "It Took A Miracle." He worked at radio station, WMBI, Chicago, 1950–55. Peterson was editor-in-chief and president of Singspiration, Inc., Grand Rapids, MI, 1955–71, and was also music director at Calvary Church, part of this time: then executive composer of Singspiration, Inc., Carefree, AZ, 1977–83. Finally, he was president of John W. Peterson Music Company, Scottsdale, AZ, 1983 on. Prostate cancer took his life after a lingering illness.

Charles U. Wagner

May 26, 1929
Detroit, Michigan

Oct. 22, 2006
Hudson, Florida

President of Northwest Baptist Seminary, Tacoma, WA, 1974–83 and Grand Rapids (MI) Baptist (Cornerstone) College and Seminary, 1983–90. After graduation from Detroit Bible College, Wagner pastored in Michigan and New Jersey. He then went to Washington state and pastored in Richland, Everett, and Temple Baptist Church in Tacoma. He married Ruth Sweetland on June 21, 1950. A recognized scholar, he wrote several books and booklets including: *The Pastor: His Life and Work,* and *Winning Words for Daily Living.* He pastored Calvary Baptist Church of Covington, KY, 1990–2001, where his memorial service was held. He died of a rare type of cancer, which precipitated a heart attack and was buried in Hudson.

James H. (Jim) Montgomery

Feb. 8, 1930
San Jose, California

Oct. 29, 2006
Colorado Springs, Colorado

Founder and director of Dawn Ministries, 1985–2005. Montgomery and his DAWN team took their strategy from country to country throughout the world. Thousands of church leaders caught the vision, resulting in untold numbers of new churches. He married Lyn White on June 7, 1955. They worked with Orient (Overseas) Crusades, 1957–85. In 1962, Montgomery challenged Filipino denominational leaders to begin planting churches everywhere, and well over fifty thousand churches were established. Then, at age 55, he started DAWN (Disciple A Whole Nation) from an office in his garage, and soon churches were springing up in many other countries of the world. He published eight books and other publications on this subject.

Allen B. Finley

Nov. 11, 1929
Charlottesville, Virginia

Oct. 30, 2006
Stallings, North Carolina

Executive Director, 1970–1976, and first president, 1976–87, of Partners. The original name of this mission board was Christian Nationals Evangelism Commission. After 1987, Finley assisted the work in various capacities for many years. He was ordained by Evangelical Church Alliance in 1952. He married Ruth Goodwin on August 14, 1953. From 1952–60, he was associated with International Students, along with his brother Bob Finley, who later started Christian Aid Mission. When Allen started his work, his office was in his home with one desk and one file cabinet. By 1987, income had grown to $5.8 million with works flourishing in 36 countries. As a missions leader, he traveled nearly three million miles. Finley was an active Presbyterian layman in several churches during his lifetime.

Donald E. Hoke

June 18, 1919
Chicago, Illinois

Nov. 15, 2006
Fort Myers, Florida

Presbyterian pastor, educator and missionary leader. Hoke gave his life to Christ at an evangelistic meeting, led by ROBERT C. MCQUILKEN at Wheaton (IL) College, in February, 1957. He married Martha Cowan on July 20, 1945. He founded and pastored the South Park Church, Park Ridge, IL, 1941–47, moving on to become assistant to MCQUILKEN at Columbia (SC) Bible College, 1947–52. He was a missionary to Japan with TEAM, 1952–73. While there, Hoke founded the Tokyo Christian University and was president, 1955–73, co-founding Japan Bible Seminary in Tokyo during this same time. In 1963, a new million dollar campus was built in the suburbs. He was the executive director of the Billy Graham International Congress on World Evangelization, Lausanne, Switzerland, 1973–79, and worked at the Billy Graham Center, Wheaton, IL, 1974–78, as the first director. Hoke then pastored the Cedar Springs Presbyterian Church of Knoxville, TN, 1978–89. He wrote four books.. He died after a lingering illness.

Gerald R. Ford

July 14, 1913
Omaha, Nebraska

Dec. 26, 2006
Rancho Mirage, California

38th President of the United States, 1974–77. Ford was the only president never elected as president or vice president. To the American people, he said, "...I ask you to confirm me as your president, with your prayers..." On Oct. 12, 1973, when Spiro T. Agnew resigned, Ford was nominated to succeed him as vice-president. Ford was a football star at the University of Michigan, captain the final year on a team that was undefeated, winning the national championship the first two years. He was center on offense, line backer on defense. He was in the Navy in many of the major battles of WWII. Ford married Elizabeth Bloomer on October 15, 1948. He became a lawyer in Grand Rapids, MI, 1941–49, then a member of Congress, 1949–74. He was elected minority leader in 1965. He was vice-president, 1973–74, and, upon RICHARD NIXON's resignation, became president on Aug. 9, 1974. Ford vetoed 48 bills in his first 21 months in office...mostly in the interest of fighting high inflation. His pardon of NIXON brought a sense of healing to a wounded nation, tainted with scandal. Ford was narrowly defeated for president by Jimmy Carter in the 1976 election (297–240) and retired to Rancho Mirage, CA, where he died in his home.

Harald Bredesen

Aug. 18, 1918
Minnesota

Dec. 29, 2006
Escondido, California

Father of the Charismatic Renewal Movement. Formerly an American Lutheran pastor, Bredesen influenced televangelists, Hollywood actors, kings and ordinary people. He moved to NYC in 1944 and launched an unconventional, far-reaching ministry. He met and married Genevieve Corrick in 1954. He pastored a Reformed Church in White Plains, NY early on, then the Trinity Christian Center in Victoria, BC. From 1972–76, he was greatly used in overseas ministries in places such as Mexico and Bangladesh. Some feel he was the original "charismatic." He had a great influence on Pat Robertson, Pat Boone, and Jack Hayford. He counseled with Anwar Sadat of Egypt and California governor, RONALD REAGAN. Bredesen was the first neo-Pentecostal from a mainline denomination, remaining in his church. On Dec. 26, he fell down the stairs in his home, fracturing his skull. He died from complications three days later. A memorial service was held, Feb. 3, 2007, at the Church of The Way, Van Nuys, California.

Tom Malone

Nov. 29, 1915
New Orleans, Louisiana

Jan. 7, 2007
Pontiac, Michigan

Outstanding preacher, pastor and educator of Pontiac, MI. Malone pastored the Emmanuel Baptist Church for some 65 years, which had 2,500 attending during its peak. He also founded Midwestern Baptist College in 1953, which had 500 attending at its peak. Malone was converted in Isbell Methodist Church, Russellville, AL in August, 1935. Upon finishing his Bob Jones College (University) education, he married his wife, Joyce Harned, on April 17, 1939. They had three children. His son, Tom Jr., died shortly after his father. In 1941, he went to Pontiac and founded the church which he pastored until 2006. He had a large radio ministry in the Detroit/Pontiac area and traveled to many conferences as a featured speaker. JOHN R. RICE called him the greatest preacher of his time. He wrote several books, beginning with *Essentials of Evangelism,* (1958), lectures at Bob Jones University.

Bruce M. Metzger

Feb. 9, 1914
Middletown, Pennsylvania

Feb. 13, 2007
Princeton, New Jersey

Outstanding scholar and author. Metzger was a leading authority on NT textual criticism through the numerous scholarly works he wrote, 1944–81. He was converted at age 14. Metzger attended Lebanon (PA) Valley College and wrote *Red Russia in Bible Prophecy* during that time. He married Isobel E. MacKay on July 7, 1944. He was a life-long professor at Princeton (NJ) Theological Seminary, 1938–84, where he was an expert in Greek biblical texts. He was editor-in-chief of the Revised Standard Version of the Bible (1990). This was a revision of the Revised Standard Version (1952). He also edited a condensed version of the Bible, published by Reader's Digest (1982). He was criticized by some as a "modernist"; however, he was a believer in the infallibility of Scripture and faith in Jesus Christ.

Gilbert E. Patterson

Sept. 22, 1939
Humboldt, Tennessee

March 20, 2007
Memphis, Tennessee

Bishop of Church of God in Christ, Memphis TN, 2000–2006. He also pastored the Temple of Deliverance there. He was converted at age 11 at his father's Holy Temple COGIC in Memphis. He was baptized in the Holy Spirit, Sept. 16, 1956 and from then on, he was much sought as an evangelist. He attended Detroit Bible Institute. Patterson married his wife, Louise, in May, 1967. He founded the Temple of Deliverance in 1975 with 436 members, which grew to 6,000, and his influence reached millions more on television. He appealed across denominational lines, both black and white, in the Pentecostal movement. Prostate cancer was discovered in 2005, but his death was attributed to heart failure. 30,000 mourners paid tribute to him: Bill Clinton and Jesse Jackson among them.

Lee Roberson

Nov. 24, 1909
English, Indiana

April 29, 2007
Chattanooga, Tennessee

Pastor and educator of large ministries in Chattanooga, TN. Roberson pastored the Highland Park Baptist Church, 1942–83. In 1955, he and the church left the Southern Baptist Convention, becoming an independent Baptist church. From 1945–55, he had led all SBC churches in baptisms. During his total ministry, some 61,000 professed faith in Jesus Christ. At age 14, Roberson became a Christian, because of his Sunday School teacher's persistance, in a church in Louisville, KY. In 1935–36, he conducted about 50 revival meetings. He married Caroline Allen on Oct. 9, 1937. From 1937–42, he pastored FBC of Fairfield, AL. After coming to Highland Park, the constant growth climaxed with a new 6,000 seat auditorium, built in 1981. In 1946, he started Tennessee Temple College (now Tennessee Temple Univ.) with 109 students. Roberson served as its first president until 1974 but retained a high-profile leadership role until his departure from the HPBC ministry in 1983. After 1983 Roberson traveled and preached in many churches and continued in a chancellor capacity with TTU until his death. The university and seminary peaked in enrollment during Roberson's watch with well over 3,000 students and continue to train men and women for ministry and career-oriented professions. He also helped found Southwide Baptist Fellowship in March, 1956. His Camp Joy, named in honor of his deceased daughter, has seen thousands of youth respond to Christ. A favorite respite for him during his later years was Temple Baptist Church of Knoxville, TN, pastored by Clarence Sexton, his former associate, who continues Roberson's emphasis and vision at this church and Crown College.

Jerry Falwell

August 11, 1933
Lynchburg, Virginia

May 15, 2007
Lynchburg, Virginia

Pastor, college president, and television evangelist. Falwell founded Thomas Road Baptist Church in 1956 with 35 members. It grew in 50 years to 24,000 members. His Old Time Gospel Hour telecast was a part of his outreach from almost the beginning. Some three million made salvation decisions as a result. Falwell started Liberty University in 1971, which has grown to 10,000 students on campus. Another 18,000 students study by extension. In 2007, there were 3,457 graduates, bringing the alumni up to 125,000. He was converted January 20, 1952, through the influence of CHARLES FULLER and the Old Fashioned Revival Hour radio broadcast. He married Macel Pate on April 12, 1958. Known for his involvement in social and political issues, he founded The Moral Majority in 1979. This political nature of his ministry was birthed in 1973 when the Supreme Court legalized abortion. Some credit the election victories of RONALD REAGAN and George Bush, Sr., as a result of these efforts. He had many enemies and sparked controversy with some conservaties and liberals. He was a historic fundamentalist and did much for his generation to bring biblical precepts to America's attention. He was found unconscious in his office and died shortly thereafter, due to heart problems. Some 10,000 attended his funeral to hear messages from Franklin Graham and Jerry Vines. He is buried on the campus, near his office.

Ruth Bell Graham

June 10, 1920
Tsing Kaing Pu, China

June 14, 2007
Montreat, North Carolina

Wife of Billy Graham, mother of five children, author. Ruth Graham died in a mountaintop cabin home that she had designed half a century earlier. Her childhood home was 300 miles north of Shanghai, where her parents had a 350-bed hospital. She attended a boarding high school in what is now North Korea. Ruth enrolled in Wheaton (IL) College in 1938, where she later met Billy Graham, a fellow student. Their first date was a Sunday afternoon sacred music concert at a Wheaton College chapel. Graduating in June, 1943, they were married August 13, 1943 at the Montreat Presbyterian Church (where her funeral was held on June 16, 2007, after nearly 64 years of marriage). They spent their seven-day, $70 dollar, honeymoon in Blowing Rock, NC and moved to Hinsdale, IL, where Graham pastored a Western Springs congregation. When he joined Youth For Christ as an evangelist, Ruth moved to Montreat, where she could be near her parents and provide a home and headquarters for her husband. In 1956, the family moved into a new home on 200 acres of mountaintop property that Graham had purchased for more privacy. Here, their five children grew up. Ruth became an accomplished electrician, plumber, painter, and seamstress. She wrote more than a dozen inspirational books, and shared with her husband the Congressional Gold Medal in 1996 for their contribution "to morality, racial equality, family and religion." Ruth became bedridden with degenerative osteoarthritis in her spine. In 2005, Billy, unable to carry on his crusades, retired to her bedside. Her funeral was attended by over 2,000 and presided upon by her pastor, Richard White. George Beverly Shea was featured at the funeral, singing at age 98. Her husband has probably been the most influential leader in the history of the Christian church since the days of MARTIN LUTHER. At 416 crusades in 195 countries, Graham preached to some 210,000,000 in person, not to mention the radio, TV and film ministry (which resulted in untold millions coming to Christ). To a great extent, this would not have been possible without Ruth, a special wife, raising his children as he was gone great periods of time. All their children carry on as able communicators of the gospel. Franklin (Samaritan's Purse) and Anne Graham-Lotz have conducted numerous evangelistic crusades. Nelson (Ned) Graham heads East Gate Ministries (distributing Bibles in China).

Tammy Faye (Bakker) Messner

March 7, 1942
International Falls, Minnesota

July 20, 2007
near Kansas City, Missouri

PTL televangelist and soloist. Tammy Messner came to prominence as co-host of *The PTL Club*, which she founded with her former husband, Jim Bakker in 1974. In 1978, they opened Heritage USA, a 2,300 acre complex designed for vacations and Christian living. In 1987 the ministry was embroiled in scandal involving her husband, who later went to prison for fraud (45-year sentence overturned in 1994). They divorced in 1992, and Tammy married Roe Messner, a longtime friend and Heritage contractor. She never left the media spotlight, even while her health deteriorated. In an effort to reach out in love, she ministered to homosexuals, though she never affirmed the gay lifestyle. Tammy and Jim participated in founding Pat Robertson's *700 Club* (CBN) and the Trinity Broadcasting Network (TBN). In 1996, Tammy was diagnosed with cancer. She fought it for almost eleven years while continuing her evangelistic work. Even as cancer racked her body, she continued to make appearances on talk shows, testifying to God's faithfulness. Just days before dying, she gave her final interview on the *Larry King Live* show. Her final words were, "I believe, when I leave this earth, because I love the Lord, I am going straight to heaven. She had two children: a son, Jay Bakker, and a daughter, Tammy Sue Chapman.

George Otis, Sr.

April 20, 1917
Payne, Ohio

July 22, 2007
Murrieta, California

Radio pioneer for Assemblies of God, founder of the Voice of Hope Radio Network. Otis launched shortwave radio stations around the globe. He also started Middle East Television, and in 1973, High Adventure Ministries, which continues to broadcast news and Bible teaching from its base in Jerusalem. Otis accepted Christ while working as a manager for Lear Corporation in California. "I discovered Jesus was high adventure; I was walking in the stars instead of having my 'lights put out,' as I had feared." Sometimes known as "the electric man," he helped lead his employer, Bill Lear, to salvation and influenced athletes, politicians and actors to accept Christ and receive the baptism of the Holy Spirit. Otis authored more than a dozen books, including his autobiography, *High Adventure*. He began advocating support for Israel in the 1970s, fearlessly spreading the gospel in the Middle East. When a suicide bomber attacked High Adventure's station there, killing four, the station went back on the air in an hour. He and his wife, Virginia were married fifty-five years and raised two sons and three daughters.

Ian Thomas

Sept. 13, 1914
Hampstead, London, England

August 1, 2007
Estes Park, Colorado

Evangelist, founder of the Torchbearers Missionary Fellowship and Capernwray Hall, a beautiful recreation center in Carnforth, England. At twelve years of age, he received Christ at a boy's camp. At 15, he decided to be a missionary and entered London University to study medicine. At age 19, he felt God wanted him to preach throughout the British Isles. From ages 25 to 32, he served in World War II as a member of the Royal Fusileers, who batled the Nazis acrosss North Africa, Italy, and Greece. He married his wife, Joan, in 1941. This evangelical statesman also helped start Bible schools and Christian conference centers around the world. Capernwray Hall, a castle-like mansion, set on 100 acres of parkland, was acquired for a conference center in 1946. From 1948–56, more than 1,250 young people from several European countries came there, and 150 students attended his two-term winter Bible school. In 1953, the movement was organized as the Capernwray Missionary Fellowship of Torchbearers. Capernwray also became a holiday center for British young people, and thousands attended Bible conferences and house parties.

Warren Webster

Feb. 17, 1928
Gary, Indiana

August 15, 2007
Wheaton, Illinois

Director of Conservative Baptist Foreign Mission Society (named World Venture in 2001). Warren and his wife, Shirley served as missionaries to Pakistan, and Warren was a keynote speaker at several Urbana missions conferences.

Fred Smith

1916
Hampstead, London, England

August 17, 2007
Estes Park, Colorado

Leadership expert, mentor to Christian business executives and ministry leaders. Smith was also president of his own food packaging company and a consultant to Mobil, Caterpillar, and a vice president at Gruen Watch. Fred's business expertise made him a popular speaker and writer. He always referred to the Bible, calling America back to the basics. He could offer criticism with wit and humor, and people welcomed it. Smith credited his success in speaking, business and leadership to his upbringing. The son of a Baptist pastor, he said he learned organization from his mother, who fed seven on $125 per month. They also taught him to share his gifts with others—which he did, helping organizations such as Christianity Today, Youth for Christ, Bill Glass Ministries, Turner Foundation, Reach International, and a Cincinnati Billy Graham Crusade, among others. Smith was married to Mary Alice for sixty-seven years and left three children.

Alphabetical Index

Aaron, Thomas L.	763
Aasgard, John A.	871
Abbadie, James	261
Abbo(n)	99
Abbot, George	208
Abbot, Robert	221
Abbott, Benjamin	296
Abbott, Edward	547
Abbott, Edwin A.	628
Abbott, Jacob	434
Abbott, Lyman	614
Abeel, David	348
Abel, Charles W.	646
Abelard, Peter	115
Aberhart, William	721
Aberly, John	854
Abernathy, Ralph D.	1062
Abraham, Dezso	1136
Absalon, Axel	123
Acacius	63
Ackerman, William	1215
Ackley, Alfred H.	829
Ackley, Bentley D.	815
Adalbert of Hamburg/Bremen	106
Adalbert of Prague	98
Adaldag	97
Adam of Marsh	129
Adam of Saint Victor	122
Adamnan,	80
Adams, Abigail Smith	315
Adams, C. C.	833
Adams, Kenneth R.	1024
Adams, Theodore F.	978
Adams, Thomas	218
Adamson, Patrick	193
Addams, Jane	673
Addicks, George B.	555
Addison, Joseph	257
Ademar	108
Adeotatus	45
Aelfric of Canterbury	99
Aelfric of York	104
Aelfric the Grammarian	101
Aethelbert of Kent	73
Aethelheard	86
Aethelnoth	103
Aethelred	119
Aethelthryth (Etheldreda)	78
Aethelwold	97
Africanus, Sextus J.	17
Afrikaner	316
Agatha	19
Aggrey, James E. K.	632
Aglipay, Labayan G.	705
Agnes	27
Agnew, David H.	478
Agnew, Eliza	449
Agricola, Johann	181
Ahlfeld, Johann F.	451
Ahnfelt, Oscar	446
Aidan	76
Ainsworth, Ariel C.	1066
Ainsworth, Henry	203
Alain	123
Alban	28
Albert	182
Albright, Jacob	306
Albright, William F.	911
Alcock, John	154
Alcuin, Flacous A	86
Alderfer, Owen H.	1072
Aldhelm	80
Aldrich, Doris Coffin	813
Aldrich, Lloyd L. (Roy)	1146
Aldridge, Dennis M.	1199
Alesius, Alexander	181
Alexander - Dixon, Helen Cadbury	892
Alexander I	3
Alexander of Alexandria	32
Alexander of Comana	18
Alexander of Hales	127
Alexander of Jerusalem	19
Alexander, Archibald	357
Alexander, Cecil Frances Humphreys	491
Alexander, Charles M.	603
Alexander, George M.	999
Alexander, James W.	371
Alexander, John W.	1192
Alexander, Joseph A.	373
Alexander, Michael S.	347
Alexander, William A.	553
Alford, Henry	401
Alfred	93
Allan, George	711

Name	Page	Name	Page
Alleine, Joseph	228	Anderson, Paul	1108
Allen, Asa A.	904	Anderson, Robert	588
Allen, Charles L.	1237	Anderson, Rufus	436
Allen, Chester G.	429	Anderson, Stuart L.	1116
Allen, George N.	429	Anderson, Theodore W.	918
Allen, Horace N.	66	Anderson, William B.	702
Allen, Paul S.	922	Anderson, William F.	728
Allen, Richard	329	Andre, John	288
Allen, William	393	Andreae, Jacob (James)	192
Allen, William H.	446	Andreae, Johann V.	218
Allenby, Edmund H. H.	680	Andreen, Gustaf A.	705
Allin, John M.	1146	Andrew of Crete,	82
Alline, Henry	289	Andrew, James O.	401
Allis, Oswald T.	921	Andrew, Samuel	266
Allshorn, Florence	760	Andrewes, Lancelot	206
Allston, Washington	342	Andrews, Charles F.	703
Alopen (Olopun)	79	Andrews, Edward G.	545
Alphege	100	Andrews, James E.	1243
Altman, Frank D.	614	Andrews, Lorrin	394
Alypius	57	Angel, Bernard	642
Amalarius	89	Angelico, Fra	150
Amandus	78	Angilbert	87
Ambrose	47	Anglin, Leslie M.	716
Ambrose, Isaac	227	Angus, Joseph	523
Ambrosiaster	47	Anicetus	6
Amburgey, Kash	1201	Ankerberg, Floyd	1126
Ames, Edward R.	432	Annand, James E.	1247
Ames, Edward S.	814	Anselm of Canterbury	110
Ames, William	209	Anselm of Laon	112
Amman, Jacob(Joseph)	251	Ansgar (Anskar)	90
Amsdorf, Nikolaus von	181	Anterus	17
Amyraut, Moise(Moses)	227	Anthony of Egypt	38
Anacletus I	2	Anthony of Kiev	106
Anastasia (1)	28	Anthony of Padua	126
Anastasia (2)	71	Anthony, Susan B.	538
Anastasia and Basilissa	1	Anthusa,	42
Anastasius (1)	19	Antipas,	2
Anastasius (2)	27	Aphraates, Jacob	39
Anastasius I	50	Apollinaris of Laodicea	45
Anatolius	62	Apollinaris, Claudius	9
Ancillon, Charles	254	Apollonia	18
Anderrson, Lars	171	Appelman, Hyman J.	1003
Andersen, Hans Christian	418	Appenzeller, Henry G.	523
Anderson (Fisher), Marian	1091	Archer, Gleason	1224
Anderson, Archer E.	962	Archer, Glenn L.	1203
Anderson, Charles W.	1071	Archer, Russell C.	1147
Anderson, Elmer G.	897	Archibald, Byran F.	1181
Anderson, Harry O.	889	Arenas, Manuel	1082
Anderson, John	328	Argue, Andrew H.	818
Anderson, Ken	1243	Aristides, Marcianus	5
Anderson, Lyle C.	1075	Aristides, Publius A.	9

Aristo	7
Arlander, Ragner A.	799
Armerding, Carl	1036
Armerding, George D.	1026
Arminius, Jacobus	198
Armitage, Thomas B.	493
Armour, Philip D.	513
Armstrong, Annie W.	696
Armstrong, C.I.	930
Armstrong, Hart R.	1103
Armstrong, Philip E.	989
Arnaud, Henri	258
Arndt, Johann	203
Arndt, William F.	805
Arne, Thomas A.	286
Arnobius the Elder	33
Arnold of Brescia	117
Arnold, Gottfried	252
Arnold, Thomas	340
Arnot, Frederick S.	573
Arnot, William	417
Arnup, Jesse H.	865
Arrowhead, Virgil	1216
Arthur, William	515
Asaph	70
Asbury, Francis	312
Ashbrook, William E.	957
Ashcroft, J. Robert	1111
Askew, Anne	169
Asser	94
Asterius,	53
Athanasius I	134
Athanasius of Alexandria	41
Athanasius the Athonite	99
Athearn, Walter S.	670
Athelbert of East Anglia	85
Athenagoras	10
Atkinson, Frederick C.	496
Atterbury, Francis	264
Atwood, Rudy	1086
Audubon, John J.	354
Auger, Wes	1130
Aughiera, Peter M.	159
Augsburger, Bryce B.	1049
Augustine of Canterbury,	72
Augustine, Aurelius	56
Autorianus, Arsenius	130
Autrey, C. Elijah	1093
Axton, John T.	688
Ayer, William W.	1023
Aylward, Gladys	900
Azariah, Vedanayagam S.	729
Babcock, Maltbie D.	517
Babson, Roger W.	877
Bach, Johann S.	271
Bach, Thomas J.	851
Backus, Isaac	304
Bacon, Francis	206
Bacon, Roger	132
Bacon, Sr., Leonard	442
Bader, Jesse M.	852
Bading, Johannes	569
Baedeker, Friedrich W.	540
Baer, John W.	651
Bagby, William B.	691
Bagger, Henry H.	878
Bailey, Nathan L.	971
Bailey, Wellesley C.	687
Baillie (1), Robert	225
Baillie (2), Robert	239
Bainton, Roland H.	1009
Baird, Jesse H.	947
Baird, Robert	379
Baker, Charles F.	1108
Baker, Daniel	368
Baker, E. Dewitt	1168
Baker, Edwin G.	833
Baker, Elizabeth V. Duncan Dawson-	577
Baker, Henry W.	425
Baker, Herman	1068
Baker, James C.	898
Baker, Mary Ann	609
Baker, Milton G.	957
Baker, Oren H.	995
Baker, Osmon C.	403
Bakewell, John	315
Balch, William	340
Baldwin I	112
Baldwin II	114
Baldwin,	122
Bale, John	179
Balfe, Christopher J.	750
Balfour, Arthur J.	646
Ball (1), John	142
Ball (2), John	211
Ball, Arthur G.	794
Ball, Henry C.	1055
Ball, William F.	1008
Ballantyne, Victor A.	1058
Balsamon, Theodore	122
Bancroft, Richard	199
Bandy, Julian A.	1149

Bangs, Nathan	377
Banks, Louis A.	665
Banneker, Benjamin	304
Baptista, Charles O.	862
Baradaeus, Jacobus	69
Barbara	29
Barber, Walter L.	1086
Barbieri, Sante U.	1068
Barbon, Praisegod	236
Barbour, Clarence A.	687
Barbour, Clifford E.	968
Barclay, Alexander	171
Barclay, John	297
Barclay, Robert	243
Bardesanes	15
Barfoot, Walter F.	965
Baring-Gould, Sabine	618
Barker, Annie H.	655
Barlow, Fred M.	1001
Barlow, Joel	309
Barnard, Charlotte Alington Pye	394
Barnard, Russell D.	1027
Barnardo, Thomas J.	535
Barnby, Joseph	493
Barnes, Albert	400
Barnes, Marion D.	1231
Barnes, Robert	165
Barnett, Lester (Les)	819
Barnett, Samuel A.	569
Barnhouse, Donald G.	831
Baron, David	629
Barraclough, Henry	1005
Barrett, Ethel Macmamee	1148
Barrett, Harold J.	1132
Barrow(e), Henry	193
Barrow, Isaac	235
Barrow, Nita	1120
Barry, Alvin L.	1178
Barstow, Robbins W.	844
Barth, Christian G.	378
Barth, Hattie M. Sexton	802
Barth, Karl	891
Barth, Paul T.	710
Bartholomew,	137
Bartleman, Frank	684
Bartlett, Eugene M.	707
Bartlett, Gene E.	1058
Bartlett, George G.	774
Bartolommeo, Fra	156
Barton, Bernard	351
Barton, Bruce	879
Barton, George A.	714
Barton, James L.	683
Barton, William E.	650
Bascom, Henry B.	354
Basham, Donald W.	1053
Bashford, James W.	596
Basil	42
Bast, Henry	1002
Bates, Carl E.	1164
Bates, Katherine L.	639
Bathurst, William H.	428
Baugh, Helen Duff	1122
Baugher, Norman J.	887
Baughman, Harry F.	981
Bauman, Louis S.	761
Bauman, Paul F.	1005
Baur, Benjamin A.	824
Bauslin, David H.	611
Baxter, Annie	1024
Baxter, George A.	339
Baxter, J. Sidlow	1164
Baxter, Jesse R.	825
Baxter, Lydia Odell	414
Baxter, Richard	244
Bayly, Joseph T.	1030
Bazar, Kenneth L.	1028
Beach, David N.	629
Beach, Harlan P.	662
Beachum, Paul F.	962
Beal, Richard S.	1059
Beam, David J.	1151
Beamer, Todd	1185
Beardslee, Jr., John W.	842
Beardslee, Sr., John W.	605
Beauchamp, Daniel E.	1030
Beausobre, Isaac de	266
Beaven, Albert W.	719
Becher, Wilhelm	597
Becker, Carl K.	1066
Becker, Elmer	897
Beckwith, Paul	943
Beddow, James	1133
Bede	82
Bedell, William	212
Bedford, James N.	900
Beebe, Joseph A.	527
Beebe, Wally	1201
Beecher, Henry W.	460
Beecher, Lyman	378
Beecher, Willis J.	564
Beers, Alexander	607

Name	Page
Beets, Henry	747
Begbie, Harold	642
Beguin, Olivier	914
Behnken, John W.	885
Belknap, Jeremy	297
Bell, B. Clayton	1169
Bell, Colin W.	1049
Bell, Eudorus B.	617
Bell, George K.A.	816
Bell, J. Leonard	1184
Bell, L. Nelson	926
Bell, William Y.	842
Bellamy, Edward	502
Bellamy, Joseph	292
Beman, Nathan S.S.	402
Bender, Harold S.	844
Benedict of Aniane	87
Benedict of Nursia	67
Benedict, Cleveland K.	677
Benezet	120
Bengel, Johann A.	273
Benham, Priscilla Patten	1166
Bennard, George	816
Benner, Hugh C.	941
Bennet, James E.	825
Bennett, Dennis F.	1076
Bennett, Sanford F.	503
Bennett, John C.	1160
Benno	109
Benson, Clarence H.	788
Benson, Edward W.	496
Benson, Joseph	317
Benson, Louis F.	648
Benson, Raymond E.	1140
Benson, Robert	1028
Bentley, John B.	1056
Bentley, Richard	267
Bentley, William H.	1093
Benton, John K.	801
Benton, Robert W.	1159
Berengar	107
Berg, Carolina Sandell, Mrs. C.Berg	527
Bergemann, Gustav E.	785
Bergendorf, Conrad J.I.	1144
Berggrav, Eivand	818
Berkeley, George	273
Berkhof, Louis	806
Berkouwer, Gerrit C.	1122
Bernall, Cassie	1157
Bernard of Clairvaux	117
Bernard of Cluny	117
Bernard of Menthon,	100
Bernard, Thomas D.	532
Bernardino,	150
Berno (Bruno)	94
Bernsten, Annie S.	1077
Berntsen, William B.	1064
Berquin, Louis de	161
Berquist, Millard J.	1062
Berry, Lelwellyn L.	789
Bersell, Petrus O.	879
Bersier, Eugene A.F.	470
Bertermann, Eugene R.	1008
Berthold von Regensburg	130
Bessmertny, Boris	1034
Bethune, George W.	377
Bethune, Mary McLeod	792
Beveridge, Thomas	411
Beveridge, William	251
Beyschlag, Willibald	512
Beza, Theodore	197
Bhengu, Nicholas B.H.	1023
Bickersteth, Jr., Edward H.	539
Bickersteth, Sr., Edward H.	353
Biederwolf, William E.	700
Biel, Gabriel	154
Bigg, Charles	547
Bihl, Carl J.	1209
Bilderdijk, Willem	329
Bilhorn, Peter P.	686
Bill, Samuel A.	717
Billings, Robert J.	1115
Billington, Dallas F.	918
Bilney, Thomas	162
Bilson, Thomas	201
Bimeler, Joseph M.	360
Bingham, Jr., Hiram	549
Bingham, Roland V.	718
Bingham, Sr., Hiram	396
Binkley, Olin T.	1160
Binney, John	569
Binney, Thomas	413
Birch, Frank R.	872
Birch, John M.	734
Bird, Milton	402
Birinus	76
Birks, Thomas R.	449
Birney, Lauress J.	689
Biscop, Benedict	79
Bishop, Bridget	245
Bishop, Tom	599
Bishop, William H.	411

Bismarck, Otto E. L.	503		Bodine, William B.	544
Bitterman, Chester	986		Boegner, Marc	907
Bjork, Carl A.	584		Boehler, Peter	285
Blaatand, Harold	97		Boehm, Martin	308
Black, Hugh	777		Boehme, Jakob	205
Black, James M.	696		Boethius, Anicius M. S.	65
Blackburn, Gideon	337		Bogard, Ben M.	766
Blackett, George M.	837		Bogatzky, Karl H.	285
Blackstone (1), William E.	287		Bogue, David	323
Blackstone (2), William E.	676		Bohemund I, Marc	111
Blackwood, Andrew W.	872		Boice, James M.	1169
Blackwood, James W.	1191		Bonar, Andrew A.	479
Blackwood R. W. Lyles, Bill	787		Bonar, Horatius	468
Blaikie, William G.	506		Bond, Jeffery	1244
Blaiklock, Edward M.	1006		Bond, Silas W.	701
Blair, James	268		Bondone, Giotto	137
Blair, Samuel	272		Bonhoeffer, Dietrich	731
Blaise,	32		Boniface I,	55
Blake, Eugene C.	1021		Boniface of Savoy	129
Blake, Robert	222		Boniface	83
Blake, Thaddeus C.	493		Bonnell, John S.	1079
Blakemore, William B.	939		Bonner, Winnie	972
Blanchard, Charles A.	626		Bonsak, Charles D.	777
Blanchard, Ferdinand Q.	886		Boon, Harold W.	1163
Blanchard, Jonathan	478		Booth, Ballington	706
Blanchard, Richard E.	1223		Booth, Catherine Mumford	472
Blandina	8		Booth, Charles B.	970
Blandy, Gray M.	1061		Booth, Evangeline C.	760
Blanton, Sankey L.	932		Booth, F. Carlton	1081
Blanton, Smiley	875		Booth, L. Venchael	1203
Blaurock, Georg	161		Booth, Maude Charlesworth	752
Blegen, Allen R.	973		Booth, W. Bramwell	640
Blinco, Joseph	888		Booth, William	566
Bliss, Daniel	584		Booth-Tucker, Frederick G.	641
Bliss, Philip P.	424		Borden, William W.	568
Blodget, Henry	527		Boreham, Frank W.	821
Blodgett, Robert	1131		Borel, Adam	228
Blom, Fredrick A.	631		Boren, Charles E.	1014
Blumhardt, Johann C.	436		Boris I	94
Boardman, Henry A.	437		Borrow, George H.	440
Boardman, Jr., George D.	526		Borthwick, Jane L.	499
Boardman, Sr., George D.	328		Boston, Thomas	264
Boardman, Richard	289		Bosworth, Edward I.	628
Boaz, Hiram A.	840		Bosworth, Fred F.	884
Boberg, Carl G.	702		Botticelli, Alessandro F.	156
Bock, Fred	1150		Bottome, Frank / Francis	486
Bockman, Marcus O.	715		Boudinot, Elias	318
Bocskay, Stephen	197		Boulter, Hugh	268
Boddie, Charles E.	1140		Bouma, Clarence	843
Bode, John E.	415		Bounds, Edward M.	569
Bodholt, Knud C.	655		Bourbon, Louis de	183

Bourgeois, Louis	178
Bowen, Arthur J.	841
Bowie, Walter R.	894
Bowlby, Harry L.	875
Bowman, Clellan A.	687
Bowman (1), Thomas A.	573
Bowman (2), Thomas	616
Bowman, John C.	648
Bowman, Rufus D.	773
Bownde, Nicholas	200
Bowring, John	408
Boyce (1), James	468
Boyce (2), James	555
Boyce, James P.	466
Boyce, William W.	931
Boyd, Myron F.	965
Boyle, Robert	245
Boyle, Samuel E.	1201
Boyum, Arne E.	569
Bracken, Archie K.	873
Bradbury, John W.	1038
Bradbury, William B.	390
Bradford, John	174
Bradford, Samuel J.	932
Bradford, William	221
Bradshaw, William	202
Bradstreet, Anne Dudley	232
Bradwardine, Thomas	138
Bradwell, Marion G.	1073
Brady, Nicholas	260
Brahms, Johannes	497
Brainerd, David	270
Bramwell, William	315
Brand, Frederick	753
Brand, Paul	1210
Brandelle, Gustaf A.	678
Branham, William M.	870
Brant, Joseph	305
Brasher, John L.	907
Brauer, Jerald C.	1162
Braun, Willys K.	1216
Braunlin, Hermann G.	1118
Bray, Billy	392
Bray, Thomas	263
Breasted, James H.	676
Breck, Carrie Elizabeth Ellis	668
Breck, James L.	421
Breckbill, William W.	934
Breckenridge, John	339
Breckenridge, Robert J.	403
Bredesen, Harold	1249

Breese, Dave	1195
Brendan	69
Brengle, Samuel L.	680
Brenner, John T.	845
Brent, Charles H.	639
Brentz, Johannes	184
Bresee, Phineas F.	581
Bretschneider, Albert	892
Brewster, David	391
Brewster, Percy S.	981
Brewster, William	213
Breyfogel, Sylvanus C.	671
Briconnet, Guillaume (William)	163
Bridgers, Luther B.	751
Bridget	140
Bridgman, Elijah C.	375
Briggs, Eugene S.	963
Bright, Bill	1211
Brigit	65
Brink, William P.	1162
Britton, Homer F.	1075
Broadus, John A.	489
Brock, Blanche Kerr	810
Brock, Jr., Fred R.	1004
Brock, Virgil P.	963
Broen, Engret M.	693
Broger, John	1242
Broman, Franklin A.	1089
Brondsema, John	1088
Bronstein, David	1024
Bronte, Anne	352
Brookes, James H.	498
Brooks, Keith L.	784
Brooks, Phillips	480
Brooks, Samuel P.	652
Brookshire, Joseph R.	1077
Broomfield, John C.	751
Brorson, Hans A.	279
Brougham, Royal	967
Brougher, J. Whitcomb	882
Broughton, Leonard G.	680
Brouwer, Arie R.	1098
Brown (1), John	291
Brown (2), John	372
Brown, Arlo A.	839
Brown, Arnold	1198
Brown, Arthur J.	848
Brown, Charles E.	911
Brown, Charles R.	762
Brown, David	498
Brown, Edith M.	803

Brown, Frank R.	1111
Brown, Fred	1085
Brown, Fred F.	829
Brown, George	403
Brown, James A.	445
Brown, Oswald E.	701
Brown, Robert M.	1185
Brown, Robert R.	855
Brown, Samuel R.	437
Brown, Sr., John E.	804
Brown, W. Shelburne	967
Brown, William	392
Browne, Robert	208
Browne, Thomas	238
Brownell, Thomas C.	383
Browning, Delmar L.	1241
Browning, Robert	470
Brownlow, William G.	426
Brownson, Truman G.	636
Brownville, C. Gordon	974
Brubaker, Henry G.	854
Brubaker, Leland S.	883
Bruce, Alexander B.	507
Bruce, Frederick F.	1065
Bruce, Walter F.	1084
Bruce, William	438
Brucioli, Antonio	172
Bruffett, Fred	907
Brully, Peter	168
Brumbaugh, Martin G.	646
Brumley, Albert E.	960
Bruno (Boniface) of Querfurt,	100
Bruno I	95
Bruno of Cologne,	109
Brushwyler, Vincent	982
Bryan, Elmer B.	670
Bryan, William J.	624
Bucer, Martin	170
Buchanan, Claudius	310
Buchanan, George	188
Buchanan, James	392
Buchman, Frank N. D.	836
Buck, Charles	311
Buck, Dudley	553
Buck-Walsh, Pearl Sydenstricker	922
Buckingham, Jamie	1079
Buckley, James M.	600
Budd, Henry H.	1159
Budde, Johann F.	263
Bude, Guillaume (Wm)	165
Buehring, Paul H.	814
Buell, Harriet E. Peck	555
Buell, Marcus D.	667
Buffum, Herbert	700
Bugenhagen, Johann	176
Buhrig, Marga	1192
Buksbazen, Victor	935
Bull, George	251
Bullinger, J. Heinrich	187
Bultema, Daniel C.	1223
Buntain, D. Mark	1056
Buntain, Daniel N.	794
Bunting, Jabez	369
Bunyan, John	242
Buonarroti, Michelangelo	180
Burckhardt, Johann L.	314
Burger, Andrew	1242
Burgess, William J.	953
Burgon, John W.	465
Burke, Daniel	901
Burkett, Larry	1210
Burkholder, Melvin I.	1042
Burleson, Rufus C.	516
Burnet, Gilbert	253
Burnett, Cordas C.	942
Burns, James D.	382
Burns, William C.	391
Burnvedt, Thorvald O.	828
Burr, Sr., Aaron	275
Burrell, David J.	629
Burris, Jackie L.	937
Burritt, Eldon G.	633
Burrough, Edward	225
Burrows, Lansing	598
Burrows, Millar	980
Burtchin, H. Lee	847
Burton, Charles E.	705
Burton, John	319
Burton, Robert	210
Bury, John B.	631
Bustin, Green T.	1116
Buswell, James O.	955
Butler, Charles W.	826
Butler, Joseph	273
Butler, William	507
Butterfield, Charles E.	979
Butterick, George A.	977
Buttz, Henry A.	603
Buxton, Barclay F.	736
Buxton, Cleo W.	1046
Buxton, Thomas F.	345
Byers, Noah E.	843

Byington, Cyrus	394
Byrer, Charles E.	722
Byrom, John	279
Byrum, Enoch E.	712
Cable, A. Mildred	771
Cadle, E. Howard	718
Cadman, Samuel P.	686
Caecilian	36
Caedmon,	78
Caird, John	503
Cairns, John	477
Caius,	26
Calamy, Edmund	228
Caldbeck, George T.	589
Calderwood, David	217
Caldwell, Frank H.	1037
Caldwell, Josiah S.	672
Calhoun, Simeon H.	424
Calixtus I	14
Calixtus, Georg	220
Calkin, John B.	534
Calvert, James	477
Calvin, John	180
Cambrensis, Giraldus	125
Cameron, Richard	237
Camp, Mabel Johnston	689
Camp, Norman H.	772
Campanius, John	239
Campbell, Alexander	386
Campbell, Duncan	916
Campbell, Henry D.	775
Campbell, Thomas	361
Campbell, William H.	473
Candler, Warren A.	710
Candlish, Robert S.	412
Cannon, Jr., James H.	727
Cannon, William R.	1134
Canstein, Karl H.	257
Cantrell, Roy H.	1144
Canute II	103
Canute IV	107
Capgrave, John	151
Capito, Wolfgang F.	166
Carey, William	332
Cargill, Donald	237
Carle, Bill J.	846
Carleton, Alfred	1005
Carlile, Wilson	716
Carlsen, John	851
Carlsen, Niels C.	758
Carlson, Frank	1037
Carlson, G. Ray	1155
Carlson, Maurice	1104
Carlson, Paul	860
Carlson, Walter	1051
Carlstadt, Andreas R. B.	166
Carmichael, Amy B.	763
Carnahan, James	370
Carnell, Edward J.	878
Carpenter, Edward D.	739
Carpenter, George L.	750
Carpenter, Mary	427
Carpenter, William B.	588
Carpzov, Johann B.	247
Carr, Benjamin	329
Carrington, William O.	916
Carroll, Benajah H.	575
Carson, Alexander	344
Carstares, William	254
Carter, Calvin G.	994
Carter, Charles	1128
Carter, George W.	646
Carter, Raymond F.	1163
Carter, Randall A.	783
Carter, Russell K.	637
Cartlidge, A. Ray	1064
Cartwright, Peter	407
Cartwright, Thomas	196
Carver, George W.	719
Carver, John	203
Carver, Loyce C.	1123
Carver, William O.	786
Carvosso, William	333
Cary, Lott	327
Cary, Maud	880
Casaubon, Isaac	200
Case, Charles C.	593
Caserta, Frederick A.	1243
Cash, Johnny	1213
Cashwell, Gaston B.	582
Cassel, Elijah Taylor.	647
Cassel, Flora Hamilton	562
Cassianus, John	58
Cassiodorus, Flavius M. A.	69
Castell, Edmund	240
Castle, Nicholas	612
Catherine of Alexandria	29
Catherine of Bologna	151
Catherine of Genoa	156
Catherine of Siena	141
Catherine of Sweden	141
Caton, William	228

Cattell, Everett L.	985
Cauthern, Baker J.	1019
Cavalier, Jean	266
Cavell, Edith L.	580
Cavert, Samuel M.	954
Cavin, David A.	1083
Cecil, Richard	307
Cecilia	16
Cedarholm, B. Myron	1135
Cedd	77
Celestine I	57
Cennick, John	274
Cerularius, Michael	105
Chad	78
Chaderton, Laurence	211
Chadwick, Samuel	659
Chafer, Lewis S.	753
Chalmers, James	516
Chalmers, Thomas	349
Chamberlain, Jacob	546
Chambers, George A.	810
Chambers, Oswald	588
Chamber, Stanley W.	1225
Chambers, Talbot W.	493
Chamier, Daniel	203
Champion, Richard	1105
Chao, Jonathan	1220
Chao, Tsu-Chen	974
Chapman, J. Wilbur	593
Chapman, James B.	746
Chapman, Vaughn	1145
Chapman, William A.	988
Chappell, Clovis G.	918
Charlemagne	86
Charles I	215
Charles IX	199
Charles VII	151
Charles, Elizabeth Rundle	494
Charles, B. Raymond	1051
Charles, Robert H.	650
Charlesworth, Vernon J.	576
Charnock, Stephen	237
Chase, Irah	382
Chase, Philander	358
Chase, Salmon P.	410
Chaucer, Geoffrey	144
Chauncy, Charles	231
Chelli, Jacob	1235
Chemnitz, Martin	190
Cheney, Charles E.	585
Cherry, Floyd B.	1233
Chesser, Hallie L.	1040
Chester, Samuel H.	703
Cheyne, Thomas K.	578
Chichele, Henry	149
Childs, John F.	730
Chillingworth, William	213
Ching-Yi, Cheng	696
Chiniquy, Charles P. T.	505
Chisholm, Thomas O.	826
Chorley, Henry F.	405
Chown, Samuel D.	661
Christensen, Bernard M.	1012
Christian II	176
Christian IV	215
Christiansen, Avis M. Burgeson	1016
Christiansen, Gottleib B.	642
Christlieb, Theodor	469
Christopher	19
Chrysologus, Peter	60
Chrysostom, John	52
Church, Richard W.	473
Churchill, Clinton H.	926
Claas, Gerhard	1044
Clap, Thomas	280
Clark, A. D.	451
Clark, Eugene L.	995
Clark, Francis E.	631
Clark, Glenn	800
Clark, Gordon H.	1018
Clark, Howard H.	1000
Clark, Isaac	591
Clark, Mary E.	1193
Clark, Nathaniel G.	492
Clark, Scott T.	958
Clark, Thomas M.	528
Clark, Walter H.	1110
Clarke, Adam	330
Clarke, George R.	478
Clarke, Harry D.	808
Clarke, John	234
Clarke, Sarah Dunn	589
Clarkson, Thomas	348
Claude, Jean	240
Claudon, David N.	745
Claybaugh, Joseph	365
Clayton, Norman J.	1082
Clearwaters, Richard V.	1127
Clement I of Rome	2
Clement of Alexandria	13
Clement, Frank G.	899
Clements, John R.	736

Clephane, Elizabeth Cecelia Douglas	395	Conder, Josiah	365
Cleveland, James L.	1068	Cone, Spencer H.	364
Clifford, John	617	Confer, Bernard	1048
Climacus, John	75	Conkey, Ithamar	388
Climenhaga, Art	1234	Conner, Benjamin C.	607
Cline, Eddy S.	1228	Conner, Walter T.	772
Clinton, Joseph J.	439	Conrad of Waldhausen	140
Clippinger, Arthur R.	814	Conrad, Arcturus Z.	688
Cloak, Frank V. C.	781	Constantine I	34
Clotilda	67	Converse, Charles C.	592
Cloud	68	Conwell, Russell H.	625
Clough, John E.	558	Conybeare, William J.	367
Clough, Samuel O. G.	554	Conzett, Jacob	580
Clovis I	64	Cook C., James	287
Clow, William M.	644	Cook, Charles	368
Clowney, Ed P.	1233	Cook, David C.	632
Coan, Titus	447	Cook, Gaines M.	1002
Cocceius, Johannes	230	Cook, George H.	749
Coder, S. Maxwell	1137	Cook, III, David C.	1062
Coe, Jack	803	Cook, J. Hubert	993
Coerper, Heinrich	683	Cook, John H. W.	716
Coffey, Rufus	1176	Cook, Robert A.	1069
Coffin, Frank G.	709	Cooke, Henry	394
Coggan, F. Donald	1168	Cookman, George C.	339
Coghill, Annie L. Walker	543	Coolidge, Calvin	661
Cohn, Joseph H.	781	Cooper, Charles M.	1087
Cohn, Leopold	692	Cooper, Clay	1105
Coillard, Francois	529	Cooper, David L.	861
Coke, Thomas	310	Cooper, Owen	1033
Cole, Azel D.	457	Coornhert, Dirck V.	192
Coleman, George W.	543	Cop, Nicholas	169
Coleman, Robert H.	737	Copping, John	189
Colgate, William	367	Corbett, W. Lynn	1075
Coligny, Gaspard de	184	Corey, Charles H.	507
Collins, Millard E.	1025	Corey, Stephen J.	845
Collins, Wendy	1174	Corlett, Lewis T.	1078
Collison, William H.	610	Cornelius,	20
Colman	78	Cornelius, Jack	1140
Columba	71	Cornell, George W.	1107
Columbanus/Columban	73	Correll, D. Sidney	1073
Columbus, Christopher	155	Corsini, Richard L.	1164
Colvin, Mrs. David L.	795	Corson, Fred P.	1017
Colwell, Ernest C.	935	Corvin, Raymond O.	992
Comber, Thomas J.	462	Cory, Bernice Tucker	924
Come, Arnold B.	1194	Cory, Julia Bulkley Cady	850
Comenius, John(Jay) A.	230	Cory, Victor E.	888
Comgall,	72	Cosin, John	231
Commodianus,	24	Cosmas and Damian	26
Compton, Henry	252	Costas, Orlando	1041
Conant, Newton C.	1133	Costen, James H.	1208
Conant, Thomas J.	475	Cotton, John	217

Cottrell, Elias	691
Couchman, Gaylord M.	942
Coughran, Murrell F.	1160
Coughlin, Joseph W.	1238
Cousin, Anne Ross	541
Coulter, S. George	1114
Court, Antoine	278
Courtney, Howard P.	1172
Coutts, Frederick	1026
Coverdale, Miles	182
Cowen, Charles E.	940
Cowman, Charles E.	622
Cowman, Leticia Burd	827
Cowper, William	299
Cox, Bonnie L.	951
Cox, Richard	188
Cox, Winifred R.	792
Coxe, Arthur C.	495
Craemer, A. Friedrich	475
Craft, Andrew C.	717
Craig, John	195
Craig, Robert J.	710
Cram, Willard G.	899
Crane, William C.	454
Cranmer, Thomas	175
Crannell, Philip W.	686
Cranston, Earl	658
Crawford, Angus	621
Crawford, Daniel	627
Crawford, Florence L. Reed	682
Crawford, Lois	1025
Crawford, Percy B.	831
Crawford, Raymond R.	867
Crawford, Robert B.	1184
Crawford-Porter, Ruth Duvall	1033
Crichton, James B.	1009
Crimm, B. B.	762
Cripps, Stafford	771
Crispell, Cornelius E.	557
Crispin and Crispinian,	25
Criswell, Wallie A.	1190
Crittendon, Charles N.	554
Croft, William	261
Croly, George	374
Cromwell, Oliver	222
Crosby, Frances J.	577
Crosby, Howard	474
Crosby, Thomas	572
Crose, Lester A.	1212
Cross, Allen E.	720
Cross, James A.	1061
Crossfield, Richard H.	767
Crouch, Philip P.	1232
Crowell, Elton	991
Crowell, Grace Noll	893
Crowell, Henry C.	869
Crowell, Henry P.	728
Crowley, Dale S.	1108
Crowley, Mary Carter	1029
Crowther, Samuel A.	476
Crozer, John P.	386
Cruden, Alexander	282
Cruger, Johann	225
Crumes, William B.	1222
Crummel, Alexander	504
Crumpler, Ambrose B.	775
Crumpton, James W.	1226
Cryderman, W. Dale	1240
Csehy, Wilmos	1098
Cudworth, Ralph	242
Culbertson, William	911
Culver, Ellsworth	1236
Cumming, John	440
Cummings, Kenneth	929
Cummins, George D.	422
Cummons, Bruce D.	1220
Cuninggim, Merrimon	1119
Cunningham, Arthur B.	1007
Cunningham, Fred	1119
Cunningham, Glenn	1043
Cunningham, Robert C.	1164
Cunningham, Robert W.	1150
Cunningham, William	375
Currie, Thomas W.	720
Currie, William E.	1169
Curry, Irwin K.	868
Cushing, William O.	524
Cushman, Ralph S.	830
Cushman, Robert E.	1093
Cuthbert of Lindisfarne	79
Cuthburt of Canterbury	84
Cutler, Anne	294
Cutler, Henry S.	525
Cutler, Timothy	280
Cutting, Churchill H.	620
Cuyler, Theodore L.	551
Cynewulf	88
Cyprian, Thascius	22
Cyril of Alexandria	59
Cyril of Jerusalem	44
Cyril of Thessalonica, Constantius	91
D'Albret, Jeanne	184

D'Aubigne, Jean H. M.	408
Da Costa, Isaak	373
Dabaro, Wandaro	1067
Dabney, Robert L.	500
Dagg, John L.	452
Daggett, Naphtali	288
Dahl, Theodore H.	615
Dahlberg, Edwin T.	1033
Dahlquist, Lloyd W.	1098
Dain, Jack	1203
Dake, Finis J.	1034
Dale, James G.	832
Dale, Robert W.	489
Damascus I,	44
Damianus	72
Danhof, Ralph J.	911
Daniel, Robert P.	884
Daniels, Elam J.	1035
Danner, William M.	776
Dante, Alighieri	136
Darbee, Lennard	1071
Darboy, Georges	402
Darby, John N.	444
Dargan, Edwin C.	649
Darling, Ed	1101
Darlington, Urban V. W.	789
Darr, Dick	1224
Darwall, John	291
Daugherty, Mary Lee	1230
Davenport, John	230
David	71
David, Christian	272
Davidson, Andrew B.	521
Davidson, Benjamin	751
Davidson, Randall T.	647
Davidson, Richard	725
Davies, Samuel	278
Davies, W. Elwyn	1008
Davis, F. Benjamin	1209
Davis, George T. B.	878
Davis, Gordon C.	839
Davis, John A.	668
Davis, Joseph A.	812
Davis, Lewis	471
Davis, Lyman E.	647
Davis, Merle L.	922
Davis, Ozora S.	651
Davis, Ralph T.	852
Davis, Raymond J.	1057
Dawson, Joseph M.	925
Day, Albert E.	927
Day, Cecil B.	968
Day, Jeremiah B.	388
Day, Lloyd R.	969
Day, Richard E.	862
Dayton, Edward R.	1190
De Armond, Lizzie	685
De Bres, Guido	102
De Haan, Martin R.	870
De Haan, Richard	1198
De Long, Russell V.	985
De Schweinitz, Edmund A.	463
Deal, Elmer G.	931
Dean, Horace F.	1000
Dean, John T.	1170
Dearmer, Percy	681
DeBlois, Austin K.	733
Decker, Rutherford L.	919
Dees, James P.	1067
Dehart, Don	1244
DeHart, William H.	582
Deindoerfer, Johannes	542
Deir, Costa	1154
Deissman, Adolf G.	688
Delitzsch, Franz J.	471
Dellenback, John R.	1204
Demaray, C. Dorr	1087
DeMarbelle, Daniel	529
Demarest, William H. S.	800
DeMent, Byron H.	663
Demetrius	16
DeMoss, Arthur S.	972
DeMoss, Ted	1141
Denck, Johannes	160
Denis	22
Denman, Harry	953
Denney, James	587
Dennis, Clyde H.	841
Dennis, Muriel Benson	1097
Dennis, Sr., Russell	1149
Denny, Robert S.	1123
Deusdedit	77
Devay, Matyas B.	167
DeVelder, Marion	1228
Deweerd, James A.	914
Dewey, Melvil	655
DeWitt, Thomas	414
Dewitt, William C.	654
Dexter, Henry M.	473
Deyneka, Jr., Peter	1174
Deyneka, Sr., Peter	1038
Dibelius, Otto F. K.	877

Name	Page
Dick, Otto E.	851
Dick, Walter J.	1200
Dickens, Charles J. H.	398
Dickey, Solomon C.	604
Dickhaut, John W.	1013
Dickinson, Jonathan	270
Dickson, John	542
Dickson, Lillian Levescente	999
Didacus,	124
Didymus	46
Diefenbaker, John G.	971
Dieter, Harold D.	753
Diffendorfer, Ralph E.	764
Dillon, William S.	1168
Dimnent, Edward D.	821
Diodati, J. Giovanni	216
Diodorus	46
Dionysius of Alexandria	22
Dionysius of Corinth	11
Dionysius of Rome	23
Dionysius the Areopagite	1
Dionysius the Carthusian	152
Disraeli, Benjamin	439
Dix, Morgan	547
Dix, William C.	504
Dixon, Amzi C.	624
Doan, Harold J.	1004
Doane, George W.	371
Doane, Marguerite T.	789
Doane, William C.	568
Doane, William H.	581
Dobbie, William G.	859
Dober, J. Leonhard	280
Dock, Christopher	282
Dodd, Damon C.	1208
Dodd, Monroe E.	773
Doddridge, Philip	272
Dodds, Gilbert L. "Gil"	955
Dodge, Ebenezer	470
Dodge, William E.	448
Dods, Marcus	552
Dolcino	133
Domitilla, Flavia	2
Donaghue, Charles C.	937
Donatus	38
Donnally, Chad (Chuck) V.	1174
Donne, John	207
Donnell, Robert	362
Donnelson, Fred	930
Doolittle, Justus	437
Dore, P. Gustave	448
Doremus, Sarah P. Haines	425
Dorner, Isaac A.	453
Dorothea (Dorothy),	31
Dorothy of Prussia,	147
Dorsey, Thomas A.	1089
Doudney, Sarah	629
Douglas, James D.	1212
Douglas, John E.	1046
Douglas, Lloyd C.	764
Douglass, Frederick	489
Douglass, Harlan P.	778
Dow, Lorenzo	331
Dowell, Bill	1195
Doyle, Bertram W.	983
Draper, Bourne H.	342
Drelincourt, Charles	230
Drew, Daniel	434
Drexler, Frederick I.	900
Driver, Samuel R.	572
Drum, Woodrow G.	1188
Drummond (1), Henry	373
Drummond (2), Henry	497
Druthmar, Christian	92
Du Moulin, Pierre	222
Du Plessis, David J.	1034
Du Toit, Jakob D.	779
DuBose, Henry W.	826
DuBose, William P.	591
Dubs, Rudolph	578
Duff, Alexander	428
Duffecy, James A.	1007
Duffield, Jr., George	465
Duggar, John W.	1151
Dulles, John F.	821
Duncan, Samuel E.	889
Duncan, William	590
Dunkin, John	1235
Dunlop, Merrill C.	1197
Dunn, Bruce	1094
Dunn, R. Willard	1111
Duns Scotus, John (Johannes)	134
Dunstan	97
Dunster, Henry	223
Durand, William	137
Durbin, John P.	423
Durer, Albrecht	161
Durham, William M.	565
Durie, John	242
Durkin, James F.	1121
Dwight (1), Timothy	313
Dwight (2), Timothy	583

Name	Page
Dye, Cecil A.	718
Dyer, John L.	517
Dyer, Mary Barret	223
Dykes, John B.	420
Dzao, Timothy S. K.	927
Eadie, John	422
Eagle, James P.	532
Earle, Absalom B.	490
Earle, Ralph	1115
Early, Henry C.	710
Eaton, Emma F.	787
Eaton, George W.	406
Eber, Paul	183
Ebers, George	503
Ebrard, Johannes H. A.	465
Eby, Enoch	556
Eckhart, Meister (Johann)	136
Eddings, Van V.	916
Eddleman, Henry L.	1116
Eddy, Sherwood	848
Edersheim, Alfred	467
Edman, V. Raymond	881
Edmeston, James	387
Edmund of Abingdon,	126
Edmund	92
Edsall, Samuel C.	586
Edson, Lewis	316
Edstrom, George L.	859
Edward I	134
Edward the Martyr	96
Edward VI	172
Edward	105
Edwards, David	422
Edwards, Gustav	751
Edwards, Jr., Jonathan	301
Edwards, Sr., Jonathan	275
Edwin	74
Eerdmans, William B.	872
Egede, Hans	276
Eggers, Teacher G.	901
Ehlert, Mack C.	865
Eidem, Erling	914
Einarsen, Gisser	190
Einhard	89
Eisenhower, Dwight D.	893
Ekberg, Einar	836
Ekings, Frank P.	830
Ekman, Erik	579
Elderdice, Hugh L.	694
Eldersveld, Peter H.	868
Eleutherius	10
Elias,	128
Eligius,	76
Eliot, John	242
Elizabeth I	196
Elizabeth	126
Eller, Paul H.	1112
Ellerton, John	481
Ellicott, Charles J.	535
Ellinwood, Frank F.	545
Elliot, Charles	394
Elliot, Jim	796
Elliott, Charlotte	403
Elliott, Emily E. Steele	499
Elliott, Errol T.	1079
Elliott, Harrison S.	766
Elliott, Paul F.	1022
Ellis, Paul N.	1208
Ellis, Vesphew B.	1045
Ellis, William	406
Ellor, James	508
Ellyson, Edgar P.	788
Elsner, Theodore	976
Elson, Edward L. R.	1096
Elvey, George J.	484
Ely, Ezra S.	375
Embury, Philip	284
Emerson, Ralph	379
Emery, Paul J.	1020
Emery, Sr., Allen	776
Emmons, Curt	1026
Emmons, Nathanael	338
Emory, John	333
Empie, Paul C.	972
Endecott(Endicott), John	227
Engebretson, Milton B.	1129
Engelhard, David	1241
Engle, Jacob	329
English, E. Schuyler	986
Engstrom, Theodore W. (Ted)	1246
Ennodius, Magnus F.	65
Entizminger, Louis	816
Ephraem, Syrus	41
Epiphanius	50
Episcopius, Simon	212
Epp, George E.	903
Epp, Theodore H.	1022
Erastus, Thomas	189
Erb, Jacob	448
Erb, Paul	1012
Erdman, Charles R.	827
Eremita, Marcus	56

Erickson, Clarence	869
Erickson, Harold W.	1139
Ernesti, Johann A.	288
Ernst, August F.	621
Ernst, Henry	641
Erny, Eugene A.	1035
Errett, Isaac	466
Erskine, Ebenezer	273
Erskine, John	193
Erskine, Thomas	320
Esbjorn, Lars P.	399
Eshelman, Ira	1238
Esher, John J.	516
Espy, R. H. Edwin	1089
Estabrook, Lizzie S. Tourjee	572
Estep, Howard C.	1030
Etter, Harold C.	845
Ettwein, John	301
Eudocia,	62
Eugenicus, Marcus (Mark)	150
Eusebius of Caesarea	35
Eusebius of Dorylaeum	61
Eusebius of Laodicea	23
Eusebius of Rome	30
Eusebius of Samosata	43
Eusebius of Vercelli	40
Eustace	3
Eustathius of Antioch,	36
Eustathius of Sebaste	42
Eustathius of Thessalonica	122
Euthymius	146
Eutychian(us)	24
Evagrius,	49
Evans, Christmas	336
Evans, James	348
Evans, Milton G.	700
Evans, Sr., Louis H.	990
Evans, William	759
Evaristus	3
Evenhouse, Henry J.	1112
Everett, Asa B.	419
Ewald, Alfred	1021
Ewing, Charles W.	1202
Ewing, Finis	39
Ewing, James C. R.	625
Excell, Edwin O.	606
Exell, Joseph S.	594
Exiguus, Dionysius	67
Eyck, Hubert van	148
Eyck, Jan van	149
Fabian	18
Fabiola	49
Fairbairn, Andrew M.	563
Fairbairn, Charles V.	938
Fairbairn, Patrick	414
Fairchild, James H.	521
Faith	26
Fakkema, Mark	905
Falconieri, Juliana	138
Falkenberg, Donald R.	936
Fallows, Samuel	613
Falwell, Jerry	1250
Fancher, Enoch L.	509
Fant, David J.	993
Faraday, Michael	388
Farel, Guillaume	181
Farmer, Blake	1151
Farragut, David G.	399
Farrar, Frederic W.	526
Fausset, Andrew R.	554
Faustus	64
Fauth, Robert T.	1112
Fawcett, John	314
Featherstone, William R.	411
Featly(Fairclougby), Daniel	213
Fehsenfeld, Jr., Del	1059
Feinberg, Charles L.	1117
Felicitas	7
Felicity	13
Felix I	24
Felix of Dunwich	75
Felix of Urgel	87
Felix of Valois	124
Fell, John	240
Fendt, Edward C.	969
Fenelon, Francois S. M.	253
Feng, Yu Hsiang	753
Fenn, William P.	1092
Fenton, Ferrar	576
Ferdinand I,	105
Ferguson, David	194
Ferguson, Manie Payne	599
Ferrar, Nicholas	210
Ferrar, Robert	174
Ferrin, Howard W.	1089
Fiacre	77
Ficino, Marsilio	154
Field, Edward P.	634
Field, John	191
Field, Richard	201
Fields, Rik	660
Fiers, Alan D.	1215

Fife, Eric S.	1165
Figgis, John N.	594
Filkin, W. Warren	1099
Fillmore, Charles M.	774
Fillmore, James H.	679
Finan	76
Findlay, George G.	599
Finley, Allen B.	1248
Finley, James B.	366
Finney, Charles G.	418
Finnian	68
Fisch, George S.	440
Fischer, William G.	566
Fisher, Edward	219
Fisher, Geoffrey F.	918
Fisher, George P.	554
Fisher, George S.	600
Fisk, Franklin W.	518
Fisk, George	957
Fisk, Pliny	322
Fisk, Wilbur	337
Fiske, Fidelia	382
Fitzwater, Perry B.	810
Flacius, Matthias	186
Flack, Elmer E.	946
Flavel, John	244
Flavian I	51
Flavian II	65
Flavian of Constantinople	59
Fleece, G. Allen	1122
Fleetwood, William	259
Fleming, George D.	1006
Fleming, Paul W.	761
Fleming, Sanford	932
Flemming, Arthur S.	1127
Flemming, Friedrich F.	309
Flenniken, Warren	357
Fletcher, Mary Bosanquet	312
Fletcher, John W.	290
Flexon, Richard G.	993
Flickinger, Daniel K.	561
Fliedner, Theodor	382
Flint, Annie Johnson	658
Flint, Robert	554
Flipper, Joseph S.	727
Flora, Delbert	1117
Florian	27
Flower, J. Roswell	904
Foelsch, Charles B.	929
Folden, Ed F.	1184
Fontaine, Tony	933
Fooks, Daniel W.	728
Force, Maynard	1006
Ford, Ernest	1076
Ford, Gerald R.	1248
Ford, Henry	743
Ford, Louis H.	1113
Ford, W. Herschel	954
Foreman, L.D.	1013
Forrest, Richard A.	817
Forrester, James	1031
Forsyth, Peter T.	608
Fortunato, Frank	1154
Fortunatus, Ventantius H. C.	73
Fosbroke, Hughell E. W.	809
Foster, Andrew J.	1042
Foster, John	342
Foster, Randolph S.	526
Foster, Richard A.	998
Foster, Stephen S.	441
Fountain, William A.	791
Fowle, James L.	967
Fowler, Charles H.	546
Fowler, Charles J.	597
Fowler, Clifton L.	865
Fowler, Frederick C.	895
Fox, George	243
Fox, Margaret Fell	247
Foxe, John	191
Francis, Mable	940
Francis of Assisi	126
Francis of Paola	155
Francke, August H.	261
Frank, Graham	787
Frank, Robert W.	966
Franklin, Garland	1121
Franklin, James H.	834
Franks, James E.	1186
Franson, Fredrik	548
Franz, Leonard J.	912
Fraser, Gordon	1061
Fraser, James O.	695
Frazer, James G.	708
Frazier, John B.	696
Frederick 1, John	173
Frederick I	163
Frederick I	121
Frederick III of Saxony	158
Frederick III	187
Frederick IV	263
Frederick IV	199
Frederick, Edward L.	1239

Name	Page
Frederick, Paul W. H.	868
Free, Joseph P.	935
Freed, Paul E.	1129
Freed, Ralph	929
Freeman, Harold F.	1195
Freeman, Thomas B.	472
Frelinghuysen, Theodore	377
Frelinghuysen, Theodorus J.	270
French, Thomas V.	476
Freylinghausen, Johann A.	266
Fridolin	70
Friedrich, Paul	1038
Frith, John	163
Fritschel, Conrad S.	510
Fritschel, Max C. E.	701
Frobel, Friedrich W. A.	357
Froment, Antoine	188
Frost, Henry W.	729
Frumentius	43
Fry, Charles W.	446
Fry, Elizabeth Gurney	346
Fry, Franklin C.	888
Fuchida, Mitsuo	948
Fuerbringer, Alfred O.	1131
Fuerbringer, Ludwig E.	744
Fulbert	102
Fulgentius	66
Fulke, William	192
Fuller, Andrew	311
Fuller, Charles E.	886
Fuller, David O.	1043
Fuller, Richard	423
Fuller, Sr., William E	811
Fuller, Thomas	224
Fulton, Charles D.	957
Fulton, Everett J.	968
Fulton, Howard C.	764
Fulton, Samuel A.	783
Funk, Isaac K.	564
Funkhouser, George A.	632
Furman, Richard	322
Gabriel, Charles H.	659
Gaebelein, Arno C.	736
Gaebelein, Frank E.	999
Gairdner, William H. T.	636
Gale, Theophilus	235
Galilei, Galileo A.	211
Gall	75
Gallaudet, Thomas H.	356
Gambrell, James B.	606
Gamertsfelder, Solomon J.	624
Gamewell, Francis D.	761
Gannett, Alden A.	1187
Gantz, Hallie G.	917
Gapp, Samuel S.	843
Gardiner, Allen F.	356
Gardiner, James	268
Gardiner, William	360
Garfield, James A.	441
Garibaldi, Guiseppe	444
Garland, Fred	1063
Garlock, George W.	770
Garman, Wilfred O. H.	1004
Garr, Alfred G.	726
Garrettson, Freeborn	326
Garrison, William L.	432
Garry, Spokane	476
Gartenhaus, Jacob	1008
Garvie, Alfred E.	730
Gaston, William T.	81
Gataker, Thomas	218
Gates, Edward P.	796
Gates, Ellen Maria Huntington	603
Gattinoni, Juan E.	901
Gauden, John E.	226
Gaulke, Maxwell R.	1084
Gausewitz, Carl F. W.	633
Gaussen, Francois S. L.	380
Gavazzi, Alessandro	466
Geddes, Janet	217
Geddie, John	404
Gee, Donald	874
Geibel, Adam	666
Geiger, Kenneth E.	1013
Geikie, John C.	538
Geiler von Kaysersberg, Johann	155
Gellert, Christian F.	281
Genevieve	64
Gennadius II	152
Geoffrey	117
George of Brandenberg	167
George, Elizabeth Davis	975
George of Polentz	170
George V	678
George VI of England	769
George	27
Gerald of Aurillac	94
Gerald of Northumbria	82
Geraldini, Alessandro	158
Gerard, Tenque	113
Gerhard, Johann	209
Gerhardt, Paul	234

Name	Page
Gerhart, Emmanuel V.	530
Gerig, Jared F.	1199
Germain of Auxerre	59
Germain of Paris	69
Germany, James H.	1179
Gertrude,	132
Gesswein, Armin	1178
Gettys, Ebenezer	989
Getz, Joe	871
Gezork, Herbert J.	1015
Giardini, Felice de	296
Gibbs, Ada Rose	533
Gibson, Christine A.	793
Gifford, Frank D.	947
Gih, Andrew	1017
Gilbert	121
Gildas	68
Giles of Provence	81
Giles, John E.	417
Gilkey, James G.	858
Gill, John	282
Gillentine, Ezra C.	806
Gillespie, George	215
Gillespie, John M.	1236
Gillespie, Thomas	284
Gilman, Daniel C.	549
Gilmore, Joseph H.	590
Gilmour, Henry L.	602
Gilmour, James	476
Gilpin, Bernard	188
Gilpin, John R.	936
Gingrich, Joseph L.	952
Ginsberg, Solomon L.	631
Girdlestone, Robert B.	615
Gladden, Washington	590
Gladstone, William E.	502
Glas(s), John	284
Glaser, Carl G.	327
Glasse, James D.	1226
Glegg, Alexander L.	940
Glen, Arthur A.	775
Glenn, Lewis	708
Glenn, Victor V.	1010
Glenny, Edward H.	626
Gloag, Paton J.	537
Glossbrenner, Jacob J.	459
Glover, Robert H.	743
Glover, Terrot R.	721
Gobat, Samuel	432
Goch, Johann	153
Gockel, Herman	1124
Godet, Frederic L.	512
Godfrey	109
Godiva, Lady	106
Goebel, Louis W.	927
Goforth, Jonathan	684
Goforth, Rosalind Bell-Smith	714
Goldberg, Louis	1201
Goldschmidt, Jenny Lind	462
Goler, William H.	738
Goltz, Carl	1212
Gomarus, Francis	211
Gomez, Walter	1156
Goodell, William	387
Goodman, Howard	1203
Goodman, Vestal	1219
Goodman, Watson	1191
Goodman, Woodrow G.	1228
Goodrich, Chauncey	625
Goodsell, Fred F.	951
Goodspeed, Edgar J.	840
Goodwin, Daniel R.	471
Goodwin, John	227
Goodwin, John W.	730
Goodwin, Thomas	236
Gordon, Adoniram Judson	488
Gordon, Ben	912
Gordon, Charles G.	454
Gordon, Charles W.	691
Gordon, Ernest B.	797
Gordon, Lynn G.	1210
Gordon, Samuel D.	682
Gore, Charles	656
Gossip, Arthur J.	786
Gossner, Johannes E.	368
Gothard, Sr., William W.	1102
Gottschalk,	91
Gottschalk, Louis M.	397
Goudie, Samuel	766
Gouge, William	218
Gough, John B.	458
Goulburn, Edward M.	498
Gould, John E.	416
Govan, John G.	634
Gowans, Walter	484
Grabau, Johannes A. A.	433
Graber, Joseph D.	962
Graeff, Frank E.	597
Graffam, Everett S.	1041
Grafton, Richard	185
Graham, Eugene	1194
Graham, Isabella Marshall	310

Graham, Morrow Coffey	989
Graham, Robert	514
Graham, Ruth Bell	1251
Graham, Thomas W.	909
Grant, Asahel	343
Grant, Frederick C.	933
Grant, Robert	336
Grant, Walter V.	999
Grape, John T.	381
Gratian	118
Gravengaard, Niels P.	750
Graves, Allen W.	1075
Graves, Arthur H.	928
Graves, Frederick A.	630
Graves, Harold K.	1139
Graves, James R.	481
Gray, Albert F.	894
Gray, Asa	464
Gray, Edward J.	533
Gray, George Z.	469
Gray, James M.	674
Gray, Robert	404
Gray, Robert L.	1160
Greatorex, Henry W.	370
Grebel, Conrad	159
Green, Ashbel	350
Green, Berryman	662
Green, Jim H.	793
Green, Keith	996
Green, Samuel G.	535
Green, William H.	509
Greene, Daniel C.	570
Greene, Elizabeth (Betty)	1133
Greene, Oliver B.	950
Greene, Sherman L.	880
Greenwell, Dora	443
Greenwood, John	193
Gregory of Nazianzus	45
Gregory of Nyssa	46
Gregory of Tours	70
Gregory of Utrecht	84
Gregory Thaumaturgus	24
Gregory the Illuminator	33
Greig II, William T.	1242
Grellet, Stephen	265
Gremmels, Charles E.	867
Grenfell, George	539
Grenfell, Wilfred T.	706
Grey, James D.	1021
Grey, Jane	173
Grier (1), Robert C.	401
Grier (2), Robert C.	885
Grier, James A.	592
Grier, William M.	507
Griffin, Edward D.	335
Griffin, Herbert M.	978
Griffin, J. Herschell	936
Griffith, Earle G.	909
Griffith, Glenn	945
Griffith, Oran H.	1221
Grigg, Joseph	281
Grimshaw, William	278
Grindal, Edmund	189
Grinnell, Josiah B.	474
Griswold, Alexander V.	341
Grocyn, William	157
Groenfeldt, John S.	1121
Groote, Gerhard	142
Grose, Howard B.	698
Grosseteste, Robert	128
Grossman, George M.	499
Grossmann, Walter	801
Grotius, Hugo	213
Groton, William M.	579
Groves, Anthony N.	359
Grubb, Norman P.	1099
Grubb, Wilifrid B.	644
Grube, Henry E.	897
Gruber, L. Franklin	711
Grundtvig, Nikolai F. S.	407
Grunewald, Matthias	161
Grunigen, Arnold J.	797
Gubelmann, Jacob S.	595
Guber, Eberhard L.	262
Guffin, Gilbert L.	1083
Guido of Arezzo	104
Guinness, Jr., Henry G.	579
Guinness, Sr., Henry G.	557
Guizot, Francois P. G.	415
Gullerud, Carl M.	1112
Gullixson, Thaddeus F.	893
Gunsaulus, Frank W.	605
Gupta, Paul	960
Gurnall, William	236
Gurney, Archer T.	460
Gurney, Joseph J.	349
Gustafson, Roy	1195
Gustavson, E. Brandt	1180
Gustavus I, Vasa	177
Gustavus II, Adolphus	208
Gutenberg, Johann	151
Guthlac	81

Guthrie, J. Louis	732
Guthrie, Thomas	409
Gutzlaff, Karl F .A.	355
Guyon, Jeanne M. B. de la Mothe	255
Haakon I	95
Haan, Bernard J.	1110
Haapanen, Alfred	837
Habegger, Tillman	1175
Habershon, Ada R.	650
Hackett, Horatio B.	419
Hadley, E. C.	990
Hadley, Sam H.	538
Haeberle, Louis	637
Hagedorn, Ivan H.	988
Hageman, Howard G.	1088
Hagenbach, Karl R.	414
Hager, Harry J.	1003
Haggard, Cornelius P.	941
Hagin, Kenneth E.	1214
Hagstrom, G. Arvid	780
Hague, Dyson	672
Hahn, Johann M.	315
Haight, Grace Woodman	794
Haldane, James A.	355
Haldane, Robert	341
Haldeman, Issac M.	667
Hale, Matthew	234
Hale, Nathan	285
Hale, Sarah J. Buell	432
Hall - Myers, Elvina M. Reynolds	468
Hall, C. Newman	521
Hall, Charles C.	546
Hall, Colby D.	852
Hall, Gordon	323
Hall, Granville S.	620
Hall, J. Lincoln	649
Hall, James J. D.	767
Hall, John	504
Hall, John V.	374
Hall, Joseph	220
Hall, Morley R.	862
Hall, Robert	329
Halleen, Erick A.	811
Haller, Berthold	164
Hallesby, Ole K.	838
Halley, Henry H.	866
Hallock, Gerhard B. F.	782
Hallock, William A.	437
Halvarson, Hilding	1070
Halverson, Richard C.	1120
Ham, Mordecai F.	838
Hamblen, Stuart	1052
Hamilton, J. Taylor	764
Hamilton, Jack	1223
Hamilton, James	389
Hamilton, Patrick	160
Hamilton, Raymond F.	1001
Hamilton, William W.	832
Hamlett, J. Arthur	841
Hamlin, Cyrus	511
Hammarskjöld, Dag	837
Hammond, Robert	1199
Hammontree, Homer A.	862
Han, Kyung Chik	1167
Hanby, William	436
Handel, George F.	277
Hanes, Leonard	1118
Hankey, Arabella C.	560
Hankins, Joseph H.	876
Hanley, C. S.	622
Hannington, James	457
Hanson, Martin G.	580
Haralson, Jonathan	565
Haraszti, Alexander S.	1145
Hardenberg, Friedrich L. Von	300
Harder, Waldo E.	948
Hardgrave, Robert	1177
Harding, Stephen	114
Hardwick, Harry T.	1039
Hardy, Chester E.	913
Hardy, Robert S.	391
Hare, Augustus W.	332
Hare, Julius C.	363
Hargis, Billy J.	1229
Hargroves, V. Carney	1029
Harkness, Georgia E.	934
Harkness, Robert	834
Harlow, R. E.	1207
Harms, George L. D. T.	385
Harms, Klaus	364
Harms, Oliver R.	980
Harner, Nevin C.	767
Harper, James	566
Harper, John	564
Harper, Redd	1079
Harrington, Karl P.	782
Harrington, W. Frank	1156
Harris, Charles U.	1186
Harris, Elmore	562
Harris, Frederick B.	905
Harris, George K.	842
Harris, Howell	283

Name	Page
Harris, Samuel	506
Harris, Thoro	791
Harrison, Benjamin	515
Harrison, Dan	1209
Harrison, Doyle	1153
Harrison, Irvine J.	917
Harrison, Norman B.	830
Harrison, Robert	190
Harrison, William K.	1037
Hart, Edward P.	596
Hart, Joseph	280
Hart, Ray	1050
Hartford, Paul C.	1134
Hartranft, Chester D.	575
Hartsough, Lewis	594
Hartsough, Palmer	659
Harvard, John	210
Harvey, William	222
Harwood, Sr., Carl C.	808
Hasbrouck, Abraham B.	431
Haskin, Dorothy C.	1051
Hasselblad, Oliver W.	1133
Hasselquist, Tuve N.	474
Hassler, Hans L.	199
Hastings, Horace L.	508
Hastings, James	613
Hastings, Selina (Shirley)	293
Hastings, Thomas	406
Hastings, Thomas S.	560
Hatch, Clarence W.	825
Hatch, Edwin	469
Hatch, John W.	818
Hatfield, Edwin F.	450
Hatton, John	294
Hauge, Hans N.	320
Haugen, Sanford	1243
Haupert, Raymond S.	920
Havelock, Henry	367
Haven, Erastus O.	440
Haven, Gilbert	435
Havens, George	1049
Havergal, Frances Ridley	433
Havner, Vance H.	1032
Haweis, Thomas	316
Hawk, Eugene B.	853
Hawkins, Mont E.	801
Hawks, Annie Sherwood	589
Hawks, Francis L.	387
Hayden, Perry	784
Haygood, Atticus G.	492
Haymaker, Willis G.	983
Hays, L. Brooks	990
Hays, William S.	543
Haywood, Garfield T.	651
Hazelius, Ernest L.	359
Head, Elrod D.	856
Headlam, Arthur C.	741
Heard, R. Dennis	1001
Hearn, Marianne	551
Heaton, C. Adrian	963
Heber, Reginald	323
Heck, Barbara Ruckle	302
Heck, J. Arthur	930
Hedberg, George E.	1155
Hedding, Elijah	357
Hedeen, Olof	682
Hedwig	127
Heemstra, Jacob	816
Hegesippus	9
Hegre, Theodore A.	1015
Heiges, Donald R.	1064
Heiler, J. Friedrich	879
Hein, Carl C.	689
Heininger, Harold R.	1000
Heinmiller, Carl	1109
Heinmiller, Gottleib	614
Heinrich	166
Heinrich, Maurice	1048
Heinz, Henry J.	596
Helena	33
Helms, Edgar J.	719
Heloise	119
Helser, Albert D.	899
Helwys, Thomas	200
Hemberger, Samuel T.	1236
Hemmeter, Henry B.	752
Hemphill, Charles R.	657
Henderson, Alexander	214
Henderson, Ebenezer	369
Hendley, Jesse	1110
Hendrix, Eugene R.	634
Hengstenberg, Ernest W.	395
Henkel, Paul	323
Henninger, Harold R.	1229
Henry I	114
Henry II	121
Henry III	104
Henry IV of France of Navarre	198
Henry IV of Germany	110
Henry of Ghent	132
Henry of Lausanne	116
Henry V	113

Henry VII	155
Henry, Carl F. H.	1218
Henry, Joseph	429
Henry, Matthew	253
Henry, Patrick	298
Henry, Paul B.	1095
Henry, Philip	246
Henson, Elmer D.	934
Henson, Josiah	448
Hepburn, Henry	779
Hepburn, James C.	559
Heraclas	18
Herbart, Johann F.	340
Herbert, George	208
Herbster, Ben M.	1015
Hering, Joshua W.	570
Herman, Nicholas	243
Hermas	5
Hermogenes	14
Heroo, Leonard W.	1031
Herrick, Everett C.	804
Herrick, Robert	233
Herring, Thomas	275
Herron, Jr., Stephen D.	1102
Hershey, Clement E	959
Hervey, James	279
Herzog, Johann J.	446
Hess, Enos H.	707
Hess, W. Jake	1219
Hess, W. Robert	1114
Hesychius	61
Heurnius, Justus	220
Heusel, Linton	1189
Heusser, Meta S.	420
Hewitt, Eliza E.	601
Heydt, Henry J.	1035
Heylyn, Peter	225
Hickey, Handley A.	1178
Hickman, Roger M.	886
Hicks, Tommy	920
Hiebert, Nicholas N.	747
Higashi, Howard	1153
Higginbottom, Samuel	813
Higgins, Edward J.	748
Higgins, Howard D.	979
Hilarion	40
Hilary of Poitiers,	40
Hilda	79
Hildebrand, Henry P.	1241
Hildegard	120
Hill, Clairborne M.	757
Hill, E. V.	1206
Hill, Rowland	330
Hill, Samuel E.	685
Hill, William E.	1007
Hill-Lutz, Grace Livingston	742
Hillis, Newell D.	638
Hillis, Richard (Dick)	1240
Hills, Aaron M.	674
Hilton, Walter	144
Hincmar of Laon	92
Hincmar of Rheims	92
Hines, Jerome	1205
Hines, John E.	1137
Hinkson, Nelson C.	1083
Hinson, Walter B.	627
Hinson, William H.	1231
Hippolytus	17
Hirt, Oscar H.	1128
Hitchcock, Benjamin F.	829
Hitchcock, Edward	381
Hitt, Russell T.	1087
Hjerpe, Eric G.	653
Hobart, John H.	328
Hobbs, Herschel H.	1120
Hochmann, Ernest C.	258
Hodder, Edwin	530
Hodge, Archibald A.	459
Hodge, Charles	430
Hodges (1), George	597
Hodges (2), George	849
Hodges, Sloan S.	1058
Hodgson, Telfair	482
Hoekema, Anthony A.	1048
Hoeksema, Homer C.	1057
Hoekstra, Ray	1142
Hoenecke, Adolf	545
Hoenecke, Edgar	1192
Hoffman, Elisha A.	643
Hoffman, Eugene A.	523
Hoffman, James E.	898
Hoffman, Joseph	366
Hoffmann, Melchior	167
Hoffman, Oswald J.	1237
Hofmann, Johann M. F. Heinrich	520
Hogan, J. Philip	1202
Hoge, Moses D.	317
Hoggard, James C.	1196
Hogue, Wilson T.	600
Hojbjerg, Carl P.	782
Hoke, Donald E.	1248
Holcomb, Jack	889

Holdcraft, J. Gordon	917
Holden, J. Stuart	667
Holden, Oliver	344
Holland, Josiah G.	442
Holm, Bernard	1170
Holman, Wilbur A.	1196
Holmes, Nicholas J.	599
Holsey, Lucius H.	602
Holt, Harry	856
Holt, Ivan L.	876
Holter, Don W.	1161
Holtzmann, Heinrich J.	558
Holwerda, Carl	1153
Holyoke, Edward	281
Homer, Cyril E.	976
Honda, Koji	1194
Hone, William	340
Honeycutt, Roy L.	1231
Honeyman, Robert M.	769
Honorius	76
Hood, E. Lyman	654
Hood, James W.	592
Hook, Walter F.	419
Hooker, Richard	195
Hooker, Thomas	214
Hooper, John	173
Hoover, Herbert C.	859
Hoover, J. Edgar	915
Hope, Johnny	1222
Hopkins, Edward J.	514
Hopkins, John H.	390
Hopkins, Mark	461
Hopkins, Samuel	302
Hopper, Edward	464
Horne, Charles S.	573
Horne, Thomas H.	376
Hornshuh, Fred L.	994
Horr, George E.	630
Horsley, Samuel	304
Hort, Fenton J. A.	479
Horton, Douglas	889
Horton, Thomas C.	657
Horton, Wade H.	1148
Hosius	38
Hoskins, Fermin L.	672
Hoskins, Fred	872
Hoste, Dixon E.	739
Hostetter, Henry N.	1152
Hostetter, Jr., Christian N.	981
Hostetter, Sr., Christian N.	785
Hotchkiss, Joe V.	1228
Hottell, William S.	866
Hough, Lynn H.	909
Houghton, Frank	912
Houghton, William H. (Will)	745
Houston, Samuel	380
Hovey, Alvah	528
Hoving, Walter	1059
How, William W.	499
Howard, Alfred T.	753
Howard, Clinton N.	791
Howard, John	291
Howard, Jr., Philip E.	854
Howard, Sr., Philip E.	739
Howe, Jacob	709
Howe, John	249
Howell, Robert B. C.	391
Howells, Rees	758
Howson, John S.	457
Howley, William	350
Hoyme, Gjermund	522
Hoyt, Herman A.	1171
Hoyt, Wayland	555
Hsaio, Samuel	855
Huarte, Myrtle Nordin	983
Hubbard, David A.	1125
Hubbert, James M.	669
Huber, Lucas C.	1107
Hubert	81
Hubert, Walter	124
Hubmaier, Balthasar	160
Hudson, Ralph E.	518
Hudson, W. Jack	1065
Huenemann, Rueben H.	1219
Huffman, John A.	1225
Huffman, Jasper A.	906
Huffman, Nyles G.	813
Hugg, George C.	549
Hugh of Cluny	111
Hugh of Grenoble	114
Hugh of Lincoln	123
Hugh of St. Victor	115
Hughes, Albert	813
Hughes, Andrew W.	1107
Hughes, Bob	951
Hughes, Edwin H.	758
Hughes, John	657
Hughes, John W.	657
Hughes, Selwin	1241
Hugo, Victor M.	455
Hulbert, Eric B.	541
Hull, James R.	913

Name	Page		Name	Page
Hultman, Johannes A.	716		Irwin, James B.	1074
Humberd, Russell I.	865		Isaac	58
Hummel, Charles E.	1227		Isbill, O. Ralph	1179
Hummel, Homer	1098		Isidore	74
Hummel, Karl D.	948		Iske, Lucy Turner	950
Humphrey, Heman	374		Islip, Simon	140
Humphrey, Laurence	192		Iverach, James	609
Hunt, John	351		Ives, Burl	1113
Hunt, Robert	198		Ivo/ Ives of Chartres,	112
Hunt, W. Holman	557		Jablonski, Daniel E.	267
Hunter, James H.	783		Jackson, Alfred R.	958
Hunter, William	427		Jackson, Andrew	345
Huntington, DeWitt C.	562		Jackson, Doss N.	891
Huntington, Frederick D.	531		Jackson, Frederick J. F.	711
Hurlburt, Charles E.	679		Jackson, Joseph H.	1064
Hurlbut, Jesse L.	647		Jackson, Mahalia	912
Hurse, John W.	675		Jackson, Paul R.	895
Hurst, John F.	527		Jackson, Robert	574
Husband, John J.	321		Jackson, Samuel M.	565
Huss, John	145		Jackson, Sheldon	552
Hussey, Jennie E.	815		Jackson, Thomas J.	379
Huston, Frank C.	823		Jacob of Edessa,	80
Hut, Hans	159		Jacob of Misa,	150
Hutchens, Paul	955		Jacob, Henry	205
Hutchings, Eric A.	997		Jacobs, Charles M.	693
Hutchins, James H.	1010		Jacobs, Henry E.	658
Hutchinson, Anne Marbury	212		Jacobson, John C.	400
Hutson, Curtis	1113		Jacobson, John H.	1232
Hutten, Ulrich von	157		Jacobus, Melanchthon W.	424
Hutter, Jacob	164		Jacopone da Todi,	133
Hutter, Leonhard	201		Jaffray, Robert A.	733
Hyde, Edwin F.	663		James I	206
Hyde, John	563		James, John A.	372
Hyde, William D.	587		Jamieson, Robert	435
Hyginus	5		Janes, Edmund S.	423
Hyles, Jack F.	1175		Janeway, Jacob J.	369
Ibas	62		Januarius	29
Ibiam, Frances A.	1111		Janz, Leo	1246
Ignatius	3		Janzen, Abraham E.	1120
Ingham, Benjamin	283		Jarman, W. Maxey	982
Ingham, John A.	724		Jarratt, Devereaux	300
Inglis, Charles	312		Jarvis, Anna M.	753
Ingraham, M. Virgil	1206		Jarvis, Fred D.	1065
Innes, T. Christe	881		Jasper, John	515
Innocent I	53		Jay, John	327
Inskip, John S.	451		Jay, William	360
Ireland, John	340		Jefferson, Charles E.	690
Irenaeus	12		Jeffrey, James N.	1072
Irion, Andreas	399		Jeffreys, George	840
Ironside, Henry A.	762		Jemison, David V.	784
Irving, Edward	333		Jenkins, Elizabeth M.	765

Jenner, Edward	319	Johnston, Julia H.	599
Jensen, Alfred	981	Johnstone, Tom	1200
Jepson, N. Alvin	765	Jonas, Justus	174
Jeremiah, James T.	1170	Jones, Abner	339
Jernigan, John C.	979	Jones, Burton R.	664
Jerome of Bethlehem,	54	Jones, Charles P.	796
Jerome of Prague,	146	Jones, Clarence W.	1028
Jess, John D.	1211	Jones, David	338
Jessup, Henry H.	556	Jones, E. Stanley	921
Jeter, Jeremiah B.	435	Jones, Edgar D.	798
Jewel, John	184	Jones, Edward P.	610
Jiagge, Annie R.	1125	Jones, George H.	596
Joachim	123	Jones, Hosea W.	587
Joan of Arc	148	Jones, James A.	875
John IV	70	Jones, John D.	713
John of Antioch	58	Jones, Jr., Bob	1142
John of Asia	70	Jones, Lewis E.	784
John of Chur	141	Jones, Robert E.	828
John of Damascus	83	Jones, Rufus	1132
John of Gaunt	144	Jones, Rufus Matthew	751
John of Jandun	137	Jones, Ruth Caye	918
John of Leyden	164	Jones, Samuel P.	540
John of Monte Corvino	136	Jones, Smith J.	996
John of Nepomuk	143	Jones, Sr., Bob	884
John of Odzun (Otzun)	81	Jones, Thomas W.	942
John of Paris	133	Jonswold, Olav M.	762
John of Salisbury	110	Jordan, Eugene	1066
John of Wesel	153	Jordan, Fred	1045
John the Constant	162	Jordan, Lewis G.	697
John, Griffith	562	Jordan, William H.	796
Johnson (1), Samuel	283	Jordanus (Jordan)	139
Johnson (2), Samuel	290	Jorgensen, Hakon	855
Johnson, Albert G.	910	Joris, Johann D.	175
Johnson, Albert M.	789	Joseph II	149
Johnson, Audrey Wetherall	1016	Joseph of Volokolamsk	456
Johnson, C. Oscar	869	Joseph	92
Johnson, David H.	890	Jovianus	39
Johnson, Erastus	552	Jovinian	51
Johnson, Gilbert H.	1118	Jowett, Benjamin	482
Johnson, Gustaf F.	819	Jowett, John H.	618
Johnson, Guy C.	1172	Joy, Vincent	874
Johnson, Herrick	571	Jud, Leo	166
Johnson, James T.(Jimmy)	1212	Judd, Walter H.	1101
Johnson, Linton C.	1198	Jude, William H.	612
Johnson, Merle (Mel)	1178	Judson, Adoniram	353
Johnson, Sherman E.	1091	Judson, Ann Hasseltine	325
Johnson, Torrey M.	1196	Judson, Emily Chubbuck	362
Johnson, Wallace E.	1045	Judson, Sarah Hall Boardman	346
Johnson, William B.	378	Julia	63
Johnson, Zachery T.	987	Juliana of Liege,	128
Johnston, Kenneth J.	1187	Juliana of Norwich,	145

Julicher, Gustav A.	694
Julius I	37
Junkin, George	392
Just, Roy	1104
Justinian I	68
Justus	74
Kagawa, Toyohiko	827
Kahn, Ida	654
Kai Shek, Madame	1217
Kai-Shek, Chiang	939
Kallenbach, Walter D.	741
Kanamori, Tsurin P.	729
Kantzer, Ken	1197
Kapiolani, Queen	320
Kaplan, Louis	1158
Kato, Byang	944
Katterjohn, Arthur D.	976
Kauffman, Daniel	723
Kauffman, Paul E.	1132
Kaufman, Edmund G.	977
Keach, Benjamin	248
Kearney, Joseph C.	984
Keaton, Everett A.	953
Keble, John	386
Keener, John C.	537
Keil, Johann K. F.	465
Keiller, James A.	1131
Keisler, Efird B.	1000
Keith, George	254
Keith, Roy	1004
Keith-Falconer, Ion G. N.	461
Kellar, Gerald D.	1181
Kellersburger, Eugene R.	871
Kelley, Alden D.	979
Kelley, Lloyd C.	795
Kellogg, Samuel H.	506
Kelly, Howard A.	718
Kelly, Thomas	364
Kelly, Thomas R.	707
Kelly, William	538
Kelso, James A.	768
Kempe, Margery Burnham	149
Kempis, Thomas a'	152
Ken, Thomas	251
Kendrick, Asahel C.	491
Kendrick, Nathaniel	351
Kennedy, Clyde J.	845
Kennedy, Gerald H.	977
Kennicott, Benjamin F.	289
Kentigern	72
Kenyon, Frederick G.	774
Kepler, Johannes	207
Kerr, Hugh T.	760
Kerr, Phil T.	830
Kerr, Robert S.	848
Kerschener, Frederick D.	798
Ketcham, Robert T.	965
Kethe, William	194
Keur, Cornelius	1095
Key, Francis S.	341
Keysor, Charles W.	1023
Khama III	616
Kibira, Josiah M.	1046
Kidd, Beresford J.	750
Kidder, Mary Ann Pepper	536
Kiffin, William	247
Kilham, Alexander	298
Kilian	79
Killman, J. Russell	1159
Kimmel, Gustav B.	698
Kimura, Henry S.	811
King, Guy E.	976
King, Jonas	395
King, Joseph H.	738
King, Jr., Martin Luther	887
King, Louis L.	1229
King, Willis J.	949
Kingsley, Calvin	398
Kinnaird, Mary J.	463
Kipling, J. Rudyard	678
Kirk, Edward N.	414
Kirkendall, Chester	1146
Kirkland, Samuel	306
Kirkpatrick, Charles D.	1019
Kirkpatrick, William J.	608
Kiser, Keith	1194
Kitagawa, Joseph M.	1085
Kitching, Wilfred	961
Kittel, Gerhard	752
Kittel, Rudolf	642
Kitto, John	363
Kivengere, Festo	1045
Klak, Harold	93
Klapstein, Harvey	1177
Klausler, Alfred P.	1077
Klein, Frederick C.	630
Klein, Henry A.	677
Kliewer, John W.	693
Kligerman, Aaron G.	883
Klopstock, Friedrich G.	301
Knapp, Albert	382
Knapp, Jacob	412

Knapp, Martin C.	520
Knapp, Phoebe Palmer	547
Knight, John L.	1183
Knight, Walter B.	1167
Knight, William A.	804
Knighton, J. Ray	1213
Knippers, Dianne	1234
Knollys, Hanserd	244
Knox, John	185
Knubel, Frederick H.	735
Knudsen, Johannes H.	998
Knudson, Albert C.	780
Knutson, Kent S.	923
Kocher, Conrad	405
Koehler, John P.	768
Kollen, Gerrit J.	580
Koller, Charles W.	1003
Konkel, Wilbur S.	1081
Koren, Ulrik V.	558
Kortz, Edwin W.	1194
Kraemer, Charles E.S.	1046
Kraft, James L.	777
Krapf, Johann L.	442
Krauth, Charles Philip	388
Krauth, Charles Porterfield	447
Krebs, John M.	389
Kremser, Edward	575
Kresge, Stanley S.	1020
Kriege, Otto E.	806
Kroeger, Hanna U. Zimmer	1148
Kromminga, John H.	1103
Kronquest, Max R.	1132
Krummacher, Friedrich W.	394
Kuehner, Fred C.	937
Kuhlman, Kathryn	946
Kuhn, Harold B.	1108
Kuhn, Isobel S. Miller	805
Kuhn, William	767
Kuhnle, William E.	989
Kuiper, Henry J.	847
Kulp, George B.	699
Kumler, Jr., Henry	445
Kumler, Sr., Henry	361
Kumm, Karl	648
Kunz, Alfred A.	955
Kunz, George J.	623
Kunze, John C.	305
Kunzmann, Jacob C.	711
Kurtz, Benjamin	385
Kurtz, Daniel W.	755
Kurtz, Johann H.	471
Kuyper, Abraham	604
Kyle, Melvin G.	665
Kyles, Lynwood W.	709
La Vastida, Bartholomew G.	1085
Labadie, Jean de	232
Lachmann, Karl K. F. W.	355
Lactantius, Firmianus	35
Lacy, Benjamin R.	988
Lacy, Floyd H.	898
Ladd, George E.	997
Ladd, William P.	709
Laestadius, Lars L.	374
Laidlaw, Robert	908
Laird, Harold S.	1038
Lake, John G.	674
Lake, Kirsopp	741
Lakin, Bascom R.	1010
Lam, Nora	1221
Lambert, Francois	161
Lambie, Thomas A.	785
Lambuth, Walter R.	608
Lamson, Byron S.	1106
Landis, Josiah P.	691
Landis, Morris D.	659
Landon, Alfred M.	1040
Landon, Warren H.	636
Landrum, Clyde	1145
Landry, Tomas (Tom)	1165
Lane, Issac	692
Lane, Ted A.	1229
Lane, Spencer	527
Lanfranc,	107
Lang, Cosmo G.	735
Lang, George A.	983
Lang, John D.	430
Lang, Walter H. J.	1226
Lange, Johann P.	453
Langford, Sidney	1172
Langford, Thomas A.	1166
Langlie, Arthur B.	874
Langmade, Nye J.	882
Lanier, Sidney	441
Lanphier, Jeremiah C.	447
Larcom, Lucy	480
Larimer, Loyal H.	842
Larkin, Clarence	619
Larrabee, Edward A.	620
Larson, Melvin G.	918
Larson, Reuben E.	991
Laski (Lasco), Jan(Johannes)	177
Latham, Lance B.	1016

Name	Page
Lathan, Robert	494
Lathbury, Mary A.	571
Latimer, Hugh	175
Latimer, James E.	453
Latimer, Samuel W.	757
LaTourette, Kenneth S.	891
Laubach, Frank C.	904
Lauby, Paul	1209
Lauer, Martin	485
Laurin, Roy L.	873
Lavater, Johann K.	300
Law, Thomas H.	618
Law, William	278
Lawrance, Marion	620
Lawrence of Canterbury,	73
Lawrence, Thomas E.	673
Lawrence of Rome	21
Lawrenz, Carl J.	1058
Laws, Curtis L.	740
Laws, Robert	669
Lawson, Robert C.	835
Lea, Henry C.	553
Leaming, Charles	1050
Leander	71
Lease, Stuart E.	1232
Leavell, Roland Q.	848
Leavitt, Joshua	408
Leber, Charles T.	822
Lee, Benjamin F.	627
Lee, Carl Q.	1082
Lee, Flavius J.	637
Lee, Jason	345
Lee, Jesse	313
Lee, Robert E.	400
Lee, Robert G.	965
Lee, Samuel	359
Lee, Witness	1136
Leech, Lida S.	841
Leete, Frederick D.	812
Lefevre D'Etaples, Jacques	165
Legge, James	500
Legters, Leonard L.	704
Lehman, Frederick M.	777
Lehman, Glen A.	1245
Lehman, Louis P.	1033
Lehmann, Leo H.	759
Lehmann, William F.	438
Leibnitz, Gottfried W.	255
Leighton, Robert	239
Leinbach, Paul S.	711
Leland, John	338
Lemmel, Helen H.	838
Lenox, James	435
Lenski, Richard C. H.	684
Leo III	83
Leonardo da Vinci	157
Leonides	12
Leontius	67
Lesemann, Louis F. W.	708
Lesesne, J. Mauldin	1094
Leslie, Charles	258
Leslie, John D.	674
LeTourneau, Richard A.	1226
LeTourneau, Robert G.	896
Levang, J. H.	1192
Levengood, Albert J.	799
Levengood, Paul M.	1001
Leverett, John	259
Levering, Joshua	675
Levin, Paul J.	1127
Lewis, Allan E.	1173
Lewis, Arthur	1233
Lewis, Clifford	1024
Lewis, Clive S.	854
Lewis, Gayle F.	977
Lewis, L. Glenn	749
Lewis, Theodore L.	819
Lewis, Thomas H.	640
Lewis, Voyle H.	1173
Lewis, Walter O.	866
Leyburn, John	481
Liberius	40
Lichtenberger, Arthur C.	890
Liddell, Eric	730
Liddell, Henry G.	501
Liddick, Alton F.	1011
Liddon, Henry P.	472
Liele, George	326
Lightfoot, John	233
Lightfoot, Joseph B.	470
Lilje, Johannes	954
Lillenas, Haldor	822
Lincoln, Abraham	383
Lincoln, William	465
Lindberg, Milton B.	1031
Lindell, Paul J.	930
Lindquist, C. Reuben	1053
Lindquist, Frank J.	1058
Lindsay, J. Gordon	923
Lindsay, Thomas M.	575
Lindsell, Harold	1144
Lindstrom, Paul	1197

Lingle, Walter L.	801
Linnaeus, Carl	286
Linton, John	861
Lintz, Harry M.	1054
Linus	1
Lioba	85
Lipphard, William B.	909
Lippi, Fra Filippo	152
Lister, Hovie F.	1189
Little, Charles J.	559
Little, Paul E.	940
Liudger	86
Livingston, John H.	321
Livingstone, David	410
Livingstone, John	231
Lloyd, Arthur S.	683
Lloyd-George, David	731
Lloyd-Jones, D. Martin	985
Lock, Walter	660
Locke, John	248
Lockhart, W. P.	481
Lockridge, Shadrach M.	1167
Lockwood, Henry	657
Lockyer, Sr., Herbert	1015
Loder, Dwight E.	1203
Loehe, Johann K. W.	404
Loes, Harry D.	863
Loftin, Bernard M.	1126
Logan, J. Sutherland	1065
Loguen, Jeremiah W.	408
Lohrenz, Henry W.	730
Long, Ernest E.	1021
Long, George A.	896
Long, Henry J.	981
Long, John W.	739
Long, Ralph H.	749
Longstaff, William D.	485
Lonie, Don	1188
Loomer, Bernard M.	1022
Lord, F. Townley	840
Lord, John	487
Lorenz, Edmund S.	715
Lorimer, George C.	531
Lotze, Rudolf H.	440
Louis I	89
Louis IX	130
Louis VII	120
Love, James F.	635
Lovejoy, Elijah P.	335
Loveless, Wendell P.	1040
Lowden, C. Harold	848
Lowe, Titus	823
Lowell, John	334
Lowell, Leroy M.	1019
Lowry, Robert C.	508
Loy, Matthias	577
Loyson, Charles	563
Lubbers, Irwin J.	1022
Lucar(is), Cyril	210
Luccock, Halford E.	831
Lucius I	20
Luckey, James S.	689
Luke, Jemima Thompson	537
Lull, Raymond	135
Lund, Conrad	995
Lund-quist, Carl E.	867
Lundmark, G. Alfred	779
Lundquist, Carl H.	1069
Lundquist, Harold L.	820
Luthardt, Christoph E.	524
Luther, Arthur A.	824
Luther, Charles C.	622
Luther, Katherine Bora	172
Luther, Martin	168
Lutkin, Peter C.	657
Luttrell, Donald D.	1037
Luwum, Janani	956
Lyles, Bill	787
Lyon, Mary	351
Lyons, Noel	823
Lyte, Henry F.	350
Lyttelton, George	284
Mac Arthur, Douglas	856
Mac Arthur, Robert S.	616
Macarius of Alexandria	51
Macarius of Egypt	45
Macarius of Jerusalem	34
MacArthur, Jack	1235
MacArtney, Clarence E.	804
MacAulay, Joseph C.	989
MacAulay, Neil	1096
MacAulay, Zachary	336
MacCorkle, Doug	1198
MacDonald, George	535
MacDonald, Thomas	963
MacDonald, Walter R.	853
MacFarlane, Peter	812
Machen, J. Gresham	687
Machlin, Abraham B.	846
Machray, Robert	530
Machtild	131
Mack, Alexander	264

Mackay, Alexander M.	471
Mackay, George L.	517
MacKay, John A.	1003
Mackay, Joy	1143
Mackay, R. P.	640
Mackay, William P.	456
Mackenzie, Charles F.	376
Mackenzie, John	505
Mackenzie, John K.	464
MacKenzie, William D.	680
Mackey, Alexander B.	927
Mackintosh, Charles H.	496
Mackintosh, Hugh R.	681
MacLaren, Alexander	556
Maclay, Robert S.	543
Maclean, Jr., John	459
MacLeod, Norman	406
MacNeill, John	688
MacPherson, Cornelius G.	505
MacPherson, Merrill T.	830
MacRae, Allen A.	1139
Madden, Darius S.	1220
Maddry, Charles E.	844
Madson, Norman A.	847
Magni, Peter	169
Magnus, Albertus	131
Mahan, Asa	468
Mahon, Edgar	678
Mahood, J. Wilmot	794
Maier, Walter A.	756
Main, Hubert P.	625
Maitland, Samuel R.	385
Majorinus	37
Makemie, Frances	250
Maker, Frederick C.	630
Malachy, O'Morgair	116
Malan, Cesar H. A.	381
Malcom, Howard	432
Malof, Basil	807
Malone, J. Walter	677
Malone, Tom	1249
Malotte, Albert M.	860
Malsbary, Dwight R.	1138
Mann, Arthur H.	643
Mann, Frank E.	1006
Manners-Sutton, Sr., Charles	326
Manning, Ernest C.	1122
Manning, James	293
Manning, William T.	755
Manson, John T.	724
Manton, Thomas	235
Manwaring, Roger	218
Manz, Feliz	160
Marahrens, August	759
Maravich, Peter	1042
Marcella,	53
Marcellinus	28
Marcellus I	30
March, Daniel	551
Marco, Anton	900
Margaret of Antioch	30
Margaret of Scotland	108
Mark	34
Markham, Charles E.	703
Markham, Oscar C.	952
Marlatt, Earl B.	948
Marlorat, Augustin	179
Marot, Clement (Clemens)	167
Marquart, W. Edward	1182
Marsden, Samuel	336
Marsh, Charles H.	799
Marsh, Simeon B.	418
Marshall, Albert B.	654
Marshall, Alexander	636
Marshall, Frederic W.	301
Marshall LeSourd, Catherine Wood	1001
Marshall, Peter	754
Marshall, Stephen	219
Marshman, Joshua	335
Marsilius,	138
Marston, Leslie R.	971
Martel, Charles	83
Martensen, Hans L.	450
Martin of Braga	69
Martin of Tours	48
Martin, Alfred	1123
Martin, Civilla Durfee	749
Martin, Edward (Eddie) W.	1134
Martin, Horace F.	785
Martin, I. G.	807
Martin, Sarah	341
Martin, Thomas T.	698
Martin, Walter R.	1056
Martin, Walter S.	677
Martin, William A. P.	585
Martin, William C.	1014
Martini, Raymond	131
Martyn, Henry	308
Martyr, Justin	6
Mason, Charles H.	838
Mason, Francis	413
Mason, Harold C.	857

Name	Page
Mason, Harry S.	860
Mason, Joe	1234
Mason, John M.	328
Mason, Lowell	406
Massee, Jasper C.	864
Masserano, Sr., Frank	991
Matamoros, Manuel	386
Mateer, Calvin W.	549
Mather, Cotton	262
Mather, Increase	259
Mather, Richard	229
Matheson, Duncan	396
Matheson, George	540
Matheson, Samuel P.	714
Mathews, Basil J.	765
Mathewson, Maynard	1199
Mathys, Jan	163
Matthew,	129
Matthews, Aaron	820
Matthews, Charles E.	802
Matthews, Mark A.	702
Matthews, Timothy R.	555
Matthews, William A.	721
Matthews, William H.	738
Matthews, William W.	1244
Matthias	143
Mattson, Karl E.	860
Mauck, David H. L.	1162
Mauer, Leon	1041
Maurer, Kenneth R.	957
Maurice Tiberius,	25
Maurice,	172
Maurus, Rabanus	90
Maury, Matthew F.	409
Maxfield, Thomas	289
Maximilla	8
Maximus	77
Maxwell, Leslie E.	1009
Mayer, Lewis	352
Mayes, Henry H.	1027
Mayhew, Experience	276
McAfee, Cleland B.	723
McAlister, Jack	1241
McAlister, Robert E.	780
McAlister, Walter E	1069
McAll, Robert W.	480
McAuley, Jeremiah (Jerry)	453
McBurney, Robert R.	504
McCaba, Joseph	921
McCall, Abner V.	1115
McCall, Druie A.	821
McCarrell, William (Billy) R.	971
McCarter, Neely D.	1245
McCarty, Elmer F.	840
McCash, Issac N.	835
McChesney, W. Renwick	725
McCheyne, Robert M.	341
McClain, Alva J.	890
McClintock, John	397
McClure, James G. K.	656
McClurkan, James O.	574
McConkey, James H.	690
McConn, William F.	892
McConnell, Francis J.	780
McConnell, James E.	787
McConnell, Lela G.	902
McCord, James I.	1061
McCormick, Cyrus H.	451
McCosh, James	487
McCoy, Issac	347
McCracken, Robert J.	923
McCrie, Thomas	333
McCulley, Theodore E.	865
McCullough, Joseph S.	1187
McCutchan, Robert G.	813
McDaniel, George W.	632
McDaniel, Rufus H.	702
McDonald, William	519
McDormand, Thomas	1049
McDowell, William F.	689
McElwain, Frank A.	808
McFarland, John T.	571
McFerrin, John B.	461
McGarvey, John W.	561
McGavran, Donald A.	1063
McGee, J. Vernon	1050
McGiffert, Art Jr.	1092
McGill, David F.	652
McGinley, James	814
McGlothin, William J.	665
McGranahan, James	543
McGready, James	314
McGuffey, William H.	410
McIlvaine, Charles P.	409
McIntire, Carl A.	1193
McIntosh, Rigdon M.	507
McKay, Arthur R.	1054
McKechnie, Don F.	1076
McKee, Arthur W.	778
McKee, Dean G.	1038
McKendree, William	333
McKibbin, William	655

Name	Page
McKinley, William	519
McKinney, Baylus B.	774
McKinney, David	668
McKnight, Donald	1072
McKnight, Robert J.	875
McKoy, Charles F.	863
McLaren, William E.	533
McLean, John K.	572
McLeish, James	1101
McLelland, Vernon	1205
McMahon, John	1139
McMaster, William	462
McMillan, John	331
McNairn, A. Stuart	778
McNaugher, John	748
McNeill, John	664
McPheeters, Julian C.	1007
McPherson, Aimme Kennedy Semple	727
McQuilken, Robert C.	772
McTyeire, Holland N.	467
Meade, Russell J. (Russ)	952
Meade, William	376
Meadows, Clyde W.	1161
Mears, Henrietta C.	849
Meck, Allen S.	946
Medford, Hampton T.	859
Medhurst, Walter H.	367
Medley, Samuel	298
Meeker, Charles P.	704
Meineke, Charles	354
Mekeel, Herbert S.	1032
Melanchthon, Philip	177
Melitius of Antioch,	43
Melitius of Lycopolis,	32
Melito	10
Mell, Patrick H.	463
Melton, Thomas A.	878
Melville, Andrew	203
Mendelssohn-Bartholdy, Felix J. L.	349
Mendenhall, William O.	814
Mercator, Gerhardus	194
Mercator, Marius	62
Mercer, Theodore C.	1028
Meredith, Isaac H.	846
Merrill, George E.	546
Merrill, Selah	550
Merrill, Stephen M.	536
Merrill, William P.	786
Merswin, Rulman	142
Meserve, Charles M.	680
Messiter, Arthur H.	583
Messner, Tammy Faye (Bakker)	1251
Metaphrastes, Simeon	100
Metcalf, Hattie A. Hackett	1136
Methodius	93
Metsker, Al	1093
Metz, Christian	387
Metzger, Bruce M.	1249
Meyer, Frederick B.	638
Meyer, Heinrich A. W.	411
Meyer, John P. C.	860
Meyer, Lucy Rider	611
Meyer, Walter	1175
Michalson, Gordon E.	1129
Michelfelder, Sylvester C.	768
Middleton, Thomas F.	319
Midura, Edward	1074
Mieir, Audrey	1121
Mierop, William A.	1210
Milburn, William H.	526
Miles, C. Austin	737
Miles, George A.	1170
Miles, William H.	479
Miley, John	492
Milicz, Jan	140
Mill, John	250
Millard, James A.	1052
Milledoler, Philip	358
Miller, Adam W.	1100
Miller, Basil W.	964
Miller, Chester I.	1211
Miller, Ernest E.	937
Miller, Gareth B.	1069
Miller, George A.	837
Miller, Hugh	366
Miller, J. Irwin	1227
Miller, James R.	565
Miller, Marlin E.	1109
Miller, Orie O.	954
Miller, Samuel	352
Miller, Samuel H.	886
Millet, Jean F.	416
Milligan, George	671
Milligan, Orlando H.	784
Milligan, Robert	417
Milligan, William	485
Milliken, William T.	841
Mills, B. Fay	583
Mills, Elizabeth King	327
Mills, Howard T.	923
Mills, Samuel J.	315
Mills, Susan Lincoln	567

Milman, Henry H.	393
Milne, William	318
Milner, George S.	901
Milner, Isaac	317
Milner, Joseph	297
Miltiades of Rome,	32
Miltiades	11
Milton, John	233
Mininger, Paul	1130
Minor, George A.	529
Mintern, Michael J.	835
Minucius, Felix M.	16
Mitchell, Andrew E.	855
Mitchell, Hubert	1119
Mitchell, John G.	1062
Mitchell, R. Bryant	1143
Mitzner, Herman D.	931
Moe, Malla P.	781
Moffat, Robert	449
Moffatt, James	725
Moffatt, James S.	610
Moffett, Samuel A.	701
Molay, Jacques de	135
Molinos, Miguel de	246
Monica	44
Monier-Williams, Sir	506
Monk, William H.	467
Monod, Adolphe T.	365
Monod, Frederic J. J.	381
Monroe, Harry	584
Monsell, John S. B.	417
Montano, Walter M.	861
Montanus	7
Montanus, Ralph J.	1031
Montgomery, Bernard L.	947
Montgomery, Carrie Judd	740
Montgomery, Granville H.	874
Montgomery, Helen Barrett	670
Montgomery, James	362
Montgomery, James H.	1248
Montgomery, Richmond A.	760
Montgomery, Riley B.	943
Moody, Dale	1078
Moody, Dwight L.	508
Moody, Emma Revell	528
Moody, May Whittle	852
Moon, Charlotte (Lottie)	567
Moon, Irwin A.	1029
Mooneyham, W. S. Stan	1072
Moore, A. B. T.	724
Moore, Arthur J.	933
Moore, Clement C.	386
Moore, George F.	652
Moore, Evelyn Underhill	709
Moore, James C.	843
Moore, John	302
Moore, John J.	485
Moore, John M.	752
Moore, Mark R.	1242
Moore, Oscar	1158
Moore, Richard V.	1101
Moore, T. Albert	703
Moore, Walter W.	628
Moorehead, William G.	572
Moorhouse, Henry (Harry)	438
More, Hannah	331
More, Henry	241
Morehead, John A.	681
Morgan, Arthur T.	882
Morgan, G. Campbell	732
Morgan, John P. (JP)	568
Morison, James	484
Morken, David	1206
Mornay, Philippe de	204
Morris, Elias C.	612
Morris, Henry M.	1242
Morris, Leila Naylor	641
Morris, Leon	1246
Morris, Samuel	480
Morris, Samuel N.	1042
Morris, Thomas A.	415
Morrison, George H.	634
Morrison, Henry C.	713
Morrison, John A.	870
Morrison, Robert	332
Morse, Jedediah	324
Morse, Samuel B. F.	405
Mortenson, P. Vernon	1168
Morton, Richard E.	1114
Moseley, Thomas	824
Moses, David G.	929
Mosheim, Johann L.	274
Mosher, Samuel J.	695
Mosiman, Samuel K.	702
Moss, Elza	1030
Moss, Robert V.	952
Mote, Edward	416
Moton, Robert R.	704
Mott, Edward	792
Mott, John R.	790
Mott, Lucretia Coffin	438
Moule, Handley C. G.	601

Moulton, James H.	586
Moulton, Richard G.	621
Moulton, Warren J.	744
Moulton, William F.	501
Mountain, James	665
Moyer, Robert L.	727
Mozley, James B.	429
Mudge, Lewis S.	732
Muehlhaeuser, Johannes	389
Muelder, Walter G.	1225
Mueller, Reuben H.	995
Muggeridge, Malcolm	1066
Muhlenberg, Frederick A. C.	300
Muhlenberg, Gotthif H. E.	311
Muhlenberg, Henry M.	291
Muhlenberg, John P. G.	305
Muhlenberg, William A.	426
Mulder, John R.	858
Mullens, Joseph	433
Muller, Friedrich M.	511
Muller, George	502
Muller, Julius	431
Mullinax, Rhett C.	1062
Mullins, Edgar Y.	638
Mullins, Rich	1138
Mumaw, John. R.	1094
Mumaw, Levi	673
Mummart, Clarence A.	824
Munhall, Leander W.	668
Munsey, William E.	427
Muntz, J. Palmer	1081
Muntzer, Thomas	159
Murch, James D.	925
Murchison, Elisha P.	1087
Murfin, Robert	1218
Murphy, Annie S.	713
Murray, Andrew	585
Murray, Billy	1230
Murray, Jack W.	1123
Murray, James R.	534
Murray, John	939
Murray, Robert	558
Murton, John	205
Muse, Daniel T.	758
Musgrave, Walter E.	759
Musser, Irvin W.	913
Myconius, Friedrich	168
Myconius, Oswald	171
Myers, Cortland	7125
Myers, Lester	1171
Myers, Paul	921
Myers, Russell	1188
Myers, Tressie V.	1049
Myland, David W.	720
Mynster, Jakob P.	361
Nagel, Charles F. K.	1138
Nageli, Johann G.	335
Nash, Charles S.	629
Nassau, Robert H.	606
Nation, Carry Moore Gloyd	561
Naumann, Oscar J.	970
Naylor (er), James	223
Naylor, Robert E.	1156
Neal, Daniel	268
Neale, John M.	387
Neander, Joachim N.	236
Neander, Johann A. W.	354
Nectarius	48
Nee, Watchman	916
Needham, George C.	520
Needham, Harold	770
Neesima, Joseph H.	470
Neff, Felix	327
Neff, Pat M.	769
Neff, William H.	966
Neighbor, Ralph W.	1173
Neighbor, Robert E. (Ralph)	729
Nelson, Clarence A.	909
Nelson, Cy	1056
Nelson, David	344
Nelson, Franklin O.	1063
Nelson, Peter C.	717
Nelson, Reuben E.	825
Nelson, Wilbur E.	1212
Nelson, William S.	956
Nemeschy, Edward	643
Neprash, Ivan V.	806
Ness, Henry H.	902
Nestle, Christopher E.	567
Nestorius	60
Nettleton, Asahel	343
Nettleton, David	1095
Neuberg, Frank J.	834
Neumeister, Erdmann	275
Neve, Juregen L.	721
Nevin, John W.	4548
Nevius, John L.	483
Nevski, Alexander	129
Newberry, Thomas	513
Newbigin, Leslie J. E.	1145
Newell, Harriet Atwood	309
Newell, Samuel	317

Name	Page
Newell, William R.	799
Newlin, Thomas	697
Newman, Albert H.	665
Newton, Benjamin W.	500
Newton, Isaac	260
Newton, John	305
Newton, Joseph F.	757
Newton, Louis D.	1029
Newton, Robert	362
Nicephorous	88
Nichol, Henry E.	628
Nicholas of Basle	144
Nicholas of Clamanges	148
Nicholas of Flue	153
Nicholas of Hereford	147
Nicholas of Myra	36
Nicholas, Robert E.	959
Nicholls, Merrill E.	986
Nichols, Decatur W.	1232
Nichols, William F.	620
Nicholson, James L.	424
Nicholson, Martha Snell	807
Nicholson, Roy S.	1091
Nicholson, William P. (Billy)	823
Nicholson, William R.	517
Nicoll, William R.	617
Niebuhr, Helmut R.	843
Nielsen, Anders S.	552
Nielsen, Fredrik K.	542
Niemoeller, Martin	1009
Nightingale, Florence	557
Nikander, Johann K.	594
Nikander, Viljo K.	902
Niles, Daniel T.	904
Nilus	56
Ninian	57
Nitobe, Inanzo O.	667
Nitschmann, David	283
Nitzsch, Karl I.	393
Nixon, Richard M.	1103
Noel, Baptist W.	409
Noetius	11
Nogaret, Guillaume	134
Nolasco, Peter	128
Nommensen, Ludwig I.	589
Norbert	114
Nordenhaug, Josef	898
Norelius, Eric	582
Norris, Buford A.	1027
Norris, J. Frank	773
Norris, John S.	544
Norris, Stuart G.	1060
North, Brownlow	419
North, Frank M.	677
North, Ian	1236
Northen, William J.	568
Northfelt, Marlyn	1092
Northrup, George W.	513
Norwood, G. Hunter	1150
Notker	101
Nott, Eliphalet	385
Nott, Henry	343
Nott, Samuel	396
Nottage, Berlin M.	872
Novatian	21
Novatus	25
Nowell, Alexander	195
Nuelsen, John L.	739
Nusbaum, Cyrus S.	692
Nutter, Edmonson J. M.	777
Nyall, David J.	736
Nygren, Anders	967
Nyman, William G.	833
O'Brian, William	390
O'Dell, Harland J.	858
O'Hair, John C.	811
O'Hanlon, Lily	992
O'Kane, Tullis C.	563
O'Kelly, James	324
Oatman, Johnson	613
Oberlin, Jean F.	323
Obookiah, Henry	314
Occom, Samson	294
Ochino, Bernardino	179
Ockenga, Harold J.	1017
Oda, Kaneo	863
Odell, John P.	1069
Odilo	103
Odle, Don	1193
Odo of Canterbury	95
Odo of Cluny	95
Odoric	137
Oecolampadius, Johannes	162
Oehler, Gustav F.	405
Oengus	89
Oesterley, William O. E.	756
Ogden, William A.	499
Ogdon, Ina Duley	856
Ohlson, Algoth	879
Ohrn, Arnold T.	852
Olaf I of Norway	98
Olaf I of Sweden	102

Name	Page
Olaf II	102
Oldcastle, John	146
Oldenbarneveldt, Johann van	202
Oldham, Dale	1222
Oldham, Earl K.	1102
Oldham, Joseph H.	895
Olevianus, Kaspar	190
Olford, Stephen	1227
Olga	96
Olin, Stephen	356
Oliver, Ernest W.	1186
Oliver, Leonard S.	1173
Olivers, Thomas	298
Olivetan, Pierre R.	165
Olsen, Betty A.	890
Olsen, Ivan E	1097
Olsen, Wesley	1099
Olshausen, Hermann	338
Olson, Arnold T.	1211
Olson, John G.	1106
Olson, Tom M.	941
Olsson, Karl A.	1125
Olsson, Olof	510
Onderdonk, Henry U.	370
Oosterzee, Johannes	445
Opper, Burton	992
Orelli, Conrad von	567
Origen	20
Ormond, Ron	987
Ormston, Mark D.	829
Orr, J. Edwin	1036
Orr, James	570
Orsborn, Albert W. T.	877
Ort, Samuel A.	559
Osborne, Byron L.	1063
Osgood, David	319
Osgood, Howard	562
Osiander, Andreas	171
Osmund	109
Ost, Axel B.	969
Ost, Daniel K.	1019
Ost, John	1245
Ost, Warren W.	1141
Osteen, John	1154
Osterwald, Jean F.	269
Ostrom, Henry	712
Oswald of Northumbria,	74
Oswald of York	98
Oswy	77
Otis, George	1252
Otterbein, Philip W.	310
Otteson, Joseph S.	960
Otto I	96
Otto II	97
Otto III	98
Otto of Bamberg	115
Otto, Milton H.	996
Overbey, Hafford H.	1106
Overholtzer, J. Irvin	793
Owen, Derwyn T.	743
Owen, John	238
Owens, James C. (Jesse)	978
Owens, Priscilla J.	545
Oxenham, John	707
Oxnam, Garfield B.	849
Pachomius	37
Packard, Joseph	520
Page, Albert J.	1087
Page, John I.	1155
Page, Kirby	809
Paget, Francis	561
Paine, Robert	446
Paine, Stephen W.	1078
Paisley, Edward B.	825
Pal, Krishan	318
Palamas, Gregory	139
Paleario, Antonio	183
Palermo, Louis	1200
Palermo, Phil	1215
Paley, William	303
Palissy, Bernard	191
Palladius of Helenopolis,	56
Palladius, Peder	177
Palmer, Albert W.	790
Palmer, Bernard	1148
Palmer, Edward H.	445
Palmer, George A.	984
Palmer, Gordon	953
Palmer, Herbert	214
Palmer, Horatio R.	544
Palmer, Phoebe Worrall	415
Palmer, Ray	460
Palmer, William	454
Pamphilus	31
Pannabecker, Sam F.	960
Pannamaker, Ray P.	1182
Pantaenus	12
Paphnutius	37
Papias	4
Pardee, Richard G.	395
Parham, Charles F.	641
Park, Edwards A.	510

Park, John E.	798		Peabody, George	396
Parker, Daniel	344		Peace, Albert L.	563
Parker, Edward J.	833		Peachey, Mark	969
Parker, Franklin N.	784		Peacock, Joseph L.	788
Parker, J. Monroe (Monk)	1106		Peake, Arthur S.	642
Parker, Joseph	525		Peale, Norman V.	1100
Parker, Matthew	186		Pearce, William	746
Parker, Peter	463		Pearsall, Kenneth H.	1161
Parkhurst, Charles H.	666		Pearse, Mark Guy	645
Parks, Henry B.	679		Pearse, Samuel	299
Parlin, Charles C.	991		Pearson, Eliphalet	324
Parris, Samuel	257		Pearson, John	240
Parrott, Grady	1224		Pearson, Roy M.	1126
Parry, Joseph	526		Peck, Francis J. W.	1226
Parsons, Levi	318		Peck, George	421
Parsons, Robert	985		Peck, Jesse T.	448
Pascal, Blaise	226		Peck, John M.	368
Passavant, William A.	486		Peck, Thomas E.	482
Paton, John G.	541		Peckham, John	132
Paton, William	721		Pedigo, Ray T.	1039
Patrick	63		Peek, Joseph Y.	560
Patrick, Simon	250		Pelagius	54
Patroclus	22		Peloubet, Francis N.	600
Patten, Bebe H.	1221		Pendelton, James M.	476
Patten, John L.	988		Penn, William	256
Patterson, Alfred L.	1047		Penn-Lewis, Jesse Jones	632
Patterson, Gilbert E.	1249		Penney, James C. (JC)	908
Patterson, James O.	1060		Pennington, Isaac	236
Patterson, Marion C.	975		Pennington, Levi T.	930
Patterson, Samuel C.	1035		Penry, John	194
Patterson, William T.	906		Pentecost, George F.	602
Patteson, John C.	402		Pepin III,	84
Pattison, Dorothy Wyndlow "Dora"	431		Percy, John O. (Jack)	1171
Patton, Francis L.	660		Perkin, Noel O.	974
Paul of Thebes	36		Perkins, Justin	397
Paul the Deacon	85		Perkins, William	195
Paul, John H.	883		Perowne, Edward H.	536
Paul, Kankarayan T.	651		Perowne, John J. S.	532
Paul, Thomas E.	892		Perpetua	13
Paula	50		Perritt, R. T.	1054
Paulinus of Nola	57		Perronet, Edward	294
Paulinus of York	75		Perry, Henry G.	945
Paulo, Karl S.	988		Perry, James D.	743
Paulson, Theodore (Ted) M	1163		Pestalozzi, Johann H.	325
Paxson, Ruth A.	755		Peter of Alexandria	31
Paxson, Stephen	439		Peter of Blois	124
Payne, Daniel A.	484		Peter of Bruys	113
Payne, Ernest A.	976		Peter the Hermit,	112
Payne, J. Barton	970		Peter the Lombard	119
Payne, Talmage	871		Peter the Venerable	118
Payson, Edward	326		Peter, Hugh	224

Peters, John L.	1089
Peters, Raymond R.	1188
Peterson, John W.	1247
Peterson, Bartlett	1047
Peterson, Paul B.	968
Pethrus, P. Lewi	934
Petrarch, Francesco	140
Petri, Laurentius	185
Petri, Olaus	170
Petrie, Arthur	882
Petrie, W. M. Flinders	715
Pettaway, Caleb D.	889
Petticord, Paul P.	941
Pettingill, William L.	761
Pew, J. Howard	911
Pfeiffer, Charles F.	949
Pfohl, J. Kenneth	882
Pfotenhauer, Frederick	700
Phaup, Bernard H.	1030
Phelps, Austin	472
Phelps, John W.	744
Phelps, Philip	495
Phelps, Sylvanus D.	491
Phelps, William L.	722
Philaster	47
Philip II	125
Philip IV	135
Philip of Hesse	182
Philip, John	356
Philips, Obbe	176
Phillips, Charles H.	765
Phillips, Frank C.	811
Phillips, James O.	1012
Phillips, John B.	996
Phillips, Philip	490
Phillips, Wendell	450
Phillips, William T.	928
Phillips, Zebarney T.	714
Philpot, Ford R.	1079
Philpott, Peter W.	805
Photius	93
Pickering, D. Ernest	1172
Pickett, Clarence E.	864
Pico della Mirandola, Giovanni	153
Pieper, Franz A. O.	652
Pieper, Reinhold	601
Pierce, Lovick	434
Pierce, Robert W.	966
Pierpont, Folliott S.	586
Pierson, Arthur T.	560
Pierson, Delavan L.	782
Pietsch, William E.	818
Pike, Clarence J.	1060
Pike, Kenneth L.	1074
Pilkington, George L.	497
Pilmore, Joseph	322
Pink, Arthur W.	772
Pipkin, Lester	1189
Pitts, William S.	591
Pius I	6
Place, Lester	1007
Place, Ted	1238
Placidus	68
Playfair, Guy W.	853
Plegmund	94
Plummer, Alfred	626
Plumptre, Edward H.	473
Plutschau, Heinrich	269
Pocahontas	202
Poling, Daniel A.	885
Pollard, Adelaide A.	672
Pollard, Ramsay	1011
Pollard, Samuel	580
Pollock, Thomas B.	497
Polk, James K.	352
Polycarp	5
Polycrates	11
Polyeuctes,	18
Pond, Enoch	443
Pontian,	17
Poole, George J.	1052
Poole, Matthew	235
Poole, William C.	756
Pope, Liston	931
Popov, Harlan	1050
Poppen, Emmanuel F.	833
Pordage, John	237
Porter, Ford	953
Porter, Noah	477
Post, George E.	553
Poteat, Edwin M.	795
Pothinus	8
Pott, Francis L. H.	742
Potter, Henry C.	547
Potter, John	270
Pounds, Jesse Brown	605
Powell, Robert L.	905
Powell, Sr., Adam Clayton	778
Powers, Hardy C.	917
Pradham, Prem	1152
Pratt, Waldo S.	699
Prentiss, Elizabeth Payson	431

Press, Samuel D.	881
Pressense, Edward D.	475
Pressly, Francis Y.	671
Pressly, John S.	380
Pressly, John T.	399
Pressly, William L.	539
Preston, Ann	539
Pretlove, Harold B.	1056
Preus, Adolph C.	430
Preus, Herman A.	486
Preus, Jacob A. O.	1107
Preus, Robert D.	1119
Price, Dolphus	1221
Price, Eugenia	1125
Price, Ira M.	700
Price, John M.	945
Price, Joseph C.	483
Prichard, Rowland H.	460
Prime, Samuel I.	456
Prince, Derek V.	1214
Prince, Green L.	802
Princell, John G.	578
Prior, Charles E.	631
Prisca (Priscilla)	8
Priscillian	43
Procopius of Caesarea	68
Procopius, Andrew	149
Proctor, Samuel D.	1135
Prosper	63
Provoost, Samuel	311
Prudentius of Troyes,	90
Prudentius, Aurelius C.	53
Prynne, William	229
Pseudo-Dionysius the Areopagite	66
Puckett, John L.	639
Pudney, Edwin J.	1044
Pugh, William B.	761
Pugmire, Ernest I.	779
Pulcheria	61
Punshon, William M.	439
Purcell, Henry	246
Purves, George T.	519
Purvey, John	148
Pyatt, Charles L.	832
Quadratus	4
Quamina, James V.	733
Queener, Dorlan H.	1022
Quillian, Joseph D.	1081
Rabaut, Paul	295
Radbertus, Paschasius	91
Rader, Paul D.	694
Radewyn, Florentius	144
Raffles, Thomas	381
Raikes, Robert	307
Rainy, Robert	541
Raleigh, Alexander	436
Raleigh, Walter	202
Ramabai, Pandita S.	611
Ramaker, Albert J.	737
Ramm, Bernard	1084
Ramsay, William M.	697
Ramsey, Arthur M.	1044
Ramsey, James	364
Ramseyer, Joseph E.	723
Ramseyer, Lloyd L.	958
Rand, William W.	551
Randall, Benjamin	306
Ranke, Leopold von	458
Rankin, Jeremiah E.	532
Rankin, Thomas	307
Ransom, Reverdy C.	820
Rasmussen, Robert	1218
Ratramnus	91
Raud, Ganz P.	781
Rauschenbusch, Augustus	508
Rauschenbusch, Walter	590
Ravenhill, Leonard	1110
Rawlinson, George	524
Raws, Addison C.	903
Raws, William	558
Ray, Percy	1070
Rayburn, James C.	907
Rayburn, Robert G.	1060
Raymond du Puy	118
Raymond of Penafort	130
Read, O. J.	836
Reade, Thaddeus C.	523
Reagan, Ronald	1225
Reahm, Duane A.	1070
Rebmann, Johannes	423
Recared I	71
Redal, Rueben H.	1245
Reddin, Abner R.	913
Rediger, C. J.	1048
Rediger, Christian E.	897
Rediger, Milo A.	1048
Redner, Lewis H.	549
Redpath, Alan	1053
Reece, Glenn A.	974
Reed, A. Brant	986
Reed, Andrew	376
Reed, Harold W.	1080

Reed, Harry L.	857
Reed, Mary	720
Reed, Walter	524
Reed, William E.	1024
Rees, Paul S.	1071
Rees, Seth C.	664
Rees, Thomas B. (Tom)	902
Reeves, Robert E.	1158
Regier, Peter K.	922
Reich, Max I	733
Reid, William J.	524
Reim, Edmund C.	897
Reinagle, Alexander R.	425
Reinartz, Eppling	966
Reinhard, Franz V.	308
Reisdorph, Rufus D.	947
Reitz, Albert S.	875
Reland, Adrian	256
Rembrandt van Rijn	229
Remigius	66
Renee	186
Renwick, James	241
Repass, Stephen A.	539
Reublin, Wilhelm	176
Reuss, Eduard G. E.	475
Reveal, Ernest I.	820
Revell, Fleming H.	654
Revels, Hiram R.	513
Reynolds, Edward	233
Reynolds, Hiram F.	694
Reynolds, John	197
Reynolds, Jr., Marion H.	1138
Reynolds, Sr., Marion H.	903
Rhee, Syngman	867
Rhoads, J. Lawrence	1216
Rice, Helen S.	980
Rice, John R.	984
Rice, Lloys Cooke	1059
Rice, Luther	334
Rice, Nathan L.	427
Rice, Robert F.	1204
Rice, Sr., William	964
Richard I	122
Richard of Chichester	127
Richard of St. Victor	119
Richard, Timothy	596
Richards, George W.	793
Richards, J. McDowell	1032
Richardson, Harry V.	1067
Richey, John R.	1011
Richey, Raymond T.	887
Richmond, Leigh	325
Richter, Christian F. G.	252
Richter, Frederick F.	670
Richter, Julius	703
Rickenbacker, Edward V.	926
Rickman, Claude R.	1222
Ridderhof, Joy F. C.	1015
Ridgaway, Henry B.	490
Ridley, John G.	952
Ridley, Nicholas	174
Riggs, Elias	513
Riggs, Ralph M.	908
Riggs, Stephen R.	449
Riley, John E.	1179
Riley, Ralph W.	820
Riley, William B.	748
Rimbault, Edward F.	423
Rimmer, Harry	770
Rinkhart, Martin	216
Rippon, John	335
Risley, Clayton A.	935
Ritter, Karl	371
Ritz, Gale	902
Roach, Corwin C.	1055
Roane, Claude A.	803
Robb, Edmund	1230
Robb, Kenneth C.	1137
Robbins, Wilford L.	633
Roberson, Lee	1250
Robert of Jumieges	104
Robert of Molesme	111
Robert of Sorbon	130
Roberts, Benjamin T.	480
Roberts, Benson H.	645
Roberts, Daniel C.	544
Roberts, Edward H.	790
Roberts, Evan J.	764
Roberts, Issachar J.	404
Roberts, Verne D.	978
Roberts, Walter N.	871
Roberts, William H.	602
Robertson, Archibald T.	669
Robertson, Frederick W.	359
Robertson, James	521
Robinson, Charles S.	505
Robinson, Edward	379
Robinson, George L.	817
Robinson, H. Wheeler	732
Robinson, John	205
Robinson, John W.	745
Robinson, Millard L.	744

Robinson, Paul M.	1187
Robinson, Reuben A. (Bud)	717
Robinson, Reuben D.	469
Robinson, Robert	292
Robinson, Stuart	441
Roch	136
Rock, Johann F.	271
Rockness, Morris	1147
Rodeheaver, Homer A.	795
Rodgers, John	308
Roe, W. Douglas	1016
Rogers, Adrian	1239
Rogers, Arthur M.	969
Rogers, Arthur S.	861
Rogers, Dale Evans	1176
Rogers, Henry	427
Rogers, John	173
Rogers, Roy	1150
Rogness, Alvin N.	1083
Rohr, Philip A.	550
Rolle de Hampole, Richard	139
Rollins, Wallace E.	824
Roloff, Lester	997
Romaine, William	295
Romauld	102
Rondthaler, Edward	650
Rood, Paul W.	798
Rooks, Albertus J.	812
Rooks, Charles S.	1180
Roosevelt, Theodore	594
Root, George F.	490
Roscellinus	113
Rose of Viterbo,	127
Rose, Hugh J.	337
Rose, Joe E.	898
Rose, Lawrence	1040
Rosell, Merve	1185
Rosenberg, Leon	879
Rosenius, Karl O.	390
Ross, Milo C.	972
Ross, Roy G.	961
Ross, Stan O.	1086
Rossetti, Christina G.	487
Rossetti, Dante	444
Rossi, Anthony T.	1090
Roth, Elton M.	768
Roth, Paul H.	876
Rothe, Johann A.	276
Rothman, Bernhard	163
Rounds, Tryphena C.	699
Rounsefell, Carrie Parker	648
Rous, Francis	223
Rouse, Bertist	1217
Rouse, Ruth	802
Routh, Eugene C.	873
Routh, Martin J.	363
Rowe, James	667
Rowley, Francis H.	769
Rowntree, Joseph	623
Royer, Galen B.	766
Rublev, Andrei	148
Rudd, Judson A.	906
Ruelke, Winfield F.	1097
Rufinus, Tyrannius	52
Rugh, William W.	686
Ruibal, Julio C.	1120
Runcie, Robert A. K.	1169
Runyan, William M.	807
Ruscoe, Alfred W.	969
Rush, Christopher	411
Rushbrooke, James H.	742
Rushdoony, Rousas J.	1176
Ruskin, John	509
Russell, Anna B.	789
Russell, Elbert	767
Russell, Howard H.	740
Rust, Eric C.	1077
Rutherford, Samuel	224
Ruysbroeck, Jan van	142
Ryerson, Adolphus E.	443
Ryland, John	322
Ryle, John C.	511
Sa'eed, Muallah M.	715
Sabas	66
Sabatier, Charles P.	635
Sacheverell, Henry	260
Sachs, Hans	187
Sacy, Louis I. L.	239
Saint, Lawrence B.	835
Saint, Nate	797
Saint, Phil	1090
Saint, Rachel B.	1109
Saker, Alfred	436
Sallman, Warner	887
Salmon, George	529
Sammis, John H.	597
Sampey, John R.	741
Sampson, Thomas	191
Sams, James C.	1020
Sancroft, William	245
Sanctis, Luigi de	397
Sanday, William	603

Name	Page
Sanden, Oscar E.	861
Sanders, Frank K.	662
Sanders, Harland	983
Sanders, J. Oswald	1086
Sanders, Terrell C.	1112
Sandys, William	413
Sangster, William E.	828
Sankey, Ira D.	548
Sanny, Loren	1233
Sanville, George W.	809
Saphir, Adolf A.	475
Sarapion	39
Saravia, Adrian	200
Sarpi, Paolo	204
Satterwhite, John H.	1055
Saulnier, Harry G.	1067
Saunders, Wilbour E.	970
Saune, Romulo	1084
Saurin, Jacques	264
Savage, Henry H.	883
Savage, James (Jim) A.	1078
Savage, Kenzy	1159
Savage, Robert C.	1041
Savile, Henry	204
Savonarola, Girolamo	154
Sawatsky, Rodney	1230
Sayce, Archibald H.	661
Sayers, Dorothy L.	809
Scarborough, Lee R.	731
Scates, Hiram S.	970
Schaeffer, Charles F.	435
Schaeffer, Charles W.	494
Schaeffer, Francis A.	1012
Schaeffer, Hermann M.	498
Schaff, David S.	708
Schaff, Philip M.	483
Schaller, Johannes	600
Schauffler, Adolf F.	595
Schauffler, Albert H.	533
Schellenberg, Abraham	601
Schellenberg, Peter E.	924
Scherer, Paul E.	893
Schereschewsky, Samuel I.	540
Schieffelin, William J.	792
Schild, Vern	1095
Schilke, Richard	1182
Schiller, Johann C. F.	303
Schilling, Henry C.	1151
Schiotz, Frederick A.	1052
Schlatter, Michael	292
Schlegel, August W. von	345
Schlegel, Katharina von	279
Schmidt, Robert O.	1102
Schmolck, Benjamin	265
Schmucker, Samuel S.	412
Schmul, Harold M.	1149
Schofield, Alfred T.	645
Schofield, Jack P.	917
Schroeder, Frederick W.	993
Schuette, Conrad H. L.	628
Schuh, Henry F.	870
Schuler, George S.	928
Schulte, George A.	582
Schultz, Earle	1132
Schultze, Augustus	593
Schultze, Henry	819
Schulz, Charles M.	1166
Schumann, Robert A.	365
Schunk, Glenn	964
Schurer, Emil	556
Schutz, Roger	1237
Schwan, Heinrich C.	534
Schwartz, Christian F.	297
Schwarz, Diebold	178
Schwarze, William N.	750
Schwedler, Johann C.	263
Schweitzer, Albert	867
Schwenkfeld, Caspar	179
Sciffi, Clara	128
Scofield, Cyrus I.	607
Scott (1), Thomas	285
Scott (1), Walter	330
Scott (2), Thomas	318
Scott (2), Walter	375
Scott, Austin	612
Scott, Carlyle	1005
Scott, Charles	483
Scott, Clara H. J.	498
Scott, Eugene C.	914
Scott, George	413
Scott, George G.	429
Scott, Peter C.	496
Scott, William A.	454
Scott, William M.	798
Scriven, Joseph M.	459
Scrivener, Frederic H. A.	476
Scroggie, William G.	817
Scudder, Ida S.	828
Scudder, John	363
Seaborg, Glen E.	1104
Seabury, Samuel	296
Seagrave, Gordon S.	864

Name	Page
Seagrave, Robert	277
Seamonds, David	1246
Sears, Barnas	437
Sears, Edmund H.	420
Sears, Gordon E.	1183
Sebastian	26
Secker, Thomas	281
Seeberg, Reinhold	675
Sehon, Edmund W.	422
Seidel, Nathaniel	289
Seiss, Joseph A.	531
Selassie, Haile	942
Selden, John	219
Sellers, Ernest O.	775
Sellew, Walter A.	638
Sellon, Priscilla L.	420
Selnecker, Nickolaus	193
Selwyn, George A.	429
Sergius of Constantinople	74
Sergius of Radonezh	143
Severus	66
Sewell, Hampton H.	688
Seybert, John	372
Seymour, William J.	613
Shaftesbury, Anthony A. C.	456
Shakarian, Demos	1094
Shakespeare, William	201
Shane, Samuel H.	998
Shank, Ezra A.	944
Shaw, Barnabas	367
Shaw, Benjamin G.	765
Shaw, Herbert B.	975
Shaw, Knowles	430
Shaw, William	408
Shedd, William G. T.	487
Sheets, Harold K.	967
Sheffield, W. Marvin	1054
Sheldon, Charles M.	737
Sheldon, Gilbert	235
Sheldon, Henry C.	636
Shelly, Andrew B.	571
Shelly, Anthony S.	635
Shelton, Lee Roy	1204
Shelton, Orman L.	819
Shengmo, Hsi	494
Shepard, Thomas	216
Shepherd, Coulson	869
Shepherd, Thomas	266
Sheppard, Franklin L.	645
Sheppard, Hugh R. L.	691
Sherlock, William	250
Sherrill, Henry K.	980
Sherrill, Lewis J.	804
Sherwin, William F.	454
Shidler, Donald P.	1039
Shields, Thomas T.	791
Shinn, Asa	359
Shires, Henry M.	982
Shoemaker, Joseph S.	679
Shoemaker, Samuel M.	853
Shoemaker, Vaughn	1074
Shooks-Jensen, Bertha T.	981
Showalter, Anthony J.	621
Shrubsole, William	303
Shuck, Daniel	512
Shufelt, J. Stratton	1039
Shuler, Jack	847
Shuler, Robert P.	868
Shultz, Frank	1047
Shultz, Joseph R.	1214
Shuman, Harry M.	877
Shurtleff, Ernest W.	588
Sibelius, Johann J.	808
Sickingen, Franz von	157
Sieck, Louis J.	775
Sievers, Ferdinand	482
Sigebert	111
Sightler, Harold B.	1118
Sigourney, Lydia H. Huntley	684
Sihler, Wilhelm	457
Simatupang, Tahib	1060
Simeon the New Theologian,	101
Simeon, Charles	334
Simmons, Loyed R.	1151
Simons, Menno	178
Simpson, Albert B.	598
Simpson, James Y.	398
Simpson, Matthew	452
Singh, Bakht	1171
Singh, Sadhu S.	640
Singleton, James	1183
Singmaster, John A.	626
Siricius	49
Sisco, Gordon A.	782
Sixtus I	3
Sixtus II	21
Sixtus III	58
Skinner, Howard	1021
Skinner, Thomas	1105
Skinner, Thomas H.	401
Slade, Harold C.	932
Slade, Mary B. C.	443

Sleeper, William T.	532
Slessor, Mary M.	576
Small, James G.	464
Smalley, John	317
Smart, Henry T.	433
Smart, John	944
Smick, Elmer B.	1110
Smith (1), George	422
Smith (2), George	647
Smith, Alfred B.	1184
Smith, Amanda B.	578
Smith, Arthur H.	658
Smith, Benjamin B.	452
Smith, Benjamin J.	959
Smith, Bernard	251
Smith, Campbell B.	839
Smith, Edwin W.	810
Smith, Egbert W.	726
Smith, Eli	366
Smith, Elias	348
Smith, Eugene L.	1026
Smith, Everett	1071
Smith, Frank W.	1141
Smith, Fred	1252
Smith, Fred B.	684
Smith, Frederick G.	744
Smith, George A.	712
Smith, Gerald L. K.	947
Smith, Gordon H.	956
Smith, Hannah H. Whitall	560
Smith, Harry R.	857
Smith, Henry B.	420
Smith, Henry P.	501
Smith, Herbert A.	770
Smith, Horace G.	885
Smith, Howard E.	591
Smith, Ida Reed	766
Smith, J. Edward	1128
Smith, J. Harold	1188
Smith, J. Taylor	692
Smith, James H.	1091
Smith, John	328
Smith, John B.	299
Smith, John C.	347
Smith, John C.	1009
Smith, John S.	334
Smith, Merlin G.	962
Smith, Noel	929
Smith, Oswald J.	1025
Smith, Paul B.	1114
Smith, R. Curtis	1055
Smith, Rodney (Gypsy)	746
Smith, Roy L.	850
Smith, Samuel F.	491
Smith, Samuel R.	584
Smith, Samuel S.	316
Smith, Thomas S.	375
Smith, Timothy L.	1130
Smith, Walter C.	549
Smith, Wilbur M.	948
Smith, William	482
Smith (1), William M.	855
Smith (2), William M.	1113
Smyth, Egbert C.	530
Smythe (Smith), John	200
Smythe, Harper G.	734
Smythe, Newman	623
Smythe, Walter H.	1217
Snead, Alfred C.	834
Snowden, James H.	686
Snyder, Jackson	1074
Snyder, Melvin H.	1010
Snyder, William T.	1097
Socrates,	58
Soderholm, Nathan	653
Sohm, Rudolph	587
Soltau, Herrietta E.	668
Sonneveldt, Jack	1179
Soren, Jose	1190
Soter	7
Soule, Joshua	388
South, Robert	255
Sower, Christopher	276
Sozomen, Salaminius H.	59
Spafford, Horatio G.	466
Spalatin, Georg	167
Spangenberg, August G.	294
Sparrow, William	413
Spaugh, R. Gordon	961
Speaks, Reuben L.	1182
Speer, J. Brock	1157
Speer, Robert E.	747
Speer, Tom	874
Spence - Jones, Henry D. M.	585
Spencer, Ivan Q.	905
Spencer, Tim	931
Spener, Philip J.	249
Spenser, Edmund	194
Sperry, Willard L.	785
Spicer, Charles W.	1240
Spiers, Joseph	550
Spitta, Karl J. P.	372

Name	Page
Spohr, Louis	372
Spooner, William A.	648
Spotswood, John	210
Spottswood, Stephen G.	936
Sprague, William B.	421
Sprecher, Samuel	492
Spreng, Samuel P.	738
Spring, Gardiner	412
Spring, Worthy A.	919
Springer, Harvey H.	873
Spurgeon, Charles H.	477
Stace, Arthur	880
Stafford, Russell H.	910
Stagg, Amos A.	864
Stagg, Frank	1181
Stainer, John	516
Stair, Fred R.	1152
Stairs, Wynn T.	996
Stalker, James	630
Stalley, Harold B.	1124
Stam, Betty Scott	671
Stam, Cornelius R.	1202
Stam, Jacob	915
Stam, John C.	671
Stamm, John S.	798
Stamps, Virgil O.	704
Standerlin, Ann Lee	290
Standish, Myles	221
Standley, Meredith G.	842
Standridge, William C.	1019
Stanger, Frank B.	1028
Stanislaus	106
Stanley, Chester G.	1070
Stanley, Edmund L.	635
Stanley, Henry M.	530
Stanphill, Ira	1100
Stapleton, Ruth Carter	1005
Staten, Walter	1045
Stauch, John	346
Stauffer, John L.	822
Staupitz, Johann von	158
Stead - Wodehouse, Louisa M. R.	585
Stealey, Sydnor L.	896
Stearns, Daniel M.	604
Stearns, Miner B.	938
Stebbins, George C.	735
Stedelbauer, Elliot	1103
Stedman, C. Ray	1085
Steele, Anne	286
Steele, Ellsworth V.	899
Steffens, Cornelius M.	661
Steffens, Nicholas M.	565
Steiner, Edward A.	800
Steiner, Leonhard	1080
Stellhorn, Frederick W.	595
Stennett, Joseph	252
Stennett, Samuel	295
Stephen I of Hungary,	103
Stephen I of Rome,	21
Stephens, Edwin W.	652
Stephens, George T.	802
Stern, Henry A.	455
Sterne, Lawrence	280
Sternhold, Thomas	169
Stevens, Charles H.	995
Stevens, Edward F.	1149
Stevens, Maurice	1031
Stevens, Lillie M. N.	573
Stevenson, John M.	795
Stevenson, Joseph R.	699
Stewart, George B.	658
Stewart, H. Ray	1141
Stewart, James	536
Stewart, James A.	941
Stewart, James S.	1063
Stewart, Lyman	617
Stewart, Payne	1162
Stidley, Leonard A.	813
Stier, Rudolf E.	378
Stigand, William	105
Stiles, Ezra	295
Stiles, Marjorie Scoville	1158
Stillingfleet, Edward	247
Stillwell, Harry E.	734
Stilwell, Albert H.	656
Stime, Eugene V.	1070
Stirrett, Andrew P.	752
Stites, Edgar P.	605
Stitt, David L.	1216
Stock, Harry T.	815
Stock, Simon	129
Stocker, Fred P.	1083
Stocking, Jay T.	679
Stockton, John H.	425
Stoddard, David T.	366
Stoddard, Solomon	262
Stoll, Charles A.	697
Stone, Barton W.	344
Stone, Ellen M.	634
Stone, John S.	443
Stone, John T.	786
Stone, Mary	790

Stone, Samuel	226		Suggs, M. Jack	1166
Stone, Samuel J.	512		Sullivan, Arthur S.	512
Stonehouse, Ned B.	846		Sullivan, James L.	1231
Storch, Nikolaus	164		Sullivan, Leon H.	1180
Storer, James W.	903		Sulpicius Severus,	55
Storm, August L.	574		Summerfield, John	322
Storrs, Richard S.	510		Sumner, John B. (1)	378
Stowe, David M.	1165		Sumner, John B. (2)	589
Stowe, Harriet Beecher	495		Sumner, John D. (J.D.)	1153
Stowell, Hugh	384		Sumrall, Lester F.	1124
Strabo, Walafrid	90		Sunday, Helen Thompson	805
Strachan, Harry	731		Sunday, William A. (Billy)	676
Strachan, John	389		Sung, John	726
Strachan, R. Kenneth	863		Surbrook, Walter L.	1043
Strand, John P.	1137		Suso, Heinrich (Henry)	139
Stratford, John	138		Sutcliffe, Bernard B.	754
Straton, John R.	643		Sutherland, Samuel H.	1101
Straughn, James H.	935		Sverdrup, Jr., George	691
Strauser, Charles E.	1096		Sverdrup, Sr., Georg	542
Strauss, Lehmann	1135		Swain, Clara A.	559
Strawbridge, Robert	288		Swanson, David R.	1176
Street, George E.	442		Swanson, Edward C.	928
Streeter, Burnett H.	690		Swanson, Everett F.	869
Strickland, Charles H.	1047		Swanson, Robert S.	817
Strohm, George D.	962		Swartz, Herman F.	915
Strom, Erwin M.	894		Sweet, William W.	817
Strong, Augustus H.	609		Sweney, John R.	506
Strong, Charles	320		Swete, Henry B.	586
Strong, James	486		Swift, Allan A.	855
Strong, Josiah	583		Swift, Elisha P.	383
Strong, Nathan	313		Swift, Jonathan	269
Strong, William M.	826		Swift, Judson	607
Stroud, Jimmy	949		Swing, David	486
Stuart, Charles M.	656		Swithun	90
Stuart, George R.	627		Sykes, Seth	756
Stuart, Moses	357		Sylvanus	7
Stuart, Robert L.	776		Sylvester I,	34
Stub, Hans G.	653		Symphorosa	4
Stuckey, Obed W.	1077		Synan, Joseph A.	1011
Studd, Charles T.	653		Synesius	53
Studdert - Kennedy, Geoffrey A.	639		Taft, Charles P.	1004
Stump, Joseph	673		Taft, George W.	696
Stumpf, Johannes	187		Tait, Archibald C.	447
Sturk, Lewis W.	793		Talbot, Louis T.	946
Sturm of Fulda	85		Tallis, Thomas	190
Sturm, Jakob	172		Talmage, Thomas D.	522
Sturm, Johannes	191		Tancred	111
Stylites, Simeon	62		Tappan, Henry P.	442
Suckau, Cornelius H.	768		Tappan, William B.	352
Suffield, Kattie L.	919		Tapper, William	812
Sugden, Howard	1098		Tassell, Paul	1197

Tate, Nahum	254
Tatian	9
Tauler, Johann	139
Tausen, Hans	178
Taverner, Richard	186
Tayler, Lewis	426
Taylor, Cary G.	783
Taylor, Charles L.	974
Taylor, Clyde W.	1046
Taylor, Dan	313
Taylor, Edward T.	401
Taylor, Ethel Robinson	763
Taylor, George F.	670
Taylor, Graham	695
Taylor, Herbert J.	964
Taylor, Isaac	384
Taylor, J. Hudson	534
Taylor, J. Randolph	1190
Taylor, J. Paul	925
Taylor, James B.	404
Taylor, Jeremy	228
Taylor, John L.	453
Taylor, Kenneth N.	1235
Taylor, Mary Dyer	399
Taylor, Nathaniel W.	368
Taylor, Walter	747
Taylor, William	522
Taylor, William H.	1208
Taylor, William M.	488
Tchaikovsky, Peter I.	484
Teegarden, Kenneth L.	1200
Telemachus,	49
Telesphorus,	4
Telford, Andrew	1128
Temple, William	728
Ten Boom, Corrie	1002
Tenison, Thomas	254
Tennent, Gilbert	279
Tennent, Jr., William	286
Tennent, Sr., William	269
Tenney, Merrill C.	1018
Tennyson, Alfred	479
Terrell, Gail	1216
Terry, Milton S.	574
Tersteegen, Gerhard	281
Tertullian,	15
Teschner, Melchior	209
Teter, Eber	636
Tharp, Zeno C.	1018
Thayer, Joseph H.	520
Theobald,	118

Theodore of Mopsuestia,	55
Theodore of Studius,	88
Theodore,	80
Theodoret,	61
Theodosius I,	47
Theodosius II,	60
Theodulf,	88
Theophanes,	87
Theophilus,	9
Theophylactus,	110
Thielicke, Helmut	1027
Thierry,	116
Thiessen, Henry C.	745
Thigpen, Jonathan	1180
Thirkield, Wilbur P.	685
Thirlwall, Connop	418
Thoburn, Isabella	518
Thoburn, James M.	614
Tholuck, Friedrich A. G.	426
Thomas of Cantelupe,	131
Thomas of Sitney,	145
Thomas, Carey S.	797
Thomas, Charles P. (Chuck)	1081
Thomas, Elver C.	1057
Thomas, Ian	1252
Thomas, John C.	832
Thomas, Painummoottil J.	1147
Thomas, Paul W.	913
Thomas, W. H. Griffith	618
Thomas, Wilbur K.	778
Thomasius, Christian	262
Thompson, Charles L.	619
Thompson, Elmer V.	1152
Thompson, Frank C.	701
Thompson, Horace E.	776
Thompson, Joseph P.	434
Thompson, Muri	1080
Thompson, Robert H.	1238
Thompson, Will L.	553
Thompson, William	467
Thompson, William P.	1244
Thomson, Edward	397
Thomson, James	361
Thomson, Mary Ann	616
Thomson, William M.	485
Thomson, William T.	545
Thorlaksson, Gudbrandur	207
Thornwell, James H.	377
Thorp, Almus M.	1154
Thorton, Leo M.	1158
Thorvaldsen, Albert B.	343

Thring, Godfrey	528
Throckmorton, Job	195
Thrupp, Dorothy A.	350
Thurstan,	115
Tibertius,	15
Tiffany, Orin E.	757
Tillet, Wilbur F.	681
Tillman, Charles D.	722
Tillotson, John	245
Tindley, Charles A.	666
Tiplady, Thomas	876
Tipple, Ezra S.	685
Tiridates III,	31
Tischendorf, Konstantin L. F. von	416
Tissot, James J. J.	523
Titcombe, Tommy	888
Titus, P.J.	1215
Tkach, Sr., Joseph W.	1117
Tobey, Charles W.	779
Todd, John	412
Toirac, Florent D.	1057
Tolbert, William R.	979
Tomer, William G.	496
Tomhave, Duane K.	1146
Tomlinson, Ambrose J.	722
Tomlinson, Homer A.	891
Tomlinson, Milton A.	1114
Tomlinson, Robert	570
Tooze, Ruby Tibbits	1082
Toplady, Augustus M.	286
Torrey, Charles T.	347
Torrey, Frank C.	998
Torrey, Joseph	390
Torrey, Reuben A.	637
Tovey, Herbert G.	914
Towner, Daniel B.	598
Townsend, Luther T.	610
Townsend, Norman S.	837
Townsend, W. Cameron	994
Tozer, Aiden W.	850
Traber, Bessie	973
Traherne, Thomas	232
Trapp, John	229
Trasher, Lillian H.	839
Travers, Walter	209
Tregelles, Samuel P.	417
Tremellius, John I.	188
Trench, Richard C.	458
Trent, William J.	851
Trimble, Henry B.	846
Trimmer, Sarah	307
Tritton, Fredrich	884
Trotman, Dawson E.	800
Trott, Norman L.	944
Trotter, Melvin E.	705
Troup, Jack	783
Trudel, Dorthea	376
Trueblood, D. Elton	1111
Truett, George W.	725
Truman, Harry S.	920
Trumbull, Charles G.	706
Trumbull, David	466
Trumbull, Henry C.	529
Trust, Harry	827
Truth, Sojourner	450
Trutza, Peter	1035
Tsai, Christiana	1013
Tsutada, David	910
Tubman, Harriet Ross	567
Tubman, William V. S.	910
Tucker, Alfred R.	573
Tucker, Henry S. G.	822
Tuinstra, Kenneth	1156
Tulga, Chester A.	945
Tullar, Grant C.	759
Tupper, Henry A.	522
Turner, Harry L.	949
Turner, Henry M.	579
Turner, Samuel H.	376
Turnwall, William	903
Tuttle, Daniel S.	616
Tweedy, Henry H.	780
Twisse, William	214
Tyconius,	50
Tyler, Bennet	369
Tyler, Herbert R.	1096
Tyler, Walter	141
Tyndale, William	164
Tyng, Stephen H.	456
Tyro, Theodore	29
Uchimura, Kanzo	646
Uemura, Masahisa	622
Ufford, Edward S.	644
Ulery, Orville B.	734
Ullmann, Karl	383
Ulrich,	96
Umbreit, Friedrich W. K.	373
Underwood, Bernard E.	1162
Underwood, Horace G.	584
Unger, Merrill F.	982
Upham, Thomas C.	405
Urban I of Rome,	16

Name	Page	Name	Page
Urban, Percy L.	933	Vaughn, Delbert P.	1157
Urshan, Nathaniel A.	1233	Vaus, Jim	1143
Ursinus, Zacharias	189	Vayhinger, Monroe	695
Ursula,	61	Vedder, Henry C.	675
Ussher, James	220	Veenstra, Johanna	663
Vadianus, Joachim	170	Veninga, Frank	1155
Vail, Silas J.	452	Venn, Henry	297
Vail, Thomas H.	469	Venn, John	309
Valdez, Alfred C.	907	Vennard, Iva Durham	734
Valentine	23	Verbeck, Guido H. F.	502
Valentine, Milton	537	Vereide, Abraham	894
Valentinian I	42	Vermigli, Pietro	179
Valentinus	63	Veronica	1
Van Andel, Jay	1230	Vick, G. Beachamp	943
Van Broekhoven, Harold	1136	Victor I	11
Van Deventer, Judson W.	698	Victoria V of England	514
Van Dyke, Henry J.	663	Vidalin, Thorkelsson	257
Van Ess, Louis	1090	Vig, Peter S.	639
Van Eyck, Hubert	148	Vigilantius	53
Van Eyck, Jan	149	Vilmar, August F. C.	393
Van Gilder, Heber O.	1034	Vincent Ferrer	147
Van Halsema, Dick	1239	Vincent of Lerins	60
Van Ruysbroeck, Jan	142	Vincent of Saragossa	28
Van Raalte, Albertus C.	424	Vincent, John H.	602
Van Steenberghe, Odiloon	844	Vincent, Marvin R.	612
Van Til, Cornelius	1036	Vine, Ebenezer G.	857
Van Valin, Clyde E.	1170	Vinet, Alexandre R.	349
Vandall, Napoleon B.	906	Vins, Georgi P.	1144
Vanderkemp, Johannes T.	308	Vinton, Francis	407
VanderMuelen, John M.	682	Viret, Pierre	184
VanderPool, Daniel I.	1044	Virgilius	85
Van Der Puy, Abe C.	1207	Visser't Hooft, Willem A.	1020
Vandersall, Stanley	796	Vitringa, Campegius	258
Van Der Veer, Raymond	1186	Vitus	25
VanDusen, Henry P.	938	Vladimir I	100
VanDyck, Cornelius V. A.	491	Voekel, Harold	1011
Vane, Henry	225	Voetius, Gisbert	234
VanKampen, Robert C.	1059	Voight, Andrew G.	660
VanKampen, Robert D.	1163	Voliva, Wilbur G.	717
Vannah, Guy L.	866	Voller, Ellwood A.	1090
Vanosdel, Oliver W.	672	Von Blomberg, Martha Louise Moenich	915
VanVliet, Adrian	402	Von Braun, Wernher	958
Varick, James	325	Vos, Gerhardus	755
Varley, Henry	564	Voskuyl, Roger J.	1239
Vasey, Thomas	325	Voss, Gerhard	215
Vassar, John E.	431	Voth, Heinrich	593
Vaughan, Charles J.	500	Wace, Henry	619
Vaughan, Henry	246	Wach, Joachim	794
Vaughan, James D.	708	Waddel, James	303
Vaughan, Robert	393	Waddell, John N.	488
Vaughan-Williams, Ralph	815	Wade, Raymond J.	901

Name	Page
Wadsworth, Benjamin	265
Wadsworth, Ernest M.	853
Waermo, Einer	937
Wagler, Elmer	993
Wagner, Charles	588
Wagner, Charles U.	1247
Wagner, Donald M.	1142
Wagner, Edmund F.	1053
Wagner, Glenn	961
Wagner, James E.	1023
Wahlstrom, Jarl	1163
Wailes, George W.	880
Wainwright, Jonathan M.	363
Wake, William	265
Walch, James	518
Waldegrave (Lord Radstock), Grandville A. W.	571
Waldenstrom, Paul P.	583
Waldo, Peter	125
Walford, William	354
Walker, John H.	950
Walker, Williston	611
Wall, E. Wayne	1219
Wallace, F. Grace	1238
Wallace, Lewis	533
Wallace, William V.	385
Wallenius, Carl G.	742
Wallin, Johan O.	337
Walls, Alice E.	803
Walls, William J.	939
Walpurgis	84
Walter the Penniless	108
Walter, Howard A.	592
Walters, Dick H.	883
Walther, Carl F. W.	461
Waltner, Orlando	1074
Walton, Brian	224
Walton, Joseph B.	850
Walton, W. Spencer	537
Walvoord, John	1204
Wanamaker, John	615
Wang, Mingdao	1073
Warburton, William	287
Ward, C. Morse	1126
Ward, Houston	1076
Ward, James T.	497
Ward, Larry	1217
Ward, Nathaniel	217
Ward, Samuel A.	528
Ward, William	319
Wardlaw, Ralph	360
Wardner, Nathan	504
Wareing, Ernest C.	724
Warfield, Benjamin B.	605
Wargelin, John	906
Waring, Anna L.	556
Warneck, Gustav A.	559
Warner, Anna B.	577
Warner, Daniel S.	492
Warner, David S.	635
Warner, George R.	933
Warner, Ira D.	857
Warner, Susan Bogert	455
Warren, Casper C.	924
Warren, George W.	521
Warren, William F.	644
Washburn, Edward A.	438
Washburn, Henry B.	842
Washington, Booker T.	581
Washington, George	299
Waterbury-Peabody, Lucy McGill	754
Waterland, Daniel	267
Waters, Ethel	959
Waters, Frances B.	391
Watson (1), Richard	312
Watson (2), Richard	330
Watson, Austin	1117
Watson, C. Hoyt	896
Watson, Charles R.	749
Watson, David C. K.	1008
Watson, John	542
Watson, William T.	987
Watters, Philip M.	627
Watts, Isaac	271
Wayland, Francis	384
Wead, Roy H.	1036
Weatherhead, Leslie D.	944
Weaver, George	1192
Weaver, Jonathan	514
Webb, George J.	462
Webb, Thomas	296
Webb, William W.	661
Webb-Peploe, Hammer W.	615
Weber, Charles V.	1220
Weber, Jaroy	1018
Weber, Karl M.	324
Webster, Daniel	358
Webster, George O.	716
Webster, Joseph P.	416
Webster, Noah	342
Webster, Warren	1252
Wedel, Cornelius H.	555
Wedel, Cynthia Clark	1032

Weeden, Winfield S.	548	Whichcote, Benjamin	238
Weems, Mason L.	321	Whipple, Henry B.	519
Weiben, William H.	1223	White, Alma Birdell	739
Weidner, Revere F.	576	White, Arthur K.	990
Weigle, Charles F.	876	White, Henry K.	304
Weigle, Luther A.	951	White, John	666
Weil, Simone	722	White, Kenneth O.	1020
Weiss, Benjamin S.	1026	White, Paul H.	1088
Weiss, G. Christian	1000	White, Reggie	1231
Welch, Dale D.	943	White, Stanley	645
Welch, Herbert	894	White, Wilbert W.	726
Welch, John W.	698	White, William	334
Weld, Theodore D.	488	White, William R.	956
Welliver, Lester A.	928	Whitefield, George	282
Wells, Amos R.	662	Whitehead, Alfred N.	748
Wells, Charles L.	693	Whitfield, Frederick	531
Wells, J. Oscar	1157	Whitfield, Henry	221
Wells, Marcus M.	490	Whitgift, John	196
Wells, Milton T.	940	Whiting, William	429
Wells, Robert J.	1207	Whitman, Marcus	350
Welsh, Wiley A.	1129	Whittaker, Frederick W.	1130
Weltz, Justinian F. von	241	Whittemore, Emma Mott	650
Wenceslaus IV,	147	Whittier, John G.	478
Wenceslaus,	95	Whittle, Daniel W.	515
Wendt, Lowell C.	1224	Whyte, Alexander	604
Weng, Armin G.	881	Wichern, Johann H.	439
Wenger, Amos D.	675	Wichers, Wyand	908
Weniger, Arno Q.	1116	Wickberg, Eric	1124
Weniger, G. Archer	997	Wickey, Gould	950
Wentz, Abdel R.	950	Widmeyer, Charles B.	936
Wesberry, James P.	1088	Wieand, Albert C.	787
Wesley, Charles	291	Wiebe, Vernon R.	1131
Wesley, John	293	Wigglesworth, Michael	249
Wesley, Samuel S.	421	Wigglesworth, Smith	742
Wesley, Sr., Samuel	265	Wilberforce, Samuel	411
Wesley, Susannah Annesley	267	Wilberforce, William	331
Wessel, Johann (John)	153	Wilbert	109
West, James C.	1245	Wilbur, Henry W.	574
West, Stephen	316	Wilder, Robert P.	693
Westcott, Brooke F.	518	Wiley, H. Orton	836
Westerhoff, Harold E.	1099	Wilfrid	82
Weston, Agnes	592	Wilhelmina, Helena	847
Weston, Frank	622	Wilkes, A. Paget	669
Weston, Henry G.	550	Wilkins, John	232
Weymouth, Richard F.	525	Willard, Frances E. C.	501
Whaling, Thorton C.	695	Willard, Joseph	302
Whatcoat, Richard	303	Willard-Yates, Emma Hart	398
Whateley, Richard	381	Willett, Herbert L.	724
Wheatley, Phyllis	290	William de la Mare	132
Wheelock, Eleazar	287	William I of England	107
Whelpton, George	649	William I of The Netherlands of Nassau	189

William I, The Pious	94
William III	248
William of Auvergne	127
William of Champeaux	113
William of Corbeil	115
William of Ockham,	138
William of St. Carilef	108
William of St. Thierry	116
William of Tyre	121
William of Wickham	145
William, Frederick	241
Williams (1), John	338
Williams (2), John	505
Williams, Aaron	285
Williams, Charles B.	771
Williams, Clara Tear	690
Williams, Colin W.	1164
Williams, Eleazar	370
Williams, Elisha	274
Williams, Ernest S.	991
Williams, George	536
Williams, Isaac	384
Williams, J. Floyd	1103
Williams, Joseph D.	754
Williams, Monier	506
Williams, Peter	296
Williams, Robert S.	656
Williams, Roger	238
Williams, Roy T.	738
Williams, Samuel W.	451
Williams, Smallwood	1073
Williams, Walter R.	926
Williams, William	292
Williams, William R.	455
Williamson, Gideon B.	992
Willibald	85
Willibrord	82
Willingham, Robert J.	575
Willingham, Theodore W.	1054
Willis, Richard S.	510
Willson, David B.	595
Willson, James R.	360
Willson, S. Bruce	1161
Wilmer, Richard H.	975
Wilson, Arthur W.	1213
Wilson, Emily Divine	714
Wilson, George M.	1159
Wilson, Grady B.	1041
Wilson, Hugh	321
Wilson, Ira B.	758
Wilson, J. Christy	924
Wilson, John	419
Wilson, John L.	458
Wilson, Joseph D.	623
Wilson, Joseph R.	525
Wilson, Robert D.	649
Wilson, Samuel B.	396
Wilson, T. Woodrow	619
Wilson, Thomas	274
Wilson, Thomas (T.W.)	1181
Wilson, Walter L.	895
Wiman, David W.	1227
Wimber, John	1142
Wimbish, John S.	997
Winchell, Richard	1147
Winchelsey, Robert	135
Winebrenner, John	373
Winer, Johann G. B.	369
Wingblade, Henry C.	961
Winger, Otho	740
Winget, Benjamin	608
Winifred	75
Winkworth, Catherine	430
Winrod, Gerald B.	809
Winsett, Robert E.	772
Winslow, Edward	219
Winston, John C.	1072
Winthrop, John	216
Wipo	104
Wise, John	260
Wishart, George	168
Witherspoon, John	295
Witmar, Safara A.	844
Woike, Richard	1051
Wolfe, Aaron R.	524
Wolfram, Donald J.	1213
Wolgemuth, Samuel F.	1191
Wood, James	626
Wood, John A.	500
Wood, John E.	644
Wood, John W.	746
Wood, Nathan E.	690
Wood, Nathan R.	834
Woodard, Nathaniel	473
Woodbridge, Charles J.	1115
Woodbury, Isaac B.	370
Woods, C. Stacey	1002
Woods, Leonard	362
Woodson, George F.	706
Woodward, Walter C.	713
Woodworth-Etter, Maria B.	621
Wooley, William L.	1105

Name	Page
Wulfstan of Worcester	108
Wurmbrand, Richard	1177
Wyatt, Thomas	856
Wycliffe, John	143
Wylie, Samuel B.	358
Wyneken, Friedrich K. D.	421
Wyrtzen, Jack	1123
Wyttenbach, Thomas	159
Yarnell, Ralph I.	1134
Yat Sen, Sun	623
Yates, John H.	511
Yates, William	346
Yeager, Waldo	1167
Yetter, Arch H.	1109
Yoakum, Finis E.	599
Yocum, William F.	609
Yoder, Sanford C.	938
Yonge, Charlotte M.	515
York, Alvin C.	858
Yost, John L.	1018
Younce, George	1234
Young, Alexander	487
Young, Andrew	610
Young, Edward	279
Young, Edward J.	885
Young, Egerton R.	550
Young, G. Douglas	980
Young, John F.	457
Young, Robert	465
Young, Samuel	1061
Youngdahl, Luther W.	964
Younger, W. Thomas	1205
Yuan, Allen	1237
Yves of Brittany	133
Zahn, Theodor	662
Zeidler, Clemens H.	977
Zeisberger, David	307
Zell, Matthew	169
Zelley, Henry J.	713
Zenos, Andreas/Andrew C.	712
Zeoli, Anthony	1014
Zephyrinus	14
Ziegenbalg, Bartholomew	256
Ziegler, Jesse H.	1177
Ziegler, Samuel G.	982
Zigabenus, Euthymius	112
Zimmerman, Henry D.	932
Zimmerman, Paul	924
Zimmerman, Thomas F.	1068
Zimmerman, Wendell	1080
Zinzendorf, Nicholas L. von	277
Zirkle, James	1140
Zizka, Jan	147
Zoller, John	973
Zondervan, Bernard D.	873
Zondervan, Peter J. (Pat)	1092
Zorn, Edwin G.	755
Zosimus	54
Zucker, Frederick	633
Zulu, Aphaeus H.	1043
Zundel, John	445
Zwemer, Samuel M.	771
Zwilling, Gabriel	175
Zwingli, Ulrich	162

OTHER INFLUENTIAL PERSONALITIES

These indexes list people not in the main body of this volume. Reasons are self-explanatory.

Within the categories there are many fine individuals and these listings are not meant in any way to cast negative implications. The editor is not an authority in these areas. It was difficult enough to select who would be included among the traditional Christian leaders for this volume. Perhaps someone can pick up the baton for these categories and further develop the various branches mentioned for their own followers.

These individuals are not portrayed or categorized by the whims of the editor. They are listed because of what history attests to them, and what these individuals have themselves declared concerning their understanding or distaste of traditional Christianity.

Page #

1.	B.C. Personalities	1308
2.	Catholics	1308
3.	Cults/Comparative World Religionists	1312
4.	Enemies of Christianity	1313
5.	Jewish Leaders	1315
6.	Liberals	1316
7.	Miscellaneous	1317
8.	Orthodox	1319
9.	Popes	1319
10.	Unitarians	1320
11.	Liberal Arts Colleges	1321
12.	World Council of Churches	1322
13.	Lack of Data	1323

1. B.C. Personalities

Those that lived during the Old Testament era and had some religious/philosophical interests, but are non-Biblical personalities. Dates are all B.C.

Name	Birth	Death	Comments	Contribution
ANAXAGORAS	c500	428	Greek philosopher	Explained eclipses
ANTISTHENES	441	371	Greek philosopher	Founder of Cynics
ARISTOTLE	384	322	Philosopher	Great thinker, scientist, teacher
AUGUSTUS, Caesar	63	14	1st Rom. Emperor	Birth of Christ during his reign
BUDDHA	563	468	Founder of Buddhism	Born in India, flourished in China
CAESAR, Julius	100	44	Roman general	Introduced the Julian calendar 46 BC
CONFUCIUS	551	479	Chinese philosopher	Trained "disciples" in literature, music and ethics
DIOGENES	412	323	Greek philosopher	Leader of Cynics, disregarded luxuries
EPICURUS	341	270	Greek philosopher	Evolutionist- held view that death ends all
HERACLITUS	540	480	Greek philosopher	Cosmologist who believed in a state of flux
MAHAVIRA	559	527	Founder of Jainism	Indian ascetic, practiced extreme asceticism
MENICIUS	371	288	Chinese philosopher	Confucian scholar
PAULUS, Aemicius	230	160	Roman general	Led in key battle over Greeks
PYTHAGORAS	580	500	Greek philosopher,	Founded a moral and religious brotherhood
SOCRATES	470	399	Greek philosopher	Discipled Plato-used inquiry and instruction
TIBERIUS, Claudius	42	37	2nd Rom. Emperor	Jesus was crucified and church born 14–37 AD
ZENO of CYPRUS	335	264	Greek philosopher	Did not believe in immortality
ZOROASTER	660	583	Persian reformer	Founder of Zoroastrianism

2. Catholic

Up to 440, we include all the bishops (popes) of Rome. Many of these early bishops (pastors at Rome) died for their faith! The word "pope" was not used in the sense of a universal leader until about the time of Leo I (ruled: 440–461). Prior to this, they did not dominate the Christian World. From 500 to 1500, we have included important Catholics, who were in the mainstream of Christianity at that time, except for cardinals and popes. From 1500 on, few Catholics are included as (in the author's opinion) the Reformation offered a viable alternative.

Name	Birth	Death	Comments	Contribution
AILLY, Pierre	1350	1420	Cardinal	French theologian, philosopher, bishop
ALACOQUE, Marguerite M.	1647	1690	French founder	"The Devotion to the Sacred Heart of Jesus"
ALBERT	1490	1545	Cardinal	Archbishop; elector of Mainz
ALVA, Fernando A.	1507	1582	Spanish General	Caused deaths of 18,000 in Netherlands
ANDREWS, Samuel J.	1817	1906	Apostolic leader	American Clergyman
ANGELA de MERICI	1474	1540	Italian/Ursulines	Taught children, aided the poor
AQUINAS, Thomas	1225	1274	Italian schoolman,	"Calvin of Catholicism", Dominican monk
ARUNDEL, Thomas	1353	1413	Arch/Cant. 1399-14	Persecuted the Lollard
ASTRUC, Jean	1684	1766	French Physician	Free thinker, denied inspiration of Scripture
BARTOLI, Daniello	1608	1685	Italian Jesuit	Preacher and historian
BEATON David	1494	1546	Scottish Cardinal	Archbishop of St. Andrews, Ireland
BECKET, Thomas A.	1118	1170	Arch/Cant. 1162-70	Murdered by King Henry II's knights
BEETHOVEN, Ludwig Van	1770	1827	German composer	Symphonies, quartets, sonatas
BELLARMINO, Roberto F. R.	1542	1621	Italian	Theologian led in condemning of Galileo
BERNADETTE	1844	1879	French visionary	Saw Virgin Mary at Lourdes
BONAVENTURA, Giovanni	1221	1274	Italian Cardinal	Mystic and saint; scholastic revitalized Franciscans
BORGIA, Cesare	1475	1507	Cardinal	Criminal, insolent; spread terror to all of Italy
BORROMEO Charles	1538	1584	Italian cardinal	Reforming influence at Council of Trent
BOSSUET, Jacques B.	1627	1704	French pulpit orator	Simplicity, piety, sincerity; attacked Quietism
BOURCHIER, Thomas	1412	1486	Arch/Cant. 1454-86	Cardinal, 1467-86
BOURDALOUE, Louis	1632	1704	French Jesuit court	Known for preaching, saintly character
BRIDAINE, Jacques	1701	1767	French Jesuit	Evangelistic preacher, admired by all
BRIDGES, Matthew	1800	1894	Song writer	Wrote "Crown Him with Many Crowns"

Name	Born	Died	Role	Description
BROWNSON, Orestus	1803	1876	Clergyman, writer	Was a Universalist before 1844
CABRINI, Frances X.	1850	1917	Founded Order	1st USA citizen to be canonized as a saint
CAJETAN, Jacopo T.	1469	1534	Italian Cardinal	Tried to reconcile Luther with the Church
CALVERT, George	1580	1632	English statesman	Planned Maryland for Catholics
CAMPANELLA, Tommaso	1568	1639	Philosopher	Italian Dominican monk
CANISIUS, Peter	1521	1597	German leader	Lead Counter Reformation, wrote catechisms
CAPISTRANO, Giovanni	1385	1456	Italian	Franciscan preacher and inquisitor
CARROLL, John	1735	1815	Prelate, Baltimore	1st Roman Catholic bishop in the US
CASWALL, Edward	1814	1878	Hymn writer	"Jesus, the Very Thought of Thee"
CATHERINE de MEDICI	1519	1589	French Queen	Married to Henry II; persuaded massacre order
CAVANAUGH, John F.	1899	1979	Educator	Notre Dame President, 1946–79
CHARLES II	1630	1685	King 1660–1685	England, Scotland, Ireland; court was dissolute
CHARLES V	1500	1558	HRE emp 1519–56	King of Spain, 1516–56; political foe of Luther
CHESTERTON, G.K.	1874	1936	English writer,	Poet, fiction, joined Catholic church in 1922
CODY, John P.	1907	1982	Cardinal	Archbishop of Chicago, 1965–1982
CHOPIN, Fred	1810	1849	Polish-French	Composer and pianist, musician
COLET, John	1466	1519	English theologian	Erasmus said "He was pious and knew Christ"
CONTARIN, Gasparo	1483	1542	Venetian Cardinal	Moderate statesman; sought reconciliation
COOK, Terence	1921	1983	Cardinal	Archbishop of New York, 1968–83
COPERNICUS, Nicolaus	1473	1543	Polish astronomer	Stated earth rotates daily, and revolves around the sun
CORREGGIO, Antonio A.	1494	1534	Italian Painter	Did many Bible frescoes and paintings
COSIMO de MEDICI	1389	1464	Florence ruler	"Despotic and cruel;" layman
COUGHLIN, Charles E.	1891	1979	Priest	Bitterly opposed F.D. Roosevelt
COURTENAY, William	1342	1396	Arch/Cant. 1381–96	Foe of Wycliffe and the Lollards
CRASHAW, Richard	1613	1649	English poet	Wrote poetry in Greek, Latin and English
CROMWELL, Thomas	1485	1540	Chancellor, politician	Died in the Catholic faith; supported Henry VIII
CUSHING, Richard James	1895	1970	Cardinal	Archbishop of Boston, 1944–70
DAMIAN, Peter	1007	1072	Cardinal, 1057	Italian bishop of Ostia; reformer, denounced vices
DAMIEN, Joseph V.	1840	1889	Belgian priest	Hawaiian Missionary; worked with lepers
DAY, Dorothy	1897	1980	Journalist, reformer	Founded Catholic Worker newspaper (1933)
DE SMET, Pierre-Jean	1801	1873	Jesuit missionary	Missionary to the Indians on the western frontier
DESCARTES, Rene	1596	1650	French philosopher	"I know, therefore I am"; attempted to unify knowledge
DOLLINGER, Johann J. I.	1799	1890	German Theologian	Leader in the Old Catholic movement; Jesuit foe
DOMINIC de GUZMAN	1170	1221	Spanish Theologian	Founder of Dominican Order
DOOLEY Thomas	1927	1961	Physician	Missionary doctor in Laos
DOUGHERTY, Dennis	1865	1951	Cardinal, 1921	Served in Philadelphia, 1918–51
DUCHESNE, Louis M.	1843	1922	French prelate	Offended conservative theologians, scholar
ECK, Johann M.	1486	1543	German theologian	In a famous debate with Luther at Leipzig in 1519
ELIOT, Thomas S.	1888	1965	British Essayist	Anglo-Catholic quest reconciling man with God
FABER, Frederik W.	1814	1863	Hymn writer	Wrote "Faith of Our Fathers"; left Anglicanism
FARLEY, John M.	1842	1918	Cardinal, 1911	Served in New York City, 1911–18
FEEHAN Patrick A.	1829	1902	Archbishop	1st Archbishop of Chicago, 1880–1902
FERDINAND V	1452	1516	King of Spain	Equipped Columbus' trip to the New World in 1492
FISHER, John	1459	1535	Bishop of Rochester	Martyred upon the word of Henry VIII
FLANAGAN, Edward	1886	1948	Clergyman	Founded BoysTown in Omaha, Nebraska area
FLECHIER, Valentine	1632	1710	French panegyrist	Bishop of Nimes; kind to Protestants
FRANCIS de SALES	1567	1622	French preacher	Humanist, declined cardinal's hat
FRANCK César A. J. G. H.	1822	1890	French composer	Wrote a mass and other church music
GERMANUS of Const.	634	732	Patriarch 715–730	Opposed Monophysites; follower of cult of Mary
GERSON, Jean C.	1363	1429	French theologian	Influenced martyrdom of Huss and Jerome

Name	Born	Died	Role	Description
GIBBONS, James	1834	1921	Cardinal of Baltmore	Leader of the Roman Catholic Church in America
GOUNOD, Charles F.	1818	1893	French composer	Wrote "Ave Maria"; majored in opera, oratorios
GRUBER, Franz	1787	1863	Austrian organist	Provided music for "Silent Night"
GUICCIARDINI, Francesco	1483	1540	Florentine statesman	Governor of papal states, liked Martin Luther
HARDING, Bernard	1912	1998	German theologian	Helped reforms of Vatican II
HAYDN, Franz J.	1732	1809	Austrian composer	Composed over 360 works for the Church
HAYDN, Johann M.	1737	1806	Austrian composer	Wrote music for "O Worship the King."
HAYES, Patrick	1867	1938	American cardinal	Founded Catholic charities in 1920; active NYC
HECKER, Isaac T.	1819	1888	Founder of Paulists	Object of his order was to convert Protestants
HEFELE, Karl J.	1809	1893	German Prelate	Helped prepare Vatican Council of 1870
HEMY, Henry F.	1818	1888	Hymn-writer	Wrote music for "Faith of Our Fathers"
HENNEPIN, Louis	1626	1705	French explorer	Discovered St. Lawrence and Mississippi River source
HUGEL, Baron F.	1852	1925	Brit. lay theologian	Liberal scholar; critic of the Bible
HUGHES, John J.	1797	1864	1st Archbishop NYC	Built more than 100 churches
HUMBERT	1000	1061	Cardinal	French reform leader, very influential
IGNATIUS of LOYOLA	1491	1556	Spanish leader	Founder of Society of Jesus (Jesuit Order)
IRELAND, John	1838	1918	Educator/reformer	Helped found the Catholic Univ. in Washington, D.C.
ISABELLA of CASTILE	1451	1504	Patron of Columbus	Married Ferdinand II; she was gentle and religious
JAMES II	1633	1701	King of England	Sought to restore Roman Catholicism in England
JANSEN, Cornelius O.	1585	1638	Dutch theologian	Opposed Jesuits; condemned by the pope
JAVOUHEY, Anne	c1780	c1852	African missionary	Trained 900 nuns
JIMENES, Franciso	1436	1517	Spanish cardinal	Preacher, Archbishop of Toledo
JOHN, Lackland	1167	1216	English	Repudiating his signature of the Magna Charta
JOHN of AVILA	1500	1569	Spanish reformer	Great preacher, loved the Bible; supported Jesuits
JOHN of the CROSS	1542	1591	Spanish mystic, poet	Carmelite order; was a reformer of the monasteries
JOLIET, Louis	c1645	1700	French explorer	With Marquette, discovered the Mississippi River
KENNEDY, John F.	1917	1963	35th President USA	First Catholic president, assassinated in Dallas
KENRICK, Francis P.	1797	1863	Archbishop (Balt)	Learned theologian; revised the Douay Bible with notes
KILMER, Joyce	1886	1918	Poet	Wrote famed "The Trees" (1914); killed in WWI
KNOX, Ronald	1888	1957	English writer	Translator of the Bible (1944–48)
LACORDAIRE, Jean B.	1802	1861	French prelate	Monk, preacher, theologian; preached liberty
LAMENNAIS, Hughes F.	1782	1854	French philospher	Broke with the Church; was religious radical.
LAMY, Jean (John)	1814	1888	American bishop	Built missions, schools, and hospitals in southwest
LANGTON, Stephen	1150	1228	English Cardinal	Arch/Cant, divided the Bible into Chapters
LASALLE, Robert	1643	1687	French explorer	Claimed Mississippi Valley for France
LAS CASAS, Bartolome de	1474	1566	Spanish missionary	Friend of American Indians in West Indies
LAUD, William	1573	1645	Arch/Cant. 1633–1645	Sought to force ritualism on Scottish Presbyterians
LAYNEZ, James	1512	1565	Spanish Jesuit	Helped shape anti-protestant canons at Trent
LESSON, Jane Eliza	1808	1882	Hymnwriter	Translated "Christ the Lord is Risen Today"
LIGOURI, Alphonsus	1696	1787	Italian theologian	Founded Redemptorist Order; preaching to the poor
LINACRE, Thomas	1460	1524	Humanist	First president of College of Physicians
LISZT, Franz	1811	1886	Hungarian pianist	Became Franciscan;wrote some sacred songs
LOISY, Alfred F.	1857	1940	French theologian	Liberal, philospher; accepted evolution
LORD, Daniel A.	1888	1955	Writer	Composer, playwright, wrote 30 books, 50 plays
LORENZO II de MEDICI	1449	1492	Florentine Ruler	Papacy opposed his power; tyrannical and immoral
LOUIS XVI	1754	1793	King of France	Devoted and sincere; wife Marie Antoinette, corrupt
MANNING, Henry E.	1808	1842	Cardinal	Archbishop of Westminster; left the Angilcanism
MARITAIN, Jacques	1882	1973	French philosopher	Defended reason opposed to subjectivism
MARQUETTE, Jacques	1637	1675	French explorer	Established Mississippi River flow
MASSILLON, Jean Baptiste	1663	1742	French preacher	Great preacher, funeral orator, moral bishop

Name	Born	Died	Role	Description
MAZARINI, Jules	1602	1661	Cardinal, 1641	French statesman; strengthened the nation
McCLOSKEY, John	1810	1885	Cardinal, 1875	1st American citizen to be a cardinal (1875)
MCGLYNN, Edward	1837	1900	Priest	Social Reformer, pastor in New York
MERTON, Thomas	1915	1968	Writer, poet	Trappist monk, mystic who died in Thailand
MILTITZ, Karl von	1480	1529	Saxon ecclesiastic	Chamberlain of Pope Leo X
MINDSZENTY, Jozsef	1892	1975	Hungarian cardinal	Prisoner of Germans in WWII
MOHLER, Johann A.	1796	1838	German historian	"Catholic Schleiermacher"; great theologian
MOHR, Joseph	1792	1848	Aussie hymn writer	Wrote words for "Silent Night" (1818)
MONTALEMBERT, Charles	1810	1870	French historian	Sought to bring Catholic faith and freedom together
MOORE, Thomas	1779	1852	Hymnwriter	Wrote "Come, Ye Disconsolate"
MORE, Sir Thomas	1478	1535	English statesman	Author; cultured, educated, honest; martyr
MORTON, John	c1420	1500	Arch/Cant. 1486–1501	Cardinal, 1493–1500
MOZART., J. C. Wolfgang	1756	1791	Austrian musician	Died at age 35; wrote 18 orchestral masses
MUNDELEIN, George W.	1872	1939	Cardinal, 1924	Cardinal in 1924; Archbishop of Chicago, 1915–39
MURILLO, Bartolome E.	1617	1682	Spanish painter	Painted religious pictures by dictates of Church
NAPOLEON I, Bonaparte	1769	1821	French Emp. 1804–14	Nominal RC until break with Pope Pius VII
NEUMANN, John N.	1811	1860	Philadelphia bishop	Saw much growth, established Sister's Organization
NEWMAN, John H.	1801	1890	Cardinal, 1879	Left Anglican Church; wrote "Lead Kindly Light"
NICHOLAS of CUSA	1400	1464	Cardinal, 1448	German scholar, philosopher; prelate
NOBILI, Robert de	1577	1656	Jesuit missionary	In Goa, India accepted Hindu customs
O'CONNELL, Daniel	1775	1847	Irish National leader	Originated Catholic Association
O'CONNOR, Flannery	1925	1964	Writer	Author of novels and short stories
OAKLEY, Frederick	1802	1880	Poet, preacher	Translated "O Come, All Ye Faithful"
OURSLER, Fulton	1893	1952	Novelist, journalist	Wrote "The Greatest Story Ever Told"
PALESTRINA, Giovanni	1525	1594	Italian composer	"The savior of church music"
PASTEUR, Louis	1822	1895	French chemist	Had profound faith; helped control many diseases
PFEFFERKORN, Johannes	1469	1524	Dominican convert	Writer; burned all Jewish books except for the OT
PHILIP II	1527	1598	King of Spain	Sought to make Catholicism supreme and Catholicism
PIRCKHEIMER, Willibald	1470	1530	German scholar	Defended Luther early on; converted to Catholicism
POLE, Reginald	1500	1558	Cardinal, 1556–58	Gave great assistance to "Bloody Mary"
PROCTOR, Adelade	1825	1864	Hymnwriter	Wrote "The Lost Chord"
QUESNEL, Pasquier	1634	1719	French Theologian	Hated by the Jesuits; embraced the entire NT
RAPHAEL, Santi	1483	1520	Italian painter	Paintings include famous Madonnas; died at 37
REUCHLIN, Johannes	1455	1522	German scholar	Champion of modern pronunciation of Greek
RICCI, Matteo	1552	1610	Italian Jesuit	Missionary to China
RICHELIEU, Arman J.	1585	1642	Cardinal, 1622	French statesman; primary political leader
ROUSSEAU, Jean J.	1712	1778	French philosopher	Proclaimed gospel of "back to nature"
RUBENS, Peter P.	1577	1640	Flemish painter	Most famous painter in Europe; educated by Jesuits
SADOLETO, Jacopo	1477	1547	Cardinal, 1536	Italian prelate, papal secretary; clashed with Calvin
SAMSON, Bernhardino	1520	1570	Swiss commissioner	Clashed with Zwingli
SARTO, Andrea del	1486	1530	Florentine artist	Painted frescoes for the Servite church
SCHALL, Johann A.	1591	1666	Missionary to China	German Jesuit translated Western astronomical books
SCHLEGEL, Karl W. F. von	1772	1829	German poet, writer	Lectured on philosophy, literature and history
SCHUBERT, Franz	1797	1828	Austrian composer	Composed operas, operattas, and chamber music
SERRA, Junipero	1713	1784	Spanish missionary	Defender of Indians in California and Mexico
SETON, Elizabeth A.	1774	1821	Founder of Sisters	Sought care of poor widows and orphans
SHEEN, Fulton	1895	1979	Mass media	Radio (1930–52) and television (1952–65)
SIGISMUND	1368	1437	King and Emperor	Betrayed Huss and Jerome
SMITH, Alfred E.	1873	1944	Candidate, 1928	1st Catholic to run for President's office
SORBON, Robert de	1201	1274	French theologian	Founder of the Sorbonne, chaplain for Louis IX

Name	Born	Died	Role	Description
SOUTHWELL, Robert	1561	1595	Poet and martyr	Hanged as traitor for undercover "missionary" zeal
SPELLMAN, Francis	1889	1967	Cardinal, 1946	Archbishop of New York (1939–46)
ST. SAENS, Camille	1835	1921	French composer	Organist and pianist; also wrote poetry and plays
STRITCH, Samuel	1887	1958	Cardinal, 1939	Served in Chicago, 1939–58
TASSO, Torquato	1544	1595	Italian poet	Became prey to morbid fancies and delusions
TEILHARD, Pierre	1881	1955	French priest	Also paleontologist and philosopher
TERESA, Mother	1910	1997	Missionary	Founder of Sisters of Charity
TERESA of AVILA	1515	1582	Spanish mystic	Founded Discalced Carmelite convents for nuns
TETZEL, Johann	1465	1519	German monk	Actions led Luther to post his Ninety-five Theses
THERESA of LISEUX	1873	1897	French Carm. nun	Developed doctrine of "little way"
TITIAN	1485	1576	Italian painter	Greatest "colorist" among painters
TOCQUEVILLE, Alexis	1805	1859	French thinker	Encouraged separation of Church and State
TOLKIEN, John R. R.	1892	1973	British writer	Writer of fantasies, including "The Hobbit" (1937)
TORQUEMADA, Tomas de	1420	1498	Spanish monk	Expelled Moors and Jews from Spain
TYRRELL, George H.	1861	1909	Irish theologian	Expelled from the Jesuits, nearly excommunicated
VALDES, Juan de	1490	1532	Spanish theologian	Also a humanist and reformer; Catholicism
VELASCO, Luis de	1511	1564	Spanish admin.	Emancipated many native Indians in Mexico
VERBIEST, Ferdinand	1623	1688	Flemish astronomer	Missionary to China; opened door for Jesuits
VILATTE, Joseph R.	1854	1925	Organizer of CC	Later returned to the Roman Catholic Church
VINCENT de PAUL	1580	1660	French Sociologist	Founded Daughters of Charity to help the poor
VON TRAPP, Maria			Austrian musician	Featured in "Sound of Music"
WADE, John Francis	1711	1786	Hymnwriter	Wrote "O Come, All Ye Faithful"
WARHAM, William	c1450	1532	Arch/Cant. 1503–32	Married Henry VIII and Cathanne of Aragon in 1509
WILLEBRANDS, Johanne	1909	1969	Dutch cardinal	Catholic Conference for Ecumenical Questions
WOLSEY, Thomas	1474	1530	English cardinal	Statesman; Henry VIII sought his help
XAVIER, Francis	1506	1552	Spanish Jesuit	Great missionary to India, Japan and China
XIMENES, D. C. Franzisco	1436	1517	Cardinal	Spanish inquisitor, patriot and statesman

3. Cultists/ Comparative World Religionists

A cult is a distortion or perversion of historic Christianity. Comparative World Religions are non-Christian religions of the world.

Name	Born	Died	Role	Description
ADLER, Felix	1851	1933	Free Thinker	Founder of Society for Ethical Culture, educator
AMALRIC of BENA	1207		French theologian	Mystical philosopher, pantheistic views
AMMONIUS SACCAS	175/242		Neo-platonism	Alexandrian philosopher
ARMSTRONG, Garner Ted	1930	2003	Cult Founder	Founder of Int. Church of God
ARMSTRONG, Herbert W.	1892	1986	Cult Founder	Founder, World-Wide Church of God
ARTEMON (Artemas)	260		Adoptionist heretic	Denied Trinity, deity of Christ
AVERROES	1126	1198	Spanish Arabian	High regard for Aristotle; nominal Muslim, philospher
BAHA-U-LAH	1817	1892	Founder of Mahaism	Sought to unite humanity under one religious faith
BALLARD, Guy W.	1878	1939	Co-foun. of "I AM"	Combination of many religions
BASILIDES	138/145		Mystic, gnostic	"Christ did not die on the cross"
BEISSEL Johann Konrad	1690	1768	Society of Ephrata	Seventh Day German Baptist; Dunkers
BERG, David	1919	1994	Cult Founder	Organization also known as The Children of God
BESANT, Annie Wood	1847	1933	British theosophist	Became nationalist political leader in India
BLAVATSKY, Helena Hahn	1831	1891	Theosophists, 1875	Mystical, philosophical cult
BOND, Ahva J. C.	1875	1958	Seventh Day Baptist	Dean of Alfred University (1935 until death)
BROWNING, Elizabeth	1806	1861	English poet, hymnist	Leaned toward spiritualism; semi-invalid
BUSH, George	1796	1859	Bible commentator	Embraced mystical doctrines of Swedenborgianism
CARPOCRATES	131/150		Greek gnostic	His followers survived until the 4th century
CERINTHUS	75/100		Gnostic leader	Also followed Jewish Ebonite teachings
DIOSCURUS	c.378	454	Greek prelate	Head of extreme Monophysite party

Name	Born	Died	Role	Description
DIVINE, Father	1880	1965	Black leader	Personified as God headqts in NYC/Philadelphia
EDDY, Mary Baker	1821	1910	Cult Founder	Founder of Christian Science Church
EPICTETUS	50	120	Greek philosopher	"Virtue-end of life"; "man is ruled by fate"
EUTYCHES	378	454	leader of monks	Human nature of Christ absorbed into the divine
FILLMORE, Charles S.	1854	1948	Cult Founder	Founder of Unity School of Christianity
FOX, Margaret	1833	1893	Spiritualist medium	"heard supernaturalist rappings"; heavy drinker
FREEMAN, Hobart	1920	1984	Faith leader	Rejected medicine-several died
GANDI, Mohandas	1869	1948	Indian Nationalist	Considered Father of his country; Hindu
GRACE, Charles M.	1881	1960	Black evangelist	Founder of United House of Prayer
HALLIWELL, Jesse			Missionary	Seventh Day Adventist missionary
HIROHITO	1901	1989	Japanese Emperor	Claimed to be a god prior to WWII, 1926
HUBBARD, Lafayette	1911	1986	Cult Founder	Scientology Founder In 1954
JONES, Jim	1931	1978	People's Temple	Led nearly 900 to death in Jonestown, Guyana
KELLOGG, John H.	1852	1943	Seventh Day Advt.	Physical and health reformer, invented corn flakes
KENYON, William	1812	1867	Seventh Day Baptist	1st president of Alfred (NY) University
KNORR, Nathan H.	1905	1977	Jehovah Witness	Rapid growth under his leadership, 1942–77
KORESH, David	1959	1993	Branch Davidian	86 of his followers died in Waco, Texas fire
MALCOLM X	1925	1965	Muslim leader	Powerful voice for Black independence
MANI	216	274	Persian sage	Founder of Manicheanism
MARCELLUS of ANCYRA	374/350		Sebellianism leader	Views similar to Samosastism; Arian opponent
MARCION	c.85	160	Marcionite	Merged gnosticism to Christianity
MILLER, William	1782	1849	Adventist advocate	Prophecied Christ's return in 1843–44
MOHAMMED	570	632	Founder of Islam	Flight to Medina in 622 begins sect
MOHAMMED, Mirza Ali	1819	1850	Moslem reformer	Shiite sect; executed by Moslems as a heretic
MUHAMMAD, Eliijah	1897	1975	Black nationalist	Headed nation of Islam in Black Muslims
NOYES, John H.	1811	1886	Oneida Community	Taught that the Kingdom of God came in 1847
OLCOTT, Henry S.	1832	1907	Theosophical society	Farmer, lawyer
PRABHUPADA, Swami	c1895	1977	Indian leader	Founded Hare Krishna movement in U.S., 1965
PRAXEAS	120	170	Heretic of Asia M.	First major advocate of modalistic Monarchianism
PURNELL. Benjamin	1861	1927	Cult founder	Founder of the Israelite House of David
QUIMBY, Phineas P.	1802	1866	Mental healing	Helped Christian Science and Unity to develop
RAPP, Johann G.	1757	1847	Harmony Society	Believed Napoleon was God's ambassador
RIGDON, Sidney	1793	1876	Mormon leader	Former Baptist and Restoration leader
ROBINSON, Frank B.	1886	1948	Founder of Psychiana	Unitarian; emphasized health, prosperity, happiness
RUSSELL, Charles T.	1852	1916	Cult Founder	Founder of Jehovah's Witnesses
RUTHERFORD, Joseph F.	1869	1942	Cult Founder	Second President of Jehovah Witnesses
SANDEMAN, Robert	1718	1771	Sandeman Church	Taught extreme election
SIMON MAGUS	20	70	Samaritan sorcerer	Founder of early form of Gnosticism
SMITH, George A.	1870	1951	Mormon leader	President of Latter Day Saints, 1945–51
SMITH, Joseph F.	1838	1918	Mormon leader	Had 42 children stated plural marriages wrong
SMITH Jr., Joseph	1832	1914	Mormon leader	Reorganized Mormon Church
SMITH Sr., Joseph	1805	1844	Mormon Founder	Authorized polygamous marriages, murdered
THOMAS, John	1805	1871	Christadelphians	Rejects all basic Christian doctrines
TINGLEY. Katherine A.	1852	1929	Theosophist	Philanthropist; led in world-wide expansion of cult
WHITE, Ellen Gould	1827	1915	Cult Founder	First called Seventh Day Adventist in 1860
YOUNG, Brigham	1801	1877	Mormon leader	In 1847, led 142 "pioneers" to Salt Lake City

4. Enemies of Christianity

Name	Born	Died	Role	Description
ANTOINETTE, Marie	1755	1793	French Queen	Her lifestyle was luxurious and extravagant
ANTONINUS PIUS	86	161	Rom. Emp. 138–161	Punished Christians after legal proceedings

Name	Born	Died	Role	Description
BAUER, Bruno	1809	1882	German theologian	Critic, historian, philosopher–"Voltaire of Germany"
CARLYLE, Thomas	1795	1881	Scottish essayist	Biographer, theist; rejected Christian dogmas
CELSUS	180		Rom. philosopher	Polemical writer against Christianity
CLAUDIUS, Tiberius	10 BC	54	Rom. Emp. 41–45	Expelled Jews from Rome; declared a god
COLLINS, Anthony	1676	1729	Deist	Denied value of Old Testament prophecies
COMTE, Isidore A.	1798	1857	French philosopher	Sociologist
CONSTANTIUS II, Flavius J.	317	361	Rom. Emp 337–361	Fanatical Arian
DARROW, Clarence	1857	1938	Lawyer	Opposed William J. Bryan in famed trial in Dayton, TN
DARWIN, Charles R.	1809	1882	English naturalist	Evolutionist-famous for defining Order of the Species
DECIUS	201	251	Rom. Emp 249–251	Made national effort to eradicate Christianity
DEWEY, John	1859	1952	Educator	Humanistic philosophy denied Christian faith
DIDEROT, Denis	1713	1784	French philosopher	"Pantheistic sensualism"-enemy of the church
DIOCLETIAN	245	313	Rom. Emp 284–305	Led in the last/severest Christian persecution
DOMITIAN	51	96	Rom. Emp 81–91	Deified himself; exiled the Apostle John to Patmos
EUNOMIUS	335	394	Leader of Arianism	Denied that Christ had any divine nature
FELIX, Antonius C.			Roman procurator	Hoped to receive bribes from Paul, Judea 52–60
FESTUS, Porcius		62	Roman procurator	Higher type of pagan official, Judea 60–62
FEURBACH, Ludwig	1804	1872	German philosopher	Influenced Karl Marx
FICHTE, Johann G.	1762	1814	German philosopher	Atheist; early interest in theology; transcendalist
FRANCK, Sebastian	1499	1543	German free thinker	Also humanist, historian, and mystic
FREDERICK II	1194	1250	HRE 1215–50	Complete denial of the Gospel
FREUD, Sigmund	1856	1939	Austrian physician	Wrote "The Interpretation of Dreams" 1900
GALERIUS	243	311	Rom. Emp 305–311	Persecuted Christians, later relented, asking for prayers
GESENIUS, Heinrich	1786	1842	German scholar	Last of the proponents of Rationalism at Halle
GIBBON Edward	1737	1794	English historian	Betrays an unfriendly animus to Christianity
GODWIN, William	1756	1836	English philosopher	Champion of Atheism
HADRIAN	76	138	Rom, Emp 117–138	Punished Christians who were convicted
HAECKEL, Ernest H.	1834	1919	German philosopher	1st German to endorse Darwin's Evolution Theory
HEGEL, George W.	1770	1831	German philosopher	Portrayed Jesus only as son of Joseph and Mary
HENRY VIII,	1491	1547	King of England	Had many wives; started Church of England
HERBERT, Edward	1589	1648	Deist	"Supernatural revelation is not necessary for religion."
HITLER, Adolf	1889	1945	Fuhrer of Germany	Enemy of freedom, Christianity, and Jews
HOBBES, Thomas	1588	1679	Philosopher, theorist	Forerunner of modern materialism, atheist
HUME, David	1711	1776	Scottish philosopher	Nothing exists but perceptions; denied miracles
HUXLEY, Thomas	1835	1895	English biologist	Foe of Christianity; an agnostic, evolutionist,
HYPATIA	355	415	Greek philosopher	Lectured on pagan theories; murdered
INGERSOLL, Robert	1833	1899	Lawyer, orator	Agnostic; attacked the Bible and Christianity
JAMES, William	1842	1910	Philosopher	Founder of pragmatism or empiricism
JULIAN the APOSTATE	332	363	Rom. Emp 361–363	Hated Christianity, yet remained tolerant
KANT, Immaunel	1724	1804	German philosopher	No place for Christ; the Bible is man-made
KIERKEGAARD, Soren A.	1813	1855	Danish philosopher	Waged war against religion; founder of Existentialism
KING, Henry C.	1858	1934	Theologian, scholar	Left Presbyterianism to avoid heresy trial
LAVEY, Anton	1930	1997	Satanist	Founder of Church of Satan in 1966
LESSING, Gotthold E.	1729	1781	German dramatist	Religion was independent of all historical revelation
LIBANIUS	314	393	Greek rhetorician	Defended paganism to the last
LOUIS XIII	1601	1643	King of France	Huguenot power was broken by him
LOUIS XIV	1638	1715	King of France	Ruled 72 years; revocated 1685 the Edict of Toleration
LOUIS XV	1710	1774	King of France	Lost Canada, Louisiana, and India; became bankrupt
LUCIAN OF SAMOSATA	120	200	Greek writer	Also a satirist, rhetorician; the "Voltaire of literature"
MACHIAVELLI, Niccolo	1469	1527	Italian statesman	Political philosopher

MARCION	c85	c160	Gnostic	Completed his own NT- God of Moses different
MARCUS AURELIUS	121	180	Rom. Emp 161–180	Justin Martyr, Polycarp of Smyrna, etc., martyred
MARX, H. Karl	1818	1883	German philosopher	Basic philosophy of communism came from him
MARY STUART	1542	1587	"Queen of Scots"	Foe of John Knox; executed for treason
MARY TUDOR	1516	1558	Queen of England	"Bloody Mary"; over 300 Protestants martyred
MAUGHAM, Somerset	1874	1965	British novelist	Agnostic, dramatist
MILL, John S.	1806	1873	English philosopher	Political economist; "no room for Christianity"
MUSSOLINI, Benito	1883	1945	Italian dictator	Ally of Hitler in WWII
NERO, Claudius C. D. G.	37	68	Rom. Emp 54–68	2/3 of Rome burned in 64; blamed Christians
NIETZSCHE, Friedrich W.	1844	1900	German philosopher	Ridiculed Christian religion and ethics
O'HARE, Madalyn	1919	1995	Atheist	Led legal efforts to eliminate God from national life.
PAINE, Thomas	1737	1809	Political philosopher	Deist who wrote "Age of Reason" against the Bible
PHILIPPO of BRUNO	1548	1600	Philosopher	Neo-platonic, humanist, pantheistic
PHILOSTORGIUS	368	439	Byzantine historian	Church historian, follower of Eunomius
PLINY the YOUNGER	62	113	Roman statesman	Despised Christianity, persecuting Christians
PLOTINUS	205	270	Philosopher, mystic	Follower of Plato; teacher of Porphyry
PORPHYRY	232	303	Greek philosopher	Wrote 15 books "Against the Christians"
RENAN, Joseph E.	1823	1892	French essayist	Said "science will replace all religion;" skeptical
ROYCE, Josiah	1855	1916	Philosopher	Wrote "The Problem of Christianity"
RUSSELL, Bertrand	1872	1970	English philosopher	Protested nuclear weapons and the Vietnam War
SCHELLING, Friedrich W. J.	1775	1854	German philosopher	Adopted many erroneous beliefs
SCHOPENHAUER, Arthur	1788	1860	German philosopher	Borrowed ideas from Kant, Plato, and Hindus
SPENCER, Herbert	1820	1903	English philosopher	Champion of evolution
SPINOZA, Baruch	1632	1677	Dutch philosopher	Pantheist; excommunicated from Judaism
STRAUSS, David F.	1808	1874	German philosopher,	Theological writer denying basic tenets of the faith
SWEDENBORG, Emmanuel	1688	1772	Philosopher	Denied the Christian basic tenets of the faith
THEOPHILUS of Alexandria	412		Greek patriarch	Banished Chrysostom; practiced violence
TINDALL, Matthew	1655	1733	Deist	Taught Christianity is to be tested by nature
TOLAND, John	1670	1722	Deist	Denied that Christianity introduced anything
TOLSTOI, Lyo (Leo)	1828	1910	Russian philosopher	Rejected all authority that would allow one person rule
TRAJAN	53	117	Rom. Emp 98–117	Legalized Christian punishment
VALENTINIAN III	419	455	Rom. Emp 425–455	Issued edict that bishop of Rome is world primate
VALENTINUS	160		Philosopher, teacher	Founder of Gnostic sect
VALERIAN	193	260	Rom. Emp 253–260	Ordered clergy banished, executed
VILLEGAIGNON, Nicolas	1510	1571	French soldier	Betrayer of French Protestant colony in Brazil
VOLTAIRE, Jean	1694	1778	French writer	Attacked Christianity and atheism
WELLS, Herbert G.	1866	1946	English author	Sociologist and historian; bitter foe of Christianity
WOOLSTON, Thomas	1669	1733	Deist	Insisted that NT miracles were symbolic, not factual

5. Jewish Leaders

ADLER, Cyrus	1863	1940	Educator	President of Jewish Theo. Sem., NYC, 1916–40
ASCH, Sholem	1880	1957	Polish playwright	Regretted Jewish-Gentile divisions
BAAL-SHEM-TOV	c1700	1760	Teacher	Founder of Hasidism
BAR KOKHBA	70	135	False Messiah	Led futile insurrection against Rome
BERGSON, Henri L.	1859	1941	French philosopher	Some called him an atheist
BUBER, Martin	1878	1965	Austrian philosopher	Relational thoughts led him to new insights
GOLDMAN, Soloman	1893	1953	Zionist leader	Leader of Conservative Judaism
HUGH of LINCOLN	1246	1255	English boy	His murder caused great political backlash
KOHLER, Kaufmann	1843	1926	Rabbi	Leader of Reformed Judaism
MAIMONIDES	1135	1204	Rabbi	Rich in honor, fame, and friends; born in Spain

PHILO of ALEXANDRIA	20 BC	50	Greek philosopher	Sought to reconcile OT with Greek philosophy
TOURO, Isaac de	1737	1784	Jeshuat Leader	First Jewish Rabbi in Americas
WISE, Isaac M.	1819	1900	Rabbi	Founder of Reformed Judaism in U.S.A.
WISE, Stephen S.	1874	1949	Rabbi	Founder of Zionist Organization of America

6. Liberals

Many entries in this book would be considered liberal, as we have tried to be fair and balanced. However, attacks on the inspiration of Scripture and/or the deity of Christ generates this list, especially if they have influence.

ADENEY, Walter F.	1849	1920	English clergy	Accepted results of Biblical criticism
AETIUS	367		Syrian heretic	Leader of extreme Arianism after Nicea
AGRICOLA, Rudolphus	1443	1485	Dutch Reformed	Scholar, man of good character, humanist
ARIUS	256	336	Founder of Arianism	Jesus could not be co-eternal with His Father
ARNAULD, Antoine	1612	1694	French Theologian	Disciple of Descartes; foe of Jesuits and Calvinists
BARCLAY, William	1907		Scotch Theologian	Universalist, doubts on virgin birth, miracles, etc.
BAUR, Ferdinand C.	1792	1860	German higher critic	Theologian and scholar; eliminated the supernatural
BEET, Joseph A.	1840	1924	Theologian, author	English Wesleyan
BERYLLUS of BOSTRA	200	245	Theologian	Denied pre-existence and deity of Christ
BOCCACCIO, Giovanni	1313	1375	Italian writer	Novelist, story teller; early humanist, scandalous life
BOWNE, Borden P.	1847	1910	Methodist, educator	He stressed the personality of Jesus as the norm
BRIGGS, Charles A.	1841	1913	Presbyterian scholar	Theologian-tried for heresy; Episcopalian
BRIGHTMAN, Edgar S.	1884	1953	Method. philosopher	Leading exponent of Browne's Personalism
BROWN, Francis	1849	1916	OT scholar	President of Union Theological Seminary
BROWN, William A.	1865	1943	Pres. theologian	Union Theological Seminary 1892–1936
BRUNNER, Emil	1889	1966	Swiss Reformed	Rejected historic orthodox view of revelation
BRUNO, Philippo G.	1548	1600	Philosopher	Pantheistic, humanist, neo-Platonic
BULTMANN, Rudolph K.	1884	1976	Theologian	Skeptical of historical contents of the gospel
BURTON, Ernest D.	1856	1925	Baptist theologian	University of Chicago educator; led many astray
BUSHNELL, Horace	1802	1876	Congregationalist	Accused of anti-Trinitarian heresy
CAMPBELL, John M.	1800	1872	Scotch theologian	Deposed by Presbyterians for heresy
CASE, Shirley J.	1872	1947	Baptist theologian	Teacher at University of Chicago, 1908–38
CHAPMAN, John	1774	1825	Humanitarian	Known as "Johnny Appleseed"
CLARKE, William N.	1841	1912	Baptist theologian	Responsible for modernism in seminaries
COE, George A.	1862	1951	Religious educator	Taught in four universities; opposed militarism
COFFIN, Henry S.	1877	1954	Presbyterian cleric	Union Theological Seminary, 1926–45
COLENSO, John W.	1814	1883	Anglican bishop	Higher critical interpretation of Bible
ELOHHORN, Johann	1752	1827	Higher critic	Defended scripture, but explained away miracles,
EUCKEN, Rudolph C.	1846	1926	German philosopher	Considered orthodox religion incapable of spiritual
EUSEBIUS of EMESA	300	359	Greek, Semi-Arian	Theologian and writer; favorite of Constantine
EUSEBIUS of NICOMEDIA	342		Syrian Arian bishop	Baptized Constantine in 337; Arian leader
FERRE, Nels	1908	1971	Theologian	Congregational Christian Church leader
FOSDICK, Harry E.	1878	1969	Pastor, teacher	At Riverside Church in New York City (1926–46)
FROUDE, Richard H.	1803	1836	Anglican churchman	Admired Catholicism; medieval church follower
GOETHE, Johann	1749	1832	German writer, poet	Developed theory of evolution prior to Darwin
GRAF, Karl H.	1815	1869	German OT Critic	Promoted post-exilic origin of Pentateuch
HARNACK, Karl G. A.	1851	1930	German Lutheran	Follower of Ritschl; leader of critical school
HARPER, William R.	1856	1906	Hebrew scholar	Authored International Critical Commentary
HASE, Karl A.	1800	1890	German historian	Opposed supernaturalism; moderately rationalistic
HERDER, Johann G.	1744	1803	German theologian	Philosopher; opposed orthodoxy
HICKS, Elias	1748	1830	Quaker	Liberal wing of Society of Friends (Hicksites)
HROMADKA, Josef	1889	1969	Czech pastor	Founder of Christian-Marxist dialogue

Name	Born	Died	Role	Description
INGE, William R.	1860	1954	Anglican divine	Known as the "gloomy dean"; prophet of doom
KING, Henry C.	1858	1934	Theologian	Educator, accepted evolution and Biblical criticism
KINGSLEY, Charles	1819	1875	Cleric, novelist	Social movement; endorsed Darwin
LECLERC, Jean	1657	1736	Swiss theologian	Denied divine inspiration of some Biblical books
LUCIAN of ANTIOCH	240	312	Presbyter of Antioch	Theologian accepting evolution and Biblical criticism
MACEDONIUS	362		Patriarch	Founder of Macedonian sect
MACINTOSH, Douglas C.	1877	1948	Canadian Baptist	Cleric, Theologian, pacifist
MADISON, James	1751	1836	4th USA President	Champion of religious freedom, but Deist
MATHEWS, Shailer	1863	1941	Baptist educator	Rejected divine origin of Bible, divinity of Christ
MAURICE, John F. D.	1805	1872	Ch. Eng. theologian	One of founders of Christian Socialist movement
McGIFFERT Sr., Arthur C.	1861	1933	Congregationalist	Left Presbyterianism to avoid heresy trial
MOMMSEN, Theodore	1817	1903	German scholar	Member of Liberal Union and German Liberal Party
MORRISON, Charles C.	1874	1966	Disciples of Christ	Editor of Christian Century (1908–47)
NIEBUHR, Reinhold N.	1892	1971	Theologian, cleric	Denied Bible inspiration and divinity of Christ
PAJON, Claude	1626	1685	French pastor	Had deist tendencies
PAUL of SAMATOSA	c200		Patriarch of Antioch	Said Christ was adopted as Son of God, not equal
PAULUS, Heinrich	1761	1851	German theologian	Said NT writers suffered hallucinations
PIKE, James A.	1913	1969	Episcopalian	Denied virgin birth, explored spiritualism
POWELL, Adam C.	1908	1972	NYC pastor	Abyssinian Baptist Church, NYC pastor, 1937–60
PUSEY, Edward B.	1800	1882	Tractarian leader	Anglo-Catholic leader; established sisterhoods
RITSCHL, Albrecht B.	1822	1889	German theologian	Opened the way for critical study of the Bible
SABATIER, Louis A.	1839	1901	French theologian	Extremely liberal; prepared the way for Modernism
SATURNINUS	120	170	Leader of Syrian sect	Denied human birth of Jesus; rejected the OT
SCHLEIERMACHER, Freidrich	1768	1834	German theologian	Denied deity of Christ, and atonement, philosopher
SEMLER, Johann	1725	1791	German rationalist	Denied inspiration of the Bible
SERVETUS, Miguel	1511	1553	Spanish physician	Anti-Trinity; advocated Arian and Anabaptist views
SMITH, Henry P.	1847	1927	Educator	Tried and suspended by Presbyterians
SMITH, William R.	1846	1894	Scottish scholar	Biblical critic; suspended from Free Church College
SOCKMAN, Ralph	1889	1970	Methodist Cleric	Liberal in preaching and writing
STANLEY, Arthur P.	1815	1881	Anglican divine	Broad Church leader; emphasis was on ethics
THEODORIC the GREAT	455	526	Ostrogoths/King	Arian in belief; killed his opponents
THEODOTUS	120	170	Byzantine theologian	Anti-Trinitarian views
THOREAU, Henry D.	1817	1862	Essayist, poet	Member of Transcendentalist group
TILLICH, Paul J.	1886	1965	Lutheran scholar	Liberal in preaching and writings
TOY, Crawford H.	1830	1919	Hebrew scholar	Rejected the Bible inspiration, accepted evolution
TROELTSCH, Ernst	1865	1923	German theologian	"Christianity is one of many good religions"
TULLOCH, John	1823	1866	Scottish theologian	Sought to awaken liberal orthodoxy in Scotland
ULFILAS	311	381	Cappadocian	Great Arian missionary; gave them the Bible
VOSSIUS, Gerhardus J.	1577	1649	Dutch humanist	Classical scholar; defended Arminianism
WEISS, Carl P. B.	1827	1918	German theologian	Conservatives critic
WELLHAUSEN, Julius	1844	1918	German theologian	Denied the inspiration of Scripture

7. Miscellaneous

Personalities who have shown some interest in Christianity, but have no evidence of acceptance. Christians whose faith was evident, but death-bed conversions, serious personal problems, lack of sufficient Christian related data, or other criteria question their inclusion in this volume.

Name	Born	Died	Role	Description
ACUFF, Roy	1903	1992	"Christian Hillbilly"	Tennessee tenor of Grand Ole Opry
ADAMS, Samuel	1722	1803	Politician	Apparent Christian; owned a brewery
ALEXANDER I	1777	1825	Czar of Russia	"Closet" Baptist, sympathized with Baptists
ATWATER, Lee	1951	1991	Politician	Republican National chairman
BARKLEY, Alben	1877	1956	Vice-pres. of U.S.	Evidently a Christian

Name	Born	Died	Role	Notes
BERNHARDT, Sarah	1844	1923	French actress	Converted from Judaism
BLANCHARD, Ferdinand Q.	1876		Cong. hymn writer	Moderator of Congregational Christian Churches
BONAPARTE, Napoleon	1769	1821	Emporer	"The external reign of Christ who is praised and living"
CHURCHILL, Winston	1874	1965	Eng. Prime Minister	Made good comments about the Bible
CLEAVER, Eldridge	1935	1998	Black Power Adv.	Fled to Algeria, Converted in 1975
CLEMENS, Samuel	1835	1410	Writer, humorist	Wrote on two religious subjects, "Joan of Arc," etc.
COBB, Ty	1886	1961	Baseball player	Converted on deathbed via Billy Graham message
CONSTANTIUS I, Flavius	250	306	Rom. Emp 305–306	Non-Christian, gave Christians protection
DICKINSON, Emily	1830	1886	American poet	Metaphysical speculation in poetry
DOLLAR, Truman	1937	1996	Baptist pastor	Personal problems led to suicide, great preacher
DOOLITTLE, Jimmy	1896		Military Hero, Pastor	Led attack on Tokyo April 15, 1942
DOWIE, John A.	1847	1907	Pastor	Founder of Christian Catholic Church
ELIOT, Thomas S.	1888	1965	British essayist	Church of England, interested in sociology and culture
ERASMUS, Desiderius	1466	1536	Dutch scholar	Prince of the humanists; Greek New Testament (1516)
ERIGENA, Johannes S.	810	877	Irish theologian	Influenced mystics/ scholastics, pantheistic leaning
FAULKNER, William	1897	1962	Novelist	Several of his books had religious themes
FRANKLIN, Benjamin	1706	1790	Inventor, statesman	Deist, believed in God and prayer, but not in Christ
FREDERICK II the GREAT	1712	1786	King of Prussia	Deist, influenced by Voltaire
GARNET, Henry	1815	1882	Radical Abolitionist	Encouraged slaves to kill their masters
GILBERT, Dan	1911	1962	Anti-Communist	Personal problems led to his murder
GRANT, Ulyssius	1822	1885	18th Pres. of USA	Methodist roots, but non-church attendee
HAWTHORNE, Nathaniel	1804	1864	Writer	Lived in Massachusetts; wrote many books and stories
JEFFERSON, Thomas	1743	1826	3rd Pres. of USA	Deist, sought for religious freedom
JOSEPHUS, Flavius	37	101	Historian	Non-Christian, but gave credence to Christ
KAISER, Henry	1882	1967	Industrialist	Construction of highways, bridges, and ships
KASHA, Al	1937		Composer	Converted from Judaism
KINNEY, Kenneth		1976	ACC Pres. 1953–55	GARB pastor; personal problems
MANTLE, Mickey	1931	1995	Baseball player	Converted via Bobby Richardson
MERRICK, Joseph	1862	1890	English oddity	Grotesque, deformed body, but was a blessing
PATON, Alan	1903	1988	South African leader	Author of "Cry the Beloved Country"
PATTON, George S.	1885	1945	Army general	Outstanding general in WWII
PRACELSUS, H. T. Bombastus	1493	1541	German philiospher	Theology based on the Bible via philosphy
PRESLEY, Elvis	1935	1977	Singer	Religious but introduces rock music age
PULITZER, Joseph	1847	1911	Journalist, publisher	Converted from Judaism; established prizes
ROCKEFELLER, John D.	1839	1937	Industrialist	Organized Standard Oil Company
SHAW, George B.	1856	1950	Playwright	Said in October, 1942 "Why not give Christianity a try?"
SHEFFEY, Robert S.			Evangelist	A 19th century circuit-riding preacher
SNIPSTEAD, Richard	1916	1998	Free Lutheran	President 1978–92; personal problems plagued him
SOONG, Charles Jones			Chinese Businessman	Daughters married Sun Yat-Sen, and Chiang Kai Shek.
SPENSER, Edward	1834	1917	Hero	Saved 17 in Lake Michigan boat mishap
STUBNER, Markus T.	1550		Radical Anabaptist	Claimed inspiration from God in every utterance
SYDEN-STRIKER, Carie			China missionary	Mother of Pearl Buck
TEMPLETON, Charles		2002	Toronto Nazarene	Former Youth for Christ enthusiast; Later Apostate
THEODORA	500	547	Byzantine Empress	Wife of Justinian I – cruel, licentious life style
WALLACE, William			Missionary	In China for 17 years with SBC
WATSON, Claude	1885		Lawyer	Free Methodist: ran for President of US in 1944
WEDGEWOOD, Josiah	1730	1795	Maker of pottery	He defended biblical truths
WOLSTON, Walter T. P.	1840	1917	English doctor	Also a preacher: wrote many books and tracts

8. Orthodox

The Orthodox Church originated in Constantinople in 1054 following a split with Rome/Catholicism

ALEXIS	1877	1970	Russian church man	Patriarch of Moscow and all Russia, 1945–70
BERDYAYEV, Nikolay	1874	1948	Russian philosopher	Critical of Marxism and Russian Orthodox Church
DOSTOYEVSKY, Fyodor	1821	1881	Russian novelist	Stories of explorations of the lives of people
HERMAN	1750	1836	Russian monk	Missionary to Alaska
INNOCENT			Russian monk	Missionary to Alaska
JOHN of KRONSTAAT	1829	1909	Russian cleric	Revitalized spirituality in the Russian Church; priest
KHOMIAKOV, Alexey	1804	1860	Russian theologian	Did not place authority in pope or Bible
KISHKOVSKY, Leonid			Pres. NCC (1988–90)	
KUDENKIN, Sergevitch			Russian Church	Foreign church relations department
MALIK, Charles	1906	1987	UN Official	President 1958–59
NICOLAI (Kasatkin), Ivan	1835	1912	Missionary to Japan	Successful Russian endeavor: 30,000 converts
NIKON, Nikita Minin	1605	1681	Patriarch of Moscow	Declared separation of church and state; imprisoned
TIKHON, Beliavin	1865	1925	Patriarch of Moscow	1st Patriarch of the Russian Church since 1700

9. Popes

There have been hundreds but these seemed to be some of the more predominant individuals.

ADRIAN IV, Nicolas Breakspear	1100	1159	Pope 1154–1159	Only Englishman to sit on the papal throne
ALEXANDER II, Anselmo Backguis		1073	Pope 1061–1073	Favored Wm. the Conq. invasion of England
ALEXANDER III, Rolando Bandinelli	1105	1181	Pope 1159–1181	Cathari excomm, Waldo forbidden to preach
ALEXANDER VI, Rodrigo Borgia	1431	1503	Pope 1492–1503	Most corrupt pope since 10th century
BENEDICT IX, Theophylactus	1012	1056	Pope 1032–45,47–48	Elected at age 21 by simony and intrigue
BENEDICT XIII, Pedro de Luna	1328	1423	Pope 1394–1417	Last of the Avignon popes in Western Schism
BONIFACE VIII, Benedetto Caetani	1235	1303	Pope 1294–1303	Had "passionate temper, was violent, faithless
CELESTINE V, Pietro di Murrhone	1209	1296	Pope 1294	Resigned after five months-liked hermit life
CLEMENT V, Bertrand de Goth	1260	1314	1st Avignon pope	Moved residence from Rome to Avignon
GREGORY I the GREAT	540	604	Pope 590–604	Greatest pope; extended influence of Church
GREGORY IX	1145	1241	Pope 1227–1241	Helped Francis of Assisi; helped develop Inquisition
GREGORY VII, Hildebrand	1020	1085	Pope 1073–1085	Pope-conflict with Henry IV of Germany
GREGORY VIII, Alberto de Morra	c1100		Pope 1187	Began preparation for 3rd Crusade
GREGORY XI, Pierre de Beaufort	1329	1378	Pope 1370–1387	Ordered Papal Bulls against Wycliffe's doctrines
GREGORY XII, Angelo Corrario	1325	1417	Pope 1406–1415	Last Roman pope in Papal Schism
GREGORY XIII, Ugo Buoncompagni	1502	1585	Pope 1572–1585	Reformed Julian calendar (added leap year)
INNOCENT III, Lotario de Conti	1161	1216	Pope 1198–1216	Added title "Vicar of God," instigated Inquisition
JOHN XII, Octavian	937	964	Pope 955–964	Pope at age 17, immoral and wicked
JOHN XXII, Jacquid D'use	1245	1334	3rd Avignon pope	Long conflict with emperor Louis of Bavaria
JOHN XXIII, Angelo Ronsalli	1881	1963	Pope 1958–1963	Called Vatican II for 1962
JOHN XXIII, Baldassare Cossa	1370	1419	Anti-Pope 1410–1417	His right of succession was challenged
JULIUS II, Giuliano Rovere	1443	1513	Pope 1503–1513	Reformer, repudiated simony, nepotism
LEO I, The Great	400	461	Pope 440–461	Created the papacy; power came from Peter
LEO III		816	Pope 795–816	Crowned Charlemagne emperor in 800
LEO IX, Bruno	1002	1054	Pope 1048–1054	Conflicts with Cerularius, 1054 schism
LEO X, Giovanni de Medici	1475	1521	Pope 1513–1521	Reformation began with Luther's rebellion
LEO XIII Gioacchino (Pecci)	1810	1903	Pope 1878–1903	Scholar and statesman, raising prestige of office
PAUL I, John (Luciani Albino)	1912	1978	Pope for 34 days	
PAUL II, John	1920	2005	Pope 1977–2005	Popular, much traveled, conservative leader.
PAUL III, Alessandro Farnese	1468	1549	Pope 1534–1549	In 1537, summoned the Council of Trent
PAUL IV, Giovanni-Caraffa	1426	1559	Pope 1555–1559	Initiated Index of Prohibited Books
PAUL VI, Giovanni-Montini	1897	1978	Pope 1963–1978	First pope to visit the U.S. (1965)

PIUS V, Mighele Ghslieri	1504	1572	Pope 1566–1572	Excommunicated Elizabeth I of England
PIUS IX, Mastai-Ferretti	1792	1878	Pope 1846–1878	Created Papal Infallibility (1870)
PIUS X, Giuseppe Sarto	1835	1914	Pope 1903–1914	Devoted to charitable work; reformer of church
PIUS XI, A. D. Achille Ratti	1857	1939	Pope 1922–1939	Condemned capitalism, Communism and Nazism
PIUS XII, Eugenio Pacelli	1876	1958	Pope 1939–1958	Proclaimed the bodily assumption of the Virgin Mary
URBAN II, Odo (Otto) de Lagny	1035	1099	Pope 1088–1099	His preaching started the Crusades
URBAN V, Guillaume de Grimoard	1309	1370	Pope 1362–1370	Best of Avignon popes; lived in Rome/France
URBAN VI, Bartolommeo Prignani	1318	1389	Pope 1378–1389	Declined to leave Rome; alienated French cardinals
URBAN VIII, Maffeo Barberini	1568	1644	Pope 1623–1644	Acted as Italian prince instead of head of Church

10. Unitarian Leaders
Unitarians believe in universal salvation.

ADAMS, John	1735	1826	2nd President	Defeated by Jefferson in 1800
ADAMS, John Q.	1767	1848	6th USA President	Defeated by Andrew Jackson in 1830
ADAMS, Sarah F.	1805	1848	Hymn writer, poet	Wrote hymn, "Nearer My God to Thee"
BALLOU I, Hosea	1771	1852	Amer. Universalist	Rejected doctrines of depravity, Hell, trinity, miracles
BALLOU II, Hosea	1796	1861	Amer. Universalist	Boston pastor, believed God saves everyone
BARTON, Clara	1821	1912	Universalist	Founder of American Red Cross
BIDDLE, John	1615	1662	British lay theologian	Founder of English Unitarianism
BRADLEY, Preston	1888	1983	Pastor	People's Church, Chicago, 1926–76
BRYANT, William C.	1794	1878	Poet and journalist	Occasionally attended traditional churches
CARY, Alice	1820	1871	Hymn writer	Universalist; wrote "Ballads, Lyrics, and Hymns"
CARY, Phoebe	1824	1871	Hymn writer	Universalist; wrote hymn "Nearer Home"
CHANNING, William E.	1780	1842	Clergyman	Pastored Federal Street Church, Boston, 1803–42
CHAPIN, Edwin	1814	1880	Universalists	Pastored at Church of Divine Paternity, New York City
CHAUNCY, Charles	1705	1787	Clergyman	Pastored First Church, Boston, 1727–87
CLARKE, James F.	1810	1888	Theologian	Pastored Church of the Disciples, Boston
COLLYER, Robert	1823	1912	Pastor	Churches in Chicago and New York City
ELLIOT, Charles W.	1834	1926	Harvard President	Educator, editor of Harvard Classics
EMERSON, Ralph W.	1803	1882	Philosopher, poet	Pastor of Second Church, Boston, 1829–32
EVERETT, Charles	1829	1900	Harvard President	Pastored Bangor, Maine, 1859–69
EVERETT, Edward	1794	1865	Educator, diplomat	Governor of Massachusetts, U.S. senator
FENN, William	1862	1932	Harvard President	1st Unitarian society, Chicago, 1891–1901
FREEMAN, James	1759	1835	Clergyman	Pastor of King's Chapel 1783–1826
HALE, Edward E.	1822	1909	Author	Pastored South Congregational Church, Boston
HANAFORD, Phoebe	1829	1921	Universalist	First woman preacher ordained in New England
HEDGE, Frederick Henry	1805	1890	Harvard Professor	Translated " A Mighty Fortress is Our God"
HOLMES, John H.	1879	1964	Hymn writer	Became an Independent after 1919
HOLMES, Oliver W.	1809	1894	Writer and physician	Rebelled against Calvinism and Puritanism
HOSMER, Fred L.	1840	1929	Hymn writer, pastor	Pastored in Mass., Illinois, Ohio, and Cal.
HOWE, Julia W.	1819	1910	Writer, lecturer	Wrote "Battle Hymn of Republic"
KIRKLAND, John T.	1770	1840	Harvard President,	Did post-grad study of liberal divines
LONGFELLOW, Henry W.	1807	1882	American poet	Wrote "I Heard the Bells on Christmas Day."
LONGFELLOW, Samuel	1819	1892	Hymn Writer	American Unitarian clergyman
LOWELL, James R.	1819	1891	Author, diplomat	Scholar, gentleman, well-read man; poet and essayist
MARTINEAU, James	1805	1900	English theologian	Taught at Manchester, preacher in Liverpool
MAYHEW, Jonathan	1720	1766	Clergyman	Pastored West Church, Boston
MURRAY, John	1741	1815	Clergyman	Founder of American Universalism Gloucester/Boston
OLIVER, Henry K.	1800	1885	Musician, Educator	Massachusetts state official, organist
PALFREY, John G.	1796	1881	Harvard President	Member of Mass. House of Representatives

PARKER, Theodore	1810	1860	Clergyman	Extremely liberal; pastored in two Boston churches
PARKMAN, Francis	1823	1893	Historian	Visited Indians on Oregon Trail, a chronic invalid
PRIESTLY, Joseph	1733	1804	English preacher	Rejected Trinity and atonement; scientist, chemist
SABELLIUS	c215	261	Roman theologian	Close to pantheism in teachings, preceded Arius
SOZZINI, Fausto P.	1539	1604	Italian theologian	Denied all the chief Christian dogmas
TARRANT, William G.	1853	1928	Hymn writer	Wrote several song books, hymn texts, and tunes
WARE, Henry	1764	1845	Clergyman	Professor of divinity at Harvard 1805–40
WHITBY, Daniel	1638	1725	Writer	Developed post-millennial views
WYETH, John	1770	1858	Hymn Writer	Wrote music for "Come Thou Fount"

11. Liberal Arts Colleges

The following liberal arts colleges of evangelical persuasion are listed in the last National Association of Evangelicals yearbook. Those people that are deceased and have served ten or more years as president are listed. Several have incomplete data in regards to birth date and/or death date.

Belhaven College, Jackson, Mississippi (United Presbyterian, USA)
    Girls College   1894–1954
    Co-ed   1954–   ~ Margaret Weathersby, Gretchen Cook, Cille J. Norman, Evelyn Tacket

Campbell University, Buies Creek, North Carolina (Southern Baptist Convention)
    James A. Campbell   1887–1934
    Leslie H. Campbell   1934–1967   ~ Diamond J. Matthews

Campbellsville University, Campbellsville, Kentucky (Southern Baptist Convention)
    Warren F. Jones   1926–30, 41–45   September 3, 1896 – June 17, 1971
    D.J. Wright   1930–1941
    John M. Carter   1948–1968

College of the Ozarks, (United Presbyterian, USA)
    High school   1906–1952
    M. Graham Clark   1952–1981   February 25, 1909 – March 15, 2001   ~ Gwen Simmons

Dallas Baptist University, Dallas, Texas (Southern Baptist Convention)   ~ Gary R. Cook

East Texas Baptist University, Marshall, Texas
    Franklin Groner   1928–1942   January 3, 1877 – November 8, 1943
    Harvey D. Bruce   1942–1960   September 29, 1895 – March 2, 1986
    Howard C. Bennett   1960–1976   June 13, 1910 – April 15, 1985   ~ Dorothy Meadows

Geneva College, Beaver Falls, Pennsylvania (Reformed Presbyterian of North America)
    Henry H. George   1872–1890   February 20, 1833 – March 25, 1914
    William P. Johnston   1890–1907   January 26, 1839 – February 6, 1920
    William H. George   1907–1916   August 18, 1878 – September 24, 1949
    McLeod M. Pearce   1923–1948   July 16, 1874 – November 22, 1948
    Edwin C. Clarke   1956–1980   October 30, 1913 – February 17, 1787
    John White   2002   ~ Mark D. Weinstein, Robert M. Copeland

Grand Canyon College, Phoenix, Arizona (Southern Baptist Convention)

Grove City College, Grove City, Pennsylvania (United Presbyterian USA)
    Isaac Ketler   1876–1913   January 21, 1853
    Weir C. Ketler   1916–1956   March 14, 1889
    John Stanley Harker   1956–1971   December 12, 1903   ~ Rhoda K. Mathias

Judson College, Elgin, Illinois (North American Baptist)   ~ James W. Didier

King College, Bristol, Tennessee
    James D. Tadlock   1867–1885   1825 – August 26, 1899
    Jesse A. Wallace   1885–1894   January 16, 1846 – June 23, 1912
    Tilden Scherer   1912–1931   December 24, 1876 – February 26, 1958
    Robert T.L. Liston   1943–1968   December 10, 1898 – December 9, 1987 ~ D. H. Filty, M. S. Peltier, W. J. Wad

Montreat College, Montreat, North Carolina (United Presbyterian, USA)
    Girls College   1916–1957
    Calvin G. Davis   1959–1972   September 15, 1906 – April 2, 1992   ~ Elizabeth Pearson, L. Nelson Bell

Palm Beach Atlantic University, West Palm Beach, Florida (Southern Baptist Convention)

Southwest Baptist University, Bolivar, Missouri (Southern Baptist Convention)
    John C. Pike   1916–1928
    Courts Redford   1930–1943
    John W. Dowdy Sr. 1949–1960   June 28, 2000
    James L. Sells   1968–1979

Sterling College, Sterling, Kansas (United Presbyterian, USA)
    High School   1899–1910
    Rose T. Campbell   1911–1934
    Hugh A. Kelsey   1934–1947
    Wm. A. McCreecy   1947–1974   January 21, 1912 – July 6, 1999   ~ Susan Cornett, Cynthia Akers, LeAnn Walker

Union University, Jackson, Tennessee (Southern Baptist Convention)
    Academy   1831–1844
    Joseph H. Eaton   1848–1859   September 10, 1812 – January 12, 1859
    George W. Jarman   1876–1890
    George M. Savage   1890–1904
    Henry E. Watters   1918–1931   September 14, 1876 – April 15, 1938
    John J. Hurt Sr.   1932–1945   March 1, 1873
    Warren F. Jones   1945–1963
    Robert E. Craig   1967–1986   ~ David S. Dockery –2002

University of Sioux Falls, Sioux Falls, South Dakota (American Baptist)
    Evan B. Meredith   1885–1894   April 19, 1853 – August 1933
    Edward F. Jorden   1904–1915   September 24, 1858 – September 26, 1927   ~ Rita Jerke

Whitworth College, Spokane, Washington (United Presbyterian, USA)
    Ward W.S. Sullivan 1929–1938   December 27, 1883
    Frank W. Warren   1940–1963   November 23, 1899
    Edward B. Lindaman 1970–1980   May 6, 1920 – August 26, 1982   ~Janet Hauck

Williams Baptist College (Southern Baptist Convention)
    H.E. Williams   1941–1973
    D. Jack Nicholas   1973–1991

12. World Council of Churches presidents

(Parenthesis means the individuals are in the main body of the book) Host city and presidents elected at these gatherings

1948–1954, Amsterdam, Netherlands   (Moderator: George Bell)
    (Boegner, Fisher, T.C. Chao, Oxnam, Eidem, Bergrav, Mott, Chakko)
    Germanos of Thyateira (1948–51)   – Sept. 15, 1882 – January 24, 1951, London, England
    Athenagoras of Thyateira (1951–54) – March 25, 1866 – July 6, 1972, Istanbul, Turkey

1954–1961, Evanston, Illinois   (Moderator: Franklin C. Fry)
    (Barbieri, Dibelius, H.K. Sherill, Mott, Bell)
    John Baillie   1886–1960
    Juhanon Mar Thoma   –1976
    Michael (1954–59)
    Iakovos (1959–61)   1911–April 10, 2005, United States

1961–1968, New Delhi, India   (Moderator: Franklin C. Fry)
    (Ramsey, Ibiam, Moses, Niemoller, Parlin, Oldham)
    Iakovos (Patriarchate of Constantinople)

1968–1975, Uppsala, Sweden   (Moderator: M.M. Thomas – May 15, 1916– ?)
    (Lilje, Niles, Payne, John Coventry Smith, Oldham, Visser't Hooft, Zulu)

    Patriarch German   –1991
    Koyoko Takeda Cho

1975–1983, Nairobi, Kenya (Moderator: Edward W. Scott – April 30, 1919 –?)
    (C. Wedel, Visser't Hooft, Jiagge, Simatupang)
    Jose Miguez-Bonino
    Nikodim   1930–September 5, 1978, Rome, Itlay
    Ilja II of Georgia (1979–83)
    Olof Sundby

1983–1991, Vancouver, BC, Canada (Moderator: Heinz J. Held)
    (Visser't Hooft, Barrow, Buhrig)
    Paulos Mar Gregorius (Malankbiza Orthodox Syrian Church)
    Johannes W. Hempel (Federation of Evangelical Churches)
    W.P. Khotso Makhulu (Church of Province of Central Africa)
    Lois M. Wilson (United Church of Canada)
    Ignatius IV (Greek Orthodox Patriarchate of Antioch)

1991–1998, Canberra, Australia (Moderator: Aram Keshishian)
    Anna Marie Aagaard
    Vinton R. Anderson
    Leslie Boseto
    Priyanka Mendis
    Eunice Santana
    Shenouda III of Alexandria
    Aaron Tolen   – April 7, 1999, Yaounde, Cameroon
    Parthenois of Alexandria

1998–2006, Harare, Zimbabwe
    Agnes Abuom (Anglican Church of Kenya)
    Jabez L. Bryce (Anglican Church of New Zealand, etc)
    Chrysostomos of Ephesus (Patriarchate of Constantinople)
    Ignatius Zakka I Iwas (Patriarchate of Syrian Orthodox Church of Antioch)
    Moon Kyu Kang (Presbyterian Church in Korea)
    Federico J. Pagura (Evangelical Church of Argentina)
    Kathryn Bannister (United Methodist Church)
    Bernice Powell-Jackson
    Eberhardt Renz (Evangelical Church in Germany)

2006–2012, Porto Alegre, Brazil
    Archbishop Anastasios of Tirana and All Albania
    John Taroani Doom
    Simon Dossou
    Soritua Nababan
    Ofelia Ortega
    Abune Paulos
    Bernice Powell Jackson
    Mary Tanner

13. Lack of data

The following individuals should be in this book but are not for lack of data. If any of our readers has data on any, please inform us for future printings.

1) Archbishops of Canterbury

AETHELRED	870 – 890
ATHELHELM (ATHELM),	914 – 923
BERTCHWALD	690 – 731

CEOLNOTH	833 – 870	
CORNWALLIS, Frederick K.	1768 – 1783	
EADSIGE,	1038 – 1051	
ESCURES, Ralph E.	1114–1123	
JAENBEORHT (JAENBERHT)	765 – 792	
REYNOLDS, Walter	1313 – 1328	
RICHARD of DOVER	1174 – 1185	
STAFFORD, John	1443 – 1452	
WULFRED	805 – 832	
WULHELM (WULFHELM)	923 – 942	

2) The following individuals qualify by nature of their organizational leadership, but information on them was not available. They were all presidents, CEOs, directors, etc. of the organization listed by their name.

Name	Organization	Dates	Birth-Death
Robert Abernathy	Rutherford Seminary (Bevard)	1861–1870	
F.C. Aldridge	Gideon's	1955–56, 68–70	Died June 13, 2000, Bradenton, FL
Virgil Arrowood	NT Association Baptist Church	1974–1989	
Ralph Baney	Holy Land Christian Mission (Children Int.)	1936–1973	
Edward T. Bartlett	Philadelphia Divinity School	1884–1900	
Elwell A. Bishop	Montpelier Seminary (Vermont College)	1881–93, 1904–13	
Kermit Black	Association of Fundamental Ministers	1969–1991	Born January 12, 1914, Batavia, IA
Ralph Boyer	Fellowship of International Missions	1960–1965	
E. S. Branch	National Baptist Convention Missions	1950–1970	
Percy Brantley	National Primitive Baptist Conventions Inc.	1956–1972	
M. L. Breeding	Christian Methodist Episcopal Church Missions	1954–1970	
John Brill	Christian Business Men's Committee	1976–1977	
Lawrence Brisbin	Pentecostal Assemblies of the World	1980–1986	
E. A. Buckels	Church of God of Apostolic Faith	1914–1939	
Cope Budge	Vanguard University	1958–1970	
Theodore Bueno	Latin America Bible Institute (California)	1951–1968	
Voy Bullen	Church of God	1969–1992	Died August 1996, Huntsville, AL
Cleo Buxton	Officers Christian Fellowship	1952–1972	
Ray Carter	Full Gospel Grace Fellowship	1954–1984	
Frank Casley	Free Gospel Church	1916–1954	Died July 10, 1954 Turtle Creek, PA
T.M. Chambers	Prog. Nat. Baptist Convention	1961–1966	
William Christian	Church of the Living God	1889–1928	
Chester Clark	African Methodist Episcopal Church Missions	1954–1968	
Uriah Cleary	Gammon Theological School	1870–1883	
I. H. Coe	American Christian Church (UCC)	1858–62, 70–78	
A.D. Cole	Somerset Chrisitan College	1975–1991	
C.D. Coleman	Christian Methodist Church	1986–1994	
Harold M. Collins	International Pentecostal Church of God	1937–1942	
Joseph Cooper	Presbyterian Church of North America	1863–1875	Born Dec. 26, 1813; Died Aug. 22, 1886
J.H. Cornelson	Bible Impact Ministries	1944–1957	
Harold Couchener	Christian Holiness Partnership	1946–1990	
James G. Craighead	Howard School of Divinity	1879–1891	
Clarence Didden	Independent Fundamental Churches of America	1957–60, 63–66	
H. J. Duckworth	Christian Union	1882–1894	
James Duffin	American Rescue Workers	1896–1956	
John R. Edwards	General Baptist Missions	1919–1936	
Char. P. Eisenmayer	Gideon's	1944–1948	

Name	Organization	Years	Notes
Franklin Ellis	Child Evangelism	1952–1959	
Albert Ericson	Swedish ME Theological Sem. (Kendall College)	1883–1909	
John L. Ewell	Howard School of Divinity	1891–1901	
H. L. Fisher	United Holy Church America	1920–1947	
J. R. Fleming	World Alliance Reformed Churches	1918–1927	
Melvin Forney	Lord's Day Alliance	1954–1963	
Simeon R. Franco	Latin American Bible Institute (California)	1939–1949	
John Frizzell	Cumberland Presbyterian Church	1872–1883	
Samuel L. Gandy	Howard School of Divinity	1964–1974	
Henry Garber	Evangelical Mennonite Mission	1934–1956	
Stuart R. Garver	Christ's Mission	1960–1978	
Maria L. Gibson	Scarritt Bible Training School (Scarritt College)	1892–1910	
C. M. Grace	United House of Prayer	1919–1960	
Sam Grey	Christian Service Brigade	1970–1991	
Francis Grim	Hospital Christian Fellowship	1936–1972	
Sam Grimes	Pentecostal Assemblies of the World	1932–1967	Born January 3, 1884, British West Indies
Holly H. Hairston	United Holy Church of America	1949–1963	
Ollie V. Hall	Church of the Living God	1939–1955	
W. H. Hamilton	World Alliance of Reformed Churches	1927–1948	
Samuel Hand	Berkley Divinity School	1908–1917	
L. Archie Hargraves	Shaw Divinity School	1971–1981	
Edwin L. Harvey	Metropolitan Church Association	1894–1926	Died January 1926
Brig. Gen. Hayes	Officers Christian Fellowship	1943–1952	
Clifton B. Hedstrom	Christian Business Men's Committee	1938–1940	
Philip Hennen	Ceylon and India Missions (SIM)	1951–1968	
George W. Hill	George Mercer Memorial School of Theology	1972–1988	
David Hoffer	National Religious Broadcasters	1976–1982	
Jerry Holbert	National Home Missionary Fellowship	1942–1972	(Association of North American Missions)
Lewis Hoskins	American Friends Service Committee	1950–1959	
Russell Howden	Ceylon and Indian Missions (SIM)	1930–1951	
Charles Hoyoheook	Metropolitan Church Association	1926–1950	
Wes Huber	Vision New England	1936–1958	
Ray Humble	Churches of Christ in Christian Union Missions	1930–1946	
J. H. Humphreys	Gideon's	1917–1923	
W.T. Ingram	Memphis Theological Seminary	1964–1978	
Fahey J. Jackson	Evangelical Church Alliance	1928–1957	Died July 23, 1957, Webster Springs, MI
Mikko Juva	Lutheran World Federation	1970–1977	
Wayne Karvonen	Finnish Lutheran Church in America	1949–1967	(Apostolic Lutheran Church of America)
Calvin Kateer	Int. Christian Literature Distributors	1961–1989	
Howard Keeley	Vision New England	1958–1967	
Reul Keith`	Virginia Theological Seminary	1923–1942	
Younge Kinderg	International Bible Society	1963–1983	
Paul L. Kindschi	National Holiness Association	1964–1968	
Herman Koch	German Seminary, Kirksville, MO	1870–1895	
C.J. Laurenz	Somerset Christian College	1965–1975	
Gleason Ledyard	Christian Literature Int.	1966–2006	
Joseph Brethren	Christian University	1980–1996	
Howard Lewis	Int Gospel League	1976–1998	
Forest Livingstone	National Primitive Baptist Convention	1972–1995	Died 1995
Paul Loth	Evangelical Teacher Training	1961–1987	

Donald MacDonald	Christian Business Men's Committee	1947–1956	
George D. Matthews	World Alliance of Reformed Churches	1888–1913	
Carl H. Mau	Lutheran World Convention	1974–1985	Died 1995
J. W. May	International Pentecostal Church of God	1942–1947	
Wm. McCullough	United House of Prayer	1960–1965	
William McElhaney	St. Paul School of Theology	1971–1985	
William McGlothlin	Vellore Christian Medical College	1948–1965	
John McNickel	Toronto Bible College	1906–1946	
Peter Meeusen	Evangelical Press Association	1975–1975	
John Mellinger	Evangelical Mennonite Missions	1914–1934	
Wayne C. Meschter	Schwenkfelder Church	1932–1958	
Thomas Mitchell	Williamson-Dickinson Sem. (Lycoming College)	1860–1869	
John H. Moore	Christian Methodist Church Missions	1914–1934	Died January 27, 1957, Mississippi
Samuel B. Morse	California College	1887–1896	(American Baptist Seminary of the West)
Stanley Nease	Naz. Theo. Sem. 1976–1980 Eastern Naz. College	1980–1989	
J. P. Nielsen	Trinity(Warthburg Theological Sem)	1929–1946	
James O'Connor	Christ's Mission	1887–1911	
Ross T. Padock	Pentecostal Assemblies of the World	1967–1974	
Josephine Patterson	Ramabai Mutki Mission	1929–1953	(Member Grace Chapel, Havertown, PA)
Arthur Penneglley	Cummins Memorial Theological Sem	1910–1930	
E. Perrot	World Alliance Reformed Churches (WARC)	1970–1989	
Howard Pierocki	Gull Lake Bible Conference	1961–1985	
Don P. Pike	American Christian Church (UCC)	1850–54, 66–76	
Richard Porter	Int. Council of Community Churches	1953–1966	
D. Butler Pratt	Howard School of Divinity	1917–1934	
Marcel Pradervamd	World Alliance of Reformed Churches	1949–1970	
James Prestley	Presbyterian Church of North America	1859–1863	
J. P. Reeder	National Baptist Convention Missions	1930–1950	
D. K. Reisinger	Evangelical Teacher Training Association	1955–1961	(Evangelical Training Association)
George Rhoad	Gospel Furthering	1935–1962	
Watkins Roberts	Bibles for the World	1958–1969	
Jasper Roby	Apostolic Overcome Holy Church of God	1973–2001	
Otto A. Ross	Mt. Hermon (CA) Bible Conference	1922–1940	
Wilson D. Samuels	American Christian Churches (UCC)	1906–1919	
Roy Sauder	American Christian Churches of Armenia	1966–1984	
Sam Sayford	Vision New England	1871–1921	
Floyd C. Scott	Church of the Living God	1955–1979	
Gene Scott	Full Gospel Fellowship Churches	1975–1984	
Charles Seidspennir	Southeastern Bible College	1945–1958	
James Seymour Jr.	Auburn Theological Seminary	1856–1891	
William Shaw	Christian Endeavor	1906–1920	
J. Harold Sherk	NSBRO/NISBCO	1958–1969	
Russel Shive	Conservative Baptist Association	1968–1987	
Carl Smith	National Religious Broadcasters		
Francis E. Smith	Pentecostal Assemblies of the World	1974–1980	
Isaac V. Smith	Christian Congregation	1887–1892	
Simeon Smith	Union Bible College	1964–1980	
Hubert Spencer	Church of Our Lord Jesus Christ	1961–1972	
Richard Steel	Auburn Theological Seminary	1823–1839, 1847–1854	
Fre Steele	Latin American Bible Institute (California)	1929–1939	

John L. Steele	D. M. Stearns Missionary Foundation	1922–1949	
Peter Stephens	Cummins Memorial Theological Seminary	1870–1910	
Harold Sterk	NISBCO	1958–1969	
Eugene Stine	Trinity Lutheran College	1944–1970	
Mr. Stone	Pacific School of Religion	1869–1880	
A. B. Stone	General Baptist Missions	1903–1919	
William R. Strassner	Shaw Divinity School	1951–1962	
W. N. Strobhar	United Holiness Church	1963–1980	
Daniel C. Suggs	Livingstone College	1916–1925	
J. L. Sullivent	Church of God of Apostolic Faith	1951–1979	
William. J. Tennison	General Baptist Missions	1903–1919	
Abe P. Thiesen	National Religious Broadcasts Early leader		
Tommy Thompson	Family of Faith Ministries	1972–2000	
Joel Torres	Latin America Bible Institute (California)	1968–1978	
M.J. Trotter	Virginia Theological Seminary	1956–1969	
Henry M. Tupper	Shaw Divinity School	1865–1893	
S. L. Umbach	Evangelical Theological Seminary	1888–1908	
Issac V. Westerberge	Gull Lake Bible Conference	1921–1941	
Jacob Vitti	Finnish Apostolic Lutheran Church in America	1929–1949	(Apostolic Lutheran Church of America)
Philip Weiss	Fellowship International Mission	1966–1982	
Doris Wheeler	Evangelical Child Welfare Agency	1972–1991	
S. L. Wiest	UEC (Methodist)	1891–1905	
Arthur P. Wilde	Interchurch Medical Assistance	1961–1980	
Finley Wilson	Reformed Prebyterian Church of NA	–1953	
Granville Woods	Virginia Theological Seminary	1969–1982	
Alex Zabriske	Virginia Theological Seminary	1940–1950	
John Zierzogle	Institue of Chinese Studies	1977–1996	

3) The following individuals also qualify because of their contributions but information and/or death dates on them was not available. Can readers help us?

Lee Amber	Jewish Evangelist	1916–
Ron Avalone	Soloist	
Harry Bristow	Christian Films	1910–1984
Arthur I Brown	Evangelist, Lecturer	1875–1947
James Calhoun	Evangelist	
George Ford	NAE Executive	
Carl Gunderson	Businessman – Wheaton, IL	
William W. Orr	BIOLA Teacher, Writer	
E. Coleman Ralston	Chapel Crusaders	
Grace Ramont	Hymn writer authority	
Harlin J. Roper	Bible teacher	
George Santa	Youth worker authority	
David Short	Black church leader	
Harry Vom Bruch	Evangelist	
G. Tom Willey	CBMC leader	
Teresa Worman	WMBI Radio children's leader	

4) Hymn or gospel song writers that I do not have data on.

Name	Dates	Title of Song
Alfred Barratt	10/2/1879	Jesus Won My Heart
Elsie Ahlwen	1905	He the Pearly Gates Will Open
Doris Akers	5/21/22	Sweet, Sweet Spirit
J.K. Alwood	1/13/1909	The Unclouded Day
Carl Blackwood		Some Golden Daybreak
Thomas Campbell	7/27/1777–6/15/1844	And Can It Be
Annie R. Cousin	1824–1906	The Sands of Time are Sinking
Sidney E. Cox		Many Choruses- Salvation Army
M. Mosley Deas		Every Time I Feel the Spirit
Lidie H. Edmunds	1849–1889	My Faith Has Found a Hiding Place
Foss Fellers	1887–1924	A Passion for Souls
Clavar A. Gabriel		Just Keep on Praying
Homer W. Grimes		Jesus Gives Me a Song
Bill Harvey		I Want that Mountain
Floyd Hawkins		I've Discovered the Way of Gladness
N.B. Hemell	1877–1954	The Unveiled Christ
R. J Hughes		The Lord is Watching Over Me
Howard Jones		The King is Coming
Albert A. Ketcham	2/12/1894	Why Do I Sing About Jesus
Scott Lawrence		He Loves Even Me
Mylon LeFevre		Without Him
Mrs. H. S. Lehman		Are You Living Where God Answers Prayers
Leila Long		Jesus Is the Sweetest Name I Know
Gene MacLellan		Put Your Hand in the Hand
Mary Maxwell		Channels Only
William E. Marks		The Last Mile of the Way
Larry McGuill		Jesus Only Jesus
Glady B. Muller		Music for all of C. Weigle's Songs
Harry K. Oliver	8/12/1885	Jesus and Shall it Ever Be?
Jean Perry	1865–1935	That Beautiful Name
H.H. Pierson		My Father Planned it All
Jean S. Pigott	1854–1882	Jesus I Am Resting
C. Luis Reichardt	4/11/1779–11/17/1826	Who Is on the Lord's Side?
George Wade Robinson	1838–1877	I am His and He is Mine
Esther K Rusthoi	1909–1962	When We See Christ
Chelsea Stockwell		So Little Time
Elwood Stakes	1815–1895	Fill Me Now
Chretian Urham	1790–1845	The Sands of Time are Sinking
Herman Voss		Every Heartbeat Brings me Nearer Home
H. Williams Walter	1825–1893	Rise up O Men of God
Anna Waterman	1874–1957	Yes, I Know
Samuel Webbe		Come Ye Disconsolate
Ensign E. Young	1895	Have I Done My Best for Jesus?

Abbreviations

AABC	American Association of Bible Colleges
AAFC	American Association of Football Conference
AATS	American Association of Theological Schools
ABC	American Baptist Convention
	American Broadcasting Company
ABCFM	American Board Commissioners for Foreign Missions
ACCC	American Council of Christian Churches
AEF	American Expeditory Forces
AFLBS	Association of Free Lutherans Bible School
AFLTS	Association of Free Lutherans Theological Seminary
AM	Amplitude Modulation
ALC	American Lutheran Church
AME	African Methodist Episcopal
AMF	American Messianic Fellowship
AMOCC	American Mission for Opening Closed Churches
ARP	Associate Reformed Presbyterian
ATS	Association of Theological Schools
BA	Bachelor of Arts
BBC	British Broadcasting Corporation
BBU	Baptist Bible Union
BC	British Columbia
BGEA	Billy Graham Evangelistic Association
BIOLA	Bible Institute of Los Angeles
BJU	Bob Jones University
BS	Bachelor of Science
BSU	Baptist Student Union
BTS	Baptist Theological Seminary
BWA	Baptist World Alliance
CBA	Christian Booksellers Association
CBFMS	Conservative Baptist Foreign Missions Society
CBMC	Christian Business Men's Committee
CBS	Columbia Broadcasting System
CCC	Civilian Conservation Corp
CEO	Chief Executive Officer
CIM	China Inland Mission
CMA	Christian and Missionary Alliance
CMEC	Christian Methodist Episcopal Church
CP	Command Post
CPA	Certified Public Accountant
CTS	Christian Theological Seminary
EC	Evangelical Church
EFC	Evangelical Free Church
EFMA	Evangelical Foreign Missions Association
ELC	Evangelical Lutheran Church
ELCA	Evangelical Lutheran Church of America
EPA	Evangelical Press Association
EUBC	Evangelical United Brethren Church
FBI	Federal Bureau of Investigation
FBC	First Baptist Church
FCA	Fellowship of Christian Athletes
FCC	Federal Council of Christian Churches
FEBC	Far East Broadcasting Company

FGBC	Fellowship of Grace Brethren Churches
FMC	First Methodist Church
FMS	Foreign Missionary Society
FPC	First Presbyterian Church
GARB	General Association of Regular Baptists
GETS	Garrett Evangelical Theological Seminary
GMC	General Motors Corporation
HCJB	Heralding Christ Jesus Blessings
HRE	Holy Roman Emperor
IBM	International Business Machines
ICC	International Council of Christian Churches
IFCA	Independent Fundamental Church of America
IFMA	Interdenominational Foreign Missions Association
JAARS	Jungle Aviation and Radio Services
KJV	King James Version
LCA	Lutheran Church America
LMS	London Missionary Society
LSD	Lysergic Acid Diethylamide
LSU	Louisiana State University
MBI	Moody Bible Institute
MD	Medical Doctor
MP	Member of Parliament
NA	North America
NAACP	National Assoc. for Advancement of Colored People
NAB	North American Baptist
NABS	North American Baptist Seminary
NACS	National Association of Christian Schools
NAE	National Association Evangelicals
NASA	National Aeronautics and Space Administration
NATO	North Atlantic Treaty Organization
NBC	National Baptist Convention
NBC	Northern Baptist Convention
NBTS	New Brunswick Theological Seminary
NCC	National Council of Churches
NFL	National Football League
NIV	New International Version
NRB	National Religious Broadcasters
NT	New Testament
NWT	Northwestern
NYC	New York City
OT	Old Testament
PC	Presbyterian Church
PCA	Presbyterian Church of America
PCUS	Presbyterian Church United States
PCUSA	Presbyterian Church USA
PE	Protestant Episcopal
PHC	Pentecostal Holiness Church
PTA	Parent Teacher Association
PTL	Pocket Testament League
PTS	Princeton Theological Seminary
PYPA	Pentecostal Young Peoples Association
RCA	Reformed Church of America
RPC	Reformed Presbyterian Church
SBC	Southern Baptist Convention
SBSS	Southern Baptist Sunday School

SCLC	Southern Christian Leadership Conference
SIL	Summer Institute Linguistics
SIM	Sudan Interior Mission
SMU	Southern Methodist University
SS	Sunday School
SVM	Student Volunteer Mission
TEAM	The Evangelical Alliance Mission
TTU	Tennessee Temple University
UCBWM	United Church Board of World Missions
UCC	United Church of Christ
UCLA	University of California, Los Angeles
UK	United Kingdom
UMC	United Methodist Church
UNLC	United Norwegian Lutheran Church
UP	United Presbyterian
UPC	United Presbyterian Church
US	United States
USA	United States of America
USO	United States Organizations
USS	Unites States Ship
UTS	United Theological Seminary
VBS	Vacation Bible School
VP	Vice President
WCC	World Council of Churches
WCFA	World Christian Fundamentalist Association
WCTU	Women's Christian Temperance Union
WEC	World Evangelization Crusade
WELS	Wisconsin Evangelical Lutheran Seminary
WWI	World War I
WWII	World War II
YFC	Youth For Christ
YFCI	Youth For Christ International
YMCA	Young Men's Christian Association
YWCA	Young Women's Christian Association

Glossary

Terms in the left column are defined in biographical sketches listed in the right column

Abbess	Caedmon
Abbey	Caedmon
Abbot	Nilus
Abolitionist Movement	Alex Crummell
Act of Supremacy	Elizabeth I
Act of Uniformity	Isaac Ambrose
Adoptionist Heresy	Alcuin
Albigensians	Philip II
Alchemist	Alain
Alemanni	Fridolin
Alexandria School of Thought	Diodorus
All Souls Day	Odilo
Allegory (ical)	Prudentius
Almshouses	William Law
Alsatian Scholar	Eduard Reuss
Amillennial	Origen
Amyraldism	Moise Amyraut
Anathematizing	Ibas
Anchoress	Juliana of Norwich
Anchorite	Alphege
Anti-Burgher	Ebenezer Erskine
Anti-Revolutionary Party	Abraham Kuyper
Antinomianism(ians)	Johann Agricola
Antiphonal Singing	Flavian I
Antipodes	Virgilius
Antipope	Hippolytus
Antiquarian	John Selden
Apartheid	John Philip
Apocryphal	Dorothea
Apollinarism	Apollinnarius
Apologist(s)	Quadratus
Apostasy	Marcellinus
Apostolic Fathers	Clement I of Rome
Aquilla Version of Bible	Aristo
Archdeacon	Berengar
Archduke	Stephen Bocskay
Areopagus	Dionysius
Arian(ism) Controversy	Alexander of Alexandria
Arteriosclerosis	Evang Booth
Assyriologist	George Smith
Augsburg Confession	Johann Bugenhagen
Augsburg Interim	Andreas Osiander
Augustinians	Bernard of Menthone
Austrasia	Vent Fortunatus
Avars	Sergius
Avigon Papacy	Guillaume Nogart
Bampton Lectures	John Bode
Barbarians	Marcella
Barbizon School	Jean Willet
Baronet	Walter Scott
Barons	Boniface of Savoy
Basilica	Macarius of Jerusalem
Basque	Amandus

Reese Chronological Encyclopedia of Christian Biographies

Beguine	Machtild
Belgic Confession	Guido De Bres
Benedictine(s) Order (Rule)	Benedict
Binomial	Carl Linnaeus
Blessed Sacrament	Juliana of Liege
Boer	Johannes Vanderkemp
Bohairic Version	F. A. Hort
Bourbon	Henry IV of France
Boxer Rebellion	Cheng
Brethren of Common Life	Gerhard Groote
Bright's Disease	Howard Cadle
Broad Church Movement	Richard Whateley
Brownists	Robert Browne
Bull	Guillaume Nogaret
Burgesses	Ebenezer Erskine
Burghers	Ebenezer Erskine
Burgundian	Clovis
Byzantine	Nilus
Cabala	Giovanni Pico
Caesar	Helena
Caliph	John of Damascus
Calixtines	Jan Zizka
Camaldoli Order	Otto III
Cambridge Synod	Thomas Shepherd
Cameronians	Rich Cameron
Camisards	Jean Cavalier
Cannibalism	Athenagoras
Canon	Adalag
Canon of the Mass	Anacletus I
Canoness	Johann Goch
Canons (Church Law)	Alypius
Canory	Marsillo Ficino
Cantonal	Nicholas of Flue
Cantor	Melchior Teschner
Capuchian Order	Bernardino Ochino
Carmelite	Simon Stock
Carolingian	Charles Martel
Carthusian	Bruno of Cologne
Catacomb(s)	Domitila
Catechetical School	Athenagoras
Catechisms (ical)	Mathew Zell
Catechumens	Cyril of Jerusalem
Cathari (ist)	Alain
Catholic Church	Ignatius
Cell	Gall
Celtic	Patrick
Chalcedonian Party	Anatolius
Chancellor	Osmund
Chorea	Vitus
Christology	Zephyrinus
Chronicler	Richard Grafton
Cistercian Order	Robert of Molense
Civil Oath	Ebenezer Erskine
Clapham Sect	Wm Wilberforce
Coadjutor	Alexander of Jerusalem

Cocceianism	Johann Cocceius
Codex	Eusebius of Vercelli
Codex Alexandrinus	Cyril Lucar
Codex D	Theo Beza
Codification	Justinian I
Coloratura	Suffiels
Commentaries	Jacob Aphraates
Commonwealth	John Fell
Concordat	Henry V
Consubstantiation	Ratramnus
Copernican System	Galileo
Corpus Christi	Juliana of Liege
Cossacks	Cyril Lucar
Council of Constance	John Huss
Council of Nicea (Nicene Council)	Alexander of Alexandria
Council of Trent	John Fredrick I
Council of Pisa	Henry Chichele
Covenanters	Alexander Henderson
Curate (cies)	Thomas Fuller
Curia	Catherine of Siena
Cyrillic	Cyril
Dean	Thomas Sampson
Declaration of Indulgences	Bunyan/Sancroft
Declaration of Rights	William III
Decree	Siricus
Deism	Ralph Cudworth
Department	Denis
Descants	Gregory of Nazianzus
Dialectics	William of Champeaux
Diet of Ratisbon	Johannes Kepler
Disputation in Heidelberg	Martin Bucer
Disruption Controversy, 1843	Thomas Chalmers
Docetist (ism)	Ignatius
Dominicans	Raymond of Penafort
Donatist(s)	Donatus
Down Grade Controversy	Spurgeon
Dragoons	Arnaud/Gardener
Druids	Patrick
Duchy	Godfrey
Duke	Vladimir I
Earl	Robert of Jumieges
Edict of Nantes	Henry IV
Edict of Ratison	Johannes Kepler
Edict of Toleration 1787	Paul Rabaut
Elector	Frederick III of Saxony
Empiricism	John Locke
Encratites	Tatian
Epigrams	Bede
Episcopal	Stephen Marshall
Episcopate	Hugh of Grenoble
Erysipelas	Mary Lyon
Essayist	Joseph Addison
Esthetics	Francis Willard
Eucharist	John of Paris
Eustathians	Flavian I

Euthychian Heresy	Flavin
Exarch	Sabas
Exegete	Hilary of Poitiers
Extorted	Sam Parris
Federal Theology	Johann Cocceius
Fellow	John Jewel
Feudal (ism)	Harold Klak
Fifth Monarchy men	Praisegod Barbon
Filioque	Leander
Formula of Concord	Martin Chemnitz
Franciscan (s)	Francis of Assisi
Franks (Frankish)	Clovis
Frescoes	Giotto Bondone
Friar	Miles Coverdale
Friary	John Capgrave
Friends of God	Johann Tauler
General Superintendent	Johann Andrae
Ghibelline	Rose of Viterbo
Glasgow Assembly	Robert Baillie
Glorious Revolution	Ed Stillingfleet
Gnostics	Polycarp
Goldsmith	Johann Gutenberg
Gothic	Fulbert
Goths	Theodosius I
Great Western Schism	Fra Angelico
Greek Canon (Music)	Andrew
Guises	Louis Bourbon
Hagiographer	Sulpicus Severus
Half Way Covenant (Stoddardeanism)	Solomon Stoddard
Hampton Court Conference	John Whitgift
Heidelberg Cathechism	Frederick III
Helvetic Confessions	Leo Jud
Heraldic	Phil Spener
Hermeneutics	Tyconius
Hexachord	Guido
Higher Criticism	Washington Gladden
Homilies	Asterius
Homoiousions	Eustathius of Sebaste
Hospice	Basil
Huguenot(s)	Louis Bourgeois
Huns	Theodosius II
Hussite	Jan Zizka
Hydrographers	Mathew Maury
Icon(s)	Theophanes
Iconoclasts (ism)	Nicephorous
Iconography	Andrei Rublev
Immaculate Conception	Aelfric
Inquisition	John of Wesel
Interdicts	Abbon
Interliner gloss	Anselm of Laon
Investiture	Henry IV
Jacobite(s) Church	Jacobus Baradaeus
Jansenism	Luis Sacy
Judaizers	Ignatius
Justicar	Hubert Walter

Kapelmeister	Johann Bach
Keeper of Seals	Thomas Trahern
Keswick Movement	Hammer Webb-People
Knights Hospitallers of John	Raymond Du Puy
Knights Templars	Baldwin II
Labadist	Jean Labadie
Lambeth Articles	John Whitgift
Lambeth Manuscripts	Sam Maitland
Landgrave	Philip of Hesse
Landmarkism	Joseph Pendelton
Laplanders	Vasa Gustavus I
Lateran	William of Tyre
League of Torgeau	John the Constant
Legate	Boniface
Leipzig Interim	Matthias Flacius
Lexicographer	Samuel Johnson
Logos Christianity	Noetius
Lollards	John Wycliffe
Lombard League	Frederick I
Lombards	Pepin III
Lord	John Erskine
Loyalists	Barbara Heck
Macedonian Heresy	Eustathius of Sebaste
Manicheanism	Priscillian
Marcionism (ites)	Polycarp
Margrave	George of Brandenberg
Marquisate	Charles Manners-Sutton
Marrowmen	Edward Fisher
Masques	Thomas Arne
Mass	Stanislaus
Master	William Fulke
Mayflower Compact	John Carver
Melitians	Melitius of Lycopolis
Mendicant Orders	Henry of Ghent
Mercerville Theology	John Nevin
Merovingian	Clovis
Metaphysical	Henry Vaughan
Metrical Versions	Thomas Sternhold
Metropolitan/Patriarch	Peter of Alexandria
Minims, Order of	Francis of Paula
Monarchians	Noetius
Monasticism	Anthony of Egypt
Monophysitism (ite)	Apollinarius
Monothelite Controversy	Sergius
Montanism (ists)	Montanus
Moors	Anthony of Padua
Motet	Nick Selnecker
National Covenant	Robert Baillie
Navarre	Ferdinand I
Neo-Orthodoxy	Karl Barth
Neo-Pentecostalism	Julio C Ruibal
Neoplatonic (ism)	Evagrius
Nephritis	Robert Moyer
Nestorianism	Nestorius
Nestorians	Justin Perkins

New Evangelical	Ed Carnell
New Hegelian Movement	John Caird
Nicene Creed	Eusebius of Caesarea
Nominalism (ist)	Roscellinus
Nonjurors	John Tillotson
Nordic	Adalbert
Normans	Hincmar of Rheims
Novatianism	Novatian
Observants	Bernardino
Oratories	Johann Bach
Oratory	Anacletus I
Orientalist	Edmund Castell
Ostrogoths	Magnus Ennodius
Oxford Movement	William Palmer
Palatinate	Frederick III
Pallium	Mark
Pantheism (istic)	Meister Eckhart
Particular Baptist	Benjamin Keach
Paschal Controversy	Claudius Apollinaris
Patriarchate	Adalbert
Patrician	Pladius
Patristic	William of St. Thierry
Patron	George
Pedagogics (ical)—Pedagogy	Johann Herbart
Pelagianism (ists)	Pelagius
Petrobrusians	Peter of Bruys
Philology (ists)	Leonhard Hutter
Picts	Ninian
Piedmont	Henri Arnauld
Pietism (ist)	Jean Labadie
Pilgrim	John Carver
Platonism	Clement of Alexandria
Polemics (ical)	Marius Mercator
Polyglot Bibles	Edmund Castell
Polytheism (ist)	Noetius
Praetorian Guard	Sebastian
Prebendary	William Grocyn
Precentor	Benedict Bishop
Prefect	Maurice Tiberius
Prelate	Adalbert
Premonstratensian Order	Norbert
Presbyter	Pantaenus
Presbytery	Francis Makemie
Primate	Laurentius Petri
Prior	Lanfranc
Prioress	Heloise
Priory	Peter Abelard
Priscillianist	Priscillian
Procurator	Faith
Prosody	Aldhelm
Provost	Henry Savile
Pulmonary disease	George Boardman
Puritans (ism)	Thomas Sampson
Quietists	Miguel Molinos
Realism	William of Champeaux

Rector	Nicholas of Clamanges
Regent	Charles IX
Regersberg Interim	Martin Bucer
Regius Professor	James Mozley
Remonstrance	David Calderwood
Remonstrant(s)	Jacobus Arminius
Restoration	Hugh Peter
Revolution of 1848	Frances Guizot
Rhenish	Dionysius the Carthusian
Rhetorician	Publius Aristides
Rye House Plot	Robert Baillie
Sabellianism (ians)	Noetius
Sacred Heart of Jesus	Gertrude
Sadhu	Sadan Singh
Sanctification	Phoebe Palmer
Sandemanians	Benjamin Ingram
Sanskrit	Fred Muller
Saracen	Charles Martel
Sarum (Salisbury Rite)	Osmund
Savoy Conference	John Gauden
Savoyards	Henri Arnauld
Saxons	Germain
Saybrook Synod	Samuel Andrew
Scevophylak	Joseph
Schismatics	Majorinus
Schmalkald War	Bernardino Ochino
Schmalkaldic League	John the Constant
Scholasticism	William of Auvergne
Sedition	Mary Dyer
See	Dionysius of Alexandria
Semantics	Dionysius of Rome
Semi-Arians	Eusebius of Caesarea
Semi-Pelagianism	Cassianus
Separatists	Al Van Raalte
Septuagint	Pamphilus
Sequential	Frank Thompson
Servite Order	Juliani Falconieri
Seven Sacraments	Peter Lombard
Sinologist	Karl Gutzlaff
Slavs/Slavic	Cyril
Social Gospel	G. Taylor
Socinians	Ed Stillingfleet
Sophist	Eudocia
Sorbonne	Robert of Sorbon
Stadholder	William III
Statecraft	Walfrid Strabo
Statues of Provisors/Praemunire	Henry Chichele
Stoddardeanism	Solomon Stoddard
Stoics (ism)	Panthaenus
Stuart	James I
Subordinationism Controversy	Dionysius of Rome
Sultan	Baldwin
Syncretism	Calixtus
Synod of Dort	Francis Gomarus
Taborites	Jan Zizka

Taxonomy	Carl Linnaeus
Tertiary	Rose of Viterbo
Teutonic	Oswy
Textus Receptus	Theo Beza
Theban Legion	Maurice Tibetius
Theosophist	Jacob Boehme
Thermodynamics	William Thompson
Thirty-nine Articles	William Bradshaw
Tiarae	Sylvester I
Toleration Act:1689	Robert South
Tome	Gratian
Tories (Tory)	William Fleetwood
Tracterian Movement	Julius Hare
Transubstantiation	Ratramnus
Treaty of Westphalia	Frederick William
Trent Affair	Charles McIlvain
Tribune	Anastasius(1)
Trinitarians	Felix of Valois
Tritheism	Damianus
Tudor	Thomas Cranmer
Tuscan	Antonio Brucioli
Unicals	F. A. Hort
Unidiomatic	John Purvey
Valentinians	Polycarp
Vandals	Fabiola
Veronica Cloth	Veronica
Vicar	Alexander Barclay
Vicar general	Bernard of Menthone
Visigoths	Ambrose
Vulgate	Ambrosiaster
Walloon	Adrian Saravia
Warden	Thomas Bilson
Wends	Adalbert
Westminster Assembly	Dan Featley
Westminster Confession	John Ball
Whig	William Fleetwood
Wittenberg Concord	Martin Bucer

Acknowledgments of Help from Christian Organizations (Material and Photos)

Many more organizations were helpful by telephone and/or sent information anonymously.

Codes are M-Missions, D-Denominations, S-Schools, O-Organizations.

Name	Code	Location	Helpful Sources
A Beka Book Publications	O	Pensacola, FL	Diana Smeltzer
ABWE (Assoc of Baptists for World Evangelism)	M	Harrisburg, PA	Mary Ann Eckman - Wendel Kempton - Harold Amstutz, Executive Administrator
Accrediting Association of Bible Colleges	O	Orlando, FL	Ralph E. Enlow, Jr., Ex Dir - Randall E. Bell, Ex Dir -Garry D. Matson
Action Int Ministries	M	Mountlake Ter, WA	Diana Morice
Acts International Ministries	M	Colorado Sp, CO	Alvin Low
ADRIS (Assoc for Dev of Rel Info Systems)	O	Nashville, TN	David O. Moberg, Coordinator
Advancing Indigenous Missions	M	San Antonio, TX	James W. Colley
Advent Christian Church	D	Charlotte, NC	David E. Ross, President
Africa Inland Mission	M	Pearl River, NY	Ted Barnett - Lynn David - Janyce Nasgowitz - Darlene Noden - A. B. Holm
Africa Inter-Mennonite Mission	M	Elkhart, IN	Edith Driver - Leona Schrag, Asst. Executive Secretary
African Enterprise	M	Monrovia, CA	Malcolm Graham, Inter Executive Officer,
African Methodist Episcopal Church	D	Washington, DC	Jacqueline Brown, Asst. Library Archivist (Wilberforce University) - Charles Freeney, Archivist
African Methodist Episcopal Church Missions	M	Washington, DC	Howard B. Gregg - R.E. Stokes Library, Wilberforce, OH- Dennis Dickerson, Nashville
African Methodist Episcopal Zion Church	D	Charlotte, NC	Phyllis H. Galloway, Director (Heritage Hall, Livingstone College, Salisbury, NC) - Stokes Resources Center Library (Wilberforce (OH) University)
African Mission Evangelism (Restoration)	M	Knoxville, TN	Carl Bridges
Alaska Bible College	S	Glenallen, AK	Sherry Nace
Albert Brumley and Sons	M	Powell, MO	Sharon K. Boles
All Nations INC	M	Colorado Sp, CO	Lois I. Watkins
Alliance Theological Seminary	S	Nyack, NY	David Hartzfeld - Esther L. Shelly, Admininstrative Asst.
Alliance World Fellowship c/o C M Alliance	O	Colorado Sp, CO	Arui Shoresh, Secretary
ALM INT (American Leprosy Missions)	M	Greenville, SC	James A. Gittings, Director - Diane C. Bryson, Ex. Asst. - Diane C. Bryson, Executive Asst.
American Advent Mission Soc.	M	Charlotte, NC	Harold R. Patterson, Charlotte, NC
American Association of Christian Counsellors	O	Forest, VA	Rick Boothe, Coordinator, Forest, VA
American Association of Christian Schools	O	Independence, MO	Gary A. Deedrick, Administrative Asst., Independence, MO
American Baptist Association	D	Texarkana, TX	I. K. Cross, Public Relations
American Baptist Assoc. Missionary Committee	M	Texarkana, TX	I.K. Cross, Public Relations
American Baptist Churches (Northern Baptist)	D	Valley Forge, PA	Beverly C. Carlson (ABHS) - Elinor T. Johnson, Ex. Sec. - Convention)- Historical Society - Charles Primavera, Office Mgr. - Deborah B. Vanbrockhoven, Ex. Dir. (Am.Bpt.Hist.Soc., Valley Forge, PA) - Betty Layton, Archivist - Stephanie
American Baptist College and Theo Seminary	S	Nashville, TN	Georgia Larnes, Registrar -Dorothy Lucas
American Baptist Foreign Mission Society	M	Valley Forge, PA	Priscilla B. Shaw, Librarian - Terry O'Connor - James R. Lynch (American Baptist Historical Society, Valley Forge, PA)
American Baptist Seminary of the West	S	Berkeley, CA	Beth Johnson -Gwen Christian, Administrative Asst.Bap. Divinity School)
American Bible Society	O	Plantation, FL	Mary Ellen Gleason, Archivist - Mary F. Cordato - Maria Deptula, NYC - Mary F. Cordato, Asst. Archivist/Historical Researcher - Maria Deptula, Asst. Archivist/ Historical Researcher

Name	Code	Location	Helpful Sources
American Christian College	S	OK City, OK	Betty Layton, Archivist
American Friends Service Committee	O	Philadelphia, PA	Chris Densmore, Jack Sutters Archives - Terry Foss, ArchivistWillie O. Reyes, Alyssa Chatten,
American Mission for Opening Churches Inc	O	Olcott, NY	Thomas J. Buckley, General Director
American Missionary Fellowship/Am. Sunday	O	Villanova, PA	Jim Gerhart - Walter W. Scott, Ex VP, Philadelphia - School Union Judy Entner
American Tract Society	O	Garland, TX	Kristen Mitrisin, Archivist - Kent Barnard
Americas Keswick Bible Conference	O	Whiting, NJ	Ruth Lockhart, Executive Secretary
AMF International	M	Lansing, IL	Mel Shelver - Robert Shuster - Lori Taber - Wes Taber - Chicago Hebrew Mission) Administrative Asst.
Anderson University	S	Anderson, IN	Margaret L. Camm, Secretary to the President - Charles T. Kendall, Archivist and Librarian - Doug Welch (School of Theology)
Andover-Newton Theological Seminary	S	Newton, MA	Diana Yount, Special Collections Librarian
Apostolic Bible Institute	S	St Paul, MN	Gerald Grant
Apostolic Christian Church (Nazarene)	D	Richmond, VA	Ted Custer
Apostolic Christian Churches of America	D	Peoria, IL	William Schlatter, National Secretary (Defiance, OH) Apostolic Faith Missions of Portland, Oregon Portland, OR Linda L. (Carver) Sheals - Karen L. Barrett, Office Manager
Apostolic Overcoming Holy Church of God	M	Mobile, AL	Juanita R. Arrington
Appalachian Bible College	S	Bradley, WV	Lee Walker
Appalachian Ministries Educational Resource	O	Berea, KY	Mary Lee Daugherty
Arab World Ministries/ North Africa Mission	M	Upper Darby, PA	Pamella J. Snyder - Alasdair McLaren, Executive Secretary - Harold Stalley - Debbie Hansell, Administrative Secretary
Asbury College	S	Wilmore, KY	Bill Kostlevy - Joseph A. Thacker, Coordinator/ Historian - Dana Moutz, Administrative Asst. to the President
Asbury Theological Seminary	S	Wilmore, KY	Scott Burson - Sheila Lovell, Executive Asst. to the President
Ashland Theological Seminary/ University	S	Ashland, OH	Brad Weidenhamer, Librarian - Frederick J. Finks, Vice President - Dave Roepe
Asian Outreach	M	Red Bank, NJ	Bonnie Kauffman
Assemblies of God	D	Springfield, MO	Glenn W. Gohr, Asst. Archivist (Flower Pentecostal Heritage Center) - Joyce Lee, Asst. Archivist (FPHC)
Assemblies of God Foreign Missions	M	Springfield, MO	Betty Jansen, Secretary
Assemblies of God Theological Seminary	S	Springfield, MO	Carol J. Stair, Secretary to the President (Evangel College) - Deloris Crawford, Secretary to the President
Associate Reformed Presbyterian Church	D	Greenville, SC	Ben Johnston, Editor - Edith M. Brawley (McCain Library, Synod) Erksine College, SC - Edward H. Mills (Hopewell, ARP church) - C.R. Beard
Associated Church Press	O	Stoughton, WS	John Stapert
Associated Mennonite Biblical Seminary	S	Elkhart, IN	Rosemary Rescaly, Administrative Secretary - Mary E. Klassen, Director of Communications
Association of Free Lutheran Congregations World	M	Minneapolis, MN	Eugene W. Enderlein, World Missions Director, Missions Minneapolis, MN
Association of Fundamental Ministers (and Churches)	O	Kansas City, MO	Joan Loulos
Association of Gospel Rescue Missions	O	Nn Kansas City, MO	Jo Rydman, Administrative Asst. - Philip W. Rydman, (Dir of Gospel Missions)
Association of Theological Schools in the U.S.	O	Pittsburgh, PA	Leon Pacala, Executive Director - Nancy Merrill, Director
Auburn Theological Seminary	S	New York, NY	Barbara G. Wheeler - Rachel Bundang, Assistant (Auburn Center) - Mark N. Wilhelm, Associate Director (Auburn Center), Ruth Tomkiss, Cameron
Aurora Mission, Inc (Bible Alliance Mission Inc)	M	Bradenton, FL	Sharon Weiner - James E. Pike - Jano E. Pike
Austin Presbyterian Theological Seminary	S	Austin, TX	Bill Broly - Robert Shelton - Peggy Cockrum, Public Relations Coordinator

Name	Code	Location	Helpful Sources
AWANA Clubs Int	O	Streamwood, IL	Art Rorheim, President
Azusa Pacific University (Pacific Bible College)	S	Azusa, CA	Donna Hays, Asst. to the President -Marilyn Schulz, Executive Secretary -Robin Dunn, Administrative Asst. to the V.P. -J. Swinney -Cliff Hamlow, Executive V.P.
Back to the Bible	M	Lincoln, NE	John Paton, Literary Director -Janet Miller, Administrative Asst.
Bangor Theological Seminary (United Church of Christ)	S	Bangor, ME	Theresa M. Morris, Registrar - Dr. G. Wayne Glick
Baptist Bible College (BBF)	S	Springfield, MO	James Sewell
Baptist Bible College of Pennsylvania	S	Clarks Summit, PA	Mr. McClain, Librarian - Kathy Compton, Secretary to the President - Barbara Trussler
Baptist Bible Fellowship (BBF)	D	Springfield, MO	Dorothy Cook, Secretary to Director
Baptist Bible Fellowship International (Mission)	M	Springfield, MO	Dorothy Cook, Secretary to Director
Baptist Church Planters	O	Elyria, OH	Wayne Ritchie
Baptist Faith Missions	M	Lexington, KY	Dave Parks
Baptist General Conference	D	Arlington Heights, IL	Dr. Diana Magnuson, Archivist (Bethel College) - Norris A. Magnuson (Bethel Theological Seminary) -Lloyd Dahlquist - Bob Putnam
Baptist General Conference, Global Missions	M	Arlington Heights, IL	Donald E. Anderson, Editor <The Standard>
Baptist International Missions (BIMI)	M	Chattanooga, TN	Clifford Huskey, Secretary/Treasurer
Baptist Mid Missions	M	Cleveland, OH	Alan E. Lewis -Jane H. Acker, Secretary to the President -Gary H. Anderson
Baptist Missionary Association of America	M	Little Rock, AR	James C. Blaylock, Director (Baptist News Service)
Baptist Missionary Association Theological Seminary	S	Jacksonville, TX	James C. Blaylock (North American Theological Seminary)
Baptist World Alliance	O	Falls Church, VA	Debbie Buie - Rubby Burke - Wendy Ryan
Baptist World Mission	M	Decatur, AL	Fred Moritz, Executive Director
Barclay College (Friends Bible College, Ev Friends Alliance)	S	Haviland, KS	Glenn W. Leppert, Registrar
Bay Ridge Christian College	S	Kendleton, TX	Robert C. Williams -Verda
Baylor University	S	Waco, TX	Ellen K. Brown, Archivist -Thomas E. Turner, Historian
BCM INT (Bible Club Movement)	M		Oscar Hirt, International Director -Phyllis Ross, Secretary to General Director
Berean Fellowship of Churches	D	Lincoln, NE	Farral Shada, Executive Secretary
Berean Mission, Inc	M	St Louis, MO	Barbara Sullivan -Jill Patrick -Kenneth A. Epp, General Director
Berkeley Divinity School (see Episcopal Church)	S	New Haven, CT	Jacqueline Corning -Jeanne Moule, Administrative Asst.
Berkshire Christian College (NE School of Theology)	S	Lenox, MA	Edna Amnott, Asst. Librarian (Aurora (IL) University) -David T. Arthur - Curator -David E. Ross
Bethany Bible College (Glad Tidings Bible Institute-	S	Scotts Valley, CA	Ed Koetitz, Reference Librarian (Assembly of God)
Bethany Fellowship Missions	M	Bloomington, MN	Catherine Brooke -Joani Brooks
Bethany Lutheran Theological Seminary (Evang Luth Synod)	S	Mankato, MN	Wilhelm W. Petersen, President -Norman Holte, Archivist - Melvina Aaberg, Secretary
Bethany Theological Seminary (CH of the Brethren)	S	Richmond, IN	Darlene A. Alman -E. Floyd McDowell, Director of Development
Bethel Christian Ministries	M	Seattle, WA	Daniel W. Peterson
Bethel College	S	Mishawaka, IN	Carol Lux, Secretary to the President
Bethel College (Gen Conf Menn)	S	North Newton, KS	James A. Lynch, Asst. Archivist
Bethel College and Theological Seminary (BGC)	S	St Paul, MN	G. David Guston, Archivist -Ruth A. Anderson, Secretary to the President -Diana L. Magnuson, Archivist
Bethel Theological Seminary (West Campus)	S	San Diego, CA	Clifford V. Anderson
Bethseda Christian University (All courses in Korean)	S	Anaheim, CA	Gary Jefferson
Bethune Cookman College	S	Daytona Beach, FL	Dr. Henderson -Lucy Jefferson
Beulah Heights Bible College - (International Pentacostal Church of Christ)	S	Altanta, GA	James B. Keiller, V.P. -Samuel R. Chand
Bible Literature Int (Bible Meditation League)	M	Columbus, OH	Bob Falkenberg
Bible Town Community Church	O	Boca Raton, FL	Evelyn C. Brower
Bible Way Church of Our Lord Jesus Christ	D	Columbia, SC	Arthurene S. Foxx, Secretary
Biblical Ministries Worldwide	M	Lawrenceville, GA	Lillian Oreutt -Susan Rodriguez – Linda Davis
Biblical Theological Seminary	S	Hatfield, PA	George Clark, Vice President
Billy Graham Center	O	Wheaton, IL	Janyce H. Nasgowitz - Wayne Webber, Archivist
Billy Graham Evangelistic Association Int Ministries	O	Minneapolis, MN	Connie Knutson, Human Resources - Ruth McKinney, Sec to S.E. Wirt - Fred L. Durston

Name	Code	Location	Helpful Sources
			– Wayne D. Weber
Biola University	S	La Mirada, CA	Robert F. Crawford -Signe Watterford, Archivist - Sue Whitehead
Bluffton College	S	Bluffton, OH	Kelly A. Smith, Asst. Archivist
Bob Jones University	S	Greenville, SC	Laura Lading -Mary Shamblin
Boston University (School of Theology - Meth)	S	Boston, MA	Susan Baker, Alumni Representative -Stephen P. Pentek, Archivist Coordinator – Kara
Brazil Gospel Fellowship Mission	M	Springfield, IL	Gerald Bergen, Executive Secretary
Brethren Church Missionary Ministries	M	Ashland, OH	Ginny Hoyt, Secretary
Brethren in Christ Church	D	Grantham, PA	A. Graybill Brubaker -E. Morris Sider, Archivist -Karen B. Haldeman, Asst. to the Executive Director -Dori I. Steckbeck, Archivist Director (Messiah College) -Kenneth O. Hoke, General Secretary -J. Wilmer Heisey, Gloria J. Stonge, Dir. Lib and Archives
Brite Divinity School (Texas Christian Univ)	S	Fort Worth, TX	Lisa Peno, Special Collections (TCU Library)
Bryan College	S	Dayton, TN	Karin J. Traylor, Administrative Asst. to the Academic Vice President -Lavonne Johnson, Librarian -Margaret A. Legg, Administrative Asst. to the President
California Baptist College	S	Riverside, CA	Janice G. Sutton, Secreatry to the President -Brenda Flowers, Director of Public Relations
Calvary Bible College and Theological Seminary	S	Kansas City, MO	Douglas Langmade, Asst. to the President -Sandra Smith, Secretary to the President
Calvin College	S	Grand Rapids, MI	Hendrina Van Spronsen, Secretary (Heritage Hall) -James De Jonge, Archivist (Heritage Hall) -Carol W. Dirske - Rich H. Harms, Archivist (Curator, Heritage Hall) – Wendy Alan Kespoor, Lib/Arch.
CAM Int (Central American Mission)	M	Dallas, TX	Jeane Olson -Carolyn Owens
Candler School of Theology (Emory University)	S	Atlanta, GA	Kathy Shoemaker, Associate Reference Archivist -Joan S. Clemens, Curator of Archives and Manuscripts
Canyonview Bible College and Seminary	S	Silverton, OR	Ernest R. Campbell, President
Carver Bible Institute and College	S	Atlanta, GA	Tim Skinner, Academic Dean -Tosha L. Bussey, Librarian
Carver Int Missions, Inc	M	Atlanta, GA	Lawanda Owens
CB Int	M	Littleton, CO	Warren Webster, General Director
Cedarville University	S	Cedarville, OH	Kenneth H. St.Clair, V.P. for Business -Ed Clark -Gary Kuhn - Alumni -Jeanne Forsyth, Archivist (Oberlin College, OH) -Lynn A. Brock, Archivist
Cedine Bible Mission, Inc	O	Spring City, TN	P. Dwight Zimmerman
Central Baptist College (Missionary Baptist)	S	Conway, AR	James C. Blaylock
Central Baptist Theological Seminary (American Baptist)	S	Kansas City, KS	Larry Blazer -Amy W. Derrick, Alumni Secretary (Southern Baptist Theological Seminary, Louisville, KY) Arel T. Lewis, Asst. Librarian -Betty S. Gibson, Executive Secretary of Development
Central Baptist Theological Seminary in Indiana	S	Indianapolis, IN	Henrietta Brown
Central Bible College	S	Springfield, MO	Joyce Lee, Asst. Archivist (Assembly of God, Springfield, MO)
Central Christian College	S	McPherson, KS	Claudine Fewell -Katie McGinn, Archivist (Marston Memorial Historical Center - Indianapolis, IN) -Beverly Kelley, Librarian
Chattanooga Bible Institute	S	Chattanooga, TN	Henry Henega
Chesapeake Theological Seminary (Presbyterian Church)	S	Linthicum, MD	John
Chicago Theological Seminary	S	Chicago, IL	Stephen J. Davidson -Herbert W. Thompson, Director of Public Relations -Joan Blocher, Asst. Librarian
Child Evangelism Fellowship, INC	O	Warrenton, MO	Alan George - Mari-Jo Vissus
Children Int (Holy Land Christian Mission)	M	Kansas City, MO	Joseph Gripkey
Children's Haven Int	M	Pharr, TX	Berverly Baerg
China Outreach Ministries	M	Mechanicsburg, PA	Donald T. McIntosh
Chosen People Ministries, Inc.	M	New York, NY	Barbara Benedict, Assistant to the President -Harold A. Sevener, President - Ben R. Alpert
Christ Community Church	D	Zion, IL	Lucy Burris, Secretary
Christ for the Nations, Inc	M	Dallas, TX	Freda Lindsay -Naomi Westbrook, Assistant to the Director
Christar International Missions (formerly Int. Missions)	M	Reading, PA	Osborne Buchanan, Jr., Asst. to the President - Bob
Christian and Missionary Alliance	D	Colorado Springs, CO	Jean Fuchs, Archivist -Peter A. Burgo, Media

Name	Code	Location	Helpful Sources
			Developer -Gilbert H. Johnson -Patty McGarvey, Asst. Archivist
Christian and Missionary Alliance Overseas Mission	M	Colorado Springs, CO	David H. Moore -Carol Hall, Secretary -Jewel Hall, Secretary -Arui Shoreski
Christian Booksellers Association	O	Colorado Springs, CO	Janice Randolph
Christian Brethren (Plymouth Brethren)	D	Wheaton, IL	Mary Ann Conlon (Interest Ministries) -Marjorie Carlson, Managing Editor <Loizeaux Bros.>
Christian Business and Professional Woman (Stonecraft Ministries)	O	Kansas City, MO	Susan Collard
Christian Business Mens Committee (CBMC)	O	Chattanooga, TN	David R. Enlow - Ruth Strothers - Clifton Headstrom - Walter McKeag -Walter C. McKeas, Chairman -Bob Tamasay - Frank Sheriff (Chicago)
Christian Church (Disciples of Christ)	D	Indianapolis, IN	David I. McWhirter, Librarian/Archivist (Disciples Historical Society, Nashville, TN) -May Reed, Asst. Librarian (Disciples Historical Society) -Patricia P. McCarty, Editor <Christian Standard> - Elaine Philpott, Researcher
Christian Church of North of America (Pentecostal)	D	Transfer, PA	Candace Tarr, Secretary
Christian Congregation	D	LaFollette, TN	Ora W. Eads
Christian Endeavor (Worlds CE Union)	O	Mount Vernon, OH	David G. Jackson, General Secretary -Jean W. Hinton, Secretary
Christian Holiness Partnership	O	Hazelton, PA	Kenneth O. Brown, Hazleton, PA
Christian Leadership Development, INC	M	Madisonville, KY	Franklin Stevenson, Treasurer
Christian Literacy Associates	M	Pittsburgh, PA	William E. Kofmehl, Jr.
Christian Literature Crusade	M	Fort Washington, PA	Ray B. Parnell -William M. Almack, Overseas Director -Robert J. Gerry
Christian Medical and Dental Association		Bristol, TN	Tracie Coppedge, Executive Asst., Bristol, TN
Christian Methodist Episcopal Church	M	Dallas, TX	Lawrence L. Reddick, III - <Christian Index> -Othel Lackey, Historian
Christian Mission for the Deaf	M	Detroit, MI	Bertha Foster, Administration
Christian Reformed Church	D	Grand Rapids, MI	Charlene Ezinga, Yearbook Manager - Richard Hamrs, Archivist
Christian Reformed World Missions	M	Grand Rapids, MI	Charlene Ezinga, Yearbook Manager
Christian Reformed World Relief Committee	M	Grand Rapids, MI	Bonnie Talsma
Christian Theological Seminary	S	Indianapolis, IN	Kathleen Bell, Administrative Asst. -Eleyce Hinant, Administrative Asst. -Paul Valliere - Professor (Butler University) -Don Haymes, Asst. Librarian
Christian Union	D	Chilicothe, OH	Robert E. Uhrig, Dean
Christian Union Bible College	S	Greenfield, OH	Robert E. Uhrig - Neal Reid, Acad Dean
Christians in Action	M	Woodlake, CA	David W. Konold, Jr., Vice President
Church Divinity School of the Pacific	S	Berkeley, CA	J.G. Rateaver -Richard E. Helmer, Asst. Archivist
Church Ministries Int	M	Rockwell, TX	Ginny Murray, Administrative Asst.
Church of God	D	Scottsville, KY	Voy M. Bullen
Church of God (Anderson, IN)	D	Anderson, IN	Lester A. Crose -Charles T. Kendall, Librarian (Anderson University) -Merle D. Strege, Archivist (AU)
Church of God (Anderson, IN) Mission Board	M	Anderson, IN	Lester A. Crose -Norman S. Patton, President
Church of God (TN)	D	Cleveland, TN	Louis F. Morgan, Archivist (Dixon Pentecostal Research)
Church of God (TN) Missions	M	Cleveland, TN	Kathy - Adrian Varlack
Church of God General Conference	D	Morrow, GA	David Krogh
Church of God Holiness	D	Overland Park, KS	William L. Hayton, C.E.O.
Church of God in Christ	D	Memphis, TN	David A. Hall -Shedrick D. Cade
Church of God of Prophecy	D	Cleveland, TN	Randy Howard, Global Outreach -Perry Gillum, Director of Public Relations
Church of God of Prophecy Missions	M	Cleveland, TN	Adrian L. Varlack, Sr.
Church of God School of Theology	S	Cleveland, TN	James M. Beaty, Academic Dean
Church of the Brethren General Board	D	Elgin, IL	Kenneth M. Shaffer, Jr., Director of Historical Library Archives
Church of the Brethren World Ministries Commission	M	Elgin, IL	Kenneth M. Shaffer, Jr.
Church of the Living God	D	Cincinnati, OH	W.E. Gumes, Chief Bishop
Church of the Nazarene	D	Kansas City, MO	Stan Ingersol, Archivist -Kara Lyons, Research Asst. -Lon E. Dagley, Curator of Manuscripts
Church of the Nazarene World Mission	M	Kansas City, MO	Stan Ingersol, Archivist -Remiss Rehfeldt -Lon E. Dagley -John Stockton -Patricia A. Braselton, Office Manager
Church of the United Brethren in Christ	D	Huntington, IN	Randy Neuman, Archivist (Huntinton College, IN)

Name	Code	Location	Helpful Sources
Church of the United Brethren in Christ Board of Missions	M	Huntington, IN	-Jane E. Mason, Archivist Jane E. Mason, Archivist (Historical Center) -Jerry F. Datema
Churches of Christ in Christian Union	D	Circleville, OH	Donald L. Seymoor, General Mission Support -Lydia Amspaugh, Secretary -Ralph Hux, Director of Communications - Robert Uttrig
Churches of God General Conference	D	Findlay, OH	Roberta G. Bakies,Reist
Churches of God General Conference Missions	M	Findlay, OH	Roberta G. Bakies
Churches Uniting in Christ	O	Lowell, MA	David W.A. Taylor
Circleville Bible College	S	Circleville, OH	David F. Van Hoose, President
Claremont School of Theology	S	Claremont, CA	Patricia E. Coats, Director of Alumni
Clear Creek Baptist Bible College	S	Pineville, KY	Bill D. Whittaker, President -Carol Wallace, Secretary for Institutional Advancement
Colgate-Rochester Divinity School (Bexley Hall) (Crozer Theological Seminary)	S	Rochester, NY	Jami Pelle, Special Collections Librarian (Kenyon College, Gambier, OH) -George Swierc, Asst. to the Dean Bonnie L. Van Delinder, Asst. Librarian -Christopher Brennan, Asst. Librarian -Sally Dodgson, Institutional Research
Colorado Chrisitan University	S	Lakewood, CO	Kelly Murphy -Gayle C. Gunderson, Reference Librarian - Jeffrey L. DeClue -Frank R. Ames, Alumni
Columbia International University and Seminary	S	Columbia, SC	Sherry D. Brown -Bob Kallgren, Executive Asst. to the President
Columbia Theological Seminary	S	Decatur, GA	Peggy Rowland, Administrative Asst. to the President
Compassion Int	M	Colorado Springs, CO	Wallace H. Erickson
Concordia Seminary	S	St Louis, MO	Roy A. Ledbetter, Research Asst.
Concordia Theological Seminary	S	FT Wayne, IN	Trudy Behning -Robert Zagore (Walther Library) -Charles W. Westby (Walther Library)
Congregational Methodist Church	D	Florence, MS	Daniel W. Coker, President
Congregational Methodist Church Div. of Foreign Missions	M	Florence, MS	Dale Owens Foreign Missions
Conservative Baptist Association of America	D	Littleton, IL	Marilyn Searle
Conservative Baptist Seminary of the East		Dresher, PA	Cheryl L. Gregg
Conservative Congregational Christian Conference	D	St Paul, MN	Clifford R. Chistensen, Conference Minister
Conservative Mennonite Board of Missions and Charities	M	Irwin, OH	Becky Roth, Secretary
Consultation on Church Union	O	Princeton, NJ	David W. P. Taylor, General Secretary, Princeton, NJ
Continental Baptist Missions	O	Rockford, MI	Dennis Hamel - Margaret Wetherington -Margaret Wetherington, Executive Secretary -Dione Russell,
Cook Communication Ministries	O	Cold Springs, CA	Carol Messina, Founding Secretary - Diane Russell
Cornerstone College (former BBC)	S	Grand Rapids, MI	John D. Elmore, Coordinator of Media Relations -Jane Slusher -Kathryn Jarke
Council for Christian Colleges (90 schools)	O	Washington, DC	Tom England
Covenant College	S	Lookout Mt, GA	Frank A. Brock, President – Susan Cardwell
Covenant Theological Seminary	S	St Louis, MO	Betty Porter -Byran Chapell
Criswell College	S	Gaston, TX	Paige Patterson, President -George B. Davis, Vice President
Crossway Books/Good News Publishers	O	Wheaton, IL	Sarah Krogh
Crown College	S	St. Boniface, MN	Angie DeWaard, Communications Secretary -Douglas P. Parkinson, College Relations
Cumberland Presbyterian Church Board of Missions	M	Memphis, TN	Joe Matlock
Cumberland Presbyterian Church of America	D	Huntsville, AL	Evelyn Walpale, General Assembly Office
D M Stearns Missionary Foundation, Inc	M	North Wales, PA	K.F. Oestreich, Secretary -Lorraine Kirk, Secretary -Elber W. Stearns, Jr.
Dallas Theological Seminary	S	Dallas, TX	John F. Walvoord - President -Brandy Freiger, Asst. Director of Alumn
Davis College	S	Bible School Park, NY	Karen Francis, Exec. Secretary – Gerald Franz, Librarian
Dayspring Enterprises Intl	M	Virginia Beach, VA	Deborah Darnell
Denver Conservative Baptist Seminary/Thomas	S	Denver, CO	Alice P. Mathews-Ginny Buk, Director of Public Relations-Sarah Miller
Detroit Baptist Theological Seminary	S	Allen Park, MI	Rolland D. McCune, President
Disciples Divinity House	S	Chicago, IL	William E. Crowl, Associate Dean
Disciples Ecumenical Consultative Council (DECC)	O	Indianapolis, IN	Paul A. Crow Jr., General Secretary
Door of Hope, Int - Evangelism to Communism	M	Pasadena, CA	Paul Popov
Dordt College	S	Sioux Center, IA	John B. Hulst, President
Drew University Theological School	S	Madison, NJ	Randall Hand, Director of Admissions-Rachel M. Jones, Archivist-Jean Schoenthaler - Archivist-Lyn Schmaltz, Asst. to the Dean

Name	Code	Location	Helpful Sources
Dubuque Theological Seminary (University of Dubuque)	S	Dubuque, IA	Betsy J. Crawford-Gore, Curator
Duke University Divinity School	S	Durham, NC	Gregory Strong, Methodist Archives-Wesley F. Brown, Director/Alumni-Greg Smith, Research Asst.-Donn Michael Farris, Librarian
Earlham School of Religion	S	Richmond, IN	Wilmer A. Cooper, Dean-Susan Kern, Secretary to the Dean-Thomas D. Hamm, Archivist, Professor of Church
Eastern Baptist Theological Seminary	S	Wynnewood, PA	Esther George
Eastern Mennonite Board of Missions and Charities	M	Salunga, PA	Ruth Sauder-J. Allen Brubaker, Director - Mary Jane
Eastern Mennonite Seminary/University	S	Harrisonburg, VA	Harold E. Huber, Asst. Librarian-Lois B. Bowman,
Eastern University	S	Wynnewood, PA	Melody Mazuk
Eastern Nazarene College	S	Quincy, MA	Jane Michaels, Secretary to the President
Eden Theological Seminary	S	St Louis, MO	Lowell H. Zuck, Archivist
Eerdmans Publishing Company	O	Grand Rapids, MI	William Eerdman, Sr.
Elim Bible Institute	S	Lima, NY	Darian Jaynes, Secretary to the President - Carlton Spencer
Elim Fellowship Missions	M	Lima, NY	Harry V. Vellekoop, Director
Emmanuel Bible College	S	Pasadena, CA	Veghia E. Babikian
Emmanuel College and School of Christian Ministries	S	Franklin Springs, GA	Beth Ward, Secretary to the President -Richard DuPont
Emmaus Bible College	S	Dubuque, IA	Laurel Rasmussen
EPC Missions	M		Merilyn Bartel
Episcopal Church	D	New York, NY	Mark J. Duffy, Archivist-Jennifer Peters, Archivist -Yogi Patel, Asst. Archivist (Austin, TX) -T. Matthew DeWelsche, Archivist (Austin, TX)
Episcopal Church in the USA	M	New York, NY	Avis E. Harvey
Episcopal Divinity School	S	Cambridge, MA	David Siegenthaler, Curator
Episcopal Theological Seminary of the SW	S	Austin, TX	Jan Wallace, Executive Secretary to the Dean -Bob Kinnly
Erksine College	S	Due West, SC	Edith Brawley (McCain Library)
Erksine Theological Seminary	S	Due West, SC	Randall T. Ruble, President
Eugene Bible College	S	Eugene, OR	Clayton E. Crymes, Dean of Academic Affairs -P. Cameron, Librarian -Dennis M. Schmidt, President (Open Bible College) - P. Cameron, Librarian - Danell L. Bemis,
European Christian Mission, Inc	M	Point Roberts, WA	Vincent C. Price, Director for North America
Evangel College University	S	Springfield, MO	Carol J. Stair, Secretary to the President
Evangelical Baptist Missions	M	Indianapolis, IN	David L. Marshall, General Director
Evangelical Child and Family Agency	O	Wheaton, IL	Rev. Milford Shoulund, Dr. Harold Lundquist, Gen William Harrison, Arthur Zahnizer, Rev. Herbert Lockyear, Rev. Robert Murfin, Doris Wheeler, Kenton J. Withrow
Evangelical Christian Publishers Association	O	Tempe, AZ	Laraine Baxter
Evangelical Church Alliance	O	Bradley, IL	Glen E. Seaborg, Executive Director -George L. Miller, Executive Director
Evangelical Church Library Association	O	Glen Ellyn, IL	Mary K. Bechtel
Evangelical Congregational Church	D	Myerstown, PA	Terry Heisey Archivist -Keith R. Miller
Evangelical Congregational Church Division of Missions	M	Myerstown, PA	David G. Hornberger, Jr.
Evangelical Covenant Church, Board of World Missions	M	Chicago, IL	Eileen Thorpe, Secretary
Evangelical Fellowship of Mission Agencies	O	Atlanta, GA	Kathi Kemp, Operations Director
Evangelical Friends Int	D	Canton, OH	Lucy M. Anderson, Administrative Asst.
Evangelical Friends Mission	M	Arvada, CO	Lucy M. Anderson – Katina McConaughey
Evangelical Lutheran Church in America (ELCA)	D	Chicago, IL	Sara Mummert - Wentz Library (Lutheran Theo Seminary, Gettysburg, PA) -Joel Thoreson, Reference Archivist Lowell G. Almen, Secretary -Steven E. Bean, Archivist -Elisabeth Wittman, Archivist
Evangelical Lutheran Church in America (ELCA)		St. Paul, MN	Paul A. Daniels, Arch Region 3
Evangelical Lutheran Church in America (ELCA)		Dubuque, IA	Robert C. Wiederaenders - Archivist -Patricia M. Region 5 GassIMissions
Evangelical Lutheran Church in America (ELCA)		Columbia, SC	James R. Crumley, Jr. Region 9 See Lutheran Theo. Southern Seminary
Evangelical Lutheran Synod	D	Mankata, MN	Walther C. Gullixson, Asst. Archivist
Evangelical Mennonite Church Missions	M	Fort Wayne, IN	Carol Strom
Evangelical Press Association (Victor Books)	O	Charlottesville, VA	Gary Warner, Executive Director -Mavis Sanders
Evangelical School of Theology	S	Myerstown, PA	Ray A. Seilhamer, President -Julie Blancaflor, Academic Secretary

Reese Chronological Encyclopedia of Christian Biographies

Name	Code	Location	Helpful Sources
Evangelical Theological Society	O	Lynchburg, VA	Richard N. Longenecker (Wycliffe College, Toronto) -Simon J. Kistemaker, Secretary/Treasurer
Evangelical Training Association	O	Wheaton, IL	Robert R. West, Vice President of Operations -Richard Patterson, President
Evangelism and Missions Information Service	M	Wheaton, IL	James W. Reapsome
Evangelistic Faith Missions Inc	M	Bedford, IN	J.B. "Juddie" Peyton, President and Director -J. Stevan Manley, President
Every Home for Christ	M	Colorado Springs, CO	Elaine West, Correspondence Secretary
Fairhaven Baptist College	S	Chesterton, IN	Roger Voegtlin, President
Faith Baptist Bible College	S	Ankeny, IA	Robert L. Domokos, President -Jeff Gates, Librarian -Lance Young
Far East Broadcasting Company, Inc	M	Lamirada, CA	Robert H. Bowman, President - Barbara Mack
Fellowship Int Mission	M	Allentown, PA	Richard R. Ruth -Paulette Grant, Secretary
Fellowship of Christian Athletes	O	Kansas City, MO	Don Hilhemloy -Clayton Ketterling, Vice President of Development
Fellowship of Grace Brethren Churches	D	Winona Lake, IN	Kenneth Koontz -Clyde K. Landrum
Florida Bible College	S	Miramir, FL	Paul C. Goody
FOCAS - Fdn of Compassionate American Samaritans	M	Cincinnati, OH	Richard P. Taylor
Free Methodist Church of North America World	M	Indianapolis, IN	Frances Haslam, Director -Cathy Fortner, Director (Marston Missions Memorial Historical Center)
Free Methodists Church of North America	D	Indianapolis, IN	Cathy Fortner -Frances Haslam
Free Will Baptist Bible College	S	Nashville, TN	Robert E. Picirilli
Friends General Conference	D	Philadelphia, PA	Chris Dinsmore, Friends Historical Library (Swarthmore [PA] College) -Elisabeth P. Brown - Quaker Bibliographer (Haverford [PA] College) -Nancy P. Speers, Archivist, Friends Historical Library
Friends United Meeting	D	Richmond, IN	Kimberly Niles -Thomas D. Hamm, Archivist (Earlham College, Richmond, IN) - Karole Cox
Friends United World Ministries	M	Richmond, IN	Thomas D. Hamm, Archivist
Friends University	S	Wichita, KS	Max M. Burson, Asst. Library Director
Friends World Committee for Consultation	O	Philadelphia, PA	Cilda Grom, Executive Secretary -Carl Williams, Associate Secretary – Thecla Geraghty, Office Manager
Frontiers	M	Mesa, AZ	Greg Livingstone
Fuller Theological Seminary	S	Pasadena, CA	Steven Pattie, Administrative Asst. to the President -Denny Miller, Coordinator (Editorial and Media)
Garrett-Evangelical Theological Seminary	S	Evanston, IL	Dorothy BorDurant, Asst. to the President -David K. Himrod, Asst. Librarian (The United Library)
General Association of General Baptists	D	Poplar Bluff, MO	Glen O. Spence, Executive Secretary
General Association of Regular Baptists	D	Schaumburg, IL	Vernon D. Miller, Executive Editor
General Baptist Foreign Mission Society	M	Poplar Bluff, MO	Charles L. Carr -Marlin Dossett
General Theological Seminary	S	New York, NY	Herbert D. Thomas -David Kisling
George Fox University	S	Newberg, OR	Frank Cole, Archivist -Richard L. Votaw, Archivist
George Mercer Jr Memorial School of Theology	S	Garden City, NY	Lloyd A. Lewis, Jr., Dean
Gideons International	O	Nashville, TN	N.A. Knudsen, Asst. to the Executive Director -Kathleen Hays, Editorial Asst.
Global Outreach Mission (Mexican Mission)	M	Buffalo, NY	Walter Gomez - Mexican Mission -James O. Blackwood, President
Go Ye Fellowship	M	Pasadena, CA	Fern Nelson - Hubert Mitchell
God's Bible School/College	S	Cincinnati, OH	Vanessa G. Heppeard, Secretary to the President
Gordon College	S	Wenham, MA	Evelyn M. Reed, Public Relations -John Beauregard, Archivist
Gordon-Conwell Theological Seminary	S	South Hamilton, MA	Scott M. Gibson, Archivist and Curator
Goshen College	S	Goshen, IN	Miriam Bontreger, Records Secretary
Gospel Communications International	O	Muskegon, MI	Lynn Morse - David R. Anderson (Films)
Gospel for Asia	M	Carrollton, TX	Kris Davis
Gospel Furthering	M	Myerstown, PA	Bruce P. Busch, General Director
Gospel Light/Regal Books	O	Ventura, CA	Chris Nelson
Gospel Mission of South America	M	Fort Lauderdale, FL	Hudson Shedd
Gospel Missionary Union	M	Kansas City, MO	Michele Phillips, Publications Editor -Carl McMindes -Carol Meyer -Dennis Smith, Secretary -Dick Darr, President -Elna M. Cook -Martha Fales, Secretary -Abe Reddekopp, Director of Public Ministries - Bunnie Foster
Gospel Recordings	M	Los Angeles, CA	Larry D. Allmon
Grace and Truth, Inc	M	Danville, IL	Sam O. Hadley

Name	Code	Location	Helpful Sources
Grace Bible College/ Ministries	S	Grand Rapids, MI	Timothy F. Conklin
Grace Brethren International Missions	M	Winona Lake, IN	Lillian Teiter, Secretary -John Zielasko
Grace College and Seminary	S	Winona Lake, IN	Homer A. Kent, Jr. -Nancy Weimer, Secretary to the President – Bill Darr – Jonathan Potter
Grace College of the Bible	S	Omaha, NE	Harold J. Berry
Great Commision Foundation, Int	M	Tuscaloosa, AL	Edwin Messerschmidt
Greater Europe Mission	M	Monument, CO	Don Brugmann, Executive Director -George Winston
Greenville College	S	Greenville, IL	M. Staer -Edith Simcoe
Haggai Institute for Advanced Leadership Training	M	Atlanta, GA	Norman M. Vaughn, Jr., Asst. to the President
Hartford Seminary Foundation	S	Hartford, CT	Edna Madden, Library Director -Ann Lana -Marion Stephens, Asst. Director of Development -Steven Blackburn, Reference Librarian
Harvard University Divinity School	S	Cambridge, MA	James W. McCarthy, Curatorial Asst. -Patrice Donaghue, Curatorial Associate -Kyle Carey, Reference Asst. -David A. Ware, Archivist Asst. -Timothy Driscoll, Curator
Harvest	M	Tempe, AZ	Bob Moffitt
HBI Global Partnership Int	M	Union Mills, NC	Chrystal Searcy, Office Administrator
Heritage Baptist University	S	Greenwood, IN	Russell Dennis, Jr., President
Hermano Pablo Ministries	M	Costa Mesa, CA	Jonathan Brown, Executive Director
Hillsdale Free Will Baptist College	S	Moore, OK	Madine Followwill. Asst. Pres.
Hispanic Baptist Theological School	S	San Antonio, TX	Edith Pefveni
Hobe Sound Bible College	S	Hobe Sound, FL	Joyce M. Movyan
Holt International Childrens Services	M	Eugene, OR	John Creby
Hood Theological Seminary	S	Salisbury, NC	Bernard W. Franklin - Reginald W. Brown
Hope College	S	Holland, MI	Russell Gasero -Larry J. Wagenaar, Associate Professor - Chad A. Boorsma – Geoffrey D. Reynolds
Houghton College	S	Houghton, NY	Dean Liddick, Director of Public Information -Stephen W. Paine -Donna Watson, Asst. Archivist -Richard J. Aldeman, Executive Director of Alumni -Linda A. Doezema, Archivist -Richard A. Gould, Asst. Archivist Bob and Ruth Luckey
Howard University/Divinity School	S	Washington, DC	Carrie M. Hackney, Divinity Librarian
Huntington College	S	Huntington, IN	Randy Neuman, Archivist -Jane E. Mason, Archivist-
Hutterian Brethren	D	Reardon, WA	Dennis Stoltz, Archivist (Goshen College, IN)
Iliff School of Theology	S	Denver, CO	Marshall Eidson, Librarian and Archivist -Donald E. Messer, President -Virginia M. Dorjahn, Executive Secretary to the President
Immanuel Lutheran College	S	Eau Claire, WI	John Lau, President
Impact International	M	Boca Raton, FL	Bruce Woodman
Independent Baptist College	S	Fort Worth, TX	Judy Myers, Secretary
Independent Board for Presbyterian Foreign Missions	M	Philadelphia, PA	Robert E. Martin, Sr., Busines Manager -William R. LeRoy, Executive Director
Independent Fundamental Churches of America	D	Grandville, MI	Mary Esther Carter, Executive Secretary - Marjorie Thomas, Adm. Ast. - Miriam Lotquist
India Rural Evangelical Fellowship	M	Park Ridge, IL	John Paul
Indian Bible College	M	Flagstaff, AZ	Helen Yazzie
Indiana Wesleyan University	S	Marion, IN	Alice Wills, Reference Librarian
Institute for International Christian Communication	M	Portland, OR	Donald K. Smith
Intercessors for America	O	Leesburg, VA	Eileen Reed
Interchurch Holiness Convention	O	Bedford, IN	Leonard Sankey
Interdenominational Foreign Missions Association of North America	O	Carol Stream, IL	Edwin L. Frizen, Jr. -Helen R. Beerley
Interdenominational Theological Center	S	Atlanta, GA	Karen L. Jefferson, Archives, Woodruff Library
International Bible College	S	San Antonio, TX	Lavonda Coble -Hope Coote
International Bible Society	O	Colorado Springs, CO	Jeanene Moore, Coordinator
International Board of Jewish Missions	M	Hixson, TN	Ormand L. Norwood
International Christian Leprosy Mission	M	Forrest Grove, OR	Daniel Pulliam, President
International Church of the Foursquare Gospel	D	Los Angeles, CA	J. Eugene Kurtz, General Supervisor - Steph Zeleny, Arch
International Church of the Foursquare Gospel,	M	Los Angeles, CA	J. Eugene Kurtz, General Supervisor Missions
International College and Grad School	S	Honolulu, HA	Carol White, Registrar
International Council of Community Churches (Long Boat Island Chapel)	D	Frankfort, IL	J. Ralph Shotwell -Carolyn M. Willey, Asst. Minister
International Gospel League	M	Pasadena, CA	Howard T. Lewis, President
International Lutheran Laymens League	M	St Louis, MO	Gerald Perschbacher -Wayne Huebner -Ronald J. Schlegel, Director -Timothy A. Daene, Archivist and

Name	Code	Location	Helpful Sources
			Research Asst.
International Ministries to Israel	O		Ralph Gade
International Pentecostal Church of Christ	D	London, OH	Erwin L. Hargrove, Treasurer
International Pentecostal Holiness Church	D	Oklahoma City, OK	Delores Cox, Secretary -Brenda Wilkins -Erica Y. Rutland, Archivist, Secretary -James B. Robinson, Archivist -Margaret Johnson
International Pentecostal Holiness Church Missions	M	Oklahoma City, OK	Delores Cox - Margarey Johnson
International Students	M	Colorado Springs, CO	Jerry Nanfelt, Administrative Asst.
International Teams	M	Elgin, IL	Mark K. Dyer, President -Debbie Dassie, Secretary -Kevin G. Dyer, President -Paula Wanden, Secretary
International Theological Seminary of California	S	Van Nuys, CA	Jamie Dezur, Vice President
Interserve	M	Upper Darby, PA	Jack Dain, President -Margaret Hobbs, Director of Servcies
Intervarsity	O	Madison, WI	Susan Pohorski, Director of Information and Services -Martha Baker -Hyvonne Vinkennuldin -William T. McConnell, Asst. to the President – Stephane Knecht
Japanese Evangelization Center	M	Pasadena, CA	John Misuki
Jerusalem University College	S	Rockford, IL	Amelia Nakai, Program Coordinator
Jews for Jesus	O	San Francisco, CA	Susan Perlman
John Wesley College (Owossa)	S	High Point, NC	Donna Watson, Archivist (Wesleyan Church) -David F. Hanson, Department Executive (St. Michael's, Lansing, MI)
John Wesley College(High Point)	S		Geneva C. Temple, Archivist
Kansas City College and Bible School	S	Overland Park, KS	Helen J. Shipman -Ray Crooks, Vice President
Kentucky Mountain Bible College	S	Van Cleve, KY	J. Eldon Neihof, President
Kentucky Mountain Holiness Association	O	Van Cleve, KY	J. Eldon Neihof, President
Kids Alive International	M	Valparaiso, IN	Louise H. Rock, Publications Editor
Kings College	S	New York, NY	Louise Arfor
L.I.F.E. Bible College (foursquare gospel)	S	San Dimas, CA	Jack E. Hamilton
Lancaster Bible College	S	Lancaster, PA	Gilbert A. Peterson, President -Carol Hofmann, Director of Public Information
Lancaster Theological Seminary	S	Lancaster, PA	Richard Glatfelter -MaryLin Siever, Secretary to the President -Dianne Russell, Researcher - Richard Berg, Archives
Larry W Jones Int Ministries (Feed the Children)	M	Oklahoma City, OK	Peggy Neel, Special Projects
Latin American Bible Institute	S	LaPuente, CA	E. Romo, Academic Secretary -Simon Melendres, President
Latin American Mission	M	Miami, FL	John Manst -Donna W. Johnson, Secretary
Lausanne Committee For World Evangelism	M	Palm Desert, CA	Paul Cedar, Chairman
Lee College	S	Cleveland, TN	Cameron Fisher, Administrative Aide to the V.P. -Myra Robertson
Lester Summerall Evangelistic Association	M	South Bend, IN	Susann Wilkeson, Secretary
LeTourneau University	S	Longview, TX	Connie Douty, Administrative Asst. to the President - Janet Ragland
Lexington Theological Seminary	S	Lexington, KY	William O. Paulsell -Betty F. Marinaro, Secretary to the President -Philip N. Dare -Boswell Library -John Charles Heaberlin
Liberty Theological Seminary	S	Lynchburg, VA	Linda Sweat, Administrative Asst. to the President - Jim Borland
Liebenzell Mission of USA Inc	M	Schooleys Mountain, NJ	Juanita Simpson, Overseas Director -Barbara Casidy, Secretary -Michael S. Galley, Director of Communications
LIFE Bible College	S		Jack E. Hamilton, President
LIFE College East	S	Christiansburg, VA	Betty W. Stickrod -William R. Mouer, Sr.
LIFE Ministries	M	San Dimas, CA	Kathy Nelson, Executive Secretary
Livingstone College	S	Salisbury, NC	Joseph Prile
LOGOI, Inc	M	Miami, FL	C. Thompson
Logos Christian College	S	Jacksonville, FL	Sophia T. Dunn, Secretary (Florida Beacon Bible College) -Dwight Martin, Academic Dean
Lord's Day Alliance	O	Atlanta, GA	Timothy A. Norton, Executive Director -James P. Westberry, Executive Director/Editor
Louisville Presbyterian Theological Seminary	S	Louisville, KY	Milton J. Coalter, Jr., Librarian -Suzanne Stowe, Office Information -John M. Mulder, President -Angela G. Morris, Reference Librarian
Luther Northwestern Theological Seminary	S	St Paul, MN	Suzanne Hequet, Asst. Archivist -Paul A. Daniels, Arvhicist (ELCA Region 3) -Lisa C. Griffin, Archivist (ELCA Region 3) -(See ELCA, Region 3)

Name	Code	Location	Helpful Sources
Lutheran Bible Institute in California	S	Irvine, CA	Ben Johnson
Lutheran Brethren Seminary	S	Fergus Falls, MN	Everald H. Strom -Kathy Garvin
Lutheran Church - Missouri Synod	D	St Louis, MO	Roy A. Ledbetter, Reference and Research Asst. -Robert Shreckhise (Concordia Historical Institute) Mark West (CHI) -Wayne Huebner -David Loy (CHI) -Christopher B. Brown (CHI), Paul M. Heerboth -Ann Porterfield
Lutheran Church - Missouri Synod Mission	M		Roy A. Ledbetter, Ref & Pres Ast
Lutheran School of Theology	S	Chicago, IL	David L. Lindberg, Archivist -William E. Lesher, President -Margaret Lillard, Alumni Supervisor -Steven E. Bean, Archivist (ELCA) -(See ELCA, Region 3)
Lutheran Southern Theological Seminary	S	Columbia, SC	Helen S. Sanders, Facilitator -Jeanette Bergeron, Lineberger Memorial Library (See ELCA, Region 9)
Lutheran Synodical Conference	O	St. Louis, MO	Paul M. Heerboth, Secretary (Lutheran Conference - Missouri Synod) -Ann Porterfield, Secretary (LC-MS)
Lutheran Theological Seminary at Gettysburg	S	Gettysburg, PA	Ruth B. Fair -Sara Mummert, Arwentz Library (See ELCA, Region 3)
Lutheran Theological Seminary at Philadelphia (Lutheran Archives Center at PA)	S	Philadelphia, PA	John A. Kaufmann -L. Walker, Asst. Librarian -Andrew Voight, Professor -John E. Peterson, Curator -Robyn A. Kulp, Asst. Curator
Lutheran World Federation	O	1211 Geneva 20,	Birgitta Kok -Ingrid Krahenbuhl -F. Andreas Muller -Mary W. Pond -Karen M. Ward (ELCA) -Delene Constante (ELCA)- Ingrid Krahenbuhl – Elizabeth Elliott – Helen Penet – Margit Eggert
M C Missions	M		Ann Colwell
Malone College	S	Canton, OH	Lucy Anderson (Evangelical Friends Church) -Eleanor J. Young, Secretary to the President
Map International	M	Brunswick, GA	Gordon F. Thompson, Vice President
Maranatha Baptist Bible College	S	Watertown, WI	Arno G. Weniger, Jr.
Maranatha Baptist Missions, Inc	M	Natchez, MS	James W. Crumpton
Masters Seminary	S	Sun Valley, CA	John R. Dunkin, President Emeritus (Masters College, Santa Clarita, CA)
McCormick Theological Seminary	S	Chicago, IL	Mary E. Hagemann, Treasurer (Trust Lane Seminary) -Martha L. Payne, Secretary/Archival Liason -Ken Sawyer
Medical Ambassadors, Int	M	Modesto, CA	Paul Calhoun, Executive Director
Memphis Theological Seminary	S	Memphis, TN	J. David Hester, President
Mennonite Brethren Biblical Seminary	S	Fresno, CA	Marilyn Lewis, Asministrative Asst. -Kevin Enns-Rempel, Archivist
Mennonite Brethren Churches	D	Hillsboro, KS	Peggy Goertzen (Tabor College)
Mennonite Brethren Missions Services (General Conferences)	M	Fresno, CA	Dennis Stoesz, Archivist -Peggy Goertzen (Tabor College) -Kevin Enns-Rempel -Jeanne Liechty , Asst. Archivist -Kaylene Unruh, Personnel Dept. -Nancy Funk, Secretary -Stanley Voth, Asst. Librarian - Marilyn Doran (Goshen,
Mennonite Central Committee	M	Akron, OH	John A. Lapp -Irene Leaman, Records/Library Archivist
Mennonite Church, the General Conference	D	Newton, KS	John D. Thiesen, Archivist (Bethel College) -Vern Preheim -David A. Haury, Archivist -Dennis Stoesz, Archivist -James R. Lynch, Asst. Archivist (Bethel College)
Mennonite Church, the General Conference Missions	M	Newton, KS	Stanley Voth -Nancy Funk
Messiah College	S	Grantham, PA	E. Morris Sider, Archivist -Henry N. Hostetter -Dori I. Steckbeck, Archives Director – Joy Houch, Inter. Director
Methodist Theological School in Ohio	S	Delaware, OH	Karen Stoner, Secretary to the President
Mid America Bible College	S	Oklahoma City, OK	Elizabeth A. Cox, Administrative Asst.
Mid America Nazarene College	S	Olathe, KS	Linda L. Baldridge, Administrative Asst.
Mid Continental Baptist Bible College	S	Mayfield, KY	Robert G. Vann
Mission America	O	Edina, MN	Jeannie
Mission Aviation Fellowship	M	Redlands, CA	Midge Huizinga, Personnel Asst.
Mission Moving Mountains	M	Savage, MN	Richard L. Patterson
Mission to Japan	M		Jow Wiegand
Mission to the Americas/Conservative Baptist Home	O	Wheaton, IL	Linda Marty, Secretary -Heidi Barz, Secretary to the General Mission Director
Missionary Church	D	Ft Wayne, IN	Wava Bueschlen, Director of the Library (Summit

Name	Code	Location	Helpful Sources
			Christian College) -Diane Norris, Secretary
Missionary Flights Int.	M	West Palm Beach, FL	Don H. Beldin, President
Missionary Gospel Fellowship	M	Turlock, CA	William C. Pietsch
Missionary Revival Crusade	M	Cedar Hill, TX	Roger West, President
Missionary TECH Team	M	Longview, TX	Birne D. Wiley
Montrose Bible Conference	O	Montrose, PA	Jim Fahringer, Executive Director
Moody Bible Institute	S	Chicago, IL	Caleb Roberts - Walster Osborn, Librarian - Elgin Moyer, Librarian – Marian Shaw, Asst. Archives
Moravian Church in America, Board of World	M	Bethlehem, PA	Hermann J. Wenlick, Publications Missions
Moravian Church in North America (Northern Province)	D	Bethlehem, PA	Hermann J. Wenlick -Vernon H. Nelson -Margaret Wilde -Susan M. Dreydoppel, Executive Director (Moravian Historical Society, Nazareth, PA)
Moravian Church in North America (Southern Province)	D	Winston-Salem, NC	Susan M. Dreydoppel, Executive Director (Moravian Historical Society, Nazareth, PA) -L. Nicole Blum, Asst. Archivist
Moravian Theological Seminary	S	Bethlehem, PA	John Thomas Minot, Librarian
Mount Vernon Nazarene College	S	Mt. Vernon, OH	E. Lebron Fairbanks, President
Mountain States Baptist College	S	Great Falls, MT	Richard Jonas, Academic Dean -Richard A. Dion, President
Multnomah Bible College and International Biblical Seminary	S	Portland, OR	Erma H. Wolever, Administrative Asst.
Mutual Faith Ministries	O	Oranda Hills, CA	Keith Hershey
Nashatah House	O	Nashatah, WI	Susan Lee Mills, Archivist -Barb Simpson, Asst. Librarian
National Association of Evangelicals	O	Azusa, CA	Billy C. Melvin - Beth Thompson
National Association of Freewill Baptist	D	Antioch, TN	Jack Williams
National Association of Freewill Baptist Foreign	M	Antioch, TN	R. Eugene Waddell, General Director -Shirley J. Lauthern Mission Board Raymond Riggs, Evangelist
National Baptist Convention of America	O	Dallas, TX	Marvin C. Griffin (Ebenezer Baptist Church, Austin, TX)
National Baptist Convention USA Inc. Foreign	M	Philadelphia, PA	William J. Harvey, III, Executive Secretary Mission Board
National Community of Churches	D		Joseph Shotwell -Carolyn M. Willey, Associate Pastor (Longboat First Chapel)
National Council of Churches	D	New York, NY	Alice Jones (Yearbook of American Churches, New York, NY) -Constant H. Jacquet, Editor of the Yearbook -Sarah Vilankulu, Director for Interpretation Resources
National Institute of Businesses Industrial Chaplains	S	Houston, TX	Diana Dale -Elizabeth F. Bureigh - Attorney at Law
National Lutheran Council (Lutheran Council in	O	New York, NY	Miriam L. Woolbert, Staff Asst. -Benjamin Bankson, Consultant for Communications -Walter R. Harrison, President (Lutheran Archives, Philadelphia, PA)
National Organization of New Apostolic Church	D	Chicago, IL	Peter Raich
Navigators	O	Colorado Springs, CO	Katie McCaffery -Rhonda Schneider
Nazarene Bible College	S	Colorado Springs, CO	W.T. Porkiser ("Called Unto Holiness"- Vol. 2) -Maryann Whitney, Secretary to the President
Nazarene Theological Seminary	S	Kansas City, MO	Carolyn Steele, Secretary to the President
New Apostolic Church of North America	D	Chicago, IL	Peter Raich
New Brunswick Theological Seminary	S	New Brunswick, NJ	Russell Gasero -John W. Beardslee, III, Archivist -Chad A. Boorsma, Research Asst. - Everett Zabriskie
New England Fellowship of Evangelicals	O	Rumney, NH	David S. Wood, President
New Orleans Baptist Theological Seminary	S	New Orleans, LA	Paul Gericke, Director of the Library -Eric Benoy, Public Service
New Tribes Mission	M	Sanford, FL	George W.E. Davison -Marilyn Meisel
New York Theological Seminary	S	New York, NY	Kathryn Ketcham, Administrative Secretary to the President
Nisco	O	Washington D.C., PA	Dean Jones, Outreach Database
North American Baptist Confederation	D	Oakbrook Terrace, IL	Berneice V. Westerman, Asst. Archivist (Heritage NAB Commission) -George A. Dunger, Archivist
North American Baptist Missions	M	Oakbrook Terrace, IL	Berneice V. Westerman, Asst. Archivist -George A. Dunger, Archivist
North American Baptist Seminary	S	Sioux Falls, SD	George A. Dunger, Archivist -Berneice V. Westerman
North Central Bible College	S	Minneapolis, MN	Don Argue, President -Cathy Anderson, Alumni Director
North Park University (Evangelical Covenant)	S	Chicago, IL	Ellen M. Engseth, Archivist
Northeastern Bible College	S	Essex Fells, NJ	Eleanor H. Keil, Registrar
Northern Baptist Theological Seminary	S	Lombard, IL	Betsy K. Dursor, Director of Publications

Name	Code	Location	Helpful Sources
Northland Baptist Bible College	S	Dunbar, WI	William G. Bellshaw, President
Northwest Bible College (Church of God)	S	Minot, ND	Louis F. Morgan, Archivist (See Church of God, Cleveland, TN)
Northwest College (Assembly of God)	S	Kirkland, WA	A.D. Millard
Northwest Nazarene University	S	Nampa, ID	Kenneth F. Watson, Asst. to the President
Northwestern College	S	Orange City, IA	Cornelia B. Kennedy, Curator (Dutch Heritage Collection)
Northwestern Collge	S	St. Paul, MN	William B. Berntsen, President -Janell L. Wojtowicz, Media and Publications
Nurses Christian Fellowship	O	Madison, WI	Mary Thompson
Nyack (Missionary) College	S	Nyack, NY	John F. Taylor, Executive Director of Alumni
Oberlin College	S	Oberlin, OH	Jeanne Forsyth, Archivist Volunteer -Carol S. Jacobs, Asst. Archivist -Valerie S. Komor, Project Archivist -Roland M. Baumann, Archivist
Officers Christian Fellowship	O	Englewood, CO	Medwyn D. Sloane, III, Administrator
Olivet Nazarene College	S	Kankakee, IL	Norman L. Moore, Archivist -Janice Royal, Secretary to the President
OMS International Inc.	O	Greenwood, IN	Edward Erny
Open Air Campaigners	O	Stuart, FL	John Cutlip, Director -David Wilson
Open Bible Standard Churches, Inc.	D	Des Moines, IA	Marian L. Smith, Secretary -Ray E. Smith, General Support
Open Bible Standard Missions, Inc.	M	Des Moines, IA	Ray E. Smith, General Support
Operation Mobilization	O	Tyrone, GA	Rita Haywood, Secretary
Oral Roberts University School of Theology	S	Tulsa, OK	Paul G. Chappell (School of Theology and Missions)
Orient Crusades (OC International)	O	Colorado Springs, CO	Mary Salter, Secretary to the President
Overseas Mission Fellowship	M	Littleton, CO	Dorcas Simpson, Secretary -Robert Shuster, Billy Graham Archivist -Patty Nelson, Graphic Design -Lindie Bacon, Administrative Asst. -Jeanne Daugherty
Pacific Lutheran Theological Seminary	S	Berkeley, CA	Wendy Eilers -Carol A. Schmalenberger, Archivist
Pacific School of Religion	S	Berkeley, CA	Joe C. Numes -Eileen M. Weston, Secretary to the
Partners Int.	M	Spokane, WA	Allen Finley - Linda Otto
Patten University	S	Oakland, CA	Susan Robinson
Payne Theological Seminary	S	Wilberforce, OH	Tracy L. Coleman, Administrative Asst.
Pentecostal Assemblies of Canada	D	Mississauga, Ontario	Marilyn Stroud, Asst. Archives
Pentecostal Church of God	D	Joplin, MO	Ronald R.Minor, General Secretary/Treasurer
Pentecostal Church of God of America World	M	Joplin, MO	Ronald R. Minor, General Secretary/Treasurer Missions Dept.
Pentecostal Fellowship of North America	O	Los Angeles, CA	Jodie Loutzenhisei, Asst. Archivist
Pentecostal Fire Baptized Holiness Church	D	La Grange, GA	W.B. Pittman, Jr.
Pentecostal Free Will Baptist Church	D	Dunn, NC	David A. Taylor (Missions)
Pentecostal World Fellowship	O	Emmetten, Switzerland	Joyce Lee, Asst. Archivist (Springfield, MO)
Perkins School of Theology	S	Dallas, TX	Kate Warnick - Bridwell Librarian -Marilyn Aldexander -Kay Bailey, Alumni Recorder
Philadelphia College of Bible	S	Langhorne, PA	Mrs. Doug Roe -William A. Mierop -Mae Stewart -S. Elizabeth Chung, Asst. to Stewart
Phillips Theological Seminary	S	Tulsa, OK	Harold Hat, Vice President and Dean -Roberta Hamburger, Director of the Library
Piedmont Baptist College	S	Winston-Salem, NC	Howard L. Wilburn, President -Roger L. Barnes, George Manuel Memorial Library
Pillar of Fire	D	Zarephath, NJ	Andrew J. Lavender – Robert Dallenbosh – Suzan Wolfram
Pillsbury Baptist Bible College	S	Owatonna, MN	Pamela S. Baines, Secretary to the President
Pioneer Bible Translators	M	Dallas, TX	Rondal B. Smith
Pioneer Clubs	O	Wheaton, IL	Judy Bryson, President – Nancy Walker
Pioneers	M	Wheaton, IL	Barbara L. Snyder
Pittsburgh Theological Seminary	S	Pittsburgh, PA	Eugene P. Degitz, Vice President -Mary Ellen Scott, Archivist -Andrew Sopko, Associate Librarian
Plymouth Brethren	D	Neptune, NJ	Marjorie Carlson -Ross McClaron (Nashville, TN -Mary Ann Conlon (Interest Ministries - Wheaton, IL) -Bruce R. McNichol (Wheaton, IL)
Pocket Testament League	M	Lititz, PA	Martha Kitchen, Editor -Nancy Knyfd, Ministry Asst. -Christine Hash, Secretary -Heather R. McCaskey, Publications Manager
Presbyterian Church in America	D	Atlanta, GA	William A. Mahlow, Sr. - Pastor Emeritas -Mary Lou Bahnsack, Administrative Asst.
Presbyterian Church in America Missions	M	Atlanta, GA	William Maalow - Mary Lou Bohnsack

Name	Code	Location	Helpful Sources
Presbyterian Church USA	M	Louisville, KY	Diana Ruby Sanderson, Research Historian (Montreat, NC) -Boyd Reese, Asst. Librarian -Owen T. Robbin, Historian/Research - William B. Bynom - William O Harris - Eileen M. Sklar - Beht Bensman - Mary Plummer
Primitive Methodist Chruch	D		Wayne Yarnall
Primitive Methodist Church in the USA, Int. Mission Board	M	Johnson City, NY	Harold J. Barrett, Asst. General Director -William L. Vasey -William H. Fudge, Executive Director
Princeton Theological Seminary and University	S	Princeton, NJ	Julie E. Dawson, Reference Librarian -Kate Skrebutenas, Reference Librarian -William O. Harris, Librarian for Archives -Christine B. Deming (Luce Library) -Carl Esche, Special Collections Asst. (Mudd Manuscript Library) Ben Primer - Kenneth Henke
Prison Fellowship	O	Washington, DC	Suzanne Walker
Progressive National Baptist Convention, Inc.	D	Washington, DC	Ishmael L. Shaw, Interim General Secretary
Project Partner with Christ	M	Springboro, OH	Ellen Haddix
Protestant Hour (Protestant Radio and TV Center)	O	Atlanta, GA	Peter Wallace, President and Executive Producer
Protestant Reformed Church in America	D	South Holland, IL	Jud Dozema
Provident Inc.	O	Franklin, TN	Andrea Walters (Benson Music Group)
Ramabai Mukti Mission	M	Clinton, NJ	Kathy R. Crivellaro, Secretary
RBM Ministries	O	Plainwell, MI	Kent Wray
Red Sea Team International	M	Saratoga, CA	John D. Condie
Reformed Bible College	S	Grand Rapids, MI	Hermina Nyhof
Reformed Church in America	D	New York, NY	Chad A. Boorsma, Research Asst. (Hope College) -Larry J. Wagenaar, Archivist (Hope College) -Russell L. Gasero, Archivist (New Brunswick Theological Seminary) -Jeff Reynolds, Archivist (Hope College, Holland, MI)
Reformed Church in the U.S.	D	Bakersfied, CA	Frank Walker
Reformed Episcopal Church	D	Blue Bell, PA	Donae L. Smith
Reformed Episcopal Seminary	S	Blue Bell, PA	Rt. Reverand Leonard W. Riches -Donae L. Smith
Reformed Presbyterian Church of North America	M	Pittsburg, PA	Robert H. Henning
Reformed Presbyterian Theological Seminary	S	Pittsburgh, PA	Rachel George, Librarian -Thomas G. Reid, Jr., Librarian -Bruce G. Stewart
Reformed Theological Seminary	S	Maitland, FL	Harold DeRoo
Reformed Theological Seminary (school)	S	Jackson, MS	Luder G. Whitlock, Jr., President -Simon J. Kistemaker, Professor of New Testament
Rio Grande Bible Institute	S	Edinburg, TX	Gordon E. Johnson -Helen L. Hanes
Ripe for Harvest OMC	M	Mesa, AZ	Tim Smith
Roberts Wesleyan College	S	Rochester, NY	Charles H. Canan, III
Romanian Missionary Society	M	Wheaton, IL	George A. Festian, Director of Special Projects -Carole A. Boy, Office Manager
Rosedale Bible College	S	Irwin, OH	Sharon Miller - Administrative Asst.
Rosedale Mennonite Missions	M	Irwin, OH	Emma G. Kauffman, Administrative Asst.
Rural Home Missionary Association	O	Morton, IL	Lynette K. Goebel, Dir. Of Operations
Saint Paul School of Theology	S	Kansas City, MO	Kimberly L. Nielon, Administrative Asst. to the President -Logan S. Wright
Salvation Army	D	Alexandria, VA	Connie J. Nelson, Asst. Archivist -Susan Mitchem, Archivist - Jenty Fairbank, Archivist – Scott Bedio, Archivist
Samaritans Purse	M	Boone, NC	Donna L. Toney
San Diego Christian College	S	San Diego, CA	Ashley Lieber, Alumni
San Francisco Theological Seminary	S	San Anselmo, CA	Paul Baird -Allan Schreiber, Librarian Asst. - George Peacock – Michael Peterson, Library – Shelley Calkins
Scripture Memory Mountain Mission	O	Emmalena, KY	Roy Hodson, Mission Director
Scripture Union	M	Wayne, PA	Whitney T. Kuniholm, President -Janet E. Marcellus, Executive Asst.
Seabury-Western Theological Seminary	S	Evanston, IL	Carol Harper, Asst. to the Dean -Newland Smith, Librarian-Elaine S. Caldbeck
Seattle Pacific University	S	Seattle, WA	C. Joyce King, Archivist -Karen Jacobson, Executive Officer -J. Ray Doerksen, Librarian -Jennifer Sigafoes, Librarian -John Glancy, Universal Communications
Send International	M	Farmington, MI	Frank M. Severn -Verona Dutton, Asst. Personnel Director
Shaw Divinity School	S	Raleigh, NC	Carolyn Baker

Name	Code	Location	Helpful Sources
SIM International	M	Fort Mill, SC	Marjory Koop -Stanley B. Willerton, Asia Area Treasurer -Ed Welch -James R. Pfeiffer-Geoffrey W. Griffith -Peter Paget -Esther L. Hutchings -Bobbie Stone -Janet Faber-Jo-Ann Brant -Bob Schultz -Bob Arnold
Simpson College	S	Redding, CA	Miles S. Campton, Librarian -Sally Voder -Marilyn Bryan (Christian and Missionary Alliance)
Slavic Gospel Association (EuroVision)	M	Loves Park, IL	Walter E. Zurfluh -Rosemary Gianesin, Vice President
Source of Light Ministries	M	Madison, GA	David G. Keener
South America Mission	M	Lake Worth, FL	Robert D. Anderson
South American Missionary Society of Episcopal Church	M	Ambridge, PA	Denise J. Cox
Southeastern Baptist College	S	Laurel, MS	James C. Blaylock
Southeastern Baptist Theological Seminary	S	Wake Forest, NC	Jan Fountain -Paul M. Debusman, Librarian -Bonnie M. Hoff, Secretary -Joan C. McGorman, Librarian and Archivist
Southeastern Bible College	S	Birmingham, AL	Evelyn Penner, Secretary (Calvary Church) -Howard F. Sugden, Pastor (South Baptist Church) -Leon W. Gillaspie, Vice President
Southeastern College of Assemblies of God	S	Lakeland, FL	Betty Futch -Gordon Miller, Executive Asst. to the
Southern Baptist Convention	D	Nashville, TN	Bill Sumners, Director and Archivist -Carol Woodfin, Publications and Archivist
Southern Baptist Convention, Foreign Mission	M	Richmond, VA	Barbara Kuntze -Dorothy Owen, Archival Asst.
Southern Baptist Theological Seminary	S	Louisville, KY	Brian J. Vickers -Bonnie M. Hoff, Secretary to the President -Paul M. Debusander, Reference Librarian Moody Brewer
Southern Nazarene University	S	Bethany, OK	W. Don Beaver, Vice President of Academic Affairs -Nelle C. Ryan, Executive Secretary -Paul Gray, Archivist
Southern Wesleyan College (formerly Central Wesleyan)	S	Central, SC	Claude R. Rickman, Asst. to the President (Central Wesleyan) -Debbie H. King, Administrative Asst. (Cent. Wes.) -John M. Newby, President (Cent. Wes.)
Southland Bible Institute	S	Ashland, KY	Arnold Adams
Southwestern Assemblies of God College	S	Waxahachie, TX	Berna Pruett, Administrative Asst. to the President
Southwestern Baptist Theological Seminary	S	Ft. Worth, TX	Mina M. Bickerstaff, Director of Personnel Services
Southwestern College of Christian Ministries	S	Bethany, OK	Wesley A. Olsen
Southwide Baptist Fellowship	O	Stockbridge, GA	Raymond L. Hancock, Secretary and Treasurer -Tom Wallace -Joan Burnett
Sovereign Grace Baptists	D	St.Croix Falls, WI	Jon Zens
Spanish World Gospel Missions	M	Winona Lake, IN	Buel R. Meadows
Spring Arbor University	S	Spring Arbor, MI	Sharon R. Pitts, Director of College Relations -Karren Reish, Librarian/Archivist -Susan M. Panak, Archivist
Spurgeon Baptist Bible College	S	Mulberry, FL	Jackie Barlow, Secretary to the President
STEER Inc.	M	Bismarck, ND	LaRue Goetz, Executive Director
Summit Christian College	S		Donald Gerig, President -See "Taylor University"
Tabernacle Baptist Bible Institute	S	Virginia Beach, VA	Edward Caughill, Dean
Tabor College	S	Hillsboro, KS	Peggy Goertzen
Talbot Theological Seminary	S	La Mirada, CA	Signe Wattenford, Archivist
Taylor University	S	Upland, IN	Dwight Mikkelson, Archivist -Miriam Jeran -Heather Kittleman, Archivist
Teen Missions International	M	Merritt Island, FL	Robert M. Bland
Tennessee Temple University	S	Chattanooga, TN	Gary Matson
The Evangelical Alliance Mission (TEAM)	M	Wheaton, IL	John A. Siewert (MARC) -Richard M. Winchell -Dorothy Vust, Secretary -C. Luke Boughter, Director of Personnel -Marianne Chantelau
Things to Come Mission	M	Indianapolis, IN	Joseph W. Watkins
Toccoa Falls College	S	Toccoa Falls, GA	Ruth A. Megill
Touch the World Ministries	O	Bergenfield, NJ	Alice Omdal, Administrative Secretary
Trans World Missions	M	Glendale, CA	John G. Olson, President -Tiffany Arbogast
Trans World Radio	M	Cary, NC	Rosemary Jaszka – Linda Sink
Trevecca Nazarene University	S	Nashville, TN	Karla Wardlow, Archivist -Delores Green, Secretary to the President
Trinity Bible Christian College	S	Miami, FL	P. Baitle -Larry McCullough
Trinity Bible College	S	Ellendale, ND	David C. Zink
Trinity College	S	Holiday, FL	Carol Grenon
Trinity Evangelical Seminary of Florida	S	Naples, FL	Larry D. McCullough, President (Miami)

Name	Code	Location	Helpful Sources
(formerly Miami Christian College)			-P. Baitle, Miami Christian College
Trinity International University	S	Deerfield, IL	Roy H. Fry, Archivist
Trinity Lutheran College	S	Issaquah, WA	Sharon Conner
Trinity Luthern Seminary	S	Columbus, OH	Jeanne H. Letcher, Asst. Archivist (ELCA, Region 6) -Donald L. Huber, Archivist and Professor -Fred W. Meuser - President of Church History -James M. Childs, Jr. -Donald Huder, Librarian -Louis Voight -J. Elen Locke, Reference Librarian
UFM International	M	Bala-Cynwyd, PA	John T. Dale -Alfred Larson, General Director -Debbie Alexander, Secretary -Leis J. Combs - T. W. Swarp, UP
Union Theological Seminary	S	New York, NY	E. Richard Knox - Ruth Tomkiss Cameron, Archivist
Union Theological Seminary in Virginia	S	Richmond, VA	Lou McKinney, Media Specialist -Heath K. Rada, President (Presbyterian School) -Martha Chycich, Asst. Librarian -Paula Skreslet, WSM Librarian -Patsy Verreault, Librarian - Robert P. Davis
United Bible Societies	O	Reading, England	Kathleen Cann, Archivist - Andrew Mathewson
United Board for Christian Higher Education in Asia	M	New York, NY	Joseph A. Sprunger
United Christian Church	D	Cleoma, PA	John P. Ludwig, President and Elder
United Church Board of Commissioners for Forgotten Miss.	M	Cleveland, OH	Emily Walhout, Houghton Reading Room (Harvard College Library, Cambridge, MA) -Carol Lea -Fujiko Kitagwa, Archivist -David M. Stone, Executive V.P.
United Church of Christ	O	Cleveland, OH	Harold F. Worthley (Cone Christian Historical Society) -Nancy Bainey, Archivist (Lancaster [PA] Theological Seminary) -Dianne Russell (E & R Historical Society) Bridgetic A. Kelly, Archives
United Library	S	Evanston, IL	Kathleen Kordesh
United Methodist Church	D	New York, NY	Scott T. Kisker, Archivist -Mary-Louise Mussell, Research Asst. -Dawn Patterson, UMC Archivist (Madison, NJ) -Mark C. Shenise, Associate Archivist - Jeanette Roberson, World Meth. - Joseph A. Stroble (Drew)
United Pentecostal Church International Missions	M	Hazelwood, MO	Virginia Rigdon, Secretary
United Pentecostal Church, International	D	Hazelwood, MO	Calvin & Virginia Rigdon (Historical Center) – Robin Johnston
United Pentecostal Church, Mission	M	Hazelwood, MO	Calvin & Virginia Rigdon (Historical Center)
United Pentecostal Churches of Christ	D	Cleveland, OH	Benjamin T. Douglass - Suffragan Bishop
United States Centre for World Mission	D		Ralph D. Winter
United Theological Seminary		Dayton, OH	Ashley D. Cox -Elmer J. O'Brien, Librarian -David P. Bunnell, Asst. Librarian
United Theological Seminary of the Twin Cities	S	New Brighton, MN	Dale Dobias, Asst. Librarian
United Wesleyan Collge	S	Allentown, PA	Donna Watson, Asst. Archivist -Kenneth Heer
United World Mission	M	Charlotte, NC	Betty J. Sadler
University of Chicago Divinity School	S	Chicago, IL	Sandy Roscoe (Special Collections Research Center) -Debra Levine (SCRC) -James Lewis
University of Dubuque		Dubuque, IA	Jim Gunn -Joel Samuels – Chas. Myers Library
University of the South School of Theology	S	Sewanee, TN	Arthur & Elizabeth Ben Chitty, Historiographer -Annie Armour, Archivist
Valley Forge Christian College	S	Phoenixville, PA	Lois Nelms, Administrative Asst. and Secretary to the President – Paul Mattias, Storm Research
Vanderbilt Divinity School	S	Nashville, TN	Teresa Gray - Harry Shipman
Vanguard University	S	Costa Mesa, CA	Patti Tyro, Executvie Administrative Asst.
Vellore Christian Medical College	M	New York, NY	Phil Ansalone -Linda L. Pierce, Executive Director
Vennard College	S	University Park, IA	W. Edward Rickman, President -Joe C. Brown -Rodney Birch, Library Director
Virginia Mennonite Board of Missions	M	Harrisonville, VA	Lois Maust
Virginia Theological Seminary	S	Alexandria, VA	Julia Randle -Mitzi J. Budde, Librarian
Vision New England	O	Acton, MA	Stephen Macchia
Volunteers of America	D	Alexandria, VA	Sue Cheveallier, Director of Ecclesiastical Affairs -Stephen Abbott, Vice President of the Committee - Sandie
Warner Pacific College	S	Portland, OR	Milo Chapman, President -Arthur M. Kelley, Exec.
Wartburg Theological Seminary	S	Dubuque, IA	Robert C. Wiederaenders, Archivist
Washington Bible College	S	Lanham, MD	Eleanor R. Bergsten, Administrative Asst. -Barbara Sherry, Librarian and Administrative Asst.
Washington Theological Consortium	S	Washington, DC	Eileen Griffin

Name	Code	Location	Helpful Sources
WEC International	M	Ft. Washington, PA	Robert Mackey -Thomas I. Marks, Jr. -Mrs.(Iris) J. V. Moules -Jacqueline Olson - Secretary
Wesley Biblical Seminary	S	Jackson, MS	Ray Fasley
Wesley College	S	Florence, MS	Frank Gilmore, Vice President
Wesley Theological Seminary	S	Washington, DC	Chip Aldridge, Director of Seminary Relations
Wesleyan Church	D	Indianapolis, IN	William C. Clark, Archivist -Ronald R. Brannon, General Secretary -Paul W. Thomas, Asst. General Secretary Donna Watson
Wesleyan Church General Department of World Missions	M	Indianapolis, IN	Donna Watson, Asst. Archivist
Wesleyan Seminary Foundation	S	Indianapolis, IN	Kenneth Heer
West Coast Bible College			Louis F. Morgan, Dixon Pentecostal Center (Cleveland,
Western (Conservative Baptist) Seminary	S	Portland, OR	Betty Lu Johnstone, Librarian
Western Baptist College	S	Salem, OR	Marie Zarfas, Administrative Asst. -Jeff James -G.A. Woolsey
Western Theological Seminary	S	Holland, MI	David Andrew, Archivist
Westminster Theological Seminary	S	Philadephia, PA	Ken Rush - Dorothy
Westmont College	S	Santa Barbara, CA	Edwin J. Potts
Wheaton College	S	Wheaton, IL	David B. Malone
William Tyndale College	S	Farmington Hills, MI	Barbara Demerest -Herbert Cocking
Winebrenner Theological Seminary	S	Findlay, OH	Jean Leathers, Archivist
Wisconsin Evangelical Lutheran Synod (World Missions)	D	Milwaukee, WI	James P. Schae -Carl H. Mischke, President - Morton A. Schroeder
Wisconsin Evangelical Lutheran Synod World Missions	M	Milwaukee, WI	Carl H. Mischke
Wisconsin Lutheran Seminary	S	Mequon, WI	Cathy Zell, Librarian -Gerry Kuhnle, Librarian – Byron R. Diring, Library
Word of Life Fellowship	O	Schroon Lake, NY	Paul L. Bubar - Cindy Baker
World Alliance of Reformed Churches	O	Geneva, Switzerland	James I. McCord (Princeton, NJ) -Edmond Perret, General Secretary -Margrethe B.J. Brown -Queenie C. McBride, Specialist (Presbyterian Church, Louisville, KY) – Penny Blachut, Asst. Gen. Secretary
World Council of Churches		Geneva, Switzerland	Richard Olson-Miriam Reidy-Prost-Laurence Diehr Stephanie Kenecht
World Evangelical Fellowship	O	Wheaton, IL	David W. Howard
World Gospel Mission	M	Marion, IN	Burnis H. Bushong
World Harvest Mission	M	Oveland, PA	Michael J. Tannous, Personnel Director
World Indigenous Missions, Inc.	M	New Braunfels, TX	Mark R. Balderson
World Methodist Council/ Museum	O	Lake Junahuska, NC	Joe Hale
World Mission Prayer League	M	Minneapolis, MN	Frances Svenson -Gary Hafvenstein, Administrative Asst.
World Missions Far Corners	M	Long Beach, CA	J. Leornard Bell, President
World Missions Fellowship	M	Oregon City, OR	Evangeline Moore -Bob Minter -George Bradley
World Opportunities	M	Hollywood, CA	Ken Phillips, VP - Roy McKeonan, President
World Radio Missionary Fellowship	M	Colorado Springs, CO	H. Susann Pile, Administrative Asst. -John J. Christiansen, Secretary -Betty Smart, Secretary
World Relief Corporation	M	Wheaton, IL	Jerry Ballard -Billy A. Melvin, Executive Director (National Asociation of Evangelicals)
World Team	M	Warrington, PA	David Melick -G.R. Larcombe -Margy Martin
World Vision, Inc.	M	Monrovia, CA	Melissa A. Lowe, Public Relations Representative -Marcia Whitehead, News and Information Services -Jim Canning
World Wide Missions	M	Redland, CA	Fred M. Johnson
World Witness	M	Greenville, SC	C.R. Beard -John E. Mariner, Executive Director
Worldwide Discipleship Association	M	Fayetteville, GA	Carl W. Wilson
Wycliffe Associates USA	M	Orange, CA	Noelle Dreiling, Communications
Wycliffe Bible Translators USA	M	Orlando, FL	Donnajean Davis, Executive Secretary -Steve Sheldon, Vice President -Nancy C. Bergman, Secretary -Ken B.
Yale University Divinity School	S	New Haven, CT	John F. Utz, Alumni Asst. -Robert Ford, Alumni -Harry B. Adams, Associate Dean -Judith Ann Schiff, Archivist -Benjamin F. Moss, Research -Danelle Moon, Archivist and Reference Manager
Young Life	O	Colorado Springs, CO	Sharon Phillips, Administrative Asst.
Youth for Christ	O	Denver, CO	June Thompson, Administrative Asst. - Earl Schultz
Zion Bible Institute	S	Barrington, RI	Patricia Pickard, Resident Historian

The following organizations were not in the original survey, but we are glad they helped us as well.

Organization	Location	Name
Baptist Union of Australia	Hawthornaust	
Benson Company	Nashville, TN	O.C. Abbott - Laura L. Benson
Bible League	Chicago, IL	
Biblical Evangelist	Murfreesboro, TN	Robert Sumner
Bowdoin College	Brunswick, ME	
Cadle Chapel	Indianapolis, IN	Ruth Wade
Calvary Baptist Church	NY, NY	Victoria Kuhl
Canadian Baptist Archives		Melissa Richer
Christian Life Missions	Wheaton, IL	Donna Hallenbeck
Christian Life Publications	Wheaton, IL	Robert Walker
Congregational Christian Churches	Oak Creek WI	Fred Rennebo
Congress of the US Washington DC		Dan Coats
Disciples of Christian History Society	Nashville, TN	May Reed
East Coast Bible College		Ron D. Martin
Full Gospel Fellowship	Irving, TX	
Harvey Cedars (NJ) Bible Conference		Al Oldham
Hymn Society of America	NY, NY	Deane Edwards
International Aid	Grand Haven, MI	Jim Franks
International Fellowship/EWHA Womans	NY, NY	TI-Yel Park University
Issachar	Lynwood, WA	Jim Moats, President
Jaars	Waxhaw, NC	Harrlette Colvin
Joyful Woman	Chattanooga, TN	Joy Martin
Literacy Int	Tulsa, OK	
Loizeaux Brothers	Neptune, NJ	Marie Lozeaux
Lutheran Bible Translators	Avora, IL	Judith Behiens
Lycoming College	Williamsport, PA	Julia E. Dougherty-Tamara Hutson
MAI	Bloomingdale, IL	Sharyl J. Sieh, Asistant to the President
Mennonite Church USA Historical Society	Goshen, IN	
Missionary Internship		Don Roberts
Moody Monthly	Chicago, IL	Cindy Goucd
Moody Press	Chicago, IL	Ella Windvall - Martha Gomes
New College		Bonnie Johnston
Others		Jim Canning Doreen Macaulay Edgar Winnipeg, Manitoba - Shockley Few, Columbia, SC
Pentecostal Assembly Canada		Marilyn Stroud
Pentecostal Research Center	Cleveland, TN	Carol Wall
Pioneer Bible Translators, Inc		Rondal B. Smith, PhD
Pioneers Sterling, VA		Barbara L. Snyder
Presbyterian Center for Mission Studies	Pasadena, CA	Lary Beckl
Presbyterian Church in Canada		Christina Trasteus
Reformed Presbyterian Church of NA Bd For Missions	Winchester, KS	Robert A. Henrey
Rodeheaver - Hall Mack Co	Winona Lake, IN	Gertrude Dye
Salem Bible College		Calley Kender
Scripture Press		Jim Adair
Speer Family	Nashville, TN	James Blackwood

Springhouse Association	Alexandria, IN	Linda Mason
Sunday School Times	Philladelphia	Philip Howard Jr.
Swiss Evangelical Alliance	Zurich, Switz	Frank Probst
Sword of the Lord	Murfreesburo, TN	Al Byers - Jim R Rice
Tuskegee Institute(AL)		Lelda B. Belton
United Church of Canada/ Victorica		Alex Thompson
University NS		
University of Edinburgh(Scotland)		J. Howard, Librarian
World Wide Pictures	Burbank, CA	Fred Stangl
YMCA of USA	Chicago, ILL	Angela M Hatseras-Jennifer Clayborne-Thorkelson
Zondervan Publishers	Grand Rapids, MI	Al Bryant

Thanks For Information

Last	First	Our Thanks for Information (P=Photo)
Aaron	Thomas L.	(P) Emmanuel College Archives
Abbott	Edward	(P) Reminesces by Lyman Abbott
Abbott	Benjamin V.	(P) Reminceses by Lyman Abbot
Abeel	David	(P) American Missionary Memorial- H.W. Berson
Aberly	John	Sarah Mummert- Wentz Library- LTS- Gettysburg, PA
Abraham	Dezso	Cynthia Csik Sarrazin, (P) Margaret Abraham- Bordentown, NJ
Ackley	Alfred H.	Gertrude Ackley Dye
Ackley	Bentley D.	Gertrude Ackley Dye, Oswald J. Smith- (P) Peoples Mag. Toronto, ONT
Adams	Theodore F.	(P) Baptist World Alliance
Adams	Kenneth R.	Mrs. William Almack- (P) Joe Baker-Lonsdale, PA
Addicks	George B.	(P) Judy Sapko
Addison	Joseph	(P) Bettman Archive
Aglipay	Labayan G.	Dana C. Ignacio - Staff Assistant, PCEC
Agricola	Johann	(P) Martin Luther by H.E. Jacobs
Aldrich	Doris Coffin	(P) Multonomah Schol of Bible-Portland, OR
Alexander	Archibald	(P) Pictorial History Protestants
Alexander	Charles M.	Hazel Thomson, Mrs. Charles Alexander- (P) Autokon 1000 news graphic system-Tewkbury, MA
Alexander	James W.	(P) Revival and Revialism
Alexander	Dixon	Helen Cadbury (P) PTL World Wide News(2)
Allan	George	Margarita Hudspith, Elsie M. Kurzhals(P) Reminiscences-George Allan
Allen	Richard	(P) Autokon 1000 News Graphics System-Tewkbury, MA
Allenby	Edmund H.	(P) Underwood & Underwood, N.Y.
Allin	John M.	(P) Episcopal Church Archives
Allis	Oswald T.	(P) Fabian Bachrach
Allshorn	Florence	(P) Florence Allshorn by Florence Allshorn
Amburgey	Kash	(P) Mrs. Amburgey – So. Lebanon, OH
Anderson	Charles W.	Kay Jaycox (P) Brookdale Baptist Bloomfield, NJ
Anderson	Elmer G.	(P) Nazarene Headquarters
Anderson	Theodore	T.W.A.
Anderson	Harry O.	Susan Hottel, Warren Young, Kenneth Shaffer
Andrews	Charles F.	(P) C. Devashayam (India)
Andrews	Samuel	(P) Cowell and Company, Yale University
Angelico	Fra	(P) Men who have walked with God by Sheldan Chainey
Anglin	Leslie M.	Mrs. Louise H. Rock - "Kid's Alive International"
Ankerberg	Floyd	F.A., Elaine Ankerberg
Appelman	Hyman J.	H.J.A.
Archer	Gleason	Greg Waybright – Bob Krapohl, Library, Trinity Evangelical University
Archer	Glen	Jeff Farmer
Archibald	Byran F.	Helen K. Mainelli - Northern Baptist Theo. Seminary
Arenas	Manuel	(P) Latin American Indian Ministries-Pasadena, CA
Armerding	Carl	(P) Gibson Studios-Chicago, IL
Armerding	George D.	Mary Jane Searle
Armitage	Thomas B.	(P) Pictorial Biog of Spurgeon-Pilgrim Pub-Pasadena, TX
Armour	Philip D.	(P) Life History of the US-Time-Life
Armstrong	Philip E.	P.E.A.(P) Far Eastern Gospel Crusade-Detroit,MI
Armstrong	Hart	Beth Ann Williamson - Christian Communications Intl. (P) Wichita,KS-My Story-Oral Roberts
Arndt	William F.	(P) Concordia Historical Society
Arnup	Jesse H.	Mrs. Hilda Gregorio - "Toronto Star Syndicate"(P) Star News Paper Service-Toronto, ONT
Arthur	William	BK Nussiai Evangafa Ozwald pg 74
Asbury	Francis	Herbert Asbury, John Chilton
Athearn	Walter S.	Stuart A. Johnston, Chris Theofanis, A. Dale Fiers(P) Christian BD of Pub
Atwood	Rudy	YFC Magazine
Auger	Wes	Rockford, ILL YFC
Augsburger	Bryce B.	B.B.A.
Augustine of Canterbury		Ron Jackson

Autrey	C. Elijah	C.E.A., Mrs. Gerry Pepitone - Home Mission Board(P) Division of Evangelism-Dallas,TX
Ayer	William W.	Mrs. Barbara E. Scofield, Victoria Kuhl(P) WA
Aylward	Gladys	(P) Guardians of Great Comission-Ruth Tucker
Azariah	Vedanayagam S.	C & Life Pg. 167
Babson	Roger W.	Don Chun
Bach	Thomas J.	(P) Tract - How I Came to Know Christ
Bacon	Francis	(P) Great Men &Famous Women-VolII
Baedeker	Friedrich W.	(P) They Knew Their God Vol 4-Harvey/Hey
Bagby	William B.	(P) 10 Famous Missionaries-Basil Miller
Baker	Charles F.	Kathy L. Molinkamp (P) Grace Bible College
Baker	Mary Ann	Alfred Epstein (P) Women's Christian Temperance Union
Baker	Edwin G.	Miss L. F. Softley (P) Sec McCullagh Studio,Toronto, ONT
Baker	Herman	Rich Baker(P) David LA Claire
Balfour	Arthur J.	(P) World 460
Ball	Henry C.	(P) Ivah Britt-Garden Grove, CA
Ball	Arthur G.	Mrs. A. G. Ball
Ballantyne	Victor A.	Mrs. Peg Ballantyne(P) Salem,OR
Bandy	Julian A.	Jennifer M. Weller
Baptista	Charles O.	(P) Sunday 5/45 p13
Barber	Walter L.	(P) A Jay Spencer
Barbour	Clifford E.	(P) Pittburgh Perspective, March 1,1960
Barlow	Fred M.	(P) Great Preaching On Soulwinning Vol XIII- Sword of the Lord
Barnard	Russell D.	Gordon Austin, Clyde K. Landrum
Barnes	Milton	Jim Allen
Barnett	Lester (Les)	Larry Hancock, Bill Weston(P) Sacred Record Jacket
Barnhouse	Donald G.	Russell T. Hitt - "Eternity"
Barrett	Harold J.	Loren Anderson
Barrow	Nita	UDFT Magazine, University of Toronto
Barstow	Robbins W.	(P) John Haley, Hartford, CT
Bartlett	George G.	(P) Archives of the Episcopal Church
Barton	George A.	Katherine Barton Platt, Flora Colton, William Manross(P) Mrs. B. Platt-Miami FL
Bast	Henry	(P) Booklet Cover-Romans
Bates	Carl E.	Jean Forbis - (P) Southern Baptist Hist. Library & Archives-TN
Bates	Katherine L.	Jean N. Berry - Wellesley College(P) Wellesley College
Baugh	Helen Duff	Helen A. Nichols - Stonecroft Ministries
Baugher	Norman J.	Howard E. Royer - General Brotherhood Board(P) Church of the Breathren
Bauman	Louis S.	(P) Kramer Photos-Long Beach CA
Bauman	Paul	(P) William and Grace Reeves
Bayly	Joseph T.	(P) J.B. David Cook Publ. Co. -Elgin, IL
Bazar	Kenneth L.	Sally McInvale
Beal	Richard S.	R.S.B., David P. Beal, Mrs. Grace Ellen Haug (P) Stoody Portraits, Tuscon, AZ-Mrs.-1963 ANNN Program
Beam	David J.	Claire H. Beam - Free Gospel Bible Institute
Becker	Elmer	Mrs. Colleen Klepser (P) Rickert
Beckwith	Paul	Katherine Koster Clark, Rev. George Bontekoe(P) Mel Troter Mission Conference Brochure
Beddow	James	LeRoy Newport, Sherry Kuntz - Bonne Terre, MO- (P) Glen H. Hackmaster Jr.- Independence, KA
Beecher	Henry W.	Blanche Gosselin, Aaron Boese
Beecher	Willis J.	(P) Nat Association of American Biography Vol. 16 James White & CO NY, NY
Beets	Henry	(P) Christian Ref. Pbl.House, Grand Rapids, MI
Behnken	John W.	(P) A. H. Schwermann
Bell	George K.A.	(P) Cover-George Beil- Ken Slack
Bennard	George	Mrs. George Bennard, D.J. Neaves
Bennet	James E.	Miss Aune H. Rees
Bennett	John C.	Mrs. Gail Bennet
Bennett	Dennis F.	D.F.B., Kevin Martin, Mrs. R. Bennet, Michael Harper(P) Cover Charisma May 1980
Benson	Robert	Robert Benson, Jr.
Benson	Clarence H.	Harold E. Garner(P) Cover-SS Promoter, May, 1943
Benson	Raymond E.	Mrs. Louvisa Benson(P) Beauerton OR
Bentley	William H.	Mrs. Ruth Bentley(P) Chicago, IL
Bergendorf	Conrad J.I.	(P) Len Brown Studio, ILL Via Augustana cull rock isc
Berkeley	George	(P) Progress of the Protestant pg. 121 John Haverstick
Berkhof	Louis	Mrs. Louis Berkhof

Bernard of Clairvaux		(P) El Greco- Men Who Walked with God- Sheldon Cheney pg 170
Berntsen	William B.	Mrs. Beryl Berntsen
Berquist	Millard J.	Judy Howie - Midwestern Seminary
Berry	Lelwellyn L.	(P) African Methodism
Bertermann	Eugene R.	Rev. Kurt A. Bodling, Rev. Les Kimball
Bhengu	Nicholas B.H.	John M. Lindner
Bickersteth, Sr.	Edward H.	(P) Gospel Hymns p399
Biederwolf	William E.	James Huffman
Bilhorn	Peter P.	G. Herbert Shorney - Hope Publishing Company
Billings	Robert J.	R.J.B. (P) Christian School Action- Washington, DC 20013
Billington	Dallas F.	(P) Unusual Films. BJU- Greenville, SC
Bingham	Roland V.	K.L. (P) Sudan Witness 8/63
Birch	John M.	Edgar C. Bundy, Arnie Smith, Wes Auger(P) Life of John Birch- Kofert Welch
Bitterman	Chester	(P) Mission Frontiers- April 1981
Black	Hugh	(P) Underwood & Underwood Studio - New York, N.Y.
Blackett	George M.	Mrs. Lucy Blackett (P) W. L. West- Regina Sask
Blackwood	Andrew W.	A.W.B. (P) AB-Lakeland, FL
Blake	Eugene C.	Miss Mabel L. Hunt(P) PresbtarianOffice of Inf. - Phill, Penn.
Blanchard	Charles A.	Larry_____, William S. Favata - Wheaton College(P) Modern Secret Societies-1943
Blanchard	Jonathan	(P) Modern Secret Societies- CB
Blegen	Allen R.	Mrs. Frances Blegen, B. Paul Blegen
Bliss	Philip P.	Glenna-Rae Boyd, Leslie B. Flynn
Blumhardt	Johann C.	(P) Mpl Journal Vol II #4, 1980 -Ministers Personal Library, Waco, TX
Boardman Jr.	George	(P) Rays of Light
Bockman	Marcus O.	(P) Luther NW Theo. Sem. Archives- St Paul, MN
Boddie	Charles E.	C.E.B.
Boegner	Marc	(P) Year (1948)
Bonar	Andrew A.	(P) Andrew A.. Bonar- Banner of Truth Trust
Bond	Silas W.	Katherine W. Lindley, Beth Edgar - Wheaton College
Bonhoeffer	Dietrich	John T. Elson
Bonnell	John S.	(P) Dale W. Hansen
Bonner	Winnie	W.B.
Boon	Harold W.	Mrs. Hazel Boon (P) Nyack Miss. College- Nyack, NY
Booth	Ballington	J. McHahon -Vols. of America, Joy Rich -Salvation Army(P) P. Waitwall
Booth	Catherine	(P) Vanderweyde
Booth	William	Gerald Wright, John D. Waldron
Booth	Evangeline C.	(P) General Evangelical Booth - by Whitwall Wilson
Booth	F. Carlton	F.C.B.(P) Fuller Theo. Sem.-Pasadena, CA
Booth	Maude Charlesworth	J. McHahon -Vols. of America, Joy Rich -Salvation Army
Borden	William W.	(P) Borden of Yale- Mrs. Howard Taylor
Boreham	Frank W.	Mary Elizabeth Barram (P) Luggage of Life
Boston	Thomas	(P) Memoirs of Th. Boston- Banner of Truth Trust
Bosworth	Fred F.	(P) Joybringer Bosworth - by Eunice Perkins
Bouma	Clarence	Mrs. Clarence Bouma
Bowen	Arthur J.	Rev. Ezra A. Shank - Africa Evangelical Fellowship
Bowlby	Harry L.	Raymond Edwin Bowlby
Bowman	C.A.	(P) United Theological Seminary
Bowman	Rufus D.	Darlene A. Almon
Boyce (1)	James	Ben Johnston
Boyd	Myron F.	(P) Cox Studio- Warsaw, IND
Bracken	Archie K.	Frances Bracken Yarbrough(P) FBY- Bethany, OK
Bradbury	John W.	Lawrence T. Slaght - The Watchman Examiner (P) WL Program 1949
Bradwell	Marion G.	(P) J. Sumter Bradwell-Atlanta, GA
Brainerd	David	Ted Miller, Malcom Stearns, Jr., James C. Hefley (P) History of Christanity in US- Mark Noll
Brand	Frederick	(P) Schmidt - St. Louis, MO
Branham	William M.	George Butler - "Times"
Brasher	John L.	Don Coughlin - "Times"
Braunlin	Hermann G.	Tina Traster Polak, Dan Kraut, George Sweeting
Bray	Billy	Dorothy C. Haskin(P) -Morgan & Scott- London, Evg
Brentz	Johannes	(P) Martin Luther- by H. E Jacobs
Bresee	Phineas F.	John Chilton - Trevecca Nazarence College

Bretschneider	Albert	Rev. G.K. Zimmerman - N. American Baptist Gen. Con.
Briggs	Eugene S.	(P) Phillips Theological Seminary- Okla City Ok- 1938 YR BK
Brock	Fred R.	Dorothy James (P) Western Baptist (Corban College), Salem OR
Brock	Virgil P.	V.P.B., Mario A. Sahagun, Ronald J. Busch
Broen	Engret M.	(P) Everald Strohm- Fergus Falls, MN
Brondsema	John	Dot Hekman - The Tract League
Bronstein	David	Mrs. Mary H. Bronstein
Brookes	James H.	(P) Great Preaching Vol XVI Curtis Hutson- Sword of the Lord
Broughton	Leonard G.	Louie D. Newton, Vivian Perkins, Edwin B. Peel (P) Talks on Home- LB- Stone Publishers, Roanoke, VA
Brown	Fred F.	Mary E. Tyler - First Baptist Church, Knoxville, TN
Brown	Arlo A.	Mrs. Betty B. Arnold - (P) Drew University
Brown	Arthur J.	(P) United Pres Ch in USA
Brown	Robert R.	Bernard Palmer, Mrs. Jack E. Bishop (P) Omaha Gospel Tabernacle- NB
Brownson	Truman G.	Jean Caspers - Linfield College, McMinnville, OR
Brownville	C. Gordon	Linda T. Hurd - Tremont Temple Baptist Church, Boston, MA
Bruce	Frederick F.	J. Harris - Tyndale House
Bruce	Walter E.	Mrs. Lois L. Bruce(P) Pearl, MS
Brumley	Albert E.	Sharon K. Boles - Albert E. Brumley & Sons
Brushwyler	Vincent	V.B., Mrs. Nan Brushwyler
Bryan	Elmer B.	George W. Bain - Ohio University
Bryan	William J.	(P) Year Inc., Los Angeles, CA (1900-50)
Buchanan	James	(P) H.B. Hall Jr., (Appletons)
Buchman	Frank N. D.	J. Blanton Belk - Moral Re-Armament
Buck-Walsh	Pearl S.	(P) Agip/Pictorial Parade- En BR 74 pg 514
Buckingham	Jamie	J.B. (P) O Happy Day- J.B.
Bugenhagen	Johann	(P) Martin Luther- by H.E. Jacobs
Bull	George	(P) Cranack Engraving
Bullinger	J. Heinrich	(P) Fridericz Roth- Scholtyii- Norimberg
Bunyan	John	Pete Adams, Grace Davis, Leslie Tarr, Tim Christoson
Burke	Daniel	Laton E. Holmgren, John Andersen, Robert T. Taylor
Burkholder	Melvin I.	(P) Huntington (IND) College
Burris	Jackie L.	Mrs. Jackie Burris, Martha Nixon
Burritt	Eldon G.	(P) Greenville College
Burrows	Millar	M.B.
Burtchin	H. Lee	Mrs. Gail McCain
Butler	Charles W.	Mrs. C.W. Butler
Butler	Joseph	(P) London & Sons, Covent Garden, London & NY
Butterfield	Charles E.	(P) NorthEast College Ass. Of God- Kirkland, WA
Buttz	Henry A.	(P) The Christian Advocate- NY
Cadle	E. Howard	E.H.C.(P) Cadle Chapel-Indianapolis, IN
Caird	John	(P) Fundamental Ideas of Christianity
Cairns	John	(P) T&R Annon, Glasgow
Caldwell	Frank H.	F.H.C.
Calvin	John	James C. Hefley (P) Religious Denominations of the World, pg345
Camp	Norman H.	Orva Koenigsberg, John M. Camp - J.M. Camp & Co.
Campbell	Henry D.	A.B. Holm, H.R. Campbell, Grace E. Barth, Lynn David
Campbell,	Thomas	(P) John B. Martin
Cannon, Jr.	James H.	(P) Foster Studio, Richmond, VA
Cantrell	Roy H.	R.H.C.(P) Curtis Studios, Oklahoma City, OK
Carlson	Frank	(P) U.S. Senator Dansa
Carlson	Maurice	(P) Youth Haven Boys Home, Muskegon, MI
Carlson	Paul	(P) Mongola Paul - by Lois Carlson
Carmichael	Amy B.	(P) G.G.Center
Carnell	Edward J.	(P) Juanita Studio- Pasadena, CA
Carrington	W.O.	(P) Funeral Brochure, AME Zion Church, Brooklyn, NY
Carter	Calvin G.	(P) Baptist Century Around the Alamo - by Edith Pegotine
Carter	Ray F.	Marcheta Carter
Cartwright	Peter	James R. Adair
Casserta	Frederick A.	Donna M. Russo, Exec. Director – Kingdom Bound
Catherine of Alexandria		(P) Christ. Hist. Issue 17
Cattell	Everett L.	(P) Malone College, Canton, OH

Cauthern	Baker J.	Rogers M. Smith - Foreign Mission Board of SBC(P) Bapt. Foreign Miss Board- VA
Cavell	Edith	(P) Year, 1950
Cavert	Samuel M.	S.M.C.
Cedarholm	Mryon	(P) Canfields
Cerularius	Michael	(P) Bible and Christianity, pg. 96
Chadwick	Samuel	(P) Pulpit Giants - by Henry James
Chafer	Lewis S.	Ann Crow, John F. Walvoord - Dallas Theo. Seminary(P) H-169
Chalmers	James	Dr. F. Boreham (P) London Missionary Society
Chamberlain	Jacob	(P) Natiional Encyclopedia of America Biography, vol. 35 pg. 300
Chambers	George A.	Mrs. R.C. Spaetzel
Champion	Richard	(P) Pent. Evang.
Chapman	James B.	John Chilton - "Holy Men of God"
Chapman	Vaughn	Mildred Jones, Shoreline, WA (P) Olan Mills
Chapman	J. Wilbur	Thomas A. Christopher - The Christopher Pub. House
Chapman	William A.	Herman A. Chapman, Bill Ackerman(P) The Sower
Chappell	Clovis G.	Gregory Strong, Mrs. Betty Warren - Abingdon Press(P) 1st Meth. Church
Charlesworth	Vernon J.	(P) Pictorial History of Spurgeon - by Bob Ross
Chase	Philander	(P) Some Am. Churches pg 53
Cherry	Floyd	Rudy Owens
Chesser	Hallie L.	Louis F. Morgan - Dixon Pentecostal Research Center
Cheyne	Thomas K.	(P) The Expositor Vol IX
Chisholm	Thomas O.	Ruth C. Blisard, Gertrude Dye
Christiansen	Avis B.	A.B.C., E. Rankin - The Moody Church
Claas	Gerhard	(P) Gen Secretary, Bapt. World Alliance
Clark	Mary	(P) Stonecraft Ministries, Kansas City, MO
Clark	Scott T.	Lois Smith, G. Leppert, Lucy Anderson, Neil Thompson
Clark	Thomas M.	(P) Episcopal Church
Clark	Gordon H.	G.H.C.
Clark	Glenn	R. MacDonald (P) MacAlister College Library, St Paul, MN
Clark	Walter H.	Carolyn Sperl - Hartford Seminary
Clark	A. D.	(P) Allegheny Theological. Seminary
Clarke	George R.	G.R.C.
Clarke	Adam	John Chilton - "holy men of God"
Clayton	Norman J.	Barbara Fulforth(P) Sydney R. Kanter, Pittsfield, Mass.
Clearwaters	Richard V.	R.V.C.(P) Zinzmasters Studios, Minneapolis, MN
Climenhaga	Arthur M.	Messiah College, Grantham, PA
Clippinger	Arthur R.	(P) Hist Soc.-EUB Church, Dayton, OH
Coder	S. Maxwell	Walter Osborn - Moody Bible Institute
Coe	Jack	Gordon Lindsay - (P) Herald of Healing, Dallas, TX
Coerper	Heinrich	Michael S. Galley - (P) Liebenzell USA Global Ministries
Cohn	Joseph H.	Clemence Earle, Rev. Daniel Fuchs
Cohn	Leopold	(P) Chosen People Ministries
Coke	Thomas	Peter W. Gentry
Colwell	Ernest C.	(P) New York Times pg 32
Confer	Bernhard	Barbara C. Johnson - Lutheran World Relief
Conwell	Russell H.	Robert Wescott
Cook	David C.	(P) Cook Publications, Colorado Springs, CO
Cook	George H.	Walter A. Quigg - St. Paul's United Methodist Church
Cook	J. Hubert	(P) Evangelical Union of South America, Anglewood, NJ
Cook	John H. W.	Carol Meyer, Elna M. Cook
Cook	Robert A.	Dr. Roy McKeown, R.B. "Jack" Turney
Cook	Gaines M.	(P) International Convention of Christian Churches, Indianapolis, IN
Cook, III	David C.	Mrs. A.W. Henning
Cooper	Clay	Eloise Eubanks
Corlett	Lewis T.	Carolyn Steele
Correll	D. Sidney	D.S.C.
Cory	Victor E.	Mrs. Ferne S. Larson, Mrs. Margaret Winkelmann(P) Scripture Press Pub., Wheaton, IL
Couchman	Gaylord	Janet Metelak - Westminster Pres Church – Myers Lib. – Un. Of Dubuque
Coughlin	James	BJ Singer, Public Dir., CSB
Coutts	Frederick	(Major) Andrew S. Miller - (P) Salvation Army, London, England
Cowen	Charles E.	Glenn D. McClure

Cowman	Charles M.	(P) Charles E. Cowman - by Mrs. L. Cowman
Cowman	Leticia Burd	Frances Black, Mervin Russell - World Gospel Crusades
Cox	Bonnie L.	(P) The Gospel Messenger Vol 52 #9
Cox	Winifred R.	Mrs. Geneva C. Temple
Coxe	Arthur C.	(P) ECBH
Craig	Robert J.	(P) Bethany Bible College, Scotts Valley, CA
Cram	Willard G.	(P) NWD Collection pg 34
Crannell	Philip W.	Mrs. Florence Crannell Means
Crawford	Lois	Ruth Keller - Boone Biblical Ministries(P) KFGQ Book Store Boone, NC
Crawford	Daniel	HCY, Akron, OH (P) Thinking Black - by D.C.
Crawford	Ruth Duvall	Donald B. Crawford - Crawford Broadcasting Company
Crichton	James B.	(P) Margaret Crighton-Germantown, TN
Crosby	Thomas	(P) The People Magazine-Canada
Crosby	Frances J.	Leslie K. Tarr, Martha Trotzke(P) D-27
Crowell	Henry C.	(P) Breakfast Table Autocrat - by R.E. Day
Crowell	Henry P.	Rev. Richard Ellsworth Day, D.D. (P) Breakfast Table Autocrat - by R.E. Day
Crowell	Elton	Mrs. Elton Crowell, Neil Fichthorn
Crowell	Grace Noll	Reid Crowell
Crowley	Dale S.	Mrs. Ruth E. Crowley
Crowley	Mary Carter	Beverly LaHaye (P) Home Interiors, Dallas, TX
Csehy	Wilmos	Gladys Csehy
Cummings	Kenneth	K.C., Mrs. Wanda Cummings Vincent(P) Conservative Baptist Foreign Missions Society, Portland, OR
Cunningham	Robert W.	Kara Lyons - Nazarene Archives Clerk
Cunningham	Fred	(P) Mrs. Fred Cunningham- Aurora, MO
Cunningham	Robert C.	(P) Assemblies of God, Sprigfield, Missouri
Currie	Thomas W.	Bill Brock, Robert M. Shelton - Austin Pres. Theo. Sem., (P) University Studio
Currie	William E.	(P) American Messianic Fellowship, Chicago, IL
Cuyler	Theodore L.	(P) Kings of the Platform, pg 369
D'Albret	Jeanne	(P) FFF
Dahlberg	Edwin T.	E.T.D., Samuel R. Binch - Delmar Baptist Church(P) CrozerTheological Seminary, Chester, PA
Dahlquist	Lloyd W.	(P) Varde Studio
Dale	James G.	Mrs. Lois J. Combs, John T. Dale - UFM International
Darbee	Lennard	Mrs. Ruth Darbee
Darby	John N.	(P) The Bible Collector #6
Davidson	Richard	Marjorie Macdonald - United Church of Canada
Davidson	Benjamin	George B. Davidson, Charles W. Chamberlin (P) Christian Life Magazine - September 1948
Davies	W. Elwyn	W.E.D., G. Ronald Slade - Bible Christian Union
Davis	Joseph A.	William T. Wiley, Andrea Schmidt - (S.A.I.M.)
Davis	Ozora S.	(P) Chicago Theo Sem.
Davis	Ralph T.	Mrs. Ellen O. Nixon
Davis	Raymond J.	Albert H. TerMeer - (P) Sudan Interior Mission, New York, NY
Davis	George T. B.	Debbie Thompson, Raymond C. Oramd
De Armond	Lizzie	Ruth Crissey
De Haan	Richard	Barton Deiters - Grand Rapids Press
De Haan	Martin R.	Leona Hertel - Radio Bible Class
Deal	Elmer G.	Ralph Deal (P) Schiavone Studio, Kalamazoo, MI
Dean	John T.	(P) Ann Dean- Jenison, MI
Dean	Horace F.	J. Borco - Philadelphia College of Bible
Decker	Rutherford L.	R.L.D.
Deir	Costa	Howard Stone
Demaray	C. Dorr	Donald Demaray- Wilmore, KY
DeMoss	Arthur S.	Mrs. Arthur S. Demoss, Jean Ann Pate - TennesseTemple Schools, Chattanooga, TN
Denman	Harry	H.D., Lou Dozier
Denney	James	(P) T&R Aman, Glasgow
Dennis	Clyde H.	Geoffry Dennis, Carl F.H. Henry, Dorothy Boggess
Dibelius	Otto K.	(P) Year, 1956
Dick	Otto E.	David Krogh
Dick	Walter	Marci Backlin
Dickhaut	John W.	Kevin L. Smith - Methodist Theological School in Ohio
Dickson	Lillian Levescente	M. D. Tank, J. Dickson, L. Nightingale, W. Barbour, Jr.
Diefendorfer	John G.	(P) Year, 1960

Diffendorfer	Ralph E.	(P) Methodist Prints - by R. Rickarby
Dillon	William S.	Mildred Dillon, Bill Dillon, Jr. (P) New Tribes Mission, Rivergrove IL
Disraeli	Benjamin	(P) World Year 1958
Doane	George W.	(P) Some American. Churchman pg 65
Dobbie	William	(P) A Very Present Help
Doddridge	Philip	(P) Awake My Soul
Dodds	Gilbert L. "Gil"	(P) Huntington College, Huntington, IL
Donaghue	Charles C.	Helen Donaghue
Donnelson	Fred	Dannah Andrews - Baptist Bible Fellowship International
Douglas	John E.	(P) World Missionary Evangelism
Douglas	Lloyd C.	(P) Bible and Christianity - by Baldwin Ward
Doyle	Bertram W.	N. Charles Thomas - General Board of Personnel Services
Drum	Woodrow	(P) Rich Dupont – Librarian, Emmanuel College, Franklin Springs, GA
Drummund	Henry	(P) Henry Drummond - by James Kennedy
Du Plessis	David J.	D.J.D.
Duggar	John W.	(P) Mrs. Jn Duggar- Little Rock, AR
Dulles	John F.	(P) Year, 1953
Dunn	Bruce	B.D.
Dunn	R. Willard	(P) Wayne Dunn- Lexington, NC
Durkin	James F.	John Gordon
Dzao	Timothy S. K.	T.S.K.D.
Eby	Enoch	(P) CU of BR
Eddings	Van V.	V.V.E., Alvin F. Lewis
Edman	V. Raymond	V.R.E., Earle E. Cairns - Mennonite Service Program (P) News Bureau- Wheaton (IL) College
Edsall	Samuel C.	(P) E.L. Sheppard, Minneapolis, MN
Edwards	David	(P) Life of Bishop Edwards - by Lewis Davis
Edwards, Jr.	Jonathan	Oren M. Watts
Ehlert	Mack C.	Doug Roeglin - Rio Grande Bible Institute
Ekberg	Einar	Brigit Dickerman, Veryl Hawes - Duluth (MN) Gospel Tabernacle
Ekings	Frank P.	Mrs. Marjorie Ekings Gorton, Thomas G. Clark
Elizabeth	Queen	(P) Zucchero, Hatfield House, England
Elliot	Jim	Mrs. Elisabeth Elliot
Elliott	Harrison S.	(P) Union Theo. Sem., New York, NY
Elliott	Paul F.	(P) Owosso (MI) College
Ellis	Franklin T.	Ruth T.
Ellyson	Edgar P.	Carolyn Davis
Emmons	Curt	Mrs. Curt Emmons
Empie	Paul C.	(P) National Lutheran Council
Engelhardt	David	Nancy W. Haynes, CRC
Epp	Theodore H.	T.H.E.
Erdman	Charles R.	(P) Orren Jack Turner, Princeton (NJ) Theological Seminary
Erickson	Clarence	Mrs. Clarence Erickson
Erickson	Harold W.	H.W.E., Stanley W. Olson, M.D. - (P) First Evang Free Church, Rockford IL
Ernst	August F.	(P) Wells Institute Journal
Ernst	Henry	Mr. Wiederaenders
Erny	Eugene A.	Miss Hilda Johnecheck - Orental Missionary Society
Errett	Isaac	(P) Discipliana
Estabrook	Lizzie S. Tourjee	Wilma R. Slaight - Wellesley College
Estep	Howard C.	Mrs. Marian F. Estep
Etter	Harold C.	Harold Etter, Jr.(P) S Surrey, BC Canada
Evans	William	(P) MBI of Chicago, IL
Evans	Milton G.	Stephen M. Reynolds - Crozer Theological Seminary
Evans	James	Richard M. Elam
Evans, Sr.	Louis H.	Kevin Evans, Jr.
Fakkema	Mark	M.F., Mrs. Harold L. Shelton, Adrian DeVos
Falkenberg	Donald R.	D.R.F., J. Falkenberg(P) Orlando, FL
Farmer	Blake	(P) Viola Holder
Fehsenfeld, Jr.	Del	Lynda Keese, Joe Tower - Life Action Ministries
Feinberg	Charles L.	Frances B. Older
Fenn	William P.	Joseph A. Sprunger
Fenton	Ferrar	S. Campbell - Destiny Publishers

Ferrin	Howard W.	(P) Barrington (RI) College
Field	E.P.	David Wilson – Open Air Campaigners
Fife	Eric S.	Barbara & Bryan Stickland, Irene Kemis(P) Joan File-Bradenton, FL Inter-Varsity, Chicago, IL
Filkin	W. Warren	(P) Maranantha, Muskegon, MI
Finney	Charles G.	Leslie K. Tarr, Lewis A. Drummond
Fisher	George S.	R.J. Reinmiller - Gospel Missionary Union(P) Boch of Barfoot
Fisk	Franklin W.	(P) Chicago Seminary Quarterly, July 1901
Fisk	George	Mary Epp, Wayne D. Weber
Fitzwater	Perry B.	(P) MBI of Chicago, IL
Fleming	Paul W.	Hildur J. Fleming, Mrs. Cherrill Fleming Northey
Fletcher	John W.	(P) Life of John Fletcher - by Joseph Benson (I. Jackson)
Flexon	Richard G.	Vanessa Whittle - God's Bible School & College
Flora	Delbert	(P) Ashland (OH) Theological Seminary
Fontaine	Tony	(P) Christian Life
Force	Maynard	Rev. Roy F. Kibler III - Lutheran Bible Institute
Forrest	Richard A.	Alice L. Barnes(P) Kelly Barnes, Toccoa Falls, GA
Forrester	James	(P) Gordon Devil. Dept.,Wenham, Mass.
Fortunato	Frank	(P) Lorraine Montanari- Woodbridge,VA
Foster	Richard	(P) Linda Davis – Biblical Ministries Worldwide
Fowle	James L.	Henry A. Henegar - Psychological Studies Institute
Fowler	Charles H.	(P) Neeleys Parliament of Religion, pg 967
Fowler	Frederick C.	F.C.F., Miss Anna-Marie Hett(P) Gallagher's Studio, Duluth, Min.
Francis of Assisi		Derek Hagland
Frank	Graham	Nell G. Gammon - Central Christian Church
Franklin	Garland	Roy Hodson - SMMM
Franks	James E.	Clarence Poel
Franson	Frederick	(P) Frederick Franson - by O.C. Graver
Frazer	James O.	(P) Behind the Ranges - by Mrs. Howard Taylor
Frazer	James G.	(P) Bible and Christianity, Year Inc, New York, NY
Frederick	Paul W. H.	(P) Region 2 Archives Evan. Luth. Church in America
Freed	Paul E.	P.E.F.(P) Trans World Radio Vol 18, No. 1 – Linda Sink
Freed	Ralph	Dick Olsen, Archives
Friederich	Paul	(P) Cranbrook Photo
Frost	Henry W.	H.W.F.
Fry	Franklin C.	Margaret Duhme - Lutheran Church in America(P) Commistion on Press, Radio & TV, NY
Fuchida	Mitsuo	Rich Shannon - Agape House Ministries
Fuerbringer	Alfred O.	(P) Edrvyn Portrait
Fuerbringer	Ludwig	(P) Concordia Historical Institute, St. Louis, MO
Fuller	Andrew	Baptist History
Fuller	David O.	D.O.F., Tom Fitzgerald
Fuller	Charles E.	C.E.F., P. Lenderman, D.P. Fuller, D. Miller, N. Rohrer
Funkhouser	George A.	(P) Bonebrake Theo. Sem. Bulletin XXIII No. 3
Gaebelein	Frank E.	(P) Christianity Today
Gambrell	James B.	(P) EBCH John Ellerton
Gapp	Solomon H.	(P) Egert, Bethlehem, PA
Garland	Fred	Louis Arnold
Garman	Wilfred O. H.	W.G., David Otis Fuller - Wealthy Street Baptist Church
Gartenhaus	Jacob	J.G., Mrs. Lillian Gartenhaus
Gaston	William T.	(P) Assembly of God Missions
Gaulke	Maxwell R.	Elizabeth A. Cox - Mid-America Bible College
Geddie	John	(P) Christian Biography Resources
Gee	Donald	D.G.
Geiger	Kenneth E.	(P) Your Worship Hour
George V		(P) Year-World 461
Gerig	Jared	(P) Clippinger Photography, Fort Wayne, IN
Gesswein	Armin	A.G.
Gettys	Ebenezer	John E. Mariner - World Witness
Gifford	Frank	David Siegenthaler, Epis. Div. School Archives – Craig Maynard
Gih	Andrew	Mrs. Rose Wang - Holy Word Children's Home (P) Century Photographers, Singapore
Gilkey	James G.	Francis R. Daugherty - Evang. & Reformed Hist. Society
Gilpin	John R.	John R. Gilpin, Jr.

Gingrich	Joseph L.	Cindy Trott
Glasse	James	Richard D. Berg, Landcaster Theo. School Archivist
Glenn	Lewis	Stanley E. Glenn
Glenn	Victor V.	Stanley E. Glenn, J.B. Peyton - (P) Evangelistic Faith Missions Inc., Bedford, IN
Glover	Robert H.	Florence G. Morrison
Goforth	Jonathan	D. Marvin, R. Ransom, E. Harrison, B. DeRemer
Gomez	Walter	El Roy Ratzlaff - MMM
Goodspeed	Edgar	(P) University of Chicago
Gordon	Charles W.	Marjorie Macdonald - United Church of Canada
Gordon	Samuel D.	Cora M. Weber - Ohio-West Virginia Area Council
Gordon	Ben	Howard Pierucki - Gull Lake Bible & Missionary Conf.
Goudie	Samuel	Ward Shantz, R.S. Reilly - United Missionary Society
Graber	Joseph D.	(P) Mennonite Board of Missions Collection, Goshen, IN
Graffam	Everett S.	Richard Alderman, W. Watson - Lancaster Presbyterian
Graham	Eugene	Lois Graham
Grant	Fred C.	(P) The Witness, February 4, 1932
Graves	Harold K.	Kathy Lee(P) Golden Gate Bapt. Church Sem, CA
Graves	Arthur H.	A.H.G. (P) New York Times
Graves	Allen W.	A.W.G., Mr. Deering (P) Golden Gate Theological Baptist Seminary, Mill Valley, CA
Graves	Harold K.	(P) Church of God Youth, Anderson, IN
Gray	Albert F.	Dan Jones - Otto F. Linn Library
Gray	George Z.	(P) Pach Bros., Cambridge, MA
Gray	James M.	(P) Moody Bible Institute - Bern Dekema
Grebel	Conrad	(P) Conrad Grebel, Son of Zurich - by John L. Ruth
Green	Keith	Betty Daffin - (P) Last Days Ministries
Greene	Elizabeth (Betty)	Helen Kooman Hosier (P) MAF- Photo Catalog
Gregory of Tours		(P) World pg 113
Gremmels	Charles E.	C.E.G., Miss G.L. Gremmels
Grenfell	George	(P) H. Coles, Watford, England
Grenfell	Wilfred T.	W.T.G.
Griffin	Herbert M.	Ivan Allbrutt (P) Moody Monthly
Griffith	Earle G.	Mrs. Louis Griffith Howell
Griffith	Glenn	John R. Brewer - WHAC
Grose	Howard	(P) Sarah H. Hanson, Archives Univ. of South Dakota
Grossmann	Walter	Rev. Bob Grossmann(P) Vermillion, SD
Groton	William M.	(P) Gutekun
Grubb	Norman P.	N.P.G.
Gruber	Franklin L.	Barry C. Hopkins, JKM Library, Chicago
Gullerud	Carl M.	(P) David Lau-Eau Claire, WV
Gullixson	Thaddeus F.	Valbarg E. Bestul, Paul Daniels - ELCA Region 3
Gupta	Paul	Chrystal Searcy - HBI Global Partners
Hagedorn	Ivan H.	Mrs. Catherine M. Hagedorm
Hagin	Ken	(P) Charisma, August 1985
Hagstrom	G. Arvid	Mrs. G. Arvid Hagstrom
Haight	Grace Woodman	Jennifer Sackett, Mary Shamblin - Bob Jones University
Hall	Granville S.	Dorothy E. Mosakowski - Clark University
Halleen	Erick A.	Elizabeth Hermanson - Evang. Free Church of America
Hallock	Gerhard B. F.	Miss Adelia Hallock, June E. Russell
Halvarson	Hilding	Trudy Halvarson
Halverson	Richard C.	R.C.H.
Ham	Mordecai F.	M.A. Buffington, R. Ham, V. Hancock, J. Truelove
Hamblen	Stuart	Lisa Hamblen Jaserie
Hamilton	Raymond F.	Miss Marianne Baltonsperger - GARBC
Hammarskjold	Dag	(P) Encyclopedia Britannica, 1960
Hammontree	Homer A.	Gerald L. Raquet, Rev. George Bontekoe
Han	Kyung Chik	Y.E. Nah - World Vision, Korea
Handel	George F.	(P) Denner
Hanes	Leonard	Gordon Johnson(P) Helen Hanes-Edingurg, TX
Harder	Waldo	(P) Grace University, Omaha, NE Catalog
Harkness	Georgia E.	G.E.H., Eileen M. Weston - Pacific School of Religion
Harms	Oliver	(P) Paul Ockrassa, St. Louis, MO

Harner	Nevin	(P) Lancaster (PA) Theological Seminary Bulletin, October 1951
Harper	Redd	R.H.
Harris	Charles U.	(P) Kathleen Kordesh, United Library
Harris	Thoro	Ruby Bailey - Circuit & Chancery Courts
Harrison	Benjamin	(P) Appletons
Harrison	Doyle	Gary DeVoe - Faith Christian Fellowship International
Hart	Edward	(P) Gould, Saratoga Springs, NY
Harwood, Sr.	Carl C.	Carl Harwood, Jr., Karen Tuinsta, Ruby Renstrom (P) Brandon, FL
Havens	George	Mrs. George Havens
Havergal	Frances Ridley	Ruth Tietje
Havner	Vance H.	James M. Robertson - CPA (P) Flynt Studios, Greensboro, NC
Hawkins	Mont E.	Agnes Hawkins, R.G. Hamman, D.D.
Hayden	Perry	Betty Sprunger
Haymaker	Willis G.	Agnes Scroggs
Hays	L. Brooks	Carole McCloskey
Head	Elrod D.	Paige Patterson - Southwestern Baptist Theo. Seminary
Heard	R. Dennis	R.D.H.
Heaton	Adrian	(P) California Baptist Theological Seminary, Covina, CA
Hedberg	George E.	Louise Rock - Kid's Alive International
Heeden	Olaf	David Pevelich, Regenstein Library, Univ. of Chicago – Diana L. Magnusson
Hegre	Theodore A.	T.A.H., Linda Foster - Bethany Fellowship International
Helms	Edgar	(P) The Good Will Man - by Beatrice Plum
Helser	Albert D.	A.D.H. (P) Orlin Kohli, Wheaton, IL
Henry	Carl	(P) Fabian Bachrach
Heroo	Leonard W.	(P) Zion Bible Institute, Providence, RI
Herring	Joseph	Barbara O'Brian, Archivist, McDaniel College
Herron, Jr.	Stephen D.	Bob Triplett - (P) Hobe Sound (FL) Bible College Brochure
Hess	W. Robert	Lucy Anderson
Heydt	Henry J.	Colleen A. Watson - Lancaster Bible College
Hill	Clairborne M.	Arthur L. Foster
Hill	Samuel F.	(P) They Stood Every Man In His Place
Hillis	Dick	(P) Overssees Crusades Brochurc, Palo Alto, CA
Hines	John E.	(P) Gittings, Dallas, TX
Hirt	Oscar H.	O.H.H., Phyllis Rast, Kent _____
Hitchcock	Benjamin F.	Eldon Hitchcock(P) Colorado Springs, CO
Hitt	Russell T.	R.T.H., Ron Wilson
Hobbs	Herschel H.	H.H.H., Bill Sumners - The Historical Commission
Hodges	Sloan S.	Tyrone S. Pitts - Baptist Convention, Inc.
Hoekesma	Homer C.	(P) Protestant Reformed Seminary- Granville, MI
Hoge	Moses D.	(P) Foster, Richmond, VA
Holdcraft	J. Gordon	J.G.H.
Holmes	Nicholas J.	Carol A. Bush - Holmes Bible College
Holt	Harry	Laura Lucas, Mrs. Bertha Holt
Holwerda	Carl	C.H., Marilyn Holwerda, Kenneth E. Floyd
Holyoke	Edward	E.H.
Homer	Cyril E.	Mrs. Ruth B. Homer
Honda	Koji	Kenny Joseph
Honeycutt	Roy	Christ Dewease, Archives, Southern Bapt. Theo. Seminary
Hoover	Herbert C.	Frank E. Mason
Hoover	J. Edgar	J.E.H., Helen W. Gandy (P) Encyclopedia Britannica, 1973
Hornshuh	Fred L.	Mrs. Carlson (P) Eugene (OR) Bible College
Hoskins	Fermin L.	(P) Mrs. Gladys Calvert, J. Ralph Pfister
Hostetter, Jr.	Christian N.	Henry Hostetter
Hottell	William S.	W.S.H. (P) Drapkin
Hough	Lynn H.	Mark C. Shenise
Houghton	Frank	F.H., Sandra Barnes
Howard, Jr.	Philip E.	H. Trumbull Howard, P.E.H., Jr.
Howard, Sr	Philip E.	P.E.H., Jr.
Howell	Rees	(P) Decision Magazine
Huarte	Mertel N.	(P) Latin American Lutheran Mission
Hubbard	David A.	D.A.H.

Huber	Lucas C.	Gail Hodel
Huffman	Jasper A.	J.A.H., Diane Norris - Missionary Church (P) Lowell Blosser, Warsaw, IN
Huffman	Nyles G.	Mrs. Nyles G. Huffman
Hughes	Andrew W.	(P) New York Times, New York, NY
Hull	James R.	(P) Fabian Bachrach
Humberd	Russell I.	R.I.H., Mrs. R.I. Humberd
Hummel	Karl D.	K.D.H., Jeane Olson
Humphrey	Heman	(P) Illustrated Book of All Religions
Hurlburt	Charles E.	Sidney Langford - Africa Inland Mission
Huss	John	Tom Rhodes
Hutchens	Paul	P.H., Bernard Palmer, Ken Anderson
Hutchings	Eric A.	E.H., George Bartram
Hutson	Curtis	(P) Sword of the Lord
Hyles	Jack F.	J.F.H., R. Anderson, E. McKinney, V. Linkletter, K. Thomas
Ignatius		(P) Schoenfield Collection from Three Lions
Iske	Lucy Turner	Linda Hilyard (P) Holiday, FL
Jackson	Doss N.	I.K. Cross - Baptist Sunday School Committee (P) Sam Fausett, Conway, AR
Jackson	Paul R.	P.R.J.
Jacobs	Charles M.	John A. Kaufmann - Lutheran Theological Seminary
Jacobson	John	Lauri Thetheway, Jeffrey D. Reynolds, Joint Archives of Holland
Jaffray	Robert A.	Arni Shareski, H. Robert Cowles, Alda E. Gruley
Janzen	Abraham E.	A.E.J.
Jarvis	Fred D.	Stanley Runnels - New Life League International
Jeffrey	James N.	Mrs. Frances W. Jeffry
Jepson	N. Alvin	Margaret L. Jepson
Johnson	David H.	D.H.J.
Johnson	Merle (Mel)	M.J., Mrs. Janet Johnson
Johnson	Torrey M.	Norma Collins
Jones	Clarence W.	C.W.J.
Jones	Rufus	Marshall Macaluso, R. Miller - Mission to the Americans
Jones	Samuel P.	J. Roy Reasonover, Miss Fairy Shappard
Jones	John D.	J.D.J.
Jones	James A.	Eleanor R. Millard
Jones	E. Stanley	(P) Methodist Prints
Jones, Jr.	Bob	Pauline Rupp, John R. Rice (P) Photographic Studios, BJU, Greenville, SC
Jones, Sr.	Bob	Harry Ward, Pauline Rupp - Bob Jones University
Jonswold	Olav M.	Gordon Johsword
Jordan	Eugene	E.J.
Jordan	William H.	(P) Phillip Kramer, Patten Library, Faith Bapt. Bible College (P) Drinkwater
Jowett	John H.	(P) Drinkwater
Joy	Vincent	Dr. Crandall, Jack Sailor - E.N.D.
Judd	Leo	(P) History of Christian Church Vol. VII - by Philip Schaff
Judd	Walter H.	W.H.J.
Judson	Adoniram	William Nigel Kerr
Kai-Shek	Chiang	James Shen - Govt. Info. Center, Republic of China
Katterjohn	Aurther	Keith Call, Special Collections, Wheaton College
Keiller	James A.	(P) Print, H&W Studios, Atlanta, GA
Kelly	Howard A.	Robert Westcott
Kelly	Thomas R.	Diana F. Peterson, Haverford, PA
Kennedy	Gerald H.	G.H.K., Mrs. Timothy Hancock
Kerr	Hugh T.	(P) Presbyterian Historical Society
Kerr	Phil T.	Mrs. Phil Kerr, Grace Ramont - Christian Etude
Ketcham	Robert T.	R.T.K.
Keysor	Charles W.	Kathleen Demaray - Asbury Theological Seminary
Killman	J. Russell	J.R.K.
Kimura	Henry J.	(P) Henry Kimura - by Moto Kichi Haseqawa
King	Joseph H.	Joseph A. Synan, Mrs. J.H. King
King, Jr.	Martin Luther	Scott McNeil - Southern Christian Leadership Conference (P)
Kinnaird	Mary J.	Ronald F.S. Hills - Bible & Medical Missionary Flwship.
Kirkendall	Chester	(P) Mapel Kirkendall- Jackson, TN
Kitto	John	(P) Illustrated History of the Bible - by John Kitto (H.W. Smith, T.B. Templeton)

Klapstin	Harvey C.	(P) Flint Studio, Eugene, OR
Kligerman	Aaron G.	(P) Presbyterian Board of National Missions
Knight	John L.	(P) Jack Rabbit Company, Spartanburg, SC
Knighton	Ray	Margie Shealy – Christian Medical Association, Bristol, TN
Knox	John	James C. Hefley, Billy Vick Bartlett, Johnn M. Linch
Knudson	Kent	(P) Lutheran Standard, April 12, 1973
Konkel	Wilbur S.	Arlene Konkel (P) Westminstier, CO
Kramer	Charles	(P) Union Theological Seminary, Richmond, VA
Kraft	James L.	Paul E. Chandler - Kraft Foods (P) Kraft Booklet, Saron Inc. - Chicago
Krauth	Charles Philip	(P) Lutherans in America - by Wolf
Kresge	Stanley S.	S.S.K., Mrs. Laura I. McMullin
Kronquest	Max R.	Vanita Kronquest(P) Palmer, Alaska
Kuhn	William	Rev. Martin L. Leuschner
Kuhn	Isobel S. Miller	Michael Jones
Kuhnle	William E.	Mrs. Edna Kuhnle
Kuyper	Henry J.	(P) Christian Reformed Publishing House
Kunz	Alfred A.	A.A.K.
Kunzman	Jacob	(P) Pacific Theo. Sem., Seattle, WA
La Vastida	Bartholomew G.	E. Thoman, Ruth La Vastida, Patrick Arnold, Bro. Melick
Lacy	Floyd H.	F.H.L.
Ladd	George E.	Nancy Goller, Asst. Archivist, Fuller Theo. Seminary
Laird	Harold S.	Mrs. Betty M. Laird, Robert Laird Harris
Lakin	Bascom R.	B.R.L.
Lambie	Thomas A.	Mrs. Irma Lambie
Lambuth	W.R.	(P) Thuss, Nashville, TN
Lamson	Bryron	(P) Cox Studio, Warsaw, IN
Landis	Morris D.	John P. Ludwig, Jr. - United Christian Church (P) Cleona, PA
Langford	Thomas A.	Reed Criswell
Langford	Sidney	S.L.
Langmade	Nye J.	(P) Winfrey - Vane Studio, St. Louis, MO
Lamphier	J.C.	(P) America's Great Revival
Larson	Reuben E.	(P) M. Wengerow Fotografo
Latham	Lance B.	Mrs. Virginia Latham, Dave Breese, Eileen Depner (P) Bolber, Chicago, IL
Lathan	Robert	(P) Marion- Chester, SC
Latimer	Samuel W.	Carol Wall - Pentecostal Research Center
Laurin	Roy L.	Robert B. Laurin (P) Ted Miller Studio, Los Angeles, CA
Lee	Witness	John Pester
Lee	Robert G.	R.G.L., Jerry Fallwell
Legters	Leonard L.	Cal Hibbard, Mrs. Beverly M. O'Brien - (P) Wycliffe Bible Translators, Santa Anna, CA
Lehman	Louis P.	L.P.L.
Lenski	Richard C. H.	Mrs. E.H. Lenski, Willard G. Books - Capital University
Leslie	John D.	(P) Mrs. Mary G. Lane - Historical Foundation, Montrcc, NC
LeTourneau	Robert G.	R.G.T., Richard, Roy, & Shirley LeTourneau, N. Yoder
Lewis	Auther	Dwaine Lind, Bethel College
Lewis	Gayle F.	Eileen F. Kuepfer, Carl G. Conner
Lewis	Clive S.	Wendy Collins, Carolyn K.
Lewis	Clifford	Marvin Lewis - GFA Missions
Lillenas	Haldor	Mrs. Lola Lillenas
Lincoln	Abraham	Mark Lenderman (P) M. P. Rice
Lindberg	Milton B.	M.B.L. (P) Maxheim Photo, Des Moines, IA
Lindquist	C. Reuben	Jim Lindquist
Lindsay	T. Gordon	(P) Christ for the Nations
Lindquist	Frank J.	J. McCabe - Central Bible College
Lindstrom	Paul	Mike McHugh
Lintz	J. McCormick	(P) Bob Jones University, Greenville, SC
Lockridge	Shadrach M.	(P) Calvary Baptist Ch- San Diego, Cal
Lockyer, Sr.	Herbert	H.L.
Loes	Harry D.	Mrs. Gertrude Draves - Moody Bible Institute
Lofton	Bernhard M.	(P) Bible Missionary Brochure
Lohrenz	Henry W.	Mrs. Mariana Lohrenz Remple
Long	Henry J.	H.J.L.

Lorimer	George C.	(P) The Galillean
Loveless	Wendell P.	W.P.L. (P) Irving Rosen, Honolulu, HI
Lubbers	Irwin J.	(P) Feiler Studio, Des Moines, IA
Luckey	James S.	Mary E. Bennett (P) Man of the Hour = by Erma Thomas
Lundmark	G. Alfred	Mrs. Ruth L. Wiener
Lundquist	Carl H.	(P) Peterson Portraits, Minneapolis, MN
Luther	Katrina	(P) Cranach
Luttrell	Donald D.	Ruth Luttrell
Lyons	Noel	Don Brugmann - Greater Europe Mission
MacArtney	Clarence E.	Albert Noble McCartney
MacAulay	Joseph C.	J.C.M. (P) Victor Aziz, London, ONT
MacAulay	Neil	N.M., Marth Nixon, Pat
MacDonald	Walter R.	Don M. Rabe, David Otis Fuller
Machen	J. Gresham	Edmund P. Clowney - Westminster Theological Seminary (P) J.G. Machen - by Ned Stonehouse
MacKay	Joy	Nancy Walker – Pioneer Clubs, Wheaton, IL – Wine Press Pub., Mukilteo, WA
Maddry	Charles E.	Miss Nell Stanley - Foreign Mission Board of the SBC (P) Foster Studio
Mahood	J. Wilmot	Jennifer Spencer, Tyndale University
Malof	Basil	Ben Wilkerson - Russian Bible Society
Malone	J. Walter	Lucy Anderson
Mann	Frank E.	Gayle Cameron(P) Niles, MI
Manning	Ernest	(P) Alberta Govt. Photo, Edmonton, ALB
Markham	Oscar C.	Carlene Farmer - KY Virtual Library
Marquart	W. Edward	Sandy Marquart(P) Glenrock, WY
Marshall	LeSourd	Catherine Wood, C.M.L. (P) Tom McKay
Marsen	Leslie	(P) Cox Studio, Warsaw, IN
Martin	I. G.	I.G.M.
Martin	Walter R.	Hendrik Hanegraaff, Raymond F. Smith
Martyn	Henry	Justin M. Hall
Matthews	Mark	David Lepse
Maurus	Rabanus	(P) Gospel in Hymns - by Albert Bailey
Mason	Joe	Don Summer, Prison Mission Associate
Massee	J.C.	(P) Pioneers in Righteousness - by J.C.M.
Mathews	Basil	(P) Diana Yount, Archives, Andover Newton Theo. Seminary
Matthews	William A.	Dr. Austel
Maxwell	Leslie E.	Paul Maxwell, Tim MacKenzie
Mayes	Henry B.	(P) Catherine Mayes- Middlesboro,KY
McAfee	Cleland B.	Miss Myrtle M. Clemmer - United Presb. Church (USA)
McCaba	Joseph	Fred Herzog
McCarrell	William R. (Billy)	Miss Alice Osborne - Christian Work Center
McCarter	Neely	Russ Schoch, Pacific School of Religion
McCheyne	Robert M.	J.D. Douglas, Bernard R. DeRemer, Don Weber
McClurkan	James O.	John Chilton - "holy men of old"
McConkey	James H.	Louise Harrison McCraw - Braille Circulating Library, Inc.
McConn	William F.	Marjorie J. Elder, John D. Mack (P) Yonohope Photo Studio, Lakeland, FL
McConnell	Lela G.	Beth duff Boggs
McCracken	Robert J.	Emily Deeter - Riverside Church
McCully	Theo E.	(P) Christian Business Men's Committee, Lombard, IL
McDaniel	William R.	McGarvey Ice – Disciples of Christ Hist. Soc.
McDormand	Thomas B.	Winnie Bodden, Vaughn Library, Acadia University
McGee	J. Vernon	Ridgely Ryan - Thru the Bible Radio (P) Witzel Studio, Los Angeles, CA
McGinlay	James	Rev. James McGinlay (son)
McGlothlin	William S.	William C. Martin, American Baptist College, Nashville, TN
McKee	Arthur W.	Mrs. A.W. McKee
McKee	Dean G.	Eleanor Soler(P) Mrs. Dean McKee- Decator, GA
McKibbin	William	Mary E. Hagemann - Lane Theological Seminary
McKnight	Donald	D.M.
McKnight	Robert J.	(P) Covenanter Ministers
McKoy	Charles F.	C.F.M. (P) Nisin, Jerusalem
McLeish	James	J.M.
McMillan	John	David W. Kraeuter - U. Grant Miller Library
McNairn	A. Stuart	J. Hubert Cook - Evangelical Union of South America

McPheeters	Julian C.	(P) Lafayette Studio, Lexington, KY
Meade	Russell J.	(P) Jeanna Wilson
McPherson	Aimme Semple	R. McPherson - Int'l Church of the Foursquare Gospel (P) Angeleno Photo Service, Los Angeles, CA
Meadows	Clyde W.	C.W.M., Mrs. Jane E. Mason, Steve Dennie(P) Mrs. C. Meadows, Columbus, OH
Mears	Henrietta C.	Mrs. Marian Morris, Cyrus N. Nelson - Light Publications
Meck	Allen S.	Dianne Russell – Evangelical and Reformed Historical Society
Mekeel	Herbert S.	Michael R. Alford - First Presbyterian Church (P) Costas Studio, Schenectady, NY
Meyer	John P. C.	J. Daniels - St. Marks
Meyer	Walter	Steve Meyer(P) Tremont, IL
Midura	Edward	Mrs. Alice Midura
Miles	George A.	Barbara Sherr - Washington Bible College
Miller	Orie O.	O.O.M., Mary Elizabeth Lutz
Miller	Adam W.	Doug Welch
Miller	Basil W.	Esther Miller Howard - World-Wide Missions
Miller	Gareth B.	Joseph E. Richter
Miller	Hugh	J.F. Miller
Miller	James R.	J.F.Miller
Milliken	William T.	Audrey Arnst - Western Seminary
Mills	Howard T.	H.T.M.
Mitchell	Hubert	H.M. (P) Edward Fox, Chicago, IL
Mitchell	John G.	Irene Scruggs
Mitzner	Herman D	.H.D.M.
Montanus	Ralph J.	R.M., Miss Joy Hoffleit
Moody	Dwight L.	Stanley N. Gundry - Moody Bible Institute
Moon	Charlotte (Lottie)	Catherine B. Allen
Moon	Irwin A.	Miss Jane Schrock
Mooneyham	W. S. Stan	W.S.M.
Moore	A. B. T.	Alanna Young
Moore	Arthur J.	(P) J. F. Knox
Moore	Mark	(P) Jan Greathouse, Trevecca Naz. University
Moore	Richard V.	Dr. Henderson
Moore	T. Albert	(P) Lord's Day Alliance Publication
Morgan	J.P.	(P) Life History, Vol. VII
Morris	Samuel	Warren Lewis - Taylor University, Fort Wayne, IN (P) March of Faith - by Lindley Baldwin
Morrison	Henry C.	Dr. Stanger, Franklin D. Morrison
Morrison	John A.	Mrs. J.A. Morrison
Moseley	Thomas	Mrs. Thomas Moseley (P) Missionary Training Institute, Nyack, NY
Moss	Elza	Sue Wilkinson(P) Sissonville, WV
Mott	John R.	Peter E. Bock
Mott	Edward	Bernard E. Mott, Sr., I.E. Pike, Estalene Harned
Moyer	Robert L.	Mrs. M. June Jenings - Northwestern College, Minneapolis, MN
Mueller	Reuben H.	Mrs. Jean Pickett
Muhlenberg	Frederick H.C.	(P) America Vol. III
Mullinax	R.C.	(P) Central Weslyan College
Mumaw	Levi	(P) Phoebe Mumaw Kolb Collection Archives, Mennonite Church, Goshen, IN
Mummart	Clarence A.	(P) Library, Huntington (IN) College
Munsay	William	(P) Sword of the Lord
Muntz	J. Palmer	J.P.M., Carole Sizemore - Cazenovia Park Baptist
Murray	Andrew	Rindi Bowman, Roy N. Davey - Africa Evang. Fellowship
Musgrave	Walter E.	(P) Rickert Studio, Huntington, IN
Musser	Irvin W.	I.W.M., Henry N. Hostetter
Myer	Tressie V.	Linda Kunz
Myers	Paul	Ella Miller, Val Hellikson - Haven of Rest (P) Victor Baldwin, Beverly Hills, CA
Nagel	Charles F. K.	Kay Raftery, Virginia Nagel Bridgman(P) Bryn Manor, PA
Naylor	Robert E.	Cory J. Hailey
Nee	Watchman	Peter D. Smith, C. McKinneay
Needham	Harold	Pam Crenshaw, Archivist, Vanguard University (P) Vanguard University Publication
Neighbor	Robert E. (Ralph)	David W. Holden - "The Granary"
Nelson	Franklin O.	Donald E. Anderson - "The Standard"
Nelson	Peter C.	Paul Nelson
Nelson	Reuben E.	Mrs. Patricia Schlosser (P) Black Stone Studio, New York, NY

Nettleton	David	D.N., Jeff Gates
Neuberg	Frank J.	R. Turek (P) Wealthy Street Church Bulletin, Grand Rapics, MI
Neve	Juregen L.	John W. Rilling - (P) Wittenberg University
Nevius	John L.	(P) Princely Men - by Harlan Beach
Newell	Harriet W.	(P) Anne Judson Biography
Newton	John	Mike Piazza, Jean Vail Jackson, Ruth Hollander
Nicholson	Martha Snell	Muriel Dennis
Nicholson	Roy S.	R.S.N.
Niemoeller	Martin	M.N.
Norris	J. Frank	Robert A. Allen, Steve Saunders
Norris	Stuart G.	Gerald Grant - Apostolic Bible Institute
Northrup	George	(P) University of Chicago Library
Norwood	G. Hunter	Mrs. Edith B. Norwood(P) Sam Daneday 1983
Nigren	Anders	Helen Putsman Penet
O'Hair	John C.	Paul R. Franzen - North Shore Church (P) Northshore Church Booklet
Ochino	Bernardino	(P) History of the Christian Church Vol. VII
Ockenga	Harold J.	H.J.O.
Oda	Kano	(P) Free Methodist
Ohlson	Algoth	Bill Lundberg - First Covenant Church
Oldham	Earl K.	(P) Arlington (TX) Baptist Schools Catalog
Oliver	Ernest W.	E.W.O., Mrs. Margaret Oliver(P) St Albans, Eng., Joe Conley(P) Deerfield Beach, FL
Olsen	Wes	(P) Carole Dibble – W.O.
Olsen	Arnold T.	(P) Evangelical Free Church, Minneapolis, MN
Orr	J. Edwin	J.E.O.
Orsborn	Albert W. T.	(Major) Andrew S. Miller - Salvation Army
Ost	Axel B.	(P) March Sumer 1985
Ost	Daniel K.	Linda West - Missionary Revival Crusade
Ost	John	Barbara English
Overbey	Hafford H.	Dave Parks(P) Lexington, KY
Overholtzer	J. Irvin	Mrs. Overholtzer, Jacob DeBruin, Jr.
Owens	James C.	Paul Neimark
Oxnam	B. Garfield	(P) Life, Vol. XII
Page	John I.	Don Englund - Kansas City College & Bible School
Paine	Stephen	(P) Roland Studio, Friendship, NY
Palmer	George A.	(P) Paul Palmer- Elkton, MD Booklet
Pannamaker	Ray	(P) Bethel College, Michawaka, IN
Parker	Franklin N.	Robert Woodruff Library – Emory Univ., Atlanta, GA
Parker	Joseph	(P) Ernest H. Mills, London, (Preachers I Have Know - by Alexander Grammie
Parker	J. Monroe	Amy J. Walton - Baptist World Mission
Parsons	Robert	Walter Osborn - Moody Bible Institute
Paton	John G.	F.W. Boreham, Clint Sauder
Patterson	Alfred L.	Randy Cloud - American Baptist Association
Patterson	Samuel C.	Stephanie Hartley, Mrs. Rogers (P) Reformed Theological Seminary, Jackson, MS
Paul	Thomas E.	(P) BD Missions-Ev Cong Ch.-Shillington, PA
Paulo	Karl S.	Rebecca Martha McKinley (P) Lela McConnell Biography
Paulson	Theodore M.	(P) M. Paulson- Stoughton, SA, CA
Paxson	Ruth A.	Le Mardred Brushwood
Paxson	Stephen	Jim Gerhart - American Missionary Fellowship (P) A.M. Markley, Philadelphia, PA
Payne	J. Barton	Mrs. Dorothy Payne Wood
Peabody	George	(P) Appletons, New York, NY
Peachey	Mark	(P) Fannie Peachey- Irwin, OH
Peale	Norman V.	N.V.P.
Pearce	William	Florence Taylor, Bob Conner
Pearsall	Kenneth H.	(P) Ruby Pearsall- Nampa, ID
Peck	John M.	(P) Heroes of the Cross in America - by Don Shelton
Pedigo	Ray T.	Rev. Joe Weigend - Missions to Japan, Inc. (P) Adventures in Faith, Campbell, CA
Penney	James C.	Mrs. Eva McLaughlin
Percy	John O. (Jack)	Mrs. Marilyn J. Percy-Sebring, FL , J. Joseph Charles
Perkin	Noel O.	Christine Carmichael - Gen. Council of Assem. of God (P) Foreign Mission Dept. AOG, Sprinfield, MO
Perritt	R. T.	Mrs. Betty Perritt(P) Clinton, OK
Perrowne	Edward H.	(P) Corpus Gallery

Peters	John L.	Pam Glyckherr - World Neighbors
Pethrus	P. Lewi	Bill Lundberg, M.E. Nelson - Philadelphia Church
Petrie	Auther	Patty McGarvey, CMA Archives
Pettaway	Caleb D.	Marvin C. Griffin - Ebenezer Baptist Church
Petticord	Paul P.	P.P.P.
Pettingill	William L.	R. Showers, W. Woods, J. Borgard, C.E. Mason, Jr. (P) J. George Nussbaumer, Buffalo, NY
Pfeiffer	Charles F.	John Beauregard - Gordon College
Phelps	Austin	Diana Yount - Andover Newton Theological School
Phelps	John W.	Mrs. Grace Lumm, Charlotte Brooks
Phillips	Frank C.	Ken F. Phillips (P) World Vision Magazine
Phillips	William T.	R.E. Harris
Philpot	Ford R.	L. Ernest Otter (P) Lafayette Studio, Lexington, KY
Philpott	Peter	(P) Mel Trotter Mission Flyer
Pierce	Robert W.	B.P.
Pierson	Arthur T.	William B. Bynum
Pietsch	William E.	Timothy Pietsch, Bro. Foxwell
Pink	Arthur W.	Mr.& Mrs. C. Pressel, I. C. Herendeen
Place	Lester	(P) Shaner Studio, Pottsdown, PA
Playfair	Guy W.	Jean Playfair, Esther L. Hutchings, Joyce M. Playfair
Poole	George J.	Margrett Poole (P) HCJB Catalog
Pope	Liston	L.P.
Popov	Harlan	H.D.
Porter	Ford	F.D., Robert Ford Porter - Lifegate
Powell	Robert	(P) GARB Fellowship
Preston	Ann	(P) An Irish Saint - by Helen Bingham
Pretlove	Harold B.	Mrs. Leona M. Pretlove
Price	Eugenia	E.P.
Price	John M.	(P) Southwestern Baptist Seminary, Fort Worth, TX
Princell	J. G.	Ellen Engseth, North Park College, Chicago
Pudney	Edwin J.	Dorothy Pudney
Pyatt	Charles L.	Walt Johnson - Lexington Theological Seminary
Quamina	James V.	Ted Smith - Fund. Baptist Msn. of Trinidad & Tobago
Rader	Paul D.	P.R., Eileen Lightfoot, Robert Shuster
Rainy	Robert	(P) Life of Principal Rainy - by P.C. Simpson
Ramabai	Pandita S.	Marian Bishop Bower (P) Devotees of Christ - by D.S. Batley
Ramsey	James	(P) J. Magee, Del - T. Sinclair, Lith.
Ramseyer	Joseph E.	Tillman Habegger
Rand	William W.	(P) Intelligincer
Raud	Ganz P.	Kenneth M. Jones, Ruth R. Rexon (P) Maurice Lehn, Brooklyn, NY
Raws	Addison C.	Ruth Lockhart - Americ
Raws	William	Ruth Lockhart - America's Keswick
Ray	Percy	Gerald Primm(P) Greensboro, NC
Rayburn	Robert G.	R.G.R.
Read	O. J.	O.J.R., Mrs. O.J. Read
Reade	Thaddeus	(P) Taylor Univ. Archives, Upland, IN
Reahm	Duane	(P) United Brethren, September 1981
Redal	Reuben H.	Michael Adams, Faith Evang. Luther. Sem. President
Rediger	Christian E.	Donald W. Roth - Evangelical Mennonite Church
Redpath	Alan	Evelyn Rankin
Reed	A. Brant	May Reedv
Reed	Harold W.	H.W.R.
Reed	William E.	Robert L. Coffman - Anderson College
Rees	Seth C.	P.S.R., Mrs. Lucile Sheehan - World Vision, Inc.
Rees	Paul S.	R.S.R., Mrs. Florence Santor
Reim	Edmund C.	Dr. Lau (P) Lutheran Spokesman, October 1969
Reveal	Ernest	(P) Olive Studio, Evansville, IN
Rhee	Syngman	(P) Year, 1948
Rice	John R.	J.R.R., Viola Walden, Timothy Reitsch (P) Unusual Films, BJU, Greenville, SC
Rice, Sr.	William	B.R. (P) Funeral Brochure
Richard I		(P) Histroy of the Crusades
Richardson	Harry V.	Cathy Lynn Mundale - Atlanta University Center

Ridderhof	Joy F. C.	Marguerite G. Carter - (P) Gospel Recording, Inc., Los Angeles, CA
Ridley	John G.	J.G.R., Ruby Burke, Keith Williams, O.C. Abbott
Riggs	Ralph	(P) Mignard, Springfield, MO (Assembly of God)
Riley	William B.	W. Bersten, A. Russell, S.E. Anderson, F.G. Kordick
Rimmer	Harry	Mrs. Mignou B. Rimmer
Ritz	Gale	Jean Leathers - Churches of God, Gen. Conf.
Roberts	Verne D.	Mrs. Jacquelin M. Fowler
Roberts	Walter N.	Mrs. Marjorie Roberts
Rockness	Morris	(P) Ann Rockness- Centerville,MA
Roe	W. Douglas	Mrs. Natalie Roe
Rogers	Dale Evans	John Mark, Alanna Young
Roloff	Lester	L.R., Alfred Edge, W.B. Cameron, W.P. Clements, Jr. (P) Roloff Evang. Enterprises, Corpus Christie, TX
Rondthaler	Edward	Bobbie H. Blackburn
Rood	Paul W.	Don B. Rood -The Pocket Testament League, Inc.
Rooks	Albertus J.	Dr. Richard H. Harms
Rosell	Merve	M.R.
Rossi	Anthony T.	Sharon K. Weaver - The Aurora Foundation
Roth	Paul	(P) Paul Daniels ELCA Region III Archives, St. Paul, Minnesota
Rudd	Judson	(P) Bryan University, Dayton, TN Catalog
Ruelke	Winfield F.	Vi Gommer(P) Sweet Vavey, PA
Ruscoe	Alfred W.	A.W.R.
Rust	Eric C.	Bill Sumner - SBC Archives
Sa'eed	Muallah M.	Jeanette Hoffner, Lorena Hyneck - Zwemer Institute
Saint	Laurence	(P) Von Trotts, Philadelphia, PA
Saint	Nate	Steve Saint
Saint	Rachel B.	R.B.S., H. Susann Pile, Roy, Edith, & Barbie Gleason
Saint	Phil	P.S.
Sanders	Harlan	(P) Testimony Tract
Saulnier	Harry G.	A.J. Vander Meulen
Savage	Henry H.	H.H.S.
Savage	James (Jim)	J.A.S.
Savage	Kenzy	Patsy Jenks, Rio Rancho, NM
Savage	Robert C.	Wilda Z. Savage
Sawatsky	Rodney	Messiah College, Grantham, PA
Scarborough	Lee	(P) Reid, Fort Worth, TX
Schlatter	Michael	(P) Bill Schlatter- Defiance, OH
Schofield	Jack P.	Miss Mary D. Cannon - Home Mission Board
Schultz	Earle	E.S., Mrs. Barbara Schultz, Wendy Collins
Schultze	Henry	Dr. Richard H. Harms
Scott	Eugene C.	E.C.S.
Scott	William M.	M.G. Miles - Florida State Primitive Baptist Convention (P) James Photo
Scudder	Ida S.	Dorothy Clarke Wilson
Seaborg	Glen E.	G.E.S.
Seagrave	Gordon	(P) Burma Surgeon = by G.S.
Scheon	E.W.	(P) Engraved Butlers EST, Philadelphia, PA
Selassie	Haile	B. Hughes - Embassy of Ethiopia
Shakarian	Demos	D.S.
Shane	Samuel	(P) Presbyterian Office Inc., Philadelphia, PA
Shank	Ezra A.	E.A.S.
Shaw	Benjamin G.	Mrs. B. Earlene Morgan, W. J. Walls
Shelly	Anthony S.	John D. Thiesen - Mennonite Library & Archives
Shelton	Leroy	Sharon Frolek
Shepherd	Coulson	C.S.
Sherrill	Lewis J.	Ernest N. White, Helen H. Sherrill
Shidler	Donald P.	D.P.S.
Shires	Henry M.	Richard Helmer - Church Divinity School of the Pacific
Shooks-Jensen	Bertha T.	B.T.S., "Mr. Charlie" Vandermeer - Children's Bible Hour (P) CBH Memorial
Shufelt	J. Stratton	Mrs. Marjory Shufelt
Shuler	Jack	J.S., Mrs. Ruth Shuler (P) Shuler Crusade Brochure, Grand Rapids, MI
Shultz	Frank	Wayne H. Ritchie (P) Galillean Baptist Mission calendar, Grand Rapids, MI
Schulz	Charles	(P) Associated Press

Shuman	Harry M.	Dori Lynn Nason, Nathan Bailey - C. M. Alliance
Sightler	Harold B.	(P) Ervin Dorn, Greenville, SC
Sisco	Gordon H.	(P) Randolph MacDonald Eatons
Skinner	Howard	H.S., Mrs. Ada Rupp Skinner
Skinner	Thomas	T.S. (P) Black and Free - by Archie Marston
Slade	H.C.	(P) American Counsel of Churches Booklet
Smart	John	Mrs. Fay Smart
Smick	Elmer B.	E.B.S., Freeman Barton - (P) Gordon-Conwell Theological Seminary, South Hamilton, MA
Smith	Everett	(P) American Bible Society Archives – Roy Lloyd – Kristin Miller
Smith	Walter	Wayne Weber, Billy Graham Archives
Smith	Wilbur M.	W.M.S.
Smith	Samuel R.	Dori I. Steckbeck
Smith	Oswald J.	O.J.S., Paul B. Smith
Smith	James H.	Mrs. Janet Smith, Earl W. Schultz - YFC/USA
Smith	J. Taylor	(P) Lafayette
Smith	Gordon H.	G.H.S.
Smith	George A.	G.A.S. (P) G.A.S. = by Lillean Smith
Smith	Frank W.	Dennis M. Schmidt - Open Bible College
Smith	Henry	(P) Gabriel Moultin Studio, San Francisco, CA
Smith	Paul B.	P.B.S., Jack McAllister, Don White, Mrs. D. Drinkwater
Smith	Rodney (Gypsy)	Stuart Conrad
Snead	Alfred C.	Mrs. Alfred C. Snead
Snyder	Melvin H.	Paul W. Thomas - Wesleyan Church
Snyder	William T.	Irene Leaman, Marilyn Langeman (P) George Martin
Spaugh	R. Gordon	(P) Flying Fotos
Speer	Robert E.	(P) United Presbyterian Church of USA
Spencer	Ivan Q.	Tery Guckenbihl - Elim Bible Institute
Spencer	Tim	Dale Bruner, Hal Spencer, Cy Jackson, Ken Phillips
Spener	Philip	(P) An Encyclopedia of the Lutheran Church, Vol. III - J. Boedensick
Sperry	Willard L.	Sandra Yenolemtz, Mr. Holden - Harvard Univ. Archives
Spicer	Charles	(P) Bobbi S. Graves, Greenwood, IN
Spring	Worthy A.	Mrs. Maxine Spring Jones, Lucy Anerson
Spurgeon	Charles H.	Earl Miller - Baptist Evangel (P) 20 Centuries of Great Preaching, Vol. VI - Pinson
Spurling	Thurl	Jennifer Pierce
Stagg	Amos A.	Stella R. Stagg, Mrs. Ann Colley
Stam	Cornelius R.	(P) Berean Society Magazine
Stam	Jacob	Gene Jordan
Stam	John C.	Theodore W. Engstrom, Ivan Allbrut
Stamps	Virgil	(P) Favorite Radio Songs, SB Music Convention
Stanphill	Ira	(P) Hymntime Harmonies
Staten	Walter	(P) Norma Staten- South Point, OH
Stearns	Daniel M.	Elber W. Stearns, Jr.(P) Kinnelon, NJ
Stebbins	George	Dick Weiss
Stedelbauer	Elliott	(P) CBMC, Chicago, IL
Stedman	C. Ray	Bro. Stedman
Steiner	Edward	(P) Scheryl Neubert, Asst. Archivist, Grinnell College
Steiner	Leonhard	Marianne Kafer-Steiner, Jakob Zopfi
Stevens	Maurice	Beverly Stevens(P) Nicholasville, KY
Stevens	Charles H.	Roger L. Barnes - George M. Manuel Memorial Library
Stewart	Lyman	Sue Whitehead
Stiles	Marjorie Scoville	Eric & Marileen Parsons
Stillwell	Harry E.	Janet Holmes, Miss E. Harlow, Mrs. Keith Daniel
Stilwell	Albert H.	Marilyn Starn, Susan M. Panak - Spring Arbor University
Stone	Barton W.	B.W.S.
Stone	John T.	Norman Swenson, J. W. McCracken
Stonehouse	Ned B.	Mrs. Margaret R. Stonehouse (P) Presbyterian Guardian, Philadelphia, PA
Strachan	Harry	Molly P. Fahringer, Mary Anne Klein - L.A.M.
Strachan	Ken	(P) Latin America Mission, Bogota, NJ
Straton	John R.	Robert H. Straton - Calvary Baptist Church
Strauser	Charles E.	Simeon Strauser - Full Gospel Assemblies International
Strohm	George D.	Joseph C. Wenninger(P) Ev Erald Strohm- Fergus Falls, MN (P) St. Paul Bible Institute Catalog

Strong	William M.	T.L. Thompson, L. Woodward, H. Shedd, N. Eggleton – William Strong, Jr
Stroud	Jimmy	(P) Westminster Films Photo, Pasadena, CA
Stuart	George R.	(P) G.R.S - by W.W. Pinson
Studd	Charles T.	Mrs. Dorothy Barclay, Norman P. Grubb
Stump	Joseph	M. JoAnn Jergenson
Sturk	L.W.	(P) Weslyan Church Headquarters
Suckau	Cornelius H.	Mrs. Edna Suckau Gustner
Sumrall	Lester F.	L.F.S., Helen K. Hosier - LeSEA Broadcasting
Sunday	William A. (Billy)	W.T. Ellis, R. Allen, R. Shuster, I.S. Yeaworth, Jr.
Surbrook	Walter L.	W.L.S.
Sutcliffe	Bernard B.	Willard M. Aldrich - Multnomah School of the Bible (P) Moody Monthly, September 1948
Swanson	Everett F.	E.F.S., Mrs. Miriam Swanson, Miss Pat Milligan
Swing	David	(P) Neelys Parliaments of Religions - by Walter Hughton
Synan	Joseph A.	J.A.S., Carol Synan
Tait	Archibald	(P) Victorian Church in Decline - by T.P. Marsh
Taft	Charles P.	C.P.T., Avis E. Harvey - Sherrill Resource Center
Talbot	Louis T.	L.T.T., Mrs. I.P. Bruechert - the Bible Institute of L.A.
Tapper	William	John Tapper
Taylor	James B.	(P) International Mission Board SBC, Richmond, VA
Taylor	J. Hudson	Samuel H. Chao, Mark Galli, Daniel H. Bays
Taylor	Clyde W.	C.W.T.
Taylor	G.W.	(P) Emmanuel College Archives
Taylor	John L.	Peg Hughes - Andover Historical Society
Taylor	Paul	(P) Cox Studio, Warsaw, IN
Taylor	Walter	Harry G. Saulnier - PGM, Jim Adair - PGM
Teegarden	Kenneth	(P) Christian Church, Indianapolis, IN
Telford	Andrew	(P) William A. Painter, Philadelphia, PA
Tenney	Merrill C.	M.C.T., Mrs. Mina G. Hill - (P) News Bureau, Wheaton (IL) College
Tennyson	Alfred Lloyd	(P) British Information Services, New York, NY
Terrell	Gail	Caroline Terrell
Tharp	Zeno C.	Z.C.T. (P) Church of God, Cleveland, TN
Thomas	Carey S.	Randall B. Kemp
Thomas	Elver C.	Mrs. E.C. Thomas, Linda Redman
Thomas	Paul W.	Lee Haines
Thompson	Elmer V.	E.V.T.
Thompson	William P.	Edna Sinnock, Presbyterian Church (USA) Info Services
Thorton	Leo M.	Dick Votaw
Tomhave	Duane K.	Mrs. Kaye Eckert - WELS
Tomlinson	Ambrose J.	Homer A. Tomlinson (P) Stanfield Studio, Cleveland, TN
Tomlinson	Homer A.	H.A.T., Mrs. H.A. Tomlinson (P) Church of God, Queensville, NY
Tomlinson	Milton A.	Perry Gillum
Torrey	Frank C.	Mrs. Lucille Torrey, Eric G. Crichton
Torrey	Rueben A.	Paul W. Schwepker - Biola College
Tovey	Herbert G.	A. Lawrence Marshburn - Biola University
Townsend	W. Cameron	Elaine Townsend, Bernie May, Harold H. Key
Tozer	Aiden W.	David R. Enlow - Christian Business Men's Comm. Int'l (P) A.W.T., 20th Century Prophey - by David Fant
Traber	Bessie	(P) Christian Life Magazine, November 1946
Trasher	Lillian H.	Christine Carmichael
Trimble	Henry B.	Elizabeth Royer - Theology Library (P) News Bureau, Emory University, Atlanta, GA
Trotman	Dawson E.	Lila Trotman
Trotter	Melvin E.	Bernard R. DeRemer
Trueblood	D. Elton	D.E.T. (P) Ralph Pyle, Richmond, IN
Truett	George W.	Melton Wright, Daniel G. Pulliam, Lynn E. May, Jr.
Trumbull	Charles G.	(P) C.G.T. - by Philip Howard
Trutza	Peter	George A. Festian - Romanian Missionary Society
Tubman	William S.	(P) Camera Press - Pictorial Parade
Tucker	Henry S. G.	(P) Church Historical Society
Tuinstra	Kenneth	(P) Daren Tuinstra- Ashland, KY
Tyler	Herbert R.	H.R.T.
Tyndale	William	Brian Money, Mary Wrucke
Uchimura	Kanzo	Elizabeth Cannon Smith - Amherst College

Unger	Merrill	J.D. Pentecost
Ursinus	Zacharias	(P) Pictorial of Protestants
Valentine	Milton	(P) W. H. Tipton
Van Gilder	Heber O.	Mrs. Lois Van Gilder (P) Western Baptist Bible College, El Cerrito, CA
Van Til	Cornelius	Grace Mullen - (P) Westminster Theological Seminary, Philadelphia, PA
VanBroekhoven	Harold	Rollin A. Van Broekhoven
Vandall	Napolean B.	Robert A. Vandall
Van Der Puy	Abe	(P) Back to the Bible, Lincoln, Nebraska
VanKampen	Robert C.	Wendy Collins
Vaughn	C.J.	(P) Kingsbury & Notcutt, Knightsbridge, South Wales
Vaus	Jim	Mary E. Craig
Vereide	Abraham	Mrs. Katherine M. Bowen
Vick	G. Beachamp	A.V. Henderson - Temple Baptist Church
Voekel	Harold	(P) World Vision Library, Monrovia, CA
Vins	Georgi	(P) Evangelical Baptist Churches in Soviet Union, Elkhart, IN
Voliva	Wilbur G.	Carl Q. Lee - The Christian Catholic Church
Von Blomberg	Martha L. Moenich	M.L.V.B.
Voskuyl	Roger	Nancy Tonn
Voth	Heinrich	Kevin Enns - Center for Mennonite Brethren Studies
Wadsworth	Ernest M.	Mrs. E.M. Wadsworth
Wagler	Elmer	(P) Rober Wagler- Tifton, GA
Wagner	Donald M.	Marcia Fuena (P) Great River Publisher, Bemidji, MI
Wagner	Edmund F.	(P) American Bible Society
Wagner	Glenn	Armond Ternak
Wahlstrom	Jarl	John R. Larsen - The Salvation Army
Walker	J.H.	(P) Church of God, Cleveland, TN
Wallace	Grace	(P) Mary Thompson - Intervarsity
Wallace	Louis	(P) Ben Hur - by L.W.
Warner	David S.	(P) Echo, 1924
Wallenius	Carl	(P) Kathleen Kordesh, United Library, Evanston, IL
Walls	William J.	W.J.W.
Waltner	Orlando	John D. Thiesen
Walton	W. Spencer	John Beauregard - Gordon College
Ward	C. M.	C.M.W., Terry Darden - Assemblies of God Archives
Wardner	Nathan	Mrs. Betty C. LaPlante
Warner	Ira D.	Ada May Warner, John H. Hess, Jr.
Warner	George R.	G.R.W. (P) World Gospel Mission, Marion, IN
Washburn	Henry B.	Bradford Washburn - Museum of Science
Washington	George	Frank D. McKay (P) Stuart Girsch, Appletons
Waterbury	Lucy McGill	Harold T. Commons
Waters	Ethel	(P) To Me Its Wonderful - by E.W.
Watson	Austin	A.W.
Watson	C. Hoyt	C.H.W. (P) Roland Studios, Seattle, WA
Watson	William T.	Robert W. Watson, Carolyn S. Miller
Watts	Isaac	Denis Applebee - World Gospel Mission
Weber	Charles	(P) Church of God, Anderson, IN
Webster	Daniel	(P) Whipple Engraving = by W. G. Jackman
Webster	George	Shirley LaForest
Weigle	Charles F.	C.F.W., Donald W. Smith, Mrs. Octavia M. Sullivan
Weiss	Benjamin	(P) Family and Freedom Digest
Weiss	G. Christian	G.C.W. (P) Edholm & Blomgren, Lincoln, NB
Welmers	Thomas E.	Judy Hilbelink - Northwestern College
Weniger	Arno Q.	(P) Hamilton Square Bapti. CH. San Francisco, CA
Wescott	Brook	(P) Elliot & Fry
White	Paul H.	P.H.W., Mrs Ruth White, R. Burrows, Heather Valentine
White	Alma Birdell	Arthur White - Pillar of Fire (P) Looking Back From Beulah - by A.W.
White	Kenneth O.	(P) Simme Studio
White	Wilbert W.	Gerald W. Gillette - The Presbyterian Historical Society (P) New York Theological Seminary, New York, NY
Whitefield	George	T.P. Weber, C. Mitchell, M. Wright, J. Hefley, B. Bartlett
Whittaker	Frederick W.	Larry Lamond - Bangor Theological Seminary
Whittemore	Emma	(P) Jerry McCauley - by R.M. Offord

Wichers	Wyand	Willard C. Wichers - The Netherlands Museum
Wickberg	Eric	E.W.
Wickey	Gould	(P) Brooks
Widmeyer	Charles B.	Mrs. Dorothy S. Widmeyer
Wieand	Albert C.	Cassel B. Wieand (P) Gospel Messanger
Wiley	H. Orton	Robert C. Woodward
Wilkes	A. Paget	Joseph H. Liversidge - Japan Evangelistic Band
Williams	Smallwood	Mrs. Arthurene S. Foxx
Williams	Roy T.	R.T. Williams, Jr. - Pasadena College
Williams	Ernest S.	E.S.W.
Williams	George	(P) GW College
Willingham	Edward B.	Ferron Okewole - International Missions
Willingham	Theodore W.	Mrs. Marilynn Falk - Church of the Nazarene (P) Stratford Studio, Kansas City, MO
Willson	S. Bruce	Tom Reid - Reformed Presbyterian Theological Seminary
Wilson	Grady B.	G.B.W.
Winrod	Gerald B.	(P) Booklet
Winthrop	John	(P) VanDyke, Girsch, (Appletons)
Witmar	Safara	(P) Masterson Studio, Fort Wayne, IN
Wolgemuth	Samuel F.	Norma Collins
Woodbridge	Charles J.	E. Lee - Moody Press Editorial
Woods	C. Stacey	C.S.W., Mrs. Yvonne K. Woods, Julian Mellows (P) Evangelical Students, Lausanne, Switzerland
Wooley	William L.	(P) Barry Wooley- Cincinnati, OH
Woolsey	Art	David C. McClain, Murphy Library, B.B. College/Seminary
Worcester	Elwood	Janice Randall – Emmanuel Church
Wright	J. Elwin	Mrs. Taylor, Harvey C. Warner, Kathryn M. Evans
Wuest	Kenneth S.	Mrs. Jeannete Wuest
Wurmbrand	Richard	M. Wurmbrand, L. Gutierrez, S. Cleary, C. Weaver
Wyatt	Thomas	T.W.
Wyrtzen	Jack	J.W., Mrs. Joan L. Wyrtzen, Barbara Fulforth
Yarnell	Ralph I.	Mrs. Ruth Heidorn (Yarnell) (P) Olan Mills
Yatsan	Sun	(P) Year, 1950
Yeager	Waldo	W.Y., Ken Anderson
Yetter	Arch H.	Gayle Gunderson - Colorado Christian University
Yocum	William F.	Heather Kittleman
York	Alvin C.	(P) Life, Vol. X
Yost	John L.	Mack C. Branham, Jr. - Lutheran Theo. Southern Sem.
Young	G. Douglas	Amelia Nakai - Jerusalem University College
Young	Robert	(P) An Analytical Concordance of the Bible
Youngdale	Luther	(P) Warolin Studio, Washington, D.C.
Zenos	Andreas	Martha L. Payne - McCormick Theological Seminary, Barry C. Hopkins
Ziegler	Jesse H.	(P) Association of Theological Schools
Zimmerman	Henry D.	Michael S. Galley - Liebenzell USA Global Ministries
Zimmerman	Thomas F.	Carl G. Conner - Gen. Council of the Assemblies of God
Zinzendorf	Nicholas L. von	C. Moore, H. Savacool, D. Van Halsema, W. Showalter
Zirkle	James	Julie Gunn
Zoller	John	J.Z., Joy
Zwemer	Samuel M.	J.C. Wilson, R.C. Douglas, C. Smith, C.A. Glasser

Organizations Which Provided Multiple Photographs

American Friends Service Committee – Philadelphia, PA
    Colin Bell, Henry Wilbur
Assembly of God—Springfield, MO
    R. Riggs, E. Williams, T. Zimmerman
Baptist Life Insurance—Buffalo, NY
    N. Macaulay, F. Woyke
Baptist World Alliance—Washington, DC
    E. Mullins, J. Nordenhaug, A. Ohrn, J.H. Rushbrooke, W. Tolbert
Bethel College – N. Newton, KS
    C. Wedel, J. Kliewer, E. Kaufmann
Bethel College – St. Paul, MN
    R. Arlander, W. Tadder, W. Turnwall
Billy Graham Evangelistic Association—Charlotte, NC
    J. Blinco, S. Fleming, W. Haymaker, J. E. Orr, C. Taylor, T. W. Wilson
Bob Jones University—Greenville, SC
    D. Billington, N. Smith
Brethren in Christ – Grantham, PA
    A. Climenhaga, R. Swatsky, S. R. Smith
Brite Divinity School – Ft. Worth, TX
    C. Hall, E. Henson, M.J. Suggs
Cedarville (OH) University bulletin
    M. R. McChesney, D. McKinney
Christian Business Men's Committee—Chicago/Lombard, IL
    R. Swanson, R. Woike, W. Yeager
Christian Church – Nashville, TN
    D.C. History Society, K. Teegarden, D. Fiers
Christian Theological Seminary – Louisville, KY
    F. Kerschner, O. L. Shelton, B. Norris
Church of God – Anderson, IN
    L. Crouse, C. Webber,
Church of God – Cleveland, TN
    F. Lee, H. Chesser, W. Horton
Disciples of Christ Historical Society – Nashville, TN
    Fiers, K. Teegarden
Emory University (Woodruff Library)—Atlanta, GA
    J. Costen, W. J. King, F. N. Parker, D. M. Watters
Evangelical Luthern Church in America—Region 3, St. Paul, MN (courtesy P. Daniels)
    B. M. Christiansen, G. Sverdrup, Jr., C. Zeidler
Faith Baptist Bible College – Ankeny, IA
    W. Jordan, J. L. Patten, S. Bradford
General Theological Seminary—New York, NY
    H. E. Fosbrooke, E. A. Hoffman, W. Robbins
Hope College – Holland, MI
    Hope College collection of the joint archives of Holland
    A.C. Van Raalte, J. Jacobson
Louisville Presbyterian Theological Seminary
    Caldwell, Hemphill, VanderMuelen
Lutheran Layman's League – St. Louis, MO
    T. Eggers, P. Friedrich

Lutheran Theological Seminary at Philadelphia
>   H.A. Bagger, H. E. Jacobs, C.W. Schaffer

Lutheran Theological Southern Seminary- Columbia, SC
>   Ed Hazelius, A. Voight, J. L. Yost, Eppling Reinartz

Lutheran World Federation (courtesy L.E. Elliot, Helen Penet)
>   A. Nygren

Maxheim Photos—Des Moines, IA
>   C. E. Fuller, S. Shufelt

McCormick Thological Seminary- Chicago, IL
>   McClure, Stone, Frank, Cotton

Mennonite Church
>   Library Archives:
>   >   Bethel College, N. Newton, KS—E. G. Kauffman, J. W. Kliewer
>   >   Elkhart, IN—C. Wedel
>   >   Goshen, IN—J. S. Shoemaker
>   >   Board of Missions (courtesy Rich Benner)—S. C. Yoder

Missionary Baptist Seminary – Little Rock, AK
>   L. Guthrey, L. D. Foreman

Moody Bible Institute—Chicago, IL
>   C. Keur, H. Lundquist, I. Moon, J. Stam

Mudd Manuscript Library – Princeton, NJ
>   J. Carnahan, J. McLean

Nazarene Archives (courtesy Stan Ingersoll)—Kansas City, MO
>   H. C. Benner, R. W. Cunningham, H. Reynolds, R. Williams

New Brunswick (NJ) Theological Seminary (Reformed Church in America)
>   W.H.S Demarest, Beardslee, H. Hageman, J. Inghman, J. Hoffman

Norwegian Lutheran Synod Who's Who
>   A. C. Preus, H. A. Preus

Pacific Garden Mission—Chicago, IL
>   E. Taylor, W. Taylor

Perkins School of Theology (SMU) – Dallas, TX
>   J. Quillan, E. Hawk, M. Cuninggim

Pillar of Fire – Zarephath, NJ
>   A.K. White, D. F. Wolfram

Presbyterian Historical Society Archives—Philadelphia, PA
>   E. C. Blake, L. Evans, L. Mudge, W. B. Pugh

Princeton Seminary – Princeton, NJ
>   E. Roberts, J. Ross Stevenson

Salvation Army Archives and Research Center
>   Bram Booth, E. Parker, E. Pubmire

Southern Baptist Archives and Historical Library (courtesy Bill Sumners)
>   Frank Stagg, James Sullivan
>   B.B. McKinney, W.O. Carver

Sword of the Lord—Murfreesboro, TN
>   H. Springer, G. A. Weninger

University of Chicago Library - Special Collections
>   B. Loomer, G.W. Northrup, J. Kitagawa

Tremont Temple - Boston, MA
>   C. Myers, L. Brougher

Troyer Studios, Inc.
>   E. E. Miller, P. Minninger

Union Theological Seminary – Richmond, VA
>   W. L. Lingle, H. W. Dubose

United Church of Christ—Cleveland, OH
    B. Herbster, D. Horton, F. Hoskins, J. E. Wagner
United Methodist Church – (Gen. Commission archives/history) – Madison, NJ
    L. Banks, U. Darlington, A. Day, H. C. Sheldon, M. Terry, H. Kumler
    T. H. Lewis, F. P. Corson, Booklet, R. L. Smith
Western Seminary – Holland, MI
    Western Seminary collection of the joint archives of Holland
    C. Crispell, C. Steffens, J. Beardslee, Sr., J. Mulder
Yale University Library – New Haven, CT (Reuben A. Holden)
    S. Andrew, E. Williams, N. Daggett, M. Burrows
Youth for Christ—Colorado Springs, CO
    B. Bessmertny, K. L. Brooks, W. Collins, M. Graham, E. Midura, J. Smith

Acknowledgements of Help from Books and Magazines (Material and Photos)

We have done our best to thank individuals and organizations for their assistance. To acknowledge each individual photo and source material is impossible. Please understand, I have done my best. I am grateful for the vast majority of organizations who responded and provided photos and data without a charge. Reasonable fees were paid to some.

For photos, we are especially indebted to *The Dictionary of American Portraits,* (Mark S. Duffy) and Appleton's *Encyclopedia of American Biography.*

For biography content, we are especially indebted to *Encyclopedia Americana* and *Who Was Who in America* (15 Vols.).

For both photos and biography content, we are greatly indebted to Reese Religious Research biography library.

The most predominant source books were:

Book Name	*Author(s)*
Adventures for God	Clarence W. Hall
Advocates of Reform	Baslie, McNeill, VanDusan
African Methodist Episcopal Zion Church, The	William J. Walls
Agents 14	Ruth Johnson
Ambassadors for Christ	John Woodbridge
American Missionary Memorial	H.W. Pierson
Appleton's Cyclopedia of American Biography Vol. 1	Wilson and Fiske
Appleton's Cyclopedia of American Biography Vol. 2	Wilson and Fiske
Appleton's Cyclopedia of American Biography Vol. 4	Wilson and Fiske
Appleton's Cyclopedia of American Biography Vol. 5	Wilson and Fiske
Appleton's Cyclopedia of American Biography Vol. 6	Wilson and Fiske
Armed with Courage	McNeer and Ward
Baptist History Workbook, The	James R. Beller
Beacon Lights of Grace	Richard E. Day
Bible and Christianity	Baldwin H. Ward
Bible Words that Guide Me	Hubert A. Elliott
Billy Graham and 7 That Were Saved	Lewis W. Gillenson
Biog. Encyclopedia Of the World	
Biographical Dictionary of Christian Missions	Gerald Anderson
Bishop's of the A.M.E. Church, The	R.R. Wright
Book of Missionary Heroes, The	Basil Mathews
Book of Protestant Saints, A	Ernest Gordon
By One Spirit	Karl A. Olsson
Cambridge Seven	J.C. Pollock
Cameos	Helen Koniman
Champions of Christianity	Silas Farmer
Changed Lives in San Quentin	Harry Howard
Changing Emphasis in American Preaching	Ernest Trice Thompson
Chart of Christian History and Culture Manual	Merril Orne Young
Christian Biographies, The	Thomas Jackson
Christian Booking and Directory	
Christian Hall of Fame, The	Elmer L. Towns
Christian Men of Science	George/Julia Mulfinger
Christians in the Arena	Allan A. Heenten

Title	Author
Chronological and Background Charts of Church History	Robert Walton
Church Federation	Elias Benjamin Sanford
Church History and Things to Come	Beka Horton
Church Year Calendar and Lectionary, The	Hight Kerr
Cleveland Colored Quartet	
Companion to Baptist Hymnal	William J. Reynolds
Cooperative Evangelism	Robert O. Ferm
Courage to Conquer	Leroy King
Crisis Experiences	V. Ray Edman
Dawn in the East	Phyllis Thompson
Day We Met Christ	Max Stilson
Deeper Experiences of Famous Christians	James G. Lawson
Devotees of Christ	D.S. Batley
Dictionary Handbook to Hymns	Don Hustad
Dictionary of Christian biography	Michael Walsh
Dictionary of Christianity in America	
Dictionary of Pentecostal and Charismatic Movements	Stanley M./Gary B. Burgess/McGee
Dictionary of the Ecumenical Movement	
Early Christian Writers	Sister Ann Carol
Eleven Christians	Various
Eminent M.E. Preachers	P. Douglass Gurrie
Encyclopedia of the Lutheran Church I, II, & III	John Bodensieck
Encyclopedia of World Methodism I	Nolan B. Harmon
Encyclopedia of World Methodism II	Nolan B. Harmon
Encyclopedia of Methodism	Matthew Simpson
Encyclopedia of Missions II	Edwin Munsell Bliss
Evangelism in Sermon and Song	Ernest O. Sellers
Faith at Work	Samuel M. Shoemaker
Faith is a Star	Roland Gammon
Faith of the Presidents, The	Anne Schraff
Family and Freedom Digest	Fletcher Brothers
Famous African Explorers and Adventurers	Charles H. Jones
Fathers of the Western Church, The	Robert Payne
Fifty-Two Story Telling Programs	Carl G. Johnson
Five Pioneer Missionaries	S.M. Houghton
Flame Touches Flame	Margaret Cropper
Forgotten Heroes	C.J. Casher
From Darkness to Light, II	Merton B. Osborn
From Jerusalem to Irian Jaya	Ruth Tucker
Giants of the Missionary Trail	Eugene M. Harrison
Goal and the Glory	Ted Simonson
God Planted Five Seeds	Jean D. Johnson
God Uses Ordinary Men	Margolyn Woods
God's Bullies	Perry Deane Young
God's Generals	Roberts Liardon
God's Prison Gang	Chaplain Ray
Good Christian Men	Martin P. Davidson
Gospel in Hymns	Albert E. Bailey
Great Conversions	Frederick S. Leahy
Great Gospel Sermons 1	
Great Gospel Sermons 2	
Great Leaders of the Christian Church	Charles Woodbridge
Great Men and Famous Women, Vols. 1-6	

Great Men of the Christian Church	Williston Walker
Great Negroes Past and Present	Russ Adams
Great Personal Workers	Faris D. Whitesell
Great Poets and Their Theology	Augustus H. Strong
Great Religious Leaders	Charles Francis Potter
Guardians of the Great Commission	Ruth Tucker
Guideposts Pocket Book of Inspiration	Norman Vincent Peale
Guideposts to a Stronger Faith	
Guideposts Treasury of Faith, The	Norman Vincent Peale
Guideposts Treasury of Hope, The	Norman Vincent Peale
He Walks With Me	David Graham
Heroes of the Cross	
Heroes of the Cross	Davenport Adams
Heroes of the Cross in America	Don O. Shelton
Heroes of the Faith	James C. Hefley
Heroes of the Faith	Gene Fedele
Heroes of Faith on Pioneer Trails	Eugene Harrison
Heroes of the Holy Life	Wesley L. Duewel
Heroic Colonial Christians	Russell Hitt
Hidden Pearls, Brentwood, TN	Blue Sky
Highways to Faith	David W. Soper
History of Fundamentalism	George W. Dollar
History of Gospel Music	The Jesse/Duane Burt/Allen
Holy Men of God	James E. Cumming
How Great Christians Met Christ	James C. Hefley
How I Found God's Will	John Sigsworth
Hymns of our Faith	William J. Reynolds
I Believe in Miracles	Kathryn Kuhlmann
I Married a Minister	Mrs. Jesse Bader
I Was Born Again	Norman A. Wingert
Illustrated Bible Church Handbook, The	Stanley I. Stuber
Illustrated History of Methodism, The	
Illustrated Minute Biographies	Nisenson & DeWitt
In God We Trust	Norman Cousins
In Spite of All	Archer Wallace
Incredible Journey	James Ray
Inside Story of the Hollywood Christian Group	J. Edwin Orr
Jews for Jesus	Ruth Rosen
Journey With the Saints, A	Thomas S. Kepler
Kings of Platform and Pulpit	Melville D. Landon
Knight's of the Labarum	Harlan P. Beach
Last Words of Saints/Sinners	Herbert Lockyer
Leaping Flame	Jack Wyrtzen
Little Pictorial Lives of the Saints	
Life and Death	Thomas Lewin
Life and Labors of Carey, Marshman and Ward	John Clark Marshman
Life and Labors of Moody and Sankey	Robert Boyd
Life of Joan of Arc and Other Biog.	Jules Michelet
Life Verses I	Frank Boreham
Life Verses II	Frank Boreham
Life Verses III	Frank Boreham
Life Verses IV	Frank Boreham
Life Verses V	Frank Boreham

Lifelines	Frank Wees
Little People Who Became Great	Laura A. Large
Lives of the Fathers Vol. 1	Frederic W. Farrar
Lives of the Reformers	
Lives that Inspire	Beatrice Plumb
Lives, Sentiment and Sufferings of Reformers and Martyrs	William Holgson
Living Biographies	Thomas, Thomas
Living the Great Adventure	Richard Engquist
Living with the Giants	Warren Wiersbe
Love Is	Don Hillis
Lutheran Cyclopedia	Erwin L. Lueker
Men and Women of Deep Piety	Clara McLeister
Men Behind Moody	Flood and Jenkins
Men of Fire	Walter R. Bowie
Men of God	Oswald J. Smith
Men Who Have Walked With God	Sheldon Cheney
Messengers of the King	David C. Hill
Missionary Crusaders for Christ	Eugene M. Harrison
Missionary Heroes and Martyrs	Lucius E. Smith
Modern Canterbury Pilgrims	James A. Pike
Modern Missionary Enterprise	Lucius E. Smith
Moody and Sankey	
Moody Bible Institute	Bernard R. DeRemer
More Story Telling Programs	Carl C. Johnson
More than Conquerors	John Woodbridge
Music in Evangelism	Phil Kerr
National Cyclopedia of American Biography, Vol. 16	
National Cyclopedia of American Biography, Vol. 30	
National Cyclopedia of American Biography, Vol. 46	
National Cyclopedia of American Biography, Vol. 50	
New Int'l Dictionary of the Christian Church, The	J. D. Douglas
New Int'l Dictionary of Pent.Charismatic Movements	Stanley M. Burgess
Not Made for Quitting	Dick Hillis
Not Somehow, But Triumphantly	V. Raymond Edman
One Hundred Bible Verses	William/Randy Peterson
One Hundred Christian Books	William/Randy Peterson
One Hundred Christian Women Who Changed the 20th Century	Helen K. Hosier
Pacts of the Church	Edwin F. Hatfield
Painted Windows	
People Who Shaped the Earth	Temple/Twitchell
Pictorial History of Protestantism	Vergilius Ferm
Pioneers of Protestantism	James Johnston
Platform Echoes	John B. Gough
Play Ball	James C. Hefley
Prayer Meetings	
Preachers I Have Heard	Alexander Grammie
Princely Men in Heavenly Kingdom	Harlan P. Beach
Princes of Christian Pulpit	Harry C. Howard
Profiles in Evangelism	Fred Barlow
Pulpit Giants	Donald E. Demaray
Quest for Reality	Merion Bosborn
Recollection of Men of Faith	Ann Rogers
Religion of the Presidents	Hampton/Judson

Religious Leaders of America	J. Gordon Melton
Religious Leaders of America	J.C. Schwarz
Religious Leaders of America- Second	J. Gordon Melton
Representation Chruchmen of 20 Centuries	Hugh Natt
Revival Times in America	Fred W. Hoffman
Ripley's Believe It Or Not series	Robert Ripley
Saint Watching	Phillis McGinley
Saints Alive	James C. Hefley
Saints Upon a Time	Joan Windham
Sawdust Trail	Gordon Langley Hall
Sea of Glory	Francis B Thorton
Seventy Great Christians	Geoffrey Hanks
Short Biographies Vol. 4	
Silhouette Women Behind Great Men	Helen W. Kooiman
Six Mighty Men	W.J. Smart
Sixty Great Founders	Geoffrey Hanks
Some American Churchmen	Frederic C. Morehouse
Some Heretics of Yesterday	
Sparks Among the Stubble	Margaret Cropper
Spiritual Lives of the Great Composers	Patrick Kavanaugh
Spiritual Secrets of Famous Christians	Anna T. McPherson
Story of Methodism	A. B. Hyde
Sunday Half Hours with Great Preachers	Jesse Lyman Hurlbut
Tell Every Man	Dorothy C. Haskin
Ten Famous Christian Athletes	Mel Larson
Ten Famous Evangelists	Basil Miller
Ten Famous Missionaries	Basil Miller
Ten Largest Sunday Schools	Elmer L. Towns
Ten Makers of Modern Protestant Thought	George L. Hunt
Ten Singers who Became Famous	Basil Miller
Ten Slave Boys and Girls	Basil Miller
Ten Torch Bearers	Dorothy Heiderstadt
Ten Who Overcame	Pat Dishman
These Sought a Country	Kenneth Scott Latourette
They Dared to Believe God	Anna Talbott McPherson
They Dared to Overcome	Anna Talbott McPherson
They Found the Secret	V. Raymond Edman
They Knew Their God, Vols. 1-4	Harvey/Hey
This I Believe About Jesus Christ	John Clover Monsma
Those Who Came Forward	Curtis Mitchell
Three Martyrs of the Nineteenth Century	Charles Rundle
Through Gates of Splendor	Elisabeth Elliott
To God Be the Glory	Roger Elwood
Travels of the Messenger, The	Grant / DiCianni
Twelve After	David A. Seamands
Twelve Famous Evangelists	James Stephen
Twelve Reformation Heroes	G. A. Neilson
Twentieth Century Christians	
Twenty Centuries of Great Preaching 1	Clyde E./William M. Fant/Pinson
Twenty Centuries of Great Preaching 2	Clyde E./William M. Fant/Pinson
Twenty Centuries of Great Preaching 3	Clyde E./William M. Fant/Pinson
Twenty Centuries of Great Preaching 4	Clyde E./William M. Fant/Pinson
Twenty Centuries of Great Preaching 5	Clyde E./William M. Fant/Pinson

Twenty Centuries of Great Preaching 6	Clyde E./William M. Fant/Pinson
Twenty Centuries of Great Preaching 7	Clyde E./William M. Fant/Pinson
Twenty Centuries of Great Preaching 8	Clyde E./William M. Fant/Pinson
Twenty Centuries of Great Preaching 9	Clyde E./William M. Fant/Pinson
Twenty Centuries of Great Preaching 10	Clyde E./William M. Fant/Pinson
Twenty Centuries of Great Preaching 11	Clyde E./William M. Fant/Pinson
Twenty Centuries of Great Preaching 12	Clyde E./William M. Fant/Pinson
Twice Born Men, The	Norman A. Wingert
Twice Born Stars	Dorothy C. Haskin
Unshackled	Bailey Price
Victorious Christians You Should Know	Warren W. Wiersbe
Voices of American Fundamentalism	C.A. Russell
Walking with the Giants	Warren Wiersbe
Webster's American Biography	Charles Van Doren
Webster's Biographical Dictionary	William Allen Neilson
When the Arrow Flies	Rosemary Cunningham
When You Need a Missionary Story	Elizabeth B. Jones
Who Was Who in Church History	Elgin S. Moyer
Who's Who in Church History	William Barker
Will To Win	James C. Hefley
Woman in Music	George P. Upton
Women of Light	Walter Russell Bowie
Words to Die For	Lawrence Kimbrough
World's Greatest Sermons, The 1	Grenville Kleiser
World's Greatest Sermons, The 2	Grenville Kleiser
World's Greatest Sermons, The 3	Grenville Kleiser
World's Greatest Sermons, The 4	Grenville Kleiser
World's Greatest Sermons, The 5	Grenville Kleiser
World's Greatest Sermons, The 6	Grenville Kleiser
World's Greatest Sermons, The 7	Grenville Kleiser
World's Greatest Sermons, The 8	Grenville Kleiser
World's Greatest Sermons, The 9	Grenville Kleiser
World's Greatest Sermons, The 10	Grenville Kleiser